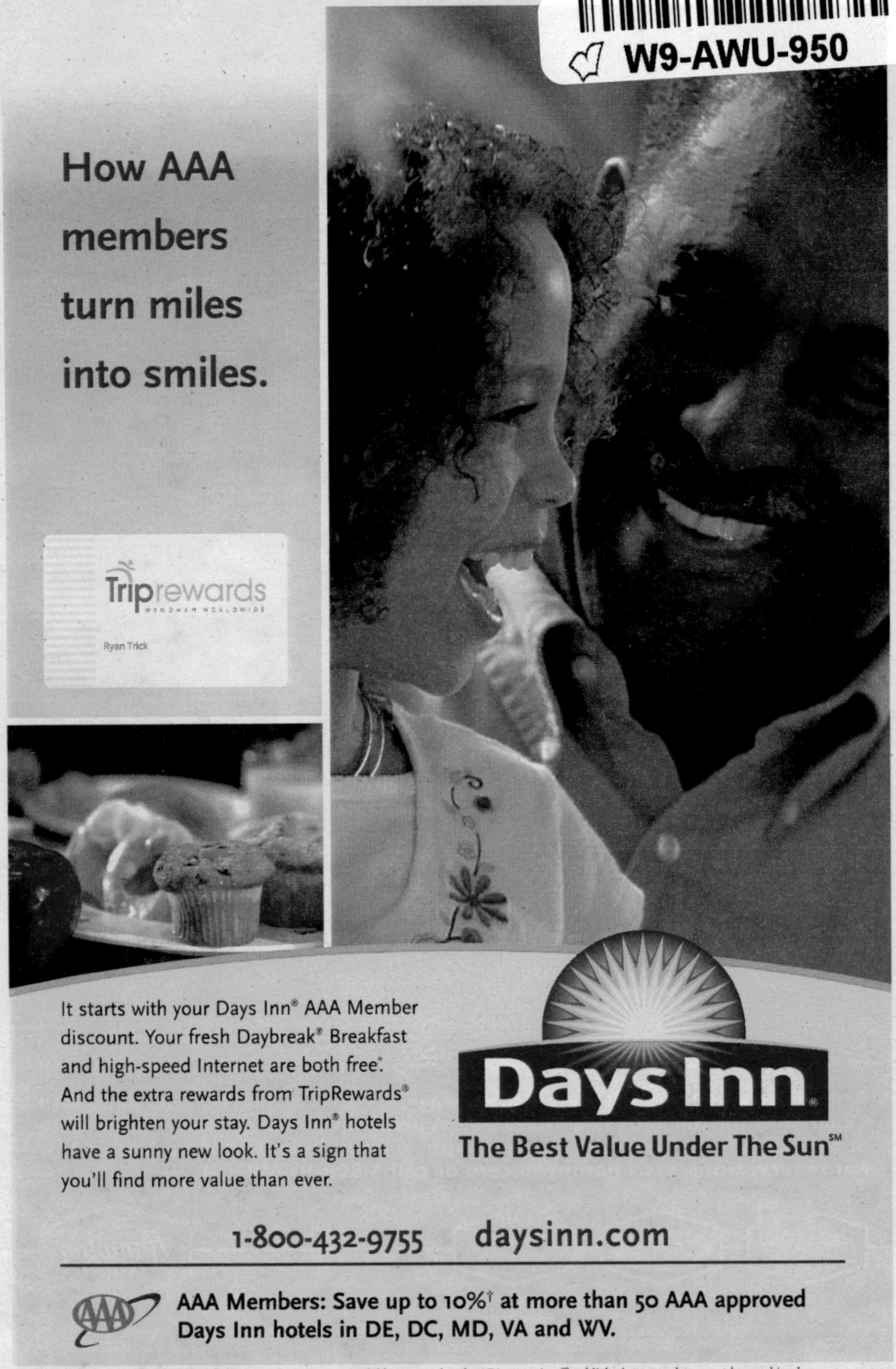
How AAA members turn miles into smiles.
Triprewards
WYNDHAM WORLDWIDE
Ryan Trick
It starts with your Days Inn® AAA Member discount. Your fresh Daybreak® Breakfast and high-speed Internet are both free*. And the extra rewards from TripRewards® will brighten your stay. Days Inn® hotels have a sunny new look. It's a sign that you'll find more value than ever.
Days Inn®
The Best Value Under The Sun℠
1-800-432-9755
daysinn.com
AAA
AAA Members: Save up to 10%† at more than 50 AAA approved Days Inn hotels in DE, DC, MD, VA and WV.

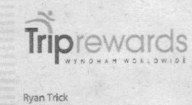

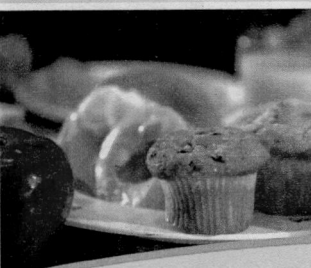

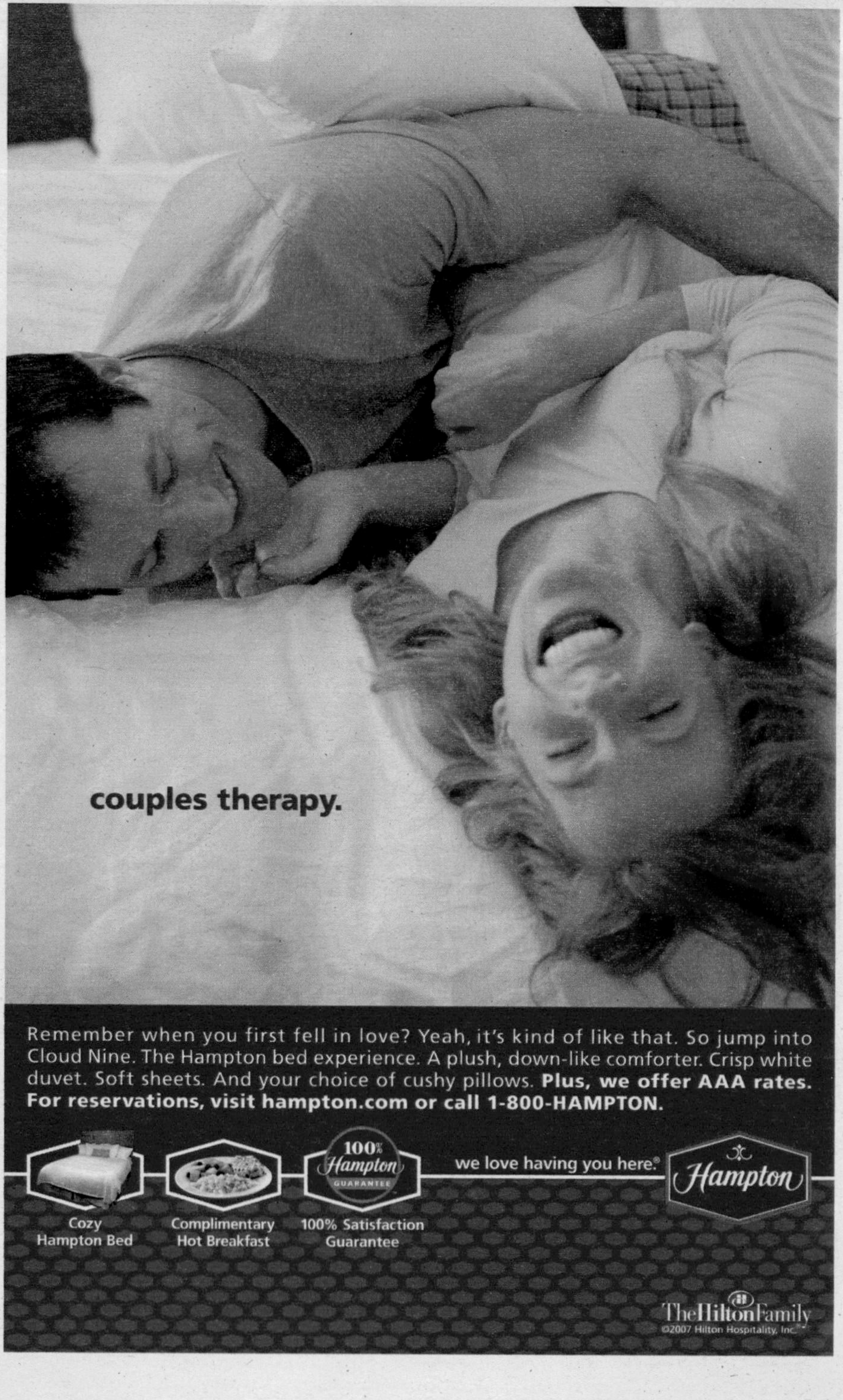

couples therapy.

Remember when you first fell in love? Yeah, it's kind of like that. So jump into Cloud Nine. The Hampton bed experience. A plush, down-like comforter. Crisp white duvet. Soft sheets. And your choice of cushy pillows. **Plus, we offer AAA rates. For reservations, visit hampton.com or call 1-800-HAMPTON.**

Cozy
Hampton Bed

Complimentary
Hot Breakfast

100% Satisfaction
Guarantee

we love having you here.®

Hampton

The Hilton Family
©2007 Hilton Hospitality, Inc.

Mid-Atlantic

Are we meeting your travel needs?
Send written comments to:

AAA Member Comments
1000 AAA Drive, Box 61
Heathrow, FL 32746-5063

Published by AAA Publishing
1000 AAA Drive
Heathrow, FL 32746-5063
Copyright AAA 2008

The publisher is not responsible for changes that occur after publication. TourBook® guides are published for the exclusive use of AAA members. Not for sale.

Advertising Rate and Circulation Information: (407) 444-8280

Printed in the USA by Quebecor World, Buffalo, NY

Photo Credit: (Cover & Title Page)
Drum Point Lighthouse,
Solomons, MD
© Kord / age fotostock

Printed on recyclable paper.
Please recycle whenever possible.

Mixed Sources
Product group from well-managed forests and other controlled sources
www.fsc.org Cert no. SW-COC-1610
© 1996 Forest Stewardship Council

Stock #4608

Mid-Atlantic

Virginia

West Virginia

Featured Information

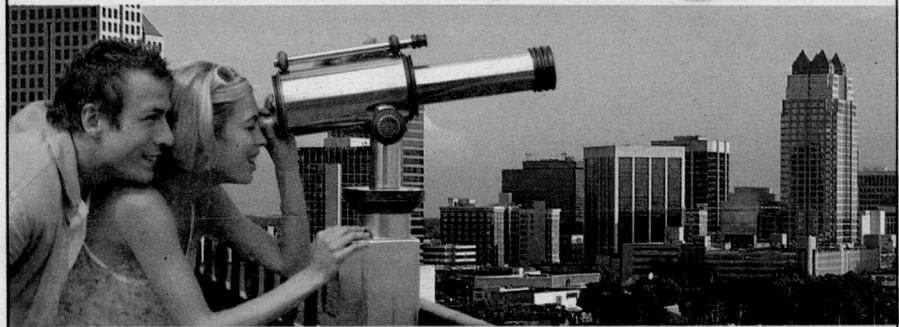

Not all online travel sites are created equal.

AAA.com offers fast, easy access to services and information not available on other Web sites:

TripTik® Travel Planner with exclusive *Modify My Route* feature lets you choose roads you prefer to travel.

AAA Diamond rated hotels and restaurants — including thousands of photos for making informed travel decisions.

Consistently lowest average hotel rates compared to Expedia, Hotels.com, and other leading travel sites according to recent surveys.

AAA.com is the only travel Web site backed by 10,000 travel professionals at more than 1,100 AAA Travel offices across the country. Make your online travel plans with confidence on AAA.com. Trust AAA's knowledgeable experts to assist with changes, questions, and additional services.

Grab your mouse and go... to AAA.com, today!

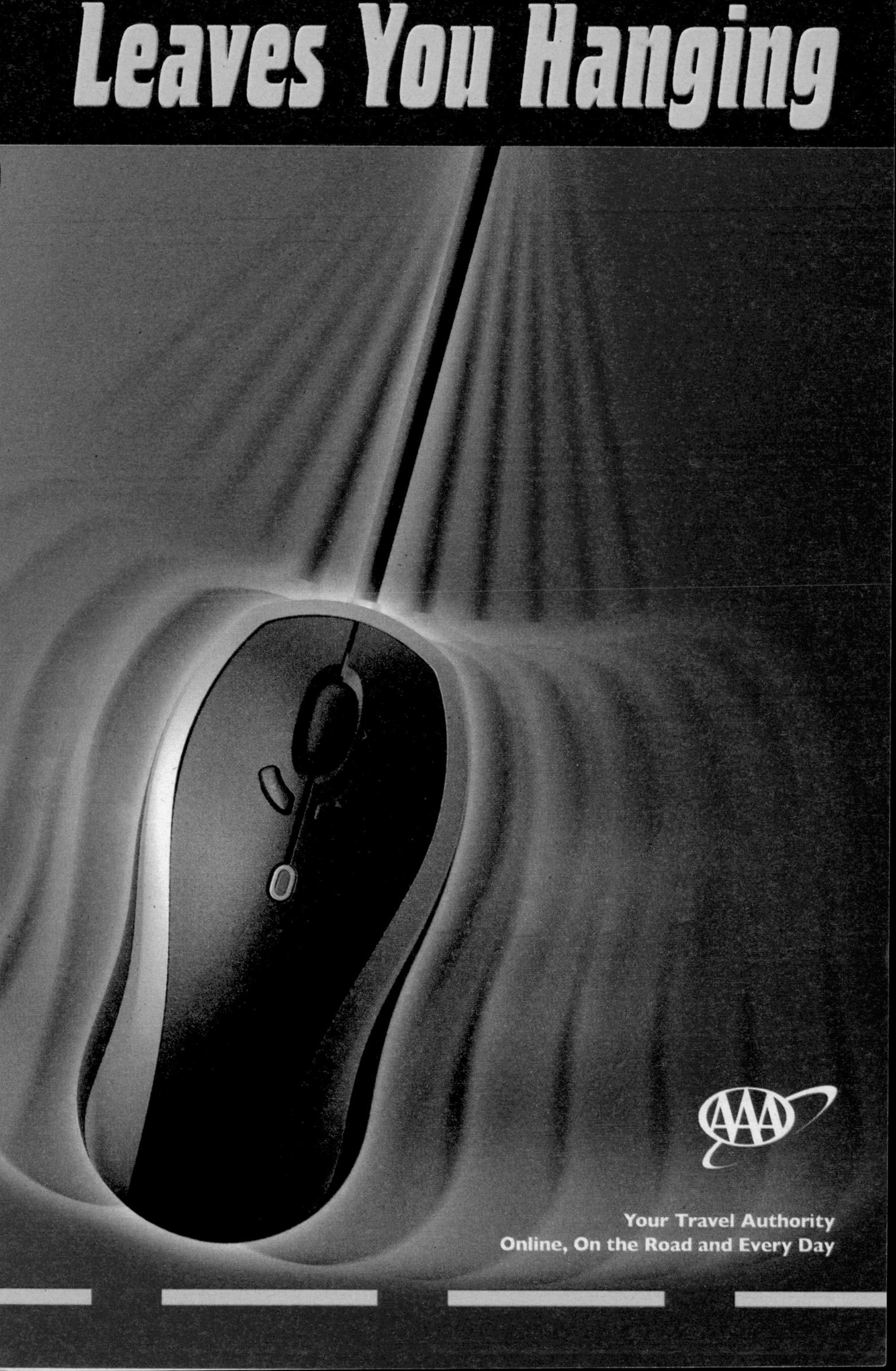
Leaves You Hanging
AAA
Your Travel Authority
Online, On the Road and Every Day

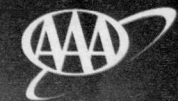

Attractions, lodgings and restaurants are listed on the basis of merit alone after careful evaluation and approval by one of AAA/CAA's full-time, professionally trained Inspectors. Evaluations are unannounced to ensure that we see an establishment just as you would see it.

An establishment's decision to advertise in the TourBook guide has no bearing on its evaluation or rating. Advertising for services or products does not imply AAA endorsement.

All information in this guide was reviewed for accuracy before publication. However, since changes inevitably occur between annual editions, we suggest you work with your AAA travel professional or check on AAA.com to confirm prices and schedules.

How the TourBook Guide is Organized

The TourBook guide is organized into three distinct sections.

The **Points of Interest** section helps you plan daily activities and sightseeing excursions and provides details about the city or attraction you are visiting.

The **Lodgings and Restaurants** section helps you select AAA Approved accommodations and dining facilities meeting your specific needs and expectations.

The **Reference** section provides indexes for locating information within this guide and items to aid the trip planning process.

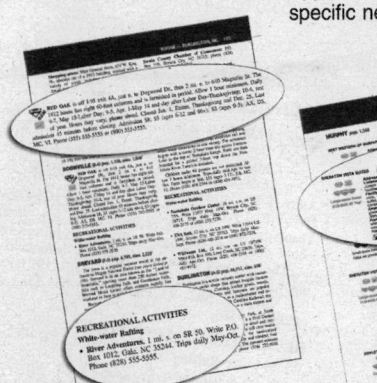

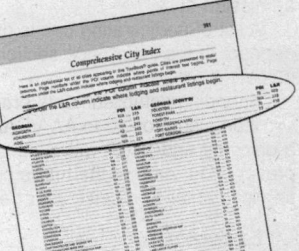

Locating the Attractions, Lodgings and Restaurants

Attractions, lodgings and restaurants are listed under the city in which they physically are located - or in some cases under the nearest recognized city. Most listings are alphabetically organized by state, province, region or island, then by city and establishment name.

A color is assigned to each state or province so that you can match the color bars at the top of the page to switch from the **Points of Interest** section to the **Lodgings and Restaurants** section.

Spotting maps help you physically locate points of interest, lodgings and restaurants in the major destinations.

The Comprehensive City Index located in the **Reference** section contains an A-to-Z list of cities.

Destination Cities and Destination Areas

Destination cities, established based on government models and local expertise, include metropolitan areas plus nearby vicinity cities. **Destination areas** are regions with broad tourist appeal; several cities will comprise the area.

If a city falls within a destination's vicinity, the city name will appear at its alphabetical location in the book, and a cross reference will give you the exact page on which listings for that city begin.

An orientation map appears at the beginning of each destination section to orient you to that destination.

Understanding the Points of Interest Listing

GEM Designation

A ☒ indicates the attraction has been rated a AAA GEM, a "must see" point of interest that offers a *Great Experience for Members®*. These attractions have been judged to be of exceptional interest and quality by AAA Inspectors.

A GEM listing page with a brief description of individual GEM attractions follows the Orientation map near the beginning of each state or province Points of Interest section. Cross-references guide the reader to the attraction's listing page.

Discount Savings

The (SAVE) icon denotes those attractions offering AAA/CAA, AAA MasterCard, AAA VISA or international Show Your Card & Save discount cardholders a discount off the attraction's standard admission. Present your card at the attraction's admission desk.

A list of participating points of interest appears in the Reference section of this guide.

Shopping establishments preceded by a (SAVE) icon also provide to AAA/CAA members a discount and/or gift with purchase; present your card at the mall's customer service center to receive your benefit.

Exceptions

- Members should inquire in advance concerning the validity of the discount for special rates.
- The (SAVE) discount may not be used in conjunction with other discounts.
- Attractions that already provide a reduced senior or child rate may not honor the (SAVE) discount for those age groups.
- All offers are subject to change and may not apply during special events, particular days or seasons or for the entire validity period of the TourBook guide.

Adventure Travel

There are inherent risks with adventure travel activities like air tours, hiking, skiing and white-water rafting. For your own safety, please read and adhere to all safety instructions. Mentions of these activities are for information only and do **not** imply endorsement by AAA.

Shopping areas: Mast General Store, 630 W. King St., operates out of a 1913 building, stocked with a variety of goods includin... Amish...

Swain
Box 5...

RED OAK is off I-95 exit 4A, just n. to Dogwoo... 1812 house has eight 60-foot columns and is furn... 9-7, May 15-Labor Day; 9-5, Apr. 1-May 14 and of year. Hours may vary; phone ahead. Closed J admission 45 minutes before closing. Admission $8; $5 MC, VI. Phone (555) 555-5555 or (800) 555-5555.

holiday...
10-18); free (on Tues.). ...

BOONVILLE (B-4) pop. 1,138, elev. 1,066′

RED OAK is off I-95 exit 4A, just n. to Dogwood Dr., then 2 mi. e. to 610 Magnolia St. The 1812 house has eight 60-foot columns and is furnished in period. Allow 1 hour minimum. Daily 9-7, May 15-Labor Day; 9-5, Apr. 1-May 14 and day after Labor Day-Thanksgiving; 10-4, rest of year. Hours may vary; phone ahead. Closed Jan. 1, Easter, Thanksgiving and Dec. 25. Last admission 45 minutes before closing. Admission $8; $5 (ages 6-12 and 66+); $3 (ages 0-5). AX, DS, MC, VI. Phone (555) 555-5555 or (800) 555-5555.

RECREATIONAL ACTIVITIES

White-water Rafting

- **River Adventures,** 1 mi. s. on SR 50. Write P.O. Box 1012, Gale, NC 35244. Trips daily May-Oct. Phone (828) 555-5555.

BREVARD (F-3) pop. 6,789, elev. 2,229′

The town is a popular summer resort at the entrance to Pisgah National Forest (*see place listing p. 166*). Brevard is in an area known as the "Land of Waterfalls," sporting more than 250 named waterfalls such as Laughing Falls and Courthouse Falls. Brevard Music Center offers concerts nightly, last weekend in June to mid-...

Brevard...
po...

RECREATIONAL ACTIVIT...

White-water Rafting

- **River Adventures,** 1 mi. s. Box 1012, Gale, NC 35244. Phone (828) 555-5555.

Directions

Unless otherwise specified, directions are given from the center of town, using the following highway designations:

I=interstate highway	**US**=federal highway
SR=state route	**CR**=county road
FM=farm to market	**FR**=forest road
Mex.=Mexican highway	**Hwy.**=Canadian or Caribbean highway

Prices and Dates of Operations

Admission prices are quoted without sales tax. Children under the lowest age specified are admitted free when accompanied by an adult. Days, months and age groups written with a hyphen are inclusive.

Prices pertaining to points of interest in the United States are quoted in U.S. dollars; points of interest in Canada are quoted in Canadian dollars; prices for points of interest in Mexico and the Caribbean are quoted as an approximate U.S. dollar equivalent.

Schedules and admission rates may change throughout the validity period of this guide. Check AAA.com for the most current information.

Credit Cards Accepted

AX=American Express	**JC**=Japan Credit Bureau
CB=Carte Blanche	**MC**=MasterCard
DC=Diners Club	**VI**=VISA
DS=Discover	

Bulleted Listings

Gambling establishments are evaluated by AAA personnel; casinos within hotels are presented for member information regardless of whether the lodging is AAA Approved.

Recreational activities of a participatory nature (requiring physical exertion or special skills) are not inspected.

Wineries are inspected by AAA Tourism Editors to ensure they meet listing requirements and offer tours.

All are presented in an abbreviated bulleted format for informational purposes.

ONE — BURLINGTON, NC   125

y Chamber of Commerce: P.O.
son City, NC 28713; phone (828)

, then 2 mi. e. to 610 Magnolia St. The
in period. Allow 1 hour minimum. Daily
after Labor Day-Thanksgiving; 10-4, rest
, Easter, Thanksgiving and Dec. 25. Last
6-12 and 66+); $3 (ages 0-5). AX, DS,

...departing
...ryson City, combines rail and
er excursions in one outing. The adventure
th a scenic 2-hour train trip across Fontana
the top of Nantahala Gorge. Rafts are then
for a guided 3-hour trip down the Nan-
ver. Lunch is included.
ren under 60 pounds are not permitted. Al-
ours minimum. Trips daily mid-Apr. to late
res begin at $66; $51 (ages 3-12). DS, MC,
ne (828) 488-2384 or (800) 451-9972.

REATIONAL ACTIVITIES
-water Rafting

atahala Outdoor Center, 26 mi. s.w. on US
J. Write 13077 Hwy. 19W, Bryson City, NC
13. Trips daily Mar.-Oct. Phone (828)
-2175 or (800) 232-7238.

5A Raft, 12 mi. s. on US 19W. Write 11044 US
W, Bryson City, NC 28713. Trips daily Mar.-
ept. Phone (828) 488-3316 or (800) 872-7238.

ildwater Ltd., 12 mi. s.w. on US 19/74W.
rite P.O. Box 309, Long Creek, SC 29658. Trips
aily Apr.-Oct. Phone (828) 488-2384 or (800)
451-9972.

URLINGTON (A-5) pop. 44,917, elev. 656'
Burlington is a textile industry center with numer-
... outlet shops that attract bargain hunters
...s. Clothing, leather goods, towels,
...ets and furniture are popular
... as a maintenance and re-
... Carolina Railroad; the
... as a train station and

S

SR 50. Write P.O.
ps daily May-Oct.

ty Park, at South
is a 1910 Dentzel
eir detail and intri-
ls still exist world-
s, the hand-carved
ffe and reindeer, four
. The carousel operates
, phone (336) 222-5030.

Local Member Value

(AAA) or (SAVE) identify hotels that offer members a rate guarantee and up to two free special amenities as part of their Official Appointment partnership with AAA. Rate guarantee: Discounted standard room rate (usually based on last standard room availability) or the lowest public rate available at time of booking for dates of stay. Free special amenity options are included in the listing and could be either: Breakfast, local telephone calls, newspaper, room upgrade, preferred room, high-speed Internet.

Diamond Rating

The number of diamonds informs you of the overall complexity of a lodging's amenities and service. Red indicates an Official Appointment lodging. An (fyi) in place of diamonds indicates the property has not been rated but is included as an "information only" service. A detailed description of each rating level appears on page 20.

Classification

All diamond rated lodgings are classified using three key elements: style of operation, overall concept and service level. See pages 22-23 for details on our classifications.

Rates

The property's standard 2-person rates and effective dates are shown.

Rates are provided to AAA by each lodging and represent the regular (rack) rate or ranges for a standard room. Rates are rounded to the nearest dollar and do not include taxes. U.S., Mexican and Caribbean rates are in U.S. dollars; rates for Canadian lodgings are in Canadian dollars.

Information about cancellation and minimum stay policies is provided in the Terms section of the property's listing.

Online Reservations

This notation indicates AAA/CAA members can conveniently check room availability, validate room rates and make reservations for this property in a secure online environment at AAA.com.

Service Availability

Unit types, amenities and room features preceded by the word "Some" indicate the item is available on a limited basis, potentially within only one unit.

MURPHY — NAGS HEAD, NC 441

Phone: 828/837-3060

Phone: 555/555-5555

Sheraton
Benefit:
ers get up to
ff, plus
od Preferred
bonuses.

business center. Cards: AX, DS, MC, VI.
d local telephone calls.
NITS FEE VCR FEE
Leisure
Business

Phone: 555/555-5555

Sheraton
nefit:
s get up to
plus
d Preferred
bonuses.

siness center. Cards: AX, DS, MC, VI.
local telephone calls.
TS FEE VCR FEE

Phone: 828/837-3400
nt-porch rocking chairs or back porch
t contribute to a diversity of entrees.
bison steak with sauteed mushrooms.
ations: suggested. Hours: 11 am-2 &
in winter. Closed: 12/25. Address: 925
, just n. Parking: on-site. Cards: AX,

Phone: 828/837-4444
oky-flavored barbecued meats are at
s and country decor. Casual dress.
ddress: 2121 US Hwy 64 W 28906
C, VI.

Phone: 828/837-4589
non, totally unexpected in this area.
r the live music. Casual dress. Bar:
d major holidays; also Sun & Mon.
Cards: AX, DS, MC, VI.

Nationwide Member Value

The blue box in the listing identifies hotel brands that offer an everyday member benefit at all AAA Approved locations. (See page 19 for additional program benefits.)

Spotting Symbol

Black ovals with white numbers are used to locate, or "spot," lodgings on maps we provide for larger cities.

Credit Cards Accepted

AX=American Express   **JC**=Japan Credit Bureau
CB=Carte Blanche   **MC**=MasterCard
DC=Diners Club   **VI**=VISA
DS=Discover

Icons

Lodging icons represent some of the member values, services and facilities offered.

Discounts

(ASK) May offer discount
S⃝D Offers minimum 10% senior discount to members over 59

Member Services

Airport transportation
Pets allowed (call property for restrictions and fees)
Restaurant on premises
Restaurant off premises (walking distance)
24-hour room service
Full bar
Child care
Accessible features (call property for available services and amenities)

Leisure Activities

Full-service casino
Pool
Health club on premises
Health club off premises
Recreational activities

In-Room Amenities

Designated non-smoking rooms
VCR
Movies
Refrigerator
Microwave
Coffee maker
No air conditioning
No TV
No cable TV
No telephones

Safety Features
(see page 24)
(Mexico and Caribbean only)

S Sprinklers
D Smoke detectors

The presence of the term **SOME UNITS** indicates that any amenity icon in that section is available on a limited basis, potentially in only one unit. The term **FEE** appearing to the left of an amenity icon indicates an extra charge applies.

Official Appointment

(AAA) or (CAA) indicates our Official Appointment (OA) restaurants. The OA program permits properties to display and advertise the AAA or CAA emblem. We highlight these properties in red to help you quickly identify them. The AAA or CAA Approved sign helps traveling members find restaurants that want member business.

Diamond Rating

The number of diamonds informs you of the overall complexity of food, presentation, service and ambience. Red indicates an Official Appointment restaurant. A detailed description of each diamond level appears on page 21.

Cuisine Type

The cuisine type helps you select a dining facility that caters to your individual taste. AAA currently recognizes more than 90 different cuisine types.

Prices

Rates shown represent the minimum and maximum entree cost per person. Exceptions may include one-of-a-kind or special market priced items. Rates are rounded to the nearest dollar and do not include taxes. U.S., Mexican and Caribbean rates are in U.S. dollars; rates for Canadian restaurants are in Canadian dollars.

Icons

Icons provide additional information about services and facilities.

[AC] No air-conditioning

[&M] Accessible features offered

(call property for available services and amenities)

[N] Designated smoking section available

Menus

This notation indicates AAA/CAA members can conveniently view the restaurant's menu in a secure online environment at AAA.com.

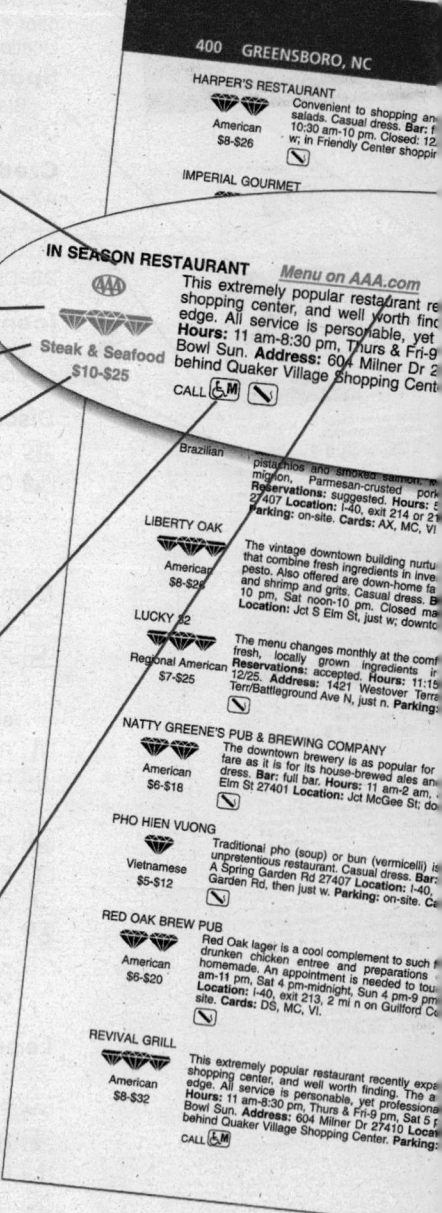

Spotting Symbol

White ovals with black numbers serve as restaurant locators and are used to locate, or "spot," restaurants on maps we provide for larger cities.

Classifications

If applicable, a restaurant may be defined as:

Classic - renowned and/or landmark restaurant in business longer than 25 years, known for unique style and ambience.

Historic - properties must meet one of the following criteria:

- Listed on the U.S. National Register of Historic Places
- Designated a U.S. National Historic Landmark
- Located in a U.S. National Register Historic District

Separate criteria designate historic properties in Canada, Mexico and the Caribbean.

Credit Cards Accepted

AX = American Express
CB = Carte Blanche
DC = Diners Club
DS = Discover
JC = Japan Credit Bureau
MC = MasterCard
VI = VISA

...ay, the casual eatery prepares tasty steak, seafood, chicken and ...ervations: accepted. **Hours:** 11:15 am-10 pm, Fri & Sat-11 pm, Sun ...s: 601 Friendly Center Rd 27408 **Location:** Jct Wendover Ave, just ...arking: on-site. **Cards:** AX, DC, DS, MC, VI.

336/547-8868

...xpanded to this newly constructed building, located behind a **Phone: 555/555-5555** ㊸ ...e atmosphere is informal, yet the menu offerings are cutting ...onal. Dressy casual. **Bar:** full bar. **Reservations:** accepted. ...: 5 pm-9 pm. Closed: 12/25; also Sun, Mon & for dinner Super ...**cation:** I-40, exit 213, 2 mi n, then just e on Hunt Club Rd; ...**ing:** on-site. **Cards:** AX, DC, DS, MC, VI. **Classic**

...ong include leg of lamb, flank steak, bacon-wrapped filet ...nd many more. Dressy casual. **Bar:** full bar. ...om. Closed: 12/25; also Sun. **Address:** 4512 W Market St ...e on Wendover Ave, exit Holden Rd, just n, then 0.8 mi w.

...ally upscale dining atmosphere. The menu features dishes **Phone: 336/273-7057** ...such as in stuffed rainbow trout and lamb with honey-mint ...ared with flair, including roasted pulled pork, fried chicken ...**Reservations:** accepted. **Hours:** 11:30 am-9:30 pm, Fri- ...s; also Sun. **Address:** 100-D W Washington St 27401 ...**g:** street. **Cards:** AX, DS, MC, VI.

...scale eatery, with the focus of the cuisine on incorporating **Phone: 336/370-0707** ...al American fare. Casual dress. **Bar:** full bar. ..., Fri & Sat-11 pm, Sun 10 am-10 pm. Closed: 11/27, ...**Location:** Wendover Ave, exit US 220 N/Westover ...ards: AX, DS, MC, VI.

...menu of burgers, wraps, sandwiches and hearty pub **Phone: 336/274-1373** ...tdoor seating is offered during warm weather. Casual ...ht. Closed: 1/1, 11/27, 12/24, 12/25. **Address:** 345 S ...arking: street. **Cards:** AX, DS, MC, VI.

...tiest and is served with a smile in the comfortable, **Phone: 336/294-5551** ...ne. **Hours:** 11 am-3:30 & 5-9:30 pm. **Address:** 4109- ...eastbound: exit 214 westbound, 1 mi ne, exit Spring ...DS, MC, VI.

...s fish and chips, gourmet sandwiches, the signature **Phone: 336/299-3649** ...Angus beef. Sauces, dressings and soups are ...e brewery. Casual dress. **Bar:** full bar. **Hours:** 11 ...11/27, 12/25. **Address:** 714 Francis King St 27410 ...just w on Hunt Club Rd, then just n. **Parking:** on-

...his newly constructed building, located behind a **Phone: 336/297-0950** ...is informal, yet the menu offerings are cutting ...casual. **Bar:** full bar. **Reservations:** accepted. ...Closed: 12/25; also Sun, Mon & for dinner Super ...exit 213, 2 mi n, then just e on Hunt Club Rd; ...ards: AX, DC, DS, MC, VI.

Lodging Rates Guaranteed

AAA/CAA members are guaranteed they will not be charged more than the maximum regular rate printed in the TourBook guide in each rate range for a standard room. Rates may vary within the range, depending on season and room type. Listed rates are usually based on last standard room availability. Obtain current AAA/CAA member rates and make reservations at AAA.com.

Discounts

Member discounts, when offered, will apply to rates quoted within the rate range and are applicable at the time of booking. Special rates used in advertising, as well as special short-term promotional rates lower than the lowest listed rate in the range, are not subject to additional member discounts.

Exceptions

Rates for properties operating as concessionaires for the U.S. National Park Service are not guaranteed due to governing regulations. Rates in the Mexico TourBook are not guaranteed and may fluctuate based on the exchange rate of the peso.

Lodgings may temporarily increase room rates, not recognize discounts or modify pricing policies during special events. Examples of special events range from Mardi Gras and the Kentucky Derby (including pre-Derby events) to college football games, holidays, holiday periods and state fairs. Although some special events are listed in AAA/CAA TourBook guides and on AAA.com, it is always wise to check in advance with AAA travel professionals for specific dates.

Get the Room You Reserved

When making your reservation, identify yourself as a AAA or CAA member and request written confirmation to guarantee: type of room, rate, dates of stay, and cancellation and refund policies. At registration, show your membership card.

When you find your room is not as specified, and you have written confirmation of reservations for a certain type of accommodation, you should be given the option of choosing a different room or finding one elsewhere. Should you choose to go elsewhere and a refund is refused or resisted, submit the matter to AAA/CAA within 30 days, along with complete documentation, including your reasons for refusing the room and copies of your written confirmation and any receipts or canceled checks associated with this problem.

If you are charged more than the maximum rate listed in the TourBook guide for a standard

room, question the additional charge. If management refuses to adhere to the published rate, pay for the room and submit your receipt and membership number to AAA/CAA within 30 days. Include all pertinent information: dates of stay, rate paid, itemized paid receipts, number of persons in your party and the room number you occupied, and list any extra room equipment used. A refund of the amount paid in excess of the stated maximum will be made if our investigation indicates that unjustified charging occurred.

Deposit, Refund and Cancellation Policies

Most establishments give full deposit refunds if they have been notified at least 48 hours before the normal check-in time. Listing prose will note if more than 48 hours' notice is required for cancellation. Some properties may charge a cancellation or handling fee. When this applies, "cancellation fee imposed" will appear in the listing. If you cancel too late, you have little recourse if a refund is denied.

When an establishment requires full or partial payment in advance and your trip is cut short, a refund may not be given.

When canceling a reservation, phone the lodging immediately. Make a note of the date and time you called, the cancellation number if there is one, and the name of the person who handled the cancellation. If your AAA/CAA club made your reservation, allow them to make the cancellation for you as well, so you will have proof of cancellation.

Check-in and Check-out Times

Check-in and check-out times are shown in the lodging listings, under Terms, only if they are before 10 a.m. or after 3 p.m. respectively.

Members Save With Our Partners

Show Your Card & Save

These National Show Your Card & Save® partners provide the listed member benefits. Admission tickets that offer greater discounts may be available for purchase at the local AAA/CAA club. A maximum of six tickets is available at the discount price at the gate. Visit AAA.com/Save to discover all the great Show Your Card & Save® discounts in your area.

SeaWorld, Busch Gardens, Sesame Place
AAA.com/SeaWorld, AAA.com/BuschGardens, AAA.com/SesamePlace

- Save on admission at the gate, at participating offices, or online
- Save 10% on up-close dining; visit Guest Relations for details

Six Flags
AAA.com/SixFlags

- Save on admission at the gate, at participating offices, or online
- Save 10% on merchandise purchases of $15 or more at in-park stores
- Save 10% on Brunch with Bugs online

Universal Orlando and Universal Studios Hollywood
AAA.com/Universal

- Save on admission at the gate, at participating offices, or online
- Save 10% on select merchandise and dining in-park and at CityWalk Orlando

Gray Line   AAA.com/GrayLine

- Save 10% on sightseeing tours of 1 day or less

Restaurant Partner Savings applies to AAA/CAA members and up to five guests.

Joe's Crab Shack

- Save 10% on food, non-alcoholic beverages and merchandise

Landry's Seafood House, The Crab House, Chart House, Muer Seafood Restaurants, and Aquarium and Downtown Aquarium Restaurants

- Save 10% on food and non-alcoholic beverages at all of the above restaurants
- Save 10% on merchandise at Aquarium and Downtown Aquarium restaurants.

Hard Rock Cafe

- Save 10% on food, non-alcoholic beverages and merchandise at all U.S. and select Canadian and international locations

Tanger Outlet Centers   www.tangeroutlet.com

- Save up to 20% on total purchase at select merchants with AAA/CAA coupon booklet
- Member BONUS: FREE $5 gift card for each additional Tanger Outlet Center visited after first within same calendar year
- Show membership card and register at the AAA customer service desk when you visit

Amtrak

- 10% discount on rail fare when booked at least 3 days in advance of travel date

Carey
AAA.com/Carey

- Save 15% on chauffeured ground transportation at over 450 locations worldwide

Grand Canyon Railway

- Save up to 20% on rail fare, hotel accommodations, restaurant and gift shop purchases

AAA Preferred Lodging Partners

EXPECT SAVINGS, SELECTION, AND SATISFACTION

- **Best AAA/CAA member rates for your dates of stay.** Provide valid membership number when placing reservation and show your card at hotel check-in.
- **Satisfaction guarantee.** Notify the property if you are dissatisfied with any part of your stay. If the matter cannot be resolved, you may be entitled to compensation (see page 17).
- **Seasonal promotions and special member offers.** Visit AAA.com to view current offers.
- **Everyday member benefit.*** Look for the blue boxes in the TourBook listings for everyday values offered at all AAA Approved locations.

Offer good at time of publication: Chains and offers may change without notice. Official Hotel Partner discounts may vary in Mexico and the Caribbean.

| Visit | Over 1,100 AAA Offices | Click | AAA.com | Call | 866-AAA-SAVE |

Understanding the Diamond Ratings

AAA/CAA Inspectors have evaluated and rated each of the 60,000 lodging and restaurant establishments in the TourBook series to ensure quality travel information for our members. All properties must meet AAA's minimum requirements (for lodgings) concerning cleanliness, comfort and security - or - AAA's minimum requirements (for restaurants) pertaining to cleanliness, food preparation and service.

Eligible applicants receive an unannounced evaluation by a AAA/CAA Inspector that includes two distinct components:

- **AAA Approval:** The Inspector first must determine whether the property meets the criteria required to be AAA Approved. Every establishment that meets these strict guidelines offers AAA members the assurance that, regardless of the diamond rating, it provides acceptable quality, cleanliness, service and value.
- **AAA Diamond Rating:** Once an establishment becomes AAA Approved, it is then assigned a rating of one to five diamonds, indicating the extensiveness of its facilities, amenities and services, from basic to moderate to luxury. These diamond ratings guide members in selecting establishments appropriately matched to their needs and expectations.

LODGINGS

1 Diamond

One diamond lodgings typically appeal to the budget-minded traveler. They provide essential, no-frills accommodations and basic comfort and hospitality.

2 Diamond

Two diamond lodgings appeal to family travelers seeking affordable yet more than the basic accommodations. Facilities, decor and amenities are modestly enhanced.

3 Diamond

Three diamond lodgings offer a distinguished style. Properties are

multi-faceted, with marked upgrades in physical attributes, amenities and guest comforts.

4 Diamond

Four diamond lodgings are refined and stylish. Physical attributes are upscale. The fundamental hallmarks at this level include an extensive array of amenities combined with a high degree of hospitality, service and attention to detail.

5 Diamond

Five diamond lodgings provide the ultimate in luxury and sophistication. Physical attributes are extraordinary in every manner. Service is meticulous, exceeding guest expectations and maintaining impeccable standards of excellence. Extensive personalized services and amenities provide first-class comfort.

fyi The lodging listings with **fyi** in place of diamonds are included as an *information only* service for members. The icon indicates that a property has not been rated for one or more of the following reasons: too new to rate, under construction, under major renovation, not evaluated, may not meet all AAA requirements.

A property not meeting all AAA requirements is included for either its member value or because it may be the only accommodation available in the area. Listing prose will give insight as to why the **fyi** designation was assigned.

4 Diamond

Four diamond restaurants provide a distinctive fine-dining experience that is typically expensive. Surroundings are highly refined with upscale enhancements throughout. Highly creative chefs use imaginative presentations to augment fresh, top-quality ingredients. A proficient service staff meets or exceeds guest expectations. A wine steward may offer menu-specific knowledge to guide selection.

5 Diamond

Five diamond restaurants are luxurious and renowned for consistently providing a world-class experience. Highly acclaimed chefs offer artistic menu selections that are imaginative and unique, using only the finest ingredients available. A maitre d' leads an expert service staff in exceeding guest expectations, attending to every detail in an effortless and unobtrusive manner.

RESTAURANTS

1 Diamond

One diamond restaurants provide simple, familiar specialty food (such as burgers, chicken, pizza or tacos) at an economical price. Often self-service, basic surroundings complement a no-nonsense approach.

2 Diamond

Two diamond restaurants offer a familiar, family-oriented experience. Menu selection includes home-style foods and family favorites, often cooked to order, modestly enhanced and reasonably priced. Service is accommodating yet relaxed, a perfect complement to casual surroundings.

fyi The restaurants with fyi in place of diamonds are included as an *information only* service for members. These listings provide additional dining choices but have not yet been evaluated.

3 Diamond

Three diamond restaurants convey an entry into fine dining and are often positioned as adult-oriented experiences. The atypical menu may feature the latest cooking trends and/or traditional cuisine. Expanded beverage offerings complement the menu. The ambience is well coordinated, comfortable and enhanced by a professional service staff.

Understanding the Lodging Classifications

To ensure that your lodging needs and preferences are met, we recommend that you consider an establishment's classification when making your travel choices. While the quality and comfort at properties with the same diamond rating should be consistent (regardless of the classification), there are differences in typical decor/theme elements, range of facilities and service levels.

Large-scale Hotel

Hotel Royal Plaza, Lake Buena Vista, FL

A multistory establishment with interior room entrances. A variety of guest unit styles is offered. Public areas are spacious and include a variety of facilities such as a restaurant, fitness center, spa, business center, shops or meeting rooms.

Small-scale Hotel

Baymont Inn, Dallas Ft. Worth-Airport N, TX

A multistory establishment typically with interior room entrances. A variety of guest unit styles is offered. Public areas are limited in size and/or the variety of facilities available.

Motel

Best Western Deltona Inn, Deltona, FL

A 1- to 3-story establishment typically with exterior room entrances facilitating convenient access to parking. The standard guest units have one bedroom with a bathroom and are typically similar in decor and design throughout. Public areas are limited in size and/or the variety of facilities available.

Country Inn

Greenville Inn, Greenville, ME

Similar in definition to a bed and breakfast but usually larger in scale, with spacious public areas offering a dining facility that serves at least breakfast and dinner.

Bed & Breakfast

1884 Paxton House Inn, Thomasville, GA

Small-scale properties emphasizing a high degree of personal touches that provide guests an "at home" feeling. Guest units tend to be individually decorated. Rooms may not include some modern amenities such as televisions and telephones, and may have a shared bathroom. Usually owner-operated with a common room or parlor separate from the innkeeper's living quarters, where guests and operators can interact during evening and breakfast hours. Evening office closures are normal. A Continental or full, hot breakfast is served and is included in the room rate.

Condominium

Sands of Kahana, Kahana, Maui, HI

Vacation-oriented or extended-stay, apartment-style accommodations that are routinely available for rent through a management company. Units vary in design and decor and often contain one or more bedrooms, a living room, full kitchen and an eating area. Studio-type models combine the sleeping and living areas into one room. Typically, basic cleaning supplies, kitchen utensils and complete bed and bath linens are supplied. The guest registration area may be located off-site.

Cabin/Cottage

Desert Rose Inn, Bluff, UT

Vacation-oriented, small-scale, freestanding houses or cabins. Units vary in design and decor and often contain one or more bedrooms, a living room, kitchen, dining area and bathroom. Studio-type models combine the sleeping and living areas into one room. Typically, basic cleaning supplies, kitchen utensils, and complete bed and bath linens are supplied. The guest registration area may be located off-site.

Ranch

Typically a working ranch with an obvious rustic, Western theme. In general, equestrian-related activities are featured, but ranches may

Lost Valley Ranch, Deckers, CO

include other animals and activities as well. A variety of guest unit styles is offered in a family-oriented atmosphere.

Vacation Home

Vacation-oriented or extended-stay, large-scale, freestanding houses that are routinely available for rent through a

ResortQuest, Hilton Head Island, SC

management company. Houses vary in design and decor and often contain two or more bedrooms, a living room, full kitchen, dining room and multiple bathrooms. Typically, basic cleaning supplies, kitchen utensils, and complete bed and bath linens are supplied. The guest registration area may be located off-site.

Lodging Subclassifications

The following are subclassifications that may appear along with the classifications listed previously to provide a more specific description of the lodging.

Casino

Extensive gaming facilities are available such as blackjack, craps, keno and slot machines. Note: This subclassification will not appear beneath its diamond rating in the listing. It will be indicated by a ⊛ icon and will be included in the row of icons immediately below the lodging listing.

Classic

Renowned and landmark properties, older than 50 years, well-known for their unique style and ambience.

Historic

These properties are typically over 75 years of age and exhibit many features of a historic nature with respect to architecture, design, furnishings, public record or acclaim. Properties must meet one of the following criteria:

- Maintained the integrity of the historical aspect
- Listed on the U.S. National Register of Historic Places
- Designated a U.S. National Historic Landmark
- Located in a U.S. National Register Historic District

Separate criteria designate historic properties in Canada, Mexico and the Caribbean.

Vacation Rental

Typically houses, condos, cottages or cabins; these properties are a "home away from home" offering more room and greater value for the money and generally provide the conveniences of home, such as full kitchens and washers/dryers. They are located in resort or popular destination areas within close proximity to major points of interest, attractions, or recreation areas. These properties may require a pre-arranged reservation and check-in at an off-site location. Housekeeping services may be limited or not included.

Resort

Recreation-oriented, geared to vacation travelers seeking a specific destination experience. Travel packages, meal plans, themed entertainment, and social and recreational programs are typically available. Recreational facilities are extensive and may include spa treatments, golf, tennis, skiing, fishing, water sports, etc. Larger resorts may offer a variety of guest accommodations.

Guest Safety

Room Security

In order to be approved for listing in AAA/CAA TourBook guides for the United States and Canada, accommodations must have dead bolt locks on all guest room entry doors and connecting room doors.

If the area outside the guest room door is not visible from inside the room through a window or door panel, viewports must be installed on all guest room entry doors. Bed and breakfast properties and country inns are not required to have viewports. Ground floor and easily accessible sliding doors must be equipped with some type of secondary security locks.

Even with those approval requirements, AAA cannot guarantee guest safety. AAA Inspectors view a percentage of rooms at each property since it is not feasible to evaluate every room in every lodging establishment. Therefore, AAA cannot guarantee that there are working locks on all doors and windows in all guest rooms.

Fire Safety

Because of the highly specialized skills needed to conduct professional fire safety inspections, AAA/CAA Inspectors cannot assess fire safety.

Properties must meet all federal, state/province and local fire codes. Each guest unit in all U.S. and Canadian lodging properties must be equipped with an operational, single-station smoke detector. A AAA/CAA Inspector has evaluated a sampling of the rooms to verify this equipment is in place.

Mexico and the Caribbean

Requirements for some features, such as door locks and smoke detectors/sprinkler systems, differ in Mexico and the Caribbean. If a property met AAA's security requirements at the time of the evaluation, the phrase "Meets AAA guest room security requirements" appears in the listing.

Service Animals

The Americans with Disabilities Act (ADA) prohibits U.S. businesses that serve the public from discriminating against persons with disabilities. Some businesses have mistakenly denied access to persons who use service animals. Businesses must permit entry to guests and their service animals, as well as allow service animals to accompany guests to all public areas of a property.

A property is permitted to ask whether the animal is a service animal or a pet, and whether the guest has a disability. The property may not, however, ask questions about the nature of the disability, the service provided by the animal, or require proof of a disability or certification that the animal is a service animal. These regulations may not apply in Canada, Mexico or the Caribbean.

No fees or deposits, even those normally charged for pets, may be charged for service animals. Service animals fulfill a critical need for their owners—they are not pets.

Frank Frand with his seeing eye dog, Cardinal.

Savings for all Seasons

Hertz rents Fords and other fine cars. ® REG. U.S PAT. OFF. © HERTZ SYSTEM INC., 1999/②406-99

No matter the season, Hertz offers AAA members exclusive discounts and benefits.

Operating in 150 countries at over 7,600 locations, Hertz makes traveling more convenient and efficient wherever and whenever you go. Hertz offers AAA members discounts up to 20% on car rentals worldwide.

To receive your exclusive AAA member discounts and benefits, mention your AAA membership card at time of reservation and present it at time of rental. **In addition**, to receive a free one car class upgrade on daily, weekly or weekend rental in the United States, Puerto Rico and Canada, mention PC# 969194 at the time of reservation. Offer is valid for vehicle pick-up on or before 12/15/08.

For reservations and program details, visit AAA.com/hertz, call your AAA Travel office or the Hertz/AAA Desk at **1-800-654-3080**.

With the AAA Visa TravelMoney® card, worry-free travel is here. Like travelers cheques, this card has replacement and refund options, emergency assistance service, zero liability, purchase security, and even luggage protection.

The next time you travel, don't forget to pack the AAA Visa TravelMoney® card.

Honey, I lost my wallet.

Without the AAA Visa TravelMoney® card, their money problems would be monumental.

* Terms and conditions apply, see detailed terms and conditions provided with your card fulfillment kit.

Visit your participating AAA office or AAA.com/travelmoney

Delaware

Fort Delaware
The pentagon-shaped building served as a prison during the Civil War

Hagley Museum
Mills along the Brandywine River recall the du Pont family's big boom

The Green
William Penn designed a patch of grass in Dover where history was later made

New Castle
Step back in time to explore restored vintage homes

Rehoboth Beach
Oceanside resorts await lovers of sun, sea and sand

Wilmington
© Andre Jenny

the first state

Winterthur Museum & Country Estate, Wilmington / © Andre Jenny / Alamy

Delaware is a mecca for history buffs. The first to ratify the Constitution, it boasts significant sites and too many restored buildings to count. From north to south reminders of the past are bound to cross your path.

Gingerbread does not go stale in Laurel; about 800 colorful Victorian houses appear much as they did in the 18th and 19th centuries.

Erected in 1638, the first log cabin sits proudly in Wilmington.

The granite, pentagon-shaped fortress of Fort Delaware looms on Pea Patch Island. Woodburn, the Dover governor's mansion since 1965, was reputed to have been a station on the Underground Railroad. And the Amish way of life is alive and well near Dover—the clop of

horses' hooves echoes along modern, blacktop roads.

Ghosts of noteworthy residents are omnipresent. Thomas McKean, a delegate to the Continental Congress of 1774, practiced law in New Castle. John Dickinson, the Penman of the American Revolution who wrote the Articles of Confederation and documents protesting British rule, lived in Dover. And the Robinson House in Wilmington served as a home for George Washington during the Revolutionary War.

The people of Delaware have meticulously preserved their past. Every footstep in Delaware is a tread back in time. So start stepping!

One way to acquaint yourself with Delaware is to rely on its oldest "residents." Restored houses and taverns, abandoned mills, groomed village greens and meticulous gardens sprinkle the state, silently declaring their chapter in history. Evidence of big events that helped shape the area turn up around every bend.

In New Castle, cobblestone roads dating from Colonial days serve as a path to the past. Dwellings that line the streets bear diverse architectural styles, mirroring the melting pot of cultures that has called the town home. The colors of Great Britain, the Netherlands, Sweden and the United States flap in the breeze over the Georgian-style courthouse; the flags represent four changes in ownership.

Great Britain gave New Castle to William Penn in 1682. Some things have changed little over time, such as the Federal-style white balustrade on the roof of the Read House, or the Victorian gardens, which appear much as they did at first planting in 1847.

If you pressed your nose against the glass of a keystone-topped window on New Castle's Amstel House in the 18th century, you may have caught a glimpse of George Washington; he attended a wedding here. Nearby, the brick Dutch House, with its steeply-pitched gambrel roof, is a memento left by the city's Dutch founders.

Turning the Wheels of Time

A water wheel on the banks of the tree-draped Brandywine River in Wilmington still turns on occasion, reminding passersby of the early importance of water power. The rushing river prompted E.I. du Pont to choose the site for his gunpowder manufacturing mill in 1802. A "form follows function" approach was taken during construction; the building consists of three stone walls and a fourth, facing the river, built of wood. In the event of an accident, the wooden wall would be blown toward the water, saving the structure and minimizing deaths.

Patches in the fourth wall grimly recall a day in March 1818 when 40 workers were not so lucky. A witness reported that the bang of the explosion "burst upon the ear like the report of a cannon," and "souls were hurled into an unknown eternity."

Henry Hudson claims the territory for the Dutch; he finds the area inhabited by Lenni Lenape Indians.

1609

© Bettmann/Corbis

Delaware falls under British rule.

1664

Inhabitants of the first European settlement are massacred by Indians.

1631

Delaware's Caesar Rodney casts the deciding vote for the Declaration of Independence.

1776

1638

Swedes establish New Sweden colony, the Delaware Valley's first permanent settlement, under leadership of Dutchman Peter Minuit.

Library of Congress

1682

William Penn arrives in New Castle and takes possession of Delaware.

Delaware Historical Timeline

Which George is it?

History oozes out of every blade of grass on The Green in Dover. The square is a spitting image of its original platting in 1722. During the Revolutionary War, the tract served as a meeting place for Delaware's Continental Regiment; they mustered here in 1775 and set out on a march to join Washington's army in the fight for independence. Blue hen chickens, noted for their pugnacious nature, waddled along to fight with the men.

One year later: The Declaration of Independence is read aloud to crowds gathered on The Green. Their enthusiasm shows in the shouts of "Freedom!" and the torching of King George III's portrait. Near The Green, a tavern now known as the Kent County Court House upheld the same independent spirit—locals maintain that it sported a sign showing the shoulders of the "Old George" and a face painted over with the likeness of the "New George."

And overlooking the square was the Golden Fleece Tavern, where, on a chilly December day in 1787, delegates to Delaware's Constitutional Congress took a deep breath and voted to ratify the Constitution, making Delaware the first state to do so. A bronze plaque commemorates the site.

Going Dutch

Coined the "first town in the first state," the harbor port of Lewes was settled by the Dutch in 1631. To commemorate its 300th anniversary, residents erected the Zwaanedael building; the elaborate stonework and ornamental gable are copies of similar features adorning a town hall in Holland.

Among brightly painted Victorian homes in Lewes stands one near-casualty of war, the cedar-shingled Cannonball House. Why the name? You guessed it—during a British bombardment in the War of 1812, a cannonball was fired at the house and lodged into the wall, becoming a permanent part of the structure. Fortunately, the naval attack resulted only in the death of a chicken and the wounding of a pig.

Through careful preservation of original architecture and landscaping, Delaware history and culture remain vital. The physical appearance of many sites, coupled with the tradition they embrace, makes for a fascinating story. And what a tale—how the First State sparked the development of a nation.

John Dickinson, Penman of the American Revolution, drafts the Articles of Confederation.
1777

Library of Congress

Salvagers retrieve the hull of the sunken HMS *DeBraak* off the coast of Lewes.
1986

Delaware becomes the first state to ratify the U.S. Constitution.
1787

1838
A railroad connecting Philadelphia and Baltimore is completed, encouraging industrial development of northern Delaware.

Office of Governor Minner

2001
Ruth Ann Minner takes office as Delaware's first female governor.

Recreation

When you're looking for recreation in Delaware, two words suffice: the beach. About 25 miles of coastline nevertheless add up to excitement.

Hang ten! Step into a wet suit and shoot the curl at the designated **surfing** zone just north of Indian River Inlet, home of the state surfing championships. The frothy waters off Rehoboth and Dewey beaches attract surfers as well.

Colorful **windsurfing** sails dot the shallow bays at Delaware Seashore State Park in Rehoboth Beach. Salty breezes cater to **sailing,** and **boaters** can explore numerous coves. Delaware Bay is another great place where first mates can cast off. **Swimmers,** boaters and even beavers feel right at home at Lums Pond State Park in Bear.

Picture yourself casually paddling amid wildflowers, lily pads and stands of bald cypress trees. It isn't paradise, just the designated wilderness **canoe** trail at Trap Pond State Park. If a wilder ride is more your style, look into **tubing** down Brandywine Creek in Wilmington.

Go Fish

The lure of the rod and reel is difficult to resist in Delaware. **Fishing** in Killens Pond State Park hooks bluegill, catfish, carp, crappie, largemouth bass, perch and pickerel. Brandywine Creek and Trap Pond state parks also attract fishing enthusiasts. Two piers make for pleasant casting at Lums Pond, where **ice fishing** is an option in winter. Those 16 years of age and older must have a license to fish freshwater ponds and non-tidal streams.

Bethany Beach, Cape Henlopen State Park, Delaware Seashore State Park and Fenwick Island are all hot spots for **surf fishing.** A permit is required to drive onto the beach; check with the park offices for more information.

Anglers frequent the banks of the Indian River Inlet and Bay, where **deep-sea fishing** charters can be arranged; catches of the day include drum, flounder, rockfish and weakfish. Fisherman's Wharf in Lewes is a starting point for excursions in search of marlin and tuna; phone (302) 645-8862.

Hikers traipse along shaded former logging paths leading to rocky outcrops at White Clay Creek State Park. The Twin Valley Trail climbs to Arc Corner Monument, where you can stand with one foot in Delaware and the other in Pennsylvania; Possum Hill hikers cross the Mason-Dixon Line on their route.

A wildlife observation tower is the terminus of a hiking trail at Fort Delaware State Park. Swamp Forest Trail at Lums Pond State Park circles the sylvan lake. While you stroll, try and catch a glimpse of those beavers!

Take your bike to Bellevue State Park in Wilmington, where you can pedal along roughly 3 miles of paved **biking** trails.

For the Birds

Make some new winged acquaintances while **birdwatching.** Grab your binoculars and climb to the top of the refurbished World War II observation tower at Cape Henlopen State Park in Rehoboth Beach for a bird's-eye view. At Gordon's Pond, toward the south end of the park, bird lovers can see osprey, as well as the endangered piping plover and American bald eagle. The dunes at Fenwick Island State Park also are home to several species of endangered seabirds, including the least tern and black skimmer.

Follow the trails on Burton's Island in Delaware Seashore State Park for a peek at noisy gulls and terns nesting in the salt marshes. Also be sure to check out the Bombay Hook National Wildlife Refuge in Smyrna; it's a habitat for migrating and wintering ducks and northbound migrating geese. The marshes of Fort Delaware State Park provide a summer home for nine species of egrets, herons and ibis.

Feeling Crabby?

Crabbing and **clamming** have long been associated with Delaware beaches, and there's a delicious reason why. The Indian River and Little Assawoman and Rehoboth bays are good places to start digging; you'll have the best luck from April to early fall. **Shellfishing** is popular from May through November.

Recreational Activities

Throughout the TourBook, you may notice a Recreational Activities heading with bulleted listings of recreation-oriented establishments listed underneath. Similar operations also may be mentioned in Destination City recreation sections. Since normal AAA inspection criteria cannot be applied, these establishments are presented only for information. Age, height and weight restrictions may apply. Reservations often are recommended and sometimes are required. Addresses and/or phone numbers are provided so visitors can contact the attraction for additional information.

Fast Facts

POPULATION: 783,600.

AREA: 2,057 square miles; ranks 49th.

CAPITAL: Dover.

HIGHEST POINT: 448 ft., near Ebright Road, Brandywine.

LOWEST POINT: Sea level, Atlantic Ocean.

TIME ZONE(S): Eastern. DST.

MINIMUM AGE FOR UNRESTRICTED DRIVER'S LICENSE: 17.

MINIMUM AGE FOR GAMBLING: 21.

SEAT BELT/CHILD RESTRAINT LAWS: Seat belts required for driver and all passengers 16 and older. Children ages 8 until 16 or over 65 pounds are required to be in a child restraint or seat belt; child restraints are required for under age 8 and less than 65 pounds.

HELMETS FOR MOTORCYCLISTS: Required for riders under 19.

RADAR DETECTORS: Permitted.

FIREARMS LAWS: Contact the Delaware State Police, Ordnance Section, 391 Clark Farm Rd. Smyrna, DE 19977; phone (302) 659-6020.

HOLIDAYS: Jan. 1; Martin Luther King Jr. Day, Jan. (3rd Mon.); Presidents Day, Feb. (3rd Mon.); Good Friday; Memorial Day, May (last Mon.); July 4; Labor Day, Sept. (1st Mon.); Columbus Day, Oct. (2nd Mon.); Veterans Day, Nov. 11; Election Day; Thanksgiving, Nov. (4th Thurs.); Christmas, Dec. 25.

TAXES: Delaware does not have a statewide sales tax, but there is an 8 percent hotel occupancy tax (10 percent in the city of Wilmington).

INFORMATION CENTERS: State welcome centers that provide details about state attractions, accommodations, historic sites, parks and events are on I-95 between exit 1 and exit 3 on the edge of Newark, phone (302) 737-4059; and at the junction of US 13 and SR 1 north of Smyrna, phone (302) 653-8910. The I-95 center is open daily 8-8; closed Dec. 25. The US 13 center is open Mon.-Fri. 7-5, Fri.-Sun. 7-7, Memorial Day-Labor Day; daily 7-5, rest of year.

FURTHER INFORMATION FOR VISITORS:

Delaware Tourism Office
99 Kings Hwy.
Dover, DE 19901
(866) 284-7483

RECREATION INFORMATION:

Delaware Division of Parks and Recreation
89 Kings Hwy.
Dover, DE 19901
(302) 739-9220 *(See color ad p. 36)*

FISHING AND HUNTING REGULATIONS:

Delaware Division of Fish and Wildlife
89 Kings Hwy.
Dover, DE 19901
(302) 739-9910

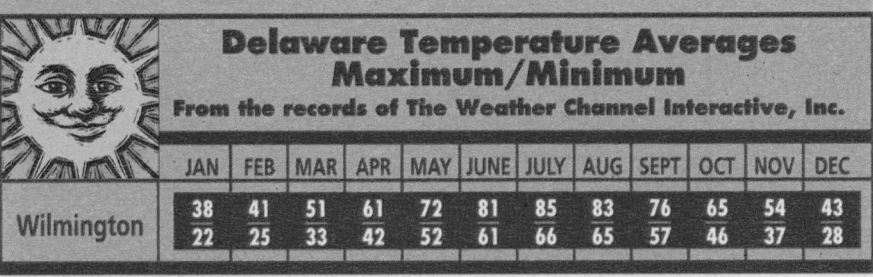

	JAN	FEB	MAR	APR	MAY	JUNE	JULY	AUG	SEPT	OCT	NOV	DEC
Wilmington	38 / 22	41 / 25	51 / 33	61 / 42	72 / 52	81 / 61	85 / 66	83 / 65	76 / 57	65 / 46	54 / 37	43 / 28

Delaware Temperature Averages Maximum/Minimum
From the records of The Weather Channel Interactive, Inc.

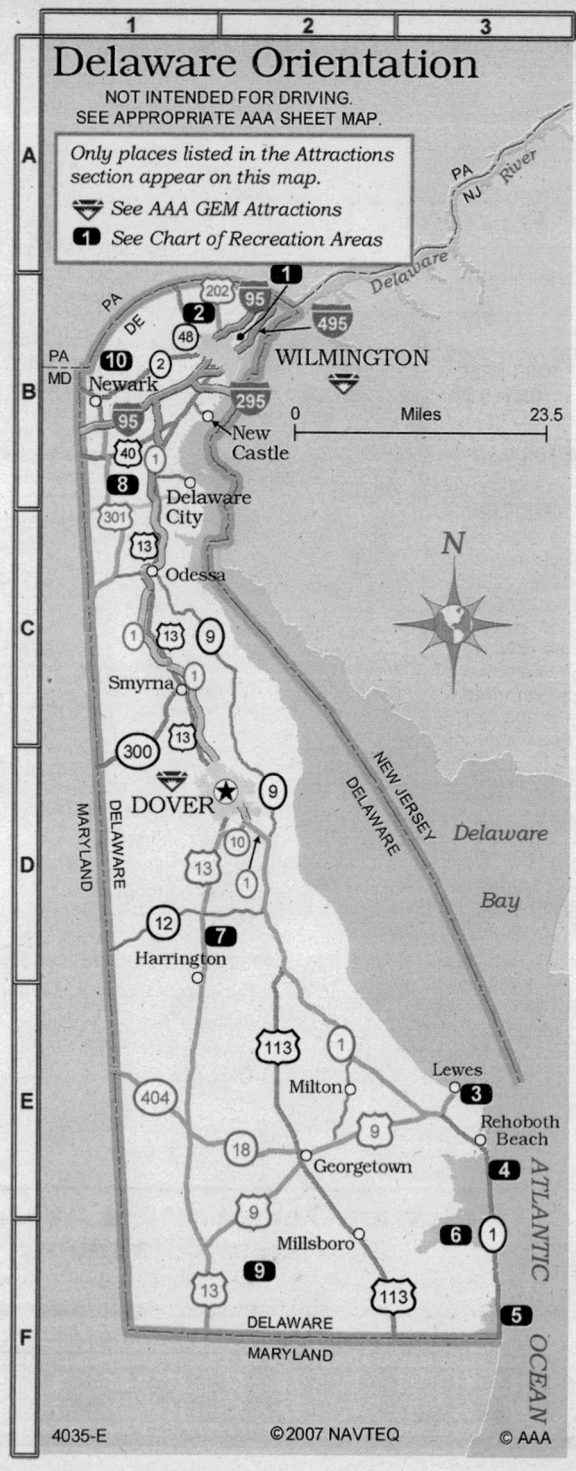

Delaware Orientation

NOT INTENDED FOR DRIVING.
SEE APPROPRIATE AAA SHEET MAP.

Only places listed in the Attractions
section appear on this map.

See AAA GEM Attractions

See Chart of Recreation Areas

WILMINGTON

Newark

New
Castle

Delaware
City

Odessa

Smyrna

DOVER

Harrington

Milton

Lewes

Rehoboth
Beach

Georgetown

Millsboro

Delaware Bay

MARYLAND

DELAWARE

NEW JERSEY

DELAWARE

ATLANTIC OCEAN

Miles
0   23.5

N

PA
NJ

Delaware River

MARYLAND
DELAWARE

4035-E   ©2007 NAVTEQ   © AAA

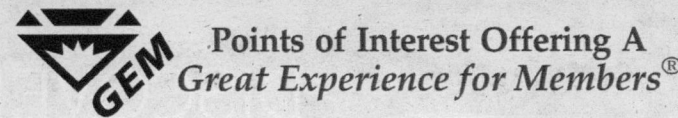

Points of Interest Offering A
Great Experience for Members®

Dover (D-1)

BIGGS MUSEUM OF AMERICAN ART—On display is Sewell C. Biggs' personal art and antiques collection, which spans 200 years and surveys major periods in American art. See p. 38.

Wilmington (B-2)

HAGLEY MUSEUM—On the site of the original du Pont gunpowder mills and estate, the museum and restored mills show the development of water power on the Brandywine River. See p. 45.

NEMOURS MANSION AND GARDENS—Built in 1909, this Louis XVI chateau contains European antiques, Oriental rugs, tapestries and 15th-century paintings. See p. 46.

WINTERTHUR MUSEUM & COUNTRY ESTATE—Galleries explore the history and development of American decorative arts, focusing on social customs, techniques, symbolism and style. See p. 46.

RECREATION AREAS

	MAP LOCATION	CAMPING	PICNICKING	HIKING TRAILS	BOATING	BOAT RAMP	BOAT RENTAL	FISHING	SWIMMING	PETS ON LEASH	BICYCLE TRAILS	WINTER SPORTS	VISITOR CENTER	LODGE/CABINS	FOOD SERVICE
STATE															
Bellevue (B-2) 329 acres 4 mi. n.e. of Wilmington off I-95. Historic. Game courts, horse trails.	1		•	•				•			•	•	•		
Brandywine Creek (B-1) 1,010 acres 9 mi. n.w. of Wilmington at jct. SRs 92 and 100 and Adams Dam Rd. Horse trails.	2		•	•				•			•	•	•	•	
Cape Henlopen (E-3) 6,000 acres 1 mi. e. of Lewes on SR 9. Historic. Nature trails. *(See Rehoboth Beach p. 43)*	3	•	•	•				•	•	•	•	•	•		
Delaware Seashore (E-3) 2,799 acres 5 mi. from Dewey Beach to Indian River Inlet off SR 1. Sailing, windsurfing. *(See Rehoboth Beach p. 43)*	4	•	•	•	•	•		•	•	•			•		
Fenwick Island (F-3) 442 acres extending from South Bethany Beach to Fenwick Island off SR 1.	5		•		•		•	•	•	•	•				
Holts Landing (F-3) 203 acres 9 mi. n.e. of Dagsboro off SR 26 on the s. shore of the Indian River. Horse trails, pier, playground.	6		•	•	•	•		•		•					
Killens Pond (D-2) 1,098 acres 12 mi. s. of Dover off US 13. Historic. Canoeing; nature trails.	7	•	•	•	•	•	•	•	•	•	•			•	
Lums Pond (B-1) 2,091 acres 10 mi. s. of Newark off SR 71. Historic. Game courts, nature trails.	8	•	•	•	•	•	•	•		•	•	•	•		
Trap Pond (F-2) 2,689 acres 6 mi. s.e. of Laurel off SR 24. Horse trails, nature trails.	9	•	•	•	•	•	•	•		•	•		•	•	•
White Clay Creek (B-1) 3,214 acres 3 mi. n. of Newark via SR 896. Historic. Horse trails.	10		•	•				•		•	•		•		

Points of Interest

DELAWARE CITY (B-1) pop. 1,453, elev. 4'

A river wharf occupied the site of Delaware City for the quarter century following 1800. In 1814 the Department of the Navy allowed the construction of a battery and fortifications on the Delaware River at what was then called Newbold's Point. Around 1825 streets were laid out at the junction of the Delaware River and the Chesapeake and Delaware Canal, which was being dug across the peninsula.

By the time the canal opened in 1829, however, railroads were handling most of the freight the canal had been built to ship. Delaware City's wide streets and grand name thus became reminders of a boom that never came.

The fortifications are gone from Newbold's Point, but Battery Park remains, offering a view of the river, Pea Patch Island and the New Jersey shoreline from the foot of Clinton Street. In the park is a restored Chesapeake and Delaware Canal lock built in 1829.

FORT DELAWARE STATE PARK is on Pea Patch Island. The park is accessible only by a ferry that departs from the dock at the foot of Clinton St. The 288-acre park features an 1859 fort, a museum displaying Civil War memorabilia, nature trails and an observation tower that provides views of nesting spots for egrets, herons and other wading birds.

Private boats are not permitted in the park. Picnicking is permitted. Allow 4 hours minimum. Wed.-Sun. and holidays 10-6, mid-June through Labor Day; Sat.-Sun. and holidays 10-6, last weekend in Apr. to mid-June and weekend after Labor Day-last weekend in Sept. Ferries to the park depart on the hour beginning at 10; the last ferry returns at 5:30. Admission (includes ferry fare) $10; $6 (ages 2-12). DS, MC, VI. Phone (302) 834-7941.

DOVER (D-1) pop. 32,135, elev. 37'

Although one early missionary feared the prevalent "bugs and mascatoes," Dover was established in 1683 as the seat of Kent County and adopted as the state capital in 1777 after British forces invaded New Castle, forcing statesmen to flee south. Delaware's deciding vote for independence from British rule had been cast in Philadelphia a year earlier by Continental Congress delegate Caesar Rodney, whose historic 80-mile ride from Dover brought him to Independence Hall just minutes before the debate closed.

The city grew quickly in the early 18th century, with stately houses built around an attractive green designed by William Penn. It was at the Golden Fleece Tavern on The Green that Delawareans voted in 1787 to ratify the Constitution, making Delaware the first of the 13 states to do so.

Dover residents were divided about the slavery issue, but many prominent families helped runaway slaves escape to the North by means of the Underground Railroad. One such station may have been Woodburn, now the governor's residence, on King's Highway south of Division Street.

Dover claims as its favorite daughter astronomer Annie Jump Cannon, who developed a prismatic technique of telescopic photography that enabled her to classify more than 400,000 stars. Her work at the Harvard Observatory during the first half of the 20th century contributed greatly to the Henry Draper Catalog, which is still used by astronomers.

Although Legislative Hall has been in use only since 1933, its 18th-century style handmade brick exterior and interior woodwork give it the same appearance as much of historic Dover. Visitors may view the governor's reception area and portraits of Delaware's governors and World War II heroes. The building is on Legislative Avenue between Duke of York and William Penn streets. Guided tours

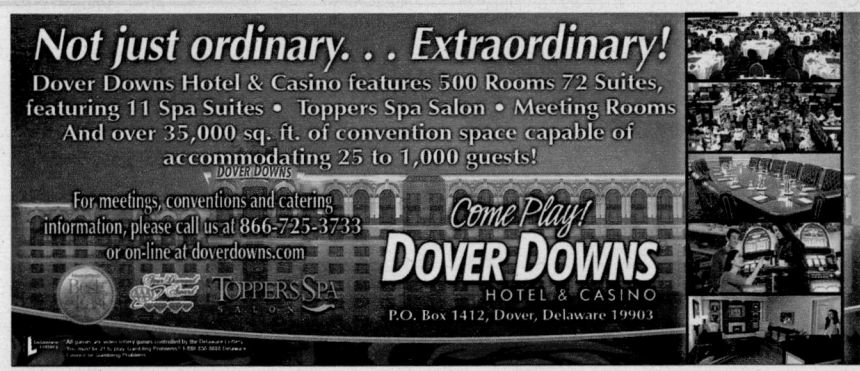

through the chambers of the 1910 Delaware Supreme Court Building at 55 The Green are available on request; phone (302) 255-0093.

Fine 18th- and 19th-century houses remain concentrated around The Green and north and south State Street. Many examples of Victorian architecture line S. State and S. Bradford streets, and 19th-century commercial structures still stand along Lockerman Street.

The Old Dover Historic District includes Christ Church, The Green, the Richardson and Robbins Complex, Wesley College and Woodburn, birthplace of Annie Jump Cannon.

Live harness racing takes place at Dover Downs on US 13 November through April; phone (302) 674-4600 or (800) 711-5882.

Note: Policies vary concerning admittance of children to pari-mutuel betting facilities. Phone for information.

Dover International Speedway at Dover Downs hosts two weekends of NASCAR racing in June and September; phone (302) 674-4600.

Central Delaware Chamber of Commerce: 435 N. DuPont Hwy. (US 13), Dover, DE 19901; phone (302) 678-0892.

Self-guiding tours: Brochures outlining tours to many of the city's most interesting buildings and attractions are available at the Delaware State Museums Visitor Center, 406 Federal St.; phone (302) 739-4266.

AIR MOBILITY COMMAND MUSEUM is off SR 1/US 113 exit 93, 1.5 mi. s., then .7 mi e. on SR 9, following signs. Vintage airplanes and military aviation artifacts are displayed in a restored World War II hangar on Dover Air Force Base. Specimens include a B-17G (Flying Fortress), a C-47 airlift aircraft, and C-124A and C-133B transports as well as jet fighters and trainers. Also available is an interactive F-106 fight simulator, the Hall of Heroes, a C-17 cockpit mock-up and exhibits of World War II airplane nose art. Allow 1 hour, 30 minutes minimum. Tues.-Sun. 9-4. Free. Phone (302) 677-5938.

BIGGS MUSEUM OF AMERICAN ART is w. on Court St., then n. to jct. of Duke of York and Federal sts. The museum contains Sewell C. Biggs' personal art and antiques collection, which was in the making for more than half a century. It is in the 1858 former Kent County Levy Court House, one of the state's first fireproof buildings.

Works spanning 200 years survey major periods in American art. Exhibits feature the paintings of regional artists and celebrated masters: Albert Bierstadt, William Merritt Chase, Childe Hassam, George Inness, Charles Willson Peale, Frank Schoonover and Gilbert Stuart. The collection also includes pastels, drawings, modern art and sculpture.

Biggs' assemblage of fine furniture and silver represents the work of some of the best Delaware

and Philadelphia craftsmen of the Colonial and Federal periods. Guided tours are available. Allow 1 hour minimum. Wed.-Fri. 10-4, Sat. and holidays 9-5, Sun. 1:30-4:30; closed Easter and Dec. 25. Free. Phone (302) 674-2111.

[SAVE] **DELAWARE AGRICULTURAL MUSEUM AND VILLAGE,** 2 mi. n. to 866 N. DuPont Hwy. (US 13) at jct. US 13 Alt., illustrates agricultural heritage and rural life. The exhibition hall houses tractors, horse-drawn equipment and farming implements dating from 1670 through the 1950s. Buildings dating from the Civil War era to about 1900 include a one-room schoolhouse, sawmill, barbershop, train station, farmhouse, general store, country church and blacksmith and wheelwright shops.

Allow 1 hour, 30 minutes minimum. Tues.-Sat. 10-4, Sun. 1-4, Apr.-Dec.; Tues.-Sat. 10-4, rest of year. Closed holidays. Admission $5; $3 (ages 6-17 and 60+). DS, MC, VI. Phone (302) 734-1618.

DELAWARE ARCHAEOLOGY MUSEUM AND MUSEUM OF SMALL TOWN LIFE, 316 S. Governor's Ave., occupies an 18th-century former Presbyterian church and chapel. The Delaware Archaeology Museum displays artifacts dating from North America's most recent ice age to the present, with emphasis on Delaware's American Indian history. The Museum of Small Town Life depicts village commerce through five re-created 19th-century shops. Exhibits chronicling the history of the phonograph are in the Johnson Victrola Museum. Allow 30 minutes minimum. Tues.-Fri. 10-3:30, Sat. and some state holidays 9-5; closed Jan. 1, Easter, Thanksgiving and Dec. 25. Free. Phone (302) 739-4266.

DELAWARE'S STATE HOUSE is on the e. side of The Green at S. State St. The restored 1792 building contains period furnishings, building artifacts and historical photographs and documents. Programs about state history and the Underground Railroad are offered. Guided tours start at the Delaware State Museums Visitor Center behind the statehouse. Allow 30 minutes minimum. Guided 30-minute tours leave Tues.-Fri. 10-4:30, Sat. and some state holidays 9-5, Sun. 1:30-4:30; closed Jan. 1, Easter, Thanksgiving and Dec. 25. Free. Phone (302) 739-4266.

DELAWARE STATE POLICE MUSEUM, 1425 N. DuPont Hwy., features uniforms, weapons, vehicles and equipment used in law enforcement. Other exhibits include an interactive mock crime scene and a police memorial. Visitors can sit at an emergency call center console. Allow 30 minutes minimum. Mon.-Fri. 9-3, third Sat. of the month 11-3; closed holidays. Free. Phone (302) 739-7700.

JOHN DICKINSON PLANTATION, 6 mi. s. on US 113, then .1 mi. e. to 340 Kitts Hummock Rd., was the boyhood home of John Dickinson, known as the Penman of the American Revolution and attributed with drafting the Articles of Confederation in 1778.

Dickinson's 1740s brick house and reconstructed farm complex exemplify area 18th-century plantation architecture. Allow 1 hour, 30 minutes minimum. Tours are available Tues.-Sat. 10-3:30 (also Sun. 1:30-4:30, Mar.-Dec.); closed holidays. Last tour begins 30 minutes before closing. Donations. Phone (302) 739-3277.

GAMBLING ESTABLISHMENTS

- **Dover Downs Hotel & Casino** is at 1131 N. DuPont Hwy. Daily 24 hours except Sun. 6 a.m.-noon; closed Easter and Dec. 25. Phone (302) 674-4600. *See color ad p. 37.*

GEORGETOWN (E-2) pop. 4,643

ELSIE WILLIAMS DOLL COLLECTION is on SR 18 (Seashore Hwy.) w. of SR 113, in the library on the Delaware Technical and Community College campus. The collection includes a wide variety of dolls by such makers as Bru, Madame Alexander and Peggy Nisbet. Allow 30 minutes minimum. Mon.-Thurs. 8 a.m.-10 p.m., Fri. 8-4:30, Sat. 9-1; closed major holidays. Hours may vary; phone ahead. Free. Phone (302) 856-9033.

[SAVE] **TREASURES OF THE SEA EXHIBIT,** on SR 18 (Seashore Hwy.) w. of SR 113, in the library on the Delaware Technical and Community College campus, displays jewels, gold and silver ingots and coins, bronze cannons and gold chains recovered from the ill-fated Spanish galleon *Nuestra Señora de Atocha*. Carrying an estimated $400 million in treasure, the ship sank in a 1622 hurricane. Videotapes chronicle the discovery of the galleon; visitors also may listen to a recording about the finding of the cannons.

Allow 1 hour minimum. Mon.-Tues. 10-4, Fri. noon-4, Sat. 9-1; closed major holidays and late Dec.-early Jan. Hours may vary; phone ahead. Admission $2.50; $2 (ages 66+); $1 (students with ID); free (ages 0-4). Phone (302) 856-5700.

HARRINGTON (D-1) pop. 3,174, elev. 63′

In central Delaware's agricultural region, Harrington is home to the Delaware State Fair. The fairgrounds complex on US 13 features Quillen Arena and an ice rink for public skating and hockey matches.

Harrington Raceway, at the fairgrounds, offers spring and fall harness racing sessions; phone (302) 398-7223.

Note: Policies vary concerning admittance of children to pari-mutuel betting facilities. Phone for information.

MESSICK AGRICULTURAL MUSEUM, 1.2 mi. w. of jct. US 13 and SR 14W on Walt Messick Rd., houses an extensive collection of early 1900s farm implements. Horse-drawn plows and vehicles, including a covered wagon, represent farm life in the 19th century. An early 20th-century kitchen and smokehouse are furnished in period. The museum has a collection of classic automobiles and trucks

spanning several decades. Allow 1 hour minimum. Mon.-Fri. 7:30-4, Sat. 7:30-noon, early Sept. to mid-Dec.; Mon.-Fri. 7:30-4, mid-July to early Sept. Free. Phone (302) 398-3729.

GAMBLING ESTABLISHMENTS

- **Midway Slots and Simulcast** is at Delaware State Fairgrounds off US 13. Daily 24 hours except Sun. 6 a.m.-noon; closed Easter and Dec. 25. Phone (888) 887-5687.

LEWES (E-3) pop. 2,932, elev. 17′

West of Cape Henlopen, Lewes (LOO-is) was founded in 1631 by a group of settlers from Hoorn, Holland. Originally called *Zwaanendael*, Valley of the Swans, the little colony intended to establish an agricultural and whaling industry, but the Siconese Indians destroyed it within a year. The interruption was brief, however. Promptly rebuilt, the town flourished, surviving pirate attacks, British bombardment in the War of 1812 and the profusion of summer vacationers to its beaches.

The DeVries Monument on Pilottown Road commemorates the early Dutch settlement. Constructed before the exact position of the Dutch fort was determined, the monument later was discovered to be on the site of the fortification's north bastion.

Lewes is the traditional home of the pilots who guide ships up Delaware Bay. This maritime orientation also makes the town a natural site for the Marine College of the University of Delaware; student enrollment is approximately 100.

Ferries connect Lewes with Cape May, N.J., daily. The 17-mile trip takes 70 minutes. For information write Cape May-Lewes Ferry, Lewes Terminal, P.O. Box 517, Lewes, DE 19958; phone (302) 644-6030 or (800) 643-3779. Cape May-Lewes ferry information also is available at AAA Mid-Atlantic, 55 Greentree Dr., in Dover; phone (302) 674-8020.

DID YOU KNOW

Delaware has tax-free shopping.

Lewes Chamber of Commerce and Visitor's Bureau: 120 Kings Hwy., Lewes, DE 19958; phone (302) 645-8073.

Self-guiding tours: Brochures and maps are available from the chamber of commerce and visitor bureau.

FISHERMAN'S WHARF CRUISES, 3 mi. e. of SR 1 on SR 9 (Anglers Rd.), just across the drawbridge, offers dolphin- and whale-watching cruises. Lighthouse and sunset cruises as well as fishing excursions also are available.

Two-hour dolphin cruises depart daily at 9 and 3, 3-hour dolphin and whale-watching cruises at 11:30, early June-early Sept. (weather permitting); dolphin cruises Sat.-Mon. at 9 and 3, dolphin and whale-watching cruise at 11:30, late May-early June. Dolphin cruise $25; $10 (ages 0-12). Dolphin and whale-watching cruise $30; $15 (ages 0-12). Hours and fares may vary; phone ahead. MC, VI. Phone (302) 645-8862.

FISHER-MARTIN HOUSE is at Kings Hwy. and Savannah Rd. The restored early 18th-century structure presents changing exhibits and houses the Lewes Chamber of Commerce and Visitor's Bureau. Allow 30 minutes minimum. Mon.-Fri. 10-4 (also Sat. 9-3, Sun. 10-2, Memorial Day weekend-Sept. 30). Free. Phone (302) 645-8073.

LEWES HISTORICAL SOCIETY COMPLEX, at Shipcarpenter and Third sts., encompasses a number of historic structures. Among the buildings are Thompson Country Store, a furnished 19th-century store moved from a site near Milford; Plank House, a tiny one-room log cabin built before 1700; and the 1789 Burton Ingraham House, furnished with Chippendale and Empire antiques. Ryves Holt House, at Second and Mulberry streets, contains the visitor center.

Allow 1 hour, 30 minutes minimum. Mon.-Sat. 11-4, Sun. 1-4, June 1-first week in Oct.; Sat. 11-4 in May. Admission $5; free (ages 0-11). Phone (302) 645-7670.

LIGHTSHIP OVERFALLS is at jct. Pilottown Rd. and Shipcarpenter St. With a 1,000-watt flashing electric lantern, a foghorn with a 5-mile range and a radio beacon capable of transmitting 25 miles, this floating lighthouse served as a navigation aid along the East Coast, first in Long Island Sound, then in Boston Harbor. Built in 1938, it was decommissioned in 1972. A tour includes the interior and exterior of the ship. Allow 1 hour minimum. Thurs.-Sat. 11-4, Sun. 1-4, July-Aug.; Fri.-Sat. 11-4, Sun. 1-4, Memorial Day-June 30 and Sept. 1-Columbus Day. Admission $2; $1 (students with ID). Phone (302) 644-8050.

SEASIDE NATURE CENTER, 1 mi. e. on US 9 past Cape May-Lewes Ferry to Cape Henlopen State Park, has several large fish aquariums, touch tanks, live snakes and turtles, and an exhibit about the

park's natural habitats. The Seaside Interpretive Trail, a self-guiding tour of the natural and human history of Cape Henlopen, leads from the center to Delaware Bay. Naturalist-led programs are offered, and guided kayak tours and rentals are available during summer months. Historic Fort Miles features a gun park, observation tower and several buildings.

Guided fort tours are available. Allow 30 minutes minimum. Daily 9-5, mid-June through Labor Day; 9-4, rest of year. Park entrance fee May-Oct. $8 (per private out-of-state vehicle); $4 (per private in-state vehicle); free (rest of year). Center free. Tour fees vary according to type of tour. Phone (302) 645-6852.

ZWAANENDAEL MUSEUM is at Savannah Rd. and Kings Hwy. This Dutch Renaissance building is an adaptation of the town hall at Hoorn in the Netherlands. Within are exhibits of historic military and maritime artifacts dating from 1631 to the War of 1812, including items from the wreckage of an 18th-century ship, the *DeBraak*, discovered off the Delaware coast in 1986. Allow 30 minutes minimum. Tues.-Sat. 10-4:30, Sun. 1:30-4:30; closed holidays. Free. Phone (302) 645-1148.

WINERIES

• **Nassau Valley Vineyards Winery and Visitors Center**, 2 mi. w. on US 9 to jct. US 404 and SR 1, then .5 mi. n. on SR 1 to overpass, then w. onto CR 14B, following signs to 33 Nassau Commons. Tues.-Sat. 11-5, Sun. noon-5. Phone (302) 645-9463.

MILLSBORO (F-2) pop. 2,360, elev. 26'

NANTICOKE INDIAN MUSEUM, at jct. SRs 24 and 5, is in a restored community schoolhouse. Exhibits interpret the history and development of the Nanticoke Indians, Delaware's first residents and its only remaining American Indian tribe. Highlights include basketwork, ceremonial dress, pottery, arrowheads and stone implements. Other collections include tribal dolls and kachinas and a reference library. Allow 30 minutes minimum. Tues.-Sat. 10-4, May-Oct.; Fri.-Sat. 10-4, in Apr. Admission $2; $1 (ages 3-11). Phone (302) 945-7022.

MILTON (E-2) pop. 1,657, elev. 13'

PRIME HOOK NATIONAL WILDLIFE REFUGE is 8 mi. n. via SR 1, then 1 mi. e. on Broadkill Beach Rd. (SR 16). Black and wood ducks, Canada geese, mallards and pintails congregate spring and fall at this 10,000-acre marsh habitat for migratory waterfowl. Indigenous mammals include red and gray foxes, white-tailed deer and the endangered Delmarva fox squirrel. A half-mile boardwalk and more than 7 miles of canoe trails are available.

Allow 1 hour, 30 minutes minimum. Refuge open daily 30 minutes before dawn-30 minutes after dusk. Refuge headquarters Mon.-Fri. 7:30-4 (also Sat.-Sun. 9-4, Apr.-Nov.). Free. Boat launch fee $1. Phone (302) 684-8419.

NEWARK (B-1) pop. 28,547, elev. 137'

Newark originated as the crossroads of two Lenni Lenape Indian trails spanning the peninsula between the Chesapeake Bay and the Delaware River. The intersection gradually matured into a village, and brickyards, mills and tanneries developed in the vicinity.

Legend maintains that in 1777 Betsy Ross' flag was flown for the first time at nearby Cooch's Bridge, the site of Delaware's only Revolutionary War battle. The Battle of Cooch's Bridge took place west off SR 896 via Welsh Tract Road or Old Baltimore Pike.

IRON HILL MUSEUM, I-95 to SR 896, then 1 mi. s. to 1355 Old Baltimore Pike, is housed in a former one-room schoolhouse built by the du Pont family in 1923. Collections include rocks, minerals, floral and faunal specimens, archeological and historical displays, mounted birds and iron exhibits. Hiking trails pass old iron ore mining pits and a replica of an early American Indian wigwam. Allow 1 hour, 30 minutes minimum. Tues.-Fri. 9-2, Sat. noon-4; closed holidays. Admission $2; free (ages 0-5 and on second Sat. of the month for Science Saturday program 10-4). Phone (302) 368-5703.

UNIVERSITY OF DELAWARE visitor center is at 196 S. College Ave. The 18,000-student campus is noted for the elm-lined mall (The Green) extending from Old College to Laurel Hall. Allow 2 hours minimum. Guided 90-minute tours are given Mon.-Fri. at 10, noon and 2; Sat. at 10 and noon. Reservations are required. Tours are not available holidays and during final exams. Free. Phone (302) 831-8123.

NEW CASTLE (B-2) pop. 4,862, elev. 17'

William Penn first set foot in North America near what is now the corner of Strand and Delaware streets. The town prospered under Penn's Quaker administration, producing two signers of the Declaration of Independence—George Read and Thomas McKean.

New Castle was a trade center until 1824 when a fire leveled the business district. Although the New Castle-Frenchtown Railroad gave New Castle new life in 1832, in the mid-19th century the main railroad lines were rerouted through Wilmington, isolating the town. New Castle's resulting seclusion has had one desirable effect: Much of its Colonial and Federal architecture remains unaltered.

The Old Library Museum, housed in a restored 1892 Victorian library designed by Philadelphia architect Frank Furness and featuring a cupola, skylight and leaded-glass doors, presents changing historic exhibits; phone (302) 322-2794.

New Castle's inhabitants own a 700-acre tract of land dating from the earliest days of Dutch settlement. Administered by the Trustees of New Castle Common instead of the municipal government, its many uses yield considerable revenue for the common good of the community.

Self-guiding tours: Brochures for the New Castle Heritage Trail walking tour are available at the New Castle Court House *(see attraction listing)* and the city administration building at the corner of Third and Delaware streets across from The Green. The tour covers historic areas and buildings dating from the mid-17th century.

AMSTEL HOUSE, 2 E. Fourth St., is an example of 18th-century Georgian architecture. The 1730s house, once the home of Governor Nicholas Van Dyke Sr., interprets life in the Colonial period through furnishings, an open-hearth kitchen and household equipment. Allow 30 minutes minimum. Wed.-Sat. 11-4, Sun. 1-4, Apr.-Dec.; by appointment rest of year. Closed holidays. Admission $4. Combination ticket with Dutch House $7. Phone (302) 322-2794.

DUTCH HOUSE, 32 E. Third St., was built in the late 17th century and is one of the oldest brick houses in the state. The structure contains decorative arts and historical artifacts, plus 17th- and 18th-century Colonial Dutch furnishings characteristic of a settler's house. Allow 30 minutes minimum. Wed.-Sat. 11-4, Sun. 1-4, Apr.-Dec.; by appointment rest of year. Closed holidays. Admission $4. Combination ticket with Amstel House $7. Phone (302) 322-2794.

THE GREEN, on Delaware St. between Third and Market sts., was laid out by Peter Stuyvesant in 1655. The Green and adjacent Market Square were the sites of fairs and weekly markets until the early 19th century. An 1809 U.S. arsenal and the 1798 New Castle Academy are on The Green.

NEW CASTLE COURT HOUSE MUSEUM is at 211 Delaware St. between Market and Third sts., Built in 1732, the courthouse was occupied by the Colonial Assembly until 1776, was the site of the adoption of Delaware's first constitution on Sept. 20, 1776, and served as the state's first capitol until 1777. It has been restored to its 1804 appearance and contains portraits, artifacts and furnishings relating to Delaware history. Allow 30 minutes minimum. Tues.-Sat. 10-3:30, Sun. 1:30-4:30; closed state holidays. Free. Phone (302) 323-4453.

NEW CASTLE PRESBYTERIAN CHURCH, 25 E. Second St., is believed to have been the direct successor of the original Dutch Reformed Church of 1657. Built in 1707, it was one of several churches forming the first presbytery in America. The cemetery contains marked graves dating from the early 1700s. Daily 8:30-12:30. Free. Phone (302) 328-3279.

ORIGINAL TICKET OFFICE, at the Battery on the s. side of Delaware St., was part of the now defunct New Castle and Frenchtown Railway. One of the first in the nation, the 1832 office marked the eastern terminus of the line. It was moved to its present site in the 1950s. Nearby is a section of reconstructed track with wooden rails pegged to stone

sleepers, the forerunner of wooden railroad ties. The interior of the structure is not accessible. Free.

READ HOUSE AND GARDENS, 42 The Strand, was built in 1801-03 by the son of George Read, one of the signers of the Declaration of Independence. A fine example of Federal architecture, the 22-room mansion is furnished in period and features carved woodwork, relief plasterwork and gilded fanlights. Tours highlight the lifestyles of three resident families. A 1.5-acre formal Victorian garden graces the grounds.

Allow 30 minutes minimum. Tues.-Fri. and Sun 11-4, Sat. 10-4, Mar.-Dec.; Sat. 10-4, Sun. 11-4, by appointment rest of year. Closed holidays. The house is open only by guided 35- to 45-minute tours; departure times vary. Last tour departs at 3:30. Admission $5; $4 (ages 13-21 and 65+); $2 (ages 6-12). MC, VI. Phone (302) 322-8411.

THE STRAND, near the river, is a block-long street bordered by shady brick walks and brick gutters. A number of townhouses dating from the 18th century survived the great fire that swept the street in 1824. The law office of Thomas McKean, a delegate to the Continental Congress of 1774, was at 22 The Strand. Packet Alley runs from The Strand to the river.

ODESSA (C-1) pop. 286, elev. 52′

With its emergence in the early 19th century as one of the area's most important grain shipping ports, the name of the town known as Cantwell's Bridge was changed to Odessa, after Russia's seaport. Farmers brought their produce to town, where it was shipped down Appoquinimink Creek to the Delaware River, then to domestic and foreign ports.

The significance of the port was eclipsed in the mid-1800s with the coming of the railroad. The railroad bypassed the city on its way through the Delmarva Peninsula and the Midwest became the nation's major grain producing region. Odessa was a primary station of the Underground Railroad prior to the outbreak of the Civil War. Well-preserved examples of 18th- and 19th-century architecture line Odessa's shaded streets.

HISTORIC HOUSES OF ODESSA, on Main and Second sts., is a cluster of 18th-century historic structures, including fine houses furnished in period. Admission is by 90-minute guided tour that departs from the visitor center in the Historic Odessa Bank, designed by Philadelphia architect Samuel Sloane and built in 1853. Brochures for self-guiding walking tours are available. Guided tours are given as needed Thurs.-Sat. 10-4, Mar.-Dec.; closed Easter, July 4, Thanksgiving and Dec. 24-25. Last tour begins 1 hour before closing. Admission $10; $8 (ages 12-17 and 60+). Phone (302) 378-4119.

The Brick Hotel, on the n. side of Main St. at Second St., is an 1822 Federal period structure that served as a hotel and tavern for nearly 100 years.

Collins-Sharp House, on Second and High sts., dates to around 1700, making it one of Delaware's oldest houses. The English gambrel-roof house was moved from Collins Beach on the Delaware River to its present location in 1962. Hearth cooking demonstrations are sometimes given.

Corbit-Sharp House, on the s. side of Main St. at Second St., is a 22-room brick Georgian house. Built in 1774 by William Corbit, a Quaker and local tanner, the home stayed in the Corbit family for more than 150 years. Period furniture and local handicrafts decorate the late 18th-century house; Colonial revival-style gardens adorn the grounds. Changing exhibits are featured.

Wilson-Warner House, next to the Corbit-Sharp House, was built by a local merchant in 1769. Fine paneling and 18th- and 19th-century furniture reflecting items recorded in the Wilson family bankruptcy sale in 1829 grace the interior. The 13-room brick Georgian house was purchased by family descendent Mary Corbit Warner and later became one of Delaware's first house museums upon her death in 1923.

REHOBOTH BEACH (E-3) pop. 1,495

Rehoboth is a biblical term meaning "room enough." Its remote location kept the beach area almost untouched until 1872 when the Rehoboth Beach Camp Meeting Association of the Methodist Episcopal Church purchased land along the sea and platted a town. Made accessible by a railroad line extended from Lewes in 1878, the town was the site of revival camp meetings until the 1880s.

When the highway replaced the railroad in the 1920s, Rehoboth Beach was well on its way to becoming a popular resort. The nearest ocean resort to the nation's capital, the town is deluged every summer by humidity-weary Washingtonians. Natives of Delaware seem scarce by comparison in the summer capital.

Clamming, crabbing, nature cruises, deep-sea and freshwater fishing, golfing, birding, sailing and swimming are some of the recreational pursuits available to visitors.

Camping is available at Delaware Seashore State Park *(see Recreation Chart and the AAA Mideastern CampBook)* on a 7-mile strip of land between the Atlantic Ocean and the Rehoboth and Indian River bays. Cape Henlopen State Park *(see Recreation Chart and the AAA Mideastern CampBook)* offers sand dunes, camping, nature trails, bathhouses, surf fishing and swimming areas where Delaware Bay meets the Atlantic Ocean.

Rehoboth Beach-Dewey Beach Chamber of Commerce and Visitor Center: Rehoboth Railroad Station, 501 Rehoboth Ave., P.O. Box 216, Rehoboth Beach, DE 19971; phone (302) 227-2233 or (800) 441-1329.

Shopping areas: SAVE Tanger Outlets on SR 1 has more than 150 outlet stores, including Ann Taylor, Bugle Boy, Izod, L.L. Bean, Oneida, Pierre Cardin, Reebok and Van Heusen.

SMYRNA (C-1) pop. 5,679, elev. 33'

BOMBAY HOOK NATIONAL WILDLIFE REFUGE, s. on US 13, e. on SR 12, s. on SR 9, then about 2.5 mi. e. on Whitehall Neck Rd., is primarily a refuge for migrating ducks, geese and shore birds, but wildlife can be seen year-round. Five walking trails and a 12-mile round-trip driving route offer opportunities to explore the 15,978-acre refuge, and observation towers provide a panorama of the area.

Refuge open daily dawn-dusk. Visitor center open Mon.-Fri. 8-4 (also Sat.-Sun. 9-5, Mar.-May and Sept. 1 to mid-Dec.). Admission $4 per private vehicle, $2 for persons arriving by bicycle or on foot. Phone (302) 653-6872.

WILMINGTON (B-2) pop. 72,664, elev. 134'

See map page 44.

Quakers laid out Wilmington in 1731. The settlement grew into an important market and shipping center. Industrial growth followed, stimulated by Wilmington's accessibility to other eastern ports and by the abundant water power in the Brandywine River Valley.

In the early 19th century Wilmington attracted Éleuthère Irénée du Pont and his two sons, who intended to finance a colony based on Utopian ideas. Seeing a need for high-quality gunpowder, however, the du Ponts abandoned their original plan, and in 1803 their new Eleuthera Mills produced the first barrel of Du Pont powder. The du Pont influence was instrumental in shaping Delaware's largest city into an industrial, financial and shipping hub.

A highlight of Wilmington's downtown renewal effort is the 1871 Grand Opera House, with its ornate cast-iron facade. The building, on the Market Street Mall, now serves as the Delaware Center for the Performing Arts. Free tours are available by reservation; phone (302) 658-7897. The Custom House, Sixth and King streets, was Wilmington's first federal building. Built in 1855, it is noted for its simple but bold exterior lines and impressive interior.

The Quaker Hill Historic District, downtown between Jefferson and Tatnall streets and Second and Eighth streets, was Wilmington's first neighborhood. It contains residences built 1745-1890, 19th-century churches and an 1816 Quaker meeting hall with a large cemetery.

The 18th-century John Chads House, built by a local innkeeper and ferry operator, is open for tours, which include a beehive oven baking demonstration.

Riverwalk is a mile-long landscaped path along the Christina River with scenic overlooks and parks as well as access to shops and cafes.

The Wilmington and Western Railroad offers 1- and 2-hour scenic rides through the Red Clay Valley area on weekends as well as seasonal specialty rides May through December. For schedule and fare information phone (302) 998-1930.

Greater Wilmington Convention and Visitors Bureau: 100 W. 10th St., Suite 20, Wilmington, DE 19801; phone (800) 489-6664.

Self-guiding tours: Maps for a self-guiding walking tour of the Quaker Hill Historic District are available from the Quaker Hill Historic Preservation Foundation at 521 N. West St.; phone (302) 658-9295.

Shopping areas: Shipyard Shops on Madison Street at the riverfront features brand-name outlet stores such as L.L. Bean and Nautica. Vendors at Riverfront Market, a European-style marketplace in a historic warehouse, sell fresh produce, meat, fish and gourmet food items.

BRANDYWINE PARK AND ZOO is at 1001 N. Park Dr. along the Brandywine River between Augustine and Market sts. The 180-acre park was designed by the creator of New York City's Central Park, Frederick Law Olmstead, and features the Josephine Garden, which has 118 Japanese cherry trees. The zoo houses Florida bobcats, Siberian tigers, small mammals and a variety of North and South American reptiles and birds.

Allow 2 hours minimum. Park daily dawn-dusk. Zoo daily 10-4. Park free. Zoo admission June-Sept. $5; $4 (ages 63+); $3 (ages 3-11). Admission rest of year $4; $2 (ages 3-11 and 63+). Phone (302) 571-7747.

[SAVE] **DELAWARE ART MUSEUM,** 2301 Kentmere Pkwy., contains a renowned collection of American paintings and illustrations by 19th-, 20th- and 21st-century artists. A 9-acre sculpture park, changing exhibits and an art research library provide further enrichment. A children's gallery features hands-on activities designed to stimulate creativity.

Allow 1 hour minimum. Tues.-Sat. 10-4, Sun. noon-4. Library available by appointment. Closed Jan. 1, Thanksgiving and Dec. 25. Admission $10; $8 (ages 60+); $5 (college students with ID); $3 (ages 7-18); free (on Sat. 10-1). AX, DS, MC, VI. Phone (302) 571-9590.

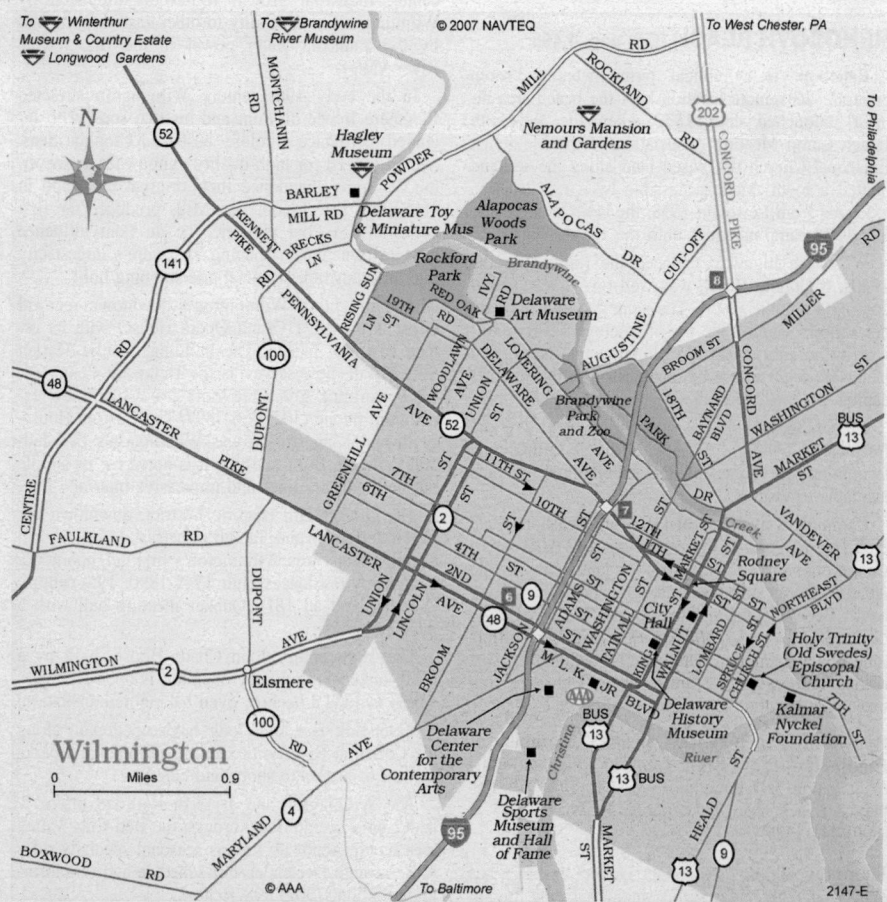

Wilmington

0   Miles   0.9

© 2007 NAVTEQ

DELAWARE CENTER FOR THE CONTEMPO-RARY ARTS is at 200 S. Madison St. Seven galleries show curated exhibits by nationally- and internationally-known artists. The facility also contains more than 20 artist studios. Allow 1 hour minimum. Tues. and Thurs.-Sat. 10-5, Wed. and Sun. noon-5; closed holidays. Admission $5; $3 (ages 65+ and students with ID); free (ages 0-11). MC, VI. Phone (302) 656-6466.

DELAWARE HISTORY MUSEUM, 504 N. Market St., features the interactive, multimedia permanent exhibition Distinctively Delaware. Changing exhibits feature art, costumes, toys, antiques, re-created scenes and historic photographs. Grandma's Attic is a learn-and-play discovery center for children. Allow 30 minutes minimum. Tues.-Fri. 11-4, Sat. 10-4; closed holidays. Phone ahead for current exhibit information. Admission $4; $3 (ages 66+ and college students and military with ID); $2 (ages 3-18). MC, VI. Phone (302) 656-0637.

SAVE **DELAWARE MUSEUM OF NATURAL HISTORY,** 5 mi. n.w. on SR 52, contains a variety of natural history exhibits in naturalistic settings, from native flora and fauna to specimens representing Africa and the Great Barrier Reef. Noteworthy are an extensive shell collection, life-size dinosaurs and a full-scale model of a giant squid, and mounted African animals and extinct birds. The Discovery Room features hands-on exhibits and activities.

Allow 1 hour, 30 minutes minimum. Mon.-Sat. 9:30-4:30, Sun. noon-4:30; closed Jan. 1, Easter, July 4, Thanksgiving and Dec. 25. Admission $6; $5 (ages 3-17); $4 (ages 60+). MC, VI. Phone (302) 658-9111.

SAVE **DELAWARE SPORTS MUSEUM AND HALL OF FAME** is off I-95 exit 6, following signs to Frawley Stadium. The museum chronicles Delaware sports history from 1860 to the present through photographs, audio- and videotape presentations, artifacts and memorabilia. Highlighted among the sports notables that represent more than 30 sports are Olympic athletes, professional players, coaches, journalists and sportscasters. A 12-minute videotape provides an overview. Allow 30 minutes minimum. Tues.-Sat. noon-5, Apr.-Oct.; by appointment rest of year Admission $4; $3 (ages 50+); $2 (ages 13-19). MC, VI. Phone (302) 425-3263.

DELAWARE TOY & MINIATURE MUSEUM is 3 mi. n. on SR 52 and .5 mi. n. to SR 141, then s. following signs to Hagley Museum *(see attraction listing).* The museum holds a collection of antique and contemporary dollhouses, miniatures and sample furniture. Featured are American and European dolls, toy trains, boats and planes from the 18th century to the present. Enameled brass figurines and miniature vases dating from 600 B.C. also are displayed.

Allow 1 hour minimum. Guided 1.5- to 2.5-hour tours are available by reservation. Open Tues.-Sat. 10-4, Sun. noon-4; closed holidays. Admission $6; $5 (ages 62+); $3 (ages 2-12). MC, VI. Phone (302) 427-8697.

GEM **HAGLEY MUSEUM,** 3 mi. n. on SR 52 and .5 mi. n. on SR 141, then s. to Old Barley Mill Rd., following signs, occupies 235 landscaped acres on the site of the original DuPont gunpowder mills, estate and gardens. Many restored mills show the development of water power on the Brandywine River.

The visitor center is in an old stone cotton-spinning mill that houses interactive science exhibits tracing DuPont Co. history, from explosives manufacturing to the development of chemical products that changed the world. Highlights include a reproduction of Jeff Gordon's #24 DuPont NASCAR race car and a space suit made of DuPont materials.

Eleutherian Mills, a Georgian house erected by Éleuthère Irénée du Pont in 1803, contains furnishings reflecting the tastes of five generations of du Ponts.

Allow 3 hours minimum. Daily 9:30-4:30, Mar. 15-Dec. 31; Sat.-Sun. 9:30-4:30, rest of year. Closed Thanksgiving and Dec. 25. Admission $11; $9 (ages 62+ and students with ID); $4 (ages 6-14). Visitor center admission $5; $2 (ages 6-14). AX, DS, MC, VI. Phone (302) 658-2400.

HOLY TRINITY (OLD SWEDES) EPISCOPAL CHURCH, 606 Church St., was built in 1698 and is one of the oldest active churches in North America. Established as a Swedish Lutheran church, Old Swedes was placed under the jurisdiction of the protestant Episcopal church in 1791. Allow 30 minutes minimum. Wed.-Sat. 10-4. Admission $2. Phone (302) 652-5629.

Hendrickson House, on Church St., is a Swedish stone farmhouse erected in Pennsylvania in 1690. Dismantled and rebuilt on the current site, the structure now houses the library, museum and office of Old Swedes Foundation. Admission included with Holy Trinity (Old Swedes) Episcopal Church.

SAVE *KALMAR NYCKEL* **FOUNDATION** is at 1124 E. Seventh St., adjacent to Fort Christina Park. The *Kalmar Nyckel* is a re-creation of the ship that brought the first European settlers to the Delaware Valley in 1638. The shipyard contains a small museum with a videotape that documents the ship's construction using Old World techniques. The ship is usually in the shipyard for maintenance November through April. During sailing season, it rotates between the shipyard and docks at Tubman-Garrett Park and Dravo Plaza in Wilmington, Del., as well as docks at Lewes, Del., and other ports along the East Coast.

Allow 30 minutes minimum. Shipyard and museum open Thurs.-Sun. 10-4, Nov.-Apr.; by appointment, rest of year. Closed holidays. Phone ahead for the ship docking schedule. Admission $5; $4 (ages 6-12). AX, DS, MC, VI. Phone (302) 429-7447.

NEMOURS MANSION AND GARDENS, 3.5 mi. n.w. to 1600 Rockland Rd., at Alapacos Rd. and SR 141, is a modified Louis XVI chateau built 1909-10 on the 300-acre estate of Alfred I. du Pont. The 47,000-square-foot mansion contains European antiques, tapestries, Oriental rugs and paintings as well as several of A.I. du Pont's innovations, such as an ice-making plant. The French-style gardens extend a third of a mile from the house. Admission, by tour only, includes rooms on three of the mansion's floors as well as a bus tour through the estate's gardens. Stairways are an essential part of the tour.

Note: The mansion and gardens are closed while the mansion undergoes renovations. Reopening is scheduled for late spring 2008. Operating schedule to be determined on reopening. Admission $12. Phone (302) 651-6912 or (800) 651-6912.

ROCKWOOD MUSEUM, off I-95 exit 9 (Marsh Rd.) at 610 Shipley Rd., is a rare example of Rural Gothic architecture. The 72-acre estate contains an 1851 manor house furnished as it was in 1895. Also on the grounds are a conservatory, the gardener's cottage, the carriage house, a lighted walking trail and six acres of gardens that exemplify fine landscape design. A gallery features rotating exhibits from the museum's collections.

Guided grounds tours and food are available. Allow 1 hour minimum. Grounds daily 6 a.m.-10 p.m. House tours Tues.-Sun. 10-3; closed major holidays. Grounds free. House tours $5; $2 (ages 2-12). Phone (302) 761-4340.

RODNEY SQUARE, bounded by Market, King, 10th and 11th sts., contains an equestrian statue of Caesar Rodney. This Delaware statesman made a hurried night ride from Dover to Philadelphia on July 2, 1776, to sway a tie vote to the side of independence.

WINTERTHUR MUSEUM & COUNTRY ESTATE is 6 mi. n.w. off I-95 exit 7 (Pennsylvania Ave.) on SR 52. The former home of Henry Francis du Pont was designed in the style of an English country estate and holds one of the richest collections of 17th-, 18th- and 19th-century American antiques. Exhibits and interactive displays explore the history and development of American decorative arts. The Campbell Collection of Soup Tureens also is displayed.

The 1,000-acre estate reflects du Pont's mastery of horticulture and includes a 60-acre naturalistic garden of native and exotic plants complemented by waterways, meadows and woodlands. Flowering plants bloom successively late January through November. A children's garden, tram rides and guided garden walks are available as are a variety of guided mansion and grounds tours lasting 45 minutes to 2 hours.

Allow 2 hours minimum. Tues.-Sun. 10-5; closed Thanksgiving and Dec. 25. Last tour ticket sold at 3:45. Admission $15; $13 (ages 12-18 and 63+); $5 (ages 2-11). Guided tours $5-$15. Reservations are recommended for tours in May and Dec. AX, DS, MC, VI. Phone (302) 888-4600, (800) 448-3883, or TTY (302) 888-4907.

GAMBLING ESTABLISHMENTS

• **Delaware Park Racetrack and Slots** is at 777 Delaware Park Blvd. Daily 24 hours except Sun. 6 a.m.-noon; closed Easter and Dec. 25. Phone (800) 417-5687.

District of Columbia

A Monumental City

The spirit of America iconized in obelisks, domes and colonnaded shrines

Our Nation's Front Yard

Open spaces, parks and grassy malls complement this federal showplace

Art and Culture

The District abounds with venerable museums, theaters and galleries

Cherry Blossoms

Trimming the Tidal Basin, to tout the natural beauty of our capital city

Historic Structures

Celebrated monuments define the history of a world power

Washington Monument
© AAA / Denise E. Campbell

the heart of the nation

Tidal Basin / © AAA / Denise E. Campbell

The District of Columbia represents America.

Tourists crouch on the ground in an attempt to snap a photo of the Washington Monument, leaving with a 3 x 5 of most of the tower and a lot of sky. Family members search in silence for names of their loved ones at the Vietnam Memorial, taking with them a name etching and a memory.

Artists and history buffs wander the hallowed halls of the Smithsonian, conjuring plans to leave their mark on this world. Parks provide a spot for ordinary people to stroll and, unfortunately, for the underprivileged to sleep. Foreign dignitaries are wined and dined, while residents meander along the streets of Georgetown, popping in and out of boutiques.

Sidewalks feel the hustling feet of VIPs. Blades of grass on the Mall are matted from the heavy footsteps of protesters. Mourners gaze at the sea of white headstones at Arlington National Cemetery. The president holds press conferences for a field of reporters amid flashing bulbs, which are in turn broadcast to a nation of viewers.

Comedians poke fun at the town, while presidents sing its glory—and opinions from citizens and foreigners fall everywhere in between.

All these ideas of what the capital is, should be or should not be help define it. Washington, D.C. is the people it represents, the freedom it stands for, the power it holds, the history it preserves and the future it promises.

From the District of Columbia pulses the heartbeat of the nation. And it pounds quickly: Policies are debated, bills are made laws, protests are staged, heroes are honored, lobbyists "do lunch" and scandals sizzle. Government, economic and social issues in the District all sprout from one seed—politics.

Politics had a hand in determining the location of the "federal city." Thomas Jefferson and Virginians wanted the permanent capital of the new nation to be along the Potomac River; to gain this demand they backed Northerner Alexander Hamilton's Assumption Bill. The final decision was conceded to George Washington, who chose what Jefferson termed "that Indian swamp in the wilderness." It's been a hotbed for debate ever since.

The task of forging a visionary capital of monuments, broad avenues and spacious circles fell upon French-born architect Pierre-Charles L'Enfant. His grandiose concept featured 100-foot-wide streets and one avenue a mile long. Some thought his plan foolhardy, but Washington endorsed it.

L'Enfant's vision included two focal points: the Capitol and the President's Mansion. He placed the two structures just far enough from each other to reinforce the separation of powers between the legislative and executive branches of government.

1600 Pennsylvania Avenue

The White House has been the scene of many events in American history, making this address a symbol of the vigor of American democracy. Outside, reporters line the avenue that fronts Lafayette Square, clamoring for the latest scoop. Camera lights shine, illuminating the stately white edifice in the background. It seems that everyone wants a glimpse into the oldest public building in Washington.

And it's no wonder. The business associated with our nation's highest office takes place behind these walls. The president conducts meetings that determine national and international policy, signs new legislation, entertains dignitaries and carries out countless other duties.

Every U.S. president since Washington has called this structure home, leaving his stamp on the nation's history. Throughout the mansion, furnishings, portraits and decor are tangible representations both of alliances with other countries and the personal touches of past residents.

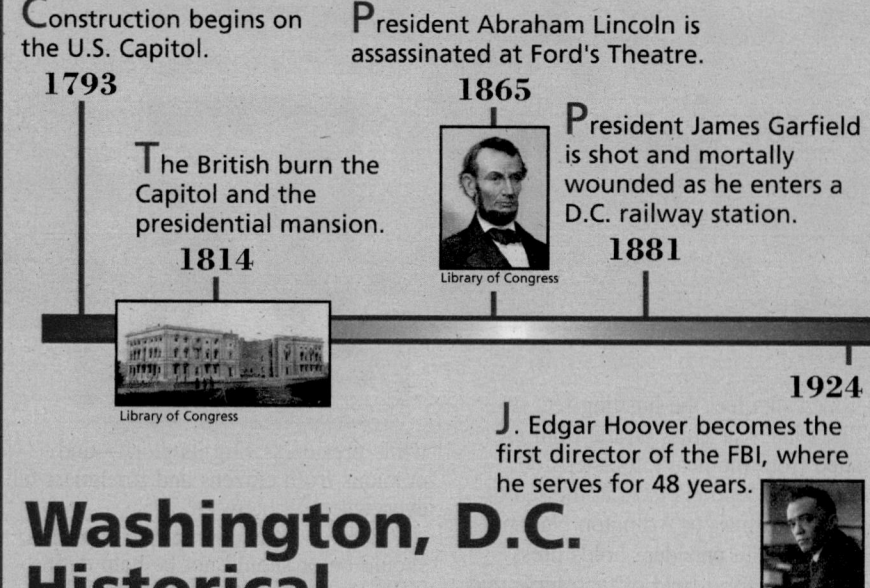

Construction begins on the U.S. Capitol.
1793

The British burn the Capitol and the presidential mansion.
1814

Library of Congress

President Abraham Lincoln is assassinated at Ford's Theatre.
1865

Library of Congress

President James Garfield is shot and mortally wounded as he enters a D.C. railway station.
1881

1924

J. Edgar Hoover becomes the first director of the FBI, where he serves for 48 years.

Library of Congress

Washington, D.C. Historical Timeline

The People's House

The nucleus of L'Enfant's design was the U.S. Capitol. Its lofty stature is not only due to its location on Capitol (formerly Jenkins) Hill; governed by tradition, it is here that congressional leaders determine the laws of the land.

Under one of the world's largest domes—the magnificent cast iron Rotunda—members of the House and Senate engage in spirited debates that have caused gavels to split and tempers to flare.

Tradition continues in the number of memorials found in Washington. Monuments and museums honor everyone from war veterans to presidents to postal workers. And among the most impressive is the monument dedicated to Thomas Jefferson.

A Renaissance Man

Architect, diplomat, horticulturist, inventor, musician, political philosopher, scientist, president—Jefferson amassed a long list of achievements during his lifetime. It's fitting that his memorial occupies a prominent site on the southeast bank of the Tidal Basin. The circular domed structure, modeled on the Pantheon in Rome, is an adaptation of the classical style of architecture that Jefferson admired. In spring the memorial is exquisitely framed by clouds of white and pink blossoms adorning the Japanese cherry trees.

A street named for the same man runs the southern length of the National Mall, that swath of green anchored at one end by the U.S. Capitol and at the other by the Washington Monument.

Surrounded by a dizzying assortment of landmarks, the Mall becomes an enormous sardine can during annual Fourth of July festivities. Political demonstrations led by suffragettes and Rev. Dr. Martin Luther King, Jr. also have attracted record crowds. In the 1980s silence fell over the Mall when it was blanketed by the Names Project Quilt, a memorial to those suffering from AIDS.

Whatever the cause, Washington opens its arms. The city that functions as national headquarters for "the land of the free and the home of the brave" honors the worthy, preserves the past, looks to the future and welcomes the visitor.

President John F. Kennedy establishes the Peace Corps.
1961

John F. Kennedy Library

Terrorists hijack American Airlines Flight 77 and crash it into the west face of the Pentagon.
2001

© Dennis Brack

Martin Luther King Jr. delivers his moving "I Have a Dream" speech on the steps of the Lincoln Memorial.
1963

© The Nobel Foundation

1995
African-American men gather on the Mall for the Million Man March to promote community activism and unity.

2004
A state funeral for former President Ronald Reagan is held at Washington National Cathedral.

1974
Richard Nixon becomes the first U.S. president to resign from office.

Recreation

While the majority of D.C. visitors focus on sightseeing, an escape from all that concrete and marble offers a welcome respite. Take a break from history and explore the present on one of the area's trails or rivers. After all, you just may find yourself unwinding alongside a local politician.

Plenty of **bicycling** trails wind their way in and around the city. Although bicycles are forbidden on Theodore Roosevelt Island—a memorial and wildlife refuge with about 2 miles of wooded **hiking** trails—the parking lot serves as a starting point for many routes.

For a "moving" monumental view, try the Potomac Tour. Start pedaling at Theodore Roosevelt Island and follow the recreation paths along the shores of the Potomac River, circling East Potomac Park. If they aren't crowded with strollers and joggers, cruise the National Mall's gravel pathways.

The 18-mile Mount Vernon Trail follows the Potomac River's Virginia border from Theodore Roosevelt Island south to Mount Vernon, George Washington's estate. It's rated the most scenic due to sweeping views of the river; quaint houses line the route as you pass through Old Town Alexandria.

Ride the Rail-Trail

Locals refer to abandoned railway paths converted to recreational trails as "rail-trails," and one in particular is not to be missed. Head east on the 4-mile-long Custis Trail to connect with the popular 45-mile Washington & Old Dominion Trail. The WOD, as locals call it, is crowded with bikers, **inline skaters** and **horseback riders.** Shady bridle paths in northern Rock Creek Park also cater to equestrians.

The towpath of the Chesapeake & Ohio (C&O) Canal follows the banks of the Potomac River for 184 miles from Washington, D.C., to Cumberland, Md.; sites along the paved route include Great Falls, the Monocacy River Aqueduct and historic Harpers Ferry. **Campers** also set up tents along the trail.

The Potomac River offers a full range of white water for paddling enthusiasts. **Kayakers** looking for a rush will want to put in just below Great Falls, where there are exciting class II and III runs. On the Maryland side, a hot spot for **canoeists** exists upstream from the Old Anglers Inn. Little Falls, inside the Beltway above Chain Bridge, is a quick but daring class IV rapid.

Leisurely paddling can be found on the Anacostia River, Swains Lock on the C&O Canal and scenic Jug Bay Wetlands Sanctuary on the Patuxent River. The tributaries, harbors and coves of Chesapeake Bay are secluded spots for exploring in a canoe or **sea kayak.** Here **anglers** can cast for bass, flounder and trout.

Boating also is popular on the bay; its largely undeveloped shoreline provides a tranquil view from the deck of a sailboat.

Winter Wonderland

When the snowflakes fall, snap those **ski** racks to the top of your car and head to the slopes. A short drive rewards you with a variety of choices: Some popular resorts are Wisp near McHenry, Md.; Bryce near Basye, Va.; Blue Knob near Claysburg, Pa.; and Timberline near Davis, W.Va.

Twirl a pirouette or take small, wobbly steps with national monuments as a backdrop—**ice skating** is an option at the National Gallery Ice Rink on the Mall, 9th Street and Constitution Avenue.

Fans of almost any professional sport have something to cheer for: In Washington, the Capitals play **hockey;** the Redskins play **football;** the Nationals play **baseball;** the United play **soccer;** and the Wizards play **basketball.** Nearby Baltimore is home to the Orioles, Ravens and Thunder, pros in **baseball, football** and **lacrosse,** respectively.

And collegiate athletics are no less important. The programs of six area universities—American, Georgetown, George Washington and Howard in the District, George Mason University in Virginia and the University of Maryland—rouse fans out of their seats.

Recreational Activities

Throughout the TourBook, you may notice a Recreational Activities heading with bulleted listings of recreation-oriented establishments listed underneath. Similar operations also may be mentioned in Destination City recreation sections. Since normal AAA inspection criteria cannot be applied, these establishments are presented only for information. Age, height and weight restrictions may apply. Reservations often are recommended and sometimes are required. Addresses and/or phone numbers are provided so visitors can contact the attraction for additional information.

Fast Facts

AREA: 67 square miles.

HIGHEST POINT: 410 ft., Tenleytown in N.W. section.

LOWEST POINT: Sea level, Atlantic Ocean.

TIME ZONE(S): Eastern. DST.

MINIMUM AGE FOR UNRESTRICTED DRIVER'S LICENSE: 18.

SEAT BELT/CHILD RESTRAINT LAWS: Seat belts are required for driver and all passengers 16 and older. Children ages 8 until 16 are required to be in a child restraint or seat belt; child restraints are required for under 8.

HELMETS FOR MOTORCYCLISTS: Required for all riders.

RADAR DETECTORS: Not permitted.

FIREARMS LAWS: Contact the D.C. Gun Control Office, 300 Indiana Ave. N.W., Washington, DC 20001; phone (202) 727-4275.

HOLIDAYS: Jan. 1; Martin Luther King Jr. Day, Jan. (3rd Mon.); Presidents Day, Feb. (3rd Mon.); Memorial Day; July 4; Labor Day; Columbus Day, Oct. (2nd Mon.); Veterans Day, Nov. 11; Thanksgiving; Christmas, Dec. 25.

INFORMATION CENTERS: Kiosks at the Ellipse, Jefferson Memorial, Lafayette Park, Lincoln Memorial, National Gallery of Art, Washington Monument and the Smithsonian Museums of Air and Space and Natural History

dispense information about places and events in the city. For information about places to visit, concerts, art shows, recreation and other activities, contact the Washington, D.C. Convention & Tourism Corp., (202) 789-7000 or (800) 422-8644; the National Capital Park Service, (202) 619-7275; and the Visitor Information Center, (202) 328-4748 or (866) 324-7386.

FURTHER INFORMATION FOR VISITORS:

D.C. Committee to Promote Washington
901 7th St. N.W., 4th floor
Washington, DC 20001
(202) 789-7000

National Park Service Public Information Office
U.S. Department of the Interior
1100 Ohio Dr. S.W.
Washington, DC 20242
(202) 619-7222

Smithsonian Information Center
Smithsonian Institution
P.O. Box 37012
SI 153, MRC 010
Washington, DC 20013

(202) 633-1000
TTY (202) 633-5285

Visitor Information Center
Ronald Reagan Building
1300 Pennsylvania Ave. N.W.
Washington, DC 20004
(202) 328-4748
(866) 324-7386

District of Columbia Temperature Averages
Maximum/Minimum
From the records of The Weather Channel Interactive, Inc.

	JAN	FEB	MAR	APR	MAY	JUNE	JULY	AUG	SEPT	OCT	NOV	DEC
Washington	43	47	55	66	76	84	89	87	80	69	58	48
	24	26	33	42	52	62	67	65	57	44	36	28

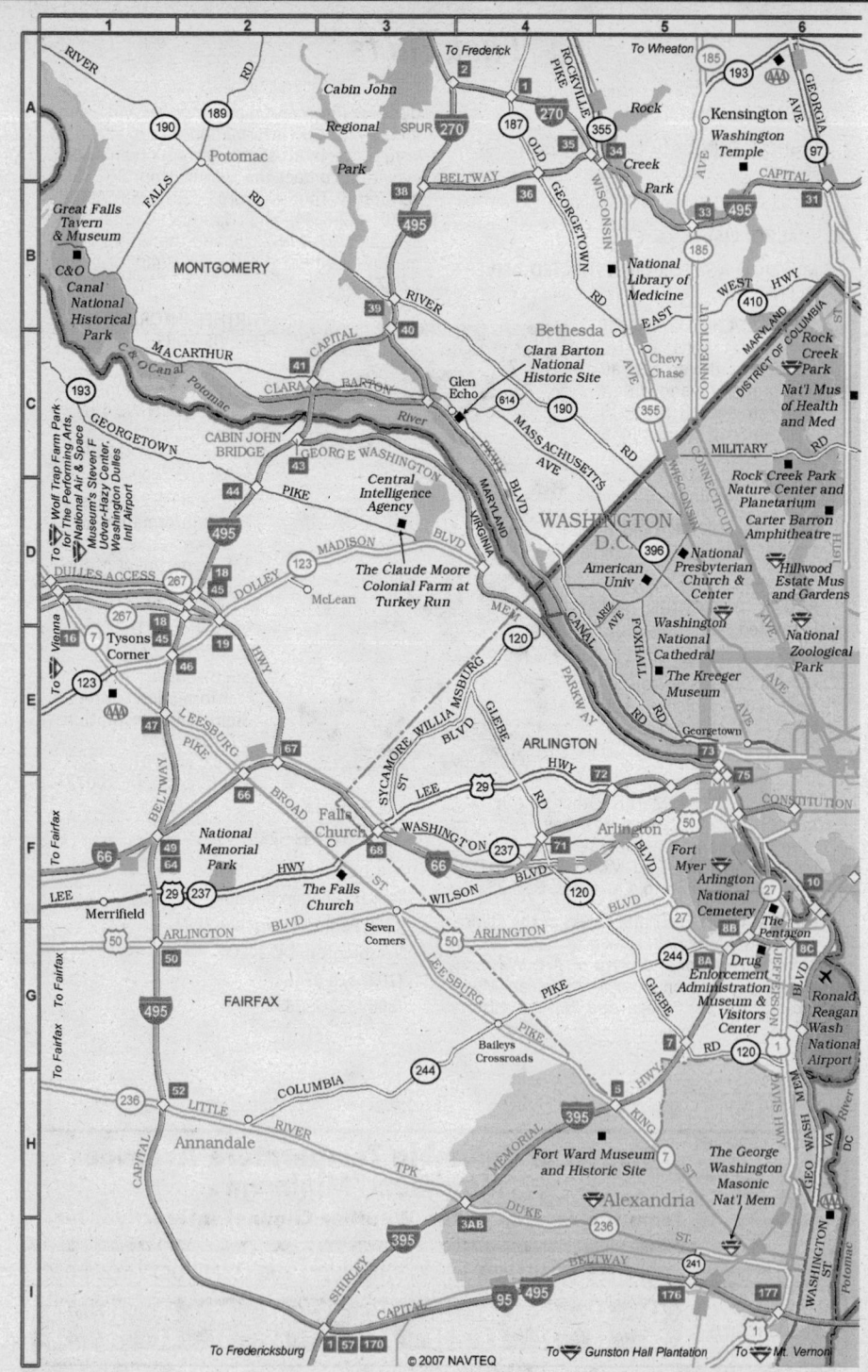

© 2007 NAVTEQ

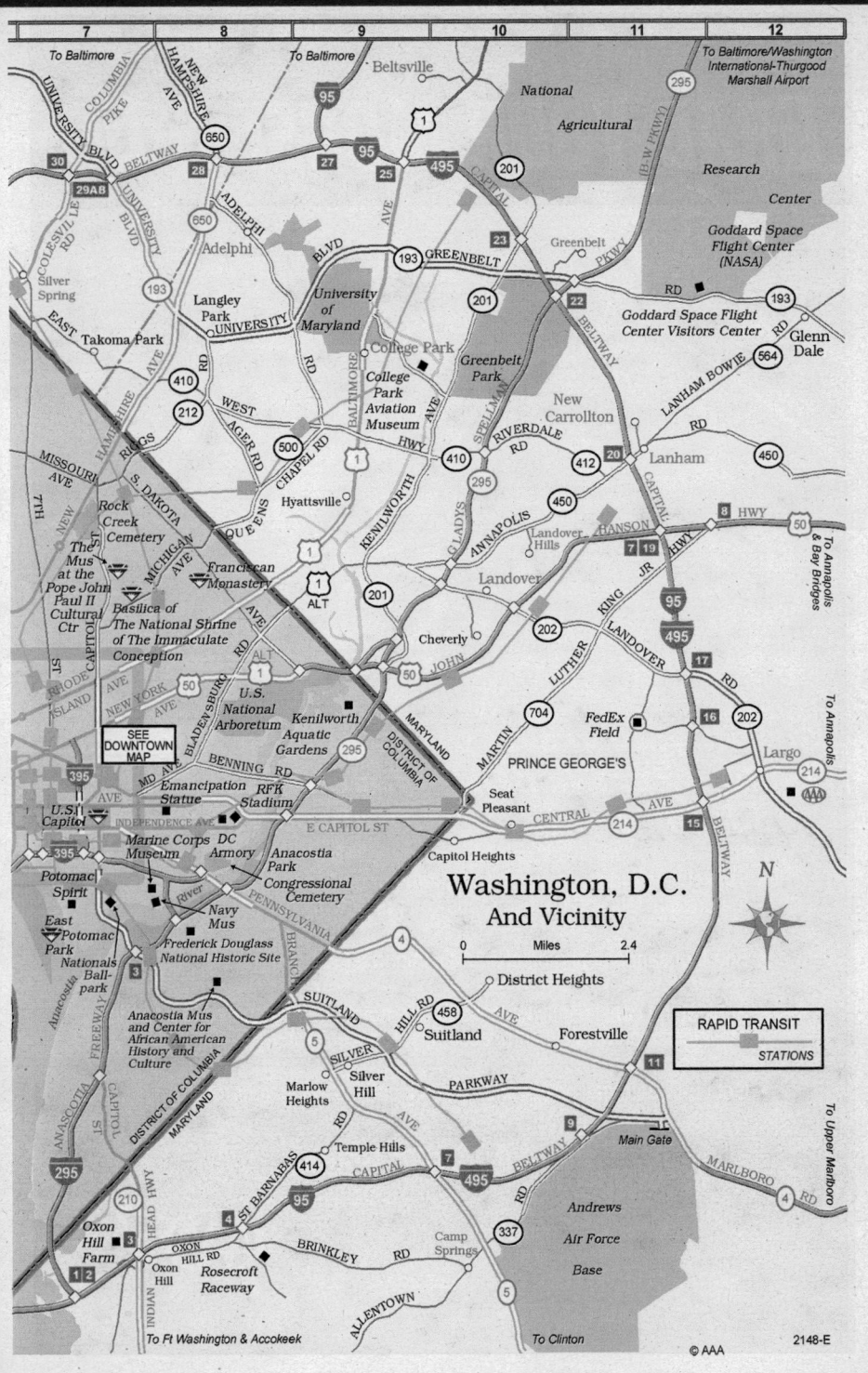

Washington, D.C.
And Vicinity

0   Miles   2.4

RAPID TRANSIT

— STATIONS

© AAA

2148-E

Points of Interest Offering A
Great Experience for Members®

Alexandria, Va. (H-5)

CHRIST CHURCH—Pew 60 of this 1773 church was purchased for 36 pounds, 10 shillings by George Washington, who was a regular attendee. See p. 119.

GEORGE WASHINGTON MA-SONIC NATIONAL MEMO-RIAL—The memorial is a 333-foot-tall landmark modeled after the ancient lighthouse at Alexandria, Egypt. See p. 120.

OLD PRESBYTERIAN MEETING HOUSE—This 1774 church was the location of George Washington's funeral. See p. 121.

Arlington National Cemetery, Va. (F-5)

ARLINGTON HOUSE, THE ROBERT E. LEE MEMO-RIAL—Built in 1802, Gen. Robert E. Lee's former home was confiscated during the war and used as a place to bury the war dead. See p. 126.

ARLINGTON NATIONAL CEMETERY—Seemingly endless rows of white headstones mark the graves of some of America's heroes, including John F. Kennedy, Rear Adm. Richard Byrd and Justice Earl Warren. See p. 126.

TOMB OF THE UNKNOWNS—Beneath the tomb made of Colorado marble rests the body of an unknown soldier from World War I. See p. 127.

Chantilly, Va.

NATIONAL AIR AND SPACE MUSEUM'S STEVEN F. UDVAR-HAZY CENTER—Discover here how man learned to slip the surly bonds of Earth. See p. 127.

Largo, Md. (E-12)

SIX FLAGS AMERICA—The park offers more than 100 ways to have fun, from thrilling roller coasters and live shows to a water park with a million-gallon wave pool. See p. 116.

Leesburg, Va.

OATLANDS—Of the 3,408 acres that originally made up this estate, only 261 remain; visitors can view the 1804 house, furnished in period. See p. 129.

Lorton, Va.

GUNSTON HALL PLANTATION—This 1755 brick Georgian residence was home to George Mason, author of the Virginia Declaration of Rights of 1776 and one of the framers of the U.S. Constitution. See p. 130.

POHICK CHURCH—Used as a stable during the Civil War, this church, where George Washington served as a vestryman for 23 years, was restored 1902-17. See p. 130.

McLean, Va. (D-2)

GREAT FALLS PARK—The Potomac River, which drops some 77 feet in thunderous rapids and falls, is a feature of this 800-acre park. See p. 131.

Mount Vernon, Va.

DONALD W. REYNOLDS MUSEUM AND EDUCA-TION CENTER—Learn how the Washington family lived as you view their personal effects and theater presentations providing unique insights. See p. 132.

GEORGE WASHINGTON'S MOUNT VERNON ESTATE & GARDENS—The final home of George Washington contains personal effects of our first president. See p. 132.

Quantico, Va.

NATIONAL MUSEUM OF THE MARINE CORPS—Learn about a Marine's role from boot camp to conflict and view aircraft, tanks, uniforms and weapons in this museum honoring the Corps' history. See p. 133.

Vienna, Va.

WOLF TRAP NATIONAL PARK FOR THE PERFORM-ING ARTS—This is the country's only national park dedicated to the performing arts. See p. 133.

Washington, D.C.

ARTHUR M. SACKLER GALLERY—Permanent collections feature paintings, sculpture, ceramics and Asian art. See p. 69.

BASILICA OF THE NATIONAL SHRINE OF THE IMMACULATE CONCEPTION—A large collection of 20th-century mosaics is housed in this Byzantine-Romanesque structure, one of the largest Roman Catholic churches in the world. See p. 73.

CORCORAN GALLERY OF ART—American paintings, sculpture and drawings from the 18th century are on display. Also featured are pottery and tapestries as well as contemporary art. See p. 74.

DEPARTMENT OF STATE—Part of the Executive Branch, the agency is responsible for formulating and implementing U.S. foreign policy. See p. 75.

FORD'S THEATRE NATIONAL HISTORIC SITE—Restored to its 1860s appearance, this is where Abraham Lincoln was fatally shot by John Wilkes Booth on April 14, 1865. See p. 76.

FRANCISCAN MONASTERY—Called Mount St. Sepulchre, the monastery features replicas of Holy Land shrines. See p. 76.

FRANKLIN DELANO ROOSEVELT MEMORIAL—Four outdoor rooms depict the 12 years that FDR served as president. See p. 76.

FREER GALLERY OF ART—The Freer features calligraphy and porcelain as well as notable collections of American paintings, Japanese art and Korean ceramics. See p. 77.

HILLWOOD ESTATE MUSEUM AND GARDENS—Cereal heiress and art connoisseur Marjorie Merriweather Post bought and expanded this mansion to house her extensive collection of decorative and fine art objects, which includes ornate Fabergé Easter eggs. See p. 77.

HIRSHHORN MUSEUM AND SCULPTURE GARDEN—American and European art spanning the 19th century to the present encompasses works by Jackson Pollock, Auguste Rodin and others. See p. 77.

INTERNATIONAL SPY MUSEUM—You won't encounter James Bond or Maxwell Smart here, but you'll see gadgets as fantastic as theirs. See p. 78.

THE JOHN F. KENNEDY CENTER FOR THE PERFORMING ARTS—American and international music, drama, dance and film are presented in the nation's memorial to President Kennedy. See p. 78.

KOREAN WAR VETERANS MEMORIAL—Erected in gratitude to those 1.5 million American personnel who served in Korea 1950-53, the memorial features statues of patrolling soldiers. See p. 78.

LIBRARY OF CONGRESS—Thomas Jefferson's personal collection of 6,000 volumes formed the basis of the national library, founded in 1800. See p. 79.

LINCOLN MEMORIAL—This inspiring marble structure features 36 columns and a colossal seated statue of Abraham Lincoln. See p. 80.

NATIONAL AIR AND SPACE MUSEUM—The museum is devoted to the history and development of air and space technology. See p. 80.

NATIONAL GALLERY OF ART—The National Gallery's East and West buildings offer an outstanding collection of painting and sculpture, from old masters to contemporary artists. See p. 82.

NATIONAL MUSEUM OF AFRICAN ART—Bronze, wood, ivory and ceramic objects depict the traditional arts of Africa. See p. 83.

NATIONAL MUSEUM OF AMERICAN HISTORY, KENNETH E. BEHRING CENTER—Displays at this museum focus on the scientific, cultural, technological and political development of the United States. See p. 83.

NATIONAL MUSEUM OF THE AMERICAN INDIAN—Native American design principles play an integral role in the Smithsonian's newest museum, an exhibition space for Indian arts, history and material culture. See p. 84.

NATIONAL MUSEUM OF NATURAL HISTORY—The multitude of exhibits at this ever-popular museum highlights natural history and human cultures. See p. 84.

NATIONAL PORTRAIT GALLERY—The gallery is devoted to portraiture of Americans who made significant contributions to the nation. See p. 85.

NATIONAL POSTAL MUSEUM—Hands-on exhibits portray the history and development of our nation's mail service. See p. 85.

NATIONAL WORLD WAR II MEMORIAL—This memorial salutes a generation of Americans who fought and helped win the most devastating conflict in world history. See p. 85.

NATIONAL ZOOLOGICAL PARK—Several thousand exotic animals, including Sumatran tigers, lowland gorillas and Komodo dragons, call this 163-acre biological park home. See p. 85.

THE PHILLIPS COLLECTION—View modern and impressionist works in a comfortable setting, or attend an artful evening or Sunday concert. See p. 87.

POPE JOHN PAUL II CULTURAL CENTER—Explore a 2,000-year-old religion in this thoroughly contemporary building. See p. 87.

POTOMAC PARK—Exceptionally beautiful in spring when the cherry trees are in bloom, this area along the Tidal Basin has facilities for outdoor recreation. See p. 88.

ROCK CREEK PARK—Acres of natural woodland in the middle of the city encompass bridle paths, trails and athletic facilities. See p. 88.

ST. MATTHEW'S CATHEDRAL—Built in 1840 in the Renaissance style, the church features an inscription in marble commemorating the funeral of John F. Kennedy. See p. 89.

CATHEDRAL OF
ST. MATTHEW
THE APOSTLE

SMITHSONIAN AMERICAN ART MUSEUM—Exhibits include the oldest national art collection, paintings, sculptures, portraits and photographs. See p. 89.

SMITHSONIAN INSTITUTION—Sixteen Washington museums and galleries comprise this complex, founded for the increase and diffusion of knowledge. See p. 90.

SUPREME COURT BUILDING—The unanimous opinion is that the interior of this 1935 building is stunning. See p. 91.

THOMAS JEFFERSON MEMORIAL—Supported by Ionic columns, this graceful, circular domed structure features panels inscribed with significant Jefferson writings as well as a large statue of the president. See p. 92.

UNITED STATES CAPITOL—One of the nation's most familiar landmarks, this imposing marble building contains about 550 rooms. See p. 92.

UNITED STATES HOLOCAUST MEMORIAL MUSEUM—The tragedy of the Holocaust is depicted through artifacts, photographs, films and oral histories. See p. 92.

U.S. BOTANIC GARDEN—Founded in 1820, this facility is dedicated to showcasing the aesthetic, cultural, economic, therapeutic and ecological importance of plants. See p. 93.

VIETNAM VETERANS MEMORIAL—A life-size statue of three servicemen stands near the V-shaped black granite walls that honor the men and women who served in the U.S. Armed Forces in Vietnam. See p. 94.

WASHINGTON MONUMENT—Honoring our first president, this marble obelisk stands 555 feet from base to tip. It rises from the center of a knoll on the National Mall, surrounded by 50 American flags. See p. 94.

WASHINGTON NATIONAL CATHEDRAL—A beautiful example of Gothic architecture, this cathedral was completed in 1990 after 83 years of construction. Statues, stained-glass windows, gardens and a carillon are among its most noteworthy features. See p. 94.

WHITE HOUSE—The executive mansion has been the home of every U.S. president except George Washington. Antiques, presidential portraits and rich decorative accents all contribute to the preservation of American history. See p. 94.

Washington, D.C.

Capitol Hill / Washington DC Convention and Tourism Corporation

City Population: 572,059 **Elevation: 25 ft.**

Editor's Picks:

Library of Congress.................(see p. 79)

Smithsonian Institution.............(see p. 90)

United States Capitol ....(see p. 92)

Find more AAA top picks at AAA.com

Getting There

By Car

Although it does not enter Washington, the Capital Beltway (I-495) encircles the city and interchanges with all major approach routes. The eastern portion is part of I-95, a major artery linking Baltimore to the north and Richmond, Va., to the south. US 1 and the Gladys Spellman Parkway (also called the Baltimore-Washington Parkway or SR 295) approach Washington from the north; US 50, SR 4 and SR 5 come from eastern and southern Maryland. Leading into the city from the south, via Alexandria and Arlington, Va., are US 1 and I-395.

The remainder of the beltway is intersected by US 29 from the Baltimore area and I-270, which links the metropolitan area with transcontinental I-70 at Frederick, Md. Interchanging with the Virginia part of I-495 are I-66 and US 50, both of which cross the Piedmont from the west and converge at the Theodore Roosevelt Bridge.

Air Travel

Visitors arriving by plane can land at Ronald Reagan Washington National Airport, Washington Dulles International Airport or Baltimore-Washington International Thurgood Marshall Airport (BWI). Frequent transportation services into town are available from all three airports.

Just across the Potomac River from the District is Ronald Reagan Washington National Airport, the most centrally located of the three major facilities serving the Washington area. To get to downtown D.C. from terminal A, B or C, follow the exit signs and take the George Washington Memorial Parkway north to the 14th Street Bridge exit (officially, the Arland D. Williams Jr. Memorial Bridge northbound and the George Mason Bridge southbound). Once across the bridge, you will be on 14th Street going north, which runs just west of the Smithsonian museums on the National Mall. To reach Arlington, Alexandria or other nearby Virginia suburbs, take the I-395 South exit off the parkway (just past the 14th Street Bridge exit).

Taxi fare from Ronald Reagan Washington National Airport into Washington averages about $12 but depends on the length of the trip. Metrobus and Metrorail both serve the airport as well. Non-rush hour fares are $1.25 and $1.35, respectively; Metrorail fares are higher during rush hours, depending upon the destination.

Washington Dulles International Airport is about 26 miles west of downtown Washington via I-66 and the Dulles Access Road (SR 267), just west of Herndon, Va. To reach downtown Washington, exit the airport terminal and take the Dulles Access Road east to I-66; continue east on I-66, which enters the District via the

Getting There — starting on this page

Getting Around — starting on p. 65

What To See — starting on p. 69

What To Do — starting on p. 95

Where To Stay — starting on p. 431

Where To Dine — starting on p. 455

Essential Experiences — visit AAA.com

Editor's Event Picks — visit AAA.com

Theodore Roosevelt Bridge. Cross the bridge and you will be on Constitution Avenue eastbound. A taxi ride into downtown from Dulles costs about $45.

Washington Flyer offers transportation between Ronald Reagan Washington National Airport, Dulles International Airport and major hotels in downtown D.C. Buses depart National for Dulles on the hour 6 a.m.-11 p.m. Mon.-Fri. The Sat.-Sun. and holiday schedule is every 2 hours 6 a.m.-2 p.m. and on the hour 2-11 p.m. From Dulles to Ronald Reagan Washington National Airport, the schedule is on the hour 5 a.m.-11 p.m. Mon.-Fri.; Sat.-Sun. and holidays, every 2 hours 5 a.m.-1 p.m. and on the hour 1-11 p.m. Inter-airport services is $16 one way, $26 round trip (MC, VI).

Washington Flyer service is available from Dulles to the West Falls Church Metro station. Buses depart every half-hour; one-way fare $8, round trip $14. For additional Washington Flyer schedule and fare information phone (703) 685-1400 or (888) 927-4359.

Baltimore-Washington International Airport is about 30 miles northeast of the city via the Gladys Spellman Parkway (SR 295). From the airport terminal area, follow the exit signs to SR 295, then take the parkway west toward the Washington area. You can either exit east or west onto the Beltway or continue into the city; the parkway ends at New York Avenue just before the District line.

Taxi service from Baltimore-Washington International Airport costs about $45, although fares depend upon the zone serviced. Rail transportation to the airport is available from Union Station in Washington. Super Shuttle provides van service from the Washington metro area to Baltimore-Washington International, Ronald Reagan Washington National and Dulles International airports, with 24-hour advance reservations recommended; phone (800) 258-3826.

Manassas / Prince William County/Manassas Convention and Visitors Bureau

Car rental agencies in Washington are numerous; most have conveniently located offices in the city and nearby Maryland and Virginia suburbs. Reservations are recommended and should be made in advance of your arrival; your local AAA/CAA club can provide this assistance or additional information.

Hertz offers discounts to AAA members; phone (800) 654-3080. For listings of other agencies check the telephone directory.

Rail Service

After falling into an advanced state of disrepair in the early 1980s, Union Station was completely renovated (with three levels of upscale shopping added) and re-opened in 1988. Trains pull into the Train Concourse at 1st Street and Massachusetts Avenue N.E. at all hours; phone (202) 906-3000. Amtrak's Metroliner travels to New York daily in about 3 hours. Trains depart for Baltimore-Washington International Airport every hour from 7:20 a.m. to 10:10 p.m. For trains that run from Baltimore-Washington International Airport, phone (800) 872-7245 for reservations.

Destination Washington, D.C.

A culturally diverse blend of young and old, rich and poor—the District of Columbia is a true representation of the United States.

America's past was charted in the hallowed halls of the same buildings that camera-laden tourists spend vacations visiting. Elegant memorials recall the deeds of our nation's founding fathers. And the country's treasures can be seen in museums and galleries lining the expanse of green known as the Mall.

© AAA
Denise E. Campbell

Renwick Gallery, Washington, D.C.
The collection of American crafts and decorative arts at Washington's first art museum, the Renwick—part of the Smithsonian Institution—are exhibited in a beautiful French Second Empire building. (See listing page 88)

© Steve Vidler
eStock Photo

Lincoln Memorial, Washington, D.C.
Daniel Chester French's monumental sculpture of Abraham Lincoln is the centerpiece of this eloquent memorial to the nation's 16th president. (See listing page 80)

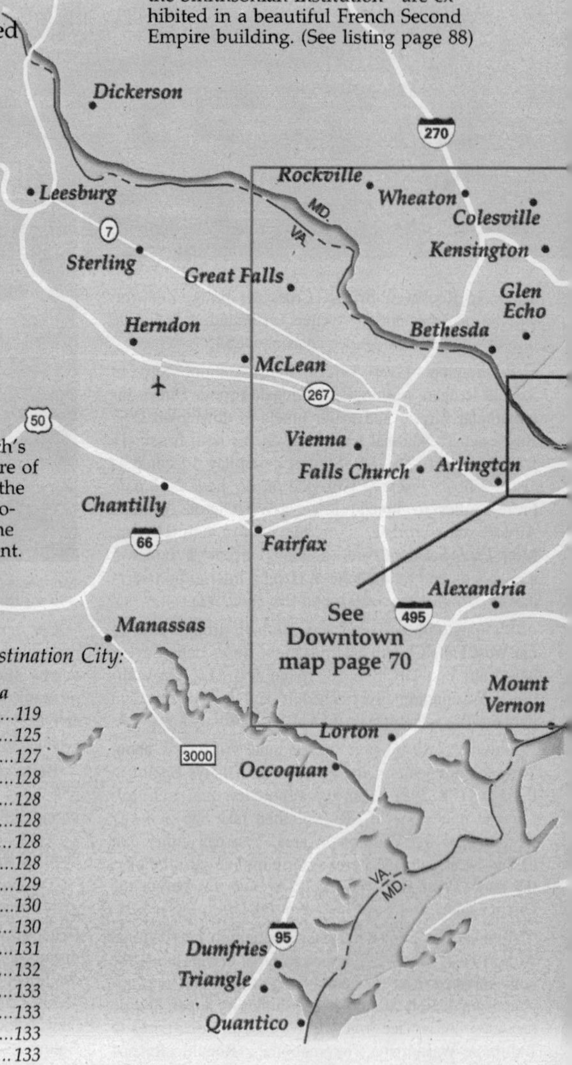

P*laces included in this AAA Destination City:*

Dickerson

270

Rockville
Leesburg
7
Sterling
Great Falls
Herndon
Wheaton
Colesville
Kensington
Glen Echo
Bethesda
McLean
267
50
Vienna
Falls Church   Arlington
Chantilly
66
Fairfax
Alexandria
Manassas
See Downtown map page 70
495
Mount Vernon
3000
Lorton
Occoquan
Dumfries
Triangle
95
Quantico

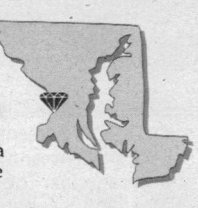

Iwo Jima Statue, Quantico, Va.
A replica of the statue depicting the raising of the American flag during the World War II battle for Iwo Jima stands at the entrance to the Marine Corps installation base in Quantico. (See listing page 133)

Prince William County/Manassas CVB

Laurel

95

1

95

College Park•

Greenbelt

Glenn Dale

Silver Spring

Washington D.C.

Bowie

50

Largo

D.C.
MD.

495

95

Oxon Hill

VA.
MD.

5

301

210

Clinton•

Fort Washington

Accokeek

See Vicinity map page 54

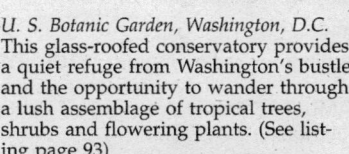

Chinatown Friendship Archway, Washington, D.C.
Myriad colorful dragons decorate this ceremonial entrance to D.C.'s Chinatown neighborhood, an eight-block-square area. (See listing page 74)

Washington DC Convention and Tourism Corp

U. S. Botanic Garden, Washington, D.C.
This glass-roofed conservatory provides a quiet refuge from Washington's bustle and the opportunity to wander through a lush assemblage of tropical trees, shrubs and flowering plants. (See listing page 93)

© Gibson Stock Photography

The Informed Traveler

Sales Tax: The District of Columbia's sales tax is 5.75 percent. There is a hotel tax of 14.5 percent and a 10 percent food and beverage tax. The sales tax in neighboring Maryland is 5 percent, in Virginia 4.5 percent; lodging taxes vary by county.

WHOM TO CALL

Emergency: 911

Police (non-emergency): (202) 727-1010

Time: (202) 844-2525 or (202) 844-1212

Temperature: (202) 936-1212

Hospitals: George Washington University Hospital, (202) 715-4000; Howard University Hospital, (202) 865-6100; Sibley Memorial Hospital, (202) 537-4000; Washington Hospital Center, (202) 877-7000.

WHERE TO LOOK

Newspapers

The major newspapers, both distributed in the morning, are *The Washington Post* and the *Washington Times*. The weekly *Washington Afro-American* is available at newsstands, as are various smaller dailies and weeklies. Events are listed in the *City Paper,* a free weekly, and the daily Style or Friday Weekend sections of the *Post*.

Radio

Washington radio station WTOP (1500 AM) is an all-news/weather station; WAMU (88.5 FM) is a member of National Public Radio.

Visitor Information

Visitor Information Center: Ronald Reagan Building, 1300 Pennsylvania Ave. N.W., Washington, DC 20005; phone (202) 328-4748 or (866) 324-7386.

The center has brochures, city guides, interactive computers, an introductory video and staff to answer questions. Those over age 15 must have ID to enter the building. Open Mon.-Fri. 8:30-5:30, Sat. 9-4, Mar. 15-Labor Day; Mon.-Fri. 9-4:30, rest of year.

Washington, D.C. Convention & Tourism Corp.: 901 7th St. N.W., 4th floor, Washington, DC 20001; phone (202) 789-7000 or (800) 422-8644.

WHAT TO PACK

Summers are warm and humid, and during spells of sweltering weather, high temperatures can hover between 95 and 100, accompanied by steamy humidity. Washingtonians anticipate the occasional brief burst of refreshing weather in July and August—sunny, breezy afternoons around 80 degrees, with low humidity and blue skies.

Washington winters can be raw, with a few nights plunging into the single digits and blustery days when the thermometer fails to rise above freezing. Some winters have practically no snow, while others can deal out several snowfalls and the occasional near blizzard. The District also is susceptible to ice storms. For winter driving, make sure your vehicle is equipped with snow tires.

Spring and fall are short but exceedingly pleasant, with daytime highs in the 60s and 70s and nighttime lows in the 40s and 50s. April, May and October are the nicest months of the year, with sunny days and low humidity. *For additional information see temperature chart p. 53.*

Casual clothes are fine for sightseeing. Comfortable walking shoes are essential. Sunglasses and a hat come in handy in summer, a hat and gloves in winter. A jacket and tie may be required or advised at some of the finer restaurants.

Buses

The Greyhound Lines Inc. bus terminal is at 1st and L streets N.E.; phone (800) 231-2222.

Getting Around

Street System

Pierre-Charles L'Enfant's plan for the capital did not take into account the demands of modern traffic. Although streets are laid out in a basic grid pattern divided into four quadrants, there are several confusing traffic circles and a number of one-way streets. An easy-to-read street map will come in handy for those unfamiliar with the city.

In the central part of the District, streets running north-south are numbered; those running east-west are designated by letters (with the exception of J, X, Y and Z). This general pattern is crisscrossed in both directions by diagonal avenues named after states. Where avenues intersect there are traffic circles and rectangular parks or squares.

North, East and South Capitol streets and the National Mall divide the diamond-shaped District of Columbia into quadrants; the Capitol is the central starting point for the street numbering system. The quadrant initials—N.W., N.E., S.W. and S.E.—are an integral part of any Washington address; they determine which of four possible locations is correct.

Southwest is by far the smallest quadrant, encompassing a few government buildings, the Tidal Basin, the Maine Avenue waterfront along the Washington Channel and Fort Lesley J. McNair, intended by L'Enfant to be the capital's chief fortification and a major 19th-century U.S. weapons arsenal. Also within Southwest is L'Enfant Plaza, bounded by D Street, the 12th Street Expressway ramp, the 9th Street Expressway and the Southwest Freeway. This example of late 1960s urban planning—a brick-paved concourse lined with office buildings that runs for a couple of blocks off Independence Avenue— is named for the man who drafted the city's blueprint.

Most of Washington's tourist attractions and its wealthiest neighborhoods are concentrated in the northwest quadrant, along with American, Georgetown, George Washington and Howard universities, the University of the District of Columbia, Rock Creek Park and Walter Reed Army Medical Center. Most of Northeast and Southeast are residential, as is the upper part of Northwest.

North of W Street, east-west streets are assigned two-syllable alphabetical names (Belmont, Quincy, Randolph), then three-syllable names (Buchanan, Hamilton, Underwood). Above Whittier Street in upper Northwest, alphabetical names shift to trees and plants with two- (Aspen), three- (Butternut) or four-syllable (Geranium) names. At this point the District ends and Maryland begins, which no doubt delighted planners.

Some illogical aspects of the city street system confuse even residents. Pennsylvania Avenue, for example, enters southeast Washington from suburban Maryland; is interrupted at Independence Avenue S.E. by the Capitol grounds; picks up again at

National Museum of the American Indian / © AAA / Denise E. Campbell

1st Street N.W.; is interrupted at 15th Street by the Ellipse; picks up again around the corner at the intersection of 15th Street and New York Avenue N.W.; and continues west past the White House into Georgetown, where it turns into M Street.

Traveling east of the Capitol on Pennsylvania can be equally confusing; once you cross 15th Street, you are on New York Avenue. And 17th Street N.W. heads north from Constitution Avenue only as far as K Street, where it then links with Connecticut Avenue.

Adding to the frustration level of drivers was the closing in 1995 of Pennsylvania Avenue to automobile traffic in front of the White House. Done for security reasons, it nevertheless created some initial havoc for the thousands of downtown workers and tourists who had daily negotiated the 2-block stretch between 15th and 17th streets N.W. Traffic engineers responded by redirecting traffic on nearby streets and installing new signals, signs and pavement markings, while inline skaters, bicyclists and strollers savored the newfound peace and quiet and the refreshing lack of exhaust fumes.

The speed limit is 25 mph or as posted; on major arteries it is usually 30 mph. A right turn on a red light is permitted unless otherwise posted. High-beam headlights are prohibited at all times.

Business areas, particularly in the downtown core, are congested throughout the day. Avoid rush hours if at all possible. If you are spending the day sightseeing but are staying in nearby Maryland or Virginia—and driving a car—leave in plenty of time to avoid the outbound exodus of city workers. The backup on I-395 southbound begins early (particularly on Fridays and the beginning of holiday weekends), and traffic soon slows to a painful crawl.

Also remember that carpooling regulations (HOV) govern the number of people in vehicles that use certain heavily traveled highways, such as I-66 and I-395 inside the Beltway. Signs denote designated HOV lanes; the restrictions apply during both morning (6:30 to 9 a.m.) and evening (4 to 6:30 p.m.) rush-hour periods.

Parking

Despite luring millions and millions of tourists annually with an abundance of sightseeing attractions, Washington is distinctly less generous in supplying them with parking spaces. On-street parking downtown is limited, particularly near the National Mall and the major museums. Violations are strictly enforced; pay close attention to all signs in the vicinity of any space you are lucky enough to find.

Meters are closely monitored, and as soon as the "expired" flag pops up in the window a vehicle is fair game to be ticketed. Most meters run for only an hour, so visitors taking in the museums along the Mall should designate someone to keep the device supplied with quarters. The problem eases on weekends, when meters are not running.

Parking is free on Jefferson and Madison drives north and south of the Mall Mon.-Fri. 10-1, but these spots are invariably filled. If you venture off the Mall looking for a space, watch for signs in residential neighborhoods; often street parking is reserved for residents, and a special zone sticker must be displayed on the front windshield. You can park on the street in such neighborhoods, but usually only for a 2-hour period. In Georgetown parking and standing are banned on M Street between 29th Street and Key Bridge, as well as on Wisconsin Avenue between K and O streets, Friday and Saturday nights from 6:30 p.m. to 4 a.m.

Be sure to park only between the marked lines on the pavement; drivers of small cars are often tempted to squeeze into a space that is not really legal. Parking is prohibited within 10 feet of a fire hydrant, 25 feet of a stop sign and 40 feet of an intersection. Parking statutes are strictly enforced by tickets, but cars are generally towed only when they endanger public safety. If your vehicle is towed Friday after 7 p.m. or anytime on weekends, you must wait until the following Monday after 9 a.m. to retrieve it.

No Standing zones also are enforced; automobiles are not permitted to be in those areas except briefly to pick up or discharge passengers. For additional details, contact the D.C. Department of Public Works; phone (202) 576-7217.

Downtown commercial lots and garages can be expensive, many charging $12 or more per day, with discounts for those arriving early in the morning or late in the afternoon. Some stores may offer shoppers a parking discount; inquire at the individual establishment. Many garages close by about 7 p.m., making them impractical for attending evening events. For a cheaper and frequently more convenient alternative, consider the Metro system (see *Public Transportation*).

Taxis & Limousines

Rather than meters, taxicabs in Washington use the zone system to determine fares. The basic zone charge is $6.25 per person, with a $1.50 surcharge for each additional person (an additional $1.50 is charged for travel to another zone). There also is a $1.25 surcharge per person (or group of persons traveling together) for weekday taxi service that commences between 4 and 6:30 p.m. The maximum basic fare for one person within the District is $13.25. Other factors, from the amount of baggage to the time of day, might increase the fare.

The rates quoted above are for cabs hailed on the street; rates increase by about $1.50 when a cab is requested by telephone. Taxi rates for trips into or from nearby points in Maryland and Virginia will vary; make sure you determine the rate with the driver in advance. Cabs with Virginia or Maryland license plates may transport passengers in and out of the District, but not between points within the District. Cab companies include Capitol, (202) 545-8900; Diamond, (202) 387-6200; Liberty,

(202) 636-1600; and Yellow, (202) 544-1212. Limousine service in and around Washington averages $50 per hour, excluding tax and tip.

Public Transportation

Washington's heavy traffic congestion and chronic lack of public parking make public transportation an enticing alternative indeed. The red, white and blue buses of the Metro system reach nearly every point in the D.C. area for $1.25, senior citizens and the physically impaired 60c. Express fare is $3. Up to two children 4 years of age and younger may ride free with each adult paying full fare; over age 4 pay the adult fare.

A regional 1-day pass offers unlimited rides on regular Metrobuses and other local buses. The fare is $3; on express buses, the pass covers $1.25 of the $3 fare. A free transfer is valid for unlimited Metrobus connections (including round trips) within a 2-hour period; ask the driver for a transfer. A free Metrorail to Metrobus transfer, available at the entrances to Metro stations, is worth 90c off the bus fare.

Metrobus operates daily 24 hours, but service intervals vary by time of day, during the week and on weekends to best meet demand. Exact fare is required. For information about special and reduced fares phone (202) 637-7000.

The red, white, black and yellow buses of the DC Circulator transit system offer service to the area's major cultural, shopping, dining and business sites. Running every 5-10 minutes daily 7 a.m.-9 p.m., the buses connect downtown Washington with Georgetown, the Washington Convention Center and the southwest waterfront. Fare is $1, senior citizens and the physically impaired 50c. Exact fare is required. Travelers can transfer from Metrobus or between Circulator buses for free. For information about routes phone (202) 962-1423.

Metrorail is a clean, architecturally striking subway that provides access to most of the city's attractions and is an efficient and economical means of getting around. Stations functioning as major transfer points between lines are Metro Center, Gallery Place-Chinatown, L'Enfant Plaza, Pentagon, Rosslyn, Stadium-Armory, King Street and Fort Totten.

The Red Line runs from Glenmont, Md., to Shady Grove, Md., via downtown Washington. The Yellow Line runs from Mt. Vernon Square in Washington to Huntington, south of Alexandria, Va., via Ronald Reagan Washington National Airport. The Blue Line connects Addison Road in Prince Georges County, Md., with the Franconia/Springfield station via downtown Washington; it is in the process of being extended to Largo, Md. The Orange Line travels between New Carrollton, Md., and Vienna, Va., via downtown Washington. The Green Line extends from Greenbelt, Md., south to Branch Avenue in Prince George's County, Md., via downtown Washington.

Maps at each station's mezzanine provide route and fare information; station managers also are available on the mezzanine. Route maps are posted near the doors of each train car. Farecard machines at each station dispense the magnetically encoded cards needed by each rider to enter and leave station faregates.

The minimum fare is $1.35; additional charges depend on the distance traveled and whether you enter the system during regular fare hours (Mon.-Fri. 5:30-9:30, 3-7 and 2 a.m.-closing) or reduced fare hours (all other times). **Note:** If using Metro in the evening, check the scheduled departure time for the last train; at many stations it departs before the system closes. Final departure times are posted in each station kiosk.

The maximum one-way fare is $3.90 during peak hours, $2.35 during off-peak hours. Two children under 5 may ride free with each paying passenger. The Metrorail One-Day Pass entitles riders to unlimited rail travel Mon.-Thurs. 9:30 a.m.-midnight, Fri. 9:30 a.m.-3 a.m., Sat. 7 a.m.-3 a.m., Sun. and holidays 7 a.m.-midnight. The fare is $6.50.

Parking lots and garages are available at most of the suburban stations, but they often are full by 8 a.m. on weekdays. Parking at Metro-operated lots is free on weekends and federal holidays. Parking fees must be paid using a SmarTrip card, sold in vending machines at stations where parking is available. These permanent, rechargeable plastic farecards also can be used in Metro stations. For SmarTrip card information phone (888) 762-7874.

Metrorail operates Mon.-Thurs. 5:30 a.m.-midnight, Fri. 5:30 a.m.-3 a.m., Sat. 7 a.m.-3 a.m., Sun. 7 a.m.-midnight. Hours are reduced on the following holidays: Jan. 1, Martin Luther King, Jr. Day, Presidents' Day, Memorial Day, July 4, Labor Day, Columbus Day, Veterans Day, Thanksgiving, and Dec. 25 and 31.

Intervals between trains vary by time and route, but are usually about 5 minutes during rush hour and 12 minutes at other times. For further information about routes and rates phone (202) 637-7000, or TTY (202) 638-3780.

One- or multiday passes and other farecards can be purchased at the Metro sales offices at 600 5th St. N.W. (Mon.-Fri. 10-3) and 12th and F streets N.W. (Mon.-Fri. 7:30-6:30), and at the Pentagon Transit Center in Arlington, Va. (Mon.-Fri. 7-6:30). Metro fare cards, tokens and passes also are available at nearly 400 participating retail outlets and at Commuter Stores in the Crystal City Underground Mall, the Ballston Common Mall and Rosslyn Center (all in Arlington).

Note: In the *Points of Interest* section attraction listings include the nearest Metrorail (M:) stop if applicable. *Also see page 72.*

What To See

AFRICAN AMERICAN CIVIL WAR MEMORIAL, Vermont and U sts. N.W. (M: U Street/African-Amer Civil War Memorial/Cardozo), is a tribute to African-Americans who served in the Union forces during the Civil War.

The 10-foot-tall bronze "Spirit of Freedom" sculpture depicts soldiers and sailors from the various armed services. Low semicircular walls bear the names of the 209,145 members of the United States Colored Troops (USCT). Allow 30 minutes minimum. Daily 24 hours. Free. Phone (202) 426-6841.

Thomas Jefferson Memorial / © AAA / Denise E. Campbell

African American Civil War Museum is at 1200 U St. N.W. Photographs, original documents, clothing, weapons and newspaper articles depict the history of African-Americans in the United States, with an emphasis on African-American participation in the Civil War. Allow 30 minutes minimum. Mon.-Fri. 10-5, Sat. 10-2; closed national holidays. Donations. Phone (202) 667-2667.

THE ALBERT EINSTEIN MEMORIAL stands in a shady grove of trees at the s.w. corner of the National Academy of Sciences, 2100 C St. N.W. (M: Foggy Bottom-GWU). Robert Berks created this 12-foot-tall seated bronze statue of the most widely known modern physicist, who also was a National Academy of Sciences member.

Einstein is casually seated on a white granite bench, while at his feet much of the known universe is depicted on a 28-foot circular sky map that shows stars to the sixth magnitude. Daily 24 hours. Free. Phone (202) 334-2000.

ANACOSTIA COMMUNITY MUSEUM of the Smithsonian Institution is at 1901 Fort Pl. S.E. (M: Anacostia; transfer to W2 or W3 bus) in Fort Stanton Park, approximately 8 mi. from the National Mall. The museum is dedicated to the documentation, preservation and interpretation of African American history and culture from a community perspective.

Its collection of objects and archival material dates from the early 1800s and focuses on such key areas as community and family history, religion and contemporary popular culture. The museum also hosts a revolving program of exhibitions and educational activities. Allow 1 hour minimum. Daily 10-5; closed Dec. 25. Free. Phone (202) 633-1000, or TTY (202) 633-5285.

ANACOSTIA PARK lies on both sides of the Anacostia River in the n.e. and s.e. sections of the city (M: Anacostia). In 1608, a year after the founding of Jamestown, Va., Capt. John Smith made his way up the Potomac River and discovered the large Indian village of Nacotchtank, which is believed to have been in the southern end of what is now Anacostia Park.

The 1,271-acre park contains tennis and basketball courts, soccer and baseball fields, a swimming pool, a skating rink, a pavilion and the Aquatic Education Center. Fishing and bicycling are permitted. Allow 30 minutes minimum. Daily 9:30-5:30. Free. Phone (202) 690-5182.

ANDERSON HOUSE, 2118 Massachusetts Ave. N.W. (M: Dupont Circle), is the headquarters, library and museum of The Society of the Cincinnati, which was founded by the officers of the Continental Army and Navy in 1783. Displays pertain to the American Revolution. European and Oriental decorative arts also are exhibited.

Allow 1 hour minimum. Museum open Tues.-Sat. 1-4. Library open Mon.-Fri. 10-4 by appointment. Closed major holidays and during society meetings. Guided tours are available Tues.-Sat. at 1:15, 2:15 and 3:15. Free. Phone (202) 785-2040.

ARTHUR M. SACKLER GALLERY of the Smithsonian Institution, 1050 Independence Ave. S.W. (M: Smithsonian), is entered from a pavilion in the Enid A. Haupt Garden, s. of the Smithsonian Institution Building (the Castle). The gallery is housed in a three-level complex that, except for the entrance pavilion, is entirely underground and connects to the Smithsonian's other Asian art museum, the Freer Gallery of Art.

The Sackler Gallery's permanent collection of art from the Mediterranean to Japan spans ancient times to the present. Included are objects in bronze, jade, silver, gold, lacquer and ceramics, as well as paintings and sculptures. The gallery also features changing exhibitions of Asian art from museums around the world. Allow 2 hours minimum. Daily 10-5:30; closed Dec. 25. Guided tours are available on selected days; phone for schedule. Free. Phone (202) 633-1000, or TTY (202) 633-5285.

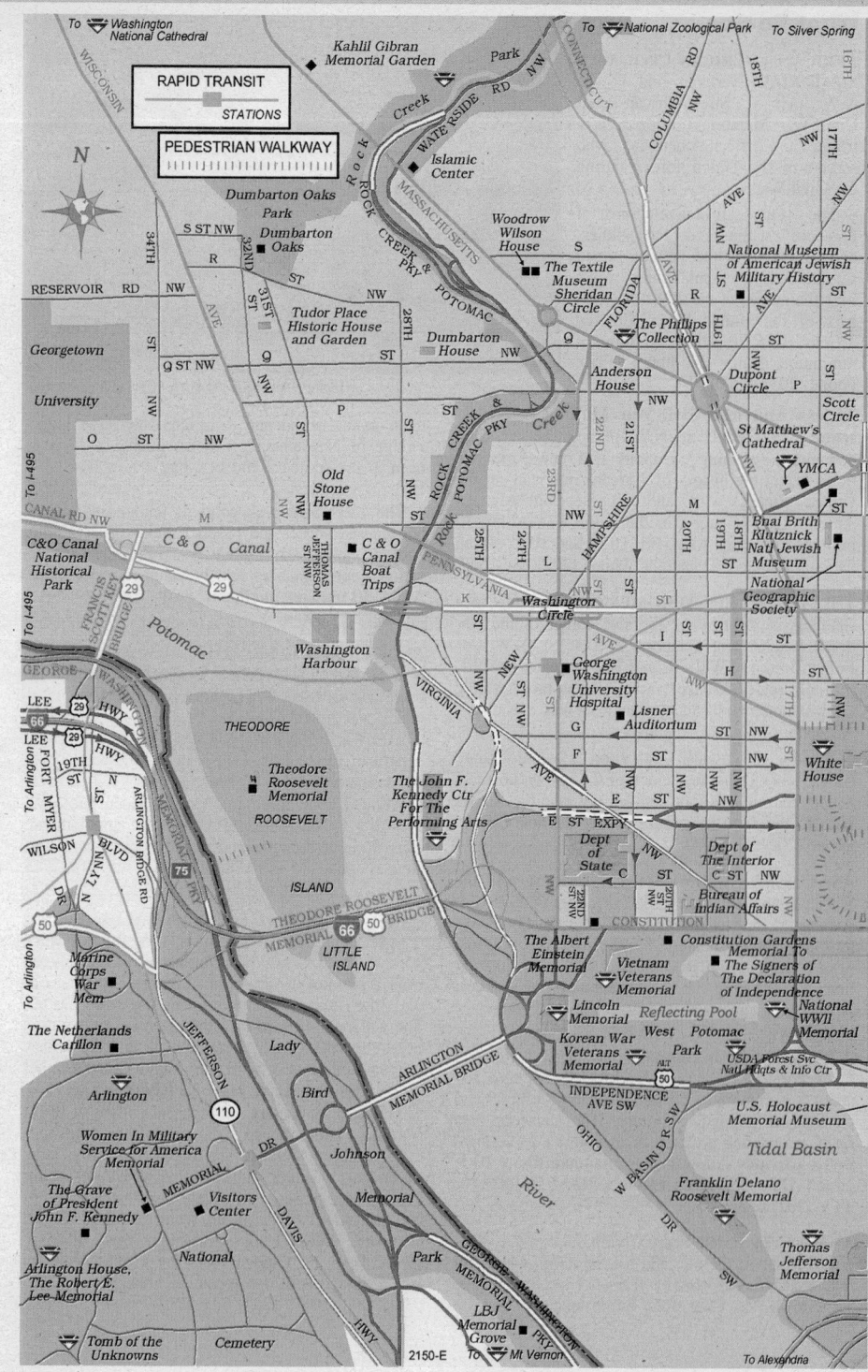

To Washington National Cathedral
To National Zoological Park
To Silver Spring

RAPID TRANSIT
STATIONS
PEDESTRIAN WALKWAY

N

Kahlil Gibran Memorial Garden

Rock Creek Park

Islamic Center

Waterside RD NW

Woodrow Wilson House

MASSACHUSETTS

National Museum of American Jewish Military History

Dumbarton Oaks Park

Dumbarton Oaks

S ST NW
R ST
32ND ST
31ST ST
34TH ST
AVE

The Textile Museum
Sheridan Circle

FLORIDA

The Phillips Collection

Tudor Place Historic House and Garden

Dumbarton House NW

Anderson House

Dupont Circle

Scott Circle

Georgetown University

RESERVOIR RD NW

POTOMAC

28TH ST

Q ST NW
P ST
O ST NW

St Matthew's Cathedral

YMCA

Old Stone House

ROCK CREEK & POTOMAC PKY

Creek

22ND
21ST
20TH
19TH
18TH

Bnai Brith Klutznick Natl Jewish Museum

CANAL RD NW

C & O Canal

23RD
25TH
24TH

National Geographic Society

C&O Canal National Historical Park

THOMAS JEFFERSON ST NW

C & O Canal Boat Trips

PENNSYLVANIA

Washington Circle

NEW HAMPSHIRE

George Washington University Hospital

17TH

White House

To I-495

FRANCIS SCOTT KEY BRIDGE

Potomac

Washington Harbour

VIRGINIA

Lisner Auditorium

THEODORE

GEORGE

LEE HWY
29
66
LEE HWY
29

WILSON

FORT MYER

Theodore Roosevelt Memorial

ROOSEVELT

The John F. Kennedy Ctr For The Performing Arts

E ST EXPY

Dept of State

Dept of The Interior

Bureau of Indian Affairs

ARLINGTON MEMORIAL PKY

ISLAND

THEODORE ROOSEVELT MEMORIAL BRIDGE
66
50

LITTLE ISLAND

CONSTITUTION

The Albert Einstein Memorial

Constitution Gardens Memorial To The Signers of The Declaration of Independence

To Arlington
50

Marine Corps War Mem

Vietnam Veterans Memorial

Lincoln Memorial

Reflecting Pool

West Potomac

National WWII Memorial

The Netherlands Carillon

Korean War Veterans Memorial

USDA Forest Svc Natl Hdqts & Info Ctr

Arlington

JEFFERSON

Lady

Bird

ARLINGTON MEMORIAL BRIDGE

INDEPENDENCE AVE SW

OHIO

U.S. Holocaust Memorial Museum

Women In Military Service for America Memorial

110

Johnson

Tidal Basin

Franklin Delano Roosevelt Memorial

The Grave of President John F. Kennedy

MEMORIAL

Visitors Center

DAVIS

Memorial

River

GEORGE WASHINGTON MEMORIAL PKY

Arlington House, The Robert E. Lee Memorial

National

Park

Thomas Jefferson Memorial

Tomb of the Unknowns

Cemetery

2150-E

LBJ Memorial Grove
To Mt Vernon

To Alexandria

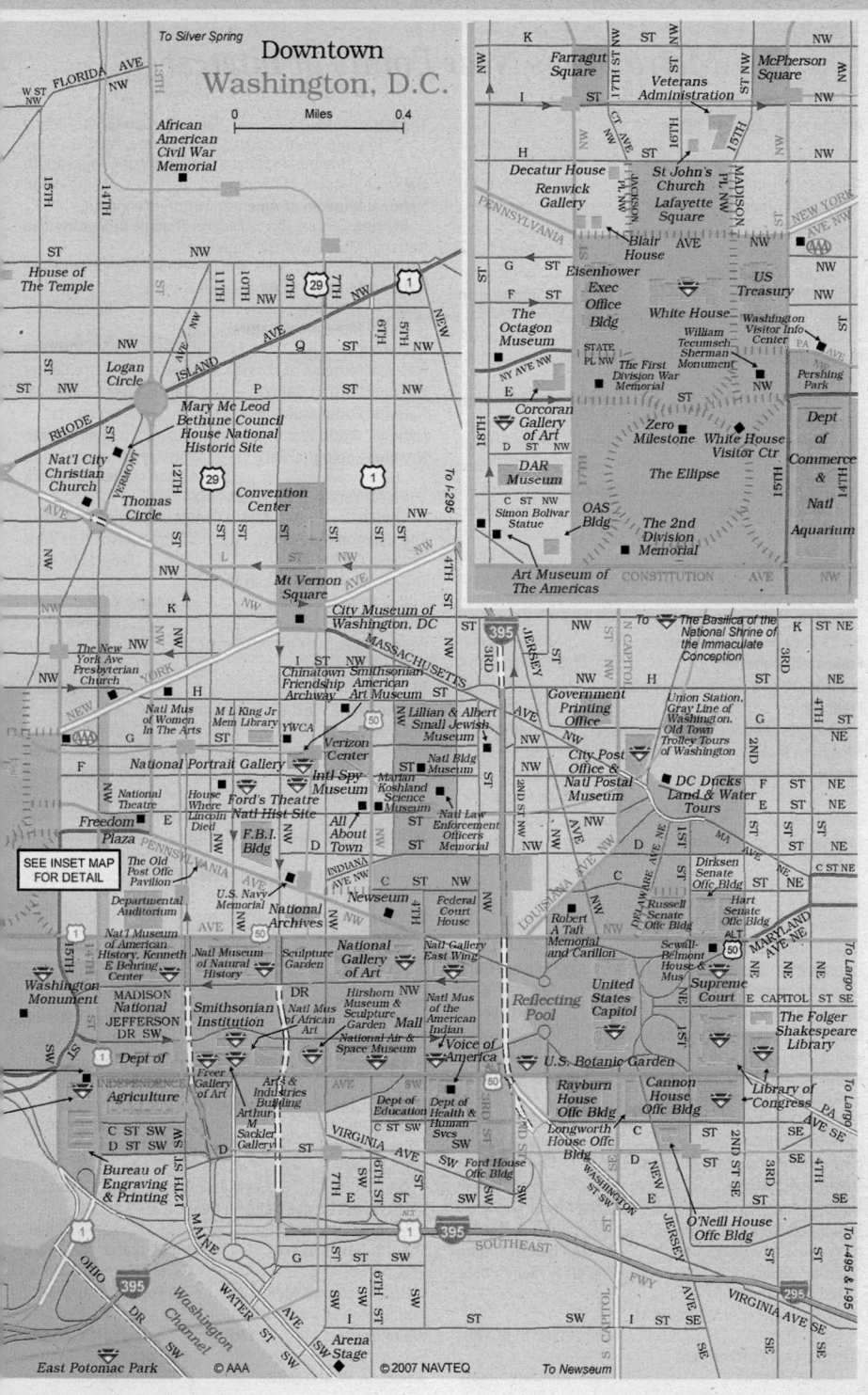

Downtown
Washington, D.C.

To Silver Spring

African American Civil War Memorial

House of The Temple

Logan Circle

Mary Mc Leod Bethune Council House National Historic Site

Nat'l City Christian Church

Thomas Circle

Convention Center

Mt Vernon Square

City Museum of Washington, DC

The New York Ave Presbyterian Church

Chinatown Friendship Archway

Smithsonian American Art Museum

Nat'l Mus of Women In The Arts

M L King Jr Mem Library

YWCA

Lillian & Albert Small Jewish Museum

Nat'l Bldg Museum

National Portrait Gallery

Verizon Center

Intl Spy Museum

Marian Koshland Science Museum

National Theatre

House Where Lincoln Died

Ford's Theatre Nat'l Hist Site

All About Town

Nat'l Law Enforcement Officers Memorial

Freedom Plaza

F.B.I. Bldg

SEE INSET MAP FOR DETAIL

The Old Post Ofc Pavilion

Departmental Auditorium

U.S. Navy Memorial

National Archives

Newseum

Federal Court House

Nat'l Museum of American History, Kenneth E Behring Center

Nat'l Museum of Natural History

Sculpture Garden

National Gallery of Art

Nat'l Gallery East Wing

Washington Monument

MADISON

NATIONAL JEFFERSON DR SW

Smithsonian Institution

Nat'l Mus of African Art

Hirshorn Museum & Sculpture Garden

Nat'l Mus of the American Indian

Dept of Agriculture

Freer Gallery of Art

Arts & Industries Building Arthur M Sackler Gallery

National Air & Space Museum

Voice of America

U.S. Botanic Garden

Bureau of Engraving & Printing

Dept of Education

Dept of Health & Human Svcs

Reflecting Pool

United States Capitol

Supreme Court

Rayburn House Offc Bldg

Cannon House Offc Bldg

Library of Congress

The Folger Shakespeare Library

Longworth House Offc Bldg

Ford House Offc Bldg

O'Neill House Offc Bldg

East Potomac Park

Washington Channel

Arena Stage

© AAA

© 2007 NAVTEQ

To Newseum

The Basilica of the National Shrine of the Immaculate Conception

Government Printing Office

Union Station, Gray Line of Washington, Old Town Trolley Tours of Washington

City Post Office & Nat'l Postal Museum

DC Ducks Land & Water Tours

Dirksen Senate Offc Bldg

Hart Senate Offc Bldg

Russell Senate Offc Bldg

Robert A Taft Memorial and Carillon

Sewall-Belmont House & Mus

Inset (top right):

Farragut Square

Veterans Administration

McPherson Square

Decatur House

Renwick Gallery

St John's Church

Lafayette Square

Blair House

Eisenhower Exec Office Bldg

US Treasury

The Octagon Museum

White House

William Tecumseh Sherman Monument

Washington Visitor Info Center

The First Division War Memorial

Pershing Park

Corcoran Gallery of Art

Zero Milestone

White House Visitor Ctr

Dept of Commerce & Natl Aquarium

DAR Museum

The Ellipse

Simon Bolivar Statue

OAS Bldg

The 2nd Division Memorial

Art Museum of The Americas

Metro Stops Near Points of Interest

African American Civil War
Memorial .... U Street/African-Amer Civil War
Memorial/Cardozo
The Albert Einstein Memorial .... Foggy Bottom-GWU
Anacostia Community Museum .... Anacostia
Anacostia Park .... Anacostia
Anderson House .... Dupont Circle
Arthur M. Sackler Gallery .... Smithsonian
Arts and Industries Building .... Smithsonian
Basilica of the National Shrine of the Immaculate
Conception .... Brookland-CUA
Bureau of Engraving and Printing .... Smithsonian
Chinatown Friendship
Archway .... Gallery Place-Chinatown
Constitution Gardens .... Smithsonian
Corcoran Gallery of Art .... Farragut North or West
DAR Museum .... Farragut North or West
Decatur House .... Farragut North or West
Department of State .... Foggy Bottom-GWU
Department of the Interior Museum ...... Farragut West
Dumbarton House .... Dupont Circle
Emancipation Statue .... Eastern Market
Folger Shakespeare Library .... Capitol South or Union
Station
Ford's Theatre National Historic Site .... Metro Center
Franciscan Monastery .... Brookland-CUA
Franklin Delano Roosevelt Memorial .... Smithsonian
Freer Gallery of Art .... Smithsonian
Hillwood Estate Museum and Gardens .... Van Ness-UDC
Hirshhorn Museum and Sculpture Garden . L'Enfant Plaza
The House of the Temple .... Dupont Circle
International Spy Museum ..... Gallery Place-Chinatown
Islamic Center .... Dupont Circle
Japanese American Memorial to Patriotism During World
War II .... Union Station
J. Edgar Hoover F.B.I. Building .... Metro Center
The John F. Kennedy Center for
the Performing Arts .... Foggy Bottom-GWU
Kenilworth Aquatic Gardens .... Deanwood
Korean War Veterans Memorial .... Foggy Bottom-GWU
Lafayette Square .... Farragut West
Library of Congress .... Capitol South
Lillian & Albert Small Jewish Museum ... Judiciary Square
Lincoln Memorial .... Foggy Bottom-GWU
Marian Koshland Science Museum ... Judiciary Square or
Gallery Place-Chinatown
Mary McLeod Bethune Council House
National Historic Site .... McPherson Square
National Air and Space Museum .... L'Enfant Plaza
National Aquarium .... Federal Triangle
National Archives .... Archives-Navy Memorial
National Building Museum .... Judiciary Square
National City Christian Church ...... McPherson Square
National Gallery of Art .... Archives-Navy Memorial or
Judiciary Square
National Geographic Museum at
Explorers Hall .... Farragut North or West
National Law Enforcement
Officers Memorial .... Judiciary Square

The National Mall .... Foggy Bottom-GWU, Federal
Triangle, Smithsonian, L'Enfant Plaza, Archives-Navy
Memorial, Federal Center SW or Capitol South
National Museum of African Art .... Smithsonian
National Museum of American History, Kenneth E.
Behring Center ...... Federal Triangle or Smithsonian
National Museum of the American
Indian .... Federal Center SW or L'Enfant Plaza
National Museum of American Jewish
Military History .... Dupont Circle
National Museum of Natural
History .... Federal Triangle or Smithsonian
National Museum of Women in the Arts ... Metro Center
National Portrait Gallery .... Gallery Place-Chinatown
National Postal Museum .... Union Station
National World War II Memorial .... Smithsonian
National Zoological Park ...... Woodley Park-Zoo/Adams
Morgan or Cleveland Park
The New York Avenue Presbyterian
Church .... Metro Center or McPherson Square
The Octagon Museum .... Farragut North or West
Old Post Office Pavilion .... Federal Triangle
Organization of American States
Building .... Farragut West or North
The Phillips Collection .... Dupont Circle
Pope John Paul II Cultural Center .... Brookland-CUA
Renwick Gallery .... Farragut West
RFK Stadium .... Stadium-Armory
The Robert A. Taft Memorial and
Carillon .... Union Station
Rock Creek Cemetery .... Fort Totten
St. John's Church .... McPherson Square
St. Matthew's
Cathedral .... Dupont Circle or Farragut North
Senate and House Office Buildings ...... Capitol South or
Union Station
Sewall-Belmont House and Museum .... Capitol South or
Union Station
Smithsonian American Art Museum .... Gallery
Place-Chinatown
Smithsonian Institution Building
(the Castle) .... Smithsonian
Supreme Court
Building .... Capitol South or Union Station
The Textile Museum .... Dupont Circle
Tudor Place Historic House and Garden .... Dupont Circle
United States Capitol .... Capitol South or Union Station
United States Holocaust Memorial
Museum .... Smithsonian
United States Navy Memorial ... Archives-Navy Memorial
U.S. Botanic
Garden .... Capitol South or Federal Center SW
USDA Forest Service National Headquarters and
Information Center .... Smithsonian
The U.S. Navy Museum ..... Eastern Market or Navy Yard
Verizon Center .... Gallery Place-Chinatown
Vietnam Veterans Memorial .... Foggy Bottom-GWU
Washington Monument .... Smithsonian
White House .... McPherson Square, Metro Center
or Federal Triangle
Woodrow Wilson House .... Dupont Circle

Enid A. Haupt Garden is above the National Museum of African Art, the Arthur M. Sackler Gallery and the S. Dillon Ripley Center. Although it is at ground level, the site is essentially a rooftop garden, with a three-story building beneath it. This 4.2-acre garden with a Victorian parterre is bordered by two thematic gardens. Among the plants on display are saucer magnolias, katsura trees and weeping beeches. Collections of 19th-century urns, benches and wickets grace the garden's brick paths.

Daily 6:30 a.m.-dusk. Guided tours are available on selected days (weather permitting), spring through fall; phone for schedule. Free. Phone (202) 633-1000, or TTY (202) 633-5285.

ARTS AND INDUSTRIES BUILDING of the Smithsonian Institution, 900 Jefferson Dr. S.W. (M: Smithsonian), was built to exhibit materials acquired from the 1876 Philadelphia Centennial Exposition. From the early 1990s through January 2004 the museum featured special changing exhibitions about art, history, science and culture.

Between the building and the Hirshhorn Museum, the Mary Livingston Ripley Garden has a variety of colorful herbaceous and woody perennials, shrubs and trees, augmented by seasonal annuals and tropical plants along a serpentine brick walkway. Along Jefferson Drive between the building and the Smithsonian Castle is the Kathrine Dulin Folger Rose Garden, where roses, annuals, perennials and woody plants are chosen to provide year-round interest.

CLOSURE INFORMATION: The Arts and Industries Building is closed in preparation for renovation. The two gardens remain open. Free guided tours of the Ripley garden are available on selected days (weather permitting), spring through fall; phone for schedule. Gardens free. Phone (202) 633-1000, or TTY (202) 633-5285.

BASILICA OF THE NATIONAL SHRINE OF THE IMMACULATE CONCEPTION, Michigan Ave. at 4th St. N.E. (M: Brookland-CUA), is said to be the largest Roman Catholic church in America and one of the largest in the world. The Crypt Church has been in use since the late 1920s; the Great Upper Church was dedicated in 1959. The shrine is Byzantine-Romanesque in style and structure. There is no steel skeleton or framework; it is made entirely of stone, brick, tile and concrete.

The shrine houses a large collection of 20th-century mosaics. Artworks include Vatican Studio mosaic reproductions of Bartolomé Esteban Murillo's "Immaculate Conception" and Titian's "Assumption" as well as a large mosaic of "Christ in Majesty" by John de Rosen. Memorial tablets cover the walls and columns of Memorial Hall, where the coronation tiara of Pope Paul VI is displayed.

Food is available. Allow 1 hour minimum. Daily 7-7, Apr.-Oct.; 7-6, rest of year. Guided tours are offered Mon.-Sat. 9-11 and 1-3, Sun. 1:30-3:30. Guest artists give organ recitals Sun. at 6 p.m., preceded

Passes and Tickets from U.S. Senators and Representatives

Passes for both the House and Senate galleries must be obtained from your senator or representative (see *United States Capitol p. 92*). Although these passes may be available on a walk-in basis, it is suggested that visitors contact their senator or representative several months in advance, because the number of passes is limited. Senator and representative names often can be found in the front matter of your telephone directory.

Requests for tours of the White House *(see attraction listing p. 94)* also must be made through your senator or representative and are accepted up to 6 months in advance; tours are scheduled approximately 1 month before the requested date.

In addition to gallery passes, your legislators can provide tickets for special tours of the F.B.I. Building, Capitol, Supreme Court, Bureau of Engraving and Printing, State Department, Kennedy Center, Treasury Department and National Archives. Tickets should be reserved as early as possible, but some facilities permit tickets to be reserved only 1, 2 or 3 months in advance because of the possibility of ceremonies or other unscheduled closings. Generally, a maximum of five tickets per facility may be issued under one name. Your legislator's office can tell you more.

To contact your legislator, phone the congressional main switchboard at (202) 224-3121, give your legislator's name and ask to be connected to his or her office. The switchboard operator may be able to answer general questions but cannot issue passes or tickets.

by a carillon recital at 5:30 on the 56-bell carillon in Knights' Tower, June-Aug. Free. Phone (202) 526-8300.

BUREAU OF ENGRAVING AND PRINTING, s. of the Washington Monument grounds at 14th and C sts. S.W. (M: Smithsonian), is the site where the U.S. government designs, engraves and prints currency, bonds and other miscellaneous items. A visitor center contains related exhibits, including various engraved cards and uncut currency sheets that may be purchased.

Note: Fluctuating security levels may affect public access; phone ahead to verify schedule. Sharp objects are not allowed in the building. Photography is not permitted. Allow 30 minutes minimum.

Visitor center open Mon.-Fri. 8:30-7:30, May-Aug.; 8:30-3:30, rest of year. Closed federal holidays and Dec. 23-Jan. 2. Guided tours are given Mon.-Fri. every 15 minutes 9-10:45 and 12:30-2 (also 5-7, May-Aug.). Same-day tickets for tours may be obtained at the booth on Raoul Wallenberg Place beginning at 8 a.m., early Mar.-late Aug.; no tickets are required rest of year. Tickets are limited, and lines often form an hour or more before ticket booth opens. One person may obtain up to four tickets Free. Phone (202) 874-2330 or (866) 874-2330.

CHINATOWN FRIENDSHIP ARCHWAY, 7th and H sts. N.W. (M: Gallery Place-Chinatown), marks the entrance to the eight-block Chinatown neighborhood, bounded by H, I, 6th and 11th streets. One of the largest single-span archways in the world, the intricate red and gold structure is decorated with

Eisenhower Executive Office Building
© AAA / Denise E. Campbell

7,000 tile and 272 painted dragons in the styles of the Ming and Kuing dynasties.

The Chinese New Year's parade passes under the archway, which was dedicated in 1986 by the mayors of Beijing, China and the District of Columbia. The parade takes place between late January and mid-February, depending on the lunar calendar.

CONGRESSIONAL CEMETERY is at 1801 E St. S.E. A number of famous and colorful figures are buried at the cemetery, including Mathew Brady, Elbridge Gerry, J. Edgar Hoover, John Philip Sousa and numerous members of Congress. Brochures outlining a self-guiding walking tour are available at the office. **Note:** Exercise caution when moving about, as the ground contains depressions, footstones and markers that may cause one to trip. Allow 1 hour minimum. Cemetery open daily dawn-dusk. Office open Mon., Wed. and Fri. 10-2, Sat. 9-1. Free. Phone (202) 543-0539.

CONSTITUTION GARDENS, just off Constitution Ave. between 17th and 26th sts. N.W. (M: Smithsonian), is a 52-acre section of the National Mall containing a 6-acre lake and a 1-acre garden. The Vietnam Veterans Memorial *(see attraction listing p. 94)* is just west of and adjacent to Constitution Gardens. This tranquil, shady retreat is especially lovely in spring. Daily 24 hours. Free. Phone (202) 426-6841.

Memorial to the Signers of the Declaration of Independence, on the lake in Constitution Gardens, consists of large granite blocks carved with replicas of the 56 signatures on the Declaration of Independence. A landscaped garden surrounds the memorial. Daily 24 hours. Free. Phone (202) 426-6841.

CORCORAN GALLERY OF ART, 17th St. between E St. and New York Ave. N.W. (M: Farragut North or Farragut West), has an extensive collection of American paintings, drawings, prints and sculpture from the 18th century to the present.

The permanent collection includes the W.A. Clark Collection of European paintings and sculpture, tapestries and pottery; the Salon Doré, an ornate example of 18th-century interior design; and American painter Albert Bierstadt's panoramic canvas "The Last of the Buffalo." There also are changing exhibits of contemporary art and works by fine art photographers and local artists.

Food is available. Sun.-Mon. and Wed.-Thurs. 10-6 (also Thurs. 6-9 p.m.), Fri.-Sat. 10-5; closed Jan. 1, Martin Luther King Jr. Day, Presidents Day, Memorial Day, Thanksgiving and Dec. 25. Guided tours are given Wed.-Sun. at noon. Admission $14; $12 (senior citizens and military); $10 (students with ID); free (ages 0-11). Phone (202) 639-1700.

DAR MUSEUM is at 1776 D St. N.W. in Memorial Continental Hall (M: Farragut North or Farragut West). Maintained by the National Society Daughters of the American Revolution, the museum consists of 33 period rooms displaying such decorative arts as furniture, ceramics, glass, paintings and silver made or used in early America. Constitution Hall, a 3,702-seat auditorium, was designed by John Russell Pope in monumental neoclassic style. It serves as a venue for special events as well as a variety of popular music concerts.

Museum open Mon.-Fri. 8:30-4, Sat. 9-5; closed federal holidays and two weeks late June-early July. Tours are given Mon.-Fri. 10-2:30, Sat. 9-4:30. Free. Phone (202) 879-3241 for the museum, (202) 628-1776 for general information or (202) 628-4780 for concert information.

DAR Library is at 1776 D St. N.W. in Memorial Continental Hall. This genealogical research facility was founded in 1896. Also housed in the building, the Americana Collection contains more than 4,000 historic manuscripts and rare imprints highlighting American life during the early republic, Colonial period and Revolutionary War era.

Library open Mon.-Fri. 8:30-4, Sat. 9-5; closed federal holidays and two weeks late June-early July. Americana Collection open Mon.-Fri. 8:30-4. Library $6. Americana Collection free. Phone (202) 879-3229 for the library, (202) 628-1776 for general information or (202) 879-3256 for Americana Collection information.

DECATUR HOUSE, entered at 1610 H St. N.W. (M: Farragut North or Farragut West), was designed by Benjamin Latrobe for naval hero Stephen Decatur and his wife Susan. Completed in 1818 shortly after the White House and St. John's Church were built, this was the first private residence on Lafayette Square *(see attraction listing p. 79).*

The house later served as the unofficial residence for a string of American and foreign dignitaries while simultaneously being occupied by slaves. Guided tours are given Tues.-Sat. 10-5, Sun. noon-4; closed major holidays. Donations. Phone (202) 842-0920.

DEPARTMENT OF STATE is at 2201 C St. N.W. (M: Foggy Bottom-GWU). It has been at this location since 1947; an extension was completed in 1961. Part of the Executive Branch, the agency is responsible for formulating and implementing U.S. foreign policy.

Forty-five-minute tours of the eighth-floor diplomatic reception rooms are available. These elaborately decorated rooms, used by the Secretary of State, the Vice President and Cabinet members to entertain dignitaries, contain furnishings dating 1750-1825. Publications and travel information are available from the Public Information Service.

Note: A photo ID is required for admittance. No strollers, backpacks or packages are permitted, and storage facilities are not available. Guided tours are offered Mon.-Fri. at 9:30, 10:30 and 2:45. Free. Tours are not recommended for children under 12. Reservations are required and should be made approximately 4 weeks in advance. Phone (202) 647-3241, TTY (202) 736-4474, or (202) 647-6575 for publications and travel information.

DEPARTMENT OF THE INTERIOR MUSEUM, 1849 C St. N.W., is in the Department of the Interior building, which covers two city blocks from C to E sts. and 18th to 19th sts. (M: Farragut West). The building contains many New Deal murals that can be viewed only by appointment. Museum exhibits illustrate the development, use and conservation of natural resources and the art and architecture of the building. Crafts by American Indians and Pacific Islanders also are on display.

Note: A photo ID is required for adult admittance. Guided tours are available. Allow 30 minutes minimum. Mon.-Fri. 8:30-4:30, third Sat. of the month 1-4; closed federal holidays. Free. Reservations are required for guided tours and viewing of the murals in restricted areas and should be made 2 weeks in advance. Phone (202) 208-4743.

[SAVE] **DUMBARTON HOUSE** is in Georgetown at 2715 Q St. N.W. (M: Dupont Circle). This Federal-period house, built about 1800, was the home of Joseph Nourse, Register of the U.S. Treasury 1781-1829. The building contains fine examples of Federal furniture, paintings, silver and Chinese export porcelain, as well as letters and documents signed by George Washington, Thomas Jefferson and Dolley Madison.

Allow 1 hour minimum. Guided 45-minute tours are given every hour Tues.-Sat. 10:15-1:15; closed most federal holidays and Dec. 24. Fee $5; free (students with ID). Phone (202) 337-2288.

DUMBARTON OAKS garden entrance is at jct. 31st and R sts. The 19th-century house contains a research center for Byzantine and medieval civilizations studies, pre-Columbian studies and the history of landscape architecture. Collections include a library of more than 100,000 volumes and an art collection representing the early Christian and Byzantine periods. The 10-acre gardens incorporate traditional French, English, and Italian design elements.

Of historical note was the 1944 Dumbarton Oaks Conversations, a series of meetings about international organization. Attended by representatives from the United States, United Kingdom, the Soviet Union and China, the conference led to the founding of the United Nations. Formal gardens designed by noted landscape architect Beatrix Jones Farrand occupy the grounds of the estate.

Note: The museum, with Byzantine and Pre-Columbian collections, is currently closed to the public and is scheduled to reopen in April 2008. Gardens open Tues.-Sun. 2-6, Mar. 15-Oct. 31; 2-5, rest of year (weather permitting). Closed federal holidays and Dec. 24. Gardens admission (Mar. 15-Oct. 31) $7; $5 (senior citizens and ages 0-11). Gardens admission (rest of year) free to all. Phone (202) 339-6401 for recorded information or (202) 339-6409 for docent tour information.

Ford's Theatre National Historic Site / © AAA / Denise E. Campbell

EMANCIPATION STATUE is at the w. end of Lincoln Park on E. Capitol St. between 11th and 13th sts. N.E. (M: Eastern Market). The sculpture, created by Thomas Ball, depicts a slave being liberated by Abraham Lincoln. It was paid for by donations from emancipated slaves and was dedicated in 1876 with Frederick Douglass in attendance. Also in Lincoln Park is the Mary McLeod Bethune Memorial.

ENID A. HAUPT GARDEN—
see *Arthur M. Sackler Gallery p. 69.*

F.B.I. BUILDING—
see *J. Edgar Hoover F.B.I. Building p. 78.*

FOLGER SHAKESPEARE LIBRARY is at 2nd and E. Capitol sts. S.E., just e. of the Library of Congress (M: Capitol South or Union Station). This neoclassic building has a Tudor-inspired interior. A permanent multimedia exhibition in the Shakespeare Gallery allows visitors to electronically browse through the library's collection and listen to music performed by the Folger Consort.

Lectures, theater programs, concerts, plays and readings of poetry and fiction are presented regularly. Changing exhibits featuring Shakespearean and Renaissance items, including paintings and rare books and manuscripts, are displayed in the Folger Great Hall.

Visitors also can view the Elizabethan Garden; it features a knot garden, herbs mentioned in Shakespeare's plays and statues by American sculptor Greg Wyatt.

Mon.-Sat. 10-4; closed federal holidays. Tours are given Mon.-Sat. at 11 (also Sat. at 1). Evening and weekend performance times vary; phone ahead for schedule. Garden tours are available at 10 and 11 on the third Sat. of each month, Apr.-Oct. Library free. Ticket prices for performances vary. Phone (202) 544-7077 for performance information.

FORD'S THEATRE NATIONAL HISTORIC SITE is at 511 10th St. N.W. (M: Metro Center). This theater, in which President Abraham Lincoln was fatally shot by John Wilkes Booth on Apr. 14, 1865, has been restored to its 1860s appearance. National Park Service rangers provide short talks recounting Washington during the Civil War era and the story of the assassination. Musical productions and plays about prominent Americans also are staged.

Allow 1 hour minimum. Theater open daily 9-5; closed Dec. 25. Ranger talks are given 9:15-noon and 2:15-4:15. Theater performances are presented Tues.-Sun. at 7:30 p.m. (also Thurs. at 1 and Sat.-Sun. at 2:30); phone ahead to confirm times. The theater closes at 12:30 before matinee performances and sometimes on short notice for rehearsals. Theater free. Ticket prices for performances vary. Phone (202) 426-6924, or (202) 347-4833 for box office.

Ford's Theatre Museum is in the basement of Ford's Theatre. Exhibits depict the assassination and display the gun that John Wilkes Booth used to kill Lincoln. Daily 9-5; closed Dec. 25. Free. Phone (202) 426-6924.

House Where Lincoln Died (Petersen House) is at 516 10th St. N.W., across from Ford's Theatre. The president was carried to this house after being shot in Ford's Theatre; he died the following morning. Built in 1849 by William Petersen, the house has been restored to its 1860s appearance. Daily 9-5; closed Dec. 25. Free. Phone (202) 426-6830 or (202) 426-6924.

FRANCISCAN MONASTERY, 14th and Quincy sts. N.E. (M: Brookland-CUA), is called Mount St. Sepulchre, The Holy Land of America. The monastery features replicas of Holy Land shrines including the Grotto of Bethlehem, Nazareth and the Holy Sepulchre in Jerusalem as well as the Roman Catacombs. Gardens surrounding the monastery offer changing seasonal flower displays. Church and gardens open daily 9-5. Tours are given Mon.-Sat. at 10, 11, 1, 2 and 3, Sun. at 1, 2 and 3. Donations. Phone (202) 526-6800.

FRANKLIN DELANO ROOSEVELT MEMORIAL is in West Potomac Park along the Tidal Basin between the Jefferson and Lincoln memorials (M: Smithsonian). Four outdoor rooms depict the 12 years (1933-45) FDR served as America's 32nd president.

The Prologue Room contains a 10-foot statue of FDR in a wheelchair. Room One focuses on Roosevelt's early presidency. Sculptural groups in Room Two include an urban bread line, a rural couple and a man listening intently to one of FDR's fireside chats. Room Three contains a statue of Roosevelt and his dog, Fala, while Room Four, where a sculptural relief of the president's funeral cortege hangs in an alcove, honors his life and legacy.

Throughout the memorial are shade trees, waterfalls, plantings and quiet alcoves, all of which lend an expansive feeling. Famous Roosevelt quotations are carved into the granite walls. Allow 1 hour minimum. Daily 24 hours; closed Dec. 25. Park rangers are available daily 9:30 a.m.-11:30 p.m. Free. Phone (202) 426-6841.

FREDERICK DOUGLASS NATIONAL HISTORIC SITE (Cedar Hill), 1411 W St. S.E., was the last home of the one-time slave, statesman and human rights activist, who died in 1895. Many of the house's 19th-century Victorian furnishings are original. The visitor center's interpretive exhibits and 17-minute film document Douglass' life. A self-guiding walking tour of the historic grounds is available.

Guided tours of the home are offered daily. Allow 1 hour minimum. Site open daily 9-5, mid-Apr. to mid-Oct.; 9-4, rest of year. Closed Jan. 1, Thanksgiving and Dec. 25. Free. Reservations for guided tours are recommended; service charge $1.50 per person. Phone (202) 426-5961, or (877) 444-6777 for guided tour reservations.

FREER GALLERY OF ART of the Smithsonian Institution is on the National Mall at Jefferson Dr. and 12th St. S.W. (M: Smithsonian). The gallery houses an Asian collection of Japanese art, Korean ceramics, Buddhist art, South Asian art, Islamic and Chinese art that includes ancient works, porcelains, calligraphy and paintings. An underground exhibition area leads to the Smithsonian's other Asian art museum, the Arthur M. Sackler Gallery *(see attraction listing p. 69).*

A collection of American paintings includes works by Thomas Wilmer Dewing, Abbott Handerson Thayer and Dwight William Tryon. "Harmony in Blue and Gold: The Peacock Room," an elaborate dining room designed and executed by James McNeill Whistler, is his only existing interior scheme. Displayed in this room is Whistler's "The Princess from the Land of Porcelain" and a collection of Chinese blue and white porcelain.

Allow 2 hours minimum. Daily 10-5:30; closed Dec. 25. Guided tours are available on selected days; phone for schedule. Free. Phone (202) 633-1000, or TTY (202) 633-5285.

HILLWOOD ESTATE MUSEUM AND GARDENS is at 4155 Linnean Ave. N.W. (M: Van Ness-UDC). This 1926 Georgianstyle mansion, former home of Post cereal heiress Marjorie Merriweather Post, contains comprehensive collections of 18th- and 19th-century imperial Russian art as well as 18th-century French decorative arts.

The Porcelain Room features china services and glassware commissioned by Catherine the Great. The Icon Room boasts rare icons, gold and silver chalices and an array of jeweled items by Carl Fabergé. The Drawing Room contains tapestries and 18th-century French furniture. A one-room *dacha,* or Russian summer house, displays changing exhibits.

Gardens on the 25-acre estate include a formal garden, a French parterre, a Japanese-style garden and a rose garden.

Guided tours and food are available. Allow 2 hours, 30 minutes minimum. Tues.-Sat. 10-5, Feb.-Dec.; closed federal holidays. Admission $12; $10 (ages 65+); $7 (students with ID); $5 (ages 6-18). Reservations are recommended. AX, MC, VI. Phone (202) 686-8507.

HIRSHHORN MUSEUM AND SCULPTURE GARDEN of the Smithsonian Institution is on the National Mall on Independence Ave. at 7th St. S.W. (M: L'Enfant Plaza). It houses a collection of international modern and contemporary art. The permanent collection includes works by Matthew Barney, Jean Dubuffet, Ann Hannah, Willem de Kooning, Jackson Pollock, Auguste Rodin and Lorna Simpson and is shown on a rotating basis.

When it opened in 1974, the cylindrical building was as controversial as many of the works it contains. The galleries on the upper two floors follow the circular contours of the walls. Across from the museum on the National Mall is a sunken outdoor garden with large sculptures.

Allow 1 hour minimum. Daily 10-5:30; closed Dec. 25. Guided tours of the museum and sculpture garden are available on selected days (weather permitting); phone for schedule. Free. Phone (202) 633-1000, or TTY (202) 633-5285.

HOLOCAUST MEMORIAL MUSEUM— *see United States Holocaust Memorial Museum p. 92.*

THE HOUSE OF THE TEMPLE is at 1733 16th St. N.W. (M: Dupont Circle). This building, modeled after the tomb of Mausolus at Halicarnassus (now Bodrum) in Asia Minor, displays a variety of museum collections that include Masonic memorabilia, works by and about Scottish poet Robert Burns and

DID YOU KNOW

President Abraham Lincoln proclaimed the first national Thanksgiving Day in 1863.

many of the personal belongings of J. Edgar Hoover. There is an extensive library of Masonic and relafed subjects. Allow 2 hours minimum. Guided tours are given Mon.-Fri. 8-2. Free. Phone (202) 232-3579.

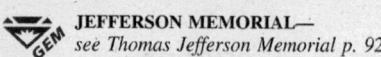 **INTERNATIONAL SPY MUSEUM** is at 800 F St. N.W. (M: Gallery Place-Chinatown). The museum houses devices related to the history and practice of espionage. Interactive exhibits provide an insider's view into the world of spying and emphasize its importance in recent history.

Food is available. Allow 2 hours minimum. Museum opens daily at 10. Closing times vary; phone ahead for schedule. Closed Jan. 1, Thanksgiving and Dec. 25. Admission $16; $15 (ages 65+); $13 (ages 5-11). Advance tickets are highly recommended Apr. 1-Labor Day, especially for weekend and holiday visits. Advance tickets are available through Ticketmaster; standard service charges apply. AX, DS, MC, VI. Phone (202) 393-7798, TTY (202) 654-2840, or (800) 551-7328 for Ticketmaster information.

ISLAMIC CENTER is at 2551 Massachusetts Ave. N.W. (M: Dupont Circle). This Islamic mosque is an institution of Muslim worship, education and culture, contains a library of works about Islam and presents changing exhibitions. The minaret, about 160 feet high, and the mosaic inscriptions in Arabic of verses from the holy Quran are noteworthy. Tours that include talks about Islam by an officer of the center are available.

Note: Female visitors must cover themselves except for their hands, face and feet. Allow 1 hour minimum. Mon.-Fri. 10-5. Donations. Phone (202) 332-8343.

J. EDGAR HOOVER F.B.I. BUILDING is on E St. between 9th and 10th sts. N.W. (M: Metro Center). Exhibits explain the history and jurisdiction of the FBI as well as the work of the FBI laboratory. Guided 1-hour tours, which begin at the 9th and E streets entrance, include a firearms demonstration.

Note: Tours have been discontinued while parts of the building are being renovated; phone ahead to confirm schedule. Tours are given Mon.-Fri. 8:45-11:45; closed holidays. Free. Phone (202) 324-3447.

JEFFERSON MEMORIAL— *see Thomas Jefferson Memorial p. 92.*

THE JOHN F. KENNEDY CENTER FOR THE PERFORMING ARTS is at jct. Rock Creek Pkwy. and New Hampshire Ave. N.W., overlooking the Potomac River just n. of the Theodore Roosevelt Bridge. Rock Creek Pkwy. S. is inaccessible during rush-hour lane closures, Mon.-Fri. 4-6:30 p.m.; follow signs from New Hampshire Ave. N.W. to entrance (M: Foggy Bottom-GWU).

Opened in 1971, the Kennedy Center is both Washington's showplace for the performing arts and a tribute to President John F. Kennedy. Kennedy was instrumental in raising funds for the National Cultural Center—a facility envisioned by President Dwight D. Eisenhower, who signed legislation to create it in 1958. Congress designated the center a "living memorial" to Kennedy 2 months after his November 1963 assassination.

American and international music, opera, dance, theater and film are presented in eight facilities: the Eisenhower Theater, the Opera House, the Concert Hall, the Terrace Theater, the Theater Lab, the Terrace Gallery, Millennium Stage and the Family Theater.

Free performances are given daily at 6 p.m. on the Millennium Stage; no tickets are required, and shows cover a range of art forms. Free 60-minute parking is available to visitors purchasing tickets at the box-office; phone ahead for specific details. Guided tours are given Mon.-Fri. 10-5, Sat.-Sun. 10-1; closed Jan. 1 and Dec. 25. Box office open Mon.-Sat. 10-9, Sun. and holidays noon-9. Performance times vary; phone ahead for schedule.

Tours free. Ticket prices for events vary. Full-time students, over 64, persons with permanent disabilities and military grades E-1 through E-4 are eligible for a limited number of half-price tickets. Event parking $15. AX, DC, MC, VI. For information or to charge tickets phone (202) 467-4600, (800) 444-1324 or TTY (202) 416-8524 daily 10-9. For guided tour information phone (202) 416-8340.

KENILWORTH AQUATIC GARDENS is w. of I-295 (Kenilworth Ave.) between Quarles and Douglas sts., on Anacostia Ave. (M: Deanwood). The gardens occupy 14 acres along the Anacostia River. Known for its bird-watching opportunities, the marsh contains 44 ponds filled with a large variety of water plants. Water lilies, lotuses, water hyacinths and other flowering plants bloom May through September; the best viewing is before 11 a.m. A boardwalk and river trail make the marsh area accessible.

Allow 1 hour, 30 minutes minimum. Gardens daily 7-4. Visitor center daily 8-4. Closed Jan. 1, Thanksgiving and Dec. 25. Free. Phone (202) 426-6905.

KOREAN WAR VETERANS MEMORIAL is near the Lincoln Memorial between the Reflecting Pool and Independence Ave. (M: Smithsonian). It was erected in gratitude to those 1.5 million American military personnel who served in Korea 1950-53. The statues of 19 poncho-clad soldiers give the impression of moving warily uphill through an unknown terrain of rice paddies, seemingly cautioning visitors who have accidentally encountered the patrol.

From a distance, the etched images on a 164-foot-long polished gray granite wall appear to be of the mountainous and rolling topography of Korea, but up close are actually military archives photographs of support forces. The memorial is in shades of black, gray and white, as are the recorded images of this forgotten war. Daily 24 hours; closed Dec. 25. Park rangers are available daily 9:30 a.m.-11:30 p.m. Free. Phone (202) 426-6841.

THE KREEGER MUSEUM is at 2401 Foxhall Rd. N.W. Designed by Philip Johnson, this impressive postmodern structure was once the residence of philanthropists David and Carmen Kreeger. The collection features 19th- and 20th-century paintings and sculptures as well as examples of traditional African and Asian sacred art. Guided tours highlight works by such artists as Joan Miró, Claude Monet and Pablo Picasso.

Note: Photography is not permitted in certain areas. Allow 1 hour, 30 minutes minimum. Guided tours are given by appointment Tues.-Fri. at 10:30 and 1:30, Sat. 10-4 (Self-guiding tours also are available Sat.), Sept.-July; closed Jan. 1, July 4, Thanksgiving, day after Thanksgiving and Dec. 25. Admission $8; $5 (ages 65+ and students with ID). Under 12 are not permitted Tues.-Fri. Phone (202) 337-3050, (877) 337-3050, or (202) 338-3552 for tour appointments.

LAFAYETTE SQUARE is n. of the White House on H St. between 15th and 17th sts. N.W. (M: McPherson Square). The major monument in Washington's best-known square is an equestrian statue of Andrew Jackson by Clark Mills. Bounded by such historic buildings as Blair House and Decatur House *(see attraction listing p. 75)*, Lafayette Square is a favored site for protests and demonstrations due to its proximity to the Executive Mansion.

LIBRARY OF CONGRESS, across from the Capitol at 1st St. and Independence Ave. S.E. (M: Capitol South), is a complex of three facilities: the James Madison Memorial Building, the John Adams Building and the Thomas Jefferson Building. The library contains 30 million books and other printed materials; more than 59 million manuscripts; and extensive files of maps, prints, photographs, musical scores, recordings, newspapers and the papers of 23 U.S. presidents.

Thomas Jefferson's personal collection of more than 6,000 volumes formed the basis of the national library. In the Thomas Jefferson Building the permanent American Treasures of the Library of Congress exhibit consists of more than 200 items relating to the country's past. Rotating exhibits are arranged in three categories: Memory (history), Reason (philosophy, law, science and geography) and Imagination (fine arts, architecture, music, literature and sports).

Note: Researchers must present a valid photo ID at the James Madison Building for access to some of the collections at the Library of Congress; phone ahead for specific details. Food is available in the Madison Building. Hours for specific reading rooms and centers vary; closed federal holidays. Free. Phone (202) 707-5000 for general information, (202) 707-8000 for recorded information or (202) 707-9779 for the visitor information office. Phone (202) 707-4604 for exhibition information.

James Madison Memorial Building is across from the Thomas Jefferson Building at 101 Independence Ave. S.E.. Opened in 1980, this contemporary structure contains reading rooms and exhibit halls. The James Madison Memorial Building also houses a permanent collection detailing jazz musician Gerry Mulligan's career. Mon.-Fri. 8:30 a.m.-9:30 p.m., Sat. 8:30-6:30; closed federal holidays. Gerry Mulligan Collection Mon.-Fri. 8:30-5. Free.

John Adams Building is behind the Thomas Jefferson Building on 2nd St. S.E. This 1939 Art Deco edifice offers a general business and science reading room that is open to researchers only. Mon. and Wed.-Thurs. 8:30 a.m.-9:30 p.m., Tues. and Fri.-Sat. 8:30-5:30; closed federal holidays. Free.

Thomas Jefferson Building is across from the Capitol at 1st St. S.E. (M: Capitol South). The first Library of Congress building, constructed in 1897, is distinguished by its richly ornamental Italian Renaissance architecture. The main halls and some of its reading rooms feature elaborately decorated vaulting; intricate sculpture; and fine paintings, murals and mosaics. The Great Hall rises 75 feet from a marble floor to a stained-glass ceiling. A visitor center offers a 12-minute orientation film.

Library and visitor center open Mon.-Sat. 10-5; closed federal holidays. Guided tours are given Mon.-Fri. at 10:30, 11:30, 1:30, 2:30 and 3:30, Sat. at 10:30, 11:30, 1:30 and 2:30. Free.

LILLIAN & ALBERT SMALL JEWISH MUSEUM is at 701 3rd St. N.W. at G St. N.W. (M: Judiciary Square). The original Adas Israel Synagogue was founded in 1876 and is the District's oldest synagogue. Guided tours cover the historic sanctuary and provide information about the history of the building. Allow 30 minutes minimum. Guided tours are offered Mon.-Thurs. by appointment; closed national and Jewish holidays. Fee $3. Phone ahead 24 hours in advance to schedule an appointment. Phone (202) 789-0900.

LINCOLN MEMORIAL is on the National Mall off 23rd St. N.W., aligned with the Capitol and the Washington Monument (M: Smithsonian). Between the Lincoln Memorial and the Washington Monument lie two reflecting pools with a combined length of 2,292 feet. The stately marble structure, designed by Henry Bacon, stands just before the approach to Arlington Memorial Bridge. Its 36 Doric columns, one for each state in existence at the time of Lincoln's death, symbolize the Union.

Dominating the interior is the colossal seated statue of Lincoln by Daniel Chester French. Two of Lincoln's more famous speeches—the eloquent Gettysburg Address and his Second Inaugural Address—are carved on the north and south walls of the memorial. Murals by Jules Guerin allegorize the themes of emancipation and reunion.

Interpretive tours are available by request. Allow 30 minutes minimum. Daily 24 hours; closed Dec.

25. Park rangers are available daily 9:30 a.m.-11:30 p.m. Free. Phone (202) 426-6841.

MARIAN KOSHLAND SCIENCE MUSEUM is at jct. 6th and E sts. N.W. (M: Judiciary Square or Gallery Place-Chinatown). On-site parking is not available. The museum contains three major exhibits focusing on such contemporary scientific issues as DNA and gene sequencing and global climate change. The sophisticated interactive displays, which incorporate findings from reports published by the National Academy of Sciences, allow visitors to examine in depth the evidence behind current scientific issues.

Allow 1 hour minimum. Wed.-Mon. 10-6; closed Jan. 1, Thanksgiving and Dec. 25. Last admission is 1 hour before closing. Admission $5; $3 (ages 5-18, ages 66+ and students and active duty military with ID). MC, VI. Phone (202) 334-1201 or (888) 567-4526.

MARY McLEOD BETHUNE COUNCIL HOUSE NATIONAL HISTORIC SITE is at 1318 Vermont Ave. N.W. (M: McPherson Square). Former home of Mary McLeod Bethune, the Victorian townhouse contains exhibits, a 20-minute video about her life and the National Archives of Black Women's History.

Bethune founded Daytona Educational and Industrial School for Negro Girls in 1904, which became Bethune-Cookman College. In 1935 she became a special advisor to President Franklin D. Roosevelt. Allow 1 hour minimum. Mon.-Sat. 10-4; closed major holidays. Free. Phone (202) 673-2402.

NATIONAL AIR AND SPACE MUSEUM of the Smithsonian Institution is on the National Mall at 7th St. and Independence Ave. S.W. (M: L'Enfant Plaza, 7th St. & Maryland Ave. exit). It is devoted to presenting the history, science and technology of air and space flight.

In the Milestones of Flight gallery, visitors can touch a moon rock and view such historically important items as Charles Lindbergh's *Spirit of St. Louis,* Chuck Yeager's Bell X-1 *Glamorous Glennis,* John Glenn's spacecraft *Friendship 7,* the Apollo 11 Command Module *Columbia,* a Viking Mars Lander and SpaceShipOne, the first privately built, piloted spacecraft to reach space. The Wright brothers' 1903 Flyer is temporarily on view in the exhibition "The Wright Brothers & The Invention of the Aerial Age."

Twenty-two other galleries deal with such subjects as early flight, jet aviation, lunar and planetary exploration, rocketry, military aircraft, computers in aerospace and aerial imaging. The How Things Fly gallery explains the principles of flight and features hands-on activities, live demonstrations and interactive stations. Space Race highlights the struggle between the United States and the former Soviet Union and the race to be first in space.

IMAX films are shown on the five-story screen in the Lockheed Martin IMAX Theater, and multimedia shows are presented in the Albert Einstein Planetarium. Various immersive flight simulator experiences are available.

Guided tours and food are available. Allow 2 hours minimum. Daily 10-5:30; closed Dec. 25. Museum free. Fees for IMAX films, planetarium shows and flight simulators vary. Phone (202) 633-1000, or TTY (202) 633-5285. For IMAX film and planetarium show information phone (877) 932-4629.

 NATIONAL AIR AND SPACE MUSEUM'S STEVEN F. UDVAR-HAZY CENTER— *see Chantilly, Va., p. 127.*

NATIONAL AQUARIUM is on the lower level of the Herbert C. Hoover Building (the Department of Commerce) at 14th St. and Constitution Ave. N.W. (M: Federal Triangle). Constructed in 1931, the aquarium is a direct descendent of the first public aquarium in the United States. It exhibits 1,200 freshwater and saltwater fish and other aquatic creatures. A touch tank for children features sting rays.

Allow 30 minutes minimum. Daily 9-5; closed Thanksgiving and Dec. 25. Feeding shows are conducted daily at 2. Last admission is 30 minutes before closing. Admission $5; $4 (ages 60+ and military with ID); $2.50 (ages 2-10). Phone (202) 482-2825.

NATIONAL ARCHIVES, Constitution Ave. between 7th and 9th sts. N.W. (M: Archives-Navy Memorial), preserves federal government records of enduring value. Visitors can see the Declaration of Independence, the Constitution, the Bill of Rights and an original copy of the Magna Carta. In the multimedia Public Vaults exhibition gallery visitors eavesdrop on presidential conversations, view newly declassified top-secret documents and investigate the sinking of the *Titanic.*

A documentary film series as well as an 11-minute introductory film about the National Archives are shown in the William G. McGowan Theater. The Lawrence F. O'Brien Gallery has changing exhibitions.

Note: All visitors and bags will be checked by security upon entrance. Allow 1 hour minimum. Exhibit halls open daily 10-9, Memorial Day weekend-Labor Day; 10-7, Apr. 1-Fri. before Memorial Day weekend; 10-5:30, rest of year. Closed Thanksgiving and Dec. 25. Free. Reservations are recommended. Phone (866) 272-6272, (202) 357-5000 for event information, or TTY (301) 837-0482.

NATIONAL BUILDING MUSEUM occupies the block on F St. between 4th and 5th sts. N.W. (M: Judiciary Square). Housed in a massive brick building completed in 1887, the museum's rotating exhibits examine various aspects of building, including architecture, design, engineering, construction and urban planning. The permanent exhibit is Washington: Symbol and City. The dramatic Great Hall, site of 15 presidential inaugural balls, contains 75-foot-tall brick Corinthian columns.

Food is available. Allow 1 hour minimum. Mon.-Sat. 10-5, Sun. 11-5; closed Jan. 1, Thanksgiving and Dec. 25. Guided 45-minute tours are offered Mon.-Wed. at 12:30, Thurs.-Sat. at 11:30, 12:30 and 1:30. Donations. Phone (202) 272-2448.

NATIONAL CITY CHRISTIAN CHURCH, 5 Thomas Cir. at Massachusetts Ave. and 14th St. N.W. (M: McPherson Square), is the national cathedral of the Christian Church (Disciples of Christ). The neoclassic sanctuary was designed by John Russell Pope in 1930. Guided tours are available by appointment. Open Mon.-Fri. 9-5, Sun. 8:30-2. Free half-hour recitals are given Thurs. at 12:15, Feb.-July and early Sept.-Dec. 31. Free. Phone (202) 232-0323.

NATIONAL GALLERY OF ART is housed in two buildings along Constitution Ave. between 3rd and 7th sts. N.W. (M: Archives-Navy Memorial or Judiciary Square). The classical West Building, designed by John Russell Pope, and the contemporary East Building, designed by I.M. Pei, are linked by a paved plaza and an underground concourse.

Donated to the nation by The Morris and Gwendolyn Cafritz Foundation, the 6.1-acre outdoor sculpture garden, with its dynamic and richly landscaped setting, includes 17 major works, including important acquisitions of post-World War II sculpture. It is adjacent to the West Building, between 7th and 9th streets and features works by such artists as Roy Lichtenstein, Claes Oldenburg and Tony Smith. The sculpture garden is the site for free jazz concerts in summer and an ice-skating rink in winter.

The West Building contains American art as well as one of the world's finest collections of western European paintings and sculpture spanning the 13th century to the present, including British, Dutch, Flemish, French, German, Italian and Spanish works. Highlights include works by Titian, Rembrandt and Anthony van Dyck, French impressionist paintings and the only painting by Leonardo da Vinci in the Western Hemisphere. The Micro Gallery offers an interactive multimedia computer.

The East Building focuses on modern and contemporary art by European and American artists and represents such major artists as Alexander Calder, Helen Frankenthaler, Henri Matisse, Joan Miró, Pablo Picasso, Jackson Pollock and Mark Rothko. The building also houses the Center for Advanced Study in the Visual Arts, a research library and an extensive photographic archive.

The gallery also exhibits 17 of the surviving 69 original wax sculptures modeled by Edgar Degas. Gifts in honor of the gallery's 50th anniversary include major works by Albert Bierstadt, Alexander Calder, Claude Monet, Clyfford Still and Andy Warhol.

Guided tours and food are available. Sign language interpretation is offered with 3 weeks' notice. Gallery open Mon.-Sat. 10-5, Sun. 11-6. Sculpture garden open Mon.-Sat. 10-7 (also Fri. 7-9:30 p.m.), Sun. 11-7, Memorial Day-Labor Day; Mon.-Sat. 10-5, Sun. 11-6, rest of year. Closed Jan. 1 and Dec. 25. East Building guided tours are given Mon.-Fri. at 11:30 and 1:30, Sat.-Sun. at 11:30 and 3:30. West Building guided tours are given Mon.-Fri. at 10:30, Sat. at 10:30 and 12:30, Sun. at 11:30 and 4:30. Lectures are given Sun. at 2 in the East Building auditorium. Concerts take place Sun. at 6:30, Oct.-June. Visitors should phone ahead to confirm tour and event times and locations.

Gallery free. Guided tours $6; $5 (ages 65+ and students with ID). Self-guiding audio tours of the permanent collection are available for $5; special exhibition audio tours vary in price. Phone (202) 737-4215, or TTY (202) 842-6176.

NATIONAL GEOGRAPHIC MUSEUM AT EXPLORERS HALL is at 17th and M sts. N.W. (M: Farragut North or Farragut West). This interactive center features changing exhibits about culture, natural history and science. Adjoining Explorers Hall is Grosvenor Auditorium, where guest lecturers present programs on a variety of subjects. Allow 1 hour minimum. Mon.-Sat. and federal holidays 9-5, Sun. 10-5; closed Dec. 25. Free. Phone (202) 857-7588, or (202) 857-7700 for lecture and film information.

NATIONAL JAPANESE AMERICAN MEMORIAL TO PATRIOTISM DURING WORLD WAR II, jct. of Louisiana and New Jersey aves. and D St. N.W. (M: Union Station), pays tribute to 120,000 Japanese-American men, women and children moved to detention camps in 1942 solely because of their ethnic roots.

Representing courage and triumph over oppression, a sculpture of two cranes struggling to break free from barbed wire is encircled by a wall engraved with the names of more than 800 Japanese-American soldiers who gave their lives during the war. Allow 30 minutes minimum. Daily 24 hours. Free. Phone (202) 530-0015.

NATIONAL LAW ENFORCEMENT OFFICERS MEMORIAL is at Judiciary Square between E and F sts. and 4th and 5th sts. N.W.; a visitor center is 2

blks. w. at 605 E St. N.W. (M: Judiciary Square). Inscribed on marble walls are the names of the more than 17,500 law enforcement officers who have died in the line of duty since the first known death in 1792. The 3-acre memorial contains landscaped gardens, symbolic bronze statues of lions, tree-lined pathways and an 80-foot reflecting pool.

The visitor center features exhibits, an interactive video kiosk and personal mementos left at the memorial. Guided tours are available by appointment. Allow 30 minutes minimum. Memorial open daily 24 hours. Visitor center open Mon.-Fri. 9-5, Sat. 10-5, Sun. noon-5; closed Jan. 1, July 4, Thanksgiving and Dec. 25. Free. Phone (202) 737-3213 for the visitor center. *See color ad p. 82.*

THE NATIONAL MALL extends from the Capitol grounds to the Lincoln Memorial (M: Federal Triangle, Smithsonian, L'Enfant Plaza, Archives-Navy Memorial, Federal Center SW and Capitol South). The rectangular area between the Capitol and the Washington Monument is a popular spot for strolling, picnicking or just relaxing on one of the many benches. This section is lined on both sides by stately American elm trees and 10 Smithsonian Institution museums.

On the east side of the Capitol Reflecting Pool, at the foot of the Capitol grounds, is the Ulysses S. Grant Memorial, a powerful sculptural group depicting the general on horseback, flanked by Union cavalry and artillery soldiers. *See sidebar p. 85 and What to Do, Walking Tours p. 101.*

NATIONAL MUSEUM OF AFRICAN ART of the Smithsonian Institution, 950 Independence Ave. S.W. (M: Smithsonian), is entered from a pavilion in the Enid A. Haupt Garden on the s. side of the Smithsonian Institution Building (the Castle). Except for the entrance pavilion, the museum is housed in a three-level complex that is entirely underground. The museum focuses on the rich artistic heritage of the African continent, presenting arts from the living traditions of diverse African cultures.

Its permanent collection of bronze, wood, ivory, cast metal and ceramic objects is an important resource for the study of African art and culture. Changing exhibitions also are presented. Open daily 10-5:30; closed Dec. 25. Free. Phone (202) 633-1000, or TTY (202) 633-5285.

NATIONAL MUSEUM OF AMERICAN HISTORY, KENNETH E. BEHRING CENTER of the Smithsonian Institution is on Constitution Ave. between 12th and 14th sts. N.W. (M: Federal Triangle or Smithsonian). The museum depicts the scientific, cultural, social, technological and political development of the United States. Venerated objects make up the collections, including the lap desk Thomas Jefferson used to draft the Declaration of Independence; an Edison light bulb; the Star-Spangled Banner, the flag that inspired the national anthem; and a Woolworth's lunch counter from segregation-era Greensboro, N.C.

The National Mall

The National Mall is the focus of many of Washington's events and celebrations, an arrival and departure point for visiting dignitaries and the location of many of the city's most famous landmarks. The Mall's swath of green between the Capitol and the Washington Monument also is a gathering place for cyclists, skaters, strollers and those just wanting to stretch out on the grass. It has become a sort of national common that visitors and locals alike can rightfully regard as their own.

The grounds of the Washington Monument divide the National Mall into two distinct sections. To the east lie the Capitol, the U.S. Botanic Garden and 10 Smithsonian museums. To the west lie the Korean War Veterans Memorial, the Lincoln Memorial, the National World War II Memorial, the Vietnam Veterans Memorial, Constitution Gardens and the Reflecting Pool, which is almost four-tenths of a mile long. The total distance from the steps of the Lincoln Memorial to the Capitol grounds is about 2 miles. A secondary axis intersects the Mall—also at the Washington Monument grounds—extending from the White House (about a half-mile north of the monument) to the Thomas Jefferson Memorial (about a half-mile south). Nearly half the attractions listed under *Points of Interest* are either on or along this cross of parkland or—like the Franklin Delano Roosevelt Memorial—a short walk from it.

If such distances seem daunting, Tourmobile shuttles and Old Town Trolley Tours link most of the major sights *(see What To Do, Sightseeing).* Parking in the area is at a premium, but several Metro stations are within a block or two of the National Mall, and the entrance to the Blue/Orange Line's Smithsonian Station is right on the Mall.

Digital Archives

AAA is a proud sponsor of the permanent exhibition America on the Move, which examines how transportation in the United States from 1876 to the present has shaped our identity from a mostly rural nation into a major economic power. The American Presidency: A Glorious Burden explores the public, personal, ceremonial and executive boundaries of the nation's highest office, while The Price of Freedom: Americans at War surveys the history of America's military from the Revolutionary War to the present conflict in Iraq.

National Museum of African Art / © AAA / Denise E. Campbell

CLOSURE INFORMATION: In the fall of 2006, the museum embarked on a dramatic transformation of its building and will be closed for renovation through 2007. It is expected to reopen in summer of 2008 with a new state-of-the art gallery for the Star-Spangled Banner, as well as improved public amenities. For additional information, visit the museum's web site at americanhistory.si.edu for renovation updates or to subscribe to a free newsletter. Phone (202) 633-1000, or TTY (202) 633-5285.

NATIONAL MUSEUM OF THE AMERICAN INDIAN of the Smithsonian Institution is on the National Mall at 4th St. and Independence Ave. S.W. (M: L'Enfant Plaza, 7th St. & Maryland Ave., or Federal Center SW), between the National Air and Space Museum and the U.S. Capitol. It is the world's premier destination for Native American art, culture and history.

· This curvilinear structure of Kasota buff-colored limestone is evocative of natural rock formations sculpted over time by wind and water. Also indicative of natural landscapes are the plantings around the building's perimeter, which suggest wetlands, meadowlands, crops and forests.

The permanent exhibitions Our Universes, Our Peoples, Our Lives, Return to a Native Place and Window on Collections chronicle arts, history and material culture from across the Western Hemisphere. Rotating contemporary art exhibitions also are presented. The museum also is a venue for performances and public programs, including films, lectures and symposia.

Food is available. Allow 2 hours minimum. Daily 10-5:30; closed Dec. 25. Guided tours are available; phone for schedule. Free. Phone (202) 633-1000, or TTY (202) 633-5285.

NATIONAL MUSEUM OF AMERICAN JEWISH MILITARY HISTORY is at 1811 R St. N.W. (M: Dupont Circle). Exhibits include photographs, bugles, binoculars, stirrups, posters, hand-painted illustrated maps of troop movements, flags and firearms from the Revolutionary War to the present.

A permanent exhibition recounts World War II hero Julius Klein's historic life and work, and changing exhibits are regularly presented. Guided 90-minute tours are available. Open Mon.-Fri. 9-5, Sun. by appointment; closed Jewish and most federal holidays. Donations. Phone (202) 265-6280.

NATIONAL MUSEUM OF HEALTH AND MEDICINE is at Georgia Ave. and Elder St. N.W. on the Walter Reed Army Medical Center campus. Although there are several gates around the campus, visitors may enter through the Elder St. gate only.

This facility was established during the Civil War as a center for the collection of specimens for research in military medicine and surgery. The museum's exhibits focus on personal and public health and promote an understanding of medicine past, present and future, with special emphasis on American military medicine.

Note: Visitors must present a valid photo ID. Allow 1 hour, 30 minutes minimum. Daily 10-5:30; closed Dec. 25. Docent-led tours begin at 1 on the second and fourth Sat. of the month. Free. Phone (202) 782-2200.

NATIONAL MUSEUM OF NATURAL HISTORY of the Smithsonian Institution, 10th St. and Constitution Ave. N.W. (M: Federal Triangle or Smithsonian), is devoted to understanding the natural world and our place in it. Permanent exhibitions include the Janet Annenberg Hooker Hall of Geology, Gems and Minerals, which showcases a collection of gemstones—including the legendary Hope Diamond —and minerals, as well as a section on mining and plate tectonics.

The Kenneth E. Behring Family Hall of Mammals features more than 270 mammals in lifelike poses that tell the 225 million-year-old story of mammal evolution and adaptation from polar regions to the Sahara Desert. "Butterflies & Plant: Partners in Evolution," opening in November 2007, will explore the ways butterflies and other animals have evolved, adapted and diversified together with their plant partners; tickets may be purchased for entrance to the Living Butterfly Pavilion, which is within the exhibition.

Opening September 2008, "Ocean Hall," a one-of-a-kind interpretive exhibition extraordinary in scale, will demonstrate how the ocean is intrinsically connected to other global systems and our daily lives. Outside, along the sidewalk between the museum and the 9th Street tunnel, is the Butterfly Habitat Garden (seasonal), a living showcase of plants that support butterflies during their life cycle.

Other highlights include the African bush elephant in the rotunda, ice age mammals and prehistoric life displays. Changing exhibitions also are presented. Hands-on learning activities are offered most days in the Discovery Room, while other popular attractions are the dinosaur exhibits and the O. Orkin Insect Zoo, which has tarantula feedings on most days.

Food is available. Museum open daily 10-5:30; closed Dec. 25. Free guided tours are available on selected days, Sept.-June; phone for schedule. Museum free. Fees for IMAX films vary. Phone (202) 633-1000, TTY (202) 633-5285, or (877) 932-4629 for IMAX film schedule and prices.

NATIONAL MUSEUM OF WOMEN IN THE ARTS is in the renovated former Masonic Grand Lodge of the National Capital at 1250 New York Ave. and 13th St. N.W. (M: Metro Center). The museum, housed in a restored 1907 Renaissance Revival structure, is dedicated to the recognition of women artists. The permanent collection includes more than 2,500 works.

Food is available. Mon.-Sat. 10-5, Sun. noon-5; closed Jan. 1, Thanksgiving and Dec. 25. Admission $10; $8 (ages 60+ and college students with ID); free (ages 0-18). Phone (202) 783-5000 or (800) 222-7270.

NATIONAL PORTRAIT GALLERY of the Smithsonian Institution is housed in the Donald W. Reynolds Center for American Art and Portraiture at 8th and F sts. N.W. (M: Gallery Place-Chinatown). The third oldest government building in Washington served as a Civil War hospital and was the scene of Abraham Lincoln's second inaugural ball. Featuring porticos modeled after the Parthenon in Athens, Greece, a curving double staircase and skylights, the facility also houses the Smithsonian American Art Museum *(see attraction listing p. 89)*.

The Portrait Gallery's collection describes the history of America through the individuals who have shaped it. Individuals represented include poets and presidents, visionaries and villains, and actors and activists. The cultural history and portrait museum also holds the nation's only complete presidential portrait collection outside the White House.

Food is available. Daily 11:30-7; closed Dec. 25. Guided tours are available on selected days; phone for schedule. Free. Phone (202) 633-1000, or TTY (202) 633-5285.

NATIONAL POSTAL MUSEUM of the Smithsonian Institution is at 2 Massachusetts Ave. N.E. (M: Union Station). This museum is housed on the lower level of the Old City Post Office, which was built in 1914. The hands-on museum offers exhibitions portraying the history of the nation's mail service and includes one of the largest collections of stamps and philatelic materials in the world.

Of note are the major galleries Binding the Nation, Customers and Communities, Moving the Mail, The Art of Cards and Letters, and the Philatelic & Rarities Galleries. The museum also houses the Library Research Center, which includes more than 40,000 volumes and manuscripts.

Guided tours are available by appointment. Sign language interpretation is offered with 3 weeks' notice. Museum open daily 10-5:30; closed Dec. 25. Library open by appointment. Free. Phone (202) 633-1000, TTY (202) 633-5285, (202) 633-5535 for guided tours and sign language interpretation, and (202) 633-5544 for the library.

 NATIONAL SHRINE OF THE IMMACULATE CONCEPTION—
see Basilica of the National Shrine of the Immaculate Conception p. 73.

NATIONAL WORLD WAR II MEMORIAL is in West Potomac Park at the e. end of the Reflecting Pool, between the Lincoln Memorial and the Washington Monument (M: Smithsonian). The 7.4-acre site honors the 16 million men and women who served in the U.S. armed forces during the war, the more than 400,000 who died and the millions who supported the war effort at home.

Two 43-foot arches at the north and south ends of the oval-shaped memorial plaza mark the war's two major theaters, Atlantic and Pacific, while 56 17-foot-tall stone pillars—representing the District of Columbia and the existing U.S. states and territories at the time of the war—form the memorial's outer boundary. Daily 24 hours; closed Dec. 25. Park rangers are available daily 9:30 a.m.-11:30 p.m. Free. Phone (202) 426-6841.

NATIONAL ZOOLOGICAL PARK of the Smithsonian Institution borders Rock Creek Park, with entrances in the 3000 blk. of Connecticut Ave., on Harvard St. and on Beach Dr. The zoo can be reached via Metrorail's Red Line (M: Woodley Park-Zoo/Adams Morgan or Cleveland Park). Connecticut Ave. bus lines stop at the zoo's main entrance.

The indoor and outdoor exhibits together house approximately 2,000 animals, including Sumatran tigers, Asian elephants, orangutans, lowland gorillas and a Komodo dragon; however, three giant pandas—adults Tian Tian and Mei Xiang and their offspring, Tai Shan—are the zoo's most noted residents. The Asia Trail exhibit features sloth bears, clouded leopards, red pandas and more.

Other highlights are the Invertebrate Exhibit; Think Tank, an animal thinking exhibit; a cheetah exhibit; and Amazonia, a replica of the Amazon rain forest.

Guided tours are available by appointment. Food is available. Grounds open daily 6 a.m.-8 p.m., Apr.-Oct.; 6-6, rest of year. Most buildings open daily 10-6, Apr.-Oct.; 10-4:30, rest of year. Closed Dec. 25. Free. Parking $4-$16. Phone (202) 633-4888, (202) 633-4800 for recorded information, (202) 633-3025 for guided tour information, or TTY (202) 673-7800.

NEWSEUM is at 555 Pennsylvania Ave. N.W. The museum takes visitors behind the scenes to illustrate how and why news is made. Featured are an interactive newsroom, two state-of-the-art broadcast studios, 15 theaters and 14 galleries along with displays and exhibits. Note: The attraction will open in early 2008; call ahead to verify schedule. Allow 1 hour minimum. Daily 9-5; closed Jan. 1, Thanksgiving and Dec. 25. Admission $17.91; $16 (ages 65+); $13 (ages 7-12). AX, MC, VI. Phone (888) 639-7386.

THE NEW YORK AVENUE PRESBYTERIAN CHURCH is at 1313 New York Ave. N.W. (M: Metro Center or McPherson Square). The church was organized in 1803; its distinguished members have included John Quincy Adams and Abraham Lincoln. The current Federal-style structure, built in 1951, contains 19 contemporary stained-glass windows.

Lincoln's pew, hitching post and the original manuscript of his proposal to abolish slavery can be seen. Church office open Tues.-Fri. 9-5, Sun. 9-1. Guided tours are offered after Sun. worship services. Free. Phone (202) 393-3700.

THE OCTAGON MUSEUM is at 1799 New York Ave. N.W. at 18th St., 2 blks. w. of the White House (M: Farragut North or Farragut West). Built 1799-1801 by architect Dr. William Thornton, this Federal-style residence served as the executive mansion for President James Madison in 1814 after the White House was burned by the British during the War of 1812. The Octagon is now a historic house museum owned by the American Architectural Foundation.

Allow 1 hour minimum. Prearranged group tours for 10-25 individuals are given during the hours of Mon.-Fri. 10-4; closed major holidays. Reservations are required. Fee $5; $3 (senior citizens and students). Phone (202) 638-3221.

OLD POST OFFICE PAVILION is at 12th St. and Pennsylvania Ave. N.W. (M: Federal Triangle). The Romanesque Revival Old Post Office was built in 1899 as the country's postal headquarters. The renovated building now contains shops and eateries. The 315-foot clock tower houses 10 bells given by Great Britain for the U.S. Bicentennial. A glass elevator connects the Pavilion and the bell-ringing chamber; another elevator continues to the 12th-floor observation deck, which offers panoramic views.

Food is available. Building open Mon.-Sat. 10-8, Sun. noon-7, Apr. 1-Labor Day; Mon.-Sat. 10-7,

Sun. noon-6, rest of year. Closed Jan. 1, Thanksgiving and Dec. 25. Tower tours are given Mon.-Sat. 9-5, Sun. 10-6. Tower closes Thurs. at 6:30. Last tour begins 15 minutes before closing. Hours may be extended; phone to confirm schedule. Free. Phone (202) 289-4224, or (202) 606-8691 for clock tower information.

ORGANIZATION OF AMERICAN STATES BUILDING, 17th St. and Constitution Ave. N.W. (M: Farragut West or Farragut North), is headquarters of the general secretariat of the Organization of American States (OAS). The building contains a tropical patio entrance hall, the Hall of Heroes and Flags, the Liberator Simón Bolívar Room, the Hall of the Americas and an Aztec Garden.

Allow 1 hour minimum. Guided tours are offered Mon.-Fri. 9-5:30 by appointment; closed federal holidays and Good Friday. Free. Phone (202) 458-3000, or (202) 458-3927 for tour appointments.

Art Museum of the Americas, 201 18th St. N.W., directly behind the Organization of American States Building, houses the OAS permanent collection of Latin American and Caribbean art. Guided tours are offered by appointment. Open Tues.-Sun. 10-5; closed federal holidays and Good Friday. Free. Phone (202) 458-6016, or (202) 458-6301 for tour appointments.

THE PHILLIPS COLLECTION is at 1600 21st St. N.W. at Q St. (M: Dupont Circle); street parking is limited. The museum is home to impressionist and modern American and European art, with works by such artists as Pierre Bonnard, Paul Cézanne, Richard Diebenkorn, Paul Klee, Henri Matisse, Georgia O'Keeffe, Pablo Picasso and Mark Rothko. The most famous work in this distinguished collection is Pierre Auguste Renoir's "Luncheon of the Boating Party." The museum regularly presents special exhibitions.

Guided tours are available. Food is available. Allow 2 hours minimum. Museum open Tues.-Sat. 10-5 (also Thurs. 5-8:30), Sun. 11-6; closed major holidays. Concerts are held Sun. at 4, Oct.-May. Artful Evenings featuring live music and gallery talks are offered Thurs. 5-8:30.

Permanent collection admission Tues.-Fri. by donation. Permanent collection admission Sat.-Sun. varies. Special exhibition admission (includes admission to the permanent collection, concerts and Artful Evenings) $12; $10 (ages 62+ and students with ID); free (ages 0-18). Special exhibition admission may vary; phone ahead. Phone (202) 387-2151.

POPE JOHN PAUL II CULTURAL CENTER is at 3900 Harewood Rd. N.E. (M: Brookland-CUA). This architecturally stunning complex explores faith and cultural diversity through interactive galleries, rotating exhibits, an orientation theater, music, lectures and cultural programs.

The Faith, Wonder, Community and Imagination galleries offer interactive exhibits. The scaled-down, hands-on Children's Gallery gives young visitors the opportunity to participate in such activities as ringing bells and creating stained-glass windows. The Papal and Polish Heritage Room contains photos and memorabilia pertaining to Pope John Paul II. Within the center's peaceful chapel is the original portrait of St. Thérèse of Lisieux painted by her sister.

Food is available. Allow 2 hours minimum. Center open Tues. and Thurs.-Sat. 10-5, Sun. noon-5; closed major holidays. Mass celebrated Tues. and Thurs.-Fri. at noon. Admission $5; $15 (family rate). Phone (202) 635-5400.

POTOMAC PARK is divided into East Potomac Park, accessed via I-395, and West Potomac Park, off Ohio Dr. via Independence Ave. N.W. Ohio Drive S.W. follows the river, the Washington Channel and the Tidal Basin. This drive is exceptionally beautiful in April, when more than 3,700 cherry trees are in bloom around the Tidal Basin and in East Potomac Park. Most trees are of the Yoshino variety, which produce single white blossoms; Kwanzan cherry trees bearing clusters of pale pink blossoms also are well-represented.

The 720-acre park is home to Constitution Gardens; the Korean War Veterans, Vietnam Veterans, Thomas Jefferson and National World War II memorials; and the Reflecting Pool. In East Potomac Park between the river and the channel lies Hains Point, where golfing, swimming and tennis can be enjoyed. Here "The Awakening," consisting of five separate sculpted pieces buried in the ground, depicts a stone giant coming out of the earth. Picnicking is permitted. Grounds daily 24 hours. Free.

RENWICK GALLERY, a branch of the Smithsonian American Art Museum, is at 17th St. and Pennsylvania Ave. N.W. (M: Farragut West). Housed in a historic architectural landmark, the Renwick collects, interprets, and exhibits the finest work in American craft. The gallery was designed in 1858 to display the art collection of William Wilson Corcoran, a prominent Washington banker. Completed in 1874, it was the city's first art museum.

Today, the Renwick exhibits contemporary American craft and decorative arts in addition to actively collecting works in clay, fiber, glass, metal, wood and mixed media. The Grand Salon, considered one of Washington, D.C.'s premier spaces, features paintings hung salon-style, re-creating the elegant setting of a 19th-century collector's picture gallery. Daily 10-5:30; closed Dec. 25. Guided tours are available on selected days; phone for schedule. Free. Phone (202) 633-1000, or TTY (202) 633-5285.

THE ROBERT A. TAFT MEMORIAL AND CARILLON stands 1 blk. n. of the Capitol on Constitution Ave. between New Jersey Ave. and 1st St. N.W. (M: Union Station). Taft was senator from Ohio 1938-53, and the son of President William Howard Taft. The memorial consists of a 100-foot-tall tower with 27 matched bells and a 10-foot-tall bronze statue.

The bells strike the hour and sound on the quarter-hour. Patriotic musical selections are played on the electronic keyboard on July 4. Free.

ROCK CREEK CEMETERY is at Rock Creek Church Rd. and Webster St. N.W. (M: Fort Totten). Established in 1719, this is Washington's oldest cemetery. St. Paul's Episcopal Church, the District's only Colonial church, is on the grounds.

One of the best-known memorials is the Adams Memorial, created by Augustus Saint-Gaudens. Others are the Ffoulke memorial "Rabboni" by Gutzon Borglum and the Boardman memorial "Journey of Life" by James Earle Fraser. Cemetery open daily 7-dusk. Office open for genealogy research Mon.-Fri. 9-5, Sat. 9-1. Phone (202) 829-0585.

ROCK CREEK PARK follows the course of Rock Creek through n.w. Washington. Its 1,754 acres of natural woodland encompass tennis courts; 29 picnic areas; a golf course; landscaped gardens; playgrounds; and hiking, biking and jogging trails. A nature center and a planetarium also are on site.

The remains of Fort De Russy, one of a circle of 68 forts that defended the city during the Civil War, stands near Oregon Avenue and Military Road and can be reached on foot. One-acre Battleground National Cemetery is at 6625 Georgia Ave. N.W. On Beach Drive north of Military Road is the log studio of eccentric poet Joaquin Miller, who wrote "Song of the Sierras."

Concerts take place at Carter Barron Amphitheatre, 16th Street and Colorado Avenue N.W., late June through late August. Park daily dawn-dusk. Park free. Phone (202) 895-6000 for park information or (202) 426-0486 for concert information.

Dumbarton Oaks Park is entered via Lovers' Ln., off R St. between Avon Pl. and 31st St. N.W.. The park occupies 27 acres of the former 50-acre estate of Robert Woods Bliss. Accessible only by foot, this wooded area with a creek running through it is most attractive from early April to late June. Allow 30 minutes minimum. Daily 8-dusk. Free. Phone (202) 895-6000.

Kahlil Gibran Memorial Garden is on Massachusetts Ave. N.W. between 30th and 34th sts. N.W., opposite the British Embassy. It is dedicated to early 20th-century Lebanese-American poet and philosopher Kahlil Gibran. Visitors follow a stone walkway across a footbridge that leads to the memorial area. Granite benches engraved with quotations surround a fountain in the center of the garden. Daily 24 hours. Free.

Old Stone House is at 3051 M St. N.W. in Georgetown. The oldest building in Washington, it dates from 1765 and is an excellent example of pre-Revolutionary architecture. Restored and furnished in period, it is open for self-guiding tours. Allow 30 minutes minimum. Wed.-Sun. noon-5; closed major holidays. Free. Phone (202) 426-6851.

Rock Creek Park Nature Center and Planetarium, near Military Rd. at 5200 Glover Rd. N.W., offers exhibits about the park's wildlife and ecosystem, a hands-on nature discovery room, ranger-guided nature walks and interpretive programs. Facilities include an auditorium, planetarium, observation beehive and self-guiding nature trails.

Allow 30 minutes minimum. Wed.-Sun. 9-5; closed Jan. 1, July 4, Thanksgiving and Dec. 25. Planetarium shows are given Wed. at 4, Sat.-Sun. at 1 and 4. Free. Ages 0-3 not permitted at planetarium shows; ages 4-7 must be with an adult. Phone (202) 895-6070 or (202) 895-6239 for recorded event information.

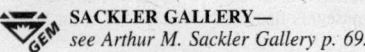 **SACKLER GALLERY—**
see Arthur M. Sackler Gallery p. 69.

ST. JOHN'S CHURCH (Episcopal) is at 16th and H sts. N.W., opposite Lafayette Square (M: McPherson Square). This is known as the Church of the Presidents because every president since its establishment in 1815 has attended one or more services. Several of the stained-glass windows are dedicated to famous statesmen. Allow 30 minutes minimum. Daily 9-3; closed federal holidays and during services. Guided tours are offered after services on the first Sun. of each month. Free. Phone (202) 347-8766.

ST. MATTHEW'S CATHEDRAL is at 1725 Rhode Island Ave. N.W. (M: Dupont Circle or Farragut North). Established in 1840, the present Renaissance-style church was completed in 1895. Both the altar and the baptismal font were gifts from India. The altar is made of white marble with colored floral insets reminiscent of decorations in India's Taj Mahal.

The work of French and Italian craftsmen is displayed in the faceted windows, frescoes, marble and mosaics throughout the church. An inscription in marble commemorates the funeral of assassinated President John F. Kennedy. Guided tours are available by appointment. Allow 30 minutes minimum. Sun.-Fri. 6:30-6:30, Sat. 7:30-6:30, holidays 7:30-1. Free. Phone (202) 347-3215.

SENATE AND HOUSE OFFICE BUILDINGS are on opposite sides of Capitol Square (M: Capitol South or Union Station). The House offices face Independence Ave. between 1st St. S.W. and 1st St. S.E. The Rayburn Building is the westernmost of the House buildings; the Longworth Building is next door; and the Cannon Building is at the junction of 1st Street S.E. and Independence Avenue S.E. Housed in the Russell, Dirksen and Hart buildings, the Senate offices are on Constitution Avenue between Delaware Avenue and 2nd Street N.E.

Senators travel from some of the office buildings to the Capitol via subways, which visitors also may use. **Note:** Fluctuating security levels may affect public access; phone ahead to verify schedule. House and Senate offices open Mon.-Sat. 9-4:30. Free. Phone (202) 225-6827 for recorded tour information.

SEWALL-BELMONT HOUSE AND MUSEUM, 144 Constitution Ave. N.E. at jct. 2nd St. (M: Capitol South or Union Station), has been the headquarters of the National Woman's Party since 1929. The original structure was built in 1750; the main house was added in 1799. It contains antique furniture, party memorabilia and portraits of women important to the women's suffrage campaign.

Guided tours are given on the hour Tues.-Fri. 11-3, Sat. 10-5, Memorial Day-Labor Day; Tues.-Fri. 11-3, Sat. noon-4, rest of year. Closed federal holidays. Last tour begins 1 hour before closing. Admission $5. Phone (202) 546-1210.

SMITHSONIAN AMERICAN ART MUSEUM of the Smithsonian Institution is at 8th and F sts. N.W. (M: Gallery Place-Chinatown). As the nation's first collection of American art, it is an unparalleled record of the American experience. The collection captures the aspirations, character and imagination of the American people over 3 centuries. Major masters are represented in the museum's collection, including Mary Cassatt, David Hockney, Edward Hopper, Georgia O'Keeffe, Robert Rauschenberg and John Singer Sargent. Artworks in the collection reveal key aspects of America's rich artistic and cultural history from the colonial period to today.

In addition to permanent collection galleries, the museum contains two innovative public spaces—the Luce Foundation Center for American Art, the first visible art storage and study center in Washington, and the Lunder Conservation Center, the first conservation facility to allow the public permanent behind-the-scenes views of the preservation work of museums.[5]

This monumental Greek Revival structure served as a hospital during the Civil War and was the scene of Abraham Lincoln's second inaugural ball. The building also houses the National Portrait Gallery

Smithsonian Institution

Congress puzzled for more than a decade over what to do with James Smithson's strange and unprecedented bequest. A wealthy British scientist, Smithson willed his entire fortune of a half-million dollars to a country he had never visited, "to found at Washington, under the name of the Smithsonian Institution an Establishment for the increase and diffusion of knowledge...." Some congressmen argued against accepting the gift at all; others proposed a university, an observatory, a school for teachers or a library. What they finally settled on in 1846 was a natural history museum and research cen-

ter of sorts, an institutional seedling that was to grow in size and scope at a remarkable rate.

The first-time visitor is often surprised to learn that nearly all of the buildings on the National Mall are Smithsonian museums: the Arthur M. Sackler Gallery; the Arts and Industries Building (closed in preparation for major renovation); the Freer Gallery of Art; the Hirshhorn Museum and Sculpture Garden; the National Air and Space Museum; the National Museum of African Art; the National Museum of American History, Kenneth E. Behring Center (closed for renovations until summer 2008); the National Museum of the American Indian; the National Museum of Natural History; and the Smithsonian Institution Building (the Castle), the original building, completed in 1855.

Other facilities include the Anacostia Community Museum; the National Portrait Gallery; the National Postal Museum; the Renwick Gallery of the Smithsonian American Art Museum; the Smithsonian American Art Museum; and the National Zoological Park. The National Air and Space Museum's Steven F. Udvar-Hazy Center is located near Washington Dulles International Airport in nearby Chantilly, Va.

(see attraction listing p. 85); the museums are collectively known as the Donald W. Reynolds Center for American Art and Portraiture.

Food is available. Daily 11:30-7; closed Dec. 25. Guided tours are available on selected days; phone for schedule. Free. Phone (202) 633-1000, or TTY (202) 633-5285.

SMITHSONIAN INSTITUTION encompasses 18 museums and galleries, including one in Chantilly, Va., and two in New York City. The National Zoological Park also is part of the Smithsonian. The Smithsonian's 19th museum, the National Museum of African American History and Culture, will be built on the National Mall. Ten of the museums line the National Mall from 3rd St. to 14th St.

They are the Arthur M. Sackler Gallery; the Arts and Industries Building (closed in preparation for renovation); the Freer Gallery of Art; the Hirshhorn Museum and Sculpture Garden; the National Air and Space Museum; the National Museum of African Art; the National Museum of American History, Kenneth E. Behring Center (closed for renovations until summer 2008); the National Museum of the American Indian; the National Museum of Natural History; and the Smithsonian Institution Building (the Castle) *(see following listing)*.

Nearby are the National Portrait Gallery, the National Postal Museum, the Renwick Gallery and the Smithsonian American Art Museum. Elsewhere in the city is the Anacostia Community Museum, and in Chantilly, Va., the National Air and Space Museum's Steven F. Udvar-Hazy Center. *See sidebar p. 90 and separate attraction listings.*

Note: Security has increased at the Smithsonian. All visitors and their belongings will be checked by security upon entrance. Because on-street parking in the vicinity of the National Mall is extremely limited, visitors are encouraged to take public transportation. Metrorail is the most convenient way to travel to the Smithsonian museums on the National Mall. For parking at off-mall museums and the National Zoological Park, *see individual attraction listings.*

Most Smithsonian museums are open daily 10-5:30; closed Dec. 25. Extended summer hours are determined annually; phone for times. Free. Phone (202) 633-1000, or TTY (202) 633-5285.

S. Dillon Ripley Center is entered through a small above-ground, glass-enclosed kiosk on Jefferson Dr. between the Freer Gallery of Art and the Smithsonian Castle (M: Smithsonian). Part of the underground complex that includes the National Museum of African Art and the Arthur M. Sackler Gallery, the center houses the International Gallery, featuring changing exhibitions, and The Smithsonian Associates and its Discovery Theater and classrooms.

Center open daily 10-5:30; closed Dec. 25. Discovery Theater show times vary; phone ahead. Center free. Theater ticket prices vary. Phone (202) 633-1000, TTY (202) 633-5285, or (202) 633-8700 (voice) for the Discovery Theater.

Smithsonian Institution Building (the Castle) is on the National Mall at 1000 Jefferson Dr. S.W. (M: Smithsonian). The Institution's first building, it was completed in 1855 and houses the Smithsonian Information Center, the administrative headquarters and the tomb of James Smithson, the Institution's benefactor.

In the Smithsonian Information Center, volunteer information specialists welcome visitors and provide information about the institution's exhibitions, activities and services. It also has interactive touch-screen programs, a scale model of the National Mall and surrounding park land and a short film that runs continuously in the orientation theater. The America's Treasure Chest exhibit in the Commons hall displays objects representing the breadth and depth of each museum's collection.

Food is available. Smithsonian Information Center open daily 8:30-5:30; closed Dec. 25. Guided tours of the Castle are available on selected days; phone for schedule. Free. Phone (202) 633-1000, or TTY (202) 633-5285.

SUPREME COURT BUILDING faces the Capitol between Maryland Ave. and E. Capitol St. N.E. (M: Capitol South or Union Station). This white marble edifice is where the country's highest judicial body holds its sessions. Exhibits and a film describing the court are presented on the ground floor. All sessions are open to the public; seating is on a first-come, first-served basis.

The richly ornamented, Corinthian Classical-style building was completed in 1935. The entrance, with the mandate on the architrave of "Equal Justice Under Law," is flanked by the statues "Contemplation of Justice" and "Authority of Law." The panels on the massive bronze doors depict the history of the development of law. The five-story, self-supporting marble and bronze spiral staircases are architectural masterpieces.

Food is available. Allow 1 hour minimum. Building open Mon.-Fri. 9-4:30; closed federal holidays, during inclement weather and occasionally for cleaning. The court often hears arguments Mon.-Wed., first Mon. in Oct.-late Apr. When it hands down opinions, these take place Mon. at 10, Oct.-June. Lectures are given in the courtroom every hour on the half-hour 9:30-3:30 when court is not sitting. Free. Phone (202) 479-3211.

THE TEXTILE MUSEUM, 2320 S St. N.W. (M: Dupont Circle), is devoted to the handmade textile arts. Changing exhibits cover both traditional techniques and modern masters. Much of the collection can be viewed on slides in The Arthur D. Jenkins Library, which has more than 20,000 books and periodicals about textiles. The Textile Learning Center shows how textiles are made and highlights their cultural and artistic significance.

Allow 1 hour minimum. Museum open Mon.-Sat. 10-5, Sun. 1-5. Library open Wed.-Fri. 10-2, Sat. 10-4. Closed federal holidays and Dec. 24. Highlight tours are given the first Wed. of the month at

Smithsonian Institution
(continued)

The Smithsonian's vast collection chronicles nearly every facet of human endeavor, from the masterful to the mundane. The Institution also encompasses research installations, observatories, libraries and facilities for preserving and restoring artifacts, and offers publications, lectures, classes and other educational programs.

Before exploring the museums, visitors are encouraged to first stop by the Smithsonian Information Center in the Castle to plan their visit. While there, be sure to give thanks to James Smithson; his tomb—rescued late 1903 by Alexander Graham Bell from an endangered cemetery in Genoa, Italy—lies in a crypt off the north entrance. It is a resting place he would surely approve of, as he would the multifarious institution he helped found for "the increase and diffusion of knowledge."

Note: The East and West Buildings of the National Gallery of Art and The John F. Kennedy Center for the Performing Arts are not administered by the Smithsonian Institution.

America on the Move

With AAA as a co-sponsor, the Smithsonian's National Museum of American History opened the largest exhibition in its 40-year history in November 2003. America on the Move immerses visitors in the history of transportation in the United States from 1876 to the present. The exhibition showcases the Smithsonian's popular transportation collections in 15 historic settings. Visitors to the exhibition will:

• Celebrate with townspeople in Santa Cruz, Calif., as they welcome a railroad to the isolated town in 1876. • Come "aboard" the 1920s U.S. Lighthouse Service Ship *Oak* in New York harbor. • Join the morning commute on the Chicago Elevated. • Watch as Horatio Nelson Jackson and Sewall K. Crocker pull their 20-horsepower 1903 Winton out of a mud hole during the first transcontinental automobile trip in 1903. • Walk 40 feet of pavement from Route 66, one of the first great interstate highways.

America on the Move thoroughly and entertainingly explores transportation's social and economic effects on our lives, communities and country. **Note:** The National Museum of American History is scheduled to reopen summer 2008.

1, Sat.-Sun. at 1:30, Sept.-May; other tours are by appointment. Admission $5. Phone (202) 667-0441.

THOMAS JEFFERSON MEMORIAL is on the s.e. side of the Tidal Basin. The monument to the author of the Declaration of Independence and the country's third president is a circular Classical dome supported by 54 Ionic columns. The central memorial room contains a 19-foot-tall bronze statue of Jefferson by Rudolph Evans; panels on the surrounding walls are inscribed with the statesman's most significant writings.

Guided tours are available by request. Allow 30 minutes minimum. Daily 24 hours; closed Dec. 25. Park rangers are available daily 9:30 a.m.-11:30 p.m.. Free. Phone (202) 426-6841.

SAVE **TUDOR PLACE HISTORIC HOUSE AND GARDEN** is in Georgetown at 1644 31st St. N.W. (M: Dupont Circle). The 1816 neoclassic house was built by Thomas Peter and his wife, Martha Custis Peter, granddaughter of Martha Washington. It reflects six generations of family life illustrated in paintings, furniture and decorative arts, including an important collection of Mount Vernon heirlooms. Visitors also may enjoy a self-guiding tour of the surrounding 5.5 acres of gardens.

Note: No cameras are permitted inside the house. Docent-led garden tours are available by appointment. Allow 1 hour minimum. Guided 45-minute house tours are offered Tues.-Fri. at 10, 11:30, 1 and 2:30, Sat. on the hour 10-3, Sun. on the hour noon-3, Feb.-Dec. Self-guiding tours of the garden are available Tues.-Sat. 10-4, Sun. noon-4, Feb.-Dec. (weather permitting). Closed major holidays. House tour $6; $5 (ages 65+); $2 (ages 6-12). Self-guiding garden tour $2. Phone (202) 965-0400.

UNITED STATES CAPITOL is on Capitol Hill in a 59-acre park (M: Capitol South or Union Station). The Capitol, based on Dr. William Thornton's 1792 design, with revisions by subsequent architects over a 200-year period, is 751 feet long and 350 feet wide, and contains about 550 rooms.

A 19.5-foot-tall statue of Freedom surmounts the dome. The two wings, constructed of marble, contain the Senate and House chambers, while the central part of the building includes the Rotunda. National Statuary Hall is a semicircular room south of the Rotunda that was the meeting place of the U.S. House of Representatives for nearly 50 years. It now contains a collection of statues.

Note: The Capitol is open to the public only by guided tour. Obtain House or Senate gallery passes from your senator or representative by phoning his/her office (*see sidebar p. 73*). Visitors from outside the United States can obtain an International Visitor's Pass by presenting a valid passport or other photo ID at the South Visitors Facility, the departure point for tours.

Tours are given Mon.-Sat. 9-4:30; closed Thanksgiving and Dec. 25. Tickets for tours are required and are available on a first-come, first-served basis (one ticket per person) beginning at 9 a.m. at the Capitol Guide Service kiosk near the intersection of 1st Street S.W. and Independence Avenue. Free. Phone (202) 225-6827 for recorded information.

UNITED STATES HOLOCAUST MEMORIAL MUSEUM has entrances on 14th St. S.W. and at 100 Raoul Wallenberg Pl. S.W. (M: Smithsonian); there is no parking at the museum and limited parking in the area. The museum presents the history of the 6 million Jews and millions of others—including Gypsies, Soviet POWs, Poles, dissidents, homosexuals, Jehovah's Witnesses and the disabled—who suffered and died at the hands of the Nazis during their rule of Germany 1933-45.

The museum serves as a memorial to these victims and teaches the implications of the Holocaust for contemporary life. The three-floor permanent exhibition depicts the story of the Holocaust through artifacts, photographs, films and oral histories. To personalize the experience, upon entry each visitor is given an identity card bearing the name and picture of a Holocaust victim. The Hall of Remembrance, a six-sided, 60-foot-high structure illuminated by a skylight, is an area for private contemplation.

The permanent exhibit also features stories of resistance and rescue, highlighting such heroes as Raoul Wallenberg, the Swedish diplomat who risked his life to hide and save Jews. The Wexner Learning Center offers a number of multimedia displays.

Note: Free timed passes, required for admission to the permanent exhibition, are available at the information desk. Passes (limited to 10 per person) are timed at 15-minute intervals between 10 and 3:45 and are available on a first-come, first-served basis. The permanent exhibition is recommended for visitors over age 11. Remember the Children: Daniel's Story is designed for over age 8. Food is available. Allow 2 hours minimum.

Museum open daily 10-5:30; closed Yom Kippur and Dec. 25. Free. Phone (202) 488-6100, TTY (202) 448-0406.

UNITED STATES NAVY MEMORIAL is on Pennsylvania Ave. between 7th and 9th sts. N.W. (M: Archives-Navy Memorial). The base is a ground-level granite map of the world 100 feet in diameter, illustrating the enormity of Earth's ocean surface compared to land areas. Surrounded by fountains, pools, flag masts and 26 bronze relief sculptures depicting naval history, the map serves as an amphitheater for free outdoor summer concerts as well as traditional Navy ceremonies. The statue of "The Lone Sailor" is emblematic of the classic U.S. Navy bluejacket.

Allow 1 hour minimum. Memorial open Mon.-Sat. 9:30-5, Mar.-Oct.; Tues.-Sat. 9:30-5, rest of year. Concerts are provided by the U.S. Navy Band and other service bands every Tues. at 8 p.m., Memorial Day-Labor Day. Free. Phone (202) 737-2300 or (800) 821-8892.

Naval Heritage Center, adjacent to the memorial, is a visitor center that includes a database listing of Navy, Marine Corps, Coast Guard and Merchant Marine men and women; a reference library; and educational displays. "Blue Angels: A Year in the Life" and "At Sea" are two Navy-related films airing in the center's 242-seat theater. Guided tours are available. Open Mon.-Sat. 9:30-5, Mar.-Oct.; Tues.-Sat. 9:30-5, rest of year. Closed Jan. 1, July 4, Thanksgiving and Dec. 25. Free. Phone (202) 737-2300 or (800) 821-8892.

U.S. BOTANIC GARDEN is on the w. side of the Capitol at 1st St. and Independence Ave. S.W. (M: Federal Center SW or Capitol South). Founded in 1820, the conservatory is a plant museum as well as a beautiful and quiet retreat from the city. Visitors enter through the Garden Court, where there are pools, benches and displays of tropical plants and flowers. The 100-foot-tall, glass-enclosed jungle room includes a canopy walk that allows visitors to view palm trees and ornamental plantings from above.

Adjacent to the conservatory is the National Garden, which sits on 3 acres and includes the Lawn Terrace, the Butterfly Garden, the Rose Garden, the First Ladies' Water Garden and the Regional Garden. Bartholdi Park, across Independence Avenue from the conservatory, contains the Bartholdi Fountain, a rock garden, and changing seasonal displays of annuals and perennials.

Note: Bartholdi Fountain is currently undergoing renovations. Street parking is metered and limited; using public transportation is encouraged. Allow 1 hour minimum. Conservatory open daily 10-5. Free. Phone (202) 225-8333.

USDA FOREST SERVICE NATIONAL HEADQUARTERS AND INFORMATION CENTER is at 201 14th St. S.W. in the Yates Federal Building (M: Smithsonian). The information center features an animatronic Smokey Bear that greets visitors, as well as interactive touch-screen exhibits, a log cabin interior with videos and historical items, and an 8-foot by 20-foot photo wall explaining the purpose of the Forest Service.

Allow 30 minutes minimum. Daily 8-4, Mar. 15-Sept. 15; Mon.-Fri. 8-4, rest of year. Closed federal holidays Sept. 16-Mar. 14. Free. Phone (202) 205-1680.

U.S. NATIONAL ARBORETUM is just e. of jct. US 50 (New York Ave.) and Bladensburg Rd. N.E.; entrances are on New York Ave. N.E. and at 24th and R sts. N.E. Shuttle service from Union Station to the arboretum aboard the X6 Metrobus is available Sat.-Sun. and holidays (except Dec. 25). Many introduced and native plants commonly found in the eastern United States grow within the arboretum's 446 acres.

A network of foot trails and 9.5 miles of roads enables visitors to observe thousands of primarily woody plants. Narrated 40-minute tram tours provide a good introduction to this peaceful refuge from hectic Washington. The National Bonsai and Penjing Museum Collection features a sampling of American, Chinese and Japanese bonsai trees.

Allow 1 hour minimum. Grounds open daily 8-5. Administration building open Mon.-Fri. 8-4:30 (also Sat.-Sun. 8-5, Mar. 1 to mid-Nov.). The National Bonsai and Penjing Museum Collection open daily 10-3:30. Closed Dec. 25. Tram tours are given Sat.-Sun. and holidays at 10:30 (if not previously booked), 11:30, 1, 2, 3 and 4, mid-Apr. to mid-Oct. Grounds free. Tram tour $4; $3 (ages 55+); $2 (ages 4-16); free (ages 0-3 on lap). Phone (202) 245-4523.

THE U.S. NAVY MUSEUM, in building 76 at the Washington Navy Yard, 11th and O sts. S.E. (M: Eastern Market or Navy Yard), presents the past and present history of the U.S. Navy. Exhibits depict important battles and early naval heroes, and trace developments in weapons and technology. Highlights include ship models, a gun deck section, a fully rigged foremast fighting top from the frigate USS *Constitution* and a submarine room with operating periscopes. Outdoor parks display guns and a cannon.

Note: Fluctuating security levels may affect public access; phone ahead to verify schedule. Guided tours are available by appointment. Allow 1 hour minimum. Mon.-Fri. 9-5, Sat.-Sun. 10-5; closed Jan. 1, Thanksgiving and Dec. 24-25. Free. Nonmilitary visitors must make a reservation 24 hours in advance. Phone (202) 433-4882.

USS *Barry* is docked at Pier 2 within the Washington Navy Yard. The destroyer, which saw action during the Cuban missile blockade and in Vietnam, was commissioned in 1956 and was decommissioned in 1982. Visitors can take a self-guiding tour of the ship. Allow 1 hour minimum. Daily 9-5; closed Thanksgiving and Dec. 25. Free. Phone (202) 433-6897.

DID YOU KNOW

Thomas Jefferson, John Adams and James Monroe all died on July 4th.

VIETNAM VETERANS MEMORIAL, near the Lincoln Memorial between the Reflecting Pool and Constitution Ave. (M: Smithsonian), honors the men and women who served in the U.S. Armed Forces in Vietnam. Its polished black granite walls are inscribed with the names of the dead listed chronologically by date of casualty; the names of the missing also are listed.

A life-size statue of three servicemen stands near the V-shaped walls; each one carries a dog tag in a different place. Wreath ceremonies take place on Memorial Day and Veterans Day. The Memorial to Honor Women Who Served in Vietnam honors the more than 265,000 women who served during the Vietnam War with a statue depicting three servicewomen coming to the aid of a wounded soldier. Allow 30 minutes minimum. Daily 24 hours; closed Dec. 25. Park rangers are available daily 9:30 a.m.-11:30 p.m. Free. Phone (202) 426-6841.

WASHINGTON MONUMENT stands near the center of the National Mall; the grounds extend from 14th to 17th sts. and from Constitution to Independence aves. N.W. (M: Smithsonian). The cornerstone for a monument to honor the first president was laid July 4, 1848, but was not completed until 1884, when a 3,300-pound marble capstone, topped with a 9-inch pyramid of cast aluminum, was set in place.

The marble obelisk rises just over 555 feet from a knoll in the center of the grounds, surrounded by 50 American flags. An elevator runs to the observation room at the 500-foot level.

Memorial to Honor Women Who Served in Vietnam, Vietnam Veteran's Memorial / © AAA / Denise E. Campbell

Allow 1 hour minimum. Daily 9-4:45; closed Dec. 25. Tickets are required and are available on a first-come, first-served basis daily 8-4:30 at the kiosk on 15th Street near Madison Drive. The line for same-day tickets forms at 7:30 or earlier, and all passes are usually distributed before 10 a.m. Tickets also are available from 24 hours to up to 5 months in advance and can be reserved by phoning the monument's toll-free number. Same-day tickets free. Advance ticket reservations $2 per ticket. Phone (202) 426-6841, or (800) 967-2283 daily 10-10 for advance tickets.

WASHINGTON NATIONAL CATHEDRAL (Episcopal) is on Mount St. Alban at Massachusetts and Wisconsin aves. N.W. Officially the Cathedral Church of St. Peter and St. Paul, this impressive example of Gothic architecture is said to be the sixth largest cathedral in the world. It was completed in 1990 after 83 years of construction. The top of the Gloria in Excelsis Central Tower, one of the last towers in the world to contain both a carillon and a 10-bell peal, is the highest point in Washington.

Decorative features include elaborate stone carvings and large stained-glass rose windows, as well as statues of Abraham Lincoln and George Washington. Notable individuals interred in the cathedral are Adm. George Dewey, secretaries of state Cordell Hull and Frank Kellogg, Helen Keller and President Woodrow Wilson.

Note: Fluctuating security levels and special cathedral services may affect public access; phone ahead to confirm schedule. Allow 1 hour minimum.

Cathedral open Mon.-Fri. 10-7:45, Sat. 10-4:30, Sun. 8-6:30, early June-Labor Day; Mon.-Fri. 10-5:30, Sat. 10-4:30, Sun. 8-6:30, rest of year. Thirty-minute guided cathedral tours departing from the west-end docent station and self-guiding audio tours are available Mon. and Wed. 10-11:30 and 1:15-3:30, Tues. and Thurs.-Sat. 10-11:30 and 12:45-3:30, Sun. 12:45-2:30. Cathedral services take place Mon.-Fri. at 7:30, noon, 2:30 and 5:30; Sat. at 7:30, noon, 2:30 and 4; Sun. at 8, 9, 10, 11, 4 and 6:30. Pipe organ demonstrations take place Mon. and Wed. at 12:30. Ringing of the peal bells occurs Tues. at 7:30 p.m. and Sun. at 12:30. Carillon recitals are given Sat. at 12:30.

Cathedral free. Half-hour guided tour $3; $2 (senior citizens and students with ID); $1 (children). Self-guiding audio tours $5. Phone (202) 537-6200, or (202) 364-6616 for a weekly listing of special events.

WHITE HOUSE is at 1600 Pennsylvania Ave. N.W. (M: McPherson Square, Metro Center or Federal Triangle); street parking in the vicinity is not available. James Hoban's design was chosen for the presidential mansion in 1792, and the building was completed in 1800. A 1948-52 renovation preserved the exterior walls and rebuilt the interior. The West Wing, the location of the President's Oval Office, was constructed in 1902. This has been the home of every president except George Washington.

Note: Self-guiding public tours of the White House are available Tues.-Sat. 7:30-12:30 for groups of 10 or more people. Tour requests must be submitted through one's member of Congress and are accepted up to 6 months in advance; contact the U.S. Capitol switchboard at (202) 224-3121 to reach your senator or representative. Tours are scheduled on a first-come, first-served basis approximately 1 month before the requested date *(see sidebar p. 73)*. Visitors requesting additional information should call the White House Visitors Office 24-hour recorded information line.

The White House Visitor Center (1450 Pennsylvania Ave., N.W.), part of President's Park, is in the historic Malcolm Baldrige Hall in the Department of Commerce building. It offers opportunities to learn more about the White House and the presidency through exhibits, artifacts, park ranger talks, special events, education programs and a 30-minute video. Visitor center open daily 7:30-4; closed Jan. 1, Thanksgiving and Dec. 25. Tours and visitor center free. Phone (202) 456-7041 for 24-hour recorded information, (202) 208-1631 for the visitor center, or TTY (202) 456-2121.

WOODROW WILSON HOUSE is at 2340 S St. N.W. (M: Dupont Circle). From 1921 until his death in 1924, former President Woodrow Wilson lived in this 1915 Georgian Revival townhouse on Embassy Row. The house is filled with personal furnishings and mementos of the 28th president's career, and is the only presidential museum in Washington. Allow 1 hour minimum. Guided tours are given Tues.-Sun. 10-4; closed federal holidays. Fee $7.50; $6.50 (ages 63+); $3 (students with ID and ages 7-18). AX, MC, VI. Phone (202) 387-4062.

What To Do

Sightseeing

Sightseeing tours cover the city and most major suburban points of interest. Your local AAA office can provide information about tours of embassies, houses and gardens that occur periodically *(see Special Events section)*. For more information visit one of the AAA Mid-Atlantic offices. Visitors can obtain access to services and tours by contacting their U.S. senators and representatives before leaving home.

Voice of America, 330 Independence Ave. S.W. (M: Federal Center SW), is a worldwide service supplying broadcasts in 44 languages. Visitors can take a 45-minute guided tour of its radio and television studios; phone (202) 203-4990.

Mount Vernon, VA / Washington DC Convention and Tourism Corp

Boat Tours

C&O CANAL BOAT TRIPS— *see Chesapeake and Ohio Canal National Historical Park, Md., p. 189.*

SPIRIT OF WASHINGTON-POTOMAC CRUISES, departing Pier 4 at 6th and Water sts. S.W. (M: Waterfront), offers a narrated cruise (90 minutes each way) on the Potomac River plus a 3.5-hour stopover at George Washington's Mount Vernon estate. Other sights include the Washington Monument, Old Town Alexandria and the Woodrow Wilson Bridge. Lunch and dinner cruises including live entertainment also are available; phone for fares and departure times.

Inquire about refund policies. Food is available. Allow 7 hours minimum. Sightseeing trips depart Tues.-Sun. and Mon. holidays at 8:30, late Mar.-day before Labor Day; Thurs.-Sun. at 8:30, mid-Mar. to late Mar.; Fri.-Sun. and Mon. holidays at 8:30, Labor Day-late Oct. Fare (includes admission to Mount Vernon) $38; $36 (ages 60+); $31 (ages 6-11). Parking $12-$15. Reservations are recommended. AX, MC, VI. Phone (202) 554-8000 or (866) 211-3811.

Bus, Limousine or Trolley Tours

Individually operated limousine tours are sold by the drivers near the various information kiosks. Most taxi companies also can provide sightseeing services. Bus tours range in price from about $10 to $65, depending on length of tour and itinerary, and include trips around Washington, Mount Vernon and all stops between. Tour companies are listed in the telephone directory.

DC DUCKS LAND & WATER TOURS begin and end at Union Station, 50 Massachusetts Ave. N.E. (M: Union Station). These nonstop, 90-minute narrated tours aboard rebuilt World War II amphibious vehicles roll past the memorials and museums along the National Mall and splash down into the Potomac River. Tours depart daily (weather permitting) 10-4, mid-Mar. through Oct. 31; closed July 4. Departure times may vary; phone ahead. Fare $32; $16 (ages 4-12). AX, DS, MC, VI. Phone (202) 832-9800.

U.S. Botanic Garden / © AAA / Denise E. Campbell

[SAVE] **GRAY LINE OF WASHINGTON** tours depart from the Gray Line Terminal, on the first parking level of Union Station, 50 Massachusetts Ave. N.E. (M: Union Station). Gray Line offers a variety of tour packages. Seasonal tours are available to Colonial Williamsburg, Busch Gardens Williamsburg, Gettysburg and Monticello. Some combination tours are available. Fares include all applicable admission charges. AX, MC, VI. Phone (202) 289-1995 or (800) 862-1400.

Interiors of Public Buildings Tour (Tour BA) departs from the Gray Line Terminal, on the first parking level of Union Station, 50 Massachusetts Ave. N.E. (M: Union Station). The 9-hour tour stops at the White House Visitor Center, Ford's Theatre National Historic Site, the National Air and Space Museum and the National World War II Memorial. A stop also is made at the U.S. Capitol.

The Supreme Court Building, the Thomas Jefferson Memorial, the Tidal Basin and a number of government buildings can be viewed from the coach. Tours depart Mon.-Sat. at 8 a.m.; closed Jan. 1, Thanksgiving and Dec. 25. Fare $48; $24 (ages 3-11). AX, MC, VI. Phone (202) 289-1995 or (800) 862-1400.

Mount Vernon & Alexandria Tour (Tour D) departs from the Gray Line Terminal, on the first parking level of Union Station, 50 Massachusetts Ave. N.E. (M: Union Station). The 4-hour tour includes a stop at Christ Church (not available during services), George Washington's place of worship in Alexandria, Va., and then continues to Mount Vernon to visit his home, gardens and farm.

Tours depart daily at 8 a.m. (also at 2, late June-early Oct.); closed Jan. 1, Thanksgiving and Dec. 25. Fare $37; $18 (ages 3-11). All-day combination tour (Tour DC) with the Washington, Embassy Row & Arlington National Cemetery Tour $60; $30 (ages 3-11). AX, MC, VI. Phone (202) 289-1995 or (800) 862-1400.

Washington After Dark Tour (Tour L) departs from the Gray Line Terminal, on the first parking level of Union Station, 50 Massachusetts Ave. N.E. (M: Union Station). The 3-hour tour features Washington's monuments and buildings illuminated by floodlights.

Stops include the Kennedy Center (as available) and the Lincoln, Vietnam Veterans, Korean War Veterans, Marine Corps War and Franklin Delano Roosevelt memorials. The U.S. Capitol, Supreme Court Building, Library of Congress, House and Senate office buildings, White House and Georgetown are seen en route.

Tours depart nightly at 7:45; closed Jan. 1, July 4, Thanksgiving, and Dec. 24-25 and 31. Fare $38; $19 (ages 3-11). AX, MC, VI. Phone (202) 289-1995 or (800) 862-1400.

Washington, Embassy Row & Arlington National Cemetery Tour (Tour C) departs from the Gray Line Terminal, on the first parking level of Union Station, 50 Massachusetts Ave. N.E. (M: Union Station). The 4-hour tour includes stops at the Lincoln, Korean War, Marine Corps and Vietnam Veterans memorials and Arlington National Cemetery for a tram tour to the Changing of the Guard ceremony and the Kennedy gravesites. Many downtown sites as well as the Pentagon, Georgetown and Embassy Row can be seen en route.

Tours depart daily at 2 (also at 8:30 a.m., late June-late Oct.); closed Jan. 1, Thanksgiving and Dec. 25. Fare $38; $19 (ages 3-11). All-day combination tour (Tour DC) with the Mount Vernon and Alexandria Tour $60; $30 (ages 3-11). AX, MC, VI. Phone (202) 289-1995 or (800) 862-1400.

OLD TOWN TROLLEY TOURS OF WASHINGTON depart from any one of 17 stops. Tickets can be purchased at Union Station, 50 Massachusetts Ave. N.E., or at the welcome center at 1001 E St. N.W. This 2-hour narrated tour passes most of Washington's major attractions, from Capitol Hill to Washington National Cathedral, and includes the Smithsonian museums, the White House and Arlington National Cemetery. Unlimited free reboarding for the day is permitted on the trolleys, which pass designated stops at least every 30 minutes.

Tours are given daily 9-5:30, Apr.-Oct.; 9-4:30, rest of year. Closed day before Memorial Day, July 4, last Sun. in Oct., Thanksgiving and Dec. 25. Fare $32; $16 (ages 4-12). AX, DS, MC, VI. Phone (202) 832-9800.

TOURMOBILE SIGHTSEEING INC. tours depart from various locations. Tickets can be purchased year-round from Tourmobile drivers, at the Tourmobile Ticket/Information booth at Arlington National Cemetery or at Union Station. The Washington Monument ticket kiosk is open seasonally. The company offers several narrated sightseeing shuttle tours around Washington landmarks, with stops at up to 21 different sights on or near the National Mall and four sites at Arlington National Cemetery.

Note: Tour itineraries, times and rates are all subject to change; phone ahead. Free all-day parking is available in the visitor parking lot near the Thomas Jefferson Memorial; free 3-hour parking is available off Ohio Drive S.W. near West Potomac Park. Paid parking also is available in the Arlington National Cemetery visitor parking lot ($1.25 per hour for first 3 hours, then $2 per hour) and at Union Station. Tours are offered daily; closed Dec. 25. Phone (202) 554-5100 or (888) 868-7707. *See color ad p. 67.*

Arlington National Cemetery Tour begins at the visitor center on Memorial Dr.; tickets are available at the Arlington National Cemetery Tourmobile ticket booth. The tour includes the Kennedy gravesites; the Tomb of the Unknowns for the Changing of the Guard ceremony; and Arlington House, the Robert E. Lee Memorial. Tours are given daily 8:30-6:30, Apr.-Sept.; 8:30-4:30, rest of year. Closed Dec. 25. Last tour begins 30 minutes before cemetery closing. Fare $7; $6 (ages 65+); $3.50 (ages 3-11). Phone (202) 554-5100 or (888) 868-7707.

Frederick Douglass Tour departs from the Arlington National Cemetery and Washington Monument ticket booths. The 2.5-hour tour includes landmarks on Capitol Hill, Cedar Hill (the former home of Frederick Douglass), the Mary McLeod Bethune Memorial and Lincoln Park.

Tours depart daily at noon, mid-June through Labor Day; closed Dec. 25. Fare $7; $3.50 (ages 3-11). Reservations in person are required and should be made 30 minutes before departure. Phone (202) 554-5100 or (888) 868-7707.

Mount Vernon Tour leaves from the Arlington National Cemetery ticket booth. The 5-hour tour includes a scenic 17-mile excursion along the George Washington Parkway via Old Town Alexandria to George Washington's estate and gardens at Mount Vernon.

Tours depart daily at 11, mid-June through Labor Day. Fare (includes admission to home, gardens and exhibits) $30; $15 (ages 3-11). Seating is available on a first-come, first-served basis. Reservations in person are required and should be made at least 30 minutes before departure. Phone (202) 554-5100 or (888) 868-7707.

Washington D.C. & Arlington National Cemetery Tour begins at sites along and near the National Mall marked by Tourmobile stop signs. This tour provides live narrated sightseeing shuttle service to 25 historic sites, including the White House Visitor Center; the Washington Monument; the Jefferson, Lincoln, Vietnam War, National World War II and Korean War memorials; the United States Holocaust Memorial Museum; the Smithsonian museums; and Arlington National Cemetery.

There is unlimited free reboarding throughout the day. Tours depart daily 9:30-4:30; closed Jan. 1 and Dec. 25. Final reboarding is at 4. Fare $25; $12 (ages 3-11). Consecutive 2-day ticket fare $35; $17 (ages 3-11). Phone (202) 554-5100 or (888) 868-7707.

Driving Tours

A 3-hour driving cassette tape tour of the District of Columbia and Mount Vernon is available by mail from CCInc. Auto Tape Tours for $12.95 (plus $2 for shipping and handling); a CD is $15.95 (plus $3 for shipping and handling). Phone (201) 236-1666.

Self-guiding Walking Tours

For those exploring the Dupont Circle area, the Dupont-Kalorama Museum Walk brochure outlines a walking tour of historic buildings near the circle. To get a copy, send a self-addressed stamped No. 10 envelope to The Textile Museum, 2320 S Street N.W., Washington, DC 20008, or pick one up at The Textile Museum *(see attraction listing p. 91)* or other sites along the tour; phone (202) 667-0441.

The Washington, D.C. Black History National Recreation Trail consists of various neighborhoods that played an important role in the community from the time of slavery to the mid-20th century. Contact the National Park Service for more information; phone (202) 619-7222.

Attraction and tour information highlighting African-American history in Washington, D.C. can be found in the "African American Heritage Trail" guide. The free booklet is available at several locations, including the Visitor Information Center in the Ronald Reagan Building, 1300 Pennsylvania Ave. N.W.; phone (202) 328-4748 for the visitor center or (202) 661-7581 for information about the guide.

AAA Walking Tours

A walk among the monuments and monumental buildings of Washington, D.C. is sure to leave a lasting impression on all but the most jaded traveler. The District's imposing white-columned facades have come to symbolize the United States, its government and its principles. America's founding fathers chose this classical motif as befitting a young republic committed to the ancient Greek ideal of democracy.

The following three tours focus on the U.S. Capitol and vicinity, the museums surrounding the Mall, and the White House and vicinity. Each tour should take 3-4 hours, depending on your pace and the number of listed sites you visit along the way. *Those that appear in bold type have detailed listings on the preceding pages. Even if you decide not to visit a site, reading the listing when you reach that point should make the tour more interesting.*

Because parking in the District is difficult even on a good day, avoid driving whenever possible. The easiest way to get around is to use Washington Metrorail. Trains run Mon.-Thurs. 5:30 a.m.-midnight, Fri. 5:30 a.m.-3 a.m., Sat. 7 a.m.-3 a.m., Sun. 7 a.m.-midnight; opening and closing times are scaled back on federal holidays. Fares range between $1.35 and $3.90, depending on distance traveled and whether you travel during regular or off-peak hours.

Dramatic spotlighting illuminates many public buildings after dusk, although most of them aren't open at this time. In good weather early evening is a pleasant time to stroll around the Capitol, the Mall museums or the White House, when otherwise stark white or gray edifices are bathed in a mellow glow.

Note: Although restrooms can be found within most public buildings around Capitol Hill and on the Mall, they may not always be convenient. It's a good idea to take advantage of the facilities whenever you get a chance.

The Capitol

See map following. From the Capitol South Metro station at 1st Street S.E. between C and D streets S.E., go north up the hill on 1st Street and cross C Street. The austere marble facade on your right belongs to the James Madison Building of the **Library of Congress,** which comprises three buildings (named for Presidents Adams, Jefferson and Madison).

By far the most elaborate of the three is the Italian Renaissance-style Jefferson Building, which will be on your right after you cross Independence Avenue. Completed in 1897 and renovated for its centennial, the building features an ornate exterior that is but a foretaste of the splendor inside.

The golden Torch of Learning atop a central cupola indicates the building's purpose. A beautiful fountain along 1st Street features the Roman god Neptune and his court. As you approach the main entrance, notice the faces set in the keystones above several first-floor windows. There are 33 in all, and each represents a different ethnic group. A little higher up, framed by circular windows, are the busts of nine important authors: Dante, Demosthenes, Ralph Waldo Emerson, Benjamin Franklin, Johann Wolfgang von Goethe, Nathaniel Hawthorne, Washington Irving, Thomas Babington Macaulay and Sir Walter Scott.

Three pairs of decorative bronze doors originally served as the building's main entrance, but now these are opened only for special occasions. Visitors must enter via the ground-floor doorway below, where stairs lead back up to the first floor's Great Hall vestibule. Here you may have to remind yourself that you're standing in a library and not a European-style palace.

Constructed of white Italian marble, this vast room features stained-glass skylights 75 feet above the multihued, brass-inlaid marble floor. The ornamental touches are almost too numerous to take in: stucco ceilings accented with gold leaf, murals, mosaics, Corinthian columns, sweeping arches and classical statues. Don't overlook the Great Hall's East Corridor, which contains two of the library's most precious items: the Giant Bible of Mainz and the Gutenberg Bible, one of only three vellum copies in existence.

Beyond the Great Hall is the Main Reading Room, which is accessible only by way of the library's free public tours during the height of tourist season in spring and early summer. Even then you are limited to seeing the room from behind the Visitors Gallery's transparent, sound-dampening walls. The view, however, is worth it.

From the base of its massive columns to the domed ceiling 160 feet above, the Main Reading Room is richly detailed. Octagonal in shape, it has walls and columns made of brown, red and cream-colored marble from three continents. Semicircular, stained-glass windows bear the seals of the 48 contiguous states. Between these windows stand eight larger than life-size statues of female allegorical figures representing religion, commerce, history, art, philosophy, poetry, law and science.

A few feet below and on either side of the figures stand 16 bronze statues of men who have distinguished themselves in those eight fields, including Moses, Christopher Columbus, Ludwig van Beethoven, William Shakespeare and Sir Isaac Newton. Murals, bas-reliefs, plaster rosettes, balustrades and baroque molding complete this impressive chamber.

If the other two library buildings look newer than the Jefferson Building, that's because they are. The Adams Building was completed in 1939, the Madison Building in 1981. Together the three contain more than 120 million items, making the Library of Congress the world's largest.

From the library's main exit on 1st Street, go right around the corner onto E. Capitol Street and cross 2nd Street S.E. Just south is the **Folger Shakespeare Library,** which houses rare books and manuscripts, paintings, engravings, costumes and musical instruments. Henry Clay Folger, who

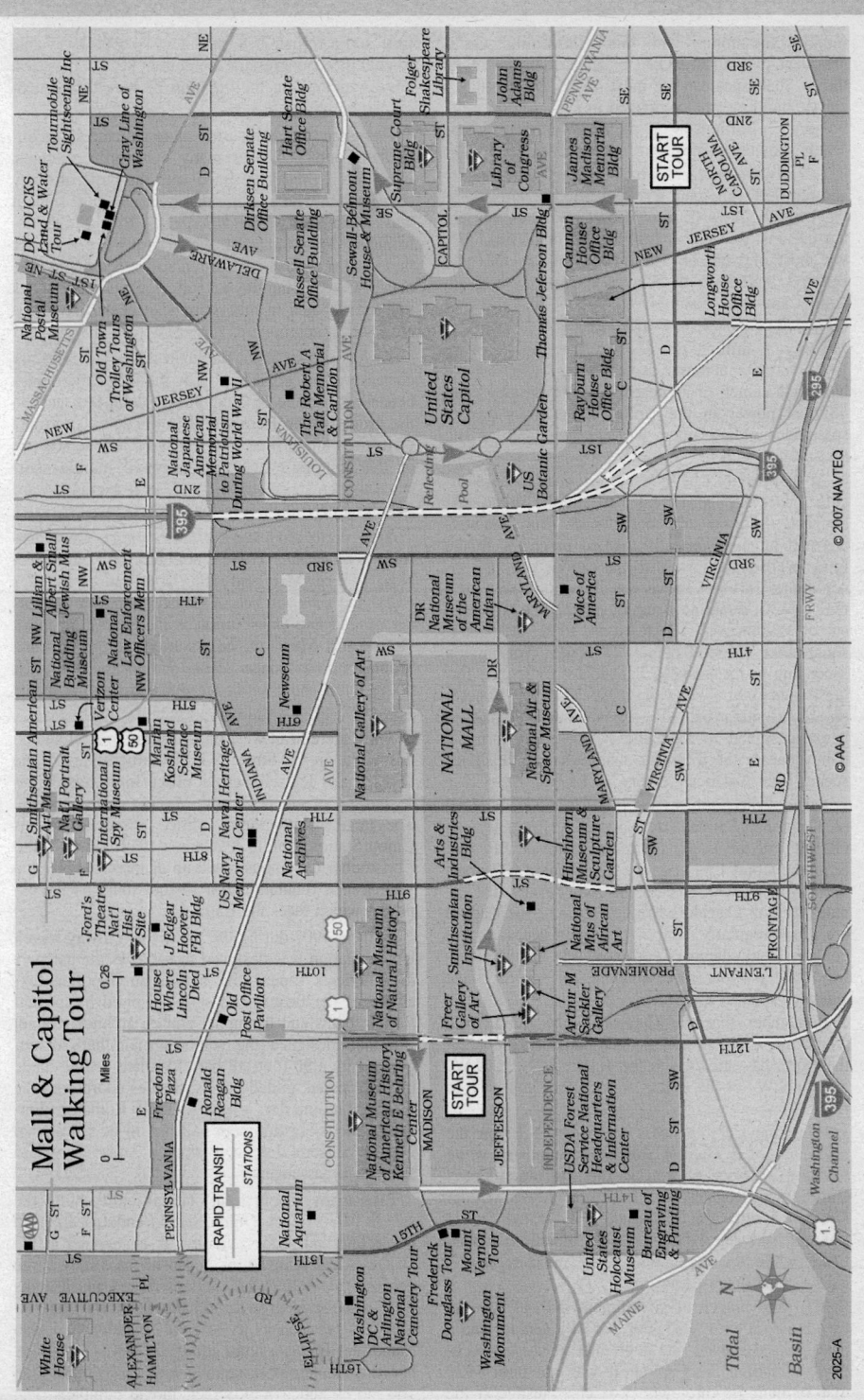

Mall & Capitol Walking Tour

RAPID TRANSIT
STATIONS

Miles 0   0.26

© 2007 NAVTEQ
© AAA
2025-A

founded the library with this wife Emily, was a president of Standard Oil Co. and a devotee of all things Shakespearean for most of his life. The neoclassic building was completed in 1932 to house the Folgers' collection; it is adorned with nine bas-reliefs showing scenes from Shakespeare's plays.

Leaving the library, return to E. Capitol Street and turn left, following it 2 blocks to the entrance of the **United States Capitol.** George Washington laid the cornerstone of this familiar landmark in 1793, but most of what is visible was built in the next century, including the Capitol's north and south wings and the distinctive 287-foot-tall cast-iron dome, all of which were added 1855-70.

Up to 5 million people visit the Capitol every year, and for obvious reasons: Not only is this the hallowed center of representative government and political power in the United States, but it is a splendid building filled with historic and artistic treasures as well.

At the Capitol's heart is the rotunda, a grand circular space 96 feet across beneath the dome that connects the north and south wings. From the statues and large, historically themed paintings on the lower walls look upward to the canopy over the inner dome, 180 feet above, which is adorned with a fresco by Constantino Brumidi titled "The Apotheosis of Washington." Restored in 1988, the 4,664-square-foot fresco depicts George Washington ascending to the heavens flanked by 15 female figures—two symbolizing Liberty and Victory, the others representing the 13 original states. A painted frieze designed to look like a bas-relief forms a band beneath the rotunda's windows and illustrates scenes from American history.

Other sights within the Capitol include the Hall of Columns; National Statuary Hall (formerly the Old Hall of the House of Representatives); the Old Supreme Court Chamber; the Old Senate Chamber; the Crypt, located beneath the rotunda; and the ornate Brumidi Corridors. Guided tours of the Capitol are given regularly; however, to gain access to the congressional chambers you must first obtain a pass from one of your representatives or senators *(see sidebar p. 73).*

Remember that the Capitol is the point from which the city's streets are numbered and lettered; therefore, pay attention to the quadrant (N.E., N.W., S.E. or S.W.) of the streets or addresses you wish to find.

From the Capitol, cross 1st Street N.E. on the north side of E. Capitol Street. The imposing white building in front of you is the **Supreme Court Building,** where the creed "Equal Justice Under Law" is written on the facade. The seated female figure to the left is titled "Contemplation of Justice," while the male counterpart opposite her is called "Guardian of Law."

The third branch of government did not have its own building until 1935. For almost a century and a half of its existence, the court met in various locations, including the Capitol. It was not until 1929 that William H. Taft—who was chief justice at the

time and a former U.S. president to boot—was able to convince Congress of the court's need for its own home, authorizing the creation of the current neoclassic building.

Designed to match surrounding structures, the Supreme Court possesses many noteworthy features, including a Great Hall lined with the busts of every chief justice who has presided over the court since it was established. The hall leads to the marble-trimmed Court Chamber, which looks like a theater thanks to the plush red curtain suspended behind the bench. Considering the weighty Constitutional issues that are debated in this room, the theaterlike ambience seems appropriate.

To learn more about the court and what cases are currently being argued, stop by the information desk beneath the statue of Chief Justice John Marshall on the ground floor. Here you'll find exhibits, portraits of justices and a film. You'll also be able to see one of the building's two, five-story-tall marble staircases that creates a striking vista as it spirals upward without a central column for support.

Turn north after leaving the Supreme Court and follow Maryland Avenue northeast to 2nd Street N.E., where Maryland and Constitution avenues meet, and go north across Constitution. On the corner of 2nd and Constitution is the **Sewall-Belmont House and Museum,** headquarters of the National Woman's Party since 1929. Within the red-brick house, built about 1700, are displays relating to the women's suffrage and equal rights movements.

From there head west on Constitution Avenue and turn right on 1st Street N.E. To either side are the Dirksen and Russell **Senate office buildings.** Cross C and D streets N.E. and Massachusetts Avenue. The large, white-granite edifice ahead of you is Union Station. Before it stands a 1912 monument to Christopher Columbus made up of three flagpoles, a semicircular fountain and a 15-foot statue of the explorer, which faces the Capitol.

Built in 1907 during the heyday of railway travel, Union Station was designed to serve as the gateway to America's capital city and is an important example of the Beaux Arts style. Inspired by ancient Roman baths and triumphal arches, architect Daniel Burnham designed the station's main hall, distinguished by a 96-foot-tall barrel-vaulted ceiling made up of recessed, gilded panels. Statues adorn both the exterior and interior; a few of the 46 Roman legionnaires encircling the main hall had to be redesigned due to concern that their skimpy uniforms would scandalize passengers.

Like many stately train stations built before the advent of air travel, Union Station endured a period of decline and decay until it was abandoned in the 1970s. When renovations began in the 1980s, large portions of ceiling had collapsed and mushrooms were discovered growing on the floor. But the station was returned to its original splendor, and also found new life as a retail and entertainment complex boasting numerous restaurants and cafes, more than 100 stores and a multiscreen movie complex. The building also houses a Metrorail station and is Amtrak's hub and headquarters.

From Union Station walk back toward the Capitol via Delaware Avenue N.E. Once you cross D Street N.E., Capitol Plaza will be on your right. If you're a shutterbug then get your camera ready. This spacious park's reflecting pool and fountain make an especially picturesque foreground for the Capitol. Just west of the plaza across New Jersey Avenue is **The Robert A. Taft Memorial and Carillon.** This 100-foot bell tower, dedicated in 1959, honors the influential Ohio senator who became known as "Mr. Republican" for his outspoken opposition to President Franklin D. Roosevelt's New Deal policies. Son of President Taft, the senator died of cancer in 1953. His statue stands before the tower.

From the Taft memorial, cross Constitution Avenue and then go immediately right across 1st Street N.W. Continuing south down 1st Street, you'll enter Union Square with its monuments and Reflecting Pool. The first memorial you'll come to is the Peace Monument, at Pennsylvania Avenue and 1st Street N.W. Dedicated to those who served at sea during the Civil War, the memorial depicts two female figures representing Grief weeping on the shoulder of History.

The next memorial honors Ulysses S. Grant, Union general and U.S. president. The central figure depicts the general on horseback impassively gazing westward. His poise contrasts sharply with the artillery and cavalry statuary groups frozen in action at either side of him. Said to be the largest equestrian statue in America, the pedestal, horse and rider together stand 65 feet tall. Dedicated in 1922, the memorial took sculptor Henry Merwin Shrady 2 decades to complete.

The James A. Garfield Monument stands at 1st Street and Maryland Avenue S.W. and honors the 20th president, who was assassinated in 1881 after serving only 4 months in office. Garfield was a brigadier general during the Civil War and held public office as both a U.S. senator and representative before being elected president. The monument features a lifelike statue of Garfield atop a cylindrical pedestal. The three figures arranged around the base represent different phases of his career: student, officer and statesman.

Just south of the Garfield Monument across Maryland Avenue S.W. is the **U.S. Botanic Garden.** Established by Congress in 1820 as a research facility to cultivate and distribute plants from around the world to benefit the American people, it has existed at its current location on the Capitol grounds since 1933. The main conservatory features soaring glass walls. Also part of the Botanic Garden is Bartholdi Park, across Independence Avenue. The centerpiece of this seasonal flower and plant garden is a fanciful cast-iron fountain complete with sea nymphs and tritons; it was designed by Frédéric Auguste Bartholdi, sculptor of the Statue of Liberty.

After leaving the Botanic Garden, turn right on 1st Street S.W. to Independence Avenue. Cross Independence and turn left, following it east across 1st Street, S. Capitol Street and New Jersey Avenue S.E. Turn right onto 1st Street S.E.; the Capitol South Metro station is 1 block south across C Street S.E. on the right.

The National Mall

See map page 99. From the Smithsonian Metro station, on the Mall opposite where 12th Street S.W. meets Jefferson Drive S.W., follow the short gravel path to the sidewalk, cross Jefferson Drive and turn left. Just ahead on the right is the **Freer Gallery of Art,** which contains Chinese paintings, Islamic metalwork, Indian sculpture, Korean ceramics and Japanese lacquer.

Although primarily dedicated to Asian art, the Freer also exhibits American paintings and prints from the late 19th century and is noted for The Peacock Room. This finely detailed interior space was designed by James McNeill Whistler 1876-77; it served as a dining room in a London mansion before being relocated to the museum's southeast corner.

Leaving the Freer, turn right, still going east on Jefferson Drive. Next door is the administrative building of the **Smithsonian Institution.** Nicknamed the Castle because of its red sandstone walls, towers, mullioned windows and Romanesque details, this 1855 structure is the work of James Renwick Jr., who also designed the Smithsonian's Renwick Gallery near the White House and St. Patrick's Cathedral in New York. The Castle houses an information center and the tomb of James Smithson, the institution's benefactor. A domed entry pavilion between the Castle and the Freer leads to the **S. Dillon Ripley Center,** a three-level underground structure built in 1987 that includes an International Gallery, offices and classrooms.

On either side of the Smithsonian Castle are the entrances to the underground **Arthur M. Sackler Gallery** and the **National Museum of African Art.** Connected to the Freer by a skylighted gallery, the Sackler continues the Smithsonian's Asian art collection, with a focus on changing exhibitions. Inside the National Museum of African Art you'll find traditional objects from the sub-Saharan continent, including highly wrought sculptures, carvings and masks.

Continue east to the **Arts and Industries Building,** which was built in 1881 to house items from the 1876 Centennial Exhibition in Philadelphia. Above the entrance, a statue grouping portrays Columbia shielding seated figures representing Science and Industry. The museum is currently closed for renovations.

What appears to be an alien spaceship next door is actually the **Hirshhorn Museum and Sculpture Garden.** In sharp contrast to the 19th-century architecture nearby, the cylindrical Hirshhorn building makes a fitting showplace for one of America's best collections of modern art. Glass-walled ambulatories overlook a central courtyard with a fountain, allowing visitors to see art pieces in natural lighting. Name a 20th-century artistic movement and it is

Lee House / © AAA / Denise E. Campbell

likely represented in the collection: Pop Art, Abstract Expressionism, Cubism, Minimalism, Surrealism and several other "isms." Unusual figure studies fill the museum's sunken outdoor sculpture garden, across the sidewalk on the building's Mall side.

Just east of the Hirshhorn across 7th Street S.W. is the capital's most visited museum, the **National Air and Space Museum.** Crowds come in droves here to see history-making flying machines dramatically suspended in cavernous exhibit spaces. From the Wright Flyer to rockets and lunar landers, the spectrum of air and spacecraft on display traces the evolution of flight, delighting busloads of tourists and school children in the process.

The high concentration of large museums will take its toll on even the most energetic of sightseers, one reason the Mall is amply lined with shaded benches for rest stops. Vendor carts also sell a variety of refreshments along the way. If you require assistance or information, visit one of the National Park Service kiosks that dot the Mall.

From the Air and Space Museum, continue down Jefferson Drive. Across 4th Street N.W. is the **National Museum of the American Indian.** The newest Smithsonian museum is distinguished by undulating walls of buff-colored limestone. Inside this cultural resource center are three permanent exhibitions as well as rotating exhibits and performance spaces.

Turn left onto 4th Street S.W. and walk toward the modern glass and concrete structure ahead on the right. This is the East Building of the **National Gallery of Art,** which features contemporary art as

well as changing exhibits. It is linked to the West Building by a paved plaza and an underground concourse. Take either one to view the gallery's world-class collection of European and American painting and sculpture.

From the West Building's Mall exit go down the large flight of stairs and turn right, going west on Madison Drive. Taking a short detour from the Mall, turn right again at 7th Street N.W. The park on your left is the National Gallery of Art's Sculpture Garden; works by Claes Oldenburg, Joan Miró and Isamu Noguchi are on display here year-round, and a jazz concert series takes place in summer.

Cross Constitution Avenue, and between 7th and 9th streets N.W. you'll come to a mammoth neoclassic building, the **National Archives.** It contains the nation's triumvirate of governmental blueprints: the Declaration of Independence, the Constitution and the Bill of Rights. At Pennsylvania Avenue and 7th Street N.W. is the **United States Navy Memorial,** which displays a ground-level granite map of the world some 100 feet in diameter.

From the Archives go back across Constitution Avenue, proceed south 1 block on 7th Street N.W., then turn west onto Madison Drive on the Mall. One block ahead on the right is the **National Museum of Natural History,** with treasures that include natural and cultural specimens ranging from the Hope Diamond to a giant squid. Enter the rotunda and prepare to be greeted by an African elephant showing off its raised trunk and lengthy tusks. Even more intimidating displays await intrepid visitors in the skeleton-crowded Dinosaur Hall.

Another block west along Madison Drive is the **National Museum of American History, Kenneth E. Behring Center,** home to such familiar objects of Americana as a covered wagon, steam locomotive and a 19th-century general store. You can see such historic items as Lewis and Clark's compass and even Cold War-era submarines, or if you're more interested in America's popular culture, there's Muhammad Ali's boxing gloves, Evel Knievel's motorcycle and Dorothy's ruby slippers from "The Wizard of Oz." Another museum highlight: a colorful collection of First Ladies' gowns. The sixth Smithsonian building on the National Mall originally opened to the public in January 1964 as the Museum of History and Technology. **Note:** The museum currently is closed for renovations and is scheduled to reopen in summer 2008.

From the museum return to Madison Drive N.W. and continue west to 14th Street. Turn left, cross Madison and go south toward Jefferson Drive. Halfway across the walkway, pause to take in the view of the Mall's tallest landmarks, the Capitol and the **Washington Monument.** Turn left at Jefferson Drive; the Smithsonian Metro station, where you began, is on the left.

The White House

See map following. Beginning at the McPherson Square Metro station's White House/Vermont Avenue exit at the corner of Vermont Avenue and I

Street N.W., go 1 block west on I Street to 16th Street N.W. Turn left and go south on 16th to the end of the block. On your left is **St. John's Church.** Painted yellow and white with a distinctive golden-roofed steeple, St. John's is known as the Church of the Presidents due to the number of commanders-in-chief who have worshiped here over the years.

Cross H Street N.W. to **Lafayette Square,** the park opposite the main entrance to the **White House.** A statue of Andrew Jackson presides over squirrels, chess players and the occasional placards and protestors. Impressive monuments at the park's four corners honor foreign-born Revolutionary War heroes: Baron von Steuben of Prussia, Brig. Gen. Thaddeus Kosciusko of Poland, Maj. Gen. Comte de Rochambeau of France and Maj. Gen. Marquis de Lafayette, the Frenchman for whom the park is named.

Go right and walk west through the park along H Street, crossing Jackson Place N.W. On the corner is **Decatur House,** which was the first private home in this part of the city.

Farther south on Jackson Place and around the corner to the right on Pennsylvania Avenue N.W. is Blair House. It was named for its original owner, Francis Preston Blair, founder of *The Washington Globe* newspaper during President Andrew Jackson's term of office and one of the founders of the Republican Party. It was in Blair House that Robert E. Lee, at President Abraham Lincoln's insistence, was offered the command of the Union army, which he declined. The house later served as a residence for President Harry S. Truman while the White House was being renovated 1948-52.

Next door is the Lee House, the former home of Blair's daughter and son-in-law. The Blair and Lee houses have been combined and serve as guest quarters for visiting dignitaries; both are closed to the public.

Next to Lee House is the **Renwick Gallery** of the Smithsonian American Art Museum, which displays changing exhibits of American decorative arts, crafts and design. The 1858 building was the first home of the Corcoran Gallery of Art and is such a splendid example of Second Empire style that its name was changed in the 1960s to honor the architect who designed it, James Renwick Jr.

Walk south across Pennsylvania Avenue N.W. and down 17th Street N.W. to the stately Old Executive Office Building, now called the Eisenhower Executive Office Building. Another example of Second Empire architecture, it was built 1871-88 to house the State, War and Navy Departments.

Cross 17th Street to the right and proceed down New York Avenue N.W. 1 block to **The Octagon Museum.** This weathered, red-brick house, really more of a hexagon than an octagon, was built 1798-1800 and was the temporary home of President and Mrs. James Madison after the White House was burned during the War of 1812. The marvelous architecture is both practical and decorative and explains why the house is now a museum of The

American Institute of Architects, whose headquarters building looms behind it.

Head 2 blocks south on 18th Street. Between C and D streets N.W. is Constitution Hall, where concerts are presented throughout the year. On the same block is the **DAR Museum** and the national headquarters of the Daughters of the American Revolution.

One block south of Constitution Hall across C Street at the corner of 18th Street and Virginia Avenue N.W. is the **Art Museum of the Americas.** This small gallery contains a collection of colorful and insightful works by Latin American artists. Across 18th Street stands a regal equestrian statue of South American revolutionary leader Simón Bolívar; the monument was a gift from Venezuela.

The art museum is a part of the **Organization of American States** (OAS) complex. The main building is entered around the corner from the museum on 17th Street N.W. Inside is a lush atrium filled with tropical foliage and centered about an Aztec-themed fountain. Busts of Latin American heroes line the walls.

Continue up 17th Street 2 blocks to E Street N.W. and the **Corcoran Gallery of Art.** Its entrance flanked by two lounging lions, this palatial Beaux Arts building has changing exhibits ranging from classic masterpieces to contemporary photography. Named for 19th-century banker and founder William Wilson Corcoran, it is one of the nation's oldest museums.

White House Walking Tour

Leaving the Corcoran's main entrance, turn right, cross 17th Street at the corner and go east along E Street, which links with West and East Executive avenues beside the White House. Opposite the south lawn of the White House is the Ellipse, where the Zero Milestone marks the original center of the city.

Originally called the President's House, the **White House** got its current name after it was painted white to cover scorch marks left after the British burned it in 1814. The White House Visitor Center on the southwest corner of 15th and E streets features exhibits and a 30-minute video that describe the history and architecture of the Executive Mansion.

Nearby on Pennsylvania Avenue N.W. between 13th and 14th streets N.W. is Freedom Plaza, made up of inlaid pieces depicting parts of Pierre-Charles L'Enfant's city plan. A time capsule filled with belongings of Martin Luther King Jr. lies buried beneath the plaza surface.

From E Street turn left onto E. Executive Avenue and follow it north. Yet another equestrian statue is on your right; this one honors Civil War Gen. William Tecumseh Sherman, remembered for his march through Georgia and capture of Savannah.

Farther on, the Treasury Building, pictured on the back of the $10 bill, is on the right opposite the White House's East Gate. Construction of this Greek Revival building, the headquarters for the Treasury Department, began in 1836 and was completed 33 years later. Inside, the Andrew Johnson Suite is where President Andrew Johnson conducted business after Lincoln's assassination. Other rooms include the Salmon P. Chase Suite; the Cash Room, where President Ulysses S. Grant's inaugural reception was held; and the 1864 burglar-proof Vault. Guided tours are available on Saturday mornings by reservation; phone (202) 622-0146.

Continue north across Pennsylvania Avenue N.W.; note that E. Executive Avenue is now called Madison Place. Follow Madison Place N.W. and cross H Street. Traveling on the left side of the street, continue north up Vermont Avenue; the McPherson Square Metro station entrance is at the end of the block on the left.

Spectator Sports

D.C. is not usually thought of as a sports-crazy town in the sense that Chicago or Pittsburgh are. However, the city still goes wild for the **Washington Redskins.** The three-time Super Bowl champions draw strength from an across-the-board contingent of fans. And major league baseball returned to the District in 2005 when the Montréal Expos moved south and became the **Washington Nationals.**

Spectators also can choose from four additional professional sports teams—basketball's **Washington Wizards,** the WNBA's (Women's National Basketball Association) **Mystics,** hockey's **Washington Capitals** and soccer's **D.C. United.** In addition, six area universities—American, Georgetown, George

Washington and Howard in the District, George Mason University in Virginia and the University of Maryland—offer intercollegiate sports action.

Baseball

The Washington Nationals played their inaugural season at venerable **RFK Stadium**, 2400 E. Capitol St. S.E. (M: Stadium-Armory). They will share the stadium with the D.C. United through 2007. A new 41,000-seat ballpark, scheduled to open in April 2008, is currently in the planning stages. The facility will rise along S. Capital Street and Potomac Avenue, less than a mile south of the U.S. Capitol dome. Single-game tickets are available; for information phone (202) 397-7328.

Basketball

Legions of local fans head to the **Verizon Center**, 7th and F streets N.W. (M: Gallery Place-Chinatown), to take in a Washington Wizards game. The Wizards are thrice Eastern Conference champs and walked away victorious over the Golden State Warriors in the 1977-78 NBA finals. The action takes place from November to April; phone (202) 628-3200. The Verizon Center also is home to the WNBA Mystics, who began play in 1998.

Impressive NCAA champions the **Hoyas** hail from Georgetown University and are widely known by hometown rooters as well as by those who follow the Division IA circuit. Basketball fans also should check out the **American University Eagles**, the **George Washington University Colonials**, the **Howard University Bison**, the **University of Maryland Terrapins** (the Terps) and the **George Mason University Patriots**. The **D.C. Armory**, 3rd and M streets N.E., offers exhibition basketball games.

Football

The Washington Redskins—who won the Super Bowl in 1983, 1988 and 1992—have an army of

---

DID YOU KNOW

The Washington Redskins' 72-41 victory over the New York Giants in 1966 was the highest scoring game in NFL history.

followers notorious for their zeal. Hear that whoosh-ing noise? It's the sound of fans sucking up every last home game ticket in town. They are more pre-cious than gold; sports fans interested in seeing the Skins play would be better served trying to track down some preseason tickets instead.

FedEx Field, off I-495/I-95 exit 15A (Central Ave. East) or 17A (Landover Rd. East) in nearby Landover, Md. (M: Morgan Boulevard), is packed with fans from September to December; phone (301) 276-6050 for ticket information or (301) 276-6248 for recorded directions. Meanwhile, the University of Maryland's football team, the Terra-pins, play their home games at **Byrd Stadium**.

Hockey

The Washington Capitals have been around since the 1974-75 season, and waged a division-winning campaign in 1999-2000. The season runs from Octo-ber through April at the Verizon Center. Various sea-son ticket plans are offered; for information phone Capitals Guest Services at (202) 266-2350.

Horse Racing

Several tracks around the District offer horse rac-ing; **Rosecroft Raceway** in Fort Washington, Md., (301) 567-4000, and **Laurel Park Race Course,** (301) 725-0400, in Laurel, Md., are the closest. All programs are flat races unless otherwise noted; dark days—days when no live racing is scheduled—are announced during the meets.

Public transportation is available from downtown D.C. to the tracks. For information contact the Maryland Transit Administration (MTA); phone (410) 539-5000 or (866) 743-3682 Mon.-Fri. 6 a.m.-7 p.m.

Track seasons are usually from early October through March at Laurel; mid-January to mid-December (for three nights a week) at Rosecroft; from mid-March to early June at **Pimlico**, near Bal-timore, (410) 542-9400; from late August to early September at **Timonium**, (301) 725-0400, also near Baltimore; and from early January to mid-December at Charles Town, W.Va.

Note: Policies concerning admittance of children to pari-mutuel betting facilities vary. Phone for information.

Soccer

D.C. also is home to Major League Soccer's D.C. United, a professional team that plays at RFK Sta-dium. For ticket information contact D.C. United customer service; phone (202) 587-5000.

Recreation

No matter what the season, activities in the Wash-ington metropolitan area are plentiful. And who knows: You may find yourself jogging, bicycling or fishing not only with the locals but with a congres-sional power broker as well. For information contact the D.C. Department of Parks and Recreation; phone (202) 673-7665.

Bicycling

Bicycling can be enjoyed along the **C&O Canal towpath** and on **Rock Creek Park** trails. The **Washington and Old Dominion Trail** (W&OD or "WOD" to locals) is an excellent 45-mile paved, multi-use path that runs from I-395 at Shirlington near the Potomac River through Leesburg, Va., me-andering through the cities of Falls Church, Vienna and Herndon, Va., to Purcellville, Va. Close to the city, the WOD overlooks busy I-66 as it winds through Arlington, Va., residential areas; the farther west you go the less crowded the trail becomes. Once past Herndon, the rural landscapes and flat ter-rain offer great bicycling.

Bicycles can be rented at **Fletcher's Boat House**, at the intersection of Reservoir and Canal roads N.W. It is open from early March through October; phone (202) 244-0461. Another in-town outlet is **Thompson's Boat Center**, Rock Creek Parkway and Virginia Avenue N.W. in Georgetown. Bikes can be rented from March through November; phone (202) 333-9543.

Bike the Sites, in the Old Post Office Pavilion at 1100 Pennsylvania Ave. N.W. (M: Federal Triangle), offers guided bicycle tours as well as mountain bike and stroller rentals. Safety equipment is included. Summer rental hours are Mon.-Sat. 9-9, Sun. 9-6; phone (202) 842-2453.

Fishing

The area's best fishing is in the **Chesapeake Bay**, the ocean and in Shenandoah mountain streams. An-glers need not be afraid to cast a line along the Maryland shore of the **Potomac River** from the Wilson Bridge south to Fort Washington Park; this once-polluted river has made a remarkable come-back. A trip to **Fletcher's Cove** on the Potomac, about a mile above Key Bridge, or to the rocky gorge at **Chain Bridge** might net a catch of white shad or herring.

Golf

Public golf courses can be found at three loca-tions in the District. Tee times are awarded on a first-come, first-served basis. Langston Golf Course is at 2600 Benning Rd. N.E.; phone (202) 397-8638. East Potomac Golf Course, 972 Ohio Dr. S.W., (202) 554-7660, has two nine-hole courses and one 18-hole course. Rock Creek Public Golf Course, 6100 Rittenhouse St. N.W., has one 18-hole course that can be played as two nine-hole courses; phone (202) 882-7332 for greens fees.

Outside the District, public 18-hole golf courses include: Falls Road Golf Course, 10800 Falls Rd., Potomac, Md., (301) 299-5156; Greendale Golf Course, 6700 Telegraph Rd., Alexandria, Va., (703) 971-6170; Herndon Centennial Golf Course, 909 Ferndale Ave., Herndon, Va., (703) 471-5769; Redgate Golf Course, 14500 Avery Rd., Rockville, Md., (240) 314-8730; Reston National Golf Course, 11875 Sunrise Valley Dr., Reston, Va., (703) 620-9333; and the University of Maryland Golf Course, University Boulevard, College Park, Md., (301) 314-4653.

Horseback Riding

Horseback riding is possible on the shady bridle paths in northern Rock Creek Park. Horses can be rented for guided rides at **Rock Creek Park Horse Center**, Military and Glover roads N.W.; phone (202) 362-0117 for fees and schedule. Other nearby stables are listed in the telephone directory.

Jogging and Walking

Using your own two feet in Washington goes beyond just the sightseeing sense; jogging and walking are almost a way of life for residents and workers. The most popular spot by far is the Mall—specifically the rectangle between 3rd and 14th streets and Constitution and Independence avenues N.W.— where you might see senators and other members of Washington's political elite burning off some extra calories and stress on this 4-mile sightseeing route. Joggers also traverse Memorial Bridge between the Lincoln Memorial and Arlington National Cemetery; the visual attraction is the Potomac and its grassy banks.

The **Mount Vernon Trail** provides two running courses. The shorter one begins near the pedestrian walkway leading to Theodore Roosevelt Island and runs south past Ronald Reagan Washington National Airport to Old Town Alexandria (a little over 3 miles). For the truly fit, a delightfully scenic 9-mile path follows the Potomac's banks from Alexandria south to Mount Vernon.

For a breathtaking outing camouflaged by nature, try the 15 miles of trails crisscrossing Rock Creek Park. One of the best runs is a 4-mile stretch paralleling the creek from Georgetown to the National Zoological Park. The gravel- and dirt-packed towpath alongside the C&O Canal offers a serene, wooded setting for short runs (about 4 miles round trip between Georgetown and Fletcher's Boat House) or really serious training—well into Maryland, if you are so inclined.

Tennis

The city offers a number of public outdoor courts to choose from. Some, however, are in less-than-desirable locations, so check out neighborhoods in advance. National Park Service courts, which do not require permits but charge a fee, are at **Hains Point** in East Potomac Park, 1090 Ohio Dr. S.W., and in Rock Creek Park near 16th and Kennedy streets N.W. Reservations are suggested.

For a complete list of court locations and information about fees and permits, write the D.C. Department of Parks and Recreation, 3149 16th St. N.W., Washington, DC 20010; phone (202) 673-7646.

Water Sports

The Potomac River is good for an invigorating powerboat ride or a soothing sail. Boats and canoes can be rented at Fletcher's and Thompson's, mentioned in the Bicycling section, and at **Jack's Boathouse**, 3500 Water St. (at the end of K Street in Georgetown, beneath the intersection of Key Bridge and the Whitehurst Freeway), (202) 337-9642; rental season is April through October. Paddleboats can be rented on the Tidal Basin's east side in front of the Thomas Jefferson Memorial.

Riding the rapids of **Great Falls** as they course between Virginia and Maryland will appeal to those with an adventurous side. Although no river wild, the Potomac does work up quite a bit of white water nevertheless. The bluffs above the river offer a fine vantage point for those who would rather watch than participate. For information, contact the ranger station at Great Falls, Va.; phone (703) 285-2966.

Swimming is available at the 34 outdoor and six indoor pools of the D.C. Department of Recreation; local YMCA and YWCA branches also have facilities. Swimmers and sunbathers with more time on their hands can try the Atlantic Ocean or Chesapeake Bay beaches, a 3- to 4-hour drive.

Winter Sports

When sightseeing becomes a bone-chilling proposition during Washington's occasional frigid winter days, spend some time ice skating at one of several area rinks. Two of the nicest spots are the **Sculpture Garden Outdoor Rink**, on Constitution Avenue between 7th and 9th streets N.W., and the **Pershing Park Ice Rink**, (202) 737-6938, on Pennsylvania Avenue between 14th and 15th streets N.W.

Shopping

The Washington metropolitan area is neither a center of manufacturing nor a region known for locally produced items. It is, however, one of the nation's most affluent areas, and as a result, there are more malls and specialized shopping districts than one could imagine. And those searching for just the right memento to commemorate their trip are definitely in luck: Washington offers a mountain of souvenirs of every stripe.

Antiques

An area with a concentration of craft and antique shops is **Howard Avenue** in Kensington, Md. Within a five-block section an array of antique furniture and decorative items is housed in more than 40 Victorian buildings. These buildings also contain numerous art galleries and craft studios.

Malls

One of the city's most elegant settings for mall shopping is at **Union Station** (M: Union Station), along Massachusetts Avenue between 1st and 2nd streets N.E. This restored 1907 train station on Capitol Hill contains not only Amtrak's headquarters and a working train station, but more than 130 shops and restaurants and a multiscreen movie complex. It features barrel-vaulted ceilings, Romanesque columns, spiral staircases, and intricate decorative painting and gold leaf. Greeting visitors who arrive by train is a bronze statue of A. Philip Randolph, founder of the Sleeping Car Porters Union and orchestrator of the 1963 March on Washington for Jobs and Freedom.

Among the three escalator-connected levels of stores are such retailers as Crabtree & Evelyn and Victoria's Secret. In the East Hall you will find expensive, high-quality items—everything from collector postage stamps to handcrafted kaleidoscopes—in a plush atmosphere accented by potted palms and mahogany kiosks. The enormous food court on the lower level has an around-the-world smorgasbord of interesting choices in addition to the usual pizza and sandwiches. It makes for a colorful scene, particularly at lunchtime when nearby office workers and Hill aides show up in droves.

Union Station / © AAA / Denise E. Campbell

The Shops at Georgetown Park occupy four stories and an entire block at 3222 M St. N.W., just off the intersection of M Street and Wisconsin Avenue. The brick exterior adheres to the Federal style characteristic of much Georgetown architecture. The interior, however, is elaborately Victorian, with more than 80 shops and restaurants situated amid wrought iron, potted parlor palms and grand chandeliers, all bathed by a huge skylight. Christian Bernard, for jewelry and fine watches, and gourmet food purveyor Dean & DeLuca are among the retailers.

A legion of suburban malls provide shopping opportunities—and crowded parking lots—galore. Just across the Potomac in Arlington, Va., is **Fashion Centre at Pentagon City**, one of the few shopping areas outside the city with its own subway stop (M: Pentagon City). A spectacular glass atrium encloses some 130 stores on four levels, among them Macy's and Nordstrom, plus a food court. Also in Arlington is **Ballston Common Mall**, 4238 Wilson Blvd. at Glebe Road (M: Ballston), with Macy's, numerous chain outlets and a fast-food court.

Springfield Mall, just east of I-95 exit 169A (M: Franconia-Springfield), is about 10 miles south of downtown D.C. There are more than 230 stores, including JCPenney and Macy's, as well as 10 movie theaters, several bookstores, restaurants and a food court.

One of the first major malls to open in the suburbs was **Tysons Corner Center**, just off the Beltway on SR 7 (Leesburg Pike). It contains five major department stores—Bloomingdale's, JCPenney, Lord & Taylor, Macy's and Nordstrom—and more than 250 smaller shops. A slightly more upscale neighbor is **Tysons Galleria**, 2001 International Dr. (across Chain Bridge Road/SR 123 from Tysons Corner Center). Macy's, Neiman Marcus and Saks Fifth Avenue anchor more than 100 specialty boutiques.

Another longtime northern Virginia mall is **Landmark Mall**, which opened in 1965. There are plans to convert the present three-level enclosed building to an outdoor town center of stores and restaurants. Another big center is **Fair Oaks Mall**, at the intersection of I-66 and SR 50 in Fairfax, Va.

Maryland malls include **Iverson Mall**, **Lakeforest Mall**, **Montgomery Mall**, **Westfield Shoppingtown** and **White Flint Mall**.

Outlets

Almost everyone, it seems, goes to **Potomac Mills**, just off I-95 (Potomac Mills exit 156), 25 miles south of Washington and about a 45-minute drive (depending on traffic). More than a mile long, it attracts busloads of D.C. area shoppers and regional bargain hunters from as far away as Pennsylvania, a popularity that leads Potomac Mills to bill itself as Virginia's biggest tourist attraction. Among the many outlets are Eddie Bauer, Guess and Saks Fifth Avenue.

Specialty Districts

Shopping in Washington offers as much variety as sightseeing. The downtown shopping area is centered on F Street near 14th Street N.W.; the landscaped section between 12th and 14th is **F Street Plaza**. Macy's, downtown's only remaining department store, offers fine clothing, linens and gifts. The grand old building at 14th and F streets, formerly occupied by Garfinckel's department store, is now home to a Borders bookstore.

The **Old Post Office Pavilion** (M: Federal Triangle), 12th Street and Pennsylvania Avenue N.W., occupies the Romanesque Revival structure that formerly housed the Old Post Office. Stylishly renovated, it has specialty stores and a food court.

The Shops at National Place (M: Metro Center), along F Street between 13th and 14th streets N.W., is a four-tiered complex of more than 80 restaurants and specialty boutiques. It extends from the National Press Building to the J.W. Marriott Pennsylvania Avenue (you can enter the shops through the hotel) and is conveniently located near the National Theatre.

For exclusive browsing, try the upper Northwest neighborhood of Chevy Chase. **Mazza Gallerie**, along Wisconsin Avenue at the D.C./Maryland border (M: Friendship Heights), is a four-level complex anchored by fashionable Neiman Marcus and supplemented by such retail outlets as the Saks Fifth Avenue Men's Store and Williams-Sonoma.

Close by at 5255 Western Ave. N.W. (near Jenifer Street) is the D.C. location of Lord & Taylor, which carries fine men's and women's clothing, shoes, linens and other items. Brooks Brothers, Gianni Versace and Saks Fifth Avenue are among the names vying for the attention of your wallet along a stretch of Wisconsin Avenue just above the District line in Montgomery County, Md.

Also in this neighborhood is **Chevy Chase Pavilion**. Situated above the Friendship Heights Metro station, it offers more mall-oriented retailers, from Ann Taylor to Pottery Barn.

Connecticut Connection, 1101 Connecticut Ave. (M: Farragut North), is a centrally located downtown shopping and dining complex. Where Connecticut Avenue intersects Massachusetts Avenue, **Dupont Circle** is an eclectic blend of embassy buildings, art galleries, bookstores and sidewalk cafes.

The **Adams-Morgan** neighborhood, bounded by Columbia Road, 16th Street and Connecticut and Florida avenues N.W., offers specialty stores, secondhand bookshops, and numerous ethnic groceries and restaurants. The shops along 18th Street N.W. from Florida Avenue north to Columbia Road are filled with funky jewelry and furniture, reggae and world music CDs, and Caribbean- and African-inspired clothing. **Note:** Parking is challenging during the day and next to impossible at night. The closest Metro station is Dupont Circle; exit at Q Street and walk up Connecticut Avenue to Columbia Road.

The **Indian Craft Shop**, inside the Department of the Interior along with the Department of the Interior Museum *(see attraction listing p. 75)*, sells exquisite handmade jewelry, pottery, beadwork, weavings, baskets, sand paintings and other crafts created by more than 45 different tribal groups. A photo ID is necessary to enter the building; the C Street entrance is open to the public. The shop is open Mon.-Fri. 8:30-4:30, third Sat. of the month 10-4.

Other treasures can be found at the **Smithsonian Institution**. Individual shops reflect the focus and collections of the world's largest complex of museums, art galleries and research facilities. They feature crafts from around the world, books, recordings, educational toys, jewelry, kites, and Smithsonian reproductions and adaptations. The shops are open daily 10-5:30 and some have extended summer hours; phone (202) 633-1000.

Despite the crowded sidewalks, a serious shortage of parking and the absence of a convenient Metro station, **Georgetown** is many Washingtonians' favorite place to shop. Perhaps the reason is that instead of wandering through the sterile, enclosed corridors of the malls you're in the fresh air, strolling charming streets through a historic neighborhood. Antiques, cookware, contemporary fashions, china and glassware, fabrics and rare books are only a few of the items to be found in the little shops along and just off Wisconsin Avenue and M Street.

As much fun as Georgetown is **Old Town Alexandria**, Va. (M: King Street). The Torpedo Factory Art Center *(see attraction listing p. 121)* offers workshops and sales outlets for local artists. The heart of Old Town is the intersection of King and Washington streets, but the shopping opportunities also include Cameron Street and Tavern Square. From the Metro station, a DASH city bus will take you to any of these areas; the fare is $1.

Performing Arts

Although the opening of **The John F. Kennedy Center for the Performing Arts** *(see attraction listing p. 78)* more than 3 decades ago was a major catalyst in heating up Washington's fine arts scene, the city is home to all sorts of venues. The Kennedy Center is the star, with its eight concert, opera and drama halls, but there are many other fine facilities.

University groups, dinner theaters and open-air facilities like Virginia's **Wolf Trap National Park for the Performing Arts** *(see attraction listing p. 133)* offer live entertainment throughout the year. And a number of performances are free, such as the National Park Service's military band concerts at various monuments during the summer months and the chamber music concerts offered by the Library of Congress.

Weekend magazine, published in the Friday edition of *The Washington Post,* gives complete listings for current and upcoming cultural events in the Washington area. *City Paper,* a free weekly available at local bookstores, newsstands and curbside vending machines, also has detailed listings for theater, music, film, dance, gallery and performance art events.

For bargain hunters, TICKETplace, 407 7th St. N.W., around the corner from the Woolly Mammoth Theatre (M: Archives or Gallery Place), sells half-price (plus a service charge equal to 12 percent of the ticket's face value) advance tickets to a variety of performing arts events in the D.C. area. Full-price, advance-sale tickets to some events are available as well. Only credit cards are accepted. The booth is open Tues.-Fri. 11-6, Sat. 10-5; phone (202) 842-5387.

Dance

The **Washington Ballet** presents works both classical and contemporary, mostly at the **Kennedy Center Opera House** but also at the center's Eisenhower Theater and other venues. Each December the company stages the holiday classic "The Nutcracker." Such prestigious companies as the Bolshoi Ballet and the American Ballet Theater give frequent Washington performances. The **Howard University Dance Ensemble** and the annual dance series presented by **Mount Vernon College** provide opportunities for visitors to attend a wide variety of modern and ethnic dance performances. The **Smithsonian Institution** frequently presents national and international dance troupes; for information phone (202) 633-1000.

Film

First-run movie theaters are plentiful in the District, although parking is not. The most readily available parking is at theaters on upper Wisconsin and Connecticut avenues. The **Cineplex Odeon Uptown**, 3246 Connecticut Ave. N.W. (M: Cleveland Park), and the **Cineplex Odeon Cinema**, 5100 Wisconsin Ave. N.W. (M: Friendship Heights), are good places to see current hits.

Foreign, art house and independent films are often shown at the **Cineplex Odeon Outer Circle**, 4849 Wisconsin Ave. N.W. (M: Tenleytown-AU), and the **Cineplex Odeon Dupont Circle**, 1350 19th St. N.W. (M: Dupont Circle). In nearby Old Town Alexandria, the **Old Town Theater**, 815 1/2 King St., screens independent and art house fare as well as current mainstream films.

The **AFI Silver Theatre and Cultural Center**, 8633 Colesville Rd. in Silver Spring, Md. (M: Silver Spring), includes a restored 1938 movie house and two contemporary stadium theaters providing state-of-the-art presentation facilities for a variety of screenings, from classics to cult films to new releases; for recorded program information phone (301) 495-6700.

Documentaries and experimental films are often shown at the **Hirshhorn Museum and Sculpture Garden** and the **National Gallery of Art's East Building**; for information about programs, contact the individual museums.

Music

The John F. Kennedy Center for the Performing Arts presents a variety of nationally and internationally acclaimed artists. Under the direction of Leonard Slatkin, the **National Symphony Orchestra** performs in the center's spacious **Concert Hall**. The season runs from September to June. Chamber music societies, choral groups and symphony orchestras from around the world perform here as well; for information phone (202) 467-4600. In the summer months the orchestra performs outdoors at Wolf Trap National Park for the Performing Arts.

Constitution Hall, at 18th and D streets N.W., focuses on musical events. **Lisner Auditorium** of George Washington University, 21st and H streets N.W., is the scene of a wider variety of concerts, recitals and sometimes opera and ballet. For information phone (202) 994-6800.

One of Washington's best bargains is the series of free chamber music concerts given by the **Library of Congress** at different theaters and auditoriums. For schedule and ticket information phone (202) 707-5502. The **Juilliard String Quartet** is in residence during October, November and December, performing on the library's rare Stradivarius instruments.

The airy **West Garden Court** in the National Gallery of Art is the scene of free concerts Sunday evenings at 7 from October through June. Programs consist of a variety of guest artists and the **National Gallery Orchestra**. Four concerts in March or April constitute a festival of American music. For program information phone (202) 842-6941.

From September through May, Sunday afternoon chamber concerts take place in the paneled **Music Room** at The Phillips Collection, 1600 21st St. N.W. (at Q Street). They begin promptly at 5 (early arrival is recommended); phone (202) 387-2151. Free lunchtime jazz concerts take place at the **Frances and Armand Hammer Auditorium** in the **Corcoran Gallery of Art** on the first and third Wednesday of the month at 12:30. Tickets are not required; for information phone (202) 639-1770.

From October to May, the **Folger Consort**, the resident Renaissance music ensemble at the Folger Shakespeare Library, presents a series of instrumental and vocal performances in the library's **Elizabethan Theatre**, 201 E. Capitol St. S.E. (M: Capitol South or Union Station); phone (202) 544-7077. Chamber music groups perform on selected Sundays from October through April at the **National Academy of Sciences** auditorium, 2101 Constitution Ave. N.W. (M: Foggy Bottom-GWU), which is celebrated for its fine acoustics. A photo ID is required to enter the building. For schedule information phone (202) 334-2436.

During summer, visitors enjoy outdoor performances at **Carter Barron Amphitheatre**, in upper northwest Washington at 16th Street and Colorado Avenue N.W. in Rock Creek Park (near the Maryland line). Events range from funk, jazz and blues bands, R & B and gospel singers, and oldies groups to performances by dance companies, the National Symphony Orchestra and the Shakespeare Theatre Company. Some shows are free, but all require tickets; phone (202) 426-0486 for information or (202) 397-7328 for advance tickets.

The John F. Kennedy Center for the Performing Arts
© Dean Fox / SuperStock

Wolf Trap is D.C.'s premier destination for "music under the stars," and is the summer home of the National Symphony Orchestra. About half of the seats in the **Filene Center** are uncovered; the stage and open-sided canopy are built to take advantage of a natural slope. Less expensive and unprotected seating is available on the lawn. From October to mid-May, performances move inside to the smaller **The Barns at Wolf Trap** *(see attraction listing p. 134)*, three-quarters of a mile south of the park at 1635 Trap Rd. The 350-seat theater features everything from chamber music and opera to folk, jazz, country and bluegrass. For ticket information phone the box office at (703) 938-2404.

Warm weather also ushers in the National Park Service's free weekly concert series, held by military bands on the steps of the U.S. Capitol and the national monuments. The U.S. Air Force Band presents a free guest artist concert series with nationally known performers at **DAR Constitution Hall**, 18th and D streets N.W., Sunday afternoons during February; phone (202) 628-4780 for schedule and ticket information.

The U.S. Marines schedule their own free parade, including band, drum and bugle corps and silent drill team, at the **Marine Barracks,** 8th and I streets S.E. (M: Eastern Market), on Fri. at 8:45 p.m. from the first weekend in May through the last weekend in August. Parking is available at Maritime Plaza, 12th and M streets S.E.; a free shuttle bus provides transportation from the plaza to the barracks and back. Reservations should be made at least 3 weeks in advance. For reservations write Protocol Officer, Marine Barracks, 8th and I streets S.E., Washington, D.C. 20390-5000; phone (202) 433-6060 for recorded information.

For something less formal and with no reservations required, the Marine Drum and Bugle Corps and Silent Drill Team present Sunset Parades every Tuesday at 7 p.m. from the first Tuesday in May to the third Tuesday in August at the Marine Corps War Memorial. Take a blanket or lawn chair; no seats are provided. Shuttle bus service to this free performance is provided from the parking lot next to the Arlington National Cemetery Visitor Center from 5-7 and 8-9 p.m.; the parking fee is $1.25 per hour for the first 3 hours, then $2 per hour.

Twilight Tattoo, another sunset parade, is performed by the U.S. Army Band and The 3rd U.S. Infantry most Wednesdays (weather permitting) at 7 p.m., May through late June on the Ellipse (M: Federal Triangle); phone (202) 685-2888.

Another great deal is the free summer concert series given June through August by military bands of the U.S. armed forces. Many of them take place at the outdoor Sylvan Theatre, just off 15th Street N.W. near the Washington Monument, as well as on the lower West Terrace of the U.S. Capitol. These traditional concerts feature occasional vocalists and include stirring patriotic marches as well as pops

and classical selections. For schedule information phone (703) 696-3399 (Army), (202) 433-2525 (Navy), (202) 767-5658 (Air Force) or (202) 433-4011 (Marines).

Opera

The Kennedy Center Opera House has three levels and a stage curtain of gold and red Japanese silk. The plush setting is utilized for seasonal performances by the **Washington Opera** that take place from November to March. Seven productions are performed in their original languages, with English supertitles. Standing-room-only tickets go on sale at the Kennedy Center box office on Saturday beginning at 10 a.m. for performances the following week. For performance and ticket information phone (202) 467-4600 or (800) 444-1324.

Theater

Washington is a theatergoer's delight. Broadway-bound plays often have their last tryouts here, and there are several excellent repertory companies. Among the Kennedy Center's venues is the **Eisenhower Theater**, where smaller-scale dramas are presented, while lavish musicals play the 2,300-seat Opera House. The **Theater Lab** features free children's programs and in the evening the long-running play "Shear Madness," a humorous murder mystery that differs every time it is presented.

The center's intimate **Terrace Theater** has a varied menu of chamber music concerts, opera, choral recitals, comedy revues and theater offerings, along with solo performances from classical violinists to multimedia performance artists. For Kennedy Center show and ticket information phone (202) 467-4600 or (800) 444-1324.

The **Warner Theatre**, 513 13th St. N.W. between E and F streets (M: Metro Center), opened in 1924 as a vaudeville house, was an old-fashioned movie palace during the 1960s and functioned mainly as a rock concert venue in the 1970s and '80s. Shut down and then reopened in 1992 following extensive renovations, it now provides an ornately decorative setting for dance performances, touring Broadway and off-Broadway shows, and popular headlining entertainers and musicians. For general information phone (202) 783-4000 Mon.-Fri. 9-6.

Ford's Theatre *(see attraction listing p. 76)* has a tragic past—it was where President Abraham Lincoln was assassinated in 1865. An October-to-July schedule of contemporary plays and musicals takes place in the theater itself, which has been carefully restored to its former appearance—although the 1860s-style chairs are of questionable comfort; phone (202) 347-4833.

Razzle-dazzle hits appear at the **National Theater**, 1321 Pennsylvania Ave. (M: Metro Center), which has operated continuously since 1835. It was lavishly renovated in the early 1980s and is managed by New York's Shubert Organization, making the National Washington's closest thing to a big, Broadway-style theater. For ticket information phone (202) 628-6161 or (800) 447-7400.

The **Arena Stage** complex, at 6th and Maine streets S.W. (M: Waterfront-SEU), is home to D.C.'s most lauded ensemble company. Founded by now-retired director Zelda Fichandler in 1950, the Arena over the years has nurtured the stage careers of such luminaries as Jane Alexander and James Earl Jones. New plays and emerging playwrights are emphasized during the September-to-June season. The facility has three stages: the Arena, a theater-in-the-round; the Kreeger, a proscenium; and the Old Vat Room, a cabaret-style space; phone (202) 488-3300.

In the Lansburgh Theatre at 450 7th St. N.W., the **Shakespeare Theatre Company** specializes, naturally, in the Bard's works. Premium productions of Shakespearean plays and other classical works also will be presented in Sidney Harman Hall, 6th and F streets N.W., scheduled to open October 2007. Backstage tours of the performance facilities are available by appointment; phone (202) 547-5688. Also offered are educational programs and special events, including the Shakespeare Theatre Company Free For All, a free outdoor production held in June. Tickets for regular performances sell out quickly; for performance information or tickets phone (202) 547-1122 or (877) 487-8849.

Smaller professional resident theaters abound. Contemporary plays—including new productions—are presented at **The Studio Theatre**, 1333 P St. N.W. (M: Dupont Circle). For box office information phone (202) 332-3300. The troupe at the tiny **Source Theatre Company**, 1835 14th St. N.W. between S and T streets (M: U Street/African-Amer Civil War Memorial/Cardozo), actively supports emerging and local playwrights and promotes new plays. For program and schedule information phone (202) 518-0152.

The **Woolly Mammoth Theatre Company**, 641 D St. N.W. (at 7th Street) has a reputation for staging some of the city's most artistically provocative productions. For ticket information phone the box office at (202) 393-3939. The **GALA Hispanic Theatre** presents works by classic and contemporary Latin and Latin-American playwrights. Productions are staged at the Warehouse Theater, 1021 7th St. N.W. (M: Mount Vernon Square-UDC); phone (202) 234-7174.

The **African Continuum Theatre Company** brings to life African and African-American themes at the **Atlas Performing Arts Center**; phone (202) 529-5763 for the theater company or (202) 399-7993 for the performing arts center.

A growing number of small professional resident theaters are developing solid reputations and provide a variety of performances year-round. The **Horizons Theatre**, 3700 South Four Mile Run in Arlington, Va., focuses on plays by and about the life experiences of women; phone (703) 578-1100. The **Round House Theatre** has two locations—in Bethesda and Silver Spring, Md.—offering new plays as well as classics. For ticket information phone (240) 644-1100.

Tidal Basin / © AAA / Denise E. Campbell

Special Events

Washington's events are almost as numerous as its bureaucrats; scarcely a week goes by without some sort of festival, celebration or show. Contact the Washington, D.C. Convention & Tourism Corp. at (202) 789-7000.

The season begins with the **Washington Antique Show** at the Omni Shoreham Hotel in early January. In mid-January **Martin Luther King Jr. Day** is celebrated throughout the metropolitan area. **Chinese New Year Festival** celebrants parade through the streets of Chinatown and enjoy the holiday menus of the area's restaurants in January and sometimes February. **Abraham Lincoln's Birthday** on Feb. 12 is commemorated at the Lincoln Memorial with a wreath ceremony and a reading of the Gettysburg Address. In February **George Washington's Birthday** festivities are held at Mount Vernon in Alexandria, Va.

The **St. Patrick's Day Parade** marches down Constitution Avenue on the Sunday closest to Mar. 17; the **Festival of St. Patrick** is celebrated throughout the city for the entire month. The Smithsonian Institution sponsors a **Kite Festival** on the Washington Monument grounds in late March or early April. Children ages 8 and younger are invited onto the White House lawn the Monday following Easter Sunday for the **Easter Egg Roll**; a special **Easter Egg Hunt for Blind Children** on the Washington Monument grounds lets children search for electronic beeping eggs that can be exchanged for prizes.

A burst of white and pale pink flowers begins one of the city's most cherished events. The ✥ **National Cherry Blossom Festival** begins late March to early April and includes a parade, music, pageants and a Japanese lantern lighting ceremony. Thousands of cherry trees that line the Tidal Basin near the Thomas Jefferson Memorial are illuminated at night during the approximately weeklong blooming season so their delicate beauty is always visible.

Also in April is the **Georgetown House Tour**, when one of the city's most fashionable neighborhoods opens its doors to the public. Serving one of

the top 10 movie markets in the country, the District's theaters participate in the **Washington, D.C. International Film Festival** in late April. The **White House Spring Garden Tour** follows later in the month, and the month ends with the Smithsonian's **Washington Craft Show** at the National Building Museum, 440 F St. N.W.

Jazz aficionados will not want to miss **Duke Ellington's Birthday Celebration**. Live performances pay tribute to this musical giant and native Washingtonian in early May.

Also in May is the **Georgetown Garden Tour** and the **Goodwill Embassy Tour**, which gives the public a chance to tour various gardens and embassies; proceeds go to Davis Memorial Goodwill Industries. In mid-May you can help Sts. Constantine and Helen Greek Orthodox Church, 4115 16th St. N.W., celebrate **Greek Spring Festival**; Greek food, music, dance and crafts are featured.

In late June more than 1 million people attend the **Smithsonian Folklife Festival**, which celebrates different regions and cultural aspects of the nation with music, crafts and food. The capital's grand party is, of course, July 4th; ✥ **Independence Day** celebrations include a noon parade, symphony concerts and events on the Mall, all followed by a huge fireworks display over the Washington Monument beginning at 9 p.m.

To spice up the end of summer, residents sample the music, cuisine and culture of Washington's Latin community during the **Latin-American Festival**, held in late July on the Mall. The **Legg Mason Tennis Classic** also heats up in late July, with the sports excitement continuing through early August.

With live entertainment and pavilions showcasing such themes as fitness, education, economic empowerment and spirituality, **The National Black Family Reunion Celebration** attracts more than 500,000 people in September. **Adams-Morgan Day** in mid-September is a colorful mix of ethnic food, music and crafts.

The **National Book Festival**, sponsored by the Library of Congress, attracts about 100,000 people to the National Mall. The September event features award-winning authors, illustrators and poets as well as family festivities and themed pavilions. Also held in September, the **Kennedy Center Prelude Festival** offers entertaining performances and previews of the center's upcoming shows.

In late October the **Washington International Horse Show** is held in the Verizon Center. Also in late October is the grueling **Marine Corps Marathon**. The ✥ **Pageant of Peace/Lighting of the National Christmas Tree** in mid-December makes the holiday season official. **Kwanzaa**, the traditional African-American celebration of the harvest, is commemorated for several days in late December at the Anacostia Community Museum.

The Washington, D.C. Vicinity

Nearby Maryland

ACCOKEEK pop. 7,349, elev. 190'

Accokeek occupies the site of the Indian village Moyaone that Capt. John Smith marked on a map. Settlers burned the village in 1622 as a reprisal during American Indian uprisings. Not all the residents were killed; the Piscataways who survived settled along Piscataway Creek. About 1,000 skeletons, some of which date from the early Christian era, as well as pottery and tools from 8000-1000 B.C. have been unearthed.

NATIONAL COLONIAL FARM, 4 mi. w. of jct. SRs 373 and 210, offers exhibits pertaining to historic agriculture in Maryland. The farm is a living-history museum that presents a glimpse at the life of a typical tobacco-planting family in Prince George's County. The area also features the Ecosystem Farm, an organic, sustainable vegetable farm.

Allow 1 hour minimum. Tues.-Sun. 10-4, mid-Mar. to mid-Dec.; Sat.-Sun. 10-4, rest of year. Closed Jan. 1, Nov. 11, Thanksgiving and Dec. 25. Guided tours of the Colonial Farm are given Sat.-Sun. at 1. Guided tours of the Ecosystem Farm are given Sat.-Sun. at 11. Admission $2; 50c (ages 3-12); $5 (family). Phone (301) 283-2113.

BETHESDA (C-5) pop. 55,277, elev. 303'

Bethesda takes its name from the 1820 Bethesda Presbyterian Church (Bethesda Meeting House) on the Georgetown-Frederick Pike (Old National Road). The city is home to the National Cancer Institute, the National Institutes of Health, the National Naval Medical Center and other research facilities, making it the second largest employment center in the state.

Greater Bethesda-Chevy Chase Chamber of Commerce: 7910 Woodmont Ave., Suite 1204, Bethesda, MD 20814; phone (301) 652-4900.

NATIONAL LIBRARY OF MEDICINE is at 8600 Rockville Pike (M: Medical Center Station). Originally established in 1836 as the Library of the Army Surgeon General's Office, the library is a source of biomedical information for health professionals and the public. One-hour guided tours begin in the visitor center, which is located in the lobby of the Lister Hill Center Building 38A. Tours include an 11-minute videotape as well as a tour of the library.

Parking is limited. Allow 1 hour minimum. Library open Mon.-Fri. 8:30-5, Sat. 8:30-2; closed federal holidays and the Sat. preceding Mon. holidays. Visitor center open Mon.-Fri. 9-4; closed federal holidays. Guided tours are given Mon.-Fri. at 1:30. Free. Phone (301) 496-6308.

BOWIE pop. 50,269, elev. 151'

Founded in 1870 and incorporated in 1916, Bowie has progressed from a small railroad stop to Maryland's fourth largest city. Originally called Huntington City, it was renamed for former governor and local resident Oden Bowie, president of the Baltimore and Potomac Railroad.

The Prince George's County Genealogical Library, 12219 Tulip Grove Dr., is a research center that houses 4,000 volumes, numerous periodicals and surname files spanning 250 years of town history; phone (301) 262-2063.

For outdoor recreation, Allen Pond Park off SR 197 allows for a variety of activities including boating, fishing, hiking and picnicking. The Bowie Ice Arena, three soccer fields, two softball fields and a playground also are on site; phone (301) 809-3011.

BELAIR MANSION is off US 50 exit 11, 1.2 mi. n. on SR 197, then .5 mi. e. to 12207 Tulip Grove Dr. This 1745 Georgian-style house on nicely landscaped grounds is the former home of Samuel Ogle, Maryland's three-time provincial governor. The house was kept in the family until 1898. It was restored and enlarged 1910-14. Antiques can be viewed throughout the rooms. Allow 30 minutes minimum. Wed.-Sun. noon-4; closed federal holidays. Donations. Phone (301) 809-3089.

Belair Stable Museum is off US 50 exit 11, 1.2 mi. n. on SR 197, then .6 mi. e. to 2835 Belair Dr. James Woodward, an occupant of Belair Mansion and president of the Hanover National Bank, built this English-style stable in 1907 for Thoroughbreds.

Several famous race horses—Gallant Fox, Nashua and Omaha, for example—came from the Woodward family's stable during the first half of the 20th century. Inside is a small apartment with period furnishings. Allow 30 minutes minimum. Wed.-Sun. noon-4; closed federal holidays. Donations. Phone (301) 809-3089.

BOWIE RAILROAD MUSEUM & CHILDREN'S HERITAGE CENTER is off US 50 exit 11, 3.1 mi. n. on SR 197, .8 mi. w. on 11th St., then just n. to 8614 Chestnut Ave. The railroad station was named for Oden Bowie, president of the Baltimore & Potomac Railroad Co. and eventually governor of Maryland, who played a major role in bringing the railroad to southern Maryland in 1872.

The museum chronicles the history of the railroad and its influence on the town. The site has two small buildings, a caboose and a children's activity center. Allow 30 minutes minimum. Tues.-Sun. 10-4; closed federal holidays. Donations. Phone (301) 809-3089.

THE RADIO & TELEVISION MUSEUM is 1.3 mi. s. of US 50 on SR 197, then 1.5 mi. w. to jct. Mitchellville and Mt. Oak rds. A docent leads visitors on a 1-hour tour through the museum, which offers a collection of vintage radios and televisions as well as broadcasting memorabilia and equipment.

Some of the first radios ever made are on display, from inventor Guglielmo Marconi's earliest wireless telegraph to primitive crystal sets from the 1920s. Early television receivers are showcased on the ground floor. Allow 1 hour minimum. Tours are given Fri. 10-5, Sat.-Sun. 1-5; closed Jan. 1 and Dec. 25. Donations. Phone (301) 390-1020.

CHESAPEAKE AND OHIO CANAL NATIONAL HISTORICAL PARK—

see Maryland p..189.

CLINTON pop. 26,064, elev. 248'

Originally named Surrattsville for John Surratt, who was appointed the town's postmaster in 1854, Clinton is off SR 5 (Branch Avenue) southeast of Washington, D.C.

John Wilkes Booth stopped at the Surratt residence after he assassinated President Abraham Lincoln. Accused of involvement in Booth's crime, Mary Surratt was found guilty by the military commission responsible for the alleged conspirators' trial and hanged. The debate over Mary Surratt's connection with Lincoln's assassination still rages.

His Lordship's Kindness, a Georgian mansion built in 1787, is on a 138-acre horse farm at 7606 Woodyard Rd. It has been the home of many dignitaries and is furnished with a variety of antique pieces and replicas; phone (301) 856-0358.

ALL ABOUT TOWN tours depart from most local hotels. Narrated half-day, full-day and 2-day sightseeing excursions are offered. The itineraries include government buildings, the National Air and Space Museum, the National Museum of Natural History, Arlington National Cemetery and Mount Vernon. Washington by Twilight tours provide views of illuminated memorials and the Capitol dome.

Morning tours, lasting a half or a full day, depart at 7:15. Afternoon tours depart at 1 and return at 5. Evening tours depart at 7 and return at 10:45. Departure times vary by location of the hotel at which you are picked up. Closed Jan. 1, Thanksgiving and Dec. 25. Fare $32-$90; $16-$45 (ages 3-11 with adult). Reservations are required. Phone (301) 856-5556.

[SAVE] **SURRATT HOUSE AND MUSEUM,** 9118 Brandywine Rd., is the restored 1852 home of Mary Surratt. Guides in period dress conduct tours of the house and tavern and explain the house's role as the first stop on John Wilkes Booth's escape route through southern Maryland. Allow 1 hour minimum. Tours are given Thurs.-Fri. 11-3, Sat.-Sun. noon-4, mid-Jan. to mid-Dec. Last tour begins 30 minutes before closing. Fee $3; $2 (ages 60+); $1 (ages 5-18). Phone (301) 868-1121.

COLESVILLE pop. 19,810, elev. 436'

NATIONAL CAPITAL TROLLEY MUSEUM is 1.4 mi. n. on SR 650 (New Hampshire Ave.), then 1.7 mi. w. to 1313 Bonifant Rd. Exhibits include the permanent display Streetcar Communities and a slide presentation about Washington, D.C., trolleys. A 1.7-mile trolley ride also is offered.

Allow 1 hour minimum. Sat.-Sun. noon-5, Jan.-Nov. (also Thurs.-Fri. 11-3, mid-June to mid-Aug., and Thurs.-Fri. 10-2, Mar. 15-May 15 and Oct. 1-Nov. 15); Sat.-Sun. 5-9, rest of year. Closed Jan. 1 and Dec. 24-25 and 31. Last trolley departs 30 minutes before closing. Museum free. Trolley $3; $2 (ages 2-17). Phone (301) 384-6088.

COLLEGE PARK (C-9) pop. 24,657, elev. 70'

Originally founded in 1856 to educate the sons of area planters, Maryland Agricultural College became home to several thousand Union troops during the Civil War. After their departure, nearly 400 Confederate soldiers camped on the school grounds before heading for Washington in an attempted raid on the Capital. Later renamed University of Maryland, the public college is now the state's flagship institution.

Alumni include journalist Connie Chung and "Seinfeld" co-creator Larry David. On campus the Jim Henson Statue and Memorial Garden pays tribute to the Alumni Hall of Fame member and his most well-known creation Kermit the Frog. The school also is home to a 318,000-square-foot performing arts center, which features concerts, dance presentations and theatrical shows.

COLLEGE PARK AVIATION MUSEUM is off I-95/495 exit 23 (Kenilworth Avenue), 1.6 mi. s. on US 1, 1 mi. e. on Paint Branch Pkwy., then just n. to 1985 Corporal Frank Scott Dr. This museum relates the history of the College Park Airport, in continuous use since 1909, using vintage aircraft, hands-on exhibits and film of early flight attempts.

An animatronic Wilbur Wright describes the pioneer aviator's adventures as a flight instructor here. Allow 30 minutes minimum. Daily 10-5; closed major holidays. Admission $4; $3 (ages 60+); $2 (ages 2-17). MC, VI. Phone (301) 864-6029.

DICKERSON elev. 338'

SUGARLOAF MOUNTAIN is approximately 13 mi. s. via I-270, on SR 109 at the Barnsville-Hyattstown exit. The isolated mountain—a public oasis on a private estate—rises about 1,281 feet above the surrounding countryside. It served as a Union Army signal station during the Civil War. Picnicking and hiking are allowed. Horses and mountain bikes are permitted on certain trails; phone for details. No fires are permitted. Daily 8 a.m.-1 hour before dusk. Free. Phone (301) 874-2024.

FORT WASHINGTON
pop. 23,845, elev. 105'

Completed in 1809, the original Fort Washington protected the District of Columbia until the defensive structure was destroyed by its own garrison in 1814. Pierre-Charles L'Enfant worked on the construction of a new fort for a short period of time but was replaced by Lieutenant Colonel Walker K. Armistead. At Fort Washington Park *(see attraction listing)* military seacoast fortifications from three different time periods can still be seen.

The thunder of hooves rather than artillery is heard year-round 4 to 5 nights a week as harness racing takes place at Rosecroft Raceway, just off exit 4A of the Beltway; phone (301) 567-4000.

Note: Policies concerning admittance of children to pari-mutuel betting facilities vary. Phone for information.

FORT WASHINGTON PARK is off I-495 exit 3; take SR 210 (Indian Head Hwy.) 4 mi. s., then 3.5 mi. s.w. on Fort Washington Rd. This imposing 1824 masonry structure overlooking the Potomac River can be entered by a drawbridge over a dry moat. Two guardrooms provide a glimpse of military life and punishment. The superb view from the front wall takes in both Washington to the north and Mount Vernon to the south. A visitor center offers exhibits and an audio-visual program.

Picnicking is permitted. Allow 1 hour minimum. Grounds daily 8:30-dusk. Fort open daily 9-5, Apr.-Sept.; 9-4:30, rest of year. Visitor center open daily 9-noon and 2-5, Apr.-Sept.; 9-noon and 2-4:30, rest of year. Closed Jan. 1, Thanksgiving and Dec. 25. Admission $5 per private vehicle (valid for 3 days); $3 per person (on foot or by bicycle or bus). Phone (301) 763-4600.

GLEN ECHO (C-4) pop. 242, elev. 153'

Glen Echo's use as a cultural and educational center by the National Chautauqua Assembly ended when a rumor of malaria began in the fall of 1891. The Washington Railway and Electric Company later purchased the land and developed it into a major amusement park. From 1900 until 1968, Washingtonians rode the streetcar from the city to Glen Echo for a day in the country.

Conference and Visitors Bureau of Montgomery County-Glen Echo: 12900 Middlebrook Rd., Germantown, MD 20874; phone (301) 916-0698 or (800) 925-0880. *See color ad p. 68.*

CLARA BARTON NATIONAL HISTORIC SITE, 5801 Oxford Rd., was the home of the founder and first president of the American Red Cross from 1897 until her death in 1912, and served as the early headquarters of that organization. Built according to the floor plan of a Red Cross relief structure used after the flood of 1889 at Johnstown, Pa., the 1891 house is furnished with some items that once belonged to Barton.

Allow 1 hour minimum. Guided tours are given daily on the hour 10-4; closed Jan. 1, Thanksgiving and Dec. 25. Last tour begins at closing. Free. Phone (301) 320-1410.

GLEN ECHO PARK is at 7300 MacArthur Blvd. More than 200 arts classes are available to the public, and an artists-in-residence program offers performances, demonstrations and workshops. Historic buildings house the working studios of glass, ceramics and metalwork artisans. Year-round highlights include a children's nature museum; The Puppet Co. and Adventure Theatre children's shows; and Spanish Ballroom Dances. A 1921 Dentzel carousel operates May through September.

Picnicking is permitted. Park open daily 6 a.m.-1 a.m.; closed Thanksgiving and Dec. 25. Nature museum open Sat.-Sun. 10-3. Children's shows are presented Wed.-Fri. at 10 and 11:30, Sat.-Sun. at 11:30, 1, 1:30 and 3:30. Dances are held Fri. 7:30-11:30 p.m., Sat. 8 p.m.-midnight, Sun. 3-6 and 7:30-10:30

p.m. Carousel operates Wed.-Fri. 10-2, Sat.-Sun. noon-6, July-Aug.; Wed.-Thurs. 10-2, Sat.-Sun. noon-6, May-June; Sat.-Sun. noon-6, in Sept. Rangers provide tours Sun. at 2. Hours may vary; phone ahead.

Park admission free. Nature museum $5. Children's shows $8. Dances $8-$15. Carousel rides $1. Phone (301) 492-6229 for visitor information, (301) 634-2222 for recorded events information or (301) 634-2226 for class information.

GLENN DALE (B-12) pop. 12,609

MARIETTA HOUSE MUSEUM is at 5626 Bell Station Rd. Built in 1813, the Federal-style plantation home belonged to Gabriel Duvall, an associate justice on the U.S. Supreme Court. The home is furnished with period pieces and reproductions that represent three generations of Duvall family occupancy. A library of county history also is on the premises. Allow 30 minutes minimum. Wed.-Fri. 11-3, Sat.-Sun. noon-4, mid-June to late Aug.; Fri. 11-3, Sat.-Sun. noon-4, rest of year. Closed major holidays. Admission $3; $2 (60+); $1 (ages 5-18). MC, VI. Phone (301) 464-5291.

GREENBELT (B-11) pop. 21,456, elev. 180′

Greenbelt was constructed 1935-38 as a planned community and garden city with funds from the New Deal administration of President Franklin Roosevelt. Depression glass and 1937 furnishings designed specifically for the Greenbelt houses are part of the glimpse of the past that can be had at the Greenbelt Museum at 10B Crescent Rd., one of the town's original houses. Guided tours of the museum are offered by reservation. Exhibitions are displayed across the street at the community center gallery; phone (301) 474-1936.

GODDARD SPACE FLIGHT CENTER VISITORS CENTER is off I 95/495 exit 22A; take SR 193 (Greenbelt Rd.) 2.1 mi. e., Soil Conservation Rd. .2 mi. n., then Explorer Rd. .2 mi. w., following signs. The center offers programs, special events and presentations pertaining to the nation's space program.

Exhibits in the Earth Science and Space Science galleries are open to the public. Model rockets are launched the first Sunday of every month at 1 p.m. Allow 30 minutes minimum. Tues.-Fri. 10-3, Sat.-Sun. noon-4, Sept.-June; Tues.-Sat. 10-5, rest of year. Closed federal holidays. Free. Phone (301) 286-9041.

KENSINGTON (A-5) pop. 1,873, elev. 301′

Kensington is best known for its array of antique shops, housed in more than 40 Victorian buildings within a five-block area along Howard Avenue. Several of the shops also contain art galleries, potters and other artisans. Working demonstrations are sometimes offered in this area, which is known as Antique Row.

Wheaton-Kensington Chamber of Commerce: 2401 Blueridge Ave., Suite 101, Wheaton, MD 20902; phone (301) 949-0080.

WASHINGTON TEMPLE AND VISITOR CENTER OF THE CHURCH OF JESUS CHRIST OF LATTER-DAY SAINTS is off I-495 exit 33; take Beach Dr. 1 mi. e., then n. to 9900 Stoneybrook Dr. The visitor center on the grounds of the white marble temple features a copy of Bertel Thorvaldsen's eight-foot statue "Christus," and offers a variety of multimedia presentations, Christmas events and films about the temple.

The temple is closed to the public. Holiday programs include decorated trees, 450,000 lights and a nativity scene nightly in December. Allow 1 hour minimum. Visitor center daily 10-9. Free. Phone (301) 587-0144.

LARGO (E-12) pop. 8,408, elev. 180′

East of Washington, D.C., this bedroom community is of interest to visitors primarily for its proximity to Six Flags America (see attraction listing).

Prince George's County Conference and Visitors Bureau: 9200 Basil Ct., Suite 101, Largo, MD 20774; phone (301) 925-8300.

SIX FLAGS AMERICA is about 5 mi. e. of Beltway (I-495/I-95) exit 15A. This 170-acre theme and water park features more than 100 rides, shows and attractions. Highlights include eight roller coasters, including Batwing, Jokers Jinx, The Wild One and Superman-Ride of Steel as well as Hurricane Harbor water park.

For non thrill-seekers there are The Penguin's River, Looney Tunes Movie Town and a variety of live shows. Hurricane Harbor features a million-gallon wave pool, Buccaneer Beach for the little ones and a variety of slides and other attractions.

Food is available. Allow 5 hours minimum. Park open daily, late May-late Aug. and Labor Day weekend; some Sat.-Sun. in Apr. and Sept.-Oct. Hours vary; phone ahead. Hurricane Harbor open Memorial Day-Labor Day; phone ahead for schedule. Admission (includes water park) $49.99; $34.99 (children under 54 inches tall); free (ages 0-3). Prices may vary; phone ahead. Parking $15. AAA members save on select services and merchandise. See guest relations for details. AX, DS, MC, VI. Phone (301) 249-1500.

LAUREL pop. 19,960

A suburb northeast of Washington, D.C., Laurel was once a small industrial center. Cotton and grain no longer draw visitors, but horse racing does from early October through March. Laurel Park has been offering Thoroughbred racing since 1911. The track features the International, a race that presents leading horses from around the world; phone (301) 725-0400.

Note: Policies concerning admittance of children to pari-mutuel betting facilities vary. Phone for information.

Baltimore/Washington Corridor Chamber of Commerce: 312 Marshall Ave., Suite 104, Laurel, MD 20707; phone (301) 725-4000 or (410) 792-9714.

Shopping areas: The main shopping complex in the area is Laurel Mall on US 1, which features JCPenney and Macy's among its 110 stores.

MONTPELIER MANSION AND CULTURAL ARTS CENTER is w. off Gladys Spellman (Baltimore-Washington) Pkwy. (I-295) Laurel-Bowie Rd. exit (SR 197), following signs to Muirkirk Rd. The center has three galleries with changing exhibits. Visitors are encouraged to watch artists, whose talents range from painting and sculpting to rug hooking and jewelry making.

The Montpelier Mansion, next to the cultural arts center, was built 1774-83 and is a fine example of Georgian architecture, complete with boxwood gardens on the grounds. Allow 30 minutes minimum. Arts center open daily 10-5. Guided tours of the mansion are given on the hour Sun.-Thurs. noon-3, Mar.-Nov.; Sun. at 1 and 2, rest of year. Arts center free. Guided tours $3; $2 (senior citizens); $1 (ages 5-18). Phone (301) 953-1993, (410) 792-0664 in Baltimore, (301) 953-1376 for mansion tour information, or TTY (301) 490-2329.

NATIONAL WILDLIFE VISITOR CENTER is 2 mi. e. on Powder Mill Rd. off the Baltimore-Washington Pkwy. to 10901 Scarlet Tanager Loop. Within the 12,750-acre Patuxent Research Refuge, the center's interactive exhibits focus on global environmental issues, migratory bird routes, wildlife habitats and endangered species recovery efforts. Surrounding forests, lakes and trails provide opportunities for recreation and educational programs. Thirty-minute guided tours aboard open-air trams also are offered.

Allow 2 hours minimum. Grounds and visitor center open daily 9-4:30; closed federal holidays. Tram tours are given Mon.-Fri. at 11:30, 1 and 2:30 (also by appointment at 10:30, 12:15 and 3:30), Sat.-Sun. at 11:30, 1, 2:30 and 3:30, late June-Sept. 30; Mon.-Fri. by reservation 10-noon, Sat.-Sun. at 11:30, 1, 2:30 and 3:30, rest of year (weather permitting). Operating hours and tram schedule may vary; phone ahead. Grounds and visitor center free. Tram tours $3; $2 (ages 55+); $1 (ages 3-12). Phone (301) 497-5763.

OXON HILL (I-8) elev. 220'

Since the 17th century Oxon Hill has been associated with the estate belonging to the Addison family, long prominent in southern Maryland history. The present manor was built in the late 1920s for Sumner Welles, President Franklin Roosevelt's undersecretary of state. It is currently closed for renovations; phone (301) 839-7782.

Fort Foote Park, 1.5 miles west off SR 210, contains the crude concrete and stone gun emplacements and earthworks of Fort Foote, built to protect Washington, D.C., during the Civil War.

OXON HILL FARM is off I-495/I-95 exit 3A and Oxon Hill Rd. Comprising 512 acres, this working early 20th-century farm also depicts agricultural practices of the 17th century to the present through displays of livestock and other animals, machinery, barns and gardens. Picnicking is permitted. Allow 1 hour minimum. Daily 8-4:30; closed Jan. 1, Thanksgiving and Dec. 25. Free. Phone (301) 839-1176, or TTY (301) 839-1176.

ROCKVILLE pop. 47,388, elev. 432'

Rockville traces its history to 1776, when irate citizens vowed to cut off all trade with England until the tea tax was lifted. A prosperous Washington suburb, Rockville's pockets of Victorian architecture, brick sidewalks and large trees help preserve some of the city's old essence amid the prevailing suburban sprawl.

The Mansion Art Gallery of Rockville, 603 Edmonston Dr., offers free art exhibitions that change monthly. The graves of F. Scott Fitzgerald, his wife and his daughter are in the cemetery of the 1817 St. Mary's Catholic Church, in one of Rockville's seven historic districts.

Rockville Chamber of Commerce: 255 Rockville Pike, Suite L 10, Rockville, MD 20850; phone (301) 424-9300.

BEALL-DAWSON HOUSE is at 103 W. Montgomery Ave. in Beall-Dawson Historical Park. This restored 1815 house is furnished in period. The Federal exterior complements its interior, which is designed in the neoclassic style of Robert Adam. Changing exhibits are displayed. The small brick building to the rear of the house was the original dairy house. Docents detail the daily life and culture of the house's upper-class Montgomery County residents and the slaves who labored there.

Allow 30 minutes minimum. Guided tours are given Tues.-Sun. noon-4; closed major holidays. Last tour begins 30 minutes before closing. Fee (includes tour of Stonestreet Museum of 19th Century Medicine) $3; $2 (senior citizens and students with ID). Phone (301) 762-1492.

Jane C. Swoon Library is at 42 Middle Ln. in the Beall-Dawson Historical Park. This library has a collection of books, maps, documents and photographs pertaining to Montgomery County history and genealogy. Tues.-Sat. 10-4, Sun. 1-4. Admission $5; $2 (senior citizens and students with ID). Phone (301) 340-2974.

Stonestreet Museum of 19th Century Medicine is on the grounds of the Beall-Dawson House at 103 W. Montgomery Ave. Included in the Beall-Dawson House tour, this 1852 one-room building exhibits antiquated medical instruments, apothecary accessories and period furniture in a former doctor's office. Guided tours are given Tues.-Sun. noon-4; closed major holidays. Last tour begins 30 minutes before closing. Admission included in fee for Beall-Dawson House. Phone (301) 762-1492.

ROCK CREEK REGIONAL PARK is 4 mi. e. on SR 28, then 2 mi. n. on Muncaster Mill Rd. to Avery Rd. The park contains hiking and bicycle trails, an archery range and golf courses. Lake Needwood offers canoe, pedal boat and rowboat rentals Memorial Day through Labor Day, and Lake Frank allows fishing. Meadowside Nature Center has interactive exhibits and nature trails. The *Needwood Queen* offers 15-minute lake cruises on weekends and holidays, May through September.

Picnicking is permitted. Park open daily dawn-dusk. Nature center open Tues.-Sat. 9-5. Closed major winter holidays. Park free. Phone (301) 948-5053, (301) 495-2525 for picnic shelter reservations, (202) 924-4141 for the nature center, or (202) 762-1888 for boating information. *See Maryland Recreation Chart.*

SILVER SPRING (B-7) pop. 76,540, elev. 340′

In 1842 *Washington Globe* editor Francis Preston Blair discovered a spring in a heavily wooded area north of Washington, D.C. He later purchased the land around the spring, built a home and named it Silver Spring after the sparkling water. By 1899 the first post office was built, and Blair became the first postmaster for the small farming community.

Greater Silver Spring Chamber of Commerce: 8601 Georgia Ave., Suite 203, Silver Spring, MD 20910; phone (301) 565-3777.

SEVENTH-DAY ADVENTIST CHURCH WORLD HEADQUARTERS is at 12501 Old Columbia Pike. The world headquarters and the estate of Ellen G. White, one of the founding members of the church, are open to the public. A visitor center presents various facets of the church's history, beliefs and activities through photographs, multimedia displays and interactive computer kiosks.

Food is available. Allow 1 hour minimum. Visitor center and Ellen White Estate open Mon.-Thurs.

8-5:30, Fri. 8-noon; closed major holidays. Thirty-minute guided tours are given Mon.-Fri. at 9. Free. Phone (301) 680-6000.

WHEATON elev. 469′

Wheaton took its name from Union general Frank Wheaton, who helped defend Washington, D.C., from his post at Fort Stevens; the fort still stands on Georgia Avenue. Wheaton also was home to Charles Francis Jenkins, owner of more than 400 patents and perfecter of the home television set; Jenkins delivered the nation's first television broadcast in 1923.

Wheaton-Kensington Chamber of Commerce: 2401 Blueridge Ave., Suite 101, Wheaton, MD 20902; phone (301) 949-0080.

BROOKSIDE GARDENS is 1 mi. n. on SR 97 (Georgia Ave.), .3 mi. n.e. on Randolph Rd., then .3 mi. e. to 1800 Glenallan Ave. It features two conservatories and 50 acres of outdoor gardens. Plantings include winter, formal, rose, fragrance and azalea gardens. Tropical plants in the conservatories accent the seasonal flower displays. There also is a horticultural library on the premises.

Guided tours and educational programs are available. Allow 30 minutes minimum in winter, 1 hour minimum rest of year. Grounds open daily dawn-dusk. Conservatories open daily 10-5. Visitor center open daily 9-5. Horticultural reference library hours vary; phone ahead. Closed Dec. 25. Free. Phone (301) 962-1400.

BROOKSIDE NATURE CENTER is 1 mi. n. on SR 97 (Georgia Ave.), .3 mi. n.e. on Randolph Rd., then .7 mi. e. to 1400 Glenallan Ave. In addition to hiking trails this wooded area offers a primitive weather station, a re-created pioneer homestead, animal exhibits and a hands-on learning center for children. Picnicking is permitted. Allow 30 minutes minimum. Nature center Tues.-Sat. 9-5, Sun. 1-5. Trails daily dawn-dusk. Closed major holidays. Free. Phone (301) 946-9071.

Nearby Virginia

ALEXANDRIA (H-5) pop. 128,283, elev. 20'

Although an integral part of the Washington, D.C., metropolitan area, Alexandria is a distinct city in its own right. It was established in 1749 by a group of Scottish merchants and named for John Alexander, who had purchased the land in 1669. During the Revolutionary period Alexandria was a principal Colonial port as well as a trade, social and political center.

George Washington maintained a town house in Alexandria. During his residence he organized the Friendship Fire Co., was elected vestryman of Christ Church Parish and was a member of the Masonic Lodge, becoming its Charter Master in 1788.

Alexandria also was the home of Revolutionary War general "Light Horse" Harry Lee, and the boyhood home of his son, Robert E. Lee. During the Civil War the city was captured and occupied by Federal forces, who used it as a base of operations for various Union campaigns in Virginia.

Through careful guardianship and planning, parts of Alexandria have managed to retain the appearance of another century. Old Town Alexandria, extending westward from the Potomac River, is the major historical area (see Alexandria Walking Tour p. 122). The city's DASH bus system connects the King Street and Braddock Road Metro stations with various Old Town locations. The base fare is $1 (exact change only), under 5 with adult free, and includes a transfer good for 4 hours for the return trip; phone (703) 370-3274 for route and schedule information.

The cruise ship Dandy, at the foot of Prince Street, is an enclosed ship offering 2-hour luncheon and 3-hour dinner-dance cruises on the Potomac River; phone (703) 683-6076 for information and reservations.

The special events hotline maintained by the Alexandria Department of Recreation, Parks and Cultural Activities provides information about local music events; phone (703) 883-4686.

Alexandria Convention and Visitors Association: 421 King St., Suite 300, Alexandria, VA 22314; phone (703) 838-4200, (800) 388-9119, or TTY (703) 838-6494.

Self-guiding tours: Among the visitors association's offerings are a walking tour brochure, Civil War walking tour and bicycle trail maps, a parking map and a parking pass good for 24 hours of free parking.

Shopping areas: Old Town Alexandria's streets are lined with galleries, antique shops and boutiques. Landmark Mall is on Duke Street; its anchor stores are Lord & Taylor, Macy's and Sears. The Torpedo Factory Art Center (see attraction listing p. 121) offers specialty items.

ALEXANDRIA BLACK HISTORY MUSEUM, 902 Wythe St., interprets the contributions of African-Americans to Alexandria's history and culture from 1749 to the present. Guided tours are available. Allow 30 minutes minimum. Tues.-Sat. 10-4; closed Jan. 1, Easter, July 4, Thanksgiving and Dec. 25. Free. Phone (703) 838-4356.

CARLYLE HOUSE is at 121 N. Fairfax St. In 1753 this stone, Georgian-Palladian mansion was the grandest in the new town of Alexandria. The house features rich architectural detail, authentic paint colors and fine furnishings, and the grounds include a garden laid out in 18th-century style, with brick walkways and boxwood parterres. Exhibits interpret the domestic life of a Colonial gentleman, his family and his slaves.

Allow 1 hour minimum. Guided tours are given every half-hour Tues.-Sat. 10-4, Sun. noon-4; closed Jan. 1, Thanksgiving and Dec. 25. Fee $4; $2 (ages 11-17). Phone (703) 549-2997.

CHRIST CHURCH (Anglican) is at 118 N. Washington St. near Columbus and Cameron sts. Built 1767-73, this Georgian-style brick church, with a Palladian chancel window unusual for its time, is in nearly original condition.

George Washington purchased Pew 60 for 36 pounds and 10 shillings when the church first opened, and he regularly attended services. Robert E. Lee, who also attended services regularly, was confirmed in the church in 1853. The cut-glass chandelier, under the gallery, represents one of the most advanced types of lighting fixtures available in the early 19th century.

Allow 30 minutes minimum. Mon.-Sat. 9-4, Sun. 2-4, except during services; closed holidays and after services Jan. 1, Thanksgiving and Dec. 25. Hours may vary; phone ahead. Donations. Phone (703) 549-1450.

COLLINGWOOD LIBRARY AND MUSEUM ON AMERICANISM is on the Potomac River at 8301 E. Boulevard Dr. The oldest part of Collingwood Mansion dates from 1783. The museum presents presidential china, American Indian artifacts and displays about Revolutionary War heroes. Books in the library, devoted exclusively to American history, can be used on the premises. Mon. and Wed.-Sat. 10-4, Sun. 1-4; closed federal holidays and Dec. 18-Jan. 4. Free. Phone (703) 765-1652.

FORT WARD MUSEUM AND HISTORIC SITE is at 4301 W. Braddock Rd., just e. of I-395 between King St. and Seminary Rd. Fort Ward sits on 45 acres and was one of the forts that formed a defensive ring around Washington during the Civil War. The museum presents changing exhibits pertaining to that conflict. Interpretive programs, an orientation videotape and lectures are offered throughout the year. Free evening concerts are held outdoors July through August; phone for information.

Picnicking is permitted. Park open daily 9-dusk. Museum open Tues.-Sat. 9-5, Sun. noon-5; closed Jan. 1, Thanksgiving and Dec. 25. Donations. A fee may be charged during special events. Phone (703) 838-4848.

FRIENDSHIP FIREHOUSE is at 107 S. Alfred St. between King and Prince sts. Established in 1774 as Alexandria's first volunteer fire company, Friendship Firehouse claims George Washington as a founding member. The current structure dates to 1855. Hand-drawn fire engines and historic firefighting apparatus are displayed, as are Victorian furnishings and ceremonial objects. Allow 30 minutes minimum. Fri.-Sat. 10-4, Sun. 1-4; closed Jan. 1 and Dec. 25. Free. Phone (703) 838-3891.

[SAVE] **GADSBY'S TAVERN MUSEUM,** 134 N. Royal St., comprises the original 1785 Georgian tavern and the 1792 City Tavern and Hotel. The tavern, with its taproom, small dining room and assembly room, and the hotel ballroom were a center for Alexandria's social and political life. Interpretive programs are offered year-round.

Tues.-Sat. 10-5, Sun.-Mon. 1-5, Apr.-Oct.; Wed.-Sat. 11-4, Sun. 1-4, rest of year. Closed Jan. 1, Thanksgiving and Dec. 25. Guided tours are given at a quarter before and a quarter past each hour. Last tour begins 15 minutes before closing. Admission $4; $2 (ages 11-17). Phone (703) 838-4242.

 GEORGE WASHINGTON MASONIC NATIONAL MEMORIAL surmounts Shooter's Hill at the w. end of King St. The 333-foot-tall landmark is modeled after the ancient lighthouse at Alexandria, Egypt. The Replica Room contains original furnishings of Alexandria Lodge No. 22, the lodge in Alexandria over which Washington was the first Worshipful Master under Virginia charter.

The nine floors of exhibits include a colossal statue of George Washington in Memorial Hall and a museum that features the Washington family Bible among numerous other artifacts. The memorial also houses a research library and is topped by a 360-degree observation deck providing a view of the metropolitan Washington area. Daily 10-4; closed Jan. 1, Thanksgiving and Dec. 25. Guided tours are given at 10, 11:30, 1:30 and 3. Free. Phone (703) 683-2007.

 GEORGE WASHINGTON'S MOUNT VERNON ESTATE & GARDENS— see Mount Vernon p. 132.

GEORGE WASHINGTON'S RIVER FARM is off George Washington Memorial Pkwy., 4 mi. s. of Old Town Alexandria, on the Potomac River at 7931 E. Boulevard Dr. George Washington bought this property in 1760, and he may also have planted the two black walnut trees that still stand in the meadow near the main buildings.

The manor house was built in the early 20th century. Now headquarters for the American Horticultural Society, the 25-acre site contains display and children's gardens. Allow 30 minutes minimum. Mon.-Fri. 9-5 (also Sat. 9-1, Apr.-Sept.); closed holidays. Free. Phone (703) 768-5700 or (800) 777-7931.

GUNSTON HALL PLANTATION— see Lorton p. 130.

LEE-FENDALL HOUSE MUSEUM, 614 Oronoco St., was built in 1785 by Alexandria civic leader Philip Richard Fendall and remained in the family

until 1903. It is furnished with period antiques, including many Lee possessions. John L. Lewis, U.S. labor leader, owned the house 1937-69. Guided tours depart on the hour Tues.-Sat. 10-3, Sun. 1-4; closed holidays. Last tour begins 1 hour before closing. Fee $4; $2 (ages 11-17). Phone (703) 548-1789.

THE LYCEUM is at 201 S. Washington St. This museum of Alexandria's history presents changing exhibits, lectures, concerts and educational programs. Built in 1839 as the city's first cultural center, the building was occupied by both Confederate and Union troops during the Civil War. Mon.-Sat. 10-5, Sun. 1-5; closed Jan. 1, Thanksgiving and Dec. 24-25. Free. Phone (703) 838-4994.

OLD PRESBYTERIAN MEETING HOUSE is at 321 S. Fairfax St. between Duke and Wolfe sts. Established in 1772, the meeting house became a gathering place for patriots during the Revolutionary War and was the site of George Washington's funeral sermons in December 1799. During the Civil War it was used briefly as a hospital.

In the churchyard is the grave of John Carlyle and the Tomb of the Unknown Revolutionary War Soldier. The old-fashioned gate pews of this still-active church have been retained. The keys to the sanctuary are available at the church office. Mon.-Fri. 8:30-4:30. Free. Phone (703) 549-6670.

POTOMAC RIVERBOAT COMPANY vessels dock at the Alexandria City Marina, Cameron and Union sts., behind the Torpedo Factory Art Center; cruises also depart from Washington Harbour at 31st and K sts. N.W. in Georgetown. Tickets are sold at the booths at the marina and harbor.

The Alexandria by Water Seaport Cruise is a 40-minute, round-trip sightseeing excursion. A guide narrates the history of the region while the boat cruises along the waterfront past historic landmarks. Other trips, including the Washington by Water Monuments Cruise and Water Taxi and George Washington's Mount Vernon by Water Cruise and Water Taxi are offered.

Alexandria by Water Seaport Cruise departs Tues.-Fri. on the hour 11-2, Sat. noon-10, Sun. noon-8, early May-Labor Day; Sat. noon-10, Sun. noon-8, day after Labor Day-early Oct.; Sat.-Sun. noon-7, in Apr. Departure times may vary; phone ahead. Alexandria by Water Seaport Cruise $12; $10 (ages 61+); $6 (ages 2-11). Phone (703) 684-0580, or (703) 548-9000 for recorded tour information.

RAMSAY HOUSE VISITORS CENTER is at 221 King St. The original Ramsay House, one of the oldest structures in the city, was moved to this site in 1749 by William Ramsay, a founder and first lord mayor of Alexandria. It burned down in 1949 and was replaced by the current building, which is staffed by Alexandria Convention and Visitors Association employees. Daily 9-5; closed Jan. 1, Thanksgiving and Dec. 25. Free. Phone (703) 838-5005.

STABLER-LEADBEATER APOTHECARY MUSEUM entrance is at 105 S. Fairfax St. Founded in 1792 by Quaker pharmacist Edward Stabler, this is said to be Alexandria's oldest mercantile establishment; George Washington, James Monroe and Robert E. Lee were patrons. Old account books, prescriptions, early medical wares and a collection of period apothecary containers can be seen in their original setting. The shop remained in the family until 1933.

Tues.-Sat. 10-5, Sun.-Mon. 1-5 (last admission at 4:45); closed major holidays. Admission $4; $2 (ages 11-17). Phone (703) 838-3852.

TORPEDO FACTORY ART CENTER is at 105 N. Union St. on the waterfront in Old Town Alexandria. Built for the manufacture of torpedo casings for World War I and World War II, the building now contains 84 studios and six galleries where visitors can watch artists and crafters at work. Works by more than 160 artists are on exhibit and for sale. The center includes the Art League School. Daily 10-5 (also 2nd Thurs. of month 6-9 p.m.); closed Jan. 1, Easter, July 4, Thanksgiving and Dec. 25. Free. Phone (703) 838-4565.

Alexandria Archaeology Museum and Laboratory is on the third floor of the Torpedo Factory Art Center. This museum displays and interprets objects from recent excavations in Alexandria. The collection has items dating from 7500 B.C. to the early 20th century. Tues.-Fri. 10-3, Sat. 10-5, Sun. 1-5; closed Jan. 1, Easter, July 4, Thanksgiving and Dec. 25. Free. Phone (703) 838-4399.

WOODLAWN PLANTATION is 7.5 mi. s. on US 1 at jct. SR 235. The land, originally part of Mount Vernon, was a gift from George Washington to his nephew, Maj. Lawrence Lewis, and Lewis's wife Eleanor "Nelly" Custis, a granddaughter of Martha Washington. Dr. William Thornton, who designed the 1805 mansion, was the first architect of the Capitol. The 19th-century period rooms and restored formal gardens are open for viewing.

Picnicking is permitted. Allow 1 hour minimum. Guided tours are given Tues.-Sun. and select holidays every 30 minutes 10-5, Mar.-Dec. Last tour begins 30 minutes before closing. Admission $7.50; $3 (students in grades K-12). Combination ticket with Frank Lloyd Wright's Pope-Leighey House $13; $5 (students in grades K-12). AX, MC, VI. Phone (703) 780-4000.

Frank Lloyd Wright's Pope-Leighey House is on the Woodlawn Plantation grounds. The Usonian house was designed by Wright and exhibits many of the significant contributions he made to contemporary architecture. The house also contains original furnishings designed by the architect.

Allow 30 minutes minimum. Guided tours are given Tues.-Sun. and select holidays every 30 minutes 10-5, Mar.-Dec. Last tour begins 30 minutes before closing. Admission $7.50; $3 (students in grades K-12). Combination ticket with Woodlawn Plantation $13; $5 (students in grades K-12). AX, MC, VI. Phone (703) 780-4000.

⚑ Walking Tour: Alexandria

See map following. This tour of Old Town takes 2-3 hours, depending on your pace and the number of listed sites you visit along the way. *Those that appear in bold type have detailed listings on the preceding pages. Even if you decide not to visit a site, reading the listing when you reach that point should make the tour more interesting.*

If you drive into Alexandria, you can pick up a free 24-hour parking proclamation from the visitor center at Ramsay House. The passes are valid only when using 2-hour metered spaces; upon arrival, you should insert enough change in the meter to give yourself time to pick up the parking pass and return to your car with it. To receive a pass, you must provide state identification and your license plate number.

Served by both the Blue and Yellow lines, the King Street Metro station is about a mile west of Ramsay House. The city's DASH bus system connects the King Street and Braddock Road Metro stations with various Old Town locations. The fare is $1 (exact change only), under 5 with adult free, and includes a transfer good for 4 hours for the return trip.

If street-side parking is at a premium—and it will be on weekdays—there are several parking garages in the area as well. The most convenient is the City Hall garage (during evenings and weekends only) at the corner of King and Fairfax streets. Other nearby garages are across Union Street from the Torpedo Factory Art Center; at 200 Queen St.; at 10 Thompson Alley; at the Courthouse, 111 S. Pitt St.; at 115 S. Union St.; and at 210 N. St. Asaph St.

Note: In keeping with Old Town's quaint ambience, many of its sidewalks are brick-paved. Watch your step or you'll risk tripping over the occasional protruding paver.

Few areas offer a more pleasant stroll into another century than Old Town Alexandria. Here visitors can enjoy shady cobblestone streets closely flanked by 18th- and 19th-century houses with leafy courtyards. Newer buildings emulate the prevailing architectural style, helping to preserve this historic district's charm.

Begin your tour at **Ramsay House**—the city's visitor center—at 221 King St., which is on the corner of King and Fairfax streets.

From the Ramsay House, walk east on King Street toward the river. Turn left at Lee Street, and follow Lee to the corner of Cameron Street for a view of Cameron Mews, mews being another word for alley or back street. This Colonial town house development exemplifies Alexandria's approach to new housing in Old Town. Turn left on Cameron Street and walk past the lovely gardens on the southwest corner of Cameron and Lee. These belong to the **Carlyle House.**

John Carlyle, a Scottish merchant and city founder, built this grand Georgian Palladian manor 1751-53. Two years after its completion,

Gen. Edward Braddock and five Colonial governors met there to discuss funding a campaign against the French during the French and Indian War. The issue of financing the war later became so contentious that it led to the American Revolution.

Continue west on Cameron, which is one of the city's most interesting shopping streets. The north side of the block between Fairfax and Royal streets has many boutiques and specialty shops. Opposite is the block-long, brick City Hall, and behind it is airy Market Square. The market held here every Saturday morning is reputed to be the nation's oldest.

The neat brick facades facing Cameron Street between Royal and Pitt streets hide Tavern Square, named for historic **Gadsby's Tavern Museum,** which forms its northeast corner. Made up of two buildings—the 1770 City Tavern and 1792 City Hotel—Gadsby's Tavern prospered due to its location along the main stage route between Williamsburg and Boston. For many years it was a center for social and political life in the city.

Proceed 1 block west on Cameron past George Washington's reconstructed town house, which is the clapboard house on the street's south side. Washington stayed here when business or bad weather prevented him from returning to his Mount Vernon estate. Like many historic homes, it is a private residence not open to the public.

Turn right on tree-lined St. Asaph Street, where the town homes are beautified by landscaped courtyards and pocket gardens. As you cross Princess Street, look left to see a section of restored cobblestone roadway between St. Asaph and Washington streets.

Make a left at Oronoco, and on the right as you approach Washington Street you'll find the boyhood home of Gen. Robert E. Lee, which is a private residence. Lee lived here from age 5 until he left to enroll at West Point when he was 18. Across the street, on the southeast corner of Oronoco and Washington, stands the 1785 **Lee-Fendall House Museum.** Home to generations of Robert E. Lee's relatives, the house contains a variety of items that once belonged to this celebrated Virginia family.

Head south on Washington Street. On the southwest corner of Queen and Washington is the 1797 Lloyd House, one of the city's best examples of late Georgian architecture. Turn left on Cameron; on your left, at 611 Cameron, is a small, red-brick house that once belonged to Revolutionary War hero Gen. Henry "Light Horse Harry" Lee. Due to financial difficulties, Lee was forced to move his family—including young son Robert Edward—to this house from their Stratford Hall Plantation *(see attraction listing in Stratford, Va., p. 308).* The Lees lived here 1810-12; it is currently a private residence.

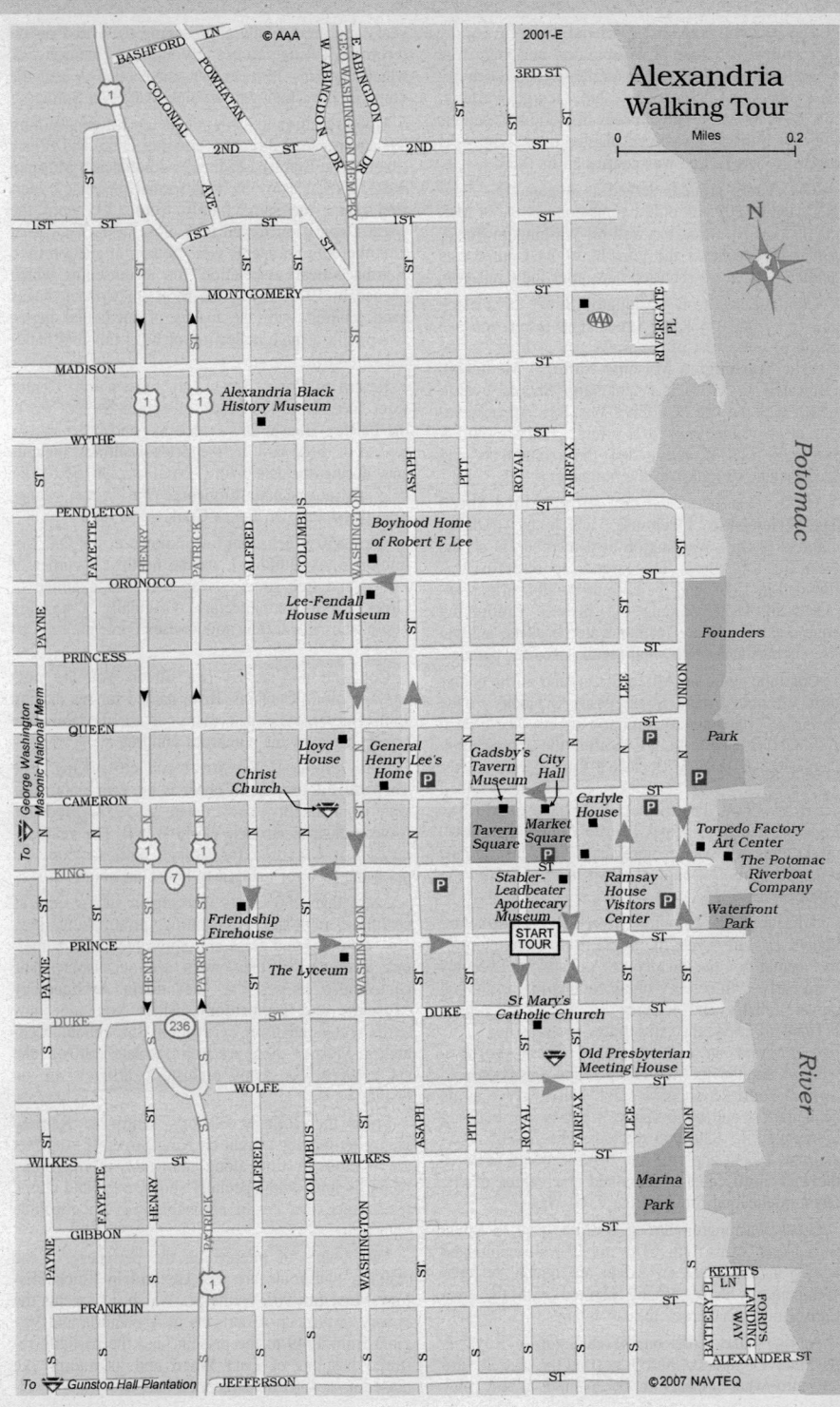

The peaceful grounds of **Christ Church** occupy the southwest corner of Washington and Cameron. Completed in 1773, the Georgian-style church remains an active house of worship. George Washington was an early parishioner; his original pew is preserved inside. A silver plaque marks the spot where Robert E. Lee was confirmed in 1853.

The church grounds served as Alexandria's cemetery until 1809; its oldest tombstone is dated Mar. 20, 1791. Just inside the wall on Washington Street, a mass grave holds the remains of 34 Confederate soldiers who were reburied here after the Civil War.

Continue south on Washington Street for a block and turn right on King Street. The tower you see ahead of you, west of the walking tour route, is the **George Washington Masonic National Memorial.** Dedicated in 1932, it stands atop Shooter's Hill, which was the site of a Civil War fort. An observation deck on the ninth level offers a fantastic bird's-eye view of Alexandria and the monuments and government buildings of the nation's capital.

Go 2 blocks west and turn left on Alfred Street. The **Friendship Firehouse,** which by tradition claimed George Washington as a member, is on the west side of Alfred. The Friendship Fire Co. was founded in 1774, and the current building was completed in 1855. Among the historic firefighting equipment inside are leather water buckets, antique fire engines and ceremonial regalia used for parades.

Continue south on Alfred Street, and at the corner turn left onto Prince Street. Walk 2 blocks to the corner of Prince and Washington streets. The bronze Confederate Statue stands within the intersection. Dedicated in 1889, it depicts a Confederate soldier gazing south with head bowed and arms folded across his chest. The memorial, the base of which is inscribed with the names of 100 Confederate dead, marks the spot where more than 700 Alexandrians left the Union-occupied city to fight for the Confederacy.

Adjacent is the two-story, Greek Revival structure known as **The Lyceum** (lie-SEE-um), an interpretive center for the history of Alexandria. Lyceums were early 19th-century organizations that promoted public debates and lectures on a host of topics. Formed in 1834, the Alexandria Lyceum hosted its first programs at a local school. These programs were so popular that the organization was soon able to fund construction of a grand hall to serve as its headquarters and main venue, which is the building (completed in 1839) you see today. Eventually Alexandrians began applying the organization's name to the hall itself, and it remained the center of the city's intellectual life until the Civil War.

Cross Washington Street, continue east to Royal Street and turn right. The neat, well-maintained homes in this block of Royal are typical restored 18th-century houses, many marked with the oval Early Buildings Survey registry plaque.

Across Duke Street on the east side of Royal is St. Mary's Catholic Church; beyond the church, turn left into what appears to be a small grassy play yard. You are actually approaching the **Old Presbyterian Meeting House** through its churchyard, which contains 18th-century grave markers and the Tomb of the Unknown Revolutionary War Soldier.

Upon reaching the front of the meetinghouse, turn left and proceed 2 blocks, crossing Duke and Prince streets. The Stabler-Leadbeater Apothecary Museum is at 105 S. Fairfax St. This former pharmacy operated under the same family from 1796 until the Great Depression forced it to close in 1933. At that time the entire contents were bought at auction by a pharmaceutical association for a museum, which opened in 1939. Inside the shop are wooden boxes hand lettered with the names of medicinal herbs, along with a huge collection of drug tins and hand-blown bottles.

Return to Prince Street and make a left. Gentry Row, along the 200 block of Prince Street, boasts the Fairfax House, 207 Prince St., and other homes typical of those built by the city's wealthiest inhabitants during the late 1700s. Number 209 next door belonged at one time to George Washington's longtime physician, Dr. James Craik.

The 1850 Athenaeum (also known as the Old Dominion Bank Building), on the northwest corner of Prince and Lee streets, is an excellent example of Greek Revival architecture. Originally a banking house, the Athenaeum now houses contemporary art shows.

Continue east across Lee Street. You are now walking along Captains' Row, named for sea captain John Harper, who had many of the Federal-style houses built for his numerous children.

Turn left on Union Street and cross King. The **Torpedo Factory Art Center** is on your right. This waterfront facility, constructed in 1918, produced torpedo casings through World War II. For years afterward it was used for storage until someone hit upon the idea for using it to house art studios.

More than 160 artists working in such media as sculpture, photography, painting, printmaking, jewelry, ceramics and glass are represented, and numerous examples of their work are on display. The center also houses the **Alexandria Archaeology Museum and Laboratory,** where you can view items recovered from excavations throughout Alexandria. Most of these are from the late 1600s to the early 1900s, but many prehistoric artifacts are on display as well.

From the Torpedo Factory, return to Ramsay House by making a right on King Street. If your feet are willing, a stroll along this main thoroughfare, which is lined with specialty shops, pubs and ethnic restaurants, can be an enjoyable way to conclude your tour.

Two points of interest on the periphery of the walking tour route are the **Alexandria Black History Museum,** 902 Wythe St., which documents the history of African-Americans in Alexandria and Virginia from 1749 to the present, and the partially restored bastions of **Fort Ward** and its interpretive museum, at 4301 W. Braddock Rd.

ARLINGTON (F-5) pop. 189,453

Arlington, on the southwest bank of the Potomac, is a suburb of Washington, D.C. One of the smallest counties in the United States, it covers 25.7 square miles, of which about 4.6 square miles are federal property. Some of the major centers of development (the county contains no incorporated communities) are Ballston, Clarendon, Columbia Pike, Crystal City, Rosslyn and Shirlington.

Within Arlington is The Pentagon, one of the world's largest office buildings. The five-sided structure, which was completed in 1943 after only 16 months of construction, covers 29 acres and houses branches of the Department of Defense.

Arlington Visitors Center: 1301 S. Joyce St., Arlington, VA 22202; (703) 228-5720 or (800) 677-6267.

Shopping areas: At the Crystal City Metro station there is a collection of underground boutiques, restaurants and clothing stores. Fashion Centre at Pentagon City, at the Pentagon City Metro station, features Macy's, Nordstrom and more than 150 other stores. For above-ground shopping Ballston Common Mall, at Wilson Boulevard and Glebe Road, offers an indoor array of more than 130 stores, including Macy's.

DRUG ENFORCEMENT ADMINISTRATION MUSEUM & VISITORS CENTER is on the ground floor of an office building at 700 Army Navy Dr. (M: Pentagon City). The DEA Museum presents the history of federal drug law enforcement, from 19th-century opium dens to today's organized drug cartels. Displays include drug paraphernalia and items—such as a helicopter and customized motorcycles—confiscated during drug raids. Street parking is limited. Allow 30 minutes minimum. Tues.-Fri. 10-4; closed federal holidays. Free. Phone (202) 307-3463.

FORT MYER is near Arlington National Cemetery, off I-395 exit 8A (Washington Blvd.), following signs. The fort is accessed via Hatfield Gate, off Washington Blvd., or Wright Gate, off Fort Myer Dr. A military post since 1863, tenants include the U.S. Army Band Pershing's Own and the 3rd Infantry (The Old Guard), whose duties include conducting ceremonies for visiting dignitaries and military funerals, serving as escort for the president and standing guard at the Tomb of the Unknowns.

Note: Visitors must show a valid photo ID, and vehicles are subject to search. Arrive early for events. Hatfield Gate open daily 24 hours. Wright Gate open daily 5 a.m.-9 p.m. Free. Phone (703) 696-3944 for information about the fort or (703) 607-8000, ext. 1, for the changing of the guard schedule.

LYNDON BAINES JOHNSON MEMORIAL GROVE is s. of Memorial Bridge along George Washington Memorial Pkwy. in Lady Bird Johnson Park, a Potomac River island. A granite memorial to President Lyndon B. Johnson on the 17-acre island is surrounded by stones inscribed with quotations from his works. Daily dawn-dusk. Free. Phone (703) 289-2500.

◥◣ ARLINGTON NATIONAL CEMETERY (F-5)

Directly across the Potomac River west of Washington (M: Arlington National Cemetery), Arlington National Cemetery was established in 1864 on the confiscated estate of Robert E. Lee. It is an impressive sight, with seemingly endless rows of simple white headstones. Imposing stones and monuments mark the graves of many individuals and groups.

Among those buried are the original owners of the estate, George Washington Parke Custis and his wife Mary Lee Fitzhugh Custis, in addition to Pierre-Charles L'Enfant, President William Howard Taft, Chief Justice Oliver Wendell Holmes Jr., Gen. John J. Pershing, Rear Adm. Robert E. Peary, three-time presidential nominee William Jennings Bryan, Rear Adm. Richard E. Byrd, Lt. Gen. Claire L. Chennault, Gen. Hoyt S. Vandenberg, Secretary of State John Foster Dulles, Gen. George C. Marshall, Chief Justice Earl Warren, President John F. Kennedy, Sen. Robert F. Kennedy, first lady Jacqueline Kennedy Onassis, Gen. Omar Bradley, Medal of Honor recipient Audie Murphy and heavyweight champion boxer Joe Louis.

The cemetery is open daily 8-7, Apr.-Sept.; 8-5, rest of year. Paid parking is available off of Memorial Drive at the visitor center; people visiting gravesites of relatives can obtain a temporary pass to drive into the cemetery.

For the general public, Tourmobiles that leave from the visitor center provide the only motorized transportation through the cemetery (see attraction listing p. 96). A 2-hour narrated tour covers all major points of interest. An interpretive audio tour also can be rented at the visitor center. Parking is $1.25 per hour for the first three hours, $2 per hour thereafter. Tourmobile fare is $6; over 64, $5; ages 3-11, $3.

In order to drive into the cemetery, individuals over 65 must present identification that verifies date of birth; the physically impaired must show their handicapped placard. Phone (703) 607-8000 for visitor information or (202) 554-5100 for Tourmobile information.

◥◣ ARLINGTON HOUSE, THE ROBERT E. LEE MEMORIAL,

off Sherman Dr. on the w. side of the cemetery, is where young Lee courted and married Mary Anna Randolph Custis and where they lived 1831-61. Mrs. Lee inherited the property from her father, George Washington Parke Custis, grandson of Martha Washington. He began building the house in 1802 on land purchased by his father, John Parke Custis. Here in 1861 Lee chose to resign his commission in the U.S. Army to defend his native state.

During the Civil War Union troops occupied the house because of its position commanding the Potomac and the capital. In 1864 the Arlington estate was confiscated on a legal technicality for nonpayment of taxes. After the war George Washington Custis Lee, Lee's eldest son, sued for return of the property. In 1882 the U.S. Supreme Court ruled in his favor, but by then thousands of graves covered the estate. Custis Lee elected to sell everything to the U.S. government for $150,000.

Administered by the National Park Service, the mansion has been restored to its 1861 appearance and contains some of the original Custis and Lee family furnishings. The grand portico faces the river and affords a splendid view of Washington. The Robert E. Lee Museum also is on site.

Note: Arlington House is currently empty of furnishings as it is undergoing restoration. The house will continue to be open to the public with some exceptions; phone ahead to ensure it will be open the day of your visit. Allow 30 minutes minimum. Grounds daily 8-7, Apr.-Sept.; 8-5, rest of year. House daily 9:30-4:30. Museum daily 8-4:30. Closed Jan. 1 and Dec. 25. Free. Phone (703) 235-1530.

CONFEDERATE MEMORIAL, on the w. side of the cemetery off McPherson Dr., was erected by the United Daughters of the Confederacy in 1914 to honor their dead and to symbolize a reunited North and South. The graves of Confederate soldiers and veterans who died in the Washington, D.C., area are arranged in concentric circles around the monument.

THE GRAVE OF PRESIDENT JOHN F. KENNEDY is on the slope below Arlington House. The site is marked by an eternal flame and excerpts from his inaugural address. Next to it is the grave of his wife Jacqueline, their infant son Patrick and an unnamed stillborn daughter. Near them is the grave of his brother, Sen. Robert F. Kennedy, also the victim of an assassin's bullet.

THE L'ENFANT MONUMENT is in front of Arlington House. French engineer Pierre-Charles L'Enfant planned the city of Washington; his original plan is on the monument. Consisting of four white marble slabs, with the upper section supported by six marble posts, the monument marks the site of L'Enfant's grave.

MARINE CORPS WAR MEMORIAL stands on a promontory at the n. end of the cemetery. The memorial is a 78-foot, 100-ton portrayal of Joseph Rosenthal's photograph of the raising of the flag on Iwo Jima during World War II. The figures were cast in bronze from a model created by Felix de Weldon. The Sunset Parade, also known as the Iwo Jima Memorial Parade, is a color ceremony featuring the Marine Silent Drill Team, Color Guard and Drum and Bugle Corps.

Parade begins Tues. at 7, second Tues. in June-third Tues. in Aug. (Aug. parades begin at 6:30). Free bus service to the ceremony runs from the Arlington National Cemetery visitors' parking area. Phone (703) 289-2500, or (202) 433-6060 for parade information.

MAST OF THE BATTLESHIP USS *MAINE* is bordered on two sides by Sigsbee Dr. The battleship was sunk in Havana Harbor on Feb. 15, 1898. The explosion was one of a series of events that led to the beginning of the Spanish-American War. The memorial is surrounded by the graves of the 62 known and 167 unknown men who died in the disaster.

MEMORIAL AMPHITHEATER, just w. of jct. Memorial and Wilson drs., is an elliptical, white marble structure honoring those who have defended the nation. It seats approximately 6,000 people. Unknowns Memorial Display Room, between the amphitheater and the Tomb of the Unknowns, contains tributes to the Unknown Dead of World Wars I and II and the Korean and Vietnam wars. Easter service begins at 6 a.m., Memorial Day and Veterans Day services begin at 11 a.m.

THE NETHERLANDS CARILLON is off US 50 just outside the n. end of the cemetery, next to the Marine Corps War Memorial. This gift from the Netherlands was in gratitude for the United States' aid during and after World War II. Each of the original 49 bells represents a different segment of the Netherlands' population. A 50th bell was added in 1995, on the 50th anniversary of the liberation of the Netherlands. Allow 30 minutes minimum. Concerts are given Sat. and federal holidays 2-4 in May and Sept.; Sat. 6-8, June-Aug. Free. Phone (703) 289-2500.

TOMB OF THE UNKNOWN DEAD OF THE CIVIL WAR is w. of Arlington House off Sherman Dr. The stone and masonry burial vault marks the mass grave of the 2,111 unidentified soldiers who died on nearby Virginia battlefields during the Civil War.

TOMB OF THE UNKNOWNS is s. of Memorial Amphitheater, just w. of jct. Memorial and Wilson drs. Striking in its simplicity, the die piece of Colorado marble on which the sculpture is carved is one of the largest blocks ever quarried. Before carving, it weighed 50 tons. Lying in a sarcophagus beneath the tomb is the body of an unknown American soldier brought back from France after World War I. In 1958 the remains of unknown American military personnel from World War II and the Korean War were interred in marked crypts at the head of the tomb.

Specially selected members of the Army's 3rd U.S. Infantry Regiment (The Old Guard) guard the tomb 24 hours a day. During the day the guard is changed every half-hour, Apr.-Sept.; every hour, rest of year. It is changed every 2 hours throughout the night, all year. Free.

WOMEN IN MILITARY SERVICE FOR AMERICA MEMORIAL, on Memorial Dr. at the entrance to the cemetery, honors women who have served in the nation's defense. The national memorial chronicles their history, beginning with the American Revolution. It includes an education center with exhibits and an interactive computer kiosk. Daily 8-7, Apr.-Sept.; 8-5, rest of year. Closed Dec. 25. Free. Phone (703) 892-2606 or (800) 222-2294.

CHANTILLY pop. 41,041

NATIONAL AIR AND SPACE MUSEUM'S STEVEN F. UDVAR-HAZY CENTER is at 14390 Air and Space Museum Pkwy., near Washington Dulles International Airport. This facility allows the public to see the 80 percent of the Smithsonian's air and space collection that is not on loan or displayed at the museum's building on the National Mall. Until the center opened in 2003, a majority of these artifacts had never before been on display.

Hundreds of famous air- and spacecraft, and thousands of small historic artifacts are displayed, including a supersonic Concorde; the B-29 Superfortress *Enola Gay*, which dropped the first atomic bomb during WWII; Global Flyer, the first airplane to be flown solo, nonstop around the globe without refueling; and the Space Shuttle *Enterprise*, the only real space shuttle on view anywhere.

Free realistic space shuttle and Mission Control simulations can be enjoyed. IMAX films are shown on a five-story theater screen, and various immersive flight simulator experiences are available.

Guided tours and food are available. Open daily 10-5:30; closed Dec. 25. Center free. Fees for IMAX films and flight simulators vary. Parking $12. Phone (202) 633-1000 or TTY (202) 633-5285.

SAVE **SULLY HISTORIC SITE** is on SR 28 about .3 mi. n. of US 50 and 5 mi. s. of the Dulles Toll Rd. at 3601 Sully Rd. This house was built in 1794 by Richard Bland Lee, uncle of Robert E. Lee and northern Virginia's first congressman. The restored house is furnished with antiques of the Federal period and appears much as it did 1795-1811. Features include the kitchen/laundry, smokehouse, stone dairy, slave quarters, and flower and vegetable gardens.

Allow 2 hours minimum. Guided 45-minute house tours are offered Wed.-Mon. on the hour 11-4. Guided outbuildings and grounds tours are given Wed.-Mon. (weather permitting) at 2, Mar. 1 to mid-Nov.; by appointment rest of year. Closed Jan. 1, Thanksgiving and Dec. 25. Hours may vary; phone ahead. Last house tour begins 1 hour before closing.

Grounds free except during events. House tour $6; $5 (students with ID and 60+); $4 (ages 5-15). House and outbuildings tour $8; $7 (students with ID and 60+); $6 (ages 5-15). Phone (703) 437-1794, or TTY (703) 803-3354.

DUMFRIES pop. 4,937

It was from the town of Dumfries in 1800 that the itinerant bookseller and former Anglican priest Parson Mason Locke Weems launched his popular biography "Life of Washington." The highly fictionalized book is best known for its story about young Washington chopping down a cherry tree and confessing to his father, "I cannot tell a lie."

The Weems-Botts Museum, 3914 Cameron St., originally served as Weems' bookshop. The property was later purchased by Benjamin Botts, a prominent defense lawyer who represented Aaron Burr in his 1807 treason trial. Picnic facilities are available; phone (703) 221-2218.

PRINCE WILLIAM FOREST PARK— *see Triangle p. 133.*

FAIRFAX pop. 21,498, elev. 365′

Located in prosperous, populous Fairfax County, Fairfax is the site of the original wills of George and Martha Washington; they are housed in the Judicial Center at 4010 Chain Bridge Rd.

Built in 1800, the original Fairfax County Courthouse at 4000 Chain Bridge Rd. has been used continuously except during the Civil War, when Union troops occupied the town and used it as a stable. A monument to the first Confederate officer killed during the Civil War stands on the courthouse grounds.

Ratcliff-Allison House (Earp's Ordinary), built in the early 1800s, is on Main Street between University Drive and SR 123. In 1820 it began operating as a post office. The original half of the building reflects specifications that were set by the Virginia Assembly for houses built in 1805.

Central Fairfax Chamber of Commerce: 3975 University Dr., Suite 350, Fairfax, VA 22030; phone (703) 591-2450.

Self-guiding tours: The Fairfax Museum and Visitors Center *(see attraction listing)* publishes and distributes an illustrated brochure about local historic buildings and sites.

Shopping areas: Fair Oaks Mall, I-66 and US 50, has more than 200 stores, including JCPenney, Lord & Taylor, Macy's and Sears.

FAIRFAX MUSEUM AND VISITORS CENTER is at 10209 Main St. Housed in the 1873 Historic Fairfax Elementary School, the museum presents changing exhibits about local history. Allow 30 minutes minimum. Daily 9-5; closed Jan. 1, Easter, Thanksgiving and Dec. 25. Free. Phone (703) 385-8414.

NATIONAL FIREARMS MUSEUM is on the main floor of the National Rifle Association's headquarters off I-66 exit 57A; take US 50 .5 mi. e., then .3 mi. n. to 11250 Waples Mill Rd. Displays include antique firearms from wars significant in America's history, as well as modern engraved handguns. Dioramas, historical replicas and guns previously belonging to celebrities also are exhibited. Daily 10-4; closed major holidays. Free. Phone (703) 267-1600.

FALLS CHURCH (F-3) pop. 10,377, elev. 364′

A Fairfax County suburb, Falls Church dates from the mid-1700s and the formation of Truro Parish, for which George Washington was a vestryman 1762-84.

Greater Falls Church Chamber of Commerce: 417 W. Broad St., Falls Church, VA 22046; phone (703) 532-1050.

Shopping areas: Tysons Galleria, SR 123 and International Drive, includes Macy's, Neiman Marcus and Saks Fifth Avenue as well as some 100 specialty shops. Bloomingdale's, JCPenney, Lord & Taylor, Macy's and Nordstrom, plus more than 200 other stores, can be found at Tysons Corner Center, off SRs 7 and 123.

THE FALLS CHURCH (Episcopal) is near jct. US 29 (Lee Hwy.) and SR 7 (Broad St.) at 115 E. Fairfax St. Founded in 1732, the first church building was erected in 1733 near a road that led to the falls of the Potomac River—hence the name that later was adopted by the town. The present building, completed in 1769, served as a recruiting station during the Revolution, and in the Civil War it was used as a Federal hospital.

Renovations to restore the structure to its 18th-century appearance were completed in 1959. Allow 30 minutes minimum. Mon.-Fri. 9-5. Free. Phone (703) 532-7600.

GREAT FALLS pop. 8,549

COLVIN RUN MILL HISTORIC SITE is on SR 7 at Colvin Run Rd., 7 mi. w. of I-495 (Capital Beltway) exit 47A. The restored 19th-century mill still grinds cornmeal and whole wheat flour, and the miller's house and barn contain historical exhibits. A general store also is on the grounds.

Allow 1 hour minimum. Grounds open Wed.-Mon. 11-5, Mar.-Dec.; 11-4, rest of year. Closed Jan. 1, Thanksgiving and Dec. 25. Guided tours are given on the hour. Mill grinds grain Sun. (weather permitting) noon-3. Last tour departs 1 hour before closing. Grounds free except during events. Guided tour $6; $5 (students with ID); $4 (ages 5-15 and 61+). Phone (703) 759-2771, or TTY (703) 324-3988.

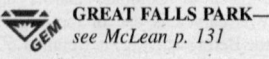 **GREAT FALLS PARK—** *see McLean p. 131*

HERNDON pop. 21,655, elev. 358′

Once a quiet vacation town for Washington's elite citizenry and a main stop on the Washington & Old Dominion Railroad, Herndon is in densely developed Fairfax County just 20 miles west of the nation's capital. The Herndon Depot Museum, maintained by the Herndon Historical Society, has a collection of railroad memorabilia, Civil War information and historic artifacts on loan from local residents. The building served as a train station until

1968 and also houses the Herndon Dulles Visitor's Center.

Herndon Dulles Visitor's Center: 717 Lynn St., Herndon, VA 20170; phone (703) 437-6366.

FRYING PAN PARK is at 2709 West Ox Rd.; take I-495 (Capital Beltway) exit 49 (I-66) w. to the Fairfax County Pkwy. (CR 7100), continue 6 mi. to West Ox Rd., then take West Ox Rd. 1.5 mi. to the park entrance. Rural community history is preserved at this 130-acre park, which contains historic buildings, a nature trail and Kidwell Farm, a 1930s-era working farm.

Visitors can view cows, sheep, goats, pigs, horses, chickens, rabbits, peacocks and a variety of antique farm equipment. Wagon rides are available March through November. Picnicking is permitted. Allow 1 hour minimum. Daily dawn-dusk. Free. Phone (703) 437-9101.

LEESBURG pop. 28,311, elev. 313′

One of the oldest towns in northern Virginia, Leesburg was an outfitting post during the French and Indian War. In 1758 the House of Burgesses passed a bill authorizing the establishment of a town at that site.

During the War of 1812, when the city of Washington was in flames, 22 wagonloads of U.S. documents, including the Declaration of Independence, the Articles of Confederation, the Constitution, much of George Washington's correspondence, and Congressional and State Department records were brought to Leesburg for safekeeping.

The fourth armed engagement of the Civil War took place northeast of Leesburg at Balls Bluff. On Oct. 21, 1861, Confederate forces inflicted devastating losses upon four Union regiments under the command of Col. Edward D. Baker. Among the injured was a 20-year-old lieutenant from Massachusetts, Oliver Wendell Holmes Jr., who later became chief justice of the United States Supreme Court.

The National Cemetery at Balls Bluff is purportedly the smallest in the nation. Surrounding the cemetery is Balls Bluff, a regional park with hiking trails and picnicking; phone (703) 737-7800.

Since 1828 a ferry has carried passengers and freight across the quarter-mile-wide Potomac between a point northeast of Leesburg and Whites Ferry, Md. The *Gen. Jubal Early* still crosses daily dawn to dusk.

Several of Leesburg's older homes are open to the public during Historic Garden Week in late April. The Loudoun Museum (*see attraction listing*) offers guided walking tours of historic Leesburg that are available by reservation May through October; phone (703) 777-7427 or (703) 777-8331.

Loudoun Convention & Visitors Association: 222 Catoctin Cir. S.E., Suite 100, Leesburg, VA 20175; phone (703) 771-2617 or (800) 752-6118.

Self-guiding tours: A walking-tour booklet of Leesburg's historic district is available from the Loudoun Museum.

LEESBURG ANIMAL PARK is at 19270 James Monroe Hwy. It is home to a variety of animals, including parrots and lemurs. Children can touch and feed domesticated animals in a petting area. Pumpkinville includes a trip to a 3-acre farm play area and pumpkin patch in addition to other park activities. Pony and wagon rides also are available.

Allow 1 hour, 30 minutes minimum. Park open Tues.-Sun. 10-3 (also Thurs.-Sun. 3-5), Apr. 1-late Sept. Pumpkinville takes place Tues.-Sun. 9-6, late Sept.-early Nov. Park admission $10. Pony rides $3. Wagon rides $1. MC, VI. Phone (703) 433-0002.

LOUDOUN MUSEUM is at 16 Loudoun St. S.W. It offers visitors a look into Loudoun County's past through displays of memorabilia. Hands-on exhibits, a children's discovery room, an audiovisual presentation, lectures and workshops. Mon. and Wed.-Sat. 10-5, Sun. 1-5; closed Jan. 1, Thanksgiving and Dec. 24-25. Museum admission $3; $1 (senior citizens, students with ID and teachers); free (military and dependents with ID and ages 0-4). Phone (703) 777-7427 or (703) 777-8331.

[SAVE] **MORVEN PARK** is w. on SR 7 Bus. Rte., then n. on Morven Park Rd. and w. on Old Waterford Rd. The gardens of this 1,200-acre estate surround the Westmoreland Davis Mansion, which contains the Museum of Hounds and Hunting. Historical tours of the grounds include such highlights as the Winmill Carriage Collection, displaying more than 70 antique carriages, and replicas of three log huts similar to those built on the property by Southern troops during the Civil War.

Note: The mansion is closed while undergoing a multiyear preservation effort that includes restoration of the interior; it is expected to reopen in 2009. While the mansion is closed for renovation, living-history programs and historic estate tours will continue to be offered Fri.-Mon. 11-4; other days by appointment. Fee $5; $1 (ages 6-12). Reservations are required for weekday tours. Phone (703) 777-2414, or (703) 777-6034 for tour information.

[GEM] **OATLANDS** is about 6 mi. s. on US 15 to 20850 Oatlands Plantation Ln. This stately 22-room, 1804 mansion combines Federal and Greek Revival styles. The house is furnished with French, English and American art and antiques. Just 261 of the plantation's original 3,408 acres remain. The grounds retain the original basic design, with 4 acres of formal gardens and an 1810 greenhouse. The surrounding fields are the setting for point-to-point races, fairs, dog shows and many other events.

Picnicking is permitted. Allow 1 hour minimum. Mon.-Sat. 10-5, Sun. 1-5, Apr. 1-Dec. 30; closed Thanksgiving and Dec. 24-25. Guided 30- to 45-minute tours are given on the hour. Last tour begins 1 hour before closing. Fee $10; $9 (ages 61+); $7 (ages 6-16). Garden tour only $7. MC, VI. Phone (703) 777-3174.

WINERIES

• **Tarara Vineyard and Winery** is 8 mi. n. on US 15 (James Monroe Hwy.), then 3 mi. e. on SR 662 (Lucketts Rd.) following signs to 13648 Tarara Ln. Daily 11-5; closed Easter, Thanksgiving and Dec. 25. Last tasting is 30 minutes before closing. Phone (703) 771-7100.

LORTON pop. 17,786, elev. 100′

Fairfax County Visitor Center: 8180-A Silverbrook Rd., Lorton, VA 22079; phone (703) 550-2450 or (800) 732-4732.

GUNSTON HALL PLANTATION is s. off US 1 via SR 242 to 10709 Gunston Rd. George Mason, the author of the Virginia Declaration of Rights of 1776 and one of the framers of the U.S. Constitution, designed and lived in this 1755 brick Georgian residence. A visitor center offers an 11-minute orientation film called "George Mason and the Bill of Rights."

English architect William Buckland also designed many elements in the home, including a variety of woodcarvings. The English and American furnishings are from the 18th century and earlier. Guided tours are given of the main floor; visitors may take a self-guiding tour of the second-story bedrooms and grounds.

Next to the main house are such reconstructed outbuildings as the kitchen, laundry, dairy, smokehouse and schoolhouse. The 18th-century gardens contain an original English boxwood allée, reconstructed pebble pathways and viewing mounds. Deer and eagle sightings are possible from a nature trail leading to the Potomac River.

Allow 1 hour minimum. Daily 9:30-5; closed Jan. 1, Thanksgiving and Dec. 25. House tours are given daily every half-hour. Last tour begins 30 minutes before closing. Admission $8; $7 (ages 60+); $4 (students in grades 1-12). Phone (703) 550-9220.

POHICK CHURCH (Episcopal) is 2 mi. s.w. on US 1 at 9301 Richmond Hwy. This was the Colonial parish church of Mount Vernon, Gunston Hall and Belvoir. George Washington chose the site and served as vestryman for 23 years. George Mason, a vestryman for 37 years, served on the building committee.

During the Civil War the original 1774 interior was torn out by Union troops and the building was used as a stable. The building was restored 1902-17. The old stone baptismal font was found many years later serving as a trough in a nearby farmyard. Mon.-Fri. 9-4:30, Sat.-Sun. 10-5. Free. Phone (703) 339-6572.

MANASSAS pop. 35,135, elev. 312′

The juncture of the Manassas Gap and the Orange & Alexandria railroads in the 1850s created the hamlet of Manassas (ma-NAS-sas). During the Civil War this tiny junction became a bloody pawn between two contending armies. Fought over and burned, Manassas was a key to the heart of Virginia and the site for hospitals, fortifications and supply depots for both North and the South.

When the war ended, the railroad became the basis of the town's economy, which was further spurred in the last half of the 20th century by the growth of the Washington, D.C. metropolitan area. The Historic Manassas Visitor Center is at 9431 West St.; phone (703) 361-6599.

Prince William County/Manassas Convention and Visitors Bureau: 8609 Sudley Rd., Suite 105, Manassas, VA 20110; phone (703) 396-7130 or (800) 432-1792.

Self-guiding tours: Brochures outlining driving and walking tours are available from the Historic Manassas Visitor Center and The Manassas Museum *(see attraction listing).*

THE MANASSAS MUSEUM is at 9101 Prince William St. The museum depicts the history and culture of Manassas and the northern Virginia Piedmont region through artifacts, photographs and videotape presentations. Highlights include 19th-century toys, a Confederate regimental flag, weapons and African-American history exhibits. Living-history programs are presented throughout the year.

Tues.-Sun. and Mon. federal holidays 10-5; closed Jan. 1, Thanksgiving and Dec. 24-25. Admission $4; $3 (ages 6-16 and 65+). Phone (703) 368-1873.

MANASSAS NATIONAL BATTLEFIELD PARK

Manassas National Battlefield Park, on SR 234 between I-66 and US 29, marks the site north of the strategically important railroad junction at Manassas where two great battles of the Civil War—the First and Second Battles of Manassas, or Bull Run—were fought.

On July 21, 1861, picnickers and other sightseers observed a well-equipped but ill-trained Union Army under Gen. Irvin McDowell as it battled the Confederate Army under Gens. Pierre Beauregard and Joseph Johnston. After 10 hours of deadly fighting it became apparent that this conflict was not going to decide the war, as most had expected. The Union army, finally broken by Confederate forces, was forced to retreat toward Washington, D.C. It was at this battle that Gen. Thomas J. Jackson earned the nickname Stonewall.

When the armies returned to the plains of Manassas in August 1862, they were no longer young recruits in colorful new uniforms. A year of war had hardened both armies and brought the Confederacy to the peak of its power, soon to be realized with the outcome of this battle. The encounter also proved to be a bloody demonstration of Robert E. Lee's genius, as he defeated the larger army of Gen. John Pope in 3 days of fighting.

A walking trail on Henry Hill offers scenic views of the first battlefield. The focal point of the hill is an equestrian statue of Gen. Stonewall Jackson. The Stone House, which served as a field hospital in both battles, is open seasonally. A driving tour of the park encompasses the main points of the second battle as well as areas involved in both engagements. Two 5-mile hikes around the battlefield are detailed in a pamphlet available at the visitor center.

The Second Manassas Expedition Guide tape and CD driving tour by TravelBrains is available at the visitor center and by mail; phone (888) 458-6475. The Henry Hill Visitor Center has a museum and theater that shows the 45-minute film "Manassas: End of Innocence"; a 3-D map illustrates the strategies of the first battle.

Grounds open daily dawn-dusk. Visitor center open daily 8:30-5; closed Thanksgiving and Dec. 25. Stone House open daily 1-4, June-Aug. Park admission $3, under 17 free. Theater admission $3, under 17 free. For information phone the visitor center at (703) 361-1339 or the park headquarters at (703) 754-1861.

McLEAN (D-2) pop. 38,929, elev. 303'

SAVE **THE CLAUDE MOORE COLONIAL FARM AT TURKEY RUN** is 2.5 mi. e. on SR 193 from I-495 exit 44 to 6310 Georgetown Pike. This is a small-scale representation of a homestead during the late Colonial period, with a costumed family performing the farm tasks. In addition to field crops, heritage breeds of cattle, chickens, turkeys and hogs are on the farm. Re-enactments of Colonial market fairs are held on the third full weekend in May, July and October.

Allow 30 minutes minimum. Wed.-Sun. 10-4:30, Apr. 1 to mid-Dec.; closed Thanksgiving. Admission $3; $2 (ages 3-12 and 61+). An additional fee may be charged during events. Phone (703) 442-7557.

GEM **GREAT FALLS PARK** is w. on SR 193 to Old Dominion Dr. Here the Potomac River plunges a total of 77 feet in a series of picturesque falls and thundering rapids. One-mile-long Mather Gorge is walled by irregular palisades. Biking, cross-country skiing and kayaking are among the possible recreational activities.

Within the 800-acre park are remnants of a skirting canal constructed about 1785 by the Patowmack Co., of which George Washington was founder and president. The canal had a series of locks that enabled boats to re-enter the river after having bypassed the falls. There is no direct access between the Virginia and Maryland sides. The Maryland side is part of Chesapeake and Ohio Canal National Historical Park *(see Chesapeake and Ohio Canal National Historical Park, Md., p. 189).*

Note: Extreme care must be taken when visiting this beautiful but hazardous natural area. Signs indicate treacherous spots. Stay on the trails and observe the signs. Picnicking is permitted, but alcoholic beverages are not. Park grounds open daily 7 a.m.-dusk. Admission $5 per private vehicle (valid for 3 days); $3 per person (on foot or horseback or by bicycle, bus or motorcycle).

Visitor Center is within walking distance of the falls overlooks at 9200 Old Dominion Dr. The center has displays, a slide show about park history and changing exhibits. Ranger-led and historical programs vary with the seasons. Picnicking is permitted. Daily 10-4; extended hours during spring and summer, call ahead. Closed Dec. 25. Phone (703) 285-2965.

THEODORE ROOSEVELT ISLAND is accessible by pedestrian bridge from the Virginia shore; a parking lot is off the northbound lane of George Washington Memorial Pkwy. just n. of the Theodore Roosevelt Bridge. The island lies in the Potomac River between Rosslyn, Va., and The John F. Kennedy Center for the Performing Arts (M: Rosslyn).

This 88.5-acre memorial honors the nation's 26th president. A massive granite monument includes a 17-foot bronze statue of Roosevelt and four towering slabs inscribed with his ideas about nature, youth, manhood and the state. More than 50 species of trees and some 200 varieties of wildflowers flourish. Wayside exhibits are in English and Spanish. Dogs on leash are permitted. Allow 30 minutes minimum. Daily dawn-dusk. Free. Phone (703) 289-2500.

MOUNT VERNON pop. 28,582

GEORGE WASHINGTON'S MOUNT VERNON ESTATE & GARDENS is at the s. end of George Washington Memorial Pkwy. overlooking the Potomac River. George Washington's residence at Mount Vernon, from 1783 until his death in 1799, was interrupted by his tenure as president. Both George and Martha Washington are buried here.

John Washington, great-grandfather of George, was granted land on the upper Potomac between Little Hunting Creek and Dogue Run, which became the Mount Vernon homesite in 1674. Washington family members occupied Mount Vernon over the years, and in 1754, George acquired the plantation, enlarging and improving the mansion and estate.

The mansion has been restored to appear as it was during the last year of Washington's life and contains much of the original furniture. Displays include the bed in which Washington died, his sword and the key to the Bastille presented to him by Marquis de Lafayette, which are in the Donald W. Reynolds Museum *(see attraction listing)*. Visitors can tour Washington's tomb, gardens and 12 outbuildings. The Pioneer Farmer site offers hands-on activities and contains a reconstruction of Washington's round barn, where horses walk the second floor threshing wheat.

Note: Baby strollers are not permitted inside the mansion. Allow 1 hour minimum. Daily 8-5, Apr.-Aug.; 9-5 in Mar. and Sept.-Oct.; 9-4, rest of year. Grounds are cleared 30 minutes after closing. Admission $13; $12 (ages 62+); $6 (ages 6-11). Combination ticket with George Washington's Gristmill $15; $7.50 (ages 6-11). AX, MC, VI. Phone (703) 780-2000, or TTY (703) 799-8697.

Donald W. Reynolds Museum and Education Center is at the s. end of George Washington Memorial Pkwy. at George Washington's Mount Vernon Estate & Gardens. Visitors can learn about George Washington in 23 galleries and theaters with interactive displays, short videos and a collection of some 700 items. Computers provide access to more than 20,000 letters penned by Washington.

Museum highlights include a bust of the first president sculpted by Jean-Antoine Houdon noted for its remarkable likeness; objects accumulated by Washington from Europe and other parts of the world; historic articles relating to Washington's military career and presidency; a gallery offering a behind-the-scenes glimpse into the daily lives of the Washington family; and a collection of books, manuscripts and maps. A gallery of changing exhibits also is on site.

The education center features original videos produced by The History Channel offering viewers a state-of-the-art theater experience depicting Washington's life story. Allow 1 hour minimum. Daily 8-5, Apr.-Aug.; 9-5 in Mar. and Sept.-Oct.; 9-4, rest of year. Admission included in ticket to George Washington's Mount Vernon Estate & Gardens. Phone (703) 780-2000.

Ford Orientation Center is at the s. end of George Washington Memorial Pkwy. at George Washington's Mount Vernon Estate & Gardens. "We Fight to be Free," a 25-minute video, provides general information about Mount Vernon as well as insight into the challenges George Washington faced during his life. In addition, visitors can explore a one-twelfth scaled replica of the Mount Vernon mansion, complete with operational windows, fireplaces and doorknobs. Allow 30 minutes minimum. Daily 8-5, Apr.-Aug.; 9-5 in Mar. and Sept.-Oct.; 9-4, rest of year. Admission included in ticket to George Washington's Mount Vernon Estate & Gardens. Phone (703) 780-2000.

George Washington's Whiskey Distillery & Gristmill is in a small park 3 mi. s. of Mount Vernon on SR 235. Demonstrations by costumed distillers take visitors through the historic process of whiskey making in this reconstruction of what is reputedly the largest 18th-century distillery in America. The distillery is adjacent to the reconstructed gristmill, a water-powered mill where guides in period garb grind corn into meal and wheat into flour just as it was done by millers more than 200 years ago. Together, these buildings showcase Washington's entrepreneurship and his vision for the nation's future.

Guided tours are available. Picnicking is permitted. Allow 1 hour minimum. Daily 10-5, Apr.-Oct. Admission $4; $2 (ages 6-11). Combination ticket with Mount Vernon Estate & Gardens $15; $7.50 (ages 6-11). Phone (703) 360-1750.

Mount Vernon Sightseeing Cruises on the Potomac River is at the s. end of George Washington Memorial Pkwy. at George Washington's Mount Vernon Estate & Gardens. Departing from Mount Vernon's wharf, the 40-minute cruise provides scenic views of the estate, with some narration provided. The boat travels just beyond Fort Washington, then turns around. Allow 45 minutes minimum. Tues.-Sun. at 10:30, 11:30, 12:30, 2 and 3, May-Aug.; Sat.-Sun. at 10:30, 11:30, 12:30, 2 and 3 in Apr. and Sept. Admission $9; $5 (ages 6-11). AX, MC, VI. Phone (703) 780-2000.

OCCOQUAN pop. 759, elev. 80′

The historic town of Occoquan, its name taken from a Dogue Indian word meaning "at the end of the water," was a recognized community in 1734. By the late 18th century the area was a thriving port and milling town dependent on the waterpower of the Occoquan River. During the Civil War Gen. Wade Hampton made his headquarters in the Hammill Hotel, today a collection of shops and offices.

One of Virginia's first cotton mills, built in 1828, hummed with 1,000 spindles before it was silenced by fire during the Civil War. The village flourished until deepening silt in the Occoquan River prevented vessels from reaching the mills.

Prince William County Visitor Information Center: 200 Mill St., Occoquan, VA 22125; phone (703) 491-4045.

Self-guiding tours: A brochure offering a walking tour of the historic district and a list of local artists and galleries is available at the visitor information center.

Shopping areas: There are more than 120 specialty shops in the compact historic district. Many are housed in original historic buildings and offer antiques and crafts. Several miles south via I-95 is Potomac Mills, which has more than 225 factory outlet stores including Benetton, Calvin Klein, IKEA, Laura Ashley, Nordstrom Rack and Sears.

QUANTICO pop. 561, elev. 35′

Quantico is one of the nation's largest Marine Corps installations and the site of the Marine Corps Combat Development Command. At the entrance is a replica of the Marine Corps War Memorial, a statue depicting the flag raising on Mount Suribachi during the World War II battle for Iwo Jima. The original stands at the north end of Arlington National Cemetery *(see place listing p. 126).*

Quantico National Cemetery is off I-95 on CR 619W. Ceremonies on Memorial Day and Veterans Day feature color guards from area veterans' organizations.

 NATIONAL MUSEUM OF THE MARINE CORPS is at 18900 Jefferson Davis Hwy.

The building's stunning design captivates visitors as they enter by way of the Leatherneck Gallery, where aircraft hang from the ceiling. Adjacent to the gallery, the Legacy Walk contains a timeline and leads to areas depicting various actions the Marines have been involved in.

Visitors can learn about Marines in boot camp, World War II, the Korean War and Vietnam as well as the role of the Marines in the global war on terrorism. A gallery of combat art contains nearly 8,000 works. Allow 4 hours minimum. Daily 9-5; closed Dec. 25. Free. Phone (877) 635-1775.

STERLING elev. 300′

LOUDOUN HERITAGE FARM MUSEUM is 2 mi. n. on SR 28, 1 mi. e. on Church Rd., then .4 mi. n. on Cascades Pkwy. to the Claude Moore Park entrance. Some 300 years of agricultural history unfold at this facility tracing the ventures of 10 generations of Loudoun County residents. Much of the original Waxpool General Store, in operation 1890-1946, has been reconstructed inside the museum. Kids also can dress up and play farmer for the day in an interactive exhibit area.

Allow 1 hour minimum. Tues.-Sat. 10-5, Sun. noon-5; closed Jan. 1 and Dec. 25. Admission $5; $4 (senior citizens); $3 (ages 2-12). DS, MC, VI. Phone (703) 421-5322.

TRIANGLE pop. 5,500, elev. 161′

PRINCE WILLIAM FOREST PARK is accessed by taking I-95 s. to exit 150B, then .2 mi. w. to Joplin Rd. (SR 619). Covering more than 15,000 acres, the park offers hikers more than 37 miles of hiking trails and 21 miles of biking trails. Cabins and camping facilities are available. Park rangers offer regularly scheduled interpretive programs. Historic and nature exhibits are displayed at the Pine Grove Visitor Center.

Only campers and cabin occupants are admitted after dark, except when there are evening programs. Park open daily dawn-dusk. Visitor center open daily 9-5. Admission (valid for 1 week) $5 per private vehicle; $3 per person (on foot or by bicycle, bus or motorcycle). Phone (703) 221-7181. *See the Virginia Recreation Chart and the AAA Mideastern CampBook.*

VIENNA pop. 14,453, elev. 345′

WOLF TRAP NATIONAL PARK FOR THE PERFORMING ARTS is off I-495 (Capital Beltway) exit 45, then SR 267 (Dulles Toll Rd.) w. to exit 15. Wolf Trap is the only national park dedicated to the performing arts. Opera, symphony, jazz, folk, musical, country, dance and popular music productions are presented from late May to early September. The Filene Center, the largest of Wolf Trap's several venues, is an open-air pavilion with a sloping lawn that can accommodate an audience of 7,028; it is situated in a setting of rolling hills and woodland.

Picnicking is permitted. Food is available. Park open daily 7 a.m.-dusk. Park closes 2 hours prior to and 1 hour following festivals and Filene Center performances. Event schedule varies; phone ahead. Park free. Lawn seating for Filene Center shows starts at $8; other ticket prices vary by performance. Check local newspapers for schedules and prices. AX, MC, VI. Phone (703) 255-1800 for general information or (877) 965-3872 daily 10-9 for ticket information.

The Barns at Wolf Trap is .25 mi. s. of Wolf Trap at 1635 Trap Rd. This 382-seat facility—Wolf Trap's indoor performance space—has superb acoustics created by the wood interior and enhanced by a state-of-the-art sound system. Bluegrass, chamber music, country, folk, jazz, zydeco and other performances take place October to mid-May; phone the Barns box office for event schedule.

Shows $16-$35. Reservations are required. MC, VI. Phone (703) 938-2404 for general information or (877) 965-3872 daily 10-9 for ticket information.

Vietnam Veterans Memorial / © AAA / Denise E. Campbell

This ends listings for the Washington, D.C. Vicinity.

Maryland

"'Nevermore,' Quoth the raven..."

Today the local Ravens and Orioles say "hike" and "play ball"

Ocean City

Ride the roller coasters, shop or eat your way along the boardwalk

"duty, honor and loyalty..."

The U.S. Naval Academy— a state-of-the-art institution, tempered by traditional values

Centuries of Sentries

Fort Frederick, Fort McHenry, Fort Washington, Antietam, Monocacy and Aberdeen

"Athens of America"

Fine Georgian buildings reflect the status of Annapolis in the early 1700s

from shore to sparkling shore

Antietam National Battlefield / © Laurence Parent

Maryland's identity is anchored in the waters that boldly sprawl across its inland mass. How could it not be? There's water all over the place!

Twenty-three principal rivers and numerous other bays infiltrate this gun-shaped state. More than 400 miles of water are tributary to the Chesapeake Bay.

Of Maryland's 23 counties, 16 border the tidal shoreline. So, too, do the state's largest city, Baltimore, and its capital, Annapolis.

It's not just simple ubiquity that makes all this water so vital; it's everything the water sustains.

The harvesting of crabs, clams and oysters provided a livelihood for

generations of watermen who plied the
Chesapeake—named for the American
Indian word *chesepiook,* meaning "great
shellfish bay"—in skipjacks.

The Port of Baltimore is a hub
of international importing and
exporting.

Central to the national defense, the
U.S. Naval Academy produces many of
the top
officers
in the U.S. Navy
and Marine Corps.

And, of course,
where there's lots of water, there's
opportunity galore for recreation.

Labor and leisure exist in harmony on
Maryland's expansive shore.

"Maryland is for crabs."

Or at least that's the tongue-in-cheek slogan a witty T-shirt manufacturer made popular in the 1970s as a parody of the motto coined by the state's southern neighbor, Virginia.

Literally speaking, the state *is* for crabs. Heck, the Maryland blue variety is the state crustacean. And it's for oysters and clams, too. It's a genuine water wonderland.

As if the fact that Maryland has a state crustacean isn't curious enough, its maritime past also is recalled via the similarly unusual claim of a state boat—the skipjack—and a state dog, the Chesapeake Bay retriever, named for a prominent tributary.

Although the Atlantic coastline stretches just 31 miles, that distance multiplies more than a hundredfold—to 3,190 miles—if you factor in the shoreline along the rivers and bays.

Exhibits at the Baltimore and Chesapeake Bay maritime museums and the Calvert Marine Museum all recall the importance of water in Maryland's history.

Even the name of one of its counties—Allegany—means "beautiful stream."

In addition to an attractive setting, the state boasts its fair share of human achievers—musicians, actors and writers who together constitute a veritable fountain of creativity.

A Cultured Pool of Talent

A grave in Mount Olivet Cemetery in Frederick serves as a lasting tribute to Francis Scott Key, who was born and buried in the same state where he composed "The Star-Spangled Banner."

Ragtime performer Eubie Blake perfected his talents in the honky-tonks of Baltimore, his hometown. Another Baltimore-born musician, Billie Holiday, gave her beautiful voice to the rich sounds of jazz and the blues.

Acclaimed Shakespearean actor Ira Aldridge, of Bel Air, performed for a U.S. president, Queen Victoria and the archduke of Chambory.

Although he never attended the U.S. Naval Academy in Annapolis, let alone served so much as a day in any branch of the service, Baltimore resident Tom Clancy is a commanding author of military drama.

A pair of Baltimore-bred writers, no doubt influenced by the city's decidedly blue-collar roots, shared a penchant for politics. Upton

Maryland Historical Timeline

1729 — Baltimore Town is established.

1784 — The Treaty of Paris, ending the Revolutionary War, is ratified at Annapolis.

1814 — Francis Scott Key writes the "Star-Spangled Banner" following the bombardment of Fort McHenry.

1845 — The U.S. Naval Academy is founded at Annapolis.

1862 — America's bloodiest battle so far is fought at Antietam during the Civil War.

© David Forbert/SuperStock

1893 — The Johns Hopkins School of Medicine opens in Baltimore.

Sinclair espoused the cause of socialism in "The Jungle," while the writings of H.L. Mencken show a libertarian lean.

It was in Baltimore that master of the macabre Edgar Allan Poe fell in love with his cousin, who was 13 when the two exchanged vows. Displays in the Enoch Pratt Free Library explore his mysterious life; Poe's grave lies in the city's Historic Westminster Hall and Burying Ground.

A formidable literary inspiration was born in Charles County. Josiah Henson, who observed the treatment of slaves, was interviewed by Harriet Beecher Stowe and inspired her novel, "Uncle Tom's Cabin."

Making Progressive Strides

Although its links to a creative past are impressive, Maryland's visionaries have had a much more definitive impact on history.

Harriett Tubman, born in Dorchester County, escaped from slavery and returned to the South to help more than 300 other slaves flee via the Underground Railroad. One of the former stops on this route now operates as the Baltimore Civil War Museum.

During a 1909 expedition, Baltimore-born Matthew A. Henson placed the Stars and Stripes at the North Pole.

Despite dropping out of school at age 12, entrepreneur Johns Hopkins amassed a fortune through hard work and wise investments. His legacy lives on in the Baltimore hospital and university that bear his name.

Baltimore native Thurgood Marshall was a highly regarded lawyer and civil rights pioneer before serving as the first African-American justice on the U.S. Supreme Court.

Although he never played for the Orioles, Baltimore native Babe Ruth propelled the game of baseball to a higher level as he unleashed the home run-hitting power that earned him the nickname "Sultan of Swat." Displays in the Babe Ruth Birthplace Museum pay tribute to him and other Maryland baseball greats, including Cal Ripken Jr.

Maryland's doors have opened wide to a long list of fascinating folks. From its rolling western mountains to its eastern coastal plain, it's ready to welcome you, too.

Maryland becomes the first state in the Union to adopt an income tax.
1938

Middle East peace talks between Israel and the Palestine Liberation Organization take place at Wye River Conference Center, resulting in the signing of the Wye River Memorandum on Oct. 23.
1998

1973
Urban renewal in Baltimore is encouraged through the "homesteading" of abandoned properties.

2000
Maryland is the first state to require built-in locks on all new handguns sold after Jan.1, 2003.

2002
By winning the lieutenant governor post, Michael Steele becomes the first African-American elected to statewide office in Maryland.

© Stefan Zaklin/epa/Corbis

Recreation

With the Atlantic Ocean lapping at its eastern shores and the Potomac River and Chesapeake Bay reaching like crooked fingers into the mainland, Maryland is a water lover's dream.

Soak up the sun, relish the scenery or go **swimming** in the breakers at Assateague Island National Seashore, near Berlin.

Once you've received permission to go **scuba diving,** slip into your wet suit and explore the underwater world of the William Houck Area in Cunningham Falls State Park, off SR 77 west of Thurmont. Phone (301) 271-7574 for details about submitting requests.

Wind surfing is good at Chesapeake Beach; Gunpowder Falls State Park, east of Chase; Kentmoor Marina on Kent Island, 5 miles south of US 50 on SR 8; and Sandy Point State Park, east of Cape St. Claire. **Sailing** is huge almost anywhere you find water. Annapolis is especially scenic.

For a rough-and-tumble adventure, check out **white-water rafting** on the Potomac and Youghiogheny (the "Yock") rivers. Runs on the latter have such colorful names as Meatcleaver and Backbender. **Canoeing** and **kayaking** trips are a peaceful diversion in the Patuxent River in Calvert County and the Patapsco River, near Ellicott City. The section of the Potomac River at Great Falls also is popular; portages are necessary at most locks.

Catch of the Day

Greenbrier Lake in Boonsboro is a big **fishing** destination because of its trout, bluegill and bass. The coffee-colored waters of the Pocomoke River near Snow Hill are home to largemouth bass, catfish and crappie. Annapolis, Crisfield, Point Lookout, Solomons and Tilghman Island are favorite starting points for bay fishing, which yields bluefish, channel bass, croakers and trout. Excellent marlin grounds lie off Ocean City.

Assawoman Bay, north of Ocean City, is a **clamming** hot spot. Popular spots for **crabbing** line the rivers and bay in southern Maryland and the eastern shore, particularly at Deal Island and Point Lookout.

Flintstone's Billmeyer/Belle Grove Wildlife Management Area—with its plentiful populations of turkeys, ruffed grouse, woodcocks, deer, squirrels and rabbits—is prime **hunting** territory. Such waterfowl as Canada geese,

wigeons, pintails, shovelers and black ducks abound at Deal Island. Contact the Maryland Department of Natural Resources for information about fishing and hunting licenses.

The Chesapeake and Ohio Canal Trail (the C & O)—a 184-mile route between Cumberland and the Georgetown neighborhood of Washington, D.C.—caters to anyone who enjoys **bicycling.** You can take a pleasant, shaded ride at the Georgetown end or, if you're up to it, tackle the entire stretch. The 15 miles of paths in Patuxent River Park, south of Upper Marlboro, challenge off-road cyclists.

Sharing the Trails with Snakes

The **hiking** trails at Cunningham Falls State Park, south of Thurmont, are tough. Although the rocky, wooded terrain makes for an exciting trek, it's also an ideal habitat for copperheads and rattlesnakes.

Stake out a spot on the water's edge and enjoy a secluded **camping** getaway in Janes Island State Park, west of Crisfield. The island is accessible only by boat.

Catch some cold-weather exercise while **cross-country skiing** in New Germany and Herrington Manor state parks, both in Garrett County; or **snowshoeing** through Catoctin Mountain Park in Thurmont. Let the chill nip at your nose as you take on the **downhill skiing** runs at Wisp Ski Resort, in McHenry, or go **snowmobiling** on the ungroomed trails in Potomac State Forest.

If you're up for an unusual pursuit, check out the state sport: **jousting.** Competitors on horseback charge through an arena and catch rings of decreasing size on a lance. Maryland's most renowned tournament is held the last Saturday in August in Port Republic.

Recreational Activities

Throughout the TourBook, you may notice a Recreational Activities heading with bulleted listings of recreation-oriented establishments listed underneath. Similar operations also may be mentioned in Destination City recreation sections. Since normal AAA inspection criteria cannot be applied, these establishments are presented only for information. Age, height and weight restrictions may apply. Reservations often are recommended and sometimes are required. Addresses and/or phone numbers are provided so visitors can contact the attraction for additional information.

Fast Facts

POPULATION: 5,296,486.

AREA: 10,577 square miles; ranks 42nd.

CAPITAL: Annapolis.

HIGHEST POINT: 3,360 ft., Backbone Mountain.

LOWEST POINT: Sea level, Atlantic Ocean.

TIME ZONE(S): Eastern. DST.

MINIMUM AGE FOR UNRESTRICTED DRIVER'S LICENSE: 17 years, 9 months.

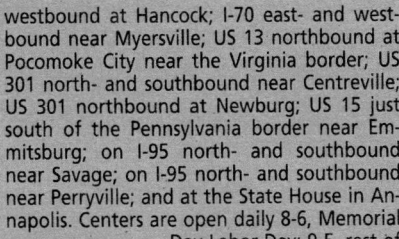

SEAT BELT/CHILD RESTRAINT LAWS: Seat belts required for driver and front-seat passengers 16 and older. Children ages 6 until 16 and over 40 lbs. are required to be in a child restraint or seat belt; child restraints required for under 6 years or less than 41 lbs.

HELMETS FOR MOTORCYCLISTS: Required for all riders.

RADAR DETECTORS: Permitted.

FIREARMS LAWS: Vary by state and/or county. Contact Maryland State Police, Handgun Permits, 1711 Belmont Ave., Baltimore, MD 21244; phone (410) 799-0191.

HOLIDAYS: Jan. 1; Martin Luther King Jr.'s Birthday, Jan. (3rd Mon.); President's Day, Feb. (3rd Mon.); Memorial Day, May (last Mon.); July 4; Labor Day, Sept. (1st Mon.); Columbus Day, Oct. (2nd Mon.); Presidential Election, Nov. (1st Tues.); Veterans Day, Nov. 11; Thanksgiving, Nov. (4th Thurs.); Day after Thanksgiving; Christmas, Dec. 25.

TAXES: Maryland's statewide sales tax is 5 percent. A 1 to 13 percent lodging and amusement tax also may be imposed. An 11.5 percent tax is imposed on short-term passenger car and recreational vehicle rentals.

INFORMATION CENTERS: State welcome centers are on I-68 eastbound from the West Virginia border near Friendsville; I-68 east- and westbound at Hancock; I-70 east- and westbound near Myersville; US 13 northbound at Pocomoke City near the Virginia border; US 301 north- and southbound near Centreville; US 301 northbound at Newburg; US 15 just south of the Pennsylvania border near Emmitsburg; on I-95 north- and southbound near Savage; on I-95 north- and southbound near Perryville; and at the State House in Annapolis. Centers are open daily 8-6, Memorial Day-Labor Day; 9-5, rest of year. Hours may vary. Centers are closed Jan. 1, Easter, Thanksgiving and Dec. 25.

AREA CODE REQUIRED: Whenever you make a local call within Maryland you must dial the area code as well as the seven-digit telephone number.

FURTHER INFORMATION FOR VISITORS:

> Maryland Office of Tourism Development
> Redwood Tower, 9th Floor
> 217 E. Redwood St.
> Baltimore, MD 21202
> (800) 394-5725 *See color ad p. 149.*

RECREATION INFORMATION:

Maryland Department of Natural Resources
State Forest and Parks Service
580 Taylor Ave.
Annapolis, MD 21401
(410) 260-8186

FISHING AND HUNTING REGULATIONS:

Fishing:

Fisheries Administration
Maryland Department of Natural Resources
580 Taylor Ave.
Annapolis, MD 21401
(800) 688-3467

Hunting:

Wildlife Division
Maryland Department of Natural Resources
Tawes State Office Bldg., Wing E1
Annapolis, MD 21401
(410) 260-8540

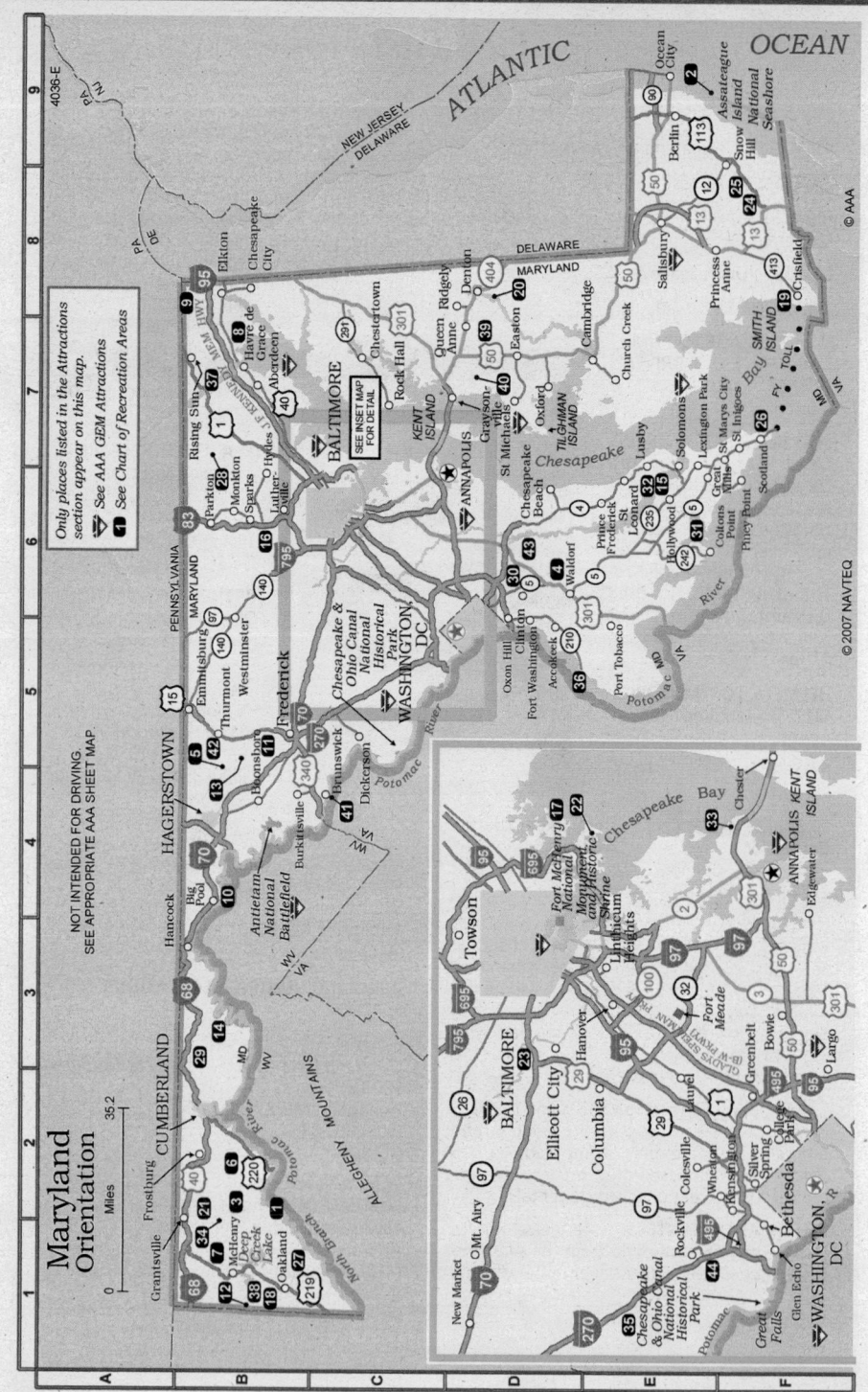

Maryland Orientation

Only places listed in the Attractions section appear on this map.

🚶 See AAA GEM Attractions
① See Chart of Recreation Areas

NOT INTENDED FOR DRIVING.
SEE APPROPRIATE AAA SHEET MAP.

© AAA

© 2007 NAVTEQ

4036-E

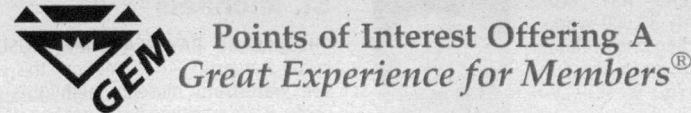

Points of Interest Offering A Great Experience for Members®

Aberdeen (B-7)

U.S. ARMY ORDNANCE MUSEUM—Trace the development of 20th-century weaponry through this collection of items from small arms to combat vehicles. See p. 179.

Annapolis (F-4)

HAMMOND-HARWOOD HOUSE—This fine example of late American Colonial architecture is furnished with Early American decorative arts pieces. See p. 180.

MARYLAND STATE HOUSE—The Treaty of Paris, which officially ended the Revolutionary War, was ratified here. See p. 181.

U.S. NAVAL ACADEMY—A military institution since 1845, the academy is the undergraduate college of the U.S. Navy and captures history in its buildings and exhibits. See p. 182.

WILLIAM PACA HOUSE AND GARDEN—After the garden was paved over with asphalt in the mid-20th century, it was reconstructed using careful research, aerial photography and the features in the background of Charles Wilson Peale's portrait of William Paca. See p. 183.

Antietam National Battlefield (B-4)

ANTIETAM NATIONAL BATTLEFIELD—On September 17, 1862, more than 126,000 Union and Confederate troops clashed at this site at Sharpsburg, resulting in so many casualties that it has been called the bloodiest day of the Civil War. See p. 161.

Baltimore (C-7)

BALTIMORE & OHIO RAILROAD MUSEUM—Visit this railroad station and view the extensive collection of locomotives and railroad memorabilia in this 40-acre indoor/outdoor museum. See p. 171.

BALTIMORE MUSEUM OF ART—More than 90,000 works of art comprise the BMA's permanent collection, which can take you from Africa to Oceania, and from Rembrandt to Andy Warhol. See p. 171.

EVERGREEN MUSEUM AND LIBRARY—This elegant mansion's collection contains more than 50,000 objects and includes a library and a theater. See p. 172.

MARYLAND HISTORICAL SOCIETY—The extensive collections in the society's museum and library help trace the link between the past and the present. See p. 174.

MARYLAND SCIENCE CENTER, IMAX THEATER AND DAVIS PLANETARIUM—Hands-on science exhibits offer educational fun for all ages at this multifaceted attraction overlooking the Inner Harbor. See p. 174.

THE MARYLAND ZOO IN BALTIMORE—On the grounds of one of the country's largest city parks, this 161-acre zoo counts a large colony of African black-footed penguins among its 2,000 animals. See p. 172.

NATIONAL AQUARIUM IN BALTIMORE—Five stories house a variety of aquatic exhibits, including a 335,000-gallon coral reef and a 1.2 million-gallon Atlantic bottlenose dolphin habitat. See p. 174.

THE WALTERS ART MUSEUM—Nearly 30,000 works of art, including one of Raphael's paintings, span 55 centuries. See p. 176.

Fort McHenry National Monument and Historic Shrine (D-4)

FORT McHENRY NATIONAL MONUMENT AND HISTORIC SHRINE—The American defense of this fort against British attack on the night and early morning of Sept. 13-14, 1814, was the inspiration for the U.S. national anthem. See p. 184.

Largo (F-3)

SIX FLAGS AMERICA—The park offers more than 100 ways to have fun, from thrilling roller coasters and live shows to a water park with a million-gallon wave pool. See District of Columbia p. 116.

St. Michaels (D-7)

CHESAPEAKE BAY MARITIME MUSEUM—From oyster harvesting to recreation, this comprehensive waterfront museum highlights the Chesapeake Bay's maritime heritage. See p. 204.

Salisbury (E-8)

THE WARD MUSEUM, SALISBURY UNIVERSITY—Discover the practical and artistic uses of decoys in what is said to be the world's most comprehensive collection of wildfowl art. See p. 205.

Solomons (E-7)

CALVERT MARINE MUSEUM—This extensive facility interprets the maritime history of the region with artifacts, displays, models, vessels and 17 aquariums. See p. 206.

Maryland Temperature Averages
Maximum/Minimum
From the records of The Weather Channel Interactive, Inc.

	JAN	FEB	MAR	APR	MAY	JUNE	JULY	AUG	SEPT	OCT	NOV	DEC
Annapolis	42 / 24	45 / 25	54 / 33	65 / 42	75 / 52	83 / 62	88 / 67	85 / 66	78 / 59	67 / 46	56 / 36	47 / 29
Baltimore	44 / 29	47 / 31	57 / 39	68 / 48	77 / 58	86 / 68	91 / 73	88 / 71	81 / 64	70 / 52	59 / 42	49 / 33
Frederick	41 / 25	46 / 27	56 / 35	67 / 44	77 / 54	85 / 62	89 / 67	87 / 66	80 / 59	68 / 47	57 / 38	46 / 30
Ocean City	44 / 28	46 / 30	53 / 35	61 / 44	70 / 53	79 / 62	84 / 67	83 / 67	78 / 62	68 / 51	58 / 41	49 / 32

RECREATION AREAS

Area	MAP LOCATION	CAMPING	PICNICKING	HIKING TRAILS	BOATING	BOAT RAMP	BOAT RENTAL	FISHING	SWIMMING	PETS ON LEASH	BICYCLE TRAILS	WINTER SPORTS	VISITOR CENTER	LODGE/CABINS	FOOD SERVICE
NATIONAL SEASHORE *(See place listing)*															
Assateague Island (F-9) 39,500 acres 8 mi. s. of Ocean City via SR 611 on Assateague Island.		•	•	•	•			•	•	•	•		•		
ARMY CORPS OF ENGINEERS															
Jennings Randolph Lake (B-2) 952 acres in Garrett County, and Mineral County, W. Va. From Bloomington take US 220 to SR 135, then 9 mi. w. to Lake Access Rd. Playground.	**1**	•	•	•	•	•	•		•				•		
STATE															
Assateague (E-9) 756 acres 6 mi. s. of Ocean City via SR 611. Crabbing; interpretive programs.	**2**	•	•		•	•	•	•	•	•			•		•
Big Run (B-2) 300 acres 11 mi. n.w. of Luke on Savage River Rd.	**3**	•	•	•	•	•	•	•		•	•				
Cedarville State Forest (D-6) 3,697 acres in Brandywine on Bee Oak Rd. Cross-country skiing, hunting; horseback riding trails.	**4**	•	•	•				•		•	•	•	•		
Cunningham Falls (B-5) 4,946 acres off US 15 at Thurmont. Historic. Lake, waterfall.	**5**	•	•	•	•	•	•	•	•	•				•	•
Dans Mountain (B-2) 481 acres 9 mi. s. of Frostburg on SR 36. Historic. Playground, pool.	**6**		•	•				•	•	•			•		•
Deep Creek Lake (B-1) 1,818 acres 2 mi. n.e. of Thayerville. Maryland's largest freshwater lake. Cross-country skiing; nature trail, snowmobile trails.	**7**	•	•	•	•	•	•	•	•	•		•	•		
Elk Neck (B-7) 2,188 acres 9 mi. s. of North East on SR 272. Scenic. Bird watching; nature trail.	**8**	•	•	•	•	•	•	•	•	•	•		•	•	•
Fair Hill NRMA (B-8) 5,613 acres in Fair Hill on SR 273 at jct. 213. Historic. Hunting; equestrian center, horseback riding trails.	**9**		•	•				•		•			•		
Fort Frederick (B-4) 561 acres in Big Pool off SR 56, 1 mi. s.w. of I-70 Big Pool exit. Historic. Nature trail. *(See Big Pool p. 188.)*	**10**	•	•	•	•	•		•		•			•		•
Gambrill (B-5) 1,137 acres 6 mi. n.w. of Frederick off I-70. Nature trail.	**11**	•	•	•				•		•					
Garrett State Forest (B-1) 7,066 acres about 5 mi. n.w. of Oakland off US 219. Cross-country skiing, hunting; horseback riding trails, snowmobile trails.	**12**	•	•	•				•		•					
Greenbrier (B-4) 1,288 acres 10 mi. e. of Hagerstown on US 40. Hunting; nature trail.	**13**	•	•	•	•	•	•	•	•				•		•
Green Ridge State Forest (B-3) 38,811 acres in eastern Allegany County, 22 mi. e. of Cumberland; exit 64 off I-68. Historic.	**14**	•	•	•	•			•		•	•	•	•		
Greenwell (E-6) 596 acres in Hollywood off SR 245 on Steerhorn Neck Rd. Cross-country skiing, hunting; horseback riding trails, playground.	**15**	•	•	•	•	•		•		•	•		•	•	
Gunpowder Falls (B-6) 13,020 acres along the Little and Big Gunpowder rivers s. of Kingsville.	**16**		•	•	•	•	•	•	•	•	•				•
Hart-Miller Island (D-4) 244 acres on the Chesapeake Bay at the mouth of Middle River.	**17**	•	•		•				•	•					
Herrington Manor (B-1) 365 acres 5 mi. n.w. of Oakland on CR 20. Cross-country skiing; nature trail, ski rentals.	**18**		•	•	•		•	•	•	•	•	•	•	•	•
Janes Island (F-8) 3,147 acres 1.5 mi. n. of Crisfield off SR 413. Crabbing.	**19**	•	•	•	•	•	•	•	•				•	•	
Martinak (D-8) 105 acres 2 mi. s. of Denton off SR 404.	**20**	•	•		•	•		•	•				•	•	
New Germany (B-2) 455 acres 5 mi. s. of Grantsville off US 40 on New Germany Rd. Cross-country skiing; nature trail.	**21**	•	•	•	•	•	•	•	•	•	•	•	•	•	•

RECREATION AREAS	MAP LOCATION	CAMPING	PICNICKING	HIKING TRAILS	BOATING	BOAT RAMP	BOAT RENTAL	FISHING	SWIMMING	PETS ON LEASH	BICYCLE TRAILS	WINTER SPORTS	VISITOR CENTER	LODGE/CABINS	FOOD SERVICE
North Point (D-4) 1,310 acres on the Chesapeake Bay in Edgemere off Old North Point Rd. Historic. Flat-water paddling.	22		•	•	•			•			•		•		
Patapsco Valley (D-3) 12,699 acres along the Patapsco River from Baltimore to Liberty Dam w. of Ellicott City on US 40.	23	•	•	•				•			•	•	•		
Pocomoke River															
Milburn Landing (F-8) 370 acres 8 mi. w. of Snow Hill off SR 12.	24	•	•	•	•	•		•		•	•				
Shad Landing (F-8) 544 acres 4 mi. s.w. of Snow Hill off US 113.	25	•	•	•	•	•	•	•	•		•		•		•
Point Lookout (F-7) 528 acres on the southern tip of the western shore on SR 5. Historic. *(See Scotland p. 205.)*	26	•	•	•	•	•	•	•	•	•	•		•	•	•
Potomac State Forest (B-1) 10,416 acres in southeastern Garrett County, off SR 135.	27	•	•	•				•	•	•		•			
Rocks (B-6) 855 acres 8 mi. n.w. of Bel Air on SR 24. Historic. Scenic. Canoeing, tubing.	28		•	•				•		•					
Rocky Gap (B-3) 3,200 acres 6 mi. e. of Cumberland on I-68. Scenic. Ice skating; nature trails.	29	•	•	•	•	•	•	•	•	•	•	•	•		
Rosaryville (D-6) 982 acres about 4 mi. s.w. of Upper Marlboro off US 301. Horseback riding trails.	30		•					•			•				
St. Clement's Island (E-6) 62 acres in the Potomac River near St. Clement's and Breton bays. Historic. Accessible only by boat.	31		•	•	•			•							
St. Mary's River (E-6) 2,176 acres 3 mi. n. of Great Mills, off SR 5 on Camp Cosoma Rd. Hunting.	32		•	•	•	•		•		•					
Sandy Point (E-4) 786 acres 7 mi. e. of Annapolis on US 50, on Chesapeake Bay. Bird watching.	33		•	•	•	•	•	•	•						•
Savage River State Forest (B-1) 52,819 acres mostly s. of I-68 and US 40 near Grantsville.	34	•	•	•	•			•		•	•	•			
Seneca Creek (E-1) 6,109 acres 2 mi. w. of Gaithersburg on SR 117.	35		•	•		•	•			•	•	•	•		
Smallwood (D-5) 629 acres in Marbury off SR 224. Historic. Marina, playground.	36	•	•	•	•	•	•	•						•	•
Susquehanna (B-7) 2,639 acres 3 mi. n. of Havre de Grace on SR 155. Historic. Scenic.	37	•	•	•	•	•		•		•	•	•			
Swallow Falls (B-1) 257 acres 9 mi. n.w. of Oakland on Herrington Manor-Swallow Falls Rd. Maryland's highest waterfall. Cross-country skiing; nature trails.	38	•	•	•				•		•	•	•			
Tuckahoe (D-7) 3,498 acres 6 mi. n. of Queen Anne off SR 404 via SR 480. Flat-water canoeing. Arboretum, lake.	39		•	•	•	•	•	•	•		•		•		
Wye Island NRMA (D-7) 2,450 acres about 11 mi. w. of Queenstown. Hunting; horseback riding trails.	40	•		•	•			•		•	•		•		
OTHER															
Brunswick Campsite (C-4) 24 acres on the C&O Canal towpath in Brunswick.	41	•	•	•	•			•		•	•				
Catoctin Mountain (B-5) 5,769 acres 2 mi. w. of Thurmont on SR 77. Cross-country skiing; bridle trail, nature trails. *(See Thurmont p. 206.)*	42	•	•	•				•				•	•	•	
Louise F. Cosca (D-6) 500 acres on Thrift Rd. near Clinton.	43	•	•	•			•	•		•					•
Rock Creek (E-1) 1,740 acres 4 mi. e. of Rockville on SR 28, then 2 mi. n. on Muncaster Mill Rd. to Avery Rd. Nature center. Archery, golf (18 holes, nine holes); nature trails. *(See Rockville in District of Columbia p. 118.)*	44		•	•	•		•	•		•	•				

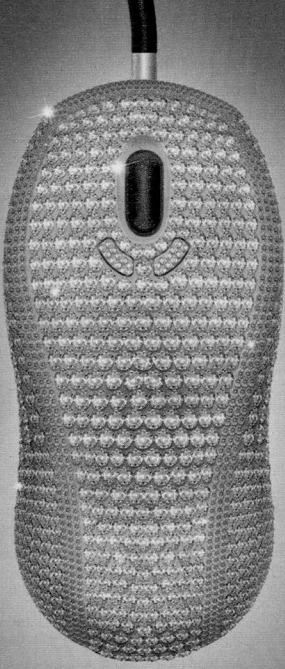

Exploring Maryland

For descriptions of places in bold type, see individual listings.

Northeast

The primary route through Cecil and Harford counties, constituting Maryland's northeast region, is I-95, which enters the state from the north about 3 miles below Newark, Del. The scant 40 miles of this route, traversing a gently rolling plain, give little hint of the attractions to be found but a short distance to either side of the expressway.

To explore the area leave I-95 at the first Cecil County interchange and take SR 279 south for about 2 miles. At SR 213 head north through Cherry Hill and on to Fair Hill. This small town is on the edge of Maryland's horse country. Fair Hill Races, where steeplechase and cross-country racing can be viewed, is a popular northeast attraction.

SR 273 westward from Fair Hill marks the beginning of a scenic drive through grain and dairy farmlands, rolling hills and ever-increasing horse farms. About a mile west of Calvert, a diverting stop can be made at the Plumpton Park Zoo. Four miles farther along SR 273 is **Rising Sun,** an early 18th-century settlement and now a trading and banking center.

Not far beyond Rising Sun SR 273 terminates at US 1. The scenic drive follows the federal highway south on through Conowingo on the banks of the Susquehanna River. As US 1 crosses the river over the Conowingo Dam the view to the north is of Conowingo Lake, a 14-mile product of the river's damming.

Crossing the Susquehanna brings you into Harford County, a pastoral Piedmont area dotted with farms and small towns. Eight miles beyond the river turn north on SR 136. Just below the Pennsylvania state line this route swings to the west and terminates at Norrisville in the county's northwest corner.

From here take SR 23 south to Madonna. Turn south onto SR 146 and go just beyond the intersection with SR 152 to reach one

Cove Point Lighthouse, near Solomons
Maryland Office of Tourism Development

Down by the Bay in Maryland

of northeast Maryland's outstanding attractions: Ladew Topiary Gardens in **Monkton.** A tour of the 15 seasonal gardens and the estate house displaying paintings, antiques and equestrian memorabilia should not be missed.

On leaving Ladew Gardens, backtrack briefly on SR 146 to SR 152. Take this south to the intersection with SR 147 where a left turn leads to Bel Air. The Hays House Museum will lure American history buffs. Several miles east at the intersection of SRs 543 and 22 stands a marker

on the side of the road to designate Tudor Hall—the house in which actor Edwin Booth and his notorious brother, John Wilkes Booth, were born.

From Bel Air take SR 24 south beyond I-95 to Edgewood to begin a tour of northeast Maryland's more industrial and urban areas. From SR 24 a short drive up US 40 takes you to **Havre de Grace** at the point where the Susquehanna meets the Chesapeake.

You will pass the entrance to the **Aberdeen** Proving Ground en route. Its chief attraction, the U.S. Army Ordnance Museum, does not open until ten but a visit could be planned following a tour of Havre de Grace. Then proceed north again on US 40.

After crossing the Susquehanna and re-entering Cecil County, a side trip into Perryville takes you by both the site of Susquehanna Lower Ferry, a crossing much used by 18th-century travelers, and the now-restored Rodgers Tavern, a favorite stopping place of George Washington. Further up US 40, a turnoff onto SR 7 leads to Charlestown, a quiet waterfront village with another restored tavern reflecting its Colonial history.

From Charlestown, SR 7 leads to North East, also an 18th-century town that early became a small manufacturing center. A basket factory and a museum displaying fishing, hunting and boating artifacts peculiar to the Upper Chesapeake region are among the area attractions.

From North East SR 7 leads to **Elkton,** which grew in the 18th century as a shipping center. The availability of waterpower soon brought in the mills that turned it

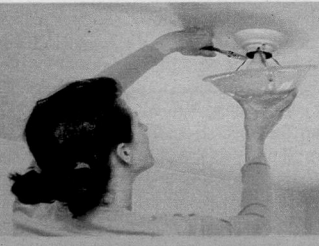

INSTEAD OF HOME REPAIR, USE YOUR VACATION DAYS FOR A LITTLE "ME REPAIR."

You work hard to earn your vacation. And Maryland helps you make the most of it. Our new Byways Book delivers the best routes to follow for all sorts of activities and interests — from hiking in Western Maryland to kicking back on the Eastern Shore. For a day or an extended stay, Maryland is the perfect fix.

For your free Travel Guide with great getaway ideas call 800.394.5725 or go to VisitMaryland.org/mag.

WELCOME

Martin O'Malley, Governor
Anthony G. Brown, Lt. Governor

AD FUNDED IN PART BY THE FEDERAL HIGHWAY ADMINISTRATION.

into a factory town. Despite commercial development a number of pre-Revolutionary homes have survived and, though private, are visible to motorists.

From Elkton proceed south on SR 213 to explore the "Chesapeake Country" section of Cecil County. Cut off on SR 285 and follow signs to the Chesapeake and Delaware Canal linking the two bays that define the Delmarva Peninsula. At the

lead to another Maryland region with a wealth of touring attractions. As you cross the Sassafras River just beyond Fredrickton you leave Cecil County behind and enter into the special charm of the Eastern Shore.

The Eastern Shore

Topography, occupational pursuits and history account for differences between the two distinct sections of the Eastern Shore: the

Kent County at Georgetown, an early 18th-century town that was almost destroyed by the British during the War of 1812. Drivers who enter Kent from the northeast on US 301 can cut off just beyond Sassafras on SR 290 to connect with SR 213 in Galena, where a turn north will lead to Georgetown. Heading south from Georgetown, SR 213 winds through rolling countryside past Locust Grove and Kennedyville, where those interested in antique farm equipment may wish to stop at the Kent Museum.

Chestertown, on the west bank of the Chester River, includes among its attractions pre-Revolutionary War homes, a restored 19th-century general store, an 18th-century tavern and Washington College. The nation's first president was one of the founders of the college.

From Chestertown, SR 20 leads to the southwestern section of the county, an area punctuated by small inlets of the bay. Turn south at Rock Hall onto SR 445 to go to the southernmost tip of the county. At this point a county road leads over to the Eastern Neck National Wildlife Refuge where hundreds of Canada geese migrate each autumn.

St. John's College, Annapolis / Annapolis & Anne Arundel County CVB

Maryland terminus is **Chesapeake City,** a 19th-century town that grew up with the canal construction industry and continues as the center for maintaining the waterway and servicing vessels using it.

Back on SR 213 proceed to Cecilton and turn west on Main Street. Four miles out is Mount Harmon Plantation. This 18th-century tobacco plantation, on the north bank of the Sassafras River, has a restored house furnished with antiques, boxwood gardens and the original tobacco press house.

From Cecilton, your visit to Maryland's northeast section can terminate with the scenic drive north on SR 213 back to I-95. A turn to the south, however, can

Upper Shore and the Southern Eastern Shore. While both include a lengthy stretch of Chesapeake Bay coastline, with fishing villages and yachting marinas, the Upper Shore is an area of farms and small-town ambience while its neighbor to the south is a flat, sandy region marked by pine forests, wetlands, shipping ports and cosmopolitan beach resorts.

The northern two of the four counties constituting Chesapeake Country, as Marylanders know the Upper Shore, are Kent and Queen Anne's. US 301 is the major route through them, but SR 213 affords a more picturesque drive with easy access to scenic and historical attractions.

Motorists coming in from Cecil County on SR 213 enter

From the refuge backtrack to Rock Hall and go north on SR 20. About 4 miles up the road is the entrance to Remington Farms, a 3,000-acre wildlife sanctuary and research area with nature trails. After 2 more miles on SR 20 a side trip on Sandy Bottom Road leads to St. Paul's Episcopal Church, Maryland's oldest continuously used Episcopal church.

Continue on SR 20 to Chestertown and take SR 213 south into Queen Anne's County. Visible on the way to Centreville are 18th-century homes still in use. In the town are several opportunities for browsing among collections of Early American memorabilia.

About 7 miles south of Centreville, SR 213 leads to **Wye Mills** *(see Queen Anne p. 202).* Wye Oak State Park is south of town on SR 662. Also on SR 662 is Old Wye Church, established in 1721. Back in town, SR 213 east leads past the Wye Grist Mill, where grain was ground for Revolutionary War troops.

East of Wye Mills SR 213 runs into SR 404. Follow this into Caroline County and proceed eastward toward **Denton.** This small manufacturing town with Colonial roots is a trading center for the surrounding rural areas.

En route to Denton you pass the entrance to Tuckahoe State Park, where an environmental education program is offered at the 500-acre arboretum. Fishing, canoeing, hiking and camping are available. South of town on SR 404 is Martinak State Park, another recreational area offering camping facilities. A museum of American Indian artifacts is among the park's attractions.

Beyond Martinak SR 16 forks off SR 404 to the southwest. This rural route through a farming area leads to Preston, a canning and marketing center, and southward to the county line. Just before leaving Chesapeake Country you pass through Linchester, one of the earliest settlements in Caroline County. A gristmill, established in 1681 and reconstructed in the early 19th century, is still in operation.

As you enter Dorchester County you begin your tour of the Southern Eastern Shore. Three miles south of the county line SR 331 cuts off to the southeast along an officially designated state scenic route. After a few miles the route switches east on SR 392, then south on SR 313 to the Nanticoke River.

Across the river the scenic route leads to Mardela Springs. At US 50 turn east for a 10-mile drive into **Salisbury,** the largest city on the Eastern Shore and the trade center for the Lower Shore. Although it was established in 1732, Salisbury lacks the Colonial appearance of Eastern Shore neighbors to the north. Because mid- and late-19th-century fires obliterated most pre-Victorian

National Shrine Grotto of Lourdes, Emmitsburg
Tourism Council of Frederick County

structures, it is decidedly a 20th-century city. A bustling commercial center, it has museums, art galleries, a zoo, fashion outlets and a riverfront park that call for a stop.

From Salisbury proceed toward the Atlantic coast on US 50 for about 20 miles. Turn onto access-controlled SR 90, which leads past Ocean Pines and over to **Ocean City.** The 10-mile long public beach, the attractions of the 3-mile boardwalk, the sport fishing opportunities and the lures of fine seafood restaurants can make an extended stay in this resort city desirable.

Leaving Ocean City take US 50 for 2 miles and turn left on SR 611 to **Assateague Island National Seashore.** Noted for its herds of free-roaming Chincoteague ponies, the park offers camping facilities, nature trails and naturalist-led demonstrations of crabbing and fishing.

From Assateague begin another of Maryland's scenic drives by backtracking on SR 611 to SR 376. Take this west and at **Berlin** go south on US 113 to **Snow Hill.** One of the Southern Eastern Shore's communities dating from the 17th century, Snow Hill has several attractions of a historical nature. Just north of town a side trip on SR 12 passes Furnace Town, a re-created early industrial village at the site of a bog-ore furnace.

Beyond Snow Hill, US 113 passes through Pocomoke River State Park, which offers a view of the Pocomoke Cypress Swamps. The stand of bald cypress is one of the northernmost in the country. At the end of US 113 take US 13 westward through Pocomoke City and into Somerset County.

Turn south at Westover to pick up SR 413 for the drive down to **Crisfield** at Maryland's southern tip. The town, which calls itself the "Seafood Capital of the World," has numerous attractions related to the seafood industry and also is the point of departure for ferry trips to **Smith Island** and Tangier Island.

Backtracking to US 13, proceed to **Princess Anne,** another pre-Revolutionary town that experienced the destruction of most of its Colonial structures by fire. A few have been preserved and can be seen along with Federal and Victorian homes on a self-guiding walking tour.

From Princess Anne follow US 13 to Salisbury and then US 50 to re-enter Dorchester County at Vienna. Leave US 50 for a leisurely drive on county roads down to the southern Dorchester fishing villages. Follow Crossroads to Henry's Crossroads, go west on Griffith Neck Road, then north on Bestpitch Ferry Road and west on Greenbrier, which curves south to merge with Maple Dam Road. Just past the junction take Key Wallace west to SR 335.

On Key Wallace you will pass the Visitor Center of the Blackwater National Wildlife Refuge, winter haven for thousands of Canada geese as well as ospreys, ducks and swans and a sanctuary for bald eagles. Admission is charged for a 5-mile tour on Wildlife Drive and use of the nature trails and observation tower.

Beyond the refuge go south on SR 335 to SR 536. A left turn on SR 536 will take you down to the far point of the area Marylanders know as the "Cape Cod of the South." Continuing on SR 335 instead, you reach the Narrow Ferry Bridge leading to the fishing villages of Hooper Island on the bay.

Coming back to the junction of SRs 335 and 536, follow 335 north to **Church Creek.** Turn right on SR 16 toward **Cambridge.** Almost immediately you will pass Old Trinity Church, one of the oldest churches in use in America. In Cambridge look for other 18th- and 19th-century buildings as well as several museums and a gallery of local arts.

Taking US 50 north from Cambridge you resume your tour of Chesapeake Country as you cross the Choptank River. About 10 miles north of the river leave US 50 and head west on Almshouse Road, a county route. This will merge with SR 333, which leads to **Oxford,** on the tip of a peninsula between the Tred Avon and Choptank rivers. This boating, shipbuilding and fishing center is one of Talbot County's principal towns.

The Oxford-Bellevue Ferry, crossing the Tred Avon, provides an attractive shortcut to **St. Michaels,** reached from Bellevue via a county road north to SR 33 and then west. This yachting and sailing center is a popular resort town and might be a spot where you'll want to arrange an extended stay.

From St. Michaels take SR 33 eastward to **Easton.** As you enter town you will pass the Third Haven Friends Meeting House, where William Penn sometimes held meetings. Although Easton was established early in the 18th century, this is the only pre-Revolutionary structure still standing. Federal period houses are much in evidence, however.

From Easton, the drive up US 50 brings the tour of the Eastern Shore to a close. Motorists who recall the old drawbridge linking the Eastern Shore mainland to **Kent Island** will find that the Kent Narrows Bridge, opened in 1990, has eliminated the traffic jams that for years impeded travel to and from the shore. Kent Island is still the Eastern Shore's most-used entry/exit point. Discount outlet centers are the attractions to be visited before the Chesapeake Bay Bridge puts the Eastern Shore behind.

Central Maryland

Annapolis, the center of the state's political life, is a well-situated spot at which to commence a tour of central Maryland. At the point where the Severn River flows into Chesapeake Bay, Maryland's capital city is easily reached from the northeast via US 301 and from the west and south by US 50 coming east from I-95.

The home of the U.S. Naval Academy, Annapolis also is a virtual museum of Colonial and 18th- and 19th-century history. As a lively social and cultural center, a sailor's mecca and an architectural show town, this small city has attractions that can claim a tourist's attention for days.

From the cradle of Maryland history a 25-mile drive across the center of Anne Arundel County and into Howard County leads to

St. Anne's Church, Annapolis / Annapolis & Anne Arundel County CVB

a city that has become a monument to late 20th-century urban planning. From Annapolis take I-97 to SR 3; go south 1 mile to SR 175 and follow this west through the Fort George Meade National Wildlife Refuge and into **Columbia.** This planned community includes a college and a hospital on 15,000 acres of what was underused farmland in the mid-1960s.

For a step back into Maryland's past, take US 29 through the countryside north of Columbia to the outskirts of **Ellicott City.** Follow Old Columbia Pike into this hilly, historic town overlooking the Patapsco River valley, which was the first terminus of the Baltimore and Ohio Railroad.

Leaving Ellicott City on SR 144 you will enter Baltimore County at Catonsville. Founded early in the 18th century, this neighbor of the city of Baltimore was the scene of historic 20th-century civil rights activity.

Beyond Catonsville continue on SR 144 into **Baltimore,** or at

Assateague Island National Seashore
Maryland Office of Tourism Development

I-695 swing up to US 40 for access to Maryland's largest city. Either route will take you into an area convenient for starting a tour of the glittering downtown business district and the entertainment arenas, architectural showpieces and cultural attractions of the Inner Harbor.

Not all the interesting sights of Baltimore are products of the urban renewal that has revolutionized the harbor area; many historic, scientific and educational sites of note are scattered throughout this, the 13th-largest city of the nation. Allow yourself more than a day or two to see it.

Wisp Ski Resort, McHenry / Maryland Office of Tourism Development

The Pimlico Race Course, on Belvedere Avenue in the northwestern section of the city, is the site of the Preakness as well as a number of other major horse races each year. It is Maryland's oldest racetrack. The Jones Falls Expressway (I-83), a good route to the north, is a short distance from the track.

Heading up I-83 and east on I-695 you see a mixture of suburban and exurban territory. Open land is interspersed with housing developments that increasingly expand from the metropolis. However, a short side trip up SR 45 to the little racetrack at Timonium reminds you that central Maryland is horse country. Worthington Valley, a short drive west of Timonium off I-795, is home to several horse farms. In late April the Maryland Hunt Club Race is held. First run in 1894, it is one of the country's most demanding steeplechases.

Heading south on I-795 to I-695 and then east brings you to **Lutherville,** home of the Fire Museum of Maryland. Continue south on SR 45 just beyond I-695 to **Towson.** Once a farm community, the city is now the site of

light manufacturing plants, corporate headquarters, some state government offices and colleges.

From Towson proceed east on I-695 to exit 31 and turn north on SR 147 for less-urban exploring. Fork left on Long Green Pike. Follow this to **Hydes** to visit the Boordy Winery. From this point take Hydes Road west to Manor Road. Go north and then west into horse country along SR 145. At SR 45 a turn northward leads up to Hereford.

At Hereford pick up the scenic drive that winds westward along the northern sector of the state. SR 137 goes over to White House, where a right turn on SR 25 takes you north to Carroll County and on to Alesia near the Pennsylvania border. The scenic route then veers to the southwest on SR 27 and at the SR 30 intersection goes north again to Melrose.

Beyond Melrose go south on SR 496 to **Westminster.** A number of historical attractions and a couple of wineries are to be found in this agricultural and light-manufacturing community and the neighboring small towns.

From Westminster the scenic route follows SR 140 up to **Emmitsburg.** In this town, 3 miles

short of the state line, you can visit historical sites related to Elizabeth Ann Seton, the first American woman canonized by the Roman Catholic Church.

From Emmitsburg a drive down US 15 leads to **Thurmont** on the edge of Catoctin Mountain Park. The nearby attractions bring the tour of central Maryland to an end. From Thurmont either continue south on US 15 to begin exploring the Capital Region or head through the mountain park to enter western Maryland via SR 77.

Western Maryland

Because **Hagerstown,** 3 miles north of I-70 and traversed by US 40 and I-81, is accessible from all directions, it is a good starting place for a tour of Maryland's western region. After exploring the town proceed west on I-70 or US 40. These roads pass through historic small towns, first in fertile valleys and then up the orchard-covered slopes that mark the early stages of the Allegheny Mountains.

At Clear Spring go south on Big Spring Road to SR 56 and turn west to Fort Frederick State Park. Visit the museum, dealing with the fort's role in the French and Indian War, the American Revolution and the Civil War, and enjoy the park's picnic facilities.

Continue northwest on SR 56, watching for signs of roadside markets as you pass through this fruit-growing region. At **Big Pool** take I-70 west to Exit 1B and follow SR 522 south to **Hancock.** The outskirts of this small manufacturing city overlook the northernmost stretch of the Potomac River. Civil War hostilities were centered nearby, and reminders of this phase of the town's history are still to be seen.

From Hancock, I-68 becomes the route to follow. It offers a scenic drive through the northern sector of forested mountains in Maryland's far western segment. At various points beyond Sideling Hill, about 6 miles out of Hancock, I-68 divides with the older, more scenic roadway paralleling the principal highway. At the first exit in Allegany County follow scenic SR 40, which winds through Piney Grove and the Bill Meyer Wildlife Management Area before returning to the through route in the midst of the Green Ridge State Forest.

Continuing west on US 40, watch for the scenic overlook a few miles beyond Flintstone. At this point the road curves down to **Cumberland.** This industrial city on the north branch of the Potomac River wraps around a peninsula-like projection of West Virginia. Because of its strategic importance in area history from days of the French and Indian War and its setting in a river valley surrounded by towering mountains, Cumberland offers numerous scenic and historic attractions, including the Western Maryland Scenic Railroad.

From Cumberland alternate US 40/Centre Street follows the route of the Indian footpath that provided the roadbed for a section of the first federally funded highway, the National Road, constructed early in the 19th century. In LaVale, it passes Maryland's first and only remaining tollgate house on the National Road. A plaque lists the original tolls for wagons, animals and pedestrians. Farther on, in Clarysville, is an inn built to serve early National Road travelers.

Another National Road inn, operated by Meshach Frost, was the establishment around which the town of **Frostburg** developed. A center of western Maryland's 19th-century coal mining industry, the picturesque mountain town is now the home of Frostburg State University.

Alternate US 40 then heads west to **Grantsville,** passing the Casselman River Bridge, a single-span stone arch built for the National Road in 1813. The town is largely populated by descendants of Amish and Mennonite farmers who moved into the area in the mid-19th century.

Annapolis & Anne Arundel County Conference and Visitors Bureau

Nearby attractions include a still-functioning 1797 gristmill and Penn Alps, a remodeled log stagecoach stop now offering demonstrations of Colonial arts and crafts.

From Grantsville alternate US 40 winds through the northern section of Savage River State Forest and on to Keysers Ridge. This is the point at which to cut south down the side of the western Maryland triangle. US 219 runs the length of the north/south plateau near the Allegheny ridges and offers easy access to the various attractions along the way.

About 4 miles south of Keysers Ridge a scenic overlook 2,800 feet above sea level offers a dramatic view of valley farmlands surrounded by mountain peaks. A few miles farther Accident/Bear Creek Road, a county route, leads off to the west. Follow this to Friendsville, south of the dam that creates the Youghiogheny Reservoir. Tours of the dam are available, and the Youghiogheny River itself is one of the protected scenic beauties of western Maryland. Trout and bass fishing opportunities abound.

From Friendsville SR 42 will take you back to US 219 a few miles north of Deep Creek Lake, the largest freshwater lake in Maryland. If downhill skiing is on your agenda, turn right on Sang Run Road in **McHenry.** This will take you to the ski area on 3,080-foot-high Marsh Mountain. For year-round outdoor activities turn left farther down US 219 on a road marked by a sign to Deep Creek Lake State Park.

About 8 miles beyond the state park US 219 brings you into **Oakland.** High on a plateau, in an area local hotels once described as the "Switzerland of America," Oakland and nearby Mountain Lake Park were popular with late 19th-century vacationers.

From Oakland, CR 20 offers access to Swallows Falls State Park and the largest waterfalls in Maryland. Beyond the park the road leads to the Cranesville Sub-Arctic Swamp on the Maryland-West Virginia border. One of the region's most unusual natural phenomena, this 5,000-acre remnant of an ice age forest produces plant life usually found only in regions close to the Arctic Circle. Unfortunately, the paved road ends before reaching the swamp, and final access is by gravel and dirt roads.

South of Oakland US 219 enters Redhouse, on the incline leading to the highest elevation in Maryland, Backbone Mountain. The 3,360-foot peak dominates the lower tip of the western Maryland triangle. From Redhouse US 50 heading east cuts through Backbone Mountain Pass to the other West Virginia boundary at Gorman.

From Gorman, SR 560 will take you back toward Oakland. At Loch Lynn Heights turn north on SR 135. Deer Park Hotel Road goes off to the right about 4 miles up SR 135. This will lead to the village of Deer Park, a favored vacation resort of Presidents Grant, Harrison and Cleveland as well as of affluent late 19th-century eastern Marylanders. The spacious house, termed a "cottage," in which Cleveland spent his honeymoon stands.

Leaving Deer Park you have a choice of routes. You can proceed on a precipitous drive on SR 135 through Altamont and the lower portion of Savage River State Forest. Beyond McCoole turn north on US 220 toward Cumberland and US 40. However, SR 135 descends the northeastern face of Backbone Mountain with a long steep pitch and presents some treacherous curves.

An alternate would be to cross SR 135 at Deer Park and return to US 219 before heading north to US 40. This will involve some backtracking, but using principal route US 40 rather than the alternate across the northern tier of the area will cut driving time and may provide views you missed initially.

Back in the Hancock area pick up I-70. At interchange #18 take SR 68 southeast for a scenic drive through Washington County. At Lappans turn south on SR 65 and proceed to the **Antietam National Battlefield** at Sharpsburg. Allow several hours to see this and the other historical sites in the area before taking SR 34 to **Boonsboro.**

From SR 34 turn east onto alternate US 40. To your left about a mile from Boonsboro is Washington Monument State Park. With the hike to the monument and the museum slide presentation, the tour of western Maryland comes to a close. Beyond the park you can begin exploration of the Greater Washington region.

Capital Region

Defining this area poses problems because of the ever-expanding nature of the metropolis it abuts. It enlarges as housing subdivisions proliferate, corporations reach out for business park space, federal agencies seek offices beyond the District of Columbia and transportation systems linking the nation's capital with outlying communities multiply.

These touring suggestions are limited to the irregularly-shaped crescent that encompasses the cities of Frederick and Washington and has its western boundary defined by the Potomac from about 3 miles northwest of **Brunswick** to a little below Accokeek. Included in this area are the southern half of Frederick County, Montgomery County and almost all of Prince George's County.

The primary routes serving the region are I-270 and I-95. Though they pass through pleasing Piedmont countryside both are heavily traveled, especially during commuter rush hours. To enjoy area attractions avoid these routes when possible.

Frederick is a good base from which to explore the surrounding area as well as to visit local attractions. When you have seen the latter take SR 144 east to **New Market** to browse at the antiques capital of Maryland. Then follow SR 75 north from New Market to Glissans Mill Road and turn east to reach Berrywine Plantations/Linganore Winecellars.

Fort McHenry National Monument and Historic Shrine
© Gibson Stock Photography

For a scenic drive along the Potomac take US 340 west from Frederick to Exit 1 and follow signs to SR 478 south. From Brunswick follow SR 464 to US 15. Take this south to Point of Rocks and turn east on SR 28. Just beyond Tuscarora turn away from the Potomac and go north on SR 85. At Lilypons Road go east not quite 2 miles and make a stop in Lilypons, Maryland's smallest town.

Lilypons is little more than a post office and the site of the Lilypons Water Gardens and Three Springs Fisheries. Ornamental aquatic plants, flashing goldfish and a variety of waterfowl and migratory birds attract visitors all year.

From Lilypons return to Frederick via SR 85 to the north or head on south into Montgomery County. For the latter, SR 28 offers a scenic alternative to I-270. Return to it from Lilypons Road; turn east and follow SR 28 into **Rockville.** Make this or any of several neighboring communities your base for exploring the Washington suburban area.

Bethesda, Chevy Chase, Gaithersburg, **Glen Echo, Kensington,** Potomac, **Rockville** and **Wheaton** have historic, scientific, scenic and educational attractions for visitors, and all can be reached easily from any lower Montgomery County AAA accommodation; see District of Columbia (West and North Region) listings. Bethesda, **Silver Spring** and Takoma Park have Metrorail stations offering convenient access to Washington attractions.

Complete your tour of Montgomery County by driving north on US 29 through an area that in the not-distant past was open countryside but now is a rapidly developing corridor of high-tech corporations and luxury condominiums. At SR 198 turn east to head into Prince George's County.

Stop in **Laurel** to see the Montpelier Mansion and the Montpelier Cultural Arts Center.

Western Maryland Scenic Railroad, Cumberland
Maryland Office of Tourism Development

You can check out the Laurel Race Track and the Laurel Raceway before taking the Baltimore-Washington Parkway south toward Beltsville. Exit at Powder Mill Road and proceed to the grounds of the Agricultural Research Center, the largest research center operated by the U.S. Department of Agriculture. Tours of the experimental farm are offered by appointment.

From the farm continue south on the Baltimore-Washington Parkway to **Greenbelt,** then take SR 193 south to SR 214. Going west toward **Largo** you will pass Six Flags America, a family theme park featuring rides, shows, games and water-related activities.

Just beyond Upper Marlboro go east on SR 4 to US 301. Take this south and turn left on SR 382. Proceed to Croom Airport Road and follow signs to Patuxent River Park, a restricted-use recreation and ecology education center where you can enjoy hiking, bird watching, canoeing, pontoon tours and exploring a restored 100-year-old village. Fishing and hunting require special permits.

Farther south on SR 382, a left turn on St. Thomas Church Road leads to the entrance of the Merkle Wildlife Sanctuary and Visitor's Center, a haven for a wide variety of migratory birds and waterfowl.

Returning toward Upper Marlboro go 5 miles west on SR 4 and take SR 223 south to **Clinton.** In the center of town turn left on Brandywine Road. At 9110 Brandywine stop for a tour of the Surratt House and Tavern, the restored home of the woman convicted of aiding John Wilkes Booth as he attempted to flee following the assassination of President Abraham Lincoln. Surratt was the first woman to be executed in the United States for complicity in a crime.

Your next stop should be **Oxon Hill.** Take SR 5 north to I-95 and I-95 west to SR 210. Go south on SR 210 to Oxon Hill Road and turn at the sign for the Oxon Hill Farm. Costumed staff at this working farm demonstrate methods of the late 19th century. Wagon rides, horseback rides and hands-on activities such as milking are special features.

From Oxon Hill take SR 210 south for about 4 miles. Turn right on Fort Washington Road to visit Fort Washington Park on the east bank of the Potomac. This 341-acre national park is on the site of the first fort built to defend the nation's capital.

Back on SR 210 continue south for 5 miles toward **Accokeek.** Turn right at Bryan Point Road, which takes you again to the Potomac shore. The road ends at the National Colonial Farm, where agricultural methods and plantation lifestyles of the mid-18th century are demonstrated.

The view of George Washington's Mount Vernon home across the river from the farm provides a fitting end to the tour of the Capital Region, so steeped in the nation's history. From Accokeek SR 373 will lead to Brandywine; take either US 301 to the northeast or SR 5 north to reach I-95. US 301 south is the turn to make to begin a tour of southern Maryland.

Southern Maryland

Starting a tour of southern Maryland on US 301 from the north you enter Charles County, the region's largest in area and population. Initially SR 5 shares the roadway with the federal highway, but as you near **Waldorf** it turns left into the town, which is bypassed by US 301. Follow SR 5 for your first touring stop in the region.

Just beyond Waldorf turn left on SR 382 and proceed to SR 232. Turn right and around the corner on SR 232 you will find The Dr. Samuel A. Mudd House Museum. This is the restored plantation home of the surgeon who, without knowing the identity of his patient, set John Wilkes Booth's broken leg following the assassination of Lincoln. Imprisoned for this act, he was later pardoned and honored for services rendered in prison during a yellow fever epidemic.

Back on SR 5 go south and turn right on SR 488. At SR 6 a right turn will take you into La-Plata, site of several notable Tidewater homes. Farther on SR 6 is **Port Tobacco,** one of the oldest continuously occupied towns in America. Fork to the left on Chapel Point Road to visit the reconstructed 1819 federal courthouse and Charles County Museum of Port Tobacco.

Back on SR 6 go west to Doncaster and turn right on SR 344, which merges with SR 224. Proceed on SR 224 to Marbury and turn right on SR 484. At Pisgah take a right again on SR 425. Follow this to SR 6; continue 1 mile farther to the Old Durham Church, attended by Gen. Smallwood and visited by Washington. Return to SR 6 and go east across the county. For a break from historical exploring you might wish to enjoy activities available at scenic 180-acre Gilbert Run Park in Dentsville.

One mile beyond Dentsville take SR 231 south to SR 234. A left turn takes you into St. Mary's County via a scenic route. Continue on SR 234 to Chaptico and turn right on SR 242 leading to **Coltons Point.** A museum in this Potomac coastal town honors the first Marylanders—settlers who landed on nearby St. Clement's Island in 1634.

Leaving Coltons Point on SR 242, turn right on SR 234, which shortly merges with SR 5. Follow this into Leonardtown, where the Old Jail Museum and a county library in a restored early 18th-century house are open to visitors.

From Leonardtown take SR 245 through **Hollywood** and out 3 more miles to Sotterley Plantation on the western shore of the Patuxent River. The restored Colonial mansion, English country gardens, slave cabin, smoke house and other original support buildings make this one of southern Maryland's most distinctive attractions.

Return to Hollywood and take SR 235 south. Pass SR 237 and, as you enter **Lexington Park,** watch for Three Notch Road on your left. This is the entrance to the Naval Air Test and Evaluation Museum. If you come to the entrance to the navy base on SR 235 you have gone a block too far; there is no access to the museum from the base.

From the museum proceed south on SR 235 to Ridge, where the route merges with SR 5. Follow this to Scotland Beach and Point Lookout State Park, at the southernmost tip of Maryland's western shore. On a site where Confederate

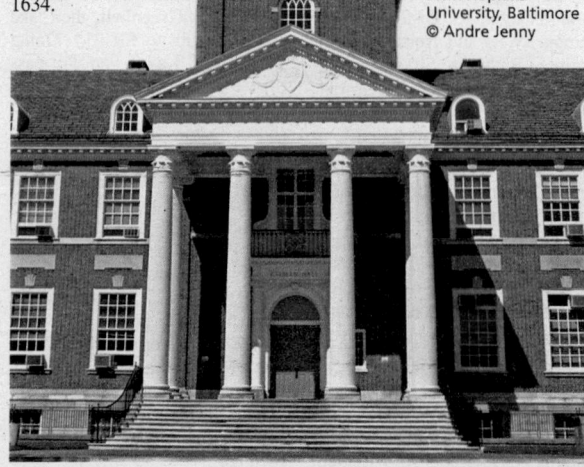

John Hopkins University, Baltimore
© Andre Jenny

prisoners were held during the Civil War, the park includes a Confederate cemetery and a museum in addition to recreational facilities.

Return to Ridge and continue on SR 5 to Maryland's first capital, **St. Mary's City.** In town follow signs for Historic St. Mary's City, a complex of exhibits and attractions spread over 800 acres. You can expect to spend a day or two seeing the reconstructed town that was settled in 1634 by Maryland's first colonists.

From St. Mary's City continue on SR 5 to Park Hall and go east on Park Hall Road to SR 235. Take this north for about 8 miles and turn right on SR 4. After passing through Town Creek you will cross the Patuxent River and enter Calvert County, at the lower tip of the peninsula between the Patuxent and the Chesapeake Bay.

The first town you enter in Calvert County is **Solomons,** a quiet waterfront community with one of North America's deepest natural ports. Visit the Calvert Marine Museum, the Drum Point Lighthouse and the nearby oyster-packing house and, if time permits, take the hour-long harbor cruise.

From Solomons follow SRs 2 and 4 north, watching for directional signs on side roads to attractions on the Chesapeake shore. SR 497 leads to Cove Point Lighthouse, the oldest tower light on the Chesapeake; other roads lead to Calvert Cliffs State Park, where fossils can be collected on the beach, and to the Calvert Cliffs Nuclear Power Plant Visitors Center. Near **Lusby** is the 327-acre Flag Ponds Nature Park, with facilities for hiking, fishing and picnicking.

Near Port Republic do not miss a side trip to the Jefferson Patterson Park and Museum. To reach this archeological and environmental preserve from SRs 2/4 take SR 264 south 2 miles, fork to the left on SR 265 and follow signs. On the way back to SRs 2/4 stop at Christ Church on SR 264 to see the garden of biblical plants.

Farther north on SRs 2/4 take SR 506 west. Turn left on Gray's Road to reach the Battle Creek Cypress Swamp Sanctuary. For information see the Points of Interest entry for **Prince Frederick.** Back on SRs 2/4 swing around Prince Frederick and proceed north to the point where the two routes diverge.

Follow SR 2 to Mount Harmony and take Mount Harmony Road east. When this runs into SR 260 continue to **Chesapeake Beach.** This community on the western shore provides a scenic climax to your tour of southern Maryland. After taking in the exhibits at the Chesapeake Beach Railway Museum you can sit on the pier, gaze across the bay, and delight in the graceful ways of the swans and geese.

When you can no longer resist the prodding to return to the workaday world take SR 260 back to Mount Harmony and then northwest to SR 4. Follow this north to US 301 or beyond to I-95 for access to your homeward route.

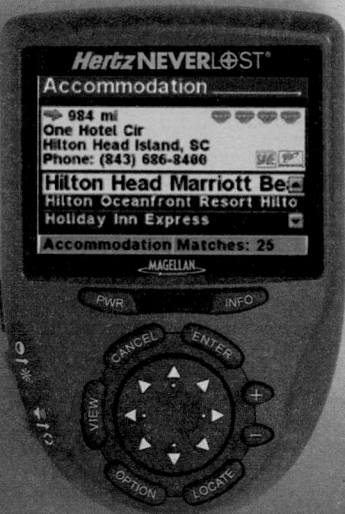

Points of Interest

ABERDEEN—*see Baltimore p. 179.*

ACCOKEEK—*see District of Columbia p. 113.*

ANNAPOLIS—*see Baltimore p. 179.*

 **ANTIETAM NATIONAL BATTLEFIELD** (B-4)

On SR 34/65 at Sharpsburg, Antietam National Battlefield is a more than 3,000-acre site where the Battle of Antietam, as it was called by the Union, or the Battle of Sharpsburg, as it was referred to by the Confederacy, took place Sept. 17, 1862.

On this bloodiest day of the Civil War, 12,410 Union and 10,700 Confederate soldiers were killed or wounded. Gen. George McClellan's 86,000 men met Gen. Robert E. Lee's 40,000 after decisive victories for the South in Virginia. Lee's objective was to invade northern home territory; this was to be his first invasion of the North. Therefore, his forced withdrawal following a tactical draw resulted in a strategic Union victory.

A Confederate victory at Antietam would have been such a blow to the Union that the momentum would have moved to the Confederacy and it probably would have won the war; thus, this victory at Antietam enabled President Abraham Lincoln to issue the Emancipation Proclamation. William S. McKinley, later president of the United States, fought at the site.

General Information and Activities

Maps, tablets and monuments mark the battlefield, and vertical cannon barrels indicate sites where three Union and three Confederate generals died. An 8.5-mile driving tour highlights historic areas of the battlefield. Allow 2 hours minimum. The battlefield is open daily dawn-dusk; closed Jan. 1, Thanksgiving and Dec. 25.

ADMISSION to the park, visitor center and cemetery is $4; free (ages 0-16); $6 (family rate).

PETS must be restricted at all times, either in vehicles or by leash, and are not allowed in public buildings.

ADDRESS inquiries to the Superintendent, Antietam National Battlefield, P.O. Box 158, Sharpsburg, MD 21782; phone (301) 432-5124.

Points of Interest

ANTIETAM NATIONAL BATTLEFIELD VISITOR CENTER, 1 mi. n. of Sharpsburg on SR 65 at the battlefield entrance, has exhibits pertaining to this significant Civil War conflict. Five oil murals by Capt. James Hope, a battle participant, illustrate various Antietam battle scenes. Interpretive talks, a 26-minute film and a 1-hour documentary about Lee's Maryland campaign are offered. An audiotape describing points of interest can be rented or purchased.

Allow 1 hour minimum. Daily 8-7, Memorial Day-Labor Day; 8:30-5, rest of year. Closed Jan. 1, Thanksgiving and Dec. 25. Talks scheduled daily, June 1-Labor Day. The 26-minute film is shown every half hour 8:30-noon and 1-4. Combined park, cemetery and visitor center admission $4; free (ages 0-16); $6 (family rate). Phone (301) 432-5124.

ANTIETAM NATIONAL CEMETERY, 1 mi. from battlefield entrance on SR 34, was established in 1866 and contains the graves of 4,776 Union soldiers and those of 261 men who fought in subsequent wars. "The Private Soldier," a monument dedicated to Civil War dead, is a notable landmark. Allow 30 minutes minimum. Daily dawn-dusk. Combined park, cemetery and visitor center admission $4; free (ages 0-16); $6 (family rate). Phone (301) 432-5124.

PRY HOUSE FIELD HOSPITAL MUSEUM, 18906 Shepherdstown Pike (SR 34) in Keedysville and affiliated with Frederick's National Museum of Civil War Medicine, chronicles the house's use as a medical facility and headquarters for the Army of the Potomac during the Battle of Antietam. President Lincoln visited the house a few weeks after the battle in 1862.

DID YOU KNOW

Including islands, the shoreline of Maryland is 4,431 miles long.

An amputation kit, a doctor's medical bag and a small household medicine chest are among the several dozen artifacts displayed. A life-sized diorama also can be seen. Allow 1 hour minimum. Daily 11-5:30, June-Oct.; Sat.-Sun. in May and Nov. Admission $2. Phone (301) 695-1864.

ASSATEAGUE ISLAND NATIONAL SEASHORE (F-9)

Eight miles south of Ocean City via SR 611, Assateague Island National Seashore encompasses 39,500 acres (19,000 of which are land), including Assateague Island and nearby small islands. Paralleling the coast of Maryland and Virginia, Assateague Island is a narrow 37-mile-long barrier island with Maryland's Assateague State Park *(see Recreation Chart and Ocean City in the AAA Mideastern CampBook)* at the northern end and the Chincoteague National Wildlife Refuge *(see Chincoteague, Va., p. 241)* at the southern end.

The island is home to Chincoteague ponies that eat marsh grass and drink from freshwater ponds. The horses reportedly are descendants of a 16th-century herd that swam ashore from a sinking Spanish galleon, although a more likely story is that they descended from local farm horses. The island is also a stop-off point during the migration of the endangered peregrine falcon and several waterfowl, including the greater snow goose.

General Information and Activities

The National Park Service operates a visitor center with exhibits at the bridge approach to the north end of the island. Allow 30 minutes minimum. Both the National Park Service and the wildlife refuge operate information centers at the southern end.

Boating, crabbing, fishing, swimming and camping opportunities are available. Naturalists conduct canoe trips, campfire talks, guided nature walks and clamming and fishing demonstrations daily mid-June through August. Because of the importance of the sand dunes to the preservation of the barrier island, visitors are asked to use the marked passageways across the dunes.

Allow 1 hour minimum to see the island. The seashore is open daily 24 hours. Visitor centers are open daily 9-5. *See Recreation Chart and the AAA Mideastern CampBook.*

ADMISSION to the park (including Chincoteague National Wildlife Refuge) is by a 7-day, $15 permit per private vehicle, or a $30 annual permit.

PETS must be restricted at all times, either in vehicles or by leash, and are not allowed in public buildings or on trails. This pet policy varies by area; phone ahead to find out where pets are not allowed.

ADDRESS inquiries to the Superintendent, Assateague Island National Seashore, 7206 National Seashore Ln., Berlin, MD 21811; phone (410) 641-1441, or (410) 641-3030 for camping information.

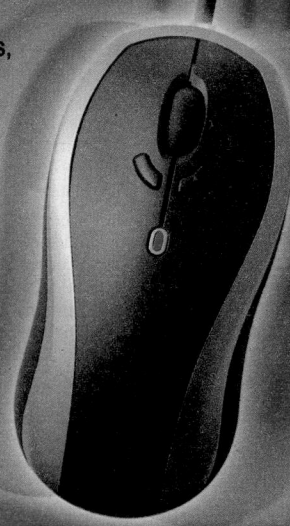

Baltimore

City Population: 651,154	Elevation: 445 ft.

Editor's Picks:

Baltimore & Ohio Railroad
Museum ....(see p. 171)

Baltimore Museum of Art .... (see p. 171)

National Aquarium in Baltimore(see p. 174)

Find more AAA top picks at AAA.com

Inner Harbor / © Kord / age fotostock

Although its proud natives may sometimes feel overshadowed by the attention paid to the power and politics of nearby Washington, D.C., Baltimore is important in its own right as the economic and educational center of Maryland.

Founded in 1729 by an act of the Provincial Assembly, the city was incorporated in 1797 with a population of 20,000. During the War of 1812 the British unsuccessfully attacked Baltimore, and Francis Scott Key wrote "The Star-Spangled Banner" while watching the bombardment from a warship anchored in Baltimore Harbor.

Baltimore's history has been a series of firsts. The Mount Clare Station at W. Pratt and Poppleton streets was the starting point for the country's first railroad, the Baltimore and Ohio, as well as the country's first railroad freight and passenger station *(see the Baltimore & Ohio Railroad Museum attraction listing p. 171)*. The first telegraphic communication—"What hath God wrought?"—was received in 1844.

The nation's oldest Catholic cathedral, the Basilica of the Assumption of the Blessed Virgin Mary, is at Mulberry and Cathedral streets; buried in the crypt is John Carroll, the country's first archbishop. Lloyd Street Synagogue, near Lombard, was the first synagogue to be built in Maryland.

Vision and vitality thrive in today's Baltimore. Johns Hopkins University, several medical schools and such colleges as the Peabody Conservatory of Music and the Maryland Institute College of Art are among the institutions that provide the city with a stimulating and innovative learning environment.

Baltimore's continuing urban renewal program is one of the most successful in the nation, and many of the city's omnipresent marble-stooped row houses have been restored or remodeled. Striking modern buildings, overhead walkways, fountains and plazas distinguish Charles Center, Baltimore's downtown business district. One Charles Center, a 24-story skyscraper of bronze glass designed by Mies van der Rohe, dominates the complex.

The Inner Harbor is an example of the pride Baltimoreans take in their city. Once home to decaying factories and warehouses, the harbor is now a showplace that attracts throngs of weekend visitors. Gleaming office buildings, the five-story National Aquarium in Baltimore and the glass-enclosed pavilions of Harborplace rise from the water's edge.

Still a major port for grain, coal and spices, the harbor also hosts many ethnic festivals and is the permanent home of the last Civil War-era vessel still afloat, the USS *Constellation (see attraction listing p. 175)*.

Baltimore's ethnic diversity and history are reflected in such venerable neighborhoods as Little Italy, Little Lithuania and H.L. Mencken's beloved Union Square. Offering a fine view of the Inner Harbor is the historic Federal Hill area, the site of a picnic where 4,000 citizens celebrated the ratification of the Constitution in 1788. Fells Point is an

Getting There — starting on p. 165

Getting Around — starting on p. 165

What To See — starting on p. 169

What To Do — starting on p. 176

Where To Stay — starting on p. 585

Where To Dine — starting on p. 591

Essential Experiences — visit AAA.com

Editor's Event Picks — visit AAA.com

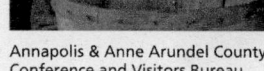

old seaport neighborhood with an international flair. National Katyn Memorial, a tribute to the thousands of Polish officers executed under Stalin at three Soviet Union concentration camps stands at the center of the traffic circle at Aliceanna and President streets. One panel describes the massacres and another explains the memorial's design.

Getting There

By Car

A network of superhighways makes Baltimore easily accessible from all directions. From the south the main approach is I-95, with access to the downtown area via I-395 and the Baltimore-Washington Parkway. Traffic from the west approaches downtown via I-70 and US 40.

Access from the north is via I-83, while traffic from the northeast arrives on I-95. The Baltimore Beltway (I-695); the four-lane Harbor Tunnel Thruway (I-895), a toll road; and the Fort McHenry Tunnel (I-95), also a toll road, combine to provide a complete bypass of the city.

Getting Around

Street System

Charles Street separates east and west Baltimore; Baltimore Street divides the city's north and south sections. Numbered streets run east and west. Except for Eutaw Street, most downtown streets are one way.

The city speed limit for most areas is 30 mph, or as posted. Rush hours are from about 7:30 to 9 a.m. and from about 4 to 6 p.m. Avoid driving during rush hours if possible. A right turn on red is permitted, unless otherwise posted.

Annapolis & Anne Arundel County Conference and Visitors Bureau

Parking

Parking on the street is controlled by meter. Many municipal metered parking lots are in and near downtown. Rates at the numerous commercial lots and garages average about $2.50 an hour.

Public Transportation

Baltimore's public transportation consists of buses, a metro subway, light rail and MARC commuter trains. Buses cover most of the city while the trains connect downtown with many surrounding areas. The fare for bus, metro subway and light rail is $1.60, with an additional 40c for express bus routes. Exact fare is required, and the fare box accepts only dollar bills and tokens. Bus and train schedules vary depending on the route and day of the week. MARC trains do not operate on weekends and most holidays. A $3.50 unlimited-use day pass is good on the bus, subway and light rail systems. MARC train fares range from $4-$14 depending on the distance.

Destination Baltimore

National Aquarium in Baltimore.
Aquatic exhibits abound at this five-story
aquarium in the Inner Harbor. (See listing
page 174)

*H*istory buffs will delight in the
many sights and sounds of
Maryland's largest city.

*R*elive the battle at Fort
McHenry that inspired Francis
Scott Key's "The Star-Spangled
Banner"; take a cruise at the
Inner Harbor; or hop aboard a
train at the B&O Railroad
Museum at Mount Clare Station,
starting point of the country's
first railroad.

© Babe Ruth Birthplace
Museum

*Babe Ruth Birth-
place Museum,
Baltimore.*
The Sultan of
Swat's birthplace
hits a home run
with visitors. (See
listing page 169)

See Baltimore-Washington
International Thurgood
Marshall Airport
map page 579

*P*laces included in this
AAA Destination City:

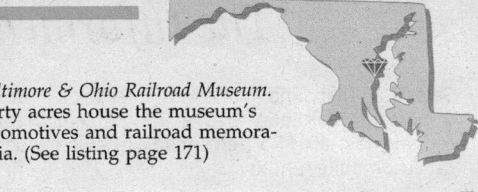

Baltimore & Ohio Railroad Museum.
Forty acres house the museum's
locomotives and railroad memorabilia. (See listing page 171)

© Ralph Krubner / Jupiter Images

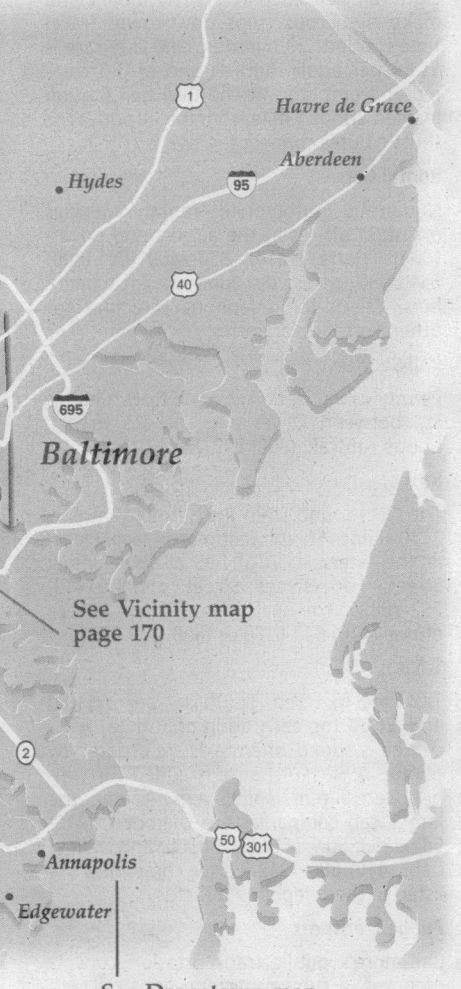

See Vicinity map
page 170

See Downtown map
page 180

Annapolis & Anne Arundel County CVB

St. Anne's Church, Annapolis.
Rebuilt in 1859, this Episcopalian
church is the third to occupy the
site since the parish was founded in
1692. (See listing page 181)

Maryland Office of Tourism
Development

*Fort McHenry National
Monument and Historic Shrine.*
It was here in 1814 that Francis Scott Key was inspired to
write "The Star-Spangled Banner." (See listing page 184)

The Informed Traveler

Sales Tax: Maryland's statewide sales tax is 5 percent; Baltimore has a 7.5 percent lodging tax; an 11.5 percent tax is levied on automobile rentals.

WHOM TO CALL

Emergency: 911

Police (non-emergency): 311 or (410) 396-2525

Time: (410) 844-1212

Temperature: (410) 936-1212

Hospitals: Franklin Square Hospital Center, (443) 777-7000; Greater Baltimore Medical Center, (443) 849-2000; Johns Hopkins Hospital, (410) 955-5000; Maryland General Hospital, (410) 225-8000; Sinai Hospital of Baltimore, (410) 601-9000; University of Maryland Medical Center, (410) 328-8667.

WHERE TO LOOK

Newspapers

The major newspaper is *The Baltimore Sun. The Baltimore Examiner* is a free newspaper available Monday through Friday; it is available Saturday in limited areas.

Radio

Radio station WBAL (1090 AM) is an all-news/weather station; WJHU (88.1 FM) is a member of National Public Radio.

Visitor Information

Baltimore Visitor Center: 401 Light St., Baltimore, MD 21202; phone (410) 837-4636 or (877) 225-8466. Visitor center hours are daily 9-6.

Monthly *Baltimore* magazine lists dining, entertainment and events information.

TRANSPORTATION

Air Travel

Baltimore/Washington International Thurgood Marshall Airport, about 10 miles south of downtown, is reached via I-195 off I-95 or SR 295 (Baltimore-Washington Parkway). Taxi fare to downtown is $2.90 for the first mile and $2 for each additional mile; phone (410) 859-1100. Shuttle service to downtown is about $21 for the first passenger and $12 per additional passenger; phone (800) 258-3826, (800) 776-0323 or (410) 381-2772. Limousine fare to principal downtown hotels is $52 (1-4 people) and $92 (up to 6 people), plus an 18 percent tip; phone (410) 519-0000.

Light rail trains depart BWI Terminal E and make numerous stops downtown; travel time is about 20 minutes. One-way fare is $1.60 per adult. Amtrak and MARC commuter trains stop at the BWI Rail Station located about 1 mile from the airport. Free shuttle buses connect the two.

Rental Cars

Numerous automobile rental agencies maintain offices at the airport and downtown. Hertz, (410) 850-7400 or (800) 654-3080, offers discounts to AAA members. Check the telephone directory for other car rental agencies.

Rail Service

Pennsylvania Station is at 1515 N. Charles St., between Oliver and Lanvale streets; phone Amtrak, (800) 872-7245.

Buses

The Greyhound Lines Inc. terminals are at 2110 Haines St. and Baltimore Travel Plaza, at the intersection of I-95 and O'Donnell Street. For Haines Street phone (410) 752-7682; for Baltimore Travel Plaza phone (410) 633-6389 or (800) 231-2222.

Taxis

Taxis are metered. The base fare is $1.80 and $1.60 for each additional mile. A $1 charge is added when taxis are ordered by phone. A 50c surcharge is added for trips between 9 p.m. and 5 a.m. Among the larger cab companies are Diamond, (410) 947-3333; Sun, (410) 235-0300; and Yellow Cab, (410) 685-1212. Other companies are listed in the telephone directory.

Public Transport

Baltimore's public transportation consists of buses, a subway system, light rail and MARC commuter trains. *See Public Transportation for details.*

Discounts are available for senior citizens, passengers with disabilities, children and regular commuters. The MTA *Ride Guide* provides information about the systems. For additional information, phone (410) 539-5000, (866) 743-3682 or TTY (410) 539-3497.

The Baltimore Metro subway system runs from downtown at Johns Hopkins Hospital northwest to Owings Mills Station at I-795 and Painters Mill Road with 14 intermediate stations. Free parking is available at some of the stations. The system operates Monday-Friday 5 a.m.-midnight and Saturday-Sunday and holidays 6 a.m.-midnight.

Light Rail service runs between Hunt Valley and Glen Burnie, with spur lines serving Baltimore/Washington International Thurgood Marshall Airport and Penn Station. There are 30 intermediate stops, and parking is available at some of the stations. Trains operate Monday-Saturday 6 a.m.-11 p.m. and Sunday and holidays 11 a.m.-7 p.m.

What To See

AMERICAN VISIONARY ART MUSEUM is at 800 Key Hwy. at jct. Covington St. This museum features the imaginative, creative and intuitive works of self-taught artists. The artists come from diverse work and cultural backgrounds and have created in various conventional and unconventional media. Of interest is the 55-foot high "Whirligig" in the outdoor Central Plaza.

Food is available. Allow 1 hour minimum. Tues.-Sun. 10-6; closed Thanksgiving and Dec. 25. Admission $12; $8 (ages 0-17, ages 55+ and students with ID). Phone (410) 244-1900.

[SAVE] **BABE RUTH BIRTHPLACE MUSEUM,** off the 600 block of W. Pratt St. at 216 Emory St., comprises four adjoining row houses, including the birthplace of the "Sultan of Swat." The museum contains numerous photographs, paintings and memorabilia associated with Babe Ruth. The furnishings are from the late 1800s. Film clips of Ruth's life are shown.

Allow 1 hour minimum. Daily 10-6 (also 6-7:30 p.m. on Orioles game days), Apr.-Oct.; Tues.-Sun. 10-5 (also 5-8 on Ravens game days), rest of year. Closed Jan. 1, Thanksgiving and Dec. 25. Admission $6; $4 (ages 60+); $3 (ages 3-12). Combination ticket with Sports Legends Museum at Camden Yards $14; $11 (ages 60+); $9 (ages 3-12). Phone (410) 727-1539.

BALLPARK TOURS-ORIOLES departs from 333 W. Camden St. Visitors will learn about the park's construction and visit the Orioles dugout, the press area, a party suite and a luxury suite.

Note: Areas on the tour may change due to facility events. Allow 1 hour, 30 minutes minimum. Tours depart Mon.-Sat. at 11, noon, 1 and 2, Sun. at 12:30, 1, 2 and 3. Tours are not given on days when an afternoon game is scheduled. Phone ahead to

Little Italy / Baltimore Area Convention and Visitors Association

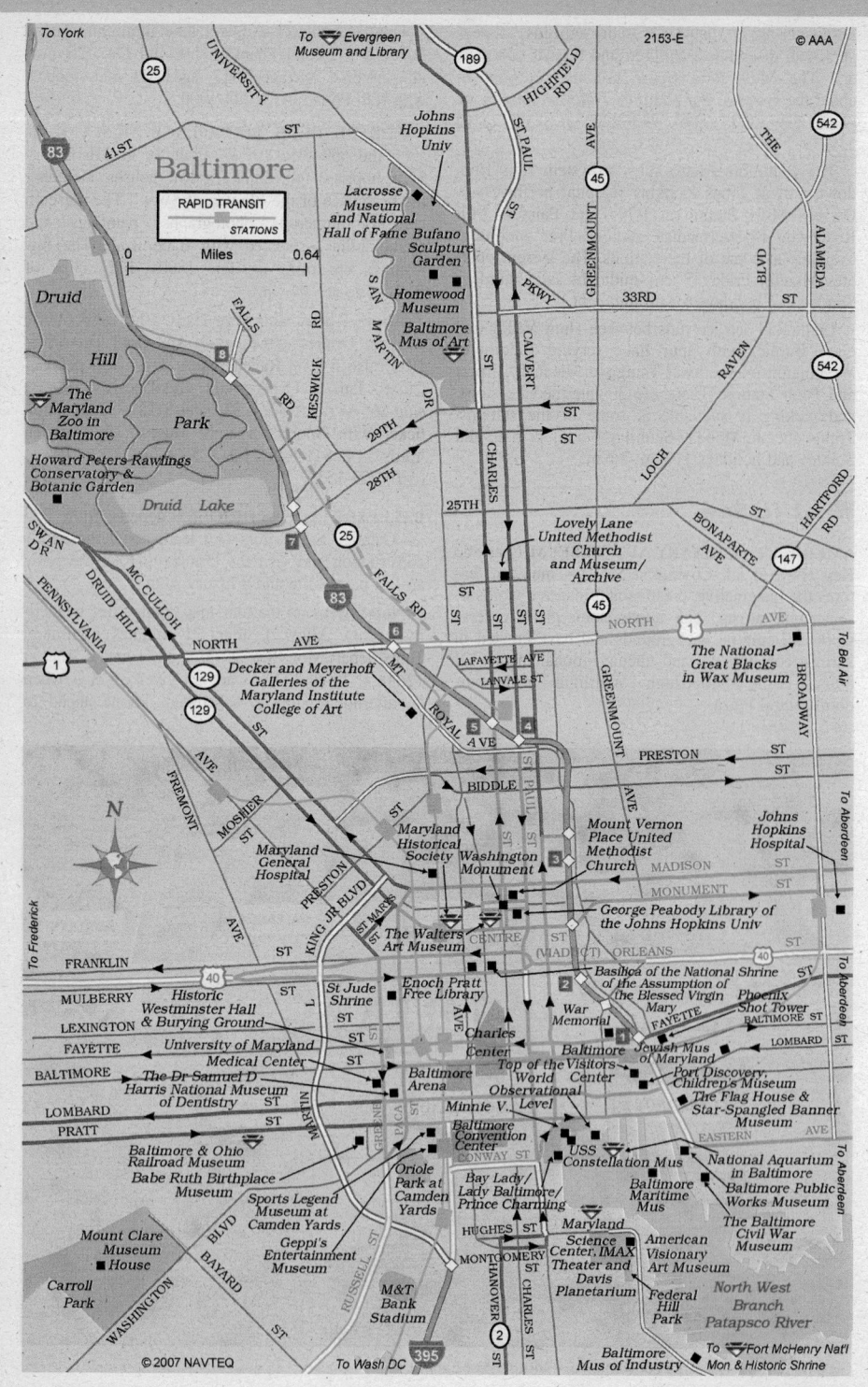

To York

To Evergreen
Museum and Library

189

2153-E   © AAA

25

UNIVERSITY

41ST   ST

83

Baltimore

RAPID TRANSIT

STATIONS

0   Miles   0.64

Johns
Hopkins
Univ

Lacrosse
Museum
and National
Hall of Fame

Bufano
Sculpture
Garden

Homewood
Museum

Baltimore
Mus of Art

Druid

Hill

Park

The
Maryland
Zoo in
Baltimore

Howard Peters Rawlings
Conservatory &
Botanic Garden

Druid   Lake

HIGHFIELD
RD

ST PAUL
ST

GREENMOUNT   AVE

542

THE   ALAMEDA

33RD

RAVEN   BLVD

542

147

LOCH   RAVEN

HARTFORD   RD

33RD

8

SWAN   DR

PENNSYLVANIA

DRUID HILL

MCCULLOH

KESWICK   RD

FALLS   RD

SAN   MARTIN

29TH   DR

28TH

25TH

CHARLES   ST

CALVERT   ST

PKWY

ST

ST

ST

7

25

83

FALLS RD

Lovely Lane
United Methodist
Church
and Museum/
Archive

45

NORTH   AVE   1

To Bel Air

1

129

129

NORTH   AVE

6

MT   ROYAL   AVE

Decker and Meyerhoff
Galleries of the
Maryland Institute
College of Art

LAFAYETTE AVE

LANVALE ST

5   4

BIDDLE   ST

The National
Great Blacks
in Wax Museum

BROADWAY

GREENMOUNT   AVE

PRESTON   ST

To Aberdeen

N

FREMONT   AVE

MOSHER   ST

PRESTON   ST

AVE

Maryland
General
Hospital

Maryland
Historical
Society

Washington
Monument

Mount Vernon
Place United
Methodist
Church

3

MADISON   ST

MONUMENT   ST

Johns
Hopkins
Hospital

To Frederick

FRANKLIN   ST

MULBERRY

40

Historic
Westminster Hall
& Burying Ground

LEXINGTON

FAYETTE

BALTIMORE

University of Maryland
Medical Center

The Dr Samuel D
Harris National Museum
of Dentistry

LOMBARD

PRATT

Baltimore & Ohio
Railroad Museum
Babe Ruth Birthplace
Museum

Mount Clare
Museum
House

Carroll
Park

KING JR BLVD

ST MARY

St Jude
Shrine

Enoch Pratt
Free Library

The Walters
Art Museum

CENTRE   ST

(VIADUCT)   ORLEANS   ST

Basilica of the National Shrine
of the Assumption of
the Blessed Virgin
Mary

2

War
Memorial

George Peabody Library of
the Johns Hopkins Univ

FAYETTE

40

To Aberdeen

Phoenix
Shot Tower

BALTIMORE   ST

LOMBARD   ST

Charles
Center

Baltimore
Arena

Baltimore
Top of the
World
Observational
Level

Visitors
Center

1

Jewish Mus
of Maryland

Port Discovery,
Children's Museum

The Flag House &
Star-Spangled Banner
Museum

Minnie V.

Baltimore
Convention
Center

CONWAY   ST

USS
Constellation Mus

Baltimore
Maritime
Mus

EASTERN   AVE

National Aquarium
in Baltimore

Baltimore Public
Works Museum

Sports Legend
Museum at Camden Yards

Geppi's
Entertainment
Museum

Oriole
Park at
Camden
Yards

Bay Lady/
Lady Baltimore/
Prince Charming

HUGHES   ST

MONTGOMERY   ST

Maryland
Science
Center, IMAX
Theater and
Davis
Planetarium

American
Visionary
Art Museum

The Baltimore
Civil War
Museum

North West
Branch
Patapsco River

RUSSELL   ST

BAYARD

WASHINGTON   BLVD

M&T
Bank
Stadium

395

2

Federal
Hill
Park

Baltimore
Mus of Industry

To Fort McHenry Nat'l
Mon & Historic Shrine

© 2007 NAVTEQ   To Wash DC

HANOVER   ST

CHARLES   ST

confirm schedule. Admission $7; $5 (ages 3-12 and 55+). Parking $5-$10. AX, DS, MC, VI. Phone (410) 547-6234.

BALTIMORE & OHIO RAILROAD MU-SEUM is at 901 W. Pratt St. The 40-acre indoor/outdoor museum's extensive collection of locomotives, both originals and replicas, dates from 1829. In addition to examples of many types of engines, the museum contains railroad china and silver, outdoor train exhibition platforms, and an exhibit about railroad time and time pieces.

The shops that once surrounded the station built thousands of cars and engines and were known as "The Railroad University." The station's focal point is the roundhouse dome covering a wooden turntable surrounded by 22 stalls that contain cars and locomotives. Train rides and a tour of the restoration facility also are available.

Food is available. Allow 2 hours, 30 minutes minimum. Mon.-Fri. 10-4, Sat. 10-5, Sun. 11-4; closed Jan. 1, Easter, Memorial Day, July 4, Labor Day, Thanksgiving, Dec. 24-25 and Dec. 31. Last admission is 30 minutes before closing. Admission $14; $12 (ages 60+); $8 (ages 2-12). Admission is half-price the first Tues. of the month. AX, DS, MC, VI. Phone (410) 752-2490 to verify schedule and prices.

THE BALTIMORE CIVIL WAR MUSEUM, 601 President St., tells the story of the first bloodshed of the Civil War that occurred in April 1861 as the Sixth Massachusetts Volunteer Militia Regiment was attacked by Southern sympathizers; five soldiers and 11 civilians were killed. The station's role in the Underground Railroad and Maryland's role as a border state in the Civil War are featured.

Allow 1 hour minimum. Thurs.-Mon. 10-5; closed Jan. 1, Thanksgiving and Dec. 25. Admission $4; $3 (ages 13-17, ages 60+ and students with ID). MC, VI. Phone (410) 385-5188.

BALTIMORE MARITIME MUSEUM, Inner Harbor at Pier 3 on Pratt St., includes the USS *Torsk,* a World War II submarine. Next to the *Torsk* is the *Chesapeake,* a floating lighthouse designed to aid shipping in the bay. Also included is the Coast Guard cutter *Taney,* the last ship afloat to have survived the attack on Pearl Harbor, and the 1856 Seven Foot Knoll Lighthouse, which stood at the entrance to Baltimore Harbor for 133 years before being moved to the Inner Harbor.

Allow 1 hour minimum. Daily 10-5, Mar.-Dec.; Fri.-Sun. 10-5, rest of year. Closed Thanksgiving and Dec. 25. Admission $8; $6 (ages 60+); $4 (ages 6-14). AX, MC, VI. Phone (410) 396-3453.

BALTIMORE MUSEUM OF ART is 3 mi. n. of the Inner Harbor on Art Museum Dr. at N. Charles and 31st sts. Designed by John Russell Pope, architect of the National Gallery of Art in Washington, D.C., the museum houses a permanent collection of more than 90,000 objects, ranging from ancient mosaics to contemporary art.

Visitors can see furniture, decorative arts, paintings, miniature and period rooms; art from Africa, the Americas and Oceania; Chinese ceramics; and eight galleries devoted to European old masters. Two sculpture gardens contain 20th-century works by artists from Rodin to Nevelson.

The Cone Collection includes paintings and sculptures by Henri Matisse, Pablo Picasso, Vincent van Gogh and other modern artists. The West Wing for Contemporary Art houses a large collection of Andy Warhol paintings. Programs, events and special exhibitions are held throughout the year.

Food is available. Wed.-Sun. 11-5 (also Sat.-Sun. 5-6); closed Jan. 1, July 4, Thanksgiving and Dec. 25. Free. Phone (443) 573-1700.

BALTIMORE MUSEUM OF INDUSTRY is at 1415 Key Hwy. Housed in an 1865 oyster cannery, the museum features exhibits about the social and economic history of Baltimore's industries. Re-creations include a print shop, a garment loft, a late 19th-century machine shop, a pharmacy and a cannery. Visitors can view the 1906 steam tug *Baltimore,* which was a common sight on the city waterfront for more than 50 years.

Allow 1 hour minimum. Tues.-Sat. 10-4, Sun. 11-4; closed Easter, Thanksgiving and Dec. 24-25. Admission $10; $6 (senior citizens); free (ages 0-3). Phone (410) 727-4808.

BALTIMORE PUBLIC WORKS MUSEUM is off E. Falls Ave. at 751 Eastern Ave. on the eastern edge of the Inner Harbor. The museum provides a behind-the-scenes and even under-the-scenes glimpse of how a large city provides necessary utility services to its citizens. Its collection of more than 2,000 items includes photographs, wooden water pipes from the early 19th century and water meters. The museum is in an architecturally striking 1912 sewage pumping station. A life-size model shows what it looks like beneath the streets. Tues.-Sun. 10-4; closed major holidays. Admission $3; $2.50 (ages 55+ students with ID); free (ages 0-5). Phone (410) 396-5565.

BASILICA OF THE NATIONAL SHRINE OF THE ASSUMPTION OF THE BLESSED VIRGIN MARY is at Cathedral and Mulberry sts. Designed by architect Benjamin Henry Latrobe and overseen by America's first bishop, John Carroll, the neoclassical basilica was begun in 1806 and completed in 1821, making it the first Roman Catholic cathedral in the country. More than 20 saints and potential saints have visited the site, including St. John Neumann, Pope John Paul II and Blessed Teresa of Calcutta. Eight Baltimore archbishops, including Carroll, are buried in the crypt. A museum features artifacts, photographs, textiles and documents.

Daily 8:30-4:30. Guided 45-minute tours depart Mon.-Sat. at 9, 11 and 1; Sun. at noon. Phone ahead to confirm Sat. tour schedule. No tours are given on major national holidays. Church free. Guided tour $2. Phone (410) 727-3565.

CYLBURN ARBORETUM, 4915 Greenspring Ave., is 207 acres and contains marked trails; a garden of the senses for the physically impaired; an all-American garden; an herb garden; the Heritage Rose Garden, which features species more than 100 years old; and a formal garden. A post-Civil War mansion can be toured; highlights include fireplaces, mosaics and tapestries. A museum interprets sights seen on the arboretum's trails. Special events are held throughout the year. Grounds daily dawn-dusk. Mansion Mon.-Fri. 7:30-3:30. Free. Phone (410) 396-0180.

DECKER AND MEYERHOFF GALLERIES OF THE MARYLAND INSTITUTE COLLEGE OF ART are in the Fox Building on Mount Royal Ave. Rotating exhibits feature works by students, faculty and national and international artists. Mon.-Sat. 10-5, Sun. noon-5. Summer hours may vary; phone ahead. Free. Phone (410) 225-2280.

[SAVE] **THE DR. SAMUEL D. HARRIS NATIONAL MUSEUM OF DENTISTRY,** an affiliate of the Smithsonian Institution, is at 31 S. Greene St. on the University of Maryland Baltimore campus. Visitors can learn about the history and importance of oral health while viewing creatively presented exhibits. MouthPower teaches good nutrition and the dangers of tobacco. Science exhibits explore saliva and forensics. Among the museum's artifacts are George Washington's denture and Queen Victoria's dental instruments.

Allow 1 hour minimum. Wed.-Sat. 10-4, Sun. 1-4; closed major holidays. Admission $6; $3 (ages 60+ and students with ID); free (ages 0-5). AX, MC, VI. Phone (410) 706-0600.

DRUID HILL PARK, n.w. section of the city at jct. Druid Park Lake Dr. and Madison Ave. This 744-acre park is one of the country's largest natural city parks and dates from 1688. Daily dawn-dusk. Free. Phone (410) 396-7900.

Howard Peters Rawlings Conservatory and Botanic Gardens, near the entrance of Druid Hill Park, was built in 1888. The display area includes the original 1888 five-story Palm House as well as the Orchid Room, Mediterranean House, Tropical House and Desert House. A 10-acre garden east of the Palm House has thousands of tulips in spring and annuals and tropical plants June through October. Plants from around the world and seasonal displays also can be seen.

Tours of the grounds and gardens are available. Tues.-Sun. 10-4; closed Dec. 25. Guided tour $4. Self-guiding tour free. Phone (410) 396-0008 to confirm schedule.

[GEM] **The Maryland Zoo in Baltimore,** in Druid Hill Park, is comprised of 161 acres with more than 2,000 birds, mammals and reptiles. A highlight is the African Journey, which includes a large breeding colony of African black-footed penguins, a troop of chimpanzees and the African Watering Hole with white rhinoceroses, zebras and ostriches.

The 8-acre children's zoo features interactive exhibits, a giant tree slide and a petting farm. The Polar Bear Watch is a state-of-the-art exhibit enabling observation of Magnet and Alaska as they swim and play underwater. Keeper Encounters allow visitors to learn about animal habits and habitats.

Picnicking is permitted. Food is available. Daily 10-4; closed 2nd Friday in June for annual fundraiser, Thanksgiving and Dec. 25. Phone ahead for Keeper Encounter program schedule. Admission $15; $12 (ages 65+); $10 (ages 2-11). Phone (410) 366-5466.

ENOCH PRATT FREE LIBRARY, 400 Cathedral St. between Franklin and Mulberry sts., is the city's principal public library and serves as Maryland's State Library Resource Center. Built in a 1930s Art Deco design, the library has a permanent display about H.L. Mencken that includes books, photos and letters. Guided tours are available by appointment. Mon.-Wed. 10-8, Thurs. 10-5:30, Fri.-Sat. 10-5, Sun. 1-5. Hours may vary; phone ahead. Phone (410) 396-5430.

[GEM] [SAVE] **EVERGREEN MUSEUM AND LIBRARY** is at 4545 N. Charles St., 1.5 blks. n. of Cold Spring Ln. This 1850s 48-room Italianate mansion was home to B&O Railroad's Garrett family 1878-1942. These two generations of discriminating collectors accumulated more than 50,000 objects. Among the items are Asian ceramics, Tiffany windows and chandeliers, Postimpressionist paintings and sculptures, and a 17th-century Belgian tapestry.

The library contains prints, manuscripts, rare books and other artifacts from around the world. The 1923 theater was created by Leon Bakst, renowned for his sets and costumes for Ballet Russes. Special events, lectures, concerts, performances, exhibitions and educational programs are scheduled throughout the year.

Allow 1 hour, 30 minutes minimum. Guided tours depart on the hour Tues.-Fri. 11-4, Sat.-Sun. noon-4; closed Jan. 1, Memorial Day, July 4, Labor Day, Thanksgiving and Dec. 25. Last tour begins 1 hour before closing. Hours may vary; phone ahead. Fee $6; $5 (senior citizens); $3 (children and students with ID); free (ages 0-6). Phone (410) 516-0341.

FEDERAL HILL PARK, Battery Ave. and Key Hwy., was the site of a Civil War fort. It provides a view of the harbor and city skyline. Picnicking is permitted; grilling requires a permit. (410) 396-7070.

FELLS POINT MARITIME MUSEUM is at 1724 Thames St. Baltimore's maritime history is chronicled through ship models, paintings, exhibits about ships and a brief film detailing the area's maritime significance. The 1859 building housed a horse-drawn trolley line and later served as a rope warehouse, which is when the freight elevator capable of carrying up to 2,000 pounds was installed.

Allow 30 minutes minimum. Thurs.-Mon. 10-5; closed major holidays. Admission $4; $3 (ages 13-17, ages 60+ and students with ID). MC, VI. Phone (410) 732-0278.

 THE FLAG HOUSE AND STAR-SPANGLED BANNER MUSEUM, off Albemarle St. at 844 E. Pratt St., was the home of Mary Pickersgill, who made the 15-star and 15-stripe American flag in 1813 that inspired Francis Scott Key to write "The Star-Spangled Banner." The flag waved above Fort McHenry during its bombardment in 1814. Guided tours of the 1793 house showcase furniture, textiles, photographs, clothing and military objects from the 17th-19th centuries.

The adjacent museum commemorates the War of 1812. The Great Flag Window made of colored panes of glass is a replica of the original flag. Tues.-Sat. 10-4; last tour begins at 3:15. Admission (includes house tour and museum) $7; $6 (senior citizens); $5 (ages 4-18). Phone (410) 837-1793.

FORT McHENRY NATIONAL MONUMENT AND HISTORIC SHRINE—
see place listing in the Vicinity section p. 184.

FREDERICK DOUGLASS-ISAAC MYERS MARITIME PARK AND MUSEUM is in Fells Point at 1417 Thames St. at jct. Caroline St. It is near the site where the Chesapeake Marine Railway and Dry Dock Co., which Myers helped found in 1866, used to be located. On the grounds is a replica of a marine railway, a device allowing boats to be pulled out of the water so they can be worked on at a dry dock. A 10-minute film shares stories about Douglass and Myers as well as Baltimore African-American history. Artifacts found in the area are displayed. A boat workshop and panoramic views of Baltimore's harbor also are featured.

Allow 45 minutes minimum. Tues.-Sun. 10-5; closed Jan. 1, Thanksgiving and Dec. 25. Admission $5; $4.50 (ages 55+); $4 (ages 6-11). AX, MC, VI. Phone (410) 685-0295.

GEORGE PEABODY LIBRARY OF THE JOHNS HOPKINS UNIVERSITY, 17 E. Mount Vernon Pl., has five ornate iron balconies surrounding a marble atrium. Tues.-Fri. 9-5, Sat. 9-1. Free. Phone (410) 659-8179.

GEPPI'S ENTERTAINMENT MUSEUM is on the second floor of Camden Station at 301 W. Camden St., adjacent to Oriole Park at Camden Yards. Pop culture and its role in advertising is celebrated with this diverse collection of memorabilia dating from 1776 to the present. Toys, comic books, music and other collectibles are displayed. Pieces relating to pop culture icons like Charlie Chaplin, Elvis Presley and The Beatles also are part of the collection.

Allow 1 hour minimum. Daily 10-6, Apr.-Sept.; Tues.-Sun. 10-5, rest of year. Closed Jan. 1, Thanksgiving and Dec. 25. Admission $10; $9 (ages 55+); $7 (ages 5-18 and students with ID). AX, MC, VI. Phone (410) 625-7060.

HAMPTON NATIONAL HISTORIC SITE—
see Towson in the Vicinity section p. 186.

HISTORIC WESTMINSTER HALL AND BURYING GROUND, W. Fayette and Greene sts., is the cemetery of the Westminster Presbyterian Church. Buried here are Edgar Allan Poe, James McHenry—U.S. Secretary of War 1797-1800—and a number of other historical figures. Churchyard and catacomb tours are available.

Cemetery open daily 8-dusk. Guided churchyard and catacomb tours the first and third Fri. of each month at 6:30 p.m., Sat. at 10 a.m., Apr.-Nov. Church and grounds free. Tours $5; $4 (ages 0-12 and 60+). Reservations are required for guided tours. Phone (410) 706-2072.

JEWISH MUSEUM OF MARYLAND, 15 Lloyd St., encompasses the 1845 Lloyd Street Synagogue, believed to be the country's third oldest surviving synagogue, and the 1876 B'nai Israel Synagogue, which still has an active congregation. The museum maintains documents, objects and photographs related to the 350-year history of Jewry in Maryland. Two exhibition galleries host changing exhibits about local and national Jewish culture and history topics.

Allow 1 hour minimum. Museum open Tues.-Thurs. and Sun. noon-4. Free guided tours are available at 1 and 2:30 and by appointment. Library by appointment. Closed holidays. Admission $8; $4 (students with ID); $3 (ages 0-12). Phone (410) 732-6400.

JOHNS HOPKINS UNIVERSITY, off N. Charles St., is a small, private liberal arts university founded in 1876. The 140-acre campus originally was the estate of Charles Carroll Jr., son of Charles Carroll, a signer of the Declaration of Independence. Today the Homewood campus has more than 4,000 undergraduates studying in top-ranked programs. Its well-known schools of medicine, public health, nursing and music are elsewhere in Baltimore.

Tours of the campus can be arranged at the Admissions Office, 140 Garland Hall. Tours depart Mon.-Fri. at 10 and 1; a tour occasionally is offered Sat. Hours may vary; phone ahead. Free. Phone (410) 516-8171.

Bufano Sculpture Garden, in Dunning Park behind Mudd Hall, is a wooded area with a paved pathway meandering among 11 sculptures of animals by Beniamino Bufano. Daily 24 hours. Free. Phone (410) 516-8171.

Homewood Museum, 3400 N. Charles St., was an 1801 wedding gift from Maryland Declaration of Independence signer Charles Carroll to his son, Charles Carroll Jr. Highlights in the restored house include intricate woodwork carvings and ornate plaster ceiling ornaments. Much of the house is furnished with period pieces, some originally owned by the Carroll family. Special events are scheduled throughout the year.

Guided tours depart Tues.-Fri. on the half-hour 11-4, Sat.-Sun. noon-4; closed Jan. 1, Memorial

Day, July 4, Labor Day, Thanksgiving and Dec. 25. Last tour begins 30 minutes before closing. Admission $6; $5 (senior citizens); $3 (children and students with ID); free (ages 0-6). Phone (410) 516-5589.

LACROSSE MUSEUM AND NATIONAL HALL OF FAME, 113 W. University Pkwy., depicts the history of this game through photographs and art, uniforms, equipment, trophies, memorabilia and documentaries that highlight the evolution of the game from the days of the American Indians to the present. Allow 30 minutes minimum. Mon.-Fri. 10-3, June-Jan.; Tues.-Sat. 10-3, rest of year. Closed holidays. Admission $3; $2 (ages 5-15). Phone (410) 235-6882.

LOVELY LANE UNITED METHODIST CHURCH AND MUSEUM/ARCHIVE, 2200 Saint Paul St., was designed by noted architect Stanford White in 1884; White is best known for the design of the Washington Arch in New York City. The museum exhibits Methodist historical materials. The archive contains extensive material used by historians and genealogists.

Church open Mon.-Fri. 9-3. Museum/Archive open Thurs.-Fri. 10-4. Guided tours of the church and museum are available Sun. at 11, July-Aug.; at noon, rest of year. Tours also are available by appointment. Donations. Phone (410) 889-1512 for the church, or (410) 889-4458 for the museum/archive.

MARYLAND HISTORICAL SOCIETY is at 201 W. Monument St. at Park Ave. Founded in 1844, the society preserves and interprets Maryland's history with a museum of more than 200,000 pieces and a library of nearly 7 million items.

One of the museum exhibits combines more than 200 images and objects with a collection of oral histories to reveal Marylanders' pursuit of liberty. A highlight is Francis Scott Key's original manuscript of "The Star-Spangled Banner." Because of its fragility the manuscript is only displayed for 10 minutes of every hour. A facsimile is displayed at all times.

A visual arts exhibit includes portraits, landscape paintings and miniatures. Some of Henry Latrobe's paintings, sketches and letter books can be seen. The museum also features furniture dating 1634-2000 as well as decorative arts, including silver. The library includes ephemera, genealogical material and photographs.

Museum open Wed.-Sun. 10-5. Library open Wed.-Sat. 10-4:30. Museum and library closed holidays. Museum admission $4; $3 (ages 13-17, ages 60+ and students with ID). Library admission $6. Phone (410) 685-3750.

MARYLAND SCIENCE CENTER, IMAX THEATER AND DAVIS PLANETARIUM, 601 Light St. at the Inner Harbor, has hands-on exhibits and live science demonstrations. The Dinosaur Mysteries exhibit features 14 full-size dinosaur skeletons and casts. The human body is featured in Your Body: The Inside Story. Newton's

Alley is an interactive exhibit dedicated to Sir Isaac Newton's principles of science. Children are encouraged to learn by playing in the Kids Room.

Multimedia presentations are offered in Davis Planetarium. An IMAX theater with a five-story screen gives visitors a larger-than-life perspective on a variety of subjects.

Allow 1 hour, 30 minutes minimum. Daily 10-6 (also Fri.-Sat. 6-8 p.m.), Memorial Day weekend-Labor Day; Mon.-Sat. 10-5 (also Sat. 5-6), Sun. 11-5, Apr. 9-day before Memorial Day weekend; Tues.-Sat. 10-5 (also Sat. 5-6), Sun. 11-5, rest of year. The IMAX Theater is open after center hours for evening shows. Closed Thanksgiving and Dec. 25. Admission $14.50; $13.50 (ages 60+); $10 (ages 3-12). IMAX admission $8. Combination tickets also available. AX, MC, VI. Phone (410) 685-5225.

THE MARYLAND ZOO IN BALTIMORE—*see Druid Hill Park p. 172.*

[SAVE] **MOUNT CLARE MUSEUM HOUSE** is in Carroll Park at 1500 Washington Blvd. between Bush and Monroe sts. The only pre-Revolutionary mansion within the city limits, this 1760 Georgian-style house was the home of Charles Carroll, barrister and Revolutionary patriot. Originally part of an 800-acre plantation, the estate once contained wheat fields, a gristmill, an ironworks, brick kilns, racing stables, a shipyard and terraced gardens. More than 85 percent of the period furnishings are Carroll family pieces.

Allow 1 hour minimum. Tues.-Sat. 10-4, Mon. by appointment; closed holidays. Guided tours are given on the hour. Last tour begins 1 hour before closing. Admission $6; $5 (ages 55+); $4 (ages 6-18). Phone (410) 837-3262.

MOUNT VERNON PLACE UNITED METHODIST CHURCH is at 10 E. Mount Vernon Pl., corner of N. Charles St. This 1872 green serpentine and gray stone church, on the site where Francis Scott Key died in 1843, exemplifies Victorian Gothic architecture. The ornately carved interior features an organ with 3,827 pipes, and a labyrinth winding two-thirds of a mile. Guided tours are available. Mon.-Thurs. 9-2:30, Fri. 9-noon; closed holidays. Donations. Phone (410) 685-5290.

NATIONAL AQUARIUM IN BALTIMORE, 501 E. Pratt St., is on Pier 3 in Baltimore's Inner Harbor. This aquarium's five-story main structure displays a collection of 16,000 aquatic animals representing more than 600 species from around the world.

Other aquatic exhibits include a 335,000-gallon Atlantic Coral Reef featuring hundreds of tropical reef fish; the Open Ocean, home to the aquarium's largest sharks; a steamy South American rain forest enclosed by a pyramid of glass; and one of the world's largest poison-dart frog collections. Animal Planet Australia: Wild Extremes, an exhibit representing Australia's northern outback, includes such animals as pig-nosed turtles, freshwater crocodiles, flying foxes and zebra finches.

The Marine Mammal Pavilion includes an educational arcade, an interactive touch pool and a 1.2 million-gallon Atlantic bottlenose dolphin habitat offering daily marine mammal presentations.

Note: Lines form early and there often is a long wait outside, so the best time to visit is before 11. Baby strollers must be checked, but backpack baby carriers are provided. Allow 2 hours, 30 minutes minimum. Daily 9-8, July 1 to mid-Aug.; daily 9-6 (also Fri. 6-8 p.m.), mid-Aug. through Aug. 31; daily 9-5 (also Fri. 5-8), Mar.-June and Sept.-Oct.; daily 10-5 (also Fri. 5-8), rest of year. The aquarium remains open 1.5 hours after the last ticket is sold. Schedule may vary; phone ahead. Closed Thanksgiving and Dec. 25.

Admission $21.95; $20.95 (ages 61+); $12.95 (ages 3-11). Aquarium and dolphin presentation $24.95; $23.95 (ages 61+); $13.95 (ages 3-11). AX, DS, MC, VI. Phone (410) 576-3800, or TTY (410) 625-0720.

THE NATIONAL GREAT BLACKS IN WAX MUSEUM, 1601 E. North Ave., is committed to the study and preservation of African-American history. More than 100 life-size wax figures portray people who had significant impact on events in ancient Africa, the Middle Passage, the Civil War, Reconstruction, the Harlem Renaissance and the modern civil rights movement. A 24-foot-by-30-foot replica of a slave ship also is featured.

Guided tours, audiotape tours, and sign language tours by reservation are available. Allow 30 minutes minimum. Tues.-Sat. 9-6, Sun. noon-6, Jan. 15-Oct. 14; Tues.-Sat. 9-5, Sun. noon-5, rest of year. Closed most federal holidays. Admission $9; $8 (ages 12-17, ages 55+ and students with ID); $6 (ages 3-11). AX, MC, VI. Phone (410) 563-3404.

PORT DISCOVERY, CHILDREN'S MUSEUM is at 35 Market Pl. in Baltimore's Inner Harbor. Educational and interactive exhibits designed for ages 2-10 include time traveling back to ancient Egypt, collecting clues and solving mysteries, climbing around a three-story urban tree house and making arts and crafts.

Allow 1 hour, 30 minutes minimum. Mon.-Sat. 10-5, Sun. noon-5, Memorial Day-Labor Day; Tues.-Fri. 9:30-4:30, Sat. 10-5, Sun. noon-5, Oct. 1-day before Memorial Day; Fri. 9:30-4:30, Sat. 10-5, Sun. noon-5, rest of year. Admission $10.75; free (ages 0-1). AX, MC, VI. Phone (410) 727-8120.

REGINALD F. LEWIS MUSEUM OF MARYLAND AFRICAN AMERICAN HISTORY & CULTURE is at 830 E. Pratt St. at jct. E. Pratt and President sts. Themed exhibits tell the story of the African-American experience in Maryland. Topics include African-Americans' work in various industries and professions, their influence in the arts and the important role that families and communities have played in their lives. Featured African-Americans include Harriet Tubman, Benjamin Banneker and Frederick Douglass.

Food is available. Allow 1 hour, 30 minutes minimum. Tues.-Sat. 10-5, Sun. noon-5; closed Jan. 1, Easter, Thanksgiving and Dec. 25. Admission $8; $6 (ages 65+ and college students with ID); free (ages 0-6). AX, DS, MC, VI. Phone (443) 263-1875.

ST. JUDE SHRINE is at 308 N. Paca St. Staffed by the Pallottine Fathers and Brothers since 1917, the St. Jude Shrine is the nationwide center of St. Jude Thaddeus devotions. Catholics pray to St. Jude, patron of the desperate and hopeless. Novena services are held. Allow 30 minutes minimum. Mon.-Fri. 6:30-4:30 (also Wed. 4:30-8:30), Sat. 7-4:30, Sun. 7-2. Free. Phone (410) 685-6026.

SAVE **SPORTS LEGENDS MUSEUM AT CAMDEN YARDS** is at 301 W. Camden St. Exhibits inside Camden Station pay tribute to local college and professional sports. Babe Ruth, Johnny Unitas and horse racing as well as the Baltimore Orioles, Ravens and Colts are among the athletes, events and teams profiled. An area is dedicated to Civil War and railroad history, including President Abraham Lincoln, who is said to have stopped at this rail station several times, once on his way to his famed Gettysburg visit.

Allow 1 hour minimum. Daily 10-6 (also 6-7:30 p.m. on Orioles game days), Apr.-Sept.; Tues.-Sun. 10-5, rest of year. Closed Jan. 1, Thanksgiving and Dec. 25. Admission $10; $8 (ages 60+); $6.50 (ages 3-12). Combination ticket with Babe Ruth Birthplace Museum $14; $11 (ages 60+); $9 (ages 3-12). Phone (410) 727-1539.

SAVE **TOP OF THE WORLD OBSERVATIONAL LEVEL** is on the 27th floor of the World Trade Center in Inner Harbor at 401 E. Pratt St. The observation level in what is said to be the world's tallest pentagonal building offers a panoramic view of the skyline, harbor and beyond. Exhibits highlight Baltimore's history, including local landmarks and city milestones.

Allow 30 minutes minimum. Daily 10-6 (also Sat. 6-8 p.m.), Memorial Day-Labor Day; Wed.-Sun. 10-6, rest of year. Closed Thanksgiving and Dec. 25. Admission $5; $4 (senior citizens and military with ID); $3 (ages 3-12). Phone (410) 837-8439.

SAVE **USS CONSTELLATION MUSEUM,** just s. of downtown on Pier 1 at 301 E. Pratt St., is the last all-sail warship built by the U.S. Navy and the only Civil War-era vessel still afloat. Artifacts displayed include a navy cutlass, leg irons and navigation instruments, while hands-on activities include setting sails and turning the capstan. A replica cannon is fired twice daily (weather permitting).

Allow 30 minutes minimum. Daily 10-5, May 1-Oct. 14; 10-4, rest of year. Closed Jan. 1, Thanksgiving and Dec. 25. Hours may vary; phone ahead. Admission (includes audio tour) $8.75; $7.50 (ages 60+); $4.75 (ages 6-14). Phone (410) 539-1797.

THE WALTERS ART MUSEUM is at jct. Centre and Cathedral sts. at 600 N. Charles St. This municipally-owned museum houses more than 28,500 works of art spanning 55 centuries. Decorative art collections include ceramics, enamels, Fabergé eggs, tapestries and jewelry. Collections include ancient art, medieval art, Renaissance and post-Renaissance sculptures and decorative arts, old masters paintings, 19th-century paintings and sculptures, Asian art, illuminated manuscripts and arms and armor.

Raphael's "Madonna of the Candelabra" was the first of his Madonna paintings to become part of an American collection. Other Renaissance and Baroque artists represented include El Greco, Giovanni Battista Tiepolo and Paolo Veronese.

Food is available. Wed.-Sun. 11-5 (also Fri. 5-8); closed Memorial Day, July 4, Labor Day, Thanksgiving and Dec. 24-25. Free. Phone (410) 547-9000.

WAR MEMORIAL overlooks Memorial Plaza and Gay and E. Fayette sts. This Greek-style memorial honors Maryland citizens killed in World War I. Free. Phone (410) 396-8013.

WASHINGTON MONUMENT, in Mount Vernon Sq. at jct. W. Pratt and N. Charles sts., is dedicated to the nation's first president. A 228-step spiral stairway leads to the top of the monument where four observation windows provide a panorama of the city. A 30-ton statue of George Washington sits atop the monument. No elevators are available. Allow 30 minutes minimum. Wed.-Sun. 10-4:30; closed holidays. Phone to verify schedule. Admission _$1. Phone (410) 396-1049.

What To Do

Sightseeing

The Baltimore Visitor Center *(see The Informed Traveler box)* offers a combination ticket called the **Harbor Pass,** which provides admission to the Maryland Science Center; National Aquarium in Baltimore; Port Discovery, Children's Museum; and Top of the World Observational Level. The pass also includes 1 day of unlimited free rides on the water taxi and numerous discounts in the area. Valid for 3 consecutive days, the Harbor Pass costs $49; $35 (ages 3-12).

Several tour companies offer guides who will accompany you on specialized tours focusing on Baltimore historical sites, architecture or art.

Tour companies include Baltimore Rent-A-Tour, (410) 464-7994; Baltimore Shuttle, (410) 254-8687; City Hall Tours, (410) 396-4947; Convention Management Services Ltd., (410) 377-8181 and Presenting Baltimore Inc., (410) 539-1344.

Boat Tours

Visitors who would rather not walk can travel between attractions at the Inner Harbor aboard water taxis that run approximately every 15 minutes in season, about every 45 minutes the rest of the year. The taxis operate Mon.-Sat. 10 a.m.-11 p.m. and

Sun. 10-9, May 1-Labor Day; daily 10-8 (also Fri.-Sat. 8-11 p.m.) in Apr. and day after Labor Day-Oct. 31; daily 11-6, rest of year. Unlimited 1-day pass $8; $4 (ages 0-10).

Stops include the Maryland Science Center, IMAX Theater and Davis Planetarium; the National Aquarium in Baltimore *(see attraction listings)*; Harborplace; Little Italy; the Rusty Scupper restaurant; the Pier 6 Concert Pavilion; and piers 5 and 6. Boats also travel to Fells Point and Canton. Phone (410) 563-3901 or (800) 658-8947.

BAY LADY/LADY BALTIMORE/PRINCE CHARMING, 561 Light St., offers narrated 2-hour lunch tours, 3-hour dinner cruises and a 3-hour Sunday brunch cruise of Baltimore's Inner Harbor and the Chesapeake Bay. A 1-hour sightseeing tour includes such sights as Ft. McHenry National Monument and Historic Shrine, National Aquarium in Baltimore and Fells Point. Moonlight and theme cruises also are available.

Lunch cruise Mon.-Sat. at noon, Apr.-Oct. Dinner cruise Mon.-Sat. at 7, Sun. at 5, Apr.-Oct. Brunch cruise Sun. at noon, Apr.-Oct. One-hour cruise daily every 90 minutes, 11:30-4, Apr.-Sept. Phone ahead to verify schedule. Fare for lunch cruise Mon. and Wed.-Fri. $32.90; $16.45 (ages 3-12). Tues. lunch cruise $26.90; $13.45 (ages 3-12). Sat. lunch cruise $36.90; $18.45 (ages 3-12). Dinner cruise $20.95-$65.90. Brunch cruise $38.90; $19.45 (ages 3-12). One-hour cruise $14.95; $10 (ages 3-12). Additional fees and service charges also apply. Reservations are recommended. AX, DS, MC, VI. Phone (410) 727-3113 or (800) 695-2628.

RIDE THE DUCKS-BALTIMORE departs from the Inner Harbor at jct. Light and Conway sts.; ticket booth is outside the Light Street Pavilion. Tours aboard a type of amphibious vehicle that was used during World War II take visitors through Baltimore's streets and on a cruise through the Inner Harbor. Among the sightseeing highlights are Oriole Park at Camden Yards, The Flag House and Star-Spangled Banner Museum, and the Washington Monument. The captain provides historical and other relevant information about the sites along the way.

Allow 1 hour, 30 minutes minimum. Tours depart daily on the hour 10-6, Apr.-Oct. Fare $24; $23 (ages 62+); $14 (ages 3-12). AX, DS, MC, VI. Phone (410) 727-3825, (877) 887-8225 or (800) 813-1637.

Walking Tours

Baltimore's old neighborhoods add much to the city's charm. A pleasant day can be spent visiting the historic areas of Federal Hill, Fells Point and Mount Vernon Place, or such ethnic neighborhoods as Little Italy.

"Urban homesteading" got its start in Baltimore's old neighborhoods. Under this program, an old house was purchased for as little as $1 with the understanding that the resident would restore or remodel it within a certain number of years. The eye-catching results can be seen in the Otterbein area on

Conway Street near Sharp Street and in the Stirling Street section off the 1000 block of Monument Street.

The city offers two free 90-minute guided walking tours departing from the Baltimore Visitor Center at 401 Light St. Heritage Walk features historical sites in the Inner Harbor, Little Italy, Jonestown and City Center, including the Flag House and Star-Spangled Banner Museum, the Carroll Mansion and the Phoenix Shot Tower. Mount Vernon Cultural Walk features such historic sites as Mount Vernon Place and Basilica of the National Shrine of the Assumption of the Blessed Virgin Mary. Brochures and trail markers allow visitors to take self-guiding tours of both routes. Each route covers about 3 miles; the guided tours cover about 1.5 miles. Comfortable walking shoes are recommended. Heritage Walk departs daily at 10, May-Oct., Sat.-Sun. at 10, in Apr. Mount Vernon Cultural Walk departs daily at noon, May-Oct., Sat.-Sun. at noon, in Apr. Phone (443) 984-3089 or (800) 343-3468.

Literature, maps and brochures for a walking tour of the city may also be obtained from the visitor center; phone (410) 659-7300 or (877) 225-8466. A variety of options are available, including heritage, ghost and architectural tours. In addition, tour information is available at the information kiosks on the west shore promenade of the Inner Harbor and at the Penn Central Railroad Station.

Sports and Recreation

Baseball attracts faithful fans in Baltimore; the Baltimore Orioles regularly draw big crowds to Oriole Park at Camden Yards; phone (410) 685-9800.

Named for Edgar Allan Poe's "The Raven," National **Football** League Super Bowl XXXV champions Baltimore Ravens compete for gridiron glory at M&T Bank Stadium; phone (410) 261-7283.

The Baltimore Blast, (410) 732-5278, play **indoor soccer** at 1st Mariner Arena. Some of the nation's top **lacrosse** players make up Baltimore's many NCAA teams, including the Johns Hopkins' Blue Jays, who compete at Homewood Field, Charles Street and University Parkway; phone (410) 235-6882. The Baltimore Bayhawks, one of Major League Lacrosse's newest teams, play outdoor lacrosse at Johnny Unitas Stadium; phone (866) 994-2957.

Horse racing is popular, and Pimlico Race Course has meets September through October; phone (410) 542-9400. The second race of the Triple Crown, The Preakness Stakes, is held at Pimlico the third weekend in May. The racetracks at Laurel and Timonium are an easy drive from the city.

Note: Policies concerning admittance of children to pari-mutuel betting facilities vary. Phone for information.

Golf can be played at Carroll Park, Monroe Street and Washington Boulevard; Clifton Park, Harford Road and St. Lo Drive; Forest Park Golf Course, 2900 Hillsdale at Forest Park Avenue; Mount Pleasant Golf Course, 6001 Hillen Rd.; and Pine Ridge Golf Course, 2001 Dulaney Valley Road in Lutherville.

Tennis players can find public courts at Clifton, Druid Hill and Patterson parks. In the winter **ice-skating** takes place at Patterson Park; phone Baltimore Recreation Department (410) 396-7900.

Boating is enjoyed at the Inner Harbor, Pratt and Light streets, and **fishing** is permitted at Loch Raven Reservoir, the city's principal water source.

Biking enthusiasts have their choice of bicycle trails in Clifton, Herring Run and Patterson parks.

Shopping

In the heart of Baltimore's revitalized financial and office district, Harborplace and The Gallery, at the corner of Light and Pratt streets overlooking the Inner Harbor, features national retailers and a variety of cafes and restaurants divided among three buildings: two glass-enclosed pavilions and, connected via an overhead skywalk, the Gallery, which offers three floors of shopping. A fourth floor consists of restaurants and shops.

A visit to one of the city's indoor food markets can be a fascinating experience. These markets are well-preserved monuments of an older Baltimore and contain aisle after aisle of stalls in which vendors offer wares ranging from meats and produce to fresh seafood from the bay. Baked goods also are available. Some of these markets have served their neighborhoods since the city's earliest days.

Two of the city's markets are located in areas often visited by tourists: Broadway Market, at Broadway and Fleet sts., and Cross Street Market, on Cross St. between Light and S. Charles sts. Broadway Market was founded in the late 18th century, and Cross Street Market began in the mid-19th century. Both are open Monday through Saturday from 7 a.m. until early evening; phone (410) 276-9498. The other markets, which are Lexington, Hollins, Avenue and Northeast, draw mostly local residents. Lexington Market, at 400 W. Lexington St., covers Lexington, Eutaw, Paca, Saratoga and Green sts. and is the largest city-operated market since 1782. It is open Monday through Saturday 8:30-6. The Arcade, a contemporary addition, offers everything from fresh produce to local seafood as well as two restaurants and a central stage area for entertainment and community use. Phone (410) 685-6169. Hollins Market is on Hollins St. between Arlington Ave. and Carrollton St., Avenue Market is at Pennsylvania and Laurens sts., and Northeast Market is at Monument and Chester sts. These began in the mid-19th century. The markets are open Monday through Saturday from 7 a.m. until early evening; Hollins Market is not open on Monday. Phone (410) 276-9498. **Note:** It is advisable to visit the markets, particularly Lexington, Hollins, Avenue and Northeast, only during daylight hours, to leave wallets and handbags in a safe place, and to travel with a partner. A renovation and revitalization of downtown Baltimore's Westside neighborhood is currently underway.

Small shops abound in Baltimore. Galleries and restaurants now occupy the elegant houses that long distinguished Charles Street.

Those in search of the unusual may want to visit Antique Row in the 700 and 800 blocks of Howard Street. Both blocks have rows of shops and galleries specializing in antiques, art and unusual gifts and collectibles. Mount Washington Village, on Kelly and Sulgrave avenues, encompasses specialty shops and boutiques within a village setting.

Cross Keys Village is a complex of shops and restaurants surrounding a parklike square on Falls Road between Northern Parkway and Cold Spring Lane. The Rotunda, north of downtown at 711 W. 40th St. near Johns Hopkins University, caters to college students and others with its 21 specialty shops.

For something different, the Historic Savage Mill in nearby Savage is an 1820s textile mill turned specialty marketplace where shoppers can find some 50 shops, eateries and art galleries in restored buildings.

Several regional malls are within the metropolitan area. One of the largest, White Marsh Mall, just north of the city off I-95 at exit 67, has a number of major stores, including JCPenney, Macy's and Sears.

Bargain hunters can find plenty of shopping territory at Arundel Mills, 10 miles south of Baltimore off I-95 exit 43 in Hanover via SR 100 E.

Other large malls include Eastpoint, I-695 exit 38W; Marley Station, via I-97 exit 14 and SR 100 exit 16 to 7900 Ritchie Hwy. (SR 2); Owings Mills, I-795 and Owings Mills Boulevard; Security Square, I-695 exit 17 to 6901 Security Blvd.; Towson Town Center, 825 Dulaney Valley Rd.; and Westview, I-695 exit 15B.

Performing Arts

The pleasures of good music can be found in the concerts, ballets and other musical programs presented by the Baltimore Symphony Orchestra. The orchestra performs throughout the season at Joseph Meyerhoff Symphony Hall, 1212 Cathedral St.; phone (410) 783-8100. The home of the Baltimore Opera Company is Lyric Opera House, a replica of Germany's Leipzig Music Hall, 140 W. Mount Royal Ave.; phone (410) 727-6000.

Throughout the summer and early fall, Pier 6 Concert Pavilion in the Inner Harbor presents R&B, rock and country acts featuring numerous individual artists; phone (410) 659-7100.

Hopkins Plaza offers free concerts once a month May through September. Concerts—some of which are free—are regularly scheduled at the acoustically superb Concert Hall of the Peabody Conservatory of Music, 21 E. Mount Vernon Pl.; phone (410) 659-8100. Cultural and sporting events take place at 1st Mariner Arena; phone (410) 347-2020.

Baltimore's major regional theater is Center Stage, 700 N. Calvert St., which produces a variety of contemporary and classic plays; phone (410) 332-0033 or TTY (410) 332-4240. Drama devotees can enjoy touring Broadway shows as well as the classics at the Hippodrome Theatre at the France-Merrick Performing Arts Center, 12 N. Eutaw St.; phone (410) 837-7400 for schedule information. Other dramatic offerings are staged at the theaters of the Arena Players, 801 McCulloch St., (410) 728-6500, and the Vagabond Players, 806 S. Broadway, (410) 563-9135.

The Theater Project, 45 W. Preston St., is the city's center for avant-garde productions; phone (410) 752-8558. The Cockpit in Court Summer Theatre of Essex Campus of the Community College of Baltimore County presents musicals, dramas and comedies throughout the summer; phone (410) 780-6369.

The Children's Theatre Association, 100 W. 22nd St., offers lighthearted dramas, classic children's literature and fairy tales; phone (410) 366-6403.

Several dinner theaters are in and around the city. Toby's Dinner Theater is in the Best Western Hotel & Conference Center at 5625 O'Donnell St.; phone (410) 995-1969 or (800) 888-6297. A second location is in Columbia at 5900 Symphony Woods Rd.; phone (410) 730-8311 or (800) 888-6297.

For schedules of current theatrical and musical offerings check the local newspapers.

Special Events

Baltimore's biggest event, The ▽ Preakness Celebration, takes place during May and culminates in the running of The Preakness Stakes at Pimlico Race Course. The celebration includes a parade, hot air balloon race and concerts.

Many of Baltimore's celebrations and festivals take place in the Inner Harbor or in the surrounding parks and plazas. The Inner Harbor also is the site of the Showcase of Nations during which colorful ethnic festivals are held each weekend from June to October; each honors a different group of settlers.

In July Mount Vernon's ▽ Artscape features such activities as continuous musical performances, indoor and outdoor visual arts exhibitions, film and theater.

Nearby Timonium hosts the Maryland State Fair in late August. The Fells Point Fun Festival attracts crowds to Baltimore's harbor area in early October. The ▽ Baltimore Book Festival is held in mid-September downtown at Mount Vernon Place. The Recreational Vehicle Show, also held in Timonium, is in mid-February.

From late April through mid-May, the Maryland House and Garden Pilgrimage opens homes and gardens in the Baltimore area and around the state for public viewing. Phone (410) 821-6933.

The Baltimore Vicinity

ABERDEEN (B-7) pop. 13,842

Aberdeen is the site of the 75,000-acre Aberdeen Proving Ground, established in 1917 to develop and test ordnance under simulated combat conditions. Outdoor displays about the federal reservation include foreign and U.S. artillery and tanks. The visitor entrance is on SR 715; a driver's license and vehicle registration are required to enter.

Harford County Tourism Council—Aberdeen: 211 W. Bel Air Ave., Aberdeen, MD 21001; phone (410) 575-7278.

U.S. ARMY ORDNANCE MUSEUM is on Aberdeen Proving Ground 2.7 mi. s. of jct. US 40 and SR 22 on SR 715. The required base day pass is issued only at the Maryland Ave. gate on SR 715. This indoor/outdoor museum contains a collection of small arms, artillery and tanks from most major nations. Displays trace the development of 20th-century weaponry. Many successful and failed prototypes can be seen on the grounds.

The museum houses a collection of American, British, French, German, Italian and Japanese artillery and tanks. An American fighting vehicle and 44,000-pound bomb also are on the grounds. "Anzio Annie," a German railroad gun that fired on Allies on the Anzio beachhead during World War II, is part of the artillery collection. Allied forces named the gun during the Italian Campaign of the war. When it was not in use, it was hidden in mountain tunnels. The gun has the capability to accurately fire about 31 miles.

Note: A driver's license and vehicle registration are required to obtain the museum pass. Daily 9-4:45; closed holidays except Armed Forces Day, Memorial Day, July 4 and Nov. 11. Free. Phone (410) 278-3602 or (410) 278-2396.

ANNAPOLIS (F-4) pop. 35,838, elev. 16'

See map page 180.

Annapolis' roots hark back to 1649 when a group of Puritan families from Virginia established the settlement of Providence on the north bank of the Severn River. Within a year a new county named after Lady Anne Arundel, the late wife of Cecil Calvert, the second Lord of Baltimore, was established. By 1684 Anne Arundel Town was laid out on 100 acres across the Severn from Providence and by 1694 the first royal assembly meeting under Governor Sir Francis Nicholson designated the settlement on the south side of the river the new capital, which was renamed Annapolis in 1695 in honor of Princess Anne, King James II's daughter and future queen of England.

The charter of 1708 makes Annapolis one of the oldest cities in the country. In 1783 and 1784 Congress assembled in Annapolis, making it the first peacetime capital of the United States.

The U.S. Naval Academy was established in Annapolis at the Army's Fort Severn in 1845. Attention focuses on the academy and city in late May during Commissioning Week, when members of the graduating class become naval officers.

In addition to its identity as a Navy center, Annapolis is distinguished by its architecture—altogether, 1,300 buildings from 15 different architectural styles earn Annapolis the title "A museum without walls." The city has the highest concentration of 18th-century Georgian-style buildings in the nation, including the homes of all four Maryland signers of the Declaration of Independence. Three of the four are open to the public: the Charles Carroll House, the Chase-Lloyd House and the William Paca House and Garden *(see attraction listing).*

The Charles Carroll House, 107 Duke of Gloucester St. behind St. Mary's Church, belonged to Carroll, one of the wealthiest men in early America and the only Catholic to sign the Declaration of Independence. Charles' grandfather built a frame house on the site, and then Charles' father built a larger brick house which joined both structures. Eventually Charles enlarged the brick house, and now only that portion remains. An 18th-century terraced garden overlooks Spa Creek. The site is open weekends June through October and other times by appointment; phone (410) 269-1737. The Chase-Lloyd House is 2 blocks east of Capitol Circle at 22 Maryland Ave. Construction began in 1769, but lawyer Samuel Chase sold it to planter and politician Edward Lloyd IV in 1771, who had the house completed three years later. In 1847, Chase's descendants acquired it but then bequeathed it to the Protestant Episcopal Church in 1888. A noteworthy historical event occurred in the residence when Francis Scott Key, author of the national anthem, was married here in 1804. Most of the house is in private use, but the first floor is open Tuesday through Saturday 2-4, Mar.-Dec.; phone (410) 263-2723.

The many public and private Colonial buildings in Annapolis exemplify the life and architecture of the pre-Revolutionary period, often referred to as the "Golden Age of Annapolis." An architectural anomaly is the executive residence, Government House, at State Circle and School Street; it was built in the late 1860s in the French Second Empire style, then one side was remodeled in the 1930s in the Georgian revival style. Guided tours of the house are offered by appointment; phone (410) 974-3531.

The waterfront, which surrounds City Dock, is one of the best preserved in the country. Historically this is the city's front door, as Annapolis was once an important seaport for trade with Great Britain, the West Indies and West Africa. Today, recreational boaters and sailing schools have made the city a major center for regattas, services and charters. Historic Waterfront Warehouse, just off Market Space at 4 Pinkney St., is a small single-room building that now displays a model representing the waterfront as it appeared in the late 1700s; phone (800) 603-4020.

A variety of tours allows visitors to explore the city and its environs. Tours originate at the Annapolis Visitor Center, 26 West St., and April through September at the information booth at the City Dock; phone (410) 280-0445 or (888) 302-2852.

"Historic Annapolis Walk with Walter Cronkite" is an audio cassette walking tour taking the listener to 18 historic sites. The tour takes about 75 minutes. "Historic Annapolis African-American Heritage Audio Walking Tour" is an audio cassette detailing a 1-hour self-guiding walking tour of historic sites that includes houses, museums, cemeteries and the dock where Kunta Kinte landed. At a fee of $5, player and cassette rentals for both tours are available at the Historic Annapolis Foundation Museum store at 77 Main St. Phone (410) 268-5576.

Ample parking is available at the Navy-Marine Corps Stadium. Shuttle trolleys run frequently to and from the downtown area daily. Fare is 75c each way.

Annapolis and Anne Arundel County Conference and Visitors Bureau: 26 West St., Annapolis, MD 21401; phone (410) 280-0445 or (888) 302-2852.

Self-guiding tours: Brochures and maps for self-guiding tours as well as tour and cruise schedules are available year-round at the Annapolis Visitor Center at 26 West St., and April through September at the City Dock information booth.

Shopping areas: Downtown Annapolis has a wealth of specialty shops and boutiques concentrated around Main Street, West Street, Maryland Avenue, the City Dock area and West Annapolis. Westfield Annapolis Mall, at the intersection of SR

450 (Crownsville Road) and US 50, includes Hecht's, JCPenney and Nordstrom. Marley Station, 10 miles north on SR 2/Ritchie Highway near Severna Park, features Hecht's, Macy's and Sears department stores.

ANNAPOLIS CARRIAGE departs from jct. Market Space and Main St. across the street from HistoryQuest. Coachmen point out historic buildings and sites where noteworthy events occurred during 25-min. and 50-min. horse-drawn carriage rides. Sights along the route include Hammond-Harwood House, Maryland State House, St. Anne's Church and the city dock. Traveling on cobblestoned streets reflects the city's appearance as it was 200 years ago.

Wed.-Sun. 11-10, mid-Mar. through Dec. 31. Schedule varies; phone ahead. Fare for 50-min. tour $35; $15 (ages 3-10). Fare for 25-min. tour $20; $10 (ages 3-10). Reservations are recommended. AX, DS, MC, VI. Phone (410) 267-6656.

BANNEKER-DOUGLASS MUSEUM is at 84 Franklin St. The museum features changing exhibits focusing on the role African-Americans have played throughout Maryland's history. Annual programs and educational events also are offered. Allow 30 minutes minimum. Tues.-Sat. 10-4. Free. Phone (410) 216-6180.

CAPITAL CITY COLONIALS departs from 36 Market Space. Guides dressed in period garb lead 1- to 2-hour walking tours to historic sites in the city, including Hammond-Harwood House, Maryland State House, St. Anne's Church, U.S. Naval Academy and William Paca House and Garden.

Note: Photo ID is required to enter the Maryland State House and U.S. Naval Academy. Departures Tues.-Sun. 10-2:30, Apr.-Oct.; Sat. 10-2:30 and by appointment, rest of year. Departure times vary depending on tour; phone ahead to confirm. Fare $10-$16, depending on tour. AX, DC, DS, MC, VI. Phone (410) 295-9715.

DISCOVER ANNAPOLIS TROLLEY TOURS departs from the Annapolis Visitor Center at 26 West St. This 1-hour narrated trolley tour introduces passengers to 350 years of local history, architecture, folklore and trivia. The tours pass residential areas and the waterfront as well as the exterior of the U.S. Naval Academy, Maryland State House and the governor's residence.

Departures daily (weather permitting), Apr.-Nov.; most weekends, rest of year. Phone for departure times and to confirm schedule. Closed Jan. 1, Thanksgiving and Dec. 25. Fare $15; $7 (ages 11-15); $3 (ages 5-10). Phone (410) 626-6000.

HAMMOND-HARWOOD HOUSE, off King George St. at 19 Maryland Ave., is a preserved Anglo-Palladian house. Built in 1774 for patriot, legislator and planter Matthias Hammond, the Palladian-style building was the last work of prominent English architect William Buckland. A museum since 1938, the house exhibits late

Annapolis

18th- and early 19th-century ceramics, enamels, furniture, glass and silver pieces.

The museum is home to a collection of paintings, many of which are portraits. More than a dozen works were done by the Peale family of artists. Eight are attributed to Charles Willson Peale, who was born in Maryland, studied painting in England and then returned to Maryland. Throughout his life he painted hundreds of portraits.

Allow 1 hour minimum. Guided 45-minute tours depart on the hour Tues.-Sun. noon-4, Apr.-Oct.; by appointment rest of year. Last tour begins 1 hour before closing. Closed Jan. 1, Thanksgiving and Dec. 25. Admission $6; $5.50 (students with ID); $3 (ages 0-10). MC, VI. Phone (410) 263-4683.

HELEN AVALYNNE TAWES GARDEN is at 580 Taylor Ave. at the Tawes State Office Building across from Navy Stadium. This 5-acre botanical garden features representations of the state's natural environmental communities, from the forested mountains of western Maryland to the sand dunes of the Eastern Shore. Shallow ponds support such wildlife as bullfrogs, ducks, fish, songbirds and turtles. An arc of cultivated plants stands opposite a stately arbor. Among the lobby's exhibits are two aquariums.

Guided tours are available by reservation. Weekdays the garden is entered through Tawes State Office Building; weekend and holiday access is between the Court of Appeals and the Department of Natural Resources buildings. Pets are not permitted. Allow 1 hour minimum. Gardens daily dawn-dusk. Lobby Mon.-Fri. 9-3. Free. Phone (410) 260-8189.

HISTORIC LONDON TOWN AND GARDENS— *see Edgewater in the Vicinity section p. 184.*

HISTORYQUEST OF THE HISTORIC ANNAPOLIS FOUNDATION is at 99 Main St. at the City Dock. This 3-story building features six rooms of exhibits about the city's history, and some artifacts can be seen. Visitors may rent a self-guiding audio tour of the city. Allow 45 minutes minimum for HistoryQuest. Daily 9:30-5 (also Fri.-Sat. 5-7, in summer); closed major holidays. Donations. Audio tour $10. Phone (410) 267-6656.

MARYLAND STATE HOUSE, on State Cir., is the oldest state capitol in continuous legislative use. It was begun in 1772 and finished 7 years later. Because of its convenient location, the State House served as capitol of the United States from Nov. 26, 1783, to Aug. 13, 1784, until a permanent location was chosen. In the Old Senate Chamber, George Washington resigned his commission as the commander in chief of the Continental Army, and Thomas Jefferson accepted his position as the first United States minister plenipotentiary to foreign governments.

The most significant event, however, took place Jan. 14, 1784, when the Continental Congress ratified the Treaty of Paris, officially ending the American Revolution.

Note: A photo ID is required to enter. Allow 1 hour minimum. Building open daily 8:30-5; closed Dec. 25. Guided tours are given daily at 11 and 3. Free. Phone (410) 974-3400.

PIRATE ADVENTURES ON THE CHESAPEAKE departs from 311 Third St. Aboard the *Sea Gypsy*, children experience a pirate excursion in Annapolis Harbor. Activities include reading a treasure map and shooting a water cannon.

Allow 1 hour, 30 minutes minimum. Tours depart daily every 90 minutes 9:30-5, mid-Apr. through Labor Day; Sat.-Sun. every 90 minutes 9:30-5 and by appointment, day after Labor Day-Oct. 31. Arrive 30 minutes prior to departure. Fare $18; $10 (ages 0-2). Reservations are recommended. AX, DS, MC, VI. Phone (410) 263-0002.

ST. ANNE'S CHURCH (Episcopal), Church Circle, was rebuilt in 1859. It is the third church on this site since the parish was founded in 1692. King William III presented the communion silver in 1695. The St. Anne's Memorial Window, by Tiffany & Co., won first prize for ecclesiastical art at the Chicago World's Fair in 1893. Daily 8-4:30. Free. Phone (410) 267-9333.

ST. JOHN'S COLLEGE, 60 College Ave., is a four-year liberal arts school enrolling 500 students. The college received its charter in 1784, succeeding the 1696 King William's School. Francis Scott Key was among the students of St. John's.

The Elizabeth Myers Mitchell Gallery displays changing exhibits during the academic year. A walking tour brochure featuring 19 buildings and monuments of historic and architectural interest is available.

DID YOU KNOW

Baltimore has won the Super Bowl with two different teams: the Baltimore Colts and the Baltimore Ravens.

Elizabeth Myers Mitchell Gallery open Tues.-Sun. noon-5 (also Fri. 7-8 p.m.) when exhibits are on view. Phone (410) 626-2556.

SCHOONER *WOODWIND* departs from Pusser's Landing at the Annapolis Marriott Waterfront Hotel, 80 Compromise St. A replica of classic, early 20th-century yachts, this 48-passenger vessel is outfitted with mahogany woodwork and gleaming chrome. A typical 2-hour cruise includes Annapolis harbor, waterfront views of the U.S. Naval Academy and a trip into the Chesapeake Bay. Guests are encouraged to help hoist the four sails or take a turn at the helm. Evening and overnight cruises also are available.

Tues.-Sun. and Mon. holidays at 11, 1:30, 4 and 6:30, Mon. at 6:30, mid-May through Labor Day; Tues.-Sun. at 10, 12:30, 3 and 5:30, early to mid-May and day after Labor Day-Sept. 30; Tues.-Sun. at 10, 12:30 and 3, mid-Apr. to late Apr. and mid-Oct. to late Oct.

Weekday daytime sightseeing fare $31; $29 (ages 61+); $20 (ages 0-11). Sunset and weekend cruise fares $34; $32 (ages 61+); $20 (ages 0-11). All ticket sales for cruises are not refundable or exchangeable unless the captain cancels the cruise due to unsafe conditions. AX, DS, MC, VI. Phone (410) 263-7837.

U.S. NAVAL ACADEMY can be accessed via entrance Gate 1 at jct. King George and Randall sts. Covering 338 acres on the south side of the Severn River, the academy is the undergraduate college of the U.S. Navy. It was established in 1845 by Navy Secretary George Bancroft on the site of old Fort Severn. Guided walking tours and information are available at the Armel-Leftwich Visitor Center, which features a film, a sample midshipman's room, the *Freedom 7* space capsule and exhibits about John Paul Jones as well as academy graduates who have gone into the space program.

The U.S. Naval Academy Museum in Preble Hall features the exhibit 100 Years & Forward, paintings, flags, medals, historical objects and personal memorabilia. Noon formation is held before Bancroft Hall, weather permitting, Monday through Friday during the school year.

Note: All visitors age 16 and older must be prepared to show a valid photo ID. Only vehicles with Department of Defense stickers or handicapped tags are permitted in the Yard. Grounds open daily 9-5; chapel and crypt of John Paul Jones close at 4. Visitor center open daily 9-5, Mar.-Dec.; 9-4, rest of year. Museum open Mon.-Sat. 9-5, Sun. 11-5. Guided walking tours depart from the visitor center daily; phone ahead for times. Visitor center and museum closed Jan. 1, Thanksgiving and Dec. 25. Tour $8.50; $7.50 (ages 62+); $6.50 (grades 1-12). Phone (410) 293-8687.

WATERMARK, departing from the city dock and from the visitor center at 26 West St., offers a walking tour and a variety of cruises (weather permitting) aboard various vessels. Ninety-minute tours

include the Severn River, Chesapeake Bay bridges and the Thomas Point Lighthouse. A 3-hour music cruise, a Pirates of the Chesapeake cruise, lighthouse tours and special event cruises also are available. Phone (410) 268-7601 to verify prices.

Annapolis Harbor Tour, departing from the city dock at the foot of Main St., offers a 40-minute cruise of Annapolis harbor, the Severn River and the banks of the U.S. Naval Academy. Departures on the hour Mon.-Fri. 11-4, Sat.-Sun. 11-7, mid-May through Labor Day; Mon.-Fri. noon-3, Sat.-Sun. 11-6, Apr. 1 to mid-May and day after Labor Day-early Oct. Phone ahead to verify schedule. Fare $10; $4 (ages 3-11). AX, DS, MC, VI. Phone (410) 268-7601 to verify prices.

Annapolis Tours By Watermark departs from two locations: the information booth at City Dock and the visitor center at 26 West St. Guides in Colonial attire conduct walking tours of historic Annapolis and the U.S. Naval Academy. Tours include interiors in the academy and the Maryland State House when accessible.

Note: Due to security concerns at sites visited, participants over age 15 must have a photo ID, and no pocket knives may be carried. Allow 2 hours, 30 minutes minimum. Tours depart daily at 10:30 from the visitor center and 1:30 from City Dock, Apr.-Oct.; Sat. at 1:30 from City Dock, rest of year. Fee $14; $7 (ages 3-11). Phone (410) 268-7601.

Day on the Bay Cruise, departing from the city dock at the foot of Main St., is a 7.5-hour tour that visits one of the following ports of call: Rock Hall or the restored fishing village of St. Michaels. There is a 3-hour stop for dining, shopping and exploring the Chesapeake Bay Maritime Museum.

St. Michaels cruises depart Sat. and Mon., mid-July to late Aug.; on Sat., late May to mid-July and late Aug.-late Sept. Schedule may vary; phone ahead. Fare for St. Michaels cruise $55-$60; $27.50-$30 (ages 0-11). Rock Hall cruise $50; $25 (ages 0-11). Lunch is not included in the fare. Reservations are recommended. Inquire about refund policies and the minimum number of passengers requirement. AX, DS, MC, VI. Phone (410) 268-7601 to verify prices.

Spa Creek Tour, departing from the city dock at the foot of Main St., is a 40-minute cruise of Annapolis harbor, including such sights as the U.S. Naval Academy and the residential areas of Spa Creek.

Cruises depart Mon.-Fri. on the half-hour 3:30-8:30, Sat.-Sun. at a quarter after and a quarter before the hour 1:15-8:15, mid-May through Labor Day; Mon.-Fri. on the half-hour 3:30-6:30, Sat.-Sun. 1:30-6:30, mid-Apr. to mid-May; Mon.-Fri. on the half-hour 3:30-6:30, Sat.-Sun. a quarter after and a quarter before the hour 1:15-7:15, day after Labor Day-early Oct. Fare $10; $4 (ages 3-11). AX, DS, MC, VI. Phone (410) 268-7601 to verify prices.

WILLIAM PACA HOUSE AND GARDEN, 186 Prince George St., was the estate of Paca, governor of Maryland and signer of the Declaration of Independence. Built 1763-65, the restored Georgian house, which combines elements of English Georgian style with progressive Maryland additions such as massive end chimneys, contains period furnishings. The restored 2-acre area includes a Chinese Chippendale bridge, a summer house, a fish-shaped pond, formal parterres and a wilderness garden. Seasonal events and lectures also are offered.

The garden was originally laid out 1765-72 and was paved over in the mid-20th century with asphalt. Research, aerial photography, and background details in Charles Wilson Peale's portrait of Paca aided in its reconstruction.

Guided 45-minute tours are available. Allow 2 hours minimum. Mon.-Sat. 10-5, Sun. noon-5, mid-Mar. through Dec. 31; Fri.-Sat. 10-5, Sun. noon-5, mid-Jan. to mid-Mar. Closed Jan. 1, Thanksgiving and Dec. 24-25. Last tour begins at 3:30, with the gardens closing at 4. Admission $8; $7 (senior citizens); $5 (ages 6-17); $25 (family rate for two adults and two children). Phone (410) 267-7619 or (800) 603-4020.

COLUMBIA (E-2) pop. 88,254

Columbia, between Washington, D.C., and Baltimore, is a planned community of villages designed to improve living and to shape urban growth. It was started in 1966 by visionary developer James Rouse and the first residents arrived in 1967. The town includes residential areas, schools, churches, hospitals, shopping centers, industries and recreation.

The Merriweather Post Pavilion, designed by noted architect Frank Gehry, presents popular music concerts in summer.

Columbia Association Welcome Center: 10221 Wincopin Cir., Columbia, MD 21044; phone (410) 715-3000.

Self-guiding tours: Columbia Lakefront Walking Tour along Lake Kittamaqundi includes such scenery as architecture, fountains, pathways, plazas and public artwork.

Shopping areas: The Mall in Columbia, which is reached via the Columbia Town Center exit off US 29, encompasses 200 shops and restaurants including Hecht's, JCPenney, Lord & Taylor, Nordstrom and Sears.

AFRICAN ART MUSEUM OF MARYLAND, .2 mi. s. off SR 175 (Little Patuxent Pkwy.) to 5430 Vantage Point Rd. in historic Oakland Manor, promotes understanding of African art and culture through lectures, exhibits, workshops and tours. Exhibits include sculptured figures, textiles, basketry, jewelry, masks and musical instruments.

Allow 30 minutes minimum. Tues.-Fri. 10-5; closed holidays. Museum also closes during new exhibit installations; phone ahead to confirm schedule.

Admission $3; $2 (senior citizens); $1 (ages 0-12). Phone ahead to verify prices. Phone (410) 730-7106.

HOWARD COUNTY CENTER OF AFRICAN-AMERICAN CULTURE is .2 mi. s. off SR 175 (Little Patuxent Pkwy.) to 5434 Vantage Point Rd. A profile of the African-American experience in Howard County since the 19th century can be seen in themed rooms displaying artifacts relating to art, collectibles, music, sports and military. A dining room, kitchen and living room are set with period pieces and furniture. A library and children's area with interactive exhibits also are featured.

Allow 30 minutes minimum. Tues.-Fri. noon-5, Sat. noon-4, Sun. by appointment; closed national holidays. Admission $3; $2 (ages 6-18). Phone (410) 715-1921.

EDGEWATER (F-3)

HISTORIC LONDON TOWN AND GARDENS, 2 mi. e. via SR 253 to 839 Londontown Rd., depicts accommodations available to the 18th-century traveler. The 1760 tavern is restored and furnished in period. The woodland gardens cover 8 acres; native plants are emphasized throughout. An archeological dig is in progress; artifacts can be seen.

Special events and programs are held during the year. Allow 1 hour minimum. Tues.-Sat. 10-3, Sun. noon-3; closed major holidays. Admission $7; $5 (ages 55+); $3 (ages 7-12). Phone (410) 222-1919.

ELLICOTT CITY (D-2) pop. 56,397, elev. 141'

The site that became Ellicott City was first known as Ellicott Mills, named for three Quaker brothers and the gristmill they established. One of the brothers, Andrew Ellicott, and Benjamin Banneker, a free black born in the area in 1731, were commissioned by George Washington to survey and lay out Washington, D.C. Banneker is said to have successfully reproduced from memory plans originally designed by Pierre L'Enfant, who was dismissed from the project.

Ellicott City became the first terminus outside Baltimore for the Baltimore and Ohio Railroad. Andrew Jackson became the first president to travel by train when he boarded a car here in 1833. Many of the stone buildings that line the narrow, winding streets above the Patapsco River have been preserved.

Another historic site, Patapsco Female Institute Historic Park, at 3691 Sarah's Ln., was one of the first schools in the nation to offer girls an academic education. Now a ruin, the school is the focal point of the park where a variety of special events are offered.

Howard County Visitor Information Center— Ellicott City: 8267 Main St., P.O. Box 9, Ellicott City, MD 21043; phone (410) 313-1900 or (800) 288-8747.

Self-guiding tours: A brochure outlining a walking tour of the historic district is available at the visitor information center and many area shops.

Shopping areas: The historic district of downtown offers a wealth of restaurants and specialty, antiques and art shops.

B&O RAILROAD MUSEUM ELLICOTT CITY STATION, 2711 Maryland Ave. at Main St., is the restored first terminus of the Baltimore & Ohio Railroad and was the destination of America's first steam engine, the "Tom Thumb," in August 1830. Display areas include the stationmaster's quarters, a waiting room, a ticket office and a freight house, which offers a model railroad display of the first 13 miles of the line and a restored 1927 caboose. Allow 1 hour minimum. Wed.-Sun. 11-4; closed major holidays. Admission $5; $4 (ages 65+); $3 (ages 0-12). Phone (410) 461-1945.

CLARK'S ELIOAK FARM, 10500 Clarksville Pike, offers a petting zoo with farm animals, including cows, ducks, donkeys, goats, horses, pigs, rabbits and an emu. Pony rides and hay rides are available for an additional fee. The farm also contains many of the large figures from the Enchanted Forest, a storybook park in Ellicott City that opened in 1955 and closed some 30 years later. A fall pumpkin patch also is offered.

Note: Food and drinks are not permitted in the petting farm area. Hand-washing stations are available. Picnicking is permitted. Allow 30 minutes minimum. Tues.-Sat. 10-4, April 1-early Nov. Admission $4.50; free (ages 0-12 months). Pony ride $2 per child. Hay ride $2; free (ages 0-12 months). Under age 12 must be with an adult. MC, VI. Phone (410) 730-4049.

FORT McHENRY NATIONAL MONUMENT AND HISTORIC SHRINE (D-4)

To reach Fort McHenry from I-95, take exit 55 (Key Hwy./Fort McHenry Monument) and follow the aqua signs on Key Highway to Lawrence Street. Turn south on Lawrence Street and then go east 1 mile on E. Fort Avenue. It also can be reached by shuttle boat service from Light St. in the Baltimore Inner Harbor.

Guardian of Baltimore's harbor, Fort McHenry was built 1798-1803. During the War of 1812, when the capture of Baltimore was a major British objective, Fort McHenry's resistance to a 25-hour bombardment saved the city from occupation and inspired the writing of the American national anthem.

Francis Scott Key, a young Georgetown lawyer, had sailed from Baltimore to secure the release of Dr. William Beanes, a friend who had earlier been seized by the British. Detained aboard an American truce ship, Key anxiously witnessed the bombardment of Fort McHenry throughout the day and into the night. After dawn on Sept. 14, 1814, the British guns ceased firing, and the sight of the 15-star, 15-stripe flag still defiantly flying over the fort inspired

Key to write the poem "The Star-Spangled Banner" which was set to the British tune "Anacreon in Heaven." It was not adopted as the national anthem until Mar. 3, 1931.

The fort never again came under attack. However, it was an active military post periodically over the next 100 years. The fort is restored to its pre-Civil War appearance. Several of the Star Fort buildings contain exhibits of historical and military memorabilia. The replica flagstaff, from which the flag flies 24 hours a day by presidential proclamation, is in the same location as the original.

Park orientation and a 15-minute movie about the Battle of Baltimore and the writing of "The Star-Spangled Banner" are offered in the visitor center. Guided activities, weekend performances by the Fort McHenry Guard (Living History unit) and special programs are given in the summer.

Allow 1 hour minimum. Daily 8-8, early June-Labor Day; 8-4:45, rest of year. Closed Jan. 1, Thanksgiving and Dec. 25. Fort admission $7; free (ages 0-15). Additional fee for shuttle boat. Phone (410) 962-4290.

FORT MEADE (E-3)

NATIONAL CRYPTOLOGIC MUSEUM is on Colony 7 Rd. at jct. SRs 32 and 295 near National Security Agency headquarters. The museum recounts the history of encryption and highlights dramatic tales from the secretive world of cryptology. Visitors can see a cipher wheel, a hands-on German enigma machine, an exhibit about the American Indian Code Talkers and recently declassified super computers.

A park honors aerial reconnaissance crew members who died in the line of duty. Allow 30 minutes minimum. Mon.-Fri. 9-4 (also first and third Sat. of the month 10-2); closed federal holidays. Free. Phone (301) 688-5849.

HANOVER (E-3) elev. 96′

Shopping areas: Arundel Mills is at jct. Baltimore Washington Parkway (SR 295) and SR 100 at 7000 Arundel Mills Cir.

MEDIEVAL TIMES DINNER AND TOURNAMENT is off I-95 exit 43, 5 mi. e. on SR 100 to exit 10A, then s. to 7000 Arundel Mills Cir. Within a building made to look like an 11th-century European castle, waiters and waitresses dressed in period servant costumes serve guests a medieval feast. Knights on Andalusian stallions compete in jousting matches and medieval games of skill just a few feet away from dining spectators. A falcon flies throughout the arena during a falconry demonstration.

Allow 2 hours minimum. Wed.-Thurs. at 7, Fri. at 7:30, Sat. at 5 and 7:30 and Sun. at 2:30 and 5. Showtimes may vary; phone ahead. Admission $48.95; $36.95 (ages 0-11). Reservations are required. AX, CB, DC, DS, JC, MC, VI. Phone (443) 755-0011 or (888) 935-6878.

HAVRE DE GRACE (B-7)
pop. 11,331, elev. 106′

Havre de Grace rose to prosperity as a mercantile center in the mid-1800s, due in large part to the town's location at the convergence of the Susquehanna River and the Chesapeake Bay. By 1836 a railroad, canal and steamship line served the city. From 1839 to the early 1900s mule-drawn barges carried coal, lumber, grains, ore and iron products between Havre de Grace and Wrightsville, Pa., 45 miles upstream.

Few buildings survived the British torch in the War of 1812. Many examples of the architectural styles favored by wealthy 19th-century merchants have been retained, however, and now serve as offices and homes. The old lock house beside the defunct Susquehanna and Tidewater Canal has been restored as a museum. The Concord Point Lighthouse is among the oldest lighthouses in continuous operation on the East Coast.

Departing the City Yacht Basin in Tydings Park, the skipjack *Martha Lewis* offers 75-minute tours of the Susquehanna Flats and upper Chesapeake Bay. Phone (410) 939-4078.

Havre de Grace Office of Tourism & Visitor Center: 450 Pennington Ave., Havre de Grace, MD 21078; phone (410) 939-2100 or (800) 851-7756.

Self-guiding tours: Maps and literature for a walking tour of the historic district are available at Havre de Grace Office of Tourism & Visitor Center.

HAVRE DE GRACE DECOY MUSEUM, off I-95 exit 89 at Market and Giles sts., exhibits displays about the folk art of decoy carving. Included are works that trace the history of the waterfowl hunting decoy and of hunting methods. The Carvers' Workshop displays tools used in the painstaking process of carving and painting, in addition to decoy models in various stages of preparation.

Guided tours are available. Allow 30 minutes minimum. Mon.-Sat. 10:30-4:30, Sun. noon-4. Admission $6; $5 (ages 62+); $2 (ages 9-18). MC, VI. Phone (410) 939-3739.

HYDES (B-7)

WINERIES

• Boordy Vineyards, 12820 Long Green Pike. Mon.-Sat. 10-5, Sun. 1-5; closed Jan. 1, Easter, July 4, Thanksgiving and Dec. 25. Phone (410) 592-5015.

LINTHICUM HEIGHTS (E-3) elev. 171′

Linthicum Heights was named for the Linthicum family, who have been property owners here since 1801. The town borders Baltimore-Washington International Airport, which provides a commercial boost for the area.

HISTORICAL ELECTRONICS MUSEUM, 1 mi. e. of SR 295 off Nursery Rd. exit to 1745 W. Nursery Rd., depicts the history of advanced electronic technology through an extensive display of equipment. Visitors can see the lunar TV camera that transmitted Neil Armstrong's first steps on the moon and the German Enigma machine that encoded messages in World War II. The Fundamentals of Electricity Gallery offers hands-on activities for children. Allow 1 hour minimum. Mon.-Fri. 9-3, Sat. 10-2; closed holidays. Donations. Phone (410) 765-3803.

LUTHERVILLE (B-6)

Named for Reformation leader Martin Luther, the town was founded by two Lutheran ministers and one Lutheran layman in 1852 as the location for a seminary for young women. Lutherville developed a reputation as a summer resort and eventually became a suburb of Baltimore. A historic district preserves 19th-century homes.

Baltimore County Conference and Visitors Bureau—Lutherville: 825 Dulaney Valley Rd., Towson, MD 21204-1010; P.O. Box 5426, Lutherville, MD 21094-5426; phone (410) 296-4886.

FIRE MUSEUM OF MARYLAND is off I-695 exit 26B at 1301 York Rd. The main exhibit has more than 40 fire engines ranging from horse-drawn wagons to contemporary vehicles. A working fire alarm office shows how fire alarms once worked. In the Discovery Room children can try on uniforms and climb on a fire engine. Also available is an audio tour of an exhibit dedicated to the Great Baltimore Fire of 1904.

Allow 1 hour minimum. Tues.-Sat. 10-4, June-Aug.; Sat. 11-4 in May and Sept.-Dec. Closed July 4 and Dec.24-25. Admission $8; $7 (ages 62+); $4 (ages 2-12). MC, VI. Phone (410) 321-7500.

MONKTON (B-6) elev. 318′

[SAVE] **LADEW TOPIARY GARDENS** is at 3535 Jarrettsville Pike. Harvey S. Ladew (1887-1976), artist and foxhunting devotee, designed and developed these 22 acres of topiary gardens. More than 100 larger-than-life topiary forms can be seen. Ladew's circa 1747 manor house contains his collections of art and English antiques as well as his foxhunting and equestrian memorabilia. A 1.5-mile nature walk includes educational stations and a boardwalk through wetlands.

Guided tours of the house are available. Allow 1 hour minimum. Mon.-Fri. and holidays 10-4, Sat.-Sun. 10:30-5, Apr.-Oct. Guided house tours depart Mon.-Fri. at 11, 12, 2 and 3; Sat.-Sun. on the half-hour 11-4. House, gardens and nature walk admission $13; $11 (ages 62+ and students with ID); $5 (ages 0-11). Gardens and nature walk admission $10; $8 (ages 62+ and students with ID); $2 (ages 0-11). MC, VI. Phone (410) 557-9466.

MOUNT AIRY (D-1) pop. 6,425

WINERIES

• **Berrywine Plantations/Linganore Winecellars** is at 13601 Glissans Mill Rd. Mon.-Fri. 10-5, Sat. 10-6, Sun. noon-6; closed major holidays. Phone (410) 795-6432, (301) 831-5889 in D.C., or (800) 514-8735.

• **Elk Run Vineyards** is at 15113 Liberty Rd. Tues.-Sat. 10-5, Sun. 1-5, Apr.-Nov.; Fri.-Sat. 10-5 (also Fri. 5-9), Sun. 1-5, rest of year. Closed major holidays. Phone (410) 775-2513.

PARKTON (B-6) elev. 420′

WINERIES

• **Woodhall Wine Cellars** is at 17912 York Rd. Mon.-Fri. 11-5, Sat. 10-5, Sun. noon-5; closed Jan. 1, Easter, Thanksgiving and Dec. 25. Phone (410) 357-8644.

SPARKS (B-6) elev. 420′

WINERIES

• **Basignani Winery** is at 15722 Falls Rd. Wed.-Sat. 11:30-5:30, Sun. noon-6. Phone (410) 472-0703.

TOWSON (D-3) pop. 51,793

Baltimore County Conference and Visitors Bureau: 825 Dulaney Valley Rd., Towson, MD 21204-1010; P.O. Box 5426, Lutherville, MD 21094-5426; phone (410) 296-4886.

Shopping areas: Towson Town Center, at 825 Dulaney Valley Rd., features Macy's and Nordstrom.

HAMPTON NATIONAL HISTORIC SITE is at 535 Hampton Ln. just off SR 146; from I-695 take exit 27B and turn immediately onto Hampton Ln. A Georgian mansion begun in 1783 by Charles Ridgely, Hampton represents post-Revolutionary War opulence. At its completion in 1790, it was the largest house in the country. The 62-acre site features a formal garden, greenhouses, an ice house, stables, slave quarters and a restored orangery.

Guided tours are available; phone ahead for details. Allow 1 hour, 30 minutes minimum. Grounds daily 9-5. Visitor Center 9:30-4. Phone ahead to verify schedule. Closed Jan. 1, Thanksgiving and Dec. 25. Free. Phone (410) 823-1309.

WESTMINSTER (B-5) pop. 16,731, elev. 700′

Originally named in 1764 for founder William Winchester, Westminster's name was changed after the beginning of the American Revolution because much of the local mail was being routed to nearby

Winchester, Va. During the Civil War the community and its resources were used by both Union and Confederate forces. Westminster's economy is primarily agricultural, with some manufacturing concerns; many residents commute to Baltimore to work.

Carroll County Visitor Center: 210 E. Main St., Westminster, MD 21157; phone (410) 848-1388 or (800) 272-1933.

CARROLL COUNTY FARM MUSEUM, 500 S. Center St., is a 142-acre tract that depicts 19th-century farm life. In addition to a farmhouse furnished in period and a barn containing old farm tools, there are 16 other buildings, nature trails and a pond. Demonstrations of quilting, spinning, weaving, blacksmithing and other crafts take place periodically.

Picnicking is permitted. Allow 1 hour minimum. Tues.-Fri. 10-4, Sat.-Sun. and some holidays noon-5, July-Aug.; Sat.-Sun. noon-5, May-June and Sept.-Oct. Admission $5; $3 (ages 7-18 and 60+). Phone (410) 386-3880.

UNION MILLS HOMESTEAD AND HOUSE MUSEUM is 7 mi. n. on SR 97 to 3311 Littlestown Pike. This large 1797 clapboard farmhouse was the home of six generations of the Shriver family, who operated milling, farming, tannery and canning businesses known collectively as "Union Mills." Furnishings, utensils and other items represent nearly two centuries of American life. Across the lane is the three-story 1797 Union Mills Grist Mill, built with bricks made on the property. Powered by a large waterwheel, the mill still operates.

Tues.-Fri. 10-4, Sat.-Sun. noon-4, June-Aug.; Sat.-Sun. noon-4 in May and in Sept. Admission (includes house and mill) $5; $3 (ages 6-12). Phone (410) 848-2288.

National Aquarium in Baltimore / © E. David Luria

This ends listings for the Baltimore Vicinity.
The following page resumes the alphabetical listings of cities in Maryland.

BERLIN (E-9) pop. 3,491, elev. 45'

CALVIN B. TAYLOR HOUSE MUSEUM, 208 N. Main St., is a restored 1832 Federal-style house furnished in period. One wing features changing exhibits of local memorabilia. Mon., Wed. and Fri.-Sat. 1-4, Memorial Day weekend-late Oct. Donations. Phone (410) 641-1019.

FRONTIER TOWN WESTERN THEME PARK, 4 mi. s. on SR 611 from US 50, depicts the era of the Wild West through staged holdups, street fights, trail rides, cancan shows and a rodeo. Daily 10-6, mid-June through Labor Day. Last admission 1 hour, 30 minutes before closing. Admission $13; $11 (ages 4-10). Phone (410) 641-0057.

BETHESDA—see District of Columbia p. 113.

BIG POOL (B-4)

FORT FREDERICK STATE PARK is off SR 56, 1 mi. s.w. of the I-70 Big Pool exit. The 1756 frontier fort protected Cumberland Valley settlers during the French and Indian War and was utilized during the Revolutionary and Civil wars. The visitor center shows a 10-minute orientation film and contains a display of military uniforms. A museum holds material explaining the fort's restoration. Barracks are furnished as they would have been in 1758. Interpreters offer information about the fort's history.

Picnicking is permitted. Food is available. Allow 1 hour minimum. Park and museum open daily 8-dusk, Apr.-Oct.; 10-dusk, rest of year. Visitor center open Mon.-Fri. 8-4, Sat.-Sun. 9-5, May-Sept. Hours may vary; phone ahead. Park closed Thanksgiving and Dec. 24-25. Park free. Museum admission $3; $2 (ages 6-12). Phone (301) 842-2155. *See Recreation Chart and the AAA Mideastern Camp Book.*

BOONSBORO (B-4) pop. 2,803, elev. 591'

Boonsboro was founded in 1792 by George and William Boone, cousins of Daniel Boone. The town prospered during the early 1800s thanks to its facilities serving the westward-bound pioneers taking the wagon road through town. The road would later become the National Pike. Stonewall Jackson and J.E.B. Stuart fought Civil War battles in the area.

WASHINGTON MONUMENT STATE PARK, 147 acres 3 mi. s.e. off US 40A, is along the Appalachian Trail. The restored 34-foot stone monument and observation tower, erected in 1827, commemorates George Washington. Visitors can go inside the tower and climb to the top. A museum contains Civil War artifacts and exhibits about the history of the monument.

Picnicking is permitted. Allow 30 minutes minimum. Park daily 8-dusk, Mar.-Nov.; 10-dusk, rest of year. Museum daily 9-5, Memorial Day-Labor Day; Sat.-Sun. 9-5, Apr. 1-day before Memorial Day and day after Labor Day-late Oct. Admission $3 per vehicle. Phone (301) 432-8065.

BOWIE—see District of Columbia p. 113.

BRUNSWICK (C-4) pop. 4,894, elev. 247'

BRUNSWICK RAILROAD MUSEUM, 40 W. Potomac St., offers an HO scale model of the B&O Metropolitan Subdivision, social history exhibits, railroad memorabilia and hands-on exhibits for children. The museum also houses the Brunswick visitor center for Chesapeake and Ohio Canal National Historic Park. Allow 30 minutes minimum. Fri. 10-2, Sat. 10-4, Sun. 1-4; closed Jan. 1, Easter, Thanksgiving and Dec. 25. Admission $6; $5.40 (ages 60+); $3 (ages 6-12); $1.25 (ages 3-5). DS, MC, VI. Phone (301) 834-7100.

RECREATIONAL ACTIVITIES
Recreational Complex

- **River and Trail Outfitters** is at 604 Valley Rd., Knoxville, MD 21758. Raft trips daily, Apr. 1-Nov. 15 (weather permitting). Hiking and biking tours Mar.-Nov. Cross-country ski trips Thurs.-Sun., late Dec.-Mar. 31. Canoe and kayak rentals and lessons; bicycle rentals. Phone (301) 695-5177 or (888) 446-7529.

BURKITTSVILLE (B-4) pop. 171

Much of Burkittsville's history is closely tied to that of George Alfred Townsend, a Civil War correspondent and novelist. In tribute to his fellow newspapermen who covered the Civil War, Townsend designed the War Correspondents Memorial. Dedicated in 1896, the memorial is now in Gathland State Park, 1 mile west of town. "The Blair Witch Project" and its sequel "Book of Shadows" were set and filmed in Burkittsville.

CAMBRIDGE (E-7) pop. 10,911, elev. 32'

Cambridge, founded in 1684, is located on the fertile bank of the Choptank River, which plays a significant role in the local economy. The area's agricultural focus has changed from tobacco to truck farming, and a farmers' market takes place every Tuesday and Friday from 8 to noon, June through September; closing time may be extended depending on number of shoppers.

Christ Episcopal Church stands on the site of the original church; its cemetery contains the graves of local Revolutionary War soldiers and several of Maryland's statesmen; phone (410) 228-3161.

The High Street Historic District, downtown, extends west from the Choptank River. The buildings in this area date from the mid-1700s and exhibit a variety of architectural styles.

Dorchester County Tourism's Visitor Center at Sailwinds Park: 2 Rose Hill Pl., Cambridge, MD 21613; phone (410) 228-1000 or (800) 522-8687.

Self-guiding tours: Walking tour maps of the historic district are available at Visitor Center at Sailwinds Park.

BLACKWATER NATIONAL WILDLIFE REFUGE is 10 mi. s. on SRs 16 and 335 at the confluence of the Blackwater and Little Blackwater rivers. The more than 27,000 acres are home to eagles, muskrats, red foxes and such migratory waterfowl as ducks, geese and swans. The best time to view waterfowl is mid-March. Ospreys hatch in late May. A 6.5-mile wildlife drive, four nature hiking trails, 26 miles of paddling trails and a bicycle route offer views. The visitor center has films, exhibits and an observatory overlooking the wetlands.

Allow 1 hour minimum. Refuge and wildlife drive open daily dawn-dusk. Visitor center open Mon.-Fri. 8-4, Sat.-Sun. 9-5; closed Thanksgiving and Dec. 25. Admission $3 per private vehicle, $1 per pedestrian or bicyclist; free (ages 0-15). Phone (410) 228-2677.

RICHARDSON MARITIME MUSEUM is at 401 High St. at jct. Locust St. and pays tribute to James Richardson, an accomplished boatbuilder who built *The Maryland Dove (see attraction listing p. 203)*; artifacts and photos chronicle his life. Boatbuilding tools, watermen equipment and models of a variety of vessels that have sailed the Chesapeake Bay and Choptank River also are displayed. Interpretive panels describe the local boating industry's history.

Allow 30 minutes minimum. Sat. 10-4, Sun. and Wed. 1-4, Mar.-Oct.; Sat.-Sun. 1-4, Mon.-Fri. by appointment, rest of year. Closed major holidays. Donations. Phone (410) 221-1871.

SPOCOTT WINDMILL, 7 mi. w. on SR 343 in Lloyds, is a 1972 reconstruction of a post windmill that was designed and built by James Richardson, an accomplished boatbuilder. This is one in a series of windmills that have occupied this site since the late 18th century. Also on the grounds are a Colonial tenant house furnished in period and an 1870s one-room Victorian schoolhouse with a fireplace as well as desks and other related artifacts. Allow 30 minutes minimum. Daily 9-5. Free. Phone (800) 522-8687.

CHESAPEAKE AND OHIO CANAL NATIONAL HISTORICAL PARK (E-1)

The Chesapeake and Ohio Canal National Historical Park follows the Maryland shore of the Potomac River from Georgetown in Washington, D.C., to Cumberland. Construction on the 184.5-mile canal began in 1828, and the canal operated 1850-1924.

Along the canal are 74 lift locks, 11 aqueducts and a number of historic lock houses. About 15 miles northwest of Washington, D.C., the Great Falls of the Potomac makes a thundering descent in a series of picturesque falls and rapids. This portion of the park, accessible via exit 41 off I-495 (Capital Beltway), is at the Great Falls Tavern Visitor Center at 11710 MacArthur Blvd.

The area is not served by public transportation, and motorized vehicles are not permitted on the towpath. Visitors can view the falls from Omsted Island Bridge near the visitor center on the Maryland side as well as from scenic overlooks on the Virginia side *(see Great Falls, Va., p. 131)*.

General Information and Activities

The Monocacy Aqueduct near Dickerson and the Paw Paw Tunnel near Paw Paw, W.Va., are major attractions. Between Georgetown and Seneca the canal has been refilled with water. A 184-mile towpath parallels the Potomac River; camping and picnic facilities are available. Hikers, bicyclists and canoeists list Great Falls as a favorite spot.

Note: The hike on the Billy Goat Trail, Section A, is strenuous over difficult and dangerous terrain. Visitors in less than optimal health, carrying small children or those who are not experienced and properly outfitted should consider trail hiking options carefully. Alcoholic beverages are not permitted in the park.

Maps and additional information are available at the park's visitor centers in Brunswick, Cumberland, Great Falls, Hancock and Williamsport, Md., and in the Georgetown section of Washington, D.C. The Williamsport Visitor Center presents an audiovisual history and displays photographs, artifacts and a boat replica.

Georgetown Visitor Center Wed.-Sun. 9-4:30, early Apr.-early Nov., hours vary rest of year; phone (202) 653-5190. Great Falls Tavern Visitor Center daily 9-4:45; phone (301) 767-3714. Williamsport Visitor Center Wed.-Sun. 9-4:30; phone (301) 582-0813. Hancock Visitor Center Fri.-Tues. 9-4:30, spring through fall; phone (301) 678-5463. Cumberland Visitor Center daily 9-5; phone (301) 722-8226. Brunswick Visitor Center Sat. 10-4, Fri. 10-2 and Sun. 1-4; phone Williamsport Visitor Center at (301) 582-0813. All visitor centers are closed Jan. 1, Thanksgiving and Dec. 25. *See the AAA Mideastern CampBook.*

ADMISSION to the Great Falls area of the park is $5 per private vehicle or $3 per person arriving on foot or by bicycle. Admission charged only at Great Falls.

PETS must be restricted at all times, either in vehicles or by leash, and are not permitted in public buildings.

ADDRESS inquiries to the Superintendent, Chesapeake and Ohio Canal National Historical Park, 1850 Dual Hwy., Suite 100, Hagerstown, MD 21740; phone (301) 739-4200.

Points of Interest

C & O CANAL BOAT TRIPS depart from two locations: in the park at Great Falls Tavern Visitor Center at 11710 MacArthur Blvd. in Potomac and 1 blk. s. of M St. between Thomas Jefferson and 30th sts. N.W. in the Georgetown section of Washington, D.C. A muledrawn replica of a 19th-century canal boat offers 1-hour tours through Georgetown's historic district and 1-hour tours along a quiet wooded section of the C & O Canal. Tickets are sold at Great Falls Tavern Visitor Center and the Georgetown Visitor Center, 1057 Thomas Jefferson St. N.W.

Trips depart Wed.-Sun. at 11, 1:30, and 3, mid-June to early Sept.; Wed.-Fri. at 11 and 3 and by reservation, Sat.-Sun. at 11, 1:30 and 3, early May to mid-June and early Sept.-early Nov. Phone ahead to verify schedule. Fare $7; $5 (ages 5-15 and 62+). MC, VI. Phone (301) 767-3714 (Potomac) or (202) 653-5190 (Georgetown).

GREAT FALLS TAVERN AND MUSEUM is 3 mi. s. on Falls Rd. then right on MacArthur Blvd., following signs to 11710 MacArthur Blvd. Built 1828-31 as a stop on the canal route, the museum houses exhibits about the history of the canal. Films about the canal are shown continuously. A variety of programs about cultural and natural history also are offered. Allow 1 hour minimum. Daily 9-4:45; closed Jan. 1, Thanksgiving and Dec. 25. Free. Phone (301) 767-3714.

CHESAPEAKE BEACH (D-6) pop. 3,180

CHESAPEAKE BEACH RAILWAY MUSEUM, .2 mi. s. of SR 260 on SR 261, chronicles the history of Chesapeake Beach, once a glittering early 20th-century resort. A diorama of the boardwalk and resort can be seen. The museum occupies the railway station, the only surviving building from the town's heyday. Exhibits include railroad equipment, rolling stock and memorabilia.

Daily 1-4 (also Sat.-Sun. 11-1 and 4-5, June-Aug.), Apr.-Oct.; Sat.-Sun. 1-4, mid-Mar. to late Mar. and in Nov. Free. Phone (410) 257-3892.

CHESAPEAKE CITY (B-8) pop. 787

Chesapeake City came into existence because of the Chesapeake & Delaware Canal, which links Delaware and Chesapeake bays across the Delmarva Peninsula. Work on the canal began in 1803, but the waterway did not open for navigation until 1829. It allows oceangoing vessels serving Baltimore and other northern ports to avoid the 296-mile trip around the peninsula.

The canal proved to be of vital strategic importance during World War II, when ships used it to escape enemy submarines in the Atlantic Ocean. Today, as an avenue for pleasure craft traveling the inland waterway, the canal is the impetus for many of Chesapeake City's businesses.

Cecil County Tourism: 1 Seahawk Dr., Suite 114, North East, MD 21901; phone (410) 996-6290 or (800) 232-4595.

C&D CANAL MUSEUM is off SR 213 at 2nd St. and Bethel Rd. Housed in the original canal pump house complex, the museum includes a working model of a water wheel and lock, paintings, maps, documents and artifacts pertaining to the history of the waterway. Allow 1 hour minimum. Mon.-Fri. 8-4:15; closed holidays. Free. Phone (410) 885-5621 or (410) 885-5622.

CHESTER (F-4) pop. 3,723, elev. 16′

The 6-mile paved Cross Island Trail Park that begins in Terrapin Nature Park in Stevensville ends in Chester. Cyclists, pedestrians and runners can experience the outdoors and enjoy the trail's natural vistas.

Queen Anne's County Office of Tourism—Chester: 425 Piney Narrows Rd., Chester, MD 21619; phone (410) 604-2100.

CHESAPEAKE EXPLORATION CENTER is off US 50 exit 41 at Kent Narrows Bridge, then just n. following signs to 425 Piney Narrows Rd. Displays and interactive exhibits tell the history of the Chesapeake Bay area. Visitors can learn how the bay was formed and what life was like for past inhabitants. Fossils and relics of the settlers' existence are included. A brief video explains the construction of the first Bay Bridge. Visitors can learn how to protect the bay. Visitor information about the region also is available.

Allow 30 minutes minimum. Mon.-Fri 8:30-4:30, Sat.-Sun. and national holidays 10-4; closed Easter and Dec. 25. Donations. Phone (410) 604-2100 or (888) 400-7787.

CHESTERTOWN (C-7) pop. 4,746, elev. 36′

A graceful town of 18th-century brick houses facing the Chester River, Chestertown began in 1706 as a port of entry for Cecil, Kent and Queen Anne's counties. During its early years it hosted horse races and traveling theatrical groups. Shipbuilding and trading were economic mainstays.

A spirit of independence prevailed in 1774 when citizens, enraged over England's tea tax, threw overboard tea brought into port by the brigantine *Geddes*. Soon after, Chestertown sent provisions to the similarly inclined town of Boston, which was suffering from the effects of the Boston Port Act.

Washington College was founded in 1782. Named after George Washington, on whom it conferred an honorary degree of doctor of laws, the college was visited by its namesake in 1784.

Kent County Visitor Center: 122 N. Cross St., Chestertown, MD 21620; phone (410) 778-9737. *See color ad p. 190.*

Self-guiding tours: Information about historical driving and walking tours can be obtained from the tourism office.

Shopping areas: The historic downtown area features some 35 shops and eateries.

CHESAPEAKE FARMS, on SR 20, is a 3,300-acre wildlife management demonstration area. Described in the tour brochure are 15 stops, each marked and labeled. The first stop is the main resting area, where as many as 10,000 geese, ducks and other waterfowl can be seen at one time. Many types of plant and animal species—including upland birds, beavers, turtles and nesting wood ducks—are found in the refuge.

Visitors are asked to remain in their vehicles throughout the tour; motorcycles and horses are not permitted. Allow 1 hour minimum. Main resting area open daily dawn-dusk. Habitat tour available Mar. 15-Oct. 10. Schedule may vary; phone ahead. Free. Phone (410) 778-8400.

CHURCH CREEK (E-7) pop. 85, elev. 57′

OLD TRINITY CHURCH is w. of US 50 on SR 16/Church Creek Rd. The restored church dates prior to 1690 and still is in use. The adjoining cemetery contains graves of the Carroll family, one of whom, Anna Ella Carroll, was such a close advisor to President Lincoln that many consider her an unofficial member of his cabinet. A brilliant military strategist, Carroll devised the Tennessee campaign, credited by some historians with securing the Union's victory in the Civil War. Church open by appointment. Cemetery open daily dawn-dusk. Free. Phone (410) 228-2940.

CLINTON—*see District of Columbia p. 114.*

COLESVILLE—*see District of Columbia p. 114.*

COLLEGE PARK—
see District of Columbia p. 115.

COLTONS POINT (E-6)

Coltons Point faces St. Clement's Island, where the *Ark* and the *Dove,* carrying the first Maryland settlers, dropped anchor on March 25, 1634. On this

The Blue Crab

To those who know the Chesapeake Bay, the blue crab symbolizes fine eating and a way of life. Ancestors of the crustacean fed the area's earliest inhabitants more than 10,000 years ago; later, Eastern Archaic and Woodlands Indians left crab shells as testaments to their feasts.

Although blue crabs are found as far north as Cape Cod, as far south as Uruguay and in such exotic places as the lakes of the Nile Delta, they thrive in greatest abundance in the Chesapeake Bay. Scientists credit the bay's varying salinity and the water's shallowness for the large harvests that

form the basis of the bay's prosperous crabbing industry.

Crab harvests vary with changing weather patterns, and some bay experts are concerned about dwindling populations, but the crab still reigns as the king of cuisine in Maryland. Baltimore crab houses fork up spicy renditions of steamed hard-shell crab, which bib-clad patrons consume with the aid of mallets and knives. Succulent crab cakes are considered by many to be the best in the world.

To some, the act of catching these crustaceans is as much fun as eating them. In the bay tributaries, crab fishers use baited trotlines. In the open bay, crab pots are baited and weighted, then cast into the water. Once a crab has entered through the one-way opening, it has no choice but to await its captor. Soft-shell crabs, considered a delicacy, are taken after the molting of one shell and before the hardening of a new one. Both hard-shell and soft-shell crabs are kept alive on ice until they are cooked. Whether served soft or hard or whole or minced, blue crabs are the pride of the Chesapeake.

Potomac River island Gov. Leonard Calvert and Jesuit Father Andrew White erected a large wooden cross and performed the first Roman Catholic Mass in the English-speaking Colonies. A replica of the *Dove* is permanently docked in St. Mary's City *(see attraction listing p. 203).*

St. Mary's County Division of Tourism—Coltons Point: 23115 Leonard Hall Dr., P.O. Box 653, Leonardtown, MD 20650; phone (301) 475-4200, ext. 1402 or (800) 327-9023.

ST. CLEMENT'S ISLAND-POTOMAC RIVER MUSEUM is at the end of SR 242 on the Potomac River facing St. Clement's Island. The museum contains exhibits about Maryland's first colonists, who arrived in 1634 and negotiated with the American Indians for settlement. Also featured is Potomac River history with exhibits featuring local watermen, a dory boat, a replica of the original lighthouse and a restored circa 1820s one-room schoolhouse. Weekend water taxi service to St. Clement's Island is available seasonally. A pier also is available.

Picnicking is permitted. Allow 1 hour minimum. Mon.-Fri. 9-5, Sat.-Sun. noon-4, Mar. 25-first weekend in Oct. Admission $3; $2 (senior citizens); $1.50 (ages 5-18). Phone (301) 769-2222.

COLUMBIA—*see Baltimore p. 183.*

CRISFIELD (F-8) pop. 2,723, elev. 5'

Crisfield is on an inlet of Tangier Sound, a part of Chesapeake Bay set off and protected by islands. The townspeople lived in relative isolation until 1867, when a railroad was extended to the harbor by John Woodland Crisfield. Said to be built almost entirely on oyster shells, the town has a number of oyster houses at its piers, where visitors can sample the fresh delicacy in season.

Ferries provide daily service to Tangier Island, Va. *(see Tangier, Va., p. 309)* and Smith Island *(see place listing p. 205).*

Crisfield Area Chamber of Commerce: 906 W. Main St., Crisfield, MD 21817; phone (410) 968-2500 or (800) 782-3913.

J. MILLARD TAWES HISTORICAL MUSEUM at 3 Ninth St. at the Somers Cove Marina reveals local history through exhibits related to the Chesapeake Bay and its watermen, the relationship between the colonists and the American Indians, the oyster and crab industry, and the history of decoy carving and painting. The late Gov. J. Millard Tawes as well as decoy carver brothers Lem and Steve Ward are profiled in some of the exhibits. A guided walking tour of the port area, which includes a stop at a crab and oyster processing facility, also is offered.

Tours can be arranged by appointment to the J. Millard Tawes Library and the Ward Brothers Workshop. Allow 30 minutes minimum for the museum. Mon.-Sat. 9-4. Guided tour departs at 10. Winter hours may vary; phone ahead. Admission $3; $1 (ages 6-12). MC, VI. Phone (410) 968-2501.

SMITH ISLAND SIGHTSEEING CRUISES departs from the Somers Cove Marina on Seventh St. The *Twister* and the *Chelsea Lane Tyler* carry passengers to Smith Island daily at 12:30 and return at 4:30, Memorial Day-Oct. 15. Fare $24; $12 (ages 3-11); phone ahead to verify fares. Reservations are required. Phone (410) 425-2771.

TANGIER ISLAND CRUISES, 1001 W. Main St., offers cruises on the *Steven Thomas* to Tangier Island. Cruises depart daily at 12:30 and return at 5:15, May 15 to mid-Oct. Fare $25; $12.50 (ages 6-12). Phone (410) 968-2338 or (800) 863-2338.

CUMBERLAND (A-2) pop. 21,518, elev. 655'

Cumberland took its name in 1787 from Fort Cumberland, the headquarters for Gen. Edward Braddock and Lt. George Washington during the French and Indian War. The one-room headquarters, where 21-year-old Washington assumed his first military command, is the only surviving structure of Fort Cumberland.

Cumberland developed as a transportation center after it was made the western terminus of the Chesapeake & Ohio Canal and the eastern terminus of the National Road—what is now alternate US 40. The first road built with federal funds, the National Road passed through the Cumberland Narrows—a natural gateway through the Appalachian Mountains into the Ohio Valley—and for a time was the main route to the Northwest Territory.

When Cumberland was at its economic peak during the late 19th century, coal and rail barons lived in ornate mansions along Washington Street. Many of these homes, which range in style from Federal to Georgian Revival, have been restored.

Allegany County Department of Tourism—Cumberland: Western Maryland Station Center, 13 Canal St., Cumberland, MD 21502; phone (301) 777-5132 or (800) 425-2067.

Self-guiding tours: Tour brochures of the Fort Cumberland Walking Trail as well as walking and driving brochures of the Washington Street Historic District are available at the department of tourism.

Shopping areas: Downtown Cumberland, a brick-lined pedestrian mall with fountains and small parks, contains shops in restored early 20th-century buildings.

CHESAPEAKE AND OHIO CANAL NATIONAL HISTORICAL PARK—*see place listing p. 189.*

BROOKE WHITING HOUSE OF ART is at 632 Washington St. This 1911 bungalow was built for the Whitings, a prominent Cumberland family. Their wealth allowed them to travel and collect various art pieces. The house displays their collections of Asian art and early American, British and European decorative arts. The Whiting Archives contain more than 1,500 volumes and ancestral documents dating since the 18th century.

Allow 30 minutes minimum. Guided tours Tues.-Sat. on the hour 10-4. Last tour begins at closing. Archives open by appointment. Admission $5. Phone (301) 777-7782.

GORDON-ROBERTS HOUSE is at 218 Washington St. This 1867 Victorian house is headquarters for the Allegany County Historical Society and features period pieces, antiques and displays depicting life in the mid-1800s. Changing exhibits feature such historical items as art, books, clothing, glassware, maps, photographs, postcards, toys and utensils. A cup of tea is offered as part of a guided tour. Allow 1 hour minimum. Guided tours Tues.-Sat. 10-4; closed Jan. 1, Thanksgiving and Dec. 25. Admission $7. Phone (301) 777-8678.

WESTERN MARYLAND SCENIC RAILROAD, departing the station center at 13 Canal St., offers 3.5-hour round-trip excursions up 1,300-foot-high Piney Mountain, through Brush Tunnel and into Frostburg aboard a train pulled by either a 1916 Baldwin steam locomotive known as "Mountain Thunder" or a restored diesel engine. Murder mystery and first-class trips also are available.

Steam locomotive excursions depart Thurs.-Sun. at 11:30 in Oct.; Fri.-Sun. at 11:30, May-Sept.; Sat.-Sun. at 11:30, Nov. 1 to mid-Dec. Diesel engine trips depart Tues.-Thurs. at 11:30, in Oct.; Thurs. at 11:30, May-Aug. Schedule may vary; phone ahead. Fare $25; $23 (ages 60+); $12 (ages 0-12); free (ages 0-1 on lap). Reservations are required. Phone (301) 759-4400 or (800) 872-4650.

DENTON (D-8) pop. 2,960, elev. 43′

MUSEUM OF RURAL LIFE & VISITOR CENTER is at 16 N. 2nd St. An 1840s log cabin of a tenant or subsistence farmer is housed in the museum, which was built around the relocated cabin. Portions of two middle-class dwellings and a wealthy farmer's brick house also can be seen. A large riverboat model represents the type of boats that once traveled in this area.

Allow 30 minutes minimum. Daily 10-5, Apr.-Nov.; Fri.-Sat. 10-3, Sun. noon-4, rest of year; other times by appointment. Closed major holidays. Hours

may vary; phone ahead. Donations. Phone (410) 479-2055.

DICKERSON—*see District of Columbia p. 115.*

EASTON (D-7) pop. 11,708, elev. 38′

Continued use of Colonial architecture is Easton's tribute to its heritage. Settled in the late 17th century, the town was an economic, governmental and cultural center for the Eastern Shore. The 1682 Third Haven Friends Meeting House was built by the Society of Friends and is one of the nation's oldest frame houses of worship. Other notable town landmarks are the 18th-century courthouse and the Tidewater Inn.

Talbot County Office of Tourism—Easton: 11 S. Harrison St., Easton, MD 21601; phone (410) 770-8000.

Self-guiding tours: Maps and brochures outlining self-guiding tours can be obtained at the Historical Society of Talbot County *(see attraction listing).*

Shopping areas: Downtown Easton, especially Washington, Harrison, Dover and Goldsborough streets, offers a wide variety of antiques stores, specialty shops and boutiques.

ACADEMY ART MUSEUM, 106 South St. at Harrison St., was founded in 1958. The permanent collection consists of works on paper by American and European masters. National and regional exhibitions as well as performances and educational programs are offered throughout the year. A juried craft show is held the second weekend in October. Mon.-Sat. 10-4, (also Tues.-Thurs. 4-8). Admission $3; free (Wed.). Phone (410) 822-2787.

HISTORICAL SOCIETY OF TALBOT COUNTY is at 25 S. Washington St. Two museum galleries showcase changing exhibitions. A guided tour features the homes of two Quaker cabinetmakers. One is a small wood frame house built in 1795 and the other is an 1805 brick Federal-style town house. The tour includes the relocated studio-museum of architect H. Chandlee Forman, a collector of Colonial antiques from the Eastern Shore. Also featured are boxwood and perennial gardens.

Allow 1 hour, 30 minutes minimum. Museum open Mon.-Sat. 10-4; closed major holidays. Guided tours are offered by appointment. Guided tour $5; $2 (children). Museum free. Phone (410) 822-0773.

PICKERING CREEK AUDUBON CENTER is 3.9 mi. n. on SR 370 from jct. SRs 33 and 370, then 2.1 mi. s. on Todds Corner Rd. and w. to 11450 Audubon Ln., following signs. Highlights include nature trails, a welcome center with pictures and historical farm implements, a children's garden and trail as well as a visitor center with taxidermic animals. The center lies within hardwood forest, bay shoreline, freshwater and brackish marsh environments, allowing ample opportunity for nature viewing, especially bird watching.

Picnicking is permitted. Allow 30 minutes minimum. Grounds daily dawn-dusk. Visitor center Mon.-Fri. 9-5, Sat. 10-4, Mar.-Dec.; Mon.-Fri. 9-5, rest of year. Closed national holidays. Free. Phone (410) 822-4903.

EDGEWATER—see Baltimore p. 184.

ELKTON (B-8) pop. 11,893, elev. 28'

Originally named Head of Elk by John Smith in 1652 because of its position at the top of the Elk River, Elkton's commercial ties were evident as early as 1683 when a gristmill was built on the Big and Little Elk Creeks. In 1786, shortly after the Revolutionary War, Head of Elk became the county seat of Cecil County, and the following year the town's name was changed to Elkton.

Cecil County Tourism: 1 Seahawk Dr., Suite 114, North East, MD 21901; phone (410) 996-6290 or (800) 232-4595.

THE HISTORICAL SOCIETY OF CECIL COUNTY, 135 E. Main St., is in a building originally constructed as a bank in 1830. In addition to a research library, the historical society features a museum with regularly changing exhibits and the Sheriff John F. DeWitt Military Museum. Mon. and Thurs. 10-5, Tues. 6-8:30 p.m., first and fourth Sat. of the month 10-2; closed holidays. Free. Phone (410) 398-1790.

ELLICOTT CITY—see Baltimore p. 184.

EMMITSBURG (B-5) pop. 2,290

Named for a local landowner, Emmitsburg is a few miles northeast of Catoctin Mountain Park *(see Thurmont p. 206)*, location of Camp David, the presidential retreat.

NATIONAL FALLEN FIREFIGHTERS MEMORIAL, off US 15 S. Seton Ave. exit, then .6 mi. w. following signs to 16825 S. Seton Ave., is on the campus of the U.S. Fire Administration's National Fire Academy and Emergency Management Institute. This 7-foot high stone monument to firefighters who have died in the line of duty is surmounted by a bronze Maltese Cross, a motif on many firefighters' badges. The eternal flame at the base of the monument symbolizes the spirit of firefighters. A memorial chapel and a brick walk of honor are on the grounds.

Allow 30 minutes minimum. Daily dawn-dusk. Free. Ages 16+ must present a photo ID for admission to the campus. Phone (301) 447-1365.

NATIONAL SHRINE GROTTO OF LOURDES, 3 mi. s. on SR 15 to 16300 Old Emmitsburg Rd., overlooks Mount St. Mary's University. The shrine, a replica of the Grotto of Lourdes in France, was established by Father John DuBois in 1805. Paved walkways wind through landscaped gardens containing stone and copper Stations of the Cross, mosaic murals depicting the Mysteries of the Rosary, a bronze statue of Mary and a campanile with Westminster chimes. Allow 30 minutes minimum. Daily dawn-dusk. Free. Phone (301) 447-5318.

NATIONAL SHRINE OF ST. ELIZABETH ANN SETON is at 333 S. Seton Ave. on the grounds of St. Joseph's Provincial House. In the early 1800s Mother Seton, founder of the Sisters of Charity of St. Joseph, opened the first free parochial school staffed by religious sisters. She was canonized in 1975, the first native-born American woman to be so honored. Her remains are buried beneath her altar in the basilica. A visitor center contains a museum and shows a 15-minute film depicting Seton's life and times every half-hour. Two historic houses, a cemetery and a mortuary chapel can be seen.

Guided tours are available by appointment. Allow 1 hour, 30 minutes minimum. Basilica open daily 10-4:30. Visitor center and other buildings open Tues.-Sun. 10-4:30. Closed major holidays, Easter and the last week in Jan. and the first week in Feb. Free. Phone (301) 447-6606.

 FORT McHENRY NATIONAL MONUMENT AND HISTORIC SHRINE—see Baltimore p. 184.

FORT MEADE—see Baltimore p. 185.

FORT WASHINGTON—
see District of Columbia p. 115.

FREDERICK (B-5) pop. 52,767, elev. 271'

Frederick was occupied by both Union and Confederate forces several times. During the Confederate advance toward Sharpsburg and the Battle of Antietam, resident Barbara Fritchie allegedly dared the marching men to shoot her rather than the Union flag she was waving, an act that caused John Greenleaf Whittier to immortalize her in his poem "Barbara Fritchie."

Confederate general Jubal Early occupied the town briefly in 1864 and levied a ransom of $200,000 against its destruction. The town government paid the ransom by borrowing from local banks, which financed the loans with a bond issue. An estimated $600,000 in interest was paid on the bonds before the loans were finally repaid in 1951.

Monocacy National Battlefield, on SR 355, is the site where Union general Lew Wallace's greatly outnumbered troops, many of whom were untried in battle, were defeated by Confederate forces led by Gen. Early on July 9, 1864. The battle, though won by the Confederates, delayed Early's advance on Washington, D.C. With the arrival of Federal reinforcements the next day, the Confederates' hope of taking Washington was thwarted. Their withdrawal into Virginia spared the national capital and marked the Confederacy's last attempt to carry the war into the North.

A visitor center, 4801 Urbana Pike (SR 355), features pamphlets outlining self-guiding tours of the battlefield, as well as an interactive system showing people who fought; phone (301) 662-3515.

Tourism Council of Frederick County Visitor Center: 19 E. Church St., Frederick, MD 21701; phone (301) 644-4047 or (800) 999-3613.

Self-guiding tours: The Visitor Center offers information about a walking tour of historic Frederick County.

Shopping areas: Francis Scott Key Mall, 5500 Buckeystown Pike, is anchored by Sears.

Specialty shops selling antiques, crafts, clothing and pottery are plentiful at Shab Row and Everedy Square on East Street. Nearly 40 antiques shops are scattered around town; a cluster of them can be found on Antique Walk, near South Carroll and East Patrick streets.

SAVE **THE CHILDREN'S MUSEUM OF ROSE HILL MANOR PARK,** 1611 N. Market St., was the retirement home of Thomas Johnson, Maryland's first elected governor. Guided tours of the 1790s house as well as the carriages and garden are available. The museum depicts 19th-century family life; a blacksmith shop and a log cabin are on the grounds.

Hands-on displays in quilt-making, carding wool and operating a beaten biscuit machine and cream separator are of special interest. Mon.-Sat. 10-4, Sun. 1-4, Apr.-Oct.; Sat. 10-4, Sun. 1-4, in Nov. Admission $5; $4 (ages 3-17 and 55+). Phone (301) 600-1650.

THE DELAPLAINE VISUAL ARTS CENTER, 40 S. Carroll St., houses works by prominent and local artists, crafts persons and photographers in seven galleries. Traveling exhibits also are featured. Allow 1 hour minimum. Mon.-Sat. 9-5, Sun. 1-4; closed federal holidays. Donations. Phone (301) 698-0656.

SAVE **HISTORICAL SOCIETY OF FREDERICK COUNTY,** 24 E. Church St., features a collection of period furnishings, art and artifacts housed in a restored 1820s Federal-style mansion. A local history and genealogical library also is on the grounds. Allow 1 hour minimum. Mon.-Sat. 10-4, Sun. 1-4. Library Tues.-Sat. 10-4. Closed holidays. Admission $3; free (ages 0-16). Phone (301) 663-1188.

MOUNT OLIVET CEMETERY, s. end of Market St., contains the graves of Francis Scott Key and his wife; at least 408 "Unknown Confederates" from the battles of Antietam and Monocacy; Barbara Fritchie; and Thomas Johnson, Maryland's first elected governor. The Revolutionary War Hessian Barracks are nearby. Daily 8-dusk. Free. Phone (301) 662-1164.

SAVE **NATIONAL MUSEUM OF CIVIL WAR MEDICINE,** just e. of SR 355/Market St. at 48 E. Patrick St., portrays how coping with sickness and death during the Civil War ushered in a new era of medical treatment. Exhibits vividly illustrate different aspects of Civil War medicine and include such re-creations as a field dressing station and field and pavilion hospitals. Other exhibits highlight nursing and embalming. Special events and educational programs also are available.

Guided tours are available. Allow 1 hour minimum. Mon.-Sat. 10-5, Sun. 11-5; closed Jan. 1, Easter, Thanksgiving and Dec. 24-25 and 31. Admission $6.50; $6 (ages 61+ and military with ID); $4.50 (ages 10-16). DS, MC, VI. Phone (301) 695-1864 or (800) 564-1864.

SCHIFFERSTADT ARCHITECTURAL MUSEUM is off US 15 Rosemont Ave. (exit 14) to 1110 Rosemont Ave. is a fine example of German Colonial architecture as well as of a fortified house from the French and Indian War era. Built in 1756, the house reveals early construction methods and is one of the oldest structures in Frederick. Allow 30 minutes minimum. Thurs.-Sun. noon-4, Apr. 1 to mid-Dec. Hours may vary; phone ahead. Closed Easter and Thanksgiving. Admission $3; free (ages 0-11). Phone (301) 663-3885.

FROSTBURG (A-2) pop. 7,873, elev. 1,920′

Frostburg owes its founding to the National Road, authorized by an act of Congress in 1806. In 1812 Meshach Frost, son of the first resident, built a log house for his bride. When stagecoach service began in 1818, the house was converted to Highland Hall Inn. Taverns, smithies and houses grew up around the inn, and the cluster of buildings was named Frostburg by the Post Office when mail service began in 1820.

By 1840 the railroad superseded the road, and the town became a commercial center for coal mining. The biggest employer is Frostburg State University, which began as a normal school in 1898; the student enrollment is 5,400. The town has returned to its roots with the restoration of The Old Depot, which dates back to 1891 and is now the destination point for the Western Maryland Scenic Railroad *(see attraction listing in Cumberland p. 193).* The depot center area also includes the Thrasher Carriage Museum *(see attraction listing).*

Allegany County Department of Tourism— Frostburg: Western Maryland Station Center, 13 Canal St., Cumberland, MD 21502; phone (301) 777-5132 or (800) 425-2067.

Self-guiding tours: Frostburg's historic district covers 3 blocks along alternate US 40; the oldest structure was built in 1846. Self-guiding tour maps are available Mon.-Fri. 8-4 at City Hall, 59 E. Main St.; phone (301) 689-6000. Information also is available in nearby Cumberland *(see place listing p. 192)* from the Allegany County Department of Tourism.

THRASHER CARRIAGE MUSEUM, Depot Center on Depot St., is in a renovated 1800s warehouse. The museum contains nearly 40 late 19th- and early 20th-century horse-drawn vehicles, including formal closed carriages, funeral wagons, sleighs, carts and milk wagons. Also displayed are carriage accessories such as hitches, saddles and lap robes. Guided tours by docents in period attire are available.

Allow 30 minutes minimum. Wed.-Sat. 10-4 (also Sun. noon-3, May-Oct.), Mar.-Dec.; by appointment rest of year. Last tour begins 1 hour before closing. Admission $4; $2 (ages 7-18). Phone (301) 689-3380.

GLEN ECHO—*see District of Columbia p. 115.*

GRANTSVILLE (A-1) pop. 619

Grantsville took its name from Daniel Grant, a Baltimorean who is said to have helped settle the area during the 1790s. The Casselman Hotel, Little Crossings Inn—now the Penn Alps—and Stanton's Mill, all founded 1797-1824, are among the buildings that remain from that era; all still are in use.

About a half-mile east of town is the Casselman Bridge, an 80-foot stone span built in 1813 for the National Road. At the time of its construction it was the country's longest single-span stone arch bridge. Nearby Casselman River Bridge State Park has picnic facilities.

Garrett County Chamber of Commerce— Grantsville: 15 Visitors Center Dr., McHenry, MD 21541; phone (301) 387-4386.

SPRUCE FOREST ARTISAN VILLAGE, .5 mi. e. on alternate US 40, has demonstrations of such Colonial and contemporary arts and crafts as bird sculpture, stained glass, loom weaving, jewelry metalwork and slate painting. The artisan village is on the grounds of the former Little Crossings Inn, a 19th-century stagecoach stop. The village includes 12 restored log houses and buildings, including a church and mill; two structures date from Revolutionary War days. Allow 1 hour minimum. Mon.-Sat. 10-5, May-Oct.; by appointment rest of year. Donations. Phone (301) 895-3332.

GRASONVILLE (C-7) pop. 2,193, elev. 16′

CHESAPEAKE BAY ENVIRONMENTAL CENTER is off US 50/301 exit 43B, then just s.e. on SR 18, then .5 mi. s. on Perry Corner Rd. to 600 Discovery Ln., following signs. Within the center's 500 acres lie 4 miles of walking trails through marshes, meadows and woodlands. The environment is ideal for bird watching; more than 200 species of birds can be seen. A boardwalk at the wetlands and observation towers provide scenic views.

Allow 2 hours minimum. Daily 9-5; closed national holidays. Admission $5; $4 (ages 55+); $2 (ages 5-18). DS, MC, VI. Phone (410) 827-6694.

GREAT FALLS—

see Chesapeake and Ohio Canal National Historical Park p. 189.

GREAT MILLS (E-6) elev. 10′

CECIL'S OLD MILL, 20854 Indian Bridge Rd., was built in 1810 as a textile mill. The soil proved unsuitable for growing cotton, so the mill was subsequently used as a grist- and sawmill that ceased operation in 1957. Inside are a grinder, bagger, wheat cleaning machine and scales. Outside is restored operational sawmill equipment. Today the mill is the focal point for 50 local craftsmen who display their works among the mill machinery.

Allow 1 hour minimum. Thurs.-Sun. 10-5 (also Mon.-Wed. 10-5, Nov.-Dec.), Apr.-Dec. Free. Phone (301) 994-1510.

GREENBELT—*see District of Columbia p. 116.*

HAGERSTOWN (A-4) pop. 36,687, elev. 547′

The Hagerstown area was wilderness when Jonathan Hager settled there in the mid-18th century. In 1762 he laid out a hamlet called Elizabeth Town on part of his land, and settlers of German descent arrived. Although Hager had named the town after his wife, it was known to the others simply as "Hager's Town," a name that was made official in 1813.

One of the first county libraries in the country was founded by local businessmen in 1901. Although residents of the predominately rural area still considered reading a luxury, the project was an instant success. A few years later, the library began the world's first bookmobile by sending a two-horse wagon equipped with bookshelves to call on isolated farms.

Hagerstown is western Maryland's largest community, noted for a mixture of old and new buildings interspersed with many trees and public parks. Among the city's highlights is the Maryland Theater on Potomac Street, a 1915 vaudeville house designed by Charles Lamb. Home to the Maryland Symphony Orchestra, the restored theater stages regular concerts, symphony productions and shows.

Hagerstown-Washington County Convention and Visitors Bureau: 16 Public Sq., Hagerstown, MD 21740; phone (301) 791-3246 or (888) 257-2600.

DISCOVERY STATION, 101 W. Washington St., features many science exhibits and interactive displays about a variety of topics, including agriculture, dinosaurs, health, space exploration and weather. Programs with audience participation are given on Saturdays. A separate gallery contains activities designed for children ages 2-5.

Allow 1 hour minimum. Tues.-Sat. 10-4 (also Sun. 2-5, Sept.-June). Programs are given Sat. at 1 and 2:30. Closed major holidays. Discovery Station and program schedules may vary; phone ahead. Admission (includes Hagerstown Aviation Museum) $7; $6 (ages 2-17); $5 (ages 55+). Phone (301) 790-0076.

Hagerstown Aviation Museum is at 101 W. Washington St. on the first floor of Discovery Station. Local aviation history of the Hagerstown area, which at one time was one of the nation's leaders in aircraft manufacturing, is shared through artifacts, exhibits and memorabilia. A highlight is a flight simulator that allows visitors to sit in the cockpit of a plane to see how all the controls and instruments operate.

Allow 30 minutes minimum. Tues.-Sat. 10-4 (also Sun. 2-5, Sept.-June); closed major holidays. Schedule may vary; phone ahead. Admission (includes Discovery Station) $7; $6 (ages 2-17); $5 (ages 55+). Phone (301) 790-0076.

HAGER HOUSE AND MUSEUM, .5 mi. s. on Virginia Ave. in Hagerstown City Park at 110 Key St., offers guided tours of the house built by town-founder Jonathan Hager in 1739. This impregnable building, erected over two springs to assure a protected water supply, served as home, fort and storehouse for its owner. The house is furnished in period; an adjacent museum has artifacts. Allow 30 minutes minimum. Tues.-Sat. 10-4, Sun. 2-5, Apr.-Dec. Admission $3; $1 (ages 6-12). Phone (301) 739-8393.

MILLER HOUSE, 135 W. Washington St., is a Federal-period town house with period furnishings and a replica of an early 19th-century garden. Doll and clock collections, Civil War artifacts, Bell pottery, Chesapeake and Ohio Canal exhibits and the first Hagerstown taxicab—a 1910 Regal—are among the displays. Allow 1 hour minimum. Wed.-Sat. 1-4, Apr.-Nov.; Wed.-Sun. 1-4 in Dec. Admission $5; $3 (ages 61+); free (ages 0-11). Phone (301) 797-8782.

DID YOU KNOW

The world's only eight-lane underwater tunnel for automobiles is Fort McHenry Tunnel.

WASHINGTON COUNTY MUSEUM OF FINE ARTS, .5 mi. s. on US 11 in Hagerstown City Park, displays sculptures and paintings as well as Asian and African decorative arts through changing exhibits. Concerts and lectures are scheduled regularly. Allow 30 minutes minimum. Tues.-Fri. 9-5, Sat. 9-4, Sun. 1-5; closed major holidays. Free. Phone (301) 739-5727.

HANCOCK (A-3) pop. 1,725, elev. 448'

SIDELING HILL EXHIBIT CENTER is on I-68, 6 mi. w. of town; go 2 mi. past exit 77. It is immediately accessible from westbound I-68; eastbound I-68 travelers must stop at the rest stop and cross to it via a pedestrian bridge. The exposure of the surface beneath the crust of the Earth that was created when I-68 was cut through this hill provides the opportunity to examine sedimentary rock types, structural features and relationships of topography.

The center has geologic exhibits including a cross-section of a 350-million-year-old rock formation, displays about indigenous animals and tourist information. Allow 30 minutes minimum. Daily 8:30-5; closed Jan. 1, Easter, Thanksgiving and Dec. 25. Donations. Phone (301) 678-5442.

HANOVER—see Baltimore p. 185.

HAVRE DE GRACE—see Baltimore p. 185.

HOLLYWOOD (E-6)

[SAVE] SOTTERLEY PLANTATION is 4 mi. n. off of SR 245 at 44300 Sotterley Ln. The 300-year-old Colonial mansion overlooks woods, pastures and the Patuxent River. Features include a Chippendale-style staircase, pine paneling with handcrafted shell alcoves, antique furnishings and Colonial Revival gardens. Original outbuildings, including 19th-century slave quarters, an 18th-century warehouse, a "necessary" and a schoolhouse, also are accessible. Guided 45-minute tours of the restored mansion are available.

Allow 1 hour minimum. Grounds open Tues.-Sat. 10-4, Sun. noon-4, year-round. Guided mansion tours Tues.-Sat. at 10:30, 11:30, 1, 2 and 3; Sun. at noon, 1, 2 and 3, May-Oct. Grounds $3. Grounds and mansion tour $10; $8 (senior citizens); $5 (ages 6-12). Phone (301) 373-2280 or (800) 681-0850.

HYDES—see Baltimore p. 185.

KENSINGTON—see District of Columbia p. 116.

KENT ISLAND (C-7)

Following his exploration of the bay in 1631, Virginian William Claiborne set up a trading post on Kent Island, the largest of the Chesapeake Bay islands. A colony developed and formed the first Anglican congregation in what is now the state of Maryland. Although Claiborne fought for possession of the island, England decreed in 1638 that it was part of Maryland and not Virginia.

The dual William Preston Lane Jr. Memorial Bridges span the Chesapeake Bay from Kent Island to Sandy Point, connecting the eastern and western shores of Maryland.

Queen Anne's County Office of Tourism— Kent Island: 425 Piney Narrows Rd., Chester, MD 21619; phone (410) 604-2100.

LARGO—see District of Columbia p. 116.

LAUREL—see District of Columbia p. 116.

LEXINGTON PARK (E-7) pop. 11,021

PATUXENT RIVER NAVAL AIR MUSEUM is outside Patuxent River Naval Air Station, adjacent to Gate 1 base access road at 22156 Three Notch Rd. (SR 235). The museum displays 20 naval aircraft, including two Joint Strike Fighter concept demonstrator aircraft, in an outdoor flight line. Indoor exhibits showcase the history of research, development, testing and evaluation of U.S. Navy aircraft. Flight simulations are available for a fee. Guided tours are available. Allow 1 hour minimum. Tues.-Sun. 10-5. Free. Phone (301) 863-7418, or (301) 866-0027 for flight simulation information.

LINTHICUM HEIGHTS—see Baltimore p. 185.

LUSBY (E-7) pop. 1,666

COVE POINT LIGHTHOUSE is 3.3 mi. e. off SR 2/4 on SR 497 to the end of Cove Point Rd. This 1828 lighthouse was automated in 1986 and is still operating today. Visitors can walk in the lighthouse base and look up the spiral staircase. Wayside panels chronicle the site's history, and a 10-minute video about the history of the lighthouse plays continuously in a one-room building on the grounds. An observation platform contains a telescope for viewing the bay and the Calvert Cliffs.

Allow 30 minutes minimum. Daily 1-4, June-Aug.; Sat.-Sun. 1-4, in May and Sept. Donations. Phone (410) 326-2042 for the Calvert Marine Museum.

FLAG PONDS NATURE PARK is 10 mi. s. on SR 2/4. The 545-acre park is a haven for native wildlife, including muskrats, otters, white-tailed deer, turkeys, foxes and pileated woodpeckers. Plant life ranges from venerable hardwoods to the blue flag iris that gives the park its name. Two ponds have observation platforms. There also are 3 miles of hiking trails with interpretive signs, a wetlands boardwalk and a beach where fossils may be collected.

Allow 1 hour minimum. Daily 9-6 (also Sat.-Sun. 6-8 p.m.), Memorial Day-Labor Day; Sat.-Sun. 9-5, rest of year. Admission $6 per private vehicle (Apr.-Sept.); $3 (rest of year). Phone (410) 586-1477.

LUTHERVILLE—*see Baltimore p. 186.*

McHENRY (B-1) elev. 2,480′

Covering nearly 3,900 acres, McHenry's Deep Creek Lake is Maryland's largest freshwater lake and offers visitors boating, camping, fishing and swimming opportunities *(see Recreation Chart and Oakland in the AAA Mideastern CampBook).*

Garrett County Chamber of Commerce—McHenry: 15 Visitors Center Dr., McHenry, MD 21541; phone (301) 387-4386.

ADVENTURE SPORTS CENTER INTERNATIONAL is at 250 Adventure Sports Way. A 2-hour guided rafting trip, a 3-hour guided climbing trip, a 3-hour guided rappelling trip and a combined guided climbing and rafting trip are offered along with a variety of non-guided recreational activities.

Note: Pregnant women are not permitted to raft. Visitors with heart problems should consult with their doctor. Allow 2 hours minimum. Wed.-Mon. 9-7, late May to early Sept. Hours vary mid-Apr. to late May and early Sept.-Oct. 31 but are generally Fri.-Mon. 9-5. Guided rafting, climbing or rappelling fee late May to early Sept. $50; guided rafting, climbing or rappelling fee mid-Apr. to late May and early Sept.-Oct. 31 $45; guided climbing and rafting fee $95. Phone for other activity fees. Reservations are recommended in summer. AX, CB, DC, DS, JC, MC, VI. Phone (301) 387-3250 or (877) 300-2724.

THE DISCOVERY CENTER AT THE DEEP CREEK LAKE RECREATION AREA is 1.5 mi. s. on US 219 to Glendale Rd., then 1.5 mi. w. to 898 State Park Rd. This interpretive, environmental center on the shore in Deep Creek Lake State Park provides hands-on exhibits for children about the natural resources of western Maryland. On-site naturalists lead daily educational programs dealing with the flora, fauna, and cultural and historical heritage of this area.

Allow 1 hour minimum. Daily 10-5, Memorial Day weekend-Labor Day; Mon.-Fri. noon-4, Sat.-Sun. 10-4, day after Labor Day-Sept. 30, Sat.-Sun. 10-4, rest of year. Free. Phone (301) 387-7067.

RECREATIONAL ACTIVITIES

Skiing

• **Wisp Ski Resort** is 1 mi. s. on US 219. Write 1388 296 Marsh Hill Rd., McHenry, MD 21541. Other activities are offered. Tues.-Sat. 9-9, Sun.-Mon. 9-5, mid-Dec. to early Mar.; Tues.-Fri. 9-9, Sun.-Mon. 9-5, in mid-Dec. and early Mar.-late Mar. Phone (301) 387-4911.

MONKTON—*see Baltimore p. 186.*

MOUNT AIRY—*see Baltimore p. 186.*

NEW MARKET (D-1) pop. 427

Founded in 1793 along what would later become the historic National Pike (US 40) between Baltimore and Frederick, New Market was an important stop for early 19th-century travelers. The proximity of the road fostered many travel-related businesses.

Travelers still favor New Market, but today's visitors are searching for bargains in the town's many antiques and craft shops. New Market's historic district includes the original plot laid out by the town's founders.

Shopping areas: Antiques enthusiasts can find more than 35 shops on Main Street.

OAKLAND (B-1) pop. 2,000, elev. 2,385′

Outdoor opportunities abound in Oakland. Herrington Manor State Park, 5 miles north on US 219, offers both summer and winter activities, including cross-country skiing and hiking. Near the confluence of Muddy Creek and the Youghiogheny River, Swallow Falls State Park, 9 miles northwest on CR 20, is home to the state's largest waterfall—Muddy Creek Falls. *See Recreation Chart and the AAA Mideastern CampBook.*

Covering some 600 acres, Cranesville Sub-Arctic Swamp was formed during the ice age. Due to the high elevation and cool climate, the swamp contains vegetation normally found in Arctic regions. The boardwalk through the bog is open during the dry season, in summer and fall.

Garrett County Chamber of Commerce—Oakland: 15 Visitors Center Dr., McHenry, MD 21541; phone (301) 387-4386.

OCEAN CITY (E-9) pop. 7,173

Ocean City is a resort town on a 10-mile barrier island bordered by the Atlantic Ocean to the east and a chain of coastal bays and the mainland to the west. The Ocean City Inlet, connecting the sea and the bays, offers sport fishing boats and pleasure boats a safe harbor with access to the ocean.

Deep-sea fishing for white and blue marlin, bigeye and yellowfin tuna, mako and dolphin can be arranged through a number of charter boat and headboat operators. Good fishing opportunities can also be found in the area, including from the piers and by surf fishing off the beaches.

Windsurfing, jet skiing, parasailing, kayaking and sailing are available. In addition to these water activities, several golf courses highlight the area's natural beauty.

The 10-mile-long public beach offers a wide sandy expanse for strolling, sunbathing and seaside recreation. Shops and restaurants line the three-mile boardwalk, which extends from the inlet to 27th Street. A boardwalk tram runs daily mid-May through September and on weekends beginning Easter weekend through mid-May and in October. Water parks, miniature golf courses and two full-scale amusement parks lend a festive atmosphere. Bicycle rental facilities also are available.

The Roland E. Powell Convention Center at 40th and Coastal Highway brings in arts and crafts shows, antique shows, car shows and conventions; phone (800) 626-2326.

Concerts are held Sunday evenings July through August at Northside Park on 125th Street.

Nearby Ocean Downs Racetrack offers harness racing late July through August, and simulcasting year-round; phone (410) 641-0600.

Note: Policies concerning admittance of children to pari-mutuel betting facilities vary. Phone for information.

Ocean City Chamber of Commerce: 12320 Ocean Gateway, Ocean City, MD 21842; phone (888) 626-3386.

Ocean City Department of Tourism and Convention and Visitors Bureau: 4001 Coastal Hwy., P.O. Box 116, Ocean City, MD 21842; phone (410) 626-2326. *See color ad.*

Ocean City Hotel, Motel & Restaurant Association: 4001 Coastal Hwy., P.O. Box 340, Ocean City, MD 21842-0340; phone (800) 626-2326.

Self-guiding tours: Walking, biking, boating and driving tour brochures are available from the Ocean City Hotel, Motel & Restaurant Association. Also offering brochures for a variety of tours as well as sightseeing publications is the Ocean City Chamber of Commerce.

Shopping areas: Ocean City Factory Outlets, 12741 Ocean Gateway, offers more than 40 stores.

[SAVE] **OCEAN CITY LIFE-SAVING STATION MUSEUM** is at the s. end of the boardwalk on the inlet. Exhibits describe the history of the 1891 station and the many area shipwrecks and rescues. There are displays of early lifesaving equipment and related memorabilia, beach sands from around the world, shipwreck artifacts and mermaid-themed objects. Models of early hotels, beach fashions and a photographic exhibit of Ocean City history also CAN be seen. An aquarium room features local marine life.

Allow 1 hour minimum. Daily 10-10, June-Sept.; daily 10-4, in May and Oct.; Sat.-Sun. 10-4, rest of year. Admission $3; $1 (ages 6-12). Phone (410) 289-4991.

WHEELS OF YESTERDAY is on US 50 at 12798 Ocean Gateway. More than 40 classic automobiles, including a fire engine, are displayed. Other historic artifacts are interspersed among the auto exhibits. Allow 30 minutes minimum. Daily 9-5 (also 5-9, June 15-Sept. 30); closed Jan. 1, Thanksgiving and Dec. 25. Admission $4; $2 (ages 0-12). DS, MC, VI. Phone (410) 213-7329.

OXFORD (D-7) pop. 771, elev. 9′

Rivaled only by Annapolis among pre-Revolutionary Maryland ports, Oxford was made an official port of entry for the colony in 1683. Prosperous London and Liverpool businesses established branch stores that exchanged goods for tobacco. But

with the rise of Baltimore as a commercial port during the Revolutionary War, Oxford lapsed into obscurity.

After the Civil War, shipbuilding, oystering and fish packing revitalized the Eastern Shore town's economy, and they have continued to sustain it. Most of the boats made in Oxford are built for fishing and pleasure.

Local attractions include a replica of the first federal customhouse, built by the collector appointed by George Washington, at the corner of Morris St. and The Strand, and the 18th-century N. Morris Street home of Robert Morris, whose son, Robert Morris Jr., was a signer of the Declaration of Independence and the finance minister for the Confederation—the initial government of the Continental Congress of the Revolutionary period.

The grave of Lt. Tench Tilghman, who carried the news of Gen. Charles Cornwallis' surrender from Yorktown, Va., to the Continental Congress in Philadelphia, is in the Oxford Cemetery.

To reach the Oxford-Bellevue Ferry follow signs to the western terminus of SR 333. The ferry was established in 1683 and is considered the oldest privately owned ferry in the country. It was propelled by oars until 1886, when powered service began. The ferry carries nine vehicles and lots of bicycles and passengers across the Tred Avon River between Oxford and Bellevue (St. Michaels area) daily April through November; phone (410) 745-9023.

Talbot County Office of Tourism—Oxford: 11 S. Harrison St., Easton, MD 21601; phone (410) 770-8000.

OXFORD MUSEUM, 101 S. Morris St., has more than 2,500 artifacts to document the town's cultural and economic history since the 17th century. Included in the artifact collection are boatbuilding tools, china, clothing, documents, furniture, paintings, photographs, pottery and American Indian items. A soda fountain adds another element of nostalgia. A small garden also is on the grounds. Holiday exhibits are displayed on weekends in December.

Allow 30 minutes minimum. Fri.-Sat. and Mon. 10-4 (also Wed. 10-4, June-Sept.), Sun. noon-4, late Apr. to mid-Nov. Admission $3; free (ages 0-12). Phone (410) 226-0191.

OXON HILL—see District of Columbia p. 117.

PARKTON—see Baltimore p. 186.

PINEY POINT (F-6) elev. 10'

PINEY POINT LIGHTHOUSE MUSEUM & PARK is 7.5 mi. s.w. off SR 5 on SR 249, then 1.3 mi. n. to 44720 Lighthouse Rd. Visitors can climb the stairs of this lighthouse that operated 1836-1964. The museum chronicles the history of the structure and a German submarine sunk off the coast as well as Piney Point, a summer destination for such notable Americans as presidents James Monroe, Franklin Pierce and Theodore Roosevelt. A maritime

exhibit in a separate building showcases Potomac fishermen and includes four wooden vessels. A pier also is available.

Picnicking is permitted. Allow 1 hour minimum. Grounds daily dawn-dusk. Museum and lighthouse Fri.-Mon. 10-5, mid-Apr. through late Oct.; Sat.-Sun. noon-4, early Nov. to mid-Dec. Admission $3; $2 (ages 60+); $1.50 (ages 6-18). MC, VI. Phone (301) 994-1471.

PORT TOBACCO (E-5) elev. 177'

Port Tobacco, originally settled by the English in 1634, became the second largest river port in Maryland. Much of the tobacco sent to England was loaded at the town dock. A severe buildup of silt in the river and the passage of the railroad through nearby La Plata eventually diminished Port Tobacco's importance. Near the end of the 19th century the county seat was moved to La Plata, and the old port languished.

Port Tobacco consists of a village green bordered by a reconstructed Federal-style courthouse, two restored 18th-century houses, one reconstructed 19th-century house and the Salt Box, a restored 1700 house on Cheapside Street. The second floor of the courthouse contains the Charles County Museum of Port Tobacco, which is open weekends and has displays and a film about the village; phone (301) 934-4313.

Charles County Office of Tourism: 200 Baltimore St., P.O. Box 2150, LaPlata, MD 20646; phone (800) 766-3386.

PRINCE FREDERICK (E-6) pop. 1,432

Named for a son of King George II, Prince Frederick has served as the seat of Calvert County since 1725. Fire destroyed the town three times: first in the 1740s, then during the War of 1812, and again in 1882.

Department of Economic Development and Tourism: 175 Main St., Prince Frederick, MD 20678; phone (410) 535-4583.

BATTLE CREEK CYPRESS SWAMP SANCTUARY AND NATURE CENTER, 4 mi. s.w. via SR 2/4 and SR 506, then s. on Gray's Rd., contains one of the nation's northernmost stands of bald cypress trees, which range from 75 to more than 500 years old. An elevated quarter-mile boardwalk angles through part of the swamp. A nature center contains natural and cultural history exhibits, including a honeybee hive. Films, demonstrations and programs are scheduled throughout the year.

Picnicking is permitted. Allow 1 hour minimum. Tues.-Sat. 10-5, Sun. 1-5, Apr.-Sept.; Tues.-Sat. 10-4:30, Sun. 1-4:30, rest of year. Trail open daily. Pets are not permitted. Free. Phone (410) 535-5327.

PRINCESS ANNE (E-8) pop. 2,313, elev. 17'

Founded at the headwaters of the Manokin River, Princess Anne is part of Somerset County, which was created by Lord Baltimore's proclamation in 1666. Several Colonial and Federal homes still stand along Mansion Street and US 13S. Of particular interest are Teackle Mansion, which is open for tours some afternoons, and the Washington Hotel.

Somerset County Tourism and Visitor Center Office—Princess Anne: 11440 Ocean Hwy., P.O. Box 243, Princess Anne, MD 21853; phone (410) 651-2968 or (800) 521-9189.

Self-guiding tours: A walking tour brochure detailing many of the town's historic buildings is available at the tourism office.

QUEEN ANNE (C-7) pop. 176, elev. 30'

About 7 miles west of Queen Anne is the town of Wye Mills, which grew up around Old Wye Mill. The mill produced flour for George Washington's troops at Valley Forge. The restored mill continues to operate and grinds and sells flour the first and third Saturday of the month; phone (410) 827-6909. Wye Church, a quarter-mile south of Wye Mills on SR 662, is a restored Colonial structure with a hanging pulpit and box pews. A reconstructed vestry house furnished in period and a parish house built in the 18th-century style are nearby.

RIDGELY (C-7) pop. 1,352, elev. 59'

ADKINS ARBORETUM is 2.3 mi. n.e. off SR 480 to 12610 Eveland Rd. Within the arboretum's 400 acres are 4 miles of trails that traverse meadows, a hardwood forest and lush bottomland. A library is housed in the visitor center. Allow 30 minutes minimum. Daily 10-4; closed Thanksgiving and Dec. 25. Admission $3; $1 (ages 6-18). AX, DS, MC, VI. Phone (410) 634-2847.

RISING SUN (B-7) pop. 1,702, elev. 387'

Originally part of Pennsylvania, Rising Sun became part of Maryland when the Mason-Dixon line was established in 1765. In the early 1700s the town was called Summer Hill and had five wagon trails leading into its center and meeting at the Rising Sun tavern; when a post office was established in 1802 the town changed its name to that of this popular meeting spot.

PLUMPTON PARK ZOO, off I-95 exit 100, 5 mi. n. on SR 272, then 1 mi. w. on SR 273 to 1416 Telegraph Rd., features more than 300 species of birds, reptiles and mammals, including North American bison, giraffes, llamas, lynx, monkeys, water buffalo, zebras and a tiger. The structures within the park, including a wooden gristmill, date to the 18th century.

Allow 1 hour minimum. Daily 10-4, Mar.-Sept.; Thurs.-Mon. 10-4, rest of year. Fall and winter hours may vary; phone ahead to confirm. Closed Thanksgiving and Dec. 25. Admission $11.95; $10.95 (ages 60+); $7.95 (ages 2-12). Phone (410) 658-6850.

ROCK HALL (C-7) pop. 1,396, elev. 10'

EASTERN NECK NATIONAL WILDLIFE REFUGE is 6.1 mi. s. off SR 20 on SR 445 at 1730 Eastern Neck Rd. Migrating and wintering waterfowl come to this 2,285-acre island refuge to feed and rest; at peak times more than 40,000 are on the grounds. Visitors can view wildlife and the bay from nearly 6 miles of roads and trails. Threatened southern bald eagles and endangered Delmarva fox squirrels can be seen. A boardwalk also is available. Allow 30 minutes minimum. Daily 7 a.m.-30 mins. after dusk. Free. Phone (410) 639-7056.

ROCKVILLE—see District of Columbia p. 117.

ST. INIGOES (F-7)

The town is home to St. Ignatius Church, built in 1785 and named for St. Ignatius Loyola, founder of the Jesuit order. Its cemetery is one of the oldest in America and contains the graves of many Jesuit priests as well as several soldiers of the American Revolution. The key to the church, which is on Villa Road, can be obtained at the Pass and Security Office of the adjacent Naval Electronics Systems Engineering Activities Station.

ST. LEONARD (E-6) pop. 536, elev. 115'

JEFFERSON PATTERSON PARK AND MUSEUM is at 10515 Mackall Rd. (SR 265), following signs. Archeology and history are showcased on 560 acres containing more than 70 recorded archeological sites. An exhibit in the visitor center chronicles 9,000 years of human occupation on this land by American Indians, plantation owners, tenants, free and enslaved Africans and indentured servants. Walking and driving trails are available. Special events are held throughout the year. Picnicking is permitted. Wed.-Sun. 10-5, Apr. 15-Oct. 15. Free. Phone (410) 586-8501.

ST. MARY'S CITY (F-7)

In March 1634 the *Ark* and the *Dove* sailed up the Potomac River and into the mouth of the St. Mary's River, carrying the first colonists to arrive in Maryland under the royal charter of Lord Baltimore. A representative government was initiated, and St. Mary's City became the first capital of Maryland. The town prospered on the impetus of government, but farming assumed priority when the capital was moved to Annapolis.

St. Mary's County Tourism: 23115 Leonard Hall Dr., P.O. Box 653, Leonardtown, MD 20650; phone (301) 475-4200, ext. 1404 or (800) 327-9023. *See color ad p. 203.*

[SAVE] **HISTORIC ST. MARY'S CITY,** off SR 5 at 18751 Hogaboom Ln., is an 800-acre outdoor museum of living history and archeology. Exhibits include a square-rigged ship, a tobacco plantation, a town center and a Woodland Indian hamlet. Costumed interpreters in re-created 17th-century settings illustrate life in Colonial Maryland. Maps, brochures and an audiotape tour are available from the museum visitor center.

Wed.-Sun. 10-5, mid-June through mid-Sept.; Tues.-Sat. 10-5, mid-Mar. through early June and late Sept.-late Nov. Complex closed Thanksgiving. Admission (includes Godiah Spray Tobacco Plantation, *The Maryland Dove,* Town Center and The Woodland Indian Hamlet) $10; $8 (ages 60+); $6 (students with ID); $3.50 (ages 6-12). DS, MC, VI. Phone (240) 895-4990 or (800) 762-1634. *See color ad.*

Godiah Spray Tobacco Plantation is at Historic St. Mary's City off Rosecroft Rd.; access begins from the visitor center off SR 5 at 18751 Hogaboom Ln. This working reconstruction of a 17th-century tobacco plantation consists of the main dwelling house, a tenant's cottage, barns, gardens and livestock. Interpreters in period attire perform the tasks that would have consumed the lives of the family and servants of Godiah Spray—a 17th-century term for an average man and similar to today's use of John Doe.

Wed.-Sun. 10-5, mid-June through mid-Sept.; Tues.-Sat. 10-5, mid-Mar. through early June and late Sept.-late Nov. Complex closed Thanksgiving. Admission (includes *The Maryland Dove,* Town Center and The Woodland Indian Hamlet) $10; $8 (ages 60+); $6 (students with ID); $3.50 (ages 6-12). DS, MC, VI. Phone (240) 895-4990 or (800) 762-1634.

The Maryland Dove is on the St. Mary's River behind the State House at Historic St. Mary's City; access begins from the visitor center off SR 5 at 18751 Hogaboom Ln. The ship is a representation of the small square-rigged ships of the 1630s that brought settlers and cargo to Maryland. Iron murtherers (breech-loading shotguns), compasses, sandglasses and log pumps are among the ship's appointments.

Wed.-Sun. 10-5, mid-June through mid-Sept.; Tues.-Sat. 10-5, mid-Mar. through early June and late Sept.-late Nov. Complex closed Thanksgiving. Admission (includes Godiah Spray Tobacco Plantation, Town Center and The Woodland Indian Hamlet) $10; $8 (ages 60+); $6 (students with ID); $3.50 (ages 6-12). DS, MC, VI. Phone (240) 895-4990 or (800) 762-1634.

Town Center is at Historic St. Mary's City off Old State House Rd.; access begins from the visitor center off SR 5 at 18751 Hogaboom Ln. The complex includes Smith's Ordinary, a reconstructed 17th-century inn; Cordea's Hope, a mercantile; several ghost frames; a reconstructed print house; and the

State House, a reconstruction of the 1676 building. Work currently is underway on the 1667 Brick Chapel.

Wed.-Sun. 10-5, mid-June through mid-Sept.; Tues.-Sat. 10-5, mid-Mar. through early June and late Sept.-late Nov. Complex closed Thanksgiving. Admission (includes Godiah Spray Tobacco Plantation, *The Maryland Dove* and The Woodland Indian Hamlet) $10; $8 (ages 60+); $6 (students with ID); $3.50 (ages 6-12). DS, MC, VI. Phone (240) 895-4990 or (800) 762-1634.

The Woodland Indian Hamlet is behind the visitor center at Historic St. Mary's City; access begins from the visitor center off SR 5 at 18751 Hogaboom Ln. Interpreters at this representation of a Yaocomaco Indian settlement demonstrate indigenous ways of life. Visitors to the hamlet can learn how Maryland's native population interacted with the English colonists.

Wed.-Sun. 10-5, mid-June through mid-Sept.; Tues.-Sat. 10-5, mid-Mar. through early June and late Sept.-late Nov. Complex closed Thanksgiving. Admission (includes Godiah Spray Tobacco Plantation, *The Maryland Dove* and Town Center) $10; $8 (ages 60+); $6 (students with ID); $3.50 (ages 6-12). DS, MC, VI. Phone (240) 895-4990 or (800) 762-1634.

LEONARD CALVERT MONUMENT, next to Historic St. Mary's City, stands on the site where Leonard Calvert signed a treaty with the Yaocomaco Indian king while buying land for the young colony.

TRINITY CHURCH, next to Historic St. Mary's City, dates from 1829 and was built with the bricks of the first state house. Daily 9-5; Sunday services at 10:30. Free. Phone (301) 862-4597.

ST. MICHAELS (D-7) pop. 1,193

About the time of the American Revolution St. Michaels began to develop as a noted shipbuilding center. During the War of 1812, St. Michaels' militia successfully repelled two British attacks. Traditional accounts of the attack on Aug. 9, 1813, credit the townspeople with extinguishing all ground lights and hanging lanterns in treetops, causing the British to shoot over the town. Because of the event, St. Michaels earned the nickname "The Town That Fooled The British."

Seafood and agricultural processing industries now sustain the economy, but the town's status as a commercial port seriously declined after the completion of the Chesapeake Bay Bridge in 1951. Visitors are rediscovering the region's unspoiled heritage, preserved by many years of near-isolation. One of the better known yachting centers on the East Coast, St. Michaels draws thousands of sailing enthusiasts each summer.

Self-guiding tours: A free brochure describing a historic walking tour down streets lined with 19th-century frame houses is available throughout the town; phone (410) 745-9535.

Shopping areas: Downtown St. Michaels, centering on Talbot Street, boasts specialty shops offering antiques, clothing and handmade items.

CHESAPEAKE BAY MARITIME MUSEUM, off SR 33 at 213 N. Talbot St., is devoted to the history and traditions of the Chesapeake Bay. Skipjacks and other bay craft, waterfowling boats, decoys, paintings, ship models and the 1879 cottage-style Hooper Strait Lighthouse are among the exhibits on this 18-acre waterfront campus on the Miles River.

Oystering is presented through artifacts, historic photographs and oyster harvesting equipment. The At Play on the Bay building explores how the bay has changed from a place of work to a place where people come to play.

Guided tours are available. Picnicking is permitted. Allow 1 hour minimum. Daily 10-6, June-Sept.; 10-5, Mar.-May and Oct.-Nov.; 10-4, rest of year. Closed Jan. 1, Thanksgiving and Dec. 25. Admission $13; $10 (ages 63+); $5 (ages 6-17). AX, DS, MC, VI. Phone (410) 745-2916.

PATRIOT OF ST. MICHAELS (Historic Miles River Cruise) departs from the maritime museum for 60- and 90-minute narrated tours of the Miles River. Summer sunset cruises also are available. One-hour tour departs daily at 11, 2:30 and 4, Apr.-Nov. Ninety-minute tour departs daily at 12:30. Fare for 60- or 90-minute tour $19.55; $15.45 (ages 63+); $15.90 (ages 0-11). Phone (410) 745-3100.

SALISBURY (E-8) pop. 23,743

Originally a settlement at the intersection of American Indian trails and the Wicomico River, Salisbury was chartered in 1732. Beginning as an important stop for freight and passenger coaches, it later became a railroad freight center.

Salisbury is the largest city and second largest port on Maryland's eastern shore as well as the trade and transportation center for the Delmarva Peninsula. Flatboat ferries still operate on the eastern shore. The Upper Ferry at Salisbury is guided by a cable and powered by a small outboard motor as it takes travelers across the Wicomico River.

Newtown Historic District, north of Salisbury Parkway (US 50), covers six blocks. The homes, which reflect several architectural styles, date from the early to late 1800s. Poplar Hill Mansion, (410) 749-1776, and the Art Institute and Gallery, (410) 546-4748, also may be visited.

Wicomico County Convention and Visitors Bureau: 8480 Ocean Hwy., Delmar, MD 21875; phone (410) 548-4914 or (800) 332-8687.

Self-guiding tours: Information and maps for tours of the historic district are available at the convention and visitors bureau.

SALISBURY ZOO is 1.5 mi. e. on US 50, .5 mi. s. on Civic Ave., w. onto Glen Ave. then s. on Memorial Plaza. Nestled on 12 acres, this zoo provides exhibits featuring specimens native to the Americas.

Among the major exhibits are jaguars, otters, monkeys and an extensive waterfowl collection. Picnicking is permitted. Allow 1 hour minimum. Daily 8-7, Memorial Day-Labor Day; 8-4:30, rest of year. Closed Thanksgiving and Dec. 25. Donations. Phone (410) 548-3188.

THE WARD MUSEUM, SALISBURY UNIVERSITY, 909 S. Schumaker Dr., displays what is considered to be the world's most comprehensive collection of wildfowl art, including antique decoys and contemporary sculptures. Galleries, displays and walk-through exhibits trace the evolution of the decoy from its origins as a hunter's tool to its status as an art form. In the Decoy Study Gallery the regional differences found in decoys are featured. A theater shows a film highlighting the importance of protecting natural wildfowl environments. Changing exhibits include works by noted wildfowl artists. A nature trail also is on the grounds.

The museum is named for Lem and Steve Ward of Crisfield, whose works helped promote the art of decoy carving. A re-creation of their workshop contains memorabilia, including some of their carvings, paintings and poetry.

Special events are held throughout the year. Flash photography is prohibited. Allow 1 hour minimum. Mon.-Sat. 10-5, Sun. noon-5; closed major holidays. Admission $7; $5 (ages 63+); $3 (grades K-12 and college students with ID); $17 (family rate). Phone ahead to verify prices. Phone (410) 742-4988, ext. 120.

SCOTLAND (F-7) elev. 10′

POINT LOOKOUT STATE PARK is 4.5 mi. s. on SR 5. A popular resort before the Civil War, the park is on a peninsula that forms the southern tip of Maryland's western shore. During the war, nearby Camp Hoffman housed more than 52,000 Confederate prisoners; more than 4,000 died from exposure, starvation and disease. There is a beach, fishing pier, picnic area and nature trails. A museum features Civil War history.

Park daily dawn-dusk. Museum hours vary; phone ahead. Day-use fee Mon.-Fri. $4 per private vehicle, Sat.-Sun. and holidays $6 per person (May-Sept.); daily $6 per private vehicle (rest of year). Phone (301) 872-5688. *See Recreation Chart and the AAA Mideastern CampBook.*

SILVER SPRING—
see District of Columbia p. 118.

SMITH ISLAND (F-7) pop. 364

Smith Island was named for Capt. John Smith, who explored the Chesapeake Bay in 1608. The island actually comprises three islands that form an area about 8 miles long and 4 miles wide. Settled in 1657 by English dissenters from Lord Baltimore's colony, Smith Island is populated by descendants of the original Colonists.

Isolation from the mainland has allowed ancient modes of speech and grammatical constructions to survive. For more than three centuries the islanders have derived their livelihoods from the surrounding bay. The three fishing villages on the island are Ewell, Rhodes Point and Tylerton.

Smith Island Center in Ewell offers tourist information as well as a small museum with exhibits relating to the island's history and the Chesapeake Bay. A 20-minute film showcases the area's history, an exhibit reveals the island residents' dialect, a genealogy database is available and a 30-foot mural by local artist Reuben Becker can be seen. The center is open daily May through October; phone (410) 425-3351 or (800) 521-9189.

Boats carry passengers to the island from Crisfield, Md. *(see place listing p. 192)*, Reedville, Va. *(see Reedville, Va. p. 285)* and from Point Lookout, Md.

SNOW HILL (F-9) pop. 2,409

Settled along the Pocomoke River in 1642, Snow Hill grew into a port town and was made a British royal port in 1694. Warehouses, shipbuilding shops and other businesses sprang up to support the expanding trade, and the town was named the Worcester County seat in 1742. Growth continued despite the decreased national reliance upon water transportation. Snow Hill still is the county seat, but commerce now centers on the agricultural interests that spawned the town.

Worcester County Tourism: 104 W. Market St., Snow Hill, MD 21863; phone (410) 632-3110 or (800) 852-0335.

Self-guiding tours: A walking tour brochure of the historic area is available from Town Hall, on the corner of Green and Bank streets, or from Purnell Museum at 208 W. Market St.; phone (410) 632-0515.

FURNACE TOWN LIVING HERITAGE MUSEUM is 5 mi. n. on SR 12, then 1 mi. w. to 3816 Old Furnace Rd. This re-created 19th-century industrial village features the Nassawango Iron Furnace, Maryland's only bog-ore furnace. A 19th-century garden kitchen, broom house, blacksmith shop, church, print shop, weaver house, woodworkers shop and museum also are on the site.

Year-round events include art, music, nature walks and living-history presentations. A nature trail winds 1 mile into the Pocomoke forest and cypress swamp. Allow 30 minutes minimum. Daily 10-5, Apr.-Oct. Admission $4; $3.50 (ages 61+); $2 (ages 2-18). Phone (410) 632-2032.

SOLOMONS (E-7) pop. 1,536, elev. 20′

The Solomons area includes Solomons Island, near the point where the Patuxent River empties into the Chesapeake Bay. The town's harbor is one of the world's deepest natural ports. Noted as a yacht and boatbuilding center, the resort affords access to fine fishing grounds.

ANNMARIE GARDEN, on Dowell Rd. .5 mi. e. of SR 2/4, is a 30-acre outdoor sculpture park featuring a meandering paved path past permanent and loaned works of sculpture. Allow 1 hour minimum. Daily 9-5. Free. Phone (410) 326-4640.

CALVERT MARINE MUSEUM is s. off SR 2/4 at Solomon's Island Rd. The museum showcases local maritime history and the environmental culture of Southern Maryland. Exhibits include vessels, models, artifacts and displays depicting the maritime history of the Chesapeake Bay and the Patuxent River area. Also featured are 17 aquariums with live specimens of various species, including the river otter. Other offerings include a touch tank and a hands-on Discovery Room.

Also on the grounds is the restored and furnished cottage-type Drum Point Lighthouse, commissioned in 1883 and moved to this site in 1975. The J.C. Lore Oyster House, one-half mile south, has exhibits and films chronicling regional fishing. One-hour harbor tours are available aboard the historic bugeye *Wm. B. Tennison.* Nearby Cove Point Lighthouse *(see attraction listing p. 198)* is open seasonally.

Special events are held throughout the year. Allow 1 hour minimum. Museum open daily 10-5; closed Jan. 1, Thanksgiving and Dec. 25. Harbor tours Wed.-Sun. at 2, May-Oct. Museum admission $7; $6 (ages .55+); $2 (ages 5-12). Harbor tour $7; $4 (ages 5-12). Phone (410) 326-2042.

SPARKS GLENCOE—*see Baltimore p. 186.*

THURMONT (B-5) pop. 5,588

Legend maintains that Jacob Weller and his family, traveling west with a wagon train, stopped at what is now Thurmont in 1751 to nurse a sick child and remained. As a result of the industries introduced by generations of Wellers, the site became a town in which most residents worked as mechanics. By 1811 the hamlet was known as Mechanicstown.

After the railroad made the area readily accessible, the town became a popular resort noted for its mountain scenery. It was renamed Thurmont, "gateway to the mountains."

Catoctin Furnace, 4 miles south via US 15, is a partially restored iron furnace that operated 1777-1903. Visitors may explore the site.

CAMP DAVID MUSEUM at 105 Frederick Rd. (SR 806) houses memorabilia relating to the presidential families, administration and guests who have visited Camp David and chronicles some of the important events that have taken place there. The museum entrance re-creates the facade of Aspen, the Presidential Cabin at Camp David, with rocking chairs on the front porch made by the same manufacturer that made President Kennedy's.

Food is available. Allow 45 minutes minimum. Mon.-Fri. 11-8, Sat.-Sun. 8-8 (also Sat. 8-9 p.m.). Donations. Phone (301) 271-7373.

CATOCTIN MOUNTAIN PARK, 2 mi. w. on SR 77, offers self-guiding nature trails, a bridle trail, picnicking, camping, fishing, cross-country skiing and snowshoeing. A visitor center just off SR 77 has information about interpretive programs. The Blue Blazes Still, a typical example of an 18th-century still used during Prohibition, can be seen. Recreational facilities also are in adjoining Cunningham Falls State Park *(see Recreation Chart and the AAA Mideastern CampBook).*

Park daily dawn-dusk. Visitor center Mon.-Fri. 10-4:30, Sat.-Sun. 8:30-5; closed federal holidays during the winter. Free. Phone (301) 663-9388. *See Recreation Chart and the AAA Mideastern Camp-Book.*

TILGHMAN ISLAND (D-7) elev. 7'

DOCKSIDE EXPRESS CRUISES AND TOURS departs from 21606 Chicken Point Rd. A marine biologist/historian conducts 90-minute narrated ecology cruises aboard a 49-passenger vessel. Sights include Colonial manor houses, working watermen and various animals such as ospreys and blue herons. Captains are native to the area. Also available are champagne sunset cruises and crabbing cruises.

Ecology and sunset cruise departures require a minimum of six passengers. Ecology cruises are offered daily, Apr. 1-early Nov. Ecology cruise $30; $15 (ages 3-12). Cruises may be preempted by charters; phone ahead. Reservations are required. AX, MC, VI. Phone (410) 886-2643 or (888) 312-7847.

TOWSON—*see Baltimore p. 186.*

WALDORF (D-6) pop. 22,312

THE DR. SAMUEL A. MUDD HOUSE MUSEUM is .4 mi. s. off Poplar Hill Rd. to 3725 Dr. Samuel A. Mudd Rd., following signs. The house is where President Abraham Lincoln's assassin, John Wilkes Booth, was treated for a broken leg the morning after the crime. Though unaware of the assassination and the identity of his patient, Dr. Mudd was convicted of complicity and sentenced to life imprisonment. He was pardoned in 1869 by President Andrew Johnson. The house contains family furnishings of the period. A farm museum and exhibit building also can be seen.

Guided tours are available. Allow 30 minutes minimum. Wed. and Sat.-Sun. 11-4, first weekend in Apr.-late Nov.; closed Easter. Last tour begins 30 minutes before closing. Admission $5; $2 (ages 6-16). Phone (301) 274-9358 or (301) 645-6870.

WESTMINSTER—*see Baltimore p. 186.*

WHEATON—*see District of Columbia p. 118.*

Virginia

Blue Ridge Splendor

Bursts of yellow, orange and red fill the winding parkway with a mosaic of color as summer turns to autumn

Civil War Battlefields

Once the site of deadly conflict, these now peaceful havens pay homage to those who fought for their beliefs

Jefferson's Virginia

From Monticello to the State Capitol, Jefferson's legacies can be seen throughout his beloved Virginia

Tidewater Delicacies

Save room to sample some of the area's succulent oysters and blue crabs

Chincoteague
© Tom Algire
Photography

yesterday and today in harmony

Peaks of Otter, Blue Ridge Parkway / © Garry Black / Masterfile

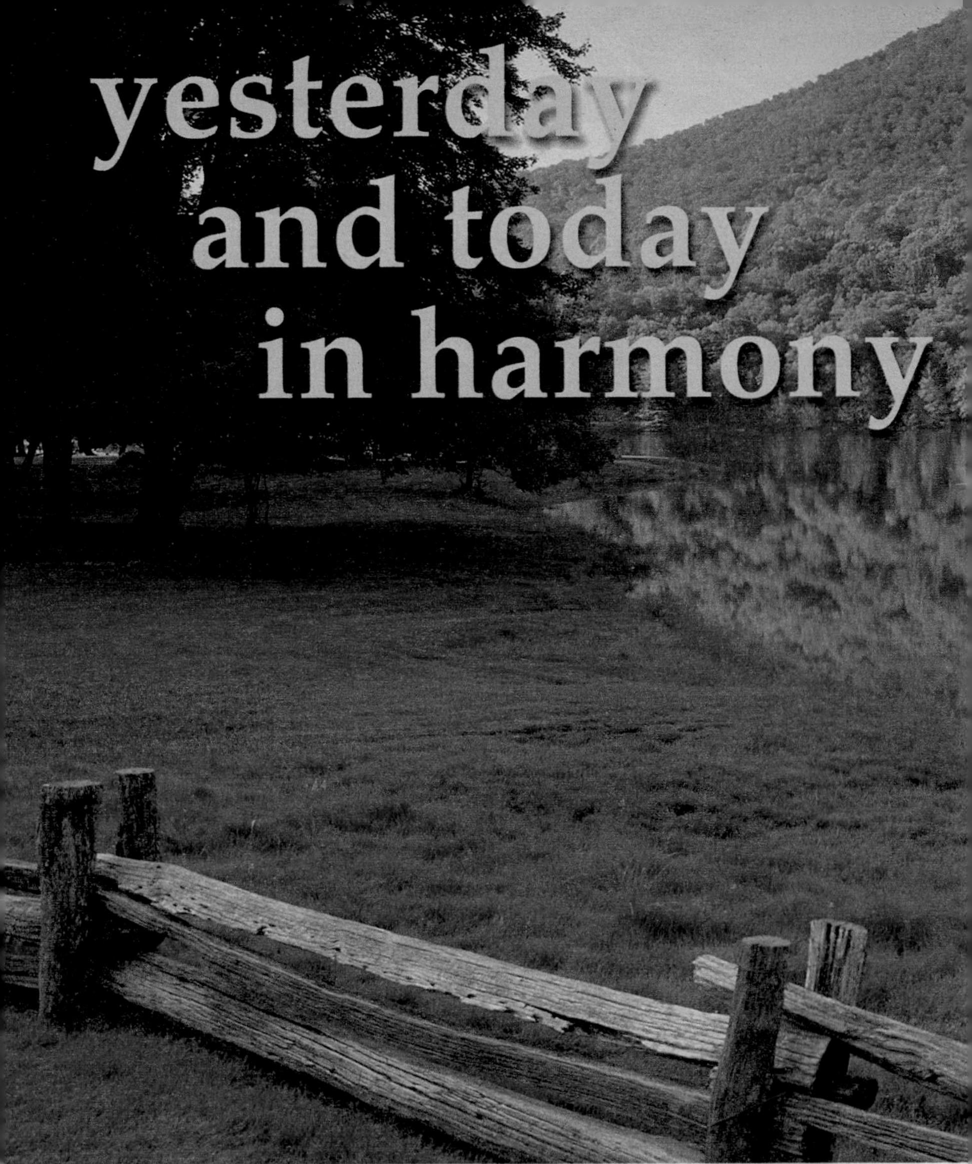

Entrenched in history and entwined with tradition, Virginia not only embraces its past, but thrives on it. Eight presidential homes, two Colonial capitals, more Civil War battlefields than any other state—only Virginia can offer such a historical legacy.

Climb aboard replicas of wooden ships or visit the ruins of Jamestown and witness archeological digs. Stroll along the streets of Colonial Williamsburg and chat with 18th-century merchants. Embrace Richmond's history and discover such treasures as the capitol designed by Thomas Jefferson, and The Museum of the Confederacy, brimming with war memorabilia. Visit Charlottesville, home of Jefferson's Monticello, and have lunch at

Michie Tavern, once an inn for the wayworn.

Follow in the footsteps of war heroes as you roam myriad battlefields, walking where valiant soldiers once fought. Travel to Manassas, site of the first Civil War battle; Chancellorsville, where Gen. Thomas J. "Stonewall" Jackson was mortally wounded; Petersburg, home of The Crater, created by a Union explosion that killed 278 Confederate soldiers; and Appomattox Court House, where Gen. Robert E. Lee surrendered to Gen. Ulysses S. Grant.

Step back in time and experience Virginia's flourishing heritage.

A trip through Virginia is a bit of a science-fiction experience. One minute, you're square in the present, sailing on the sparkling waters of Chesapeake Bay. The next, you've stumbled back into the past, amid figures in Colonial attire atop horse-drawn carriages on cobbled streets.

So it is in the Old Dominion, where a quick, 5-mile drive easily can become a journey to a different period in time.

Set the dial in the time capsule to "today," and you're loaded with options.

Hop in the car and head for the mountains. The scenery along Skyline Drive and the Blue Ridge Parkway—both meandering, two-lane roads—is breathtaking. If you prefer to have your breath taken in a more jarring way, buckle yourself into the seat of a theme park roller-coaster.

Start with a lesson about agriculture and finish with a taste test at one of the many wineries that proliferate in northern Virginia.

Experience real-world art. Mother Nature's hands shape limestone like molding clay to create striking natural wonders. The vivid colors of gargantuan formations reflect off the surface of still pools in the chambers of caverns in Front Royal, Luray and New Market.

Natural Bridge, an impressive 215-foot arch, spans Cedar Creek. Its subterranean equivalent, which carves through Powell's Mountain and emerges in a natural amphitheater, is in Natural Tunnel State Park in Duffield.

Succumb to the lure of the sea. Observe the denizens of a wildlife refuge, visit a museum to trace the ocean's impact on the culture or just wade out into the surf, where modest breakers may dampen your swimwear but never your spirits.

If none of that appeals to you, then go take a hike. The Appalachian Trail sets the standard for outdoor adventure.

Through the Pages of History

Turn the time dial backward and explore intriguing eras in history.

Crank it way back and experience what life was like when the first permanent English settlers came to North America. Costumed interpreters at Jamestown Settlement demonstrate how the adventurous colonists coped with the hardships of life in the New World.

To get a little closer to the real thing, cruise to the romantic destination of Tangier Island. Life on the largely unspoiled island is

North America's first permanent English colony is founded at Jamestown.
1607

Jamestown-Yorktown Foundation

The seat of government is moved to Williamsburg; Richmond becomes the capital in 1779.
1699

Virginia becomes the 10th state in the Union.
1788

1775
Virginia patriot Patrick Henry makes his famous "Give me liberty or give me death" speech in Richmond.

Library of Congress

1781
British general Charles Cornwallis surrenders to Gen. George Washington at Yorktown, ending the Revolutionary War.

Virginia Historical Timeline

a radical departure from the hustle and bustle on the mainland. Residents who live and work along the quaint, narrow streets speak in a lingering Elizabethan dialect and adhere to the customs of a bygone era.

Learn something about an American leader by paying a visit to a presidential home. Virginia is the birthplace of eight presidents: George Washington, Thomas Jefferson, James Madison, James Monroe, William Henry Harrison, John Tyler, Zachary Taylor and Woodrow Wilson.

One of Washington's legacies lives on in Winchester. Although his act of leveling a cherry tree often is detailed in lore, lesser known is his requirement that tenants in the Shenandoah Valley plant 4 acres of apple trees. Orchards now envelop the town.

Hub of the Civil War

Bloody battlefields transformed the countryside during the Civil War. Fredericksburg, Manassas, Petersburg, Spotsylvania and Yorktown all suffered the ravages of bitter fighting. Richmond, capital of the Confederacy, was left a smoking ruin.

Born on a Stratford plantation, Robert E. Lee left footprints all over the state as he led the Army of Northern Virginia during the war. He chalked up victories at Richmond and Chancellorsville and tasted defeat at Gettysburg and Appomattox Court House, the site of his surrender to Gen. Ulysses S. Grant. Lee's body is buried beneath a chapel on the campus of Washington and Lee University in Lexington.

Booker T. Washington was among those who laid the framework on which the civil rights movement was built. Born a slave, the Virginia native advised presidents, inspired such philanthropists as Andrew Carnegie and John D. Rockefeller, and founded the Tuskegee Normal and Industrial Institute in Alabama. A national monument southeast of Roanoke pays tribute to his accomplishments.

The state strikes a wide balance between today and yesterday. Whether you're into nature, recreation or exploring the past, you'll have a healthy range of choices here.

If Virginia isn't part of your present, consider it as part of your future.

Confederate general Robert E. Lee surrenders to Union general Ulysses S. Grant at Appomattox.

1865

L. Douglas Wilder becomes the nation's first elected African-American governor.

1989

© Wally McNamee/Corbis

Library of Congress

The Lewis and Clark Bicentennial is launched at Monticello, honoring the expedition's Virginian sponsor and leaders.

2003

1917

Congress commissions a naval station at Hampton Roads, which will become home to one of the world's largest military installations.

1996

Archeologists uncover the remains of the original James Fort, abandoned for three centuries.

2007

Fifty years after her first visit, Queen Elizabeth II returns to Jamestown to help celebrate the 400th anniversary of the New World's first permanent English settlement.

Recreation

From the sandy shores of Virginia Beach to the hundreds of remote hiking trails in the state's western mountains, Virginia's recreational activities are as varied as its landscape.

Mountain Escapes

The majestic Allegheny, Appalachian, Blue Ridge and Shenandoah mountains, standing like sentinels over western Virginia, offer a wealth of outdoor opportunities. Scenic Skyline Drive, winding along the crest of the Blue Ridge Mountains, runs the length of Shenandoah National Park and provides the perfect backdrop for **bicycling.** Crisp autumn days, with trees ablaze with fiery red and yellow leaves, are ideal for two-wheeling it along the 105 miles of twisting roadway. Frequent overviews allow for breathtaking scenery.

For the more adventurous, **mountain biking** is a popular pastime. Thrillseekers might want to try cruising down the mountain bike trails in Mount Rogers National Recreation Area, home to Virginia's highest elevation.

Grab your **hiking** boots and head to Shenandoah National Park, where more than 500 miles of trails lead trekkers through havens abloom in the spring with azaleas, dogwood and mountain laurel; if you're lucky you might happen upon a chipmunk or deer. Some popular hikes include the Whiteoak Canyon Trail and five nature trails: Fox Hollow, Loft Mountain Deadening, Mathews Arm Traces, Stony Man Mountain and Story of the Forest.

After an action-packed day of romping through the woods, a night of sound slumber beneath the twinkling stars just might be what you need. **Camping** in this pristine wilderness can do wonders for the soul. There are several developed campgrounds available. Some 535 miles of the Appalachian Trail traverses Virginia, offering numerous opportunities for primitive camping. Keep in mind that a backcountry permit is required.

Taking to the slopes can be quite rewarding. **Skiing** and **snowboarding** at Virginia's four resorts—Bryce Resort in Basye, The Homestead in Hot Springs, Massanutten near Harrisonburg and Wintergreen Resort near Waynesboro—can be indulged from December to March.

Major **hunting** grounds for deer and turkey are the national forests, game management areas and two military reservations, A.P. Hill and Quantico, which collectively provide more than 2 million acres of public land. Remember that a valid license is required and can be obtained from the Virginia Department of Game and Inland Fisheries; phone (804) 367-1000.

Coastal Connections

The Tidewater area is a great place for frolicking in the water. Boats can be launched, sails can be hoisted and swimmers can take to the inviting ocean waters. Shipwrecks off the coast entice experienced **scuba divers** to explore the mysterious depths.

Virginia's many rivers, streams and lakes provide countless hours of **swimming, rafting, canoeing** and **kayaking.** For an active outing, canoe down the remote, tree-lined Shenandoah River or take to the rapids on the James River in downtown Richmond, with the city's skyline towering in the background. The Chesapeake Bay is the perfect backdrop for a day of **sailing.**

Mountain streams and inland rivers provide the backdrop for excellent **freshwater fishing.** Several large reservoirs include Lake Anna, Claytor Lake, Smith Mountain Lake, Philpott Reservoir and Kerr Lake. State fish hatcheries help keep the lakes, rivers and streams stocked with trout and bass. Anglers can reel in more than 25 species of fish. Don't forget your valid license.

Saltwater fishing is good at Chincoteague and other barrier islands. The Atlantic Ocean is home to such catches as blue marlin, dolphins, flounder, wahoo, white marlin and yellowfin tuna. The Chesapeake Bay is popular for sport fishing, with some catches weighing in anywhere from 50 to 100 pounds. If the rod and reel are not your style, try scooping up some of the bay's delectable crabs and oysters.

Recreational Activities

Throughout the TourBook, you may notice a Recreational Activities heading with bulleted listings of recreation-oriented establishments listed underneath. Similar operations also may be mentioned in Destination City recreation sections. Since normal AAA inspection criteria cannot be applied, these establishments are presented only for information. Age, height and weight restrictions may apply. Reservations often are recommended and sometimes are required. Addresses and/or phone numbers are provided so visitors can contact the attraction for additional information.

Fast Facts

POPULATION: 7,078,515.

AREA: 40,817 square miles; ranks 36th.

CAPITAL: Richmond.

HIGHEST POINT: 5,729 ft., Mount Rogers.

LOWEST POINT: Sea level, Atlantic Ocean.

TIME ZONE(S): Eastern. DST.

MINIMUM AGE FOR UNRESTRICTED DRIVER'S LICENSE: 18

SEAT BELT/CHILD RESTRAINT LAWS: Seat belts required for driver and front-seat passengers over age 15. Children ages 8-15 required to be in a child restraint or seat belt; child restraints required for under age 8.

HELMETS FOR MOTORCYCLISTS: Required for all riders.

RADAR DETECTORS: Not permitted.

FIREARMS LAWS: Vary by state and/or county. Contact Firearms Transactions Office, Virginia State Police, P.O. Box 85608, Richmond, VA 23285-5608; phone (804) 674-2292.

HOLIDAYS: Jan. 1; Lee-Jackson-King Day, Jan. (3rd Mon.); Washington's Birthday, Feb. (3rd Mon.); Memorial Day; July 4; Labor Day; Columbus Day, Oct. (2nd Mon.); Election Day; Veterans Day, Nov. 11; Thanksgiving; Christmas, Dec. 25.

TAXES: The Virginia statewide sales tax is 5 percent, with cities and counties imposing an additional 1 percent increment. Local options also allow admission, lodgings and restaurant taxes of varying increments.

INFORMATION CENTERS: State welcome centers are on US 13S near New Church, just south of the Maryland border; on I-64E southwest of Callaghan, just east of the West Virginia border; on I-66W near Manassas; on I-81S south of the West Virginia border, near Stephenson; on I-81N at the Tennessee border, near Bristol; on I-85N at the North Carolina border, south of Bracey; on I-77 at Lambsburg; on I-77 near Rocky Gap; on I-95N at the North Carolina border, south of Skippers; and on I-95S near Fredericksburg.

FURTHER INFORMATION FOR VISITORS:

Virginia Tourism Corp.
901 E. Byrd St.
Richmond, VA 23219
(804) 786-2051
(800) 847-4882

FISHING AND HUNTING REGULATIONS:

Virginia Department of Game & Inland Fisheries
4010 W. Broad St.
Richmond, VA 23230
(804) 367-1000

NATIONAL FOREST INFORMATION:

Southern Region Information Office
1720 Peachtree Rd., Suite 760S
Atlanta, GA 30309
(404) 347-4177
(877) 444-6777 (reservations)
National Park Service/D.C. Region
1100 Ohio Dr. S.W.
Washington, DC 20242
(202) 619-7222

RECREATION INFORMATION:

Virginia State Parks
Department of Conservation & Recreation
203 Governor St., Suite 213
Richmond, VA 23219
(804) 786-1712
(800) 933-7275 (reservations)

Virginia Temperature Averages Maximum/Minimum
From the records of The Weather Channel Interactive, Inc.

	JAN	FEB	MAR	APR	MAY	JUNE	JULY	AUG	SEPT	OCT	NOV	DEC
Norfolk	48/34	51/35	59/42	68/50	76/59	83/68	88/73	86/72	80/67	70/55	61/46	53/38
Richmond	45/28	49/30	58/37	69/45	76/55	84/63	88/68	86/67	80/60	69/47	60/38	50/31
Roanoke	45/27	49/29	58/36	68/44	76/52	83/60	88/65	86/63	79/57	69/45	58/37	49/30

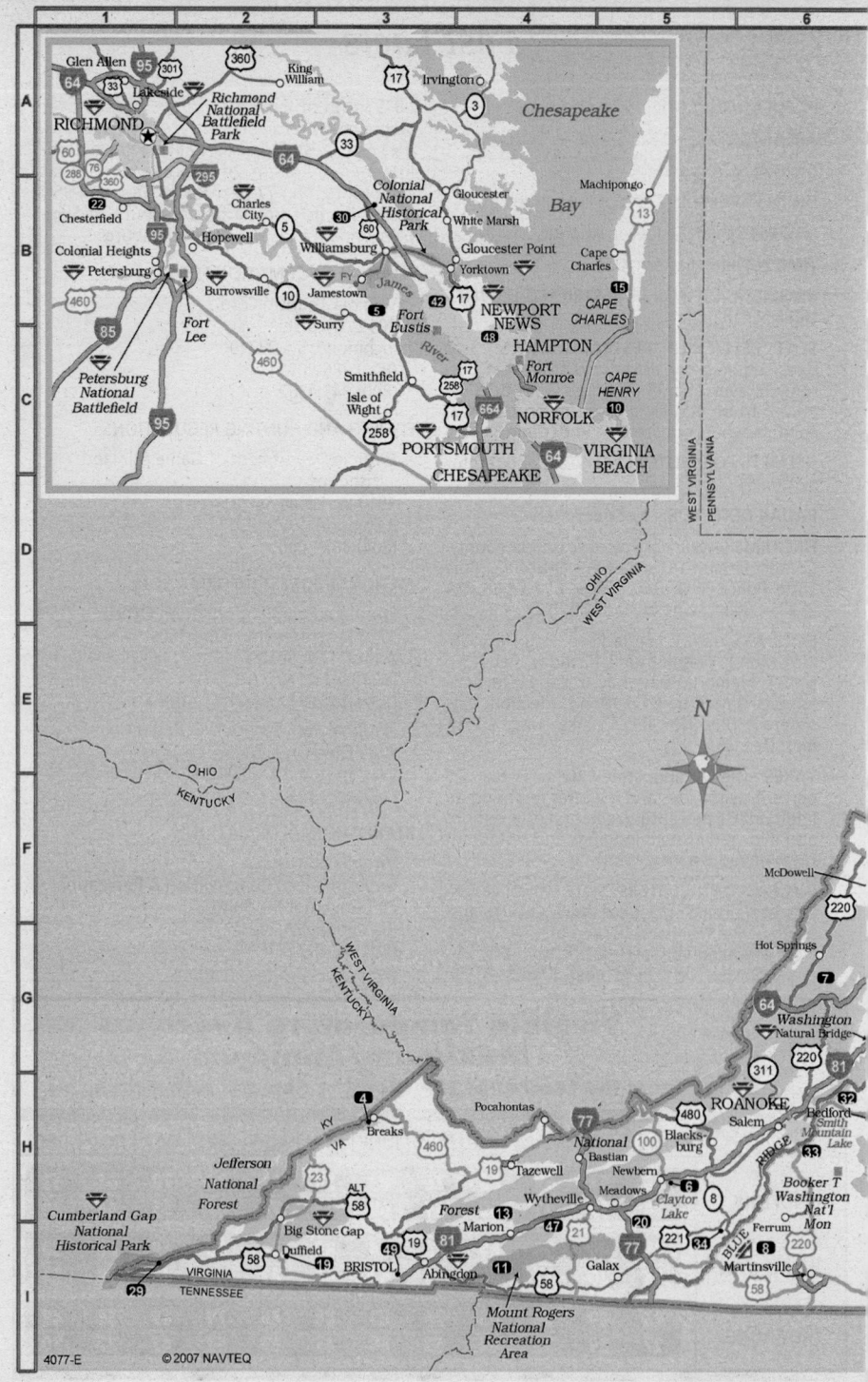

© 2007 NAVTEQ

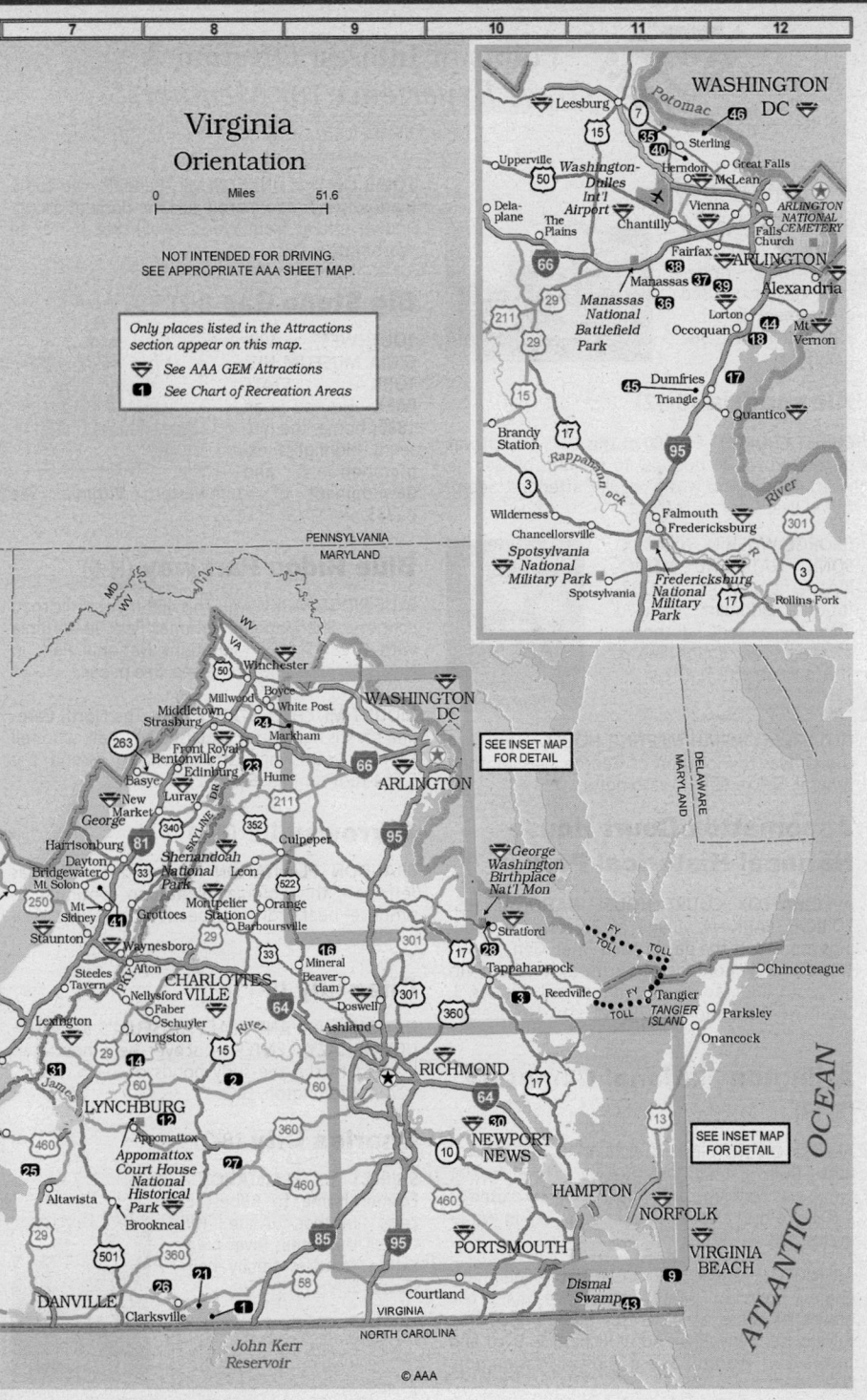

Virginia
Orientation

0   Miles   51.6

NOT INTENDED FOR DRIVING.
SEE APPROPRIATE AAA SHEET MAP.

Only places listed in the Attractions
section appear on this map.
☞ See AAA GEM Attractions
❶ See Chart of Recreation Areas

PENNSYLVANIA
MARYLAND

WASHINGTON
DC

Leesburg
Potomac
46
35
7
Upperville   Washington-   40   Sterling   Great Falls
50   Dulles   Herndon   McLean
Dela-   Int'l   Vienna   ARLINGTON
plane   Airport   Chantilly   NATIONAL
The   CEMETERY
Plains   Fairfax   Falls ARLINGTON
66   Manassas   38   Church
                                    37   39
211   Manassas   36   Lorton   Alexandria
29   National   Occoquan   44   Mt
              Battlefield   18   Vernon
15   Park
                            45   Dumfries   17
                                    Triangle
Brandy   Quantico
Station   17   95
3   Falmouth
Wilderness   Fredericksburg   301
              Chancellorsville
Spotsylvania
National   Fredericksburg   3
Military Park   Spotsylvania   National   Rollins Fork
                            Military   17
                            Park

Winchester
50
Millwood   Boyce
Middletown   White Post
Strasburg   24   Markham
263   Front Royal
Bentonville   23   Hume
Basye   Edinburg
New   Luray
Market
George
Harrisonburg   81
Dayton   340
Bridgewater   333   Shenandoah
Mt Solon   National   Leon
250   Mt   Park   522
Sidney   Montpelier   Orange
Staunton   Grottoes   Station   Barboursville
Waynesboro   29   33
Steeles   Afton   Mineral   16
Tavern   Nellysford CHARLOTTES-   Beaver   301
Lexington   Faber VILLE   dam
Schuyler   64   Doswell
Lovingston   Ashland
31   29   15
60
LYNCHBURG   60
Appomattox
Appomattox   27
Court House
National   460
Historical
Park
Altavista   Brookneal
29
501   360   21
DANVILLE   26
Clarksville

WASHINGTON
DC
66
ARLINGTON
95

SEE INSET MAP
FOR DETAIL

George
Washington
Birthplace
Nat'l Mon
Stratford
301   17   23
Tappahannock
360
3   Reedville
Tangier
TANGIER
ISLAND

MARYLAND
DELAWARE

Chincoteague
Parksley
Onancock

RICHMOND
64   17
30
NEWPORT
10   NEWS
13
HAMPTON
460
NORFOLK
85   95
PORTSMOUTH
VIRGINIA
BEACH
58   Courtland   Dismal
Swamp   43
VIRGINIA
NORTH CAROLINA
John Kerr
Reservoir
9

SEE INSET MAP
FOR DETAIL

ATLANTIC OCEAN

© AAA

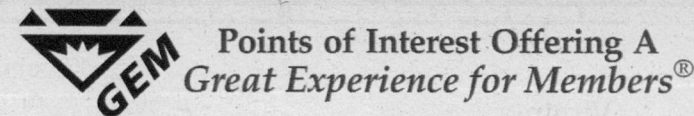

Points of Interest Offering A
Great Experience for Members®

Abingdon (I-3)

BARTER THEATRE— During the Depression, food, rather than cash, was used as payment for theater tickets. See p. 231.

Alexandria (B-12)

CHRIST CHURCH—Pew 60 of this 1773 church was purchased for 36 pounds, 10 shillings by George Washington, who was a regular attendee. See p. 119 in Washington, D.C.

GEORGE WASHINGTON MASONIC NATIONAL MEMORIAL—The memorial is a 333-foot-tall landmark modeled after the ancient lighthouse at Alexandria, Egypt. See p. 120 in Washington, D.C.

OLD PRESBYTERIAN MEETING HOUSE—This 1774 church was the location of George Washington's funeral. See p. 121 in Washington, D.C.

Appomattox Court House National Historical Park (H-7)

APPOMATTOX COURT HOUSE NATIONAL HISTORICAL PARK—A village of 27 restored buildings represents the day in 1865 when Gen. Robert E. Lee and the Confederate Army of Northern Virginia surrendered to Union general Ulysses S. Grant in the parlor of the McLean House. See p. 232.

Arlington National Cemetery (B-12)

ARLINGTON HOUSE, THE ROBERT E. LEE MEMORIAL—Built in 1802, Gen. Robert E. Lee's former home was confiscated during the war and used as a place to bury the war dead. See p. 126 in Washington, D.C.

ARLINGTON NATIONAL CEMETERY—Seemingly endless rows of white headstones mark the graves of some of America's heroes, including John F. Kennedy, Rear Adm. Richard E. Byrd and Justice Earl Warren. See p. 126 in Washington, D.C.

TOMB OF THE UNKNOWNS—Beneath the tomb made of Colorado marble lies the body of an unknown soldier from World War I. See p. 127 in Washington, D.C.

Big Stone Gap (I-2)

SOUTHWEST VIRGINIA MUSEUM HISTORICAL STATE PARK—Housed in an 1880s home, the museum highlights exploration and development of southwestern Virginia. See p. 233.

Blue Ridge Parkway (H-6)

BLUE RIDGE PARKWAY—This 469-mile scenic road connects Shenandoah National Park in Virginia with Great Smoky Mountains National Park in North Carolina and Tennessee. See p. 234.

MOUNT MITCHELL STATE PARK—The North Carolina park is named for Dr. Elisha Mitchell, who fell to his death while attempting to ascend the 6,684-foot summit. See p. 236.

Burrowsville (B-2)

BRANDON PLANTATION—Designed by Thomas Jefferson, this Colonial plantation continues to produce beef, corn, soybeans and wheat. See p. 238.

Chantilly (B-11)

NATIONAL AIR AND SPACE MUSEUM'S STEVEN F. UDVAR-HAZY CENTER—Discover here how man learned to slip the surly bonds of Earth. See p. 127 in Washington, D.C.

Charles City (B-2)

SHIRLEY PLANTATION—Former home to Robert E. Lee's mother, Anne Hill Carter, this James River plantation features family heirlooms. See p. 313.

Charlottesville (G-8)

ASH LAWN-HIGHLAND—James Monroe, America's fifth president, lived at this 535-acre estate. See p. 239.

MICHIE TAVERN—Scotsman William Michie built this inn about 1784 as a rest stop for weary travelers. See p. 240.

MONTICELLO—Thomas Jefferson's mountaintop estate reflects his era, accomplishments and diverse interests. See p. 240.

UNIVERSITY OF VIRGINIA—Designed in the neoclassical style by Thomas Jefferson, this university boasts such former students as Edgar Allan Poe and Woodrow Wilson. See p. 241.

Cumberland Gap National Historical Park (I-1)

CUMBERLAND GAP NATIONAL HISTORICAL PARK—The gap, now within a 20,444-acre park, provides a natural passageway through the mountains into Tennessee, western Virginia and Kentucky. See p. 243.

Doswell (G-9)

KINGS DOMINION—More than 50 rides and shows are presented in eight thematic areas of this 400-acre amusement park. See p. 301.

Fredericksburg (D-11)

JAMES MONROE MUSEUM AND MEMORIAL LIBRARY—This property was owned by James Monroe 1786-92 and today is home to one of the largest collections of Monroe memorabilia in the country. See p. 249.

KENMORE PLANTATION & GARDENS—This Tidewater mid-Georgian manor house was the home of George Washington's sister, Betty Washington Lewis. See p. 249.

MARY WASHINGTON HOUSE—It was from this house that George Washington, the newly elected president, left for his inauguration after receiving his mother's blessing. See p. 249.

RISING SUN TAVERN—This 1760 house was built for Charles Washington, brother of our first president. See p. 250.

Fredericksburg and Spotsylvania National Military Park (D-11)

FREDERICKSBURG AND SPOTSYLVANIA NATIONAL MILITARY PARK—This 8,400-acre area comprises four great Civil War battlegrounds: Chancellorsville, Fredericksburg, Spotsylvania Court House and the Wilderness. See p. 250.

Front Royal (E-8)

SKYLINE CAVERNS—These caves feature rare calcite formations known as anthodites, or cave flowers. See p. 252.

George Washington Birthplace National Monument (F-10)

GEORGE WASHINGTON BIRTHPLACE NATIONAL MONUMENT—On the south side of the Potomac River, the monument contains a replica of an 18th-century plantation home furnished with antiques from Washington's era. See p. 253.

Jamestown (B-3)

HISTORIC JAMESTOWNE—More than a million artifacts have been excavated at this archeological site, which preserves the foundations and ruins of the 17th-century Jamestown settlement. See p. 316.

JAMESTOWN SETTLEMENT—This living-history museum re-creates early life at Jamestown through interactive exhibits and three outdoor areas, including James Fort, the river dock and a Powhatan Indian village. See p. 319.

Lakeside (A-1)

LEWIS GINTER BOTANICAL GARDEN—Filled with exquisite plants and flowers, several themed gardens attract birds and butterflies as well as scores of two-legged creatures. See p. 301.

Leesburg (A-11)

OATLANDS—Of the 3,408 acres that originally made up this estate, only 261 remain; visitors can view the 1804 house furnished in period. See p. 129 in Washington, D.C.

Lexington (G-7)

LEE CHAPEL & MUSEUM—The 1867 chapel on the campus of Washington and Lee University now is a shrine to Gen. Robert E. Lee. See p. 274.

Lorton (B-12)

GUNSTON HALL PLANTATION—This 1755 brick Georgian residence was home to George Mason, author of the Virginia Declaration of Rights of 1776 and one of the framers of the U.S. Constitution. See p. 130 in Washington, D.C.

POHICK CHURCH—Used as a stable during the Civil War, this church, where George Washington served as a vestryman for 23 years, was restored 1902-17. See p. 130 in Washington, D.C.

Luray (F-8)

LURAY CAVERNS—The Cathedral Room of these caves features unusually formed stalactites that can produce beautiful music. See p. 275.

McLean (A-12)

GREAT FALLS PARK—The Potomac River, which drops some 77 feet in thunderous rapids and falls, is a feature of this 800-acre park. See p. 131 in Washington, D.C.

Montpelier Station (F-8)

JAMES MADISON'S MONTPELIER—This former residence of James Madison depicts the lifestyle and history of the Father of the United States Constitution and his family. See p. 279.

Mount Vernon (B-12)

DONALD W. REYNOLDS MUSEUM AND EDUCATION CENTER—Learn how the Washington family lived as you view their personal effects and theater presentations providing unique insights. See p. 132 in Washington, D.C.

GEORGE WASHINGTON'S MOUNT VERNON ESTATE & GARDENS—The final home of George Washington contains personal effects of our first president. See p. 132 in Washington, D.C.

Natural Bridge (G-6)

THE NATURAL BRIDGE OF VIRGINIA—Supporting US 11, this limestone arch spans Cedar Creek. See p. 279.

New Market (F-7)

ENDLESS CAVERNS—These caves feature stalagmites, stalactites and various other formations. See p. 280.

NEW MARKET BATTLEFIELD STATE HISTORICAL PARK—A self-guiding tour covers the battlefield where 257 Virginia Military Institute cadets fought in a Union victory on May 15, 1864. See p. 281.

SHENANDOAH CAVERNS—A mile-long guided tour offers spectacular views of cave formations. See p. 281.

Newport News (B-4)

THE MARINERS' MUSEUM—Situated in a 550-acre park, this museum is dedicated to preserving and interpreting the heritage of the sea. See p. 261.

USS *MONITOR* CENTER—Artifacts, multimedia presentations and interactive exhibits highlight the legacy of one of the Civil War's ironclad warships. See p. 261.

VIRGINIA LIVING MUSEUM—From the ocean to the mountains, this museum explores Virginia's natural heritage, ecosystems, plants and animals. See p. 262.

Norfolk (C-4)

CHRYSLER MUSEUM OF ART—Some 30,000 pieces of art include works by Mary Cassatt, Pablo Picasso and Andy Warhol. See p. 263.

GENERAL DOUGLAS MACARTHUR MEMORIAL—The general's trademark cap is among the items on display in galleries chronicling the military leader's life and career. See p. 264.

NAUTICUS—High-tech, interactive exhibits focus on such nautical themes as shipbuilding and navigation. See p. 264.

NORFOLK BOTANICAL GARDEN—Stroll the 155-acre site, which features a variety of plants, or take a tram or boat ride through the gardens. See p. 265.

Petersburg (B-1)

PAMPLIN HISTORICAL PARK AND THE NATIONAL MUSEUM OF THE CIVIL WAR SOLDIER—Centered on a Civil War battlefield, the museum explores the plight of the common soldier through multimedia exhibits. See p. 283.

Petersburg National Battlefield (C-1)

PETERSBURG NATIONAL BATTLEFIELD—An important holding spot to Richmond, Petersburg saw 10 months of brutal Civil War fighting before falling to the Union army. See p. 284.

Portsmouth (C-3)

CHILDREN'S MUSEUM OF VIRGINIA—More than 90 hands-on exhibits allow children to explore science, nature, art and music. See p. 266.

CHILDREN'S MUSEUM
OF VIRGINIA

Quantico (C-12)

NATIONAL MUSEUM OF THE MARINE CORPS—Learn about a Marine's role from boot camp to conflict and view aircraft, tanks, uniforms and weapons in this museum honoring the history of the Corps. See p. 133 in Washington, D.C.

Richmond (G-9)

AGECROFT HALL—Originally built during the 15th century, this Tudor-style house is surrounded by 23 acres of gardens. See p. 291.

AGECROFT HALL—15TH CENTURY ENGLISH MANOR HOUSE

MAYMONT—This 100-acre Victorian country estate features the 1893 Maymont House, formal gardens, an arboretum, a carriage house and a petting zoo. See p. 294.

THE MUSEUM OF THE CONFEDERACY—Founded in 1890, this museum contains one of the largest collections of Civil War artifacts in the country. See p. 294.

VALENTINE RICHMOND HISTORY CENTER—The story of Richmond is told through an extensive collection of artifacts and displays; a tour of the 1812 Wickham House is offered. See p. 295.

VIRGINIA HISTORICAL SOCIETY & MUSEUM—Seven galleries exhibit treasures from Virginia. See p. 295.

VIRGINIA MUSEUM OF FINE ARTS—Fabergé jeweled eggs are just some of the art treasures found in this museum. See p. 296.

VIRGINIA STATE CAPITOL—Designed by Thomas Jefferson, the commonwealth's capitol is modeled after a Roman temple in France. See p. 296.

WHITE HOUSE OF THE CONFEDERACY—This Victorian-style mansion served as home to Confederate President Jefferson Davis during the Civil War. See p. 294.

Roanoke (H-6)

CENTER IN THE SQUARE—Several cultural attractions share this restored 1914 warehouse, including the Art Museum of Western Virginia; the History Museum and Historical Society of Western Virginia; and the Science Museum of Western Virginia and Hopkins Planetarium. See p. 303.

Shenandoah National Park (F-8)

SKYLINE DRIVE—Some 105 miles of scenic highway traverse Shenandoah National Park. See p. 306.

Staunton (F-7)

FRONTIER CULTURE MUSEUM—This living-history farm depicts the Appalachian frontier and the European heritage of its immigrant settlers. See p. 307.

Stratford (F-10)

STRATFORD HALL PLANTATION—THE BIRTHPLACE OF ROBERT E. LEE—Built in the shape of an H, this Colonial-style estate has been home to four generations of the Lee family. See p. 308.

Stratford Hall
PLANTATION

Surry (B-3)

SURRY NUCLEAR INFORMATION CENTER—Innovative exhibits illuminate the science behind nuclear-generated electricity. See p. 268.

Vienna (B-11)

WOLF TRAP NATIONAL PARK FOR THE PERFORMING ARTS—This is the country's only national park dedicated to the performing arts. See p. 133 in Washington, D.C.

Virginia Beach (C-5)

VIRGINIA AQUARIUM & MARINE SCIENCE CENTER—Hands-on exhibits explore Virginia's marine environment. See p. 270.

Waynesboro (G-7)

P. BUCKLEY MOSS MUSEUM—Amish and Mennonite people are portrayed in the works of this local artist. See p. 310.

Williamsburg (B-3)

BUSCH GARDENS EUROPE—More than 100 rides, shows and exhibits portray the cultures of England, Ireland, Scotland, France, Germany and Italy. See p. 322.

COLONIAL WILLIAMSBURG HISTORIC AREA—This expansive living-history site, with restored buildings and costumed interpreters, depicts the 18th-century Colonial capital. See p. 322.

Colonial Williamsburg

THE DEWITT WALLACE DECORATIVE ARTS MUSEUM—More than 10,000 decorative items portray area history. See p. 324.

GOVERNOR'S PALACE—The palace is a reconstruction of the 1722 building that served as executive mansion to Virginia's first two governors, Patrick Henry and Thomas Jefferson. See p. 324.

WATER COUNTRY USA—Wave pools, water slides and a high-dive show are just some of the attractions offered at this water park. See p. 325.

Winchester (E-8)

MUSEUM OF THE SHENANDOAH VALLEY—The complex's regional history museum, opulent 1700s mansion and 6 acres of manicured gardens bring the rich history of the Shenandoah Valley alive. See p. 328.

Yorktown (B-4)

YORKTOWN VICTORY CENTER—Costumed interpreters and exhibits recall the events of the American Revolution. See p. 327.

RECREATION AREAS

	MAP LOCATION	CAMPING	PICNICKING	HIKING TRAILS	BOATING	BOAT RAMP	BOAT RENTAL	FISHING	SWIMMING	PETS ON LEASH	BICYCLE TRAILS	WINTER SPORTS	VISITOR CENTER	LODGE/CABINS	FOOD SERVICE
NATIONAL PARKS *(See place listings)*															
Shenandoah (F-8) 197,412 acres. Western Virginia. Horse rental.		•	•	•				•		•			•	•	•
NATIONAL FORESTS *(See place listings)*															
George Washington and Jefferson 1,800,000 acres. Western Virginia and eastern edge of West Virginia.		•	•	•	•	•	•	•	•	•	•	•			
NATIONAL RECREATION AREAS *(See place listings)*															
Mount Rogers (I-3) 200,000 acres in southwestern Virginia.		•	•	•				•	•	•	•	•		•	•
ARMY CORPS OF ENGINEERS															
John H. Kerr Reservoir (I-8) 106,860 acres off SR 4 near Boydton. Water skiing.	❶	•	•	•	•	•	•	•	•	•		•	•		
STATE															
Bear Creek Lake (G-8) 326 acres 5 mi. w. of Cumberland off US 60. Horseback riding trails.	❷	•	•	•	•	•	•	•	•	•	•	•			•
Belle Isle (B-10) 733 acres on SR 683 near Litwalton. Saltwater fishing; paddleboats, playground.	❸	•	•	•	•	•	•	•		•	•	•		•	
Breaks Interstate (H-3) 4,500 acres 7 mi. e. of Breaks on SR 80. Scenic. Horse rental. *(See Breaks p. 237)*	❹	•	•	•				•	•	•	•	•	•	•	•
Chippokes Plantation (B-3) 1,683 acres on the James River 1.5 mi. e. of Surry via SR 10, then 3 mi. n. on CR 634. Historic. *(See Surry p. 268)*	❺		•	•				•	•	•	•	•	•		
Claytor Lake (H-5) 472 acres 4 mi. s. of Radford via I-81, then 2 mi. s. on SR 660. Horse rental.	❻	•	•	•	•	•	•	•	•	•	•		•	•	•
Douthat (G-6) 4,493 acres 6 mi. n. of Clifton Forge on SR 629.	❼	•	•	•	•	•	•	•	•	•	•		•	•	•
Fairy Stone (I-6) 4,750 acres 8 mi. w. of Bassett on SR 57.	❽	•	•	•	•	•	•	•	•	•	•		•	•	•
False Cape (I-11) 4,321 acres s.e. of Sandbridge via signs to Little Island Recreation Area. (Accessible only by foot, bicycle or boat.)	❾	•	•	•	•			•		•	•		•		
First Landing (C-5) 2,888 acres at Cape Henry on US 60.	❿	•	•	•	•			•	•	•	•		•	•	•
Grayson Highlands (I-4) 4,754 acres w. of Volney on US 58. Horseback riding trails.	⓫	•	•	•				•		•	•	•	•		
Holliday Lake (H-8) 250 acres 6 mi. n.e. of Appomattox on SR 24, then 4 mi. e. via SR 626/629.	⓬	•	•	•	•	•	•	•	•	•	•		•		•

RECREATION AREAS

	MAP LOCATION	CAMPING	PICNICKING	HIKING TRAILS	BOATING	BOAT RAMP	BOAT RENTAL	FISHING	SWIMMING	PETS ON LEASH	BICYCLE TRAILS	WINTER SPORTS	VISITOR CENTER	LODGE/CABINS	FOOD SERVICE
Hungry Mother (H-4) 2,215 acres 3 mi. n.e. of Marion on SR 16.	13	•	•	•	•	•	•	•	•	•			•	•	•
James River (G-7) 1,500 acres on CR 606 near Norwood. Canoeing, kayaking; bicycle rentals, horseback riding trails.	14	•	•	•	•	•	•	•		•	•				
Kiptopeke (B-5) 540 acres 3 mi. n. of the Chesapeake Bay Bridge Tunnel from Virginia Beach on US 13, then w. on SR 704.	15	•	•			•		•	•	•					•
Lake Anna (G-9) 2,304 acres 25 mi. s.w. of Fredericksburg off SR 208.	16		•	•	•	•	•	•	•	•	•				
Leesylvania (C-12) 508 acres 3 mi. e. of Woodbridge off I-95 exit 156.	17		•	•	•	•		•		•			•		
Mason Neck (B-12) 1,814 acres 5 mi. n. of Woodbridge on US 1, then 5.5 mi. e. on SR 242.	18		•	•				•		•			•		
Natural Tunnel (I-3) 850 acres .4 mi. s. of Duffield on US 23, then 4.2 mi. e. on Daniel Boone Tr. *(See Duffield p. 246)*	19	•	•	•				•	•	•			•		
New River Trail (H-5) 765 acres off I-77 exit 24, then 1.5 mi. n. on US 52 in Wytheville. Historic. Canoe rental. *(See Wytheville p. 330)*	20	•	•	•	•	•	•	•		•	•		•		
Occoneechee (I-8) 2,698 acres 1.5 mi. e. of Clarksville on US 58.	21	•	•	•	•	•	•	•		•			•		
Pocahontas (B-1) 7,625 acres 4 mi. s.w. of Chesterfield off SR 655.	22	•	•	•	•		•	•	•	•	•				•
Raymond R. "Andy" Guest Jr. Shenandoah River (E-8) 1,604 acres 8 mi. s. of Front Royal off US 340. Horse rental.	23	•	•	•	•			•		•					
Sky Meadows (E-8) 1,862 acres 5.1 mi. n. of Delaplane off US 17. Scenic. *(See Delaplane p. 245)*	24	•	•	•				•		•			•		
Smith Mountain Lake (H-6) 22,000 acres 26 mi. s. of Bedford via SR 122 to SR 608 to SR 626.	25	•	•	•	•	•	•	•	•	•			•	•	•
Staunton River (I-8) 1,597 acres 9 mi. s.e. of Scottsburg on SR 344.	26	•	•	•	•	•		•	•	•				•	•
Twin Lakes (H-8) 425 acres 3 mi. n.e. of Green Bay off US 360 to SR 613.	27	•	•	•	•		•	•	•	•				•	•
Westmoreland (G-10) 1,299 acres 5 mi. n.w. of Montross on SR 3. Swimming pool.	28	•	•	•	•	•	•	•	•	•				•	•
Wilderness Road (I-1) 200 acres 5 mi. w. of Ewing at US 58 and SR 690. Historic home.	29		•	•						•			•		•
York River (B-3) 2,550 acres 3.1 mi. n. of I-64 exit 234B, then 1.2 mi. w. to 5526 Riverview Rd. in Williamsburg. *(See Williamsburg p. 326)*	30		•	•	•	•		•		•	•		•		
BLUE RIDGE PARKWAY															
Otter Creek (G-7) 552 acres at Milepost 61.	31	•	•	•				•		•					•
Peaks of Otter (H-6) 4,150 acres at Milepost 86.	32	•	•	•				•		•			•	•	•
Roanoke Mountain (H-6) 65 acres at Milepost 121.	33	•	•	•						•					
Rocky Knob (I-5) 4,200 acres at Milepost 169.	34	•	•	•				•		•			•	•	•
OTHER															
Algonkian Regional Park (A-11) 500 acres 11 mi. e. of Leesburg and 3 mi. n. of SR 7. Golf, miniature golf; playground.	35		•			•				•				•	•
Bull Run Regional Park (B-11) 1563 acres 3 mi. w. of Centreville off US 29. Miniature golf, skeet and trap shooting; playground.	36	•	•	•						•	•		•		•
Burke Lake Park (B-11) 888 acres 6 mi. s.w. of I-495 exit 5W via CR 620, CR 645 and SR 123. Golf; carousel, miniature train.	37	•	•	•	•	•	•	•		•	•		•		•
Ellanor C. Lawrence Park (B-11) 640 acres .5 mi. n. from I-66 exit 53 via SR 28. Historic.	38		•	•					•				•		•

RECREATION AREAS	MAP LOCATION	CAMPING	PICNICKING	HIKING TRAILS	BOATING	BOAT RAMP	BOAT RENTAL	FISHING	SWIMMING	PETS ON LEASH	BICYCLE TRAILS	WINTER SPORTS	VISITOR CENTER	LODGE/CABINS	FOOD SERVICE
Lake Accotink Park (B-12) 479 acres 3 mi. from I-495 exit 5E via CR 620 and Heming Ave. Canoeing, miniature golf; carousel, playground.	**39**		●	●	●	●	●	●			●	●			●
Lake Fairfax Park (A-11) 479 acres 7 mi. w. of I-495 exit 10W via SR 7 and CR 606. Cross-country skiing; athletic fields, carousel, miniature train.	**40**	●	●	●	●			●	●	●	●	●			●
Natural Chimneys (F-7) 150 acres .5 mi. n.w. on SR 731 following signs. *(See Mount Solon p. 279)*	**41**	●	●	●				●	●	●	●		●		
Newport News (B-3) 8,000 acres on SR 143, then .5 mi. w. of jct. SR 105 in Newport News. Golf, jogging; archery range. *(See Newport News p. 262)*	**42**	●	●	●	●		●	●		●	●	●	●		●
Northwest River Park (I-11) 763 acres 7.4 mi. s. of Chesapeake on Battlefield Blvd. S., then 3.8 mi. e. on Indian Creek Rd. Miniature golf; playground. *(See Chesapeake p. 255)*	**43**	●	●	●	●		●	●			●	●			●
Pohick Bay Regional Park (B-12) 1,003 acres 1 mi. s.w. of Lorton on US 1, then 3.2 mi. s.e. on Gunston Rd. Golf, miniature golf.	**44**	●	●	●	●	●	●	●					●		●
Prince William Forest (C-11) 15,000 acres off I-95 exit 150, then .2 mi. w. on Joplin Rd. (SR 619). *(See Triangle in the District of Columbia p. 133)*	**45**	●	●	●				●			●	●	●	●	●
Riverbend Park (A-12) 409 acres 10 mi. w. of I-495 exit 13 via SR 193, CR 603 and Jeffrey Rd. (CR 1268). Nature center.	**46**		●	●		●		●					●	●	
Rural Retreat Lake (I-4) 350 acres 4 mi. s.w. of Rural Retreat off I-81 exit 60, 4 mi. e. on CR 749, then 1 mi. s. on CR 677.	**47**	●	●	●	●	●	●	●	●	●					
Sandy Bottom Nature Park (C-4) 456 acres off I-64 at 1255 Big Bethel Rd. in Hampton. Nature center, playground.	**48**	●	●	●	●			●			●	●		●		
Sugar Hollow (I-3) 500 acres in Bristol off Lee Hwy. via I-81 exit 7. Golf; driving range, swimming pool.	**49**	●	●	●							●				●	

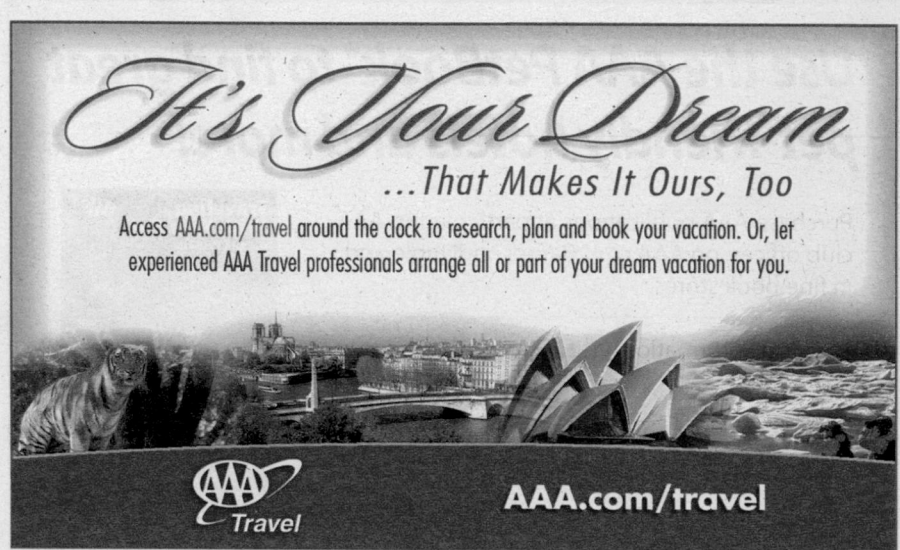

Exploring Virginia

For descriptions of places in bold type, see individual listings.

The Eastern Shore

Tales of Blackbeard, herds of wild ponies, secluded fishing villages and unspoiled beaches lend to the romantic atmosphere of Virginia's Eastern Shore.

In 1965 the almost 18-mile Chesapeake Bay Bridge-Tunnel opened, linking mainland Virginia to the southern tip of the Delmarva Peninsula (parts of the peninsula belong to *Dela*ware, *Mary*land and *Virgin*ia) at Cape Charles. Called one of the world's most incredible engineering feats, the bridge-tunnel dips into the water and carries motorists under massive, ocean-bound freighters. The bridge holds a scenic stop, fishing pier and restaurant and connects US 13 from the mainland to the peninsula where it becomes the main run.

Bounded by wetlands, barrier islands and the Atlantic Ocean on the east and the Chesapeake Bay on the west, the 70-mile Delmarva Peninsula and several barrier islands constitute what is called Virginia's Eastern Shore. Capt. John Smith and his exploring party were the first Europeans to visit the area when they mapped the Chesapeake Islands in 1608. In 1614 the Jamestown government purchased the land; 6

years later the English colonized the peninsula.

The grave of John Custis IV lies near **Cape Charles** on the peninsula's bay side. The tomb for this ancestor of the Virginia Custis family bears an epitaph evidently intended to be the last

Colonial Williamsburg Foundation

Virginia's Past is Ever Present

word in a lifelong quarrel with his wife.

Farther north on US 13 is Eastville, a town with a 1644 debtor's prison and the country's oldest standing courthouse. The building contains the nation's earliest continuous court records, dating from 1632, including the first account of an American dramatic performance—the 1665 play "The Bear and the Cub"— and the only record of a local court's declaration that the English Parliament's Stamp Act was unconstitutional.

Onancock's deep harbor offers docking for any size craft. Passenger ferries leave Onancock for

Tangier Island, in the heart of Chesapeake Bay. In 1814 the British established headquarters on Tangier and swayed the young island men into service. But the night before the recruits were to sail with the British, the Tangier women sank their small boats, and the British had to sail without them.

Tangier Island seems untouched by time. Most of the denizens still speak with Elizabethan idioms and accents, and many customs remain. There is no industry on the island, and its two main roads are 8 to 10 feet wide.

Near the Maryland border, SR 175 branches off US 13 to the east. The NASA Visitor Center is on SR 175, 6 miles east of US 13.

As many remember, Marguerite Henry's famed pony, Misty, was from **Chincoteague**. The ponies are an island trademark; according to local legend they descended from mine horses that swam ashore from a wrecked Spanish galleon centuries ago. Most historians, however, believe the original herd was brought over by the first English colonists who turned them loose on Assateague and Chincoteague in the late 1600s when the ponies began to damage mainland Virginia's crops.

The ponies are rounded up at their home on the southern end of Assateague Island to swim at slack tide (when the tide is changing and there is no movement) across the narrow channel

Mabry Mill, Blue Ridge Parkway / Tim Thompson / VA Tourism Corp

Roanoke, once called Big Lick because of salt marshes that attracted herds of game, is cradled between the Blue Ridge Mountains to the east and the Allegheny Mountains to the west. I-81 and the Blue Ridge Parkway flank the city. Twenty miles southeast of Roanoke, the **Booker T. Washington National Monument** re-creates the small tobacco plantation where the educator and advisor to presidents was born a slave.

Just south of **Lexington** is one of the seven natural wonders of the world, **Natural Bridge.** The 23-story arch is a product of limestone substratum erosion. The Monocan Indians worshiped "The Bridge of God," and George Washington carved his still-visible initials into the stone. Natural Bridge spans Cedar Creek and supports US 11 but cannot be seen from the highway.

Near Lexington I-81 runs north through the George Washington and Jefferson National Forests. One of the first national forests established in the East, it includes the largest public hunting ground in the region; the main marks are white-tailed deer, wild turkeys, black bears and some smaller game. Fishing for trout, bass and bluegill is excellent.

The forest's 1 million acres are divided into three chief parts: The largest is in the Allegheny and Shenandoah mountains along the West Virginia border; another is southwest of **Shenandoah National Park,** along the Blue Ridge Parkway and the Appalachian Trail; the third is Massanutten Mountain, between **Front Royal** and **Harrisonburg.**

Scenic I-64 disjoints at I-81 near **Staunton,** resumes farther south near Lexington and continues westward through the Alleghenies and into West Virginia.

Roadside stands with vendors peddling Virginia apples and cider speckle the Shenandoah Valley from Roanoke to **Winchester.** When George Washington owned farmland near Winchester, he required his tenants to plant 4 acres

to Chincoteague to be auctioned; the unsold ponies swim back to Assateague. This annual July event draws tens of thousands of spectators.

The Highlands and the Great Valley

Carved by the Shenandoah and James rivers, the Shenandoah Valley is nestled between the Blue Ridge Mountains on the east and the Allegheny Mountains on the west. Conifers and such hardwoods as hickory and walnut dot the valley; copious broomsedge, crabgrass and wire grass that once made this region impassable to frontiersmen blanket the land.

The majestic Blue Ridge, Shenandoah, Allegheny and Cumberland mountains frame Virginia's western border and exhibit some of the most spectacular scenery in the nation. Many of the region's routes are AAA designated scenic byways: the **Blue Ridge Parkway,** Skyline Drive, I-81, I-77 and I-64.

Shawnee Indians lived in villages along the riverbanks of the

Shenandoah and the James. In the 1720s the region was settled by people of German, Scottish, Irish and English descent. In 1750 Daniel Boone crossed the valley on his way to find the Cumberland Gap, thereby opening the door to westward expansion beyond the Appalachians into the Mississippi region.

From the southwest corner of the state to the northern border of the mountainous region, I-81 runs parallel to the ranges through the 200-mile patchworklike Shenandoah Valley. **George Washington and Jefferson National Forests,** with miles of trails and numerous trout streams, stretches through 1.8 million acres of Virginia's Blue Ridge and Allegheny mountains. The forest has deer, turkey, grouse and squirrel hunting, many campgrounds and fishing and swimming lakes.

South of **Marion** on SR 16 is **Mount Rogers National Recreation Area,** containing the highest point in the state at 5,729 feet. I-77 bisects the forest and connects I-81 to the Blue Ridge Parkway and the West Virginia border.

of apple trees in the rich limestone soil, fostering the current production of 5 million bushels of apples a year.

Blue Ridge Parkway and Skyline Drive are actually one road. Skyline Drive runs 105 miles through Shenandoah National Park; at the southern terminus of Skyline Drive the Blue Ridge Parkway begins and heads toward the North Carolina border and on to Great Smoky Mountains National Park. These routes are winding two-lane roads intended for leisurely travel. They do not go to or through any towns, and lodging and food availability are limited. The speed limit on Skyline Drive is always 35 mph.

Skyline Drive runs for 105 miles from Front Royal south to Rockfish Gap, twisting its way through Shenandoah National Park. More than 70 overlooks provide views of the Shenandoah River Valley to the west and the Piedmont to the east. Skyline Drive can be accessed from four points: near **Front Royal** on US 340; at Swift Run Gap, between Stanardsville and Elkton on US 33; at Rockfish Gap, between **Charlottesville** and **Waynesboro** on US 250 near I-64; and at Thornton Gap, between **Luray** and Sperryville on US 211.

Near Thornton Gap Skyline Drive runs through an unusual 610-foot tunnel in the solid granodiorite of Marys Rock. Outside the park underground caverns at Luray are a natural wonder produced when the region's limestone soil eroded. The caverns contain thousands of massive colored formations. Cathedral Room has an unusual "Stalacpipe Organ" using specially tuned stalactites to produce music of almost symphonic quality.

The Blue Ridge Parkway continues Skyline Drive 469 miles from Shenandoah National Park to Great Smoky Mountains National Park in North Carolina. A ride along the parkway reveals weathered farmhouses and barns and miles of split-rail fences. Mountain flowers color the meadows in spring and early summer.

Dogwoods bloom in early May, and in the cool, clear June air mountain laurel, azaleas and rhododendron burgeon. From mid-October through November hickory, maple and sassafras trees burst into fiery flames of gold and red. In winter the parkway offers solitude and crisp beauty.

The parkway ribbons along the natural contours of the southern Appalachian Mountains' crests, granting picturesque overlooks and many natural attractions: Humpback Rocks, Otter Creek, Peaks of Otter (with a 360-degree panorama), Smart View, Roanoke Mountain and Rocky Knob.

The parkway's average elevation is 3,000 feet, and the speed limit is 45 mph with few opportunities to pass, making it truly a scenic route unsuitable for those in a hurry. The parkway is always open, but weather conditions affect the accessibility of certain sections of the road.

Northern Virginia

Northern Virginia, from the Potomac River south to **Fredericksburg** and west to the fall line, is the most diversified region in the state. While much of it borders the District of Columbia—a bustling, cosmopolitan city revolving around the politics and business of the nation's capital—northern Virginia's roots are still deeply planted in the past.

The District's mien spills over into **Arlington** and **Alexandria,** which at one time were part of the capital

city. Alexandria, a metropolitan suburb of Washington, is almost wholly contained by I-95/495 (the Capital Beltway) and I-395 (the Shirley Memorial Highway).

Few areas offer a more pleasant trip into an earlier time than Old Town Alexandria, where more than 400 early buildings remain, including the Boyhood Home of Robert E. Lee (a private residence) and Christ Church, where George Washington and Lee worshiped. Lining the cobblestone streets are 18th- and 19th-century town houses, some of which have been converted into Colonial-era shops and restaurants.

Eight miles south of Alexandria at the southern end of the George Washington Memorial Parkway, a AAA designated scenic byway, is the impressive estate and burial place of George Washington—**Mount Vernon.**

Arlington is north of Alexandria on the southwest bank of the Potomac via the George Washington Memorial Parkway. One of the smallest counties in the United States, this capital suburb

Old Cape Henry Lighthouse, Virginia Beach
© Jeff Greenberg / Lonely Planet Images

Monticello, Charlottesville / Jack Hollingsworth / Virginia Tourism Corporation

covers only 25.7 square miles, much of it federal property.

Directly across the Potomac from Washington, on the confiscated estate of Robert E. Lee, is **Arlington National Cemetery** with rows of uniform white headstones. At the north end of the cemetery is the Marine Corps War Memorial, an immense bronze depiction of U.S. Marines raising the American flag on Mount Suribachi during the World War II battle for Iwo Jima.

West on I-66 and then west on US 29 is **Falls Church,** named after the 1734 church built near the Little Falls of the Potomac River. George Washington was a vestryman in this Georgian church 1762-84. In a park south of West Street is the original stone marker that was to indicate the western boundary of the District of Columbia, as first conceived in 1791. It marks where Falls Church meets Arlington and Fairfax counties.

North of Falls Church, Old Dominion Drive terminates at Great Falls Park, which straddles the Potomac with one leg in Maryland and the other in Virginia. Near Washington Dulles International Airport is **Chantilly** and Historic Sully Plantation. This virtually unchanged 1794 home belonged to Richard Bland Lee, who was a member of the first U.S. Congress and instrumental in relocating the nation's capital to Washington in 1800.

West on SR 236 (Little River Turnpike) off I-495 is **Fairfax,** a residential community that holds George and Martha Washington's wills in its Judicial Center on Chain Bridge Road. Fairfax is home to George Mason University.

West on US 50 is historic **Middleburg,** where steeplechase races and fox hunts are still enjoyed. This rural village is in the heart of the John S. Mosby Heritage Area, which lies north and south of US 50 from SR 17 to CR 600; US 50 is a Virginia scenic byway. Three AAA designated scenic byways traverse this region: I-66 from Skyline Drive to its junction with CR 647 near Marshall; SR 7 from its junction with CR 662 west to Berryville; and SR 9 from the West Virginia border to its junction with CR 662. The Appalachian Trail crosses all three of these scenic routes. Audiotapes of a self-guiding driving tour are available at local visitor centers.

SR 28 from Chantilly leads into SR 29 via I-66 and to **Manassas National Battlefield Park,** where the Civil War battles of the First and Second Manassas, or Bull Run, were fought. Picnickers and other sightseers came out to see this "Sunday afternoon skirmish" that was thought would determine the outcome of the war. "Stonewall" Jackson received his nickname during the first conflict when Confederate general Barnard Bee rallied his men by pointing out, "There is Jackson standing like a stone wall. Let us determine to die here, and we will conquer."

East of the battlefield and 2 miles southwest of **Lorton** stands the 1774 Pohick Church. Gunston Hall, on SR 242, is the home of George Mason, author of the Virginia Declaration of Rights and the Virginia Constitution of 1776. Close by is **Occoquan,** and farther south on I-95 is **Quantico,** one of the largest Marine Corps installations in the nation and home of the Marine Corps Air-Ground Museum.

Farther south is Fredericksburg, which Washington called "the place of my growing infancy." It also is the place where the cherry tree legend originated. Four major Civil War battles were fought in this area, and Fredericksburg changed hands between Confederate and Union forces seven times. The battlefields are preserved in nearby **Fredericksburg and Spotsylvania National Military Park.**

Other area highlights include the 40-block historic district, one of the country's largest collections of 18th- and 19th-century buildings; James Monroe Museum and Memorial Library; Kenmore Plantation & Gardens, the home of Washington's sister and her family; Mary Washington House, Washington's mother's home; and Rising Sun Tavern, a place where rebel patriots gathered before the Revolutionary War.

In 1777 **Culpeper** citizens responded to Gov. Patrick Henry's call to arms. Almost 100 years later the homes, churches and buildings of Culpeper's residents were used as hospitals during several Civil War battles. And later, Culpeper was the Union Army's headquarters. The town is northwest of Fredericksburg via SR 3.

The Piedmont

From the Blue Ridge Mountains near **Charlottesville** to the fall line near I-95 and south to the North Carolina border is Virginia's heartland. South-central Virginia's serene beauty is manifested in low rolling hills and water rapids, in meadows and pine and hardwood forests, and in clay and limestone covered with broomsedge, crabgrass and wire grass.

The area's scenic routes include I-64 from Charlottesville to Staunton and I-77 in the southwestern corner of the region, extending from I-81 and into North Carolina.

Soon after Tidewater plantations and townsites were developed, Virginia's Colonial population swelled and settlers moved into the Piedmont area. Some people brought Tidewater grace and etiquette; others arrived with only their independent spirit.

Thomas Jefferson built his grand Monticello near Charlottesville in the foothills of the Blue Ridge Mountains, which Jefferson called "the Eden of the United States." Charlottesville also is home to the University of Virginia, chartered in 1819. The university was a dream of Jefferson, who insisted that religious freedom be an absolute: "The institution will be based on the illimitable freedom of the human mind."

East of Charlottesville via I-64 is historic **Richmond,** once capital of the Confederate States of America and site of Patrick Henry's proclamation, "I know not what course others may take; but as for me, give me liberty or give me death!" The Museum of the Confederacy, next to the White House of the Confederacy at 12th

Godspeed & Discovery, Jamestown Settlement / © Gibson Stock Photography

and E. Clay streets, honors the Confederacy.

South of Richmond on I-95 or I-295 and then east on SR 10 is **Hopewell,** an outgrowth of City Point. Weston Manor, a three-story, 18th-century Georgian mansion at Weston Lane and 21st Avenue, was built in 1789 by local plantation owners William and Christian Eppes Gilliam.

Farther south on I-95 is **Petersburg.** By 1850 Petersburg was a major tobacco and industrial port where skilled tradesmen were more valuable than slaves. Black workers often earned wages sufficient to purchase their freedom, thus creating the largest free black population in the antebellum South. **Petersburg National Battlefield** is nearby.

US 29 from Charlottesville leads to **Lynchburg,** once a tobacco town that now offers sightseeing tours of its 19th-century historic areas. Thomas Jefferson's personal haven, Poplar Forest, is

southwest of Lynchburg, while the last home of his political adversary, Patrick Henry, is a modest frame dwelling called Red Hill at Brookneal approximately 35 miles southeast of Lynchburg on CR 600.

US 460 meets SR 24 at Appomattox, the center of Virginia's heartland. **Appomattox Court House National Historical Park,** 3 miles northeast of Appomattox on SR 24, commemorates the site where Gen. Robert E. Lee's 28,231 remaining Confederate soldiers found themselves surrounded by Bluecoats. Lee surrendered, bringing the Civil War to an end.

The Virginia Civil War Trails are self-guiding driving tours that allow visitors to retrace the steps taken by both Union and Confederate troops during the Civil War. Red, white and blue interpretive signs throughout the state mark the routes, mostly roads used by the soldiers, and provide historical backgrounds. The "Lee vs. Grant: The 1864 Campaign" route covers some 150 miles and visits more than 30 historical sites starting in Germanna Ford on the Rapidan River and ending in Petersburg. The "Lee's Retreat" trail cover the final days of the Civil War from Petersburg to Appomattox and features 18 historic sites. Other routes include the "1862 Peninsula Campaign," "Shenandoah Valley" and "Northern Virginia." For further information phone (888) 248-4592.

Danville is quartered by north-south US 29 and east-west US 58 near the North Carolina border. The last capital of the Confederacy, it was at Danville that Jefferson Davis received word that Lee had surrendered at Appomattox. The city is still a tobacco town that sells the leaf in loose piles.

Tidewater

Tidewater Virginia, the coastal plain region from the Potomac River south to North Carolina, was the first area on the continent settled by English-speaking people. The Potomac, Rappahannock, James and York rivers cut the northern and central Tidewater into fingers. The Chesapeake Bay and Eastern Shore protect the three narrow peninsulas, or necks. Early settlement naturally took place along these sheltered estuaries, which were means of commerce and transportation. The area's land is flat, but rich in nutrients as well as history.

Colonial Parkway, a AAA designated scenic route, connects **Jamestown, Williamsburg** and **Yorktown** in the southernmost neck of the Tidewater region. **Colonial National Historical Park** encompasses Historic Jamestowne, the site of the first permanent English settlement, founded in 1607, and Yorktown Battlefield, where the last important conflict of the Revolutionary War was fought.

At the intersection of US 60 and the parkway is Williamsburg. Originally an outpost of Jamestown called Middle Plantation, Williamsburg was renamed in 1699 and replaced Jamestown as the capital of Virginia. An earlier era is re-created in the nation's largest restored 18th-century town through Colonial shops, artisans demonstrating Colonial crafts, taverns that serve authentic Colonial-era foods and citizens dressed in the attire of the day.

On SR 5 near **Charles City** are several antebellum plantations majestically lining the James River. Among them are Berkeley Plantation, site of the first official Thanksgiving in 1619, and Shirley Plantation, Robert E. Lee's ancestors' home.

Yorktown, at the eastern terminus of Colonial Parkway, is best known as the site of the British surrender that ended the American Revolution. The battlefield surrounds the town.

I-64 intersects the Colonial Parkway, continues east to **Newport News,** on to **Hampton, Norfolk** and then around **Portsmouth** to the west. These cities also share the world's largest natural harbor, Hampton Roads.

In the shipbuilding business since 1886, Newport News preserves its maritime heritage through The Mariners' Museum on US 60. Hampton is America's oldest continuously English-speaking settlement. Norfolk remains a major shipping port and because of its superior harbor is the headquarters for the U.S. Navy Atlantic Fleet. Nauticus, Norfolk's renovated waterfront and downtown add to the city's nautical charm. Portsmouth is a harbor town across Hampton Roads from Newport News and separated from Norfolk on the east by the Elizabeth River.

The Virginia Beach-Norfolk Expressway extends from the junction of I-264 and I-64 to the coast. **Virginia Beach** has become a family vacation hot spot with 28 miles of golden beaches, excellent fishing, a variety of water sports and local seafood.

Just south of Portsmouth, **Dismal Swamp** stretches over more than 223,000 acres of southeastern Virginia and northeastern North Carolina. Surrounding Lake Drummond is the Great Dismal Swamp National Wildlife Refuge, which shelters black bears, wildcats and thousands of birds in its dense forests, vine and brier thickets and peat bogs.

Manassas National
Battlefield Park
© Jeff Gnass

Points of Interest

ABINGDON (I-3) pop. 7,780, elev. 2,057'

Abingdon was founded in 1778 at the junction of two American Indian trails on a site where Daniel Boone had camped some years before. Abingdon is one of the oldest English-speaking towns in the Blue Ridge Mountains.

The Virginia Creeper National Recreation Trail follows one of the traditional footpaths for 34 miles along a former railbed of the Virginia-Carolina Railroad. Beginning in Abingdon, the trail is popular with hikers, bicyclists, runners and horseback riders. A 15-mile section provides an easy hike on winding trails leading to Damascus.

Abingdon's 20-square-block historic district contains many 19th-century buildings, including museums, craft shops, art studios, galleries and historic lodgings. The area is a thriving arts community with the Arts Depot on Depot Square, offering changing exhibits. Lasting from late July to early August, the ▼ Virginia Highlands Festival offers an antiques market and a variety of art competitions.

Abingdon Convention and Visitors Bureau: 335 Cummings St., Abingdon, VA 24210; phone (276) 676-2282 or (800) 435-3440.

Self-guiding tours: A brochure detailing a walking tour of Abingdon's historic district is available from the convention and visitors bureau.

Shopping areas: Dixie Pottery, off I-81 on SR 11, features 100,000 square feet of housewares, including pottery, baskets, arts and craft supplies and kitchenware. The Cave House Craft Shop, 279 E. Main St., offers regionally made wares.

BARTER THEATRE is off I-81 exit 17 at 127 W. Main St. One of the country's oldest professional regional theaters, the "State Theatre of Virginia" was founded in 1933 on the theory that drama could be bartered for food. During the Depression, Robert Porterfield convinced 22 Broadway actors that it was better to eat in Virginia than to starve in New York. Though cash is now the accepted medium of payment, Porterfield's original theater offered tickets in exchange for milk, ham, chicken and other provisions.

Dramas, comedies and musicals are presented on two stages; spring, summer and fall repertories allow patrons to see four shows in 2 days. Performances Wed.-Thurs. at 7:45, Fri.-Sat. at 8:15, Sun. at 7, with matinees Wed.-Thurs. and Sat. at 2 and Sun. at 3, Feb.-Dec. Performance tickets $22-$38. Reservations are recommended. DS, MC, VI. Phone (276) 628-3991.

FIELDS-PENN 1860 HOUSE MUSEUM is at 208 W. Main St. Guided tours of this historic house museum offer a glimpse of 19th-century life. Exhibits include period room settings, decorative arts authentic to the era and a permanent collection of regional pottery, furniture, textiles, metal works and basketry. Tours are given every 30 minutes Wed. 11-4, Thurs.-Sat. 1-4, Apr.-Dec. Fee $3. Phone (276) 676-0216 or (800) 435-3440.

WILLIAM KING REGIONAL ARTS CENTER is at 415 Academy Dr. Museum galleries showcase art of the region and the world. On the grounds are resident artist studios and an outdoor sculpture garden. Allow 30 minutes minimum. Tues.-Sat. 10-5 (also Tues. 5-9), Sun. 1-5; closed major holidays. Free. Phone (276) 628-5005.

AFTON (G-7) elev. 1,360'

WINERIES

- **Afton Mountain Vineyards** is 1.1 mi. s.w. on Afton Mountain Rd. (SR 151), 1.2 mi. w. on Mountain Rd., then just e. to 234 Vineyard Ln. Wed.-Mon. 10-6, Mar.-Oct.; Wed.-Mon. 10-5, Nov.-Dec.; Fri.-Mon. 11-5, rest of year. Closed Jan. 1, Easter, Thanksgiving and Dec. 25. Phone (540) 456-8667.

- **Cardinal Point Vineyard and Winery** is 3.1 mi. s. on Afton Mountain Rd. (SR 151), .9 mi. s.e. on Avon Rd., then .4 mi. e. on Batesville Rd. Daily 11-5:30; closed Jan. 1, Easter, Thanksgiving and Dec. 25. Phone (540) 456-8400.

- **Veritas Vineyard & Winery** is 1.8 mi. s. on Afton Mountain Rd. (SR 151), then just e. to 145 Saddleback Farm. Mon.-Fri. 9:30-5, Sat.-Sun. 11-5; closed Jan. 1, Thanksgiving and Dec. 25. Phone (540) 456-8000.

ALEXANDRIA—*see District of Columbia p. 119.*

ALTAVISTA (H-7) pop. 3,425, elev. 596'

A relatively young town by Virginia standards, Altavista was founded in 1905 by three Lane brothers who purchased 2,000 acres in Campbell County during construction of the Virginia Railway. In 1912 the Lane family opened a box plant, today known for its cedar chests and furniture.

Altavista Area Chamber of Commerce: 414 Washington St., P.O. Box 606, Altavista, VA 24517; phone (434) 369-6665.

AVOCA MUSEUM is at 1514 Main St. Housed in the 1901 country Victorian home of Revolutionary patriot Col. Charles Lynch, the museum features American Indian artifacts and Civil War items. An arboretum, an antique log cabin and a cemetery are on the grounds. Thurs.-Sat. 11-3, Sun. 1:30-4:30, mid-Apr. to mid-Oct. Admission $5; $4 (ages 66+); $2 (ages 6-18). Phone (434) 369-1076.

APPOMATTOX COURT HOUSE NATIONAL HISTORICAL PARK (H-7)

Three miles northeast of Appomattox on SR 24, Appomattox Court House National Historical Park is a 1,744-acre site. On April 9, 1865, Gen. Robert E. Lee's weakened and outnumbered Confederate Army of Northern Virginia was cut off at Appomattox Court House by Gen. Ulysses S. Grant. The two commanders met in the parlor of a house owned by Wilmer McLean—and the Army of Northern Virginia was surrendered to Grant.

Markers designate Grant's and Lee's headquarters, the site of the last shots fired by the Confederate artillery and infantry, and the road where the arms were laid down.

The courthouse building burned in 1892, and a new one was built at the location of the present town of Appomattox. A speculator razed the McLean House in 1893 with the intention of rebuilding it in Washington, D.C. This project failed and the materials, left exposed to the ravages of decay and souvenir hunters, soon were lost. The McLean House was reconstructed on the original site by the National Park Service.

A village of 27 structures has been restored to its 1865 appearance. Among the buildings open to visitors are Clover Hill Tavern, a county jail, a guest house, Jones Law Office, a kitchen, McLean House, Meeks General Store and Woodson Law Office.

Exterior restorations include Isbell House, Mariah Wright House and Peers House. The reconstructed courthouse serves as a visitor center and has a museum and an auditorium where audiovisual programs are shown every half-hour.

Living-history programs are presented in summer. Costumed interpreters portraying Confederate and Union soldiers and village residents answer visitors' questions. Area information is available at the visitor information center in the railroad depot on Main Street in the town of Appomattox.

The park and buildings are open daily 8:30-5; closed Jan. 1, Thanksgiving and Dec. 25. Admission (Memorial Day weekend-Labor Day) is $4 ($10 maximum per private vehicle), under 16 free. Admission (rest of year) is $3 ($5 maximum per private vehicle), under 16 free. Phone (434) 352-8987 for park information, or (434) 352-2621 for area information.

ARLINGTON—*see District of Columbia p. 125.*

ARLINGTON NATIONAL CEMETERY—

see District of Columbia p. 126.

ASHLAND—*see Richmond p. 300.*

BARBOURSVILLE (F-8) elev. 510'

Among his many interests, Thomas Jefferson hoped to establish vineyards in America to rival those of Europe. He employed an Italian viticulturist to plant vines at Monticello and along the mountain slopes toward Barboursville, but disease killed the vines before they could mature. Jefferson remained convinced that the region was ideal for winemaking. Successful vineyards were re-established here in the 1970s.

In his spare time, Jefferson designed a plantation home for his friend James Barbour, who served as governor of Virginia, U.S. senator and secretary of war. The mansion with its octagonal parlor was completed in 1822. After Barbour's death, a Christmas fire destroyed the estate. The ruins are visible on the grounds of the Barboursville Vineyard.

WINERIES

- **Barboursville Vineyard** is near jct. SR 20/US 33 at 17655 Winery Rd. Tastings Mon.-Sat. 10-5, Sun. 11-5. Guided tours Sat.-Sun. noon-4. Closed Jan. 1, Thanksgiving and Dec. 25. Phone (540) 832-3824.

BASTIAN (H-4) elev. 2,180'

The Wolf Creek Railroad came to Bastian in 1914 to serve a growing logging industry, and the Virginia Hardwood Lumber Mill opened here in 1927. Thanks to the mill, Bastian was the first town in Bland County to receive electricity. During the Great Depression, thousands of young men worked at a model camp established in Bastian by the Civilian Conservation Corps. The mill and railroad closed after World War II.

WOLF CREEK INDIAN VILLAGE & MUSEUM is off I-77 exit 58, then just n. on US 52 at 6394 N. Scenic Hwy. Interpretive guides conduct hands-on tours of a re-created American Indian village that stands near an actual archeological site. Museum displays include excavated artifacts. Nature trails also are on the grounds. Picnicking is permitted. Allow 1 hour minimum. Daily 9-5; closed Jan. 1, Thanksgiving and Dec. 24-25. Admission $8; $7 (senior citizens); $5 (ages 5-16). DS, MC, VI. Phone (276) 688-3438.

BASYE (F-7) pop. 986, elev. 1,325'

RECREATIONAL ACTIVITIES

Skiing and Snowboarding

- **Bryce Resort** is at 1982 Fairway Dr. Write P.O. Box 3, Basye, VA 22810. Daily 9-4:30 (also Tues.-Sat. 4:30-9:30), mid-Dec. to mid.-Mar. Hours may vary; phone ahead. Phone (540) 856-2121 or (800) 821-1444.

BEAVERDAM—*see Richmond p. 300.*

BEDFORD (H-7) pop. 6,299

Founded as the town of Liberty in 1782, Bedford soon was renamed after the Fourth Duke of Bedford. The town is home to many historic structures, including Avenel, a former 1838 plantation manor house that once welcomed such visitors as Gen.

Robert E. Lee and writer Edgar Allan Poe. Tours are available by appointment; phone (540) 586-1814.

Bedford Area Welcome Center: 816 Burks Hill Rd., Bedford, VA 24523; phone (540) 587-5681 or (877) 447-3257.

Shopping areas: The Bedford Farmers Market, downtown on Washington Street, offers fresh fruits and vegetables and homemade wares Tuesday, Friday and Saturday.

BEDFORD CITY/COUNTY MUSEUM is at 201 E. Main St. This former Masonic Lodge built in 1895 houses permanent and changing exhibits related to city and county history, Bedford County Indian artifacts, Civil War relics and local genealogy information. Mon.-Fri. 10-5; closed major holidays. Donations. Phone (540) 586-4520.

THE NATIONAL D-DAY MEMORIAL is at 3 Overlord Cir. The monument pays tribute to the troops who, fighting for the liberation of Europe, stormed the beaches of Normandy on June 6, 1944. Allow 30 minutes minimum. Daily 10-5; closed Jan. 1, Thanksgiving and Dec. 25. Admission $5; $3 (ages 6-16). AX, DS, MC, VI. Phone (540) 586-3329 or (800) 351-3329.

POPLAR PARK is off Smith St. on Grand Arbre Dr. The 1.5-acre park is home to one of the world's largest yellow poplar trees and the largest tree in Virginia. Also known as a tulip tree, this national champion stands more than 145 feet high. Picnicking is permitted. Open daily dawn-dusk. Free. Phone (540) 587-6061.

BENTONVILLE (F-8) elev. 754'

RECREATIONAL ACTIVITIES

Canoeing

• **Downriver Canoe Co.** is at 884 Indian Hollow Rd. Write P.O. Box 10, Bentonville, VA 22610. Mon.-Fri. 9-6, Sat.-Sun. 7-7, Apr.-Oct. Phone (540) 635-5526 or (800) 338-1963.

BIG STONE GAP (I-2)
pop. 4,856, elev. 1,334'

Big Stone Gap is at the junction of three forks of the Powell River, which has created a pass through Stone Mountain. This mountain country provided the inspiration and setting for novelist John Fox Jr.'s "The Trail of the Lonesome Pine."

Heart of Appalachia Tourism Authority: 112 Shawnee Ave., P.O. Box 207, Big Stone Gap, VA 24219; phone (276) 523-2005.

THE HARRY W. MEADOR JR. COAL MUSEUM is at jct. E. Third St. and Shawnee Ave. In addition to displays about the coal-mining industry, the museum also features collections of medical and dental equipment, cash registers and antique office machines. Wed.-Sat. 10-5, Sun. 1-5; closed major holidays. Free. Phone (276) 523-9209.

JUNE TOLLIVER HOUSE is at Jerome and Clinton sts. June Tolliver, the real-life heroine of John Fox Jr.'s book "The Trail of the Lonesome Pine," lived in this 1896 house while she attended school. It is furnished in period and features school memorabilia. Guided tours Tues.-Sat. 10-5, Sun. 2-5, May 1 to mid-Dec. (also Thurs.-Sat. 5-9, July-Aug.). Free. Phone (276) 523-4707.

[SAVE] **John Fox Jr. Museum** is at 117 Shawnee Ave. E. This is the 1888 family home of novelist John Fox Jr. The 22-room house contains original furnishings and memorabilia. It was here that Fox wrote "The Trail of the Lonesome Pine" and other works inspired by life in the Appalachian Mountains. Guided tours are available. Allow 30 minutes minimum. Wed.-Sat. 2-5, Memorial Day-Labor Day; by appointment rest of year. Closed holidays. Admission $3; $2 (ages 56+); $1 (ages 0-17). Phone (276) 523-2747.

[SAVE] **"The Trail of the Lonesome Pine"** is performed at the June Tolliver Playhouse on Clinton St. Telling the story of a Virginia mountain girl who falls in love with a mining engineer from the east, this production is the state's official historical outdoor drama. Inquire about weather policies. Shows are given Thurs.-Sat. at 8 p.m., late June-late Aug. Admission $15; $12 (ages 56+); $8 (ages 0-12). Phone (276) 523-1235 or (800) 362-0149.

[GEM] **SOUTHWEST VIRGINIA MUSEUM HISTORICAL STATE PARK** is at 10 W. First St. near Wood Ave. An 1880s house contains exhibits relating to the exploration and development of southwestern Virginia and the lives of the early settlers of that region.

The first floor of the museum features exhibits about the area's coal and iron ore deposits and their part in the town's "boom and bust" mining past. Second- and third-floor displays offer Victorian and pioneer memorabilia including a quilt exhibit, tools, household furnishings and American Indian artifacts.

Guided tours are available by appointment. Open Tues.-Thurs. 10-4 (also Mon. 10-4, Memorial Day-Labor Day), Fri. 9-4, Sat. 10-5, Sun. 1-5, Mar.-Dec.; closed Thanksgiving and Dec. 25. Admission $3; $2 (ages 6-12). MC, VI. Phone (276) 523-1322.

BLACKSBURG (H-5) pop. 39,573, elev. 2,135'

Blacksburg originally was founded as the Draper's Meadow Settlement in 1748 by a group of German, English and Scot-Irish farmers. The settlement was short-lived, however, when only four people survived a 1755 Shawnee Indian attack in what became known as the Draper's Meadow Massacre. In 1798 the present town was established on land donated by William Black.

Huckleberry Trail, a recreational pathway popular with bicyclists, walkers, runners and inline skaters, connects Blacksburg and Christiansburg, a 6-mile distance. The trail winds along the Huckleberry Rail Line, used by Virginia Tech to transport cadets in the early 1900s.

Montgomery County Chamber of Commerce: 612 New River Rd., Christiansburg, VA 24073; phone (540) 382-4010.

(SAVE) **HISTORIC SMITHFIELD** is w. off US 460 bypass exit to US 314, on the edge of the Virginia Tech campus at 1000 Smithfield Plantation Rd. Smithfield was built in the 1770s by noted surveyor and patriot Col. William Preston and named for his wife, Susanna Smith. This original frame house was the birthplace of two Virginia governors and the home of a third. The 1,900-acre plantation was one of the earliest and largest estates west of the Blue Ridge Mountains. A demonstration kitchen garden is on the grounds.

Guided tours are given every 30 minutes Mon.-Tues. and Thurs.-Sat. 10-5, Sun. 1-5, Apr. 1-first weekend in Dec. Last tour begins 30 minutes before closing. Fee $6; $4 (ages 12-17 and college students with ID); $3 (ages 5-11). Phone (540) 231-3947.

VIRGINIA POLYTECHNIC INSTITUTE AND STATE UNIVERSITY is 7.8 mi. n.w. of I-81 exit 118 (US 460W bypass), then .5 mi. e. on Southgate Dr. to the visitor center at jct. Duckpond Dr. Founded in 1872, Virginia Tech is one of the largest university in the state, with more than 26,000 students and 379 buildings. The 2,600-acre campus blends modern structures with beautiful old buildings built from native Hokie stone, a variety of limestone rich in calcium and magnesium. Maps, parking passes and information about tours are available at the visitor center. Visitor center open Mon.-Fri. 8-5. Free. Phone (540) 231-3548 for the visitor center.

▼ BLUE RIDGE PARKWAY

The Blue Ridge Parkway connects Shenandoah National Park in Virginia *(see place listing p. 305, Recreation Chart and the AAA Mideastern Camp-Book)* and Great Smoky Mountains National Park in North Carolina and Tennessee. The 469-mile scenic road follows the crest of the Blue Ridge and other ranges at elevations from 649 to 6,047 feet. Only 800 feet wide at certain points, the parkway is constructed free of billboards and with little residential encroachment, allowing for leisurely drives and enjoyment of the surrounding area.

The concept for the construction of the parkway began during Franklin D. Roosevelt's administration in the 1930s. The project, in addition to creating a scenic route linking the two new national parks and spurring tourism, was a way to provide jobs for many of those left unemployed during the peak of the Great Depression. Begun in 1935, the dedication of the completed parkway did not take place until 1987, although sections of the road have been enjoyed by travelers for many years.

The parkway offers panoramas of the Southern Highlands. Among the areas of outstanding scenic interest are Humpback Rocks, Otter Creek, Peaks of Otter, Roanoke Mountain, Rocky Knob and Smart View in Virginia; and Crabtree Meadows, Craggy Gardens, Cumberland Knob, Doughton Park, E.B. Jeffress Park, Julian Price, Linville Falls and Moses H. Cone memorial parks, Mount Pisgah and Waterrock Knob in North Carolina. Wildflowers are in bloom mid-May through August; fall foliage is at its peak in October.

Hiking trails, varying in length from short strolls to the lengthy and strenuous Appalachian Trail, can be reached from many overlooks and parking areas; information can be obtained at parkway visitor centers. During the summer season craft demonstrations and ranger programs at various points along the parkway provide insights into the everyday life and culture of mountain residents.

Concrete mileposts help keep track of mileage along the road, beginning at Milepost 0 at the northern portion and concluding at Milepost 469 at its southern terminus at Great Smoky Mountains National Park. The speed limit of 45 mph is enforced. To drive the entire length, plan on 3 to 5 days at an average speed of 30 mph. For weather and other information contact Blue Ridge Parkway, 199 Hemphill Knob Rd., Asheville, NC 28803.

The Travel Narrator Audio Driving Tour, covering Mileposts 390-469, is available at the Folk Art Center *(see attraction listing p. 236)*. This 90-minute narrated driving tour of the Blue Ridge Parkway from Asheville to Cherokee explores the region's history, people and lore; phone (770) 594-7842.

Food is available at Crabtree Meadows, Doughton Park, Mabry Mill, Mount Pisgah, Otter Creek and Peaks of Otter. There are overnight facilities at Peaks of Otter Lodge, housekeeping cabins at Rocky Knob and lodges at Doughton Park and Mount Pisgah. Other accommodations are nearby but off the parkway.

Pets are permitted if confined or leashed; they are prohibited in overnight facilities. Picnic spots and drinking water are available at intervals along the parkway. Hunting is prohibited.

The parkway is open all year, but sections of the road may be closed during icy or snowy weather. Most park facilities close November through April. Phone (828) 298-0398 for weather or other information or, for emergencies, (800) 727-5928 in North Carolina or Virginia.

North Carolina High Country Host: 1700 Blowing Rock Rd., Boone, NC 28607; phone (828) 264-1299 or (800) 438-7500.

Note: *The points of interest below are listed in order, from north to south according to their nearness to the northern terminus of the road at Shenandoah National Park.*

HUMPBACK ROCKS VISITOR CENTER is at Milepost 5.8, 6 mi. s.e. of Afton. The center features an outdoor museum comprised of 1890s farm buildings. Allow 1 hour minimum. Daily 9-5, May-Oct. Hours may vary; phone ahead. Free. Phone (540) 943-4716.

JAMES RIVER VISITOR CENTER is at Milepost 63.6, 3 mi. n. of Big Island. Exhibits chronicle the story of the James River and the Kanawha Canal. A pedestrian walkway crossing the river leads to a restored canal lock. Open daily 9-5, Memorial Day-Nov. 1. Free. Phone (434) 299-5496.

PEAKS OF OTTER VISITOR CENTER is at Milepost 86, 10 mi. n.w. of Bedford. Exhibits focus on forest ecology and the history of the Peaks of Otter area. Nearby is an 1830s cabin that sheltered early travelers. A historic farm offers living-history demonstrations. Daily shuttle-bus trips to the summit of Sharp Top Mountain as well as a walking trail to the summit are available.

Allow 1 hour minimum. Visitor center daily 9-5, Memorial Day-Oct. 31. Shuttle bus departs daily on the hour 10-5 (weather permitting), late May-Oct. 31. Farm and trail hours vary; phone ahead. Visitor center free. One-way bus fare $5; $4 (ages 0-11). Round-trip bus fare $8; $6 (ages 0-11). Phone (540) 586-4496 or (540) 586-4357. *See Recreation Chart.*

ROCKY KNOB VISITOR CENTER is at Milepost 169, 8 mi. n.e. of Meadows of Dan. The center provides information about the Rocky Knob recreation area, which covers more than 4,000 acres. Daily 9-5, May-Oct. Free. Phone (540) 745-9662. *See Recreation Chart and the AAA Mideastern CampBook.*

MABRY MILL is at Milepost 176.1, just n. of jct. US 58, 1 mi. n.w. of Meadows of Dan. A display of pioneer items includes a blacksmith shop, gristmill, sawmill and sorghum press. Food is available. Allow 1 hour minimum. Daily 8-6, last weekend in April-early Nov. Free. Phone (276) 952-2947.

CUMBERLAND KNOB VISITORS CENTER is at Milepost 217.5 near the state border in N.C. The Civilian Conservation Corps began construction on the parkway here in 1935. Picnic facilities and hiking trails are available. Daily 9-5, May-Oct. Free.

BLUE RIDGE MOUNTAIN FRESCOES are at Milepost 259 in Glendale Springs, N.C., 3 mi. n. of the parkway's jct. with SR 16; and in West Jefferson, N.C., following signs from jct. US 221 Bus. Rte. and SR 194. North Carolina artist Ben Long painted these religious artworks in two Episcopal churches, Holy Trinity in Glendale Springs and St. Mary's in West Jefferson. Taped narratives describe their history. Allow 1 hour minimum. Daily 24 hours. Donations. Phone (336) 982-3076.

PARKWAY CRAFT CENTER is at Milepost 294, 3 mi. w. of Blowing Rock, N.C. In the former manor house at Moses H. Cone Memorial Park, the center is operated by the Southern Highland Craft Guild. Cone, a wealthy textile manufacturer, built his country estate at the turn of the 20th century. Mountain crafts are demonstrated. Allow 30 minutes minimum. Daily 9-5, Mar. 15-Nov. 30. Free. Phone (828) 295-7938.

LINN COVE VIADUCT AND VISITORS CENTER is at Milepost 304.4, 5 mi. n.e. of Linville, N.C. Completed in 1983, the Linn Cove Viaduct is one of the most complicated concrete spans ever built. The quarter-mile bridge skirting the rugged perimeter of Grandfather Mountain was designed for minimal environmental impact. The visitor center has a scale model and a hiking trail leading under the viaduct for a closer look. Daily 9-5, May-Oct. Free. Phone (828) 733-1354.

LINVILLE FALLS RECREATION AREA is at Milepost 316.4, 2 mi. n.w. of Linville Falls, N.C. Trails lead to the pedestrian overlooks of Linville Falls and Linville Gorge. The park includes picnic facilities and a campground. Fishing is permitted in the

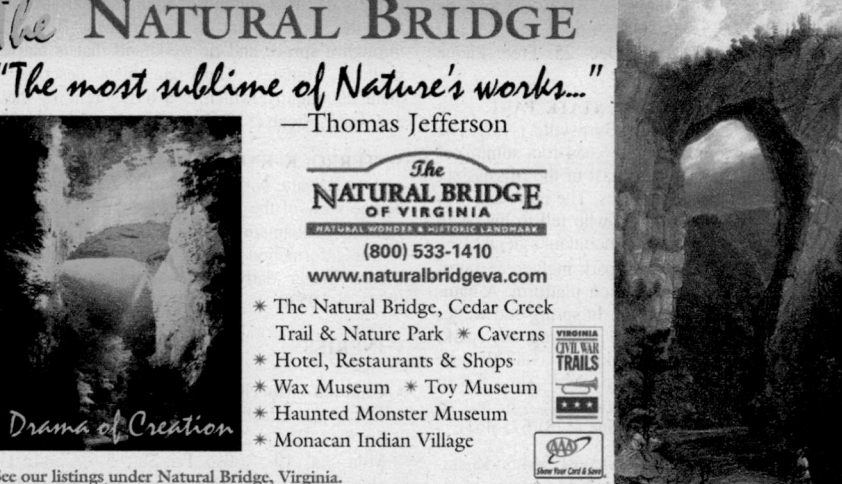

Linville River. Park open daily 24 hours. Visitor center open daily 9-5, May-Oct. Free. Phone (828) 765-1045. *See Blue Ridge Parkway in the AAA Southeastern CampBook.*

Linville Gorge is a scenic chasm within Linville Falls Recreation Area at Milepost 316.4 in N.C. Linville Gorge Wilderness, below the falls, is part of Pisgah National Forest and has been set aside for scientific and recreational use. Wiseman's View observation point on the west overlooks the gorge. Paths to the falls and to lookouts have been cut through great jungles of rhododendron. **Note:** The area is reached only by trail or cross-country travel. A few steep trails are moderately difficult and require some hiking skill.

Hunting and fishing are permitted in season. Permits are available at the district ranger's office in the library building in Marion. Camping is available year-round; permits are required Sat.-Sun. and holidays, May-Oct. Free. Phone (828) 652-2144.

LINVILLE CAVERNS is at Milepost 317 at Linville Falls, N.C., then 4 mi. s. on US 221. In 1822 the spectacle of trout swimming in and out of the mountainside led settlers on a torch-lit expedition inside the caves. Ever since, their discovery has been a source of fascination and sometimes shelter. During the Civil War, deserting soldiers from both armies sought refuge among the cathedral-like arches, columns and deep passageways. The underground temperature is a constant 52 F.

A jacket and comfortable walking shoes are recommended. Guided 30-minute tours daily 9-6, June 1-Labor Day; daily 9-5, Apr.-May and day after Labor Day-Oct. 31; daily 9-4:30 in Nov. and Mar.; Sat.-Sun. 9-4:30, rest of year. Fee $6; $4.50 (ages 63+); $4 (ages 5-12). Phone (800) 419-0540.

MUSEUM OF NORTH CAROLINA MINERALS is at Milepost 331 on SR 226, 5 mi. s. of Spruce Pine, N.C. The museum displays samples of many rocks and minerals found in the area. Allow 30 minutes minimum. Daily 9-5, May-Oct.; 9-noon and 1-5, rest of year. Closed Jan. 1 and Dec. 25. Free. Phone (828) 765-2761.

MOUNT MITCHELL STATE PARK is at Milepost 355, near Burnsville, N.C. The park encompasses the 6,684-foot summit of Mount Mitchell, highest peak east of the Mississippi River, and a portion of its slopes. The mountain was named for Dr. Elisha Mitchell, who fell to his death while attempting to prove the mountain's height.

Facilities at this 1,946-acre park include an interpretive center and an observation platform. A naturalist is on duty in the summer. In spring and winter check road conditions before entering the park. Food is available May-Oct. Parking is available near the summit. Daily 8 a.m.-9 p.m., May-Aug.; 8-8 in Apr. and Sept.; 8-7 in Mar. and Oct.; 8-6, rest of year. Closed Dec. 25. Free. Phone (828) 675-4611.

CRAGGY GARDENS is at Milepost 364.6, 18 mi. n.e. of Asheville, N.C. The Craggy Mountains, at elevations of 5,500-6,000 feet, are a colorful sight when the rhododendrons bloom around mid-June. Trails, picnic facilities and a visitor center are available. Daily 9-5, May-Oct. Hours may vary; phone ahead. Free. Phone (828) 298-0398.

FOLK ART CENTER is at Milepost 382, 5 mi. n.e. of Asheville, N.C., via I-40 to US 70W exit 55. Operated by the Southern Highland Craft Guild, the center celebrates the tradition of craft work in the southern Appalachian region through demonstrations, special events and three galleries of historic and contemporary Southern Highlands crafts.

A Blue Ridge Parkway information center is in the facility. Allow 30 minutes minimum. Daily 9-6, Apr.-Dec.; 9-5, rest of year. Closed Jan. 1, Thanksgiving and Dec. 25. Free. Phone (828) 298-7928.

THE NORTH CAROLINA ARBORETUM is at Milepost 393, 9 mi. s. of Asheville, N.C. Surrounded by the Southern Appalachian Mountains, the 434-acre arboretum offers 65 acres of cultivated gardens, 10 miles of forested hiking and biking trails, a visitor education center, a state-of-the-art greenhouse production facility and one of the finest bonsai collections in the southeastern United States.

Allow 30 minutes minimum. Grounds daily 8 a.m.-9 p.m., Apr.-Oct.; 8-7, rest of year. Closed Dec. 25. Visitor center Mon.-Sat. 9-5, Sun. noon-5. Greenhouse Mon.-Fri. 8-2; closed holidays. Free. Parking $6. Phone (828) 665-2492.

MOUNT PISGAH is at Milepost 408.6. Walking trails lead to the 5,721-foot summit. Educational programs are presented in an outdoor amphitheater some evenings June through October. Picnicking is permitted. Food is available. Free. Phone (828) 235-8228.

RICHLAND BALSAM is near Milepost 431, 12 mi. n.e. of Balsam, N.C. A 1.5-mile walking trail winds to the 6,047-foot summit of Richland Balsam Mountain, the highest point on the parkway. Hikers pass through a spruce and fir woodland that is native to northern climates. Trail pamphlets describe this plant community, which is a living relic of the ice age. Free. Phone (828) 298-0398 or (828) 456-9530.

WATERROCK KNOB is at Milepost 451.2, 8 mi. n.w. of Balsam, N.C. The summit commands a 360-degree view of the main ranges of the southern Appalachian Mountains from a 6,000-foot elevation. A visitor information center is in the parking area. Visitor center daily 10-5, May-Oct. Free. Phone (828) 456-9530.

WINERIES

- **Château Morrisette Winery** is at Milepost 171.5, exit Black Ridge Rd. (SR 726), then s.w. on SR 777 to 287 Winery Rd. S.W. in Floyd. Mon.-Sat. 10-5 (also Fri.-Sat. 5-6), Sun. 11-5; closed Jan. 1, Thanksgiving and Dec. 24-25. Phone (540) 593-2865.

BOOKER T. WASHINGTON NATIONAL MONUMENT (H-6)

Booker T. Washington National Monument is 30 miles southeast of Roanoke via US 220 south to Rocky Mount, then north on SR 122. The 239-acre site commemorates Booker T. Washington's first 9 years in slavery by re-creating the environment of his childhood at Burroughs Plantation.

Freed at the end of the Civil War, Booker T. Washington rose from his impoverished childhood to found Tuskegee Normal and Industrial Institute in Alabama and to receive international recognition as an educator, advisor to President Roosevelt, speaker and African-American leader. He graduated from Hampton Institute in 1875 and received honorary degrees from Harvard and Dartmouth.

A visitor center offers exhibits and a 15-minute videotape presentation about Washington's life. Crops and farm animals can be seen from the quarter-mile Plantation Trail. Tours, special events and educational programs are offered.

Picnic facilities are available. Allow 1 hour minimum. Daily 9-5; closed Jan. 1, Thanksgiving and Dec. 25. Free. Phone (540) 721-2094.

BOYCE (E-8) pop. 426, elev. 572′

THE STATE ARBORETUM OF VIRGINIA is 1.3 mi. e. of US 340 on US 50. Some 170 acres of maintained landscapes and gardens can be explored on foot, on horseback or by car. More than 1,000 varieties of plants, flowers and trees are on the grounds. A trail winds through an area of native Virginian plants. Picnicking is permitted. Allow 30 minutes minimum. Daily dawn-dusk. Free. Phone (540) 837-1758.

BRANDY STATION (F-9) elev. 350′

Some 17,000 mounted soldiers fought at the Battle of Brandy Station, making it the largest cavalry engagement of the Civil War. On June 9, 1863, Major Gen. J.E.B. Stuart and his cavalry division were screening the northern movement of Confederate troops toward Pennsylvania. Union forces led by Brigadier Gen. Alfred Pleasonton launched a surprise attack near Brandy Station. The day-long battle was considered a draw, but it would mark the high point of the Confederate cavalry in the east. Brandy Station became the opening battle of Lee's Gettysburg Campaign. The town got its name from a stagecoach stop that served apply brandy.

THE GRAFFITI HOUSE is at 19484 Brandy Rd. The 1858 house, once a Civil War field hospital, serves as an information center for the nearby Brandy Station Battlefield. Modern renovations led to the discovery of charcoal etchings made on the upstairs walls by recovering soldiers. Exhibits depict area Civil War history. Allow 1 hour minimum. Wed. and Fri.-Sun. 11-4, Apr.-Nov.; Wed. and Sat. 11-4, rest of year. Closed major holidays. Free. Phone (540) 727-7718.

BREAKS (H-3) elev. 1,470′

The town of Breaks is named for one of the longest and deepest gorges east of the Mississippi River, a 5-mile-rift carved by the Big Sandy River through Pine Mountain. Daniel Boone is said to have discovered The Breaks in 1767 while forging trails into Kentucky. Few visitors saw the remote "Grand Canyon of the South" until after World War II, when coal roads were built into the mountains.

BREAKS INTERSTATE PARK is off SR 80 on the eastern edge of the Cumberland Mountain Plateau. Along the Kentucky-Virginia border, the Russell Fork of the Big Sandy River has cut a "break," a 1,600-foot-deep gorge known as the Grand Canyon of the South, through Pine Mountain.

A paved road leads to the canyon rim; overlooks provide excellent views of the gorge, rock formations, caves, springs and vibrant rhododendron. Natural science and historical displays are housed at the visitor center, which provides self-guiding maps of 13 miles of nature and hiking trails.

Park open daily 7 a.m.-11 p.m., Apr.-Dec.; 7:30-6, rest of year. Visitor center open daily 9-5, May-Oct.; 8-4, in Apr. Overnight facilities, with the exception of vacation cottages, closed late Dec.-Mar. 31. Admission $1 per private vehicle. Phone (276) 865-4413 or (800) 982-5122. *See Recreation Chart and the AAA Mideastern CampBook.*

BRIDGEWATER (F-7) pop. 5,203, elev. 1,982′

Originally known as Magill's Ford, this crossing place on the North River was later called Bridgeport. By the time a charter was granted in 1835, the town had adopted its present name. Bridgewater College was established in 1880 by Daniel Christian Flory, a young leader of the Church of the Brethren.

REUEL B. PRITCHETT MUSEUM is on the Bridgewater College campus, 402 E. College St., in Cole Hall. The Rev. Pritchett, a minister of the Church of the Brethren, donated his collection of historic articles to the school in 1954. Today the museum contains more than 10,000 items; highlights include some 1,000 bottles and glassware, a saber-toothed tiger skull, rare books and Bibles, currency and antique weapons. Allow 1 hour minimum. Mon.-Fri. 1-4:30; closed major holidays. Free. Phone (540) 828-5462.

BRISTOL (I-3) pop. 17,367, elev. 1,680′

State Street, Bristol's main thoroughfare, is bisected by the Tennessee/Virginia border. Brass markers down the street's center denote the dividing line. Although each side has its own government and city services, together they form an important industrial center, which manufactures metal goods, textiles and electronic products.

Evan Shelby, noted for battling American Indians and founding what became the city of Bristol, built a stockade here in 1776. Daniel Boone and many other distinguished pioneers bartered in Bristol and planned the campaign that defeated the British at the Battle of Kings Mountain in South Carolina.

The city has a theater, an arts center and a ballet company. Recreational activities on the Tennessee side are provided by Steele Creek Park and South Holston Dam and Lake. Sugar Hollow Park is on the Virginia side.

The Bristol Motor Speedway, a half-mile race-track 5 miles south on US 11E, is on the NASCAR circuit; phone (423) 764-1161. Scenic I-81 passes through Bristol and continues 88 miles south to the I-40 junction.

Bristol Convention and Visitors Bureau: P.O. Box 519, Bristol, VA 24203; phone (423) 989-4850.

SAVE **BRISTOL CAVERNS** is 5.5 mi. s.e. on SR 435 and 2.5 mi. s. on US 421. The caverns have many unusual formations; visitors walk along the banks of an underground river. A lighted asphalt trail traverses several levels, with guided 1-hour tours descending 180 feet below ground.

Picnicking is permitted. Tours are given every 20 minutes Mon.-Sat. 9-5, Sun. 12:30-5, Mar.-Nov.; Mon.-Sat. 10-4, Sun. 12:30-4:30, rest of year. Closed Easter, Thanksgiving and Dec. 24-25. Fee $11; $9 (ages 62+); $5.50 (ages 5-12). Phone (423) 878-2011.

BROOKNEAL (H-7) pop. 1,259, elev. 537′

One of the smallest incorporated towns in central Virginia, Brookneal was founded in 1802 upon the marriage of two landowners, John Brook and Sarah Neal. Patrick Henry, the state's first elected governor, had retired to the area in 1794, spending the last 5 years of his life at Red Hill plantation, which he called "the garden spot of the world." Fire destroyed the manor home in 1919.

RED HILL—PATRICK HENRY NATIONAL MEMORIAL is 5 mi. e. on SR 40, following signs to 1250 Red Hill Rd. The site preserves the last home and burial place of Patrick Henry, the Virginia patriot who said, "Give me liberty or give me death!" The main building has been reconstructed and contains Henry family furnishings. Henry's grave and law office, a coachman's cabin, a blacksmith shop, a kitchen and boxwood and herb gardens can be seen. An orientation and introductory videotape begin the tour at the museum and visitor center.

Mon.-Sat. 9-5, Sun. 1-5, Mar.-Oct.; Tues.-Sat. 9-4, Sun. 1-4, Mon. by appointment, rest of year. Closed Jan. 1, Thanksgiving and Dec. 25. Admission $6; $2 (ages 5-17). Phone (434) 376-2044.

BULL RUN—

see Manassas National Battlefield Park in the District of Columbia p. 131.

BURROWSVILLE (B-2) elev. 70′

The first land grant in Prince George County was deeded in 1616 to Captain John Martin, one of the founders of Jamestown. A grandson of William

Shakespeare was one of several absentee owners before the 7,000-acre property, known as Brandon, passed from Benjamin Harrison III to his sons, Nathanial and William, in 1720. The Brandon Plantation at Burrowsville remains in operation as a working farm, one of the oldest in the country.

GEM **BRANDON PLANTATION** is 5.5 mi. n.e. on CR 611 (Brandon Rd.). Designed by Thomas Jefferson and built by Nathaniel Harrison in the mid-18th century, the red brick house remained in the Harrison family until 1926. The gardens of the Colonial plantation extend to the James River. The portico bears reminders of two wars—a British ship during the Revolutionary War opened fire from the river, and Union soldiers during the Civil War fired upon and then occupied the house.

The parklike grounds contain old trees and expanses of lawn. The garden is the original plan; plantings include perennials, ornamentals, bulbs and trees native to the area. Brandon Plantation is still a working farm. The principal crops are corn, soybeans and wheat. Beef cattle also are raised on the plantation. Grounds and gardens open daily 9-5. House open by appointment. Grounds and gardens admission $8. House additional $2. Phone (757) 866-8486.

CAPE CHARLES (B-5) pop. 1,134, elev. 7′

This planned community on the Eastern Shore was incorporated in 1886. With its deep harbor, Cape Charles served as a railroad terminus for ferries carrying freight and passengers from Little Creek. Development slowed after the last ferry terminal closed in 1950. One of the town founders, Alexander Cassatt, was the brother of impressionist painter Mary Cassatt.

Most of the original town has been preserved as a historic district, with houses reflecting Victorian, Colonial Revival, Craftsman and neoclassic styles. Contemporary residences dot the landscape at the 1,700-acre Bay Creek Resort and Marina, which features golf courses designed by Jack Nicklaus and Arnold Palmer.

EASTERN SHORE OF VIRGINIA NATIONAL WILDLIFE REFUGE is at 5003 Hallett Cir. The 2,972-acre refuge protects four habitats: the Chesapeake Bay, barrier islands, salt marshes and upland forests. Songbirds, raptors and monarch butterflies assemble on the peninsula for the fall migration. Fisherman Island, a military installation during World Wars I and II, is home to brown pelicans and royal terns. A visitor center, wildlife exhibits, trails and an observation deck also are featured. Peak wildlife viewing time is from late August to early November.

Allow 1 hour minimum. Refuge open daily 30 minutes before dawn-30 minutes after dusk. Visitor center open daily 9-4, Apr.-Nov.; daily 10-2 in Mar. and Dec.; Fri.-Sun. 10-2, rest of year. Closed Jan. 1

and Dec. 25. Guided 3-hour tours of Fisherman Island are offered Sat. at 9, Oct.-Mar. Free. Reservations are required for guided tour. Phone (757) 331-2760.

CHANCELLORSVILLE (D-10)

Twelve miles west of Fredericksburg on SR 3, Chancellorsville Battlefield is part of Fredericksburg and Spotsylvania National Military Park *(see place listing p. 250).*

The battles of Chancellorsville and Salem Church, April 27 through May 6, 1863, were among the most important engagements of the Civil War. The Confederate Army of Northern Virginia, under the command of Gen. Robert E. Lee, numbered approximately 60,000. Maj. Gen. Joseph Hooker directed about 134,000 Union troops.

Hooker crossed the Rappahannock River and entrenched his army along a 6-mile line centered at an inn known as Chancellorsville. Lee sent Gen. Thomas J. "Stonewall" Jackson to attack the right wing of the Union line, driving it back to Chancellorsville. That evening Jackson's own men accidentally shot him; a week later he died of pneumonia.

The next day Lee attacked, forcing Hooker to withdraw. The result was a brilliant victory for the South that sparked Lee's invasion of Pennsylvania.

The national park visitor center offers exhibits and a 12-minute slide show. A 6-mile, self-guiding driving tour of the battlefield begins near the visitor center parking lot. Another way to tour the battlefield is by following a 3-hour audiotape tour, available for sale or rent at the visitor center.

The park is open daily 8:30-6:30, mid-June through Labor Day; Mon.-Fri. 9-5, Sat.-Sun. 9-6, Apr. 1 to mid-June and day after Labor Day-Oct. 31; daily 9-5, rest of year. Closed Jan. 1 and Dec. 25. Walking tours led by park rangers are conducted in summer. Phone (540) 786-2880.

CHANTILLY—*see District of Columbia p. 127.*

CHARLES CITY—
see Virginia's Historic Triangle p. 312.

CHARLOTTESVILLE (G-8)
pop. 45,049, elev. 480'

Historic Charlottesville, in the foothills of the Blue Ridge Mountains, was the home of Thomas Jefferson and James Monroe. The University of Virginia, founded and designed by Jefferson and first governed by a board whose membership included Jefferson, James Monroe and James Madison, enhances the city.

Meriwether Lewis, who with William Clark was sent on an expedition to explore the Louisiana Purchase, was born near Charlottesville. Frontiersman George Rogers Clark, William Clark's brother, also was born near Charlottesville.

Many old homes and estates in the surrounding countryside reveal Jefferson's architectural influence; the Old Courthouse is a notable example. Albemarle County is known for its horses, dogs and fox hunting as well as its peach and apple orchards. The Albemarle Pippin apple was developed in the area.

Charlottesville-Albemarle County Convention and Visitors Bureau: Monticello Visitors Center, SR 20S, P.O. Box 178, Charlottesville, VA 22902; phone (434) 977-1783 or (877) 386-1102.

Self-guiding tours: Brochures outlining self-guiding walking tours of Charlottesville's historic downtown and the University of Virginia are available at the convention and visitors bureau, and at the downtown visitor center at 100 5th St. NE; phone (434) 977-6100 or (434) 293-6789.

Shopping areas: Barracks Road Shopping Center, jct. Emmer Street and Barracks Road, features some 80 upscale stores. Charlottesville Fashion Square, jct. US 29 and E. Rio Road, features more than 70 stores, including Belk, Eddie Bauer, JCPenney and Sears. Charlottesville Historic Downtown Pedestrian Mall offers art galleries, restaurants and various specialty shops.

ASH LAWN-HIGHLAND is off I-64 exit 121, .5 mi. s. on SR 20, 3 mi. e. on SR 53, then .5 mi. s. on CR 795. The 535-acre estate once was owned by James Monroe, fifth president of the United States. His neighbor Thomas Jefferson personally selected the site and sent his gardeners to plant orchards. Monroe and his wife moved to their tobacco plantation in 1799. Ash Lawn-Highland today retains the feel of an early 1800s working plantation.

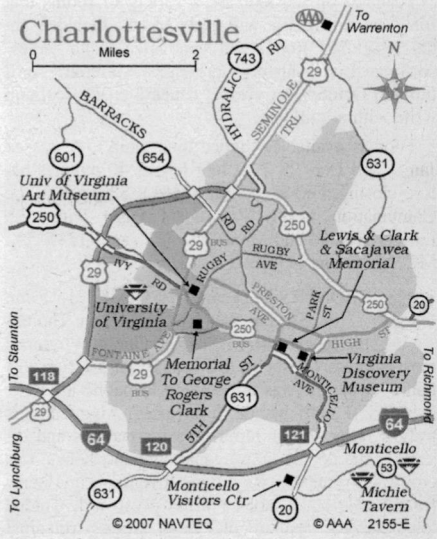

© 2007 NAVTEQ   © AAA   2155-E

Guided tours of the main house, which contains many Monroe possessions, are available daily. Periodic cooking and spinning demonstrations and other activities are offered. The tour also includes the overseer's house and slave quarters. To celebrate the 250th anniversary of Monroe's birth, special events and exhibits also will be offered throughout 2008.

The boxwood gardens feature resident peacocks and a statue of Monroe by Attilio Piccirilli. The Blue Ridge Mountains are visible on the horizon. Picnicking is permitted. Allow 1 hour minimum. Daily 9-6, Apr.-Oct.; 11-5, rest of year. Closed Jan. 1, Thanksgiving and Dec. 25. Admission $10; $9 (ages 60+); $5 (ages 6-11). Combination ticket (President's Pass) with Michie Tavern and Monticello $27 (ages 12+). DS, MC, VI. Phone (434) 293-9539.

JAMES MADISON'S MONTPELIER— *See Montpelier Station p. 279.*

LEWIS AND CLARK AND SACAJAWEA MEMORIAL is in Midway Park at Ridge and Main sts. The statue honors Louisiana Purchase explorers Meriwether Lewis and William Clark and their American Indian guide Sacajawea.

MEMORIAL TO GEORGE ROGERS CLARK is on W. Main St., just e. of the University of Virginia. Clark, elder brother of William Clark, is known for his exploration of the Northwest Territory.

MICHIE TAVERN is .5 mi. s. of I-64 on SR 20, then 1 mi. e. on Thomas Jefferson Pkwy. Established by Scotsman William Michie, the 1784 tavern accommodated travelers with food, drink and lodging. In 1927 the inn was moved 17 miles to its present location as part of the 1920s Preservation Movement.

Featured on the tour are a variety of rooms that focus on tavern life and early travel. Included are the Assembly Room and gentlemen's and ladies' parlors. Living-history programs, offered April through October, let visitors dance a tavern reel and write with a quill pen.

Food is available. Guided tours daily 9-5; closed Jan. 1 and Dec. 25. Last tour begins 40 minutes before closing. Fee $8; $7 (ages 66+); $3 (ages 6-11). Combination ticket (President's Pass) with Ash Lawn-Highland and Monticello $27 (ages 12+). AX, MC, VI. Phone (434) 977-1234.

MONTICELLO is off I-64 exit 121, .5 mi. s. on SR 20, then 1.5 mi. e. on Thomas Jefferson Pkwy. (SR 53). One of Virginia's most impressive estates, this was Thomas Jefferson's home—when he was not serving in public affairs—from 1770 until his death in 1826. Monticello is truly a reflection of Jefferson's innovations and diversity; the domed house contains maps, books, scientific instruments, time-saving inventions and items from Lewis and Clark's journey westward. Guided tours include ten of the main floor's principal

rooms, in which the statesman's furniture and personal effects are displayed.

Jefferson died at Monticello July 4, 1826, exactly 50 years after the adoption of the Declaration of Independence. The estate was sold at auction to pay his debts. His grave is in the family cemetery on the grounds, which also include dependencies, slave quarters, a garden terrace, an 8-acre fruit orchard and two vineyards.

Note: Monticello will remain open while a new visitor and education center is constructed near the main visitor parking area; work on the project began in 2006 and will continue through 2008. Tickets are purchased at a shuttle station a half-mile from the mansion. Shuttle buses provide transportation to the house. Backpacks are not permitted beyond the shuttle station, and photography is not allowed inside the house. Allow 3 hours minimum.

Daily 8-5, Mar.-Oct.; 9-4:30, rest of year. Guided 30-minute tours of the house depart approximately every 5 minutes. Garden and grounds tours are given daily every hour 9:15-4:15, Apr.-Oct. Plantation Community Tours depart daily every hour 10-3, Apr.-Oct. Children's tours depart daily every hour 10-3, mid-June to late Aug. (except July 4). Closed Dec. 25.

Admission $15; $7 (ages 6-11). Combination ticket with Montalto Tours $26; $12 (ages 6-11). Combination ticket (President's Pass) with Ash Lawn-Highland and Michie Tavern $27 (ages 12+). To avoid long lines and guarantee a tour of the house, reservations are advised. AX, MC, VI. Phone (434) 984-9822.

Montalto Tours departs from the Monticello shuttle station off I-64 exit 121, .5 mi. s. on SR 20, then 1.5 mi. e. on Thomas Jefferson Pkwy (SR 53). In 1777 Thomas Jefferson purchased 574 acres on a neighboring mountain, ensuring that all the land he viewed from his Virginia estate would be his own. Montalto ("high mountain") rises about 400 feet above Monticello ("little mountain"). Guided 60-minute bus tours describe Jefferson's dreams for the land, allowing visitors to climb to the summit for a view of his estate.

Guided tours are given daily at 10 and 1, Apr.-Oct. (weather permitting). Fee $13; $7 (ages 6-11). Combination ticket with Monticello $26; $12 (ages 6-11). Reservations are advised. Phone (434) 984-9822.

Monticello Visitors Center is off I-64 exit 121, then s. on SR 20 to 600 College Dr., approximately 2 miles below the mountain estate. An exhibit, Thomas Jefferson at Monticello, focuses on Jefferson's domestic life and includes about 400 objects and artifacts, many of which were uncovered during archeological excavations at Monticello. The exhibit complements guided tours of the house and grounds as well as a 38-minute film, "Thomas Jefferson: The Pursuit of Liberty."

Visitors center daily 9-5:30, Mar.-Oct.; 9-5, rest of year. Film shown daily on the hour 10-4, June

15-Labor Day; at 11 and 2, rest of year. Closed Dec. 25. Visitors center free. Phone (434) 984-9822.

UNIVERSITY OF VIRGINIA is in the center of town on US 29 and US 250 Bus. Rtes. Thomas Jefferson founded this "academical village" in 1819 and devoted his final years to its design, construction and curriculum. The state university opened in 1825 with 123 students and a hand-picked faculty of American and European scholars.

Seeking to create an environment in which learning infused daily life, Jefferson planned the school with ten pavilions built around an expansive lawn. Each pavilion contained a professor's home, students' quarters and classrooms. At the heart of the campus was the Rotunda, a domed library modeled after the Pantheon in Rome. The university design is considered an outstanding accomplishment in American architecture. Edgar Allan Poe was among the students who attended dinner at Monticello before Jefferson's death in 1826.

Parking is available for a fee at the Central Grounds parking lot at Emmet Street and Ivy Road. Guided tours of the Rotunda and lawn are given daily at 10, 11, 2, 3 and 4, Sept.-Apr.; tours of the Rotunda only are given at 10, 11, 2, 3 and 4, rest of year. No tours are given during exam periods. Tours free. Phone (434) 924-7969.

Kluge-Ruhe Aboriginal Art Collection is 4 mi. e. on US 250 toward Pantops Mountain, then s. at Peter Jefferson Place to 400 Worrell Dr. The university of Virginia gallery features an extensive collection of Australian Aboriginal art. Allow 30 minutes minimum. Tues.-Sat. 9-3. Free. Phone (434) 244-0234.

University of Virginia Art Museum is n. of US 250 (University Ave.) in the Bayly Building at 155 Rugby Rd. First opened in 1935, this fine arts museum displays works from the 15th century through the present with an emphasis on American art and art from the Jefferson era. Other highlights include pre-Columbian, African, American Indian, Asian and Oceanic art. Allow 1 hour minimum. Tues.-Sun. 1-5; closed major holidays. Free. Phone (434) 924-3592.

VIRGINIA DISCOVERY MUSEUM is at the e. end of the downtown pedestrian mall off Main St. The museum, geared toward children ages 1-10 and their families, invites learning through hands-on activities. Highlights include an art studio; a reconstructed 18th-century pioneer log cabin; a take-apart table, which enables young visitors to see what makes things work; a children's carousel; and a special room for toddlers. Tues.-Sat. 10-5, Sun. 1-5; closed major holidays. Admission $4; free (under 1). Phone (434) 977-1025.

WINERIES

- **First Colony Winery** is off I-64 exit 121, 11 mi. s. on SR 20, then 1 mi. w. on CR 720 to 1650 Harris Creek Rd. Mon.-Fri. 9-5, Sat.-Sun. 11-5; closed Jan. 1, Thanksgiving and Dec. 25. Phone (434) 979-7105.

- **Jefferson Vineyards** is off I-64 exit 121A, .7 mi. s. on SR 20, then 2 mi. e. on SR 53 to 1353 Thomas Jefferson Pkwy. Daily 10-6; closed Jan. 1, Thanksgiving and Dec. 25. Phone (434) 977-3042 or (800) 272-3042.

- **Oakencroft Vineyard and Winery** is 3.5 mi. w. of US 29 on Barracks/Garth Rd. Daily 11-5, Apr.-Dec.; Sat.-Sun. 11-5, rest of year. Closed Jan. 1 and Dec. 25. Phone (434) 296-4188.

CHESAPEAKE—*see Hampton Roads Area p. 254.*

CHESTERFIELD—*see Richmond p. 300.*

CHINCOTEAGUE (G-12) pop. 4,317

Local legends say that Chincoteague (SHIN-ko-teeg) ponies, an island trademark, are descendants of mine horses that survived the shipwreck of a 16th-century Spanish galleon. Most historians, however, agree that the ponies were brought over by the first English colonists, who turned the herds loose on Assateague and Chincoteague in the late 1600s when the horses began to damage their crops.

Off the Eastern Shore in Chincoteague Bay, the 7-mile-long, 1.5-mile-wide island is connected to the mainland by a causeway and bridges. Assateague Island, which includes Assateague Island National Seashore *(see place listing in Md. p. 162)*, shields Chincoteague from the sea. Serpentine waterways, called "guts" by the islanders, punctuate Chincoteague's flat expanses of salt marsh and scrub-pine woods. Duck and goose hunting and deep-sea or channel fishing are excellent.

Chincoteague oysters and clams constitute the island's second-greatest industry, after tourism. The local watermen cultivate oysters and clams on the leased tideflats, or "rocks," surrounding the island and in the inlet. Crabbing is a popular pastime, particularly in the early summer when the blue crabs are out of their hibernation in the Chincoteague Bay mud.

The Chincoteague Pony Penning, held the last consecutive Wednesday and Thursday in July, probably originated from the colonists' practice of rounding up foals and yearlings to renew their supply of workhorses. On these days the partly wild ponies are rounded up from their home on the southern end of Assateague Island to swim at slack tide (when the tide is changing and there is no movement) across the narrow channel to Chincoteague. Foals are sold at auction; the rest swim back to Assateague. The island's ponies were made famous by Marguerite Henry's book, "Misty of Chincoteague."

Chincoteague Chamber of Commerce: 6733 Maddox Blvd., P.O. Box 258, Chincoteague, VA 23336; phone (757) 336-6161.

CHINCOTEAGUE NATIONAL WILDLIFE REFUGE occupies the Virginia portion of Assateague Island and several barrier islands along the Atlantic coast. Chincoteague ponies and other wildlife can be observed at the 14,000-acre refuge, which protects beaches, dunes, marshes and maritime forests. Sightings of migratory birds include snow geese, great blue herons, sanderlings, peregrine falcons and bald eagles. A 3.2-mile wildlife trail is open to walkers and bicyclists; vehicles are permitted from 3 p.m. until dusk.

The 5-mile beach at Toms Cove offers surf casting, shell collecting, swimming and picnicking. Nesting areas for piping plovers are closed March 15 through August 31. Visitor centers provide marine exhibits. One-hour wildlife and lighthouse tours of areas that are normally restricted to visitors are available.

Pets are not permitted. Refuge open daily 5 a.m.-10 p.m., May-Sept.; 6 a.m.-8 p.m. in Apr. and Oct.; 6-6, rest of year. Hours may vary; phone ahead. Guided tours are offered Fri.-Sun. 9-3, Easter weekend-Thanksgiving. Admission (good for 7 days) $10 per private vehicle. Phone (757) 336-6122, or (757) 336-3696 for guided tour information.

NASA WALLOPS FLIGHT FACILITY VISITOR CENTER is off SR 13, then 5 mi. e. on SR 175. The center has an exhibit hall focusing on NASA's spaceflight and scientific research programs. Hands-on displays and audiovisual presentations also are offered. Public programs are offered on weekends.

Picnicking is permitted. Allow 30 minutes minimum. Daily 10-4, July 4-Labor Day; Thurs.-Mon. 10-4, Mar. 1-July 3 and day after Labor Day-Nov. 30; Mon.-Fri. 10-4, rest of year. Closed federal holidays except Memorial Day, July 4 and Labor Day. Free. Phone (757) 824-2298 or (757) 824-1344.

CLARKSVILLE (I-8) pop. 1,329, elev. 1,468'

Clarksville was established in 1818 at the crossroads of several Occoneechee Indian trading trails. By the mid-19th century, it had become a major tobacco production center. With the damming of the Roanoke River in 1952, Clarkesville became the only town on the newly formed Buggs Island Lake.

PRESTWOULD PLANTATION is 2 mi. n. on US 15, overlooking Buggs Island Lake. Built in 1795 by Sir Peyton Skipwith, the plantation house has original furnishings, rare vintage wallpaper and a library. Docents conduct tours of the house, restored outbuildings and gardens. Allow 1 hour minimum. Guided tours Mon.-Sat. 12:30-3:30, Sun. 1:30-3:30, Apr. 15-Oct. 31. Guided tour $8; $6 (ages 66+); $3 (ages 6-12). Grounds admission only $3. Phone (434) 374-8672.

COLONIAL HEIGHTS (B-1) pop. 16,897

This area gained its name during the Revolutionary War when Colonial forces led by the Marquis de Lafayette established a garrison on the heights above Petersburg. During the Civil War, Gen. Robert E. Lee made this town his headquarters for the

siege of 1864. He arrived in June, setting up a post at the estate known as Violet Bank. The falling leaves of autumn exposed his position to the enemy, making it necessary for him to move his encampment elsewhere.

Colonial Heights Chamber of Commerce: 201 Temple Ave., Suite E, Colonial Heights, VA 23834; phone (804) 526-5872.

VIOLET BANK MUSEUM is at 303 Virginia Ave. This Federal-style plantation house served as Gen. Robert E. Lee's headquarters for 5 months in 1864 during the siege of Petersburg. Civil War weapons and memorabilia, furniture, textiles and ceramics are displayed. Noted for its plaster ornamentation, the house retains its original woodwork, fireplaces and floors. On the front lawn is an enormous "cucumber tree," actually a variety of magnolia, said to be more than 2 centuries old. Tues.-Sat. 10-5, Sun. 1-6. Free. Phone (804) 520-9395.

COLONIAL NATIONAL HISTORICAL PARK—see Virginia's Historic Triangle p. 316.

COURTLAND (I-10) pop. 1,270, elev. 32'

Originally named Jerusalem, this settlement was founded in 1791 on 10 acres along the Nottoway River. On Aug. 22, 1831 it experienced one of the nation's bloodiest slave revolts, the Nat Turner Rebellion. When the violent 3-day siege ended, more than 150 people were dead. Turner survived the insurrection and escaped, but was captured 2 months later and quickly convicted. While awaiting execution Turner told his story to attorney Thomas Gray, who later published the account as "The Confessions of Nat Turner." In 1888 the town's name was changed to Courtland. Today it serves as the county seat for Southampton County.

SOUTHAMPTON AGRICULTURE & FORESTRY MUSEUM AND HERITAGE VILLAGE is at 26135 Heritage Ln. The village pays tribute to the area's past with antique farming equipment, American Indian artifacts and an old-time country store.

Guided tours wind through re-created farm outbuildings, including a smokehouse, a sawmill, a one-room schoolhouse, a country farmhouse, a blacksmith's shop, a doctor's office and an icehouse. Allow 1 hour minimum. Wed. and Sat.-Sun. 1-5, Mar.-Nov.; closed Easter, second Sun. in May and third Sun. in June. Admission $2. Phone (757) 653-9554.

CULPEPER (F-9) pop. 9,664, elev. 423'

It was here in 1749 that 17-year-old George Washington received his surveyor's license and began work for the proprietor Lord Thomas Fairfax.

As the Revolution became imminent, the Culpeper Minute Men were organized in 1775. Two years later, with volunteers from Fauquier and Orange counties, they marched to Williamsburg in answer to Gov. Patrick Henry's call to arms. Their flag depicted a coiled rattlesnake with the defiant legends "Don't tread on me" and "Liberty or Death." During the Civil War, the wounded from the battles of Cedar Mountain, Kelly's Ford and Brandy Station were treated in makeshift hospitals set up in many Culpeper residences, churches and vacant buildings. The Union Army later established its headquarters at the old Virginia Hotel.

Culpeper County Visitor Center: 109 S. Commerce St., Culpeper, VA 22701; phone (540) 825-8628 or (888) 285-7373.

MUSEUM OF CULPEPER HISTORY is at 803 S. Main St. Exhibits depict local history, beginning with dinosaur tracks made 215 million years ago. Displays include American Indian artifacts and battle relics from the American Revolution and the Civil War. On the grounds is a restored 18th-century log cabin, the Burgandine House. Guided tours are available by appointment. Open Mon.-Sat. 10-5, Sun. 1-5. Admission $3; free (ages 0-17). Guided tour $5. Phone (540) 829-1749.

CUMBERLAND GAP NATIONAL HISTORICAL PARK (I-1)

Elevations in the park range from 1,660 ft. at the Cumberland Gap to 3,513 ft. at White Rocks. Refer to AAA maps for additional elevation information.

At the convergence of Kentucky, Tennessee and Virginia, Cumberland Gap National Historical Park covers 20,444 acres of heavily forested, rugged mountains honoring the historic pass.

The gap provides a natural doorway through the mountains. It was first used by migratory animals as a seasonal thoroughfare, then by American Indians, whose footpaths followed the buffalo and deer trails. The westward movement of settlers seemed barred by the Allegheny Ridge until April 1750, when Dr. Thomas Walker discovered the gap while seeking the fabled land to the west, the "Kentucke" of American Indian lore.

Daniel Boone passed through with a hunting party in 1769, and in 1775 he blazed a trail called the Wilderness Road. For the next 20 years, the gap could only be traversed by those on foot or horseback, and although no wagon traveled over it during this period, more than 200,000 people made their way through the gap into Kentucky and beyond.

A strategic point during the Civil War, Cumberland Gap changed hands several times without any major battles. Some of the earthwork fortifications remain.

General Information and Activities

With the opening of the Cumberland Gap Highway Tunnel and the rerouting of US 25E through the tunnel, Cumberland Gap and the Wilderness Road have been returned to their late 1700s appearance.

Pinnacle Overlook, providing a view into the gap as well as affording views of the mountain range and parts of three states, is accessible via a 4-mile paved road from the visitor center. No trailers or vehicles more than 20 feet long are allowed.

Still a wild area, the park has almost 70 miles of hiking trails ranging from relatively easy nature trails to those requiring an overnight trek. Many park features, including Sand Cave, a multicolored sandstone overhang, and White Rocks, a prominent sandstone outcropping, can be reached only by trail. Ridge Trail, a 19-mile-long route offering panoramas of the valley, approaches five primitive campsites, all accessible by foot. The park also has 160 developed campsites; 41 sites have 50-amp hookups.

Hensley Settlement can be reached by an all-day hike or, during the summer, by a shuttle. Phone ahead for shuttle service; reservations are recommended. A reconstruction of a community that was occupied 1903-51, the settlement sits atop a mountain in the eastern end of the park. With more than 70 acres of land under cultivation, it has several reconstructed log houses, barns and outbuildings. Reminiscent of a time much earlier than that from which it actually dates, Hensley seems like a community of the late 1700s or early 1800s.

It is not advisable to hike alone; overnight camping requires a permit. Trail guides and other information can be obtained at the visitor center, where two films are offered. The visitor center also contains a museum with weapons and tools dating from the pioneer and Civil War eras. Throughout the year, ranger-led programs suitable for the entire family introduce visitors to the historical, cultural and natural aspects of the park; phone for a schedule of events. *See the AAA Southeastern CampBook.*

The park is open daily 9-dusk. The visitor center at the park entrance is open daily 8-5; closed Dec. 25.

ADMISSION to the park is free.

PETS must be restricted at all times, either in vehicles or by leash, and are not allowed in public buildings.

ADDRESS inquiries to the Superintendent, Cumberland Gap National Historical Park, Box 1848, Middlesboro, KY 40965; phone (606) 248-2817.

Points of Interest

GAP CAVE is .25 mi. s. of Middlesboro on US 25E in Cumberland Gap National Historical Park. Guided 2-hour tours of the cave, discovered in 1750, are conducted by lantern light. Rooms and walls are covered with stalactites and stalagmites. Wildlife, including bats and salamanders, can be seen, as can the names of Civil War soldiers carved on the walls.

Note: The guided tour includes 183 steps. Visitors are advised to wear good walking shoes. Tours are given daily at 10 and 2, late May-Labor Day; Mon.-Fri. at 10, Sat.-Sun. at 10 and 2, Apr. 1-late

May and day after Labor Day-Dec. 31; Sat.-Sun. at 10 and 2, rest of year. Tickets must be purchased at the park visitor center 30 minutes in advance of the tour. Fee $8; $4 (ages 5-12). Under 5 are not allowed on cave tours. Reservations are recommended. AX, DC, DS, MC. Phone (606) 248-2817.

DANVILLE (I-7) pop. 48,411, elev. 565′

The auction method of selling tobacco in piles of loose leaves originated at Neal's Warehouse in Danville in 1858. Large tobacco processing plants such as Dimon Inc. are in the area. Danville also is the home of Dan River Inc., the largest single-unit textile mill in the world; their factory outlet offers bed and bath linens.

Danville was the last capital of the Confederacy; President Jefferson Davis and his cabinet officers moved to the town after the evacuation of Richmond on April 3, 1865. Davis wrote his last proclamation as president in Danville. At the Sutherlin House, 975 Main St., Davis received the news that Gen. Robert E. Lee had surrendered at Appomattox. The Sutherlin House is now Danville Museum of Fine Arts and History (see attraction listing).

Lady Astor, the first female member of the British Parliament, was born as Nancy Witcher Langhorne in Danville in 1879. Her cottage birthplace at 117 Broad St. is open by appointment. Information is available at the visitor center; phone (434) 836-6990.

The railroad accident that inspired the popular folk ballad "Wreck of the Old 97" occurred in the town on Sept. 27, 1903, killing nine people. A commemorative marker is on US 58W.

Reflecting Danville's prosperous tobacco and textile heritage, Millionaires Row Historic District along Main Street boasts fine examples of Victorian and Edwardian residential architecture. A few of these private homes are open to the public during the Christmas Walking Tour held the second Sunday in December.

Danville Area Chamber of Commerce and Visitor Center: 635 Main St., Danville, VA 24541; phone (434) 836-6990.

Self-guiding tours: Brochures outlining a walking tour of Millionaires Row and a driving tour of Civil War sites as well as schedules, maps and tours of auction warehouses in the historic district are available from the chamber of commerce and visitor center.

Shopping areas: Piedmont Mall, on Piedmont Drive off the US 29 bypass, has more than 70 stores, including Belk, JCPenney and Sears. The Danville Community Market, at 626 Craghead St., offers fresh produce, baked goods, crafts, artisans and a welcome center on Saturdays, April through December.

[SAVE] **AAF TANK MUSEUM** is at 3401 US 29B. The museum's collection includes tanks, uniforms, medals, weapons, artillery and military memorabilia. Allow 1 hour minimum. Mon.-Sat. 10-5; closed Thanksgiving and Dec. 25. Admission $10; $9.50 (ages 0-11 and 61+). MC, VI. Phone (434) 836-5323.

DANVILLE MUSEUM OF FINE ARTS & HISTORY is at 975 Main St. Built in the Italianate style in 1859 by tobacco merchant Maj. William T. Sutherlin, the museum contains original and period furnishings as well as changing art exhibits. Open Tues.-Fri. 10-5, Sat.-Sun. 2-5; closed major holidays. Free. Phone (434) 793-5644.

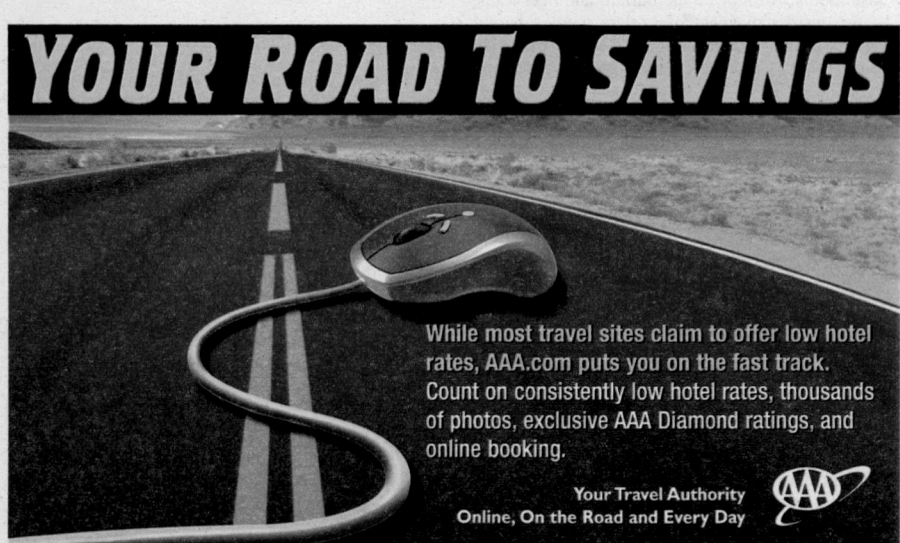

SAVE **DANVILLE SCIENCE CENTER** is at 677 Craghead St. Housed in an 1899 train station, the science center features interactive exhibits, the Womack Natural History Collection, events and touring displays, a computer lab and an early childhood gallery. Mon.-Sat. 9:30-5, Sun. 1-5; closed Thanksgiving and Dec. 25. Admission $5; $4 (ages 4-12, ages 60+ and students with ID). MC, VI. Phone (434) 791-5160.

DAYTON (F-7) pop. 1,344, elev. 1,230′

Daniel Harrison, brother of the founder of the town of Harrisonburg, built his home along Cook's Creek just north of town. The Daniel Harrison House also is known as Fort Harrison due to its solid stone structure with an underground passage to a well and a stockade that once surrounded the home, protecting it from American Indian attacks. Visitors can tour the 18th-century home; phone (540) 879-2280.

HARRISONBURG-ROCKINGHAM HISTORICAL SOCIETY HERITAGE CENTER is at 382 High St. Documents and artifacts of the Shenandoah Valley include a permanent exhibit titled Invincible Spirit: History in the Heart of the Shenandoah. The museum also focuses on one of the area's major historical events, Gen. Thomas J. "Stonewall" Jackson's Valley Campaign of 1862.

Displays include Civil War artifacts, documents and photographs as well as folk art encompassing works in ceramics, textiles, wood and metals. Allow 30 minutes minimum. Mon.-Sat. 10-4; closed major holidays and the last week in Dec. Admission $5; $1 (ages 5-18). MC, VI. Phone (540) 879-2681.

DELAPLANE (B-10) elev. 460′

On July 19, 1861, Gen. Thomas J. "Stonewall" Jackson marched the new recruits of Virginia's First Brigade toward Delaplane, then known as Piedmont Station. Some 10,000 soldiers boarded freight and cattle cars to reach the first major battle of the Civil War, First Manassas. The use of the railroad for large-scale troop movement marked a new era in military transport. The battle 2 days later was a decisive victory for the South.

SKY MEADOWS STATE PARK is 5.1 mi. n. off US 17. This 1,862-acre park offers rolling pastures and woodlands, scenic views, access to the Appalachian Trail, picnic facilities, and hiking and horseback riding trails. Hike-in primitive camping is available; reservations are required. Mount Bleak House is furnished to resemble a middle-class farmhouse circa 1860. From mid-April through October tours are offered on weekends and holidays.

Park open daily 8-dusk. Admission $3 (per private vehicle Mon.-Fri.); $4 (per private vehicle Sat.-Sun. and holidays). Phone (540) 592-3556 or (800) 933-7275. *See Recreation Chart.*

DISMAL SWAMP (I-11)

In southeastern Virginia and northeastern North Carolina, the Great Dismal Swamp is characterized by forested peat soils and a dense undergrowth of briars and vines. The 223,000-acre area is threaded by canals and ditches, many of which have grown over to resemble green tunnels.

Col. William Byrd of Virginia surveyed the swamp in 1728 and named it Great Dismal. George Washington explored it in 1763, saw its possibilities as a timber producer and commercial canal and formed a company known as The Adventurers for Draining the Great Dismal Swamp. Much of the refuge was once owned by Washington, Patrick Henry and other prominent Virginians. The original swamp area is believed to have covered 2,200 square miles.

Remnants of an Atlantic white cedar forest still can be found. Commercially valuable trees include cypress, juniper, red maple and yellow poplar; however, the peat soils make lumbering difficult. The Great Dismal Swamp National Wildlife Refuge was established in 1973.

Lake Drummond, a circular lake covering 3,000 acres, is in the heart of the swamp. Its average depth is 6 feet, and the unusually pure water is preserved by the tannic acids from the bark of the cypress, juniper and gum trees. Gnarled cypress trees, moss and the dense growth surrounding the lake give it an eerie appearance. The coffee-colored lake has a sandy bottom and is unusual in that it is not formed in a basin, but rather on a gently sloping hillside.

Boat access is available via a launch on US 17 at the mouth of the feeder ditch, a 3-mile-long shallow waterway connecting the lake with the Dismal Swamp Canal. To enter the lake, boats must be transported across the Corps of Engineers spillway at the head of the feeder ditch via a small motorized tram (1,000-pound weight limit).

The 22-mile canal, part of the Atlantic Intracoastal Waterway, is the oldest man-made waterway in the country. Locks open four times daily to accommodate yachts and private boats. A wildlife canoe trail provides access for small, portable watercraft. The Dismal Swamp Canal Welcome Center is 3 miles south of the state line on US 17 in South Mills, North Carolina. A 4.5-mile paved trail along the canal is open to walkers, bicyclists and birdwatchers. The welcome center is open daily 9-5, Memorial Day-Oct. 31, Tues.-Sat. 9-5, rest of year. Phone (252) 771-8333 or (877) 771-8333.

GREAT DISMAL SWAMP NATIONAL WILDLIFE REFUGE is off SR 32 in Suffolk; the refuge headquarters is at 3100 Desert Rd. The refuge preserves 111,000 acres of forested wetlands surrounding Lake Drummond. Inhabitants include black bears, white-tailed deer, bobcats, otters and more than 200 recorded species of birds.

Visitors to the refuge can hike or bicycle on several miles of unpaved trails. Interpretive boardwalks along the Washington and West ditches traverse a variety of swamp habitats. Boating, fishing and picnicking are permitted. Trails open daily dawn-dusk.

Refuge headquarters Mon.-Fri. 7:30-4; closed federal holidays. Free. Phone (757) 986-3705.

DOSWELL—*see Richmond p. 301.*

DUFFIELD (I-2) pop. 62

NATURAL TUNNEL STATE PARK is .4 mi. s. on US 23, then 4.2 mi. e. on Daniel Boone Tr. An 850-foot tunnel has been carved through solid limestone by the waters of Stock Creek. The tunnel emerges in a natural amphitheater measuring more than a half-mile around and rising 400 feet above the tunnel entrance.

Seven trails, one of which leads to the summit of Lover's Leap, weave through the park. The park has a swimming pool, a chairlift, a visitor center that features interpretive exhibits and a conference center with lodges and a re-created blockhouse.

Camping is permitted. Allow 1 hour minimum. Trails open 8 a.m.-dusk. Visitor center open daily 10-5 (also Sat.-Sun. 5-6), Memorial Day-Labor Day; Sat.-Sun. 10-4, early Mar.-day before Memorial Day and day after Labor Day-late Oct. Chairlift open daily 10-5 (also Sat.-Sun. and holidays 5-6), Memorial Day-Labor Day. Pool open daily 10-6 (also Sat.-Sun. 6-7 p.m.), Memorial Day weekend-Labor Day.

Admission $2 (per private vehicle Mon.-Fri.); $3 (per private vehicle Sat.-Sun.). Chairlift $3; free (ages 0-5). Pool $3; $2 (ages 3-12). MC, VI. Phone (276) 940-2674, or (800) 933-7275 for camping reservations. *See Recreation Chart.*

DUMFRIES—*see District of Columbia p. 128.*

EDINBURG (E-8) pop. 813

Nestled in the Shenandoah Valley, Edinburg was founded by German and Swiss immigrants in the late 18th century. The fertile region became known as the "Breadbasket of the Confederacy" during the Civil War. After his soldiers destroyed barns, livestock and crops across the valley in 1864, Union general Philip Sheridan boasted that the Shenandoah was so bare, "a crow would be well advised to take its own provisions."

Shenandoah County Travel Council: 600 N. Main St., Woodstock, VA 22664; phone (540) 459-6227.

WINERIES

• **Shenandoah Vineyards** is off I-81 exit 279, w. on Stony Creek Rd., then 1.5 mi. n. on S. Ox Rd. Daily 10-6, Mar.-Nov.; 10-5, rest of year. Closed Jan. 1, Thanksgiving and Dec. 25. Phone (540) 984-8699.

FABER (G-8) elev. 587′

WINERIES

• **Delfosse Vineyards and Winery** is 2.3 mi. w. on SR 616. Wed.-Sun. 11-5; closed Jan. 1, Easter,

Thanksgiving and Dec. 24-25. Phone (434) 263-6100.

FAIRFAX—*see District of Columbia p. 128.*

FALLS CHURCH—
see District of Columbia p. 128.

FALMOUTH (D-11) pop. 3,624

Chartered in 1720, Falmouth once rivaled Fredericksburg in commercial importance. During the Revolution, James Hunter's ironworks ran full tilt to supply the American Army and Navy with such articles as camp kettles, bayonets and anchors. Tapping into Falmouth's thriving industry, resident Basil Gordon became one of America's first millionaires.

Falmouth is now a subdued but charming relic of its past. George Washington reportedly received his primary education in the town. Noted Falmouth natives include Confederate Secretary of War James Alexander Seddon, and Dr. Kate Waller Barrett, a staunch crusader for social reform. Falmouth served as the headquarters for the Federal Army before and after the Battle of Fredericksburg.

BELMONT, THE GARI MELCHERS HOME AND STUDIO is s.w. of jct. US 1 and US 17N at 224 Washington St. (SR 1001). The 18th-century manor house, set on 27 acres overlooking the Rappahannock River, is preserved as a memorial to its former owner Gari Melchers, an American artist who died in 1932. The house is furnished with antiques and art collected by Melchers and his wife. More than 75 of his paintings are displayed in his studio, which also hosts special exhibitions regularly.

A visitor center, located in the former carriage house, offers an orientation videotape. Allow 1 hour minimum. Mon.-Sat. 10-5, Sun. 1-5, Apr.-Nov.; Mon.-Sat. 10-4, Sun. 1-4, rest of year. Closed Jan. 1, Thanksgiving and Dec. 24-25 and 31. Admission $10; $5 (ages 6-18). MC, VI. Phone (540) 654-1015.

SAVE **WHITE OAK CIVIL WAR MUSEUM** is at 985 White Oak Rd. Located in a renovated 1912 schoolhouse, the museum contains battlefield relics such as buttons, buckles and more than 90,000 bullets. Also displayed are bottles; soldiers' equipment; and replicas of campsite huts, which housed soldiers during the winter. Wed.-Sun. 10-5; closed Dec. 25. Admission $4; $2 (ages 13-17 and 66+); $1 (ages 7-12). Phone (540) 371-4234.

FERRUM (I-6) pop. 1,313, elev. 1,300′

Ferrum College was founded in 1913 by the Woman's Missionary Union of the Methodist Church.

BLUE RIDGE INSTITUTE AND MUSEUM is on SR 40W on the campus of Ferrum College. Preserving the heritage of the Blue Ridge region, the museum houses changing exhibits about Blue Ridge folklife. A re-created German-American farm illustrates early 19th-century life complete with period furnishings and costumed interpreters. The Blue Ridge Folklife Festival, the fourth Saturday in October, showcases the region's folk culture.

Allow 2 hours minimum. Museum Mon.-Sat. 10-4; closed Thanksgiving and Dec. 25. Museum free. Farm $5; $4 (ages 6-14 and 61+). Phone (540) 365-4416.

FORT LEE (B-2) elev. 165′

Fort Lee, 2 miles east of Petersburg, is the only U.S. Army Quartermaster installation and training center in the nation. Formed in 1775, the Quartermaster Corps is a combat support branch responsible for providing food, fuel and field services to army soldiers.

ARMY WOMEN'S MUSEUM is at 2100 Adams Ave. Women's contributions to the U.S. Army are depicted through interactive exhibits, artifacts and a collection of films. Allow 30 minutes minimum. Tues.-Fri. 10-5, Sat.-Sun. 11-5; closed Jan. 1, Thanksgiving and Dec. 25. Free. Phone (804) 734-4327.

U.S. ARMY QUARTERMASTER MUSEUM is 1 blk. inside the main gate of Fort Lee. The army's oldest logistic branch, the Quartermaster Corps has fed, clothed and equipped American soldiers since 1775. A variety of exhibits portraying the corps' mission are featured as well as presidential flags, Civil War memorabilia, Gen. George S. Patton's jeep, Gen. Dwight D. Eisenhower's uniforms and Gen. Ulysses S. Grant's saddle. Tues.-Fri. 10-5, Sat.-Sun. 11-5; closed Jan. 1, Thanksgiving and Dec. 25. Donations. Phone (804) 734-4203.

FREDERICKSBURG (D-11)
pop. 19,279, elev. 69′
See map page 248.

Fredericksburg was officially founded and given its present name in 1728, even though settlers had built a fort as early as 1676. Its location in a valley at the head of navigation on the Rappahannock River led to the city's emergence as a prosperous port.

Fredericksburg was George Washington's boyhood home, his mother's last home and the home of his sister, Betty Washington Lewis. James Monroe set up his first law office in the city in 1786.

Between 1861 and 1865 Fredericksburg was an armed camp and the scene of violent battles. By the end of the Civil War it was desolate, its houses torn by shot and shell and the dead buried in its streets.

The Battle of Fredericksburg was fought on Dec. 13, 1862. The Union Army of 142,551 under Gen. Ambrose Everett Burnside camped on Stafford Heights on the north side of the river. The Confederate force of 91,760 under Gen. Robert E. Lee was entrenched west and south of the town.

The Union troops made repeated unsuccessful attacks on the Confederate fortifications, resulting in Burnside's retreat across the river. On the Union side the dead and wounded numbered 12,653; Confederate casualties totaled 5,309.

After the Battle of Chancellorsville the city served as a hospital for the Confederate wounded; it provided a similar service for the Union forces after the Battle of the Wilderness. The Gothic Revival Fredericksburg Courthouse, erected 1851-52, is still in use today. Its historic documents include the will of Mary Washington. The bell was made by the Paul Revere foundry.

From Fredericksburg SR 3 leads down the historic Northern Neck past such sites as George Washington Birthplace National Monument, Robert E. Lee's birthplace at Stratford and George Washington's mother's birthplace near Lancaster.

Another historic, scenic route is US 17, which follows the Rappahannock River to Tappahannock and Gloucester, crosses the York River to Yorktown and the Colonial Parkway, and continues to Williamsburg.

Fredericksburg Visitor Center: 706 Caroline St., Fredericksburg, VA 22401; phone (540) 373-1776 or (800) 678-4748. *See color ad.*

Self-guiding tours: Brochures and maps outlining self-guiding tours of historic Fredericksburg and the area are available from the visitor center, where a 14-minute orientation film is shown. Brochures, maps and area information as well as a 10-minute

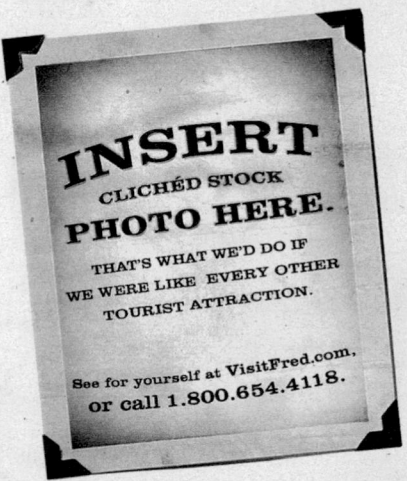

orientation film also are available at the Spotsylvania Visitor Center, 4704 Southpoint Pkwy.; phone (540) 891-8687 or (800) 654-4118.

Shopping areas: Old Town Fredericksburg boasts an array of boutiques and more than 120 antiques dealers. Spotsylvania Mall, I-95 and SR 3, has more than 120 stores, including five department stores.

BELMONT, THE GARI MELCHERS HOME AND STUDIO—*see Falmouth p. 246.*

[SAVE] **CIVIL WAR LIFE-THE SOLDIER'S MUSEUM** is at 4712 Southpoint Pkwy. adjacent to the Spotsylvania Visitor Center. Depicting the life of a typical Civil War soldier, the collection includes original weapons, military gear, life-size dioramas and interactive touch screen programs. A 3-D Civil War slide show also is presented. Daily 9-5, Apr. 2-Labor Day; 10-5, Feb. 1-Apr. 1 and day after Labor Day-Dec. 20. Admission $5; $4.50 (senior citizens); $3 (military with ID); $2.50 (children). Slide show $3. DS, MC, VI. Phone (540) 834-1859.

[SAVE] **FREDERICKSBURG AREA MUSEUM & CULTURAL CENTER** is at 907 Princess Anne St. This 1816 building was once the town hall and market house. A decorative arts exhibit tells the personal stories of area residents through the craftsmanship of local cabinetmakers, silversmiths and

painters. Also on display is a collection of rare Masonic artifacts from George Washington's era. Changing displays on the first floor depict the region's heritage.

Allow 30 minutes minimum. Mon.-Sat. 10-5, Sun. 1-5, Mar.-Nov.; Mon.-Sat. 10-4, Sun. 1-4, rest of year. Closed Jan. 1, Thanksgiving and Dec. 24-25 and 31. Admission $7; $5.50 (active military with ID); $2 (students with ID); free (ages 0-6). Phone (540) 371-3037.

GEORGE WASHINGTON'S FERRY FARM is 1.5 mi. e. on SR 3 to 268 Kings Hwy. Though no buildings remain from the Washington family era, archeological excavations are ongoing. It was here on his father's 600-acre tobacco and corn plantation that Washington learned his skills as a surveyor. The farm was also the fabled setting of the cherry tree, created by an early biographer to illustrate young George's honesty.

In summer a demonstration garden features plants typical of those grown on the original plantation. Open daily 10-5; closed Jan. 1, Thanksgiving and Dec. 24-25 and 31. Admission $5; $3 (ages 6-17). Phone (540) 370-0732.

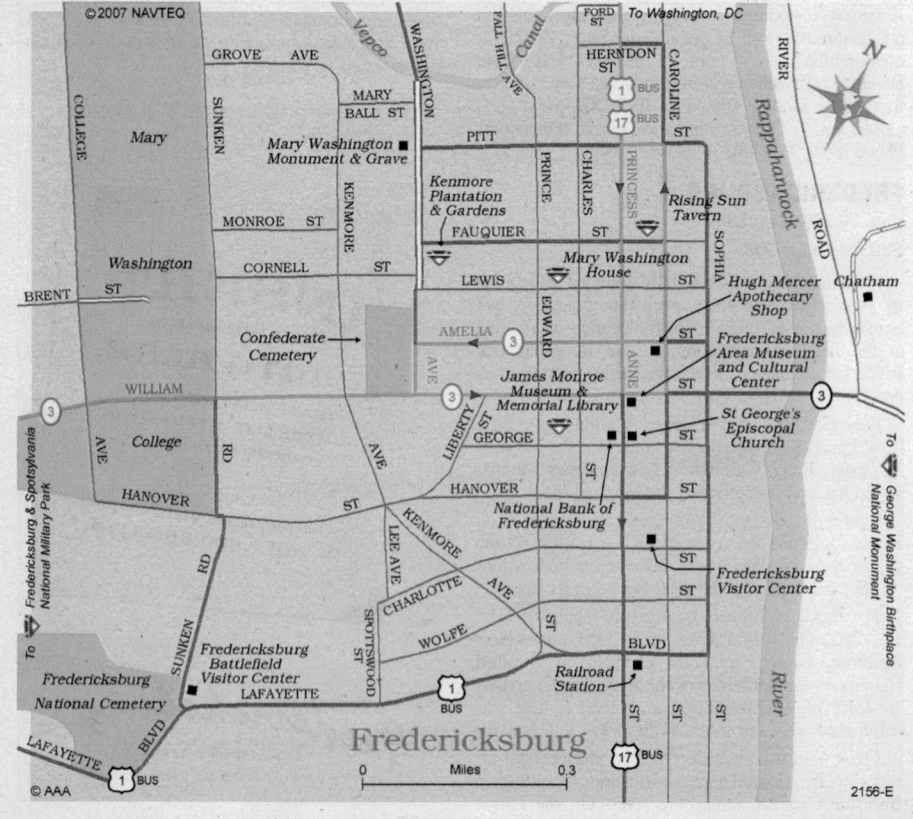

SAVE **HUGH MERCER APOTHECARY SHOP** is at
Caroline and Amelia sts. Displays include
18th-century medicinal and surgical supplies, such
as leeches, lancets, blisters, purges and herbs.
Living-history presentations demonstrate various
practices. A physic garden of medicinal herbs adjoins the building where Dr. Hugh Mercer worked
prior to joining the Continental Army as a brigadier
general in 1776.

Allow 30 minutes minimum. Mon.-Sat. 9-5, Sun.
11-5, Mar.-Nov.; Mon.-Sat. 10-4, Sun. noon-4, rest
of year. Closed Jan. 1, Thanksgiving and Dec. 24-25
and 31. Admission $5; $2 (ages 6-18). Phone (540)
373-3362.

GEM **JAMES MONROE MUSEUM AND MEMO-
RIAL LIBRARY** is at 908 Charles St. Monroe owned this property 1786-92 and
SAVE probably used it while practicing law as a
young attorney in Fredericksburg. The museum contains what is said to be the largest collection of
Monroe-related material in the country, including
belongings of President and Mrs. Monroe and the
Louis XVI furniture they bought in Paris when he
was minister to France 1794-97.

The collection includes the desk on which Monroe prepared his 1823 address to Congress; a section
of this speech became known as the Monroe Doc-
trine. Also displayed are gems owned by Elizabeth
Monroe. A library contains historical manuscripts relating to the president and his era. A bronze bust of
the fifth president is in the walled garden.

Allow 30 minutes minimum. Mon.-Sat. 10-5,
Sun. 1-5, Mar.-Nov.; Mon.-Sat. 10-4, Sun. 1-4, rest
of year. Closed Jan. 1, Thanksgiving and Dec. 24-25
and 31. Admission $5; $1 (ages 6-18). Phone (540)
654-1043.

GEM **KENMORE PLANTATION & GARDENS**
is at 1201 Washington Ave. Kenmore was
the home of Col. Fielding Lewis and his
wife, Betty Washington Lewis, sister of George
Washington. Built in 1775, this Colonial home is an
example of a Georgian manor house. The building
was used as a hospital during the Civil War. The
house is noted for the elaborate, decorative plasterwork on its ceilings and over its fireplaces.

The Bissell Gallery offers an exhibit about
Virginia-made furnishings, portraits and a diorama
of Fredericksburg in the late 1700s. Restoration and
archeological research is ongoing. The grounds also
include a wilderness walking trail. Allow 1 hour
minimum. Daily 10-5; closed Jan. 1, Thanksgiving
and Dec. 24-25 and 31. Admission $8; $4 (students
with ID). MC, VI. Phone (540) 373-3381.

GEM **MARY WASHINGTON HOUSE** is at 1200
Charles St. George Washington bought the
house in 1772 for his mother, Mary Ball
SAVE Washington, who lived here until her death
in 1789. It was from this house that Washington left
for his inauguration after having received his mother's blessing. The home contains some of Mrs.
Washington's favorite possessions.

Combination Tickets

The Pass to Historic Fredericksburg
includes admission to Fredericksburg
area battlefields, the Fredericksburg
Area Museum & Cultural Center,
George Washington's Ferry Farm, Hugh
Mercer Apothecary Shop, James Monroe Museum and Memorial Library,
Kenmore Plantation & Gardens, Mary
Washington House, Rising Sun Tavern
and Belmont, the Gari Melchers Home
and Studio (in Falmouth). The combined admission is $29; ages 6-18,
$9.50.

Another discount option is the Pick
Four ticket, which includes any four
attractions listed above for a combined
admission of $18; ages 6-18, $7.

Passes are available at any of the
above attractions and at the Fredericksburg or Spotsylvania visitor centers.
Phone (800) 654-4118.

Note: It is a good idea to verify hours
and admission fees in advance.

The old English garden is especially beautiful; some of the first boxwoods Mrs. Washington planted remain, and her sundial still marks the hours. Allow 30 minutes minimum. Mon.-Sat. 9-5, Sun. 11-5, Mar.-Oct.; Mon.-Sat. 10-4, Sun. noon-4, rest of year. Closed Jan. 1, Thanksgiving and Dec. 24-25 and 31. Admission $5; $2 (ages 6-18). Phone (540) 373-1569.

MARY WASHINGTON MONUMENT AND GRAVE is on Washington Ave. at the end of Pitt St. The first president's mother was buried here in 1789. Andrew Jackson laid the cornerstone for a marble monument to "the Mother of Washington" in 1833. It was never completed, and during the bombardment of Fredericksburg in 1862 it was scarred badly by shellfire. In 1894 President Grover Cleveland dedicated the present marker, a 40-foot granite shaft.

NATIONAL BANK OF FREDERICKSBURG is at 900 Princess Anne St. Built in 1820, the Federal-style Farmers' Bank building contains a restored banking room and local banking artifacts including a scale for weighing gold dust, a counterfeit bank note from the 1800s and bank certificates and correspondence from the 1860s. Allow 30 minutes minimum. Mon.-Fri. 9-2. Free. Phone (540) 899-3243.

RISING SUN TAVERN is at 1306 Caroline St. The house was built about 1760 for Charles Washington, brother of George Washington. It later served as a coach stop. Costumed tavern wenches give living-history tours. Night tours are available through the Fredericksburg Visitor Center. Allow 30 minutes minimum. Mon.-Sat. 9-5, Sun. 11-5, Mar.-Nov.; Mon.-Sat. 10-4, Sun. noon-4, rest of year. Closed Jan. 1, Thanksgiving and Dec. 24-25 and 31. Admission $5; $2 (ages 6-18). Phone (540) 371-1494, or (800) 678-4748 for night tour information.

ST. GEORGE'S EPISCOPAL CHURCH is at Princess Anne and George sts. The original church was built on this site in 1732; the present structure dates from 1849. It contains a memorial window to Mary Washington and three original Louis Comfort Tiffany windows. In the churchyard are buried William Paul, brother of Revolutionary War hero John Paul Jones, and John Dandridge of New Kent, father of Martha Washington. Daily 9-5. Guided tours are offered Mon.-Fri. 10-3, day after Memorial Day-day before Labor Day. Free. Phone (540) 373-4133.

FREDERICKSBURG AND SPOTSYLVANIA NATIONAL MILITARY PARK (D-11)

In and around Fredericksburg, the park covers about 8,400 acres and includes four great battlefields of the Civil War: Chancellorsville *(see place listing p. 239)*, Fredericksburg, Spotsylvania Court House *(see Spotsylvania p. 306)* and the Wilderness *(see place listing p. 310)*.

Due to its strategic location halfway between Richmond and Washington, D.C., Fredericksburg

and the surrounding area were of prime military importance to both sides. The intense and continuous fighting resulted in the estimated loss of 65,000 Union soldiers and 40,000 Confederate fighters.

Walking trails from the Fredericksburg Battlefield Visitor Center on US 1 lead to the Sunken Road, Marye's Heights and the Fredericksburg National Cemetery. The Kirkland Monument honors a 19-year-old Confederate sergeant who risked his life to give water to the wounded and dying of the Union Army. Old Salem Church, which served as a refuge for civilians fleeing the city during the Battle of Fredericksburg, is within the park. The church, also the site of a battle during the Chancellorsville campaign, later was used by the Confederates to tend to the wounded of both sides. Also on the grounds is Ellwood, a house standing in the middle of the Wilderness Battlefield that once served as a hospital for Confederates.

All of the battlefields are in a 17-mile radius of Fredericksburg. Exhibits, paintings, interpretive trails, historic buildings, narrative markers and maps identify Union and Confederate lines and relate the stories of the battles. Roads lead to the battlefields, earthworks and other points of historic interest.

The TravelBrains Fredericksburg Expedition Guide is available at the national park bookstore. This package includes multimedia resources, a self-guiding walking tour on audio CD and a guide book featuring maps of battle sites, photographs and information about armies, monuments, memorials and soldiers. In-depth driving tours of each battlefield also are available on audio CD or cassette.

The park is open daily 8:30-6:30, Memorial Day-Labor Day; 9-5, rest of year. Closed Jan. 1 and Dec. 25. Park admission is free. The TravelBrains Fredericksburg Expedition Guide is $24.95. Phone (540) 371-0802.

CHANCELLORSVILLE BATTLEFIELD VISITOR CENTER is 8 mi. w. of I-95 on SR 3 at 9001 Plank Rd. The center offers a 22-minute film and displays about the battle in the spring of 1863. Four walking trails with battle paintings and troop maps traverse the battlefield. A 7-mile driving tour begins at the center with roadside tour markers and informational signs describing the battle. Seasonal walking tours lead to the place where Gen. Thomas J. "Stonewall" Jackson was shot; phone ahead for schedule.

Allow 1 hour minimum. Daily 8:30-6:30, mid-June through Labor Day; Mon.-Fri. 9-5, Sat.-Sun. 9-6, Apr. 1 to mid-June and day after Labor Day-Oct. 31; daily 9-5, rest of year. Closed Jan. 1, Thanksgiving and Dec. 25. Visitor center free. Film $2; $1 (ages 62+); free (ages 0-9). CD detailing a 3-hour self-guiding tour $12.95 (to purchase); $4.95 (to rent). Phone (540) 786-2880.

CHATHAM is .5 mi. e. across the Rappahannock River off SR 212 at 120 Chatham Ln. The 18th-century Georgian mansion served as Union headquarters and a field hospital during the Civil War. From its front terrace, officers had a clear view of the city and points along the river where Northern engineers built pontoon bridges for the Battle of Fredericksburg.

Clara Barton was among those who provided care for wounded soldiers here. A film and a museum relate the story of Chatham and the role it played in the war. Daily 9-4:30; closed Jan. 1, Thanksgiving and Dec. 25. Free. Phone (540) 654-5121.

FREDERICKSBURG BATTLEFIELD VISITOR CENTER is at 1013 Lafayette Blvd. (US 1) on the Sunken Road. The center presents a 22-minute film and museum exhibits about the battle that occurred on Dec. 13, 1862. Walking trails lead to Marye's Heights and the Fredericksburg National Cemetery. A 12-mile driving tour starts and ends at the center, covering the majority of the battlefield. Historians lead seasonal walking tours along the Sunken Road; phone for schedule.

Allow 1 hour minimum. Daily 8:30-6:30, mid-June through Labor Day; Mon.-Fri. 9-5, Sat.-Sun. 9-6, Apr. 1 to mid-June and day after Labor Day-Oct. 31; daily 9-5, rest of year. Closed Jan. 1, Thanksgiving and Dec. 25. Visitor center free. Film $2; $1 (ages 62+); free (ages 0-9). CD detailing a 3-hour self-guiding tour $12.95 (to purchase); $4.95 (to rent). Phone (540) 373-6122.

FREDERICKSBURG NATIONAL CEMETERY is on Lafayette Blvd. (US 1) atop Marye's Heights. More than 15,000 U.S. veterans are buried here, the majority of whom are Union soldiers who died in the nearby battles of Fredericksburg, Chancellorsville, Spotsylvania Court House and the Wilderness. More than 80 percent of the soldiers are unknown. The Fredericksburg Battlefield Visitor Center keeps a record of identified soldiers. Grounds open daily dawn-dusk. Free. Phone (540) 373-4510 or (540) 373-6122.

"STONEWALL" JACKSON SHRINE is 15 mi. s. of Fredericksburg via I-95, US 1 or SR 2, then by CR 606 to Guinea Station. On the night of May 2, 1863, Gen. Thomas J. "Stonewall" Jackson was mistakenly shot by his own men at Chancellorsville, losing an arm. The Confederate general was moved by order of Gen. Robert E. Lee to recover at Fairfield Plantation. With the main house already filled with injured soldiers, Jackson's doctors settled him in the plantation office. The room where he died a week later has been preserved.

Daily 9-5, mid-June through Labor Day; Fri.-Tues. 9-5, Apr. 1 to mid-June and day after Labor Day-Oct. 31; Sat.-Mon. 9-5, rest of year. Closed Jan. 1 and Dec. 25. Free. Phone (804) 633-6076.

FRONT ROYAL (E-8) pop. 13,589, elev. 565'

Front Royal began as Lehew Town, a frontier village on the packhorse road to the east. According to local lore, its current name derives from the command by frustrated military officers for unruly troops to "front the royal oak," which once stood in the public square.

Belle Boyd, the Confederate spy who charmed military secrets out of her Union suitors, used Front Royal as one of her most effective bases. On May 15, 1862, Boyd overheard plans that the Union troops were exiting Front Royal, leaving behind a small force. Boyd relayed this information to Gen. Thomas J. "Stonewall" Jackson, and on May 23, Jackson led his troops into town and the Battle of Front Royal ended with the capture of 750 of the 1,000 Union soldiers. No remains of the battlefield exist.

A popular stopping point for visitors bound for the Skyline Drive (*see attraction listing p. 306*), Front Royal has preserved some of its 19th-century atmosphere on Chester Street, in the historic district. The 1787 Balthis House is the oldest building in town.

Front Royal Visitor Center: 414 E. Main St., Front Royal, VA 22630; phone (540) 635-5788 or (800) 338-2576.

Self-guiding tours: Brochures describing a walking tour of the historic district are available at the visitor center in the Southern Railway Train Station.

BALTHIS HOUSE is at 55 Chester St.; tickets can be purchased at the Ivy Lodge Museum. Built before the town of Front Royal was chartered, the Balthis house dates to 1787. It is one of few in the historic district to retain its original dependencies, including a smokehouse, a separate kitchen and a workshop. Guided tours detail the region's Colonial history. Allow 30 minutes minimum. Mon.-Fri. 10-4, Mar.-Oct. Closed major holidays. Admission $3; free (ages 0-9). Phone (504) 636-1446.

BELLE BOYD COTTAGE is at 101 Chester St.; tickets can be purchased at the Ivy Lodge Museum. The 1860s middle-class home was used by the Confederate spy Belle Boyd. Furnished in period, the cottage contains memorabilia depicting the Civil War era. Mon.-Fri. 10-4; closed major holidays. Admission $3; free (ages 0-9). Phone (540) 636-1446.

IVY LODGE MUSEUM is at 101 Chester St. Exhibits in this former private residence include artifacts chronicling the history of Front Royal and Warren County. The lodge is headquarters of the Warren Heritage Society. Allow 30 minutes minimum. Mon.-Fri. 9:30-4; closed major holidays. Free. Phone (504) 636-1446.

SKYLINE CAVERNS are on US 340, approximately 1 mi. s. of the entrance to Skyline Drive and 1.5 mi. s. of jct. SR 55. The caverns contain calcite formations known as anthodites or cave flowers, found in few caves worldwide. Subterranean streams and cascades are of interest. Indirect illumination is provided. Also offered is the Enchanted Dragon Mirror Maze and a .5-mile tour of the grounds aboard a miniature train (weather permitting).

Guided cavern tours are given every 15-20 minutes daily 9-6, June 15-Labor Day; Mon.-Fri. 9-5, Sat.-Sun. 9-6, Mar. 15-June 14 and day after Labor Day-Nov. 14; daily 9-4, rest of year. Cavern tour $16; $14 (ages 62+); $8 (ages 7-13). Maze $5. Train fare $3; free (ages 0-2). AX, MC, VI. Phone (540) 635-4545 or (800) 296-4545.

"WARREN RIFLES" CONFEDERATE MUSEUM is at 95 Chester St. The museum houses documents, guns, pictures, letters from Confederate soldiers and personal items of Belle Boyd, a Confederate spy, and Gens. Thomas J. "Stonewall" Jackson, Robert E. Lee and Turner Ashby. The "Warren Rifles" were an infantry brigade formed in Front Royal in 1861. Mon.-Sat. 9-4, Sun. noon-4, Apr. 15-Nov. 1; by appointment rest of year. Admission $5; free (ages 0-11 and students and active military with ID). Prices may vary; phone ahead. Phone (540) 636-6982 or (540) 635-2219.

GALAX (I-5) pop. 6,837, elev. 2,382'

Tucked in the Blue Ridge Mountains on the North Carolina state line, Galax is noted for its pristine beauty. The town is named for the leaf of the galax, a plant indigenous to the area. The terrain is popular with mountain bikers, horseback riders and hikers, while placid rivers and streams draw angles, canoeists and kayakers.

Every Friday evening at 8, a weekly radio show featuring regional bluegrass bands is broadcast live from the historical Rex Theatre at 113 E. Grayson St.

Director of Tourism: 111 E. Grayson St., Galax, VA 24333; phone (276) 238-8130.

JEFF MATTHEWS MEMORIAL MUSEUM is at 606 W. Stuart Dr. An eclectic collection includes photographs of Civil War veterans, a covered wagon, a coin collection, medical and dental equipment, farm implements, musical instruments and more than 50 big-game mounted heads and animal-skin rugs.

Two restored log cabins also are on the grounds. Jeff Matthews, one of Galax's first settlers, established the museum with a friend, combining their collections of American Indian artifacts and other memorabilia. Wed.-Sat. 11-4; closed major holidays. Donations. Phone (276) 236-7874.

GEORGE WASHINGTON AND JEFFERSON NATIONAL FORESTS

Elevations in the forests range from 600 ft. near Covington to 5,729 ft. Mount Rogers in the Mount Rogers National Recreation Area. Refer to AAA maps for additional elevation information.

Stretching from Big Stone Gap to Winchester, the George Washington and Jefferson National Forests contain some 1.8 million acres.

The northern end of the forest, known as the George Washington National Forest, extends more than 1 million acres across the Blue Ridge, Massanutten, Shenandoah and Allegheny mountain ranges into West Virginia. Towering over all these ranges is 4,463-foot Elliott Knob, just west of Staunton.

Among the major recreation areas are Brandywine and Todd lakes, respectively west and southwest of Harrisonburg; Elizabeth Furnace, south of Waterlick; Trout Pond, west of Woodstock; Sherando Lake, near Waynesboro; and Lake Moomaw, southwest of Warm Springs.

More than 950 miles of trails wind through the George Washington National Forest leading to scenic views of mountains, valleys and rivers. A portion of the Appalachian Trail traverses the forest, and another trail leads to Crabtree Falls, five cascading waterfalls that are the highest in the Blue Ridge.

A 5-mile loop trail winds gradually to the top of Pompey Mountain and Mount Pleasant. Popular because it is not steep, the trail provides scenic vistas of the Blue Ridge Mountains. Also noteworthy is The Highlands Scenic Tour, a 20-mile scenic drive through the mountains along a steep, twisting road. The Massanutten Gap Visitor Center is on US 211 at New Market Gap, west of Luray.

The southern end of the forest, known as Jefferson National Forest, embraces approximately 710,000 acres in west-central Virginia. A 300-mile portion of the Appalachian Trail runs through the forest; trail shelters are provided.

Jefferson National Forest has more than 1,100 miles of trails, 500 miles of trout streams, 24 developed campgrounds, 25 picnic areas and six fishing and four swimming lakes, some of which have bathhouses. The Cascades National Recreation Trail is a scenic 4-mile hike leading to a 66-foot waterfall. The 4-mile John's Creek Mountain Trail offers panoramic views as it intersects the Appalachian Trail.

Beginning near Wytheville, Big Walker Mountain Scenic Byway winds 16 miles through forested countryside past old farm homesteads, hiking trails, fishing ponds, picnic areas, campgrounds and beautiful mountain vistas. The byway leads up the mountain to Big Walker Lookout, which features a visitor center, swinging bridge and an observation tower, all open daily April through October. Another scenic route, Mount Rogers Scenic Byway, passes through valleys and over mountains rich in the ever-changing colors of leaves and wildflowers.

Nearby are the towns of Abingdon *(see place listing p. 231)*, Big Stone Gap *(see place listing p. 233)*, Blacksburg *(see place listing p. 233)*, Natural Bridge *(see place listing p. 279)*, Roanoke *(see place listing p. 303)*, Winchester *(see place listing p. 328)* and Wytheville *(see place listing p. 330)*.

The main recreation season for George Washington and Jefferson National Forests is April through November. Fees are charged at some sites. For more information contact the Forest Supervisor, 5162 Valleypointe Pkwy., Roanoke, VA 24019; phone (888) 265-0019. *See Recreation Chart and the AAA Mideastern CampBook.*

CAVE MOUNTAIN LAKE RECREATION AREA is 8 mi. s.e. of Natural Bridge. The park contains a 7-acre lake with a beach and bathhouse, hiking trails, picnic facilities, and tent and trailer camping areas. A scenic drive past Cave Mountain Lake climbs Wildcat Mountain, where it forks; the left spur leads to Sunset Field, where it connects with Blue Ridge Parkway. Daily 6 a.m.-11 p.m., Apr.-Oct. Day-use fee $5 per private vehicle. Camping $15 per night. Phone (540) 291-2188.

GEORGE WASHINGTON BIRTHPLACE NATIONAL MONUMENT (F-10)

On the south side of the Potomac River, 38 miles east of Fredericksburg off SR 3 on SR 204, George Washington Birthplace National Monument includes 550 acres and a portion of the old Washington Plantation. John, the first Washington to settle in the

area, arrived about 1657. In 1731 his grandson Augustine married Mary Ball of Epping Forest. He brought her to his home on Popes Creek, and there George Washington was born in 1732.

The house, built by Augustine 1722-26, was destroyed by fire on Christmas Day in 1779. Excavations have revealed five original foundations. Since the exact appearance of the original is not known, a memorial house was built to represent an 18th-century plantation home.

Native clay was used to make the bricks for the building, which is furnished with antiques carefully selected to reflect the period of Washington's boyhood. The grounds include a kitchen and garden.

The Colonial Living Farm re-creates some of the farm scenes of young Washington's environment. The livestock, gardens and crops are historical varieties raised by methods common during the Colonial period.

Also on the grounds is a cemetery containing the graves of 32 members of the family, including George's father, grandfather and great-grandfather. Picnic facilities are available. The house and grounds are open daily 9-5; closed Jan. 1, Thanksgiving and Dec. 25. Admission is $4, under 17 free. Phone (804) 224-1732.

GLEN ALLEN—*see Richmond p. 301.*

GLOUCESTER—*see Hampton Roads Area p. 255.*

GLOUCESTER POINT—
see Hampton Roads Area p. 257.

GREAT FALLS—*see District of Columbia p. 128.*

GROTTOES (F-8) pop. 2,114

Known in its early history as Liola and then Shendun, this area was settled around 1735 with a land grant of 60,000 acres on the Shenandoah River. The Grottoes Co. was formed in 1889 to develop the local caves and mineral resources; the enterprise folded 4 years later. The town adopted its present name in 1912.

(SAVE) **GRAND CAVERNS REGIONAL PARK** is off I-81 exit 235, then 6 mi. e. on SR 256. One of the country's oldest show caverns, the Grottoes cave was discovered in 1804 and opened to the public 2 years later. At different times both Union and Gen. Thomas J. "Stonewall" Jackson's Confederate troops visited the Great Cathedral Hall and Grand Ballroom. Signatures of soldiers from both armies are visible on cave walls. Unusual cave formations include calcite shields.

Nature trails, fishing, picnicking, tennis, swimming and miniature golf are offered. Guided cave tours are given daily every 45 minutes 9-5, Apr.-Oct.; Sat.-Sun. 9-5, rest of year. Fee $16; $15 (ages 61+ and military with ID); $9 (ages 3-12). MC, VI. Phone (540) 249-5705.

HAMPTON—*see Hampton Roads Area p. 257.*

Hampton Roads Area

Norfolk / © Buddy Mays Travel Stock Photography

When the *Susan Constant*, the *Godspeed* and the *Discovery* landed at Chesapeake Bay in 1607, our nation's history began. The travelers, led by John Smith, bestowed the name Cape Henry on the site before continuing their journey along the James River and establishing the first permanent English colony in America at Jamestown.

Settlement quickly pushed outward from the James River. The site of present-day Newport News was settled in 1621, with Norfolk following suit in 1682. The Revolutionary War reached the region in 1776 when Norfolk was bombarded by the British; citizens burned the remains of the town to the ground to prevent the enemy's return.

Steeped in the history of the Colonial era, Hampton Roads also holds importance as the site of two key Civil War events. The naval engagement between the CSS *Virginia (Merrimac)* and the USS *Monitor*—the first duel between ironclad warships—was fought in 1862 in the harbor at the mouth of the James River. Three years later Abraham Lincoln and Confederate representatives met aboard the *River Queen,* where unsuccessful negotiations to end the war were conducted.

Virginia Beach was a desolate strip of sand in the 1870s—its only notoriety being that of a graveyard for ships lost along the Atlantic coast—when Congress authorized the construction of four lifesaving stations in the area. Seatack Lifesaving Station developed into the community of Virginia Beach.

The area's ties to the sea were further strengthened when the Newport News Shipbuilding and Dry Dock Co., a leader in the production of ocean liners as well as military vessels, was established in 1886. Soldiers leaving for both world wars embarked from this city; those returning from World War I were honored with the Victory Arch on 25th Street, commemorating all American veterans.

Norfolk, with one of the finest harbors in the world, accommodates the largest ships, including supercarriers, merchant ships and U.S. Navy vessels. The Norfolk Naval Shipyard in nearby Portsmouth and the Naval Station and Naval Air Station in Norfolk constitute one of the largest naval facilities in the world.

A merger of Virginia Beach with Princess Anne County created a city with a 29-mile-long coastline. The resort offers an excellent beach and 3 miles of boardwalk. Surf swimming is probably the favorite sport, complemented by aquaplaning, water skiing and boating on inland waters. Fishing also is prime here, and the region is noted for seafood, especially the Lynnhaven oyster.

The term Hampton Roads has come to include the section of southeastern Virginia encompassing Norfolk, Virginia Beach, Newport News, Hampton, Portsmouth and other surrounding towns as well as Williamsburg, Jamestown and Yorktown. Historically the name refers to the place of safe harbor off the Virginia peninsula between the James, Elizabeth and Nansemond rivers and Chesapeake Bay named after the third Earl of Southampton. A "road," in the nautical sense, is a place where ships can safely anchor.

CHESAPEAKE (C-4) pop. 199,184

Nestled in the southeast corner of the commonwealth in the heart of the Tidewater/Hampton Roads region, Chesapeake was created in 1963 following the merger of Norfolk County and the city of Norfolk. Though relatively new as a city, Chesapeake was one of the first areas explored by Capt. John Smith in the 1600s. During the Revolutionary War, American and British forces clashed here in the Battle of Great Bridge.

Two branches of the Atlantic Intracoastal Waterway stretch southward from Chesapeake, providing boaters with a choice of two scenic routes to Florida.

An untamed wilderness is nearby at the Dismal Swamp *(see place listing p. 245).* Boating access to Lake Drummond in the Great Dismal Swamp National Wildlife Refuge is available at the Chesapeake ramp off US 17 at Ballahack Road and west to the junction of George Washington Highway. Birds and birdwatchers share common ground on the South Chesapeake Loop of the Virginia Birding and Wildlife Trail.

Chesapeake Conventions & Tourism: 3815 Bainbridge Blvd., Chesapeake, VA 23324; phone (757) 502-4898 or (888) 889-5551. *See color ad p. 745.*

Shopping areas: Area malls include Chesapeake Square Mall, at the corner of Portsmouth Boulevard and Taylor Road, and Greenbrier Mall, off I-64 exit 289B (Greenbrier Parkway South). Chesapeake Square has Dillard's, Hecht's, JCPenney and Sears; Greenbrier Mall features Dillard's, Hecht's and Sears. Antique Alley, an eclectic group of stores, auctions and flea markets, is at South Military Highway and Canal Drive.

GREAT BRIDGE LOCKS PARK is off SR 168 (Great Bridge Bypass) at SR 190, then s. on Battlefield Blvd. to 100 Locks Rd. The park sits on the Atlantic Intracoastal Waterway where the Albemarle and Chesapeake Canal meets the Elizabeth River. Thousands of luxury yachts and pleasure boats make their way into the Chesapeake watershed from here.

A viewing area allows visitors to sit and watch lock operations. The park also includes a boat ramp, fishing and crabbing spots, a playground, nature trails and picnic facilities. Daily dawn-dusk. Free. Phone (757) 382-6411.

NORTHWEST RIVER PARK is 7.4 mi. s. on Battlefield Blvd. S., then 3.8 mi. e. to 1733 Indian Creek Rd. This 763-acre park on the Northwest River offers natural recreation areas, camping and picnic facilities, a fragrance garden for the blind, an equestrian area for horse owners and more than 7 miles of hiking trails. A freshwater lake is stocked with bass, bluegill, crappie, catfish, and trout. Canoes, johnboats, paddleboats and fishing poles are available for rent. Daily 9-dusk. Free. Phone (757)

Peninsula Fine Arts Center
Newport News Tourism Development Office

421-7151. *See Recreation Chart and the AAA Mideastern CampBook.*

PORTLOCK GALLERIES AT SONO is at 3815 Bainbridge Blvd. Housed in the historic Portlock School, this contemporary art gallery features work by local and regional artists. Tues.-Fri. 10-5, Sat.-Sun. 1-5; closed major holidays. Free. Phone (757) 502-4901.

GLOUCESTER (B-4) elev. 75′

Gloucester (GLOSS-ter), in Tidewater Virginia, is noted for its many historical landmarks that have remained undisturbed. The 1766 Courthouse, on the Court Green, is enclosed by a brick wall. The Old Debtors Prison dates from the mid-18th century. Several old estates are in this region near Gloucester and near White Marsh *(see place listing p. 270)*. Long Bridge Ordinary, a stagecoach tavern built in 1732, is open during Garden Week in late April. Dr. Walter Reed, instrumental in the eradication of yellow fever, was born in nearby Belroi.

Destination Hampton Roads Area

L et the outstanding maritime museums in Norfolk and Newport News set the tone for your visit. But don't be surprised if you find more than nautical landmarks and seafaring lore in the Hampton Roads Area.

© Gibson Stock Photography

The Mariners' Museum, Newport News. This museum is dedicated to preserving and interpreting marine heritage. (See listing page 261)

N orfolk also is home to the Chrysler Museum of Art; nearby Portsmouth boasts the Children's Museum of Virginia; and historic houses and old churches are in almost every community.

© Streano, Havens Jupiter Images

Virginia Zoo, Norfolk. Visitors are captivated by more than 300 animals, including this Siberian tiger. (See listing page 265)

• Gloucester

White Marsh •

17

64

Gloucester Point

See Vicinity map pages 258 & 259

13

© Gibson Stock Photography

Hampton Roads Area

Surry •

10

Newport News

17

Hampton

Fort Monroe

Smithfield •

258

32

664

Norfolk

Isle of Wight

460   258

Portsmouth

64

13

264

Virginia Beach

Chesapeake

460   64

58

13

17

168

Virginia Air & Space Center, Hampton. A model space shuttle is among the spacecraft and aircraft displayed here. (See listing page 260)

- -
VA.
N.C.

P laces included in this AAA Destination Area:

Gloucester Chamber of Commerce: P.O. Box 296, Gloucester, VA 23061; phone (804) 693-2425.

GLOUCESTER POINT (B-4) pop. 9,429

Located on the York River, Gloucester Point has been a strategic town throughout its history. The town originally was called Tyndall's Point in honor of an early mapmaker.

VIRGINIA INSTITUTE OF MARINE SCIENCE is off US 17, .8 mi. n. of Coleman Bridge over the York River. This research institute and graduate school of the College of William and Mary maintains eight aquariums containing saltwater fish indigenous to the area. Exhibits include a living oyster reef. Mon.-Fri. 9-4:30; closed Jan. 1-2, Memorial Day, Thanksgiving, day after Thanksgiving and Dec. 24-31. Free. Phone (804) 684-7000.

HAMPTON (C-4) pop. 146,437, elev. 3′

Settled in 1610, Hampton is the oldest continuously English-speaking settlement still in existence in the nation. In 1619 it was one of the original boroughs in the Virginia Legislature.

One of the first battles of the Revolutionary War in Virginia was fought in Hampton in October 1775. Hampton again was invaded and partially burned by British forces in 1813. The first planned land battle of the Civil War was fought at Big Bethel in Hampton in 1861. In August 1861 the town was burned again, this time by Confederates.

Fort Monroe at Hampton was one of the few forts in the South not captured by the Confederates at the outbreak of hostilities. The fortification was an important base in the Chesapeake Bay for the Union Army and Navy during the Civil War. The world's first conflict between two ironclad vessels took place here in 1862 when the Confederate ironclad CSS *Virginia (Merrimac)* attacked the Union fleet and its defending ironclad, the USS *Monitor.* Each failed to pierce the other's armor, but the *Virginia* destroyed two other ships, the *Congress* and the *Cumberland.*

North off SR 134 is Langley Air Force Base, headquarters for the 1st Fighter Wing and a number of other units. The nearby NASA Langley Research Center served as the original training site for the nation's first seven astronauts; the U.S. space program was founded in Hampton and NASA Langley remains active in aeronautical research.

The Hampton area is the center of Virginia's fishing industry. Oysters and Chesapeake Bay blue crabs are of particular importance. Public beach areas include Buckroe Beach, a bayside vacation area reached via Pembroke Avenue, and Grandview, north off Beach Road. Shops, restaurants and museums line the downtown waterfront along Settlers Landing Road, where visitors can watch the traffic of fishing boats, ferries and sightseeing charters. The antique Hampton Carousel, with hand-carved horses and an original band organ, has its own harborside pavilion; rides are offered from late April through October.

Virginia Air & Space Center / Hampton Convention & Visitors Bureau

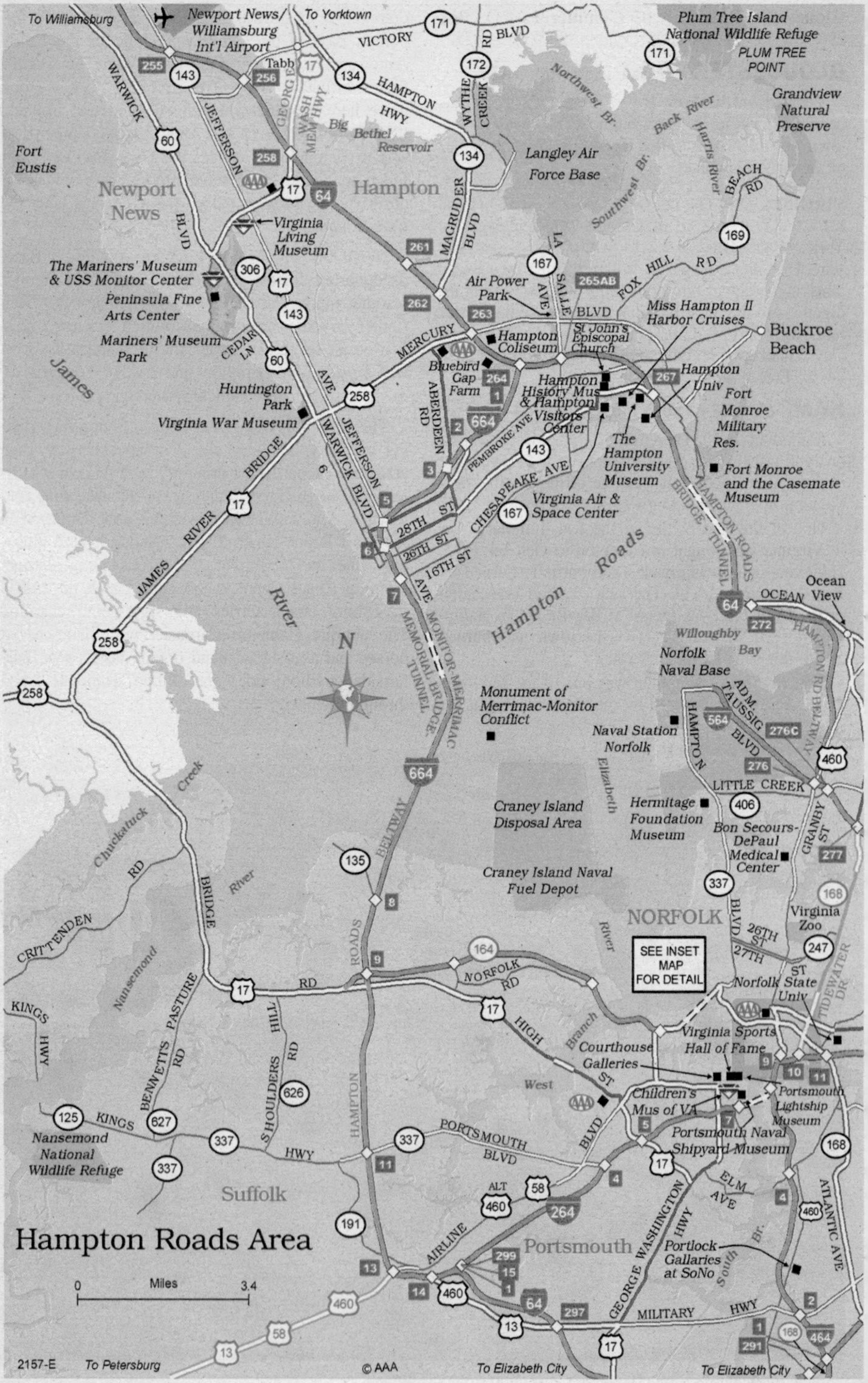
Hampton Roads Area
To Williamsburg
Newport News/ Williamsburg Int'l Airport
To Yorktown
Plum Tree Island National Wildlife Refuge
PLUM TREE POINT
Grandview Natural Preserve
Fort Eustis
Newport News
Hampton
Big Bethel Reservoir
Langley Air Force Base
Virginia Living Museum
The Mariners' Museum & USS Monitor Center
Peninsula Fine Arts Center
Mariners' Museum Park
Air Power Park
Hampton Coliseum
St John's Episcopal Church
Miss Hampton II Harbor Cruises
Buckroe Beach
Bluebird Gap Farm
Hampton History Mus & Hampton Visitors Center
Hampton Univ
Fort Monroe Military Res.
The Hampton University Museum
Fort Monroe and the Casemate Museum
Virginia Air & Space Center
Huntington Park
Virginia War Museum
James River
Hampton Roads
HAMPTON ROADS BRIDGE - TUNNEL
MONITOR-MERRIMAC MEMORIAL BRIDGE-TUNNEL
Ocean View
Willoughby Bay
Norfolk Naval Base
Naval Station Norfolk
Monument of Merrimac-Monitor Conflict
Craney Island Disposal Area
Craney Island Naval Fuel Depot
Hermitage Foundation Museum
Bon Secours-DePaul Medical Center
Virginia Zoo
NORFOLK
SEE INSET MAP FOR DETAIL
Norfolk State Univ
Virginia Sports Hall of Fame
Courthouse Galleries
Children's Mus of VA
Portsmouth Lightship Museum
Portsmouth Naval Shipyard Museum
Portlock Gallaries at SoNo
Portsmouth
Suffolk
Nansemond National Wildlife Refuge
Chuckatuck Creek
Nansemond River
VICTORY BLVD
HAMPTON HWY
WARWICK BLVD
JEFFERSON AVE
MERCURY BLVD
JAMES RIVER BRIDGE
CHESAPEAKE AVE
MAGRUDER BLVD
FOX HILL RD
LA SALLE AVE
LITTLE CREEK
GRANBY ST
HAMPTON BLVD
NORFOLK RD
HIGH ST
PORTSMOUTH BLVD
AIRLINE
GEORGE WASHINGTON HWY
MILITARY HWY
ATLANTIC AVE
TIDEWATER DR
PORTSMOUTH HWY
KINGS HWY
CRITTENDEN RD
BENNETT'S PASTURE RD
SHOULDERS HILL RD
Miles
0
3.4
2157-E
To Petersburg
© AAA
To Elizabeth City
To Elizabeth City

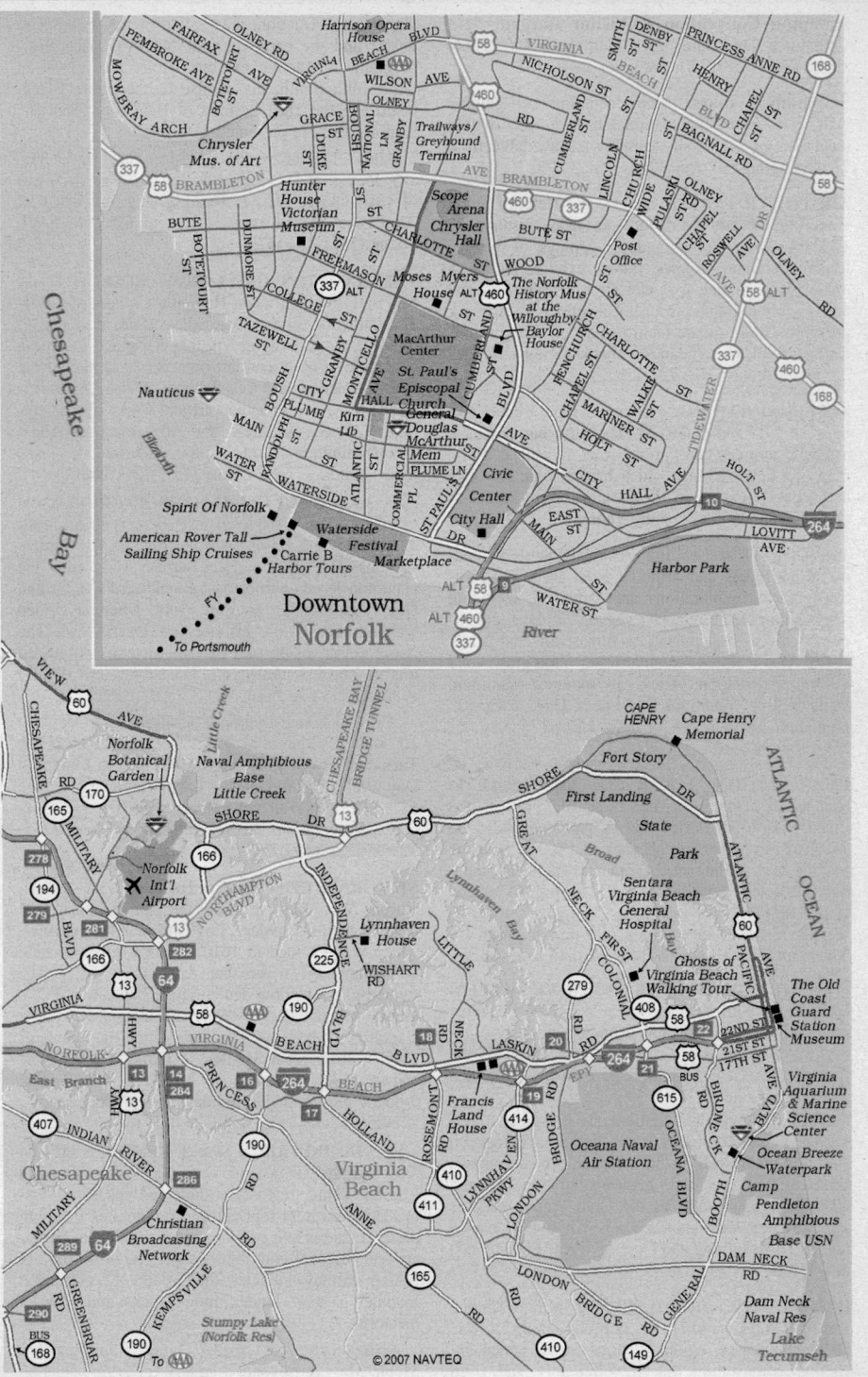

Downtown
Norfolk

Hampton Convention & Visitor Bureau: 1919 Commerce Dr., Suite 290, Hampton, VA 23666; phone (757) 728-5330. *See color ad p. 318.*

Self-guiding tours: Maps detailing self-guiding walking tours of five national historic sites within the Hampton University campus are available from The Hampton University Museum.

AIR POWER PARK is at 413 W. Mercury Blvd. Honoring the city's aviation and space history, the 15-acre park features outdoor displays of vintage jets, rockets and missiles. Indoor exhibits include a model wind tunnel, a model aircraft collection and archive photographs from local military bases. A playground and picnic facilities are on the grounds. Daily 9-4:30; closed Jan. 1, Thanksgiving and Dec. 25. Free. Phone (757) 727-1163.

BLUEBIRD GAP FARM is at 60 Pine Chapel Rd. between I-64 and Queen St. The farm has domestic and wild animals and various fowl as well as a display of farm machines and a barn. Picnic facilities and a play area are on the grounds. Wed.-Sun. 9-5; closed major holidays. Free. Phone (757) 727-6739.

THE COUSTEAU SOCIETY is at 710 Settlers Landing Rd. Models and artifacts from Jacques Cousteau's marine explorations are displayed, including re-creations of the research vessels *Calypso* and *Alcyone*, diving equipment, a hovercraft and shark cages. Also featured are underwater photographs and a film presentation. Allow 30 minutes minimum. Daily 9:30-4, Memorial Day-Labor Day; Tues.-Sat. 10-4, Sun. noon-3, rest of year. Closed major holidays. Free. Phone (757) 722-9300.

EMANCIPATION OAK is near the entrance to Hampton University at the corner of Tyler St. and Emancipation Dr. Former slaves gathered under the shade of this sprawling live oak in 1863 to hear the South's first reading of the Emancipation Proclamation. Hampton Institute opened here in 1868 as one of the first colleges for blacks; alumnus Booker T. Washington returned to teach in a new program for American Indian students from Western reservations.

FORT MONROE AND THE CASEMATE MUSEUM is at 20 Bernard Rd. Named in honor of President James Monroe, the fort has been continuously occupied since 1823. A water-filled moat surrounds the structure, which is in the shape of a seven-pointed star.

After the Civil War, Confederate President Jefferson Davis was confined here until 1867. Visitors can view his prison cell at the museum, which contains exhibits about the battle between the ironclads and other important events of the Civil War as well as army artillery memorabilia. Daily 10:30-4:30; closed Jan. 1, Thanksgiving and Dec. 25. Free. Phone (757) 788-3391.

HAMPTON HISTORY MUSEUM is in the Hampton Visitor Center building at 120 Old Hampton Ln. Four centuries of regional history are presented, including colonization, the Revolutionary and Civil wars, Reconstruction, the growth of the seafood industry and the early days of NASA's space flight program. Interactive exhibits depict the arrival of Capt. John Smith, the demise of the pirate Blackbeard and the 1861 burning of Hampton. Changing exhibits also are presented.

Allow 1 hour minimum. Mon.-Sat. 10-5, Sun. 1-5, Memorial Day-Labor Day; Mon.-Sat. 10-5, rest of year. Closed Jan. 1, Thanksgiving and Dec. 25. Admission $5; $4 (ages 4-12 and 62+). MC, VI. Phone (757) 727-1610.

THE HAMPTON UNIVERSITY MUSEUM is off I-64 exit 267 then w. on Hampton University's Tyler St., following signs. Founded in 1868, it is one of the oldest museums in Virginia. Displays include a collection of traditional art objects and artifacts from North America and sub-Saharan Africa. Also featured are American Indian art and works by contemporary African-American and African artists. Allow 1 hour minimum. Mon.-Fri. 8-5, Sat. noon-4; closed major holidays. Free. Phone (757) 727-5308.

[SAVE] **MISS HAMPTON II HARBOR CRUISES** departs from the Cousteau Society U.S. headquarters on the Hampton waterfront at 710 Settlers Landing Rd. The narrated cruise sails into the Hampton Roads harbor past Blackbeard's Point and Old Point Comfort to Fort Wool, where a guided walking tour of the historic fort is provided. The cruise continues on past the aircraft carriers, guided missile cruisers, destroyers and submarines docked at Norfolk Naval Base.

Allow 3 hours minimum. Cruises depart daily at 10 and 2, Memorial Day weekend-Labor Day; Tues.-Sat. at 10, early Apr. to day before Memorial Day weekend and day after Labor Day-Oct. 31. Fare $21; $19 (ages 61+ and military with ID); $10 (ages 6-12). Reservations are recommended. Phone (757) 722-9102 or (888) 757-2628.

ST. JOHN'S EPISCOPAL CHURCH is at 100 W. Queens Way. Built in 1728, the church houses one of the nation's oldest English-speaking parishes, which was founded in 1610. Its most precious relic is Communion silver that dates from 1618. The stained-glass window depicting the baptism of Pocahontas was donated by American Indian students at Hampton University. The parish museum contains artifacts from previous sites, including a 1599 Bible and a 1632 prayer book. Mon.-Fri. 9-3:30, Sat. 9-noon; closed major holidays. Free. Phone (757) 722-2567.

[SAVE] **VIRGINIA AIR & SPACE CENTER** is off I-64 exit 267, then 1 mi. w. to 600 Settlers Landing Rd. The center features aircraft and spacecraft suspended from a 94-foot ceiling. Adventures in Flight presents interactive exhibits about the Wright Brothers and regional contributions to aviation history. A NASA display includes the Apollo 12 command module, a lunar lander, moon rocks and a Mars meteorite.

Also on-site are Space Quest: Exploring the Moon, Mars & Beyond, a gallery featuring hands-on displays; an IMAX theater; and a seven-story observation deck providing panoramic views.

Daily 10-5 (also Thurs.-Sun. 5-7), Memorial Day-Labor Day; Mon.-Sat. 10-5; Sun. noon-5, rest of year. Closed Thanksgiving and Dec. 25. Center admission $9; $8 (ages 65+ and military with ID); $7 (ages 3-18). IMAX 45-minute presentation $8; $7 (ages 65+ and military with ID); $6.75 (ages 3-18). Combination ticket $14; $13 (ages 65+ and military with ID); $11 (ages 3-18). Other combination tickets are available. MC, VI. Phone (757) 727-0900 or (800) 296-0800.

ISLE OF WIGHT (C-3) elev. 60'

Colonists from Jamestown established the Isle of Wight Plantation on the James River in 1619. Some of its original settlers may have come from the English island of the same name. Villagers traded peacefully with the Worrosquoyacke and Nottoway Indians until 1622, when the Powhatan Confederacy launched a series of attacks against dozens of James River settlements. Nearly a third of all Virginia colonists were killed; most local tribes were driven from their lands in reprisal.

Smithfield and Isle of Wight Convention and Visitors Bureau: 335 Main St., P.O. Box 37, Smithfield, VA 23431; phone (757) 357-5182 or (800) 365-9339.

BOYKINS TAVERN is at 17130 Monument Cir. Built in 1762 by Maj. Francis Boykin, the tavern served as a gathering spot for travelers and those conducting business at the nearby courthouse and jail. It remained in the Boykin family until 1831. Two downstairs rooms and a basement kitchen recreate the original tavern surroundings. Other rooms feature period antiques and artifacts. Guided tours are available. Allow 30 minutes minimum. Thurs.-Sat. 11-4, Sun. 1-4; closed major holidays. Free. Phone (757) 365-9771 or (800) 365-9339.

JAMESTOWN—

see Virginia's Historic Triangle p. 316.

NEWPORT NEWS pop. 180,150

It is said this city gained its name when the Jamestown settlers, ready to abandon their colony, met Capt. Christopher Newport on the James River. The captain's ship was carrying supplies and reinforcements from England, hence "Newport's good news." The captain played a key role in the permanent settlement of Virginia, making five transatlantic voyages between 1607 and 1619.

Newport News Visitor Center: 13560 Jefferson Ave., Newport News, VA 23603; phone (757) 886-7777 or (888) 493-7386. *See color ad p. 922.*

[SAVE] **ENDVIEW PLANTATION** is at 362 Yorktown Rd. Over the span of three conflicts—the American Revolution, the War of 1812 and the Civil War—the plantation served as a military hospital and training grounds. Water from a spring attracted more than 3,000 militia during the Revolutionary War. Visitors may explore the cemetery and battlefield on the grounds.

Guided tours are available. Allow 30 minutes minimum. Mon. and Wed.-Sat. 10-4, Sun. 1-5, Apr.-Dec.; Mon. and Thurs.-Sat. 10-4, Sun. 1-5, rest of year. Closed Jan. 1, Easter, Thanksgiving and Dec. 24-25. Admission $6; $5 (ages 62+); $4 (ages 7-18). Combination ticket with the Lee Hall Mansion and the Virginia War Museum $15; $12 (ages 62+); $9 (ages 7-18). Phone (757) 887-1862.

[SAVE] **LEE HALL MANSION** is at 163 Yorktown Rd. The Italianate mansion was built in 1859 by Richard Decauter Lee, a wealthy tobacco planter. Confederate general John Magruder used the house as his headquarters during the Warwick River siege of the 1862 Peninsula Campaign initiated by Union general George McClellan. An exhibit about the campaign is featured.

Allow 30 minutes minimum. Tours are given every 30 minutes Mon. and Wed.-Sat. 10-4, Sun. 1-5, Tues. by appointment, Apr.-Dec.; Mon. and Thurs.-Sat. 10-4, Sun. 1-5, Tues. by appointment, rest of year. Closed Jan. 1, Easter, Thanksgiving and Dec. 24-25. Last tour begins 30 minutes before closing. Fee $6; $5 (ages 62+); $4 (ages 7-18). Combination ticket with the Endview Plantation and the Virginia War Museum $15; $12 (ages 62+); $9 (ages 7-18). MC, VI. Phone (757) 888-3371.

[GEM] **THE MARINERS' MUSEUM** is off I-64 exit 258A, following US 17S to 100 Museum Dr. Dedicated to preserving and interpreting the heritage of the sea, the museum [SAVE] features some 35,000 maritime artifacts, including figureheads, scrimshaw, decorative arts, rare books, maps and navigational instruments. The Defending the Seas gallery explores the history of the U.S. Navy using re-created sections of military ships, including the ready room of an aircraft carrier and the helm section of a submarine.

Other exhibits include the Chesapeake Bay Gallery, the Crabtree Collection of Miniature Ships, the Great Hall of Steam and the USS *Monitor* Center. The museum is in a 550-acre park with a picnic area, a 5-mile walking trail and a fishing lake.

Food is available. Allow 2 hours minimum. Museum Mon.-Sat. 10-5, Sun. noon-5; closed Thanksgiving and Dec. 25. Walking trail daily 10-8:30. Museum tours are given Mon.-Fri. at 11 and 1:30. Tour schedule may vary; phone ahead. Admission (includes the USS *Monitor* Center) $12.50; $11.50 (ages 65+ and military with ID); $7.25 (ages 6-17). AX, MC, VI. Phone (757) 596-2222 or (800) 581-7245. *See color ad p. 318.*

[GEM] USS *Monitor* **Center** is at The Mariners' Museum at 100 Museum Dr. The facility houses such artifacts as the gun turret and the steam engine from the USS *Monitor,* an ironclad warship that came head to head with the CSS *Virginia* during the Battle of Hampton Roads. Videos depict the personal experiences of crew members, while interactive exhibits allow visitors to maneuver a sailing frigate in battle, walk through re-creations of the *Monitor's* living quarters and feel the action of the Civil War skirmish in the Battle Theater.

Allow 1 hour minimum. Mon.-Sat. 10-5, Sun. noon-5; closed Thanksgiving and Dec. 25. Admission included with The Mariners' Museum. AX, MC, VI. Phone (757) 596-2222 or (800) 581-7245.

NEWPORT NEWS PARK is on SR 143, .5 mi. w. of jct. SR 105. The 8,000-acre woodland park includes nature trails and facilities for jogging, fishing, boating, canoeing, paddleboating, bicycling, camping, picnicking, archery, horseback riding and golf.

Confederate gun positions, Union trenches and a dam built to halt Gen. George McClellan's march toward Richmond are visible. The discovery center offers programs and exhibits about the natural features and history of the park. Park daily dawn-dusk. Discovery center Wed.-Sun. 10-6, Memorial Day-Labor Day; Sat.-Sun. 9-5, rest of year. Free. Phone (757) 886-7912 or (800) 203-8322. *See Recreation Chart.*

PENINSULA FINE ARTS CENTER is at 101 Museum Dr. The center offers changing exhibits from Richmond's Virginia Museum of Fine Arts *(see attraction listing p. 296)* as well as art classes, workshops and special events. Hands-On For Kids, an interactive art gallery, is available. Allow 1 hour minimum. Tues.-Sat. 10-5, Sun. 1-5. Admission $5; $4 (students and active military with ID and senior citizens); $3 (ages 4-15). Phone (757) 596-8175.

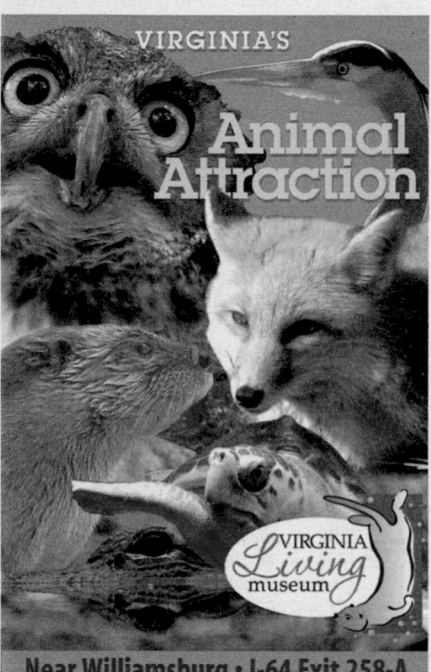

Near Williamsburg • I-64 Exit 258-A
757-595-1900 • www.thevlm.org

U.S. ARMY TRANSPORTATION MUSEUM AT FORT EUSTIS is s.w. of I-64 exit 250A. During World War I Fort Eustis was established at Newport News as a school for Railway Artillery Fire. Today the fort is the home of the U.S. Army Transportation Corps.

The museum displays miniature models and dioramas as well as full-size vehicles, helicopters, winged aircraft, trains and marine vessels. Exhibits pertaining to World War II, Korea and Vietnam include a L-19 airplane, a H-19 helicopter and a Huey helicopter. Tues.-Sun. 9-4:30; closed federal holidays. Free. Phone (757) 878-1115.

VIRGINIA LIVING MUSEUM is at 524 J. Clyde Morris Blvd., off I-64 exit 258A between SR 143 and US 60. Virginia's natural heritage is explored through indoor and outdoor exhibits that highlight regional geography, geology, ecosystems, plants and animals. An elevated boardwalk winds through a 10-acre nature area, offering views of red wolves, bobcats, eagles, deer and coyotes. Interactive discovery centers invite visitors to handle natural science specimens and live animals.

The Coastal Plain Gallery presents marine life from the Chesapeake Bay estuary. Gems, fossils and cave-dwelling creatures are found in the Virginia Underground Gallery. The James River ecosystem is depicted in the Piedmont and Mountains Gallery. Ghost crabs, sharks, flying squirrels and other live nocturnal animals dwell within the Virginia's World of Darkness Gallery.

Allow 2 hours minimum. Daily 9-6, Memorial Day-Labor Day; Mon.-Sat. 9-5, Sun. noon-5, rest of year. Closed Jan. 1, Thanksgiving and Dec. 24-25. Museum admission $13; $10 (ages 3-12). Planetarium $3. Combination ticket $15; $12 (ages 3-12). Under 3 are not permitted at some planetarium shows. DS, MC, VI. Phone (757) 595-1900. *See color ad.*

VIRGINIA WAR MUSEUM is at 9285 Warwick Blvd. in Huntington Park. More than 60,000 artifacts document U.S. military history from 1775 to the present. Exhibits include propaganda posters, uniforms, vehicles, weapons and accouterments. The museum also has educational programs, a military history film collection and a research library. The park facilities also include a picnic area and tennis courts.

Allow 1 hour minimum. Museum open Mon.-Sat. 9-5, Sun. 1-5; closed Jan. 1, Thanksgiving and Dec. 24-25. Library open by appointment. Admission $6; $5 (ages 62+ and military with ID); $4 (ages 7-18). Combination ticket with the Endview Plantation and the Lee Hall Mansion $15; $12 (ages 62+); $9 (ages 7-18). Phone (757) 247-8523.

NORFOLK pop. 234,403

In 1680 the General Assembly of Virginia authorized the purchase of a 50-acre tract along the Elizabeth River for "The Towne of Lower Norfolk County." The seller, Nicholas Wise Jr., received 10,000 pounds of tobacco for his land.

Choral groups, Celtic dancers, color guards, marching bands and military drill teams embody the ◆ Virginia International Tattoo, which takes place in mid-April. In early June the downtown waterfront is bursting with activity during ◆ Harborfest.

Norfolk Convention & Visitors Bureau: 232 E. Main St., Norfolk, VA 23510; phone (757) 664-6620 or (800) 368-3097. *See color ad.*

AMERICAN ROVER **TALL SAILING SHIP CRUISES** departs from the Waterside on Waterside Dr. Guests can work the sails, take a turn at the helm or just relax aboard the 135-foot-long, three-mast topsail schooner as it cruises the historic Hampton Roads harbor. The ship is modeled after the cargo schooners that plied the waters of Chesapeake Bay during the 1800s. Narrated 2-hour harbor and 3-hour naval base cruises are offered. Sunset cruises also are available.

Food is available. Cruises depart daily at 3 and 6:30 p.m. (also Wed.-Sat. at 11:30), late May to early Sept.; daily at 3 (also Fri.-Sun. at 6 p.m.), mid-Apr. to late May and early Sept.-late Oct. Hours may vary; phone ahead. Fares $12-$22; $8-$12 (ages 0-11). MC, VI. Phone (757) 627-7245.

CARRIE B. **HARBOR TOURS** departs from the Waterside on Waterside Dr. Narrated 3-hour cruises aboard the *Carrie B.*—a replica of a double-decked, 19th-century Mississippi riverboat—pass Navy ships

and submarines, commercial freighters and shipyards. Food is available. Cruises depart daily at 11 and 2, Apr. 1 to mid-Oct. Hours may vary; phone ahead. Fare $18; $9 (ages 0-11). Phone (757) 393-4735.

CHRYSLER MUSEUM OF ART is 3 blks. w. at Olney Rd. and W. Virginia Beach Blvd. Comprising 30,000 pieces, the museum's diverse collection includes art treasures from ancient Greece, Rome, the Orient and pre-Columbian America; European and American paintings and sculpture; and decorative arts from the 12th century to the present.

Among artists represented are Mary Cassatt, Edgar Degas, Paul Gauguin, Winslow Homer, Henri Matisse, Pablo Picasso, Jackson Pollock, Pierre Auguste Renoir, Auguste Rodin, Mark Rothko and Andy Warhol. A photography gallery features images of 19th-century pioneers and contemporary artists.

One of the country's most comprehensive glass collections includes more than 8,000 pieces of carved and blown sculptural works. Major pieces by Emile Galle, Rene Lalique and Louis Comfort Tiffany also are on display.

Lectures, films and concerts are scheduled regularly. Food is available. Allow 2 hours minimum. Wed.-Sat. 10-5 (also Wed. 5-9), Sun. 1-5; closed major holidays. Admission $7; $5 (ages 66+ and

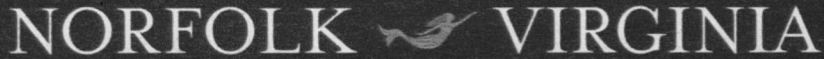

teachers and military with ID); free (ages 0-17 and college students with ID); by donation (on Wed.). Phone (757) 664-6200.

GENERAL DOUGLAS MacARTHUR MEMORIAL is on City Hall Ave. Nine galleries in the former 1847 city hall portray the general's life and military career through displays of gifts, art objects, maps, murals, pictures, models and mementos. MacArthur's trademark military cap, corncob pipe and sunglasses and his 1950 Chrysler Imperial limousine are among the artifacts. The general's books and an extensive collection of correspondence, photographs, scrapbooks and newspapers are housed in a library and archives.

In the main rotunda, the tomb containing MacArthur and his wife is surrounded by inscriptions and flags from the general's military career. A 24-minute documentary is shown continuously. Open Mon.-Sat. 10-5, Sun. 11-5; closed Jan. 1, Thanksgiving and Dec. 25. Donations. Phone (757) 441-2965.

[SAVE] **HERMITAGE FOUNDATION MUSEUM** is at 7637 N. Shore Rd. on the Lafayette River. Contemporary art exhibitions, multimedia art classes and seasonal events are offered at this early 20th-century estate of the Sloane family. Docent-led tours describe the art, architecture and natural features of the estate; visitors may stroll the waterfront and 12-acre gardens.

Picnicking is permitted. Allow 1 hour minimum. Mon.-Tues. and Thurs.-Sat. 10-5, Sun. 1-5; closed Jan. 1, Memorial Day, Thanksgiving and Dec. 24-25 and 31. Guided 30-minute house tours depart on the hour. Last tour begins 1 hour before closing. Admission $5; $3 (college students with ID); $2 (ages 6-18); free (military with ID). Phone (757) 423-2052.

HUNTER HOUSE VICTORIAN MUSEUM is at 240 W. Freemason St. The 1894 Romanesque mansion was built for merchant and banker James Wilson Hunter. The house displays the family's Victorian furnishings, stained-glass windows and a collection of medical memorabilia, including an early 20th-century electrocardiograph machine. Allow 1 hour minimum. Guided tours Wed.-Sat. 10-3:30, Sun. 12:30-3:30, Apr.-Dec.; closed holidays. Fee $5; $4 (ages 61+); $1 (ages 6-18). Phone (757) 623-9814.

MOSES MYERS HOUSE is at Freemason and Bank sts. An example of Federal Period architecture, the 1792 townhouse was built for one of the nation's first millionaires. The restored home contains original furniture as well as artwork by Gilbert Stuart and Thomas Sully. Its furnishings reflect the lifestyle and religious practices of this late 18th-century Jewish merchant family.

Allow 1 hour minimum. Wed.-Sat. 10-4, Sun. 1-4, with extended hours in summer; closed major holidays. Tours are given on the hour. Last tour begins 1 hour before closing. Free. Phone (757) 441-1526.

NAUTICUS is at One Waterside Dr., downtown on the Elizabeth River. The Norfolk waterfront maritime science museum features hands-on exhibits that explore the naval, economic and natural power of the sea. Visitors can feel the texture of a nurse shark's skin, touch a tornado, participate in a naval battle simulation and see digital high-definition films on a giant screen.

On the second floor, the Hampton Roads Naval Museum examines two centuries of naval activity in and around the harbor. The museum manages the day-to-day operations of the Battleship *Wisconsin*, which is berthed at Nauticus. A chronology of the ship's history is presented in "Wisky Walk: 50 Years of Service."

Food is available. Allow 1 hour minimum. Daily 9-5, Memorial Day-Labor Day; Tues.-Sat. 10-5, Sun. noon-5, rest of year. Closed Jan. 1, Thanksgiving and Dec. 24-25. Admission $10.95; $9.95 (ages 55+ and military with ID); $8.50 (ages 4-12). AX, MC, VI. Phone (757) 664-1000 or (800) 664-1080. *See color ad.*

Battleship *Wisconsin* is at Nauticus on Waterside Dr. One of the last and largest battleships built by the U.S. Navy, this vessel was used in World War II, the Korean War and Operation Desert Storm. A self-guiding tour of the main deck includes interactive exhibits depicting the history of the ship and life on

board. Audiotape tours are available. Allow 1 hour minimum. Daily 10-5, Memorial Day-Labor Day; Tues.-Sat. 10-5, Sun. noon-5, rest of year. Closed Jan. 1, Thanksgiving and Dec. 24-25. Admission included with Nauticus. Phone (757) 664-1000 or (800) 664-1080.

NAVAL STATION NORFOLK offers tours that originate at the information center at 9079 Hampton Blvd. The 45-minute bus tours visit sites that include the naval station, piers and the waterfront area. Narrated by U.S. Navy personnel, tours pass by cruisers, destroyers, aircraft carriers and frigates as well as historic homes. The base is home port to more than 100 ships of the Atlantic fleet.

Bus tours depart daily on the half-hour 10-2:30, late May-early Sept.; on the hour 11-2, early Sept. to mid-Oct. and late Mar.-late May; at noon and 1, mid-Oct. to late Dec. and late Feb.-late Mar.; at 1:30, rest of year. Hours may vary; phone ahead. Fee $7.50; $5 (ages 3-11 and 61+); free (military with ID). Phone (757) 444-7955.

NORFOLK BOTANICAL GARDEN is next to Norfolk International Airport at 6700 Azalea Garden Rd. The 155-acre garden includes one of the largest collections of azaleas, camellias, rhododendrons and roses on the East Coast. The climate-controlled Tropical Pavilion houses over 100 varieties of plants from tropical regions around the world. Visitors may tour the gardens by foot on over 12 miles of pathways; guided tours are offered aboard trams and boats.

Food is available. Grounds open daily 9-7, Apr. 1 to mid-Oct.; 9-5, rest of year. Closed Jan. 1, Thanksgiving and Dec. 25. Boat and tram tours are offered daily, Apr. 1 to mid-Oct.; Sat.-Sun., rest of year (weather permitting). Departure times for boat and tram tours vary; phone ahead. Admission $7; $6 (ages 63+ and military with ID); $5 (ages 3-18). Boat tour $4; $2 (ages 3-12). Tram tour free with admission. Phone (757) 441-5830.

THE NORFOLK HISTORY MUSEUM AT THE WILLOUGHBY-BAYLOR HOUSE is at 601 E. Freemason St. This collection of thematic exhibitions focuses on the history of Hampton Roads. Displays include maritime artifacts and decorative arts from the archives of the Chrysler Museum of Art. A Colonial garden with period oyster-shell paving surrounds the restored Willoughby-Baylor House, which was built around 1794. Wed.-Sat. 10-4, Sun. 1-4; closed major holidays. Guided tours are given on the hour. Last tour begins 1 hour before closing. Free. Phone (757) 441-1526.

ST. PAUL'S EPISCOPAL CHURCH is at St. Paul's Blvd. and City Hall Ave. Built in 1739 on the site of a 1641 church known as The Chapel of Ease, the present structure was the only building left after the burning of Norfolk in 1776. A cannonball fired from a British ship is embedded in its wall. The church cemetery contains graves dating from the 17th century. Allow 30 minutes minimum. Tues.-Fri. 10-4;

closed federal holidays. Donations. Phone (757) 627-4353.

SPIRIT OF NORFOLK departs from Otter Berth at the Waterside on Waterside Dr. Two-hour narrated lunch cruises of the Elizabeth River and the Hampton Roads Harbor include the Norfolk Naval Base and local points of interest. Dinner and moonlight cruises also are available. Lunch cruise Tues.-Fri. noon-2, Sat. 11:30-1:30, Sun. 1-3. Boarding is 30 minutes prior to departure. Schedule may vary. Two-hour lunch cruise $35; $17 (ages 0-12). Fares may vary. Reservations are required. AX, DS, MC, VI. Phone (866) 211-3803.

[SAVE] **VIRGINIA ZOO** is at 3500 Granby St. The zoo is home to more than 300 animals in such exhibits as a farmyard, a waterfowl pond, an environment for large mammals and a building housing small mammals. A botanical conservatory is on the grounds. Daily 10-5; closed Jan. 1, Thanksgiving and Dec. 24-25. Admission $7; $6 (ages 62+); $5 (ages 2-11). Phone (757) 624-9937.

PORTSMOUTH (C-3) pop. 100,565, elev. 11′

Because of the location's accessibility to water and a ready supply of timber for shipbuilding, Portsmouth earned a king's grant for settlement in 1620. Ownership alternated between the crown and mariners until it was re-patented in 1716 by Col. William Crawford, presiding justice of Norfolk County. Crawford donated the four corners of High and Court streets for a market, a jail, a courthouse and a church. The restored 1762 Trinity Episcopal Church is the town's oldest building.

Portsmouth was a strategic military objective in early U.S. conflicts. During the Revolution, after seven British vessels had bombarded and set fire to Portsmouth and the surrounding Tidewater areas, Benedict Arnold set up headquarters and the British line of defense on Hospital Point, then called Fort Nelson.

During the early months of the Civil War the Virginia Militia wrested control of the naval shipyard from the Union. After the Federal troops burned and abandoned Portsmouth, the Confederates raised the frigate *Merrimac* and turned it into the world's first ironclad battleship, the CSS *Virginia*.

Beginning as a marine yard in 1767, the Norfolk Naval Shipyard is the largest in the world. Besides the CSS *Virginia*, the shipyard produced the *Chesapeake*, the sister of the *Constitution* and one of the Navy's first warships.

Trolley tours highlight the Olde Towne Historic District, which is distinguished by a fine collection of period homes with a rich diversity of architectural styles. One of 45 sites along the tour, the Hill House, 221 North St., is an 1800s English basement dwelling containing its original furnishings; phone (757) 393-5111 or (757) 393-5327. The Art Deco marquee of the Commodore Theatre at 421 High St. is a local landmark. The theater, which was built in 1945, features first-run films and dining; phone (757) 393-6962.

Ferry service between Norfolk and Portsmouth resumed on the Elizabeth River in the early 1980s; the river was first crossed in 1636 by North America's first pedestrian ferry. The ferry is operated by Hampton Roads Transit; an information station is at North Landing, 6 Crawford Parkway.

Portsmouth Convention and Visitors Bureau: 505 Crawford St., Suite 2, Portsmouth, VA 23704; phone (757) 393-5327 or (800) 767-8782. *See color ad.*

Self-guiding tours: A brochure describing a walking tour of Olde Towne's historic district is available at the visitor center on the waterfront; phone (757) 393-5111.

Shopping areas: The Olde Towne Historic District offers various small specialty shops including antiques stores.

CHILDREN'S MUSEUM OF VIRGINIA is at 221 High St. More than 90 hands-on displays challenge the imagination of both children and adults. Exhibits focus on science, art, music, communications, cultural diversity and technology.

Among the learning stations are the Bubbles area, where children can study refraction, reflection, geometry and surface tension by using wands to create bubbles; The City, which features role-playing; and

Every Body, which teaches about health and physiology. A 64-seat planetarium presents changing shows. Also featured is the Lancaster Train and Toy Collection.

Allow 1 hour minimum. Mon.-Sat. 9-5, Sun. 11-5, Memorial Day-Labor Day; Tues.-Sat. 9-5, Sun. 11-5, rest of year. Closed Jan. 1, Thanksgiving and Dec. 25. Admission $6; $5 (military with ID and senior citizens); free (ages 0-1). Combination ticket (good for 1 visit to each attraction for 90 days) with the Courthouse Galleries, the *Portsmouth* Lightship Museum and the Portsmouth Naval Shipyard Museum $9; $6 (children). Phone (757) 393-5258 or (800) 767-8782.

COURTHOUSE GALLERIES is at High and Court sts. Visitors to the restored 1846 courthouse can view modern cultural works and changing exhibits from international and regional artists. Mon.-Sat. 10-5, Sun. 1-5, Memorial Day-Labor Day; Tues.-Sat. 10-5, Sun. 1-5, rest of year. Closed Jan. 1, Thanksgiving and Dec. 25. Admission $3; free (ages 0-1). Combination ticket (good for 1 visit to each attraction for 90 days) with the Children's Museum of Virginia, the *Portsmouth* Lightship Museum and the Portsmouth Naval Shipyard Museum $9; $6 (children). Phone (757) 393-8543.

PORTSMOUTH LIGHTSHIP MUSEUM adjoins the Portsmouth Naval Shipyard Museum. This former

Coast Guard lightship was one of many used to assist mariners in navigating dangerous shoals at night. With lights attached to their masts, lightships were anchored in strategic locations off the coast. Museum exhibits include artifacts relating to lightship service, photographs, uniforms and Coast Guard equipment as well as realistically appointed officers' and crews' quarters.

Mon.-Sat. 10-5, Sun. 1-5, Memorial Day-Labor Day; Sat. 10-5, Sun. 1-5, Mar. 1-day before Memorial Day and day after Labor Day-Nov. 30. Admission (includes the Portsmouth Naval Shipyard Museum) $3. Combination ticket (good for 1 visit to each attraction for 90 days) with the Children's Museum of Virginia, the Courthouse Galleries and the Portsmouth Naval Shipyard Museum $9; $6 (children). Phone (757) 393-8741.

PORTSMOUTH NAVAL SHIPYARD MUSEUM is at the foot of High St. on the Elizabeth River waterfront. Paintings, models and exhibits trace the history of the U.S. Navy, with emphasis on the Portsmouth-Norfolk area's role. Noteworthy are the models of the CSS *Virginia*, the U.S. *Delaware*, and the nation's first dry-docked ship.

Mon.-Sat. 10-5, Sun. 1-5, Memorial Day-Labor Day; Tues.-Sat. 10-5, Sun. 1-5, rest of year. Closed Jan. 1, Thanksgiving and Dec. 25. Admission (includes the *Portsmouth* Lightship Museum) $3. Combination ticket (good for 1 visit to each attraction for 90 days) with the Children's Museum of Virginia, the Courthouse Galleries and the *Portsmouth* Lightship Museum $9; $6 (children). Phone (757) 393-8591.

SAVE **VIRGINIA SPORTS HALL OF FAME** is at 206 High St. Displays include photographs, plaques, personal equipment and biographical sketches of noted Virginia athletes as well as information about college, Olympic and professional inductees. Interactive exhibits focus on such topics as health in sports, NASCAR, football, soccer, basketball and baseball. Allow 1 hour minimum. Mon.-Sat. 9-5 (also Fri.-Sat. 5-7), Sun. 11-5, Memorial Day-Labor Day; Tues.-Sat. 9-5 (also Fri.-Sat. 5-7), Sun. 11-5, rest of year. Admission $7; $6 (military with ID and senior citizens); free (ages 0-2). MC, VI. Phone (757) 393-8031.

SMITHFIELD (C-3) pop. 6,324

Known internationally for its hams, Smithfield is one of Virginia's best preserved Colonial seaports. The town's Old Courthouse of 1750 (*see attraction listing*), still stands on Main Street not far from the 1752 Smithfield Inn. The downtown historic district features more than 60 buildings that represent Colonial, Federal and Victorian architectural styles.

Smithfield & Isle of Wight Convention and Visitors Bureau: 335 Main St., P.O. Box 37, Smithfield, VA 23431; phone (757) 357-5182 or (800) 365-9339.

Self-guiding tours: Old Town Walking Tour maps detail 65 historic points of interest and are available at the convention and visitors bureau.

Shopping areas: The Smithfield Historic District offers antique shops, art galleries and specialty stores.

FORT BOYKIN HISTORIC PARK is n. on CR 674, then e. on CR 673 to 7410 Fort Boykin Tr. The park preserves the remains of a fort erected in 1623 to protect American colonists. Built in the shape of a seven-pointed star, the fort was used in every major military campaign fought on American soil.

"The Castle" was renamed for Gen. Francis Boykin during the Revolutionary War. On the bluffs above the James River, the park features gardens, views of the Atlantic fleet and a trail with markers. Picnicking is permitted. Open daily 8-dusk (weather permitting). Free. Phone (757) 357-2291.

HISTORIC ST. LUKE'S CHURCH is 2 mi. s.e. on SR 10 at 14477 Benn's Church Blvd. The Old Brick Church is said to be among the oldest church of English foundation standing in America. A brick dated 1632 was found in the original walls and is displayed. Artwork and paneling have been restored. The Gothic church's 1630 English chamber organ is purported to be the oldest of its type in the United States. Confederate soldiers camped in the church cemetery during the Civil War.

Tues.-Sat. 9:30-5, Sun. 1-5, Apr.-Oct.; Tues.-Sat. 9:30-4, Sun. 1-4, Feb.-Mar. and Nov.-Dec. Closed July 4, Thanksgiving and Dec. 24-25 and 31. Last tour begins 30 minutes before closing. Free. Phone (757) 357-3367.

ISLE OF WIGHT MUSEUM is at 103 Main St. The history of the Smithfield ham is among the local exhibits at the museum, which features Civil War memorabilia, American Indian artifacts and archeological items. Tues.-Sat. 10-4, Sun. 1-5; closed Jan. 1, Thanksgiving and Dec. 25. Free. Phone (757) 357-7459.

OLD COURTHOUSE OF 1750 is at 130 Main St. Designed after the Colonial Capitol in Williamsburg, the original part of this building was constructed in 1750. Legal disputes of the day were settled here until 1800. The three-room building was then renovated and expanded into a 10-room, three-story mansion. The main courtroom has been restored to period. Guided tours are available. Allow 30 minutes minimum. Tues.-Sat. 10-4, Sun. 1-4; closed major holidays. Free. Phone (757) 356-9016 or (800) 365-9339.

SURRY (B-3) pop. 262

Capt. William Powell obtained a land grant along the Chippokes Creek in 1619. The property passed to Col. Henry Bishop, who expanded the plantation to its present 1,400 acres. It is said the Chippokes mansion survived the Civil War because its owner supplied liquor to both sides.

BACON'S CASTLE is 7 mi. e. on SR 10 following signs. The 1665 house is one of few surviving examples of Jacobean architecture in America. Its Flemish curvilinear gables, triple chimney stacks and cruciform design are architectural features that are virtually extinct. A 17th-century garden is next to the castle. A 13-minute videotape explains the history of the house, which is furnished with 17th- and 18th-century antiques.

Guided tours are available. Open Tues.-Sat. 10-4, Sun. noon-4, Apr.-Oct.; Sat. 10-4, Sun. noon-4 in Mar. and Nov. Admission $7; $5 (ages 65+); $4 (ages 6-18). Phone (757) 357-5976.

CHIPPOKES PLANTATION STATE PARK is 1.5 mi. e. via SR 10, then 3 mi. n. on CR 634. A working farm since the early 1600s, this estate on the James River retains a plantation atmosphere. Old mulberry trees, remnants of America's attempt to establish a silk industry, grow throughout the park. An interpretive tour road and hiking and bicycle trails explore the grounds. A museum contains antique farm and forestry equipment that help detail the area's history.

Tours of the 1854 mansion are given Fri.-Mon. 1-5, Memorial Day-Labor Day; Sat.-Sun. 1-5, first weekend in Apr.-day before Memorial Day and day after Labor Day-last weekend in Oct. Museum open Wed.-Sun. and holidays 10-5, Memorial Day-Labor Day; Sat.-Sun. 10-5, first weekend in Apr.-day before Memorial Day and day after Labor Day-last weekend in Oct.

Park admission $2 (per private vehicle Mon.-Fri.); $3 (per private vehicle Sat.-Sun.). Mansion $4; $2 (ages 6-12). Museum $3; $2 (ages 6-12). Combination ticket for mansion and museum $6; $3 (ages 6-12). Admission may vary during special events. Phone (757) 294-3625. *See Recreation Chart.*

SMITH'S FORT PLANTATION is across the river from Jamestown on SR 31, about 2 mi. from the ferry. Capt. John Smith built a fort on this site in 1609. The house was built in the 18th century on land that Powhatan gave John Rolfe when Rolfe married Pocahontas. A footpath leads to the original fort site. Tues.-Sat. 10-4, Sun. noon-4, Apr.-Oct.; Sat. 10-4, Sun. noon-4 in Mar. and Nov. Admission $7; $5 (ages 65+); $4 (ages 6-17 and college students with ID). Phone (757) 294-3872.

SURRY NUCLEAR INFORMATION CENTER is 10 mi. e. on SR 10 to SR 650, then 5 mi. n. Innovative displays and hands-on exhibits illuminate the science behind nuclear-generated electricity. Using muscle power, visitors produce electricity with a bicycle generator; measure radioactivity with a Geiger counter; and learn about nuclear power from uranium mining to electricity generation.

Environmental exhibits focus on the James River and area wildlife. Film topics include electrical safety, nuclear technology and the safe storage of nuclear fuel. Mon.-Fri. 9-4; closed holidays. Free. Phone (757) 357-5410.

VIRGINIA BEACH pop. 425,257

The Jamestown settlers first made landfall on this windswept beach at the mouth of Chesapeake Bay on April 26, 1607. The Old Cape Henry Lighthouse, one of the first public works facilities authorized by Congress, was built here 1781-92. Its replacement, the 1881 New Lighthouse, is one of the tallest cast-iron lighthouses in the United States.

Despite beacons and bonfires, hundreds of ships foundered offshore in the 19th century, prompting the construction of four lifesaving stations. In 1891 visitors watched in horror as rescuers struggled to save the crew of the Norwegian bark *Dictator.* The captain's wife and young son were among the dead. The Norwegian Lady, on 25th Street facing the sea, is a 9-foot bronze figurehead commemorating the shipwreck; a twin statue stands in Moss, Norway.

In September the Virginia Beach Neptune Festival features an air show, an arts show, wine tasting and the King Neptune's Grand Parade.

Virginia Beach Visitor Information Center: 2100 Parks Ave., Virginia Beach, VA 23451; phone (757) 437-4882 or (800) 822-3224. *See color ad p. 781.*

BACK BAY NATIONAL WILDLIFE REFUGE is at 4005 Sandpiper Rd. The 9,000-acre wildlife preserve is bordered by the Atlantic Ocean on the east side and by Back Bay on the west. Several trails, some decked, are available for hikers and bicyclists; a tram occasionally runs along the trails. A variety of waterfowl and other wildlife can be seen.

Allow 30 minutes minimum. Refuge open daily half-hour before dawn to half-hour after dusk; some trails are closed seasonally. Visitor contact station open Mon.-Fri. 8-4 (also Sat. 9-4, Apr.-Oct.), Sun. 9-4; closed holidays. Admission (Apr.-Oct.) $5 (per private vehicle); $2 (per person arriving by other means). Admission (rest of year) free. Phone (757) 721-2412.

CAPE HENRY MEMORIAL is within the Fort Story Military Reservation. The stone cross commemorates the Jamestown settlers' landfall in the New World. After exploring the cape, christened after Henry, Prince of Wales, the settlers erected a wooden cross and sailed up the James River. The site is part of Colonial National Historical Park *(see place listing p. 316).*

Two other monuments honor the Battle of the Capes, fought offshore between French and British naval forces in 1781. The British defeat played a key role in Washington's victory at Yorktown a month later. Phone (757) 898-2410.

CHESAPEAKE BAY BRIDGE-TUNNEL carries US 13 across the mouth of Chesapeake Bay from Virginia Beach to Virginia's Eastern Shore. This travel convenience and tourist attraction offers a spectacular panoramic view of the bay. The 17.6-mile bridge-tunnel is unusual in its combination of different types of major structures in one crossing, including bridges, tunnels and four man-made islands.

After its completion in 1964, the bridge-tunnel was named "one of the seven engineering wonders of the modern world." The southernmost island features visitor facilities, a restaurant and a fishing pier. One-way toll $12 per private vehicle. Phone (757) 331-2960.

CHRISTIAN BROADCASTING NETWORK is off I-64 exit 286B, then .5 mi. s.e. on Indian River Rd. to the Studio Headquarters Building. Highlights include tours of the production studios of the Christian Broadcasting Network (CBN) television shows. A collection of paintings and sculptures depicting biblical scenes is displayed. Visitors also can view the taping of "The 700 Club" show. Allow 1 hour minimum. Mon.-Fri. 8-5. Guided tours are given at 10 and 2. Show taping begins at 9 a.m.; seating is at 8:30 a.m. Free. Reservations are required to attend taping. Phone (757) 226-2745.

FRANCIS LAND HOUSE is at 3131 Virginia Beach Blvd. Guides in period dress tell the story of six generations of the Land family and their home, which was built by a wealthy planter around 1810. Nature trails also are on the grounds. Guided tours Tues.-Sat. 9-5, Sun. 11-5. Last tour begins 30 minutes before closing. Fee $4; $3 (ages 62+); $2 (ages 6-12). Phone (757) 431-4000.

GHOSTS OF VIRGINIA BEACH WALKING TOUR departs from the Courtyard by Marriott at 2501 Atlantic Ave. This 90-minute walk explores local haunts along the boardwalk and city streets. Stories depict the exploits of the pirate Blackbeard and the Witch of Pungo, the ghostly sentry at the Old Coast Guard Station and the spirits of Ferry Plantation. Tours depart nightly at 8, Memorial Day-Labor Day and Halloween. Reservations are recommended. Fee $15; $7 (ages 6-12). MC, VI. Phone (757) 498-2127.

LYNNHAVEN HOUSE is n. on Independence Blvd. (SR 225), then e. to 4405 Wishart Rd. The 1725 English-style, brick house is situated on 5 wooded acres that feature a small cemetery, native plant beds and an 18th-century kitchen garden. Tours are conducted by interpreters in period dress. Allow 1 hour, 30 minutes minimum. Guided tours Tues.-Sat. 10-4, Sun. noon-4. Last tour begins 30 minutes before closing. Fee $3; $3 (ages 60+); $2 (ages 6-19 and students with ID). Phone (757) 460-7109.

SAVE **OCEAN BREEZE WATERPARK** is at 849 General Booth Blvd. This Caribbean-themed destination features 16 water slides, a million-gallon wave pool and the Buccaneer Bay water playground. Open daily 10-6 (also Fri.-Sat. 6-8 p.m.), Memorial Day-Labor Day. Hours may vary; phone ahead. Admission $21.95; $15.95 (ages 3-9 and 55+). AX, DS, MC, VI. Phone (757) 422-4444 or (800) 678-9453.

SAVE **THE OLD COAST GUARD STATION MUSEUM** is at 24th St. and Atlantic Ave. Housed in a restored 1903 lifesaving station, the museum traces the history of the United States Life-Saving Service, now known as the Coast Guard. Special exhibits chronicle the shipwrecks that occurred off the Virginia coast. An interactive video monitoring system enables visitors to see the ocean and beach from a tower where early lifesavers were stationed. A touch-screen computer system identifies vessels that come into port.

Mon.-Sat. 10-5, Sun. noon-5, day after Memorial Day-Sept. 30; Tues.-Sat. 10-5, Sun. noon-5, rest of year. Closed Jan. 1, Thanksgiving and Dec. 25 and 31. Admission $4; $3 (ages 61+ and military with ID); $2 (ages 6-18). Phone (757) 422-1587.

DID YOU KNOW

Hampton Roads is home to the world's largest naval station.

VIRGINIA AQUARIUM & MARINE SCI- ENCE CENTER is 1 mi. s. of Rudee Inlet Bridge at 717 General Booth Blvd. Hands-on exhibits, live animal displays and a multitude of aquariums spotlight Virginia's marine environment. The Norfolk Canyon Aquarium features sharks and other large ocean creatures. Other highlights include a harbor seal habitat, a floor-to-ceiling sea turtle aquarium, a sea turtle hatchling laboratory, an artificial reef touch-tank and an IMAX theater presenting 3-D marine science and nature films.

A nature trail skirts the edge of Owls Creek Salt Marsh and includes a river otter habitat, an aviary and other marsh animal exhibits. Whale-watching, dolphin-watching and salt marsh creek boat trips are available; phone for schedule.

Daily 9-7, Memorial Day-Labor Day; 9-5, rest of year. Closed Thanksgiving and Dec. 25. Aquarium admission $11.95; $10.95 (ages 62+); $7.95 (ages 3-11). IMAX film $7.50; $6.75 (ages 62+); $6.50 (ages 3-11). Combination ticket $16.95; $15.95 (ages 62+); $12.95 (ages 3-11). MC, VI. Phone (757) 385-3474 for recorded information, (757) 437-2628 for boat trips, or TTY (757) 427-4305.

WHITE MARSH (B-4) elev. 55'

Archeological evidence dates the earliest settlements of coastal Virginia Indians to 8,000 B.C. By the time the Jamestown colonists arrived in 1607, some 15,000 Powhatans inhabited the Chesapeake Bay region, led by Wahunsunacock, or Chief Powhatan. In 2003, researchers announced the discovery of the lost village of Werowocomoco—the chief's home and the first known capital of Virginia—on a farm near White Marsh. Thousands of artifacts have been found on the 50-acre site; excavations are ongoing.

ABINGDON EPISCOPAL CHURCH is just n. of the Coleman Bridge on US 17. The first house of worship on this site was built about 1655 on land donated by Col. Augustine Warner, maternal grandfather of George Washington. The present brick structure, dating from 1755, is considered one of the largest Colonial churches in Virginia. It was used as a Union hospital during the Civil War, and many soldiers are buried in the surrounding cemetery. Depending on staff availability, tours are offered Mon.-Thurs. 9-2. Hours may vary; phone ahead. Free. Phone (804) 693-3035.

WILLIAMSBURG—

see Virginia's Historic Triangle p. 320.

YORKTOWN—

see Virginia's Historic Triangle p. 326.

Endview Plantation / Newport News Tourism Development Office

This ends listings for the Hampton Roads Area.
The following page resumes the alphabetical listings of cities in Virginia.

HARRISONBURG (F-7)
pop. 40,468, elev. 1,338'

Harrisonburg was named after founder Thomas Harrison, who settled at the crossroads of an American Indian path and the Spotswood Trail about 1739. Supplying lands for municipal expansion, Harrison's two sons followed a tradition set by their father when he donated land to Rockingham County for the erection of a courthouse in 1779.

Gen. Turner Ashby, one of the most respected Confederate officers of the Valley Campaign, fell in battle at Harrisonburg on June 6, 1862, while protecting Gen. Thomas J. "Stonewall" Jackson's approach to Port Republic. Of Ashby, Jackson wrote, "As a partisan officer, I never knew his superior. His daring proverbial, his powers of endurance almost incredible…"

Harrisonburg lies in the heart of the Shenandoah Valley noted for its deep agrarian roots, vistas, many caverns and prime fishing waters. The cave nearest town is Endless Caverns in New Market *(see place listing p. 280)*, 11 miles north on US 11. The Shenandoah River, Lake Shenandoah and Silver Lake are known for their trout and bass fishing. Developed recreational areas of the George Washington and Jefferson National Forests *(see place listing p. 252)* are nearby.

The arts flourish in Harrisonburg. Court Square Theater, on Court Square, opens its doors for various plays, films and concerts; phone (540) 433-9189. The Blue Ridge Theatre Festival is a professional theater company that presents musicals, comedies and dramas at the Court Square Theater; phone (540) 564-1998.

Harrisonburg Tourism and Visitor Services: 212 S. Main St., Harrisonburg, VA 22801; phone (540) 432-8935. *See color ad.*

Self-guiding tours: Brochures and audio CDs describing self-guiding driving tours and walking tours are available from the tourism and visitor services center.

Shopping areas: Valley Mall, off US 33, is anchored by Belk and JCPenney.

VIRGINIA QUILT MUSEUM is off I-81 exit 245, just w. on Port Republic Rd., then 1 mi. n. to 301 S. Main St. (US 11). Antique and contemporary quilts are displayed in the 1856 Warren-Sipe House. Guided tours are available. Allow 30 minutes minimum. Mon. and Thurs.-Sat. 10-4, Sun. 1-4; closed major holidays. Admission $5; $3 (students with ID); $2 (ages 5-11). Phone (540) 433-3818.

RECREATIONAL ACTIVITIES
Skiing and Snowboarding
- **Massanutten** is 3.1 mi. s.e. on E. Market St., 8.8 mi. s.e. on Spotswood Tr. (US 33), then 1.7 mi. n. on Resort Dr. Write P.O. Box 1227, Harrisonburg, VA 22803. Daily 9 a.m.-10 p.m., mid-Dec. to mid.-Mar. Phone (540) 289-4954 or (800) 207-6277.

HERNDON—*see District of Columbia p. 128.*

HOPEWELL (B-2) pop. 22,354, elev. 5'

Hopewell is an outgrowth of old City Point, which was founded in 1613 by Sir Thomas Dale. In 1622 the town was wiped out by an American Indian attack, and not until the Civil War did the community revive. Its deep-water access made City Point a natural supply base, which Gen. Ulysses S. Grant transformed into a vast base of operations for his siege of Petersburg. From June 1864 to April 1865, the busy seaport supplied some 100,000 soldiers and served as the nerve center of the Union war effort.

At the close of the Civil War, City Point returned to being a hamlet. The modern successor to City Point emerged with the building of a dynamite factory by E.I. du Pont on the site of Hopewell Farms in 1911. World War I sparked a boom that evaporated by 1920, with Hopewell again becoming a quiet village. Diversified industry once more has brought prosperity to this seaport.

Merchant's Hope Church, 6 miles southeast on SR 10, then a half-mile west on SR 641, is an example of 1657 Colonial architecture.

Hopewell Visitors Center: 4100 Oaklawn Blvd., Hopewell, VA 23860; phone (804) 541-2461 or (800) 863-8687. *See color ad.*

Self-guiding tours: A brochure detailing a walking tour of the City Point National Historic District is available at the visitor center. A dozen audiovisual exhibits lining the streets depict the 10-month period General Grant occupied the area. The center also offers walking and driving tour brochures of the Crescent Hills area, where some 42 Sears ready-to-assemble homes built 1926-37 can be seen.

CITY POINT EARLY HISTORY MUSEUM AT ST. DENNIS CHAPEL is at 609 Brown Ave. Artifacts and exhibits depict Colonial, Civil War and early 20th-century history of the village of City Point. An archeological exhibit from Kippax Plantation, the home of Pocahontas' granddaughter, is displayed. Allow 30 minutes minimum. Mon.-Sat. 10-4:30, Sun. 1-4:30, Apr.-Oct. Admission $3; free (ages 0-11 with adult). Combination ticket with Weston Manor $7. Phone (804) 458-2564.

GRANT'S HEADQUARTERS AT CITY POINT is at Cedar Ln. and Pecan Ave. Eight miles behind Union lines, City Point served as Gen. Ulysses S. Grant's command post during the siege of Petersburg and was the location of one of the largest supply bases of the Civil War. The unit is part of Petersburg National Battlefield *(see place listing p. 284).*

The visitor contact station is in a 1763 plantation house owned by the Eppes family for about 215 years. During the siege of Petersburg, the home served as headquarters for Quartermaster General Rufus Ingalls.

When Grant arrived on June 15, 1864, he set up a tent on the east lawn. A cabin was later built for Grant, who directed the Union war effort here until April 2, 1865. President Abraham Lincoln visited City Point twice and spent 2 of the last 3 weeks of his life here. Daily 9-5; closed Jan. 1, Thanksgiving and Dec. 25. Free. Phone (804) 458-9504.

WESTON MANOR is on Weston Ln. and 21st Ave. Overlooking the Appomattox River, this 18th-century home has retained much of its original interior woodwork, and its 12 rooms are furnished with period antiques. Union general Philip Sheridan purportedly occupied the house during the Civil War. The grounds and gardens also are open to the public. Guided tours are available. Allow 1 hour minimum. Mon.-Sat. 10-4:30, Sun. 1-4:30, Apr.-Oct. Admission $5; free (ages 0-11 with adult). Combination ticket with City Point Early History Museum at St. Dennis Chapel $7. Phone (804) 458-4682.

HOT SPRINGS (G-6) elev. 2,195'

Hot Springs is in a scenic valley surrounded by forested mountains. The medicinal springs have made it a health resort for generations. Summer and winter sports facilities are available.

Bath County Chamber of Commerce: P.O. Box 718, Hot Springs, VA 24445; phone (540) 839-5409 or (800) 628-8092.

RECREATIONAL ACTIVITIES

Skiing and Snowboarding

- **The Homestead** is off SR 220. Write P.O. Box 2000, Hot Springs, VA 24445. Mon.-Fri. 9-5, Sat.-Sun. 8-5, mid-Dec. to mid-Mar. Phone (540) 839-7721 or (800) 838-1766.

HUME (E-8) elev. 80'

WINERIES

- **Oasis Winery** is off I-66 exit 27, 4.8 mi. s.w. on SR 647, then 10.7 mi. w. on SR 635. Daily 10-5. Guided tours are given daily at 1. Closed Jan. 1, Thanksgiving and Dec. 25. Phone (540) 635-7627.

IRVINGTON (A-3) pop. 673

At the end of the Northern Neck peninsula between the Rappahannock and Potomac rivers, Irvington long has been associated with Tides Inn, a golf and water sports resort that has been open since 1947. Cruises of the Rappahannock and the coves of Carter's Creek are available.

Irvington Chamber of Commerce: P.O. Box 282, Irvington, VA 22480; phone (804) 438-6230 or (804) 438-5447.

HISTORIC CHRIST CHURCH is 2.5 mi. n. on SR 200, then 1 mi. w. on CR 646 following signs. The ornate tomb of Robert "King" Carter, who financed and built the church in 1735, is on the grounds. The brick church stands as it was built, without heat or electricity. Of interest is a marble baptismal font, a three-decker pulpit, a Queen Anne holy table and original communion silver. Carter Reception Center and Museum offers a videotape presentation and guided tours.

Guided tours are available. Church open Mon.-Sat. 10-4, Sun. 2-5, Apr.-Nov.; Mon.-Fri. 8:30-4:30, rest of year. Closed Jan. 1, Thanksgiving, day after Thanksgiving and Dec. 24-25 and 29. Museum open Mon.-Sat. 10-4, Sun. 2-5, Apr.-Nov. Donations. Phone (804) 438-6855.

ISLE OF WIGHT—

see Hampton Roads Area p. 261.

JAMESTOWN—

see Virginia's Historic Triangle p. 316.

JEFFERSON NATIONAL FOREST—

see George Washington and Jefferson National Forests p. 252.

KING WILLIAM elev. 142′

Archeological evidence of the Pamunkey Indians in the area dates back 10,000 years. An English treaty signed by King Charles II in 1677 established articles of peace and a tribal territory that remains in existence today. The Pamunkey Indian Reservation encompasses some 1,200 acres in King William County.

PAMUNKEY INDIAN MUSEUM is on SR 30 past jct. SR 30/SR 633. The museum displays artifacts and exhibits about the Pamunkey Indians, once part of the Powhatan Confederacy. Tues.-Sat. 10-4, Sun. 1-4. Admission $2.50; $1.75 (ages 55+); $1.25 (ages 7-15). Phone (804) 843-4792.

LAKESIDE—*see Richmond p. 301.*

LEESBURG—*see District of Columbia p. 129.*

LEON (F-8) elev. 560′

WINERIES

• **Prince Michel Vineyards** is 10 mi. s. on US 29. Daily 10-5 (also Fri.-Sun. 5-6); closed Jan. 1,

Thanksgiving and Dec. 25. Phone (540) 547-3707 or (800) 800-9463.

LEXINGTON (G-7) pop. 6,867, elev. 1,100′

Four American generals—George Washington, Robert E. Lee, Thomas J. "Stonewall" Jackson and George C. Marshall—have played major roles in historic Lexington. The two Confederate heroes had homes and are buried in the historic town.

Restored downtown includes the Alexander-Withrow House, one of the few buildings that survived the 1796 fire that raged through town. Lawyers' Row and Court House Square were laid out as part of the original town in 1778.

Just beyond Lexington, the Theater at Lime Kiln presents plays and concerts from Memorial Day through Labor Day. The Virginia Horse Center, off SR 39, offers horse shows, workshops and seminars.

Of scenic interest is rugged Goshen Pass Natural Area, 15 miles northwest on SR 39. Here the southwest face of Little North Mountain drops sharply from 3,600 feet to the Maury River, about 1,800 feet below. Rhododendrons, mountain laurels, pines and dogwoods grow profusely along the river and the surrounding mountains. Traversed by stagecoaches in the 19th century, Goshen Pass is enjoyed today for the recreational activities it provides.

A 7-mile stretch of railbed between Lexington and Buena Vista has been developed into the Chessie Nature Trail. The trail is designed for pedestrians who enjoy hiking, bird-watching, running, fishing, cross-country skiing and picnicking. Vehicles, including bicycles, are not allowed on the trail.

Lexington Visitor Center: 106 E. Washington St., Lexington, VA 24450; phone (540) 463-3777 or (877) 453-9822.

Self-guiding tours: A brochure with information about several walking tours is available at the visitor center.

SAVE **"STONEWALL" JACKSON HOUSE** is at 8 E. Washington St. This was the home of Gen. Thomas J. "Stonewall" Jackson from 1859 until his death in 1863, a result of wounds received at the Battle of Chancellorsville. The house and garden are restored and furnished with many original pieces. Jackson's personal effects also are exhibited. Guided tours are available. Open Mon.-Sat. 9-5, Sun. 1-5; closed Jan. 1, Easter, Thanksgiving and Dec. 25. Last tour begins 30 minutes before closing. Admission $6; $3 (ages 6-17). MC, VI. Phone (540) 463-2552.

VIRGINIA MILITARY INSTITUTE is off Main St. Founded in 1839, this was the nation's first state-supported military college. On the National Register of Historic Districts, VMI is noted for its military and academic programs; the Barracks is a National Historic Landmark. Alumni include Gen. George C. Marshall, Adm. Richard E. Byrd and Lt. Gen. Lewis B. "Chesty" Puller.

Allow 1 hour minimum. Daily 9-5; closed Jan. 1-4, week of Thanksgiving and Dec. 20-31. Guided post tours (departing from the VMI Museum) are given Mon.-Fri. at 11:15 and 3:15. No tours are given during exam periods. Free. Phone (540) 464-7334.

George C. Marshall Museum and Library is at the w. end of the Virginia Military Institute parade ground. The building houses the World War II chief of staff's papers and material relating to U.S. military and diplomatic history through much of the 20th century.

An electric map with narration traces the developments of World War II. Displayed are the Nobel Peace Prize awarded Marshall in 1953 and the Academy Award presented to Gen. Frank McCarthy, the VMI graduate who produced the movie "Patton." Daily 9-5; closed Jan. 1, Thanksgiving and Dec. 25. Admission $3; $2 (ages 63+); free (ages 0-17). Phone (540) 463-7103.

Jackson Memorial Hall is off Main St. on Letcher Ave. at the Virginia Military Institute. The cadet assembly hall is dominated by an oil painting depicting the VMI cadet charge at the Battle of New Market. It was painted by Benjamin West Clinedinst, class of 1880. The flags around the hall represent the 26 states in the Union when VMI was founded Nov. 11, 1839. Allow 30 minutes minimum. Daily 9-5; closed Jan. 1, Thanksgiving and Dec. 24-31. Free. Phone (540) 464-7232.

VMI Museum is in Jackson Memorial Hall, off Main St. on Letcher Ave. at the Virginia Military Institute. One of the state's oldest museums, it houses items illustrating the history and traditions of the nation's first state military college. Gen. Thomas J. "Stonewall" Jackson's uniform, his bullet-pierced raincoat from Chancellorsville, and the mounted hide of his horse, Little Sorrel, are displayed.

A replica of a barracks room depicts cadet life. Visitors also can view the Robert Rayburn Civil War art collection. Allow 1 hour minimum. Daily 9-9; closed Thanksgiving and Dec. 24-Jan. 1. Free. Phone (540) 464-7232.

WASHINGTON AND LEE UNIVERSITY is at 204 W. Jefferson St. A white colonnaded building houses the college, which dates from the 1749 founding of Augusta Academy. Later known as Liberty Hall, the academy was endowed by George Washington and renamed Washington Academy in 1796. Gen. Robert E. Lee was president of the college from the end of the Civil War until his death in 1870, after which the university took its present name. Phone (540) 458-8400.

Lee Chapel & Museum is on the historic Front Campus of Washington and Lee University. Built in 1867 under Lee's supervision, the Victorian-style chapel now stands as a shrine to the general. It preserves Lee's office much as he left it on Sept. 28, 1870, only 2 weeks before his death. Edward Valentine's recumbent statue of Lee is at the far end of the chapel. Lee and his family are buried beneath the chapel on the museum level. The museum traces the history of the university, focusing on the heritage of its namesakes. The Washington-Custis-Lee Collection of portraits includes Charles Willson Peale's portrait of Washington.

Allow 1 hour minimum. Mon.-Sat. 9-5, Sun. 1-5, Apr.-Oct.; Mon.-Sat. 9-4, Sun. 1-4, rest of year. Closed Thanksgiving, day after Thanksgiving, Dec. 24-Jan. 1 and school holidays. Donations. Phone (540) 458-8768.

LORTON—*see District of Columbia p. 130.*

LOVINGSTON (G-8) elev. 745'

Lovingston, the county seat for Nelson County, offers a historic district featuring what is said to be the oldest courthouse in continuous use in the state. Surrounded by oak-hickory forests and prairie grass, a 5.3-mile hiking trail at Fortune's Cove Preserve, 1627 Fortune's Cove Ln., affords opportunities for wildlife viewing. Black bear, bobcat, white-tailed deer, quail and blue-winged warblers frequent this 755-acre expanse.

Nelson County Convention & Visitors Bureau: 8519 Thomas Nelson Hwy., P.O. Box 636, Lovingston, VA 22949; phone (800) 282-8223.

WINERIES

- **Mountain Cove Vineyards & Wine Garden** is .6 mi. n. on Thomas Nelson Hwy. (US 29), 1.6 mi. s.w. on Mountain Cove Rd., then 1.4 mi. n. to 1362 Fortunes Cove Ln. Wed.-Sun. noon-6, Mar.-Oct.; 2-5, rest of year. Closed Thanksgiving and Dec. 25. Phone (434) 263-5392.

DID YOU KNOW

More than half of all Civil War battles were fought in Virginia.

LURAY (F-8) pop. 4,871, elev. 819′

Luray was settled by a group of German-Swiss at the base of Massanutten Mountain along the South Fork of the Shenandoah River. Laid out in 1812, Luray was close enough to Virginia's untamed wilderness that some of its early homes contained thick stone forts within their walls to guard against the constant threat of American Indian attacks. These forts, usually in the basement, were kept supplied with firewood and food and often included a tunnel that connected with a well.

Hiking, fishing and boating can be enjoyed in developed recreational areas of George Washington and Jefferson National Forests *(see place listing p. 252 and the AAA Mideastern CampBook)* and in Shenandoah National Park *(see place listing p. 305)*, to the east.

Page County Chamber of Commerce: 46 E. Main St., Luray, VA 22835; phone (540) 743-3915.

LURAY CAVERNS is 1 mi. w. on US 211 and 340 bypass. The massive chambers, 30 to 140 feet high, contain a variety of formations all in beautiful natural color. In the Cathedral Room is the Stalacpipe Organ, which is purported to be the world's largest musical instrument. It uses specially tuned stalactites to produce music of symphonic quality. Lighted and paved walkways lead visitors past towering stone columns and crystal pools.

Guided 1-hour tours depart every 20 minutes daily 9-7, June 15-Labor Day; daily 9-6, Apr.1-June 14 and day after Labor Day-Oct. 31; Mon.-Fri. 9-4, Sat.-Sun. 9-5, rest of year. Fee (includes Car and Carriage Caravan) $19; $16 (ages 62+); $9 (ages 6-12). AX, DS, MC, VI. Phone (540) 743-6551. *See color ad.*

Car and Carriage Caravan is 1 mi. w. on US 211 and 340 bypass near the entrance to Luray Caverns. The progress of transportation is depicted through carriage and automobile exhibits. Among the more than 140 items on display are an 1892 Benz, a 1904 Cadillac, a 1935 Hispano-Suiza and many early Ford models. Daily 9-8:30, June 15-Labor Day; daily 9-7:30, Apr. 1-June 14 and day after Labor Day-Oct. 31; Mon.-Fri. 9-5:30, Sat.-Sun. 9-6:30, rest of year. Hours may vary; phone ahead. Admission included with Luray Caverns. Phone (540) 743-6551.

The Garden Maze is at 970 US 211W at Luray Caverns. Visitors must navigate a half-mile path through 8-foot-high arborvitae trees by solving riddles along the way. The 1-acre ornamental garden features misting fog, fountains and a cave. Allow 30 minutes minimum. Daily 9:30-7, June 15-Labor Day; daily 9:30-6, Apr. 1-June 14 and day after Labor Day-Oct. 31; Mon.-Fri. 9:30-4, Sat.-Sun. 9:30-5, rest of year. Admission $6; $5 (ages 7-13). AX, DS, MC, VI. Phone (540) 843-0769.

Singing Tower is 1 mi. w. on US 211 at the entrance to Luray Caverns. Situated in a parklike setting, the Belle Brown Northcott Memorial is built of

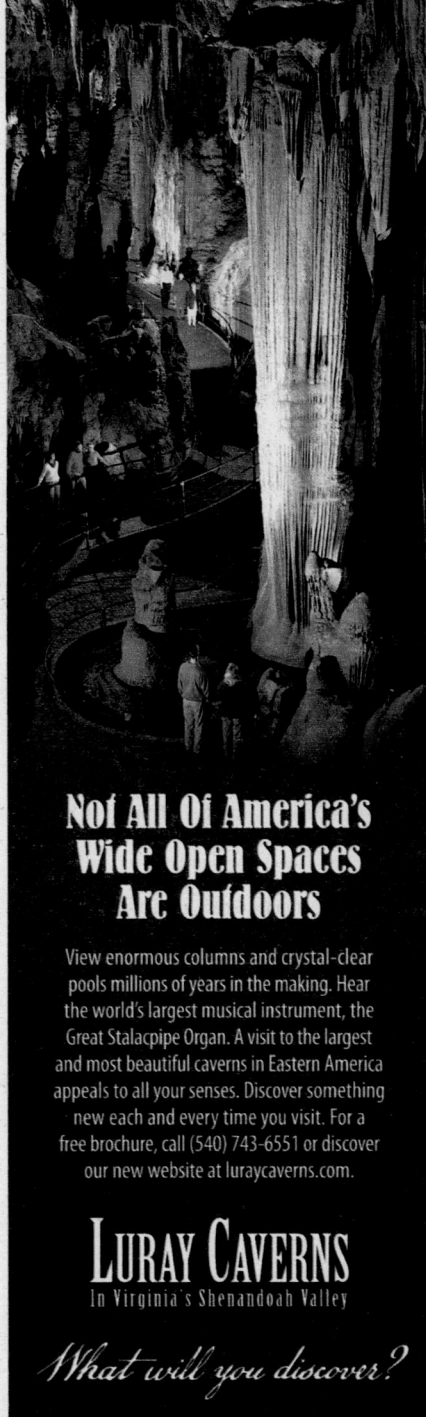

sandstone from Massanutten Mountain. The 117-foot carillon, 25 feet square at the base, contains 47 bells; the largest weighs 7,640 pounds, the smallest 12.5 pounds. Recitals, which last about 45 minutes, are given Tues., Thurs. and Sat.-Sun. at 8 p.m., June-Aug.; Sat.-Sun. at 2, Apr.-May and Sept.-Oct. Free. Phone (540) 743-6551.

RECREATIONAL ACTIVITIES

Canoeing

- **Shenandoah River Outfitters Inc.** is at 6502 S. Page Valley Rd., Luray, VA 22835. Daily 8-5, Apr.-Nov. Phone (540) 743-4159 or (800) 622-6632.

LYNCHBURG (H-7) pop. 65,269, elev. 517′

A ferry established by John Lynch in 1757 was the nucleus of the original settlement that became Lynchburg, laid out on 45 acres of Lynch's land. He built the region's first tobacco warehouse in 1785.

During the Civil War the city was a supply base for the Confederate Army. It was for the possession of these stores that the Battle of Lynchburg was fought June 18, 1864, when Union general David Hunter made an unsuccessful attempt to capture the city from Confederates commanded by Gen. Jubal A. Early. Throughout the Civil War Lynchburg served as a major hospital center.

Lynchburg has several 19th- and early 20th-century residential districts. Five hills in the "City of Seven Hills" are National Register Historic Districts. Court House Hill is home of Lynchburg Museum at the Old Courthouse *(see attraction listing)* and is named after the first courthouse built in 1813. Diamond and Garland hills represent the wealth of the tobacco era with magnificent residences of wealthy citizens. Federal Hill was Lynchburg's first suburb. On Daniel's Hill, Cabell Street is reminiscent of the Victorian elegance in the 1890s.

Lynchburg salutes the James River in mid-June with the Bateau Festival. It kicks off an 8-day trek in which flat-bottomed boats, once used to transport tobacco and other goods, pole their way from Lynchburg to Richmond.

Lynchburg Regional Convention and Visitors Bureau: 216 Twelfth St., Bateau Landing, Lynchburg, VA 24504; phone (434) 847-1811 or (800) 732-5821.

Self-guiding tours: Brochures outlining walking and driving tours of Lynchburg's historic areas are available from the visitors bureau.

(SAVE) **AMAZEMENT SQUARE—THE RIGHTMIRE CHILDREN'S MUSEUM** is at 27 Ninth St. This dynamic learning environment encourages children to play, learn and solve problems through four floors of hands-on exhibits. Visitors can explore global and regional topics, the arts and humanities, history, culture, science, health and technology.

Allow 1 hour minimum. Tues.-Sat. 10-5, Sun.-Mon. 1-5, Memorial Day-Labor Day; Tues.-Sat. 10-5, Sun. 1-5, rest of year. Closed Jan. 1, Easter, July 4, Thanksgiving and Dec. 25. Admission $7; $6 (ages 60+); free (ages 0-1). MC, VI. Phone (434) 845-1888.

THE LEGACY MUSEUM OF AFRICAN-AMERICAN HISTORY is at 403 Monroe St. The galleries feature rotating exhibits targeting the history and culture of local African-Americans in central Virginia. Guided tours are available. Picnicking is permitted. Allow 30 minutes minimum. Wed.-Sat. noon-4, Sun. 2-4; closed major holidays. Admission $5; $3 (ages 7-17 and senior citizens). Phone (434) 845-3455.

LYNCHBURG MUSEUM AT THE OLD COURTHOUSE is at 901 Court St. Exhibits detail the history of Lynchburg. Built in 1855, the Greek Revival court building houses displays of Monacan Indian artifacts, Quaker relics and Civil War memorabilia. Exhibits also chronicle Lynchburg's transition from a tobacco trading center in the early 1800s to a modern industrial city. Allow 30 minutes minimum. Mon.-Sat. 10-4, Sun. noon-4; closed Jan. 1, Thanksgiving and Dec. 24-25. Admission $4; free (ages 0-6). Phone (434) 455-6226.

MAIER MUSEUM OF ART is off Rivermont Ave. at 1 Quinlan St. on the campus of Randolph College. The museum's permanent collection focuses on American paintings of the 19th and 20th centuries. The galleries display works by such artists as Thomas Hart Benton, Mary Cassatt, Childe Hassam, Georgia O'Keeffe and Jamie Wyeth. Changing exhibits also are displayed. Allow 30 minutes minimum. Tues.-Sun. 1-5, late Aug.-late May; Wed.-Sun. 1-4, rest of year. Closed holidays and mid- to late Dec. Free. Phone (434) 947-8136.

OLD CITY CEMETERY is at 401 Taylor St. Established in 1806, the 26-acre "grave garden" is noted for its antique rose and daffodil collections and an arboretum of more than 100 tree varieties. The Confederate section contains the graves of 2,200 Civil War soldiers. Five small museums on the grounds interpret local history and funereal customs. The Pest House Medical Museum stands on the site of Lynchburg's first hospital and house of quarantine.

Guided cemetery tours are available by appointment. Brochures for self-guiding tours are available at the gate. Grounds open daily dawn-dusk (weather permitting). Visitor center open daily 11-3, Mar.-Oct.; Mon.-Sat. 11-3, rest of year. Cemetery free. Guided tour $5. Phone (434) 847-1465.

POINT OF HONOR is at 112 Cabell St. The 1815 mansion was the home of one of Lynchburg's most prominent citizens, Dr. George Cabell Sr., physician and friend to Patrick Henry. The distinctive octagon-bay facade overlooks the James River. The dwelling's interior woodwork, furnishings and other appointments have been restored to their Federal period appearance. Re-created kitchen and stable buildings provide glimpses into early 19th-century lifestyles.

Allow 30 minutes minimum. Guided tours Mon.-Sat. 10-4, Sun. noon-4; closed Jan. 1, Thanksgiving and Dec. 24-25. Fee $6; $5 (ages 60+); $2 (ages 6-16). Phone (434) 455-6226 or (434) 847-1867.

THOMAS JEFFERSON'S POPLAR FOREST is off US 460, n. on SR 811, then e. on SR 661. The brick octagonal villa, one of only two homes that Jefferson designed for himself, was his retreat when he visited his working plantations in Bedford County. The Palladian-style house is undergoing restoration. Displays and guided 40-minute tours explain the restoration process as well as plantation life. Guided tours Wed.-Mon. 10-4, Apr.-Nov.; closed Thanksgiving. Fee $9; $7.50 (ages 61+); $1 (ages 6-16). Phone (434) 525-1806.

MACHIPONGO (B-5) elev. 40′

This barrier island on the Atlantic Ocean is part of Virginia's Eastern Shore, famed for its natural beauty, abundant wildlife, bountiful fishing and rural charm.

EASTERN SHORE OF VIRGINIA BARRIER ISLANDS VISITOR CENTER is at 7295 Young St. Exhibits and artifacts depict significant events, landmarks and people who played a role in the history of the state's barrier islands. The museum is in a restored 19th-century building on the Historic Almshouse Farm, which was established in 1803 to care for the destitute. Guided tours are available. Allow 30 minutes minimum. Tues.-Sat. 10-4, Sun. 1-5; closed holidays. Admission $4; $3 (ages 60+); $2 (ages 6-17 and students with ID). Phone (757) 678-5550.

MANASSAS — see District of Columbia p. 130.

MANASSAS NATIONAL BATTLEFIELD PARK —
see District of Columbia p. 131.

MARION (I-4) pop. 6,349

Marion was named for Gen. Francis Marion, known as the "Swamp Fox" during the Revolution because of the guerilla warfare tactics he used against the British in South Carolina. A popular vacation base, Marion is surrounded by the George Washington and Jefferson National Forests (see place listing p. 252) and is near Hungry Mother State Park (see Recreation Chart and the AAA Mideastern CampBook).

Chamber of Commerce of Smyth County: 214 W. Main St., P.O. Box 924, Marion, VA 24354; phone (276) 783-3161.

STATE TROUT CULTURE STATION is 2 mi. s. on SR 16. Trout hatched and raised in the State Fish Hatchery stock waterways throughout Virginia. Guided tours are available by appointment. Open daily 8-3:30. Free. Phone (276) 782-9314.

MARKHAM (E-8)

WINERIES

- **Naked Mountain Vineyard** is off I-66 exit 18, then 1.5 mi. n. on Leeds Manor Rd. Daily 11-5. Phone (540) 364-1609.

MARTINSVILLE (I-6) pop. 15,416

> **MARTINSVILLE SPEEDWAY** is 1 mi. n. of jct. US 220/58 bypass and US 220 Bus. Rte. at 340 Speedway Rd. This is the only original NASCAR-sanctioned track still hosting NEXTEL Cup events—at slightly more than a half-mile in length, the track is the circuit's shortest. Events taking place at Martinsville include the Modified 300, Bailey's 300, Kroger 200 and Subway 500. The race season extends from March to late Oct. The speedway is open to visitors Mon.-Fri. 9-5. Phone (877) 722-3849 for tickets and information.

© International Speedway Corporation
AAA is the Official Motor Club of Martinsville Speedway.

VIRGINIA MUSEUM OF NATURAL HISTORY is at 21 Starling Ave. This state-of-the-art facility offers walk-through exhibits and hands-on experiences relating to the natural world and Virginia's ancient past. A collection of fossils includes a towering allosaurus skeleton and re-creations of important geologic sites. A behind-the-scenes look at research projects and objects in storage lets visitors see how a natural history museum works.

Picnicking is permitted. Food is available. Allow 2 hours minimum. Mon.-Sat. 9-5:30, Sun. noon-5:30; closed Jan. 1, Thanksgiving and Dec. 25. Admission $7; $6 (college students with ID and senior citizens); $5 (ages 3-18). AX, DS, MC, VI. Phone (276) 666-8600.

MAX MEADOWS (H-5) pop. 512, elev. 2,028′

[SAVE] **FORT CHISWELL ANIMAL PARK** is 1.5 mi. s. on US 52S off I-81 exit 80, then just e. at 569 Red Hollow Rd. The 45-acre park is home to creatures from Africa, Asia, Australia, Europe, North America and South America. A petting zoo and narrated bus tours allow visitors to learn about different species of animals.

Food is available. Allow 1 hour, 30 minutes minimum. Daily 10-4 (also Fri.-Sun. 4-6), Memorial Day-Labor Day; Fri.-Sun. 10-6, Apr. 1-day before Memorial Day and day after Labor Day-Nov. 30. Guided bus tours depart on the hour beginning at 11. Last tour begins 1 hour before closing. Admission $10; $8 (ages 3-12). MC, VI. Phone (276) 637-6754.

WINERIES

- **West Wind Farm Vineyard & Winery** is off I-81 exit 80, then 3.8 mi. s. on US 52 to 2228 Fort Chiswell Rd. Mon.-Sat. 11-6, Sun. 1-6. Phone (276) 699-2020.

McDOWELL (F-6) elev. 2,107'

On the eastern edge of McDowell, on US 250, a sign and monument identify McDowell Battlefield, where Gen. Thomas J. "Stonewall" Jackson turned back a Federal attack. At Sitlington's Hill the second battle and first victory of Jackson's Valley Campaign took place. Nearby McDowell Presbyterian Church was used as a hospital during the war; soldiers are buried in the cemetery.

Highland County Chamber of Commerce: P.O. Box 223, Monterey, VA 24465; phone (540) 468-2550.

McLEAN—*see District of Columbia p. 131.*

MIDDLETOWN (E-8) pop. 1,015, elev. 660'

The Battle of Cedar Creek took place October 19, 1864, when Confederate general Jubal Early executed a surprise attack on Gen. Philip Sheridan's army encamped on Cedar Creek, south of Middletown. Sheridan was at Winchester when the firing began, and he raced to the scene of the battle. Meeting the retreating soldiers about a mile north of Middletown, he not only halted the flight of his troops but also galvanized them to attack and defeat Early.

The Wayside Theater, which gives matinee performances Wednesday and Saturday and evening performances Wednesday through Friday, is one of the oldest professional theaters in Virginia. The theater is well-known for comedies, musicals and farces; phone (540) 869-1776 for schedules.

For those interested in one of America's favorite snack foods, visit the Route 11 Potato Chip Factory at 7815 Main St. Purportedly the smallest chip factory in the country, it has a viewing area where visitors can watch production of the handmade chips. The best viewing is before 11 a.m.; phone (540) 869-0104.

[SAVE] **BELLE GROVE PLANTATION** is 1 mi. s. on US 11, then .5 mi. w. on Belle Grove Rd. Maj. Isaac Hite Jr. acquired the 483-acre parcel in 1783, the same year he married Nelly Conway Madison, sister of the future president. During the Civil War, Union troops repeatedly occupied the estate, which was the focus of the Battle of Cedar Creek in October 1864. On the grounds of the limestone manor house are gardens, orchards, an overseer's house, a slave cemetery and original outbuildings.

Allow 2 hours minimum. Grounds Mon.-Sat. 10-4, Sun. 1-5, Mar.-Dec. Guided house tours Mon.-Sat. 10:15-3:15, Sun. 1:15-4:15, Apr.-Oct.; Sat. 10:15-3:15, Sun. 1:15-4:15, in Nov. Tour schedule may vary; phone ahead. Admission $8; $7 (ages 65+); $4 (ages 6-12). Admission may vary during special events. AX, DS, MC, VI. Phone (540) 869-2028.

CEDAR CREEK BATTLEFIELD VISITORS CENTER is at 8437 Valley Pike. Overlooking the Civil War battlefield, the center offers a brief description of the Battle of Cedar Creek via interpretive displays, films and a driving tour. Thousands of participants gather for the annual battle re-enactment, which takes place the third weekend in October. Open Mon.-Sat. 10-4, Sun. 1-4, Apr.-Oct. Free. Phone (540) 869-2064.

MILLWOOD (E-8) elev. 520'

Millwood lies near the Shenandoah River. Descendants of Tidewater aristocrat Robert "King" Carter built several large estates in and around Millwood in the late 18th century. One of these wealthy settlers, Nathaniel Burwell, built Carter Hall 1790-98. Among Carter Hall's guests were Gen. Thomas J. "Stonewall" Jackson and Edmund Randolph.

Before completing Carter Hall, Burwell had become partners with Gen. Daniel Morgan in building a mill. Morgan, who had been one of the Revolutionary War's most brilliant leaders, supervised the construction of the mill and its first years of operation. The Burwell-Morgan Mill remained a vital outlet for its wheat-growing neighbors until 1953, surviving not only the Civil War but also several changes of ownership.

BURWELL-MORGAN MILL is off SR 255 at 15 Tannery Ln. Built in 1785, the mill once processed 60,000 bushels of wheat per year. The restored works include an interior waterwheel that powers the grinding of corn into meal. The process is demonstrated on Saturdays. Picnicking is permitted. Open Thurs.-Sat. 10-5, Sun. noon-5, Apr.-Oct. Donations. Phone (540) 837-1799 or (540) 955-2600.

HISTORIC LONG BRANCH is off SR 624 at 830 Long Branch Ln. This 1805 Greek revival mansion sits on 400 rolling acres. Situated in the midst of Virginia hunt country, the estate once was owned by Lord Fairfax and Robert "King" Carter. Visitors may take a self-guiding tour of the Sheila MacQueen Gardens or picnic on the grounds; the house is open on weekends for guided tours. A stable on the estate is home to retired Thoroughbreds and saddle horses.

Grounds open daily 8-6. Guided mansion tours are offered Sat.-Sun. noon-4, Apr.-Oct. Grounds free. Mansion tour $8; $6 (ages 65+); $4 (ages 0-11). Phone (540) 837-1856 or (888) 558-5567.

MINERAL (G-9) pop. 424, elev. 463'

Originally known as Tollersville, the town of Mineral was renamed in 1890 after deposits of copper, gold, mica and sulfur were discovered in the area.

NORTH ANNA NUCLEAR INFORMATION CENTER is 2.5 mi. e. on CR 618, then 6.3 mi. n. on CR 700. Maintained by Dominion Virginia Power, the center offers displays about the development and operation of nuclear power plants and the generation of electricity. Films, slide shows and lectures complement the displays. Picnicking is permitted.

Allow 30 minutes minimum. Guided information center tours Mon.-Fri. 9-4; closed major holidays. Free. Phone (804) 771-3200.

MONTICELLO—

see Charlottesville p. 240.

MONTPELIER STATION (F-8) elev. 492'

JAMES MADISON'S MONTPELIER is at 11407 Constitution Hwy. (SR 20). Owned by the Madison family 1723-1844, the property was the lifelong home of James Madison, fourth president of the United States and Father of the Constitution. The 2,700-acre estate includes more than 130 buildings, extensive gardens and forests and a steeplechase course. Madison and his wife, Dolley—America's "first" First Lady—are buried in the family cemetery.

A visitor center houses a theater, which presents an orientation film, and the Joe and Marge Grills Gallery. Next door, the William duPont Gallery pays tribute to William and Annie duPont, Montpelier's inhabitants during most of the 20th century. Personal mementos, photographs and trophies belonging to the duPonts—who established a successful Thoroughbred training farm—are displayed. Also on the grounds is the Gilmore Cabin, open on weekends from April through October. The restored structure was built in 1872 by George Gilmore, a freed Montpelier slave.

The mansion is undergoing an extensive restoration that will return the home to its original 1820s appearance. Behind-the-scenes tours and special exhibits invite visitors to witness the work in progress. Archeological excavations continue to uncover details of plantation life. Montpelier exhibits include items belonging to the Madisons, historic room recreations and a collection of Madison furniture.

Note: The mansion will remain open during restoration, which is scheduled for completion in 2009. Guided tours are available. Picnicking is permitted. Open daily 9:30-5:30, Apr.-Oct.; 9:30-4:30, rest of year. Closed Thanksgiving and Dec. 25. Admission $12; $6 (ages 6-14). MC, VI. Phone (540) 672-2728.

MOUNT ROGERS NATIONAL RECREATION AREA (I-4)

The visitor center for the Mount Rogers National Recreation Area, in the highlands of southwestern Virginia, is at 3714 SR 16. The 200,000-acre recreation area is part of George Washington and Jefferson National Forests *(see place listing p. 252).* Mount Rogers is the highest point in the state at 5,729 feet; a trail to the top begins at Grindstone Campground and Grayson Highlands State Park *(see Recreation Chart and the AAA Mideastern CampBook).*

Broad mountain meadows and forests of spruce, fir and northern hardwood provide settings for seven developed campgrounds, six of which are open April through October while the other one is open year-round.

A network of trails includes a 60-mile segment of the Appalachian Trail and others suitable for cross-country skiing. Three primitive horse camps adjoin the Virginia Highlands Horse Trail. The area offers good trout fishing and deer and turkey hunting.

The visitor center is open Mon.-Fri. 8-4:30, Sat. 10-4, Memorial Day to mid-Oct.; Mon.-Fri. 8-4:30, rest of year. Phone (276) 783-5196 or (800) 628-7202. *See Recreation Chart.*

MOUNT SIDNEY (F-7) elev. 1,309'

AUGUSTA MILITARY ACADEMY ALUMNI HOUSE/MUSEUM is 1.7 mi. s.w. on Lee Hwy. in Fort Defiance The museum depicts cadet life and the history of the school that operated 1874-1984. Chronological exhibits are presented in the restored 1870s Roller House, which features Victorian furnishings, a cadet barracks and classroom. Exhibits contain military uniforms, artifacts and memorabilia. Allow 30 minutes minimum. Tues.-Sun. 10-4; closed Jan. 1, Thanksgiving and Dec. 24-25. Free. Phone (540) 248-3007.

MOUNT SOLON (F-7) elev. 1,322'

NATURAL CHIMNEYS REGIONAL PARK is .5 mi. n.w. on SR 731, following signs. The park comprises seven natural limestone towers. Nature trails, a swimming pool, campgrounds and picnic areas are available. The park hosts an annual jousting tournament in August and is home to the National Jousting Hall of Fame.

Sun.-Wed. 9-5, Thurs. and Sat. 9-6, Fri. 9-8, May 31-Aug. 31; daily 9-5, mid-Apr. through May 30 and Sept.-Oct.; Sat.-Sun. 9-5, Mar. 1 to mid-Apr.; by appointment rest of year. Admission $8 (per private vehicle); $4 (per person arriving by other means). Swimming pool $3; $2.75 (ages 4-12). Phone (540) 350-2510 or (888) 430-2267. *See Recreation Chart.*

MOUNT VERNON—

see District of Columbia p. 132.

NATURAL BRIDGE (G-6) elev. 1,078'

Historic Natural Bridge, in the heart of the Blue Ridge Mountains, is home to the "rock bridge" (the county's namesake) and adjacent to George Washington and Jefferson National Forests *(see place listing p. 252).* Natural Bridge became a retreat when Thomas Jefferson built a two-room log cabin for guests. By the 19th century, the railway dropped off thousands of people at Natural Bridge station for a mountain respite, during which they would view the renowned "rock bridge"—now known as The Natural Bridge of Virginia—that Jefferson called "the most sublime of nature's works."

THE NATURAL BRIDGE OF VIRGINIA is off I-81 exit 175 or 180 on US 11 at SR 130, or off the Blue Ridge Pkwy. Mileposts 61.6 and 63.7 (SR 130/US 501). The 215-foot tall limestone arch spanning Cedar Creek, known by the Monacan Indians as The Bridge of God, is an ancient natural wonder and Virginia Civil War Trails site; it was purchased in 1774 by Thomas Jefferson, and surveyed by George Washington.

In early American history the Natural Bridge ranked with Niagara Falls in the top tier of the country's natural wonders and continues to inspire awe today. Visitors also can experience the Cedar Creek Trail & Nature Park. "The Drama of Creation," with lighting effects and music, is presented beneath the bridge.

Picnicking is permitted. Food is available. Allow 1 hour minimum. Bridge open daily 8-dusk. Nature park open daily 8-dusk. Drama presentations are given daily at dusk, Apr.-Oct.; Sat. at dusk, rest of year. Admission (includes Monacan Indian Living History Village) $12; $6 (ages 5-12). Combination ticket with Natural Bridge Caverns and Natural Bridge Wax Museum and Factory Tour $23; $12 (ages 5-12). AX, DS, MC, VI. Phone (800) 533-1410. *See color ad p. 235.*

Monacan Indian Living History Village is on US 11 at the Natural Bridge. This re-created 17th-century village features Monacan interpreters in period costume and demonstrations of rope making, weaving, meal preparation, wigwam building, hide tanning and other activities. Monacans have lived in the area for 1,500 years; their first known encounter with Europeans was with Capt. John Smith in 1608. Guided tours are available. Allow 1 hour minimum. Daily 10-5, Apr.-Nov.; closed Thanksgiving. Admission included with The Natural Bridge of Virginia. Phone (800) 533-1410. *See color ad p. 235.*

Natural Bridge Caverns is on US 11. Guided 45-minute tours highlight the cavern stalagmites, stalactites, underground streams and waterfall. The temperature in the caverns is a constant 54 F. Allow 1 hour minimum. Tours depart daily every 20 minutes 10-5, Mar.-Oct. Fee $10; $6 (ages 5-12). Combination ticket with The Natural Bridge of Virginia and Natural Bridge Wax Museum and Factory Tour $23; $12 (ages 5-12). AX, DS, MC, VI. Phone (540) 291-2482 or (800) 533-1410. *See color ad p. 235.*

SAVE **Natural Bridge Wax Museum and Factory Tour** is on US 11. More than 150 life-size replicas of historical figures are featured in scenes depicting the history of the Shenandoah Valley, American Indian legends and folklore. Guided tours take visitors through the wax museum factory to see how the figures are made.

Daily 9-9, Mar.-Aug.; 10-6, Sept.-Oct.; Sat.-Sun. 10-5, rest of year. Hours may vary; phone ahead. Admission $10; $6 (ages 5-12). Combination ticket with The Natural Bridge of Virginia and the Natural Bridge Caverns $23; $12 (ages 5-12). MC, VI. Phone (540) 291-2426. *See color ad p. 235.*

VIRGINIA SAFARI PARK is at 229 Safari Ln. This 180-acre, drive-through zoo permits close contact with free-roaming buffalo, elk, zebras and other large herd animals. Buckets of feed are available for purchase. Safari wagon rides also are available. Allow 1 hour minimum. Daily 9-6, Memorial Day-Labor Day; 9-5, Mar. 1-day before Memorial Day

and day after Labor Day-Nov. 30. Closed Thanksgiving. Admission $12; $11 (ages 65+); $8 (ages 3-12). MC, VI. Phone (540) 291-3205.

NELLYSFORD (G-7) elev. 673′

RECREATIONAL ACTIVITIES
Skiing and Snowboarding
• **Wintergreen Resort** is 3 mi. s.w. on Patrick Henry Hwy. (SR 151), then 4.5 mi. n.w. on Beech Grove Pkwy. Write P.O. Box 706, Wintergreen, VA 22958. Daily 9 a.m.-10 p.m. (also Fri.-Sat. 10-11 p.m.), mid-Dec. to mid.-Mar. Phone (434) 325-2100.

WINERIES
• **Hill Top Berry Farm & Winery** is 2.5 mi. n.e. on SR 151, .5 mi. e. on Virginia Ln., then just e. to 2800 Berry Hill Rd. Wed.-Sat. 11-5, Sun. 1-5; closed Jan. 1, Easter, Thanksgiving and Dec. 24-25. Phone (434) 361-1266.
• **Wintergreen Vineyard & Winery** is .25 mi. w. on SR 664 from jct. SR 151. Daily 10-6, Apr.-Oct.; 10-5, rest of year. Closed Jan. 1, Thanksgiving and Dec. 25. Phone (434) 361-2519.

NEWBERN (H-5) elev. 2,136′
SAVE **WILDERNESS ROAD REGIONAL MUSEUM** is off I-81 exit 98 following brown signs. The museum preserves several early 19th-century log buildings that were part of a planned community on the Wilderness Road. Exhibits include regional artifacts, photographs and furniture. A brochure detailing a walking tour of Newbern's historic district is available at the museum. Allow 30 minutes minimum. Mon.-Sat. 10:30-4:30, Sun. 1:30-4:30. Admission $2; $1 (ages 6-12). Phone (540) 674-4835.

NEW MARKET (F-7) pop. 1,637, elev. 1,060′
One of the more spectacular events of the Civil War occurred during the Battle of New Market on May 15, 1864. Compelled by necessity, Gen. John Breckinridge ordered 257 cadets from Virginia Military Institute to confront the Union forces under Gen. Franz Sigel. The boys were to be kept in reserve until needed to fill a gap in the advancing line, but in the confusion of battle, they were accidentally put on the front line. Ten were killed and 45 wounded. The cadets' heroism in holding the line helped to defeat Sigel's seasoned troops, who then retreated north.

Shenandoah Valley Travel Association: P.O. Box 1040, New Market, VA 22844; phone (540) 740-3132.

Self-guiding tours: A walking tour brochure is available from the travel association, off I-81 exit 264.

ENDLESS CAVERNS is off I-81 exit 264; take US 211 .2 mi. e., US 11 3.1 mi. s.w., then Endless Caverns Rd. 1.8 mi. s.e. No end has been discovered to these caverns, which include an impressive array of stalactites, stalagmites, giant columns, flowstone and limestone pendants, and such chambers as Snowdrift, Fairyland and Grand Canyon.

Picnicking is permitted. Allow 1 hour, 30 minutes minimum. Guided tours daily 9:30-6, June 15-Labor Day; 9-5, Mar. 15-June 14 and day after Labor Day-Oct. 31; 9:30-4, rest of year. Closed Jan. 1, Thanksgiving and Dec. 25. Fee $16; $8 (ages 4-12). AX, DS, MC, VI. Phone (540) 896-2283.

NEW MARKET BATTLEFIELD STATE HISTORICAL PARK is off I-81 exit 264 at 8895 Collins Dr. On May 15, 1864, 257 cadets from the Virginia Military Institute aided veteran Confederate troops in victory over Union forces here. The cadets' courage is commemorated with exhibits and the Emmy-winning 45-minute film, "Field of Lost Shoes." A hall with models and dioramas presents a chronological overview of the Civil War.

On the park grounds is the historic Bushong farm, dating from the early 1800s; two original houses and eight re-created dependencies also are on the property. A brochure describing a self-guiding walking tour of the battlefield is available at the park visitor center.

Allow 1 hour minimum. Daily 9-5; closed Jan. 1, Thanksgiving and Dec. 24-25. Admission (includes The Hall of Valor, the Bushong farm complex and the battlefield walking tour) $9; $8 (ages 60+ and military with ID); $5 (ages 6-17). Phone (866) 515-1864.

SHENANDOAH CAVERNS is 1 mi. w. of I-81 exit 269 at 261 Caverns Rd. Local legend says that two boys descended into these caverns after railroad workers broke through the limestone ceiling. American Indians had sought shelter in the underground passages for centuries. The cave opened to the public in 1922, providing natural air-conditioning to a hotel that was formerly located at the entrance.

A guided 1-hour tour begins with an elevator descent to the cave's subterranean entrance hall. Colorful and pure-white formations are visible in 17 rooms, which are connected by a mile of level pathways. Fault lines are visible in the ceilings of many of the rooms since the caverns were largely formed by earthquake movement.

Among the highlights are the crystal-laden Diamond Cascade, the Bacon Formations, the Grotto of the Gods and the Oriental Garden. The temperature in the caverns remains a constant 56 F.

Relating the area's agricultural and rural heritage is The Yellow Barn at Shenandoah Caverns; exhibits include arts and crafts, restored farm vehicles, a mineral cave and an indoor beehive.

Picnicking is permitted. Food is available June-Aug. A jacket and comfortable walking shoes are recommended. Guided cave tours daily 9-6:15, June 16-Sept. 1; 9-5:15, Apr. 15-June 15 and Sept. 2-Oct. 31; 9-4:15, rest of year. The Yellow Barn daily 9-5. Closed Dec. 25. Fee (includes American Celebration on Parade, Main Street of Yesteryear and The Yellow Barn) $22; $19 (ages 62+); $10 (ages 6-14). AX, DS, MC, VI. Phone (540) 477-3115 or (888) 422-8376 for Shenandoah Caverns or (540) 477-2432 for The Yellow Barn. *See color ad.*

American Celebration On Parade is at 397 Caverns Road at Shenandoah Caverns. A 40,000-square-foot exhibit hall contains a collection of parade floats, props and stage settings from America's entertainment and political history, including the Rose Parade, presidential inaugurations, the Miss America pageant, Thanksgiving parades and world summit meetings. Guided 30-minute tours daily 9-6:15, June 16-Sept. 1; 9-5:15, Apr. 15-June 15 and Sept. 2-Oct. 31; 9-4:15, rest of year. Closed Dec. 25. Fee included with Shenandoah Caverns. Phone (540) 477-4300. *See color ad.*

Main Street of Yesteryear is at Shenandoah Caverns. Antique, animated window displays that appeared in famous department stores include Cinderella at the ball, a 100-figure circus parade, toy soldiers and a miniature presidential inaugural parade. Daily 9-5; closed Dec. 25. Admission included with Shenandoah Caverns. Phone (540) 477-3115.

NEWPORT NEWS—
see Hampton Roads Area p. 261.

NORFOLK—*see Hampton Roads Area p. 262.*

OCCOQUAN—*see District of Columbia p. 133.*

ONANCOCK (G-11) pop. 1,525, elev. 20′

This waterfront village was established in 1680 on the Chesapeake Bay's eastern shore. The name is said to come from an American Indian word meaning "a foggy place."

KER PLACE is at 69 Market St. The Federal-style mansion was built in 1799 by merchant John Shepherd Ker. Visitors can view rooms furnished in period. Allow 30 minutes minimum. Tues.-Sat. 10-4, Mar. 1-Dec. 20. Admission $5; $2 (ages 0-17). Phone (757) 787-8012.

TANGIER ISLAND CRUISES departs from 2 Market St. A 1.5-hour trip crosses the Chesapeake Bay to the tiny island of Tangier *(see place listing p. 309)*, where visitors can stroll the narrow streets of the quaint town. Cruises depart Tues.-Sun. at 10 and return at 3:30, Memorial Day weekend-Oct. 15. Fare $25; $12.50 (ages 4-12). Phone (757) 891-2240.

ORANGE (F-8) pop. 4,123

Settled in 1734, Orange was home to Col. James Taylor II, great-grandfather to two American presidents, James Madison and Zachary Taylor. Robert E. Lee worshiped at St. Thomas Episcopal Church on Caroline Street during the winter of 1863-64; the tree where he tied his horse, Traveler, is marked.

Orange County Visitors Center: 122 E. Main St., Orange, VA 22960; phone (540) 672-1653.

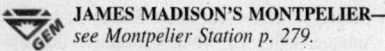 **JAMES MADISON'S MONTPELIER—** *see Montpelier Station p. 279.*

[SAVE] **JAMES MADISON MUSEUM** is at 129 Caroline St. The museum honors James Madison, the fourth president of the United States and chief architect of the Constitution. Exhibits detail his life and contributions to the American political system and include such items as Madison memorabilia, antique tools and agricultural implements. Quarterly changing exhibits highlight local history and culture. Mon.-Fri. 9-5, Sat. 10-5, Sun. 1-5; closed Jan. 1, Easter, Thanksgiving and Dec. 25. Admission $4; $3 (ages 61+); $1 (ages 6-16). Phone (540) 672-1776.

PARKSLEY (G-12) pop. 837, elev. 43′

Henry R. Bennett, a traveling salesman, laid out the town of Parksley in 1884 during construction of the Eastern Shore Railway. In the 160-acre planned community, selling liquor meant the immediate loss of one's property. Benjamin Parks, upon whose farm Parksley was built, soon fled the constraints of town life for a new seaside home.

EASTERN SHORE RAILWAY MUSEUM is at 18468 Dunne Ave. A train depot houses railroad memorabilia and a model train exhibit. Visitors may tour antique railroad cars. Allow 30 minutes minimum. Wed.-Sun. noon-4 and by appointment; closed Jan. 1, Thanksgiving and Dec. 25. Admission $2; free (ages 0-12). Phone (757) 665-7245.

PETERSBURG (B-1) pop. 33,740, elev. 100′

Petersburg began in 1645 as Fort Henry, a frontier fort and trading post. In 1781 a British force under generals William Phillips and Benedict Arnold marched on the town, which was inadequately garrisoned by 1,000 men under Gen. Friedrich von Steuben. After a short skirmish to cover his retreat, von Steuben withdrew across Pocahontas Bridge, burning it behind him. Later the Marquis de Lafayette bombarded the city. It was in Petersburg that Gen. Charles Cornwallis gathered British troops for the Yorktown campaign.

By the time it was incorporated as a city in 1850, Petersburg had become a thriving industrial and commercial center, with tobacco warehouses, cotton and flour mills and iron foundries. Economic success was followed by a cultural blossoming; schools, colleges, churches and theaters flourished.

Unfortunately, Petersburg's importance as an industrial and transportation center of the Confederacy made it a prime target for Gen. Ulysses S. Grant's armies. In the summer of 1864 the surrounding countryside turned into a battlefield. Stray shells struck 800 homes. For 10 months the city suffered hunger and cannon bombardment before it fell to the Union near the close of the Civil War *(see Petersburg National Battlefield p. 284).*

Not long after the war's end, Mary Logan, wife of Union commander Gen. John A. Logan, witnessed a group of schoolgirls placing flowers on the graves of Petersburg defenders at the Old Blandford Church. Deeply moved when she saw the ritual repeated the next year, she related the story to her husband, who took steps that ultimately led to the observance of Memorial Day as a national holiday.

Petersburg Visitor Center: 425 Cockade Alley, Petersburg, VA 23803; phone (804) 733-2400 or (800) 368-3595.

Self-guiding tours: The visitor center offers a variety of maps outlining tours of Petersburg and its Old Towne historic district as well as Lee's Retreat. This 26-stop driving tour through seven counties connecting Petersburg to Appomattox follows the route of Gen. Robert E. Lee at the end of the Civil War.

Petersburg's African-American heritage is one of the oldest in the country. By the mid-19th century, the area had one of the largest free black populations in the state. A brochure outlining a self-guiding tour of Petersburg's African-American historic sites is available at the visitor center and at Petersburg museums.

BLANDFORD CHURCH AND RECEPTION CENTER is at 319 S. Crater Rd. in Blandford Cemetery. Known in Colonial times as the Brick Church on Well's Hill, the church was built 1735-37. Its 15 stained-glass windows by Tiffany Studios are memorials donated by the Confederate States. Blandford Cemetery contains the graves of 30,000 Confederate soldiers and the unmarked grave of British general William Phillips.

Guided tours leave from the reception center at 111 Rochelle Lane inside the cemetery. Open daily 10-5; closed Jan. 1, Thanksgiving and Dec. 24-25. Admission $5; $4 (ages 6-11, ages 60+ and military with ID). Phone (804) 733-2396.

CENTRE HILL MANSION is on Centre Hill Ct. off Franklin St. Extensive renovations to this 1823 Federal-style mansion took place in the 1840s and again in 1901, thereby depicting the architectural evolution that paralleled the Victorian era. Period antiques include a rare 1886 Knabe Art grand piano that is 9 feet long. Daily 10-5; closed Jan. 1, Thanksgiving and Dec. 24-25. Admission $5; $4 (ages 6-11, ages 61+ and military with ID). Phone (804) 733-2400.

PAMPLIN HISTORICAL PARK AND THE NATIONAL MUSEUM OF THE CIVIL WAR SOLDIER is off I-85 exit 63A to 6125 Boydton Plank Rd. A premier Civil War history destination, this 422-acre park features three antebellum homes, four museums and daily living-history demonstrations. The park is also the site of the Breakthrough Battle of April 2, 1865, a decisive point in the Petersburg Campaign that led to Gen. Robert E. Lee's retreat from Richmond.

Appealing to casual visitors, serious students of Civil War history and families, the park explores the experiences of common soldiers and life in the antebellum South. The National Museum of the Civil War Soldier displays more than 3,000 artifacts, supplying visitors with personal audio players to follow the true-life stories of individuals who fought in the conflict.

The site includes a military encampment, slave quarters, fortifications and nearly a mile of original earthworks. The Battlefield Center features artifacts and a special exhibit about African-Americans in the Civil War.

Picnicking is permitted. Food is available. Allow 3 hours minimum. Daily 9-5; closed Jan. 1, Thanksgiving and Dec. 25. Admission $15; $13.50 (ages 65+ and military with ID); $9 (ages 6-12). AX, DS, MC, VI. Phone (804) 861-2408 or (877) 726-7546.

SIEGE MUSEUM is at 15 W. Bank St. The human side of the Civil War is presented through exhibits depicting the lives of the citizens of Petersburg while under siege. A 20-minute film shows the contrast between the city before the war and as it was during the 10 months preceding Lee's surrender. Daily 10-5; closed Jan. 1, Thanksgiving and Dec. 24-25. Admission $5; $4 (ages 7-12, ages 60+ and military with ID). Phone (804) 733-2404 or (800) 368-3595.

PETERSBURG NATIONAL BATTLEFIELD (C-1)

The 2,659-acre Petersburg National Battlefield, 2 miles east of Petersburg via Washington/Oaklawn St. (SR 36), was established to preserve and interpret the battlefields where 10 months of grim trench warfare sapped the strength of Gen. Robert E. Lee's Confederate army and led to the fall of Richmond.

Petersburg was an important point through which supplies moved to Richmond, as five railroads converged at Petersburg with only one line leading to the capital city.

Despite disastrous losses at Wilderness, Spotsylvania Court House and Cold Harbor, Gen. Ulysses S. Grant moved on from Richmond, intending to cut off its line of communication with the South at Petersburg and compel the evacuation of the Confederate capital. Four days of furious fighting—June 15-18, 1864—forced the Confederate line back about a mile, where the armies entrenched and Grant began his siege.

Between June 25 and July 23, Union volunteers, including many Pennsylvania coal miners, dug a 511-foot-long mine shaft that ended beneath the Confederate line. Quietly carrying out tons of soil in cracker boxes, the Union men packed the shaft with 4 tons of black powder which, when ignited, created a 170- by 60-foot crater 30 feet deep. The blast produced 278 casualties. Only faulty Union plans in the following battle and the prompt action of Confederate troops saved the city. The deep depression created by the explosion is called The Crater.

Confederate lines stretched farther south and west as the soldiers were forced to defend both the eastern and western sectors against the Union's attempt to take the city. On April 3, 1865, Lee evacuated Petersburg and Richmond, an action that culminated 1 week later in his surrender at Appomattox Court House. About 42,000 Union and 28,000 Confederate soldiers were casualties in the Petersburg Campaign.

The park includes miles of original earthworks. Outstanding features are The Crater; Battery Five, where Grant's army first struck and from which he later shelled Petersburg with a 17,000-pound seacoast mortar known as "The Dictator"; Fort Stedman, where Lee's last grand offensive failed; the site of Fort Morton, near which the concentration of Union artillery used at the Battle of The Crater was stored; City Point, the Union supply center and logistics base where Grant and President Lincoln conferred for 2 weeks near the end of the siege (see Hopewell p. 272); Five Forks Battlefield, about 17 miles southwest of Petersburg, site of the last major battle for the South Side Railroad on April 1, 1865; and Poplar Grove National Cemetery, where 6,000 Union soldiers are buried.

The 4-mile self-guiding Battlefield Tour begins at the Eastern Front Visitor Center; part of the tour road is reserved for hikers and cyclists. From four points on the tour road, walks lead to major battle sites. The 16-mile Siege Line Tour picks up where the Battlefield Tour ends and leads to park areas south and west of Petersburg. The park is open daily 8-dusk; closed Jan. 1, Thanksgiving and Dec. 25.

EASTERN FRONT VISITOR CENTER is at the entrance to Petersburg National Battlefield off Oaklawn St. (SR 36). The Petersburg campaign is depicted through exhibits, battlefield relics, maps and models. Self-guiding tour maps and a recorded narration of the 37-mile driving tour of the battlefield (available on audiotape or CD-ROM) are available.

Visitor center open daily 9-5; closed Jan.1, Thanksgiving and Dec. 25. Admission (good for 7 days) $5 (per private vehicle); $3 (per person arriving by other means). Driving tour $7.50 (audiotape); $13.95 (CD-ROM). Phone (804) 732-3531.

POCAHONTAS (H-4) pop. 441, elev. 2,300′

In 1873 Maj. Jed Hotchkiss hired a surveyor to explore a 500,000-acre tract along the Bluestone River. The report noted a coal bed used for fuel by a local blacksmith, and Hotchkiss brought the discovery to the attention of investors. A railroad was built to the site, and the first shipment of "smokeless" Pocahontas coal was delivered to Norfolk in 1883. When the original shaft was depleted decades later, the company town turned it into a show mine.

SAVE **POCAHONTAS EXHIBITION COAL MINE AND MUSEUM** is off SR 102 and CR 644, on CR 659. The museum preserves the history of the Pocahontas Coal Mine, which opened in 1883 and operated for 73 years. Visitors also may view the renowned Pocahontas #3 coal seam, which is more than 10 feet high.

DID YOU KNOW

The Battle of Chancellorsville was considered Gen. Robert E. Lee's greatest victory.

Demonstrations include coal cutting, blasting and loading as well as the old method of hand undercutting. The mine maintains a constant 52 F temperature. Guided tours are available. Allow 30 minutes minimum. Mon.-Sat. 10-5, Sun. 1-6, Apr.-Oct. Admission $7; $4.50 (ages 6-12). AX, DS, MC, VI. Phone (276) 945-2134.

PORTSMOUTH—
see Hampton Roads Area p. 265.

QUANTICO—*see District of Columbia p. 133.*

REEDVILLE (G-11) elev. 10′

Reedville's history is intertwined with that of the Potomac River and Chesapeake Bay. On Virginia's Northern Neck, the city was the home of wealthy fishermen and factory owners whose fortunes were made from the menhaden that populated those waters. Their Victorian mansions can be seen along Main Street. Reedville retains its ties to the water, as fishing charters and cruises to nearby Smith and Tangier islands are popular with visitors.

REEDVILLE FISHERMEN'S MUSEUM is on US 360 in the historic district. The museum comprises Walker House, a restored fisherman's home, and Covington Building, which contains two galleries— one with the permanent collection and the other with rotating exhibits. An outside exhibit features traditional boats and equipment. Allow 30 minutes

minimum. Daily 10:30-4:30, May-Oct.; Fri.-Sun. 10:30-4:30, Nov. 1 to mid-Jan.; Sat.-Sun. 10:30-4:30, mid-Mar. through Apr. 30. Admission $5; $3 (ages 65+); free (ages 0-11). Phone (804) 453-6529.

SMITH ISLAND CRUISES operates from the Chesapeake Bay/Smith Island KOA Campground, 2 mi. n.e. of jct. US 360 and CR 650 (Sunnybank Rd.). The narrated 13.5-mile cruise across the Chesapeake Bay to Smith Island, Md. *(see place listing p. 205)*, takes 1.5 hours each way. Upon arrival, visitors embark on a narrated bus tour of remote Ewell Village, the largest of three settlements on the island. Lunch at a restaurant in the village is optional.

Cruises depart Tues.-Sun. at 10 (based on demand and weather permitting) and return at 3:45, May 15-Oct. 15. Fare $25; $12.50 (ages 3-12). Reservations are required. Phone (804) 453-3430 or (804) 453-4051.

TANGIER & CHESAPEAKE CRUISES departs from Buzzard's Point Marina at 468 Buzzard Point Rd. The narrated boat trip to quaint Tangier Island *(see place listing p. 309)* crosses the Chesapeake Bay, taking 1.5 hours each way. Passengers are given 2.5 hours on the island. Cruises depart daily at 10 and return at 3:45, May 1-Oct. 15. Fare $25; $13 (ages 4-12). Reservations are required. Phone (804) 453-2628.

Richmond

City Population: 197,790 **Elevation:** 15 ft.

Editor's Picks:

Maymont...........................*(see p. 294)*

The Museum of the
 Confederacy ....*(see p. 294)*

Virginia State Capitol ....*(see p. 296)*

The capital of Virginia, Richmond combines the atmosphere of a gracious cultural center, the legacy of an absorbing past and the technological drive of a progressive city.

From its founding, Richmond has been linked with the activities of patriots, presidents of both the United and the Confederate States, and several authors. Many historical shrines and reminders of the events Richmond has witnessed are found throughout the city.

In 1609 Capt. John Smith bought from the Indian chief Powhatan a tract of land near the present site of Richmond and founded a settlement he called "None Such." The city was laid out in 1737 by Col. William Byrd and designated the state capital in 1779.

In 1775 the Virginia Convention met at St. John's Church. The roster, a "Who's Who" of Colonial days, contains the names of Benjamin Harrison, Thomas Jefferson, Richard Henry Lee, Edmund Pendleton, Peyton Randolph, George Washington and George Wythe. Patrick Henry made his speech, proclaiming, "I know not what course others may take; but as for me, give me liberty or give me death!"

In 1861 the Ordinance of Secession was passed, and Richmond soon became the capital of the Confederate States of America. Gen. Irvin McDowell, Gen. George McClellan, Gen. Ambrose Everett Burnside, Gen. Joseph Hooker, Gen. George Meade and Gen. Ulysses S. Grant in succession failed to subdue the Southern capital.

Grant finally succeeded, but not by capturing the city itself. In 1864, after the Battle of Cold Harbor near Mechanicsville, Grant abandoned the project of taking Richmond directly and started the siege of Petersburg, which ended in the Confederacy's downfall. When Richmond was evacuated, Confederate

James River / Buddy Mays / Virginia Tourism Corporation

troops burned the government warehouse; the spreading flames destroyed most of the city.

The Governor's Mansion on the northeast corner of Capitol Square dates 1811-13. On the site have lived four U.S. presidents; three of them—Thomas Jefferson, James Monroe and John Tyler—also served as governors of Virginia, and William Henry Harrison lived here while his father was governor.

The renovation of several historic districts has brought new vitality to the downtown area. Court End, just north of Capitol Square, was named for its attorney residents and nearby legal buildings. The neighborhood is home to some of the city's most notable architectural and historic landmarks.

Shockoe Slip, between the financial district and the James River, was the center for the milling and tobacco industries in the 19th century. The warehouses have been restored, the narrow streets have been re-cobbled and the neighborhood is now a highlight of Richmond's dining and night life; boutiques, restaurants, craft shops, office buildings and residences fill the street.

Shockoe Bottom, just past the slip along E. Cary, E. Franklin and E. Main streets between 17th and 25th streets, also has been developed into a lively

Getting There — *starting on p. 290*

Getting Around — *starting on p. 290*

What To See — *starting on p. 291*

What To Do — *starting on p. 297*

Where To Stay — *starting on p. 856*

Where To Dine — *starting on p. 858*

area of restaurants, nightclubs, art galleries, shops, warehouse apartments and a farmers' market. Past flooding of the James River prohibited restoration of the area until a floodwall was built, spurring restoration of the historic neighborhood. The 17th-century Farmer's Market on Main and 17th streets is home to summertime produce and autumn pumpkins. A downtown landmark, Main Street Station, has been restored and once again welcomes daily train travelers to the city.

Church Hill, on the East End above Shockoe Bottom, is poised above the James River. The area is home to tree-lined streets and renovated townhouses.

Named for the layout of streets that fan out toward the west, the Fan District is bordered by Belvidere Street on the east, Boulevard on the west, Monument Avenue on the north and Main Street on the south. Within the Fan's boundaries are late 19th-century town houses with interesting architectural features as well as the academic campus of Virginia Commonwealth University. VCU's Medical College of Virginia campus is 1.5 miles east in the downtown area. Other institutions of higher learning in the Richmond area include Virginia Union University on North Lombardy Street; the University of Richmond in West End; Randolph-Macon College in nearby Ashland; and Virginia State University in Ettrick.

The statues along Monument Avenue were originally laid out in 1890 with the dedication of the Lee Monument. Graced by a diverse mix of slate-roofed Classical Revival mansions, churches, apartments and stately oak and maple trees, the avenue is considered one of America's most beautiful. It is purported to be the only U.S. street to be designated a

Science Museum of Virginia
Richmond Metropolitan Convention and Visitors Bureau

historic landmark. The 7-mile-long stretch begins at Lombardy Street and runs to Horsepen Road/Glenside Drive in Henrico County. Only the easternmost mile contains statues, beginning west to east with the most recent addition, tennis great Arthur Ashe, who was born and raised in the city. Ashe's statue is at Roseneath Avenue. The statue of Civil War naval officer Matthew Fontaine Maury, inventor of the electronic torpedo, followed by other Civil War heroes including Thomas J. "Stonewall" Jackson, Jefferson Davis, Robert E. Lee and J.E.B. Stuart.

Jackson Ward on the north side of Broad Street is a historic African-American district with Federal and Greek Revival houses; the nation's first African-American-owned bank and insurance companies were chartered in this area. There also is a monument to Bill "Bojangles" Robinson, who was born in Richmond.

Destination Richmond

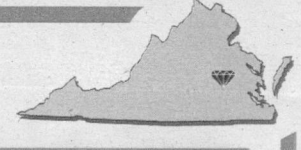

What has *not* changed in Richmond speaks of its progress. With a reverence for the past and an eye to the future, preservationists have ensured that historic treasures will be enjoyed by generations to come. Here's how to see them:

Gaze out over Capitol Square from the observation deck atop city hall. Take a walking tour of a historic neighborhood. Or cruise up and down the James River.

Richmond Metropolitan CVB

Science Museum of Virginia, Richmond. Hands-on exhibits focus on space exploration and the progress of science. (See listing page 295)

Virginia Tourism Corp

Tredegar Iron Works, Richmond National Battlefield Park. Observe the waterwheel and iron works before entering the adjacent visitor center. (See listing page 302)

© Gibson Stock Photography

Beaverdam • 684

Doswell

95

Ashland

Glen Allen • **See Downtown map page 291**

64

295

Lakeside •

360

Richmond

60

150

76

64

Kings Dominion, Doswell. Thrill-seekers will find plenty of adventure on the twists and turns of the park's roaring coasters. (See listing page 301)

Agecroft Hall, Richmond. The Knot Garden is just one of the elegant landscaping features surrounding the Tudor manor house. (See listing page 291)

360 Chesterfield • 288

295

95

© Gibson Stock Photography

Places included in this AAA Destination City:

The Informed Traveler

Sales Tax: Virginia levies a 5 percent sales tax with cities and counties imposing an additional 1 percent increment. The Richmond area has a lodging tax of 10.5 percent.

WHOM TO CALL

Emergency: 911

Fire: (804) 780-6663

Police (non-emergency): (804) 646-5100

Time and Temperature: (804) 732-2121

Hospitals: Bon Secours-Richmond Community Hospital, (804) 225-1700; Bon Secours St Mary's Hospital, (804) 285-2011; CJW Johnston-Willis Hospital, (804) 330-2000; CJW Medical Center, (804) 320-3911; Henrico Doctors' Hospital, (804) 289-4500; Retreat Hospital, (804) 254-5100; and VCU Health System, (804) 828-9000.

WHERE TO LOOK

Newspapers

The daily newspaper is the *Richmond Times-Dispatch.*

Radio

Richmond radio station WRVA (1140 AM) is all news/talk stations; WCVE (88.9 FM) is a member of National Public Radio.

Visitor Information

Richmond Metropolitan Convention & Visitors Bureau: 401 N. Third St., Richmond, VA 23219; phone (804) 783-7450 or (888) 742-4666.

Walk-in visitor centers are off I-95 exit Fifth St. at 405 N. Third St.; on the Canal Walk at 470 Tredegar St.; and at the Richmond International Airport.

TRANSPORTATION

Air Travel

The Richmond International Airport, off I-64 exit 197A, is served by American Airlines, (800) 433-7300; Continental Airlines, (800) 525-0280; Delta Airlines, (800) 221-1212; Northwest Airlines, (800) 225-2525; United Airlines, (800) 241-6522; and US Airways, (800) 245-4882.

Limousine service is available between the greater Richmond area and the airport; phone (804) 222-7226.

Rental Cars

Hertz, at Richmond International Airport, offers discounts to AAA members; phone (804) 222-7228 or (800) 654-3080. For listings of other agencies check the telephone directory.

Rail Service

The Amtrak Train Station is at 7519 Staples Mill Rd.; phone (800) 872-7245.

Buses

The Greyhound Lines Inc. bus terminal is at 2910 N. Boulevard St. across from The Diamond baseball field; phone (804) 254-5938 or (800) 231-2222.

Taxis

Some of the larger cab companies include Acton, (804) 360-7106; Yellow, (804) 222-7300; and Metro (804) 353-5000. Base fare is $2.50 for the first one-fifth mile, $1.50 per each additional mile and 30c for each minute of delay, including traffic. Base fare rises $1 for each additional passenger over age 6 and for rides between 9 p.m. and 6 a.m.

Public Transport

The Greater Richmond Transit Co. (GRTC) operates buses throughout most of the city and parts of Henrico County. The base fare is $1.25; transfers cost 15c. A Super Saver Ticket is $10 per book of 10; senior citizens $5. Phone (804) 358-4782 for information.

At Byrd and 12th streets are canal locks built in 1854 as part of a canal system George Washington proposed to complete between the Tidewater region and the Kanawha River. A self-guiding tour and an outdoor museum border the canal; the canal area offers concerts, boat tours and recreational activities.

Getting There

By Car

Richmond is served by numerous highways, including two major interstates. To the southwest, I-295 misses Richmond by sprouting off I-95 in Petersburg and catches up with I-95 north of Richmond in northern Henrico County; I-295 continues westward until it dead-ends into I-64 near Short Pump. The 3rd Street approach offers access to downtown on I-95 (Richmond-Petersburg Turnpike) from the north; take Broad Street if entering from the south.

East-west I-64 from Williamsburg enters the city from the southeast, joins up with I-95 downtown and then re-emerges south of Dumbarton near Joseph Bryan Park to continue its trek northwest toward Charlottesville. The 3rd Street exit off I-64 provides access to downtown if coming from the west; the 5th Street exit off I-64 takes you downtown from the east.

SR 150 semicircles the western side of the city, coming in from the south as the Chippenham Parkway on the James River in eastern Chesterfield County, crossing the James River to the west of Richmond as Parham Road, crossing I-64 northwest of the city and joining US 301/Chamberlayne Road north of Richmond near I-295.

US 1/301 enters the city from the south as Jefferson Davis Highway, crosses the James River over the Robert E. Lee Bridge, becomes Belvidere Street as it runs through downtown, and splits just north of I-95 (Richmond-Petersburg Parkway) with US 1 heading north as Brook Road and US 301 heading northeast as Chamberlayne Road.

Getting Around

Street System

Downtown Richmond is bounded by the James River to the south and I-95 to the north and east. Belvidere Street (US 1/301) is roughly the eastern edge of downtown. Broad Street (US 250) bisects the area.

Richmond resembles a grid pattern. Numbered streets 1st through 40th fall either in the East End (in the Church Hill and Shockoe Bottom area) or on the South Side (in the Forest Hill and Brainbridge area). Some streets change names, including Monument Avenue, which becomes W. Franklin Street at Stuart Circle; Malvern becomes Westwood as it crosses Broad Street; and The Boulevard flows into Hermitage Road northbound and Westover Hill Boulevard southbound as it traverses the river (it changes again to Belt Boulevard as it crosses Midlothian Turnpike).

Virginia State Capitol / Douglas Peebles / Virginia Tourism Corporation

Six bridges cross the James River east to west: I-95/Richmond-Petersburg Turnpike, Mayo's Bridge (US 360), Manchester Bridge (US 60), Robert E. Lee Bridge (US 1/301/Belvidere Street), Boulevard Bridge (SR 161) and Powhite Parkway (SR 76).

Many of the roads throughout Richmond are toll roads, including the Boulevard Bridge (SR 161) over the James River; SR 195/Downtown Expressway from Powhite Parkway to I-95; and the Powhite Parkway Bridge over the James River.

The city speed limit is 30 mph, or as posted. Rush hours are usually 7:30-9 a.m. and 4-6 p.m. Unless otherwise posted, a right turn on red is permitted.

Parking

Like any big city, Richmond has some downtown street parking; metered parking is limited and strictly monitored. If your car is towed from a downtown street, phone police information at (804) 646-5100. Numerous parking lots and garages are available throughout the city. Hourly rates vary from 50c-$2.50.

What To See

AGECROFT HALL is at 4305 Sulgrave Rd. in Windsor Farms. Built in the late 15th century in Lancashire, England, this Tudor manor house was dismantled in the late 1920s and shipped to its present location overlooking the James River.

Outstanding features include the original hand-carved oak paneling, leaded-glass windows and furnishings from the Tudor and early Stuart periods (1580-1640). The house is surrounded by 23 acres of lawns, woodlands and several Elizabethan gardens.

Tours begin with a 10-minute film portraying the home in its English location and its shipment to this country. Allow 1 hour minimum. Tues.-Sat. 10-4, Sun. 12:30-5; closed national holidays. Admission $8; $7 (ages 65+); $5 (students with ID); free (ages 0-5 and military with ID). Phone (804) 353-4241.

BETH AHABAH MUSEUM & ARCHIVES is at 1109 W. Franklin St. Virginia's museum of Jewish

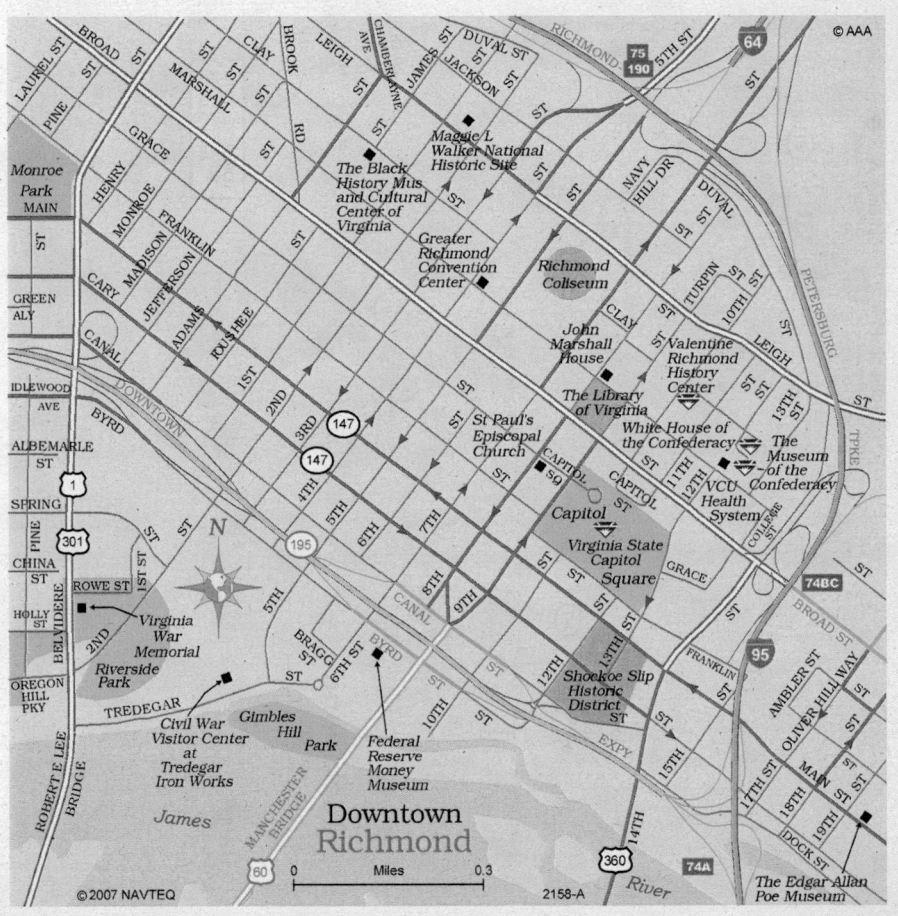

Downtown
Richmond

© 2007 NAVTEQ
2158-A

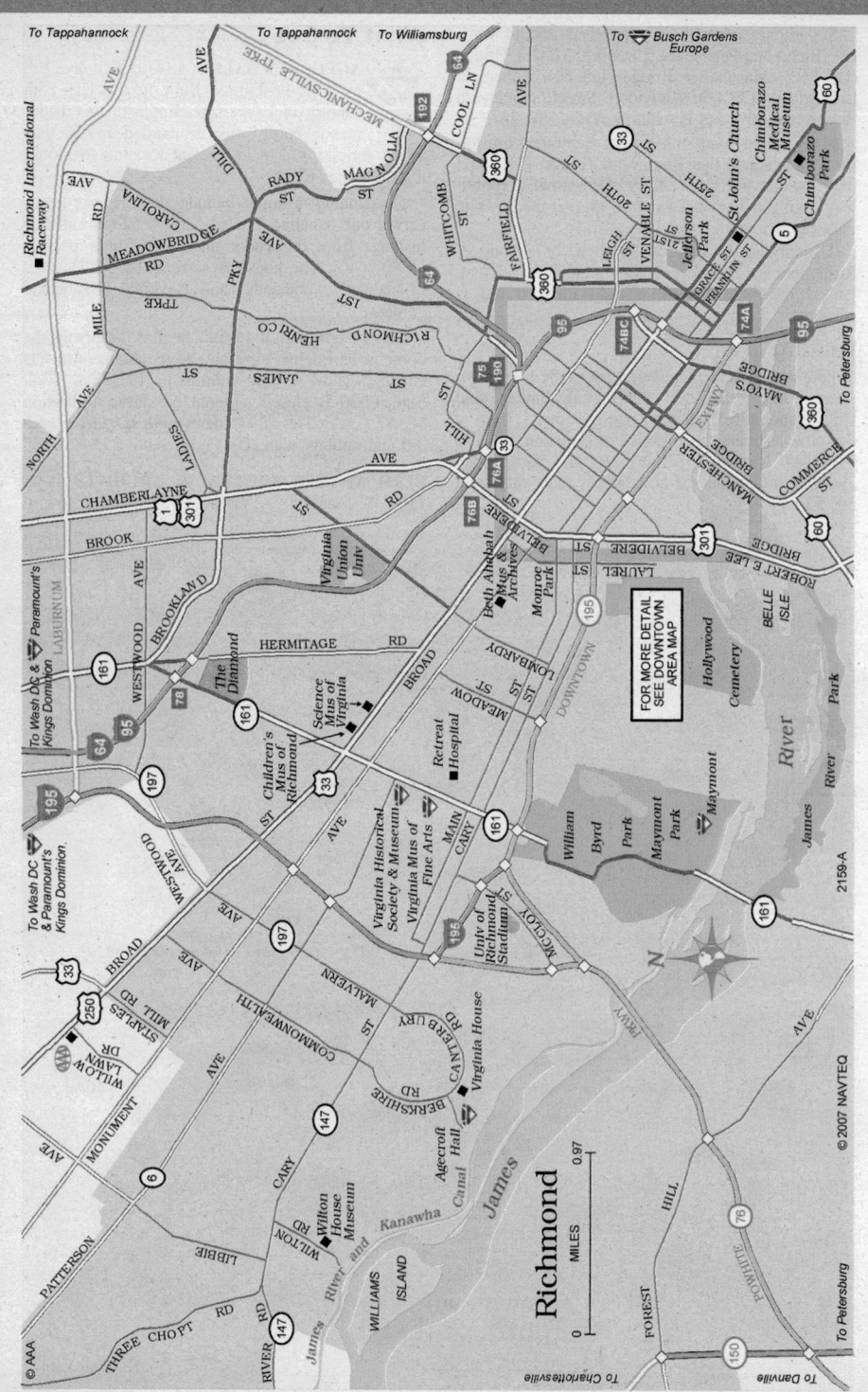

To Tappahannock
To Tappahannock
To Williamsburg
To Busch Gardens Europe

Richmond International Raceway

MECHANICSVILLE TPKE

AVE
AVE
AVE
DILL
RADY ST
MAGNOLIA ST
WHITCOMB ST
COOL LN
FAIRFIELD
AVE

CAROLINA RD
MEADOWBRIDGE RD
PKY
1ST
RICHMOND
HENRY CO
JAMES ST
ST
HILL ST

33
ST
30TH ST
VENABLE ST
21ST ST
25TH ST
St. John's Church
Chimborazo Medical Museum
Chimborazo Park
60
5

LEIGH
Jefferson Park
GRACE ST
FRANKLIN ST

360
360
95
74BC
74A

MILE TPKE
NORTH AVE
LADIES ST
CHAMBERLAYNE
BROOK
WESTWOOD AVE
BROOKLAND

ST
ST
AVE
RD

78
190
76A
33
76B
BELVIDERE ST

LAUREL ST
Beth Ahabah Mus & Archives
Monroe Park
ROBERT E LEE BRIDGE
BELVIDERE ST
LAUREL ST
301
60

MAYO'S BRIDGE
MANCHESTER BRIDGE
COMMERCE ST
360

BELLE ISLE

1
301

161
64
95
78

LABURNUM

The Diamond
HERMITAGE RD
Science Mus of Virginia
Children's Mus of Richmond
Retreat Hospital
LOMBARDY ST
MEADOW ST
BROAD
DOWNTOWN
195

FOR MORE DETAIL SEE DOWNTOWN AREA MAP

Hollywood Cemetery

William Byrd Park
Maymont Park
Maymont

River

James River Park

To Wash DC & Paramount's Kings Dominion

197
195
33

WESTWOOD AVE
161

AVE
ST
33
AVE
MAIN
CARY
Virginia Historical Society & Museum
Virginia Mus of Fine Arts
Univ of Richmond Stadium
195
McCLOY ST

161

161

2159-A

197
BROAD
STAPLES MILL RD
250
WILLOW LAWN DR

AVE
AVE
MALVERN
COMMONWEALTH
CANTERBURY RD
BERKSHIRE RD
Virginia House
147

MONUMENT AVE
6
CARY
Agecroft
Canal Hall
WILTON RD
Wilton House Museum
James River and Kanawha

PATTERSON AVE
LIBBIE
THREE CHOPT RD
RIVER RD
147

WILLIAMS ISLAND

James

Richmond
MILES
0.97
0

N

FOREST HILL
76
150

To Charlottesville
To Danville
To Petersburg

© 2007 NAVTEQ
© AAA

history and culture features a collection passed down from one of the oldest Jewish congregations in America. The museum houses changing exhibits of documents, historical photographs and religious objects. An archival collection may be used for historical and genealogical research. Allow 30 minutes minimum. Sun.-Thurs. 10-3; closed Jan. 1, Memorial Day, July 4, Labor Day, Thanksgiving and Jewish holidays. Admission $5. Phone (804) 353-2668.

THE BLACK HISTORY MUSEUM AND CULTURAL CENTER OF VIRGINIA is at 00 Clay St. Housed in an 1832 Federal and Greek Revival building in the historic Jackson Ward district, the museum is a repository for artifacts detailing the lives of African-Americans in Virginia. Displays include fine art objects, traditional African artifacts and oral history records. Tues.-Sat. 10-5; closed holidays. Admission $5; $4 (students with ID and senior citizens); $3 (ages 0-12). Phone (804) 780-9093.

CAPITOL SQUARE lies between 9th and Governor sts. and Broad and Bank sts. surrounding the Virginia State Capitol. At the heart of the square is the Washington Monument, a 60-foot-high equestrian statue surrounded by patriots of the American Revolution. To the east is the Executive Mansion, the official residence of Virginia's governors since 1813. To the north is the 1894 Old City Hall. The new City Hall across the street offers a 19th-floor observation deck. The 1824 Bell Tower houses a state visitor center.

Visitors may take a self-guiding tour of the grounds. Capitol Square open daily 7 a.m.-11 p.m. Free. Phone (804) 698-1788 for the Capitol or (804) 545-5586 for the state visitor center and Bell Tower.

SAVE **CHILDREN'S MUSEUM OF RICHMOND** is at 2626 W. Broad St. Interactive exhibits allow children to learn about the human body, discover river ecosystems, work in a grocery store, experiment in the Inventor's Laboratory and create artwork. Allow 30 minutes minimum. Tues.-Sat. 9:30-5 (also Mon. 9:30-5, Memorial Day-Labor Day), Sun. noon-5; closed Jan. 1, Thanksgiving and Dec. 25. Admission $7; $6 (senior citizens); free (ages 0-1). Phone (804) 474-7000 or (877) 295-2667.

SAVE **THE EDGAR ALLAN POE MUSEUM** is at 1914 E. Main St. Although Poe never resided in the 1737 Old Stone House—Richmond's oldest residence—he lived and worked in the area for much of his life. The museum features a complex of four buildings that house Poe's personal memorabilia and rare first editions, a gallery with James Carling illustrations inspired by "The Raven," and a large-scale model of early 19th-century Richmond focusing on Poe's life in the city.

Tues.-Sat. 10-5, Sun. 11-5; closed major holidays. Guided tours are given on the hour. Admission $6; $5 (ages 60+ and students with ID). AX, MC, VI. Phone (804) 648-5523.

FEDERAL RESERVE MONEY MUSEUM is at 701 E. Byrd St. More than 500 items depict the history of currency and coins. The museum contains such items as compressed tea bricks that could be spent or brewed; and a coin from the Kingdom of Lydia, the birthplace of coinage. **Note:** The museum is closed for renovations through 2009; phone ahead for updates. Free. Reservations are required. Phone (804) 697-8110.

HOLLYWOOD CEMETERY is at the n. end of Robert E. Lee Bridge at 412 S. Cherry St. and Albemarle St. Several noted Virginians are buried here, including Presidents John Tyler and James Monroe, Confederate President Jefferson Davis, Gen. Fitzhugh Lee, John Randolph, Gen. J.E.B. Stuart, Gov. William Smith and Gen. George E. Pickett. A 90-foot-high granite pyramid honors 18,000 buried Confederate soldiers. The cemetery, which opened in 1849, is named for its holly trees.

Self-guiding maps and historical brochures are available for a fee at the cemetery office. Grounds daily 8-6, mid-Mar. to early Nov.; 8-5, rest of year. Office Mon.-Fri. 8:30-4:30. Guided walking tours are given Mon.-Sat. at 10, Apr.-Oct. Cemetery free. Guided walking tour $10. Phone (804) 648-8501 for the office or (804) 649-0711 for tour information.

JOHN MARSHALL HOUSE is at 818 E. Marshall St. The house was built in 1790 for Chief Justice Marshall, who occupied it until his death in 1835.

The residence retains the original woodwork, paneling and many furnishings.

Guided tours Tues.-Sat. 10-5, Sun. noon-5; closed major holidays. Last tour begins 45 minutes before closing. Fee $6; $5 (ages 66+); $4 (ages 4-18). Combination ticket (includes Valentine Richmond History Center and Wickham House and, on weekends May though October, Monumental Church at 1224 E. Broad St.) $10; $7 (ages 4-18, students with ID and senior citizens). Phone (804) 648-7998.

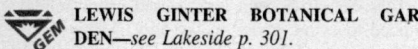 **LEWIS GINTER BOTANICAL GARDEN—**see Lakeside p. 301.

THE LIBRARY OF VIRGINIA is at 800 E. Broad St. Treasures from the library's extensive collection of books, manuscripts, maps and artwork—the commonwealth's records from the colony's founding through the present—are displayed to the public. Research facilities are available. Allow 30 minutes minimum. Mon.-Sat. 9-5; closed holidays. Free. Phone (804) 692-3500.

MAGGIE L. WALKER NATIONAL HISTORIC SITE is at 600 N. 2nd St. The daughter of a former slave, Maggie Lena Walker rose to prominence in Richmond as a businesswoman and community leader in the early 1900s. Among her many accomplishments was the founding of the St. Luke Penny Savings Bank, the first chartered bank in the country started by a woman.

Her home in the Jackson Ward district has been restored to its 1930s appearance. A visitor center offers an audiovisual presentation and exhibits. Allow 30 minutes minimum. House tours depart Mon.-Sat. every 30 minutes 9-5; closed Jan. 1, Thanksgiving and Dec. 25. Free. Phone (804) 771-2017.

MAYMONT is at 2201 Shields Lake Dr. This 100-acre, late-Victorian country estate typifies Gilded Age opulence. Built in 1893 by Maj. and Mrs. James Dooley, the 33-room mansion overlooks the James River. The estate features the Maymont House Museum, original outbuildings, gardens and a collection of period carriages. Twelve restored rooms of the mansion, furnished with original pieces, are open to guided tours. The basement includes a domestic service exhibit.

The Robins Nature & Visitor Center includes giant aquariums, interactive exhibits and a 20-foot waterfall. Some 700 animals are presented at the native Virginia wildlife exhibits, the children's farm and the nature center. Tram, carriage and hay wagon rides are offered.

Food is available. Grounds open daily 10-7, Apr.-Oct.; 10-5, rest of year. Closed Jan. 1, Thanksgiving and Dec. 25. Guided mansion tours are offered Tues.-Sun. noon-4:30. Tram and carriage ride hours vary; private rides by appointment. Hay wagon rides are offered Sat.-Sun. 1-4, June-Aug. Mansion $5. Nature center $4. Children's Farm $2. Tram, carriage or hay wagon ride $3; $2 (ages 0-11). Phone (804) 358-7166.

MEADOW FARM MUSEUM—
see Glen Allen p. 301.

THE MUSEUM OF THE CONFEDERACY is 2 blks. n. of Broad St. at 1201 E. Clay St. Founded in 1890, the museum interprets the Civil War through one of the largest collections of Confederate artifacts, paintings and documents.

Some 15,000 artifacts include military equipment and clothing that belonged to Confederate leaders, among them Jefferson Davis, Robert E. Lee, J.E.B. Stuart and Thomas J. "Stonewall" Jackson; artifacts documenting the lives of free and enslaved African-Americans; art illustrating the Confederate experience; and flags relating to the Confederate armed forces and government. On display is the 1869 painting "The Last Meeting of Lee and Jackson," a 15-foot painting depicting the moment Jackson went off to Chancellorsville, where he was mortally wounded.

Free parking is available at the Medical College of Virginia Hospital visitor/patient parking deck on Clay St. (museum will validate parking slip). Allow 1 hour minimum. Mon.-Sat. 10-5, Sun. noon-5; closed Jan. 1, Thanksgiving and Dec. 25. Admission $8; $7 (ages 62+); $4 (ages 7-13); free (military with ID). Combination ticket with the White House of the Confederacy $11; $10 (ages 62+); $6 (ages 7-13). AX, MC, VI. Phone (804) 649-1861.

White House of the Confederacy is next to The Museum of the Confederacy at 1201 E. Clay St. This was the executive mansion of President Jefferson Davis and his family during the Civil War. The house was saved from demolition by the Confederate Memorial Literary Society in 1890 and served as the Confederate Museum until the mid-1970s. After 10 years of restoration and the return of many of its original furnishings, the mansion has regained its Victorian opulence. Eleven period rooms are on exhibit. Guided tours start in the basement and explore the first and second floors.

Allow 1 hour minimum. Guided tours Mon.-Sat. 10-5, Sun. noon-5, Mar.-Dec.; closed Thanksgiving and Dec. 25. Last tour begins 1 hour before closing. Fee $8; $7 (ages 62+); $4 (ages 7-13); free (military with ID). Combination ticket with The Museum of the Confederacy $11; $10 (ages 62+); $6 (ages 7-13). Phone (804) 649-1861.

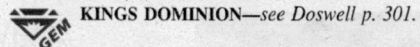 **KINGS DOMINION—**see Doswell p. 301.

ST. JOHN'S CHURCH is at 2401 E. Broad St. Erected in 1741, the church was the site from which Patrick Henry delivered his "Liberty or Death" speech in favor of independence. The Second Virginia Convention is re-enacted Sunday at 2 p.m., Memorial Day weekend-Labor Day weekend. The surrounding burial ground contains the graves of George Wythe, the first Virginia signer of the Declaration of Independence, and Elizabeth Arnold Poe, mother of Edgar Allan Poe.

Guided tours Mon.-Sat. 10-4:30, Sun. 1-4:30, Memorial Day weekend-Labor Day; Mon.-Sat. 10-3:30, Sun. 1-3:30, rest of year. Closed Jan. 1, Easter, Thanksgiving and Dec. 24-25 and 31. Last tour begins at closing. Fee $6; $5 (ages 63+); $4 (ages 7-18). Phone (804) 648-5015.

ST. PAUL'S EPISCOPAL CHURCH is at Grace and 9th sts. President Jefferson Davis and Gen. Robert E. Lee worshiped here. Nearly everything in the church, including the windows commemorating Lee, is a memorial. Mon.-Sat. 10-4, Sun. 8-3; closed holidays. Free. Phone (804) 643-3589.

SCIENCE MUSEUM OF VIRGINIA is off US 95 and US 64, at 2500 W. Broad St. The museum, in a former 1919 train station, offers more than 250 hands-on exhibits as well as demonstrations, displays and touring exhibitions. A planetarium with an IMAX theater features large-format films and multimedia shows.

Mon.-Sat. 9:30-5, Sun. 11:30-5; closed Thanksgiving and Dec. 25. IMAX schedule varies; phone ahead. Museum admission $10; $9 (ages 4-12, ages 60+ and military with ID). IMAX film $8.50; free (ages 0-3 with adult). Combination ticket $17.50; $16.50 (ages 4-12, ages 60+ and military with ID). MC, VI. Phone (804) 864-1400 or (800) 659-1727.

THREE LAKES NATURE CENTER AND AQUARIUM is off I-95N, 1.7 mi. n.e. on Chamberlayne Ave./US 301, .9 mi. s.e. on Wilkinson Rd., then .1 mi. w. to 400 Sausiluta Dr. The 132-acre park features a 50,000-gallon freshwater aquarium. Exhibits pertain to the park's three lakes, wetlands, forest and animal life. Hands-on activities are offered as well as nature trails and fishing.

Picnicking is permitted. Allow 30 minutes minimum. Tues.-Fri. 10-4:30, Sat.-Sun. noon-4:30, June-Aug.; Tues.-Sun. noon-4:30, Mar.-May and Sept.-Nov.; Sat.-Sun. noon-4:30, rest of year. Free. Phone (804) 262-5055.

UNIVERSITY OF RICHMOND is off I-64 exit 183A; take Glenside Dr. (SR 356) 1.2 mi. s., Three Chopt Rd. .5 mi. s.e., Boatwright Dr. .3 mi. w., then Campus Dr. .2 mi. s., following signs to the main entrance. Information sessions and campus tours depart from the admissions office in Brunet Hall, just s. of the main entrance. An admissions officer outlines the university's academic programs and environment, followed by a student-guided campus tour.

Tours are offered twice a day, Mon.-Fri. (also on Sat. some weeks during the academic year); closed major holidays and university breaks. Hours vary; phone ahead. Free. Phone (804) 289-8640 or (800) 700-1662.

Harnett Museum of Art is on the first floor of the Modlin Center for the Arts on the University of Richmond campus. The gallery, a forum for the visual arts, offers a permanent collection as well as exhibitions, concerts, lectures, workshops and other programs. Allow 30 minutes minimum. Tues.-Sun.

1-5; closed major holidays and university breaks. Free. Phone (804) 289-8276.

Lora Robins Gallery of Design from Nature is in the lower level of the Boatwright Memorial Library on the University of Richmond campus. Collections represent cultures and countries throughout the world and range from ancient works to contemporary art. Highlights include a 2,400-carat blue topaz, a dinosaur fossil reputed to be 165 million years old, a 150-pound giant clamshell and a selection of minerals, fossils, gemstones and shells. Allow 30 minutes minimum. Tues.-Fri. 11-5, Sat.-Sun. 1-5; closed major holidays and university breaks. Free. Phone (804) 289-8276.

VALENTINE RICHMOND HISTORY CENTER is at 1015 E. Clay St. The museum's founder, Mann S. Valentine Jr., bequeathed his personal collection of art and artifacts to the city in 1892, along with ownership of the 1812 Wickham House. With its focus on the history of Richmond and the people who shaped it, the center offers changing exhibits from its extensive holdings.

Displays include decorative and industrial arts, paintings, prints, manuscripts and books. Complementing these artifacts are more than half a million photographs of the city and the surrounding area.

The 1812 Wickham House was built by John and Elizabeth Wickham, one of Richmond's wealthiest couples. Guided tours interpret the lives of 31 residents, black and white, including the Wickhams' many children. The elegant house, with its magnificent freestanding stairway, rare neo-classical wall paintings and carved ornamentation, typifies late Federal architecture.

Food is available. Open Tues.-Sat. 10-5, Sun. noon-5; closed Jan. 1, Thanksgiving and Dec. 24-25. Admission (includes John Marshall House and Wickham House and, on weekends May though October, Monumental Church at 1224 E. Broad St.) $10; $7 (ages 4-18, students with ID and senior citizens). AX, DS, MC, VI. Phone (804) 649-0711.

VIRGINIA AVIATION MUSEUM is at Richmond International Airport, off I-64E exit 197, following signs to 5701 Huntsman Rd. The museum offers a tour through aviation history with planes from World Wars I and II. Included are a late 1920s open cockpit mail plane and a plane belonging to Virginia native Adm. Richard E. Byrd. Other displays include aviation artifacts, flying clothes and equipment. Virginia's Aviation Hall of Fame is in the museum.

Allow 1 hour minimum. Mon.-Sat. 9:30-5, Sun. noon-5; closed Thanksgiving and Dec. 25. Admission $6; $5 (ages 4-12 and 60+). MC, VI. Phone (804) 236-3622.

VIRGINIA HISTORICAL SOCIETY & MUSEUM is at 428 N. Boulevard. Museum galleries exhibit rare Virginia treasures. The Story of Virginia, an American Experience explores the development of Virginia from the Colonial period and the Civil War through World Wars I and II to the present. Highlights include such early archeological specimens as a 17th-century Virginia dug-out canoe, an 18th-century smokehouse and kitchen, a re-creation of Francis Lightfoot Lee's dining room, a Conestoga wagon and a Richmond streetcar.

A library, Civil War murals and Confederate-made weapons also are featured. Battle Abbey, the original building, is a memorial to the Confederate soldier. Picnicking is permitted. Allow 1 hour minimum. Mon.-Sat. 10-5, Sun. 1-5; closed Jan. 1, Easter, July 4, Thanksgiving and Dec. 24-25 and 31. Admission $5; $4 (ages 55+); $3 (students with ID); $2 (ages 55+ on Tues.); free (ages 0-18 and on Sun.). Combination ticket with Virginia House $6; $5 (ages 60+); $4 (students with ID); free (ages 0-18). Phone (804) 358-4901.

VIRGINIA HOLOCAUST MUSEUM is in Shockoe Bottom at 2000 E. Cary St. The museum contains memorabilia, archives, audiovisual presentations and re-creations of scenes related to the Holocaust. A special exhibit is dedicated to the Ipps family, who fled from the Kovno Ghetto in Lithuania and survived in an underground bunker for 6 months. Visitors can climb into a model of the 9-by-12-foot hiding place, which sheltered 13 people.

Allow 1 hour minimum. Mon.-Fri. 9-5, Sat.-Sun. 11-5; closed Jan. 1, Thanksgiving, Dec. 25 and Jewish holidays. Donations. Not recommended for children under 9. Phone (804) 257-5400.

VIRGINIA HOUSE is at 4301 Sulgrave Rd. This American adaptation of an English country estate was home to U.S. ambassador Alexander Weddell and his wife, Virginia. Reconstructed from a centuries-old English manor, the house is furnished with Elizabethan oak furniture and Spanish Colonial art. Landscape architect Charles Gillette designed the gardens.

Picnicking is permitted. Allow 1 hour minimum. Grounds Mon.-Sat. 10-4, Sun. 12:30-5; closed major holidays. Guided house tours depart on the hour Fri.-Sat. 10-4, Sun. 12:30-5; otherwise by appointment. Last tour begins 1 hour before closing. Admission $5; $4 (ages 60+); $3 (ages 2-18 and students with ID). Combination ticket with Virginia Historical Society & Museum $6; $5 (ages 60+); $4 (students with ID); free (ages 0-18). Phone (804) 353-4251.

VIRGINIA MUSEUM OF FINE ARTS is at 200 N. Boulevard. Ancient to contemporary art is represented in collections of paintings, prints, jewelry, decorative arts and sculpture at the museum, one of the largest of its kind in the South. Among the highlights are Fabergé jeweled objects, including five Russian Imperial Easter eggs, and a life-size marble statue dating from the first-century reign of the Roman emperor Caligula.

The museum features fine collections of the art of India, Nepal and Tibet; British sporting art; French impressionist and post-impressionist art; art nouveau; art deco; and furniture. Among artists with works on display are Edgar Degas, Francisco Goya, Claude Monet and John Singer Sargent. **Note:** Some galleries will be closed due to museum expansion through 2008; phone ahead for updates. Food is available. Open Wed.-Sun. 11-5; closed Jan. 1, July 4, Thanksgiving and Dec. 25. Donations. Fee charged for special exhibits. Phone (804) 340-1400 or TTY (804) 340-1401.

VIRGINIA STATE CAPITOL is on Capitol Square with a pedestrian entrance on Bank St. near 10th St. Designed by Thomas Jefferson, this "Temple on the Hill" has been occupied since 1788 and is home to America's oldest ongoing legislature.

The U.S. Bill of Rights was ratified here in 1791. Among other significant American events, former vice president Aaron Burr was tried for treason at the Capitol in 1807, and Robert E. Lee received his commission as commander of the Virginia forces in 1861. Winston Churchill addressed the Virginia Assembly in 1946, and L. Douglas Wilder was sworn in as the country's first elected African-American governor in 1990.

Visitors will find important historical statuary and paintings, rare exhibit objects and beautifully restored old and new legislative chambers. A magnificent statue of George Washington stands under the interior dome of the two-story rotunda, surrounded by marble busts of seven other Virginia-born presidents.

Metered street parking and parking garages are nearby. Guided tours Mon.-Sat. 9-5, Sun. 1-4; closed some state and federal holidays. Last tour begins 1 hour before closing. Free. Phone (804) 698-1788.

VIRGINIA WAR MEMORIAL is at the n. end of Robert E. Lee Bridge at 621 S. Belvidere St. (US 1). The memorial honors American veterans and particularly those Virginians killed in World War II, Korea, Vietnam and the Persian Gulf. The names of more than 11,600 soldiers are engraved on the marble walls of the Shrine of Memory. Site open daily 24 hours. Visitor center Mon.-Sat. 9-4, Sun. noon-4. Donations. Phone (804) 786-2050.

WILLIAM BYRD PARK is at the s. end of Boulevard at Idlewood Ave. The park contains the Christopher Columbus Monument, the World War I Memorial with its 56-bell carillon, and Dogwood Dell Amphitheatre. The Festival of Arts, featuring ballets, plays and musical performances, takes place at the amphitheater from mid-June to mid-August. Phone (804) 646-3355.

[SAVE] **WILTON HOUSE MUSEUM** is at 215 S. Wilton Rd. off Cary St. Built in 1753, Wilton was the home of William Randolph III, cousin to Thomas Jefferson. Before the house was moved in 1934, it stood on the banks of the James River about 7 miles east of Richmond, making it Richmond's only James River plantation home. Portraits of members of the Randolph family and period furnishings fill the spacious rooms.

Guided tours Tues.-Fri. 1-4:30, Sat. 10:30-4:30, Sun. 1:30-4:30, Mar.-Jan.; otherwise by appointment. Closed holidays. Last tour begins 45 minutes before closing. Fee $10; $6 (senior citizens); free (ages 0-5). Phone (804) 282-5936.

What To Do

Sightseeing

Walking Tours

Historic Richmond Tours, a service of the Valentine Richmond History Center, offers guided walking tours of the downtown area on Sunday afternoons April through October. The tour covers such historic areas as the Riverfront, Hollywood Cemetery, Shockoe Bottom, Church Hill, the Court End, Jackson Ward and Richmond's Wall Street. Year-round specialty bus tours also are offered; phone (804) 649-0711.

Richmond Discoveries offers guided walking tours of Hollywood Cemetery on the last Sunday of each month March through October. Tours are $7; phone (804) 222-8595.

Visitors can view remnants of the James River and Kanawha Canal that once flowed westward 197 miles to the Allegheny Mountains. Highlights along the 1.5-mile walk, which runs between 7th and 12th streets, include views of Belle Isle, Brown's Island, Tredegar Iron Works, and the James River and Kanawha Tidewater Connection Locks.

Belle Isle, once home to a Civil War prison camp, can be reached by the pedestrian bridge under the Lee Bridge at 7th and Tredegar streets. A 1-mile walking trail allows visitors to walk along the falls and view the historic earthworks. Brown's Island is the former site of the Confederate Laboratory that exploded in 1863, killing some 50 workers.

Visitors can view remnants of the buildings of Tredegar Iron Works, the most important iron works in the South during the Civil War. The armor used for the CSS *Virginia*, formerly the USS *Merrimac*, was manufactured at this plant. Historical markers along the river recall the area's history.

Running along the James River, the Richmond Floodwall is a 1-mile-long concrete levee that varies in height from 7 feet to 30 feet. Self-guiding tour brochures are available for 50c from the Richmond Metropolitan Convention & Visitors Bureau Information Center at 405 N. Third St. Highlights of the walk atop the levee include views of the river where walkers can spot various wildlife, including blue herons, Canada geese and turtles.

Sports and Recreation

Centrally located, Richmond offers a wealth of recreational opportunities. To the west are the Blue Ridge and Shenandoah mountains and the chance for such winter sports as **skiing** and **sledding**. To the east are Chesapeake Bay and the Atlantic Ocean where anglers and water sports enthusiasts alike can revel in the miles of shoreline.

The James River is a great place to lure in smallmouth bass; catfish, bream, largemouth bass and muskie also can be caught. Saltwater **fishing** can be found nearby in the Hampton Roads area and in Chesapeake Bay. For information about fishing licenses contact the Virginia Department of Game and Inland Fisheries; phone (804) 367-1000.

White-water **rafting, kayaking, tubing** and **canoeing** also are available on the James River. White-water canoe trips depart from James River Park, 22nd Street and Riverside Drive. The Richmond Raft Co., 4400 E. Main St., offers guided rafting trips on the James; phone (804) 222-7238. Adventure Challenge offers kayaking and tubing trips; phone (804) 276-7600.

Some 60 parks can be found throughout the greater Richmond area. Some of the activities available at the parks include **tennis, bicycling, hiking,** picnicking, **swimming, boating** and **horseback riding.** For information contact the Department of Parks, Recreation and Community Facilities; phone (804) 780-5733 in Richmond, (804) 748-1623 in Chesterfield County, (804) 501-7275 in Henrico County or (804) 365-4695 in Hanover County.

James River Park, at 22nd Street and Riverside Drive, is a good place to fish or hike. As part of the park, Belle Isle is reached via a footbridge on Tredegar Street or from the parking lot on 22nd Street. The island has walking trails with interpretive signs, a floating fishing pier and the opportunity for kayaking, canoeing, bicycling and **rock climbing.**

Pocahontas State Park, in nearby Chesterfield, offers more than 7,000 acres of outdoor opportunities for **camping,** swimming, hiking, boating and fishing.

More than 20 public and private **golf** courses can be found within the Richmond area. Some of the public and semi-private courses are Birkdale, (804) 739-8800, 8511 Royal Birkdale Dr. in Chesterfield; The Crossings, (804) 261-0000, 800 Virginia Center Pkwy. in Glen Allen; Glenwood, (804) 226-1793, 3100 Creighton Rd.; The Hollows, (804) 798-2949, 14501 Greenwood Church Rd. in Montpelier; River's Bend, (804) 530-1000, 11700 Hogan's Alley Dr.; and Sycamore Creek, (804) 784-3544, 1991 Manakin Rd. in Manakin-Sabot.

Spectator sports abound in Richmond. **Baseball** fans can cheer on the Richmond Braves, a minor league team of the Atlanta Braves. The Braves play ball from April through September at The Diamond on the Boulevard; phone (804) 359-4444 for ticket information.

Ice hockey fans can be found downtown at the Richmond Coliseum where the Richmond River-Dogs play in the United Hockey League; phone (804) 225-7825 for ticket information.

The Richmond Kickers play **soccer** in the United States Interregional Soccer League at the University of Richmond Stadium at Douglas Avenue and McCloy Street; phone (804) 644-5425 for schedule and tickets.

AAA and Motorsports

AAA, a pioneer in the development and growth of auto racing during the first half of the 20th century, has returned to the racetrack. Today the association is the "Official Motor Club" and "Official Roadside Assistance Provider" of 11 tracks owned and operated by the International Speedway Corporation (ISC), which hosts the NASCAR NEXTEL Cup Series and Indy Racing League (IRL) events.

As part of an agreement with ISC, AAA's widely recognized logo appears on track safety and recovery vehicles as well as on track signs, in racing programs and at other promotional venues. ISC, a leading promoter of motorsports activities in the United States, conducts more than 100 events annually. ISC/AAA facilities include California Speedway in Fontana, Calif.; Darlington Raceway in Darlington, S.C.; Daytona International Speedway in Daytona Beach, Fla.; Homestead-Miami Speedway in Homestead, Fla.; Kansas Speedway in Kansas City, Kan.; Martinsville Speedway in Martinsville, Va.; Michigan International Speedway in Cambridge Junction, Mich.; Phoenix International Raceway in Phoenix, Ariz.; Richmond International Raceway in Richmond, Va.; Talladega Superspeedway in Talladega, Ala.; and Watkins Glen International in Watkins Glen, N.Y.

© International Speedway Corporation

RICHMOND INTERNATIONAL RACEWAY is at 600 E. Laburnum Ave. Reputedly the only track to hold all of its major events "under the lights," the raceway hosts two NASCAR NEXTEL Cup Series races and two NASCAR Busch Series events, an IRL Indy-Car Series event, a USAC National Sprint Car Series event and a USAC Silver Crown Series race. The season spans May to Sept. Phone (866) 455-7223 for tickets or information.

© International Speedway Corporation
AAA is the Official Motor Club of Richmond International Raceway.

With four major colleges and universities in the area, Richmond is home to many rivalrous collegiate games. **Basketball** and **football** are popular at the University of Richmond where the Spiders play ball in Robins Center and UR Stadium, respectively; phone (804) 289-8363. The Virginia Commonwealth University Rams play baseball and basketball; phone (804) 828-1726. The Panthers at Virginia Union University play football on campus at Hovey Field and basketball at the Arthur Ashe Center near The Diamond; phone (804) 342-1484. A variety of sports is offered at Randolph-Macon College in Ashland, including basketball, football and both men's and women's soccer, baseball, **lacrosse** and **field hockey;** phone (804) 752-7223.

Richmond is home to the Richmond International Raceway (RIR), which hosts several NASCAR **automobile racing** events throughout the year. Located at the Richmond Raceway Complex, the raceway houses some 105,000 reserved seats; phone (804) 345-7223 for tickets and information.

Shopping

From Americana antiques to trendy boutiques, Richmond offers a wealth of shopping experiences. For those searching for a taste of the past, Shockoe Slip is a three-block area on Cary Street where cobblestone streets and brick buildings house boutiques, shops and eateries in renovated tobacco buildings and warehouses. This area near the river once was the city's commercial center. Just a few blocks east is another rejuvenated area, Shockoe Bottom. Dating to 1737, the 17th Street Farmers' Market at Main Street is one of the oldest public marketplaces in the country. Local produce is offered during the summer months.

West of Shockoe Slip is the Sixth Street Marketplace, stretching from Grace Street to the Richmond Coliseum. This emporium blends historic buildings and modern specialty shops as well as restaurants and food booths. Another noteworthy shopping area is Carytown, a nine-block area of Cary Street between Nansemond and Boulevard known for its eclectic shops and sidewalk cafes.

Some 45 specialty shops are available on Libbie and Grove Avenues in the West End. Sycamore Square, off Midlothian Turnpike in Chesterfield County, offers Colonial-style buildings housing boutiques and galleries. Numerous antiques shops are located throughout the area, including several downtown off Broad Street.

Area malls include Chesterfield Towne Center, US 60 and Huguenot Road; Cloverleaf, Chippenham Parkway and US 60; Regency Square, Parham and Quioccasin roads; Shops at Willow Lawn, Willow Lawn Drive and Broad Street; Stony Point Fashion Park, off I-95 at Chippenham Pkwy.; and Virginia Center Commons, I-95 and I-295 exit 43C (US 1).

Performing Arts

Built upon a rich history, Richmond's cultural scene began in 1786 with the opening of the city's first theater. The Landmark Theater, 6 N. Laurel St., was formerly known as the Mosque because of its resemblance to a Moslem Temple. Built in 1926 by the Shriners, the 3,500-seat theater today offers performances by national touring companies; phone (804) 646-4213. The 2,040-seat Loew's Theatre, later re-named the Carpenter Center for the Performing Arts, will reopen in fall 2009 after a $25 million renovation; phone (804) 225-9000 for ticket and event information.

The Theatre IV building at 114 W. Broad St. originally was founded in 1911 as the Empire Theatre and underwent restoration in the early 1990s. It is now home to a children's theater; phone (804) 344-8040. The historic Barksdale Theatre was founded as Richmond's first dinner theater. The theater is now in The Shops at Willow Lawn and presents classical and contemporary performances; phone (804) 282-2620. Another historic theater, the Byrd Theatre, 2908 W. Cary St., was built in 1928 and offers contemporary movies; phone (804) 353-9911.

Offering five major concerts and several smaller venues, the Richmond Symphony is for classical music lovers; phone (804) 788-1212. The Richmond Philharmonic also presents four concerts a year throughout town; phone (804) 673-7400 for information. Concerts by top-name performers regularly take place at the Richmond Coliseum, 601 E. Leigh St.; phone (804) 780-4956 for event information.

The Richmond Ballet, the commonwealth's only professional troupe, performs year-round and travels throughout Virginia presenting its repertoire of both classical and contemporary works; phone (804) 344-0906.

Special Events

February is a busy month in Richmond with the Camping/RV Show early in the month, the Boat Show mid-month and the Home and Garden Show rounding out February; all three events take place at the Richmond Raceway Complex. The Maymont Flower and Garden Show is held in the middle of the month at the Greater Richmond Convention Center.

The Strawberry Hill Races are held in early April and feature a steeplechase race. Historic Garden Week takes place throughout the state at various times in April. During this special event, special homes and gardens are opened up to the public for viewing.

The Virginia State Horse Shows take place in mid-April, late June and August. In early May Byrd Park is home to Arts in the Park, one of the largest outdoor craft shows on the East Coast.

Mid-July brings the Big Gig music festival held at various locations downtown and the World Gardenfest for Children in Lewis Ginter Botanical Garden.

Confederate sailors and Marine troops portray life at Fort Darling at the height of the Civil War during the Living History Encampment at Drewry's Bluff in mid-October. In November the Richmond Centre presents the Hand Workshop's Craft and Design Show where more than 200 craftspeople display their wares.

The Richmond Vicinity

ASHLAND (G-9) pop. 6,619, elev. 221'

This turn-of-the-20th-century railroad town originally was developed as a resort for Richmond residents. The village grew and later assumed the name of Henry Clay's Kentucky estate. When the railroad company gave land to the Methodist Church in 1866, the church moved its Randolph-Macon College to Ashland. The town has various Victorian houses.

Ashland Visitor Center: 112 N. Railroad Ave., Ashland, VA 23005; phone (804) 752-6766 or (800) 897-1479.

Self-guiding tours: The information center, located in the 1923 train depot on Railroad Avenue, provides information about self-guiding tours; guided walking tours also are offered.

 KINGS DOMINION—*see Doswell p. 301.*

BEAVERDAM (G-9) elev. 290'

SCOTCHTOWN is 1.3 mi. s.e. on Beaverdam School Rd., 8 mi. s. on Teman Rd. (Coatesville Rd.), then 1.2 mi. n.e. on Scotchtown Rd. Scotchtown was built by Col. Charles Chiswell in 1719 and is one of the state's oldest surviving plantations. Dolley Payne, who would later marry James Madison, visited the manor as a child. Scotchtown is best known as the home of Patrick Henry, who owned the house 1771-78. It was from Scotchtown that Henry rode to Richmond to deliver his famous "Liberty or Death" speech at St. John's Church in 1775.

Mon. and Thurs.-Sat. 10-4:30, Sun. 1:30-4:30, Apr.-Oct.; Sat. 10-4:30, Sun. 1:30-4:30, Nov.-Dec. Closed Easter, second Sun. in May and July 4. Admission $7; $5 (ages 56+); $4 (ages 6-12 and students with ID). Phone (804) 227-3500.

CHESTERFIELD (B-1) elev. 209'

A number of the earliest land grants to English colonists lay along the south side of the James River and were recorded in Chesterfield's courthouse. During the American Revolution the courthouse served as the headquarters for Baron von Steuben. The importance of this training facility provoked the British—with the aid of Benedict Arnold—to burn the courthouse in 1781.

SAVE **CHESTERFIELD COUNTY MUSEUM** is on SR 10 in the Courthouse Complex. The history of Chesterfield County is chronicled through a variety of exhibits from prehistoric times into the 20th century. Built as a replica of the 1750 courthouse, the museum displays ancient tools, American Indian artifacts, Civil War items and a 19th-century country store.

Allow 30 minutes minimum. Tues.-Fri. 10-4, Sat. 10-2, in summer; otherwise varies. Closed holidays. Phone ahead to confirm schedule. Admission (includes Magnolia Grange) $5; $4 (senior citizens); $3 (students with ID). Phone (804) 777-9663.

SAVE **HENRICUS HISTORICAL PARK** is off I-95 exit 61A, following signs on Old Stage Rd. Site of the second successful English settlement in the New World, Henricus was established by Sir Thomas Dale in 1611. Interpreters dressed in period costume re-enact everyday tasks and provide insight about life in the early 1600s. A hiking trail runs through the Dutch Gap Conservation Area.

Allow 1 hour minimum. Tues.-Sun. 10-5; closed Jan. 1, Thanksgiving and Dec. 25. Admission $6; $5 (senior citizens); $4 (ages 3-12). MC, VI. Phone (804) 706-1340.

MAGNOLIA GRANGE is on SR 10 across from the Courthouse Complex. The 1822 Federal-style plantation home, furnished in period, boasts distinctive architecture, ornate ceiling medallions and sophisticated carvings on the mantels, doorways and window frames.

Guided tours are available: Allow 30 minutes minimum. Tues.-Fri. 10-4, Sat. 10-2, in summer; otherwise varies. Closed holidays. Phone ahead to confirm schedule. Admission (includes the Chesterfield County Museum) $5; $4 (senior citizens); $3 (students with ID). Phone (804) 796-1479.

DOSWELL (G-9) elev. 145′

Originally known as Hanover, the town was the home of James Doswell, a Revolutionary War veteran. His estate, Bullfield, was noted for its winning racehorses. Hanover was renamed in the 1890s in honor of Maj. Thomas Doswell, who returned from the Civil War to open a hotel and continue the family's horse-breeding business.

KINGS DOMINION is .5 mi. e. off I-95 exit 98 on SR 30. A 300-foot replica of the Eiffel Tower stands at the gates to this 400-acre theme park, which features live shows, thrill and family rides and a water park. KidZville and Nickelodeon Central are areas designed for the younger set. Among a dozen roller-coasters are Shockwave, a stand-up, looping steel coaster; Hypersonic XLC, an air-launched ride that goes from 0 to 80 mph in 1.8 seconds; and Flight of Fear, an indoor coaster that runs in total darkness. Scooby-Doo! and the Haunted Mansion is an interactive, animated ride geared to families. Volcano, The Blast Coaster rockets out of a volcanic crater.

Tomb Raider: Firefall is a multisensory adventure combining an environmental theme with special effects. Swimsuits are required at WaterWorks, where the main attractions are Pipeline Peak, purported to be the world's tallest enclosed dark water slide; Big Wave Bay, a 650,000-gallon wave pool; and Surf City Splash House, a family play station.

Park open daily, Memorial Day-Labor Day; Sat.-Sun., late March-day before Memorial Day and first Sat. after Labor Day-late Oct. WaterWorks open daily, early May-Labor Day. Hours of operation vary depending on the season; phone ahead. Admission $49.95; $24.95 (ages 62+ and 0-47 inches tall). Parking $10. DS, MC, VI. Phone (804) 876-5000.

GLEN ALLEN (A-1) pop. 12,562, elev. 855′

First called Mountain Road Crossing, this settlement on the Chickahominy River became known as Glen Allen for an early resident, Benjamin Allen. In 1713, William Sheppard received a land grant for Meadow Farm, which remained in his family until 1993.

MEADOW FARM MUSEUM is off I-295 exit 45; take Woodman Rd. .1 mi. s., then Mountain Rd. 2.1 mi. w. to General Sheppard Crump Memorial Park entrance, following signs. This living-history farm and museum, once the home of a 19th-century doctor and his family, presents programs and exhibits about rural Southern culture. On some weekends, costumed interpreters demonstrate the day-to-day activities of the 1800s in the on-site barns, blacksmith forge, doctor's office, farmhouse and fields.

An orientation center features rotating exhibits. A fishing pond, nature trails and a playground also are offered. Park open daily dawn-dusk. Farmhouse and orientation center open Tues.-Sun. noon-4, Mar.-Nov.; Sat.-Sun. noon-4, rest of year. Closed Thanksgiving and Dec. 22-25. Free. Phone (804) 501-5520.

LAKESIDE (A-1) pop. 11,157, elev. 190′

LEWIS GINTER BOTANICAL GARDEN is 1.5 mi. n. of I-95 exit 80 (Lakeside Ave./Hilliard Rd.) at 1800 Lakeside Ave. This popular garden offers year-round beauty on a historic property of more than 40 landscaped acres. A classical domed conservatory contains changing displays, including more than 200 orchids in bloom. More than a dozen themed gardens include the Asian Valley, featuring plants native to East Asia; a sunken garden; the Flagler Perennial Garden, a 3-acre expanse with winding paths enhanced by perennials, shrubs, trees and bulbs; a rose collection; a Victorian garden; and a water-rich environment inhabited by the fauna and flora of wetlands, explored via bridges and boardwalks.

Also on-site is a children's garden, which offers a wheelchair-accessible tree house, an adventure pathway, an international village, and sand and water play areas. Food is available. Open daily 9-5; closed Jan. 1, Thanksgiving and Dec. 24-25. Admission $10; $9 (ages 56+); $6 (ages 3-12) MC, VI. Phone (804) 262-9887.

RICHMOND NATIONAL BATTLEFIELD PARK (A-2)

Headquartered in Richmond with battlefields in Hanover, Henrico and Chesterfield counties, the park commemorates the struggle for possession of the Confederate capital. Seven Federal attacks on Richmond took place during the Civil War. The park, consisting of 13 units, preserves the sites of the two efforts that came close to success—Gen. George McClellan's Peninsula Campaign of 1862 and Gen. Ulysses S. Grant's Overland Campaign in 1864. Completely touring the park involves a 60-mile drive.

Of McClellan's campaign, the park includes the sites of the important Seven Days' Battles at Beaver Dam Creek, Gaines' Mill at Glendale and Malvern Hill. Grant's campaign is represented by the battlefield at Cold Harbor, where on June 3, 1864, Grant hurled his army at strongly fortified Confederate positions, resulting in nearly 5,000 casualties. That September, Grant also made several more attacks across the James River on Confederates at Fort Harrison and New Market Heights.

Several Confederate strongholds, including Fort Harrison and Drewry's Bluff (Fort Darling), and Union-built Fort Brady are in the park. Living-history programs are presented in summer. The park's units are open daily dawn-dusk; closed Jan. 1, Thanksgiving and Dec. 25. Free. Phone (804) 226-1981.

CHIMBORAZO MEDICAL MUSEUM is at 3215 E. Broad St. in Richmond National Battlefield Park. The massive Chimborazo Hospital, built in 1861, treated more than 76,000 Confederate patients during the Civil War. The 40-acre hilltop site was said to be named by a Richmond traveler for a volcano in Ecuador. Exhibits and a film tell the story of hospital life and the Confederate Medical Service. Daily 9-5; closed Jan. 1, Thanksgiving and Dec. 25. Phone (804) 226-1981.

CIVIL WAR VISITOR CENTER AT TREDEGAR IRON WORKS is at 470 Tredegar St. The main visitor center to Richmond National Battlefield Park contains three floors of audiovisual presentations and exhibits about Richmond's role in the Civil War. Park maps are offered at the center, which is the beginning point for a self-guiding driving tour of the 1862 Seven Days' Battles and 1864 Overland Campaign sites. Daily 9-5; closed Jan. 1, Thanksgiving and Dec. 25. Free. Phone (804) 771-2145.

COLD HARBOR BATTLEFIELD VISITOR CENTER is 5 mi. s.e. of Mechanicsville on SR 156. This facility serves as the starting point for tours of the Cold Harbor and Gaines' Mill battlefields within Richmond National Battlefield Park. The center contains exhibits and an electronic battle map for both engagements. Daily 9-5; closed Jan. 1, Thanksgiving and Dec. 25. Phone (804) 730-5025.

FORT HARRISON VISITOR CENTER is off SR 5 on Battlefield Park Rd. This summer facility for Richmond National Battlefield Park offers brochures and exhibits. A walking trail leads through the remains of the fort, which was captured by 2,500 union soldiers on Sept. 29, 1864. Visitor center daily 9-5, June-Aug. Trail daily dawn-dusk.

GLENDALE/MALVERN HILL BATTLEFIELDS VISITOR CENTER is on SR 156 at the Glendale National Cemetery on Willis Church Rd. Part of Richmond National Battlefield Park, this center features exhibits and an electronic battle map about the Glendale and Malvern Hill battles of the 1862 Seven Days Campaign. Daily 9-5, June-Aug. Phone (804) 795-5017.

Capitol Square / © Lynn Seldon / Danita Delimont Stock Photography

This ends listings for the Richmond Vicinity.
The following page resumes the alphabetical listings of cities in Virginia.

RICHMOND NATIONAL BATTLEFIELD PARK—*see Richmond p. 301.*

ROANOKE (H-6) pop. 94,911, elev. 940´

Roanoke, the commercial and medical center of southwest Virginia, is rich in history and Virginia tradition. Diverse products manufactured include railroad cars, fabricated steel, electronic components, furniture, plastics, textiles and clothing.

Surrounding lakes, state parks and national forests offer recreational opportunities, including hiking, picnicking and camping along the Appalachian Trail and the Blue Ridge Parkway *(see place listing p. 234).* Fishing and boating are popular activities at nearby Smith Mountain Lake *(see Recreation Chart).*

Downtown Roanoke boasts many historic landmarks, including a 1907 fire station, a historic farmers' market and the Tudor-style Hotel Roanoke. The city's farmers' market was first opened in 1882; it still operates Monday through Saturday on the same site, downtown on Market Square. A city landmark, the 100-foot-tall Roanoke Star was erected on top of Mill Mountain in 1949; the star is illuminated each night, and the site offers a scenic overlook of the Roanoke Valley.

Roanoke Valley Convention & Visitors Bureau: 101 Shenandoah Ave., Roanoke, VA 24016; phone (540) 342-6025 or (800) 635-5535. *See color ad.*

Self-guiding tours: A downtown visitor center on Shenandoah Avenue offers a visitors guide, which includes a walking tour of downtown Roanoke.

Shopping areas: Valley View Mall, I-581 exit 3E, offers more than 100 stores, including Belk, Hecht's, JCPenney and Sears.

 CENTER IN THE SQUARE is off I-581 downtown at One Market Sq. This restored 1914 warehouse is adjacent to Roanoke's historic farmers' market. The center houses seven independent cultural organizations, including Mill Mountain Theatre, a professional theater featuring musicals, comedies, dramas and family productions. Also on-site are art, history and science museums as well as a planetarium. Phone (540) 342-5700 for the center, or (540) 342-5740 or (800) 317-6455 for theater information.

Art Museum of Western Virginia is off I-581 downtown at One Market Sq. in Center in the Square. The museum houses a permanent collection of American art and decorative arts from the 19th and 20th centuries. Modern, contemporary and changing exhibitions also are featured. Art Venture, an interactive gallery and art center, offers visitors a hands-on experience.

Note: The museum will close in summer 2008 in order to relocate to a new facility on Salem Avenue, between Market Street and Williamson Road; reopening is scheduled for November 2008. Phone

ahead for updates. Guided tours are available. Open Tues.-Sat. 10-5, Sun. 1-5; closed major holidays. Admission $3; free (ages 0-11). Art Venture $3. Phone (540) 342-5760.

History Museum and Historical Society of Western Virginia is off I-581 downtown at One Market Sq. in Center in the Square. Historical collections pertain to the history of western Virginia. Hands-on exhibits and a display titled Crossroads of History help guests learn about Virginia's past. Another gallery contains relics, costumes and photographs relating the history of Roanoke's theaters. Also featured are a research library and rotating exhibits. Tues.-Sat. 10-4 (also Sat. 4-5), Sun. 1-5. Library open by appointment. Closed holidays. Admission $3; $2 (ages 6-17 and 60+). Phone (540) 342-5770.

Science Museum of Western Virginia and Hopkins Planetarium is off I-581 downtown at One Market Sq. in Center in the Square. Interactive exhibits explore the wonders of science. Exhibits are devoted to light, sound, geology, the human body, animals and weather. Traveling exhibits also are featured. Hopkins Planetarium presents programs related to stars, planets and galaxies. The museum also offers the MegaDome Theatre, featuring large-screen films.

Tues.-Sat. 10-5, Sun. 1-5; closed major holidays. Exhibits only $8; $7 (ages 60+); $6 (ages 3-12). Exhibits and planetarium $10; $9 (ages 60+); $8 (ages 3-12). Exhibits, planetarium and MegaDome Theatre $13; $12 (ages 60+); $7 (ages 3-12). Prices may vary; phone ahead. Phone (540) 342-5726 or (540) 342-5710.

HARRISON MUSEUM OF AFRICAN AMERICAN CULTURE is off I-581 exit 4W, then 5 blks. s. to 523 Harrison Ave. Housed in Harrison School—the first public high school for African-American students in southwestern Virginia—the museum displays artifacts and memorabilia that preserve and interpret African-American heritage. Changing art exhibits feature local, regional and national artists. Tues.-Sat. 1-5; closed holidays. Free. Phone (540) 345-4818.

MILL MOUNTAIN is off Jefferson St. at Walnut Ave., following signs. Rising about 1,000 feet within the city limits, the mountain is topped by a city park and Mill Mountain Zoological Park. At the crest is the 88-foot-high Roanoke Star, which is illuminated at night. City park open daily 6 a.m.-11 p.m. Free.

SAVE **MILL MOUNTAIN ZOOLOGICAL PARK** is at the top of Mill Mountain; take Walnut Ave. (Fishburn Pkwy.) 1.7 mi. s.w., then Prospect Rd. .4 mi. n. More than 35 species of animals include mountain lions, red pandas, snow leopards and wolverines. Several vantage points offer incredible views of the surrounding area. Miniature train rides also are available seasonally (weather permitting). Allow 30 minutes minimum. Daily 10-5; closed Dec. 25. Admission $6.75; $6.07 (ages 61+); $4.50

(ages 3-11). Miniature train ride $2. DS, MC, VI. Phone (540) 343-3241.

O. WINSTON LINK MUSEUM is at 101 Shenandoah Ave. The museum is dedicated to O. Winston Link, whose black and white photographs documented the final days of railroad steam engines. Many works captured Norfolk & Western Railway trains as they passed through Virginia, Maryland and North Carolina 1955-60. Displays of photographic equipment and railway artifacts also are presented. Allow 1 hour minimum. Daily 10-5; closed Jan. 1, Easter, Thanksgiving and Dec. 25. Admission $5; $4.50 (ages 65+); $4 (ages 3-11). AX, DS, MC, VI. Phone (540) 982-5465.

SAVE **VIRGINIA MUSEUM OF TRANSPORTATION** is at 303 Norfolk Ave. A historic freight station houses steam, electric and diesel locomotives, railcars and cabooses; a large two-tier, O-gauge model train layout; a model circus; antique carriages, automobiles and trucks; and aviation equipment. The museum collection includes more than 50 pieces of rolling stock. Star Station offers interactive exhibits for children. Mon.-Sat. 10-5, Sun. 1-5; closed some holidays. Admission $8; $7 (ages 61+); $6 (ages 3-11). MC, VI. Phone (540) 342-5670. *See color ad p. 303.*

SAVE **VIRGINIA'S EXPLORE PARK** is e. on Roanoke River Pkwy. from Blue Ridge Pkwy. Milepost 115. The 1,100-acre living-history recreational park includes a 1671 American Indian village; a 1757 frontier fort; and an 1850s area with a farmstead, barns, a working gristmill and a one-room schoolhouse. Interpreters in period dress staff the facilities.

For nature enthusiasts, the park offers miles of hiking and mountain-biking trails and fishing, canoeing and kayaking on the Roanoke River. Food is available. Allow 2 hours minimum. Wed.-Sat. 10-5, Sun. noon-5, first Wed. in Apr.-third Sun. in Nov. Hours may vary; phone ahead Admission $9; $7 (ages 56+); $5 (ages 4-15). Prices may vary. MC, VI. Phone (540) 427-1800 or (800) 842-9163.

ROLLINS FORK (D-12) elev. 174′

WINERIES

• **Ingleside Vineyards** is 3.5 mi. e. on SR 3, .4 mi. n. on James Monroe Hwy., then just e. on CR 638 (Leedstown Rd.) in Oak Grove. Mon.-Sat. 10-5, Sun. noon-5; closed Jan. 1, Easter, Thanksgiving and Dec. 25. Phone (804) 224-8687.

SALEM (H-6) pop. 24,747

Fort Lewis was built near present-day Salem in 1752 to protect area settlers. The town was chartered in 1802 upon land previously owned by the son of Gen. Andrew Lewis, the fort's namesake. Roanoke College, then a Lutheran men's school, moved to Salem in 1847. After the Civil War, the growing town marketed itself as the "Switzerland of the South." A major blizzard devastated the local economy in 1890.

Salem Visitor's Center: 1001 Boulevard, Salem, VA 24153; phone (540) 375-4044 or (888) 827-2536.

DIXIE CAVERNS is off I-81 exit 132 to 5753 W. Main St. Guided 45-minute tours take visitors through still-growing caverns that go up into the mountain instead of down into the earth. Allow 1 hour minimum. Daily 9:30-6, June-Sept.; 9:30-5, rest of year. Closed Dec. 25. Admission $10; $5 (ages 5-12). AX, DS, MC, VI. Phone (540) 380-2085. *See color ad p. 303.*

THE SALEM MUSEUM is off I-81 exit 140, then .5 mi. e. to 801 E. Main St. The restored Williams-Brown House served as a residence, a post office and a general store during the Civil War. Built in 1845, the house sits on the Great Wagon Road where stage coaches, pioneers on horseback and Confederate soldiers traveled.

Exhibits include a collection of local American Indian artifacts and displays that trace Salem's history from its early settlement to present day. Guided tours are available. Allow 30 minutes minimum. Tues.-Fri. 10-4, Sat. noon-5. Donations. Phone (540) 389-6760.

SCHUYLER (G-8) elev. 400'

It was in Schuyler, in the foothills of the Blue Ridge Mountains, that author Earl Hamner Jr. grew up and recorded his childhood memories in journals that were to be the basis for the popular television show "The Waltons."

WALTON'S MOUNTAIN MUSEUM is on SR 617. The museum is in the Schuyler Elementary School, across the street from the boyhood home of Earl Hamner Jr., creator of "The Waltons." Re-creations of sets include John-Boy's bedroom, the family kitchen and living room and Ike Godsey's store. The Baldwin sisters' "recipe" machine is among show memorabilia on display. A 30-minute audiovisual presentation precedes the self-guiding tour.

Allow 1 hour, 30 minutes minimum. Daily 10-4, first Sat. in March-last Sun. in Nov.; closed Easter, last Sat. in Sept. and Thanksgiving. Admission $6; free (ages 0-5). Phone (434) 831-2000.

SHENANDOAH NATIONAL PARK (F-8)

Elevations in the park range from 600 ft. at the north entrance to 4,050 ft. at the summit of Hawksbill Peak. Refer to AAA maps for additional elevation information.

The park extends approximately 105 miles along the crest of the Blue Ridge Mountains, between Front Royal on the north and Waynesboro on the south. In one of the most beautiful and historic regions of the East, Shenandoah National Park embraces one of the highest and most scenic portions of the Blue Ridge. Shenandoah, an American Indian name, is thought to mean "Daughter of the Stars."

Spur ridges from the mountain crest blend into the rolling land of the Shenandoah Valley on the west and the wooded hills, orchards and fields of the Piedmont on the east. Between these ridges are deep, timbered hollows and cascading streams.

The 4,050-foot Hawksbill Peak and the 4,010-foot Stony Man are among the highest points in northern Virginia. Notable among the passes through the Blue Ridge are Thornton, Swift Run and Rockfish gaps, which form three of the four primary entrances into the park.

The park's 197,412 acres contain hundreds of miles of hiking trails and scenic viewpoints and are home to many species of plant and animal life. The park is a wildlife sanctuary harboring about 50 varieties of mammals, from chipmunks and groundhogs to deer and bears. Some 200 kinds of birds and a number of reptiles have been observed. The only poisonous snakes are rattlesnakes and copperheads, neither of which is encountered often. It is illegal to feed or harm wild animals.

There are nearly 100 species of trees. Most common are the hardwoods, which produce the annual blaze of autumn color; their height of brilliance usually occurs from mid- to late October. About 1,100 species of flowering plants have been identified. Wildflowers typically bloom from May through late fall. Azaleas and mountain laurel are strikingly beautiful in late spring; redbud and dogwood trees also flower at lower elevations in early spring.

General Information and Activities

Shenandoah National Park is open all year, although facilities close in winter. Permits for backcountry camping are required and are available free of charge at the park headquarters, entrance stations and visitor centers.

Free guided hikes and walks, slide shows and campfire programs are available; schedules are posted on park bulletin boards and published in "The Overlook," a park guide.

Information is available on weekdays at park headquarters, approximately 4 miles west of Thornton Gap on US 211.

The Harry F. Byrd Sr. Visitor Center, at Big Meadows (Milepost 51), offers interactive exhibits and films about the park. Dickey Ridge Visitor Center (Milepost 4.6) offers an orientation program and exhibits. Both centers are open daily 9-5, early spring through late fall, with extended hours during summer weekends.

Hiking trails within the park cover more than 500 miles, including a 101-mile section of the Appalachian Trail, the mountain footpath from Maine to Georgia. Among the most popular trails are the Whiteoak Canyon Trail and several shorter trails, including Limberlost, Stony Man and Frazier Discovery. Trail maps are available at park entrance stations, visitor centers and concession units.

One- and 2.5-hour guided horseback rides leave May through October from Skyland.

Free picnic grounds with water, fireplaces, tables and restrooms are found at Dickey Ridge, Elkwallow, Pinnacles, Big Meadows, Lewis Mountain and South River. *See Recreation Chart and the AAA Mideastern CampBook.*

ADMISSION to the park is $15 per private vehicle or $5 per person arriving by bicycle, bus, motorcycle or on foot. Permits are good for 7 days. An annual pass is $30.

PETS are permitted in the park only if they are leashed, crated or otherwise restricted at all times. Some trails are closed to pets.

ADDRESS inquiries to the Superintendent, Shenandoah National Park, 3655 US 211E, Luray, VA 22835; phone (540) 999-3500.

Points of Interest

SKYLINE DRIVE runs along the ridgecrest the entire length of the park and can be entered at four points: near Front Royal on US 340; at Thornton Gap between Luray and Sperryville on US 211; at Swift Run Gap between Stanardsville and Elkton on US 33; and at Rockfish Gap between Charlottesville and Waynesboro on US 250/I-64. The speed limit is 35 mph.

The 105-mile drive is one of the most spectacular scenic highways in the East. Parking overlooks offer views of the Piedmont to the east and the Shenandoah Valley to the west. Across the Shenandoah Valley rise Massanutten Mountain and, farther away, the Allegheny Mountains.

Not far from Thornton Gap is a 610-foot tunnel through the solid granodiorite of Marys Rock. The highest point on the road is at the north entrance to Skyland, where the elevation is 3,680 feet. Blue Ridge Parkway *(see place listing p. 234)* extends 469 miles from the southern end of Skyline Drive to Great Smoky Mountains National Park in North Carolina and Tennessee.

An audio tour running from north to south describes the highlights, features and history of the Skyline Drive; it is available for $10 at the two northernmost entrance stations, Front Royal and Thornton Gap, and at concessioners and park visitor centers. Phone (540) 999-3582 to order audio tour.

SMITHFIELD—*see Hampton Roads Area p. 267.*

SPOTSYLVANIA (D-11) pop. 3,833

The Battle of Spotsylvania Court House was fought May 8-21, 1864. The site is preserved as part of Fredericksburg and Spotsylvania National Military Park *(see place listing p. 250).*

In spite of losing about 17,000 men in the Battle of the Wilderness, Gen. Ulysses S. Grant pressed on toward Richmond. On May 8, north of Spotsylvania, the Union Army of the Potomac met Lee's Confederate Army of Northern Virginia. Fighting continued for 2 weeks, resulting in approximately 30,000 casualties; among them was Union general John Sedgwick, who was killed by a sharpshooter.

The fighting reached its zenith May 12 when Union and Confederate armies struggled for 20 hours over a turn in the Confederate logworks known as the Bloody Angle. Though neither side could claim victory, Grant continued toward Richmond.

Spotsylvania County Visitor Center: 4704 Southpoint Pkwy., Fredericksburg, VA 22407; phone (540) 891-8687 or (800) 654-4118.

STAUNTON (F-7) pop. 23,853, elev. 1,382′

One of the oldest cities west of the Blue Ridge Mountains, Staunton (STAN-tun) was settled by John Lewis in 1732. It was named for Lady Rebecca Staunton, the wife of Gov. William Gooch. The town was laid out in 1747, and by 1800 its population had reached 1,000. Staunton's growth was aided by the opening of rail service in 1854 and its proximity to extensive mining operations.

Because it remained largely unscathed during the Civil War, Staunton has one of Virginia's finest collections of 19th-century architecture. Trinity Episcopal Church on Beverley Street was built in 1855 on the site of the building in which the Virginia Assembly took refuge in 1781, after escaping the British. Visitors can view 12 Tiffany stained-glass windows in the church.

Staunton also is noted as the early home of Woodrow Wilson, the most recent of the eight Virginia-born presidents. Free guided walking tours of the historic town depart from the Woodrow Wilson Presidential Library and Museum *(see attraction listing)* on Saturday at 10, May through October.

Staunton-Augusta Travel Information Center: 1290 Richmond Rd., Staunton, VA 24401; phone (540) 332-3972 or (800) 332-5219. *See color ad p. 307.*

Self-guiding tours: The travel information center has maps detailing a walking tour of Staunton, which features five National Historic Districts: Beverley, Gospel Hill, Newtown, Stuart Addition and The Wharf. The brochure also is available at the Downtown Staunton Visitors Center at 35 S. New St.; phone (540) 332-3971.

AMERICAN SHAKESPEARE CENTER— BLACKFRIARS PLAYHOUSE is at 10 S. Market St. The company presents Elizabethan plays and other works at the Blackfriars Playhouse, modeled after Shakespeare's original indoor theater. In 17th-century tradition the audience closely surrounds the stage and often interacts with the performers. Pre-show lectures and educational programs also are offered.

Allow 1 hour minimum for guided tours. Guided theater tours are given Mon.-Fri. at 11 and 2, Sat. at 11, year-round. Evening and matinee performances are presented Wed.-Sun., 51 weeks per year. Performance times vary; phone ahead. Guided tour $5. Performance tickets $30-$32; $26-$28 (ages 65+ and students with ID); $22-$24 (ages 7-12). Prices may vary for performances. Under 7 are not permitted to performances. AX, DS, MC, VI. Phone (540) 851-1733 or (877) 682-4236.

FRONTIER CULTURE MUSEUM is off I-81 exit 222, then .3 mi. w. on US 250.

The living-history facility features reconstructed working farms of the 17th, 18th and 19th centuries. Costumed interpreters depict life in Germany, Northern Ireland and England. Living-history demonstrations at two American farms show a rich European influence on Appalachian cultural traditions.

Typical farms from Germany, England, Northern Ireland and the Shenandoah Valley have been moved and re-assembled at the museum. Many of Virginia's early colonists were representative of the farmers who occupied these historic homes. A short film about the development of the museum project is available. Changing exhibits focus on European and American culture. The self-guiding tour covers five-eighths of a mile.

Allow 2 hours minimum. Daily 9-5, mid-Mar. through Nov. 30; 10-4, rest of year. Closed Jan. 1, Thanksgiving and Dec. 25. Admission $10; $9.50 (ages 61+); $6 (ages 6-12). AX, DS, MC, VI. Phone (540) 332-7850.

SUNSPOTS STUDIOS is at 202 S. Lewis St. Working artisans at this commercial studio demonstrate the techniques they use to blow molten glass into handcrafted decorative objects. Allow 1 hour minimum. Mon.-Sat. 9:30-5:30 (also Fri.-Sat. 5:30-9, in July), Sun. 11:30-5. Free. Phone (540) 885-0678.

SAVE **WOODROW WILSON PRESIDENTIAL LIBRARY AND MUSEUM**, 18-24 N. Coalter and Frederick sts., is dedicated to the life and legacy of the 28th president of the United States. Exhibit galleries and archives in a restored 1855 mansion also interpret Wilson's other roles: scholar, university president and New Jersey governor.

Also offered are guided tours of his birthplace, the Presbyterian Manse, a Greek Revival house adjacent to the museum. The home has been restored to depict the Wilsons' family life in the Shenandoah

Valley before the Civil War. A Victorian garden also is on the grounds.

Allow 1 hour minimum. Museum and library Mon.-Sat. 9-5, Sun. noon-5, Mar.-Oct.; Mon.-Sat. 10-4, Sun. noon-4, rest of year. Closed Jan. 1, Easter, Thanksgiving and Dec. 25. Presbyterian Manse tours are given Mon.-Sat. 10-5, Sun. 12:30-5, Mar.-Oct.; Mon.-Sat. 10-4, Sun. noon-4, rest of year. Last tour begins 45 minutes before closing. Admission $10; $5 (ages 13-18 and college students with ID); $3 (ages 6-12). MC, VI. Phone (540) 885-0897 or (888) 496-6376.

STEELES TAVERN (G-7) elev. 1,680'

David Steele settled here in 1781, offering lodging to travelers on the road between Staunton and Lexington. The village that grew up around the tavern would be the birthplace of two revolutionary labor-saving devices, the Gibbs sewing machine and the McCormick reaper.

WALNUT GROVE (McCORMICK'S FARM) is off I-81 exit 205, then about 1 mi. e. on SR 606. Cyrus McCormick and his father perfected and marketed the first mechanical grain reaper here in 1831. Cyrus' smithy, now a museum, contains an original reaper. Daily 8-5, Apr.-Dec.; Mon.-Fri. 8-5, rest of year (weather permitting). Free. Phone (540) 377-2255.

STERLING—see District of Columbia p. 133.

STRASBURG (E-8) pop. 4,017, elev. 637'

German settlers were drawn to the Bavarian-like countryside around Strasburg in the late 1700s. Beginning in the 19th century, pottery-making rose to such prominence that the community was dubbed "Pot Town." By 1908, however, its six potteries had closed. Strasburg's economy is based primarily on printing and the manufacture of automotive parts. The city also is a favorite stop for antique hunters.

Strasburg Chamber of Commerce: 105 Stony Pointe Way, Suite 204, P.O. Box 42, Strasburg, VA 22657; phone (540) 465-3187. *See color ad p. 904.*

Self-guiding tours: A self-guiding walking tour brochure is available from the chamber of commerce.

Shopping areas: Strasburg Antique Emporium, 150 North Massanutten St., features a multitude of vendors specializing in Civil War memorabilia, furniture, vintage clothing, reproductions and art.

[SAVE] **CRYSTAL CAVERNS AT HUPP'S HILL** is off I-81 exit 298, then .5 mi. s. on Old Valley Pike (US 11). The caverns, once used by both Shawnee Indians and Civil War soldiers, contain formations such as terraced flowstone. Allow 1 hour, 30 minutes minimum. Tours are given daily at 11, 12:30, 2 and 3:30. Fee $10; $8 (ages 7-17 and 65+). MC, VI. Phone (540) 465-5884.

THE JEANE DIXON MUSEUM & LIBRARY is at 132 N. Massanutten St. A collection of personal possessions, documents and furnishings depict the life of psychic Jeane Dixon, perhaps best known for her prediction of the 1963 Kennedy assassination. Exhibits illustrate her accomplishments and predictions as well as skeptics' attempts to debunk her work. Allow 1 hour minimum. Sat.-Sun. 10-5, June-Aug.; otherwise by appointment. Tours are given at 10 and 2. Admission $5; $4 (ages 6-18, ages 62+ and students with ID). MC, VI. Phone (540) 465-5999.

[SAVE] **THE MUSEUM OF AMERICAN PRESIDENTS** is off I-81 exit 298, then 2 mi. s. on US 11 to 130 N. Massanutten St. Highlights include the desk on which James Madison drafted the Federalist Papers, White House doors, a reproduction of Washington's Rising Sun chair, a variety of handwritten letters of the presidents and presidential portraits. A one-room schoolhouse offers hands-on activities for children. Allow 30 minutes minimum. Sat.-Sun. 10-5, June-Aug.; otherwise by appointment. Admission $5; $4 (ages 6-18, ages 62+ and students with ID). MC, VI. Phone (540) 465-5999.

DID YOU KNOW

America's first peanuts were grown in Virginia.

[SAVE] **"STONEWALL" JACKSON MUSEUM** is off I-81 exit 298, then .5 mi. s. on Old Valley Pike (US 11) at Hupp's Hill. This 18-acre site played a role in the 1864 Battle of Hupp's Hill and other campaigns. A half-mile walking trail highlights lunettes and trenches built by Gen. Philip Sheridan's troops.

Exhibits detail Gen. Thomas J. "Stonewall" Jackson's campaign with maps, photographs, original artifacts and hands-on reproductions. Children can dress in Civil War garb while playing in a mock encampment. Daily 10-5; closed Jan. 1, Easter, Thanksgiving and Dec. 24-25 and 31. Admission $5; $4 (ages 7-17 and 56+). MC, VI. Phone (540) 465-5884.

STRASBURG MUSEUM is 2 blks. e. of jct. US 11 and E. King St. on SR 55. The town's old railroad station houses a pottery collection, toys, apparel, home implements, farm tools and shop machines that date from the mid-1800s. Settings include Colonial and Victorian rooms and cooper's, potter's and blacksmith's shops. Civil War exhibits also are featured. Daily 10-4, May-Oct. Admission $3; $1 (ages 13-18); 50c (ages 0-12). Phone (540) 465-3175.

STRATFORD (F-10)

The land for Stratford Hall Plantation was purchased in 1717 by Thomas Lee, president of the Council of Virginia and acting governor 1749-50. The manor he built overlooking the Potomac River would be home to four generations of the Lee family, including Gen. Robert E. Lee, who was born there in 1807. Thomas' sons, Richard Henry and Francis Lightfoot, were the only brothers to sign the Declaration of Independence. "Light Horse" Harry Lee, Robert E. Lee's father, was a Revolutionary War general.

[GEM] **STRATFORD HALL PLANTATION—THE BIRTHPLACE OF ROBERT E. LEE** is off SR 3 to SR 214, then 1 mi. following signs. Owned by the Lee family 1717-1822, the plantation still is operated in the manner of that era. Visitors can wander more than 1,600 acres of woods, meadows, gardens and cultivated fields. The house, built in 1730 in the shape of an H, is among the finest examples of Colonial architecture in the United States. The visitor center offers a museum.

Auxiliary buildings include an 18th-century kitchen and a coach house. A reconstructed mill grinds corn, wheat, oats and barley (weather permitting) on the first full weekend of each month. More than two miles of nature trails crisscross the plantation. Food is available daily 11-3. Grounds daily 9:30-4; closed Jan. 1, Thanksgiving and Dec. 24-25 and 31. House tours are offered daily 10-4. Admission $10; $9 (ages 61+); $5 (ages 6-11). Phone (804) 493-8371.

SURRY—*see Hampton Roads Area p. 267.*

TANGIER (G-11) pop. 604

Discovered and named in 1608 by Capt. John Smith, Tangier Island was settled in 1686 by John Crockett and his sons' families. In 1814 it was headquarters of a British fleet that ravaged the Chesapeake Bay. Until recently it had few visitors because of its inaccessibility. Many customs and much of the appearance of an earlier era remain. Natives of the island still speak with a trace of an Elizabethan accent.

Since the 1800s Tangier's fishermen have supplied the Eastern Shore of Maryland with crabs and oysters. Crab farms lie along the island's shore and in open tanks perched on pilings in the harbor, which is crowded with fishing craft and sailboats. Duck hunting, fishing and swimming are permitted.

There are only a few cars and trucks on the island; bicycles and motor scooters are popular means of transportation. The island's two streets are only 8 to 10 feet wide.

Boat trips to the island depart from Onancock (*see place listing p. 282*) and Reedville (*see place listing p. 285*) as well as Crisfield, Md. (*see place listing in Maryland p. 192*). Reservations are required.

TAPPAHANNOCK (G-10) pop. 2,068

In 1680 the General Assembly passed an act for "cohabitation," creating Tappahannock and 15 other towns. The act was vetoed by King Charles II, but later revived under William and Mary. Despite these delays in sanctioning its existence, Tappahannock grew into a prosperous Colonial port and county seat.

Tappahannock-Essex County Chamber of Commerce: P.O. Box 481, Tappahannock, VA 22560; phone (804) 443-5241.

RAPPAHANNOCK RIVER CRUISES departs from the foot of the Hoskins Creek Bridge, just s. of jct. US 17 and US 360. An all-day cruise travels from the Hoskins Creek Bridge up the Rappahannock River to Ingleside Plantation Vineyards (*see Rollins Fork p. 304*); tours and tastings are included. Cruises depart daily at 10 and return at 4, May 1-Oct. 15. Fare $25; $13 (ages 4-12). Reservations are required. Phone (804) 453-2628.

TAZEWELL (H-4) pop. 4,206, elev. 2,372'

Settled in 1799, the village was named for Henry Tazewell, a member of the Virginia House of Burgesses and later a state senator.

Tazewell County Visitor Center: 200 Sanders Ln., Bluefield, VA 24605; phone (276) 322-1345.

SAVE **CRAB ORCHARD MUSEUM AND PIONEER PARK**, 4 mi. w. on US 19/460, highlights Appalachian heritage, pioneer life, the Revolutionary and Civil wars and animals of Southwest Virginia.

Items on display include a horse-drawn hearse and a Model T ford as well as 18th- and 19th-century weapons, tools and furnishings. Within the park is a settlement containing 14 log and stone buildings and a 500-year-old Indian village.

Tues.-Sat. 9-5, Sun. 1-5, Memorial Day-Labor Day; Tues.-Sat. 9-5, rest of year. Closed Thanksgiving and Dec. 24-Jan. 1. Admission $4; $3 (ages 61+); $2 (ages 7-11). DS, MC, VI. Phone (276) 988-6755.

THE PLAINS (B-10) pop. 266, elev. 605′

In the heart of hunt country, The Plains is home to Great Meadow, a 250-acre site for horse-racing and steeplechase events. The Virginia Gold Cup, a spring tradition since 1922, is held on the first Saturday in May and draws some 45,000 spectators.

WINERIES

• **Piedmont Vineyards** is at 2546D Halfway Rd. Daily 11-6, Apr.-Oct.; 11-5, rest of year. Closed Jan. 1, Thanksgiving, and Dec. 24-25 and 31. Phone (540) 687-5528.

TRIANGLE—see District of Columbia p. 133.

UPPERVILLE (A-10) elev. 537′

TRINITY EPISCOPAL CHURCH is at 9108 John Mosby Hwy. Architect H. Page Cross adapted the style of 12th- and 13th-century French country churches for his 1955 design. Most of the stone and wood used in the church was fashioned by local men who made their cutting tools in a forge on the grounds. Of interest are the sculptured ornamentations on the pews, pulpit and columns, and the windows of the nave and choir, which were made in Amsterdam. Daily 9-4. Free. Phone (540) 592-3343.

VIENNA—see District of Columbia p. 133.

VIRGINIA BEACH—
see Hampton Roads Area p. 268.

WAYNESBORO (G-7) pop. 19,520

Located in the Shenandoah Valley, Waynesboro was the site of the last major Civil War battle in central Virginia. The area offers visitors a variety of historical and natural attractions as well as many recreational opportunities found along Skyline Drive (*see attraction listing p. 306*) and the Blue Ridge Parkway (*see place listing p. 234*).

P. BUCKLEY MOSS MUSEUM is off I-64 exit 94 at 150 P. Buckley Moss Dr. The museum houses the permanent collection of renowned artist Patricia. Buckley Moss. A retrospect of Moss's life and art is represented on the main floor, while third floor pieces feature historic Virginia locations and religious themes. Works also reflect the cultural heritage of the Shenandoah Valley

and the Amish and Mennonite people of the area. Guided tours are available by appointment. Allow 1 hour minimum. Mon.-Sat. 10-6, Sun. 12:30-5:30. Free. Phone (540) 949-6473 or (800) 343-8643.

WHITE HALL (F-8) elev. 722′

WINERIES

• **White Hall Vineyards** is 8 mi. w. of US 29 on Barracks/Garth Rd., then 1.5 mi. n. w. to 5282 Sugar Ridge Rd. Wed.-Sun. 11-5; closed major holidays. Phone (434) 823-8615.

WHITE MARSH—
see Hampton Roads Area p. 270.

WHITE POST (E-8) elev. 607′

White Post takes its name from the white post erected by surveyor George Washington to mark the route to Lord Thomas Fairfax's wilderness manor, Greenway Court. A white post on SR 277 still points the way to Fairfax's estate, torn down in 1858.

Following his residency at Belvoir with his cousin William Fairfax, Lord Thomas Fairfax moved to White Post in 1748 and built Greenway Court, where he threw lavish parties for his male acquaintances. He lived at Greenway Court until his death at the age of 91. Legend has it that Fairfax, a loyal Tory, took to his bed and died soon after he learned of Gen. Charles Cornwallis' surrender.

DINOSAUR LAND is at 3848 Stonewall Jackson Hwy. Life-size reproductions of dinosaurs are displayed, including the tyrannosaurus, velociraptor, apatosaurus and more. Many photo opportunities exist at this family-oriented attraction. Allow 1 hour minimum. Daily 9:30-6:30, Memorial Day-Labor Day; 9:30-5:30, Mar. 1-day before Memorial Day and day after Labor Day-Oct. 31; 9:30-5, Nov.-Dec. Admission $5; $4 (ages 2-10). AX, DS, MC, VI. Phone (540) 869-2222.

WILDERNESS (D-10) elev. 247′

The Wilderness, a region of dense thickets south of the Rapidan River, is where Gen. Ulysses S. Grant opened his 1864 campaign. In the Battle of the Wilderness, beginning on May 5, Grant's troops met Gen. Robert E. Lee's Confederates, and fighting raged for 2 days.

Fierce attacks and counterattacks swept through the Wilderness. The woods caught fire, making an inferno in which many of the wounded perished. By the end of the second day neither side had gained the advantage. On May 7 Grant again started his army toward Richmond, but he met Confederate resistance at Spotsylvania Court House (*see Spotsylvania p. 306*).

The Wilderness is now part of Fredericksburg and Spotsylvania National Military Park (*see place listing p. 250*).

Williamsburg, Jamestown and Yorktown

Virginia's Historic Triangle

Colonial Williamsburg Historic Area
© Medford Taylor / SuperStock

Williamsburg began as Middle Plantation, an outpost of Jamestown, in 1633. It was adjacent to a palisade that the settlers built across the peninsula between the James and York rivers.

Because of its strategic location and the strength of its defenses, Middle Plantation soon became important to the colony. In 1676 rebel Nathaniel Bacon and his followers held a convention here, and a year later the General Assembly met after Bacon burned the statehouse at Jamestown.

When the capital of the colony was removed from Jamestown in 1699, a new planned city was laid out at Middle Plantation named Williamsburg in honor of King William III. For 81 years it was the seat of government and the social and cultural center of Virginia. In 1780 Gov. Thomas Jefferson relocated the capital to Richmond, 50 miles to the west at the fall line of the James River.

CHARLES CITY (B-2) elev. 45′

Charles City County, established in 1616, is wedged in between the James and Chickahominy Rivers. From its very beginning the area has been tied to America's history. Chief Powhatan and his daughter Pocahontas were early residents; they were followed by Benjamin Harrison, presidents William Henry Harrison and John Tyler, and Robert E. Lee. Their tobacco farms and plantations lined the James River, on or just off scenic SR 5, near the Colonial capitals of Williamsburg and Jamestown and convenient to the later capital, Richmond.

[SAVE] **BERKELEY PLANTATION** is 6.5 mi. w. on SR 5, then 1 mi. s. to 12602 Harrison Landing Rd. The 1726 Georgian mansion is the birthplace of both Benjamin Harrison V, a signer of the Declaration of Independence, and William Henry Harrison, ninth U.S. president. "Taps" was composed here while Gen. George McClellan used Berkeley as a Civil War headquarters.

The grounds feature five terraces that contain restored boxwood and flower gardens along the James

River. Costumed guides lead tours. Open daily 9-4:30; closed Thanksgiving and Dec. 25. Admission $11; $7.50 (ages 13-16); $6 (ages 6-12). MC, VI. Phone (804) 829-6018 or (888) 466-6018.

EDGEWOOD PLANTATION is on SR 5 at 4800 John Tyler Memorial Hwy. The restored 7,000-square-foot Gothic mansion, built by Spenser Rowland in 1849, features a freestanding, winding, three-story staircase as well as 10 fireplaces. Guided tours take in 11 rooms containing antique furnishings, Victorian memorabilia and period clothing.

Two gazebos, formal gardens, slave quarters and a 1725 gristmill are on the grounds. A tea lunch is available by reservation. Special events and educational programs also are offered, including Victorian Christmas, held mid-November through December 31, and Charles Dickens Candlelight Tours, available mid-November through January 1.

Daily 11-4; closed major holidays. Admission $10; $5 (ages 7-10). A grounds and gardens combination ticket with North Bend Plantation, Piney Grove at Southall's Plantation and Westover is available. Fees for special events and educational programs vary; phone ahead. Phone (804) 829-2962.

NORTH BEND PLANTATION is 1 mi. e. on SR 5, then 1 mi. s. on CR 619 to 12200 Weyanoke Rd. The 1819 Greek Revival-style house was built by John Minge for his wife Sarah Harrison, sister of William Henry Harrison. Other original buildings on the grounds include a dairy barn and a smokehouse. Guided house tours are available by appointment. Grounds open daily 9-5. Admission $3; $1 (ages 8-18). A grounds and gardens combination ticket with Edgewood Plantation, Piney Grove at

Southall's Plantation and Westover is available. Phone (804) 829-5176.

SAVE **PINEY GROVE AT SOUTHALL'S PLANTATION** is .1 mi. e. on SR 5, then 6 mi. n. on CR 615 to 16920 Southall Plantation Ln. A collection of buildings that exemplify regional architectural styles includes Piney Grove, a late 18th-century log house built on site by Furneau Southall. Among the structures moved to the grounds are a modest 1835 plantation house and an 1857 post-and-beam residence. Gardens and a nature trail also are on the property.

Allow 30 minutes minimum. Grounds daily 9-5. Admission $3. A grounds and gardens combination ticket with Edgewood Plantation, North Bend Plantation and Westover is available. Phone (804) 829-2480.

GEM **SHIRLEY PLANTATION** is 9.5 mi. w. via SR 5 to 501 Shirley Plantation Rd.
SAVE The plantation has been owned by the Hill and Carter families since 1638 and is purported to be the oldest continuously owned family business in the United States. The present mansion, built in 1723, was the birthplace of Anne Hill Carter and the setting for her marriage to "Light Horse" Harry Lee. In later years their son, Gen. Robert E. Lee, was a frequent visitor.

Docents highlight family portraits, silver and furniture—items handed down for 11 generations—on tours of the mansion, which sits on a bluff of the James River. A carved-walnut staircase rises three stories without visible support and is said to be the only one of its kind in America. Self-guiding tours of the plantation grounds, which also includes four brick outbuildings set in a Queen Anne-style courtyard, are available. A stable, smokehouse and dovecote are other original structures.

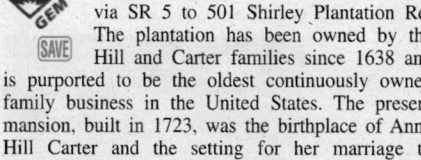

Williamsburg / © Bill Bachmann
Danita Delimont Stock Photography

Allow 1 hour minimum. Grounds daily 9-5; closed Thanksgiving and Dec. 25. Last house tour begins 15 minutes before closing. Admission $11; $10 (ages 61+); $7.50 (ages 6-18); $5 (military with ID). MC, VI. Phone (804) 829-5121 or (800) 232-1613.

WESTOVER is off SR 5 at 7000 Westover Rd. An outstanding example of Georgian architecture, this plantation home was built about 1730 by Richmond founder William Byrd II. The house is closed to the public, but visitors can stroll the grounds where tulip poplars and formal gardens overlook the James River. Brochures for a self-guiding walking tour are available at the gate.

Grounds daily 9-6. Admission $2. A grounds and gardens combination ticket with Edgewood Plantation, North Bend Plantation and Piney Grove at Southall's Plantation is available. Phone (804) 829-2882.

Destination Williamsburg Jamestown & Yorktown

Visiting this historic area is like taking a refresher course in American History 101. Places and faces here have popped right off the pages of textbooks.

Study the 17th-century site of the first Thanksgiving and see its faithful re-creation, Jamestown Settlement. Talk with colonists in 18th-century Colonial Williamsburg. But don't dwell on the past—20th-century theme parks also are memory makers.

© Gibson Stock Photography

College of William and Mary, Williamsburg. Thomas Jefferson, James Monroe and John Tyler are among the alumni of the second oldest college in America. (See listing page 322)

Douglas Peebles
Virginia Tourism
Corp

Governor's Palace in Colonial Williamsburg. The reconstructed palace served as the executive mansion for governors Patrick Henry and Thomas Jefferson. (See listing page 324)

© SuperStock

James Fort at Jamestown Settlement. Wattle-and-daub structures topped with thatched roofs reflect the time period from 1610-1614. (See listing page 319)

Williamsburg Area

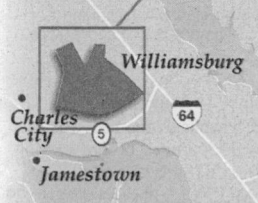

See Area map page 315

17

Williamsburg

Charles City

64

5

Jamestown

Yorktown

105

17

Virginia Tourism Corp

Yorktown Battlefield. Peruse the battlefield grounds to encounter siege works and encampment areas. (See listing page 326)

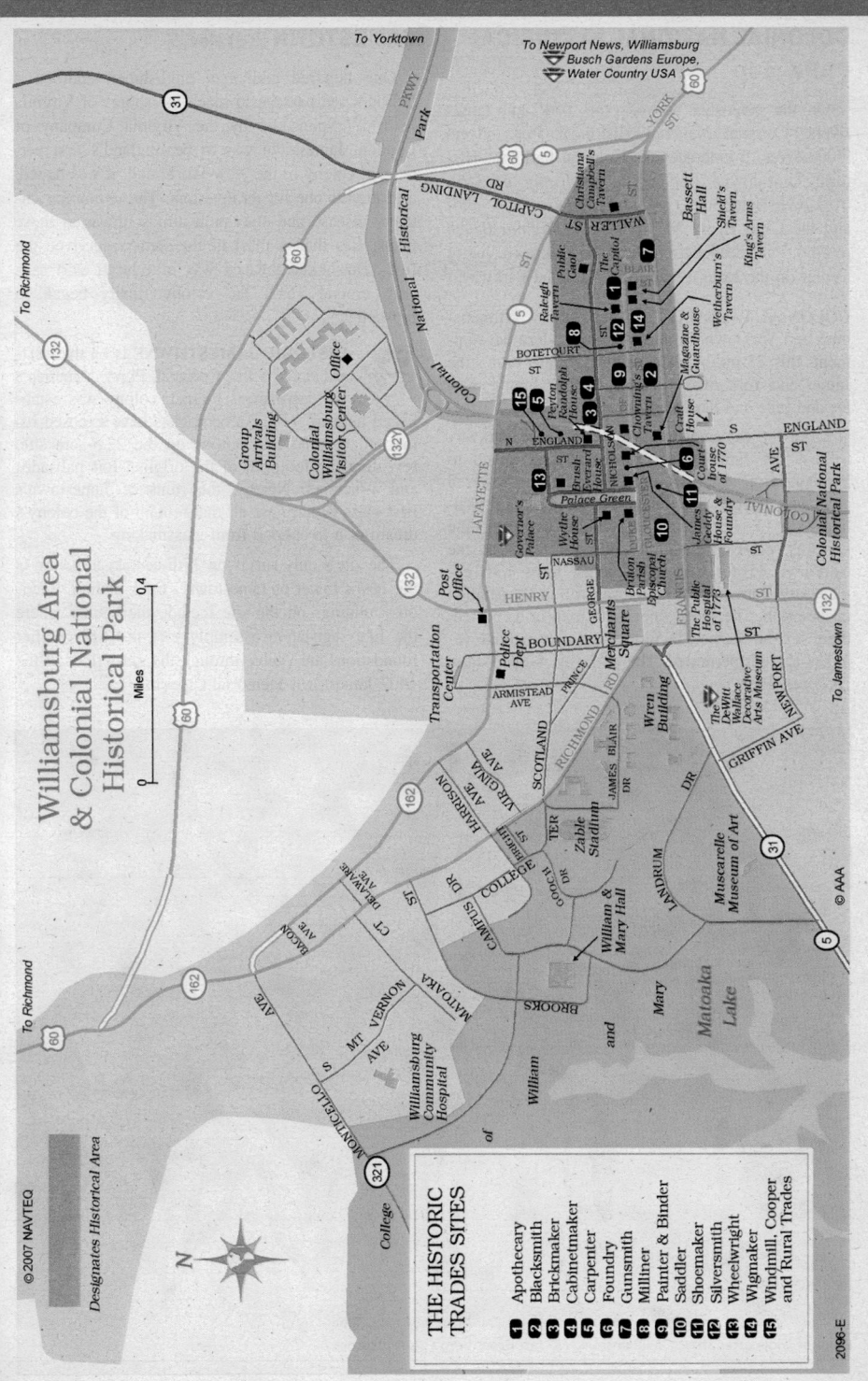

Williamsburg Area
& Colonial National
Historical Park

Designates Historical Area

© 2007 NAVTEQ

To Yorktown

To Newport News, Williamsburg
Busch Gardens Europe,
Water Country USA

To Richmond

To Richmond

To Jamestown

Group Arrivals Building

Colonial Williamsburg Visitor Center

Post Office

Police Dept

Transportation Center

Williamsburg Community Hospital

Matoaka Lake

Mary and

William of College

Musearelle Museum of Art

William & Mary Hall

Zable Stadium

Wren Building

The DeWitt Wallace Decorative Arts Museum

The Public Hospital of 1773

Bruton Parish Episcopal Church

Wythe House

Governor's Palace

Palace Green

Brush Everard House

Merchants Square

Peyton Randolph House

Raleigh Tavern

Public Gaol

The Capitol

Christiana Campbell's Tavern

Bassett Hall

Shield's Tavern

King's Arms Tavern

Wetherburn's Tavern

Magazine & Guardhouse

Craft House

Chowning's Tavern

James Geddy House & Foundry

Court House of 1770

Miles   0   0.4

N

© AAA

2096-E

THE HISTORIC TRADES SITES

1 Apothecary
2 Blacksmith
3 Brickmaker
4 Cabinetmaker
5 Carpenter
6 Foundry
7 Gunsmith
8 Milliner
9 Painter & Binder
10 Saddler
11 Shoemaker
12 Silversmith
13 Wheelwright
14 Wigmaker
15 Windmill, Cooper and Rural Trades

COLONIAL NATIONAL HISTORICAL PARK (B-3)

On the peninsula between the York and James rivers, Colonial National Historical Park covers 9,000 acres. It embraces the Colonial Parkway, Historic Jamestowne *(see attraction listing p. 316),* Yorktown Battlefield *(see attraction listing p. 326)* and the Cape Henry Memorial *(see Virginia Beach p. 269).* Park headquarters is in the Yorktown Visitor Center on the eastern end of the Colonial Parkway.

COLONIAL PARKWAY links Jamestown, Williamsburg and Yorktown. Protected from modern development, this 23-mile scenic highway winds along the James and York rivers, passing through tidal estuaries and pine and hardwood forests.

From the Jamestown Visitor Center the parkway follows the James River before turning inland to Williamsburg, where it tunnels under the restored city. Just beyond the tunnel is the Colonial Williamsburg Visitor Center. Traveling overland, the parkway passes plantation sites and ends at the Yorktown Visitor Center. Turnouts, most with explanatory markers, allow pauses for more detailed observation. The speed limit is 45 mph or as posted; there are no service facilities, and commercial vehicles are not permitted. The parkway is open daily 24 hours. Free.

JAMESTOWN (B-3) elev. 5′

One hundred and four Englishmen endured a 5-month sea passage to reach the shores of Virginia in 1607. Sponsored by the Virginia Company of London, Jamestown was to be England's first permanent colony in the New World and, it was hoped, a profitable one for its investors. The unfamiliar climate, disease and starvation almost thwarted those plans; less than a third of the settlers survived the first year. When tobacco was introduced as a cash crop around 1613, the colony finally began to prosper.

HISTORIC JAMESTOWNE is on the western end of the Colonial Pkwy. America's first permanent English colony was established here in 1607. Archeologists have exposed ruins and original foundations on the 22.5-acre site, revealing the footprint of the original fort palisades and structures. Nearby, the ruins of Jamestown's first glass furnace are all that remain of the colony's dream of a livelihood from glassmaking.

The site's only surviving 17th-century structure is the 1690s tower of Jamestown's brick church. Previous buildings on the site include the church where the first legislative assembly met in 1619. Earlier foundations are visible through the glass floor of the 1907 Jamestown Memorial Church.

Duke of Gloucester Street, Williamsburg / © Jeff Greenberg / age fotostock

Foundations of homes, taverns and shops built after 1620 can be seen in the New Towne section, which includes the 18th-century Ambler Mansion. Costumed interpreters lead living-history tours in the summer, and ranger-led walking tours are available all year (weather permitting). A 5-mile driving tour features interpretive waysides and views of the island's natural environment.

The site is administered jointly by the National Park Service and the Association for the Preservation of Virginia Antiquities (APVA). Allow 2 hours minimum. Entrance station open daily 9-5; closed Jan. 1 and Dec. 25. Archeological site and tour road remain open until dusk. Admission (good for 7 days) includes Yorktown Battlefield *(see attraction listing p. 326)* $10; free (ages 0-15). Phone (757) 229-1733.

Historic Jamestowne Visitor Center and Archaearium is on the western end of the Colonial Pkwy. An immersion theater experience and exhibits portray the story of Historic Jamestowne. The Archaearium museum displays some of the more than 1 million artifacts that have been excavated at the site, including weapons, tools, ceramics and the personal belongings of Jamestown's earliest colonists. By looking through special viewers, visitors can see a virtual 17th-century landscape.

In addition a walking trail leads to the re-created glasshouse, where costumed interpreters demonstrate early glassblowing techniques. Open daily 9-5; closed Dec. 25. Admission included with Historic Jamestowne. Phone (757) 229-1733.

JAMESTOWN SETTLEMENT is on SR 31 next to Historic Jamestowne. This living history museum was established in 1957 to celebrate the 350th anniversary of Jamestown's founding. Gallery exhibits and a 15-minute film trace the settlement's origins in England and its first century in America. Also explored is the influence of the European, African and Powhatan Indian cultures that shaped the colony's development.

Costumed interpreters provide a glimpse of life during the early 1600s at three outdoor living history areas. The palisaded structure that was home to the first Jamestown colonists is re-created at James Fort. Wattle-and-daub buildings include a church, the governor's house, a storehouse and an armory. Visitors can climb aboard a 17th-century sailing vessel on the James River, where reproductions of the *Discovery, Godspeed* and *Susan Constant* are moored. The Powhatan Indian Village, with several houses, a garden and a ceremonial dance circle, is based on archeological findings and eyewitness accounts of the period.

Food is available. Allow 2 hours minimum. Museum and outdoor exhibits open daily 9-6, June 15-Aug. 15; 9-5, rest of year. Closed Jan. 1 and Dec.

Colonial Williamsburg Visitor Center

Northeast of the Governor's Palace, the Colonial Williamsburg Visitor Center is open daily 8:45-5:45. Holiday hours may vary. Go to the center first for tickets and information. Streets in the Historic Area are closed to automobiles. Park at the visitor center; shuttle buses leave for the historic area every few minutes.

Several combination tickets for Colonial Williamsburg are available. All passes include the Revolutionary City, the Colonial Williamsburg bus system and an orientation film. The Capital City Pass (1 day) includes most Colonial Williamsburg Historic Area buildings,

gardens and museums (excludes the Governor's Palace). The Governor's Key-to-the-City Pass (good for 2 consecutive days) and the Colonial Williamsburg Freedom Pass (good for 1 year) include admission to all Colonial Williamsburg exhibition buildings and museums. The 1-day Capital City Pass is $36; ages 6-17, $18. The 2-day Governor's Key-to-the-City Pass is $49; ages 6-17, $24. The annual Freedom Pass is $59; ages 6-17, $29.

Note: It is a good idea to verify hours and admission fees in advance.

Further information about Colonial Williamsburg's points of interest can be obtained by writing The Colonial Williamsburg Foundation, P.O. Box 1776, Williamsburg, VA 23187; phone (800) 447-8679.

25. Hours may vary; phone ahead. Admission $13.50; $6.25 (ages 6-12). Combination ticket with Yorktown Victory Center *(see attraction listing p. 327)* $19.25; $9.25 (ages 6-12). Other combination tickets are available. Phone (757) 253-4838 or (888) 593-4682. *See color ad p. 317.*

WILLIAMSBURG (B-3) pop. 11,998, elev. 78'

"That the future may learn from the past" is the theme for the Colonial Williamsburg Foundation, which operates this restoration project. Through extensive research, the 301-acre Colonial area of the city has been restored as nearly as possible to its 18th-century appearance.

Within this historic area are 88 buildings that survived from the 1700s. In addition more than 400 others have been faithfully rebuilt on their original sites.

Stately public buildings and a variety of Colonial homes, shops, taverns and gardens are on or just off historic Duke of Gloucester Street, the main thoroughfare of the city.

Interpreters dressed in 18th-century attire populate the historic area. Fife and drum parades take place April through October. In early December Grand Illumination Festivities herald the beginning of the Christmas season. Candles light up the regal homes of the historic district as fireworks streak across the night sky.

The Historic Triangle Shuttle, a bus linking Jamestown, Colonial Williamsburg and Yorktown, costs $1 per one-way trip for ages 7 and above, plus 25c for transfers to another route line; phone (757) 898-2410.

Greater Williamsburg Chamber & Tourism Alliance: 421 N. Boundary St., P.O. Box 3595, Williamsburg, VA 23187; phone (757) 229-6511 or (800) 368-6511.

Shopping areas: Merchants Square, on Gloucester Street near the College of William and Mary, is a downtown specialty shopping hub. It includes four Colonial Williamsburg stores including Craft House, which features antique-reproduction furniture and decorative accessories.

Bargain hunters find more than 90 upscale retailers, including Coach, Eddie Bauer, Jones New York and Nautica, at the Prime Outlets at Williamsburg on Richmond Road. The Williamsburg Outlet Mall, also on Richmond Road, offers more than 40 discount stores including Bass, Dockers and Farberware.

Some 400 antique vendors display their wares at the Williamsburg Antique Mall on Lightfoot Road. Handcrafted Colonial-style candles are available at the Williamsburg Candle Factory on US 60W; and the Williamsburg Pottery Factory, 5 miles west on US 60, offers woven baskets, brass pieces, china and crystal as well as pottery.

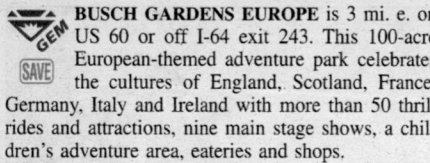 **BUSCH GARDENS EUROPE** is 3 mi. e. on US 60 or off I-64 exit 243. This 100-acre European-themed adventure park celebrates the cultures of England, Scotland, France, Germany, Italy and Ireland with more than 50 thrill rides and attractions, nine main stage shows, a children's adventure area, eateries and shops.

Griffon, one of the world's tallest floorless dive coasters, thrills riders with two Immelmann loops, dramatic drops and speeds of up to 75 mph as it climbs 205 feet, then dives 90 degrees straight down. The hypercoaster Apollo's Chariot takes riders over nine camelback humps, while the inverted steel coaster Alpengeist propels "skiers" on a dynamic, high-speed journey. The Big Bad Wolf coaster sends guests "howling" through a Bavarian village, and Loch Ness Monster, named after Scotland's serpent, hurls passengers through double interlocking loops.

Curse of DarKastle sends guests aboard gravity-defying sleighs careening through the dark and mysterious corridors of a Bavarian castle. Roman Rapids is a white-water raft ride, and Escape from Pompeii, with an erupting Mt. Vesuvius, results in a wet retreat from the volcano. Jack Hanna's Wild Reserve offers guests up-close encounters with a variety of wildlife. Visitors can kick up their heels at Emerald Beat, an Irish dance extravaganza.

Park opens daily at 10, Mar.-Oct.; days and closing times vary. Phone ahead to confirm schedule. Admission $56.95; $49.95 (ages 3-6). Multiday and combination tickets with Water Country USA are available. Rates may vary; phone ahead. Parking $10-$15. AX, DS, MC, VI. Phone (800) 343-7946.

COLLEGE OF WILLIAM AND MARY is at the w. end of Duke of Gloucester St. Harvard is the only U.S. college older than William and Mary. Chartered by King William III and Queen Mary II of England in 1693, the state university numbers among its alumni four presidents—George Washington, Thomas Jefferson, James Monroe and John Tyler. Phone (757) 221-4000.

Muscarelle Museum of Art is on Jamestown Rd. (SR 31) at the College of William and Mary. The museum hosts traveling exhibits and contains a permanent collection of some 4,000 paintings, graphics and sculpture.

The collection includes work from American artists such as Milton Avery, Paul Cadmus, Jasper Cropsey, Hans Hofmann, Jacob Lawrence, Georgia O'Keeffe, John Frederick Peto and Henry Ossawa Tanner. Wed. and Sat.-Sun. noon-4, Thurs.-Fri. 10-4:45; closed holidays. Galleries free. Special exhibitions $5; free (ages 0-11). Phone (757) 221-2700.

Wren Building is at the w. end of Duke of Gloucester St. at the College of William and Mary. The design of the building, which dates from 1695, has been attributed to English architect Sir Christopher Wren. Although damaged by three fires, the outer walls are still largely original. The chapel, great hall, convocation room and a classroom have been furnished to appear as they probably did in the 18th century. This is said to be the oldest academic building still in use in the United States. Mon.-Fri. 10-5, Sat. 9-5, Sun. noon-5. Free. Phone (757) 221-3278.

 COLONIAL WILLIAMSBURG HISTORIC AREA is off I-64 exit 238, following signs. This 301-acre, outdoor living-history museum re-creates the spirit and culture of everyday life in the 18th-century capital of Virginia.

After 1780, when Richmond became Virginia's capital, Williamsburg reverted to the status of a quiet college town. Fearing that many of its historic buildings would be lost, a local minister persuaded John D. Rockefeller Jr. to finance the restoration of the Colonial town. In 1926 the two men embarked on an ambitious project with architects, archeologists and historians to preserve some 70 structures.

Colonial Williamsburg is a step back in time to the 18th century, where costumed interpreters—tradespeople, housewives, slaves, freemen, governmental officials and soldiers—go about their everyday duties. Many of the buildings can be visited on self-guiding tours, while others are open for guided tours only.

Revolutionary City is a live outdoor theater experience re-creating the struggle for American independence 1774-1781. The program is staged over 2 days, focusing on the collapse of the royal government and the colonies at war. Events take place daily in the east end of the historic area; hours vary seasonally.

Pets on leashes are permitted in some outdoor areas. Historic area buildings open daily 9-5. Museums and The Public Hospital open daily 10-7. Hours vary seasonally; phone ahead. Various performances depicting aspects of Colonial life take place daily throughout the historic area. Admission tickets, which are required to enter most buildings and to ride the shuttle, are available at the Colonial Williamsburg Visitor Center (*see Visitor Center box*), the Greenhow Lumber House ticket office on Duke of Gloucester Street and at the Merchants Square Information Station. Phone (757) 220-7645 or (800) 447-8679.

The Abby Aldrich Rockefeller Folk Art Museum is at 325. W. Francis St. The institution is dedicated to the collection and preservation of American folk art. Eleven galleries display items from the 18th century to the present. Exhibits include carvings, embroideries, paintings, toys and weather vanes. Phone (757) 220-7724.

Bassett Hall is at 522 E. Francis St. This was the Williamsburg home of John D. and Abby Aldrich Rockefeller. The 18th-century house is named for Martha Washington's nephew, Burwell Bassett, who owned it 1800-39. It is furnished to reflect the Rockefellers' lifestyle during the 1930s when they were instrumental in restoring Colonial Williamsburg. A 10-minute videotape presentation precedes a tour of the house and grounds. Allow 30 minutes minimum.

TONIGHT, WHY NOT DINE WITH THE COLONISTS?

Experience the SIGHTS, SOUNDS, SCENTS, *and* TASTES of the 18th century in Colonial Williamsburg's historic taverns.

Enjoy colonial fare in our taverns located throughout the picturesque Historic Area. Dinner reservations are recommended for King's Arms and Christiana Campbell's Taverns, and casual attire is appropriate. Children's menus and vegetarian dishes are available. We accept all major credit cards. Smoking is not permitted in the taverns.

View our full menus at www.ColonialWilliamsburg.com.

～ FULL-SERVICE ～

KING'S ARMS TAVERN®
Where the Finest Gentry Dine

Relish generous cuts of prime aged beef, tender pork, and lamb served in the King's grand tradition! It's the Historic Area's finest dining experience.
416 East Duke of Gloucester Street

CHRISTIANA CAMPBELL'S TAVERN®
George Washington's Favorite for Seafood

Dine on regional specialties at Colonial Williamsburg's premier seafood tavern. Parking available behind the tavern.
101 South Waller Street

～ CASUAL DINING ～

CHOWNING'S TAVERN®
Traditional-Style Pit BBQ

Savor the great tastes of BBQ! Pulled pork, ribs, and chicken. A local favorite! Get it to go. Enjoy Gambols in the evenings. Tavern parking available in Francis Street lot.
198 East Duke of Gloucester Street

SHIELDS TAVERN®
18th-Century-Style Coffeehouse

This tavern takes on a new life as an 18th-century-style coffeehouse. Enjoy all-day, walk-in convenience for beverage and light food choices. Eat in or carry out. Tavern parking available in Francis Street lot.
422 East Duke of Gloucester Street

FOR RESERVATIONS, CALL 1-800-TAVERNS (1-800-828-3767)

Colonial Williamsburg Taverns

Bruton Parish Episcopal Church is at the n.w. corner of Duke of Gloucester St. and the Palace Green. Dr. W.A.R. Goodwin, rector of this church in the early 1900s, approached John D. Rockefeller with the idea of preserving Colonial Williamsburg. The church itself was erected 1712-15 to replace an earlier building and has been restored. The bell in the tower, rung for many important events since 1761, still rings for services.

Guided tours are offered Mon.-Sat. 9-5 (also Thurs. at 8 p.m., in summer), Sun. 1-5. Candlelight recitals are offered Tues. and Sat. at 8 p.m., in summer. Hours may vary; phone ahead. Free. Phone (757) 229-2891.

The Capitol is at the e. end of Duke of Gloucester St. The current structure represents the first capitol, which was built in 1701 and reconstructed during the 1930s. The Capitol was the site of many important political events. The most significant of these took place May 15, 1776, when Virginia's legislators—nearly two months before the Continental Congress adopted the Declaration of Independence in Philadelphia—voted for delegates in Philadelphia to introduce a resolution declaring the Colonies' independence from England. Dancing, entertainment and other evening programs take place on a varying schedule.

Courthouse of 1770 is on Duke of Gloucester St., e. of the Palace Green. Costumed interpreters demonstrate the workings of local 18th-century government and justice, culminating in a re-enactment of a typical courtroom proceeding. A brief background of Colonial law and the building's history also is provided.

The DeWitt Wallace Decorative Arts Museum, 325 W. Francis St., houses British and American decorative arts dating from 1600 through 1830. An impressive assembly of furniture is on display, including what is said to be the world's largest collection of Virginia furniture.

DID YOU KNOW

Silk was supposed to be Jamestown's chief export, but tobacco proved more profitable.

In addition to maps, paintings, prints and textiles, the museum features a fine assortment of English pottery. Food is available. Phone (757) 220-7724.

 Governor's Palace faces the Palace Green. When it was completed in 1722, the residence of Virginia's royal governor was considered one of the finest structures in British North America. The elegant and imposing residence has been the home of seven royal governors and the commonwealth's first two state governors. The current building was reconstructed on the original foundations; it opened to the public in April 1934.

The Palace complex also includes a stable and elaborate gardens. Admission to palace included with Colonial Williamsburg multiple-day tickets (not included with 1-day pass). Gardens admission included with Colonial Williamsburg multiple admission tickets.

The Historic Trades Sites are throughout Colonial Williamsburg. Twenty-two trade sites are in operation in the historic area; collectively, the practiced trades replicate an 18th-century production system. Nearly 90 artisans—including brickmakers, coopers, milliners and silversmiths—offer insights into early American society and technology. Hours vary seasonally. Some trades are demonstrated outdoors (weather permitting).

James Geddy House and Foundry is at 117 W. Duke of Gloucester St. and the Palace Green. The house was built in the 1760s. James Geddy Jr. operated a silversmith business here; a foundry and 18th-century furnishings can be seen. At this trade site, skilled artisans cast objects in brass, bronze, pewter and silver.

Magazine and Guardhouse is on Market Square. The storehouse for arms and ammunition was built in 1715. The magazine displays firearms and military artifacts.

Peyton Randolph House, on Nicholson St. facing Market Square, is the restored 18th-century home of the first president of the Continental Congress. Outbuildings, including a granary, storehouses and a smokehouse, also are on-site.

Public Gaol is at 461 E. Nicholson St., near The Capitol. This 1704 jail with later additions is completely restored and includes an early form of indoor plumbing and cells for criminals. Its most infamous occupants were 15 of the pirate Blackbeard's henchmen, caught in 1718, and Henry "Hair Buyer" Hamilton, a British lieutenant governor who allegedly offered bounties for patriots' scalps.

The Public Hospital is at 325. W. Francis St. This building was reconstructed on the original site of the Public Hospital for Persons of Insane and Disordered Minds. Opened in 1773, it was the first public institution in the English Colonies devoted solely to the treatment of mental illness. An exhibit on the first floor focuses on the history of the hospital. Other subjects addressed are the underlying reasons for the facility's establishment, its doctors, patients and methods of treatment. Phone (757) 220-7724.

Raleigh Tavern is on Duke of Gloucester St. near the Capitol. First established around 1717, the tavern became a center of social and political life during the 18th century. George Washington, Thomas Jefferson and Patrick Henry are a few of the patriots who helped make history here. It was in the Apollo Room that students from the College of William and Mary are said to have founded the Phi Beta Kappa Society in 1776. The building was reconstructed after a fire destroyed it in 1859.

Wetherburn's Tavern, on the s. side of Duke of Gloucester St. near The Capitol, owned by Henry Wetherburn, figured prominently in the commercial life of Williamsburg in the 1750s. The tavern is furnished in period.

Wythe House is s. of Prince George St. facing the Palace Green. Built in the mid 18th century, the attractive Georgian-style structure was the home of George Wythe, one of the period's most prominent lawyers. He was a scholar who mentored Thomas Jefferson, a signer of the Declaration of Independence and the first law professor at the College of William and Mary.

THE ORIGINAL GHOSTS OF WILLIAMSBURG CANDLELIGHT TOUR departs from Barnes & Noble on Duke of Gloucester St. Guided tours explore the streets of Williamsburg by lantern. Based on the works of author L.B. Taylor Jr., the narrative incorporates folklore and local history. Allow 1 hour, 30 minutes minimum. Tours depart nightly at 8 (also at 8:45 p.m., June-Aug.); closed major holidays. Fee $10; free (ages 0-9). Reservations are required. AX, DS, MC, VI. Phone (757) 253-1058 or (877) 624-4678.

PRESIDENTS PARK is off I-64 exit 242B at 211 Water Country Pkwy. This outdoor museum features 16- to 18-foot-tall busts of the American presidents, presented with biographical information, events and accomplishments. The park also chronicles defining moments in the country's history, from the American Revolution to the civil rights movement to Sept. 11. The museum is home base for the American Presidents Experience, whose exhibits include replicas of Air Force One, the Oval Office, a presidential limousine and gowns worn by First Ladies.

Food is available. Allow 1 hour minimum. Daily 9-8, Apr.-Aug.; daily 9-5, rest of year. Closed Jan. 1, Thanksgiving and Dec. 25. Admission $16; $15 (ages 55+); $10 (ages 6-17). AX, DS, MC, VI. Phone (757) 259-1121 or (800) 588-4327.

WATER COUNTRY USA is 3 mi. w. off I-64 exit 242B on SR 199. This 320-acre water park features more than 35 water rides and slides as well as live entertainment. The park blends high-tech thrills, water elements and an interactive children's play area with a 1950s and 1960s surf theme.

Hubba Hubba Highway is a free-floating interactive river ride where coconuts, cactus and geysers provide a drenching experience. Meltdown takes riders on a high-speed toboggan race down a flume full of twists, turns and banks.

Visitors can experience the rush of a thrilling wipe-out on Malibu Pipeline or take a special-effects family white-water rafting ride aboard Aquazoid. Racers can see who passes the finish line first on Nitro Racer, a super-speed slide.

Other rides include Jet Scream; Rampage; Surfer's Bay, a wave pool; and a water-soaked children's area with H_2O UFO, Kritter Koral and Cow-A-Bunga. The Island Quest dive show is a 20-minute

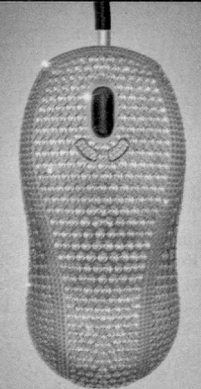

spectacular featuring divers, acrobats and trampoline artists.

Food is available. Park open daily at 10, May-Sept. Days and closing times vary; phone ahead to confirm schedule. Admission $39.95; $32.95 (ages 3-6). Multiday and combination tickets with Busch Gardens Europe are available. Rates may vary; phone ahead. Parking $10-$15. AX, DS, MC, VI. Phone (800) 343-7946.

YORK RIVER STATE PARK is 3.1 mi. n. on New-man Rd. off I-64 exit 234B, then 1.2 mi. w. to 5526 Riverview Rd. The 2,550-acre park is part of coastal Virginia's system of estuaries. Guided canoe and kayak trips begin at the visitor center, which contains exhibits focusing on the delicate estuarine environment where freshwater and saltwater meet to create a habitat rich in marine plant and animal life.

The park offers picnic facilities and more than 25 miles of hiking, bicycling and equestrian trails; paddleboats, johnboats, canoes, kayaks and bicycles are available for rent during the main season. Park open daily 8 a.m.-dusk. Visitor center open daily 8-4, Apr.-Oct. Admission $2 (per private vehicle Mon.-Fri.); $3 (per private vehicle Sat.-Sun.). Reservations are suggested for interpretive tours. Phone (757) 566-3036. *See Recreation Chart.*

WINERIES

• **Williamsburg Winery** is off I-64 exit 242A (SR 199), .5 mi. n.w. to Brookwood Ln. following signs to 5800 Wessex Hundred. Mon.-Sat. 10-6, Sun. 11-6, Apr.-Oct.; Mon.-Sat. 10-5, Sun. 11-5, rest of year. Closed Jan. 1, Thanksgiving and Dec. 25. Guided tour $7. Phone (757) 229-0999.

YORKTOWN (B-4) pop. 203, elev. 12′

Yorktown, founded in 1691, was a busy 18th-century tobacco port. The town is best remembered for the Battle of Yorktown, which effectively ended the Revolutionary War. Less than 100 years later, Yorktown was embroiled in another major battle when Union general George McClellan landed his troops at Fort Monroe in 1862 and opened the Peninsular Campaign.

Gen. John Magruder, commanding the Confederate forces, fortified Yorktown and threw a line of trenches from town to the James River. Magruder marched his outnumbered forces back and forth behind the fortifications and convinced McClellan that he was facing a force twice the size of his own.

So convincing was Magruder's charade that the Union forces slowed their advance and began to besiege the town. Rather than having his troops risk being bottled up in Yorktown, Gen. Joseph Johnston, replacing Magruder, moved them toward Williamsburg. The Union forces moved into Yorktown and retained control throughout the rest of the war.

Nine 18th-century buildings survived the 1781 Battle of Yorktown and can still be seen. While most are private, several are open to the public, including Nelson House and Moore House. The restored Somerwell House, at Main and Church

streets, was once an 18th-century inn and is now a private residence.

The 1693 Sessions House, the oldest house in Yorktown, was used by Gen. James Negley as headquarters during the Federal occupation. The Sessions and Somerwell houses are closed to the public.

The headquarters and one of the visitor centers for the Colonial National Historical Park *(see place listing p. 316)* are on the northeast edge of town at the end of the Colonial Parkway. For further information about the park and homes phone (757) 898-3400.

York County Public Information Office: 224 Ballard St., P.O. Box 532, Yorktown, VA 23690-0532; phone (757) 890-3300.

GRACE EPISCOPAL CHURCH is on the eastern end of the Colonial Pkwy. at 111 Church St. Built of native marl about 1697, the church was used as a magazine during the siege of Yorktown. It was burned partially in 1814 but later rebuilt. Communion silver dating from 1649 is still in use. Among the graves in the churchyard is that of Thomas Nelson Jr., a signer of the Declaration of Independence. Daily 9-3. Free. Phone (757) 898-3261.

SWAN TAVERN GROUP is at Main and Ballard sts. The original 18th-century buildings—a tavern, kitchen, smokehouse and stable—were destroyed when a Union Army powder magazine in the York County Courthouse across the street exploded in December 1863. These reconstructions are of interest for their exterior appearance.

WATERMEN'S MUSEUM is e. on SR 238 to 309 Water St. Five galleries portray the history of Virginia's watermen, who worked on or with the waters of the Chesapeake Bay and its tributaries. Exhibits include ship models, paintings, dioramas, photographs and tools. Tues.-Sat. 10-4, Sun. 1-4, Apr. 1-Thanksgiving; Sat. 10-4, Sun. 1-4, rest of year. Hours may vary; phone ahead. Admission $4; $1 (ages 6-18). Phone (757) 887-2641.

YORKTOWN BATTLEFIELD is on the eastern end of the Colonial Pkwy. The last major battle of the Revolutionary War was fought here in 1781, when Gen. Charles Cornwallis sought to establish a British naval port at Yorktown with 8,300 soldiers. Gen. George Washington moved his American army into Virginia to reinforce the Marquis de Lafayette's allied forces; the French fleet blockaded Chesapeake Bay. Under siege by 17,600 Continental troops, Cornwallis surrendered.

The battlefield is administered by Colonial National Historical Park *(see place listing p. 316)*. Two driving tours begin at the visitor center. The 7-mile Battlefield Tour Road includes earthworks, redoubts and siege lines. At Moore House, officers met to negotiate terms of surrender. The 9-mile Encampment Tour Road passes allied camps and Washington's Headquarters. Other stops include the French Cemetery, the Civil War-era National Cemetery and Historic Yorktown.

Roads open daily 8-dusk. Admission (good for 7 days) includes Historic Jamestowne *(see attraction listing p. 316)* $10; free (ages 0-15). Battlefield Tour Road narrated driving tour $3.95 (audiotape); $4.95 (CD-ROM). Phone (757) 898-2410.

Yorktown Visitor Center is .75 mi. s. of Yorktown on the edge of town, at the e. end of the Colonial Pkwy. The center includes an observation deck, a re-constructed section of a gun deck and a British Frigate captain's cabin. A 16-minute film relates the events of the siege. Driving tours begin at this point; self-guiding tour leaflets and taped tours of the battlefield are available. Daily 9-5; closed Dec. 25. Admission included with Yorktown Battlefield. Phone (757) 898-2410.

YORKTOWN VICTORY CENTER is off I-64 exit 247 on SR 1020 near the Colonial Pkwy. and US 17. This museum of the American Revolution chronicles the events leading up to the colonists' declaration of independence from Britain—and the impact of the war upon ordinary lives.

The Witnesses to Revolution gallery presents the stories of 10 individuals who lived during this turbulent time. Converging on Yorktown describes the multinational nature of forces that met here in 1781. Yorktown's Sunken Fleet reveals the history of the *Betsy* and other British ships scuttled or lost during the siege. Children's Kaleidoscope is a discovery room that provides opportunities for interactive learning and play.

Daily life during the Revolution is re-created in an outdoor Continental Army encampment and a 1780s farm where costumed interpreters fire muskets, tend crops and discuss medical practices of the day. Other exhibits relate the experiences of Revolutionary soldiers and describe the final step in America's journey to nationhood—the development of the Constitution and Bill of Rights.

Allow 2 hours minimum. Daily 9-6, June 15-Aug. 15; 9-5, rest of year. Closed Jan. 1 and Dec. 25. Admission $9.25; $5 (ages 6-12). Combination ticket with Jamestown Settlement *(see attraction listing p. 319)* $19.25; $9.25 (ages 6-12). Other combination tickets are available. Phone (757) 253-4838 or (888) 593-4682. *See color ad p. 317.*

Yorktown Victory Center, Yorktown / Jeff Greenberg / Virginia Tourism Corporation

This ends listings for Williamsburg, Jamestown and Yorktown. The following page resumes the alphabetical listings of cities in Virginia.

WINCHESTER (E-8) pop. 23,585, elev. 717′

Established in 1732 by German, Scottish and Irish settlers heading south from Pennsylvania, Winchester played a major part in the French and Indian and Civil wars. It was in Winchester in that a young George Washington established his surveying career. He also built Fort Loudoun and had his headquarters in the town as commander on the Virginia frontier 1755-58. In addition, Washington was elected in Winchester to the Virginia House of Burgesses in 1758 and 1761.

During the Civil War, the town changed hands at least 72 times, including 13 times in a day. The First, Second and Third battles of Winchester occurred in 1862, 1863 and 1864. The Confederate and National cemeteries contain the bodies of 7,500 Union and Confederate soldiers. The 55-acre Mount Hebron Cemetery, E. Boscawen St. in the historic district, includes the Stonewall Confederate Cemetery and two original church cemeteries. Among its monuments is one dedicated to 829 unknown Confederate dead.

An early landlord in the Shenandoah Valley, George Washington required each tenant to plant 4 acres of apples. As a result extensive orchards surround Winchester. In early May the ☙ Apple Blossom Festival features dances, live music, parades and various competitions.

Lower Shenandoah Valley history is preserved in books, manuscripts and archives at the Handley Regional Library, an elaborate 1908 beaux-arts structure at the corner of Braddock and Picadilly streets; phone (540) 662-9041.

Winchester-Frederick County Convention and Visitor Bureau: 1360 S. Pleasant Valley Rd., Winchester, VA 22601; phone (540) 542-1326 or (877) 871-1326.

Self-guiding tours: The convention and visitor bureau, housed in a restored gristmill, has brochures detailing walking and driving tours as well as videotape presentations about the area.

[SAVE] **ABRAM'S DELIGHT MUSEUM** is 1 blk. n. of US 50 at 1340 S. Pleasant Valley Rd. The oldest house in Winchester, this two-story limestone structure was built in 1754 by an early Quaker, Isaac Hollingsworth. His father, Abraham, had declared the property "a delight to behold." Furnished in period, the house contains a large center hall and an open-hearth kitchen. Furnishings and artwork from the 18th and 19th centuries are exhibited.

Allow 30 minutes minimum. Guided tours Mon.-Sat. 10-4, Sun. noon-4, Apr.-Oct. Fee $5; $4.50 (ages 61+); $2.50 (ages 7-18). Combination ticket with George Washington's Office Museum and "Stonewall" Jackson's Headquarters $10; $9 (ages 61+); $4 (ages 7-18); $20 (family). Phone (540) 662-6519 or (540) 662-6550.

CHRIST EPISCOPAL CHURCH is at Washington and Boscawen sts. In the courtyard is the tomb of Lord Thomas Fairfax, proprietor of the Northern Neck of Virginia, who lived near Winchester at Greenway Court 1739-82 *(see White Post p. 310).* Courtyard open daily 24 hours. Free. Phone (540) 662-5843.

[SAVE] **GEORGE WASHINGTON'S OFFICE MUSEUM** is s. on US 11 at jct. S. Braddock and W. Cork sts. This small log building served as Washington's office 1755-56 while he built Fort Loudoun. Visitors can see some of Washington's personal effects and related artifacts, including rare surveying instruments.

Mon.-Sat. 10-4, Sun. noon-4, Apr.-Oct. Admission $5; $4.50 (ages 61+); $2.50 (ages 7-18); $12 (family). Combination ticket with Abram's Delight Museum and "Stonewall" Jackson's Headquarters $10; $9 (ages 61+); $4 (ages 7-18); $20 (family). Phone (540) 662-4412.

◤GEM◢ **MUSEUM OF THE SHENANDOAH VALLEY** is at 901 Amherst St. (SR 50W). Designed by architect Michael Graves, the [SAVE] 50,000-square-foot regional history museum contains three exhibition galleries dedicated to interpreting the art, history and culture of the Shenandoah Valley. The complex includes the Glen Burnie Historic House, built in 1794 by Robert Wood, son of Winchester founder Col. James Wood. It is furnished with 18th- and 19th-century antiques, paintings and decorative objects collected by Julian Wood Glass Jr., the last family descendent to reside there. Temporary exhibitions also are offered.

The property's 6 acres of manicured grounds include formal Chinese, water, rose, parterre, herb and vegetable gardens with fountains, statues and shady passages made from flowering crab apple trees. A 1-hour, self-guiding audiotape tour of the gardens is available.

Food is available Tues.-Sun. 11-4. Allow 2 hours minimum. Museum open Tues.-Sun. 10-4. House and gardens open Tues.-Sun. 10-4, Mar.-Nov. Closed major holidays. Guided house tours are given Tues.-Sun. every 30 minutes 10-4, Mar.-Nov. Last house tour begins 30 minutes before closing.

Museum or house and gardens admission $8; $6 (ages 7-18 and senior citizens). Gardens only $6; $5 (ages 7-18 and senior citizens). Combination ticket for museum and gardens $10; $9 (ages 7-18 and senior citizens). Combination ticket for museum, house and gardens $12; $10 (ages 7-18 and senior citizens). Self-guiding audiotape tour of gardens $2. MC, VI. Phone (540) 662-1473 or (888) 556-5799.

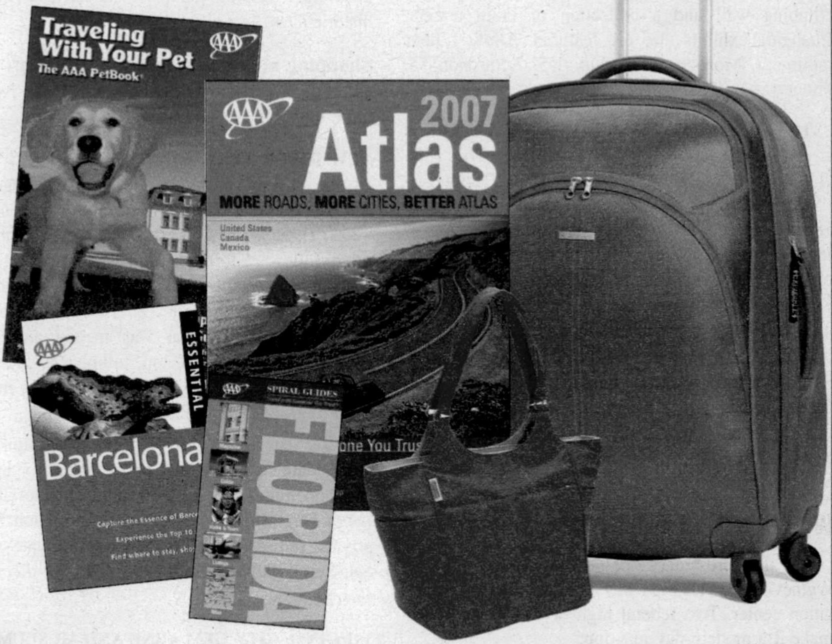

SHENANDOAH VALLEY DISCOVERY MUSEUM is at 54 S. Loudon St. Appealing to all ages are exhibits based on science, math and art. Highlights include an American Indian longhouse, an art room, a climbing wall and a collection of brain teasers. Changing exhibits also are featured. Allow 1 hour minimum. Mon.-Sat. 9-5, Sun. 1-5. Admission $5. Phone (540) 722-2020.

"STONEWALL" JACKSON'S HEADQUARTERS is s. on US 11 at 415 N. Braddock St. The 1854 Gothic Revival house served as Gen. Thomas J. "Stonewall" Jackson's headquarters from November 1861 to March 1862. The house contains many of Jackson's possessions, prints, pictures and artifacts of the Civil War. Also displayed are items that belonged to topographer Jed Hotchkiss and cavalry general Turner Ashby.

Allow 30 minutes minimum. Mon.-Sat. 10-4, Sun. noon-4, Apr.-Oct. Admission $5; $4.50 (ages 61+); $2.50 (ages 7-18); $12 (family). Combination ticket with Abram's Delight Museum and George Washington's Office Museum $10; $9 (ages 61+); $4 (ages 7-18); $20 (family). Phone (540) 667-3242.

WYTHEVILLE (H-4) pop. 7,804, elev. 2,230'

At the crossroads of early pioneer routes, Wytheville (WITH-vill) was a 19th-century transportation center. Two federal highways, I-77 and I-81, make it a modern-day junction.

Founded in 1790, Wythe County was named for Virginia's first signer of the Declaration of Independence, George Wythe. The town was the site of several Civil War skirmishes, including a July 1863 attack by Union forces under Col. John Toland. The mountain town in the Blue Ridge Highlands later became a summer resort due to its cool climate and "healing waters." The second wife of President Woodrow Wilson, Edith Bolling Galt, was born in Wytheville, the daughter of a local judge.

The surrounding Jefferson National Forest *(see place listing p. 252)*, Big Walker Mountain Scenic Byway, New River Trail State Park and the historic New River offer vast recreational opportunities including hiking, bicycling, fishing, camping, boating and picnicking. A 100-foot observation tower on top of Big Walker Mountain offers a panoramic view of the surrounding mountains. Numerous sites on Virginia's Birding Trails and Virginia's Civil War Trails can also be explored.

Wytheville Convention & Visitors Bureau: 975 Tazewell St., P.O. Box 533, Wytheville, VA 24382; phone (276) 223-3355 or (877) 347-8307.

Self-guiding tours: A walking tour of the town showcases more than 50 historic structures, beginning downtown at Wytheville's Heritage Preservation Center at 115 Spiller St. The tour is detailed in a brochure and on an audio cassette; both are available from the heritage center as well as the convention and visitors bureau. Also available is a brochure detailing a driving tour of local African-American historic sites.

Shopping areas: Four antique malls within a mile are collectively known as Collectors Lane, featuring more than 300 dealers.

NEW RIVER TRAIL STATE PARK is off I-77 exit 24, then 1.5 mi. n. on US 52. Virginia's longest linear park parallels the New River for 37 of its 57 miles. The trail for walkers, bicyclists and horseback riders follows a former railroad track through Grayson, Carroll, Wythe and Pulaski counties. A fortress-like shot tower, built in 1807, was used to make lead ammunition. Metal was melted and poured through sieves from the top, falling 150 feet into a kettle of water. The 75-foot-tall tower was made of local limestone; its walls are 2 feet thick.

Note: The tower is closed for renovations, with no set date for reopening; phone ahead for updates. Park open daily 8 a.m.-10 p.m., Memorial Day-Labor Day; 8-dusk, rest of year. Admission $2 (per private vehicle Mon.-Fri.); $3 (per private vehicle Sat.-Sun.). Phone (276) 699-6778. *See Recreation Chart.*

VIRGINIA CITY GEM MINE AND MUSEUM is off I-77 exit 47; take Krenning Rd. 4.2 mi. w., then US 52 1 mi. n. This museum town includes educational displays as well as a saw mill, a grist mill, a general store, a town hall and a city jail. Visitors also may mine for gems. Trails are available for hiking, horse riding and mountain biking. Picnicking is permitted. Allow 1 hour minimum. Daily 10-6, mid-Apr. through Oct. 31. Admission by donation. Gem mining equipment $7.50. Phone (276) 223-1873.

WYTHEVILLE'S HERITAGE PRESERVATION CENTER, 115 Spiller St., is in a former schoolhouse; the site encompasses a visitor orientation area, a genealogical library and two historic houses. The Thomas J. Boyd Museum features an interactive exhibit about the 1950s polio epidemic, Civil War displays and local history exhibits. The Haller-Gibboney Rock House Museum, the former home of Wytheville's first resident physician, focuses on 19th-century family life and early medicine.

Preservation center Mon.-Fri. 10-5, third Sat. of the month 10-4. Guided tours are given on the hour. Last tour begins 1 hour before closing. Preservation center free. Admission to both museums $6; $3 (children). Phone (276) 223-3330.

YORKTOWN—

see Virginia's Historic Triangle p. 326.

West Virginia

Rapidly Flowing Rivers

Rushing waters beckon adventurers to the New, Gauley and Cheat rivers

Pottery, Baskets and Woodcrafts

The arts, crafts and music of the state are synonymous with its mountain culture

Harpers Ferry

Some say the Civil War began here when John Brown made a stand against slavery

The Mountain State

Backpacking, hiking, skiing, biking, fishing— there's plenty to do in West Virginia's mountains

Blazing a Trail

Pioneer forts are testaments to the rigors of frontier life in early settlements

Monongahela National Forest
© Laurence Parent

"almost heaven"

John Brown's Fort, Harpers Ferry National Historical Park / © Alan Briere / SuperStock

Rocky peaks receding toward a mist-dimmed horizon. Rivers churned to a froth, rushing through narrow canyons. Waterfalls tumbling down steep hills into secluded alpine valleys. Vast forests ablaze with autumn color. These images only begin to describe West Virginia.

Born during a war that nearly destroyed the nation, the Mountain State has endured a troubled history of Civil War battles, mountaineer feuds and coal mining labor disputes. But thanks to abundant highland beauty, the state has left its past difficulties far behind to become a playground for skiers, white-water rafters, hikers and anyone else who loves the outdoors.

This is not to say that West Virginians have forgotten their heritage.

Descendants of self-reliant pioneers still craft objects that were once necessities of frontier life. Shops selling quilts, pottery, baskets, woodwork, hand-crafted furniture and other homemade items are easy to find.

What's more, carefully restored sites like Harpers Ferry, Blennerhassett Island and Wheeling's Independence Hall show how seriously the locals take their history. Honoring the past and enjoying the spectacular scenery of the present are clearly a source of mountaineer pride. One visit and you'll understand why.

If you closed your eyes and ran a finger along a 3-D map of West Virginia, one trait would be immediately noticeable: mountains. Like raised bumps in a Braille book, the state's rugged terrain explains a lot about it.

"Mountaineers Are Always Free"

If it weren't for mountains, West Virginia might not exist as a separate state at all. Originally part of Virginia, this remote inland region was settled later and placed very different demands on its inhabitants than the benign coastal plain. This resulted in a rift between the highland pioneers and their wealthier tidewater relatives. By the time the Civil War broke out, the split was so vast that when Virginia seceded from the Union, several western counties seceded from *it,* thus giving birth to West Virginia.

Aptly named, the Mountain State is indeed the most mountainous east of the Mississippi. Blanketed with trees and cut through by swift-flowing streams, the chain of craggy peaks—part of the ancient Appalachians—stretches along West Virginia's entire eastern border. This may once have been the capital of coal country, but today the most used natural resources are above ground. West Virginia's scenic grandeur and recreation destinations draw hundreds of thousands of tourists each year.

Tops on their list are ski slopes renowned for being some of the best east of the Rockies; names like Timberline, Canaan Valley and Snowshoe come to mind. An ever-growing number of white-water rafters challenge the rapids of the New, Gauley and Cheat rivers.

The thrill of these sports is intensified by the scenery. One sight to behold is the 1,000-foot-deep canyons of the New River Gorge National River, most dazzlingly viewed from the bridge perched above its raging waters. And although no one rafts down the plummeting streams of Blackwater, Hill Creek and Holly River falls, their beauty still draws tourists from all over.

Perhaps the greatest natural assets are stunning mountain vistas like those at Spruce Knob, the highest point in West Virginia. Located in the extensive Monongahela National Forest, this peak is in Spruce Knob-Seneca Rocks National Recreation Area, one of the most popular rock climbing areas in the East.

Colonial governor William Berkeley sends an expedition to the West Virginia region.
1669

The first permanent settler, Morgan Morgan, moves to Bunker Hill in Berkeley County.
1726

The last battle of the Revolutionary War is fought at Fort Henry in Wheeling.
1782

1742
Coal is discovered in Kanawha County.

West Virginia Historical Timeline

Library of Congress

1859
John Brown and a small band of abolitionists raid the federal arsenal at Harpers Ferry.

Scenic Railways and Fall Foliage

Part of a once-extensive railway network for transporting lumber, the Cass Scenic Railroad carries passengers to a viewing area just below lofty Bald Knob for breathtaking views of the surrounding countryside. In fall, the landscape blazes with color as untold millions of leaves change hue. Similarly, West Virginia's many picturesque covered bridges were originally built for practical reasons but are now the focus of the pleasantly impractical endeavor of sightseeing.

Other man-made attractions also are worth seeking out. Victorian historic districts in Parkersburg, Wheeling and Charleston, the state capital, evoke the coal boom era. You'll also want to see the capitol building and its impressive 293-foot-tall golden dome.

And as if West Virginia weren't hilly enough, the Adena culture created artificial hillocks 2,000 years ago near Moundsville as vertical graveyards for the dead. Are you more interested in the future than the past? Tour the National Radio Astronomy Observatory, perched in the mountains near Green Bank. Here astronomers tune in to galactic noise to learn more about the universe.

At the opposite end of the elevation spectrum is West Virginia's lowest point, Harpers Ferry. But the town's biggest claim to fame is abolitionist John Brown's 1859 raid on the federal arsenal. He was defeated after considerable bloodshed and hanged, but the incident inflamed tensions between North and South and brought the nation closer to civil war. Nearby Harpers Ferry National Historical Park preserves the scene of the conflict.

The state's dramatic scenery continues underground thanks to the many caves scattered throughout the highlands. In Greenbrier Valley, Lost World Caverns features huge subterranean rooms and waterfalls up to 235 feet below the surface. And even if you can't tell the difference between a stalagmite and a stalactite you'll still enjoy Smoke Hole Caverns west of Petersburg and Seneca Caverns near Riverton, which have both.

Today bathers in search of therapeutic balm still flock to White Sulphur Springs and Berkeley Springs. The warm, mineral-laden waters bubbling up from these depths were discovered by American colonists more than 200 years ago. You won't want to linger long in the tub, though; a state filled with such spectacular sights just begs to be explored.

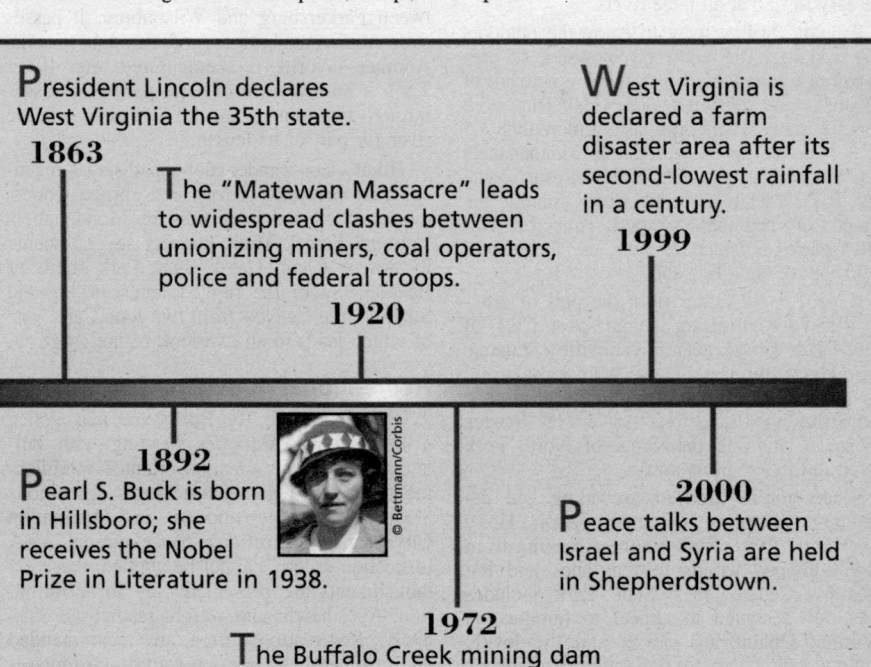

President Lincoln declares West Virginia the 35th state.
1863

The "Matewan Massacre" leads to widespread clashes between unionizing miners, coal operators, police and federal troops.
1920

West Virginia is declared a farm disaster area after its second-lowest rainfall in a century.
1999

1892
Pearl S. Buck is born in Hillsboro; she receives the Nobel Prize in Literature in 1938.

© Bettmann/Corbis

2000
Peace talks between Israel and Syria are held in Shepherdstown.

1972
The Buffalo Creek mining dam collapses, killing 118 people and leaving thousands homeless.

Recreation

Although West Virginia was once isolated from the rest of the country by rugged Appalachian peaks, these same mountains now lure outdoor enthusiasts in droves. For travelers who enjoy alfresco activities—be they with paddles or pedals—the Mountain State is paradise.

Go With the Flow

If **white-water rafting** floats your boat, remember these names: Gauley, Cheat and New. The big three of West Virginia rafting rivers enjoy a world-wide reputation for superior white water. The Gauley River has 100 major rapids on a 25-mile course. Be forewarned: The Upper Gauley is not for the faint of heart. This Class V river challenges even expert river guides. Exciting boulder-strewn rapids also characterize the Cheat River, but because there are no dams controlling its flow, suitable water levels are limited to spring.

Despite its name, the New River is one of the oldest in North America. Here you'll find a full range of white-water rafting options. The Lower New has swirling Class IV and V rapids, while the Upper New features calmer water. Both have plenty of lovely scenery, from lush forest to rugged canyon. Professional outfitters are easy to find at all three rivers.

Another thrilling way to enjoy the outdoors here is **skiing.** The renowned Snowshoe ski area on top of Cheat Mountain features a network of 57 slopes and trails including Cupp Run, with its 1,500-foot vertical drop lasting more than 1.5 miles. On the northern edge of Monongahela National Forest, Canaan Valley Resort State Park has 37 interconnecting slopes running the gamut from beginner to expert. Timberline Resort features Salamander Run, the longest ski trail south of New England.

If you would rather fight the pull of gravity, then **rock climbing** is your sport. Cliffs at New River Gorge near Fayetteville challenge even expert climbers. Those who are unafraid of heights will be amply rewarded after a climb up the sandstone tower of Seneca Rocks; a stunning panorama of North Fork River and its environs awaits.

When you're tired of ascending and descending, **camping** is a great option. Holly River State Park offers facilities ranging from fully equipped cabins to tent sites and RV hookups. Cedar Creek State Park includes amenities designed to appeal to families on vacation. Quaint log cabins and the lovely Glade Creek Grist Mill distinguish Babcock State Park, while Pipestem Resort State Park, located on Bluestone Gorge, attracts campers with its dramatic views.

Avid anglers won't have any trouble finding a spot to cast a lure in West Virginia. Places such as Laura Anderson Lake are stocked with trout and are open for **fishing** year-round. Middle Island Creek, which is more river than creek, teems with large mouth bass and channel catfish. Named after the state's favorite son, Stonewall Jackson Lake occupies the center of Stonewall Resort State Park. Catches to brag about here are bass, crappie and walleye.

West Virginians put their lakes to other uses as well. Tygart Lake State Park is great for **boating, swimming** and **water skiing.** The calm waters of Summersville Lake also make it perfect for water skiing.

Happy Trails to You

Many of the railways that carried lumber and coal from West Virginia's highlands have been converted to **hiking, biking** and **horseback riding** trails. The state has more than 300 miles of rails-to-trails paths offering a range of scenic treks. For more information about these, phone (800) 225-5982.

One standout is North Bend Rail Trail, which ascends to the Wolf Summit terminus of the old rail line. Stretching 72 miles between Parkersburg and Wilsonburg, it passes over numerous bridges and through tunnels. Another favorite is scenic Greenbrier River Trail, a narrow strip of state park that passes through two tunnels and follows alongside the river for part of its length.

Hikers can wander along paths that meander past hemlock groves, red spruce woods, moors, bogs and waterfalls in Monongahela National Forest. Trails connect several scenic locales at Camp Creek State Park south of Beckley. Savor the rugged landscape around Smoke Hole Canyon from two loop trails, one of which leads to an overlook of the gorge.

Recreational Activities

Throughout the TourBook, you may notice a Recreational Activities heading with bulleted listings of recreation-oriented establishments listed underneath. Similar operations also may be mentioned in Destination City recreation sections. Since normal AAA inspection criteria cannot be applied, these establishments are presented only for information. Age, height and weight restrictions may apply. Reservations often are recommended and sometimes are required. Addresses and/or phone numbers are provided so visitors can contact the attraction for additional information.

Fast Facts

POPULATION: 1,808,344.

AREA: 24,232 square miles; ranks 41st.

CAPITAL: Charleston.

HIGHEST POINT: 4,861 ft., Spruce Knob.

LOWEST POINT: 240 ft., Potomac River at Harpers Ferry.

TIME ZONE(S): Eastern. DST.

MINIMUM AGE FOR UNRESTRICTED DRIVER'S LICENSE: 17.

MINIMUM AGE FOR GAMBLING: 21.

SEAT BELT/CHILD RESTRAINT LAWS: Seat belts required for driver and front-seat passengers over age 7 and ages 8-17 in all seats; under age 8 and over 4'9" must be in a seat belt or child restraint; child restraints required for under age 8 and under 4'9".

HELMETS FOR MOTORCYCLISTS: Required for driver and all passengers.

RADAR DETECTORS: Permitted.

FIREARMS LAWS: Vary by state and/or county. Contact the West Virginia State Police, 725 Jefferson Rd., South Charleston, WV 25309; phone (304) 746-2100.

HOLIDAYS: Jan. 1; Martin Luther King Jr. Day, Jan. (3rd Mon.); Lincoln's Birthday, Feb. 12; Presidents Day, Feb. (3rd Mon.); Memorial Day, May (last Mon.); West Virginia Day, June 20; July 4; Labor Day, Sept. (1st Mon.); Columbus Day, Oct. (2nd Mon.); Veterans Day, Nov. 11; Thanksgiving; Dec. 24; Christmas, Dec. 25.

TAXES: West Virginia's statewide sales tax is 6 percent. Cities and counties may impose lodgings taxes of up to 3 percent.

INFORMATION CENTERS: State welcome centers are on US 340 at Harpers Ferry; on I-64 westbound at White Sulphur Springs and eastbound at Huntington; on I-77 north- or southbound at Princeton (exit 9), northbound at Milepost 18 near Princeton, northbound near Mahan, southbound at Beckley and north- or southbound at Williamstown; on I-70 westbound near the Pennsylvania state line, close to Valley Grove; on I-79 southbound north of Morgantown; and on I-81 northbound 2 miles north of the Virginia state line near Ridgeway, and southbound 1 mile south of the Maryland state line near Williamsport. Most centers are open daily 9-5, with extended hours during the summer; closed major holidays.

FURTHER INFORMATION FOR VISITORS:

> West Virginia Division of Tourism
> 90 MacCorkle Ave. S.W.
> South Charleston, WV 25303
> (800) 225-5982

RECREATION INFORMATION:

West Virginia Division of Tourism
90 MacCorkle Ave. S.W.
South Charleston, WV 25303
(800) 225-5982

FISHING AND HUNTING REGULATIONS:

West Virginia Division of Natural Resources
State Capitol Complex
Building 3, Room 624
Charleston, WV 25305
(304) 558-2771

NATIONAL FOREST INFORMATION:

U.S. Forest Service
200 Sycamore St.
Elkins, WV 26241-9505
(304) 636-1800
(877) 444-6777 (reservations)

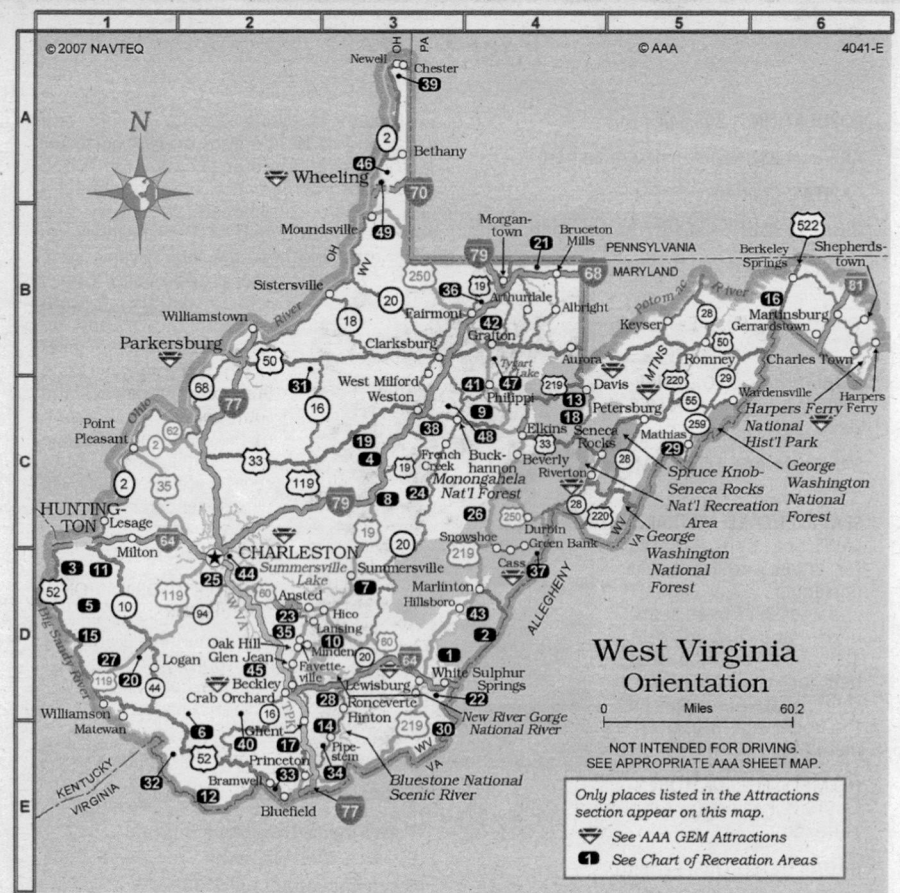

West Virginia Temperature Averages
Maximum/Minimum
From the records of The Weather Channel Interactive, Inc.

	JAN	FEB	MAR	APR	MAY	JUNE	JULY	AUG	SEPT	OCT	NOV	DEC
Charleston	45/28	47/28	55/34	66/44	76/53	82/61	85/64	83/63	79/57	68/46	55/36	46/29
Huntington	47/28	49/29	57/34	69/44	79/53	86/62	88/66	88/65	82/58	71/46	58/36	48/30
Parkersburg	43/26	47/27	53/33	65/43	75/53	83/62	86/65	85/64	79/57	68/46	54/35	44/28
Wheeling	38/21	42/23	51/31	63/39	73/50	82/59	85/64	84/63	77/56	66/43	54/35	42/27

Points of Interest Offering A *Great Experience for Members*®

Beckley (D-2)

THEATRE WEST VIRGINIA—The story of the infamous feud between the Hatfields and McCoys is the theme of one of the musical productions presented outdoors in a cliffside amphitheater. See p. 343.

Cass (D-4)

CASS SCENIC RAILROAD STATE PARK—Steam locomotives once used to haul logs now transport passengers past panoramic mountain scenery to the top of 4,800-foot-tall Bald Knob. See p. 346.

Charleston (D-2)

WEST VIRGINIA STATE CAPITOL—A golden dome tops the Mountain State's capitol, designed by renowned architect Cass Gilbert; the building is a landmark along the Kanawha River. See p. 347.

Davis (C-4)

BLACKWATER FALLS STATE PARK—Observation points allow for scenic views of amber water plunging 65 feet into a deep gorge; stairways leading to the base of the falls provide a closer look. See p. 349.

Harpers Ferry National Historical Park (C-6)

HARPERS FERRY NATIONAL HISTORICAL PARK—Exhibits and museums in more than two dozen restored 19th-century buildings reflect historical events, including legendary abolitionist John Brown's arsenal raid. See p. 352.

Lewisburg (D-3)

LOST WORLD CAVERNS—Flowstone formations, stalactites and stalagmites are some of the natural wonders to be seen in the cave's 52 F environment. See p. 355.

Parkersburg (B-1)

BLENNERHASSETT ISLAND HISTORICAL STATE PARK—The park is home to a reconstructed Palladian-style mansion originally built in 1798 by aristocrat Harman Blennerhassett, who later fled the island after a treasonous plot with Aaron Burr was revealed. See p. 360.

Petersburg (C-5)

SMOKE HOLE CAVERNS—Legend has it the caverns were formerly used by American Indians to smoke meat and by settlers to make moonshine; today they're explored for their underground beauty. See p. 360.

Riverton (C-4)

SENECA CAVERNS—Cave coral, rimstone and travertine are just a few of the subterranean rock formations in these caverns originally used by the Seneca Indians for ceremonial rituals. See p. 362.

Wheeling (A-3)

OGLEBAY RESORT—Formal gardens, a cascading water fountain, a glass museum and a historic mansion grace the grounds of this 1,750-acre park; golf, tennis, swimming and fishing are among the recreational activities available. See p. 366.

OGLEBAY'S GOOD ZOO—Animals native to North America, South America and Africa live in natural habitats at this 30-acre zoo; an 1863 train takes visitors on a 1.5-mile trip through the wildlife park. See p. 366.

RECREATION AREAS

	MAP LOCATION	CAMPING	PICNICKING	HIKING TRAILS	BOATING	BOAT RAMP	BOAT RENTAL	FISHING	SWIMMING	PETS ON LEASH	BICYCLE TRAILS	WINTER SPORTS	VISITOR CENTER	LODGE/CABINS	FOOD SERVICE
NATIONAL FORESTS *(See place listings)*															
Monongahela 909,000 acres in eastern West Virginia.		•	•	•	•	•	•	•	•	•		•	•		
Blue Bend (D-3) 4 mi. w. of Alvon off SR 92.	1	•	•	•				•	•				•		
Lake Sherwood (D-4) 11 mi. n.e. of Neola on SR 14.	2	•	•	•	•	•	•	•	•	•		•	•		
NATIONAL RECREATION AREAS *(See place listings)*															
Spruce Knob-Seneca Rocks (C-4,C-5) Eastern West Virginia.		•	•	•				•	•	•			•		
NATIONAL RIVERS															
Bluestone National Scenic River (E-3) 4,300 acres on SR 20 s. of Hinton in Bluestone State Park.			•	•	•			•					•	•	
New River Gorge (E-3) 62,000 acres between Fayetteville and Hinton. *(See place listing p. 358)*		•	•	•				•	•	•			•		
ARMY CORPS OF ENGINEERS															
Beech Fork Lake (D-1) 720 acres about 15 mi. s.e. of Huntington on SR 152.	3	•	•	•	•	•	•	•	•	•			•		•
Burnsville Lake (C-3) 970 acres just off I-79 Burnsville exit. Water skiing.	4	•	•	•	•	•	•	•	•	•			•		
East Lynn Lake (D-1) 1,005 acres 10 mi. s. of Wayne on SR 37. Water skiing.	5	•	•	•	•	•	•	•	•	•			•		•
R.D. Bailey Lake (E-2) 630 acres 30 mi. e. of Williamson. Water skiing.	6	•	•		•	•	•	•	•	•			•		
Summersville Lake (D-3) 2,798 acres 7 mi. s. of Summersville off US 19 on SR 129. Scuba diving, water skiing.	7	•	•	•	•	•	•	•	•	•		•	•		
Sutton Lake (C-3) 1,440 acres 5 mi. n.e. of Sutton. Water skiing.	8	•	•	•	•	•	•	•	•	•					•
STATE															
Audra (C-4) 355 acres 10 mi. w. of Belington off CR 11. Playground.	9	•	•	•					•						•
Babcock (D-3) 4,127 acres 4 mi. s.w. of Clifftop on SR 41. Nature programs. Scenic. Gristmill, horse rental. Boats with motors not permitted.	10	•	•	•	•			•	•	•			•	•	
Beech Fork (D-1) 3,981 acres 15 mi. s.e. of Huntington on SR 152. Playground.	11	•	•	•	•	•	•	•	•	•			•	•	•
Berwind Lake (E-2) 18,093 acres 17 mi. s. of Welch off SR 16.	12	•	•	•	•	•		•	•						
Blackwater Falls (C-4) 1,688 acres about .25 mile s.w. of Davis off SR 32 via signs. Nature programs. Scenic. Cross-country skiing, horse rental. *(See Davis p. 349)*	13	•	•	•	•			•	•	•		•	•	•	•
Bluestone (E-3) 2,155 acres 4 mi. s. of Hinton on SR 20. Water skiing.	14	•	•	•	•	•	•	•	•	•			•	•	
Cabwaylingo (D-1) 8,123 acres 5 mi. s.e. of Dunlow off SR 152. Hunting.	15	•	•					•	•					•	
Cacapon Resort (B-6) 6,115 acres 10 mi. s. of Berkeley Springs on US 522. Golf (18-hole); horse rental, playground.	16		•	•	•			•	•				•	•	•
Camp Creek (E-2) 5,897 acres 3 mi. n.w. of Camp Creek.	17	•	•	•				•				•			
Canaan Valley Resort (C-4) 6,015 acres 10 mi. s. of Davis on SR 32. Cross-country and downhill skiing, golf (18-hole); bicycle rental, summer chairlift rides. *(See Davis p. 348)*	18	•	•	•				•	•			•	•	•	•
Cedar Creek (C-3) 2,443 acres 8 mi. s. of Glenville off US 33.	19	•	•	•	•			•	•						
Chief Logan (D-1) 3,303 acres 3 mi. n. of Logan off SR 10. Outdoor drama. *(See Logan p. 355)*	20	•	•	•				•	•	•				•	•
Coopers Rock (B-4) 12,713 acres 8 mi. w. of Bruceton Mills on I-68. *(See Bruceton Mills p. 346)*	21	•	•	•				•					•		

RECREATION AREAS

RECREATION AREAS	MAP LOCATION	CAMPING	PICNICKING	HIKING TRAILS	BOATING	BOAT RAMP	BOAT RENTAL	FISHING	SWIMMING	PETS ON LEASH	BICYCLE TRAILS	WINTER SPORTS	VISITOR CENTER	LODGE/CABINS	FOOD SERVICE
Greenbrier (D-4) 5,130 acres 4 mi. s.w. of White Sulphur Springs via US 60 and Harts Run Rd. Nature programs.	**22**	•	•	•					•					•	
Hawks Nest (D-2) 276 acres 1.75 mi. w. on US 60 in Ansted. Historic. Scenic. Golf. *(See Ansted p. 342)*	**23**		•	•	•	•	•	•	•				•	•	•
Holly River (C-3) 8,292 acres 2 mi. n. of Hacker Valley off SR 20.	**24**	•	•	•					•	•				•	•
Kanawha (D-2) 9,302 acres 12 mi. s. of Charleston on Kanawha Forest Dr. Hunting; horse rental.	**25**	•	•	•					•	•				•	
Kumbrabow (C-4) 9,474 acres 5 mi. w. of Elkwater off US 219. Hunting.	**26**	•	•	•					•					•	
Laurel Lake (D-1) 12,851 acres 7 mi. n.e. of Lenore off SR 65.	**27**		•	•	•	•			•		•				
Little Beaver (D-3) 562 acres 10 mi. s.e. of Beckley on I-64 to SR 9, following signs.	**28**	•	•	•	•		•	•	•	•					
Lost River (C-5) 3,712 acres 4 mi. w. of Mathias on SR 259 and CR 12, following signs. *(See Mathias p. 356)*	**29**	•	•	•					•	•	•	•	•		•
Moncove Lake (E-3) 896 acres 6 mi. n. of SR 3 on SR 8 near Gap Mills.	**30**	•	•	•	•	•		•	•	•					
North Bend (C-2) 1,405 acres 2 mi. e. of Cairo off SR 31. Nature programs. Miniature golf, tennis; bicycle rental.	**31**	•	•	•	•		•	•	•	•	•			•	•
Panther (E-1) 7,810 acres 3 mi. s. of Panther, following signs.	**32**	•	•	•					•	•					
Pinnacle Rock (E-2) 396 acres 5 mi.s.e. of Bramwell on US 52. *(See Bramwell p. 346)*	**33**		•	•	•	•			•			•	•	•		
Pipestem Resort (E-3) 4,023 acres on SR 20. Nature programs. Scenic. Golf (18-hole), tennis; horse rental. *(See Pipestem p. 361)*	**34**	•	•	•	•		•	•	•	•			•	•	•	•
Plum Orchard Lake (D-2) 3,201 acres e. off I-77 exit 54 or 60 on CR 23 between Mount Hope and Oak Hill.	**35**	•	•	•	•	•	•	•	•	•					
Pricketts Fort (B-3) 188 acres about 2.5 mi. w. off I-79 exit 139 n. of Fairmont. *(See Fairmont p. 350)*	**36**		•	•	•						•		•		•
Seneca (D-4) 11,684 acres 4 mi. s.w. of Dunmore off SR 28.	**37**	•	•	•					•	•		•		•	
Stonewall Resort (C-3) more than 2,000 acres 2 mi. e. of I-79 near Weston. Golf (18-hole).	**38**	•	•	•	•				•	•				•	•	•
Tomlinson Run (A-3) 1,398 acres 2 mi. n. of New Manchester off SR 8. Tent and camping gear rental.	**39**	•	•	•	•	•		•	•	•	•				
Twin Falls Resort (E-2) 3,776 acres 8 mi. n.e. of Pineville. Nature programs. Golf (18-hole), tennis.	**40**	•	•	•					•				•	•	•	•
Tygart Lake (C-4) 2,134 acres 2 mi. s. of Grafton on CR 44 along e. bank of Tygart River Reservoir. Scuba diving, water skiing.	**41**	•	•	•	•	•	•	•	•	•			•	•	•	•
Valley Falls (B-4) 1,145 acres 9 mi. s. of Fairmont off I-79 exit 137 on SR 310. *(See Fairmont p. 350)*	**42**		•	•					•	•		•	•			
Watoga (D-4) 10,100 acres 10 mi. s. of Huntersville (turn at park sign on SR 39, then 10 mi. s.). Nature programs. Horse rental.	**43**	•	•	•	•		•	•	•	•			•		•	•
OTHER															
Coonskin Park (D-2) 1,200 acres 5 mi. n. of Charleston on SR 114. Golf, swimming, tennis.	**44**	•	•	•					•	•			•	•		•
Lake Stephens (D-2) 2,500 acres 9 mi. w. of Beckley on SR 3.	**45**	•	•	•	•	•		•	•	•					•
Oglebay Resort (A-3) 1,650 acres in Wheeling 5 mi. n.e. on SR 88. Horse rental, zoo. *(See Wheeling p. 366)*	**46**		•	•	•				•	•		•	•	•	•	•
Pleasants Creek (C-4) 3,373 acres 10 mi. n. of Philippi off US 119/250.	**47**	•			•	•		•							
Pringle Tree (C-4) 4.5 acres 2 mi. n. of Buckhannon off US 119 and SR 20.	**48**		•		•	•		•		•					
Wheeling Park (B-3) 406 acres in Wheeling 4 mi. e. on US 40 at 1801 National Rd. *(See Wheeling p. 366)*	**49**		•		•				•	•		•	•		•

Points of Interest

ALBRIGHT (B-4) pop. 247, elev. 1,291'

RECREATIONAL ACTIVITIES
White-water Rafting

- **Laurel Highlands River Tours** departs from SR 26. Write P.O. Box 107, Ohiopyle, PA 15470. Trips run daily, Apr.-June. Phone (724) 329-8531 or (800) 472-3846.

- **Mountain Streams & Trails Outfitters** departs from SR 26. Write 235 Quarry Run Rd., Morgantown, WV 26508. Cheat River trips depart daily, mid-Mar. to mid-Sept. Cheat Narrows trips depart daily, May-Sept. Big Sandy River and Tygart River trips depart Sat.-Sun., mid-Mar. to mid-May. Phone (304) 594-0333 or (800) 723-8669.

- **White Water Adventures Inc.** departs from SR 26. Write P.O. Box 31, Ohiopyle, PA 15470. Cheat River trips depart daily, mid-Mar. to mid-June. Phone (724) 329-8850 or (800) 992-7238.

- **Wilderness Voyageurs Inc.** departs .75 mi. n. on SR 26. Write P.O. Box 97, Ohiopyle, PA 15470. Trips depart daily, Mar.-Oct. Reservations are required for Cheat River trips. Phone (724) 329-1000 or (800) 272-4141.

ANSTED (D-2) pop. 1,576, elev. 1,312'

Ansted, originally settled by Baptists in 1790, was named New Haven by a group of New England Spiritualists who came to the town in 1830. The following year it was renamed after British scientist David T. Ansted, who had interested English investors in building coal-mining operations. On a knoll overlooking the town, Westlake Cemetery contains

---

DID YOU KNOW

Berkeley Springs was established as a health resort in 1776; George Washington was an early visitor.

---

the grave of Julia Jackson Woodson, Gen. Thomas "Stonewall" Jackson's mother.

CONTENTMENT is .75 mi. n.w. on US 60. Confederate colonel George Imboden's antebellum home, built in 1830, has been restored. A museum and one-room country schoolhouse are on the grounds. Wed.-Sat. 10-4, June-Aug.; by appointment in May. Admission $3; $1 (ages 0-11). Phone (304) 658-5695.

HAWKS NEST STATE PARK is 1.75 mi. w. on US 60. The 276-acre park is named for a sweeping lookout point above the New River. A nature center, open May through October, has hands-on displays. Hiking trails of varying lengths and intensity lead to scenic views and overlooks. Food is available. Park open daily 24 hours. Free. Phone (304) 658-5212 or (800) 225-5982. *See Recreation Chart.*

Hawks Nest Canyon Tramway runs from the park lodge to the marina. The aerial tram descends 446 feet to the bottom of the New River Gorge. The tramway operates Mon.-Tues. and Thurs.-Fri. 11-4:45, Sat.-Sun. 9-6:45, June-Aug.; Mon.-Tues. and Thurs.-Fri. 11-4:45, Sat.-Sun. 11-6:45, in Oct.; Sat.-Sun. 11-6:45 in May and Sept. Round-trip fare $3; $2 (ages 5-12 and 60+). AX, MC, VI .

NEW RIVER JETBOATS departs from the dock in Hawks Nest State Park; passengers must take the Hawks Nest Canyon Tramway from the park lodge to reach the dock. A 6-mile, 45-minute round-trip takes passengers upstream to the New River Gorge Bridge on the *Miss M. Rocks,* providing scenic views of the New River Valley and opportunities to see wildlife.

Mon.-Tues. and Thurs.-Fri. 11-4, Sat.-Sun. 9-6, June-Aug.; Mon.-Tues. and Thurs.-Fri. 11-4, Sat.-Sun. 11-6, in Oct.; Sat.-Sun. 11-6 in May and Sept. Fare (including tram) $18; $16 (ages 60+); $7 (ages 5-16). AX, MC, VI. Phone (304) 469-2525.

ARTHURDALE (B-4) elev. 1,780'

The homestead community of Arthurdale was created in 1934 by the federal government. Eleanor Roosevelt guided the New Deal project that helped displaced coal miners and their families start a new life during the Great Depression. The First Lady was a frequent visitor to the town; her husband made his only presidential graduation address there in 1938.

ARTHURDALE HERITAGE NEW DEAL MUSEUM is at jct. Q and A rds. Unveiled by Eleanor Roosevelt in the 1930s, the 165 buildings of the first New Deal homestead include houses, schools, a health clinic, a community center and a dairy farm. Visitors may tour the administration building museum, a 1935 homestead, a blacksmith's forge, a vintage service station and the historic Center Hall. A self-guiding driving tour brochure is available.

Guided tours are available. Allow 1 hour minimum. Tues.-Sun. noon-4, May-Oct.; Tues.-Fri. noon-4, rest of year. Admission $5; $4 (ages 55+); $3 (elementary school students). DS, MC, VI. Phone (304) 864-3959.

AURORA (B-4) elev. 2,641'

Aurora is in a region where West Virginia's state tree, the sugar maple, is plentiful. American Indians once collected the sap, which runs in early spring, in wooden troughs and heated it with hot stones. The sap, now gathered using metal buckets or networks of plastic tubing that lead to large tanks, is then processed in modern evaporating plants.

Cathedral State Park, 1 mile east on SR 50, comprises 133 acres of virgin timber and offers 5 miles of walking trails, a nature area and picnic facilities; for further information phone (304) 735-3771.

BECKLEY (D-2) pop. 17,254, elev. 2,300'

Beckley is the center of southern West Virginia's smokeless coal region. The bituminous coal mined in this area is a higher grade of coal that produces less smoke when burned.

Beckley is the northern anchor of the Coal Heritage Trail which winds its way past company stores, miners' houses, railroad yards, coal tipples and 500 small company towns on its way south to Bluefield; follow SR 16 southwest to US 52, which heads south and east to Bluefield, the end of the trail. Mile markers along the way indicate points of interest. Another scenic drive runs south along US 19 in Bluestone Canyon.

Southern West Virginia Convention & Visitors Bureau: 221 George St., Suite 2, Beckley, WV 25801; phone (304) 252-2244 or (800) 847-4898. *See color ad.*

Shopping areas: Crossroads Mall, at SR 16 and US 19 in north Beckley, houses such stores as Belk, JCPenney and Sears. Raleigh Mall, on US 19, features Elder-Beerman.

BECKLEY EXHIBITION COAL MINE is at 513 Ewart Ave. adjacent to New River Park. Veteran miners lead 45-minute underground tours of a vintage coal mine, providing visitors an opportunity to see how a turn-of-the-20th-century mine operated. A coal mining museum and coal camp homes, schools, a miner's shanty and churches provide a glimpse into life in a typical coal camp. Bring a jacket, as the mine is a constant 58 F.

Picnicking is permitted. Allow 1 hour, 30 minutes minimum. Daily 10-6, Apr.-Oct. Admission (includes Youth Museum of Southern West Virginia & Mountain Homestead) $15; $13 (ages 55+); $10 (ages 4-12). MC, VI. Phone (304) 256-1747.

TAMARACK is off I-64/77 exit 45. This showcase for the state's cultural heritage and traditions displays West Virginia-made juried arts, foods and agricultural products. The facility also has nature trails, gardens, a fine arts gallery and a theater. Demonstration areas allow visitors to see artisans at work creating such items as pottery, glass, woodcrafts and quilts. Allow 30 minutes minimum. Daily 8-8, Apr.-Dec.; 8-7, rest of year. Closed Dec. 25. Free. Phone (304) 256-6843 or (888) 262-7225.

THEATRE WEST VIRGINIA is 15 mi. e. on I-64 to exit 129B at Grandview. Outdoor dramas are presented at the Cliffside Amphitheatre on the New River Gorge National River. "Hatfields and McCoys" is a musical drama about the infamous feuding families, and "Honey in the Rock" tells the story of the state's Civil War birth. A different Broadway musical is featured each summer.

Inquire about weather policies. Shows are presented Tues.-Sun. at 8:15, mid-June to late Aug. Admission $16; $14 (senior citizens); $8 (ages 0-11). Reservations are recommended. MC, VI. Phone (304) 256-6800 or (800) 666-9142 for reservations.

YOUTH MUSEUM OF SOUTHERN WEST VIRGINIA & MOUNTAIN HOMESTEAD, 509 Ewart Ave. in New River Park, features a planetarium and changing displays about science and the arts, including interactive exhibits about color, electricity and magnetism.

The Mountain Homestead features traditional craft demonstrations in an Appalachian pioneer village complete with a log house and barn, a one-room schoolhouse, a weaver's shed, a blacksmith shop, a moonshine still and a country store.

Allow 1 hour minimum. Mon.-Sat. 10-6, Apr.-Oct.; Tues.-Sat. 10-5, rest of year. Phone for planetarium show schedule. Admission (includes Beckley Exhibition Coal Mine) $15; $13 (ages 55+); $10 (ages 4-12). Phone (304) 252-3730.

BERKELEY SPRINGS (B-6)
pop. 663, elev. 612′

The Berkeley Springs, famous for their supposed curative properties, were a haven for American Indians long before Europeans discovered their soothing waters. A thriving community had been established by the time George Washington arrived in 1748 to survey the area for its owner, Lord Thomas Fairfax. In 1776, Washington assisted in establishing the town as a health resort under the name of Bath, which remains its official name.

More than a dozen members of the Colonial elite were among original lot owners—George and Martha Washington bought property in the area. The springs continue to flow from five main sources at the rate of 1,000-1,500 gallons per minute; the water maintains a uniform temperature of 74 F.

Though known for its spas, Berkeley Springs is also gaining notice as an arts community. The town is home to a growing number of art and craft galleries and shows. Ten miles south, Cacapon Resort State Park *(see Recreation Chart)* offers an 18-hole golf course, a lodge, a lake beach and trails to the top of Cacapon Mountain.

Berkeley Springs-Morgan County Chamber of Commerce: 127 Fairfax St., Berkeley Springs, WV 25411; phone (304) 258-9147 or (800) 447-8797.

BERKELEY SPRINGS STATE PARK is near the center of town at 2 S. Washington St. Several bathhouses offer a variety of baths, massages and other heat treatments. The historic Roman Bath House has been in use since 1815.

Allow 1 hour minimum. Main building open daily 10-6 (also Fri. 6-9 p.m., Apr.-Oct.); closed Jan. 1, Easter, Thanksgiving and Dec. 25. Old Roman Bath House open daily 10-6 (also Fri. 6-8 p.m., Apr.-Oct.). Swimming pool open daily, Memorial Day weekend-Labor Day.

Bath and massage Mon.-Thurs. $40; $36 (senior citizens). Bath and massage Fri.-Sun. and holidays $45; $40.50 (senior citizens). Bath and shower $25. Bath $20. Pool $3; $2.50 (senior citizens); $2 (ages 0-11). Reservations are recommended 1 month in advance; a deposit is required. AX, MC, VI. Phone (304) 258-2711 or (800) 225-5982.

BETHANY (A-3) pop. 985, elev. 818′

Bethany centers on Bethany College, a liberal arts school chartered in 1840 by Alexander Campbell, a leader of religious and educational reform in the 19th century. The son of a Presbyterian minister, Campbell sailed from Scotland to the United States

in 1809. He became the principal founder of one of the largest religious movements in the United States, from which developed the Christian Churches, the Christian Church (Disciples of Christ) and the Churches of Christ.

Self-guiding tours: Tour maps and brochures are available at Historic Bethany Center on the Bethany College campus. Sights include the Campbell Mansion and cemetery, Old Main, Delta Tau Delta Founder's House and Museum, and Old Bethany Meeting House. More extensive tours are available upon request; phone (304) 829-4258.

CAMPBELL MANSION is .75 mi. e. on SR 67. Alexander Campbell's 24-room home was host to such noted historic figures as Henry Clay, Jefferson Davis and President James Garfield. Eighteen rooms of the late 1700s homestead are furnished in period and include Campbell's hexagonal brick study and a schoolroom. A springhouse is on the grounds. The Campbell family cemetery is nearby.

Allow 1 hour minimum. Guided tours Mon.-Fri. 10-noon and 1-4, Sat.-Sun. by appointment; closed holidays and commencement day. Last tour begins 1 hour before closing. Admission $4; $2 (ages 6-17). AX, DS, MC, VI. Phone (304) 829-4258.

BEVERLY (C-4) pop. 651, elev. 1,946'

Originally christened Edmunton in honor of Virginia governor Edmund Randolph, Beverly was later renamed after the governor's mother. The town was chartered in 1790. During the Civil War, the Battle of Rich Mountain brought the area under Union control, and federal troops occupied the town for 2 years. Beverly served as the county seat until 1899, when the Western Maryland Railroad established the community of Elkins to the north.

Rich Mountain/Historic Beverly Visitor Center: 4 Court St., P.O. Box 227, Beverly, WV 26253; phone (304) 637-7424.

Self-guiding tours: A self-guiding walking tour brochure of the Beverly historic district and a driving tour of Civil War sites along the Beverly-Fairmont Turnpike are available from the visitor center on the town square.

RICH MOUNTAIN BATTLEFIELD is 5 mi. w. on Rich Mountain Rd. On July 11, 1861, General George McClellan's Union troops routed the Confederates who controlled the Staunton-Parkersburg Pike across Rich Mountain. Confederate earthworks, a homestead site and inscriptions carved by soldiers are visible. A visitor center is housed in the Bushrod Crawford Store, which served as McClellan's headquarters.

Allow 30 minutes minimum. Mon.-Sat. 9-dusk, June-Aug.; Mon.-Fri. 9-4, rest of year. Closed Memorial Day, July 4 and Labor Day. Donations. Phone (304) 637-7424.

BLUEFIELD (E-2) pop. 11,451, elev. 2,560'

Founded in 1889 as the regional headquarters of the Norfolk & Western Railway, remnants of the natural-gravity switching yards remain in Bluefield. Named for the many chicory flowers growing wild along the hillsides, the town attracted many industries, including coal mining.

South of town, the border between the two Virginias is on the crest of East River Mountain. A sister city, Bluefield, Va., lies to the southwest. The West Virginia city's original municipal building, built in 1924, now houses the Bluefield Area Arts Center, an active center for visual and performing arts.

Bluefield is the southern anchor of the Coal Heritage Trail which winds its way past company stores, miners' houses, railroad yards, coal tipples and 500 small company towns on its way north to Beckley; follow US 52 northwest to SR 16, which meanders north and east to Beckley. Mile markers along the way indicate points of interest.

Baseball comes to Bluefield in mid-June when the minor league Bluefield Orioles, part of the Appalachian League, play ball at Bowen Field in City Park.

Mercer County Convention and Visitors Bureau: 704 Bland St., P.O. Box 4088, Bluefield, WV 24701; phone (304) 325-8438 or (800) 221-3206. *See color ad p. 345.*

Self-guiding tours: Examples of historic Victorian architecture can be seen on a walking tour of downtown Bluefield. Brochures are available at the convention and visitors bureau and chamber of commerce offices on Bland Street.

Shopping areas: Mercer Mall, at US 460 and SR 25, has more than 70 stores, including Belk, JCPenney and Sears.

EASTERN REGIONAL COAL ARCHIVES is at 600 Commerce St. in the Craft Memorial Library. The collection of coal mining memorabilia includes artifacts, diaries, photographs, mining equipment, films and research materials. Allow 30 minutes minimum. Mon.-Fri. 9:30-5; closed major holidays. Free. Phone (304) 325-3943.

BRAMWELL (E-2) pop. 426, elev. 2,253′

Its economy fired by the nearby coal fields, Bramwell was once considered the richest town in the country, having 19 millionaires. The symbol of its wealth, the Bramwell Bank, gained fame when it floated the largest Liberty Bond during World War I, resulting in the commonly used 1920s phrase "solid as the Bank of Bramwell."

The Depression brought an end to prosperity and closed the bank, but many of the structures representative of West Virginia's gilded age have been preserved in the town's historic district. And the bank, complete with its elegant period details, is once again open.

Pinnacle Rock State Park, 5 miles southeast on US 52, is known for its namesake 3,100-foot sandstone formation. Picnicking, hiking and fishing can be enjoyed at this scenic park. *See Recreation Chart and the AAA Mideastern CampBook.*

Self-guiding tours: Walking tour maps are available at city hall and the Coal Heritage Trail Southern Interpretive Center. The sights include several mansions and buildings in the business district. For more information contact the Bramwell Town Hall; phone (304) 248-7114.

BRUCETON MILLS (B-4)
pop. 74, elev. 1,527′

COOPERS ROCK STATE FOREST is 8 mi. w. on I-68 at exit 15 (CR 73/12). The park comprises 12,713 acres of mountainous woodland. Among the forest's features are miles of nature and cross-country skiing trails and an overlook with a view of the 1,200-foot-deep Cheat River Gorge. Camping, fishing, hunting, mountain bicycling, picnicking and rock climbing are popular activities. Food is available April through November. Park open daily 8-dusk. Free. Phone (304) 594-1561. *See Recreation Chart and the AAA Mideastern CampBook.*

Henry Clay Iron Furnace is accessible from a 1-mi. trail off CR 73/12. One of the few surviving examples of an early 19th-century iron furnace, the 30-foot-high square stack was built from local stone in the 1830s and operated through the 1840s. Except for a small glade, the surrounding forest shows no sign of the community that flourished for 12 years, shipping pig iron as far away as St. Louis.

BUCKHANNON (C-4) pop. 5,725, elev. 1,433′

RECREATIONAL ACTIVITIES

Hot Air Ballooning

- **Mountain Air Balloons** is at 100 Woodall Ln., Buckhannon, WV 26201. Transportation is provided to the departure point. Tours depart daily at 6 a.m. and 5 p.m., May-Nov. (weather permitting). Reservations are required. Phone (304) 472-0792.

CASS (D-4) elev. 2,437′

Once a large lumbering community, Cass retains the history of its greatness at the beginning of the 20th century. The Cass Country Store is in the former West Virginia Pulp and Paper General Store, purported to have been the largest company store in the world.

The Historical Museum houses a collection of photographs and relics pertaining to the logging industry, including one of the largest band saws in the world. The Cass Showcase is a historic diorama depicting the Cass Railroad in its lumbering days and includes a reproduction of the town during the lumber boom at the beginning of the 19th century.

CASS SCENIC RAILROAD STATE PARK departs from the downtown depot. Passenger trains make several runs with the old steam Shay and Heisler locomotives that once hauled logging trains up the steep slopes of Cheat Mountain.

The rail excursions, which offer scenic mountain vistas, include an 8-mile, 2-hour round-trip to Whittaker Station and a 22-mile, 4.5-hour round-trip excursion to the top of Bald Knob. Also available is a 4.5-hour trip to Spruce, an abandoned logging town along Shavers Fork of the Cheat River. Trips are preceded by a free show that includes a diorama and audiovisual orientation film that relate the town's lumbering history. Other trips, including dinner trains and caboose rides, also are available.

The 2-hour trip runs daily at noon and 2:30, Memorial Day weekend-Labor Day and late Sept.-late Oct.; Fri.-Sun. at noon and 2:30, day after Labor Day-late Sept. and in late Oct. The 4.5-hour trip to Bald Knob departs Tues.-Sun. and holidays at 11, Memorial Day weekend-Labor Day and late Sept.-late Oct.; Sat.-Sun. at 11, day after Labor Day-late Sept. and in late Oct. The 4.5-hour trip to Spruce departs Fri. at 11, Memorial Day weekend-late Oct. Schedules may vary; phone ahead.

Fare Memorial Day weekend-Labor Day for 2-hour trip, Mon.-Fri. $15; $10 (ages 5-12). Sat.-Sun. and holidays $18; $13 (ages 5-12). Fare Memorial Day weekend-Labor Day for either 4.5-hour trip, Tues.-Fri. $21; $14 (ages 5-12). Sat.-Sun. and holidays $24; $17 (ages 5-12). Fare rest of season for 2-hour trip, Mon.-Fri. $20; $14 (ages 5-12). Sat.-Sun. and holidays $23; $17 (ages 5-12). Fare rest of season for 4.5-hour trip, Tues.-Fri. $26; $18 (ages 5-12). Sat.-Sun. $29; $21 (ages 5-12). Guaranteed reserved seat $4. Reservations are recommended. AX, DS, MC, VI. Phone (304) 456-4300 or (800) 225-5982.

CHARLESTON (D-2) pop. 53,421, elev. 601′

Capital of the state, Charleston was founded in 1794. From 1788-95, Daniel Boone lived across the river. He served in the Virginia Assembly in 1791. Remains of an American Indian burial ground are in South Charleston at MacCorkle Avenue and D Street.

Serving as a regional cultural center, Clay Center for the Arts & Sciences houses a performance hall and a black box theater as well as museums and a planetarium. Off I-64 exit 100 (Leon Sullivan Way), the center is home to the West Virginia Symphony Orchestra.

The Midland Trail Scenic Highway/US 60 travels from Charleston to White Sulphur Springs (see place listing p. 367) through pastoral scenery and past the rugged New River Gorge.

Appalachian music, ethnic and traditional foods, West Virginia arts and crafts, dancing, storytelling and contests are part of the Vandalia Gathering, held on the Capitol lawn and in the Cultural Center on Memorial Day weekend. Vandalia, proposed as the 14th colony during the late 1760s, had many backers, including Benjamin Franklin; the new colony's boundaries would have encompassed most of present-day West Virginia, in addition to much of what is now Kentucky. However, because of the strained relations between the fledgling American colonies and Great Britain, the plan never came to fruition.

For racing fans, Tri-State Racetrack and Gaming Center, 12 miles west of Charleston off I-64 exit 47, offers greyhound racing. The glass-enclosed facility has more than 4,000 seats and a clubhouse; phone (800) 224-9683.

Note: Policies concerning admittance of children to pari-mutuel betting facilities vary. Phone for information.

Charleston Convention and Visitors Bureau: 200 Civic Center Dr., Charleston, WV 25301; phone (304) 344-5075 or (800) 733-5469.

Shopping areas: Charleston Town Center, downtown between Quarrier and Lee streets, has more than 130 stores including JCPenney, Macy's, Sears and numerous specialty shops. Capitol Street, the main street of Old Charleston, offers shops and restaurants housed in 19th-century buildings.

Open daily year-round, the Capitol Market at 800 Smith St. offers both indoor and outdoor shopping. The restored former Kanawha and Michigan Railway Depot now houses specialty shops and eateries, and an outdoors farmer's market provides fresh local produce as well as flowers, shrubs and trees.

[SAVE] **AVAMPATO DISCOVERY MUSEUM,** downtown at 300 Leon Sullivan Way at the Clay Center, has interactive science exhibits, an art gallery and a theater with a planetarium and large-format films. Science galleries include The Gizmo Factory's physical science exhibits; Earth City, which explores the forces that shaped the state; a gallery about health and wellness; and a fanciful space for children under 6. The art museum's primary focus is on 19th- and 20th-century paintings.

Food is available. Allow 1 hour, 30 minutes minimum. Museum open Wed.-Sat. 10-5, Sun. noon-5. Planetarium shows and films are offered several times daily. Admission (includes museum, planetarium and film) $12.50; $10 (ages 3-18 and senior citizens). Admission to individual attractions and other combination admissions also are available. AX, DS, MC, VI. Phone (304) 561-3575.

CRAIK-PATTON HOUSE is at 2809 Kanawha Blvd. E. in Daniel Boone Park. Built in 1834 by James Craik, the house later was purchased by George Smith Patton, a Confederate colonel and grandfather of World War II Gen. George S. Patton. The restored house, which was moved from its original location on Virginia Street, is furnished true to mid-19th-century style.

Landscaped grounds feature herb and boxwood gardens. Allow 1 hour minimum. Tues.-Thurs. 9-4:30, otherwise by appointment. Admission $3; $2 (children). Phone (304) 925-5341.

CULTURAL CENTER is in the West Virginia State Capitol Complex at Greenbrier and Washington sts. The center houses a 500-seat theater, reference library, archives and art exhibits. Mon.-Thurs. 9-8, Fri.-Sat. 9-6, Sun. noon-6. Free. Phone (304) 558-0162.

[GEM] **WEST VIRGINIA STATE CAPITOL** is on Kanawha Blvd. E., facing the Kanawha River. This masterpiece of architect Cass Gilbert was completed in 1932. The outstanding feature is the rotunda's gold-tone dome, 180 feet above the main floor. From its center hangs a 2-ton rock crystal chandelier, 8 feet in diameter. The second-floor ceiling is decorated with a panel design showing leaves of West Virginia's native trees.

The building's office wings house the state administrative departments, including the Supreme Court and Law Library. The governor's mansion is next door. Guided tours are available. Capitol open Mon.-Fri. 9-3:30, Sat. 9-7, Sun. noon-7. The governor's mansion is open Thurs.-Fri. 9:30-11:30. Both buildings closed Jan. 1, Thanksgiving and Dec. 25. Reservations are required for the governor's mansion and are suggested for other areas. Free. Phone (304) 558-4839.

CHARLES TOWN (B-6) pop. 2,907, elev. 513'

Charles Town was named for George Washington's brother, who laid out the town in 1786. Streets bear the names of Washington's family members. After his raid on Harpers Ferry, John Brown was tried and hanged for treason in Charles Town.

Automobile races take place nearby at Summit Point Raceway, April through October; phone (304) 725-8444. Thoroughbred horse racing has drawn crowds since 1786. Charles Town Races, 1 mile east on US 340, is open all year; phone (304) 725-7001 or (800) 795-7001.

Note: Policies concerning admittance of children to pari-mutuel betting facilities vary. Phone for information.

Charles Town marks the West Virginia terminus of the scenic portion of SR 9, which runs eastward into Virginia. From Charles Town it is 6 miles to the Virginia border.

Jefferson County Chamber of Commerce: 29 Keyes Ferry Rd., Suite 200, P.O. Box 426, Charles Town, WV 25414; phone (304) 725-2055 or (800) 624-0577.

JEFFERSON COUNTY COURTHOUSE is at George and Washington sts. The original one-room courthouse, built in 1803 on land donated by Charles Washington, was incorporated into the present building. The room where John Brown was tried is open to the public. Mon.-Fri. 9-5 (also Fri. 5-7). Free. Phone (304) 728-3240.

JEFFERSON COUNTY MUSEUM is at 200 E. Washington St. in the lower level of the Charles Town Library. Displays include memorabilia of the Washington family and John Brown, Jefferson County historical relics and many Civil War items. Tues.-Sat. 11-4, Apr.-Nov. Admission $3; free (ages 0-17). Phone (304) 725-8628.

GAMBLING ESTABLISHMENTS

• **Charles Town Races & Slots** is 1 mi. e. on US 340. Daily 7 a.m.-4 a.m.; closed Dec. 25. Phone (304) 725-7001 or (800) 795-7001.

CHESTER (A-3) pop. 2,592, elev. 705'

GAMBLING ESTABLISHMENTS

• **Mountaineer Race Track and Gaming Resort** is on SR 2. Daily 7 a.m.-4 a.m. Phone (800) 804-0468.

CLARKSBURG (B-3) pop. 16,743, elev. 1,034'

From 1861 until the first battle of Bull Run, Clarksburg was the headquarters for Gen. George B. McClellan. It also served as a Union supply depot throughout the war. Gen. William E. Jones' Confederate cavalry passed through in 1863 on the raid that destroyed military points on the B & O Railroad.

Clarksburg was the birthplace in 1824 of Gen. Thomas J. "Stonewall" Jackson, hero of the Confederacy. The site is marked by a bronze plate at 326-328 W. Main St. An equestrian statue of Jackson is on the northeast corner of the Court House Plaza. The military leader spent most of his boyhood 20 miles south at Jackson's Mill *(see Weston p. 364)*.

More than 100,000 visitors come to Clarksburg over Labor Day weekend to join in the merriment of the West Virginia Italian Heritage Festival. The 3-day street festival features name entertainment, traditional Italian foods, a children's area, a parade and a homemade wine contest.

Greater Bridgeport Conference & Visitors Center: 164 W. Main St., Bridgeport, WV 26330; phone (304) 842-7272 or (800) 368-4324.

Shopping areas: Meadowbrook Mall, off I-79 exit 121, has Elder-Beerman, JCPenney and Sears among its stores.

CRAB ORCHARD (D-2)
pop. 2,761, elev. 2,292'

WINERIES

• **Daniel Vineyards** is at 200 Twin Oaks Rd. Tours and tastings Mon.-Sat. 10-5, Sun. 1-5; closed major holidays. Phone (304) 252-9750 or (877) 378-1990.

DAVIS (C-4) pop. 624, elev. 3,200'

Incorporated in 1885, Davis was born of the lumber boom. Today the area is a mecca for mountain bikers and rafters. Ten miles south, Canaan Valley Resort State Park *(see Recreation Chart)* is an all-year resort and conference center. Downhill and cross-country skiing are popular in winter; golf on an 18-hole championship course, hiking, tennis and swimming prevail during the summer. Deer often cross the golf course early and late in the day. Other privately operated resorts and camping facilities also are available in the Canaan (ka-NAIN) valley.

Of historical significance is the Fairfax Stone, 7 miles north of town off US 219, which marked the western boundary of Lord Fairfax's lands. Under the terms of the grant issued by the king of England,

Lord Fairfax owned all the lands between the Potomac and the Rappahannock rivers, and this marker served as the base point for the boundary between Maryland and Virginia (now West Virginia).

Tucker County Convention and Visitors Bureau: William Avenue at 4th Street, P.O. Box 565, Davis, WV 26260; phone (304) 259-5315 or (800) 782-2775.

BLACKWATER FALLS STATE PARK is about .25 mi. s.w. off SR 32, following signs. The scenic Blackwater Falls are 65 feet high, and the gorge below is more than 525 feet deep. An observation point is on the gorge's rim; stairways descend to the foot of the falls. Recreational activities include cross-country skiing, paddleboating, hiking, horseback riding, picnicking, swimming, tennis, bicycling, sledding, volleyball and nature programs.

Food is available. Park open daily 6 a.m.-10 p.m. Waterfall accessible 6 a.m.-dusk. Campgrounds available last week in Apr.-Oct. 31; cabins and lodge facilities are available all year. Free. Phone (304) 259-5216. *See Recreation Chart.*

RECREATIONAL ACTIVITIES
Skiing
- **Timberline Resort** is 6 mi. s. on SR 32, then 3.5 mi. e. on Timberline Rd. Write HC 70, Box 488, Davis, WV 26260. Daily early Dec.-early Apr. Phone (304) 866-4801 or (800) 766-9464.

DURBIN (C-4) pop. 262, elev. 2,753′

CHEAT MOUNTAIN SALAMANDER departs from the station on Red Run Rd., .5 mi. n. of the Shavers Fork River on US 250. Three-hour trips, in a replica of a 1922 Edwards Railway motor car, take passengers through the rugged, scenic mountains. The High Falls trip runs past rock walls and tight curves to a waterfall on the Cheat River. The Spruce trip runs through spruce forests and the historic district of the town of Spruce to a hand-dug notch called "Big Cut." There are half-hour layovers at High Falls and Spruce.

Allow 3 hours minimum. Departures to High Falls Thurs.-Sun. at 11, to Spruce at 2:30, in Oct.; Thurs.-Sat., late June-Aug. 31 and in late Sept.; Fri.-Sat., Memorial Day weekend-late June; Sat., May 1-day before Memorial Day weekend and Sept. 1-late Sept. A combination trip is available. Fare $25; $23 (ages 60+); $17 (ages 4-11). Reservations are recommended. AX, DS, MC, VI. Phone (877) 686-7245.

DURBIN ROCKET departs from US 250 (Staunton-Parkersburg Tpke.). Powered by a restored 1910 steam locomotive, the 10.5-mile, 2.5-hour trip travels through the Greenbrier River wilderness providing both scenic mountain and river views as the train makes its way through the Monongahela National Forest. Passengers have a choice of riding in one of two 1920s cabooses or in an open-air car. A 30-minute stop is made at a picnic area at Piney Island.

Allow 3 hours minimum. Departures Thurs.-Sun. (and Columbus Day) at 11:30 and 3, late June-early Sept. and in Oct.; Sat.-Sun. at 11:30 and 3, early Sept.-Sept. 30; Sat.-Sun. at 11:30, May 1-late June. Fare $20; $18 (ages 60+); $11 (ages 4-11). AX, DS, MC, VI. Phone (877) 686-7245.

ELKINS (C-4) pop. 7,032, elev. 1,940′

Elkins, on the Tygart Valley River in the Potomac Highlands, is in a region that contains many of West Virginia's highest mountains. Named for Stephen B. Elkins, secretary of war and U.S. senator 1895-1911, the city was a center for railroad, timber and coal operations. The mountains provide a variety of recreational opportunities. Ski areas are nearby in the Monongahela National Forest *(see place listing p. 356)*, which maintains its headquarters in Elkins.

Elkins is at the crossroads of three scenic highways. From Fairmont to the north, the scenic section of US 250 passes through, running south to Huttonsville. US 219 runs south jointly with US 250 to Huttonsville and then continues on to White Sulphur Springs. US 33 crosses them in Elkins, following the Tygart River into town before heading east into some of the region's most spectacular scenery. The Stuart Memorial Drive, which passes Stuart Recreation Area and 4,020-foot Bickles Knob, runs between Elkins and Alpena.

Elkins-Randolph County Chamber of Commerce: 200 Executive Plaza, Elkins, WV 26241; phone (304) 636-2717.

NEW TYGART FLYER departs from the depot on Railroad Ave. A 4-hour, 46-mile round-trip takes passengers by train through the Cheat River Mountain canyons and the Tygart Valley, past waterfalls, through an "S" curve tunnel and across a bridge over the Cheat River. A parlor car, available at an additional cost, includes food. Other excursions also are offered.

Allow 4 hours minimum. Departures Thurs.-Sun. at 11, in Oct.; Fri.-Sun. at 11, late June-late Aug.; select Sat. and Sun. at 11, May 1-late June, late Aug.-Sept. 30 and in early Nov. Other departures may be available; phone ahead. Coach fare $30; $26 (ages 60+); $22 (ages 4-11). Reservations are recommended. AX, DS, MC, VI. Phone (304) 456-4935 or (877) 686-7245.

FAIRMONT (B-3) pop. 19,097, elev. 884′

Fairmont occupies the steep hills surrounding the Monongahela River, which divides the town into east and west sections. Originally two towns, Palatine and Middletown, Fairmont was incorporated in 1843. Ferries shuttled people and supplies across the river until 1852, when a suspension bridge unified the town.

During the 1850s railroad access encouraged the development of coal mines in the area. While coal continues to be a source of employment, today the town is on a high-tech corridor with a NASA software facility and a software consortium. Other Fairmont products include mine machinery and aluminum.

Fifteen miles south off SR 310, Valley Falls State Park features a series of waterfalls generated by the Tygart Valley River. The park's 1,145 acres are popular with anglers, picnickers and hikers *(see Recreation Chart)*. Fairmont is the northern end of the scenic section of US 250, which runs 73 miles to Huttonsville and continues as US 219 to Lewisburg.

Convention and Visitors Bureau of Marion County: 110 Adams St., Fairmont, WV 26554; phone (304) 368-1123 or (800) 834-7365.

PRICKETTS FORT STATE PARK, about 2.5 mi. w. off I-79 exit 139, contains a reconstructed log fort similar to one built in 1774 to protect settlers from American Indian attacks. The museum captures West Virginia's 18th-century lifestyle through costumed interpreters and craft demonstrations.

The visitor center offers exhibits about the Monongahela Valley's history. The park also has a nature trail and a hiking trail that follows a converted rail bed to Fairmont.

Picnicking is permitted. Allow 2 hours minimum. Park open daily 6 a.m.-10 p.m. year-round. Historical attractions open Mon.-Sat. 10-4:30, Sun. noon-4:30, Memorial Day-Labor Day; Wed.-Sat. 10-4:30, Sun. noon-4:30, mid-Apr. through day before Memorial Day and day after Labor Day-Oct. 31. Park free. Historical attractions admission $6; $5 (ages 56+); $3 (ages 6-12). Phone (304) 363-3030. *See Recreation Chart.*

FAYETTEVILLE (D-2)
pop. 2,754, elev. 1,750'

Settled in 1818, Fayetteville was named for Marquis de Lafayette in 1837. A historical marker on the town lawn identifies Fayetteville as the site where the military tactic of indirect firing—the shooting over friendly troops into enemy positions beyond—was first used during the Civil War.

Fayetteville's proximity to the New and Gauley rivers has made it a center for recreation. Both these rivers are famous for their challenging white-water rapids, which are considered some of the best in the country.

Northeast of Fayetteville is the New River Gorge Bridge, one of the longest steel-arch span bridges in the world and one of the highest bridges in the nation. The arch spans 1,700 feet, while the bridge itself stretches 3,030 feet across the gorge. At 876 feet, it is 321 feet higher than the Washington Monument.

Extreme sports fanatics gather in Fayetteville the third Saturday in October for the ☞ New River Gorge Bridge Day. Close to 200,000 spectators watch as hundreds of BASE jumpers, rappel teams

and high line riders leap, jump and descend from the bridge.

Fayetteville lies along scenic US 19, which runs 45 miles from the West Virginia Turnpike/I-77 at Bradley to I-79 near Sutton.

Fayetteville Convention & Visitors Bureau: 310 N. Court St., Fayetteville, WV 25840; phone (888) 574-1500.

RECREATIONAL ACTIVITIES
Horseback Riding

- **Canyon Rim Ranch** is off US 19, s. on Court St. (CR 16) to Gatewood Rd., then 3 mi. on Cunard Rd. Write R.R. 1, Box 601B, Fayetteville, WV 25840. Other activities are offered. Daily, Apr.-Nov. Phone (304) 574-3111.

White-water Rafting

- **Cantrell Ultimate Rafting** is w. on Court St. (CR 16), then .5 mi. s. on Gatewood Rd. following signs. Write Rt. 4, Box 2, Fayetteville, WV 25840. Other activities are offered. Trips on the New and Gauley rivers depart daily, Mar.-Oct. Phone (304) 574-2500 or (800) 470-7238.

- **Passages to Adventure** is at US 19 and Maple Ln. Write P.O. Box 71, Fayetteville, WV 25840. Other activities are offered. Trips on the Gauley and Lower New River run late Mar. to mid-Oct. Phone (304) 574-1037 or (800) 634-3785.

- **Raft West Virginia Inc.** is off US 19 on Whitewater Ave. Write Rt. 3, Box 459A, Fayetteville, WV 25840. Other activities are offered. New River trips depart daily, Mar.-Oct. Gauley River trips depart daily, Sept.-Oct. Phone (304) 574-1004 or (800) 782-7238.

- **Rivers Whitewater Rafting** is .5 mi. w. off US 19 on Fayette Station Rd. Write P.O. Box 39, Lansing, WV 25862. Other activities are offered. Trips depart Mar.-Oct. Phone (304) 574-3834 or (800) 879-7483.

- **USA Raft** is at jct. SR 16 and Appalachian Dr. Write P.O. Box 277, Rowlesburg, WV 26425. New and Gauley river trips depart Mar.-Oct. Phone (304) 454-2475 or (800) 872-7238.

FRENCH CREEK (C-3) elev. 1,500'

French Creek was first settled in 1808 by a party from Massachusetts. The name came from a local legend about three Frenchmen who prospected for gold in the area in 1725.

WEST VIRGINIA STATE WILDLIFE CENTER is s. on SR 20 at CR 11. The center exhibits native and introduced animals and birds in natural settings. Among the animals exhibited are bison, elk, mountain lions, snakes, river otters, timber wolves, white-tailed deer and wild turkeys. Food and picnic facilities are available. Allow 2 hours minimum. Daily 9-6, May-Aug.; 9-5, rest of year (weather permitting). Admission $3; $1.50 (ages 3-15). Phone (304) 924-6211.

GEORGE WASHINGTON AND JEFFERSON NATIONAL FORESTS—

see place listing in Virginia p. 252.

GERRARDSTOWN (B-6) elev. 676′

Gerrardstown, in the Eastern Panhandle, was first settled in 1742 by 14 Baptist families from New Jersey. In 1787 the town was founded and named for the Rev. David Gerrard, who enlarged the town by platting 100 lots of his own property to be sold to new settlers. The many older buildings in the village have led to its being described as "a 19th-century community restored."

Gerrard House, in the center of the village, is one of the oldest known buildings in West Virginia. Built in 1743 by John Hays, it was later the home of David Gerrard. The two-story stone house, heavily constructed for protection not only from the elements but also from the American Indians, retains much of its original woodwork; it is not open to the public. For additional information contact the Berkeley County Historical Society at (304) 267-4713.

GHENT (E-2) elev. 2,986′

RECREATIONAL ACTIVITIES
Skiing

- **Winterplace Ski Resort** is .7 mi. s. on US 19, then .9 mi. s. on Flat Top Mountain Rd. Write 100 Old Flat Top Mountain Rd., Ghent, WV 25843. Daily, early Dec.-late Mar. Phone (304) 787-3221 or (800) 607-7669.

GLEN JEAN (D-2) elev. 1,600′

RECREATIONAL ACTIVITIES
White-water Rafting

- **West Virginia Adventures** is off US 19 on Wood Mountain Rd. Write P.O. Box 243, Glen Jean, WV 25846. Rafting trips on the New and Gauley rivers depart daily, Mar.-Oct. Phone (304) 465-2025 or (800) 292-0880.

GRAFTON (B-4) pop. 5,489, elev. 1,002′

While still a part of Virginia, Grafton was incorporated in 1856. The town was a key point in the Civil War because of its location on the B&O Railroad. At the beginning of the war, Confederate colonel George A. Porterfield and a small contingent established a base in Grafton. Bailey Brown, who during the Battle of Philippi became the first Union soldier killed by Confederate forces, is buried in Grafton National Cemetery at 431 Walnut St.

Grafton-Taylor County Convention and Visitors Bureau: P.O. Box 513, Grafton, WV 26354; phone (304) 265-1589.

SAVE **THE ANNA JARVIS BIRTHPLACE MUSEUM** is 4 mi. s. on US 119. The 1854 two-story home was the birthplace of Anna Jarvis, the founder of Mother's Day. The establishment of this holiday was a fervent wish of Ms. Jarvis' mother.

Gen. George McClellan used the house as his headquarters during the Civil War while planning the war's first land battle. The museum contains more than 5,500 artifacts relating to Ms. Jarvis and the war. Allow 30 minutes minimum. Tues.-Sun. 10-4, Apr.-Dec.; closed Dec. 25 and 31. Admission $5; free (ages 0-12). Phone (304) 265-5549.

THE INTERNATIONAL MOTHER'S DAY SHRINE is at 11 E. Main St. Andrews Methodist Episcopal Church was the site of the first observance of Mother's Day, May 10, 1908. Tues.-Sat. 10-4, Sun.-Mon. by appointment, mid-Apr. to late Oct. Donations. Phone (304) 265-1589.

TYGART RIVER DAM AND LAKE is 2 mi. s., following signs from US 50 or US 119. The dam was built to control floods on the Monongahela River and reduce the crest of the Ohio River during flood times. The dam is 207 feet thick at the base, 1,921 feet long and 230 feet high. The reservoir, which covers 3,440 acres and has a 32-mile shoreline, provides opportunities for swimming, fishing and hiking. Phone (304) 265-6144 or (800) 225-5982. *See Recreation Chart and the AAA Mideastern CampBook.*

GREEN BANK (D-4) elev. 2,700′

NATIONAL RADIO ASTRONOMY OBSERVATORY is on SR 92 in Deer Creek Valley. Guided tours of the radio astronomy research center include a 15-minute slide show followed by a narrated bus ride to see the radio telescopes. The science center also includes exhibits and educational demonstrations.

Food is available. Allow 1 hour minimum. Open daily 8:30-7, Memorial Day weekend-Labor Day; Wed.-Sun. 8:30-7, day after Labor Day-Oct. 31; Wed.-Sun. 10-5, rest of year. Closed Jan. 1, Easter, Thanksgiving and Dec. 25. Tours are given on the hour 9-6, Memorial Day weekend-Oct. 31; at 11, 1 and 3, rest of year. Free. Phone (304) 456-2150.

HARPERS FERRY (C-6) pop. 307, elev. 282′

The town of Harpers Ferry is at the confluence of the Potomac and Shenandoah rivers, separating Maryland, Virginia and West Virginia. The federal arsenal and armory built in 1796 manufactured many of the muskets and rifles used in the War of 1812 and the Civil War. These buildings were the targets of abolitionist John Brown's notorious raid.

On the night of Oct. 16, 1859, Brown, accompanied by 18 members of his 21-man "army," surprised and captured the armory and arsenal. His intent was to incite the slaves to insurrection and arm them from the government stores. After considerable bloodshed, the raiders were captured by U.S. Marines under Col. Robert E. Lee. Brown and six of his followers were tried for treason, convicted and hanged at Charles Town.

During the Civil War, Harpers Ferry was regarded by the Union command as a key to the safety of Washington, D.C. In 1861 the small federal garrison abandoned the town before a force of Virginians, but destroyed the arsenal before leaving. It was never rebuilt. The following year Gen. Thomas "Stonewall" Jackson captured the federal garrison after a terrific bombardment, taking 12,500 Union soldiers as prisoners before moving on to join Lee at Antietam.

The Appalachian Trail passes nearby, and the Shenandoah and Potomac rivers offer opportunities for fishing, canoeing and rafting.

Jefferson County Convention & Visitors Bureau: 37 Washington Ct., Harpers Ferry, WV 25425; phone (304) 535-1813 or (866) 435-5698.

JOHN BROWN WAX MUSEUM is at 168 High St. Life-size figures depict the life of John Brown. Daily 9-5, Mar. 15-Dec. 1. Admission $7; $6 (ages 60+); $5 (ages 6-12). DS, MC, VI. Phone (304) 535-6342.

RECREATIONAL ACTIVITIES
White-water Rafting

- **River Riders Inc.** is s. off US 340 on Millville Rd., following signs to 408 Alstadts Hill Rd., Harpers Ferry, WV 25425. Other activities are offered. Trips depart daily, Apr.-Oct. Phone (304) 535-2663 or (800) 326-7238.

⬥GEM HARPERS FERRY NATIONAL HISTORICAL PARK (C-6)

Harpers Ferry National Historical Park borders US 340 at the scenic confluence of the Shenandoah and Potomac rivers. The 2,505-acre park is comprised of several areas: the Lower Town Historic District, Maryland Heights, Loudoun Heights, Bolivar Heights, Cavalier Heights, Short Hill and Virginius Island. Maps and guides are available at the park visitor center on Cavalier Heights, about 1 mile west of the Shenandoah River bridge.

Congress authorized a national monument here in 1944, and the area was declared a National Historical Park in 1963. Shuttle buses connect the visitor center with the Lower Town Historic District, the site where George Washington persuaded the federal government to construct a national armory and arsenal and where John Brown led his famous raid in 1859.

Park exhibits and museums in more than two dozen restored 19th-century buildings, including John Brown's fort, John Brown Museum, the Provost Marshal office, Civil War Museum, Industry Museum and Restoration Museum, reflect the diverse historical events that shaped the region: the first successful application of interchangeable manufacture; the arrival of the first successful American railroad; John Brown's attack on slavery; the largest surrender of Federal troops during the Civil War; and the education of former slaves at Storer College, one of the earliest integrated schools in the United States.

Guided tours are available throughout the summer. Hiking trails lead to Maryland Heights, 1,448 feet above the rivers, where remnants of Civil War

fortifications and campsites are visible. A walking tour of Virginius Island on the banks of the Shenandoah River reveals the ruins of a once-thriving industrial community. The foundries, mills and factories that survived the war were leveled by record floods in 1870 and 1889.

The park and visitor center are open daily 8-5; closed Jan. 1, Thanksgiving and Dec. 25. Admission (valid for 3 days) is $6 per private vehicle; $4 for individuals. Phone (304) 535-6029.

HARPER HOUSE is accessible via stone steps leading uphill from High St. The lower level of this 1782 home, the oldest surviving structure in Harpers Ferry, exhibits an armory worker's apartment.

JOHN BROWN MONUMENT stands by the B&O Railroad. The granite monument marks the original site of the firehouse where Brown and his men made their stand.

JOHN BROWN'S FORT is on Arsenal Square. The 1848 brick armory firehouse was the scene of Brown's capture. Dismantled and moved to Chicago after the Civil War, the building was later restored to a site 150 feet east of its original location.

HICO (D-3) elev. 2,056′

Hico received its name in 1895 when the postmaster moved the post office from his house to a nearby store. The store sold a brand of tobacco called Hico, and the post office was named for it.

Hico is at the intersection of two scenic highways. US 60 passes Hico on its 71-mile run between White Sulphur Springs and Gauley Bridge, and US 19 passes Hico about halfway along its 45-mile scenic stretch from Bradley to Sutton.

RECREATIONAL ACTIVITIES
White-water Rafting

- [SAVE] **Adventures Mountain River** is at US 60 and US 19 on Sunday Rd. Write P.O. Box 88, Hico, WV 25854. Other activities are offered. New River and Gauley River trips run late Mar.-late Oct. Phone (304) 658-5266 or (800) 822-1386.

- **North American River Runners** is .2 mi. w. of US 19 on US 60. Write P.O. Box 81, Hico, WV 25854. Other activities are offered. Trips depart Mar.-Oct. Phone (304) 658-5276 or (800) 950-2585.

HILLSBORO (D-3) pop. 243, elev. 2,303′

As with many frontier towns, Hillsboro was established by a man who was running from his past. In 1765 John McNeil fled into the wilderness believing he had killed a man in a boxing match. Two brothers, Charles and Jacob Kinnison, found him during an expedition and gave McNeil news of his opponent's recovery. McNeil would not be swayed to return with them, but he persuaded the Kinnisons to stay and help build a new settlement.

From Huttonsville to the north, scenic SR 55/US 219 runs 86 miles to Lewisburg, traversing Hillsboro near Watoga State Park *(see Recreation Chart and the AAA Mideastern CampBook)*.

DROOP MOUNTAIN BATTLEFIELD STATE PARK is 4.1 mi. s.w. on US 219. The 287-acre park was the scene of a Civil War battle that ended the last serious Confederate resistance in the state. Seven different hiking trails, an observation tower, a cemetery and several monuments are on the grounds. A log cabin museum contains Civil War memorabilia. Picnicking is permitted. Allow 30 minutes minimum. Park open daily 6 a.m.-10 p.m. Museum 10-2. Free. Phone (304) 653-4254.

PEARL S. BUCK BIRTHPLACE MUSEUM is .5 mi. n. on US 219. The restored 1892 home in which the Nobel Prize-winning author was born is furnished in period and contains some original pieces and memorabilia. On the grounds is the boyhood home of Buck's father, Absalom Sydenstricker. Picnicking is permitted. Guided 45-minute tours are offered Mon.-Sat. and holidays 9-4:30, May-Oct. Admission $6; $5 (senior citizens); $1 (ages 6-18). Phone (304) 653-4430.

HINTON (D-3) pop. 2,880, elev. 1,372′

Hinton, a historic railroad town on the New River, was once the main terminal for the Chesapeake & Ohio Railway. Ten miles north via SR 26 (River Road) is Sandstone Falls, a noted spot among anglers for catfish and bass. West on SR 20, the New River Gorge National River's Sandstone Visitor Center *(see attraction listing p. 359)* features interactive exhibits.

Bluestone Dam, 1 mile south via SR 20 on the New River, forms 2,040-acre Bluestone Lake, providing recreational options such as boating, fishing and picnicking; phone (304) 466-1234 for information.

Hinton Visitors Center: 206 Temple St., Hinton, WV 25951; phone (304) 466-5420.

Self-guiding tours: Brochures outlining a walking tour of Hinton's historic district, with more than 200 buildings of historic and architectural interest, are available at the convention and visitors bureau.

HINTON RAILROAD MUSEUM is at 206 Temple St. This museum displays artifacts of the Chesapeake & Ohio Railway. The John Henry Woodcarving exhibit features wood sculptures by folk artist Charlie Permelia. In one display 98 figurines represent every railroad job that existed in 1870. Allow 30 minutes minimum. Mon.-Sat. 10-4. Donations. Phone (304) 466-1433.

HUNTINGTON (C-1) pop. 51,475, elev. 565′

Huntington lies in a semicircle between low hills and the Ohio River. Eleven miles of floodwalls protect the city. Founded in 1871 by Collis P. Huntington, who was then president of the Chesapeake & Ohio Railroad, the city has become a busy industrial center and trans-shipping point. Among the products manufactured in the area are chemicals, clothing, glass and steel.

The city's Civic Center, One Civic Center Plaza, draws convention business to Huntington and plays host to entertainment events. Marshall University offers guided campus tours through its Welcome Center; phone (304) 696-6833 or (800) 642-3499.

The rose garden in Ritter Park, on McCoy Road between 8th and 12th streets, displays four species and 87 varieties of roses. Virginia Point, a park at the mouth of the Big Sandy River, has a boat-launching ramp and a camping area. The Ohio River also offers recreational opportunities. Public launching ramps and a marina provide boaters access to the river.

Camden Park, an amusement park just west of the city on US 60, offers 27 rides, including two wooden roller coasters and a 1907 carousel, as well as shows by nationally known recording artists; phone (304) 429-4321 or (866) 822-6336.

Cabell-Huntington Convention and Visitors Bureau: 763 3rd Ave., P.O. Box 347, Huntington, WV 25708; phone (304) 525-7333 or (800) 635-6329.

Shopping areas: Huntington Mall, off I-64 exit 20B, contains JCPenney, Macy's and Sears among its stores. Heritage Village, a restored railway yard at 11th Street and Veterans Memorial Boulevard, offers shops and restaurants housed in old warehouses and boxcars.

HERITAGE FARM MUSEUM AND VILLAGE is off I-64 exit 8 (5th St.), 1 mi. w. on Johnstown Rd., then 1.7 mi. s. to 3300 Harvey Rd. Appalachian heritage is preserved in more than 12 restored buildings, including a sawmill, blacksmith shop, country store, one-room school and log church. A petting zoo, animal barn and nature walk are featured. Museum displays include farm machinery, steam tractors, covered wagons, early automobiles and home technology.

Allow 1 hour minimum. Mon.-Sat. 10-3; closed holidays. Guided 2-hour tours $8; $7 (ages 65+); $6 (ages 3-12). Guided 1-hour tour $6; $5 (ages 3-12 and 65+). Petting zoo/nature walk (with tour) $3. Petting zoo only $5. AX, DS, MC, VI. Phone (304) 522-1244.

HUNTINGTON MUSEUM OF ART is at 2033 McCoy Rd. in Park Hills. Collections include 19th- and 20th-century sculpture, 19th-century French and English paintings, Ohio Valley glass, decorative arts, Georgian silver, plants and firearms. Also available are special exhibits and a children's art museum. Marked nature trails are on the grounds.

Food is available. Allow 1 hour minimum. Wed.-Sat. 10-5 (also Tues. 5-9), Sun. noon-5; closed Jan. 1, Thanksgiving and Dec. 24-25. Admission $5; $18 (family rate for four or more people); free (Tues.). Phone (304) 529-2701.

KEYSER (B-5) pop. 5,303, elev. 809′

The country around Keyser was a frequent battleground during the Civil War. A supply point for both armies, the community changed hands 14 times during the war. Nancy Hanks, mother of Abraham Lincoln, was born nearby on Doll Farm at Mikes Run.

Fort Ashby, on SR 46 near its intersection with SR 28, was built in 1755 and is the only remaining fort of the 69 that George Washington built to protect western Virginians. The fort is open by appointment; phone (304) 298-3836 or (304) 298-4776.

Mineral County Convention and Visitors Bureau: Grand Central Business Center, Suite 2011, Keyser, WV 26726; phone (304) 788-2513.

LANSING (D-3) elev. 1,864′

Along with nearby Fayetteville and Hico *(see place listings p. 350 and p. 352)*, Lansing serves as a base of operations for outfitters offering trips down the New River. The Canyon Rim Visitor Center *(see attraction listing p. 359)* provides information about the New River Gorge National River.

RECREATIONAL ACTIVITIES
White-water Rafting

- **Class VI River Runners** is .1 mi. n. of the New River Gorge Bridge exit off US 19, then .5 mi. w. on Ames Heights Rd.; bear left at the fork in the road. Write P.O. Box 78, Lansing, WV 25862. Trips depart daily, Apr.-Oct. Phone (304) 574-0704 or (800) 252-7784.

- **New and Gauley River Adventures** is off US 19 exit Lansing Rd. Write P.O. Box 44, Lansing, WV 25862. Other activities are offered. Trips on the New and Gauley rivers depart daily, Mar.-Oct. Phone (304) 574-3008 or (800) 759-7238.

DID YOU KNOW

June 20, the date West Virginia entered the Union in 1863, is a state holiday.

- **Wildwater Expeditions Unlimited** is 1.25 mi. n. of the New River Gorge Bridge at jct. US 19 and Milroy Grose Rd. Write P.O. Box 155, Lansing, WV 25862. Other activities are offered. Trips depart daily, Apr.-Oct. Phone (304) 658-4007 or (800) 982-7238.

LESAGE (C-1) pop. 2,273, elev. 565′

THE JENKINS PLANTATION MUSEUM is .2 mi. n. on SR 2 to 8814 Ohio River Rd. This two-story brick house on the banks of the Ohio River, built in 1835 by Capt. William Jenkins, also was home to former U.S. congressman and Confederate brigadier general Albert Gallatin Jenkins. Restored to its mid-19th-century appearance, the house relates the story of the Jenkins family and the 50 slaves who worked on their 4,000-acre plantation. Allow 30 minutes minimum. Tues.-Sat. 10-4. Free. Phone (304) 762-1059.

LEWISBURG (D-3) pop. 3,624, elev. 2,300′

Lewisburg's name was changed from Camp Union to honor Gen. Andrew Lewis, who organized the Virginia militia in 1774 for a campaign against the Shawnee. Lewis led his frontiersmen to victory at the Battle of Point Pleasant, said to be the first battle of the American Revolution. Andrew Lewis Park on N. Jefferson Street was the site where the militia assembled for the historic campaign.

The Civil War made yet another battleground out of Lewisburg. On May 23, 1862, the Confederate forces of Henry Heth clashed with the Union troops of George Crook, who later would win renown as the captor of Apache chief Geronimo. Although the Union force was victorious, Lewisburg remained a Confederate outpost for most of the war.

Some of Lewisburg's old buildings still bear scars of the battle, and a cross-shaped mass grave on McElhenny Road holds the remains of 95 unknown Confederate soldiers killed during the Battle of Lewisburg.

Carnegie Hall, 105 Church St., was a 1902 gift from Andrew Carnegie to the Lewisburg Female Institute, later known as Greenbrier College. The building now serves as an arts and education center; phone (304) 645-7917 for information about performances and exhibits.

Professional theatrical productions are staged by Greenbrier Valley Theatre. Musicals, dramas, comedies, children's plays, musical concerts, and literary and poetry readings are offered year-round; phone (304) 645-3838 for information.

The Greenbrier River Trail, a 79-mile pathway for hikers and bicyclers, runs along the Greenbrier River from Caldwell to Cass *(see place listing p. 346)*; the entrance to the trail at Caldwell is 3 miles east via US 60. The trail, originally part of the Chesapeake & Ohio rail system, provides access to the river for fishing, canoeing and cross-country skiing.

Greenbrier County Visitors Center—Lewisburg: 540 N. Jefferson St., Lewisburg, WV 24901; phone (304) 645-1000 or (800) 833-2068.

Self-guiding tours: Booklets outlining tours of the Battle of Lewisburg and the 236-acre historic district, containing more than 60 18th- and 19th-century buildings of historic and architectural interest, are available at local lodgings and at the visitors center. Brochures containing information about self-guiding tours of the county's covered bridges, scenic overlooks and historic sites also are available at the visitors center.

LOST WORLD CAVERNS is 1.5 mi. n. via Court St. (which changes names to Fairview Rd.). Discovered in 1942 by speleologists from Virginia Polytechnic Institute, the caves contain a number of large rooms with stalactite, stalagmite and flowstone formations as well as impressive displays of pure calcite. One formation is more than 40 feet high and has a circumference of 25 feet. The caverns' temperature is a constant 52 F.

Picnicking is permitted. Warm clothing is recommended. Allow 1 hour minimum. Self-guiding tours daily 9-7, May 15-Labor Day; 9-5, Apr. 1-May 14 and day after Labor Day-Thanksgiving; 10-4, rest of year. Closed Jan.1, Easter, Thanksgiving and Dec. 25. Last admission 45 minutes before closing. Admission $10; $5 (ages 6-12). AX, DS, MC, VI. Phone (304) 645-6677 or (866) 228-3778.

[SAVE] NORTH HOUSE MUSEUM is .5 mi. w. on US 60 to 301 W. Washington St. The restored 1820 house displays antiques and artifacts dating from the early 1700s to the late 1800s, including Civil and Revolutionary war items and a Conestoga wagon. The library and its archives contain documents and family records from the same period.

Allow 30 minutes minimum. Mon.-Sat. 10-4; closed Jan. 1, Memorial Day, July 4, Labor Day, Thanksgiving and Dec. 25. Admission $5; $4.50 (ages 56+); $2 (ages 6-17). Phone (304) 645-3398.

OLD STONE CHURCH is 2 blks. s.w. of US 60 and US 219 on Church St. Built to replace a log structure, the church was constructed of native stone by Scottish settlers in 1796. The original slave balcony and hand-hewn woodwork are noteworthy. The church is home to one of the earliest Presbyterian congregations in the state. Mon.-Fri. 9-4. Free. Phone (304) 645-2676.

LOGAN (D-2) pop. 1,630, elev. 671'

Logan, named after a chief of the Cayuga tribe, is the burial site of "Devil Anse" Hatfield; the family leader in the infamous feud with the McCoys lies south of Logan on SR 44 at Sarah Ann. A life-size statue imported from Italy marks his grave. The grave site is on private property.

An outdoor amphitheater at Chief Logan State Park presents "The Aracoma Story," a play based on a local American Indian legend, and other dramas. In addition to recreational offerings such as a swimming pool, hiking trails and horseback riding,

the park also has a wildlife exhibit with animals native to West Virginia and a museum with artwork and historical artifacts. *See Recreation Chart and the AAA Mideastern CampBook.*

Logan County Chamber of Commerce: 214 Stratton St., P.O. Box 218, Logan, WV 25601; phone (304) 752-1324.

MARLINTON (D-3) pop. 1,204, elev. 2,127'

Marlinton was named after Jacob Marlin, one of its early settlers. The town is known as "the birthplace of rivers" because eight major rivers—the Cheat, Cranberry, Elk, Greenbrier, Shaver's Fork, Williams, Tygart and the Gauley and its tributaries—have their sources in the area. It also is a noted hunting area: Bears, deer, ruffed grouse and wild turkeys are plentiful in the region.

Marlinton marks an approximate halfway point along the scenic portion of SR 55/US 219, a scenic highway which runs 86 miles. The town also lies midway along the 76-mile Greenbrier River Trail, a hiking, bicycling and cross-country skiing trail that runs between North Caldwell and Cass.

Pocahontas County Tourism Commission Visitor Center: 700 4th Ave., P.O. Box 275, Marlinton, WV 24954; phone (304) 799-4636 or (800) 336-7009.

POCAHONTAS COUNTY HISTORICAL MUSEUM is .25 mi. s. on US 219 from jct. SR 39. A 1904 house contains documents, photographs, implements, clothes and other items depicting county history. Of particular interest is a Swiss music box that plays 36 tunes. Mon.-Sat. 11-5, Sun. 1-5, Memorial Day weekend-Labor Day. Admission $2; $1 (ages 12-18). Phone (304) 799-6659.

MARTINSBURG (B-6) pop. 14,972, elev. 457'

Founded in the 18th century, Martinsburg developed into an important shipping center with the construction of the Baltimore & Ohio Railroad in the 1850s. During the late 19th century orchards were planted in surrounding areas, and today Martinsburg has become a distribution center for apples and peaches. The preparation of these fruits for shipment can be viewed at Jefferson Orchards on SR 9 in Kearneysville, about 10 miles southeast of town.

Martinsburg was torn apart by the Civil War because of Union and Confederate occupation, internal strife and the proximity of many battles. The town was the home of Belle Boyd, a beautiful 17-year-old Confederate spy who shot a Union soldier in her parents' home after he had made threats against her mother.

Martinsburg-Berkeley County Convention and Visitors Bureau: 229A E. Martin St., Martinsburg, WV 25401; phone (304) 264-8801 or (800) 498-2386.

Shopping areas: Anchor shops at the Martinsburg Mall, between I-81 exits 12 and 13, are The Bon-Ton, JCPenney and Sears.

MATEWAN (E-1) pop. 498, elev. 700'

The infamous Hatfield and McCoy feud started in the Tug River Valley near present-day Matewan on Aug. 7, 1882, when Ellison Hatfield was killed by three McCoy brothers. The argument was said to have originated over a stolen hog, although court records indicate trouble between the families of William Anderson "Devil Anse" Hatfield and Randolph McCoy as early as the Civil War. The violence lasted only 6 years, but the press continued to sensationalize the feud for many years afterward.

The town of Matewan was established in 1895 with the extension of the Norfolk and Western Railway and the opening of the Williamson Coalfield. In 1920, as the United Mine Workers of America attempted to organize miners, a strike led to an armed confrontation in which 10 people died. The Matewan Massacre, as the incident came to be known, led to widespread clashes between miners and coal operators, police and federal troops.

MATEWAN WALKING TOUR begins at the replica of the Matewan Depot on Mate St. An exhibit features early photographs of the area and its citizens. The self-guiding tour route traces Matewan's history as evidenced by buildings from the late 1800s to early 1900s. Sites include locations immortalized by the Hatfield and McCoy feud and the Matewan Massacre. Brochures are available. Guided tours are given by appointment. Allow 30 minutes minimum. Daily 10-5. Free. Phone (304) 426-4522.

MATHIAS (C-5) elev. 1,531'

LOST RIVER STATE PARK is 4 mi. w. of SR 259 on CR 12, following signs. The park encompasses 3,712 acres of woodlands, part of which is virgin timber. The park was once a portion of the resort known as Lee's Sulphur Springs, which was developed by the Lee family. The springs were a part of the land grant awarded to Henry "Light Horse Harry" Lee, father of Robert E. Lee. Henry Lee's restored summer cabin, now a museum, is on the grounds.

Swimming and horseback riding are available. Allow 1 hour minimum. Park open daily 8-dusk. Museum open by appointment. Free. Phone (304) 897-5372 or (800) 225-5982. *See Recreation Chart.*

MILTON (D-1) pop. 2,206, elev. 586'

BLENKO GLASS CO., off I-64 exit 28 to US 60, then w. to Fairgrounds Rd., is known for handmade contemporary tableware and stained glass. A visitor center houses displays and a museum containing early glassware, glassmaking equipment, military uniforms and historic documents.

Visitors may view artisans using the earliest-known techniques of glass blowing. A pond-side floral garden contains stained-glass pieces. Allow 30 minutes minimum. Observation area and guided tours Mon.-Thurs. 8-3; closed holidays, the first 2 weeks in July and mid-Dec. through Jan. 1. Visitor center Mon.-Fri. 8-5, Sat. 9-5, Sun. noon-5. Free. Phone (304) 743-9081.

MINDEN (D-2) elev. 1,572'

RECREATIONAL ACTIVITIES

White-water Rafting

- **Ace Adventure Center** is off Minden Rd., following signs. Write P.O. Box 1168, Oak Hill, WV 25901. Other activities are offered. Trips on the New and Gauley rivers depart Mar.-Nov. Phone (304) 469-2651 or (888) 223-7238.

MONONGAHELA NATIONAL FOREST

Elevations in the forest range from 900 ft. at Petersburg to 4,861 ft. at Spruce Knob. Refer to AAA maps for additional elevation information.

Monongahela National Forest encompasses ten West Virginia counties in the Allegheny Mountains. Noted for its rugged terrain, highland bogs, blueberry thickets and vistas of exposed rocks, the forest was established in 1911 after widespread cutting of eastern forests. Many of the 909,000-acre forest's natural attractions are visible from the summit of 4,861-foot Spruce Knob *(see Spruce Knob-Seneca Rocks National Recreation Area p. 363).*

The Cranberry Glades Botanical Area, four bogs just north of the Cranberry Mountain Nature Center *(see attraction listing)* that can be seen from a half-mile-long boardwalk; Seneca Rocks *(see Spruce Knob-Seneca Rocks National Recreation Area p. 363)*; and July-blooming rhododendrons are among the region's highlights.

Many good routes traverse the forest; some provide picturesque drives. The 43-mile Highland Scenic Highway between Richwood and US 219 follows SR 39/55 for 21 miles, then SR 150 for 22 miles, offering spectacular views of the Allegheny Highlands. US 250 offers some exceptional scenery. Between Huttonsville and the Virginia line the highway crosses 4,353-foot Top of Allegheny. A 60-mile section of US 33 from Elkins east to Franklin also offers splendid vistas.

Bears, deer, grouse, rabbits, squirrels and turkeys can be hunted in season. The forest contains 129 miles of warm-water fishing and 576 miles of trout streams. Gaudineer Scenic Area, off US 250 north of Durbin, protects 140 acres of virgin red spruce. The Dolly Sods Wilderness Area, 10,215 acres west of Hopeville, offers wide views and upland bogs with unusual plants. In the 20,000 acres of Otter Creek Wilderness Area hiking trails thread through mountainous terrain. Fernow Experimental Forest, administered by the U.S. Forest Service, adjoins Otter Creek; hunting is permitted in season.

Other wilderness areas within the forest are Cranberry, Laurel Fork North and Laurel Fork South. The forest is traversed by some 500 miles of hiking trails and an extensive backwoods road and trail system for hiking, mountain biking and horseback riding. An excellent hiking guide to the forest is available for a fee from the West Virginia Highlands Conservancy, P.O. Box 306, Charleston, WV 25321.

For further information contact the Forest Supervisor, Monongahela National Forest, 200 Sycamore St., Elkins, WV 26241; phone (304) 636-1800, voice and TTY. *See Recreation Chart and the AAA Mideastern CampBook.*

CRANBERRY MOUNTAIN NATURE CENTER is 23 mi. e. of Richwood on SR 39 at SR 150. Forest ecology, history and wildlife are depicted through exhibits and lectures. A self-guiding nature trail winds through the forest. A boardwalk provides access to the Cranberry Glades Botanical Area, which contains bog vegetation that is far south of its normal range. Daily 9-4:30, May-Oct.; Thurs.-Sun. 9-4:30 in Apr. and Nov. Free. Phone (304) 653-4826.

MORGANTOWN (B-4) pop. 26,809, elev. 869′

Morgantown, on the east bank of the Monongahela River, is the seat of Monongalia County and the home of West Virginia University. Near the Evansdale campus is the WVU Health Sciences Center.

Cooper's Rock State Forest *(see Bruceton Mills p. 346)*, 13 miles east off I-68, offers 12,713 acres of forest, interesting rock formations, hiking trails, cross-country ski trails, camping and picnic areas, a 19th-century iron furnace and a spectacular view of the Cheat River Valley. Swimming and boating are popular activities at Cheat Lake, just east of town on I-68.

A 52-mile section of the West Virginia Rail Trail follows the Monongahela River through Morgantown. Ideal for walking, bicycling, jogging and in-line skating, the trail is paved within city limits. Morgantown is at the western end of the scenic portion of I-68, which runs east to Hancock, Md.

Greater Morgantown Convention and Visitors Bureau: 68 Donley St., Morgantown, WV 26501; phone (304) 292-5081 or (800) 458-7373.

Shopping areas: Morgantown Mall, at the junction of I-79 exit 152 and US 19, features Belk, Elder-Beerman, JCPenney and Sears as well as more than 75 specialty shops. Seneca Center, in the old Seneca Glass Factory at 709 Beechurst Ave., contains specialty shops.

CORE ARBORETUM is on Monongahela Blvd. just s. of the WVU Coliseum. Some 3 miles of trails wind past hundreds of species of trees, shrubs and native wildflowers (some labeled) in this 91-acre classroom. The arboretum serves as a research facility and outdoor classroom for West Virginia University. Allow 1 hour minimum. Daily dawn-dusk. Free. Phone (304) 293-5201.

PERSONAL RAPID TRANSIT (PRT) connects the Evansdale and downtown WVU campuses with the central business district. This computer-operated transit system, launched in 1975, includes five stations along a 9-mile corridor and carries up to 15,000 riders per day. The automated "people mover" serves as a transportation laboratory for engineering students and urban planners. Guided tours are available by reservation.

System operates Mon.-Fri. 6:30 a.m.-10:15 p.m., Sat. 9:30-5, late Aug.-late May; Mon.-Fri. 6:30 a.m.-6:15 p.m., Sat. 9:30-5, rest of year. Closed university holidays. Fare 50c. Phone (304) 293-5011.

MOUNDSVILLE (B-3) pop. 9,998, elev. 647′

Moundsville, first known as Grave Creek, started as a cabin built in 1771 by Joseph, Samuel and James Tomlinson about 300 yards from the Grave Creek Burial Mound. In 1865 the town consolidated with Mound City and was named after the large prehistoric burial mound from the Adena Indian culture.

Marshall County Chamber of Commerce: 609 Jefferson Ave., Moundsville, WV 26041; phone (304) 845-2773.

FOSTORIA GLASS MUSEUM is at 6th St. and Tomlinson Ave. The museum, in an early 20th-century house, exhibits examples of the blown, etched and pressed glass pieces produced by the Fostoria Glass Co., which operated in Moundsville from the early 1900s through 1986.

At one time the company was the nation's largest producer of handmade glassware. Glassware from the company was ordered by all U.S. presidents from Dwight Eisenhower through Ronald Reagan. Allow 45 minutes minimum. Wed.-Sat. 1-4, Mar.-Nov.; closed major holidays. Admission $4. Phone (304) 845-9188.

GRAVE CREEK MOUND ARCHAEOLOGY COMPLEX is at 801 Jefferson Ave. and 8th St. via SR 2. Considered the largest prehistoric Indian burial mound of its kind, the 69-foot mound was built more than 2,000 years ago and was originally surrounded by a moat. The Delf Norona Museum contains a collection of artifacts of the Adena period (approximately 1000 B.C. to beyond A.D. 1). Allow 1 hour minimum. Mon.-Sat. 10-4:30, Sun. 1-5; closed major holidays. Admission $3; $2 (ages 6-16). Phone (304) 843-4128.

THE OFFICIAL MARX TOY MUSEUM is at 915 2nd St. Louis Marx created the Louis Marx Toy Co. in 1919, and before long it claimed the title of world's largest toy company. During its 5 decades of operation, the plant in nearby Glen Dale produced toys that should be familiar to most baby boomers.

The museum's decor, designed to highlight the 1950s, displays the company's most memorable toys: Rock'em, Sock'em Robots; big wheels; Johnny West figures; and themed plastic play sets, such as Fort Apache, Roy Rogers, Dodge City and Davy Crockett. Food is available. Allow 1 hour minimum. Thurs.-Sun. 11-5, Apr.-Dec. Admission $6.50; $6 (senior citizens); $4.25 (ages 6-17). MC, VI. Phone (304) 845-6022.

WEST VIRGINIA PENITENTIARY is at 818 Jefferson Ave. This Gothic-style fortress was built by convict labor in 1867 as the state's first territorial prison. Guided 90-minute tours allow visitors to step inside a 5-foot-by-7-foot cell and see the electric chair, the gallows and North Hall, where inmates were confined 22 hours a day. Hand-painted murals adorn the walls.

Tours depart on the hour Tues.-Sun. 10-4, Apr.-Nov.; closed major holidays. Admission $10; $8 (senior citizens); $5 (ages 6-10). MC, VI. Phone (304) 845-6200.

NEWELL (A-3) pop. 1,602, elev. 691'

THE HOMER LAUGHLIN CHINA CO. is on SR 2, 1 mi. s. of the Newell Bridge at the Ohio River. Said to be the largest American maker of domestic and hotel china, the company claims to have produced one-third of all the china sold in the United States. The company was founded in 1871 and introduced the popular Fiesta line of china in 1936. Guided tours are preceded by a slide presentation.

Allow 1 hour minimum. Open Mon.-Sat. 9:30-5, Sun. noon-5; closed major holidays. Tours are given Mon.-Fri. at 10:30 and 12:30. Free. Reservations are required for tours. Phone (304) 387-1300.

NEW RIVER GORGE NATIONAL RIVER (D-4)

The New River Gorge National River encompasses 53 miles of the New River and its narrow gorge that wind through the Appalachian Mountains from Hinton to the New River Gorge Bridge (US 19) near Fayetteville. Contrary to its name, the New is believed to be one of the oldest rivers in North America; it was part of the ancient Teays River system, which originated more than 65 million years ago.

The river's human history began about 12,000 years ago when prehistoric Indians lived and hunted in the area. The portion of the river within the park, however, was largely unsettled due to the dangerous and often impassable rapids and steep gorge walls. In 1873 the C&O Railroad was completed through the gorge and provided access to the exposed rich seams of coal in the mountains.

For the next 80 years the area was a booming industrial center, whose heart was the 18-odd communities in the lower canyon from Prince to Fayette Station. But as the mines were worked out, people began to leave the gorge's coal towns. Forest has since reclaimed most of the towns and mine sites.

General Information and Activities

The New is regarded as one of the best rivers in the state for small-mouth bass fishing. In addition, muskellunge, walleye, catfish and carp test the skill of anglers. Some of the river's tributaries are stocked with trout. The most popular portion of the New for fishing is the upper section from Hinton to McCreery.

The New River is said to rival the Colorado for its white-water rafting opportunities. The 30 miles of the lower portion from McCreery to the New River Gorge Bridge draw white-water rafting enthusiasts each year from early April to mid-October. Many outfitters with highly skilled guides provide both scenic and white-water trips through the gorge and are primarily located at the northern end of the river.

The sandstone cliffs along the New River, which range up to 120 feet tall, have become well-known among rock climbing enthusiasts. The peak climbing season runs from April through November.

Other popular recreational activities within the park include picnicking, camping, hiking, mountain biking, canoeing, kayaking and horseback riding. *See Recreation Chart.*

ADDRESS inquiries to the Superintendent, New River Gorge National River, National Park Service, Box 246, Glen Jean, WV 25846. Phone (304) 465-0508.

VISITOR CENTERS include locations on US 19 n. of Fayetteville, SR 20 n. of I-64 exit 139 in Sandstone, SR 25 in the Thurmond railroad depot and SR 9 in Grandview. Each center offers brochures, maps and historic background on the river and the surrounding area; park rangers provide information and orientation services. Grandview's center is noted for its overlooks, trails and spring display of rhododendrons. The Fayetteville and Sandstone visitor centers are open year-round; all others are open seasonally.

Canyon Rim Visitor Center is 2 mi. n. of Fayetteville on US 19. Panoramic views of the gorge and the New River Gorge Bridge are offered at the center, which also features exhibits and a slide presentation. Daily 9-5; closed Jan. 1, Thanksgiving and Dec. 25. Free. Phone (304) 574-2115.

Sandstone Visitor Center, just n. on SR 20 from jct. I-64 exit 139, was designed and built using "green" concepts. It features information and interactive exhibits about the river's natural and cultural history as well as a 10-minute video presentation about ecology and the New River Valley. Picnicking is permitted. Allow 30 minutes minimum. Daily 9-5; closed Jan. 1, Thanksgiving and Dec. 25. Free. Phone (304) 466-0417.

OAK HILL (D-2) pop. 7,589, elev. 2,014'

Though not the county seat, Oak Hill is Fayette County's largest city. The Coal Miner's Memorial Statue, at the visitor center on Oyler Avenue, stands as a reminder of the area's coal mining heritage; visitors are welcome to take a piece of coal as a souvenir. White-water rafting opportunities are numerous due to the city's proximity to the New River Gorge.

New River Convention and Visitors Bureau: 310 Oyler Ave., Oak Hill, WV 25901; phone (304) 465-5617 or (800) 927-0263.

RECREATIONAL ACTIVITIES
White-water Rafting

- **Appalachian Wildwaters Inc.** is 3.3 mi. n. on US 19, e. on Appalachian Dr., s. on SR 16, then just e. on Broadway Ave. Write P.O. Box 100, Rowlesburg, WV 26425. Trips on the New and Gauley rivers depart Mar.-Oct. Phone (304) 454-2475 or (800) 624-8060.

PARKERSBURG (B-1) pop. 33,099, elev. 151'

Parkersburg's strategic location at the confluence of the Little Kanawha and Ohio rivers aided its development as an industrial center. An early visitor was George Washington, who surveyed land above the city on the Ohio River. In 1810 the Virginia legislature passed an act to found the town, known as Neal's Station and Newport prior to being incorporated as Parkersburg. Improved transportation modes and routes to the area soon followed. West Virginia's first oil wells were drilled nearby in 1860, which made Parkersburg the supply and shipping point for the "black gold" fields.

The region also was blessed with natural gas fields, and gas soon became the major source of fuel for the growing number of industrial plants. More than 100 industries produce chemicals, glass, metals, plastics and other products.

Visitors interested in architecture, history and literature can find all three at Trans Allegheny Books, downtown at 725 Green St. West Virginia's largest used bookstore, which carries more than 500,000 volumes in addition to West Virginia titles, is in the restored 1905 former Carnegie Library. The building's vintage wrought iron and brass spiral staircase, stained glass windows and hand-carved wooden staircases are grand surroundings for the books as well as items hand-crafted in the state.

A rails-to-trails conversion, the North Bend Rail Trail extends for 72 miles from its trailhead near Parkersburg to Wolf Summit near Clarksburg. The scenic trail runs through 10 tunnels constructed by the Baltimore and Ohio Railroad 1853-57 and crosses 36 bridges.

Parkersburg/Wood County Convention and Visitors Bureau: 350 Seventh St., Parkersburg, WV 26101; phone (304) 428-1130 or (800) 752-4982.

DID YOU KNOW

Nearly 80 percent of
West Virginia
is forest land.

Self-guiding tours: Brochures outlining a walking tour of historic buildings are available at the convention and visitors bureau.

BLENNERHASSETT ISLAND HISTORICAL STATE PARK is in the Ohio River, reached by stern-wheeler from Point Park at Second and Ann sts. Harman Blennerhassett, an Irish aristocrat, built his island mansion in 1798. He became involved with Aaron Burr in an alleged plot to establish an empire in the Southwest and was forced to flee the island with his family in 1806 when the conspiracy came to light. Both men were eventually acquitted of treason, but their lives were ruined.

Fire destroyed the abandoned mansion in 1811. The Palladian-style house has been reconstructed upon its original foundation, and guided tours of the interior are offered. Narrated horse-drawn wagon rides recount the island's history.

Picnic facilities and food are available. Allow 3 hours minimum. Tues.-Fri. 10-5:30, Sat. 11-5:30, Sun. noon-5:30, May 1-early June; Tues.-Sat. 11-5:30, Sun. noon-5:30, early June-Labor Day; Thurs.-Sat. 11-4:30, Sun. noon-4:30, day after Labor Day-Oct. 31. Park admission free. Mansion tour $3; $2 (ages 3-12). Wagon rides $5; $3 (ages 3-12). Phone (304) 420-4800 or (800) 225-5982.

Blennerhassett Museum is downtown at Second and Juliana sts. Three floors are dedicated to archeological and historical exhibits. A 12-minute videotape reveals the history of the Blennerhassett family and its island.

Allow 30 minutes minimum. Tues.-Fri. 9:30-5, Sat. 10-6, Sun. 11-6, May 1-early June; Tues.-Fri. 10-5, Sat. 10-6, Sun. 11-6, early June-Labor Day; Tues.-Sat. 10-5, Sun. 11-5, day after Labor Day-Oct. 31; Tues.-Sat. 11-5, Sun. 1-5, late Mar.-Apr. 30 and Nov.-Dec.; Sat. 11-5, Sun. 1-5, rest of year. Closed Dec. 24-31. Admission $2; $1 (ages 3-12). Phone (304) 420-4800 or (800) 225-5982.

Stern-wheelers depart for the island from Point Park at Second and Ann sts. Trips run Tues.-Fri. 10-4, Sat. 11-4, Sun. noon-4, May 1-Labor Day; Thurs.-Sat. on the hour 10-3, Sun. noon-4:30, day after Labor Day-Oct. 31. To tour the mansion, depart from Point Park no later than 3 p.m.; the last shuttle leaves the island at 5:30 p.m. Fare $8; $7 (ages 3-12). AX, CB, DS, MC, VI. Phone (740) 423-7268.

OIL AND GAS MUSEUM, downtown at 119 Third St., commemorates the historical significance of those industries to West Virginia and southeastern Ohio through displays, exhibits and historic photographs. The museum also chronicles the city's history and culture. Allow 45 minutes minimum. Mon.-Sat. 10-5, Sun. noon-5; closed major holidays. Admission $2; $1 (ages 1-12). Phone (304) 485-5446.

THE PARKERSBURG ART CENTER is at 725 Market St. The center presents changing visual art displays of work by nationally known and local artists

as well as traveling exhibitions. Guided tours are available by appointment. Open Tues.-Sat. 10-5, Sun. 1-5; closed major holidays. Admission $2; $1 (children). Phone (304) 485-3859.

PETERSBURG (C-5) pop. 2,423, elev. 937'

On the south branch of the Potomac River, Petersburg was settled in 1745. It was named after German colonist Jacob Peterson, who established the town's first store. During the Civil War the town served as a Union outpost along the contested border between the North and South. Nearby earthworks were constructed by troops from Illinois and Ohio in 1863.

Because it is near the entrance to Monongahela National Forest and Spruce Knob-Seneca Rocks National Recreation Area (*see place listings p. 356 and p. 363*), Petersburg is considered a recreation center, and calls itself the "Home of the Golden Trout." Area outfitters provide information, equipment and guides for hunting, fishing and canoeing trips into the surrounding wilderness.

PETERSBURG GAP is e. on US 220 and SR 55. The South Branch of the Potomac River breaks through Orr's Mountain at this point. The cliffs on the south side rise to a height of 800 feet. The "Pictured Rocks" are where figures of a fox and an ox or buffalo appear to have been carved into the cliffs.

SMOKE HOLE CAVERNS is 8 mi. s.w. on SR 28/55. Unusual formations include one of the world's longest ribbon stalactites and an underground lake and stream. The caverns were reportedly used by American Indians to smoke meat and by enterprising settlers to make "moonshine." A 19th-century still is displayed. A wildlife museum is on the grounds. The caverns maintain a constant temperature of 56 F.

Picnic facilities are available. Guided tours daily every half-hour 9-5. Admission $10; $9 (senior citizens); $5.50 (ages 5-12). AX, DC, DS, MC, VI. Phone (304) 257-4442 or (800) 828-8478.

PHILIPPI (C-4) pop. 2,870, elev. 1,247'

The first land battle of the Civil War occurred at Philippi (FIL-uh-pee) on June 3, 1861. Col. B.F. Kelley and a detachment of Federal troops from George McClellan's army surprised and routed the newly recruited Confederates under the command of Col. George Alexander Porterfield.

Spanning the Tygart River is a covered bridge that was originally built in 1852 and was used by both Confederate and Union forces during the battles. The bridge burned in 1989 but has been completely restored and is the only covered bridge still in use as a federal highway. From Fairmont to the north, the scenic portion of US 250 passes through Philippi on its 73-mile journey to Huttonsville.

Barbour County Chamber of Commerce: P.O. Box 5000, Philippi, WV 26416; phone (304) 457-1958.

SAVE **ADALAND MANSION AND HISTORICAL BARN** is 4 mi. n. on US 119 to SR 76, then 1 mi. n. to Adaland Rd. This 1870 brick mansion features Neo-Greek architecture, period wallpaper and antique furnishings. Details include woodwork of native hardwood, double porches, an outside walnut stairway, travelers' rooms and a metal roof with handmade brackets. A restored 1850 barn houses a display of early farm tools.

Guided tours are offered. Allow 1 hour minimum. Wed.-Thurs. and Sat. 11-5, Sun. 1-5, May-Dec.; closed Thanksgiving and Dec. 25. Mansion admission $5; free (ages 0-11). Admission to mansion and barn $7. AX, DS, MC, VI. Phone (304) 457-1587.

BARBOUR COUNTY HISTORICAL MUSEUM is at 200 N. Main St. Housed in a renovated railroad station, the museum features Civil War memorabilia, antiques, books and two mummies. Mon.-Sat. 11-4, Sun. 1-4, May 15-Oct. 15; Fri.-Sat. 11-4, Sun. 1-4, rest of year. Museum free. Mummy exhibit $1. Phone (304) 457-4846.

PIPESTEM (E-3) elev. 2,389′

PIPESTEM RESORT STATE PARK is on SR 20. The 4,024-acre park covers a broad plateau overlooking the Bluestone River Gorge. The resort offers camping, canoeing, cross-country skiing, golfing, horseback riding, swimming, tennis and rental paddleboats. Nature programs also are offered. Plays and concerts are presented in the summer. An aerial tram, ascending 3,600 feet, departs from the visitor center.

Food is available. Allow 1 hour minimum for aerial tram. Park open daily 6 a.m.-10 p.m., year-round. Tram daily 7 a.m.-midnight (closed Tues. and Thurs. 1-4), May-Oct. Park free. Tram $5; $4.50 (ages 5-12). Phone (304) 466-1800 or (800) 225-5982. *See Recreation Chart and the AAA Mideastern CampBook.*

POINT PLEASANT (C-1)
pop. 4,637, elev. 561′

Point Pleasant is in a growing resort area near the confluence of the Kanawha and Ohio rivers. It is said that when George Washington surveyed this area in the 1740s, he referred to it as the Pleasant Point.

A reconstruction of Fort Randolph, the best known of the town's forts, is in Krodel Park. A showplace for many of the town's events, the fort is open from mid-April through October on weekends. The 44-acre park also contains campsites, paddleboats, a playground and a miniature golf course, and allows fishing; phone (304) 675-2360.

The 11,164-acre Chief Cornstalk Public Hunting and Fishing Area, southeast of town, is accessible via a hard-surfaced road that branches west off SR 35 near Southside.

Mason County Area Chamber of Commerce: 305 Main St., Point Pleasant, WV 25550; phone (304) 675-1050.

C.F. McCLINTIC WILDLIFE MANAGEMENT AREA is 5 mi. n. on SR 62, then 1 mi. e. on Potters Creek Rd. (CR 11). Hunting for deer, grouse, quails, rabbits and waterfowl is popular in the 3,566-acre area. More than 30 impoundments allow for warm-water fishing for a wide variety of species, including bluegill, bass, catfish and northern pike.

While there are neither marked hiking trails nor visitor centers, primitive campsites are available. Open daily 24 hours. Office hours Mon.-Fri. 8:30-4:30. Admission free. Camping $5. Phone (304) 675-0871.

POINT PLEASANT RIVER MUSEUM is at 28 Main St., across from Tu-Endie-Wei State Park. In a building that has been associated in some way with river traffic since 1854, the museum has interactive exhibits about life and commerce along the Ohio and Kanawha rivers, including displays about a bridge disaster and a flood, shipbuilding, and shantyboats. A highlight is a working model of a pilot house.

Allow 30 minutes minimum. Tues.-Fri. 10-3, Sat. 11-4, Sun. 1-5; closed Jan. 1, Thanksgiving and Dec. 25. Admission $4; $3.50 (ages 55+); $1 (ages 6-18). MC, VI. Phone (304) 674-0144.

TU-ENDIE-WEI STATE PARK is at the southern end of town at 1 Main St. and jct. Ohio and Kanawha rivers. The land was named "tu-endie-wei" or "the point between two waters" by the Wyandotte Indians. At this site on Oct. 10, 1774, Gen. Andrew Lewis and about 1,100 Virginia frontiersmen were attacked by Shawnee chief Cornstalk and a like number of American Indians.

The day-long battle at the site is said to have been the opening engagement of the American Revolution. Park open Mon.-Sat. 10-4:30, Sun. 1-4:30, May-Oct. Free. Phone (304) 675-0869.

Mansion House is in the park at 1 Main St. Built by Walter Newman in 1796 as a public inn, the building is the oldest in the Kanawha Valley. Constructed of hewn logs, it has two fireplaces and contains local Colonial furniture and heirlooms as well as relics from the Battle of Point Pleasant. Mon.-Sat. 10-4:30, Sun. 1-4:30, May-Oct. Free.

WEST VIRGINIA STATE FARM MUSEUM is 4 mi. n. on SR 62 to Fairgrounds Rd., following signs. This 50-acre museum features log cabins built in the early 1800s, a replica of an old Lutheran church, a one-room schoolhouse built around 1870, a print shop, a taxidermy collection, a doctor's office, a country store, farm equipment including a collection of tractors, a working blacksmith shop, an herb garden, railroad cars and a barn. Picnicking is permitted. Allow 1 hour, 30 minutes minimum. Tues.-Sat. 9-5, Sun. 1-5, Apr. 1-Nov. 15. Donations. Phone (304) 675-5737.

PRINCETON (E-2) pop. 6,347, elev. 2,460'

Mercer County, at the southern tip of West Virginia, bears the name of General Hugh Mercer, a Revolutionary War hero who was mortally wounded in 1777 at the Battle of Princeton in New Jersey. The county seat, Princeton, honors the place where he died.

Princeton-Mercer County Chamber of Commerce: 1522 N. Walker St., Princeton, WV 24740; phone (304) 487-1502.

THOSE WHO SERVED WAR MUSEUM is at 1500 W. Main St. This museum houses more than 750 war relics and personal effects, the majority from World War II, with additional displays dating from the Civil War to Operation Enduring Freedom. Allow 30 minutes minimum. Mon.-Fri. 10-4; closed holidays. Free. Phone (304) 487-8397 or (304) 487-3670.

RIVERTON (C-4) elev. 1,809'

SENECA CAVERNS is 3 mi. e. of US 33 via Seneca Caverns Rd. to German Valley Rd. Visitors travel along a .75-mile passage through the caverns at a depth ranging from 25-165 feet below ground level. Lighted trails provide access to the caverns' unusual mineral formations including cave coral, rimstone, stalactites, stalagmites and travertine.

Other formations include Mirror Lake, a reflective underground pool, and the Grand Ballroom, featuring a natural balcony. The caverns served as a refuge for the Seneca Indians from cold winters and for ceremonial rituals during the 1600s and 1700s. Gemstone mining is available.

Picnicking is permitted. Food is available. Warm clothing and comfortable walking shoes are recommended. Allow 1 hour minimum. Guided 55-minute tours depart every 20 minutes daily 9-6:45, June-Aug.; 10-4:45, Sept.-Oct.; 10-4, rest of year. Admission $10; $8.25 (ages 63+); $5.50 (ages 6-12). AX, DS, MC, VI. Phone (304) 567-2691 or (800) 239-7647.

ROMNEY (B-5) pop. 1,940, elev. 820'

Incorporated in 1762, Romney is one of the oldest settlements in West Virginia. During the Civil War, the town is said to have changed hands at least 56 times. The West Virginia State Schools for the Deaf and Blind were established at Romney in 1870.

Departing from the Romney Station, 1.5 miles north on SR 28, the Potomac Eagle Scenic Railroad offers narrated 3-hour excursions through scenic mountain valleys. Bald eagles are often sighted on the trips, which run on Saturday, May through September, and daily in October; phone (304) 424-0736.

Hampshire County Chamber of Commerce: 91 S. High St., Taggart Hall, Romney, WV 26757; phone (304) 822-7221.

TAGGART HALL CIVIL WAR MUSEUM AND VISITOR'S CENTER is .1 mi. s. on US 50 at 91 S. High St. In a clapboard house built 1795-98 by Quaker Francis Taggart, the museum features artifacts from the Civil War and the French and Indian War as well as historical items from Hampshire County. The building also houses the county visitor center. Allow 30 minutes minimum. Mon.-Sat. 9-4, Sun. noon-4; closed Dec. 25. Donations. Phone (304) 822-7221.

RONCEVERTE (D-3) pop. 1,557, elev. 1,676'

ORGAN CAVE is 5 mi. s. on US 219/SR 63, then .5 mi. e. on SR 63. Ninety-minute walking tours of the cave, discovered in 1704, feature fossils, stalactites, stalagmites and a Civil War refinery used by the Confederates to produce saltpeter. More than 200 passages have yet to be mapped. The cave, left as unaltered as possible, has more than 45 miles of passageways and maintains a constant temperature of 48 F.

Picnicking is permitted. Food is available. Allow 1 hour, 30 minutes minimum. Tours are given every half-hour Mon.-Tues. and Thurs.-Sat. 9:30-5:30, Wed. 9:30-4, Sun. 1:30-4, Memorial Day-early Sept.; Mon.-Fri. at 10, noon and 2, Sat. 10-4, early Sept.-Oct. 31; Mon.-Sat. at 10, noon and 2, Apr. 1-day before Memorial Day (weather permitting); Mon.-Sat. at noon and 2, rest of year (weather permitting). Closed Thanksgiving, day after Thanksgiving and Dec. 24-26. Admission $14; $7 (ages 6-12). AX, DS, MC, VI. Phone (304) 645-7600.

SENECA ROCKS (C-4) elev. 1,568'

SENECA ROCKS DISCOVERY CENTER is at jct. US 33 and SR 28. At the base of the massive Seneca Rocks formation *(see Spruce Knob-Seneca Rocks National Recreation Area)*, the discovery center has audiovisual presentations and interactive displays and offers hikes and outdoor interpretive programs. Nearby is the Sites Homestead, an 1839 log home with heirloom gardens. Picnicking is permitted. Thurs.-Sun. 9-4:30, Apr.-Oct. Free. Phone (304) 567-2827.

SHEPHERDSTOWN (B-6)
pop. 803, elev. 402'

The site of one of the earliest settlements in West Virginia, Shepherdstown was established by English and German farmers who had crossed the river from Pennsylvania into this area before 1730. The legal grant to the land was purchased by Thomas Shepherd in 1732.

Originally named Mecklenburg, the name was changed to Shepherdstown in 1798. While living in Shepherdstown in 1787, James Rumsey gave the first public exhibition of his steamboat. A monument on the banks of the Potomac commemorates this successful demonstration. On German Street are Shepherd College, built in 1871, and the Entler Hotel, built in 1786.

Shepherdstown Visitors Center: 102 E. German St., P.O. Box 329, Shepherdstown, WV 25443-0329; phone (304) 876-2786.

SISTERSVILLE (B-2) pop. 1,588, elev. 590'

Charles Wells settled Sistersville in the early 19th century. In 1839 the town was incorporated and named in honor of his daughters Sarah and Deliah, the 18th and 19th of his 22 children.

Sistersville's relatively quiet posture as a farming and trade community on the Ohio River changed dramatically in 1889 with the discovery of oil on an area farm. Oil barons descended upon the town, building unsightly rigs as well as many stately homes and a striking business district along Wells Street. The oil boom ended in 1915, returning the town to its earlier lifestyle but leaving a legacy of handsome buildings that represent a variety of architectural styles.

A ferry takes passengers from Sistersville across the Ohio River to Fly, Ohio. The ferry, which can hold up to eight automobiles, operates Mon.-Fri. 6-6, Sat.-Sun. 9-6.

Self-guiding tours: A brochure outlining a walking tour past many historic buildings is available at The Wells Inn, 316 Charles St., Sistersville, WV 26175; phone (304) 652-1312.

SNOWSHOE (C-4)

RECREATIONAL ACTIVITIES

Skiing

- **Snowshoe Mountain Resort** is off US 219 at SR 66. Write P.O. Box 10, Snowshoe, WV 26209. Other activities are offered. Skiing daily, Thanksgiving-early Apr. Phone (304) 572-1000 or (877) 441-4386.

SPRUCE KNOB-SENECA ROCKS NATIONAL RECREATION AREA (C-5)

The Spruce Knob-Seneca Rocks National Recreation Area is composed of two sections within the Monongahela National Forest *(see place listing p. 356)*. The larger Seneca Rocks unit is especially noted for rugged terrain and white-water boating and rock-climbing opportunities. Camping, fishing and hiking are popular during spring and summer. Hunting is permitted in season. Cross-country skiers prefer the higher elevations in the Spruce Knob unit, where trails are plentiful. For further information, phone (304) 257-4488. *See Recreation Chart.*

SENECA ROCKS is off US 33 and SR 28 at the town of Seneca Rocks. Rising above the North Fork River, this 900-foot-tall mass of intricately eroded quartzite sandstone is one of the most impressive rock formations in the East and is considered to be an excellent rock-climbing area.

According to legend, Snow Bird, the beautiful daughter of Seneca chief Bald Eagle, held a contest to decide who should be her husband. The first warrior to scale the mighty cliff, which she had been able to climb since her early childhood, was eligible to marry her.

SMOKE HOLE lies along Smoke Hole Rd. n. of Upper Tract in the Seneca Rocks unit; take FR 79 s. from jct. SR 28 at Cabins. The half-mile-deep gorge was formed by the south branch of the Potomac River as it ran between North and Cave mountains. A road leads northwest from US 220, traverses a portion of the gorge and ends at the Big Bend Campground. Among Smoke Hole's notable formations is Eagle Rock, which towers upward from the river.

SPRUCE KNOB is w. of US 33 by a forest road about 2.5 mi. s. of Riverton. Spruce Knob is the highest point in West Virginia at 4,861 feet *(see Monongahela National Forest p. 356)*. Numerous overlooks provide scenic views on the road to the summit, which features an observation tower and an interpretive trail.

Nearby Spruce Knob Lake is stocked with trout and offers good fishing, especially during the spring and fall. **Note:** Since the partially paved road has unprotected shoulders at some points, caution is advised. The road should not be attempted by inexperienced drivers or during hazardous driving conditions. Camping is available.

SUMMERSVILLE (D-3)
pop. 3,294, elev. 1,926'

Nancy Hart, a Confederate spy, led an attack on Summersville in 1861. During the battle a Union force was captured, and the town was burned. Hart escaped to Confederate lines but returned after Gen. Robert E. Lee's surrender.

US 19, a 45-mile scenic highway linking I-79 at Sutton and the West Virginia Turnpike at Bradley, passes Summersville near Summersville Lake *(see Recreation Chart and the AAA Mideastern Camp-Book)*. The lake, West Virginia's largest with 60 miles of shoreline and more than 2,800 acres of water, offers swimming, fishing, boating, hiking and picnicking opportunities. Summersville serves as the county seat for Nicholas County.

The Gauley River National Recreation Area, between Summersville and Swiss, protects 25 miles of the Gauley River and 6 miles of its tributary, the Meadow River. The Gauley is known for its rapids, white-water rafting and fishing opportunities. The recreation area can be reached from Carnifex Ferry Battlefield State Park *(see attraction listing)* or Summersville Dam off SR 129 and from SR 39. Information is available at park headquarters, P.O. Box 246, Glen Jean, WV 25846; phone (304) 465-0508.

Summersville Area Chamber of Commerce: 1 Wilderness Rd., P.O. Box 567, Summersville, WV 26651; phone (304) 872-1588 or (800) 760-6158.

CARNIFEX FERRY BATTLEFIELD STATE PARK is 5.6 mi. s. on US 19, 5.2 mi. w. on SR 129, then .9 mi. s. on Carnifex Ferry Rd. (CR 23). A Civil War engagement was fought on this 156-acre site Sept. 10, 1861. The Patterson House Museum contains Civil War relics from the battle. A Civil War battle re-enactment weekend takes place in September of odd-numbered years. Park open daily dawndusk. Museum open Sat.-Sun. and holidays 10-5, Memorial Day weekend-Labor Day. Free. Phone (304) 872-0825.

WINERIES

• **Kirkwood Winery and Isaiah Morgan Distillery** is 2.7 mi. n.e. on SR 41, 1.1 mi. n. on US 19, then .5 mi. e. on CR 8 (Phillips Run Rd.), following signs. Tours and tastings Mon.-Sat. 9-5:30, Sun. 1-5:30; closed Jan. 1, Thanksgiving and Dec. 25. Phone (304) 872-7332 or (888) 498-9463.

WARDENSVILLE (C-5) pop. 246, elev. 1,011′

The Lost River, west of Wardensville along SR 55/259, vanishes many times during its course, appearing and disappearing close to the highway. About 4.3 miles southwest of town, the river flows under Sandy Ridge, emerging on the other side to form the Cacapon River. Lost River State Park *(see attraction listing p. 356)* is 23 miles south in Mathias.

WEST MILFORD (C-3) pop. 651, elev. 980′

WATTERS SMITH MEMORIAL STATE PARK is 2 mi. s. on Duck Creek Rd., following signs. The park contains a replica of a log cabin built in 1796 by Watters Smith, the first pioneer in this area. The Smith family lived on the site until 1948. The park also includes a museum with historical items and memorabilia of the Smith family, a residence built in 1876, a blacksmith shop and several barns. Hiking trails, a swimming pool and mountain biking are available.

Picnicking is permitted. Park daily 7-dusk, Memorial Day weekend-Labor Day. Museum daily noon-5. Pool Thurs.-Tues. 11-7. Admission $3; $2 (ages 4-11). Phone (304) 745-3081.

WESTON (C-3) pop. 4,317, elev. 982′

Weston serves as a commercial center for an agricultural area and supports glass industries. Surveyed by Thomas "Stonewall" Jackson's grandfather, the town contains several rambling Victorian-era homes. The former Weston State Hospital is surrounded by vast landscaped grounds. The main building, begun in 1860 and completed in 1865, has 9 acres of floor space and is said to be the largest hand-cut stone building in the United States.

The Citizens Bank Building at 201 Main Ave. is noted among devotees of classic Art Deco architecture. Built 1928-30, this 54-foot tall Indiana limestone structure is believed to be the tallest singlestory building in the United States; the wrought-iron

work is by the noted artist Samuel Yellen. Inside, the woodwork is hand-carved American walnut, and the 45-foot suspended plaster ceiling has a relief of the Great Seal of West Virginia. Also of interest in town is the West Virginia Genealogical and Historical Library and Museum, which is open to the public for research; phone (304) 269-7091.

Nearby Stonewall Resort State Park surrounds the state's second-largest lake. This park offers many recreational opportunities and facilities. For more information phone (304) 269-0523. *See Recreation Chart.*

In recent years Weston has gained recognition for its unusual Christmas lights display on Main Street. Called "Dancing Snowflakes," this computerized light show includes 32 snowflakes that dance down the street in more than 15 pattern variations. The snowflakes are accompanied by Santa and his nine reindeer, which prance on the rooftops. The 39-minute show runs continuously daily from dusk to 1 a.m., day after Thanksgiving through January 1.

Lewis County Convention & Visitors Bureau: 499 US 33E, Suite 102, Weston, WV 26452; phone (304) 269-7328.

WVU JACKSON'S MILL STATE 4-H CAMP is about 4 mi. n. on US 19. In 1921 Jackson's Mill became the first state 4-H camp in the nation. The 523-acre site includes an amphitheater, livestock pavilions, gardens, recreation facilities and hiking trails. The site is the setting for the Lewis County Fair, Stonewall Jackson Heritage Arts and Crafts Jubilee and the West Virginia Storytelling Festival. Camp open Mon.-Fri. 8-4:30. Free. Phone (800) 287-8206.

Historic Area at WVU Jackson's Mill is at WVU Jackson's Mill 4-H Camp. The historic area, on the original 5 acres of Thomas "Stonewall" Jackson's boyhood home, features the mill building from Jackson's time, which is now a museum. Gristmill and water-driven sawmill components, farm implements, weaving equipment and blacksmithing and carpentry tools are displayed. Other buildings include log cabins from the 1700s and 1800s and a working gristmill from the late 18th century.

Demonstrations and guided tours are available. Open Tues.-Sun. 10-5, Memorial Day-Labor Day; Thurs.-Sun. 10-5, Apr. 1-day before Memorial Day and day after Labor Day-Oct. 31. Admission $6; $5 (senior citizens); $3 (ages 4-12). AX, DS, MC, VI. Phone (800) 287-8206, ext. 158.

WHEELING (A-3) pop. 31,419, elev. 645′

Wheeling lies along the scenic portion of I-70, which continues into Pennsylvania to the east and Ohio to the west. The last battle of the American Revolution was fought in Wheeling Sept. 11-13, 1782, when Fort Henry was attacked by a force of 40 British soldiers and 260 Indians. The news of the peace had not yet reached this outpost. Ebenezer and Silas Zane, who founded the city in 1769, led the defending forces. Their sister, Betty, brought powder from the Zane cabin to the fort; her efforts saved the garrison. The site of the fort is marked by a memorial stone on Main Street.

When Virginia seceded from the Union, delegates from the western counties met at Wheeling and set up the "Restored Government of Virginia," with Wheeling as the capital. After West Virginia was formally admitted to the Union in 1863, Wheeling was the capital until 1870 and again 1875-85.

The 1,010-foot-long Wheeling Suspension Bridge, built in 1849, is one of the world's longest of its kind. Henry Clay, while visiting Wheeling a year after the bridge opened, described it as "a rainbow to behold."

Wheeling's history as a frontier port where the National Road met the Ohio River is evident in the Old Town section; some of the buildings are open to the public by tour. Victorian Homes Tour, which departs from Eckhart House at 810 Main St., offers tours of some of the historic houses; phone (304) 232-5439 or (888) 700-0118.

From June through August the Wheeling Heritage Port hosts Wheeling's Waterfront Wednesdays where free concerts are featured. Greyhound racing takes place Wednesday through Monday throughout the year at Wheeling Island Racetrack & Gaming Center; phone (304) 232-5050 or (877) 946-4373.

Note: Policies concerning admittance of children to pari-mutuel betting facilities vary. Phone for information.

Wheeling Visitors Center: 1401 Main St., Wheeling, WV 26003; phone (304) 233-7709 or (800) 828-3097.

Shopping areas: Eight miles west on I-70 in nearby St. Clairsville, Ohio, is Ohio Valley Mall, whose more than 150 stores include Elder-Beerman, JCPenney, Macy's and Sears. North Main Street's Victorian Wheeling (Old Town) has antique and specialty shops; from I-70 exit 1A go north on Main Street. Wheeling's Historic Centre Market, 2200 Market St., features antique and craft shops in and around the refurbished Centre Market House.

SAVE **THE ECKHART HOUSE VICTORIAN HOME TOURS & TEAS** is at 810 Main St. The 18-room 1892 Queen Anne town home maintains many original features, such as stained glass, fretwork, mantles, inlaid floors, pocket doors and electric and gas light fixtures. Parlor talks and tours provide information about area history and the home's living and servants' quarters. Parlor teas include high tea in the home's elegant parlor presided over by a costumed hostess.

Allow 1 hour minimum. Parlor talks and tours are given Wed.-Sat. 1-4, May-Dec. Last tour begins 30 minutes before closing. Teas require a minimum of six people. Fee for parlor talks and tours $3; $2.50 (ages 6-18). Teas $15. Reservations are required for teas. DS, MC, VI. Phone (304) 232-5439 or (888) 700-0118.

[SAVE] THE KRUGER STREET TOY & TRAIN MUSEUM is off I-70 exit 5, .1 mi. w. on US 40, then .2 mi. s. to 144 Kruger St. Housed in a restored 1906 three-story Victorian school building, the museum contains 10 themed rooms with model trains; toy trucks, cars, aircraft and boats; toy firearms and military equipment; dolls and doll houses; play sets; household items; riding toys; and photographs and memorabilia relating to toy manufacturing. Many displays are interactive.

Guided tours are available. Daily 9-5, Memorial Day-Dec. 31; Sat.-Sun. 9-5, rest of year. Hours may vary; phone ahead. Closed Jan. 1, Easter, Thanksgiving and Dec. 25. Last tour begins 1 hour before closing. Admission $8; $7 (ages 65+); $5 (ages 10-18). MC, VI. Phone (304) 242-8133 or (877) 242-8133.

[GEM] OGLEBAY RESORT is off I-70 at US 40, then 3 mi. n. on SR 88. This 1,750-acre parklike resort offers gardens, nature trails, stables, a zoo, shops and two museums. Activities include golf, tennis, swimming, trail rides, pedalboating and fishing.

Cascading Waters on Schenk Lake are displayed twice nightly during the summer in a computerized light and sound show. In November and December a million holiday lights decorate the park for the ☃ Winter Festival of Lights.

Food is available. Park open daily 9-dusk. All-day pass (excluding rental equipment) for zoo, museums, par 3 golf, miniature golf, tennis, fishing, pedal boats, train, trolley, and outdoor pool $12.50, Memorial Day weekend-Labor Day. Festival of Lights $10 per private vehicle, $6 per person for trolley rides. AX, DC, MC, VI. Phone (304) 243-4000 or (800) 624-6988. *See Recreation Chart.*

Bissonnette Gardens covers 16 acres between the park museums. Formal and herb gardens, an arboretum, landscape lighting and water displays are featured in this re-creation of gardens that existed at the turn of the 20th century. Spring arrives with tulips, summer offers displays of annuals, and mums are a fall highlight. Audio tour stations are located along brick paths. Picnicking is permitted. Daily 9-dusk, mid-Apr. to late Oct. Gardens free. Phone (304) 243-4010 or (800) 624-6988.

Carriage House Glass Museum is on a hilltop in the park. The museum houses a large collection of glassware produced 1817-1939. Exhibits include flint glass, lead crystal, cut glass and a 21-gallon Sweeney punch bowl. Also featured are glass-blowing demonstrations and a videotape about the history of glassmaking in the valley.

Allow 30 minutes minimum. Museum open Mon.-Sat. 10-5, Sun. noon-5, June-Aug; hours vary rest of year. Admission $6; free (ages 0-12). AX, MC, VI. Phone (304) 243-4340 or (800) 624-6988.

Henry Stifel Schrader Environmental Education Center, within Oglebay Resort, offers three nature trails that cover almost 5 miles, featuring overlooks, wildlife observation areas and waterfalls. More than 130 species of butterflies can be found in the flower gardens. Mon.-Sat. 10-5, Sun. noon-5. Free. Phone (304) 242-6855.

Mansion Museum, within Oglebay Resort, contains historical material and is furnished with items reflecting Ohio Valley life in the early days. The mansion, the former summer home of Col. and Mrs. Earl W. Oglebay, is furnished to represent different eras of Wheeling's past. Changing exhibits are presented. Mon.-Sat. 10-5, Sun. noon-5. Admission $6; free (ages 0-12). AX, DC, MC, VI. Phone (304) 242-7272 or (800) 624-6988.

[GEM] Oglebay's Good Zoo, within Oglebay Resort, is named in memory of 7-year-old Philip Mayer Good, a young boy who loved nature and visiting Oglebay Park. The 30-acre zoo provides natural settings for 85 North American species as well as animals from South America and Africa.

The Discovery Lab offers hands-on exhibits for children, while a planetarium provides shows for all ages. A wetlands exhibit has bald eagles and other animals and plants native to such regions. An 1863 train tours the zoo along a 1.5-mile track. An O-gauge model train is part of an indoor display.

Lorikeet Landing is an Australian walk-through aviary where cups of nectar can be hand-fed to the colorful birds who perch right on visitors' hands. A children's farm, a goat contact area, the Colors of Nature exhibit and a natural science theater also are available.

Daily 10-5, June-Aug; hours vary rest of year. Lorikeet Landing daily 11-4. Admission $6.50; $5.25 (ages 3-12). Train ride $1.25. AX, DC, MC, VI. Phone (304) 243-4030 or (800) 624-6988.

[SAVE] WEST VIRGINIA INDEPENDENCE HALL MUSEUM is at 16th and Market sts. This former Custom House is considered to be the Civil War birthplace of West Virginia. The state's separation from Virginia was the only change in the map of the United States resulting from the Civil War.

Restored rooms and a film interpret the building's history. A permanent exhibit of 3-D maps, artifacts and audiovisual displays depicts the rise to statehood and the war in West Virginia. Allow 30 minutes minimum. Mon.-Sat. 10-4; closed major holidays. Admission $3; $2 (students with ID); free (ages 0-5). Phone (304) 238-1300.

WHEELING PARK is 4 mi. e. on US 40 at 1801 National Rd. The 406-acre park contains paddleboating facilities, a covered ice-skating rink, indoor and outdoor tennis courts, a miniature golf course, a nine-hole golf course, a swimming pool and waterslide. Food is available. Daily 10-7, late May-early Sept. Daily passes start at $8 (Tues.-Sun. and holidays); $7 (Mon.). AX, DC, DS, MC, VI. Phone (304) 243-4085. *See Recreation Chart.*

GAMBLING ESTABLISHMENTS

- **Wheeling Island Racetrack and Gaming Center** is off I-70 eastbound exit 225 or off I-70 westbound exit 0 at 1 S. Stone St. Daily 7 a.m.-4 a.m. Phone (304) 232-5050 or (877) 946-4373.

WHITE SULPHUR SPRINGS (D-4)
pop. 2,315, elev. 1,917′

White Sulphur Springs was a fashionable health and pleasure resort as early as 1778. It was named after its mineral springs, which are said to possess curative qualities. The site of the original spring is on the grounds of the Greenbrier Hotel.

From the time America entered World War II until July 1942, Axis diplomats and their dependents who had been stationed in Washington, D.C., were interned in the Greenbrier until they could be exchanged for American diplomats and their dependents who were in the Axis countries. For the duration of the war the hotel was used as a soldiers' hospital; it also served as a hospital during the Civil War. In 1948 the 6,500-acre estate reopened as a luxury hotel.

Nearby are the 5,130-acre Greenbrier State Forest for camping, hiking and swimming *(see Recreation Chart and the AAA Mideastern CampBook)*; Greenbrier River Trail for bicycling, cross-country skiing and hiking; and the southern terminus of the 330-mile Allegheny Trail for hikers.

Greenbrier County Visitors Center—White Sulphur Springs: 540 N. Jefferson St., Lewisburg, WV 24901; phone (304) 645-1000 or (800) 833-2068.

WHITE SULPHUR SPRINGS NATIONAL FISH HATCHERY is on US 60. Several thousand rainbow trout are distributed annually from the facility to streams in the Monongahela National Forest *(see place listing p. 356)*. A visitor center houses aquariums and displays describing some of the hatchery's activities. A self-guiding tour of the hatchery is available year-round. Guided tours are available by request.

Allow 1 hour minimum. Hatchery Mon.-Fri. 7-3:30. A guided tour is given Fri. at 2, May-Nov. Visitor center Mon.-Fri. 7-3:30, Memorial Day weekend-Labor Day. Free. Phone (304) 536-1361.

WILLIAMSON (D-1) pop. 3,414, elev. 600′

Williamson is the business center for the vast coalfields of the Tug Valley area in West Virginia and Kentucky. Symbolic of coal's importance to the region is the Tug Valley Chamber of Commerce Building at Second Avenue and Court Street. Known as the Coal House, it was built in 1933 from 65 tons of locally mined coal.

Tug Valley Chamber of Commerce: P.O. Box 376, Williamson, WV 25661; phone (304) 235-5240.

WILLIAMSTOWN (B-2) pop. 2,996, elev. 610′

FENTON GLASS MUSEUM is just off I-77 exit 185 following signs to 420 Caroline Ave.; it also is reached via SR 2/14/31 or US 50. The museum exhibits more than 1,500 examples of Fenton glass and glass produced in Ohio Valley plants from 1880 to the present. A 22-minute video about the making of Fenton glass is shown regularly.

Mon.-Fri. 8-8, Sat. 8-5, Sun. noon-5, June-Aug.; Mon.-Fri. 8-7, Sat. 8-5, Sun. noon-5, Apr.-May and Sept.-Dec.; Mon.-Sat. 8-5, Sun. noon-5, rest of year. Closed Jan. 1, Easter, Thanksgiving and Dec. 25. Schedule may vary; phone ahead. Free. Phone (304) 375-7772.

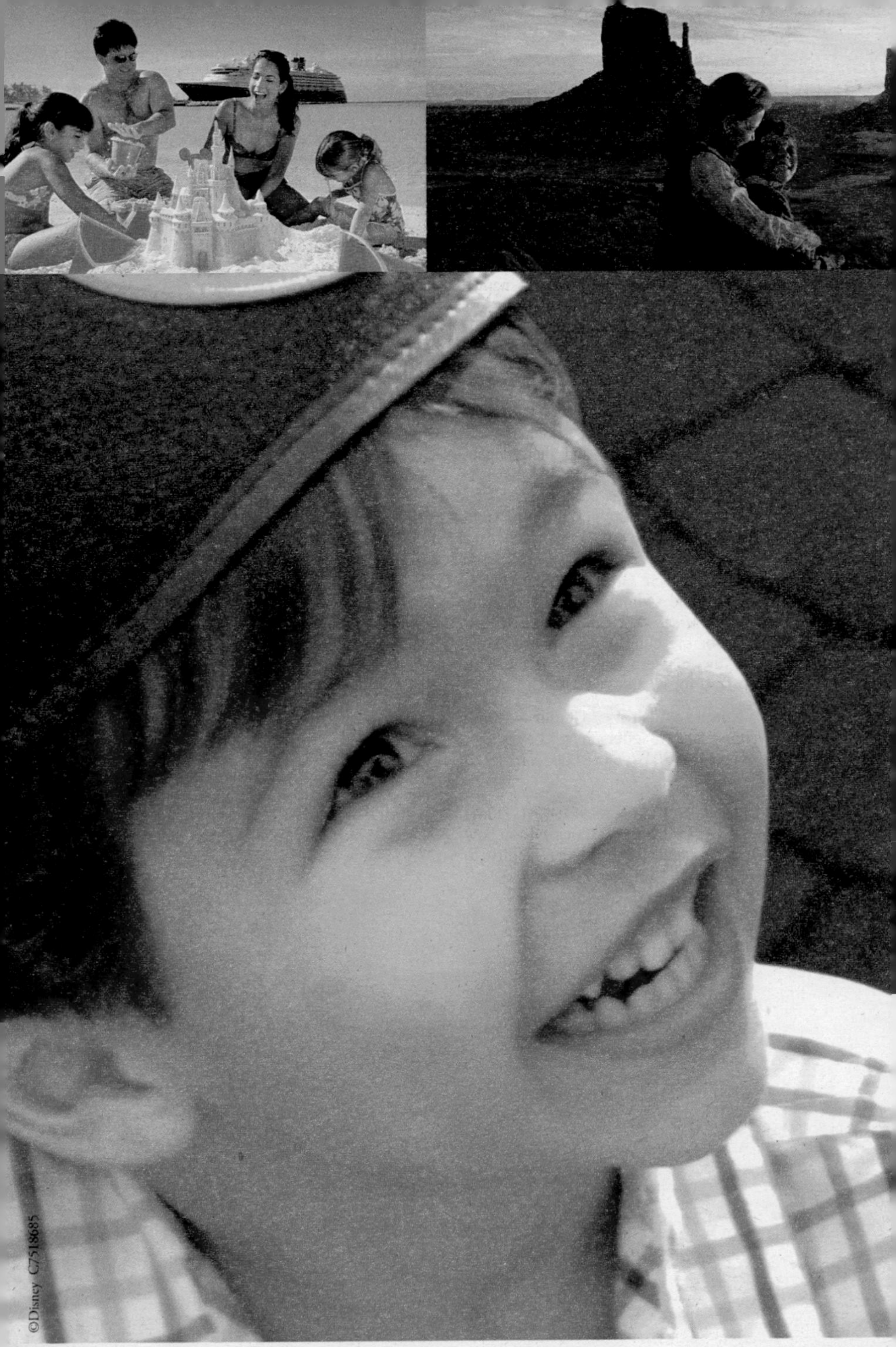
©Disney C7518685

AAA CAA®

No matter the Disney destination,
the smiles are always the same.

Let a AAA/CAA Travel professional help you get there.

A Disney vacation can take you to the world's greatest Theme Parks, *Walt Disney World*® Resort in Florida and *Disneyland*® Resort in California, and much, much more. Chart a course for magic on *Disney Cruise Line*, featuring fun for every member of the family. Or immerse your family in the stories of some of the world's greatest destinations with *Adventures by Disney*. A brand-new way for you to travel the globe.

Whatever you choose, make sure you book through your AAA/CAA Travel professional to receive exclusive benefits.

Where dreams come true

*Because the voyage of your dreams
just happens to be theirs, too.*

*AAA/CAA Travel adds special
benefits to your Disney dreams.*

On a *Disney Cruise Line*
vacation, you'll find something
enchanting for everyone of
every age—it's the kind of
magic only Disney can create.
And when you book through
AAA/CAA Travel, you'll enjoy
many special benefits! So call
or stop by your AAA/CAA
Travel Office today.

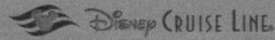

As to properties artwork © Disney C-056579 Ships' Registry: The Bahamas
CST # 1022229-50

Delaware

Wilmington
© Andre Jenny

BEAR pop. 17,593

———— WHERE TO STAY ————

AMERICINN LODGE & SUITES BEAR/WILMINGTON   *Book at AAA.com*   **Phone:** 302/326-2500

WWWW
Small-scale Hotel
Rates not provided

Address: 875 Pulaski Hwy 19701 **Location:** I-95, exit 4, 3.3 mi se on SR 1, exit 160, then just e on US 40. **Facility:** 75 units. 69 one-bedroom standard units, some with whirlpools. 6 one-bedroom suites, some with whirlpools. 3 stories, interior corridors. *Bath:* combo or shower only. **Parking:** on-site. **Amenities:** high-speed Internet, dual phone lines, voice mail, safes (fee), irons, hair dryers. **Pool(s):** heated indoor. **Leisure Activities:** sauna, whirlpool, exercise room. **Guest Services:** valet and coin laundry. **Business Services:** meeting rooms, business center.

[⊓⊤+] CALL [&M] [🏊] [✕] [🐾] [▭] / SOME UNITS [✕] FEE [VCR] [🔒] [📷]

BETHANY BEACH pop. 903

———— WHERE TO STAY ————

HOLIDAY INN EXPRESS BETHANY BEACH   *Book at AAA.com*   **Phone:** (302)541-9200

WWWW
Small-scale Hotel
$84-$304 3/1-10/15
$74-$119 10/16-2/28

Address: 710 S Coastal Hwy 19930 **Location:** On SR 1, 0.5 mi s of jct SR 26. **Facility:** Smoke free premises. 100 one-bedroom standard units, some with whirlpools. 4 stories, interior corridors. *Bath:* combo or shower only. **Parking:** on-site. **Terms:** 7 day cancellation notice-fee imposed. **Amenities:** dual phone lines, voice mail, irons, hair dryers. **Pool(s):** outdoor. **Leisure Activities:** limited exercise equipment. **Guest Services:** coin laundry, wireless Internet. **Business Services:** meeting rooms, administrative services. **Cards:** AX, DC, DS, MC, VI.

[ASK] [S/D] [⊓⊤+] CALL [&M] [🏊] [✕] [🐾] [🔒] [📷] [▭]

———— *The following lodgings were either not evaluated or did not* ————
meet AAA rating requirements but are listed for your information only.

RESORT QUEST AT BEAR TRAP   **Phone:** 302/537-8888

[fyi]   Not evaluated. **Address:** Marketplace at Sea Colony 19930 **Location:** Off SR 1, just s of jct SR 26. Facilities, services, and decor characterize a mid-range property.

SEA COLONY BEACH COMMUNITY BY RESORT QUEST   **Phone:** 302/537-8888

[fyi]   Not evaluated. **Address:** Marketplace at Sea Colony 19930 **Location:** Oceanfront. Off SR 1, just s of jct SR 26. Facilities, services, and decor characterize a mid-range property.

SEA COLONY TENNIS COMMUNITY BY RESORT QUEST   **Phone:** 302/537-8888

[fyi]   Not evaluated. **Address:** Marketplace at Sea Colony 19930 **Location:** Off SR 1, just s of jct SR 26. Facilities, services, and decor characterize a mid-range property.

——— WHERE TO DINE ———

PHO SAIGON

American
$6-$20

Phone: 302/539-8710
Traditional American cuisine served in a casual comfortable dining atmosphere. The staff is friendly and helpful, the atmosphere is suitable for families and the menu ranges from chicken, beef, seafood and pasta. Casual dress. **Bar:** Full bar. **Reservations:** not accepted. **Hours:** 11 am-9 pm, Fri & Sat 10 am-10 pm; 11 am-10 pm, Fri-11 pm, Sat & Sun 8 am-11 pm 3/30-9/5. Closed: 11/27, 12/25. **Address:** Rt 1, Hickmans Beach Plaza 19930 **Location:** On SR 1, 0.7 mi s of jct SR 26. **Parking:** on-site. **Cards:** AX, DC, MC, VI.

SEDONA *Menu on AAA.com*

American
$26-$39

Phone: 302/539-1200
Creative American cuisine is offered in this stylish little restaurant. The staff is friendly and helpful. The kitchen displays their talents with each dish served. Casual dress. **Bar:** Full bar. **Reservations:** suggested. **Hours:** Open 4/1-10/31; 5 pm-10 pm. Closed: call for days. **Address:** 26 Pennsylvania Ave 19930 **Location:** Just e of SR 1. **Parking:** street. **Cards:** AX, DS, MC, VI.

CLAYMONT pop. 9,220

——— WHERE TO STAY ———

HOLIDAY INN SELECT WILMINGTON *Book great rates at AAA.com*

Large-scale Hotel
$109-$145 All Year

Phone: (302)792-2700
Address: 630 Naamans Rd 19703 **Location:** I-95, exit 11, just w on SR 92; I-495, exit 6 (Naamans Rd). **Facility:** 189 units. 186 one-bedroom standard units. 3 one-bedroom suites. 8 stories, interior corridors. *Bath:* combo or shower only. **Parking:** on-site. **Amenities:** high-speed Internet, dual phone lines, voice mail, irons, hair dryers. **Pool(s):** outdoor. **Leisure Activities:** limited exercise equipment. **Guest Services:** valet laundry. **Business Services:** meeting rooms, business center. **Cards:** AX, DC, DS, MC, VI. *(See color ad p 390)*

DEWEY BEACH pop. 301

——— WHERE TO STAY ———

ATLANTIC OCEANSIDE MOTEL

Motel
$45-$269 3/14-11/16

Phone: 302/227-8811
Address: 1700 Hwy 1 19971 **Location:** Jct SR 1 and McKinley St. **Facility:** 63 one-bedroom standard units, some with efficiencies. 3 stories (no elevator), exterior corridors. *Bath:* combo or shower only. **Parking:** on-site. **Terms:** open 3/14-11/16, 2-3 night minimum stay - seasonal and/or weekends, 7 day cancellation notice-fee imposed. **Amenities:** hair dryers. **Pool(s):** heated outdoor. **Leisure Activities:** sun deck. **Business Services:** fax (fee). **Cards:** AX, DC, DS, MC, VI.

ATLANTIC VIEW HOTEL

Motel
Rates not provided

Phone: 302/227-3878
Address: 2 Clayton St 19971 **Location:** Oceanfront. Jct SR 1 and Clayton St, just s. **Facility:** Smoke free premises. 35 one-bedroom standard units. 4 stories (no elevator), interior corridors. **Parking:** on-site. **Terms:** open 3/1-12/3 & 2/2-2/28, office hours 8 am-11 pm. **Amenities:** irons, hair dryers. **Pool(s):** outdoor. **Guest Services:** coin laundry. **Business Services:** fax (fee).

BELLBUOY MOTEL

Motel
$55-$375 4/20-11/1

Phone: 302/227-6000
Address: 21 Van Dyke St 19971 **Location:** SR 1, on oceanside block of Van Dyke St. **Facility:** 16 one-bedroom standard units, some with kitchens. 3 stories (no elevator), exterior corridors. **Parking:** on-site. **Terms:** open 4/20-11/1, 2 night minimum stay - seasonal and/or weekends, 3 day cancellation notice-fee imposed. **Amenities:** safes. **Cards:** AX, DS, MC, VI.

BEST WESTERN GOLD LEAF *Book great rates at AAA.com*

Small-scale Hotel
Rates not provided

Phone: 302/226-1100
Address: 1400 Hwy 1 19971 **Location:** On SR 1; center. **Facility:** 76 one-bedroom standard units, some with whirlpools. 4 stories, interior corridors. **Parking:** on-site. **Amenities:** voice mail, safes, irons, hair dryers. **Pool(s):** outdoor. **Guest Services:** coin laundry, wireless Internet. **Business Services:** meeting rooms, fax (fee). **Free Special Amenities:** expanded continental breakfast and high-speed Internet. *(See color ad p 383)*

AAA Benefit:
Members save 10% everyday, plus an exclusive frequent stay program.

SEA-ESTA MOTEL I

Motel
$49-$199 5/1-10/13

Phone: (302)227-7666

Address: 2306 Hwy 1 19971 **Location:** SR 1 at Houston St. **Facility:** 30 one-bedroom standard units. 3 stories (no elevator), exterior corridors. **Parking:** on-site. **Terms:** open 5/1-10/13, 2 night minimum stay - seasonal and/or weekends. **Amenities:** hair dryers. **Business Services:** fax (fee). **Cards:** AX, CB, DC, DS, MC, VI. **Free Special Amenities: local telephone calls and newspaper.**

SEA-ESTA MOTEL III

Motel
$55-$229 3/1-10/15
$69 10/16-2/28

Phone: (302)227-4343

Address: 1409 Hwy 1 19971 **Location:** Jct SR 1 and Rodney St. **Facility:** 33 one-bedroom standard units with efficiencies (no utensils). 3 stories, exterior corridors. **Terms:** 2 night minimum stay - seasonal and/or weekends. **Amenities:** irons, hair dryers. **Business Services:** fax (fee). **Cards:** AX, CB, DC, DS, MC, VI. **Free Special Amenities: local telephone calls and newspaper.**

THE SURF CLUB HOTEL

Condominium
$75-$225 3/1-9/15
$75-$140 9/16-2/28

Phone: 302/227-7059

Address: 1 Read St 19971 **Location:** Just e of SR 1; center. **Facility:** 49 units. 48 one-bedroom standard units with efficiencies. 1 vacation home. 4 stories (no elevator), exterior corridors. **Parking:** on-site. **Terms:** office hours 8 am-10 pm. **Amenities:** video library, CD players, voice mail. **Pool(s):** outdoor. **Leisure Activities:** sauna, whirlpool, bicycles. **Guest Services:** coin laundry. **Business Services:** fax (fee). **Cards:** AX, DS, MC, VI.

——— WHERE TO DINE ———

CRABBER'S COVE

American
$12-$25

Phone: 302/227-6444

All-you-can-eat crabs are the specialty at this family-oriented restaurant, which has a menu that centers on seafood but also includes steak, rib and chicken choices. A lobster tank and picture windows that look out on the bay carry out the nautical feel. Weather permitting, the windows are retracted to allow an open-air ambience. That combined with plastic patio furniture gives diners the feel of participating in a large picnic. Viewing evening sunsets is an added attraction. Casual dress. **Bar:** Full bar. **Reservations:** not accepted. **Hours:** Open 5/15-9/12; 4 pm-9 pm, Fri & Sat-10 pm. **Address:** 113 Dickinson St 19971 **Location:** SR 1; center; in Rudder Towne complex. **Parking:** on-site. **Cards:** AX, DC, DS, MC, VI,

RUSTY RUDDER

Steak & Seafood
$7-$29

Phone: 302/227-3888

On the bay one block from the beach, this casual, nautically themed restaurant builds its menu around prime rib and seafood. An all-you-can-eat land and sea buffet is laid out daily during the summer and on Friday the rest of the year. The lunch menu is served until 4 pm. Casual dress. Entertainment. **Bar:** Full bar. **Hours:** 11:30 am-10 pm. Closed: 12/25; also Mon-Wed 10/31-3/15. **Address:** 113 Dickinson St 19971 **Location:** SR 1; center; in Rudder Towne complex. **Parking:** on-site. **Cards:** AX, DC, DS, MC, VI.

DOVER pop. 32,135

——— WHERE TO STAY ———

COMFORT INN-DOVER

Book great rates at AAA.com

Motel
$89-$129 3/1-10/31
$89-$109 11/1-2/28

Phone: (302)674-3300

Address: 222 S DuPont Hwy 19901 **Location:** SR 1, exit 95, 2 mi n on US 13, then 0.3 mi n on US 13. Located in a commercial area. **Facility:** 94 one-bedroom standard units. 2 stories (no elevator), exterior corridors. **Parking:** on-site. **Amenities:** voice mail, safes (fee), irons, hair dryers. **Pool(s):** outdoor. **Leisure Activities:** limited exercise equipment. **Guest Services:** valet and coin laundry, wireless Internet. **Business Services:** PC. **Cards:** AX, DC, DS, MC, VI. **Free Special Amenities: expanded continental breakfast and high-speed Internet.**

COMFORT SUITES-DOVER

Book at AAA.com

Small-scale Hotel
$100-$170 All Year

Phone: (302)736-1204

Address: 1654 N DuPont Hwy 19901 **Location:** SR 1, exit 104, 0.3 mi s on US 13. **Facility:** 64 units. 58 one-bedroom standard units, some with whirlpools. 6 one-bedroom suites with whirlpools. 3 stories, interior corridors. **Bath:** combo or shower only. **Parking:** on-site. **Amenities:** safes (fee), irons, hair dryers. *Some:* dual phone lines. **Pool(s):** outdoor. **Guest Services:** valet and coin laundry, wireless Internet. **Business Services:** meeting rooms, fax (fee). **Cards:** AX, CB, DC, DS, JC, MC, VI.

COUNTRY INN & SUITES BY CARLSON DOVER

fyi

Small-scale Hotel
$125-$400 3/1-9/30
$125-$200 10/1-2/28

Phone: 302/677-0505

Too new to rate. **Address:** 764 Dover Leipsic Rd 19901 **Location:** SR 1, exit 104. **Amenities:** 89 units, coffeemakers, microwaves, refrigerators, pool. **Cards:** AX, DS, MC, VI.

DAYS INN DOVER

Motel
Rates not provided

Book great rates at AAA.com

Phone: 302/674-8002

Address: 272 N DuPont Hwy 19901 **Location:** SR 1, exit 104, 2.8 mi s on US 13. Located in a commercial area. **Facility:** 81 one-bedroom standard units, some with efficiencies (no utensils). 1 story, exterior corridors. **Parking:** on-site. **Amenities:** voice mail, safes, irons, hair dryers. *Some:* high-speed Internet. **Guest Services:** coin laundry, wireless Internet. **Business Services:** fax (fee). **Free Special Amenities: expanded continental breakfast.**

DOVER DOWNS HOTEL & CASINO

Large-scale Hotel
$145-$800 All Year

Book great rates at AAA.com

Phone: (302)674-4600

Address: 1131 N DuPont Hwy 19903 **Location:** SR 1, exit 104, 1.9 mi s on US 13. Located adjacent to Dover Downs Race Track. **Facility:** A full-service hotel offering handsome, comfortable guest rooms and inviting public spaces, the property is attached to a casino. 232 units. 207 one-bedroom standard units. 25 one-bedroom suites, some with whirlpools. 10 stories, interior corridors. *Bath:* combo or shower only. **Parking:** on-site and valet. **Terms:** check-in 4 pm, cancellation fee imposed. **Amenities:** video games (fee), dual phone lines, voice mail, safes, honor bars, irons, hair dryers. *Some:* CD players. **Dining:** 4 restaurants, entertainment. **Pool(s):** heated indoor. **Leisure Activities:** whirlpool, steamrooms, exercise room. **Guest Services:** valet laundry, wireless Internet. **Business Services:** conference facilities, business center. **Cards:** AX, DS, MC, VI. *(See color ad p 37)*

FAIRFIELD INN & SUITES BY MARRIOTT-DOVER

Small-scale Hotel
$110-$141 All Year

Book great rates at AAA.com

Phone: 302/677-0900

Address: 655 N DuPont Hwy 19901 **Location:** SR 1, exit 104, 2.7 mi s on US 13. Located in a commercial area. **Facility:** Smoke free premises. 77 units. 58 one-bedroom standard units. 19 one-bedroom suites. 4 stories, interior corridors. *Bath:* combo or shower only. **Parking:** on-site. **Amenities:** high-speed Internet, dual phone lines, voice mail, irons, hair dryers. *Some:* CD players. **Pool(s):** heated indoor. **Leisure Activities:** whirlpool, sun deck, limited exercise equipment. **Guest Services:** valet and coin laundry, wireless Internet. **Business Services:** PC, fax. **Cards:** AX, DC, DS, MC, VI. **Free Special Amenities: expanded continental breakfast and high-speed Internet.**

AAA Benefit:

Members save 5% off of the best available rate.

HAMPTON INN-DOVER

Small-scale Hotel
Rates not provided

Book great rates at AAA.com

Phone: 302/736-3500

Address: 1568 N DuPont Hwy 19901 **Location:** SR 1, exit 104, 1 mi s. Located in a commercial area. **Facility:** 81 units. 78 one-bedroom standard units, some with whirlpools. 3 one-bedroom suites with whirlpools. 4 stories, interior corridors. *Bath:* combo or shower only. **Parking:** on-site. **Amenities:** voice mail, irons, hair dryers. **Pool(s):** outdoor. **Leisure Activities:** limited exercise equipment. **Guest Services:** valet laundry, wireless Internet. **Business Services:** business center.

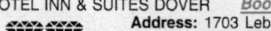

HOLIDAY INN EXPRESS HOTEL & SUITES DOVER

Small-scale Hotel
$109-$199 All Year

Book at AAA.com

Phone: (302)678-0600

Address: 1780 N DuPont Hwy 19901 **Location:** SR 1, exit 104, just s on US 13. **Facility:** 81 units. 73 one-bedroom standard units, some with whirlpools. 8 one-bedroom suites with whirlpools. 5 stories, interior corridors. *Bath:* combo or shower only. **Parking:** on-site. **Terms:** cancellation fee imposed. **Amenities:** high-speed Internet, dual phone lines, voice mail, irons, hair dryers. **Pool(s):** outdoor. **Leisure Activities:** exercise room. **Guest Services:** valet and coin laundry, wireless Internet. **Business Services:** meeting rooms, business center. **Cards:** AX, CB, DC, DS, JC, MC, VI.

MICROTEL INN & SUITES DOVER

Small-scale Hotel
$95-$189 All Year

Book at AAA.com

Phone: (302)674-3800

Address: 1703 Lebanon Rd 19901 **Location:** SR 1, exit 95, just w on SR 10. Near Dover Airforce Base. **Facility:** 70 one-bedroom standard units. 3 stories, interior corridors. *Bath:* combo or shower only. **Parking:** on-site. **Amenities:** safes (fee), irons, hair dryers. **Leisure Activities:** limited exercise equipment. **Guest Services:** coin laundry, wireless Internet. **Business Services:** meeting rooms, administrative services. **Cards:** AX, DC, DS, MC, VI.

SHERATON DOVER HOTEL

Large-scale Hotel
Rates not provided

Book great rates at AAA.com

Phone: 302/678-8500

Address: 1570 N DuPont Hwy 19901 **Location:** SR 1, exit 104, 1 mi s on US 13. Located in a commercial area. **Facility:** 152 units. 149 one-bedroom standard units, some with whirlpools. 3 one-bedroom suites with whirlpools. 7 stories, interior corridors. **Parking:** on-site. **Amenities:** video games (fee), high-speed Internet, dual phone lines, voice mail, irons, hair dryers. **Dining:** Chops Grille, see separate listing. **Pool(s):** heated indoor. **Leisure Activities:** whirlpool, exercise room. **Guest Services:** valet and coin laundry, area transportation, wireless Internet. **Business Services:** conference facilities, business center.

AAA Benefit:

Members get up to 15% off, plus Starwood Preferred Guest® bonuses.

——— **WHERE TO DINE** ———

CHOPS GRILLE

American
$8-$28

Phone: 302/678-8500

Serving contemporary American cuisine in a casual, comfortable atmosphere. Chicken Chesapeake — hand-seared chicken breast with jumbo lump crabmeat — is just one of several popular specialties of the house, as well as the French onion soup. Casual dress. **Bar:** Full bar. **Reservations:** accepted. **Hours:** 6:30 am-3 & 5-10:30 pm, Sun-2 pm. Closed: 12/25. **Address:** 1570 N DuPont Hwy 19901 **Location:** SR 1, exit 104, 1 mi s on US 13; in Sheraton Dover Hotel. **Parking:** on-site. **Cards:** AX, CB, DC, DS, MC, VI.

SHUCKER'S PIER 13

Seafood
$5-$30

Phone: 302/674-1190

This casual restaurant is popular with the locals. The menu offers seafood, pasta and meat dishes. Casual dress. **Bar:** Full bar. **Reservations:** accepted, Sun-Thurs. **Hours:** 11 am-10 pm, Fri & Sat-11 pm, Sun 11:30 am-9:30 pm. Closed: 3/23, 11/27, 12/25. **Address:** 889 N DuPont Hwy 19901 **Location:** SR 1, exit 104, 2.8 mi s on US 13. **Parking:** on-site. **Cards:** AX, DC, DS, MC, VI.

FENWICK ISLAND pop. 342

——— **WHERE TO STAY** ———

ATLANTIC COAST INN

Motel
$59-$199 4/25-9/21

Phone: 302/539-7673

Address: 37558 Lighthouse Rd & Coastal Hwy 19944 **Location:** Jct SR 1 and 54. **Facility:** 54 units. 52 one-bedroom standard units, some with efficiencies. 2 two-bedroom suites with kitchens. 2 stories (no elevator), exterior corridors. **Bath:** combo or shower only. **Parking:** on-site. **Terms:** open 4/25-9/21, 2 night minimum stay - seasonal and/or weekends, 7 day cancellation notice-fee imposed. **Pool(s):** outdoor. **Guest Services:** coin laundry. **Business Services:** fax (fee). **Cards:** AX, DS, MC, VI.

——— **WHERE TO DINE** ———

HARPOON HANNAS
Seafood
$5-$24

Phone: 302/539-3095

Looking for a fun, energetic come-as-you-are crowd and a nautical view? Hannas menu offers tempting choices such as crab imperial, Maryland style crab cakes, fried or broiled and surf n' turf (lobster and a charbroiled filet mignon). There's even a tiki bar. Casual dress. Entertainment. **Bar:** Full bar. **Reservations:** not accepted. **Hours:** 11 am-1 am, Sun from 10 am. **Address:** SR 54 & Bay 19944 **Location:** SR 54, 0.8 mi w of Coastal Hwy. **Parking:** on-site. **Cards:** DS, MC, VI.

NANTUCKETS
Seafood
$30-$50

Phone: 302/539-2607

The restaurant offers a bit of New England on the Eastern shore, with a menu of fresh seafood, crab cakes and black Angus steak. The walls of the charming old beach cottage, which was converted into this fine dining establishment, are adorned with original artwork. Dressy casual. **Bar:** Full bar. **Reservations:** suggested. **Hours:** 4 pm-10 pm, Fri & Sat-midnight. **Address:** Rt 1 & Atlantic Ave 19944 **Location:** On SR 1, just n of jct W SR 54. **Parking:** on-site and street. **Cards:** AX, CB, DC, DS, MC, VI.

GEORGETOWN pop. 4,643

——— **WHERE TO STAY** ———

COMFORT INN & SUITES-GEORGETOWN   *Book great rates at AAA.com*

Phone: 302/854-9400

Small-scale Hotel
$90-$280 All Year

Address: 20530 DuPont Blvd 19947 **Location:** On US 113, 0.5 mi n of jct SR 404. **Facility:** 71 one-bedroom standard units, some with whirlpools. 2 stories (no elevator), interior corridors. **Parking:** on-site. **Terms:** 3 day cancellation notice-fee imposed. **Amenities:** high-speed Internet, irons, hair dryers. **Pool(s):** outdoor. **Leisure Activities:** limited exercise equipment. **Guest Services:** wireless Internet. **Business Services:** meeting rooms, administrative services (fee), PC. **Cards:** AX, DC, DS, MC, VI. **Free Special Amenities: continental breakfast and high-speed Internet.**

HARRINGTON pop. 3,174

——— **WHERE TO STAY** ———

AMERICINN LODGE & SUITES OF HARRINGTON   *Book at AAA.com*

Phone: (302)398-3900

Small-scale Hotel
$99-$139 All Year

Address: 1259 Corn Crib Rd 19952 **Location:** On US 13, 0.6 mi s of jct SR 14. **Facility:** 70 units. 66 one-bedroom standard units, some with whirlpools. 4 one-bedroom suites. 2 stories, interior corridors. **Bath:** combo or shower only. **Parking:** on-site. **Amenities:** irons, hair dryers. **Pool(s):** heated indoor. **Leisure Activities:** whirlpool, exercise room. **Guest Services:** coin laundry, wireless Internet. **Business Services:** meeting rooms, administrative services (fee), PC. **Cards:** AX, DS, MC, VI.

HOLIDAY INN EXPRESS HOTEL & SUITES-HARRINGTON   *Book great rates at AAA.com*

Phone: 302/398-8800

Small-scale Hotel
$119-$149 3/1-10/31
$99-$109 11/1-2/28

Address: 17271 S DuPont Hwy 19952 **Location:** Jct SR 14, on US 13. **Facility:** 86 one-bedroom standard units. 3 stories, interior corridors. **Bath:** combo or shower only. **Parking:** on-site. **Amenities:** dual phone lines, voice mail, irons, hair dryers. **Pool(s):** heated outdoor. **Leisure Activities:** exercise room. **Guest Services:** valet laundry, wireless Internet. **Business Services:** meeting rooms, administrative services, PC. **Cards:** AX, DC, DS, MC, VI. **Free Special Amenities: expanded continental breakfast and high-speed Internet.**

LEWES pop. 2,932

——— WHERE TO STAY ———

THE HERITAGE INN AND GOLF CLUB   *Book great rates at AAA.com*
Phone: (302)644-0600

AAA [SAVE]

▼▼▼

Small-scale Hotel
$79-$219 All Year

Address: 2 Postal Ln 19958 **Location:** 1.5 mi s on SR 1. Located in a commercial area. **Facility:** Smoke free premises. 90 units. 85 one-bedroom standard units, some with whirlpools. 5 one-bedroom suites with whirlpools. 4 stories, interior corridors. *Bath:* combo or shower only. **Parking:** on-site. **Terms:** 2 night minimum stay - seasonal, 3 day cancellation notice. **Amenities:** voice mail, irons, hair dryers. **Pool(s):** outdoor. **Leisure Activities:** limited exercise equipment. *Fee:* golf-9 holes. **Guest Services:** coin laundry, wireless Internet. **Business Services:** meeting rooms. **Cards:** AX, DS, MC, VI. **Free Special Amenities: continental breakfast and high-speed Internet.**

🍴 CALL 🅜 🏊 ✕ 🎦 🖥 🖨 / SOME UNITS 🐾

HOTEL BLUE
Phone: 302/645-4880

AAA [SAVE]

▼▼▼

Small-scale Hotel
$120-$310 All Year

Address: 110 Anglers Rd, Suite 107 19958 **Location:** Over SR 9 bridge, just w; in historic Lewes. **Facility:** Smoke free premises. 16 units. 12 one-bedroom standard units. 4 one-bedroom suites. 3 stories, interior corridors. **Parking:** on-site. **Terms:** office hours 9 am-10 pm, age restrictions may apply, 7 day cancellation notice-fee imposed. **Amenities:** voice mail, safes, irons, hair dryers. *Some:* DVD players. **Pool(s):** heated outdoor. **Leisure Activities:** exercise room. *Fee:* massage. **Guest Services:** wireless Internet. **Business Services:** meeting rooms, administrative services (fee). **Cards:** AX, MC, VI. **Free Special Amenities: local telephone calls and high-speed Internet.**

CALL 🅜 🏊 ✕ 🎦 🖥 🖨 🖨

THE INN AT CANAL SQUARE
Phone: 302/644-3377

AAA [SAVE]

▼▼▼

Small-scale Hotel
$105-$300 All Year

Address: 122 Market St 19958 **Location:** On the canal. **Facility:** Smoke free premises. 24 units. 20 one-bedroom standard units, some with whirlpools. 2 one- and 2 two-bedroom suites, some with kitchens and/or whirlpools. 4 stories, interior corridors. *Bath:* combo or shower only. **Parking:** on-site. **Terms:** office hours 7 am-11 pm, 2 night minimum stay - weekends, 7 day cancellation notice-fee imposed. **Amenities:** dual phone lines, voice mail, irons, hair dryers. *Some:* CD players, honor bars. **Leisure Activities:** exercise room. *Fee:* massage. **Guest Services:** valet laundry, wireless Internet. **Business Services:** meeting rooms, PC, fax (fee). **Cards:** AX, MC, VI. **Free Special Amenities: expanded continental breakfast and high-speed Internet.**

🅢 🍴 ✕ 🎦 🖥 🖨 / SOME UNITS 🐾 🖨

SLEEP INN & SUITES   *Book great rates at AAA.com*
Phone: (302)645-6464

AAA [SAVE]

▼▼

Small-scale Hotel
$59-$259 All Year

Address: 18451 Coastal Hwy 19958 **Location:** On SR 1, 1.5 mi s. Located in a commercial area. **Facility:** 81 one-bedroom standard units, some with whirlpools. 4 stories, interior corridors. *Bath:* combo or shower only. **Parking:** on-site. **Terms:** cancellation fee imposed. **Amenities:** dual phone lines, voice mail, safes (fee), irons, hair dryers. **Pool(s):** heated outdoor. **Leisure Activities:** limited exercise equipment. **Guest Services:** coin laundry, wireless Internet. **Business Services:** meeting rooms, administrative services (fee). **Cards:** AX, DS, MC, VI. **Free Special Amenities: expanded continental breakfast and high-speed Internet.**

🅢 🍴 CALL 🅜 🏊 🎦 🖥 🖨 🖨 / SOME UNITS FEE 🐾 ✕

——— WHERE TO DINE ———

THE BUTTERY   *Menu on AAA.com*
Phone: 302/645-7755

AAA

▼▼▼

American
$10-$36

In the heart of the historic shopping and gallery district, the quaint, converted residence provides a charming setting for casual lunches and more formal dinners. The kitchen is skilled in preparing such dishes as veal, grilled duck breast and jumbo lump crab cakes. The staff is friendly and professional. Dressy casual. **Bar:** Full bar. **Reservations:** suggested. **Hours:** 11 am-2:30 & 5-9 pm, Fri & Sat-10 pm, Sun 10:30 am-2:30 & 5-9 pm. Closed: 1/1, 12/25. **Address:** 102 2nd St 19958 **Location:** 2nd and Savannah sts (US 9 business route). **Parking:** street. **Cards:** DS, MC, VI.

LIGHTHOUSE RESTAURANT AT LEWES
Phone: 302/645-6271

▼▼▼

Seafood
$4-$26

A basic, family-style seafood establishment, the canal-front restaurant features such choices as Chesapeake crab soup and a teriyaki-marinated grilled tuna sandwich. The complimentary after-dinner cruises, available during the summer, are a big draw. Casual dress. **Bar:** Full bar. **Hours:** 7 am-9 pm, Fri & Sat-9:30 pm. Closed: 11/27, 12/25; also Tues & Wed 3/1-3/7 & 10/19-2/28. **Address:** Savannah & Anglers Rd 19958 **Location:** N of US 9 business route, just e. **Parking:** on-site. **Cards:** MC, VI.

LITTLE CREEK pop. 195

——— WHERE TO DINE ———

VILLAGE INN RESTAURANT
Phone: 302/734-3245

▼▼▼

Steak & Seafood
$18-$32

After savoring one of the house specialties, such as crab imperial, guests should save room for homemade strawberry shortcake. The decor is decidedly Early American, with framed pictures depicting Colonial times. The atmosphere is casual and the service friendly. Casual dress. **Bar:** Full bar. **Reservations:** accepted. **Hours:** 4 pm-9 pm, Fri & Sat-10 pm, Sun 2 pm-7 pm. Closed: 11/27, 12/25; also Mon & Tues. **Address:** Rt 9, S Little Creek Rd 19961 **Location:** On SR 9, just s. **Parking:** on-site. **Cards:** AX, MC, VI.

LONG NECK pop. 1,629

——— WHERE TO STAY ———

SEA ESTA II
Phone: (302)945-5900

AAA [SAVE]

▼▼ ▼▼

Motel
$49-$169 3/1-10/15
$49-$69 10/16-2/28

Address: A19 Long Neck Rd 19966 **Location:** On SR 23, 1.1 mi s of jct SR 24, 5 and 23. **Facility:** 32 one-bedroom standard units. 1 story, exterior corridors. **Parking:** on-site. **Terms:** 2-3 night minimum stay - seasonal and/or weekends. **Amenities:** irons, hair dryers. **Pool(s):** outdoor. **Business Services:** fax (fee). **Cards:** AX, CB, DC, DS, MC, VI. **Free Special Amenities: local telephone calls and newspaper.**

🍴 🏊 ✕ 🎦 🖥 🖨 🖨 / SOME UNITS FEE 🐾

MIDDLETOWN pop. 6,161

――――― WHERE TO STAY ―――――

HAMPTON INN MIDDLETOWN *Book great rates at AAA.com*

Phone: 302-378-5656

▼▼▼▼
Small-scale Hotel
Rates not provided

Address: 117 Sandhill Dr 19709 **Location:** SR 1, exit 136, 3.2 mi on SR 299. **Facility:** 72 one-bedroom standard units, some with efficiencies. 6 one-bedroom suites. 4 stories, interior corridors. *Bath:* combo or shower only. **Parking:** on-site. **Amenities:** voice mail, irons, hair dryers. **Pool(s):** heated indoor. **Leisure Activities:** whirlpool, exercise room. **Guest Services:** valet and coin laundry, wireless Internet. **Business Services:** meeting rooms, business center.

MILFORD pop. 6,732

――――― WHERE TO STAY ―――――

AMERICINN LODGE & SUITES *Book at AAA.com*

Phone: (302)839-5000

▼▼▼▼
Small-scale Hotel
$109-$289 3/1-9/30
$99-$169 10/1-2/28

Address: 699 N DuPont Blvd 19963 **Location:** SR 1, s to US 113 S. **Facility:** 57 units. 51 one-bedroom standard units, some with whirlpools. 6 one-bedroom suites. 3 stories, interior corridors. *Bath:* combo or shower only. **Parking:** on-site. **Terms:** 2 night minimum stay - seasonal, cancellation fee imposed. **Amenities:** high-speed Internet, dual phone lines, voice mail, irons, hair dryers. *Some:* DVD players (fee). **Pool(s):** heated indoor. **Leisure Activities:** whirlpool, exercise room. **Guest Services:** coin laundry, wireless Internet. **Business Services:** meeting rooms, PC. **Cards:** AX, DC, DS, MC, VI.

――――― WHERE TO DINE ―――――

SAIL LOFT RESTAURANT

Phone: 302/422-5858

▼▼ ▼▼
American
$7-$40

The most popular selections are prime rib and seafood although chicken, veal and beef are also offered. Tempting desserts are homemade. The nautical-style decor and pleasant service complement the casual atmosphere. Dressy casual. **Bar:** Full bar. **Reservations:** suggested. **Hours:** 11:30 am-2:30 & 4:30-9 pm, Sat from 4:30 pm, Sun noon-8 pm. Closed major holidays. **Address:** 1517 Bay Rd 19963 **Location:** US 113, 1.5 mi n of jct SR 1. **Parking:** on-site. **Cards:** AX, DS, MC, VI.

MILLSBORO pop. 2,360

――――― WHERE TO STAY ―――――

ATLANTIC INN-MILLSBORO

Phone: 302/934-6711

▼▼ ▼▼
Motel
$69-$189 3/1-9/30
$65-$119 10/1-2/28

Address: 210 E DuPont Hwy 19966 **Location:** US 113, just s of SR 24. **Facility:** 82 one-bedroom standard units. 2 stories (no elevator), exterior corridors. **Parking:** on-site. **Amenities:** *Some:* irons. **Pool(s):** outdoor. **Leisure Activities:** limited exercise equipment. *Fee:* game room. **Guest Services:** coin laundry, wireless Internet. **Business Services:** meeting rooms, administrative services (fee). **Cards:** AX, DC, DS, MC, VI.

NEWARK pop. 28,547

――――― WHERE TO STAY ―――――

COMFORT SUITES-NEWARK/WILMINGTON *Book at AAA.com*

Phone: (302)266-6600

▼▼▼▼
Small-scale Hotel
$99-$299 All Year

Address: 56 S Old Baltimore Pike 19702 **Location:** I-95, exit 3A northbound; exit 3 southbound, 0.8 mi e on SR 273 E. **Facility:** 66 units. 65 one-bedroom standard units, some with whirlpools. 1 one-bedroom suite with whirlpool. 3 stories, interior corridors. *Bath:* combo or shower only. **Parking:** on-site. **Terms:** 7 day cancellation notice-fee imposed. **Amenities:** voice mail, irons, hair dryers. **Pool(s):** heated indoor. **Leisure Activities:** limited exercise equipment. **Guest Services:** wireless Internet. **Business Services:** meeting rooms, PC. **Cards:** AX, CB, DC, DS, MC, VI.

COUNTRY INN & SUITES BY CARLSON NEWARK/WILMINGTON *Book at AAA.com*

Phone: 302/266-6400

▼▼▼▼
Small-scale Hotel
Rates not provided

Address: 1024 Old Churchmans Rd 19713 **Location:** I-95, exit 4B, 0.3 mi n on SR 7, exit 166, then 0.4 mi w on SR 58 (Churchmans Rd). **Facility:** 58 units. 53 one-bedroom standard units, some with whirlpools. 5 one-bedroom suites, some with efficiencies and/or whirlpools. 3 stories, interior corridors. *Bath:* combo or shower only. **Parking:** on-site. **Amenities:** high-speed Internet, dual phone lines, voice mail, irons, hair dryers. **Leisure Activities:** limited exercise equipment. **Guest Services:** valet and coin laundry. **Business Services:** meeting rooms, business center.

COURTYARD BY MARRIOTT-NEWARK AT THE UNIVERSITY OF DELAWARE

Book great rates at AAA.com

Phone: 302/737-0900

Small-scale Hotel
$188-$229 All Year

Address: 400 Pencader Way 19716 **Location:** I-95, exit 1B, from the University of Delaware campus, 0.6 mi n on SR 896. **Facility:** Smoke free premises. 126 units. 122 one-bedroom standard units, some with whirlpools. 4 one-bedroom suites. 4 stories, interior corridors. *Bath:* combo or shower only. **Parking:** on-site. **Amenities:** high-speed Internet, voice mail, irons, hair dryers. **Pool(s):** heated indoor. **Leisure Activities:** whirlpool, exercise room. **Guest Services:** valet and coin laundry, area transportation, wireless Internet. **Business Services:** meeting rooms. **Cards:** AX, DC, DS, MC, VI.

AAA Benefit:
Members save 5% off of the best available rate.

COURTYARD BY MARRIOTT-WILMINGTON NEWARK/CHRISTIANA MALL

Book great rates at AAA.com

Phone: 302/456-3800

Small-scale Hotel
$210-$240 All Year

Address: 48 Geoffrey Dr 19713 **Location:** I-95, exit 4B, 0.3 mi n on SR 7, exit 166, then just e on SR 58 (Churchmans Rd). Located adjacent to shopping complex. **Facility:** Smoke free premises. 152 units. 140 one-bedroom standard units. 12 one-bedroom suites. 4 stories, interior corridors. *Bath:* combo or shower only. **Parking:** on-site. **Amenities:** high-speed Internet, dual phone lines, voice mail, irons, hair dryers. **Pool(s):** heated indoor. **Leisure Activities:** whirlpool, exercise room. **Guest Services:** valet and coin laundry, wireless Internet. **Business Services:** meeting rooms, business center. **Cards:** AX, DC, DS, JC, MC, VI.

AAA Benefit:
Members save 5% off of the best available rate.

DAYS INN WILMINGTON/NEWARK

Book great rates at AAA.com

Phone: 302/368-2400

Motel
Rates not provided

Address: 900 Churchmans Rd 19713 **Location:** I-95, exit 4B, 0.3 mi n on SR 7, exit 166, then 0.3 mi w on SR 58 (Churchmans Rd). **Facility:** 142 one-bedroom standard units, some with whirlpools. 3 stories, exterior corridors. **Parking:** on-site. **Amenities:** voice mail, safes (fee), hair dryers. *Some:* irons. **Pool(s):** outdoor. **Guest Services:** valet and coin laundry, wireless Internet. **Business Services:** meeting rooms, PC, fax (fee). **Free Special Amenities:** expanded continental breakfast and high-speed Internet.

DELAWARE INN & CONFERENCE CENTER

Book at AAA.com

Phone: 302/738-3400

Small-scale Hotel
Rates not provided

Address: 260 Chapman Rd 19702 **Location:** I-95, exit 3 southbound; exit 3A northbound, 0.3 mi e on SR 273 E, then just n. **Facility:** 95 one-bedroom standard units. 2 stories (no elevator), interior corridors. **Parking:** on-site. **Amenities:** high-speed Internet, voice mail, irons, hair dryers. **Pool(s):** outdoor. **Guest Services:** valet and coin laundry. **Business Services:** meeting rooms, PC.

ECONO LODGE

Book at AAA.com

Phone: 302/453-9100

Motel
$72-$225 All Year

Address: 100 McIntosh Plaza 19713 **Location:** I-95, exit 3 southbound; exit 3B northbound, 0.4 mi w on SR 273. **Facility:** 103 units. 101 one-bedroom standard units. 2 one-bedroom suites with whirlpools. 2 stories (no elevator), interior/exterior corridors. *Bath:* combo or shower only. **Parking:** on-site. **Terms:** cancellation fee imposed. **Amenities:** high-speed Internet, safes, irons, hair dryers. *Some:* DVD players. **Leisure Activities:** putting green, limited exercise equipment. **Guest Services:** coin laundry, wireless Internet. **Business Services:** fax (fee). **Cards:** AX, DC, DS, MC, VI.

EMBASSY SUITES NEWARK/WILMINGTON SOUTH

Book at AAA.com

Phone: 302/368-8000

Large-scale Hotel
Rates not provided

Address: 654 S College Ave 19713 **Location:** I-95, exit 1B southbound; exit 1 northbound, 0.8 mi n on SR 896. Located opposite the University of Delaware stadium. **Facility:** 154 one-bedroom suites. 6 stories, interior corridors. *Bath:* combo or shower only. **Parking:** on-site. **Amenities:** video games (fee), dual phone lines, voice mail, safes, irons, hair dryers. **Pool(s):** heated indoor. **Leisure Activities:** whirlpool, exercise room. **Guest Services:** valet and coin laundry, area transportation, wireless Internet. **Business Services:** conference facilities, business center.

FAIRFIELD INN BY MARRIOTT NEWARK/WILMINGTON

Book great rates at AAA.com

Phone: 302/292-1500

Motel
$122-$152 3/1-11/3
$111-$141 11/4-2/28

Address: 65 Geoffrey Dr 19713 **Location:** I-95, exit 4B, 0.3 mi n on SR 7, exit 166, then just e on SR 58 (Churchmans Rd). Located in a shopping complex. **Facility:** Smoke free premises. 133 one-bedroom standard units. 3 stories, interior/exterior corridors. *Bath:* combo or shower only. **Parking:** on-site. **Amenities:** voice mail, irons, hair dryers. **Pool(s):** heated outdoor. **Leisure Activities:** limited exercise equipment. **Guest Services:** valet laundry, wireless Internet. **Business Services:** PC, fax (fee). **Cards:** AX, DC, DS, JC, MC, VI.

AAA Benefit:
Members save 5% off of the best available rate.

HAMPTON INN NEWARK/WILMINGTON

Book great rates at AAA.com

Phone: 302/737-3900

Small-scale Hotel
Rates not provided

Address: 3 Concord Ln 19713 **Location:** I-95, exit 3 southbound; exit 3B northbound, 0.5 mi w on SR 273. **Facility:** 120 one-bedroom standard units. 4 stories, interior corridors. **Parking:** on-site. **Amenities:** video games (fee), voice mail, irons, hair dryers. **Pool(s):** outdoor. **Leisure Activities:** exercise room. **Guest Services:** valet and coin laundry, wireless Internet. **Business Services:** administrative services (fee).

HILTON WILMINGTON/CHRISTIANA

Book great rates at AAA.com

Phone: 302/454-1500

Large-scale Hotel
Rates not provided

Address: 100 Continental Dr 19713 **Location:** I-95, exit 4B, 0.3 mi n on SR 7, exit 166, then 0.4 mi w on SR 58 (Churchmans Rd). Located in a business park area. **Facility:** 266 units. 263 one-bedroom standard units. 3 one-bedroom suites. 4 stories, interior corridors. **Parking:** on-site. **Amenities:** high-speed Internet (fee), dual phone lines, voice mail, irons, hair dryers. **Pool(s):** outdoor. **Leisure Activities:** whirlpool, exercise room. **Guest Services:** valet and coin laundry, area transportation. **Business Services:** conference facilities, business center.

HOMESTEAD STUDIO SUITES HOTEL-NEWARK/CHRISTIANA

Book at AAA.com

Phone: (302)283-0800

Small-scale Hotel
$114-$124 All Year

Address: 333 Continental Dr 19713 **Location:** I-95, exit 4B, 0.3 mi n on SR 7, exit 166, then 0.4 mi w on SR 58 (Churchmans Rd). Located at rear of Christiana Executive Campus. **Facility:** 141 one-bedroom standard units with efficiencies. 3 stories, interior corridors. *Bath:* combo or shower only. **Parking:** on-site. **Terms:** office hours 6:30 am-11 pm. **Amenities:** voice mail, irons, hair dryers. *Some:* DVD players (fee). **Guest Services:** valet and coin laundry, wireless Internet. **Business Services:** administrative services (fee). **Cards:** AX, DC, DS, JC, MC, VI.

HOMEWOOD SUITES BY HILTON NEWARK/WILMINGTON SOUTH

Book at AAA.com

Phone: 302/453-9700

Small-scale Hotel
Rates not provided

Address: 640 S College Ave 19713 **Location:** I-95, exit 1B southbound; exit 1 northbound, 0.8 mi n on SR 896. **Facility:** 91 units. 22 one-bedroom standard units with efficiencies. 57 one- and 12 two-bedroom suites with efficiencies. 6 stories, interior corridors. *Bath:* combo or shower only. **Parking:** on-site. **Amenities:** video games (fee), high-speed Internet, dual phone lines, voice mail, safes, irons, hair dryers. *Some:* DVD players. **Pool(s):** heated indoor. **Leisure Activities:** exercise room. **Guest Services:** valet and coin laundry, area transportation, wireless Internet. **Business Services:** meeting rooms, business center.

HOWARD JOHNSON INN & SUITES - WILMINGTON/NEWARK

Book great rates at AAA.com

Phone: 302/368-8521

Small-scale Hotel
Rates not provided

Address: 1119 S College Ave 19713 **Location:** I-95, exit 1B southbound; exit 1 northbound, 0.3 mi n on SR 896. **Facility:** 142 one-bedroom standard units, some with whirlpools. 2 stories (no elevator), interior corridors. **Parking:** on-site. **Amenities:** voice mail, safes (fee), irons, hair dryers. **Pool(s):** outdoor. **Leisure Activities:** limited exercise equipment. **Guest Services:** coin laundry, wireless Internet. **Business Services:** meeting rooms, fax (fee). **Free Special Amenities:** expanded continental breakfast and newspaper.

QUALITY INN UNIVERSITY

Book great rates at AAA.com

Phone: (302)368-8715

Motel
$59-$349 All Year

Address: 1120 S College Ave 19713 **Location:** I-95, exit 1B southbound; exit 1 northbound, 0.3 mi n on SR 896. **Facility:** 102 one-bedroom standard units. 2 stories (no elevator), exterior corridors. *Bath:* combo or shower only. **Parking:** on-site. **Amenities:** voice mail, irons, hair dryers. **Pool(s):** outdoor. **Leisure Activities:** limited exercise equipment. **Guest Services:** valet and coin laundry, wireless Internet. **Business Services:** meeting rooms, administrative services (fee), PC. **Cards:** AX, DC, DS, MC, VI. *(See color ad p 381)*

RED ROOF INN-WILMINGTON

Book at AAA.com

Phone: 302/292-2870

Motel
Rates not provided

Address: 415 Stanton Christiana Rd 19713 **Location:** I-95, exit 4B, 0.5 mi n on SR 7. **Facility:** 119 one-bedroom standard units. 3 stories, exterior corridors. *Bath:* combo or shower only. **Parking:** on-site. **Amenities:** video games (fee), voice mail. **Guest Services:** wireless Internet. **Business Services:** fax (fee).

RESIDENCE INN BY MARRIOTT

Book great rates at AAA.com

Phone: 302/453-9200

Small-scale Hotel
$219-$230 All Year

Address: 240 Chapman Rd 19702 **Location:** I-95, exit 3 southbound; exit 3A northbound, 0.3 mi w on SR 273 E, then 0.5 mi s. **Facility:** Smoke free premises. 120 units. 112 one-bedroom standard units with kitchens. 8 one-bedroom suites with kitchens. 2 stories (no elevator), exterior corridors. *Bath:* combo or shower only. **Parking:** on-site. **Amenities:** voice mail, irons, hair dryers. **Pool(s):** heated outdoor. **Leisure Activities:** whirlpool, limited exercise equipment, sports court. **Guest Services:** valet and coin laundry, area transportation, wireless Internet. **Business Services:** meeting rooms, administrative services (fee). **Cards:** AX, DC, DS, MC, VI.

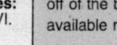

AAA Benefit:
Members save 5% off of the best available rate.

SLEEP INN-NEWARK *Book great rates at AAA.com* **Phone:** (302)453-1700

Small-scale Hotel
$89-$129 All Year

Address: 630 S College Ave 19713 **Location:** I-95, exit 1B southbound; exit 1 northbound, 0.8 mi n on SR 896. Located opposite the University of Delaware stadium. **Facility:** 96 one-bedroom standard units. 3 stories, interior corridors. *Bath:* combo or shower only. **Parking:** on-site. **Amenities:** voice mail, irons, hair dryers. **Leisure Activities:** limited exercise equipment. **Guest Services:** valet and coin laundry, wireless Internet. **Business Services:** meeting rooms, fax (fee). **Cards:** AX, DC, DS, MC, VI. **Free Special Amenities: continental breakfast and high-speed Internet.**

STAYBRIDGE SUITES-NEWARK/WILMINGTON *Book at AAA.com* **Phone:** (302)366-8097

Small-scale Hotel
$190-$200 All Year

Address: 270 Chapman Rd 19702 **Location:** I-95, exit 3 southbound; exit 273 E, then just n. **Facility:** 73 units. 45 one-bedroom standard units with efficiencies. 23 one- and 5 two-bedroom suites with efficiencies. 4 stories, interior corridors. *Bath:* combo or shower only. **Parking:** on-site. **Amenities:** DVD players, high-speed Internet, dual phone lines, voice mail, irons, hair dryers. **Pool(s):** outdoor. **Leisure Activities:** barbecue grills. **Guest Services:** valet and coin laundry. **Business Services:** meeting rooms, business center. **Cards:** AX, CB, DC, DS, MC, VI.

TOWNEPLACE SUITES BY MARRIOTT-WILMINGTON/NEWARK *Book great rates at AAA.com* **Phone:** 302/369-6212

Small-scale Hotel
$158-$193 All Year

Address: 410 Eagle Run Rd 19702 **Location:** I-95, exit 3 southbound; exit 3A northbound, just e. **Facility:** Smoke free premises. 73 units. 70 one-bedroom standard units with efficiencies. 3 one-bedroom suites with efficiencies. 4 stories, interior corridors. *Bath:* combo or shower only. **Parking:** on-site. **Amenities:** dual phone lines, voice mail, irons, hair dryers. **Pool(s):** outdoor. **Leisure Activities:** limited exercise equipment. **Guest Services:** valet and coin laundry, wireless Internet. **Business Services:** meeting rooms, business center. **Cards:** AX, DC, DS, JC, MC, VI. **Free Special Amenities: full breakfast and high-speed Internet.**

AAA Benefit:
Members save 5% off of the best available rate.

▼ See AAA listing p 380 ▼

——— WHERE TO DINE ———

ALI BABA RESTAURANT Phone: 302/738-1111

Middle Eastern
$4-$13

Patrons can sample Middle Eastern cuisine made from Moroccan and Lebanese recipes. The traditional Moroccan atmosphere incorporates tapestries and sofa seating in the back room and traditional seating in the front. Casual dress. **Bar:** Full bar. **Reservations:** accepted. **Hours:** 11:30 am-9:30 pm, Fri-10:30 pm, Sat 4:30 pm-11 pm, Sun 4:30 pm-9:30 pm. Closed major holidays. **Address:** 175 E Main St 19711 **Location:** I-95, exit 1B, 2.5 mi n on SR 896, 0.5 mi e on E Delaware Ave, then just w; downtown. **Parking:** street. **Cards:** MC, VI.

CAFFE GELATO RESTAURANT *Menu on AAA.com* Phone: 302/738-5811

(AAA)

Mediterranean
$6-$24

On bustling Main St., near the University of Delaware, this intimate cafe prepares Mediterranean cuisine with a Northern Italian influence. The kitchen creates a wide range of daily specials in addition to the regular menu items. The lunch menu is available till 5pm and offers salads, soups, panini and pasta dishes. Save room for gelato, it's homemade and a rainbow of flavors are offered. In addition to beer and wine, after dinner cordials are available. Dressy casual. **Bar:** Beer & wine. **Reservations:** suggested. **Hours:** 11 am-9:30 pm, Fri & Sat-10 pm, Sun 10:30 am-3 pm. Closed: 3/23, 11/27; also 12/24-1/1. **Address:** 90 E Main St 19711 **Location:** I-95, exit 1B, 2.5 mi n on SR 896, 0.5 mi e on E Delaware Ave, then just w; downtown. **Parking:** on-site. **Cards:** AX, DS, MC, VI.

IRON HILL BREWERY & RESTAURANT Phone: 302/266-9000

American
$7-$27

Handcrafted beers made on the premises match with the innovative American cuisine. The downtown dining room is casual, comfortable and friendly. Light fare is available throughout the day, and the dinner menu begins at 5 pm. Casual dress. **Bar:** Full bar. **Reservations:** accepted. **Hours:** 11:30 am-close, Sun 11 am-2 & 4-close; Sunday brunch. Closed: 11/27, 12/25; also for dinner 12/24. **Address:** 147 E Main St 19711 **Location:** I-95, exit 1B, 2.5 mi n on SR 896, 0.5 mi e on E Delaware Ave, then just w; downtown. **Parking:** street. **Cards:** AX, DC, DS, MC, VI.

LA CASA PASTA RESTAURANT Phone: 302/738-9935

Italian
$7-$32

For more than 20 years, the unpretentious restaurant has served fresh seafood, veal and pasta dishes. Casual dress. **Bar:** Full bar. **Reservations:** suggested. **Hours:** 11 am-10 pm, Mon-9 pm, Fri & Sat-11 pm, Sun noon-10 pm. Closed: 11/27, 12/25. **Address:** Rt 896 & Four Seasons Pkwy 19702 **Location:** I-95, exit 1A southbound; exit 1 northbound, 1.5 mi s. **Parking:** on-site. **Cards:** AX, DC, DS, MC, VI.

MICHAEL'S FAMILY RESTAURANT & PUB Phone: 302/368-4230

American
$4-$24

Buffet choices in the upscale, contemporary restaurant include prime rib, huge mussels and snow crab legs. The regular menu focuses primarily on sandwiches, burgers and seafood. Neon lighting, glass blocks and skylights all lend to the contemporary feel. Casual dress. **Bar:** Full bar. **Hours:** 8 am-10 pm, Fri & Sat-11† pm. Closed: 12/25. **Address:** 1000 Churchmans Rd 19713 **Location:** I-95, exit 4B, 0.3 mi n on SR 7, exit 166, then 0.4 mi w. **Parking:** on-site. **Cards:** AX, DS, MC, VI.

MORELIA MEXICIAN RESTAURANT & BAR Phone: 302/369-6888

Mexican
$5-$13

In a shopping plaza, the casual restaurant offers a comfortable setting, efficient service and a nice selection of Mexican dishes, ranging from tacos and burritos to steak and shrimp dishes. Casual dress. **Bar:** Full bar. **Reservations:** accepted. **Hours:** 11 am-9 pm, Fri & Sat-10 pm. Closed: 12/25. **Address:** 4617 Stanton Ogletown Rd 19713 **Location:** I-95, exit 4B, 0.3 mi n on SR 7, exit 166, 0.8 mi w on SR 58 (Churchman's Rd), then 0.7 mi s on SR 4; in The Omega Shop. **Parking:** on-site. **Cards:** AX, DS, MC, VI.

NONNA RISTORANTE Phone: 302/737-9999

Italian
$6-$32

The small, shopping plaza restaurant prepares consistently good Northern and Southern Italian cooking. Offerings on the varied menu range from veal and seafood to pasta and pizza. The wine list offers a nice selection, including many by-the-glass choices. Casual dress. **Bar:** Beer & wine. **Reservations:** accepted, Sun-Thurs. **Hours:** 11 am-10 pm, Sat & Sun from noon; Sat & Sun from 3 pm 5/31-9/6. Closed major holidays. **Address:** 4621 Stanton Ogletown Rd 19713 **Location:** I-95, exit 4B, 0.3 mi n on SR 7, exit 166, 0.8 mi w on SR 58 (Churchmans Rd), then 0.7 mi s on SR 4; in The Omega Shop. **Parking:** on-site. **Cards:** AX, MC, VI.

NEW CASTLE pop. 4,862

——— WHERE TO STAY ———

QUALITY INN SKYWAYS *Book great rates at AAA.com* Phone: (302)328-6666

(AAA) [SAVE]

Motel
$109-$184 All Year

Address: 147 N DuPont Hwy 19720 **Location:** I-95, exit 5A, 0.8 mi s on SR 141, exit 1B, 0.5 mi s on US 13, 40 and 301; I-295, exit New Castle Airport/US 13 S, 1.8 mi s on US 13, 40 and 301. Located in a commercial area next to the airport. **Facility:** 142 units. 102 one-bedroom standard units, some with kitchens. 40 one-bedroom suites, some with whirlpools. 1-2 stories (no elevator); interior/exterior corridors. **Bath:** combo or shower only. **Parking:** on-site. **Amenities:** voice mail, irons, hair dryers. *Some:* safes. **Pool(s):** outdoor. **Leisure Activities:** picnic area, barbecue grill. **Guest Services:** valet and coin laundry, area transportation-within 10 mi, wireless Internet. **Business Services:** meeting rooms, PC. **Cards:** AX, CB, DC, DS, JC, MC, VI. **Free Special Amenities:** local telephone calls and high-speed Internet.

SUPER 8 MOTEL *Book at AAA.com* Phone: 302/322-9480

Motel
Rates not provided

Address: 215 S DuPont Hwy 19720 **Location:** I-95, exit 3A, 4.3 mi e on SR 273, then 0.8 mi s on US 13. **Facility:** 59 one-bedroom standard units. 3 stories, interior corridors. **Parking:** on-site. **Amenities:** safes (fee), hair dryers. **Guest Services:** coin laundry, wireless Internet. **Business Services:** fax (fee).

─── WHERE TO DINE ───

AIR TRANSPORT COMMAND RESTAURANT

American
$8-$40

Phone: 302/328-3527

Authentic World War II memorabilia decorates the restaurant inside and out. Entree selections center on prime rib, steak, filet mignon, seafood, veal and chicken. The wait staff provides prompt, pleasant service. Guests can order from the lunch menu until 3 pm, Sunday brunch is served from 10 am to 2 pm. Casual dress. **Bar:** Full bar. **Reservations:** suggested, weekends. **Hours:** 11 am-10 pm, Fri & Sat-11 pm, Sun 10 am-10 pm. **Address:** 121 N DuPont Hwy 19720 **Location:** US 13, 0.3 mi s of Wilmington Airport entrance. **Parking:** on-site. **Cards:** AX, CB, DC, DS, MC, VI.

THE ARSENAL AT OLD NEW CASTLE

American
$9-$25

Phone: 302/328-1290

In an 1809 former militia barracks in the heart of the historic district, the restaurant serves traditional American fare. Attired in faux colonial garb, the staff reinforces the history themes employed in the inn's various rooms. The tavern has a Civil War theme, and the upstairs function room is decorated in colonial fashion. The elegant Federal decor of the main dining room conjures visions of the War of 1812 era. Casual dress. **Bar:** Full bar. **Reservations:** suggested. **Hours:** 11:30 am-9 pm, Fri & Sat-10 pm, Sun 11 am-3 pm. Closed: 12/25; also Mon. **Address:** 30 Market St 19720 **Location:** Center of historic district; directly behind courthouse. **Parking:** street. **Cards:** AX, DC, DS, MC, VI.

JESSOP'S TAVERN & COLONIAL RESTAURANT

American
$6-$22

Phone: 302/322-6111

American and English pub fare is served in hearty portions amid the ambience of a 1724 Colonial brick home. The crab chowder, chicken pot pie and fish & chips are popular choices. Both Swedish and Dutch culinary influences also reflect New Castle's early heritage. Casual dress. **Bar:** Full bar. **Reservations:** not accepted. **Hours:** 11 am-10 pm, Fri & Sat-11 pm, Sun noon-8 pm. Closed: 12/25. **Address:** 114 Delaware St 19720 **Location:** In downtown historic district. **Parking:** street. **Cards:** AX, CB, DC, DS, MC, VI. **Historic**

POLIDORO ITALIAN GRILL

Italian
$7-$25

Phone: 302/322-1500

The contemporary decor with the 2-story ceiling, decorative lighting and black and white pictures of Italy set a casual, comfortable atmosphere for any occasion. The staff is friendly and helpful. The menu offers a nice selection of pasta, beef and seafood dishes. Casual dress. **Bar:** Full bar. **Reservations:** suggested, weekends. **Hours:** 11 am-10 pm, Sat 2 pm-11 pm, Sun noon-9 pm. Closed: 12/25. **Address:** 129 N DuPont Hwy 19720 **Location:** I-95, exit 5A, 0.8 mi s on SR 141, exit 1B, then 0.6 mi s on US 13, 40 and 301; I-295, exit New Castle Airport/US 13 S, 1.8 mi s on US 13, 40 and 301. **Parking:** on-site. **Cards:** AX, DC, DS, MC, VI.

CALL Ⓖ Ⓜ

REHOBOTH BEACH pop. 1,495

─── WHERE TO STAY ───

ADMIRAL HOTEL

AAA SAVE

Motel
$139-$409 5/23-2/28
$89-$249 3/1-5/22

Phone: 302/227-2103

Address: 2 Baltimore Ave 19971 **Location:** Just off the boardwalk. **Facility:** 73 units. 72 one-bedroom standard units. 1 one-bedroom suite. 5 stories, exterior corridors. Bath: combo or shower only. **Parking:** on-site. **Terms:** 2 night minimum stay - seasonal and/or weekends, 7 day cancellation notice-fee imposed. **Amenities:** voice mail, irons, hair dryers. Some: DVD players. **Pool(s):** heated indoor. **Leisure Activities:** whirlpool. **Guest Services:** wireless Internet. **Business Services:** fax (fee). **Cards:** AX, DS, MC, VI. **Free Special Amenities:** local telephone calls and high-speed Internet.

🍽 🏊 🛗 🖨 🖵 / SOME UNITS ✖ VCR

AMERICINN LODGE & SUITES OF REHOBOTH BEACH   *Book at AAA.com*

Small-scale Hotel
$69-$249 All Year

Phone: (302)226-0700

Address: 329Z Airport Rd 19971 **Location:** Just w of SR 1; just w on Miller Rd, then just s. Located in the outlet mall area. **Facility:** 49 units. 45 one-bedroom standard units, some with whirlpools. 4 one-bedroom suites, some with whirlpools. 2 stories (no elevator), interior corridors. Bath: combo or shower only. **Parking:** on-site. **Terms:** 2 night minimum stay - weekends. **Amenities:** irons, hair dryers. Some: DVD players (fee). **Pool(s):** heated indoor. **Leisure Activities:** whirlpool. **Guest Services:** coin laundry, wireless Internet. **Business Services:** meeting rooms, PC, fax (fee). **Cards:** AX, CB, DC, DS, MC, VI.

ASK S/D 🍽 CALL ⒼⓂ 🏊 🐾 🛗 🖨 🖵 / SOME UNITS FEE 🐕 ✖ FEE VCR

▼ See AAA listing p 373 ▼

THE ATLANTIS INN

Phone: 302/227-9446

Motel
$85-$275 3/7-11/1

Address: 154 Rehoboth Ave 19971 **Location:** At Rehoboth Ave and 2nd St; downtown. **Facility:** Smoke free premises. 94 units. 89 one-bedroom standard units, some with kitchens. 5 one-bedroom suites, some with kitchens. 4 stories, exterior corridors. **Parking:** on-site. **Terms:** open 3/7-11/1, 2 night minimum stay - weekends, 7 day cancellation notice-fee imposed. **Pool(s):** outdoor. **Guest Services:** coin laundry, wireless Internet. **Business Services:** fax (fee). **Cards:** AX, DS, MC, VI.

ASK SD TI+ ⇆ X / SOME UNITS FEE 🐾 🗑 🖥 📺

BAYSIDE INN & SUITES

Phone: (302)227-0401

Motel
$79-$249 3/1-10/1
$39-$199 10/2-2/28

Address: 4353 Hwy 1 19971 **Location:** SR 1, 1.3 mi s of jct SR 24. Located in the outlet area. **Facility:** 73 units. 39 one- and 27 two-bedroom standard units. 7 one-bedroom suites. 2 stories (no elevator), exterior corridors. **Parking:** on-site. **Pool(s):** outdoor. **Business Services:** fax (fee). **Cards:** AX, DS, MC, VI. **Free Special Amenities: continental breakfast and local telephone calls.**

SD TI+ ⇆ 🗑 🖥 / SOME UNITS X

BOARDWALK PLAZA HOTEL   *Book great rates at AAA.com*

Phone: (302)227-7169

Small-scale Hotel
$99-$599 All Year

Address: Oceanfront at Olive Ave 19971 **Location:** Oceanfront. Just n of Rehoboth Ave. Located on the boardwalk. **Facility:** A Victorian ambience pervades this beachfront hotel set on the boardwalk and offering some guest rooms overlooking the ocean. Smoke free premises. 84 units. 39 one-bedroom standard units, some with whirlpools. 42 one- and 3 two-bedroom suites, some with efficiencies, kitchens and/or whirlpools. 4 stories, interior corridors. *Bath:* combo or shower only. **Parking:** on-site and valet. **Terms:** 1-4 night minimum stay - seasonal and/or weekends, 3 day cancellation notice. **Amenities:** video library (fee), DVD players, CD players, high-speed Internet, dual phone lines, voice mail, irons, hair dryers. *Some:* honor bars. **Dining:** Victoria's, see separate listing. **Leisure Activities:** whirlpool, exercise room. **Guest Services:** wireless Internet. **Business Services:** meeting rooms. *Fee:* PC, fax. **Cards:** AX, DC, DS, MC, VI. **Free Special Amenities: local telephone calls and newspaper.** *(See color ad below)*

SD TI Y CALL 🖥 X 📺 / SOME UNITS FEE VCR 🗑 🖥

THE BREAKERS HOTEL & SUITES   *Book at AAA.com*

Phone: 302/227-6688

Motel
Rates not provided

Address: 105 2nd St 19971 **Location:** Just n of Rehoboth Ave. **Facility:** 98 units. 60 one-bedroom standard units. 36 one- and 2 two-bedroom suites, some with whirlpools. 5 stories, exterior corridors. **Parking:** on-site. **Terms:** open 3/1-1/1 & 2/1-2/28. **Amenities:** voice mail, safes (fee). **Pool(s):** heated indoor/outdoor. **Leisure Activities:** limited exercise equipment. **Business Services:** meeting rooms, fax (fee).

TI+ ⇆ X 🗑 🖥 📺 / SOME UNITS FEE 🐾

BRIGHTON SUITES HOTEL   *Book great rates at AAA.com*

Phone: 302/227-5780

Small-scale Hotel
Rates not provided

Address: 34 Wilmington Ave 19971 **Location:** Just s of Rehoboth Ave. **Facility:** Designated smoking area. 66 units. 3 one-bedroom standard units. 63 one-bedroom suites. 4 stories, interior corridors. **Parking:** on-site. **Amenities:** video library, DVD players, dual phone lines, safes, irons, hair dryers. **Pool(s):** heated indoor. **Leisure Activities:** limited exercise equipment. **Guest Services:** area transportation-within 5 mi, wireless Internet. **Business Services:** meeting rooms, fax (fee). **Free Special Amenities: local telephone calls and newspaper.** *(See color ad p 385)*

TI CALL 🖥 ⇆ X 🗑 🖥 📺

COMFORT INN REHOBOTH BEACH *Book great rates at AAA.com*   Phone: (302)226-1515

Small-scale Hotel
$109-$299 All Year

Address: 19210 Coastal Hwy 19971 **Location:** On SR 1, 1.5 mi n. Located in the outlet mall area. **Facility:** 96 units. 93 one-bedroom standard units, some with whirlpools. 3 one-bedroom suites with whirlpools. 3 stories, interior corridors. *Bath:* combo or shower only. **Parking:** on-site. **Terms:** check-in 4 pm, 2-3 night minimum stay - seasonal and/or weekends, cancellation fee imposed. **Amenities:** irons, hair dryers. **Pool(s):** outdoor. **Leisure Activities:** limited exercise equipment. **Guest Services:** valet and coin laundry, wireless Internet. **Business Services:** meeting rooms, administrative services, PC. **Cards:** AX, DC, DS, MC, VI. **Free Special Amenities: expanded continental breakfast and high-speed Internet.** *(See color ad p 386)*

DELAWARE INN AT REHOBOTH   Phone: 302/227-6031

Bed & Breakfast
$150-$275 All Year

Address: 55 Delaware Ave 19971 **Location:** Jct Delaware Ave and 2nd St, just e; downtown. **Facility:** This traditional beach cottage dating from 1930 is furnished with varied antiques and reproductions. Smoke free premises. 7 one-bedroom standard units. 3 stories (no elevator), interior corridors. *Bath:* some shared or private, combo or shower only. **Parking:** on-site. **Terms:** office hours 8 am-10 pm, 2 night minimum stay - seasonal and/or weekends, age restrictions may apply, 10 day cancellation notice-fee imposed. **Amenities:** video library, irons, hair dryers. *Some:* DVD players. **Leisure Activities:** bicycles. **Guest Services:** wireless Internet. **Business Services:** fax. **Cards:** DS, MC, VI.

ECONO LODGE *Book great rates at AAA.com*   Phone: (302)227-0500

Motel
$60-$300 3/1-10/1
$40-$200 10/2-2/28

Address: 19540 Hwy 19971 **Location:** SR 1, 1.3 mi s of jct SR 24. **Facility:** 123 units. 98 one- and 2 two-bedroom standard units, some with efficiencies and/or whirlpools. 23 one-bedroom suites. 3-4 stories, interior/exterior corridors. **Parking:** on-site. **Terms:** check-in 4 pm, 2-3 night minimum stay - seasonal and/or weekends. **Amenities:** *Some:* hair dryers. **Pool(s):** outdoor. **Leisure Activities:** picnic benches. **Guest Services:** coin laundry. **Business Services:** meeting rooms, fax (fee). **Cards:** AX, DC, DS, MC, VI. **Free Special Amenities: continental breakfast and room upgrade (subject to availability with advance reservations).**

HAMPTON INN REHOBOTH BEACH/LEWES *Book great rates at AAA.com*   Phone: 302/645-8003

Small-scale Hotel
Rates not provided

Address: 4529 Hwy 1 19971 **Location:** On SR 1, 2 mi n. Located in the outlet mall area. **Facility:** 85 one-bedroom standard units, some with whirlpools. 4 stories, interior corridors. *Bath:* combo or shower only. **Parking:** on-site. **Amenities:** video games (fee), high-speed Internet, voice mail, irons, hair dryers. *Some:* dual phone lines. **Pool(s):** heated indoor. **Leisure Activities:** limited exercise equipment. **Guest Services:** coin laundry, wireless Internet. **Business Services:** meeting rooms, business center.

▼ See AAA listing p 384 ▼

HENLOPEN HOTEL

Small-scale Hotel
$69-$429 4/1-10/31

Phone: (302)227-2551

Address: 511 N Boardwalk 19971 **Location:** 0.5 mi n on 1st St from Rehoboth Ave. **Facility:** 93 units. 87 one-bedroom standard units. 6 one-bedroom suites, some with efficiencies. 8 stories, exterior corridors. **Parking:** on-site. **Terms:** open 4/1-10/31, check-in 4 pm, 2 night minimum stay - weekends, 7 day cancellation notice. **Guest Services:** wireless Internet. **Business Services:** meeting rooms, fax (fee). **Cards:** AX, DS, MC, VI. **Free Special Amenities: continental breakfast.**
(See color ad below)

HOLIDAY INN EXPRESS-REHOBOTH BEACH   *Book at AAA.com*

Small-scale Hotel
$69-$350 All Year

Phone: (302)227-4030

Address: 4289 Hwy 1 19971 **Location:** On SR 1, just n. Located in a commercial area. **Facility:** 81 one-bedroom standard units. 4 stories, interior corridors. *Bath:* combo or shower only. **Parking:** on-site. **Terms:** 2-3 night minimum stay - weekends, 7 day cancellation notice-fee imposed. **Amenities:** voice mail, irons, hair dryers. **Pool(s):** outdoor. **Leisure Activities:** limited exercise equipment. **Guest Services:** coin laundry, wireless Internet. **Business Services:** meeting rooms, PC, fax (fee). **Cards:** AX, CB, DC, DS, JC, MC, VI.

THE OCEANUS MOTEL

Motel
$69-$249 3/14-11/2

Phone: 302/227-8200

Address: 6 2nd St 19971 **Location:** Just s of Rehoboth Ave. **Facility:** 38 one-bedroom standard units. 3 stories (no elevator), exterior corridors. **Parking:** on-site. **Terms:** open 3/14-11/2, 2 night minimum stay - seasonal and/or weekends, 7 day cancellation notice-fee imposed. **Amenities:** irons, hair dryers. **Pool(s):** outdoor. **Guest Services:** coin laundry, wireless Internet. **Cards:** AX, DS, MC, VI. **Free Special Amenities: continental breakfast and high-speed Internet.**

QUALITY INN & SUITES OF REHOBOTH   *Book at AAA.com*

Small-scale Hotel
$79-$349 All Year

Phone: (302)226-2400

Address: 3100 Hwy 1 19971 **Location:** 1 mi s. **Facility:** 70 units. 62 one-bedroom standard units. 8 one-bedroom suites. 4 stories, interior corridors. *Bath:* combo or shower only. **Parking:** on-site. **Terms:** 2-3 night minimum stay - seasonal, cancellation fee imposed. **Amenities:** voice mail, irons, hair dryers. **Pool(s):** heated indoor. **Leisure Activities:** limited exercise equipment. **Guest Services:** coin laundry, wireless Internet. **Business Services:** meeting rooms, business center. **Cards:** AX, DC, DS, MC, VI.

SEA-ESTA IV

Motel
$47-$189 3/1-10/15
$47-$69 10/16-2/28

Phone: (302)227-5882

Address: 3101 Hwy 1 19971 **Location:** 1 mi s. **Facility:** 36 one-bedroom standard units. 3 stories, exterior corridors. **Parking:** on-site. **Terms:** 2 night minimum stay - seasonal and/or weekends. **Amenities:** irons, hair dryers. **Pool(s):** heated outdoor. **Business Services:** fax (fee). **Cards:** AX, CB, DC, DS, MC, VI. **Free Special Amenities:** local telephone calls and newspaper.

SEA WITCH, BEWITCHED & BEDAZZLED

Bed & Breakfast
Rates not provided

Phone: 302/226-9482

Address: 771 Lake Ave 19971 **Location:** Jct Rehoboth Ave, just ne. **Facility:** Just outside of downtown, the B&B offers distinct experiences in each home; hot tubs, an outdoor changing room and a massage parlor are on site. Smoke free premises. 17 one-bedroom standard units, some with whirlpools. 2 stories (no elevator), interior corridors. *Bath:* combo or shower only. **Parking:** on-site. **Terms:** office hours 7 am-9:30 pm, age restrictions may apply. **Amenities:** video library, high-speed Internet, irons, hair dryers. *Some:* DVD players, voice mail. **Leisure Activities:** whirlpools, beach chairs & towels. *Fee:* massage. **Guest Services:** valet laundry, wireless Internet. **Business Services:** meeting rooms, PC, fax (fee). **Free Special Amenities:** full breakfast and high-speed Internet.

——— WHERE TO DINE ———

1776 EASTERN SHORE STEAKHOUSE

Steak & Seafood
$15-$40

Phone: 302/645-9355

Dry-aged steaks are the house specialty, but the extensive seafood offerings shouldn't be overlooked. The shopping plaza restaurant has developed a strong local following. Service is professional and friendly, and the atmosphere is comfortable albeit a little loud. Dressy casual. **Bar:** Full bar. **Reservations:** suggested. **Hours:** 5 pm-10 pm. Closed major holidays. **Address:** 4590 Hwy 1 19971 **Location:** On SR 1, 2.5 mi n; in Midway Shopping Center. **Parking:** on-site. **Cards:** AX, CB, DC, DS, MC, VI.

ABSTRACTIONS SUSHI BAR AND RESTAURANT

Sushi
$19-$34

Phone: 302/226-0877

Just a few blocks from the boardwalk, the cozy restaurant and sushi bar displays a hip interior. For those who can't decide, there are chef's sampler selections of sushi and sashimi. Anyone with an aversion to raw fish will be more than satisfied with one of the cooked entrees, such as Thai curry, sesame-dusted salmon or filet mignon. Also served are varied creative martinis and decadent desserts. Casual dress. **Bar:** Full bar. **Reservations:** suggested. **Hours:** 5 pm-close. Closed major holidays; also Mon. **Address:** 203 Rehoboth Ave 19971 **Location:** Corner of 2nd St and Rehoboth Ave. **Parking:** street. **Cards:** AX, DS, MC, VI.

ADRIATICO RISTORANTE & SEAFOOD CAFE

Italian
$10-$28

Phone: 302/227-9255

In the heart of downtown, the cozy Italian restaurant specializes in veal, seafood, chicken and pasta; seasonal patio dining is available. Casual dress. **Bar:** Full bar. **Reservations:** accepted. **Hours:** Open 4/1-1/31; 4:30 pm-10 pm. Closed: Mon & Tues 9/5-5/28. **Address:** 30 Baltimore 19971 **Location:** Corner of 1st St and Baltimore; center. **Parking:** street. **Cards:** AX, DS, MC, VI.

ADRIATICO RISTORANTE & SEAFOOD CAFE

Italian
$10-$25

Phone: 302/645-6160

Tucked away in this shopping plaza this Italian restaurant offers an upscale, yet relaxed setting, attentive professional service and very good Northern Italian cooking. A couple of Chef DiLeo house specialties include Lobster Fra Diablo and Bone-in Filet Mignon. The menu offers a nice selection of meat, fish and pasta dishes. Limousine service available within 15 miles to/from local hotels. Casual dress. **Bar:** Full bar. **Reservations:** accepted. **Hours:** 4:30 pm-9 pm; to 10 pm 5/29-9/4. Closed: 3/23, 12/25. **Address:** 22 Midway Shopping Center 19971 **Location:** 2.5 mi n on SR 1; in Midway Shopping Center. **Parking:** on-site. **Cards:** AX, DC, DS, MC, VI.

BIG FISH GRILL

Seafood
$10-$30

Phone: 302/227-3474

The main attraction is fresh seafood, which is prepared using original recipes and fresh, homemade ingredients. Beef and pasta dishes appeal to those looking for something different. The casual, loud and comfortable restaurant is popular with locals and tourists alike. In summer, don't be surprised by an hour wait for a table. Casual dress. **Bar:** Full bar. **Reservations:** not accepted. **Hours:** 5 pm-9 pm, Fri 4:30 pm-9:30 pm, Sat 4 pm-9:30 pm, Sun 4 pm-9 pm. Closed: 3/23, 11/27, 12/25. **Address:** 4117 Hwy One 19971 **Location:** Just s. **Parking:** on-site. **Cards:** AX, DS, MC, VI.

BLUE MOON RESTAURANT

American
$26-$50

Phone: 302/227-6515

Less than two blocks from the ocean and inside a striking beach house, this restaurant specializes in modern American cuisine with international influences. The wine selection is impressive. Casual dress. **Bar:** Full bar. **Reservations:** suggested. **Hours:** Open 3/1-1/6 & 2/1-2/28; 6 pm-10 pm, Sun also 10:30 am-2 pm. **Address:** 35 Baltimore Ave 19971 **Location:** Between 1st and 2nd sts. **Parking:** street. **Cards:** AX, CB, DC, DS, MC, VI.

CELSIUS RESTAURANT & TAPAS BAR

Mediterranean
$15-$22

Phone: 302/227-5767

The two chef-owners combine their talents in the delightful Mediterranean restaurant. The fine-dining atmosphere is cozy. A good selection of daily specials complements the seasonally changing menu. The wine list is extensive. Casual dress. **Bar:** Full bar. **Reservations:** accepted. **Hours:** 5 pm-9 pm, Fri-10 pm, Sat-11 pm. Closed: 11/24. **Address:** 50-C Wilmington Ave 19971 **Location:** Jct 2nd St and Wilmington Ave, just e; downtown. **Parking:** street. **Cards:** AX, CB, DC, DS, MC, VI.

CHEZ LA MER RESTAURANT   *Menu on AAA.com*

Continental
$19-$36

Phone: 302/227-6494

Conveniently located just a block from the main street of this beachfront resort community, this charmingly renovated house is marked by a rustic stone fireplace, an open-air rooftop deck, an enclosed sun porch and a country French dining room. Bouillabaisse is one specialty, as are the house pate, mussels and crab imperial. The wine list is extensive. Dressy casual. **Bar:** Full bar. **Reservations:** accepted. **Hours:** Open 4/15-10/15; 5:30 pm-9 pm, Fri & Sat-10 pm. **Address:** 210 2nd St 19971 **Location:** Corner of 2nd St and Wilmington Ave. **Parking:** street. **Cards:** AX, DC, DS, MC, VI.

THE CULTURED PEARL

Phone: 302/227-8493

Asian

$17-$32

Guests can listen to birds chirping as they dine in the Japanese garden setting at a table or the sushi bar. Patio seating under the stars is available, weather permitting. The kitchen is skillful in preparing Japanese, Thai and American dishes. Casual dress. **Bar:** Full bar. **Reservations:** suggested. **Hours:** Open 3/1-12/31 & 2/1-2/28; 5 pm-10 pm; Thurs-Sun to 9 pm 9/7-5/29. Closed: 11/27, 12/25; also Mon-Wed 9/7-5/29. **Address:** 19 Wilmington Ave 19971 **Location:** Just w of the boardwalk. **Parking:** street. **Cards:** DS, MC, VI.

ESPUMA

Phone: 302/227-4199

Mediterranean

$24-$36

The chef/owner prepares sophisticated Mediterranean cuisine with a Spanish influence. The Paella, a traditional Spanish entree, is wonderfully prepared, using an abundance of fresh shell fish. The wine selection is well thought out and compliments the cooking very nicely. The dining room offers a fun, colorful atmosphere, with original artwork displayed. Casual dress. **Bar:** Full bar. **Reservations:** suggested. **Hours:** 6 pm-10 pm. Closed: 12/25. **Address:** 28 Wilmington Ave 19971 **Location:** At 1st St. **Parking:** street. **Cards:** AX, DC, DS, MC, VI.

FUSION

Phone: 302/226-1940

American

$20-$34

Artistically presented, innovative American cuisine with Pan-Asian influences served in simple, but elegantly upscale contemporary atmosphere. Casual dress. **Bar:** Full bar. **Reservations:** suggested. **Hours:** 5:30 pm-close. Closed: 11/27, 12/25; also Sun-Wed 1/2-4/1. **Address:** 50 Wilmington Ave 19971 **Location:** Jct 2nd St and Wilmington Ave, just e; downtown. **Parking:** street. **Cards:** AX, DC, DS, MC, VI.

JAKE'S SEAFOOD HOUSE

Phone: 302/227-6237

Seafood

$5-$30

Located downtown, the casual restaurant offers seafood with an Old Baltimore taste. Casual dress. **Bar:** Full bar. **Reservations:** not accepted. **Hours:** 11:30 am-9 pm, Fri & Sat-10 pm. Closed: 11/27, 12/24, 12/25. **Address:** 29 Baltimore Ave 19971 **Location:** Corner of 1st St and Baltimore; center. **Parking:** on-site and street. **Cards:** AX, DC, DS, MC, VI.

JAKE'S SEAFOOD HOUSE RESTAURANT

Phone: 302/644-7711

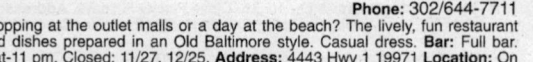

American

$5-$34

Looking for a bite to eat after shopping at the outlet malls or a day at the beach? The lively, fun restaurant offers a nice selection of seafood dishes prepared in an Old Baltimore style. Casual dress. **Bar:** Full bar. **Hours:** 11:30 am-10 pm, Fri & Sat-11 pm. Closed: 11/27, 12/25. **Address:** 4443 Hwy 1 19971 **Location:** On SR 1, 1.5 mi n. **Parking:** on-site. **Cards:** AX, DS, MC, VI.

JUST IN THYME

Phone: 302/227-3100

American

$15-$35

This comfortable, homey atmosphere is suitable for any occasion. Dishes prepared by the chef/owner blend a Continental influence with American style. A notable local favorite is carpetbagger steak, a black Angus filet mignon stuffed with Saga blue cheese and jumbo lump crabmeat. Dressy casual. **Bar:** Full bar. **Reservations:** suggested. **Hours:** 5 pm-10 pm. Closed: 12/25. **Address:** 31 Robinson Dr & Hwy 1 19971 **Location:** 1.1 mi s on SR 1. **Parking:** on-site. **Cards:** AX, CB, DC, DS, MC, VI.

LA LA LAND RESTAURANT & BAR

Phone: 302/227-3887

International

$20-$33

The highest-quality seafood and meats are prepared imaginatively to reflect international influences that draw from Asia, India, France and America. The eclectic, colorfully decorated restaurant is just steps from the boardwalk. Casual dress. **Bar:** Full bar. **Reservations:** suggested. **Hours:** Open 4/15-12/31; 6 pm-11 pm. **Address:** 22 Wilmington Ave 19971 **Location:** Just w of boardwalk. **Parking:** street. **Cards:** AX, DC, DS, MC, VI.

OCEAN POINT GRILL

Phone: 302/227-1127

American

$5-$18

The family restaurant offers a casual setting in which patrons can enjoy the varied menu selections, which range from salads and sandwiches to beef, seafood and pasta dishes. Some breakfast items are served all day. Casual dress. **Reservations:** accepted. **Hours:** 7 am-9 pm; 6:30 am-10 pm 5/29-9/4. Closed: 12/25. **Address:** 17 Market Place 19971 **Location:** 1.4 mi n on SR 1; in Food Lion shopping center. **Parking:** on-site. **Cards:** AX, DS, MC, VI.

RAMS HEAD BEACH HOUSE

Phone: 302/227-0807

International

$14-$34

Less than a block from the boardwalk is the tavern, which dishes up sumptuous fare and frothy beer. This place is part of a collection of eateries and entertainment venues in Maryland and Delaware. For starters, try beer-battered shrimp or steak chili. Entree offerings include something for everyone, including fish tacos, pasta, cioppino, jambalaya, crab cakes, burgers and sandwiches, including one with fried oysters. Casual dress. **Bar:** Full bar. **Reservations:** accepted. **Hours:** 4 pm-1 am, Sat from 11 am, Sun from 10 am; Sunday brunch. **Address:** 15 Wilmington Ave 19971 **Location:** Corner of 1st St and Willington Ave, just e; just w of the boardwalk. **Parking:** on-site (fee). **Cards:** AX, DS, MC, VI.

RISTORANTE ZEBRA

Phone: 302/226-1160

Northern Italian

$16-$36

The restaurant has a strong local following due to its consistent Italian cooking. The skilled kitchen uses only fresh ingredients in preparing its seasonally changing menu, which lists a nice selection of pasta, veal, beef, chicken and seafood dishes. The setting is casually upscale with exotic decor in the three dining rooms; hand-painted walls and artwork reflect the animals of Africa. Patrons may elect to dine inside or on the open porch. Dressy casual. **Bar:** Full bar. **Reservations:** required, weekends in summer. **Hours:** Open 3/28-1/31; 5:30 pm-10 pm. Closed: 12/25; also Mon-Wed 4/27-5/28 & 9/3-1/1. **Address:** 32 Lake Ave 19971 **Location:** Jct Rehoboth Ave, just ne. **Parking:** street. **Cards:** AX, MC, VI.

VICTORIA'S

Phone: 302/227-0615

Continental

$8-$36

Your dining experience begins with an ocean view amid traditional Victorian decor. Attractive presentations and well-prepared dishes are consistent from appetizer to dessert. The outdoor patio is open seasonally. Sunday brunch is available off season. Dressy casual. **Bar:** Full bar. **Reservations:** suggested. **Hours:** 7 am-10 pm, Fri & Sat-11 pm. **Address:** Olive Ave & Boardwalk 19971 **Location:** Just n of Rehoboth Ave; in Boardwalk Plaza Hotel. **Parking:** on-site (fee). **Cards:** AX, CB, DC, DS, MC, VI.

SEAFORD pop. 6,699

———— **WHERE TO STAY** ————

COMFORT SUITES

AAA SAVE

▽▽▽

Small-scale Hotel
$79-$249 All Year

Book great rates at AAA.com   **Phone:** (302)628-5400
Address: 550 N Dual Hwy 19973 **Location:** On SR 13, just n jct SR 20. **Facility:** Smoke free premises. 69 one-bedroom standard units. 4 stories, interior corridors. *Bath:* combo or shower only. **Parking:** on-site. **Amenities:** voice mail, irons, hair dryers. **Pool(s):** heated indoor. **Leisure Activities:** limited exercise equipment. **Guest Services:** coin laundry, wireless Internet. **Business Services:** meeting rooms, administrative services (fee), PC. **Cards:** AX, CB, DC, DS, MC, VI. **Free Special Amenities:** expanded continental breakfast and high-speed Internet.

[icons]

HAMPTON INN SEAFORD

▽▽▽

Small-scale Hotel
$99-$199 All Year

Book great rates at AAA.com   **Phone:** 302/629-4500
Address: 799 N Dual Hwy 19973 **Location:** 1.5 mi n on US 13 from SR 20. Located adjacent to a shopping plaza. **Facility:** 66 one-bedroom standard units. 3 stories, interior corridors. *Bath:* combo or shower only. **Parking:** on-site. **Amenities:** high-speed Internet, dual phone lines, voice mail, irons, hair dryers. **Pool(s):** heated indoor. **Leisure Activities:** wireless Internet. **Guest Services:** valet and coin laundry, wireless Internet. **Business Services:** meeting rooms, business center. **Cards:** AX, DC, DS, MC, VI.

[icons] / SOME UNITS

HOLIDAY INN EXPRESS-SEAFORD

▽▽▽

Small-scale Hotel
$100-$250 All Year

Book at AAA.com   **Phone:** (302)629-2000
Address: 210 N Dual Hwy 19973 **Location:** On US 13, just s of SR 20 W. **Facility:** 81 one-bedroom standard units, some with whirlpools. 4 stories, interior corridors. *Bath:* combo or shower only. **Parking:** on-site. **Amenities:** dual phone lines, voice mail, irons, hair dryers. **Pool(s):** outdoor. **Leisure Activities:** exercise room. **Guest Services:** valet and coin laundry, wireless Internet. **Business Services:** meeting rooms, business center. **Cards:** AX, DS, MC, VI.

[icons] / SOME UNITS

———— **WHERE TO DINE** ————

BON APPETIT RESTAURANT

AAA

▽▽▽

French
$8-$25

Menu on AAA.com   **Phone:** 302/629-3700
The chef-owner changes the intimate downtown restaurant's menu monthly. Comfort characterizes the setting, which includes white tableclothe, candlelit tables and fresh flowers at lunch or dinner. A five-course selection is available. Dressy casual. **Bar:** Full bar. **Reservations:** suggested. **Hours:** noon-2:30 & 5-9 pm, Sat from 5 pm. Closed: 1/1, 11/27, 12/24, 12/25; also Sun, Mon & 6/26-7/7. **Address:** 312 High St 19973 **Location:** 1.2 mi w on Middleford Rd from jct US 13; downtown. **Parking:** street. **Cards:** AX, DC, DS, MC, VI.

SMYRNA pop. 5,679

———— **WHERE TO DINE** ————

THE THOMAS ENGLAND HOUSE RESTAURANT

▽▽▽

Continental
$12-$30

Phone: 302/653-1420
Each of the five casually, elegant dining rooms in this 1711 Greek Colonial mansion is expertly staffed with servers displaying a good knowledge of the Continental menu. Seafood, beef, veal and poultry are mainstays, with the crab imperial a most popular choice. Casual dress. **Bar:** Full bar. **Reservations:** accepted. **Hours:** 4 pm-9 pm, Fri & Sat-10 pm. Closed: Sun 5/1-9/30. **Address:** 1165 S DuPont Hwy 19977 **Location:** Off US 1, exit 114, 1 mi s on US 13. **Parking:** on-site. **Cards:** AX, DS, MC, VI. **Historic**

WILMINGTON pop. 72,664

───── WHERE TO STAY ─────

BEST WESTERN BRANDYWINE VALLEY INN *Book great rates at AAA.com* **Phone:** (302)656-9436

Small-scale Hotel
$99-$117 All Year

Address: 1807 Concord Pike 19803 **Location:** I-95, exit 8, 1 mi n on US 202. Located in a commercial area. **Facility:** 94 units. 92 one-bedroom standard units, some with whirlpools. 2 one-bedroom suites. 2 stories (no elevator), exterior corridors. **Parking:** on-site. **Amenities:** video library, high-speed Internet, voice mail, irons, hair dryers. *Some:* DVD players. **Pool(s):** outdoor. **Leisure Activities:** whirlpool, limited exercise equipment. **Guest Services:** valet laundry, area transportation-within 25 mi, wireless Internet. **Business Services:** meeting rooms, administrative services. **Cards:** AX, CB, DC, DS, JC, MC, VI. **Free Special Amenities: expanded continental breakfast and high-speed Internet.** *(See color ad below)*

AAA Benefit:
Members save 10%
everyday, plus an
exclusive frequent
stay program.

BRANDYWINE SUITES-CLARION COLLECTION *Book great rates at AAA.com* **Phone:** (302)656-9300

Small-scale Hotel
$190-$210 All Year

Address: 707 N King St 19801 **Location:** Between 7th and 8th sts; downtown. **Facility:** 49 one-bedroom suites. 4 stories, interior corridors. **Parking:** on-site (fee). **Amenities:** high-speed Internet, voice mail, irons, hair dryers. **Leisure Activities:** limited exercise equipment. **Guest Services:** valet laundry. **Business Services:** meeting rooms, PC, fax (fee). **Cards:** AX, DC, JC, MC, VI.

───── ▼ See AAA listing above ▼ ─────

BRANDYWINE VALLEY INN'S *GETAWAY PACKAGES*

LONGWOOD, WINTERTHUR & HAGLEY MUSEUM
Deluxe guestroom for 3 days and 2 nights plus 2 general admission tickets to Longwood Gardens, Winterthur & Hagley Museum

$252 per couple

We customize Getaway Packages just for you!

In the heart of the Brandywine Valley just minutes from Longwood Gardens, Winterthur, Hagley, Nemours, Rockwood and Brandywine River (Wyeth) Museums.

For information and reservations call:
1-800-537-7772
www.brandywineinn.com
manager@brandywineinn.com

COURTYARD BY MARRIOTT-DOWNTOWN

Book great rates at AAA.com

Phone: 302/429-7600

Small-scale Hotel
$230-$241 All Year

Address: 1102 West St 19801 **Location:** I-95, exit 7, 0.3 mi e; between 11th and 12th sts; downtown. **Facility:** Smoke free premises. 123 one-bedroom standard units, some with whirlpools. 10 stories, interior corridors. *Bath:* combo or shower only. **Parking:** on-site (fee). **Amenities:** high-speed Internet, dual phone lines, voice mail, irons, hair dryers. **Leisure Activities:** exercise room. **Guest Services:** valet and coin laundry, wireless Internet. **Business Services:** meeting rooms, fax (fee). **Cards:** AX, DC, DS, JC, MC, VI.

AAA Benefit:
Members save 5% off of the best available rate.

COURTYARD BY MARRIOTT WILMINGTON/BRANDYWINE

Book great rates at AAA.com

Phone: 302/477-9500

Small-scale Hotel
$198-$241 All Year

Address: 320 Rocky Run Pkwy 19803 **Location:** I-95, exit 8, 3.8 mi n; just off US 202. Located in a commercial area. **Facility:** Smoke free premises. 78 units. 75 one-bedroom standard units. 3 one-bedroom suites. 3 stories, interior corridors. *Bath:* combo or shower only. **Parking:** on-site. **Amenities:** high-speed Internet, dual phone lines, voice mail, irons, hair dryers. **Pool(s):** heated indoor. **Leisure Activities:** whirlpool, limited exercise equipment. **Guest Services:** valet and coin laundry, wireless Internet. **Business Services:** meeting rooms, administrative services (fee). **Cards:** AX, DC, DS, JC, MC, VI. **Free Special Amenities: full breakfast and high-speed Internet.**

AAA Benefit:
Members save 5% off of the best available rate.

 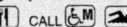

DAYS INN WILMINGTON

Book great rates at AAA.com

Phone: 302/478-0300

Motel
Rates not provided

Address: 5209 Concord Pike 19803 **Location:** I-95, exit 8, 4 mi n on US 202; jct SR 92 (Naamans Rd). **Facility:** 98 one-bedroom standard units. 2 stories (no elevator), exterior corridors. *Bath:* combo or shower only. **Parking:** on-site. **Amenities:** high-speed Internet, voice mail, safes (fee), irons, hair dryers. **Guest Services:** valet and coin laundry, wireless Internet. **Business Services:** PC, fax (fee). **Free Special Amenities: expanded continental breakfast and high-speed Internet.**

DOUBLETREE HOTEL WILMINGTON

Book great rates at AAA.com

Phone: 302/478-6000

Large-scale Hotel
Rates not provided

Address: 4727 Concord Pike, Rt 202 19803 **Location:** I-95, exit 8, 3.8 mi n on US 202. Located adjacent to Concord Shopping Mall. **Facility:** 244 units. 236 one-bedroom standard units. 8 one-bedroom suites. 5-7 stories, interior corridors. *Bath:* combo or shower only. **Parking:** on-site. **Amenities:** dual phone lines, voice mail, irons, hair dryers. *Fee:* video games, high-speed Internet. **Pool(s):** heated indoor. **Leisure Activities:** whirlpool, exercise room. **Guest Services:** valet and coin laundry, area transportation, wireless Internet. **Business Services:** conference facilities, business center.

THE DOUBLETREE HOTEL-WILMINGTON DOWNTOWN

Book great rates at AAA.com

Phone: 302/655-0400

Large-scale Hotel
Rates not provided

Address: 700 N King St 19801 **Location:** King and 7th sts; downtown. **Facility:** 215 units. 211 one-bedroom standard units. 4 one-bedroom suites. 9 stories, interior corridors. *Bath:* combo or shower only. **Parking:** on-site (fee). **Amenities:** voice mail, irons, hair dryers. *Fee:* video games, high-speed Internet. **Pool(s):** heated indoor. **Leisure Activities:** exercise room. **Guest Services:** valet laundry, area transportation. **Business Services:** conference facilities, PC, fax (fee).

▼ *See AAA listing p 373* ▼

HOMEWOOD SUITES BY HILTON BRANDYWINE VALLEY   *Book at AAA.com*

Phone: 302/479-2000

Small-scale Hotel
Rates not provided

Address: 350 Rocky Run Pkwy 19803 **Location:** I-95, exit 8, 3.8 mi n; just off US 202. Located in a commercial area. **Facility:** 113 units. 105 one- and 8 two-bedroom suites with efficiencies. 4 stories, interior corridors. *Bath:* combo or shower only. **Parking:** on-site. **Amenities:** video games (fee), dual phone lines, voice mail, safes, irons, hair dryers. *Some:* DVD players. **Pool(s):** heated outdoor. **Leisure Activities:** hiking trails, jogging, exercise room. **Guest Services:** valet and coin laundry, area transportation, wireless Internet. **Business Services:** meeting rooms, business center.

🍽️✚ CALL 🛅M 🏊 ✗ 🎦 ⬛ 📷 📺 / SOME UNITS ✗ VCR

HOTEL DU PONT   *Book great rates at AAA.com*

Phone: (302)594-3100

Large-scale Hotel
$457-$565 All Year

Address: 1007 Market St 19801 **Location:** I-95, exit 7, 0.5 mi se; downtown at 11th St. **Facility:** Opened in 1918, this luxury hotel has ornately decorated public areas and spacious guest units with plush, upholstered seating. 217 units. 206 one-bedroom standard units, some with whirlpools. 9 one- and 2 two-bedroom suites with whirlpools. 13 stories, interior corridors. **Parking:** on-site (fee) and valet. **Terms:** cancellation fee imposed. **Amenities:** video games (fee), high-speed Internet, dual phone lines, voice mail, safes, honor bars, irons, hair dryers. *Some:* DVD players (fee). **Dining:** 2 restaurants, also, The Green Room, see separate listing. **Leisure Activities:** sauna, exercise room. *Fee:* massage. **Guest Services:** valet laundry, area transportation-within city limits, beauty salon, wireless Internet. **Business Services:** conference facilities, business center. **Cards:** AX, CB, DC, DS, JC, MC, VI. Affiliated with A Preferred Hotel.

FEE ✈ 🍽️ 24 🍸 🏋️ CALL 🛅M ✗ 🎦 📷 / SOME UNITS 🛏️ ✗ VCR 📷

INN AT WILMINGTON   *Book great rates at AAA.com*

Phone: (302)479-7900

Small-scale Hotel
$129-$189 All Year

Address: 300 Rocky Run Pkwy 19803 **Location:** I-95, exit 8, 3.8 mi n; just off US 202. Located in a commercial area. **Facility:** 71 units. 69 one-bedroom standard units. 2 one-bedroom suites. 4 stories, interior corridors. *Bath:* combo or shower only. **Parking:** on-site. **Amenities:** high-speed Internet, voice mail, irons, hair dryers. **Leisure Activities:** limited exercise equipment. **Guest Services:** valet laundry, wireless Internet. **Business Services:** administrative services (fee). **Cards:** AX, DC, DS, MC, VI. **Free Special Amenities:** continental breakfast and high-speed Internet. *(See color ad below)*

S🅳 🍽️✚ CALL 🛅M 🎦 / SOME UNITS ✗ 📷 📷

QUALITY INN & SUITES   *Book great rates at AAA.com*

Phone: (302)478-2222

Small-scale Hotel
$89-$139 All Year

Address: 4000 Concord Pike 19803 **Location:** I-95, exit 8, 3 mi n on US 202. Located in a commercial area. **Facility:** 138 one-bedroom standard units. 2 stories (no elevator), exterior corridors. *Bath:* combo or shower only. **Parking:** on-site. **Amenities:** video games (fee), dual phone lines, voice mail, irons, hair dryers. **Pool(s):** outdoor. **Guest Services:** valet and coin laundry, wireless Internet. **Business Services:** meeting rooms, administrative services, PC. **Cards:** AX, DC, DS, JC, MC, VI. **Free Special Amenities:** continental breakfast and high-speed Internet.

S🅳 🍽️ 🍸 CALL 🛅M 🏊 ♿ 🎦 📷 / SOME UNITS ✗ FEE 📷 FEE 📷

SHERATON SUITES WILMINGTON   *Book great rates at AAA.com*

Phone: (302)654-8300

Large-scale Hotel
$209-$330 All Year

Address: 422 Delaware Ave 19801 **Location:** I-95, exit 7, 0.3 mi e; downtown. **Facility:** 223 one-bedroom suites. 16 stories, interior corridors. **Parking:** on-site (fee). **Amenities:** voice mail, irons, hair dryers. *Fee:* video games, high-speed Internet. *Some:* CD players, dual phone lines, fax. **Pool(s):** heated indoor. **Leisure Activities:** sauna, exercise room. **Guest Services:** valet and coin laundry. **Business Services:** conference facilities, business center. **Cards:** AX, CB, DC, DS, JC, MC, VI. **Free Special Amenities:** newspaper and early check-in/late check-out.

S🅳 🍽️ 🍸 CALL 🛅M 🏊 🎦 📷 📷 📷 / SOME UNITS 🛏️ ✗

S Sheraton
HOTELS & RESORTS

AAA Benefit:
Members get up to 15% off, plus Starwood Preferred Guest® bonuses.

▼ *See AAA listing above* ▼

—— **WHERE TO DINE** ——

821 MARKET STREET BISTRO
Phone: 302/652-8821

American
$8-$29

Innovative American cuisine reflecting Italian and French influences is what diners find at the casually upscale restaurant. The chef uses only the freshest, highest-quality ingredients to prepare delightful creations that change monthly. Four- and six-course chef's tasting menus can be paired with wines. Valet parking is available after 5:30 p.m. Dressy casual. **Bar:** Full bar. **Reservations:** suggested. **Hours:** 11:30 am-2 & 5:30-9 pm, Fri & Sat-10 pm. Closed major holidays; also Sun. **Address:** 821 N Market St 19801 **Location:** Between 8th and 9th sts; downtown; across from Grand Opera House. **Parking:** no self-parking. **Cards:** AX, CB, DC, DS, MC, VI.

CALL ⑤Ⓜ

CAFE MEZZANOTTE
Phone: 302/658-7050

Italian
$8-$39

In the heart of the downtown business district, this Italian restaurant has an upscale, relaxing atmoshpere, as well as a popular Martini bar. The menu offers a nice selection of homemade pasta, meat and seafood dishes. Everything is prepared fresh in the kitchen, sauces, soups, bread and desserts. Dressy casual. **Bar:** Full bar. **Reservations:** required. **Hours:** 11 am-2:30 & 5-10 pm, Sat 4 pm-11 pm, Sun-9 pm. Closed major holidays. **Address:** 1007 Orange St 19801 **Location:** Jct 11th and Tatnall sts. **Parking:** no self-parking. **Cards:** AX, DS, MC, VI.

CALL ⑤Ⓜ

CONLEY WARD'S STEAKHOUSE
Phone: 302/658-6626

Steak & Seafood
$8-$37

Guests can sit on the seasonal outdoor deck to savor great steaks, chops and entrees as attentive servers gladly guide them through their meal. A large wine list complements the menu. Good-size desserts are tasty. Dressy casual. **Bar:** Full bar. **Reservations:** suggested. **Hours:** noon-10 pm, Fri & Sat-11 pm, Sun-9 pm. Closed: 3/23, 11/27, 12/25. **Address:** 110 S West St 19801 **Location:** I-95, exit 6, 0.4 mi s on Jackson St, 0.4 mi e on Martin Luther King Jr Blvd, then just s. **Parking:** on-site. **Cards:** AX, CB, DC, DS, MC, VI.

CALL ⑤Ⓜ

DEEP BLUE BAR & GRILL
Phone: 302/777-2040

Seafood
$8-$28

For diners in the mood for seafood, the contemporary downtown bistro is just the place. The kitchen staff is skilled and innovative, which is evident in the taste of such dishes as seared tuna over wasabi mashed potatoes and truffle-crusted salmon. The raw bar comprises oysters from around the world. Dressy casual. **Bar:** Full bar. **Reservations:** accepted. **Hours:** 11:30 am-3 & 5:30-10 pm, Fri-11 pm, Sat 5 pm-11 pm. Closed major holidays; also Sun. **Address:** 111 W 11th St 19801 **Location:** Jct of 11th and Tatnall sts. **Parking:** on-site (fee). **Cards:** AX, CB, DC, DS, MC, VI.

CALL ⑤Ⓜ

THE GREEN ROOM
Phone: 302/594-3155

Continental
$12-$32

This formal dining room has large windows with ornate draperies overlooking the bustling downtown Wilmington scene. Its beautiful dark wood wall columns and ceiling beams, masterful gold leaf embellishments, massive chandeliers and mezzanine piano balcony offers up a glorious feast for the eyes to match the elegantly presented Continental dishes including seafood, lamb and filet mignon. Dressy casual. **Bar:** Full bar. **Reservations:** suggested. **Hours:** 6:30-11 am, 11:30-2 & 5:30-10:30 pm, Sun 10 am-2 & 5-10:30 pm. **Address:** 1007 Market St 19801 **Location:** I-95, exit 7, 0.5 mi se; downtown at 11th St; in Hotel du Pont. **Parking:** on-site (fee) and valet. **Cards:** AX, CB, DC, DS, JC, MC, VI.

CALL ⑤Ⓜ

HARRY'S SAVOY GRILL & BALLROOM
Phone: 302/475-3000

Steak & Seafood
$8-$35

Casual and fun, the bustling restaurant boasts a menu of such specialties as prime rib, horseradish-crusted salmon and creme brulee. French posters, a vivid mural and cozy fireplaces add to the comfortable feel. Service is swift and friendly. Dressy casual. **Bar:** Full bar. **Reservations:** suggested. **Hours:** 11:30 am-10 pm, Fri-11 pm, Sat 4:30 pm-11 pm, Sun noon-9 pm. Closed: 12/25. **Address:** 2020 Naamans Rd 19810 **Location:** I-95, exit 11, 2.5 mi w on SR 92 (Naamans Rd). **Parking:** on-site. **Cards:** AX, DC, DS, MC, VI.

HARRY'S SEAFOOD GRILL
Phone: 302/777-1500

American
$9-$33

On the riverfront, the restaurant has become a favorite with locals. Innovative American cuisine emphasizes fresh seafood, which is updated daily. The extensive wine selection includes 50 wines by the glass. The atmosphere is fun and the staff friendly and attentive. When the weather is appropriate, the riverside patio is a popular seating option. Dressy casual. **Bar:** Full bar. **Reservations:** suggested. **Hours:** 11 am-3 & 5-10 pm, Fri-11 pm, Sat 11 am-3 & 4:30-11 pm, Sun noon-9 pm. Closed: 11/27, 12/25. **Address:** 101 S Market St 19801 **Location:** I-95, exit 6, 0.7 mi to Riverfront Market. **Parking:** on-site. **Cards:** AX, DC, DS, MC, VI.

CALL ⑤Ⓜ

IRON HILL BREWERY & RESTAURANT

American
$7-$20

Phone: 302/472-2739

Hand-crafted beers made on the premises match with the innovative American cuisine. Along the riverfront, the setting is casual and comfortable. Seasonal outdoor seating is an option. Casual dress. **Bar:** Full bar. **Reservations:** accepted, for lunch and brunch. **Hours:** 11:30 am-close, Sun 11 am-2 & 4-close; Sunday brunch. Closed: 11/27, 12/25; also for dinner 12/24 & for lunch 1/1. **Address:** 710 S Madison St 19810 **Location:** I-95, exit 6, just s; at the riverfront area. **Parking:** on-site. **Cards:** AX, DC, DS, MC, VI.

CALL 🛆M

PAN TAI RESTAURANT

Asian
$5-$19

Phone: 302/652-6633

The menu features selections of Southeast Asian cuisine — Thai, Vietnamese and Indonesian — all served in an intimate atmosphere. A few of the local favorites include hot and sour shrimp soup, pad Thai noodles and the kung pao shrimp. Casual dress. **Bar:** Full bar. **Reservations:** suggested. **Hours:** 11:30 am-2:30 & 5-10 pm, Fri-10:30 pm, Sat 5 pm-10:30 pm. Closed major holidays; also Sun. **Address:** 837 N Union St 19805 **Location:** I-95, exit 7, 0.8 mi n on SR 52, then 0.3 mi w. **Parking:** street. **Cards:** AX, MC, VI.

TOSCANA

Northern Italian
$8-$25

Phone: 302/654-8001

Tuscan cooking is expertly prepared and complemented by an extensive wine selection. The casually upscale cafe is comfortable, and service is friendly and attentive. Patio seating is available when the weather cooperates. Live jazz is featured Wednesday nights. Dressy casual. **Bar:** Full bar. **Hours:** 11:30 am-2 & 5-10 pm, Wed-Fri to 11 pm, Sat 5 pm-11 pm, Sun 5 pm-9 pm. Closed major holidays. **Address:** 1412 N DuPont St 19806 **Location:** I-95, exit 7, just n on SR 52 to Delaware Ave, 0.5 mi n, then just w. **Parking:** on-site. **Cards:** AX, CB, DC, DS, MC, VI.

WALTER'S STEAKHOUSE

Steak House
$20-$32

Phone: 302/652-6780

Aged Certified Angus Beef rules the menu in the cozy atmosphere of the upscale, yet casual, steakhouse. The restaurant also serves veal and lamb, along with two of the most popular seafood-oriented house specials: crab imperial and Norwegian salmon. Casual dress. **Bar:** Full bar. **Reservations:** suggested. **Hours:** 5 pm-11 pm, Sun 4 pm-10 pm. Closed: 1/1, 11/27, 12/25; also 7/3-7/10. **Address:** 802 N Union St 19805 **Location:** I-95, exit 7, 0.8 mi n on SR 52, then just w. **Parking:** on-site. **Cards:** AX, DC, DS, MC, VI.

District of Columbia

Washington Monument
© AAA / Denise E.
Campbell

District of Columbia and Maryland Orientation Map to Destinations

Major destinations are color-coded to index boxes, which display vicinity communities you will find listed within that destination's section of the book.
Cities outside major destination vicinities are listed in alphabetical order throughout the book. Use the Comprehensive City Index at the back of this book to find every city's listing locations.

Destination Washington, D.C.

pop. 572,059

Transformed from a swampy bog along the Potomac River into the capital city of a fledgling nation by Pierre-Charles L'Enfant's visionary planning, Washington, D.C., is the seat of federal government and power.

Movers and shakers reside here. National policy is determined. History is created. Yet amidst the politics and power struggles, everyday life exists as well. Residents and visitors alike enjoy the culture, recreation and shopping that a world-class city provides.

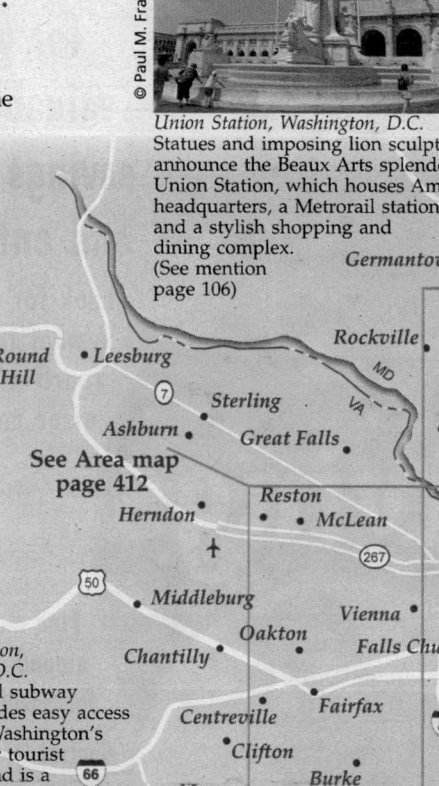

Union Station, Washington, D.C.
Statues and imposing lion sculptures announce the Beaux Arts splendor of Union Station, which houses Amtrak's headquarters, a Metrorail station and a stylish shopping and dining complex.
(See mention page 106)

© Paul M. Franklin

See Area map page 412

Metrorail station, Washington, D.C.
The Metrorail subway system provides easy access to many of Washington's most popular tourist attractions and is a convenient way for visitors to avoid dealing with the city's heavy traffic congestion and notorious lack of public parking spaces.

Washington D.C.
Convention and Tourism
Corp

Places included in this AAA Destination City:

Hirshhorn Museum and Sculpture Garden, Washington, D.C.
More than 60 intriguing figure studies and other sculptural works of art grace the sunken outdoor garden behind the Smithsonian's Hirshhorn Museum. (See listing page 77)

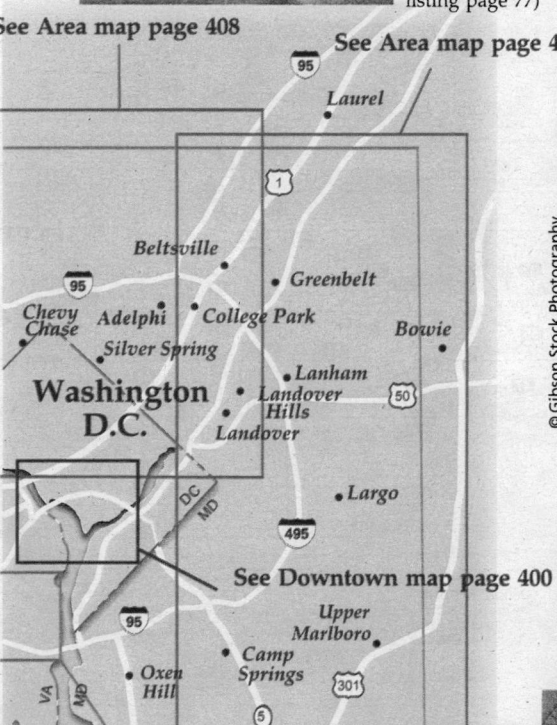

See Area map page 408

See Area map page 428

Laurel

Beltsville

Greenbelt

Chevy Chase
Adelphi
College Park
Silver Spring

Bowie

Washington D.C.

Lanham
Landover Hills
Landover

Largo

See Downtown map page 400

Upper Marlboro

Camp Springs

Oxen Hill

Clinton

See Area map page 426

See Area map page 428

The Shops at Georgetown Park, Washington, D.C.
Four levels of retailers make up this shopping complex in the heart of Georgetown, just a stone's throw from the intersection of M Street and Wisconsin Avenue. (See mention page 107)

Eastern Market, Washington, D.C.
One of the District's few public markets, this Capitol Hill institution offers a seasonal weekend farmers market as well as an indoor market of greengrocers, fishmongers, bakeries and other tempting food stalls.

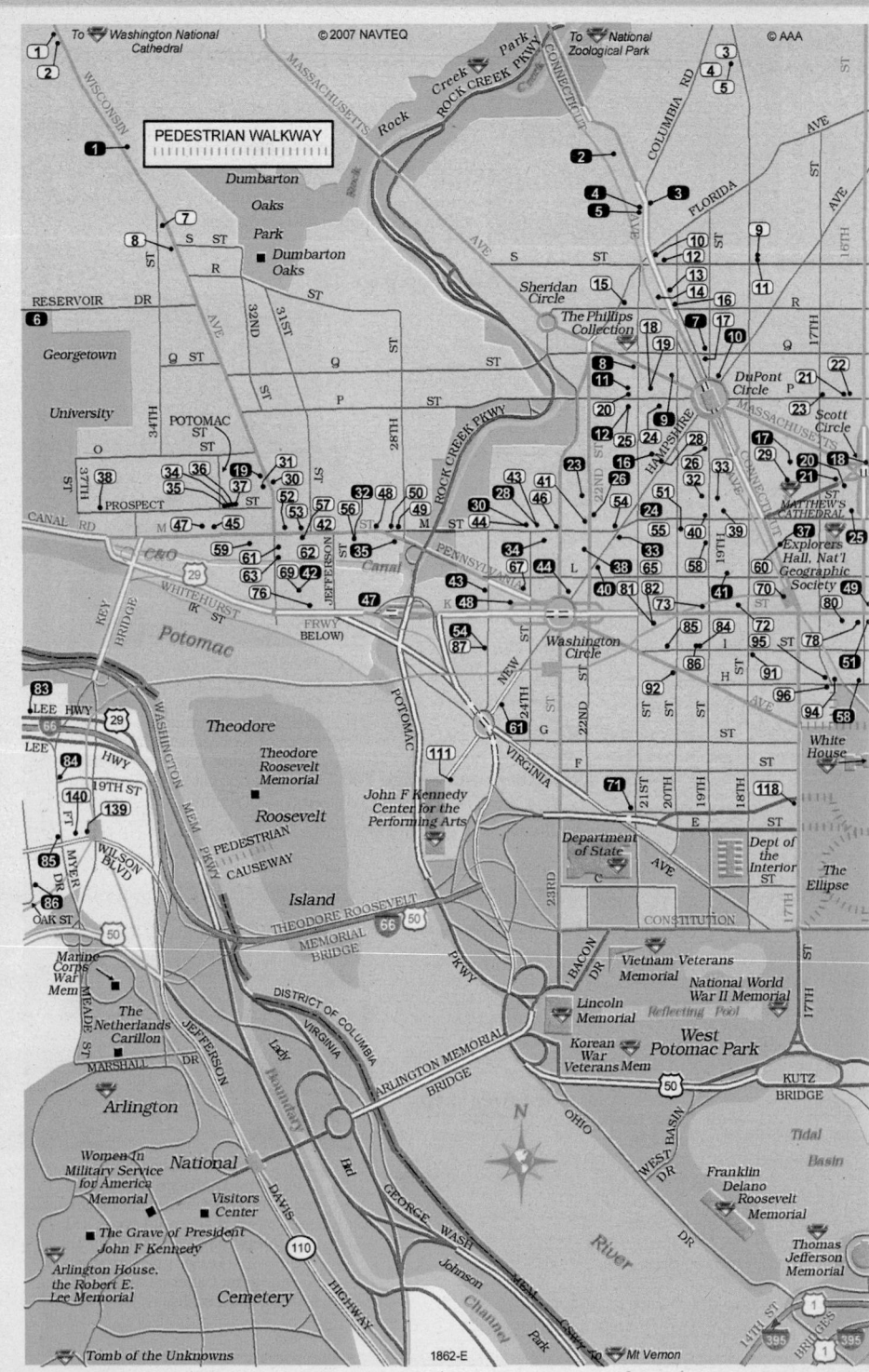

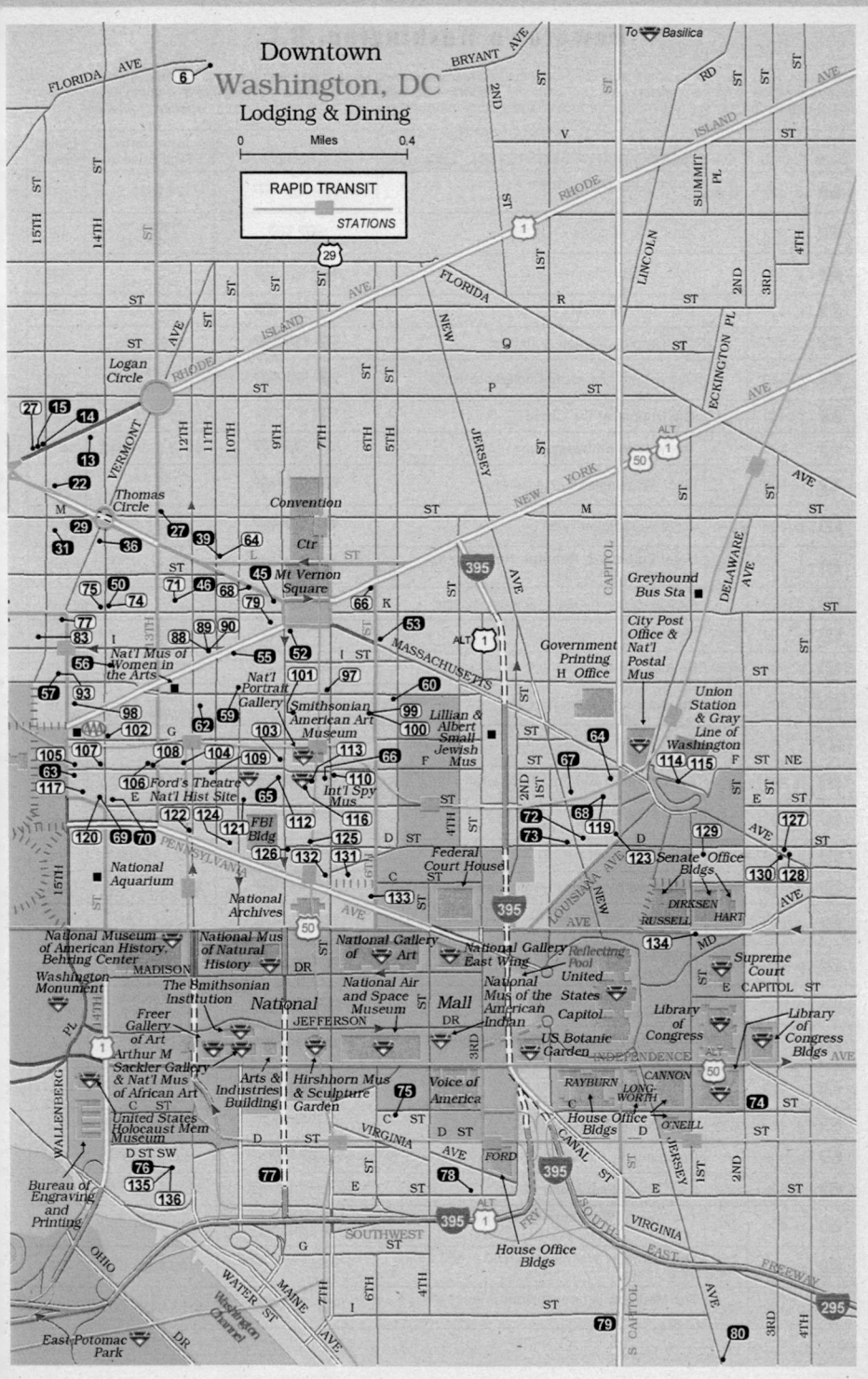

Downtown
Washington, DC
Lodging & Dining

0 — Miles — 0.4

RAPID TRANSIT
STATIONS

Downtown Washington, D.C.

This index helps you "spot" where approved lodgings and restaurants are located on the corresponding detailed maps. Lodging daily rate range is for comparison only and show the property's high season. Restaurant rate range is a combination of lunch and/or dinner. Turn to the listing page for more detailed rate information and consult display ads for special promotions.

Spotter/Map Page Number	OA	DOWNTOWN WASHINGTON - Lodgings	Diamond Rating	Rate Range High Season	Listing Page
1 / p. 400	AAA	Holiday Inn Georgetown - see color ad p 445	◆◆◆	$129-$329 SAVE	444
2 / p. 400		Jurys Normandy Inn	◆◆	Rates not provided	446
3 / p. 400		Hilton Washington	◆◆◆	Rates not provided	442
4 / p. 400		The Churchill Hotel	◆◆◆	$99-$429	434
5 / p. 400		Courtyard by Marriott-Northwest	◆◆◆	$252-$340	438
6 / p. 400		Georgetown University Conference Hotel	◆◆◆	Rates not provided	441
7 / p. 400	AAA	The Dupont at the Circle	◆◆◆	$160-$370 SAVE	439
8 / p. 400	AAA	The Westin Embassy Row	◆◆◆	$219-$759 SAVE	453
9 / p. 400		Hilton Washington Embassy Row	◆◆◆	Rates not provided	443
10 / p. 400		Jurys Washington Hotel	◆◆◆	Rates not provided	447
11 / p. 400	AAA	Hotel Palomar-A Kimpton Hotel - see color ad starting on p 436	◆◆◆	$319-$549 SAVE	446
12 / p. 400		Residence Inn by Marriott-Dupont Circle	◆◆◆	$307-$373	451
13 / p. 400	AAA	Hotel Helix - see color ad starting on p 436	◆◆◆	$139-$389 SAVE	445
14 / p. 400	AAA	Holiday Inn-Central - see color ad p 444	◆◆◆	$129-$259 SAVE	443
15 / p. 400	AAA	DoubleTree Washington, D.C.	◆◆◆	Rates not provided SAVE	439
16 / p. 400	AAA	Hotel Madera - see color ad starting on p 436	◆◆◆	$149-$429 SAVE	445
17 / p. 400	AAA	Topaz Hotel - see color ad starting on p 436	◆◆◆	$139-$409 SAVE	452
18 / p. 400	AAA	Hotel Rouge - see color ad starting on p 436	◆◆◆	$139-$389 SAVE	446
19 / p. 400		The Georgetown Inn	◆◆◆	$129-$409	440
20 / p. 400	AAA	Courtyard by Marriott-Embassy Row	◆◆◆	$307-$362 SAVE	438
21 / p. 400	AAA	Beacon Hotel and Corporate Quarters - see color ad p 434	◆◆◆	$435 SAVE	431
22 / p. 400		Homewood Suites by Hilton Washington DC/Thomas Circle	◆◆◆	Rates not provided	444
23 / p. 400		Embassy Suites Hotel-Washington DC-Downtown	◆◆◆	Rates not provided	439
24 / p. 400	AAA	St. Gregory Luxury Hotel & Suites - see color ad p 434	◆◆◆	$399-$579 SAVE	451
25 / p. 400		The Jefferson	fyi	Rates not provided	446
26 / p. 400	AAA	Washington Marriott Hotel	◆◆◆	$318-$384 SAVE	452
27 / p. 400		Comfort Inn Convention Center	◆◆	$99-$319	434
28 / p. 400	AAA	Park Hyatt Washington, D.C.	◆◆◆◆	$249-$599 SAVE	449
29 / p. 400	AAA	The Westin Washington DC City Center Hotel	◆◆◆	$119-$439 SAVE	454
30 / p. 400	AAA	The Fairmont Washington, D.C. - see color ad p 439	◆◆◆◆	$189-$699 SAVE	439
31 / p. 400	AAA	The Madison, a Loews Hotel - see color ad p 431	◆◆◆	$189-$459 SAVE	447

Spotter/Map Page Number	OA	**DOWNTOWN WASHINGTON - Lodgings (continued)**	Diamond Rating	Rate Range High Season	Listing Page
32 / p. 400	AAA	**Latham Hotel Georgetown**	◇◇◇	$189-$409 SAVE	447
33 / p. 400	AAA	**Renaissance M Street Hotel**	◇◇◇	$373-$417 SAVE	450
34 / p. 400		The Westin Grand	◇◇◇	$189-$569	454
35 / p. 400	AAA	**Four Seasons Hotel Washington D.C.**	◆◆◆◆◆	$725 SAVE	440
36 / p. 400		Residence Inn by Marriott-Washington DC-Vermont Ave	◇◇◇	$307-$373	451
37 / p. 400	AAA	**The Mayflower, A Renaissance Hotel - see color ad p 448**	◇◇◇◇	$428-$483 SAVE	448
38 / p. 400		The Ritz-Carlton, Washington, DC	◆◆◆◆◆	Rates not provided	451
39 / p. 400		Morrison-Clark Historic Inn and Restaurant	◇◇◇	$319-$389	448
40 / p. 400	AAA	**Best Western-Georgetown Hotel & Suites - see color ad p 435**	◇◇	Rates not provided SAVE	433
41 / p. 400		The Quincy - see color ad p 449	◇◇	$139-$289	450
42 / p. 400		The Ritz-Carlton, Georgetown	◆◆◆◆◆	Rates not provided	451
43 / p. 400	AAA	**Washington Suites Georgetown - see color ad p 453**	◇◇◇	$169-$394 SAVE	453
44 / p. 400		One Washington Circle Hotel - see color ad p 449	◇◇◇	Rates not provided	448
45 / p. 400		Henley Park Hotel	◇◇◇	$350-$389	442
46 / p. 400	AAA	**Four Points Sheraton Washington DC Downtown**	◇◇◇	$355 SAVE	440
47 / p. 400		Georgetown Suites	◇◇	$195-$355	441
48 / p. 400	AAA	**The Melrose Hotel, Washington DC**	◇◇◇	$189-$449 SAVE	448
49 / p. 400		Capital Hilton	◆◆◆	Rates not provided	434
50 / p. 400		Hamilton Crowne Plaza Hotel Washington DC - see color ad p 441	◇◇◇	$99-$650	441
51 / p. 400	AAA	**St. Regis, Washington, D.C.**	fyi	$795 SAVE	452
52 / p. 400	AAA	**Renaissance Washington DC Hotel**	◇◇◇	$384-$439 SAVE	450
53 / p. 400		Hampton Inn Washington DC Convention Center	◇◇◇	Rates not provided	442
54 / p. 400		The River Inn	◇◇◇	Rates not provided	451
55 / p. 400		Embassy Suites Washington DC Convention Center	◇◇◇	Rates not provided	439
56 / p. 400		Hilton Garden Inn Washington DC Downtown	◇◇◇	Rates not provided	442
57 / p. 400		Sofitel Lafayette Square Washington DC	◆◆◆◆	Rates not provided	452
58 / p. 400		The Hay-Adams	◇◇◇◇	$800-$6600	442
59 / p. 400	AAA	**Grand Hyatt Washington at Washington Center - see color ad p 440**	◇◇◇	$169-$539 SAVE	441
60 / p. 400		Red Roof Inn Downtown Washington, D.C.	◇◇	Rates not provided	450
61 / p. 400		DoubleTree Guest Suites, Washington DC	◇◇◇	Rates not provided	438
62 / p. 400		Marriott at Metro Center	◇◇◇	$406-$439	447
63 / p. 400		Hotel Washington	◇◇	Rates not provided	446
64 / p. 400	AAA	**Phoenix Park Hotel**	◇◇◇	$159-$479 SAVE	449
65 / p. 400		Courtyard by Marriott-Convention Center	◇◇◇	$318-$395	438

Spotter/Map Page Number	OA	**DOWNTOWN WASHINGTON - Lodgings (continued)**	Diamond Rating	Rate Range High Season	Listing Page
66 / p. 400	AAA	**Hotel Monaco Washington DC -** see color ad starting on p 436	◈ ◈ ◈ ◈	$169-$1200 SAVE	446
67 / p. 400		The Washington Court Hotel	◈ ◈ ◈	Rates not provided	452
68 / p. 400	AAA	**The Hotel George -** see color ad starting on p 436	◈ ◈ ◈	$169-$529 SAVE	445
69 / p. 400		The Willard InterContinental	◈ ◈ ◈ ◈	$299-$879	454
70 / p. 400		JW Marriott Pennsylvania Ave	◈ ◈ ◈	$439-$494	447
71 / p. 400		State Plaza Hotel	◈ ◈	Rates not provided	452
72 / p. 400		Holiday Inn Washington DC on The Hill (Now Known as Affinia-Washington D.C.)	◈ ◈ ◈	Rates not provided	444
73 / p. 400	AAA	**Hyatt Regency Washington On Capitol Hill -** see color ad p 440	◈ ◈ ◈	$109-$499 SAVE	446
74 / p. 400	AAA	**Capitol Hill Suites**	◈ ◈	$365-$449 SAVE	434
75 / p. 400	AAA	**Holiday Inn Capitol -** see color ad p 443	◈ ◈ ◈	$149-$399 SAVE	443
76 / p. 400		Mandarin Oriental, Washington D.C.	◈ ◈ ◈ ◈	$495-$8000	447
77 / p. 400		L'Enfant Plaza Hotel	◈ ◈ ◈	$109-$409	447
78 / p. 400		Residence Inn by Marriott Capitol	◈ ◈ ◈	$285-$362	450
79 / p. 400	AAA	**Best Western Capitol Skyline -** see color ad p 433	◈ ◈	$109-$269 SAVE	432
80 / p. 400		Courtyard by Marriott Capitol Hill/Navy Yard	◈ ◈ ◈	$285-$318	438
		DOWNTOWN WASHINGTON - Restaurants			
1 / p. 400	AAA	**Old Europe**	◈ ◈	$8-$23	466
2 / p. 400		Heritage India	◈ ◈ ◈	$7-$28	461
3 / p. 400		Leftbank	◈ ◈	$10-$19	463
4 / p. 400	AAA	**The Grill from Ipanema**	◈ ◈	$13-$22	461
5 / p. 400		Felix Restaurant and The Spy Lounge	◈ ◈	$14-$24	460
6 / p. 400		Florida Avenue Grill	◈	$5-$14	460
7 / p. 400		Cafe Divan	◈ ◈	$7-$20	457
8 / p. 400		Bistrot Lepic and Wine Bar	◈ ◈ ◈	$14-$25	456
9 / p. 400		Lauriol Plaza	◈ ◈	$8-$17	462
10 / p. 400		Ruth's Chris Steak House	◈ ◈ ◈	$19-$37	468
11 / p. 400		Rosemary's Thyme Bistro	◈ ◈	$7-$24	467
12 / p. 400	AAA	**Thaiphoon**	◈ ◈	$6-$15	469
13 / p. 400		Anna Maria's Restaurant	◈ ◈	$7-$29	455
14 / p. 400		Bistrot du Coin	◈ ◈	$10-$21	456
15 / p. 400		Nora	◈ ◈ ◈	$24-$68	465
16 / p. 400		La Tomate	◈ ◈	$11-$24	462
17 / p. 400		Raku-An Asian Diner	◈ ◈	$9-$14	467
18 / p. 400		Obelisk	◈ ◈ ◈	$65-$65	465
19 / p. 400		Pizzeria Paradiso	◈	$8-$17	467
20 / p. 400		Urbana	◈ ◈ ◈	$7-$34	469
21 / p. 400		Skewers	◈ ◈	$8-$20	468
22 / p. 400		BUA	◈ ◈	$7-$13	457

Spotter/Map Page Number	OA	**DOWNTOWN WASHINGTON - Restaurants (continued)**	Diamond Rating	Rate Range High Season	Listing Page
(23) / p. 400		Sushi Taro	◆◆	$8-$40	468
(24) / p. 400		Pesce Bistro	◆◆	$8-$31	466
(25) / p. 400		Mimi's American Bistro	◆◆	$12-$27	464
(26) / p. 400		Levante's	◆◆	$8-$25	463
(27) / p. 400		15 ria	◆◆◆	$7-$23	455
(28) / p. 400	AAA	**Firefly**	◆◆◆	$12-$26	460
(29) / p. 400		Iron Gate Restaurant	◆◆	$13-$33	461
(30) / p. 400		Paolo's Ristorante	◆◆	$8-$28	466
(31) / p. 400		Neyla-A Mediterranean Grill	◆◆◆	$16-$40	465
(32) / p. 400	AAA	**I Ricchi**	◆◆◆	$12-$31	461
(33) / p. 400		Palm Restaurant	◆◆◆	$13-$52	466
(34) / p. 400		Cafe Milano	◆◆◆	$9-$39	458
(35) / p. 400		Peacock Cafe	◆◆	$8-$39	466
(36) / p. 400		Bangkok Bistro	◆◆	$8-$19	456
(37) / p. 400		Morton's Steakhouse	◆◆◆	$25-$44	465
(38) / p. 400		1789 Restaurant	◆◆◆	$18-$38	455
(39) / p. 400		Penang	◆◆	$9-$22	466
(40) / p. 400		Sam & Harry's	◆◆◆	$34-$52	468
(41) / p. 400		Asia Nora	◆◆◆	$22-$28	456
(42) / p. 400		Miss Saigon	◆◆	$7-$30	464
(43) / p. 400		Blue Duck Tavern	◆◆◆	$14-$35	456
(44) / p. 400		Juniper	◆◆◆	$16-$35	462
(45) / p. 400		Fettoosh	◆◆	$10-$19	460
(46) / p. 400		Thai Kitchen	◆◆	$7-$18	469
(47) / p. 400		Aditi Indian Cuisine	◆◆	$8-$16	455
(48) / p. 400		Mendocino Grille & Wine Bar	◆◆◆	$19-$40	464
(49) / p. 400		Zed's Ethiopian Cuisine	◆◆	$7-$20	470
(50) / p. 400		La Chaumiere	◆◆◆	$13-$32	462
(51) / p. 400		Vidalia	◆◆◆	$16-$40	469
(52) / p. 400		Old Glory, All American Bar-B-Que	◆	$9-$25	466
(53) / p. 400		Mie N Yu	◆◆◆	$9-$48	464
(54) / p. 400		Meiwah Restaurant	◆◆	$10-$24	464
(55) / p. 400		David Greggory Restau Lounge	◆◆◆	$11-$29	459
(56) / p. 400		Michel Richard Citronelle	◆◆◆◆	$95-$155	464
(57) / p. 400	AAA	**Bistro Francais**	◆◆	$8-$25	456
(58) / p. 400		Famous Luigi's	◆◆	$8-$18	460
(59) / p. 400		Clyde's of Georgetown	◆◆	$8-$23	459
(60) / p. 400		Cafe Promenade	◆◆◆	$12-$30	458
(61) / p. 400		Filomena Ristorante	◆◆◆	$8-$40	460
(62) / p. 400		Sea Catch Restaurant	◆◆◆	$14-$49	468
(63) / p. 400		Ching Ching CHA	◆	$5-$12	459

Spotter/Map Page Number	OA	DOWNTOWN WASHINGTON - Restaurants (continued)	Diamond Rating	Rate Range High Season	Listing Page
64 / p. 400		Morrison-Clark Restaurant	◆◆◆	$24-$36	465
65 / p. 400		Galileo	◆◆◆	$14-$40	460
66 / p. 400		Marrakesh	◆◆	$30-$30	463
67 / p. 400		Marcel's	◆◆◆◆	$29-$42	463
68 / p. 400		Coeur de Lion	◆◆◆	$10-$36	459
69 / p. 400		Fahrenheit	◆◆◆◆	$15-$38	460
70 / p. 400		Morton's The Steakhouse	◆◆◆	$13-$42	465
71 / p. 400		Corduroy	◆◆◆	$10-$32	459
72 / p. 400		Restaurant Kolumbia	◆◆◆	$15-$35	467
73 / p. 400		Teatro Goldoni	◆◆◆	$13-$44	468
74 / p. 400		14K	◆◆	$8-$36	455
75 / p. 400		DC Coast	◆◆◆	$13-$30	459
76 / p. 400		Tony & Joe's Seafood Place	◆◆	$9-$36	469
77 / p. 400		Gerard's Place	◆◆◆◆	$23-$37	461
78 / p. 400		Olives	◆◆◆	$14-$41	466
79 / p. 400		Acadiana	◆◆◆	$14-$29	455
80 / p. 400		McCormick & Schmick's Seafood Restaurant	◆◆◆	$12-$36	464
81 / p. 400		The Prime Rib	◆◆◆	$12-$44	467
82 / p. 400		Bombay Palace Restaurant	◆◆◆	$13-$25	456
83 / p. 400		Georgia Brown's	◆◆◆	$15-$32	461
84 / p. 400		Kaz Sushi Bistro	◆◆	$6-$27	462
85 / p. 400		Primi Piatti	◆◆	$13-$34	467
86 / p. 400		Aroma Indian Restaurant	◆◆	$10-$18	456
87 / p. 400	AAA	**Dish**	◆◆◆	$7-$30	459
88 / p. 400		Luigino	◆◆	$9-$29	463
89 / p. 400		Haad Thai	◆◆	$8-$17	461
90 / p. 400		Sushi Aoi	◆	$7-$25	468
91 / p. 400		Taberna Del Alabardero	◆◆◆	$20-$45	468
92 / p. 400		Kinkead's Restaurant	◆◆◆	$16-$37	462
93 / p. 400		Cafe 15	◆◆◆	$15-$32	457
94 / p. 400		The Bombay Club	◆◆◆	$13-$24	456
95 / p. 400		Equinox	◆◆◆	$18-$36	460
96 / p. 400		The Oval Room	◆◆◆	$12-$32	466
97 / p. 400		Capital Q	◆	$8-$15	458
98 / p. 400		Bobby Van's Steakhouse	◆◆◆	$11-$35	456
99 / p. 400		Kanlaya Thai Cuisine	◆◆	$8-$16	462
100 / p. 400		Burma	◆	$7-$11	457
101 / p. 400		Zaytinya	◆◆◆	$5-$27	470
102 / p. 400		CEIBA	◆◆◆	$13-$29	458
103 / p. 400		McCormick & Schmick's Seafood Restaurant	◆◆◆	$12-$36	463
104 / p. 400	AAA	**The Oceanaire Seafood Room**	◆◆◆	$12-$35	465

Spotter/Map Page Number	OA	DOWNTOWN WASHINGTON - Restaurants (continued)	Diamond Rating	Rate Range High Season	Listing Page
(105) / p. 400		Old Ebbitt Grill	◈◈	$11-$26	465
(106) / p. 400		Finemondo Italian Country Kitchen	◈◈◈	$12-$34	460
(107) / p. 400		Butterfield 9	◈◈◈	$10-$36	457
(108) / p. 400		M & S Grill	◈◈◈	$8-$37	463
(109) / p. 400		Tosca	◈◈◈	$15-$40	469
(110) / p. 400		Rosa Mexicano	◈◈	$10-$24	467
(111) / p. 400		Roof Terrace Restaurant & Bar at The Kennedy Center	◈◈	$27-$34	467
(112) / p. 400		Gordon Biersch Brewery Restaurant	◈◈	$7-$26	461
(113) / p. 400		Zola	◈◈◈	$10-$29	470
(114) / p. 400		B. Smiths Restaurant	◈◈◈	$12-$30	457
(115) / p. 400		America	◈◈	$8-$20	455
(116) / p. 400	⏣	**Poste—Moderne Brasserie**	◈◈◈	$10-$28	467
(117) / p. 400		Occidental Restaurant	◈◈◈	$16-$39	465
(118) / p. 400		Cafe des Artistes	◈◈	$10-$15	457
(119) / p. 400		Bistro Bis	◈◈◈	$14-$32	456
(120) / p. 400		The Willard Room	◈◈◈◈	$23-$37	469
(121) / p. 400		Hard Rock Cafe	◈◈	$7-$25	461
(122) / p. 400		Les Halles	◈◈	$13-$26	463
(123) / p. 400		Johnny's Half Shell	◈◈◈	$10-$28	462
(124) / p. 400		TenPenh Restaurant	◈◈◈	$13-$36	468
(125) / p. 400		Cafe Atlantico	◈◈◈	$10-$28	457
(126) / p. 400		The Caucus Room	◈◈◈	$15-$35	458
(127) / p. 400		Two Quail	◈◈	$7-$28	469
(128) / p. 400		Cafe Berlin	◈◈	$7-$22	457
(129) / p. 400	⏣	**The Monocle on Capitol Hill**	◈◈	$10-$35	464
(130) / p. 400		The White Tiger	◈◈	$9-$25	469
(131) / p. 400		Le Paradou	◈◈◈	$28-$60	463
(132) / p. 400		701 Pennsylvania Avenue	◈◈◈	$12-$33	455
(133) / p. 400		The Capital Grille	◈◈◈	$8-$36	458
(134) / p. 400		Charlie Palmer Steak	◈◈◈	$18-$40	458
(135) / p. 400		Cafe MoZu	◈◈◈	$14-$35	458
(136) / p. 400	⏣	**CityZen**	◈◈◈◈◈	$80-$105	459
		ARLINGTON - Lodgings			
(83) / p. 400	⏣	**Key Bridge Marriott Hotel**	◈◈◈	Rates not provided (SAVE)	515
(84) / p. 400		Holiday Inn Rosslyn	◈◈	$99-$189	514
(85) / p. 400	⏣	**Hyatt Arlington at Key Bridge**	◈◈◈	$126-$398 (SAVE)	515
(86) / p. 400		Residence Inn by Marriott Arlington At Rosslyn	◈◈◈	$296-$362	515
		ARLINGTON - Restaurants			
(139) / p. 400	⏣	**Tom Sarris' Orleans House**	◈◈	$7-$23	522
(140) / p. 400		Tivoli Restaurant	◈◈◈	$11-$33	522

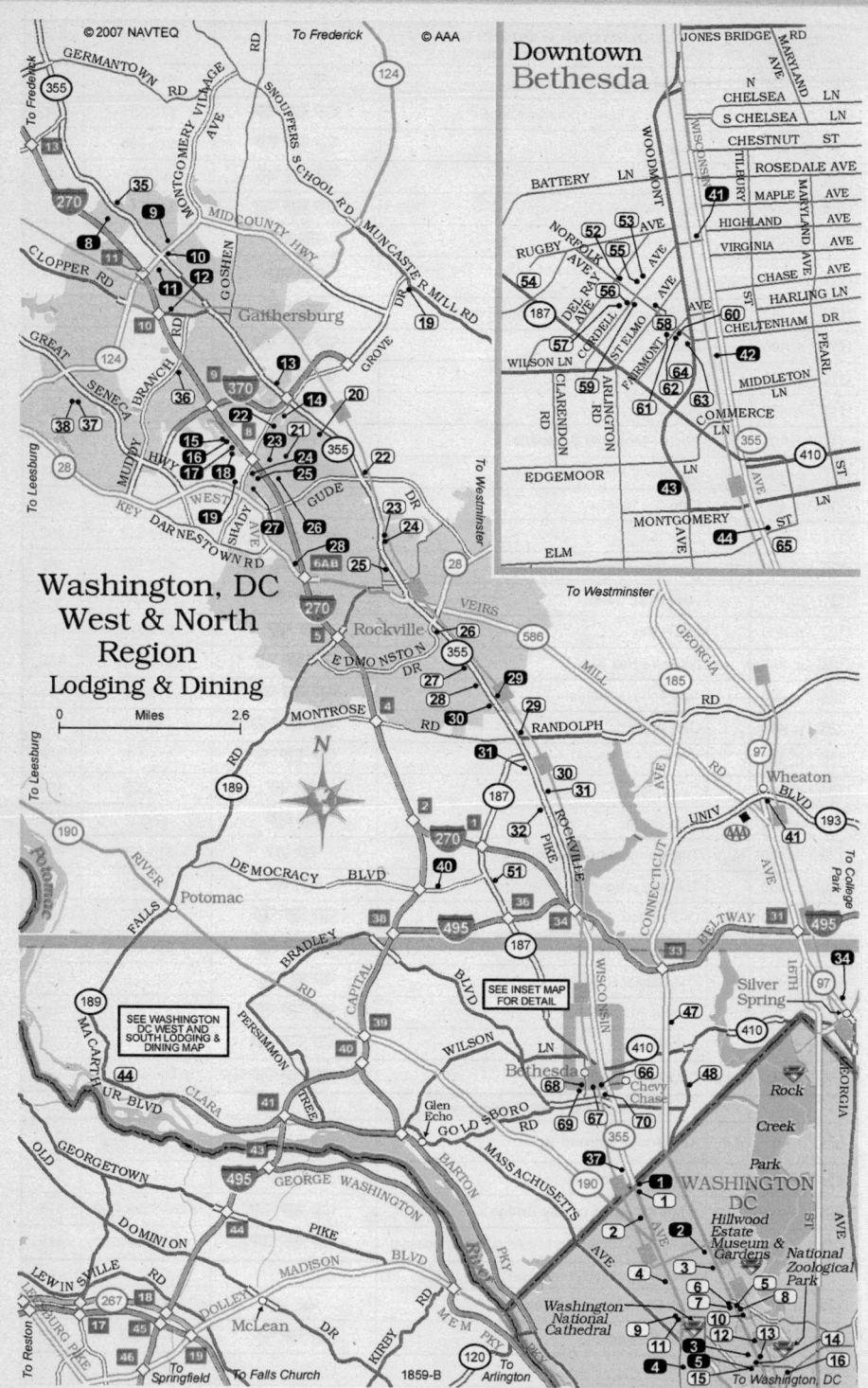

© 2007 NAVTEQ To Frederick © AAA

Downtown Bethesda

Washington, DC West & North Region
Lodging & Dining

0 Miles 2.6

SEE WASHINGTON DC WEST AND SOUTH LODGING & DINING MAP

SEE INSET MAP FOR DETAIL

WASHINGTON DC

Hillwood Estate Museum & Gardens

National Zoological Park

Washington National Cathedral

Rock Creek Park

1859-B

Washington, D.C. West & North Region

This index helps you "spot" where approved lodgings and restaurants are located on the corresponding detailed maps. Lodging daily rate range is for comparison only and show the property's high season. Restaurant rate range is a combination of lunch and/or dinner. Turn to the listing page for more detailed rate information and consult display ads for special promotions.

Spotter/Map Page Number	OA	WASHINGTON (WEST AND NORTH REGION) - Lodgings	Diamond Rating	Rate Range High Season	Listing Page
1 / p. 408	◬◬◬	Embassy Suites Hotel at The Chevy Chase Pavilion	▽▽▽	Rates not provided SAVE	470
2 / p. 408	◬◬	Connecticut Ave Days Inn - see color ad p 471	▽▽	$152-$169 SAVE	470
3 / p. 408		Marriott Wardman Park Hotel	▽▽▽	Rates not provided	472
4 / p. 408		The Savoy Suites Hotel	▽▽	$169-$429	472
5 / p. 408	◬◬◬	Omni Shoreham Hotel	▽▽▽▽	$199-$529 SAVE	472
		WASHINGTON (WEST AND NORTH REGION) - Restaurants			
1 / p. 408		Maggiano's Little Italy	▽▽▽	$7-$37	473
2 / p. 408		Matisse	▽▽▽	$11-$50	473
3 / p. 408		Charlie Chiang's Restaurant	▽▽	$7-$20	473
4 / p. 408		Cafe' Ole'	▽	$5-$8	472
5 / p. 408		Palena	▽▽▽	$57-$75	473
6 / p. 408		Yenching Palace	▽▽	$6-$27	474
7 / p. 408		Nam-Viet Pho-79	▽	$7-$18	473
8 / p. 408		Lavandou	▽▽	$10-$24	473
9 / p. 408		2 Amy's	▽	$8-$13	472
10 / p. 408		Ardeo Restaurant	▽▽▽	$8-$23	472
11 / p. 408		Cactus Cantina	▽▽	$8-$17	472
12 / p. 408		Pesto Ristorante	▽▽	$11-$20	474
13 / p. 408		Petits Plats	▽▽	$16-$28	474
14 / p. 408		New Heights	▽▽▽	$17-$30	473
15 / p. 408		Robert's Restaurant	▽▽▽	$8-$32	474
16 / p. 408		Cashion's Eat Place	▽▽▽	$19-$30	473
		GAITHERSBURG - Lodgings			
8 / p. 408		Extended Stay Deluxe-Washington, DC-Gaithersburg	▽▽	$119-$129	482
9 / p. 408		Courtyard by Marriott-Gaithersburg/Lake Forest	▽▽▽	$208-$241	482
10 / p. 408	◬◬◬	Holiday Inn-Gaithersburg - see color ad p. 483	▽▽▽	$180-$219 SAVE	483
11 / p. 408	◬◬◬	Hilton Washington DC North/Gaithersburg	▽▽▽	Rates not provided SAVE	483
12 / p. 408		TownePlace Suites by Marriott-Gaithersburg	▽▽▽	$89-$239	484
13 / p. 408	◬◬◬	Hyatt Summerfield Suites-Gaithersburg	▽▽▽	$119-$399 SAVE	484
14 / p. 408	◬◬◬	Comfort Inn Shady Grove	▽▽▽	$69-$149 SAVE	482
15 / p. 408		Courtyard By Marriott Gaithersburg Washingtonian Center	▽▽▽	$241-$285	482
16 / p. 408		Gaithersburg Marriott Washingtonian Center	▽▽▽	Rates not provided	482
17 / p. 408		Residence Inn by Marriott-Gaithersburg	▽▽▽	$227-$277	484

Spotter/Map Page Number	OA	GAITHERSBURG - Lodgings (continued)	Diamond Rating	Rate Range High Season	Listing Page
⑱ / p. 408	◬	Gaithersburg SpringHill Suites by Marriott	◊◊◊	Rates not provided [SAVE]	483
⑲ / p. 408		Homestead Studio Suites Hotel-Gaithersburg/Rockville	◊◊	$119-$129	483
		GAITHERSBURG - Restaurants			
㉟ / p. 408		Flaming Pit	◊◊	$6-$37	484
㊱ / p. 408		Il Porto Restaurant	◊◊	$8-$17	485
㊲ / p. 408		Mediterranean Grill	◊◊	$5-$23	485
㊳ / p. 408		HaKuBa Japanese Cuisine	◊◊	$6-$23	485
		ROCKVILLE - Lodgings			
㉒ / p. 408		Red Roof Inn-Rockville	◊◊	Rates not provided	494
㉓ / p. 408		Sheraton Rockville	◊◊◊	Rates not provided	495
㉔ / p. 408	◬	Crowne Plaza Washington DC-Rockville - see color ad p 431, p 432	◊◊◊	$99-$289 [SAVE]	494
㉕ / p. 408	◬	Sleep Inn-Rockville - see color ad p 431, p 432	◊◊	$89-$149 [SAVE]	495
㉖ / p. 408	◬	Woodfin Suites Hotel	◊◊◊	$159 [SAVE]	495
㉗ / p. 408	◬	Courtyard by Marriott-Rockville	◊◊◊	Rates not provided [SAVE]	494
㉘ / p. 408	◬	Best Western Washington Gateway Hotel & Suites - see color ad p 493	◊◊◊	$90-$170 [SAVE]	493
㉙ / p. 408	◬	Hilton Hotel & Executive Meeting Center Rockville	◊◊◊	Rates not provided [SAVE]	494
㉚ / p. 408	◬	Legacy Hotel - see color ad p 494	◊◊	$314-$349 [SAVE]	494
㉛ / p. 408		Bethesda North Marriott Hotel & Conference Center	◊◊◊	Rates not provided	493
		ROCKVILLE - Restaurants			
⑲ / p. 408		Ceviche House Restaurant	◊◊	$9-$18	495
⑳ / p. 408		Nick's Chophouse	◊◊◊	$8-$40	496
㉑ / p. 408		Thai Farm Restaurant	◊◊	$6-$16	497
㉒ / p. 408		Il Pizzico Ristorante	◊◊◊	$10-$26	496
㉓ / p. 408		Caribbean Feast	◊	$4-$13	495
㉔ / p. 408	◬	Cuban Corner Restaurant	◊	$9-$15	496
㉕ / p. 408		Taste of Saigon	◊◊	$6-$24	496
㉖ / p. 408		Benjarong Thai Restaurant	◊◊	$7-$22	495
㉗ / p. 408		A & J Restaurant	◊	$8-$14	495
㉘ / p. 408		Mykonos Grill	◊◊	$8-$25	496
㉙ / p. 408		Timpano Italian Chophouse	◊◊	$10-$36	497
㉚ / p. 408		Il Pinito Trattoria	◊◊	$7-$20	496
㉛ / p. 408		Dave and Busters	◊◊	$8-$19	496
㉜ / p. 408		Addie's	◊◊◊	$7-$27	495

Spotter/Map Page Number	OA	SILVER SPRING - Lodgings	Diamond Rating	Rate Range High Season	Listing Page
34 / p. 408	◆◆◆	**Crowne Plaza Washington, D.C.-Silver Springs**	◆◆◆	$129-$299 SAVE	497
		CHEVY CHASE - Lodgings			
37 / p. 408		Holiday Inn-Washington/Chevy Chase	◆◆◆	Rates not provided	480
		CHEVY CHASE - Restaurants			
47 / p. 408		Tavira	◆◆◆	$7-$25	480
48 / p. 408	◆◆◆	**La Ferme Restaurant**	◆◆◆	$12-$37	480
		BETHESDA - Lodgings			
40 / p. 408		Marriott Suites Bethesda	◆◆◆	Rates not provided	476
41 / p. 408		DoubleTree Hotel Bethesda	◆◆◆	Rates not provided	476
42 / p. 408		Golden Tulip Bethesda Court Hotel	◆◆	$109-$195	476
43 / p. 408	◆◆◆	**Hyatt Regency Bethesda**	◆◆◆	$144-$462 SAVE	476
44 / p. 408		Residence Inn by Marriott-Bethesda Downtown	◆◆◆	Rates not provided	477
		BETHESDA - Restaurants			
51 / p. 408		Jean-Michel Restaurant	◆◆◆	$11-$28	477
52 / p. 408		Bacchus Restaurant	◆◆	$8-$17	477
53 / p. 408		Grapeseed-American Bistro & Wine Bar	◆◆◆	$20-$30	477
54 / p. 408		Le Vieux Logis	◆◆◆	$24-$33	478
55 / p. 408		Cesco Trattoria	◆◆◆	$9-$30	477
56 / p. 408		Passage to India	◆◆◆	$7-$26	478
57 / p. 408	◆◆◆	**Tragara**	◆◆◆	$10-$32	478
58 / p. 408		La Miche	◆◆◆	$20-$33	478
59 / p. 408		Matuba Japanese Restaurant	◆	$6-$20	478
60 / p. 408		Haandi	◆◆	$5-$20	477
61 / p. 408		Rio Grande Cafe	◆◆	$5-$19	478
62 / p. 408		Sweet Basil	◆◆	$9-$22	478
63 / p. 408		Foong Lin Restaurant	◆◆	$5-$16	477
64 / p. 408		Black's Bar & Kitchen	◆◆◆	$7-$27	477
65 / p. 408		Ruth's Chris Steak House	◆◆◆	$18-$36	478
66 / p. 408		Thyme Square Cafe	◆◆	$8-$23	478
67 / p. 408		Cameron's Seafood Market	◆	$6-$14	477
68 / p. 408		Penang	◆	$6-$20	478
69 / p. 408		Bethesda Crab House	◆	$20-$25	477
70 / p. 408		Persimmon	◆◆◆	$8-$27	478
		WHEATON - Restaurant			
41 / p. 408		Dusit Thai Cuisine	◆	$8-$12	499
		POTOMAC - Restaurant			
44 / p. 408		Old Anglers Inn	◆◆◆	$15-$45	492

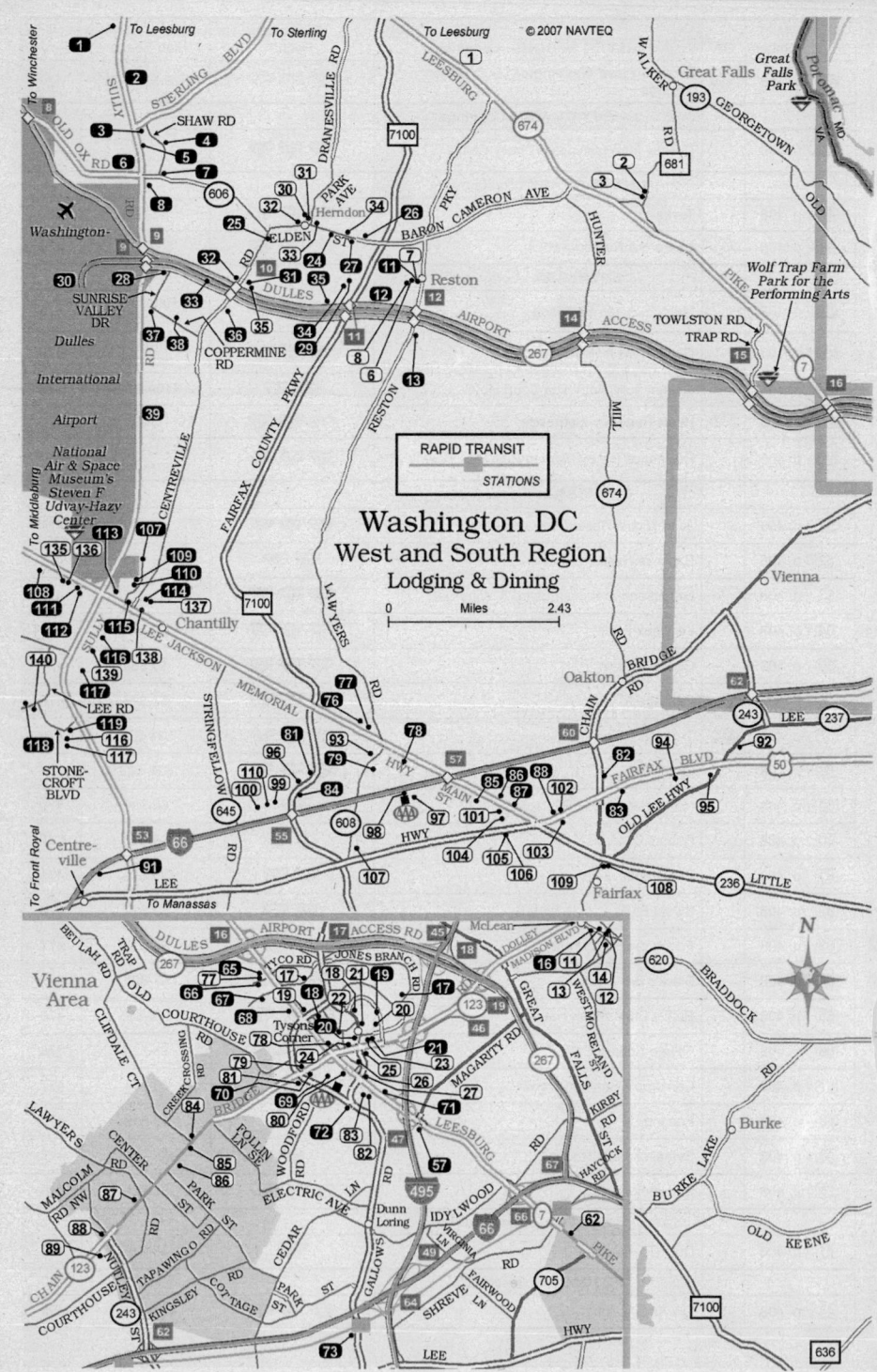

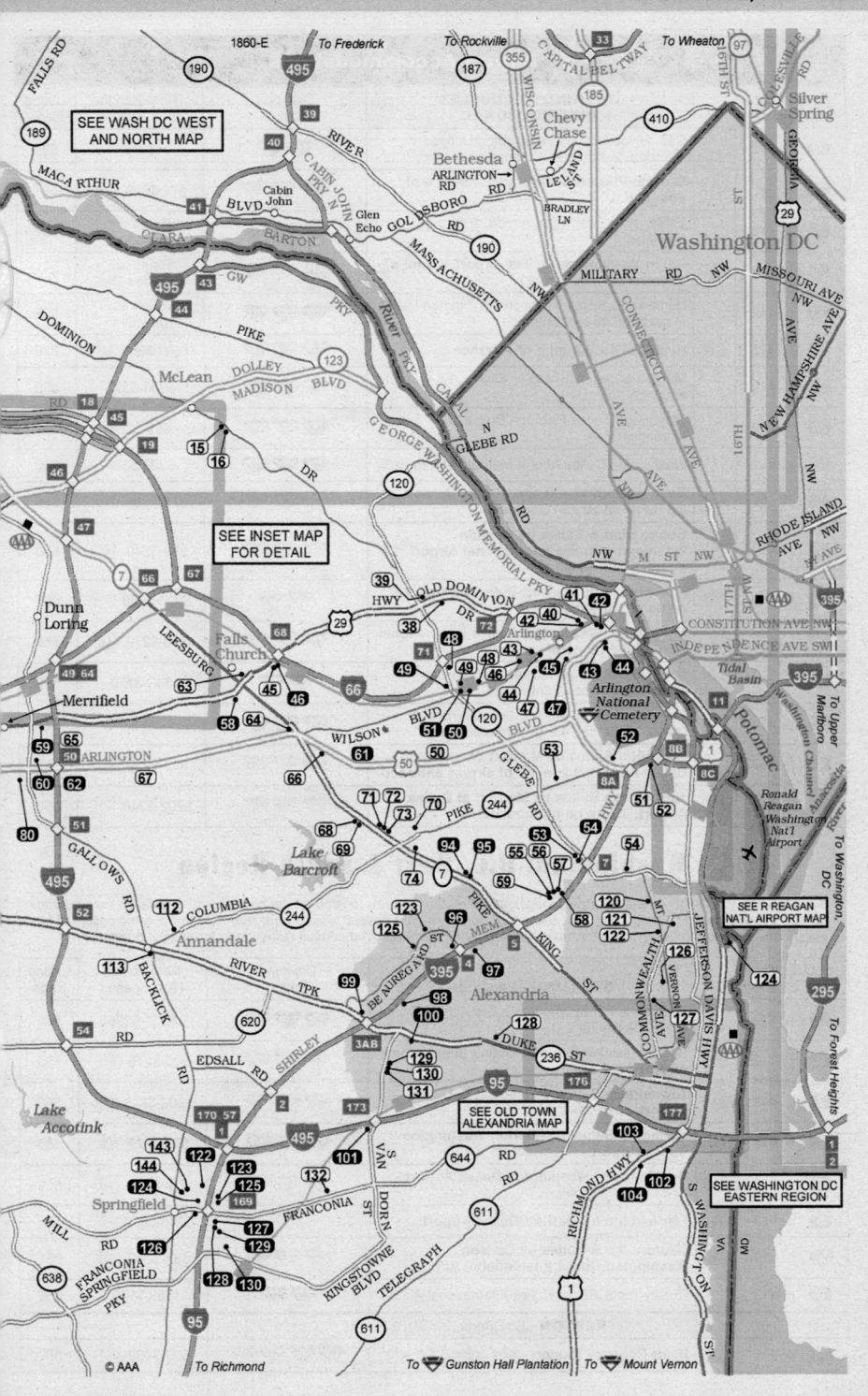

✈ Airport Accommodations

Spotter/Map Page Number	OA	WASHINGTON DULLES INTERNATIONAL	Diamond Rating	Rate Range High Season	Listing Page
37 / p. 412		Candlewood Suites Washington-Dulles Herndon, 2.4 mi e of entrance	▽▽	$215	537
32 / p. 412	AAA	Crowne Plaza Dulles Airport, 1.9 mi e of entrance	▽▽▽	$79-$349 SAVE	537
36 / p. 412		Embassy Suites Dulles Airport, 2 mi e of entrance	▽▽▽	Rates not provided	537
39 / p. 412	AAA	Hilton Washington Dulles Airport, 4.5 mi s of entrance	▽▽▽	Rates not provided SAVE	538
33 / p. 412		Homewood Suites by Hilton Washington-Dulles Airport, 2.6 mi e of entrance	▽▽▽	Rates not provided	538
28 / p. 412	AAA	Hyatt Dulles, 3.4 mi e of entrance	▽▽▽	$100-$380 SAVE	539
31 / p. 412		Marriott Suites Washington-Dulles, 1.9 mi e of entrance	▽▽▽	$351-$373	539
38 / p. 412		Staybridge Suites Herndon Dulles, 3 mi e of entrance	▽▽▽	$89-$284	539
30 / p. 412		Washington Dulles Airport Marriott, at airport	▽▽▽	$296-$329	540
5 / p. 412	AAA	Best Western Washington-Dulles Airport, 3.3 mi ne of airport entrance	▽▽▽	$79-$189 SAVE	556
7 / p. 412	AAA	Country Inn & Suites by Carlson Washington-Dulles International Airport, 1.6 mi ne of entrance	▽▽▽	$89-$249 SAVE	556
6 / p. 412	AAA	Fairfield Inn by Marriott-Dulles Airport, 1.6 mi ne of entrance	▽▽	$208-$230 SAVE	557
2 / p. 412	AAA	Holiday Inn Washington Dulles International Airport, 3.3 mi ne of entrance	▽▽▽	$99-$279 SAVE	559
8 / p. 412		Quality Inn & Suites Dulles International Airport, 1.6 mi ne of entrance	▽▽	$89-$170	559
1 / p. 412		Residence Inn by Marriott Dulles Airport @ Dulles 28 Center, 4.2 mi n of entrance	▽▽▽	$274-$296	559
4 / p. 412	AAA	SpringHill Suites by Marriott Washington Dulles Airport, 3.2 mi ne of airport entrance	▽▽▽	$99-$229 SAVE	560
3 / p. 412	AAA	TownePlace Suites by Marriott at Dulles Airport, 3.3 mi ne of entrance	▽▽▽	$202-$246 SAVE	560

Washington, D.C. West & South Region

This index helps you "spot" where approved lodgings and restaurants are located on the corresponding detailed maps. Lodging daily rate range is for comparison only and show the property's high season. Restaurant rate range is a combination of lunch and/or dinner. Turn to the listing page for more detailed rate information and consult display ads for special promotions.

Spotter/Map Page Number	OA	STERLING - Lodgings	Diamond Rating	Rate Range High Season	Listing Page
1 / p. 412		Residence Inn by Marriott Dulles Airport @ Dulles 28 Center	▽▽▽	$274-$296	559
2 / p. 412	AAA	Holiday Inn Washington Dulles International Airport - see color ad p 538	▽▽▽	$99-$279 SAVE	559
3 / p. 412	AAA	TownePlace Suites by Marriott at Dulles Airport - see color ad p 560	▽▽▽	$202-$246 SAVE	560
4 / p. 412	AAA	SpringHill Suites by Marriott Washington Dulles Airport - see color ad p 560	▽▽▽	$99-$229 SAVE	560
5 / p. 412	AAA	Best Western Washington-Dulles Airport - see color ad p 556	▽▽▽	$79-$189 SAVE	556
6 / p. 412	AAA	Fairfield Inn by Marriott-Dulles Airport	▽▽	$208-$230 SAVE	557
7 / p. 412	AAA	Country Inn & Suites by Carlson Washington-Dulles International Airport	▽▽▽	$89-$249 SAVE	556
8 / p. 412		Quality Inn & Suites Dulles International Airport	▽▽	$89-$170	559
		RESTON - Lodgings			
11 / p. 412	AAA	Hyatt Regency Reston - see color ad p 440	▽▽▽▽	$99-$499 SAVE	552

Spotter/Map Page Number	OA	RESTON - Lodgings (continued)	Diamond Rating	Rate Range High Season	Listing Page
12 / p. 412		Homestead Studio Suites Hotel-Reston	◆◆	$164-$174	552
13 / p. 412	AAA	**Sheraton Reston Hotel**	◆◆◆	$399 SAVE	552
		RESTON - Restaurants			
6 / p. 412		Paolo's Ristorante	◆◆	$8-$24	552
7 / p. 412		Market Street Bar & Grill	◆◆◆	$8-$36	552
8 / p. 412		Clyde's of Reston	◆◆	$8-$23	552
		MCLEAN - Lodgings			
16 / p. 412	AAA	**Staybridge Suites-McLean/Tysons Corner**	◆◆◆	$229-$289 SAVE	548
17 / p. 412		Hilton McLean Tysons Corner	◆◆◆	Rates not provided	548
18 / p. 412		Best Western Tysons Westpark Hotel	◆◆	Rates not provided	547
19 / p. 412		The Ritz-Carlton, Tysons Corner	◆◆◆◆	Rates not provided	548
20 / p. 412	AAA	**Crowne Plaza Tysons Corner** - see color ad p 547	◆◆◆	$89-$369 SAVE	548
21 / p. 412	AAA	**Courtyard by Marriott, Tysons Corner** - see color ad p 547	◆◆◆	$89-$329 SAVE	547
		MCLEAN - Restaurants			
11 / p. 412		Pulcinella The Italian Host	◆◆	$5-$19	550
12 / p. 412		Cafe Taj	◆◆	$8-$20	549
13 / p. 412		The Greek Taverna	◆◆	$8-$22	549
14 / p. 412		Kazan Restaurant	◆◆	$8-$25	549
15 / p. 412		Tachibana	◆◆	$7-$30	550
16 / p. 412		Cafe Oggi	◆◆◆	$12-$20	548
17 / p. 412		eCitie Restaurant & Bar	◆◆◆	$16-$29	549
18 / p. 412		P.F. Chang's China Bistro	◆◆◆	$7-$18	550
19 / p. 412		McCormick & Schmick's	◆◆◆	$8-$30	550
20 / p. 412		Palm Restaurant at Tysons II	◆◆◆	$13-$52	550
21 / p. 412		Maggiano's Little Italy	◆◆◆	$7-$30	550
22 / p. 412		Taste of Saigon	◆◆	$6-$15	551
23 / p. 412		Flemming's Prime Steakhouse and Wine Bar	◆◆◆	$19-$40	549
24 / p. 412		Da Domenico	◆◆	$6-$31	549
25 / p. 412	AAA	**Bistro 123**	◆◆◆	$9-$40	548
26 / p. 412	AAA	**J.R.'s Stockyards Inn**	◆◆	$8-$25	549
27 / p. 412		The Capital Grille	◆◆◆	$10-$36	549
		HERNDON - Lodgings			
24 / p. 412	AAA	**Holiday Inn Express-Reston/Herndon** - see color ad p 538	◆◆	$79-$239 SAVE	538
25 / p. 412		Extended StayAmerica-Herndon	◆◆	$164-$174	537
26 / p. 412	AAA	**Comfort Inn Dulles International Airport**	◆◆	$169-$209 SAVE	537
27 / p. 412		Residence Inn by Marriott-Herndon/Reston	◆◆◆	$269	539
28 / p. 412	AAA	**Hyatt Dulles** - see color ad p 440	◆◆◆	$100-$380 SAVE	539
29 / p. 412		SpringHill Suites by Marriott Herndon/Reston	◆◆◆	$241-$285	539
30 / p. 412		Washington Dulles Airport Marriott	◆◆◆	$296-$329	540

Spotter/Map Page Number	OA	HERNDON - Lodgings (continued)	Diamond Rating	Rate Range High Season	Listing Page
31 / p. 412		Marriott Suites Washington-Dulles	◆◆◆	$351-$373	539
32 / p. 412	AAA	**Crowne Plaza Dulles Airport**	◆◆◆	$79-$349 SAVE	537
33 / p. 412		Homewood Suites by Hilton Washington-Dulles Airport	◆◆◆	Rates not provided	538
34 / p. 412		Hawthorn Suites Herndon	◆◆◆	Rates not provided	537
35 / p. 412		Courtyard by Marriott/Herndon-Reston	◆◆◆	$252-$285	537
36 / p. 412		Embassy Suites Dulles Airport	◆◆◆	Rates not provided	537
37 / p. 412		Candlewood Suites Washington-Dulles Herndon	◆◆	$215	537
38 / p. 412		Staybridge Suites Herndon Dulles	◆◆◆	$89-$284	539
39 / p. 412	AAA	**Hilton Washington Dulles Airport**	◆◆◆	Rates not provided SAVE	538
		HERNDON - Restaurants			
30 / p. 412		Russia House Restaurant	◆◆◆	$12-$30	540
31 / p. 412	AAA	**Zeffirelli Ristorante Italiano**	◆◆◆	$11-$31	541
32 / p. 412		Ice House Cafe	◆◆	$7-$26	540
33 / p. 412		The Tortilla Factory Restaurant	◆	$6-$16	541
34 / p. 412		Harvest of India	◆◆	$8-$20	540
35 / p. 412		Supper Club of India	◆◆◆	$10-$25	540
		ARLINGTON - Lodgings			
42 / p. 412		Courtyard by Marriott-Arlington/Rosslyn	◆◆◆	$241-$285	511
43 / p. 412	AAA	**Best Western Rosslyn/Iwo Jima** - see color ad p 510	◆◆	$89-$259 SAVE	510
44 / p. 412		The Virginian Suites - see color ad p 517	◆◆	$139-$229	517
45 / p. 412		Hilton Garden Inn Arlington/Courthouse Plaza	◆◆◆	Rates not provided	514
46 / p. 412	AAA	**Econo Lodge-Metro Arlington** - see color ad p 512	◆◆	$110-$219 SAVE	512
47 / p. 412	AAA	**Arlington Residence Court a Clarion Collection** - see color ad p 432	◆◆◆	$99-$399 SAVE	509
48 / p. 412	AAA	**Comfort Inn Ballston**	◆◆	$189-$259 SAVE	510
49 / p. 412	AAA	**Holiday Inn Arlington** - see color ad p 513	◆◆◆	$89-$349 SAVE	514
50 / p. 412	AAA	**Hilton Arlington**	◆◆◆	Rates not provided SAVE	513
51 / p. 412		The Westin Arlington Gateway	◆◆◆	$139-$499	518
52 / p. 412	AAA	**Sheraton National Hotel** - see color ad p 516	◆◆◆	$329 SAVE	517
53 / p. 412	AAA	**Best Western-Pentagon/Reagan Airport** - see color ad p 435	◆◆	$89-$169 SAVE	510
54 / p. 412	AAA	**Comfort Inn Pentagon** - see color ad p 510	◆◆◆	$99-$229 SAVE	511
		ARLINGTON - Restaurants			
38 / p. 412		Cafe Parisien Express	◆	$3-$16	519
39 / p. 412		Metro 29 Diner	◆◆	$5-$20	520
40 / p. 412		Guajillo	◆	$5-$20	520
41 / p. 412		Cafe Asia	◆◆	$4-$14	518
42 / p. 412		Village Bistro	◆◆	$10-$25	522
43 / p. 412		Mexicali Blues	◆	$5-$13	520

Spotter/Map Page Number	OA	**ARLINGTON - Restaurants (continued)**	Diamond Rating	Rate Range High Season	Listing Page
44 / p. 412		Harry's Tap Room	◆◆◆	$10-$26	520
45 / p. 412		La Cote D'or Cafe	◆◆◆	$6-$29	520
46 / p. 412		Queen Bee Restaurant	◆◆	$4-$10	521
47 / p. 412		El Pollo Rico	◆	$4-$12	519
48 / p. 412		Cafe Tirolo	◆	$7-$19	519
49 / p. 412		Rio Grande Cafe	◆◆	$9-$25	521
50 / p. 412		Crystal Thai Restaurant	◆◆	$7-$14	519
51 / p. 412		Thaiphoon	◆◆	$7-$16	522
52 / p. 412		Sin e Irish Pub and Restaurant	◆◆	$7-$17	521
53 / p. 412		Matuba	◆	$6-$19	520
54 / p. 412		El Cuscatleco Restaurant	◆	$5-$20	519
55 / p. 412		Extra Virgin	◆◆◆	$8-$24	519
56 / p. 412	AAA	**T.H.A.I. in Shirlington**	◆◆	$7-$16	521
57 / p. 412		Bistro Bistro	◆◆	$5-$22	518
58 / p. 412		Carlyle	◆◆◆	$8-$22	519
59 / p. 412		Aroma Indian Cuisine	◆◆	$9-$18	518
		FALLS CHURCH - Lodgings			
57 / p. 412		The Westin Tysons Corner	◆◆◆	$289	534
58 / p. 412	·	TownePlace Suites by Marriott-Falls Church	◆◆	$230-$252	534
59 / p. 412		Homewood Suites by Hilton-Falls Church	◆◆◆	Rates not provided	533
60 / p. 412		Residence Inn by Marriott Fairfax-Merrifield	◆◆◆	$296-$318	533
61 / p. 412		Comfort Inn Arlington Boulevard-DC Gateway	◆◆	$159-$229	533
62 / p. 412		Fairview Park Marriott	◆◆◆	$318-$340	533
		FALLS CHURCH - Restaurants			
62 / p. 412		Haandi	◆◆	$5-$20	535
63 / p. 412		Argia's	◆◆	$8-$34	534
64 / p. 412		Pistone's Italian Inn	◆◆	$7-$30	535
65 / p. 412		2941 Restaurant	◆◆◆◆	$12-$49	534
66 / p. 412		Mark's Duck House	◆◆	$5-$29	535
67 / p. 412		Celebrity Delly	◆	$5-$15	534
68 / p. 412		Mint Thai Cuisine	◆◆	$5-$25	535
69 / p. 412		Peking Gourmet Inn	◆◆	$7-$36	535
70 / p. 412		Flavors Soul Food	◆	$6-$11	534
71 / p. 412		Rabieng	◆◆	$7-$21	535
72 / p. 412		Duangrat's	◆◆◆	$8-$29	534
73 / p. 412		Raaga	◆◆◆	$9-$18	535
74 / p. 412		City Diner	◆◆	$8-$22	534
		VIENNA - Lodgings			
65 / p. 412	AAA	**Sheraton Premiere At Tysons Corner**	◆◆◆	$349 [SAVE]	564
66 / p. 412		Residence Inn by Marriott-Tysons Corner	◆◆◆	$287-$317	563

Spotter/Map Page Number	OA	VIENNA - Lodgings (continued)	Diamond Rating	Rate Range High Season	Listing Page
67 / p. 412	AAA	**Comfort Inn Tysons Corner** - see color ad p 431	◆◆	$79-$199 SAVE	562
68 / p. 412		Embassy Suites Hotel Tysons Corner	◆◆◆	Rates not provided	562
69 / p. 412		Hilton Garden Inn Tysons Corner	◆◆◆	Rates not provided	562
70 / p. 412		Residence Inn by Marriott Tysons Corner Mall	◆◆◆	$296-$362	563
71 / p. 412		Tysons Corner Marriott Hotel	◆◆◆	$296-$318	564
72 / p. 412		Homestead Studio Suites Hotel-Tysons Corner	◆◆	$174-$184	562
73 / p. 412		Courtyard by Marriott Dunn Loring Fairfax	◆◆◆	$241-$307	562
		VIENNA - Restaurants			
77 / p. 412		Bombay Tandoor	◆◆	$9-$19	564
78 / p. 412		Clyde's of Tysons Corner	◆◆	$8-$23	565
79 / p. 412		Hunan Lion	◆◆◆	$5-$25	565
80 / p. 412		Konami Japanese Restaurant	◆◆	$8-$25	565
81 / p. 412		Paya Thai	◆◆	$8-$17	566
82 / p. 412		Morton's-The Steakhouse	◆◆◆	$13-$40	565
83 / p. 412		Chutzpah of Tysons-A Real New York Deli	◆	$9-$15	565
84 / p. 412	AAA	**Ristorante Bonaroti**	◆◆◆	$12-$29	566
85 / p. 412		Le Canard	◆◆◆	$10-$29	565
86 / p. 412	AAA	**Cafe Renaissance**	◆◆◆	$12-$35	564
87 / p. 412		Marco Polo Restaurant & Caterers	◆◆	$9-$27	565
88 / p. 412		Nizam's Restaurant	◆◆◆	$8-$22	565
89 / p. 412		Sunflower Vegetarian Restaurant	◆◆	$6-$11	566
		FAIRFAX - Lodgings			
76 / p. 412		Hilton Garden Inn Fairfax - see color ad p 529	◆◆◆	Rates not provided	529
77 / p. 412		Extended Stay Deluxe Fairfax	◆◆	$164-$174	529
78 / p. 412		Fairfax Marriott at Fair Oaks	◆◆◆	$241-$285	529
79 / p. 412		Homestead Studio Suites Hotel-Fair Oaks	◆◆	$144-$154	530
80 / p. 412		Homestead Studio Suites Hotel-Falls Church/Merrifield	◆◆	$149-$159	530
81 / p. 412		Residence Inn by Marriott-Fair Lakes	◆◆◆	$252-$274	530
82 / p. 412	AAA	**Best Western Fairfax** - see color ad p 435	◆◆	$69-$189 SAVE	528
83 / p. 412		Holiday Inn Express Fairfax	◆◆	$89-$189	530
84 / p. 412	AAA	**Hyatt Fair Lakes**	◆◆◆	$99-$349 SAVE	530
85 / p. 412		Candlewood Suites Fairfax-Washington, D.C.	◆◆	$179	528
86 / p. 412		Courtyard by Marriott-Fair Oaks	◆◆◆	$230-$274	529
87 / p. 412	AAA	**Comfort Inn University Center** - see color ad p 528	◆◆◆	$129-$179 SAVE	528
88 / p. 412		Hampton Inn-Fairfax	◆◆◆	Rates not provided	529
		FAIRFAX - Restaurants			
92 / p. 412		Jaipur Royal Indian Cuisine	◆◆◆	$8-$18	532
93 / p. 412		Chutzpah, A Real New York Deli	◆	$9-$15	531

Spotter/Map Page Number	OA	FAIRFAX - Restaurants (continued)	Diamond Rating	Rate Range High Season	Listing Page
94 / p. 412	AAA	**The Espositos Italian Restaurant**	▽▽	$5-$16	531
95 / p. 412		Arties	▽▽	$8-$29	530
96 / p. 412		Blue Iguana	▽▽	$9-$26	531
97 / p. 412		Coastal Flats	▽▽	$8-$25	531
98 / p. 412		Ruth's Chris Steak House	▽▽▽	$25-$65	532
99 / p. 412		Tsunami	▽▽	$8-$38	533
100 / p. 412		Tony's New York Pizza	▽	$6-$12	533
101 / p. 412		Bravo's Italian Cafe	▽▽	$8-$23	531
102 / p. 412		Dolce Vita	▽▽	$6-$25	531
103 / p. 412		Piano Grill	▽▽	$6-$20	532
104 / p. 412		The Lamplighter Restaurant	▽▽	$9-$32	532
105 / p. 412		Pad Thai	▽▽	$7-$24	532
106 / p. 412		Arigato Sushi	▽▽	$8-$35	530
107 / p. 412		Sakoontra	▽▽	$6-$13	532
108 / p. 412		Bellissimo	▽▽▽	$12-$32	531
109 / p. 412		La Rue 123 Restaurant at Bailiwick Inn	▽▽▽	$14-$30	532
110 / p. 412		Star Thai	▽▽	$6-$15	532
		CENTREVILLE - Lodgings			
91 / p. 412		SpringHill Suites by Marriott Centreville/Chantilly	▽▽▽	$208-$230	523
		CENTREVILLE - Restaurants			
116 / p. 412		Fiora's	▽▽	$6-$25	523
117 / p. 412		Blue Water Grille	▽▽	$7-$18	523
		ALEXANDRIA - Lodgings			
94 / p. 412		Homewood Suites by Hilton-Alexandria	▽▽▽	Rates not provided	502
95 / p. 412		Hampton Inn-Alexandria	▽▽▽	$149-$299	501
96 / p. 412		Hilton Alexandria Mark Center	▽▽▽	Rates not provided	501
97 / p. 412		Courtyard by Marriott Alexandria Pentagon South	▽▽▽	$230-$285	500
98 / p. 412		Hawthorn Suites LTD-Alexandria	▽▽	$210-$240	501
99 / p. 412		Extended StayAmerica-Washington, DC-Alexandria	▽▽	$164-$174	501
100 / p. 412	AAA	**Washington Suites-Alexandria** - see color ad p 504	▽▽▽	$159-$409 [SAVE]	505
101 / p. 412		Comfort Inn Alexandria	▽▽	$99-$105	500
102 / p. 412		Hampton Inn Alexandria/Old Town Area-South	▽▽▽	$129-$209	501
103 / p. 412	AAA	**Travelers Motel**	▽▽	$69-$89 [SAVE]	503
104 / p. 412		Red Roof Inn-Alexandria	▽▽	Rates not provided	503
		ALEXANDRIA - Restaurants			
120 / p. 412		RT's Restaurant	▽▽	$8-$29	507
121 / p. 412		Chez Andree	▽▽	$8-$27	505
122 / p. 412		Bombay Curry Company	▽▽	$5-$12	505
123 / p. 412		Clyde's at Mark Center	▽▽	$6-$26	505

Spotter/Map Page Number	OA	**ALEXANDRIA - Restaurants (continued)**	Diamond Rating	Rate Range High Season	Listing Page
(124) / p. 412		Indigo Landing	◆◆◆	$8-$29	506
(125) / p. 412		Illusions Thai Cafe	◆◆	$6-$15	506
(126) / p. 412		Evening Star Cafe'	◆◆	$7-$25	506
(127) / p. 412		Monroe's-An American Trattoria	◆◆	$6-$20	507
(128) / p. 412		Tempo Restaurant	◆◆	$10-$18	508
(129) / p. 412		Satay Sarinah	◆	$6-$17	507
(130) / p. 412		Akasaka	◆◆	$8-$20	505
(131) / p. 412		Savio's Italian Restaurant and Bar	◆◆	$7-$22	508
(132) / p. 412		Paradiso Ristorante Italiano	◆◆	$11-$20	507
		CHANTILLY - Lodgings			
(107) / p. 412		Wingate Inn Dulles Airport-Chantilly	◆◆◆	$145-$269	526
(108) / p. 412	ⒶⒶⒶ	**Hampton Inn Washington Dulles International Airport South -** see color ad p 558	◆◆◆	$79-$239 [SAVE]	525
(109) / p. 412		TownePlace Suites by Marriott-Chantilly	◆◆	$186-$208	526
(110) / p. 412	ⒶⒶⒶ	**Staybridge Suites Hotel Chantilly/Dulles International Airport**	◆◆◆	$79-$229 [SAVE]	525
(111) / p. 412		Extended StayAmerica-Chantilly	◆◆	$154-$164	524
(112) / p. 412		Residence Inn by Marriott Chantilly Dulles South	◆◆◆	$252-$274	525
(113) / p. 412		Fairfield Inn by Marriott-Chantilly/Dulles South	◆◆	$197-$230	524
(114) / p. 412		Comfort Suites Chantilly-Dulles Airport	◆◆◆	$79-$229	524
(115) / p. 412		Courtyard by Marriott-Dulles Airport	◆◆◆	$241-$263	524
(116) / p. 412		Holiday Inn Select Chantilly-Dulles Expo Center	◆◆◆	Rates not provided	525
(117) / p. 412		Extended Stay Deluxe Chantilly	◆◆	$164-$174	524
(118) / p. 412	ⒶⒶⒶ	**Westfields Marriott**	◆◆◆◆	$362-$384 [SAVE]	526
(119) / p. 412	ⒶⒶⒶ	**Hyatt Place Chantilly/Dulles Airport-South**	◆◆◆	$99-$299 [SAVE]	525
		CHANTILLY - Restaurants			
(135) / p. 412		Thai Basil	◆◆	$7-$14	527
(136) / p. 412	ⒶⒶⒶ	**Picante! The Real Taco**	◆◆	$8-$15	527
(137) / p. 412		Backyard Grill and Bar	◆◆	$6-$20	526
(138) / p. 412		Otani Japanese Steak House	◆◆	$7-$33	526
(139) / p. 412		Willard's Real Pit BBQ	◆	$5-$13	527
(140) / p. 412		Palm Court at Westfields Marriott	◆◆◆	$18-$40	526
		SPRINGFIELD - Lodgings			
(122) / p. 412		TownePlace Suites by Marriott Springfield	◆◆	$210-$241	554
(123) / p. 412		Courtyard by Marriott-Springfield	◆◆◆	$221-$251	553
(124) / p. 412		Holiday Inn Express Springfield	◆◆	$79-$209	554

Spotter/Map Page Number	OA	SPRINGFIELD - Lodgings (continued)	Diamond Rating	Rate Range High Season	Listing Page
125 / p. 412	AAA	Best Western Springfield - see color ad p 435	◆◆	$130-$170 [SAVE]	553
126 / p. 412		Red Roof Inn Springfield	◆◆	Rates not provided	554
127 / p. 412		Hampton Inn Washington DC/Springfield	◆◆◆	Rates not provided	553
128 / p. 412		Comfort Inn Washington DC/Springfield	◆◆	$99-$149	553
129 / p. 412	AAA	Hilton Springfield - see color ad p 554	◆◆◆	Rates not provided [SAVE]	554
130 / p. 412		Extended StayAmerica-Washington, DC-Springfield	◆◆	$164-$174	553
		SPRINGFIELD - Restaurants			
143 / p. 412		Mike's American Grill	◆◆	$9-$28	555
144 / p. 412		Manila Cafe	◆	$6-$13	555
		GREAT FALLS - Restaurants			
1 / p. 412		Flore di Luna	◆◆◆	$9-$19	536
2 / p. 412		Serbian Crown Restaurant	◆◆◆	$8-$38	536
3 / p. 412		Dante Ristorante	◆◆◆	$8-$32	536
		ANNANDALE - Restaurants			
112 / p. 412		Silverado	◆◆	$8-$26	509
113 / p. 412		Ribster's	◆◆	$10-$20	509

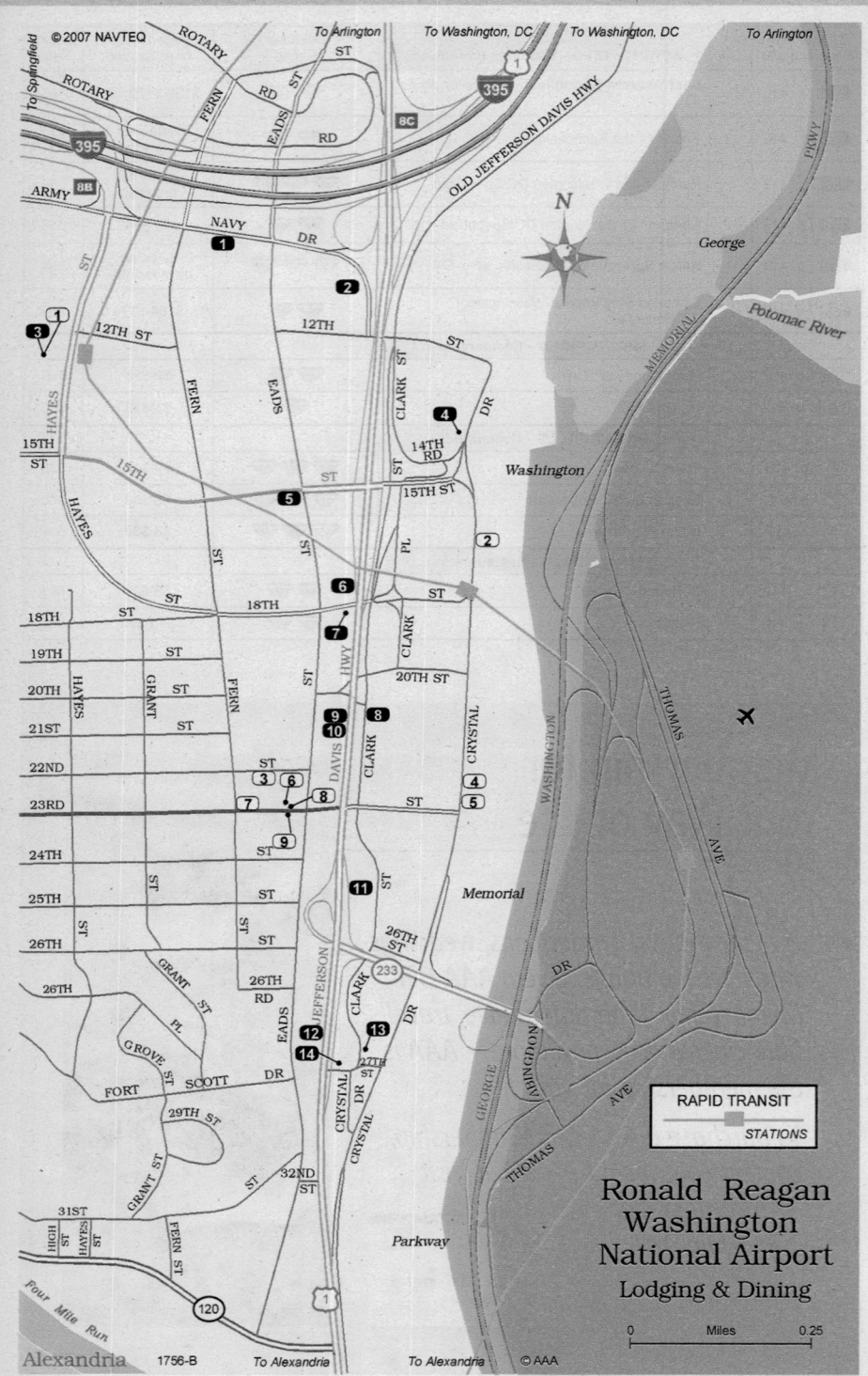

© 2007 NAVTEQ

To Springfield
To Arlington
To Washington, DC
To Washington, DC
To Arlington

ROTARY
ROTARY
ST
FERN
RD
ST
EADS
RD

I-395
I-395
8C

ARMY
ST
8B

NAVY
DR

OLD JEFFERSON DAVIS HWY

N

George

Potomac River

MEMORIAL

12TH ST
12TH
ST

HAYES

FERN
EADS
CLARK ST
ST
DR

4
14TH
RD

Washington

15TH
ST
15TH
ST
ST
15TH ST
2

HAYES
5
PL
ST

6
ST

18TH
ST
18TH
7
CLARK

19TH
ST
20TH ST

20TH
HAYES
GRANT
FERN
HWY
9
8

21ST
ST

22ND
ST
3
6
DAVIS
CLARK
CRYSTAL
4

23RD
7
8
ST
5
9

24TH
ST

25TH
ST
ST
11
ST

26TH
ST
ST
Memorial
26TH
ST

26TH
GRANT
ST
26TH
RD
EADS
CLARK
233

GROVE
ST
JEFFERSON
DR
THOMAS
DR
ABINGDON
AVE

FORT
SCOTT
DR
12
13

29TH ST
14
27TH
ST
CRYSTAL
DR
CRYSTAL
DR

GRANT
ST
32ND
ST

31ST
HIGH
ST
HAYES
ST
FERN ST

RAPID TRANSIT

STATIONS

Ronald Reagan Washington National Airport
Lodging & Dining

Four Mile Run
120

0   Miles   0.25

Alexandria
1756-B
To Alexandria
To Alexandria
© AAA

✈ Airport Accommodations

Spotter/Map Page Number	OA	RONALD REAGAN WASHINGTON NATIONAL	Diamond Rating	Rate Range High Season	Listing Page
14 / p. 422		Courtyard by Marriott Crystal City, 0.5 mi nw of airport	▽▽▽	$275-$296	511
4 / p. 422	AAA	**Crowne Plaza Hotel Washington National Airport, 1.5 mi nw of airport**	▽▽▽	$99-$399 SAVE	511
8 / p. 422	AAA	**Crystal City Marriott at Reagan National Airport, 1 mi nw of airport**	▽▽▽	$285-$340 SAVE	511
6 / p. 422		Crystal Gateway Marriott Hotel, 1 mi nw of airport	▽▽▽	$340-$351	512
2 / p. 422		DoubleTree Hotel-Crystal City, 1.5 mi n of airport	▽▽▽	Rates not provided	512
5 / p. 422		Embassy Suites Hotel Crystal City, 1.5 mi nw of airport	▽▽▽	Rates not provided	512
11 / p. 422		Hilton Crystal City at Reagan National Airport, 0.7 mi nw of airport	▽▽▽	Rates not provided	513
12 / p. 422	AAA	**Holiday Inn National Airport, 0.5 mi nw of airport**	▽▽▽	$89-$299 SAVE	514
13 / p. 422	AAA	**Hyatt Regency Crystal City at Reagan National Airport, 0.5 mi n of airport**	▽▽▽	$89-$439 SAVE	515
10 / p. 422		Radisson Hotel Reagan National Airport, 0.8 mi nw of airport	▽▽▽	$99-$259	515
1 / p. 422	AAA	**Residence Inn by Marriott-Pentagon City, 1.7 mi n of airport**	▽▽▽	$329-$351 SAVE	516
3 / p. 422		The Ritz-Carlton, Pentagon City, 1.8 mi n of airport	▽▽▽▽	Rates not provided	516
7 / p. 422	AAA	**Sheraton Crystal City Hotel, 1 mi nw of airport**	▽▽▽	$109-$319 SAVE	516
52 / p. 412	AAA	**Sheraton National Hotel, 1.3 mi w of airport**	▽▽▽	$329 SAVE	517

Ronald Reagan Washington National Airport

This index helps you "spot" where approved lodgings and restaurants are located on the corresponding detailed maps. Lodging daily rate range is for comparison only and show the property's high season. Restaurant rate range is a combination of lunch and/or dinner. Turn to the listing page for more detailed rate information and consult display ads for special promotions.

Spotter/Map Page Number	OA	ARLINGTON - Lodgings	Diamond Rating	Rate Range High Season	Listing Page
1 / p. 422	AAA	**Residence Inn by Marriott-Pentagon City**	▽▽▽	$329-$351 SAVE	516
2 / p. 422		DoubleTree Hotel-Crystal City	▽▽▽	Rates not provided	512
3 / p. 422		The Ritz-Carlton, Pentagon City	▽▽▽▽	Rates not provided	516
4 / p. 422	AAA	**Crowne Plaza Hotel Washington National Airport**	▽▽▽	$99-$399 SAVE	511
5 / p. 422		Embassy Suites Hotel Crystal City	▽▽▽	Rates not provided	512
6 / p. 422		Crystal Gateway Marriott Hotel	▽▽▽	$340-$351	512
7 / p. 422	AAA	**Sheraton Crystal City Hotel**	▽▽▽	$109-$319 SAVE	516
8 / p. 422	AAA	**Crystal City Marriott at Reagan National Airport**	▽▽▽	$285-$340 SAVE	511
9 / p. 422	AAA	**Hampton Inn & Suites Reagan National Airport**	▽▽▽	Rates not provided SAVE	513

Spotter/Map Page Number	OA	**ARLINGTON** - Lodgings (continued)	Diamond Rating	Rate Range High Season	Listing Page
10 / p. 422		Radisson Hotel Reagan National Airport	◆◆◆	$99-$259	515
11 / p. 422		Hilton Crystal City at Reagan National Airport	◆◆◆	Rates not provided	513
12 / p. 422	◬	**Holiday Inn National Airport** - see color ad p 514	◆◆◆	$89-$299 SAVE	514
13 / p. 422	◬	**Hyatt Regency Crystal City at Reagan National Airport** - see color ad p 440	◆◆◆	$89-$439 SAVE	515
14 / p. 422		Courtyard by Marriott Crystal City	◆◆◆	$275-$296	511
		ARLINGTON - Restaurants			
1 / p. 422		The Grill	◆◆◆	$12-$33	519
2 / p. 422		Morton's The Steakhouse	◆◆◆	$32-$59	521
3 / p. 422	◬	**Athena Pallas**	◆◆	$6-$20	518
4 / p. 422		Ruth's Chris Steak House	◆◆◆	$16-$43	521
5 / p. 422		Jaleo	◆◆◆	$6-$20	520
6 / p. 422	◬	**Top Thai Restaurant**	◆	$7-$14	522
7 / p. 422		Urban Thai	◆◆	$6-$15	522
8 / p. 422		Cafe Italia	◆◆	$6-$21	518
9 / p. 422		The Portofino Restaurant	◆◆	$10-$25	521

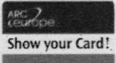

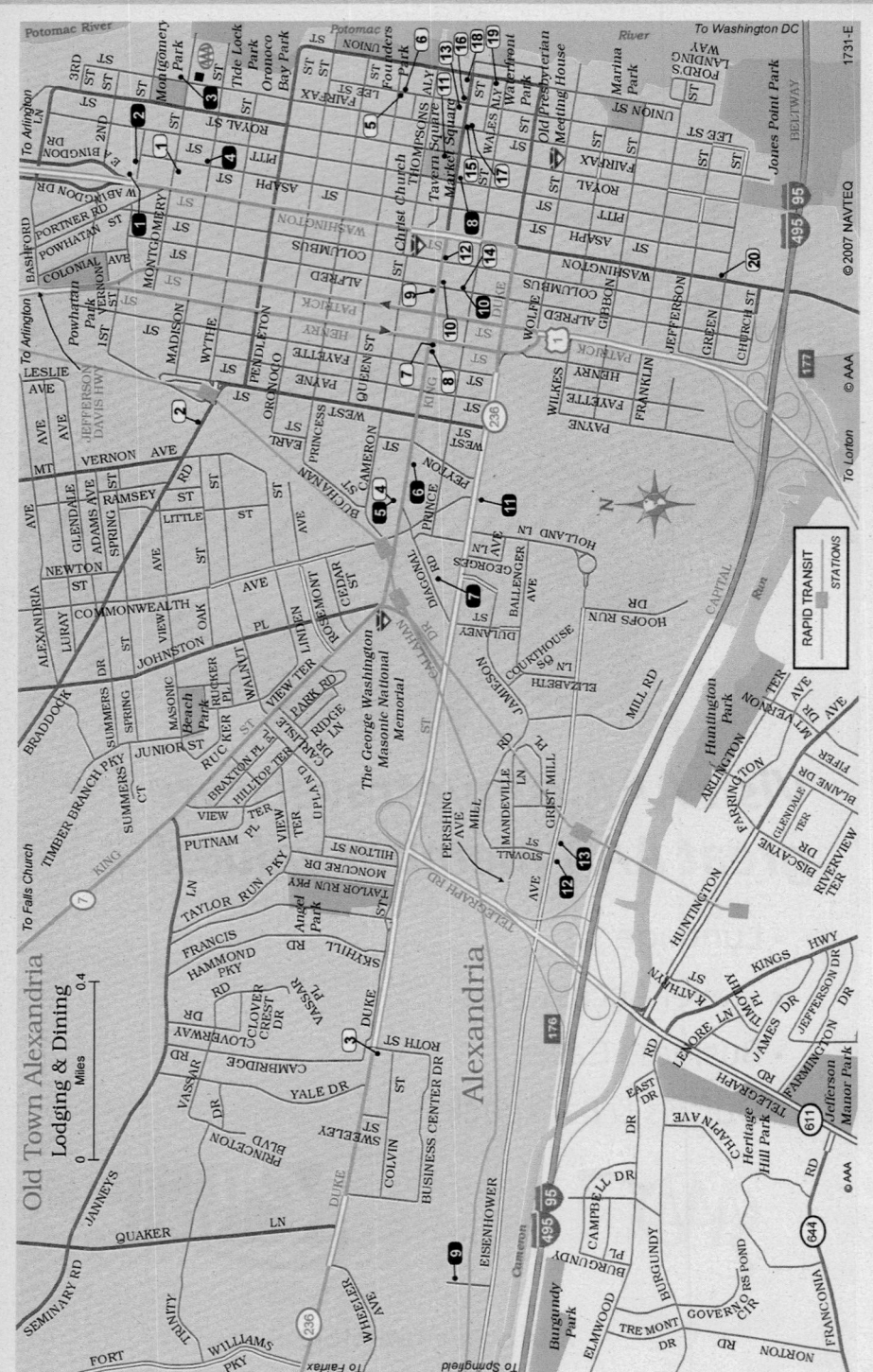

Old Town Alexandria

This index helps you "spot" where approved lodgings and restaurants are located on the corresponding detailed maps. Lodging daily rate range is for comparison only and show the property's high season. Restaurant rate range is a combination of lunch and/or dinner. Turn to the listing page for more detailed rate information and consult display ads for special promotions.

Spotter/Map Page Number	OA	**ALEXANDRIA - Lodgings**	Diamond Rating	Rate Range High Season	Listing Page
1 / p. 426	⏺	**Best Western-Old Colony Inn**	◈◈	$139-$199 SAVE	500
2 / p. 426		Holiday Inn Hotel & Suites-Historic District Alexandria	◈◈◈	$119-$259	502
3 / p. 426		The Crowne Plaza Old Town Alexandria	◈◈◈	$109-$329	500
4 / p. 426	⏺	**Sheraton Suites Old Town Alexandria** - see color ad p 503	◈◈◈	$119-$379 SAVE	503
5 / p. 426		Hilton Alexandria Old Town	◈◈◈	Rates not provided	501
6 / p. 426		Hampton Inn Old Town King Street Metro	◈◈◈	$179-$309	501
7 / p. 426		Embassy Suites-Alexandria-Old Town	◈◈◈	Rates not provided	500
8 / p. 426		Hotel Monaco Alexandria	[fyi]	$149-$459	502
9 / p. 426		Homestead Studio Suites Hotel-Alexandria	◈◈	$164-$174	502
10 / p. 426	⏺	**Morrison House** - see color ad p 502	◈◈◈◈	$169-$469 SAVE	502
11 / p. 426		Residence Inn by Marriott Alexandria-Old Town	◈◈◈	$307-$340	503
12 / p. 426		Courtyard by Marriott-Alexandria	◈◈◈	$263-$318	500
13 / p. 426		Holiday Inn Eisenhower Metro	◈◈	$190-$220	501
		ALEXANDRIA - Restaurants			
(1) / p. 426		The Stardust Restaurant & Lounge	◈◈	$7-$29	508
(2) / p. 426		La Piazza	◈	$6-$16	507
(3) / p. 426		Generous George's Positive Pizza & Pasta Place	◈	$7-$15	506
(4) / p. 426		Seagar's	◈◈◈	$10-$33	508
(5) / p. 426		Bilbo Baggins	◈◈	$8-$24	505
(6) / p. 426	⏺	**La Bergerie**	◈◈◈	$13-$35	507
(7) / p. 426		Le Gaulois	◈◈◈	$8-$25	507
(8) / p. 426		Vermilion	◈◈◈	$14-$50	509
(9) / p. 426		The Majestic	◈◈◈	$9-$22	507
(10) / p. 426	⏺	**Taverna Cretekou**	◈◈	$8-$25	508
(11) / p. 426		Gadsby's Tavern	◈◈	$8-$36	506
(12) / p. 426		Geranio Restaurant	◈◈◈	$8-$30	506
(13) / p. 426		Two Nineteen Restaurant	◈◈	$10-$29	508
(14) / p. 426		The Grille	◈◈◈	$23-$36	506
(15) / p. 426		Warehouse Bar & Grill	◈◈◈	$8-$29	509
(16) / p. 426		Il Porto Ristorante	◈◈	$8-$22	506
(17) / p. 426		Thai Old Town Restaurant	◈◈	$7-$15	508
(18) / p. 426		Landini Brothers	◈◈	$17-$30	507
(19) / p. 426		Union Street Public House	◈◈	$7-$25	509
(20) / p. 426		Southside 815	◈◈	$6-$18	508

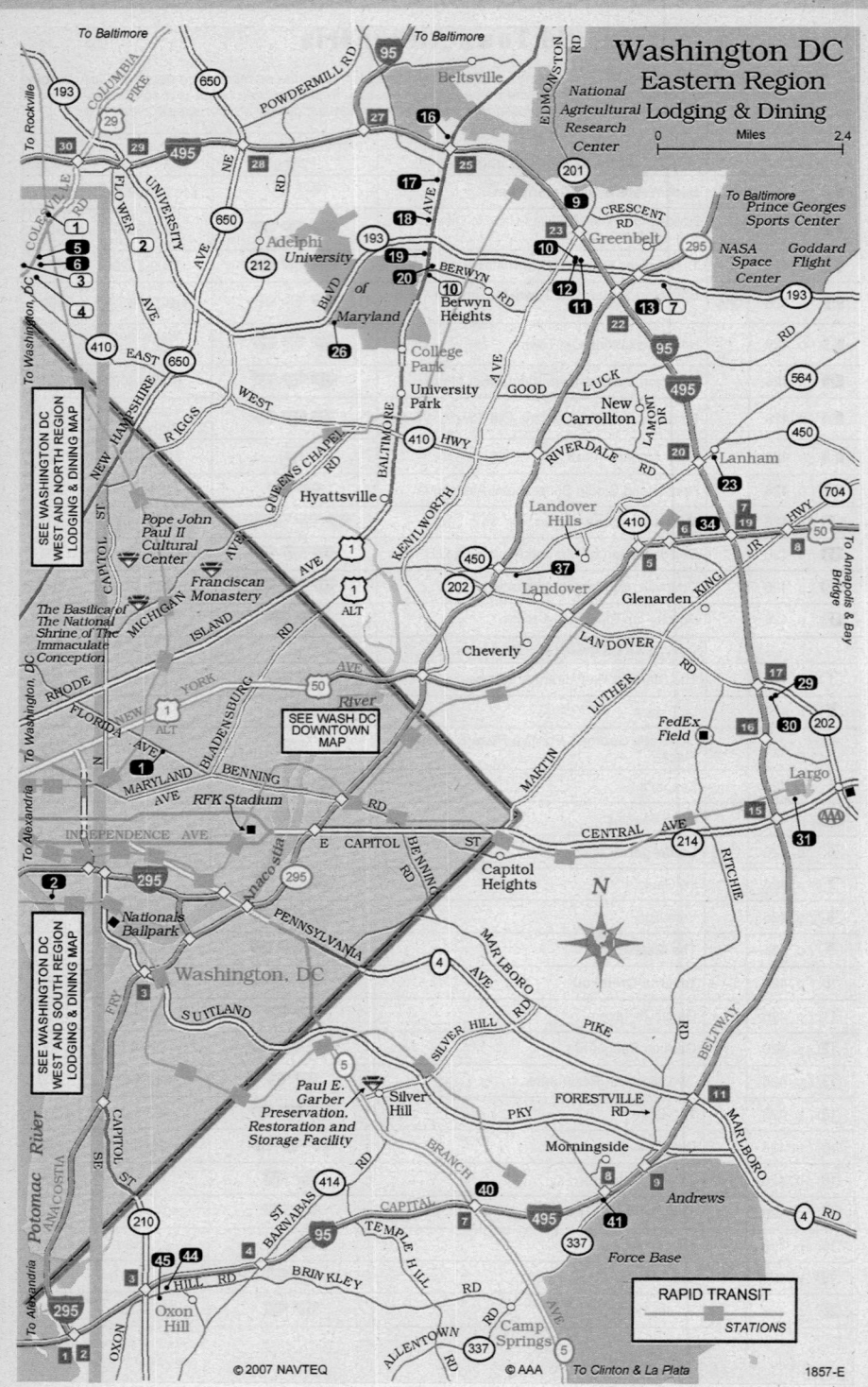

Washington, D.C. Eastern Region

This index helps you "spot" where approved lodgings and restaurants are located on the corresponding detailed maps. Lodging daily rate range is for comparison only and show the property's high season. Restaurant rate range is a combination of lunch and/or dinner. Turn to the listing page for more detailed rate information and consult display ads for special promotions.

Spotter/Map Page Number	OA	WASHINGTON (EASTERN REGION) - Lodgings	Diamond Rating	Rate Range High Season	Listing Page
1 / p. 428		Kellogg Conference Hotel at Gallaudet University	◈◈	Rates not provided	474
2 / p. 428		Channel Inn Hotel	◈◈	$175-$185	474
		SILVER SPRING - Lodgings			
5 / p. 428	AAA	**Hilton Washington DC/Silver Spring -** see color ad p 498	◈◈◈	$116-$296 SAVE	498
6 / p. 428		Courtyard by Marriott-Silver Spring Downtown	◈◈◈	Rates not provided	497
		SILVER SPRING - Restaurants			
① / p. 428		Mrs. K's Toll House	◈◈◈	$11-$34	499
② / p. 428		El Gavilan	◈	$5-$14	499
③ / p. 428		Cubano's	◈◈	$11-$27	499
④ / p. 428		Bombay Gaylord	◈◈	$5-$12	499
		GREENBELT - Lodgings			
9 / p. 428	AAA	**The Greenbelt Marriott**	◈◈◈	Rates not provided SAVE	487
10 / p. 428	AAA	**Residence Inn by Marriott-Greenbelt**	◈◈◈	Rates not provided SAVE	488
11 / p. 428		Hilton Garden Inn Washington DC/Greenbelt	◈◈◈	$249	487
12 / p. 428		Courtyard by Marriott-Greenbelt	◈◈◈	$219-$241	487
13 / p. 428	AAA	**Holiday Inn-Greenbelt-NASA Area -** see color ad p 487	◈◈◈	$129-$179 SAVE	488
		GREENBELT - Restaurant			
⑦ / p. 428	AAA	**Royal Jade**	◈◈	$6-$20	488
		COLLEGE PARK - Lodgings			
16 / p. 428	AAA	**Holiday Inn-College Park**	◈◈◈	$109-$189 SAVE	481
17 / p. 428		Hampton Inn-College Park	◈◈◈	Rates not provided	481
18 / p. 428		Super 8 Motel-College Park	◈	Rates not provided	481
19 / p. 428		Comfort Inn & Suites College Park	◈◈	$89-$199	481
20 / p. 428	AAA	**Clarion Inn & Fundome**	◈◈	$99-$169 SAVE	481
		COLLEGE PARK - Restaurant			
⑩ / p. 428		Seven Seas	◈◈	$6-$14	482
		LANHAM - Lodgings			
23 / p. 428	AAA	**Days Inn-Lanham -** see color ad p 489	◈◈	Rates not provided SAVE	489
		ADELPHI - Lodgings			
26 / p. 428		University of Maryland University College Inn & Conference Ctr by Marriott	◈◈◈	Rates not provided	475
		LARGO - Lodgings			
29 / p. 428	AAA	**Holiday Inn Express Hotel & Suites I-95 Capital Beltway**	◈◈◈	$129-$289 SAVE	490

Spotter/Map Page Number	OA	**LARGO - Lodgings (continued)**	Diamond Rating	Rate Range High Season	Listing Page
30 / p. 428		Radisson Hotel Largo/Washington, D.C.	◆◆◆	$139-$179	490
31 / p. 428	AAA	**Hampton Inn-Washington, DC/I-95 - see color ad p 442**	◆◆◆	$169-$179 [SAVE]	490
		LANDOVER - Lodgings			
34 / p. 428		Courtyard by Marriott-New Carrollton-Landover	◆◆◆	Rates not provided	488
		LANDOVER HILLS - Lodgings			
37 / p. 428		Comfort Inn-Landover Hills	◆◆	$99	489
		CAMP SPRINGS - Lodgings			
40 / p. 428		Country Inn & Suites by Carlson Camp Springs	◆◆◆	$129-$159	480
41 / p. 428	AAA	**Quality Inn Camp Springs**	◆◆	$89-$149 [SAVE]	480
		OXON HILL - Lodgings			
44 / p. 428	AAA	**Comfort Inn Oxon Hill**	◆◆	$89-$179 [SAVE]	492
45 / p. 428	AAA	**Potomac View Lexington Hotel**	◆◆	Rates not provided [SAVE]	492

▼ *See AAA listing p 444* ▼

DOWNTOWN WASHINGTON (See map and index starting on p. 400)

———— WHERE TO STAY ————

BEACON HOTEL AND CORPORATE QUARTERS   *Book great rates at AAA.com*   **Phone:** (202)296-2100   **21**

Small-scale Hotel
$435 All Year

Address: 1615 Rhode Island Ave NW 20036 **Location:** 17th St and Rhode Island Ave NW; just w of Scott Circle. **Facility:** 199 units. 174 one-bedroom standard units, some with efficiencies. 25 one-bedroom suites with efficiencies. 9 stories, interior corridors. *Bath:* combo or shower only. **Parking:** valet. **Terms:** cancellation fee imposed. **Amenities:** CD players, dual phone lines, voice mail, irons, hair dryers. *Fee:* video games, high-speed Internet. *Some:* DVD players (fee). **Leisure Activities:** exercise room. **Guest Services:** valet laundry, wireless Internet. **Business Services:** meeting rooms, business center. **Cards:** AX, CB, DC, DS, MC, VI. **Free Special Amenities:** newspaper and room upgrade (subject to availability with advance reservations). *(See color ad p 434)*

(See map and index starting on p. 400)

BEST WESTERN CAPITOL SKYLINE   *Book great rates at AAA.com*   Phone: (202)488-7500

Small-scale Hotel
$109-$269 3/1-7/31
$89-$269 8/1-2/28

Address: 10 I St SW 20024 **Location:** I-395, exit S Capitol St; S Capitol and I sts NW. **Facility:** 203 units. 197 one-bedroom standard units. 6 one-bedroom suites. 7 stories, interior corridors. *Bath:* combo or shower only. **Parking:** on-site (fee). **Terms:** cancellation fee imposed. **Amenities:** voice mail, safes, irons, hair dryers. **Pool(s):** outdoor. **Guest Services:** valet and coin laundry, area transportation-Metro Station & Smithsonian Museums, wireless Internet. **Business Services:** meeting rooms, PC (fee). **Cards:** AX, CB, DC, DS, MC, VI. **Free Special Amenities:** local telephone calls and high-speed Internet. *(See color ad p 433)*

AAA Benefit:
Members save 10% everyday, plus an exclusive frequent stay program.

  CALL   / SOME UNITS FEE

▼ See AAA listing p 509 ▼

(See map and index starting on p. 400)

BEST WESTERN-GEORGETOWN HOTEL & SUITES *Book great rates at AAA.com* **Phone:** 202/457-0565

Small-scale Hotel
Rates not provided

AAA Benefit:
Members save 10% everyday, plus an exclusive frequent stay program.

Address: 1121 New Hampshire Ave NW 20037 **Location:** Just ne of 22nd St; between L and M sts NW. **Facility:** Smoke free premises. 76 units. 68 one-bedroom standard units. 8 one-bedroom suites. 8 stories, interior corridors. *Bath:* combo or shower only. **Parking:** on-site (fee). **Amenities:** voice mail, irons, hair dryers. **Guest Services:** valet and coin laundry, wireless Internet. **Business Services:** meeting rooms, PC. **Free Special Amenities: expanded continental breakfast and high-speed Internet.** *(See color ad p 435)*

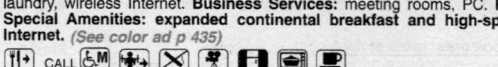
▼ See AAA listing p 432 ▼

(See map and index starting on p. 400)

CAPITAL HILTON

Book great rates at AAA.com   **Phone:** 202/393-1000   49

Large-scale Hotel
Rates not provided

Address: 1001 16th St NW 20036 **Location:** 16th and K sts NW. **Facility:** 544 units. 531 one-bedroom standard units. 12 one- and 1 two-bedroom suites, some with whirlpools. 12 stories, interior corridors. **Parking:** valet. **Amenities:** dual phone lines, voice mail, irons, hair dryers. *Fee:* video games, high-speed Internet. *Some:* CD players. **Leisure Activities:** steamrooms, spa. **Guest Services:** valet laundry, wireless Internet. **Business Services:** conference facilities, business center.

CAPITOL HILL SUITES

Book great rates at AAA.com   **Phone:** (202)543-6000   74

Small-scale Hotel
$365-$449 9/1-2/28
$289-$449 3/1-8/31

Address: 200 C St SE 20003 **Location:** 2 blks from Capitol grounds; at 2nd and C sts SE. Located in a residential area. **Facility:** 152 units. 121 one-bedroom standard units. 31 one-bedroom suites. 5 stories, interior corridors. *Bath:* combo or shower only. **Parking:** valet. **Terms:** 1-7 night minimum stay, cancellation fee imposed. **Amenities:** dual phone lines, voice mail, irons, hair dryers. *Some:* high-speed Internet (fee). **Guest Services:** valet and coin laundry, wireless Internet. **Business Services:** meeting rooms, PC (fee). **Cards:** AX, CB, DC, DS, JC, MC, VI. **Free Special Amenities:** expanded continental breakfast and newspaper.

THE CHURCHILL HOTEL

Book great rates at AAA.com   **Phone:** (202)797-2000   4

Small-scale Hotel
$99-$429 All Year

Address: 1914 Connecticut Ave NW 20009 **Location:** Just n of Dupont Circle. **Facility:** 144 units. 106 one-bedroom standard units. 38 one-bedroom suites. 9 stories, interior corridors. *Bath:* combo or shower only. **Parking:** valet. **Terms:** cancellation fee imposed. **Amenities:** video games (fee), voice mail, irons, hair dryers. *Some:* dual phone lines. **Leisure Activities:** exercise room. **Guest Services:** valet laundry, wireless Internet. **Business Services:** meeting rooms, PC (fee). **Cards:** AX, DC, DS, MC, VI.

COMFORT INN CONVENTION CENTER

Book great rates at AAA.com   **Phone:** (202)682-5300   27

Small-scale Hotel
$99-$319 All Year

Address: 1201 13th St NW 20005 **Location:** Jct 13th and M sts NW. **Facility:** 100 one-bedroom standard units. 9 stories, interior corridors. *Bath:* combo or shower only. **Parking:** valet. **Terms:** cancellation fee imposed. **Amenities:** high-speed Internet, voice mail, irons, hair dryers. **Leisure Activities:** limited exercise equipment. **Guest Services:** valet and coin laundry, wireless Internet. **Business Services:** meeting rooms, PC. **Cards:** AX, CB, DC, DS, MC, VI.

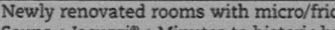

(See map and index starting on p. 400)

COURTYARD BY MARRIOTT CAPITOL HILL/NAVY YARD

 *Book great rates at AAA.com*   **Phone:** 202/479-0027   **80**

Small-scale Hotel
$285-$318 All Year

Address: 140 L St SE 20003 **Location:** I-395, exit Maine Ave SW (which becomes M St SW) and M St SE, 1.1 mi e. **Facility:** Smoke free premises. 204 units. 192 one-bedroom standard units. 12 one-bedroom suites. 14 stories, interior corridors. *Bath:* combo or shower only. **Parking:** on-site (fee). **Amenities:** high-speed Internet, dual phone lines, voice mail, irons, hair dryers. **Pool(s):** heated indoor. **Leisure Activities:** whirlpool, exercise room. **Guest Services:** valet and coin laundry, wireless Internet. **Business Services:** meeting rooms, business center. **Cards:** AX, DC, DS, MC, VI.

AAA Benefit:
Members save 5% off of the best available rate.

COURTYARD BY MARRIOTT-CONVENTION CENTER

Book great rates at AAA.com   **Phone:** 202/638-4600   **65**

Small-scale Hotel
$318-$395 3/1-9/8
$307-$395 9/9-2/28

Address: 900 F St NW 20004 **Location:** At 9th and F sts NW. Located in Penn Quarter area, near Verizon Center. **Facility:** Smoke free premises. 188 units. 179 one-bedroom standard units, some with whirlpools. 9 one-bedroom suites. 10 stories, interior corridors. *Bath:* combo or shower only. **Parking:** valet. **Amenities:** high-speed Internet, dual phone lines, voice mail, irons, hair dryers. **Pool(s):** heated indoor. **Leisure Activities:** whirlpool, exercise room. **Guest Services:** valet and coin laundry, wireless Internet. **Business Services:** meeting rooms, PC (fee). **Cards:** AX, DC, DS, MC, VI.

AAA Benefit:
Members save 5% off of the best available rate.

COURTYARD BY MARRIOTT-EMBASSY ROW

Book great rates at AAA.com   **Phone:** 202/293-8000   **20**

Small-scale Hotel
$307-$362 3/1-9/8
$285-$362 9/9-2/28

Address: 1600 Rhode Island Ave NW 20036 **Location:** 16th and Rhode Island Ave NW, at Scott Circle. **Facility:** Smoke free premises. 158 units. 151 one-bedroom standard units, some with whirlpools. 7 one-bedroom suites. 8 stories, interior corridors. *Bath:* combo or shower only. **Parking:** valet. **Amenities:** video games (fee), high-speed Internet, dual phone lines, voice mail, safes, irons, hair dryers. *Some:* CD players. **Pool(s):** heated indoor. **Leisure Activities:** whirlpool, exercise room. **Guest Services:** valet and coin laundry, wireless Internet. **Business Services:** meeting rooms, business center. **Cards:** AX, DC, DS, JC, MC, VI. **Free Special Amenities:** newspaper and high-speed Internet.

AAA Benefit:
Members save 5% off of the best available rate.

COURTYARD BY MARRIOTT-NORTHWEST

Book great rates at AAA.com   **Phone:** 202/332-9300   **5**

Small-scale Hotel
$252-$340 All Year

Address: 1900 Connecticut Ave NW 20009 **Location:** Just n of Dupont Circle. **Facility:** Smoke free premises. 147 units. 145 one-bedroom standard units. 2 one-bedroom suites, some with whirlpools. 9 stories, interior corridors. *Bath:* combo or shower only. **Parking:** valet. **Amenities:** high-speed Internet, voice mail, safes, irons, hair dryers. **Pool(s):** outdoor. **Leisure Activities:** exercise room. **Guest Services:** valet and coin laundry. **Business Services:** meeting rooms, business center. **Cards:** AX, DC, DS, MC, VI.

AAA Benefit:
Members save 5% off of the best available rate.

DOUBLETREE GUEST SUITES, WASHINGTON DC

Book great rates at AAA.com   **Phone:** 202/785-2000   **61**

Small-scale Hotel
Rates not provided

Address: 801 New Hampshire Ave NW 20037 **Location:** Just sw at Washington Circle. Located in the Foggy Bottom area. **Facility:** 105 units. 103 one- and 2 two-bedroom suites with efficiencies. 10 stories, interior corridors. *Bath:* combo or shower only. **Parking:** valet. **Amenities:** video games (fee), dual phone lines, voice mail, irons, hair dryers. **Pool(s):** outdoor. **Guest Services:** valet and coin laundry, wireless Internet.

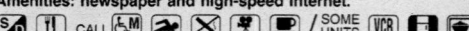

(See map and index starting on p. 400)

DOUBLETREE WASHINGTON, D.C. *Book great rates at AAA.com* Phone: 202/232-7000 **15**

Small-scale Hotel
Rates not provided

Address: 1515 Rhode Island Ave NW 20005 **Location:** Off Scott Circle. **Facility:** 220 units. 211 one-bedroom standard units. 9 one-bedroom suites. 8 stories, interior corridors. *Bath:* combo or shower only. **Parking:** valet. **Amenities:** video games (fee), dual phone lines, voice mail, safes, irons, hair dryers. *Some:* high-speed Internet (fee). **Dining:** 15 ria, see separate listing. **Leisure Activities:** exercise room. **Guest Services:** valet laundry, area transportation-within 5 blks, wireless Internet. **Business Services:** meeting rooms, business center.

THE DUPONT AT THE CIRCLE Phone: (202)332-5251 **7**

Historic Bed
& Breakfast
$160-$370 All Year

Address: 1604 19th St NW 20009 **Location:** Just n of Dupont Circle. **Facility:** These restored 1885 Victorian town homes just off Dupont Circle have wireless Internet, antiques, bathrobes and 400-600 thread count bed linens. Smoke free premises. 10 units. 9 one-bedroom standard units, some with whirlpools. 1 one-bedroom suite with kitchen. 3 stories (no elevator), interior corridors. **Parking:** on-site (fee). **Terms:** office hours 10 am-6 pm, age restrictions may apply, 7 day cancellation notice-fee imposed. **Amenities:** video library, voice mail, hair dryers. *Some:* DVD players, CD players. **Guest Services:** wireless Internet. **Business Services:** meeting rooms. **Cards:** AX, CB, DC, DS, MC, VI. **Free Special Amenities:** expanded continental breakfast and high-speed Internet.

EMBASSY SUITES HOTEL-WASHINGTON DC-DOWNTOWN *Book at AAA.com* Phone: 202/857-3388 **23**

Large-scale Hotel
Rates not provided

Address: 1250 22nd St NW 20037 **Location:** Between M and N sts NW. Located in the West End. **Facility:** 318 units. 316 one- and 2 two-bedroom suites, some with whirlpools. 9 stories, interior corridors. *Bath:* combo or shower only. **Parking:** on-site (fee). **Terms:** check-in 4 pm. **Amenities:** dual phone lines, voice mail, irons, hair dryers. *Fee:* video games, high-speed Internet. **Pool(s):** heated indoor. **Leisure Activities:** sauna, whirlpool, exercise room. *Fee:* game room. **Guest Services:** valet and coin laundry, wireless Internet. **Business Services:** conference facilities, business center.

EMBASSY SUITES WASHINGTON DC CONVENTION CENTER *Book at AAA.com* Phone: 202/739-2001 **55**

Large-scale Hotel
Rates not provided

Address: 900 10th St NW 20001 **Location:** Between K St NW and New York Ave NW. **Facility:** 384 units. 383 one- and 1 two-bedroom suites, some with whirlpools. 14 stories, interior corridors. *Bath:* combo or shower only. **Parking:** valet. **Terms:** check-in 4 pm. **Amenities:** video games (fee), high-speed Internet, dual phone lines, voice mail, safes, irons, hair dryers. **Pool(s):** heated indoor. **Leisure Activities:** whirlpool, exercise room. **Guest Services:** valet and coin laundry, wireless Internet. **Business Services:** meeting rooms, business center.

THE FAIRMONT WASHINGTON, D.C. *Book great rates at AAA.com* Phone: (202)429-2400 **30**

Large-scale Hotel
$189-$699 All Year

Address: 2401 M St NW 20037 **Location:** 24th and M sts NW. Located in the West End. **Facility:** In the West End near Georgetown, the luxury hotel has spacious, well-appointed rooms and suites with ample work space, a sunlit lobby and health club. 415 units. 396 one-bedroom standard units. 19 one-bedroom suites, some with whirlpools. 10 stories, interior corridors. *Bath:* combo or shower only. **Parking:** valet. **Terms:** check-in 4 pm, cancellation fee imposed. **Amenities:** video library, CD players, dual phone lines, voice mail, safes, honor bars, irons, hair dryers. *Fee:* video games, high-speed Internet. *Some:* DVD players. **Dining:** Juniper, see separate listing, entertainment. **Leisure Activities:** saunas, whirlpool, steamroom. *Fee:* squash/racketball court, aerobic and spinning instruction, massage. **Guest Services:** valet laundry, area transportation (fee)-downtown, tanning facilities, wireless Internet. **Business Services:** conference facilities, business center. **Cards:** AX, CB, DC, DS, JC, MC, VI. *(See color ad below)*

(See map and index starting on p. 400)

FOUR POINTS SHERATON WASHINGTON DC DOWNTOWN
Book great rates at AAA.com   Phone: (202)289-7600   **46**

Small-scale Hotel
$355 All Year

Address: 1201 K St NW 20005 **Location:** 12th and K sts NW. Located near the Convention Center. **Facility:** Smoke free premises. 265 units. 263 one-bedroom standard units. 2 one-bedroom suites with whirlpools. 10 stories, interior corridors. *Bath:* combo or shower only. **Parking:** valet. **Terms:** office hours 7 am-11 pm, cancellation fee imposed. **Amenities:** video games (fee), high-speed Internet, dual phone lines, voice mail, safes, irons, hair dryers. *Some:* CD players, fax. **Dining:** Corduroy, see separate listing. **Pool(s):** heated indoor. **Leisure Activities:** sun deck, exercise room. **Guest Services:** valet and coin laundry, wireless Internet. **Business Services:** conference facilities, business center. **Cards:** AX, CB, DC, DS, MC, VI.

FOUR ∗ POINTS
BY SHERATON

AAA Benefit:
Members get up to 15% off, plus Starwood Preferred Guest® bonuses.

FOUR SEASONS HOTEL WASHINGTON D.C.
Book great rates at AAA.com   Phone: (202)342-0444   **35**

Large-scale Hotel
$725 1/1-2/28
$695 3/1-12/31

Address: 2800 Pennsylvania Ave NW 20007 **Location:** In Georgetown. **Facility:** This service-oriented hotel in the heart of bustling Georgetown has an ambience of understated elegance. 211 units. 151 one-bedroom standard units. 60 one-bedroom suites. 6 stories, interior corridors. *Bath:* combo or shower only. **Terms:** cancellation fee imposed. **Amenities:** DVD players, CD players, high-speed Internet (fee), dual phone lines, voice mail, safes, honor bars, irons, hair dryers. *Some:* fax. **Leisure Activities:** saunas, whirlpool, steamrooms, jogging, spa. *Fee:* aerobic instruction. **Guest Services:** valet laundry, area transportation-limo within the district, personal trainer, wireless Internet. **Business Services:** conference facilities, business center. **Cards:** AX, DC, DS, JC, MC, VI.

THE GEORGETOWN INN
Book at AAA.com   Phone: 202/333-8900   **19**

Small-scale Hotel
$129-$409 All Year

Address: 1310 Wisconsin Ave NW 20007 **Location:** Wisconsin Ave and N St NW; just n of M St NW. Located in Georgetown. **Facility:** 96 units. 86 one-bedroom standard units. 10 one-bedroom suites. 6 stories, interior corridors. *Bath:* combo or shower only. **Parking:** valet. **Terms:** cancellation fee imposed. **Amenities:** video games (fee), voice mail, irons, hair dryers. *Some:* CD players. **Leisure Activities:** limited exercise equipment. **Guest Services:** valet laundry, wireless Internet. **Business Services:** meeting rooms, business center. **Cards:** AX, DC, DS, MC, VI.

(See map and index starting on p. 400)

GEORGETOWN SUITES
Book great rates at AAA.com Phone: (202)298-1600 **47**

Small-scale Hotel
$195-$355 All Year

Address: 1000 29th St NW 20007 **Location:** Jct K and 29th sts. Located in Georgetown. **Facility:** 221 units. 102 one-bedroom standard units with efficiencies. 111 one- and 8 two-bedroom suites with kitchens. 6-7 stories, interior corridors. **Parking:** on-site (fee). **Amenities:** CD players, voice mail, safes, irons, hair dryers. *Some:* DVD players. **Leisure Activities:** exercise room. **Guest Services:** valet and coin laundry, wireless Internet. **Business Services:** meeting rooms, business center. **Cards:** AX, CB, DC, DS, JC, MC, VI.

ASK SD [†¦] CALL M 🎥 🛏 📷 💻 / SOME UNITS ✕ VCR

GEORGETOWN UNIVERSITY CONFERENCE HOTEL
Book great rates at AAA.com Phone: 202/687-3200 **6**

Small-scale Hotel
Rates not provided

Address: 3800 Reservoir Rd NW 20057 **Location:** On the campus of Georgetown University; entrance 1, follow signs for the conference center. **Facility:** Smoke free premises. 146 one-bedroom standard units. 5 stories, interior corridors. **Bath:** combo or shower only. **Parking:** on-site (fee). **Amenities:** high-speed Internet (fee), dual phone lines, voice mail, irons, hair dryers. **Leisure Activities:** limited exercise equipment. **Guest Services:** valet and coin laundry. **Business Services:** conference facilities, business center. Affiliated with Marriott Hotels, Resorts and Suites.

Marriott
HOTELS & RESORTS

AAA Benefit:
Members save 5% off of the best available rate.

[†¦] CALL M ✕ 🎥 💻 / SOME UNITS 🛏 📷

GRAND HYATT WASHINGTON AT WASHINGTON CENTER
Book great rates at AAA.com Phone: (202)582-1234 **59**

AAA SAVE

Large-scale Hotel
$169-$539 All Year

Address: 1000 H St NW 20001 **Location:** Jct 11th and H sts NW. **Facility:** Smoke free premises. 888 units. 873 one-bedroom standard units. 15 one-bedroom suites, some with whirlpools. 13 stories, interior corridors. *Bath:* some combo or shower only. **Parking:** on-site (fee) and valet. **Terms:** cancellation fee imposed. **Amenities:** voice mail, honor bars, irons, hair dryers. *Some:* DVD players, dual phone lines, safes. **Dining:** 4 restaurants. **Pool(s):** heated indoor. **Leisure Activities:** *Fee:* saunas, steamrooms, aerobic instruction, massage. **Guest Services:** valet laundry, wireless Internet. **Business Services:** conference facilities, business center. **Cards:** AX, CB, DC, DS, JC, MC, VI. *(See color ad p 440)*

HYATT
HOTELS & RESORTS®

AAA Benefit:
Ask for the AAA rate and save 10%.

SD [†¦] Y [fi] CALL M 🏊 FEE🐾 ✕ ✕ 🎥 💻 / SOME UNITS FEE VCR 🛏 📷

HAMILTON CROWNE PLAZA HOTEL WASHINGTON DC
Book great rates at AAA.com Phone: (202)682-0111 **50**

Large-scale Hotel
$99-$650 All Year

Address: 1001 14th St NW 20005 **Location:** 14th and K sts NW. Located opposite Franklin Park. **Facility:** 318 units. 301 one-bedroom standard units. 17 one-bedroom suites. 13 stories, interior corridors. *Bath:* combo or shower only. **Parking:** valet. **Terms:** cancellation fee imposed. **Amenities:** CD players, dual phone lines, voice mail, safes, irons, hair dryers. *Some:* fax. **Dining:** 14K, see separate listing. **Leisure Activities:** exercise room. **Guest Services:** valet laundry, wireless Internet. **Business Services:** conference facilities, business center. **Cards:** AX, CB, DC, DS, JC, MC, VI. *(See color ad below)*

ASK SD [†¦] CALL M 🎥 💻 / SOME UNITS FEE🐾 ✕ 🛏

───── ▼ *See AAA listing above* ▼ ─────

(See map and index starting on p. 400)

HAMPTON INN WASHINGTON DC CONVENTION CENTER *Book great rates at AAA.com*

Phone: 202/842-2500 **53**

Small-scale Hotel
Rates not provided

Address: 901 6th St NW 20001 **Location:** Jct 6th St and Massachusetts Ave NW. Located two blocks from the Verizon Center and the convention center. **Facility:** 228 units. 218 one-bedroom standard units. 10 one-bedroom suites. 13 stories, interior corridors. *Bath:* combo or shower only. **Parking:** valet. **Terms:** check-in 4 pm. **Amenities:** video games (fee), high-speed Internet, dual phone lines, voice mail, safes, irons, hair dryers. **Pool(s):** heated indoor. **Leisure Activities:** whirlpool, exercise room. **Guest Services:** valet and coin laundry, wireless Internet. **Business Services:** meeting rooms, business center.

[icons] ⫩ CALL ⑤M ➳ ▣ 🖥 🖥 / SOME UNITS ✕

THE HAY-ADAMS *Book at AAA.com*

Phone: (202)638-6600 **58**

Classic Historic
Small-scale Hotel
$800-$6600 10/1-2/28
$700-$6400 3/1-9/30

Address: 800 16th St NW 20006 **Location:** 16th and H sts NW; just n of the White House. Located across Lafayette Park from the White House. **Facility:** Less than two blocks from the McPherson Square Metro Station, the 1927 hotel offers a refined setting; several rooms boast views of the White House. 145 units. 131 one-bedroom standard units. 14 one-bedroom suites. 8 stories, interior corridors. *Bath:* combo or shower only. **Parking:** valet. **Terms:** cancellation fee imposed. **Amenities:** CD players, high-speed Internet, dual phone lines, voice mail, safes, honor bars, irons, hair dryers. **Guest Services:** valet laundry, area transportation, wireless Internet. **Business Services:** meeting rooms, business center. **Cards:** AX, DC, DS, JC, MC, VI.

[icons] ⫩ 24 Y ⑤ CALL ⑤M FEE ➳ / SOME UNITS ✕ ▣

HENLEY PARK HOTEL *Book at AAA.com*

Phone: (202)638-5200 **45**

Historic
Small-scale Hotel
$350-$389 All Year

Address: 926 Massachusetts Ave NW 20001 **Location:** 10th St and Massachusetts Ave NW. Located near the convention center. **Facility:** This 1918 Tudor-style building offers tastefully furnished accommodations near the convention center, business district, Verizon Center and metro. Smoke free premises. 96 units. 95 one-bedroom standard units. 1 one-bedroom suite. 9 stories, interior corridors. **Parking:** valet. **Terms:** cancellation fee imposed. **Amenities:** dual phone lines, voice mail, safes, honor bars, irons, hair dryers. **Dining:** Coeur de Lion, see separate listing. **Guest Services:** valet laundry, area transportation (fee), wireless Internet. **Business Services:** meeting rooms. **Cards:** AX, CB, DC, DS, JC, MC, VI.

[icons] ASK S⑤ ⫩ 24 ➳ ✕ ▣

HILTON GARDEN INN WASHINGTON DC DOWNTOWN *Book great rates at AAA.com*

Phone: 202/783-7800 **56**

Small-scale Hotel
Rates not provided

Address: 815 14th St NW 20005 **Location:** Between H and I sts NW. **Facility:** 300 one-bedroom standard units. 14 stories, interior corridors. *Bath:* combo or shower only. **Parking:** valet. **Amenities:** high-speed Internet, dual phone lines, voice mail, irons, hair dryers. **Pool(s):** heated indoor. **Leisure Activities:** exercise room. **Guest Services:** valet and coin laundry, wireless Internet. **Business Services:** meeting rooms, business center.

[icons] ⫩ CALL ⑤M ➳ ▣ 🖥 🖥 / SOME UNITS ✕

HILTON WASHINGTON *Book great rates at AAA.com*

Phone: 202/483-3000 **3**

Large-scale Hotel
Rates not provided

Address: 1919 Connecticut Ave NW 20009 **Location:** Just n of Dupont Circle at T St NW. **Facility:** 1119 units. 1078 one-bedroom standard units. 41 one-bedroom suites, some with whirlpools. 10 stories, interior corridors. *Bath:* combo or shower only. **Parking:** on-site (fee). **Amenities:** dual phone lines, voice mail, irons, hair dryers. *Fee:* video games, high-speed Internet. *Some:* DVD players. **Pool(s):** heated outdoor. **Leisure Activities:** steamrooms. *Fee:* 3 lighted tennis courts, massage. **Guest Services:** valet laundry, wireless Internet. **Business Services:** conference facilities, business center.

[icons] FEE ✛ ⫩ Y ⑤ CALL ⑤M ➳ FEE ➳ ✕ ▣ / SOME UNITS ✕ FEE ▣

▼ See AAA listing p 490 ▼

(See map and index starting on p. 400)

HILTON WASHINGTON EMBASSY ROW   *Book great rates at AAA.com*   Phone: 202/265-1600

Small-scale Hotel
Rates not provided

Address: 2015 Massachusetts Ave NW 20036 **Location:** Just nw of Dupont Circle. **Facility:** 193 units. 192 one-bedroom standard units. 1 one-bedroom suite. 9 stories, interior corridors. *Bath:* combo or shower only. **Parking:** valet. **Amenities:** video games (fee), dual phone lines, voice mail, safes, irons, hair dryers. *Some:* CD players. **Pool(s):** outdoor. **Leisure Activities:** exercise room. **Guest Services:** valet laundry, wireless Internet. **Business Services:** conference facilities, business center.

HOLIDAY INN CAPITOL   *Book great rates at AAA.com*   Phone: (202)479-4000

Large-scale Hotel
$149-$399 3/1-11/21
$109-$349 11/22-2/28

Address: 550 C St SW 20024 **Location:** Corner of 6th and C sts SW. **Facility:** 532 units. 519 one-bedroom standard units. 13 one-bedroom suites. 9 stories, interior corridors. *Bath:* combo or shower only. **Parking:** on-site (fee). **Amenities:** high-speed Internet, dual phone lines, voice mail, irons, hair dryers. **Dining:** 3 restaurants. **Pool(s):** outdoor. **Leisure Activities:** exercise room. **Guest Services:** valet and coin laundry, wireless Internet. **Business Services:** conference facilities, business center. **Cards:** AX, CB, DC, DS, MC, VI. **Free Special Amenities:** newspaper and high-speed Internet. *(See color ad below)*

HOLIDAY INN-CENTRAL   *Book great rates at AAA.com*   Phone: (202)483-2000

Small-scale Hotel
$129-$259 All Year

Address: 1501 Rhode Island Ave NW 20005 **Location:** Just e of Scott Circle. **Facility:** 212 one-bedroom standard units. 10 stories, interior corridors. *Bath:* combo or shower only. **Parking:** on-site (fee). **Amenities:** video games (fee), dual phone lines, voice mail, irons, hair dryers. **Pool(s):** heated outdoor. **Leisure Activities:** exercise room. *Fee:* game room. **Guest Services:** complimentary and valet laundry, wireless Internet. **Business Services:** meeting rooms, PC (fee). **Cards:** AX, CB, DC, DS, JC, MC, VI. **Free Special Amenities:** newspaper and high-speed Internet. *(See color ad p 444)*

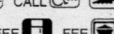 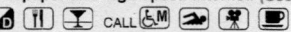

(See map and index starting on p. 400)

HOLIDAY INN GEORGETOWN   *Book great rates at AAA.com*   Phone: (202)338-4600

Large-scale Hotel
$129-$329 All Year

Address: 2101 Wisconsin Ave NW 20007 **Location:** In upper Georgetown area. **Facility:** 285 units. 281 one-bedroom standard units. 4 one-bedroom suites. 7 stories, interior corridors. *Bath:* combo or shower only. **Parking:** on-site (fee). **Terms:** check-in 4 pm. **Amenities:** video games (fee), high-speed Internet, voice mail, irons, hair dryers. **Pool(s):** outdoor. **Leisure Activities:** exercise room. **Guest Services:** valet and coin laundry, area transportation-Foggy Bottom Metro Station. **Business Services:** meeting rooms, business center. **Cards:** AX, CB, DC, DS, JC, MC, VI. **Free Special Amenities: newspaper and high-speed Internet.** *(See color ad p 445)*

HOLIDAY INN WASHINGTON DC ON THE HILL
(NOW KNOWN AS AFFINIA-WASHINGTON D.C.)   *Book great rates at AAA.com*   Phone: 202/638-1616   **72**

Large-scale Hotel
Rates not provided

Address: 415 New Jersey Ave NW 20001 **Location:** On Capitol Hill. **Facility:** 343 one-bedroom standard units. 10 stories, interior corridors. *Bath:* combo or shower only. **Parking:** on-site (fee). **Amenities:** video games (fee), high-speed Internet, dual phone lines, voice mail, irons, hair dryers. *Some:* safes. **Pool(s):** outdoor. **Leisure Activities:** exercise room. **Guest Services:** valet and coin laundry. **Business Services:** conference facilities, business center. *(See color ad p 430)*

HOMEWOOD SUITES BY HILTON WASHINGTON
DC/THOMAS CIRCLE   *Book at AAA.com*   Phone: 202/265-8000   **22**

Small-scale Hotel
Rates not provided

Address: 1475 Massachusetts Ave NW 20005 **Location:** Just nw of Thomas Circle, on service road. **Facility:** 175 one-bedroom suites with efficiencies. 8 stories, interior corridors. *Bath:* combo or shower only. **Parking:** valet. **Terms:** check-in 4 pm. **Amenities:** video games (fee), high-speed Internet, dual phone lines, voice mail, irons, hair dryers. *Some:* DVD players. **Leisure Activities:** exercise room. **Guest Services:** valet and coin laundry, wireless Internet. **Business Services:** meeting rooms, business center.

(See map and index starting on p. 400)

THE HOTEL GEORGE *Book great rates at AAA.com*   **Phone:** (202)347-4200   **68**

(AAA) (SAVE)

▼▼▼▼▼

Small-scale Hotel
$169-$529 All Year

Address: 15 E St NW 20001 **Location:** On Capitol Hill, just n of Capitol grounds. **Facility:** Smoke free premises. 139 units. 138 one-bedroom standard units. 1 one-bedroom suite with whirlpool. 8 stories, interior corridors. *Bath:* combo or shower only. **Parking:** valet. **Amenities:** DVD players, CD players, high-speed Internet, dual phone lines, voice mail, safes, honor bars, irons, hair dryers. **Dining:** Bistro Bis, see separate listing. **Leisure Activities:** steamrooms, exercise room. **Guest Services:** valet laundry, wireless Internet. **Business Services:** meeting rooms, PC, fax (fee). **Cards:** AX, CB, DC, DS, JC, MC, VI. **Free Special Amenities:** newspaper and early check-in/late check-out.
(See color ad starting on p 436)

🍽 ⊡ 🏋 CALL &M ⊠ 👫 / SOME UNITS 🐾 🛢 🖼

HOTEL HELIX *Book great rates at AAA.com*   **Phone:** (202)462-9001   **13**

(AAA) (SAVE)

▼▼▼▼▼

Small-scale Hotel
$139-$389 All Year

Address: 1430 Rhode Island Ave NW 20005 **Location:** Just e of Scott Circle. **Facility:** Smoke free premises. 178 units. 160 one-bedroom standard units. 18 one-bedroom suites. 10 stories, interior corridors. *Bath:* combo or shower only. **Parking:** valet. **Terms:** cancellation fee imposed. **Amenities:** video games (fee), CD players, dual phone lines, voice mail, safes, honor bars, irons, hair dryers. **Leisure Activities:** exercise room. **Guest Services:** valet laundry, wireless Internet. **Business Services:** meeting rooms, business center. *(See color ad starting on p 436)*

S/D 🍽 🏋 CALL &M ⊠ 👫 🛢 💻 / SOME UNITS 🐾 🖼

HOTEL MADERA *Book great rates at AAA.com*   **Phone:** (202)296-7600   **16**

(AAA) (SAVE)

▼▼▼▼▼

Small-scale Hotel
$149-$429 All Year

Address: 1310 New Hampshire Ave NW 20036 **Location:** Between 20th and N sts NW. **Facility:** Smoke free premises. 82 one-bedroom standard units. 10 stories, interior corridors. *Bath:* combo or shower only. **Parking:** valet. **Terms:** cancellation fee imposed. **Amenities:** video games (fee), CD players, high-speed Internet, dual phone lines, voice mail, safes, honor bars, irons, hair dryers. *Some:* DVD players. **Dining:** Firefly, see separate listing. **Guest Services:** valet laundry, wireless Internet. **Business Services:** meeting rooms, PC. **Cards:** AX, DC, DS, MC, VI. **Free Special Amenities:** newspaper and early check-in/late check-out. *(See color ad starting on p 436)*

S/D 🍽 CALL &M FEE 👫 ⊠ 👫 / SOME UNITS 🐾 🛢 🖼

▼ See AAA listing p 444 ▼

(See map and index starting on p. 400)

HOTEL MONACO WASHINGTON DC
Book great rates at AAA.com   **Phone:** (202)628-7177   66

AAA SAVE

WWWW

Historic
Small-scale Hotel
$169-$1200 All Year

Address: 700 F St NW 20004 **Location:** Between 7th and 8th sts NW. Located opposite the National Portrait Gallery in Penn Quarter area. **Facility:** This boutique hotel, in the historic 1839 Tariff Building, has a sophisticated charm; colorful and luxurious rooms range from spacious to cozy. Smoke free premises. 183 units. 163 one-bedroom standard units, some with whirlpools. 20 one-bedroom suites with whirlpools. 4 stories, interior corridors. *Bath:* combo or shower only. **Parking:** valet. **Terms:** cancellation fee imposed. **Amenities:** video games (fee), CD players, high-speed Internet, dual phone lines, voice mail, safes, honor bars, irons, hair dryers. *Some:* DVD players. **Dining:** Poste—Moderne Brasserie, see separate listing. **Leisure Activities:** pool privileges, exercise room. **Guest Services:** valet laundry, wireless Internet. **Business Services:** meeting rooms, business center. **Cards:** AX, CB, DC, DS, JC, MC, VI. *(See color ad starting on p 436)*

HOTEL PALOMAR-A KIMPTON HOTEL
Book great rates at AAA.com   **Phone:** (202)448-1800   11

AAA SAVE

WWWW

Small-scale Hotel
$319-$549 All Year

Address: 2121 P St NW 20037 **Location:** Between 21st and 22nd sts NW; just w of Dupont Circle. **Facility:** 335 units. 295 one-bedroom standard units. 32 one- and 8 two-bedroom suites. 10 stories, interior corridors. *Bath:* combo or shower only. **Parking:** valet. **Terms:** cancellation fee imposed. **Amenities:** DVD players, video games (fee), CD players, high-speed Internet, dual phone lines, voice mail, safes, honor bars, irons, hair dryers. **Dining:** Urbana, see separate listing. **Pool(s):** heated outdoor. **Leisure Activities:** rooftop sun deck, exercise room. **Guest Services:** valet laundry, wireless Internet. **Business Services:** meeting rooms, business center. **Cards:** AX, CB, DC, DS, JC, MC, VI. **Free Special Amenities:** newspaper and high-speed Internet. *(See color ad starting on p 436)*

HOTEL ROUGE
Book great rates at AAA.com   **Phone:** (202)232-8000   18

AAA SAVE

WWWW

Small-scale Hotel
$139-$389 All Year

Address: 1315 16th St NW 20036 **Location:** Just n of Scott Circle. **Facility:** Smoke free premises. 137 one-bedroom standard units. 10 stories, interior corridors. *Bath:* combo or shower only. **Parking:** valet. **Terms:** cancellation fee imposed. **Amenities:** video games (fee), CD players, high-speed Internet, dual phone lines, voice mail, safes, honor bars, irons, hair dryers. *Some:* DVD players. **Leisure Activities:** limited exercise equipment. **Guest Services:** valet laundry, wireless Internet. **Business Services:** meeting rooms, PC. **Cards:** AX, DC, DS, MC, VI. *(See color ad starting on p 436)*

HOTEL WASHINGTON
Book great rates at AAA.com   **Phone:** 202/638-5900   63

WWW

Historic
Large-scale Hotel
Rates not provided

Address: 515 15th St NW 20004 **Location:** 1 blk e of the White House at Pennsylvania Ave and 15th St NW; 2 blks from Metro Center. **Facility:** Near the White House and Metro Center, the 1918 hotel boasts a classic lobby, rooftop dining and a lounge with a view of the Washington Monument. Smoke free premises. 344 units. 328 one-bedroom standard units. 16 one-bedroom suites. 10 stories, interior corridors. *Bath:* combo or shower only. **Parking:** on-site (fee). **Terms:** check-in 4 pm. **Amenities:** video games (fee), voice mail, irons, hair dryers. **Leisure Activities:** saunas, exercise room. **Guest Services:** valet laundry, wireless Internet. **Business Services:** conference facilities, business center.

HYATT REGENCY WASHINGTON ON CAPITOL HILL
Book great rates at AAA.com **Phone:** (202)737-1234   73

AAA SAVE

WWWW

Large-scale Hotel
$109-$499 All Year

Address: 400 New Jersey Ave NW 20001 **Location:** On Capitol Hill. **Facility:** 834 units. 802 one-bedroom standard units. 32 one-bedroom suites. 11 stories, interior corridors. *Bath:* combo or shower only. **Parking:** valet. **Terms:** cancellation fee imposed. **Amenities:** dual phone lines, voice mail, irons, hair dryers. *Some:* CD players. **Pool(s):** heated indoor. **Leisure Activities:** sun deck. *Fee:* massage. **Guest Services:** valet laundry, airport transportation (fee)-Baltimore-Washington, Washington Dulles Int'l & National airports, wireless Internet. **Business Services:** conference facilities, business center. **Cards:** AX, CB, DC, DS, JC, MC, VI. *(See color ad p 440)*

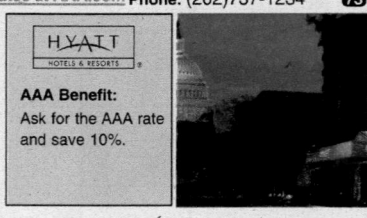

HYATT HOTELS & RESORTS ®

AAA Benefit:
Ask for the AAA rate and save 10%.

THE JEFFERSON
  Phone: 202/347-2200   25

[fyi]

Small-scale Hotel
Rates not provided

Under major renovation, scheduled to be completed December 2008. **Last rated:** WWWW **Address:** 1200 16th St NW 20036 **Location:** 16th and M sts NW. **Facility:** 100 units. 70 one-bedroom standard units. 30 one-bedroom suites, some with kitchens (no utensils) and/or whirlpools. 8 stories, interior corridors. *Bath:* combo or shower only. **Parking:** valet. **Terms:** open 3/1-9/1. **Amenities:** CD players, dual phone lines, voice mail, safes, honor bars, irons, hair dryers. *Fee:* video games, high-speed Internet. *Some:* DVD players. **Leisure Activities:** exercise room, spa. **Guest Services:** valet laundry, wireless Internet. **Business Services:** meeting rooms, business center.

JURYS NORMANDY INN
Book at AAA.com   **Phone:** 202/483-1350   2

WW

Small-scale Hotel
Rates not provided

Address: 2118 Wyoming Ave NW 20008 **Location:** Just w of Connecticut Ave. Located in residential/Embassy area. **Facility:** 75 one-bedroom standard units. 6 stories, interior corridors. *Bath:* combo or shower only. **Parking:** on-site (fee). **Amenities:** high-speed Internet, dual phone lines, voice mail, safes, irons, hair dryers. **Leisure Activities:** exercise room privileges. **Guest Services:** valet and coin laundry, wireless Internet.

(See map and index starting on p. 400)

JURYS WASHINGTON HOTEL   *Book at AAA.com*   Phone: 202/483-6000    **10**

Large-scale Hotel
Rates not provided

Address: 1500 New Hampshire Ave NW 20036 **Location:** At Dupont Circle, Connecticut and Massachusetts aves NW. **Facility:** Smoke free premises. 314 units. 308 one-bedroom standard units. 6 one-bedroom suites. 8 stories, interior corridors. *Bath:* combo or shower only. **Parking:** valet. **Amenities:** high-speed Internet, dual phone lines, voice mail, safes, honor bars, irons, hair dryers. **Leisure Activities:** exercise room. **Guest Services:** valet laundry, wireless Internet. **Business Services:** conference facilities, business center.

JW MARRIOTT PENNSYLVANIA AVE   *Book great rates at AAA.com*   Phone: 202/393-2000   **70**

Large-scale Hotel
$439-$494 3/1-9/8
$406-$494 9/9-2/28

Address: 1331 Pennsylvania Ave NW 20004 **Location:** 14th St and Pennsylvania Ave. Connected to a shopping mall. **Facility:** Smoke free premises. 772 units. 759 one-bedroom standard units. 13 one-bedroom suites, some with whirlpools. 18 stories, interior corridors. *Bath:* combo or shower only. **Parking:** valet. **Terms:** check-in 4 pm. **Amenities:** voice mail, safes, honor bars, irons, hair dryers. *Fee:* video games, high-speed Internet. *Some:* CD players. **Pool(s):** heated indoor. **Leisure Activities:** saunas, whirlpool, exercise room. *Fee:* massage. **Guest Services:** valet laundry, wireless Internet. **Business Services:** conference facilities, business center. **Cards:** AX, DC, DS, JC, MC, VI.

LATHAM HOTEL GEORGETOWN   *Book great rates at AAA.com*   Phone: 202/726-5000   **32**

Small-scale Hotel
$189-$409 3/1-6/30
$129-$349 7/1-2/28

Address: 3000 M St NW 20007 **Location:** Between 30th and 31st sts NW. Located in Georgetown. **Facility:** 142 units. 133 one-bedroom standard units. 9 one-bedroom suites. 10 stories, interior corridors. *Bath:* combo or shower only. **Parking:** valet. **Terms:** cancellation fee imposed. **Amenities:** video games (fee), voice mail, irons, hair dryers. *Some:* dual phone lines. **Dining:** Michel Richard Citronelle, see separate listing. **Pool(s):** outdoor. **Leisure Activities:** exercise room. **Guest Services:** valet laundry, wireless Internet. **Business Services:** meeting rooms, PC. **Cards:** AX, DC, DS, MC, VI.

L'ENFANT PLAZA HOTEL   *Book at AAA.com*   Phone: (202)484-1000   **77**

Large-scale Hotel
$109-$409 All Year

Address: 480 L'Enfant Plaza SW 20024 **Location:** I-395, exit L'Enfant Plaza/12th St. **Facility:** Smoke free premises. 370 one-bedroom standard units. 15 stories, interior corridors. *Bath:* combo or shower only. **Parking:** valet. **Terms:** cancellation fee imposed. **Amenities:** high-speed Internet (fee), dual phone lines, voice mail, safes, irons, hair dryers. *Some:* DVD players, CD players. **Pool(s):** heated indoor/outdoor. **Leisure Activities:** *Fee:* massage. **Guest Services:** valet laundry, wireless Internet. **Business Services:** conference facilities, business center. **Cards:** AX, CB, DC, DS, JC, MC, VI.

THE MADISON, A LOEWS HOTEL   *Book great rates at AAA.com*   Phone: (202)862-1600   **31**

Large-scale Hotel
$189-$459 All Year

Address: 1177 15th St NW 20005 **Location:** 15th and M sts NW. **Facility:** 353 units. 340 one-bedroom standard units. 13 one-bedroom suites, some with whirlpools. 14 stories, interior corridors. *Bath:* combo or shower only. **Parking:** valet. **Terms:** cancellation fee imposed. **Amenities:** dual phone lines, voice mail, safes, irons, hair dryers. *Fee:* video games, high-speed Internet. *Some:* CD players. **Dining:** 2 restaurants. **Leisure Activities:** saunas, steamroom, exercise room. *Fee:* massage. **Guest Services:** valet laundry, wireless Internet. **Business Services:** conference facilities, business center. **Cards:** AX, CB, DC, DS, JC, MC, VI. *(See color ad p 431)*

MANDARIN ORIENTAL, WASHINGTON D.C.   *Book at AAA.com*   Phone: (202)554-8588   **76**

Large-scale Hotel
$495-$8000 ·All Year

Address: 1330 Maryland Ave SW 20024 **Location:** Jct Independence Ave SW, just s on 12th St SW. **Facility:** Surroundings at this luxury hotel are sophisticated and elegant, and the staff displays exceptional attention to detail. 400 units. 347 one-bedroom standard units. 53 one-bedroom suites, some with whirlpools. 10 stories, interior corridors. *Bath:* combo, shower or tub only. **Parking:** valet. **Terms:** cancellation fee imposed. **Amenities:** video library, DVD players, CD players, high-speed Internet (fee), dual phone lines, voice mail, safes, honor bars, irons, hair dryers. **Dining:** Cafe MoZu, CityZen, see separate listings. **Pool(s):** heated indoor. **Leisure Activities:** sauna, whirlpools, steamrooms, exercise room, spa. **Guest Services:** valet laundry, area transportation, wireless Internet. **Business Services:** conference facilities, business center. **Cards:** AX, DC, DS, JC, MC, VI.

MARRIOTT AT METRO CENTER   *Book great rates at AAA.com*   Phone: 202/737-2200   **62**

Large-scale Hotel
$406-$439 3/1-9/8
$362-$439 9/9-2/28

Address: 775 12th St NW 20005 **Location:** Jct 12th and H sts NW; at Metro Center, metro stop. **Facility:** Smoke free premises. 456 units. 454 one-bedroom standard units. 2 one-bedroom suites, some with whirlpools. 14 stories, interior corridors. *Bath:* combo or shower only. **Parking:** valet. **Terms:** check-in 4 pm. **Amenities:** voice mail, irons, hair dryers. *Fee:* video games, high-speed Internet. **Pool(s):** heated indoor. **Leisure Activities:** sauna, whirlpool. **Guest Services:** valet and coin laundry, wireless Internet. **Business Services:** conference facilities, business center. **Cards:** AX, DC, DS, JC, MC, VI.

Marriott
HOTELS & RESORTS

AAA Benefit:
Members save 5% off of the best available rate.

(See map and index starting on p. 400)

THE MAYFLOWER, A RENAISSANCE HOTEL
Book great rates at AAA.com 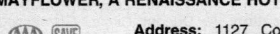 **Phone: 202/347-3000** **37**

AAA Benefit:
Members save 5% off of the best available rate.

Classic Historic Large-scale Hotel
$428-$483 3/1-9/8
$406-$483 9/9-2/28

Address: 1127 Connecticut Ave NW 20036 **Location:** Just n of K St NW; in business district. **Facility:** Smoke free premises. 657 units. 583 one-bedroom standard units. 74 one-bedroom suites. 10 stories, interior corridors. *Bath:* combo or shower only. **Parking:** valet. **Amenities:** high-speed Internet (fee), dual phone lines, voice mail, honor bars, irons, hair dryers. *Some:* CD players. **Dining:** Cafe Promenade, see separate listing, entertainment. **Leisure Activities:** exercise room, in-room exercise equipment. **Guest Services:** valet laundry, wireless Internet. **Business Services:** conference facilities, business center. **Cards:** AX, DC, DS, JC, MC, VI. *(See color ad below)*

THE MELROSE HOTEL, WASHINGTON DC
Book great rates at AAA.com **Phone: (202)955-6400** **48**

Small-scale Hotel
$189-$449 All Year

Address: 2430 Pennsylvania Ave NW 20037 **Location:** Between 24th and 25th sts NW. **Facility:** 240 units. 205 one-bedroom standard units. 35 one-bedroom suites, some with efficiencies and/or whirlpools. 8 stories, interior corridors. *Bath:* combo or shower only. **Parking:** valet. **Terms:** cancellation fee imposed. **Amenities:** dual phone lines, voice mail, safes, honor bars, irons, hair dryers. *Fee:* video games, high-speed Internet. *Some:* CD players. **Leisure Activities:** exercise room. **Guest Services:** valet laundry. **Business Services:** meeting rooms, business center. **Cards:** AX, CB, DC, DS, JC, MC, VI.

MORRISON-CLARK HISTORIC INN AND RESTAURANT
Book at AAA.com **Phone: (202)898-1200** **39**

Historic Small-scale Hotel
$319-$389 All Year

Address: 1015 L St NW 20001 **Location:** 11th and L sts NW; just n of Massachusetts Ave. Located near the Convention Center. **Facility:** The 1865 townhouses were the Soldiers, Sailors, Marines and Airmen's Club and now offer varied rooms, some with balconies overlooking a courtyard. Smoke free premises. 54 units. 41 one-bedroom standard units. 13 one-bedroom suites. 5 stories, interior/exterior corridors. **Parking:** valet. **Terms:** cancellation fee imposed. **Amenities:** voice mail, honor bars, irons, hair dryers. **Dining:** restaurant, see separate listing. **Leisure Activities:** limited exercise equipment. *Fee:* massage. **Guest Services:** valet laundry, area transportation, wireless Internet. **Business Services:** meeting rooms, PC. **Cards:** AX, CB, DC, DS, JC, MC, VI.

ONE WASHINGTON CIRCLE HOTEL
Book great rates at AAA.com **Phone: 202/872-1680** **44**

Small-scale Hotel
Rates not provided

Address: One Washington Circle NW 20037 **Location:** Between 23rd St and New Hampshire Ave NW. Located opposite George Washington University Hospital. **Facility:** 151 units. 101 one-bedroom standard units, some with efficiencies. 50 one-bedroom suites with kitchens. 9 stories, interior corridors. *Bath:* combo or shower only. **Parking:** valet. **Amenities:** video games (fee), CD players, high-speed Internet, dual phone lines, voice mail, safes, irons, hair dryers. **Pool(s):** outdoor. **Leisure Activities:** exercise room. **Guest Services:** valet laundry, wireless Internet. **Business Services:** meeting rooms. *(See color ad p 449)*

(See map and index starting on p. 400)

PARK HYATT WASHINGTON, D.C. *Book great rates at AAA.com* **Phone:** (202)789-1234 28

AAA SAVE

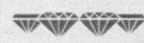

Large-scale Hotel
$249-$599 All Year

Address: 1201 24th St NW 20037 **Location:** 24th and M sts NW. Located in the West End. **Facility:** 215 units. 195 one-bedroom standard units. 20 one-bedroom suites. 10 stories, interior corridors. *Bath:* combo or shower only. **Parking:** valet. **Terms:** cancellation fee imposed. **Amenities:** high-speed Internet, dual phone lines, voice mail, safes, honor bars, hair dryers. **Dining:** Blue Duck Tavern, see separate listing. **Pool(s):** heated indoor. **Leisure Activities:** whirlpool. *Fee:* in-room spa services, massage. **Guest Services:** valet laundry, airport transportation (fee)-Ronald Reagan Washington National Airport, area transportation-within 3 mi, wireless Internet. **Business Services:** conference facilities, business center. **Cards:** AX, CB, DC, DS, JC, MC, VI.

FEE CALL / SOME UNITS FEE

HYATT HOTELS & RESORTS

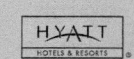

AAA Benefit:
Ask for the AAA rate and save 10%.

PHOENIX PARK HOTEL *Book great rates at AAA.com* **Phone:** (202)638-6900 64

AAA SAVE

Historic
Small-scale Hotel
$159-$479 All Year

Address: 520 N Capitol St NW 20001 **Location:** Just n of Capitol grounds. **Facility:** Near the Capitol and Union Station, the hotel is a small, European-style hotel with Celtic-style ambience; while rooms are tasteful, some are compact. 149 units. 143 one-bedroom standard units. 6 one-bedroom suites. 9 stories, interior corridors. *Bath:* combo or shower only. **Parking:** valet. **Terms:** cancellation fee imposed. **Amenities:** dual phone lines, voice mail, irons, hair dryers. *Fee:* video games, high-speed Internet. *Some:* honor bars. **Dining:** entertainment. **Leisure Activities:** exercise room. **Guest Services:** valet laundry, wireless Internet. **Business Services:** meeting rooms, business center. **Cards:** AX, DC, DS, MC, VI.

CALL / SOME UNITS

▼ See AAA listing p 448 ▼

▼ See AAA listing p 450 ▼

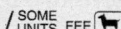

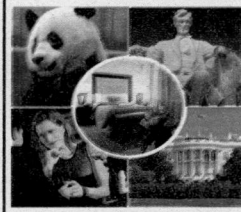

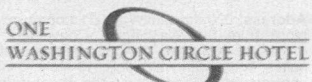

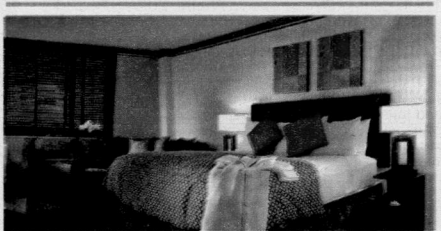

(See map and index starting on p. 400)

THE QUINCY   *Book great rates at AAA.com*   Phone: (202)223-4320   [41]

Small-scale Hotel
$139-$289 3/1-10/31
$109-$289 11/1-2/28

Address: 1823 L St NW 20036 **Location:** Between 18th and 19th sts NW. **Facility:** 99 one-bedroom standard units, some with kitchens. 10 stories, interior corridors. *Bath:* combo or shower only. **Parking:** on-site (fee). **Terms:** cancellation fee imposed. **Amenities:** video games (fee), high-speed Internet, voice mail, safes, irons, hair dryers. *Some:* CD players. **Guest Services:** valet and coin laundry, wireless Internet. **Business Services:** meeting rooms, PC. **Cards:** AX, DC, DS, MC, VI. *(See color ad p 449)*

   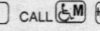   

RED ROOF INN DOWNTOWN WASHINGTON, D.C.   *Book at AAA.com*   Phone: 202/289-5959   [60]

Small-scale Hotel
Rates not provided

Address: 500 H St NW 20001 **Location:** At 5th and H sts NW; in Chinatown. **Facility:** 196 one-bedroom standard units. 10 stories, interior corridors. *Bath:* combo or shower only. **Parking:** on-site (fee). **Amenities:** video games (fee), voice mail, irons, hair dryers. **Leisure Activities:** sauna, limited exercise equipment. **Guest Services:** valet and coin laundry, wireless Internet.

RENAISSANCE M STREET HOTEL   *Book great rates at AAA.com*   Phone: 202/775-0800   [33]

Large-scale Hotel
$373-$417 3/1-9/8
$329-$417 9/9-2/28

Address: 1143 New Hampshire Ave NW 20037 **Location:** Just e of 22nd and M sts NW. **Facility:** Smoke free premises. 355 units. 347 one-bedroom standard units. 8 one-bedroom suites. 9 stories, interior corridors. *Bath:* combo or shower only. **Parking:** valet. **Amenities:** dual phone lines, voice mail, safes, irons, hair dryers. *Fee:* video games, high-speed Internet. **Leisure Activities:** exercise room. **Guest Services:** valet laundry, wireless Internet. **Business Services:** conference facilities, business center. **Cards:** AX, DC, DS, MC, VI. **Free Special Amenities: newspaper and room upgrade (subject to availability with advance reservations).**

AAA Benefit: Members save 5% off of the best available rate.

RENAISSANCE WASHINGTON DC HOTEL   *Book great rates at AAA.com*   Phone: 202/898-9000   [52]

Large-scale Hotel
$384-$439 3/1-9/8
$373-$439 9/9-2/28

Address: 999 9th St NW 20001 **Location:** 9th and K sts NW. Located one block from the Washington Convention Center. **Facility:** Smoke free premises. 807 units. 794 one-bedroom standard units. 16 one-bedroom suites, some with whirlpools. 16 stories, interior corridors. *Bath:* combo or shower only. **Parking:** on-site (fee) and valet. **Amenities:** high-speed Internet (fee), voice mail, irons, hair dryers. **Dining:** 2 restaurants. **Leisure Activities:** steamrooms, aerobic instruction. *Fee:* massage. **Guest Services:** valet laundry, wireless Internet. **Business Services:** conference facilities, business center. **Cards:** AX, DC, DS, JC, MC, VI. **Free Special Amenities: newspaper.**

AAA Benefit: Members save 5% off of the best available rate.

RESIDENCE INN BY MARRIOTT CAPITOL   *Book great rates at AAA.com*   Phone: 202/484-8280   [78]

Small-scale Hotel
$285-$362 All Year

Address: 333 E St SW 20024 **Location:** Between 3rd and 4th sts SW. **Facility:** Smoke free premises. 233 units. 102 one-bedroom standard units with efficiencies. 107 one- and 24 two-bedroom suites, some with efficiencies or kitchens. 13 stories, interior corridors. *Bath:* combo or shower only. **Parking:** on-site (fee). **Terms:** check-in 4 pm. **Amenities:** video games (fee), high-speed Internet, dual phone lines, voice mail, safes, irons, hair dryers. **Pool(s):** heated indoor. **Leisure Activities:** whirlpool, exercise room. **Guest Services:** valet and coin laundry, wireless Internet. **Business Services:** meeting rooms, business center. **Cards:** AX, DS, MC, VI.

AAA Benefit: Members save 5% off of the best available rate.

(See map and index starting on p. 400)

RESIDENCE INN BY MARRIOTT-DUPONT CIRCLE

Book great rates at AAA.com   **Phone:** 202/466-6800   **12**

Small-scale Hotel
$307-$373 3/1-9/8
$285-$373 9/9-2/28

Address: 2120 P St NW 20037 **Location:** Between 21st and 22nd sts NW; just w of Dupont Circle. **Facility:** Smoke free premises. 107 units. 48 one-bedroom standard units with efficiencies. 43 one- and 16 two-bedroom suites, some with efficiencies or kitchens. 10 stories, interior corridors. *Bath:* combo or shower only. **Parking:** on-site (fee). **Amenities:** video games (fee), high-speed Internet, dual phone lines, voice mail, irons, hair dryers. **Leisure Activities:** exercise room. **Guest Services:** valet and coin laundry, wireless Internet. **Business Services:** meeting rooms, PC. **Cards:** AX, DC, DS, JC, MC, VI.

AAA Benefit:
Members save 5% off of the best available rate.

(ASK) (S) (T+) CALL (M) (X) (📷) (🔲) (🔲) (🔲) / SOME UNITS FEE (🐾)

RESIDENCE INN BY MARRIOTT-WASHINGTON DC-VERMONT AVE

Book great rates at AAA.com   **Phone:** 202/898-1100   **36**

Small-scale Hotel
$307-$373 3/1-9/8
$296-$373 9/9-2/28

Address: 1199 Vermont Ave NW 20005 **Location:** Jct 14th St and Vermont Ave NW, at Thomas Circle. **Facility:** Smoke free premises. 202 units. 182 one-bedroom standard units with efficiencies. 20 one-bedroom suites, some with efficiencies or kitchens. 12 stories, interior corridors. *Bath:* combo or shower only. **Parking:** valet. **Terms:** check-in 4 pm. **Amenities:** video games (fee), high-speed Internet, voice mail, irons, hair dryers. **Leisure Activities:** exercise room. **Guest Services:** valet and coin laundry. **Business Services:** meeting rooms, business center. **Cards:** AX, DC, DS, JC, MC, VI.

AAA Benefit:
Members save 5% off of the best available rate.

(ASK) (S) (T+) CALL (M) (X) (📷) (🔲) (🔲) (🔲) / SOME UNITS FEE (🐾)

THE RITZ-CARLTON, GEORGETOWN

Book at AAA.com   **Phone:** 202/912-4100   **42**

Small-scale Hotel
Rates not provided

Address: 3100 South St NW 20007 **Location:** Just s of jct M St and Wisconsin Ave; off Wisconsin Ave, just e; in Georgetown. **Facility:** Smoke free premises. 86 units. 52 one-bedroom standard units. 34 one-bedroom suites, some with whirlpools. 5-6 stories, interior corridors. *Bath:* combo or shower only. **Parking:** valet. **Amenities:** video library, DVD players, CD players, dual phone lines, voice mail, safes, honor bars, irons. *Fee:* video games, high-speed Internet. **Dining:** Fahrenheit, see separate listing. **Leisure Activities:** saunas, steamrooms, exercise room, spa. **Guest Services:** valet laundry, area transportation, wireless Internet. **Business Services:** meeting rooms, business center.

(🍴) (24) (Y) (🏃) CALL (M) (X) (X) (📷) / SOME UNITS FEE (🐾) (🔲) (🔲)

THE RITZ-CARLTON, WASHINGTON, DC

Book at AAA.com   **Phone:** 202/835-0500   **38**

Large-scale Hotel
Rates not provided

Address: 1150 22nd St NW 20037 **Location:** At 22nd and M sts NW. **Facility:** Smoke free premises. 300 units. 268 one-bedroom standard units. 32 one-bedroom suites, some with whirlpools. 11 stories, interior corridors. *Bath:* combo or shower only. **Parking:** on-site (fee) and valet. **Amenities:** CD players, dual phone lines, voice mail, safes, honor bars, irons, hair dryers. *Fee:* video games, high-speed Internet. *Some:* DVD players, fax. **Pool(s):** heated indoor. **Leisure Activities:** spa. *Fee:* saunas, steamrooms, exercise classes, yoga, spinning. **Guest Services:** valet laundry, area transportation, beauty salon, wireless Internet. **Business Services:** conference facilities, business center.

(🍴) (24) (Y) (🏃) CALL (M) (🏊) FEE (✚) (X) (X) (📷) (🔲) / SOME UNITS FEE (🐾) (VCR)

THE RIVER INN

Book great rates at AAA.com   **Phone:** 202/337-7600   **54**

Small-scale Hotel
Rates not provided

Address: 924 25th St NW 20037 **Location:** Between K and I sts NW. Located in the Foggy Bottom area. **Facility:** 125 units. 97 one-bedroom standard units with efficiencies. 28 one-bedroom suites with efficiencies. 9 stories, interior corridors. **Parking:** valet. **Amenities:** video games (fee), high-speed Internet, dual phone lines, voice mail, safes, irons, hair dryers. *Some:* DVD players, CD players. **Dining:** Dish, see separate listing. **Leisure Activities:** limited exercise equipment. **Guest Services:** valet and coin laundry, wireless Internet. **Business Services:** meeting rooms, business center.

(🍴) CALL (M) (📷) (🔲) (🔲) (🔲) / SOME UNITS FEE (🐾) (X) (VCR)

ST. GREGORY LUXURY HOTEL & SUITES

Book great rates at AAA.com   **Phone:** (202)530-3600   **24**

(AAA) (SAVE)

Small-scale Hotel
$399-$579 3/1-12/31
$389-$559 1/1-2/28

Address: 2033 M St NW 20036 **Location:** Jct M and 21st sts NW. **Facility:** Smoke free premises. 154 units. 54 one-bedroom standard units, some with kitchens. 9 stories, interior corridors. *Bath:* combo or shower only. **Parking:** valet. **Amenities:** CD players, dual phone lines, voice mail, irons, hair dryers. *Fee:* video games, high-speed Internet. *Some:* honor bars. **Leisure Activities:** exercise room. **Guest Services:** valet and coin laundry, wireless Internet. **Business Services:** meeting rooms, business center. **Cards:** AX, CB, DC, DS, MC, VI. **Free Special Amenities:** newspaper and room upgrade (subject to availability with advance reservations). *(See color ad p 434)*

(S) (🍴) (Y) CALL (M) (📷) (🔲) (🔲) / SOME UNITS FEE (X) (VCR) (🔲)

(See map and index starting on p. 400)

ST. REGIS, WASHINGTON, D.C.

Phone: (202)638-2626 **51**

AAA SAVE fyi
Historic
Large-scale Hotel
$795 All Year

Under major renovation, scheduled to be completed September 2007. Last rated: ▼▼▼▼ **Address:** 923 16th St NW 20006 **Location:** 16th and K sts; just n of the White House. **Facility:** Find an aura of opulence at the 1926 luxury hotel near the White House, with tasteful rooms, marble bathrooms, quality amenities and turndown service. 193 units. 178 one-bedroom standard units. 15 one-bedroom suites. 8 stories, interior corridors. **Parking:** valet. **Terms:** cancellation fee imposed. **Amenities:** high-speed Internet (fee), dual phone lines, voice mail, safes, honor bars, hair dryers. *Some:* DVD players, CD players, fax. **Guest Services:** valet laundry, area transportation-within 7-10 blks. **Business Services:** conference facilities, business center. **Cards:** AX, DC, MC, VI. **Free Special Amenities:** newspaper.

ST. REGIS HOTELS & RESORTS
AAA Benefit:
Luxury at a preferred rate for members only.

[icons: 🍴 24🈁 🍸 📶 CALL 🅼 FEE 🏋 📽 / SOME UNITS FEE 🐕 ✖ VCR]

SOFITEL LAFAYETTE SQUARE WASHINGTON DC   *Book at AAA.com*

Phone: 202/730-8800 **57**

▼▼▼▼
Small-scale Hotel
Rates not provided

Address: 806 15th St NW 20005 **Location:** Jct 15th and H sts NW. **Facility:** Blocks from the White House, the intimate hotel has rich public areas, an attentive staff, dining and exercise rooms and well-appointed rooms. 237 units. 220 one-bedroom standard units. 17 one-bedroom suites, some with whirlpools. 12 stories, interior corridors. *Bath:* combo or shower only. **Parking:** valet. **Amenities:** high-speed Internet (fee), dual phone lines, voice mail, safes, honor bars, irons, hair dryers. *Some:* DVD players (fee), fax. **Dining:** Cafe 15, see separate listing. **Leisure Activities:** exercise room. **Guest Services:** valet laundry, wireless Internet. **Business Services:** meeting rooms, business center.

[icons: 🍴 24🈁 🍸 📶 CALL 🅼 📽 / SOME UNITS 🐕 ✖ FEE VCR]

STATE PLAZA HOTEL   *Book at AAA.com*

Phone: 202/861-8200 **71**

▼▼▼
Small-scale Hotel
Rates not provided

Address: 2117 E St NW 20037 **Location:** Between 21st St and Virginia Ave NW. **Facility:** Smoke free premises. 228 units. 173 one-bedroom standard units with efficiencies. 55 one-bedroom suites with kitchens. 8 stories, interior corridors. **Parking:** on-site (fee). **Amenities:** dual phone lines, voice mail, safes, honor bars, irons, hair dryers. *Fee:* video games, high-speed Internet. **Leisure Activities:** exercise room. **Guest Services:** valet laundry. **Business Services:** meeting rooms, business center.

[icons: 🍴 CALL 🅼 ✖ 📽 🛗 ☕ / SOME UNITS 🍽]

TOPAZ HOTEL   *Book great rates at AAA.com*

Phone: (202)393-3000 **17**

AAA SAVE
▼▼▼▼
Small-scale Hotel
$139-$409 All Year

Address: 1733 N St NW 20036 **Location:** Just e of Connecticut Ave. **Facility:** Smoke free premises. 99 one-bedroom standard units. 10 stories, interior corridors. *Bath:* combo or shower only. **Parking:** valet. **Terms:** cancellation fee imposed. **Amenities:** CD players, dual phone lines, voice mail, safes, honor bars, irons, hair dryers. *Some:* DVD players. **Guest Services:** valet laundry, wireless Internet. **Business Services:** meeting rooms, PC (fee). **Cards:** AX, DC, DS, MC, VI.
(See color ad starting on p 436)

[icons: 🆂ⅅ 🍴 🍸 CALL 🅼 FEE 🏋 ✖ 📽 / SOME UNITS 🐕]

THE WASHINGTON COURT HOTEL   *Book at AAA.com*

Phone: 202/628-2100 **67**

▼▼▼
Large-scale Hotel
Rates not provided

Address: 525 New Jersey Ave NW 20001 **Location:** 3 blks from Capitol grounds. **Facility:** Smoke free premises. 267 units. 263 one-bedroom standard units. 4 one-bedroom suites, some with whirlpools. 16 stories, interior corridors. *Bath:* combo or shower only. **Parking:** valet. **Terms:** check-in 4 pm. **Amenities:** dual phone lines, voice mail, irons, hair dryers. *Fee:* video games, high-speed Internet. *Some:* DVD players, CD players. **Leisure Activities:** exercise room. **Guest Services:** valet laundry, wireless Internet. **Business Services:** conference facilities, business center.

[icons: 🍴 🍸 CALL 🅼 ✖ 📽 ☕ / SOME UNITS VCR FEE 🛗]

WASHINGTON MARRIOTT HOTEL   *Book great rates at AAA.com*

Phone: 202/872-1500 **26**

AAA SAVE
▼▼▼▼
Large-scale Hotel
$318-$384 3/1-9/8
$296-$384 9/9-2/28

Address: 1221 22nd St NW 20037 **Location:** 22nd and M sts NW. Located in the west end. **Facility:** Smoke free premises. 418 units. 415 one-bedroom standard units. 3 one-bedroom suites. 9 stories, interior corridors. *Bath:* combo or shower only. **Parking:** on-site (fee). **Terms:** check-in 4 pm. **Amenities:** voice mail, irons, hair dryers. *Fee:* video games, high-speed Internet. **Pool(s):** heated indoor. **Leisure Activities:** sauna, whirlpool, locker rooms, exercise room. **Guest Services:** complimentary and valet laundry, wireless Internet. **Business Services:** conference facilities, business center. **Cards:** AX, DC, DS, JC, MC, VI. **Free Special Amenities:** newspaper.

Marriott HOTELS & RESORTS
AAA Benefit:
Members save 5% off of the best available rate.

[icons: 🆂ⅅ 🍴 🍸 CALL 🅼 🏊 ✖ ✖ 📽 ☕ / SOME UNITS 🛗]

(See map and index starting on p. 400)

WASHINGTON SUITES GEORGETOWN

Book great rates at AAA.com

Phone: (202)333-8060

Small-scale Hotel
$169-$394 All Year

Address: 2500 Pennsylvania Ave NW 20037 **Location:** Jct 25th St NW and Pennsylvania Ave; 2 blks from Foggy Bottom metro station. **Facility:** 124 one-bedroom suites with kitchens. 10 stories, interior corridors. *Bath:* combo or shower only. **Parking:** valet. **Amenities:** video games (fee), high-speed Internet, dual phone lines, voice mail, irons, hair dryers. **Leisure Activities:** limited exercise equipment. **Guest Services:** valet and coin laundry. **Business Services:** *Fee:* PC, fax. **Cards:** AX, DC, DS, MC, VI. **Free Special Amenities: expanded continental breakfast and high-speed Internet.** *(See color ad below)*

THE WESTIN EMBASSY ROW

Phone: (202)293-2100

Small-scale Hotel
$219-$759 All Year

Address: 2100 Massachusetts Ave NW 20008 **Location:** Just w of Dupont Circle; at 21st St. **Facility:** Smoke free premises. 207 units. 174 one-bedroom standard units. 33 one-bedroom suites, some with whirlpools. 8 stories, interior corridors. *Bath:* combo or shower only. **Parking:** valet. **Terms:** cancellation fee imposed. **Amenities:** dual phone lines, voice mail, safes, honor bars, irons, hair dryers. *Fee:* video games, high-speed Internet. *Some:* DVD players (fee), CD players, fax. **Leisure Activities:** saunas, exercise room. *Fee:* massage. **Guest Services:** valet laundry, wireless Internet. **Business Services:** conference facilities, business center. **Cards:** AX, DC, DS, JC, MC, VI. **Free Special Amenities: newspaper.**

WESTIN
HOTELS & RESORTS

AAA Benefit:
Members get up to 15% off, plus Starwood Preferred Guest® bonuses.

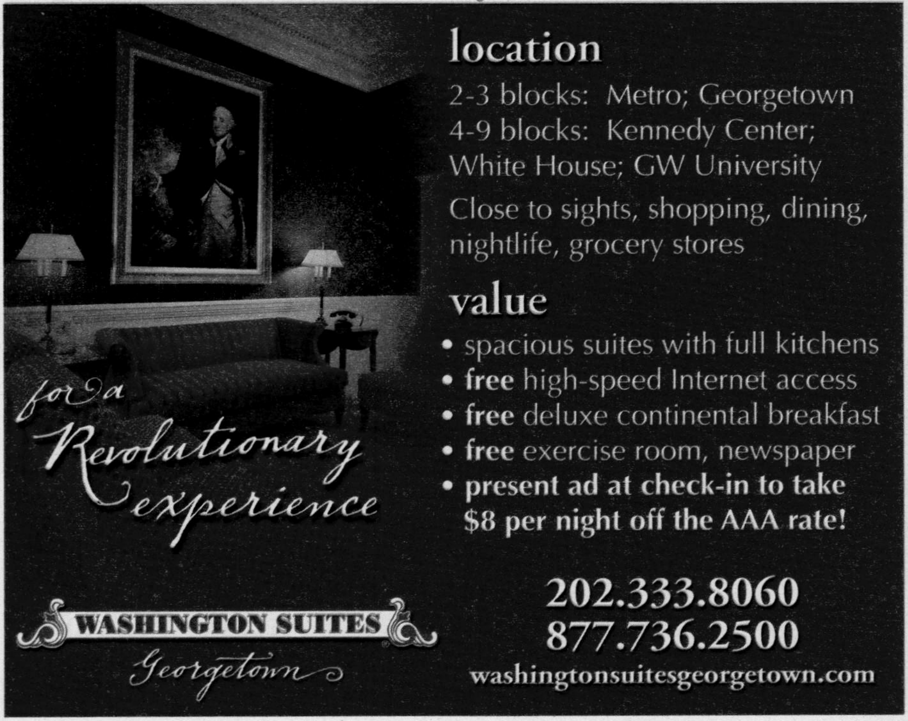

(See map and index starting on p. 400)

THE WESTIN GRAND   *Book great rates at AAA.com*   Phone: (202)429-0100   **34**

Large-scale Hotel
$189-$569 1/1-2/28
$179-$549 3/1-12/31

Address: 2350 M St NW 20037 **Location:** 24th and M sts NW. Located in the West End. **Facility:** Smoke free premises. 263 units. 258 one-bedroom standard units, some with whirlpools. 5 one-bedroom suites with whirlpools. 8 stories, interior corridors. *Bath:* combo or shower only. **Parking:** on-site (fee) and valet. **Terms:** 3 day cancellation notice-fee imposed. **Amenities:** CD players, high-speed Internet (fee), dual phone lines, voice mail, safes, honor bars, irons, hair dryers. *Some:* fax. **Pool(s):** heated outdoor. **Leisure Activities:** exercise room. **Guest Services:** valet laundry, wireless Internet. **Business Services:** conference facilities, business center. **Cards:** AX, DS, MC, VI.

THE WESTIN WASHINGTON DC CITY CENTER
HOTEL   *Book great rates at AAA.com*   Phone: (202)429-1700   **29**

Large-scale Hotel
$119-$439 All Year

Address: 1400 M St NW 20005 **Location:** Just w of Thomas Circle. **Facility:** Smoke free premises. 406 units. 399 one-bedroom standard units. 7 one-bedroom suites, some with whirlpools. 14 stories, interior corridors. *Bath:* combo or shower only. **Parking:** valet. *Some:* video games, high-speed Internet. *Some:* DVD players, CD players, fax. **Dining:** 2 restaurants. **Leisure Activities:** exercise room. **Guest Services:** valet laundry, wireless Internet. **Business Services:** conference facilities, business center. **Cards:** AX, MC, VI. **Free Special Amenities:** newspaper.

Phone lines, voice mail, safes, honor bars, irons, hair dryers. **Fee:** video games, high-speed Internet.

THE WILLARD INTERCONTINENTAL   *Book at AAA.com*   Phone: (202)628-9100   **69**

Classic Historic
Large-scale Hotel
$299-$879 All Year

Address: 1401 Pennsylvania Ave NW 20004 **Location:** Just e of the White House. **Facility:** This luxury hotel features an eye-catching architectural design; it is conveniently close to the White House. Smoke free premises. 332 units. 292 one-bedroom standard units. 40 one-bedroom suites, some with whirlpools. 12 stories, interior corridors. *Bath:* combo or shower only. **Parking:** valet. **Terms:** cancellation fee imposed. **Amenities:** video library, CD players, high-speed Internet (fee), dual phone lines, voice mail, safes, honor bars, irons, hair dryers. *Some:* DVD players. **Dining:** The Willard Room, see separate listing. **Leisure Activities:** saunas, steamrooms, exercise room, spa. **Guest Services:** valet laundry, personal trainers, wireless Internet. **Business Services:** conference facilities, business center. **Cards:** AX, CB, DC, DS, JC, MC, VI.

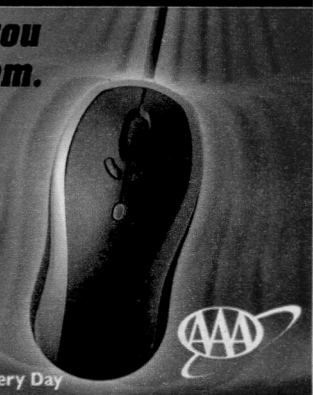

(See map and index starting on p. 400)

———— WHERE TO DINE ————

14K

American
$8-$36

Phone: 202/682-0111   ⑦④

The hotel restaurant sustains a casual, comfortable dining atmosphere. Seasonal sidewalk seating overlooks Franklin Park. The menu centers on well-prepared beef, seafood and pasta dishes. Casual dress. **Bar:** Full bar. **Reservations:** accepted. **Hours:** 6:30 am-10 pm. **Address:** 1001 14th St NW 20005 **Location:** 14th and K sts NW; in Hamilton Crowne Plaza Hotel Washington DC. **Parking:** valet. **Cards:** AX, DC, DS, JC, MC, VI.

CALL   🅼

15 RIA

American
$7-$23

Phone: 202/521-7101   ②⑦

The hotel restaurant has a soothing, stylish dining room and a talented kitchen staff. The chef uses fresh ingredients to prepare contemporary American cuisine and offers daily specials popular with the regulars. The service is professional and efficient. Casual dress. **Bar:** Full bar. **Reservations:** suggested. **Hours:** 6:30 am-2 & 5:30-11 pm, Sat & Sun from 7 am. **Address:** 1515 Rhode Island Ave NW 20005 **Location:** Off Scott Circle; in DoubleTree Washington, D.C. **Parking:** valet. **Cards:** AX, CB, DC, DS, MC, VI.

CALL   🅼

1789 RESTAURANT

American
$18-$38

Phone: 202/965-1789   ③⑧

Nestled among narrow streets and busy sidewalks near the university, the restaurant employs a chef who uses fresh local produce to prepare creative American regional dishes with an upscale touch. Prices are reasonable for this level of quality, but diners who find them too steep might opt instead for the prix-fixe selection offered before 6:45 pm. Waiters aren't the only ones who must dress up, as the formal dress code requires men to don jackets. Formal attire. **Bar:** Full bar. **Reservations:** suggested. **Hours:** 6 pm-10 pm, Fri-11 pm, Sat 5:30 pm-11 pm, Sun 5:30 pm-10 pm. Closed: 7/4, 12/25. **Address:** 1226 36th St NW 20007 **Location:** In Georgetown; just e of Georgetown University. **Parking:** valet. **Cards:** AX, CB, DC, DS, MC, VI.

701 PENNSYLVANIA AVENUE

American
$12-$33

Phone: 202/393-0701   ①③②

The upscale dining room and seasonal outdoor seating area overlook the Naval Memorial. Service is professional and attentive. Although the menu of contemporary American dishes—including preparations of fresh seafood, beef and lamb—changes seasonally, the tuna tartare appetizer is a tradition. Valet parking is available for a fee during dinner. Dressy casual. **Bar:** Full bar. **Reservations:** suggested. **Hours:** 11:30 am-3 & 5:30-10:30 pm, Fri-11:30 pm, Sat 5:30 pm-11:30 pm, Sun 5 pm-9:30 pm. Closed major holidays. **Address:** 701 Pennsylvania Ave NW 20004 **Location:** Market Square; adjacent to the US Navy Memorial, between 7th and 9th sts NW. **Parking:** no self-parking. **Cards:** AX, CB, DC, DS, MC, VI.

ACADIANA

South American
$14-$29

Phone: 202/408-8848   ⑦⑨

Cultural and flavorful describes the Louisiana dishes created under the direction of Chef Tunks. The menu balances seafood and premium meats using a variety of cooking techniques reflective of the area. The comfortable, upscale setting suits most any occasion. Valet parking is available at dinner for a fee. Casual dress. **Bar:** Full bar. **Reservations:** suggested. **Hours:** 11:30 am-2:30 & 5:30-10:30 pm, Fri-11 pm, Sat 5:30 pm-11 pm. Closed major holidays; also Sun. **Address:** 901 New York Ave NW 20001 **Location:** Between 9th and 10th sts. **Parking:** no self-parking. **Cards:** AX, DC, DS, MC, VI.

ADITI INDIAN CUISINE

Indian
$8-$16

Phone: 202/625-6825   ④⑦

In a two-story townhouse on bustling M Street, the restaurant presents a menu with a wide range of traditional tandoori dishes, as well as a large selection of curries. Choose from lamb, beef, chicken and vegetarian entrees. Casual dress. **Bar:** Full bar. **Reservations:** suggested, weekends. **Hours:** 11:30 am-2:30 & 5:30-10 pm, Fri & Sat-10:30 pm, Sun noon-2:30 & 5:30-10 pm. Closed: 7/4, 11/27; also for lunch 12/25 & 1/1. **Address:** 3299 M St NW 20007 **Location:** Just e of Key Bridge. **Parking:** no self-parking. **Cards:** AX, CB, DC, DS, MC, VI.

AMERICA

American
$8-$20

Phone: 202/682-9555   ①①⑤

The unusual Union Station setting—with seating in the bi-level dining room, train station lobby or along the outdoor sidewalk—complements the casual atmosphere. The menu lists an extensive selection of items from full dinners to sandwiches, soups and salads. Casual dress. **Bar:** Full bar. **Reservations:** accepted. **Hours:** 11:30 am-10 pm. Closed: 12/25. **Address:** 50 Massachusetts Ave NE 20002 **Location:** Just e of N Capitol St; in the west hall of Union Station. **Parking:** on-site (fee). **Cards:** AX, DC, DS, MC, VI.

AMMA VEGETARIAN KITCHEN

Indian
$6-$8

Phone: 202/625-6625

The simple, second-floor spot is not much to look at, but that isn't the case for the view of Virginia's skyline from the window tables. The house's best bets are the two samplers, in which diners can taste Northern or Southern vegetarian curries along with tandoori oven breads. Casual dress. **Bar:** Beer & wine. **Reservations:** accepted. **Hours:** 11:30 am-2:30 & 5:30-10 pm, Fri-10:30 pm, Sat 11:30 am-3:30 & 5:30-10:30 pm, Sun noon-3:30 & 5:30-10 pm. Closed: 7/4, 11/27; also for lunch 1/1 & 12/25. **Address:** 3291-A M St NW 20007 **Location:** At 33rd St; in Georgetown. **Parking:** no self-parking. **Cards:** DS, MC, VI.

ANNA MARIA'S RESTAURANT

Italian
$7-$29

Phone: 202/667-1444   ①③

Established in the late 1950s, this neighborhood restaurant offers dishes from the north and south of Italy. Veal is the house specialty, with a variety of different preparations. The pasta is made fresh daily. Photographs of celebrities who have dined here over the years adorn the dining room walls. Casual dress. **Bar:** Full bar. **Reservations:** accepted. **Hours:** 11 am-11 pm, Fri-1 am, Sat 5 pm-1 am, Sun 5 pm-11 pm. Closed major holidays. **Address:** 1737 Connecticut Ave NW 20009 **Location:** 2 blks from Dupont Circle Metro Station. **Parking:** street. **Cards:** AX, MC, VI.

(See map and index starting on p. 400)

AROMA INDIAN RESTAURANT
Indian
$10-$18

Phone: 202/833-4700 [86]

The menu offers authentic, creative tandoori (type of Indian oven) barbecue dishes of lamb, chicken and beef, along with vegetarian selections in an intimate dining atmosphere with banquettes. The portions are manageable and reasonably priced; the service is attentive. Casual dress. **Bar:** Full bar. **Reservations:** accepted. **Hours:** 11:30 am-2:30 & 5:30-10 pm, Sat from noon; Saturday brunch. Closed: Sun & for lunch 12/25 & 1/1. **Address:** 1919 I St NW 20006 **Location:** Between 19th and 20th sts NW. **Parking:** no self-parking. **Cards:** AX, DC, DS, MC, VI.

ASIA NORA
Asian
$22-$28

Phone: 202/797-4860 [41]

A soft, subtle ambience pervades the intimate, bi-level dining room. Decorated with Asian artwork. The creatively prepared cuisine, which uses only certified organic meats, fish and vegatables, includes tempting choices blending Asian and American influences. Dressy casual. **Bar:** Full bar. **Reservations:** suggested. **Hours:** 5:30 pm-10 pm, Fri & Sat-10:30 pm. Closed: 12/25; also Sun & last 2 weeks of Aug. **Address:** 2213 M St NW 20037 **Location:** Between 22nd and 23rd sts NW. **Parking:** valet. **Cards:** AX, DS, MC, VI.

BANGKOK BISTRO
Thai
$8-$19

Phone: 202/337-2424 [36]

The plentiful selections range from vegetarian dishes to those made with beef, chicken, pork, duck and seafood. Thai fried rice is heaped high on a bisected fresh pineapple. In good weather, outdoor seating lines the front sidewalk. The decor is stylish, the servers accommodating and the prices reasonable. Casual dress. **Bar:** Full bar. **Reservations:** suggested, weekends. **Hours:** 11:30 am-10:30 pm, Fri & Sat-11:30 pm. Closed: 11/27, 12/25. **Address:** 3251 Prospect St 20007 **Location:** Between 33rd St and Wisconsin Ave; in Georgetown. **Parking:** street. **Cards:** AX, CB, DC, DS, MC, VI.

BISTRO BIS
French
$14-$32

Phone: 202/661-2700 [119]

Just off the lobby of Hotel George, the stylish bistro serves breakfast, lunch and dinner. French fare—such as duck confit with roasted potatoes and seared scallops Provencal with garlic—reflects American influences. Dressy casual. **Bar:** Full bar. **Reservations:** suggested. **Hours:** 7-10:30 am, 11:30-2:30 & 5:30-10:30 pm. Closed: 12/25. **Address:** 15 E St NW 20001 **Location:** On Capitol Hill, just n of Capitol grounds; in The Hotel George. **Parking:** on-site (fee). **Cards:** AX, DC, DS, MC, VI.

BISTRO FRANCAIS
AAA
French
$8-$25

Phone: 202/338-3830 [57]

A casual, Parisian brassiere atmosphere. The banquette seating is rather intimate. Huge menu offers beef, veal, pate, veal kidneys, mussels and seafood, as well as homemade pastries. A couple of the restaurant signature dishes are the minute steak, steak tartar and rotisserie chicken. Casual dress. **Bar:** Full bar. **Reservations:** accepted. **Hours:** 11 am-3 am, Fri & Sat-4 am. Closed: 12/25; also for dinner 12/24. **Address:** 3128 M St NW 20007 **Location:** In Georgetown. **Parking:** no self-parking. **Cards:** AX, CB, DC, MC, VI.

BISTROT DU COIN
French
$10-$21

Phone: 202/234-6969 [14]

The Parisian-style bistro lives up to its "French, fun and friendly" motto. Closely spaced tables contribute to the loud, spirited atmosphere. Guests can sample homemade pates, foie gras and mussels, among other tasty selections. Casual dress. **Bar:** Full bar. **Reservations:** suggested. **Hours:** 11:30 am-11 pm, Thurs & Fri-1 am, Sat 11 am-1 am, Sun 11 am-11 pm. Closed: 9/1. **Address:** 1738 Connecticut Ave NW 20009 **Location:** Jct Florida Ave NW, 3 blks n of Dupont Circle. **Parking:** no self-parking. **Cards:** AX, DS, MC, VI.

BISTROT LEPIC AND WINE BAR
French
$14-$25

Phone: 202/333-0111 [8]

In Georgetown, there is a French resurtant that serves classical and regional cuisine. Menu changes seasonally, but a favorite dish that is on all menus is the La grande salade de Volaille Tiede(organic chicken with poached egg and balsamic vinaigrette). Desserts are made fresh daily. Reservations are required. Semi-formal attire. **Bar:** Full bar. **Reservations:** suggested, required on weekends. **Hours:** 11:30 am-2:30 & 5:30-10 pm, Fri & Sat-10:30 pm, Sun-9:30 pm. Closed major holidays. **Address:** 1736 Wisconsin Ave NW 20007 **Location:** In Upper Georgetown. **Parking:** street. **Cards:** AX, CB, DC, DS, MC, VI.

BLUE DUCK TAVERN
American
$14-$35

Phone: 202/419-6755 [43]

Bar: Full bar. **Reservations:** suggested. **Hours:** 11:30 am-2:30 & 5:30-10:30 pm. **Address:** 1201 24th St NW 20037 **Location:** 24th and M sts NW; in Park Hyatt Washington DC. **Parking:** valet. **Cards:** AX, DC, DS, JC, MC, VI.

BOBBY VAN'S STEAKHOUSE
Steak House
$11-$35

Phone: 202/589-0060 [98]

The steakhouse prepares one of the best porterhouse steaks in town. Beef is dry-aged on the premises. Seafood lovers will find large lobsters and other seafood dishes. An award-winning wine selection is available. Dressy casual. **Bar:** Full bar. **Reservations:** suggested. **Hours:** 11:30 am-10 pm, Sat from 5 pm, Sun 5 pm-9 pm. Closed: 1/1, 11/27, 12/25. **Address:** 809 15th St NW 20005 **Location:** Between H and I sts NW. **Parking:** no self-parking. **Cards:** AX, DC, DS, MC, VI.

THE BOMBAY CLUB
Indian
$13-$24

Phone: 202/659-3727 [94]

The decor is tropical and elegant in the theme of the British Officer's clubs of Colonial India. Cuisine represents the regions and cultures of India, such as Moghul, Goa and the Northwest Frontier. Other items are prepared in the tandoor, a clay oven. The sidewalk cafe is a delightful spot on sunny days. Valet parking is available for dinner. Dressy casual. Entertainment. **Bar:** Full bar. **Reservations:** suggested. **Hours:** 11:30 am-2:30 & 5:30-10:30 pm, Fri-11 pm, Sat 5:30 pm-11 pm, Sun 11:30 am-2:30 & 5:30-9 pm. Closed major holidays. **Address:** 815 Connecticut Ave NW 20006 **Location:** Between H and I sts; just n of the White House. **Parking:** no self-parking. **Cards:** AX, DC, DS, MC, VI.

BOMBAY PALACE RESTAURANT
Northern Indian
$13-$25

Phone: 202/331-4200 [82]

Moghul-type cuisine, including tandoori chicken, salmon, lamb chops and jumbo shrimp, is cooked in a charcoal pit oven and served in the downtown restaurant's stylish and upscale dining room. The menu also lists curries, pilafs, biryanis and vindaloos. Etched glass, mirrors and a large fish tank set the tone. Complimentary valet parking is available from 5:30 p.m. Semi-formal attire. **Bar:** Full bar. **Reservations:** suggested. **Hours:** 11:30 am-2:30 & 5:30-10 pm, Fri-10:30 pm, Sat noon-2:30 & 5:30-10:30 pm, Sun noon-2:30 & 5:30-10 pm. Closed: 1/1; also for lunch 12/25. **Address:** 2020 K St NW 20006 **Location:** Between 20th and 21st sts NW. **Parking:** no self-parking. **Cards:** AX, DC, DS, MC, VI.

(See map and index starting on p. 400)

B. SMITHS RESTAURANT
Phone: 202/289-6188 (114)

Regional American
$12-$30

Guests can experience graceful, Southern-style dining in a beaux arts setting off the lobby of Union Station. The menu centers on Creole recipes and other Southern dishes. Brunch is served on weekends. Dressy casual. **Bar:** Full bar. **Reservations:** suggested. **Hours:** 11:30 am-3 & 5-9 pm, Fri-10 pm, Sat noon-3 & 5-10 pm, Sun 11:30 am-9 pm; Saturday & Sunday brunch. Closed: 12/25. **Address:** 50 Massachusetts Ave NE 20002 **Location:** At N Capitol St; in Union Station. **Parking:** on-site (fee). **Cards:** AX, DC, DS, MC, VI.

BUA
Phone: 202/265-0828 (22)

Thai
$7-$13

The pleasant but simple dining room on the second floor of a restored townhouse is a great spot in which to enjoy a meal of well-prepared dishes of yellow, red and green curries, noodles and tasty appetizers. This is a great place to meet friends after work for a casual but very good meal. Casual dress. **Bar:** Full bar. **Reservations:** suggested. **Hours:** 11:30 am-3 & 5-10:30 pm, Fri-11 pm, Sat noon-4 & 5-11 pm, Sun noon-10:30 pm. Closed: 11/27. **Address:** 1635 P St NW 20036 **Location:** Between 16th and 17th sts. **Parking:** street. **Cards:** AX, DC, DS, MC, VI.

BURMA
Phone: 202/638-1280 (100)

Burmese
$7-$11

The Chinatown restaurant prepares Burmese cooking. The menu lists a nice selection of vegetarian, beef, chicken and fish choices, as well as an extensive array of salads and noodle dishes. The simple, second-floor dining rooms are decorated with Burmese and Asian artwork. Casual dress. **Bar:** Full bar. **Reservations:** accepted. **Hours:** 11 am-3 & 6-10 pm, Sat & Sun from 6 pm. Closed: 11/27, 12/25. **Address:** 740 6th St NW 20001 **Location:** Between H and G sts NW; upstairs; in Chinatown. **Parking:** no self-parking. **Cards:** AX, CB, DC, DS, MC, VI.

BUSARA
Phone: 202/337-2340

Thai
$6-$16

Contemporary furnishings and creative lighting give the restaurant a light, fun atmosphere. The menu offers a nice selection of appetizers, soups, salads and entrees. Siamese cooking is creative and consistent. Vegetarian selections are also available. Pad Thai noodles are a popular favorite, and sticky rice and mangos, along with an espresso or cappuccino, is a delightful conclusion to the meal. Casual dress. **Bar:** Full bar. **Reservations:** suggested, weekends. **Hours:** 11:30 am-3 & 5-10:30 pm, Fri-11:30 pm, Sat 11:30 am-4 & 5-11:30 pm, Sun 11:30 am-4 & 5-10:30 pm. Closed: 11/27; also for lunch 7/4 & 12/25. **Address:** 2340 Wisconsin Ave NW 20007 **Location:** In Upper Georgetown area. **Parking:** no self-parking. **Cards:** AX, CB, DC, DS, MC, VI.

BUTTERFIELD 9
Phone: 202/289-8810 (107)

American
$10-$36

The stylish dining room—with high ceilings, soft earth tones, large glass windows, black and white artwork and white tablecloths—nurtures an upscale air. The seasonally changing menu focuses on contemporary American cuisine. The staff provides knowledgeable, attentive service. Dressy casual. **Bar:** Full bar. **Reservations:** suggested. **Hours:** 11:30 am-2:30 & 5:30-10 pm, Fri-11 pm, Sat 5:30 pm-11 pm, Sun 5:30 pm-10 pm. Closed major holidays. **Address:** 600 14th St NW 20005 **Location:** Between G and F sts NW. **Parking:** no self-parking. **Cards:** AX, CB, DC, DS, MC, VI.

CAFE 15
Phone: 202/730-8700 (93)

French
$15-$32

Off the lobby of the Sofitel Lafayette Square Hotel is an intimate, upscale dining room offering wonderful Contemporary French cuisine. The kitchen displays it's talents with each dish. The prepartion is simplistic yet sophiscated. The wait staff is professional and attentive and will see to your needs. Dressy casual. **Bar:** Full bar. **Reservations:** suggested. **Hours:** 6:30-10:30 am, 11-2:30 & 6-10:30 pm, Sat & Sun 6:30 am-10:30 & 6-10:30 pm. **Address:** 806 15th St NW 20005 **Location:** Jct 15th and H sts NW; in Sofitel Lafayette Square Washington DC. **Parking:** valet. **Cards:** AX, CB, DC, DS, JC, MC, VI.

CALL

CAFE ATLANTICO
Phone: 202/393-0812 (125)

Latino
$10-$28

Nuevo Latin American cuisine is rich with Latin American and Caribbean spices. The colorful, lively, multilevel dining room is set in the heart of downtown. Casual dress. **Bar:** Full bar. **Reservations:** suggested. **Hours:** 11:30 am-2:30 & 5-10 pm, Fri & Sat-11 pm. Closed major holidays. **Address:** 405 8th St NW 20004 **Location:** Between D and E sts NW. **Parking:** no self-parking. **Cards:** AX, DC, DS, MC, VI.

CAFE BERLIN
Phone: 202/543-7656 (128)

German
$7-$22

New German and continental are Cafe Berlin's hallmark cuisines. Start with a herring appetizer then move on to a sauerbraten and red cabbage entree. Top it off with one of a variety of creative and homemade desserts. Outdoor dining is available in season. Casual dress. **Bar:** Full bar. **Reservations:** suggested. **Hours:** 11:30 am-10 pm, Fri-11 pm, Sat noon-11 pm, Sun 4 pm-10 pm. Closed: 7/4. **Address:** 322 Massachusetts Ave NE 20002 **Location:** Between 3rd and 4th sts NE. **Parking:** street. **Cards:** AX, DC, DS, MC, VI.

CAFE DES ARTISTES
Phone: 202/639-1786 (118)

American
$10-$15

Primarily a casual place for soup and sandwiches, the relaxed bistro-style cafe is popular with the business lunch crowd. The menu changes periodically depending on events in the art gallery. Choirs and gospel groups perform at the Sunday brunch. Casual dress. **Bar:** Beer & wine. **Hours:** 11 am-3 pm, Thurs also 5 pm-8 pm; Sunday brunch 10:30 am-2 pm. Closed: 1/1, 11/27, 12/25; also Mon & Tues. **Address:** 500 17th St NW 20006 **Location:** 1 blk from the White House on 17th St; in the lobby of Corcoran Gallery of Art. **Parking:** no self-parking. **Cards:** AX, CB, DC, DS, MC, VI.

CAFE DIVAN
Phone: 202/338-1747 (7)

Turkish
$7-$20

Adding to the stylish cafe's visual appeal are Brazilian wood floors, Italian wood furniture and glass windows all around. The menu centers on Turkish cooking, including such specialties as doner kebab: thin, marinated lamb and veal strips served over pita bread with yogurt. The lunch menu is presented until 4 pm. Casual dress. **Bar:** Full bar. **Reservations:** suggested, weekends. **Hours:** 11 am-10:30 pm, Fri & Sat-11 pm. Closed: 1/1, 12/25. **Address:** 1834 Wisconsin Ave NW 20007 **Location:** Jct 34th St NW; in upper Georgetown. **Parking:** no self-parking. **Cards:** AX, MC, VI.

(See map and index starting on p. 400)

CAFE MILANO

Italian
$9-$39

Phone: 202/333-6183 (34)
A bright, busy atmosphere punctuates this trendy, contemporary cafe, where diners often retreat to the sidewalk to sip an espresso and nibble on biscotti. The seasonally changing menu offers a good selection of pasta, pizza, salad and dinners. Lunch menu served until 4 pm. Dressy casual. **Bar:** Full bar. **Reservations:** suggested. **Hours:** 11:30 am-1 am, Thurs-Sat to 2 am. Closed: 11/27, 12/25. **Address:** 3251 Prospect St NW 20007 **Location:** Off Wisconsin Ave; just n of M St NW. **Parking:** on-site. **Cards:** AX, CB, DC, DS, MC, VI.

CAFE MOZU

Asian
$14-$35

Phone: 202/554-8588 (135)
Bar: Full bar. **Reservations:** suggested. **Hours:** 6:30 am-10:30 pm, Sun from 7 am. **Address:** 1330 Maryland Ave SW 20024 **Location:** Jct Independence Ave SW, just s on 12th St SW; in Mandarin Oriental, Washington D.C. **Parking:** valet. **Cards:** AX, CB, DC, DS, JC, MC, VI.

CAFE PROMENADE

Mediterranean
$12-$30

Phone: 202/347-3000 (60)
Taste the flavors of the Mediterranean in the dining room at the Mayflower Hotel. The service is professional and attentive from the staff in white jackets. The spacious dining room is a comfortable setting for any occasion. A Sunday Brunch is offered 11 am-3 pm. Dressy casual. **Bar:** Full bar. **Reservations:** suggested. **Hours:** 6:30 am-11 pm. **Address:** 1127 Conneticut Ave NW 20036 **Location:** Just n of K St NW; in business district; in Renaissance Mayflower Hotel. **Parking:** on-site (fee). **Cards:** AX, CB, DC, DS, JC, MC, VI.

THE CAPITAL GRILLE

Steak House
$8-$36

Phone: 202/737-6200 (133)
Cherry wood and red leather assist in making this "clubby" dining room a beautiful spot to dine on excellent cuts of dry-aged beef. The staff is highly attentive and knowledgeable. Dressy casual. **Bar:** Full bar. **Reservations:** suggested. **Hours:** 11:30 am-3 & 5-10 pm, Thurs-Sat to 11 pm, Sun 5 pm-10 pm. Closed major holidays. **Address:** 601 Pennsylvania Ave NW 20004 **Location:** Jct 6th St NW. **Parking:** no self-parking. **Cards:** AX, DS, MC, VI.

CALL

CAPITAL Q

Barbecue
$8-$15

Phone: 202/347-8396 (97)
The Chinatown restaurant prepares Texas-style barbecue and offers cafeteria-style service. Beef brisket is a specialty, and jalapeno cornbread is popular. Casual dress. **Bar:** Full bar. **Reservations:** not accepted. **Hours:** 11 am-10 pm. Closed major holidays; also Sun. **Address:** 707 H St NW 20001 **Location:** At 7th and H sts NW. **Parking:** no self-parking. **Cards:** AX, DC, DS, MC, VI.

CAPITOL CITY BREWING CO CAPITOL HILL

American
$5-$25

Phone: 202/842-2337
The fare is simple and wholesome, and the surroundings plain and comfortable. You can find good plated full meals, or more basic and quick food while on your busy schedule. Casual dress. **Bar:** Full bar. **Reservations:** not accepted. **Hours:** 11 am-11 pm, Fri & Sat-midnight. Closed: 11/27, 12/25. **Address:** 2 Massachusetts Ave NE 20002 **Location:** At Postal Museum, next to Union Station. **Parking:** no self-parking. **Cards:** AX, DC, DS, MC, VI.

CAPITOL CITY BREWING COMPANY-DOWNTOWN

American
$8-$16

Phone: 202/628-2222
The fare is simple and wholesome, and the surroundings plain and comfortable. You can find good plated full meals, or more basic and quick food while on your busy schedule. Casual dress. **Bar:** Full bar. **Hours:** 11 am-11 pm, Fri & Sat-midnight. Closed: 11/27, 12/25. **Address:** 1100 New York Ave NW 20005 **Location:** Between 11th and 12th sts; south side of building; 1 blk n of Metro Center subway stop. **Parking:** no self-parking. **Cards:** AX, DS, MC, VI.

CALL

THE CAUCUS ROOM

American
$15-$35

Phone: 202/393-1300 (126)
Rich cherry wood paneling, polished brass and marble lend to the clubby atmosphere. The kitchen prepares generous portions of prime aged beef and fresh seafood. Don't be surprised to see Democratic and Republican politicians dining at adjacent tables in the bipartisan establishment. The staff is professional and friendly. Valet parking is available during dinner service for a fee. Semi-formal attire. **Bar:** Full bar. **Reservations:** suggested. **Hours:** 11:30 am-2:30 & 5:30-10:30 pm, Sat from 5:30 pm. Closed major holidays; also Sun. **Address:** 401 9th St NW 20004 **Location:** 9th and D sts NW; in Market Square North. **Parking:** no self-parking. **Cards:** AX, DC, DS, MC, VI.

CALL

CEIBA

Latino
$13-$29

Phone: 202/393-3983 (102)
Pronounced "SAY-ba," the restaurant carries out a Latin American theme. The dining room is decorated with fabrics, wood and tile from Latin American countries. The menu reflects influences from a variety of regions in Mexico, as well as the Yucatan, Brazil, Argentina and the Caribbean. Dressy casual. **Reservations:** suggested. **Hours:** 11:30 am-2:30 & 5:30-10:30 pm, Fri-11 pm, Sat 5:30 pm-11 pm. Closed major holidays; also Sun. **Address:** 701 14th St NW 20005 **Location:** At 14th and G sts NW. **Parking:** valet. **Cards:** AX, CB, DC, DS, MC, VI.

CALL

CHARLIE PALMER STEAK

Steak House
$18-$40

Phone: 202/547-8100 (134)
The comfortable, upscale Capitol Hill steakhouse looks out over Constitution Avenue and the Capitol grounds. The kitchen prepares progressive American cuisine with finesse. In addition to quality steaks, the menu lists lobster, duck, chicken and fresh fish dishes. An extensive selection of domestic wines is available. Valet parking is an option for dinner. Dressy casual. **Bar:** Full bar. **Reservations:** suggested. **Hours:** 11:30 am-2:30 & 5:30-10 pm, Sat 5 pm-10:30 pm, Sun 5 pm-10 pm. Closed: 12/25. **Address:** 101 Constitution Ave NW 20001 **Location:** On Capitol Hill; at jct 1st St and Constitution Ave NW. **Parking:** no self-parking. **Cards:** AX, CB, DC, MC, VI.

CALL

(See map and index starting on p. 400)

CHING CHING CHA
Phone: 202/333-8288

Chinese
$5-$12

Tea connoisseurs will fall in love with the adorable tea shop and its wide array of Asian infusions. While sipping a soothing brew, patrons can munch on dumplings, curry rolls, a subtle egg flower soup or a bento box of ginger salmon, chicken, beef or tofu. Casual dress. **Reservations:** accepted, Tues-Fri. **Hours:** 11:30 am-9 pm, Sun-7 pm. Closed: 1/1, 11/27, 12/25; also Mon. **Address:** 1063 Wisconsin Ave NW 20007 **Location:** Between K and M sts; in Georgetown. **Parking:** no self-parking. **Cards:** AX, DS, MC, VI.

CITYZEN
Phone: 202/787-6868

American
$80-$105

The setting is modern and cutting-edge at this new spot; choose a table overlooking the open-kitchen where the star West Coast chef presides over a talented staff who turn out a seasonal menu of the finest culinary offerings. Dressy casual. **Bar:** Full bar. **Reservations:** suggested. **Hours:** 5:30 pm-10 pm. Closed major holidays; also Sun & Mon. **Address:** 1330 Maryland Ave SW 20024 **Location:** Jct Independence Ave SW, just s on 12th St SW; in Mandarin Oriental, Washington D.C. **Parking:** valet. **Cards:** AX, CB, DC, DS, JC, MC, VI.

CALL 🔈 M

CLYDE'S OF GEORGETOWN
Phone: 202/333-9180

American
$8-$23

In the heart of Georgetown, the popular saloon has numerous dining rooms in which diners may enjoy a changing selection of consistently good American fare. Casual dress. **Bar:** Full bar. **Reservations:** suggested. **Hours:** 11 am-10:30 pm, Fri-1 am, Sat 10 am-1 am, Sun 9 am-midnight. Closed: 12/25. **Address:** 3236 M St NW 20007 **Location:** Just w of jct Wisconsin Ave NW. **Parking:** no self-parking. **Cards:** AX, DC, DS, MC, VI.

COEUR DE LION
Phone: 202/414-0500

Continental
$10-$36

Located in the heart of the capital city inside the historic Henley Park Hotel, the Coeur de Lion offers upscale Continental dining. The dining rooms here are each distinct, but the level of elegance, while understated, never waivers. The atrium roof and creative lighting provides for the most romantic of evenings. Enjoy your dinner while listening to live entertainment, Thursday-Saturday nights. Dressy casual. Entertainment. **Bar:** Full bar. **Reservations:** suggested. **Hours:** 6:30-10:30 am, and 11:30-2:30 & 6-10:30 pm, Sun 6:30 am-11 & 11:30-2:30 pm. **Address:** 926 Massachusetts Ave NW 20001 **Location:** 10th St and Massachusetts Ave NW; in Henley Park Hotel. **Parking:** valet. **Cards:** AX, CB, DC, DS, MC, VI. **Historic**

CORDUROY
Phone: 202/589-0699

American
$10-$32

The New American cuisine of chef Tom Power has brought the hotel dining room to life. The menu changes seasonally using the freshest market ingredients. The wine list offers a nice selection, with a very extensive offering of half bottles. Limited valet parking is available, validated for 2 hours for lunch, 3 hours for dinner. Dressy casual. **Bar:** Full bar. **Reservations:** suggested. **Hours:** noon-2:30 & 5:30-10:30 pm, Sat 5 pm-11 pm. Closed: Sun. **Address:** 1201 K St NW 20005 **Location:** 12th and K sts NW; in Four Points Sheraton Washington DC Downtown. **Parking:** valet. **Cards:** AX, DC, DS, MC, VI.

DAVID GREGGORY RESTAU LOUNGE
Phone: 202/872-8700

American
$11-$29

Two chefs share a single vision for creating "American retro forward" cuisine from fresh local and organic ingredients. The light, airy dining atmosphere is enhanced by creative styling and the work of local artists. Sidewalk tables are offered seasonally. Dressy casual. **Bar:** Full bar. **Reservations:** suggested. **Hours:** 11:30 am-2:30 & 5:30-10 pm, Fri-11 pm, Sat 5:30 pm-11 pm. Closed major holidays; also Sun. **Address:** 2030 M St NW 20036 **Location:** Jct 21st and M sts NW. **Parking:** no self-parking. **Cards:** AX, CB, DC, DS, MC, VI.

DC COAST
Phone: 202/216-5988

American
$13-$30

Casually upscale Beaux Arts styling in the two-story dining room and on the small, glassed-in balcony concentrates on the details. So does Chef Tunks in preparing modern American cuisine. Preparation for the dishes, many of which emphasize seafood, reflects influences from the Southern, Southwestern and Mid-Atlantic areas of the country, as well as the Pacific Rim. Valet parking is available from 5:30 pm for a fee. Dressy casual. **Bar:** Full bar. **Reservations:** suggested. **Hours:** 11:30 am-2:30 & 5:30-10:30 pm, Fri-11 pm, Sat 5:30 pm-11 pm. Closed major holidays; also Sun. **Address:** 1401 K St NW 20005 **Location:** Jct of 14th and K sts NW; in the Tower Building, ground floor. **Parking:** no self-parking. **Cards:** AX, CB, DC, DS, MC, VI.

DISH
Phone: 202/338-8707

American
$7-$30

The stylish cafe provides a simple setting for enjoying classic American cooking. The chef regularly changes the menu, which is driven by the availability of fresh, local Mid-Atlantic ingredients. Casual dress. **Bar:** Full bar. **Reservations:** suggested. **Hours:** 7-10 am, 11:30-2:30 & 5-10 pm, Fri-11 pm, Sat 8 am-10 & 5-11 pm, Sun 8 am-10 & 5-10 pm. Closed: 1/1, 11/27, 12/24, 12/25. **Address:** 924 25th St NW 20037 **Location:** Between K and I sts NW; in The River Inn. **Parking:** valet. **Cards:** AX, DC, MC, VI.

DISTRICT CHOPHOUSE & BREWERY
Phone: 202/347-3434

American
$10-$55

A half-block from Verizon Center, Shakespeare Theater and the Gallery Place/Chinatown metro station, the restored building maintains a nostalgic air. The mezzanine level is a great place to relax and play billiards while sampling a fine, hand-crafted beer from the property's on-site micro-brew vats. The menu offers traditional chophouse fare, with a variety of juicy steaks, brick-oven pizzas, sandwiches and salads. Casual dress. **Bar:** Full bar. **Reservations:** accepted. **Hours:** 11 am-11 pm, Thurs-Sat to midnight. Closed: 11/27, 12/25. **Address:** 509 7th St NW 20004 **Location:** Between E and F sts NW; just s of MCI center. **Parking:** no self-parking. **Cards:** AX, DC, DS, MC, VI.

(See map and index starting on p. 400)

EQUINOX

American
$18-$36

Phone: 202/331-8118 ⑨⑤

A few blocks from the White House, the restaurant's dining room provides a simple, soothing, upscale setting. Shaded by umbrellas, the sidewalk terrace is a wonderful spot for lunch. Chef Todd Gray prepares simple, yet sophisticated, contemporary American fare that can be savored in three- to six-course tasting menus. The bar menu focuses on a la carte selections. The seasonally changing menu is driven by the availability of farm-fresh ingredients. Friendly servers are helpful and attentive. **Reservations:** suggested. **Hours:** 11:30 am-2 & 5:30-10 pm, Fri-10:30 pm, Sat 5:30 pm-10:30 pm, Sun 5 pm-9 pm. Closed major holidays. **Address:** 818 Connecticut Ave NW 20006 **Location:** Between H and I sts NW. **Parking:** valet. **Cards:** AX, CB, DC, DS, JC, MC, VI.

FAHRENHEIT

Nouvelle American
$15-$38

Phone: 202/912-4110 ⑥⑨

In the fascinatingly restored former Georgetown incinerator, the restaurant exhibits sharp, modern decor and features exposed brick, soaring ceilings, fiery orange glasses and a dominating view of its smokestack. The seasonally changing menu focuses on regional American fare. Dressy casual. **Bar:** Full bar. **Reservations:** suggested. **Hours:** 6:30 am-2:30 & 6-10 pm, Fri-11 pm, Sat 7 am-2:30 & 6-11 pm, Sun 7-10 am, 11-2:30 & 6-10 pm. **Address:** 3100 South St 20007 **Location:** Just s of jct M St and Wisconsin Ave; off Wisconsin Ave, just e; in The Ritz-Carlton, Georgetown. **Parking:** valet. **Cards:** AX, CB, DC, DS, JC, MC, VI.

CALL ♿Ⓜ

FAMOUS LUIGI'S

Italian
$8-$18

Phone: 202/331-7574 ⑤⑧

Operated by the same family since its opening in 1943, the restaurant serves Italian food in a traditional setting with red and white checked tablecloths. Service is friendly. Casual dress. **Bar:** Full bar. **Reservations:** not accepted. **Hours:** 11 am-midnight, Sun from noon. Closed: 11/27, 12/25. **Address:** 1132 19th St NW 20036 **Location:** Between M and N sts. **Parking:** no self-parking. **Cards:** AX, DC, DS, MC, VI.

FELIX RESTAURANT AND THE SPY LOUNGE

American
$14-$24

Phone: 202/483-3549 ⑤

The chic, lounge-style restaurant nurtures a cosmopolitan ambience. The talented kitchen prepares full dinners and modern American tapas with Mediterranean influences. Seared tuna, grilled meats and vegetarian selections are just a few of the offered choices. Dressy casual. **Bar:** Full bar. **Reservations:** suggested. **Hours:** 5 pm-10:30 pm, Fri & Sat-11 pm. Closed: 1/1, 11/27. **Address:** 2406 18th St NW 20009 **Location:** Jct 18th St NW and Belmont Rd; in Adams Morgan area. **Parking:** street. **Cards:** AX, CB, DC, MC, VI.

FETTOOSH
Lebanese
$10-$19

Phone: 202/342-1199 ㊺

The food is good and the service prompt in the comfortable Lebanese restaurant. Vegetarians will find options galore. Casual dress. **Bar:** Full bar. **Reservations:** suggested, weekends. **Hours:** 11 am-midnight, Fri & Sat-5 am. **Address:** 3277 M St NW 20007 **Location:** In Georgetown. **Parking:** no self-parking. **Cards:** AX, CB, DC, DS, MC, VI.

FILOMENA RISTORANTE

Italian
$8-$40

Phone: 202/338-8800 ⑥①

This restaurant has a loyal local following, and for good reasons: exceptional food and quality service. The menu features homemade pasta, seafood, meat and poultry, and buffets are laid out Friday, Saturday and Sunday for brunch. The atmosphere blends Old World and garden influences. Dressy casual. **Bar:** Full bar. **Reservations:** suggested. **Hours:** 11:30 am-11 pm. Closed: 1/1, 11/27, 12/25; also evening of 12/24. **Address:** 1063 Wisconsin Ave NW 20027 **Location:** Between K and M sts; in Georgetown. **Parking:** no self-parking. **Cards:** AX, DC, DS, MC, VI.

CALL ♿Ⓜ

FINEMONDO ITALIAN COUNTRY KITCHEN

Italian
$12-$34

Phone: 202/737-3100 ⑩⑥

The kitchen prepares good country-style recipes from all regions of Italy. Spit-roasted meats, fish and poultry are seared in their own juices to create a wonderful flavor and are served with traditional sauces and side dishes. The atmosphere is comfortable, and service is professional. Casual dress. **Bar:** Full bar. **Reservations:** suggested. **Hours:** 11:30 am-2:30 & 5:30-10:30 pm, Sat from 5:30 pm. Closed major holidays; also Sun. **Address:** 1319 F St NW 20004 **Location:** Between 13th and 14th sts NW. **Parking:** no self-parking. **Cards:** AX, DC, DS, MC, VI.

CALL ♿Ⓜ

FIREFLY
 ⒶⒶⒶ

American
$12-$26

Phone: 202/861-1310 ㉘

Contemporary American cuisine makes up the seasonally changing menu, which is influenced by both regional and international recipes. The stylish dining room has a floor-to-ceiling firefly tree with candlelit lanterns dangling from the branches. An exhibition kitchen is tucked behind a rustic stone wall. Casual dress. **Bar:** Full bar. **Reservations:** suggested. **Hours:** 7-10 am, 11:30-2:30 & 5:30-10:30 pm, Sat 7 am-10 & 5:30-10:30 pm, Sun 11 am-2 & 5:30-10:30 pm. Closed major holidays. **Address:** 1310 New Hampshire Ave NW 20036 **Location:** Between 20th and N sts NW; in Hotel Madera. **Parking:** no self-parking. **Cards:** AX, DC, DS, MC, VI.

FLORIDA AVENUE GRILL
Soul Food
$5-$14

Phone: 202/265-1586 ⑥

Since the 1940s, the famed diner has served delicious soul food and Southern specialties to a host of the famous and infamous whose autographed photographs line the walls. Casual dress. **Hours:** 8 am-9 pm, Sun-4:30 pm. Closed major holidays; also Mon. **Address:** 1100 Florida Ave NW 20009 **Location:** Jct 11th St. **Parking:** street. **Cards:** AX, DC, DS, MC, VI.

GALILEO

Northern Italian
$14-$40

Phone: 202/293-7191 ⑥⑤

The stylish eatery prepares artful dishes from only fresh ingredients. It's worth splurging on the simply delicious tiramisu. Some private dining rooms allow for an intimate meal. Valet parking is offered during the evening, except on Sundays. Dressy casual. **Bar:** Full bar. **Reservations:** suggested. **Hours:** 11:30 am-2 & 5:30-10 pm, Fri-10:30 pm, Sat 5:30 pm-10:30 pm, Sun 5 pm-10 pm. Closed major holidays. **Address:** 1110 21st St NW 20036 **Location:** Between L and M sts NW. **Parking:** valet. **Cards:** AX, DC, DS, JC, MC, VI.

(See map and index starting on p. 400)

GEORGIA BROWN'S

Phone: 202/393-4499   [83]

Regional American
$15-$32

The tasty fare at the stylish cafe, a hot spot with the political crowd, reflects the culinary traditions of the South, particularly the Lowcountry of South Carolina. The menu shows flair and inventiveness. Blues and jazz artists perform at Sunday brunch. Guests can pay for valet service from 6 p.m. Dressy casual. **Bar:** Full bar. **Reservations:** suggested. **Hours:** 11:30 am-10 pm, Fri-11 pm, Sat 5 pm-11 pm, Sun 10 am-2:15 & 5:30-10 pm. Closed major holidays. **Address:** 950 15th St NW 20005 **Location:** At McPherson Square; between K and I sts NW. **Parking:** no self-parking. **Cards:** AX, CB, DC, DS, MC, VI.

GERARD'S PLACE

Phone: 202/737-4445   [77]

French
$23-$37

Opposite McPherson Square, the small, intimate restaurant with a subtle upscale ambience offers a menu centered around contemporary French cuisine. Chef/owner Gerard Pangaud uses fresh ingredients in such expertly prepared selections as the signature lobster dish, presented in two services-the body first, followed by the claws. Desserts are prepared "a la commande," which requires a 25-minute preparation time. A three-course, prix fixe menu is available for lunch in addition to a la carte selections. Options for dinner include a la carte selections and a five-course tasting menu, which can be paired with appropriate wines. Semi-formal attire. **Bar:** Full bar. **Reservations:** suggested. **Hours:** 11:30 am-2 & 5:30-9 pm, Fri-9:30 pm, Sat 5:30 pm-9:30 pm. Closed major holidays; also Sun. **Address:** 915 15th St NW 20005 **Location:** At McPherson Square. **Parking:** no self-parking. **Cards:** AX, DC, MC, VI.

GORDON BIERSCH BREWERY RESTAURANT

Phone: 202/783-5454   [112]

American
$7-$26

Everything about this place is big: Tall ceilings with elaborate molding, huge marble pillars and lots of floor space all remain from a former life as a bank. Added are the towering steel fermentation tanks, which are part of the brewery. Some dishes are Asian-influenced, but you'll also find pastas, roast chickens, grilled steaks, seafood and the like. It's loud, it's fun, and the bar is usually crowded. Casual dress. **Bar:** Full bar. **Reservations:** accepted. **Hours:** 11 am-11 pm, Fri & Sat-midnight, Sun-10 pm. Closed: 11/27, 12/25. **Address:** 900 F St NW 20004 **Location:** Corner of 9th St. **Parking:** no self-parking. **Cards:** AX, DC, DS, MC, VI.

THE GRILL FROM IPANEMA

Phone: 202/986-0757   [4]

Brazilian
$13-$22

You'll enjoy the popular, chic, lively atmosphere, with close table spacing. The menu offers an extensive selection of Brazilian dishes and specialties, including moqueca (a seafood stew) and feijoada (a bean pork casserole). Sidewalk dining is seasonal. Casual dress. **Bar:** Full bar. **Reservations:** accepted. **Hours:** 5 pm-11 pm, Fri-11:30 pm, Sat noon-11:30 pm, Sun noon-10 pm. Closed: 7/4, 11/27, 12/25. **Address:** 1858 Columbia Rd NW 20009 **Location:** Between 18th St and Belmont Rd. **Parking:** no self-parking. **Cards:** AX, DC, DS, MC, VI.

HAAD THAI

Phone: 202/682-1111   [89]

Thai
$8-$17

Just north of Metro Center on the subway, the eatery is convenient. Although this place bustles at lunch, the atmosphere is more subdued in the evening, when tablecloths are used and some extra tables are removed. Tom kha is nicely spiced, and chicken satay is as good as it looks. Also among the entrees are pad Thai, panang gai and honey roast duck. No monosodium glutamate is used, and dishes can be spiced to taste. Casual dress. **Bar:** Full bar. **Reservations:** suggested. **Hours:** 11:30 am-2:30 & 5-10:30 pm, Sat noon-10:30 pm, Sun 5 pm-10:30 pm. Closed: 7/4, 11/27. **Address:** 1100 New York Ave NW 20005 **Location:** Between 11th and 12th sts, on east side of building, 1 blk n of Metro Center subway stop. **Parking:** no self-parking. **Cards:** AX, DC, MC, VI.

CALL

HARD ROCK CAFE

Phone: 202/737-7625   [121]

American
$7-$25

Rock 'n' roll memorabilia decorates the walls of the popular theme restaurant. Live music on the weekends contributes to the bustling atmosphere. On the menu is a wide variety of American cuisine—from burgers and sandwiches to seafood, steaks and pasta. Casual dress. **Bar:** Full bar. **Reservations:** not accepted. **Hours:** 11 am-close. **Address:** 999 E St NW 20004 **Location:** At 9th and E sts NW. **Parking:** no self-parking. **Cards:** AX, DC, DS, JC, MC, VI.

HERITAGE INDIA

Phone: 202/333-3120   [2]

Indian
$7-$28

The upscale dining room, with Indian photos and artwork, provides a comfortable atmosphere in which patrons can sample superb Indian cooking. The chef blends herbs and spices to create subtle, balanced flavors. Semi-formal attire. **Bar:** Full bar. **Reservations:** suggested, required weekends. **Hours:** 11:30 am-2:30 & 5:30-10:30 pm, Fri & Sat-11 pm. **Address:** 2400 Wisconsin Ave NW 20007 **Location:** In the Glover Park area. **Parking:** valet. **Cards:** AX, DC, DS, MC, VI.

I RICCHI

Phone: 202/835-0459   [32]

Regional Italian
$12-$31

The wait staff's inspiring description of the menu is not only informative but also accurate. Tuscan specialties are served in traditional trattoria surroundings. A favorite is the tortellini sage butter. Valet parking is offered after 5:30 pm. Dressy casual. **Bar:** Full bar. **Reservations:** suggested. **Hours:** 11:30 am-1:45 & 5:30-9:45 pm, Fri-10 pm, Sat 5:30 pm-10 pm. Closed major holidays; also Sun. **Address:** 1220 19th St NW 20036 **Location:** Between M and N sts NW. **Parking:** on-site (fee). **Cards:** AX, DC, MC, VI.

IRON GATE RESTAURANT

Phone: 202/737-1370   [29]

Mediterranean
$13-$33

A cozier place can hardly be imagined; the restaurant is comfortably worn and radiates warmth and intimacy, with nooks for couples and booths for friends. Occasionally someone stokes the wood-burning fireplace which continuously crackles. It seems secret and poetic, well away from the modern world. Warmer months find elegant courtyard dining under an arbor of heavy grape vines. Dressy casual. **Bar:** Full bar. **Reservations:** suggested. **Hours:** 11:30 am-2:15 & 5:30-10 pm, Sat from 5:30 pm. Closed: 9/1; also Sun, Thanksgiving & Christmas weeks. **Address:** 1734 N St NW 20036 **Location:** Between 17th and 18th sts. **Parking:** no self-parking. **Cards:** AX, DC, DS, MC, VI.

(See map and index starting on p. 400)

JALEO
Spanish
$7-$17

Phone: 202/628-7949

In a popular spot near Verizon Center, the bustling Spanish restaurant offers an extensive menu of tapas as well as full meals. The staff is friendly, and the atmosphere is lively and fun. Casual dress. **Bar:** Full bar. **Reservations:** accepted. **Hours:** 11:30 am-10 pm, Tues-Thurs to 11:30 pm, Fri & Sat-midnight. Closed: 11/27, 12/24, 12/25. **Address:** 480 7th St NW 20004 **Location:** Jct 7th and E St NW; 3 blks n off Pennsylvania Ave NW; 1 blk s of Verizon Center. **Parking:** no self-parking. **Cards:** AX, DC, DS, MC, VI.

JOHNNY'S HALF SHELL
Seafood
$10-$28

Phone: 202/737-0400   123

Enjoy the casual but upscale atmosphere for lunch or dinner. Crabcakes are their specialty here along with several specialty drinks from the bar. Casual dress. **Bar:** Full bar. **Reservations:** accepted. **Hours:** 11:30 am-2:30 & 4:30-10 pm, Fri-11 pm, Sat 5 pm-11 pm. Closed: 1/1, 11/27, 12/25; also Sun. **Address:** 400 N Capitol St NW 20001 **Location:** Just n of capitol grounds. **Parking:** no self-parking. **Cards:** AX, MC, VI.

J. PAUL'S
American
$9-$23

Phone: 202/333-3450

In the heart of Georgetown is the popular dining saloon. It's noisy and the tables are spaced closely, but it's casual, fun and lively. On the menu are traditional dishes, including hickory spare ribs, bayou salmon and Eastern Shore rotisserie chicken. Casual dress. **Bar:** Full bar. **Reservations:** accepted. **Hours:** 11:30 am-2 am, Fri & Sat-3 am, Sun 10:30 am-2 am. Closed: 12/25. **Address:** 3218 M St NW 20007 **Location:** Just w of jct Wisconsin Ave NW. **Parking:** no self-parking. **Cards:** AX, DC, DS, MC, VI.

JUNIPER
American
$16-$35

Phone: 202/457-5020   44

The fine-dining establishment sustains an upscale, relaxed setting in which guests can savor breakfast, lunch or dinner. The chef uses fresh ingredients from the Mid-Atlantic region to make many of the tasty dishes. The patio opens seasonally. Dressy casual. **Bar:** Full bar. **Reservations:** suggested. **Hours:** 6:30 am-10 pm. **Address:** 2401 M St NW 20037 **Location:** 24th and M sts NW; in The Fairmont Washington, D.C. **Parking:** valet. **Cards:** AX, CB, DC, DS, MC, VI.

CALL ⚡M

KANLAYA THAI CUISINE
Thai
$8-$16

Phone: 202/393-0088   99

The simple, contemporary dining room provides a nice setting for Thai cuisine. The menu lines up a large selection of vegetarian dishes, as well as traditional recipes. Casual dress. **Bar:** Full bar. **Reservations:** accepted. **Hours:** 11:30 am-10 pm, Fri & Sat-10:30 pm. **Address:** 740 6th St NW 20001 **Location:** Jct H St NW, just s; in Chinatown. **Parking:** no self-parking. **Cards:** DS, MC, VI.

KAZ SUSHI BISTRO
Japanese
$6-$27

Phone: 202/530-5500   84

Chef-owner Kazuhiro Okochi originated a concept he calls "free-style Japanese cuisine," a combination of a relaxed restaurant atmosphere with modern Japanese influences. Employing only the freshest seasonal ingredients, he creates innovative dishes that delight both the eye and palate. Try the tempura bento, grilled baby octopus with seaweed salad. Casual dress. **Bar:** Beer & wine. **Reservations:** suggested, dinner. **Hours:** 11:30 am-2 & 6-10 pm, Sat from 6 pm. Closed major holidays; also Sun. **Address:** 1915 I St NW 20006 **Location:** Between 19th and 20th sts. **Parking:** no self-parking. **Cards:** AX, CB, DC, DS, JC, MC, VI.

KINKEAD'S RESTAURANT
American
$16-$37

Phone: 202/296-7700   92

The cuisine here is New American with emphasis on seafood. The bi-level restaurant, with a cafe and lounge on the lower level and a pleasant, upscale atmosphere and open kitchen on the top level, is inviting. Valet parking is complimentary during dinner. Dressy casual. Entertainment. **Bar:** Full bar. **Reservations:** suggested. **Hours:** 11:30 am-2:30 & 5:30-10 pm, Fri-10:30 pm, Sat 5:30 pm-10:30 pm, Sun 5:30 pm-10 pm. Closed major holidays. **Address:** 2000 Pennsylvania Ave NW 20006 **Location:** Between 20th and 21st sts NW. **Parking:** valet and street. **Cards:** AX, DC, DS, MC, VI.

LA CHAUMIERE
French
$13-$32

Phone: 202/338-1784   50

A consistently popular operation, the established restaurant, with its open-hearth fireplace, exudes the ambience of a secluded country inn. Baked onion soup is subtle and sweet, and pike dumplings in lobster sauce is a local favorite. On Wednesday, the chef prepares wonderful couscous with a spicy combination of boiled beef, lamb, chicken, vegetables and chickpeas with semolina and harissa. Two-hour parking at the Four Seasons Hotel is validated. Dressy casual. **Bar:** Full bar. **Reservations:** suggested. **Hours:** 11:30 am-2:30 & 5:30-10:30 pm, Sat from 5:30 pm. Closed major holidays; also Sun. **Address:** 2813 M St NW 20007 **Location:** In Georgetown; opposite Four Seasons Hotel. **Parking:** street. **Cards:** AX, CB, DC, MC, VI.

LA TOMATE
Italian
$11-$24

Phone: 202/667-5505   16

The bistro's location on a prominent street corner in a popular neighborhood makes it a nice stop for people-watching. Specialties include smoked trout and salmon, plus a wide variety of pasta dishes. The patio is open seasonally. Valet parking is available after 6 pm for a fee. Casual dress. **Bar:** Full bar. **Reservations:** suggested. **Hours:** 11:30 am-10:30 pm, Thurs-11 pm, Fri & Sat-11:30 pm, Sun-10 pm. Closed: 12/25; also for lunch 1/1. **Address:** 1701 Connecticut Ave NW 20009 **Location:** Jct R St NW. **Parking:** no self-parking. **Cards:** AX, DS, MC, VI.

LAURIOL PLAZA
Latino
$8-$17

Phone: 202/387-0035   9

The stylish dining room comprises three levels of open, airy ambience. Sidewalk dining is a nice option when the weather cooperates. The menu incorporates a selection of Mexican and Spanish dishes, from tacos and fajitas to seafood, chicken and beef dishes. The kitchen is reliable. Casual dress. **Bar:** Full bar. **Hours:** 11:30 am-11 pm, Fri & Sat-midnight. Closed: 11/27. **Address:** 1835 18th St NW 20009 **Location:** Jct 18th and T sts NW. **Parking:** on-site. **Cards:** AX, DC, DS, MC, VI.

(See map and index starting on p. 400)

LEFTBANK
Phone: 202/464-2100 (3)

American
$10-$19

In the heart of Adams Morgan, the casual, contemporary bistro prepares such creative small plates as crispy calamari and seared scallops, as well as large plates of fresh fish, roasted chicken breast and New York strip steak. Diners can sample sushi in the sushi bar at the rear of the dining room. Dressy casual. **Bar:** Full bar. **Reservations:** suggested, weekends. **Hours:** 5 pm-2 am, Sat 10 am-3 am; Sunday brunch. Closed: 12/25. **Address:** 2424 18th St NW 20009 **Location:** In Adams Morgan. **Parking:** on-site (fee). **Cards:** AX, DS, MC, VI.

LEGAL SEA FOODS
Phone: 202/496-1111

Seafood
$9-$58

Legal prides itself on a reputation for freshness and consistency. More than 40 varieties of seafood can be grilled, broiled, fried or prepared Cajun style. Try the clam chowder that has been served at every presidential inauguration since 1981. The nautically inspired dining room is upscale and attractive with its rich cherry wood paneling and intricately detailed model ships. Casual dress. **Bar:** Full bar. **Reservations:** accepted. **Hours:** 11:30 am-10 pm, Fri-10:30 pm, Sat 4 pm-10:30 pm. Closed major holidays; also Sun. **Address:** 2020 K St NW 20006 **Location:** Between 20th and 21st sts NW. **Parking:** no self-parking. **Cards:** AX, DC, DS, MC, VI.

CALL

LE PARADOU
Phone: 202/347-6780 (131)

French
$28-$60

The dining room's subtle elegance sets the tone for your experience at Le Paradou. An award-winning wine list complements gracious, professional service and excellent contemporary French cooking. Together they create a wonderful dining experience. The chef uses only fresh ingredients in creating dishes with masterfully bold flavors. During lunch, a pre fixe, three-course menu is available. A la carte and tasting menus with six and nine courses are available for dinner, as is valet parking. Semi-formal attire. **Bar:** Full bar. **Reservations:** suggested, weekends. **Hours:** noon-2 & 5:30-10 pm, Sat 5:30 pm-10 pm. Closed major holidays; also Sun. **Address:** 678 Indiana Ave NW 20004 **Location:** On Indiana Ave NW between 6th and 7th sts NW; center. **Parking:** no self-parking. **Cards:** AX, CB, DC, DS, JC, MC, VI.

LES HALLES
Phone: 202/347-6848 (122)

French
$13-$26

In a brasserie setting, the steakhouse prepares American beef with a French flair. The seasonal heated sidewalk terrace is a popular spot to dine and people watch, and the lively bistro atmosphere suits social and business gatherings. The Pennsylvania Avenue spot is just blocks from the White House. Professional, efficient service is the norm. Casual dress. **Bar:** Full bar. **Reservations:** suggested. **Hours:** 11:30 am-midnight. **Address:** 1201 Pennsylvania Ave NW 20004 **Location:** Between 12th and 13th sts. **Parking:** no self-parking. **Cards:** AX, DC, DS, JC, MC, VI.

LEVANTE'S
Phone: 202/293-3244 (26)

Mediterranean
$8-$25

Mediterranean coast colors of cobalt blue and yellow project an upbeat mood. Greek- and Turkish-inspired dishes are accented with exotic spices. Casual dress. **Bar:** Full bar. **Reservations:** accepted. **Hours:** 11 am-10 pm, Fri & Sat-11 pm; Saturday & Sunday brunch. Closed: 11/27, 12/25. **Address:** 1320 19th St NW 20036 **Location:** Just s of Dupont Circle. **Parking:** no self-parking. **Cards:** AX, DC, DS, MC, VI.

LUIGINO
Phone: 202/371-0595 (88)

Italian
$9-$29

With all glass walls, the corner location affords a good view of busy sidewalk traffic. Those who are in a hurry can eat at the dining bar with a full view of the kitchen. The selection of well-prepared and flavorful pasta, meat and seafood preparations is good. Service is timely but somewhat impersonal during lunch. Casual dress. **Bar:** Full bar. **Reservations:** suggested. **Hours:** 11:30 am-10:30 pm, Fri-11:30 pm, Sat 5 pm-11:30 pm, Sun 5 pm-10:30 pm. Closed: 9/1, 12/25. **Address:** 1100 New York Ave NW 20005 **Location:** Corner of H and 12th sts NW. **Parking:** on-site (fee). **Cards:** AX, DS, MC, VI.

M & S GRILL
Phone: 202/347-1500 (108)

Steak & Seafood
$8-$37

This place is steeped in the tradition that defines "restaurant." The staff is friendly, and the chefs prepare tasty dishes using fresh seafood and USDA prime beef. Casual dress. **Bar:** Full bar. **Reservations:** accepted. **Hours:** 11:30 am-11 pm, Sat 4 pm-11 pm, Sun 4 pm-10 pm, Mon 11:30 am-10 pm. **Address:** 600 13th St NW 20005 **Location:** At E St NW; metro stop; Metro Center. **Parking:** no self-parking. **Cards:** AX, DC, DS, MC, VI.

MARCEL'S
Phone: 202/296-1166 (67)

French
$29-$42

Chef Robert Wiedmainer and his talented kitchen prepare wonderful French cuisine with Belgian influences. The availability of fresh ingredients drives the seasonally changing menu choices. In addition to a la carte selections, three-, four- and six-course tasting menus are available, as is a pre-theater menu presented from 5:30 to 7 p.m. Professional, attentive servers see to every need, and a wine steward assists with wine selections. Valet parking is provided for a fee. Dressy casual. **Bar:** Full bar. **Reservations:** suggested. **Hours:** 5:30 pm-10 pm, Fri & Sat-11 pm, Sun 5 pm-10 pm. Closed major holidays. **Address:** 2401 Pennsylvania Ave NW 20037 **Location:** 1.5 blks nw of Washington Circle. **Parking:** no self-parking. **Cards:** AX, CB, DC, DS, MC, VI.

MARRAKESH
Phone: 202/393-9393 (66)

Moroccan

It's well worth taking the time to experience the seven-course Moroccan food and memorable ambience here. Besides the lively belly dancing during dinner, there's also valet parking from 6 pm. No credit cards are accepted. Dressy casual. Entertainment. **Bar:** Full bar. **Reservations:** required. **Hours:** 6 pm-11 pm, Sat & Sun from 5 pm. Closed: 11/27. **Address:** 617 New York Ave NW 20001 **Location:** Between 6th and 7th sts NW. **Parking:** valet.

MCCORMICK & SCHMICK'S SEAFOOD RESTAURANT
Phone: 202/639-9330 (103)

Seafood
$12-$36

This place is all about seafood, which is imported from all over the world. Among good choices are Washington state oysters, Maine clams, delicate Hawaiian escolar and tuna from Ecuador. The clublike decor is cozy, and expert staff provide able assistance. Dressy casual. **Bar:** Full bar. **Reservations:** suggested. **Hours:** 11:30 am-11 pm, Fri-midnight, Sat 4 pm-midnight, Sun 4 pm-10 pm, Mon 11:30 am-10 pm. **Address:** 901 F St NW 20004 **Location:** Between 9th and 10th sts NW; metro stop; Gallery Pl/Chinatown. **Parking:** street. **Cards:** AX, DC, DS, MC, VI.

CALL

(See map and index starting on p. 400)

MCCORMICK & SCHMICK'S SEAFOOD RESTAURANT

Phone: 202/861-2233   ⑧⓪

Seafood
$12-$36

This place is all about seafood, which is imported from all over the world. Among good choices are Washington state oysters, Maine clams, delicate Hawaiian escolar and tuna from Ecuador. The clublike decor is cozy, and expert staff provide able assistance. Casual dress. **Bar:** Full bar. **Reservations:** suggested. **Hours:** 11 am-11 pm, Fri-midnight, Sat 2 pm-midnight, Sun 4 pm-10 pm. **Address:** 1652 K St NW 20006 **Location:** Between 16th and 17th sts. **Parking:** valet and street. **Cards:** AX, DC, DS, MC, VI.

CALL

MEIWAH RESTAURANT

Phone: 202/833-2888   ⑤④

Chinese
$10-$24

The bi-level dining room offers a comfortable, relaxing atmosphere. Photographs of the many politicians who have dined at Meiwah decorate the walls. Sidewalk dining, weather permitting. The food is very well prepared, one of many tasty dishes is the Crispy shredded beef with fried strands of meat and vegetables, the chilies are tamed by caramelized sugar. Casual dress. **Bar:** Full bar. **Reservations:** accepted. **Hours:** 11:30 am-10:30 pm, Sat noon-11 pm, Sun noon-10:30 pm. Closed: 11/27. **Address:** 1200 New Hampshire Ave NW 20036 **Location:** Jct M St and New Hampshire Ave NW. **Parking:** no self-parking. **Cards:** AX, DC, DS, MC, VI.

CALL

MENDOCINO GRILLE & WINE BAR

Phone: 202/333-2912   ④⑧

American
$19-$40

A relative newcomer to the Georgetown dining scene, the bistro-style eatery features a wide selection of premium wines by the glass. The weekend a la carte brunch is popular. Among lunch offerings are Thai snapper club, grilled organic Kobe burger and crispy soft-shell crab. Dinner is more formal, with entrees ranging from seared Alaskan halibut to pan-roasted venison to roasted organic chicken. Any of the extensive list of cheese plates, paired with wine, is a great way to end a meal. Dressy casual. **Bar:** Full bar. **Reservations:** suggested. **Hours:** 11:30 am-3 & 5:30-10 pm, Sat-11 pm, Sun 5:30 pm-10 pm. Closed: 11/27; also 12/24. **Address:** 2917 M St NW 20007 **Location:** Between 29th and 30th sts; in Georgetown. **Parking:** on-site (fee). **Cards:** AX, DC, DS, MC, VI.

MICHEL RICHARD CITRONELLE

Phone: 202/625-2150   ⑤⑥

French
$95-$155

Guest watch skilled chef Michel Richard create French cuisines with a California influence from an open kitchen as changing colored lights dance along another wall; upscale and relaxing with sophisticated table settings and attentive servers. Jeans are not permitted. Formal attire. **Bar:** Full bar. **Reservations:** required. **Hours:** 6 pm-10 pm. Closed: 1/1, 5/26, 9/1; also Sun 7/4-9/7. **Address:** 3000 M St NW 20007-3701 **Location:** Between 30th and 31st sts NW; in Latham Hotel Georgetown. **Parking:** valet. **Cards:** AX, CB, DC, DS, MC, VI.

MIE N YU

Phone: 202/333-6122   ⑤③

American
$9-$48

A small Buddha fountain in the window serves as a glimpse into the show inside: glowing lanterns, cushions, draped fabric, dining nooks, distressed wood and the exotic surroundings of the Silk Road, with Moroccan, baroque and Venetian rooms. The contemporary American cuisine picks up on the same influences. Dressy casual. **Bar:** Full bar. **Reservations:** suggested. **Hours:** 11:30 am-11 pm, Fri & Sat-midnight, Sun 11 am-11 pm, Mon & Tues 4 pm-11 pm. Closed: 12/25. **Address:** 3125 M St NW 20007 **Location:** Just w of 31st NW; in Georgetown. **Parking:** no self-parking. **Cards:** AX, DS, MC, VI.

MIMI'S AMERICAN BISTRO

Phone: 202/464-6464   ②⑤

American
$12-$27

The dining room at this theater-oriented restaurant offers a casual, comfortable atmosphere, and sidewalk dining is available seasonally. Mediterranean cuisine employs fresh, locally grown produce and organic eggs and meats, and the menu offers a nice selection of salads, sandwiches and entrees. Sunday brunch is offered from 10-3, and singing waiters are a highlight Wednesday-Sunday beginning at 7:30 pm. Casual dress. **Bar:** Full bar. **Reservations:** accepted. **Hours:** 11:30 am-midnight, Sat & Sun from 10 am. Closed: 11/27, 12/25. **Address:** 2120 P St NW 20037 **Location:** Just w of Dupont Circle. **Parking:** no self-parking. **Cards:** AX, DC, DS, MC, VI.

MISS SAIGON

Phone: 202/333-5545   ④②

Vietnamese
$7-$30

The devoted and loyal fan base know that this frequently lauded charmer serves fragrant, zesty, well-seasoned dishes. The wonton soup, rich with tender dumplings, roast pork and onion crisps in a satisfying broth, sauteed steak marinated in wine butter and garlic, light and crispy golden crepes and hearty caramel shrimp with onion and lemongrass are a sampling. Palm trees strung with white lights and soft, silky background music create a friendly setting for the meal. Casual dress. **Bar:** Full bar. **Reservations:** accepted. **Hours:** 11:30 am-10:30 pm, Fri & Sat noon-11 pm, Sun noon-10:30 pm. Closed: 7/4, 11/27, 12/25. **Address:** 3057 M St NW 20007 **Location:** Between 30th and 31st sts. **Parking:** no self-parking. **Cards:** AX, DC, MC, VI.

THE MONOCLE ON CAPITOL HILL

Phone: 202/546-4488   ⑫⑨

American
$10-$35

Established in 1960, the converted Colonial-style townhouse has a casual atmosphere, and pictures of the many politicians who have dined here adorn the walls. The upbeat, friendly restaurant features selections of aged beef, fresh seafood, pasta and crab cakes. Dressy casual. **Bar:** Full bar. **Reservations:** suggested. **Hours:** 11:30 am-midnight. Closed major holidays; also Sat & Sun. **Address:** 107 D St NE 20002 **Location:** Just n of the Capitol. **Parking:** no self-parking. **Cards:** AX, CB, DC, MC, VI.

(See map and index starting on p. 400)

MORRISON-CLARK RESTAURANT   **Phone:** 202/898-1200   64

American
$24-$36

Although many publications have bestowed accolades on the upscale restaurant, the food speaks for itself. The kitchen prepares excellent contemporary American fare in a Victorian setting. Dressy casual. **Bar:** Full bar. **Reservations:** suggested. **Hours:** 7 am-10:30 & 6-10 pm, Sun 11:30 am-2:30 pm. Closed major holidays; also Mon. **Address:** 1015 L St NW 20001 **Location:** 11th and L sts NW; just n of Massachusetts Ave; in Morrison-Clark Historic Inn and Restaurant. **Parking:** valet. **Cards:** AX, CB, DC, DS, MC, VI. **Historic**

MORTON'S STEAKHOUSE   **Phone:** 202/342-6258   37

Steak House
$25-$44

Patrons should make sure to reserve ahead for the popular, well-known steak house. Large portions, including huge cuts of fine beef and plentiful seafood, are the norm. Even the vegetables are oversized, with baked potatoes big enough for sharing. Dressy casual. **Bar:** Full bar. **Reservations:** suggested, weekends. **Hours:** 5:30 pm-11 pm, Sun 5 pm-10 pm. Closed major holidays. **Address:** 3251 Prospect St NW 20007 **Location:** At Wisconsin and Prospect sts NW. **Parking:** valet. **Cards:** AX, DC, MC, VI.

MORTON'S THE STEAKHOUSE   **Phone:** 202/955-5997   70

Steak & Seafood
$13-$42

Patrons should make sure to reserve ahead for the popular, well-known steak house. Large portions, including huge cuts of fine beef and plentiful seafood, are the norm. Even the vegetables are oversized, with baked potatoes big enough for sharing. Dressy casual. **Bar:** Full bar. **Reservations:** suggested. **Hours:** 11:30 am-11 pm, Sat from 5:30 pm, Sun 5 pm-10 pm. Closed major holidays. **Address:** 1050 Connecticut Ave 20036 **Location:** Jct L St NW; on Terrace Level of The Washington Square office building. **Parking:** on-site (fee). **Cards:** AX, DC, MC, VI.

CALL 👍M 🚷

NEYLA-A MEDITERRANEAN GRILL   **Phone:** 202/333-6353   31

Mediterranean
$16-$40

A Mediterranean grill with much of it's heart in the middle east, offering the hip crowds mezze platters of fattoush, hommus, baba ghannoug, grape leaves, falafel, and the like, and beef or lamb kebabs, shish taouk, and lamb chops while the more Mediterranean choices are fried calamari with cilantro infused tahini, seafood salad, grilled spiced tuna, porcini scented sea bass, and other less middle eastern dishes like them. Dressy casual. **Bar:** Full bar. **Reservations:** suggested. **Hours:** 5 pm-10:30 pm, Fri & Sat-11:30 pm. Closed: 1/1, 12/25. **Address:** 3206 N St NW 20007 **Location:** Just w of Wisconsin Ave NW; in Georgetown. **Parking:** no self-parking. **Cards:** AX, DC, DS, MC, VI.

🚷

NORA   **Phone:** 202/462-5143   15

American
$24-$68

The tranquil, rustic setting has brick walls, beamed ceilings and hand-crafted quilts displayed. Creative American cuisine is prepared with only organic ingredients—from the flour and sugar to the meats and poultry. Chef Nora Pouillon has received certification from Oregon Tilth, which verifies that 95 percent of ingredients come from certified organic farmers, growers and suppliers. Casual dress. **Bar:** Full bar. **Reservations:** suggested. **Hours:** 5:30 pm-10 pm, Fri & Sat-10:30 pm. Closed: Sun & last 2 weeks of Aug. **Address:** 2132 Florida Ave NW 20008 **Location:** Corner of R St and Florida Ave NW; between 21st St and Florida Ave. **Parking:** on-site (fee) and valet. **Cards:** AX, MC, VI.

OBELISK   **Phone:** 202/872-1180   18

Northern Italian

The prix fixe five-course menu at Obelisk changes every day and is driven by the availability of fresh market ingredients. This intimate, well established, chef-owned restaurant employs a knowledgeable, capable and kitchen-smart service staff. Casual dress. **Bar:** Full bar. **Reservations:** suggested. **Hours:** 1st seating 6 pm, 6:30 pm & 7 pm; 2nd seating 8:30 pm, 9 pm & 9:30 pm. Closed major holidays; also Sun & Mon. **Address:** 2029 P St NW 20036 **Location:** Just w of Dupont Circle. **Parking:** street. **Cards:** DC, MC, VI.

OCCIDENTAL RESTAURANT   **Phone:** 202/783-1475   117

American
$16-$39

Just a block and a half from the White House and adjacent to The Willard Inter-Continental Hotel, the clubby dining room originally opened in 1912 and operated until 1972. The restaurant reopened in 1986, and through extensive research, the owners were able to recover most of the original photo collection. An endless list of politicians and other celebrities have dined here, and the walls display more than 3,000 framed black-and-white pictures of the many political movers and shakers who have dined here over the years. The fare is contemporary American cuisine; find a nice fish selection as well as grilled meats. The menu offers salads, sandwiches and full meals. A friendly staff provides professional service. Dressy casual. **Bar:** Full bar. **Reservations:** suggested. **Hours:** 11:30 am-3 & 5-10 pm, Sat from 5 pm, Sun 5 pm-9 pm. Closed: 5/26, 11/27, 12/24, 12/25. **Address:** 1475 Pennsylvania Ave NW 20004 **Location:** 1.5 blks from the White House; adjacent to Willard Intercontinental. **Parking:** no self-parking. **Cards:** AX, DC, MC, VI.

CALL 👍M

THE OCEANAIRE SEAFOOD ROOM   *Menu on AAA.com*   **Phone:** 202/347-2277   104

(AAA)

Seafood
$12-$35

Fresh fish and shellfish are flown in daily from around the globe. The sleek, handsomely designed dining room has a raw bar and is tastefully appointed in an art deco/nautical theme. The menu notes the seafood available daily and the varied preparation styles, such as broiled, grilled and blackened. Dressy casual. **Bar:** Full bar. **Reservations:** suggested. **Hours:** 11:30 am-10 pm, Fri-11 pm, Sat 5 pm-11 pm, Sun 5 pm-9 pm. Closed major holidays. **Address:** 1201 F St NW 20004 **Location:** Between 12th and 13th sts NW. **Parking:** no self-parking. **Cards:** AX, MC, VI.

CALL 👍M 🚷

OLD EBBITT GRILL   **Phone:** 202/347-4800   105

American
$11-$26

Around the corner from the White House, the historic downtown eatery is popular with the locals. Uniformed servers are friendly and professional. The menu blends a nice selection of American dishes, raw bar items and creative desserts. Brunch is served on weekends from 8:30 am to 4 pm. Casual dress. **Bar:** Full bar. **Reservations:** suggested. **Hours:** 7:30 am-midnight, Sat & Sun from 8:30 am. Closed: 12/25. **Address:** 675 15th St NW 20005 **Location:** 1 blk from the White House, 2 blks from Metro Center, exit 13th St. **Parking:** no self-parking. **Cards:** AX, DC, DS, MC, VI.

(See map and index starting on p. 400)

OLD EUROPE   *Menu on AAA.com*   **Phone:** 202/333-7600   ①

German
$8-$23

The acclaimed restaurant, which exudes the atmosphere of a German gasthaus, booms with business. Among well-prepared meals is the delicious sauerbraten with red cabbage and dumplings. Veteran servers in Bavarian dress are friendly and thoughtful. Casual dress. **Bar:** Full bar. **Reservations:** suggested, weekends. **Hours:** 11:30 am-3 & 5-9 pm, Fri & Sat-10 pm, Sun 1 pm-3:30 & 4-8 pm. Closed: 7/4; also 12/24 & Mon. **Address:** 2434 Wisconsin Ave NW 20007 **Location:** In Upper Georgetown. **Parking:** street. **Cards:** AX, CB, DC, MC, VI.

OLD GLORY, ALL AMERICAN BAR-B-QUE   **Phone:** 202/337-3406   52

American
$9-$25

The noisy, rustic roadhouse packs them in each night with its well-prepared entrees and frequent live entertainment. The barbecue spare ribs, leg of lamb and Sunday country brunch are among the most popular offerings. Service is friendly and casual. Casual dress. **Bar:** Full bar. **Reservations:** accepted, Sun-Thurs. **Hours:** 11:30 am-11 pm, Fri & Sat-midnight, Sun 11 am-11 pm. Closed: 11/27, 12/25. **Address:** 3139 M St NW 20007 **Location:** Corner of M St and Wisconsin Ave NW. **Parking:** no self-parking. **Cards:** AX, CB, DC, DS, MC, VI.

OLIVES   **Phone:** 202/452-1866   78

Regional Italian
$14-$41

The contemporary Italian cooking uses the freshest ingredients in its seasonally changing menu. The wood-grilled sea bass on horseradish mashed potatoes, has become popular with the locals. The stylish street level dining room offers a casual air, with more formal setting on the lower level. Pay valet parking is available for dinner. Dressy casual. **Bar:** Full bar. **Reservations:** suggested. **Hours:** 11:30 am-2:30 & 5:30-10:30 pm, Sat from 5:30 pm. Closed major holidays; also Sun. **Address:** 1600 K St NW 20006 **Location:** At 16th and K sts NW. **Parking:** no self-parking. **Cards:** AX, DC, DS, MC, VI.

THE OVAL ROOM   **Phone:** 202/463-8700   96

American
$12-$32

A location convenient to the White House and Farragut Square accounts for the elegantly sophisticated restaurant's popularity with politicians, journalists, lawyers and former presidents. The chef prepares seasonal contemporary American cuisine in a chic atmosphere. Favorites include golden cod cakes and hand-harvested sea scallops with caramelized cauliflower and baby bok choy. The flower-bedecked patio offers another seating option. Dressy casual. **Bar:** Full bar. **Reservations:** suggested. **Hours:** 11:30 am-3 & 5:30-10 pm, Fri-10:30 pm, Sat 5:30 pm-10:30 pm. Closed major holidays; also Sun. **Address:** 800 Connecticut Ave NW 20006 **Location:** Between H and I sts. **Parking:** no self-parking. **Cards:** AX, DC, DS, MC, VI.

PALM RESTAURANT   **Phone:** 202/293-9091   33

American
$13-$52

This bustling restaurant is noted for prime, dry-aged steaks and Nova Scotia lobsters, huge portions are delivered by an attentive staff in an atmosphere that is fun and lively. At the end of the meal, servers present tempting pastries tableside. Caricature-lined walls lend to the feeling that patrons are dining in an art gallery. Even if you bring a big appetite you still may leave with a doggy bag. Casual dress. **Bar:** Full bar. **Reservations:** suggested. **Hours:** 11:45 am-10:30 pm, Sat from 5:30 pm, Sun 5:30 pm-9:30 pm. Closed major holidays. **Address:** 1225 19th St NW 20036 **Location:** Between M and N sts NW. **Parking:** no self-parking. **Cards:** AX, CB, DC, DS, JC, MC, VI.

PAOLO'S RISTORANTE   **Phone:** 202/333-7353   30

Italian
$8-$28

In the heart of Georgetown, the busy restaurant presents a menu of pasta, seafood, steak, veal chops and pizza. The brick oven and open kitchen add an informal feel to the setting. The place is fun and energetic and the service staff pleasant and prompt. Casual dress. **Bar:** Full bar. **Reservations:** suggested, weekends. **Hours:** 11:30 am-11:30 pm, Fri & Sat-12:30 am, Sun 11 am-11:30 pm. Closed: 12/25. **Address:** 1303 Wisconsin Ave NW 20007 **Location:** Just n of M St NW; in Georgetown. **Parking:** no self-parking. **Cards:** AX, CB, DC, DS, MC, VI.

PEACOCK CAFE   **Phone:** 202/625-2740   35

American
$8-$39

In the heart of Georgetown, the hip, trendy cafe is known locally for its full-service fresh fruit and vegetable juice bar, the first of its kind in the city, as well as its weekend brunch. Menu offerings range from meatloaf and ravioli to seared peppered tuna and veggie burgers. Guests can order from the dinner menu after 5 pm. Sidewalk seating opens seasonally. Casual dress. **Bar:** Full bar. **Reservations:** suggested. **Hours:** 11:30 am-10:30 pm, Fri-11 pm, Sat 9 am-11 pm, Sun 9 am-10:30 pm. Closed: 11/27, 12/25. **Address:** 3251 Prospect St NW 20007 **Location:** Jct Prospect and Wisconsin sts; in Georgetown. **Parking:** no self-parking. **Cards:** AX, DC, DS, MC, VI.

PENANG   **Phone:** 202/822-8773   39

Indonesian
$9-$22

Malaysian fare with flair is on hand at the upper-level bistro. The menu lists exotic preparations of Indian-style roti canai, satays, noodles, rices and curries. Food is served family-style. Casual dress. **Bar:** Full bar. **Reservations:** accepted. **Hours:** 11:30 am-11 pm, Thurs-midnight, Fri & Sat-1 am, Sun-10 pm. Closed: 11/27, 12/25. **Address:** 1837 M St NW 20036 **Location:** At 19th St. **Parking:** no self-parking. **Cards:** AX, DC, DS, MC, VI.

PESCE BISTRO   **Phone:** 202/466-3474   24

Seafood
$8-$31

Fresh seafood, expertly prepared in eye-appealing presentations, is the draw at the compact, popular bistro. Palate-pleasing creations change daily. The no-reservations policy can be challenging. Casual dress. **Bar:** Beer & wine. **Hours:** 11:30 am-2:30 & 5:30-10 pm, Fri-10:30 pm, Sat 5:30 pm-10:30 pm, Sun 5 pm-9:30 pm. Closed: 1/1, 11/27, 12/25. **Address:** 2016 P St NW 20036 **Location:** Between Hopkins and 20th sts, just w of Dupont Circle. **Parking:** no self-parking. **Cards:** AX, DC, DS, MC, VI.

(See map and index starting on p. 400)

PHILLIPS FLAGSHIP

Phone: 202/488-8515

Seafood
$14-$27

A large, casual waterfront restaurant overlooking the Washington Channel. They offer an extensive all-you-can-eat buffet, with traditional Maryland seafood, carving table, sushi bar, pasta & salad bar. The house specilty is the crabcakes, using a recipe dating back to 1956. Menu service is also available. Casual dress. **Bar:** Full bar. **Hours:** 11 am-9 pm, Fri & Sat-10 pm, Sun 10 am-9 pm. Closed: 12/25. **Address:** 900 Water St SW 20024 **Location:** I-395, exit Maine Ave, just e. **Parking:** on-site (fee). **Cards:** AX, CB, DC, DS, MC, VI.

PIZZERIA PARADISO

Phone: 202/223-1245   19

Pizza
$8-$17

The dining room is always hopping at the popular pizzeria. The menu is not extensive—listing mainly pizza, salads and panini—but the fresh ingredients are the draw. Sandwiches are made with homemade focaccia rolls, and pizzas are produced in a wood-burning oven. Casual dress. **Bar:** Beer & wine. **Reservations:** not accepted. **Hours:** 11:30 am-11 pm, Fri & Sat-midnight, Sun noon-10 pm. Closed major holidays. **Address:** 2029 P St NW 20036 **Location:** Just w of Dupont Circle. **Parking:** no self-parking. **Cards:** AX, DC, DS, MC, VI.

POSTE—MODERNE BRASSERIE

Phone: 202/783-6060   116

American
$10-$28

The stylish bistro, in the courtyard at the Hotel Monaco, nurtures a bustling, chic atmosphere. The kitchen skillfully prepares modern American cuisine along the lines of braised short ribs and mushroom risotto. The service staff is friendly and efficient. Casual dress. **Bar:** Full bar. **Reservations:** suggested. **Hours:** 7-10 am, 11:30-2:30, & 5-10 pm, Sat 9 am-2 & 5-10 pm, Sun 9 am-2 & 5-9 pm. Closed major holidays. **Address:** 555 8th St NW 20004 **Location:** Between 7th and 8th sts NW; in Hotel Monaco Washington DC. **Parking:** valet. **Cards:** AX, CB, DC, DS, JC, MC, VI.

THE PRIME RIB

Phone: 202/466-8811   81

Steak & Seafood
$12-$44

Well-prepared beef and seafood highlight the menu, but as the name suggests, aged, roast prime rib is the specialty. Nicely appointed dining rooms exude a supper club ambience. Good service rounds out the experience. Complimentary valet parking is available for dinner. Formal attire. Entertainment. **Bar:** Full bar. **Reservations:** suggested. **Hours:** 11:30 am-3 & 5-11 pm, Fri-11:30 pm, Sat 5 pm-11:30 pm. Closed: 1/1, 11/27, 12/25; also Sun & for lunch 7/4. **Address:** 2020 K St NW 20006 **Location:** Between 20th and 21st sts NW. **Parking:** no self-parking. **Cards:** AX, CB, DC, MC, VI.

PRIMI PIATTI

Phone: 202/223-3600   85

Northern Italian
$13-$34

The noisy, bustling trattoria offers a fine selection of pasta, seafood and meat dishes as well as a memorable tiramisu. Italian music and European decor characterize the main dining room; a breezy feel envelops the sidewalk dining area. Dressy casual. **Bar:** Full bar. **Reservations:** suggested. **Hours:** 11:30 am-2:30 & 5:30-10:30 pm, Sat from 5:30 pm. Closed major holidays; also Sun. **Address:** 2013 I St NW 20006 **Location:** Off Pennsylvania Ave; between 20th and 21st sts NW. **Parking:** no self-parking. **Cards:** AX, DC, JC, MC, VI.

RAKU-AN ASIAN DINER

Phone: 202/265-7258   17

Asian
$9-$14

Just off Dupont Circle you'll find this casual Asian Diner. The menu offers a nice selection of dishes from a variety of Asian countries. Casual dress. **Bar:** Full bar. **Reservations:** not accepted. **Hours:** 11:30 am-10 pm, Fri & Sat-11 pm. Closed: 12/25. **Address:** 1900 Q St NW 20009 **Location:** Jct 19th and Q sts NW. **Parking:** no self-parking. **Cards:** AX, MC, VI.

RESTAURANT KOLUMBIA

Phone: 202/331-5551   72

American
$15-$35

The stylish dining room provides a comfortable setting for any occasion. Finesse and artistry go into the chef/owner's seasonally changing preparations of modern American cuisine. A chef's tasting menu can be sampled with or without wine pairings, but diners also have the option to order a la carte. Dressy casual. **Bar:** Full bar. **Reservations:** suggested. **Hours:** 11:30 am-2 & 5:30-10 pm, Fri-11 pm, Sat 5:30 pm-11 pm. Closed major holidays; also Sun except holidays. **Address:** 1801 K St NW 20006 **Location:** At 18th St. **Parking:** no self-parking. **Cards:** AX, DC, DS, MC, VI.

ROOF TERRACE RESTAURANT & BAR AT THE
KENNEDY CENTER

Phone: 202/416-8555   111

Regional American
$27-$34

A special-occasion destination, the versatile restaurant looks out over the Potomac River. High ceilings and huge windows with floor-to-ceiling drapes set a romantic tone. Worth trying are sea bass and rack of lamb entrees and the sinful molten chocolate cake for dessert. Dressy casual. **Bar:** Full bar. **Reservations:** suggested. **Hours:** 5 pm-8 pm; open only when there are major performances. Closed: for dinner 7/4. **Address:** 2700 F St NW 20566 **Location:** On the roof terrace level at The Kennedy Center. **Parking:** on-site (fee). **Cards:** AX, CB, DC, DS, MC, VI.

ROSA MEXICANO

Phone: 202/783-5522   110

Mexican
$10-$24

Classic Mexican cuisine is served in a relaxed and casual atmosphere. Tableside guacamole preparation and a lively service staff enhance the experience. Casual dress. **Bar:** Full bar. **Hours:** 11:30 am-3 & 5-11 pm, Sat from 11 am, Sun 11 am-3 pm, Mon 11:30 am-3 & 5-10 pm. Closed: 12/25. **Address:** 575 7th St NW 20004 **Location:** Corner of 7th and F sts; center; in Penn Quarter area, opposite MCI Center. **Parking:** street. **Cards:** AX, CB, DC, DS, JC, MC, VI.

ROSEMARY'S THYME BISTRO

Phone: 202/332-3200   11

Mediterranean
$7-$24

A neighborhood restaurant serving Mediterranean cuisine using fresh market ingredients. The menu offers a nice selection appetizers, pasta, meat and seafood dishes. Seasonal sidewalk dining available when the weather is appropriate. Casual dress. **Bar:** Full bar. **Reservations:** suggested, weekends. **Hours:** 5 pm-11 pm, Fri & Sat 11 am-midnight, Sun 11 am-10 pm. Closed: 11/27, 12/25. **Address:** 1801 18th St NW 20009 **Location:** Jct S St NW. **Parking:** street. **Cards:** AX, DC, DS, MC, VI.

(See map and index starting on p. 400)

RUTH'S CHRIS STEAK HOUSE

Steak House
$19-$37

Phone: 202/797-0033   (10)

The main fare is steak, which is prepared from several cuts of prime beef and cooked to perfection, but the menu also lists lamb, chicken and seafood dishes. Guests should come hungry because the side dishes, which are among the a la carte offerings, could make a meal in themselves. Dressy casual. **Bar:** Full bar. **Reservations:** suggested. **Hours:** 5 pm-10 pm, Fri & Sat-10:30 pm, Sun-9 pm. Closed: 11/27, 12/25. **Address:** 1801 Connecticut Ave 20009 **Location:** At S St NW; metro stop, Dupont Circle. **Parking:** valet. **Cards:** AX, DC, DS, MC, VI.

SAM & HARRY'S

Steak House
$34-$52

Phone: 202/296-4333   (40)

A jazz theme echoes in the restaurant's friendly, clubby atmosphere. The house specialty is prime, aged beef, but the menu also features three- to four-pound lobsters, veal, seafood, chicken, pork and lamb—all in generous portions. Complimentary valet parking is available for dinner. Dressy casual. **Bar:** Full bar. **Reservations:** suggested. **Hours:** 5:30 pm-10 pm. Closed major holidays; also Sun. **Address:** 1200 19th St NW 20036 **Location:** Between M and N sts NW. **Parking:** valet. **Cards:** AX, CB, DC, DS, MC, VI.

SEA CATCH RESTAURANT

Seafood
$14-$49

Phone: 202/337-8855   (62)

Set along the C&O canal, in the Canal Square complex. The building orginally constructed in 1842, is the birthplace of the first computer. A punched card tabulating machine, designed to be used in the 1890 census. The restaurant specialty is fish. The raw bar offerings are wonderful; enormous, plump and juicy shrimp and at least three types of oysters. The kitchen is very skilled in the preparation of the seafood dishes. Lamb, veal chops, beef and chicken are also available. Dressy casual. **Bar:** Full bar. **Reservations:** suggested. **Hours:** noon-3 & 5:30-10 pm. Closed major holidays; also Sun. **Address:** 1054 31st St NW 20007 **Location:** Just s of M St; at Canal Square; in Georgetown. **Parking:** on-site. **Cards:** AX, CB, DC, DS, MC, VI.

SKEWERS

Middle Eastern
$8-$20

Phone: 202/387-7400   (21)

Middle Eastern fare is the cuisine of choice at the casual eatery. Curried dishes, falafel and meze specials all are tasty. Casual dress. **Bar:** Full bar. **Reservations:** accepted. **Hours:** 11:30 am-10 pm, Fri & Sat-11 pm. Closed: 11/27, 12/25. **Address:** 1633 P St NW 20036 **Location:** Between 16th and 17th sts NW. **Parking:** street. **Cards:** AX, DC, DS, MC, VI.

SUSHI AOI

Japanese
$7-$25

Phone: 202/408-7770   (90)

The cozy restaurant serves well-prepared, familiar Japanese dishes and a number of creative specialties and features contemporary yet casual decor and, of course, a sushi bar. Casual dress. **Bar:** Full bar. **Reservations:** accepted. **Hours:** 11:30 am-2:30 & 5-10:30 pm, Sat & Sun from 5 pm. Closed: 7/4, 11/27, 12/25. **Address:** 1100 New York Ave NW 20005 **Location:** At 11th St. **Parking:** no self-parking. **Cards:** AX, DC, MC, VI.

SUSHI TARO

Japanese
$8-$40

Phone: 202/462-8999   (23)

Skilled Japanese chefs prepare sushi, sashimi and tempura. Guests may choose seating in a dining room with standard chairs and tables or in a re-created traditional tatami room with the low tables for which Japan is known. Casual dress. **Bar:** Full bar. **Reservations:** suggested. **Hours:** 11:30 am-2 & 5:30-10 pm, Fri-10:30 pm, Sat 5:30 pm-10:30 pm. Closed major holidays; also Sun. **Address:** 1503 17th St NW 20036 **Location:** Jct 17th NW and P sts. **Parking:** no self-parking. **Cards:** AX, CB, DC, DS, JC, MC, VI.

TABERNA DEL ALABARDERO

Spanish
$20-$45

Phone: 202/429-2200   (91)

The menu spotlights cuisine from the Basque region of northern Spain. Beautiful 19th-century Spanish decor lends character to the dining area. Well-prepared entrees of fresh seafood, paella, meat and game are notable. Parking in the adjacent garage is validated. Dressy casual. **Bar:** Full bar. **Reservations:** suggested. **Hours:** 11:30 am-2:30 & 5:30-10 pm, Sat from 5:30 pm. Closed major holidays; also Sun. **Address:** 1776 I St NW 20006 **Location:** Entrance on 18th St NW. **Parking:** no self-parking. **Cards:** AX, CB, DC, DS, MC, VI.

TEATRO GOLDONI

Italian
$13-$44

Phone: 202/955-9494   (73)

Chef Fabrizio Aielli's kitchen prepares delicious Italian cuisine with a Venetian influence, in a theatrical, contemporary setting. In addition to the ala carte menu, prix-fixed lunch and dinner menu's are available. Extensive selection of wines by the glass. Pay valet parking available for dinner. Dressy casual. **Bar:** Full bar. **Reservations:** suggested. **Hours:** 11:30 am-2 & 5:30-10 pm, Fri-11 pm, Sat 5 pm-11 pm. Closed major holidays; also Sun. **Address:** 1909 K St NW 20006 **Location:** Between 19th and 20th sts NW. **Parking:** no self-parking. **Cards:** AX, CB, DC, DS, JC, MC, VI.

CALL 🚹M

TENPENH RESTAURANT

Pacific Rim
$13-$36

Phone: 202/393-4500   (124)

The cuisine of Chef Tunks is Asian-Pacific inspired, with contemporary preparation of indigenous ingredients from the Pacific Rim and Southeast Asia. The striking interior reflects an Asian influence, with statues, teak tables and chairs and fine fabrics. Valet parking is available during dinner. Dressy casual. **Bar:** Full bar. **Reservations:** suggested. **Hours:** 11:30 am-2:30 & 5:30-10:30 pm, Fri-11 pm, Sat 5:30 pm-11 pm. Closed major holidays; also Sun. **Address:** 1001 Pennsylvania Ave NW 20004 **Location:** At 10th St and Pennsylvania Ave NW. **Parking:** no self-parking. **Cards:** AX, DC, DS, MC, VI.

CALL 🚹M

(See map and index starting on p. 400)

THAI KITCHEN

Thai
$7-$18

Phone: 202/452-6090 46

In the West End, the basement-level Thai restaurant serves traditional Thai dishes along the lines of crispy whole flounder, scallops and snow peas, curries, noodles, fried rice and vegetarian dishes. Casual dress. **Bar:** Full bar. **Reservations:** accepted. **Hours:** 11 am-10:30 pm, Sat noon-10 pm, Sun 4:30 pm-10 pm. Closed: 7/4, 11/27, 12/25. **Address:** 2311 M St NW 20037 **Location:** Between 23rd and 24th sts NW. **Parking:** no self-parking. **Cards:** AX, MC, VI.

THAIPHOON

Thai
$6-$15

Phone: 202/667-3505 12

Good Thai food is served in the intimate, contemporary restaurant just north of Dupont Circle. Listed on the extensive menu are beef, chicken, seafood, noodle and vegetarian dishes. The degree of spiciness is shown on the menu by the number of peppers next to each item. Casual dress. **Bar:** Full bar. **Reservations:** suggested, weekends. **Hours:** 11:30 am-10:30 pm, Fri & Sat-11 pm. Closed: 11/27, 12/25. **Address:** 2011 S St NW 20009 **Location:** 3 blks n of Dupont Circle, just off Connecticut Ave NW. **Parking:** no self-parking. **Cards:** AX, DC, DS, MC, VI.

TONY & JOE'S SEAFOOD PLACE
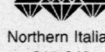
Seafood
$9-$36

Phone: 202/944-4545 76

Overlooking the scenic Potomac River, the bright, open dining room is the highlight of the casual, bustling restaurant. The outdoor terrace is a great spot to relax and watch boats drive by and crew teams train. The extensive menu offers a wide variety of fresh fish, but beef and chicken selections are also available. Casual dress. **Bar:** Full bar. **Reservations:** suggested. **Hours:** 11 am-10 pm, Fri & Sat-midnight. Closed: 12/25. **Address:** 3000 K St NW, Suite 10 20007 **Location:** In Georgetown; at Washington Harbour Complex. **Parking:** on-site (fee). **Cards:** AX, CB, DC, DS, MC, VI.

TOSCA

Northern Italian
$15-$40

Phone: 202/367-1990 109

The restaurant has a sophisticated design, formally attired wait staff and a contemporary Northern Italian menu. The staff is knowledgeable about wines and menu items. At dinner, valets provide parking service for a fee. Dressy casual. **Bar:** Full bar. **Reservations:** suggested, weekends. **Hours:** 11:30 am-2:30 & 5:30-10:30 pm, Fri-11 pm, Sat 5:30 pm-11 pm. Closed major holidays; also Sun. **Address:** 1112 F St NW 20004 **Location:** Just e of the White House; between 11th and 12th sts. **Parking:** no self-parking. **Cards:** AX, DC, DS, MC, VI.

TWO QUAIL

American
$7-$28

Phone: 202/543-8030 127

On the outside, the restaurant is classic Capitol Hill row house and is mere blocks from the Capitol; on the inside, it's reminiscent of Grandma's dining room, with Victorian touches, flowery fabrics and knickknacks throughout. The menu lists innovative American cuisine that changes with the seasons. Efficient servers take care of business in the dining room and on the seasonal dining patio. Horse-drawn carriage rides around the historic area can be arranged, but reservations are limited. Dressy casual. **Bar:** Full bar. **Reservations:** suggested. **Hours:** 11:30 am-2:30 & 5-10 pm, Fri-11 pm, Sat 5 pm-11 pm, Sun 5 pm-10 pm. Closed: 1/1, 7/4; also for lunch most national holidays. **Address:** 320 Massachusetts Ave NE 20002 **Location:** Between 3rd and 4th sts NE. **Parking:** street. **Cards:** AX, DC, DS, MC, VI.

URBANA
American
$7-$34

Phone: 202/448-1800 20

Bar: Full bar. **Reservations:** suggested. **Hours:** 6 am-midnight. **Address:** 2121 P St NW 20037 **Location:** Between 21st and 22nd sts NW, just w of Dupont Cir; in Hotel Palomar A Kimpton Hotel. **Parking:** valet. **Cards:** AX, CB, DC, DS, JC, MC, VI.

VIDALIA
Regional American
$16-$40

Phone: 202/659-1990 51

Diners will find a contemporary atmosphere as they step into this basement-level dining room in the heart of downtown along bustling M Street. Here, American cuisine reflects a distinctively Southern accent. Skilled cooks consistently prepare sophisticated, complex dishes that change with the season. Among the chef's tempting signature dishes are shrimp and grits, but many selections on the varied menu will satisfy any appetite. Valet parking is available during dinner. Dressy casual. **Bar:** Full bar. **Reservations:** suggested. **Hours:** 11:30 am-2:30 & 5:30-10 pm, Fri-10:30 pm, Sat 5:30 pm-10:30 pm, Sun 5 pm-9:30 pm. Closed major holidays. **Address:** 1990 M St NW 20036 **Location:** Between 19th and 20th sts. **Parking:** no self-parking. **Cards:** AX, DC, DS, MC, VI.

THE WHITE TIGER

Indian
$9-$25

Phone: 202/546-5900 130

A rare creature in nature, the white tiger was chosen to be emblematic of the restaurant's distinctive position among Indian restaurants. While listing traditional cuisine, the menu is innovative in appealing to Western palates. Among offerings are Cajun salmon and crabettes—jumbo lump crab cakes done in Indian fashion—and marinated filet mignon, the rare beef dish for an Indian eatery. Offerings also include Sunday brunch and a $9.95 weekday lunch buffet. Hand-carved figurines accent the decor. Dressy casual. **Bar:** Full bar. **Reservations:** suggested. **Hours:** 11:30 am-2:30 & 5-10 pm, Fri-10:30 pm, Sat 5 pm-10:30 pm. Closed: 12/25. **Address:** 301 Massachusetts Ave NE 20002 **Location:** Jct Massachusetts Ave NE and 3rd St. **Parking:** street. **Cards:** AX, CB, DC, DS, MC, VI.

THE WILLARD ROOM

French
$23-$37

Phone: 202/637-7440 120

A stately, elegant dining room with exquisite woodwork. The setting is formal, as jacket and tie are recommended. The contemporary American cuisine is superbly prepared. The chef demonstrates his skills in each dish he creates. The seafood selections are some of his best work. Complimentary valet parking is provided for dinner guests. Semi-formal attire. **Bar:** Full bar. **Reservations:** suggested. **Hours:** Open 3/1-7/31 & 9/2-2/28; 7:30-10 am, 11:30-2 & 6-10 pm, Fri 7:30-10 am, 11:30-2 & 5:30-10 pm, Sat 8 am-noon & 5:30-10 pm, Sun 11 am-3 pm. Closed: 9/1; also 1/2-1/8. **Address:** 1401 Pennsylvania Ave NW 20004 **Location:** Just e of the White House; in The Willard InterContinental. **Parking:** valet. **Cards:** AX, CB, DC, DS, JC, MC, VI. **Historic**

CALL

(See map and index starting on p. 400)

ZAYTINYA

Mediterranean
$5-$27

Phone: 202/638-0800 (101)

The restaurant is a place to see and be seen among the young but not too young. A large, glass-enclosed fish tank of a dining room—with polished gray marble, dark wood accents and upbeat, flattering Euro-music—lends a vibrant mood to an already energetic crowd. The bar is large and just as swank, a great place to meet for drinks. An abundant and varied menu of beautifully presented and flavorful Turkish, Lebanese and Greek meze is full of opportunity. Dressy casual. **Bar:** Full bar. **Hours:** 11:30 am-11:30 pm, Fri & Sat-midnight, Sun & Mon-10 pm; Saturday & Sunday brunch. Closed: 1/1, 11/27, 12/24, 12/25. **Address:** 701 9th St NW 20001 **Location:** Between F St and G Pl NW; Gallery Place/Chinatown metro stop (exit 9 and G). **Parking:** no self-parking. **Cards:** AX, CB, DC, DS, MC, VI.

ZED'S ETHIOPIAN CUISINE

Ethiopian
$7-$20

Phone: 202/333-4710 (49)

Zed's has been a Georgetown favorite for over 10 years but has a bright new corner spot offering up two cozy floors with large windows overlooking the street. They serve up authentic cuisine; both meat and Vegetarian dishes stewed with exotic spices. The fun is in the eating; all is served tableside onto large platters and then diners scoop up items with Injera, a spongy flatbread used in place of utensils. Casual dress. **Bar:** Full bar. **Hours:** 11 am-11 pm. Closed: 11/27, 12/25. **Address:** 1201 28th St NW 20007 **Location:** Jct M and 28th sts NW; in Georgetown. **Parking:** no self-parking. **Cards:** AX, DC, MC, VI.

ZOLA

American
$10-$29

Phone: 202/654-0999 (113)

The influence of the International Spy Museum can be felt in the ambience of its restaurant neighbor. Sleek and sophisticated with a touch of intrigue, this place presents a menu of inventive American cuisine. Valet parking is available in the evening, from 5 pm, at a fee. Casual dress. **Bar:** Full bar. **Reservations:** suggested. **Hours:** 11:30 am-3 & 5-10 pm, Fri-11 pm, Sat 5 pm-11 pm, Sun 5 pm-9 pm. Closed: 1/1, 11/27, 12/25. **Address:** 800 F St NW 20004 **Location:** At 8th and F sts NW. **Parking:** no self-parking. **Cards:** AX, DC, DS, MC, VI.

---

*The following restaurants have not been evaluated by AAA
but are listed for your information only.*

BRICKSKELLER

[fyi]

Phone: 202/293-1885

Not evaluated. Established in 1957, Brickskeller is a tavern with more than 800 brands of American and imported beers. The menu offers traditional American fare, from pizza to South Dakota buffalo steaks and burgers. **Address:** 1523 22nd St NW 20037 **Location:** Between P and Q sts NW.

SPY CITY CAFE

[fyi]

Phone: 202/654-0995

Not evaluated. Museum visitors will appreciate the made-to-order salads, homemade soups and hot and cold offerings in the cafeteria-style eatery. **Address:** 800 F St NW 20004 **Location:** Jct of F and 8th sts NW.

SUSHI-KO

[fyi]

Phone: 202/333-4187

Not evaluated. Traditional sushi is the showcase for lunch, but the chef pulls out his inventive Western-influenced Asian dishes, paired with fine French wines, in the evening. **Address:** 2309 Wisconsin Ave NW 20007 **Location:** S of Calvert St.

WASHINGTON (WEST AND NORTH REGION) (See map and index starting on p. 408)

--- **WHERE TO STAY** ---

CONNECTICUT AVE DAYS INN *Book great rates at AAA.com*

AAA SAVE

Small-scale Hotel
$152-$169 3/1-10/31
$89-$99 11/1-2/28

Phone: (202)244-5600 **2**

Address: 4400 Connecticut Ave NW 20008 **Location:** 1.2 mi n of the National Zoo. **Facility:** 155 one-bedroom standard units. 6 stories, interior corridors. *Bath:* combo or shower only. **Parking:** on-site (fee). **Amenities:** voice mail, irons, hair dryers. *Fee:* video games, safes. **Guest Services:** wireless Internet. **Business Services:** meeting rooms, PC (fee). **Cards:** AX, DC, DS, MC, VI. **Free Special Amenities:** newspaper. *(See color ad p 471)*

[SD] [TI] CALL [GM] FEE [icons] / SOME UNITS [X] FEE [icon] FEE [icon]

**EMBASSY SUITES HOTEL AT THE CHEVY CHASE
PAVILION** *Book great rates at AAA.com*

AAA SAVE

Small-scale Hotel
Rates not provided

Phone: 202/362-9300 **1**

Address: 4300 Military Rd NW 20015 **Location:** SR 355; at Friendship Heights Metro Station. Located opposite the Mazza Gallery Shopping Mall. **Facility:** 198 one-bedroom suites. 9 stories, interior corridors. *Bath:* combo or shower only. **Parking:** on-site (fee). **Amenities:** dual phone lines, voice mail, irons, hair dryers. *Fee:* video games, high-speed Internet. **Pool(s):** heated indoor. **Leisure Activities:** saunas, whirlpool. *Fee:* massage. **Guest Services:** valet and coin laundry, wireless Internet. *Fee:* personal trainers. **Business Services:** meeting rooms, business center. **Free Special Amenities:** full breakfast and newspaper.

[TI] CALL [GM] [icons] [X] [icons] / SOME UNITS [X]

▼ *See AAA listing p 470* ▼

(See map and index starting on p. 408)

MARRIOTT WARDMAN PARK HOTEL   *Book great rates at AAA.com*   Phone: 202/328-2000   **3**

Large-scale Hotel
Rates not provided

Address: 2660 Woodley Rd NW 20008 **Location:** Just w of Connecticut Ave; at Woodley Park/Zoo Metro Station. **Facility:** Smoke free premises. 1334 units. 1247 one-bedroom standard units. 77 one-, 9 two- and 1 three-bedroom suites. 8-10 stories, interior corridors. *Bath:* combo or shower only. **Parking:** on-site (fee) and valet. **Terms:** check-in 4 pm. **Amenities:** high-speed Internet (fee), dual phone lines, voice mail, irons, hair dryers. **Pool(s):** outdoor. **Leisure Activities:** steamrooms, exercise room. *Fee:* massage. **Guest Services:** valet laundry, wireless Internet. **Business Services:** conference facilities, business center.

Marriott
HOTELS & RESORTS

AAA Benefit:
Members save 5% off of the best available rate.

OMNI SHOREHAM HOTEL   *Book great rates at AAA.com*   Phone: (202)234-0700   **5**

Historic
Large-scale Hotel
$199-$529 All Year

Address: 2500 Calvert St NW 20008 **Location:** Just w of Connecticut Ave. Adjacent to Rock Creek Park; 1 blk from Woodley Park/Zoo Metro Station. **Facility:** Crystal chandeliers add grandeur to the lobby of this beautifully restored 1930s hotel overlooking Rock Creek Park; guest rooms are well appointed. 834 units. 809 one-bedroom standard units. 24 one- and 1 two-bedroom suites, some with whirlpools. 5-8 stories, interior corridors. *Bath:* combo or shower only. **Parking:** on-site (fee) and valet. **Terms:** cancellation fee imposed. **Amenities:** video games (fee), dual phone lines, voice mail, honor bars, irons, hair dryers. *Some:* high-speed Internet. **Dining:** Robert's Restaurant, see separate listing, entertainment. **Pool(s):** heated outdoor. **Leisure Activities:** whirlpool, wildlife observation deck;, jogging, spa. *Fee:* saunas, swimming instruction, jogging strollers, lawn games, bicycles. **Guest Services:** valet laundry, wireless Internet. **Business Services:** conference facilities, business center. **Cards:** AX, CB, DC, DS, MC, VI.

THE SAVOY SUITES HOTEL   *Book great rates at AAA.com*   Phone: (202)337-9700   **4**

Small-scale Hotel
$169-$429 All Year

Address: 2505 Wisconsin Ave NW 20007 **Location:** In upper Georgetown area; 0.3 mi s of Massachusetts Ave NW. Located in a residential area. **Facility:** 152 one-bedroom standard units, some with efficiencies and/or whirlpools. 8 stories, interior corridors. *Bath:* combo or shower only. **Parking:** on-site. **Terms:** cancellation fee imposed. **Amenities:** dual phone lines, voice mail, irons, hair dryers. *Some:* DVD players. **Guest Services:** valet and coin laundry, area transportation, wireless Internet. **Business Services:** meeting rooms, fax. **Cards:** AX, MC, VI.

--------- **WHERE TO DINE** ---------

2 AMY'S   Phone: 202/885-5700   **9**

Pizza
$8-$13

Pizza, Pizza, Pizza, if that is what you are looking for then this is the place to be. A variety of specialty pizzas along with salads, and other dishes makes this a great night for pizza lovers. Casual dress. **Bar:** Full bar. **Reservations:** not accepted. **Hours:** 11 am-10 pm, Sun noon-10 pm, Mon 5 pm-10 pm. Closed: 1/1, 11/27, 12/25. **Address:** 3715 Macomb St NW 20016 **Location:** Cleveland Park; just w of Wisconsin Ave NW. **Parking:** on-site (fee) and street. **Cards:** MC, VI.

ARDEO RESTAURANT   Phone: 202/244-6750   **10**

American
$8-$23

The trendy bistro offers diners a delectable selection of freshly prepared dishes that may include pan-fried rockfish, crab bisque and wonderful homemade desserts. Dressy casual. **Bar:** Full bar. **Reservations:** suggested. **Hours:** 5:30 pm-10:30 pm, Fri & Sat-11:30 pm, Sun 11 am-3 & 5:30-10:30 pm; Sunday brunch. Closed: 1/1, 12/25. **Address:** 3311 Connecticut Ave NW 20008 **Location:** At Macomb St NW; metro stop; Cleveland Park. **Parking:** street. **Cards:** AX, CB, DC, DS, MC, VI.

CACTUS CANTINA   Phone: 202/686-7222   **11**

Tex-Mex
$8-$17

The Tex-Mex cantina is fun, lively and popular with the locals. A great example of the flavorful dishes cooked over a mesquite-wood fire is steak fajitas with fresh vegetables. Crispy chips and salsa are good palate preppers. Outdoor dining is available in season. Casual dress. **Bar:** Full bar. **Reservations:** not accepted. **Hours:** 11 am-11 pm, Fri & Sat-midnight, Sun 10:30 am-11 pm. Closed: 11/27, 12/25. **Address:** 3300 Wisconsin Ave NW 20016 **Location:** Jct Macomb St. **Parking:** street. **Cards:** AX, CB, DC, DS, MC, VI.

CAFE' OLE'   Phone: 202/244-1330   **4**

Mediterranean
$5-$8

The menu outlines an interesting variety of Mediterranean dishes and flavors in appetizer-size servings (meze)—from Moroccan lamb tagine to Tel Aviv nachos to Sicilian tuna kebab. The price-range reflects the price of meze, with two or three typically making an entree or meal. Some meze can be served as roll-ups rather than in a dish. The menu also lists panini. Casual dress. **Bar:** Full bar. **Reservations:** not accepted. **Hours:** 11 am-10 pm, Fri & Sat-11 pm. Closed major holidays. **Address:** 4000 Wisconsin Ave NW 20016 **Location:** Jct Upton St; in Tenleytown area. **Parking:** on-site (fee). **Cards:** AX, DC, DS, MC, VI.

(See map and index starting on p. 408)

CASHION'S EAT PLACE

American
$19-$30

Phone: 202/797-1819 ⟨16⟩

The hand-written menu changes frequently based on the availability of fresh ingredients. The kitchen displays its skill in preparing a variety of dishes with influences from the American South, Italy, France, Spain and Asia. Attentive, helpful staffers will be happy to make recommendations. Dressy casual. **Bar:** Full bar. **Reservations:** suggested. **Hours:** 5:30 pm-11 pm, Sun 11:30 am-2:30 & 5:30-10 pm, Tues 5:30 pm-10 pm; Sunday brunch. Closed major holidays; also Mon. **Address:** 1819 Columbia Rd NW 20009 **Location:** Between 18th St and Belmont Rd NW; in Adams Morgan area. **Parking:** no self-parking. **Cards:** AX, MC, VI.

CHARLIE CHIANG'S RESTAURANT

Chinese
$7-$20

Phone: 202/966-1916 ⟨3⟩

The popular Chinese restaurant offers Hunan and Szechuan dishes, such as the popular General Tso's chicken and delicious dumplings. The simple, contemporary dining room looks out onto busy Connecticut Avenue. Casual dress. **Bar:** Full bar. **Reservations:** accepted. **Hours:** 10:30 am-10:30 pm. Closed: 11/27. **Address:** 4250 Connecticut Ave NW 20008 **Location:** Jct Connecticut Ave and Windom Pl. **Parking:** on-site. **Cards:** AX, DC, DS, MC, VI.

LAVANDOU

South French
$10-$24

Phone: 202/966-3002 ⟨8⟩

Provencal French fare, extensive menu selections and daily specials make the restaurant popular. The cozy bistro, which exudes a country air, features preparations of seafood, chicken and beef, including such specialties as lobster, North Sea shrimp and scallop gratinee and boeuf bourguignon, a beef stew in red wine . Casual dress. **Bar:** Full bar. **Reservations:** suggested. **Hours:** 11:30 am-10 pm, Sat from 5 pm, Sun 5 pm-9 pm. Closed major holidays. **Address:** 3321 Connecticut Ave NW 20008 **Location:** Jct Macomb St NW; in Cleveland Park area. **Parking:** on-site (fee) and street. **Cards:** AX, CB, DC, DS, MC, VI.

LEBANESE TAVERNA

Lebanese
$10-$20

Phone: 202/265-8681

A devoted local following frequents this friendly restaurant. Menu offerings include rotisserie-grilled beef and marinated lamb with potatoes and radishes, as well as a variety of mezza—appetizers hearty enough to serve as a full meal. Casual dress. **Bar:** Full bar. **Reservations:** accepted, prior to 6:30 pm, prior to 6 pm weekends. **Hours:** 11:30 am-2:30 & 5:30-10:30 pm, Fri-11 pm, Sat noon-3 & 5:30-11 pm, Sun 4:30 pm-9:30 pm. Closed major holidays. **Address:** 2641 Connecticut Ave NW 20008 **Location:** Between Woodley Rd and Calvert St. **Parking:** on-site. **Cards:** AX, DC, DS, MC, VI.

MAGGIANO'S LITTLE ITALY

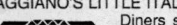

Italian
$7-$37

Phone: 202/966-5500 ⟨1⟩

Diners savor scrumptious, traditional favorites served in a bustling atmosphere reminiscent of Little Italy. The dining area projects an early-20th-century feel; loud conversations bouncing off high ceilings evoke a sense of the Roaring 20s. Casual dress. **Bar:** Full bar. **Reservations:** suggested. **Hours:** 11:30 am-10 pm, Fri & Sat-11 pm, Sun noon-10 pm. Closed: 12/25. **Address:** 5333 Wisconsin Ave NW 20015 **Location:** On SR 355; in Chevy Chase area; opposite the Mazza Galleries. **Parking:** no self-parking. **Cards:** AX, CB, DC, DS, MC, VI.

MATISSE

French
$11-$50

Phone: 202/244-5222 ⟨2⟩

The kitchen prepares French and modern American cuisine with Mediterranean influences. Among dishes are duo of duck, which includes a leg confit and a seared breast; rack of lamb crusted with mustard and fresh herbs; and pan-seared tuna steak. The casual yet fine-dining atmosphere offers a comfortable setting for any occasion. Dressy casual. **Bar:** Full bar. **Reservations:** suggested, weekends. **Hours:** 11:30 am-2:30 & 5:30-10 pm, Fri-11 pm, Sat 5:30 pm-11 pm, Sun 11 am-3 & 5:30-9:30 pm, Mon 5:30 pm-10 pm; Sunday brunch. Closed major holidays. **Address:** 4934 Wisconsin Ave NW 20016 **Location:** Jct Fessenden St NW; 1.8 mi n. **Parking:** on-site. **Cards:** AX, MC, VI.

NAM-VIET PHO-79

Thai
$7-$18

Phone: 202/237-1015 ⟨7⟩

Overflowing dishes arrive at tables with loyal locals eager to delve into fragrant dishes of fresh flavors. Impressive-looking flash-fried whole fish, noodle soups chock full of goodies, aromatic curries and grilled entrees galore are popular with patrons who know a good thing when they taste it. Perfect for families as there is space, portions are generous, and the digs are casual. Casual dress. **Bar:** Full bar. **Reservations:** accepted. **Hours:** 11 am-10 pm, Fri & Sat-11 pm. Closed: 11/27, 12/25. **Address:** 3419 Connecticut Ave NW 20008 **Location:** Between Newark and Macomb sts. **Parking:** no self-parking. **Cards:** AX, DC, DS, MC, VI.

NEW HEIGHTS

American
$17-$30

Phone: 202/234-4110 ⟨14⟩

Opposite Rock Creek Park is the comfortable, second-floor dining room and seasonal patio seating area. The kitchen prepares seasonally changing offerings of New American cuisine reliant on the availability of fresh local ingredients. Casual dress. **Bar:** Full bar. **Reservations:** suggested. **Hours:** 5:30 pm-10 pm, Fri & Sat-11 pm, Sun also 11 am-2:30 pm; Sunday brunch. Closed major holidays. **Address:** 2317 Calvert St NW 20008 **Location:** Just w of Connecticut Ave NW; opposite Rock Creek Park. **Parking:** on-site (fee) and valet. **Cards:** AX, DC, DS, MC, VI.

CALL

PALENA

Mediterranean
$57-$75

Phone: 202/537-9250 ⟨5⟩

Chef Ruta creates wonderful Mediterranean cuisine with French and American influences. The preparation is simple yet sophisticated, and the three-, four- and five-course menu selections change frequently. Service is professional, and the setting is upscale and relaxing. Dressy casual. **Bar:** Full bar. **Reservations:** suggested. **Hours:** 5:30 pm-10 pm. Closed major holidays; also Sun & Mon. **Address:** 3529 Connecticut Ave NW 20008 **Location:** 0.5 mi nw of the National Zoo; in Cleveland Park area. **Parking:** street. **Cards:** AX, DS, MC, VI.

(See map and index starting on p. 408)

PESTO RISTORANTE

Phone: 202/332-8300   12

Italian
$11-$20

The intimate cafe has Tuscan yellow walls, white table linens and soft lighting. The chef-owner prepares homemade Northern and Southern Italian dishes. Seasonal patio seating is available. Casual dress. **Bar:** Full bar. **Reservations:** accepted. **Hours:** 5 pm-10 pm. Closed: 11/27, 12/25; also Sun. **Address:** 2915 Connecticut Ave NW 20008 **Location:** Just s of the National Zoo. **Parking:** no self-parking. **Cards:** AX, DC, DS, MC, VI.

PETITS PLATS

Phone: 202/518-0018   13

French
$16-$28

Mellow, magnolia-colored walls beckon patrons to relax and enjoy delicious French-inspired cuisine. Seafood is prepared every way imaginable, and rack of lamb, veal, duck and beef dishes also tempt the palate. Sidewalk seating is open seasonally. Casual dress. **Bar:** Full bar. **Reservations:** accepted. **Hours:** 11 am-3 & 5-10 pm, Fri-10:30 pm, Sat 11 am-3:30 & 5-10:30 pm, Sun 11 am-3:30 & 5-10 pm. Closed major holidays. **Address:** 2653 Connecticut Ave NW 20008 **Location:** At Calvert St. **Parking:** no self-parking. **Cards:** AX, DS, MC, VI.

ROBERT'S RESTAURANT

Phone: 202/756-5300   15

American
$8-$32

The dining room at the Omni Shoreham Hotel offers upscale setting with a casual air. The outdoor terrace offers a wonderful view of the landscaped grounds and Rock Creek Park. The menu changes with the seasons, though a couple of the chefs signature dishes include the crab cakes and the Vidalia onion soup. Casual dress. **Bar:** Full bar. **Reservations:** suggested. **Hours:** 6:30 am-3 & 5-10:30 pm. **Address:** 2500 Calvert St NW 20008 **Location:** Just w of Connecticut Ave; in Omni Shoreham Hotel. **Parking:** valet. **Cards:** AX, CB, DC, DS, JC, MC, VI.

YENCHING PALACE

Phone: 202/362-8200   6

Chinese
$6-$27

The current owner's uncle opened here in 1955. In addition to being one of the first restaurants to serve Peking duck without advance notice, this is said to be the place where U.S. and Soviet envoys met to defuse the Cuban missile crisis. The fare is traditional Chinese, heavy on Szechuan and Hunan dishes, but guests just might hear some ask for the menu written for Chinese Embassy regulars. The Sunday buffet is set up from noon to 2:30 pm. Casual dress. **Bar:** Full bar. **Reservations:** accepted. **Hours:** 11:30 am-11 pm, Fri & Sat-11:30 pm, Sun noon-11 pm. **Address:** 3524 Connecticut Ave NW 20008 **Location:** Jct Connecticut Ave NW and Porter St NW; Cleveland Park Metro Stop, west exit. **Parking:** on-site. **Cards:** AX, DC, DS, MC, VI.

WASHINGTON (EASTERN REGION)   (See map and index starting on p. 428)

——— WHERE TO STAY ———

CHANNEL INN HOTEL

Book at AAA.com

Phone: (202)554-2400   2

Small-scale Hotel
$175-$185 All Year

Address: 650 Water St SW 20024 **Location:** I-395, exit Maine Ave, just e. **Facility:** Smoke free premises. 100 units. 98 one-bedroom standard units. 2 one-bedroom suites. 3 stories, interior corridors. **Parking:** on-site. **Amenities:** voice mail, irons, hair dryers. **Pool(s):** outdoor. **Guest Services:** valet laundry, wireless Internet. **Business Services:** meeting rooms, fax (fee). **Cards:** AX, CB, DC, DS, JC, MC, VI.

KELLOGG CONFERENCE HOTEL AT GALLAUDET
   UNIVERSITY

Phone: 202/651-6000   1

Small-scale Hotel
Rates not provided

Address: 800 Florida Ave NE 20002-3695 **Location:** 0.6 mi se from US 50 (New York Ave). Located on the campus of Gallaudet University. **Facility:** Smoke free premises. 93 units. 87 one-bedroom standard units. 6 one-bedroom suites. 5 stories, interior corridors. **Bath:** combo or shower only. **Parking:** on-site (fee). **Amenities:** high-speed Internet, voice mail, irons, hair dryers. **Leisure Activities:** exercise room. **Guest Services:** area transportation, wireless Internet. **Business Services:** conference facilities, business center.

The Washington, D.C. Vicinity

Nearby Maryland

ADELPHI pop. 14,998   (See map and index starting on p. 428)

———— WHERE TO STAY ————

UNIVERSITY OF MARYLAND UNIVERSITY COLLEGE
INN & CONFERENCE CTR BY MARRIOTT   *Book great rates at AAA.com*   Phone: 301/985-7300

Large-scale Hotel
Rates not provided

Address: 3501 University Blvd E 20783 **Location:** I-495, exit 29 eastbound; exit 29B westbound, 3.9 mi e on SR 193; 1.8 mi w on SR 193 from jct US 1. Located on the grounds of University of Maryland. **Facility:** Smoke free premises. 237 units. 231 one-bedroom standard units. 6 one-bedroom suites. 5 stories, interior corridors. *Bath:* combo or shower only. **Parking:** on-site (fee). **Amenities:** high-speed Internet, voice mail, irons, hair dryers. **Leisure Activities:** exercise room. **Guest Services:** valet laundry, area transportation. **Business Services:** conference facilities, business center.

Marriott.
HOTELS & RESORTS

AAA Benefit:
Members save 5%
off of the best
available rate.

BELTSVILLE pop. 15,690

———— WHERE TO STAY ————

FAIRFIELD INN BY MARRIOTT-CAPITAL
BELTWAY/I-95   *Book great rates at AAA.com*   Phone: 301/572-7100

Small-scale Hotel
$164-$197 All Year

Address: 4050 Powder Mill Rd 20705 **Location:** I-95, exit 29B, just w on SR 212. Located adjacent to a small shopping plaza. **Facility:** Smoke free premises. 169 units. 168 one-bedroom standard units. 1 one-bedroom suite. 2-4 stories, interior corridors. *Bath:* combo or shower only. **Parking:** on-site. **Amenities:** video games (fee), CD players, voice mail, irons, hair dryers. **Pool(s):** outdoor. **Leisure Activities:** whirlpool, exercise room. *Fee:* game room. **Guest Services:** valet and coin laundry, area transportation, wireless Internet. **Business Services:** meeting rooms, PC. **Cards:** AX, DC, DS, MC, VI. **Free Special Amenities:** expanded continental breakfast and high-speed Internet.

FAIRFIELD
INN
Marriott

AAA Benefit:
Members save 5%
off of the best
available rate.

▼ See AAA listing p 476 ▼

SHERATON COLLEGE PARK HOTEL   *Book great rates at AAA.com*   Phone: (301)937-4422

AAA SAVE

▼▼▼

Small-scale Hotel
$99-$249 All Year

Address: 4095 Powder Mill Rd 20705 **Location:** I-95, exit 29B, just w on SR 212; 2 mi n of I-495 (Capital Beltway). **Facility:** 205 one-bedroom standard units, some with whirlpools. 9 stories, interior corridors. *Bath:* combo or shower only. **Parking:** on-site. **Terms:** cancellation fee imposed. **Amenities:** dual phone lines, voice mail, irons, hair dryers. *Fee:* video games, high-speed Internet. *Some:* safes. **Pool(s):** outdoor. **Leisure Activities:** exercise room. **Guest Services:** valet and coin laundry, area transportation-within 5 mi, & Greenbelt metro. **Business Services:** meeting rooms, business center. **Cards:** AX, CB, DC, DS, MC, VI. **Free Special Amenities: continental breakfast and newspaper.** *(See color ad p 475)*

⑤ Sheraton
HOTELS & RESORTS

AAA Benefit:
Members get up to
15% off, plus
Starwood Preferred
Guest® bonuses.

🔲 🍴 🍸 CALL ⚑M 🏊 📺 💻 / SOME UNITS 🐾 ✕ FEE 🔌 FEE 🖥

——— WHERE TO DINE ———

TJ'S OF CALVERTON   Phone: 301/572-7117

▼▼

American
$6-$19

In a shopping center, the casual eatery has been pleasing families and diners out for social events since 1985. On the menu is a nice selection of salads, sandwiches, burgers and full dinners. Casual dress. **Bar:** Full bar. **Reservations:** accepted. **Hours:** 11 am-9 pm, Fri & Sat-10 pm, Sun noon-9 pm. Closed: 11/27, 12/25. **Address:** 11607 Beltsville Rd 20705 **Location:** I-95, exit 29B, just w; in Calverton Shopping Center. **Parking:** on-site. **Cards:** AX, MC, VI.

BETHESDA pop. 55,277   (See map and index starting on p. 408)

——— WHERE TO STAY ———

DOUBLETREE HOTEL BETHESDA   *Book great rates at AAA.com*   Phone: 301/652-2000   **41**

▼▼▼

Large-scale Hotel
Rates not provided

Address: 8120 Wisconsin Ave 20814 **Location:** I-495, exit 34, 2 mi s on SR 355. Located in a commercial area. **Facility:** 269 units. 263 one-bedroom standard units. 6 one-bedroom suites, some with whirlpools. 16 stories, interior corridors. *Bath:* combo or shower only. **Parking:** on-site (fee). **Terms:** check-in 4 pm. **Amenities:** high-speed Internet, voice mail, safes, irons, hair dryers. **Pool(s):** outdoor. **Leisure Activities:** exercise room. **Guest Services:** valet and coin laundry, area transportation, wireless Internet. **Business Services:** conference facilities, business center.

🍴 🍸 CALL ⚑M 🏊 📺 💻 / SOME UNITS ✕ FEE 🔌 FEE 🖥

GOLDEN TULIP BETHESDA COURT HOTEL   *Book great rates at AAA.com*   Phone: (301)656-2100   **42**

▼▼

Small-scale Hotel
$109-$195 All Year

Address: 7740 Wisconsin Ave 20814 **Location:** I-495, exit 34, 2.2 mi s on SR 355. Located in a commercial area. **Facility:** 74 one-bedroom standard units. 3 stories, interior/exterior corridors. *Bath:* combo or shower only. **Parking:** on-site (fee). **Terms:** cancellation fee imposed. **Amenities:** video games (fee), dual phone lines, voice mail, safes, irons, hair dryers. *Some:* fax. **Leisure Activities:** limited exercise equipment. **Guest Services:** valet and coin laundry, area transportation, wireless Internet. **Cards:** AX, DC, JC, MC, VI.

ASK 🔲 🍴 CALL ⚑M 📺 🔌 💻 / SOME UNITS ✕

HYATT REGENCY BETHESDA   *Book great rates at AAA.com*   Phone: (301)657-1234   **43**

AAA SAVE

▼▼▼

Large-scale Hotel
$144-$462 All Year

Address: One Bethesda Metro Center 20814 **Location:** I-495, exit 34, 2.5 mi s on SR 355; jct Wisconsin Ave and Old Georgetown Rd. Located in a commercial area, at metro stop. **Facility:** 390 units. 384 one-bedroom standard units. 6 one-bedroom suites, some with whirlpools. 12 stories, interior corridors. *Bath:* combo or shower only. **Parking:** on-site (fee) and valet. **Terms:** cancellation fee imposed. **Amenities:** dual phone lines, voice mail, irons, hair dryers. *Some:* CD players, high-speed Internet (fee). **Dining:** 2 restaurants. **Pool(s):** heated indoor. **Leisure Activities:** saunas, whirlpool, exercise room. **Guest Services:** valet laundry, wireless Internet. **Business Services:** conference facilities, business center. **Cards:** AX, DC, DS, JC, MC, VI.

HYATT
HOTELS & RESORTS

AAA Benefit:
Ask for the AAA rate
and save 10%.

🍴 🍸 CALL ⚑M 🏊 ✕ 📺 💻 / SOME UNITS ✕ VCR 🔌

MARRIOTT SUITES BETHESDA   *Book great rates at AAA.com*   Phone: 301/897-5600   **40**

▼▼▼

Large-scale Hotel
Rates not provided

Address: 6711 Democracy Blvd 20817 **Location:** I-495, exit 36, 0.6 mi n on SR 187; 0.8 mi e of I-270 spur, exit 1. **Facility:** Smoke free premises. 272 one-bedroom suites. 11 stories, interior corridors. *Bath:* combo or shower only. **Parking:** on-site (fee). **Terms:** check-in 4 pm. **Amenities:** voice mail, safes, irons, hair dryers. *Fee:* video games, high-speed Internet. *Some:* CD players. **Pool(s):** heated indoor/outdoor. **Leisure Activities:** whirlpool, exercise room. **Guest Services:** valet and coin laundry, area transportation. **Business Services:** meeting rooms, business center.

Marriott
HOTELS & RESORTS

AAA Benefit:
Members save 5%
off of the best
available rate.

🍴 CALL ⚑M 🏊 ✕ 📺 🔌 💻 / SOME UNITS 🖥

(See map and index starting on p. 408)

RESIDENCE INN BY MARRIOTT-BETHESDA
DOWNTOWN   *Book great rates at AAA.com*   Phone: 301/718-0200   **44**

Small-scale Hotel
Rates not provided

Address: 7335 Wisconsin Ave 20814 **Location:** I-495, exit 34, 2.5 mi s on SR 355; entrance on Waverly St. Located in a commercial area. **Facility:** Smoke free premises. 177 units. 177 one- and 10 two-bedroom suites, some with efficiencies or kitchens. 13 stories, interior corridors. *Bath:* combo or shower only. **Parking:** valet. **Amenities:** video games (fee), high-speed Internet, dual phone lines, voice mail, irons, hair dryers. **Pool(s):** outdoor. **Leisure Activities:** saunas, exercise room. **Guest Services:** valet and coin laundry. **Business Services:** meeting rooms.

AAA Benefit:
Members save 5% off of the best available rate.

─────── **WHERE TO DINE** ───────

BACCHUS RESTAURANT
Phone: 301/657-1722   **52**

Lebanese
$8-$17

Lebanese menu selections vary here, from eggplant dip and hummus to "fatte" - a signature casserole made with your choice of lamb, chicken or eggplant and beef. In keeping with the cuisine, the decor is Middle Eastern. Dressy casual. **Bar:** Full bar. **Reservations:** suggested, weekends. **Hours:** noon-2 & 5:30-10:30 pm, Sat & Sun from 5:30 pm. Closed: 1/1, 11/27, 12/25. **Address:** 7945 Norfolk Ave 20814 **Location:** Just w on Cordell Ave, from jct SR 355, just n. **Parking:** street. **Cards:** AX, DC, DS, MC, VI.

BETHESDA CRAB HOUSE
Phone: 301/652-3382   **69**

Seafood
$20-$25

Operating for more than 40 years in the same location, the casual, traditional crab house serves large steamed crabs, jumbo spiced shrimp and jumbo lump crab cakes. Guests can dine in the dining room or, weather permitting, on the canopied patio with picnic tables. Casual dress. **Bar:** Beer & wine. **Reservations:** accepted, 10/1-5/31. **Hours:** 9 am-11 pm, Fri & Sat-midnight, Sun 10 am-11 pm. **Address:** 4958 Bethesda Ave 20814 **Location:** Jct Arlington Rd and Bethesda Ave, just w. **Parking:** street. **Cards:** MC, VI.

BLACK'S BAR & KITCHEN
Phone: 301/652-6278   **64**

Seafood
$7-$27

The owners of the well-known Addies have a new spot here, where Gulf Coast-style seafood is prepared with just a touch of Asian influences. Prime spots on the patio are much coveted. Casual dress. **Bar:** Full bar. **Reservations:** suggested. **Hours:** 11:30 am-2:30 & 5:30-10 pm, Fri-11 pm, Sat 5:30 pm-11 pm, Sun 5:30 pm-9:30 pm. Closed: 12/25. **Address:** 7750 Woodmont Ave 20814 **Location:** 1 blk w of Wisconsin Ave (SR 355). **Parking:** no self-parking. **Cards:** AX, CB, DC, DS, MC, VI.

CAMERON'S SEAFOOD MARKET
Phone: 301/951-1000   **67**

Seafood
$6-$14

For diners who have a craving for fresh seafood, the small eatery is worth the quick stop. Casual dress. **Bar:** Beer & wine. **Reservations:** not accepted. **Hours:** 9 am-9:30 pm, Fri & Sat-10:30 pm, Sun-9 pm. **Address:** 4831 Bethesda Ave 20814 **Location:** I-495, exit 34, 2.5 mi s on Wisconsin Ave. **Parking:** street. **Cards:** AX, MC, VI.

CESCO TRATTORIA
Phone: 301/654-8333   **55**

Northern Italian
$9-$30

Simple, comfortable decor suggests an Italian villa, and the covered sidewalk patio is a perfect venue for sipping, dining and people-watching. Award-winning Chef Ricchi prepares traditional Tuscan cuisine, including a wide selection of pasta entrees, as well as veal, beef and seafood dishes. Valet parking is available for a fee in the evening. Dressy casual. **Bar:** Full bar. **Reservations:** suggested. **Hours:** 11:30 am-2:30 & 5:30-10 pm, Fri & Sat 5:30 pm-10:30 pm, Sun 5 pm-10 pm. Closed major holidays. **Address:** 4871 Cordell Ave 20814 **Location:** 0.3 mi w of Wisconsin Ave. **Parking:** no self-parking. **Cards:** AX, DC, MC, VI.

FOONG LIN RESTAURANT
Phone: 301/656-3427   **63**

Chinese
$5-$16

A favorite of locals, this Chinese restaurant offers an extensive menu featuring regional Hunan, Szechuan and Cantonese cuisine. Casual dress. **Bar:** Full bar. **Reservations:** suggested. **Hours:** 11 am-10:30 pm, Fri & Sat-11 pm, Sun 11:30 am-10 pm. Closed: 11/27. **Address:** 7710 Norfolk Ave 20814 **Location:** 1 blk w of SR 355, jct Fairmont St. **Parking:** street. **Cards:** AX, MC, VI.

GRAPESEED-AMERICAN BISTRO & WINE BAR
Phone: 301/986-9592   **53**

American
$20-$30

Innovative American cuisine is complemented by an award-winning wine selection. The menu indicates appropriate wine-food matches. Guests can select a half glass, full glass or bottle. A limited selection of cocktails is available. Casual dress. **Bar:** Full bar. **Reservations:** suggested. **Hours:** 5 pm-10 pm, Fri & Sat-11 pm, Sun-9 pm. Closed: 11/27, 12/25. **Address:** 4865 Cordell Ave 20814 **Location:** 0.3 mi w of Wisconsin Ave. **Parking:** valet. **Cards:** AX, DC, DS, MC, VI.

HAANDI
Phone: 301/718-0121   **60**

Indian
$5-$20

With an upscale, cheerfully bright decor, the storefront eatery has earned the distinction of serving top-notch Indian cuisine and with good reason. The menu lists well-prepared and flavorful chicken, lamb, seafood and vegetarian entrees. Casual dress. **Bar:** Full bar. **Reservations:** suggested, weekends. **Hours:** 11:30 am-2:30 & 5:10 pm, Fri-10:30 pm, Sat noon-3 & 5-10:30 pm, Sun noon-3 & 5-10 pm. Closed: 11/27. **Address:** 4904 Fairmont Ave 20814 **Location:** Just w on Cheltenham Dr; from SR 355, just nw on Norfolk Ave, then just w. **Parking:** street. **Cards:** AX, CB, DC, MC, VI.

JEAN-MICHEL RESTAURANT
Phone: 301/564-4910   **51**

French
$11-$28

This restaurant is well-known for its friendly service and classic French cuisine. Dressy casual. **Bar:** Full bar. **Reservations:** suggested. **Hours:** 11:30 am-2:30 & 5:30-9:30 pm, Sat from 5:30 pm, Sun 5 pm-8 pm. Closed major holidays; also Sun 7/1-8/31. **Address:** 10223 Old Georgetown Rd 20814 **Location:** Jct SR 187 (Old Georgetown Rd) and Democracy Blvd; in Wildwood Shopping Center. **Parking:** on-site. **Cards:** AX, DC, DS, MC, VI.

(See map and index starting on p. 408)

LA MICHE

French
$20-$33

Phone: 301/986-0707   **58**

Country French cuisine and a decidedly similar decor of earth tones, antiques and hanging baskets add to the dining experience at the comfortably sophisticated restaurant. Popular menu choices include sauteed lobster with pasta and white wine sauce; escargot in garlic and butter; and dessert souffles. Semi-formal attire. **Bar:** Full bar. **Reservations:** suggested. **Hours:** 5 pm-10 pm, Sun 11:30 am-2 pm; Sunday brunch. **Address:** 7905 Norfolk Ave 20814 **Location:** 0.5 mi sw on Woodmont Ave, from SR 355, just w on St Elmo Ave. **Parking:** valet. **Cards:** AX, DS, MC, VI.

LE VIEUX LOGIS

French
$24-$33

Phone: 301/652-6816   **54**

The cozy cottage stands out with its hand-painted murals along the outside. The intimate dining room has a country air, with flowers and greenery all around. The kitchen prepares delicious French fare. Casual dress. **Bar:** Full bar. **Reservations:** suggested. **Hours:** 5 pm-9 pm. Closed: 5/26, 7/4, 9/1; also Sun & Mon. **Address:** 7925 Old Georgetown Rd 20814 **Location:** 3 blks w of SR 355; I-495, exit 36, 2.2 mi s on SR 187. **Parking:** valet. **Cards:** AX, CB, DC, DS, MC, VI.

MATUBA JAPANESE RESTAURANT

Japanese
$6-$20

Phone: 301/652-7449   **59**

Diners can name their favorites from an extensive variety of sushi and rolls: octopus, salmon, sea urchin, crab or numerous other seafood items. The energetic restaurant also provides efficient service although at times there can be a language barrier. Casual dress. **Bar:** Beer & wine. **Hours:** 11:30 am-2 & 5-10 pm, Fri-10:30 pm, Sat noon-2:30 & 5-10:30 pm, Sun 5 pm-9:30 pm. Closed: 11/27. **Address:** 4918 Cordell Ave 20814 **Location:** 0.3 mi w of SR 355. **Parking:** street. **Cards:** AX, MC, VI.

PASSAGE TO INDIA

Indian
$7-$26

Phone: 301/656-3373   **56**

The chef-owner uses fresh ingredients to prepare an array of Indian dishes. The comfortable setting has an upscale air. Efficient, professional servers are helpful with the menu. On Friday and Saturday nights, valet parking is available for a fee. Dressy casual. **Bar:** Full bar. **Reservations:** suggested. **Hours:** 11:30 am-2:30 & 5:30-close. **Address:** 4931 Cordell Ave 20814 **Location:** 3 blks w of SR 355; I-495, exit 36, 2.3 mi s on SR 187. **Parking:** valet and street. **Cards:** AX, DS, MC, VI.

PENANG

Asian
$6-$20

Phone: 301/657-2878   **68**

Malysian cuisine is served in the large converted warehouse setting. Extensive menu that serves vegetarian dishes. Sit and relax by the soothing sound of water flowing down one of the walls. Casual dress. **Bar:** Full bar. **Reservations:** accepted. **Hours:** 11:30 am-10 pm. Closed: 11/27. **Address:** 4933 Bethesda Ave 20814 **Location:** Just w of jct Arlington Rd and Bethesda Ave. **Parking:** on-site. **Cards:** AX, DC, DS, MC, VI.

PERSIMMON

American
$8-$27

Phone: 301/654-9860   **70**

A neighborhood restaurant serving contemporary American cuisine. The chef/owner uses fresh ingredients in preparing each dish. The kitchen is creative, the staff is professional and friendly and the setting is colorful and intimate. Casual dress. **Bar:** Full bar. **Reservations:** suggested. **Hours:** 11:30 am-2 & 5-10 pm, Sat & Sun from 5 pm. Closed: 11/27, 12/25. **Address:** 7003 Wisconsin Ave 20815 **Location:** I-495, exit 34, 2.8 mi s on SR 355. **Parking:** on-site (fee). **Cards:** AX, DC, MC, VI.

RIO GRANDE CAFE

Mexican
$5-$19

Phone: 301/656-2981   **61**

A loud, energetic cantina design provides a fun and festive dining atmosphere. Mesquite-grilled fajitas and stuffed jumbo shrimp are menu favorites. Casual dress. **Bar:** Full bar. **Reservations:** not accepted. **Hours:** 11 am-10:30 pm, Fri & Sat-11:30 pm. Closed: 11/27, 12/25; also for dinner 12/24. **Address:** 4870 Bethesda Ave 20814 **Location:** 2 blks w of SR 355; downtown. **Parking:** on-site (fee). **Cards:** AX, CB, DC, DS, MC, VI.

RUTH'S CHRIS STEAK HOUSE

Steak House
$18-$36

Phone: 301/652-7877   **65**

The main fare is steak, which is prepared from several cuts of prime beef and cooked to perfection, but the menu also lists lamb, chicken and seafood dishes. Guests should come hungry because the side dishes, which are among the a la carte offerings, could make a meal in themselves. Dressy casual. **Bar:** Full bar. **Reservations:** suggested. **Hours:** 5 pm-10:30 pm, Sun 4 pm-9:30 pm. Closed: 11/27, 12/25. **Address:** 7315 Wisconsin Ave 20814 **Location:** On SR 355. **Parking:** valet. **Cards:** AX, DC, DS, MC, VI.

SWEET BASIL

Thai
$9-$22

Phone: 301/657-7997   **62**

The kitchen's signature dishes include sweet basil lamb and sweet basil eggplant. Although these selections are distinctive, many other offerings are traditional Thai staples. Patrons' preferences for spiciness are taken into account. Casual dress. **Bar:** Full bar. **Reservations:** accepted. **Hours:** 11:30 am-10 pm, Sun from noon. Closed: 11/27. **Address:** 4910 Fairmont Ave 20814 **Location:** I-495, exit 36, 2.3 mi s on SR 187; 2 blks w of SR 355. **Parking:** street. **Cards:** AX, DC, DS, MC, VI.

TARA THAI

Thai
$6-$14

Phone: 301/657-0488

The stylish cafe's sea motif is one aspect of its contemporary atmosphere. Specialties include whole fresh rockfish and skewered chicken, just to mention two. Most notable is the nicely presented goong phu-ket and pad thai noodles. Portion sizes are ample. Casual dress. **Bar:** Full bar. **Reservations:** suggested, weekends. **Hours:** 11:30 am-10 pm, Fri-11 pm, Sat noon-11 pm, Sun noon-10 pm. Closed: 11/27; also for lunch 12/25 & 1/1. **Address:** 4828 Bethesda Ave 20814 **Location:** 2 blks w of SR 355; downtown. **Parking:** on-site (fee). **Cards:** AX, DC, DS, MC, VI.

THYME SQUARE CAFE

American
$8-$23

Phone: 301/657-9077   **66**

Stylish, imaginative presentation marks the upscale cafe's organic fare, much of which is vegetarian. Artsy touches give the place an upbeat feel. A juice bar is at the center of the dining area. Dressy casual. **Bar:** Full bar. **Reservations:** suggested, weekends. **Hours:** 11:30 am-9:30 pm, Fri & Sat-10:30 pm. Closed major holidays; also 12/24. **Address:** 4735 Bethesda Ave 20814 **Location:** Corner of Woodmont Ave; downtown. **Parking:** on-site (fee). **Cards:** AX, DS, MC, VI.

TRAGARA   *Menu on AAA.com*

Northern Italian
$10-$32

Phone: 301/951-4935   **57**

Intimate, handsome and elegant, this restaurant is a popular place for romance. Authentic homemade pasta, seafood and meat dishes include such specialties as red snapper with herbs and veal shanks braised in tomato sauce. The homemade ice cream is a treat. Complimentary valet parking for dinner. Dressy casual. **Bar:** Full bar. **Reservations:** suggested. **Hours:** 11:30 am-2:30 & 5:30-10 pm, Fri-10:30 pm, Sat 5:30 pm-10:30 pm, Sun 5 pm-9 pm. Closed major holidays. **Address:** 4935 Cordell Ave 20814 **Location:** 3 blks w of SR 355; I-495, exit 36, 2.3 mi s on SR 187. **Parking:** on-site (fee). **Cards:** AX, CB, DC, MC, VI.

(See map and index starting on p. 408)

──────── *The following restaurants have not been evaluated by AAA* ────────
but are listed for your information only.

POSITANO RISTORANTE ITALIANO　　　　　　　　　　　　　　**Phone:** 301/654-1717

[fyi]　　Not evaluated. A local favorite since 1977, the restaurant serves good preparations of seafood, veal, lamb and pasta. **Address:** 4940-48 Fairmont Ave 20814 **Location:** I-495, exit 36, 2.3 mi w on SR 187; 2 blks w of SR 355.

TAKO GRILL　　　　　　　　　　　　　　　　　　　　　　**Phone:** 301/652-7030

[fyi]　　Not evaluated. The restaurant's most popular entrees include octopus. Among other choices are offerings from the sushi and sake bar. **Address:** 7756 Wisconsin Ave 20814 **Location:** I-495, exit 34, 2 mi s on SR 355.

BOWIE pop. 50,269

──────── **WHERE TO STAY** ────────

COMFORT INN HOTEL & CONFERENCE
CENTER-BOWIE　　*Book at AAA.com*　　　　　　　　　　**Phone:** (301)464-0089

Small-scale Hotel
$130-$163 All Year

Address: 4500 NW Crain Hwy 20716 **Location:** US 50, exit 13A, jct US 50/301 and SR 3. Located next to a shopping center. **Facility:** 186 units. 166 one-bedroom standard units, some with whirlpools. 20 one-bedroom suites, some with whirlpools. 4-6 stories, interior corridors. *Bath:* combo or shower only. **Parking:** on-site. **Amenities:** voice mail, safes, irons, hair dryers. *Some:* dual phone lines. **Pool(s):** outdoor. **Leisure Activities:** limited exercise equipment. **Guest Services:** coin laundry, wireless Internet. **Business Services:** conference facilities, business center. **Cards:** AX, CB, DC, DS, JC, MC, VI.

  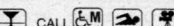 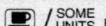

HAMPTON INN-BOWIE　　*Book great rates at AAA.com*　　　　**Phone:** 301/809-1800

[AAA] [SAVE]

Small-scale Hotel
Rates not provided

Address: 15202 Major Lansdale Blvd 20716 **Location:** US 50, exit 11, 0.4 mi s on SR 197. Located next to a movie theater complex and near shopping mall. **Facility:** 103 one-bedroom standard units. 3 stories, interior corridors. *Bath:* combo or shower only. **Parking:** on-site. **Amenities:** video games (fee), voice mail, irons, hair dryers. **Pool(s):** outdoor. **Leisure Activities:** limited exercise equipment. **Guest Services:** valet and coin laundry, wireless Internet. **Business Services:** PC. **Free Special Amenities:** expanded continental breakfast and high-speed Internet.

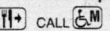   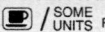

──────── **WHERE TO DINE** ────────

GLORY DAYS GRILL, BOWIE　　　　　　　　　　　　　　**Phone:** 301/805-5299

American
$7-$18

Lending to the casual restaurant's sports-themed atmosphere are memorabilia decorating the dining area and 25 TVs with control centers at each table and booth. Food selections range from wings and ribs to seafood, beef and pasta dishes. Casual dress. **Bar:** Full bar. **Reservations:** not accepted. **Hours:** 4 pm-midnight, Fri & Sat from 11:30 am, Sun 11:30 am-11 pm. Closed: 11/27, 12/25. **Address:** 15505 Annapolis Rd 20715 **Location:** US 50, exit 11, 1.4 mi n on SR 197, then 1.4 mi e on SR 450; in Jemals Bowie Market Place. **Parking:** on-site. **Cards:** AX, DS, MC, VI.

GRACE'S FORTUNE RESTAURANT　　*Menu on AAA.com*　　　　**Phone:** 301/805-1108

[AAA]

Chinese
$6-$24

Set in a small neighborhood shopping plaza, the comfortable restaurant has a koi pond and aquariums that contribute to a soothing atmosphere. The menu offers consistently good selections from various regions of China, all served in large portions. Casual dress. **Bar:** Full bar. **Reservations:** not accepted. **Hours:** 11 am-10 pm, Fri & Sat-10:30 pm, Sun 11:30 am-10 pm. Closed: 11/27. **Address:** 15500 Annapolis Rd 20715 **Location:** US 50, exit 11, 1.4 mi n on SR 197, 1.4 mi e on SR 450; in Free State Mall. **Parking:** on-site. **Cards:** AX, MC, VI.

CAMP SPRINGS pop. 17,968   (See map and index starting on p. 428)

——— WHERE TO STAY ———

COUNTRY INN & SUITES BY CARLSON CAMP
SPRINGS   *Book at AAA.com*   Phone: (240)492-1070   **40**

▼▼▼

Small-scale Hotel
$129-$159 All Year

Address: 4950 Mercedes Blvd 20746 **Location:** I-95/495, exit 7B, just e to Auth Rd, then just n. **Facility:** 95 units. 89 one-bedroom standard units. 6 one-bedroom suites. 3 stories, interior corridors. *Bath:* combo or shower only. **Parking:** on-site. **Amenities:** video games (fee), high-speed Internet, voice mail, irons, hair dryers. **Leisure Activities:** exercise room. **Guest Services:** coin laundry, wireless Internet. **Business Services:** meeting rooms, PC. **Cards:** AX, DC, DS, MC, VI.

(ASK) (SD) CALL (M) 🐾 🖵 / SOME UNITS ✕ 🛗 🖨

QUALITY INN CAMP SPRINGS   *Book great rates at AAA.com*   Phone: (301)420-2800   **41**

(AAA) (SAVE)

▼▼▼

Small-scale Hotel
$89-$149 All Year

Address: 4783 Allentown Rd 20746 **Location:** I-95/495, exit 9. Located across from the Air Force base. **Facility:** 151 one-bedroom standard units. 2-3 stories, interior/exterior corridors. *Bath:* combo or shower only. **Parking:** on-site. **Amenities:** video games (fee), high-speed Internet, dual phone lines, voice mail, irons, hair dryers. **Leisure Activities:** exercise room. **Guest Services:** valet and coin laundry, wireless Internet. **Business Services:** meeting rooms, fax (fee). **Cards:** AX, CB, DC, DS, MC, VI. **Free Special Amenities: continental breakfast and high-speed Internet.**

(SD) (🍴) CALL (M) 🐾 🛗 🖨 🖵 / SOME UNITS ✕

CHEVY CHASE pop. 9,381   (See map and index starting on p. 408)

——— WHERE TO STAY ———

HOLIDAY INN-WASHINGTON/CHEVY CHASE   *Book at AAA.com*   Phone: 301/656-1500   **37**

▼▼▼

Small-scale Hotel
Rates not provided

Address: 5520 Wisconsin Ave 20815 **Location:** Jct SR 191, 0.8 mi s on SR 355. Located in a commercial area with shopping and business's. **Facility:** Smoke free premises. 214 units. 203 one-bedroom standard units. 11 one-bedroom suites. 12 stories, interior corridors. **Parking:** on-site (fee). **Amenities:** high-speed Internet, voice mail, irons, hair dryers. *Some:* dual phone lines. **Pool(s):** heated outdoor. **Leisure Activities:** exercise room. **Guest Services:** valet and coin laundry. **Business Services:** meeting rooms.

(🍴) CALL (M) 🏊 ✕ 🐾 🖵 / SOME UNITS FEE 🛗 FEE 🖨

——— WHERE TO DINE ———

LA FERME RESTAURANT   Phone: 301/986-5255   **48**

(AAA)

▼▼◆

French
$12-$37

The decor in this restored farmhouse is comfortable, romantic country French. Caesar salad, soft-shelled crab, filet mignon, fricassee of lobster and Grand Marnier souffle prove to be discerning choices. Chateaubriand is a house special. Deck dining is available in season. Dressy casual. Entertainment. **Bar:** Full bar. **Reservations:** suggested. **Hours:** 11:30 am-2 & 6-10 pm, Sat from 6 pm, Sun 11:30 am-2 & 5-9 pm; Sunday brunch. **Address:** 7101 Brookville Rd 20815 **Location:** Chevy Chase Circle, just e on Western Ave, 1 mi ne. **Parking:** on-site. **Cards:** AX, CB, DC, DS, MC, VI.

TAVIRA   Phone: 301/652-8684   **47**

▼▼◆

Portuguese
$7-$25

The fine-dining restaurant is tucked away on the lower level of the Chevy Chase bank building. The kitchen prepares wonderful Portuguese dishes, as well as other Mediterranean dishes, including Spanish and Italian selections. Complimentary garage parking is available during dinner. Dressy casual. **Bar:** Full bar. **Reservations:** suggested. **Hours:** 11:30 am-2:30 & 5:30-9 pm, Fri-10 pm, Sat 5:30 pm-10 pm, Sun 5 pm-9 pm. Closed: 1/1, 7/4, 12/25. **Address:** 8401 Connecticut Ave 20815 **Location:** I-495, exit 33, 0.7 mi s on SR 185 (Connecticut Ave); in Chevy Chase Bank Building, lower level. **Parking:** on-site (fee). **Cards:** AX, MC, VI.

CLINTON pop. 26,064

——— WHERE TO STAY ———

COLONY SOUTH HOTEL & CONFERENCE CENTER   *Book great rates at AAA.com*   Phone: (301)856-4500

(AAA) (SAVE)

▼▼▼

Small-scale Hotel
$119-$249 All Year

Address: 7401 Surratts Rd 20735 **Location:** I-95/495, exit 7A, 5 mi s on SR 5; 1.2 mi s of jct SR 223. Located adjacent to Southern Maryland Hospital Center. **Facility:** Smoke free premises. 195 units. 187 one-bedroom standard units. 8 one-bedroom suites, some with whirlpools. 3 stories, interior corridors. *Bath:* combo or shower only. **Parking:** on-site. **Amenities:** high-speed Internet, voice mail, irons, hair dryers. *Some:* dual phone lines. **Dining:** The Wayfarer Restaurant, see separate listing. **Pool(s):** heated indoor. **Leisure Activities:** saunas, whirlpool, water aerobics, 2 lighted tennis courts, racquetball courts, picnic area, sun deck, jogging, spa. *Fee:* aerobics instruction. **Guest Services:** valet and coin laundry, airport transportation-Ronald Reagan Washington National Airport, area transportation-Branch Ave Metro, beauty salon, tanning facilities. **Business Services:** conference facilities. **Cards:** AX, DC, DS, MC, VI. **Free Special Amenities: newspaper and early check-in/late check-out.**

(SD) (✈) (🍴) (🍸) CALL (M) 🏊 (♨) ✕ ✕ 🐾 🖵 / SOME UNITS FEE 🛗 FEE 🖨

COMFORT INN AT ANDREWS AIR FORCE BASE   *Book great rates at AAA.com*   Phone: (301)856-5200

(AAA) (SAVE)

▼▼▼

Small-scale Hotel
$129-$159 All Year

Address: 7979 Malcolm Rd 20735 **Location:** I-95/495, exit 7A, 3.2 mi s on SR 5. **Facility:** Smoke free premises. 94 one-bedroom standard units. 3 stories, interior corridors. **Parking:** on-site. **Amenities:** dual phone lines, voice mail, safes (fee), irons, hair dryers. *Some:* DVD players. **Leisure Activities:** gas grill, exercise room. **Guest Services:** valet and coin laundry, wireless Internet. **Business Services:** meeting rooms, PC. **Cards:** AX, CB, DC, DS, JC, MC, VI. **Free Special Amenities: expanded continental breakfast and high-speed Internet.**

(SD) (🍴) CALL (M) ✕ 🐾 🛗 🖨 🖵 / SOME UNITS (VCR)

------ WHERE TO DINE ------

THE WAYFARER RESTAURANT
Phone: 301/856-3343

AAA

▽▽ ▽▽

Northern Italian

$13-$29

The attractive, smoke-free dining room exudes country-style ambience with vaulted beamed ceilings and an inviting fireplace. The menu showcases a nice selection of pasta dishes, beef, fresh seafood and poultry. A lunch buffet is available Monday-Friday. Casual dress. **Bar:** Full bar. **Reservations:** suggested, weekends. **Hours:** 6-10 am, 11:30-2:30 & 5:30-10 pm, Sun-9 pm. Closed: for lunch & dinner 12/25. **Address:** 7401 Surratts Rd 20735 **Location:** I-95/495, exit 7A, 5 mi s on SR 5; 1.2 mi s of jct SR 223; in Colony South Hotel & Conference Center. **Parking:** on-site. **Cards:** AX, CB, DC, DS, MC, VI.

COLLEGE PARK pop. 24,657   (See map and index starting on p. 428)

------ WHERE TO STAY ------

CLARION INN & FUNDOME
Phone: (301)474-2800   **20**

AAA SAVE

▽▽ ▽▽

Small-scale Hotel

$99-$169 All Year

Address: 8601 Baltimore Ave 20740 **Location:** I-95/495, exit 25 northbound; exit 25B southbound, 1.5 mi s on US 1. Located near the University of Maryland-College Park Campus. **Facility:** 118 one-bedroom standard units. 2 stories (no elevator), interior/exterior corridors. **Bath:** combo or shower only. **Parking:** on-site. **Amenities:** high-speed Internet, voice mail, safes (fee), irons, hair dryers. **Pool(s):** heated indoor. **Leisure Activities:** sauna, whirlpool, putting green, enclosed recreation area, limited exercise equipment, shuffleboard. **Guest Services:** valet and coin laundry, area transportation-College Park Metro, wireless Internet. **Business Services:** meeting rooms. **Cards:** AX, DC, DS, MC, VI. **Free Special Amenities: continental breakfast and high-speed Internet.**

COMFORT INN & SUITES COLLEGE PARK   *Book at AAA.com*
Phone: (301)441-8110   **19**

▽▽ ▽▽

Small-scale Hotel

$89-$199 All Year

Address: 9020 Baltimore Ave 20740 **Location:** I-95/495, exit 25 northbound; exit 25B southbound, 1.3 mi s on US 1. Located near the University of MD-College Park campus. **Facility:** 125 units. 92 one-bedroom standard units. 33 one-bedroom suites. 8 stories, interior corridors. **Bath:** combo or shower only. **Parking:** on-site. **Terms:** cancellation fee imposed. **Amenities:** voice mail, safes (fee), irons, hair dryers. *Some:* high-speed Internet, dual phone lines. **Pool(s):** outdoor. **Leisure Activities:** limited exercise equipment. **Guest Services:** valet and coin laundry, area transportation, wireless Internet. **Business Services:** meeting rooms, PC. **Cards:** AX, DC, DS, JC, MC, VI.

HAMPTON INN-COLLEGE PARK   *Book great rates at AAA.com*
Phone: 301/345-2200   **17**

▽▽ ▽▽ ▽▽

Small-scale Hotel

Rates not provided

Address: 9670 Baltimore Ave 20740 **Location:** I-95/495, exit 25 northbound; exit 25B southbound, 0.3 mi s on US 1. **Facility:** 80 units. 75 one-bedroom standard units, some with whirlpools. 5 one-bedroom suites. 6 stories, interior corridors. **Bath:** combo or shower only. **Parking:** on-site. **Amenities:** high-speed Internet, dual phone lines, voice mail, irons, hair dryers. **Pool(s):** heated indoor. **Leisure Activities:** exercise room. **Guest Services:** valet and coin laundry, wireless Internet. **Business Services:** meeting rooms, business center.

HOLIDAY INN-COLLEGE PARK   *Book great rates at AAA.com*
Phone: (301)345-6700   **16**

AAA SAVE

▽▽ ▽▽ ▽▽

Small-scale Hotel

$109-$189 All Year

Address: 10000 Baltimore Ave 20740 **Location:** I-95/495, exit 25 northbound; exit 25A southbound, just n on US 1. **Facility:** 222 one-bedroom standard units. 4-5 stories, interior corridors. **Bath:** combo or shower only. **Parking:** on-site. **Amenities:** voice mail, irons, hair dryers. **Pool(s):** heated indoor. **Leisure Activities:** sauna, whirlpool, limited exercise equipment. **Guest Services:** valet and coin laundry, area transportation-Greenbelt Metro & within 5 mi, wireless Internet. **Business Services:** conference facilities, PC. **Cards:** AX, DC, DS, MC, VI.

SUPER 8 MOTEL-COLLEGE PARK   *Book at AAA.com*
Phone: 301/474-0894   **18**

▽▽

Small-scale Hotel

Rates not provided

Address: 9150 Baltimore Ave 20740 **Location:** I-95/495, exit 25 northbound; exit 25B southbound, 0.9 mi s on US 1. **Facility:** 51 one-bedroom standard units. 3 stories, interior corridors. **Parking:** on-site. **Amenities:** safes (fee), hair dryers. **Guest Services:** wireless Internet.

------ WHERE TO DINE ------

94TH AERO SQUADRON
Phone: 301/699-9400

▽▽ ▽▽

American

$6-$49

Overlooking the small airstrip of College Park Airport, the restaurant exudes a casual atmosphere that reflects the mood of an 1800s French farmhouse. World War II memorabilia decorates the inside and out. Prime rib and crabcakes are long-time favorites. Beer cheese soup is a staple. Items from the lunch menu are served until 3 pm. Casual dress. **Bar:** Full bar. **Reservations:** suggested. **Hours:** 11 am-10 pm, Fri & Sat-11 pm, Sun 10 am-3 & 4-10 pm. Closed: 1/1. **Address:** 5240 Paint Branch Pkwy 20740 **Location:** I-95/495, exit 23, 2.5 mi sw (towards Bladensburg) on SR 201, then 0.3 mi n. **Parking:** on-site. **Cards:** AX, DC, DS, MC, VI.

HARD TIMES CAFE
Phone: 301/474-8880

▽▽ ▽▽

American

$6-$15

The hot and spicy, down-home operation knocks your socks off with an impressive variety of chilies, cooked in styles ranging from Cincinnati to Texas and vegetarian. Casual dress. **Bar:** Full bar. **Reservations:** not accepted. **Hours:** 11 am-1 am. **Address:** 4738 Cherry Hill Rd 20740 **Location:** I-95/495, exit 25 northbound; exit 25B southbound, just s on US 1 to Cherry Hill Rd; in The College Park Marketplace. **Parking:** on-site. **Cards:** AX, MC, VI.

(See map and index starting on p. 428)

SEVEN SEAS

Chinese
$6-$14

Phone: 301/345-5808 ⑩

The menu lists a selection of Chinese-American and Chinese dishes, as well as Japanese sushi, sashimi and tempura preparations. Popular choices are rice-wine-cooked chicken and seasoned, sliced beef. A sushi bar offers an alternative to sitting in the simple, comfortable dining room. Casual dress. **Bar:** Full bar. **Reservations:** accepted. **Hours:** 11:30 am-10:30 pm, Fri & Sat-11 pm. Closed: 11/27. **Address:** 8503 Baltimore Blvd 20740 **Location:** I-95/495, exit 25 northbound; exit 25B southbound, 1.6 mi s on US 1. **Parking:** on-site. **Cards:** AX, DC, DS, MC, VI.

GAITHERSBURG pop. 52,613   (See map and index starting on p. 408)

─────── **WHERE TO STAY** ───────

COMFORT INN SHADY GROVE   *Book great rates at AAA.com*

Small-scale Hotel
$69-$149 All Year

Phone: (301)330-0023 ⑭

Address: 16216 Frederick Rd 20877 **Location:** I-270, exit 8, 1 mi e on Shady Grove Rd at SR 355. Located in a commercial area. **Facility:** 127 one-bedroom standard units. 7 stories, interior corridors. **Parking:** on-site. **Amenities:** voice mail, irons, hair dryers. *Fee:* video games, safes. **Pool(s):** heated outdoor. **Leisure Activities:** picnic tables, grill, exercise room, horseshoes. **Guest Services:** valet and coin laundry, area transportation-Shady Grove Metro & local restaurants, wireless Internet. **Business Services:** meeting rooms, business center. **Cards:** AX, CB, DC, DS, JC, MC, VI. **Free Special Amenities: full breakfast and high-speed Internet.**

COURTYARD BY MARRIOTT-GAITHERSBURG/LAKE FOREST   *Book great rates at AAA.com*

Small-scale Hotel
$208-$241 All Year

Phone: 301/670-0008 ⑨

Address: 805 Russell Ave 20879 **Location:** I-270, exit 11, 0.5 mi e. Located in a commercial area near a shopping mall. **Facility:** Smoke free premises. 203 units. 202 one-bedroom standard units. 1 one-bedroom suite with whirlpool. 7 stories, interior corridors. **Parking:** on-site. **Amenities:** high-speed Internet, voice mail, irons, hair dryers. **Pool(s):** outdoor. **Leisure Activities:** sauna, whirlpool, lighted tennis court, limited exercise equipment. **Guest Services:** valet and coin laundry, area transportation. **Business Services:** meeting rooms, PC. **Cards:** AX, DC, DS, MC, VI.

AAA Benefit:
Members save 5% off of the best available rate.

COURTYARD BY MARRIOTT GAITHERSBURG WASHINGTONIAN CENTER   *Book great rates at AAA.com*

Small-scale Hotel
$241-$285 All Year

Phone: 301/527-9000 ⑮

Address: 204 Boardwalk Pl 20878 **Location:** I-270, exit 9B (I-370/Sam Eig Hwy), just w to Washingtonian Blvd, then 0.4 mi s on Washingtonian Blvd. Located in a restaurant/shopping complex. **Facility:** Smoke free premises. 210 units. 203 one-bedroom standard units. 7 one-bedroom suites. 9 stories, interior corridors. *Bath:* combo or shower only. **Parking:** on-site. **Amenities:** video games (fee), high-speed Internet, dual phone lines, voice mail, irons, hair dryers. **Pool(s):** heated indoor. **Leisure Activities:** whirlpool, exercise room. **Guest Services:** valet and coin laundry. **Business Services:** meeting rooms, PC. **Cards:** AX, DC, DS, JC, MC, VI.

AAA Benefit:
Members save 5% off of the best available rate.

EXTENDED STAY DELUXE-WASHINGTON, DC-GAITHERSBURG   *Book at AAA.com*

Small-scale Hotel
$119-$129 All Year

Phone: (301)963-3539 ⑧

Address: 201 Professional Dr 20879 **Location:** I-270, exit 11, 0.4 mi e, then 0.9 mi n on SR 355. **Facility:** 88 units. 87 one-bedroom standard units with efficiencies. 1 two-bedroom suite with efficiency. 3 stories, interior corridors. *Bath:* combo or shower only. **Parking:** on-site. **Terms:** office hours 7 am-11 pm. **Amenities:** DVD players, voice mail, irons, hair dryers. **Leisure Activities:** limited exercise equipment. **Guest Services:** coin laundry, wireless Internet. **Business Services:** meeting rooms. **Cards:** AX, DC, DS, JC, MC, VI.

GAITHERSBURG MARRIOTT WASHINGTONIAN CENTER   *Book great rates at AAA.com*

Large-scale Hotel
Rates not provided

Phone: 301/590-0044 ⑯

Address: 9751 Washingtonian Blvd 20878 **Location:** I-270, exit 9B (I-370/Sam Eig Hwy), just w to Fields Rd, 0.8 mi w, then 0.3 mi ne. Located adjacent to a restaurant/shopping complex. **Facility:** Smoke free premises. 284 units. 283 one-bedroom standard units. 1 one-bedroom suite. 11 stories, interior corridors. *Bath:* combo or shower only. **Parking:** on-site. **Terms:** check-in 4 pm. **Amenities:** voice mail, irons, hair dryers. *Fee:* video games, high-speed Internet. **Pool(s):** heated indoor. **Leisure Activities:** saunas, whirlpool, jogging, limited exercise equipment. **Guest Services:** valet laundry, area transportation. **Business Services:** conference facilities, business center.

Marriott
HOTELS & RESORTS
AAA Benefit:
Members save 5% off of the best available rate.

(See map and index starting on p. 408)

GAITHERSBURG SPRINGHILL SUITES BY MARRIOTT
Book great rates at AAA.com

Phone: 301/987-0900  **18**

Small-scale Hotel
Rates not provided

Address: 9715 Washingtonian Blvd 20878 **Location:** I-270, exit 9B (I-370/Sam Eig Hwy), just w to Fields Rd, 0.8 mi se, then ne. Located near shopping complex. **Facility:** Smoke free premises. 162 one-bedroom standard units. 6 stories, interior corridors. *Bath:* combo or shower only. **Parking:** on-site. **Amenities:** high-speed Internet, dual phone lines, voice mail, irons, hair dryers. **Pool(s):** heated indoor. **Leisure Activities:** whirlpool, exercise room. **Guest Services:** valet and coin laundry. **Business Services:** meeting rooms, PC. **Free Special Amenities:** expanded continental breakfast and high-speed Internet.

AAA Benefit:
Members save 5% off of the best available rate.

HILTON WASHINGTON DC NORTH/GAITHERSBURG
Book great rates at AAA.com

Phone: 301/977-8900 **11**

Large-scale Hotel
Rates not provided

Address: 620 Perry Pkwy 20877 **Location:** I-270, exit 11, then e. Located in a commercial area near shopping mall. **Facility:** 301 units. 299 one-bedroom standard units. 2 one-bedroom suites. 3-12 stories, interior corridors. *Bath:* combo or shower only. **Parking:** on-site. **Amenities:** dual phone lines, voice mail, irons, hair dryers. *Some:* high-speed Internet. **Pool(s):** heated indoor/outdoor. **Leisure Activities:** whirlpool, exercise room. **Guest Services:** complimentary and valet laundry, area transportation-within 5 mi, wireless Internet. **Business Services:** conference facilities, business center.

HOLIDAY INN-GAITHERSBURG
Book great rates at AAA.com

Phone: (301)948-8900 **10**

Large-scale Hotel
$180-$219 3/1-7/1
$129-$179 7/2-2/28

Address: 2 Montgomery Village Ave 20879 **Location:** I-270, exit 11, 0.3 mi e. Located in a commercial area near shopping mall. **Facility:** 301 units. 299 one-bedroom standard units. 2 one-bedroom suites. 7-8 stories, interior corridors. *Bath:* combo or shower only. **Parking:** on-site. **Terms:** cancellation fee imposed. **Amenities:** high-speed Internet, voice mail, irons, hair dryers. **Pool(s):** heated indoor. **Leisure Activities:** whirlpool, sun deck, limited exercise equipment. *Fee:* game room. **Guest Services:** valet and coin laundry, area transportation-within 5 mi, wireless Internet. **Business Services:** meeting rooms, business center. **Cards:** AX, CB, DC, DS, JC, MC, VI. **Free Special Amenities:** room upgrade (subject to availability with advance reservations) and high-speed Internet. *(See color ad below)*

HOMESTEAD STUDIO SUITES HOTEL-GAITHERSBURG/ROCKVILLE
Book at AAA.com

Phone: (301)987-9100 **19**

Small-scale Hotel
$119-$129 All Year

Address: 2621 Research Blvd 20850 **Location:** I-270, exit 8, just w, then just n. **Facility:** 134 units. 128 one-bedroom standard units with efficiencies. 6 one-bedroom suites with efficiencies. 3 stories, interior corridors. *Bath:* combo or shower only. **Parking:** on-site. **Amenities:** voice mail, irons. *Some:* hair dryers. **Guest Services:** coin laundry, wireless Internet. **Cards:** AX, DC, DS, JC, MC, VI.

(See map and index starting on p. 408)

HYATT SUMMERFIELD SUITES-GAITHERSBURG   *Book great rates at AAA.com*   Phone: (301)527-6000

Small-scale Hotel
$119-$399 All Year

Address: 200 Skidmore Blvd 20877 **Location:** I-370, exit SR 355, just n to Westland Rd. Located in a commercial/residential area. **Facility:** 140 units. 82 one- and 58 two-bedroom suites with kitchens. 2-3 stories (no elevator); exterior corridors. *Bath:* combo or shower only. **Parking:** on-site. **Terms:** check-in 4 pm, cancellation fee imposed. **Amenities:** video library (fee), DVD players, dual phone lines, voice mail, irons, hair dryers. **Pool(s):** outdoor. **Leisure Activities:** whirlpool, barbecue grill, picnic area, exercise room, sports court. **Guest Services:** valet and coin laundry, area transportation-within 5 mi, wireless Internet. **Business Services:** meeting rooms, business center. **Cards:** AX, CB, DC, DS, JC, MC, VI.

HYATT SUMMERFIELD SUITES

AAA Benefit:
Ask for the AAA rate and save 10%.

[icons] CALL, some units fee

RESIDENCE INN BY MARRIOTT-GAITHERSBURG   *Book great rates at AAA.com*   Phone: 301/590-3003   **17**

Small-scale Hotel
$227-$278 All Year

Address: 9721 Washingtonian Blvd 20878 **Location:** I-270, exit 9B (I-370/Sam Eig Hwy), just w to Fields Rd, 0.8 mi se, then just ne. Located near shopping center. **Facility:** Smoke free premises. 132 units. 57 one-bedroom standard units, some with efficiencies or kitchens. 51 one- and 24 two-bedroom suites, some with efficiencies or kitchens. 3 stories, interior corridors. *Bath:* combo or shower only. **Parking:** on-site. **Amenities:** voice mail, irons, hair dryers. **Pool(s):** outdoor. **Leisure Activities:** whirlpool, jogging, exercise room, sports court. **Guest Services:** valet and coin laundry, area transportation, wireless Internet. **Business Services:** meeting rooms. **Cards:** AX, DC, DS, JC, MC, VI.

Residence Inn Marriott

AAA Benefit:
Members save 5% off of the best available rate.

[icons] ASK, CALL, some units fee

TOWNEPLACE SUITES BY MARRIOTT-GAITHERSBURG   *Book great rates at AAA.com*   Phone: (301)590-2300   **12**

Small-scale Hotel
$89-$239 All Year

Address: 212 Perry Pkwy 20877 **Location:** I-270, exit 10 northbound, just e; exit 11 southbound, just e on SR 124 to SR 355, 0.3 mi s, then 0.5 mi sw. Located in a business park. **Facility:** Smoke free premises. 91 units. 60 one-bedroom standard units with efficiencies. 5 one- and 26 two-bedroom suites with kitchens. 3-4 stories, interior corridors. *Bath:* combo or shower only. **Parking:** on-site. **Terms:** cancellation fee imposed. **Amenities:** high-speed Internet, dual phone lines, voice mail, irons, hair dryers. **Pool(s):** heated outdoor. **Leisure Activities:** limited exercise equipment. **Guest Services:** valet and coin laundry, wireless Internet. **Business Services:** PC. **Cards:** AX, CB, DC, DS, JC, MC, VI.

TownePlace Suites Marriott

AAA Benefit:
Members save 5% off of the best available rate.

[icons] ASK, CALL, some units fee

──────── **WHERE TO DINE** ────────

CANTINA D'ITALIA   Phone: 301/948-8858

Italian
$5-$24

Good Italian fare is on the menu at Cantina D' Italia, from veal to pasta and pizza to seafood. The atmosphere is suitable for any occasion, from family dining to a business meal. Casual dress. **Bar:** Full bar. **Reservations:** accepted. **Hours:** 11 am-10 pm, Fri & Sat-11 pm, Sun noon-10 pm. Closed: 12/25. **Address:** 285 Kentlands Blvd 20878 **Location:** Jct SR 124 (Quince Orchard Rd) and Great Seneca Hwy; in Kentlands Shopping Center. **Parking:** on-site. **Cards:** AX, CB, DC, DS, MC, VI.

CHICKEN OUT ROTISSERIE   Phone: 301/975-0100

American
$5-$10

Chicken Out Rotisserie uses only fresh all natural ingredients. The chicken is chemical and hormone free. Choose from salads and sandwiches to wraps and picaccias, as well as rotisserie chicken and roast beef. Casual dress. **Reservations:** not accepted. **Hours:** 11 am-9 pm, Fri & Sat-9:30 pm. Closed: 11/27, 12/25. **Address:** 245 Kentlands Blvd 20878 **Location:** Jct SR 124 (Quince Orchard Rd) and Great Seneca Hwy; in Kentlands Shopping Center. **Parking:** on-site. **Cards:** AX, DS, MC, VI.

CALL

CHICKEN OUT ROTISSERIE   Phone: 301/921-9119

American
$5-$10

Chicken Out Rotisserie uses only fresh all natural ingredients. The chicken is chemical and hormone free. Choose from salads and sandwiches to wraps and picaccias, as well as rotisserie chicken and roast beef. Casual dress. **Reservations:** not accepted. **Hours:** 11 am-9:30 pm, Sun-8:30 pm. Closed: 11/27, 12/25. **Address:** 15780 Shady Grove Rd 20877 **Location:** I-270, exit 8, just e; in 270 Center. **Parking:** on-site. **Cards:** AX, DS, MC, VI.

CALL

FLAMING PIT   Phone: 301/977-0700   **35**

Steak & Seafood
$6-$37

The restaurant's rustic ambience is carried from the stone exterior to the stucco and wood trim dining room. The menu offers a good selection of meats and seafood, including house specialties prime rib and king crab legs. The piano lounge offers entertainment nightly and the crowd gets lively as diners are encouraged to join in song. Dressy casual. **Bar:** Full bar. **Reservations:** suggested. **Hours:** 11:30 am-11 pm, Fri-11 pm, Sat 4 pm-11 pm, Sun 5 pm-10 pm. Closed major holidays. **Address:** 18701 N Frederick Ave 20879 **Location:** I-270, exit 11, 0.3 mi e, then 1 mi n on SR 355. **Parking:** on-site. **Cards:** AX, CB, DC, DS, MC, VI.

(See map and index starting on p. 408)

HAKUBA JAPANESE CUISINE

Japanese
$6-$23

Phone: 301/947-1283   **38**

In a Main Street-like setting, the restaurant serves well-prepared Japanese food, from sushi and sashimi to teriyaki and tempura full meals. Casual dress. **Bar:** Beer & wine. **Reservations:** accepted. **Hours:** 11:30 am-2:30 & 4:30-9:30 pm, Fri & Sat-10:30 pm, Sun 5 pm-9 pm. Closed major holidays. **Address:** 706 Center Point Way 20878 **Location:** Jct of SR 124 (Quince Orchard Rd) and Great Seneca Hwy; in Market Square area of Kentlands Shopping Center. **Parking:** on-site. **Cards:** AX, DS, MC, VI.

CALL [&M]

IL PORTO RESTAURANT

Italian
$8-$17

Phone: 301/590-0735   **36**

The small shopping-plaza restaurant lets guests choose from selections of pizza, pasta, veal and seafood. A hand-painted Venetian wall mural sets the scene in the casual cafe, which is comfortable for families. Casual dress. **Bar:** Full bar. **Reservations:** accepted. **Hours:** 11:30 am-10 pm, Sat from noon, Sun noon-9 pm. Closed: 11/27, 12/25. **Address:** 245 Muddy Branch Rd 20878 **Location:** I-270, exit 9B (I-370/Sam Eig Hwy), 0.8 mi w, 0.3 mi n on Diamondback Dr, then 1.2 mi e; in Festival Shopping Plaza. **Parking:** on-site. **Cards:** AX, DS, MC, VI.

MEDITERRANEAN GRILL

Mediterranean
$5-$23

Phone: 301/963-3773   **37**

The kitchen prepares wonderful Southern Mediterranean dishes that reflect Greek, Turkish, Lebanese and Israeli influences. On the menu is a nice selection of mezza, kebabs and main courses. The relaxed dining room occupies a Main Street-type setting. Casual dress. **Bar:** Full bar. **Reservations:** accepted. **Hours:** 11 am-2:30 & 5-10 pm, Fri-11 pm, Sat 11 am-11 pm, Sun 11 am-9 pm. Closed major holidays. **Address:** 644 Center Point Way 20878 **Location:** Jct SR 124 (Quince Orchard Rd) and Great Seneca Hwy; in Market Square area of Kentlands Shopping Center. **Parking:** on-site. **Cards:** AX, DS, MC, VI.

CALL [&M]

SILVER DINER

American
$7-$13

Phone: 740/632-2900

The eatery with its chrome and glass plate exterior and the glow of neon, provides the traditional diner setting. Booths with juke boxes, counter service and friendly wait staff add to the diner experience. The menu is extensive with salads, sandwiches and full meals. The desserts are made fresh and the fountain treats, shakes, floats and malts make for a great ending. Breakfast is available all day. Casual dress. **Bar:** Beer & wine. **Reservations:** not accepted. **Hours:** 8 am-10 pm, Fri & Sat-midnight. Closed: 12/25. **Address:** 701 Russell Ave, Space E-149 20877 **Location:** I-270, exit 11, 0.7 mi e; in Lakeforest Mall. **Parking:** on-site. **Cards:** AX, DC, DS, MC, VI.

TARA THAI

Thai
$6-$13

Phone: 301/947-8330

The stylish cafe's sea motif is one aspect of its contemporary atmosphere. Specialties include whole fresh rockfish and skewered chicken, just to mention two. Most notable is the nicely presented goong phu-ket and pad thai noodles. Portion sizes are ample. Formal attire. **Bar:** Full bar. **Reservations:** accepted. **Hours:** 11:30 am-2:30 & 4:30-10 pm, Fri-11 pm, Sat noon-11 pm, Sun noon-10 pm. **Address:** 9811 Washingtonian Blvd 20878 **Location:** I-270, exit 9B (I-370/Sam Eig Hwy), 0.3 mi w, then s; in Rio Entertainment Center. **Parking:** on-site. **Cards:** AX, DC, DS, MC, VI.

———— *The following restaurant has not been evaluated by AAA* ————
but is listed for your information only.

HUNAN PALACE

[fyi]

Phone: 301/977-8600

Not evaluated. Locals favor this Chinese restaurant, which is known for its Shanghai and Taiwanese dishes. **Address:** 9011 Gaither Rd 20877 **Location:** I-270, exit 8, just e; in Shady Grove Center.

GERMANTOWN pop. 55,419

─────── WHERE TO STAY ───────

EXTENDED STAYAMERICA-WASHINGTON, DC-GERMANTOWN *Book at AAA.com*

Phone: (301)540-9369

Small-scale Hotel
$94-$104 All Year

Address: 12450 Milestone Center Dr 20876 **Location:** I-270, exit 16, 0.6 mi e on SR 27 (Father Hurley Blvd), 0.7 mi n on Observation Dr, then just w. **Facility:** 104 one-bedroom standard units with efficiencies. 3 stories, interior corridors. *Bath:* combo or shower only. **Parking:** on-site. **Terms:** office hours 7 am-11 pm. **Amenities:** voice mail, irons. **Guest Services:** coin laundry, wireless Internet. **Cards:** AX, DC, DS, JC, MC, VI.

FAIRFIELD INN & SUITES BY MARRIOTT-GERMANTOWN/GAITHERSBURG *Book great rates at AAA.com*

Phone: 301/916-0750

Small-scale Hotel
$148-$181 All Year

Address: 20025 Century Blvd 20874 **Location:** I-270, exit 15B (SR 118 S/Germantown Rd), just w on SR 118. Located in commercial area with restaurants and a movie theater. **Facility:** Smoke free premises. 87 one-bedroom standard units, some with whirlpools. 5 stories, interior corridors. *Bath:* combo or shower only. **Parking:** on-site. **Amenities:** high-speed Internet, dual phone lines, voice mail, irons, hair dryers. *Some:* DVD players, CD players. **Pool(s):** heated indoor. **Leisure Activities:** whirlpool, exercise room. **Guest Services:** valet and coin laundry, wireless Internet. **Business Services:** meeting rooms, PC. **Cards:** AX, DS, MC, VI.

AAA Benefit:
Members save 5% off of the best available rate.

HAMPTON INN GERMANTOWN/GAITHERSBURG *Book great rates at AAA.com*

Phone: 301/428-1300

Small-scale Hotel
Rates not provided

Address: 20260 Goldenrod Ln 20876 **Location:** I-270, exit 15A, just e on SR 118. **Facility:** 178 units. 160 one-bedroom standard units, some with whirlpools. 18 one-bedroom suites with kitchens, some with whirlpools. 6 stories, interior corridors. **Parking:** on-site. **Amenities:** voice mail, irons, hair dryers. **Pool(s):** outdoor. **Leisure Activities:** exercise room. **Guest Services:** valet and coin laundry, area transportation, wireless Internet. **Business Services:** meeting rooms.

HOMESTEAD STUDIO SUITES HOTEL-GERMANTOWN *Book at AAA.com*

Phone: (301)515-4500

Motel
$94-$104 All Year

Address: 20141 Century Blvd 20874 **Location:** I-270, exit 15B (SR 118 S/Germantown Rd), just w to Aircraft Dr, then just n. **Facility:** 131 one-bedroom standard units with efficiencies. 2 stories (no elevator), exterior corridors. *Bath:* combo or shower only. **Parking:** on-site. **Terms:** office hours 6:30 am-9 pm. **Amenities:** voice mail, irons. **Leisure Activities:** limited exercise equipment. **Guest Services:** coin laundry, wireless Internet. **Cards:** AX, DC, DS, JC, MC, VI.

─────── WHERE TO DINE ───────

CHICKEN OUT ROTISSERIE

Phone: 301/540-2400

American
$5-$10

Chicken Out Rotisserie uses only fresh all natural ingredients. The chicken is chemical and hormone free. Choose from salads and sandwiches to wraps and picaccias, as well as rotisserie chicken and roast beef. Casual dress. **Reservations:** not accepted. **Hours:** 11 am-9 pm, Fri & Sat-9:30 pm, Sun-8:30 pm. Closed: 11/27, 12/25. **Address:** 20940-F Frederick Rd 20876 **Location:** I-270, exit 16A, 0.9 mi e on SR 27 to SR 355, then just s on SR 355; in Neelsville Village Center at Milestone Center. **Parking:** on-site. **Cards:** AX, DS, MC, VI.

GLORY DAYS GRILL, GERMANTOWN

Phone: 301/528-2662

American
$7-$18

Lending to the casual restaurant's sports-themed atmosphere are memorabilia decorating the dining area and 25 TVs with control centers at each table and booth. Food selections range from wings and ribs to seafood, beef and pasta dishes. Casual dress. **Bar:** Full bar. **Reservations:** not accepted. **Hours:** 4 pm-midnight, Fri & Sat from 11:30 am, Sun 11:30 am-11 pm. Closed: 11/27, 12/25. **Address:** 10850 Mateny Rd 20874 **Location:** Just s of jct Clopper Rd; in Cloppers Mill Village Shopping Center. **Parking:** on-site. **Cards:** AX, DS, MC, VI.

GREENBELT pop. 21,456   (See map and index starting on p. 428)

──────── WHERE TO STAY ────────

COURTYARD BY MARRIOTT-GREENBELT   *Book great rates at AAA.com*

Phone: 301/441-3311

Small-scale Hotel
$219-$241 All Year

Address: 6301 Golden Triangle Dr 20770 **Location:** I-95/495, exit 23, 0.5 mi sw of jct SR 201; off SR 193, just n on Walker Dr. Located in a business park area. **Facility:** Smoke free premises. 152 units. 140 one-bedroom standard units. 12 one-bedroom suites. 4 stories, interior corridors. *Bath:* combo or shower only. **Parking:** on-site. **Amenities:** high-speed Internet, voice mail, irons, hair dryers. **Pool(s):** heated indoor. **Leisure Activities:** whirlpool, limited exercise equipment. **Guest Services:** valet and coin laundry. **Business Services:** meeting rooms, PC. **Cards:** AX, DC, DS, JC, MC, VI.

AAA Benefit:
Members save 5% off of the best available rate.

(ASK) (S₀) (🍴) CALL (⟵M) (🏊) (✕) (🎥) (💻) / SOME UNITS (🛗) (📠)

THE GREENBELT MARRIOTT   *Book great rates at AAA.com*

Phone: 301/441-3700

Large-scale Hotel
Rates not provided

Address: 6400 Ivy Ln 20770 **Location:** I-95/495, exit 23, 0.3 mi ne on SR 201. **Facility:** Smoke free premises. 287 one-bedroom standard units. 17 stories, interior corridors. *Bath:* combo or shower only. **Parking:** on-site. **Terms:** check-in 4 pm. **Amenities:** dual phone lines, voice mail, safes, irons, hair dryers. **Pool(s):** outdoor, heated indoor. **Leisure Activities:** sauna, whirlpool, 2 lighted tennis courts, exercise room. **Guest Services:** valet and coin laundry, area transportation-Greenbelt Metro. **Business Services:** conference facilities, business center. **Free Special Amenities:** newspaper and preferred room (subject to availability with advance reservations).

Marriott
HOTELS & RESORTS

AAA Benefit:
Members save 5% off of the best available rate.

(🍴) (🍽) CALL (⟵M) (🏊) (✕) (✕) (🎥) (🛗) (💻) / SOME UNITS (📠)

HILTON GARDEN INN WASHINGTON DC/GREENBELT   *Book great rates at AAA.com*

Phone: (301)474-7400

Small-scale Hotel
$249 All Year

Address: 7810 Walker Dr 20770 **Location:** I-95/495, exit 23, 0.5 mi sw of jct SR 201, off SR 193, just n on Walker Dr. **Facility:** 155 units. 145 one-bedroom standard units, some with whirlpools. 10 one-bedroom suites. 6 stories, interior corridors. **Parking:** on-site. **Amenities:** video games (fee), high-speed Internet, dual phone lines, voice mail, irons, hair dryers. **Pool(s):** heated indoor. **Leisure Activities:** whirlpool, exercise room. **Guest Services:** valet and coin laundry, area transportation, wireless Internet. **Business Services:** meeting rooms, business center. **Cards:** AX, DC, DS, MC, VI.

(ASK) (S₀) (🍴) CALL (⟵M) (🏊) (🎥) (🛗) (📠) (💻) / SOME UNITS (✕)

▼ See AAA listing p 488 ▼

(See map and index starting on p. 428)

HOLIDAY INN-GREENBELT-NASA AREA   *Book great rates at AAA.com*   Phone: (301)982-7000

Small-scale Hotel
$129-$179 All Year

Address: 7200 Hanover Dr 20770 **Location:** I-95/495, exit 22A, 0.3 mi e; 0.3 mi s of Baltimore-Washington Pkwy and SR 193 (Greenbelt Rd). **Facility:** 205 units. 203 one-bedroom standard units. 2 one-bedroom suites. 7 stories, interior corridors. *Bath:* combo or shower only. **Parking:** on-site. **Amenities:** video games (fee), dual phone lines, voice mail, irons, hair dryers. **Pool(s):** outdoor. **Leisure Activities:** exercise room, volleyball. **Guest Services:** valet and coin laundry, wireless Internet. **Business Services:** meeting rooms, PC. **Cards:** AX, DS, MC, VI. **Free Special Amenities:** newspaper and high-speed Internet.
(See color ad p 487)

RESIDENCE INN BY MARRIOTT-GREENBELT   *Book great rates at AAA.com*   Phone: 301-982-1600

Small-scale Hotel
Rates not provided

Address: 6320 Golden Triangle Dr 20770 **Location:** I-95/495, exit 23, 0.5 mi sw of jct SR 201; off SR 193, just n on Walker Dr. **Facility:** Smoke free premises. 120 units. 48 one-bedroom standard units with efficiencies. 52 one- and 20 two-bedroom suites, some with efficiencies or kitchens. 4 stories, interior corridors. *Bath:* combo or shower only. **Parking:** on-site. **Amenities:** video library (fee), high-speed Internet, dual phone lines, voice mail, irons, hair dryers. **Pool(s):** outdoor. **Leisure Activities:** whirlpool, limited exercise equipment, sports court. **Guest Services:** valet and coin laundry, area transportation-Greenbelt Metro. **Business Services:** meeting rooms, business center. **Free Special Amenities:** full breakfast and high-speed Internet.

AAA Benefit:
Members save 5% off of the best available rate.

----------- WHERE TO DINE -----------

ROYAL JADE   *Menu on AAA.com*   Phone: 301/441-8880   ⑦

Chinese
$6-$20

On the ground floor of an office building, the popular neighborhood restaurant prepares tasty Szechuan, Hunan, Mandarin and vegetarian dishes—all of which can be eaten in the dining room or taken out. Casual dress. **Bar:** Full bar. **Reservations:** accepted. **Hours:** 11 am-10 pm, Fri-11 pm, Sat noon-11 pm, Sun noon-10 pm. Closed: 11/27. **Address:** 7701 Greenbelt Rd 20770 **Location:** I-95/495, exit 22A, 0.3 mi s of jct Baltimore-Washington Pkwy and SR 193 (Greenbelt Rd). **Parking:** on-site. **Cards:** AX, DS, MC, VI.

SILVER DINER   Phone: 301/220-0028

American
$7-$13

The eatery with its chrome and glass plate exterior and the glow of neon, provides the traditional diner setting. Booths with juke boxes, counter service and friendly wait staff add to the diner experience. The menu is extensive with salads, sandwiches and full meals. The desserts are made fresh and the fountain treats, shakes, floats and malts make for a great ending. Breakfast is available all day. Casual dress. **Bar:** Beer & wine. **Reservations:** not accepted. **Hours:** 7 am-midnight, Fri & Sat-3 am. Closed: for dinner 12/25. **Address:** 6040 Greenbelt Rd 20770 **Location:** I-95/495, exit 23, 0.5 mi w on SR 201, then 0.6 mi w on SR 193 (Greenbelt Rd). **Parking:** on-site. **Cards:** AX, DC, DS, MC, VI.

LANDOVER   (See map and index starting on p. 428)

----------- WHERE TO STAY -----------

COURTYARD BY MARRIOTT-NEW
CARROLLTON-LANDOVER   *Book great rates at AAA.com*   Phone: 301/577-3373   ㉞

Small-scale Hotel
Rates not provided

Address: 8330 Corporate Dr 20785 **Location:** I-95/495, exit 19B, 0.3 mi w on US 50, follow signs to New Carrollton Train Station, then just e. Located in a business park area. **Facility:** Smoke free premises. 150 units. 136 one-bedroom standard units. 14 one-bedroom suites. 3-4 stories, interior corridors. *Bath:* combo or shower only. **Parking:** on-site. **Amenities:** high-speed Internet, dual phone lines, voice mail, irons, hair dryers. **Pool(s):** heated indoor. **Leisure Activities:** whirlpool, exercise room. **Guest Services:** valet and coin laundry, area transportation, wireless Internet. **Business Services:** meeting rooms, business center.

AAA Benefit:
Members save 5% off of the best available rate.

LANDOVER HILLS pop. 1,534   (See map and index starting on p. 428)

——— WHERE TO STAY ———

COMFORT INN-LANDOVER HILLS   *Book at AAA.com*   Phone: (301)322-6000   **37**

Small-scale Hotel
$99 All Year

Address: 6205 Annapolis Rd 20784 **Location:** SR 450, 0.3 mi s of jct Baltimore-Washington Pkwy. Located in a commercial area. **Facility:** 89 one-bedroom standard units, some with whirlpools. 5 stories, interior corridors. **Parking:** on-site. **Terms:** cancellation fee imposed. **Amenities:** high-speed Internet, safes (fee), irons, hair dryers. **Leisure Activities:** limited exercise equipment. **Cards:** AX, DC, DS, MC, VI.

LANHAM   (See map and index starting on p. 428)

——— WHERE TO STAY ———

DAYS INN-LANHAM   *Book great rates at AAA.com*   Phone: 301/459-6600   **23**

Small-scale Hotel
Rates not provided

Address: 9023 Annapolis Rd 20706 **Location:** I-95/495, exit 20A, just e on SR 450. Located adjacent to railroad tracks. **Facility:** 112 one-bedroom standard units, some with whirlpools. 3 stories, interior corridors. *Bath:* combo or shower only. **Parking:** on-site. **Amenities:** voice mail, safes, irons, hair dryers. **Leisure Activities:** limited exercise equipment. **Guest Services:** coin laundry, wireless Internet. **Business Services:** meeting rooms. **Free Special Amenities:** newspaper. *(See color ad below)*

——— ▼ See AAA listing above ▼ ———

LARGO pop. 8,408   (See map and index starting on p. 428)

———— WHERE TO STAY ————

HAMPTON INN-WASHINGTON, DC/I-95   *Book great rates at AAA.com*   Phone: (301)499-4600   **31**

(AAA) (SAVE)

▼▼▼▼▼

Small-scale Hotel

$169-$179 All Year

Address: 9421 Largo Dr W 20774 **Location:** I-95/495, exit 17A (SR 202), just e to Lottsford Rd, 1.3 mi s, then just e. **Facility:** 127 one-bedroom standard units. 6 stories, interior corridors. **Parking:** on-site. **Amenities:** video games (fee), voice mail, irons, hair dryers. **Pool(s):** heated indoor. **Leisure Activities:** exercise room. **Guest Services:** valet laundry, area transportation-Largo Metro Station, shopping mall, wireless Internet. **Business Services:** meeting rooms, business center. **Cards:** AX, CB, DS, MC, VI. **Free Special Amenities:** full breakfast and high-speed Internet. *(See color ad p 442)*

 [icon row]

HOLIDAY INN EXPRESS HOTEL & SUITES I-95 CAPITAL BELTWAY   *Book great rates at AAA.com*   Phone: 301/636-6090   **29**

(AAA) (SAVE)

▼▼▼▼▼

Small-scale Hotel

$129-$289 All Year

Address: 9101 Basil Ct 20774 **Location:** I-95/495, exit 17A (SR 202), just se. Located in business park area. **Facility:** 89 units. 70 one-bedroom standard units. 19 one-bedroom suites, some with whirlpools. 4 stories, interior corridors. *Bath:* combo or shower only. **Parking:** on-site. **Amenities:** high-speed Internet, dual phone lines, voice mail, irons, hair dryers. **Pool(s):** heated indoor. **Leisure Activities:** whirlpool, limited exercise equipment. **Guest Services:** valet and coin laundry, area transportation-within 5 mi & Largo Towncenter Metro, wireless Internet. **Business Services:** meeting rooms, business center. **Cards:** AX, DC, DS, MC, VI. **Free Special Amenities: expanded continental breakfast and high-speed Internet.**

[icon row]

RADISSON HOTEL LARGO/WASHINGTON, D.C.   *Book at AAA.com*   Phone: (301)773-0700   **30**

▼▼▼▼

Small-scale Hotel

$139-$179 3/1-10/31

$119-$159 11/1-2/28

Address: 9100 Basil Ct 20774 **Location:** I-95/495, exit 17A (SR 202); off Capital Beltway. Located in a business park area. **Facility:** 184 units. 183 one-bedroom standard units. 1 one-bedroom suite with whirlpool. 6 stories, interior corridors. *Bath:* combo or shower only. **Parking:** on-site. **Amenities:** voice mail, irons, hair dryers. *Some:* high-speed Internet. **Pool(s):** heated indoor. **Leisure Activities:** exercise room. **Guest Services:** valet laundry, area transportation, wireless Internet. **Business Services:** meeting rooms, business center. **Cards:** AX, CB, DC, DS, JC, MC, VI.

[icon row]

LAUREL pop. 19,960

———— WHERE TO STAY ————

COMFORT SUITES LAUREL LAKES   *Book great rates at AAA.com*   Phone: (301)206-2600

(AAA) (SAVE)

▼▼▼▼

Small-scale Hotel

$89-$179 3/1-11/14

$79-$159 11/15-2/28

Address: 14402 Laurel Pl 20707 **Location:** On US 1, 0.9 mi s of jct SR 198. Located adjacent to Laurel Lakes Mall. **Facility:** 119 one-bedroom standard units. 5 stories, interior corridors. **Parking:** on-site. **Amenities:** voice mail, irons, hair dryers. *Fee:* video games, safes. **Pool(s):** heated indoor. **Leisure Activities:** whirlpool, sun deck, limited exercise equipment. **Guest Services:** valet and coin laundry, wireless Internet. **Business Services:** meeting rooms, PC. **Cards:** AX, CB, DC, DS, MC, VI. **Free Special Amenities: expanded continental breakfast and high-speed Internet.**

[icon row]

DAYS INN & SUITES LAUREL   *Book at AAA.com*   Phone: 301/725-0769

▼▼▼▼

Small-scale Hotel

Rates not provided

Address: 9860 Washington Blvd N 20723 **Location:** Jct SR 198, 1.5 mi n on US 1. **Facility:** 85 one-bedroom standard units, some with whirlpools. 2-3 stories, interior/exterior corridors. *Bath:* combo or shower only. **Parking:** on-site. **Amenities:** voice mail, safes (fee), irons, hair dryers. *Some:* high-speed Internet. **Leisure Activities:** limited exercise equipment. **Guest Services:** valet and coin laundry, wireless Internet. **Business Services:** meeting rooms, PC.

[icon row]

▼ See AAA listing p 491 ▼

ECONO LODGE LAUREL   *Book great rates at AAA.com*

Motel
$63-$90 All Year

Phone: 301/776-8008

Address: 9700 Washington Blvd 20723 **Location:** Jct SR 198, 1.8 mi n on US 1. Located in a commercial area. **Facility:** 50 one-bedroom standard units. 2 stories (no elevator), exterior corridors. **Parking:** on-site. **Terms:** 29 day cancellation notice. **Amenities:** high-speed Internet, irons, hair dryers. **Guest Services:** wireless Internet. **Cards:** AX, DC, DS, JC, MC, VI. **Free Special Amenities: continental breakfast and high-speed Internet.**

FAIRFIELD INN BY MARRIOTT-LAUREL   *Book great rates at AAA.com*

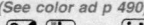

Small-scale Hotel
$153-$186 All Year

Phone: 301/498-8900

Address: 13700 Baltimore Ave 20707 **Location:** Jct SR 198, 1.7 mi s on US 1. **Facility:** Smoke free premises. 109 one-bedroom standard units. 5 stories, interior corridors. *Bath:* combo or shower only. **Parking:** on-site. **Amenities:** video games (fee), voice mail, safes, irons, hair dryers. **Pool(s):** outdoor. **Leisure Activities:** whirlpool, limited exercise equipment. **Guest Services:** valet and coin laundry, wireless Internet. **Business Services:** meeting rooms. **Cards:** AX, DC, DS, MC, VI. **Free Special Amenities: continental breakfast and high-speed Internet.**
(See color ad p 490)

AAA Benefit:
Members save 5% off of the best available rate.

HOLIDAY INN LAUREL-WEST   *Book great rates at AAA.com*

Small-scale Hotel
$119-$159 3/1-10/31
$99-$129 11/1-2/28

Phone: (301)776-5300

Address: 15101 Sweitzer Ln 20707 **Location:** I-95, exit 33B, just w on SR 198. **Facility:** 207 one-bedroom standard units. 6 stories, interior/exterior corridors. *Bath:* combo or shower only. **Parking:** on-site. **Amenities:** video games (fee), voice mail, irons, hair dryers. **Pool(s):** heated indoor. **Leisure Activities:** exercise room. **Guest Services:** valet and coin laundry, wireless Internet. **Business Services:** meeting rooms, business center. **Cards:** AX, DC, DS, MC, VI. **Free Special Amenities: local telephone calls and high-speed Internet.**

QUALITY INN & SUITES LAUREL   *Book great rates at AAA.com*

Small-scale Hotel
$99-$199 3/1-10/31
$79-$179 11/1-2/28

Phone: (301)725-8800

Address: One Second St 20707 **Location:** On US 1, 0.5 mi n of jct SR 198. **Facility:** 96 units. 86 one-bedroom standard units, some with whirlpools. 10 one-bedroom suites, some with whirlpools. 5 stories, interior/exterior corridors. *Bath:* combo or shower only. **Parking:** on-site. **Terms:** cancellation fee imposed. **Amenities:** voice mail, safes (fee), irons, hair dryers. **Pool(s):** outdoor. **Leisure Activities:** limited exercise equipment. **Guest Services:** coin laundry, wireless Internet. **Business Services:** meeting rooms, PC. **Cards:** AX, CB, DC, DS, JC, MC, VI. **Free Special Amenities: expanded continental breakfast and high-speed Internet.** *(See color ad below)*

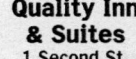

——— WHERE TO DINE ———

BAY 'N SURF SEAFOOD RESTAURANT

Phone: 301/776-7021

Seafood

$7-$43

Well-established since its opening in 1965, this rustic, nautical-themed restaurant offers good food presented in old Baltimore style. Featuring traditional jumbo lump crab cakes, crab Imperial and fresh fin fish from around the world. The cream of crab soup is a house favorite. Chicken and beef dishes are also available. Casual dress. **Bar:** Full bar. **Reservations:** suggested, weekends. **Hours:** 11 am-9 pm, Fri-10 pm, Sat noon-10 pm, Sun 1 pm-9 pm. Closed major holidays; also Super Bowl Sun. **Address:** 14411 Baltimore Ave 20707 **Location:** Jct SR 198, 1.4 mi s on US 1. **Parking:** on-site. **Cards:** AX, CB, DC, DS, MC, VI.

HARD TIMES CAFE

Phone: 301/604-7400

American

$6-$15

The hot and spicy, down-home operation knocks your socks off with an impressive variety of chilies, cooked in styles ranging from Cincinnati to Texas and vegetarian. Casual dress. **Bar:** Full bar. **Reservations:** not accepted. **Hours:** 11 am-1 am. **Address:** 1021 Washington Blvd 20707 **Location:** On US 1, just s, jct SR 198; in Laurel Shopping Center. **Parking:** on-site. **Cards:** AX, MC, VI.

PASTA PLUS RESTAURANT

Phone: 301/498-5100

Italian

$5-$20

A nondescript exterior belies the warmth and charm of the small restaurant, a favorite neighborhood haunt for homemade pasta and sauces, veal, fresh seafood and pizza cooked in a wood-burning oven. Service is friendly, efficient and knowledgeable. They operate the carryout market adjacent to the restaurant where diners can take home some real treats. Casual dress. **Bar:** Beer & wine. **Reservations:** accepted, for lunch. **Hours:** 11:30 am-2 & 5-9:30 pm, Fri-10 pm, Sat 5 pm-10 pm, Sun 4 pm-9 pm. Closed major holidays. **Address:** 209 Gorman Ave 20707 **Location:** US 1, jct SR 198; in Gorman Plaza Shopping Center. **Parking:** on-site. **Cards:** AX, CB, DC, DS, MC, VI.

SILVER DINER

Phone: 301/470-6080

American

$7-$15

The eatery with its chrome and glass plate exterior and the glow of neon, provides the traditional diner setting. Booths with juke boxes, counter service and friendly wait staff add to the diner experience. The menu is extensive with salads, sandwiches and full meals. The desserts are made fresh and the fountain treats, shakes, floats and malts make for a great ending. Breakfast is available all day. Casual dress. **Bar:** Beer & wine. **Reservations:** not accepted. **Hours:** 7 am-midnight, Fri & Sat-3 am. Closed: 12/25; also for dinner 11/20 and 1/1. **Address:** 14550 Baltimore Ave 20707 **Location:** On US 1, 0.9 mi s of jct SR 198. **Parking:** on-site. **Cards:** AX, DC, DS, MC, VI.

CALL

OXON HILL   (See map and index starting on p. 428)

——— WHERE TO STAY ———

COMFORT INN OXON HILL   *Book great rates at AAA.com*

Phone: (301)839-0001   44

Small-scale Hotel

$89-$179 3/1-7/31

$79-$179 8/1-2/28

Address: 6363 Oxon Hill Rd 20745 **Location:** I-95/495, exit 3B northbound; exit 3 southbound, 0.3 mi e on SR 414. **Facility:** 123 one-bedroom standard units. 5 stories, interior corridors. *Bath:* combo or shower only. **Parking:** on-site. **Terms:** 30 day cancellation notice-fee imposed. **Amenities:** high-speed Internet, voice mail, irons, hair dryers. **Pool(s):** outdoor. **Leisure Activities:** limited exercise equipment. **Guest Services:** coin laundry. **Business Services:** meeting rooms, PC. **Cards:** AX, CB, DC, DS, JC, MC, VI. **Free Special Amenities: expanded continental breakfast and high-speed Internet.**

GAYLORD NATIONAL RESORT & CONVENTION CENTER ON THE POTOMAC

Phone: 301/965-2000

[fyi]

Large-scale Hotel

Under construction, scheduled to open April 2008. **Address:** 201 Waterfront St 20745 **Location:** I-95/495, exit 2. **Amenities:** coffeemakers, pool.

POTOMAC VIEW LEXINGTON HOTEL   *Book great rates at AAA.com*

Phone: 301/749-9400   45

Small-scale Hotel

Rates not provided

Address: 6400 Oxon Hill Rd 20745 **Location:** I-95/495, exit 3B, just e. **Facility:** 194 units. 178 one-bedroom standard units. 16 one-bedroom suites. 8 stories, interior corridors. **Parking:** on-site. **Amenities:** high-speed Internet, voice mail, irons, hair dryers. **Pool(s):** heated indoor. **Leisure Activities:** saunas, exercise room. **Guest Services:** valet laundry. **Business Services:** meeting rooms, PC. **Free Special Amenities: continental breakfast and high-speed Internet.**

POTOMAC pop. 44,822   (See map and index starting on p. 408)

——— WHERE TO DINE ———

OLD ANGLERS INN

Phone: 301/365-2425   44

American

$15-$45

Country setting. You enter into the lounge with the ambience of a cozy living room. The stone fireplace roars when the weather is chilly. The dining room, on the second level is accessed by a narrow, spiral staircase. The rustic atmosphere continues in the dining room, with an upscale air. When the weather cooperates, lunch service is offered on the charming slate patio shaded by mature trees and green/white umbrellas around a small fountain. The chef is skilled; dishes are prepared ala-minute. Semi-formal attire. **Bar:** Full bar. **Reservations:** suggested, for dinner. **Hours:** noon-2:30 & 5:30-10 pm, Sun-9:30 pm. Closed major holidays; also Mon. **Address:** 10801 MacArthur Blvd 20854 **Location:** I-495, exit 41, 3 mi w via Clara Barton Pkwy and MacArthur Blvd. **Parking:** on-site. **Cards:** AX, CB, DC, MC, VI.

ROCKVILLE pop. 47,388   (See map and index starting on p. 408)

——— WHERE TO STAY ———

BEST WESTERN WASHINGTON GATEWAY HOTEL & SUITES   *Book great rates at AAA.com*

Phone: (301)424-4940   **28**

AAA SAVE

Small-scale Hotel
$90-$170 All Year

Address: 1251 W Montgomery Ave 20850 **Location:** I-270, exit 6B, just w on SR 28. **Facility:** 160 units. 140 one-bedroom standard units. 20 one-bedroom suites. 7 stories, interior corridors. *Bath:* combo or shower only. **Parking:** on-site. **Amenities:** high-speed Internet, dual phone lines, voice mail, irons, hair dryers. **Pool(s):** outdoor. **Leisure Activities:** exercise room. **Guest Services:** valet and coin laundry, area transportation-Rockville Metro & local businesses, wireless Internet. **Business Services:** meeting rooms, business center. **Cards:** AX, CB, DC, DS, JC, MC, VI. **Free Special Amenities:** newspaper and room upgrade (subject to availability with advance reservations). *(See color ad below)*

AAA Benefit:
Members save 10% everyday, plus an exclusive frequent stay program.

    CALL

BETHESDA NORTH MARRIOTT HOTEL & CONFERENCE CENTER   *Book great rates at AAA.com*

Phone: 301/822-9200   **31**

Large-scale Hotel
Rates not provided

Address: 5701 Marinelli Rd 20852 **Location:** I-270, exit 4A (Montrose Rd), 2 mi e, then 0.5 mi s on SR 355. Located across the street from White Flint Metro. **Facility:** Smoke free premises. 225 one-bedroom standard units. 10 stories, interior corridors. *Bath:* combo or shower only. **Parking:** on-site (fee). **Terms:** check-in 4 pm. **Amenities:** CD players, high-speed Internet (fee), dual phone lines, voice mail, irons, hair dryers. **Pool(s):** heated indoor. **Leisure Activities:** exercise room. **Guest Services:** valet laundry. **Business Services:** conference facilities, business center.

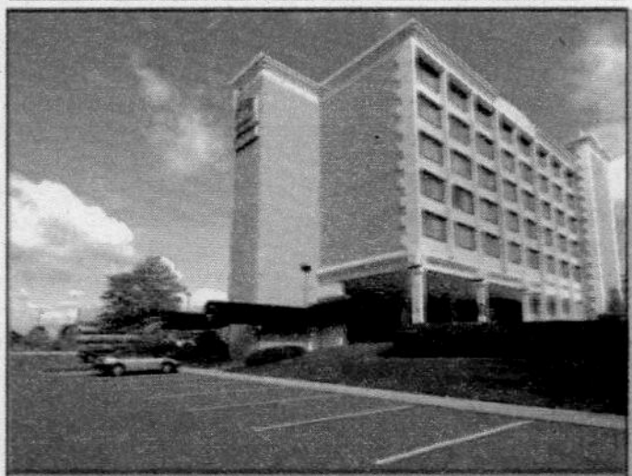

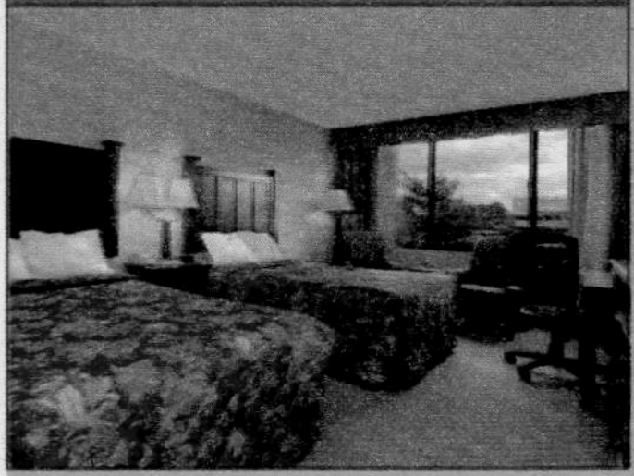

AAA Benefit:
Members save 5% off of the best available rate.

CALL

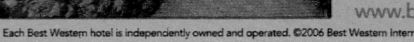

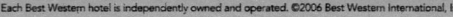

(See map and index starting on p. 408)

COURTYARD BY MARRIOTT-ROCKVILLE *Book great rates at AAA.com* Phone: 301/670-6700

 Small-scale Hotel
Rates not provided

Address: 2500 Research Blvd 20850 **Location:** I-270, exit 8 (Shady Grove Rd), 0.4 mi w. Located in business park area. **Facility:** Smoke free premises. 147 units. 134 one-bedroom standard units. 13 one-bedroom suites. 3 stories, interior corridors. *Bath:* combo or shower only. **Parking:** on-site. **Amenities:** high-speed Internet, dual phone lines, voice mail, irons, hair dryers. **Pool(s):** heated indoor. **Leisure Activities:** whirlpool, sun deck, limited exercise equipment. **Guest Services:** valet and coin laundry, wireless Internet. **Business Services:** meeting rooms, PC. **Free Special Amenities:** newspaper and high-speed Internet.

AAA Benefit:
Members save 5% off of the best available rate.

CROWNE PLAZA WASHINGTON DC-ROCKVILLE *Book great rates at AAA.com* Phone: (301)840-0200 24

 Small-scale Hotel
$99-$289 All Year

Address: 3 Research Ct 20850 **Location:** I-270, exit 8 (Shady Grove Rd), just sw. Located in a business area. **Facility:** 150 units. 125 one-bedroom standard units. 25 one-bedroom suites. 3 stories, interior corridors. *Bath:* combo or shower only. **Parking:** on-site. **Terms:** check-in 4 pm. **Amenities:** video games (fee), high-speed Internet, voice mail, irons, hair dryers. **Pool(s):** outdoor. **Leisure Activities:** yoga room, exercise room. **Guest Services:** valet laundry, area transportation-Shady Grove Metro Station, within 3 mi, wireless Internet. **Business Services:** conference facilities, business center. **Cards:** AX, CB, DC, DS, JC, MC, VI. **Free Special Amenities:** early check-in/late check-out. *(See color ad p 431 & p 432)*

HILTON HOTEL & EXECUTIVE MEETING CENTER
ROCKVILLE *Book great rates at AAA.com* Phone: 301/468-1100 29

Large-scale Hotel
Rates not provided

Address: 1750 Rockville Pike 20852 **Location:** SR 355, 2 mi s of jct SR 28. Located opposite Twinbrook Metro Stop. **Facility:** 315 units. 298 one-bedroom standard units. 8 one-bedroom suites. 8 stories, interior corridors. *Bath:* combo or shower only. **Parking:** on-site (fee). **Amenities:** high-speed Internet (fee), voice mail, irons, hair dryers. **Pool(s):** heated indoor/outdoor. **Leisure Activities:** whirlpool, exercise room. **Guest Services:** valet laundry, area transportation (fee), wireless Internet. **Business Services:** conference facilities, business center. **Free Special Amenities:** newspaper.

LEGACY HOTEL *Book great rates at AAA.com* Phone: (301)881-2300 30

Small-scale Hotel
$315-$349 3/1-3/15
$225-$249 3/16-2/28

Address: 1775 Rockville Pike 20852 **Location:** On SR 355, 2 mi s of jct SR 28. Located in a commercial area. **Facility:** 161 one-bedroom standard units. 7 stories, interior corridors. *Bath:* combo or shower only. **Parking:** on-site. **Terms:** cancellation fee imposed. **Amenities:** high-speed Internet, voice mail, irons, hair dryers. **Guest Services:** valet laundry, area transportation-within 5 mi, wireless Internet. **Business Services:** meeting rooms, business center. **Cards:** AX, CB, DC, DS, MC, VI. **Free Special Amenities:** newspaper. *(See color ad below)*

RED ROOF INN-ROCKVILLE *Book at AAA.com* Phone: 301/987-0965 22

Small-scale Hotel
Rates not provided

Address: 16001 Shady Grove Rd 20850 **Location:** I-270, exit 8 (Shady Grove Rd), 0.5 mi e. Located in a commercial area. **Facility:** 188 one-bedroom standard units. 2 stories (no elevator), exterior corridors. *Bath:* combo or shower only. **Parking:** on-site. **Amenities:** video games (fee), voice mail. **Guest Services:** area transportation, wireless Internet.

▼ *See AAA listing above* ▼

(See map and index starting on p. 408)

SHERATON ROCKVILLE   *Book great rates at AAA.com*   Phone: 240/912-8200

Small-scale Hotel
Rates not provided

Address: 920 King Farm Blvd 20850 **Location:** I-270, exit 8 northbound (Redland Rd), left on Piccard, then left on King Farm Blvd. **Facility:** 155 one-bedroom standard units. 5 stories, interior corridors. *Bath:* combo or shower only. **Parking:** on-site. **Amenities:** high-speed Internet (fee), voice mail, irons, hair dryers. **Pool(s):** heated indoor. **Leisure Activities:** whirlpool, exercise room. **Guest Services:** valet and coin laundry, area transportation, wireless Internet. **Business Services:** meeting rooms, business center.

AAA Benefit:
Members get up to 15% off, plus Starwood Preferred Guest® bonuses.

SLEEP INN-ROCKVILLE   *Book great rates at AAA.com*   Phone: (301)948-8000   ㉕

Small-scale Hotel
$89-$149 All Year

Address: 2 Research Ct 20850 **Location:** I-270, exit 8 (Shady Grove Rd), just sw. Located in a business area. **Facility:** 107 one-bedroom standard units. 3 stories, interior corridors. *Bath:* combo or shower only. **Parking:** on-site. **Amenities:** video games (fee), high-speed Internet, voice mail, irons, hair dryers. **Leisure Activities:** pool & exercise room privileges. **Guest Services:** valet and coin laundry, area transportation-Shady Grove Metro Station, wireless Internet. **Business Services:** PC (fee). **Cards:** AX, CB, DC, DS, JC, MC, VI. **Free Special Amenities: continental breakfast and early check-in/late check-out.** *(See color ad p 431 & p 432)*

WOODFIN SUITES HOTEL   *Book great rates at AAA.com*   Phone: (301)590-9880   ㉖

Small-scale Hotel
$159 All Year

Address: 1380 Piccard Dr 20850 **Location:** I-270, exit 8 (Shady Grove Rd), 0.3 mi s; 1 mi w of SR 355 via Redland Rd. Located in a business park area. **Facility:** 203 units. 18 one-bedroom standard units. 167 one- and 18 two-bedroom suites, some with efficiencies or kitchens. 3 stories, exterior corridors. *Bath:* combo or shower only. **Parking:** on-site. **Terms:** check-in 4 pm, 3 day cancellation notice-fee imposed. **Amenities:** video library, DVD players, CD players, voice mail, safes, irons, hair dryers. *Some:* high-speed Internet (fee). **Pool(s):** outdoor. **Leisure Activities:** whirlpool, limited exercise equipment, basketball. **Guest Services:** valet and coin laundry, area transportation-metro & within 5 mi, wireless Internet. **Business Services:** meeting rooms, business center. **Cards:** AX, DC, DS, MC, VI. **Free Special Amenities: continental breakfast and newspaper.**

—— WHERE TO DINE ——

A & J RESTAURANT   Phone: 301/251-7878   ㉗

Chinese
$8-$14

For those who like dim sum, the Northern Chinese version is worth a try. There are more than 60 items that are spicier and have larger portions of soups and meats than the Cantonese version. Casual dress. **Reservations:** not accepted. **Hours:** 11:30 am-9 pm, Sat & Sun from 10 am. Closed: for dinner 11/27. **Address:** 1319-C Rockville Pike 20852 **Location:** On SR 355, just s of Woodmont Country Club. **Parking:** on-site.

ADDIE'S   Phone: 301/881-0081   ㉜

American
$7-$27

Set back off a busy commercial area, the colorful, fine-dining establishment is one of the most popular in town. Casual dress. **Bar:** Beer & wine. **Reservations:** suggested. **Hours:** 11 am-2:30 & 5:30-9:30 pm, Fri-10 pm, Sat noon-2:30 & 5:30-10 pm, Sun 5 pm-9 pm. Closed major holidays. **Address:** 11120 Rockville Pike 20852 **Location:** I-270, exit 4A (Montrose Rd), 1.9 mi e, then 1.1 mi s on SR 355. **Parking:** on-site. **Cards:** AX, DC, DS, MC, VI.

BENJARONG THAI RESTAURANT   Phone: 301/424-5533   ㉖

Thai
$7-$22

The shopping plaza restaurant offers Thai cuisine in a contemporary atmosphere. Thai artwork decorates the dining room. Casual dress. **Bar:** Full bar. **Reservations:** accepted, Sun-Thurs. **Hours:** 11:30 am-3 & 5-10 pm, Fri & Sat 11:30 am-10:30 pm, Sun noon-10 pm. Closed major holidays. **Address:** 885 Rockville Pike 20852 **Location:** On SR 355; in Wintergreen Plaza. **Parking:** on-site. **Cards:** AX, DC, DS, MC, VI.

BOMBAY BISTRO   Phone: 301/762-8798

Indian
$7-$14

Consistently well-prepared cuisine is what the kitchen prepares. The setting is simple, and service is efficient. Casual dress. **Bar:** Beer & wine. **Reservations:** not accepted. **Hours:** 11:30 am-2:30 & 5-10 pm, Fri-10:30 pm, Sat noon-3 & 5-10:30 pm, Sun noon-3 & 5-10 pm. Closed: lunch 12/25. **Address:** 98 W Montgomery Ave 20850 **Location:** 0.5 mi w of SR 355, just n of jct of Washington St. **Parking:** on-site. **Cards:** AX, DC, DS, MC, VI.

CARIBBEAN FEAST   Phone: 301/315-2668   ㉓

Jamaican
$4-$13

Perfect for a quick bite of the warmth of Jamaica, the restaurant offers a choice of either hot or mild jerk seasoning. Casual dress. **Hours:** 11 am-9 pm, Fri & Sat-9:30 pm. Closed: 1/1, 11/27, 12/25; also Sun. **Address:** 823 Hungerford Dr 20850 **Location:** I-270, exit 6A, 1.2 mi e on SR 28, then 1.4 mi n on SR 355; in Saah Plaza. **Parking:** on-site. **Cards:** AX, MC, VI.

CEVICHE HOUSE RESTAURANT   Phone: 301/330-0402   ⑲

Peruvian
$9-$18

Peruvian and Latin American cooking is what you'll find at Ceviche House. The kitchen prepares dishes such as churrasco a la parrilla or poll a la parrilla con salsa de champignons to mention a couple items. Casual dress. **Bar:** Full bar. **Reservations:** accepted. **Hours:** 11 am-10 pm, Sun-9 pm. Closed: 7/4, 11/27, 12/25. **Address:** 7236 Muncaster Mill Rd 20855 **Location:** I-270, exit 8 (Shady Grove Rd), 3.3 mi e to SR 115, then just se; in Red Mill Shopping Center. **Parking:** on-site. **Cards:** AX, DS, MC, VI.

(See map and index starting on p. 408)

CHICKEN OUT ROTISSERIE
Phone: 301/230-2020

American
$5-$10

Chicken Out Rotisserie uses only fresh all natural ingredients. The chicken is chemical and hormone free. Choose from salads and sandwiches to wraps and picaccias, as well as rotisserie chicken and roast beef. Casual dress. **Reservations:** not accepted. **Hours:** 11 am-9:30 pm, Sun-9 pm. Closed: 12/25. **Address:** 1560 Rockville Pike 20852 **Location:** On SR 355, 1.7 mi s of jct SR 28. **Parking:** on-site. **Cards:** AX, DS, MC, VI.

CALL 🚹M

CUBAN CORNER RESTAURANT
Phone: 301/279-0310   [24]

AAA

Cuban
$9-$15

Cuban cooking is served in this small, popular restaurant. A local favorite dish is ropa vieja: shredded, stewed flank steak served with rice. Casual dress. **Bar:** Beer & wine. **Hours:** 10:30 am-9 pm, Fri & Sat-10 pm, Sun noon-8 pm. Closed major holidays; also Sun. **Address:** 825 Hungerford Dr 20850 **Location:** On SR 355; 1 mi n of jct SR 28; in Saah Plaza. **Parking:** on-site. **Cards:** AX, DS, MC, VI.

DAVE AND BUSTERS
Phone: 301/230-5151   [31]

American
$8-$19

Dave and Busters comprises 60,000 square feet of high-tech gaming, billiards and shuffleboard. The menu at this busy establishment offers American fare. Casual dress. **Bar:** Full bar. **Reservations:** not accepted. **Hours:** 11:30 am-midnight, Thurs-Sat to 1 am. **Address:** 11301 Rockville Pike 20895 **Location:** On SR 355; in White Flint Mall. **Parking:** on-site. **Cards:** AX, DC, DS, MC, VI.

CALL 🚹M

IL PINITO TRATTORIA
Phone: 301/881-0086   [30]

Italian
$7-$20

Traditional dishes are served at the family restaurant. The atmosphere is casual and relaxed, allowing for a comfortable family outing. Casual dress. **Bar:** Beer & wine. **Reservations:** accepted. **Hours:** 11 am-2:30 & 5-10 pm, Sat & Sun 5 pm-9 pm. Closed major holidays. **Address:** 5071 Nicholson Ln 20852 **Location:** SR 355 S, 0.5 mi e. **Parking:** on-site. **Cards:** AX, DS, MC, VI.

IL PIZZICO RISTORANTE
Phone: 301/309-0610   [22]

Italian
$10-$26

This local favorite, family-owned restaurant offers consistently good Italian fare. Menu offers a wide variety of pasta dishes, fresh seafood, veal and prime steak. Service is professional and ambience is comfortable, simple and tasteful. Dressy casual. **Bar:** Beer & wine. **Reservations:** not accepted. **Hours:** 11 am-2:30 & 5-9:30 pm, Fri-10 pm, Sat 5 pm-10 pm. Closed major holidays; also Sun. **Address:** 15209 Frederick Rd 20850 **Location:** On SR 355, 2 mi n of jct SR 28. **Parking:** on-site. **Cards:** AX, MC, VI.

MYKONOS GRILL
Phone: 301/770-5999   [28]

Greek
$8-$25

Slate floors, colorful artwork and white stucco walls with blue trim create a delightful Greek atmosphere. Dishes are prepared from fresh meats, fish and produce. Dressy casual. **Bar:** Full bar. **Reservations:** suggested, Thurs-Sat. **Hours:** 11:30 am-9:30 pm, Fri-10:30 pm, Sat noon-10:30 pm, Sun noon-9:30 pm. Closed major holidays; also Mon. **Address:** 121 Congressional Ln 20852 **Location:** Jct SR 28, 2 mi s on SR 355; in Congressional Shopping Plaza. **Parking:** on-site. **Cards:** AX, DC, DS, MC, VI.

NICK'S CHOPHOUSE
Phone: 301/926-8869   [20]

Steak & Seafood
$8-$40

This sophisticated, upscale steakhouse is on the ground level of an office building, with patio dining when the weather cooperates. On the menu is a nice selection of Certified Angus beef and seafood. Professional staffers provide attentive, friendly service. Dressy casual. **Bar:** Full bar. **Reservations:** suggested. **Hours:** 11:30 am-2:30 & 5:30-10 pm, Fri-11 pm, Sat 5:30 pm-11 pm, Sun 4:30 pm-9 pm. Closed: 1/1, 12/25. **Address:** 700 King Farm Blvd 20850 **Location:** I-270, exit 8 (Shady Grove Rd), 0.5 mi e, then 0.6 mi s on Gaither Rd. **Parking:** on-site. **Cards:** AX, DS, MC, VI.

SILVER DINER
Phone: 301/770-2828

American
$7-$13

The eatery with its chrome and glass plate exterior and the glow of neon, provides the traditional diner setting. Booths with juke boxes, counter service and friendly wait staff add to the diner experience. The menu is extensive with salads, sandwiches and full meals. The desserts are made fresh and the fountain treats, shakes, floats and malts make for a great ending. Breakfast is available all day. Casual dress. **Bar:** Beer & wine. **Reservations:** not accepted. **Hours:** 7 am-2 am, Fri & Sat-3 am. Closed: 12/25. **Address:** 11806 Rockville Pike 20852 **Location:** Just s of jct Montrose Rd; in Mid-Pike Plaza. **Parking:** on-site. **Cards:** AX, DC, DS, MC, VI.

CALL 🚹M

TARA THAI
Phone: 301/231-9899

Thai
$7-$14

The stylish cafe's sea motif is one aspect of its contemporary atmosphere. Specialties include whole fresh rockfish and skewered chicken, just to mention two. Most notable is the nicely presented goong phu-ket and pad thai noodles. Portion sizes are ample. Casual dress. **Bar:** Full bar. **Reservations:** accepted. **Hours:** 11:30 am-3 & 5-10 pm, Fri-11 pm, Sat noon-3:30 & 5-11 pm, Sun noon-3:30 & 5-10 pm. Closed: 11/27; also for lunch 12/25 & for lunch 1/1. **Address:** 12071 Rockville Pike 20852 **Location:** I-270, exit 4A (Montrose Rd), 2 mi e, then just n on SR 355; in Montrose Crossing Shopping Plaza. **Parking:** on-site. **Cards:** AX, DC, DS, MC, VI.

TASTE OF SAIGON
Phone: 301/424-7222   [25]

Vietnamese
$6-$24

The kitchen has maintained a consistent reputation for its preparations of Vietnamese dishes. Black pepper shrimp, lightly breaded in black pepper sauce and served with steamed rice, is a local favorite. In business since 1990, the family-run restaurant tucks behind an office building. Service is efficient both in the dining room and on the seasonal patio. Casual dress. **Bar:** Full bar. **Reservations:** accepted. **Hours:** 11 am-10 pm, Fri & Sat-11 pm, Sun-9:30 pm. Closed: 11/27, 12/25. **Address:** 410 Hungerford Dr 20850 **Location:** On SR 355, 0.5 mi n of SR 28. **Parking:** on-site. **Cards:** AX, DC, DS, MC, VI.

(See map and index starting on p. 408)

THAI FARM RESTAURANT   **Phone: 301/258-8829**

Thai
$6-$16
The colorful, green/yellow dining room, set on the ground floor of an office building, is decorated with muraled walls and lacquered table tops with rice farmers in the field. The kitchen uses fresh ingredients and does not use MSG. Menu selections allow diners to mix meats and seafood, as well as offers vegetarian dishes. Casual dress. **Bar:** Full bar. **Reservations:** accepted. **Hours:** 11:30 am-10 pm, Fri & Sat-10:30 pm, Sun 5 pm-10 pm. Closed major holidays. **Address:** 800 King Farm Blvd 20850 **Location:** I-270, exit 8 (Shady Grove Rd), 0.5 mi e, 0.6 mi s on Gaither Rd, then just w. **Parking:** on-site and street. **Cards:** AX, CB, DC, MC, VI.

TIMPANO ITALIAN CHOPHOUSE   **Phone: 301/881-6939**

Italian
$10-$36
The bi-level dining room is decorated in the theme of a classic, mid-50s, New York chophouse. Among specialties are one-pound center-cut pork chops and bone-in New York strip. Pasta, beef and seafood are prepared with an Italian touch. The lunch menu is presented until 4 pm. Dressy casual. **Bar:** Full bar. **Reservations:** suggested. **Hours:** 11 am-10 pm, Wed-Sat to 11 pm. Closed: 11/27. **Address:** 12021 Rockville Pike 20852 **Location:** I-270, exit 4A (Montrose Rd), 2 mi e, then just n on SR 355; in Montrose Crossing Shopping Plaza. **Parking:** on-site. **Cards:** AX, CB, DC, DS, MC, VI.

――――― *The following restaurant has not been evaluated by AAA* ―――――
but is listed for your information only.

SEVEN SEAS   **Phone: 301/770-5020**

[fyi]
Not evaluated. The restaurant specializes in northern Chinese cuisine with a flair of Taiwanese style. The menu has a variety of seafood, chicken, beef and noodle dishes to satisfy any appetite. **Address:** 1776 E Jefferson St 20852 **Location:** In Federal Plaza, around the back.

SILVER SPRING pop. 76,540   (See maps and indexes starting on p. 408, 428)

――――― **WHERE TO STAY** ―――――

COURTYARD BY MARRIOTT-SILVER SPRING   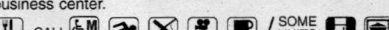   **Phone: 301/680-8500**

Small-scale Hotel
Rates not provided
Address: 12521 Prosperity Dr 20904 **Location:** I-95, exit 29B, just e of US 29 off Cherry Hill Rd, 1 mi sw on SR 212, then 1.8 mi w on Cherry Hill Rd; I-495, exit 30A, 4.3 mi n. **Facility:** Smoke free premises. 146 units. 134 one-bedroom standard units. 12 one-bedroom suites. 3 stories, interior corridors. *Bath:* combo or shower only. **Parking:** on-site. **Amenities:** high-speed Internet, voice mail, irons, hair dryers. **Pool(s):** heated indoor. **Leisure Activities:** whirlpool, exercise room. **Guest Services:** valet and coin laundry, wireless Internet. **Business Services:** meeting rooms, business center.

AAA Benefit:
Members save 5% off of the best available rate.

COURTYARD BY MARRIOTT-SILVER SPRING DOWNTOWN      **Phone: 301/589-4899**

Small-scale Hotel
Rates not provided
Address: 8506 Fenton St 20910 **Location:** I-495, exit 31B, 1.5 mi s on SR 97 (Georgia Ave), then just e on Wayne St; downtown. **Facility:** Smoke free premises. 179 units. 174 one-bedroom standard units, some with whirlpools. 5 one-bedroom suites. 10 stories, interior corridors. *Bath:* combo or shower only. **Parking:** on-site (fee). **Amenities:** video games (fee), high-speed Internet, voice mail, irons, hair dryers. **Pool(s):** heated indoor. **Guest Services:** valet and coin laundry, area transportation. **Business Services:** meeting rooms, PC.

AAA Benefit:
Members save 5% off of the best available rate.

CROWNE PLAZA WASHINGTON, D.C.-SILVER SPRINGS      **Phone: 301/589-0800**

[AAA] [SAVE]

Large-scale Hotel
$129-$299 All Year
Address: 8777 Georgia Ave 20910 **Location:** I-495, exit 31B, 1 mi s. Located in a commercial area. **Facility:** 231 units. 220 one-bedroom standard units. 11 one-bedroom suites. 16 stories, interior corridors. *Bath:* combo or shower only. **Parking:** on-site (fee) and valet. **Terms:** cancellation fee imposed. **Amenities:** CD players, dual phone lines, voice mail, irons, hair dryers. **Pool(s):** outdoor. **Leisure Activities:** exercise room. **Guest Services:** valet and coin laundry, area transportation-Silver Spring Metro & Walter Reed Medical Center, within 3 mi, wireless Internet. **Business Services:** conference facilities, business center. **Cards:** AX, CB, DC, DS, JC, MC, VI.

(See maps and indexes starting on p. 408, 428)

HILTON GARDEN INN

Small-scale Hotel

Under construction, scheduled to open October 2008. **Address:** 2200 Broadbirch Dr 20904 **Location:** On SR 29 (Columbia Pike), just s of jct Cherry Hill Rd. **Amenities:** microwaves, refrigerators, pool.

HILTON WASHINGTON DC/SILVER SPRING *Book great rates at AAA.com* **Phone:** (301)589-5200 **5**

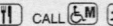  

Large-scale Hotel
$116-$296 3/1-11/30
$99-$260 12/1-2/28

Address: 8727 Colesville Rd 20910 **Location:** I-495, exit 30B, 1.5 mi s on US 29. Located in a commercial area. **Facility:** 263 units. 224 one-bedroom standard units. 39 one-bedroom suites. 11-13 stories, interior corridors. *Bath:* combo or shower only. **Parking:** valet. **Terms:** cancellation fee imposed. **Amenities:** video games (fee), high-speed Internet, dual phone lines, voice mail, irons, hair dryers. **Dining:** 2 restaurants. **Pool(s):** heated indoor. **Leisure Activities:** sauna, exercise room. **Guest Services:** valet laundry, area transportation-within 3 mi, Metro & Walter Reed Medical Center, wireless Internet. **Business Services:** conference facilities, business center. **Cards:** AX, CB, DC, DS, MC, VI. **Free Special Amenities:** newspaper and high-speed Internet. *(See color ad below)*

RESIDENCE INN BY MARRIOTT SILVER SPRING *Book great rates at AAA.com* **Phone:** 301/572-2322

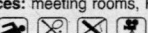

Small-scale Hotel
Rates not provided

Address: 12000 Plum Orchard Dr 20904 **Location:** I-95, exit 29B, 1.2 mi w on SR 212, then 1 mi n on Cherry Hill Rd. **Facility:** Smoke free premises. 130 units. 83 one-bedroom standard units with kitchens. 32 one- and 15 two-bedroom suites, some with efficiencies or kitchens. 4 stories, interior corridors. *Bath:* combo or shower only. **Parking:** on-site. **Amenities:** high-speed Internet, voice mail, irons, hair dryers. **Pool(s):** outdoor. **Leisure Activities:** whirlpool, limited exercise equipment, sports court. **Guest Services:** valet and coin laundry, wireless Internet. **Business Services:** meeting rooms, PC.

AAA Benefit:
Members save 5% off of the best available rate.

▼ *See AAA listing above* ▼

(See maps and indexes starting on p. 408, 428)

──────── WHERE TO DINE ────────

BOMBAY GAYLORD   Phone: 301/565-2528   ④

Indian
$5-$12

Authentic Indian cusine is offerd at this downtown Silver Spring restaurant. Tandoori specialties are some of the more popular selections, though the Chicken Tikka Masala and Butter Chicken are worth trying. Casual dress. **Bar:** Beer & wine. **Reservations:** accepted. **Hours:** 11:30 am-3 & 5-9:30 pm, Sat & Sun from noon. Closed: 1/1, 11/27, 12/25. **Address:** 8401 Georgia Ave 20910 **Location:** I-495, exit 31, 1.6 mi s on SR 97, just s of jct US 29 (Colesville Rd); downtown. **Parking:** no self-parking. **Cards:** AX, MC, VI.

CUBANO'S   Phone: 301/563-4020   ③

Cuban
$11-$27

The kitchen prepares authentic Cuban fare, with dishes such as the Cuban favorite, Ropa Vieja "Old Clothes" or Filete de Pescado a la Varadero. The setting is comfortable, with sidewalk walk dining available seasonally and the service is professional and efficient. Casual dress. **Bar:** Full bar. **Reservations:** suggested. **Hours:** 11:30 am-9 pm, Fri-10 pm, Sat noon-10 pm, Sun noon-9 pm. Closed: 11/27. **Address:** 1201 Fidler Ln 20910 **Location:** I-495, exit 31B, 1 mi s on SR 97, then 1 blk w. **Parking:** on-site (fee). **Cards:** AX, CB, DS, MC, VI.

EL GAVILAN   Phone: 301/587-4197   ②

Salvadoran
$5-$14

A favorite among the Salvadoran folks in town for ceviche and whole crispy fish, as well as a number of interesting combination platters featuring typical dishes as well as grilled shrimp, pork ribs and fajitas. Casual dress. **Bar:** Full bar. **Reservations:** accepted. **Hours:** 11 am-11 pm, Fri & Sat-12:30 am. **Address:** 8805 Flower Ave 20901 **Location:** Just n of jct SR 320 (Piney Branch Rd). **Parking:** on-site. **Cards:** AX, DC, DS, MC, VI.

MRS. K'S TOLL HOUSE   Phone: 301/589-3500   ①

American
$11-$34

Patrons first are struck by the charming atmosphere in the quaint, converted toll house. This well-established spot is attractive to a mixed crowd. The wait staff is efficient and gracious when serving the various prix fixe and a la carte menu selections. Dressy casual. **Bar:** Full bar. **Reservations:** suggested. **Hours:** 11:30 am-2:30 & 5-9 pm, Fri & Sat 11:30 am-2:30 & 4:30-9:30 pm, Sun 10:30 am-3 & 5-8 pm; Sunday brunch. Closed: 1/1, 7/4, 12/25; also Mon except Dec. **Address:** 9201 Colesville Rd 20910 **Location:** I-495, exit 30B, 0.8 mi s on US 29. **Parking:** on-site. **Cards:** AX, DC, DS, MC, VI. **Historic**

WHEATON   (See map and index starting on p. 408)

──────── WHERE TO DINE ────────

DUSIT THAI CUISINE   Phone: 301/949-4140   ㊶

Thai
$8-$12

The menu is long and the relative spiciness of each item is indicated. Among offerings are curries with or without coconut milk, fried rice, pad Thai and crispy whole fish. Casual dress. **Bar:** Full bar. **Reservations:** accepted. **Hours:** 11:30 am-10 pm, Fri & Sat-11 pm. Closed major holidays. **Address:** 2404 University Blvd W 20902 **Location:** Just e of jct SR 97 (Georgia Ave), on SR 193. **Parking:** on-site (fee). **Cards:** AX, DC, DS, MC, VI.

Nearby Virginia

ALEXANDRIA pop. 128,283   (See maps and indexes starting on p. 412, 426)

——— WHERE TO STAY ———

BEST WESTERN-OLD COLONY INN   *Book great rates at AAA.com*   **Phone:** (703)739-2222

Small-scale Hotel
$139-$199 All Year

Address: 1101 N Washington St 22314 **Location:** George Washington Memorial Pkwy; jct Second and Washington sts. **Facility:** 49 one-bedroom standard units. 2 stories (no elevator), interior corridors. **Parking:** on-site. **Terms:** cancellation fee imposed. **Amenities:** video library, DVD players, high-speed Internet, irons, hair dryers. **Leisure Activities:** sauna, whirlpool, exercise room. **Guest Services:** valet laundry, airport transportation-Ronald Reagan Washington National Airport, area transportation-King St & metro. **Business Services:** meeting rooms, business center. **Cards:** AX, DC, DS, MC, VI. **Free Special Amenities:** full breakfast and high-speed Internet.

AAA Benefit:
Members save 10% everyday, plus an exclusive frequent stay program.

COMFORT INN ALEXANDRIA   *Book great rates at AAA.com*   **Phone:** (703)922-9200   **101**

Small-scale Hotel
$99-$105 3/1-10/31
$79-$89 11/1-2/28

Address: 5716 S Van Dorn St 22310 **Location:** I-95/495, exit 173, 2 mi e of jct I-395 and 495. **Facility:** 169 units. 151 one-bedroom standard units. 18 one-bedroom suites, some with whirlpools. 9 stories, interior corridors. **Parking:** on-site. **Terms:** 45 day cancellation notice. **Amenities:** voice mail, safes (fee), irons, hair dryers. *Some:* high-speed Internet, dual phone lines. **Pool(s):** outdoor. **Leisure Activities:** limited exercise equipment. **Guest Services:** valet and coin laundry, area transportation, wireless Internet. **Business Services:** meeting rooms. **Cards:** AX, DC, DS, MC, VI.

COURTYARD BY MARRIOTT-ALEXANDRIA   *Book great rates at AAA.com*   **Phone:** 703/329-2323   **12**

Small-scale Hotel
$263-$318 All Year

Address: 2700 Eisenhower Ave 22314 **Location:** I-95/495, exit 174 (Eisenhower Ave Connector), just n, then 1.7 mi e of Telegraph Rd. **Facility:** Smoke free premises. 176 one-bedroom standard units. 8 stories, interior corridors. *Bath:* combo or shower only. **Parking:** on-site. **Amenities:** high-speed Internet, voice mail, irons, hair dryers. **Leisure Activities:** exercise room. **Guest Services:** valet and coin laundry, area transportation. **Business Services:** meeting rooms, PC. **Cards:** AX, DC, DS, MC, VI.

AAA Benefit:
Members save 5% off of the best available rate.

COURTYARD BY MARRIOTT ALEXANDRIA PENTAGON SOUTH   *Book great rates at AAA.com*   **Phone:** 703/751-4510   **97**

Small-scale Hotel
$230-$285 All Year

Address: 4641 Kenmore Ave 22304 **Location:** I-395, exit 4, 0.8 mi s of jct SR 7. **Facility:** Smoke free premises. 203 units. 196 one-bedroom standard units. 7 one-bedroom suites. 11 stories, interior corridors. *Bath:* combo or shower only. **Parking:** on-site (fee). **Amenities:** dual phone lines, voice mail, irons, hair dryers. **Pool(s):** heated indoor. **Leisure Activities:** whirlpool, exercise room. **Guest Services:** valet and coin laundry, area transportation, wireless Internet. **Business Services:** meeting rooms, PC. **Cards:** AX, DC, DS, JC, MC, VI.

AAA Benefit:
Members save 5% off of the best available rate.

THE CROWNE PLAZA OLD TOWN ALEXANDRIA   *Book great rates at AAA.com*   **Phone:** (703)683-6000   **3**

Large-scale Hotel
$109-$329 All Year

Address: 901 N Fairfax St 22314 **Location:** Between 1st St and Montgomery. Located in Old Town. **Facility:** 253 units. 249 one-bedroom standard units. 4 one-bedroom suites. 12 stories, interior corridors. *Bath:* combo or shower only. **Parking:** on-site (fee). **Amenities:** high-speed Internet, dual phone lines, voice mail, irons, hair dryers. **Pool(s):** outdoor. **Leisure Activities:** exercise room. **Guest Services:** valet laundry, area transportation, wireless Internet. **Business Services:** conference facilities, PC (fee). **Cards:** AX, CB, DC, DS, JC, MC, VI.

EMBASSY SUITES-ALEXANDRIA-OLD TOWN   *Book at AAA.com*   **Phone:** 703/684-5900   **7**

Large-scale Hotel
Rates not provided

Address: 1900 Diagonal Rd 22314 **Location:** I-95/495, exit 176, 0.5 mi n on SR 241 N, then 0.5 mi e on SR 236. Located opposite Amtrak and King St Metro Station, in Old Town. **Facility:** 268 units. 266 one- and 2 two-bedroom suites. 8 stories, interior corridors. *Bath:* combo or shower only. **Parking:** on-site (fee). **Amenities:** dual phone lines, voice mail, irons, hair dryers. *Fee:* video games, high-speed Internet. **Pool(s):** heated indoor. **Leisure Activities:** sauna, whirlpool, exercise room. **Guest Services:** valet and coin laundry, area transportation, wireless Internet. **Business Services:** conference facilities, PC.

(See maps and indexes starting on p. 412, 426)

EXTENDED STAYAMERICA-WASHINGTON, DC-ALEXANDRIA   *Book at AAA.com*   Phone: (703)941-9440   **99**

Small-scale Hotel
$164-$174 All Year

Address: 205 N Breckinridge Pl 22312 Location: I-395, exit 3B, 0.3 mi w on SR 236, 0.4 mi ne on Beauregard St, just e on Gloucester Rd, then just s. Located near a shopping center. Facility: 104 one-bedroom standard units with efficiencies. 3 stories, interior corridors. Parking: on-site. Terms: office hours 7 am-11 pm. Amenities: voice mail, irons, hair dryers. Guest Services: coin laundry, wireless Internet. Cards: AX, DC, DS, JC, MC, VI.

HAMPTON INN-ALEXANDRIA   *Book great rates at AAA.com*   Phone: (703)671-4800   **95**

Small-scale Hotel
$149-$299 All Year

Address: 4800 Leesburg Pike 22302 Location: I-395, exit 5, 1 mi w on SR 7; in Baileys Crossroads area. Located in a commercial area. Facility: 130 one-bedroom standard units. 4 stories, interior corridors. Parking: on-site. Amenities: video games (fee), dual phone lines, voice mail, irons, hair dryers. Pool(s): heated outdoor. Leisure Activities: exercise room. Guest Services: valet laundry, wireless Internet. Business Services: business center. Cards: AX, CB, DC, DS, MC, VI.

HAMPTON INN ALEXANDRIA/OLD TOWN AREA-SOUTH   *Book great rates at AAA.com*   Phone: (703)329-1400   **102**

Small-scale Hotel
$129-$209 All Year

Address: 5821 Richmond Hwy 22303 Location: I-95/495, exit 177A, just s on US 1. Facility: 156 one-bedroom standard units, some with whirlpools. 7 stories, interior corridors. Bath: combo or shower only. Parking: on-site. Amenities: high-speed Internet, dual phone lines, voice mail, irons, hair dryers. Pool(s): outdoor. Leisure Activities: exercise room. Guest Services: valet and coin laundry, area transportation, wireless Internet. Business Services: meeting rooms, business center. Cards: AX, CB, DC, DS, MC, VI.

HAMPTON INN OLD TOWN KING STREET METRO   *Book great rates at AAA.com*   Phone: (703)299-9900   **6**

Small-scale Hotel
$179-$309 All Year

Address: 1616 King St 22314 Location: I-95/495, exit 176B, 0.5 mi n on SR 241, 0.5 mi e on SR 236, then just ne on Diagonal Rd. Located in Old Town. Facility: 80 units. 75 one-bedroom standard units. 5 one-bedroom suites. 6 stories, interior corridors. Bath: combo or shower only. Parking: on-site (fee). Terms: cancellation fee imposed. Amenities: video games (fee), dual phone lines, voice mail, irons, hair dryers. Pool(s): outdoor. Leisure Activities: limited exercise equipment. Guest Services: valet and coin laundry, wireless Internet. Business Services: meeting rooms, business center. Cards: AX, CB, DC, DS, MC, VI.

HAWTHORN SUITES LTD-ALEXANDRIA   *Book at AAA.com*   Phone: (703)370-1000   **98**

Small-scale Hotel
$210-$240 3/1-7/31
$180-$210 8/1-2/28

Address: 420 N Van Dorn St 22304 Location: I-395, exit 3A, 0.3 mi e on SR 236 to S Van Dorn St, then 0.5 mi n. Facility: 185 units. 89 one-bedroom standard units with efficiencies. 88 one- and 8 two-bedroom suites. 9 stories, interior corridors. Bath: combo or shower only. Parking: on-site. Terms: cancellation fee imposed. Amenities: CD players, voice mail, irons, hair dryers. Pool(s): outdoor. Leisure Activities: exercise room. Guest Services: valet and coin laundry, area transportation, wireless Internet. Business Services: meeting rooms, PC. Cards: AX, DC, DS, MC, VI.

HILTON ALEXANDRIA MARK CENTER   *Book great rates at AAA.com*   Phone: 703/845-1010   **96**

Large-scale Hotel
Rates not provided

Address: 5000 Seminary Rd 22311 Location: I-395, exit 4, just w. Facility: 496 units. 482 one-bedroom standard units, some with whirlpools. 14 one-bedroom suites, some with whirlpools. 5-30 stories, interior corridors. Bath: combo or shower only. Parking: on-site (fee) and valet. Amenities: video games (fee), dual phone lines, voice mail, irons, hair dryers. Some: high-speed Internet (fee). Pool(s): heated indoor/outdoor. Leisure Activities: jogging, exercise room. Guest Services: valet laundry, area transportation, barber shop, wireless Internet. Business Services: conference facilities, business center.

HILTON ALEXANDRIA OLD TOWN   *Book great rates at AAA.com*   Phone: 703/837-0440   **5**

Large-scale Hotel
Rates not provided

Address: 1767 King St 22314 Location: I-95/495, exit 176B, 0.5 mi n on SR 241, 0.5 mi e on SR 236, then just ne on Diagonal Rd. Located adjacent to Amtrak and Metro Station, in Old Town. Facility: 247 units. 228 one-bedroom standard units. 19 one-bedroom suites, some with whirlpools. 7 stories, interior corridors. Bath: combo or shower only. Parking: on-site (fee). Terms: check-in 4 pm. Amenities: video games (fee), high-speed Internet, dual phone lines, voice mail, safes, irons, hair dryers. Dining: Seagar's, see separate listing. Pool(s): heated indoor. Leisure Activities: sauna, exercise room. Guest Services: valet laundry, wireless Internet. Business Services: conference facilities, business center.

HOLIDAY INN EISENHOWER METRO   *Book at AAA.com*   Phone: (703)960-3400   **13**

Small-scale Hotel
$190-$220 All Year

Address: 2460 Eisenhower Ave 22314 Location: I-95/495, exit 176B, just e on Pershing Ave, then s on Stovall Rd; jct Telegraph Rd (SR 214 N) and I-95/495. Facility: 196 one-bedroom standard units. 10 stories, interior corridors. Bath: combo or shower only. Parking: on-site. Amenities: voice mail, irons, hair dryers. Pool(s): heated indoor. Leisure Activities: exercise room. Guest Services: valet and coin laundry, area transportation, wireless Internet. Business Services: meeting rooms, PC (fee). Cards: AX, CB, DC, DS, JC, MC, VI.

(See maps and indexes starting on p. 412, 426)

**HOLIDAY INN HOTEL & SUITES-HISTORIC
DISTRICT ALEXANDRIA** *Book great rates at AAA.com*   **Phone:** (703)548-6300

Small-scale Hotel
$119-$259 All Year

Address: 625 First St 22314 **Location:** George Washington Memorial Pkwy, just e of jct First and Washington sts. Located in Old Town. **Facility:** 178 units. 161 one-bedroom standard units. 17 one-bedroom suites, some with whirlpools. 4 stories, interior corridors. *Bath:* combo or shower only. **Parking:** on-site (fee). **Amenities:** video games (fee), voice mail, irons, hair dryers. **Pool(s):** heated indoor/outdoor. **Leisure Activities:** saunas, whirlpool, exercise room. **Guest Services:** valet and coin laundry, area transportation, wireless Internet. **Business Services:** conference facilities, business center. **Cards:** AX, CB, DC, DS, JC, MC, VI.

HOMESTEAD STUDIO SUITES HOTEL-ALEXANDRIA *Book at AAA.com*   **Phone:** (703)329-3399 9

Small-scale Hotel
$164-$174 All Year

Address: 200 Bluestone Rd 22304 **Location:** I-95/495, exit 174 (Eisenhower Ave Connector), just n to Eisenhower Ave, then 1.2 mi e. **Facility:** 132 one-bedroom standard units with efficiencies. 3 stories, interior corridors. *Bath:* combo or shower only. **Parking:** on-site. **Terms:** office hours 7 am-11 pm. **Amenities:** voice mail, irons, hair dryers. **Guest Services:** coin laundry, wireless Internet. **Business Services:** meeting rooms. **Cards:** AX, DC, DS, JC, MC, VI.

HOMEWOOD SUITES BY HILTON-ALEXANDRIA *Book at AAA.com*   **Phone:** 703/671-6500 94

Small-scale Hotel
Rates not provided

Address: 4850 Leesburg Pike 22302 **Location:** I-395, exit 5, 1 mi w on SR 7; in Baileys Crossroads area. Located in a commercial area. **Facility:** 105 units. 98 one- and 7 two-bedroom suites with efficiencies, some with whirlpools. 5 stories, interior corridors. *Bath:* combo or shower only. **Parking:** on-site. **Amenities:** video games (fee), high-speed Internet, dual phone lines, voice mail, irons, hair dryers. **Pool(s):** outdoor. **Leisure Activities:** whirlpool, exercise room. **Guest Services:** valet and coin laundry, wireless Internet. **Business Services:** meeting rooms, business center.

HOTEL MONACO ALEXANDRIA   **Phone:** (703)549-6080 8

[fyi]
Large-scale Hotel
$149-$459 All Year

Under major renovation, scheduled to be completed October 2007. **Last rated:** ♥♥♥ **Address:** 480 King St 22314 **Location:** On SR 7; between S Pitt and S Royal sts; just sw of City Hall. Located in Old Town. **Facility:** 241 units. 229 one-bedroom standard units. 12 one-bedroom suites, some with whirlpools. 6 stories, interior corridors. *Bath:* combo or shower only. **Parking:** valet. **Terms:** cancellation fee imposed. **Amenities:** DVD players, dual phone lines, voice mail, safes, honor bars, irons, hair dryers. *Some:* high-speed Internet. **Pool(s):** heated indoor. **Leisure Activities:** bicycles, exercise room. **Guest Services:** valet laundry, area transportation, wireless Internet. **Business Services:** conference facilities, business center. **Cards:** AX, CB, DC, DS, MC, VI.

MORRISON HOUSE *Book great rates at AAA.com*   **Phone:** (703)838-8000 10

(AAA) [SAVE]
♥♥♥ ♥♥♥
Small-scale Hotel
$169-$469 All Year

Address: 116 S Alfred St 22314 **Location:** Jct King and S Alfred sts, just s; in Old Town. **Facility:** The elegant, Federal-style hotel provides a comfortable setting for overnight guests; rooms have period reproductions and marble baths. Smoke free premises. 45 units. 42 one-bedroom standard units. 3 one-bedroom suites. 5 stories, interior corridors. **Parking:** valet. **Terms:** cancellation fee imposed. **Amenities:** safes, hair dryers. *Some:* DVD players, irons. **Dining:** The Grille, see separate listing. **Guest Services:** valet laundry, wireless Internet. **Business Services:** meeting rooms. **Fee:** PC, fax. **Cards:** AX, CB, DC, DS, MC, VI. *(See color ad below)*

(See maps and indexes starting on p. 412, 426)

RED ROOF INN-ALEXANDRIA   *Book at AAA.com*   Phone: 703/960-5200   104

Motel
Rates not provided

Address: 5975 Richmond Hwy 22303 **Location:** I-95/495, exit 177A, 0.5 mi s on US 1. **Facility:** 115 one-bedroom standard units. 3 stories, exterior corridors. **Bath:** combo or shower only. **Parking:** on-site. **Amenities:** video games (fee), voice mail. *Some:* irons. **Guest Services:** coin laundry, wireless Internet.

RESIDENCE INN BY MARRIOTT ALEXANDRIA-OLD TOWN   *Book great rates at AAA.com*   Phone: 703/548-5474   11

Small-scale Hotel
$307-$340 All Year

Address: 1456 Duke St 22314 **Location:** I-95/495, exit 176, 0.5 mi n on SR 241, then 0.7 mi e on SR 236. Located in Old Town. **Facility:** Smoke free premises. 240 units. 114 one-bedroom standard units with efficiencies. 108 one- and 18 two-bedroom suites, some with efficiencies or kitchens. 8 stories, interior corridors. **Bath:** combo or shower only. **Parking:** on-site (fee). **Amenities:** video games (fee), high-speed Internet, dual phone lines, voice mail, irons, hair dryers. **Pool(s):** heated indoor. **Leisure Activities:** exercise room. **Guest Services:** valet and coin laundry, area transportation. **Business Services:** meeting rooms. **Cards:** AX, DC, DS, JC, MC, VI.

AAA Benefit:
Members save 5% off of the best available rate.

SHERATON SUITES OLD TOWN ALEXANDRIA   *Book great rates at AAA.com*   Phone: (703)836-4700   4

Small-scale Hotel
$119-$379 All Year

Address: 801 N St Asaph St 22314 **Location:** Just e of Washington St. Located in Old Town. **Facility:** 247 one-bedroom suites. 10 stories, interior corridors. **Bath:** some combo or shower only. **Parking:** on-site (fee). **Terms:** cancellation fee imposed. **Amenities:** voice mail, irons, hair dryers. *Fee:* video games, high-speed Internet. *Some:* dual phone lines, fax. **Pool(s):** heated indoor. **Leisure Activities:** whirlpool, sun deck, exercise room. **Guest Services:** complimentary and valet laundry, airport transportation-Ronald Reagan Washington National Airport, area transportation-National Airport Metro, wireless Internet. **Business Services:** meeting rooms, PC (fee). **Cards:** AX, CB, DC, DS, MC, VI. *(See color ad below)*

AAA Benefit:
Members get up to 15% off, plus Starwood Preferred Guest® bonuses.

TRAVELERS MOTEL   *Book great rates at AAA.com*   Phone: 703/329-1310   103

Motel
$69-$89 All Year

Address: 5916 Richmond Hwy 22303 **Location:** I-95/495, exit 177A, just s on US 1. **Facility:** 29 one-bedroom standard units. 1 story, exterior corridors. **Parking:** on-site. **Amenities:** high-speed Internet. **Guest Services:** area transportation-Huntington Metro, wireless Internet. **Cards:** AX, CB, DC, DS, MC, VI. **Free Special Amenities:** high-speed Internet.

▼ *See AAA listing above* ▼

▼ See AAA listing p 505 ▼

(See maps and indexes starting on p. 412, 426)

WASHINGTON SUITES-ALEXANDRIA *Book great rates at AAA.com*   **Phone:** (703)370-9600   100

Small-scale Hotel
$159-$409 All Year

Address: 100 S Reynolds St 22304 **Location:** I-395, exit 3A, 0.8 mi e on SR 236 E (Duke St), then just s; near a shopping center. **Facility:** 224 units. 68 one-bedroom standard units with kitchens. 124 one- and 32 two-bedroom suites with kitchens. 9 stories, interior corridors. *Bath:* combo or shower only. **Parking:** on-site. **Terms:** cancellation fee imposed. **Amenities:** high-speed Internet, dual phone lines, voice mail, irons, hair dryers. **Pool(s):** outdoor. **Leisure Activities:** putting green, sun deck, exercise room. **Guest Services:** valet and coin laundry, area transportation-within 1 mi, Van Dorn Metro & Landmark Mall, wireless Internet. **Business Services:** meeting rooms, business center. **Cards:** AX, CB, DC, DS, JC, MC, VI. **Free Special Amenities:** expanded continental breakfast and high-speed Internet.
(See color ad p 504)

THE WESTIN ALEXANDRIA   **Phone:** 703/253-8600

(fyi)
Small-scale Hotel
$399 All Year

Too new to rate, opening scheduled for November 2007. **Address:** 400 Courthouse Square 22314 **Location:** I-495, exit 1. **Amenities:** 319 units, pets, coffeemakers, refrigerators, pool. **Terms:** cancellation fee imposed. **Cards:** AX, DC, DS, JC, MC, VI.

WESTIN
HOTELS & RESORTS

AAA Benefit:
Members get up to 15% off, plus Starwood Preferred Guest® bonuses.

——— WHERE TO DINE ———

AKASAKA   **Phone:** 703/751-3133   130

Japanese
$8-$20

Tucked in the South Van Dorn Street Station shopping plaza, the little Japanese gem specializes in sushi prepared from fresh fish, with selections varying based on availability. Crisply fried tempura, buckwheat noodles and teriyaki dishes are other options. Casual dress. **Bar:** Beer & wine. **Reservations:** accepted. **Hours:** 11:30 am-2:30 & 5-10 pm, Fri-10:30 pm, Sat noon-10:30 pm, Sun 4:30 pm-9:30 pm. Closed major holidays. **Address:** 514-C S Van Dorn St 22304 **Location:** I-95/495, exit 173, 1 mi n on SR 613; in Van Dorn Station Shopping Plaza. **Parking:** on-site. **Cards:** AX, DC, MC, VI.

AUSTIN GRILL   **Phone:** 703/684-8969

Regional Mexican
$7-$19

This Old Town restaurant prepares its many Tex-Mex selections from scratch, such as delicious enchiladas, burritos and fajitas. The fun and lively atmosphere starts in the lounge and at times spills over into the dining room. Casual dress. **Bar:** Full bar. **Hours:** 11:30 am-11 pm, Fri-midnight, Sat 11 am-midnight, Sun 11 am-10:30 pm, Mon 11:30 am-10:30 pm. Closed: 11/27, 12/25; also for dinner 12/24. **Address:** 801 King St 22314 **Location:** Just w of Washington St; in Old Town. **Parking:** street. **Cards:** AX, DC, DS, MC, VI.

BILBO BAGGINS   **Phone:** 703/683-0300   5

International
$8-$24

The menu features a nice selection of salad, pasta, full meals and homemade dessert, in addition to a variety of wines and micro-brewed beers. The casual and cozy dining rooms occupy three row houses and portray a rustic, intimate atmosphere inside. Casual dress. **Bar:** Full bar. **Hours:** 11:30 am-2:30 & 5:30-10:30 pm, Fri & Sat 11 am-midnight, Sun 11 am-9:30 pm. Closed: 7/4, 11/27, 12/25. **Address:** 208 Queen St 22314 **Location:** Between Fairfax and Lee sts; in Old Town. **Parking:** street. **Cards:** AX, CB, DC, DS, MC, VI.

BOMBAY CURRY COMPANY   **Phone:** 703/836-6363   122

Indian
$5-$12

The neighborhood restaurant is simple in appearance but rich in menu complexity. Piquant flavors tinge the well-prepared dishes, ranging from curries to kabobs. The fresh-baked bread is worth the extra cost. A lunch buffet is served on Sunday. Casual dress. **Bar:** Beer & wine. **Reservations:** accepted. **Hours:** 11:30 am-2:30 & 5:30-9:30 pm, Fri-10 pm, Sat 11:30 am-2:30 & 5-10 pm, Sun 11:30 am-2:30 & 5-9:30 pm. Closed: 11/27, 12/25. **Address:** 3110 Mt Vernon Ave 22305 **Location:** Jct W Glebe Rd and Mt Vernon Ave; at Calvert Apartment Building. **Parking:** on-site. **Cards:** AX, CB, DC, DS, MC, VI.

CHEZ ANDREE   **Phone:** 703/836-1404   121

French
$8-$27

The classic, family-owned French restaurant has been pleasing locals for more than 40 years. A French feel punctuates the comfortable setting. Food is well prepared, and servers are friendly. Dressy casual. **Bar:** Full bar. **Reservations:** suggested. **Hours:** 11 am-2:30 & 5-9:30 pm, Sat from 5 pm. Closed major holidays; also Sun. **Address:** 10 E Glebe Rd 22305 **Location:** 0.4 mi w of US 1. **Parking:** on-site. **Cards:** AX, CB, DC, MC, VI.

CLYDE'S AT MARK CENTER   **Phone:** 703/820-8300   123

American
$6-$26

Ideal for any occasion, Clyde's at Mark Center offers three different settings, as well as outdoor dining, weather permitting. The menu ranges from soups and salads to sandwiches and full meals. Casual dress. **Bar:** Full bar. **Reservations:** suggested. **Hours:** 11 am-10 pm, Fri & Sat-midnight, Sun 4 pm-10 pm. Closed: 12/25. **Address:** 1700 N Beauregard St 22311 **Location:** I-395, exit 4, 0.3 mi w on Seminary Rd, then 0.3 mi s. **Parking:** on-site. **Cards:** AX, DC, DS, MC, VI.

(See maps and indexes starting on p. 412, 426)

EVENING STAR CAFE'
Phone: 703/549-5051

American
$7-$25

The neighborhood restaurant nurtures a funky, eclectic air, with red laminated tabletops, black-and-white-checkered floor tiles and exposed ceiling ducts. The kitchen prepares modern American dishes, which the chef changes seasonally. Casual dress. **Bar:** Full bar. **Reservations:** not accepted. **Hours:** 11:30 am-2:30 & 5:30-10 pm, Fri & Sat-11 pm, Sun 10 am-3 & 5:30-10 pm, Mon 5:30 pm-10 pm; Sunday brunch. Closed major holidays. **Address:** 2000 Mt. Vernon Ave 22301 **Location:** Just n of jct Monroe Ave; in the Del Ray area. **Parking:** street. **Cards:** AX, DC, DS, MC, VI.

GADSBY'S TAVERN
Phone: 703/548-1288 (11)

American
$8-$36

Experience Colonial dining in an 18th-century tavern at this quaint restaurant. A strolling minstrel performs on the lute or violin as servers in period attire cater attentively to diners' needs. The George Washington duck and prime rib are exquisite. Dressy casual. **Bar:** Full bar. **Reservations:** suggested. **Hours:** 11:30 am-3 & 5:30-10 pm, Sun from 11 am; Sunday brunch. Closed: 1/1, 12/25. **Address:** 138 N Royal St 22314 **Location:** Just n of King St; in Old Town. **Parking:** street. **Cards:** AX, DS, MC, VI. **Historic**

GENEROUS GEORGE'S POSITIVE PIZZA & PASTA PLACE
Phone: 703/370-4303 (3)

Italian
$7-$15

Bring the family and a smile to this bright, eclectic and lively eatery boasting 1970s kitchen tables with mismatched chairs. The pizza overflows with your choice of toppings and the pasta is notable. The service staff is young, efficient and friendly. Casual dress. **Bar:** Beer & wine. **Hours:** 11 am-10 pm, Fri & Sat-11 pm. Closed: 11/27, 12/25. **Address:** 3006 Duke St 22314 **Location:** I-95/495, exit 176, 0.7 mi n on SR 241 (Telegraph Rd), then 0.4 mi w on SR 236. **Parking:** on-site. **Cards:** AX, DS, MC, VI.

GERANIO RESTAURANT
Phone: 703/548-0088 (12)

Italian
$8-$30

Freshly cut roses, fireside tables and candlelight dining all contribute to a romantic and beautiful fine-dining atmosphere. The menu is varied and the servers knowledgeable. Dressy casual. **Bar:** Full bar. **Reservations:** suggested. **Hours:** 11:30 am-2:30 & 6-10:30 pm, Sat from 6 pm, Sun 5:30 pm-9:30 pm. Closed: 1/1, 11/27, 12/25. **Address:** 722 King St 22314 **Location:** Just w of Washington St; in Old Town. **Parking:** street. **Cards:** AX, DC, DS, MC, VI.

THE GRILLE
Phone: 703/838-8000 (14)

American
$23-$36

Inside the elegant 18th-century-style Morrison House in the Old Town area, the restaurant displays a Federalist period style, with individually lit paintings and high-quality table settings and linens. The kitchen skillfully prepares seasonally changing American cuisine. Professional servers make guests feel relaxed and see to their needs. Dressy casual. **Bar:** Full bar. **Reservations:** suggested. **Hours:** 7 am-10 & 6-9 pm, Fri-10 pm, Sat 8 am-10 & 6-10 pm, Sun 8 am-10 & 6-9 pm. **Address:** 116 S Alfred St 22314 **Location:** Jct King and S Alfred sts, just s; in Old Town; in Morrison House. **Parking:** on-site (fee) and valet. **Cards:** AX, CB, DC, DS, JC, MC, VI.

HARD TIMES CAFE
Phone: 703/837-0050

American
$6-$15

The hot and spicy, down-home operation knocks your socks off with an impressive variety of chilies, cooked in styles ranging from Cincinnati to Texas and vegetarian. Casual dress. **Bar:** Full bar. **Hours:** 11 am-1 am. **Address:** 1404 King St 22314 **Location:** 2 blks w of US 1; in Old Town. **Parking:** street. **Cards:** AX, MC, VI.

ILLUSIONS THAI CAFE
Phone: 703/575-1999 (125)

Thai
$6-$15

In a shopping plaza, the moderately tropical dining room has hand-painted walls and a glowing blacklight ceiling. The menu lists many traditional Thai favorites, and panang salmon is a specialty. The staff is friendly and attentive. Casual dress. **Bar:** Full bar. **Reservations:** suggested. **Hours:** 11:30 am-3 & 5-10 pm, Fri-11 pm, Sat noon-11 pm, Sun 1 pm-10 pm. Closed: 7/4, 11/27, 12/25. **Address:** 1472 N Beauregard St 22311 **Location:** I-395, exit 4, 0.3 mi w on Seminary Rd, then 0.4 mi s; in The Shops at Mark Center. **Parking:** on-site. **Cards:** AX, DC, MC, VI.

IL PORTO RISTORANTE
Phone: 703/836-8833 (16)

Northern Italian
$8-$22

Serving traditional Italian dishes for more than 20 years, the local favorite offers pasta, veal and seafood selections in a rustic cafe setting. Casual dress. **Bar:** Full bar. **Reservations:** suggested. **Hours:** 11 am-10 pm, Fri & Sat-midnight. Closed: 11/27. **Address:** 121 King St 22314 **Location:** At N Lee St; in Old Town. **Parking:** street. **Cards:** AX, DS, MC, VI.

INDIGO LANDING
Phone: 703/548-0001 (124)

American
$8-$29

Diners can watch jets take off and land at Ronald Reagan Washington National Airport or gaze out at the Potomac River as they eat. The kitchen prepares regional American cooking, focusing on the Lowcountry cuisine distinctive to South Carolina. Ingredients are fresh and authentic. The staff is helpful and attentive, and the setting is comfortable with a stylish design. Dressy casual. **Bar:** Full bar. **Reservations:** suggested. **Hours:** 11:30 am-3 & 5-10 pm, Fri & Sat-11 pm, Sun 10 am-3 & 5-9 pm. Closed major holidays. **Address:** 1 Marina Dr 22314 **Location:** On George Washington Memorial Pkwy, at Washington Sailing Marina; 1 mi n of Old Town; 3.8 mi s of 14th Street Bridge. **Parking:** on-site. **Cards:** AX, MC, VI.

KING STREET BLUES
Phone: 703/313-0400

American
$7-$15

The shopping center eatery sustains a roadhouse atmosphere, with colorful characters hanging from the walls and ceilings. Examples of Southern comfort food include smoked ribs, barbecue pork and chicken, meatloaf, fried chicken and real po' boys. Chips are made fresh and fried in peanut oil, and hand-cut fries also boast above-average freshness. Casual dress. **Bar:** Full bar. **Reservations:** accepted, weekdays. **Hours:** 11 am-10 pm, Fri & Sat-11 pm, Sun-9:30 pm. Closed: 7/4, 11/27, 12/25. **Address:** 5810 Kingstowne Center 22315 **Location:** I-95/495, exit 173, 1.6 mi s of S Van Dorn St; in Kingstowne Center. **Parking:** on-site. **Cards:** AX, DC, DS, MC, VI.

CALL

(See maps and indexes starting on p. 412, 426)

KING STREET BLUES   Phone: 703/836-8800

American
$7-$18

Tasty Southern cooking is the specialty at the bi-level townhouse, which was a fun, roadhouse-style atmosphere. The Elwood, with smoked shredded pork barbecue, is a favorite. Casual dress. **Bar:** Full bar. **Reservations:** accepted. **Hours:** 11:30 am-10 pm, Fri & Sat-11 pm, Sun 11 am-10 pm. **Address:** 112 N St. Asaph St 22314 **Location:** Just n of King St; in Old Town. **Parking:** street. **Cards:** AX, DS, MC, VI.

LA BERGERIE   Phone: 703/683-1007   6

French
$13-$35
The well-established French restaurant is on the second floor of a historic brick warehouse in Old Town. The dining room, with its brick walls and fresh flowers, sustains an intimate atmosphere. Among specialties are lobster bisque, veal chops and Maryland wild rockfish. Dessert souffles are worth saving room for. Semi-formal attire. **Bar:** Full bar. **Reservations:** suggested. **Hours:** 11:30 am-2:30 & 5:30-9:30 pm, Fri & Sat-10:30 pm, Sun 5 pm-9 pm. Closed major holidays. **Address:** 218 N Lee St 22314 **Location:** 2 blks n of King St; in Old Town. **Parking:** street. **Cards:** AX, CB, DC, DS, MC, VI.

LANDINI BROTHERS   Phone: 703/836-8404   18

Italian
$17-$30
Family owned and operated, this restaurant has been a fixture of Old Alexandria for years. Guests are wise to come with an appetite, as the food is dished in plentiful portions. Desserts also merit consideration. The lunch menu is presented until 3 pm. Dressy casual. **Bar:** Full bar. **Reservations:** suggested. **Hours:** 11:30 am-10 pm. Closed major holidays. **Address:** 115 King St 22314 **Location:** In Old Town. **Parking:** street. **Cards:** AX, CB, DC, DS, MC, VI.

LA PIAZZA   Phone: 703/519-7711   2
Italian
$6-$16
Generous portions of home-style Southern Italian cooking is available to locals and commuters for dine-in or take-out. Light and fluffy involtini, with delicately balanced marinara is a favorite. Add a crisp, fresh salad and oven-baked garlic bread for a casual, simply delicious meal. Casual dress. **Bar:** Beer & wine. **Hours:** 11:30 am-3 & 5-9:30 pm. Closed major holidays; also 12/25-1/2. **Address:** 535 E Braddock Rd 22314 **Location:** At West St; opposite Braddock Rd metro station. **Parking:** on-site. **Cards:** DS, MC, VI.

LE GAULOIS   Phone: 703/739-9494   7
French
$8-$25
The intimate restaurant nurtures the mood of a French country cafe with its cozy fireplace and many plants. Set between two row houses, the outdoor garden area evokes a European air. The menu lists an extensive selection of hearty dishes. The lunch menu is presented until 4 pm. Casual dress. **Bar:** Full bar. **Reservations:** suggested, weekends. **Hours:** 11:30 am-10:30 pm, Fri & Sat-11 pm, Sun-9:30 pm. Closed: 12/25; also for lunch 1/1. **Address:** 1106 King St 22314 **Location:** Just w of US 1 S; in Old Town. **Parking:** street. **Cards:** AX, CB, DC, DS, MC, VI.

THE MAJESTIC   Phone: 703/837-9117   9
American
$9-$22
In the heart of Old Town, The Majestic provides very well-prepared, modern American cuisine. Casual dress. **Bar:** Full bar. **Reservations:** suggested, weekends. **Hours:** 11:30 am-2:30 & 5:30-10 pm, Fri-11 pm, Sat 5:30 pm-11 pm, Sun 11 am-2:30 & 5:30-10 pm. Closed major holidays. **Address:** 911 King St 22314 **Location:** Between Alfred and Patrick sts; in Old Town. **Parking:** no self-parking. **Cards:** AX, DC, DS, MC, VI.

MONROE'S-AN AMERICAN TRATTORIA   Phone: 703/548-5792   127
American
$6-$20
This neighborhood restaurant is a favorite of the locals. The menu offers a nice selection of pizzas & pastas, as well as seafood, lamb, veal and chicken dishes. In addition the kitchen prepares a extensive selection of daily specials. Wines selections are extensive and many kinds can be ordered by the glass. Casual dress. **Bar:** Full bar. **Reservations:** accepted. **Hours:** 5 pm-9:30 pm, Fri & Sat-10:30 pm, Sun 9:30 am-2 & 5-9 pm. Closed major holidays; also 12/24. **Address:** 1603 Commonwealth Ave 22301 **Location:** 0.6 mi e of US 1; 1 mi n of King St metro; in Del Ray area. **Parking:** street. **Cards:** AX, DS, MC, VI.

PARADISO RISTORANTE ITALIANO   Phone: 703/922-6222   132
Italian
$11-$20
Suitable for any occasion, the restaurant combines a comfortable setting with friendly, efficient service and well-prepared Italian cuisine. Offerings include homemade soups, salads, pasta and pizza, as well as chicken, fish and veal dishes. A distinctive feature is the Kids Dining Room, a supervised area with plastic picnic tables, a children's menu and Disney cartoons shown on a big-screen TV. The lunch buffet is set up until 2 p.m., and Sunday brunch can be had from 10 a.m. to 3 p.m. Dressy casual. **Bar:** Full bar. **Reservations:** suggested. **Hours:** 11:30 am-10 pm, Fri-11 pm, Sat 4 pm-11 pm, Sun 10 am-10 pm. Closed: 12/25. **Address:** 6124 Franconia Rd 22310 **Location:** I-95/495, exit 173, 0.6 mi s on SR 613, 0.7 mi w on SR 644; I-95, exit 169A, 1.7 mi e on SR 644. **Parking:** on-site. **Cards:** AX, DS, MC, VI.

RT'S RESTAURANT   Phone: 703/684-6010   120
Regional American
$8-$29
The friendly, casual neighborhood restaurant prepares many Creole and Cajun specialties, including Jack Daniels shrimp, spicy she-crab soup, Cajun veal Oscar and the popular crawfish etouffee. Casual dress. **Bar:** Full bar. **Reservations:** suggested. **Hours:** 11 am-10:30 pm, Fri & Sat-11 pm, Sun 4 pm-9 pm. Closed major holidays. **Address:** 3804 Mt Vernon Ave 22305 **Location:** 0.3 mi s of Glebe Rd. **Parking:** street. **Cards:** AX, CB, DC, DS, MC, VI.
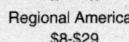

SATAY SARINAH   Phone: 703/370-4313   129
Indonesian
$6-$17
In the Van Dorn Station shopping center, the small, unassuming restaurant specializes in satay offerings. Also on the extensive menu are other preparations of meat, chicken, seafood, rice and noodles, as well as vegetarian dishes. Casual dress. **Bar:** Beer & wine. **Reservations:** accepted. **Hours:** 11:30 am-3 & 5-10 pm, Fri-11 pm, Sat 5 pm-11 pm, Sun noon-9 pm. Closed: 11/27, 12/25. **Address:** 512-A S Van Dorn St 22304 **Location:** I-95/495, exit 173, 1 mi n on SR 613; in Van Dorn Metro Station Shopping Plaza. **Parking:** on-site. **Cards:** AX, MC, VI.

(See maps and indexes starting on p. 412, 426)

SAVIO'S ITALIAN RESTAURANT AND BAR
Phone: 703/212-9651 (131)

Italian
$7-$22

In a shopping plaza, the restaurant builds its menu on both Northern and Southern Italian cooking. In addition to pasta and pizza, selections center on fish or meat. Desserts are homemade. Casual dress. **Bar:** Full bar. **Reservations:** accepted, weekends. **Hours:** 11 am-10 pm, Fri-11 pm, Sat noon-11 pm, Sun noon-9:30 pm. Closed: 7/4, 11/27, 12/25. **Address:** 516 S Van Dorn St 22304 **Location:** I-95/495, exit 173, 1 mi n on SR 613; in Van Dorn Metro Station Shopping Plaza. **Parking:** on-site. **Cards:** AX, CB, DC, DS, MC, VI.

SEAGAR'S
Phone: 703/837-0440 (4)

American
$10-$33

Just off the lobby of the Hilton Hotel, in Old Town you'll find the hotels dining room. The atmoshpere is suitable for any occasion with an upscale yet casual air. The menu offers quality beef and seafood dishes, prepared in the exhibition kitchen. Casual dress. **Bar:** Full bar. **Reservations:** suggested. **Hours:** 6 am-3 & 5:30-10 pm, Fri-11 pm, Sat 6:30 am-3 & 5-11 pm, Sun 6:30 am-3 & 5-10 pm. **Address:** 1767 King St 22314 **Location:** I-95/495, exit 176B, 0.5 mi n on SR 241, 0.5 mi e on SR 236, then just ne on Diagonal Rd; in Hilton Alexandria Old Town. **Parking:** on-site. **Cards:** AX, CB, DC, DS, MC, VI.

CALL

SOUTHSIDE 815
Phone: 703/836-6222 (20)

Southern
$6-$18

Great Southern cooking ranges from Lowcountry shrimp and sausage served over creamy grits to jambalaya pasta, gumbo and po'boys. The atmosphere is casual and lively. Casual dress. **Bar:** Full bar. **Hours:** 11:30 am-10:30 pm, Fri & Sat-11 pm. Closed: 11/27, 12/25. **Address:** 815 S Washington St 22314 **Location:** 0.6 mi s of jct King St. **Parking:** street. **Cards:** AX, CB, DC, DS, MC, VI.

THE STARDUST RESTAURANT & LOUNGE
Phone: 703/548-9864 (1)

American
$7-$29

The neighborhood favorite dining choice features eclectic choices. European/Asian influences lend to food that is as tasty as it is interesting. Casual dress. **Bar:** Full bar. **Reservations:** suggested. **Hours:** 11:30 am-10:30 pm, Fri-11 pm, Sat 5 pm-11 pm, Sun 4:30 pm-9 pm. Closed major holidays. **Address:** 608 Montgomery St 22314 **Location:** Between Washington and St Asaph sts. **Parking:** street. **Cards:** AX, DC, DS, MC, VI.

TAVERNA CRETEKOU
Phone: 703/548-8688 (10)

Greek
$8-$25

The restaurant offers a wide assortment of appetizers—as well as lamb, chicken and seafood dishes—in a Greek tavern setting. The Tuesday-Friday lunch buffet, at which diners can sample two or three Greek entrees with salad and soup, is a popular draw. The courtyard terrace is open seasonally, and live music is offered Thursday nights. Dressy casual. **Bar:** Full bar. **Reservations:** suggested, for dinner. **Hours:** 11:30 am-2:30 & 5-10 pm, Sat noon-10:30 pm, Sun 11 am-3 & 5-9:30 pm; Sunday brunch. Closed major holidays; also Mon. **Address:** 818 King St 22314 **Location:** On SR 7, just e of US 1; in Old Town. **Parking:** street. **Cards:** AX, DS, MC, VI.

TEMPO RESTAURANT
Phone: 703/370-7900 (128)

Italian
$10-$18

The chef prepares innovative Northern Italian dishes that reflect a blend of French influences. A nice selection of pasta, meat and seafood dishes makes decisions difficult. The setting is casual and comfortable, with a fine-dining air. Dressy casual. **Bar:** Full bar. **Reservations:** suggested, weekends. **Hours:** 11:30 am-2:30 & 5:30-10 pm, Sun-9 pm. Closed major holidays. **Address:** 4231 Duke St 22304 **Location:** I-395, exit 3A, 1.9 mi e on SR 236. **Parking:** on-site. **Cards:** AX, DC, DS, MC, VI.

THAI OLD TOWN RESTAURANT
Phone: 703/684-6503 (17)

Thai
$7-$15

In the heart of Old Town, the casual restaurant provides a comfortable dining setting. Guests should let the wait staff know the degree of spiciness—mild to extra-hot—they prefer. Casual dress. **Bar:** Full bar. **Reservations:** accepted. **Hours:** 11 am-10:30 pm, Sat noon-10:45 pm, Sun noon-10 pm. Closed: 12/25. **Address:** 300 King St 22314 **Location:** In Old Town; jct Fairfax St. **Parking:** no self-parking. **Cards:** AX, MC, VI.

TWO NINETEEN RESTAURANT
Phone: 703/549-1141 (13)

Regional American
$10-$29

Fine New Orleans Creole cuisine is served in three formal Victorian-style dining rooms, on the heated terrace or in the casual Bayou Room on the basement level. Evenings from Tuesday through Saturday, patrons are treated to professional jazz entertainment in the upstairs lounge. The menu lists seafood, beef, chicken and vegetarian dishes. The house specialty Cajun she-crab soup is delicious, as are New Orleans barbecued shrimp. Semi-formal attire. Entertainment. **Bar:** Full bar. **Reservations:** suggested. **Hours:** 11 am-10:30 pm, Fri & Sat-11 pm, Sun 10 am-10:30 pm. **Address:** 219 King St 22314 **Location:** In Old Town. **Parking:** street. **Cards:** AX, DC, DS, MC, VI.

(See maps and indexes starting on p. 412, 426)

UNION STREET PUBLIC HOUSE

Phone: 703/548-1785

American
$7-$25

Consistently well-prepared food and good service make the restaurant a popular operation for families and social gatherings. The atmosphere is pub-like, and the fare mainly Southern regional with an emphasis on New Orleans. Offerings range from soup, salad and sandwiches to full meals. Casual dress. **Bar:** Full bar. **Reservations:** not accepted. **Hours:** 11:30 am-midnight, Fri & Sat-1 am, Sun 11 am-midnight. Closed: 11/27, 12/25; also for dinner 12/24. **Address:** 121 S Union St 22314 **Location:** Just s of jct King and Union sts; in Old Town. **Parking:** street. **Cards:** AX, CB, DC, DS, MC, VI.

CALL

VERMILION

Phone: 703/684-9669

American
$14-$50

Contemporary American cuisine is prepared with taste, elegance and simplicity and complemented by a superb wine list. The surroundings are cozy. Casual dress. **Bar:** Full bar. **Reservations:** suggested. **Hours:** 11:30 am-3 & 5:30-10 pm, Fri & Sat-11 pm. Closed: 12/25. **Address:** 1120 King St 22314 **Location:** Between Henry and Fayette sts; center; in Old Town Alexandria. **Parking:** street. **Cards:** AX, DS, MC, VI.

WAREHOUSE BAR & GRILL

Phone: 703/683-6868

Regional American
$8-$29

New Orleans-style Cajun and Creole cuisine such as light, flaky rockfish breaded with diced pecans and served with a flavorful, mildly spicy white sauce is hard to resist. Equally tempting is warm bread pudding with whipped cream. On Saturday, the lunch menu is presented until 4 p.m. Sunday brunch is offered from 10 a.m. to 4 p.m. Dressy casual. **Bar:** Full bar. **Reservations:** suggested. **Hours:** 11 am-4 & 5-10:30 pm, Fri-11 pm, Sat 8:30 am-10:30 & 11-11 pm, Sun 10 am-9:30 pm. Closed: 1/1, 11/27, 12/25. **Address:** 214 King St 22314 **Location:** Between Fairfax and Lee sts; in Old Town. **Parking:** street. **Cards:** AX, CB, DC, DS, MC, VI.

The following restaurant has not been evaluated by AAA
but is listed for your information only.

AL'S STEAK HOUSE

Phone: 703/836-9443

[fyi]

Not evaluated. Hungry folks hankering for a great steak and cheese sandwich can grab one to go at this casual spot, which offers no seating. **Address:** 1504 Mt. Vernon Ave 22301 **Location:** 0.5 mi e of US 1; in Del Ray area.

ANNANDALE   pop. 54,994   (See map and index starting on p. 412)

——— **WHERE TO DINE** ———

RIBSTER'S

Phone: 703/750-2751

Barbecue
$10-$20

On a commercial strip, the neighborhood restaurant offers a relaxed atmosphere. This place is known for its nice selection of ribs, including baby back, beef or spare ribs, as well as barbecue sandwiches and traditional chicken and beef dishes. Casual dress. **Bar:** Full bar. **Reservations:** not accepted. **Hours:** 11 am-11 pm, Sat from noon, Sun noon-10 pm. Closed: 11/27, 12/25. **Address:** 7243 Little River Tpke 22003 **Location:** I-495, exit 52B, 1.1 mi e on SR 236. **Parking:** on-site. **Cards:** AX, DC, DS, MC, VI.

SILVERADO

Phone: 703/354-4560

American
$8-$26

This popular neighborhood restaurant provides a taste of the American Southwest. The atmosphere if fun, lively and friendly with the Southwest and cowboy niknaks decorating the restaurant and friendly, upbeat staff always visable and helpful. Casual dress. **Bar:** Full bar. **Reservations:** accepted. **Hours:** 11 am-11 pm, Fri & Sat-midnight, Sun & Mon-10 pm. Closed: 11/27, 12/25. **Address:** 7052 Columbia Pike 22003 **Location:** I-495, exit 52B, 1.6 mi e on SR 236, then 0.3 mi n on John Marr Dr; from Baily's Crossroads, 3.4 mi w on SR 244 from jct of SR 7; in Annandale Shopping Center. **Parking:** on-site. **Cards:** AX, DS, MC, VI.

ARLINGTON   pop. 189,453   (See maps and indexes p. 400-407, 412-417, 422-424)

——— **WHERE TO STAY** ———

ARLINGTON RESIDENCE COURT A CLARION COLLECTION

Book great rates at AAA.com   Phone: (703)524-4000

[AAA] [SAVE]

Small-scale Hotel
$99-$399 All Year

Address: 1200 N Courthouse Rd 22201 **Location:** 1.5 mi sw of Theodore Roosevelt Bridge on US 50. **Facility:** 187 units. 113 one-bedroom standard units with efficiencies. 30 one-, 37 two- and 7 three-bedroom suites, some with efficiencies or kitchens. 10 stories, interior corridors. *Bath:* combo or shower only. **Parking:** on-site (fee). **Terms:** cancellation fee imposed. **Amenities:** video games (fee), high-speed Internet, dual phone lines, voice mail, safes, irons, hair dryers. **Leisure Activities:** billiards, exercise room. **Guest Services:** valet and coin laundry, area transportation-courthouse metro, wireless Internet. **Business Services:** meeting rooms, business center. **Cards:** AX, CB, DC, DS, JC, MC, VI. **Free Special Amenities:** full breakfast and high-speed Internet. *(See color ad p 432)*

(See maps and indexes p. 400-407, 412-417, 422-424)

BEST WESTERN-PENTAGON/REAGAN AIRPORT   *Book great rates at AAA.com*   Phone: (703)979-4400   53

 (AAA) (SAVE)

Motel
$89-$169 All Year

Address: 2480 S Glebe Rd 22206 **Location:** I-395, exit 7B northbound; exit 7 southbound, 3.2 mi s of 14th St Bridge. **Facility:** Smoke free premises. 205 units. 203 one-bedroom standard units. 2 one-bedroom suites. 2 stories (no elevator), exterior corridors. *Bath:* combo or shower only. **Parking:** on-site. **Terms:** cancellation fee imposed. **Amenities:** voice mail, safes (fee), irons, hair dryers. *Some:* high-speed Internet. **Pool(s):** outdoor. **Leisure Activities:** exercise room. **Guest Services:** valet and coin laundry, airport transportation-Ronald Reagan Washington National Airport, area transportation-Pentagon City Metro, wireless Internet. **Business Services:** meeting rooms, business center. **Cards:** AX, DC, DS, MC, VI. **Free Special Amenities: early check-in/late check-out and high-speed Internet.** *(See color ad p 435)*

 Best Western

AAA Benefit:
Members save 10% everyday, plus an exclusive frequent stay program.

BEST WESTERN ROSSLYN/IWO JIMA   *Book great rates at AAA.com*   Phone: (703)524-5000   43

 (AAA) (SAVE)

Small-scale Hotel
$89-$259 All Year

Address: 1501 Arlington Blvd 22209 **Location:** 1 mi w of Theodore Roosevelt Bridge on US 50. **Facility:** 141 one-bedroom standard units. 2-3 stories, interior/exterior corridors. *Bath:* combo or shower only. **Parking:** on-site. **Terms:** cancellation fee imposed. **Amenities:** voice mail, irons, hair dryers. *Some:* high-speed Internet. **Pool(s):** heated indoor. **Leisure Activities:** limited exercise equipment. **Guest Services:** valet and coin laundry, wireless Internet. **Business Services:** meeting rooms, PC. **Cards:** AX, CB, DC, DS, JC, MC, VI. **Free Special Amenities: local telephone calls and high-speed Internet.** *(See color ad below)*

 Best Western

AAA Benefit:
Members save 10% everyday, plus an exclusive frequent stay program.

COMFORT INN BALLSTON   *Book great rates at AAA.com*   Phone: (703)247-3399   48

 (AAA) (SAVE)

Small-scale Hotel
$189-$259 3/1-6/30
$99-$195 7/1-2/28

Address: 1211 N Glebe Rd 22201 **Location:** I-66, exit 71, jct SR 120. **Facility:** Smoke free premises. 126 units. 124 one-bedroom standard units. 2 one-bedroom suites. 3 stories, interior corridors. **Parking:** on-site. **Terms:** cancellation fee imposed. **Amenities:** voice mail, safes (fee), irons, hair dryers. **Leisure Activities:** exercise room. **Guest Services:** valet laundry, wireless Internet. **Business Services:** meeting rooms, PC. **Cards:** AX, DC, DS, MC, VI. **Free Special Amenities: continental breakfast and high-speed Internet.**

(See maps and indexes p. 400-407, 412-417, 422-424)

COMFORT INN PENTAGON *Book great rates at AAA.com* **Phone:** (703)682-5500 **54**

AAA SAVE

Small-scale Hotel
$99-$229 All Year

Address: 2480 S Glebe Rd 22206 **Location:** I-395, exit 7B northbound; exit 7 southbound, 3.2 mi s of 14th St Bridge, on SR 120. **Facility:** Smoke free premises. 120 one-bedroom standard units. 7 stories, interior corridors. *Bath:* combo or shower only. **Parking:** on-site. **Amenities:** dual phone lines, voice mail, safes (fee), irons, hair dryers. *Some:* high-speed Internet. **Leisure Activities:** pool privileges, limited exercise equipment. **Guest Services:** valet and coin laundry, airport transportation-Ronald Reagan Washington National Airport, area transportation-Pentagon City Metro, wireless Internet. **Business Services:** meeting rooms, PC. **Cards:** AX, CB, DC, DS, MC, VI. **Free Special Amenities: continental breakfast and high-speed Internet.** *(See color ad p 510)*

COURTYARD BY MARRIOTT-ARLINGTON/ROSSLYN *Book great rates at AAA.com* **Phone:** 703/528-2222 **42**

Small-scale Hotel
$241-$285 All Year

Address: 1533 Clarendon Blvd 22209 **Location:** I-66, exit 73, 0.3 mi s on Ft Meyer Dr, 0.3 mi w on Wilson Blvd, just s on N Pierce St, then just e; 3 blks from Rosslyn metro station. Located in Rosslyn area. **Facility:** Smoke free premises. 162 units. 144 one-bedroom standard units. 18 one-bedroom suites. 10 stories, interior corridors. *Bath:* combo or shower only. **Parking:** on-site (fee). **Amenities:** high-speed Internet, dual phone lines, voice mail, irons, hair dryers. **Pool(s):** heated indoor. **Leisure Activities:** whirlpool, exercise room. **Guest Services:** valet and coin laundry, area transportation. **Business Services:** meeting rooms, PC. **Cards:** AX, DC, DS, MC, VI.

AAA Benefit:
Members save 5% off of the best available rate.

   CALL   / SOME UNITS

COURTYARD BY MARRIOTT CRYSTAL CITY *Book great rates at AAA.com* **Phone:** 703/549-3434 **14**

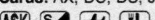
Large-scale Hotel
$275-$296 9/10-2/28
$252-$296 3/1-9/9

Address: 2899 Jefferson Davis Hwy 22202 **Location:** 2 mi s of 14th St Bridge on US 1; just s of jct SR 233. Located in the Crystal City area. **Facility:** Smoke free premises. 272 units. 271 one-bedroom standard units. 1 one-bedroom suite. 14 stories, interior corridors. *Bath:* combo or shower only. **Parking:** on-site (fee). **Amenities:** video games (fee), voice mail, irons, hair dryers. **Pool(s):** heated indoor. **Leisure Activities:** whirlpool, exercise room. **Guest Services:** valet and coin laundry, area transportation, wireless Internet. **Business Services:** meeting rooms, PC. **Cards:** AX, DC, DS, JC, MC, VI.

AAA Benefit:
Members save 5% off of the best available rate.

   CALL   / SOME UNITS

CROWNE PLAZA HOTEL WASHINGTON NATIONAL AIRPORT *Book great rates at AAA.com* **Phone:** (703)416-1600 **4**

AAA SAVE

Large-scale Hotel
$99-$399 All Year

Address: 1480 Crystal Dr 22202 **Location:** I-395, exit 8C, 1 mi s of 14th St Bridge off US 1, exit 15th St, then n. Located in Crystal City area. **Facility:** 308 units. 296 one-bedroom standard units. 12 one-bedroom suites. 12 stories, interior corridors. *Bath:* combo or shower only. **Parking:** on-site (fee). **Terms:** cancellation fee imposed. **Amenities:** CD players, high-speed Internet (fee), dual phone lines, voice mail, irons, hair dryers. **Dining:** 2 restaurants. **Pool(s):** outdoor. **Leisure Activities:** exercise room. **Guest Services:** valet laundry, airport transportation-Ronald Reagan Washington National Airport, area transportation-within Crystal City. **Business Services:** conference facilities, business center. **Cards:** AX, CB, DC, DS, JC, MC, VI. **Free Special Amenities: newspaper and high-speed Internet.**

CRYSTAL CITY MARRIOTT AT REAGAN NATIONAL AIRPORT *Book great rates at AAA.com* **Phone:** 703/413-5500 **8**

AAA SAVE

Large-scale Hotel
$285-$340 9/10-2/28
$274-$340 3/1-9/9

Address: 1999 Jefferson Davis Hwy 22202 **Location:** US 1, 1.2 mi s of 14th St Bridge; entrance on Bell St. Located in the Crystal City area. **Facility:** Smoke free premises. 343 units. 333 one-bedroom standard units. 10 one-bedroom suites. 11 stories, interior corridors. *Bath:* combo or shower only. **Parking:** on-site (fee) and valet. **Terms:** check-in 4 pm. **Amenities:** voice mail, irons, hair dryers. *Fee:* video games, high-speed Internet. **Pool(s):** heated indoor. **Leisure Activities:** sauna, whirlpool, exercise room. **Guest Services:** valet and coin laundry, airport transportation-Ronald Reagan Washington National Airport, wireless Internet. **Business Services:** conference facilities, business center. **Cards:** AX, DC, DS, JC, MC, VI. **Free Special Amenities: newspaper.**

Marriott
HOTELS & RESORTS

AAA Benefit:
Members save 5% off of the best available rate.

    CALL   / SOME UNITS

(See maps and indexes p. 400-407, 412-417, 422-424)

CRYSTAL GATEWAY MARRIOTT HOTEL *Book great rates at AAA.com* Phone: 703/920-3230 6

Large-scale Hotel
$340-$351 9/10-2/28
$274-$351 3/1-9/9

Address: 1700 Jefferson Davis Hwy 22202 **Location:** 1.3 mi s of 14th St Bridge on US 1; entrance just w on S Eads St. Located in the Crystal City area. **Facility:** Smoke free premises. 697 units. 630 one-bedroom standard units. 67 one-bedroom suites. 18 stories, interior corridors. *Bath:* combo or shower only. **Parking:** on-site (fee) and valet. **Terms:** check-in 4 pm. **Amenities:** dual phone lines, voice mail, irons, hair dryers. *Fee:* video games, high-speed Internet. **Pool(s):** heated indoor/outdoor. **Leisure Activities:** whirlpool, exercise room. **Guest Services:** valet and coin laundry, wireless Internet. **Business Services:** conference facilities, business center. **Cards:** AX, DC, DS, JC, MC, VI.

DOUBLETREE HOTEL-CRYSTAL CITY *Book great rates at AAA.com* Phone: 703/416-4100 2

Large-scale Hotel
Rates not provided

Address: 300 Army Navy Dr 22202 **Location:** I-395, exit 8C, 0.8 mi s of 14th St Bridge, jct I-395 and US 1. Located in Crystal City area. **Facility:** 631 units. 619 one-bedroom standard units. 12 one-bedroom suites with whirlpools. 15 stories, interior corridors. *Bath:* combo or shower only. **Parking:** on-site (fee) and valet. **Amenities:** video games (fee), voice mail, irons, hair dryers. *Some:* high-speed Internet (fee), dual phone lines. **Pool(s):** heated indoor. **Leisure Activities:** exercise room. **Guest Services:** valet and coin laundry, area transportation, wireless Internet. **Business Services:** conference facilities, business center.

ECONO LODGE-METRO ARLINGTON *Book great rates at AAA.com* Phone: (703)538-5300 46

Small-scale Hotel
$110-$219 3/1-10/31
$80-$199 11/1-2/28

Address: 6800 Lee Hwy 22213 **Location:** I-66, exit 69, jct US 29 and SR 237, Washington Blvd and Lee Hwy. **Facility:** Smoke free premises. 47 one-bedroom standard units, some with kitchens and/or whirlpools. 3 stories (no elevator), interior corridors. **Parking:** on-site. **Amenities:** irons, hair dryers. **Guest Services:** coin laundry, wireless Internet. **Business Services:** PC. **Cards:** AX, CB, DC, DS, JC, MC, VI. **Free Special Amenities:** continental breakfast and high-speed Internet.
(See color ad below)

EMBASSY SUITES HOTEL CRYSTAL CITY *Book at AAA.com* Phone: 703/979-9799 5

Large-scale Hotel
Rates not provided

Address: 1300 Jefferson Davis Hwy 22202 **Location:** I-395, exit 8C, just s on Eads St, entrance on Eads St; 1 mi s of 14th St Bridge. Located in Crystal City area. **Facility:** 267 units. 265 one- and 2 two-bedroom suites. 11 stories, interior corridors. *Bath:* combo or shower only. **Parking:** on-site (fee). **Amenities:** video games (fee), dual phone lines, voice mail, irons, hair dryers. *Some:* CD players, high-speed Internet (fee). **Pool(s):** heated indoor. **Leisure Activities:** whirlpool, exercise room. **Guest Services:** valet and coin laundry, area transportation, wireless Internet. **Business Services:** meeting rooms, PC (fee).

(See maps and indexes p. 400-407, 412-417, 422-424)

HAMPTON INN & SUITES REAGAN NATIONAL AIRPORT

Small-scale Hotel
Rates not provided

Phone: 703/418-8181   **9**

Address: 2000 Jefferson Davis Hwy 22202 **Location:** I-395, exit 8C, 1.5 mi s of 14th St Bridge on US 1. Located in Crystal City area. **Facility:** 161 units. 147 one-bedroom standard units. 14 one-bedroom suites. 10 stories, interior corridors. *Bath:* combo or shower only. **Parking:** on-site (fee). **Amenities:** video games (fee), high-speed Internet, dual phone lines, voice mail, irons, hair dryers. **Pool(s):** heated indoor. **Leisure Activities:** exercise room. **Guest Services:** valet and coin laundry, airport transportation-Ronald Reagan Washington National Airport, area transportation-shopping mall & metro, wireless Internet. **Business Services:** meeting rooms, business center. **Free Special Amenities: expanded continental breakfast and high-speed Internet.**

HILTON ARLINGTON

Book great rates at AAA.com

Small-scale Hotel
Rates not provided

Phone: 703/528-6000   **50**

Address: 950 N Stafford St 22203 **Location:** I-66, exit 71 (Glebe Rd/SR 120), 0.3 mi e of jct SR 120 and 237 (Glebe Rd and Fairfax Dr). Connected to Ballston Commons Mall via a skywalk. **Facility:** Smoke free premises. 209 units. 204 one-bedroom standard units. 5 one-bedroom suites, some with whirlpools. 7 stories, interior corridors. *Bath:* combo or shower only. **Parking:** on-site (fee). **Amenities:** video games (fee), dual phone lines, voice mail, irons, hair dryers. **Guest Services:** valet laundry, wireless Internet. **Business Services:** conference facilities, business center. **Free Special Amenities: preferred room (subject to availability with advance reservations).**

HILTON CRYSTAL CITY AT REAGAN NATIONAL AIRPORT   *Book great rates at AAA.com*

Large-scale Hotel
Rates not provided

Phone: 703/418-6800   **11**

Address: 2399 Jefferson Davis Hwy 22202 **Location:** 1.8 mi s of 14th St Bridge on US 1. Located in the Crystal City area. **Facility:** 386 units. 384 one-bedroom standard units. 2 one-bedroom suites. 14 stories, interior corridors. *Bath:* combo or shower only. **Parking:** on-site (fee) and valet. **Amenities:** video games (fee), dual phone lines, voice mail, irons, hair dryers. **Pool(s):** heated indoor. **Leisure Activities:** saunas, exercise room. **Guest Services:** valet laundry, area transportation, wireless Internet. **Business Services:** conference facilities, business center.

▼ *See AAA listing p 514* ▼

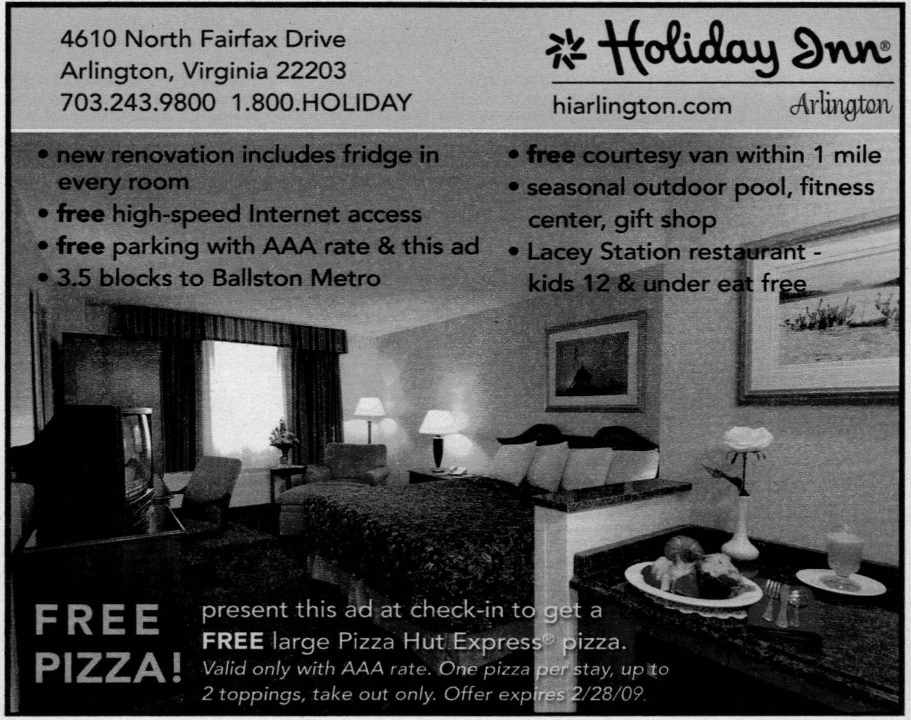

(See maps and indexes p. 400-407, 412-417, 422-424)

HILTON GARDEN INN ARLINGTON/COURTHOUSE
PLAZA *Book great rates at AAA.com* Phone: 703/528-4444 **45**

Small-scale Hotel
Rates not provided

Address: 1333 N Courthouse Rd 22201 **Location:** 1.5 mi sw of Theodore Roosevelt Bridge, off US 50, then n. **Facility:** 189 one-bedroom standard units. 8 stories, interior corridors. *Bath:* combo or shower only. **Parking:** on-site (fee). **Amenities:** video games (fee), high-speed Internet, dual phone lines, voice mail, irons, hair dryers. **Leisure Activities:** exercise room. **Guest Services:** valet laundry, area transportation, wireless Internet. **Business Services:** meeting rooms, business center.

HOLIDAY INN ARLINGTON *Book great rates at AAA.com* Phone: (703)243-9800 **49**

Small-scale Hotel
$89-$349 All Year

Address: 4610 N Fairfax Dr 22203 **Location:** I-66, exit 71 (Glebe Rd/SR 120); 2 blks from Ballston Metro Station. Located in the Ballston area. **Facility:** 221 units. 219 one-bedroom standard units. 2 one-bedroom suites. 9 stories, interior corridors. *Bath:* combo or shower only. **Parking:** on-site (fee). **Terms:** cancellation fee imposed. **Amenities:** video games (fee), high-speed Internet, voice mail, irons, hair dryers. **Pool(s):** outdoor. **Leisure Activities:** exercise room. **Guest Services:** valet and coin laundry, area transportation-within 1 mi & metro, wireless Internet. **Business Services:** conference facilities. **Cards:** AX, CB, DC, DS, JC, MC, VI. **Free Special Amenities: newspaper and high-speed Internet.** *(See color ad p 513)*

HOLIDAY INN NATIONAL AIRPORT *Book great rates at AAA.com* Phone: (703)684-7200 **12**

Large-scale Hotel
$89-$299 All Year

Address: 2650 Jefferson Davis Hwy 22202 **Location:** 2 mi s of 14th St Bridge on US 1, jct SR 233. Located in the Crystal City area. **Facility:** 280 units. 279 one-bedroom standard units. 1 one-bedroom suite. 17 stories, interior corridors. *Bath:* combo or shower only. **Parking:** on-site (fee). **Terms:** check-in 4 pm, 1-3 night minimum stay - seasonal, cancellation fee imposed. **Amenities:** high-speed Internet, dual phone lines, voice mail, irons, hair dryers. **Dining:** 2 restaurants. **Pool(s):** outdoor. **Leisure Activities:** exercise room. **Guest Services:** valet and coin laundry, airport transportation-Ronald Reagan Washington National Airport, area transportation-shopping mall & metro station, wireless Internet. **Business Services:** conference facilities, business center. **Cards:** AX, CB, DC, DS, JC, MC, VI. **Free Special Amenities: newspaper and high-speed Internet.** *(See color ad below)*

HOLIDAY INN ROSSLYN *Book great rates at AAA.com* Phone: (703)807-2000 **84**

Large-scale Hotel
$99-$189 All Year

Address: 1900 N Fort Myer Dr 22209 **Location:** I-66, exit 73, just sw of Key Bridge. Located in the Rosslyn area. **Facility:** Smoke free premises. 307 units. 279 one-bedroom standard units. 28 one-bedroom suites. 19 stories, interior corridors. *Bath:* combo or shower only. **Parking:** on-site. **Amenities:** dual phone lines, voice mail, safes, irons, hair dryers. **Pool(s):** heated indoor. **Leisure Activities:** exercise room. **Guest Services:** valet and coin laundry, wireless Internet. **Business Services:** conference facilities, PC. **Cards:** AX, CB, DC, DS, JC, MC, VI.

(See maps and indexes p. 400-407, 412-417, 422-424)

HYATT ARLINGTON AT KEY BRIDGE · *Book great rates at AAA.com* · Phone: (703)525-1234 · 85

Large-scale Hotel
$126-$398 All Year

Address: 1325 Wilson Blvd 22209 **Location:** I-66, exit 73, just sw of Key Bridge. Located in the Rosslyn area across from the metro. **Facility:** 304 units. 293 one-bedroom standard units. 11 one-bedroom suites, some with whirlpools. 15 stories, interior corridors. *Bath:* combo or shower only. **Parking:** on-site (fee) and valet. **Terms:** cancellation fee imposed. **Amenities:** dual phone lines, voice mail, irons, hair dryers. *Some:* safes. **Leisure Activities:** exercise room. **Guest Services:** complimentary and valet laundry, wireless Internet. **Business Services:** conference facilities, business center. **Cards:** AX, DC, DS, JC, MC, VI.

AAA Benefit: Ask for the AAA rate and save 10%.

HYATT REGENCY CRYSTAL CITY AT REAGAN NATIONAL AIRPORT · *Book great rates at AAA.com* · Phone: (703)418-1234 · 13

Large-scale Hotel
$89-$439 All Year

Address: 2799 Jefferson Davis Hwy 22202 **Location:** 2 mi s of 14th St Bridge on US 1, jct SR 233; entrance just e of US 1 on Clark St. Located in the Crystal City area. **Facility:** Smoke free premises. 685 units. 683 one-bedroom standard units. 2 one-bedroom suites. 13 stories, interior corridors. *Bath:* combo or shower only. **Parking:** valet. **Terms:** cancellation fee imposed. **Amenities:** dual phone lines, voice mail, irons, hair dryers. *Some:* CD players. *Fee:* high-speed Internet. **Dining:** 2 restaurants. **Pool(s):** heated outdoor. **Leisure Activities:** whirlpool, exercise room. **Guest Services:** valet laundry, airport transportation-Ronald Reagan Washington National Airport, area transportation-Crystal City Metro, wireless Internet. **Business Services:** conference facilities, business center. **Cards:** AX, DC, DS, JC, MC, VI. *(See color ad p 440)*

AAA Benefit: Ask for the AAA rate and save 10%.

KEY BRIDGE MARRIOTT HOTEL · *Book great rates at AAA.com* · Phone: 703/524-6400 · 83

Large-scale Hotel
Rates not provided

Address: 1401 Lee Hwy 22209 **Location:** I-66, exit 73, just sw of Key Bridge. Located in the Rosslyn area. **Facility:** Smoke free premises. 582 units. 574 one-bedroom standard units. 8 one-bedroom suites. 13 stories, interior corridors. *Bath:* combo or shower only. **Parking:** on-site (fee). **Terms:** check-in 4 pm. **Amenities:** voice mail, irons, hair dryers. *Fee:* video games, high-speed Internet. **Pool(s):** heated indoor/outdoor. **Leisure Activities:** saunas, whirlpool, exercise room. **Guest Services:** valet and coin laundry. **Business Services:** conference facilities, business center. **Free Special Amenities:** newspaper.

Marriott
HOTELS & RESORTS

AAA Benefit: Members save 5% off of the best available rate.

RADISSON HOTEL REAGAN NATIONAL AIRPORT · *Book great rates at AAA.com* · Phone: (703)920-8600 · 10

Small-scale Hotel
$99-$259 All Year

Address: 2020 Jefferson Davis Hwy 22202 **Location:** I-395, exit 8C, 1.5 mi s of 14th St Bridge on US 1. Located in Crystal City area. **Facility:** 244 units. 236 one-bedroom standard units. 8 one-bedroom suites. 8 stories, interior corridors. *Bath:* combo or shower only. **Parking:** on-site (fee). **Terms:** cancellation fee imposed. **Amenities:** high-speed Internet, dual phone lines, voice mail, irons, hair dryers. **Pool(s):** outdoor. **Leisure Activities:** exercise room. **Guest Services:** valet and coin laundry, area transportation, wireless Internet. **Business Services:** meeting rooms, business center. **Cards:** AX, CB, DC, DS, MC, VI.

RESIDENCE INN BY MARRIOTT ARLINGTON AT ROSSLYN · *Book great rates at AAA.com* · Phone: 703/812-8400 · 86

Small-scale Hotel
$297-$362 All Year

Address: 1651 N Oak St 22209 **Location:** I-66, exit 73, 0.3 mi s on Fort Myer Dr, 0.3 mi w on Wilson Blvd to N Pierce St, then 2 blks e on Clarendon Blvd; 2 blks from Rosslyn Metro Station. Located in the Rosslyn area. **Facility:** Smoke free premises. 176 units. 69 one-bedroom standard units with efficiencies. 96 one- and 11 two-bedroom suites, some with efficiencies or kitchens. 12 stories, interior corridors. *Bath:* combo or shower only. **Parking:** on-site (fee). **Amenities:** video games (fee), high-speed Internet, dual phone lines, voice mail, safes, irons, hair dryers. **Leisure Activities:** limited exercise equipment. **Guest Services:** valet and coin laundry, wireless Internet. **Business Services:** meeting rooms, PC. **Cards:** AX, DC, DS, JC, MC, VI.

AAA Benefit: Members save 5% off of the best available rate.

(See maps and indexes p. 400-407, 412-417, 422-424)

RESIDENCE INN BY MARRIOTT-PENTAGON CITY   *Book great rates at AAA.com*   Phone: 703/413-6630

 (AAA) (SAVE)

Small-scale Hotel
$329-$351 All Year

Address: 550 Army Navy Dr 22202 **Location:** I-395, exit 8C, just 1 mi s of 14th St Bridge. Located near Fashion Centre Shopping Complex. **Facility:** Smoke free premises. 299 units. 271 one-bedroom standard units with efficiencies. 28 two-bedroom suites with kitchens. 16 stories, interior corridors. *Bath:* combo or shower only. **Parking:** on-site (fee). **Amenities:** high-speed Internet, voice mail, irons, hair dryers. **Pool(s):** heated indoor. **Leisure Activities:** whirlpool, sun deck, exercise room. **Guest Services:** valet and coin laundry, airport transportation-Ronald Reagan Washington National Airport, area transportation-within 1 mi, wireless Internet. **Business Services:** meeting rooms, PC (fee). **Cards:** AX, DC, DS, JC, MC, VI. **Free Special Amenities: full breakfast and high-speed Internet.**

AAA Benefit:
Members save 5% off of the best available rate.

THE RITZ-CARLTON, PENTAGON CITY   *Book at AAA.com*   Phone: 703/415-5000   3

Large-scale Hotel
Rates not provided

Address: 1250 S Hayes St 22202 **Location:** 1 mi s of 14th St Bridge. Located adjacent to the Fashion Centre Shopping Complex. **Facility:** Smoke free premises. 366 units. 345 one-bedroom standard units. 21 one-bedroom suites, some with whirlpools. 18 stories, interior corridors. *Bath:* combo or shower only. **Parking:** valet. **Amenities:** CD players, dual phone lines, voice mail, safes, honor bars, irons, hair dryers. *Fee:* video games, high-speed Internet. *Some:* DVD players. **Dining:** The Grill, see separate listing. **Pool(s):** heated indoor. **Leisure Activities:** saunas, whirlpool, steamrooms. *Fee:* massage, personal trainer. **Guest Services:** valet laundry, wireless Internet. **Business Services:** conference facilities, business center.

SHERATON CRYSTAL CITY HOTEL   *Book great rates at AAA.com*   Phone: (703)486-1111   7

(AAA) (SAVE)

Large-scale Hotel
$109-$319 All Year

Address: 1800 Jefferson Davis Hwy 22202 **Location:** I-395, exit 8C, 1.4 mi s of 14th St Bridge on US 1; hotel entrance, corner of Eads St. Located in Crystal City area. **Facility:** Designated smoking area. 210 one-bedroom standard units. 15 stories, interior corridors. *Bath:* combo or shower only. **Parking:** on-site (fee). **Terms:** cancellation fee imposed. **Amenities:** voice mail, irons, hair dryers. *Fee:* video games, high-speed Internet. *Some:* dual phone lines. **Pool(s):** outdoor. **Leisure Activities:** sauna, exercise room. **Guest Services:** valet laundry, airport transportation-Ronald Reagan Washington National Airport, area transportation-shopping mall, wireless Internet. **Business Services:** conference facilities, business center. **Cards:** AX, DC, DS, MC, VI.

(S) **Sheraton**
HOTELS & RESORTS

AAA Benefit:
Members get up to 15% off, plus Starwood Preferred Guest® bonuses.

▼ *See AAA listing p 517* ▼

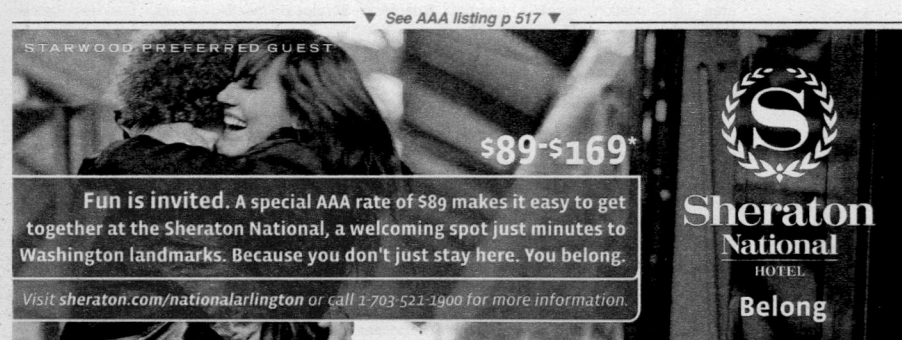

(See maps and indexes p. 400-407, 412-417, 422-424)

SHERATON NATIONAL HOTEL *Book great rates at AAA.com* Phone: (703)521-1900 **52**

Large-scale Hotel
$329 All Year

Address: 900 S Orme St 22204 **Location:** I-395, exit 8A, at SR 27 and 244; 1.3 mi s of 14th St Bridge. **Facility:** 408 units. 391 one-bedroom standard units. 17 one-bedroom suites. 5-17 stories, interior corridors. *Bath:* combo or shower only. **Parking:** on-site (fee). **Amenities:** dual phone lines, voice mail, irons, hair dryers. *Fee:* video games, high-speed Internet. **Pool(s):** heated indoor. **Leisure Activities:** sun deck, exercise room. **Guest Services:** valet laundry, airport transportation-Ronald Reagan Washington National Airport, area transportation-Pentagon City metro & Pentagon, wireless Internet. **Business Services:** conference facilities, business center. **Cards:** AX, DC, DS, JC, MC, VI. *(See color ad p 516)*

Sheraton
HOTELS & RESORTS

AAA Benefit:
Members get up to 15% off, plus Starwood Preferred Guest® bonuses.

THE VIRGINIAN SUITES *Book great rates at AAA.com* Phone: (703)522-9600 **44**

Small-scale Hotel
$139-$229 All Year

Address: 1500 Arlington Blvd 22209 **Location:** 1 mi w of Theodore Roosevelt Bridge on US 50. **Facility:** 261 units. 165 one-bedroom standard units with efficiencies. 94 one- and 2 two-bedroom suites with kitchens. 10 stories, interior corridors. **Parking:** on-site (fee). **Terms:** 2-4 night minimum stay - seasonal. **Amenities:** video games (fee), high-speed Internet, voice mail, safes, irons, hair dryers. **Pool(s):** outdoor. **Leisure Activities:** saunas, limited exercise equipment. **Guest Services:** valet and coin laundry, area transportation, wireless Internet. **Business Services:** meeting rooms, PC (fee). **Cards:** AX, DC, DS, MC, VI. *(See color ad below)*

(See maps and indexes p. 400-407, 412-417, 422-424)

THE WESTIN ARLINGTON GATEWAY   *Book great rates at AAA.com*   **Phone:** (703)717-6200   **51**

Large-scale Hotel
$139-$499 All Year

Address: 801 N Glebe Rd 22203 **Location:** I-66, exit 71, just e on Fairfax Dr to Vermont Ave; just n of jct SR 120 and Wilson Blvd; 2 blks from metro station. Located in the Ballston area. **Facility:** Smoke free premises. 336 units. 324 one-bedroom standard units. 12 one-bedroom suites. 15 stories, interior corridors. *Bath:* combo or shower only. **Parking:** valet. **Terms:** cancellation fee imposed. **Amenities:** dual phone lines, voice mail, safes, honor bars, irons, hair dryers. *Fee:* video games, high-speed Internet. **Pool(s):** heated indoor. **Leisure Activities:** whirlpool, exercise room. **Guest Services:** valet laundry, wireless Internet. **Business Services:** conference facilities, business center. **Cards:** AX, CB, DC, DS, JC, MC, VI.

AAA Benefit:
Members get up to 15% off, plus Starwood Preferred Guest® bonuses.

The following lodging was either not evaluated or did not meet AAA rating requirements but is listed for your information only.

HOTEL PALOMAR ARLINGTON AT WATERVIEW   **Phone:** 703/351-9170
fyi   Not evaluated. **Address:** 1121 N 19th St 22209 **Location:** I-66, exit 73, just sw of Key Bridge; in the Rosslyn area. Facilities, services, and decor characterize a mid-range property.

--- **WHERE TO DINE** ---

ALADDIN'S EATERY   **Phone:** 703/894-4401

Lebanese
$5-$10

The Lebanese restaurant features an extensive selection of vegetarian dishes, but a few chicken, lamb and ground beef dishes also are available. The atmosphere is casual and comfortable, and the seasonal sidewalk tables are popular. Casual dress. **Bar:** Full bar. **Reservations:** accepted. **Hours:** 11 am-10 pm, Fri & Sat-10:30 pm. Closed: 11/27, 12/25. **Address:** 4044 S 28th St 22206 **Location:** I-395, exit 6 northbound; exit 7 southbound, just w; at the Village of Shirlington. **Parking:** on-site. **Cards:** AX, DS, MC, VI.

AROMA INDIAN CUISINE   **Phone:** 703/575-8800   **59**

Indian
$9-$18

The menu offers an extensive selection of authentic Indian cooking with Tandoori and curry dishes. The dining room is attractive with Indian artwork and tables with pink tablecloths. Casual dress. **Bar:** Full bar. **Reservations:** accepted. **Hours:** 11:30 am-10 pm, Fri & Sat-10:30 pm, Sun noon-10 pm. **Address:** 4052 S 28th St 22206 **Location:** I-395, exit 6 northbound; exit 7 southbound, then just w; at the Village of Shirlington. **Parking:** on-site and street. **Cards:** AX, CB, DC, DS, MC, VI.

CALL ⑤Ⓜ

ATHENA PALLAS   **Phone:** 703/521-3870   **3**

ⒶⒶⒶ

Greek
$6-$20

Tucked in the back of the Restaurant Row area on 23rd St. is a casual, family owned and operated Greek restaurant. The kitchen prepares a nice selection of traditional and regional Greek foods. When the weather cooperates an outdoor deck is available for seating. Casual dress. **Bar:** Full bar. **Reservations:** suggested. **Hours:** 11 am-10 pm, Sat from 5 pm. Closed major holidays; also Sun. **Address:** 556 22nd St S 22202 **Location:** Just s of jct S Eads St; in Crystal City area. **Parking:** on-site. **Cards:** AX, CB, DC, DS, MC, VI.

BISTRO BISTRO   **Phone:** 703/379-0300   **57**

American
$5-$22

The lively cafe, which has seasonal sidewalk seating, boasts a changing menu of innovative cuisine, ranging from salad and sandwiches to complete dinners. Servers are friendly and knowledgeable. The Sunday brunch is popular. Casual dress. **Bar:** Full bar. **Reservations:** suggested, weekends. **Hours:** 11:30 am-10 pm, Fri & Sat-11 pm, Sun 10 am-10 pm. Closed: 12/25. **Address:** 4021 S 28th St 22206 **Location:** I-395, exit 6 northbound; exit 7 southbound, just w; at the Village of Shirlington. **Parking:** on-site. **Cards:** AX, DC, DS, MC, VI.

CAFE ASIA   **Phone:** 703/741-0870   **41**

Asian
$4-$14

At Cafe Asia you'll find a wide variety of Asian dishes. The menu reflects recipes from Thailand, Vietnam, Indonesia, China and Japan. The casual dining room with high ceilings, floor to ceiling windows and blonde wood tables and chairs has become a popular spot with the locals. The sushi bar is available for those in the mood for sushi. Dressy casual. **Bar:** Full bar. **Reservations:** suggested. **Hours:** 11 am-midnight, Sun noon-11 pm. **Address:** 1550 Wilson Blvd 22209 **Location:** Jct Pierce St and Wilson Blvd; on ground floor of office building; in Rosslyn area. **Parking:** on-site and street. **Cards:** AX, DC, DS, MC, VI.

CAFE ITALIA   **Phone:** 703/521-2565   **8**

Italian
$6-$21

The neighborhood Italian restaurant has been family owned and operated for years. Red checkered tablecloths and oversized kitchen utensils hanging from the beamed ceiling lend to the quaint, casual atmosphere. A covered sidewalk dining section is available. The menu is oriented toward Southern Italian cooking, with an extensive selection of pasta, veal and chicken dishes. Casual dress. **Bar:** Full bar. **Reservations:** accepted, to 8 pm. **Hours:** 11 am-10 pm, Sat-Mon from 5 pm. Closed major holidays. **Address:** 519 S 23rd St 22202 **Location:** 1.5 blks w of US 1; in Crystal City area. **Parking:** street. **Cards:** AX, DS, MC, VI.

(See maps and indexes p. 400-407, 412-417, 422-424)

CAFE PARISIEN EXPRESS

French
$3-$16

Phone: 703/525-3332 (38)

A little slice of Paris is set amid a block of specialty shops. The casually refined eatery treats diners to house-prepared breakfast, lunch and dinner entrees of traditional French fare, including omelets, onion soup and quiches, as well as wonderfully fresh croissants, crepes and brioche, all baked on site. Casual dress. **Bar:** Beer & wine. **Hours:** 8 am-9:30 pm, Sun 9 am-3 pm. Closed major holidays. **Address:** 4520 Lee Hwy 22207 **Location:** 0.5 mi n on Glebe Rd (SR 120), then 0.5 mi n on US 29. **Parking:** street. **Cards:** MC, VI.

CAFE TIROLO

Italian
$7-$19

Phone: 703/528-7809 (48)

In a tidy little corner of a Ballston office building and behind Tara Thai, the cafe whips up tasty Italian and Austrian offerings, including in-house-prepared pasta. The tiny restaurant's tables are at a premium at the noon hour, when the business-lunch crowd is known to frequent, but it's well worth the wait. Casual dress. **Bar:** Beer & wine. **Reservations:** not accepted. **Hours:** 11 am-2:30 & 5-9 pm, Fri-2:30 pm. Closed major holidays; also Sat & Sun. **Address:** 4001 N Fairfax Dr 22203 **Location:** Corner of N Fairfax Dr and Quincy St; behind Tara Thai. **Parking:** street. **Cards:** AX, DS, MC, VI.

CAPITOL CITY BREWING CO SHIRLINGTON

American
$9-$19

Phone: 703/578-3888

The fare is simple and wholesome, and the surroundings plain and comfortable. You can find good plated full meals, or more basic and quick food while on your busy schedule. Casual dress. **Bar:** Full bar. **Reservations:** accepted. **Hours:** 11 am-11 pm, Fri & Sat-midnight. Closed: 11/27, 12/25. **Address:** 2700 S Quincy St 22206 **Location:** I-395, exit 6 northbound; exit 7 southbound, just w; at the Village of Shirlington. **Parking:** on-site. **Cards:** AX, DC, DS, MC, VI.

CARLYLE

American
$8-$22

Phone: 703/931-0777 (58)

Innovative American cuisine is why this bustling bistro attracts the locals. Menu offerings change seasonally. The staff is friendly and efficient, and the atmosphere casual and fun. Casual dress. **Bar:** Full bar. **Hours:** 11 am-11 pm, Fri & Sat-midnight, Sun 9:30 am-11 pm. Closed: 11/27, 12/25. **Address:** 4000 S 28th St 22206 **Location:** I-395, exit 6 northbound; exit 7 southbound, just w; at the Village of Shirlington. **Parking:** on-site. **Cards:** AX, DC, DS, MC, VI.

CHICKEN OUT ROTISSERIE

American
$5-$10

Phone: 703/358-5678

Chicken Out Rotisserie uses only fresh all natural ingredients. The chicken is chemical and hormone free. Choose from salads and sandwiches to wraps and picaccias, as well as rotisserie chicken and roast beef. Casual dress. **Reservations:** not accepted. **Hours:** 11 am-9:30 pm, Fri & Sat-10 pm. Closed: 12/25. **Address:** 4238 Wilson Blvd 22203 **Location:** In Ballston Common Mall; at Wilson Blvd and Glebe Rd (SR 120). **Parking:** on-site (fee). **Cards:** AX, DS, MC, VI.

CALL

CRYSTAL THAI RESTAURANT

Thai
$7-$14

Phone: 703/522-1311 (50)

Tucked in a small shopping plaza, the Thai restaurant has developed a strong local following. A big draw here are soft-shell crabs, which are prepared several ways. Also on the extensive menu are beef, chicken, fish and vegetarian selections. Casual dress. **Bar:** Full bar. **Reservations:** accepted. **Hours:** 11:30 am-10 pm, Sun from noon. Closed: 7/4, 11/27, 12/25; also for lunch 1/1. **Address:** 4819 Arlington Blvd 22203 **Location:** 1 mi w of jct SR 120, off US 50 at Park Dr; in Arlington Forest Shopping Center. **Parking:** on-site. **Cards:** AX, DC, DS, MC, VI.

EL CUSCATLECO RESTAURANT

Spanish
$5-$20

Phone: 703/519-8875 (54)

The vaired menu at El Cuscatleco is dominated by Latin American dishes with Salvadoran and Peruvian recipes, however Italian selections are also available. The atmosphere, in the shopping center restaurant, is casual and relaxed and service is efficient. Casual dress. **Bar:** Full bar. **Hours:** 11 am-10 pm, Fri & Sat 10 am-11 pm, Sun 10 am-10 pm. **Address:** 2927 S Glebe Rd 22206 **Location:** I-395, exit 7B northbound; exit 7 southbound, 1 mi s; 3.2 mi s of 14th St Bridge. **Parking:** on-site. **Cards:** AX, DS, MC, VI.

EL POLLO RICO

Peruvian
$4-$12

Phone: 703/522-3220 (47)

The first signs guests are in for a great meal are the overflowing parking lot and the great aromas emanating from the tiny spot. Selections are limited to succulent Peruvian roast chicken with mild or spicy dipping sauces, but there are a few choices among the desserts, such as cookies or flan. Casual dress. **Reservations:** not accepted. **Hours:** 11 am-10 pm. Closed: 1/1, 11/27, 12/25. **Address:** 932 N Kenmore St 22201 **Location:** Between Wilson Blvd and Fairfax Dr. **Parking:** on-site.

EXTRA VIRGIN

Italian
$8-$24

Phone: 703/998-8474 (55)

Modern Italian cuisine makes up a diverse menu that incorporates many homemade pasta and dessert choices. Casual dress. **Bar:** Full bar. **Reservations:** suggested, weekends. **Hours:** 11 am-4 & 5-10 pm, Sat & Sun-11 pm. Closed: 12/25. **Address:** 4053 28th St S 22206 **Location:** I-395, exit 6 northbound; exit 7 southbound, then just w; at the Village of Shirlington. **Parking:** street. **Cards:** AX, MC, VI.

THE GRILL

Continental
$12-$33

Phone: 703/412-2760 (1)

The elegantly traditional restaurant, which sustains a quiet, refined ambience, presents an appetizing menu of sophisticated American and northern European fare. The presentation displays a high degree of imagination, and preparation reveals a trained palate for complementary flavors. The professional and attentive service staff sees to patrons' needs. Semi-formal attire. **Bar:** Full bar. **Reservations:** suggested. **Hours:** 6:30 am-10:30 pm. **Address:** 1250 S Hayes St 22202 **Location:** 1 mi s of 14th St Bridge; in The Ritz-Carlton, Pentagon City. **Parking:** valet. **Cards:** AX, CB, DC, DS, JC, MC, VI.

CALL

(See maps and indexes p. 400-407, 412-417, 422-424)

GUAJILLO
Phone: 703/807-0840   40

Mexican
$5-$20

Hot tamales and a spicy and fun atmosphere merge at the restaurant. Guests can nibble on chips and black bean salsa while appreciating the friendly service. Casual dress. **Bar:** Full bar. **Reservations:** accepted. **Hours:** 11 am-10 pm, Fri-11 pm, Sat 5 pm-11 pm, Sun noon-10 pm. Closed: 12/25. **Address:** 1727 Wilson Blvd 22201 **Location:** I-66, exit 73, just s on Fort Myer Dr, then 0.4 mi w; in shopping plaza. **Parking:** on-site. **Cards:** AX, DS, MC, VI.

HARD TIMES CAFE
Phone: 703/528-2233

American
$6-$15

The hot and spicy, down-home operation knocks your socks off with an impressive variety of chilies, cooked in styles ranging from Cincinnati to Texas and vegetarian. Casual dress. **Bar:** Full bar. **Reservations:** not accepted. **Hours:** 11 am-1 am. **Address:** 3028 Wilson Blvd 22201 **Location:** Jct Highland St; opposite Clarendon Metro Station. **Parking:** street. **Cards:** AX, MC, VI.

HARRY'S TAP ROOM
Phone: 703/778-7788   44

American
$10-$26

Fresh, high quality food sets the tone here at Harry's Tap Room. The bi-level dining room offers an upscale, relaxed atmosphere suitable for any occasion, it's even kid friendly. The servers are friendly and helpful and will see to your needs. Casual dress. **Bar:** Full bar. **Reservations:** accepted. **Hours:** 11:30 am-3 & 5:30-10 pm, Fri-11 pm, Sat 10 am-3 & 5:30-11 pm, Sun 10 am-3 & 5:30-10 pm; Saturday and Sunday brunch. Closed: 12/25. **Address:** 2800 Clarendon Blvd 22201 **Location:** 0.4 mi n of N Courthouse Rd. **Parking:** on-site and street. **Cards:** AX, DS, MC, VI.

CALL

JALEO
Phone: 703/413-8181   5

Spanish
$6-$20

Brightly decorated with various colorful glass mosaics and a vibrant mural over the bar, this hip fun spot also serves up a fantastic assortment of traditional Spanish tapas, or small plates which are perfect for sharing. Specialties include garlic shrimp, a heavenly gazpacho and a variety of housemade sausages. Paella is also offered in the evening. Casual dress. **Bar:** Full bar. **Reservations:** accepted, until 7 pm. **Hours:** 11 am-10 pm, Wed-Fri to 11 pm, Sat noon-11 pm, Sun noon-10 pm. Closed: 11/27, 12/24, 12/25. **Address:** 2250A Crystal Dr 22202 **Location:** 1.6 mi s of 14th St Bridge; just e of US 1; in Crystal City Shops. **Parking:** on-site (fee). **Cards:** AX, CB, DC, DS, JC, MC, VI.

LA COTE D'OR CAFE
Phone: 703/534-8059   45

French
$6-$29

Diners enjoy intimate dining in a country atmosphere. The skilled kitchen prepares dishes from all regions of France, and the chef makes seasonal changes to the menu. Specialty desserts—such as luscious tarte tatin (apple tart) and raspberries baked with hot caramel sauce—are a delicious way to complete a meal. Casual dress. **Bar:** Full bar. **Reservations:** suggested. **Hours:** 11:30 am-3 & 5-10 pm, Sun 11 am-3 & 5-9 pm. Closed: 1/1, 12/25. **Address:** 6876 Lee Hwy 22213 **Location:** I-66, exit 69, just s on US 29. **Parking:** street. **Cards:** AX, DC, MC, VI.

LEBANESE TAVERNA
Phone: 703/415-8681

Lebanese
$6-$20

Seating can be requested in the charming dining room or on the al fresco patio when the weather cooperates. The kitchen uses traditional Middle Eastern ingredients in preparing Lebanese fare. Casual dress. **Bar:** Full bar. **Reservations:** accepted, until 6:30 pm & 6 pm on Sat. **Hours:** 11:30 am-3 & 5-10 pm, Fri-10:30 pm, Sat 11:30 am-10:30 pm, Sun noon-9 pm. Closed major holidays. **Address:** 1101 S Joyce St, Suite B30 22202 **Location:** I-395, exit 8C, just s off Army Navy Dr; in Pentagon Row. **Parking:** on-site (fee). **Cards:** AX, DC, DS, MC, VI.

CALL

LEGAL SEA FOODS
Phone: 703/415-1200

Seafood
$8-$30

Legal prides itself on a reputation for freshness and consistency. More than 40 varieties of seafood can be grilled, broiled, fried or prepared Cajun style. Try the clam chowder that has been served at every presidential inauguration since 1981. The nautically inspired dining room is upscale and attractive with its rich cherry wood paneling and intricately detailed model ships. Casual dress. **Bar:** Full bar. **Reservations:** suggested, weekends. **Hours:** 11 am-10 pm, Fri & Sat-11 pm, Sun noon-9 pm. **Address:** 2301 Jefferson Davis Hwy 22202 **Location:** At 23rd St S and Jefferson Davis Hwy. **Parking:** street. **Cards:** AX, CB, DC, DS, MC, VI.

MATUBA
Phone: 703/521-2811   53

Japanese
$6-$19

The small store front looks like less than it is but people crowd the small unassuming dining room for well-prepared typical dishes of tempura, teriyaki, sushi, sashimi and the assorted bento box lunches. A small salad bar is a pleasant surprise. Casual dress. **Bar:** Beer & wine. **Hours:** 11:30 am-2 & 5:30-10 pm, Fri-10:30 pm, Sat 5 pm-10:30 pm. Closed: 11/27; also Sun. **Address:** 2915 Columbia Pike 22204 **Location:** On SR 244 (Columbia Pike), just w of jct S Walter Reed Dr. **Parking:** street. **Cards:** AX, MC, VI.

METRO 29 DINER
Phone: 703/528-2464   39

American
$5-$20

The shiny chrome diner is just what guests might expect. Extensive menu offerings include breakfast items served all day, as well as salads, sandwiches, full meals and a seemingly endless selection of desserts, including cakes and pies made here in the kitchen. Casual dress. **Bar:** Full bar. **Reservations:** not accepted. **Hours:** 6 am-1 am, Fri & Sat-3 am. Closed: 12/25. **Address:** 4711 Lee Hwy 22207 **Location:** I-66, exit 71, 0.5 mi n on Glebe Rd (SR 120) at US 29. **Parking:** on-site. **Cards:** AX, CB, DC, DS, MC, VI.

MEXICALI BLUES
Phone: 703/812-9352   43

Mexican
$5-$13

The small corner restaurant prepares some solid Mexican, and a few El Salvadoran, dishes at a good value. It's nothing fancy inside, but the service is friendly and attentive. Casual dress. **Bar:** Full bar. **Reservations:** not accepted. **Hours:** 11 am-10 pm, Fri & Sat-11 pm; Saturday and Sunday brunch. Closed major holidays. **Address:** 2933 Wilson Blvd 22201 **Location:** Jct N Garfield St. **Parking:** street. **Cards:** AX, MC, VI.

(See maps and indexes p. 400-407, 412-417, 422-424)

MORTON'S THE STEAKHOUSE
Steak House
$32-$59

Phone: 703/418-1444   [2]

Patrons should make sure to reserve ahead for the popular, well-known steak house. Large portions, including huge cuts of fine beef and plentiful seafood, are the norm. Even the vegetables are oversized, with baked potatoes big enough for sharing. Dressy casual. **Bar:** Full bar. **Reservations:** suggested. **Hours:** 5:30 pm-11 pm, Sun 5 pm-10 pm. Closed major holidays. **Address:** 1631 Crystal Square Arcade, Suite 54 22202 **Location:** 1.2 mi s of 14th St Bridge; in the underground of Crystal City Shopping Complex. **Parking:** on-site (fee) and valet. **Cards:** AX, CB, DC, DS, JC, MC, VI.

THE PORTOFINO RESTAURANT
Northern Italian
$10-$25

Phone: 703/979-8200   [9]

Established in 1970 this family owned and operated Northern Italian restaurant serves a fine selection of veal, seafood, chicken, beef and pasta dishes. Service is professional with waiters attired in tuxedos. Dressy casual. **Bar:** Full bar. **Reservations:** suggested. **Hours:** 11 am-2 & 5-10 pm, Sat & Sun from 5 pm. Closed major holidays. **Address:** 526 S 23rd St 22202 **Location:** 1.5 blks w of US 1; in Crystal City area. **Parking:** on-site. **Cards:** AX, DC, DS, MC, VI.

QUEEN BEE RESTAURANT
Vietnamese
$4-$10

Phone: 703/527-3444   [46]

A dependable kitchen as the popular, neighborhood restaurant delivers with such dishes as Hanoi-grilled pork, soft-shell crabs and grilled fish. Vietnamese paintings and silk flowers create a comfortable, relaxing atmosphere. Casual dress. **Bar:** Beer & wine. **Reservations:** accepted. **Hours:** 11 am-10 pm. Closed: 7/4, 11/27, 12/25. **Address:** 3181 Wilson Blvd 22201 **Location:** Jct Washington and Wilson blvds; opposite Clarendon Metro Station. **Parking:** street. **Cards:** AX, DC, MC, VI.

RIO GRANDE CAFE
Mexican
$9-$25

Phone: 703/528-3131   [49]

A loud, energetic cantina atmosphere—characterized by a warehouse look with raw floors and Mexican music gives this fun and festive restaurant its heart. The mesquite-grilled fajitas and stuffed jumbo shrimp are menu favorites. Sidewalk patio dining when the weather cooperates. Casual dress. **Bar:** Full bar. **Hours:** 11 am-10:30 pm, Fri & Sat-11:30 pm; Sunday brunch. Closed: 11/27, 12/25; also for dinner 12/24. **Address:** 4301 N Fairfax Dr 22203 **Location:** I-66, exit 71, 0.3 mi e of jct SR 120 and 237 (Glebe Rd and Fairfax Dr); in the Ballston area. **Parking:** street. **Cards:** AX, DC, DS, MC, VI.

RUTH'S CHRIS STEAK HOUSE
Steak House
$16-$43

Phone: 703/979-7275   [4]

The main fare is steak, which is prepared from several cuts of prime beef and cooked to perfection, but the menu also lists lamb, chicken and seafood dishes. Guests should come hungry because the side dishes, which are among the a la carte offerings, could make a meal in themselves. Dressy casual. **Bar:** Full bar. **Reservations:** suggested. **Hours:** 11:30 am-10 pm, Sat 5 pm-10:30 pm, Sun 4 pm-9 pm. Closed: 11/27, 12/25. **Address:** 2231 Crystal Dr 22202 **Location:** 1.6 mi s of 14th St Bridge, just e of US 1; in Crystal Park Building 3, on 11th floor; in Crystal City. **Parking:** on-site (fee). **Cards:** AX, CB, DC, DS, MC, VI.

SILVER DINER
American
$9-$15

Phone: 703/812-8600

The eatery with its chrome and glass plate exterior and the glow of neon, provides the traditional diner setting. Booths with juke boxes, counter service and friendly wait staff add to the diner experience. The menu is extensive with salads, sandwiches and full meals. The desserts are made fresh and the fountain treats, shakes, floats and malts make for a great ending. Breakfast is available all day. Casual dress. **Bar:** Beer & wine. **Reservations:** not accepted. **Hours:** 7 am-2 am, Fri & Sat-4 am. Closed: 11/27. **Address:** 3200 Wilson Blvd 22201 **Location:** Jct Irving St; just w of Clarendon Metro Station. **Parking:** on-site. **Cards:** AX, DS, MC, VI.

SIN E IRISH PUB AND RESTAURANT
Irish
$7-$17

Phone: 703/415-4420   [52]

Representative of typical fare are shepherd's pie, corned beef and cabbage and Irish lamb stew, as well as seafood pasta, pecan-encrusted chicken and Gaelic steak. The decor is authentic, with all but the flooring coming from Ireland. "Snugs," Irish for booths, are private, and one room has a large fireplace. Access to the Pentagon City metro stop is directly through the mall. Casual dress. **Bar:** Full bar. **Reservations:** accepted. **Hours:** 11 am-10 pm, Fri & Sat-midnight. Closed: 11/27, 12/25. **Address:** 1301 S Joyce St 22202 **Location:** Just n of 15th St; behind Fashion Centre at Pentagon City Mall; in Pentagon Row. **Parking:** on-site (fee). **Cards:** AX, DC, DS, MC, VI.

CALL (EM)

TARA THAI
Thai
$6-$13

Phone: 703/908-4999

The stylish cafe's sea motif is one aspect of its contemporary atmosphere. Specialties include whole fresh rockfish and skewered chicken, just to mention two. Most notable is the nicely presented goong phu-ket and pad thai noodles. Portion sizes are ample. Casual dress. **Bar:** Full bar. **Reservations:** suggested. **Hours:** 11:30 am-3 & 5-10 pm, Fri-11 pm, Sat noon-3:30 & 5-11 pm, Sun noon-3:30 & 5-10 pm. Closed: 11/27; also 12/31 & for lunch 1/1. **Address:** 4001 N Fairfax Dr 22203 **Location:** I-66, exit 71, 0.4 mi e of jct SR 120 (Glebe Rd) and 237 (Fairfax Dr). **Parking:** street. **Cards:** AX, DC, DS, MC, VI.

T.H.A.I. IN SHIRLINGTON   *Menu on AAA.com*
Thai
$7-$16

Phone: 703/931-3203   [56]

Part of a main street setting in the Shirlington area, the stylish Thai restaurant offers tasty authentic dishes and seasonal menu additions. Casual dress. **Bar:** Full bar. **Reservations:** accepted. **Hours:** 11:30 am-10 pm, Fri & Sat-11 pm. Closed: 11/27; also 9/6 & for lunch 12/25. **Address:** 4029 S 28th St 22206 **Location:** I-395, exit 6 northbound; exit 7 southbound, just w; in the Village of Shirlington. **Parking:** on-site. **Cards:** AX, CB, DC, DS, MC, VI.

(See maps and indexes p. 400-407, 412-417, 422-424)

THAIPHOON

Thai
$7-$16

Phone: 703/413-8200   51

Set off the plaza at Pentagon Row, the colorful, trendy Thai cafe prepares food ranging from mild to spicy. Beef "kapow" leaves mouths tingling. Mango and sticky rice is a popular dessert. Casual dress. **Bar:** Full bar. **Reservations:** accepted. **Hours:** 11:30 am-10:30 pm, Fri & Sat-11 pm. Closed: 11/27, 12/24, 12/25. **Address:** 1301 S Joyce St 22202 **Location:** I-395, exit 8C, just s on Army Navy Dr; in Pentagon Row. **Parking:** on-site and street. **Cards:** AX, CB, DC, DS, MC, VI.

TIVOLI RESTAURANT

Northern Italian
$11-$33

Phone: 703/524-8900   140

An upscale ambience pervades the contemporary dining room, where patrons order from a seasonally changing menu of fresh pasta dishes and tempting homemade pastries. The large wine selection is housed in a glass cellar in the middle of the dining area. Complimentary garage parking is available after 5 pm. Parking is validated for one hour at lunch. Dressy casual. **Bar:** Full bar. **Reservations:** suggested. **Hours:** 11:30 am-2:30 & 5:30-10 pm, Sat from 5:30 pm. Closed major holidays; also Sun. **Address:** 1700 N Moore St 22209 **Location:** At Rosslyn Metro Station. **Parking:** on-site (fee). **Cards:** AX, CB, DC, DS, MC, VI.

TOM SARRIS' ORLEANS HOUSE

Phone: 703/524-2929   139

American
$7-$23

An old New Orleans atmosphere—with quaint balconies and Tiffany lamps—pervades the low-key restaurant. Prime rib is the primary specialty, but the sinful desserts, such as chocolate pie and chocolate bourbon pecan pie, have a fan base all their own. Casual dress. **Bar:** Full bar. **Reservations:** accepted. **Hours:** 11 am-10 pm, Fri-11 pm, Sat 4 pm-11 pm, Sun 4 pm-10 pm. Closed: 11/27, 12/25. **Address:** 1213 Wilson Blvd 22209 **Location:** I-66, exit 73, 2 blks sw of Key Bridge; in Rosslyn area. **Parking:** on-site. **Cards:** AX, CB, DC, DS, MC, VI.

TOP THAI RESTAURANT

Phone: 703/521-1305   6

Thai
$7-$14

The Crystal City restaurant prepares Thai cuisine in modest surroundings. On the menu is a wide variety, including curry, meat and seafood dishes, along with noodle and vegetarian selections. The sidewalk deck is popular when the weather cooperates. Casual dress. **Bar:** Beer & wine. **Reservations:** accepted. **Hours:** 11 am-3 & 5-10 pm, Sat & Sun from noon. **Address:** 523 23rd St S 22202 **Location:** 1.5 blks w of US 1; in Crystal City area. **Parking:** street. **Cards:** AX, DS, MC, VI.

URBAN THAI

Thai
$6-$15

Phone: 703/979-0777   7

In the Crystal City area of Arlington, Urban Thai, prepares modern Thai cuisine using fresh ingredients, no MSG added. The menu offers a nice selection of traditional Thai entrees, as well as noodles, rice, curry and vegetarian dishes. Little red chilies on the menu indicate the degree of spicyness of the dish. Big bowl lunch specials are available from 11 am-3 pm. Casual dress. **Bar:** Full bar. **Reservations:** accepted. **Hours:** 11 am-10 pm, Fri & Sat-11 pm. Closed: 11/27, 12/25. **Address:** 561 S 23rd St 22202 **Location:** 2 blks w of US 1; in Crystal City area. **Parking:** street. **Cards:** AX, DS, MC, VI.

CALL &M

VILLAGE BISTRO

Continental
$10-$25

Phone: 703/522-0284   42

Gourmet French food with a touch of Italian gives this restaurant a busy night. Casual atmosphere draws in people walking by or the shopping plaza. Pasta, fish, and meat dishes are on the menu. Save room for dessert or an after dinner beverage. Casual dress. **Bar:** Full bar. **Reservations:** suggested. **Hours:** 11:30 am-2:30 & 5-10 pm, Fri-10:30 pm, Sat 5 pm-10:30 pm, Sun 5 pm-10 pm. Closed major holidays. **Address:** 1723 Wilson Blvd 22209 **Location:** I-66, exit 73, just s on Fort Myer Dr, then 0.4 mi w; in shopping plaza. **Parking:** on-site. **Cards:** AX, DC, DS, MC, VI.

ASHBURN

———— WHERE TO STAY ————

EMBASSY SUITES HOTEL DULLES-NORTH   *Book great rates at AAA.com*   **Phone: 703/723-5300**

AAA SAVE

Small-scale Hotel
Rates not provided

Address: 44610 Waxpool Rd 20147 **Location:** 1.7 mi w of jct SR 28 and Waxpool Rd (SR 625); SR 7, 3.4 mi s on Loudoun County Pkwy (CR 607), 0.3 mi w. **Facility:** 154 units. 153 one- and 1 two-bedroom suites, some with whirlpools. 6 stories, interior corridors. *Bath:* combo or shower only. **Parking:** on-site. **Amenities:** dual phone lines, voice mail, irons, hair dryers. *Fee:* video games, high-speed Internet. **Pool(s):** heated indoor. **Leisure Activities:** whirlpool, pool privileges, exercise room. **Guest Services:** valet and coin laundry, airport transportation-Washington Dulles International Airport, area transportation-within 5 mi, wireless Internet. **Business Services:** conference facilities, business center. **Free Special Amenities: full breakfast and newspaper.**

HOMEWOOD SUITES BY HILTON/DULLES NORTH   *Book great rates at AAA.com*   **Phone: 703/723-7500**

AAA SAVE

Small-scale Hotel
Rates not provided

Address: 44620 Waxpool Rd 20147 **Location:** 1.7 mi w of jct SR 28 and Waxpool Rd (SR 625); SR 7, 3.4 mi s on Loudoun County Pkwy (CR 607), 0.3 mi w. **Facility:** 90 units. 22 one-bedroom standard units with efficiencies. 57 one- and 11 two-bedroom suites, some with efficiencies or kitchens. 3 stories, interior corridors. *Bath:* combo or shower only. **Parking:** on-site. **Amenities:** video games (fee), CD players, high-speed Internet, dual phone lines, voice mail, safes, irons, hair dryers. *Some:* DVD players. **Pool(s):** outdoor. **Leisure Activities:** barbecue grill, exercise room. **Guest Services:** valet and coin laundry, airport transportation-Washington Dulles International Airport, area transportation-within 5 mi, wireless Internet. **Business Services:** meeting rooms, business center. **Free Special Amenities: full breakfast and high-speed Internet.**

──── **WHERE TO DINE** ────

TIJUANA FLATS   **Phone:** 703/724-4474

Tex-Mex
$5-$9

The quick-serve Tex-Mex eatery sets up a distinctive hot sauce bar to accompany its burritos, chimichangas, tacos and enchiladas. Guests can expect a line out the door at lunch. Casual dress. **Bar:** Beer & wine. **Reservations:** not accepted. **Hours:** 10:30 am-10 pm. Closed major holidays. **Address:** 20020 Ashbrook Commons Plaza, Suite 117 20147 **Location:** From SR 7, just s on Ashburn Village Blvd; in Ashbrook Commons Plaza. **Parking:** on-site. **Cards:** AX, MC, VI.

BURKE

──── **WHERE TO DINE** ────

ANITA'S   **Phone:** 703/455-3466

Mexican
$5-$14

This small chain is locally popular for their signature "New Mexico" style dishes. The menu features a good variety of tacos, burritos and enchiladas. If you're in the mood for a Mexican breakfast, this is the place. Casual dress. **Bar:** Full bar. **Reservations:** accepted. **Hours:** 8 am-9:30 pm, Fri-10 pm, Sat 6 am-10 pm, Sun 6 am-9 pm. Closed: 1/1, 11/27, 12/25. **Address:** 9278 Old Keene Mill Rd 22015 **Location:** 1.3 mi e from jct SR 7100 (Fairfax County Pkwy); in Rolling Valley Shopping Center. **Parking:** on-site. **Cards:** AX, DC, DS, MC, VI.

GLORY DAYS GRILL   **Phone:** 703/866-1911

American
$7-$18

Lending to the casual restaurant's sports-themed atmosphere are memorabilia decorating the dining area and 25 TVs with control centers at each table and booth. Food selections range from wings and ribs to seafood, beef and pasta dishes. Casual dress. **Bar:** Full bar. **Reservations:** not accepted. **Hours:** 4 pm-midnight, Fri & Sat from 11:30 am, Sun 11:30 am-11 pm. Closed: 11/27, 12/25. **Address:** 9526-C Old Keene Mill Rd 22015 **Location:** 0.9 mi e of jct SR 7100 (Fairfax County Pkwy); jct Lee Chapel and Old Keene Mill Rds; in Burke Town Plaza. **Parking:** on-site. **Cards:** AX, DS, MC, VI.

CENTREVILLE pop. 48,661 (See map and index starting on p. 412)

──── **WHERE TO STAY** ────

EXTENDED STAYAMERICA-CENTREVILLE   *Book at AAA.com*   **Phone:** (703)988-9955

Small-scale Hotel
$119-$129 All Year

Address: 5920 Fort Dr 20121 **Location:** I-66, exit 53, 0.9 mi s on SR 28; off SR 28, 0.3 mi s of jct US 29. **Facility:** 95 one-bedroom standard units with efficiencies. 6 stories, interior corridors. **Bath:** combo or shower only. **Parking:** on-site. **Terms:** office hours 7 am-11 pm. **Amenities:** dual phone lines, voice mail, irons. **Guest Services:** coin laundry, wireless Internet. **Cards:** AX, DC, DS, JC, MC, VI.

SPRINGHILL SUITES BY MARRIOTT
CENTREVILLE/CHANTILLY   *Book great rates at AAA.com*   **Phone:** 703-815-7800   **91**

Small-scale Hotel
$208-$230 All Year

Address: 5920 Trinity Pkwy 20120 **Location:** I-66, exit 52, just n on US 29. Located in a commerical shopping/business area. **Facility:** Smoke free premises. 136 one-bedroom standard units. 4 stories, interior corridors. **Bath:** combo or shower only. **Parking:** on-site. **Amenities:** high-speed Internet, dual phone lines, voice mail, irons, hair dryers. **Pool(s):** heated indoor. **Leisure Activities:** whirlpool, exercise room. **Guest Services:** valet and coin laundry. **Business Services:** meeting rooms, business center. **Cards:** AX, DC, DS, MC, VI.

AAA Benefit:
Members save 5% off of the best available rate.

──── **WHERE TO DINE** ────

BLUE WATER GRILLE   **Phone:** 703-803-1040   **117**

American
$7-$18

The casual eatery's American cuisine reflects a Mediterranean influence. A large deck is open during the warmer months, and a roaring fireplace blazes in the dining room when it's cold. Casual dress. **Bar:** Full bar. **Reservations:** accepted. **Hours:** 11 am-11 pm, Sun from 10 am. Closed: 1/1, 12/25. **Address:** 5127 Westfields Blvd 20120 **Location:** I-66, exit 53, 2 mi n on SR 28, then just w on Westfield Blvd; 1.7 mi s of jct SR 28 and US 50; in Sully Station Shopping Center. **Parking:** on-site. **Cards:** AX, CB, DC, DS, MC, VI.

FIORA'S   **Phone:** 703-803-2800   **116**

South Italian
$6-$25

The shopping plaza restaurant offers a varied menu of Southern Italian selections, which range from pasta and veal to chicken, steak and seafood dishes, as well as sandwiches and pizza. Casual dress. **Bar:** Full bar. **Reservations:** suggested. **Hours:** 11 am-10 pm, Sun 4 pm-9 pm. Closed major holidays. **Address:** 5081 Westfield Blvd 20120 **Location:** 1.7 mi s of jct SR 28 and US 50; in Sully Station Shopping Center. **Parking:** on-site. **Cards:** AX, DC, DS, MC, VI.

GLORY DAYS GRILL, CENTREVILLE   **Phone:** 703/266-4100

American
$7-$18

Lending to the casual restaurant's sports-themed atmosphere are memorabilia decorating the dining area and 25 TVs with control centers at each table and booth. Food selections range from wings and ribs to seafood, beef and pasta dishes. Casual dress. **Bar:** Full bar. **Reservations:** not accepted. **Hours:** 4 pm-midnight, Fri & Sat from 11:30 am, Sun 11:30 am-11 pm. Closed: 11/27, 12/25. **Address:** 13850 Braddock Rd 20121 **Location:** Off US 29, just e of jct SR 28; in Old Centreville Crossing Shopping Plaza. **Parking:** on-site. **Cards:** AX, DS, MC, VI.

(See map and index starting on p. 412)

SWEETWATER TAVERN   **Phone:** 703/449-1100

American
$8-$25

Casual dress. **Bar:** Full bar. **Hours:** 11 am-11 pm, Fri & Sat-midnight, Sun & Mon-10 pm. Closed: 11/27, 12/25. **Address:** 14250 Sweetwater Ln 20121 **Location:** I-66, exit 53A, 1.1 mi s on SR 28; 0.4 mi s on SR 28 from jct US 29; in Centre Ridge Marketplace. **Parking:** on-site. **Cards:** AX, DS, MC, VI.

CALL

CHANTILLY pop. 41,041 (See map and index starting on p. 412)

——— WHERE TO STAY ———

COMFORT SUITES CHANTILLY-DULLES AIRPORT   *Book at AAA.com*   **Phone:** (703)263-2007 **114**

Small-scale Hotel
$79-$229 All Year

Address: 13980 Metrotech Dr 20151 **Location:** Jct SR 28, 0.5 mi e on US 50. Located behind the Sully Plaza Shopping Center. **Facility:** 89 one-bedroom standard units, some with whirlpools. 4 stories, interior corridors. *Bath:* combo or shower only. **Parking:** on-site. **Amenities:** high-speed Internet, dual phone lines, voice mail, irons, hair dryers. *Some:* DVD players. **Pool(s):** heated indoor. **Leisure Activities:** sauna, limited exercise equipment. **Guest Services:** valet and coin laundry, area transportation, wireless Internet. **Business Services:** meeting rooms, business center. **Cards:** AX, CB, DC, DS, JC, MC, VI.

COURTYARD BY MARRIOTT-DULLES AIRPORT   *Book great rates at AAA.com*   **Phone:** 703/709-7100 **115**

Small-scale Hotel
$241-$263 All Year

Address: 3935 Centerview Dr 20151 **Location:** Jct SR 28, just e on US 50. **Facility:** Smoke free premises. 149 units. 137 one-bedroom standard units. 12 one-bedroom suites. 3 stories, interior corridors. *Bath:* combo or shower only. **Parking:** on-site. **Amenities:** video games (fee), high-speed Internet, dual phone lines, voice mail, irons, hair dryers. **Pool(s):** heated indoor. **Leisure Activities:** whirlpool, exercise room. **Guest Services:** valet and coin laundry. **Business Services:** meeting rooms, PC. **Cards:** AX, DC, DS, JC, MC, VI.

AAA Benefit:
Members save 5% off of the best available rate.

EXTENDED STAYAMERICA-CHANTILLY   *Book at AAA.com*   **Phone:** (703)263-7173 **111**

Small-scale Hotel
$154-$164 All Year

Address: 14420 Chantilly Crossing Ln 20151 **Location:** On US 50, 0.4 mi w of jct SR 28; at Chantilly Crossing Shopping Complex. **Facility:** 104 one-bedroom standard units with efficiencies. 3 stories, interior corridors. *Bath:* combo or shower only. **Parking:** on-site. **Terms:** office hours 7 am-11 pm. **Amenities:** voice mail, irons. **Guest Services:** coin laundry, wireless Internet. **Cards:** AX, DC, DS, JC, MC, VI.

EXTENDED STAY DELUXE CHANTILLY   *Book at AAA.com*   **Phone:** (703)263-7200 **117**

Small-scale Hotel
$164-$174 All Year

Address: 4506 Brookfield Corporate Dr 20151 **Location:** I-66, exit 53, 3 mi n on SR 28; 1 mi s of jct SR 28 and US 50. **Facility:** 88 one-bedroom standard units with efficiencies. 3 stories, interior corridors. *Bath:* combo or shower only. **Amenities:** DVD players, dual phone lines, voice mail, safes, irons, hair dryers. **Pool(s):** heated outdoor. **Leisure Activities:** limited exercise equipment. **Guest Services:** valet and coin laundry, wireless Internet. **Cards:** AX, DC, DS, JC, MC, VI.

FAIRFIELD INN BY MARRIOTT-CHANTILLY/DULLES
SOUTH   *Book great rates at AAA.com*   **Phone:** 703/435-1111 **113**

Small-scale Hotel
$197-$230 All Year

Address: 3960 Corsair Ct 20151 **Location:** Jct SR 28, just e on US 50. **Facility:** Smoke free premises. 85 one-bedroom standard units, some with whirlpools. 3 stories, interior corridors. *Bath:* combo or shower only. **Parking:** on-site. **Amenities:** dual phone lines, voice mail, irons, hair dryers. **Pool(s):** heated indoor. **Leisure Activities:** whirlpool, limited exercise equipment. **Guest Services:** valet and coin laundry, area transportation, wireless Internet. **Business Services:** PC. **Cards:** AX, DC, DS, JC, MC, VI.

AAA Benefit:
Members save 5% off of the best available rate.

(See map and index starting on p. 412)

HAMPTON INN WASHINGTON DULLES INTERNATIONAL AIRPORT SOUTH

Book great rates at AAA.com

Phone: (703)818-8200   108

Small-scale Hotel
$79-$239 All Year

Address: 4050 Westfax Dr 20151 **Location:** 1 mi w on US 50 from jct SR 28. **Facility:** 137 one-bedroom standard units. 7 stories, interior corridors. *Bath:* combo or shower only. **Parking:** on-site. **Amenities:** video games (fee), voice mail, irons, hair dryers. **Pool(s):** heated indoor. **Leisure Activities:** whirlpool, sun deck, limited exercise equipment. **Guest Services:** valet and coin laundry, airport transportation-Washington Dulles International Airport, area transportation-within 3 mi, wireless Internet. **Business Services:** meeting rooms, PC. **Cards:** AX, CB, DC, DS, MC, VI. **Free Special Amenities:** expanded continental breakfast and high-speed Internet. *(See color ad p 558)*

HOLIDAY INN SELECT CHANTILLY-DULLES EXPO CENTER

Book at AAA.com

Phone: 703/815-6060   116

Large-scale Hotel
Rates not provided

Address: 4335 Chantilly Shopping Center 20151 **Location:** I-66, exit 53, 3 mi n on SR 28; 1 mi s of jct US 50 and SR 28. Located adjacent to Dulles Expo Center. **Facility:** 232 units. 220 one-bedroom standard units. 12 one-bedroom suites. 6 stories, interior corridors. *Bath:* combo or shower only. **Parking:** on-site. **Amenities:** high-speed Internet, dual phone lines, voice mail, safes, irons, hair dryers. **Pool(s):** outdoor. **Leisure Activities:** whirlpool, exercise room. **Guest Services:** complimentary and valet laundry, area transportation, wireless Internet. **Business Services:** meeting rooms, business center.

HYATT PLACE CHANTILLY/DULLES AIRPORT-SOUTH

Book great rates at AAA.com

Phone: (703)961-8160   119

Small-scale Hotel
$99-$299 All Year

Address: 4994 Weststone Plaza Dr 20151 **Location:** I-66, exit 53, 2 mi n on SR 28, then just w on Westfields Blvd; 1.7 mi s of jct SR 28 and US 50. Located adjacent to shopping plaza. **Facility:** 122 one-bedroom standard units. 6 stories, interior corridors. *Bath:* combo or shower only. **Parking:** on-site. **Terms:** cancellation fee imposed. **Amenities:** high-speed Internet, voice mail, irons, hair dryers. **Pool(s):** outdoor. **Leisure Activities:** limited exercise equipment. **Guest Services:** valet and coin laundry, airport transportation-Washington Dulles International Airport. **Business Services:** meeting rooms, business center. **Cards:** AX, CB, DC, DS, JC, MC, VI. **Free Special Amenities:** full breakfast and high-speed Internet.

HYATT PLACE
AAA Benefit:
Ask for the AAA rate and save 10%.

RESIDENCE INN BY MARRIOTT CHANTILLY DULLES SOUTH

Book great rates at AAA.com

Phone: 703/263-7900   112

Small-scale Hotel
$252-$274 All Year

Address: 14440 Chantilly Crossing Ln 20151 **Location:** I-66, exit 57B, on US 50, just w of jct SR 28. Located next to a shopping center. **Facility:** Smoke free premises. 123 units. 81 one-bedroom standard units, some with efficiencies or kitchens. 30 one- and 12 two-bedroom suites, some with efficiencies or kitchens. 4 stories, interior corridors. *Bath:* combo or shower only. **Parking:** on-site. **Terms:** check-in 4 pm. **Amenities:** high-speed Internet, voice mail, irons, hair dryers. **Pool(s):** heated outdoor. **Leisure Activities:** whirlpool, exercise room, sports court. **Guest Services:** valet and coin laundry. **Business Services:** meeting rooms. **Cards:** AX, DC, DS, JC, MC, VI.

Residence
AAA Benefit:
Members save 5% off of the best available rate.

STAYBRIDGE SUITES HOTEL CHANTILLY/DULLES INTERNATIONAL AIRPORT

Book great rates at AAA.com

Phone: (703)435-8090   110

Small-scale Hotel
$79-$229 All Year

Address: 3860 Centerview Dr 20151 **Location:** Jct SR 28, just e on US 50. **Facility:** 142 units. 62 one-bedroom standard units with efficiencies. 64 one- and 16 two-bedroom suites with efficiencies. 4 stories, interior corridors. *Bath:* combo or shower only. **Parking:** on-site. **Terms:** cancellation fee imposed. **Amenities:** video library (fee), DVD players, CD players, high-speed Internet, dual phone lines, voice mail, safes, irons, hair dryers. **Pool(s):** heated indoor. **Leisure Activities:** exercise room. **Guest Services:** complimentary and valet laundry, airport transportation-Washington Dulles International Airport, wireless Internet. **Business Services:** meeting rooms, business center. **Cards:** AX, CB, DC, DS, JC, MC, VI. **Free Special Amenities:** full breakfast and high-speed Internet.

(See map and index starting on p. 412)

TOWNEPLACE SUITES BY MARRIOTT-CHANTILLY *Book great rates at AAA.com* Phone: 703/709-0453 109

Small-scale Hotel
$186-$208 All Year

Address: 14036 Thunderbolt Pl 20151 **Location:** Jct SR 28, just e on US 50. **Facility:** Smoke free premises. 94 units. 68 one-bedroom standard units with kitchens. 4 one- and 22 two-bedroom suites with kitchens. 3 stories, interior corridors. *Bath:* combo or shower only. **Parking:** on-site. **Amenities:** high-speed Internet, dual phone lines, voice mail, irons, hair dryers. **Pool(s):** heated outdoor. **Leisure Activities:** limited exercise equipment. **Guest Services:** valet and coin laundry. **Business Services:** PC. **Cards:** AX, DC, DS, JC, MC, VI.

AAA Benefit:
Members save 5% off of the best available rate.

WESTFIELDS MARRIOTT *Book great rates at AAA.com* Phone: 703/818-0300 118

Large-scale Hotel
$362-$384 All Year

Address: 14750 Conference Center Dr 20151 **Location:** I-66, exit 53, 2 mi n on SR 28, just w on Westfields Blvd, then 0.5 mi n on Stonecraft Blvd; 1.7 mi s of jct SR 28 and US 50. **Facility:** Smoke free premises. 336 units. 332 one-bedroom standard units. 4 one-bedroom suites. 4 stories, interior corridors. *Bath:* combo or shower only. **Parking:** on-site and valet. **Terms:** check-in 4 pm. **Amenities:** dual phone lines, voice mail, irons, hair dryers. *Fee:* video games, high-speed Internet. *Some:* DVD players, CD players. **Dining:** Palm Court at Westfields Marriott, see separate listing. **Pool(s):** heated outdoor, heated indoor. **Leisure Activities:** saunas, whirlpools, steamroom, 8 lighted tennis courts, jogging, spa, basketball, volleyball. *Fee:* golf-18 holes, bicycles. **Guest Services:** valet laundry, wireless Internet. *Fee:* airport transportation-Washington Dulles International Airport, area transportation-Westfields Business Park & golf course. **Business Services:** conference facilities, business center. **Cards:** AX, DC, DS, JC, MC, VI. **Free Special Amenities:** newspaper and high-speed Internet.

Marriott.
HOTELS & RESORTS

AAA Benefit:
Members save 5% off of the best available rate.

WINGATE INN DULLES AIRPORT-CHANTILLY *Book at AAA.com* Phone: (571)203-0999 107

Small-scale Hotel
$145-$269 All Year

Address: 3940 Centerview Dr 20151 **Location:** Jct SR 28, just e on US 50. **Facility:** 131 one-bedroom standard units, some with whirlpools. 4 stories, interior corridors. *Bath:* combo or shower only. **Parking:** on-site. **Terms:** cancellation fee imposed. **Amenities:** video games (fee), high-speed Internet, dual phone lines, voice mail, safes, irons, hair dryers. **Pool(s):** heated indoor. **Leisure Activities:** whirlpool, limited exercise equipment. **Guest Services:** valet and coin laundry, area transportation, wireless Internet. **Business Services:** meeting rooms, business center. **Cards:** AX, CB, DC, DS, JC, MC, VI.

——— WHERE TO DINE ———

ANITA'S Phone: 703/378-1717

Mexican
$5-$15

This small chain is locally popular for their signature "New Mexico" style dishes. The menu features a good variety of tacos, burritos and enchiladas. If you're in the mood for a Mexican breakfast, this is the place. Casual dress. **Bar:** Full bar. **Reservations:** accepted. **Hours:** 4:30 am-9 pm, Fri-Sun to 10 pm. Closed: 11/27, 12/25. **Address:** 13921 Lee Jackson Hwy 20151 **Location:** On US 50, 0.4 mi e of jct SR 28. **Parking:** on-site. **Cards:** AX, DC, DS, MC, VI.

BACKYARD GRILL AND BAR Phone: 703/802-6400 137

American
$6-$20

Selections on the restaurant's menu range from salads and sandwiches to steaks and pasta. Seating on the covered patio is an option during good weather. Casual dress. **Bar:** Full bar. **Reservations:** accepted. **Hours:** 11 am-11 pm, Fri & Sat-midnight, Sun-10 pm. Closed: 12/25. **Address:** 13999 Metrotech Dr 20151 **Location:** Jct SR 28, 0.5 mi e on US 50; in Sully Plaza. **Parking:** on-site. **Cards:** AX, CB, DC, DS, MC, VI.

OTANI JAPANESE STEAK HOUSE Phone: 703/802-3400 138

Japanese
$7-$33

Hibachi cooking makes for a delicious and entertaining meal. The chef prepares food with a showy display of his skill with knives. A sushi buffet is available for lunch. The shopping plaza setting allows for ample parking. Casual dress. **Bar:** Full bar. **Reservations:** accepted. **Hours:** 11:30 am-2 & 5-9:30 pm, Fri-10:30 pm, Sat 5 pm-10:30 pm, Sun 4 pm-9:30 pm. Closed: 7/4, 11/27, 12/25; also Super Bowl Sun. **Address:** 13952 Lee Jackson Memorial Hwy 20151 **Location:** Jct SR 28, 0.5 mi e on US 50; in Sully Plaza. **Parking:** on-site. **Cards:** AX, DC, DS, MC, VI.

PALM COURT AT WESTFIELDS MARRIOTT Phone: 703/818-3522 140

American
$18-$40

The full-service dining room is an elegant setting for any occasion. Professional staff members provide attentive service. The kitchen changes the American menu seasonally to incorporate the freshest available ingredients. Dressy casual. **Bar:** Full bar. **Reservations:** suggested. **Hours:** 6:30 am-2 & 6-10 pm, Sun 6:30 am-2 pm. **Address:** 14750 Conference Center Dr 20151 **Location:** I-66, exit 53, 2 mi n on SR 28, just w on Westfields Blvd, then 0.5 mi n on Stonecraft Blvd; 1.7 mi s of jct SR 28 and US 50; in Westfields Marriott. **Parking:** valet. **Cards:** AX, CB, DC, DS, MC, VI.

(See map and index starting on p. 412)

PICANTE! THE REAL TACO

Mexican
$8-$15

Phone: 703/222-2323   136

Traditional Mexician cooking is offered at this casual family oriented restaurant. The menu offers a nice selection of tacos, enchiladas, burritos and full dinners. Casual dress. **Bar:** Full bar. **Reservations:** not accepted. **Hours:** 11 am-10 pm, Fri & Sat-10:30 pm, Sun-9 pm. Closed major holidays. **Address:** 14511B-C Lee Jackson Hwy 20151 **Location:** US 50, 0.6 mi w of jct SR 28; in Chantilly Park Shopping Center. **Parking:** on-site. **Cards:** AX, DC, DS, MC, VI.

THAI BASIL

Thai
$7-$14

Phone: 703/631-8277   135

Tucked in a little shopping plaza, the quaint restaurant presents a menu of skillfully prepared cuisine that is flavored to the guest's preference for spiciness. Pad Thai noodles are a signature dish. Casual dress. **Bar:** Beer & wine. **Reservations:** accepted. **Hours:** 11 am-3 & 5-10 pm. Closed major holidays. **Address:** 14511-P Lee Jackson Hwy 20151 **Location:** US 50, 0.6 mi w of jct SR 28; in Chantilly Park shopping center. **Parking:** on-site. **Cards:** AX, CB, DC, DS, MC, VI.

WILLARD'S REAL PIT BBQ

Barbecue
$5-$13

Phone: 703/488-9970   139

In a small strip mall, the restaurant is reminiscent of barbecue joints found throughout the south. Barbecue is slowly smoked over oak and hickory hard woods, creating a moist, delicious flavor. Nothing here is fried, and desserts are made on the premises. Casual dress. **Bar:** Beer only. **Reservations:** not accepted. **Hours:** 11 am-9 pm, Sun 11:30 am-8 pm. Closed: 11/27, 12/25. **Address:** 4300 Chantilly Shopping Center #1A 20151 **Location:** 1 mi s on SR 28; from jct US 50, just e on Willard Rd; in Chantilly Shopping Center, adjacent to Dulles Expo Center. **Parking:** on-site. **Cards:** AX, MC, VI.

CALL ⟨⅏M⟩

CLIFTON pop. 185

——— **WHERE TO DINE** ———

HEART IN HAND

American
$9-$29

Phone: 703/830-4111

On the National Register of Historic Places, the restaurant sits in a rural setting and exudes a country atmosphere. Southern touches are evident in much of the cuisine, such as Tennessee ham and bean soup. Taste the homemade raspberry ice cream. Casual dress. **Bar:** Full bar. **Reservations:** suggested. **Hours:** 11 am-2:30 & 5-9 pm, Fri 5 pm-9:30 pm, Sat 11 am-3 & 5-9:30 pm, Sun 11 am-3 & 5-8 pm. Closed major holidays; also Mon. **Address:** 7145 Main St 20124 **Location:** US 29 and 211, 4.5 mi s on CR 645 (Clifton Rd). **Parking:** on-site. **Cards:** AX, CB, DC, DS, MC, VI. **Historic**

THE HERMITAGE INN RESTAURANT
Continental
$18-$33

Phone: 703/266-1623

Delicious French/Mediterranean cuisine is showcased in a restored historic hostelry. The rural setting is tranquil. Three-course prix fixe meals include soup, salad or appetizer, entree and dessert. Dressy casual. **Bar:** Full bar. **Reservations:** suggested. **Hours:** 5:30 pm-8:30 pm, Sun also 11 am-2:30 pm. Closed: 1/1, 7/4; also Mon, Tues & Super Bowl Sun. **Address:** 7134 Main St 20124 **Location:** US 29, 211 and CR 645 (Clifton Rd), 4.5 mi s on CR 645 (Clifton Rd). **Parking:** on-site. **Cards:** AX, DC, DS, MC, VI. **Historic**

⟨◣⟩

DUMFRIES pop. 4,937

——— **WHERE TO STAY** ———

COMFORT INN DUMFRIES/QUANTICO

Small-scale Hotel
$99-$139 3/1-10/31
$79-$109 11/1-2/28

Book at AAA.com   Phone: (703)445-8070

Address: 16931 Old Stage Rd 22025 **Location:** I-95, exit 152B, 0.5 mi w on SR 234. **Facility:** 80 one-bedroom standard units, some with whirlpools. 4 stories, interior corridors. *Bath:* combo or shower only. **Parking:** on-site. **Terms:** check-in 4 pm. **Amenities:** voice mail, irons, hair dryers. *Some:* high-speed Internet. **Pool(s):** heated indoor. **Leisure Activities:** limited exercise equipment. **Guest Services:** valet laundry, wireless Internet. **Business Services:** meeting rooms, PC. **Cards:** AX, CB, DC, DS, MC, VI.

ASK S⟨⅏⟩ Ⓨ CALL ⟨⅏M⟩ ⟨∼⟩ ⟨✦⟩ ▤ ▣ ▨ / SOME UNITS ⊗

HAMPTON INN-DUMFRIES/QUANTICO
Small-scale Hotel
Rates not provided

Book great rates at AAA.com   Phone: 703/441-9900

Address: 16959 Old Stage Rd 22025 **Location:** I-95, exit 152B, 0.4 mi w on SR 234. **Facility:** 78 units. 73 one-bedroom standard units. 5 one-bedroom suites with whirlpools. 4 stories, interior corridors. *Bath:* combo or shower only. **Parking:** on-site. **Amenities:** dual phone lines, voice mail, irons, hair dryers. **Pool(s):** heated indoor. **Leisure Activities:** whirlpool, limited exercise equipment. **Guest Services:** valet laundry, wireless Internet. **Business Services:** meeting rooms, business center.

Ⓨ CALL ⟨⅏M⟩ ⟨∼⟩ ⟨✦⟩ ▤ ▣ ▨ / SOME UNITS ⊗

HOLIDAY INN DUMFRIES QUANTICO CENTER
Small-scale Hotel
$129 3/1-11/1
$109 11/2-2/28

Book at AAA.com   Phone: (703)441-9001

Address: 3901 Fettler Park Dr 22026 **Location:** I-95, exit 152B, 0.5 mi w on SR 234. **Facility:** 107 one-bedroom standard units. 4 stories, interior corridors. *Bath:* combo or shower only. **Parking:** on-site. **Terms:** cancellation fee imposed. **Amenities:** high-speed Internet, voice mail, irons, hair dryers. **Pool(s):** outdoor. **Leisure Activities:** sauna, limited exercise equipment. **Guest Services:** valet and coin laundry, wireless Internet. **Business Services:** meeting rooms, PC. **Cards:** AX, DC, DS, MC, VI.

ASK S⟨⅏⟩ Ⓨ CALL ⟨⅏M⟩ ⟨∼⟩ ⟨✦⟩ ▤ ▣ ▨ / SOME UNITS ⊗

SLEEP INN QUANTICO *Book great rates at AAA.com* **Phone:** (703)445-0900

AAA SAVE

Small-scale Hotel
$70-$109 3/1-9/30
$60-$100 10/1-2/28

Address: 17470 Jefferson Davis Hwy 22026 **Location:** I-95, exit 152A, 0.5 mi e on SR 234, then just s on US 1. Located in a commercial area. **Facility:** 56 one-bedroom standard units. 3 stories, interior corridors. *Bath:* combo or shower only. **Parking:** on-site. **Amenities:** irons, hair dryers. **Leisure Activities:** sauna, limited exercise equipment. **Guest Services:** wireless Internet. **Cards:** AX, DC, DS, JC, MC, VI. **Free Special Amenities: continental breakfast and high-speed Internet.**

CALL / SOME UNITS

FAIRFAX pop. 21,498 (See map and index starting on p. 412)

WHERE TO STAY

BEST WESTERN FAIRFAX *Book great rates at AAA.com* **Phone:** (703)591-5500 **82**

AAA SAVE

Small-scale Hotel
$69-$189 All Year

Address: 3535 Chain Bridge Rd 22030 **Location:** I-66, exit 60, 0.5 mi s on SR 123; jct US 29/50. **Facility:** 127 units. 125 one-bedroom standard units. 2 one-bedroom suites. 2-3 stories (no elevator), exterior corridors. **Parking:** on-site. **Amenities:** voice mail, irons, hair dryers. **Pool(s):** outdoor. **Leisure Activities:** limited exercise equipment. **Guest Services:** valet and coin laundry, wireless Internet. **Business Services:** meeting rooms, PC. **Cards:** AX, CB, DC, DS, MC, VI. **Free Special Amenities: local telephone calls and high-speed Internet.**
(See color ad p 435)

CALL / SOME UNITS

Best Western
AAA Benefit:
Members save 10% everyday, plus an exclusive frequent stay program.

CANDLEWOOD SUITES FAIRFAX-WASHINGTON, D.C. *Book at AAA.com* **Phone:** (703)359-4490 **85**

Small-scale Hotel
$179 All Year

Address: 11400 Random Hills Rd 22030 **Location:** I-66, exit 57A, 0.5 mi e on US 50, just s on Waples Mill Rd, then 0.4 mi w. **Facility:** 122 units. 98 one-bedroom standard units with efficiencies. 24 one-bedroom suites with efficiencies. 3 stories, interior corridors. *Bath:* combo or shower only. **Parking:** on-site. **Terms:** office hours 7 am-11 pm. **Amenities:** video library, DVD players, CD players, high-speed Internet, voice mail, irons, hair dryers. **Leisure Activities:** exercise room. **Guest Services:** complimentary and valet laundry. **Cards:** AX, DC, DS, MC, VI.

ASK CALL VCR / SOME UNITS FEE

COMFORT INN UNIVERSITY CENTER *Book great rates at AAA.com* **Phone:** (703)591-5900 **87**

AAA SAVE

Small-scale Hotel
$129-$179 3/1-10/31
$109-$139 11/1-2/28

Address: 11180 Fairfax Blvd 22030 **Location:** I-66, exit 57A, 0.8 mi se on US 50, then 0.5 mi nw of jct US 29. Located near shopping center. **Facility:** 204 one-bedroom standard units, some with efficiencies (utensils extra charge) and/or whirlpools. 6 stories, interior corridors. **Parking:** on-site. **Terms:** 45 day cancellation notice-fee imposed. **Amenities:** video games (fee), voice mail, irons, hair dryers. *Some:* CD players. **Pool(s):** heated indoor. **Leisure Activities:** sun deck, exercise room. *Fee:* game room. **Guest Services:** valet and coin laundry, beauty salon, wireless Internet. **Business Services:** meeting rooms, PC. **Cards:** AX, DC, DS, MC, VI. **Free Special Amenities: expanded continental breakfast and high-speed Internet.** *(See color ad below)*

/ SOME UNITS

▼ See AAA listing above ▼

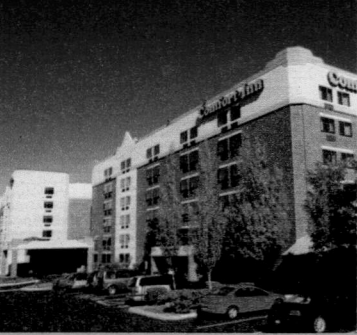

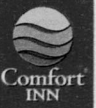

(See map and index starting on p. 412)

COURTYARD BY MARRIOTT-FAIR OAKS   *Book great rates at AAA.com*   Phone: 703/273-6161   86

Small-scale Hotel
$230-$274 All Year

Address: 11220 Lee Jackson Hwy 22030 **Location:** I-66, exit 57A, 0.5 mi se on US 50; 0.8 mi nw of jct US 29. Located across from shopping center. **Facility:** Smoke free premises. 144 units. 132 one-bedroom standard units. 12 one-bedroom suites. 3 stories, interior corridors. *Bath:* combo or shower only. **Parking:** on-site. **Amenities:** high-speed Internet, dual phone lines, voice mail, irons, hair dryers. **Pool(s):** heated indoor. **Leisure Activities:** whirlpool, exercise room. **Guest Services:** valet and coin laundry, wireless Internet. **Business Services:** meeting rooms, PC. **Cards:** AX, DC, DS, JC, MC, VI.

AAA Benefit:
Members save 5% off of the best available rate.

ASK SD ⑪ CALL GM ⌂ ✕ ▣ ▣ / SOME UNITS ▣ ▣

EXTENDED STAY DELUXE FAIRFAX   *Book at AAA.com*   Phone: (703)359-5000   77

Small-scale Hotel
$164-$174 All Year

Address: 3997 Fair Ridge Dr 22033 **Location:** I-66, exit 57B, 1.2 mi w on US 50. Located near shopping mall. **Facility:** 94 one-bedroom standard units with efficiencies. 3 stories, interior corridors. *Bath:* combo or shower only. **Parking:** on-site. **Amenities:** DVD players, dual phone lines, voice mail, irons, hair dryers. **Pool(s):** heated outdoor. **Leisure Activities:** limited exercise equipment. **Guest Services:** coin laundry, wireless Internet. **Cards:** AX, DC, DS, JC, MC, VI.

ASK SD ⑪ CALL GM ⌂ ✴ ▣ ▣ ▣ / SOME UNITS FEE 🐾 ✕

FAIRFAX MARRIOTT AT FAIR OAKS   *Book great rates at AAA.com*   Phone: 703/352-2525   78

Large-scale Hotel
$241-$285 All Year

Address: 11787 Lee Jackson Memorial Hwy 22033 **Location:** I-66, exit 57B, jct US 50. Located adjacent to Fair Oaks Mall. **Facility:** Smoke free premises. 310 units. 306 one-bedroom standard units. 4 one-bedroom suites. 6 stories, interior corridors. *Bath:* combo or shower only. **Parking:** on-site. **Terms:** check-in 4 pm. **Amenities:** dual phone lines, voice mail, irons, hair dryers. **Pool(s):** heated indoor. **Leisure Activities:** whirlpool, exercise room. **Guest Services:** complimentary and valet laundry, wireless Internet. **Business Services:** conference facilities, business center. **Cards:** AX, DS, MC, VI.

AAA Benefit:
Members save 5% off of the best available rate.

ASK SD ⑪ Ⓨ CALL GM ⌂ ✕ ▣ ▣
/ SOME UNITS FEE ▣ FEE ▣

HAMPTON INN-FAIRFAX   *Book great rates at AAA.com*   Phone: 703/385-2600   88

Small-scale Hotel
Rates not provided

Address: 10860 Fairfax Blvd 22030 **Location:** I-66, exit 60, 0.7 mi s on SR 123, then 0.7 mi w on US 50/29. Located in a commercial area. **Facility:** 86 one-bedroom standard units. 5 stories, interior corridors. **Parking:** on-site. **Amenities:** video games (fee), dual phone lines, voice mail, irons, hair dryers. **Leisure Activities:** limited exercise equipment. **Guest Services:** valet laundry, wireless Internet. **Business Services:** meeting rooms, fax (fee).

⑪ CALL GM ✴ ▣ / SOME UNITS ✕ FEE ▣ FEE ▣

HILTON GARDEN INN FAIRFAX   *Book great rates at AAA.com*   Phone: 703/385-7774   76

Small-scale Hotel
Rates not provided

Address: 3950 Fair Ridge Dr 22033 **Location:** I-66, exit 57B, 1 mi w on US 50. Located near shopping mall. **Facility:** Smoke free premises. 149 one-bedroom standard units. 5 stories, interior corridors. *Bath:* combo or shower only. **Parking:** on-site. **Amenities:** high-speed Internet, dual phone lines, voice mail, irons, hair dryers. **Pool(s):** heated indoor. **Leisure Activities:** whirlpool, exercise room. **Guest Services:** valet and coin laundry, area transportation, wireless Internet. **Business Services:** meeting rooms, business center. *(See color ad below)*

⑪ CALL GM ⌂ ✕ ✴ ▣ ▣ ▣

─────── ▼ *See AAA listing above* ▼ ───────

(See map and index starting on p. 412)

HOLIDAY INN EXPRESS FAIRFAX — *Book great rates at AAA.com*
Phone: (703)359-2888   83

Small-scale Hotel
$89-$189 All Year

Address: 10327 Fairfax Blvd 22030 **Location:** I-66, exit 60, 0.7 mi s on SR 123, then 0.3 mi e on US 29/50. **Facility:** 79 one-bedroom standard units. 4 stories, interior corridors. *Bath:* combo or shower only. **Parking:** on-site. **Terms:** 2-3 night minimum stay - seasonal. **Amenities:** high-speed Internet, voice mail, irons, hair dryers. **Leisure Activities:** limited exercise equipment. **Guest Services:** valet laundry, wireless Internet. **Business Services:** PC. **Cards:** AX, DS, MC, VI.

HOMESTEAD STUDIO SUITES HOTEL-FAIR OAKS — *Book at AAA.com*
Phone: (703)273-3444   79

Small-scale Hotel
$144-$154 All Year

Address: 12104 Monument Dr 22033 **Location:** I-66, exit 57B, 0.8 mi w on US 50, 0.3 mi s on SR 620 (West Ox Rd), then just se. Located adjacent to Fair Oaks Mall. **Facility:** 134 one-bedroom standard units with efficiencies. 2 stories (no elevator), exterior corridors. *Bath:* combo or shower only. **Parking:** on-site. **Amenities:** voice mail, irons, hair dryers. **Guest Services:** coin laundry, wireless Internet. **Cards:** AX, DC, DS, JC, MC, VI.

HOMESTEAD STUDIO SUITES HOTEL-FALLS CHURCH/MERRIFIELD — *Book at AAA.com*
Phone: (703)204-0088   80

Motel
$149-$159 All Year

Address: 8281 Willow Oaks Corporate Dr 22031 **Location:** I-495, exit 50A, just w on US 50 to Gallows Rd, then just s. **Facility:** 128 one-bedroom standard units with efficiencies. 2 stories (no elevator), exterior corridors. *Bath:* combo or shower only. **Parking:** on-site. **Amenities:** voice mail, irons, hair dryers. **Guest Services:** complimentary laundry, wireless Internet. **Cards:** AX, DC, DS, JC, MC, VI.

HYATT FAIR LAKES — *Book great rates at AAA.com*
Phone: (703)818-1234   84

Large-scale Hotel
$99-$349 All Year

Address: 12777 Fair Lakes Cir 22033 **Location:** I-66, exit 55 (Fairfax County Pkwy N); in Fair Lakes Shopping Center. **Facility:** 316 units. 315 one-bedroom standard units. 1 one-bedroom suite. 13 stories, interior corridors. *Bath:* combo or shower only. **Parking:** on-site. **Terms:** cancellation fee imposed. **Amenities:** dual phone lines, voice mail, irons, hair dryers. *Some:* CD players. **Pool(s):** heated indoor. **Leisure Activities:** whirlpool, men & women's locker room, billiards, jogging, exercise room, basketball. **Guest Services:** valet laundry, area transportation-within 1.5 mi, metro & Fair Oaks Mall, wireless Internet. **Business Services:** conference facilities, business center. **Cards:** AX, CB, DC, DS, JC, MC, VI.

HYATT
HOTELS & RESORTS
AAA Benefit:
Ask for the AAA rate and save 10%.

RESIDENCE INN BY MARRIOTT-FAIR LAKES — *Book great rates at AAA.com*
Phone: 703/266-4900   81

Small-scale Hotel
$252-$274 All Year

Address: 12815 Fair Lakes Pkwy 22033 **Location:** I-66, exit 55 (Fairfax County Pkwy N), just w. Located near shopping center and business area. **Facility:** Smoke free premises. 114 units. 30 one-bedroom standard units with efficiencies. 63 one- and 21 two-bedroom suites, some with efficiencies or kitchens. 3 stories, interior corridors. *Bath:* combo or shower only. **Parking:** on-site. **Amenities:** video games (fee), high-speed Internet, voice mail, irons, hair dryers. **Pool(s):** outdoor. **Leisure Activities:** whirlpool, exercise room, sports court. **Guest Services:** valet and coin laundry. **Business Services:** meeting rooms, PC, fax (fee). **Cards:** AX, DC, DS, JC, MC, VI.

Residence Inn Marriott
AAA Benefit:
Members save 5% off of the best available rate.

——— WHERE TO DINE ———

ANITA'S
Phone: 703/385-2965

Mexican
$5-$15

This small chain is locally popular for their signature "New Mexico" style dishes. The menu features a good variety of tacos, burritos and enchiladas. If you're in the mood for a Mexican breakfast, this is the place. Casual dress. **Bar:** Full bar. **Reservations:** accepted. **Hours:** 5 am-9:30 pm, Fri & Sat-10:30 pm, Sun 6 am-9 pm. Closed: 11/27, 12/25. **Address:** 10880 Lee Hwy 22030 **Location:** I-66, exit 60, 0.7 mi s on SR 123, then 0.7 mi w on US 50/29. **Parking:** on-site. **Cards:** AX, DC, DS, MC, VI.

ARIGATO SUSHI
Phone: 703/352-9338   106

Japanese
$8-$35

The Japanese restaurant sustains a simple yet stylish atmosphere. In addition to sushi, the menu lists a nice selection of beef, chicken and seafood dishes prepared using teriyaki, tempura or simple grilling. An all-you-can-eat sushi lunch is offered weekdays. Casual dress. **Bar:** Beer & wine. **Reservations:** accepted. **Hours:** 11:30 am-2:30 & 5-10 pm, Fri-10:30 pm, Sat noon-3 & 5-10:30 pm, Sun 4:30 pm-9:30 pm. Closed major holidays. **Address:** 11199-A Lee Hwy 22030 **Location:** Jct US 50, 29 and SR 236, 0.6 mi sw on US 29. **Parking:** on-site. **Cards:** AX, DC, DS, MC, VI.

ARTIES
Phone: 703/273-7600   95

American
$8-$29

A lively and energetic atmosphere is what patrons find at the popular restaurant, which attracts families and the young professional crowd. Fresh fish, filet mignon, smoked baby back ribs and jambalaya are among favorite dishes. Casual dress. **Bar:** Full bar. **Hours:** 11:30 am-10 pm, Tues-Thurs to 11 pm, Fri-midnight, Sat 10:30 am-midnight, Sun 10 am-10 pm. Closed: 11/27, 12/25. **Address:** 3260 Old Lee Hwy 22030 **Location:** US 50, at Fairfax Circle Centre. **Parking:** on-site. **Cards:** AX, DC, DS, MC, VI.

(See map and index starting on p. 412)

BELLISSIMO

Northern Italian
$12-$32

Phone: 703/293-2368   108

In the heart of the city, the intimate Northern Italian restaurant prepares mouthwatering dishes using veal, seafood, chicken, beef and pasta. Dressy casual. **Bar:** Full bar. **Reservations:** suggested. **Hours:** 11:30 am-2 & 5-10:30 pm, Sat 5 pm-10 pm. Closed: 1/1, 11/27, 12/25; also Sun. **Address:** 10403 Main St 22030 **Location:** On SR 236, just e of jct SR 123. **Parking:** no self-parking. **Cards:** AX, MC, VI.

BLUE IGUANA

American
$9-$26

Phone: 703/502-8108   96

Tucked in a small shopping plaza, the restaurant and bar serves creative American cuisine in a casual, comfortable setting. The lunch menu is presented until 4 pm. Sunday brunch hours are from 10 am to 2 pm. Casual dress. **Bar:** Full bar. **Reservations:** suggested, weekends. **Hours:** 11:30 am-10 pm, Fri-11 pm, Sat noon-11 pm, Sun 10 am-10 pm. **Address:** 12727 Shoppes Ln 22033 **Location:** I-66, exit 55 (Fairfax County Pkwy N), 0.3 mi n, then just w. **Parking:** on-site. **Cards:** AX, DC, DS, MC, VI.

BOMBAY BISTRO

Indian
$8-$14

Phone: 703/359-5810

The quaint, little restaurant prepares Indian cuisine in serene surroundings. Lamb vindaloo is a good choice to wake up the taste buds. Casual dress. **Bar:** Full bar. **Hours:** 11:30 am-2:30 & 5-10 pm, Fri-10:30 pm, Sat noon-3 & 5-10:30 pm, Sun noon-3 & 5-10 pm. Closed: for lunch 12/25. **Address:** 3570 Chain Bridge Rd 22030 **Location:** I-66, exit 60, 0.3 mi s on SR 123; just n of jct SR 123 and US 50. **Parking:** on-site. **Cards:** AX, CB, DC, DS, MC, VI.

BRAVO'S ITALIAN CAFE

Italian
$8-$23

Phone: 703/352-0260   101

The atmosphere is casual and comfortable, suitable for social, family or business meals. The menu features homemade pasta, fresh seafood, wood-fire pizza and the kitchens creations of chicken, veal and beef dishes. Casual dress. **Bar:** Full bar. **Reservations:** accepted. **Hours:** 11:30 am-2:30 & 5:30-10:30 pm, Fri & Sat-9 pm, Sun 5 pm-9 pm. Closed: 11/27, 12/25. **Address:** 11250 James Swart Cir 22030 **Location:** I-66, exit 57A, 0.5 mi e on US 50; in Fairfax Court Shopping Plaza. **Parking:** on-site. **Cards:** AX, DC, DS, MC, VI.

CANTINA D'ITALIA

Italian
$5-$23

Phone: 703/631-2752

Casual dress. **Bar:** Full bar. **Reservations:** suggested, weekends. **Hours:** 11 am-10 pm, Fri & Sat-11 pm. Closed: 7/4, 11/27, 12/25. **Address:** 13015 Fair Lakes Shopping Center 22033 **Location:** I-66, exit 55 (Fairfax County Pkwy N), 0.3 mi n on CR 7100, then 0.5 mi w on Fair Lakes Pkwy; in Fair Lakes Shopping Center. **Parking:** on-site. **Cards:** AX, DS, MC, VI.

CALL

CHICKEN OUT ROTISSERIE

American
$5-$10

Phone: 703/988-9130

Chicken Out Rotisserie uses only fresh all natural ingredients. The chicken is chemical and hormone free. Choose from salads and sandwiches to wraps and picaccias, as well as rotisserie chicken and roast beef. Casual dress. **Reservations:** not accepted. **Hours:** 11 am-8:30 pm, Fri & Sat-8 pm, Sun noon-8 pm; 11 am-9 pm 4/1-9/30. Closed: 11/27, 12/25. **Address:** 12955 Fair Lakes Pkwy 22033 **Location:** I-66, exit 55 (Fairfax County Pkwy N), 0.3 mi n, then 0.5 mi w. **Parking:** on-site. **Cards:** AX, DS, MC, VI.

CALL

CHUTZPAH, A REAL NEW YORK DELI

Deli/Subs
Sandwiches
$9-$15

Phone: 703/385-8883   93

The popular delicatessen fits all the requirements of a traditional New York deli. It offers freshly prepared corned beef, chopped liver, brisket and salads, just to mention a few items. Sandwiches are overstuffed, and soups are delicious. Casual dress. **Bar:** Beer only. **Reservations:** not accepted. **Hours:** 7 am-9 pm, Sat from 8 am, Sun 9 am-3 pm. Closed: 11/27, 12/25; also Yom Kippur. **Address:** 12214 Fairfax Towne Center 22033 **Location:** I-66, exit 57B, 0.7 mi w on US 50; in Fairfax Towne Center. **Parking:** on-site. **Cards:** AX, DS, MC, VI.

COASTAL FLATS

South American
$8-$25

Phone: 571/522-6300   97

The charm of 1950s Florida awaits in the popular Northern Virginia eatery. Savory dishes, including rock shrimp fritters and Key lime roast chicken, line the comfortable seafood house's menu. Call-ahead seating is available. Casual dress. **Bar:** Full bar. **Reservations:** not accepted. **Hours:** 11 am-11 pm, Fri & Sat-midnight, Sun & Mon-10 pm. Closed: 11/27, 12/25. **Address:** 11901 Grand Commons Ave 22030 **Location:** US 50, just w on West Ox Rd (SR 608), 0.8 mi e on Monument Dr; in Fairfax Corner. **Parking:** on-site. **Cards:** AX, DC, DS, MC, VI.

CALL

DOLCE VITA

Italian
$6-$25

Phone: 703/385-1530   102

The small neighborhood restaurant is popular with locals for its reliably good food. Lining the menu is a nice selection of pizza cooked in a wood-burning brick oven, pasta selections and veal, chicken and seafood dishes. Hand-painted murals decorate the otherwise simple dining room. Service is friendly and efficient. Packaged foods, sandwiches and full meals can be had in the adjacent Italian market. Casual dress. **Bar:** Beer & wine. **Hours:** 11:30 am-2:30 & 5-9:30 pm, Fri-10:30 pm, Sat noon-2:30 & 5-10:30 pm, Sun 5 pm-9:30 pm. Closed major holidays. **Address:** 10824 Lee Hwy 22030 **Location:** I-66, exit 60, 0.7 mi s on SR 123, then 0.7 mi w on US 50/29. **Parking:** on-site. **Cards:** CB, DC, DS, MC, VI.

THE ESPOSITOS ITALIAN RESTAURANT

Italian
$5-$16

Phone: 703/385-5912   94

Good food is prepared in a casual setting that's comfortable for families. Menu choices range from pizza and pasta to veal and chicken dishes. Casual dress. **Bar:** Beer & wine. **Reservations:** accepted. **Hours:** 11:30 am-2:30 & 5-10:30 pm, Fri & Sat-11:30 pm, Sun noon-10 pm. Closed: 1/1, 11/27, 12/25. **Address:** 9917 Lee Hwy 22030 **Location:** On US 50 and 20; 0.7 mi w of Fairfax Circle. **Parking:** on-site. **Cards:** AX, CB, DC, DS, MC, VI.

(See map and index starting on p. 412)

GLORY DAYS GRILL, FAIRFAX
Phone: 703/204-0900

American
$7-$18

Lending to the casual restaurant's sports-themed atmosphere are memorabilia decorating the dining area and 25 TVs with control centers at each table and booth. Food selections range from wings and ribs to seafood, beef and pasta dishes. Casual dress. **Bar:** Full bar. **Reservations:** not accepted. **Hours:** 4 pm-midnight, Fri & Sat from 11:30 am, Sun 11:30 am-11 pm. Closed: 11/27, 12/25. **Address:** 3059 Nutley St 22031 **Location:** I-66, exit 62, 0.6 mi s on Nutley St (SR 243); in Pan Am Shopping Center. **Parking:** on-site. **Cards:** AX, DS, MC, VI.

JAIPUR ROYAL INDIAN CUISINE
Phone: 703/766-1111   92

Indian
$8-$18

The dining room adorned in colorful window treatments, wood panel and Indian artwork creates a relaxing dining atmosphere. The menu offers a large selection of Northern Indian dishes, with a variety of preparations of lamb, chicken, seafood and vegetarian dishes. Lunch buffet is available daily. Dressy casual. **Bar:** Full bar. **Reservations:** suggested. **Hours:** 11:30 am-2:30 & 5:30-10 pm. Closed: for dinner 11/25, for lunch 12/25 & 1/1. **Address:** 9401 Lee Hwy, Unit 105 22031 **Location:** I-66, exit 62, 0.5 mi s on Nutley St (SR 243), then 0.5 mi s on US 29; 0.5 mi n on US 29, jct US 50 from Fairfax Circle; at Circle Towers Apartment/Office Building. **Parking:** on-site. **Cards:** AX, DC, DS, MC, VI.

THE LAMPLIGHTER RESTAURANT
Phone: 703/273-9300   104

Continental
$9-$32

This Continental restaurant has a menu that blends Greek, French, Italian and American selections. The setting is comfortable and slightly upscale. Piano entertainment is provided every night except Sunday. Dressy casual. Entertainment. **Bar:** Full bar. **Reservations:** suggested, weekends. **Hours:** 11 am-2:30 & 5-10 pm, Fri & Sat from 11:30 am, Sun 11 am-2:30 & 5-9 pm, Mon 5 pm-9 pm. Closed: 1/1. **Address:** 4068 Jermantown Rd 22030 **Location:** I-66, exit 57A, 0.5 mi se on US 50; 0.8 mi nw of jct US 29; in Fairfax Court Shopping Plaza. **Parking:** on-site. **Cards:** AX, DC, DS, MC, VI.

LA RUE 123 RESTAURANT AT BAILIWICK INN
Phone: 703/691-2266   109

French
$14-$30

In the heart of Old Town Fairfax City, the restaurant prepares very good French cuisine in the intimate setting of the Bailiwick Inn. Driven by the availability of fresh ingredients, the menu changes monthly. Dressy casual. **Bar:** Full bar. **Reservations:** suggested. **Hours:** 11:30 am-2 & 5:30-9 pm, Fri-9:30 pm, Sat 5:30 pm-9:30 pm. Closed major holidays; also Sun. **Address:** 4023 Chain Bridge Rd 22030 **Location:** I-66, exit 60, 1.5 mi s; SR 123, just s of jct SR 236; in Bailiwick Inn. **Parking:** on-site. **Cards:** AX, DC, MC, VI.

PAD THAI
Phone: 703/591-2525   105

Thai
$7-$24

The small, storefront restaurant serves traditional dishes in a simple, comfortable dining room. Casual dress. **Bar:** Beer & wine. **Reservations:** accepted. **Hours:** 11 am-3:30 & 4:30-9:30 pm, Fri-10 pm, Sat noon-10 pm, Sun 4:30 pm-9:30 pm. Closed: 11/27, 12/25. **Address:** 11199 E Lee Hwy 22030 **Location:** On US 29; 0.6 mi sw from jct US 50/29 and SR 236. **Parking:** on-site. **Cards:** AX, MC, VI.

PIANO GRILL
Phone: 703/273-3508   103

Mediterranean
$6-$20

The menu lists a good selection of Mediterranean and Middle Eastern dishes and kebabs; lamb, beef, chicken and seafood preparations; and a few American selections. Belly dancers perform on Friday and Saturday. Casual dress. **Bar:** Full bar. **Reservations:** accepted. **Hours:** 11:30 am-9:30 pm, Fri & Sat-midnight. Closed: 11/27; also Mon. **Address:** 10801 Fairfax Blvd 22030 **Location:** I-66, exit 60, 0.7 mi s on SR 123, then 0.6 mi w on US 50/129. **Parking:** on-site. **Cards:** AX, DS, MC, VI.

RUTH'S CHRIS STEAK HOUSE
Phone: 703/266-1004   98

Steak House
$25-$65

The main fare is steak, which is prepared from several cuts of prime beef and cooked to perfection, but the menu also lists lamb, chicken and seafood dishes. Guests should come hungry because the side dishes, which are among the a la carte offerings, could make a meal in themselves. Dressy casual. **Bar:** Full bar. **Reservations:** suggested. **Hours:** 5 pm-10 pm, Fri & Sat-10:30 pm, Sun 4 pm-9 pm. Closed: 11/27, 12/25. **Address:** 4100 Monument Corner Dr 22030 **Location:** US 50, just w on West Ox Rd (SR 608), 0.8 mi e on Monument Dr; in Fairfax Corner. **Parking:** valet. **Cards:** AX, DC, DS, JC, MC, VI.

SAKOONTRA
Phone: 703/818-8886   107

Thai
$6-$13

The shopping plaza restaurant has a colorful, casual atmosphere and serves traditional Thai dishes. The menu blends a nice selection of curries, vegetarian, beef, chicken and seafood dishes. Casual dress. **Bar:** Full bar. **Reservations:** accepted. **Hours:** 11:30 am-10 pm, Fri & Sat-10:30 pm. Closed major holidays. **Address:** 12300-C Price Club Plaza 22030 **Location:** Just n on CR 608 from US 29; 1.9 mi s on CR 608 from jct US 50; in shopping plaza. **Parking:** on-site. **Cards:** AX, DC, MC, VI.

CALL [&M]

SILVER DINER
Phone: 703/359-5941

American
$9-$15

The eatery with its chrome and glass plate exterior and the glow of neon, provides the traditional diner setting. Booths with juke boxes, counter service and friendly wait staff add to the diner experience. The menu is extensive with salads, sandwiches and full meals. The desserts are made fresh and the fountain treats, shakes, floats and malts make for a great ending. Breakfast is available all day. Casual dress. **Bar:** Beer & wine. **Reservations:** not accepted. **Hours:** 7 am-midnight, Fri & Sat-2 am. Closed: 12/25. **Address:** 12250 Fair Lakes Pkwy 22033 **Location:** 0.7 mi s on CR 608 from jct US 50, at jct West Ox Rd and Fair Lakes Pkwy. **Parking:** on-site. **Cards:** AX, DC, DS, MC, VI.

CALL [&M]

STAR THAI
Phone: 703/222-5452   110

Thai
$6-$15

The shopping plaza restaurant has developed a strong local following for its reliable kitchen and intimate atmosphere. A simplistic, contemporary design characterizes the dining room. Service is friendly and efficient. Casual dress. **Bar:** Full bar. **Reservations:** accepted. **Hours:** 11:30 am-3 & 4:30-10 pm, Fri-10:30 pm, Sat noon-10:30 pm, Sun noon-10 pm. Closed: 11/27; also for lunch 12/25. **Address:** 13046 Fair Lakes Shopping Ctr 22033 **Location:** I-66, exit 55 (Fairfax County Pkwy N), 0.3 mi n, then 0.5 mi w on Fair Lakes Pkwy; in Fair Lakes Shopping Center. **Parking:** on-site. **Cards:** AX, MC, VI.

(See map and index starting on p. 412)

TIJUANA FLATS

Tex-Mex
$5-$9

Phone: 703/267-6525

The quick-serve Tex-Mex eatery sets up a distinctive hot sauce bar to accompany its burritos, chimichangas, tacos and enchiladas. Guests can expect a line out the door at lunch. Casual dress. **Bar:** Beer & wine. **Reservations:** not accepted. **Hours:** 10:30 am-10 pm. Closed major holidays. **Address:** 11725 Lee Hwy, Suite 815 22030 **Location:** On US 29, 1.5 mi s of jct US 50 and SR 236; in Lee Plaza. **Parking:** on-site. **Cards:** AX, MC, VI.

CALL 🅫M

TONY'S NEW YORK PIZZA

Italian
$6-$12

Phone: 703/222-5452 🔟🄾

Need a break from shopping or a quick bite to eat, this is the place. Locals have made this a popular place to get a great pizza, by the slice or the whole pie, as well as sandwiches and full meals from veal to chicken and seafood. Casual dress. **Bar:** Beer & wine. **Reservations:** not accepted. **Hours:** 11 am-11 pm. Closed: 12/25. **Address:** 13087 Fair Lakes Shopping Center 22033 **Location:** I-66, exit 55 (Fairfax County Pkwy N), 0.3 mi n, then 0.5 mi w on Fair Lakes Pkwy; in Fair Lakes Shopping Center. **Parking:** on-site. **Cards:** AX, DS, MC, VI.

TSUNAMI

Japanese
$8-$38

Phone: 703/449-8404 🄿🄿

In the Fairlakes shopping complex, the Japanese restaurant sustains a simple yet stylish atmosphere. In addition to sushi, the menu lists a nice selection of beef, chicken and seafood dishes prepared using teriyaki, tempura or simple grilling. An all-you-can-eat sushi lunch is offered on weekdays. Casual dress. **Bar:** Full bar. **Reservations:** accepted. **Hours:** 11:30 am-2:30 & 5-10 pm, Fri-10:30 pm, Sat noon-3 & 5-10:30 pm, Sun 4:30 pm-9:30 pm. Closed major holidays. **Address:** 13039 Fair Lakes Center 22033 **Location:** I-66, exit 55 (Fairfax County Pkwy N), 0.3 mi n, then 0.5 mi w on Fair Lakes Pkwy; in Fair Lakes Shopping Center. **Parking:** on-site. **Cards:** AX, MC, VI.

FALLS CHURCH pop. 10,377 (See map and index starting on p. 412)

——— WHERE TO STAY ———

COMFORT INN ARLINGTON BOULEVARD-DC GATEWAY   *Book great rates at AAA.com*

Small-scale Hotel
$159-$229 All Year

Phone: (703)534-9100 🄑🄸

Address: 6111 Arlington Blvd 22044 **Location:** 5.5 mi w of Theodore Roosevelt Bridge on US 50; 0.5 mi e of jct SR 7. Located in a commercial area opposite shopping center. **Facility:** 111 units. 110 one-bedroom standard units. 1 one-bedroom suite. 3 stories, interior corridors. **Bath:** combo or shower only. **Parking:** on-site. **Amenities:** voice mail, safes (fee), irons, hair dryers. **Some:** high-speed Internet, dual phone lines. **Pool(s):** outdoor. **Leisure Activities:** limited exercise equipment. **Guest Services:** valet laundry, area transportation, wireless Internet. **Business Services:** meeting rooms, PC. **Cards:** AX, DC, DS, MC, VI.

   CALL 🅫M / SOME UNITS

FAIRVIEW PARK MARRIOTT   *Book great rates at AAA.com*

Large-scale Hotel
$318-$340 All Year

Phone: 703/849-9400 🄒🄸

Address: 3111 Fairview Park Dr 22042 **Location:** I-495, exit 50B, just se of US 50 via Fairview Park Dr S. **Facility:** Smoke free premises. 395 units. 390 one-bedroom standard units. 5 one-bedroom suites. 15 stories, interior corridors. **Bath:** combo or shower only. **Parking:** on-site. **Terms:** check-in 4 pm. **Amenities:** voice mail, irons, hair dryers. **Fee:** video games, high-speed Internet. **Pool(s):** heated indoor/outdoor. **Leisure Activities:** saunas, whirlpool, jogging, exercise room. **Guest Services:** complimentary and valet laundry, area transportation, wireless Internet. **Business Services:** conference facilities, business center. **Cards:** AX, DC, DS, JC, MC, VI.

Marriott
HOTELS & RESORTS

AAA Benefit:
Members save 5% off of the best available rate.

ASK 🆂🄳 🍴 🍸 CALL 🅫M 🔗 🔀 🔲 🎥 🖥
/ SOME UNITS 🅱 🖼

HOMEWOOD SUITES BY HILTON-FALLS CHURCH   *Book at AAA.com*

Small-scale Hotel
Rates not provided

Phone: 703/560-6644 🄑🄾

Address: 8130 Porter Rd 22042 **Location:** I-495, exit 50A, just w to SR 650; 0.4 mi n of SR 650. Located in a commercial area. **Facility:** 107 units. 102 one- and 5 two-bedroom suites, some with efficiencies or kitchens. 7 stories, interior corridors. **Bath:** combo or shower only. **Parking:** on-site. **Amenities:** video games (fee), high-speed Internet, dual phone lines, voice mail, irons, hair dryers. **Some:** DVD players. **Pool(s):** heated indoor. **Leisure Activities:** whirlpool, limited exercise equipment. **Guest Services:** valet and coin laundry, area transportation. **Business Services:** meeting rooms, business center.

 CALL 🅫M 🎥 🅱 🖼 🖥 / SOME UNITS FEE 🐾 🔀 🆅🄲🅁

RESIDENCE INN BY MARRIOTT FAIRFAX-MERRIFIELD   *Book great rates at AAA.com*

Small-scale Hotel
$296-$318 All Year

Phone: 703/573-5200 🄒🄾

Address: 8125 Gatehouse Rd 22042 **Location:** I-495, exit 50A, just w to SR 640 N. Located in a commercial area. **Facility:** Smoke free premises. 159 units. 80 one-bedroom standard units with efficiencies. 48 one- and 31 two-bedroom suites, some with efficiencies or kitchens. 4 stories, interior corridors. **Bath:** combo or shower only. **Parking:** on-site. **Amenities:** high-speed Internet, voice mail, irons, hair dryers. **Pool(s):** heated outdoor. **Leisure Activities:** whirlpool, limited exercise equipment, sports court. **Guest Services:** valet and coin laundry. **Business Services:** meeting rooms, PC. **Cards:** AX, DC, DS, JC, MC, VI.

Residence Inn by Marriott

AAA Benefit:
Members save 5% off of the best available rate.

ASK 🆂🄳 🍴 CALL 🅫M 🔗 🔀 🔲 🎥 🅱 🖼 🖥
/ SOME UNITS FEE 🐾

(See map and index starting on p. 412)

TOWNEPLACE SUITES BY MARRIOTT-FALLS
CHURCH   *Book great rates at AAA.com*

Small-scale Hotel
$230-$252 3/1-12/31
$166-$196 1/1-2/28

Phone: 703/237-6172   **58**

Address: 205 Hillwood Ave 22046 **Location:** I-495, exit 50B, 2.5 mi e on US 50, 0.6 mi n on Annandale Rd, then e; just s of US 29. **Facility:** Smoke free premises. 127 units. 91 one-bedroom standard units with kitchens. 6 one- and 30 two-bedroom suites with kitchens. 4 stories, interior corridors. **Bath:** combo or shower only. **Parking:** on-site. **Amenities:** high-speed Internet, voice mail, irons, hair dryers. **Pool(s):** outdoor. **Leisure Activities:** limited exercise equipment. **Guest Services:** valet and coin laundry. **Business Services:** PC, fax (fee). **Cards:** AX, DC, DS, JC, MC, VI.

AAA Benefit:
Members save 5% off of the best available rate.

THE WESTIN TYSONS CORNER   *Book great rates at AAA.com*

Large-scale Hotel
$289 All Year

Phone: (703)893-1340   **57**

Address: 7801 Leesburg Pike 22043 **Location:** I-495, exit 47B, just e on SR 7. **Facility:** Smoke free premises. 405 units. 394 one-bedroom standard units. 11 one-bedroom suites. 9-11 stories, interior corridors. **Bath:** combo or shower only. **Parking:** on-site and valet. **Terms:** cancellation fee imposed. **Amenities:** high-speed Internet (fee), dual phone lines, voice mail, safes, irons, hair dryers. **Pool(s):** heated indoor. **Leisure Activities:** whirlpool, exercise room. **Guest Services:** valet laundry, area transportation, wireless Internet. **Business Services:** conference facilities, business center. **Cards:** AX, CB, DC, DS, JC, MC, VI.

WESTIN
HOTELS & RESORTS

AAA Benefit:
Members get up to 15% off, plus Starwood Preferred Guest® bonuses.

WHERE TO DINE

2941 RESTAURANT

American
$12-$49

Phone: 703/270-1500   **65**

The stylish, upscale dining room, with floor-to-ceiling windows reaching up 30 feet, looks out over a man-made lake. The chef/owner creates wonderful seasonally changing French and American dishes using the freshest ingredients available. In addition to the a la carte menu is a five-course tasting menu. The professional and attentive wait staff sees to diners' needs as they relax and enjoy the dining experience. Dressy casual. **Bar:** Full bar. **Reservations:** suggested. **Hours:** 11:30 am-2 & 5-10 pm, Sat from 4:30 pm, Sun 5 pm-9 pm. Closed major holidays. **Address:** 2941 Fairview Park Dr 22042 **Location:** I-495, exit 50B to Fairview Park Dr, 0.3 mi n. **Parking:** valet. **Cards:** AX, DC, DS, MC, VI.

ARGIA'S

Italian
$8-$34

Phone: 703/534-1033   **63**

A hand-painted mural and family portraits adorn the walls. Varied Italian dishes are served in large portions. The staff is friendly and knowledgeable. Casual dress. **Bar:** Full bar. **Reservations:** not accepted. **Hours:** 11:30 am-9:30 pm, Fri & Sat-10:30 pm, Sun 5 pm-9 pm. Closed: 12/25. **Address:** 124 N Washington St 22046 **Location:** I-66, exit 69, 1.5 mi s on US 29; just n of jct US 29 and SR 7. **Parking:** on-site. **Cards:** AX, DC, DS, MC, VI.

CELEBRITY DELLY

Deli/Subs
Sandwiches
$5-$15

Phone: 703/573-9002   **67**

This New York-style delicatessen has been a favorite of locals since 1975. Patrons can surf the 'net with free wireless access while digging in to overstuffed sandwiches, salads and all-day breakfast items. Casual dress. **Bar:** Beer & wine. **Reservations:** not accepted. **Hours:** 9 am-9 pm, Sun-4 pm. Closed: 12/25. **Address:** 7263-A Arlington Blvd 22042 **Location:** I-495, exit 50B, 1.3 mi e on US 50; in Loehmann's Plaza Shopping Center. **Parking:** on-site. **Cards:** AX, CB, DC, DS, MC, VI.

CITY DINER

American
$8-$22

Phone: 703/671-4108   **74**

A wide selection of dishes—from salads and sandwiches to full meals—makes up the diner's menu. Greek, Italian and American dishes make appearances. Breakfast is served all day. Casual dress. **Bar:** Beer & wine. **Reservations:** not accepted. **Hours:** 6 am-10 pm, Fri & Sat-11 pm. **Address:** 5616 Leesburg Pike 22041 **Location:** I-395, exit 5, 1.8 mi w on SR 7; in Baileys Crossroads area. **Parking:** on-site. **Cards:** AX, DC, DS, MC, VI.

DUANGRAT'S

Thai
$8-$29

Phone: 703/820-5775   **72**

The casually elegant restaurant does a booming business, in part because it serves ample portions of well-seasoned food. The professional, thoughtful service staff doesn't hurt, either. Thai artwork and headdresses decorate the dining room. Dressy casual. **Bar:** Full bar. **Reservations:** suggested. **Hours:** 11:30 am-2:30 & 5-10 pm, Fri-10:45 pm, Sat 11 am-10:45 pm, Sun 11 am-10 pm. Closed: 11/27. **Address:** 5878 Leesburg Pike 22041 **Location:** I-395, exit 5, 2.5 mi w on SR 7; in Bailey's Crossroads area. **Parking:** on-site. **Cards:** AX, CB, DC, DS, MC, VI.

FLAVORS SOUL FOOD

Soul Food
$6-$11

Phone: 703/379-4411   **70**

The restaurant is a favorite stop of those in the mood for soul food. Presentations are simple and the atmosphere modest; it's the food that's the focus. Fried chicken and fish, as well as the meaty ribs, keep people coming back. Casual dress. **Bar:** Full bar. **Reservations:** not accepted. **Hours:** 11:30 am-2:30 & 5:30-9 pm, Sat 2 pm-9 pm, Sun 1 pm-7 pm. Closed major holidays; also Mon, Mothers Day & Fathers Day. **Address:** 3420 Carlyn Hill Dr 22041 **Location:** Off SR 244, just n of jct SR 7; at Bailys Crossroads area. **Parking:** on-site. **Cards:** AX, DS, MC, VI.

(See map and index starting on p. 412)

HAANDI

Phone: 703/533-3501   62

Indian
$5-$20

Soft pastels, cut-glass chandeliers and window boxes with Indian paintings create a comfortable dining atmosphere that complements a varied menu of vegetarian, seafood, chicken and lamb selections. Notable is the south Indian specialty vindaloo, chunks of lamb and potato in a spicy curry sauce. Casual dress. **Bar:** Full bar. **Reservations:** accepted, Sun-Thurs. **Hours:** 11:30 am-2:30 & 5-10 pm, Fri & Sat-10:30 pm. Closed: 11/27, 12/25. **Address:** 1222 W Broad St 22046 **Location:** I-66, exit 66A westbound; exit 66 eastbound, 2.5 mi w on SR 7 from jct US 50. **Parking:** on-site. **Cards:** AX, DC, DS, MC, VI.

MARK'S DUCK HOUSE

Phone: 703/532-2125   66

Chinese
$5-$29

The well-established, Hong Kong-style restaurant has an overwhelming menu, with an extensive selection of seafood, some rare and exotic dishes, and delightful Peking duck. Dim sum is served daily from 10 a.m. to 3 p.m. It's a good idea to make reservations on weekends, as a line often forms for dim sum. Casual dress. **Bar:** Beer & wine. **Reservations:** accepted. **Hours:** 10 am-11 pm, Fri & Sat-midnight. Closed: 7/28-8/10. **Address:** 6184-A Arlington Blvd 22044 **Location:** 5.7 mi w of Theodore Roosevelt Bridge on US 50, 0.4 mi e of jct SR 7. **Parking:** on-site. **Cards:** MC, VI.

MINT THAI CUISINE

Phone: 703/671-4658   68

Thai
$5-$25

The small restaurant has a style all its own. In a contemporary, colorful, cavelike setting, the distinctive atmosphere is inviting. Thai cooking is consistent, as the kitchen uses fresh ingredients and makes its own sauces. Casual dress. **Bar:** Full bar. **Reservations:** accepted. **Hours:** 11:30 am-3:30 & 5-10 pm, Fri-11 pm, Sat noon-3:30 & 5-11 pm, Sun noon-3:30 & 5-10 pm. Closed: 11/27; also for lunch 12/25 & 1/1. **Address:** 6037 Leesburg Pike 22041 **Location:** SR 7, at jct Glen Carlyn Rd; in Culmore Shopping Center. **Parking:** on-site. **Cards:** AX, DC, DS, MC, VI.

PEKING GOURMET INN

Phone: 703/671-8088   69

Chinese
$7-$36

Decorated with a traditional Oriental flair, the busy family eatery is known for its pan-fried dumplings, tableside-carved Peking duck and Szechuan beef proper, which is "surf fried" until golden brown then sprinkled with toasted sesame seeds. Casual dress. **Bar:** Full bar. **Reservations:** suggested, weekends. **Hours:** 11 am-10:30 pm, Fri & Sat-midnight. Closed: 11/27. **Address:** 6029 Leesburg Pike 22041 **Location:** SR 7, at Glen Carlyn Rd; in Culmore Shopping Center. **Parking:** on-site. **Cards:** AX, MC, VI.

PISTONE'S ITALIAN INN

Phone: 703/533-1885   64

Italian
$7-$30

The restaurant has a wonderful family atmosphere, great food on a diverse menu and friendly service. Casual dress. **Bar:** Full bar. **Reservations:** suggested, weekends. **Hours:** 11 am-11 pm, Fri & Sat-11:30 pm, Sun noon-10 pm. Closed: 11/27, 12/25. **Address:** 6320 Arlington Blvd 22044 **Location:** I-395, exit 5, 3 mi e on SR 7, then just n; jct SR 7 & US 50; in the Seven Corners area. **Parking:** on-site. **Cards:** AX, CB, DC, MC, VI.

RAAGA

Phone: 703/998-7000   73

Indian
$9-$18

Butter yellow walls, Indian artwork and cloth tablecloths set a comfortable dining atmosphere that's suitable for any occasion. Lining the menu is a nice selection of Northern Indian dishes and tandoori cooking. Dressy casual. **Bar:** Full bar. **Reservations:** suggested. **Hours:** 11:30 am-2:30 & 5-10 pm, Sat noon-3 & 5-10:30 pm, Sun noon-3 & 5-10 pm. Closed: 11/27, 12/25. **Address:** 5872 Leesburg Pike 22041 **Location:** I-395, exit 5, 2.5 mi w on SR 7; in Bailey's Crossroads area. **Parking:** on-site. **Cards:** AX, DC, DS, MC, VI.

RABIENG

Phone: 703/671-4222   71

Thai
$7-$21

Excellent reputations are hard to live up to but they do a fine job pleasing and surprising guests with dishes that light up diners' palates. Chicken in a coconut peanut curry sauce with basil, delectable crisp-fried catfish with basil and Japanese eggplant and chili peppers are fragrant with fresh herbs and spices, flavors married so well you may smile. The sticky rice with coconut milk and mango is a special, perfect conclusion to a wonderful meal. Casual and no-nonsense with sumptuous food. Casual dress. **Bar:** Full bar. **Reservations:** not accepted. **Hours:** 11:30 am-10 pm, Fri & Sat-10:30 pm. Closed: 11/27. **Address:** 5892 Leesburg Pike 22041 **Location:** I-395, exit 5, 2.5 mi e on SR 7; in Bailey's Crossroads area. **Parking:** on-site. **Cards:** AX, DC, DS, MC, VI.

SILVER DINER

Phone: 703/204-0816

American
$7-$15

The eatery with its chrome and glass plate exterior and the glow of neon, provides the traditional diner setting. Booths with juke boxes, counter service and friendly wait staff add to the diner experience. The menu is extensive with salads, sandwiches and full meals. The desserts are made fresh and the fountain treats, shakes, floats and malts make for a great ending. Breakfast is available all day. Casual dress. **Bar:** Beer & wine. **Reservations:** not accepted. **Hours:** 7 am-midnight, Fri & Sat-3 am. Closed: 12/25; also for dinner 11/22. **Address:** 8150 Porter Rd 22042 **Location:** I-495, exit 50A, just w to SR 650, then 0.4 mi n on SR 650. **Parking:** on-site. **Cards:** AX, DS, MC, VI.

CALL 〔M〕

SWEETWATER TAVERN

Phone: 703/645-8100

American
$8-$25

Casual dress. **Bar:** Full bar. **Reservations:** accepted, 1 pm-6 pm & Mon. **Hours:** 11 am-11 pm, Fri & Sat-midnight. Closed: 11/27, 12/25. **Address:** 3066 Gatehouse Plaza 22042 **Location:** I-495, exit 50B, jct US 50 and Gallows Rd. **Parking:** on-site. **Cards:** AX, DS, MC, VI.

CALL 〔M〕

TARA THAI

Phone: 703/506-9788

Thai
$6-$13

The stylish cafe's sea motif is one aspect of its contemporary atmosphere. Specialties include whole fresh rockfish and skewered chicken, just to mention two. Most notable is the nicely presented goong phu-ket and pad thai noodles. Portion sizes are ample. Casual dress. **Bar:** Full bar. **Reservations:** suggested. **Hours:** 11:30 am-3 & 5-10 pm, Fri-11 pm, Sat noon-3:30 & 5-11 pm, Sun noon-3:30 & 5-10 pm. **Address:** 7501-E Leesburg Pike 22043 **Location:** I-495, exit 47B, 0.9 mi e on SR 7; in Idylwood Plaza. **Parking:** on-site. **Cards:** AX, DC, DS, MC, VI.

GREAT FALLS pop. 8,549   (See map and index starting on p. 412)

—— WHERE TO DINE ——

DANTE RISTORANTE   Phone: 703/759-3131   ③

Northern Italian
$8-$32

Fine northern Italian cuisine is prepared in the intimate setting of a Victorian-era building. A typical dining experience might include a prosciutto and honeydew appetizer, then veal shank with a lovely, memorable sauce. Dressy casual. **Bar:** Full bar. **Reservations:** suggested. **Hours:** 11:30 am-2:30 & 5-10:30 pm, Sat from 5 pm, Sun 4 pm-9 pm. Closed major holidays. **Address:** 1148 Walker Rd 22066 **Location:** SR 743, 0.5 mi n of jct SR 7; 2 mi s of jct SR 193 and 743. **Parking:** on-site. **Cards:** AX, DS, MC, VI.

FLORE DI LUNA   Phone: 703/444-4060   ①

Northern Italian
$9-$19

Upscale and elegant surroundings, a fine menu, a large wine list and formally attired staffers add up to a pleasant dining experience. Dressy casual. **Bar:** Full bar. **Hours:** 11:30 am-2:30 & 5:30-10 pm, Sat from 5:30 pm, Sun 5 pm-9 pm. Closed: 12/25; also Mon. **Address:** 1025-I Seneca Rd 22066 **Location:** SR 743, 0.5 mi n; jct SR 7, just n. **Parking:** on-site. **Cards:** AX, CB, DC, DS, JC, MC, VI.

L'AUBERGE CHEZ FRANCOIS   Phone: 703/759-3800

French
$58-$70

Narrow, rolling roads lead to the charming restaurant, which serves country French cuisine. Alsatian specialties and wonderful classics line the six-course menu. The terrace opens when the weather cooperates. Background music adds to the sophistication, as do knowledgeable, trained staff members who ably assist with wine and entree selections. Jackets or ties are appreciated. Semi-formal attire. **Bar:** Full bar. **Reservations:** required, weekends. **Hours:** 5:30 pm-9:30 pm, Sun 1:30 pm-8 pm. Closed: 1/1, 7/4, 12/25; also Mon. **Address:** 332 Springvale Rd 22066 **Location:** 2.2 mi n of SR 193. **Parking:** on-site. **Cards:** AX, CB, DC, DS, MC, VI.

CALL ⓖⓂ

SERBIAN CROWN RESTAURANT   Phone: 703/759-4150   ②

International
$8-$38

In the heart of Great Falls is this fabulous place serving Serbian, Russian and French cuisine. The Russian appetizer affords several types of smoked fish, and charlotte russe is wonderful. Exotic game dishes, such as preparations of kangaroo or bear, are available seasonally. The vodka menu incorporates a wide selection of imported and flavored varieties. Semi-formal attire. **Bar:** Full bar. **Reservations:** suggested. **Hours:** 11:30 am-2:30 & 5:30-10 pm. Closed major holidays. **Address:** 1141 Walker Rd 22066 **Location:** SR 743, 0.5 mi n of jct SR 7; 2 mi s of jct SR 193 and 743. **Parking:** on-site. **Cards:** AX, CB, DC, DS, MC, VI.

HERNDON   pop. 21,655   (See map and index starting on p. 412)

─────── WHERE TO STAY ───────

CANDLEWOOD SUITES WASHINGTON-DULLES HERNDON   *Book at AAA.com*   Phone: (703)793-7100   37

Small-scale Hotel
$215 3/1-10/31
$207 11/1-2/28

Address: 13845 Sunrise Valley Dr 20171 **Location:** SR 28, 0.4 mi e on Frying Pan Rd, 0.7 mi nw. Located in residental/business area. **Facility:** 133 units. 109 one-bedroom standard units with kitchens. 24 one-bedroom suites with efficiencies. 4 stories, interior corridors. *Bath:* combo or shower only. **Parking:** on-site. **Terms:** office hours 7 am-11 pm. **Amenities:** video library, DVD players, CD players, high-speed Internet, dual phone lines, voice mail, irons, hair dryers. **Leisure Activities:** exercise room. **Guest Services:** complimentary and valet laundry. **Cards:** AX, CB, DC, DS, MC, VI.

COMFORT INN DULLES INTERNATIONAL AIRPORT   *Book great rates at AAA.com*   Phone: (703)437-7555   26

Small-scale Hotel
$169-$209 All Year

Address: 200 Elden St 20170 **Location:** Just w on CR 606 from jct CR 7100 (Fairfax County Pkwy). **Facility:** 104 one-bedroom standard units. 3 stories, interior corridors. *Bath:* combo or shower only. **Parking:** on-site. **Terms:** cancellation fee imposed. **Amenities:** voice mail, safes (fee), irons, hair dryers. *Some:* high-speed Internet, dual phone lines. **Leisure Activities:** exercise room. **Guest Services:** valet and coin laundry, airport transportation-Washington Dulles International Airport, area transportation-within 2 mi, wireless Internet. **Business Services:** PC. **Cards:** AX, DC, DS, MC, VI. **Free Special Amenities: expanded continental breakfast and high-speed Internet.**

COURTYARD BY MARRIOTT/HERNDON-RESTON   *Book great rates at AAA.com*   Phone: 703/478-9400   35

Small-scale Hotel
$252-$285 All Year

Address: 533 Herndon Pkwy 20170 **Location:** SR 267, exit 11, CR 7100 (Fairfax County Pkwy), just n to Spring St exit, just s to CR 606 (Herndon Pkwy), then 0.3 mi. Located in an office park. **Facility:** Smoke free premises. 146 units. 134 one-bedroom standard units. 12 one-bedroom suites. 3 stories, interior corridors. *Bath:* combo or shower only. **Parking:** on-site. **Amenities:** high-speed Internet, dual phone lines, voice mail, irons, hair dryers. **Pool(s):** heated indoor. **Leisure Activities:** whirlpool, exercise room. **Guest Services:** valet and coin laundry. **Business Services:** meeting rooms, PC. **Cards:** AX, DC, DS, MC, VI.

AAA Benefit:
Members save 5% off of the best available rate.

CROWNE PLAZA DULLES AIRPORT   *Book great rates at AAA.com*   Phone: (703)471-6700   32

Large-scale Hotel
$79-$349 All Year

Address: 2200 Centreville Rd 20170 **Location:** Jct SR 267 (Dulles Toll Rd), exit 10. **Facility:** 328 units. 327 one-bedroom standard units. 1 one-bedroom suite. 7 stories, interior corridors. *Bath:* combo or shower only. **Parking:** on-site. **Terms:** cancellation fee imposed. **Amenities:** CD players, voice mail, irons, hair dryers. *Some:* dual phone lines, fax. **Pool(s):** heated indoor. **Leisure Activities:** whirlpool, exercise room. **Guest Services:** valet laundry, airport transportation-Washington Dulles International Airport, area transportation-Air & Space Museum, within 5 mi, wireless Internet. **Business Services:** conference facilities, business center. **Cards:** AX, CB, DC, DS, JC, MC, VI. **Free Special Amenities: newspaper and high-speed Internet.**

EMBASSY SUITES DULLES AIRPORT   *Book at AAA.com*   Phone: 703/464-0200   36

Small-scale Hotel
Rates not provided

Address: 13341 Woodland Park Rd 20171 **Location:** SR 267 (Dulles Toll Rd), exit 10, just s. **Facility:** 150 one-bedroom suites. 6 stories, interior corridors. *Bath:* combo or shower only. **Parking:** on-site. **Amenities:** high-speed Internet (fee), dual phone lines, voice mail, irons, hair dryers. **Pool(s):** heated indoor. **Leisure Activities:** whirlpool, exercise room. **Guest Services:** valet laundry, area transportation. **Business Services:** meeting rooms, business center.

EXTENDED STAYAMERICA-HERNDON   *Book at AAA.com*   Phone: (703)481-5363   25

Small-scale Hotel
$164-$174 All Year

Address: 1021 Elden St 20170 **Location:** 0.8 mi n on SR 657 from jct SR 267 (Dulles Toll Rd), exit 10. **Facility:** 104 one-bedroom standard units with efficiencies. 3 stories, interior corridors. *Bath:* combo or shower only. **Parking:** on-site. **Terms:** office hours 7 am-11 pm. **Amenities:** voice mail, irons, hair dryers. **Guest Services:** coin laundry, wireless Internet. **Cards:** AX, DC, DS, JC, MC, VI.

HAWTHORN SUITES HERNDON   *Book at AAA.com*   Phone: 703/437-5000   34

Small-scale Hotel
Rates not provided

Address: 467 Herndon Pkwy 20170 **Location:** SR 267 (Dulles Toll Rd), exit 11 CR 7100 (Fairfax County Pkwy), just n to Spring St exit, just s to Herndon Pkwy (CR 606), just w on CR 606. Located in office park area. **Facility:** 104 units. 45 one-bedroom standard units with efficiencies. 22 one- and 37 two-bedroom suites, some with efficiencies or kitchens. 4 stories, interior corridors. *Bath:* combo or shower only. **Parking:** on-site. **Amenities:** video library (fee), dual phone lines, voice mail, irons, hair dryers. **Pool(s):** outdoor. **Leisure Activities:** whirlpool, exercise room, sports court. **Guest Services:** valet and coin laundry, area transportation, wireless Internet. **Business Services:** meeting rooms, PC.

(See map and index starting on p. 412)

HILTON WASHINGTON DULLES AIRPORT
Book great rates at AAA.com   Phone: 703/478-2900   **39**

Large-scale Hotel
Rates not provided

Address: 13869 Park Center Rd 20171 **Location:** SR 267 (Dulles Toll Rd), exit 9, 3 mi s on SR 28; at McLearen Blvd (SR 668). Located in business park area. **Facility:** 449 units. 448 one-bedroom standard units, some with whirlpools. 1 one-bedroom suite with whirlpool. 5 stories, interior corridors. *Bath:* combo or shower only. **Parking:** on-site. **Amenities:** dual phone lines, voice mail, irons, hair dryers. *Fee:* video games, high-speed Internet. **Dining:** 2 restaurants. **Pool(s):** outdoor, heated indoor. **Leisure Activities:** whirlpool, exercise room, spa. **Guest Services:** valet laundry, airport transportation-Washington Dulles International Airport, area transportation-within 3 mi, wireless Internet. **Business Services:** conference facilities, business center. **Free Special Amenities:** newspaper.

HOLIDAY INN EXPRESS-RESTON/HERNDON
Book great rates at AAA.com   Phone: (703)478-9777   **24**

Small-scale Hotel
$79-$239 All Year

Address: 485 Elden St 20170 **Location:** 0.6 mi w on CR 606 from jct CR 7100 (Fairfax County Pkwy). Located in a commercial area. **Facility:** 115 one-bedroom standard units. 4 stories, interior corridors. *Bath:* combo or shower only. **Parking:** on-site. **Amenities:** high-speed Internet, voice mail, irons, hair dryers. **Leisure Activities:** limited exercise equipment. **Guest Services:** valet laundry, airport transportation-Washington Dulles International Airport, area transportation-local businesses, within 3 mi, wireless Internet. **Business Services:** business center. **Cards:** AX, CB, DC, DS, JC, MC, VI. **Free Special Amenities:** expanded continental breakfast and high-speed Internet. *(See color ad below)*

HOMEWOOD SUITES BY HILTON WASHINGTON-DULLES AIRPORT
Book at AAA.com   Phone: 703/793-1700   **33**

Small-scale Hotel
Rates not provided

Address: 13460 Sunrise Valley Dr 20171 **Location:** SR 267 (Dulles Toll Rd), exit 10, 0.5 mi s on SR 657, then just w. **Facility:** 109 units. 104 one- and 5 two-bedroom suites with efficiencies. 7 stories, interior corridors. *Bath:* combo or shower only. **Parking:** on-site. **Amenities:** video games (fee), high-speed Internet, voice mail, irons, hair dryers. **Pool(s):** heated indoor. **Leisure Activities:** whirlpool, limited exercise equipment. **Guest Services:** valet and coin laundry, area transportation, wireless Internet. **Business Services:** meeting rooms, business center.

(See map and index starting on p. 412)

HYATT DULLES   *Book great rates at AAA.com*   Phone: (703)713-1234

Large-scale Hotel
$100-$380 All Year

Address: 2300 Dulles Corner Blvd 20171 **Location:** Jct SR 657 and 267 (Dulles Toll Rd), exit 10, 0.5 mi s on Centreville Rd (SR 657), then 1.1 mi w on Fox Mill Rd. **Facility:** 316 units. 315 one-bedroom standard units. 1 one-bedroom suite. 13 stories, interior corridors. *Bath:* combo or shower only. **Parking:** on-site. **Terms:** cancellation fee imposed. **Amenities:** dual phone lines, voice mail, irons, hair dryers. *Fee:* video games, high-speed Internet. *Some:* CD players, safes. **Pool(s):** heated indoor. **Leisure Activities:** whirlpool, sun deck, putting green, exercise room. **Guest Services:** valet laundry, airport transportation-Washington Dulles International Airport, area transportation-within 3 mi, wireless Internet. **Business Services:** conference facilities, business center. **Cards:** AX, CB, DC, DS, JC, MC, VI. *(See color ad p 440)*

AAA Benefit:
Ask for the AAA rate and save 10%.

MARRIOTT SUITES WASHINGTON-DULLES   *Book great rates at AAA.com*   Phone: 703/709-0400

Large-scale Hotel
$351-$373 All Year

Address: 13101 Worldgate Dr 20170 **Location:** Jct SR 657 and 267 (Dulles Toll Rd), exit 10. **Facility:** Smoke free premises. 253 one-bedroom suites. 11 stories, interior corridors. *Bath:* combo or shower only. **Parking:** on-site. **Amenities:** voice mail, irons, hair dryers. *Fee:* video games, high-speed Internet. **Pool(s):** heated indoor/outdoor. **Leisure Activities:** saunas, whirlpool, exercise room. **Guest Services:** complimentary and valet laundry, area transportation. **Business Services:** meeting rooms. **Cards:** AX, DC, DS, JC, MC, VI.

AAA Benefit:
Members save 5% off of the best available rate.

RESIDENCE INN BY MARRIOTT-HERNDON/RESTON   *Book great rates at AAA.com*   Phone: (703)435-0044

Small-scale Hotel
$269 3/23-2/28
$249 3/1-3/22

Address: 315 Elden St 20170 **Location:** 0.4 mi w on CR 606 from jct CR 7100 (Fairfax County Pkwy). Located in a commercial area. **Facility:** Smoke free premises. 168 units. 126 one-bedroom standard units with kitchens. 42 two-bedroom suites with kitchens. 2 stories (no elevator), interior corridors. *Bath:* combo or shower only. **Parking:** on-site. **Terms:** cancellation fee imposed. **Amenities:** high-speed Internet, voice mail, irons, hair dryers. **Pool(s):** heated outdoor. **Leisure Activities:** whirlpool, playground, sports court. **Guest Services:** valet and coin laundry. **Business Services:** meeting rooms, PC. **Cards:** AX, DS, JC, MC, VI.

AAA Benefit:
Members save 5% off of the best available rate.

SPRINGHILL SUITES BY MARRIOTT HERNDON/RESTON   *Book great rates at AAA.com*   Phone: 703/435-3100

Small-scale Hotel
$241-$285 All Year

Address: 138 Spring St 20170 **Location:** SR 267 (Dulles Toll Rd), exit 11 (Fairfax County Pkwy); CR 7100, just n to Spring St exit, then just s. **Facility:** Smoke free premises. 136 one-bedroom standard units. 4 stories, interior corridors. *Bath:* combo or shower only. **Parking:** on-site. **Amenities:** high-speed Internet, dual phone lines, voice mail, irons, hair dryers. *Some:* CD players. **Pool(s):** heated indoor. **Leisure Activities:** whirlpool, exercise room. **Guest Services:** valet and coin laundry, wireless Internet. **Business Services:** PC. **Cards:** AX, DC, DS, JC, MC, VI.

AAA Benefit:
Members save 5% off of the best available rate.

STAYBRIDGE SUITES HERNDON DULLES   *Book at AAA.com*   Phone: (703)713-6800

Small-scale Hotel
$89-$284 All Year

Address: 13700 Coppermine Rd 20171 **Location:** SR 267 (Dulles Toll Rd), exit 10, 0.7 mi s on Centreville Rd (SR 657), then 0.4 mi w. Located in a business/residential area. **Facility:** 112 units. 47 one- and 65 two-bedroom suites with kitchens. 2 stories (no elevator), exterior corridors. **Parking:** on-site. **Terms:** check-in 4 pm, cancellation fee imposed. **Amenities:** DVD players, CD players, high-speed Internet, voice mail, irons, hair dryers. **Pool(s):** outdoor. **Leisure Activities:** whirlpool, exercise room, sports court. **Guest Services:** complimentary and valet laundry, area transportation, wireless Internet. **Business Services:** meeting rooms, PC. **Cards:** AX, CB, DC, DS, JC, MC, VI.

(See map and index starting on p. 412)

WASHINGTON DULLES AIRPORT MARRIOTT   *Book great rates at AAA.com*   **Phone:** 703/471-9500

▼▼▼▼

Large-scale Hotel
$296-$329 All Year

Address: 45020 Aviation Dr 20166 **Location:** At Washington Dulles International Airport. **Facility:** Smoke free premises. 368 units. 364 one-bedroom standard units. 4 one-bedroom suites. 3 stories, interior corridors. *Bath:* combo or shower only. **Parking:** on-site. **Amenities:** voice mail, irons, hair dryers. *Fee:* video games, high-speed Internet. *Some:* dual phone lines. **Pool(s):** outdoor, heated indoor. **Leisure Activities:** whirlpool, 2 lighted tennis courts, exercise room, basketball, horseshoes, volleyball. **Guest Services:** valet and coin laundry, area transportation, wireless Internet. **Business Services:** conference facilities, business center. **Cards:** AX, DC, DS, JC, MC, VI.

Marriott
HOTELS & RESORTS

AAA Benefit:
Members save 5% off of the best available rate.

(ASK) ⓢ➋ ✈ 🍴 ⊤ CALL ⑤Ⓜ 🏊 ⊠ ✕ 🎏 🖥
/ SOME UNITS 🅗 📺

───── **WHERE TO DINE** ─────

ANITA'S   **Phone:** 703/481-1441

▼

Mexican
$5-$15

This small chain is locally popular for their signature "New Mexico" style dishes. The menu features a good variety of tacos, burritos and enchiladas. If you're in the mood for a Mexican breakfast, this is the place. Casual dress. **Bar:** Full bar. **Reservations:** accepted. **Hours:** 5 am-9:30 pm, Fri & Sat-10 pm, Sun-9 pm. Closed: 11/27, 12/25. **Address:** 701 Elden St 20170 **Location:** Jct Elden and Montroe sts; center. **Parking:** on-site. **Cards:** AX, DC, DS, MC, VI.

CANTINA D'ITALIA   **Phone:** 703/318-7171

▼▼

Italian
$7-$20

Casual dress. **Bar:** Full bar. **Reservations:** suggested, weekends. **Hours:** 11 am-10 pm, Fri & Sat-11 pm, Sun noon-10 pm. Closed: 1/1, 11/27, 12/25. **Address:** 150 Elden St 20170 **Location:** Just w on CR 606 from jct CR 7100 (Fairfax County Pkwy); in Eden Plaza. **Parking:** on-site. **Cards:** AX, CB, DC, DS, MC, VI.

GLORY DAYS GRILL, HERNDON/RESTON   **Phone:** 703/390-5555

▼▼

American
$7-$18

Lending to the casual restaurant's sports-themed atmosphere are memorabilia decorating the dining area and 25 TVs with control centers at each table and booth. Food selections range from wings and ribs to seafood, beef and pasta dishes. Casual dress. **Bar:** Full bar. **Reservations:** not accepted. **Hours:** 4 pm-midnight, Fri & Sat from 11:30 am, Sun 11:30 am-11 pm. Closed: 11/27, 12/25. **Address:** 2567 John Milton Dr 20171 **Location:** 0.9 mi e on CR 665 (Fox Mill Rd); from jct CR 7100 (Fairfax County Pkwy); in Fox Mill Shopping Center. **Parking:** on-site. **Cards:** AX, DS, MC, VI.

HARD TIMES CAFE   **Phone:** 703/318-8941

▼▼

American
$6-$15

The hot and spicy, down-home operation knocks your socks off with an impressive variety of chilies, cooked in styles ranging from Cincinnati to Texas and vegetarian. Casual dress. **Bar:** Full bar. **Reservations:** not accepted. **Hours:** 11 am-1 am. **Address:** 428 Elden St 20170 **Location:** 0.4 mi w on CR 606 from jct CR 7100 (Fairfax County Pkwy); in Herndon Center. **Parking:** on-site. **Cards:** AX, MC, VI.

CALL ⑤Ⓜ

HARVEST OF INDIA   **Phone:** 703/471-8149   ㉞

▼▼

Indian
$8-$20

Lamb and chicken vindaloo give diners a piquant jolt of spice, but many of the shopping center eatery's other dishes are more subdued. The kitchen prepares a wide selection of chicken, lamb, seafood and vegetarian fare, some of which is prepared tandoori style. The setting exudes comfort. Casual dress. **Bar:** Full bar. **Reservations:** accepted. **Hours:** 11:30 am-2 & 5:30-10 pm. **Address:** 364 Elden St 20170 **Location:** 1.4 mi w on CR 606 from jct CR 7100 (Fairfax County Pkwy); in Herndon Centre. **Parking:** on-site. **Cards:** AX, DC, DS, MC, VI.

CALL ⑤Ⓜ

ICE HOUSE CAFE   **Phone:** 703/437-4500   ㉜

▼▼

American
$7-$26

The focal point of the rustic, lively cafe is an oyster bar that resembles a turn-of-the-20th-century saloon. Signature crab cakes are mixed with scallions and peppers. The chocolate Sheba dessert is decadent. Jazz entertainers perform on weekends. Dressy casual. **Bar:** Full bar. **Reservations:** suggested, for dinner. **Hours:** 11:30 am-2:30 & 5-10 pm, Fri-10:30 pm, Sat 5 pm-10:30 pm, Sun 5 pm-9 pm. Closed major holidays. **Address:** 760 Elden St 20170 **Location:** Center. **Parking:** street. **Cards:** AX, DC, DS, MC, VI.

RUSSIA HOUSE RESTAURANT   **Phone:** 703/787-8880   ㉚

▼▼▼

Russian
$12-$30

Traditional cuisine—such as beef stroganoff, steak Nicolai flambeau and veal Orloff—is well-prepared and flavorful. Colorful Russian artwork decorates the attractive, elegant dining room, where strolling musicians perform on weekends. Nightly specials are well-thought-out. Dressy casual. **Bar:** Full bar. **Reservations:** suggested, weekends. **Hours:** 11:30 am-2:30 & 5:30-10 pm, Sat 5:30 pm-10:30 pm, Sun 5 pm-9 pm, Mon 5:30 pm-10 pm. Closed major holidays. **Address:** 790 Station St 20170 **Location:** Center. **Parking:** street. **Cards:** AX, MC, VI.

SUPPER CLUB OF INDIA   **Phone:** 703/736-0466   ㉟

▼▼▼

Indian
$10-$25

In a shopping complex near hotels, the restaurant's intimate setting offers a comfortable dining atmosphere, and the menu shows a nice selection of traditional Indian dishes using lamb, chicken, seafood and vegetables. Tandoori selections also are available. Dressy casual. **Bar:** Full bar. **Reservations:** suggested. **Hours:** 11:30 am-2:30 & 5:30-10 pm. **Address:** 13055 Worldgate Dr 20170 **Location:** Jct SR 657 and 267 (Dulles Toll Rd), exit 10; in Worldgate Centre. **Parking:** on-site. **Cards:** AX, DC, DS, MC, VI.

CALL ⑤Ⓜ ◥

(See map and index starting on p. 412)

THE TORTILLA FACTORY RESTAURANT   Phone: 703/471-1156 ③③

Mexican
$6-$16

Locals have frequented the restaurant since 1972. Sonoran specialties are made from only fresh chilies and spices from New Mexico and Arizona. Among other offerings are traditional Mexican selections, vegetarian items and such dishes as carne asada, carne machaca and chimichangas. A children's menu is available. Casual dress. **Bar:** Full bar. **Hours:** 11 am-9 pm, Tues-Thurs to 9:30 pm, Fri & Sat-10 pm, Sun noon-9 pm. Closed major holidays. **Address:** 648 Elden St 20170 **Location:** Center; in The Pines Center. **Parking:** on-site. **Cards:** AX, CB, DC, DS, MC, VI.

ZEFFIRELLI RISTORANTE ITALIANO   *Menu on AAA.com*   Phone: 703/318-7000 ③①

Italian
$11-$31

A friendly atmosphere and knowledgeable staff are two of the restaurant's strong points. Another is the award-winning veal chop entree, a favorite on the hugely varied menu. Dressy casual. **Bar:** Full bar. **Reservations:** suggested. **Hours:** 11:30 am-2:30 & 5-10 pm, Fri-10:30 pm, Sat 5 pm-10:30 pm, Sun 5 pm-9:30 pm. Closed major holidays. **Address:** 728 Pine St 20170 **Location:** Center. **Parking:** on-site. **Cards:** AX, CB, DC, DS, MC, VI.

LEESBURG pop. 28,311

——— WHERE TO STAY ———

BEST WESTERN LEESBURG HOTEL &
   CONFERENCE CENTER   *Book great rates at AAA.com*   Phone: (703)777-9400

Small-scale Hotel
$89-$149 All Year

Address: 726 E Market St 20176 **Location:** 0.5 mi e on SR 7 business route. Located in a commercial area. **Facility:** 99 one-bedroom standard units. 2 stories, interior corridors. **Parking:** on-site. **Amenities:** voice mail, safes (fee), irons, hair dryers. *Some:* high-speed Internet. **Pool(s):** heated outdoor. **Leisure Activities:** barbecue grill & picnic tables, limited exercise equipment. **Guest Services:** valet and coin laundry, airport transportation-Washington Dulles International Airport, area transportation-within 10 mi, wireless Internet. **Business Services:** meeting rooms, business center. **Cards:** AX, CB, DC, DS, JC, MC, VI. **Free Special Amenities:** full breakfast and high-speed Internet.

AAA Benefit:
Members save 10% everyday, plus an exclusive frequent stay program.

     / SOME UNITS FEE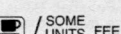

COMFORT SUITES LEESBURG   *Book at AAA.com*

▼▼▼

Small-scale Hotel
$109-$159 3/1-10/31
$99-$159 11/1-2/28

Phone: (703)669-1650

Address: 80 Prosperity Ave SE 20175 **Location:** Off SR 7, just w of jct US 15. Located in a commercial area. **Facility:** Smoke free premises. 80 units. 71 one-bedroom standard units. 9 one-bedroom suites with efficiencies and whirlpools. 4 stories, interior corridors. *Bath:* combo or shower only. **Parking:** on-site. **Terms:** check-in 4 pm. **Amenities:** high-speed Internet, dual phone lines, voice mail, safes, irons, hair dryers. *Some:* DVD players, CD players. **Pool(s):** heated indoor. **Leisure Activities:** whirlpool, limited exercise equipment. **Guest Services:** valet and coin laundry, area transportation, wireless Internet. **Business Services:** meeting rooms, business center. **Cards:** AX, CB, DC, DS, JC, MC, VI.

ASK SD ⊕ ↟↟ 🏊 ✕ 🎥 FEE ▯ 🖨 ▣

HAMPTON INN & SUITES LEESBURG

▼▼▼

Small-scale Hotel
Rates not provided

Phone: 703/669-8640

Address: 117 Ft Evans Rd NE 20176 **Location:** Off SR 7, just w of jct SR 15. **Facility:** 101 one-bedroom standard units. 4 stories, interior corridors. *Bath:* combo or shower only. **Parking:** on-site. **Amenities:** video games (fee), high-speed Internet, dual phone lines, voice mail, irons, hair dryers. **Pool(s):** heated indoor. **Leisure Activities:** whirlpool, limited exercise equipment. **Guest Services:** valet and coin laundry, area transportation. **Business Services:** meeting rooms.

⊕ ↟↟ CALL 🛗M 🏊 🎥 ▣ / SOME UNITS ✕ ▯ 🖨

HOLIDAY INN LEESBURG   *Book great rates at AAA.com*

AAA SAVE

▼▼▼

Small-scale Hotel
$169 1/1-2/28
$149 3/1-12/31

Phone: 703/771-9200

Address: 1500 E Market St 20176 **Location:** 2 mi e on SR 7. **Facility:** 126 units. 121 one-bedroom standard units. 5 one-bedroom suites. 2 stories (no elevator), interior corridors. *Bath:* combo or shower only. **Parking:** on-site. **Amenities:** video games (fee), high-speed Internet, dual phone lines, voice mail, irons, hair dryers. **Pool(s):** outdoor. **Leisure Activities:** exercise room. **Guest Services:** valet and coin laundry, airport transportation-Washington Dulles International Airport, wireless Internet. **Business Services:** meeting rooms, PC. **Cards:** AX, CB, DC, DS, JC, MC, VI. **Free Special Amenities:** local telephone calls and newspaper.

SD ⊕ ↟↟ 🍽 CALL 🛗M 🏊 🎥 ▣ / SOME UNITS FEE 🐾 ✕ FEE ▯ FEE 🖨

LANSDOWNE RESORT   *Book great rates at AAA.com*

AAA SAVE

▼▼▼▼

Resort
Large-scale Hotel
$179-$1200 All Year

Phone: 703/729-8400

Address: 44050 Woodridge Pkwy 20176 **Location:** SR 7, 3.6 mi w of jct SR 28; 4.4 mi e of jct US 15. **Facility:** Along the Potomac River, the resort is styled in a Frank Lloyd Wright theme and affords beautiful views of the river and a nearby golf course. Designated smoking area. 296 units. 292 one-bedroom standard units, some with whirlpools. 4 one-bedroom suites. 9 stories, interior corridors. *Bath:* combo or shower only. **Parking:** on-site and valet. **Terms:** check-in 4 pm, 3 day cancellation notice-fee imposed. **Amenities:** high-speed Internet (fee), dual phone lines, voice mail, irons, hair dryers. *Some:* CD players. **Dining:** 3 restaurants, also, On The Potomac, Riverside Hearth, see separate listings. **Pool(s):** 2 outdoor, 2 heated outdoor, heated indoor. **Leisure Activities:** saunas, whirlpools, steamrooms, waterslide, putting green, racquetball court, jogging, playground, spa, basketball, horseshoes, volleyball. *Fee:* golf-45 holes, driving range, 3 lighted tennis courts, children's program weekends, culinary school, bicycles, fitness classes. **Guest Services:** valet laundry, airport transportation (fee)-Washington Dulles International Airport, beauty salon, wireless Internet. **Business Services:** conference facilities, business center. **Cards:** AX, CB, DC, DS, JC, MC, VI. **Free Special Amenities:** local telephone calls and newspaper. *(See color ad p 541)*

SD FEE ⊕ ↟↟ 🍽 CALL 🛗M 🏊 ♿ ✕ ✕ 🎥 ▣ / SOME UNITS ▯

THE NORRIS HOUSE INN

▼▼ ▼▼

Historic Bed
& Breakfast
$95-$190 3/1-12/31
$85-$150 1/1-2/28

Phone: 703/777-1806

Address: 108 Loudoun St SW 20175 **Location:** Just s of SR 7; between Wirt and Liberty sts; center; in historic district. **Facility:** In historic Leesburg, The Norris House Inn offers individually decorated guest rooms with beds ranging from canopy, to brass, to feather. Smoke free premises. 6 one-bedroom standard units, some with whirlpools. 3 stories (no elevator), interior corridors. *Bath:* combo or shower only. **Parking:** street. **Terms:** office hours 9 am-6 pm, check-in 4 pm, age restrictions may apply, 3 day cancellation notice-fee imposed. **Amenities:** hair dryers. **Guest Services:** wireless Internet. **Business Services:** meeting rooms. **Cards:** AX, MC, VI.

↟↟ ✕ 🎦 ☎

——— WHERE TO DINE ———

BLUE RIDGE GRILL

▼▼

American
$7-$21

Phone: 703/669-5505

Locals have made the grill an area favorite. Menu choices range from sandwiches and salads to such entrees as certified Angus beef, crab cakes and baby back ribs. Tried-and-true dishes line the children's menu. Desserts, sauces and dressings are made on site. Casual dress. **Bar:** Full bar. **Hours:** 11 am-10 pm, Fri & Sat-11 pm. Closed: 11/27, 12/25. **Address:** 955 Edwards Ferry Rd 20176 **Location:** 0.7 mi n on US 15 from jct SR 7; in Leesburg Park. **Parking:** on-site. **Cards:** AX, DC, DS, MC, VI.

CALL 🛗M

EIFFEL TOWER CAFE

▼▼▼

French
$6-$29

Phone: 703/777-5142

The Eiffel Tower Cafe combines a wonderful mix of French and American cuisine as well as offering a soothing, relaxing atmosphere in which to dine. Dressy casual. **Bar:** Full bar. **Reservations:** suggested, weekends. **Hours:** 11:30 am-2:30 & 5:30-9:30 pm, Sun-2:30 pm. Closed major holidays; also Mon. **Address:** 107 Loudoun St SW 20175 **Location:** Just s of SR 7; between Wirt and Liberty sts; center. **Parking:** street. **Cards:** AX, CB, DC, MC, VI.

✈

G G CAFE

South Italian
$9-$24

Phone: 703/669-8600

The cafe prepares Southern Italian cuisine in a quaint setting with murals. Staff members are friendly. Casual dress. **Bar:** Full bar. **Hours:** 11 am-10 pm, Sat & Sun-11 pm. Closed: 11/27, 12/25. **Address:** Two W Market St 20176 **Location:** Just s of SR 7; between Wirt and Market sts; center. **Parking:** valet and street. **Cards:** AX, CB, DC, DS, MC, VI.

LIGHTFOOT

American
$7-$34

Phone: 703/771-2233

The chic, colorful bistro is best known for preparing and serving imaginative seasonal fare, including many specialty items. Style and ambiance are big assets. Smoking is permitted in the lounge. Casual dress. **Bar:** Full bar. **Reservations:** accepted. **Hours:** 11:30 am-2:30 & 5:30-11 pm, Fri & Sat-midnight, Sun 11:30 am-3 & 5:30-10 pm; Sunday brunch. Closed major holidays. **Address:** 11 N King St 20176 **Location:** SR 7 business route, just n on US 15; center. **Parking:** on-site. **Cards:** AX, DS, MC, VI.

ON THE POTOMAC   *Menu on AAA.com*

American
$13-$30

Phone: 703/729-4073

Overlooking the Virginia countryside, the comfortably elegant restaurant is best known for its quality steaks. This spot is great for either a quick lunch or leisurely meal. Couples and resort guests are the standard clientele. Dressy casual. **Bar:** Full bar. **Reservations:** suggested. **Hours:** 6 pm-10 pm, Sun brunch 11 am-2 pm. **Address:** 44050 Woodridge Pkwy 20176 **Location:** SR 7, 3.6 mi w of jct SR 28; 4.4 mi e of jct US 15; in Lansdowne Resort. **Parking:** on-site. **Cards:** AX, CB, DC, DS, JC, MC, VI.

RIVERSIDE HEARTH

American
$19-$35

Phone: 703/729-4105

Patrons can enjoy "upscale" buffet dining or a la carte selections for breakfast, lunch and dinner. Add in a panoramic view of Sugarloaf and the Potomac countryside for a nice experience in fine dining. In the Lansdowne Resort, the restaurant focuses on classic American fare and a high level of service. Dressy casual. **Bar:** Full bar. **Reservations:** suggested. **Hours:** 6:30-10:30 am, 11-2 & 6-10 pm. **Address:** 44050 Woodbridge Pkwy 20176 **Location:** SR 7, 3.6 mi w of jct SR 28; 4.4 mi e of jct US 15; in Lansdowne Resort. **Parking:** on-site. **Cards:** AX, CB, DC, DS, JC, MC, VI.

TUP TIM THAI RESTAURANT   *Menu on AAA.com*

Thai
$8-$18

Phone: 703/777-0097

Casual dress. **Bar:** Full bar. **Reservations:** accepted. **Hours:** 11 am-3:30 & 5-10 pm, Fri-11 pm, Sat & Sun noon-10 pm. Closed: 11/27, 12/25. **Address:** 17 Catoctin Cir 20175 **Location:** Just e of jct S King St. **Parking:** on-site. **Cards:** AX, DC, DS, MC, VI.

CALL

TUSCARORA MILL RESTAURANT

American
$7-$31

Phone: 703/771-9300

Diversity, atmosphere and polished service await diners at the downtown restaurant. The converted working mill from before the turn of the 20th century has hardwood floors and a deep wooden texture to the walls and tables. Classic American cuisine has wide appeal. Casual dress. **Bar:** Full bar. **Reservations:** suggested. **Hours:** 11:30 am-11 pm, Fri & Sat-midnight, Sun-9 pm. Closed major holidays. **Address:** 203 Harrison St SE 20175 **Location:** Just s of SR 7; corner of Loudoun and Harrison sts; center; in Market Station. **Parking:** on-site. **Cards:** AX, DC, DS, MC, VI. **Historic**

LORTON pop. 17,786

——— **WHERE TO STAY** ———

COMFORT INN GUNSTON CORNER   *Book great rates at AAA.com*

Small-scale Hotel
$109-$129 3/1-7/26
$99-$119 7/27-2/28

Phone: (703)643-3100

Address: 8180 Silverbrook Rd 22079 **Location:** I-95, exit 163, just w. **Facility:** 129 one-bedroom standard units. 4 stories, interior corridors. *Bath:* combo or shower only. **Parking:** on-site. **Amenities:** video games (fee), voice mail, irons, hair dryers. **Pool(s):** heated outdoor. **Leisure Activities:** limited exercise equipment. *Fee:* game room. **Guest Services:** valet and coin laundry, area transportation-within 5 mi, wireless Internet. **Business Services:** meeting rooms. **Cards:** AX, DS, MC, VI. **Free Special Amenities:** expanded continental breakfast and high-speed Internet.

——— **WHERE TO DINE** ———

POLO GRILL

American
$6-$20

Phone: 703/550-0002

The Polo Grill is a popular sports bar and a casual family spot offering tasty pasta, seafood and burgers as well as a handful of items sporting a Cajun/Creole accent. The friendly service won't disappoint and neither will the varied wine list. Casual dress. **Bar:** Full bar. **Reservations:** accepted. **Hours:** 11 am-10:30 pm, Fri & Sat-11 pm, Sun 10 am-9:30 pm. Closed major holidays. **Address:** 7784 Gunston Plaza Dr 22079 **Location:** I-95, exit 163, 0.7 mi e on SR 642, just s on Armistead Rd, then just e on Richmond Hwy; in Gunston Plaza Shopping Center. **Parking:** on-site. **Cards:** AX, CB, DC, DS, MC, VI.

MANASSAS pop. 35,135

———— WHERE TO STAY ————

BEST WESTERN BATTLEFIELD INN   *Book great rates at AAA.com*

Small-scale Hotel
Rates not provided

Address: 10820 Balls Ford Rd 20109 **Location:** I-66, exit 47A westbound; exit 47 eastbound, just s on SR 234 business route. Located in a commercial area. **Facility:** 125 one-bedroom standard units. 2 stories (no elevator), exterior corridors. *Bath:* combo or shower only. **Parking:** on-site. **Amenities:** high-speed Internet, voice mail, safes (fee), irons, hair dryers. **Pool(s):** outdoor. **Guest Services:** valet and coin laundry. **Business Services:** meeting rooms, PC. **Free Special Amenities: full breakfast and newspaper.**

Phone: 703/361-8000

AAA Benefit:
Members save 10% everyday, plus an exclusive frequent stay program.

BEST WESTERN MANASSAS   *Book great rates at AAA.com*

Small-scale Hotel
Rates not provided

Address: 8640 Mathis Ave 20110 **Location:** I-66, exit 53 (SR 28 S), 5 mi s to Manassas Dr, then just e. Located in a commercial area. **Facility:** 60 one-bedroom standard units, some with whirlpools. 2 stories (no elevator), interior corridors. *Bath:* combo or shower only. **Parking:** on-site. **Amenities:** voice mail, irons, hair dryers. *Some:* high-speed Internet. **Leisure Activities:** sauna, whirlpool, exercise bicycle. **Guest Services:** coin laundry, wireless Internet. **Business Services:** PC. **Free Special Amenities: continental breakfast and high-speed Internet.**
(See color ad p 435)

Phone: 703/368-7070

AAA Benefit:
Members save 10% everyday, plus an exclusive frequent stay program.

COMFORT SUITES MANASSAS   *Book at AAA.com*

Small-scale Hotel
$99-$149 All Year

Phone: (703)686-1100

Address: 7350 Williamson Blvd 20109 **Location:** I-66, exit 47A westbound; exit 47 eastbound, 0.5 mi s on SR 234 business route, then just e. **Facility:** Smoke free premises. 138 units. 137 one-bedroom standard units, some with whirlpools. 1 one-bedroom suite with whirlpool. 4 stories, interior corridors. *Bath:* combo or shower only. **Parking:** on-site. **Amenities:** video games (fee), high-speed Internet, voice mail, irons, hair dryers. **Pool(s):** heated indoor. **Leisure Activities:** whirlpool, exercise room. *Fee:* game room. **Guest Services:** valet and coin laundry, wireless Internet. **Business Services:** meeting rooms, PC. **Cards:** AX, CB, DC, DS, JC, MC, VI.

COUNTRY INN & SUITES BY CARLSON   *Book great rates at AAA.com*

Small-scale Hotel
$169-$186 3/1-8/31
$149-$164 9/1-2/28

Phone: (703)393-9797

Address: 10810 Battleview Pkwy 20109 **Location:** I-66, exit 47 eastbound; exit 47B westbound, just n on SR 234, then just e. **Facility:** 75 units. 42 one-bedroom standard units, some with whirlpools. 33 one-bedroom suites. 3 stories, interior corridors. *Bath:* combo or shower only. **Parking:** on-site. **Amenities:** video games (fee), voice mail, irons, hair dryers. **Pool(s):** heated indoor. **Leisure Activities:** whirlpool, limited exercise equipment. *Fee:* game room. **Guest Services:** valet and coin laundry, wireless Internet. **Business Services:** meeting rooms, PC. **Cards:** AX, CB, DC, DS, JC, MC, VI. *(See color ad below)*

COURTYARD BY MARRIOTT
MANASSAS-BATTLEFIELD PARK *Book great rates at AAA.com*

Phone: 703/335-1300

Small-scale Hotel
$166-$196 All Year

Address: 10701 Battleview Pkwy 20109 **Location:** I-66, exit 47 eastbound; exit 47B westbound, just n on SR 234, then just e. **Facility:** Smoke free premises. 149 units. 137 one-bedroom standard units. 12 one-bedroom suites. 3 stories, interior corridors. *Bath:* combo or shower only. **Parking:** on-site. **Amenities:** high-speed Internet, voice mail, irons, hair dryers. **Pool(s):** heated indoor. **Leisure Activities:** whirlpool, exercise room. **Guest Services:** valet and coin laundry, wireless Internet. **Business Services:** meeting rooms, PC (fee). **Cards:** AX, DC, DS, JC, MC, VI.

AAA Benefit:
Members save 5% off of the best available rate.

FAIRFIELD INN & SUITES BY MARRIOTT *Book great rates at AAA.com*

Phone: 703/393-9966

Small-scale Hotel
$148-$181 All Year

Address: 6950 Nova Way 20109 **Location:** I-66, exit 47 eastbound; exit 47B westbound, just n on SR 234, then just e. **Facility:** Smoke free premises. 80 one-bedroom standard units. 3 stories, interior corridors. *Bath:* combo or shower only. **Parking:** on-site. **Amenities:** video games (fee), high-speed Internet, voice mail, irons, hair dryers. *Some:* CD players. **Pool(s):** heated indoor. **Leisure Activities:** whirlpool, exercise room. **Guest Services:** valet and coin laundry, wireless Internet. **Business Services:** PC. **Cards:** AX, DC, DS, JC, MC, VI.

AAA Benefit:
Members save 5% off of the best available rate.

   CALL   / SOME UNITS

FOUR POINTS BY SHERATON MANASSAS
BATTLEFIELD

Phone: (703)335-0000

Small-scale Hotel
$95-$149 3/1-12/15
$85-$119 12/16-2/28

Address: 10800 Vandor Ln 20109 **Location:** I-66, exit 47 eastbound; exit 47B westbound, just n on SR 234, then just e. **Facility:** 158 one-bedroom standard units. 5 stories, interior corridors. *Bath:* combo or shower only. **Parking:** on-site. **Terms:** cancellation fee imposed. **Amenities:** video games (fee), dual phone lines, voice mail, irons, hair dryers. **Pool(s):** outdoor, heated indoor. **Leisure Activities:** exercise room. **Guest Services:** complimentary and valet laundry, wireless Internet. **Business Services:** meeting rooms, PC. **Cards:** AX, DS, MC, VI. **Free Special Amenities:** early check-in/late check-out and high-speed Internet.

AAA Benefit:
Members get up to 15% off, plus Starwood Preferred Guest® bonuses.

   CALL   / SOME UNITS

HAMPTON INN *Book great rates at AAA.com*

Phone: 703/369-1100

Small-scale Hotel
Rates not provided

Address: 7295 Williamson Blvd 20109 **Location:** I-66, exit 47A westbound; exit 47 eastbound, 0.5 mi s on SR 234 business route. Located in a commercial shopping area. **Facility:** 125 units. 120 one-bedroom standard units. 5 one-bedroom suites. 6 stories, interior corridors. *Bath:* combo or shower only. **Parking:** on-site. **Amenities:** dual phone lines, voice mail, irons, hair dryers. *Some:* DVD players. **Pool(s):** outdoor. **Leisure Activities:** limited exercise equipment. **Guest Services:** valet and coin laundry, wireless Internet. **Business Services:** meeting rooms, PC. **Free Special Amenities:** expanded continental breakfast and high-speed Internet.

QUALITY INN MANASSAS *Book great rates at AAA.com*

Phone: (703)368-2800

Motel
$79-$139 All Year

Address: 10653 Balls Ford Rd 20109 **Location:** I-66, exit 47A westbound; exit 47 eastbound, just s on SR 234 business route, then just e. **Facility:** 120 one-bedroom standard units. 2 stories (no elevator), exterior corridors. *Bath:* combo or shower only. **Parking:** on-site. **Amenities:** voice mail, irons, hair dryers. **Pool(s):** outdoor. **Guest Services:** coin laundry, wireless Internet. **Cards:** AX, CB, DC, DS, MC, VI.

 CALL FEE   / SOME UNITS

RED ROOF INN-MANASSAS *Book at AAA.com*

Phone: 703/335-9333

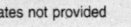
Motel
Rates not provided

Address: 10610 Automotive Dr 20109 **Location:** I-66, exit 47 eastbound; exit 47A westbound, just s on SR 234 business route, then just e on Balls Ford Rd. **Facility:** 119 one-bedroom standard units. 3 stories, exterior corridors. *Bath:* combo or shower only. **Parking:** on-site. **Amenities:** video games (fee), voice mail. **Guest Services:** wireless Internet.

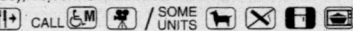

RESIDENCE INN BY MARRIOTT MANASSAS
BATTLEFIELD   *Book great rates at AAA.com*

Phone: 703/330-8808

Small-scale Hotel
$169-$206 All Year

Address: 7345 Williamson Blvd 20109 **Location:** I-66, exit 47A westbound; exit 47 eastbound, 0.5 mi s on SR 234 business route, then just e. **Facility:** Smoke free premises. 107 units. 43 one-bedroom standard units with efficiencies. 44 one- and 20 two-bedroom suites, some with efficiencies or kitchens. 3 stories, interior corridors. *Bath:* combo or shower only. **Parking:** on-site. **Amenities:** high-speed Internet, voice mail, irons, hair dryers. **Pool(s):** heated indoor. **Leisure Activities:** whirlpool, exercise room, sports court. **Guest Services:** valet and coin laundry, wireless Internet. **Business Services:** meeting rooms, PC. **Cards:** AX, DC, DS, JC, MC, VI.

AAA Benefit:
Members save 5% off of the best available rate.

────── **WHERE TO DINE** ──────

CARMELLO'S & LITTLE PORTUGAL

Phone: 703/368-5522

Northern Italian
$9-$30

Lunch and dinner menus feature both Italian and Portuguese cooking, with pasta, veal, chicken, beef and seafood dishes. Some desserts and breads are prepared on the premises. Knowledgeable, professional servers circulate in the cozy dining room. Casual dress. **Bar:** Full bar. **Reservations:** suggested. **Hours:** 5 pm-10 pm, Thurs & Fri also 11:30 am-2:30 pm, Sun 4 pm-9 pm. Closed major holidays. **Address:** 9108 Center St 20110 **Location:** At Center and Battle sts; in Historic Old Town. **Parking:** street. **Cards:** AX, DC, DS, MC, VI.

CASA CHIMAYO

Phone: 703/369-2523

Mexican
$8-$11

The restaurant takes diners back to old Mexico via a wonderful setting. Fresh chips and salsa complement a wide variety of traditional dishes. The staff is exceptionally friendly. Casual dress. **Bar:** Full bar. **Hours:** 11 am-10 pm, Fri & Sat-11 pm, Sun noon-10 pm. Closed: 12/25. **Address:** 8209 Sudley Rd 20109 **Location:** I-66, exit 47 eastbound; exit 47A westbound, 1.9 mi s on SR 234 business route. **Parking:** on-site. **Cards:** AX, DC, DS, MC, VI.

CITY SQUARE CAFE

Phone: 703/369-6022

Mediterranean
$7-$24

City Square Cafe is a family operated restaurant that serves a variety of Inetrnational and American cuisines. A Euro-styles sidewalk cafe when weather permits. Casual dress. **Bar:** Full bar. **Reservations:** accepted. **Hours:** 11 am-9 pm, Fri-10 pm, Sat 8:30 am-10 pm, Sun 8:30 am-3 pm. Closed major holidays. **Address:** 9428 Battle St 20110 **Location:** I-66, exit 47, in Historic Old Town; opposite train station. **Parking:** street. **Cards:** AX, DC, DS, MC, VI.

FOSTER'S GRILLE

Phone: 703/393-2427

American
$6-$10

The eatery is home to the charburger and freshly cut fries. Although the menu may be limited, the staff's enthusiasm is far from it. Casual dress. **Bar:** Beer only. **Reservations:** accepted. **Hours:** 11 am-9 pm, Fri & Sat-10 pm. Closed: 3/23, 11/27, 12/25. **Address:** 7817 Sudley Rd 20109 **Location:** I-66, exit 47A westbound; exit 47 eastbound, 1 mi s on SR 234 business route; in Sudley Manor Square. **Parking:** on-site. **Cards:** AX, DS, MC, VI.

GLORY DAYS GRILL, MANASSAS

Phone: 703/361-9040

American
$7-$18

Lending to the casual restaurant's sports-themed atmosphere are memorabilia decorating the dining area and 25 TVs with control centers at each table and booth. Food selections range from wings and ribs to seafood, beef and pasta dishes. Casual dress. **Bar:** Full bar. **Reservations:** not accepted. **Hours:** 4 pm-midnight, Fri & Sat from 11:30 am, Sun 11:30 am-11 pm. Closed: 11/27, 12/25. **Address:** 9516 Liberia Ave 20110 **Location:** Jct Signal Hill Rd; in Signal Hill Shopping Center. **Parking:** on-site. **Cards:** AX, DS, MC, VI.

OKRA'S LOUISIANA BISTRO

Phone: 703/330-2729

Regional American
$7-$25

Shoppers in Olde Town Manassas can refuel at this restaurant, which prepares such traditional Louisiana-style fare as shrimp Creole, chicken gumbo, gator bites and crawfish etouffee. Bright colors, Mardi Gras beads and murals line the comfortable eatery's walls. Desserts are worthy of high praise. Casual dress. **Bar:** Full bar. **Hours:** 11 am-9:30 pm, Thurs-Sat to 10:30 pm. Closed major holidays; also Sun. **Address:** 9110 Center St 20110 **Location:** Jct Battle St; in Historic Old Town. **Parking:** street. **Cards:** AX, DC, DS, MC, VI.

O'MEARA'S RESTAURANT & PUB

Phone: 703/369-1469

American
$7-$22

In historic Old Town Manassas, the restaurant presents a full menu of salads, hot and cold sandwiches, burgers and such entrees as cedar-plank salmon, stuffed chicken and corned beef and cabbage. When the weather cooperates, the patio opens for dining. After 10 pm, the pub livens up with a DJ playing music and dancing. Casual dress. **Bar:** Full bar. **Reservations:** accepted. **Hours:** 11 am-11 pm. **Address:** 8971 Center St 20110 **Location:** Jct Zebedee St; in Old Town area. **Parking:** on-site. **Cards:** AX, DS, MC, VI.

MCLEAN pop. 38,929 (See map and index starting on p. 412)

—— WHERE TO STAY ——

BEST WESTERN TYSONS WESTPARK HOTEL *Book great rates at AAA.com* Phone: 703/734-2800

Large-scale Hotel
Rates not provided

Address: 8401 Westpark Dr 22102 **Location:** I-495, exit 47A, 1.3 mi w on SR 7. **Facility:** 301 units. 287 one-bedroom standard units. 14 one-bedroom suites. 8 stories, interior corridors. *Bath:* combo or shower only. **Parking:** on-site. **Amenities:** voice mail, irons, hair dryers. *Some:* high-speed Internet. **Pool(s):** heated indoor. **Leisure Activities:** exercise room. *Fee:* game room. **Guest Services:** valet and coin laundry, area transportation, wireless Internet. **Business Services:** conference facilities, business center.

  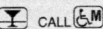

COURTYARD BY MARRIOTT, TYSONS CORNER *Book great rates at AAA.com* Phone: (703)790-0207 21

Small-scale Hotel
$89-$329 3/1-11/1
$69-$329 11/2-2/28

Address: 1960A Chain Bridge Rd 22102 **Location:** I-495, exit 46A, 0.5 mi s on SR 123, just nw on International Dr, then just se on Greensboro Dr. Located near two shopping malls & many business offices. **Facility:** Smoke free premises. 229 units. 213 one-bedroom standard units, some with whirlpools. 16 one-bedroom suites. 11 stories, interior corridors. *Bath:* combo or shower only. **Parking:** on-site. **Terms:** cancellation fee imposed. **Amenities:** high-speed Internet, dual phone lines, voice mail, irons, hair dryers. **Pool(s):** heated indoor. **Leisure Activities:** whirlpool, exercise room. **Guest Services:** valet and coin laundry, area transportation-within 3 mi, wireless Internet. **Business Services:** meeting rooms, business center. **Cards:** AX, CB, DC, DS, MC, VI. *(See color ad below)*

——— ▼ See AAA listing above ▼ ———

——— ▼ See AAA listing p 548 ▼ ———

(See map and index starting on p. 412)

CROWNE PLAZA TYSONS CORNER

Phone: (703)893-2100 ⑳

Large-scale Hotel
$89-$369 3/1-11/1
$69-$359 11/2-2/28

Address: 1960 Chain Bridge Rd 22102 **Location:** I-495, exit 46A, 0.5 mi s on SR 123, just nw on International Dr, then just sw on Greensboro Dr. Located in business and shopping area. **Facility:** 316 units. 314 one-bedroom standard units. 2 one-bedroom suites. 3-9 stories, interior corridors. *Bath:* combo or shower only. **Parking:** on-site. **Terms:** cancellation fee imposed. **Amenities:** high-speed Internet, voice mail, irons, hair dryers. *Some:* dual phone lines. **Pool(s):** heated indoor. **Leisure Activities:** whirlpool, sun deck, limited exercise equipment. **Guest Services:** valet and coin laundry, area transportation-within 2 mi & metro, wireless Internet. **Business Services:** conference facilities, business center. **Cards:** AX, CB, DC, DS, MC, VI. **Free Special Amenities: local telephone calls and newspaper.**
(See color ad p 547)

HILTON MCLEAN TYSONS CORNER *Book great rates at AAA.com*
Phone: 703/847-5000 ⑰

Large-scale Hotel
Rates not provided

Address: 7920 Jones Branch Dr 22102 **Location:** I-495, exit 46A, 0.3 mi s on SR 123, just nw on Tysons Blvd, 0.4 mi ne on Galleria/Westpark Dr, then just s. Located in a business park. **Facility:** 458 units. 453 one-bedroom standard units. 5 one-bedroom suites. 9 stories, interior corridors. *Bath:* combo or shower only. **Parking:** on-site. **Amenities:** video games (fee), dual phone lines, voice mail, irons, hair dryers. *Some:* high-speed Internet (fee). **Pool(s):** heated indoor. **Leisure Activities:** exercise room. **Guest Services:** valet laundry, area transportation, wireless Internet. **Business Services:** conference facilities, business center.

THE RITZ-CARLTON, TYSONS CORNER *Book at AAA.com*
Phone: 703/506-4300 ⑲

Large-scale Hotel
Rates not provided

Address: 1700 Tysons Blvd 22102 **Location:** I-495, exit 46A, 0.3 mi sw on SR 123, then just nw. Connected to The Galleria at Tysons II. **Facility:** Smoke free premises. 398 units. 365 one-bedroom standard units. 33 one-bedroom suites, some with whirlpools. 24 stories, interior corridors. *Bath:* combo or shower only. **Parking:** on-site (fee) and valet. **Amenities:** CD players, dual phone lines, voice mail, safes, honor bars, irons, hair dryers. *Fee:* video games, high-speed Internet. *Some:* DVD players. **Pool(s):** heated indoor. **Leisure Activities:** saunas, whirlpool, steamrooms, jogging, spa. **Guest Services:** valet laundry, area transportation, beauty salon, personal trainer, wireless Internet. **Business Services:** conference facilities, business center.

STAYBRIDGE SUITES-MCLEAN/TYSONS CORNER *Book great rates at AAA.com* Phone: (703)448-5400 ⑯

Small-scale Hotel
$229-$289 All Year

Address: 6845 Old Dominion Dr 22101 **Location:** I-495, exit 46B, 2 mi n on SR 123, then 0.3 mi e on SR 309. Located in a commercial area. **Facility:** Smoke free premises. 143 units. 34 one-bedroom standard units with efficiencies. 86 one- and 23 two-bedroom suites with efficiencies. 5 stories, interior corridors. *Bath:* combo or shower only. **Parking:** on-site. **Amenities:** video library (fee), high-speed Internet, dual phone lines, voice mail, irons, hair dryers. **Pool(s):** outdoor. **Leisure Activities:** gas grill, exercise room. **Guest Services:** complimentary and valet laundry, area transportation-within 5 mi. **Business Services:** meeting rooms, business center. **Cards:** AX, CB, DC, DS, JC, MC, VI. **Free Special Amenities: expanded continental breakfast and newspaper.**

------- WHERE TO DINE -------

BISTRO 123
Phone: 703-288-1369 ㉕

French
$9-$40

Chef-owned and operated, the restaurant lets patrons sample French cooking prepared with flair. The chef changes the menu seasonally. An afternoon tea is offered daily from 2 to 4 pm, and Sunday brunch is served from 11 am to 4 pm Guests can order from the lunch menu until 4 pm. Casual dress. **Bar:** Full bar. **Reservations:** suggested. **Hours:** 11 am-10 pm, Fri & Sat-11 pm; Sunday brunch. **Address:** 1961 Chain Bridge Rd 22102 **Location:** I-495, exit 46A, at Tysons Corner Shopping Mall outside entrance; opposite Circuit City. **Parking:** on-site. **Cards:** AX, DS, MC, VI.

BUSARA
Phone: 703/356-2288

Thai
$10-$26

Diners can enjoy the "zest" of expertly prepared Thai dishes at this restaurant, which offers noodle, vegetarian, seafood and meat dishes. A great start is kanon jeeb—delicious pork and crabmeat dumplings served with soy sauce. Sticky rice and mangoes or Thai custard are mouthwatering endings. Casual dress. **Bar:** Full bar. **Reservations:** accepted. **Hours:** 11:30 am-3 & 5-10:30 pm, Fri-11 pm, Sat 11:30 am-4 & 5-11 pm, Sun 11:30 am-4 & 5-10:30 pm. Closed: 7/4, 11/27; also for lunch 12/25 & 1/1. **Address:** 8142 Watson St 22102 **Location:** I-495, exit 47A, 0.6 mi s on SR 123 to International Dr, then just sw. **Parking:** on-site. **Cards:** AX, DC, DS, MC, VI.

CAFE OGGI
Phone: 703/442-7360 ⑯

Italian
$12-$20

The kitchen prepares good Italian cooking. On the menu is a selection of pasta dishes, as well as meats and fish. The comfortable dining room carries out an upscale, contemporary, art-deco look, with mirrored walls and glass blocks. Dressy casual. **Bar:** Full bar. **Reservations:** suggested. **Hours:** 11:30 am-2:30 & 5:30-10 pm, Fri & Sat-10:30 pm. **Address:** 6671 Old Dominion Dr 22101 **Location:** Jct SR 123, 0.6 mi e on SR 309. **Parking:** on-site. **Cards:** AX, DC, DS, MC, VI.

(See map and index starting on p. 412)

CAFE TAJ

Indian
$8-$20

Phone: 703/827-0444 ⑫

Locals have frequented the small, attractive Indian restaurant for more than a dozen years. The lunch buffet offers a variety of choices. The menu lists tandoori barbecue and kebabs, lamb, chicken, fish and vegetarian selections. Casual dress. **Bar:** Full bar. **Reservations:** not accepted. **Hours:** 11:30 am-2:30 & 5:30-10 pm, Fri & Sat-10:30 pm, Sun 5:30 pm-10 pm. Closed: 7/4, 11/27, 12/25; also for lunch 1/1. **Address:** 1379 Beverly Rd 22101 **Location:** I-495, exit 46B, 2 mi n on SR 123, then 0.3 mi e on SR 309; in Market Place Complex. **Parking:** on-site. **Cards:** AX, DC, DS, MC, VI.

THE CAPITAL GRILLE

Steak & Seafood
$10-$36

Phone: 703/448-3900 ㉗

Cherry wood and red leather assist in making this "clubby" dining room a beautiful spot to dine on excellent cuts of dry-aged beef. The staff is highly attentive and knowledgeable. Dressy casual. **Bar:** Full bar. **Reservations:** suggested. **Hours:** 11:30 & 5-10 pm, Fri-11 pm, Sun 4 pm-9 pm. Closed major holidays. **Address:** 1861 International Dr 22102 **Location:** I-495, exit 47A, 0.5 mi w on SR 7; on ground floor of office building. **Parking:** valet. **Cards:** AX, CB, DC, DS, MC, VI.

CALL

DA DOMENICO

Italian
$6-$31

Phone: 703/790-9000 ㉔

In a commercial area opposite two malls and convenient to the interstate, this family-run restaurant serves homemade pasta, fresh seafood and the succulent house specialty: marinated veal chops. The professional, helpful staff makes diners feel welcomed and sees to their needs. Open since 1980, the casual, friendly setting is comfortable for families, social or business meetings. Casual dress. **Bar:** Full bar. **Reservations:** suggested, weekends. **Hours:** 11:30 am-11 pm, Sat from 5 pm. Closed major holidays; also Sun. **Address:** 1992 Chain Bridge Rd 22102 **Location:** I-495, exit 46A, 0.7 mi s on SR 123; jct SR 123 and 7. **Parking:** on-site. **Cards:** AX, CB, DC, DS, MC, VI.

ECITIE RESTAURANT & BAR

American
$16-$29

Phone: 703/760-9000 ⑰

Lending to a fine-dining experience are a stylish bar, great artwork and an upscale menu and wine list. Casual dress. **Bar:** Full bar. **Reservations:** suggested, weekends. **Hours:** 5 pm-10 pm, Fri & Sat-11 pm. Closed: 12/25; also Sun. **Address:** 1524 Spring Hill Rd L-M 22102 **Location:** I-495, exit 46A, 0.5 mi s on SR 123, just n on International Dr, just w on Greensboro Dr, then just n. **Parking:** valet and street. **Cards:** AX, CB, DC, DS, JC, MC, VI.

FLEMMING'S PRIME STEAKHOUSE AND WINE BAR

Steak House
$19-$40

Phone: 703/442-8384 ㉓

The warm, clubby atmosphere is the ideal setting for perfectly grilled steaks and seafood. Side dishes come in hearty portions, and salads are fresh and crisp. More than 100 wine selections are available. Dressy casual. **Bar:** Full bar. **Reservations:** suggested. **Hours:** 5 pm-10 pm, Fri & Sat-11 pm. Closed: 11/27, 12/25. **Address:** 1960A Chainbridge Rd 22102 **Location:** I-495, exit 46A, 0.5 mi s on SR 123, just nw on International Dr, then se on Greensboro Dr; adjacent to Courtyard by Marriott-Tysons Corner. **Parking:** valet. **Cards:** AX, MC, VI.

CALL

THE GREEK TAVERNA

Greek
$8-$22

Phone: 703/556-0788 ⑬

Traditional Greek cooking served in a comfortable setting with slate floor, white washed walls and Greek artwork, recreating a Taverna atmosphere. Casual dress. **Bar:** Full bar. **Reservations:** accepted. **Hours:** 11:30 am-2:30 & 5-10 pm, Fri-10:30 pm, Sat 5 pm-10:30 pm, Sun 5 pm-9 pm. Closed major holidays. **Address:** 6828-C Old Dominion Dr 22101 **Location:** I-495, exit 46B, 2 mi n on SR 123, then 0.3 mi e on SR 309; in Market Place Complex. **Parking:** on-site. **Cards:** AX, MC, VI.

J.R.'S STOCKYARDS INN
 Menu on AAA.com

Steak & Seafood
$8-$25

Phone: 703/893-3390 ㉖

Rustic wood paneling, wagon wheels with lanterns and white tablecloths set the atmosphere in this steakhouse, which has been in operation since 1975. House specialties include aged and marinated beef, prime rib and lobster tail. Dressy casual. **Bar:** Full bar. **Reservations:** suggested. **Hours:** 11:30 am-2:30 & 5-10 pm, Fri-10:30 pm, Sat 5 pm-10:30 pm, Sun 5 pm-9 pm. Closed major holidays. **Address:** 8130 Watson St 22102 **Location:** I-495, exit 47A, 0.6 mi s on SR 123 to International Dr, then just sw. **Parking:** on-site. **Cards:** AX, DC, DS, MC, VI.

KAZAN RESTAURANT
Turkish
$8-$25

Phone: 703/734-1960 ⑭

This Turkish restaurant offers a light, airy dining atmosphere with seasonal sidewalk dining. The house specialty is the lamb kabob; however, do not overlook the rest of the menu with fresh seafood, chicken and vegetarian selections. Doner Kebab, a rare treat, is offered only on Wednesday, Friday and Saturday. Casual dress. **Bar:** Full bar. **Reservations:** suggested, weekends. **Hours:** 11:30 am-2:30 & 5:30-10 pm, Sat from 5:30 pm. Closed: Sun. **Address:** 6813 Redmond Dr 22101 **Location:** 0.5 mi e of jct SR 123 and 309; in McLean Shopping Center. **Parking:** on-site. **Cards:** AX, DC, MC, VI.

LEBANESE TAVERNA
Lebanese
$5-$20

Phone: 703/847-5244

This well-loved local chain has debuted a new spot with a more modern and trendy feel at this upscale mall. Shoppers and local workers crowd the bar and tables to share a wide variety of Middle Eastern tapas, or small bites. specialties include lamb, housemade-hot-from-the-oven pita bread, hummus, and stuffed grape leaves. Casual dress. **Bar:** Full bar. **Hours:** 11:30 am-10 pm, Fri & Sat-10:30 pm, Sun noon-9 pm. Closed: 1/1, 11/27, 12/25. **Address:** 1840-G International Dr 22102 **Location:** I-495, exit 46A, 0.3 mi sw on SR 123, just nw; in The Galleria at Tysons II. **Parking:** on-site. **Cards:** AX, DC, DS, MC, VI.

CALL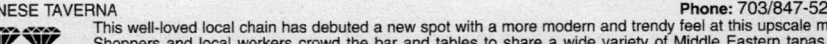

(See map and index starting on p. 412)

LEGAL SEA FOODS

Seafood
$10-$30

Phone: 703/827-8900

Legal prides itself on a reputation for freshness and consistency. More than 40 varieties of seafood can be grilled, broiled, fried or prepared Cajun style. Try the clam chowder that has been served at every presidential inauguration since 1981. The nautically inspired dining room is upscale and attractive with its rich cherry wood paneling and intricately detailed model ships. Casual dress. **Bar:** Full bar. **Hours:** 11 am-10 pm, Fri & Sat-10:30 pm, Sun noon-9 pm. Closed: 11/27, 12/25. **Address:** 2001 International Dr 22102 **Location:** I-495, exit 46A, 0.3 mi sw on SR 123, then just nw; in The Galleria at Tysons II. **Parking:** on-site. **Cards:** AX, CB, DC, DS, JC, MC, VI.

CALL

MAGGIANO'S LITTLE ITALY

Italian
$7-$30

Phone: 703/356-9000   ㉑

Diners savor scrumptious, traditional favorites served in a bustling atmosphere reminiscent of Little Italy. The dining area projects an early-20th-century feel; loud conversations bouncing off high ceilings evoke a sense of the Roaring 20s. Casual dress. **Bar:** Full bar. **Reservations:** suggested. **Hours:** 11 am-10 pm, Fri & Sat-11 pm. Closed: 12/25. **Address:** 2001 International Dr 22102 **Location:** I-495, exit 46A, 0.3 mi sw on SR 123; in The Galleria at Tysons II. **Parking:** on-site. **Cards:** AX, CB, DC, DS, MC, VI.

MCCORMICK & SCHMICK'S

Seafood
$8-$30

Phone: 703/848-8000   ⑲

This place is all about seafood, which is imported from all over the world. Among good choices are Washington state oysters, Maine clams, delicate Hawaiian escolar and tuna from Ecuador. The clublike decor is cozy, and expert staff provide able assistance. Dressy casual. **Bar:** Full bar. **Reservations:** suggested. **Hours:** 11 am-11 pm, Sun-10 pm. **Address:** 8484 Westpark Dr 22102 **Location:** I-495, exit 47A, 1.3 mi w on SR 7; in Ernst & Young Building. **Parking:** on-site (fee). **Cards:** AX, CB, DC, DS, MC, VI.

CALL

NEISHA THAI CUISINE

Thai
$6-$25

Phone: 703/883-3588

Glittering, cavelike walls, a small pond with a footbridge and an open kitchen set the tone for the stylish Thai restaurant. The kitchen prepares many wonderful dishes, such as passion beef with fresh ginger. Casual dress. **Bar:** Full bar. **Reservations:** suggested. **Hours:** 11 am-10 pm, Fri & Sat-11 pm. Closed: 11/27. **Address:** 7924 LB Tysons Corner Center 22102 **Location:** I-495, exit 46A; at Tysons Corner Shopping Mall, outside entrance, opposite Circuit City. **Parking:** on-site. **Cards:** AX, DC, DS, MC, VI.

PALM RESTAURANT AT TYSONS II

Steak & Seafood
$13-$52

Phone: 703/917-0200   ⑳

This bustling restaurant is noted for prime, dry-aged steaks and Nova Scotia lobsters, huge portions are delivered by an attentive staff in an atmosphere that is fun and lively. At the end of the meal, servers present tempting pastries tableside. Caricature-lined walls lend to the feeling that patrons are dining in an art gallery. Even if you bring a big appetite you still may leave with a doggy bag. Dressy casual. **Bar:** Full bar. **Reservations:** suggested. **Hours:** 11:30 am-10:30 pm, Sat from 5 pm, Sun 5 pm-9:30 pm. Closed major holidays. **Address:** 1750 Tysons Blvd 22102 **Location:** I-495, exit 46A, 0.3 mi sw on SR 123, just nw. **Parking:** valet. **Cards:** AX, CB, DC, DS, JC, MC, VI.

P.F. CHANG'S CHINA BISTRO

Chinese
$7-$18

Phone: 703/734-8996   ⑱

Trendy, upscale decor provides a pleasant backdrop for New Age Chinese dining. Appetizers, soups and salads are a meal by themselves. Vegetarian plates and sides, noodles, meins, chicken and meat dishes are created from exotic, fresh ingredients. Casual dress. **Bar:** Full bar. **Reservations:** suggested. **Hours:** 11 am-10:30 pm, Fri & Sat-11:30 pm. Closed: 11/27, 12/25. **Address:** 1716-M International Dr 22102 **Location:** I-495, exit 46A, 0.3 mi sw on SR 123; in The Galleria at Tysons II. **Parking:** on-site. **Cards:** AX, DC, DS, MC, VI.

PULCINELLA THE ITALIAN HOST

Regional Italian
$5-$19

Phone: 703/893-7777   ⑪

The popular, neighborhood restaurant serves southern Italian dishes—primarily fresh, homemade pasta and pizza made in a wood-burning oven—in ample portions. Dessert consists of traditional offerings. The staff is menu-smart and capable. Casual dress. **Bar:** Full bar. **Reservations:** not accepted. **Hours:** 11:30 am-10:30 pm, Sat from noon, Sun noon-9:30 pm. Closed: 11/27, 12/25. **Address:** 6852 Old Dominion Dr 22101 **Location:** On SR 309, just e of jct SR 123. **Parking:** on-site. **Cards:** AX, DC, MC, VI.

SILVER DINER

American
$7-$13

Phone: 703/821-3570

The eatery with its chrome and glass plate exterior and the glow of neon, provides the traditional diner setting. Booths with juke boxes, counter service and friendly wait staff add to the diner experience. The menu is extensive with salads, sandwiches and full meals. The desserts are made fresh and the fountain treats, shakes, floats and malts make for a great ending. Breakfast is available all day. Casual dress. **Bar:** Beer & wine. **Hours:** 7 am-midnight, Fri & Sat-3 am. Closed: Thanksgiving to 2 pm. **Address:** 8101 Fletcher Ave 22102 **Location:** I-495, exit 47A, 0.6 mi s on SR 123, to International Dr, then just sw. **Parking:** on-site. **Cards:** AX, DC, DS, MC, VI.

CALL

TACHIBANA
Japanese
$7-$30

Phone: 703/847-1771   ⑮

Looking for the some of the best sushi in the area, then Tachibana is the place. The menu also offers tempura, teriyaki and noodle dishes. Casual dress. **Bar:** Full bar. **Reservations:** not accepted, weekends. **Hours:** 11:30 am-2 & 5-10 pm, Fri-10:30 pm, Sat noon-2:30 & 5-10:30 pm, Sun noon-2:30 & 5-9:30 pm. Closed: 1/1, 11/27, 12/25. **Address:** 6715 Lowell Ave 22101 **Location:** Jct SR 123, 0.6 mi e on SR 309, just s. **Parking:** on-site. **Cards:** AX, DC, DS, MC, VI.

(See map and index starting on p. 412)

TASTE OF SAIGON   Phone: 703/790-0700   (22)

Vietnamese
$6-$15

The kitchen has established a consistent reputation for its Vietnamese cooking. The wide-ranging menu lists seafood, chicken, noodle, rice and vegetarian dishes. The setting is contemporary and the staff efficient. Casual dress. **Bar:** Full bar. **Reservations:** accepted. **Hours:** 11 am-10 pm, Fri & Sat-11 pm, Sun-9:30 pm. Closed: 7/4, 11/27, 12/25. **Address:** 8201 Greensboro Dr 22102 **Location:** I-495, exit 46A, 0.5 mi s on SR 123, just nw on International Dr, then just sw. **Parking:** on-site. **Cards:** AX, DC, DS, MC, VI.

CALL

MIDDLEBURG pop. 632

——— **WHERE TO STAY** ———

MIDDLEBURG COUNTRY INN   Phone: 540/687-6082

Historic Bed
& Breakfast
$150-$300 All Year

Address: 209 E Washington St 20118 **Location:** Just e on US 50. **Facility:** Canopy beds and fireplaces are featured in every room of this former Episcopal rectory, built sometime between 1820 and 1850. Smoke free premises. 8 one-bedroom standard units, some with whirlpools. 3 stories (no elevator), interior corridors. **Parking:** on-site. **Terms:** 10 day cancellation notice-fee imposed. **Amenities:** video library, high-speed Internet, voice mail, irons, hair dryers. **Guest Services:** wireless Internet. **Business Services:** meeting rooms. **Cards:** AX, DS, MC, VI.

——— **WHERE TO DINE** ———

HIDDEN HORSE TAVERN   Phone: 540/687-3828

American
$8-$35

Seafood specialties are served in the pleasant, informal atmosphere of a 200-year-old building. Corn and crab chowder and a tasty crab cake sandwich make a good lunch. Casual to dressy-casual attire is the norm in the dining room, which displays horse-lovers of bygone eras on the walls. Patio seating is available. Casual dress. **Bar:** Full bar. **Reservations:** suggested, weekends. **Hours:** 11 am-2:30 & 5:30-9 pm, Sun 11 am-2:30 & 5-8 pm, Mon-2:30 pm. Closed: 11/27, 12/25. **Address:** 7 W Washington St 20118 **Location:** On US 50; center. **Parking:** on-site. **Cards:** MC, VI. Historic

RED FOX INN   Phone: 540/687-6301

American
$9-$36

In the center of hunt country, the historic building now houses an attractive bistro that affords good views of the mountains and downtown. Deep wood-grain textures add to the sophisticated feel of the dining room. Uniformed servers are pleasant and offer many suggestions. Peanut soup is among the well-prepared and presented food. Casual dress. **Bar:** Full bar. **Reservations:** suggested. **Hours:** 11 am-3 & 5-9 pm, Sat-9:30 pm, Sun 11 am-8 pm; Sunday brunch. **Address:** 2 E Washington St 20117 **Location:** On US 50; center. **Parking:** on-site. **Cards:** AX, DC, DS, MC, VI. Historic

MONTCLAIR

——— **WHERE TO DINE** ———

GIORGIO'S   Phone: 703/580-8500

Italian
$6-$22

In a small strip mall not far off the interstate, the family restaurant serves well-prepared Italian, Greek and American selections. On the menu are submarine and other sandwiches, pizza, pasta and full dinners, including selections such as veal piccata and grilled New Zealand rack of lamb. Casual dress. **Bar:** Beer & wine. **Reservations:** accepted. **Hours:** 11 am-9:30 pm, Fri & Sat-10 pm. Closed: 1/1, 12/25; also Sun. **Address:** 4394 Kevin Walker Dr 22026 **Location:** I-95, exit 152B, 2 mi n on SR 234; in Montclair Shopping Plaza. **Parking:** on-site. **Cards:** DS, MC, VI.

CALL

MOUNT VERNON pop. 28,582

——— **WHERE TO DINE** ———

THE MOUNT VERNON INN   Phone: 703/780-0011

American
$6-$25

Roaring fireplaces, attractive murals and servers dressed in Colonial-era attire set a quaint mood in this charming restaurant. Regional and game specialties, such as venison with peppercorn sauce and peanut-chestnut soup, make up the varied menu. Casual dress. **Bar:** Full bar. **Reservations:** suggested, for dinner. **Hours:** 11 am-3:30 & 5-9 pm, Sun-3:30 pm; 11:30 am-2:30 pm, Sat & Sun-3:30 pm in winter. Closed: 12/25; also for dinner 7/4 & 12/24. **Address:** 3200 George Washington Memorial Pkwy 22121 **Location:** SR 235 and George Washington Memorial Pkwy; at George Washington's Mount Vernon Estate. **Parking:** on-site. **Cards:** AX, DS, MC, VI.

OAKTON

——— **WHERE TO DINE** ———

CHICKEN OUT ROTISSERIE   Phone: 703/319-8646

American
$5-$10

Chicken Out Rotisserie uses only fresh all natural ingredients. The chicken is chemical and hormone free. Choose from salads and sandwiches to wraps and picaccias, as well as rotisserie chicken and roast beef. Casual dress. **Reservations:** not accepted. **Hours:** 11 am-9 pm. Closed: 11/27, 12/25. **Address:** 2946-L Chain Bridge Rd 22124 **Location:** I-66, exit 60, 0.8 mi n on SR 123; in Hunter Mill Plaza. **Parking:** on-site. **Cards:** AX, DS, MC, VI.

CALL

RESTON pop. 56,407   (See map and index starting on p. 412)

──────── WHERE TO STAY ────────

HOMESTEAD STUDIO SUITES HOTEL-RESTON   *Book at AAA.com*   **Phone:** (703)707-9700   [12]

Motel
$164-$174 All Year

Address: 12190 Sunset Hills Rd 20190 **Location:** SR 267 (Dulles Toll Rd), exit 12 (Reston Pkwy), just n, then just w. **Facility:** 149 one-bedroom standard units with efficiencies. 2 stories (no elevator), exterior corridors. *Bath:* combo or shower only. **Parking:** on-site. **Amenities:** voice mail, irons, hair dryers. **Guest Services:** coin laundry, wireless Internet. **Cards:** AX, DC, DS, JC, MC, VI.

HYATT REGENCY RESTON   *Book great rates at AAA.com*   **Phone:** (703)709-1234   [11]

Large-scale Hotel
$99-$499 All Year

Address: 1800 Presidents St 20190 **Location:** SR 267 (Dulles Toll Rd), exit 12 (Reston Pkwy); center. Located in a shopping/restaurant complex. **Facility:** Smoke free premises. 518 units. 516 one-bedroom standard units. 2 one-bedroom suites. 15 stories, interior corridors. *Bath:* combo or shower only. **Terms:** cancellation fee imposed. **Amenities:** dual phone lines, voice mail, safes, irons, hair dryers. *Some:* DVD players. **Dining:** Market Street Bar & Grill, see separate listing. **Pool(s):** heated indoor. **Leisure Activities:** whirlpool, sun deck. *Fee:* saunas, massage. **Guest Services:** valet laundry, airport transportation-Washington Dulles International Airport, wireless Internet. **Business Services:** conference facilities, business center. **Cards:** AX, CB, DC, DS, JC, MC, VI. *(See color ad p 440)*

HYATT
HOTELS & RESORTS ®

AAA Benefit:
Ask for the AAA rate
and save 10%.

SHERATON RESTON HOTEL   *Book great rates at AAA.com*   **Phone:** (703)620-9000   [13]

Large-scale Hotel
$399 All Year

Address: 11810 Sunrise Valley Dr 20191 **Location:** SR 267 (Dulles Toll Rd), exit 12 (Reston Pkwy), just s. **Facility:** 301 units. 295 one-bedroom standard units. 6 one-bedroom suites. 6 stories, interior corridors. *Bath:* combo or shower only. **Parking:** on-site. **Terms:** cancellation fee imposed. **Amenities:** dual phone lines, voice mail, irons, hair dryers. *Fee:* video games, high-speed Internet. **Pool(s):** outdoor. **Leisure Activities:** exercise room. **Guest Services:** valet laundry, airport transportation-Washington Dulles International Airport, area transportation-within 2 mi, wireless Internet. **Business Services:** conference facilities, business center. **Cards:** AX, CB, DC, DS, MC, VI.

Ⓢ Sheraton
HOTELS & RESORTS

AAA Benefit:
Members get up to
15% off, plus
Starwood Preferred
Guest® bonuses.

──────── WHERE TO DINE ────────

CLYDE'S OF RESTON   **Phone:** 703/787-6601   [8]

American
$8-$23

A varied menu of sandwiches, salads and full meals is served in the comfortable dining room, which sustains a clubby atmosphere. Parmesan-crusted trout, crab cakes and cannelloni are house specialties at the busy eatery, which also prepares some lighter fare. Sidewalk seating can be requested seasonally. Casual dress. **Bar:** Full bar. **Reservations:** suggested. **Hours:** 11 am-10 pm, Fri & Sat-midnight, Sun 10 am-10 pm. Closed: 12/25. **Address:** 11905 Market St 20190 **Location:** SR 267 (Dulles Toll Rd), exit 12 (Reston Pkwy), 0.3 mi n; in Reston Town Center. **Parking:** on-site. **Cards:** AX, DC, DS, MC, VI.

MARKET STREET BAR & GRILL   **Phone:** 703/925-8250   [7]

American
$8-$36

The upscale open-kitchen establishment is characterized by distinctive artwork and high-quality furnishings. The spacious dining room allows for easy conversation in a romantic setting. Such offerings as house-cured and smoked salmon and other globally influenced dishes centered on fresh ingredients make up the nicely eclectic, seasonally changing menu. Creative presentations further enhance the food. Live jazz adds to the mood Thursday through Saturday night. Dressy casual. **Bar:** Full bar. **Reservations:** suggested. **Hours:** 6:30 am-2:30 & 5:30-10 pm, Fri & Sat-10:30 pm, Sun-9:30 pm. **Address:** 1800 Presidents St 20190 **Location:** SR 267 (Dulles Toll Rd), exit 12 (Reston Pkwy); center; in Hyatt Regency Reston. **Parking:** valet. **Cards:** AX, CB, DC, DS, JC, MC, VI.

PAOLO'S RISTORANTE   **Phone:** 703/318-8920   [6]

Italian
$8-$24

This busy restaurant presents a menu of pasta, seafood, steak, veal chops and pizza. The brick pizza oven and open kitchen add an informal feel to the setting. The place is fun and energetic and the service staff pleasant and prompt. Casual dress. **Bar:** Full bar. **Reservations:** accepted. **Hours:** 11 am-10 pm, Fri & Sat-midnight. Closed: 11/27, 12/25. **Address:** 11898 Market St 20190 **Location:** SR 267 (Dulles Toll Rd), exit 12 (Reston Pkwy), 0.3 mi n; in Reston Town Center. **Parking:** on-site. **Cards:** AX, CB, DC, DS, MC, VI.

SILVER DINER   **Phone:** 703/742-0804

American
$7-$13

The eatery with its chrome and glass plate exterior and the glow of neon, provides the traditional diner setting. Booths with juke boxes, counter service and friendly wait staff add to the diner experience. The menu is extensive with salads, sandwiches and full meals. The desserts are made fresh and the fountain treats, shakes, floats and malts make for a great ending. Breakfast is available all day. Casual dress. **Bar:** Beer & wine. **Reservations:** not accepted. **Hours:** 7 am-midnight, Fri & Sat-3 am. Closed: 12/25. **Address:** 11951 Killingswort Ave 20194 **Location:** Off Baron Cameron Ave (CR 606), just e of jct CR 7100 (Fairfax County Pkwy). **Parking:** on-site. **Cards:** AX, DC, DS, MC, VI.

ROUND HILL pop. 500

-------- WHERE TO STAY --------

WEONA VILLA MOTEL

Phone: 540/338-7000

(AAA) [SAVE]

Motel
$55-$75 3/1-12/31

Address: 36147 E Loudoun St 20142 **Location:** Just e on SR 7 business route. **Facility:** 8 one-bedroom standard units. 1 story, exterior corridors. *Bath:* combo or shower only. **Parking:** on-site. **Terms:** open 3/1-12/31. **Cards:** AX, MC, VI. **Free Special Amenities: local telephone calls.**

[icons]

SPRINGFIELD pop. 14,100   (See map and index starting on p. 412)

-------- WHERE TO STAY --------

BEST WESTERN SPRINGFIELD   *Book great rates at AAA.com*

Phone: (703)922-6100   **125**

(AAA) [SAVE]

Small-scale Hotel
$130-$170 All Year

Address: 6721 Commerce St 22150 **Location:** I-95, exit 169A, just e on SR 644 E, then n; jct I-395 and 495, 0.8 mi s. **Facility:** Smoke free premises. 177 one-bedroom standard units. 6 stories, interior corridors. *Bath:* combo or shower only. **Parking:** on-site. **Terms:** 7 day cancellation notice-fee imposed. **Amenities:** voice mail, safes, irons, hair dryers. **Pool(s):** outdoor. **Leisure Activities:** exercise room. **Guest Services:** valet laundry, area transportation-within 3 mi & Springfield Metro, wireless Internet. **Business Services:** meeting rooms, business center. **Cards:** AX, CB, DC, DS, JC, MC, VI. **Free Special Amenities: expanded continental breakfast and high-speed Internet.** *(See color ad p 435)*

AAA Benefit:
Members save 10% everyday, plus an exclusive frequent stay program.

[icons]

COMFORT INN WASHINGTON DC/SPRINGFIELD   *Book at AAA.com*

Phone: (703)922-9000   **128**

Small-scale Hotel
$99-$149 All Year

Address: 6560 Loisdale Ct 22150 **Location:** I-95, exit 169A, just e on SR 644 E; jct I-395 and 495, 0.8 mi s. Located adjacent to Springfield Mall. **Facility:** 112 one-bedroom standard units. 5 stories, interior corridors. *Bath:* combo or shower only. **Parking:** on-site. **Amenities:** high-speed Internet, dual phone lines, voice mail, safes (fee), irons, hair dryers. **Guest Services:** valet and coin laundry, area transportation, wireless Internet. **Business Services:** meeting rooms, PC. **Cards:** AX, DC, DS, MC, VI.

[icons]

COURTYARD BY MARRIOTT-SPRINGFIELD   *Book great rates at AAA.com*

Phone: 703/924-7200   **123**

Small-scale Hotel
$221-$251 All Year

Address: 6710 Commerce St 22150 **Location:** I-95, exit 169A, just e on SR 644, then n; jct I-395 and 495, 0.8 mi s. Located in business and shopping area. **Facility:** Smoke free premises. 191 units. 184 one-bedroom standard units. 7 one-bedroom suites. 4 stories, interior corridors. *Bath:* combo or shower only. **Parking:** on-site. **Amenities:** high-speed Internet, dual phone lines, voice mail, irons, hair dryers. **Pool(s):** heated indoor. **Leisure Activities:** whirlpool, exercise room. **Guest Services:** valet and coin laundry. **Business Services:** meeting rooms, PC. **Cards:** AX, DC, DS, JC, MC, VI.

AAA Benefit:
Members save 5% off of the best available rate.

[icons]

EXTENDED STAYAMERICA-WASHINGTON, DC-SPRINGFIELD   *Book at AAA.com*

Phone: (703)822-0992   **130**

Small-scale Hotel
$164-$174 All Year

Address: 6800 Metropolitan Center Dr 22150 **Location:** I-95, exit 169A, just e on SR 644, 0.6 mi s on Loisdale Rd, then just e. **Facility:** 126 one-bedroom standard units with efficiencies. 5 stories, interior corridors. *Bath:* combo or shower only. **Parking:** on-site. **Terms:** office hours 7 am-11 pm. **Amenities:** voice mail, irons, hair dryers. **Pool(s):** outdoor. **Leisure Activities:** limited exercise equipment. **Guest Services:** coin laundry, wireless Internet. **Cards:** AX, DC, DS, JC, MC, VI.

[icons]

HAMPTON INN WASHINGTON DC/SPRINGFIELD   *Book great rates at AAA.com*

Phone: 703/924-9444   **127**

Small-scale Hotel
Rates not provided

Address: 6550 Loisdale Ct 22150 **Location:** I-95, exit 169A, just e on SR 644 E; jct I-395 and 495, 0.8 mi s. Located adjacent to Springfield Mall. **Facility:** 153 one-bedroom standard units. 7 stories, interior corridors. *Bath:* combo or shower only. **Parking:** on-site. **Amenities:** high-speed Internet, dual phone lines, voice mail, irons, hair dryers. **Pool(s):** outdoor. **Guest Services:** valet laundry, area transportation. **Business Services:** business center.

[icons]

(See map and index starting on p. 412)

HILTON SPRINGFIELD
Book great rates at AAA.com   **Phone: 703/971-8900**   129

Large-scale Hotel
Rates not provided

Address: 6550 Loisdale Rd 22150 **Location:** I-95, exit 169A, just e on SR 644 E; jct I-395 and 495, 0.7 mi s. Located adjacent to Springfield Mall. **Facility:** 244 one-bedroom standard units. 12 stories, interior corridors. *Bath:* combo or shower only. **Parking:** on-site. **Amenities:** video games (fee), dual phone lines, voice mail, irons, hair dryers. **Pool(s):** heated indoor. **Leisure Activities:** exercise room. **Guest Services:** valet and coin laundry, area transportation-Springfield Metro, wireless Internet. **Business Services:** conference facilities, business center. **Free Special Amenities:** newspaper and high-speed Internet. *(See color ad below)*

HOLIDAY INN EXPRESS SPRINGFIELD
Book great rates at AAA.com   **Phone: (703)644-5555**   124

Small-scale Hotel
$79-$209 All Year

Address: 6401 Brandon Ave 22150 **Location:** I-95, exit 169B, just nw of SR 644; jct I-395 and 495, 0.8 mi s. Located in a business and shopping area. **Facility:** 194 one-bedroom standard units. 10 stories, interior corridors. **Parking:** on-site. **Amenities:** dual phone lines, voice mail, irons, hair dryers. *Some:* CD players, high-speed Internet. **Pool(s):** outdoor. **Guest Services:** valet laundry, area transportation, wireless Internet. **Business Services:** meeting rooms, PC. **Cards:** AX, DS, MC, VI.

RED ROOF INN SPRINGFIELD
Book at AAA.com   **Phone: 703/644-5311**   126

Small-scale Hotel
Rates not provided

Address: 6868 Springfield Blvd 22150 **Location:** I-95, exit 169B, just sw of SR 644; jct I-395 and 495, 0.8 mi s. **Facility:** 190 one-bedroom standard units. **Bath:** combo or shower only. **Parking:** on-site. **Amenities:** video games (fee), voice mail. *Some:* irons, hair dryers. **Guest Services:** valet and coin laundry, wireless Internet. **Business Services:** meeting rooms.

TOWNEPLACE SUITES BY MARRIOTT SPRINGFIELD
Book great rates at AAA.com   **Phone: 703/569-8060**   122

Small-scale Hotel
$210-$241 All Year

Address: 6245 Brandon Ave 22150 **Location:** I-95, exit 169B, just nw of SR 644; jct I-395 and 495, 0.8 mi s. Located in a commercial and shopping area. **Facility:** Smoke free premises. 148 units. 104 one-bedroom standard units with kitchens. 14 one- and 30 two-bedroom suites with kitchens. 4 stories, interior corridors. *Bath:* combo or shower only. **Parking:** on-site. **Amenities:** high-speed Internet, voice mail, irons, hair dryers. *Some:* dual phone lines. **Pool(s):** heated outdoor. **Leisure Activities:** exercise room. **Guest Services:** valet and coin laundry, wireless Internet. **Business Services:** meeting rooms, PC. **Cards:** AX, DC, DS, MC, VI.

AAA Benefit:
Members save 5% off of the best available rate.

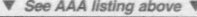

(See map and index starting on p. 412)

——— WHERE TO DINE ———

AUSTIN GRILL

Tex-Mex
$7-$17

Phone: 703/644-3111

The shopping center restaurant prepares its many Tex-Mex selections from scratch. Guests sit down to delicious enchiladas, burritos and fajitas, as well as some great slow-smoked barbecue pork ribs. Texas rock music enhances the casually lively atmosphere. Casual dress. **Bar:** Full bar. **Reservations:** not accepted. **Hours:** 11:30 am-10:30 pm, Fri-11:30 pm, Sat 11 am-11:30 pm, Sun 10 am-9:30 pm. Closed: 11/27, 12/25. **Address:** 8430-A Old Keene Mill Rd 22152 **Location:** I-95, exit 169B, 3 mi w on SR 644; at jct Rolling Rd; in Old Keene Mill Center. **Parking:** on-site. **Cards:** AX, DS, MC, VI.

CALL &M

MANILA CAFE
Philippine
$6-$13

Phone: 703/644-5825   (144)

Located in a busy shopping area, this modest little restaurant offers authentic Philippine cooking. An all-you-can-eat buffet is available daily. Casual dress. **Bar:** Beer & wine. **Reservations:** accepted. **Hours:** 11 am-9 pm, Fri & Sat-10 pm. Closed: 1/1, 12/25; also for dinner 11/20. **Address:** 7020 Commerce St 22150 **Location:** I-95, exit 169B southbound, just w; exit 169A northbound, just w on SR 644; jct of Amherst and Commerce sts; in Commerce Plaza. **Parking:** on-site. **Cards:** MC, VI.

MIKE'S AMERICAN GRILL
American
$9-$28

Phone: 703/644-7100   (143)

The restaurant has casual yet stylish atmosphere, with brick walls, decorative lighting and numerous private booths. The staff is friendly, energetic and efficient. The menu features certified Angus beef, fresh seafood, pasta and chicken. This restaurant is very popular with the locals. They do not take reservations, but you may call ahead to get on the list. Casual dress. **Bar:** Full bar. **Hours:** 11 am-11 pm, Fri & Sat-midnight, Sun-10:30 pm. Closed: 11/27, 12/25. **Address:** 6210 Backlick Rd 22150 **Location:** I-95, exit 169B southbound; exit 169A northbound, just w on SR 644, then just n on SR 617. **Parking:** on-site. **Cards:** AX, CB, DC, DS, MC, VI.

SILVER DINER
American
$7-$13

Phone: 703/924-1701

The eatery with its chrome and glass plate exterior and the glow of neon, provides the traditional diner setting. Booths with juke boxes, counter service and friendly wait staff add to the diner experience. The menu is extensive with salads, sandwiches and full meals. The desserts are made fresh and the fountain treats, shakes, floats and malts make for a great ending. Breakfast is available all day. Casual dress. **Bar:** Beer & wine. **Reservations:** not accepted. **Hours:** 7 am-midnight, Fri & Sat-3 am. Closed: 12/25. **Address:** 6592 Springfield Mall 22150 **Location:** I-95, exit 169A, 0.5 mi e on SR 644; adjacent to Springfield Mall. **Parking:** on-site. **Cards:** AX, DC, DS, MC, VI.

CALL &M

STERLING   (See map and index starting on p. 412)

———— WHERE TO STAY ————

BEST WESTERN WASHINGTON-DULLES AIRPORT

Phone: (703)471-8300   **5**

Small-scale Hotel
$79-$189 All Year

Address: 45440 Holiday Dr 20166 **Location:** 1.7 mi n on SR 28 from jct SR 267 (Dulles Toll Rd), just e on CR 846, then just s on Shaw Rd. **Facility:** 122 one-bedroom standard units. 2 stories (no elevator), exterior corridors. *Bath:* combo or shower only. **Parking:** on-site. **Amenities:** high-speed Internet, voice mail, irons, hair dryers. **Leisure Activities:** pool privileges, exercise room. **Guest Services:** valet and coin laundry, airport transportation-Washington Dulles International Airport, wireless Internet. **Business Services:** meeting rooms, business center. **Cards:** AX, DC, DS, MC, VI.

AAA Benefit: Members save 10% everyday, plus an exclusive frequent stay program.

Free Special Amenities: expanded continental breakfast and high-speed Internet.
(See color ad below)

CANDLEWOOD SUITES WASHINGTON DULLES/STERLING   *Book at AAA.com*

Phone: (703)674-2288

Small-scale Hotel
$65-$289 All Year

Address: 45520 E Severn Way 20166 **Location:** 1.6 mi s on SR 28 from jct SR 7, 0.3 mi e. **Facility:** 121 units. 97 one-bedroom standard units with efficiencies. 24 one-bedroom suites with efficiencies. 4 stories, interior corridors. *Bath:* combo or shower only. **Parking:** on-site. **Terms:** office hours 7 am-11 pm, cancellation fee imposed. **Amenities:** video library, DVD players, CD players, high-speed Internet, dual phone lines, voice mail, irons, hair dryers. **Leisure Activities:** exercise room. **Guest Services:** complimentary and valet laundry, area transportation. **Business Services:** meeting rooms. **Cards:** AX, CB, DC, DS, MC, VI.

COUNTRY INN & SUITES BY CARLSON WASHINGTON-DULLES INTERNATIONAL AIRPORT   *Book great rates at AAA.com*

Phone: (703)435-2700   **7**

Small-scale Hotel
$89-$249 All Year

Address: 45620 Falke Plaza 20166 **Location:** 1 mi n on SR 28 from jct SR 267 (Dulles Toll Rd), just e on SR 606. **Facility:** 59 units. 47 one-bedroom standard units, some with whirlpools. 12 one-bedroom suites. 3 stories, interior corridors. *Bath:* combo or shower only. **Parking:** on-site. **Amenities:** high-speed Internet, dual phone lines, voice mail, irons, hair dryers. **Leisure Activities:** exercise room. **Guest Services:** valet and coin laundry, airport transportation-Washington Dulles International Airport, wireless Internet. **Business Services:** business center. **Cards:** AX, DC, DS, JC, MC, VI. **Free Special Amenities: expanded continental breakfast and high-speed Internet.**

▼ *See AAA listing above* ▼

(See map and index starting on p. 412)

COURTYARD BY MARRIOTT DULLES TOWN CENTER *Book great rates at AAA.com*

Phone: 571/434-6400

Small-scale Hotel
$230-$285 All Year

Address: 45500 Majestic Dr 20166 **Location:** 0.4 mi e on SR 7 from jct SR 28, just s on CR 1582 (Algonkian Pkwy). Adjacent to Dulles Town Center shopping mall. **Facility:** Smoke free premises. 157 units. 149 one-bedroom standard units, some with whirlpools. 8 one-bedroom suites, some with whirlpools. 4 stories, interior corridors. *Bath:* combo or shower only. **Parking:** on-site. **Amenities:** CD players, high-speed Internet, dual phone lines, voice mail, safes, irons, hair dryers. **Pool(s):** heated indoor. **Leisure Activities:** whirlpool, exercise room. **Guest Services:** valet and coin laundry, area transportation, wireless Internet. **Business Services:** meeting rooms, PC. **Cards:** AX, DC, DS, JC, MC, VI.

AAA Benefit:
Members save 5% off of the best available rate.

EXTENDED STAYAMERICA-STERLING   *Book at AAA.com*   Phone: (703)444-7240

Small-scale Hotel
$154-$164 All Year

Address: 46001 Waterview Plaza 20166 **Location:** 1.3 mi e on SR 7 from jct SR 28. **Facility:** 101 one-bedroom standard units with efficiencies. Interior corridors. *Bath:* combo or shower only. **Parking:** on-site. **Terms:** office hours 7 am-11 pm. **Amenities:** voice mail, irons, hair dryers. **Guest Services:** coin laundry, wireless Internet. **Cards:** AX, DC, DS, JC, MC, VI.

FAIRFIELD INN BY MARRIOTT-DULLES AIRPORT   *Book great rates at AAA.com*   Phone: 703/435-5300

Small-scale Hotel
$208-$230 All Year

Address: 23000 Indian Creek Dr 20166 **Location:** 1 mi n on SR 28 from jct SR 267 (Dulles Toll Rd), just w on SR 606, then just n on Pacific Blvd. **Facility:** Smoke free premises. 106 one-bedroom standard units, some with whirlpools. 3 stories, interior corridors. *Bath:* combo or shower only. **Parking:** on-site. **Amenities:** voice mail, irons, hair dryers. **Pool(s):** heated indoor. **Leisure Activities:** sun deck, exercise room. **Guest Services:** valet laundry, airport transportation-Washington Dulles International Airport, wireless Internet. **Business Services:** PC. **Cards:** AX, DC, DS, MC, VI. **Free Special Amenities:** expanded continental breakfast and local telephone calls.

AAA Benefit:
Members save 5% off of the best available rate.

HAMPTON INN & SUITES DULLES AIRPORT   Phone: 703/537-7800

[fyi]

Small-scale Hotel
$109-$259 All Year

Too new to rate, opening scheduled for October 2007. **Address:** 22700 Holiday Park Dr 20166 **Location:** Jct SR 28 and Sterling Blvd. **Amenities:** 170 units, coffeemakers, microwaves, refrigerators, pool. **Cards:** AX, CB, DC, DS, JC, MC, VI. *(See color ad p 558)*

(See map and index starting on p. 412)

HAMPTON INN-DULLES/CASCADES   *Book great rates at AAA.com*   Phone: (703)450-9595

Small-scale Hotel
$219-$249 All Year

Address: 46331 McClellan Way 20165 **Location:** 1.7 mi e on SR 7, from jct SR 28, 0.5 mi n on CR 1794 (Cascades Pkwy) to Palisade Pkwy, just, e, then 0.4 mi s on Whitfield Pl. Adjacent to shopping area. **Facility:** 152 one-bedroom standard units, some with whirlpools. 6 stories, interior corridors. *Bath:* combo or shower only. **Parking:** on-site. **Terms:** cancellation fee imposed. **Amenities:** high-speed Internet, dual phone lines, voice mail, irons, hair dryers. **Pool(s):** heated indoor. **Leisure Activities:** whirlpool, limited exercise equipment, sports court. **Guest Services:** valet and coin laundry, airport transportation-Washington Dulles International Airport, area transportation-within 4 mi, wireless Internet. **Business Services:** meeting rooms, business center. **Cards:** AX, DS, MC, VI. **Free Special Amenities:** expanded continental breakfast and high-speed Internet. *(See color ad below)*

   CALL   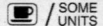 / SOME UNITS

(See map and index starting on p. 412)

HOLIDAY INN WASHINGTON DULLES INTERNATIONAL AIRPORT   *Book great rates at AAA.com*

Large-scale Hotel
$99-$279 All Year

Phone: (703)471-7411

Address: 1000 Sully Rd 20166 **Location:** 1.7 mi n on SR 28 from jct SR 267 (Dulles Toll Rd), just e on CR 846, then just s on Shaw Rd. **Facility:** 297 one-bedroom standard units, some with whirlpools. 2 stories, interior/exterior corridors. *Bath:* combo or shower only. **Parking:** on-site. **Amenities:** high-speed Internet, voice mail, irons, hair dryers. **Pool(s):** heated indoor. **Leisure Activities:** whirlpool, indoor recreation area. *Fee:* game room. **Guest Services:** valet and coin laundry, airport transportation-Washington Dulles International Airport, area transportation-within 5 mi, wireless Internet. **Business Services:** conference facilities, business center. **Cards:** AX, CB, DC, DS, JC, MC, VI. **Free Special Amenities: newspaper and early check-in/late check-out.** *(See color ad p 538)*

HOTEL SIERRA WASHINGTON DULLES

[fyi]
Small-scale Hotel
$109-$269 All Year

Phone: 703/435-9002

Too new to rate. **Address:** 45520 Dulles Plaza 20166 **Location:** 2 mi n of Washington Dulles International Airport, off SR 28. **Amenities:** 162 units, coffeemakers, microwaves, refrigerators, pool. **Cards:** AX, CB, DC, DS, JC, MC, VI.

HYATT PLACE STERLING/DULLES AIRPORT-NORTH   *Book great rates at AAA.com*

Small-scale Hotel
$99-$299 All Year

Phone: (703)444-3909

HYATT
PLACE

AAA Benefit:
Ask for the AAA rate
and save 10%.

Address: 21481 Ridgetop Cir 20166 **Location:** 1.3 mi e on SR 7 from jct SR 28. Located in shopping and business area. **Facility:** 134 one-bedroom standard units. 6 stories, interior corridors. *Bath:* combo or shower only. **Parking:** on-site. **Terms:** cancellation fee imposed. **Amenities:** video games (fee), dual phone lines, voice mail, irons, hair dryers. *Some:* high-speed Internet. **Pool(s):** outdoor. **Leisure Activities:** exercise room. **Guest Services:** valet laundry, airport transportation-Washington-Dulles International Airport, area transportation-within 5 mi, wireless Internet. **Business Services:** meeting rooms, business center. **Cards:** AX, CB, DC, DS, JC, MC, VI. **Free Special Amenities: continental breakfast and high-speed Internet.**

QUALITY INN & SUITES DULLES INTERNATIONAL AIRPORT   *Book at AAA.com*

Small-scale Hotel
$89-$170 3/1-11/20
$89-$150 11/21-2/28

Phone: (703)471-5005

Address: 45515 Dulles Plaza 20166 **Location:** 1 mi n on SR 28 from jct SR 267 (Dulles Toll Rd); just e on SR 606. **Facility:** 104 one-bedroom standard units. 3 stories, interior corridors. *Bath:* combo or shower only. **Parking:** on-site. **Amenities:** high-speed Internet, voice mail, irons, hair dryers. **Leisure Activities:** limited exercise room. **Guest Services:** coin laundry, wireless Internet. **Business Services:** PC. **Cards:** AX, CB, DC, DS, MC, VI.

RESIDENCE INN BY MARRIOTT DULLES AIRPORT @ DULLES 28 CENTER   *Book great rates at AAA.com*

Small-scale Hotel
$274-$296 All Year

Phone: 703/421-2000

Residence Inn Marriott

AAA Benefit:
Members save 5%
off of the best
available rate.

Address: 45250 Monterey Pl 20166 **Location:** SR 28, exit CR 625 (Waxpool Rd), just w, just n on Pacific Blvd, then just e on Commercial Dr. **Facility:** Smoke free premises. 151 units. 83 one-bedroom standard units with efficiencies. 45 one- and 23 two-bedroom suites, some with efficiencies or kitchens. 4 stories, interior corridors. *Bath:* combo or shower only. **Parking:** on-site. **Amenities:** high-speed Internet, dual phone lines, voice mail, safes, irons, hair dryers. **Pool(s):** heated indoor. **Leisure Activities:** whirlpool, putting green, exercise room. **Guest Services:** valet and coin laundry, area transportation, wireless Internet. **Business Services:** meeting rooms, PC. **Cards:** AX, DC, DS, JC, MC, VI.

(See map and index starting on p. 412)

SPRINGHILL SUITES BY MARRIOTT WASHINGTON DULLES AIRPORT   *Book great rates at AAA.com*

Phone: (703)444-3944   **4**

AAA SAVE
▼▼▼▼▼

Small-scale Hotel
$99-$229 All Year

Address: 22595 Shaw Rd 20166 **Location:** 1.7 mi n on SR 28 from jct SR 267 (Dulles Toll Rd), just e on CR 864. **Facility:** Smoke free premises. 158 one-bedroom standard units. 6 stories, interior corridors. *Bath:* combo or shower only. **Parking:** on-site. **Terms:** cancellation fee imposed. **Amenities:** high-speed Internet, voice mail, irons, hair dryers. **Pool(s):** heated indoor. **Leisure Activities:** whirlpool, sun deck, putting green, exercise room, sports court. **Guest Services:** valet and coin laundry, airport transportation-Washington Dulles International Airport, area transportation-within 3 mi, wireless Internet. **Business Services:** meeting rooms, business center. **Cards:** AX, CB, DC, DS, JC, MC, VI.
(See color ad below)

AAA Benefit:
Members save 5% off of the best available rate.

SUBURBAN EXTENDED STAY HOTEL WASHINGTON-DULLES/STERLING   *Book at AAA.com*

Phone: (703)674-2299

▼▼ ▼▼

Small-scale Hotel
$55-$179 All Year

Address: 45510 Severn Way 20166 **Location:** 1.6 mi s on SR 28 from jct SR 7, 0.3 mi e. **Facility:** 132 units. 128 one-bedroom standard units with efficiencies. 4 one-bedroom suites with efficiencies. 5 stories, interior corridors. *Bath:* combo or shower only. **Parking:** on-site. **Terms:** cancellation fee imposed. **Amenities:** CD players, high-speed Internet, voice mail. *Some:* irons. **Leisure Activities:** limited exercise equipment. **Guest Services:** valet and coin laundry, area transportation. **Business Services:** meeting rooms. **Cards:** AX, CB, DC, DS, MC, VI.

ASK   / SOME UNITS FEE

TOWNEPLACE SUITES BY MARRIOTT AT DULLES AIRPORT   *Book great rates at AAA.com*

Phone: 703/707-2017   **3**

AAA SAVE
▼▼▼▼▼

Small-scale Hotel
$202-$247 All Year

Address: 22744 Holiday Park Dr 20166 **Location:** 1.7 mi n on SR 28 from jct SR 267 (Dulles Toll Rd), just e on CR 846, then just s on Shaw Rd. **Facility:** Smoke free premises. 95 units. 69 one-bedroom standard units with efficiencies. 4 one- and 22 two-bedroom suites with kitchens. 3 stories, interior corridors. *Bath:* combo or shower only. **Parking:** on-site. **Amenities:** high-speed Internet, dual phone lines, voice mail, irons, hair dryers. **Pool(s):** heated outdoor. **Leisure Activities:** barbecue grill, limited exercise equipment. **Guest Services:** valet and coin laundry, airport transportation-Washington Dulles International Airport, wireless Internet. **Business Services:** PC. **Cards:** AX, DC, DS, JC, MC, VI. **Free Special Amenities:** local telephone calls and high-speed Internet.
(See color ad below)

AAA Benefit:
Members save 5% off of the best available rate.

/ SOME UNITS FEE

(See map and index starting on p. 412)

TOWNEPLACE SUITES BY MARRIOTT STERLING   *Book great rates at AAA.com*   Phone: 703/421-1090

Small-scale Hotel
$236-$256 3/1-12/15
$214-$234 12/16-2/28

Address: 21123 Whitfield Pl 20165 **Location:** 1.7 mi e on SR 7 from jct SR 28, 0.5 mi n on SR 1794 (Cascades Pkwy) to Palisades Pkwy, just e, then just s. **Facility:** Smoke free premises. 95 units. 69 one-bedroom standard units with kitchens. 4 one- and 22 two-bedroom suites with kitchens. 3 stories, interior corridors. *Bath:* combo or shower only. **Parking:** on-site. **Amenities:** voice mail, irons, hair dryers. **Pool(s):** heated outdoor. **Leisure Activities:** limited exercise equipment. **Guest Services:** valet and coin laundry, wireless Internet. **Business Services:** PC. **Cards:** AX, DC, DS, JC, MC, VI. **Free Special Amenities: continental breakfast and local telephone calls.**

AAA Benefit:
Members save 5% off of the best available rate.

——— WHERE TO DINE ———

4912 THAI CUISINE   Phone: 703/433-9720

Thai
$7-$13

Adjacent to a movie theater, the restaurant presents a menu that lists a nice variety of Thai dishes, with notations of items that are spicy. One pepper designates "American" spicy, while two peppers represents "Thai" spicy. Selections range from salads, noodles and fried rice dishes to vegetarian offerings, curry recipes and beef, chicken, pork and seafood dishes. The patio opens seasonally. Casual dress. **Bar:** Full bar. **Reservations:** suggested, weekends. **Hours:** 11:30 am-10 pm, Fri & Sat-11 pm. Closed: 11/27. **Address:** 45965 Regal Plaza 20165 **Location:** Off SR 7, 1 mi e of jct SR 28; in Regal Center Shopping Plaza. **Parking:** on-site. **Cards:** AX, DS, MC, VI.

GLORY DAYS GRILL, STERLING   Phone: 703/430-3456

American
$7-$18

Lending to the casual restaurant's sports-themed atmosphere are memorabilia decorating the dining area and 25 TVs with control centers at each table and booth. Food selections range from wings and ribs to seafood, beef and pasta dishes. Casual dress. **Bar:** Full bar. **Reservations:** not accepted. **Hours:** 4 pm-midnight, Fri & Sat from 11:30 am, Sun 11:30 am-11 pm. Closed: 11/27, 12/25. **Address:** 21800 Towncenter Plaza 20164 **Location:** Jct SR 7 and Dranesville Rd (SR 228); in Towncenter Plaza Shopping Center. **Parking:** on-site. **Cards:** AX, DS, MC, VI.

PACIFIC   Phone: 703/404-5500

Pacific Rim
$7-$26

Diners unwind in an exotic setting to enjoy the varied tastes of Pacific Rim cuisine. The patio area, reminiscent of a Japanese garden setting, opens when the weather is appropriate. The menu reflects each dish's origin and degree of spiciness. Casual dress. **Bar:** Full bar. **Reservations:** not accepted. **Hours:** 11:30 am-10 pm, Fri-11 pm, Sat noon-11 pm, Sun 11:30 am-10 pm. Closed: 7/4, 11/27. **Address:** 46240 Potomac Run Plaza 20164 **Location:** On SR 7, jct Cascades Pkwy; in Potomac Run Shopping Plaza. **Parking:** on-site. **Cards:** AX, CB, DC, MC, VI.

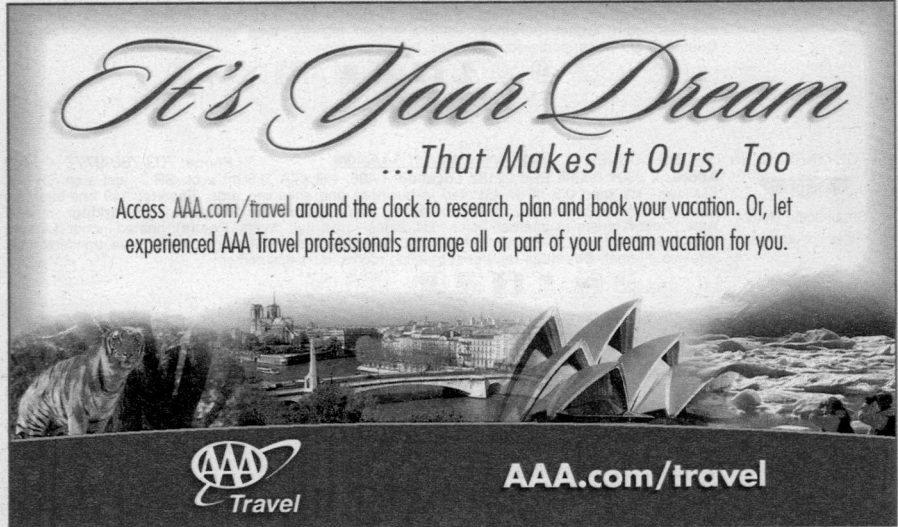

(See map and index starting on p. 412)

SWEETWATER TAVERN   Phone: 571/434-6500

American
$8-$24

Casual dress. **Bar:** Full bar. **Hours:** 11 am-10 pm, Tues-Thurs to 11 pm, Fri & Sat-midnight. Closed: 11/27, 12/25. **Address:** 45980 Waterview Plaza 20166 **Location:** 1.2 mi e on SR 7 from jct SR 28. **Parking:** on-site. **Cards:** AX, DC, DS, MC, VI.

CALL

VIENNA pop. 14,453   (See map and index starting on p. 412)

———— WHERE TO STAY ————

COMFORT INN TYSONS CORNER   *Book great rates at AAA.com*   Phone: (703)448-8020   **67**

Motel
$79-$199 All Year

Address: 1587 Spring Hill Rd 22182 **Location:** I-495, exit 47A, 1.8 mi w on SR 7, then just s; just e of jct SR 267 (Dulles Toll Rd). Located in a commercial/business area. **Facility:** 251 units. 248 one-bedroom standard units. 3 one-bedroom suites. 3 stories, exterior corridors. **Parking:** on-site. **Amenities:** high-speed Internet, voice mail, irons, hair dryers. *Fee:* video games, safes. **Pool(s):** outdoor. **Guest Services:** valet and coin laundry, airport transportation-Washington Dulles International Airport, area transportation-within 3 mi & Dunn Loring Metro, wireless Internet. **Business Services:** meeting rooms, business center. **Cards:** AX, CB, DC, DS, JC, MC, VI. **Free Special Amenities: continental breakfast and early check-in/late check-out.** *(See color ad p 431)*

COURTYARD BY MARRIOTT DUNN LORING
FAIRFAX   *Book great rates at AAA.com*   Phone: 703/573-9555   **73**

Small-scale Hotel
$241-$307 All Year

Address: 2722 Gallows Rd 22180 **Location:** I-495, exit 50A, just w to SR 650; 1 mi n on SR 650; 0.4 mi n of jct US 29. Located adjacent to Dunn Loring Metro Station. **Facility:** Smoke free premises. 206 units. 197 one-bedroom standard units. 9 one-bedroom suites. 10 stories, interior corridors. *Bath:* combo or shower only. **Parking:** on-site. **Amenities:** high-speed Internet, dual phone lines, voice mail, irons, hair dryers. *Some:* CD players. **Pool(s):** heated indoor. **Leisure Activities:** whirlpool, exercise room. **Guest Services:** valet and coin laundry, wireless Internet. **Business Services:** meeting rooms, PC. **Cards:** AX, DC, DS, MC, VI.

COURTYARD
Marriott

AAA Benefit:
Members save 5%
off of the best
available rate.

EMBASSY SUITES HOTEL TYSONS CORNER   *Book at AAA.com*   Phone: 703/883-0707   **68**

Large-scale Hotel
Rates not provided

Address: 8517 Leesburg Pike 22182 **Location:** I-495, exit 47A, 1.7 mi w on SR 7; 0.3 mi e of jct SR 267 (Dulles Toll Rd). Located in a commercial and corporate area. **Facility:** 234 units. 14 one-bedroom standard units. 220 one-bedroom suites. 8 stories, interior corridors. *Bath:* combo or shower only. **Parking:** on-site. **Amenities:** video games (fee), dual phone lines, voice mail, safes, irons, hair dryers. *Some:* high-speed Internet (fee). **Pool(s):** heated indoor. **Leisure Activities:** sauna, whirlpool, exercise room. **Guest Services:** valet and coin laundry, area transportation, wireless Internet. **Business Services:** conference facilities, business center.

HILTON GARDEN INN TYSONS CORNER   *Book great rates at AAA.com*   Phone: 703/760-9777   **69**

Small-scale Hotel
Rates not provided

Address: 8301 Boone Blvd 22182 **Location:** I-495, exit 47A, 0.5 mi w on SR 7, just s on SR 650 (Gallows Rd), then 0.3 mi w. Located in business and shopping area. **Facility:** 149 one-bedroom standard units. 9 stories, interior corridors. *Bath:* combo or shower only. **Parking:** on-site. **Amenities:** high-speed Internet, voice mail, safes, irons, hair dryers. **Pool(s):** heated indoor. **Leisure Activities:** whirlpool, exercise room. **Guest Services:** valet and coin laundry, area transportation, wireless Internet. **Business Services:** meeting rooms, business center.

HOMESTEAD STUDIO SUITES HOTEL-TYSONS
CORNER   *Book at AAA.com*   Phone: (703)356-6300   **72**

Small-scale Hotel
$174-$184 All Year

Address: 8201 Old Courthouse Rd 22182 **Location:** I-495, exit 47A, 0.6 mi w on SR 7, then just s on Gallows Rd. Located in a commercial business/shopping area. **Facility:** 106 one-bedroom standard units with efficiencies. 3 stories, interior corridors. *Bath:* combo or shower only. **Parking:** on-site. **Amenities:** voice mail, irons, hair dryers. **Guest Services:** valet and coin laundry, wireless Internet. **Business Services:** meeting rooms. **Cards:** AX, DC, DS, JC, MC, VI.

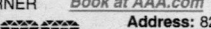

(See map and index starting on p. 412)

RESIDENCE INN BY MARRIOTT-TYSONS CORNER

 *Book great rates at AAA.com*   Phone: 703/893-0120   66

Small-scale Hotel
$287-$317 All Year

Address: 8616 Westwood Center Dr 22182 **Location:** I-495, exit 47A, 1.9 mi w on SR 7, then just s. Located in a commercial/business area. **Facility:** Smoke free premises. 96 units. 88 one-bedroom standard units with kitchens. 8 two-bedroom suites with kitchens. 2 stories (no elevator), exterior corridors. **Parking:** on-site. **Amenities:** voice mail, irons, hair dryers. **Pool(s):** outdoor. **Leisure Activities:** whirlpool, exercise room, sports court. **Guest Services:** valet and coin laundry, wireless Internet. **Cards:** AX, DC, DS, JC, MC, VI.

AAA Benefit:
Members save 5% off of the best available rate.

RESIDENCE INN BY MARRIOTT TYSONS CORNER
MALL   *Book great rates at AAA.com*

Phone: 703/917-0800   70

Small-scale Hotel
$297-$362 All Year

Address: 8400 Old Courthouse Rd 22182 **Location:** I-495, exit 46A, 1.1 mi s on SR 123; 0.3 mi s of jct SR 7 and 123. Located in a commercial business/shopping area. **Facility:** Smoke free premises. 121 units. 120 one-bedroom standard units with efficiencies. 1 one-bedroom suite with kitchen. 6 stories, interior corridors. *Bath:* combo or shower only. **Parking:** on-site. **Amenities:** video games (fee), CD players, dual phone lines, voice mail, irons, hair dryers. **Pool(s):** outdoor. **Leisure Activities:** limited exercise equipment. **Guest Services:** valet and coin laundry, area transportation, wireless Internet. **Business Services:** meeting rooms, PC. **Cards:** AX, DC, DS, JC, MC, VI.

AAA Benefit:
Members save 5% off of the best available rate.

(See map and index starting on p. 412)

SHERATON PREMIERE AT TYSONS CORNER *Book great rates at AAA.com* Phone: (703)448-1234 ⑥⑤

AAA ⑤ⓐⓥⓔ
▽▼▲▽▲▽
Large-scale Hotel
$349 All Year

Address: 8661 Leesburg Pike 22182 **Location:** SR 7, just e of jct SR 267 (Dulles Toll Rd). Located in a commerical area. **Facility:** 443 units. 441 one-bedroom standard units. 2 one-bedroom suites. 3-24 stories, interior corridors. *Bath:* combo or shower only. **Parking:** on-site. **Terms:** cancellation fee imposed. **Amenities:** video games (fee), dual phone lines, voice mail, irons, hair dryers. *Some:* high-speed Internet (fee). **Pool(s):** outdoor, heated indoor. **Leisure Activities:** saunas, whirlpool, racquetball courts, racquetball equipment, exercise room. *Fee:* massage. **Guest Services:** valet laundry, area transportation-Tysons malls, beauty salon, wireless Internet. **Business Services:** conference facilities, business center. **Cards:** AX, CB, DC, DS, JC, MC, VI.

⑤ Sheraton
HOTELS & RESORTS
AAA Benefit:
Members get up to 15% off, plus Starwood Preferred Guest® bonuses.

🍽 🍸 CALL ⑤ 🐬 ✕ 📹 💻 /SOME UNITS 🐾 ✕ 🔧

TYSONS CORNER MARRIOTT HOTEL *Book great rates at AAA.com* Phone: 703/734-3200 ⑦①

▽▼▲▽▲▽
Large-scale Hotel
$296-$318 All Year

Address: 8028 Leesburg Pike 22182 **Location:** I-495, exit 47B, just w on SR 7. Located adjacent to Tysons Corner Shopping Mall. **Facility:** Smoke free premises. 390 units. 388 one-bedroom standard units. 2 one-bedroom suites. 15 stories, interior corridors. *Bath:* combo or shower only. **Parking:** on-site. **Terms:** check-in 4 pm. **Amenities:** dual phone lines, voice mail, irons, hair dryers. *Fee:* video games, high-speed Internet. **Pool(s):** heated indoor. **Leisure Activities:** sauna, whirlpool, exercise room. **Guest Services:** complimentary and valet laundry, area transportation. **Business Services:** conference facilities, business center. **Cards:** AX, DC, DS, JC, MC, VI.

Marriott.
HOTELS & RESORTS
AAA Benefit:
Members save 5% off of the best available rate.

ⒶⓈⓀ ⑤ 🍽 🍸 CALL ⑤ 🏊 ✕ ✕ 📹 💻 / SOME UNITS 🔧

———— WHERE TO DINE ————

AMMA VEGETARIAN KITCHEN Phone: 703/938-5328

▲▽▲▽
Vegetarian
$4-$10

A modest little restaurant offering Indian vegetarian selections. It's self-service, it's simple but the food is good. Casual dress. **Reservations:** not accepted. **Hours:** 11:30 am-2:30 & 5:30-9:30 pm, Fri-Sun 11:30 am-3 & 5:30-10 pm. Closed: 12/25. **Address:** 344-A Maple Ave E 22180 **Location:** SR 123, 1.8 mi s of jct SR 7. **Parking:** on-site. **Cards:** AX, DS, MC, VI.

ANITA'S Phone: 703/255-1001

▲▽▲▽ ▲▽▲▽
Mexican
$5-$15

This small chain is locally popular for their signature "New Mexico" style dishes. The menu features a good variety of tacos, burritos and enchiladas. If you're in the mood for a Mexican breakfast, this is the place. Casual dress. **Bar:** Full bar. **Reservations:** accepted. **Hours:** 6 am-9:30 pm, Fri & Sat-10 pm, Sun-9 pm. Closed: 11/27, 12/25. **Address:** 521 E Maple Ave 22180 **Location:** SR 123, 1.5 mi s of jct SR 7. **Parking:** on-site. **Cards:** AX, MC, VI.

BOMBAY TANDOOR Phone: 703/734-2202 ⑦⑦

▲▽▲▽ ▲▽▲▽
Indian
$9-$19

Lamb chops masala, one of the chef's recommendations, can be enjoyed mild or spicy. The kitchen prepares a wide selection of Indian recipes, from vegetarian to lamb dishes. A buffet is set up daily at lunchtime. Casual dress. **Bar:** Full bar. **Reservations:** accepted. **Hours:** 11:30 am-2:30 & 5:30-10 pm, Fri-10:30 pm, Sat & Sun noon-3 & 5:30-10 pm. Closed: for lunch 1/1 & for dinner 7/4. **Address:** 8603 Westwood Center Dr 22182 **Location:** 0.3 mi s of jct SR 7 and 123; in Westwood 1 Complex. **Parking:** on-site. **Cards:** AX, CB, DC, DS, MC, VI.

CAFE RENAISSANCE Phone: 703/938-3311 ⑧⑥

ⒶⒶⒶ
▽▼▲▽▲▽
Continental
$12-$35

Tucked away to the side in this shopping plaza is a delightful little dining room serving both French and Italian food. The setting is casual yet has a formality to it with white table linen, shaded candles, flowers at each table and large oil paintings adorning the walls. The staff is professional and friendly. The kitchen is consistent and has pleased locals for over 10 years. Semi-formal attire. **Reservations:** accepted. **Hours:** 11:30 am-2:30 & 5-10 pm, Sat from 5 pm, Sun 5 pm-9 pm. Closed major holidays. **Address:** 163 Glyndon St 22180 **Location:** SR 123, 2 mi s of jct SR 7; in Glyndon Plaza. **Parking:** on-site. **Cards:** AX, DC, DS, MC, VI.

(See map and index starting on p. 412)

CHUTZPAH OF TYSONS-A REAL NEW YORK DELI
Phone: 703/556-3354   83

Deli/Subs
Sandwiches
$9-$15

Casual dress. **Bar:** Beer only. **Reservations:** not accepted. **Hours:** 7 am-4 pm, Sat & Sun 9 am-3 pm. Closed: 11/27, 12/25; also Yom Kippur. **Address:** 8100 Boone Blvd 22182 **Location:** I-495, exit 47A, 0.5 mi w on SR 7; opposite Tysons Corner Shopping Mall, on ground floor of an office building. **Parking:** on-site. **Cards:** AX, DS, MC, VI.

CALL

CLYDE'S OF TYSONS CORNER
Phone: 703/734-1901   78

American
$8-$23

This casual restaurant is a popular gathering spot for trendy professionals. Sandwiches, pizza, pasta, steak and seafood are among choices that make up the often-changing menu. Service is efficient and professional. Casual dress. **Bar:** Full bar. **Reservations:** suggested. **Hours:** 11 am-2 am. Closed: 7/4, 12/25. **Address:** 8332 Leesburg Pike 22182 **Location:** SR 7, just w of SR 123. **Parking:** on-site and valet. **Cards:** AX, CB, DC, DS, MC, VI.

HUNAN LION
Phone: 703/734-9828   79

Chinese
$5-$25

Shoppers ready to take a break from trolling the nearby malls often stop in for Hunan specialties that include General Tso's chicken, orange beef and Peking duck. Lunch service continues until 4 pm but is not offered on Sunday. Casual dress. **Bar:** Full bar. **Reservations:** suggested. **Hours:** 11:30 am-10:30 pm, Fri & Sat-11 pm. Closed: 11/27; also for lunch 12/25 & 1/1. **Address:** 2070 Chain Bridge Rd 22182 **Location:** I-495, exit 46A on SR 123, 0.3 mi s of jct SR 7. **Parking:** on-site. **Cards:** AX, CB, DC, DS, MC, VI.

KONAMI JAPANESE RESTAURANT
Phone: 703/821-3400   80

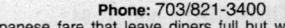
Japanese
$8-$25

The local favorite has an intimate interior and delicious Japanese fare that leave diners full but wanting more. Casual dress. **Bar:** Full bar. **Reservations:** accepted. **Hours:** 11:30 am-2:30 & 5-10:30 pm, Fri-11 pm, Sat noon-3 & 5-11 pm, Sun noon-3 & 5-10:30 pm. Closed: 1/1, 11/27, 12/25. **Address:** 8221 Leesburg Pike 22182 **Location:** I-495, exit 47A, 0.8 mi w on SR 7. **Parking:** on-site. **Cards:** AX, DC, DS, MC, VI.

CALL

LE CANARD
Phone: 703/281-0070   85

French
$10-$29

Tucked in the corner of a little shopping plaza, the quaint and romantic French restaurant presents a menu of duck, veal and fresh seafood. The staff is professional and helpful with the menu. Dressy casual. Entertainment. **Bar:** Full bar. **Reservations:** suggested. **Hours:** 11:30 am-2:30 & 5:30-10:30 pm, Fri-11 pm, Sat 5:30 pm-11 pm, Sun 5 pm-9 pm. **Address:** 132 Branch Rd SE 22180 **Location:** Off SR 123, 1.7 mi s of jct SR 7; in shopping plaza. **Parking:** on-site. **Cards:** AX, DC, DS, MC, VI.

MARCO POLO RESTAURANT & CATERERS
Phone: 703/281-3922   87

Italian
$9-$27

This is a family run operation that has been in business for more than 25 years. You will find plenty of continental and Italian selections on the menu. The pasta and sauce are made fresh on the premises. A lunch buffet is available Tuesday-Friday. Dressy casual. **Bar:** Full bar. **Reservations:** suggested, weekends. **Hours:** 11 am-10 pm, Fri & Sat-11 pm; Sunday brunch 10:30 am-2:30 pm. Closed: 1/1, 9/1, 12/25; also Mon & Tues. **Address:** 245 Maple Ave W 22180 **Location:** SR 123, 0.3 mi ne of jct SR 243. **Parking:** on-site. **Cards:** AX, CB, DC, MC, VI.

MORTON'S-THE STEAKHOUSE
Phone: 703/883-0800   82

Steak House
$13-$40

Patrons should make sure to reserve ahead for the popular, well-known steak house. Large portions, including huge cuts of fine beef and plentiful seafood, are the norm. Even the vegetables are oversized, with baked potatoes big enough for sharing. Dressy casual. **Bar:** Full bar. **Reservations:** suggested. **Hours:** 11:30 am-2:30 & 5:30-11 pm, Sat from 5:30 pm, Sun 5 pm-10 pm. Closed major holidays. **Address:** 8075 Leesburg Pike 22182 **Location:** I-495, exit 47A, 0.4 mi w on SR 7; opposite Tysons Corner Shopping Mall; in Fairfax Square. **Parking:** on-site. **Cards:** AX, DC, MC, VI.

NIZAM'S RESTAURANT
Phone: 703/938-8948   88

Turkish
$8-$22

Servers in vests and bow ties and a crisp dining room give the established restaurant a graceful air. The menu specializes in lamb with an extensive selection of kebabs, including the house specialty doner kebab, available only Tuesday, Friday, Saturday and Sunday. Fresh fish selections are also available. Casual dress. **Bar:** Full bar. **Reservations:** suggested, weekends. **Hours:** 11 am-3 & 5:30-10 pm, Fri-11 pm, Sat 5 pm-11 pm, Sun 4 pm-9 pm. Closed: 12/25; also Mon. **Address:** 523 Maple Ave W 22180 **Location:** SR 123, 0.3 mi s of jct SR 243. **Parking:** on-site. **Cards:** AX, DS, MC, VI.

(See map and index starting on p. 412)

PAYA THAI

Thai
$8-$17

Phone: 703/883-3881 ⑧⑴

The small restaurant boasts an award-winning wine selection to go with its beef, chicken, noodle, seafood and vegetarian selections. The kitchen respects guests' desired degree of spiciness. Casual dress. **Bar:** Full bar. **Reservations:** accepted. **Hours:** 11:30 am-3 & 5-10 pm, Fri-10:30 pm, Sat noon-10:30 pm, Sun noon-10 pm. Closed: 11/27; also 12/25 for lunch. **Address:** 8417 Old Courthouse Rd 22182 **Location:** I-495, exit 46A, 1.1 mi s on SR 123; 0.3 mi s of jct SR 123 and 7. **Parking:** on-site. **Cards:** AX, DS, MC, VI.

RISTORANTE BONAROTI

Northern Italian
$12-$29

Phone: 703/281-7550 ⑧④

Pleasing locals since 1982, the restaurant employs servers who display an excellent knowledge of the menu, which includes offerings such as fried calamari, tender veal and scampi stuffed with crab over risotto in a light, creamy sauce. Tastefully decorated in muted tones, the upscale dining room is a perfect setting for a intimate, relaxed dining experience. Dressy casual. **Bar:** Full bar. **Reservations:** suggested. **Hours:** 11:30 am-2:30 & 5:30-10:30 pm, Sat 5 pm-11 pm. Closed major holidays; also Sun, except major holidays. **Address:** 428 E Maple Ave 22180 **Location:** SR 123, 1.5 mi s of jct SR 7. **Parking:** on-site. **Cards:** AX, CB, DC, MC, VI.

SUNFLOWER VEGETARIAN RESTAURANT

Vegetarian
$6-$11

Phone: 703/319-3888 ⑧⑨

The vegetarian menu blends Japanese, Chinese and Continental dishes. The kitchen uses only fresh ingredients and organic flavor enhancers—never monosodium glutamate—to prepare each item. Casual dress. **Reservations:** not accepted. **Hours:** 11:30 am-10 pm, Sun from noon. Closed: 11/27, 12/24, 12/25. **Address:** 2531 Chain Bridge Rd 22181 **Location:** On SR 123, just s of jct SR 243. **Parking:** on-site. **Cards:** AX, CB, DC, DS, MC, VI.

TARA THAI

Thai
$6-$13

Phone: 703/255-2467

The stylish cafe's sea motif is one aspect of its contemporary atmosphere. Specialties include whole fresh rockfish and skewered chicken, just to mention two. Most notable is the nicely presented goong phu-ket and pad thai noodles. Portion sizes are ample. Casual dress. **Bar:** Full bar. **Reservations:** suggested, weekends. **Hours:** 11:30 am-3 & 5-10 pm, Fri-11 pm, Sat noon-3:30 & 5-11 pm, Sun noon-3:30 & 5-10 pm. Closed: 11/27; also for lunch 12/25 & 1/1. **Address:** 226 Maple Ave W 22180 **Location:** SR 123, 0.3 mi ne of jct SR 243. **Parking:** on-site. **Cards:** AX, DC, DS, MC, VI.

WOODBRIDGE pop. 31,941

—— **WHERE TO STAY** ——

BEST WESTERN POTOMAC MILLS   *Book great rates at AAA.com*

Small-scale Hotel
Rates not provided

Phone: 703/494-4433

Address: 14619 Potomac Mills Rd 22192 **Location:** I-95, exit 156, 0.5 mi w. Located in a commercial shopping area. **Facility:** 172 units. 152 one-bedroom standard units. 20 one-bedroom suites. 9 stories, interior corridors. *Bath:* combo or shower only. **Parking:** on-site. **Amenities:** voice mail, safes, irons, hair dryers. **Pool(s):** outdoor. **Leisure Activities:** exercise room. **Guest Services:** valet and coin laundry, wireless Internet. **Business Services:** meeting rooms, PC. **Free Special Amenities:** expanded continental breakfast and high-speed Internet.

(See color ad p 435)

COURTYARD BY MARRIOTT POTOMAC MILLS/WOODBRIDGE   *Book great rates at AAA.com*

Small-scale Hotel
$145-$175 3/1-7/31
$132-$153 8/1-2/28

Phone: 703/491-4525

Address: 14300 Crossing Pl 22192 **Location:** I-95, exit 158B, 0.5 mi sw on Prince William Pkwy. Located in shopping area. **Facility:** Smoke free premises. 118 units. 114 one-bedroom standard units. 4 one-bedroom suites. 4 stories, interior corridors. *Bath:* combo or shower only. **Parking:** on-site. **Amenities:** high-speed Internet, voice mail, irons, hair dryers. **Pool(s):** heated indoor. **Leisure Activities:** whirlpool, exercise room. **Guest Services:** valet and coin laundry, wireless Internet. **Business Services:** meeting rooms, PC. **Cards:** AX, DS, MC, VI.

FAIRFIELD INN BY MARRIOTT POTOMAC MILLS   *Book great rates at AAA.com*

Small-scale Hotel
$119-$159 3/1-11/15
$109-$139 11/16-2/28

Phone: (703)497-4000

Address: 2610 Prince William Pkwy 22192 **Location:** I-95, exit 158B (Prince William Pkwy), 0.8 mi w. Located in a commercial shopping area. **Facility:** Smoke free premises. 85 one-bedroom standard units, some with whirlpools. 3 stories, interior corridors. *Bath:* combo or shower only. **Parking:** on-site. **Terms:** cancellation fee imposed. **Amenities:** irons, hair dryers. **Pool(s):** heated indoor. **Leisure Activities:** limited exercise equipment. **Guest Services:** valet and coin laundry, wireless Internet. **Business Services:** meeting rooms, PC. **Cards:** AX, CB, DC, DS, JC, MC, VI.

HAMPTON INN-POTOMAC MILLS/WOODBRIDGE — *Book great rates at AAA.com*

Phone: (703)490-2300

Small-scale Hotel
$119-$179 3/1-11/15
$109-$159 11/16-2/28

Address: 1240 Annapolis Way 22191 **Location:** I-95, exit 161 southbound, 1.2 mi sw on US 1, then 0.3 mi n on SR 123; exit 160A northbound. **Facility:** 87 one-bedroom standard units. 4 stories, interior corridors. *Bath:* combo or shower only. **Parking:** on-site. **Terms:** cancellation fee imposed. **Amenities:** dual phone lines, voice mail, irons, hair dryers. **Pool(s):** heated indoor. **Leisure Activities:** whirlpool, limited exercise equipment. **Guest Services:** valet and coin laundry, wireless Internet. **Business Services:** PC. **Cards:** AX, CB, DC, DS, JC, MC, VI.

HOLIDAY INN EXPRESS HOTEL & SUITES-WOODBRIDGE — *Book at AAA.com*

Phone: (703)576-1600

Small-scale Hotel
$130-$190 All Year

Address: 14030 Telegraph Rd 22192 **Location:** I-95, exit 158B (Prince William Pkwy), 0.8 mi w. Located in a commercial shopping area. **Facility:** 84 units. 81 one-bedroom standard units, some with whirlpools. 3 one-bedroom suites. 4 stories, interior corridors. *Bath:* combo or shower only. **Parking:** on-site. **Amenities:** high-speed Internet, dual phone lines, voice mail, irons, hair dryers. **Pool(s):** heated indoor. **Guest Services:** valet and coin laundry. **Business Services:** PC. **Cards:** AX, DC, DS, MC, VI.

RESIDENCE INN BY MARRIOTT POTOMAC MILLS — *Book great rates at AAA.com*

Phone: 703/490-4020

Small-scale Hotel
$189-$219 All Year

Address: 14301 Crossing Pl 22192 **Location:** I-95, exit 158B (Prince William Pkwy), 0.5 mi sw. Located in a shopping area. **Facility:** Smoke free premises. 107 units. 43 one-bedroom standard units, some with efficiencies or kitchens. 40 one- and 24 two-bedroom suites, some with efficiencies or kitchens. 4 stories, interior corridors. *Bath:* combo or shower only. **Parking:** on-site. **Amenities:** high-speed Internet, dual phone lines, voice mail, irons, hair dryers. **Pool(s):** heated indoor. **Leisure Activities:** whirlpool, exercise room, basketball. **Guest Services:** valet and coin laundry, wireless Internet. **Business Services:** meeting rooms, PC. **Cards:** AX, DC, DS, JC, MC, VI.

AAA Benefit:
Members save 5% off of the best available rate.

SLEEP INN WOODBRIDGE — *Book great rates at AAA.com*

Phone: (703)580-9200

Small-scale Hotel
$109-$125 3/1-10/31
$99-$109 11/1-2/28

Address: 14080 Shoppers Best Way 22192 **Location:** I-95, exit 158B (Prince William Pkwy), 1.2 mi w. Located in a commercial shopping area. **Facility:** 61 one-bedroom standard units, some with whirlpools. 2 stories, interior corridors. *Bath:* combo or shower only. **Parking:** on-site. **Terms:** cancellation fee imposed. **Amenities:** high-speed Internet, voice mail, irons, hair dryers. **Leisure Activities:** limited exercise equipment. **Guest Services:** coin laundry, wireless Internet. **Business Services:** PC. **Cards:** AX, CB, DC, DS, MC, VI. **Free Special Amenities:** expanded continental breakfast and high-speed Internet.

WYTESTONE SUITES OF POTOMAC MILLS — *Book great rates at AAA.com*

Phone: (703)490-4100

Small-scale Hotel
$135-$170 3/1-10/31
$120-$155 11/1-2/28

Address: 14525 Gideon Dr 22192 **Location:** I-95, exit 156, 0.5 mi w. Located in a commercial shopping area. **Facility:** Smoke free premises. 85 one-bedroom suites. 5 stories, interior corridors. *Bath:* combo or shower only. **Parking:** on-site. **Amenities:** high-speed Internet, dual phone lines, voice mail, safes, irons, hair dryers. **Pool(s):** heated indoor. **Leisure Activities:** limited exercise equipment. **Guest Services:** valet and coin laundry, wireless Internet. **Business Services:** meeting rooms. **Cards:** AX, CB, DC, DS, MC, VI. **Free Special Amenities:** full breakfast and high-speed Internet. *(See color ad below)*

▼ *See AAA listing above* ▼

─────── **WHERE TO DINE** ───────

GLORY DAYS GRILL, WOODBRIDGE
Phone: 703/730-3663

American

$7-$18

Lending to the casual restaurant's sports-themed atmosphere are memorabilia decorating the dining area and 25 TVs with control centers at each table and booth. Food selections range from wings and ribs to seafood, beef and pasta dishes. Casual dress. **Bar:** Full bar. **Reservations:** not accepted. **Hours:** 4 pm-midnight, Fri & Sat from 11:30 am, Sun 11:30 am-11 pm. Closed: 11/27, 12/25. **Address:** 13800 Smoketown Rd 22192 **Location:** I-95, exit 158B (Prince William Pkwy), 1.3 mi w, then just n; in Smoketown Plaza. **Parking:** on-site. **Cards:** AX, DS, MC, VI.

HARD TIMES CAFE
Phone: 703/492-2950

American

$6-$15

The hot and spicy, down-home operation knocks your socks off with an impressive variety of chilies, cooked in styles ranging from Cincinnati to Texas and vegetarian. Casual dress. **Bar:** Full bar. **Reservations:** not accepted. **Hours:** 11 am-1 am. **Address:** 14389 Potomac Mills Rd 22192 **Location:** I-95, exit 156, 0.5 mi w; in Potomac Festival Shopping Center. **Parking:** on-site. **Cards:** AX, MC, VI.

SILVER DINER
Phone: 703/491-7376

American

$9-$15

The eatery with its chrome and glass plate exterior and the glow of neon, provides the traditional diner setting. Booths with juke boxes, counter service and friendly wait staff add to the diner experience. The menu is extensive with salads, sandwiches and full meals. The desserts are made fresh and the fountain treats, shakes, floats and malts make for a great ending. Breakfast is available all day. Casual dress. **Bar:** Beer & wine. **Reservations:** not accepted. **Hours:** 7 am-midnight, Fri & Sat-3 am. Closed: 12/25. **Address:** 14375 Smoketown Rd 22192 **Location:** I-95, exit 156, 0.7 mi sw to Smoketown Rd. **Parking:** on-site. **Cards:** AX, DS, MC, VI.

TIGER THAI RESTAURANT
Phone: 703/499-8424

Thai

$8-$14

The shopping plaza restaurant offers good Thai cooking. The menu is extensive,with beef, seafood, vegetarian, noodle and curry dishes. One of the staff suggestions is Tiger Thai Beef. Casual dress. **Reservations:** accepted. **Hours:** 11:30 am-10 pm, Fri & Sat-10:30 pm, Sun-9:30 pm. Closed: 11/27, 12/25; also for lunch 1/1. **Address:** 14443 Potomac Mills Rd 22192 **Location:** I-95, exit 156, 0.5 mi w; in Potomac Festival Shopping Center. **Parking:** on-site. **Cards:** AX, MC, VI.

Vietnam Veterans Memorial / © AAA / Denise E. Campbell

This ends listings for the Washington, D.C. Vicinity.

Maryland

Chesapeake and Ohio
Canal National Historical
Park / © Tom Algire
Photography

ABERDEEN —*See Baltimore p. 600.*

ACCIDENT pop. 353

--------- **WHERE TO DINE** ---------

BUMBLE Q'S RESTAURANT   Phone: 301/387-7667

A local favorite, the restaurant pleases diners with a widely varied menu and friendly service. Don't pass on the ribs. Casual dress. **Reservations:** accepted. **Hours:** 11 am-2 pm, Fri-8 pm, Sat 8 am-8 pm, Sun 8 am-2 pm. **Address:** 145 Bumble Bee Rd 21520 **Location:** 2 mi s on SR 219, then 3 mi e. **Parking:** on-site.

American
$4-$18

ADELPHI —*See District Of Columbia p. 475.*

ANNAPOLIS —*See Baltimore p. 602.*

ANNAPOLIS JUNCTION —*See Baltimore p. 608.*

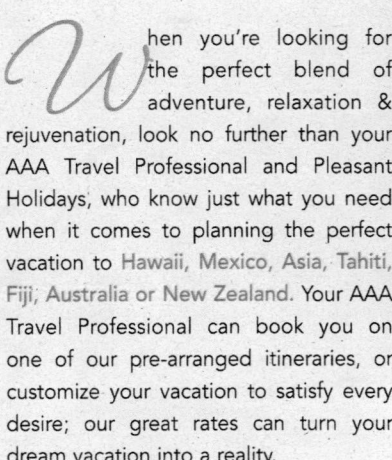

Destination Baltimore
pop. 651,154

*F*rom spectacular sports to classical culture, Baltimore has something for everyone.

*C*heer on baseball's Orioles in Oriole Park at Camden Yards. Place your bets on your favorite Thoroughbred in May's Preakness at Pimlico Race Course. Or sit back and enjoy the sounds of the Baltimore Symphony Orchestra.

© Gibson Stock Photography

Lexington Market, Baltimore.
This market has been in operation sinc 1782. (See mention page 177)

© SCPhotos / Alamy

Oriole Park at Camden Yards, Baltimore.
This is where Baltimore's baseball fans come to cheer for the hometown team. (See mention page 177)

*P*laces included in this AAA Destination City:

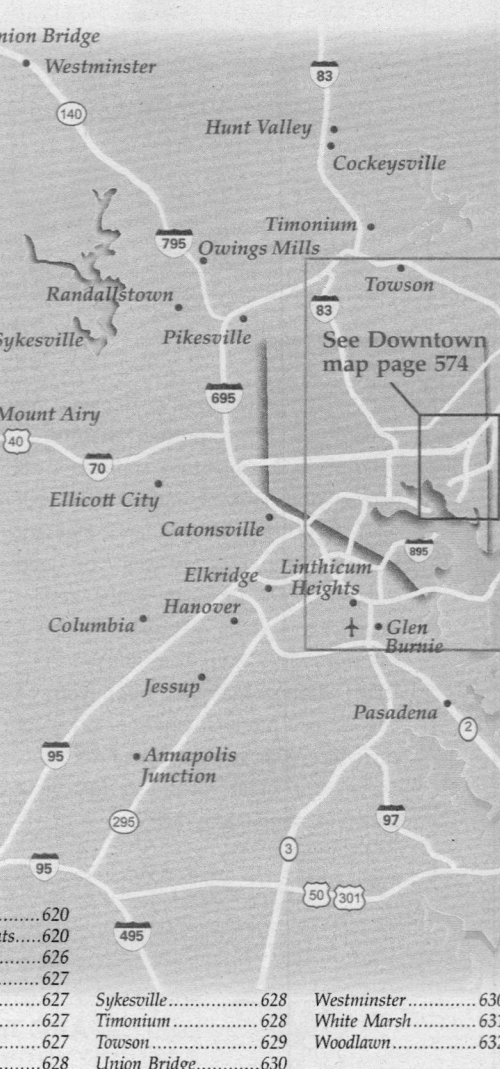

Union Bridge
Westminster
83
140
Hunt Valley
Cockeysville
795 Owings Mills
Timonium
Randallstown
Towson
83
Sykesville
Pikesville

See Downtown map page 574

695
Mount Airy
40
70
Ellicott City
Catonsville
895
Elkridge
Linthicum Heights
Hanover
Columbia
Glen Burnie
Jessup
Pasadena
2
95
Annapolis Junction
97
295
3
95
50 301
495

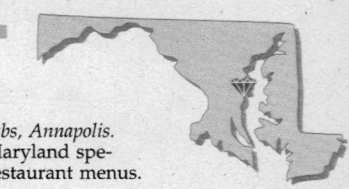

Dining on blue crabs, Annapolis. You'll find this Maryland specialty on many restaurant menus.

Woodlawn

Havre de Grace

Aberdeen

Fallston

Belcamp

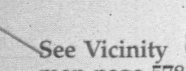
Edgewood

Joppa

White Marsh

osedale

Essex

Baltimore

Shopping in Fells Point in Baltimore. Copper pots sparkle in this old seaport neighborhood with an international flair.

See Vicinity map page 578

Baltimore Area Convention and Visitors Association

nnapolis

Tall ships in Baltimore's Inner Harbor. Entertainment and sightseeing can be found here at one of Baltimore's most popular spots.

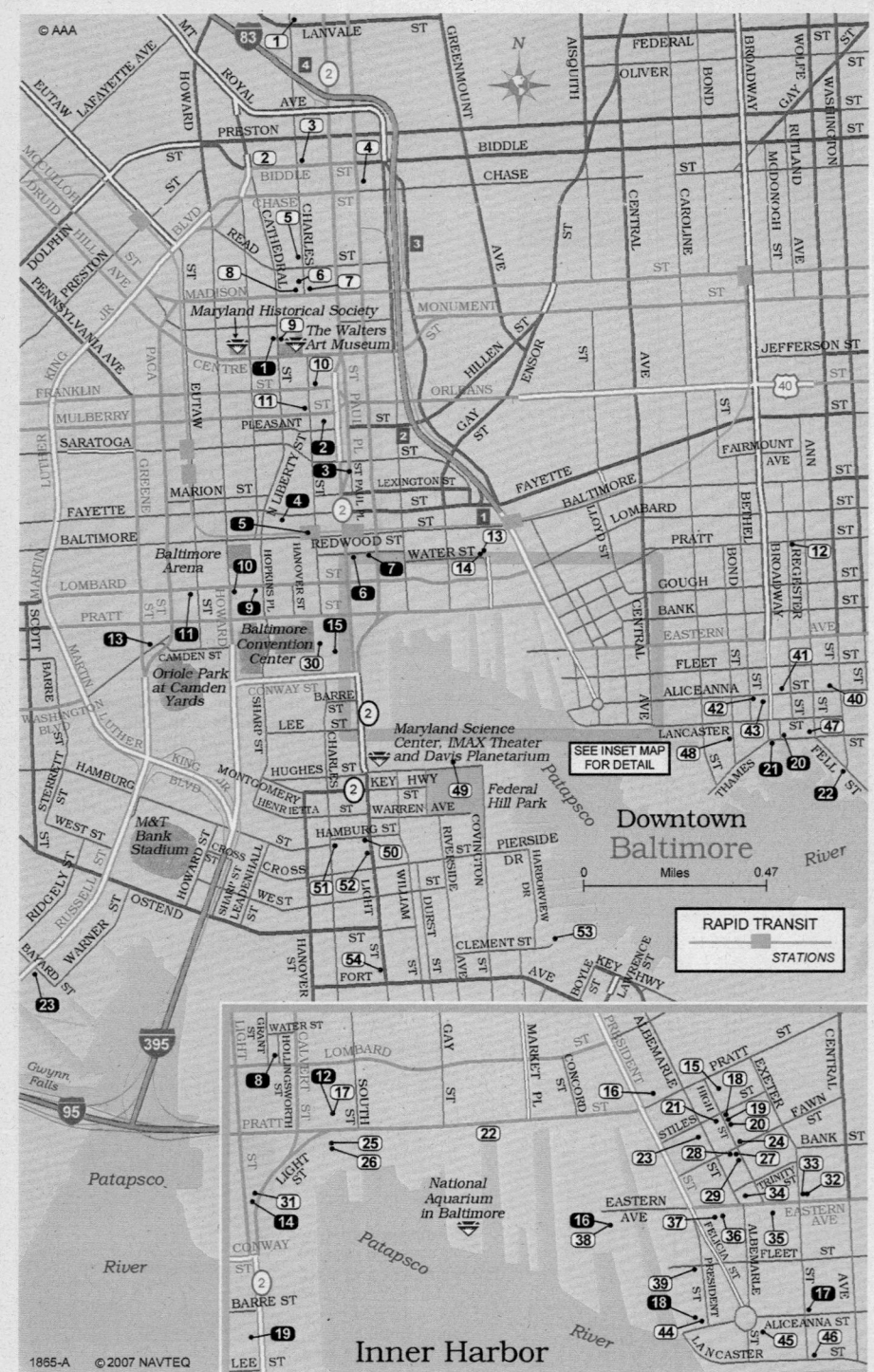

© AAA

Maryland Historical Society

The Walters Art Museum

Baltimore Arena

Baltimore Convention Center

Oriole Park at Camden Yards

M&T Bank Stadium

Maryland Science Center, IMAX Theater and Davis Planetarium

Federal Hill Park

Downtown

Baltimore

0   Miles   0.47

RAPID TRANSIT

STATIONS

Gwynn Falls

Patapsco River

National Aquarium in Baltimore

Patapsco River

Inner Harbor

1865-A   © 2007 NAVTEQ

Downtown Baltimore

This index helps you "spot" where approved lodgings and restaurants are located on the corresponding detailed maps. Lodging daily rate range is for comparison only and show the property's high season. Restaurant rate range is a combination of lunch and/or dinner. Turn to the listing page for more detailed rate information and consult display ads for special promotions.

Spotter/Map Page Number	OA	DOWNTOWN BALTIMORE - Lodgings	Diamond Rating	Rate Range High Season	Listing Page
1 / p. 574	AAA	**Peabody Court-A Clarion Hotel** - see color ad p 585	▽▽▽	$199-$309 SAVE	589
2 / p. 574		Baltimore's Tremont Park Hotel	▽▽	Rates not provided	586
3 / p. 574		Baltimore's Tremont Plaza Hotel	▽▽▽	Rates not provided	586
4 / p. 574		Sheraton Baltimore City Center Hotel	▽▽▽	$380	591
5 / p. 574	AAA	**Radisson Plaza Lord Baltimore** - see color ad p 589	▽▽▽	$139-$339 SAVE	590
6 / p. 574		Residence Inn by Marriott-Baltimore Downtown/Inner Harbor	▽▽▽	$243-$273	591
7 / p. 574	AAA	**Hampton Inn & Suites Baltimore Inner Harbor**	▽▽▽	Rates not provided SAVE	586
8 / p. 574		Brookshire Suites	▽▽▽	$129-$249	586
9 / p. 574	AAA	**Days Inn Inner Harbor Baltimore** - see color ad p 587	▽▽	$119-$299 SAVE	586
10 / p. 574	AAA	**Holiday Inn-Inner Harbor**	▽▽▽	$129-$329 SAVE	587
11 / p. 574		The Baltimore Marriott Inner Harbor at Camden Yards	▽▽▽	$364-$394	585
12 / p. 574	AAA	**Renaissance Baltimore Harborplace Hotel** - see color ad p 590	▽▽▽▽	$364-$394 SAVE	590
13 / p. 574	AAA	**Hampton Inn Baltimore-Camden Yards**	▽▽▽	Rates not provided SAVE	587
14 / p. 574	AAA	**Hyatt Regency Baltimore** - see color ad p 588	▽▽▽▽	$199-$409 SAVE	588
15 / p. 574	AAA	**Sheraton Inner Harbor Hotel**	▽▽▽	$199-$285 SAVE	591
16 / p. 574		Pier 5 Hotel	▽▽▽	$179-$299	589
17 / p. 574		Courtyard by Marriott Downtown Inner Harbor	▽▽▽	$276-$296	586
18 / p. 574		Baltimore Marriott Waterfront Hotel	▽▽▽▽	Rates not provided	585
19 / p. 574	AAA	**InterContinental Harbor Court**	▽▽▽▽	Rates not provided SAVE	589
20 / p. 574		Celie's Waterfront Inn	▽▽▽	$169-$349	586
21 / p. 574		Admiral Fell Inn	▽▽▽	$149-$269	585
22 / p. 574		The Inn at Henderson's Wharf - see color ad p 588	▽▽▽	$199-$369	588
23 / p. 574		Holiday Inn Express Baltimore at the Stadiums	▽▽▽	$169-$309	587
		DOWNTOWN BALTIMORE - Restaurants			
① / p. 574		Tapas Teatro	▽▽	$7-$22	596
② / p. 574	AAA	**Abacrombie Fine Food and Accommodations**	▽▽▽	$18-$25	591
③ / p. 574		Thai Landing	▽▽	$9-$17	597
④ / p. 574		The Prime Rib	▽▽▽	$21-$41	596
⑤ / p. 574		Brass Elephant	▽▽▽	$20-$35	592

Spotter/Map Page Number	OA	DOWNTOWN BALTIMORE - Restaurants (continued)	Diamond Rating	Rate Range High Season	Listing Page
⑥ / p. 574		The Helmand Restaurant	◆◆	$12-$18	594
⑦ / p. 574		Akbar Restaurant	◆◆	$8-$19	591
⑧ / p. 574		Saffron	◆◆◆	$18-$30	596
⑨ / p. 574	AAA	**George's on Mt. Vernon Square** - see color ad p 585	◆◆	$8-$40	593
⑩ / p. 574		Tio Pepe Restaurant	◆◆◆	$11-$35	597
⑪ / p. 574		Sotto Sopra	◆◆◆	$10-$35	596
⑫ / p. 574		Obrycki's Crab House and Seafood Restaurant	◆◆	$6-$30	595
⑬ / p. 574		Mondo Bondo Italian Bistro	◆◆	$7-$15	595
⑭ / p. 574		Babalu Grill	◆◆◆	$14-$31	592
⑮ / p. 574		Da Mimmo	◆◆	$7-$30	593
⑯ / p. 574		Velleggia's	◆◆	$12-$31	597
⑰ / p. 574		Windows	◆◆◆	$13-$32	597
⑱ / p. 574		Caesar's Den	◆◆	$9-$34	592
⑲ / p. 574		Chiapparelli's	◆◆	$8-$30	593
⑳ / p. 574		Amicci's	◆◆	$7-$19	591
㉑ / p. 574		Ciao Bella Restaurant	◆◆	$7-$25	593
㉒ / p. 574		Hard Rock Cafe	◆◆	$7-$25	594
㉓ / p. 574		La Tavola Ristorante Italiano	◆◆◆	$7-$24	594
㉔ / p. 574		Sabatino's	◆◆	$10-$35	596
㉕ / p. 574		M & S Grill	◆◆◆	$9-$26	595
㉖ / p. 574		Tir na Nog Irish Bar & Grill	◆◆	$9-$26	597
㉗ / p. 574		Germano's Trattoria	◆◆◆	$6-$19	593
㉘ / p. 574		Rocco's Capriccio	◆◆	$10-$47	596
㉙ / p. 574		Aldo's Ristorante Italiano	◆◆◆	$19-$45	591
㉚ / p. 574		Morton's The Steakhouse	◆◆◆	$25-$46	595
㉛ / p. 574		Pisces	◆◆◆	$35-$40	595
㉜ / p. 574	AAA	**La Scala Ristorante Italiano**	◆◆◆	$13-$32	594
㉝ / p. 574		Luigi Petti	◆◆◆	$10-$30	594
㉞ / p. 574		Mo's Crab and Pasta Factory	◆◆	$7-$28	595
㉟ / p. 574		Boccaccio Restaurant	◆◆◆	$12-$35	592
㊱ / p. 574		Dalesio's Restaurant of Little Italy	◆◆◆	$7-$32	593
㊲ / p. 574	AAA	**Della Notte Ristorante**	◆◆◆	$10-$39	593
㊳ / p. 574		Ruth's Chris Steak House-Pier 5	◆◆◆	$19-$39	596
㊴ / p. 574		James Joyce Irish Pub & Restaurant	◆◆	$8-$22	594
㊵ / p. 574		Pierpoint Restaurant & Bar	◆◆	$6-$25	595

Spotter/Map Page Number	OA	DOWNTOWN BALTIMORE - Restaurants (continued)	Diamond Rating	Rate Range High Season	Listing Page
41 / p. 574		Louisiana Restaurant	◈◈◈	$20-$30	594
42 / p. 574		Blue Moon Cafe'	◈◈	$5-$15	592
43 / p. 574		Bertha's	◈◈	$7-$22	592
44 / p. 574		Roy's	◈◈◈	$19-$38	596
45 / p. 574	AAA	**The Oceanaire Seafood Room**	◈◈◈	$17-$70	595
46 / p. 574		Charleston	◈◈◈◈	$67-$102	593
47 / p. 574		John Steven LTD	◈◈	$8-$29	594
48 / p. 574		The Black Olive	◈◈◈	$12-$34	592
49 / p. 574		The Rusty Scupper Resturant	◈◈	$8-$44	596
50 / p. 574		Ten-O-Six Restaurant	◈◈	$11-$22	597
51 / p. 574		Banjara Restaurant	◈◈	$8-$19	592
52 / p. 574		Blue Agave Restaurant	◈◈◈	$12-$28	592
53 / p. 574		Little Havana	◈	$6-$20	594
54 / p. 574		The Bicycle	◈◈◈	$15-$30	592

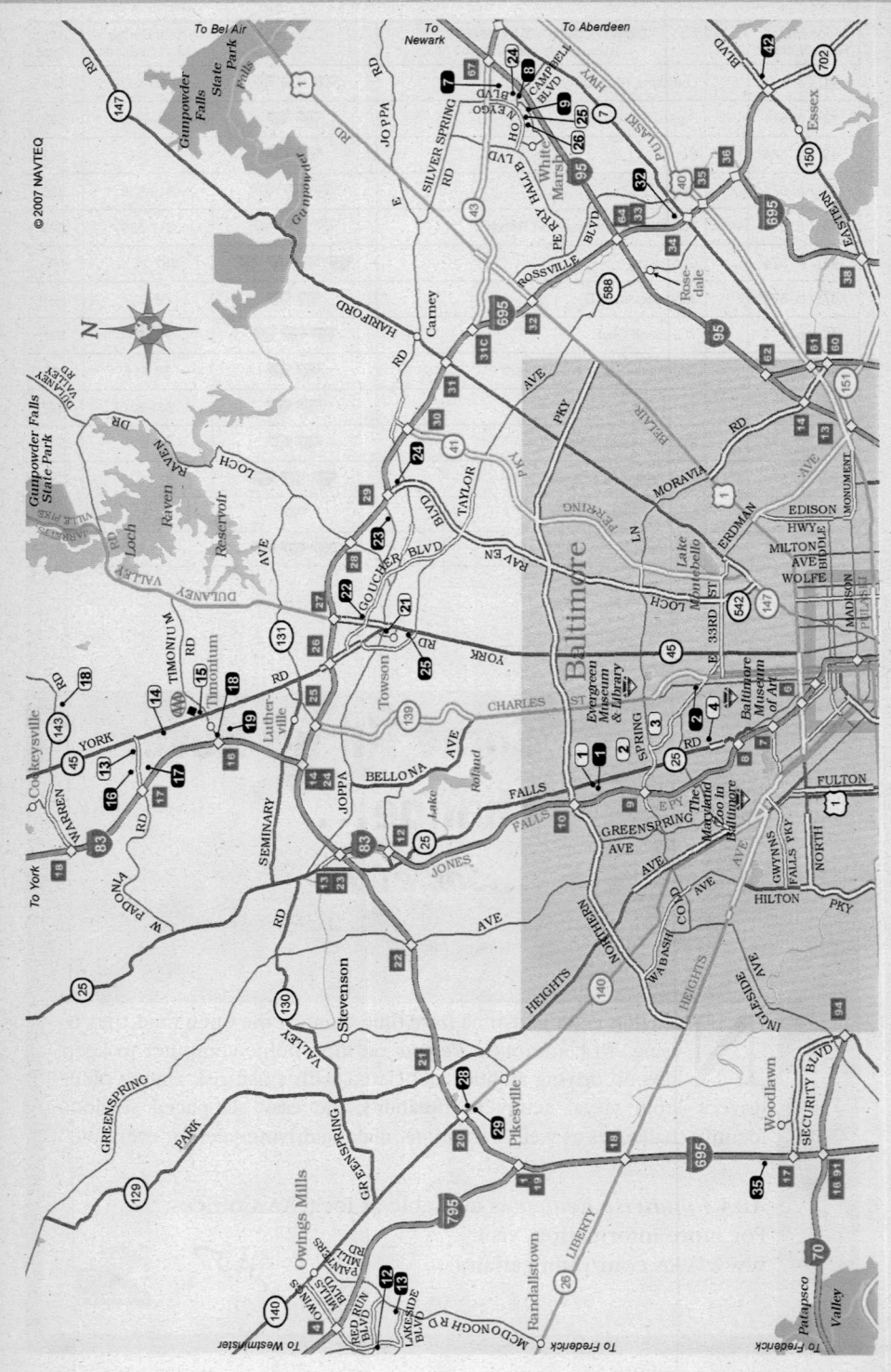

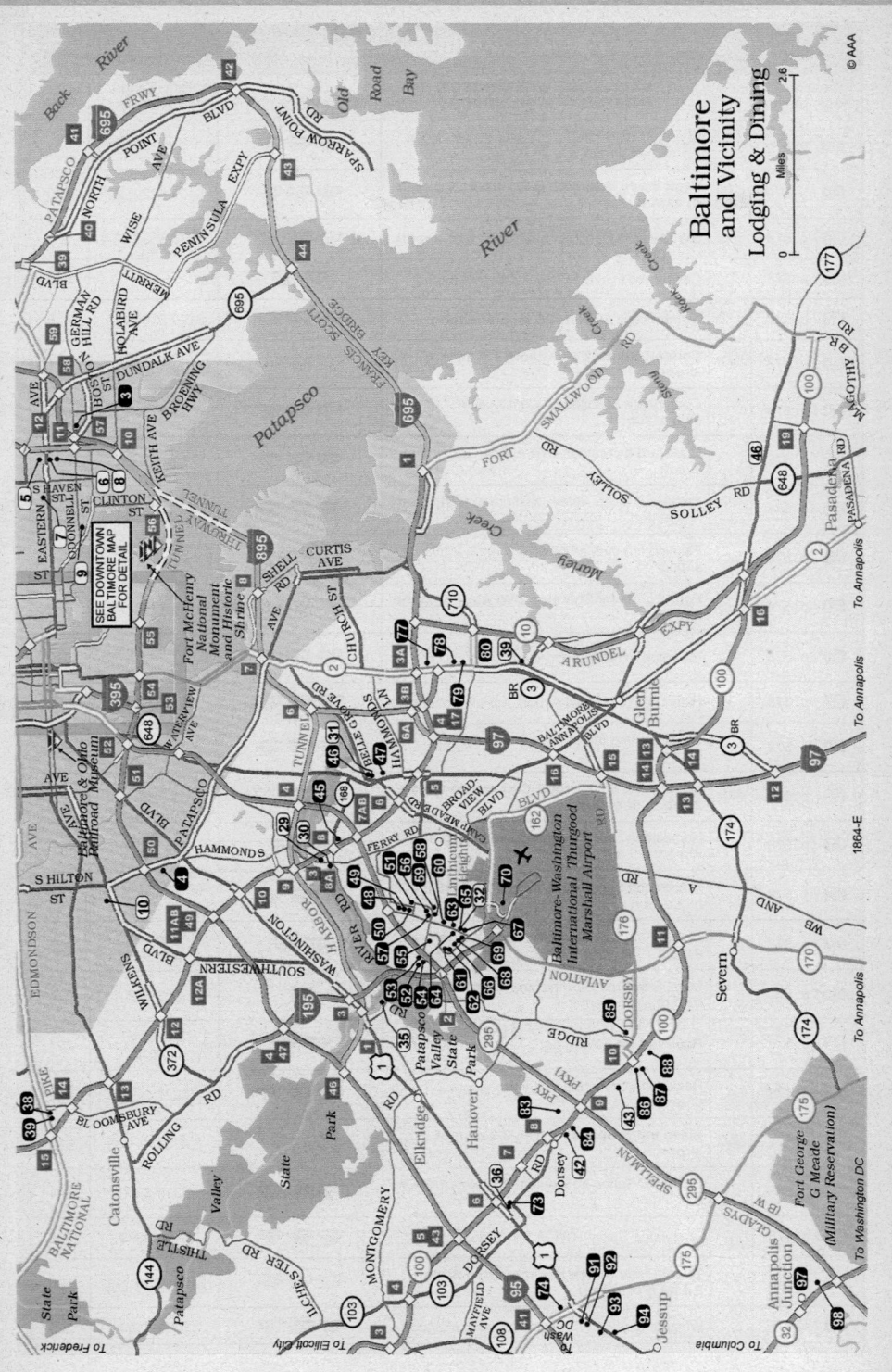

Baltimore
and Vicinity
Lodging & Dining

© AAA

✈ Airport Accommodations

Spotter/Map Page Number	OA	BALTIMORE-WASHINGTON INTERNATIONAL AIRPORT	Diamond Rating	Rate Range High Season	Listing Page
52 / p. 578		Sheraton Baltimore Washington Airport Hotel, 2.5 mi n of airport	◆◆◆	$269-$289	624
50 / p. 578	AAA	**Hyatt Place Baltimore BWI Airport, 2.5 mi n of airport**	◆◆◆	$109-$229 SAVE	623
65 / p. 578	AAA	**BWI Airport Marriott Hotel, 2 mi n of airport**	◆◆◆	$276-$338 SAVE	620
55 / p. 578		Candlewood Suites-BWI, 2.5 mi n of airport	◆◆	$135	620
47 / p. 578	AAA	**Comfort Inn Airport, 3.9 mi n of airport**	◆◆◆	$129-$189 SAVE	620
69 / p. 578	AAA	**Comfort Suites-BWI Airport, 1.8 mi w of airport**	◆◆◆	Rates not provided SAVE	621
63 / p. 578		Country Inn & Suites by Carlson BWI Airport, 2 mi n of airport	◆◆◆	$179-$199	621
60 / p. 578		Courtyard by Marriott-BWI Airport, 2.3 mi n of airport	◆◆◆	$242-$263	621
53 / p. 578		Embassy Suites Hotel Baltimore at BWI, 2.8 mi n of airport	◆◆◆	Rates not provided	621
64 / p. 578		Fairfield Inn by Marriott-BWI Airport, 2 mi n of airport	◆◆	$139-$169	621
70 / p. 578	AAA	**Four Points by Sheraton BWI Airport, at the airport**	◆◆◆	$103-$240 SAVE	622
66 / p. 578		Hampton Inn BWI Airport, 2 mi n of airport	◆◆◆	Rates not provided	622
67 / p. 578		Hilton Baltimore BWI Airport, 1.8 mi n of airport	◆◆◆	$149-$499	622
49 / p. 578		Hilton Garden Inn at BWI, 2.5 mi n of the airport	◆◆◆	Rates not provided	622
62 / p. 578	AAA	**Holiday Inn-BWI Airport Conference Center, 2.4 mi n of airport**	◆◆◆	$109-$229 SAVE	623
51 / p. 578		Homestead Studio Suites Hotel-Baltimore-BWI Airport, 2.5 mi n of airport	◆◆	$109-$119	623
58 / p. 578		Homewood Suites by Hilton-BWI Airport, 2.4 mi n of airport	◆◆◆	Rates not provided	623
57 / p. 578		Microtel Inn & Suites-BWI Airport, 2.4 mi n of airport	◆◆	Rates not provided	624
45 / p. 578		Motel 6 Baltimore-Linthicum Heights #1201, 4.6 mi n of airport terminal	◆	$68-$78	624
68 / p. 578		Red Roof Inn-BWI Airport, 1.8 mi n of airport	◆◆	Rates not provided	624
56 / p. 578		Residence Inn by Marriott-BWI Airport, 2.4 mi n of airport	◆◆◆	$227-$277	624
46 / p. 578	AAA	**Sleep Inn & Suites Airport, 3.9 mi n of airport**	◆◆	$99-$189 SAVE	624
61 / p. 578		SpringHill Suites by Marriott-BWI Airport, 2.5 mi n of airport	◆◆◆	$210-$240	624
54 / p. 578		Staybridge Suites BWI, 2.5 mi n of airport	◆◆◆	$169-$699	625
59 / p. 578	AAA	**TownePlace Suites Baltimore/BWI Airport, 2.4 mi n of airport**	◆◆◆	$109-$299 SAVE	625
48 / p. 578		Wingate Inn at BWI Airport, 2.5 mi n of airport	◆◆◆	$129-$199	626

Baltimore and Vicinity

This index helps you "spot" where approved lodgings and restaurants are located on the corresponding detailed maps. Lodging daily rate range is for comparison only and show the property's high season. Restaurant rate range is a combination of lunch and/or dinner. Turn to the listing page for more detailed rate information and consult display ads for special promotions.

Spotter/Map Page Number	OA	**BALTIMORE - Lodgings**	Diamond Rating	Rate Range High Season	Listing Page
1 / p. 578		The Inn at Cross Keys	▽▽▽	$185	598
2 / p. 578	AAA	**DoubleTree Inn At The Colonnade-A Hilton Hotel**	▽▽▽	$109-$309 SAVE	598
3 / p. 578	AAA	**Best Western Hotel & Conference Center -** see color ad p 598	▽▽▽	Rates not provided SAVE	598
4 / p. 578		Quality Inn Harbor South	▽▽	$99-$119	598
		BALTIMORE - Restaurants			
① / p. 578		Donna's Coffee Bar and Cafe	▽▽	$8-$20	599
② / p. 578		Petit Louis Bistro	▽▽▽	$11-$24	599
③ / p. 578		Loco Hombre	▽▽▽	$8-$19	599
④ / p. 578		Cafe Hon	▽▽	$6-$15	599
⑤ / p. 578		Acropolis Restaurant	▽▽	$6-$20	599
⑥ / p. 578		Ikaros Restaurant	▽▽	$6-$20	599
⑦ / p. 578		Eastern House Restaurant	▽▽	$5-$26	599
⑧ / p. 578		Samos Restaurant	▽▽	$5-$23	599
⑨ / p. 578		Nacho Mama's	▽▽	$6-$14	599
⑩ / p. 578		Kibby's Restaurant	▽	$5-$38	599
		WHITE MARSH - Lodgings			
7 / p. 578		Residence Inn by Marriott Baltimore/White Marsh	▽▽▽	$165-$196	631
8 / p. 578		Hilton Garden Inn-White Marsh	▽▽▽	Rates not provided	631
9 / p. 578		Hampton Inn at White Marsh	▽▽▽	Rates not provided	631
		WHITE MARSH - Restaurants			
㉔ / p. 578		Red Brick Station	▽▽	$7-$30	632
㉕ / p. 578		Strapazza	▽▽	$5-$23	632
㉖ / p. 578		Bayou Cafe	▽▽	$7-$27	631
		OWINGS MILLS - Lodgings			
12 / p. 578		Hilton Garden Inn-Owings Mills	▽▽▽	Rates not provided	627
13 / p. 578	AAA	**Hyatt Place Baltimore/Owings Mills**	▽▽▽	$109-$229 SAVE	627
		TIMONIUM - Lodgings			
16 / p. 578		Extended StayAmerica-Timonium	▽▽	$114-$124	628
17 / p. 578		Days Hotel & Conference Center Baltimore North	▽▽	Rates not provided	628
18 / p. 578		Red Roof Inn-Timonium	▽▽	Rates not provided	629
19 / p. 578		Holiday Inn Select Baltimore North	▽▽▽	$119-$189	628
		TIMONIUM - Restaurants			
⑬ / p. 578		Christopher Daniel	▽▽▽	$9-$30	629

Spotter/Map Page Number	OA	TIMONIUM - Restaurants (continued)	Diamond Rating	Rate Range High Season	Listing Page
14 / p. 578		An Poitin Stil	◆◆	$5-$22	629
15 / p. 578		Michael's Cafe	◆◆	$7-$28	629
		TOWSON - Lodgings			
22 / p. 578	AAA	**Sheraton Baltimore North Hotel**	◆◆◆	$233-$259 SAVE	630
23 / p. 578	AAA	**Holiday Inn Baltimore-Towson**	◆◆◆	$109-$179 SAVE	629
24 / p. 578	AAA	**Comfort Inn Towson**	◆◆	Rates not provided SAVE	629
25 / p. 578		Burkshire Marriott Conference Hotel	◆◆◆	$243-$273	629
		TOWSON - Restaurant			
21 / p. 578		Cafe Troia	◆◆◆	$9-$33	630
		PIKESVILLE - Lodgings			
28 / p. 578		Ramada Inn Baltimore West	◆◆	$98-$109	627
29 / p. 578		Hilton Pikesville	◆◆◆	Rates not provided	627
		ROSEDALE - Lodgings			
32 / p. 578	AAA	**La Quinta Inn & Suites Baltimore North**	◆◆	$139-$169 SAVE	628
		WOODLAWN - Lodgings			
35 / p. 578	AAA	**Best Western Baltimore West**	◆◆	Rates not provided SAVE	632
		CATONSVILLE - Lodgings			
38 / p. 578		Days Inn Catonsville	◆◆	$104-$115	609
39 / p. 578	AAA	**Comfort Inn Baltimore West**	◆◆	$90-$160 SAVE	609
		ESSEX - Lodgings			
42 / p. 578		Super 8 Motel Baltimore/Essex	◆	Rates not provided	615
		LINTHICUM HEIGHTS - Lodgings			
45 / p. 578		Motel 6 Baltimore-Linthicum Heights #1201	◆	$68-$78	624
46 / p. 578	AAA	**Sleep Inn & Suites Airport**	◆◆	$99-$189 SAVE	624
47 / p. 578	AAA	**Comfort Inn Airport**	◆◆◆	$129-$189 SAVE	620
48 / p. 578		Wingate Inn at BWI Airport	◆◆◆	$129-$199	626
49 / p. 578		Hilton Garden Inn at BWI	◆◆◆	Rates not provided	622
50 / p. 578	AAA	**Hyatt Place Baltimore BWI Airport**	◆◆◆	$109-$229 SAVE	623
51 / p. 578		Homestead Studio Suites Hotel-Baltimore-BWI Airport	◆◆	$109-$119	623
52 / p. 578		Sheraton Baltimore Washington Airport Hotel	◆◆◆	$269-$289	624
53 / p. 578		Embassy Suites Hotel Baltimore at BWI	◆◆◆	Rates not provided	621
54 / p. 578		Staybridge Suites BWI	◆◆◆	$169-$699	625
55 / p. 578		Candlewood Suites-BWI	◆◆	$135	620
56 / p. 578		Residence Inn by Marriott-BWI Airport	◆◆◆	$227-$277	624
57 / p. 578		Microtel Inn & Suites-BWI Airport	◆◆	Rates not provided	624
58 / p. 578		Homewood Suites by Hilton-BWI Airport	◆◆◆	Rates not provided	623

Spotter/Map Page Number	OA	LINTHICUM HEIGHTS - Lodgings (continued)	Diamond Rating	Rate Range High Season	Listing Page
59 / p. 578	AAA	TownePlace Suites Baltimore/BWI Airport - see color ad p 625	▽▽▽	$109-$299 SAVE	625
60 / p. 578		Courtyard by Marriott-BWI Airport	▽▽▽	$242-$263	621
61 / p. 578		SpringHill Suites by Marriott-BWI Airport	▽▽▽	$210-$240	624
62 / p. 578	AAA	Holiday Inn-BWI Airport Conference Center	▽▽▽	$109-$229 SAVE	623
63 / p. 578		Country Inn & Suites by Carlson BWI Airport	▽▽▽	$179-$199	621
64 / p. 578		Fairfield Inn by Marriott-BWI Airport	▽▽	$139-$169	621
65 / p. 578	AAA	BWI Airport Marriott Hotel	▽▽▽	$276-$338 SAVE	620
66 / p. 578		Hampton Inn BWI Airport	▽▽▽	Rates not provided	622
67 / p. 578		Hilton Baltimore BWI Airport - see color ad p 623	▽▽▽	$149-$499	622
68 / p. 578		Red Roof Inn-BWI Airport	▽▽	Rates not provided	624
69 / p. 578	AAA	Comfort Suites-BWI Airport	▽▽▽	Rates not provided SAVE	621
70 / p. 578	AAA	Four Points by Sheraton BWI Airport - see color ad p 622	▽▽▽	$103-$240 SAVE	622
		LINTHICUM HEIGHTS - Restaurants			
29 / p. 578		Snyder's Willow Grove	▽▽	$8-$31	626
30 / p. 578		G & M Restaurant	▽▽	$4-$29	626
31 / p. 578	AAA	The Rose Restaurant LTD	▽▽▽	$6-$24	626
32 / p. 578		Moniker's Grille	▽▽	$11-$29	626
		ELKRIDGE - Lodgings			
73 / p. 578	AAA	Best Western BWI Airport	▽▽▽	$99-$159 SAVE	613
74 / p. 578		Comfort Suites-Columbia Gateway	▽▽▽	$99-$249	613
		ELKRIDGE - Restaurants			
35 / p. 578	AAA	The Elkridge Furnace Inn	▽▽▽	$9-$36	614
36 / p. 578		House of Welsh	▽▽	$7-$25	614
		GLEN BURNIE - Lodgings			
77 / p. 578	AAA	Holiday Inn-Baltimore South	▽▽	$89-$159 SAVE	616
78 / p. 578		Days Inn-Glen Burnie	▽▽	Rates not provided	616
79 / p. 578	AAA	Hampton Inn Baltimore/Glen Burnie - see color ad p 616	▽▽▽	$99-$126 SAVE	616
80 / p. 578		Extended StayAmerica Baltimore-Glen Burnie	▽▽	$129-$139	616
		GLEN BURNIE - Restaurant			
39 / p. 578		The Olive Tree Restaurant	▽▽	$7-$24	616
		HANOVER - Lodgings			
83 / p. 578		Ramada Inn BWI Airport Conference Center	▽▽	$103-$122	617
84 / p. 578		Red Roof Inn-BWI Parkway	▽▽	Rates not provided	617
85 / p. 578		Holiday Inn Express-BWI Airport	▽▽▽	$145-$169	617
86 / p. 578		Hampton Inn & Suites-Arundel Mills/BWI	▽▽▽	$109-$299	617
87 / p. 578		Residence Inn by Marriott-Arundel Mills/BWI	▽▽▽	$207-$253	617

Spotter/Map Page Number	OA	**HANOVER** - Lodgings (continued)	Diamond Rating	Rate Range High Season	Listing Page
88 / p. 578		SpringHill Suites by Marriott-Arundel Mills/BWI	◆◆◆	$187-$229	617
		HANOVER - Restaurants			
42 / p. 578		Gunning's Seafood Restaurant	◆◆	$7-$40	617
43 / p. 578		Remomo Cafe Italia	◆◆	$7-$24	618
		JESSUP - Lodgings			
91 / p. 578		Fairfield Inn by Marriott-Columbia/Jessup	◆◆	$129-$159	619
92 / p. 578		Red Roof Inn-Columbia/Jessup	◆◆	Rates not provided	619
93 / p. 578	AAA	**Super 8 Motel**	◆	Rates not provided SAVE	620
94 / p. 578	AAA	**Sleep Inn Jessup**	◆◆	$100-$150 SAVE	620
		ANNAPOLIS JUNCTION - Lodgings			
97 / p. 578		TownePlace Suites by Marriott-Baltimore/Ft. Meade	◆◆	$158-$193	608
98 / p. 578		Courtyard by Marriott Ft. Meade @ National Business Park	◆◆◆	$231-$274	608
		COCKEYSVILLE - Restaurant			
18 / p. 578		Patrick's of Cockeysville	◆◆◆	$6-$30	609
		PASADENA - Restaurant			
46 / p. 578		Bella Napoli Italian Restaurant	◆◆◆	$8-$20	627

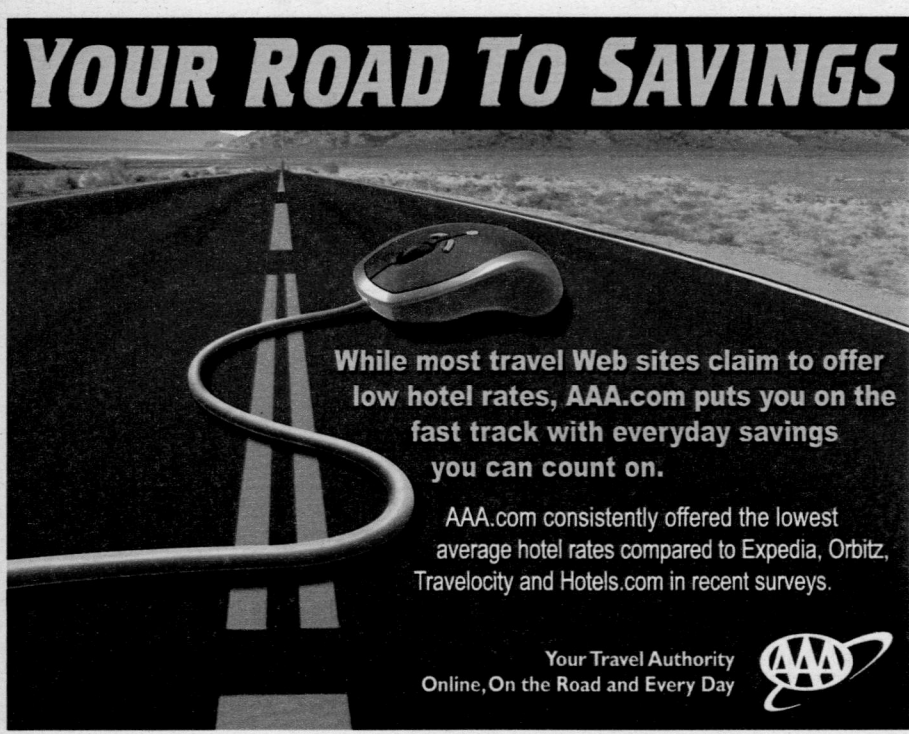

DOWNTOWN BALTIMORE   (See map and index starting on p. 574)

─────── **WHERE TO STAY** ───────

ADMIRAL FELL INN

Book at AAA.com   **Phone:** (410)522-7377   **21**

Historic
Small-scale Hotel
$149–$269 All Year

Address: 888 S Broadway St 21231 **Location:** Corner of Broadway and Thames sts; facing the waterfront. Located in historic Fells Point. **Facility:** Period pieces, including several canopy beds, decorate some guest rooms in this 1790s inn, which is made up of eight buildings. 80 one-bedroom standard units, some with whirlpools. 5 stories, interior corridors. *Bath:* combo or shower only. **Parking:** on-site (fee) and valet. **Terms:** check-in 4 pm, cancellation fee imposed. **Amenities:** voice mail, irons, hair dryers. *Fee:* video games, high-speed Internet. **Guest Services:** valet laundry, area transportation, wireless Internet. **Business Services:** meeting rooms, PC. **Cards:** AX, CB, DC, DS, MC, VI.

**THE BALTIMORE MARRIOTT INNER HARBOR AT
CAMDEN YARDS**   *Book great rates at AAA.com*   **Phone:** 410/962-0202   **11**

Large-scale Hotel
$364–$394 3/1–11/16
$275–$296 11/17–2/28

Address: 110 S Eutaw St 21201 **Location:** Pratt and Eutaw sts. Located across from Orioles Park at Camden Yards. **Facility:** Smoke free premises. 524 one-bedroom standard units. 10 stories, interior corridors. *Bath:* combo or shower only. **Parking:** on-site (fee). **Terms:** check-in 4 pm. **Amenities:** dual phone lines, voice mail, safes, honor bars, irons, hair dryers. *Fee:* video games, high-speed Internet. *Some:* CD players. **Pool(s):** heated indoor. **Leisure Activities:** whirlpool, exercise room. **Guest Services:** valet and coin laundry, wireless Internet. **Business Services:** conference facilities, business center. **Cards:** AX, DC, DS, MC, VI.

Marriott.
HOTELS & RESORTS

AAA Benefit:
Members save 5% off of the best available rate.

BALTIMORE MARRIOTT WATERFRONT HOTEL   *Book great rates at AAA.com*   **Phone:** 410/385-3000   **18**

Large-scale Hotel
Rates not provided

Address: 700 Aliceanna St 21202 **Location:** Center. Located in the Harbor East section of The Inner Harbor. **Facility:** Smoke free premises. 753 units. 747 one-bedroom standard units, some with whirlpools. 6 one-bedroom suites with whirlpools. 32 stories, interior corridors. *Bath:* combo or shower only. **Parking:** on-site (fee) and valet. **Terms:** check-in 4 pm. **Amenities:** high-speed Internet (fee), dual phone lines, voice mail, safes, honor bars, irons, hair dryers. *Some:* CD players. **Pool(s):** heated indoor. **Leisure Activities:** saunas, exercise room. *Fee:* massage. **Guest Services:** valet laundry, wireless Internet. **Business Services:** conference facilities, business center.

Marriott.
HOTELS & RESORTS

AAA Benefit:
Members save 5% off of the best available rate.

▼ See AAA listing p 589 ▼
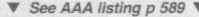

(See map and index starting on p. 574)

BALTIMORE'S TREMONT PARK HOTEL
 *Book great rates at AAA.com*
Phone: 410/576-1200 **2**

Small-scale Hotel
Rates not provided

Address: 8 E Pleasant St 21202 **Location:** Just s of US 40 E, off Charles St. **Facility:** 58 units. 26 one-bedroom standard units with efficiencies. 32 one-bedroom suites with efficiencies. 13 stories, interior corridors. *Bath:* combo or shower only. **Parking:** on-site (fee) and valet. **Terms:** check-in 4 pm. **Amenities:** high-speed Internet, dual phone lines, voice mail, irons, hair dryers. *Some:* DVD players (fee). **Leisure Activities:** exercise room. **Guest Services:** valet and coin laundry, area transportation, wireless Internet. **Business Services:** business center.

BALTIMORE'S TREMONT PLAZA HOTEL
Book great rates at AAA.com
Phone: 410/727-2222 **3**

Large-scale Hotel
Rates not provided

Address: 222 St Paul Pl 21202 **Location:** At St Paul Pl and Saratoga St. **Facility:** Smoke free premises. 303 units. 185 one-bedroom standard units. 106 one- and 12 two-bedroom suites. 37 stories, interior corridors. *Bath:* combo or shower only. **Parking:** on-site (fee) and valet. **Terms:** check-in 4 pm. **Amenities:** high-speed Internet, dual phone lines, voice mail, irons, hair dryers. *Some:* DVD players (fee). **Pool(s):** outdoor. **Leisure Activities:** saunas, exercise room. **Guest Services:** valet and coin laundry, area transportation, wireless Internet. **Business Services:** conference facilities, business center.

BROOKSHIRE SUITES
Book at AAA.com
Phone: (410)625-1300 **8**

Small-scale Hotel
$129-$249 All Year

Address: 120 E Lombard St 21202 **Location:** Corner of Calvert and Lombard sts. **Facility:** 97 units. 43 one-bedroom standard units. 54 one-bedroom suites. 13 stories, interior corridors. *Bath:* combo or shower only. **Parking:** valet. **Terms:** check-in 4 pm, cancellation fee imposed. **Amenities:** high-speed Internet (fee), dual phone lines, voice mail, honor bars, irons, hair dryers. **Leisure Activities:** exercise room. **Guest Services:** valet laundry, wireless Internet. **Business Services:** meeting rooms, PC (fee). **Cards:** AX, CB, DC, DS, MC, VI.

CELIE'S WATERFRONT INN
Phone: 410/522-2323 **20**

Bed & Breakfast
$169-$349 All Year

Address: 1714 Thames St 21231 **Location:** In historic Fells Point area. **Facility:** This B&B, which includes an answering machine in each room, is walking distance to many shops and restaurants; check-in must be pre-arranged. Smoke free premises. 9 one-bedroom standard units, some with whirlpools. 3 stories (no elevator), interior corridors. *Bath:* combo or shower only. **Parking:** on-site (fee). **Terms:** office hours 7 am-5 pm, age restrictions may apply, 15 day cancellation notice-fee imposed. **Amenities:** irons, hair dryers. *Some:* CD players. **Guest Services:** wireless Internet. **Business Services:** fax. **Cards:** AX, DS, MC, VI.

COURTYARD BY MARRIOTT DOWNTOWN INNER HARBOR
Book great rates at AAA.com
Phone: 443/923-4000 **17**

Small-scale Hotel
$276-$296 3/1-11/18
$230-$241 11/19-2/28

Address: 1000 Aliceanna St 21202 **Location:** On east side of Inner Harbor. **Facility:** Smoke free premises. 205 units. 195 one-bedroom standard units, some with whirlpools. 10 one-bedroom suites. 14 stories, interior corridors. *Bath:* combo or shower only. **Parking:** on-site (fee). **Amenities:** video games (fee), dual phone lines, voice mail, irons, hair dryers. *Some:* CD players. **Pool(s):** heated indoor. **Leisure Activities:** whirlpool, exercise room. **Guest Services:** valet and coin laundry, wireless Internet. **Business Services:** meeting rooms, PC. **Cards:** AX, DC, DS, JC, MC, VI.

AAA Benefit:
Members save 5% off of the best available rate.

DAYS INN INNER HARBOR BALTIMORE
Book great rates at AAA.com
Phone: (410)576-1000 **9**

Small-scale Hotel
$119-$299 3/1-11/20
$99-$169 11/21-2/28

Address: 100 Hopkins Pl 21201 **Location:** Opposite First Mariner Arena; 1 blk from Baltimore Convention Center. **Facility:** Smoke free premises. 250 one-bedroom standard units. 9 stories, interior corridors. *Bath:* combo or shower only. **Parking:** on-site (fee). **Amenities:** voice mail, irons, hair dryers. *Fee:* video games, safes. **Pool(s):** outdoor. **Leisure Activities:** exercise room. **Guest Services:** valet and coin laundry, wireless Internet. **Business Services:** meeting rooms, business center. **Cards:** AX, CB, DC, DS, JC, MC, VI. *(See color ad p 587)*

HAMPTON INN & SUITES BALTIMORE INNER HARBOR
Phone: 410/539-7888 **7**

Small-scale Hotel
Rates not provided

Address: 131 E Redwood St 21202 **Location:** Between Lombard and Baltimore sts; corner of Calvert and E Redwood sts. **Facility:** 116 one-bedroom standard units, some with whirlpools. 7 stories, interior corridors. *Bath:* combo or shower only. **Parking:** valet. **Amenities:** video games (fee), high-speed Internet, voice mail, irons, hair dryers. **Pool(s):** heated indoor. **Leisure Activities:** limited exercise equipment. **Guest Services:** valet and coin laundry, wireless Internet. **Business Services:** meeting rooms, business center. **Free Special Amenities:** full breakfast and high-speed Internet.

(See map and index starting on p. 574)

HAMPTON INN BALTIMORE-CAMDEN YARDS
Book great rates at AAA.com   **Phone:** 410/685-5000 🔟**13**

AAA SAVE
▽▽◇▽▽
Small-scale Hotel
Rates not provided

Address: 550 Washington Blvd 21230 **Location:** Jct Russell St and Washington Blvd; opposite Camden Yards. **Facility:** 126 one-bedroom standard units. 8 stories, interior corridors. *Bath:* combo or shower only. **Parking:** valet. **Amenities:** high-speed Internet, voice mail, irons, hair dryers. **Pool(s):** heated indoor. **Leisure Activities:** whirlpool, exercise room. **Guest Services:** complimentary and valet laundry, area transportation-within 1 mi, wireless Internet. **Business Services:** meeting rooms, business center. **Free Special Amenities: continental breakfast and high-speed Internet.**

HOLIDAY INN EXPRESS BALTIMORE AT THE STADIUMS
Book great rates at AAA.com   **Phone:** (410)727-1818 **23**

▽▽◇▽▽
Small-scale Hotel
$169-$309 All Year

Address: 1701 Russell St 21230 **Location:** I-95, exit 52 (Russell St) northbound, then just n; southbound, exit I-395, follow signs to Russell St, then just s. **Facility:** 123 units. 120 one-bedroom standard units. 3 one-bedroom suites with whirlpools. 4 stories, interior corridors. *Bath:* combo or shower only. **Parking:** on-site (fee). **Terms:** cancellation fee imposed. **Amenities:** high-speed Internet, voice mail, irons, hair dryers. **Pool(s):** outdoor. **Leisure Activities:** exercise room. **Guest Services:** valet and coin laundry, area transportation, wireless Internet. **Business Services:** meeting rooms, business center. **Cards:** AX, DC, DS, MC, VI.

HOLIDAY INN-INNER HARBOR
Book great rates at AAA.com   **Phone:** (410)685-3500 🔟**10**

AAA SAVE
▽▽◇▽▽
Large-scale Hotel
$129-$329 All Year

Address: 301 W Lombard St 21201 **Location:** Just w of Camden Yards. **Facility:** 375 one-bedroom standard units, some with whirlpools. 10-13 stories, interior corridors. *Bath:* combo or shower only. **Parking:** check-in 4 pm, cancellation fee imposed. **Amenities:** video games (fee), dual phone lines, voice mail, irons, hair dryers. **Pool(s):** heated indoor. **Leisure Activities:** sauna, exercise room. **Guest Services:** valet and coin laundry, wireless Internet. **Business Services:** conference facilities, PC, fax. **Cards:** AX, CB, DC, DS, JC, MC, VI.

▼ *See AAA listing p 586* ▼

(See map and index starting on p. 574)

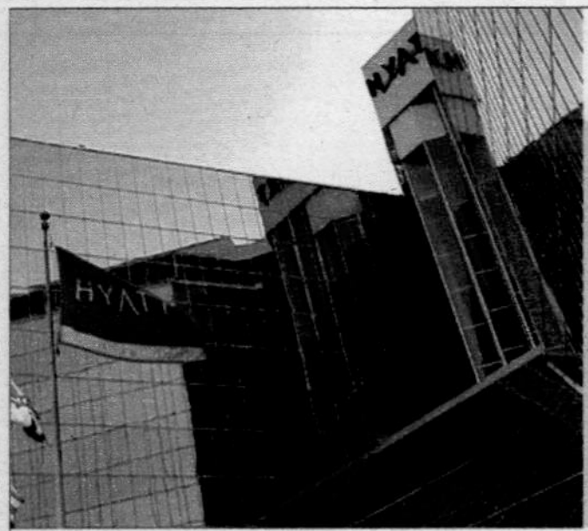

HYATT REGENCY BALTIMORE   *Book great rates at AAA.com*   Phone: (410)528-1234   **14**

 (SAVE)
▼▼▼ ▼▼▼
Large-scale Hotel
$199-$409 All Year

Address: 300 Light St 21202 **Location:** Facing Harborplace. **Facility:** 488 units. 486 one-bedroom standard units. 2 one-bedroom suites. 15 stories, interior corridors. *Bath:* combo or shower only. **Parking:** on-site (fee) and valet. **Terms:** check-in 4 pm, cancellation fee imposed. **Amenities:** voice mail, safes, honor bars, irons, hair dryers. *Some:* DVD players. **Dining:** Pisces, see separate listing. **Pool(s):** outdoor. **Leisure Activities:** whirlpool, 2 tennis courts, jogging, exercise room, basketball. **Guest Services:** valet laundry, wireless Internet. **Business Services:** conference facilities, business center. **Cards:** AX, CB, DC, DS, JC, MC, VI. *(See color ad below)*

HYATT
HOTELS & RESORTS®

AAA Benefit:
Ask for the AAA rate
and save 10%.

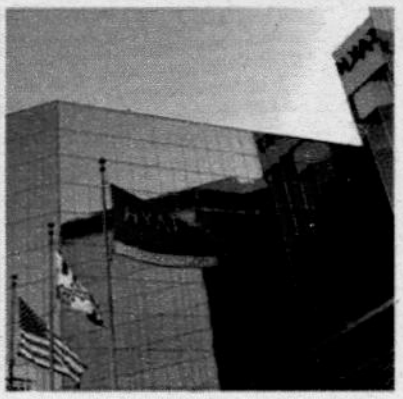

[icons]

THE INN AT HENDERSON'S WHARF   *Book great rates at AAA.com*   Phone: (410)522-7777   **22**

▼▼▼
Historic
Small-scale Hotel
$199-$369 All Year

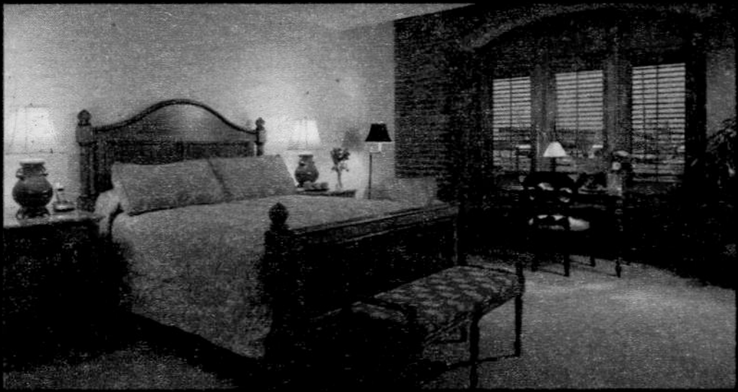

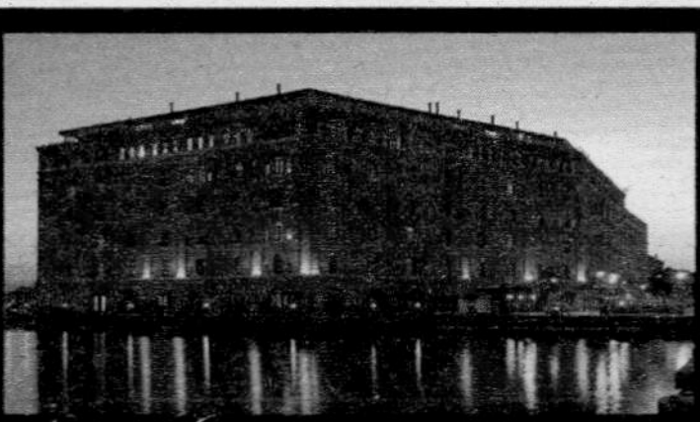

Address: 1000 Fell St 21231 **Location:** On waterfront. Located in historic Fells Point area. **Facility:** Formerly a tobacco warehouse, this hotel offers tastefully appointed rooms, some with water views and a warm ambience. 38 one-bedroom standard units. 6 stories, interior corridors. **Parking:** on-site. **Terms:** cancellation fee imposed. **Amenities:** voice mail, irons, hair dryers. *Some:* DVD players. **Leisure Activities:** exercise room. *Fee:* marina. **Guest Services:** valet laundry, wireless Internet. **Business Services:** meeting rooms, business center. **Cards:** AX, DC, DS, MC, VI. *(See color ad below)*

[icons]

(See map and index starting on p. 574)

INTERCONTINENTAL HARBOR COURT *Book great rates at AAA.com* Phone: 410/234-0550 **19**

AAA SAVE

▽▽▽ ▽▽▽
Large-scale Hotel
Rates not provided

Address: 550 Light St 21202 **Location:** Facing Inner Harbor. **Facility:** A spiral staircase in the lobby of the Harbor Court Hotel leads to two restaurants; a fitness center is available. 195 units. 187 one-bedroom standard units. 8 one-bedroom suites. 8 stories, interior corridors. **Parking:** on-site (fee) and valet. **Amenities:** CD players, high-speed Internet (fee), dual phone lines, voice mail, safes, honor bars, irons, hair dryers. **Dining:** entertainment. **Pool(s):** heated indoor. **Leisure Activities:** saunas, whirlpool, tennis court, racquetball court, aerobics, yoga. *Fee:* massage. **Guest Services:** valet laundry, tanning facilities, personal trainer, wireless Internet. **Business Services:** conference facilities, business center. **Free Special Amenities:** newspaper. Affiliated with Inter-Continental Hotels.

[icons] ⟨† 24† ⟨ ⟨† CALL &M ⟨ ⟨† ⟨ ⟨ ⟨ / SOME UNITS ⟨ FEE VCR

PEABODY COURT-A CLARION HOTEL *Book great rates at AAA.com* Phone: (410)727-7101 **1**

AAA SAVE

▽▽▽
Historic
Small-scale Hotel
$199-$309 3/1-11/15
$149-$199 11/16-2/28

Address: 612 Cathedral St 21201 **Location:** Cathedral St and Mt Vernon Square. **Facility:** This vintage hotel dates from 1924; its public spaces are limited. Smoke free premises. 104 units. 102 one-bedroom standard units. 2 one-bedroom suites, some with whirlpools. 13 stories, interior corridors. *Bath:* combo or shower only. **Parking:** valet. **Terms:** cancellation fee imposed. **Amenities:** high-speed Internet, dual phone lines, voice mail, irons, hair dryers. *Fee:* video games, safes. **Dining:** George's on Mt. Vernon Square, see separate listing. **Leisure Activities:** exercise room. **Guest Services:** valet laundry, wireless Internet. **Business Services:** meeting rooms, business center. **Cards:** AX, CB, DC, DS, JC, MC, VI. *(See color ad p 585)*

[icons] S⌀ ⟨† CALL &M ⟨ ⟨† ⟨ ⟨ / SOME UNITS FEE ⟨

PIER 5 HOTEL *Book at AAA.com* Phone: (410)539-2000 **16**

▽▽▽
Small-scale Hotel
$179-$299 All Year

Address: 711 Eastern Ave 21202 **Location:** On the Inner Harbor, at Pier 5. **Facility:** Smoke free premises. 66 one-bedroom standard units, some with whirlpools. 3 stories, interior corridors. *Bath:* combo or shower only. **Parking:** on-site (fee) and valet. **Terms:** check-in 4 pm, cancellation fee imposed. **Amenities:** CD players, high-speed Internet (fee), dual phone lines, voice mail, safes, irons, hair dryers. **Guest Services:** valet laundry. **Business Services:** meeting rooms, PC (fee). **Cards:** AX, CB, DC, DS, MC, VI.

[icons] ASK S⌀ ⟨† CALL &M FEE ⟨ ⟨ ⟨† ⟨ ⟨ / SOME UNITS FEE ⟨ ⟨

▼ See AAA listing p 590 ▼

(See map and index starting on p. 574)

RADISSON PLAZA LORD BALTIMORE   *Book great rates at AAA.com*   Phone: (410)539-8400

Large-scale Hotel
$139-$339 3/1-6/30
$109-$339 7/1-2/28

Address: 20 W Baltimore St 21201 **Location:** At Baltimore and Hanover sts. **Facility:** 440 one-bedroom standard units. 23 stories, interior corridors. *Bath:* combo or shower only. **Parking:** on-site (fee) and valet. **Amenities:** dual phone lines, voice mail, irons, hair dryers. *Some:* CD players. **Leisure Activities:** saunas, whirlpool, exercise room. **Guest Services:** valet laundry, wireless Internet. **Business Services:** conference facilities, business center. **Cards:** AX, CB, DC, DS, MC, VI. **Free Special Amenities:** newspaper and high-speed Internet.
(See color ad p 589)

RENAISSANCE BALTIMORE HARBORPLACE HOTEL   *Book great rates at AAA.com*   Phone: 410/547-1200

Large-scale Hotel
$364-$394 3/1-11/17
$318-$329 11/18-2/28

Address: 202 E Pratt St 21202 **Location:** Opposite Inner Harbor. Located adjacent to a multi-level shopping mall. **Facility:** Smoke free premises. 622 units. 618 one-bedroom standard units, some with whirlpools. 4 one-bedroom suites, some with whirlpools. 12 stories, interior corridors. *Bath:* combo or shower only. **Parking:** on-site (fee) and valet. **Terms:** check-in 4 pm. **Amenities:** high-speed Internet (fee), dual phone lines, voice mail, honor bars, irons, hair dryers. *Some:* CD players. **Dining:** Windows, see separate listing. **Pool(s):** heated indoor. **Leisure Activities:** sauna, whirlpool, sun deck, exercise room. *Fee:* massage. **Guest Services:** valet laundry, wireless Internet. **Business Services:** conference facilities, business center. **Cards:** AX, DC, DS, JC, MC, VI. *(See color ad below)*

RENAISSANCE.
HOTELS & RESORTS

AAA Benefit:
Members save 5% off of the best available rate.

▼ See AAA listing above ▼

(See map and index starting on p. 574)

RESIDENCE INN BY MARRIOTT-BALTIMORE DOWNTOWN/INNER HARBOR

Book great rates at AAA.com

Phone: 410/962-1220

Small-scale Hotel
$243-$273 3/1-11/11
$198-$219 11/12-2/28

Address: 17 Light St 21202 **Location:** Between Mercer and E Redwood sts. **Facility:** Smoke free premises. 188 units. 85 one-bedroom standard units with efficiencies. 86 one- and 17 two-bedroom suites, some with efficiencies or kitchens. 15 stories, interior corridors. *Bath:* combo or shower only. **Parking:** on-site (fee) and valet. **Terms:** check-in 4 pm. **Amenities:** video games (fee), high-speed Internet, voice mail, irons, hair dryers. **Leisure Activities:** exercise room. **Guest Services:** valet and coin laundry, wireless Internet. **Business Services:** meeting rooms, PC. **Cards:** AX, DS, MC, VI.

AAA Benefit:
Members save 5% off of the best available rate.

SHERATON BALTIMORE CITY CENTER HOTEL

Book great rates at AAA.com

Phone: (410)752-1100 **4**

Large-scale Hotel
$380 All Year

Address: 101 W Fayette St 21201 **Location:** Between Charles and Liberty sts. **Facility:** 706 one-bedroom standard units, some with whirlpools. 23-27 stories, interior corridors. *Bath:* combo or shower only. **Parking:** on-site (fee) and valet. **Terms:** check-in 4 pm, cancellation fee imposed. **Amenities:** voice mail, irons, hair dryers. *Fee:* video games, high-speed Internet. **Pool(s):** outdoor. **Leisure Activities:** exercise room. **Guest Services:** valet and coin laundry, area transportation, wireless Internet. **Business Services:** conference facilities, business center. **Cards:** AX, CB, DC, DS, JC, MC, VI.

AAA Benefit:
Members get up to 15% off, plus Starwood Preferred Guest® bonuses.

SHERATON INNER HARBOR HOTEL

Book great rates at AAA.com

Phone: (410)962-8300 **15**

Large-scale Hotel
$199-$285 All Year

Address: 300 S Charles St 21201 **Location:** At Conway St. **Facility:** Smoke free premises. 337 units. 336 one-bedroom standard units. 1 one-bedroom suite. 14 stories, interior corridors. *Bath:* combo or shower only. **Parking:** on-site (fee) and valet. **Terms:** cancellation fee imposed. **Amenities:** video games (fee), dual phone lines, voice mail, irons, hair dryers. *Some:* CD players. **Dining:** Morton's The Steakhouse, see separate listing. **Pool(s):** heated indoor. **Leisure Activities:** saunas, exercise room. **Guest Services:** valet laundry, wireless Internet. **Business Services:** conference facilities, business center. **Cards:** AX, CB, DC, DS, JC, MC, VI.

AAA Benefit:
Members get up to 15% off, plus Starwood Preferred Guest® bonuses.

———— WHERE TO DINE ————

ABACROMBIE FINE FOOD AND ACCOMMODATIONS

Phone: 410/837-3630 **2**

American
$18-$25

Fine gourmet seafood, chicken and rack of lamb can be savored in the elegant dining room. The restaurant is on the lower level of a historic inn across from Meyerhoff Symphony Hall. Dressy casual. **Bar:** Full bar. **Reservations:** suggested. **Hours:** 5 pm-10 pm, Fri & Sat-11 pm, Sun noon-8 pm. Closed: 12/25; also Mon, Tues & 1st 2 weeks in Aug. **Address:** 58 W Biddle St 21201 **Location:** Corner Chase and W Biddle sts. **Parking:** street. **Cards:** AX, CB, DC, DS, MC, VI.

AKBAR RESTAURANT

Phone: 410/539-0944 **7**

Indian
$8-$19

A local favorite since 1986, the restaurant uses authentic Indian spices and cooking techniques to prepare the lamb, chicken, seafood and vegetarian dishes. The basement level dining room provides an intimate and comfortable setting to enjoy lunch or dinner. A lunch buffet is available every day. Casual dress. **Bar:** Full bar. **Reservations:** accepted. **Hours:** 11:30 am-11 pm, Fri & Sat-11:30 pm. Closed: 11/27. **Address:** 823 N Charles St 21201 **Location:** Between Reed and Madison sts. **Parking:** street. **Cards:** AX, DC, DS, MC, VI.

ALDO'S RISTORANTE ITALIANO

Phone: 410/727-0700 **29**

Italian
$19-$45

A true complement to Baltimore's Little Italy, the eatery definitely is worth a visit. Superb food served with expertise and personality in elegant surroundings captures the dining experience in a nutshell. To avoid a parking nightmare, use valet service. Dressy casual. **Bar:** Full bar. **Reservations:** suggested. **Hours:** 5 pm-11 pm, Fri & Sat-midnight, Sun-10 pm. Closed: 1/1, 11/27, 12/25. **Address:** 306 S High St 21202 **Location:** In Little Italy area. **Parking:** valet and street. **Cards:** AX, DC, DS, JC, MC, VI.

AMICCI'S

Phone: 410/528-1096 **20**

Italian
$7-$19

Amicci's is a very casual eatery located in the heart of the Little Italy section of Baltimore. All the classic Italian favorites along with friendly service. Do not miss the chance to order the signature Penne Amicci. Casual dress. **Bar:** Full bar. **Reservations:** accepted. **Hours:** 11:30 am-10 pm, Fri & Sat-11 pm. Closed: 11/27, 12/24, 12/25. **Address:** 231 S High St 21202 **Location:** In Little Italy area. **Parking:** street. **Cards:** AX, CB, DC, DS, MC, VI.

(See map and index starting on p. 574)

BABALU GRILL — **Phone:** 410/234-9898 (14)

Cuban
$14-$31

Just a couple blocks from the Inner Harbor is a lively, fun Cuban restaurant. The menu offers both Cuban and Latin American dishes prepared from family recipes. They have sidewalk dining seasonally and valet parking is available Sunday through Thursday. Casual dress. **Bar:** Full bar. **Reservations:** suggested. **Hours:** 5 pm-10 pm, Fri & Sat-11 pm. Closed: 1/1, 11/27, 12/25; also Sun & Mon. **Address:** 32 Market Pl 21202 **Location:** 2 blks w of Pratt St; at Powerplant Live Complex. **Parking:** valet. **Cards:** AX, DC, DS, MC, VI.

CALL M

BANJARA RESTAURANT — **Phone:** 410/962-1554 (51)

Indian
$8-$19

Very well prepared Northern Indian cuisine is served in this family-owned and -operated restaurant. A lunch buffet is available daily. Casual dress. **Bar:** Full bar. **Reservations:** suggested, weekends. **Hours:** 11:30 am-2:30 & 5-10 pm, Fri-11 pm, Sat noon-3 & 5-11 pm, Sun noon-3 & 5-10 pm. Closed: 7/4, 11/27, 12/25; also for lunch Mon. **Address:** 1017 S Charles St 21230 **Location:** Between W Cross and W Hamburg sts. **Parking:** street. **Cards:** AX, MC, VI.

BERTHA'S — **Phone:** 410/327-5795 (43)

Seafood
$7-$22

Patrons find a laid-back style at the popular landmark. The menu lists seafood and meat entrees, but this place is best known for its mussels, which can be eaten with a choice of eight sauces. Casual dress. **Bar:** Full bar. **Hours:** 11:30 am-10 pm, Fri-Sun to 11 pm. Closed major holidays. **Address:** 734 S Broadway 21231 **Location:** At Broadway and Lancaster sts; in Fells Point. **Parking:** on-site (fee). **Cards:** AX, MC, VI.

THE BICYCLE — **Phone:** 410/234-1900 (54)

American
$15-$30

This modern spot creatively fuses influences from Asia to Europe with American fresh market ingredients for a cuisine style that is uniquely their own. Try to secure a table in the cozy rear dining room that overlooks a walled garden romantically lit with twinkling lights. Dressy casual. **Bar:** Beer & wine. **Reservations:** suggested. **Hours:** 5:30 pm-10 pm, Fri & Sat-10:45 pm, Sun 5 pm-8:30 pm. Closed major holidays; also Mon. **Address:** 1444 Light St 21230 **Location:** Jct Fort Ave; in Federal Hill. **Parking:** street. **Cards:** AX, DC, MC, VI.

THE BLACK OLIVE — **Phone:** 410/276-7141 (48)

Greek
$12-$34

The family-owned restaurant serves exotic fresh fish, including numerous varieties from around the world. Choices are filleted at tableside. Also on the menu are beef and vegetarian dishes. The friendly staff is professional. Casual dress. **Bar:** Full bar. **Reservations:** suggested. **Hours:** noon-2 & 5-10 pm, Sun-9 pm. Closed: 11/27, 12/25. **Address:** 814 S Bond St 21231 **Location:** In Fells Point area. **Parking:** street. **Cards:** AX, CB, DC, DS, MC, VI.

BLUE AGAVE RESTAURANT — **Phone:** 410/576-3938 (52)

Mexican
$12-$28

Great Mexican cuisine pairs with a vast array of fine quality tequilas. The atmosphere is upbeat, and service is casual and attentive. Casual dress. **Bar:** Full bar. **Reservations:** required, Fri & Sat. **Hours:** 5 pm-close. Closed: 1/1, 12/25; also Mon. **Address:** 1032 Light St 21230 **Location:** At Poultney St; in Federal Hill area. **Parking:** street. **Cards:** AX, DS, MC, VI.

BLUE MOON CAFE' — **Phone:** 410/522-3940 (42)

American
$5-$15

The basic, cozy cafe enjoys a huge following, which means guests should expect a wait for a table. Everything is homemade, and the portions are large and reasonably priced. On Friday and Saturday, this place reopens at 11 pm and serves straight through the night. Casual dress. **Reservations:** not accepted. **Hours:** 7 am-3 pm, Fri & Sat also 11 pm-3 am. Closed: 1/1, 12/25. **Address:** 1621 Aliceanna St 21231 **Location:** At Fells Point. **Parking:** street. **Cards:** AX, DS, MC, VI.

BOCCACCIO RESTAURANT — **Phone:** 410/234-1322 (35)

Northern Italian
$12-$35

A subtle formality marks the tastefully decorated dining rooms, while the clublike lounge shows a different face. The beef carpaccio appetizer is flavorful, as is the veal chops entree. Servers in tuxedos are knowledgeable, attentive and prompt. Dressy casual. **Bar:** Full bar. **Reservations:** suggested. **Hours:** 11:30 am-2:30 & 5-10 pm, Sat from 5 pm, Sun 4 pm-9 pm. Closed: 7/4, 11/27, 12/24, 12/25. **Address:** 925 Eastern Ave 21202 **Location:** Between Exeter and Albemarle sts; in Little Italy area. **Parking:** valet and street. **Cards:** AX, DC, MC, VI.

BRASS ELEPHANT — **Phone:** 410/547-8480 (5)

American
$20-$35

Exceptionally well-prepared and creatively presented New American cuisine is served in the richly decorated, 18th-century townhouse. Flaky and flavorful, the salmon served over vodka beet sauce is a work of art. An extensive wine list is provided. Dressy casual. **Bar:** Full bar. **Reservations:** suggested. **Hours:** 5:30 pm-9:30 pm, Fri & Sat-10:30 pm, Sun 4:30 pm-9 pm. Closed major holidays; also Super Bowl Sun. **Address:** 924 N Charles St 21201 **Location:** Between E Eager and E Read sts. **Parking:** valet. **Cards:** AX, DC, DS, MC, VI.

CAESAR'S DEN — **Phone:** 410/547-0820 (18)

Italian
$9-$34

In the heart of the Little Italy, the eatery prepares first-rate Italian cuisine, including pasta, veal and seafood dishes, salads and homemade desserts. A nice wine selection complements the food offerings. Casual dress. **Bar:** Full bar. **Reservations:** suggested, weekends. **Hours:** 11:30 am-3 & 5-11 pm, Sun 3 pm-10 pm. Closed: 11/27, 12/25. **Address:** 223 S High St 21202 **Location:** In Little Italy area; jct Stiles St. **Parking:** street. **Cards:** AX, DC, DS, MC, VI.

CAPITOL CITY BREWING CO-BALTIMORE — **Phone:** 410/539-7468

American
$7-$24

The fare is simple and wholesome, and the surroundings plain and comfortable. You can find good plated full meals, or more basic and quick food while on your busy schedule. Casual dress. **Bar:** Full bar. **Reservations:** accepted. **Hours:** 11 am-11 pm, Fri & Sat-midnight. Closed: 11/27, 12/25. **Address:** 301 S Light St 21202 **Location:** I-95, exit 53, 1.6 mi se; Inner Harbor. **Parking:** no self-parking. **Cards:** AX, DC, DS, MC, VI.

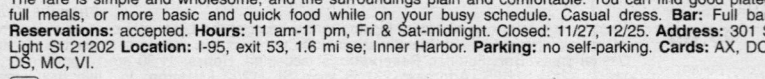

(See map and index starting on p. 574)

CHARLESTON

Regional American
$67-$102

Phone: 410/332-7373 46

American cuisine prepared from modern and traditional Southern Lowcountry recipes forges an exciting and creative menu. Guests build their own three- to six-course tasting menu from an extensive selection of hot and cold appetizers, seasonal selections, fish and shellfish, bird and game dishes, as well as meats. The skilled kitchen staff artistically presents and expertly prepares each choice, which can be paired with selections from the ample, well-chosen wine list. Dressy casual. **Bar:** Full bar. **Reservations:** suggested. **Hours:** 5:30 pm-10 pm. Closed major holidays; also Sun. **Address:** 1000 Lancaster St 21202 **Location:** Inner Harbor E; jct S Exeter and Lancaster sts; on ground floor of Sylvan Building. **Parking:** valet. **Cards:** AX, CB, DC, DS, MC, VI.

CHIAPPARELLI'S

South Italian
$8-$30

Phone: 410/837-0309 19

Established in the 1940s, the Little Italy restaurant is a longstanding favorite of the local crowd. Examples of house specials include wedding soup, Momma Chiapparelli's ravioli, veal cacciatore and homemade tiramisu. Entrees come with a large house salad. Brick walls and soft lighting lend to a comfortable atmosphere for family dining or business or social events. At dinner, valet service is offered for a fee. This place is smoke-free on Friday and Saturday. Casual dress. **Bar:** Full bar. **Reservations:** suggested, weekends. **Hours:** 11 am-10 pm, Fri & Sat-midnight. Closed: 11/27, 12/25. **Address:** 237 S High St 21202 **Location:** In Little Italy area; jct of Fawn St. **Parking:** street. **Cards:** AX, CB, DC, DS, MC, VI.

CIAO BELLA RESTAURANT

Italian
$7-$25

Phone: 410/685-7733 21

Northern and Southern Italian cuisine in the serene setting of Ciao Bella Restaurant. Many wine selections and homemade desserts. Ciao Bella means hello beautiful, and that is what you'll say when you see the food. Dressy casual. **Bar:** Full bar. **Reservations:** suggested, weekends. **Hours:** 11:30 am-10 pm, Fri & Sat-11 pm, Sun-9 pm. Closed: 1/1, 12/25. **Address:** 236 S High St 21202 **Location:** In Little Italy area. **Parking:** street. **Cards:** AX, CB, DC, DS, MC, VI.

DALESIO'S RESTAURANT OF LITTLE ITALY

Northern Italian
$7-$32

Phone: 410/539-1965 36

Friendly servers display excellent knowledge of the diverse menu, which includes many types of pasta and sauces combined in delicious dishes. Also listed are veal, chicken, beef and seafood dishes. The atmosphere is cozy. Casual dress. **Bar:** Full bar. **Reservations:** suggested, weekends. **Hours:** 11:30 am-3 & 5-10 pm, Fri-11 pm, Sat noon-3 & 5-11 pm, Sun 4 pm-9 pm. Closed: 1/1, 11/27. **Address:** 829 Eastern Ave 21202 **Location:** Between Exeter and Albermatte sts; in Little Italy area. **Parking:** street. **Cards:** AX, MC, VI.

DA MIMMO

Italian
$7-$30

Phone: 410/727-6876 15

In business since the early 1980s, the cozy restaurant invites guests to an intimate, candlelight experience. On the menu is an extensive selection of homemade pasta, fresh seafood and veal preparations, including the house specialty veal chop. Among other favorites are lobster Tetrazzini and tortellini Pavarotti. Dressy casual. **Bar:** Full bar. **Reservations:** suggested. **Hours:** 11:30 am-11 pm, Fri & Sat-midnight. Closed: 11/27, 12/25. **Address:** 217 S High St 21202 **Location:** In Little Italy area. **Parking:** on-site. **Cards:** AX, DC, DS, MC, VI.

DELLA NOTTE RISTORANTE

Italian
$10-$39

Phone: 410/837-5500 37

At the border of Little Italy, the restaurant treats patrons to views of the Inner Harbor and the city skyline. Creatively presented veal, chicken, pasta and seafood dishes are as much a feast for the eyes as for the palate. Patrons also savor the in-house-baked breads and pastries and choices from the vast wine list. A semicircular area in the large dining room exudes sophistication in feel and design. Trained servers in uniform share their knowledge of the menu as they offer suggestions. Dressy casual. Entertainment. **Bar:** Full bar. **Reservations:** suggested. **Hours:** 11 am-10 pm, Fri & Sat-midnight. Closed: 12/25. **Address:** 801 Eastern Ave 21202 **Location:** Jct President and Eastern aves; in Little Italy area. **Parking:** on-site. **Cards:** AX, DC, DS, MC, VI.

ESPN ZONE

American
$8-$18

Phone: 410/685-3776

This lively and popular tourist spot at Inner Harbor serves traditional American fare. The decor is accented with sports memorabilia. Casual dress. **Bar:** Full bar. **Reservations:** not accepted. **Hours:** 11:30 am-11 pm. Closed: 12/25. **Address:** 601 E Pratt St 21202 **Location:** At Inner Harbor. **Parking:** no self-parking. **Cards:** AX, DS, MC, VI.

GEORGE'S ON MT. VERNON SQUARE

American
$8-$40

Phone: 410/727-1314 9

Historic Mount Vernon Square is the backdrop for casual dining. This place has a full bar area and many dessert and appetizer choices. Casual dress. **Bar:** Full bar. **Reservations:** suggested. **Hours:** 6:30 am-10 pm. **Address:** 612 Cathedral St 21201 **Location:** Cathedral St and Mount Vernon Square; in Peabody Court-A Clarion Hotel. **Parking:** valet and street. **Cards:** AX, CB, DC, DS, JC, MC, VI.
(See color ad p 585)

GERMANO'S TRATTORIA

Regional Italian
$6-$19

Phone: 410/752-4515 27

Family owned since the 1970s, the relaxed, two-story restaurant has three dining areas decorated with turn-of-the-20th-century posters. Excellent entrees are topped by such decadent, made-on-the-premises desserts as tiramisu and Tuscan Napoleon. From 5 pm, valets will park your vehicle for a fee. Casual dress. **Bar:** Full bar. **Reservations:** suggested. **Hours:** 11:30 am-10 pm, Fri & Sat-11 pm. Closed: 11/27, 12/25. **Address:** 300 S High St 21202 **Location:** At S High and Fawn sts; in Little Italy area. **Parking:** street. **Cards:** AX, DC, DS, MC, VI.

(See map and index starting on p. 574)

HARD ROCK CAFE

American
$7-$25

Phone: 410/347-7625   **22**

Rock 'n' roll memorabilia decorates the walls of the popular theme restaurant. Live music on the weekends contributes to the bustling atmosphere. On the menu is a wide variety of American cuisine—from burgers and sandwiches to seafood, steaks and pasta. Casual dress. **Bar:** Full bar. **Hours:** 11 am-close. **Address:** 601 E Pratt St 21202 **Location:** At the Inner Harbor. **Parking:** no self-parking. **Cards:** AX, DC, DS, JC, MC, VI.

THE HELMAND RESTAURANT

Afghan
$12-$18

Phone: 410/752-0311   **6**

Well-prepared Afghan cuisine is served in an intimate and tasteful setting. The menu lists beef, lamb, chicken and seafood dishes, as well as extensive vegetarian selections. Succulent rack of lamb is offered Friday and Saturday evenings. Casual dress. **Bar:** Full bar. **Reservations:** suggested, weekends. **Hours:** 5 pm-10 pm, Fri & Sat-11 pm. Closed major holidays. **Address:** 806 N Charles St 21201 **Location:** Between Madison and Read sts; in Mount Vernon area. **Parking:** street. **Cards:** AX, DC, MC, VI.

JAMES JOYCE IRISH PUB & RESTAURANT

Irish
$8-$22

Phone: 410/727-5107   **39**

The home of Irish hospitality in Baltimore is the James Joyce Irish Pub & Restaurant. No need to be a writer to get great service. Casual dress. **Bar:** Full bar. **Reservations:** accepted. **Hours:** 11 am-1 am, Sun-midnight. Closed: 11/27, 12/24, 12/25. **Address:** 616 S President St 21202 **Location:** Jct President St and Eastern Ave; in Inner Harbor area. **Parking:** street. **Cards:** AX, CB, DC, DS, MC, VI.

JOHN STEVEN LTD

Steak & Seafood
$8-$29

Phone: 410/327-5561   **47**

This popular harbor tavern offers a lively bar area, which is a favorite place to dine on the house specialty of steam shrimp while chatting with friends. The more formal dining room lends to the romantic with a view of the courtyard and a comfortable setting to enjoy the popular filet mignon and lump crab cakes. Casual dress. **Bar:** Full bar. **Reservations:** accepted. **Hours:** 11 am-10 pm. Closed: 11/27, 12/25. **Address:** 1800 Thames St 21231 **Location:** Corner of S Ann and Thames sts; in Historic Fells Point area. **Parking:** street. **Cards:** AX, CB, DC, DS, MC, VI.

J. PAUL'S

American
$9-$24

Phone: 410/659-1889

In the Light Street Pavilion, the waterfront saloon affords great harbor views. The Prohibition-era dining room opens into a greenhouse area and outdoor patio. On the menu is a nice selection of salads, sandwiches and full meals. Regional barbecue dishes are a house specialty. Casual dress. **Bar:** Full bar. **Reservations:** accepted. **Hours:** 11 am-10 pm, Fri & Sat-midnight. Closed: 11/27, 12/25. **Address:** 301 Light St 21202 **Location:** At Inner Harbor; in Light Street Pavilion. **Parking:** no self-parking. **Cards:** AX, DC, DS, MC, VI.

LA SCALA RISTORANTE ITALIANO
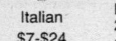
Italian
$13-$32

Phone: 410/783-9209   **32**

Innovative specials, daily seafood specials and Italian cooking at it's finest will be found at la Scala Ristorante Italiano. Do not miss the cannoli at the end of the meal. Casual dress. **Bar:** Full bar. **Reservations:** suggested. **Hours:** 4:30 pm-10 pm, Fri & Sat-11 pm, Sun 2 pm-10 pm. Closed: 1/1, 11/27, 12/24, 12/25. **Address:** 1012 Eastern Ave 21202 **Location:** Between S Exeter and S Central sts; in Little Italy area. **Parking:** street. **Cards:** AX, DC, DS, MC, VI.

LA TAVOLA RISTORANTE ITALIANO

Italian
$7-$24

Phone: 410/685-1859   **23**

Diners savor homemade pasta, breads and desserts in an elegant atmosphere. Valet parking is an option Friday and Saturday from 5 p.m. Dressy casual. **Bar:** Full bar. **Reservations:** suggested, weekends. **Hours:** 11:30 am-10 pm, Fri & Sat-10:30 pm. Closed: 1/1, 12/25; also Mon. **Address:** 248 Albemarle St 21202 **Location:** In Little Italy area. **Parking:** street. **Cards:** AX, DC, DS, MC, VI.

LITTLE HAVANA

Cuban
$6-$20

Phone: 410/837-9903   **53**

The dockside restaurant has the feel of a Caribbean island bar and an evening atmosphere to match. Among menu items are ceviche de atun (marinated tuna), camarones en salsa de langosts (shrimp in lobster broth) and oxtail pie. Guests can choose seating in a booth, at a table or on the seasonal patio. Casual dress. **Bar:** Full bar. **Reservations:** accepted. **Hours:** 4 pm-10 pm, Fri & Sat 11 am-11 pm, Sun 11 am-10 pm. Closed major holidays; also 1/1-1/7. **Address:** 1325 Key Hwy 21230 **Location:** Jct Webster St. **Parking:** on-site. **Cards:** AX, MC, VI.

LOUISIANA RESTAURANT

French
$20-$30

Phone: 410/327-2610   **41**

In the heart of Fells Point, the restaurant offers elegant dining on two levels. Carefully prepared and artfully presented menu selections fuse French and Creole flavors. Servers are knowledgeable, attentive and friendly. Dressy casual. **Bar:** Full bar. **Reservations:** suggested. **Hours:** 5 pm-10 pm, Fri & Sat-11 pm, Sun 4 pm-10 pm. Closed major holidays; also Mon. **Address:** 1708 Aliceanna St 21231 **Location:** At Fells Point. **Parking:** on-site (fee) and valet. **Cards:** AX, DC, DS, MC, VI.

LUIGI PETTI

Italian
$10-$30

Phone: 410/685-0055   **33**

The restaurant mixes elements of casual and elegant dining. On the diverse menu are many seafood and pasta choices, as well as homemade desserts. Casual dress. **Bar:** Full bar. **Reservations:** accepted. **Hours:** 11:30 am-10 pm, Fri & Sat-midnight. Closed: 11/27, 12/25. **Address:** 1002 Eastern Ave 21202 **Location:** Jct of S Exeter St; in Little Italy area. **Parking:** street. **Cards:** AX, MC, VI.

(See map and index starting on p. 574)

M & S GRILL

American
$9-$26

Phone: 410/547-9333 ㉕
This place is all about seafood, which is imported from all over the world. Among good choices are Washington state oysters, Maine clams, delicate Hawaiian escolar and tuna from Ecuador. The clublike decor is cozy, and expert staff provide able assistance. Casual dress. **Bar:** Full bar. **Reservations:** accepted. **Hours:** 11 am-11 pm, Fri & Sat-midnight; to 10 pm, Fri & Sat-11 pm in winter. **Address:** 201 E Pratt St 21202 **Location:** Just e of Light St; at Harborplace. **Parking:** no self-parking. **Cards:** AX, DC, DS, MC, VI.

MONDO BONDO ITALIAN BISTRO

Italian
$7-$15

Phone: 410/244-8080 ⑬
The intimate Italian bistro offers salads, pizza, pasta and sandwiches; sidewalk dining is available seasonally. Casual dress. **Bar:** Full bar. **Reservations:** suggested, weekends. **Hours:** 11 am-10 pm, Fri & Sat-1 am; closing hours may vary in winter. Closed major holidays. **Address:** 30 Market Pl 21202 **Location:** 2 blks w of Pratt St; at Powerplant Live Complex. **Parking:** no self-parking. **Cards:** AX, DS, MC, VI.

MORTON'S THE STEAKHOUSE

Steak House
$25-$46

Phone: 410/547-8255 ㉚
Patrons should make sure to reserve ahead for the popular, well-known steak house. Large portions, including huge cuts of fine beef and plentiful seafood, are the norm. Even the vegetables are oversized, with baked potatoes big enough for sharing. Dressy casual. **Bar:** Full bar. **Reservations:** suggested. **Hours:** 5:30 pm-11 pm, Sun 5 pm-10 pm. Closed: 1/1, 12/25. **Address:** 300 S Charles St 21201 **Location:** At Conway St; in Sheraton Inner Harbor Hotel. **Parking:** on-site (fee) and valet. **Cards:** AX, DC, MC, VI.

MO'S CRAB AND PASTA FACTORY

Seafood
$7-$28

Phone: 410/837-1600 ㉞
Mama mia! Portions of the yummy lasagna are enormous, and the same goes for other pasta, beef and chicken selections. A perfect accompaniment to any dish is the fresh salad with tasty Parmesan dressing. Casual dress. **Bar:** Full bar. **Reservations:** suggested. **Hours:** 11 am-1 am. Closed: 11/27, 12/25. **Address:** 502 Albemarle St 21202 **Location:** Just s of corner of Albemarle St and Eastern Ave. **Parking:** street. **Cards:** AX, CB, DC, DS, MC, VI.

OBRYCKI'S CRAB HOUSE AND SEAFOOD RESTAURANT

Seafood
$6-$30

Phone: 410/732-6399 ⑫
A warm, inviting atmosphere pervades the energetic restaurant, decorated with brick floors and pillars. The specialty and main attraction is steamed crabs, served on the brown-paper-covered tabletop. Casual dress. **Bar:** Full bar. **Reservations:** accepted. **Hours:** Open 3/15-11/15; 11:30 am-11 pm, Sun-9:30 pm. Closed: 3/23, 5/26, 9/1. **Address:** 1727 E Pratt St 21231 **Location:** Just e of S Broadway. **Parking:** on-site (fee). **Cards:** AX, CB, DC, DS, MC, VI.

THE OCEANAIRE SEAFOOD ROOM   *Menu on AAA.com*

Seafood
$17-$70

Phone: 443/872-0000 ㊺
Fresh fish and shellfish are flown in daily from around the globe. The sleek, handsomely designed dining room has a raw bar and is tastefully appointed in an art deco/nautical theme. The menu notes the seafood available daily and the varied preparation styles, such as broiled, grilled and blackened. Dressy casual. **Bar:** Full bar. **Reservations:** suggested. **Hours:** 5 pm-10 pm, Fri & Sat-11 pm. Closed major holidays. **Address:** 801 Aliceanna St 21202 **Location:** Jct Presidents St; in Harbor East section of the Inner Harbor. **Parking:** on-site (fee) and valet. **Cards:** AX, DS, MC, VI.

PHILLIPS HARBORPLACE

Seafood
$7-$29

Phone: 410/685-6600
In the hub of the Inner Harbor area, the busy restaurant serves an extensive selection of fresh seafood and treats diners to great harbor views. The atmosphere is festive and inviting thanks to the piano bar. A terrace opens seasonally. Casual dress. Entertainment. **Bar:** Full bar. **Reservations:** accepted. **Hours:** 11 am-10 pm, Fri & Sat-11 pm. Closed: 12/25. **Address:** 301 Light St 21202 **Location:** At Inner Harbor. **Parking:** no self-parking. **Cards:** AX, DC, DS, MC, VI.

PIERPOINT RESTAURANT & BAR

Regional American
$6-$25

Phone: 410/675-2080 ㊵
Local ingredients are what make the restaurant's creative, contemporary dishes noteworthy. The owner/chef prepares excellent smoked crab cakes and smoked corn chowder. The small neighborhood eatery buzzes with a busy cafe atmosphere. Casual dress. **Bar:** Full bar. **Reservations:** suggested, for lunch. **Hours:** 11:30 am-2 & 5-9:30 pm, Fri-10:30 pm, Sat 5:30 am-10:30 pm, Sun 10:30 am-1:30 & 4-9 pm; Sunday brunch. Closed: 1/1, 11/27, 12/25; also Mon. **Address:** 1822 Aliceanna St 21231 **Location:** In Fells Point area. **Parking:** street. **Cards:** AX, DC, DS, MC, VI.

PISCES

Seafood
$35-$40

Phone: 410/605-2835 ㉛
The big draw in the intimate rooftop restaurant is the dramatic panoramic view of the Inner Harbor. Servers are smartly attired, knowledgeable and professional. Dressy casual. **Bar:** Full bar. **Reservations:** suggested. **Hours:** 6 pm-10 pm; Sunday brunch 10 am-2 pm. Closed: 1/1, 12/25; also Mon. **Address:** 300 Light St 21202 **Location:** Facing Harborplace; in Hyatt Regency Baltimore. **Parking:** on-site and valet. **Cards:** AX, CB, DC, DS, MC, VI.

(See map and index starting on p. 574)

THE PRIME RIB

Steak & Seafood
$21-$41

Phone: 410/539-1804   ④

Generous portions of Chicago aged beef and Chesapeake Bay seafood are professionally and expertly served in an upscale and formal setting. Smoking is permitted in the lounge. Jackets are required. Semi-formal attire. Entertainment. **Bar:** Full bar. **Reservations:** suggested. **Hours:** 5 pm-11 pm, Sun 4 pm-10 pm. Closed: 11/27, 12/25. **Address:** 1101 N Calvert St 21202 **Location:** Jct of Calvert and Chase sts; in the Horizon House Building. **Parking:** valet. **Cards:** AX, CB, DC, MC, VI.

ROCCO'S CAPRICCIO

Northern Italian
$10-$47

Phone: 410/685-2710   ㉘

Soft lighting, hand-painted walls and a professionally attired staff set the tone at this intimate restaurant. The staff is versed in the preparation of such menu selections as the house specialty veal chop, which is marinated with fresh herbs, broiled and served in its natural juices. A flavorful tomato and meat sauce tops the tortellini. Dressy casual. **Bar:** Full bar. **Reservations:** suggested, weekends. **Hours:** 5 pm-11:30 pm, Sat & Sun 11:30 am-12:30 am. Closed: 11/27, 12/25. **Address:** 846 Fawn St 21202 **Location:** In Little Italy area. **Parking:** street. **Cards:** AX, CB, DC, DS, MC, VI.

ROY'S

Hawaiian
$19-$38

Phone: 410/659-0099   ㊹

Enjoy fusion of fresh Pacific seafood, French sauces and Asian seasonings. The ever-changing menu has many entrees, grilled salmon, barbecue lamb rack and signature dessert, chocolate souffle. Dressy casual. **Bar:** Full bar. **Reservations:** suggested. **Hours:** 5:30 pm-10:30 pm, Sat from 5 pm, Sun 5 pm-9 pm. Closed: 11/27, 12/25. **Address:** 720 B Aliceanna St 21202 **Location:** Jct Presidents St. **Parking:** on-site (fee) and valet. **Cards:** AX, CB, DC, DS, JC, MC, VI.

CALL

THE RUSTY SCUPPER RESTURANT

American
$8-$44

Phone: 410/727-3678   ㊺

Guests enjoy incredible Inner Harbor views from the dining area. This place is known for seafood, particularly the not-to-be-missed crab cakes. Brunch is served Sundays from 11 am to 2 pm. Casual dress. **Bar:** Full bar. **Reservations:** suggested. **Hours:** 11:30 am-10 pm, Fri & Sat-11 pm. Closed: 12/25. **Address:** 402 Key Hwy 21230 **Location:** In Inner Harbor. **Parking:** on-site (fee). **Cards:** AX, CB, DC, DS, JC, MC, VI.

RUTH'S CHRIS STEAK HOUSE-PIER 5

Steak House
$19-$39

Phone: 410/230-0033   ㊳

The main fare is steak, which is prepared from several cuts of prime beef and cooked to perfection, but the menu also lists lamb, chicken and seafood dishes. Guests should come hungry because the side dishes, which are among the a la carte offerings, could make a meal in themselves. Dressy casual. **Bar:** Full bar. **Reservations:** suggested. **Hours:** 5 pm-10 pm, Fri & Sat-11 pm, Sun 4 pm-9 pm. Closed: 1/1, 11/27, 12/25; also Super Bowl Sun. **Address:** 711 Eastern Ave 21202 **Location:** In Inner Harbor, at Pier 5. **Parking:** on-site (fee) and valet. **Cards:** AX, DC, DS, MC, VI.

CALL

SABATINO'S

Italian
$10-$35

Phone: 410/727-2667   ㉔

Excellent wine, rich desserts and flavorful veal are among offerings at the cozy, warm restaurant. Attentive, friendly staff members are familiar both with the menu and the locals who frequent the place. Those with lighter appetites may request half-orders at lunch. Casual dress. **Bar:** Full bar. **Reservations:** suggested, weekends. **Hours:** noon-midnight, Fri & Sat-3 am. Closed: 11/27, 12/25. **Address:** 901 Fawn St 21202 **Location:** Fawn and S High sts; in Little Italy. **Parking:** on-site (fee) and street. **Cards:** AX, CB, DC, DS, MC, VI.

SAFFRON

Indian
$18-$30

Phone: 410/528-1616   ⑧

The setting is sultry and exotic with walls draped in rich reds and ceilings of flying carpets; the cuisine is equally imaginative as the chef fuses classic Indian influences with modern American and French flavors and techniques. Dressy casual. **Bar:** Full bar. **Reservations:** suggested. **Hours:** 5 pm-9 pm, Fri & Sat-10 pm. Closed major holidays; also Mon. **Address:** 802 N Charles St 21201 **Location:** Just n of E Madison St. **Parking:** street. **Cards:** AX, DC, DS, MC, VI.

SOTTO SOPRA

Italian
$10-$35

Phone: 410/625-0534   ⑪

Striking features of the stylish, Renaissance-style dining room include full-wall murals and framed mirrors. The owner/chef's imagination is evident in well-prepared dishes, such as poppy/sesame seed-crusted tuna. Desserts here are wonderful. Valet parking service is offered at dinnertime for a fee. Dressy casual. **Bar:** Full bar. **Reservations:** suggested. **Hours:** 11:30 am-2:30 & 5:30-9:30 pm, Tues-Thurs to 10:30 pm, Fri-11:30 pm, Sat 5:30 pm-11:30 pm, Sun 5 pm-9 pm. Closed: 5/26, 7/4. **Address:** 405 N Charles St 21201 **Location:** Between Mulberry and Franklin sts; in the Mount Vernon area. **Parking:** street. **Cards:** AX, DC, DS, MC, VI.

TAPAS TEATRO

Spanish
$7-$22

Phone: 410/332-0110   ①

With its location adjacent to the Charles Theater, this is a popular pre and post movie spot for locals. The smell of popcorn from next door competes with attention for the scents from the open kitchen. The menu here is all appetizer-sized portions, so get set to sample. Many dishes are authentic Spanish, but flavors from Mediterranean and Asian cuisines show up also. Casual dress. **Bar:** Full bar. **Hours:** 5 pm-11 pm, Fri-midnight, Sat 4 pm-midnight, Sun 4 pm-11 pm. Closed major holidays; also Mon. **Address:** 1711 N Charles St 21201 **Location:** Jct E Lanvale St. **Parking:** street. **Cards:** AX, MC, VI.

(See map and index starting on p. 574)

TEN-O-SIX RESTAURANT

Thai

$11-$22

Phone: 410/528-2146   50

Since 1999 this chef-owned Thai restaurant has attracted the locals. The kitchen staff is skilled in both Thai and American cooking, offering dishes such as drunken noodles, Thai orange chicken, wild Alaskan king salmon and rack of wild boar, to mention a few. Diners may request the degree of spiciness from a range of 1-6, with 6 being Native Thai. Casual dress. **Bar:** Beer & wine. **Reservations:** suggested, weekends. **Hours:** 5 pm-10 pm, Sat-10:30 pm, Sun 4 pm-9 pm. Closed: 11/27; also Mon. **Address:** 1006 Light St 21230 **Location:** Between E Hamburg and Poultney sts. **Parking:** street. **Cards:** MC, VI.

THAI LANDING

Thai

$9-$17

Phone: 410/727-1234   3

Guests of the unpretentious little restaurant are greeted with a warm welcome by friendly servers who are willing to assist with menu choices. Good food descriptions indicate the degree of spiciness of each item. Vegetarian dishes are available. Casual dress. **Bar:** Full bar. **Hours:** 11:30 am-3 & 5-10 pm, Fri & Sat 5 pm-10:30 pm. Closed major holidays; also Sun. **Address:** 1207 N Charles St 21201 **Location:** Jct W Biddle St, just n. **Parking:** street. **Cards:** MC, VI.

TIO PEPE RESTAURANT

Spanish

$11-$35

Phone: 410/539-4675   10

Locals are attracted to the Spanish cuisine, which is served in basement-level dining rooms of the row house Tio Pepe calls home. The house specialty is suckling pig, but almost any of the menu choices is well worth a try. Service is attentive. Semi-formal attire. **Bar:** Full bar. **Reservations:** required, for dinner. **Hours:** 11:30 am-2:30 & 5-10 pm, Fri-11 pm, Sat 5 pm-11:30 pm, Sun 4 pm-10 pm. Closed major holidays. **Address:** 10 E Franklin St 21202 **Location:** Just e of N Charles St. **Parking:** street. **Cards:** AX, DC, DS, MC, VI.

TIR NA NOG IRISH BAR & GRILL

Irish

$9-$26

Phone: 410/483-8968   26

Casual dress. **Bar:** Full bar. **Reservations:** suggested. **Hours:** 11 am-11 pm, Sat & Sun from 10 am. Closed: 11/27, 12/25. **Address:** 201 E Pratt St 21202 **Location:** At Harborplace; in Pratt Street Pavilion. **Parking:** no self-parking. **Cards:** AX, DS, MC, VI.

VELLEGGIA'S

Italian

$12-$31

Phone: 410/685-2620   16

In business since the mid-1930s, the simple, comfortable restaurant mixes a contemporary feel with Old World charm. Pasta dishes, homemade from family recipes, are at the heart of the traditional menu. The wait staff is knowledgeable and friendly. The parking lot is small. Casual dress. **Reservations:** suggested, weekends. **Hours:** 11 am-11 pm, Fri & Sat-midnight, Sun 10 am-11 pm. Closed: 12/24, 12/25. **Address:** 829 E Pratt St 21202 **Location:** Corner of E Pratt and Albemarle sts; in Little Italy area. **Parking:** street. **Cards:** AX, DS, MC, VI.

CALL ⓔⓜ ⬛

WINDOWS

American

$13-$32

Phone: 410/685-8439   17

The contemporary, smoke-free dining room affords a spectacular view of the Inner Harbor. Although crab dishes are the specialty, the menu also lists chicken, beef, pasta and fresh fish preparations. There's also a breakfast and lunch buffet. Casual dress. **Bar:** Full bar. **Reservations:** suggested. **Hours:** 6:30 am-10 pm. **Address:** 202 E Pratt St, Fl 5 21202 **Location:** Opposite Inner Harbor; in Renaissance Baltimore Harborplace Hotel. **Parking:** on-site (fee) and valet. **Cards:** AX, CB, DC, DS, JC, MC, VI.

———— *The following restaurant has not been evaluated by AAA* ————
but is listed for your information only.

MATSURI

fyi

Phone: 410/752-8561

Not evaluated. Matsuri offers traditional Japanese Cuisine featuring sushi and sashimi. Friendly atmosphere and wait staff. **Address:** 1105 S Charles St 21230 **Location:** Center.

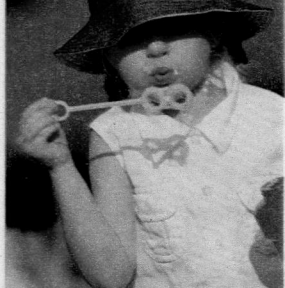

BALTIMORE pop. 651,154 (See map and index starting on p. 578)

------- WHERE TO STAY -------

BEST WESTERN HOTEL & CONFERENCE CENTER · *Book great rates at AAA.com* · Phone: 410/633-9500 · **3**

AAA SAVE
▽▽▽
Small-scale Hotel
Rates not provided

Address: 5625 O'Donnell St 21224 **Location:** I-95, exit 57, just e. Located at the north side of Ft McHenry Tunnel. **Facility:** 175 units. 172 one-bedroom standard units. 3 one-bedroom suites with whirlpools. 12 stories, interior corridors. *Bath:* combo or shower only. **Parking:** on-site. **Amenities:** voice mail, safes (fee), irons, hair dryers. **Pool(s):** heated indoor. **Leisure Activities:** sauna, whirlpool, exercise room. **Guest Services:** valet and coin laundry, area transportation-Inner Harbor, wireless Internet. **Business Services:** conference facilities, business center. **Free Special Amenities: expanded continental breakfast and high-speed Internet.** *(See color ad below)*

AAA Benefit:
Members save 10% everyday, plus an exclusive frequent stay program.

DOUBLETREE INN AT THE COLONNADE-A HILTON HOTEL · *Book great rates at AAA.com* · Phone: (410)235-5400 · **2**

AAA SAVE
▽▽▽
Small-scale Hotel
$109-$309 All Year

Address: 4 W University Pkwy 21218 **Location:** I-83, exit 9A, 0.5 mi e on Cold Springs Ln to Roland Ave/University Pkwy, then 1 mi s. **Facility:** Smoke free premises. 125 units. 89 one-bedroom standard units. 34 one- and 2 two-bedroom suites, some with whirlpools. 11 stories, interior corridors. *Bath:* combo or shower only. **Parking:** on-site (fee) and valet. **Amenities:** video games (fee), dual phone lines, voice mail, irons, hair dryers. **Pool(s):** heated indoor. **Leisure Activities:** whirlpools, sun decks, exercise room. **Guest Services:** valet laundry, wireless Internet. **Business Services:** conference facilities, business center. **Cards:** AX, DC, DS, MC, VI. **Free Special Amenities: newspaper and high-speed Internet.**

HILTON GARDEN INN · Phone: 410/234-0065

[fyi]
Small-scale Hotel
Rates not provided

Too new to rate, opening scheduled for September 2007. **Address:** 625 S President St 21202 **Location:** Located in the Harbor East section of the Inner Harbor. **Amenities:** 183 units.

HOMEWOOD SUITES · Phone: 410/234-0999

[fyi]
Small-scale Hotel
Rates not provided

Too new to rate. **Address:** 625 S President St 21202 **Location:** Located in the Harbor East section of the Inner Harbor. **Amenities:** 165 units.

THE INN AT CROSS KEYS · *Book at AAA.com* · Phone: (410)532-6900 · **1**

▽▽▽
Small-scale Hotel
$185 All Year

Address: 100 Village Sq 21210 **Location:** I-83, exit 10A (Northern Pkwy), just e, then 0.4 mi s on Falls Rd; in Village of Cross Keys. **Facility:** 147 units. 146 one-bedroom standard units. 1 one-bedroom suite. 4 stories, interior corridors. *Bath:* combo or shower only. **Terms:** cancellation fee imposed. **Amenities:** video games (fee), voice mail, irons, hair dryers. **Pool(s):** outdoor. **Leisure Activities:** jogging, exercise room. **Guest Services:** valet laundry, area transportation, wireless Internet. **Business Services:** conference facilities, PC (fee). **Cards:** AX, CB, DC, DS, JC, MC, VI.

QUALITY INN HARBOR SOUTH · *Book great rates at AAA.com* · Phone: (410)646-1700 · **4**

▽▽ ▽▽
Motel
$99-$119 3/1-9/30
$89-$99 10/1-2/28

Address: 1401 Bloomfield Ave 21227 **Location:** I-95, exit 50A, just e. **Facility:** 177 one-bedroom standard units. 4 stories, exterior corridors. *Bath:* combo or shower only. **Parking:** on-site. **Terms:** cancellation fee imposed. **Amenities:** voice mail, safes (fee), irons, hair dryers. *Some:* high-speed Internet. **Pool(s):** outdoor. **Leisure Activities:** limited exercise equipment. **Guest Services:** valet laundry, wireless Internet. **Business Services:** meeting rooms. **Cards:** AX, DC, DS, JC, MC, VI.

▼ *See AAA listing above* ▼

(See map and index starting on p. 578)

———— **WHERE TO DINE** ————

ACROPOLIS RESTAURANT
Phone: 410/675-7882   ⑤

Greek
$6-$20

Friendly, efficient servers deliver generous portions of such Greek favorites as spanakopita (spinach pie) and roast lamb. Those with a sweet tooth might want to try baklava for dessert; the thin layers of phyllo pastry drenched in spiced honey syrup are a real treat. Casual dress. **Bar:** Full bar. **Reservations:** accepted. **Hours:** 11 am-10 pm, Fri & Sat-11 pm. **Address:** 4718 Eastern Ave 21224 **Location:** Jct Oldham St. **Parking:** street. **Cards:** AX, CB, DC, DS, MC, VI.

CAFE HON
Phone: 410-243-1230   ④

American
$6-$15

Nostalgia and kitsch intermingle in this neighborhood spot which celebrates the women of the city, the "hons." Sample fresh-cut fries in gravy, "better than Mom's" meatloaf and fresh-baked desserts including coconut cake and fruit crumble pies. Casual dress. **Bar:** Full bar. **Hours:** 7 am-9 pm, Fri-10 pm, Sat 9 am-10 pm, Sun 9 am-8 pm. Closed major holidays. **Address:** 1002 W 36th St 21211 **Location:** Just e of jct Roland Ave; in Hampden. **Parking:** street. **Cards:** AX, DC, DS, MC, VI.

DONNA'S COFFEE BAR AND CAFE
Phone: 410-532-7611   ①

Mediterranean
$8-$20

This trendy cafe specializes in stylish Mediterranean fare including roasted vegetable sandwiches on olive bread and walnut-crusted chicken breasts with Gorgonzola sauce. Casual dress. **Bar:** Full bar. **Reservations:** not accepted. **Hours:** 9 am-9 pm, Fri-10 pm, Sat 10 am-10 pm, Sun 10 am-9 pm. Closed: 11/27, 12/25. **Address:** 40 Village Sq 21210 **Location:** I-83, exit 10A, just e, then 0.4 mi s on Falls Rd; in Village of Cross Keys. **Parking:** on-site. **Cards:** AX, CB, DC, MC, VI.

EASTERN HOUSE RESTAURANT
Phone: 410/342-7117   ⑦

American
$5-$26

The popular neighborhood eatery serves large portions, which keep guests coming back. Dishes include soups, salads, seafood, chicken, pork and beef. Service is friendly and efficient. Booth and table seating are available. Casual dress. **Bar:** Full bar. **Reservations:** accepted. **Hours:** 8 am-9 pm, Fri & Sat-10 pm. Closed: 1/1. **Address:** 3706 Eastern Ave 21224 **Location:** Jct Conkling St, just e. **Parking:** street. **Cards:** AX, DC, DS, MC, VI.

IKAROS RESTAURANT
Phone: 410/633-3750   ⑥

Greek
$6-$20

The well-established, urban, neighborhood restaurant offers a number of beef and seafood selections, along with homemade Greek pastry. Guests can't go wrong when ordering the Greek salad, an enormous helping traditionally prepared with feta and olives. Casual dress. **Bar:** Full bar. **Hours:** 11 am-10 pm, Fri & Sat-11 pm. Closed: 11/27, 12/25; also Tues. **Address:** 4805 Eastern Ave 21224 **Location:** I-95, exit 59, 1.3 mi w; jct Oldham St. **Parking:** street. **Cards:** AX, CB, DC, DS, MC, VI.

KIBBY'S RESTAURANT
Phone: 410/644-8716   ⑩

American
$5-$38

A simple, pleasant experience awaits diners at the casual, comfortable restaurant. French onion soup is loaded with onions and smothered in cheese, and the tasty sour beef is served with a dumpling. Servers are friendly and knowledgeable. Casual dress. **Bar:** Full bar. **Reservations:** accepted. **Hours:** 11 am-10 pm, Fri & Sat-midnight. Closed: 7/4, 11/27, 12/25. **Address:** 3450 Wilkens Ave 21229 **Location:** I-695, exit 12B (Wilkens Ave), 1.5 mi e; I-95, exit 50B (Caton Ave), 0.3 mi n to Wilkens Ave, then w. **Parking:** on-site. **Cards:** AX, DC, DS, MC, VI.

LOCO HOMBRE
Phone: 410/889-2233   ③

Mexican
$8-$19

Located in the Roland Park neighborhood, the popular family restaurant offers a diverse menu of Mexican entrees as well as Tex-Mex nouvelle entrees like southwestern chicken salad and Baja fish taco. Casual dress. **Bar:** Full bar. **Reservations:** not accepted. **Hours:** 11 am-10 pm, Fri & Sat-11 pm. Closed: 11/27, 12/25. **Address:** 413 W Cold Spring Ln 21210 **Location:** I-83, exit 9A-B, 0.9 mi e. **Parking:** on-site. **Cards:** AX, DS, MC, VI.

NACHO MAMA'S
Phone: 410/675-0898   ⑨

Mexican
$6-$14

The little restaurant has a big menu that lists chili, quesadillas, burritos, enchiladas, fajitas and tacos. Also featured are salads, wings, burgers, sandwiches and ribs. Service is fast and friendly. Casual dress. **Bar:** Full bar. **Reservations:** not accepted. **Hours:** 11 am-12:30 am, Fri & Sat-1 am. Closed: 3/23, 12/25. **Address:** 2907 O'Donnell St 21224 **Location:** Opposite Canton Square. **Parking:** street. **Cards:** AX, MC, VI.

PETIT LOUIS BISTRO
Phone: 410/366-9393   ②

French
$11-$24

Petit Louis is a fine French Bistro with an amazing menu and wine selections. Order more Bread when you go. Casual dress. **Bar:** Full bar. **Reservations:** suggested, weekends. **Hours:** 11:30 am-2 & 5-10 pm, Fri-11 pm, Sat 5 pm-11 pm, Sun 10:30 am-2 & 5-9 pm, Mon 5 pm-10 pm. Closed: 12/25. **Address:** 4800 Roland Ave 21210 **Location:** I-83, exit 9, 1.2 mi e on Cold Spring Ln, then 1 mi n. **Parking:** on-site. **Cards:** AX, DC, DS, MC, VI.

SAMOS RESTAURANT
Phone: 410/675-5292   ⑧

Greek
$5-$23

The popular Greek restaurant has a casual feel. All items are made from scratch and served in ample portions. Prices are reasonable. Casual dress. **Hours:** 10 am-9 pm. Closed major holidays; also Sun. **Address:** 600 Oldham St 21224 **Location:** Corner of Fleet St E. **Parking:** street.

The Baltimore Vicinity

ABERDEEN pop. 13,842

——— **WHERE TO STAY** ———

CLARION ABERDEEN   *Book great rates at AAA.com*   **Phone:** (410)273-6300

(AAA) (SAVE)

▼▼ ▼▼
Small-scale Hotel
$89-$119 All Year

Address: 980 Hospitality Way 21001 **Location:** I-95, exit 85, just e on SR 22. Located near shopping center. **Facility:** 134 units. 131 one-bedroom standard units. 3 one-bedroom suites. 4 stories, interior corridors. **Parking:** on-site. **Amenities:** video games (fee), high-speed Internet, dual phone lines, voice mail, irons, hair dryers. **Pool(s):** outdoor. **Leisure Activities:** limited exercise equipment, volleyball. **Guest Services:** valet and coin laundry. **Business Services:** conference facilities, business center. **Cards:** AX, CB, DC, DS, JC, MC, VI. **Free Special Amenities: full breakfast and early check-in/late check-out.**

[S/D] [¶↑] [Y] CALL [&M] [≈] [✸] [☐] [⊟] [▭] / SOME UNITS [🛏] [✕]

COURTYARD BY MARRIOTT-ABERDEEN   **Phone:** 410/273-9228

(fyi)
Small-scale Hotel
$129-$159 All Year

Too new to rate. **Address:** 630 Long Dr 21001 **Location:** I-95, exit 85, 0.5 mi w on SR 22. **Amenities:** 120 units, coffeemakers, microwaves. **Cards:** AX, DS, MC, VI.

AAA Benefit:
Members save 5% off of the best available rate.

HOLIDAY INN CHESAPEAKE HOUSE   *Book great rates at AAA.com*   **Phone:** (410)272-8100

(AAA) (SAVE)

▼▼▼ ▼▼▼
Small-scale Hotel
$135-$200 All Year

Address: 1007 Beards Hill Rd 21001 **Location:** I-95, exit 85, just e on SR 22. **Facility:** 120 one-bedroom standard units. 5 stories, interior corridors. *Bath:* combo or shower only. **Parking:** on-site. **Amenities:** voice mail, irons, hair dryers. *Some:* high-speed Internet. **Pool(s):** heated indoor. **Leisure Activities:** sun deck, limited exercise equipment. **Guest Services:** valet and coin laundry, wireless Internet. **Business Services:** conference facilities, business center. **Cards:** AX, CB, DC, DS, MC, VI. **Free Special Amenities: full breakfast and newspaper.**

[S/D] [¶↑] [Y] CALL [&M] [≈] [✸] [☐] [⊟] [▭] / SOME UNITS [✕]

LA QUINTA INN ABERDEEN   *Book great rates at AAA.com*   **Phone:** (410)272-6000

(AAA) (SAVE)

▲▼▲ ▲▼▲
Small-scale Hotel
$100-$130 All Year

Address: 793 W Bel Air Ave 21001 **Location:** I-95, exit 85, just e. Located in a commercial area. **Facility:** 112 units. 102 one-bedroom standard units. 10 one-bedroom suites, some with whirlpools. 2 stories (no elevator), interior corridors. *Bath:* combo or shower only. **Parking:** on-site. **Amenities:** high-speed Internet, voice mail, irons, hair dryers. **Pool(s):** outdoor. **Leisure Activities:** exercise room. **Guest Services:** valet and coin laundry, wireless Internet. **Business Services:** meeting rooms. **Cards:** AX, DC, DS, MC, VI. **Free Special Amenities: expanded continental breakfast and high-speed Internet.**

[S/D] [¶↑] [Y] CALL [&M] [≈] [✸] [▭] / SOME UNITS [🛏] [✕] [☐] [⊟]

LaQUINTA
INNS & SUITES
AAA Benefit:
Members save 10% everyday.

▼ See AAA listing p 613 ▼

RED ROOF INN   *Book at AAA.com*   Phone: 410/273-7800

Motel
Rates not provided

Address: 988 Hospitality Way 21001 **Location:** I-95, exit 85, just e on SR 22. **Facility:** 109 one-bedroom standard units. 2 stories (no elevator), exterior corridors. *Bath:* combo or shower only. **Parking:** on-site. **Amenities:** voice mail. **Guest Services:** wireless Internet.

RESIDENCE INN-ABERDEEN   Phone: 410/273-9226

[fyi]
Small-scale Hotel
$154-$189 All Year

Too new to rate. **Address:** 630 Long Dr 21001 **Location:** I-95, exit 85, 0.5 mi w on SR 22. **Amenities:** 78 units, pets, coffeemakers, microwaves, refrigerators. **Cards:** AX, DS, MC, VI.

AAA Benefit:
Members save 5% off of the best available rate.

SUPER 8 MOTEL ABERDEEN   *Book great rates at AAA.com*   Phone: 410/272-5420

Small-scale Hotel
Rates not provided

Address: 1008 Beards Hill Rd 21001 **Location:** I-95, exit 85, just e on SR 22. **Facility:** 62 one-bedroom standard units. 3 stories (no elevator), interior corridors. **Parking:** on-site. **Amenities:** safes (fee), hair dryers. **Guest Services:** wireless Internet.

——————— **WHERE TO DINE** ———————

LEE'S HUNAN RESTAURANT   Phone: 410/272-6611
Chinese
$5-$16

Although "Hunan" stakes its place in the restaurant's name, this shopping-plaza spot also turns out Szechuan and Cantonese dishes. Efficient, helpful servers circulate through the comfortable setting. Sprawling buffets are set up Tuesday through Friday from 11 a.m. to 2 p.m. and Sunday from noon to 3 p.m. Casual dress. **Bar:** Full bar. **Reservations:** accepted. **Hours:** 11 am-9:30 pm, Fri-10:30 pm, Sat noon-10:30 pm, Sun noon-9:30 pm. Closed: 11/27. **Address:** 971 G Beards Hill Rd 21001 **Location:** I-95, exit 85, just e; in Center at Beards Hill. **Parking:** on-site. **Cards:** AX, DC, DS, MC, VI.

THE OLIVE TREE RESTAURANT   Phone: 410/272-6217
Italian
$7-$25

Convenient to the interstate, the casual restaurant maintains the air of Italy. The bountiful offerings the kitchen concocts range from homemade pasta to veal, seafood and poultry selections. Save room for the tempting homemade desserts. Casual dress. **Bar:** Full bar. **Reservations:** accepted. **Hours:** 11 am-10:30 pm, Fri & Sat-11 pm. Closed: 12/25. **Address:** 1005 Beards Hill Rd 21001 **Location:** I-95, exit 85, just e on SR 22. **Parking:** on-site. **Cards:** AX, DS, MC, VI.

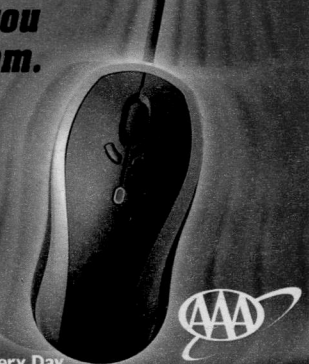

ANNAPOLIS pop. 35,838

——— **WHERE TO STAY** ———

ANNAPOLIS COMFORT INN   *Book at AAA.com*   **Phone:** (410)757-8500

Small-scale Hotel
$100-$175 3/1-11/30
$95-$150 12/1-2/28

Address: 76 Old Mill Bottom Rd N 21409 **Location:** 4 mi e on US 50 and 301, exit 28, 0.3 mi n to Old Mill Bottom Rd N, then just e; 3 mi w of Bay Bridge. Located in a semi-rural area. **Facility:** 59 one-bedroom standard units, some with whirlpools. 2 stories (no elevator), interior corridors. **Parking:** on-site. **Terms:** 2-4 night minimum stay - seasonal and/or weekends. **Amenities:** high-speed Internet, irons, hair dryers. **Leisure Activities:** limited exercise equipment. **Guest Services:** coin laundry. **Business Services:** fax (fee). **Cards:** AX, CB, DC, DS, JC, MC, VI.

ANNAPOLIS MARRIOTT WATERFRONT HOTEL   *Book great rates at AAA.com*   **Phone:** 410/268-7555

Large-scale Hotel
$263-$351 All Year

Address: 80 Compromise St 21401 **Location:** At the city dock. **Facility:** Smoke free premises. 150 one-bedroom standard units, some with whirlpools. 6 stories, interior corridors. *Bath:* combo or shower only. **Parking:** valet. **Terms:** check-in 4 pm. **Amenities:** CD players, high-speed Internet (fee), voice mail, irons, hair dryers. **Dining:** Pusser's Caribbean Grill, see separate listing. **Leisure Activities:** exercise room. *Fee:* marina. **Guest Services:** valet laundry, airport transportation (fee)-Baltimore-Washington International Airport. **Business Services:** conference facilities, business center. **Cards:** AX, DC, DS, JC, MC, VI.

Marriott
HOTELS & RESORTS

AAA Benefit:
Members save 5%
off of the best
available rate.

▼ *See AAA listing p 604* ▼

BEST WESTERN ANNAPOLIS

Book great rates at AAA.com

Phone: 410/224-2800

Motel
Rates not provided

Address: 2520 Riva Rd 21401 **Location:** 2.3 mi e on US 50 and 301, exit 22, just e. Located in a commercial area, near shopping center. **Facility:** 151 one-bedroom standard units. 2 stories (no elevator), interior/exterior corridors. **Bath:** combo or shower only. **Parking:** on-site. **Amenities:** voice mail, irons, hair dryers. *Fee:* video games, safes. *Some:* high-speed Internet. **Pool(s):** outdoor. **Leisure Activities:** limited exercise equipment. **Guest Services:** coin laundry, wireless Internet. **Business Services:** meeting rooms. *(See color ad below)*

AAA Benefit:
Members save 10% everyday, plus an exclusive frequent stay program.

COUNTRY INN & SUITES BY CARLSON-ANNAPOLIS

Book at AAA.com

Phone: (410)571-6700

Small-scale Hotel
$170-$189 All Year

Address: 2600 Housley Rd 21401 **Location:** US 50 and 301, exit 23 eastbound; exit 23B westbound, 1 mi w on SR 450. Located opposite shopping center. **Facility:** 100 units. 45 one-bedroom standard units, some with whirlpools. 55 one-bedroom suites. 4 stories, interior corridors. **Bath:** combo or shower only. **Parking:** on-site. **Amenities:** video library, DVD players, voice mail, irons, hair dryers. **Pool(s):** heated indoor. **Leisure Activities:** whirlpool, exercise room. **Guest Services:** valet and coin laundry, area transportation, wireless Internet. **Business Services:** meeting rooms, PC. **Cards:** AX, CB, DC, DS, JC, MC, VI.

COURTYARD BY MARRIOTT ANNAPOLIS

Book great rates at AAA.com

Phone: 410/266-1555

Small-scale Hotel
$144-$174 All Year

Address: 2559 Riva Rd 21401 **Location:** 2.3 mi sw on US 50 and 301, exit 22, 0.3 mi s. **Facility:** Smoke free premises. 149 units. 137 one-bedroom standard units. 12 one-bedroom suites. 3 stories, interior corridors. **Bath:** combo or shower only. **Parking:** on-site. **Amenities:** high-speed Internet, voice mail, irons, hair dryers. **Pool(s):** heated indoor. **Leisure Activities:** whirlpool, limited exercise equipment. **Guest Services:** valet and coin laundry. **Business Services:** meeting rooms, PC (fee). **Cards:** AX, DC, DS, JC, MC, VI.

AAA Benefit:
Members save 5% off of the best available rate.

DOUBLETREE HOTEL ANNAPOLIS

Book great rates at AAA.com

Phone: 410/224-3150

Small-scale Hotel
Rates not provided

Address: 210 Holiday Ct 21401 **Location:** 2.3 mi sw on US 50 and 301, exit 22 to Riva Rd, 0.3 mi n. Located in a commercial area, near shopping center. **Facility:** 219 one-bedroom standard units. 3-6 stories, interior corridors. **Bath:** combo or shower only. **Parking:** on-site. **Terms:** check-in 4 pm. **Amenities:** video games (fee), dual phone lines, voice mail, irons, hair dryers. **Pool(s):** outdoor. **Leisure Activities:** exercise room. **Guest Services:** valet laundry, area transportation-within 5 mi, wireless Internet. **Business Services:** conference facilities, business center.

EXTENDED STAYAMERICA-ANNAPOLIS/NAVAL ACADEMY

Book at AAA.com

Phone: (410)571-9988

Small-scale Hotel
$134-$144 3/1-11/1
$95-$105 11/2-2/28

Address: 1 Womack Dr 21401 **Location:** 2.3 mi sw on US 50 and 301, exit 22, just s on Admiral Cochrane Dr, then just n on Spruill Rd. Located in business park area. **Facility:** 101 one-bedroom standard units with efficiencies. 3 stories, interior corridors. **Bath:** combo or shower only. **Parking:** on-site. **Terms:** office hours 7 am-11 pm. **Amenities:** voice mail, irons. **Guest Services:** coin laundry, wireless Internet. **Cards:** AX, DC, DS, JC, MC, VI.

▼ *See AAA listing above* ▼

HAMPTON INN & SUITES-ANNAPOLIS

Phone: 410/571-0200

Small-scale Hotel
Rates not provided

Address: 124 Womack Dr 21401 **Location:** 2.3 mi sw on US 50 and 301, exit 22, just s, then just e on Admiral Cochrane Dr, just n on Spruill Rd, then just w. Located in a business park. **Facility:** 117 units. 86 one-bedroom standard units. 31 one-bedroom suites with efficiencies. 5 stories, interior corridors. *Bath:* combo or shower only. **Parking:** on-site. **Amenities:** video games (fee), dual phone lines, voice mail, irons, hair dryers. **Pool(s):** heated outdoor. **Leisure Activities:** exercise room. **Guest Services:** valet and coin laundry, wireless Internet. **Business Services:** meeting rooms, business center.

HILTON GARDEN INN ANNAPOLIS   *Book great rates at AAA.com*

Phone: 410/266-9006

Small-scale Hotel
Rates not provided

Address: 305 Harry S. Truman Pkwy 21401 **Location:** 2.3 mi sw on US 50 and 301, 0.4 mi s. **Facility:** 126 units. 122 one-bedroom standard units. 4 one-bedroom suites with whirlpools. 4 stories, interior corridors. *Bath:* combo or shower only. **Parking:** on-site. **Amenities:** DVD players, voice mail, safes, irons, hair dryers. **Pool(s):** outdoor. **Leisure Activities:** whirlpool, exercise room. **Guest Services:** complimentary and valet laundry, wireless Internet. **Business Services:** meeting rooms, business center.

HISTORIC INNS OF ANNAPOLIS   *Book at AAA.com*

Phone: (410)263-2641

Historic
Small-scale Hotel
$139-$259 All Year

Address: 58 State Circle 21401 **Location:** Facing the State Capitol; in historic district. **Facility:** Three historic buildings comprise the property; some rooms feature antiques and period pieces, and others boast flat-panel, LCD televisions. Smoke free premises. 124 units. 116 one-bedroom standard units. 8 one-bedroom suites, some with whirlpools. 3-4 stories, interior corridors. *Bath:* combo or shower only. **Parking:** valet. **Terms:** cancellation fee imposed. **Amenities:** CD players, voice mail, irons, hair dryers. *Some:* high-speed Internet. **Dining:** The Treaty of Paris, see separate listing. **Guest Services:** valet laundry, area transportation, wireless Internet. **Business Services:** meeting rooms. **Cards:** AX, DC, DS, MC, VI.

HOLIDAY INN EXPRESS HOTEL & SUITES
ANNAPOLIS   *Book great rates at AAA.com*

Phone: 410/224-4317

Small-scale Hotel
Rates not provided

Address: 2451 Riva Rd 21401 **Location:** 2.3 mi sw on US 50 and 301, exit 22 to Riva Rd, then 0.5 mi n. Located in a commercial area. **Facility:** 79 one-bedroom standard units, some with whirlpools. 2 stories, interior corridors. *Bath:* combo or shower only. **Parking:** on-site. **Amenities:** high-speed Internet, voice mail, safes (fee), irons, hair dryers. **Leisure Activities:** limited exercise equipment. **Guest Services:** valet laundry. **Business Services:** business center. *(See color ad below)*

HOMESTEAD STUDIO SUITES HOTEL-ANNAPOLIS   *Book at AAA.com*

Phone: (410)571-6600

Small-scale Hotel
$144-$154 3/1-11/1
$100-$110 11/2-2/28

Address: 120 Admiral Cochrane Dr 21401 **Location:** 2.3 mi sw on US 50 and 301, exit 22, just s, then just e. Located in business park area. **Facility:** 98 units. 81 one-bedroom standard units with efficiencies. 17 one-bedroom suites with efficiencies. 3 stories, interior corridors. *Bath:* combo or shower only. **Terms:** office hours 7 am-11 pm. **Amenities:** dual phone lines, voice mail, irons, hair dryers. **Leisure Activities:** limited exercise equipment. **Guest Services:** coin laundry, wireless Internet. **Business Services:** meeting rooms. **Cards:** AX, DC, DS, JC, MC, VI.

LOEWS ANNAPOLIS HOTEL   *Book great rates at AAA.com*

Phone: (410)263-7777

Large-scale Hotel
$143-$323 All Year

Address: 126 West St 21401 **Location:** US 50 and 301, exit 24 eastbound; exit 24A westbound, 1.4 mi s on SR 70, just sw on Calvert St, then just w. **Facility:** The historic district may be reached on foot or by shuttle from this full-service hotel offering guest rooms with traditional decor. 217 units. 211 one-bedroom standard units. 6 one-bedroom suites. 6 stories, interior corridors. *Bath:* combo or shower only. **Parking:** on-site (fee) and valet. **Amenities:** CD players, dual phone lines, voice mail, irons, hair dryers. *Fee:* video games, high-speed Internet. *Some:* DVD players (fee). **Dining:** Breeze, see separate listing. **Leisure Activities:** exercise room, spa. **Guest Services:** valet laundry, wireless Internet. **Business Services:** conference facilities, business center. **Cards:** AX, CB, DC, DS, JC, MC, VI. **Free Special Amenities:** newspaper. *(See color ad p 602)*

THE O'CALLAGHAN ANNAPOLIS HOTEL   *Book great rates at AAA.com*

Phone: (410)263-7700

Small-scale Hotel
$199-$369 3/1-12/22 &
12/26-2/28

Address: 174 West St 21401 **Location:** US 50 and 301, exit 22 eastbound; exit 24 westbound, 1.4 mi s on SR 70, just sw on Calvert St, then 0.3 mi w. **Facility:** Designated smoking area. 119 units. 117 one-bedroom standard units. 2 one-bedroom suites. 5 stories, interior corridors. *Bath:* combo or shower only. **Parking:** valet. **Terms:** open 3/1-12/22 & 12/26-2/28, cancellation fee imposed. **Amenities:** video games (fee), high-speed Internet, voice mail, safes, irons, hair dryers. **Leisure Activities:** limited exercise equipment. **Guest Services:** valet laundry, area transportation-within 4 mi. **Business Services:** meeting rooms, business center. **Cards:** AX, CB, DC, DS, JC, MC, VI.
(See color ad below)

RESIDENCE INN BY MARRIOTT-ANNAPOLIS   *Book great rates at AAA.com*

Phone: 410/573-0300

Small-scale Hotel
$176-$207 All Year

Address: 170 Admiral Cochrane Dr 21401 **Location:** 2.3 mi sw on US 50 and 301, exit 22 to Riva Rd, just s on Riva Rd, then just e. Located in a business park area. **Facility:** Smoke free premises. 102 units. 78 one-bedroom standard units with kitchens. 24 two-bedroom suites with kitchens. 2 stories (no elevator), exterior corridors. *Bath:* combo or shower only. **Parking:** on-site. **Amenities:** high-speed Internet, voice mail, irons, hair dryers. **Pool(s):** outdoor. **Leisure Activities:** whirlpool, exercise room, sports court. **Guest Services:** valet and coin laundry. **Business Services:** meeting rooms. **Cards:** AX, DC, DS, JC, MC, VI.

AAA Benefit:
Members save 5% off of the best available rate.

SHERATON ANNAPOLIS HOTEL   *Book great rates at AAA.com*   Phone: (410)266-3131

Large-scale Hotel
$369 All Year

Address: 173 Jennifer Rd 21401 **Location:** North side of US 50 and 301, exit 23B westbound; exit 23 eastbound. Located opposite Annapolis Westfield Shopping Town. **Facility:** 196 units. 189 one-bedroom standard units. 7 one-bedroom suites. 6 stories, interior corridors. *Bath:* combo or shower only. **Parking:** on-site. **Terms:** cancellation fee imposed. **Amenities:** high-speed Internet, dual phone lines, voice mail, irons, hair dryers. *Some:* safes. **Pool(s):** heated indoor. **Leisure Activities:** whirlpool, exercise room. **Guest Services:** valet laundry, area transportation-within 5 mi, wireless Internet. **Business Services:** conference facilities, business center. **Cards:** AX, DC, DS, MC, VI. **Free Special Amenities: room upgrade (subject to availability with advance reservations) and high-speed Internet.**

AAA Benefit:
Members get up to 15% off, plus Starwood Preferred Guest® bonuses.

  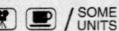

SPRINGHILL SUITES BY MARRIOTT ANNAPOLIS   *Book great rates at AAA.com*   Phone: 443/321-2500

Small-scale Hotel
$155-$185 All Year

Address: 189 Admiral Cochrane Dr 21401 **Location:** 2.3 mi sw on US 50 and 301, exit 22 to Riva Rd, just s on Riva Rd, then 0.3 mi e. **Facility:** Smoke free premises. 120 one-bedroom standard units, some with whirlpools. 4 stories, interior corridors. *Bath:* combo or shower only. **Parking:** on-site. **Amenities:** video games (fee), high-speed Internet, voice mail, safes, irons, hair dryers. **Pool(s):** heated indoor. **Leisure Activities:** whirlpool, exercise room. **Guest Services:** valet and coin laundry. **Business Services:** meeting rooms, business center. **Cards:** AX, DC, DS, JC, MC, VI.

AAA Benefit:
Members save 5% off of the best available rate.

SUPER 8 MOTEL ANNAPOLIS   Phone: 410/757-2222

Motel
Rates not provided

Address: 74 Old Mill Bottom Rd N 21409 **Location:** 4 mi e on US 50 and 301, exit 28, 0.3 mi n to Old Mill Bottom Rd N, then just e; 3 mi w of Bay Bridge. Located in semi-rural area. **Facility:** 39 one-bedroom standard units. 2 stories (no elevator), exterior corridors. *Bath:* combo or shower only. **Parking:** on-site. **Amenities:** irons, hair dryers. **Guest Services:** wireless Internet. **Business Services:** fax (fee).

WILLIAM PAGE INN   Phone: (410)626-1506

Historic Bed
& Breakfast

$205-$300 3/1-11/30
$190-$250 12/1-2/28

Address: 8 Martin St 21401-1716 **Location:** 3 blks se of State Circle; corner of East and Martin sts. Located in Historic Annapolis. **Facility:** A porch provides a place to catch the breeze at this in-town 1908 home. Smoke free premises. 5 one-bedroom standard units, some with whirlpools. 3 stories (no elevator), interior corridors. *Bath:* some shared or private, combo or shower only. **Parking:** on-site. **Terms:** office hours 10 am-8 pm, check-in 4 pm, 2 night minimum stay - seasonal and/or weekends, age restrictions may apply, 10 day cancellation notice. **Amenities:** CD players. *Some:* DVD players, hair dryers. **Guest Services:** wireless Internet. **Cards:** MC, VI.

——— WHERE TO DINE ———

AQUA TERRA OF ANNAPOLIS   Phone: 410/263-1985

American
$22-$38

The talented chef-owner operates this stylish restaurant in the heart of historic Annapolis. Creative cooking reflects influences from both Europe and Asia and fresh ingredients from both the land and sea. Casual dress. **Bar:** Full bar. **Reservations:** suggested. **Hours:** 5:30 pm-10 pm, Fri & Sat-11 pm, Sun 5 pm-9 pm, Mon 5:30 pm-9 pm. Closed major holidays. **Address:** 164 Main St 21401 **Location:** In Historic Annapolis; just nw of Church Circle. **Parking:** street. **Cards:** AX, MC, VI.

BREEZE   Phone: 410/295-3232

American
$8-$35

Off the lobby of Loews Annapolis Hotel, the dining room sustains a casually upscale atmosphere. The kitchen prepares some distinctive Chesapeake Bay specialties. Casual dress. **Bar:** Full bar. **Reservations:** suggested, for dinner. **Hours:** 6:30 am-2 & 5-10 pm. **Address:** 126 West St 21401 **Location:** US 50 and 301, exit 24 eastbound; exit 24A westbound, 1.4 mi s on SR 70, just sw on Calvert St, then just w; in Loews Annapolis Hotel. **Parking:** valet. **Cards:** AX, CB, DC, DS, MC, VI.

BUDDY'S CRABS & RIBS   Phone: 410/626-1100

Seafood
$8-$25

Nestled in the heart of this naval community, this second floor restaurant overlooks merchant activity from above. Enjoy either the raw bar choices of clams, mussels, crawfish and more or the cooked variety featuring crab. An eager staff is at your beck and call to please you while you enjoy good food and conversation. Casual dress. **Bar:** Full bar. **Reservations:** not accepted. **Hours:** 11:30 am-10 pm, Fri & Sat-11 pm, Sun 8:30 am-10 pm. **Address:** 100 Main St 21401 **Location:** Just nw of State Circle. **Parking:** street. **Cards:** AX, CB, DC, DS, MC, VI.

CARROL'S CREEK CAFE   Phone: 410/263-8102

Seafood
$7-$30

The comfortable, upscale dining room overlooks the historic Annapolis skyline, harbor and marina. On the menu is a nice selection of fresh fish, as well as beef, lamb and duck. The cafe has been a favorite of locals since 1984. Casual dress. **Bar:** Full bar. **Reservations:** accepted, weekdays. **Hours:** 11:30 am-4 & 5-10 pm, Sun 10 am-1:30 & 3-10 pm. **Address:** 410 Severn Ave 21403 **Location:** 0.3 mi e on 6th St crossing Eastport Bridge, just n; in Eastport. **Parking:** on-site. **Cards:** AX, DC, DS, MC, VI.

HARRY BROWNE'S
Phone: 410/263-4332

Continental
$9-$35

A favorite of locals and statesmen since 1979, the restaurant prepares Continental fare, such as Maryland crab cakes served with sauteed spinach, roasted red pepper coulis and sweet onion marmalade, and rack of lamb with potatoes Dauphinoise, caponata and rosemary demi-glace. Service is professional and friendly. Dressy casual. **Bar:** Full bar. **Reservations:** suggested. **Hours:** 11 am-3 & 5:30-10 pm, Fri & Sat-11 pm, Sun 4:30 pm-9 pm; Sunday brunch 10 am-3 pm. Closed: 1/1, 7/4, 12/25. **Address:** 66 State Circle 21401 **Location:** In historic district facing the State Capitol. **Parking:** street. **Cards:** AX, DC, DS, MC, VI.

INDIA'S RESTAURANT
Phone: 410/263-7900

Indian
$12-$25

Representative of Indian cuisine is a nice selection of chicken, lamb and vegetarian dishes. The setting is simple yet comfortable. The $10.95 lunch buffet fills up guests on weekdays. Casual dress. **Bar:** Full bar. **Reservations:** suggested, weekends. **Hours:** 11:30 am-2:30 & 5-10 pm, Fri & Sat-10:30 pm. Closed: 11/27, 12/25. **Address:** 257 West St 21401 **Location:** 0.5 mi w of Church Circle. **Parking:** on-site. **Cards:** AX, DS, MC, VI.

THE ITALIAN MARKET AND RESTAURANT
Phone: 410/224-1330

Italian
$5-$18

The casual eatery is a mixture of an Italian restaurant and market. Homemade items such as tomato sauce, sausage and gelato are served and sold in the small market. On the eatery's menu are foods ranging from pizza by the slice to calamari alla marinara. This is a nice place to bring the family for a tasty, inexpensive meal. Casual dress. **Bar:** Beer & wine. **Reservations:** not accepted. **Hours:** 10 am-10 pm, Fri & Sat-11 pm, Sun-9 pm. Closed: 7/4, 11/27, 12/25. **Address:** 126 Defense Hwy 21401 **Location:** US 50 and 301, exit 23 eastbound; exit 23B westbound, 0.5 mi w on SR 450. **Parking:** on-site. **Cards:** AX, CB, DC, DS, MC, VI.

JALAPENOS RESTAURANT
Phone: 410/266-7580

Spanish
$8-$24

In a nondescript shopping center is a wonderful restaurant that offers both Spanish and Mexican dishes. Some diners make a complete meal from the extensive selection of tapas. Also appealing are such entrees as rack of lamb rubbed with rosemary and served with black mole and large shrimp wrapped in serrano ham with chipotle sauce and served on a skewer. Casual dress. **Bar:** Full bar. **Reservations:** suggested. **Hours:** 11:30 am-2:30 & 5-10 pm, Sun 11 am-2 & 4-9 pm. Closed major holidays. **Address:** 85 Forest Dr 21401 **Location:** Just s of Riva Rd; in Forest Plaza Shopping Center. **Parking:** on-site. **Cards:** AX, DC, MC, VI.

CALL 🦽M

LES FOLIES
Phone: 410/573-0970

French
$7-$34

The chef-owned restaurant sustains a brasserie atmosphere. The kitchen is skillful in French cooking, and raw-bar selections and souffles are among offerings. Cell phone use is not permitted in the dining room. Casual dress. **Bar:** Full bar. **Reservations:** suggested. **Hours:** 11:30 am-2:30 & 5:30-10:30 pm, Sat from 5:30 pm, Sun 5 pm-9 pm. Closed major holidays. **Address:** 2552 Riva Rd 21401 **Location:** 2.3 mi sw on US 50 and 301, exit 22. **Parking:** on-site. **Cards:** AX, CB, DC, DS, MC, VI.

LEWNES' STEAK HOUSE
Phone: 410/263-1617

Steak & Seafood
$19-$39

Prime beef is served in generous portions, crab cakes are made with jumbo lump crab meat, and whole Maine lobsters weigh at least three pounds. The neighborhood restaurant has a bar at the entrance and its main dining room upstairs. Casual dress. **Bar:** Full bar. **Reservations:** suggested. **Hours:** 5 pm-10 pm, Fri & Sat-10:30 pm, Sun 4 pm-10 pm. Closed: 1/1, 11/27, 12/25. **Address:** 401 Fourth St 21403 **Location:** At 4th and Severn sts; in Eastport section. **Parking:** street. **Cards:** AX, DC, MC, VI.

MARIA'S SICILIAN RISTORANTE & CAFE
Phone: 410/268-2112

Italian
$7-$38

At the city dock in historic Annapolis, the family-run restaurant provides an intimate setting for a relaxing meal. The kitchen prepares Sicilian cuisine from family recipes. Casual dress. **Bar:** Full bar. **Reservations:** suggested. **Hours:** 11 am-11 pm. Closed: 11/27, 12/25. **Address:** 12 Market Space 21401 **Location:** In the historic district at city dock. **Parking:** on-site (fee). **Cards:** AX, MC, VI.

MIDDLETON TAVERN
Phone: 410/263-3323

American
$8-$35

Classic American cuisine exudes a Maryland flavor at the rustic, nautically themed, historic tavern. Diners can treat themselves to a great view of the harbor, either from the second floor or from the seasonal deck. The raw bar offers an array of fresh shellfish. Casual dress. Entertainment. **Bar:** Full bar. **Reservations:** not accepted. **Hours:** 11:30 am-10:30 pm, Sun from 10:30 am. **Address:** 2 Market Space 21401 **Location:** In the historic district at city dock. **Parking:** street. **Cards:** AX, DC, DS, MC, VI. **Historic**

NORTHWOODS
Phone: 410/268-2609

Continental
$23-$29

A soft, comfortable ambience envelops the restaurant, where cozy couples often visit for upscale, candlelight dining. The complete dinner, which includes appetizer or soup, house salad, entree and a selection from the extensive dessert cart, is an excellent value, but guests also have the option to order a la carte. Dressy casual. **Bar:** Full bar. **Reservations:** suggested. **Hours:** 5:30 pm-10 pm, Sun 5 pm-9 pm. Closed major holidays; also 12/24 & Mon. **Address:** 609 Melvin Ave 21401 **Location:** Just e of SR 70 (Rowe Blvd); 0.8 mi se of US 50, exit 24A. **Parking:** on-site. **Cards:** AX, CB, DC, DS, MC, VI.

PHILLIPS ANNAPOLIS HARBOR
Phone: 410/990-9888

Seafood
$7-$30

The popular seafood restaurant with a casual atmosphere overlooks the many boats at the City Dock. The menu centers on fresh seafood, beef and chicken dishes. On weekends, only the dinner menu is presented. Kids can order from the children's menu. Casual dress. **Bar:** Full bar. **Reservations:** suggested. **Hours:** 11 am-9 pm, Fri & Sat-10 pm; hours may vary in season. Closed: 12/25. **Address:** 12 Dock St 21401 **Location:** At the city dock. **Parking:** on-site (fee). **Cards:** AX, DC, DS, MC, VI.

PUSSER'S CARIBBEAN GRILL

Phone: 410/626-0004

Steak & Seafood
$10-$25

Eclectic cuisine spans from Maryland seafood specialties to West Indian favorites. Large, fresh oysters with zesty sauce and an entree of Creole crawfish pasta are excellent choices. The outdoor seating area opens seasonally. Casual dress. **Bar:** Full bar. **Reservations:** suggested. **Hours:** 6:30 am-11 pm; Fri & Sat-midnight 5/15-10/5. **Address:** 80 Compromise St 21401 **Location:** At the city dock; in Annapolis Marriott Waterfront Hotel. **Parking:** valet. **Cards:** AX, CB, DC, DS, MC, VI.

RAMS HEAD TAVERN

Phone: 410/268-4545

American
$8-$33

In the historic area, the brew-pub serves good American fare in a friendly, lively setting. An extensive selection of beers, including the ones brewed here, is available. The concert hall offers nationally known entertainment. Casual dress. **Bar:** Full bar. **Reservations:** accepted. **Hours:** 11 am-11 pm, Sun from 10 am; Sunday brunch. **Address:** 33 West St 21401 **Location:** Just off Church Circle. **Parking:** street. **Cards:** AX, DS, MC, VI.

THE TREATY OF PARIS

Phone: 410/216-6340

Continental
$8-$30

In the historic Maryland Inn building of the Historic Inns of Annapolis, the comfortably upscale restaurant prepares Continental cuisine with a mix of European and American cooking styles. The basement-level dining room has a historic air, with brick walls and beamed ceilings. Dressy casual. **Bar:** Full bar. **Reservations:** suggested. **Hours:** 7:30-10:30 am, 11:30-2:30 & 5:30-9:30 pm, Fri & Sat-10 pm, Sun 10 am-2 & 5:30-9:30 pm; Sunday brunch. **Address:** 16 Church Circle 21401 **Location:** In historic district; at Historic Inns of Annapolis. **Parking:** street. **Cards:** AX, CB, DC, DS, MC, VI. **Historic**

ANNAPOLIS JUNCTION   (See map and index starting on p. 578)

─────── WHERE TO STAY ───────

COURTYARD BY MARRIOTT FT. MEADE @
NATIONAL BUSINESS PARK   *Book great rates at AAA.com*

Phone: 301/498-8400   [98]

Small-scale Hotel
$231-$274 All Year

Address: 2700 Hercules Rd 20701 **Location:** I-95, exit 38A, 2.5 mi e on SR 32 to exit 11 (Dorsey Run Rd), then 1.2 mi e. **Facility:** Smoke free premises. 140 units. 136 one-bedroom standard units. 4 one-bedroom suites. 5 stories, interior corridors. *Bath:* combo or shower only. **Parking:** on-site. **Amenities:** video games (fee), high-speed Internet, dual phone lines, voice mail, safes, irons, hair dryers. **Pool(s):** heated indoor. **Leisure Activities:** whirlpool, exercise room. **Guest Services:** valet and coin laundry, wireless Internet. **Business Services:** meeting rooms, business center. **Cards:** AX, DS, MC, VI.

AAA Benefit:
Members save 5% off of the best available rate.

TOWNEPLACE SUITES BY
MARRIOTT-BALTIMORE/FT. MEADE   *Book great rates at AAA.com*

Phone: 301/498-7477   [97]

Small-scale Hotel
$158-$193 All Year

Address: 120 National Business Pkwy 20701 **Location:** I-95, exit 38A, 2.5 mi e on SR 32 to exit 11 (Dorsey Run Rd), then 1.3 mi e. **Facility:** Smoke free premises. 95 units. 67 one-bedroom standard units with kitchens. 4 one- and 24 two-bedroom suites with kitchens. 3 stories, interior corridors. *Bath:* combo or shower only. **Parking:** on-site. **Amenities:** voice mail, irons, hair dryers. **Pool(s):** outdoor. **Leisure Activities:** limited exercise equipment. **Guest Services:** valet and coin laundry, wireless Internet. **Business Services:** PC. **Cards:** AX, DC, DS, JC, MC, VI.

AAA Benefit:
Members save 5% off of the best available rate.

BELCAMP

─────── WHERE TO STAY ───────

COUNTRY INN & SUITES BY CARLSON   *Book at AAA.com*

Phone: (410)297-9444

Small-scale Hotel
$121-$139 3/1-10/31
$99-$124 11/1-2/28

Address: 1435 Handlir Dr 21015 **Location:** I-95, exit 80 (SR 543), just e. **Facility:** 81 units. 65 one-bedroom standard units, some with whirlpools. 16 one-bedroom suites. 3 stories, interior corridors. *Bath:* combo or shower only. **Parking:** on-site. **Amenities:** high-speed Internet, voice mail, irons, hair dryers. *Some:* DVD players. **Pool(s):** outdoor. **Leisure Activities:** exercise room. **Guest Services:** valet and coin laundry. **Business Services:** meeting rooms, PC. **Cards:** AX, CB, DC, DS, JC, MC, VI.

EXTENDED STAYAMERICA-BEL AIR   *Book at AAA.com*

Phone: (410)273-0194

Small-scale Hotel
$114-$124 All Year

Address: 1361 James Way 21015 **Location:** I-95, exit 80 (SR 543), just ne. **Facility:** 101 one-bedroom standard units with efficiencies. 3 stories, interior corridors. *Bath:* combo or shower only. **Parking:** on-site. **Terms:** office hours 7 am-11 pm. **Amenities:** voice mail, irons. **Guest Services:** coin laundry, wireless Internet. **Cards:** AX, DC, DS, JC, MC, VI.

SPRINGHILL SUITES BY MARRIOTT *Book great rates at AAA.com* Phone: 410/297-4970

Small-scale Hotel
$116-$146 All Year

Address: 1420 Handlir Dr 21015 **Location:** I-95, exit 80 (SR 543), just e to SR 7/Philadelphia Rd N. **Facility:** Smoke free premises. 119 one-bedroom standard units, some with whirlpools. 3 stories, interior corridors. *Bath:* combo or shower only. **Parking:** on-site. **Amenities:** video games (fee), high-speed Internet, dual phone lines, voice mail, irons, hair dryers. **Pool(s):** heated indoor. **Leisure Activities:** whirlpool, sun deck, barbecue grill, limited exercise equipment. **Guest Services:** valet and coin laundry. **Business Services:** meeting rooms, business center. **Cards:** AX, DC, DS, JC, MC, VI. **Free Special Amenities: expanded continental breakfast and room upgrade (subject to availability with advance reservations).**

AAA Benefit:
Members save 5% off of the best available rate.

WINGATE INN ABERDEEN *Book great rates at AAA.com* Phone: (410)272-2929

Small-scale Hotel
$99-$119 All Year

Address: 1326 Policy Dr 21017 **Location:** I-95, exit 80 (SR 543), 0.3 mi s on SR 543. **Facility:** 107 units. 106 one-bedroom standard units, some with whirlpools. 1 one-bedroom suite with whirlpool. 3 stories, interior corridors. *Bath:* combo or shower only. **Parking:** on-site. **Terms:** cancellation fee imposed. **Amenities:** video games (fee), high-speed Internet, dual phone lines, voice mail, safes, irons, hair dryers. **Pool(s):** heated indoor. **Leisure Activities:** whirlpool, sun deck, exercise room. **Guest Services:** valet and coin laundry, wireless Internet. **Business Services:** meeting rooms, business center. **Cards:** AX, DC, DS, JC, MC, VI. **Free Special Amenities: expanded continental breakfast and high-speed Internet.**

CATONSVILLE pop. 39,820 (See map and index starting on p. 578)

——— WHERE TO STAY ———

COMFORT INN BALTIMORE WEST *Book great rates at AAA.com* Phone: (410)744-5000 **39**

Small-scale Hotel
$90-$160 3/1-11/30
$80-$140 12/1-2/28

Address: 5801 Baltimore National Pike 21228 **Location:** I-695, exit 15A, just e on US 40. **Facility:** 92 one-bedroom standard units, some with whirlpools. 3 stories (no elevator), interior/exterior corridors. **Parking:** on-site. **Amenities:** voice mail, safes (fee), irons, hair dryers. **Leisure Activities:** limited exercise equipment. **Guest Services:** coin laundry, wireless Internet. **Business Services:** PC. **Cards:** AX, DC, DS, MC, VI. **Free Special Amenities: continental breakfast and high-speed Internet.**

DAYS INN CATONSVILLE *Book at AAA.com* Phone: (410)747-8900 **38**

Small-scale Hotel
$104-$116 3/1-8/31
$80-$89 9/1-2/28

Address: 5701 Baltimore National Pike 21228 **Location:** I-695, exit 15A, just e on US 40. Located in a commerical area; opposite shopping center. **Facility:** 124 one-bedroom standard units, some with whirlpools. 8 stories, interior corridors. **Parking:** on-site. **Amenities:** irons, hair dryers. **Pool(s):** outdoor. **Leisure Activities:** exercise room. **Guest Services:** coin laundry, wireless Internet. **Business Services:** meeting rooms, business center. **Cards:** AX, DC, DS, JC, MC, VI.

COCKEYSVILLE pop. 19,388 (See map and index starting on p. 578)

——— WHERE TO DINE ———

PATRICK'S OF COCKEYSVILLE Phone: 410/683-0604 **18**

American
$6-$30

In a suburban shopping center, the restaurant is both casual and appropriate for fine dining. A European influence is evident in traditional Maryland dishes on a menu that changes seasonally. Shrimp in garlic sauce is a local favorite, as is pine nut cake. Dressy casual. **Bar:** Full bar. **Reservations:** suggested, in fine dining area. **Hours:** 11:30 am-11:30 pm. Closed: 12/25. **Address:** 550 Cranbrook Rd 21030 **Location:** 1 mi e of York Rd; in Cranbrook Shopping Center. **Parking:** on-site. **Cards:** AX, DS, VI.

COLUMBIA pop. 88,254

——— WHERE TO STAY ———

COURTYARD BY MARRIOTT-COLUMBIA *Book great rates at AAA.com* Phone: 410/290-0002

Small-scale Hotel
$220-$263 All Year

Address: 8910 Stanford Blvd 21045 **Location:** I-95, exit 41B, 1.3 mi w on SR 175 (Little Patuxent Pkwy), 0.5 mi s on Snowden River Pkwy, just w on McGaw Rd, then 0.4 mi nw. **Facility:** Smoke free premises. 152 units. 140 one-bedroom standard units. 12 one-bedroom suites. 4 stories, interior corridors. *Bath:* combo or shower only. **Parking:** on-site. **Amenities:** high-speed Internet, voice mail, irons, hair dryers. **Pool(s):** heated indoor. **Leisure Activities:** whirlpool, limited exercise equipment. **Guest Services:** valet and coin laundry, wireless Internet. **Business Services:** meeting rooms, PC. **Cards:** AX, DC, DS, MC, VI.

AAA Benefit:
Members save 5% off of the best available rate.

EXTENDED STAYAMERICA-COLUMBIA 100 PARKWAY
Book at AAA.com

Small-scale Hotel
$119-$129 All Year

Phone: (410)772-8800

Address: 8870 Columbia 100 Pkwy 21045 **Location:** I-95, exit 43B, 4 mi w on SR 100, exit 1B, then just e. **Facility:** 104 one-bedroom standard units with efficiencies. 3 stories, interior corridors. *Bath:* combo or shower only. **Parking:** on-site. **Terms:** office hours 7 am-11 pm. **Amenities:** voice mail, irons. **Guest Services:** coin laundry, wireless Internet. **Cards:** AX, DC, DS, JC, MC, VI.

(ASK) (S) CALL (M) 🎥 🖥 📷 💻 / SOME UNITS FEE 🐾 ✕

EXTENDED STAY DELUXE COLUMBIA CORPORATE PARK
Book at AAA.com

Small-scale Hotel
$129-$139 All Year

Phone: (410)872-2994

Address: 8890 Stanford Blvd 21045 **Location:** I-95, exit 41B, 1.3 mi w on SR 175 (Little Patuxent Pkwy), 0.5 mi s on Snowden River Pkwy, just w on McGaw Rd, then 0.3 mi nw. **Facility:** 131 one-bedroom standard units with efficiencies. 3 stories, interior corridors. *Bath:* combo or shower only. **Parking:** on-site. **Terms:** office hours 7 am-11 pm, cancellation fee imposed. **Amenities:** DVD players, video games (fee), dual phone lines, voice mail, irons, hair dryers. **Pool(s):** heated outdoor. **Leisure Activities:** limited exercise equipment. **Guest Services:** coin laundry, wireless Internet. **Cards:** AX, DC, DS, JC, MC, VI.

(ASK) (S) (🛏) CALL (M) 🏊 🎥 🖥 📷 💻 / SOME UNITS FEE 🐾 ✕

HAMPTON INN COLUMBIA
Book great rates at AAA.com

Small-scale Hotel
Rates not provided

Phone: 410/997-8555

Address: 8880 Columbia 100 Pkwy 21045 **Location:** I-95, exit 43B, 4 mi w on SR 100, exit 1B. **Facility:** 83 one-bedroom standard units, some with whirlpools. 4 stories, interior corridors. *Bath:* combo or shower only. **Parking:** on-site. **Amenities:** high-speed Internet, dual phone lines, voice mail, irons, hair dryers. **Pool(s):** heated indoor. **Leisure Activities:** whirlpool, exercise room. **Guest Services:** valet laundry, wireless Internet. **Business Services:** meeting rooms, business center.

(🛏) CALL (M) 🏊 🎥 🖥 📷 💻 / SOME UNITS ✕

HILTON COLUMBIA
Book great rates at AAA.com

(AAA) (SAVE)

Small-scale Hotel
$109-$229 All Year

Phone: (410)997-1060

Address: 5485 Twin Knolls Rd 21045 **Location:** Just e on SR 175 (Little Patuxent Pkwy) from jct US 29, just s on Thunder Hill Rd, then 0.3 mi w on Twin Knolls Rd, 5th entrance. **Facility:** 152 units. 146 one-bedroom standard units. 6 one-bedroom suites. 4 stories, interior corridors. *Bath:* combo or shower only. **Parking:** on-site. **Terms:** cancellation fee imposed. **Amenities:** dual phone lines, voice mail, irons, hair dryers. **Pool(s):** heated indoor. **Leisure Activities:** saunas, whirlpool, limited exercise equipment. **Guest Services:** valet laundry, area transportation-within 5 mi, wireless Internet. **Business Services:** conference facilities, business center. **Cards:** AX, CB, DC, DS, JC, MC, VI.

(S) (🍴) (Y) CALL (M) 🏊 ✕ 🎥 💻 / SOME UNITS ✕ FEE 🖥 FEE

HILTON GARDEN INN COLUMBIA
Book great rates at AAA.com

Small-scale Hotel
Rates not provided

Phone: 410/750-3700

Address: 8241 Snowden River Pkwy 21045 **Location:** I-95, exit 43, 2 mi w on SR 100 to exit 3, then just s. Located in a business area. **Facility:** 98 units. 78 one-bedroom standard units. 20 one-bedroom suites. 4 stories, interior corridors. *Bath:* combo or shower only. **Parking:** on-site. **Amenities:** video games (fee), high-speed Internet, dual phone lines, voice mail, irons, hair dryers. **Pool(s):** heated indoor. **Leisure Activities:** whirlpool, exercise room. **Guest Services:** valet and coin laundry, wireless Internet. **Business Services:** meeting rooms, business center.

(🍴) CALL (M) 🏊 🎥 🖥 📷 💻 / SOME UNITS ✕

▼ See AAA listing p 614 ▼

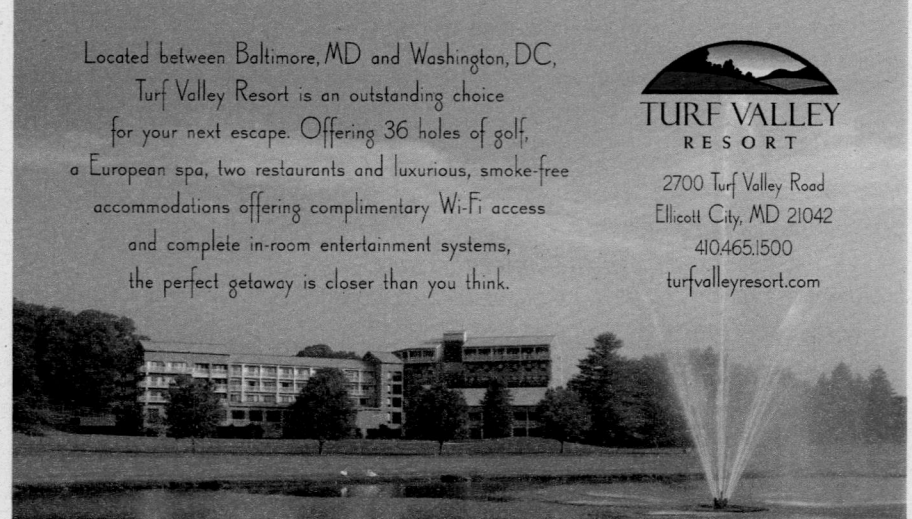

HOMEWOOD SUITES BY HILTON COLUMBIA — *Book at AAA.com*

Small-scale Hotel
Rates not provided

Phone: 410/872-9200

Address: 8320 Benson Dr 21045 **Location:** I-95, exit 41B, 0.5 mi w on SR 175 (Little Patuxent Pkwy), just nw on SR 108, then just w on Lark Brown Rd. **Facility:** 150 units. 23 one-bedroom standard units with efficiencies. 103 one- and 24 two-bedroom suites with efficiencies. 4 stories, interior corridors. *Bath:* combo or shower only. **Parking:** on-site. **Terms:** check-in 4 pm. **Amenities:** high-speed Internet, dual phone lines, voice mail, irons, hair dryers. **Pool(s):** heated outdoor. **Leisure Activities:** whirlpool, exercise room, sports court. **Guest Services:** valet and coin laundry, wireless Internet. **Business Services:** meeting rooms, business center.

SHERATON COLUMBIA HOTEL — *Book great rates at AAA.com*

Large-scale Hotel
$279-$314 All Year

Phone: (410)730-3900

Address: 10207 Wincopin Cir 21044 **Location:** 1.2 mi w on SR 175 (Little Patuxent Pkwy) from jct US 29, then just s; center. **Facility:** 288 units. 286 one-bedroom standard units. 2 one-bedroom suites. 3-10 stories, interior corridors. *Bath:* combo or shower only. **Parking:** on-site. **Terms:** cancellation fee imposed. **Amenities:** video games (fee), dual phone lines, voice mail, irons, hair dryers. **Dining:** Waterside Restaurant, see separate listing. **Pool(s):** outdoor. **Leisure Activities:** jogging, exercise room. **Guest Services:** valet and coin laundry, area transportation, wireless Internet. **Business Services:** conference facilities, business center. **Cards:** AX, DC, DS, MC, VI.

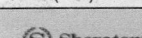
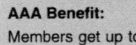

AAA Benefit:
Members get up to 15% off, plus Starwood Preferred Guest® bonuses.

STAYBRIDGE SUITES BALTIMORE-COLUMBIA — *Book at AAA.com*

Small-scale Hotel
$205-$226 All Year

Phone: (410)964-9494

Address: 8844 Columbia 100 Pkwy 21045 **Location:** I-95, exit 43B, 4 mi w on SR 100, exit 1B, then just e. Located in a residential/business park area. **Facility:** 118 units. 66 one-bedroom standard units with efficiencies. 29 one- and 23 two-bedroom suites with kitchens. 3 stories, interior corridors. *Bath:* combo or shower only. **Parking:** on-site. **Terms:** check-in 4 pm, cancellation fee imposed. **Amenities:** video library (fee), DVD players, high-speed Internet, dual phone lines, voice mail, irons, hair dryers. **Pool(s):** outdoor. **Leisure Activities:** exercise room, sports court. **Guest Services:** complimentary and valet laundry, area transportation. **Business Services:** meeting rooms, business center. **Cards:** AX, CB, DC, DS, MC, VI.

STUDIOPLUS COLUMBIA GATEWAY DRIVE — *Book at AAA.com*

Small-scale Hotel
$124-$134 All Year

Phone: (410)312-1557

Address: 6620 Eli Whitney Dr 21046 **Location:** I-95, exit 41, 1 mi w on SR 175, then just se on Columbia Gateway Dr. **Facility:** 95 one-bedroom standard units with efficiencies. 3 stories, interior corridors. *Bath:* combo or shower only. **Parking:** on-site. **Terms:** office hours 7 am-11 pm. **Amenities:** dual phone lines, voice mail, irons. **Leisure Activities:** limited exercise equipment. **Guest Services:** coin laundry, wireless Internet. **Cards:** AX, DC, DS, JC, MC, VI.

-------- **WHERE TO DINE** --------

BOMBAY PEACOCK GRILL

Indian
$7-$19

Phone: 410/381-7111

Peacock feathers and exotic statues are among features that give the restaurant its Indian feel. Fresh vegetable samosa, a deep-fried pastry filled with spiced potatoes and peas, is flavorful and filling. The lunch buffet is a popular choice. Dressy casual. **Bar:** Full bar. **Reservations:** suggested. **Hours:** 11:30 am-10 pm, Fri & Sat-11 pm. Closed: 12/25. **Address:** 10005 Old Columbia Rd 21046 **Location:** I-95, exit 38B, 2 mi w on SR 32 to Shaker Dr/Eden Brook exit, just s, then just e. **Parking:** on-site. **Cards:** AX, CB, DC, DS, MC, VI.

CHICKEN OUT ROTISSERIE

American
$5-$10

Phone: 410/872-8600

Chicken Out Rotisserie uses only fresh all natural ingredients. The chicken is chemical and hormone free. Choose from salads and sandwiches to wraps and picaccias, as well as rotisserie chicken and roast beef. Casual dress. **Reservations:** not accepted. **Hours:** 11 am-9:30 pm, Sun-8:30 pm. Closed: 12/25. **Address:** 6270 Columbia Crossing 21045 **Location:** I-95, exit 41B, 2.1 mi w on SR 175; in Columbia Crossing Shopping Complex. **Parking:** on-site. **Cards:** AX, DS, MC, VI.

CLYDE'S OF COLUMBIA

American
$7-$24

Phone: 410/730-2829

In Columbia Town Center, the popular tavern—with white tablecloths, a vintage Victorian bar and a view of the lake—is a great place to grab a bite. The staff is friendly and swift, and the food is good. Classic American fare ranges from burgers, sandwiches and salads to full dinners. Scrumptious desserts are splurge-worthy. Casual dress. **Bar:** Full bar. **Reservations:** accepted. **Hours:** 11:30 am-midnight, Fri & Sat-1 am, Sun 10 am-midnight. Closed: 12/25. **Address:** 10221 Wincopin Cir 21044 **Location:** 1.2 mi w on SR 175 (Little Patuxent Pkwy) from jct US 29, then just s; center. **Parking:** on-site. **Cards:** AX, DC, DS, MC, VI.

DONNA'S

American
$6-$18

Phone: 410/465-2399

The casual cafe is great place to have a bite to eat. The lunch and dinner menu comprises salads, sandwiches, pizza and burgers. A nice selection of entrees also comes into play at dinnertime. The staff is friendly and efficient and the atmosphere comfortable. Casual dress. **Bar:** Full bar. **Reservations:** accepted. **Hours:** 11 am-9 pm, Fri & Sat-10 pm, Sun 10 am-9 pm. Closed: 11/27, 12/25. **Address:** 5850 Waterloo Rd 21045 **Location:** I-95, exit 43, 2 mi w on SR 100 to exit 3, then just s. **Parking:** on-site. **Cards:** AX, DC, DS, MC, VI.

JESSE WONG'S HONG KONG

Chinese
$6-$28

Phone: 410/964-9088

The lakefront restaurant serves Cantonese cuisine, Hong Kong dishes and dim sum, which is shuttled on a cart through the dining area on Saturdays and Sundays. On weekdays, guests can sample from the lunch buffet. Casual dress. **Bar:** Full bar. **Reservations:** suggested, weekends. **Hours:** 11 am-10 pm, Fri & Sat-11 pm. Closed: Mon. **Address:** 10215 Wincopin Cir 21044 **Location:** 1.2 mi w on SR 175 (Little Patuxent Pkwy); from jct US 29, just s; center. **Parking:** on-site. **Cards:** AX, DS, MC, VI.

THE KINGS CONTRIVANCE

American
$14-$32

Phone: 410/995-0500

A favorite for special occasions, the restored 19th-century mansion is attractively decorated and decidedly suburban. Representative of the cuisine, American with a Continental flair, are such dishes as grilled venison and duck. Bread and pastries are baked on the premises. The early-bird menu is not offered in December. Semi-formal attire. **Bar:** Full bar. **Reservations:** suggested. **Hours:** 5:30 pm-8 pm, Fri & Sat from 5 pm, Sun from 4 pm. Closed major holidays; also Super Bowl Sun. **Address:** 10150 Shaker Dr 21046 **Location:** E of jct US 29 and SR 32; exit Shaker Dr off SR 32; I-95, exit 38B, 2 mi w on SR 32. **Parking:** on-site. **Cards:** AX, DC, DS, MC, VI.

THE TOMATO PALACE

Italian
$8-$17

Phone: 410/715-0211

On the edge of a lake in Columbia Town Center, the popular, casual and colorful cafe is ideal for family dining. The kitchen prepares 15 varieties of pizza and 15 pasta dishes, as well as sandwiches, salads and daily specials. Tasty meal toppers include traditional tiramisu and chocolate bread pudding. The staff is friendly and efficient. The seasonal patio includes an area for smokers. Casual dress. **Bar:** Full bar. **Reservations:** accepted. **Hours:** 11:30 am-10 pm, Fri & Sat-10:30 pm. Closed: 11/27, 12/25; also Super Bowl Sun. **Address:** 10221 Wincopin Cir 21044 **Location:** Off SR 175 (Little Patuxent Pkwy), 1.5 mi w of jct US 29; center. **Parking:** on-site. **Cards:** AX, DC, DS, MC, VI.

WATERSIDE RESTAURANT

American
$8-$25

Phone: 410/730-3900

Overlooking Lake Kittamaqundi, the restaurant offers indoor and outdoor dining in a tranquil, intimate setting. Crab cakes served with a remoulade sauce are a favorite. Casual dress. **Bar:** Full bar. **Reservations:** accepted. **Hours:** 6:30 am-10 pm. **Address:** 10207 Wincopin Cir 21044 **Location:** 1.2 mi w on SR 175 (Little Patuxent Pkwy) from jct US 29, just s; center; in Sheraton Columbia Hotel. **Parking:** on-site. **Cards:** AX, DC, DS, MC, VI.

EDGEWOOD pop. 23,378

—— WHERE TO STAY ——

BEST WESTERN INVITATION INN

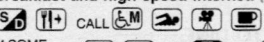
Book great rates at AAA.com

Phone: (410)679-9700

Motel
$75-$119 3/1-10/31
$69-$119 11/1-2/28

Address: 1709 Edgewood Rd 21040 **Location:** I-95, exit 77A, just e on SR 24. **Facility:** 158 one-bedroom standard units. 2 stories (no elevator), exterior corridors. **Bath:** combo or shower only. **Parking:** on-site. **Amenities:** voice mail, irons, hair dryers. *Fee:* video games, safes. *Some:* high-speed Internet. **Pool(s):** outdoor. **Leisure Activities:** limited exercise equipment. *Fee:* game room. **Guest Services:** valet and coin laundry, wireless Internet. **Business Services:** meeting rooms. **Cards:** AX, CB, DC, DS, JC, MC, VI. **Free Special Amenities:** expanded continental breakfast and high-speed Internet. *(See color ad below)*

AAA Benefit:
Members save 10% everyday, plus an exclusive frequent stay program.

DAYS INN-EDGEWOOD   *Book great rates at AAA.com*

Motel
Rates not provided

Phone: 410/671-9990

Address: 2116 Emmorton Park Rd 21040 **Location:** I-95, exit 77A, just e on SR 24. **Facility:** 72 one-bedroom standard units. 2 stories (no elevator), exterior corridors. *Bath:* combo or shower only. **Parking:** on-site. **Amenities:** voice mail, irons, hair dryers. **Guest Services:** coin laundry, wireless Internet. **Business Services:** PC. **Free Special Amenities:** continental breakfast and high-speed Internet.

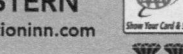

HOLIDAY INN EXPRESS

Book great rates at AAA.com

Small-scale Hotel
$125 All Year

Phone: 410/612-1200

Address: 2118 Emmorton Park Rd 21040 **Location:** I-95, exit 77A, just e on SR 24. **Facility:** 92 one-bedroom standard units, some with whirlpools. 3 stories, interior corridors. *Bath:* combo or shower only. **Parking:** on-site. **Amenities:** dual phone lines, voice mail, irons, hair dryers. **Pool(s):** heated indoor. **Leisure Activities:** whirlpool, limited exercise equipment. **Guest Services:** valet and coin laundry, wireless Internet. **Business Services:** meeting rooms, PC. **Cards:** AX, CB, DC, DS, JC, MC, VI. **Free Special Amenities:** expanded continental breakfast and high-speed Internet.

RAMADA CONFERENCE CENTER

Book great rates at AAA.com

Small-scale Hotel
$75-$119 3/1-10/31
$69-$119 11/1-2/28

Phone: (410)679-0770

Address: 1700 Van Bibber Rd 21040 **Location:** I-95, exit 77A, just e on SR 24. **Facility:** 152 units. 150 one-bedroom standard units. 2 one-bedroom suites. 2 stories (no elevator), exterior corridors. *Bath:* combo or shower only. **Parking:** on-site. **Amenities:** high-speed Internet, voice mail, irons, hair dryers. *Fee:* video games, safes. **Pool(s):** outdoor. **Leisure Activities:** exercise room. **Guest Services:** valet and coin laundry, wireless Internet. **Business Services:** conference facilities, business center. **Cards:** AX, CB, DC, DS, JC, MC, VI. **Free Special Amenities:** continental breakfast and high-speed Internet. *(See color ad p 600)*

SLEEP INN & SUITES

Book great rates at AAA.com

Small-scale Hotel
$79-$179 All Year

Phone: (410)679-4700

Address: 1807 Edgewood Rd 21040 **Location:** I-95, exit 77A, just e on SR 24. **Facility:** 84 units. 68 one-bedroom standard units. 16 one-bedroom suites, some with whirlpools. 3 stories, interior corridors. *Bath:* combo or shower only. **Parking:** on-site. **Terms:** cancellation fee imposed. **Amenities:** voice mail, safes (fee), irons, hair dryers. **Pool(s):** heated indoor. **Leisure Activities:** limited exercise equipment. **Guest Services:** valet and coin laundry, wireless Internet. **Business Services:** meeting rooms. **Cards:** AX, CB, DC, DS, JC, MC, VI. **Free Special Amenities:** expanded continental breakfast and high-speed Internet.

──── WHERE TO DINE ────

VENETIAN PALACE

Italian
$5-$20

Phone: 410/679-2330

Locals are attracted to the restaurant for good food from a wide-ranging menu that spans from sandwiches and pizza to pasta, beef and fish dishes. Families feel at home in the casual, comfortable setting. Service is relaxed yet attentive. Casual dress. **Bar:** Full bar. **Reservations:** accepted. **Hours:** 7 am-11 pm. Closed: 11/27, 12/25. **Address:** 1901 Treetop Dr 21040 **Location:** I-95, exit 77A, 1 mi e on SR 24, then 1 mi w on US 40. **Parking:** on-site. **Cards:** AX, DS, MC, VI.

VITALI'S

Italian
$6-$21

Phone: 410/671-9800

Convenient to the interstate and numerous motels, the simple, casual dining room is tended by friendly, efficient servers. On the menu is a nice selection of Italian dishes, as well as Maryland crab cakes, Certified Angus steaks, nightly specials and house specialties, which are highlighted. Casual dress. **Bar:** Full bar. **Hours:** 11:30 am-10 pm. Closed: 11/27, 12/25; also for dinner 12/24. **Address:** 1709 Edgewood Rd 21040 **Location:** I-95, exit 77A, just e on SR 24. **Parking:** on-site. **Cards:** AX, CB, DC, DS, MC, VI.

ELKRIDGE pop. 22,042 (See map and index starting on p. 578)

──── WHERE TO STAY ────

BEST WESTERN BWI AIRPORT

Book great rates at AAA.com

Small-scale Hotel
$99-$159 All Year

Phone: (410)796-3300 **73**

Address: 6755 Dorsey Rd 21075 **Location:** I-95, exit 43A, 0.7 mi e on SR 100, exit 6A, 0.3 mi s on US 1, then just e on SR 103. **Facility:** 133 one-bedroom standard units. 4 stories, interior corridors. *Bath:* combo or shower only. **Parking:** on-site. **Amenities:** high-speed Internet, voice mail, irons, hair dryers. **Pool(s):** heated indoor. **Leisure Activities:** sauna, whirlpool, sun deck, exercise room. **Guest Services:** valet laundry, airport transportation-Baltimore-Washington International Airport, area transportation-Arundel Mills Mall, Light Rail Amtrak station, wireless Internet. **Business Services:** meeting rooms, PC. **Cards:** AX, DC, DS, MC, VI. **Free Special Amenities:** expanded continental breakfast and high-speed Internet.

AAA Benefit:
Members save 10% everyday, plus an exclusive frequent stay program.

COMFORT SUITES-COLUMBIA GATEWAY

Book great rates at AAA.com

Small-scale Hotel
$99-$249 All Year

Phone: (410)799-9525 **74**

Address: 7146 Old Waterloo Rd 21075 **Location:** I-95, exit 41A, 0.6 mi n on SR 175, then just n on US 1 to Port Capital Dr. **Facility:** 83 one-bedroom suites, some with whirlpools. 4 stories, interior corridors. *Bath:* combo or shower only. **Parking:** on-site. **Terms:** cancellation fee imposed. **Amenities:** high-speed Internet, dual phone lines, voice mail, irons, hair dryers. **Pool(s):** heated indoor. **Leisure Activities:** whirlpool, exercise room. **Guest Services:** valet and coin laundry, wireless Internet. **Business Services:** meeting rooms, business center. **Cards:** AX, DC, DS, MC, VI.

HOLIDAY INN EXPRESS

[fyi]

Small-scale Hotel

Under construction, scheduled to open October 2008. **Address:** 6070 Marshal Lee Dr 21075 **Location:** I-95, exit 43, 1.5 mi w on SR 100 to exit 4 (SR 103), then just e. **Amenities:** microwaves, refrigerators, pool.

(See map and index starting on p. 578)

──────── WHERE TO DINE ────────

THE ELKRIDGE FURNACE INN

Continental
$9-$36

Phone: 410/379-9336 ㉟

On 16 acres of land, the restored circa 1744 tavern retains many original features of the Federal/Greek Revival building. The dining room is cozy. On the eclectic menu are smoked duck and preparations of beef and fish. Dressy casual. **Bar:** Full bar. **Reservations:** suggested. **Hours:** 11:30 am-2 & 5-9 pm, Sat 5 pm-10 pm, Sun 10 am-2 & 4-8 pm. Closed: 3/23, 11/27, 12/24, 12/25; also Mon. **Address:** 5745 Furnace Ave 21075 **Location:** Jct Main St and Furnace Ave, 0.5 mi s. **Parking:** on-site. **Cards:** AX, MC, VI. **Historic**

HOUSE OF WELSH

American
$7-$25

Phone: 410/796-7775 ㊱

The casual restaurant offers a comfortable dining atmosphere for any occasion. On the menu is a wide selection of beef and seafood dishes, as well as pasta. Casual dress. **Bar:** Full bar. **Reservations:** suggested, weekends. **Hours:** 11 am-10 pm. Closed: 1/1, 12/25. **Address:** 6751 Dorsey Rd 21075 **Location:** I-95, exit 43A, 0.7 mi e on SR 100, exit 6A, 0.3 mi s on US 1, then just e on SR 103. **Parking:** on-site. **Cards:** AX, DC, DS, MC, VI.

ELLICOTT CITY pop. 56,397

──────── WHERE TO STAY ────────

RESIDENCE INN BY MARRIOTT COLUMBIA *Book great rates at AAA.com*

Small-scale Hotel
$231-$252 All Year

Address: 4950 Beaver Run Way 21043 **Location:** I-95, exit 43B, 4 mi w on SR 100, exit 1B (Executive Park Dr). **Facility:** Smoke free premises. 108 units. 45 one-bedroom standard units with efficiencies. 42 one- and 21 two-bedroom suites, some with efficiencies or kitchens. 3 stories, interior corridors. *Bath:* combo or shower only. **Parking:** on-site. **Amenities:** video games (fee), high-speed Internet, voice mail, irons, hair dryers. **Pool(s):** outdoor. **Leisure Activities:** whirlpool, limited exercise equipment, sports court. **Guest Services:** valet and coin laundry, wireless Internet. **Business Services:** meeting rooms. **Cards:** AX, DC, DS, JC, MC, VI.

Phone: 410/997-7200

AAA Benefit:
Members save 5% off of the best available rate.

TURF VALLEY RESORT *Book great rates at AAA.com*

Resort
Large-scale Hotel
$110 All Year

Address: 2700 Turf Valley Rd 21042 **Location:** I-70, exit 82 eastbound, 1.5 mi e on US 40; exit 83 westbound, 0.6 mi s on Marriottsville Rd, then 0.8 mi e on US 40. **Facility:** In addition to its impressive meeting facilities, the resort offers many recreational activities, including a fine golf course. Smoke free premises. 171 units. 143 one-bedroom standard units, some with whirlpools. 27 one- and 2 two-bedroom suites. 7 stories, interior corridors. *Bath:* combo or shower only. **Parking:** on-site. **Terms:** check-in 4 pm, 3 day cancellation notice. **Amenities:** voice mail, irons, hair dryers. **Dining:** 2 restaurants. **Pool(s):** outdoor, heated indoor. **Leisure Activities:** saunas, whirlpool, 3 tennis courts (1 lighted), jogging, spa, basketball. *Fee:* golf-36 holes, driving range. **Guest Services:** valet laundry, airport transportation-Baltimore-Washington International Airport, area transportation (fee), wireless Internet. **Business Services:** conference facilities, PC. **Cards:** AX, CB, DC, DS, JC, MC, VI. **Free Special Amenities: continental breakfast and room upgrade (subject to availability with advance reservations).** *(See color ad p 610)*

Phone: (410)465-1500

──────── WHERE TO DINE ────────

THE CRAB SHANTY

Seafood
$7-$45

Phone: 410/465-9660

Guests can savor good-quality, simply prepared dishes served in ample portions. The interesting decor includes lots of wood and antiques. Some alternatives to seafood are offered. Booth or table seating can be requested, and the lounge is separate from the dining room. Casual dress. **Bar:** Full bar. **Reservations:** accepted. **Hours:** 11:30 am-2:30 & 5-9 pm, Wed & Thurs-10 pm, Sat 5 pm-10 pm, Sun 11 am-9 pm. Closed: 1/1, 11/27, 12/25. **Address:** 3410 Plumtree Dr 21042 **Location:** US 40, 1 mi w of jct US 29. **Parking:** on-site. **Cards:** AX, CB, DC, DS, MC, VI.

EGGSPECTATION

American
$7-$20

Phone: 410/750-3115

The menu lists dozens of all-day breakfast possibilities, including eggs in a bagel, Bretonne-style crepes, eggs Benedict, pancakes, French toast and waffles. Salads, burgers, sandwiches, pasta, chicken, fish and steak, as well as specialty coffees and a variety of freshly squeezed juices, round out the offerings. Casual dress. **Bar:** Full bar. **Reservations:** not accepted. **Hours:** 7 am-10 pm, Sun-9 pm. Closed: 11/27, 12/25. **Address:** 6010 University Blvd 21043 **Location:** I-95, exit 43, 2 mi w on SR 100, exit 3, then just s. **Parking:** on-site. **Cards:** AX, DC, DS, MC, VI.

CALL

KELSEY'S RESTAURANT

Phone: 410/418-9076

American
$6-$20

All the finest traditions of an Irish pub can be found at Kelsey's Restaurant: great food, a family-oriented dining room and a cozy pub. Casual dress. **Bar:** Full bar. **Reservations:** accepted. **Hours:** 11:30 am-11 pm, Thurs-midnight, Fri & Sat-1 am. Closed: 1/1, 12/25. **Address:** 8480 Baltimore National Pike 21043 **Location:** On US 40, 0.7 mi e of jct US 29; in Normandy Shopping Center. **Parking:** on-site. **Cards:** AX, DS, MC, VI.

TERSIGUEL'S FRENCH COUNTRY RESTAURANT

Phone: 410/465-4004

French
$9-$36

The established restaurant blends French-style cooking and rustic country fare using fresh seasonal items including such popular dishes as veal medallions with wild mushrooms, crispy duck with plum sauce and roast pheasant. Dressy casual. **Bar:** Full bar. **Reservations:** suggested. **Hours:** 11:30 am-2:30 & 5-9 pm, Fri & Sat-10 pm, Sun 10:30 am-2:30 & 5-9 pm. Closed: 1/1, 7/4, 12/25. **Address:** 8293 Main St 21043 **Location:** Downtown. **Parking:** street. **Cards:** AX, DC, DS, MC, VI.

ESSEX pop. 39,078 (See map and index starting on p. 578)

———— WHERE TO STAY ————

SUPER 8 MOTEL BALTIMORE/ESSEX *Book at AAA.com*

Phone: 410/780-0030 42

Small-scale Hotel
Rates not provided

Address: 98 Stemmers Run Rd 21221 **Location:** I-695, exit 36 (SR 702 S) to SR 150 E (Chase exit). Located in a commercial area. **Facility:** 48 one-bedroom standard units. 3 stories, interior corridors. **Parking:** on-site. **Amenities:** safes (fee), hair dryers. **Guest Services:** coin laundry, wireless Internet.

 CALL ⊗M ☎ / SOME UNITS FEE ☜ ✕ ⊟ ⊡

FALLSTON pop. 8,427

———— WHERE TO DINE ————

JOSEF'S COUNTRY INN

Phone: 410/877-7800

Continental
$8-$28

The restaurant's Continental menu offers a nice selection of beef, chicken and seafood dishes as well as a traditional German favorite, Wiener Schnitzel, served in generous portions with spaetzle. The staff is friendly and helpful. Dressy casual. **Bar:** Full bar. **Reservations:** suggested. **Hours:** 11:30 am-2:30 & 5-10 pm, Fri-11 pm, Sat 5 pm-11 pm, Sun noon-9 pm. Closed: 1/1, 12/25. **Address:** 2410 Pleasantville Rd 21047 **Location:** Just w of SR 152; 3.7 mi n of jct SR 147 and 152. **Parking:** on-site. **Cards:** AX, DC, DS, MC, VI.

GLEN BURNIE pop. 38,922   (See map and index starting on p. 578)

——— WHERE TO STAY ———

DAYS INN-GLEN BURNIE   *Book at AAA.com*   **Phone:** 410/761-8300   **78**

Small-scale Hotel
Rates not provided

Address: 6600 Ritchie Hwy 21061 **Location:** I-695, exit 3B eastbound; exit 2 westbound, 0.5 mi s on SR 2. Located in a commercial area. **Facility:** 100 one-bedroom standard units. 3 stories, exterior corridors. *Bath:* combo or shower only. **Parking:** on-site. **Amenities:** voice mail, safes (fee), irons, hair dryers. **Pool(s):** outdoor. **Leisure Activities:** limited exercise equipment. **Guest Services:** valet laundry, wireless Internet. **Business Services:** meeting rooms, business center.

**EXTENDED STAYAMERICA BALTIMORE-GLEN
BURNIE**   *Book at AAA.com*   **Phone:** (410)761-2708   **80**

Small-scale Hotel
$129-$139 All Year

Address: 104 Chesapeake Centre Ct 21061 **Location:** I-695, exit 3B, 0.9 mi s on SR 2, just e on E Ordance Rd, then just s. **Facility:** 101 one-bedroom standard units with efficiencies. 3 stories, interior corridors. *Bath:* combo or shower only. **Parking:** on-site. **Terms:** office hours 7 am-11 pm. **Amenities:** voice mail, irons. **Guest Services:** coin laundry, wireless Internet. **Cards:** AX, DC, DS, JC, MC, VI.

HAMPTON INN BALTIMORE/GLEN BURNIE   *Book great rates at AAA.com*   **Phone:** (410)761-7666   **79**

(AAA) (SAVE)

Small-scale Hotel
$99-$126 All Year

Address: 6617 Ritchie Hwy 21061 **Location:** I-695, exit 3B eastbound; exit 2 westbound, 0.5 mi s on SR 2. Located adjacent to Governor Plaza Shopping Center. **Facility:** 116 units. 110 one-bedroom standard units. 6 one-bedroom suites. 5 stories, interior corridors. **Parking:** on-site. **Terms:** 1-3 night minimum stay - weekends, 3 day cancellation notice-fee imposed. **Amenities:** voice mail, irons, hair dryers. **Guest Services:** valet laundry, airport transportation-Baltimore-Washington International Airport, area transportation-within 5 mi, wireless Internet. **Business Services:** meeting rooms, PC. **Cards:** AX, DC, DS, MC, VI. **Free Special Amenities:** expanded continental breakfast and high-speed Internet. *(See color ad below)*

HOLIDAY INN-BALTIMORE SOUTH   *Book great rates at AAA.com*   **Phone:** (410)636-4300   **77**

(AAA) (SAVE)

Small-scale Hotel
$89-$159 All Year

Address: 6323 Ritchie Hwy 21061 **Location:** I-695, exit 3A eastbound; exit 2 westbound, jct SR 2. **Facility:** 127 one-bedroom standard units. 4 stories, interior corridors. *Bath:* combo or shower only. **Parking:** on-site. **Terms:** cancellation fee imposed. **Amenities:** voice mail, irons, hair dryers. **Pool(s):** outdoor. **Leisure Activities:** limited exercise equipment. **Guest Services:** valet and coin laundry, wireless Internet. **Business Services:** meeting rooms, PC. **Cards:** AX, CB, DC, DS, JC, MC, VI.

——— WHERE TO DINE ———

GLORY DAYS GRILL, PASADENA   **Phone:** 443/749-4376

American
$7-$18

Lending to the casual restaurant's sports-themed atmosphere are memorabilia decorating the dining area and 25 TVs with control centers at each table and booth. Food selections range from wings and ribs to seafood, beef and pasta dishes. Casual dress. **Bar:** Full bar. **Reservations:** not accepted. **Hours:** 4 pm-midnight, Fri & Sat from 11:30 am, Sun 11:30 am-11 pm. Closed: 11/27, 12/25. **Address:** 7939 Ritchie Hwy 21061 **Location:** SR 2; at Marley Station Shopping Center. **Parking:** on-site. **Cards:** AX, DS, MC, VI.

THE OLIVE TREE RESTAURANT   **Phone:** 410/761-8237   **39**

Italian
$7-$24

The restaurant is suitable for any occasion: business, social or a family night out. The kitchen prepares traditional Italian dishes, including a nice selection of seafood, chicken, veal and beef preparations. Hand-painted wall murals add to the dining room's comfortable atmosphere. The lunch menu is presented until 3 p.m. Casual dress. **Bar:** Full bar. **Reservations:** accepted. **Hours:** 11 am-10 pm, Fri & Sat-11 pm. Closed: 12/25. **Address:** 7005 Ritchie Hwy 21061 **Location:** I-695, exit 3B eastbound; exit 2 westbound, 1.4 mi s on SR 2. **Parking:** on-site. **Cards:** AX, DC, DS, MC, VI.

▼ *See AAA listing above* ▼

HANOVER   (See map and index starting on p. 578)

------ WHERE TO STAY ------

HAMPTON INN & SUITES-ARUNDEL MILLS/BWI

Phone: (410)540-9225   **86**

Small-scale Hotel
$109-$299 All Year

Address: 7027 Arundel Mills Cir 21076 **Location:** I-95, exit 43A, 3.6 mi e on SR 100, exit 10A (Arundel Mills Blvd). Located adjacent to shopping mall. **Facility:** 131 one-bedroom standard units. 5 stories, interior corridors. *Bath:* combo or shower only. **Parking:** on-site. **Amenities:** video games (fee), high-speed Internet, dual phone lines, voice mail, irons, hair dryers. **Pool(s):** outdoor. **Leisure Activities:** limited exercise equipment. **Guest Services:** complimentary and valet laundry, area transportation, wireless Internet. **Business Services:** meeting rooms, business center. **Cards:** AX, CB, DC, DS, JC, MC, VI.

HOLIDAY INN EXPRESS-BWI AIRPORT   *Book at AAA.com*

Phone: (410)684-3388   **85**

Small-scale Hotel
$145-$169 All Year

Address: 7481 Ridge Rd 21076 **Location:** 1 mi e of SR 295, exit SR 100 E to exit 10B; just e of jct SR 176 and 713. **Facility:** 159 one-bedroom standard units. 5 stories, interior corridors. *Bath:* combo or shower only. **Parking:** on-site. **Amenities:** video games (fee), voice mail, irons, hair dryers. **Pool(s):** heated outdoor. **Leisure Activities:** exercise room. **Guest Services:** valet and coin laundry, area transportation, wireless Internet. **Business Services:** meeting rooms, PC. **Cards:** AX, DC, DS, MC, VI.

RAMADA INN BWI AIRPORT CONFERENCE CENTER   *Book at AAA.com*

Phone: (410)712-4300   **83**

Small-scale Hotel
$103-$122 All Year

Address: 7253 Parkway Dr 21076 **Location:** I-95, exit 43A, 2 mi e on SR 100, exit 8 (Coca-Cola Dr), 0.3 mi n, 0.4 mi e on Park Circle Dr, then just s. Located in business area. **Facility:** 130 one-bedroom standard units. 7 stories, interior corridors. **Parking:** on-site. **Terms:** cancellation fee imposed. **Amenities:** voice mail, safes (fee), irons, hair dryers. **Pool(s):** heated outdoor. **Leisure Activities:** limited exercise equipment. **Guest Services:** valet and coin laundry, area transportation, wireless Internet. **Business Services:** conference facilities. **Cards:** AX, CB, DC, DS, JC, MC, VI.

RED ROOF INN-BWI PARKWAY   *Book at AAA.com*

Phone: 410/712-4070   **84**

Motel
Rates not provided

Address: 7306 Parkway Dr S 21076 **Location:** I-95, exit 43A, 2 mi e on SR 100, exit 8 (Coca-Cola Dr), then 0.5 mi se. Located in business park setting. **Facility:** 108 one-bedroom standard units. 2 stories (no elevator), exterior corridors. *Bath:* combo or shower only. **Parking:** on-site. **Amenities:** voice mail. **Guest Services:** wireless Internet.

RESIDENCE INN BY MARRIOTT-ARUNDEL MILLS/BWI   *Book great rates at AAA.com*

Phone: 410/799-7332   **87**

Small-scale Hotel
$207-$253 All Year

Address: 7035 Arundel Mills Cir 21076 **Location:** I-95, exit 43A, 3.6 mi e on SR 100, exit 10A (Arundel Mills Blvd). Located adjacent to shopping mall. **Facility:** Smoke free premises. 131 units. 53 one-bedroom standard units with efficiencies. 56 one- and 22 two-bedroom suites, some with efficiencies or kitchens. 4 stories, interior corridors. *Bath:* combo or shower only. **Parking:** on-site. **Amenities:** video games (fee), high-speed Internet, dual phone lines, voice mail, irons, hair dryers. **Pool(s):** outdoor. **Leisure Activities:** whirlpool, exercise room, sports court, volleyball. **Guest Services:** complimentary and valet laundry, area transportation. **Business Services:** meeting rooms, business center. **Cards:** AX, DC, DS, JC, MC, VI.

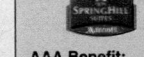

AAA Benefit:
Members save 5% off of the best available rate.

SPRINGHILL SUITES BY MARRIOTT-ARUNDEL MILLS/BWI   *Book great rates at AAA.com*

Phone: 410/799-7100   **88**

Small-scale Hotel
$188-$229 All Year

Address: 7544 Teague Rd 21076 **Location:** I-95, exit 43A, 3.6 mi e on SR 100; exit 10A (Arundel Mills Blvd), 0.4 mi s to SR 713. Located near a shopping mall. **Facility:** Smoke free premises. 128 one-bedroom standard units, some with whirlpools. 5 stories, interior corridors. *Bath:* combo or shower only. **Parking:** on-site. **Amenities:** video games (fee), high-speed Internet, voice mail, irons, hair dryers. **Pool(s):** heated indoor. **Leisure Activities:** whirlpool, limited exercise equipment. **Guest Services:** complimentary and valet laundry, area transportation, wireless Internet. **Business Services:** meeting rooms, PC. **Cards:** AX, DC, DS, MC, VI.

AAA Benefit:
Members save 5% off of the best available rate.

------ WHERE TO DINE ------

GUNNING'S SEAFOOD RESTAURANT

Phone: 410/712-9404   **42**

American
$7-$40

Gunning's Seafood Restaurant boasts of Baltimore's Best Crabs, well they are right up there. A fun and casual setting with great seafood and other menu choices. Casual dress. **Bar:** Full bar. **Hours:** 11 am-10 pm, Fri-11 pm, Sat noon-11 pm, Sun noon-10 pm. Closed: 11/27, 12/25; also Super Bowl Sun. **Address:** 7304 Parkway Dr 21076 **Location:** 0.7 mi w of SR 295, exit 100, w to exit 8, then 0.5 mi e. **Parking:** on-site. **Cards:** AX, DC, MC, VI.

(See map and index starting on p. 578)

REMOMO CAFE ITALIA   **Phone:** 410/579-6666

Italian
$7-$24

The cafe is a wonderful place to dine before or after shopping or seeing a movie. Traditional Italian dishes share menu space with modern American selections. Families enjoy the lively, colorful and friendly atmosphere. All sauces, pasta, breads and desserts are made on the premises. Casual dress. **Bar:** Full bar. **Reservations:** not accepted. **Hours:** 11:30 am-10 pm, Fri & Sat-11 pm, Sun-9 pm. Closed: 11/27, 12/25. **Address:** 7000 Arundel Mills Cir, Suite R3 21076 **Location:** I-95, exit 43A, 3.6 mi e on SR 100, exit 10A (Arundel Mills Blvd); in Arundel Mills Mall. **Parking:** on-site. **Cards:** AX, CB, DC, DS, MC, VI.

CALL 🅶ᴹ ⬛

HAVRE DE GRACE pop. 11,331

─────── **WHERE TO STAY** ───────

VANDIVER INN   **Phone:** (410)939-5200

Historic Bed
& Breakfast
$119-$169 All Year

Address: 301 S Union Ave 21078 **Location:** I-95, exit 89, 2.5 mi e on SR 155 to Otsego St, 3 blks e to Union Ave, then s to jct S Union Ave and Fountain St. **Facility:** The inn is made up of three houses dating from 1886, each offering individually decorated rooms with private baths. Smoke free premises. 18 units. 17 one-bedroom standard units, some with whirlpools. 1 two-bedroom suite with kitchen. 2 stories (no elevator), interior/exterior corridors. *Bath:* combo or shower only. **Parking:** on-site. **Terms:** 10 day cancellation notice. **Amenities:** voice mail, irons, hair dryers. *Some:* DVD players, CD players. **Leisure Activities:** croquet, parlor games. **Guest Services:** wireless Internet. **Business Services:** meeting rooms. **Cards:** AX, DC, DS, MC, VI. **Free Special Amenities: expanded continental breakfast and high-speed Internet.**

 🆂ᴰ 🗙 / SOME UNITS ⓋⒸⓇ 🔲 🖼 🖥

─────── **WHERE TO DINE** ───────

THE BAYOU RESTAURANT   **Phone:** 410/939-3565

American
$6-$25

Popular with local residents, the restaurant features seafood and veal specialties as well as homemade bread and pie. All-you-can-eat buffets are served for weekday lunches. Service is friendly and attentive, and this a great spot for a family night out. Casual dress. **Bar:** Full bar. **Reservations:** suggested, weekends. **Hours:** 11:30 am-10 pm; last seating 9 pm. Closed: 12/24-12/26; also Mon. **Address:** 927 Pulaski Hwy 21078 **Location:** I-95, exit 89, 2 mi e on SR 155, then 0.3 mi w on US 40. **Parking:** on-site. **Cards:** AX, DS, MC, VI.

MACGREGOR'S   **Phone:** 410/939-3003

American
$6-$25

Seafood is the specialty at the casually elegant restaurant, which has a two-tiered, glass dining room that overlooks the Susquehanna River. A collection of decoys—fitting for a town that proclaims itself the "decoy capital of the world"—is one facet of the eclectic decor. A covered deck opens seasonally. Leave room for one of the tempting desserts. Casual dress. **Bar:** Full bar. **Reservations:** suggested, weekends. **Hours:** 11 am-10 pm, Fri & Sat-11 pm, Sun 10 am-10 pm. **Address:** 331 St. John St 21078 **Location:** I-95, exit 89, 2.5 mi e on SR 155, 0.5 mi e on SR 7 (Otsego St which becomes Union Ave), bear left on St. John St at Statue of Lafayette. **Parking:** on-site. **Cards:** AX, DS, MC, VI.

⬛

TIDEWATER GRILLE   **Phone:** 410/939-3313

American
$7-$30

Location, location, location. That's just what the restaurant can brag about deservedly from its prime perch on the banks of the Susquehanna River. Guests can take a seat in the casual, comfortable dining room or enjoy outdoor dining on open or covered decks. Casual dress. **Bar:** Full bar. **Hours:** 11 am-9 pm, Fri & Sat-10 pm. Closed: 11/27, 12/25. **Address:** 300 Foot of Franklin St 21078 **Location:** I-95, exit 89, 2.5 mi e on SR 155, then 0.5 mi e on SR 7 (Otsego St which becomes Union Ave). **Parking:** on-site. **Cards:** AX, DC, MC, VI.

⬛

HUNT VALLEY

─────── **WHERE TO STAY** ───────

COURTYARD BY MARRIOTT HUNT VALLEY   *Book great rates at AAA.com*   **Phone:** 410/584-7070

Small-scale Hotel
$154-$186 All Year

Address: 221 International Cir 21030 **Location:** I-83, exit 20A (Shawan Rd), just ne. **Facility:** Smoke free premises. 146 units. 134 one-bedroom standard units. 12 one-bedroom suites. 3 stories, interior corridors. *Bath:* combo or shower only. **Parking:** on-site. **Amenities:** high-speed Internet, dual phone lines, voice mail, irons, hair dryers. **Pool(s):** heated indoor. **Leisure Activities:** whirlpool, exercise room. **Guest Services:** valet and coin laundry, wireless Internet. **Business Services:** meeting rooms, PC. **Cards:** AX, DC, DS, JC, MC, VI.

AAA Benefit:
Members save 5% off of the best available rate.

   CALL 🅶ᴹ 🗙 🖥 / SOME UNITS 🔲 🖼

EMBASSY SUITES BALTIMORE NORTH/HUNT
VALLEY   *Book at AAA.com*   **Phone:** 410/584-1400

Large-scale Hotel
Rates not provided

Address: 213 International Cir 21030 **Location:** I-83, exit 20A (Shawan Rd), just e. **Facility:** 223 one-bedroom suites. 8 stories, interior corridors. *Bath:* combo or shower only. **Parking:** on-site. **Terms:** check-in 4 pm. **Amenities:** video games (fee), high-speed Internet, dual phone lines, voice mail, irons, hair dryers. **Pool(s):** heated indoor. **Leisure Activities:** sauna, whirlpool, exercise room. **Guest Services:** valet and coin laundry, area transportation, wireless Internet. **Business Services:** conference facilities, business center.

HAMPTON INN HUNT VALLEY   *Book great rates at AAA.com*
Phone: 410/527-1500

Small-scale Hotel
Rates not provided

Address: 11200 York Rd 21030 **Location:** I-83, exit 20A (Shawan Rd), 2 mi se to SR 45, then just s. Located in a commercial area. **Facility:** 125 one-bedroom standard units. 7 stories, interior corridors. **Parking:** on-site. **Amenities:** video games (fee), dual phone lines, voice mail, irons, hair dryers. **Leisure Activities:** limited exercise equipment. **Guest Services:** valet laundry, area transportation, wireless Internet. **Business Services:** meeting rooms, PC.

MARRIOTT HUNT VALLEY   *Book great rates at AAA.com*
Phone: 410/785-7000

Large-scale Hotel
$158-$193 All Year

Address: 245 Shawan Rd 21031 **Location:** I-83, exit 20A (Shawan Rd), just e. **Facility:** Smoke free premises. 393 units. 392 one-bedroom standard units. 1 one-bedroom suite. 4 stories, interior corridors. *Bath:* combo or shower only. **Parking:** on-site. **Amenities:** voice mail, irons, hair dryers. **Pool(s):** heated indoor/outdoor. **Leisure Activities:** saunas, whirlpool, 2 tennis courts, exercise room. *Fee:* massage. **Guest Services:** valet laundry, area transportation, wireless Internet. **Business Services:** conference facilities, business center. **Cards:** AX, DC, DS, JC, MC, VI.

Marriott.
HOTELS & RESORTS

AAA Benefit:
Members save 5% off of the best available rate.

——— WHERE TO DINE ———

THE OREGON GRILLE
Phone: 410/771-0505

American
$6-$36

Decorated with horse-racing pictures, dark-wood paneling and candlelit tables, the upscale restaurant is known for the innovative dishes—such as lobster corn cakes and pan-fried rockfish—its talented chef creates. Beef is another strength. The staff is professional and attentive. Jackets are required after 5 pm. Monday through Saturday and after 4 pm on Sunday. Semi-formal attire. **Bar:** Full bar. **Reservations:** suggested. **Hours:** 11:30 am-4 & 5-10 pm, Fri & Sat-11 pm, Sun 11 am-3 & 4-10 pm. Closed: 12/25, 12/26. **Address:** 1201 Shawan Rd 21030 **Location:** I-83, exit 20B, 1 mi w. **Parking:** on-site. **Cards:** AX, CB, DC, DS, MC, VI.

JESSUP pop. 7,865   (See map and index starting on p. 578)

——— WHERE TO STAY ———

COMMODORE JOSHUA BARNEY HOUSE B & B
Phone: 301/362-1900

Historic Bed
& Breakfast
$175-$225 All Year

Address: 7912 Savage Gilford Rd 20763 **Location:** I-95, exit 38A, 1.5 mi e on SR 32, just s on US 1, 0.5 mi w on Howard St, then 1.1 mi n. Located in residential area. **Facility:** A building of historic significance, the Commodore House is a cozy B&B on six landscaped acres in a residential setting. Smoke free premises. 4 one-bedroom standard units. 3 stories (no elevator), interior corridors. *Bath:* combo or shower only. **Terms:** office hours 9 am-9 pm, check-in 4 pm, age restrictions may apply. **Amenities:** video library, high-speed Internet, hair dryers. *Some:* CD players. **Leisure Activities:** basketball, horseshoes. **Business Services:** meeting rooms.

EXTENDED STAYAMERICA-JESSUP   *Book at AAA.com*
Phone: (301)725-3877

Small-scale Hotel
$124-$134 All Year

Address: 8550 Washington Blvd 20794 **Location:** I-95, exit 38A, 1.4 mi e on SR 32, 0.5 mi n on US 1. **Facility:** 104 one-bedroom standard units with efficiencies. 3 stories, interior corridors. *Bath:* combo or shower only. **Parking:** on-site. **Terms:** office hours 7 am-11 pm. **Amenities:** voice mail, irons. **Guest Services:** coin laundry, wireless Internet. **Cards:** AX, DC, DS, JC, MC, VI.

FAIRFIELD INN BY MARRIOTT-COLUMBIA/JESSUP   *Book great rates at AAA.com*   **Phone: (410)799-1500**   91

Small-scale Hotel
$129-$159 All Year

Address: 7300 Crestmount Rd 20794 **Location:** I-95, exit 41A; just s of jct US 1 and SR 175. **Facility:** Smoke free premises. 105 one-bedroom standard units. 4 stories, interior corridors. *Bath:* combo or shower only. **Parking:** on-site. **Amenities:** video games (fee), voice mail, irons, hair dryers. **Leisure Activities:** limited exercise equipment. **Guest Services:** valet and coin laundry, wireless Internet. **Business Services:** PC. **Cards:** AX, DC, DS, MC, VI.

FAIRFIELD
Marriott

AAA Benefit:
Members save 5% off of the best available rate.

RED ROOF INN-COLUMBIA/JESSUP   *Book at AAA.com*
Phone: 410/796-0380   92

Motel
Rates not provided

Address: 8000 Washington Blvd 20794 **Location:** I-95, exit 41A; 0.3 mi s of jct US 1 and SR 175. **Facility:** 108 one-bedroom standard units. 3 stories, exterior corridors. *Bath:* combo or shower only. **Parking:** on-site. **Amenities:** video games (fee), voice mail. **Guest Services:** coin laundry, wireless Internet.

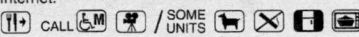

(See map and index starting on p. 578)

SLEEP INN JESSUP

AAA SAVE

Small-scale Hotel
$100-$150 All Year

Book great rates at AAA.com   Phone: (410)799-7794   **94**

Address: 8145 Washington Blvd 20794 **Location:** I-95, exit 41, just e to US 1, then 0.6 mi s on US 1. **Facility:** 54 one-bedroom standard units. 3 stories, interior corridors. *Bath:* combo or shower only. **Parking:** on-site. **Amenities:** high-speed Internet, voice mail, irons, hair dryers. **Leisure Activities:** limited exercise equipment. **Guest Services:** wireless Internet. **Business Services:** PC. **Cards:** AX, DS, MC, VI. **Free Special Amenities:** continental breakfast and high-speed Internet.

SUPER 8 MOTEL

AAA SAVE

Motel
Rates not provided

Phone: 410/796-0400   **93**

Address: 8094 Washington Blvd 20794 **Location:** I-95, exit 41A; 0.5 mi s of jct US 1 and SR 175. **Facility:** 35 one-bedroom standard units, some with whirlpools. 2 stories (no elevator), exterior corridors. **Parking:** on-site. **Amenities:** irons. **Guest Services:** wireless Internet.

JOPPA

—— WHERE TO STAY ——

SUPER 8 JOPPA MOTEL

AAA SAVE

Small-scale Hotel
Rates not provided

Book great rates at AAA.com   Phone: 410/676-2700

Address: 1015 Pulaski Hwy 21085 **Location:** I-95, exit 74, 1 mi s on SR 152, then just w on US 40. **Facility:** 55 one-bedroom standard units. 2 stories (no elevator), interior/exterior corridors. **Parking:** on-site. **Amenities:** safes (fee), hair dryers. **Guest Services:** wireless Internet. **Free Special Amenities:** expanded continental breakfast and high-speed Internet.

LINTHICUM HEIGHTS   (See map and index starting on p. 578)

—— WHERE TO STAY ——

BWI AIRPORT MARRIOTT HOTEL

AAA SAVE

Large-scale Hotel
$277-$338 All Year

Book great rates at AAA.com   Phone: 410/859-8300   **65**

Address: 1743 W Nursery Rd 21240 **Location:** I-695, exit 7A, 1 mi s on SR 295, then 1.2 mi e. **Facility:** Smoke free premises. 309 one-bedroom standard units, some with whirlpools. 10 stories, interior corridors. *Bath:* combo or shower only. **Parking:** on-site. **Amenities:** voice mail, irons, hair dryers. *Fee:* high-speed Internet. **Dining:** Moniker's Grille, see separate listing. **Pool(s):** heated indoor. **Leisure Activities:** whirlpool, sun deck, exercise room. **Guest Services:** valet and coin laundry, airport transportation-Baltimore-Washington International Airport, area transportation-Amtrak station & light rail, wireless Internet. **Business Services:** conference facilities, business center. **Cards:** AX, DC, DS, MC, VI. **Free Special Amenities:** newspaper.

Marriott
HOTELS & RESORTS

AAA Benefit:
Members save 5% off of the best available rate.

CANDLEWOOD SUITES-BWI

AAA

Small-scale Hotel
$135 All Year

Book at AAA.com   Phone: 410/850-9214   **55**

Address: 1247 Winterson Rd 21090 **Location:** I-695, exit 7A, 1 mi s on SR 295, 1.3 mi e on W Nursery Rd, then 0.3 mi w. **Facility:** 125 units. 101 one-bedroom standard units with efficiencies. 24 one-bedroom suites with efficiencies. 4 stories, interior corridors. *Bath:* combo or shower only. **Parking:** on-site. **Terms:** cancellation fee imposed. **Amenities:** video library, DVD players, CD players, high-speed Internet, dual phone lines, voice mail, irons, hair dryers. **Leisure Activities:** exercise room. **Guest Services:** complimentary and valet laundry. **Cards:** AX, DC, MC, VI.

COMFORT INN AIRPORT

AAA SAVE

Small-scale Hotel
$129-$189 All Year

Book great rates at AAA.com   Phone: (410)789-9100   **47**

Address: 6921 Baltimore Annapolis Blvd 21225 **Location:** I-695, exit 6A eastbound; exit 5 westbound, at SR 170 and 648. **Facility:** 188 one-bedroom standard units, some with whirlpools. 6 stories, interior corridors. *Bath:* combo or shower only. **Parking:** on-site. **Amenities:** dual phone lines, voice mail, irons, hair dryers. *Fee:* video games, safes. **Dining:** The Rose Restaurant LTD, see separate listing. **Leisure Activities:** sauna, whirlpool, exercise room. **Guest Services:** valet and coin laundry, airport transportation-Baltimore-Washington International Airport, area transportation-Amtrak station & light rail, wireless Internet. **Business Services:** meeting rooms, business center. **Cards:** AX, DS, MC, VI. **Free Special Amenities:** full breakfast and high-speed Internet.

(See map and index starting on p. 578)

COMFORT SUITES-BWI AIRPORT   *Book great rates at AAA.com*   Phone: 410/691-1000 69

Small-scale Hotel
Rates not provided

Address: 815 Elkridge Landing Rd 21090 **Location:** I-695, exit 7A, 1 mi s on SR 295, then 1.3 mi e on W Nursery Rd. **Facility:** 137 units. 136 one-bedroom standard units. 1 one-bedroom suite with whirlpool. 5 stories, interior corridors. *Bath:* combo or shower only. **Parking:** on-site. **Amenities:** high-speed Internet, dual phone lines, voice mail, irons, hair dryers. *Fee:* video games, safes. **Leisure Activities:** limited exercise equipment. **Guest Services:** valet and coin laundry, airport transportation-Baltimore-Washington International Airport, area transportation-Amtrak station, light rail & local restaurants, wireless Internet. **Business Services:** meeting rooms, business center. **Free Special Amenities: continental breakfast and high-speed Internet.**

COUNTRY INN & SUITES BY CARLSON BWI
AIRPORT   *Book at AAA.com*   Phone: (443)577-1036 63

Small-scale Hotel
$180-$199 All Year

Address: 1717 W Nursery Rd 21090 **Location:** I-695, exit 7A, 1 mi s on SR 295, then 1.2 mi e. **Facility:** 107 units. 81 one-bedroom standard units, some with whirlpools. 26 one-bedroom suites. 5 stories, interior corridors. *Bath:* combo or shower only. **Parking:** on-site. **Amenities:** high-speed Internet, voice mail, irons, hair dryers. **Pool(s):** heated indoor. **Leisure Activities:** whirlpool, exercise room. **Guest Services:** valet and coin laundry, area transportation, wireless Internet. **Business Services:** meeting rooms, PC. **Cards:** AX, CB, DC, DS, JC, MC, VI.

COURTYARD BY MARRIOTT-BWI AIRPORT   *Book great rates at AAA.com*   Phone: 410/859-8855 60

Small-scale Hotel
$242-$263 All Year

Address: 1671 W Nursery Rd 21090 **Location:** I-695, exit 7A, 1 mi s on SR 295, then 0.8 mi e. **Facility:** Smoke free premises. 149 units. 137 one-bedroom standard units. 12 one-bedroom suites. 3 stories, interior corridors. **Parking:** on-site. **Amenities:** high-speed Internet, voice mail, irons, hair dryers. **Pool(s):** heated indoor. **Leisure Activities:** whirlpool, limited exercise equipment. **Guest Services:** valet and coin laundry, area transportation. **Business Services:** meeting rooms, business center. **Cards:** AX, DC, DS, JC, MC, VI.

AAA Benefit:
Members save 5% off of the best available rate.

EMBASSY SUITES HOTEL BALTIMORE AT BWI   *Book at AAA.com*   Phone: 410/850-0747 53

Large-scale Hotel
Rates not provided

Address: 1300 Concourse Dr 21090 **Location:** I-695, exit 7A, 1 mi s on SR 295, 0.7 mi e on W Nursery Rd, then 0.5 mi w on Winterson. **Facility:** 251 units. 250 one- and 1 two-bedroom suites, some with whirlpools. 8 stories, interior corridors. *Bath:* combo or shower only. **Parking:** on-site. **Amenities:** video games (fee), dual phone lines, voice mail, irons, hair dryers. **Pool(s):** heated indoor. **Leisure Activities:** saunas, whirlpool, jogging, exercise room. **Guest Services:** valet laundry, area transportation, wireless Internet. **Business Services:** conference facilities, PC (fee).

FAIRFIELD INN BY MARRIOTT-BWI AIRPORT   *Book great rates at AAA.com*   Phone: (410)859-2333 64

Small-scale Hotel
$139-$169 All Year

Address: 1734 W Nursery Rd 21090 **Location:** SR 295, exit Nursery Rd, 1.2 mi e. **Facility:** Smoke free premises. 130 one-bedroom standard units. 5 stories, interior corridors. *Bath:* combo or shower only. **Parking:** on-site. **Amenities:** voice mail, irons, hair dryers. **Pool(s):** outdoor. **Leisure Activities:** limited exercise equipment. **Guest Services:** valet and coin laundry, wireless Internet. **Business Services:** PC (fee). **Cards:** AX, DC, DS, MC, VI.

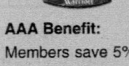

AAA Benefit:
Members save 5% off of the best available rate.

(See map and index starting on p. 578)

FOUR POINTS BY SHERATON BWI AIRPORT   *Book great rates at AAA.com*   Phone: (410)859-3300 70

 (AAA) (SAVE)

Small-scale Hotel
$103-$240 3/1-11/15
$98-$240 11/16-2/28

Address: 7032 Elm Rd 21240 **Location:** I-195, exit 1A, 0.5 mi n on SR 170, then just e. **Facility:** 201 units. 200 one-bedroom standard units. 1 one-bedroom suite. 2 stories, interior corridors. *Bath:* combo or shower only. **Parking:** on-site. **Terms:** cancellation fee imposed. **Amenities:** high-speed Internet, dual phone lines, voice mail, irons, hair dryers. **Pool(s):** outdoor. **Leisure Activities:** exercise room. **Guest Services:** valet laundry, airport transportation-Baltimore-Washington International Airport, area transportation-Amtrak station & light rail. **Business Services:** conference facilities, business center. **Cards:** AX, CB, DC, DS, JC, MC, VI. **Free Special Amenities:** newspaper and high-speed Internet. *(See color ad below)*

FOUR POINTS BY SHERATON

AAA Benefit:
Members get up to 15% off, plus Starwood Preferred Guest® bonuses.

[icons] SD · CALL · M · FEE UNITS · FEE

HAMPTON INN BWI AIRPORT   *Book great rates at AAA.com*   Phone: 410/850-0600 66

Small-scale Hotel
Rates not provided

Address: 829 Elkridge Landing Rd 21090 **Location:** I-695, exit 7A, 1 mi s on SR 295, 1.3 mi e on W Nursery Rd, then just w. **Facility:** 182 one-bedroom standard units. 5 stories, interior corridors. *Bath:* combo or shower only. **Parking:** on-site. **Amenities:** high-speed Internet, voice mail, irons, hair dryers. **Leisure Activities:** exercise room. **Guest Services:** complimentary and valet laundry, area transportation, wireless Internet. **Business Services:** meeting rooms, PC.

[icons] CALL · M · SOME UNITS FEE

HILTON BALTIMORE BWI AIRPORT   *Book great rates at AAA.com*   Phone: (410)694-0808 67

Large-scale Hotel
$149-$499 All Year

Address: 1739 W Nursery Rd 21090 **Location:** I-695, exit 7A, 1 mi s on SR 295, then 1.2 mi e. **Facility:** 280 units. 276 one-bedroom standard units. 4 one-bedroom suites, some with whirlpools. 11 stories, interior corridors. *Bath:* combo or shower only. **Parking:** on-site and valet. **Terms:** cancellation fee imposed. **Amenities:** video games (fee), high-speed Internet, dual phone lines, voice mail, safes, honor bars, irons, hair dryers. **Pool(s):** heated indoor. **Leisure Activities:** whirlpool, exercise room. **Guest Services:** valet and coin laundry, area transportation, wireless Internet. **Business Services:** conference facilities, business center. **Cards:** AX, DC, DS, JC, MC, VI.
(See color ad p 623)

[icons] A$K · 24 · CALL · M · SOME UNITS

HILTON GARDEN INN AT BWI   *Book great rates at AAA.com*   Phone: 410/691-0500 49

Small-scale Hotel
Rates not provided

Address: 1516 Aero Dr 21090 **Location:** I-695, exit 7A, 1 mi s on SR 295, 0.6 mi e on W Nursey Rd, then just n. **Facility:** 158 units. 150 one-bedroom standard units. 8 one-bedroom suites, some with whirlpools. 5 stories, interior corridors. *Bath:* combo or shower only. **Parking:** on-site. **Amenities:** video games (fee), high-speed Internet, dual phone lines, voice mail, irons, hair dryers. **Pool(s):** heated indoor. **Leisure Activities:** whirlpool, exercise room. **Guest Services:** valet and coin laundry, area transportation, wireless Internet. **Business Services:** meeting rooms, business center.

[icons] CALL · M · SOME UNITS

(See map and index starting on p. 578)

HOLIDAY INN-BWI AIRPORT CONFERENCE
CENTER   *Book great rates at AAA.com*   Phone: (410)859-8400   [62]

AAA [SAVE]

Large-scale Hotel
$109-$229 All Year

Address: 890 Elkridge Landing Rd 21090 **Location:** I-695, exit 7A, 1 mi s on SR 295, 1.3 mi e on W Nursery Rd, then 0.5 mi w. **Facility:** 260 units. 259 one-bedroom standard units. 1 one-bedroom suite. 7 stories, interior corridors. *Bath:* combo or shower only. **Parking:** on-site. **Amenities:** dual phone lines, voice mail, irons, hair dryers. **Pool(s):** outdoor. **Leisure Activities:** exercise room, sports court. **Guest Services:** valet and coin laundry, airport transportation-Baltimore-Washington International Airport, area transportation-Amtrak station & light rail, wireless Internet. **Business Services:** conference facilities, business center. **Cards:** AX, CB, DC, DS, JC, MC, VI.

[icons]

HOMESTEAD STUDIO SUITES
HOTEL-BALTIMORE-BWI AIRPORT   *Book at AAA.com*   Phone: (410)691-2500   [51]

Motel
$109-$119 All Year

Address: 939 International Dr 21090 **Location:** I-695, exit 7A, 1 mi s on SR 295, then 0.6 mi e on W Nursery Rd. **Facility:** 138 one-bedroom standard units with efficiencies. 2 stories (no elevator), exterior corridors. *Bath:* combo or shower only. **Parking:** on-site. **Terms:** office hours 7 am-11 pm. **Amenities:** voice mail, irons, hair dryers. **Guest Services:** valet and coin laundry, wireless Internet. **Cards:** AX, DC, DS, JC, MC, VI.

[icons]

HOMEWOOD SUITES BY HILTON-BWI AIRPORT   *Book at AAA.com*   Phone: 410/684-6100   [58]

Small-scale Hotel
Rates not provided

Address: 1181 Winterson Rd 21090 **Location:** I-695, exit 7A, 1 mi s on SR 295, 0.7 mi e on W Nursery Rd, then just n. **Facility:** 147 units. 140 one- and 7 two-bedroom suites with efficiencies. 4 stories, interior corridors. *Bath:* combo or shower only. **Parking:** on-site. **Amenities:** video games (fee), high-speed Internet, dual phone lines, voice mail, irons, hair dryers. **Pool(s):** heated indoor. **Leisure Activities:** whirlpool, exercise room. **Guest Services:** valet and coin laundry, area transportation. **Business Services:** meeting rooms, business center.

[icons]

HYATT PLACE BALTIMORE BWI AIRPORT   *Book great rates at AAA.com*   Phone: (410)859-3366   [50]

AAA [SAVE]

Small-scale Hotel
$109-$229 All Year

Address: 940 International Dr 21090 **Location:** I-695, exit 7A, 1 mi s on SR 295, then just e on W Nursery Rd. **Facility:** 128 one-bedroom standard units. 6 stories, interior corridors. *Bath:* combo or shower only. **Parking:** on-site. **Terms:** cancellation fee imposed. **Amenities:** voice mail, safes, irons, hair dryers. *Some:* dual phone lines. **Pool(s):** heated indoor. **Leisure Activities:** exercise room. **Guest Services:** valet and coin laundry, airport transportation-Baltimore-Washington International Airport, area transportation-within 5 mi, wireless Internet. **Business Services:** meeting rooms, PC. **Cards:** AX, CB, DC, DS, JC, MC, VI. **Free Special Amenities:** continental breakfast and high-speed Internet.

HYATT
PLACE

AAA Benefit:
Ask for the AAA rate
and save 10%.

[icons]

▼ See AAA listing p 622 ▼

(See map and index starting on p. 578)

MICROTEL INN & SUITES-BWI AIRPORT *Book great rates at AAA.com* Phone: 410/865-7500 **57**

Small-scale Hotel
Rates not provided

Address: 1170 Winterson Rd 21090 **Location:** I-695, exit 7A, 1 mi s on SR 295, 0.7 mi e on W Nursery Rd, then just n. **Facility:** 110 one-bedroom standard units. 3 stories, interior corridors. *Bath:* combo or shower only. **Parking:** on-site. **Amenities:** video games (fee), voice mail, irons, hair dryers. *Some:* high-speed Internet. **Leisure Activities:** exercise room. **Guest Services:** coin laundry, area transportation, wireless Internet. **Business Services:** meeting rooms, PC.

MOTEL 6 BALTIMORE-LINTHICUM HEIGHTS #1201 *Book at AAA.com* Phone: 410/636-9070 **45**

Motel
$68-$78 5/29-2/28
$65-$75 3/1-5/28

Address: 5179 Raynor Ave 21090 **Location:** I-695, exit 8, just e on SR 168. **Facility:** 136 one-bedroom standard units. 3 stories, exterior corridors. *Bath:* shower only. **Parking:** on-site. **Pool(s):** outdoor. **Guest Services:** coin laundry.

RED ROOF INN-BWI AIRPORT *Book at AAA.com* Phone: 410/850-7600 **68**

Motel
Rates not provided

Address: 827 Elkridge Landing Rd 21090 **Location:** I-695, exit 7A, 1 mi s on SR 295, 1.3 mi e on W Nursery Rd, then just w. **Facility:** 131 one-bedroom standard units. 3 stories, exterior corridors. **Parking:** on-site. **Amenities:** voice mail. **Guest Services:** coin laundry, area transportation, wireless Internet. **Business Services:** meeting rooms.

RESIDENCE INN BY MARRIOTT-BWI AIRPORT *Book great rates at AAA.com* Phone: 410/691-0255 **56**

Small-scale Hotel
$227-$278 All Year

Address: 1160 Winterson Rd 21090 **Location:** I-695, exit 7A, 1 mi s on SR 295, 0.7 mi e on W Nursery Rd, then just n. **Facility:** Smoke free premises. 120 units. 44 one-bedroom standard units with efficiencies. 52 one- and 24 two-bedroom suites, some with efficiencies or kitchens. 3 stories, interior corridors. *Bath:* combo or shower only. **Amenities:** video games (fee), high-speed Internet, voice mail, irons, hair dryers. *Some:* dual phone lines. **Pool(s):** outdoor. **Leisure Activities:** whirlpool, exercise room, sports court. **Guest Services:** valet and coin laundry, area transportation. **Business Services:** meeting rooms. **Cards:** AX, DS, MC, VI.

AAA Benefit:
Members save 5% off of the best available rate.

SHERATON BALTIMORE WASHINGTON AIRPORT
HOTEL *Book great rates at AAA.com* Phone: (443)577-2100 **52**

Small-scale Hotel
$269-$289 3/1-11/1
$219-$239 11/2-2/28

Address: 1100 Old Elkridge Landing Rd 21090 **Location:** I-695, exit 7A, 1 mi s on SR 295, 1.3 mi e on W Nursery Rd, then 0.4 mi w on Winterson Rd. **Facility:** Smoke free premises. 203 units. 193 one-bedroom standard units. 10 one-bedroom suites. 6 stories, interior corridors. *Bath:* combo or shower only. **Parking:** on-site. **Amenities:** high-speed Internet (fee), dual phone lines, voice mail, safes, irons, hair dryers. **Pool(s):** heated indoor. **Leisure Activities:** whirlpool, exercise room. **Guest Services:** valet and coin laundry, wireless Internet. **Business Services:** meeting rooms, business center. **Cards:** AX, CB, DC, DS, JC, MC, VI.

Sheraton
HOTELS & RESORTS
AAA Benefit:
Members get up to 15% off, plus Starwood Preferred Guest® bonuses.

SLEEP INN & SUITES AIRPORT *Book great rates at AAA.com* Phone: (410)789-7223 **46**

Small-scale Hotel
$99-$189 All Year

Address: 6055 Belle Grove Rd 21225 **Location:** I-695, exit 6A eastbound; exit 5 westbound, 0.3 mi n to jct SR 170/648. **Facility:** 145 one-bedroom standard units, some with whirlpools. 7 stories, interior corridors. *Bath:* combo or shower only. **Parking:** on-site. **Amenities:** dual phone lines, voice mail, irons, hair dryers. *Fee:* video games, safes. **Leisure Activities:** exercise room. **Guest Services:** valet and coin laundry, airport transportation-Baltimore-Washington International Airport, area transportation-Amtrak station & light rail, wireless Internet. **Business Services:** meeting rooms, business center. **Cards:** AX, DS, MC, VI. **Free Special Amenities: continental breakfast and high-speed Internet.**

SPRINGHILL SUITES BY MARRIOTT-BWI AIRPORT *Book great rates at AAA.com* Phone: 410/694-0555 **61**

Small-scale Hotel
$210-$240 3/1-11/17
$209-$229 11/18-2/28

Address: 899 Elkridge Landing Rd 21090 **Location:** I-95 to I-195, e to exit 1A, s on Elm Rd, then sw. **Facility:** Smoke free premises. 133 one-bedroom standard units. 4 stories, interior corridors. *Bath:* combo or shower only. **Parking:** on-site. **Amenities:** video games (fee), dual phone lines, voice mail, irons, hair dryers. **Pool(s):** heated indoor. **Leisure Activities:** whirlpool, exercise room. **Guest Services:** valet and coin laundry, area transportation, wireless Internet. **Business Services:** meeting rooms, business center. **Cards:** AX, DC, DS, MC, VI.

AAA Benefit:
Members save 5% off of the best available rate.

(See map and index starting on p. 578)

STAYBRIDGE SUITES BWI   *Book at AAA.com*   Phone: (410)850-5666

Small-scale Hotel
$169-$699 All Year

Address: 1301 Winterson Rd 21090 **Location:** I-695, exit 7A, 1 mi s on SR 295, 1.3 mi e on Nursery Rd, then 0.4 mi w. **Facility:** 104 units. 69 one-bedroom standard units with efficiencies. 25 one- and 10 two-bedroom suites with efficiencies. 5 stories, interior corridors. *Bath:* combo or shower only. **Parking:** on-site. **Amenities:** DVD players, high-speed Internet, voice mail, safes, irons, hair dryers. **Pool(s):** outdoor. **Leisure Activities:** limited exercise equipment. **Guest Services:** complimentary and valet laundry, area transportation, wireless Internet. **Business Services:** meeting rooms, business center. **Cards:** AX, DC, DS, MC, VI.

   CALL   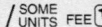 / SOME UNITS FEE

TOWNEPLACE SUITES BALTIMORE/BWI AIRPORT   *Book great rates at AAA.com*   Phone: 410/694-0060   59

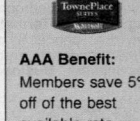
Small-scale Hotel
$109-$299 All Year

Address: 1171 Winterson Rd 21090 **Location:** I-695, exit 7A, 1 mi s on SR 295, 0.7 mi e on W Nursery Rd, then just n. **Facility:** Smoke free premises. 136 units. 113 one-bedroom standard units with efficiencies. 6 one- and 17 two-bedroom suites with kitchens. 4 stories, interior corridors. *Bath:* combo or shower only. **Parking:** on-site. **Terms:** cancellation fee imposed. **Amenities:** high-speed Internet, voice mail, irons, hair dryers. *Some:* DVD players. **Pool(s):** outdoor. **Leisure Activities:** grill, limited exercise equipment. **Guest Services:** valet and coin laundry, airport transportation-Baltimore-Washington International Airport, wireless Internet. **Business Services:** meeting rooms, PC. **Cards:** AX, CB, DC, DS, JC, MC, VI. **Free Special Amenities:** full breakfast and high-speed Internet. *(See color ad below)*

AAA Benefit:
Members save 5% off of the best available rate.

  CALL   / SOME UNITS FEE

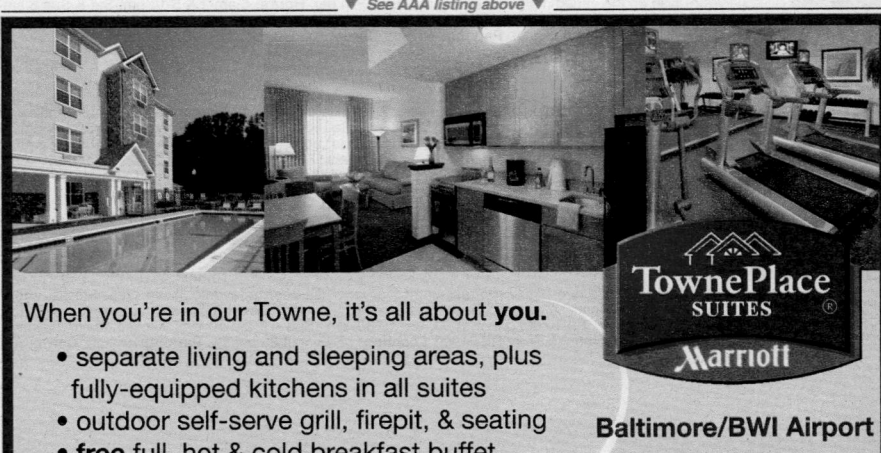

(See map and index starting on p. 578)

THE WESTIN-BALTIMORE WASHINGTON AIRPORT

Phone: 443/577-2300

[fyi]

Small-scale Hotel
$309-$329 3/1-11/1
$289-$309 11/2-2/28

Too new to rate, opening scheduled for October 2007. **Address:** 1110 Old Elkridge Landing Rd 21090 **Location:** I-95/295. **Amenities:** 261 units, coffeemakers, pool. **Cards:** AX, CB, DC, DS, JC, MC, VI.

WESTIN
HOTELS & RESORTS

AAA Benefit:
Members get up to
15% off, plus
Starwood Preferred
Guest® bonuses.

WINGATE INN AT BWI AIRPORT · *Book great rates at AAA.com*

Phone: (410)859-0003 [48]

▼▼▼

Small-scale Hotel
$129-$199 3/1-11/1
$119-$199 11/2-2/28

Address: 1510 Aero Dr 21090 **Location:** 1 mi s on SR 295, 0.6 mi e on W Nursery Rd, then just n. **Facility:** 129 one-bedroom standard units. 5 stories, interior corridors. *Bath:* combo or shower only. **Parking:** on-site. **Terms:** cancellation fee imposed. **Amenities:** video games (fee), high-speed Internet, dual phone lines, voice mail, safes, irons, hair dryers. **Pool(s):** heated indoor. **Leisure Activities:** whirlpool, exercise room. **Guest Services:** valet and coin laundry, area transportation, wireless Internet. **Business Services:** meeting rooms, business center. **Cards:** AX, DC, DS, JC, MC, VI.

(ASK) (S/D) (✈) (¶↑) CALL (&M) (🛋) (❄) (🖥) (📷) (💻) / SOME UNITS (✖)

------- **WHERE TO DINE** -------

G & M RESTAURANT

Phone: 410/636-1777 [30]

▼▼ ▼▼

American
$4-$29

If you like crab cakes, you'll love G & M Restaurant. Family oriented atmosphere and they will ship crab cakes nationwide. Casual dress. **Bar:** Full bar. **Hours:** 11 am-11 pm. Closed: 11/27, 12/25. **Address:** 804 N Hammonds Ferry Rd 21090 **Location:** I-695, exit 8, just w. **Parking:** on-site. **Cards:** AX, DS, MC, VI.

(✎)

MONIKER'S GRILLE

Phone: 410/859-8300 [32]

▼▼ ▼▼

American
$11-$29

The casual Moniker's Grille opens to the lobby of the BWI Airport Marriott Hotel. Crab cakes are the signature dish on the varied menu. Casual dress. **Bar:** Full bar. **Hours:** 6 am-2 & 5-10 pm, Sat & Sun 6 am-noon & 5-10 pm. **Address:** 1743 W Nursery Rd 21240 **Location:** I-695, exit 7A, 1 mi s on SR 295, then 1.2 mi e; in BWI Airport Marriott Hotel. **Parking:** on-site. **Cards:** AX, CB, DC, DS, JC, MC, VI.

THE ROSE RESTAURANT LTD

Phone: 410/636-0300 [31]

(AAA)

▼▼ ▼▼ ▼▼

Continental
$6-$24

Patrons can relax in the comfortable, quiet atmosphere while perusing a menu of freshly made Continental cuisine. The piano bar offers entertainment Fridays and Saturdays. Service in the pub is available from 11 am to midnight. Dressy casual. **Bar:** Full bar. **Reservations:** accepted. **Hours:** 6:30-10 am, 10:30-2 & 5-10 pm, Sat 7 am-2 & 5-10 pm, Sun 7 am-2 & 4-9 pm. **Address:** 6075 Belle Grove Rd 21225 **Location:** I-695, exit 6A eastbound; exit 5 westbound, at SR 170 and 648; in Comfort Inn Airport. **Parking:** on-site. **Cards:** AX, DC, DS, MC, VI.

(✎)

SNYDER'S WILLOW GROVE

Phone: 410/789-1149 [29]

▼▼ ▼▼

American
$8-$31

Snyder's Willow Grove is a family run restaurant that long has been a favorite in the area. Steaks, chops and all sorts of seafood selections. Casual dress. **Bar:** Full bar. **Reservations:** suggested, weekends. **Hours:** 9 am-10 pm, Fri-10:30 pm, Sat 11 am-10:30 pm, Sun 11 am-10 pm. Closed major holidays. **Address:** 841 N Hammonds Ferry Rd 21090 **Location:** I-695, exit 8, just sw. **Parking:** on-site. **Cards:** AX, DC, DS, MC, VI.

(✎)

MOUNT AIRY pop. 6,425

------- **WHERE TO DINE** -------

BRICK RIDGE RESTAURANT

Phone: 301/829-8191

▼▼ ▼▼ ▼▼

American
$12-$24

The old-time house has brick walls and lovely hardwood floors. On the menu are many classic American beef and seafood favorites. Casual dress. **Bar:** Full bar. **Hours:** 5 pm-9 pm, Fri & Sat-10 pm, Sun 11 am-2 & 4-9 pm; Sunday brunch. Closed: 12/25; also Mon. **Address:** 6212 Ridge Rd 21771 **Location:** I-70, exit 68, 3.5 mi n on SR 27. **Parking:** on-site. **Cards:** AX, DC, DS, MC, VI.

FOUR SEASONS RESTAURANT

Phone: 301/829-2320

▼▼ ▼▼

American
$5-$12

The Four Seasons Restaurant is a family-run business with a huge local following; it is well worth a quick stop off the interstate. Casual dress. **Hours:** 6 am-9 pm. Closed major holidays. **Address:** 4506 Old National Pike 21771 **Location:** I-70, exit 68, just s. **Parking:** on-site. **Cards:** AX, DS, MC, VI.

OWINGS MILLS pop. 20,193 (See map and index starting on p. 578)

——— WHERE TO STAY ———

HILTON GARDEN INN-OWINGS MILLS *Book great rates at AAA.com*   Phone: 410/654-0030   🔢12

Small-scale Hotel
Rates not provided

Address: 4770 Owings Mills Blvd 21117 **Location:** I-795, exit 4 (Owings Mills Blvd), 0.7 mi s. Located near shopping mall. **Facility:** 160 one-bedroom standard units. 6 stories, interior corridors. *Bath:* combo or shower only. **Parking:** on-site. **Amenities:** video games (fee), high-speed Internet, dual phone lines, voice mail, irons, hair dryers. **Pool(s):** heated indoor. **Leisure Activities:** whirlpool, exercise room. **Guest Services:** valet and coin laundry, wireless Internet. **Business Services:** meeting rooms, business center.

HYATT PLACE BALTIMORE/OWINGS MILLS *Book great rates at AAA.com*   Phone: (410)998-3630   🔢13

Small-scale Hotel
$109-$229 All Year

Address: 4730 Painters Mill Rd 21117 **Location:** I-795, exit 4 (Owings Mills Blvd), 0.5 mi s, then 0.7 mi e on Red Run Blvd. **Facility:** 124 one-bedroom standard units. 7 stories, interior corridors. *Bath:* combo or shower only. **Parking:** on-site. **Terms:** cancellation fee imposed. **Amenities:** dual phone lines, voice mail, safes, irons, hair dryers. **Pool(s):** heated indoor. **Leisure Activities:** limited exercise equipment. **Guest Services:** valet and coin laundry, area transportation-within 5 mi, wireless Internet. **Business Services:** meeting rooms, PC. **Cards:** AX, CB, DC, DS, JC, MC, VI. **Free Special Amenities:** full breakfast and high-speed Internet.

HYATT PLACE™

AAA Benefit:
Ask for the AAA rate
and save 10%.

——— WHERE TO DINE ———

LIBERATORE'S BISTRO   Phone: 410/356-3100

Italian
$8-$35

Italian cuisine is served in a charming Mediterranean setting. The family-run bistro lists homemade items galore on its menu. Casual dress. **Bar:** Full bar. **Reservations:** suggested. **Hours:** 11 am-10 pm, Fri & Sat-11 pm, Sun 4 pm-9 pm, Mon 11 am-9 pm. Closed major holidays. **Address:** 9712 Groffs Mill Dr 21117 **Location:** I-795, exit 4 (Owings Mills Blvd), 0.9 mi on S Owings Mills Blvd, then 0.9 mi w on Lakeside Blvd; in New Town Village Center. **Parking:** on-site. **Cards:** AX, DS, MC, VI.

PASADENA pop. 12,093 (See map and index starting on p. 578)

——— WHERE TO DINE ———

BELLA NAPOLI ITALIAN RESTAURANT   Phone: 410/255-9400   🔢46

Italian
$8-$20

Dishes are based on classic Italian recipes. Great murals and background music contribute to the setting. Casual dress. **Bar:** Full bar. **Reservations:** accepted. **Hours:** 11 am-9:30 pm, Fri & Sat-10:30 pm, Sun-8 pm. Closed: 12/25. **Address:** 350 Mountain Rd, Suite G 21122 **Location:** 1 mi n on SR 2, 2 mi e. **Parking:** on-site. **Cards:** AX, DC, DS, MC, VI.

PIKESVILLE pop. 29,123 (See map and index starting on p. 578)

——— WHERE TO STAY ———

HILTON PIKESVILLE *Book great rates at AAA.com*   Phone: 410/653-1100   🔢29

Small-scale Hotel
Rates not provided

Address: 1726 Reisterstown Rd 21208-2984 **Location:** I-695, exit 20, just s. **Facility:** 171 one-bedroom standard units. 5 stories, interior corridors. *Bath:* combo or shower only. **Parking:** on-site. **Amenities:** dual phone lines, voice mail, irons, hair dryers. **Pool(s):** outdoor. **Leisure Activities:** saunas. *Fee:* 6 lighted indoor tennis courts, massage. **Guest Services:** valet laundry, area transportation, wireless Internet. **Business Services:** conference facilities, business center.

RAMADA INN BALTIMORE WEST *Book at AAA.com*   Phone: (410)486-5600   🔢28

Small-scale Hotel
$98-$109 All Year

Address: 1721 Reisterstown Rd 21208 **Location:** I-695, exit 20, just e on US 140. **Facility:** 105 one-bedroom standard units, some with whirlpools. 2 stories (no elevator), exterior corridors. *Bath:* combo or shower only. **Parking:** on-site. **Amenities:** voice mail, safes (fee), irons, hair dryers. **Pool(s):** outdoor. **Leisure Activities:** limited exercise equipment. **Guest Services:** valet and coin laundry, wireless Internet. **Business Services:** meeting rooms. **Cards:** AX, CB, DC, DS, JC, MC, VI.

RANDALLSTOWN pop. 30,870

——— WHERE TO DINE ———

MANGIA ITALIAN GRILL   Phone: 410/461-2900

Italian
$7-$23

Mangia Italian Grill has huge selection of pasta and sauce that are lovingly prepared and served by an excellent staff. Casual dress. **Bar:** Full bar. **Reservations:** accepted. **Hours:** 11 am-10 pm, Fri & Sat-11 pm. Closed: 12/25. **Address:** 10795 Birmingham Way 21163 **Location:** I-70, exit 83, just n, then 0.4 mi e on Warwick Way; in Waverly Woods Village Center. **Parking:** on-site. **Cards:** AX, DC, DS, MC, VI.

ROSEDALE pop. 19,199 (See map and index starting on p. 578)

──────── WHERE TO STAY ────────

LA QUINTA INN & SUITES BALTIMORE NORTH *Book great rates at AAA.com*   Phone: (410)574-8100   [32]

Small-scale Hotel
$139-$169 All Year

Address: 4 Philadelphia Ct 21237 **Location:** I-695, exit 34, just n. Located in a business/shopping area. **Facility:** Smoke free premises. 131 one-bedroom standard units. 5 stories, interior corridors. *Bath:* combo or shower only. **Parking:** on-site. **Amenities:** video games (fee), voice mail, irons, hair dryers. **Pool(s):** outdoor. **Leisure Activities:** limited exercise equipment. **Guest Services:** coin laundry, wireless Internet. **Business Services:** meeting rooms, PC. **Cards:** AX, DC, DS, MC, VI. **Free Special Amenities:** expanded continental breakfast and high-speed Internet.

LAQUINTA
INNS & SUITES
AAA Benefit:
Members save 10% everyday.

SYKESVILLE pop. 4,197

──────── WHERE TO STAY ────────

INN AT NORWOOD   Phone: 410/549-7868

Historic Bed
& Breakfast
$130-$220 All Year

Address: 7514 Norwood Ave 21784 **Location:** I-70, exit 80 (SR 32), 8 mi n, just w on Main St, then just w on Church St. **Facility:** This appealing B&B, with a relaxing porch and garden, is located in the historic area close to many shops and Civil War sites. 6 one-bedroom standard units with whirlpools. 3 stories (no elevator), interior corridors. **Parking:** on-site. **Terms:** age restrictions may apply, 7 day cancellation notice. **Amenities:** irons, hair dryers. *Some:* DVD players, CD players. **Leisure Activities:** *Fee:* game room. **Guest Services:** wireless Internet. **Business Services:** PC, fax (fee). **Cards:** AX, MC, VI.

──────── WHERE TO DINE ────────

BALDWIN'S STATION   Phone: 410/795-1041

American
$8-$25

The converted train station still sits yards away from working trains. Yesteryear ambience and wide menu variety await. Casual dress. **Bar:** Full bar. **Hours:** 11 am-9:30 pm, Sun-8:30 pm. Closed: 12/25; also Mon. **Address:** 7618 Main St 21784 **Location:** I-70, exit 80, 7.6 mi n on SR 32. **Parking:** on-site. **Cards:** AX, CB, DC, DS, JC, MC, VI.

E. W. BECK'S   Phone: 410/795-1001

American
$6-$18

A Sykesville tradition, the restaurant serves homespun charm with its ice cream and varied dishes. Casual dress. **Bar:** Full bar. **Hours:** 11:30 am-1 am, Sat noon-10 pm, Sun noon-9 pm. Closed: 12/25. **Address:** 7565 Main St 21784 **Location:** I-70, exit 80, 7.7 mi n on SR 32. **Parking:** on-site and street. **Cards:** AX, CB, DC, DS, JC, MC, VI.

TIMONIUM (See map and index starting on p. 578)

──────── WHERE TO STAY ────────

DAYS HOTEL & CONFERENCE CENTER BALTIMORE NORTH   *Book at AAA.com*   Phone: 410/560-1000   [17]

Small-scale Hotel
Rates not provided

Address: 9615 Deereco Rd 21093 **Location:** I-83, exit 17, just e. Located in a commercial area. **Facility:** 145 units. 141 one-bedroom standard units, some with efficiencies. 4 one-bedroom suites, some with efficiencies. 7 stories, interior corridors. **Parking:** on-site. **Amenities:** voice mail, irons, hair dryers. **Pool(s):** outdoor. **Leisure Activities:** limited exercise equipment. **Guest Services:** complimentary and valet laundry, wireless Internet. **Business Services:** meeting rooms, PC.

EXTENDED STAYAMERICA-TIMONIUM   *Book at AAA.com*   Phone: (410)628-1088   [16]

Small-scale Hotel
$114-$124 All Year

Address: 9704 Beaver Dam Rd 21093 **Location:** I-83, exit 17, just e, follow signs to Beaver Dam Rd. **Facility:** 104 one-bedroom standard units with efficiencies. 3 stories, interior corridors. *Bath:* combo or shower only. **Parking:** on-site. **Terms:** office hours 7 am-11 pm. **Amenities:** voice mail, irons, hair dryers. **Guest Services:** coin laundry, wireless Internet. **Cards:** AX, DC, DS, JC, MC, VI.

HOLIDAY INN SELECT BALTIMORE NORTH   *Book at AAA.com*   Phone: (410)252-7373   [19]

Small-scale Hotel
$119-$189 3/1-11/15
$109-$159 11/16-2/28

Address: 2004 Greenspring Dr 21093 **Location:** I-83, exit 16A northbound; exit 16 southbound, 0.3 mi se. **Facility:** 246 units. 244 one-bedroom standard units. 2 one-bedroom suites. 5 stories, interior corridors. *Bath:* combo or shower only. **Parking:** on-site. **Amenities:** voice mail, irons, hair dryers. **Pool(s):** heated indoor/outdoor. **Leisure Activities:** whirlpool, exercise room. *Fee:* game room. **Guest Services:** valet and coin laundry, area transportation, wireless Internet. **Business Services:** conference facilities, PC. **Cards:** AX, CB, DC, DS, JC, MC, VI.

(See map and index starting on p. 578)

RED ROOF INN-TIMONIUM   *Book at AAA.com*   Phone: 410/666-0380   [18]

▼▼ ▼▼
Motel
Rates not provided

Address: 111 W Timonium Rd 21093 **Location:** I-83, exit 16A northbound; exit 16 southbound, just e. Located in a commercial area. **Facility:** 137 one-bedroom standard units. 3 stories, exterior corridors. **Parking:** on-site. **Amenities:** video games (fee), voice mail. **Guest Services:** wireless Internet.

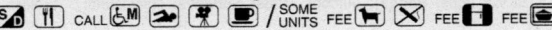

——— **WHERE TO DINE** ———

AN POITIN STIL   Phone: 410/560-7900   [14]

▼▼ ▼▼
Irish
$5-$22

The bustling Irish pub sticks with the tried and true, including corned beef and cabbage, Irish stew and fish and chips. Plenty of American selections also are available. The atmosphere is lively and fun. Casual dress. Entertainment. **Bar:** Full bar. **Reservations:** accepted. **Hours:** 11 am-midnight, Fri & Sat-1 am. Closed: 12/25. **Address:** 2323 York Rd 21093 **Location:** I-83, exit 16A northbound; exit 16 southbound, 0.6 mi e on Timonium Rd, then 0.7 mi n on SR 45. **Parking:** on-site. **Cards:** AX, DS, MC, VI.

CHRISTOPHER DANIEL   Phone: 410/308-1800   [13]

▼▼ ▼▼
Steak House
$9-$30

The trendy casual steakhouse offers a bevy of prime cut steaks and sauces including port wine reduction, bearnaise, demiglaze and bourbon. Other dishes include the popular surf and turf, roast chicken and pan seared yellow-fin tuna. Casual dress. **Bar:** Full bar. **Reservations:** accepted. **Hours:** 11 am-3 & 5-10 pm, Fri & Sat-11 pm. Closed: 11/27, 12/25. **Address:** 106 W Padonia Rd 21093 **Location:** I-83, exit 17, 1 mi e; in Padonia Park Shopping Center. **Parking:** on-site. **Cards:** AX, MC, VI.

MICHAEL'S CAFE   Phone: 410/252-2022   [15]

▼▼ ▼▼
American
$7-$28

Paraphernalia of sports heroes and movie stars hangs on the walls of the popular restaurant. Maryland jumbo lump crab cakes are the top seller on a menu that also lists chicken, veal, steak and pasta selections. Don't overlook the raw bar. Lighter fare appeals to diners with smaller appetites. Casual dress. **Bar:** Full bar. **Reservations:** accepted. **Hours:** 10:30 am-midnight, Fri & Sat-12:30 am. Closed: 12/25. **Address:** 2119 York Rd 21093 **Location:** I-83, exit 16A northbound; exit 16 southbound, 0.6 mi e on Timonium Rd, then just n on SR 45. **Parking:** on-site. **Cards:** AX, DC, DS, MC, VI.

TOWSON pop. 51,793   (See map and index starting on p. 578)

——— **WHERE TO STAY** ———

BURKSHIRE MARRIOTT CONFERENCE HOTEL   *Book great rates at AAA.com*   Phone: 410/324-8100   [25]

▼▼ ▼▼ ▼
Small-scale Hotel
$243-$273 All Year

Address: 10 W Burke Ave 21204 **Location:** I-695, exit 27A (Dulaney Valley Rd), 0.8 mi s on SR 146 (Dulaney Valley Rd), then 0.5 mi s on SR 45 (York Rd). Located on Towson University campus. **Facility:** Smoke free premises. 137 units. 72 one-, 59 two- and 6 three-bedroom suites with kitchens. 17 stories, interior corridors. *Bath:* combo or shower only. **Parking:** on-site. **Terms:** check-in 4 pm. **Amenities:** high-speed Internet, voice mail, irons, hair dryers. **Leisure Activities:** exercise room. **Guest Services:** valet laundry. **Business Services:** conference facilities, business center. **Cards:** AX, DC, DS, JC, MC, VI.

Marriott
HOTELS & RESORTS

AAA Benefit:
Members save 5% off of the best available rate.

COMFORT INN TOWSON   *Book great rates at AAA.com*   Phone: 410/882-0900   [24]

(AAA) SAVE
▼▼ ▼▼
Small-scale Hotel
Rates not provided

Address: 8801 Loch Raven Blvd 21286 **Location:** I-695, exit 29B, just e. Located in a commercial area. **Facility:** 185 one-bedroom standard units, some with whirlpools. 5 stories, interior corridors. **Parking:** on-site. **Amenities:** voice mail, safes (fee), irons, hair dryers. **Pool(s):** outdoor. **Leisure Activities:** limited exercise equipment. **Guest Services:** valet and coin laundry, wireless Internet. **Business Services:** meeting rooms, PC. **Free Special Amenities:** expanded continental breakfast and high-speed Internet.

HOLIDAY INN BALTIMORE-TOWSON   *Book great rates at AAA.com*   Phone: (410)823-4410   [23]

(AAA) SAVE
▼▼ ▼▼
Small-scale Hotel
$109-$179 All Year

Address: 1100 Cromwell Bridge Rd 21286 **Location:** I-695, exit 29A, just s. **Facility:** 139 one-bedroom standard units. 6 stories, interior corridors. *Bath:* combo or shower only. **Parking:** on-site. **Terms:** cancellation fee imposed. **Amenities:** dual phone lines, voice mail, irons, hair dryers. **Pool(s):** outdoor. **Leisure Activities:** exercise room. **Guest Services:** valet and coin laundry, wireless Internet. **Business Services:** meeting rooms, PC. **Cards:** AX, CB, DC, DS, JC, MC, VI.

(See map and index starting on p. 578)

SHERATON BALTIMORE NORTH HOTEL *Book great rates at AAA.com* Phone: (410)321-7400 22

Large-scale Hotel
$233-$259 All Year

Address: 903 Dulaney Valley Rd 21204 **Location:** I-695, exit 27A, 0.3 mi s. Connected to Towson Town Center Mall via skywalk. **Facility:** 283 one-bedroom standard units. 12 stories, interior corridors. **Parking:** on-site and valet. **Terms:** cancellation fee imposed. **Amenities:** voice mail, irons, hair dryers. **Pool(s):** heated indoor. **Leisure Activities:** whirlpool, exercise room. **Guest Services:** valet and coin laundry, area transportation-within 5 mi, wireless Internet. **Business Services:** conference facilities, business center. **Cards:** AX, CB, DC, DS, JC, MC, VI. **Free Special Amenities:** high-speed Internet.

S **⊙** **¶** **Y** CALL **M** **⊃** **¶** **▣** / SOME UNITS **🐾** **✕** **🔓**

Ⓢ Sheraton
HOTELS & RESORTS

AAA Benefit:
Members get up to 15% off, plus Starwood Preferred Guest® bonuses.

——— **WHERE TO DINE** ———

CAFE TROIA

Italian
$9-$33

Phone: 410/337-0133 21

Nestled in a row of shops in the downtown area, the chic cafe features a relaxing and romantic ambiance while serving up a creative menu of Italian favorites like pasta, seafood, beef and veal. Dressy casual. **Bar:** Full bar. **Reservations:** suggested, weekends. **Hours:** 11:30 am-3 & 5-10 pm, Sat 5 pm-11:30 pm. Closed major holidays; also Sun. **Address:** 28 W Allegheny Ave 21204 **Location:** I-695, exit 26A, 1.1 mi se on York Rd, then just w. **Parking:** street. **Cards:** AX, CB, DC, DS, MC, VI.

⬍

GLORY DAYS GRILL, TOWSON

American
$7-$18

Phone: 443/901-0270

Lending to the casual restaurant's sports-themed atmosphere are memorabilia decorating the dining area and 25 TVs with control centers at each table and booth. Food selections range from wings and ribs to seafood, beef and pasta dishes. Casual dress. **Bar:** Full bar. **Reservations:** not accepted. **Hours:** 4 pm-midnight, Fri & Sat from 11:30 am, Sun 11:30 am-11 pm. Closed: 11/27, 12/25. **Address:** 1220 E Joppa Rd 21286 **Location:** I-695, exit 29B, just s to E Joppa Rd, then w at jct LaSalle Rd. **Parking:** on-site. **Cards:** AX, DS, MC, VI.

⬍

UNION BRIDGE pop. 989

——— **WHERE TO STAY** ———

WOOD'S GAIN BED & BREAKFAST

Historic Bed
& Breakfast
$105-$175 All Year

Phone: (410)775-0308

Address: 421 McKinstry's Mill Rd 21791 **Location:** Just e on SR 75, then just s. **Facility:** A B&B in the historic village of Linwood near several Civil War sites, Wood's Gain entices guests with pleasant parlor rooms and a scenic garden. 4 units. 3 one-bedroom standard units, some with whirlpools. 1 cottage. 2 stories (no elevator), interior/exterior corridors. *Bath:* shower or tub only. **Parking:** on-site. **Terms:** check-in 4 pm, 7 day cancellation notice. **Amenities:** hair dryers. *Some:* CD players. **Leisure Activities:** whirlpool, exercise room. **Cards:** MC, VI.

(ASK) CALL **M** **✕** **W** **Z** / SOME UNITS **🔓** **▣**

WESTMINSTER pop. 16,731

——— **WHERE TO STAY** ———

BEST WESTERN WESTMINSTER CATERING AND CONFERENCE CENTER *Book great rates at AAA.com*

Phone: 410/857-1900

Small-scale Hotel
Rates not provided

Address: 451 WMC Dr 21158 **Location:** 1.7 mi w on SR 140 from jct SR 27. **Facility:** 101 one-bedroom standard units, some with whirlpools. 2 stories (no elevator), interior corridors. *Bath:* combo or shower only. **Parking:** on-site. **Amenities:** voice mail, irons, hair dryers. *Some:* high-speed Internet, wireless Internet. **Business Services:** meeting rooms, PC. **Pool(s):** outdoor. **Guest Services:** valet and coin laundry, wireless Internet.

¶ CALL **M** **⊃** **♦** **¶** **🔓** **▤** **▣** / SOME UNITS **✕**

AAA Benefit:
Members save 10% everyday, plus an exclusive frequent stay program.

THE BOSTON INN

Motel
$59-$75 All Year

Phone: 410/848-9095

Address: 533 Baltimore Blvd 21157 **Location:** 0.9 mi se on SR 97/140 from jct SR 27. Located in a commercial area, adjacent to shopping plaza. **Facility:** 118 one-bedroom standard units, some with whirlpools. 1-2 stories (no elevator), exterior corridors. **Parking:** on-site. **Amenities:** hair dryers. *Some:* irons. **Pool(s):** outdoor. **Guest Services:** coin laundry, wireless Internet. **Cards:** AX, DS, MC, VI.

(ASK) **S** **⊙** **¶** **⊃** **¶** **🔓** **▣** / SOME UNITS FEE **🐾** **✕** **(VCR)**

—— WHERE TO DINE ——

BAUGHER'S RESTAURANT

American
$3-$13

Phone: 410/848-7413

The well-established, family-owned restaurant has offered traditional country foods since 1948. The ice cream and pies are homemade. An adjacent farm market sells fruit and vegetables from the family orchards and gardens. Casual dress. **Hours:** 7:30 am-9 pm. Closed major holidays. **Address:** 289 W Main St 21158 **Location:** Jct SR 31 and 32. **Parking:** on-site. **Cards:** DS, MC, VI.

JOHANSSONS DINING HOUSE

American
$7-$25

Phone: 410/876-0101

Fine and casual dining are offered along with Westminster's original brewing company. Casual dress. **Bar:** Full bar. **Reservations:** suggested. **Hours:** 11 am-10 pm, Fri & Sat-11 pm. Closed major holidays. **Address:** 4 W Main St 21157 **Location:** Just w; center. **Parking:** street. **Cards:** AX, DS, MC, VI.

WHITE MARSH pop. 8,485   (See map and index starting on p. 578)

—— WHERE TO STAY ——

HAMPTON INN AT WHITE MARSH   *Book great rates at AAA.com*
Small-scale Hotel
Rates not provided

Phone: 410/931-2200   **9**

Address: 8225 Town Center Dr 21236 **Location:** I-95, exit 67B, 0.5 mi w on SR 43 (White Marsh Blvd), then 0.5 mi s on Honeygo Blvd. Located in a shopping/business area. **Facility:** 127 units. 121 one-bedroom standard units. 6 one-bedroom suites. 4 stories, interior corridors. **Bath:** combo or shower only. **Parking:** on-site. **Amenities:** video games (fee), dual phone lines, voice mail, irons, hair dryers. **Pool(s):** outdoor. **Leisure Activities:** limited exercise equipment. **Guest Services:** complimentary and valet laundry, area transportation, wireless Internet. **Business Services:** meeting rooms, business center.

HILTON GARDEN INN-WHITE MARSH   *Book great rates at AAA.com*
Small-scale Hotel
Rates not provided

Phone: 410/427-0600   **8**

Address: 5015 Campbell Blvd 21236 **Location:** I-95, exit 67B, 0.5 mi w on SR 43 (White Marsh Blvd), then 0.5 mi s on Honeygo Blvd. Located in a shopping/business area. **Facility:** 155 units. 145 one-bedroom standard units. 10 one-bedroom suites. 6 stories, interior corridors. **Bath:** combo or shower only. **Parking:** on-site. **Amenities:** video games (fee), high-speed Internet, dual phone lines, voice mail, irons, hair dryers. **Pool(s):** heated indoor. **Leisure Activities:** whirlpool, limited exercise equipment. **Guest Services:** complimentary and valet laundry, area transportation, wireless Internet. **Business Services:** meeting rooms, business center.

RESIDENCE INN BY MARRIOTT BALTIMORE/WHITE MARSH   *Book great rates at AAA.com*
Small-scale Hotel
$165-$196 All Year

Phone: 410/933-9554   **7**

Address: 4980 Mercantile Rd 21236 **Location:** I-95, exit 67B, 0.5 mi w on SR 43 (White Marsh Blvd), just s to Mercantile Rd, then just e. Located in a shopping/business area. **Facility:** Smoke free premises. 131 units. 54 one-bedroom standard units with efficiencies. 56 one- and 21 two-bedroom suites, some with efficiencies or kitchens. 4 stories, interior corridors. **Bath:** combo or shower only. **Parking:** on-site. **Amenities:** video games (fee), high-speed Internet, voice mail, irons, hair dryers. *Some:* dual phone lines. **Pool(s):** heated outdoor. **Leisure Activities:** whirlpool, exercise room, sports court. **Guest Services:** complimentary and valet laundry, area transportation. **Business Services:** meeting rooms, business center. **Cards:** AX, DC, DS, JC, MC, VI.

AAA Benefit:
Members save 5% off of the best available rate.

SPRINGHILL SUITES

Small-scale Hotel

Under construction, scheduled to open November 2008. **Address:** 10465 Philadelphia Rd 21162 **Location:** I-95, exit 67A, just e on SR 43, then just s on CR 7. **Amenities:** coffeemakers, microwaves, refrigerators, pool.

AAA Benefit:
Members save 5% off of the best available rate.

—— WHERE TO DINE ——

BAYOU CAFE
American
$7-$27

Phone: 410/931-2583   **26**

Patrons can let the good times roll at the cafe, which combines classic American favorites with bayou seasonings. Casual dress. **Bar:** Full bar. **Reservations:** accepted. **Hours:** 11 am-10 pm, Fri & Sat-11 pm, Sun 10 am-9 pm. Closed: 11/27, 12/25. **Address:** 8133 Honeygo Blvd 21236 **Location:** I-95, exit 67B, 0.5 mi w on SR 43 (White Marsh Blvd), then 0.6 mi s; in The Avenue at White Marsh. **Parking:** on-site. **Cards:** AX, DS, MC, VI.

(See map and index starting on p. 578)

RED BRICK STATION — Phone: 410/931-7827 (24)

American
$7-$30

Those seeking a break from shopping or driving will find a nice spot to relax at the comfortable restaurant, which is suitable for single diners and families alike. Beers brewed on the premises taste great with homemade soups, salads, sandwiches, burgers and full dinners of beef, chicken and seafood. Also making a strong menu presence is English pub fare, such as bangers and mash, fish and chips, and roast beef and Yorkshire. The pub area encourages socialization. Casual dress. **Bar:** Full bar. **Hours:** 11 am-11 pm, Fri & Sat-1 am. Closed: 11/27, 12/25. **Address:** 8149 Honeygo Blvd 21236 **Location:** I-95, exit 67B, 0.5 mi w on SR 43 (White Marsh Blvd), then 0.6 mi s; in The Avenue at White Marsh. **Parking:** on-site. **Cards:** AX, DS, MC, VI.

CALL

STRAPAZZA — Phone: 410/931-3177 (25)

Italian
$5-$23

Offering many Italian "pastabilities," the restaurant bills itself as the "Eatalian choice." Good background music and a knowledgeable wait staff await. Casual dress. **Bar:** Full bar. **Reservations:** accepted, weekdays. **Hours:** 11 am-9:30 pm, Sun from noon. Closed: 3/23, 11/27, 12/25. **Address:** 8145 Honeygo Blvd 21236 **Location:** I-95, exit 67B, 0.5 mi w on SR 43 (White Marsh Blvd), then 0.6 mi s; in The Avenue at White Marsh. **Parking:** on-site. **Cards:** AX, MC, VI.

WOODLAWN (See map and index starting on p. 578)

WHERE TO STAY

BEST WESTERN BALTIMORE WEST *Book great rates at AAA.com* — **Phone:** 410/265-1400 (35)

SAVE

Small-scale Hotel
Rates not provided

Address: 1800 Belmont Ave 21244 **Location:** I-695, exit 17, 0.3 mi nw. **Facility:** 129 one-bedroom standard units. 2 stories (no elevator), exterior corridors. *Bath:* combo or shower only. **Parking:** on-site. **Amenities:** high-speed Internet, voice mail, irons, hair dryers. **Pool(s):** outdoor. **Leisure Activities:** limited exercise equipment. **Guest Services:** valet and coin laundry, area transportation-within 3 mi. **Business Services:** meeting rooms, PC. **Free Special Amenities: expanded continental breakfast and local telephone calls.**

CALL / SOME UNITS FEE FEE

AAA Benefit:
Members save 10% everyday, plus an exclusive frequent stay program.

National Aquarium in Baltimore / © E. David Luria

This ends listings for the Baltimore Vicinity.
The following page resumes the alphabetical listings of cities in Maryland.

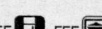

BELCAMP —*See Baltimore p. 608.*

BELTSVILLE —*See District Of Columbia p. 475.*

BERLIN pop. 3,491

———— **WHERE TO DINE** ————

**ASSATEAGUE CRAB HOUSE &
CARRYOUT**   *Menu on AAA.com*   **Phone:** 410/641-4330

Seafood
$9-$26

It's back to the basics at this informal crab house with painted cement floors, paneled walls and nautical decor. What's important though is the size of the appetite you bring to the all-you-can-eat crab special, which includes corn on the cob and more. Casual dress. **Bar:** Beer & wine. **Hours:** Open 5/25-10/31; noon-9 pm; Fri-Sun 4 pm-9 pm 9/6-10/31 & 5/25-6/15. **Address:** 7635 Stephen Decatur Rd 21811 **Location:** 2 mi s on SR 611 from jct SR 376. **Parking:** on-site. **Cards:** AX, DS, MC, VI.

RUTH'S CHRIS STEAK HOUSE   **Phone:** 410/213-9444

Steak House
$10-$39

The main fare is steak, which is prepared from several cuts of prime beef and cooked to perfection, but the menu also lists lamb, chicken and seafood dishes. Guests should come hungry because the side dishes, which are among the a la carte offerings, could make a meal in themselves. Dressy casual. **Bar:** Full bar. **Reservations:** suggested. **Hours:** 11 am-11 pm. Closed: 12/24, 12/25. **Address:** 11501 Maid At Arms Ln 21811 **Location:** Off US 50, 3.2 mi w of the Ocean City Bridge; in Glenriddle Clubhouse. **Parking:** on-site. **Cards:** AX, DS, MC, VI.

CALL &M ⬟

BETHESDA —*See District Of Columbia p. 476.*

BOONSBORO pop. 2,803

———— **WHERE TO DINE** ————

OLD SOUTH MOUNTAIN INN   **Phone:** 301/432-6155

American
$9-$32

Civil War buffs up to see Antietam will revel in the Early American atmosphere, circa 1732, and the popular Victorian-style addition. However, it's the strikingly fine food that put the restaurant on the epicurean's map. Terrace seating is a summer option. Dressy casual. **Bar:** Full bar. **Reservations:** suggested. **Hours:** 5 pm-9 pm, Sat 11:30 am-2:30 & 4-10 pm, Sun 10:30 am-8 pm. Closed: 12/25; also Mon. **Address:** 6132 Old National Pike 21713 **Location:** US 40 Alternate Rt, 1.8 mi e of jct SR 67. **Parking:** on-site. **Cards:** AX, DC, MC, VI. **Historic**

BOWIE —*See District Of Columbia p. 479.*

CAMBRIDGE pop. 10,911

——— WHERE TO STAY ———

DAYS INN & SUITES OF CAMBRIDGE   *Book at AAA.com*   **Phone:** 410/228-4444

Small-scale Hotel
Rates not provided

Address: 2917 Ocean Gateway 21613 **Location:** On US 50, 0.5 mi e of jct SR 16. **Facility:** 50 one-bedroom standard units, some with whirlpools. 2 stories (no elevator), interior corridors. **Parking:** on-site. **Amenities:** high-speed Internet, irons, hair dryers. **Pool(s):** heated outdoor. **Leisure Activities:** limited exercise equipment. **Guest Services:** coin laundry, wireless Internet.

HOLIDAY INN EXPRESS-CAMBRIDGE   *Book at AAA.com*   **Phone:** 410/221-9900

Small-scale Hotel
Rates not provided

Address: 2715 Ocean Gateway 21613 **Location:** US 50, 1.2 mi e of Frederick C Malkus Jr Bridge. **Facility:** 86 one-bedroom standard units, some with whirlpools. 4 stories, interior corridors. *Bath:* combo or shower only. **Parking:** on-site. **Amenities:** dual phone lines, voice mail, irons, hair dryers. **Pool(s):** heated indoor. **Leisure Activities:** whirlpool. **Guest Services:** valet laundry, wireless Internet. **Business Services:** meeting rooms, PC.

**HYATT REGENCY CHESAPEAKE BAY GOLF
RESORT, SPA AND MARINA**   *Book great rates at AAA.com*   **Phone:** (410)901-1234

Resort
Large-scale Hotel
$169-$419 All Year

AAA Benefit:
Ask for the AAA rate
and save 10%.

Address: 100 Heron Blvd 21613 **Location:** US 50 E, 1.2 mi e of Frederick C Malkus Jr Bridge. **Facility:** 400 units. 386 one-bedroom standard units. 14 one-bedroom suites, some with whirlpools. 6 stories, interior corridors. *Bath:* combo or shower only. **Parking:** on-site and valet. **Terms:** check-in 4 pm, 3 day cancellation notice-fee imposed. **Amenities:** dual phone lines, voice mail, safes, irons, hair dryers. *Fee:* video games, high-speed Internet. **Dining:** 4 restaurants, also, The Water's Edge Grill, see separate listing. **Pool(s):** 2 heated outdoor, heated indoor. **Leisure Activities:** saunas, whirlpool, steamrooms, waterslide, lifeguard on duty, miniature golf, 6 lighted tennis courts, recreation programs, natural wildlife preserve, tetherball, hiking trails, jogging, playground, spa, basketball, volleyball. *Fee:* paddleboats, sailboats, marina, charter fishing, boat tours, crabbing, kayaks, fly fishing instructions, golf-18 holes, driving range, skeet shooting, game room. **Guest Services:** valet and coin laundry, wireless Internet. **Business Services:** conference facilities, business center. **Cards:** AX, DC, DS, MC, VI. *(See color ad below)*

——— WHERE TO DINE ———

PLAZA TAPATIA   **Phone:** 410/228-7808

Mexican
$5-$17

The restaurant is a great stop for those in the mood for something with a south-of-the-border flavor. Appointed with Mexican decorations, the casual dining room is comfortable for any occasion. The kitchen prepares authentic Mexican recipes. Casual dress. **Bar:** Beer & wine. **Reservations:** accepted. **Hours:** 11 am-10 pm, Sat from noon, Sun noon-9 pm. Closed: 1/1, 12/25. **Address:** 315 Sunburst Hwy 21613 **Location:** On US 50, 0.4 mi se of Frederick C Malkus Jr Bridge. **Parking:** on-site. **Cards:** AX, MC, VI.

—— ▼ *See AAA listing above* ▼ ——

THE WATER'S EDGE GRILL

Phone: 410/901-1234

American
$10-$43

This full-service restaurant serves creative American cuisine that emphasizes fresh Eastern Shore ingredients. The staff is friendly and attentive. Views from the floor-to-ceiling windows skim over the pools and the Choptank River. Casual dress. **Bar:** Full bar. **Reservations:** accepted. **Hours:** 6:30-11 am, 11:30-3 & 5-10 pm; seasonal hours may vary. **Address:** 100 Heron Blvd 21613 **Location:** US 50 E, 1.2 mi e of Frederick C Malkus Jr Bridge; in Hyatt Regency Chesapeake Bay Golf Resort, Spa and Marina. **Parking:** on-site. **Cards:** AX, CB, DC, DS, JC, MC, VI.

CALL

CAMP SPRINGS —*See District Of Columbia p. 480.*

CATONSVILLE —*See Baltimore p. 609.*

CHESAPEAKE BEACH pop. 3,180

——— **WHERE TO STAY** ———

CHESAPEAKE BEACH RESORT AND SPA

Book great rates at AAA.com

Phone: (410)257-5596

(AAA) (SAVE)

Small-scale Hotel
$150-$425 3/1-10/31
$130-$425 11/1-2/28

Address: 4165 Mears Ave 20732 **Location:** Jct SR 261 and Mears Ave. Located on the Chesapeake Bay. **Facility:** Smoke free premises. 72 one-bedroom standard units, some with whirlpools. 4 stories, interior corridors. *Bath:* combo or shower only. **Parking:** on-site and valet. **Terms:** 2 night minimum stay - seasonal and/or weekends, 3 day cancellation notice-fee imposed. **Amenities:** high-speed Internet, dual phone lines, voice mail, irons, hair dryers. **Dining:** Rod 'N' Reel Restaurant, see separate listing. **Pool(s):** heated indoor. **Leisure Activities:** saunas, exercise room, spa. *Fee:* marina, charter fishing, game room. **Guest Services:** coin laundry. **Business Services:** meeting rooms, business center. **Cards:** AX, DC, DS, MC, VI. **Free Special Amenities: continental breakfast and high-speed Internet.** *(See color ad below)*

  CALL   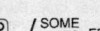 / SOME UNITS FEE

——— **WHERE TO DINE** ———

ROD 'N' REEL RESTAURANT

Phone: 301/855-8351

Seafood
$9-$40

Specializing in seafood since 1946, the waterfront eatery always has a supply of fresh fish on hand. Crab cakes are a local favorite, but much also can be said of the flavorful blackened rockfish supplied in generous portions. Ample parking, including valet parking for a fee, is available. Casual dress. **Bar:** Full bar. **Reservations:** suggested, weekends. **Hours:** 11 am-10 pm, Sat from 8 am, Sun 8 am-9 pm, Mon 11 am-9 pm. Closed: 12/25. **Address:** Rt 261 & Mears Ave 20732 **Location:** Jct SR 261 and Mears Ave; in Chesapeake Beach Resort and Spa. **Parking:** on-site. **Cards:** AX, DS, MC, VI.

CHESAPEAKE CITY pop. 787

——— **WHERE TO STAY** ———

INN AT THE CANAL

Phone: (410)885-5995

Historic Bed
& Breakfast
$95-$250 All Year

Address: 104 Bohemia Ave 21915-0187 **Location:** Bohemia Ave and 2nd St. Located in historic village. **Facility:** This 1870 inn features individually decorated guest rooms with private baths. Smoke free premises. 7 units. 6 one-bedroom standard units. 1 one-bedroom suite. 3 stories (no elevator), interior corridors. *Bath:* combo or shower only. **Parking:** on-site. **Terms:** 2 night minimum stay - seasonal, age restrictions may apply, 10 day cancellation notice-fee imposed. **Amenities:** irons, hair dryers. *Some:* DVD players. **Guest Services:** wireless Internet. **Business Services:** meeting rooms, fax (fee). **Cards:** AX, CB, DC, DS, MC, VI.

(ASK)   / SOME UNITS (VCR)

—————— **WHERE TO DINE** ——————

BAYARD HOUSE RESTAURANT   Phone: 410/885-5040

American
$10-$39

Along the banks of the Chesapeake and Delaware Canal, the gracious inn has a colorful history dating back to the 1870s. Guests in the dining rooms and on the popular enclosed porch enjoy great views of the canal and passing boats. The accomplished kitchen prepares a wide range of dishes, from spicy stuffed Anaheim peppers to traditional Maryland crab cakes. Maryland crab soup has become a local favorite. Casual dress. **Bar:** Full bar. **Reservations:** suggested, weekends. **Hours:** 11:30 am-3 & 4:30-9 pm, Fri & Sat 11:30 am-3:30 & 4:30-10 pm, Sun 11:30 am-3:30 pm & 4:30-9 pm. Closed: 3/23, 12/25; also for dinner 12/24. **Address:** 11 Bohemia Ave 21915 **Location:** Alongside Chesapeake and Delaware Canal; in historic district. **Parking:** street. **Cards:** AX, CB, DC, DS, MC, VI. **Historic**

CHESAPEAKE INN RESTAURANT & MARINA   Phone: 410/885-2040

American
$6-$29

Along the waterfront, the restaurant affords spectacular marina views. Guests can unwind in a relaxing atmosphere with great food, live entertainment and dancing. Casual dress. Entertainment. **Bar:** Full bar. **Reservations:** suggested, weekends. **Hours:** 11 am-10 pm, Fri & Sat-11 pm. **Address:** 605 Second St 21915 **Location:** Along side Chesapeake and Delaware Canal; in historic district. **Parking:** on-site. **Cards:** AX, DC, DS, MC, VI.

CHESTERTOWN pop. 4,746

—————— **WHERE TO STAY** ——————

COMFORT SUITES-CHESTERTOWN   *Book at AAA.com*   Phone: (410)810-0555

Small-scale Hotel
$90-$150 All Year

Address: 160 Scheeler Rd 21620 **Location:** 0.4 mi ne of jct SR 213 and 291. **Facility:** Smoke free premises. 53 one-bedroom standard units, some with whirlpools. 3 stories, interior corridors. *Bath:* combo or shower only. **Parking:** on-site. **Terms:** 7 day cancellation notice. **Amenities:** voice mail, safes (fee), irons, hair dryers. **Pool(s):** heated indoor. **Guest Services:** coin laundry, wireless Internet. **Business Services:** meeting rooms. **Cards:** AX, DC, DS, MC, VI.

ASK SD TI+ CALL &M FEE X B

—————— **WHERE TO DINE** ——————

THE FRONT ROOM AT THE IMPERIAL HOTEL   Phone: 410/778-5000

American
$8-$32

The historic hotel dining room offers a seasonally changing menu of innovative American cuisine that emphasizes fresh, local ingredients. The crab cake is popular, and lamb chops are the house specialty. Dressy casual. **Bar:** Full bar. **Reservations:** suggested, for dinner. **Hours:** 11:30 am-3 & 5-9 pm, Sun 10:30 am-3 pm. Closed: 11/27, 12/25; also Mon. **Address:** 208 High St 21620 **Location:** Cross St, just w to High St, then just s, SR 213 to SR 289; in historic district; in The Imperial Hotel. **Parking:** street. **Cards:** AX, MC, VI.

CHEVY CHASE —*See District Of Columbia p. 480.*

CLINTON —*See District Of Columbia p. 480.*

COCKEYSVILLE —*See Baltimore p. 609.*

COLLEGE PARK —*See District Of Columbia p. 481.*

COLUMBIA —*See Baltimore p. 609.*

CRISFIELD pop. 2,723

—————— **WHERE TO DINE** ——————

WATERMEN'S INN   Phone: 410/968-2119

Steak & Seafood
$4-$24

The atmosphere of the cozy bistro is enhanced by light music and fresh flowers. The menu comprises crabmeat dishes, regional cuisine and seasonal specials such as soft-shell crabs with artichokes and the hand cut grilled rib eye is a local favorite. Casual dress. **Bar:** Full bar. **Reservations:** suggested, weekends. **Hours:** 11 am-9 pm, Sat & Sun from 8 am; hours may vary in winter. Closed: 11/27; also Mon, Tues, 12/24-12/30 & Wed, 3/26-9/1. **Address:** 901 W Main St 21817 **Location:** Center. **Parking:** street. **Cards:** AX, DS, MC, VI.

CUMBERLAND pop. 21,518

———— WHERE TO STAY ————

HOLIDAY INN   *Book at AAA.com*   Phone: (301)724-8800

Small-scale Hotel
$109-$159 All Year

Address: 100 S George St 21502 **Location:** I-68, exit 43C, just n; downtown. **Facility:** 130 one-bedroom standard units. 6 stories, interior corridors. *Bath:* combo or shower only. **Parking:** on-site. **Terms:** 3 day cancellation notice-fee imposed. **Amenities:** video games, dual phone lines, voice mail, irons, hair dryers. *Some:* high-speed Internet. **Pool(s):** outdoor. **Guest Services:** valet and coin laundry, wireless Internet. **Business Services:** meeting rooms, fax (fee). **Cards:** AX, DC, DS, MC, VI.

INN AT WALNUT BOTTOM   Phone: (301)777-0003

Historic Bed
& Breakfast
$117-$220 3/1-12/23
$112-$220 12/26-2/28

Address: 120 Greene St 21502 **Location:** I-68, exit 43A, follow signs; between Winton Pl and Smallwood St, guest parking via Winton Pl. **Facility:** This B&B is made up of two adjacent townhouses dating from 1820 and 1890; both are furnished with antiques and period reproductions. Smoke free premises. 12 units. 10 one- and 2 two-bedroom standard units. 2-3 stories (no elevator), interior corridors. *Bath:* some shared or private, combo or shower only. **Parking:** open 3/1-12/23 & 12/26-2/28, 2 night minimum stay - seasonal and/or weekends, 10 day cancellation notice. **Amenities:** hair dryers. *Some:* DVD players. **Leisure Activities:** bicycles. *Fee:* massage. **Guest Services:** wireless Internet. **Cards:** AX, DS, MC, VI.

ROCKY GAP LODGE & GOLF RESORT   *Book great rates at AAA.com*   Phone: (301)784-8400

Resort
Large-scale Hotel
$115-$239 All Year

Address: 16701 Lakeview Rd NE 21530 **Location:** I-68, exit 50, just n. Located in a quiet area. **Facility:** In the mountains on a lake, the stylish resort is an updated version of a rustic lodge; find walking trails, grade-A golf and dining and water sports. 215 one-bedroom standard units, some with whirlpools. 6 stories, interior corridors. *Bath:* combo or shower only. **Parking:** on-site and valet. **Terms:** 3 day cancellation notice-fee imposed. **Amenities:** video games, high-speed Internet, voice mail, safes, honor bars, irons, hair dryers. **Dining:** 2 restaurants, also, Lakeside Restaurant, see separate listing. **Pool(s):** heated indoor/outdoor. **Leisure Activities:** whirlpool, limited beach access, rental boats, canoeing, paddleboats, sailboats, fishing, kayak, 2 lighted tennis courts, cross country skiing, recreation programs, rock climbing, hiking trails, jogging, playground, exercise room, spa, yoga classes, basketball, horseshoes, volleyball. *Fee:* golf-18 holes, driving range, bicycles, horseback riding. **Guest Services:** valet laundry, wireless Internet. **Business Services:** conference facilities, fax (fee). **Cards:** AX, CB, DC, DS, JC, MC, VI. *(See color ad below)*

———— WHERE TO DINE ————

GEATZ'S RESTAURANT   Phone: 301/724-2223

American
$7-$21

A city tradition for many generations, the restaurant serves dishes in large portions. The friendly staff enhances the dining experience. Casual dress. **Bar:** Full bar. **Hours:** 11 am-10 pm. Closed: 12/25; also Sun. **Address:** 206 Pala St 21502 **Location:** I-68, exit 43A, between Winton Pl and Pala St; center. **Parking:** on-site. **Cards:** AX, CB, DC, DS, JC, MC, VI.

▼ See AAA listing above ▼

LAKESIDE RESTAURANT

Phone: 301/784-8400

American
$7-$29

In Rocky Gap Lodge, the restaurant affords incredible lake views. Friendly, fast service is a staple. Casual dress. **Bar:** Full bar. **Hours:** 11:30 am-2 & 5-11 pm. **Address:** 16701 Lakeview Rd NE 21530 **Location:** I-68, exit 50, just n; in Rocky Gap Lodge & Golf Resort. **Parking:** on-site. **Cards:** AX, CB, DC, DS, JC, MC, VI.

DELMAR pop. 1,859

——— WHERE TO STAY ———

HOLIDAY INN EXPRESS HOTEL & SUITES *Book great rates at AAA.com*

Phone: (410)896-9633

Small-scale Hotel
$99-$189 All Year

Address: 30232 Lighthouse Square Dr 21875 **Location:** On US 13, 1.1 mi s of SR 54; 2.8 mi of jct US 50. **Facility:** 79 one-bedroom standard units. 3 stories, interior corridors. *Bath:* combo or shower only. **Parking:** on-site. **Amenities:** high-speed Internet, voice mail, irons, hair dryers. **Pool(s):** outdoor. **Leisure Activities:** limited exercise equipment. **Guest Services:** valet laundry, wireless Internet. **Business Services:** meeting rooms, PC. **Cards:** AX, DC, DS, MC, VI. **Free Special Amenities: continental breakfast and high-speed Internet.**

DENTON pop. 2,960

——— WHERE TO STAY ———

BEST WESTERN DENTON INN *Book great rates at AAA.com*

Phone: (410)479-8400

Small-scale Hotel
$89-$179 All Year

Address: 521 Fleetwood Rd 21629 **Location:** Jct SR 404 and 313. **Facility:** 60 one-bedroom standard units, some with whirlpools. 2 stories, interior corridors. *Bath:* combo or shower only. **Parking:** on-site. **Amenities:** high-speed Internet, voice mail, irons, hair dryers. **Pool(s):** outdoor. **Guest Services:** coin laundry, wireless Internet. **Business Services:** PC. **Cards:** AX, DC, DS, MC, VI. **Free Special Amenities: continental breakfast and local telephone calls.**

AAA Benefit:

Members save 10% everyday, plus an exclusive frequent stay program.

EASTON pop. 11,708

——— WHERE TO STAY ———

COMFORT INN EASTON *Book at AAA.com*

Phone: 410/820-8333

Motel
$69-$113 All Year

Address: 8523 Ocean Gateway 21601 **Location:** US 50, 0.7 mi n of jct SR 331. **Facility:** 84 one-bedroom standard units. 2 stories (no elevator), exterior corridors. **Parking:** on-site. **Amenities:** irons, hair dryers. **Pool(s):** outdoor. **Leisure Activities:** whirlpool. **Guest Services:** wireless Internet. **Business Services:** meeting rooms, PC. **Cards:** AX, DC, DS, MC, VI.

HAMPTON INN EASTON *Book great rates at AAA.com*

Phone: 410/822-2200

Small-scale Hotel
Rates not provided

Address: 8058 Ocean Gateway 21601 **Location:** US 50, just se of jct SR 331. **Facility:** 74 one-bedroom standard units. 4 stories, interior corridors. *Bath:* combo or shower only. **Parking:** on-site. **Amenities:** video games (fee), high-speed Internet, voice mail, irons, hair dryers. **Pool(s):** heated indoor. **Leisure Activities:** limited exercise equipment. **Guest Services:** valet and coin laundry, wireless Internet. **Business Services:** meeting rooms, PC.

HOLIDAY INN EXPRESS-EASTON *Book at AAA.com*

Phone: 410/819-6500

Small-scale Hotel
Rates not provided

Address: 8561 Ocean Gateway 21601 **Location:** US 50, 0.7 mi n of jct SR 331. **Facility:** 73 one-bedroom standard units. 4 stories, interior corridors. *Bath:* combo or shower only. **Parking:** on-site. **Amenities:** dual phone lines, voice mail, irons, hair dryers. **Pool(s):** heated indoor. **Leisure Activities:** whirlpool, exercise room. **Guest Services:** valet laundry, wireless Internet. **Business Services:** meeting rooms, PC.

——— WHERE TO DINE ———

OUT OF THE FIRE

Phone: 410/770-4777

Mediterranean
$6-$26

The small cafe and wine bar is in the city's historic district. The stone-hearth oven is the focal point of the dining room and open kitchen. On the menu are stone-hearth pizzas, homemade desserts and entrees that reflect global influences. Guests may dine at the open-kitchen counter or at the wine bar or may enjoy a glass of wine and dessert in the lounge. The cafe occasionally features live entertainment on the weekends. Casual dress. **Bar:** Full bar. **Reservations:** suggested. **Hours:** 11:30 am-2 & 5-9 pm, Fri-10 pm, Sat 5 pm-10 pm. Closed major holidays; also Sun & 12/24. **Address:** 22 Goldsborough St 21601 **Location:** Between Harrison and Washington sts. **Parking:** street. **Cards:** AX, MC, VI.

PLAZA TAPATIA
Phone: 410/770-8550

Mexican
$5-$17

If your tastebuds are looking for something with a South of the Border flavor, then this is the place. The casual atmosphere with Mexican decorations is comfortable for any occasion. The food is prepared using authentic Mexican recipes. Casual dress. **Bar:** Full bar. **Hours:** 11 am-10 pm, Sat from noon, Sun noon-9 pm. Closed major holidays. **Address:** 7813 Ocean Gateway 21601 **Location:** US 50, 0.5 mi s of jct Dover St. **Parking:** on-site. **Cards:** AX, MC, VI.

RUSTIC INN RESTAURANT
Phone: 410/820-8212

American
$5-$46

Freshly prepared dishes, such as veal, blackened prime rib and crab cakes, make up the menu in the friendly neighborhood restaurant. A hand-painted mural of waterfront life on the Eastern shore decorates the dining room. Patrons can order from the early-bird menu weekdays between 4:30 and 6 p.m. Casual dress. **Bar:** Full bar. **Reservations:** suggested, weekends. **Hours:** 11:30 am-2 & 4:30-9 pm, Sat from 5 pm, Sun 4 pm-9 pm. Closed: 7/4, 11/27, 12/25; also for lunch Mon & Wed, for dinner 12/24 & Super Bowl Sun. **Address:** Harrison St 21601 **Location:** In Talbottown Shopping Center. **Parking:** on-site. **Cards:** AX, MC, VI.

EDGEWOOD —*See Baltimore p. 612.*

ELKRIDGE —*See Baltimore p. 613.*

ELKTON pop. 11,893

——— **WHERE TO STAY** ———

DAYS INN ELKTON
(AAA) (SAVE)
◆
Motel
Rates not provided

Book great rates at AAA.com
Phone: 410/392-5010
Address: 311 Belle Hill Rd 21921 **Location:** I-95, exit 109A, just e. **Facility:** 59 one-bedroom standard units. 2 stories (no elevator); exterior corridors. **Parking:** on-site. **Amenities:** high-speed Internet, irons, hair dryers. **Guest Services:** coin laundry, wireless Internet. **Business Services:** PC.

ELK FORGE INN & SPA
◆◆◆◆
Bed & Breakfast
$99-$329 All Year

Book at AAA.com
Phone: (410)392-9007
Address: 807 Elk Mills Rd 21921 **Location:** I-95, exit 109B, 1 mi w on SR 279 to Fletchwood Rd, then 2 mi s on Fletchwood Rd (SR 277). **Facility:** Nestled on five acres of woods and gardens, this retreat and spa offers a gentle oasis to relax and re-energize. Smoke free premises. 12 units. 8 one-bedroom standard units, some with whirlpools. 4 one-bedroom suites with whirlpools. 3 stories (no elevator); interior/exterior corridors. *Bath:* combo or shower only. **Parking:** on-site. **Terms:** 7 day cancellation notice-fee imposed. **Amenities:** video library, CD players, high-speed Internet, voice mail, irons, hair dryers. **Leisure Activities:** whirlpool, putting green, hiking trails, jogging, exercise room, spa, horseshoes, volleyball. **Guest Services:** valet laundry, wireless Internet. **Business Services:** meeting rooms, PC. **Cards:** AX, DS, MC, VI.

HAMPTON INN ELKTON
◆◆◆
Small-scale Hotel
$119-$219 All Year

Book great rates at AAA.com
Phone: 410/398-7777
Address: 2 Warner Rd 21921 **Location:** I-95, exit 109A, just e. **Facility:** 71 units. 67 one-bedroom standard units, some with whirlpools. 4 one-bedroom suites. 4 stories, interior corridors. *Bath:* combo or shower only. **Parking:** on-site. **Terms:** 30 day cancellation notice-fee imposed. **Amenities:** high-speed Internet, dual phone lines, voice mail, irons, hair dryers. *Some:* DVD players. **Pool(s):** heated indoor. **Leisure Activities:** whirlpool, limited exercise equipment. **Guest Services:** valet and coin laundry. **Business Services:** meeting rooms, business center. **Cards:** AX, CB, DC, DS, JC, MC, VI.

HAWTHORN SUITES
(AAA) (SAVE)
◆◆◆
Small-scale Hotel
Rates not provided

Book great rates at AAA.com
Phone: 410/620-9494
Address: 304 Belle Hill Rd 21921 **Location:** I-95, exit 109A, just e. **Facility:** 70 one-bedroom standard units. 4 stories, interior corridors. *Bath:* combo or shower only. **Parking:** on-site. **Amenities:** high-speed Internet, dual phone lines, voice mail, safes (fee), irons, hair dryers. **Pool(s):** heated indoor. **Leisure Activities:** limited exercise equipment. **Guest Services:** valet and coin laundry, wireless Internet. **Business Services:** meeting rooms, PC. **Free Special Amenities:** full breakfast and high-speed Internet.

SUTTON MOTEL
◆
Motel
$50-$55 All Year

Phone: 410/398-3830
Address: 405 E Pulaski Hwy 21921 **Location:** US 40, 0.8 mi e of jct SR 213. Located in a commercial area. **Facility:** Smoke free premises. 11 one-bedroom standard units. 1 story, exterior corridors. *Bath:* shower only. **Parking:** on-site.

ELLICOTT CITY —*See Baltimore p. 614.*

EMMITSBURG pop. 2,290

---------- WHERE TO STAY ----------

SLEEP INN & SUITES IN EMMITSBURG   *Book great rates at AAA.com*   **Phone:** (301)447-0044

 AAA [SAVE]

Small-scale Hotel
$75-$199 All Year

Address: 501 Silo Hill Pkwy 21727 **Location:** US 15, exit SR 140, just w, then just n on Silo Hill Pkwy. **Facility:** 79 one-bedroom standard units, some with whirlpools. 3 stories, interior corridors. *Bath:* combo or shower only. **Parking:** on-site. **Amenities:** video games, high-speed Internet, voice mail, safes (fee), irons, hair dryers. **Pool(s):** heated indoor. **Leisure Activities:** exercise room. **Guest Services:** coin laundry, wireless Internet. **Business Services:** meeting rooms. **Cards:** AX, CB, DC, DS, JC, MC, VI. **Free Special Amenities: expanded continental breakfast and high-speed Internet.**

---------- WHERE TO DINE ----------

CARRIAGE HOUSE INN   *Menu on AAA.com*   **Phone:** 301/447-2366

AAA

American
$6-$25

For a tasty treat, try seafood scampi—shrimp, scallops and crab arranged on angel hair pasta. At lunch, there's a wide variety of sandwiches and always a tempting tableside dessert display. Dining in the 1857 building is comfortable and relaxed. Casual dress. **Bar:** Full bar. **Reservations:** suggested, weekends. **Hours:** 11 am-9 pm, Fri & Sat-10 pm. Closed: 12/25. **Address:** 200 S Seton Ave 21727 **Location:** 1 mi w of US 15. **Parking:** on-site. **Cards:** AX, DS, MC, VI. **Historic**

ESSEX —*See Baltimore p. 615.*

FALLSTON —*See Baltimore p. 615.*

FREDERICK pop. 52,767

---------- WHERE TO STAY ----------

BEST WESTERN HISTORIC FREDERICK   *Book great rates at AAA.com*   **Phone:** 301/695-6200

 AAA [SAVE]

Small-scale Hotel
Rates not provided

Address: 420 Prospect Blvd 21701 **Location:** US 15, exit Jefferson St, just se. **Facility:** 118 one-bedroom standard units. 2 stories (no elevator), interior corridors. **Parking:** on-site. **Amenities:** high-speed Internet, voice mail, irons, hair dryers. **Pool(s):** outdoor. **Leisure Activities:** barbecue grills, picnic tables, exercise room. **Guest Services:** coin laundry, wireless Internet. **Business Services:** meeting rooms, PC, fax (fee). **Free Special Amenities: expanded continental breakfast and high-speed Internet.**

Best Western

AAA Benefit:
Members save 10% everyday, plus an exclusive frequent stay program.

COMFORT INN   *Book at AAA.com*   **Phone:** 301/668-7272

Small-scale Hotel
$99-$129 All Year

Address: 7300 Executive Way 21704 **Location:** I-270, exit 31B, 0.9 mi sw on SR 85. **Facility:** 73 one-bedroom standard units, some with whirlpools. 3 stories, interior corridors. *Bath:* combo or shower only. **Parking:** on-site. **Terms:** cancellation fee imposed. **Amenities:** high-speed Internet, dual phone lines, voice mail, irons, hair dryers. **Leisure Activities:** exercise room. **Guest Services:** valet and coin laundry, wireless Internet. **Business Services:** meeting rooms, PC, fax (fee). **Cards:** AX, DC, DS, MC, VI. *(See color ad below)*

COMFORT INN RED HORSE FREDERICK *Book great rates at AAA.com* Phone: (301)662-0281

Small-scale Hotel
$89-$139 All Year

Address: 998 W Patrick St 21703 **Location:** Jct US 15, just w on US 40. **Facility:** 69 one-bedroom standard units, some with whirlpools. 2-4 stories, interior corridors. *Bath:* combo or shower only. **Parking:** on-site. **Terms:** 7 day cancellation notice. **Amenities:** high-speed Internet, voice mail, irons, hair dryers. **Leisure Activities:** exercise room. **Business Services:** meeting rooms, PC, fax (fee). **Cards:** AX, DC, DS, MC, VI. *(See color ad below)*

DAYS INN *Book great rates at AAA.com* Phone: 301/694-6600

Small-scale Hotel
Rates not provided

Address: 5646 Buckeystown Pike 21704 **Location:** I-270, exit 31A, 0.5 mi e on SR 85; I-70, exit 54, 0.5 mi w. **Facility:** 119 one-bedroom standard units. 2 stories (no elevator), exterior corridors. **Parking:** on-site. **Amenities:** safes (fee), irons. *Some:* irons. **Pool(s):** outdoor. **Leisure Activities:** playground. **Guest Services:** wireless Internet. **Business Services:** fax. **Free Special Amenities: continental breakfast and high-speed Internet.**

ECONO LODGE *Book great rates at AAA.com* Phone: (301)698-0555

Small-scale Hotel
$69-$99 3/1-11/1
$62-$92 11/2-2/28

Address: 6021 Francis Scott Key Dr 21704 **Location:** Jct SR 85 and 355. Located behind the Exxon station. **Facility:** 96 one-bedroom standard units. 1 story, exterior corridors. **Parking:** on-site. **Terms:** cancellation fee imposed. **Amenities:** safes (fee), hair dryers. **Guest Services:** wireless Internet. **Business Services:** meeting rooms, PC. **Cards:** AX, CB, DC, DS, JC, MC, VI. **Free Special Amenities: continental breakfast and high-speed Internet.**

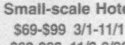

EXTENDED STAYAMERICA-FREDERICK-WESTVIEW DR *Book at AAA.com* Phone: (301)668-0808

Motel
$119-$129 All Year

Address: 5240 Westview Dr 21703 **Location:** I-270, exit 31B, 0.5 mi sw on SR 85, 0.5 mi n. **Facility:** 101 one-bedroom standard units with kitchens. 3 stories, interior corridors. *Bath:* combo or shower only. **Parking:** on-site. **Terms:** office hours 7 am-11 pm. **Amenities:** irons. **Guest Services:** coin laundry, wireless Internet. **Business Services:** fax (fee). **Cards:** AX, DC, DS, JC, MC, VI.

FAIRFIELD INN BY MARRIOTT *Book great rates at AAA.com* Phone: 301/631-2000

Small-scale Hotel
$144-$174 All Year

Address: 5220 Westview Dr 21703 **Location:** I-270, exit 31B, 0.5 mi sw on SR 85, then 0.3 mi n on Crestwood Blvd. **Facility:** Smoke free premises. 105 one-bedroom standard units. 3 stories, interior corridors. *Bath:* combo or shower only. **Amenities:** high-speed Internet, voice mail, irons, hair dryers. **Pool(s):** indoor. **Leisure Activities:** whirlpool, exercise room. **Guest Services:** valet laundry. **Business Services:** PC, fax (fee). **Cards:** AX, DC, DS, JC, MC, VI.

AAA Benefit:
Members save 5% off of the best available rate.

FREDERICK COURTYARD BY MARRIOTT

Book great rates at AAA.com

Phone: 301/631-9030

Small-scale Hotel
$177-$208 All Year

Address: 5225 Westview Dr 21703 **Location:** I-270, exit 31B, 0.5 mi sw on SR 85, then 0.3 mi n on Crestwood Blvd. **Facility:** Smoke free premises. 90 one-bedroom standard units, some with whirlpools. 3 stories, interior corridors. *Bath:* combo or shower only. **Parking:** on-site. **Amenities:** high-speed Internet, voice mail, irons, hair dryers. **Pool(s):** heated indoor. **Leisure Activities:** whirlpool, exercise room. **Guest Services:** valet and coin laundry, wireless Internet. **Business Services:** meeting rooms, business center. **Cards:** AX, DC, DS, MC, VI.

AAA Benefit:
Members save 5% off of the best available rate.

FREDERICK RESIDENCE INN BY MARRIOTT

Book great rates at AAA.com

Phone: 301/360-0010

Small-scale Hotel
$188-$219 All Year

Address: 5230 Westview Dr 21703 **Location:** I-270, exit 31B, 0.5 mi sw on SR 85, then 0.3 mi n on Crestwood Blvd. **Facility:** Smoke free premises. 90 one-bedroom standard units with kitchens. 4 stories, interior corridors. *Bath:* combo or shower only. **Parking:** on-site. **Amenities:** dual phone lines, voice mail, irons, hair dryers. **Pool(s):** heated indoor. **Leisure Activities:** whirlpool, exercise room, sports court, basketball, game room. **Guest Services:** valet and coin laundry, wireless Internet. **Business Services:** meeting rooms, PC, fax (fee). **Cards:** AX, DC, DS, JC, MC, VI.

AAA Benefit:
Members save 5% off of the best available rate.

HAMPTON INN

Book great rates at AAA.com

Phone: (301)698-2500

Small-scale Hotel
$89-$139 All Year

Address: 5311 Buckeystown Pike (SR 85) 21704 **Location:** I-270, exit 31B, 0.6 mi w. **Facility:** 161 one-bedroom standard units. 6 stories, interior corridors. *Bath:* combo or shower only. **Parking:** on-site. **Amenities:** video games, high-speed Internet, voice mail, irons, hair dryers. **Pool(s):** outdoor. **Leisure Activities:** exercise room. **Guest Services:** coin laundry, wireless Internet. **Business Services:** meeting rooms, business center. **Cards:** AX, CB, DC, DS, JC, MC, VI. **Free Special Amenities:** expanded continental breakfast and high-speed Internet.** *(See color ad below)*

HAMPTON INN & SUITES-FREDERICK

Phone: (301)696-1565

Small-scale Hotel
$99-$154 All Year

Address: 1565 Opossumtown Pike 21702 **Location:** I-70, exit 52B (US 15 N), exit 18 (Opossumtown Pike), 0.3 mi on left. **Facility:** 104 one-bedroom standard units. 5 stories, interior corridors. *Bath:* combo or shower only. **Parking:** on-site. **Amenities:** video games, high-speed Internet, dual phone lines, voice mail, irons, hair dryers. **Pool(s):** heated indoor. **Leisure Activities:** whirlpool, exercise room. **Guest Services:** valet and coin laundry, wireless Internet. **Business Services:** meeting rooms, business center. **Cards:** AX, DC, DS, MC, VI. **Free Special Amenities: full breakfast and high-speed Internet.** *(See color ad p 643)*

▼ See AAA listing above ▼

HILTON GARDEN INN FREDERICK

Book great rates at AAA.com   Phone: 240/566-1500

Small-scale Hotel
Rates not provided

Address: 7226 Corporate Ct 21703 **Location:** I-270, exit 31B, 0.5 mi s on SR 85, 0.4 mi nw on Grestwood Blvd, then just e. **Facility:** 143 one-bedroom standard units. 5 stories, interior corridors. *Bath:* combo or shower only. **Parking:** on-site. **Amenities:** video games, high-speed Internet, dual phone lines, voice mail, irons, hair dryers. **Pool(s):** heated indoor. **Leisure Activities:** whirlpool, exercise room. **Guest Services:** valet and coin laundry, wireless Internet. **Business Services:** meeting rooms, business center.

HOLIDAY INN & CONFERENCE CENTER

Book at AAA.com   Phone: 301/694-7500

Small-scale Hotel
$139-$199 All Year

Address: 5400 Holiday Dr 21703 **Location:** I-270, exit 31A, just se of SR 85. Located adjacent to shopping mall. **Facility:** 155 one-bedroom standard units. 2 stories (no elevator), interior corridors. *Bath:* combo or shower only. **Parking:** on-site. **Amenities:** video games, high-speed Internet, dual phone lines, voice mail, irons, hair dryers. **Pool(s):** heated indoor. **Leisure Activities:** saunas, whirlpool, miniature golf, exercise room. *Fee:* game room. **Guest Services:** valet and coin laundry, wireless Internet. **Business Services:** conference facilities, PC, fax (fee). **Cards:** AX, CB, DC, DS, JC, MC, VI.

HOLIDAY INN EXPRESS-FSK MALL

Book at AAA.com   Phone: 301/695-2881

Small-scale Hotel
Rates not provided

Address: 5579 Spectrum Dr 21703 **Location:** I-270, exit 31A, just e on SR 85. Located in Francis Scott Key Mall. **Facility:** 100 one-bedroom standard units. 2 stories (no elevator), interior corridors. *Bath:* combo or shower only. **Parking:** on-site. **Amenities:** high-speed Internet, voice mail, irons, hair dryers. **Guest Services:** valet and coin laundry, wireless Internet. **Business Services:** meeting rooms, PC, fax (fee).

MAINSTAY SUITES

Book great rates at AAA.com   Phone: (301)668-4600

Small-scale Hotel
$100-$149 All Year

Address: 7310 Executive Way 21704 **Location:** I-270, exit 31B, 0.7 mi sw on SR 85. **Facility:** 72 one-bedroom standard units. 3 stories, interior corridors. *Bath:* combo or shower only. **Parking:** on-site. **Amenities:** high-speed Internet, voice mail, irons, hair dryers. **Pool(s):** heated indoor. **Leisure Activities:** whirlpool, exercise room. **Guest Services:** coin laundry, wireless Internet. **Business Services:** fax (fee). **Cards:** AX, CB, DC, DS, JC, MC, VI. **Free Special Amenities:** expanded continental breakfast and high-speed Internet. *(See color ad p 640)*

SLEEP INN

Book great rates at AAA.com   Phone: (301)668-2003

Small-scale Hotel
$89-$159 All Year

Address: 5361 Spectrum Dr 21703 **Location:** I-270, exit 31A, just se of SR 85. **Facility:** 85 one-bedroom standard units. 4 stories, interior corridors. *Bath:* combo or shower only. **Parking:** on-site. **Amenities:** video games, high-speed Internet, voice mail, irons, hair dryers. **Leisure Activities:** exercise room. **Guest Services:** valet laundry. **Business Services:** meeting rooms, fax (fee). **Cards:** AX, DC, DS, MC, VI.

TRAVELODGE FREDERICK

Book great rates at AAA.com   Phone: 301/663-0500

Small-scale Hotel
Rates not provided

Address: 200 E Walser Dr 21704 **Location:** I-70, exit 54, just n. **Facility:** 122 one-bedroom standard units, some with whirlpools. 4 stories, interior corridors. **Parking:** on-site. **Amenities:** safes, hair dryers. *Some:* irons. **Guest Services:** coin laundry, wireless Internet. **Business Services:** meeting rooms, fax (fee). **Free Special Amenities:** continental breakfast and high-speed Internet.

▼ See AAA listing p 642 ▼

——— **WHERE TO DINE** ———

BARBARA FRITCHIE CANDYSTICK RESTAURANT   Phone: 301/662-2500

American
$5-$15

Named after a Civil War heroine, the restaurant has been a local favorite since 1910. Guests can expect good food fast. Casual dress. **Hours:** 7 am-10 pm. Closed: 12/25. **Address:** 1513 W Patrick St 21702 **Location:** I-70, exit 48, just n. **Parking:** on-site. **Cards:** MC, VI.

BUSH WALLER'S   Phone: 301/695-6988

American
$6-$20

Bush Waller's is an American Irish Pub with a huge selection of beers and a wide ranging menu. Casual dress. **Bar:** Full bar. **Hours:** 3 pm-2 am, Sat & Sun from 11 am. Closed: 12/25. **Address:** 209 N Market St 21701 **Location:** 0.3 mi n; center. **Parking:** street. **Cards:** AX, CB, DC, DS, JC, MC, VI.

DOUBLE TT DINER   Phone: 301/620-8797

American
$5-$20

Casual dress. **Bar:** Beer & wine. **Hours:** 6 am-10 pm. Closed: 12/25. **Address:** 5617 Spectrum Dr 21703 **Location:** I-270, exit 31A, just se of SR 85. **Parking:** on-site. **Cards:** AX, CB, DC, DS, JC, MC, VI.

DUTCH'S DAUGHTER   Phone: 301/668-9500

American
$7-$25

The casually formal restaurant prepares many beef and seafood favorites. Private rooms can accommodate up to 300. Casual dress. **Bar:** Full bar. **Reservations:** suggested. **Hours:** 11:30 am-9:30 pm, Fri-10 pm, Sat 3 pm-10 pm, Sun 10 am-9 pm; Sunday brunch. Closed: 12/25. **Address:** 581 Himes Ave 21703 **Location:** Jct US 15, just w on US 40. **Parking:** on-site. **Cards:** AX, CB, DC, DS, MC, VI.

FIRESTONE'S   Phone: 301/663-0330

American
$7-$20

The atmosphere inside the historic building is casual. World-class appetizers and specialty soups are among offerings. Casual dress. **Bar:** Full bar. **Hours:** 11 am-1:30 am. Closed: 12/25; also Mon. **Address:** 105 N Market St 21701 **Location:** Between Church and Patrick sts; downtown. **Parking:** on-site. **Cards:** AX, CB, DC, DS, JC, MC, VI.

LA PAZ MEXICAN RESTAURANT   Phone: 301/694-8980

Mexican
$7-$20

A local favorite since 1978, the restaurant serves fine Mexican food and homemade desserts. Casual dress. **Bar:** Full bar. **Hours:** 11 am-11 pm, Sun 3 pm-10 pm. Closed: 12/25. **Address:** 18 Market Space 21701 **Location:** Between Pine and Church sts; downtown. **Parking:** on-site. **Cards:** AX, CB, DC, DS, JC, MC, VI.

MAY'S RESTAURANT   Phone: 301/662-4233

American
$7-$22

The family-run restaurant has long been known for fresh seafood and a nice atmosphere. Casual dress. **Bar:** Full bar. **Hours:** 11:30 am-9:30 pm, Fri & Sat-10 pm, Sun-9 pm. Closed: 12/25, 12/26. **Address:** 5640 Urbana Pike (Rt 355) 21704 **Location:** I-270, exit 31A, 1 mi e on SR 85, 1 mi n on Grand Rd, then just w. **Parking:** on-site. **Cards:** MC, VI.

MOUNTAIN VIEW DINER RESTAURANT   Phone: 301/696-1300

American
$6-$18

Mountain View Diner Restaurant offers a huge variety for breakfast, lunch and dinner. The service and decor will remind you of simplier and friendlier days gone by. Casual dress. **Hours:** 6 am-11 pm. Closed: 12/25. **Address:** 1300 W Patrick St 21703 **Location:** 1.2 mi w of US 40 from jct US 15. **Parking:** on-site. **Cards:** MC, VI.

PARGO'S   Phone: 301/698-1800

American
$8-$20

Businesspeople, mall employees and shoppers love the bustling eatery, as evidenced by the long lines that often wait for seating. The menu offers standard favorites, such as pasta and steak, in plentiful portions. Casual dress. **Bar:** Full bar. **Hours:** 11 am-11 pm, Fri & Sat-midnight, Sun-10 pm. Closed: 11/27, 12/25, 12/26. **Address:** 5597 Spectrum Dr 21703 **Location:** I-270, exit 31A, just e on SR 85; in Francis Scott Key Mall. **Parking:** on-site. **Cards:** AX, DC, DS, MC, VI.

RED HORSE STEAK HOUSE   Phone: 301/663-3030
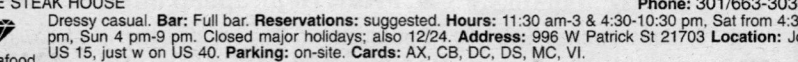
Steak & Seafood
$8-$32

Dressy casual. **Bar:** Full bar. **Reservations:** suggested. **Hours:** 11:30 am-3 & 4:30-10:30 pm, Sat from 4:30 pm, Sun 4 pm-9 pm. Closed major holidays; also 12/24. **Address:** 996 W Patrick St 21703 **Location:** Jct US 15, just w on US 40. **Parking:** on-site. **Cards:** AX, CB, DC, DS, MC, VI.

FROSTBURG pop. 7,873

———— WHERE TO STAY ————

DAYS INN & SUITES

AAA SAVE

Small-scale Hotel
Rates not provided

Book great rates at AAA.com
Phone: 301/689-2050
Address: 11100 New Georges Creek Rd 21532 **Location:** I-68, exit 34, 1 mi n on SR 36. **Facility:** 91 one-bedroom standard units, some with whirlpools. 2 stories (no elevator), interior corridors. **Parking:** on-site. **Amenities:** high-speed Internet, irons, hair dryers. **Leisure Activities:** saunas, exercise room. **Guest Services:** coin laundry, wireless Internet. **Business Services:** meeting rooms, business center. **Free Special Amenities:** expanded continental breakfast and high-speed Internet.

CALL (&M) 🐾 🖪 🖾 🖵 / SOME UNITS FEE 🐕 ✕

HAMPTON INN

Small-scale Hotel
$99-$169 All Year

Book great rates at AAA.com
Phone: (301)689-1998
Address: 11200 New Georges Creek Rd 21532 **Location:** I-68, exit 34, 1 mi n on SR 36. **Facility:** 72 one-bedroom standard units, some with whirlpools. 3 stories, interior corridors. *Bath:* combo or shower only. **Parking:** on-site. **Amenities:** video games, high-speed Internet, dual phone lines, voice mail, irons, hair dryers. **Pool(s):** indoor. **Leisure Activities:** whirlpool, exercise room. **Guest Services:** coin laundry, wireless Internet. **Business Services:** fax. **Cards:** AX, CB, DC, DS, JC, MC, VI.

ASK SD CALL (&M) 🏊 🐾 🖪 🖾 🖵 / SOME UNITS ✕

———— WHERE TO DINE ————

ACROPOLIS RESTAURANT & LOUNGE

Greek
$13-$27

Phone: 301/689-8277
Acropolis Restaurant & Lounge combines Greek and American cuisine in an elegant setting, offering knowledgeable wait staff and wonderful background music. Casual dress. **Bar:** Full bar. **Hours:** 4 pm-10 pm. Closed: 12/25; also Sun & Mon. **Address:** 45 E Main St 21532 **Location:** I-68, exit 34, 1.5 mi n on SR 36, then 0.9 mi w on US 40 Alternate Rt and SR 36; center. **Parking:** street. **Cards:** AX, CB, DC, DS, JC, MC, VI.

🔌

AU PETIT PARIS

AAA

French
$14-$32

Phone: 301/689-8946
Family owned and operated since 1960, the small, cozy restaurant is known for expert preparations of such seafood as fresh salmon, as well as beef, veal, lamb, venison and duck. The knowledgeable, experienced wait staff gives personalized attention. Dressy casual. **Bar:** Full bar. **Reservations:** suggested. **Hours:** 6 pm-9:30 pm. Closed: 1/1, 11/27, 12/24, 12/25; also Sun & Mon. **Address:** 86 E Main St 21532 **Location:** I-68, exit 34, 1.5 mi n on SR 36, then 1 mi w on US 40 Alternate Rt and SR 36; center. **Parking:** street. **Cards:** AX, CB, DC, DS, MC, VI.

CALL (&M) 🔌

GIUSEPPE'S ITALIAN RESTAURANT

Italian
$12-$22

Phone: 301/689-2220
Giuseppe's Italian Restaurant combines a bi-level dining room with knowledgeable service and wonderful cuisine. Casual dress. **Bar:** Full bar. **Hours:** 4:30 pm-11 pm, Fri & Sat from 3 pm. Closed: 12/25. **Address:** 11 Bowery St 21532 **Location:** I-68, exit 34, 1.5 mi n on SR 36, then 1 mi w on US 40 Alternate Rt and SR 36; center. **Parking:** on-site and street. **Cards:** AX, CB, DC, DS, JC, MC, VI.

🔌

FRUITLAND pop. 3,774

———— WHERE TO DINE ————

ADAM'S THE PLACE FOR RIBS

American
$8-$20

Phone: 410/749-6961
This local favorite naturally specializes in "finger licking good" ribs, but don't overlook the other menu offerings, which include, beef, chicken and seafood dishes. A children's menu is also available. Casual dress. **Bar:** Full bar. **Reservations:** accepted. **Hours:** 11 am-10 pm, Fri & Sat-11 pm. Closed: 11/27, 12/25. **Address:** 219 N Fruitland Blvd 21826 **Location:** On Business Rt 13, just s of Salisbury. **Parking:** on-site. **Cards:** AX, MC, VI.

🔌

GAITHERSBURG —See District Of Columbia p. 482.

GERMANTOWN —See District Of Columbia p. 486.

GLEN BURNIE —See Baltimore p. 616.

GRANTSVILLE pop. 619

———— WHERE TO STAY ————

THE STONEBOW INN

Bed & Breakfast
$155-$195 All Year

Phone: 301/895-4250
Address: 146 Casselman Rd 21536 **Location:** I-68, exit 22 westbound, 0.5 mi n on US 219, then 2.1 mi w on US 40; exit 19 eastbound, just n, then 0.9 mi e on US 40; behind Penn Alps Restaurant. Located in a quiet area. **Facility:** On 7 acres on the Casselman River, the 1870 Victorian mountain inn features a deck overlooking the river and garden; rooms have old-time furnishings. Smoke free premises. 9 one-bedroom standard units. 1-2 stories (no elevator), interior/exterior corridors. *Bath:* combo or shower only. **Parking:** on-site. **Terms:** age restrictions may apply, 14 day cancellation notice-fee imposed. *Some:* CD players. **Leisure Activities:** sauna, fishing. **Fee:** massage. **Guest Services:** wireless Internet. **Cards:** AX, DS, MC, VI.

ASK 🍽️ ✕ ✕ VCR 🖪 🖵 / SOME UNITS 🐕 🖾

——— WHERE TO DINE ———

PENN ALPS RESTAURANT *Menu on AAA.com*

American
$6-$16

Phone: 301/895-5985

The family-oriented restaurant offers traditionally prepared meals, including a nice prime rib and steamed shrimp buffet Friday and Saturday. In keeping with the chalet-like structure, the establishment is conveniently located at Artisan Village. Casual dress. **Hours:** 7 am-8 pm; to 7 pm, Sun-3 pm 11/1-5/27. **Closed:** 1/1, 12/24, 12/25. **Address:** 125 Casselman Rd 21536 **Location:** I-68, exit 22 westbound, 1 mi on Chestnut Ridge Rd, then 2 mi w on US 40 alternate route; exit 19 eastbound, 0.3 mi n on CR 495, 1 mi e on US 40 alternate route. **Parking:** on-site. **Cards:** DS, MC, VI.

GRASONVILLE pop. 2,193

——— WHERE TO STAY ———

BEST WESTERN KENT NARROWS INN *Book great rates at AAA.com*

Motel
$79-$219 All Year

Phone: (410)827-6767

Address: 3101 Main St 21638 **Location:** US 50 and 301, exit 42; at Kent Narrows Bridge. **Facility:** 92 one-bedroom standard units, some with kitchens and/or whirlpools. 4 stories, exterior corridors. **Parking:** on-site. **Amenities:** voice mail, irons, hair dryers. **Pool(s):** heated indoor. **Leisure Activities:** sauna, whirlpool, sun deck, limited exercise equipment. **Guest Services:** coin laundry, wireless Internet. **Business Services:** meeting rooms, PC. **Cards:** AX, CB, DC, DS, JC, MC, VI. **Free Special Amenities: expanded continental breakfast and high-speed Internet.**

AAA Benefit:
Members save 10% everyday, plus an exclusive frequent stay program.

HILTON GARDEN INN-KENT ISLAND *Book great rates at AAA.com*

Small-scale Hotel
Rates not provided

Phone: 410/827-3877

Address: 3206 Main St 21638 **Location:** US 50 and 301, exit 42; at Kent Narrows Bridge. **Facility:** 90 units. 80 one-bedroom standard units. 10 one-bedroom suites. 5 stories, interior corridors. *Bath:* combo or shower only. **Parking:** on-site. **Amenities:** video games (fee), high-speed Internet, voice mail, irons, hair dryers. **Pool(s):** heated indoor. **Leisure Activities:** whirlpool, exercise room. *Fee:* boat dock. **Guest Services:** valet and coin laundry, wireless Internet. **Business Services:** meeting rooms, business center.

HOLIDAY INN EXPRESS-ANNAPOLIS/KENT ISLAND *Book at AAA.com*
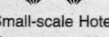
Small-scale Hotel
Rates not provided

Phone: 410/827-4454

Address: 1020 Kent Narrows Rd 21638 **Location:** US 50 and 301, exit 42; at Kent Narrows Bridge. **Facility:** 76 one-bedroom standard units, some with whirlpools. 3 stories, interior corridors. *Bath:* combo or shower only. **Parking:** on-site. **Amenities:** dual phone lines, voice mail, irons, hair dryers. **Pool(s):** outdoor. **Guest Services:** valet and coin laundry, wireless Internet. **Business Services:** meeting rooms.

SLEEP INN *Book great rates at AAA.com*

Small-scale Hotel
$89-$159 3/1-10/14
$69-$159 10/15-2/28

Phone: (410)827-5555

Address: 101 VFW Ave 21638 **Location:** US 50 and 301, exit 44A westbound; exit 43B eastbound, 0.7 mi ne. **Facility:** 59 one-bedroom standard units, some with whirlpools. 2 stories (no elevator), interior corridors. *Bath:* combo or shower only. **Parking:** on-site. **Terms:** cancellation fee imposed. **Amenities:** voice mail, safes (fee), irons, hair dryers. **Pool(s):** outdoor. **Guest Services:** wireless Internet. **Business Services:** meeting rooms, PC. **Cards:** AX, CB, DC, DS, JC, MC, VI. **Free Special Amenities: continental breakfast and high-speed Internet.** *(See color ad below)*

——— **WHERE TO DINE** ———

ANNIE'S PARAMOUNT STEAK & SEAFOOD HOUSE Phone: 410/827-7103

Steak & Seafood
$7-$30

Since 1992, this family owned and operated restaurant has pleased the locals. The menu features Certified Angus Beef, Seafood and Mediterranean dishes. The staff is professional, friendly and eager to please. Casual dress. **Bar:** Full bar. **Reservations:** suggested. **Hours:** 11 am-10 pm, Fri & Sat-11 pm, Sun 9 am-10 pm; Sunday brunch. Closed: 12/25. **Address:** 500 Kent Narrows Way N 21638 **Location:** US 50 and 301, exit 42, just n, follow signs. **Parking:** on-site. **Cards:** AX, DC, DS, MC, VI.

FISHERMAN'S CRAB DECK Phone: 410/827-6666

Seafood
$7-$26

The waterside restaurant provides a lively, casual setting and is perfect for families. If crabs are what you're looking for, then this is the place. Diners can choose from the Steamed Crab Pot, the Variety Pot or Steamed Lobster Pot, as well as a variety of crab, shrimp and scallop dishes. For those in the mood for something from the land, they offer chicken and steak as well. They also offer a good selection of ice cream drinks and frozen drinks. Casual dress. **Bar:** Full bar. **Reservations:** not accepted. **Hours:** Open 4/15-11/30; 11 am-10 pm. **Address:** 3032 Kent Narrows Way S 21638 **Location:** US 50 and 301, exit 42, at Kent Narrows Bridge. **Parking:** on-site. **Cards:** AX, DC, DS, MC, VI.

CALL

FISHERMAN'S INN Phone: 410/827-8807

Seafood
$7-$30

Families are welcomed at the casual and lively restaurant, where guests can order from the lunch menu until 4 pm. Although seafood is the specialty, crab soup is a favorite on a diverse menu. **Bar:** Full bar. **Reservations:** not accepted. **Hours:** 11 am-10 pm. Closed: 12/24, 12/25. **Address:** 3116 Main St 21638 **Location:** US 50 and 301, exit 42; at Kent Narrows Bridge. **Parking:** on-site. **Cards:** AX, DC, DS, MC, VI.

THE NARROWS Phone: 410/827-8113
Seafood
$7-$30

Windows wrap-around three sides of the tastefully decorated dining area, which looks out on the harbor. The screened porch is popular during mild weather. The cream of crab soup is a favorite on a diverse menu of seafood, beef, lamb, pork and chicken. Lunch menu available to 4 pm. Casual dress. **Bar:** Full bar. **Reservations:** suggested, weekends. **Hours:** 11 am-9 pm, Fri & Sat-10 pm. Closed: 12/24, 12/25. **Address:** 3023 Kent Narrows Way S 21638 **Location:** US 50 and 301, exit 42, 0.3 mi s. **Parking:** on-site. **Cards:** AX, CB, DC, DS, MC, VI.

GREENBELT —*See District Of Columbia p. 487.*

HAGERSTOWN pop. 36,687

——— **WHERE TO STAY** ———

BEST WESTERN GRAND VENICE HOTEL *Book great rates at AAA.com* Phone: (301)733-0830
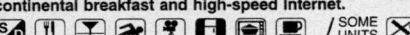

Small-scale Hotel
$89-$189 All Year

Address: 431 Dual Hwy 21740 **Location:** I-70, exit 32B, 2.7 mi w on US 40. **Facility:** 86 one-bedroom standard units, some with whirlpools. 5 stories, interior corridors. **Parking:** on-site. **Amenities:** voice mail, irons, hair dryers. **Pool(s):** outdoor. **Leisure Activities:** exercise room. **Guest Services:** wireless Internet. **Business Services:** conference facilities, business center. **Cards:** AX, DS, JC, MC, VI. **Free Special Amenities:** continental breakfast and high-speed Internet.

AAA Benefit:
Members save 10% everyday, plus an exclusive frequent stay program.

COMFORT SUITES *Book great rates at AAA.com* Phone: (301)791-8100

Small-scale Hotel
$79-$129 All Year

Address: 1801 Dual Hwy 21740 **Location:** I-70, exit 32B, 0.8 mi w on US 40. **Facility:** 75 one-bedroom standard units, some with whirlpools. 3 stories, interior corridors. *Bath:* combo or shower only. **Parking:** on-site. **Amenities:** high-speed Internet, dual phone lines, voice mail, safes, irons, hair dryers. **Pool(s):** heated indoor. **Leisure Activities:** whirlpool, exercise room. **Guest Services:** coin laundry, wireless Internet. **Business Services:** meeting rooms, business center. **Cards:** AX, DC, DS, JC, MC, VI. **Free Special Amenities:** expanded continental breakfast and high-speed Internet.

COUNTRY INN & SUITES BY CARLSON *Book at AAA.com* Phone: (301)582-5003

Small-scale Hotel
$104-$144 All Year

Address: 17612 Valley Mall Rd 21740 **Location:** I-81, exit 5A, just e. **Facility:** 85 one-bedroom standard units, some with whirlpools. 4 stories, interior corridors. *Bath:* some combo or shower only. **Parking:** on-site. **Amenities:** CD players, high-speed Internet, voice mail, safes, irons, hair dryers. **Pool(s):** heated indoor. **Leisure Activities:** sauna, whirlpool, exercise room. **Guest Services:** valet and coin laundry, wireless Internet. **Business Services:** meeting rooms, business center. **Cards:** AX, DC, DS, MC, VI.

FOUR POINTS BY SHERATON HAGERSTOWN

Book great rates at AAA.com

Phone: (301)790-3010

(AAA) SAVE

Small-scale Hotel
$79-$119 All Year

Address: 1910 Dual Hwy 21740 **Location:** I-70, exit 32B, 0.5 mi n. **Facility:** 108 one-bedroom standard units, some with whirlpools. 2 stories (no elevator), interior corridors. *Bath:* combo or shower only. **Parking:** on-site. **Amenities:** video games, high-speed Internet, voice mail, irons, hair dryers. **Dining:** Nicholas, see separate listing. **Pool(s):** outdoor. **Leisure Activities:** exercise room. **Guest Services:** wireless Internet. **Business Services:** meeting rooms, business center. **Cards:** AX, DC, DS, MC, VI. **Free Special Amenities: expanded continental breakfast and high-speed Internet.**

FOUR POINTS BY SHERATON

AAA Benefit:
Members get up to 15% off, plus Starwood Preferred Guest® bonuses.

HALFWAY HAGERSTOWN SUPER 8

Book at AAA.com

Phone: (301)582-1992

Small-scale Hotel
$63-$71 All Year

Address: 16805 Blake Rd 21740 **Location:** I-81, exit 5B, just w. **Facility:** 62 one-bedroom standard units, some with whirlpools. 2 stories (no elevator), interior corridors. *Bath:* combo or shower only. **Parking:** on-site. **Amenities:** hair dryers. **Guest Services:** coin laundry, wireless Internet. **Cards:** AX, DC, DS, MC, VI.

HAMPTON INN HAGERSTOWN

Book great rates at AAA.com

Phone: 301/739-6100

(AAA) SAVE

Small-scale Hotel
Rates not provided

Address: 1716 Dual Hwy 21740 **Location:** I-70, exit 32B, 1 mi w on US 40. **Facility:** 118 one-bedroom standard units. 4 stories, interior corridors. *Bath:* combo or shower only. **Parking:** on-site. **Amenities:** high-speed Internet, voice mail, irons, hair dryers. **Pool(s):** heated outdoor. **Leisure Activities:** exercise room. **Guest Services:** valet laundry, wireless Internet. **Business Services:** meeting rooms, PC. **Free Special Amenities: full breakfast and high-speed Internet.**

HAMPTON INN HAGERSTOWN/MAUGANSVILLE

Book great rates at AAA.com

Phone: (240)420-1970

(AAA) SAVE

Small-scale Hotel
$99-$139 All Year

Address: 18300 Peak Cir 21742 **Location:** I-81, exit 9, just e. **Facility:** 118 one-bedroom standard units. 3 stories, interior corridors. *Bath:* combo or shower only. **Parking:** on-site. **Amenities:** high-speed Internet, voice mail, irons, hair dryers. **Pool(s):** heated indoor. **Leisure Activities:** exercise room. **Guest Services:** valet laundry, area transportation-within 10 mi, wireless Internet. **Business Services:** meeting rooms, business center. **Cards:** AX, DC, DS, MC, VI. **Free Special Amenities: expanded continental breakfast and high-speed Internet.**

HOLIDAY INN EXPRESS HOTEL & SUITES

Book great rates at AAA.com

Phone: (301)745-5644

(AAA) SAVE

Small-scale Hotel
$114-$147 All Year

Address: 241 Railway Ln 21740 **Location:** I-81, exit 5A. **Facility:** 84 one-bedroom standard units, some with whirlpools. 3 stories, interior corridors. *Bath:* combo or shower only. **Parking:** on-site. **Amenities:** high-speed Internet, voice mail, irons, hair dryers. **Pool(s):** heated indoor. **Leisure Activities:** whirlpool, exercise room. **Guest Services:** valet and coin laundry, wireless Internet. **Business Services:** meeting rooms, business center. **Cards:** AX, CB, DC, DS, JC, MC, VI. **Free Special Amenities: expanded continental breakfast and high-speed Internet.** *(See color ad below)*

MICROTEL INN & SUITES-HAGERSTOWN MD   *Book at AAA.com*   Phone: (240)527-2700

Small-scale Hotel
$49-$99 All Year

Address: 13726 Oliver Dr 21740 **Location:** I-81, exit 9, just w. **Facility:** 53 one-bedroom standard units, some with whirlpools. 3 stories, interior corridors. *Bath:* combo or shower only. **Parking:** on-site. **Amenities:** *Some:* high-speed Internet. **Guest Services:** coin laundry, wireless Internet. **Cards:** AX, DS, MC, VI.

PLAZA HOTEL   *Book great rates at AAA.com*   Phone: (301)797-2500

Small-scale Hotel
$78-$97 All Year

Address: 1718 Underpass Way 21740 **Location:** I-81, exit 5, 0.3 mi e; 0.5 mi n of jct I-81 and 70. **Facility:** 162 one-bedroom standard units, some with whirlpools. 6 stories, interior corridors. **Parking:** on-site. **Amenities:** high-speed Internet, voice mail, irons, hair dryers. *Some:* CD players. **Pool(s):** heated indoor. **Leisure Activities:** sauna, whirlpool, exercise room. **Guest Services:** valet and laundry, airport transportation-Hagerstown Airport, wireless Internet. **Business Services:** meeting rooms, PC. **Cards:** AX, CB, DC, DS, MC, VI. **Free Special Amenities:** local telephone calls and high-speed Internet. *(See color ad below)*

SLEEP INN & SUITES   *Book great rates at AAA.com*   Phone: (301)766-9449

Small-scale Hotel
$95-$169 All Year

Address: 18216 Col Henry K Douglas Dr 21740 **Location:** I-70, exit 29, just s. **Facility:** 96 one-bedroom standard units, some with whirlpools. 4 stories, interior corridors. *Bath:* combo or shower only. **Parking:** on-site. **Terms:** cancellation fee imposed. **Amenities:** high-speed Internet, safes (fee), irons, hair dryers. **Pool(s):** heated indoor. **Leisure Activities:** whirlpool, exercise room. **Guest Services:** coin laundry, wireless Internet. **Business Services:** meeting rooms. **Cards:** AX, DC, DS, JC, MC, VI. **Free Special Amenities:** continental breakfast and high-speed Internet.

SPRINGHILL SUITES BY MARRIOTT HAGERSTOWN   *Book great rates at AAA.com*   Phone: 301/582-0011

Small-scale Hotel
$116-$146 All Year

Address: 17280 Valley Mall Rd 21740 **Location:** I-81, exit 5A, just e. **Facility:** Smoke free premises. 104 one-bedroom standard units, some with whirlpools. 6 stories, interior corridors. *Bath:* combo or shower only. **Parking:** on-site. **Amenities:** video games, high-speed Internet, dual phone lines, voice mail, irons, hair dryers. *Some:* DVD players. **Pool(s):** heated indoor. **Leisure Activities:** whirlpool, exercise room. **Guest Services:** valet and coin laundry, wireless Internet. **Business Services:** meeting rooms, business center. **Cards:** AX, DS, MC, VI.

AAA Benefit:
Members save 5% off of the best available rate.

SUPER 8 MOTEL HAGERSTOWN   *Book at AAA.com*   Phone: (301)739-5800

Motel
$57-$72 All Year

Address: 1220 Dual Hwy 21740 **Location:** I-70, exit 32B, 2.1 mi nw on US 40. **Facility:** 61 one-bedroom standard units. 3 stories (no elevator), interior corridors. **Parking:** on-site. **Amenities:** hair dryers. **Guest Services:** wireless Internet. **Cards:** AX, DC, DS, MC, VI.

——— WHERE TO DINE ———

AL POMODORO RISTORANTE
Phone: 301/739-0440
South Italian
$8-$22
The flavors of Southern Italy come alive in Neapolitan dishes put together with slick plate presentations. The staff is lively. Casual dress. **Bar:** Full bar. **Hours:** 11 am-10 pm, Sat from 4 pm. Closed: 12/25; also Sun. **Address:** 1101 Opal Ct 21740 **Location:** I-70, exit 32B, 2.3 mi w on US 40, then 0.3 mi e on Eastern Blvd. **Parking:** on-site. **Cards:** AX, CB, DC, DS, JC, MC, VI.

BURHANS STATION
Phone: 301/790-3000
American
$6-$21
At the converted train station, guests can step back into yesteryear and savor classic American favorites. Casual dress. **Bar:** Full bar. **Hours:** 11 am-10 pm. Closed: 12/25. **Address:** 301 S Burhans Blvd 21740 **Location:** I-81, exit 5, 0.3 mi e, 2.5 mi n on Wessel, then 0.5 mi w. **Parking:** on-site. **Cards:** AX, MC, VI.

FIRESIDE RESTAURANT & LOUNGE   *Menu on AAA.com*
Phone: 301/733-4800
AAA
American
$7-$27
A huge fireplace, from which the restaurant derives its name, is the center of attention in the dining room. Service is friendly, and portions are large. Casual dress. **Bar:** Full bar. **Hours:** 6:30-10:30 am, 11-1:30 & 5-9 pm, Sat & Sun from 7 am. Closed major holidays. **Address:** 1716 Underpass Way 21740 **Location:** I-81, exit 5, 0.3 mi e, then 0.5 mi n of jct I-81 and I-70. **Parking:** on-site. **Cards:** AX, CB, DC, DS, JC, MC, VI.

FRATELLI PIZZERIA & GRILL
Phone: 301/393-8733
Pizza
$6-$15
Pasta and specialty pizzas are favorite choices at the family-owned-and-run restaurant, which nurtures a wholesome atmosphere. Casual dress. **Bar:** Beer & wine. **Hours:** 11 am-10 pm, Sun noon-9 pm. Closed: 1/1, 12/25. **Address:** 120 E Oak Ridge Dr 21740 **Location:** I-70, exit 29, 1.4 mi n on SR 65, then 0.8 mi e. **Parking:** on-site. **Cards:** AX, CB, DC, DS, JC, MC, VI.

THE GRILL AT PARK CIRCLE
Phone: 301/797-9100
American
$6-$20
A Hagerstown tradition for many years. The Grill at Park Circle combines elegantly prepared food with a casual fun atmosphere. Casual dress. **Bar:** Full bar. **Reservations:** accepted, weekends. **Hours:** 11:30 am-11 pm, Sat from 4:30 pm. Closed: Sun & Mon. **Address:** 325 Virginia Ave 21740 **Location:** I-81, exit 5, 2.9 mi e. **Parking:** on-site. **Cards:** AX, DC, DS, MC, VI.

MALOO'S PUB & GRILL
Phone: 301/790-0077
American
$6-$16
Guests kick back in a festive and lively atmosphere. Many beer selections complement choices on the varied pub menu. Casual dress. **Bar:** Full bar. **Hours:** 11 am-2 am, Sat from noon. Closed: 12/25; also Sun. **Address:** 11353 Robinwood Dr 21742 **Location:** I-70, exit 32B, 1.1 mi w on US 40, 2.1 mi e on Edgewood Dr, then just s. **Parking:** on-site. **Cards:** AX, CB, DC, DS, JC, MC, VI.

NICHOLAS
Phone: 301/790-3640
American
$6-$20
The good variety of well-prepared food is certainly commendable, namely offerings on the Tuesday-Friday lunch buffet. Pasta, seafood, meat, poultry and Greek specialties are foremost on the menu. Service is prompt, knowledgeable and friendly. Casual dress. **Bar:** Full bar. **Reservations:** suggested. **Hours:** 6:30 am-2 & 5-10 pm, Sun 7 am-9 pm. Closed: 12/25. **Address:** 1910 Dual Hwy 21740 **Location:** I-70, exit 32B, 0.5 mi n; in Four Points by Sheraton Hagerstown. **Parking:** on-site. **Cards:** AX, DC, DS, MC, VI.

RED HORSE STEAK HOUSE
Phone: 301/733-3788
Steak & Seafood
$12-$33
Dressy casual. **Bar:** Full bar. **Reservations:** accepted. **Hours:** 4 pm-10 pm, Sun-9 pm. Closed major holidays. **Address:** 1800 Dual Hwy 21740 **Location:** I-70, exit 32B, 1 mi nw on US 40. **Parking:** on-site. **Cards:** AX, DC, MC, VI.

RICHARDSON'S RESTAURANT
Phone: 301/733-3660
American
$5-$24
Richardson's Restaurant is a culinary landmark in Hagerstown. Family oriented and run for three generations. Value priced with friendly service. Casual dress. **Bar:** Full bar. **Reservations:** accepted. **Hours:** 7 am-9:30 pm. Closed: 12/25; also for dinner 12/24. **Address:** 710 Dual Hwy 21740 **Location:** I-70, exit 32B, 2.3 mi w on US 40. **Parking:** on-site. **Cards:** DS, MC, VI.

SCHMANKERL STUBE BAVARIAN RESTAURANT
Phone: 301/797-3354
German
$7-$25
Translated as "Bavarian specialty room," Schmankerl Stube delivers as such. Well-groomed servers are knowledgeable about the German cuisine. Casual dress. **Bar:** Full bar. **Reservations:** suggested, weekends. **Hours:** 11 am-9 pm. Closed: 1/1, 12/25; also Mon. **Address:** 58 S Potomac St 21740 **Location:** Jct Potomac and Antietam sts; center of downtown. **Parking:** street. **Cards:** AX, CB, DC, DS, JC, MC, VI.

HANCOCK pop. 1,725

---- WHERE TO STAY ----

SUPER 8 MOTEL *Book great rates at AAA.com* Phone: 301/678-6101
(AAA) SAVE
Small-scale Hotel
Rates not provided

Address: 118 Limestone Rd 21750 **Location:** I-70, exit 1B, just s. **Facility:** 50 one-bedroom standard units, some with whirlpools. 2 stories (no elevator), interior/exterior corridors. **Parking:** on-site. **Amenities:** hair dryers. **Guest Services:** valet laundry, wireless Internet. **Business Services:** fax (fee). **Free Special Amenities:** continental breakfast and high-speed Internet.

---- WHERE TO DINE ----

WEAVER'S RESTAURANT & BAKERY Phone: 301/678-6346
American
$5-$16

At Weaver's you'll find homemade soups, sandwiches and desserts. Home town American pride translates to very friendly service. Casual dress. **Hours:** 11 am-8 pm, Fri-Sun from 7 am. Closed: 11/27, 12/25. **Address:** 77 W Main St 21750 **Location:** I-70, exit 1B, just s. **Parking:** street. **Cards:** MC, VI.

HANOVER —See Baltimore p. 617.

HAVRE DE GRACE —See Baltimore p. 618.

HUNT VALLEY —See Baltimore p. 618.

INDIAN HEAD pop. 3,422

---- WHERE TO STAY ----

SUPER 8 MOTEL *Book great rates at AAA.com* Phone: 301/753-8100
(AAA) SAVE
Small-scale Hotel
Rates not provided

Address: 4694 Indian Head Hwy 20640 **Location:** SR 210, 0.6 mi s of jct SR 225. **Facility:** 44 one-bedroom standard units. 3 stories, interior corridors. **Parking:** on-site. **Amenities:** irons, hair dryers. **Guest Services:** coin laundry, wireless Internet. **Business Services:** fax (fee).

JESSUP —See Baltimore p. 619.

JOPPA —See Baltimore p. 620.

LANDOVER —See District Of Columbia p. 488.

LANDOVER HILLS —See District Of Columbia p. 489.

LANHAM —See District Of Columbia p. 489.

LA PLATA pop. 6,551

---- WHERE TO STAY ----

BEST WESTERN LA PLATA INN *Book great rates at AAA.com* Phone: (301)934-4900
(AAA) SAVE
Small-scale Hotel
$119-$139 3/1-10/31
$109-$139 11/1-2/28

Address: 6900 Crain Hwy 20646 **Location:** Jct SR 6, 0.4 mi s on US 301. **Facility:** 73 units. 65 one-bedroom standard units. 8 one-bedroom suites. 2 stories (no elevator), interior corridors. **Parking:** on-site. **Terms:** 7 day cancellation notice. **Amenities:** dual phone lines, voice mail, irons, hair dryers. *Some:* high-speed Internet. **Pool(s):** outdoor. **Leisure Activities:** exercise room. **Guest Services:** coin laundry, wireless Internet. **Business Services:** meeting rooms, PC. **Cards:** AX, CB, DC, DS, JC, MC, VI. **Free Special Amenities:** expanded continental breakfast and high-speed Internet.

AAA Benefit:
Members save 10% everyday, plus an exclusive frequent stay program.

SLEEP INN & SUITES OF LA PLATA *Book great rates at AAA.com* Phone: (301)392-0065
Small-scale Hotel
$99-$189 3/1-10/31
$89-$129 11/1-2/28

Address: 6860 Crain Hwy 20646 **Location:** Jct SR 6, just s on US 301. **Facility:** Smoke free premises. 69 units. 62 one- and 4 two-bedroom standard units, some with whirlpools. 3 one-bedroom suites. 4 stories, interior corridors. *Bath:* combo or shower only. **Parking:** on-site. **Amenities:** CD players, high-speed Internet, dual phone lines, voice mail, safes (fee), irons, hair dryers. **Pool(s):** heated indoor. **Leisure Activities:** whirlpool, limited exercise equipment. **Guest Services:** valet and coin laundry, wireless Internet. **Business Services:** meeting rooms, PC. **Cards:** AX, DC, DS, MC, VI.

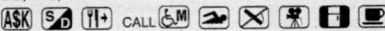

——— WHERE TO DINE ———

THE CROSSING AT CASEY JONES

American
$6-$29

The dining room of the well-established, family-run restaurant has a casual, comfortable feel. The exhibition kitchen enables diners to watch as dishes from the seasonally changing menu are prepared. A nice wine selection is available. Dressy casual. **Bar:** Full bar. **Reservations:** suggested. **Hours:** 11 am-2:30 & 5-9:30 pm, Fri-10 pm, Sat 5 pm-10 pm. Closed: 1/1, 9/1, 12/25; also Sun. **Address:** 417 E Charles St 20646 **Location:** Just e of US 301. **Parking:** on-site. **Cards:** AX, DC, DS, MC, VI.

Phone: 301/932-6226

LARGO —*See District Of Columbia p. 490.*

LAUREL —*See District Of Columbia p. 490.*

LA VALE pop. 4,613

——— WHERE TO STAY ———

BEST WESTERN BRADDOCK MOTOR INN   *Book great rates at AAA.com*

Small-scale Hotel
$74-$124 All Year

Phone: (301)729-3300

Address: 1268 National Hwy 21502 **Location:** On US 40, jct SR 53, adjacent to I-68, exit 39W/40E. **Facility:** 104 one-bedroom standard units, some with whirlpools. 3 stories (no elevator), interior corridors. *Bath:* combo or shower only. **Parking:** on-site. **Amenities:** voice mail, irons, hair dryers. *Some:* high-speed Internet. **Pool(s):** indoor. **Leisure Activities:** whirlpool, exercise room. **Guest Services:** valet laundry, area transportation-within 25 mi, wireless Internet. **Business Services:** meeting rooms, fax (fee). **Cards:** AX, CB, DC, DS, MC, VI. **Free Special Amenities: continental breakfast and local telephone calls.**

AAA Benefit:
Members save 10% everyday, plus an exclusive frequent stay program.

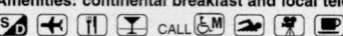

COMFORT INN & SUITES   *Book at AAA.com*

Small-scale Hotel
$89-$119 All Year

Phone: (301)729-6400

Address: 1216 National Hwy 21502 **Location:** I-68, exit 40 eastbound, 0.4 mi n; exit 39 westbound, 1 mi n. **Facility:** 67 one-bedroom standard units, some with whirlpools. 3 stories, interior corridors. *Bath:* combo or shower only. **Parking:** on-site. **Terms:** cancellation fee imposed. **Amenities:** high-speed Internet, voice mail, irons, hair dryers. **Pool(s):** heated indoor. **Leisure Activities:** whirlpool, exercise room. **Guest Services:** valet and coin laundry, wireless Internet. **Business Services:** meeting rooms. **Cards:** AX, CB, DC, DS, MC, VI.

RED ROOF INN   *Book great rates at AAA.com*

Small-scale Hotel
Rates not provided

Phone: 301/729-6700

Address: 12310 Winchester Rd SW 21502 **Location:** I-68, exit 40, 0.6 mi s. **Facility:** 82 one-bedroom standard units. 3 stories, interior/exterior corridors. *Bath:* combo or shower only. **Parking:** on-site. **Amenities:** hair dryers. *Some:* irons. **Leisure Activities:** exercise room. **Guest Services:** coin laundry, wireless Internet. **Business Services:** meeting rooms, business center. **Free Special Amenities: continental breakfast and high-speed Internet.**

SUPER 8 MOTEL   *Book at AAA.com*

Motel
Rates not provided

Phone: 301/729-6265

Address: 1301 National Hwy 21502 **Location:** I-68, exit 40, 0.4 mi n. **Facility:** 63 one-bedroom standard units. 3 stories, interior corridors. **Parking:** on-site. **Amenities:** safes (fee).

——— WHERE TO DINE ———

D'ATRI RESTAURANT

American
$6-$19

Phone: 301/729-2774

This restaurant is family owned and operated and they take pride in fresh ingredients and prompt service. Casual dress. **Hours:** 5:30 am-10 pm, Sun noon-7 pm. Closed: 12/25. **Address:** 1118 National Hwy 21502 **Location:** I-68, exit 40 eastbound, 0.9 mi s; exit 39 westbound, just n. **Parking:** on-site. **Cards:** AX, CB, DC, DS, JC, MC, VI.

PENNY'S DINER

American
$5-$15

Phone: 301/729-6700

The diner is a reminder of a memorable era in American history. Appointed in a '50s theme, the restaurant has many wonderful, tempting items, along with genuinely friendly service. Casual dress. **Hours:** 24 hours. **Address:** 12310 Winchester Rd 21502 **Location:** I-68, exit 40, 0.6 mi s. **Parking:** on-site. **Cards:** AX, DS, MC, VI.

LEONARDTOWN pop. 1,896

——— WHERE TO DINE ———

CAFE DES ARTISTES

French
$8-$27

Phone: 301/997-0500

A brasserie atmosphere thrives in this spot in the heart of historic Leonardtown. The chef/owner prepares wonderful French dishes, such as tenderloin Wellington and grilled lamb top round. Specials supplement the menu, and eggs Benedict is served until 2 pm on Sundays. Sidewalk tables open seasonally. Casual dress. **Bar:** Full bar. **Reservations:** suggested. **Hours:** 11 am-2 & 5-9 pm, Sat from 5 pm, Sun noon-8 pm. Closed: 1/1, 12/25; also Mon. **Address:** 41655 Fenwick St 20650 **Location:** On Business Rt SR 5; on the square in historic Leonardtown. **Parking:** street. **Cards:** AX, DC, DS, MC, VI.

LEXINGTON PARK pop. 11,021

——— WHERE TO STAY ———

EXTENDED STAYAMERICA LEXINGTON PARK-PAX RIVER   *Book at AAA.com*

Phone: (240)725-0100

Small-scale Hotel
$114-$124 All Year

Address: 46565 Expedition Park Dr 20653 **Location:** SR 235, just s to Lexington Park. Located near Patuxent Naval Station, Gate 1. **Facility:** 98 one-bedroom standard units with efficiencies. 3 stories, interior corridors. *Bath:* combo or shower only. **Parking:** on-site. **Terms:** office hours 7 am-11 pm. **Amenities:** voice mail, irons. *Some:* hair dryers. **Guest Services:** coin laundry, wireless Internet. **Cards:** AX, DC, DS, JC, MC, VI.

FAIRFIELD INN BY MARRIOTT LEXINGTON PARK - PATUXENT NAVAL STATION   *Book great rates at AAA.com*

Phone: 301/863-0203

Small-scale Hotel
$118-$145 All Year

Address: 22119 Three Notch Rd 20653 **Location:** On SR 235, 0.9 mi n of jct SR 246. Located opposite Patuxent Naval Station, Gate 1. **Facility:** Smoke free premises. 78 one-bedroom standard units, some with whirlpools. 4 stories, interior corridors. *Bath:* combo or shower only. **Parking:** on-site. **Amenities:** CD players, high-speed Internet, voice mail, irons, hair dryers. **Pool(s):** heated indoor. **Leisure Activities:** whirlpool, sun deck, limited exercise equipment. **Guest Services:** valet and coin laundry, wireless Internet. **Cards:** AX, DC, DS, JC, MC, VI. **Free Special Amenities: expanded continental breakfast and high-speed Internet.**

AAA Benefit:
Members save 5% off of the best available rate.

HAMPTON INN LEXINGTON PARK   *Book great rates at AAA.com*

Phone: 301/863-3200

Small-scale Hotel
Rates not provided

Address: 22211 Three Notch Rd 20653 **Location:** On SR 235, 0.9 mi n of jct SR 246. Located opposite Patuxent Naval Station, Gate 1. **Facility:** 101 one-bedroom standard units. 10 one-bedroom suites. 5 stories, interior corridors. *Bath:* combo or shower only. **Parking:** on-site. **Amenities:** voice mail, irons, hair dryers. **Pool(s):** outdoor. **Leisure Activities:** limited exercise equipment. **Guest Services:** coin laundry, wireless Internet. **Business Services:** meeting rooms, business center.

SLEEP INN & SUITES LEXINGTON PARK/SOLOMONS   *Book great rates at AAA.com*

Phone: (301)737-0000

Small-scale Hotel
$94-$206 All Year

Address: 23428 Three Notch Rd 20619 **Location:** SR 235, 0.5 mi n of jct SR 4. Located opposite the shopping center. **Facility:** 81 one-bedroom standard units, some with whirlpools. 3 stories, interior corridors. *Bath:* combo or shower only. **Amenities:** high-speed Internet, dual phone lines, voice mail, irons, hair dryers. **Pool(s):** heated indoor. **Leisure Activities:** whirlpool, exercise room. **Guest Services:** valet and coin laundry. **Business Services:** PC. **Cards:** AX, CB, DC, DS, JC, MC, VI. **Free Special Amenities: expanded continental breakfast and high-speed Internet.**

SUPER 8 MOTEL   *Book at AAA.com*

Phone: 301/862-9822

Small-scale Hotel
Rates not provided

Address: 22801 Three Notch Rd 20619 **Location:** On SR 235, 3.3 mi n of jct SR 246. **Facility:** 61 one-bedroom standard units. 3 stories (no elevator), interior corridors. **Parking:** on-site. **Amenities:** safes (fee), hair dryers. **Guest Services:** coin laundry, wireless Internet.

——— WHERE TO DINE ———

THE TIDES RESTAURANT AND OYSTER BAR

Phone: 301/862-5303

American
$10-$37

An upscale atmosphere punctuates the sophisticated restaurant, where diners rely on fresh fish, beef, veal and lamb dishes and a wine list with both domestic and international choices, as well as by-the-glass options. The chef changes the menu seasonally to reflect the freshest market ingredients. Service is efficient and friendly. Dressy casual. **Bar:** Full bar. **Reservations:** suggested. **Hours:** 11 am-9 pm, Fri-10 pm, Sat 5 pm-10 pm. Closed major holidays; also closed Sun except on holidays. **Address:** 46580 Expedition Dr 20653 **Location:** On SR 235, 0.9 mi n of jct SR 246. **Parking:** on-site. **Cards:** AX, MC, VI.

LINTHICUM HEIGHTS —See Baltimore p. 620.

MCHENRY

——— WHERE TO STAY ———

COMFORT INN AT DEEP CREEK   *Book at AAA.com*

Phone: (301)387-4200

Small-scale Hotel
$90-$170 All Year

Address: 2704 Deep Creek Dr 21541 **Location:** 1 mi s on US 219 from jct SR 42. **Facility:** 75 one-bedroom standard units, some with whirlpools. 4 stories (no elevator), interior corridors. **Parking:** on-site. **Terms:** check-in 4 pm, 2 night minimum stay - seasonal. **Amenities:** high-speed Internet, irons, hair dryers. **Pool(s):** outdoor. **Leisure Activities:** exercise room. **Guest Services:** coin laundry, wireless Internet. **Business Services:** business center. **Cards:** AX, DC, DS, MC, VI.

WISP MOUNTAIN RESORT/HOTEL & CONFERENCE CENTER — Book at AAA.com

Resort
Small-scale Hotel
$99-$369 12/15-2/28
$89-$229 3/1-12/14

Phone: (301)387-5581

Address: 290 Marsh Hill Rd 21541 **Location:** 1 mi s on US 219 from jct SR 42, just w on Sang Run Rd, then 0.3 mi s. **Facility:** Located by the Deep Creek Lake area, this is a resort for all seasons, with recreational opportunities?especially skiing and golf?for all ages. 168 one-bedroom standard units. 3-7 stories, interior corridors. *Bath:* combo or shower only. **Parking:** on-site. **Terms:** 2 night minimum stay - seasonal, 14 day cancellation notice-fee imposed. **Amenities:** dual phone lines, voice mail, irons, hair dryers. **Pool(s):** indoor. **Leisure Activities:** whirlpool, 2 lighted tennis courts, racquetball court, hiking trails, playground, exercise room, basketball, horseshoes, volleyball. *Fee:* golf-18 holes, downhill skiing, bicycles, massage. **Guest Services:** coin laundry, wireless Internet. **Business Services:** conference facilities, business center. **Cards:** AX, DC, DS, MC, VI.

 CALL / SOME UNITS FEE

——— WHERE TO DINE ———

PINE LODGE STEAKHOUSE

American
$7-$30

Phone: 301/387-6500

Around the picturesque Deep Creek Lake area, the steakhouse presents a varied menu. Views are great, and the staff is professional. Casual dress. **Bar:** Full bar. **Reservations:** suggested, weekends. **Hours:** 11 am-midnight. Closed: 11/27, 12/25. **Address:** 1520 Deep Creek Dr 21541 **Location:** 1.2 mi s on US 219 from jct SR 42. **Parking:** on-site. **Cards:** AX, CB, DC, DS, JC, MC, VI.

SANTE FE GRILLE

Mexican
$9-$21

Phone: 301/387-2182

Southwestern style is in abundance at the Sante Fe Grille, where smartly attired staffers serve classic Mexican cuisine. Casual dress. **Bar:** Full bar. **Hours:** 11 am-10 pm. Closed: 12/25. **Address:** 75 Visitors Center Dr 21541 **Location:** 1 mi s on US 219 from jct SR 42. **Parking:** on-site. **Cards:** AX, CB, DC, DS, JC, MC, VI.

MOUNT AIRY —See Baltimore p. 626.

NEW MARKET pop. 427

——— WHERE TO DINE ———

MEALEY'S RESTAURANT

American
$8-$20

Phone: 301/865-5488

Prime rib is the specialty, but the menu also lists many fish entrees and homemade soup and dessert. The cozy setting, with areas of the building dating back to 1793, also is the site of a Sunday brunch featuring grilled trout and pork tenderloin. Casual dress. **Bar:** Full bar. **Reservations:** suggested. **Hours:** 3 pm-9 pm, Fri & Sat 11:30 am-2 & 3-9 pm, Sun noon-8 pm; Sunday brunch 10 am-2 pm. Closed: 7/4, 12/24, 12/25; also Mon. **Address:** 8 Main St 21774 **Location:** I-70, exit 62, 0.3 mi n on SR 75, then 0.7 mi w on SR 144; in historic district. **Parking:** on-site. **Cards:** AX, DS, MC, VI. **Historic**

MORGAN'S AMERICAN GRILL — Menu on AAA.com

American
$7-$25

Phone: 301/865-8100

The grill combines a sleek, contemporary dining environment with a well-balanced menu of seafood, beef, chicken and pork. Casual dress. **Bar:** Full bar. **Hours:** 11 am-10 pm. Closed: 1/1, 12/25; also Mon. **Address:** 11717 Old National Pike 21774 **Location:** I-70, exit 62, just n. **Parking:** on-site. **Cards:** AX, CB, DC, DS, JC, MC, VI.

NORTH EAST pop. 2,733

——— WHERE TO STAY ———

COMFORT INN & SUITES NORTH EAST

Small-scale Hotel
$89-$189 All Year

Phone: (410)287-7100

Address: 1 Center Dr 21901 **Location:** I-95, exit 100 southbound; exit 100A northbound, just e on SR 272. **Facility:** 92 units. 91 one-bedroom standard units, some with whirlpools. 1 one-bedroom suite. 2 stories (no elevator), interior corridors. *Bath:* combo or shower only. **Parking:** on-site. **Amenities:** video library (fee), voice mail, irons, hair dryers. *Some:* DVD players. **Pool(s):** heated indoor. **Leisure Activities:** whirlpool, limited exercise equipment. **Guest Services:** coin laundry, wireless Internet. **Business Services:** meeting rooms, PC. **Cards:** AX, DS, MC, VI.

 CALL / SOME UNITS FEE

HOLIDAY INN EXPRESS HOTEL & SUITES — Book at AAA.com

Small-scale Hotel
$109-$139 3/1-8/31
$99-$119 9/1-2/28

Phone: 410/287-0008

Address: 101 Hotel Plaza 21901 **Location:** I-95, exit 100 southbound, just e on SR 272; exit 100A northbound, just e on SR 272. **Facility:** 71 one-bedroom standard units, some with whirlpools. 4 stories, interior corridors. *Bath:* combo or shower only. **Parking:** on-site. **Terms:** cancellation fee imposed. **Amenities:** high-speed Internet, voice mail, irons, hair dryers. **Pool(s):** heated outdoor. **Leisure Activities:** whirlpool, limited exercise equipment. **Guest Services:** valet laundry, wireless Internet. **Business Services:** meeting rooms, PC. **Cards:** AX, DC, DS, MC, VI.

CALL / SOME UNITS

—— WHERE TO DINE ——

WOODY'S CRAB HOUSE
Phone: 410/287-3541

The laid-back restaurant is on Main St. in the historic downtown of North East. The dining room has all the accouterments of a traditional crab house: brown paper covers the tables, a roll of paper towels serves as a centerpiece and servings of peanuts ready to have their shells tossed on the floor. Besides crab, the restaurants offers shrimp, Alaskan snow crab, and chicken and beef dishes. Casual dress. **Bar:** Full bar. **Hours:** 11:30 am-9 pm, Fri & Sat-10 pm; seasonal hours may vary. Closed major holidays. **Address:** 29 S Main St 21901 **Location:** I-95, exit 100, 2 mi e on SR 272. **Parking:** street. **Cards:** AX, CB, DC, DS, MC, VI.

Seafood
$5-$35

OAKLAND pop. 2,000

—— WHERE TO STAY ——

HALEY FARM B & B SPA AND RETREAT CENTER
Phone: 301/387-9050

Address: 16766 Garrett Hwy 21550 **Location:** 4 mi n on SR 219. **Facility:** This rural, relaxing B&B has manicured gardens, good views of the surrounding hills, gourmet breakfasts and an on-site massage therapist. 10 one-bedroom standard units, some with kitchens and/or whirlpools. 1 story, interior/exterior corridors. *Bath:* combo or shower only. **Parking:** on-site. **Terms:** 2 night minimum stay - seasonal and/or weekends, cancellation fee imposed. **Amenities:** DVD players, CD players, high-speed Internet, irons, hair dryers. **Leisure Activities:** sauna. *Fee:* massage.

Bed & Breakfast
$150-$235 All Year

SUITES AT SILVER TREE
Phone: 301/387-0650

Address: 565 Glendale Rd 21550 **Location:** 2.1 mi e on Glendale Rd, from US 219. Located on Deep Creek Lake. **Facility:** 51 one-bedroom standard units. 3 stories, interior corridors. **Parking:** on-site. **Terms:** check-in 4 pm, 14 day cancellation notice. **Amenities:** voice mail, irons, hair dryers. *Some:* DVD players. **Leisure Activities:** playground, exercise room. **Guest Services:** wireless Internet. **Business Services:** meeting rooms. **Cards:** AX, DS, MC, VI.

Small-scale Hotel
$77-$278 All Year

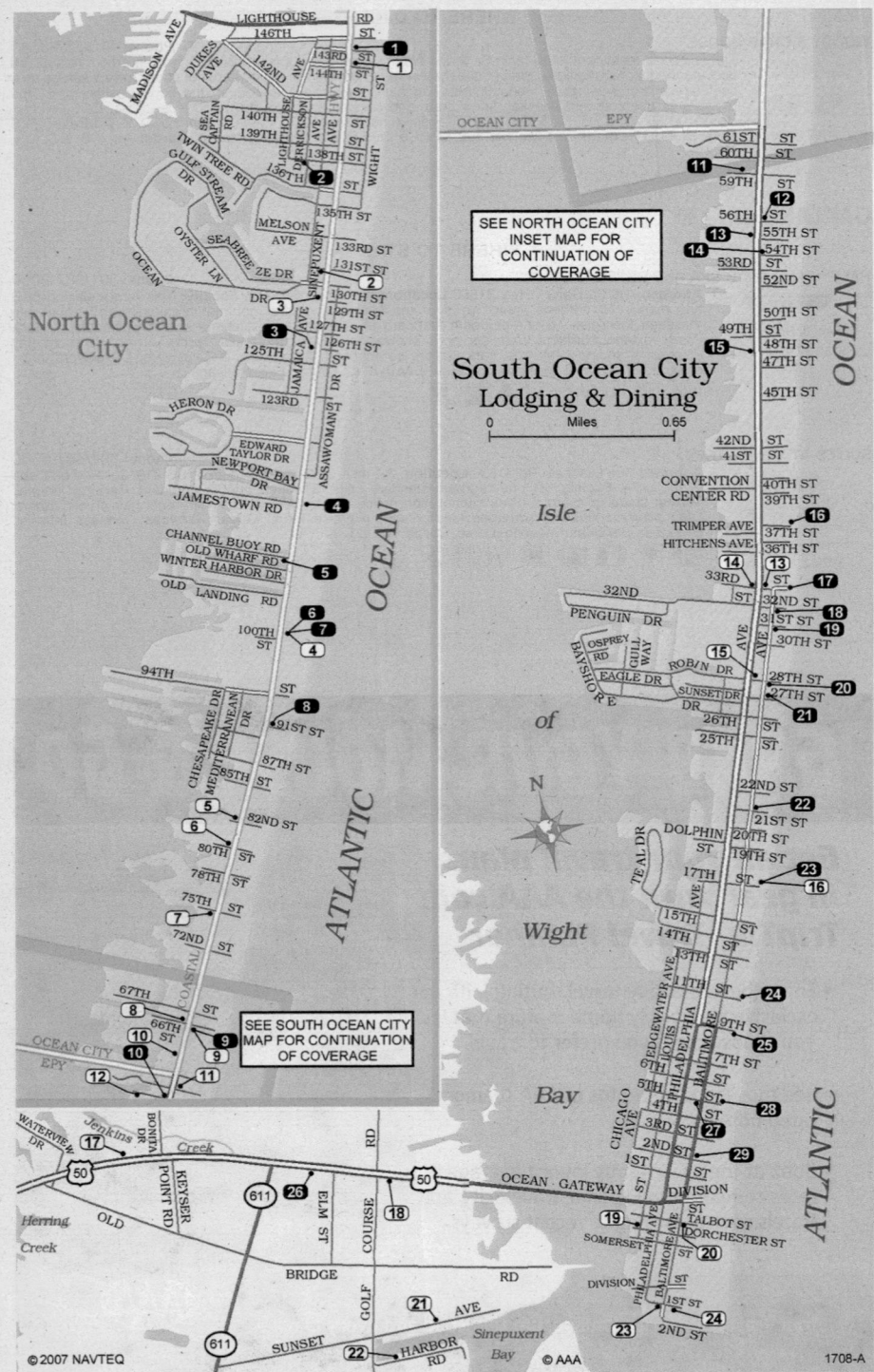

North Ocean City

South Ocean City
Lodging & Dining

0   Miles   0.65

Isle

of

Wight

Bay

N

SEE NORTH OCEAN CITY
INSET MAP FOR
CONTINUATION OF
COVERAGE

SEE SOUTH OCEAN CITY
MAP FOR CONTINUATION
OF COVERAGE

OCEAN

ATLANTIC

OCEAN

ATLANTIC

© 2007 NAVTEQ

© AAA

1708-A

Ocean City

This index helps you "spot" where approved lodgings and restaurants are located on the corresponding detailed maps. Lodging daily rate range is for comparison only and show the property's high season. Restaurant rate range is a combination of lunch and/or dinner. Turn to the listing page for more detailed rate information and consult display ads for special promotions.

Spotter/Map Page Number	OA	OCEAN CITY - Lodgings	Diamond Rating	Rate Range High Season	Listing Page
1 / p. 656		Econo Lodge Oceanblock	◆◆	$40-$265	663
2 / p. 656	AAA	Fenwick Inn	◆◆	$49-$259 SAVE	664
3 / p. 656	AAA	Holiday Inn Express Hotel & Suites	◆◆◆	$60-$300 SAVE	665
4 / p. 656	AAA	Carousel Resort Hotel & Condominiums - see color ad p 661	◆◆	Rates not provided SAVE	660
5 / p. 656		Comfort Inn Gold Coast	◆◆	Rates not provided	662
6 / p. 656	AAA	Marigot Beach Condominiums - see color ad p 667	◆◆◆	$159-$536 SAVE	666
7 / p. 656	AAA	Clarion Resort Fontainebleau Hotel - see color ad p 662	◆◆◆	$89-$399 SAVE	661
8 / p. 656		Princess Royale Oceanfront Family Resort & Condominiums	◆◆◆	$59-$565	668
9 / p. 656	AAA	Holiday Inn Oceanfront - see color ad p 666	◆◆◆	$59-$349 SAVE	665
10 / p. 656	AAA	Sea Bay Hotel - see color ad p 660	◆◆	$49-$249 SAVE	668
11 / p. 656	AAA	Coconut Malorie Resort	◆◆◆	$109-$295 SAVE	661
12 / p. 656	AAA	The Lighthouse Club Hotel & The Edge at Fager's Island	◆◆◆	$79-$425 SAVE	666
13 / p. 656	AAA	Best Western Ocean City Hotel & Suites - see color ad p 660	◆◆	$59-$299 SAVE	659
14 / p. 656	AAA	Quality Inn-Oceanfront 54th Street - see color ad p 668	◆◆	$49-$324 SAVE	668
15 / p. 656		Princess Bayside Beach Hotel	◆◆	$49-$299	667
16 / p. 656	AAA	Castle in the Sand Hotel	◆◆	$69-$359 SAVE	660
17 / p. 656	AAA	Quality Inn & Suites Beachfront - see color ad p 659	◆◆◆	$69-$450 SAVE	668
18 / p. 656	AAA	Hilton Suites Ocean City Oceanfront - see color ad p 664	◆◆◆	$109-$499 SAVE	664
19 / p. 656	AAA	Flamingo Motel - see color ad p 663	◆◆	$44-$249 SAVE	664
20 / p. 656	AAA	Dunes Manor Hotel - see color ad p 663	◆◆◆	$49-$299 SAVE	663
21 / p. 656	AAA	Dunes Motel	◆◆	$39-$299 SAVE	663
22 / p. 656	AAA	Grand Hotel	◆◆	$39-$339 SAVE	664
23 / p. 656	AAA	Holiday Inn Hotel & Suites Ocean City - see color ad p 665	◆◆◆	$99-$425 SAVE	665
24 / p. 656		Howard Johnson Oceanfront Plaza Hotel	◆◆	Rates not provided	666
25 / p. 656	AAA	Paradise Plaza Inn	◆◆	$59-$429 SAVE	666
26 / p. 656		Comfort Suites Ocean City	◆◆◆	$69-$500	662
27 / p. 656		Atlantic House Bed and Breakfast	◆◆	Rates not provided	659
28 / p. 656		Comfort Inn Boardwalk	◆◆	$39-$325	662
29 / p. 656	AAA	Park Place Hotel - see color ad p 667	◆◆	$105-$295 SAVE	667
		OCEAN CITY - Restaurants			
1 / p. 656		Nick's Original House of Ribs	◆◆	$13-$25	671

Spotter/Map Page Number	OA	OCEAN CITY - Restaurants (continued)	Diamond Rating	Rate Range High Season	Listing Page
② / p. 656		J/R's The Place For Ribs	▽▽	$11-$23	670
③ / p. 656		Tequila Mockingbird Mexican Bar & Grill	▽▽	$7-$16	672
④ / p. 656	AAA	Horizons Restaurant & Ocean Club Nightclub	▽▽▽	$7-$35	670
⑤ / p. 656		Fresco's	▽▽▽	$15-$34	670
⑥ / p. 656	AAA	La Hacienda	▽▽	$10-$24	670
⑦ / p. 656		BJ's on the Water	▽▽	$6-$50	669
⑧ / p. 656		Galaxy 66 Bar & Grille	▽▽▽	$7-$36	670
⑨ / p. 656	AAA	Reflections	▽▽▽	$20-$48	671
⑩ / p. 656		Castaway's	▽▽	$7-$29	669
⑪ / p. 656		J/R's The Place For Ribs	▽▽	$12-$25	670
⑫ / p. 656	AAA	Fager's Island	▽▽▽	$8-$36	670
⑬ / p. 656		Tutti Gusti	▽▽	$16-$29	672
⑭ / p. 656		Ristorante Antipasti	▽▽	$20-$32	672
⑮ / p. 656		Coins Pub & Restaurant	▽	$4-$24	669
⑯ / p. 656	AAA	The Coral Reef Restaurant	▽▽▽	$7-$26	669
⑰ / p. 656		Alex's Fine Dining	▽▽▽	$17-$35	669
⑱ / p. 656		Marlin Moon Grille	▽▽▽	$19-$36	671
⑲ / p. 656		Marina Deck Restaurant	▽▽	$5-$37	671
⑳ / p. 656		Little Italy on the Shore	▽▽	$14-$23	671
㉑ / p. 656		Sunset Grille	▽▽▽	$7-$34	672
㉒ / p. 656		Captain's Galley II	▽▽	$5-$29	669
㉓ / p. 656		Adolfo's	▽▽	$7-$24	669
㉔ / p. 656	AAA	Harrison's Harbor Watch	▽▽	$14-$48	670

OCEAN CITY pop. 7,173 (See map and index starting on p. 656)

——— WHERE TO STAY ———

ATLANTIC HOUSE BED AND BREAKFAST

Phone: 410/289-2333 **27**

Bed & Breakfast
Rates not provided

Address: 501 N Baltimore Ave 21842 **Location:** 5th St and Baltimore Ave. **Facility:** Smoke free premises. 11 units. 10 one-bedroom standard units. 1 two-bedroom suite with kitchen. 4 stories (no elevator), interior corridors. *Bath:* some shared or private, combo or shower only. **Parking:** on-site. **Terms:** open 5/3-10/14, office hours 8 am-7 pm, age restrictions may apply. **Leisure Activities:** whirlpool, indoor pool facilities privileges.

BEST WESTERN OCEAN CITY HOTEL & SUITES

Book great rates at AAA.com **Phone:** (443)664-4001 **13**

Small-scale Hotel
$59-$299 All Year

Address: 5501 Coastal Hwy 21842 **Location:** 55th St and Coastal Hwy. **Facility:** 72 units. 36 one-bedroom standard units with whirlpools. 36 one-bedroom suites with whirlpools. 4 stories, interior corridors. *Bath:* combo or shower only. **Parking:** on-site. **Terms:** 2 night minimum stay, 3 day cancellation notice. **Amenities:** high-speed Internet, voice mail, irons, hair dryers. *Some:* DVD players. **Leisure Activities:** limited exercise equipment. **Guest Services:** coin laundry, wireless Internet. **Cards:** AX, DS, MC, VI. **Free Special Amenities:** continental breakfast and high-speed Internet. *(See color ad p 660)*

AAA Benefit:
Members save 10% everyday, plus an exclusive frequent stay program.

▼ See AAA listing p 668 ▼

(See map and index starting on p. 656)

CAROUSEL RESORT HOTEL & CONDOMINIUMS

Large-scale Hotel
Rates not provided

Book great rates at AAA.com   Phone: 410/524-1000   **4**

Address: 11700 Coastal Hwy 21842 **Location:** Oceanfront. At 117th St and oceanfront. **Facility:** 338 units. 210 one- and 15 two-bedroom standard units, some with whirlpools. 15 one-, 73 two- and 25 three-bedroom suites, some with kitchens. 21 stories, interior corridors. **Parking:** on-site. **Terms:** check-in 4 pm. **Amenities:** voice mail, irons, hair dryers. **Pool(s):** outdoor, heated indoor. **Leisure Activities:** saunas, whirlpool, lighted tennis court, recreation programs in summer, pool table, exercise room. *Fee:* ice skating, ice skates, game room. **Guest Services:** wireless Internet. **Business Services:** conference facilities. **Free Special Amenities:** newspaper. *(See color ad. p 661)*

CASTLE IN THE SAND HOTEL

Small-scale Hotel
$69-$359 3/1-11/2

Book great rates at AAA.com   Phone: 410/289-6846   **16**

Address: 3701 Atlantic Ave 21842 **Location:** Oceanfront. 37th and oceanfront. **Facility:** 180 units. 96 one-bedroom standard units, some with efficiencies. 48 one- and 7 two-bedroom suites with kitchens. 29 cottages. 2-5 stories, interior/exterior corridors. *Bath:* combo or shower only. **Parking:** on-site. **Terms:** open 3/1-11/2, 2-3 night minimum stay - seasonal and/or weekends, 14 day cancellation notice. **Amenities:** video library, irons. *Some:* DVD players, CD players, safes, hair dryers. **Pool(s):** outdoor. **Leisure Activities:** seasonal children activities, volleyball. *Fee:* game room. **Guest Services:** coin laundry. **Business Services:** meeting rooms. **Cards:** AX, DS, MC, VI. **Free Special Amenities:** preferred room (subject to availability with advance reservations) and high-speed Internet.

(See map and index starting on p. 656)

CLARION RESORT FONTAINEBLEAU HOTEL *Book great rates at AAA.com* **Phone:** (410)524-3535 **7**

AAA SAVE

Large-scale Hotel

$89-$399 All Year

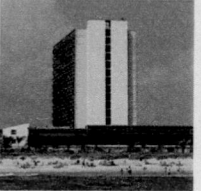

Address: 10100 Coastal Hwy 21842 **Location:** Oceanfront. 101st St and the ocean. **Facility:** 250 one-bedroom standard units. 15 stories, interior corridors. *Bath:* combo or shower only. **Parking:** on-site. **Terms:** check-in 4 pm, 2-3 night minimum stay - seasonal, 3 day cancellation notice. **Amenities:** dual phone lines, voice mail, safes, irons, hair dryers. **Dining:** Horizons Restaurant & Ocean Club Nightclub, see separate listing, entertainment. **Pool(s):** heated indoor. **Leisure Activities:** *Fee:* sauna, whirlpool, steamroom, beach concessions, eucalyptus room. **Guest Services:** valet laundry, area transportation (fee)-within town, tanning facilities, wireless Internet. **Business Services:** conference facilities, business center. **Cards:** AX, CB, DC, DS, JC, MC, VI. **Free Special Amenities: newspaper and high-speed Internet.**
(See color ad p 662)

FEE CALL FEE / SOME UNITS FEE FEE VCR

COCONUT MALORIE RESORT **Phone:** 410/723-6100 **11**

AAA SAVE

Condominium

$109-$295 All Year

Address: 200 59th St 21842 **Location:** 59th St in-the-Bay. **Facility:** Overlooking the bay, these luxuriously appointed studios and one-bedroom suites feature Caribbean-style decor. 85 units. 33 one-bedroom standard units with efficiencies and whirlpools. 52 one-bedroom suites with efficiencies and whirlpools. 5 stories, interior corridors. **Parking:** on-site. **Terms:** check-in 4 pm, cancellation fee imposed. **Amenities:** DVD players, voice mail, irons, hair dryers. **Pool(s):** heated outdoor. **Leisure Activities:** whirlpool, billiards, library, limited exercise equipment. *Fee:* game room. **Guest Services:** coin laundry. **Business Services:** meeting rooms, PC, fax. **Cards:** AX, DS, MC, VI. **Free Special Amenities: local telephone calls and high-speed Internet.**

/ SOME UNITS FEE VCR

▼ *See AAA listing p 660* ▼

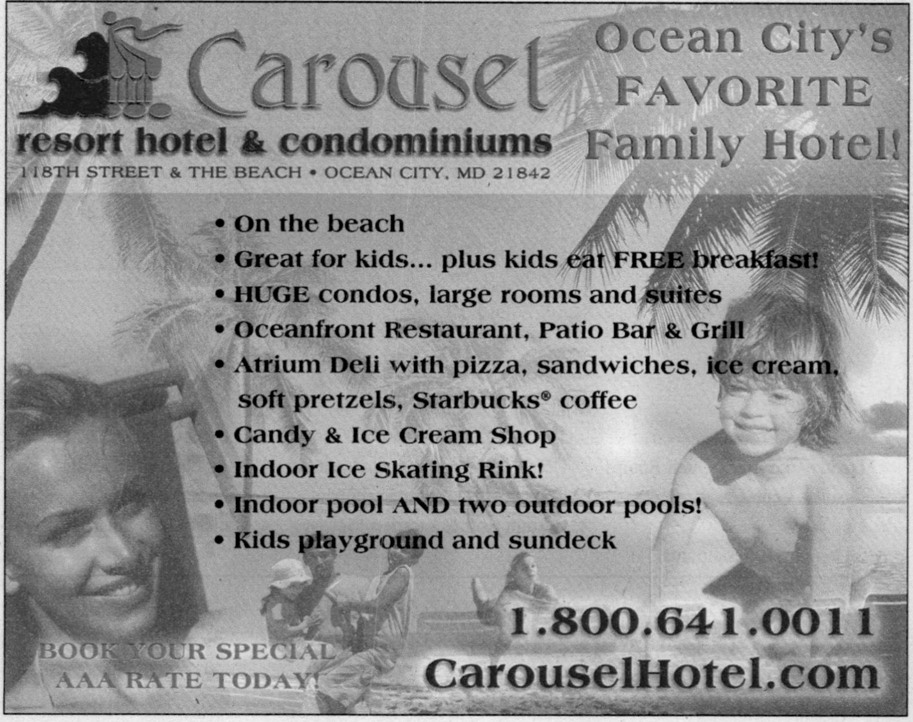

(See map and index starting on p. 656)

COMFORT INN BOARDWALK

Small-scale Hotel
$39-$325 3/1-11/30
$39-$135 2/6-2/28

Book at AAA.com   **Phone:** (410)289-5155   **28**

Address: 507 Atlantic Ave 21842 **Location:** Oceanfront. 5th St and The Boardwalk. **Facility:** 84 one-bedroom standard units, some with efficiencies. 5 stories, interior corridors. **Parking:** on-site. **Terms:** open 3/1-11/30 & 2/6-2/28, 2-3 night minimum stay - seasonal and/or weekends, 7 day cancellation notice. **Amenities:** voice mail, safes (fee), irons, hair dryers. **Pool(s):** outdoor, heated indoor. **Guest Services:** wireless Internet. **Cards:** AX, CB, DC, DS, JC, MC, VI.

COMFORT INN GOLD COAST

Small-scale Hotel
Rates not provided

Book at AAA.com   **Phone:** 410/524-3000   **5**

Address: 11201 Coastal Hwy 21842 **Location:** 112th St and Coastal Hwy; bayside. Located adjacent to movie theaters and shopping plaza. **Facility:** 201 one-bedroom standard units, some with whirlpools. 5 stories, interior corridors. **Parking:** on-site. **Terms:** check-in 4 pm. **Amenities:** voice mail, irons, hair dryers. **Pool(s):** heated indoor. **Leisure Activities:** whirlpool, exercise room. **Guest Services:** coin laundry, wireless Internet. **Business Services:** meeting rooms.

COMFORT SUITES OCEAN CITY

Small-scale Hotel
$69-$500 All Year

Book at AAA.com   **Phone:** (410)213-7171   **26**

Address: 12718 Ocean Gateway 21842 **Location:** US 50; 0.7 mi w of Ocean City Bridge. Located in west Ocean City in a commercial area. **Facility:** Smoke free premises. 85 one-bedroom standard units, some with whirlpools. 3 stories, interior corridors. *Bath:* combo or shower only. **Parking:** on-site. **Terms:** cancellation fee imposed. **Amenities:** high-speed Internet, dual phone lines, voice mail, safes (fee), irons, hair dryers. **Pool(s):** heated outdoor. **Leisure Activities:** playground, exercise room. *Fee:* game room. **Guest Services:** coin laundry, wireless Internet. **Business Services:** PC. **Cards:** AX, DS, MC, VI.

(See map and index starting on p. 656)

DUNES MANOR HOTEL

Phone: (410)289-1100

Small-scale Hotel
$49-$299 3/1-8/23
$49-$279 8/24-2/28

Address: 2800 Baltimore Ave 21842 **Location:** Oceanfront. 28th St and oceanfront. **Facility:** 170 units. 164 one-bedroom standard units, some with efficiencies. 6 one-bedroom suites with efficiencies. 11 stories, interior corridors. **Parking:** on-site. **Terms:** 2 night minimum stay - seasonal and/or weekends, 3 day cancellation notice-fee imposed. **Amenities:** voice mail, irons, hair dryers. **Pool(s):** heated indoor/outdoor. **Leisure Activities:** whirlpool, limited exercise equipment. **Guest Services:** meeting rooms. **Business Services:** meeting rooms. **Cards:** AX, DS, MC, VI. *(See color ad below)*

DUNES MOTEL

Phone: 410/289-4414

Motel
$39-$299 3/1-10/12
$29-$169 2/13-2/28

Address: 2700 Baltimore Ave 21842 **Location:** 27th St and oceanfront. **Facility:** 111 units. 109 one-bedroom standard units, some with efficiencies. 2 two-bedroom suites with kitchens. 3-5 stories, exterior corridors. *Bath:* combo or shower only. **Parking:** on-site. **Terms:** open 3/1-10/12 & 2/13-2/28, 2 night minimum stay - seasonal and/or weekends, 3 day cancellation notice-fee imposed. **Amenities:** voice mail. **Pool(s):** outdoor. **Business Services:** fax (fee). **Cards:** AX, DC, DS, MC, VI.

ECONO LODGE OCEANBLOCK

Book at AAA.com

Phone: (410)250-1155 ❶

Small-scale Hotel
$40-$265 3/14-10/12

Address: 14502 Coastal Hwy 21842 **Location:** 145th St and Coastal Hwy. Located at the northern end of Ocean City. **Facility:** 88 one-bedroom standard units with efficiencies. 4 stories, interior corridors. **Parking:** on-site. **Terms:** open 3/14-10/12, 7 day cancellation notice-fee imposed. **Amenities:** safes (fee). **Pool(s):** heated outdoor. **Guest Services:** wireless Internet. **Cards:** AX, CB, DC, DS, JC, MC, VI.

(See map and index starting on p. 656)

FENWICK INN *Book great rates at AAA.com* **Phone:** (410)250-1100 ❷

Small-scale Hotel
$49-$259 6/27-2/28
$79-$189 3/1-6/26

Address: 13801 Coastal Hwy 21842 **Location:** 138th St and Coastal Hwy. **Facility:** 201 units. 200 one-bedroom standard units. 1 one-bedroom suite. 8 stories, interior corridors. **Parking:** on-site. **Terms:** check-in 4 pm, 3 day cancellation notice-fee imposed. **Pool(s):** heated indoor. **Leisure Activities:** whirlpool. *Fee:* game room. **Business Services:** meeting rooms. **Cards:** AX, CB, DC, DS, MC, VI. **Free Special Amenities: early check-in/late check-out and room upgrade (subject to availability with advance reservations).**

FLAMINGO MOTEL *Book great rates at AAA.com* **Phone:** 410/289-6464 ❿

Small-scale Hotel
$44-$249 3/1-10/13

Address: 3100 Baltimore Ave 21842 **Location:** Oceanside at 31st St. **Facility:** 112 units. 104 one-bedroom standard units, some with efficiencies. 8 one-bedroom suites. 3-5 stories, interior/exterior corridors. **Parking:** on-site. **Terms:** open 3/1-10/13, 2-3 night minimum stay - seasonal and/or weekends, 3 day cancellation notice. **Pool(s):** outdoor, heated indoor. **Guest Services:** wireless Internet. **Cards:** AX, DS, MC, VI. **Free Special Amenities: local telephone calls and high-speed Internet.** *(See color ad p 663)*

GRAND HOTEL *Book great rates at AAA.com* **Phone:** (410)289-6191 ㉒

Large-scale Hotel
$39-$339 3/1-9/1
$39-$259 9/2-2/28

Address: 2100 Baltimore Ave 21842 **Location:** Oceanfront. 21st St and The Boardwalk. **Facility:** 251 units. 249 one- and 2 two-bedroom standard units, some with whirlpools. 12 stories, interior corridors. *Bath:* combo or shower only. **Parking:** on-site. **Terms:** check-in 4 pm, 3 day cancellation notice-fee imposed. **Amenities:** voice mail, irons, hair dryers. **Pool(s):** outdoor, heated indoor. **Leisure Activities:** saunas, pool table, exercise room. *Fee:* massage, game room. **Guest Services:** coin laundry, beauty salon, wireless Internet. **Business Services:** meeting rooms. **Cards:** AX, CB, DC, DS, MC, VI. **Free Special Amenities: newspaper and room upgrade (subject to availability with advance reservations).**

HILTON SUITES OCEAN CITY OCEANFRONT *Book great rates at AAA.com* **Phone:** (410)289-6444 ⓲

Large-scale Hotel
$109-$499 All Year

Address: 3200 Baltimore Ave 21842 **Location:** Oceanfront. At 32nd St and the ocean. **Facility:** 225 one-bedroom suites with kitchens, some with whirlpools. 12 stories, interior corridors. *Bath:* combo or shower only. **Parking:** on-site. **Terms:** 1-3 night minimum stay - seasonal and/or weekends, 3 day cancellation notice-fee imposed. **Amenities:** video library, DVD players, video games (fee), high-speed Internet, dual phone lines, voice mail, safes, irons, hair dryers. **Dining:** 2 restaurants. **Pool(s):** 2 heated outdoor, heated indoor. **Leisure Activities:** whirlpool, waterslide, lifeguard on duty, beach access, recreation programs, exercise room. *Fee:* massage, game room. **Guest Services:** complimentary and valet laundry, wireless Internet. **Business Services:** meeting rooms, business center. **Cards:** AX, CB, DC, DS, JC, MC, VI. **Free Special Amenities: local telephone calls and high-speed Internet.** *(See color ad below)*

(See map and index starting on p. 656)

HOLIDAY INN EXPRESS HOTEL & SUITES

Book great rates at AAA.com   Phone: (410)250-7800   **3**

AAA SAVE

Small-scale Hotel
$60-$300 All Year

Address: 12601 Coastal Hwy 21842 **Location:** Bayside at 127th St. **Facility:** 122 units. 118 one-bedroom standard units. 4 one-bedroom suites with whirlpools. 5 stories, interior corridors. *Bath:* combo or shower only. **Parking:** on-site. **Terms:** check-in 4 pm, 3 day cancellation notice-fee imposed. **Amenities:** dual phone lines, voice mail, irons, hair dryers. **Pool(s):** outdoor, heated indoor. **Leisure Activities:** whirlpool. **Guest Services:** coin laundry, wireless Internet. **Cards:** AX, CB, DC, DS, JC, MC, VI. **Free Special Amenities: continental breakfast and high-speed Internet.**

HOLIDAY INN HOTEL & SUITES OCEAN CITY

Book great rates at AAA.com   Phone: 410/289-7263   **23**

AAA SAVE

Large-scale Hotel
$99-$425 6/29-2/28
$129-$409 3/1-6/28

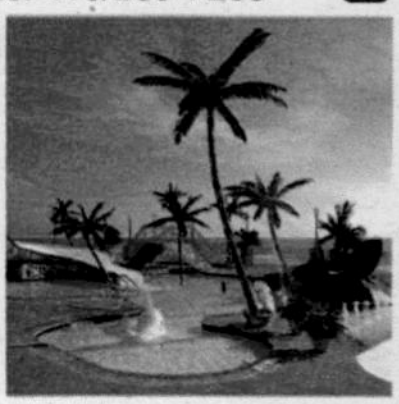

Address: 1701 Atlantic Ave 21842 **Location:** Oceanfront. 17th St and The Boardwalk. **Facility:** 210 units. 209 one- and 1 two-bedroom suites with kitchens, some with whirlpools. 13 stories, interior corridors. *Bath:* combo or shower only. **Parking:** on-site. **Terms:** 2-3 night minimum stay - seasonal and/or weekends, 3 day cancellation notice-fee imposed. **Amenities:** DVD players, high-speed Internet, dual phone lines, voice mail, irons, hair dryers. **Dining:** The Coral Reef Restaurant, see separate listing. **Pool(s):** outdoor, heated outdoor, heated indoor. **Leisure Activities:** whirlpool, exercise room. *Fee:* game room. **Guest Services:** complimentary laundry, wireless Internet. **Business Services:** meeting rooms. **Cards:** AX, CB, DC, DS, JC, MC, VI. **Free Special Amenities: local telephone calls and high-speed Internet.**
(See color ad below)

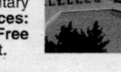

HOLIDAY INN OCEANFRONT

Book great rates at AAA.com   Phone: (410)524-1600   **9**

AAA SAVE

Large-scale Hotel
$59-$349 3/1-9/4
$59-$259 9/5-2/28

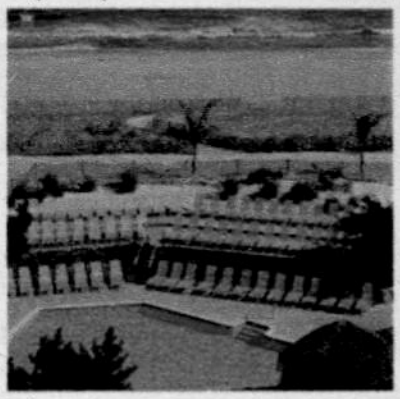

Address: 6600 Coastal Hwy 21842 **Location:** Oceanfront. 67th St and oceanfront. **Facility:** 216 one-bedroom standard units with efficiencies. 8 stories, interior corridors. *Bath:* combo or shower only. **Parking:** on-site. **Terms:** 2-3 night minimum stay - seasonal and/or weekends, 3 day cancellation notice-fee imposed. **Amenities:** DVD players, high-speed Internet, voice mail, irons, hair dryers. *Some:* safes. **Dining:** Reflections, see separate listing. **Pool(s):** outdoor, heated indoor. **Leisure Activities:** sauna, whirlpools, tennis court, recreation programs, pool table, exercise room, shuffleboard. *Fee:* game room. **Guest Services:** complimentary laundry, tanning facilities, wireless Internet. **Business Services:** conference facilities, PC. **Cards:** AX, CB, DC, DS, JC, MC, VI. **Free Special Amenities: local telephone calls and high-speed Internet.**
(See color ad p 666)

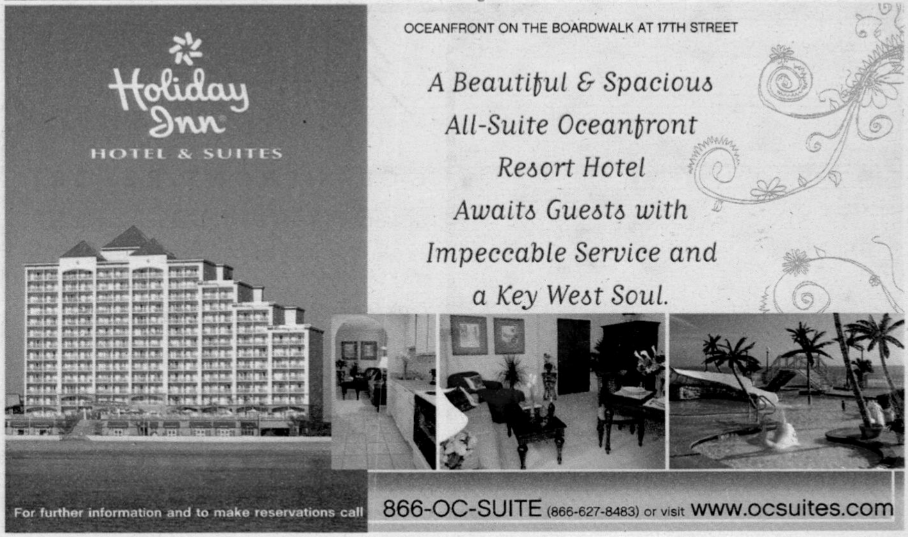

(See map and index starting on p. 656)

HOWARD JOHNSON OCEANFRONT PLAZA HOTEL   *Book great rates at AAA.com*   Phone: 410/289-7251   **24**

Small-scale Hotel
Rates not provided

Address: 1109 Atlantic Ave 21842 **Location:** Oceanfront. 12th St and The Boardwalk. **Facility:** 90 one-bedroom standard units. 8 stories, interior corridors. *Bath:* combo or shower only. **Parking:** on-site. **Amenities:** voice mail, safes (fee), irons, hair dryers. **Pool(s):** outdoor, heated indoor. **Leisure Activities:** saunas, whirlpool, limited exercise equipment. *Fee:* bicycles. **Guest Services:** valet laundry, wireless Internet. **Business Services:** meeting rooms.

THE LIGHTHOUSE CLUB HOTEL & THE EDGE AT
FAGER'S ISLAND   Phone: (410)524-5400   **12**

Small-scale Hotel
$79-$425 All Year

Address: 56th St in-the-Bay 21842 **Location:** Bayfront. **Facility:** 35 units. 33 one- and 2 two-bedroom standard units with whirlpools. 3-4 stories (no elevator), interior corridors. **Parking:** on-site. **Terms:** office hours 7 am-11 pm, check-in 4 pm, 2 night minimum stay - weekends, age restrictions may apply, 3 day cancellation notice-fee imposed. **Amenities:** voice mail, irons, hair dryers. *Some:* DVD players, CD players, safes. **Dining:** Fager's Island, see separate listing. **Pool(s):** heated outdoor. **Guest Services:** wireless Internet. **Cards:** AX, CB, DC, DS, MC, VI. **Free Special Amenities: continental breakfast and high-speed Internet.**

MARIGOT BEACH CONDOMINIUMS   *Book great rates at AAA.com*   Phone: (410)524-3535   **6**

Condominium
$159-$536 All Year

Address: 10100 Coastal Hwy 21842 **Location:** Oceanfront. 101st St and the ocean. **Facility:** The one-, two- and three-bedroom oceanfront condominiums all have balconies and washer/dryer units; registration is handled at adjacent Clarion Hotel. 73 units. 15 one-, 45 two- and 13 three-bedroom suites with kitchens. 13 stories, interior corridors. **Parking:** on-site. **Terms:** check-in 4 pm, 3-7 night minimum stay - seasonal, 30 day cancellation notice. **Amenities:** DVD players, voice mail, safes, irons, hair dryers. **Pool(s):** heated indoor. **Leisure Activities:** sauna, whirlpool, facility privileges. *Fee:* game room. **Guest Services:** valet laundry, area transportation (fee)-within town, wireless Internet. **Cards:** AX, CB, DC, DS, JC, MC, VI. *(See color ad p 667)*

PARADISE PLAZA INN   *Book great rates at AAA.com*   Phone: (410)289-6381   **25**

Small-scale Hotel
$59-$429 All Year

Address: 3 9th St 21842 **Location:** Oceanfront. 9th St and The Boardwalk. Located in a commercial area. **Facility:** 88 units. 80 one- and 4 two-bedroom standard units, some with whirlpools. 4 one-bedroom suites, some with whirlpools. 8 stories, interior corridors. *Bath:* combo or shower only. **Parking:** on-site. **Terms:** check-in 4 pm, 3 day cancellation notice-fee imposed. **Amenities:** dual phone lines, voice mail, safes (fee), irons, hair dryers. **Pool(s):** outdoor. **Guest Services:** coin laundry, wireless Internet. **Business Services:** meeting rooms. **Cards:** AX, DS, MC, VI. **Free Special Amenities: preferred room (subject to availability with advance reservations) and high-speed Internet.**

▼ *See AAA listing p 665* ▼

(See map and index starting on p. 656)

PARK PLACE HOTEL

Small-scale Hotel
$105-$295 3/1-12/7 &
2/6-2/28

Phone: 410/289-6440 [29]

Address: 208 N Baltimore Ave 21842 **Location:** Oceanfront. Between 2nd and 3rd sts. Located on The Boardwalk. **Facility:** 89 one-bedroom standard units, some with whirlpools. 6 stories, interior corridors. **Bath:** combo or shower only. **Parking:** on-site. **Terms:** open 3/1-12/7 & 2/6-2/28, 2-3 night minimum stay - seasonal and/or weekends, 5 day cancellation notice-fee imposed. **Amenities:** voice mail, safes, irons, hair dryers. *Some:* DVD players (fee). **Pool(s):** heated outdoor. **Leisure Activities:** *Fee:* game room. **Guest Services:** coin laundry, wireless Internet. **Business Services:** PC. **Cards:** AX, DC, DS, MC, VI. **Free Special Amenities:** high-speed Internet. *(See color ad below)*

PRINCESS BAYSIDE BEACH HOTEL   *Book at AAA.com*

Small-scale Hotel
$49-$299 All Year

Phone: (410)723-2900 [15]

Address: 4801 Coastal Hwy 21842 **Location:** 48th St and Coastal Hwy; bayside. **Facility:** 194 one-bedroom standard units, some with efficiencies and/or whirlpools. 5 stories, interior corridors. **Parking:** on-site. **Terms:** check-in 4 pm, 2-3 night minimum stay - seasonal and/or weekends, 7 day cancellation notice-fee imposed. **Amenities:** safes (fee), irons, hair dryers. **Pool(s):** heated outdoor, heated indoor. **Guest Services:** coin laundry, wireless Internet. **Business Services:** meeting rooms. **Cards:** AX, DS, MC, VI.

(See map and index starting on p. 656)

PRINCESS ROYALE OCEANFRONT FAMILY RESORT & CONDOMINIUMS *Book at AAA.com* Phone: (410)524-7777 **8**

Large-scale Hotel
$59-$565 All Year

Address: 9100 Coastal Hwy 21842 **Location:** Oceanfront. 91st St and oceanfront. **Facility:** 334 units. 306 one-, 23 two- and 5 three-bedroom suites with kitchens, some with whirlpools. 5-10 stories, interior corridors. **Parking:** on-site. **Terms:** check-in 4 pm, 2-3 night minimum stay - seasonal and/or weekends, 7 day cancellation notice-fee imposed. **Amenities:** voice mail, safes (fee), irons, hair dryers. **Pool(s):** heated indoor. **Leisure Activities:** saunas, whirlpools, 2 lighted tennis courts, exercise room, volleyball. *Fee:* massage, game room. **Guest Services:** coin laundry, wireless Internet. **Business Services:** conference facilities. **Cards:** AX, DC, DS, MC, VI.

QUALITY INN & SUITES BEACHFRONT *Book great rates at AAA.com* Phone: (410)289-1234 **17**

Small-scale Hotel
$69-$450 All Year

Address: 3301 Atlantic Ave 21842 **Location:** Oceanfront. 33rd St and oceanfront. **Facility:** 110 units. 99 one-bedroom standard units, some with efficiencies and/or whirlpools. 11 one-bedroom suites with efficiencies, some with whirlpools. 8 stories, interior/exterior corridors. **Parking:** on-site. **Terms:** 3 day cancellation notice-fee imposed. **Amenities:** irons, hair dryers. **Pool(s):** outdoor, heated indoor. **Leisure Activities:** sauna, whirlpool, exercise room. *Fee:* game room. **Guest Services:** valet and coin laundry, tanning facilities, wireless Internet. **Cards:** AX, CB, DC, DS, MC, VI. *(See color ad p 659)*

QUALITY INN-OCEANFRONT 54TH STREET *Book great rates at AAA.com* Phone: (410)524-7200 **14**

Small-scale Hotel
$49-$324 7/13-2/28
$49-$299 3/1-7/12

Address: 5400 Coastal Hwy 21842 **Location:** Oceanfront. At 54th St. **Facility:** 130 one-bedroom standard units, some with efficiencies. 3-5 stories, interior/exterior corridors. *Bath:* combo or shower only. **Parking:** on-site. **Terms:** 1-3 night minimum stay - weekends, 3 day cancellation notice. **Amenities:** video library, hair dryers. *Some:* DVD players, safes, irons. **Pool(s):** outdoor, heated indoor. **Leisure Activities:** saunas, whirlpool, tennis court, children's play area, playground, limited exercise equipment. *Fee:* game room. **Guest Services:** complimentary laundry, tanning facilities, wireless Internet. **Cards:** AX, CB, DC, DS, JC, MC, VI. **Free Special Amenities:** local telephone calls and high-speed Internet. *(See color ad below)*

SEA BAY HOTEL Phone: 410/524-6100 **10**

Small-scale Hotel
$49-$249 All Year

Address: 6007 Coastal Hwy 21842 **Location:** At 60th St and Coastal Hwy. **Facility:** Smoke free premises. 157 one-bedroom standard units. 5 stories, interior corridors. **Parking:** on-site. **Terms:** 2-3 night minimum stay - weekends, 3 day cancellation notice. **Amenities:** voice mail, irons. **Pool(s):** outdoor. **Guest Services:** coin laundry, wireless Internet. **Business Services:** meeting rooms. **Cards:** AX, DS, MC, VI. **Free Special Amenities:** newspaper and high-speed Internet. *(See color ad p 660)*

▼ See AAA listing above ▼

(See map and index starting on p. 656)

──────── *The following lodgings were either not evaluated or did not* ────────
meet AAA rating requirements but are listed for your information only.

LIGHTHOUSE POINT VILLAS
Phone: 410/723-3747

[fyi]

Condominium

Did not meet all AAA rating requirements for some guest rooms at time of last evaluation on 11/02/2005. **Address:** 14409 Lighthouse Rd 21842 **Location:** Just w of Coastal Hwy at 145th St. Facilities, services, and decor characterize a basic property.

MARLIN COVE II
Phone: 410/723-3747

[fyi]

Condominium

Did not meet all AAA rating requirements for some guest rooms at time of last evaluation on 11/02/2005. **Address:** Edward Taylor Rd 21842 **Location:** Just w of Coastal Hwy at 120th St. Facilities, services, and decor characterize a basic property.

OCEAN HIGH
Phone: 410/723-3747

[fyi]

Condominium

Did not meet all AAA rating requirements for some guest rooms at time of last evaluation on 01/04/2005. **Address:** 502 32nd St 21842 **Location:** Just w of Coastal Hwy at 32nd St. Facilities, services, and decor characterize a basic property.

──────── **WHERE TO DINE** ────────

ADOLFO'S
Phone: 410/289-4001 [23]

Italian
$7-$24

The intimate dining room and enclosed porch provide a comfortable setting to dine on the plentiful Italian fare. The menu offers a nice selection of pasta, meat, seafood and chicken dishes. Casual dress. **Bar:** Full bar. **Reservations:** suggested. **Hours:** 5 pm-10 pm; to 9 pm off season. Closed: 12/15-12/30 & Sun-Tues 10/1-5/1. **Address:** 806 S Baltimore Ave 21842 **Location:** 0.5 mi s of US 50; at the inlet. **Parking:** on-site. **Cards:** DS, MC, VI.

ALEX'S FINE DINING
Phone: 410/213-7717 [17]

Italian
$17-$35

The setting is intimate, the service efficient and the food delicious at the upscale spot. Preparations of Angus beef, veal, chicken, fresh fish and pasta make up much of the menu. Tableside preparation of such dishes as Caesar salad, steak Diane and lobster Chantilly is handled expertly. Dressy casual. **Bar:** Full bar. **Reservations:** suggested, in season. **Hours:** 5 pm-10 pm; to 9 pm 10/1-5/14. Closed: 11/27, 12/25; also Wed 10/1-5/14. **Address:** 12445 Ocean Gateway, Unit 1-6 21842 **Location:** US 50, 1.3 mi w of the Ocean City bridge; in West Ocean City. **Parking:** on-site. **Cards:** AX, DC, DS, MC, VI.

BJ'S ON THE WATER
Phone: 410/524-7575 [7]

American
$6-$50

Located on the bay, the restaurant has been in operation for more than 25 years. The atmosphere is casual and lively, with a saloon-like bar and an enclosed porch with hanging plants and a bay view. The food ranges from soups and salads to overstuffed sandwiches and complete entrees. The 1 pm duck feeding attracts an abundance of wild ducks. Casual dress. **Bar:** Full bar. **Reservations:** not accepted. **Hours:** 11 am-1:30 am. Closed: 12/24, 12/25. **Address:** 115 75th St 21842 **Location:** 75th St and the bay. **Parking:** on-site. **Cards:** AX, CB, DC, DS, MC, VI.

CAPTAIN'S GALLEY II
Phone: 410/213-2525 [22]

Seafood
$5-$29

Set on the harbor, this casual restaurant has been a favorite of locals for years. They are known for their fresh seafood. The crab cakes, one of the house specialties, is all lump crabmeat, definitely worth checking out. A comfortable atmosphere for families. Casual dress. **Bar:** Full bar. **Reservations:** not accepted. **Hours:** Open 3/15-1/2; 11:30 am-10 pm. Closed: 11/27, 12/25. **Address:** 12817 Harbor Rd 21842 **Location:** 0.7 mi s on Golf Course Rd from jct US 50; in West Ocean City. **Parking:** on-site. **Cards:** AX, DC, DS, MC, VI.

CASTAWAY'S
Phone: 410/524-9090 [10]

American
$7-$29

The casual restaurant's tropical dining area and outside deck overlook the bay. On the menu are steaks, chicken, seafood and some pasta dishes. Entertainment is scheduled daily in season and less regularly in the off-season. Casual dress. **Bar:** Full bar. **Reservations:** accepted. **Hours:** Open 3/15-1/1; 11 am-1 am. Closed: 12/25. **Address:** 105 64th St 21842 **Location:** At 64th St and the bay. **Parking:** on-site. **Cards:** AX, DC, DS, MC, VI.

CALL [&M]

COINS PUB & RESTAURANT
Phone: 410/289-3100 [15]

American
$4-$24

Popular with the locals, the little, pub-like restaurant serves consistent American fare. The house specialty is the crab cake. Casual dress. **Bar:** Full bar. **Hours:** 11 am-11 pm. Closed: 11/27, 12/25. **Address:** 2820 Coastal Hwy 21842 **Location:** In 28th St Plaza. **Parking:** on-site. **Cards:** DS, MC, VI.

THE CORAL REEF RESTAURANT   *Menu on AAA.com*
Phone: 410/289-6388 [16]

AAA

American
$7-$26

Off the lobby, just beyond the indoor pool and cafe, you'll find an intimate, upscale dining room with an island plantation ambiance. The menu tempts you with a variety of flavors. Carribbean dishes, such as island barbecued pork chops, citrus chicken penne and Jamaican grouper, treat you to the spices of the islands. Chicken Chesapeake, soft shell crabs and fried Chesapeake oysters give you the flavor of the Eastern Shore. They use only certified Angus beef and certified blue crab. Casual dress. **Bar:** Full bar. **Reservations:** accepted. **Hours:** 7 am-10 pm, Fri & Sat-11 pm; to 9 pm, Fri & Sat-10 pm off season. **Address:** 1701 Atlantic Ave 21842 **Location:** 17th St and The Boardwalk; in Holiday Inn Hotel & Suites Ocean City. **Parking:** on-site and street. **Cards:** AX, DS, MC, VI.

(See map and index starting on p. 656)

FAGER'S ISLAND

Phone: 410/524-5500   [12]

American
$8-$36

As the sun sets, the strains of Tchaikovsky's 1812 Overture rise, just as they have every night since the mid-1970s. The busy, bayfront restaurant serves casual meals all day and shifts to a more fine-dining mode from 5 pm to 10 pm. An award-winning wine selection and exotic microbrewed beers enhance creative menu selections. Entertainment is nightly in season and on weekends in the off-season. Casual dress. Entertainment. **Bar:** Full bar. **Reservations:** suggested, for dinner. **Hours:** 11 am-midnight. Closed: 12/25; also for dinner 12/24. **Address:** 201 60th St 21842 **Location:** Bayfront; at The Lighthouse Club Hotel & The Edge at Fager's Island. **Parking:** on-site. **Cards:** AX, CB, DC, DS, MC, VI.

FRESCO'S

Phone: 410/524-8202   [5]

American
$15-$34

The casually upscale dining room overlooks the bay. Chef Pino Tomasello's American cuisine is prepared with Mediterranean influences. Selections range from pasta and seafood to beef and chicken. Casual dress. **Bar:** Full bar. **Reservations:** suggested. **Hours:** 4:30 pm-10 pm, Fri & Sat-11 pm. Closed: 11/27, 12/24, 12/25. **Address:** 8203 Coastal Hwy 21842 **Location:** Jct 83rd St and Coastal Hwy. **Parking:** on-site. **Cards:** AX, DC, DS, MC, VI.

GALAXY 66 BAR & GRILLE

Phone: 410/723-6762   [8]

American
$7-$36

At this bayside restaurant, diners will discover a seasonally changing menu of creative, contemporary American cuisine creatively prepared using fresh ingredients. The atmosphere is modern and stylish, with a casual, yet still upscale, air. Find an open kitchen and a rooftop bar area, which is open seasonally. In addition, the upstairs dining room offers bay and ocean views. The staff is friendly, professional and attentive. In the summer months, a light fare menu is available until midnight. Casual dress. **Bar:** Full bar. **Reservations:** suggested. **Hours:** 11:30 am-10 pm. Closed: 11/27, 12/24-12/26. **Address:** 6601 Coastal Hwy 21842 **Location:** 66th St and Coastal Hwy. **Parking:** on-site. **Cards:** AX, DC, DS, MC, VI.

HARRISON'S HARBOR WATCH   *Menu on AAA.com*

Phone: 410/289-5121   [24]

Seafood
$14-$48

Seafood rules at the laid-back restaurant, which affords a great view of the inlet. Not only are there daily specials and an extensive selection of fresh fish, but the menu also includes steak and pasta offerings to appeal to landlubbers. The raw bar is open from 11:30 am to 10 pm. An elevator provides access to the second floor. Casual dress. **Bar:** Full bar. **Reservations:** suggested. **Hours:** 5 pm-10 pm. **Address:** 806 S Boardwalk & The Inlet 21842 **Location:** At Inlet Village; south end of boardwalk; 0.5 mi s of US 50 bridge. **Parking:** on-site (fee). **Cards:** AX, DC, DS, MC, VI.

HORIZONS RESTAURANT & OCEAN CLUB NIGHTCLUB   *Menu on AAA.com*

Phone: 410/524-3535   [4]

American
$7-$35

This oceanfront restaurant offers a nice selection of seafood, meat and pasta dishes as well as an award-winning wine list to complement the meal. After dinner, enjoy live entertainment. Casual dress. Entertainment. **Bar:** Full bar. **Reservations:** suggested, in season. **Hours:** 6:30 am-2 & 5-10 pm. **Address:** 10100 Coastal Hwy 21842 **Location:** 101st St and the ocean; in Clarion Resort Fontainebleau Hotel. **Parking:** on-site. **Cards:** AX, CB, DC, DS, JC, MC, VI.

J/R'S THE PLACE FOR RIBS

Phone: 410/250-3100   [2]

American
$11-$23

Be sure to try the excellent onion loaf with any one of the featured menu items, including barbecue baby back ribs, chicken, prime rib, steak and fresh seafood. The atmosphere is casual and family-oriented with a Western decor; the service is attentive. Casual dress. **Bar:** Full bar. **Reservations:** not accepted. **Hours:** Open 3/1-12/31 & 2/14-2/28; 4 pm-10:30 pm, Sun from 3 pm; Thurs-Sun to 9:30 pm 2/14-3/30. Closed: 11/27, 12/25; also Sun-Thurs 2/14-3/30. **Address:** 131 Coastal Hwy 21842 **Location:** 131st St and Coastal Hwy. **Parking:** on-site. **Cards:** AX, DS, MC, VI.

J/R'S THE PLACE FOR RIBS

Phone: 410/524-7427   [11]

American
$12-$25

A favorite choice at the popular, energetic eatery is the barbecue baby back ribs. Also on the menu are chicken, prime rib, steak and seafood dishes and an excellent onion loaf. The atmosphere is family-oriented. Smoking is permitted in the lounge. Casual dress. **Bar:** Full bar. **Hours:** Open 3/1-12/3 & 1/14-2/28; 4 pm-10:30 pm, Sun from 3 pm. Closed: 11/27, 12/25; also Mon-Thurs 1/14-3/16 & 11/1-11/30. **Address:** 6104 Coastal Hwy 21842 **Location:** 62nd St and Coastal Hwy. **Parking:** on-site. **Cards:** AX, DS, MC, VI.

LA HACIENDA   *Menu on AAA.com*

Phone: 410/524-8080   [6]

Mexican
$10-$24

In the mood for something from south of the border. This casual Mexican restaurant is popular with locals and tourists alike. The food is good and the service is friendly and efficient. Casual dress. **Bar:** Full bar. **Reservations:** not accepted. **Hours:** 5 pm-9:30 pm. Closed: 11/27, 12/25; also Mon & Tues 12/1-2/28. **Address:** 8003 Coastal Hwy 21842 **Location:** At 81st St. **Parking:** on-site. **Cards:** AX, MC, VI.

LIGHTHOUSE SOUND RESTAURANT

Phone: 410/352-5250

American
$6-$36

The dining room at The Links at Lighthouse Sound overlooks Assawoman Bay and off in the distance is the skyline of Ocean City. Suitable for any occasion, the dining room is comfortable and casual. The menu offers creatively prepared American dishes using fresh ingredients. Casual dress. **Bar:** Full bar. **Reservations:** suggested. **Hours:** 7 am-3 & 5-10 pm; hours may vary off season. Closed: 12/25; also for dinner 12/24. **Address:** 12723 St. Martin's Neck Rd 21813 **Location:** Just across SR 90 bridge from Ocean City; 1.3 mi n of jct SR 90; at Lighthouse Sound Clubhouse. **Parking:** on-site. **Cards:** AX, DS, MC, VI.

CALL

(See map and index starting on p. 656)

LITTLE ITALY ON THE SHORE
Phone: 410/289-0505   ⟨20⟩

Italian
$14-$23

At the southern end of the city, the chef-owned Italian restaurant presents a menu that includes pasta, meat and seafood dishes. The atmosphere is casual and comfortable. Casual dress. **Bar:** Full bar. **Reservations:** accepted. **Hours:** Open 5/1-12/31; 4:30 pm-11 pm. Closed: 3/23, 11/27, 12/25. **Address:** 215 S Baltimore Ave 21842 **Location:** 2 blks s of jct US 50. **Parking:** street. **Cards:** AX, DC, DS, MC, VI.

MARINA DECK RESTAURANT
Phone: 410/289-4411   ⟨19⟩

American
$5-$37

Established in the late 1970s, the relaxed bayfront restaurant treats guests to beautiful views of the sunset from the dining room and the enclosed terrace. Casual dress. **Bar:** Full bar. **Reservations:** accepted. **Hours:** Open 4/4-10/15; 11 am-11 pm. **Address:** 306 Dorchester St 21842 **Location:** Just s of US 50. **Parking:** on-site. **Cards:** AX, DS, MC, VI.

MARLIN MOON GRILLE
Phone: 410/213-1618   ⟨18⟩

American
$19-$36

Off the lobby of a hotel, the dining room carries off a nautical atmosphere in a comfortable, casual fine-dining setting. The menu lists a nice selection of meat and fish dishes. Dressy casual. **Bar:** Full bar. **Hours:** 5 pm-10 pm; off season hours vary. Closed: 11/27, 12/24, 12/25. **Address:** 12806 Ocean Gateway 21842 **Location:** On US 50, 0.5 mi w of the US 50 Bridge; in West Ocean City; in Francis Scott Key Hotel. **Parking:** on-site. **Cards:** AX, DC, DS, MC, VI.

NICK'S ORIGINAL HOUSE OF RIBS
Phone: 410/250-1984   ⟨1⟩

American
$13-$25

The casual restaurant offers a comfortable setting for all age groups. Guests who shy away from the specialty barbecued baby back ribs have plenty of other choices, including preparations of Black Angus beef, chicken, shrimp and flounder. Little ones can choose from children's meals. Casual dress. **Bar:** Full bar. **Reservations:** not accepted. **Hours:** 4 pm-10 pm, Sat & Sun from noon. Closed: 11/27, 12/24, 12/25. **Address:** 14410 Coastal Hwy 21842 **Location:** 145th St and Coastal Hwy. **Parking:** on-site. **Cards:** AX, DC, DS, MC, VI.

PHILLIPS BY THE SEA
Phone: 410/289-9121

Seafood
$4-$35

The boardwalk restaurant's Old World atmosphere is evidenced by the semiformal Victorian dining room and charming piano bar. The evening menu features fresh seafood specials, including stuffed flounder. For breakfast, try the flavorful malt waffles. Casual dress. Entertainment. **Bar:** Full bar. **Reservations:** accepted. **Hours:** Open 3/15-1/2; 8 am-11 & 5-10 pm, Sat & Sun 8 am-1 & 5-10 pm. **Address:** 1301 Atlantic Ave 21842 **Location:** 13th St and The Boardwalk. **Parking:** on-site. **Cards:** AX, DC, MC, VI.

PHILLIPS CRAB HOUSE
Phone: 410/289-6821

Seafood
$6-$35

The crab imperial—jumbo lump crabmeat mixed with mayonnaise and seafood seasoning, baked, then topped with cheddar cheese—is the hands-down favorite at this loud, busy restaurant. A local hot spot since 1957. A seafood buffet is offered nightly, in season. Casual dress. **Bar:** Full bar. **Reservations:** not accepted. **Hours:** Open 3/30-10/31; 11:45 am-11 pm, closing hours may vary. Closed: Mon-Thurs 4/11-5/12. **Address:** 2004 Philadelphia Ave 21842 **Location:** 21st and Philadelphia Ave. **Parking:** on-site. **Cards:** AX, DC, DS, MC, VI.

PHILLIPS SEAFOOD HOUSE
Phone: 410/250-1200

Seafood
$7-$30

Popular with diners of all ages, you'll love the Eastern-shore ambience created by the rustic wood paneling and brick walls, carousel horses, stained-glass panels and Tiffany-style lights. Both a seafood buffet and a la carte menu are offered. Casual dress. **Bar:** Full bar. **Reservations:** not accepted. **Hours:** Open 3/1-11/30 & 2/18-2/28; noon-10 pm; closing hours may vary. Closed: Mon & Tues 2/18-5/31, also Wed & Thurs 2/18-4/15. **Address:** 14101 Coastal Hwy 21842 **Location:** 141st St and Coastal Hwy. **Parking:** on-site. **Cards:** AX, DC, DS, MC, VI.

PLANTATION HOUSE BAR & GRILLE   *Menu on AAA.com*
Phone: 410/213-7786

AAA
Steak & Seafood
$6-$40

In West Ocean City, the restaurant prepares a nice selection of fresh seafood and Choice Mid-Western aged beef. Friendly, attentive staffers provide service in the comfortable setting. Casual dress. **Bar:** Full bar. **Reservations:** accepted. **Hours:** 11:30 am-10 pm. Closed: 11/27, 12/25. **Address:** 12308 Ocean Gateway, Suite 8 21842 **Location:** In West Ocean City; US 50, 1.7 mi w of the Ocean City Bridge; in Thee Gina Renee Plaza. **Parking:** on-site. **Cards:** AX, DS, MC, VI.

CALL

REFLECTIONS   *Menu on AAA.com*
Phone: 410/524-5252   ⟨9⟩

AAA
American
$20-$48

Although its location may seem ordinary, there's little typical about the experience here. Noteworthy features include an attractive, bilevel dining room attended by crisp, attentive servers. Representative of the flavorful, creative dishes are Thai curry shrimp and steak Diane prepared tableside. Early-bird specials are available from 5 to 6 p.m. Casual dress. **Bar:** Full bar. **Reservations:** suggested, for dinner. **Hours:** 7 am-11 & 5-10 pm. **Address:** 6600 Coastal Hwy 21842 **Location:** 67th St and oceanfront; in Holiday Inn Oceanfront. **Parking:** on-site. **Cards:** AX, DC, DS, MC, VI.

(See map and index starting on p. 656)

RISTORANTE ANTIPASTI
Phone: 410/289-4588

Italian
$20-$32

The chef/owner has developed a strong local following for such preparations as gnocchi alla contadina, garlic steak and homemade pasta. The staff is efficient and friendly and the setting relaxing and comfortable. Dressy casual. **Bar:** Full bar. **Reservations:** suggested, in season. **Hours:** 5 pm-10:30 pm; to 11 pm 6/1-9/30. Closed: 1/1, 11/27, 12/25. **Address:** 3101 Coastal Hwy 21842 **Location:** 33rd St and Coastal Hwy. **Parking:** on-site. **Cards:** AX, DC, DS, MC, VI.

SUNSET GRILLE
Phone: 410/213-8110

American
$7-$34

The restaurant provides a nice setting for any occasion. The kitchen prepares a nice selection of salads, sandwiches and entrees, such as tempura fried lobster tails and Memphis baby back ribs. Casual dress. **Bar:** Full bar. **Reservations:** accepted. **Hours:** 11 am-10 pm, Fri & Sat-11 pm. Closed: 11/27, 12/25. **Address:** 12933 Sunset Ave 21842 **Location:** In West Ocean City; 0.6 mi s on Golf Course Rd from jct US 50, just e; at Sunset Marina. **Parking:** on-site. **Cards:** AX, DC, DS, MC, VI.

CALL

TEQUILA MOCKINGBIRD MEXICAN BAR & GRILL
Phone: 410/250-4424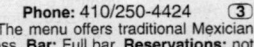

Mexican
$7-$16

This casual shopping plaza restaurant offers a lively, fun atmosphere. The menu offers traditional Mexican fare with tacos, burritos, enchilada and some speciality items. Casual dress. **Bar:** Full bar. **Reservations:** not accepted. **Hours:** noon-midnight. Closed: 11/27, 12/25; also Tues & Wed 11/1-3/31. **Address:** 12919 Coastal Hwy 21842 **Location:** At 130th St. **Parking:** on-site. **Cards:** AX, DS, MC, VI.

TUTTI GUSTI
Phone: 410/289-3318

Northern Italian
$16-$29

Salmon-painted walls, white tablecloths and candlelit tables set a sophisticated atmosphere in the charming, little restaurant. The menu comprises specialties of the northern region, mostly veal, chicken, seafood and pasta. Pasta is made fresh daily. Saturday night osso buco served over risotto is a favorite choice. Dressy casual. **Bar:** Full bar. **Reservations:** suggested. **Hours:** Open 3/1-12/31 & 2/10-2/28; 5 pm-11 pm. Closed: 11/27, 12/25. **Address:** 3322 Coastal Hwy 21842 **Location:** 33rd St and Coastal Hwy. **Parking:** on-site. **Cards:** AX, DS, MC, VI.

The following restaurant has not been evaluated by AAA but is listed for your information only.

SEACRETS BAR & GRILL
Phone: 410/524-4900

[fyi]

Not evaluated. The tropical atmosphere, outside dining and bayside location will remind you of a Jamaican beach party. Full lunch and dinner menus are available off season, while only light fare is served in season. A cover charge is in effect after 4 pm in season. **Address:** 117 W 49th St 21842 **Location:** 49th St and the Bay.

OWINGS MILLS —*See Baltimore p. 627.*

OXON HILL —*See District Of Columbia p. 492.*

PASADENA —*See Baltimore p. 627.*

PERRYVILLE pop. 3,672

—— WHERE TO STAY ——

RAMADA PERRYVILLE   *Book great rates at AAA.com*   **Phone:** (410)642-2866

(AAA) SAVE
▼▼▼▼▼
Motel
$79-$87 3/1-10/31
$75-$83 11/1-2/28

Address: 61 Heather Ln 21903 **Location:** I-95, exit 93, just e. Adjacent to outlet mall. **Facility:** 104 one-bedroom standard units. 2 stories (no elevator), exterior corridors. **Parking:** on-site. **Amenities:** voice mail, safes (fee), irons, hair dryers. **Leisure Activities:** limited exercise equipment. **Guest Services:** valet and coin laundry, wireless Internet. **Business Services:** meeting rooms. **Cards:** AX, CB, DC, DS, JC, MC, VI. **Free Special Amenities:** expanded continental breakfast and high-speed Internet. *(See color ad below)*

[S] [¶↑] CALL [M] / SOME UNITS FEE [icons]

PIKESVILLE —*See Baltimore p. 627.*

POCOMOKE CITY pop. 4,098

—— WHERE TO STAY ——

HOLIDAY INN EXPRESS-POCOMOKE   *Book at AAA.com*   **Phone:** 410/957-6444

▼▼▼▼
Small-scale Hotel
Rates not provided

Address: 125 Newtowne Blvd 21851 **Location:** On SR 756 at US 13, 0.8 mi nw on US 13 from jct US 113. **Facility:** 66 one-bedroom standard units, some with whirlpools. 3 stories, interior corridors. *Bath:* combo or shower only. **Parking:** on-site. **Terms:** check-in 4 pm. **Amenities:** high-speed Internet, dual phone lines, voice mail, irons, hair dryers. **Pool(s):** heated indoor. **Leisure Activities:** limited exercise equipment. **Guest Services:** coin laundry, wireless Internet. **Business Services:** meeting rooms, PC.

[¶↑] CALL [M] [icons] / SOME UNITS [X]

POTOMAC —*See District Of Columbia p. 492.*

PRINCE FREDERICK pop. 1,432

—— WHERE TO STAY ——

HOLIDAY INN EXPRESS PRINCE FREDERICK   *Book great rates at AAA.com*   **Phone:** 410/535-6800

(AAA) SAVE
▼▼▼▼▼
Small-scale Hotel
$100-$200 All Year

Address: 355 Merrimac Ct 20678 **Location:** SR 2/4; center. Located near a shopping plaza. **Facility:** 70 one-bedroom standard units, some with whirlpools. *Bath:* combo or shower only. **Parking:** on-site. **Amenities:** dual phone lines, voice mail, irons, hair dryers. *Some:* CD players. **Guest Services:** valet and coin laundry, wireless Internet. **Business Services:** meeting rooms, PC. **Cards:** AX, DS, MC, VI. **Free Special Amenities:** expanded continental breakfast and high-speed Internet.

[S] CALL [M] FEE [icons] / SOME UNITS [X]

SPRINGHILL SUITES BY MARRIOTT PRINCE FREDERICK   *Book great rates at AAA.com*   **Phone:** 410/414-5217

▼▼▼▼
Small-scale Hotel
Rates not provided

Address: 75 Sherry Ln 20678 **Location:** Off SR 2/4. **Facility:** Smoke free premises. 87 one-bedroom standard units. 4 stories, interior corridors. *Bath:* combo or shower only. **Parking:** on-site. **Amenities:** high-speed Internet, voice mail, irons, hair dryers. **Pool(s):** heated indoor. **Leisure Activities:** whirlpool, limited exercise equipment. **Guest Services:** valet and coin laundry, wireless Internet. **Business Services:** meeting rooms, business center.

AAA Benefit:
Members save 5% off of the best available rate.

[¶↑] CALL [M] [icons]

—— WHERE TO DINE ——

ADAM'S THE PLACE FOR RIBS

American
$8-$24

Phone: 410/586-0001

This local favorite naturally specializes in "finger licking good" ribs, but don't overlook the other menu offerings, which include, beef, chicken and seafood dishes. A children's menu is also available. Casual dress. **Bar:** Full bar. **Reservations:** not accepted. **Hours:** 11 am-9 pm, Fri-10 pm. Closed: 3/23, 11/27, 12/25. **Address:** 2200 Solomons Island Rd 20678 **Location:** On SR 2/4, 2.7 mi s of jct SR 231. **Parking:** on-site. **Cards:** AX, MC, VI.

OLD FIELD INN

American
$8-$30

Phone: 410/535-1054

In the heart of town, the chef-owned spot provides a comfortable setting for any occasion. Inside the Victorian-style house are three dining rooms, each with its own distinct decor. The kitchen prepares a nice selection of fresh seafood and hand-cut steaks. Dressy casual. **Bar:** Full bar. **Reservations:** suggested. **Hours:** 11 am-2 & 5-9 pm, Fri-9:30 pm, Sat 5 pm-9:30 pm, Sun 5 pm-8 pm. Closed major holidays. **Address:** 485 Main St 20678 **Location:** On SR 765; center. **Parking:** on-site. **Cards:** AX, DS, MC, VI.

RANDALLSTOWN —See Baltimore p. 627.

ROCK HALL pop. 1,396

—— WHERE TO STAY ——

INN AT HUNTINGFIELD CREEK

Bed & Breakfast
$149-$269 All Year

Phone: 410/639-7779

Address: 4928 Eastern Neck Rd 21661 **Location:** 1.8 mi s on SR 445 from jct SR 20. Located in a quiet rural area. **Facility:** Attractively decorated guest rooms and a cottage unit with a gas fireplace make up the converted farmhouse, part of a 70-acre working farm. Smoke free premises. 8 units. 5 one-bedroom standard units, some with whirlpools. 3 cottages. 2 stories (no elevator), interior/exterior corridors. *Bath:* combo, shower or tub only. **Parking:** on-site. **Terms:** office hours 7 am-9 pm, 14 day cancellation notice. **Amenities:** *Some:* DVD players, irons, hair dryers. **Pool(s):** outdoor. **Leisure Activities:** fishing, bicycles, hiking trails. **Business Services:** meeting rooms. **Cards:** AX, MC, VI.

MARINERS MOTEL

Motel
$70-$85 All Year

Phone: 410/639-2291

Address: 5681 S Hawthorne Ave 21661 **Location:** 0.3 mi e of SR 20. **Facility:** 12 one-bedroom standard units. 1 story, exterior corridors. **Parking:** on-site. **Terms:** office hours 8 am-9 pm, cancellation fee imposed. **Pool(s):** outdoor. **Leisure Activities:** playground, horseshoes. **Guest Services:** coin laundry. **Cards:** AX, DS, MC, VI.

ROCKVILLE —See District Of Columbia p. 493.

ROSEDALE —See Baltimore p. 628.

ST. MICHAELS pop. 1,193

—— WHERE TO STAY ——

BEST WESTERN ST. MICHAELS MOTOR INN

Motel
$98-$169 3/1-11/15
$98-$115 11/16-2/28

Book great rates at AAA.com

Phone: (410)745-3333

Address: 1228 S Talbot St 21663 **Location:** 1 mi s on SR 33. **Facility:** 93 one-bedroom standard units. 2 stories (no elevator), interior/exterior corridors. **Parking:** on-site. **Amenities:** irons, hair dryers. **Pool(s):** 2 outdoor. **Guest Services:** wireless Internet. **Business Services:** meeting rooms. **Cards:** AX, CB, DC, DS, JC, MC, VI. **Free Special Amenities:** continental breakfast and high-speed Internet.

AAA Benefit:
Members save 10% everyday, plus an exclusive frequent stay program.

THE PARSONAGE INN

Historic Bed
& Breakfast
Rates not provided

Phone: 410/745-5519

Address: 210 N Talbot St 21663 **Location:** 0.3 mi w on SR 33. **Facility:** Brass beds, floral linens, antique furnishings and fireplaces add to the romantic ambience of the lodgings in this 1883 Victorian house. Smoke free premises. 8 units. 7 one-bedroom standard units. 1 one-bedroom suite. 1-2 stories (no elevator), interior/exterior corridors. *Bath:* combo or shower only. **Parking:** on-site. **Terms:** office hours 10 am-8 pm. **Leisure Activities:** pool & whirlpool privileges, picnic area, bicycles.

ST. MICHAELS HARBOUR INN, MARINA & SPA   *Book great rates at AAA.com*   Phone: 410/745-9001

Small-scale Hotel
$159-$525 All Year

Address: 101 N Harbor Rd 21663 **Location:** 0.3 mi e on SR 33, just n on Seymour Ave, then just w on Meadow St. **Facility:** 46 units. 14 one-bedroom standard units, some with whirlpools. 32 one-bedroom suites, some with whirlpools. 3 stories, interior corridors. **Parking:** on-site. **Terms:** check-in 4 pm, 3 day cancellation notice-fee imposed. **Amenities:** video library (fee), DVD players, voice mail, irons, hair dryers. **Dining:** Shore Restaurant & Lounge, see separate listing. **Pool(s):** outdoor. **Leisure Activities:** whirlpool, rental canoes, bicycles, exercise room, spa. *Fee:* paddleboats, marina, kayaks, water taxi. **Guest Services:** valet and coin laundry, airport transportation (fee)-Easton Airport, area transportation-within St. Michaels, wireless Internet. **Business Services:** meeting rooms, PC. **Cards:** DS, MC, VI. **Free Special Amenities:** newspaper.

The following lodging was either not evaluated or did not meet AAA rating requirements but is listed for your information only.

THE INN AT PERRY CABIN
Phone: 410/745-2200

fyi

Small-scale Hotel

Did not meet all AAA rating requirements for locking devices in some guest rooms at time of last evaluation on 04/02/2007. **Address:** 308 Watkins Ln 21663 **Location:** 0.5 mi w on SR 33. Located on the Miles River. Facilities, services, and decor characterize a mid-range property.

─── WHERE TO DINE ───

208 TALBOT RESTAURANT & WINE BAR
Phone: 410/745-3838

American
$23-$34

The restaurant's full menu features fresh seafood, local products and homemade dessert. A prix fixe menu is available only on Saturday. Dressy casual. **Bar:** Full bar. **Reservations:** suggested. **Hours:** 5 pm-10 pm; seasonal hours may vary. Closed: 1/1, 11/27, 12/24, 12/25; also Mon, Tues 11/1-4/30. **Address:** 208 N Talbot St 21663 **Location:** 0.3 mi w on SR 33. **Parking:** on-site. **Cards:** AX, DS, MC, VI.

CARPENTER STREET SALOON
Phone: 410/745-5111

American
$6-$17

Nestled among downtown shops, the casual, old-time eatery has an eclectic interior marked by an overhead circling train, decoys and interesting artwork On the menu are fresh local seafood dishes, including crab combinations and seaskin cheese and crab on potato skins. Guests can relax and enjoy friendly service while keeping an eye on the foot traffic nearby. Casual dress. **Bar:** Full bar. **Reservations:** accepted. **Hours:** 8-11 am, 11:30-2:30 & 4-9:30 pm. Closed: for breakfast & lunch 12/25. **Address:** 113/115 S Talbot St 21663 **Location:** On SR 33; center. **Parking:** no self-parking. **Cards:** DS, MC, VI.

THE CRAB CLAW
Phone: 410/745-2900

Seafood
$10-$25

A popular choice for crabs, this restaurant overlooks the harbor and specializes in Chesapeake Bay seafood. Casual dress. **Bar:** Full bar. **Reservations:** suggested, in season. **Hours:** Open 3/4-12/15; 11 am-10 pm; seasonal hours vary. Closed: 1/1, 11/27, 12/25. **Address:** 304 Mill St 21663 **Location:** On the harbor; adjacent to the Chesapeake Bay Maritime Museum. **Parking:** on-site.

SHERWOOD'S LANDING
Phone: 410/745-2200

Continental
$14-$40

The elegant dining room overlooks the Miles River and is perfect for any occasion: a business meeting, romantic getaway or family gathering. The professional, attentive staff displays excellent knowledge of the menu and wine selections. Creative and artfully prepared dishes use only the freshest local and international ingredients. Dressy casual. **Bar:** Full bar. **Reservations:** suggested, weekend nights. **Hours:** 7 am-10, noon-2:30 & 6-10 pm. **Address:** 308 Watkins Ln 21663 **Location:** 0.5 mi w on SR 33; in The Inn at Perry Cabin. **Parking:** valet. **Cards:** AX, CB, DC, DS, MC, VI.

SHORE RESTAURANT & LOUNGE
Phone: 410/924-4769

American
$7-$32

The casually elegant dining room overlooks the harbor, making the view here almost as good as the eclectic American cuisine. The chef/owner changes the menu monthly to take advantage of the availability of fresh market and local ingredients. Dressy casual. **Bar:** Full bar. **Reservations:** suggested. **Hours:** 11:30 am-2:30 & 6-10 pm, Sun from 10 am. **Address:** 101 N Harbor Rd 21663 **Location:** 0.3 mi e on SR 33, just n on Seymour Ave, then just w on Meadow St; in St. Michaels Harbour Inn, Marina & Spa. **Parking:** on-site. **Cards:** AX, MC, VI.

The following restaurant has not been evaluated by AAA but is listed for your information only.

BISTRO ST. MICHAELS
Phone: 410/745-9111

fyi

Not evaluated. The food at this bistro is prepared with finesse and the setting is comfortable. Don't miss the wonderful soft-shell crab sandwich. **Address:** 403 S Talbot St 21663 **Location:** On SR 33; center.

SALISBURY pop. 23,743

———— WHERE TO STAY ————

BEST WESTERN SALISBURY PLAZA — *Book great rates at AAA.com*

Phone: (410)546-1300

Motel
$55-$135 5/1-2/28
$55-$110 3/1-4/30

Address: 1735 N Salisbury Blvd 21801 **Location:** US 13 business route, 0.5 mi s of US 50 Bypass. Located in a commercial area. **Facility:** 101 one-bedroom standard units. 2 stories (no elevator), exterior corridors. **Parking:** on-site. **Amenities:** irons, hair dryers. *Some:* high-speed Internet. **Pool(s):** outdoor. **Leisure Activities:** limited exercise equipment. **Guest Services:** coin laundry, wireless Internet. **Business Services:** meeting rooms, business center. **Cards:** AX, DC, DS, MC, VI. **Free Special Amenities: room upgrade (subject to availability with advance reservations).** *(See color ad below)*

AAA Benefit:
Members save 10% everyday, plus an exclusive frequent stay program.

COMFORT INN SALISBURY — *Book great rates at AAA.com*

Phone: (410)543-4666

Small-scale Hotel
$49-$159 5/24-2/28
$49-$119 3/1-5/23

Address: 2701 N Salisbury Blvd 21801 **Location:** US 13, 0.5 mi n of jct US 13 business route and Bypass. **Facility:** 96 units. 93 one-bedroom standard units, some with whirlpools. 3 one-bedroom suites with whirlpools. 2 stories (no elevator), interior corridors. **Parking:** on-site. **Amenities:** safes (fee), irons, hair dryers. **Leisure Activities:** picnic area with table & grill, volleyball. **Guest Services:** valet and coin laundry, wireless Internet. **Business Services:** meeting rooms, PC. **Cards:** AX, CB, DC, DS, MC, VI. **Free Special Amenities: continental breakfast and high-speed Internet.**

COUNTRY INN & SUITES BY CARLSON OF SALISBURY — *Book at AAA.com*

Phone: (410)742-2688

Small-scale Hotel
$189-$209 All Year

Address: 1804 Sweetbay Dr 21804 **Location:** Off US 50 business route, just w of jct US 13. **Facility:** Smoke free premises. 77 units. 65 one-bedroom standard units, some with whirlpools. 12 one-bedroom suites. 3 stories, interior corridors. *Bath:* combo or shower only. **Parking:** on-site. **Amenities:** high-speed Internet, voice mail, irons, hair dryers. **Pool(s):** heated indoor. **Leisure Activities:** whirlpool, exercise room. **Guest Services:** coin laundry, wireless Internet. **Business Services:** PC (fee). **Cards:** AX, CB, DC, DS, MC, VI.

COURTYARD BY MARRIOTT SALISBURY — *Book great rates at AAA.com*

Phone: 410/742-4405

Small-scale Hotel
$100-$130 All Year

Address: 128 Troopers Way 21804 **Location:** On US 13; 1.5 mi n of jct US 50 Bypass. **Facility:** Smoke free premises. 106 units. 102 one-bedroom standard units. 4 one-bedroom suites. 4 stories, interior corridors. *Bath:* combo or shower only. **Parking:** on-site. **Amenities:** high-speed Internet, voice mail, irons, hair dryers. *Some:* dual phone lines. **Pool(s):** heated indoor. **Leisure Activities:** whirlpool, exercise room. **Guest Services:** valet and coin laundry, wireless Internet. **Business Services:** meeting rooms, business center. **Cards:** AX, DC, DS, MC, VI. **Free Special Amenities: newspaper and high-speed Internet.**

AAA Benefit:
Members save 5% off of the best available rate.

HAMPTON INN-SALISBURY   *Book great rates at AAA.com*
Phone: (410)334-3080

AAA SAVE
▽▽▽
Small-scale Hotel
$94-$189 3/1-10/23
$94-$129 10/24-2/28

Address: 121 E Naylor Mill Rd 21804 **Location:** US 13, 0.5 mi n of jct US 50 Bypass. **Facility:** 150 one-bedroom standard units, some with whirlpools. 5 stories, interior corridors. *Bath:* combo or shower only. **Parking:** on-site. **Amenities:** video games (fee), voice mail, irons, hair dryers. **Pool(s):** heated indoor. **Leisure Activities:** whirlpool, exercise room. *Fee:* game room. **Guest Services:** valet and coin laundry, wireless Internet. **Business Services:** meeting rooms, PC. **Cards:** AX, CB, DC, DS, MC, VI. **Free Special Amenities:** newspaper and high-speed Internet.

MICROTEL INN & SUITES SALISBURY/OCEAN CITY   *Book at AAA.com*
Phone: (410)742-2626

▽▽
Small-scale Hotel
$59-$199 All Year

Address: 3050 Merritt Mill Rd 21804 **Location:** Off US 50 business route; just w of jct US 13. **Facility:** 59 one-bedroom standard units. 3 stories, interior corridors. *Bath:* combo or shower only. **Parking:** on-site. **Terms:** 3 day cancellation notice. **Amenities:** irons, hair dryers. **Guest Services:** coin laundry, wireless Internet. **Business Services:** PC. **Cards:** AX, DC, DS, MC, VI.

RAMADA INN AND CONFERENCE CENTER   *Book at AAA.com*
Phone: 410/546-4400

▽▽
Large-scale Hotel
Rates not provided

Address: 300 S Salisbury Blvd 21801 **Location:** US 13 business route, 0.4 mi s of jct Business US 50; downtown. Located in a commercial area. **Facility:** 156 units. 155 one-bedroom standard units. 1 one-bedroom suite. 5 stories, interior corridors. **Parking:** on-site. **Amenities:** voice mail, safes (fee), irons, hair dryers. **Pool(s):** heated indoor. **Leisure Activities:** limited exercise equipment. **Guest Services:** valet laundry, wireless Internet. **Business Services:** conference facilities, PC.

RESIDENCE INN BY MARRIOTT SALISBURY   *Book great rates at AAA.com*
Phone: 410/543-0033

▽▽▽
Small-scale Hotel
$111-$141 All Year

Address: 140 Centre Rd 21801 **Location:** Just off US 13 business route at US 50. **Facility:** Smoke free premises. 84 units. 41 one-bedroom standard units with efficiencies. 35 one- and 8 two-bedroom suites, some with efficiencies or kitchens. 3 stories, interior corridors. *Bath:* combo or shower only. **Parking:** on-site. **Amenities:** high-speed Internet, dual phone lines, voice mail, irons, hair dryers. **Pool(s):** outdoor. **Leisure Activities:** whirlpool, exercise room, sports court. **Guest Services:** valet and coin laundry, wireless Internet. **Business Services:** meeting rooms, PC. **Cards:** AX, DC, DS, JC, MC, VI.

AAA Benefit:
Members save 5% off of the best available rate.

SLEEP INN-SALISBURY   *Book great rates at AAA.com*
Phone: (410)572-5516

AAA SAVE
▽▽▽
Small-scale Hotel
$65-$159 All Year

Address: 406 Punkin Ct 21804 **Location:** US 50 business route; just w of jct US 13. **Facility:** 78 one-bedroom standard units, some with whirlpools. 3 stories, interior corridors. *Bath:* combo or shower only. **Parking:** on-site. **Terms:** cancellation fee imposed. **Amenities:** voice mail, irons, hair dryers. **Pool(s):** outdoor. **Leisure Activities:** limited exercise equipment. **Guest Services:** wireless Internet. **Business Services:** PC. **Cards:** AX, CB, DC, DS, JC, MC, VI. **Free Special Amenities:** continental breakfast and high-speed Internet.

———— WHERE TO DINE ————

BREW RIVER RESTAURANT & BAR
Phone: 410/677-6757

▽▽
American
$7-$29

In the heart of town and overlooking the Wicomico River, the casual restaurant appeals to all age groups. The menu leans to seafood but doesn't stop there, as beef, chicken and pasta dishes also make appearances. Casual dress. **Bar:** Full bar. **Reservations:** accepted. **Hours:** 11 am-11 pm, Sun from 10 am. **Address:** 502 W Main St 21801 **Location:** US 50, 1 blk s; on Wicomico River. **Parking:** on-site. **Cards:** AX, DS, MC, VI.

CACTUS TAVERNA
Phone: 410/548-1254

▽▽
International
$7-$25

On a busy highway and opposite the Salisbury Mall, this shopping plaza restaurant offers a casual, comfortable atmosphere with a Mexican vibe. The kitchen prepares a wide array of dishes, from traditional Mexican selections to South American, Spanish and Mediterranean fare. Beef and seafood specialties get top billing. Casual dress. **Bar:** Full bar. **Reservations:** suggested. **Hours:** 4 pm-10 pm, Fri & Sat-11 pm. Closed: 11/27, 12/25. **Address:** 2420 N Salisbury Blvd 21801 **Location:** On US 13, just n of jct US 50 Bypass. **Parking:** on-site. **Cards:** AX, DS, MC, VI.

GOIN' NUTS CAFE
Phone: 410/860-1164

▽▽
International
$6-$20

The casual restaurant serves international samplings of cuisine from Jamaica, Mexico, Italy, France and the good ol' U.S.A. Servers are friendly and attentive. During warm weather, the patio is a nice spot to relax. Live music provides seasonal entertainment on Wednesday, Thursday and Sunday. Casual dress. **Bar:** Full bar. **Reservations:** accepted. **Hours:** 11 am-11 pm, Sun-10 pm. Closed major holidays. **Address:** 947 Mount Hermon Rd 21804 **Location:** Just se of jct US 50 and E Main St, on SR 350; in Market Place East Professional. **Parking:** on-site. **Cards:** AX, MC, VI.

SILVER SPRING —See District Of Columbia p. 497.

SNOW HILL pop. 2,409

———— **WHERE TO STAY** ————

RIVER HOUSE INN

(AAA) (SAVE)

▽▽▽▽

Bed & Breakfast
$125-$300 3/1-11/30

Phone: (410)632-2722
Address: 201 E Market St 21863 **Location:** 1 mi w on SR 394 from jct SR 113. **Facility:** The B&B offers tastefully decorated cottages set on landscaped grounds that slope down to the Pocomoke River. Smoke free premises. 4 units. 3 one-bedroom standard units with whirlpools. 1 two-bedroom suite with kitchen. 1-2 stories (no elevator), interior/exterior corridors. **Parking:** on-site. **Terms:** open 3/1-11/30, office hours 7 am-9 pm, 2 night minimum stay - seasonal and/or weekends, 7 day cancellation notice. **Amenities:** video library, DVD players, irons, hair dryers. **Pool(s):** heated outdoor. **Guest Services:** wireless Internet. **Cards:** AX, MC, VI. **Free Special Amenities:** full breakfast and high-speed Internet.

SOLOMONS pop. 1,536

———— **WHERE TO STAY** ————

HILTON GARDEN INN SOLOMONS   *Book great rates at AAA.com*   **Phone:** 410/326-0303

▽▽▽▽

Small-scale Hotel
Rates not provided

Address: 13100 Dowell Rd 20629 **Location:** Off SR 2/4; 1.4 mi n of the bridge. **Facility:** 100 units. 94 one-bedroom standard units. 6 one-bedroom suites with whirlpools. 3 stories, interior corridors. *Bath:* combo or shower only. **Parking:** on-site. **Amenities:** high-speed Internet, voice mail, irons, hair dryers. **Pool(s):** outdoor, heated indoor. **Leisure Activities:** whirlpool, exercise room. **Guest Services:** coin laundry, wireless Internet. **Business Services:** meeting rooms, business center.

HOLIDAY INN SELECT SOLOMONS HOTEL   *Book at AAA.com*   **Phone:** 410/326-6311

▽▽▽▽

Large-scale Hotel
Rates not provided

Address: 155 Holiday Dr 20688 **Location:** SR 2/4; center. **Facility:** 326 units. 319 one-bedroom standard units, some with efficiencies. 7 one-bedroom suites with efficiencies. 4-5 stories, interior corridors. **Parking:** on-site. **Amenities:** voice mail, irons, hair dryers. **Pool(s):** outdoor. **Leisure Activities:** sauna, 2 tennis courts, exercise room. *Fee:* marina, massage. **Guest Services:** valet and coin laundry, wireless Internet. **Business Services:** conference facilities, business center.

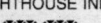

———— **WHERE TO DINE** ————

THE C D CAFE

▽▽ ▽▽

American
$9-$25

Phone: 410/326-3877
The simple cafe has great food and a casual atmosphere. The chef/owners prepare an eclectic selection of American dishes, from seafood to vegetarian. Creme brulee has become the chef's signature dessert. Casual dress. **Bar:** Full bar. **Reservations:** not accepted. **Hours:** 11:30 am-2:30 & 5:30-9:30 pm, Sun 9:30 am-2:30 & 5:30-9 pm. Closed: 11/27, 12/25. **Address:** 14350 Solomons Island Rd 20688 **Location:** 0.5 mi s on SR 2 from Solomons Bridge. **Parking:** on-site. **Cards:** MC, VI.

THE DRY DOCK RESTAURANT

▽▽ ▽▽

American
$8-$30

Phone: 410/326-4817
The menu changes daily at the marina-front restaurant. The kitchen's creativity is reflected in such dishes as crab-stuffed lobster drizzled with lemon dill hollandaise and ginger-seared scallops with spicy Oriental sauce. The second-level dining room, as well as the popular seasonal balcony, provides a great view of the marina. Casual dress. **Bar:** Full bar. **Reservations:** suggested. **Hours:** 5 pm-9 pm, Fri & Sat-9:30 pm, Sun 10 am-2 & 5-9 pm. Closed: 1/1, 11/27, 12/25. **Address:** 245 C St 20688 **Location:** 0.3 mi s on SR 2 from Solomons Bridge, just e on C St; at Zahnisers Marina. **Parking:** on-site. **Cards:** AX, MC, VI.

LIGHTHOUSE INN

▽▽ ▽▽

Seafood
$15-$29

Phone: 410/326-2444
Seafood—most notably crabcakes—is the specialty at the two-story restaurant that looks out on Solomons Harbor and the Patuxent River. A skipjack boat replica serves as the bar. Depending on the night, the mood can range from romantic to buzzing. Casual dress. **Bar:** Full bar. **Reservations:** suggested. **Hours:** 5 pm-9 pm, Fri & Sat-10 pm, Sun 4 pm-8 pm. Closed: 11/27, 12/25. **Address:** 14636 Solomons Island Rd S 20688 **Location:** 1 mi s on SR 2 from Solomons Bridge. **Parking:** on-site. **Cards:** AX, DC, DS, MC, VI.

STEVENSVILLE pop. 5,880

———— **WHERE TO STAY** ————

KENT MANOR INN   *Book at AAA.com*   **Phone:** (410)643-5757

▽▽▽▽

Historic
Country Inn
$160-$345 All Year

Address: 500 Kent Manor Dr 21666 **Location:** US 50/301, exit 37, just s on SR 8; 0.5 mi e of Bay Bridge. **Facility:** Victorian reproductions furnish the individually decorated guest rooms in this 1820 inn set well back from the road. Designated smoking area. 24 units. 23 one- and 1 two-bedroom standard units. 3 stories (no elevator), interior corridors. **Parking:** on-site. **Terms:** office hours 7:30 am-9 pm, 3 day cancellation notice. **Amenities:** hair dryers. **Pool(s):** outdoor. **Leisure Activities:** paddleboats, boat dock, fishing, bicycles, horseshoes, volleyball. **Guest Services:** wireless Internet. **Business Services:** meeting rooms. **Cards:** AX, DC, DS, MC, VI.

——— WHERE TO DINE ———

KENTMORR RESTAURANT & CRAB HOUSE   *Menu on AAA.com*

Phone: 410/643-2263

Seafood
$7-$27

The atmosphere is casual and family-oriented at the restaurant, where steamed crabs, fried oysters and a great view of the bay are featured presentations. Pasta and beef dishes also are available. An outdoor dining area provides seasonal seating. Casual dress. **Bar:** Full bar. **Reservations:** suggested. **Hours:** 11:30 am-9 pm. Closed: 12/24-12/26. **Address:** 910 Kentmorr Rd 21666 **Location:** 5 mi s on SR 8 from jct US 50/301, exit 37, 0.6 mi w. **Parking:** on-site. **Cards:** AX, DS, MC, VI.

SWANTON

——— WHERE TO STAY ———

CARMEL COVE INN

Phone: (301)387-0067

Bed & Breakfast
$175-$195 All Year

Address: 105 Monastery Way 21561 **Location:** 2.5 mi e on Glendale Rd from US 219. Located on Deep Creek Lake. **Facility:** Close to the Deep Creek Lake area and originally constructed as a retreat for Carmelite Order priests, the B&B has sections built in 1945 and 1960. Smoke free premises. 10 one-bedroom standard units, some with whirlpools. 2 stories (no elevator), interior corridors. *Bath:* combo or shower only. **Parking:** on-site. **Terms:** check-in 4 pm, 2-3 night minimum stay - seasonal and/or weekends, age restrictions may apply, 5 day cancellation notice. **Amenities:** video library, DVD players, CD players, hair dryers. **Leisure Activities:** canoeing, paddleboats, fishing, tennis court, bicycles, horseshoes. **Guest Services:** wireless Internet. **Business Services:** meeting rooms. **Cards:** DS, MC, VI.

SYKESVILLE —*See Baltimore p. 628.*

THURMONT pop. 5,588

——— WHERE TO STAY ———

COZY COUNTRY INN

Phone: 301-271-4301

Country Inn
$67-$155 All Year

Address: 103 Frederick Rd 21788 **Location:** US 15, just e to SR 806, 0.4 mi n. **Facility:** Family owned since 1929, the inn's rooms are named for former presidents and other dignitaries who have visited the inn or nearby Camp David. 21 one-bedroom standard units, some with whirlpools. 1-2 stories (no elevator), exterior corridors. *Bath:* combo or shower only. **Parking:** on-site. **Terms:** cancellation fee imposed. **Amenities:** voice mail, irons, hair dryers. *Some:* DVD players. **Dining:** Cozy Restaurant, see separate listing. **Leisure Activities:** sports equipment on loan. **Business Services:** meeting rooms. **Cards:** AX, DS, MC, VI. **Free Special Amenities: continental breakfast and local telephone calls.**

RAMBLER INN

Phone: (301)271-2424

Motel
$30-$95 All Year

Address: 426 N Church St 21788 **Location:** US 15 at SR 550. **Facility:** 30 one-bedroom standard units. 1 story, interior/exterior corridors. **Parking:** on-site. **Guest Services:** coin laundry. **Business Services:** fax. **Cards:** AX, DC, DS, MC, VI. **Free Special Amenities: early check-in/late check-out and high-speed Internet.**

SUPER 8 MOTEL-THURMONT   *Book at AAA.com*

Phone: 301-271-7888

Motel
Rates not provided

Address: 300 Tippin Dr 21788 **Location:** US 15, just w on SR 806. **Facility:** 46 one-bedroom standard units. 2 stories (no elevator), interior corridors. **Parking:** on-site. **Amenities:** high-speed Internet, safes (fee), hair dryers. **Guest Services:** wireless Internet. **Business Services:** meeting rooms.

——— WHERE TO DINE ———

COZY RESTAURANT

Phone: 301-271-7373

American
$7-$20

As the name implies, the restaurant is cozy. Guests can choose from a huge selection of entrees and salads, as well as desserts from the buffet. Casual dress. **Bar:** Full bar. **Hours:** 11 am-9 pm, Sat & Sun from 8 am. Closed: 12/24, 12/25. **Address:** 105 Frederick Rd 21788 **Location:** US 15, just e to SR 806, 0.4 mi n; in Cozy Country Inn. **Parking:** on-site. **Cards:** AX, MC, VI.

MOUNTAIN GATE FAMILY RESTAURANT

Phone: 301-271-4373

American
$5-$12

Families and seniors keep the popular restaurant bustling. Extensive buffets line up such tantalizing fare as ham and cabbage, lasagna and slippery chicken pot pie. Breakfast from the menu can be ordered all day. Casual dress. **Hours:** 5 am-11 pm, Fri & Sat-midnight. Closed: 12/25; also for dinner 12/24. **Address:** 133 Frederick Rd 21788 **Location:** 1.5 mi s on SR 806; just n on SR 806 (Thurmont exit) off US 15. **Parking:** on-site. **Cards:** DS, MC, VI.

SHAMROCK RESTAURANT *Menu on AAA.com*   **Phone:** 301/271-2912

Appealing to locals and travelers on their way to and from Gettysburg, the restaurant has a definite Irish theme. The food is a mixture of salads, mostly seafood appetizers, and steak, seafood and some poultry dishes. Casual dress. **Bar:** Full bar. **Reservations:** suggested, weekends. **Hours:** 11 am-10 pm, Sun noon-9 pm. Closed: 1/1, 12/25. **Address:** 7701 Fitzgerald Rd 21788 **Location:** 1 mi n on US 15 from jct SR 550. **Parking:** on-site. **Cards:** MC, VI.

Steak & Seafood
$6-$21

TILGHMAN ISLAND

——— WHERE TO STAY ———

CHESAPEAKE WOOD DUCK INN   **Phone:** (410)886-2070

Address: 21490 Gibsontown Rd 21671 **Location:** SR 33, 0.4 mi w of Knapps Narrows Drawbridge, just s. **Facility:** The guest rooms are individually decorated in this 1890 historic house, which affords nice views of sunsets on the water. Smoke free premises. 7 units. 6 one-bedroom standard units. 1 one-bedroom suite. 3 stories (no elevator), interior corridors. *Bath:* combo or shower only. **Parking:** on-site. **Terms:** office hours 8 am-9 pm, check-in 4 pm, 2 night minimum stay - weekends, age restrictions may apply, 7 day cancellation notice-fee imposed. **Amenities:** CD players. **Guest Services:** wireless Internet. **Business Services:** fax (fee). **Cards:** MC, VI. **Free Special Amenities: full breakfast and high-speed Internet.**

Historic Bed & Breakfast
$129-$259 All Year

THE INN AT KNAPP'S NARROW MARINA   **Phone:** 410/886-2720

Address: 6176 Tilghman Island Rd 21671 **Location:** On SR 33, east side of the bridge. **Facility:** 20 units. 19 one-bedroom standard units. 1 one-bedroom suite. 3 stories, exterior corridors. **Parking:** on-site. **Terms:** office hours 8 am-9 pm, 2 night minimum stay - seasonal and/or weekends, 7 day cancellation notice-fee imposed. **Amenities:** voice mail, hair dryers. **Pool(s):** outdoor. **Guest Services:** coin laundry, wireless Internet. **Business Services:** meeting rooms. **Cards:** DS, MC, VI.

Motel
$120-$170 3/1-11/20
$80-$120 11/21-2/28

——— WHERE TO DINE ———

THE TILGHMAN ISLAND INN   **Phone:** 410/886-2141

This restaurant is located on an isolated island separated only by a drawbridge from the mainland. Dine inside or out; either formal dining areas with tablecloth or casual dining tables with logo umbrellas viewing the passing boats. Enjoy creative selections of seafood with some twists and some land animal choices. Lunch has some classic options of Rueben, soft-shell crab in season, and other creative options. Casual dress. **Bar:** Full bar. **Reservations:** suggested. **Hours:** Open 3/1-1/1 & 1/27-2/28; noon-4 & 6-9 pm, Fri & Sat-10 pm, Sun noon-4 & 5-9 pm. Closed: Wed. **Address:** 21384 Coopertown Rd 21671 **Location:** Just n of Knapps Narrows Drawbridge. **Parking:** on-site. **Cards:** AX, DS, MC, VI.

American
$8-$35

TIMONIUM —*See Baltimore p. 628.*

TOWSON —*See Baltimore p. 629.*

UNION BRIDGE —*See Baltimore p. 630.*

WALDORF pop. 22,312

———— **WHERE TO STAY** ————

COMFORT SUITES WALDORF *Book great rates at AAA.com*   **Phone:** (301)932-4400

AAA SAVE

Small-scale Hotel
$99-$189 3/1-10/31
$89-$129 11/1-2/28

Address: 11765 Business Park Dr 20601 **Location:** Just off US 301; 1 mi n of jct SR 5 business route. Located in a commercial area. **Facility:** Smoke free premises. 69 one-bedroom standard units, some with whirlpools. 2 stories, interior corridors. *Bath:* combo or shower only. **Parking:** on-site. **Amenities:** high-speed Internet, dual phone lines, voice mail, safes (fee), irons, hair dryers. **Pool(s):** heated indoor. **Guest Services:** coin laundry. **Business Services:** meeting rooms, PC. **Cards:** AX, DC, DS, MC, VI. **Free Special Amenities:** full breakfast and high-speed Internet.

COUNTRY INN & SUITES BY CARLSON WALDORF   *Book at AAA.com*   **Phone:** (301)645-6595

Small-scale Hotel
$119-$149 3/1-10/31
$99-$129 11/1-2/28

Address: 2555 Business Park Ct 20601 **Location:** Just off US 301; 1 mi n of jct SR 5 business route. Located in a commercial area. **Facility:** Smoke free premises. 66 units. 50 one-bedroom standard units, some with whirlpools. 16 one-bedroom suites. 3 stories, interior corridors. *Bath:* combo or shower only. **Parking:** on-site. **Amenities:** CD players, high-speed Internet, dual phone lines, voice mail, safes, irons, hair dryers. **Pool(s):** heated indoor. **Leisure Activities:** whirlpool, limited exercise equipment. **Guest Services:** valet and coin laundry, wireless Internet. **Business Services:** PC. **Cards:** AX, CB, DC, DS, JC, MC, VI.

COURTYARD BY MARRIOTT

[fyi]
Small-scale Hotel

Under construction, scheduled to open September 2008. **Address:** 3145 Craine Hwy 20602 **Location:** On US 301, just s of jct SR 228. **Amenities:** coffeemakers, microwaves, refrigerators, pool.

AAA Benefit:
Members save 5% off of the best available rate.

HAMPTON INN WALDORF   *Book great rates at AAA.com*   **Phone:** 301/632-9600

Small-scale Hotel
$119-$189 All Year

Address: 3750 Crain Hwy 20603 **Location:** On US 301; opposite St Charles Towne Plaza. Located opposite a shopping center. **Facility:** 100 one-bedroom standard units, some with whirlpools. 3 stories, interior corridors. *Bath:* combo or shower only. **Parking:** on-site. **Amenities:** dual phone lines, voice mail, irons, hair dryers. **Pool(s):** outdoor. **Leisure Activities:** limited exercise equipment. **Guest Services:** coin laundry, wireless Internet. **Business Services:** meeting rooms, PC. **Cards:** AX, CB, DC, DS, JC, MC, VI.

HOLIDAY INN WALDORF   *Book at AAA.com*   **Phone:** 301/645-8200

Small-scale Hotel
Rates not provided

Address: 45 St Patrick Dr 20603 **Location:** 0.7 mi s on US 301 from jct SR 228. Located adjacent to shopping mall. **Facility:** 191 one-bedroom standard units, some with efficiencies and/or whirlpools. 3 stories, interior corridors. *Bath:* combo or shower only. **Parking:** on-site. **Amenities:** voice mail, irons, hair dryers. **Pool(s):** outdoor. **Leisure Activities:** limited exercise equipment. **Guest Services:** valet and coin laundry, beauty salon, wireless Internet. **Business Services:** meeting rooms.

LA QUINTA INN WALDORF   *Book great rates at AAA.com*   **Phone:** (301)645-0022

AAA SAVE

Small-scale Hotel
$100-$130 All Year

Address: 11770 Business Park Dr 20601 **Location:** 1 mi n on US 301 from jct SR 228. **Facility:** 87 units. 85 one-bedroom standard units. 2 one-bedroom suites with whirlpools. 2 stories (no elevator), interior corridors. *Bath:* combo or shower only. **Parking:** on-site. **Amenities:** voice mail, irons, hair dryers. **Guest Services:** coin laundry, wireless Internet. **Business Services:** PC. **Cards:** AX, DC, DS, MC, VI. **Free Special Amenities:** expanded continental breakfast and high-speed Internet.

AAA Benefit:
Members save 10% everyday.

——— **WHERE TO DINE** ———

SILVER SKEWERS RESTAURANT

Persian
$8-$17

Phone: 301/396-5758

Set back off the main road, the small, casual restaurant prepares a variety of delicious kebabs: beef, lamb, chicken, shrimp and salmon in combination or alone. Casual dress. **Reservations:** accepted. **Hours:** 11:30 am-9 pm, Fri & Sat-10 pm. Closed major holidays; also Sun. **Address:** 2788 Old Washington Rd 20601 **Location:** Just e of US 301, jct Central Ave. **Parking:** on-site. **Cards:** MC, VI.

WESTMINSTER —See Baltimore p. 630.

WHEATON —See District Of Columbia p. 499.

WHITEHAVEN

——— **WHERE TO DINE** ———

THE RED ROOST

Steak & Seafood
$11-$40

Phone: 410/546-5443

An eastern shore tradition for more than 30 years, the restaurant offers an adventurous dining experience. Tucked away off a gravel country road, it's anything but quiet. Guests should be prepared to swing a mallet when ordering the all-you-can-eat crab dinner. Heaping helpings and fun make this place popular. Casual dress. **Bar:** Full bar. **Hours:** Open 3/16-10/30; 5:30 pm-10 pm, Sat from 3 pm, Sun 3 pm-9 pm. Closed: Mon & Tues 3/16-5/21 & 9/2-10/30. **Address:** 2670 Clara Rd 21856 **Location:** From SR 352, follow signs. **Parking:** on-site. **Cards:** AX, DC, MC, VI.

WHITE MARSH —See Baltimore p. 631.

WILLIAMSPORT pop. 1,868

——— **WHERE TO STAY** ———

RED ROOF INN

Small-scale Hotel
$50-$80 All Year

Book great rates at AAA.com

Phone: (301)582-3500

Address: 310 E Potomac St 21795 **Location:** I-81, exit 2, 0.3 mi sw on US 11. **Facility:** 108 one-bedroom standard units. 2 stories (no elevator), exterior corridors. **Parking:** on-site. **Leisure Activities:** picnic tables. **Guest Services:** coin laundry, wireless Internet. **Cards:** AX, CB, DC, DS, MC, VI.

WOODLAWN —See Baltimore p. 632.

Virginia

Chincoteague
© Tom Algire
Photography

Virginia Orientation Map To Destinations

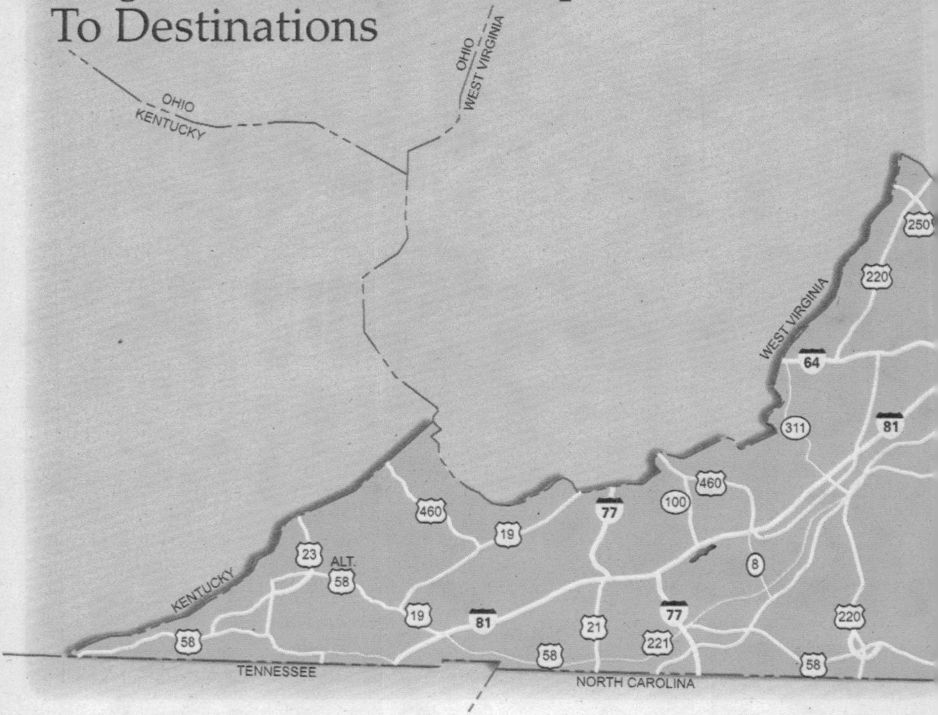

OHIO
WEST VIRGINIA

OHIO
KENTUCKY

250

220

WEST VIRGINIA

64

311

81

460

100

460

77

460

19

77

8

23

ALT.
58

KENTUCKY

19

81

21

77

220

58

58

221

TENNESSEE

58

NORTH CAROLINA

58

Major destinations are color-coded to index boxes, which display vicinity communities you will find listed within that destination's section of the book.

Cities outside major destination vicinities are listed in alphabetical order throughout this book.

Use the *Comprehensive City Index* at the back of this book to find every city's listing location.

ABINGDON pop. 7,780

——— WHERE TO STAY ———

ALPINE MOTEL

Motel
$49-$79 3/1-10/31
$39-$59 11/1-2/28

Phone: (276)628-3178
Address: 882 E Main St 24210 **Location:** I-81, exit 19 (US 11), 0.5 mi w. **Facility:** 19 one-bedroom standard units. 1 story, exterior corridors. **Parking:** on-site. **Terms:** cancellation fee imposed. **Cards:** AX, DS, MC, VI. **Free Special Amenities:** continental breakfast and high-speed Internet.

COMFORT INN ABINGDON   *Book at AAA.com*

Small-scale Hotel
Rates not provided

Phone: 276/676-2222
Address: 170 Jonesboro Rd 24210 **Location:** I-81, exit 14, just n. **Facility:** 80 one-bedroom standard units. 2 stories (no elevator), interior corridors. **Parking:** on-site. **Amenities:** high-speed Internet, irons, hair dryers. **Pool(s):** heated outdoor. **Guest Services:** valet laundry, wireless Internet.

HAMPTON INN ABINGDON   *Book great rates at AAA.com*

Small-scale Hotel
Rates not provided

Phone: 276/619-4600
Address: 340 Commerce Dr 24211 **Location:** I-81, exit 17, just e. **Facility:** 68 one-bedroom standard units, some with whirlpools. 3 stories, interior corridors. *Bath:* combo or shower only. **Parking:** on-site. **Terms:** check-in 4 pm. **Amenities:** video games, high-speed Internet, voice mail, irons, hair dryers. **Pool(s):** heated outdoor. **Leisure Activities:** exercise room. **Guest Services:** valet laundry, wireless Internet. **Business Services:** meeting rooms, PC.

HOLIDAY INN EXPRESS   *Book great rates at AAA.com*

Small-scale Hotel
$89-$129 All Year

Phone: (276)676-2829
Address: 940 E Main St 24210 **Location:** I-81, exit 19 (US 11), just w. **Facility:** 81 one-bedroom standard units, some with whirlpools. 3 stories, interior corridors. *Bath:* combo or shower only. **Parking:** on-site. **Amenities:** video games, high-speed Internet, voice mail, irons, hair dryers. **Pool(s):** outdoor. **Guest Services:** valet and coin laundry, wireless Internet. **Business Services:** business center. **Cards:** AX, DC, DS, MC, VI. **Free Special Amenities:** expanded continental breakfast and high-speed Internet.

INN ON TOWN CREEK

Bed & Breakfast
$120-$145 All Year

Phone: (276)628-4560
Address: 445 E Valley St 24210 **Location:** I-81, exit 17, 0.8 mi w on Cummings St, then 0.8 mi n. **Facility:** On 4 acres of manicured grounds, this brick home with a slate roof offers a solarium as well as rooms furnished with antiques and reproductions. Smoke free premises. 5 one-bedroom standard units. 3 stories (no elevator), interior corridors. *Bath:* some shared or private. **Parking:** on-site. **Terms:** age restrictions may apply, 7 day cancellation notice-fee imposed. **Amenities:** DVD players, irons, hair dryers. **Leisure Activities:** whirlpool. **Cards:** AX, DS, MC, VI.

THE MARTHA WASHINGTON INN & SPA   *Book at AAA.com*

Classic Historic
Small-scale Hotel
$200-$450 All Year

Phone: (276)628-3161
Address: 150 W Main St 24210 **Location:** I-81, exit 17, 0.7 mi n on Cummings St, then just e. **Facility:** Built in 1832 as a private home which later served as a women's college, this red-brick Federalist mansion is set amid landscaped grounds. 62 one-bedroom standard units, some with whirlpools. 3 stories, interior corridors. *Bath:* combo or shower only. **Parking:** on-site. **Terms:** 2 night minimum stay - weekends, cancellation fee imposed. **Amenities:** video games, CD players, high-speed Internet, voice mail, irons, hair dryers. *Some:* DVD players. **Dining:** The Dining Room, see separate listing. **Pool(s):** heated indoor. **Leisure Activities:** whirlpool, exercise room, spa. **Guest Services:** valet laundry, area transportation, wireless Internet. **Business Services:** meeting rooms, PC, fax. **Cards:** AX, DS, MC, VI.

QUALITY INN & SUITES OF ABINGDON   *Book at AAA.com*

Small-scale Hotel
Rates not provided

Phone: 276/676-9090
Address: 930 E Main St 24210 **Location:** I-81, exit 19 (US 11), just w. **Facility:** 75 one-bedroom standard units, some with whirlpools. 4 stories, interior corridors. *Bath:* combo or shower only. **Parking:** on-site. **Amenities:** high-speed Internet, voice mail, irons, hair dryers. **Pool(s):** outdoor. **Leisure Activities:** exercise room. **Guest Services:** valet laundry, wireless Internet. **Business Services:** meeting rooms, business center.

SUMMERFIELD INN BED AND BREAKFAST

Historic Bed
& Breakfast
$165-$210 All Year

Phone: 276/628-5905
Address: 101 W Valley St 24210 **Location:** I-81, exit 17, 0.8 mi w on Cummings St, then just n. **Facility:** Spacious public areas, a huge front porch and a carriage house enhance this 1920s Colonial Revival home with antique furnishings and modern amenities. Smoke free premises. 7 one-bedroom standard units, some with whirlpools. 1-2 stories (no elevator), interior corridors. *Bath:* combo or shower only. **Parking:** on-site. **Terms:** check-in 4 pm. **Amenities:** hair dryers. **Guest Services:** wireless Internet.

SUPER 8 MOTEL OF ABINGDON   *Book at AAA.com*   **Phone:** 276/676-3329

Motel

Rates not provided

Address: 298 Towne Centre Dr 24210 **Location:** I-81, exit 17, just ne. **Facility:** 51 one-bedroom standard units. 3 stories (no elevator), interior corridors. **Parking:** on-site. **Amenities:** safes (fee), hair dryers. **Guest Services:** valet laundry, wireless Internet.

VICTORIA & ALBERT INN   **Phone:** 276/623-1281

Historic Bed & Breakfast

$125-$165 All Year

Address: 224 Oak Hill St 24210 **Location:** I-81, exit 17, 0.8 mi w on Cummings St, 0.3 mi e on Valley St, then just n. Located in a quiet residential area. **Facility:** In a neighborhood setting within walking distance to the famous Barter Theatre, the 1892 Victorian features a pretty porch and garden areas. Smoke free premises. 5 one-bedroom standard units, some with whirlpools. 3 stories (no elevator), interior corridors. **Parking:** on-site. **Terms:** check-in 3:30 pm, 2 night minimum stay - seasonal and/or weekends, age restrictions may apply, 3 day cancellation notice. **Amenities:** video library, CD players, hair dryers. *Some:* irons. **Leisure Activities:** *Fee:* massage. **Business Services:** PC, fax. **Cards:** AX, DS, MC, VI.

WHITE BIRCHES INN   **Phone:** 276/676-2140

Historic Bed & Breakfast

$149-$175 All Year

Address: 268 Whites Mill Rd 24210 **Location:** I-81, exit 17, 0.8 mi w on Cummings St, 0.7 mi n on Valley St, then just n. **Facility:** Find icon art throughout this 1901 Cape Cod-style house with a library, elegant breakfast area, fine parlors and rooms with four-poster beds. Designated smoking area. 5 one-bedroom standard units, some with whirlpools. 2 stories (no elevator), interior corridors. *Bath:* combo or shower only. **Parking:** on-site. **Terms:** 2-3 night minimum stay - weekends, age restrictions may apply, 10 day cancellation notice-fee imposed. **Amenities:** video library, CD players, high-speed Internet, irons, hair dryers. **Guest Services:** wireless Internet. **Cards:** MC, VI.

─── WHERE TO DINE ───

ALISON'S RESTAURANT   **Phone:** 276/628-8002

American

$6-$21

The restaurant blends hometown cooking with friendly, delightful service. The menu selection is huge. Casual dress. **Hours:** 11 am-9 pm. Closed: 12/25. **Address:** 1220 W Main St 24210 **Location:** I-81, exit 14, just w. **Parking:** on-site. **Cards:** MC, VI.

BELLA'S   **Phone:** 276/628-8101

American

$6-$19

Patrons can look forward to a fun dining experience. Western New York recipes resurface here in the lower Shenandoah Valley. Quality and consistency are hallmarks. Casual dress. **Bar:** Beer only. **Hours:** 11 am-11 pm. **Address:** 872 E Main St 24210 **Location:** I-81, exit 19 (US 11), just w. **Parking:** on-site. **Cards:** MC, VI.

THE DINING ROOM   **Phone:** 276/628-9151

Regional American

$8-$32

In a pre-Civil War mansion that later served as a girl's college, the moderately upscale restaurant serves fine cuisine with elements of Southern tradition. Those who visit on Friday might opt for the seafood buffet. Dressy casual. **Bar:** Full bar. **Reservations:** suggested. **Hours:** 7-10 am, 11:30-2 & 5-9 pm; Sunday brunch. Closed: 12/25. **Address:** 150 W Main 24210 **Location:** I-81, exit 17, 0.7 mi n on Cummings St, then just e; in The Martha Washington Inn & Spa. **Parking:** on-site. **Cards:** AX, DC, DS, MC, VI. **Historic**

THE PEPPERMILL RESTAURANT & LOUNGE   **Phone:** 276/623-0530

American

$8-$22

Innovative cuisine in a casual atmosphere with good artwork and background music. The Peppermill Restaurant & Lounge has a diverse menu and good wine list. Casual dress. **Bar:** Full bar. **Hours:** 11 am-9 pm. Closed: 12/25; also Sun. **Address:** 967 W Main St 24210 **Location:** I-81, exit 14, just n. **Parking:** on-site. **Cards:** AX, CB, DC, DS, JC, MC, VI.

THE TAVERN   **Phone:** 276/628-1118

American

$16-$32

A restored 1779 stagecoach stop, the dark tavern has brick floors and historic decor. Much of the seating is in the enclosed rear patio or on the second-floor porch. An eclectic selection of beers complements a mix of American and German dishes. Casual dress. **Bar:** Full bar. **Reservations:** suggested. **Hours:** 5 pm-10 pm. Closed major holidays; also Sun. **Address:** 222 E Main St 24210 **Location:** I-81, exit 17, 0.7 mi n on Cummings St, then 0.5 mi e. **Parking:** street. **Cards:** AX, DS, MC, VI. **Historic**

WITHERS HARDWARE RESTAURANT   *Menu on AAA.com*   **Phone:** 276/628-1111

American

$5-$24

The restored 1895 hardware store features turn-of-the-20th-century, Victorian-style decor and lots of brass, greenery and dark wood. The restaurant is known for prime rib, fresh seafood and attentive servers. The atmosphere is quiet, relaxed and cozy. Casual dress. **Bar:** Full bar. **Hours:** 11 am-10 pm. Closed: 12/25. **Address:** 260 W Main St 24210 **Location:** I-81, exit 17, 1.2 mi n on US 11; center. **Parking:** street. **Cards:** AX, CB, DC, DS, JC, MC, VI. **Historic**

ALEXANDRIA —*See District Of Columbia p. 500.*

ALTAVISTA pop. 3,425

———— WHERE TO STAY ————

COMFORT INN   *Book at AAA.com*   Phone: (434)369-4000

Small-scale Hotel
$63-$200 All Year

Address: 1558 Main St 24517 **Location:** US 29 business route, at jct US 29. **Facility:** 65 one-bedroom standard units, some with whirlpools. 2 stories (no elevator), interior corridors. **Parking:** on-site. **Amenities:** high-speed Internet, dual phone lines, irons, hair dryers. **Pool(s):** outdoor. **Leisure Activities:** miniature golf, horseshoes. **Guest Services:** valet and coin laundry, wireless Internet. **Business Services:** fax. **Cards:** AX, DS, MC, VI.

ASK S⊘ ⛉ ⛵ ⊞ ⛺ ⊟ ⊡ ⊑ / SOME UNITS FEE ⌂ ✕ FEE VCR

HOLIDAY INN EXPRESS   *Book at AAA.com*   Phone: 434/369-4070

Small-scale Hotel
$78-$99 All Year

Address: 1557 Main St 24517 **Location:** US 29 business route, at jct US 29. **Facility:** 66 one-bedroom standard units, some with whirlpools. 2 stories (no elevator), interior corridors. **Bath:** combo or shower only. **Parking:** on-site. **Amenities:** high-speed Internet, dual phone lines, voice mail, irons, hair dryers. **Leisure Activities:** exercise room. **Guest Services:** valet and coin laundry, wireless Internet. **Business Services:** meeting rooms, business center. **Cards:** AX, CB, DC, DS, MC, VI.

ASK S⊘ CALL ⊛M ⛺ ⊑ / SOME UNITS ✕ ⊟ ⊡

———— WHERE TO DINE ————

BETTY'S KITCHEN   Phone: 434/369-5363

Regional American
$5-$10

The restaurant offers a true Southern home-style dining experience and serves such favorites as country-fried steak, cornbread and, on Mondays, chicken and dumplings. For pure refreshment, it's hard to beat a cool glass of sweet tea with a slice of one of the fine pies. A collection of nostalgic tin advertising signs from the '40s and '50s decks the walls of the simple spot. Casual dress. **Hours:** 7 am-8 pm, Fri & Sat-8:30 pm. Closed: 11/27, 12/25. **Address:** 534 Main St 24517 **Location:** Center. **Parking:** on-site. **Cards:** AX, DS, MC, VI.

AMELIA

———— WHERE TO STAY ————

WINTERHAM PLANTATION   Phone: 804/561-4519

Historic Bed
& Breakfast
$99-$247 All Year

Address: 11441 Grub Hill Church Rd 23002 **Location:** 1.7 mi n on SR 609 from US 360. **Facility:** This 1840 historic farmhouse, with original wood plank floors, sits amid rolling hills along General Lee's retreat route and features Civil War relics. Smoke free premises. 4 units. 3 one- and 1 two-bedroom standard units, some with whirlpools. 1 two-bedroom suite. 2 stories, interior corridors. **Bath:** combo or shower only. **Parking:** on-site. **Terms:** check-in 4 pm, cancellation fee imposed. **Amenities:** *Some:* hair dryers.

✕ ☎ / SOME UNITS VCR ⊟ ⊡

ANNANDALE —See District Of Columbia p. 509.

APPOMATTOX pop. 1,761

———— WHERE TO STAY ————

THE BABCOCK HOUSE   Phone: 434/352-7532

Historic Bed
& Breakfast
$105-$140 All Year

Address: 250 Oakleigh Ave 24522 **Location:** US 460 business route, just s. **Facility:** Featuring a grand second-floor veranda, this restored turn-of-the-20th-century inn offers spacious lodgings with fine antiques and wide-plank floors. Smoke free premises. 6 units. 5 one-bedroom standard units. 1 one-bedroom suite. 2 stories (no elevator), interior corridors. **Bath:** combo or shower only. **Parking:** on-site. **Terms:** 3 day cancellation notice-fee imposed. **Amenities:** hair dryers. **Dining:** restaurant, see separate listing. **Cards:** AX, DS, MC, VI.

S⊘ ⦀ ✕ ⊑ / SOME UNITS VCR

SUPER 8 MOTEL   *Book at AAA.com*   Phone: 434/352-2339

Motel
Rates not provided

Address: 7571 Richmond Hwy 24522 **Location:** US 460, just w of jct US 26. **Facility:** 44 one-bedroom standard units. 2 stories (no elevator), interior corridors. **Parking:** on-site. **Amenities:** high-speed Internet, safes (fee), hair dryers. **Guest Services:** wireless Internet. **Business Services:** meeting rooms.

⦀ ⛺ ⊟ / SOME UNITS ✕ ⊡

———— WHERE TO DINE ————

THE BABCOCK HOUSE   Phone: 434/352-7532

Regional American
$5-$19

The charming historic inn prepares such lunch choices as fresh salads, sandwiches and daily soups. Desserts, especially hummingbird cake, are a highlight not to be missed. Finer entrees and a more romantic mood appear for evening meals. Casual dress. **Bar:** Beer & wine. **Reservations:** required, for dinner. **Hours:** 11 am-1:30 pm, Sun-2 pm; Tues-Sat dinner by reservation. Closed: Mon & for lunch Sat. **Address:** 106 Oakleigh Ave 24522 **Location:** US 460 business route, just s; in The Babcock House. **Parking:** on-site. **Cards:** AX, DS, MC, VI.

AC

ARLINGTON —See District Of Columbia p. 509.

ASHBURN —See District Of Columbia p. 522.

ASHLAND —*See Richmond p. 872.*

ATKINS pop. 1,138

——— WHERE TO STAY ———

COMFORT INN

AAA SAVE
◈◈◈ ◈◈◈

Small-scale Hotel
$80 All Year

Book great rates at AAA.com   **Phone:** 276/783-2144

Address: 5558 Lee Hwy 24311 **Location:** I-81, exit 50, just w, then just n on US 11. **Facility:** 50 one-bedroom standard units. 2 stories (no elevator), interior corridors. **Parking:** on-site. **Amenities:** high-speed Internet, irons, hair dryers. **Guest Services:** wireless Internet. **Cards:** AX, CB, DC, DS, JC, MC, VI.

[icons]

——— WHERE TO DINE ———

ATKINS DINER

◈

American
$4-$12

Phone: 276/783-8091

Southern hospitality and comfort food in a relaxed setting with easy access off the Interstate await at the Atkins Diner. Casual dress. **Hours:** 7 am-7 pm. Closed: 11/27, 12/25; also Sun. **Address:** 5315 Lee Hwy 24311 **Location:** I-81, exit 50, just w, then just s on US 11. **Parking:** on-site.

BARBOURSVILLE

——— WHERE TO DINE ———

BLACKHAWK GRILL

◈◈◈

American
$15-$32

Phone: 304/736-9494

Appointed in an English style, the restaurant's dining room is bathed in light that streams in through stained-glass windows. Creativity marks the entrees, as well as the gourmet desserts. Casual dress. **Bar:** Full bar. **Reservations:** suggested. **Hours:** 5 pm-10 pm. Closed: 3/23; also Sun & Mon. **Address:** 646 Central Ave 25504 **Location:** I-64, exit 18, just n. **Parking:** street. **Cards:** AX, MC, VI.

[icon]

BEDFORD pop. 6,299

——— WHERE TO STAY ———

SUPER 8 MOTEL

◈◈

Small-scale Hotel
Rates not provided

Book at AAA.com   **Phone:** 540/587-0100

Address: 842 Sword Beach Ln 24523 **Location:** 1.5 mi w on US 221 and 460. **Facility:** 58 one-bedroom standard units, some with whirlpools. 2 stories (no elevator), interior corridors. *Bath:* combo or shower only. **Parking:** on-site. **Amenities:** hair dryers. **Business Services:** meeting rooms.

[icons]

BIG STONE GAP pop. 4,856

——— WHERE TO STAY ———

COMFORT INN

◈◈◈

Small-scale Hotel
$85-$250 3/1-8/31
$85-$160 9/1-2/28

Book at AAA.com   **Phone:** (276)523-5911

Address: 1928B Wildcat Rd 24219 **Location:** US 23, just n. **Facility:** 61 one-bedroom standard units, some with whirlpools. 3 stories, interior corridors. *Bath:* combo or shower only. **Parking:** on-site. **Amenities:** irons, hair dryers. **Pool(s):** heated indoor. **Leisure Activities:** exercise room. **Guest Services:** coin laundry, wireless Internet. **Business Services:** meeting rooms. **Cards:** AX, CB, DC, DS, JC, MC, VI.

[icons]

COUNTRY INN MOTEL

AAA SAVE
◈

Motel
$45-$52 All Year

Phone: (276)523-0374

Address: 627 Gilley Ave 24219 **Location:** US 23, 1 mi w on US 23 business route and 58A. **Facility:** 42 one-bedroom standard units. 2 stories (no elevator), exterior corridors. **Parking:** on-site. **Leisure Activities:** basketball, horseshoes. **Cards:** AX, DC, DS, MC, VI. **Free Special Amenities:** local telephone calls and early check-in/late check-out.

[icons]

BLACKSBURG pop. 39,573

——— WHERE TO STAY ———

COMFORT INN

AAA SAVE
◈◈◈

Small-scale Hotel
$100-$160 3/1-11/30
$80-$100 12/1-2/28

Book great rates at AAA.com   **Phone:** 540/951-1500

Address: 3705 S Main St 24060 **Location:** 3.5 mi s on US 460, jct US 460 Bypass. **Facility:** 80 one-bedroom standard units, some with whirlpools. 4 stories, interior corridors. **Parking:** on-site. **Terms:** 7 day cancellation notice. **Amenities:** high-speed Internet, voice mail, safes, irons, hair dryers. **Pool(s):** heated outdoor. **Leisure Activities:** exercise room. **Guest Services:** valet laundry, wireless Internet. **Business Services:** meeting rooms. **Cards:** AX, DC, DS, MC, VI. **Free Special Amenities:** expanded continental breakfast and high-speed Internet.

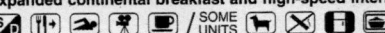

HAWTHORN SUITES BLACKSBURG/UNIVERSITY   *Book at AAA.com*   Phone: 540/552-5636

Small-scale Hotel
Rates not provided

Address: 1020 Plantation Rd 24060 **Location:** I-81, exit 118 (US 460 Bypass), follow signs for Virginia Tech, pass main entrance, right on Prices Fork Rd (SR 412). **Facility:** 94 one-bedroom standard units. 5 stories, interior corridors. *Bath:* combo or shower only. **Parking:** on-site. **Terms:** check-in 4 pm. **Amenities:** video games, high-speed Internet, voice mail, irons, hair dryers. **Pool(s):** indoor. **Leisure Activities:** exercise room. **Guest Services:** valet and coin laundry, wireless Internet. **Business Services:** meeting rooms, business center.

CALL ⬛M 🏊 ✕ 📷 🛢 🖥 🖵 / SOME UNITS VCR

HOLIDAY INN BLACKSBURG   *Book at AAA.com*   Phone: (540)552-7001

Small-scale Hotel
$99-$199 3/1-11/23
$89-$159 11/24-2/28

Address: 900 Prices Fork Rd 24060 **Location:** 0.7 mi e on Prices Fork Rd (SR 412) from jct US 460 Bypass. Located adjacent to Virginia Tech campus. **Facility:** 148 one-bedroom standard units. 2 stories (no elevator), interior corridors. *Bath:* combo or shower only. **Parking:** on-site. **Amenities:** high-speed Internet, dual phone lines, voice mail, safes (fee), irons, hair dryers. **Pool(s):** heated indoor/outdoor. **Leisure Activities:** tennis court, exercise room, horseshoes, volleyball. **Guest Services:** valet and coin laundry, wireless Internet. **Business Services:** meeting rooms, business center. **Cards:** AX, DS, MC, VI.

ASK S🅳 🅳 🍴 Ⅱ CALL ⬛M 🏊 ✕ 📷 🛢 🖥 🖵 / SOME UNITS ✕

——— WHERE TO DINE ———

BACKSTREETS RESTAURANT   Phone: 540/552-6712

American
$7-$20

Specialties at the neighborhood restaurant include Tuscan shrimp, chicken Marsala, pizza and tiramisu. Casual dress. **Bar:** Beer only. **Hours:** 11 am-11 pm, Fri & Sat-midnight. Closed major holidays. **Address:** 207 S Main St 24060 **Location:** Center. **Parking:** on-site. **Cards:** AX, DS, MC, VI.

🚬

BOUDREAUX'S CAJUN RESTAURANT   Phone: 540/961-2330

Cajun
$5-$18

Cajun dishes are the rage in the simple setting. The kitchen accommodates requests for extra-hot food. Casual dress. **Bar:** Beer only. **Hours:** 11 am-11 pm. Closed major holidays. **Address:** 205 N Main St 24060 **Location:** Center. **Parking:** on-site. **Cards:** AX, DC, DS, MC, VI.

🚬

MAXWELL'S   Phone: 540/552-3300

American
$10-$26

Maxwell's offers a handsome, relaxed and cozy atmosphere. Modern plate presentations, taste and an award winning chef. Casual dress. **Bar:** Full bar. **Reservations:** suggested, weekends. **Hours:** 11:30 am-10 pm, Sat from 5 pm. Closed: 12/25; also Sun. **Address:** 1204 N Main St 24060 **Location:** 0.5 mi n; between Northview and Patrick Henry sts; center. **Parking:** on-site. **Cards:** AX, CB, DC, DS, JC, MC, VI.

🚬

NERV RESTAURANT & LOUNGE   Phone: 540/961-3004

American
$7-$25

The modern, sophisticated restaurant and lounge nurtures an upscale atmosphere. Eclectic menu choices are moderately priced. Casual dress. **Bar:** Full bar. **Reservations:** suggested, weekends. **Hours:** 11 am-10 pm, Fri & Sat-11 pm. Closed: 12/25. **Address:** 221 Progress St NE 24060 **Location:** On Progress St NE; between Main and South sts; center. **Parking:** on-site. **Cards:** AX, CB, DC, DS, JC, MC, VI.

🚬

VINCENT'S RISTORANTE   Phone: 540/552-9000

Italian
$6-$22

The family-operated Italian eatery prepares many pasta selections, fresh salads, bread and desserts in a setting that emanates Old World charm. Casual dress. **Bar:** Full bar. **Reservations:** suggested. **Hours:** 4:30 pm-9:30 pm, Fri 11:30 am-10 pm, Sat 4:30 pm-10 pm, Sun 4 pm-9 pm. Closed: Mon. **Address:** 1200 S Main St 24060 **Location:** Jct US 460 and 460 business route, 2.1 mi w on US 460 business route. **Parking:** on-site. **Cards:** AX, DS, MC, VI.

ZEPPOLI'S ITALIAN RESTAURANT   Phone: 540/953-2000

Italian
$6-$20

The sauces, the bread, the pasta and the sausage are all made on the premises to ensure absolute freshness. Casual dress. **Bar:** Full bar. **Hours:** 11 am-10 pm, Sat from 4 pm. Closed: 12/24, 12/25. **Address:** 810 University City Blvd 24060 **Location:** 0.6 mi e on Prices Fork Rd (SR 412) from jct US 460 Bypass. **Parking:** on-site. **Cards:** AX, DS, MC, VI.

BLUEFIELD pop. 5,078

——— WHERE TO STAY ———

COMFORT INN-BLUEFIELD   *Book great rates at AAA.com*   Phone: (276)326-3688

AAA SAVE

Small-scale Hotel
$67-$115 All Year

Address: 38769 Govenor G C Peery Hwy 24605 **Location:** I-77, exit 1, 2.7 mi nw on SR 52, then 9.7 mi w on US 460. **Facility:** 61 one-bedroom standard units. 2 stories (no elevator), interior corridors. **Parking:** on-site. **Amenities:** voice mail, irons, hair dryers. **Pool(s):** heated outdoor. **Leisure Activities:** picnic tables, basketball. *Fee:* golf privileges. **Guest Services:** wireless Internet. **Cards:** AX, CB, DC, DS, JC, MC, VI. **Free Special Amenities:** expanded continental breakfast and high-speed Internet.

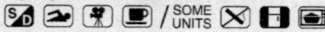

S🅳 🏊 📷 🖵 / SOME UNITS ✕ 🛢 🖥

BRIDGEWATER pop. 5,203

––––––– **WHERE TO DINE** –––––––

BOB-A-REA'S

Italian
$6-$18

Phone: 540/828-3433

The family-operated hometown pasta place offers a fun, casual setting ideal for families. Homemade specials make menu appearances daily. Casual dress. **Bar:** Beer only. **Hours:** 6 am-10 pm, Sun from 1 pm. Closed: 12/25; also Mon. **Address:** 305 N Main St 22812 **Location:** Just n. **Parking:** on-site. **Cards:** AX, CB, DC, DS, JC, MC, VI.

NORTH RIVER GRILL

American
$6-$20

Phone: 540/828-0700

North River Grill features favorites from the Shenandoah Valley like fried chicken and peanut soup. Casual dress. **Bar:** Full bar. **Hours:** 11 am-10 pm. Closed: 1/1, 11/27, 12/25; also Mon. **Address:** 101 N Main St 22812 **Location:** Center. **Parking:** street. **Cards:** AX, CB, DC, DS, JC, MC, VI.

BRISTOL pop. 17,367

––––––– **WHERE TO STAY** –––––––

BUDGET HOST INN

(AAA) [SAVE]

Motel
$42-$195 All Year

Phone: 276/669-5187

Address: 1209 W State St 24201 **Location:** I-81, exit 1, 2 mi s on SR 421. **Facility:** 23 one-bedroom standard units, some with whirlpools. 1 story, exterior corridors. **Parking:** on-site. **Cards:** AX, DS, MC, VI. **Free Special Amenities: local telephone calls and early check-in/late check-out.**

COURTYARD BY MARRIOTT   *Book great rates at AAA.com*

(AAA) [SAVE]

Small-scale Hotel
$105-$135 All Year

Phone: 276/591-4400

Address: 3169 Linden Dr 24202 **Location:** I-81, exit 7, just w. **Facility:** Smoke free premises. 175 one-bedroom standard units, some with whirlpools. 5 stories, interior corridors. **Bath:** combo or shower only. **Parking:** on-site. **Amenities:** video games, high-speed Internet, dual phone lines, voice mail, irons, hair dryers. **Pool(s):** heated indoor. **Leisure Activities:** whirlpool, exercise room. **Guest Services:** valet and coin laundry, wireless Internet. **Business Services:** meeting rooms, business center. **Cards:** AX, DC, DS, MC, VI. **Free Special Amenities: newspaper and high-speed Internet.**

AAA Benefit:
Members save 5% off of the best available rate.

ECONO LODGE   *Book great rates at AAA.com*

(AAA) [SAVE]

Motel
$79-$109 3/1-9/30
$69-$99 10/1-2/28

Phone: (276)466-2112

Address: 912 Commonwealth Ave 24201 **Location:** I-81, exit 3, 1.5 mi e. Located in a commercial area. **Facility:** 47 one-bedroom standard units. 2 stories (no elevator), exterior corridors. **Parking:** on-site. **Amenities:** safes (fee). *Some:* irons, hair dryers. **Guest Services:** wireless Internet. **Cards:** AX, DC, DS, MC, VI. **Free Special Amenities: continental breakfast and high-speed Internet.**

HOLIDAY INN HOTEL & SUITES   *Book at AAA.com*

Large-scale Hotel
$104 All Year

Phone: (276)466-4100

Address: 3005 Linden Dr 24202 **Location:** I-81, exit 7, just w. **Facility:** 226 one-bedroom standard units, some with whirlpools. 10 stories, interior corridors. **Bath:** combo or shower only. **Parking:** on-site. **Amenities:** voice mail, irons, hair dryers. *Some:* high-speed Internet. **Pool(s):** heated outdoor. **Leisure Activities:** whirlpool, exercise room. **Guest Services:** valet and coin laundry, wireless Internet. **Business Services:** conference facilities, PC, fax (fee). **Cards:** AX, CB, DC, DS, JC, MC, VI.

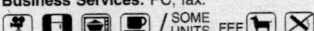

KNIGHTS INN   *Book at AAA.com*

Motel
Rates not provided

Phone: 276/591-5090

Address: 2221 Euclid Ave 24201 **Location:** I-81, exit 1, just e. **Facility:** 38 one-bedroom standard units. 2 stories (no elevator), exterior corridors. **Parking:** on-site. **Amenities:** *Some:* irons, hair dryers. **Business Services:** PC, fax.

LA QUINTA INN BRISTOL   *Book great rates at AAA.com*

Phone: (276)669-9353

AAA SAVE

Small-scale Hotel
$89-$129 All Year

Address: 1014 Old Airport Rd 24201 **Location:** I-81, exit 7, just e. **Facility:** 123 one-bedroom standard units. 4 stories, exterior corridors. *Bath:* combo or shower only. **Parking:** on-site. **Amenities:** video games, high-speed Internet, voice mail, irons, hair dryers. **Pool(s):** outdoor. **Guest Services:** valet laundry, wireless Internet. **Business Services:** meeting rooms, business center. **Cards:** AX, DC, DS, MC, VI. **Free Special Amenities: expanded continental breakfast and high-speed Internet.**

LA QUINTA
INNS & SUITES

AAA Benefit:
Members save 10%
everyday.

MICROTEL INN & SUITES   *Book at AAA.com*

Phone: (276)669-8164

Small-scale Hotel
$75-$260 All Year

Address: 131 Bristol Rd E 24201 **Location:** I-81, exit 7 northbound, just w; exit southbound, just e. **Facility:** 65 one-bedroom standard units, some with whirlpools. 3 stories, interior corridors. **Parking:** on-site. **Amenities:** high-speed Internet. **Pool(s):** heated indoor. **Leisure Activities:** whirlpool. **Guest Services:** wireless Internet. **Cards:** AX, DS, MC, VI.

MOTEL 6 #4125

Phone: 276/466-6060

Small-scale Hotel
$58-$75 All Year

Address: 21561 Clear Creek Rd 24202 **Location:** I-81, exit 7, 0.3 mi w. **Facility:** 53 one-bedroom standard units. 3 stories, interior corridors. *Bath:* combo or shower only. **Parking:** on-site. **Terms:** cancellation fee imposed. **Amenities:** high-speed Internet. **Guest Services:** coin laundry, wireless Internet. **Cards:** AX, DS, MC, VI.

SUPER 8 MOTEL   *Book great rates at AAA.com*

Phone: 276/466-8800

AAA SAVE

Small-scale Hotel
Rates not provided

Address: 2139 Lee Hwy 24201 **Location:** I-81, exit 5, just s. **Facility:** 62 one-bedroom standard units. 3 stories (no elevator), interior corridors. **Parking:** on-site. **Guest Services:** wireless Internet. **Free Special Amenities: continental breakfast and high-speed Internet.**

———— WHERE TO DINE ————

ATHEN'S STEAK HOUSE

Phone: 276/466-8271

Steak House
$13-$23

The flavors of America and Greece mingle in selections on the restaurant's tempting menu. Most popular are the steaks and homemade desserts, such as baklava and apple pie. Parquet and carpet floors, along with candles and light music, create ambience. Casual dress. **Bar:** Full bar. **Reservations:** accepted. **Hours:** 4 pm-10 pm. Closed: 1/1, 11/27, 12/25; also Sun. **Address:** 105 Goodson St 24201 **Location:** I-81, exit 3, 2.6 mi s to State St, 0.6 mi e, then just n. **Parking:** on-site. **Cards:** AX, MC, VI.

LOS ARCOS

Phone: 276/591-3180

Mexican
$6-$15

Meticulously prepared Mexican cuisine is served with a smile and a heaping helping of piping hot chips and salsa. Casual dress. **Bar:** Full bar. **Hours:** 11 am-9 pm. Closed: 12/25. **Address:** 3175 Linden Dr 24201 **Location:** I-81, exit 7, just w. **Parking:** on-site. **Cards:** AX, CB, DC, DS, JC, MC, VI.

BROADWAY pop. 2,192

———— WHERE TO DINE ————

FRANCESCO'S RISTORANTE ITALIANO

Phone: 540/901-9799

Italian
$8-$20

The casual restaurant's Italian atmosphere and cuisine are enjoyable. On the menu are many specialty pastas and pizzas. Casual dress. **Bar:** Full bar. **Hours:** 10:30 am-9 pm. Closed: 1/1, 12/25. **Address:** 116 S Main St 22815 **Location:** I-81, exit 257, 4.1 mi w on SR 259, then just s on SR 42. **Parking:** on-site. **Cards:** AX, CB, DC, DS, JC, MC, VI.

BUCHANAN pop. 1,233

———— WHERE TO STAY ————

WATTSTULL INN

Phone: 540/254-1551

AAA SAVE

Small-scale Hotel
$55-$68 All Year

Address: 130 Arcadia Rd 24066 **Location:** I-81, exit 168, just e on SR 614. Located in a quiet rural area. **Facility:** 26 one-bedroom standard units. 1 story, exterior corridors. **Parking:** on-site. **Terms:** 7 day cancellation notice-fee imposed. **Pool(s):** outdoor. **Cards:** DS, MC, VI.

——— **WHERE TO DINE** ———

COPPER TOP

American
$6-$18

Phone: 540/254-6005

Hometown pride and friendliness combine with homemade recipes to give patrons a nice dining experience. Casual dress. **Bar:** Full bar. **Hours:** 11 am-10 pm. Closed: 11/27, 12/25. **Address:** 630 Lowe St 24066 **Location:** Just w; center. **Parking:** on-site.

FANZARELLI'S

Italian
$9-$20

Phone: 540/254-3070

The aromas of garlic and bread and wonderful murals on the wall heighten the senses. The pasta is fresh and the people genuinely friendly. Casual dress. **Bar:** Full bar. **Hours:** 11 am-9 pm. Closed: 12/25; also Mon. **Address:** 19857 Main St 24066 **Location:** I-81, exit 167, 2.1 mi s on US 11. **Parking:** on-site. **Cards:** AX, CB, DC, DS, JC, MC, VI.

THE OLD BUCHANAN FAMILY RESTAURANT

American
$6-$18

Phone: 540/254-1600

In the center of historic downtown, the family restaurant is known for great food, warm people and homemade pies. Casual dress. **Hours:** 11 am-8 pm, Sun-3 pm. Closed: 1/1, 11/27, 12/25; also Mon. **Address:** 19758 Main St 24066 **Location:** Center. **Parking:** on-site. **Cards:** MC, VI.

BURKE —See District Of Columbia p. 523.

BURKEVILLE pop. 489

——— **WHERE TO STAY** ———

COMFORT INN BURKEVILLE   *Book at AAA.com*

Small-scale Hotel
$72-$121 All Year

Phone: (434)767-3750

Address: 419 N Agnew St 23922 **Location:** On US 460, just e of jct US 360. **Facility:** 60 one-bedroom standard units, some with whirlpools. 2 stories, interior corridors. *Bath:* combo or shower only. **Parking:** on-site. **Amenities:** high-speed Internet, dual phone lines, voice mail, irons, hair dryers. **Pool(s):** heated indoor. **Leisure Activities:** exercise room. *Fee:* game room. **Guest Services:** coin laundry. **Business Services:** meeting rooms, fax. **Cards:** AX, DC, DS, MC, VI.

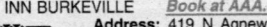

CAPE CHARLES pop. 1,134

——— **WHERE TO STAY** ———

SUNSET BEACH RESORT

Small-scale Hotel
$79-$109 All Year

Phone: 757/331-1776

Address: 32246 Lankford Hwy 23310 **Location:** US 13, just n of the Chesapeake Bay Bridge Tunnel. **Facility:** 73 units. 65 one-bedroom standard units. 8 one-bedroom suites. 2 stories (no elevator), exterior corridors. *Bath:* combo or shower only. **Parking:** on-site. **Terms:** cancellation fee imposed. **Amenities:** high-speed Internet, irons, hair dryers. **Dining:** 2 restaurants. **Pool(s):** outdoor. **Leisure Activities:** fishing, sea kayak, playground, horseshoes, volleyball. **Guest Services:** coin laundry, wireless Internet. **Business Services:** meeting rooms, business center. **Cards:** AX, DS, MC, VI. **Free Special Amenities:** full breakfast and local telephone calls.

——— **WHERE TO DINE** ———

**MARIAH'S AT TOWER HILL BED &
BREAKFAST INN**   *Menu on AAA.com*

American
$18-$28

Phone: 757/331-1700

Guests can dine in Colonial elegance in the main dining room or in the romantic wine cellar at the elegant inn. The chef masterfully combines his fine training with fresh local produce and Chesapeake Bay seafood. Casual dress. **Bar:** Full bar. **Reservations:** suggested. **Hours:** 5:30 pm-9 pm. Closed: 12/24, 12/25; also Sun & Mon. **Address:** 3018 Bowden Landing 23310 **Location:** US 13, just w on SR 184 to Parsons Circle, just n; in Tower Hill Estates, follow signs; in Tower Hill Bed Breakfast & Inn. **Parking:** on-site. **Cards:** AX, MC, VI. **Country Inn**

STINGRAY'S RESTAURANT

Seafood
$4-$23

Phone: 757/331-2505

Guests can fill up the car at the gas station, then come inside to fill up themselves. Locals and travelers alike flock to the crowded spot for local seafood and Southern favorites cooked the old-fashioned way. Prices are reasonable. Casual dress. **Bar:** Beer & wine. **Hours:** 6 am-9 pm. Closed: 11/27, 12/24, 12/25. **Address:** 26507 Lankford Hwy 23310 **Location:** US 13. **Parking:** on-site. **Cards:** DS, MC, VI.

CENTRAL WILLIAMSBURG —See Williamsburg, Jamestown & Yorktown p. 928.

CENTREVILLE —See District Of Columbia p. 523.

CHANTILLY —See District Of Columbia p. 524.

CHARLES CITY —See Williamsburg, Jamestown & Yorktown p. 949.

CHARLOTTESVILLE pop. 45,049

─── WHERE TO STAY ───

BEST WESTERN-CAVALIER INN   *Book great rates at AAA.com*   Phone: 434/296-8111

AAA SAVE
◊◊◊
Small-scale Hotel
Rates not provided

Address: 105 N Emmet St 22903 **Location:** Jct US 29 and 250 Bypass, 1.3 mi s on US 29 business route. **Facility:** 118 one-bedroom standard units. 5 stories, interior/exterior corridors. **Parking:** on-site. **Amenities:** high-speed Internet, voice mail, irons, hair dryers. **Pool(s):** outdoor. **Guest Services:** valet laundry, area transportation-University of Virginia Hospital, wireless Internet. **Business Services:** meeting rooms, business center. **Free Special Amenities:** continental breakfast and local telephone calls. *(See color ad below)*

AAA Benefit:
Members save 10% everyday, plus an exclusive frequent stay program.

[CALL] [&M] [🏊] [🚐] [🎬] [💻] / SOME UNITS [✕] [🔒] [📠]

BOAR'S HEAD INN

AAA SAVE
◊◊◊◊
Resort
Large-scale Hotel
$185-$425 3/1-11/30
$175-$425 12/1-2/28

Book great rates at AAA.com   Phone: (434)296-2181
Address: Rt 250 W 22903 **Location:** Jct US 29 Bypass, 1 mi w on US 250. Located in a quiet area. **Facility:** On 53 acres in the Blue Ridge foothills, this country-style resort offers traditional rooms, some of which overlook a lake with swans. 171 one-bedroom standard units, some with whirlpools. 3 stories, interior/exterior corridors. *Bath:* combo or shower only. **Parking:** on-site. **Terms:** check-in 4 pm, 7 day cancellation notice-fee imposed. **Amenities:** video games, CD players, high-speed Internet, voice mail, safes, irons, hair dryers. **Dining:** 4 restaurants, also, The Old Mill Room, see separate listing. **Pool(s):** 3 outdoor. **Leisure Activities:** saunas, whirlpool, steamrooms, fishing, driving range, recreation programs, bicycles, hiking trails, playground, spa, sports court, basketball, volleyball. *Fee:* golf-18 holes, 26 tennis courts (12 indoor, 12 lighted), racquetball courts, aerobics. **Guest Services:** valet laundry, area transportation-University of Virginia, wireless Internet. **Business Services:** conference facilities, business center. **Cards:** AX, DC, DS, MC, VI. **Free Special Amenities:** room upgrade (subject to availability with advance reservations) and high-speed Internet.

[S/D] [✈] [🍴] [Y] [♿] CALL [&M] [🚐] [🚐] [✕] [🎬] [🔒] [💻] / SOME UNITS [✕] [📠]

BUDGET INN

Motel
$46-$105 All Year

Phone: (434)293-5141

Address: 140 Emmet St N 22903 **Location:** Jct US 29 and 250 Bypass, 1.3 mi s on US 29 business route. **Facility:** 37 one-bedroom standard units. 2 stories (no elevator), exterior corridors. *Bath:* combo or shower only. **Parking:** on-site. **Terms:** 2 night minimum stay - seasonal, 7 day cancellation notice-fee imposed. **Amenities:** high-speed Internet. **Guest Services:** coin laundry. **Cards:** AX, DS, MC, VI. **Free Special Amenities: continental breakfast and high-speed Internet.** *(See color ad p 694)*

CHARLOTTESVILLE NORTH COURTYARD BY MARRIOTT   *Book great rates at AAA.com*

Small-scale Hotel
$118-$145 All Year

Phone: 434/973-7100

Address: 638 Hillsdale Dr 22901 **Location:** US 29, 1.4 mi n of US 250 Bypass. **Facility:** Smoke free premises. 150 one-bedroom standard units. 2-3 stories, interior corridors. *Bath:* combo or shower only. **Parking:** on-site. **Amenities:** high-speed Internet, voice mail, irons, hair dryers. **Pool(s):** heated indoor. **Leisure Activities:** whirlpool, exercise room. **Guest Services:** coin laundry, wireless Internet. **Business Services:** meeting rooms, fax (fee). **Cards:** AX, DC, DS, MC, VI. **Free Special Amenities: full breakfast and high-speed Internet.**

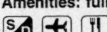 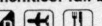

AAA Benefit:
Members save 5% off of the best available rate.

COMFORT INN   *Book great rates at AAA.com*

Small-scale Hotel
$72-$129 All Year

Phone: (434)293-6188

Address: 1807 Emmet St 22901 **Location:** Jct US 250 Bypass, just n on US 29. **Facility:** 64 one-bedroom standard units. 4 stories, interior corridors. *Bath:* combo or shower only. **Amenities:** high-speed Internet, voice mail, safes (fee), irons, hair dryers. **Pool(s):** outdoor. **Guest Services:** valet and coin laundry, wireless Internet. **Business Services:** PC, fax (fee). **Cards:** AX, CB, DC, DS, JC, MC, VI. **Free Special Amenities: expanded continental breakfast and high-speed Internet.**

COMFORT INN MONTICELLO   *Book great rates at AAA.com*

Small-scale Hotel
$59-$299 All Year

Phone: (434)977-3300

Address: 2097 Inn Dr 22911 **Location:** I-64, exit 124 (US 250 E). **Facility:** 99 one-bedroom standard units, some with whirlpools. 2 stories (no elevator), interior corridors. **Parking:** on-site. **Amenities:** high-speed Internet, voice mail, irons, hair dryers. **Pool(s):** outdoor. **Leisure Activities:** miniature golf, exercise room. **Guest Services:** coin laundry, wireless Internet. **Business Services:** meeting rooms, business center. **Cards:** AX, CB, DC, DS, JC, MC, VI. **Free Special Amenities: expanded continental breakfast and high-speed Internet.** *(See color ad below)*

COURTYARD BY MARRIOTT UNIVERSITY MEDICAL CENTER   *Book great rates at AAA.com*

Small-scale Hotel
$111-$141 All Year

Phone: 434/977-1700

Address: 1201 W Main St 22903 **Location:** I-64, exit 120, 2 mi n on 5th St, then left. **Facility:** Smoke free premises. 137 one-bedroom standard units, some with whirlpools. 4 stories, interior corridors. *Bath:* combo or shower only. **Parking:** on-site. **Amenities:** video games, high-speed Internet, voice mail, irons, hair dryers. **Pool(s):** indoor. **Leisure Activities:** whirlpool, exercise room. **Guest Services:** valet and coin laundry, wireless Internet. **Business Services:** meeting rooms, business center. **Cards:** AX, DC, DS, JC, MC, VI.

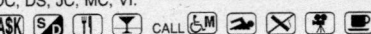
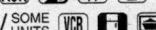

AAA Benefit:
Members save 5% off of the best available rate.

DOUBLETREE HOTEL CHARLOTTESVILLE

Book great rates at AAA.com

Phone: 434/973-2121

 **AAA** SAVE

▼▼▼▼

Small-scale Hotel
Rates not provided

Address: 990 Hilton Heights Rd 22901 **Location:** I-64, exit 118B (US 29), 4 mi n of jct US 250 Bypass. **Facility:** 240 one-bedroom standard units, some with whirlpools. 9 stories, interior corridors. *Bath:* combo or shower only. **Parking:** on-site. **Amenities:** video games, high-speed Internet, voice mail, irons, hair dryers. **Pool(s):** heated outdoor, heated indoor. **Leisure Activities:** whirlpools, 2 tennis courts, exercise room, horseshoes, volleyball. **Guest Services:** valet laundry, airport transportation-Charlottesville/Albemarle Airport, area transportation-within 4 mi, wireless Internet. **Business Services:** conference facilities, business center. **Free Special Amenities: local telephone calls and high-speed Internet.**

ECONO LODGE-NORTH

Book at AAA.com

Phone: 434/295-3185

▼▼▼ ▼▼▼

Small-scale Hotel
Rates not provided

Address: 2014 Holiday Dr 22901 **Location:** US 29, just n of jct US 250 Bypass, then just e. **Facility:** 47 one-bedroom standard units. 2 stories (no elevator), exterior corridors. **Parking:** on-site. **Guest Services:** wireless Internet.

ENGLISH INN OF CHARLOTTESVILLE

Phone: (434)971-9900

AAA SAVE

▼▼▼▼

Small-scale Hotel
$80-$200 3/1-10/31
$90-$180 11/1-2/28

Address: 2000 Morton Dr 22903 **Location:** US 29 business route, just s of jct US 29 and 250 Bypass. **Facility:** Smoke free premises. 88 one-bedroom standard units. 3 stories, interior corridors. **Parking:** on-site. **Amenities:** high-speed Internet, voice mail, irons, hair dryers. **Pool(s):** heated indoor. **Leisure Activities:** sauna, exercise room. **Guest Services:** valet laundry, area transportation-hospital, Amtrak & bus station, wireless Internet. **Business Services:** meeting rooms, fax (fee). **Cards:** AX, DC, DS, MC, VI. **Free Special Amenities: full breakfast and high-speed Internet.** *(See color ad below)*

FAIRFIELD INN BY MARRIOTT

Book great rates at AAA.com

Phone: (434)964-9411

▼▼▼▼

Small-scale Hotel
$94-$109 All Year

Address: 577 Branchlands Blvd 22901 **Location:** US 29 (Emmet St), 1.3 mi n of US 250 Bypass. **Facility:** Smoke free premises. 121 one-bedroom standard units. 3 stories, interior corridors. *Bath:* combo or shower only. **Parking:** on-site. **Terms:** 3 day cancellation notice. **Amenities:** high-speed Internet, voice mail, irons, hair dryers. **Pool(s):** outdoor. **Leisure Activities:** whirlpool. **Guest Services:** valet laundry, wireless Internet. **Business Services:** PC, fax (fee). **Cards:** AX, CB, DC, DS, JC, MC, VI.

AAA Benefit:
Members save 5% off of the best available rate.

THE FOXFIELD INN

Phone: 434/923-8892

▼▼▼

Bed & Breakfast
$175-$275 All Year

Address: 2280 Garth Rd 22901 **Location:** US 250 Bypass, 5.4 mi nw on Barracks Rd (which becomes Garth Rd). Located in a rural area. **Facility:** Find hand-crafted furnishings, flower beds, a pond, hammocks and modern conveniences at this restored, 50-year-old inn near the university. Smoke free premises. 5 one-bedroom standard units, some with whirlpools. 1 story, interior corridors. **Parking:** on-site. **Terms:** check-in 4 pm, 2 night minimum stay - weekends, age restrictions may apply, 14 day cancellation notice-fee imposed. **Amenities:** CD players, irons, hair dryers. **Leisure Activities:** whirlpool. **Business Services:** meeting rooms. **Cards:** MC, VI.

HAMPTON INN & SUITES-CHARLOTTESVILLE AT THE UNIVERSITY MEDICAL CENTER

Phone: 434/923-8600

Small-scale Hotel
Rates not provided

Address: 900 W Main St 22903 **Location:** US 29 (Emmet St), 1.4 mi e on US 250 (University Ave). **Facility:** 100 one-bedroom standard units, some with kitchens. 5 stories, interior corridors. *Bath:* combo or shower only. **Parking:** on-site. **Amenities:** high-speed Internet, voice mail, irons, hair dryers. *Some:* DVD players, CD players. **Leisure Activities:** exercise room. **Guest Services:** valet and coin laundry, wireless Internet. **Business Services:** meeting rooms, business center.

HAMPTON INN OF CHARLOTTESVILLE   *Book great rates at AAA.com*

Phone: 434/978-7888

Small-scale Hotel
Rates not provided

Address: 2035 India Rd 22901 **Location:** I-64, exit 118B (US 29), 4 mi on US 29 N/250 Bypass to Washington exit, then 0.5 mi on US 29 N. Located at Seminole Square Shopping Center. **Facility:** 123 one-bedroom standard units. 5 stories, interior corridors. *Bath:* combo or shower only. **Parking:** on-site. **Amenities:** high-speed Internet, voice mail, irons, hair dryers. **Pool(s):** outdoor. **Guest Services:** valet laundry, area transportation, wireless Internet. **Business Services:** meeting rooms, business center.

HILTON GARDEN INN CHARLOTTESVILLE   *Book great rates at AAA.com*

Phone: 434/979-4442

Small-scale Hotel
Rates not provided

Address: 1793 Richmond Rd 22911 **Location:** I-64, exit 124, just n. **Facility:** 124 one-bedroom standard units, some with whirlpools. 4 stories, interior corridors. *Bath:* combo or shower only. **Parking:** on-site. **Amenities:** video games, high-speed Internet, dual phone lines, voice mail, irons, hair dryers. **Pool(s):** heated indoor. **Leisure Activities:** whirlpool, exercise room. **Guest Services:** valet and coin laundry, wireless Internet. **Business Services:** meeting rooms, business center.

HOLIDAY INN-MONTICELLO/CHARLOTTESVILLE   *Book at AAA.com*

Phone: 434/977-5100

Large-scale Hotel
$88-$199 3/1-11/30
$84-$199 12/1-2/28

Address: 1200 5th St SW 22902 **Location:** I-64, exit 120, just n on SR 631. **Facility:** 131 one-bedroom standard units. 6 stories, interior corridors. **Parking:** on-site. **Terms:** check-in 4 pm. **Amenities:** video games, voice mail, irons, hair dryers. **Pool(s):** outdoor. **Leisure Activities:** exercise room. *Fee:* game room. **Guest Services:** coin laundry, wireless Internet. **Business Services:** meeting rooms, business center. **Cards:** AX, CB, DC, DS, JC, MC, VI.

HOLIDAY INN UNIVERSITY AREA & CONFERENCE CENTER   *Book at AAA.com*

Phone: (434)977-7700

Small-scale Hotel
$99-$249 All Year

Address: 1901 Emmet St 22901 **Location:** Jct US 250 Bypass, 0.3 mi n on US 29. **Facility:** 170 one-bedroom standard units. 7 stories, interior corridors. *Bath:* combo or shower only. **Parking:** on-site. **Amenities:** video games, high-speed Internet, voice mail, irons, hair dryers. **Pool(s):** heated indoor. **Leisure Activities:** exercise room. **Guest Services:** valet and coin laundry, area transportation, wireless Internet. **Business Services:** conference facilities, business center. **Cards:** AX, CB, DC, DS, JC, MC, VI.

THE INN AT MONTICELLO

Phone: 434/979-3593

Bed & Breakfast
$145-$245 All Year

Address: 1188 Scottsville Rd (Rt 20) 22902 **Location:** I-64, exit 121, 0.8 mi s on SR 20. Located in a quiet area. **Facility:** In a hilly area near Monticello, this mid-1800s manor home offers relaxing grounds boasting beautiful views in all directions. Smoke free premises. 5 one-bedroom standard units. 2 stories (no elevator), interior corridors. **Parking:** on-site. **Terms:** check-in 4 pm, age restrictions may apply, 10 day cancellation notice-fee imposed. **Amenities:** CD players, high-speed Internet, irons, hair dryers. **Business Services:** meeting rooms. **Cards:** AX, MC, VI. **Free Special Amenities:** full breakfast and high-speed Internet.

OMNI CHARLOTTESVILLE HOTEL   *Book great rates at AAA.com*

Phone: (434)971-5500

Large-scale Hotel
$199-$299 All Year

Address: 235 W Main St 22902 **Location:** I-64, exit 120, 2.3 mi n on SR 631; downtown. Located in historic area. **Facility:** 208 one-bedroom standard units. 7 stories, interior corridors. **Parking:** on-site. **Amenities:** video games, high-speed Internet, voice mail, honor bars, irons, hair dryers. **Dining:** The Pointe Restaurant & Lounge, see separate listing. **Pool(s):** outdoor, heated indoor. **Leisure Activities:** saunas, whirlpool, exercise room. **Guest Services:** valet laundry, wireless Internet. **Business Services:** conference facilities, business center. **Cards:** AX, CB, DC, DS, JC, MC, VI.

QUALITY INN-UNIVERSITY AREA   *Book at AAA.com*

Phone: 434/971-3746

Small-scale Hotel
$89-$169 4/1-2/28
$84-$129 3/1-3/31

Address: 1600 Emmet St 22901 **Location:** US 29 (Emmet St), just n of jct US 250 Bypass, then just e on Holiday Dr. **Facility:** 69 one-bedroom standard units. 3 stories, exterior corridors. **Parking:** on-site. **Amenities:** high-speed Internet, irons, hair dryers. **Guest Services:** valet laundry, wireless Internet. **Business Services:** PC. **Cards:** AX, DC, DS, JC, MC, VI.

RED ROOF INN OF CHARLOTTESVILLE   *Book at AAA.com*

Phone: 434/295-4333

Small-scale Hotel
Rates not provided

Address: 1309 W Main St 22903 **Location:** US 29 (Emmet St), 1 mi e on US 250 (University Ave). **Facility:** 135 one-bedroom standard units. 8 stories, interior corridors. *Bath:* combo or shower only. **Parking:** on-site. **Amenities:** video games, high-speed Internet, voice mail, irons, hair dryers. **Guest Services:** coin laundry, wireless Internet. **Business Services:** meeting rooms.

RESIDENCE INN BY MARRIOTT *Book great rates at AAA.com*

Small-scale Hotel
$143-$174 All Year

Phone: 434/923-0300

Address: 1111 Millmont St 22903 **Location:** I-64, exit 118B (US 29), 2.5 mi n on US 29/250 E, just s on Barracks Rd, then just se. **Facility:** Smoke free premises. 108 one-bedroom standard units with kitchens. 3 stories, interior corridors. *Bath:* combo or shower only. **Parking:** on-site. **Amenities:** high-speed Internet, voice mail, irons, hair dryers. **Pool(s):** heated outdoor. **Leisure Activities:** whirlpool, playground, exercise room, basketball, volleyball. **Guest Services:** valet and coin laundry, wireless Internet. **Business Services:** PC, fax (fee). **Cards:** AX, DC, DS, JC, MC, VI.

AAA Benefit:
Members save 5% off of the best available rate.

ASK SD ʸ⁺ CALL &M ⇨ ✗ ✗ 📽 🖥 🖼 🖵
/ SOME UNITS FEE 🐾

SILVER THATCH INN

Historic
Country Inn
$170-$210 All Year

Phone: 434/978-4686

Address: 3001 Hollymead Dr 22911-7422 **Location:** 5 mi n on US 29 (Emmet St), then 0.5 mi e on SR 1520. **Facility:** In a serene setting near the Charlottesville airport, this 1780 clapboard inn has a modern section with furnishings complementing the original design. Smoke free premises. 7 one-bedroom standard units. 2 stories (no elevator), interior corridors. *Bath:* combo or shower only. **Parking:** on-site. **Terms:** age restrictions may apply, 7 day cancellation notice. **Amenities:** CD players, irons, hair dryers. **Dining:** restaurant, see separate listing. **Pool(s):** outdoor. **Guest Services:** wireless Internet. **Business Services:** meeting rooms. **Cards:** AX, CB, DC, DS, MC, VI.

ʸ⁺ ⇨ ✗ 📽 ℤ

SLEEP INN & SUITES MONTICELLO *Book great rates at AAA.com*

(AAA) SAVE

Small-scale Hotel
$89-$239 All Year

Phone: (434)244-9969

Address: 1185 5th St 22902 **Location:** I-64, exit 120, just n. **Facility:** 76 one-bedroom standard units. 3 stories, interior corridors. *Bath:* combo or shower only. **Parking:** on-site. **Amenities:** high-speed Internet, voice mail, safes, irons, hair dryers. **Pool(s):** heated indoor. **Leisure Activities:** whirlpool, exercise room. **Guest Services:** valet and coin laundry, wireless Internet. **Business Services:** meeting rooms, fax (fee). **Cards:** AX, CB, DC, DS, JC, MC, VI. **Free Special Amenities: expanded continental breakfast and high-speed Internet.**

SD CALL &M ⇨ 🛏 🖵 / SOME UNITS FEE 🐾 ✗ 🖥 🖼

─────── **WHERE TO DINE** ───────

ABERDEEN BARN

(AAA)

Steak & Seafood
$17-$42

Phone: 434/296-4630

Known for its slow-roasted prime rib of beef prepared on an open charcoal hearth, this rustic steakhouse features post-and-beam construction and attractive barn decor. Other USDA Corn Fed Angus Beef selections, fresh local seafood and mouthwatering desserts round out the menu. Dressy casual. Entertainment. **Bar:** Full bar. **Reservations:** suggested, Fri & Sat. **Hours:** 5 pm-11 pm, Sun-10 pm. Closed: 11/27, 12/25. **Address:** 2018 Holiday Dr 22901 **Location:** I-64, exit 118B (US 29), just n of jct US 250 Bypass, then just e. **Parking:** on-site. **Cards:** AX, CB, DC, MC, VI.

🚫

BLUE LIGHT GRILL & RAW BAR

Seafood
$10-$20

Phone: 434/295-1223

Fresh seafood is prepared with a flair. The fun, casual restaurant employs a friendly staff. Casual dress. **Bar:** Full bar. **Hours:** 5:30 pm-10 pm. Closed: 1/1, 12/25. **Address:** 120 E Main St 22902 **Location:** I-64, exit 120, 2.6 mi n on SR 631; in downtown mall area. **Parking:** street. **Cards:** AX, CB, DC, DS, JC, MC, VI.

🚫

CASSIS

American
$17-$32

Phone: 434/979-0188

The warm and charming restaurant presents a seasonally influenced menu. Servers are friendly. Casual dress. **Bar:** Full bar. **Hours:** 5 pm-10 pm, Sun 11 am-3 pm. Closed: 1/1, 12/25; also Mon. **Address:** 210 W Water St 22902 **Location:** I-64, exit 120, 2.3 mi n on SR 631, then just e; in downtown mall area. **Parking:** street. **Cards:** AX, CB, DC, DS, JC, MC, VI.

CHRISTIAN'S PIZZERIA

Pizza
$5-$16

Phone: 434/977-9688

Voted the best pizza in Charlottesville almost annually with pizza whole or by the slice and a very upbeat staff. Casual dress. **Bar:** Beer only. **Hours:** 11 am-10 pm. Closed: 12/25. **Address:** 118 N Main St 22902 **Location:** I-64, exit 120, 2.3 mi n on SR 631, then just w. **Parking:** street.

🚫

COPACABANA BRAZILIAN INTERNATIONAL

Brazilian
$7-$24

Phone: 434/973-1177

Unusual sauces flavor excellent preparations of Brazilian cuisine, including fabulous veal medallions in lemon sauce. The atmosphere is informal. The restaurant is a great alternative for diners who can't get to Rio de Janeiro. Casual dress. **Bar:** Full bar. **Reservations:** suggested, for dinner. **Hours:** 11 am-2:30 & 5-11 pm, Sun from 5 pm. Closed: 11/27, 12/25. **Address:** 400 Shoppers World Ct 22901 **Location:** US 29 (Emmet St), 1.6 mi n of jct US 250 Bypass; in Shopper's World Shopping Center. **Parking:** on-site. **Cards:** AX, DC, MC, VI.

🚫

THE DOWNTOWN GRILLE

(AAA)

American
$13-$26

Phone: 434/817-7080

The restaurant combines elegant dining surroundings with a wonderful wine list and superior menu. Casual dress. **Bar:** Full bar. **Reservations:** suggested, weekends. **Hours:** 5 pm-10 pm, Fri & Sat-11 pm, Sun-9 pm. Closed: 12/25. **Address:** 201 W Main St 22902 **Location:** I-64, exit 120, 2.5 mi n on SR 631; downtown mall area. **Parking:** street. **Cards:** AX, CB, DC, DS, JC, MC, VI.

🚫

ESCAFE

American
$8-$17

Phone: 434/295-8668

Escafe has a wonderful setting with outdoor dining when weather permits and a whimsical atmosphere. The varied menu is complemented well by the knowledgeable servers. Casual dress. **Bar:** Full bar. **Reservations:** accepted. **Hours:** 5:30 pm-11 pm, Sun 4:30 pm-9:30 pm. Closed: Mon. **Address:** 227 W Main St 22902 **Location:** I-64, exit 120, 2.4 mi n on SR 361; in downtown mall area. **Parking:** street. **Cards:** AX, DS, MC, VI.

FLAMING WOK

Chinese
$7-$16

Menu on AAA.com   **Phone: 434/974-6555**

Experience the ancient method of cooking on a stone over hot coals while enjoying good Chinese, Japanese and Korean cuisine. A daily lunch buffet (also featuring the stone grill) is laden with a plentiful variety of standard favorites, including sushi. Background music makes guests feel as though they are in the Orient. Casual dress. **Bar:** Full bar. **Reservations:** required. **Hours:** 11:30 am-10 pm, Fri & Sat-11 pm. Closed: 11/27. **Address:** 1305 Seminole Tr 22901 **Location:** US 29 (Emmet St), 1 mi n of jct US 250 Bypass. **Parking:** on-site. **Cards:** AX, DC, DS, MC, VI.

HAMILTON'S AT FIRST AND MAIN

American
$8-$24

Phone: 434/295-6649

This restaurant has a cheerful cozy atmosphere, attentive service and a diverse menu. Casual dress. **Bar:** Full bar. **Hours:** 11:30 am-3 & 5:30-10 pm. Closed: 12/25; also Sun. **Address:** 101 W Main St 22902 **Location:** I-64, exit 120, 2.3 mi n on SR 631, then just w; in downtown mall area. **Parking:** street. **Cards:** AX, CB, DC, DS, JC, MC, VI.

THE IVY INN RESTAURANT

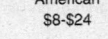

American
$19-$32

Phone: 434/977-1222

In a converted 1816 inn-like residence, the restaurant provides a richly historical and elegant atmosphere for fine dining. Fresh, local ingredients and a great wine list enhance the epicurean aspect, while hardwood floors, wine racks and wonderful paintings add to the ambience. The daily changing menu focuses on extraordinary American cuisine. Dressy casual. **Bar:** Full bar. **Reservations:** required. **Hours:** 5 pm-9:30 pm. Closed: 1/1, 12/24, 12/25; also Sun. **Address:** 2244 Old Ivy Rd 22903 **Location:** 0.5 mi w on Ivy Rd from US 29 business route, then just n on SR 601. **Parking:** on-site. **Cards:** AX, DC, MC, VI. **Historic**

L'ETOILE

French
$8-$30

Phone: 434/979-7957

The combination of French culinary techniques with Virginian style results in amazing cuisine choices. A large wine list and trained wait staff await. Casual dress. **Bar:** Full bar. **Reservations:** suggested, weekends. **Hours:** 11 am-2:30 pm, Wed-Fri also 5:30 pm-11 pm, Sat from 5:30 pm. Closed: 12/25; also Sun & Mon. **Address:** 817 W Main St 22903 **Location:** US 29 (Emmet St), 1.5 mi e on US 250. **Parking:** on-site. **Cards:** AX, CB, DC, DS, JC, MC, VI.

LORD HARDWICK'S

British
$7-$22

Phone: 434/295-6668

Lord Hardwick's is a classic British style pub with Fish and Chips and lots of British ambience. Casual dress. **Bar:** Full bar. **Reservations:** suggested, weekends. **Hours:** 11 am-10 pm. Closed: 12/25. **Address:** 1248 Emmet St 22901 **Location:** US 29 business route, just s of jct US 29 (Emmet St) and 250 Bypass. **Parking:** on-site. **Cards:** AX, CB, DC, DS, JC, MC, VI.

LUDWIG'S SCHNITZELHOUSE RESTAURANT

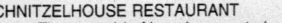

German
$15-$27

Phone: 434/293-7185

The owner/chef here has created varied menu selections specializing in tasty, traditional favorites, especially veal dishes, homemade salad dressing and dessert. Swiss cuisine is also featured. Many half-portion and light fare items also are available. Quaint setting, very relaxed atmosphere. Very friendly management and service staff. Soothing background music. Casual dress. **Bar:** Full bar. **Reservations:** suggested, weekends. **Hours:** 5 pm-9 pm. Closed: 11/27, 12/25; also Sun & Mon. **Address:** 2208 Fontaine Ave 22903 **Location:** 0.5 mi s on US 29 business route; just s of University of Virginia. **Parking:** on-site. **Cards:** AX, MC, VI.

MICHIE TAVERN CA 1784

American
$18

Phone: 434/977-1234

Diners are hard-pressed to find a better Colonial-style lunch buffet served in the true Southern tradition. Fried chicken can be savored with a rich array of traditional sides, including stewed tomatoes, black-eyed peas and cornbread. The atmosphere takes its cue from the 200-year-old log cabin setting. Don't miss the walk alongside the mill. The tavern evokes the feel of yesteryear. Casual dress. **Bar:** Beer & wine. **Hours:** 11:30 am-3 pm. Closed: 1/1, 12/25. **Address:** 683 Thomas Jefferson Pkwy 22902 **Location:** I-64, exit 121A, just s on SR 20, then 1 mi e on SR 53. **Parking:** on-site. **Cards:** AX, MC, VI. **Historic**

MONO LOCO

Latino
$7-$20

Phone: 434/979-0688

The friendly staff serves creative and festive menu selections in a quaint and cozy setting. Casual dress. **Bar:** Full bar. **Hours:** 11:30 am-2:30 & 5:30-11 pm, Sun-2:30 pm. Closed: 12/25. **Address:** 200 W Water St 22902 **Location:** I-64, exit 120, 2.3 mi n on SR 631, then just e; in downtown mall area. **Parking:** street. **Cards:** AX, CB, DC, DS, JC, MC, VI.

THE NOOK

American
$7-$19

Phone: 434/295-6665

The family-operated restaurant's menu centers on Mom's home cooking. Breakfast is served all day. Casual dress. **Bar:** Beer only. **Hours:** 7 am-7 pm. Closed: 1/1, 12/25. **Address:** 415 E Main St 22902 **Location:** I-64, exit 120, 2.7 mi n on SR 631; in downtown mall area. **Parking:** street. **Cards:** AX, CB, DC, DS, JC, MC, VI.

THE OLD MILL ROOM   *Menu on AAA.com*   **Phone:** 434/972-2230

An Early American atmosphere pervades the restored grist mill, a city fixture since 1834. Gentle rolling hills surround the restaurant. The menu, which changes slightly each night, showcases local ingredients blended in imaginative ways and with a hint of traditional Southern influence. The staff is pleasant and attentive. Top off the meal with the chocolate shining star. Semi-formal attire. Entertainment. **Bar:** Full bar. **Reservations:** suggested. **Hours:** 7 am-10:30, noon-2 & 6-9:30 pm, Fri-9:30 pm, Sat & Sun 7 am-10:30 & 6-9:30 pm. **Address:** Rt 250 W 22903 **Location:** Jct US 29 Bypass, 1 mi w on US 250; in Boar's Head Inn. **Parking:** on-site. **Cards:** AX, CB, DC, DS, MC, VI. **Historic**

Regional American
$10-$40

OXO   **Phone:** 434/977-8111

Guests relax in a soothing white setting with plenty of pillows and nice background music. The menu centers on eclectic nouvelle French cuisine. Casual dress. **Bar:** Full bar. **Reservations:** suggested, weekends. **Hours:** 5:30 pm-9:30 pm, Fri & Sat-10 pm, Sun-9 pm. Closed: 12/25. **Address:** 215 W Water St 22902 **Location:** I-64, exit 120, 2.3 mi n on SR 631, then just e; in downtown mall area. **Parking:** street. **Cards:** AX, CB, DC, DS, JC, MC, VI.

French
$24-$35

THE POINTE RESTAURANT & LOUNGE   **Phone:** 434/971-5500

Patrons might start a meal with an appetizer of eggplant Napoleon, then savor grilled salmon with steamed vegetables and couscous. Virginia wine is featured. The decor is airy and light. Casual dress. **Bar:** Full bar. **Reservations:** accepted. **Hours:** 6:30 am-9:30 pm, Fri & Sat-10 pm. **Address:** 235 W Main St 22902 **Location:** I-64, exit 120, 2.3 mi n on SR 631; downtown; in Omni Charlottesville Hotel. **Parking:** on-site. **Cards:** AX, CB, DC, DS, JC, MC, VI.

Regional American
$8-$25

RAGAZZI'S   **Phone:** 434/973-5940

Contemporary cuisine brings together many Italian and American classics, including many types of pasta. A popular choice is the longtime favorite lasagna. Casual dress. **Bar:** Full bar. **Hours:** 11 am-10 pm, Sun-9 pm. Closed major holidays. **Address:** 900 Shoppers World Ct 22901 **Location:** US 29 (Emmet St), 1.5 mi n of US 29 Bypass. **Parking:** on-site. **Cards:** AX, MC, VI.

Italian
$6-$15

RHETT'S RIVER GRILL AND RAW BAR   **Phone:** 434/974-7818

This restaurant is pure fun in a casual place combining great food and personable staff for a fun dining experience. Casual dress. **Bar:** Full bar. **Hours:** 11:30 am-2 & 5:30-10 pm, Fri & Sat-10:30 pm, Sun 10 am-2 pm. Closed major holidays. **Address:** 2335 Seminole Trail, Suite 100 22901 **Location:** I-64, exit 118B (US 29), 3.9 mi n of jct US 250 Bypass. **Parking:** on-site. **Cards:** AX, MC, VI.

American
$6-$21

RISTORANTE AL DENTE   **Phone:** 434/295-9922

Ristorante al Dente offers an elegant dining haven with amazing Italian cuisine, large wine list and homemade desserts. Casual dress. **Bar:** Full bar. **Hours:** 5 pm-10 pm. Closed: 12/25; also Mon. **Address:** 225 W Main St 22902 **Location:** I-64, exit 120, 2.4 mi n on SR 631; in downtown mall area. **Parking:** street. **Cards:** AX, CB, DC, DS, JC, MC, VI.

Italian
$18-$26

ROCOCO'S   **Phone:** 434/971-7371

The high-energy restaurant is known for chic and sophisticated food, such as rich, homemade pasta, excellent pizza and decadent dessert made on the premises. The sauteed escarole appetizer, house salad and chicken lasagna entree are flavorful. Casual dress. **Bar:** Full bar. **Hours:** 11 am-10 pm, Sat from 5 pm, Sun 11 am-3 & 5-10 pm. Closed: 12/25. **Address:** 2001 Commonwealth Dr 22901 **Location:** I-64, exit 118 (US 29), 0.3 mi n from jct US 250 Bypass, then 0.4 mi w on Hydraulic Rd; in Village Green Shopping Center. **Parking:** on-site. **Cards:** AX, DS, MC, VI.

Italian
$6-$20

ST. MAARTEN CAFE   **Phone:** 434/293-2233

St. Maarten Cafe offers eclectic Americn Cuisine in a fun Caribbean atmosphere close to the University of Virginia campus. Casual dress. **Bar:** Full bar. **Hours:** 11 am-11 pm. Closed: 12/25. **Address:** 1400 Wertland Ave 22903 **Location:** US 29 (Emmet St), 1.5 mi e on US 250. **Parking:** street. **Cards:** AX, CB, DC, DS, JC, MC, VI.

American
$6-$20

SAM'S KITCHEN   **Phone:** 434/977-1619

A fun atmosphere prevails in the friendly restaurant. Good food is prepared with a home-style influence. Casual dress. **Hours:** 11 am-3 & 5-midnight. Closed: 11/27, 12/25. **Address:** 1403 Emmet St 22903 **Location:** Just s of US 250 Bypass. **Parking:** on-site. **Cards:** AX, DS, MC, VI.

American
$6-$12

THE SHEBEEN   **Phone:** 434/296-3185

The Shebeen is a South African style pub with many unique cuisine selections from Africa and a huge beer and wine list. Casual dress. **Bar:** Full bar. **Hours:** 11 am-10 pm, Sun from 10:30 am. Closed: 12/25. **Address:** 247 Ridge-McIntire Rd 22903 **Location:** I-64, exit 120, 2.5 mi n on SR 631; in downtown mall area. **Parking:** street. **Cards:** AX, CB, DC, DS, JC, MC, VI.

South African
$10-$25

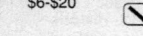

THE SILVER THATCH INN DINING ROOM

Phone: 434/978-4686

American
$19-$34

Contemporary cuisine shows the kitchen's flair for creative sauces and stylish presentation. Patrons visit the historic inn for a distinctive fine-dining experience. The excellent wine list incorporates a good selection of Virginia vintages. Dressy casual. **Bar:** Full bar. **Reservations:** suggested. **Hours:** 5:30 pm-9 pm. Closed: Sun & Mon. **Address:** 3001 Hollymead Dr 22911-7422 **Location:** 5 mi n on US 29 (Emmet St), 0.5 mi e on SR 1520; in Silver Thatch Inn. **Parking:** on-site. **Cards:** AX, CB, DC, MC, VI.

STICKS KABOB SHOP

Phone: 434/295-5262

American
$6-$12

High-velocity healthy food on a stick comes in many varieties and with homemade sauces at the fun and casual spot. Casual dress. **Hours:** 11 am-9 pm, Sun noon-8 pm. Closed: 12/25. **Address:** 917 Preston Ave 22903 **Location:** I-64, exit 118B, 2.4 mi e on US 250 Bypass, just s on US 29, then 1.7 mi e. **Parking:** on-site. **Cards:** MC, VI.

TIFFANY'S SEAFOOD RESTAURANT

Phone: 434/293-5000

American
$6-$18

The seafood restaurant specializes in steamed and spiced shrimp. In addition to selections such as seafood with pasta, the menu lists beef dishes. Casual dress. **Bar:** Full bar. **Hours:** 11:30 am-10:30 pm, Sun 5 pm-10 pm. Closed major holidays. **Address:** 155 Seminole Ct 22901 **Location:** US 29 (Emmet St), 0.6 mi n of jct US 250 Bypass. **Parking:** on-site. **Cards:** AX, DS, MC, VI.

TIP TOP RESTAURANT

Phone: 434/244-3424

American
$6-$18

On the menu is a nice selection of American dishes. Hillside views are attractive, and servers are friendly. Casual dress. **Hours:** 6 am-10 pm. Closed: 12/25. **Address:** 1420 Richmond Rd 22911 **Location:** I-64, exit 124, just n. **Parking:** on-site. **Cards:** MC, VI.

THE VIRGINIAN

Phone: 434/984-4667

American
$6-$20

Near the University of Virginia, the city's oldest restaurant thrives on tradition and a broad menu. Casual dress. **Bar:** Full bar. **Hours:** 10 am-10 pm. Closed: 12/25. **Address:** 1521 University Ave 22903 **Location:** US 29 (Emmet St), 0.7 mi e on US 250 (University Ave). **Parking:** street. **Cards:** AX, CB, DC, DS, JC, MC, VI.

WEST MAIN

Phone: 434/293-2605

American
$7-$20

West Main offers a casual American theme with a children's menu, fresh salads, Angus beef and a light atmosphere. Casual dress. **Bar:** Full bar. **Hours:** 11 am-2 am, Sun from 10 am. Closed: 12/25. **Address:** 333 W Main St 22903 **Location:** I-64, exit 120, 2.3 mi n on SR 631, then just w. **Parking:** on-site. **Cards:** AX, CB, DC, DS, JC, MC, VI.

WHITE ORCHID

Phone: 434/297-4400

Vietnamese
$8-$20

Fine Vietnamese cuisine is served in a cozy and contemporary setting. The staff focuses on friendliness. Casual dress. **Bar:** Full bar. **Hours:** 11:30 am-2 & 5:30-10 pm. Closed: Mon. **Address:** 420 W Main St 22902 **Location:** I-64, exit 120, 2.3 mi n on SR 631, then just w. **Parking:** on-site and street. **Cards:** AX, CB, DC, DS, JC, MC, VI.

WILD GREENS

Phone: 434/296-9453

American
$7-$22

Wonderful murals, beautiful background music and stylish dish presentation are hallmarks of the fine-dining establishment. Each entree includes the signature wild greens salad, a treat not to be missed. Fresh ingredients and a nice wine list are other pluses. Casual dress. **Bar:** Full bar. **Hours:** 11:30 am-9:30 pm, Fri & Sat-10 pm, Sun 11 am-9 pm. Closed major holidays. **Address:** 2162 Barracks Rd 22903 **Location:** 0.5 mi w on Barracks Rd from US 29 (Emmet St). **Parking:** on-site. **Cards:** AX, MC, VI. **Historic**

ZO CA LO

Phone: 434/977-4944

Latino
$10-$22

Latin cuisine is served in a quaint atmosphere characterized by distinctive artwork. The staff is knowledgeable and friendly. Casual dress. **Bar:** Full bar. **Hours:** 5:30 pm-10 pm. Closed: 12/25; also Mon. **Address:** 201 E Main St, Suite E 22902 **Location:** I-64, exit 120, 2.5 mi n on SR 631; in downtown mall area. **Parking:** street. **Cards:** AX, CB, DC, DS, JC, MC, VI.

CHESAPEAKE —See Hampton Roads Area p. 745.

CHESTER —See Richmond p. 873.

CHESTERFIELD —See Richmond p. 875.

CHILHOWIE pop. 1,827

——— **WHERE TO DINE** ———

TOWN HOUSE GRILL

Phone: 276/646-8787

American
$7-$26

Guests experience fine dining in a relaxed atmosphere. An expanded wine list is presented, and friendly staffers are a staple. Casual dress. **Bar:** Full bar. **Hours:** 11 am-2 & 5-9 pm. Closed: 12/25; also Sun & Mon. **Address:** 132 E Main St 24319 **Location:** I-81, exit 35, just w. **Parking:** on-site. **Cards:** AX, CB, DC, DS, JC, MC, VI.

CHINCOTEAGUE pop. 4,317

—— **WHERE TO STAY** ——

AMERICAS BEST VALUE INN & SUITES   *Book great rates at AAA.com*   Phone: (757)336-6562

Motel
$65-$199 3/1-8/31
$65-$75 9/1-2/28

Address: 6151 Maddox Blvd 23336 **Location:** 0.5 mi n on N Main St, just e. **Facility:** 26 units. 23 one-bedroom standard units, some with whirlpools. 1 one-bedroom suite. 2 cottages. 1 story, exterior corridors. **Parking:** on-site. **Terms:** office hours 8 am-midnight, 2-3 night minimum stay - seasonal, 10 day cancellation notice. **Amenities:** high-speed Internet, hair dryers. *Some:* irons, hair dryers. *Some:* irons. **Pool(s):** outdoor. **Leisure Activities:** barbecue grill, picnic area. **Guest Services:** wireless Internet. **Cards:** AX, DS, MC, VI. **Free Special Amenities:** continental breakfast and local telephone calls.

ASSATEAGUE INN   Phone: 757/336-3738

Small-scale Hotel
$55-$150 All Year

Address: 6570 Coachs Ln 23336 **Location:** 0.5 mi n on Main St, 0.8 mi e on Maddox Blvd, then just s on CR 2102 to Chicken City Rd, follow signs. Located in a rustic area. **Facility:** 24 units. 6 one-bedroom standard units. 18 one-bedroom suites with kitchens. 3 stories, interior/exterior corridors. **Parking:** on-site. **Terms:** office hours 8 am-10 pm, 3 day cancellation notice. **Amenities:** high-speed Internet, hair dryers. *Some:* DVD players. **Pool(s):** outdoor. **Leisure Activities:** crabbing dock, exercise room. **Guest Services:** wireless Internet. **Cards:** AX, DS, MC, VI. **Free Special Amenities:** continental breakfast and high-speed Internet.

BEST WESTERN CHINCOTEAGUE ISLAND   *Book great rates at AAA.com*   Phone: (757)336-6557

Small-scale Hotel
$69-$209 All Year

Address: 7105 Maddox Blvd 23336 **Location:** 0.5 mi n on N Main St, 1.5 mi e on Maddox Blvd/Beach Rd; at entrance to Assateague National Seashore. **Facility:** Smoke free premises. 52 units. 50 one- and 2 two-bedroom standard units, some with whirlpools. 3 stories, interior/exterior corridors. **Parking:** on-site. **Terms:** 2 night minimum stay - seasonal and/or weekends, 3 day cancellation notice. **Amenities:** high-speed Internet, irons, hair dryers. *Some: Fee:* DVD players. **Pool(s):** heated outdoor. **Leisure Activities:** barbecue grill. **Guest Services:** coin laundry, wireless Internet. **Business Services:** business center. **Cards:** AX, DC, DS, MC, VI. **Free Special Amenities:** full breakfast and high-speed Internet.

AAA Benefit:
Members save 10% everyday, plus an exclusive frequent stay program.

BIRCHWOOD MOTEL   Phone: 757/336-6133

Motel
$75-$155 5/1-10/15

Address: 3650 Main St 23336 **Location:** 0.8 mi s. **Facility:** 21 one-bedroom standard units, some with efficiencies. 1 story, exterior corridors. **Parking:** on-site. **Terms:** open 5/1-10/15, office hours 8 am-11 pm, 2-4 night minimum stay - weekends, 3 day cancellation notice-fee imposed. **Amenities:** voice mail. **Pool(s):** outdoor. **Leisure Activities:** bicycles. **Guest Services:** coin laundry, wireless Internet. **Business Services:** meeting rooms. **Cards:** AX, DS, MC, VI.

CHINCOTEAGUE INN   Phone: 757/336-6415

Motel
Rates not provided

Address: 4417 Deep Hole Rd 23336 **Location:** 0.5 mi n on N Main St, just e on Maddox Blvd. **Facility:** 70 one-bedroom standard units. 3 stories (no elevator), exterior corridors. **Parking:** on-site. **Terms:** open 4/15-10/15, office hours 8 am-midnight. **Amenities:** high-speed Internet, voice mail. *Some:* irons, hair dryers. **Pool(s):** outdoor. **Leisure Activities:** volleyball. **Guest Services:** wireless Internet.

COMFORT SUITES   *Book great rates at AAA.com*   Phone: (757)336-3700

Small-scale Hotel
$80-$399 All Year

Address: 4195 N Main St 23336 **Location:** Just n. **Facility:** Smoke free premises. 87 one-bedroom standard units, some with whirlpools. 3 stories, interior corridors. *Bath:* combo or shower only. **Parking:** on-site. **Amenities:** high-speed Internet, voice mail, safes (fee), irons, hair dryers. *Some:* DVD players, dual phone lines. **Pool(s):** heated outdoor, heated indoor. **Leisure Activities:** whirlpool, exercise room. *Fee:* game room. **Guest Services:** coin laundry, wireless Internet. **Business Services:** meeting rooms, business center. **Cards:** AX, CB, DC, DS, JC, MC, VI.

HAMPTON INN & SUITES   Phone: 757/336-1616

Small-scale Hotel
Rates not provided

Address: 4179 Main St 23336 **Location:** Just n of downtown. **Facility:** 59 one-bedroom standard units, some with whirlpools. 3 stories, interior corridors. *Bath:* combo or shower only. **Parking:** on-site. **Amenities:** high-speed Internet, voice mail, irons, hair dryers. **Pool(s):** heated indoor. **Leisure Activities:** whirlpool, exercise room. **Guest Services:** coin laundry, wireless Internet. **Business Services:** meeting rooms, business center.

THE INN AT POPLAR CORNER   Phone: (757)336-6115

Bed & Breakfast
$149-$219 4/1-10/31

Address: 4248 Main St 23336 **Location:** Just n of downtown. **Facility:** Guests gain a vantage point on the surrounding town from this elegant inn's wraparound porch; rooms feature whirlpool baths and other luxuries. Smoke free premises. 4 one-bedroom standard units with whirlpools. 3 stories (no elevator), interior corridors. **Parking:** on-site. **Terms:** open 4/1-10/31, age restrictions may apply, 14 day cancellation notice-fee imposed. **Amenities:** high-speed Internet. **Leisure Activities:** bicycles. **Guest Services:** wireless Internet. **Cards:** AX, DS, MC, VI.

ISLAND MOTOR INN RESORT

▼▼▼

Small-scale Hotel
$68-$195 All Year

Phone: 757-336-3141
Address: 4391 Main St 23336 **Location:** 0.8 mi n. **Facility:** 60 one-bedroom standard units. 3 stories, interior/exterior corridors. **Parking:** on-site. **Terms:** office hours 6 am-1 am, check-in 4 pm, 2-3 night minimum stay - seasonal and/or weekends, 7 day cancellation notice-fee imposed. **Amenities:** high-speed Internet. *Some:* hair dryers. **Pool(s):** outdoor, heated indoor. **Leisure Activities:** whirlpool, boat dock, fishing, exercise room, facials. *Fee:* massage. **Guest Services:** complimentary laundry, personal trainer, tanning facilities, wireless Internet. **Business Services:** meeting rooms. **Cards:** AX, DC, DS, MC, VI.

REFUGE INN

Book great rates at AAA.com

AAA SAVE
▼▼▼
Small-scale Hotel
$100-$320 3/1-8/31
$89-$290 9/1-2/28

Phone: (757)336-5511
Address: 7058 Maddox Blvd 23336 **Location:** 0.5 mi n on N Main St, 1.5 mi e on Maddox Blvd/Beach Rd. **Facility:** 72 units. 70 one-bedroom standard units. 2 one-bedroom suites with whirlpools. 2 stories (no elevator), interior corridors. **Parking:** on-site. **Terms:** office hours 7:30 am-10 pm, check-in 4 pm, 2 night minimum stay - seasonal and/or weekends, 7 day cancellation notice. **Amenities:** high-speed Internet, dual phone lines, voice mail. **Pool(s):** heated indoor/outdoor. **Leisure Activities:** sauna, whirlpool, observation deck, hiking trails, playground, exercise room. *Fee:* bicycles. **Guest Services:** coin laundry, wireless Internet. **Business Services:** meeting rooms, PC (fee). **Cards:** AX, DC, DS, MC, VI. **Free Special Amenities:** expanded continental breakfast and high-speed Internet.

SEA SHELL MOTEL

▼▼▼
Motel
$59-$225 3/21-10/13

Phone: 757/336-6589
Address: 3720 Willow St 23336 **Location:** Just s on S Main St, e on Cleveland Ave. **Facility:** 40 units. 36 one-bedroom standard units, some with efficiencies. 4 one-bedroom suites with kitchens. 2 stories (no elevator), exterior corridors. *Bath:* combo or shower only. **Parking:** on-site. **Terms:** open 3/21-10/13, office hours 9 am-9 pm, 2 night minimum stay - seasonal and/or weekends, 7 day cancellation notice. **Amenities:** *Some:* DVD players. **Pool(s):** outdoor. **Guest Services:** wireless Internet. **Cards:** AX, DS, MC, VI.

SUNRISE MOTOR INN

▼▼▼
Motel
$45-$85 3/14-11/2

Phone: 757/336-6671
Address: 4491 Chicken City Rd 23336 **Location:** 0.5 mi n on N Main St, 0.8 mi e on Maddox Blvd, then just s on CR 2102. **Facility:** 24 units. 22 one-bedroom standard units. 1 one- and 1 two-bedroom suites with kitchens. 1 story, exterior corridors. **Parking:** on-site. **Terms:** open 3/14-11/2, office hours 7 am-10 pm, 2 night minimum stay - seasonal and/or weekends. **Pool(s):** outdoor. **Cards:** AX, DC, DS, MC, VI.

WATERSIDE INN

Book great rates at AAA.com

AAA SAVE
▼▼▼
Small-scale Hotel
$78-$200 All Year

Phone: 757/336-3434
Address: 3761 S Main St 23336 **Location:** 0.5 mi s. **Facility:** 49 units. 45 one-bedroom standard units. 4 two-bedroom suites with kitchens. 3 stories, exterior corridors. **Parking:** on-site. **Terms:** office hours 7 am-10 pm, 2 night minimum stay - seasonal, 3 day cancellation notice-fee imposed. **Amenities:** high-speed Internet, voice mail, irons, hair dryers. **Pool(s):** heated outdoor. **Leisure Activities:** whirlpool, marina, fishing, tennis court, exercise room. **Guest Services:** coin laundry, wireless Internet. **Business Services:** meeting rooms, business center. **Cards:** AX, CB, DC, DS, MC, VI. **Free Special Amenities:** expanded continental breakfast and high-speed Internet.

THE WATSON HOUSE

▼▼▼
Historic Bed
& Breakfast
$130-$160 3/1-1/3 &
2/14-2/28

Phone: 757/336-1564
Address: 4240 Main St 23336 **Location:** Just n of downtown. **Facility:** This restored 1898 Victorian with the look of a dollhouse offers service-oriented lodgings complemented by authentic period details. Smoke free premises. 4 one-bedroom standard units. 2 stories (no elevator), interior corridors. *Bath:* combo or shower only. **Parking:** on-site. **Terms:** open 3/1-1/3 & 2/14-2/28, 2 night minimum stay - seasonal and/or weekends, age restrictions may apply, 14 day cancellation notice. **Amenities:** high-speed Internet, hair dryers. **Leisure Activities:** bicycles. **Guest Services:** wireless Internet. **Cards:** MC, VI.

------ **WHERE TO DINE** ------

AJ'S..ON THE CREEK

▼▼▼
American
$5-$30

Phone: 757/336-1539
Dine on sauteed flounder, smothered with scallops, shrimp and crab, amid an intimate, romantically lit setting. Along with fresh grilled fish and seafood, steak, veal and pasta also grace the extensive menu. Screened porch dining is available in summer. Casual dress. **Bar:** Full bar. **Reservations:** not accepted. **Hours:** 11:30 am-9 pm, Fri & Sat-10 pm. Closed: 11/27, 12/25; also Sun. **Address:** 6585 Maddox Blvd 23336 **Location:** 0.5 mi n on Main St, 1 mi e. **Parking:** on-site. **Cards:** AX, DC, DS, MC, VI.

BILL'S SEAFOOD RESTAURANT

AAA
▼▼▼
Seafood
$4-$25

Phone: 757/336-5831
The fact that the owner also owns a bakery is evident in the exceptional bread found at the casual restaurant. The focus is basic, regional seafood—served grilled, fried or broiled—although a sprinkling of beef and poultry dishes also dots the menu. Casual dress. **Bar:** Full bar. **Reservations:** suggested, weekends. **Hours:** 6 am-close. Closed: 12/25. **Address:** 4040 Main St 23336 **Location:** 0.5 mi s. **Parking:** on-site. **Cards:** AX, DC, DS, MC, VI.

DON'S SEAFOOD RESTAURANT

Seafood
$4-$19

Phone: 757/336-5715
Casual dress. **Bar:** Full bar. **Hours:** 11 am-9 pm. **Address:** 4113 Main St 23336 **Location:** Center. **Parking:** on-site. **Cards:** MC, VI.

ETTA'S CHANNEL SIDE RESTAURANT
Seafood
$8-$20

Phone: 757/336-5644
Overlooking the Assateague channel, the restaurant offers views of the lighthouse in the distance. Diners can expect the freshest local seafood, including flounder stuffed with crab imperial, fried oysters, crab cakes and daily catch specials. Pasta, pork and chicken dishes round out the menu. Casual dress. **Bar:** Beer & wine. **Hours:** Open 3/24-11/27; 4 pm-9 pm, Sun from noon; hours vary off season. **Address:** 7452 E Side Rd 23336 **Location:** From Main St, just e on Church St to East Side Rd, then just s. **Parking:** on-site. **Cards:** AX, DS, MC, VI.

SAIGON VILLAGE
Vietnamese
$6-$12

Phone: 757/336-7299
In the center of town, the tiny spot serves fresh Vietnamese specialties, such as grilled shrimp with rice noodles, steamed rice paper rolls, midget wonton soup and barbecue pork over rice noodles or broken rice. Casual dress. **Hours:** 11 am-9:30 pm. Closed major holidays. **Address:** 4069 Main St 23336 **Location:** Downtown. **Parking:** street. **Cards:** MC, VI.

STEAMERS
Seafood
$10-$28

Phone: 757/336-5478
A favorite of locals, Steamers is always packed in season. No one can deny the more than hearty portions and a casual atmosphere for you to enjoy it in. Fresh seafood from local waters, much of it served in all-you-can-eat platters like crabs and steamed shrimp make this spot a must. Casual dress. **Bar:** Full bar. **Reservations:** accepted. **Hours:** Open 3/1-11/30; 4:30 pm-10 pm, Sat & Sun from 4 pm; hours vary off season. **Address:** 6251 Maddox Blvd 23336 **Location:** 0.5 mi n from stop light, 0.3 mi e. **Parking:** on-site. **Cards:** AX, DS, MC, VI.

THE VILLAGE RESTAURANT
Steak & Seafood
$10-$32

Phone: 757/336-5120
Overlooking the wetlands, the relaxed setting is built to resemble a small village from the outside and cozy and romantic once inside. The menu takes advantage of the freshest local Chesapeake Bay and Atlantic Ocean seafood such as crab, shrimp, flounder, and shellfish. Excellent Crab Imperial. Casual dress. **Bar:** Full bar. **Reservations:** suggested, in season. **Hours:** 5 pm-9 pm. Closed: 1/1, 12/24-12/26. **Address:** 6576 Maddox Blvd 23336 **Location:** 0.5 mi n on Main St, 1 mi e. **Parking:** on-site. **Cards:** AX, DS, MC, VI.

The following restaurants have not been evaluated by AAA but are listed for your information only.

SEA STAR CAFE
(fyi)

Phone: 757/336-5442
Not evaluated. Set downtown in a former mobile ice cream stand, Sea Star Cafe is the spot where locals love to pick up fresh salads and gourmet sandwiches when on the run. **Address:** 4121 Main St 23336 **Location:** Center.

SUGARBAKER'S
(fyi)

Phone: 757/336-3712
Not evaluated. Sugarbaker's is a charming bakery in the center of town. Stop at breakfast for donuts, bagels and pastry or at lunch for large salad and overstuffed sandwiches on a variety of fresh-baked bread such as eight-grain or French baguette. **Address:** 4095 Main St 23336 **Location:** Downtown.

CHRISTIANSBURG pop. 16,947

--- WHERE TO STAY ---

ECONO LODGE
Motel
$53-$179 3/1-11/30
$49-$89 12/1-2/28

Book great rates at AAA.com
Phone: (540)382-6161
Address: 2430 Roanoke St 24073 **Location:** I-81, exit 118, just w on US 11/460. **Facility:** 72 one-bedroom standard units. 2 stories (no elevator), exterior corridors. **Parking:** on-site. **Amenities:** irons, hair dryers. **Pool(s):** outdoor. **Guest Services:** wireless Internet. **Cards:** AX, DC, DS, MC, VI. **Free Special Amenities: continental breakfast and high-speed Internet.**

FAIRFIELD INN & SUITES BY MARRIOTT
Small-scale Hotel
$75-$92 All Year

Book great rates at AAA.com
Phone: 540/381-9596
Address: 2659 Roanoke St 24073 **Location:** I-81, exit 118C, just e. **Facility:** Smoke free premises. 87 one-bedroom standard units. 3 stories, interior corridors. *Bath:* combo or shower only. **Parking:** on-site. **Amenities:** high-speed Internet, voice mail, irons, hair dryers. *Some:* CD players. **Pool(s):** outdoor. **Leisure Activities:** whirlpool, exercise room. **Guest Services:** coin laundry, wireless Internet. **Business Services:** meeting rooms, business center. **Cards:** AX, DC, DS, JC, MC, VI. **Free Special Amenities: expanded continental breakfast and high-speed Internet.**

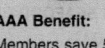

HAMPTON INN CHRISTIANSBURG/BLACKSBURG

Book great rates at AAA.com Phone: 540/381-5874

Small-scale Hotel
Rates not provided

Address: 380 Arbor Dr 24073 **Location:** I-81, exit 118B, 4 mi w on US 460 Bypass, just n on Peppers Ferry Rd, then just w. **Facility:** 119 one-bedroom standard units, some with whirlpools. 5 stories, interior corridors. *Bath:* combo or shower only. **Parking:** on-site. **Amenities:** video games, high-speed Internet, voice mail, irons, hair dryers. *Some:* CD players. **Pool(s):** outdoor. **Leisure Activities:** exercise room. **Guest Services:** coin laundry, wireless Internet. **Business Services:** meeting rooms, business center.

HOLIDAY INN EXPRESS HOTEL & SUITES
CHRISTIANSBURG/BLACKSBURG

Book great rates at AAA.com Phone: (540)382-6500

Small-scale Hotel
$92-$199 7/1-2/28
$89-$189 3/1-6/30

Address: 2725 Roanoke St 24073 **Location:** I-81, exit 118C, just e. **Facility:** 74 one-bedroom standard units, some with whirlpools. 4 stories, interior corridors. *Bath:* combo or shower only. **Parking:** on-site. **Terms:** cancellation fee imposed. **Amenities:** high-speed Internet, voice mail, irons, hair dryers. **Pool(s):** heated indoor. **Leisure Activities:** exercise room. **Guest Services:** coin laundry, wireless Internet. **Business Services:** meeting rooms, business center. **Cards:** AX, CB, DC, DS, JC, MC, VI. **Free Special Amenities: continental breakfast and high-speed Internet.**

MICROTEL INN & SUITES

Book at AAA.com Phone: (540)381-0500

Small-scale Hotel
$50-$70 All Year

Address: 135 Ponderosa Dr 24073 **Location:** I-81, exit 118B, 3 mi w on US 460, then just n; off Arbor Rd. Located in the New River Valley Mall. **Facility:** 86 one-bedroom standard units. 3 stories, interior corridors. *Bath:* combo or shower only. **Parking:** on-site. **Amenities:** voice mail. **Leisure Activities:** exercise room. **Guest Services:** coin laundry. **Business Services:** meeting rooms, fax (fee). **Cards:** AX, DS, MC, VI.

THE OAKS VICTORIAN INN

Phone: (540)381-1500

Historic Bed
& Breakfast
$110-$200 All Year

Address: 311 E Main St 24073 **Location:** I-81, exit 114, 2 mi w. **Facility:** Large guest rooms reflect period ambience but offer modern conveniences at this 1893 Queen Anne Victorian inn, where huge oak trees line the grounds. Smoke free premises. 7 units. 6 one-bedroom standard units, some with whirlpools. 1 cottage. 3 stories (no elevator), interior corridors. *Bath:* combo or shower only. **Parking:** on-site. **Terms:** check-in 4 pm, 1-2 night minimum stay - seasonal, 10 day cancellation notice-fee imposed. **Amenities:** video library, DVD players, CD players, high-speed Internet, voice mail, hair dryers. **Leisure Activities:** whirlpool. *Fee:* bicycles, massage. **Guest Services:** valet laundry, wireless Internet. **Business Services:** meeting rooms, fax (fee). **Cards:** DS, MC, VI. **Free Special Amenities: full breakfast and high-speed Internet.**

QUALITY INN

Book great rates at AAA.com Phone: (540)382-2055

Small-scale Hotel
$69-$170 All Year

Address: 50 Hampton Blvd 24073 **Location:** I-81, exit 118C, just e. **Facility:** 124 one-bedroom standard units, some with whirlpools. 2 stories (no elevator), exterior corridors. **Parking:** on-site. **Amenities:** voice mail, safes (fee), irons, hair dryers. *Some:* high-speed Internet. **Pool(s):** outdoor. **Leisure Activities:** whirlpool, exercise room. **Guest Services:** valet and coin laundry, wireless Internet. **Business Services:** meeting rooms, business center. **Cards:** AX, DS, MC, VI. **Free Special Amenities: expanded continental breakfast and high-speed Internet.**

SUPER 8 MOTEL-CHRISTIANSBURG EAST

Book great rates at AAA.com Phone: 540/382-7421

Motel
Rates not provided

Address: 2780 Roanoke Rd 24073 **Location:** I-81, exit 118C, just e. **Facility:** 63 one-bedroom standard units. 1 story, exterior corridors. **Parking:** on-site. **Pool(s):** outdoor.

SUPER 8 MOTEL-CHRISTIANSBURG WEST

Book at AAA.com Phone: 540/382-5813

Small-scale Hotel
Rates not provided

Address: 55 Laurel St NE 24073 **Location:** I-81, exit 118, 1 mi w on US 11/460, then 3.5 mi nw on US 460 Bypass; jct SR 114. **Facility:** 49 one-bedroom standard units. 2 stories (no elevator), interior corridors. **Parking:** on-site. **Amenities:** safes (fee), hair dryers. **Guest Services:** wireless Internet. **Business Services:** fax (fee).

------- **WHERE TO DINE** -------

BEAMER'S

Phone: 540/381-0233

American
$7-$20

Both original and traditional American dishes are served in an upbeat and smoke-free setting. Casual dress. **Bar:** Full bar. **Hours:** 11 am-11 pm. Closed major holidays. **Address:** 2509 Market St 24073 **Location:** I-81, exit 118B, 3 mi w on US 460, then just n; at New River Valley Marketplace. **Parking:** on-site. **Cards:** AX, CB, DC, DS, JC, MC, VI.

THE FARMHOUSE

Phone: 540/382-4253

American
$15-$26

Meals are served in a 19th-century farmhouse attractively styled with cozy and private high-backed wood booths. Since 1963, the restaurant has been known for its prime rib, steak, seafood, pasta and chicken dishes, as well as pleasant, dependable service. Casual dress. **Bar:** Full bar. **Hours:** 5 pm-9:45 pm, Sun noon-8:45 pm. Closed: 1/1, 12/24, 12/25. **Address:** 285 Ridinger St 24073 **Location:** 2 mi w on US 460, 0.3 mi s on Cambria St. **Parking:** on-site. **Cards:** AX, DC, DS, MC, VI.

GENNARO'S

Pizza
$6-$17
Phone: 540/381-9690
A taste of Italy finds its way to southwest Virginia via this restaurant's food, which gets its pop from homemade sauces. For dessert, guests can choose from a huge variety of pies. Casual dress. **Bar:** Beer only. **Hours:** 11 am-11 pm. Closed: 12/25. **Address:** 613 New River Rd 24073 **Location:** I-81, exit 118, 1 mi w on US 11/460, 3.2 mi nw on US 460 Bypass, then just w. **Parking:** on-site. **Cards:** MC, VI.

CHURCHVILLE

─── **WHERE TO DINE** ───

T-BONE TOOTER RESTAURANT
American
$6-$16
Phone: 540/337-6500
Casual dress. **Bar:** Full bar. **Hours:** 8 am-8 pm, Sun-3 pm. Closed: 1/1, 11/27, 12/25; also Mon. **Address:** Rt 250 W 24421 **Location:** I-81, exit 225, 5.1 mi w on SR 250. **Parking:** on-site. **Cards:** MC, VI.

CLARKSVILLE pop. 1,329

─── **WHERE TO STAY** ───

BEST WESTERN ON THE LAKE   *Book great rates at AAA.com*   **Phone:** (434)374-5023

AAA SAVE
Small-scale Hotel
$89-$124 3/1-10/31
$76-$99 11/1-2/28

Address: 103 Second St 23927 **Location:** Just n of US 58 business route. Located on lake. **Facility:** 70 units. 66 one-bedroom standard units. 4 one-bedroom suites. 2 stories (no elevator), interior corridors. **Parking:** on-site, winter plug-ins. **Terms:** 2 night minimum stay - seasonal and/or weekends, 3 day cancellation notice. **Amenities:** high-speed Internet, voice mail, irons, hair dryers. *Some:* dual phone lines. **Pool(s):** outdoor. **Leisure Activities:** boat dock. **Guest Services:** wireless Internet. **Business Services:** meeting rooms, business center. **Cards:** AX, DC, DS, JC, MC, VI. **Free Special Amenities: high-speed Internet.**

AAA Benefit:
Members save 10% everyday, plus an exclusive frequent stay program.

CLIFTON —*See District Of Columbia p. 527.*

COLLINSVILLE pop. 7,777

─── **WHERE TO STAY** ───

KNIGHTS INN   *Book great rates at AAA.com*   **Phone:** 276/647-3716

AAA SAVE
Motel
Rates not provided

Address: 2357 Virginia Ave 24078 **Location:** Jct US 58, 3 mi n on US 220 business route. **Facility:** 40 one-bedroom standard units. 1-2 stories (no elevator), exterior corridors. **Parking:** on-site. **Pool(s):** outdoor. **Free Special Amenities: local telephone calls and early check-in/late check-out.**

QUALITY INN-DUTCH INN HOTEL AND
    CONVENTION CENTER   *Book at AAA.com*   **Phone:** (276)647-3721

Small-scale Hotel
$80-$300 All Year

Address: 2360 Virginia Ave 24078 **Location:** Jct US 58, 3 mi n on US 220 business route. **Facility:** 148 one-bedroom standard units. 2 stories (no elevator), exterior corridors. **Parking:** on-site. **Terms:** cancellation fee imposed. **Amenities:** high-speed Internet, voice mail, irons, hair dryers. **Pool(s):** outdoor. **Leisure Activities:** whirlpool, exercise room. **Guest Services:** valet and coin laundry, wireless Internet. **Business Services:** meeting rooms, PC, fax (fee). **Cards:** AX, CB, DC, DS, JC, MC, VI.

COLONIAL HEIGHTS —*See Richmond p. 875.*

COVINGTON pop. 6,303

─── **WHERE TO STAY** ───

BEST WESTERN MOUNTAIN VIEW   *Book great rates at AAA.com*   **Phone:** 540/962-4951

Small-scale Hotel
Rates not provided

Address: 820 E Madison St 24426 **Location:** I-64, exit 16, just n. **Facility:** 76 one-bedroom standard units. 2 stories (no elevator), exterior corridors. **Parking:** on-site. **Amenities:** high-speed Internet, irons, hair dryers. **Pool(s):** outdoor. **Guest Services:** coin laundry, wireless Internet. **Business Services:** meeting rooms.

AAA Benefit:
Members save 10% everyday, plus an exclusive frequent stay program.

COMPARE INN & SUITES

Small-scale Hotel
$103-$115 5/1-2/28
$98-$105 3/1-4/30

Phone: (540)962-2141
Address: 203 Interstate Dr 24426 **Location:** I-64, exit 16, just sw. **Facility:** 98 one-bedroom standard units. 2 stories (no elevator), interior corridors. **Parking:** on-site. **Amenities:** irons, hair dryers. **Pool(s):** outdoor. **Leisure Activities:** whirlpool. **Guest Services:** coin laundry, wireless Internet. **Business Services:** meeting rooms, fax. **Cards:** AX, CB, DC, DS, MC, VI.

HOLIDAY INN EXPRESS   *Book at AAA.com*

Small-scale Hotel
$109-$259 All Year

Phone: 540/962-1200
Address: 701 Carlyle St 24426 **Location:** I-64, exit 16, just n, then 0.3 mi w. **Facility:** 63 one-bedroom standard units, some with whirlpools. 4 stories, interior corridors. *Bath:* combo or shower only. **Parking:** on-site. **Amenities:** high-speed Internet, voice mail, irons, hair dryers. **Pool(s):** heated indoor. **Leisure Activities:** whirlpool, exercise room. **Guest Services:** coin laundry, wireless Internet. **Business Services:** meeting rooms, business center. **Cards:** AX, CB, DC, DS, JC, MC, VI.

WHERE TO DINE

THE BRASS LANTERN

American
$8-$15

Phone: 540/962-4951
Preset and ready for patrons, the elegant dining room affords wonderful scenic views of the mountains. The focus of the menu is on classic American cuisine. A local favorite for lunch or dinner, this place is well worth the stop off the interstate. Casual dress. **Bar:** Full bar. **Hours:** 6 am-10 & 5-9 pm, Fri-9:30 pm, Sat 7 am-10 & 5-9:30 pm, Sun 7 am-10 & 5-9 pm. **Address:** 820 E Madison St 24426 **Location:** I-64, exit 16, 0.3 mi n. **Parking:** on-site. **Cards:** AX, DC, DS, MC, VI.

CUCCI'S

Italian
$6-$15

Phone: 540/962-3964
Cucci's is a family friendly restaurant with many pasta and pizza chocies. Try the famous turnovers. Casual dress. **Bar:** Beer & wine. **Hours:** 11 am-11 pm, Fri & Sat-midnight. Closed major holidays; also Sun. **Address:** 566 E Madison Ave 24426 **Location:** I-64, exit 16, just n. **Parking:** on-site. **Cards:** AX, MC, VI.

CULPEPER pop. 9,664

WHERE TO STAY

BEST WESTERN CULPEPER INN   *Book great rates at AAA.com*

Small-scale Hotel
Rates not provided

Phone: 540/825-1253
Address: 791 Madison Rd 22701 **Location:** Jct US 29, 2 mi s on US 29 business route. **Facility:** 158 one-bedroom standard units. 2 stories (no elevator), exterior corridors. *Bath:* combo or shower only. **Parking:** on-site. **Amenities:** high-speed Internet, voice mail, irons, hair dryers. **Pool(s):** outdoor. **Leisure Activities:** exercise room. **Guest Services:** coin laundry, wireless Internet. **Business Services:** meeting rooms. **Free Special Amenities:** local telephone calls and high-speed Internet.

AAA Benefit:
Members save 10% everyday, plus an exclusive frequent stay program.

COMFORT INN-CULPEPER   *Book at AAA.com*

Small-scale Hotel
$90-$100 All Year

Phone: (540)825-4900
Address: 890 Willis Ln 22701 **Location:** 2 mi s on US 29 business route; jct US 29, then just e. **Facility:** 49 one-bedroom standard units. 2 stories (no elevator), exterior corridors. *Bath:* combo or shower only. **Parking:** on-site. **Amenities:** high-speed Internet, irons, hair dryers. *Fee:* safes. **Pool(s):** outdoor. **Guest Services:** valet laundry, wireless Internet. **Cards:** AX, CB, DC, DS, JC, MC, VI.

FOUNTAIN HALL BED & BREAKFAST

Historic Bed
& Breakfast
$125-$200 All Year

Phone: (540)825-8200
Address: 609 S East St 22701 **Location:** Just e of S Main St (US 29 business route) via Chandler St, then just s at Asher St; center. **Facility:** This 1859 Colonial Revival mansion offers three units with private balconies; breakfast is prepared on site. Smoke free premises. 6 one-bedroom standard units, some with whirlpools. 2 stories (no elevator), interior corridors. *Bath:* combo or shower only. **Parking:** on-site. **Terms:** 7 day cancellation notice-fee imposed. **Amenities:** CD players, hair dryers. *Some:* DVD players, high-speed Internet, safes, irons. **Guest Services:** valet laundry, wireless Internet. **Business Services:** meeting rooms, fax (fee). **Cards:** AX, DS, MC, VI.

WHERE TO DINE

FOTI'S RESTAURANT

Mediterranean
$18-$35

Phone: 540/829-8400
Dressy casual. **Bar:** Full bar. **Reservations:** suggested. **Hours:** 5 pm-9:30 pm. Closed: 7/4, 12/25; also Sun & Mon. **Address:** 219 E Davis St 22701 **Location:** Just e on Davis St; center. **Parking:** street. **Cards:** AX, CB, DC, DS, JC, MC, VI.

HAZEL RIVER INN RESTAURANT

Phone: 540/825-7148

American
$7-$30

Guests can enjoy a fine-dining experience in elegant surroundings. The menu lists a wonderful blend of choices. Casual dress. **Bar:** Full bar. **Reservations:** suggested, weekends. **Hours:** 11:30 am-9 pm. Closed: 12/25. **Address:** 195 E Davis St 22701 **Location:** Just e; center. **Parking:** on-site and street. **Cards:** AX, CB, DC, DS, JC, MC, VI.

IT'S ABOUT THYME

Phone: 540/825-4264

American
$5-$28

The fun and casual downtown restaurant has beautiful murals, friendly people and a dash of European country cuisine. Casual dress. **Bar:** Full bar. **Hours:** 11 am-3 & 5:30-10 pm. Closed major holidays; also Sun & Mon. **Address:** 128 E Davis St 22701 **Location:** Just e; center. **Parking:** street. **Cards:** AX, CB, DC, DS, JC, MC, VI.

LUCIO

Phone: 540/829-9788

Italian
$10-$25

European flavors, hand-made pastas and elegant dining surroundings await at the comfortable restaurant. Casual dress. **Bar:** Full bar. **Reservations:** suggested, weekends. **Hours:** 11:30 am-2:30 & 5-10 pm, Sun-8 pm. Closed: 12/25; also Mon & Tues. **Address:** 702 S Main St 22701 **Location:** 1.5 mi s on Main St (US 29 business route). **Parking:** on-site. **Cards:** AX, CB, DC, DS, JC, MC, VI.

PANCHO VILLA MEXICAN RESTAURANT

Phone: 540/825-5268

Mexican
$6-$19

A huge assortment of drink and dessert specialties complements the widely varied choices. Hot chips and salsa prime the palate for a Mexican feast. Casual dress. **Bar:** Full bar. **Hours:** 11 am-10 pm. Closed: 12/25. **Address:** 910 S Main St 22701 **Location:** Just s on Main St (US 29 business route). **Parking:** on-site. **Cards:** AX, MC, VI.

DAHLGREN pop. 997

———— WHERE TO STAY ————

COMFORT INN-DAHLGREN   *Book at AAA.com*

Phone: (540)663-3060

Small-scale Hotel
$83-$89 All Year

Address: 4661 James Madison Pkwy 22485 **Location:** US 301; 2 mi s of entrance to US Navy Surface Weapons Center; 4 mi s of Potomac River Bridge. **Facility:** 59 one-bedroom standard units, some with whirlpools. 2 stories (no elevator), interior corridors. *Bath:* combo or shower only. **Parking:** on-site. **Amenities:** high-speed Internet, irons, hair dryers. *Some:* dual phone lines. **Pool(s):** outdoor. **Leisure Activities:** whirlpool, limited exercise equipment. **Guest Services:** wireless Internet. **Business Services:** fax. **Cards:** AX, CB, DC, DS, JC, MC, VI.

HOLIDAY INN EXPRESS   *Book at AAA.com*

Phone: (540)644-1500

Small-scale Hotel
$90-$105 3/1-9/30
$80-$95 10/1-2/28

Address: 4755 James Madison Pkwy 22485 **Location:** US 301, 4.2 mi s of Potomac River Bridge, 2 mi s of entrance to US Navy Surface Weapons Center. **Facility:** 60 one-bedroom standard units, some with whirlpools. 2 stories (no elevator), interior corridors. *Bath:* combo or shower only. **Parking:** on-site. **Amenities:** high-speed Internet, dual phone lines, voice mail, irons, hair dryers. **Pool(s):** outdoor. **Guest Services:** wireless Internet. **Business Services:** meeting rooms, fax. **Cards:** AX, CB, DC, DS, JC, MC, VI.

DALEVILLE pop. 1,454

———— WHERE TO STAY ————

ECONO LODGE-ROANOKE/DALEVILLE   *Book great rates at AAA.com*

Phone: 540/992-3000

Motel
$57-$85 All Year

Address: 446 Roanoke Rd 24083 **Location:** I-81, exit 150B, just nw on US 220. **Facility:** 66 one-bedroom standard units. 2 stories (no elevator), interior corridors. **Parking:** on-site. **Pool(s):** outdoor. **Leisure Activities:** basketball. **Guest Services:** coin laundry. **Cards:** AX, DC, DS, MC, VI. **Free Special Amenities: continental breakfast and high-speed Internet.**

HOWARD JOHNSON EXPRESS INN   *Book at AAA.com*

Phone: 540/992-1234

Small-scale Hotel
Rates not provided

Address: 437 Roanoke Rd 24083 **Location:** I-81, exit 150B, just nw on US 220. **Facility:** 94 one-bedroom standard units. 1-2 stories (no elevator), exterior corridors. **Parking:** on-site. **Amenities:** safes (fee), irons, hair dryers. **Pool(s):** outdoor. **Leisure Activities:** horseshoes, volleyball. **Guest Services:** coin laundry, wireless Internet. **Business Services:** meeting rooms.

———— WHERE TO DINE ————

THREE LI'L PIGS BARBEQUE

Phone: 540/966-0165

Barbecue
$5-$14

This restaurant has a catchy name and fresh quality barbeque. Three Li'l Pigs Barbeque hickory smokes it's pork and slow cooks it for fine flavor. Casual dress. **Bar:** Beer & wine. **Hours:** 11 am-10 pm. Closed: 12/25, 12/26; also Sun. **Address:** 120 Kingston Dr 24083 **Location:** I-81, exit 150, just w on US 220. **Parking:** on-site. **Cards:** DS, MC, VI.

DAMASCUS pop. 981

———— WHERE TO STAY ————

APPLE TREE B & B

Bed & Breakfast
$75-$95 All Year

Phone: 276/475-5261
Address: 115 E Laurel Ave 24236 **Location:** Town center. **Facility:** On the Appalachian Trail in a quaint town with antiques shops and restaurants, the 1904 B&B boasts a wrap-around porch and rooms with antiques. Smoke free premises. 4 units. 3 one-bedroom standard units. 1 one-bedroom suite. 1-2 stories (no elevator), interior corridors. *Bath:* combo or shower only. **Parking:** on-site. **Terms:** 2 night minimum stay - weekends, 3 day cancellation notice-fee imposed. **Amenities:** video library, hair dryers. *Some:* DVD players. **Cards:** MC, VI.

DANVILLE pop. 48,411

———— WHERE TO STAY ————

BEST WESTERN WINDSOR INN & SUITES   *Book great rates at AAA.com*

Small-scale Hotel
$79-$89 All Year

Phone: (434)483-5000
Address: 1292 S Boston Rd 24540 **Location:** On US 58, 1 mi e of jct US 29. **Facility:** 74 one-bedroom standard units, some with whirlpools. 3 stories, interior corridors. *Bath:* combo or shower only. **Parking:** on-site. **Amenities:** high-speed Internet, dual phone lines, voice mail, irons, hair dryers. **Pool(s):** heated indoor. **Leisure Activities:** whirlpool, exercise room. **Guest Services:** valet and coin laundry, wireless Internet. **Business Services:** meeting rooms, business center. **Cards:** AX, DS, MC, VI.

AAA Benefit:
Members save 10% everyday, plus an exclusive frequent stay program.

COMFORT INN & SUITES   *Book at AAA.com*

Small-scale Hotel
$79-$139 All Year

Phone: (434)793-2000
Address: 100 Tower Dr 24540 **Location:** US 58, just w of jct US 29 business route. Located adjacent to the mall. **Facility:** 118 one-bedroom standard units, some with whirlpools. 6 stories, interior corridors. **Parking:** on-site. **Terms:** 14 day cancellation notice. **Amenities:** high-speed Internet, voice mail, irons, hair dryers. **Pool(s):** outdoor. **Guest Services:** valet and coin laundry, wireless Internet. **Business Services:** meeting rooms, business center. **Cards:** AX, DC, DS, MC, VI.

COURTYARD BY MARRIOTT   *Book great rates at AAA.com*

Small-scale Hotel
$99-$114 All Year

Phone: (434)791-2661
Address: 2136 Riverside Dr 24540 **Location:** On US 58, just w of jct US 29 business route. **Facility:** Smoke free premises. 92 units. 89 one-bedroom standard units. 3 one-bedroom suites. 3 stories, interior corridors. *Bath:* combo or shower only. **Parking:** on-site. **Terms:** 3 day cancellation notice. **Amenities:** video games (fee), high-speed Internet, dual phone lines, voice mail, irons, hair dryers. **Pool(s):** heated outdoor. **Leisure Activities:** whirlpool, exercise room. **Guest Services:** valet and coin laundry. **Business Services:** meeting rooms, business center. **Cards:** AX, CB, DC, DS, JC, MC, VI.

AAA Benefit:
Members save 5% off of the best available rate.

HAMPTON INN RIVERSIDE   *Book great rates at AAA.com*

Small-scale Hotel
Rates not provided

Phone: 434/793-1111
Address: 2130 Riverside Dr 24540 **Location:** US 58, 0.5 mi e of jct US 86 and 29. **Facility:** 58 one-bedroom standard units, some with whirlpools. 3 stories, interior corridors. *Bath:* combo or shower only. **Parking:** on-site. **Amenities:** high-speed Internet, voice mail, irons, hair dryers. **Pool(s):** outdoor. **Leisure Activities:** exercise room. **Guest Services:** valet and coin laundry, wireless Internet. **Business Services:** meeting rooms, business center.

HOLIDAY INN EXPRESS DANVILLE   *Book at AAA.com*

Small-scale Hotel
$85-$104 All Year

Phone: (434)793-4000
Address: 2121 Riverside Dr 24541 **Location:** US 58, 0.5 mi e of jct US 86 and 29. **Facility:** 98 one-bedroom standard units, some with whirlpools. 3 stories, interior/exterior corridors. **Parking:** on-site. **Terms:** 3 day cancellation notice. **Amenities:** high-speed Internet, voice mail, irons, hair dryers. **Pool(s):** outdoor. **Leisure Activities:** fishing. **Guest Services:** valet laundry, wireless Internet. **Business Services:** meeting rooms, business center. **Cards:** AX, CB, DC, DS, JC, MC, VI.

INNKEEPER DANVILLE NORTH   *Book at AAA.com*

Motel
$50-$65 All Year

Phone: (434)836-1700
Address: 1030 Piney Forest Rd 24540 **Location:** US 29 N business route, 0.5 mi n of US 58. **Facility:** 52 one-bedroom standard units. 2 stories (no elevator), exterior corridors. **Parking:** on-site. **Terms:** 3 day cancellation notice. **Amenities:** high-speed Internet. **Pool(s):** outdoor. **Guest Services:** valet laundry, wireless Internet. **Business Services:** fax. **Cards:** AX, CB, DC, DS, JC, MC, VI.

INNKEEPER DANVILLE WEST
Small-scale Hotel
$50-$71 All Year

Book at AAA.com
Phone: (434)799-1202
Address: 3020 Riverside Dr 24541 **Location:** US 58 W, just w of jct US 29. **Facility:** 117 units. 114 one-bedroom standard units, some with whirlpools. 3 one-bedroom suites. 2 stories (no elevator), interior/exterior corridors. **Parking:** on-site. **Terms:** 3 day cancellation notice. **Pool(s):** outdoor. **Business Services:** fax. **Cards:** AX, CB, DC, DS, JC, MC, VI.

[ASK] [S/D] [Y] [swim] [icons] / SOME UNITS [X] FEE [icon] FEE [icon]

SLEEP INN & SUITES
(AAA) [SAVE]
Small-scale Hotel
$89-$250 3/1-10/31
$79-$250 11/1-2/28

Book great rates at AAA.com
Phone: (434)793-6090
Address: 1483 S Boston Rd 24540 **Location:** On US 58, 1.3 mi e of jct US 29. Located across from Danville Regional Airport. **Facility:** 76 units. 70 one-bedroom standard units. 6 one-bedroom suites. 3 stories, interior corridors. *Bath:* combo or shower only. **Parking:** on-site. **Amenities:** high-speed Internet, dual phone lines, voice mail, irons, hair dryers. **Pool(s):** heated outdoor. **Leisure Activities:** whirlpool, exercise room. **Guest Services:** valet and coin laundry, wireless Internet. **Business Services:** business center. **Cards:** AX, CB, DC, DS, MC, VI. **Free Special Amenities:** expanded continental breakfast and high-speed Internet.

[S/D] [Y] CALL [icon] [icons] / SOME UNITS [X] FEE [icon] FEE [icon]

SUPER 8 MOTEL
Motel
Rates not provided

Book at AAA.com
Phone: 434/799-5845
Address: 2385 Riverside Dr 24541 **Location:** On US 58, just e of jct US 29 business route. **Facility:** 57 one-bedroom standard units. 3 stories, interior corridors. **Parking:** on-site. **Amenities:** high-speed Internet, safes (fee), irons, hair dryers. **Guest Services:** wireless Internet.

[Y] [icons] [icon] / SOME UNITS FEE [icon] [X] [VCR] [icon]

——— **WHERE TO DINE** ———

EL VALLARTA RESTAURANTE MEXICANO
Mexican
$4-$12

Phone: 434/799-0506
With TVs tuned to sports in every corner, the large, friendly spot serves such favorites as fajitas, burritos, tacos with a twist and, for the truly adventurous, menudo. Casual dress. **Bar:** Full bar. **Hours:** 11 am-10 pm, Fri & Sat 11:45 am-10:30 pm, Sun 11:45 am-9 pm. Closed: 11/27, 12/25. **Address:** 418 Westover Pl 24541 **Location:** 1 mi n of US 58 via Piedmont Dr. **Parking:** on-site. **Cards:** AX, DS, MC, VI.

CALL [icon]

THE GALLERY RESTAURANT
(AAA)
American
$6-$20

Phone: 434/793-2500
With cozy booths, Early American decor accents and a pianist in the clubby lounge, the dining room strikes a more formal atmosphere than other spots in town. Built on seafood, steaks and some Italian offerings, the traditional menu has changed little in years. Casual dress. **Bar:** Full bar. **Hours:** 7 am-2 pm, Fri & Sat also 5 pm-10 pm. Closed: 12/25. **Address:** 2500 Riverside Dr 24540 **Location:** US 58, just e of jct US 29 business route; in Stratford Inn. **Parking:** on-site. **Cards:** AX, CB, DC, DS, MC, VI.

JOE & MIMMA'S ITALIAN RESTAURANT
Italian
$4-$18

Phone: 434/799-5763
This is a casual dining spot, offering traditional and "new" Italian pasta, veal and seafood dishes as well as calzone and pizza. Of note is a flavorful "penne rustica" in a creamy tomato sauce with a blend of mushrooms, spinach, and sun-dried tomatoes. Casual dress. **Bar:** Beer & wine. **Reservations:** suggested, weekends. **Hours:** 11 am-9:30 pm, Fri & Sat-10 pm. Closed: Sun & Mon. **Address:** 3336 Riverside Dr 24541 **Location:** On US 58; just w of jct W US 29 business route; in Riverside Shopping Center, rear corner. **Parking:** on-site. **Cards:** AX, DC, DS, MC, VI.

CALL [icon]

MARY'S DINER
Southern
$5-$10

Phone: 434/836-0132
The Southern cafeteria is a favorite for locals who rave that its fried chicken is the best. Other specialties include collard greens, cornbread and chicken livers. Folks on the run can take advantage of the drive-through menu. Casual dress. **Hours:** 11 am-9 pm. Closed: 12/24-12/26. **Address:** 1203 Piney Forest Rd 24540 **Location:** US 29 N, 2.7 mi n of US 58. **Parking:** on-site. **Cards:** AX, DS, MC, VI.

DAYTON pop. 1,344

——— **WHERE TO DINE** ———

LA CASITA RESTAURANT
Mexican
$6-$15

Phone: 540/879-2455
Diners nibble on great chips and salsa before digging into Mexican favorites. The mood here is friendly. Casual dress. **Bar:** Beer only. **Hours:** 8 am-8 pm. Closed: 12/25; also Sun. **Address:** 270 Dingledine Rd 22821 **Location:** Just s on US 11; center. **Parking:** on-site. **Cards:** AX, DS, MC, VI.

[icon]

THOMAS HOUSE RESTAURANT
American
$5-$14

Phone: 540/879-2181
Thomas House Restaurant offers home-spun charm and elegance as well as country home cooked favoraites. Casual dress. **Hours:** 6 am-8 pm. Closed: 1/1, 11/27, 12/25; also Sun. **Address:** 222 Main St 22821 **Location:** Center. **Parking:** on-site.

DINWIDDIE (See map and index starting on p. 854)

——— WHERE TO STAY ———

HOLIDAY INN EXPRESS HOTEL & SUITES   *Book great rates at AAA.com*   **Phone:** (804)518-1515   [22]

(AAA) (SAVE)

▽▽▽▽▽

Small-scale Hotel
$105-$133 3/1-11/2
$105-$114 11/3-2/28

Address: 5679 Boydton Plank Rd 23803 **Location:** I-85, exit 63A, just s. **Facility:** 67 one-bedroom standard units, some with whirlpools. 3 stories, interior corridors. *Bath:* combo or shower only. **Parking:** on-site. **Amenities:** dual phone lines, voice mail, irons, hair dryers. *Some:* DVD players (fee). **Pool(s):** outdoor. **Leisure Activities:** limited exercise equipment. **Guest Services:** valet laundry, wireless Internet. **Business Services:** meeting rooms, business center. **Cards:** AX, DC, DS, MC, VI. **Free Special Amenities: continental breakfast and high-speed Internet.** *(See color ad p 839)*

🅂🄳 🍴 CALL 🛗M 🏊 🎦 🛏 🖥 🍷 / SOME UNITS ✕

——— WHERE TO DINE ———

THE HOME PLACE RESTAURANT   **Phone:** 804/469-9596

(AAA)

▽▽▽

Southern
$4-$13

Nestled on 76 acres of beautiful, rustic surroundings and renowned as the birthplace of General Winfield Scott, the name says it all: Southern-style food and friendly service in a converted barn. A great place to have a good meal in a scenic spot. Casual dress. **Bar:** Beer & wine. **Reservations:** suggested, Fri & Sat. **Hours:** 7 am-8 pm, Fri & Sat-9 pm. Closed: 12/25. **Address:** 14712 Spring Creek Rd 23841 **Location:** I-85, exit 53, 1 mi w on SR 703, 1 mi s on US 1, then e. **Parking:** on-site. **Cards:** MC, VI.

CALL 🛗M 🖊

DOSWELL —See Richmond p. 876.

DUBLIN pop. 2,228

——— WHERE TO STAY ———

HAMPTON INN   *Book great rates at AAA.com*   **Phone:** 540/674-5700

(AAA) (SAVE)

▽▽▽▽

Small-scale Hotel
Rates not provided

Address: 4420 Cleburne Blvd 24084 **Location:** I-81, exit 98, just s. **Facility:** 63 one-bedroom standard units. 3 stories, interior corridors. *Bath:* combo or shower only. **Parking:** on-site. **Amenities:** high-speed Internet, voice mail, irons, hair dryers. **Pool(s):** heated indoor. **Leisure Activities:** exercise room. **Guest Services:** coin laundry, wireless Internet. **Business Services:** meeting rooms, business center. **Free Special Amenities: expanded continental breakfast and high-speed Internet.**

CALL 🛗M 🏊 🛏 🖥 🍷 / SOME UNITS ✕

HOLIDAY INN EXPRESS   *Book great rates at AAA.com*   **Phone:** (540)674-1600

(AAA) (SAVE)

▽▽▽▽

Small-scale Hotel
$84-$150 All Year

Address: 4428 Cleburne Blvd 24084 **Location:** I-81, exit 98, just e. **Facility:** 62 one-bedroom standard units, some with whirlpools. 3 stories, interior corridors. *Bath:* combo or shower only. **Parking:** on-site. **Amenities:** high-speed Internet, voice mail, irons, hair dryers. **Pool(s):** heated indoor. **Leisure Activities:** whirlpool, exercise room. **Guest Services:** valet and coin laundry, wireless Internet. **Business Services:** business center. **Cards:** AX, CB, DC, DS, MC, VI. **Free Special Amenities: continental breakfast and high-speed Internet.**

🅂🄳 CALL 🛗M 🏊 🎦 🛏 🖥 🍷 / SOME UNITS ✕

SLEEP INN & SUITES   *Book great rates at AAA.com*   **Phone:** (540)674-4099

(AAA) (SAVE)

▽▽▽▽

Small-scale Hotel
$79-$200 All Year

Address: 5094 State Park Rd 24084 **Location:** I-81, exit 101, just e. **Facility:** 67 one-bedroom standard units, some with whirlpools. 3 stories, interior corridors. *Bath:* combo or shower only. **Parking:** on-site. **Amenities:** high-speed Internet, voice mail, irons, hair dryers. **Pool(s):** heated indoor. **Leisure Activities:** whirlpool, exercise room. **Guest Services:** coin laundry, wireless Internet. **Business Services:** meeting rooms, business center. **Cards:** AX, CB, DC, DS, JC, MC, VI.

🅂🄳 CALL 🛗M 🏊 🎦 🍷 / SOME UNITS ✕ 📼 🛏 🖥

SUPER 8 MOTEL-DUBLIN   *Book at AAA.com*   **Phone:** 540/674-1951

▽▽

Small-scale Hotel
Rates not provided

Address: 4600 Cleburne Blvd 24084 **Location:** I-81, exit 98, just w. **Facility:** 46 one-bedroom standard units, some with whirlpools. 2 stories (no elevator), interior corridors. **Parking:** on-site. **Amenities:** irons, hair dryers. **Guest Services:** coin laundry, wireless Internet. **Business Services:** PC.

🎦 / SOME UNITS ✕

DUMFRIES —See District Of Columbia p. 527.

EASTVILLE pop. 203

——— WHERE TO DINE ———

EASTVILLE INN   **Phone:** 757/678-5745

▽▽▽▽

American
$6-$22

In the middle of town since the 1800s, the historic building has been painstakingly restored to house a restaurant and small museum. Fresh Chesapeake Bay seafood is the specialty on a menu with crab cakes, fried flounder, scallops in creamy cognac sauce, shrimp and cucumber cocktail, and oyster stew. Also offered are Greek salads, burgers, sandwiches and steaks. Casual dress. **Bar:** Full bar. **Reservations:** suggested. **Hours:** 11 am-9 pm. Closed: 11/27, 12/25; also Tues & Wed. **Address:** 16422 Courthouse Rd 23347 **Location:** From US 13, 0.5 mi w on SR 631; center. **Parking:** on-site. **Cards:** AX, MC, VI.

CALL 🛗M

ELKTON pop. 2,042

------ WHERE TO DINE ------

LOG CABIN BARBECUE

Barbecue
$5-$12

Casual dress. **Hours:** 11 am-9 pm. Closed: 7/4, 11/27, 12/25. **Address:** 11672 Spotswood Trail 22827 **Location:** 2 mi w on US 33. **Parking:** on-site. **Cards:** MC, VI.

Phone: 540/289-9400

EMPORIA pop. 5,665

------ WHERE TO STAY ------

BEST WESTERN EMPORIA   *Book great rates at AAA.com*

Phone: 434/634-3200

Small-scale Hotel
Rates not provided

Address: 1100 W Atlantic St 23847 **Location:** I-95, exit 11B, just w on US 58. **Facility:** 97 one-bedroom standard units, some with whirlpools. 2 stories (no elevator), exterior corridors. *Bath:* combo or shower only. **Parking:** on-site. **Amenities:** high-speed Internet, irons, hair dryers. **Pool(s):** outdoor. **Leisure Activities:** exercise room. **Guest Services:** wireless Internet. **Business Services:** business center. **Free Special Amenities:** expanded continental breakfast and high-speed Internet. *(See color ad below)*

 CALL   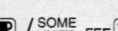 / SOME UNITS FEE

DAYS INN-EMPORIA   *Book great rates at AAA.com*

Phone: 434/634-9481

Small-scale Hotel
Rates not provided

Address: 921 W Atlantic St 23847 **Location:** I-95, exit 11B, just w on US 58. **Facility:** 119 one-bedroom standard units. 2 stories (no elevator), exterior corridors. **Parking:** on-site. **Amenities:** high-speed Internet, safes (fee), hair dryers. **Pool(s):** outdoor. **Guest Services:** coin laundry, wireless Internet. **Business Services:** PC. **Free Special Amenities:** continental breakfast and high-speed Internet.

    / SOME UNITS FEE

FAIRFIELD INN & SUITES EMPORIA/I-95

 *Book great rates at AAA.com*

Phone: 434/348-3800

Small-scale Hotel
$88-$108 All Year

Address: 104 W Cloverleaf Dr 23847 **Location:** I-95, exit 11A, just e. **Facility:** Smoke free premises. 82 one-bedroom standard units. 3 stories, interior corridors. *Bath:* combo or shower only. **Parking:** on-site. **Amenities:** high-speed Internet, dual phone lines, voice mail, irons, hair dryers. *Some:* CD players. **Pool(s):** heated indoor. **Leisure Activities:** whirlpool, exercise room. **Guest Services:** valet and coin laundry, wireless Internet. **Business Services:** meeting rooms, business center. **Cards:** AX, DC, DS, JC, MC, VI.

(ASK) (SD) (TI+) CALL (&M) (≈) (✕) (🎬) (▣)
/ SOME UNITS FEE (📷) FEE (🖨)

AAA Benefit:
Members save 5%
off of the best
available rate.

HAMPTON INN

Book great rates at AAA.com

Phone: 434/634-9200

(AAA) (SAVE)

Small-scale Hotel
Rates not provided

Address: 898 Wiggins Rd 23847 **Location:** I-95, exit 11B (US 58), just w. **Facility:** 85 units. 81 one-bedroom standard units. 4 one-bedroom suites. 5 stories, interior corridors. *Bath:* combo or shower only. **Parking:** on-site. **Amenities:** high-speed Internet, voice mail, irons, hair dryers. **Pool(s):** heated indoor. **Leisure Activities:** exercise room. **Guest Services:** valet laundry, wireless Internet. **Business Services:** meeting rooms, business center. **Free Special Amenities:** expanded continental breakfast and high-speed Internet. *(See color ad below)*

(TI+) CALL (&M) (≈) (🎬) (📷) (🖨) (▣) / SOME UNITS (🐾) (✕)

HOLIDAY INN EXPRESS HOTEL & SUITES

Book great rates at AAA.com

Phone: (434)336-9999

(AAA) (SAVE)

Small-scale Hotel
$89-$119 3/1-9/30
$79-$109 10/1-2/28

Address: 1350 W Atlantic St 23847 **Location:** I-95, exit 11B, just w on US 58. **Facility:** 78 one-bedroom standard units. 3 stories, interior corridors. *Bath:* combo or shower only. **Parking:** on-site. **Terms:** cancellation fee imposed. **Amenities:** high-speed Internet, dual phone lines, voice mail, irons, hair dryers. **Pool(s):** heated indoor. **Leisure Activities:** whirlpool, exercise room. **Guest Services:** coin laundry, wireless Internet. **Business Services:** meeting rooms, business center. **Cards:** AX, CB, DC, DS, MC, VI. **Free Special Amenities:** full breakfast and high-speed Internet. *(See color ad p 712)*

(SD) (TI+) CALL (&M) (≈) (🎬) (📷) (🖨) (▣) / SOME UNITS (✕)

▼ See AAA listing above ▼

▼ See AAA listing p 714 ▼

QUALITY INN *Book great rates at AAA.com* Phone: (434)348-8888

Small-scale Hotel
$65-$99 All Year

Address: 1207 W Atlantic St 23847 **Location:** I-95, exit 11B, just w on US 58. **Facility:** 115 one-bedroom standard units. 2 stories (no elevator), exterior corridors. **Parking:** on-site. **Amenities:** high-speed Internet, dual phone lines, voice mail, irons, hair dryers. **Pool(s):** outdoor. **Guest Services:** valet laundry, wireless Internet. **Business Services:** meeting rooms. **Cards:** AX, DC, DS, MC, VI. **Free Special Amenities: continental breakfast and high-speed Internet.**

SUPER 8 *Book great rates at AAA.com* Phone: (434)348-3282

Small-scale Hotel
$60-$79 All Year

Address: 1411 Skippers Rd 23847 **Location:** I-95, exit 8, just e on US 301. **Facility:** 96 one-bedroom standard units. 2 stories (no elevator), exterior corridors. **Parking:** on-site. **Amenities:** high-speed Internet, irons, hair dryers. **Pool(s):** outdoor. **Leisure Activities:** playground. **Guest Services:** wireless Internet. **Cards:** AX, DC, DS, MC, VI. **Free Special Amenities: continental breakfast and high-speed Internet.** *(See color ad p 713)*

——— WHERE TO DINE ———

PUEBLO VIEJO MEXICAN RESTAURANT Phone: 434/348-0362

Mexican
$4-$11

Interstate travelers have found a welcome refuge from fast food at this bright new spot. On the menu are tasty dishes served in combination plates, as well as such specialties as marinated shrimp cocktail, chile poblanos and carne asada. Casual dress. **Bar:** Full bar. **Reservations:** accepted. **Hours:** 11 am-10 pm, Sat from noon, Sun noon-9 pm. Closed major holidays. **Address:** 931 W Atlantic St 23847 **Location:** I-95, exit 11B, just w on US 58. **Parking:** on-site. **Cards:** AX, DS, MC, VI.

EXMORE pop. 1,136

——— WHERE TO STAY ———

BEST WESTERN EASTERN SHORE INN *Book great rates at AAA.com* Phone: (757)442-7378

Small-scale Hotel
$75-$107 All Year

Address: 2543 Lankford Hwy 23350 **Location:** US 13, just n of SR 178. **Facility:** 52 one-bedroom standard units, some with whirlpools. 2 stories (no elevator), interior/exterior corridors. **Bath:** combo or shower only. **Parking:** on-site. **Amenities:** high-speed Internet, irons, hair dryers. **Pool(s):** heated outdoor. **Guest Services:** coin laundry, wireless Internet. **Business Services:** PC, fax. **Cards:** AX, DS, MC, VI. **Free Special Amenities: continental breakfast and preferred room (subject to availability with advance reservations).**

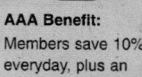

AAA Benefit:
Members save 10% everyday, plus an exclusive frequent stay program.

——— WHERE TO DINE ———

THE TRAWLER SEAFOOD RESTAURANT Phone: 757/442-2092

Seafood
$5-$25

Dark woods, decoys and ocean pictures contribute to the nautical mood in the simple seafood restaurant. All the basics are here: broiled, fried, steamed and blackened. Fresh ingredients make the difference for selections such as the homemade clam chowder. Casual dress. **Entertainment. Bar:** Full bar. **Reservations:** suggested, weekends. **Hours:** 11 am-8 pm, Fri-Sun to 9 pm. Closed: 11/27, 12/25. **Address:** 2555 Lankford Hwy 23350 **Location:** Just n on US 13. **Parking:** on-site. **Cards:** AX, DS, MC, VI.

FAIRFAX —*See District Of Columbia p. 528.*

FAIRFIELD

——— WHERE TO DINE ———

WHISTLE STOP CAFE Phone: 540/377-9492

American
$5-$18

Shenandoah hospitality at its finest. This quaint and cozy little cafe offers all the classic American Cuisine favorites as well as a mini-train running overhead. Casual dress. **Bar:** Beer & wine. **Hours:** 11 am-9 pm. Closed: 12/25; also Mon. **Address:** 33 Soapy Pl 24435 **Location:** I-81, exit 200, just e. **Parking:** on-site. **Cards:** DS, MC, VI.

FALLS CHURCH —*See District Of Columbia p. 533.*

FANCY GAP pop. 260

——— WHERE TO STAY ———

DAYS INN *Book at AAA.com*

Small-scale Hotel
Rates not provided

Phone: 276/728-5101
Address: 142 Kelly Rd 24328 **Location:** I-77, exit 8, 0.3 mi w; on top of the hill. Located behind Exxon. **Facility:** 60 one-bedroom standard units. 2 stories (no elevator), interior/exterior corridors. **Parking:** on-site. **Amenities:** hair dryers. **Leisure Activities:** exercise room. **Guest Services:** valet laundry. **Business Services:** fax (fee).

FARMVILLE pop. 6,845

——— WHERE TO STAY ———

COMFORT INN-FARMVILLE *Book at AAA.com*

Small-scale Hotel
$60-$136 All Year

Phone: (434)392-8163
Address: 2108 S Main St 23901 **Location:** Jct US 460 Bypass and US 15, exit Keysville. **Facility:** 51 one-bedroom standard units, some with whirlpools. 2 stories (no elevator), interior corridors. *Bath:* combo or shower only. **Parking:** on-site. **Amenities:** high-speed Internet, safes (fee), irons, hair dryers. **Pool(s):** outdoor. **Guest Services:** wireless Internet. **Business Services:** fax. **Cards:** AX, CB, DC, DS, JC, MC, VI.

HAMPTON INN *Book great rates at AAA.com*

Small-scale Hotel
$89-$169 All Year

Phone: (434)392-8826
Address: 300 Sunchase Blvd 23901 **Location:** 1.3 mi se on E 3rd St (US 460 Business route). **Facility:** 72 one-bedroom standard units. 4 stories, interior corridors. *Bath:* combo or shower only. **Parking:** on-site. **Amenities:** video games (fee), high-speed Internet, voice mail, irons, hair dryers. **Pool(s):** outdoor. **Leisure Activities:** exercise room. **Guest Services:** wireless Internet. **Business Services:** meeting rooms. **Cards:** AX, CB, DC, DS, MC, VI. **Free Special Amenities:** newspaper and high-speed Internet.

——— WHERE TO DINE ———

THE BAKERY

Deli/Subs
Sandwiches
$5-$9

This tiny spot serves delicious omelets, pate, Brie and French baguette sandwiches, such as tuna with mascarpone. The pastry window displays scrumptious treats, including chocolate-filled croissants. Gourmet grocery options and a small wine shop are also offered. Casual dress. **Bar:** Beer & wine. **Hours:** 7 am-6 pm, Sat from 8 am. Closed major holidays; also Sun & Mon. **Address:** 218 N Main St 23901 **Location:** Center. **Parking:** street. **Cards:** MC, VI.

CAFE ZELIA

American
$5-$8

Main Street shoppers often refuel at the cozy Farmville haunt. Guests can choose from a spectacularly wide variety of salads, soups and sandwiches at more than reasonable prices. Daily changing dessert offerings might include freshly baked pies, cakes and cookies. Casual dress. **Bar:** Beer & wine. **Hours:** 8:30 am-4 pm. Closed major holidays; also Sun. **Address:** 214 N Main St 23901 **Location:** Between 2nd and 3rd sts; downtown. **Parking:** street. **Cards:** MC, VI.

CHARLEY'S WATERFRONT CAFE

American
$6-$19

Overlooking a river, the former tobacco warehouse is rustic in appearance, with the centerpiece being a huge scale once used for tobacco. The diverse menu comprises potato skins, spiced wings, blackened tuna Caesar, a great sandwich selection, pasta dishes and perhaps a stir-fry option. Dessert is made from scratch. The casual experience is great for families. Casual dress. **Bar:** Full bar. **Reservations:** accepted. **Hours:** 11 am-10 pm; Sunday brunch. Closed: 1/1, 11/27, 12/24, 12/25. **Address:** 201 B Mill St 23901 **Location:** Just n on Mill St/US 15 N; downtown. **Parking:** on-site. **Cards:** AX, DS, MC, VI.

MACADO'S

American
$6-$8

The lively student hangout is well-loved for its lengthy list of imaginative overstuffed sandwiches and wraps. Macaroni and cheese, chili and oversized ice cream desserts also are popular. Casual dress. **Hours:** 8 am-12:30 am, Fri & Sat-1:30 am. Closed: 12/25. **Address:** 200 3rd St 23901 **Location:** Just e of Main St. **Parking:** on-site. **Cards:** AX, CB, DC, DS, JC, MC, VI.

FINCASTLE pop. 359

——— WHERE TO DINE ———

CAPTAIN'S TAVERN SEAFOOD RESTAURANT & LOUNGE

Seafood
$6-$25

Phone: 540-473-2299
To ensure freshness, seafood is prepared after guests order. The menu comprises a wide variety of dishes. Service is friendly. Casual dress. **Bar:** Full bar. **Hours:** 11:30 am-2:30 & 4-9:30 pm, Sat & Sun 11:30 am-9:30 pm. Closed major holidays; also Mon. **Address:** US 220 N 24090 **Location:** On US 220 N, 1 mi n. **Parking:** on-site. **Cards:** MC, VI.

FISHERSVILLE pop. 4,998

——— WHERE TO STAY ———

HAMPTON INN WAYNESBORO/STUARTS DRAFT
Book great rates at AAA.com
Phone: (540)213-9500

AAA [SAVE]
◆◆◆

Small-scale Hotel
$179-$199 5/1-2/28
$114-$139 3/1-4/30

Address: 15 Four Square Ln 22939 **Location:** I-64, exit 91, just n. **Facility:** 66 one-bedroom standard units. 4 stories, interior corridors. *Bath:* combo or shower only. **Parking:** on-site. **Terms:** 2 night minimum stay - seasonal and/or weekends. **Amenities:** voice mail, irons, hair dryers. *Some:* high-speed Internet. **Pool(s):** heated indoor. **Leisure Activities:** exercise room. **Guest Services:** valet laundry, wireless Internet. **Business Services:** meeting rooms, fax (fee). **Cards:** AX, DC, DS, MC, VI. **Free Special Amenities:** full breakfast and high-speed Internet.

[icons] CALL [icons] / SOME UNITS [X]

FLINT HILL

——— WHERE TO DINE ———

FOUR AND TWENTY BLACKBIRDS
Phone: 540/675-1111

◆◆◆

American
$20-$30

Not only is its name distinctive, but the restaurant blends unusual ingredients into memorably good appetizers and entrees. Servers are outgoing. Casual dress. **Bar:** Full bar. **Reservations:** suggested, weekends. **Hours:** 5:30 pm-9 pm; Sunday brunch 10 am-2 pm. Closed: 9/1, 12/25; also Mon, Tues, 8/3-8/20 & 12/31-1/14. **Address:** 650 Zachary Taylor Hwy 22627 **Location:** Center. **Parking:** on-site. **Cards:** MC, VI.

GRIFFIN TAVERN & RESTAURANT
Phone: 540/675-3227

AAA
◆◆

American
$6-$21

The new establishment gives patrons a choice of outdoor seating (weather permitting) or cozy, wood-grained surroundings. A griffin collection is on display. Casual dress. **Bar:** Full bar. **Hours:** 11 am-10 pm. Closed: 12/25. **Address:** 659 Zachary Taylor Hwy 22627 **Location:** Center. **Parking:** on-site. **Cards:** AX, CB, DC, DS, JC, MC, VI.

FRANKLIN pop. 8,346

——— WHERE TO STAY ———

COMFORT INN
Book at AAA.com
Phone: 757/569-0018

◆◆◆

Small-scale Hotel
$67-$90 All Year

Address: 1620 Armory Dr 23851 **Location:** Jct US 58 Bypass and SR 671. **Facility:** 77 units. 75 one-bedroom standard units, some with whirlpools. 2 one-bedroom suites with whirlpools. 2 stories (no elevator), exterior corridors. *Bath:* combo or shower only. **Parking:** on-site. **Amenities:** high-speed Internet, irons, hair dryers. **Pool(s):** outdoor. **Leisure Activities:** limited exercise equipment. **Guest Services:** coin laundry, wireless Internet. **Business Services:** meeting rooms, PC. **Cards:** AX, DC, DS, MC, VI.

[ASK] [icons] CALL [icons] / SOME UNITS [X]

SUPER 8 MOTEL
Book at AAA.com
Phone: 757/562-2888

◆

Motel
Rates not provided

Address: 1599 Armory Dr 23851 **Location:** Jct US 58 Bypass and SR 671. **Facility:** 52 one-bedroom standard units. 2 stories (no elevator), interior corridors. **Parking:** on-site. **Amenities:** high-speed Internet, safes (fee). **Guest Services:** coin laundry, wireless Internet. **Business Services:** fax.

[icons] CALL [icons] / SOME UNITS [X] FEE [icon]

——— WHERE TO DINE ———

GREY FOX RESTAURANT
Phone: 757/516-8877

◆◆

American
$6-$18

The charming downtown spot has a warm Southern character and serves regional American cuisine that picks up on influences from Creole to the Southwest. Specialties includes crab Louie, she-crab soup, blackened tilapia and roasted pork tenderloin. Casual dress. **Bar:** Full bar. **Reservations:** accepted. **Hours:** 11:30 am-2:30 & 5-9 pm, Sat from 5 pm, Sun noon-3 & 5-8 pm. Closed major holidays; also Wed. **Address:** 401 N Main St 23851 **Location:** Jct 4th Ave; downtown. **Parking:** street. **Cards:** AX, MC, VI.

FREDERICKSBURG pop. 19,279

——— WHERE TO STAY ———

BEST WESTERN CENTRAL PLAZA
Book great rates at AAA.com
Phone: 540/786-7404

AAA [SAVE]
◆◆

Motel
Rates not provided

Address: 3000 Plank Rd 22401 **Location:** I-95, exit 130B on SR 3. Located adjacent to Spotsylvania Mall. **Facility:** 76 one-bedroom standard units. 3 stories (no elevator), exterior corridors. **Parking:** on-site. **Amenities:** high-speed Internet, voice mail, irons, hair dryers. **Guest Services:** valet and coin laundry. **Business Services:** fax. **Free Special Amenities:** continental breakfast and high-speed Internet.

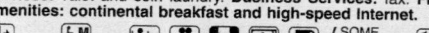

[icons] CALL [icons] FEE [icons] / SOME UNITS FEE [icons] [X]

AAA Benefit:
Members save 10% everyday, plus an exclusive frequent stay program.

BEST WESTERN FREDERICKSBURG

Book great rates at AAA.com

Phone: (540)371-5050

Small-scale Hotel
$79-$89 3/1-10/31
$69-$79 11/1-2/28

Address: 2205 William St 22401 **Location:** I-95, exit 130A, 0.3 mi e on SR 3. **Facility:** 108 one-bedroom standard units. 2 stories (no elevator), exterior corridors. **Parking:** on-site. **Amenities:** high-speed Internet, voice mail, irons, hair dryers. **Pool(s):** outdoor. **Guest Services:** valet and coin laundry. **Business Services:** meeting rooms, fax. **Cards:** AX, CB, DC, DS, JC, MC, VI. **Free Special Amenities: expanded continental breakfast and high-speed Internet.** *(See color ad below)*

AAA Benefit:
Members save 10% everyday, plus an exclusive frequent stay program.

COMFORT INN FREDERICKSBURG SOUTHPOINT

Book great rates at AAA.com

Phone: (540)898-5550

Small-scale Hotel
$91 All Year

Address: 5422 Jefferson Davis Hwy 22407 **Location:** I-95, exit 126 (Massaponax), just s on US 1; exit 126B northbound; in Southpoint. **Facility:** 125 one-bedroom standard units. 5 stories, interior corridors. **Parking:** on-site. **Amenities:** high-speed Internet, voice mail, irons, hair dryers. **Pool(s):** heated indoor. **Leisure Activities:** sauna, exercise room. **Business Services:** meeting rooms, PC, fax. **Cards:** AX, CB, DC, DS, MC, VI. **Free Special Amenities: expanded continental breakfast and local telephone calls.**

COMFORT SUITES

Phone: 540/322-4700

[fyi]

Small-scale Hotel
$89-$132 All Year

Too new to rate. **Address:** 541 Warrenton Rd 22406 **Location:** I-95, exit 133. **Amenities:** 77 units, coffeemakers, microwaves, refrigerators, pool. **Cards:** AX, DC, DS, MC, VI.

COUNTRY INN & SUITES FREDERICKSBURG

Book great rates at AAA.com

Phone: (540)898-1800

Small-scale Hotel
$98-$108 All Year

Address: 5327 Jefferson Davis Hwy 22408 **Location:** I-95, 126 southbound; exit 126A nortbound; just n on US 1. **Facility:** Smoke free premises. 119 units. 101 one-bedroom standard units. 18 one-bedroom suites with efficiencies. 4 stories, interior corridors. *Bath:* combo or shower only. **Parking:** on-site. **Amenities:** high-speed Internet, voice mail, irons, hair dryers. **Pool(s):** outdoor. **Leisure Activities:** exercise room. **Guest Services:** valet and coin laundry, wireless Internet. **Business Services:** meeting rooms, business center. **Cards:** AX, DC, DS, MC, VI.

DUNNING MILLS INN ALL SUITES HOTEL

Phone: 540/373-1256

Condominium
$69-$89 3/1-10/31
$59-$79 11/1-2/28

Address: 2305-C Jefferson Davis Hwy 22401 **Location:** I-95, exit 126, 3 mi n on US 1. **Facility:** 54 one-bedroom standard units with kitchens. 2 stories (no elevator), exterior corridors. **Terms:** office hours 8 am-midnight, cancellation fee imposed. **Amenities:** high-speed Internet, irons, hair dryers. **Pool(s):** outdoor. **Guest Services:** coin laundry, wireless Internet. **Business Services:** fax. **Cards:** AX, DC, DS, MC, VI. **Free Special Amenities: local telephone calls and high-speed Internet.**

▼ *See AAA listing above* ▼

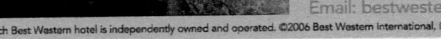

FAIRFIELD INN OF FREDERICKSBURG   *Book great rates at AAA.com*

Phone: 540/891-9100

Small-scale Hotel
$87-$109 All Year

Address: 10330 Spotsylvania Ave 22408 **Location:** I-95, exit 126 southbound; exit 126A northbound, just n on US 1, just e to Market St, then just s. **Facility:** Smoke free premises. 74 one-bedroom standard units. 3 stories, interior corridors. **Bath:** combo or shower only. **Parking:** on-site. **Amenities:** high-speed Internet, irons, hair dryers. **Pool(s):** heated indoor. **Leisure Activities:** exercise room. **Guest Services:** valet laundry, wireless Internet. **Business Services:** fax (fee). **Cards:** AX, DC, DS, MC, VI.

AAA Benefit:
Members save 5% off of the best available rate.

FREDERICKSBURG HOSPITALITY HOUSE & CONFERENCE CENTER   *Book great rates at AAA.com*

Phone: (540)786-8321

Large-scale Hotel
$129 3/1-12/31
$119 1/1-2/28

Address: 2801 Plank Rd 22401 **Location:** I-95, exit 130B, on SR 3. Located in Central Park, a shopping complex. **Facility:** 194 units. 188 one- and 1 two-bedroom standard units, some with whirlpools. 5 one-bedroom suites. 3 stories, interior corridors. **Bath:** combo or shower only. **Parking:** on-site. **Amenities:** video games (fee), dual phone lines, voice mail, irons, hair dryers. **Dining:** 2 restaurants. **Pool(s):** outdoor. **Leisure Activities:** exercise room. **Guest Services:** valet and coin laundry, wireless Internet. **Business Services:** conference facilities, business center. **Cards:** AX, CB, DC, DS, JC, MC, VI. **Free Special Amenities:** newspaper and high-speed Internet.

HAMPTON INN & SUITES OF FREDERICKSBURG   *Book great rates at AAA.com*

Phone: (540)898-5000

Small-scale Hotel
$109-$129 All Year

Address: 4800 Market St 22408 **Location:** I-95, exit 126 southbound; exit 126A northbound, just n on US 1, then just e to Market St. **Facility:** 121 one-bedroom standard units. 5 stories, interior corridors. **Bath:** combo or shower only. **Parking:** on-site. **Terms:** 20 day cancellation notice. **Facility:** 148 units. **Amenities:** video games (fee), high-speed Internet, voice mail, irons, hair dryers. **Pool(s):** heated indoor. **Leisure Activities:** whirlpool, exercise room. **Fee:** game room. **Guest Services:** valet and coin laundry, wireless Internet. **Business Services:** meeting rooms, business center. **Cards:** AX, CB, DC, DS, MC, VI. **Free Special Amenities:** newspaper and high-speed Internet.

HILTON GARDEN INN   *Book great rates at AAA.com*

Phone: 540/548-8822

Small-scale Hotel
Rates not provided

Address: 1060 Hospitality Ln 22401 **Location:** I-95, exit 130B (SR 3), just w to Carl D Silver Pkwy, then 2 mi n; adjacent to Expo Center. Located in Central Park, a shopping complex. **Facility:** 148 units. 147 one-bedroom standard units, some with whirlpools. 1 one-bedroom suite with whirlpool. 5 stories, interior corridors. **Bath:** combo or shower only. **Amenities:** high-speed Internet, dual phone lines, voice mail, irons, hair dryers. **Pool(s):** heated indoor. **Leisure Activities:** whirlpool, exercise room. **Guest Services:** valet and coin laundry, wireless Internet. **Business Services:** meeting rooms, business center.

HOLIDAY INN-FREDERICKSBURG NORTH   *Book great rates at AAA.com*

Phone: (540)371-5550

Small-scale Hotel
$85-$115 3/1-10/31
$75-$100 11/1-2/28

Address: 564 Warrenton Rd 22405 **Location:** I-95, exit 133, just nw on US 17. **Facility:** 149 one-bedroom standard units. 2 stories (no elevator), exterior corridors. **Bath:** combo or shower only. **Parking:** on-site. **Amenities:** high-speed Internet, dual phone lines, voice mail, irons, hair dryers. **Pool(s):** outdoor, heated indoor. **Leisure Activities:** whirlpool, exercise room. **Fee:** game room. **Guest Services:** valet and coin laundry. **Business Services:** meeting rooms, business center. **Cards:** AX, CB, DC, DS, JC, MC, VI. **Free Special Amenities:** newspaper and high-speed Internet.

▼ See AAA listing p 719 ▼

QUALITY INN CENTRAL PARK

 Book great rates at AAA.com

Phone: (540)371-0330

Small-scale Hotel
$75-$125 All Year

Address: 2310 William St 22401 **Location:** I-95, exit 130A on SR 3 E. **Facility:** 166 one-bedroom standard units. 2 stories (no elevator), exterior corridors. **Parking:** on-site. **Amenities:** high-speed Internet, voice mail, irons, hair dryers. **Pool(s):** outdoor. **Guest Services:** valet and coin laundry, wireless Internet. **Business Services:** meeting rooms, fax. **Cards:** AX, CB, DC, DS, JC, MC, VI. **Free Special Amenities: expanded continental breakfast and high-speed Internet.**

QUALITY INN FREDERICKSBURG

 Book great rates at AAA.com

Phone: (540)373-0000

Small-scale Hotel
$69-$109 3/1-8/31
$59-$79 9/1-2/28

Address: 543 Warrenton Rd 22406 **Location:** I-95, exit 133, just n on US 17. **Facility:** 61 one-bedroom standard units. 2 stories (no elevator), exterior corridors. **Parking:** on-site. **Amenities:** high-speed Internet, irons, hair dryers. **Guest Services:** wireless Internet. **Business Services:** PC, fax. **Cards:** AX, CB, DC, DS, MC, VI. **Free Special Amenities: full breakfast and high-speed Internet.**

RAMADA INN SOUTH

Book great rates at AAA.com

Phone: 540/898-1102

Small-scale Hotel
Rates not provided

Address: 5324 Jefferson Davis Hwy 22408 **Location:** I-95, exit 126, just n on US 1. **Facility:** 198 one-bedroom standard units. 2 stories (no elevator), interior/exterior corridors. **Parking:** on-site. **Amenities:** high-speed Internet, voice mail, irons, hair dryers. *Fee:* video games, safes. **Dining:** entertainment. **Pool(s):** heated indoor. **Leisure Activities:** sauna, whirlpool, exercise room. *Fee:* game room. **Guest Services:** valet and coin laundry, wireless Internet. **Business Services:** meeting rooms, PC (fee), fax. **Free Special Amenities: newspaper and room upgrade (subject to availability with advance reservations).**

ROYAL INN MOTEL

Phone: (540)891-2700

Motel
$45-$70 3/1-8/31
$40-$60 9/1-2/28

Address: 5309 Jefferson Davis Hwy 22408 **Location:** I-95, exit 126, 0.5 mi ne on US 1. Located in a commercial area. **Facility:** 27 one-bedroom standard units. 2 stories (no elevator), exterior corridors. **Parking:** on-site. **Business Services:** fax. **Cards:** AX, CB, DC, DS, MC, VI. **Free Special Amenities: local telephone calls and high-speed Internet.**

SLEEP INN

Book great rates at AAA.com

Phone: (540)372-6868

Small-scale Hotel
$79-$109 3/1-10/31
$69-$99 11/1-2/28

Address: 595 Warrenton Rd 22406 **Location:** I-95, exit 133, just w. **Facility:** 68 one-bedroom standard units. 2 stories (no elevator), interior corridors. *Bath:* combo or shower only. **Parking:** on-site. **Amenities:** high-speed Internet, irons, hair dryers. **Guest Services:** coin laundry, wireless Internet. **Business Services:** fax (fee). **Cards:** AX, CB, DC, DS, JC, MC, VI.

SLEEP INN SOUTHPOINT

Book great rates at AAA.com

Phone: (540)710-5500

Small-scale Hotel
$72-$98 All Year

Address: 5400 Southpoint Blvd 22407 **Location:** I-95, exit 126 southbound; exit 126B northbound; on US 1 S. **Facility:** 67 one-bedroom standard units. 3 stories, interior corridors. *Bath:* combo or shower only. **Parking:** on-site. **Amenities:** high-speed Internet, dual phone lines, voice mail, irons, hair dryers. **Pool(s):** heated outdoor. **Leisure Activities:** exercise room. **Guest Services:** valet and coin laundry, wireless Internet. **Business Services:** meeting rooms, fax. **Cards:** AX, DC, DS, MC, VI. **Free Special Amenities: continental breakfast and high-speed Internet.** *(See color ad p 718)*

▼ See AAA listing p 720 ▼

TOWNEPLACE SUITES BY MARRIOTT

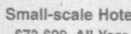

Book great rates at AAA.com

Phone: 540/891-0775

Small-scale Hotel
$73-$90 All Year

Address: 4700 Market St 22408 **Location:** I-95, exit 126 southbound; exit 126A northbound, just n on US 1, then just e. **Facility:** Smoke free premises. 93 units. 70 one-bedroom standard units with kitchens. 10 one- and 13 two-bedroom suites with kitchens. 3 stories, interior corridors. *Bath:* combo or shower only. **Parking:** on-site. **Amenities:** high-speed Internet, voice mail, irons, hair dryers. **Pool(s):** heated outdoor. **Leisure Activities:** exercise room. **Guest Services:** valet and coin laundry, wireless Internet. **Business Services:** meeting rooms, business center. **Cards:** AX, DC, DS, JC, MC, VI. **Free Special Amenities: continental breakfast and local telephone calls.**

AAA Benefit:
Members save 5% off of the best available rate.

WINGATE INN

Book at AAA.com

Phone: (540)368-8000

Small-scale Hotel
$99-$129 All Year

Address: 20 Sanford Dr 22406 **Location:** I-95, exit 133, just s. **Facility:** 129 one-bedroom standard units, some with whirlpools. 4 stories, interior corridors. *Bath:* combo or shower only. **Parking:** on-site. **Amenities:** video games (fee), high-speed Internet, dual phone lines, voice mail, safes, irons, hair dryers. **Pool(s):** heated indoor. **Leisure Activities:** whirlpool, exercise room. **Guest Services:** valet and coin laundry, wireless Internet. **Business Services:** conference facilities, business center. **Cards:** AX, CB, DC, DS, JC, MC, VI.

WYTESTONE SUITES OF FREDERICKSBURG

Book great rates at AAA.com

Phone: (540)891-1112

Small-scale Hotel
$135-$150 3/1-10/31
$95-$110 11/1-2/28

Address: 4615 Southpoint Pkwy 22407 **Location:** I-95, exit 126 (Spotsylvania), just s on US 1; exit 126B northbound, in Southpoint. **Facility:** Smoke free premises. 85 one-bedroom suites. 5 stories, interior corridors. *Bath:* combo or shower only. **Parking:** on-site. **Amenities:** high-speed Internet, dual phone lines, voice mail, safes, irons, hair dryers. **Pool(s):** heated indoor. **Leisure Activities:** exercise room. **Guest Services:** valet and coin laundry. **Business Services:** meeting rooms, business center. **Free Special Amenities: full breakfast and high-speed Internet.** *(See color ad p 719)*

WHERE TO DINE

ALLMAN'S BARBECUE

Barbecue
$5-$11

Phone: 540-373-9881

For more than 40 years, the same cook has prepared pork barbecue with a sweet peppery sauce at this local institution. The cole slaw recipe is a family secret that dates back 100 years. Casual dress. **Hours:** 11 am-8:30 pm. Closed major holidays; also Sun. **Address:** 1299 Jefferson Davis Hwy 22401 **Location:** On US 1 (Jefferson Davis Hwy), just n of jct SR 3. **Parking:** on-site.

BANGKOK CAFE

Thai
$6-$14

Phone: 540-373-0745

This casual spot offers authentic Thai cuisine, such as crispy whole fish with basil, pad Thai noodles, four curry varieties, and vegetarian stir fry. The desserts are unusual, using tropical fruits and sweet rice. Thai tea and coffee also are available. Casual dress. **Bar:** Beer & wine. **Hours:** 11:30 am-9 pm, Wed from 4 pm, Fri & Sat 11:30 am-9:30 pm. Closed: Tues. **Address:** 825 Caroline St 22401 **Location:** Just n of Visitor's Center; in Olde Towne. **Parking:** street. **Cards:** CB, DC, DS, MC, VI.

BAREFOOT GREENS SEAFOOD MARKET

Seafood
$7-$15

Phone: 540-373-2012

Down by the river, the tiny, bare-bones seafood market prepares excellent fresh grilled and fried fish, whole crabs, steamed shrimp and more, with tasty homemade coleslaw and hushpuppies on the side. Casual dress. **Bar:** Beer & wine. **Hours:** 11 am-9 pm. **Address:** 1017 Sophia St 22401 **Location:** In Olde Towne on the riverfront. **Parking:** on-site. **Cards:** MC, VI.

BISTRO BETHEM

American
$7-$28

Phone: 540-371-9999

In a sleek and modern setting with walls that serve as a showcase for rotating displays of artwork, a talented young chef creates a seasonally changing menu of exciting modern American dishes with a Southern flair. Try such specialties as asparagus soup with stilton, chile-roasted salmon and grilled romaine salad. Wine selections are intelligent and thoughtful. Casual dress. **Bar:** Full bar. **Reservations:** suggested. **Hours:** 11:30 am-2:30 & 5-10 pm, Sun-9 pm; Sunday brunch. Closed: 1/1, 12/25; also Mon. **Address:** 309 William St 22401 **Location:** Jct with Caroline St; in Olde Towne. **Parking:** street. **Cards:** AX, CB, DC, DS, JC, MC, VI.

BONEFISH GRILL

Seafood
$13-$18

Phone: 540/548-1984

Fish is the house specialty, and the menu and nightly specials offer a variety of choices. Well-prepared food is cooked to perfection. Service is casual in nature, and the staff is skilled and attentive. Casual dress. **Bar:** Full bar. **Reservations:** accepted. **Hours:** 4 pm-10:30 pm, Fri-11:30 pm, Sat 2 pm-11:30 pm, Sun noon-10 pm. Closed: 11/27, 12/25. **Address:** 1779 Carl D Silver Pkwy 22401 **Location:** I-95, exit 130B, just n; in Central Park. **Parking:** on-site. **Cards:** AX, DS, MC, VI.

BROCKS RIVERSIDE GRILL

American
$6-$28

Phone: 540-370-1820

There's a large, friendly lounge in the front of this riverside spot and a cozy back room with a large hearth for more intimate dining. Traditional dishes are prepared from scratch with fine ingredients. Specialties include black Angus beef, blackened tuna and crab cakes. Casual dress. **Bar:** Full bar. **Reservations:** accepted. **Hours:** 11 am-9 pm, Thurs-Sat to 10 pm. Closed: 1/1, 12/25. **Address:** 503 Sophia St 22401 **Location:** In Olde Towne, on the riverfront. **Parking:** on-site. **Cards:** AX, MC, VI.

BURGER & KABAB PLACE

Phone: 540/370-1878

Pakistani
$5-$13

Casual dress. **Hours:** 11 am-9 pm, Fri-10 pm, Sat noon-10 pm, Sun noon-8 pm. Closed major holidays. **Address:** 367 Warrenton Rd 22405 **Location:** I-95, exit 133, just e; in Olde Forge Plaza. **Parking:** on-site. **Cards:** MC, VI.

CALL

CAROLINE STREET CAFE

Phone: 540/654-9180

Deli/Subs
Sandwiches
$7-$8

A father-and-son team at the tiny cafe turns out tasty favorites, such as white chicken chili, roasted top round of beef or smoked turkey sandwiches and delectable desserts, including creme brulee blossoms and chocolate confusion brownies. Casual dress. **Bar:** Beer & wine. **Hours:** 10 am-4 pm, Sun from 11 am. Closed major holidays. **Address:** 1002 Caroline St 22401 **Location:** Jct William St; in Olde Towne. **Parking:** street. **Cards:** MC, VI.

CASTIGLIA'S ITALIAN RESTAURANT & PIZZERIA

Phone: 540/373-6650

Italian
$8-$14

Watch the streetscape from the small, unassuming spot, which has booths next to large picture windows. The menu of mostly Italian dishes lists varied pasta dishes, seafood and some good veal preparations. Also offered are a few Latino appetizers. The far-from-pretentious setting is comfortably accommodating. Casual dress. **Bar:** Full bar. **Hours:** 11 am-10 pm, Fri & Sat-11 pm, Sun-9 pm. **Address:** 324 William St 22401 **Location:** Jct Charles St; in Olde Towne. **Parking:** street. **Cards:** AX, DC, DS, MC, VI.

CLAIBORNE'S

Phone: 540/371-7080

Steak House
$5-$34

Sleek sophistication marks the early 1900s train station, decorated with rich wood, historic prints, candlelight and a glowing fireplace. The menu is a showcase for fine steak and low-country specialties, such as shrimp and grits. An extensive list of wines and liquors is offered. The atmosphere is city chic and romantic. Dressy casual. **Bar:** Full bar. **Reservations:** suggested. **Hours:** 5 pm-9 pm, Fri & Sat-10 pm, Sun 11 am-2 & 5-9 pm. Closed major holidays. **Address:** 200 Lafayette Blvd 22401 **Location:** In Olde Towne; at train station. **Parking:** on-site. **Cards:** AX, DS, MC, VI.

CUZCO CHICKEN RUN

Phone: 540/548-0008

Peruvian
$6-$20

This simple spot serves succulent charcoal-grilled chicken and other traditional Peruvian favorites, such as seviche, fried plantains, steak churrasco, whole fried red snapper and tamales steamed in banana leaves. Casual dress. **Bar:** Full bar. **Reservations:** not accepted. **Hours:** 10 am-10 pm, Fri & Sat-11 pm. **Address:** 1632 Carl D Silver Pkwy 22401 **Location:** I-95, exit 130B (SR 3), 0.5 mi n; in Central Park. **Parking:** on-site. **Cards:** MC, VI.

GARNJANA THAI

Phone: 540/891-0280

Thai
$6-$13

Traditional fresh Thai specialties are served in a small but comfortable setting. Among choices are regional curry preparations, shrimp in a blanket and crispy soft-shell crabs. Many dishes are infused with exotic spices and tropical flavors, such as coconut, pineapple and mango. Casual dress. **Bar:** Beer & wine. **Hours:** 11 am-9 pm, Fri & Sat-10 pm. Closed major holidays; also Sun. **Address:** 4416 Lafayette Blvd 22408 **Location:** I-95, exit 126A, just n to Lafayette Blvd; Lafayette Junction. **Parking:** on-site. **Cards:** AX, DC, DS, MC, VI.

GOOLRICK'S

Phone: 540/373-9878

American
$3-$7

Nostalgic pharmacy lunch counter with the oldest operating soda fountain in the country serving up traditional egg creams, milkshakes, and ice cream sodas. Lunch offerings include sandwiches, daily soups, and chili on Saturday. Casual dress. **Hours:** 9 am-6 pm, Sat-4 pm. Closed major holidays; also Sun. **Address:** 901 Caroline St 22401 **Location:** Jct George St; in Olde Towne. **Parking:** street. **Cards:** MC, VI.

GURU INDIAN CUISINE

Phone: 540/548-1011

Indian
$8-$15

Once inside guests are lulled into a sense of calm by the cool sounds of the rock waterfall and the rich colors and gold. The menu offers specialties from the tandoor oven including a variety of great breads, curries, and vegetarian offerings. Casual dress. **Bar:** Full bar. **Hours:** 11:30 am-2:30 & 5-9:30 pm, Fri-10 pm, Sat 11:30 am-3 & 5-10 pm, Sun 11:30 am-3 & 5-9:30 pm. Closed major holidays. **Address:** 1320 Central Park Blvd 22401 **Location:** I-95, exit 130B, just w on SR 3, then just n; in Uptown Central Park. **Parking:** on-site. **Cards:** AX, DC, DS, MC, VI.

CALL

LA PETITE AUBERGE

Phone: 540/371-2727

French
$7-$26

This charming restaurant with a cafe setting offers traditional French dishes, all excellent (most notably the vegetarian plate with rice, red and black beans and ratatouille). The lunch menu also features sandwiches, soup and salad and other treats. Dressy casual. **Bar:** Full bar. **Reservations:** required. **Hours:** 11:30 am-2:30 & 5:30-10 pm, Sat 11:30 am-2:15 & 5:30-10 pm. Closed major holidays; also Sun. **Address:** 311 William St 22401 **Location:** Just e of corner William and Charles sts; in Olde Towne. **Parking:** street. **Cards:** AX, DC, MC, VI.

OLDE TOWNE STEAK AND SEAFOOD

Phone: 540/371-8020

Steak & Seafood
$22-$35

The setting is warm with wood paneling and roaring fireplaces crowned with stag's heads. The large steaks arrive on sizzling platters and the shrimp are amply stuffed with crabmeat. Casual dress. **Bar:** Full bar. **Reservations:** suggested. **Hours:** 4 pm-10 pm, Sun-9 pm. Closed major holidays; also Mon. **Address:** 1612 Caroline St 22401 **Location:** 0.5 mi n of jct William St; in Olde Towne. **Parking:** on-site. **Cards:** AX, DC, MC, VI.

OLDE TOWNE WINE & CHEESE DELI
Phone: 540/373-7877

Deli/Subs Sandwiches
$5-$10

The popular and friendly lunch spot is known for specialty sandwiches, daily soup and local microbrews. **Casual dress. Bar:** Beer & wine. **Hours:** 11 am-4 pm, Sun noon-3 pm. Closed: 3/23, 11/27, 12/25. **Address:** 707 Caroline St 22401 **Location:** Between Hanover and Charlotte sts; in Olde Towne. **Parking:** street. **Cards:** AX, DS, MC, VI.

OLD TOWN GRILL & CAFE
Phone: 540/899-9199

American
$5-$10

Reminiscent of lunch counters of days gone by this small spot serves gourmet updates of old favorites such as burgers with roasted garlic spread, grilled tuna salad, corn fries, salads, and more. **Casual dress. Bar:** Beer & wine. **Hours:** 8 am-5 pm. Closed major holidays; also Sun. **Address:** 722 Caroline St 22401 **Location:** S of jct William St; in Olde Towne. **Parking:** street. **Cards:** AX, DS, MC, VI.

PANCHO VILLA MEXICAN RESTAURANT
Phone: 540/710-9999

Mexican
$5-$14

In a Southwestern setting with stone hearths, antler chandeliers and historic black-and-white prints, the restaurant lets guests sample standard favorites, from fajitas to burritos, with frosty margaritas. **Casual dress. Bar:** Full bar. **Hours:** 11 am-10 pm, Fri-11 pm, Sun-9 pm. Closed major holidays. **Address:** 10500 Spotsylvania Ave 22408 **Location:** I-95, exit 126A, just n on US 1; adjacent to Lee's Hill Shopping Center. **Parking:** on-site. **Cards:** AX, DC, DS, MC, VI.

PHO SAIGON
Phone: 540/891-2400

Vietnamese
$7-$12

Sample the light and fresh flavors of Vietnam at this cozy family spot named for a favored noodle soup of the country. Other specialties include garden rolls, a un-fried version of spring rolls, braised quail, and rice vermicelli noodles with grilled meats or seafood. **Casual dress. Bar:** Beer & wine. **Hours:** 10 am-9 pm, Fri & Sat-10 pm, Sun 11 am-8 pm. Closed: 12/25; also Tues. **Address:** 10705 Courthouse Rd, Suite 102 22407 **Location:** I-95, exit 126B, 1 mi n on US 1, then 0.9 mi w; in Breezewood Station. **Parking:** on-site. **Cards:** MC, VI.

CALL &M

POPPY HILL TUSCAN KITCHEN
Phone: 540/373-2035

Italian
$7-$28

Stone steps lead downstairs from the sidewalk and into this cozy, low-ceilinged spot. The Italian menu lists specialties of daily made pasta, crab crostini, tomato basil bisque and roasted salmon over risotto cakes. Dishes incorporate fresh local farm-raised produce. **Casual dress. Bar:** Beer & wine. **Reservations:** accepted. **Hours:** 11:30 am-2:30 & 5-9 pm, Fri & Sat-10 pm, Mon & Tues 5 pm-9 pm. Closed major holidays; also Sun. **Address:** 1000 Charles St 22401 **Location:** Jct William St; in Olde Towne. **Parking:** street. **Cards:** AX, DS, MC, VI.

RISTORANTE RENATO
Phone: 540/371-8228

AAA

Italian
$8-$27

The menu showcases authentic Northern Italian cuisine such as fresh pasta, beef and seafood specialties. Dessert selections — cannoli, stromboli, cheesecake and spumoni — are all homemade. Classical guitar entertainment is offered Friday and Saturday. **Casual dress. Bar:** Full bar. **Reservations:** accepted. **Hours:** 11:30 am-2 & 4:30-10 pm, Sat from 4:30 pm, Sun 4:30 pm-9 pm. Closed: 1/1, 11/27, 12/25. **Address:** 422 William St 22401 **Location:** I-95, exit 130A, 2 mi e on SR 3 business route; corner of William and Prince Edward sts; downtown. **Parking:** on-site. **Cards:** AX, DC, DS, MC, VI.

SAKURA JAPANESE STEAK AND SEAFOOD HOUSE
Phone: 540/786-8100

Japanese
$14-$23

Watching Japanese chefs in action at the lively spot is as good as eating the food. Guests can sample stir-fried shrimp, steak and more that's even better when paired with delicacies from the sushi bar, a popular dining spot in its own right. **Casual dress. Bar:** Full bar. **Reservations:** accepted. **Hours:** 4:30 pm-9:30 pm, Sat 2 pm-10 pm, Sun noon-9 pm. Closed major holidays. **Address:** 4540 Plank Rd 22407 **Location:** I-95, exit 130B (SR 3), 0.6 mi w. **Parking:** on-site. **Cards:** AX, DS, MC, VI.

CALL &M

SAMMY T'S
Phone: 540/371-2008

AAA

American
$6-$18

The specialties are freshly made soup, salad, plus a wide variety of vegan, vegetarian entrees, pasta and excellent burgers. A tasty choice is the black bean soup and vegan wrap with spinach and hummus. Try apple crisp, a homemade dessert. Sidewalk dining is available. **Casual dress. Bar:** Full bar. **Hours:** 11 am-9 pm. Closed major holidays. **Address:** 801 Caroline St 22401 **Location:** Jct Hanover St, just n of Visitor's Center; in Olde Towne. **Parking:** street. **Cards:** AX, DS, MC, VI.

THE SOUP & TACO ETC..
Phone: 540/899-0969

Mexican
$5-$9

The tiny Olde Towne spot serves fresh beef, chicken, fish and vegetable soft tacos with its signature creamy sauce. Daily changing soup specials often feature local farm market produce. Delicious fresh guacamole and chips also are available. **Casual dress. Hours:** 11 am-9 pm, Mon-5 pm. Closed major holidays; also Sun. **Address:** 813 Caroline St 22401 **Location:** In Olde Towne. **Parking:** street. **Cards:** MC, VI.

SUNSET THAI
Phone: 540/786-0044

Thai
$9-$25

Classic Thai dishes, such as pad thai, satays, coconut soup and red curries, are served in a soothing atmosphere with a small pond and scenic footbridge in the center of the room. **Casual dress. Bar:** Beer & wine. **Reservations:** accepted. **Hours:** 11 am-9:30 pm, Fri & Sat-10:30 pm. Closed: 11/27. **Address:** 1885 Carl D. Silver Pkwy 22401 **Location:** I-95, exit 130 (SR 130), 0.6 mi n in Central Park. **Parking:** on-site. **Cards:** AX, DS, MC, VI.

FRONT ROYAL pop. 13,589

——— WHERE TO STAY ———

BUDGET INN

Motel
$45-$65 All Year

Phone: (540)635-2196
Address: 1122 N Royal Ave 22630 **Location:** I-66, exit 6, 2.2 mi s on US 340/522 and SR 55. **Facility:** 21 one-bedroom standard units. 1 story, exterior corridors. **Parking:** on-site. **Cards:** AX, DS, MC, VI. **Free Special Amenities: continental breakfast and local telephone calls.**

CENTER CITY MOTEL

Motel
$35-$85 All Year

Phone: (540)635-4050
Address: 416 S Royal Ave 22630 **Location:** I-66, exit 6, 3.5 mi s on US 340. Located in historic Front Royal. **Facility:** 14 one-bedroom standard units. 1 story, exterior corridors. **Parking:** on-site. **Cards:** AX, DS, MC, VI. **Free Special Amenities: local telephone calls and preferred room (subject to availability with advance reservations).**

HAMPTON INN/FRONT ROYAL

Book great rates at AAA.com

Small-scale Hotel
Rates not provided

Phone: 540/635-1882
Address: 9800 Winchester Rd 22630 **Location:** I-66, exit 6, just s. **Facility:** 75 one-bedroom standard units, some with whirlpools. 4 stories, interior corridors. *Bath:* combo or shower only. **Amenities:** high-speed Internet, dual phone lines, voice mail, irons, hair dryers. **Pool(s):** outdoor. **Leisure Activities:** exercise room. **Guest Services:** valet and coin laundry, wireless Internet. **Business Services:** meeting rooms, business center.

RELAX INN

Motel
$50-$75 3/1-11/15
$45-$59 11/16-2/28

Phone: (540)635-4101
Address: 1801 Shenandoah Ave 22630 **Location:** I-66, exit 6, 1.5 mi s on US 340/522. Located in historic Front Royal. **Facility:** 20 one-bedroom standard units. 1 story, exterior corridors. **Parking:** on-site. **Pool(s):** outdoor. **Leisure Activities:** picnic area, playground. **Cards:** AX, DS, MC, VI. **Free Special Amenities: continental breakfast and local telephone calls.**

TWI-LITE MOTEL

Motel
$39-$89 All Year

Phone: (540)635-4148
Address: 53 W 14th St 22630 **Location:** I-66, exit 6, 2.3 mi s on US 340/522. **Facility:** 19 one-bedroom standard units, some with whirlpools. 1 story, exterior corridors. **Parking:** on-site. **Terms:** cancellation fee imposed. **Pool(s):** outdoor. **Cards:** AX, DS, MC, VI. **Free Special Amenities: continental breakfast and high-speed Internet.**

——— WHERE TO DINE ———

DEAN'S STEAKHOUSE

Steak House
$7-$22

Phone: 540/635-1780
Great steaks, great atmosphere and a friendly wait staff are what is offered at Dean's Steakhouse. A Front Royal tradition. Casual dress. **Bar:** Full bar. **Reservations:** suggested, weekends. **Hours:** 11 am-10 pm. Closed: 12/25. **Address:** 708 S Royal Ave 22630 **Location:** I-66, exit 6, 3.9 mi s on US 340. **Parking:** on-site. **Cards:** AX, CB, DC, DS, JC, MC, VI.

JALISCO MEXICAN RESTAURANT

Mexican
$6-$20

Phone: 540/635-7348
Mexican entrees are bookended by super chips and salsa and homemade desserts. The dining room displays south-of-the-border decor, and the hospitality shows the same influence. The family-owned and operated restaurant has four locations throughout the Shenandoah Valley. Casual dress. **Bar:** Full bar. **Hours:** 11 am-10 pm. Closed: 12/25. **Address:** 1303 N Royal Ave 22630 **Location:** I-66, exit 6, 2.2 mi s on US 340/522. **Parking:** on-site. **Cards:** AX, CB, DC, DS, JC, MC, VI.

JIMBO'S RESTAURANT

American
$5-$12

Phone: 540/635-3466
Home-style cooking and friendliness abound. All-day breakfast items are among choices on the varied menu. Casual dress. **Hours:** 7 am-8 pm. Closed: 12/25. **Address:** 1411 Shenandoah Ave 22630 **Location:** I-66, exit 6, 2.1 mi s on US 340/522. **Parking:** on-site. **Cards:** MC, VI.

ROYAL OAK TAVERN

American
$6-$20

Phone: 540/551-9953
The atmosphere is fun and light at the laid-back restaurant. On the menu are classic American favorites and a wide variety of dessert choices. Casual dress. **Bar:** Full bar. **Reservations:** suggested. **Hours:** 11 am-midnight, Sun noon-10 pm. **Address:** 101 W 14th St 22630 **Location:** I-66, exit 6, 2.2 mi s on US 340/522. **Parking:** on-site. **Cards:** AX, CB, DC, DS, JC, MC, VI.

SOUTH STREET GRILLE

American
$5-$15

South Street Grille is a trip back in time with a 50's nostalgia decor theme, real hamburgers and shakes, and friendly service. Casual dress. **Hours:** 7 am-9 pm. Closed: 12/25. **Address:** 424A South St 22630 **Location:** I-66, exit 6, 3.3 mi s on US 522. **Parking:** on-site. **Cards:** MC, VI.

Phone: 540/636-6654

GAINESVILLE pop. 4,382

—————— WHERE TO DINE ——————

GLORY DAYS GRILL

American
$7-$21

Lending to the casual restaurant's sports-themed atmosphere are memorabilia decorating the dining area and 25 TVs with control centers at each table and booth. Food selections range from wings and ribs to seafood, beef and pasta dishes. Casual dress. **Bar:** Full bar. **Reservations:** not accepted. **Hours:** 4 pm-midnight, Fri & Sat from 11:30 am, Sun 11:30 am-11 pm. Closed: 11/27, 12/25. **Address:** 7581 Somerset Crossing Dr 20155 **Location:** I-66, exit 43A, 2.1 mi s on US 29; in Somerset Crossing Shopping Ctr. **Parking:** on-site. **Cards:** AX, DC, DS, MC, VI.

Phone: 571/261-1500

GALAX pop. 6,837

—————— WHERE TO DINE ——————

BOGEY'S

American
$8-$25

Bogey's is a relaxed, fun eatery with great golf course views and a wide and diverse menu with an upbeat staff. Casual dress. **Bar:** Full bar. **Hours:** 11 am-9:30 pm. Closed: 12/25; also Mon. **Address:** 103 Country Club Ln 24333 **Location:** I-77, exit 14, 8.1 mi w on US 58, then just n. **Parking:** on-site. **Cards:** AX, CB, DC, DS, JC, MC, VI.

Phone: 276/236-0060

THE GALAX SMOKEHOUSE

Barbecue
$5-$14

Great sauces flavor the smokehouse's award-winning barbecue, which also comes with tasty sides. The staff is friendly. Casual dress. **Hours:** 11 am-9 pm, Sun-3 pm. Closed: 12/25. **Address:** 101 N Main St 24333 **Location:** 2 mi n; center of downtown. **Parking:** on-site. **Cards:** MC, VI.

Phone: 276/236-1000

GLADE SPRING pop. 1,374

——— WHERE TO STAY ———

SWISS INN MOTEL & SUITES

AAA SAVE

Motel
$39-$79 All Year

Phone: (276)429-5191

Address: 33361 Lee Hwy 24340 **Location:** I-81, exit 29, just e. **Facility:** 32 one-bedroom standard units, some with whirlpools. 2 stories (no elevator), exterior corridors. *Bath:* combo or shower only. **Parking:** on-site. **Terms:** cancellation fee imposed. **Amenities:** hair dryers. **Guest Services:** valet laundry, wireless Internet. **Cards:** AX, DS, MC, VI. **Free Special Amenities: continental breakfast and high-speed Internet.**

SD CALL &M / SOME UNITS FEE

GLEN ALLEN —*See Richmond p. 876.*

GLOUCESTER —*See Hampton Roads Area p. 749.*

GLOUCESTER POINT —*See Hampton Roads Area p. 750.*

GOOCHLAND —*See Richmond p. 879.*

GORDONSVILLE pop. 1,498

——— WHERE TO STAY ———

SHENANDOAH CROSSING RESORT   *Book great rates at AAA.com*

AAA SAVE

Large-scale Hotel
$39-$69 All Year

Phone: 540/832-9400

Address: 174 Horseshoe Cir 22942 **Location:** 2.8 mi e on US 33. **Facility:** 181 units. 48 one-bedroom standard units. 14 two-bedroom suites with kitchens. 119 cabins. 2 stories (no elevator), interior/exterior corridors. **Parking:** on-site. **Terms:** 3 day cancellation notice. **Amenities:** voice mail, irons, hair dryers. *Some:* CD players. **Pool(s):** 2 outdoor, heated indoor. **Leisure Activities:** saunas, whirlpools, canoeing, paddleboats, marina, fishing, miniature golf, 2 lighted tennis courts, recreation programs, radio control car park, softball diamond, archery, hiking trails, playground, exercise room, basketball, horseshoes, volleyball. *Fee:* horseback riding, massage, game room. **Guest Services:** coin laundry, wireless Internet. **Business Services:** meeting rooms, business center. **Cards:** AX, DS, MC, VI. *(See color ad below)*

/ SOME UNITS

▼ See AAA listing above ▼

GREAT FALLS —See District Of Columbia p. 536.

GREENVILLE pop. 886

——— WHERE TO STAY ———

BUDGET HOST-HISTORIC HESSIAN HOUSE   *Book great rates at AAA.com*   **Phone:** (540)337-1231

AAA [SAVE]

Small-scale Hotel
$55-$85 3/1-11/2
$49-$59 11/3-2/28

Location: I-81, exit 213, 0.3 mi e. Located in a quiet area. **Facility:** 32 one-bedroom standard units. 2 stories (no elevator), exterior corridors. **Parking:** on-site. **Terms:** 3 day cancellation notice. **Leisure Activities:** picnic area, playground, basketball. **Cards:** AX, DS, MC, VI. **Free Special Amenities:** continental breakfast and local telephone calls.

⟨icons⟩ [SD] [†|→] [⊠] [▣] [📞] / SOME UNITS FEE [🛏] [⊠] [📷]

——— WHERE TO DINE ———

EDELWEISS RESTAURANT   **Phone:** 540/337-1203

German
$7-$18

On the menu are tasty traditional favorites, from schnitzels and spaetzle to Black Forest cake. The unusual pine log cabin setting is cozy and relaxed. A nice wine list includes a sampling of German selections. Casual dress. **Bar:** Beer & wine. **Reservations:** suggested, weekends. **Hours:** 11:30 am-9 pm, Sun-8 pm. Closed: 11/27, 12/25; also Mon. **Location:** I-81, exit 213 northbound; exit 213A southbound, just e on US 11, then just n on US 340. **Parking:** on-site. **Cards:** AX, DC, DS, MC, VI.

[⊘]

GRUNDY pop. 1,105

——— WHERE TO STAY ———

COMFORT INN   *Book at AAA.com*   **Phone:** (276)935-5050

Small-scale Hotel
$74-$175 All Year

Address: 22006 Riverside Dr 24614 **Location:** On US 460, 0.5 mi e. **Facility:** 70 units. 68 one-bedroom standard units. 2 one-bedroom suites. 4 stories, interior corridors. *Bath:* combo or shower only. **Parking:**- on-site. **Amenities:** high-speed Internet, voice mail, irons, hair dryers. **Leisure Activities:** exercise room. **Guest Services:** coin laundry, wireless Internet. **Business Services:** meeting rooms. **Cards:** AX, CB, DC, DS, JC, MC, VI.

[ASK] [SD] [†|→] CALL [⑤M] [⊠] [▣] / SOME UNITS FEE [🛏] [⊠] [VCR] [📞] [📷]

HALIFAX pop. 1,389

——— WHERE TO DINE ———

MOLASSES GRILL   **Phone:** 434/476-6265

American
$15-$23

The chef's European heritage mixes with local Southern traditions at this elegant spot in a small, quaint town. Among creative specialties are sweet potato-crusted salmon, bourbon-molasses grilled pork loin and grilled steaks. The sophisticated Sunday brunch includes such Southern choices as shrimp and grits and crab gratin. Casual dress. **Bar:** Full bar. **Reservations:** accepted. **Hours:** 5 pm-10 pm. Closed major holidays; also Sun & Mon. **Address:** 63 S Main St 24558 **Location:** Center; across from county courthouse. **Parking:** street. **Cards:** AX, MC, VI.

[⊘]

HAMPTON —See Hampton Roads Area p. 750.

Destination Hampton Roads Area

Hampton Roads, the passage between Chesapeake Bay and the James River, has drawn maritime adventurers from the 1607 arrival of the English colonists to the 20th-century installation of U.S. naval facilities.

Find your own excitement in or near the waters of this "safe harbor." There are rivers to cruise, beaches to ramble, bases to tour and a very unusual bridge-tunnel to cross.

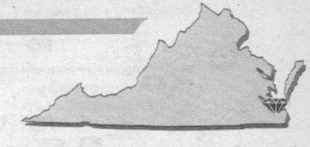

© M. Gibson / Robertstock

Virginia Beach Oceanfront. Catch a glimpse of visitors floating the days away along this sandy coast.

Olde Towne Historic District, Portsmouth. Antique stores and vintage homes dot this quaint section of town. (See mention page 266)

© Gibson Stock Photography

© Gibson Stock Photography

American Rover Tall Sailing Ship Cruises, Norfolk. Guests can pitch in and work the sails while enjoying the harbor tour on this tall ship. (See listing page 263)

Shopping in Smithfield. Visitors can pick up a renowned Smithfield ham or other specialty items while perusing area shops.

Hampton Roads Area

- Gloucester
- Gloucester Point
- See Area map page 728
- Surry
- Newport News
- Hampton
- Smithfield
- Norfolk
- See Area map page 734
- Portsmouth
- Chesapeake
- Virginia Beach
- Suffolk
- See Area map page 738

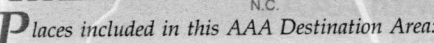
VA.
N.C.

Places included in this AAA Destination Area:

Virginia Tourism Corp

NO KIDDING
AAA SAVES YOU 5-15% with AAA's Preferred Lodging Partners!
— see page 19 for full details.

Visit Over 1,100 AAA Offices **Click** AAA.com **Call** 1-866-AAA-SAVE

Hampton Roads Area (Newport News)

This index helps you "spot" where approved lodgings and restaurants are located on the corresponding detailed maps. Lodging daily rate range is for comparison only and show the property's high season. Restaurant rate range is a combination of lunch and/or dinner. Turn to the listing page for more detailed rate information and consult display ads for special promotions.

Spotter/Map Page Number	OA	NEWPORT NEWS - Lodgings	Diamond Rating	Rate Range High Season	Listing Page
❶ / p. 728	AAA	**Comfort Suites Airport**	◇◇◇	$89-$209 SAVE	754
❷ / p. 728		Travelodge	◇	Rates not provided	756
❸ / p. 728		StudioPLUS-Newport News	◇◇	$95-$155	756
❹ / p. 728		Comfort Inn	◇◇◇	$109-$149	754
❺ / p. 728		Hampton Inn	◇◇◇	Rates not provided	754
❻ / p. 728		Hampton Inn & Suites	◇◇◇	Rates not provided	755
❼ / p. 728		Hilton Garden Inn	◇◇◇	Rates not provided	755
❽ / p. 728		Microtel Inn	◇◇	$59-$109	755
❾ / p. 728	AAA	**Best Western Newport News Inn & Suites**	◇◇◇	Rates not provided SAVE	754
❿ / p. 728		Sleep Inn & Suites	◇◇◇	$69-$149	756
⓫ / p. 728		Crestwood Suites	◇◇	$65-$130	754
⓬ / p. 728	AAA	**Country Inn & Suites by Carlson**	◇◇◇	$139-$149 SAVE	754
⓭ / p. 728	AAA	**Host Inn**	◇	$45-$59 SAVE	755
⓮ / p. 728	AAA	**Point Plaza-Suites at City Center**	◇◇◇	$69-$139 SAVE	756
⓯ / p. 728	AAA	**Super 8 Motel**	◇	Rates not provided SAVE	756
⓰ / p. 728		Holiday Inn Hotel & Suites	◇◇◇	$129-$219	755
⓱ / p. 728	AAA	**Omni Newport News Hotel**	◇◇◇	$136-$159 SAVE	756
⓲ / p. 728	AAA	**Days Inn-Oyster Point at City Center**	◇◇	$99-$119 SAVE	754
⓳ / p. 728		Newport News Marriott at City Center	◇◇◇	$148-$180	755
⓴ / p. 728		Extended StayAmerica Newport News-Oyster Point	◇◇	$77-$145	754
		NEWPORT NEWS - Restaurants			
① / p. 728		Plaza Azteca Restaurante Mexicano	◇	$5-$14	758
② / p. 728		Wok & Roll	◇	$5-$13	758
③ / p. 728		Kyung Sung Korean Restaurant	◇	$6-$16	757
④ / p. 728		Samurai Sushi & Hibachi Restaurant	◇◇	$8-$28	758
⑤ / p. 728		Kappo Nara Seafood & Sushi Restaurant	◇◇	$5-$20	757
⑥ / p. 728		Plaza Azteca	◇	$6-$13	758
⑦ / p. 728		Aromas	◇	$5-$11	756
⑧ / p. 728		Fab Foods at Medik's Market	◇	$6-$9	757
⑨ / p. 728		The Jamestown Pie Company	◇	$5-$18	757
⑩ / p. 728		The Lunch Bell	◇	$5-$8	757
⑪ / p. 728		Light	◇◇◇	$9-$33	757
⑫ / p. 728		Schlesinger's Chophouse	◇◇◇	$7-$55	758
⑬ / p. 728		Al Fresco Ristorante	◇◇	$7-$19	756
⑭ / p. 728		El Mariachi Restaurant & Cantina	◇	$3-$15	757

Spotter/Map Page Number	OA	NEWPORT NEWS - Restaurants (continued)	Diamond Rating	Rate Range High Season	Listing Page
⑮ / p. 728		Mike's Place	◆	$5-$16	757
⑯ / p. 728		Rocky Mount Barbecue	◆	$5-$10	758
⑰ / p. 728		99 Main	◆◆◆	$16-$30	756
⑱ / p. 728		The Crab Shack	◆◆	$6-$18	757
		YORKTOWN - Lodgings			
㉓ / p. 728		Days Inn	◆◆	Rates not provided	951
㉔ / p. 728	ⒶⒶⒶ	**TownePlace Suites by Marriott**	◆◆	$154-$185 SAVE	952
㉕ / p. 728		Courtyard by Marriott	◆◆◆	$143-$174	951
㉖ / p. 728		Candlewood Suites-Yorktown	◆◆	Rates not provided	951
		YORKTOWN - Restaurants			
㉑ / p. 728		Spring Garden	◆	$5-$13	953
㉒ / p. 728		The Glass Pheasant English Tea Room	◆◆	$5-$9	952
㉓ / p. 728		Empress Restaurant	◆	$6-$13	952
		HAMPTON - Lodgings			
㉙ / p. 728		Candlewood Suites	◆◆	Rates not provided	750
㉚ / p. 728		Country Inn & Suites Hampton	◆◆◆	$79-$149	750
㉛ / p. 728	ⒶⒶⒶ	**Clarion Hotel-Hampton Roads Convention Center**	◆◆◆	$89-$159 SAVE	750
㉜ / p. 728	ⒶⒶⒶ	**Holiday Inn Hampton Hotel & Conference Center**	◆◆◆	$104-$159 SAVE	751
㉝ / p. 728		Quality Inn	◆◆◆	$94-$159	751
㉞ / p. 728		Comfort Inn	◆◆	$79-$149	750
㉟ / p. 728		Courtyard By Marriott	◆◆◆	$142-$164	751
㊱ / p. 728		Ramada Hampton Coliseum & Convention Center	◆◆	Rates not provided	751
㊲ / p. 728	ⒶⒶⒶ	**Embassy Suites Hampton Roads Hotel, Spa, and Convention Center**	◆◆◆	Rates not provided SAVE	751
㊳ / p. 728		Extended StayAmerica-Hampton Coliseum	◆◆	$77-$140	751
㊴ / p. 728		Super 8 Motel	◆	Rates not provided	752
		HAMPTON - Restaurants			
㉖ / p. 728		El Azteca Restaurante Mexicano	◆	$4-$12	752
㉗ / p. 728		Harpoon Larry's Oyster Bar	◆	$7-$35	752
㉘ / p. 728		Pho 79	◆	$6-$9	753
㉙ / p. 728		McFadden's Saloon	◆◆	$7-$27	753
㉚ / p. 728		Tommy's Restaurant	◆	$3-$9	753
㉛ / p. 728		Marker 20	◆◆	$6-$16	752
㉜ / p. 728		La Bodega Hampton	◆	$4-$7	752
㉝ / p. 728		Musasi Japanese Restaurant	◆◆	$7-$18	753
㉞ / p. 728		The Grey Goose	◆◆	$5-$10	752
㉟ / p. 728		Mama Rosa's	◆◆	$6-$15	752
㊱ / p. 728		Surfrider Bluewater	◆◆	$6-$20	753

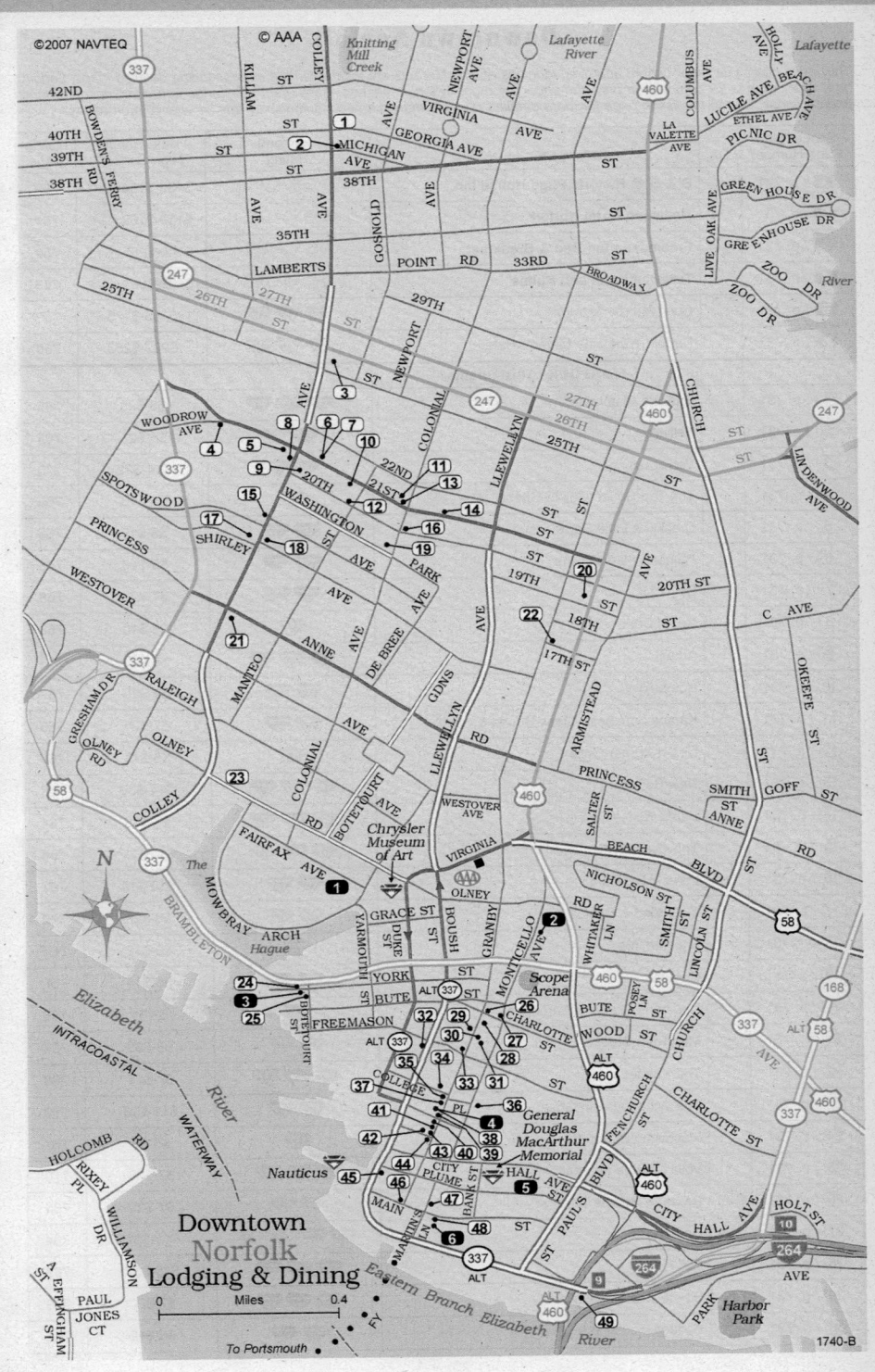

©2007 NAVTEQ

© AAA

Downtown
Norfolk
Lodging & Dining

1740-B

Downtown Norfolk

This index helps you "spot" where approved lodgings and restaurants are located on the corresponding detailed maps. Lodging daily rate range is for comparison only and show the property's high season. Restaurant rate range is a combination of lunch and/or dinner. Turn to the listing page for more detailed rate information and consult display ads for special promotions.

Spotter/Map Page Number	OA	NORFOLK - Lodgings	Diamond Rating	Rate Range High Season	Listing Page
1 / p. 731	AAA	**B & B @ Historic Page House Inn**	◆◆◆◆	$139-$154 SAVE	759
2 / p. 731	AAA	**Radisson Hotel Norfolk**	◆◆◆	$139-$169 SAVE	761
3 / p. 731	AAA	**Freemason Inn Bed & Breakfast**	◆◆◆	$145-$255 SAVE	760
4 / p. 731	AAA	**Tazewell Hotel and Suites**	◆◆◆	$109-$269 SAVE	763
5 / p. 731		Courtyard by Marriott	◆◆◆	$153-$175	759
6 / p. 731		Norfolk Waterside Marriott Hotel	◆◆◆	$207-$253	760
		NORFOLK - Restaurants			
① / p. 731		Enrico's Ristorante	◆◆◆	$6-$23	765
② / p. 731		Fellini's	◆◆	$5-$20	765
③ / p. 731		Velvet Lounge	◆◆	$14-$22	770
④ / p. 731		The Tap House Grill in Ghent	◆	$5-$13	769
⑤ / p. 731		Cracker's Little Bar & Bistro	◆◆	$5-$19	765
⑥ / p. 731		Rajput Indian Cuisine	◆◆	$9-$16	768
⑦ / p. 731		Siam 21	◆◆	$7-$20	768
⑧ / p. 731		Nazef Char-grill	◆	$5-$10	768
⑨ / p. 731		Amalfi	◆◆◆	$6-$23	763
⑩ / p. 731		Kotobuki	◆◆	$9-$20	767
⑪ / p. 731		Katana Japanese Steak House & Sushi	◆◆	$7-$25	766
⑫ / p. 731		Dog-n-Burger Grille	◆	$5-$15	765
⑬ / p. 731		New Belmont	◆◆◆	$14-$30	768
⑭ / p. 731		Bardo Edibles & Elixirs	◆◆◆	$7-$18	764
⑮ / p. 731		The Green Onion	◆◆◆	$14-$20	766
⑯ / p. 731		Luna Maya Cantina	◆◆	$10-$14	767
⑰ / p. 731		Zio's Vino & Cucina	◆◆	$8-$20	770
⑱ / p. 731		The Ten Top	◆	$6-$12	769
⑲ / p. 731		Cogan's	◆◆	$5-$15	765
⑳ / p. 731		Doumar's Cones & Barbecue	◆	$2-$4	765
㉑ / p. 731	AAA	**Magnolia Steak**	◆◆	$8-$33	767
㉒ / p. 731		The Painted Lady	◆◆◆	$7-$28	768
㉓ / p. 731		The Winehouse in Ghent	◆◆	$13-$26	770
㉔ / p. 731		Machismo Burrito Bar	◆	$5-$8	767
㉕ / p. 731		Voila Cuisine International	◆◆◆	$7-$36	770
㉖ / p. 731	AAA	**Baxter's Sports Lounge**	◆◆	$7-$20	764
㉗ / p. 731	AAA	**Bobbywood**	◆◆◆◆	$18-$32	764
㉘ / p. 731		456 Fish	◆◆◆	$15-$37	763
㉙ / p. 731		Sirena Cucina Italiana	◆◆◆	$7-$20	768
㉚ / p. 731		Bodega	◆◆	$6-$12	764

Spotter/Map Page Number	OA	**NORFOLK - Restaurants (continued)**	Diamond Rating	Rate Range High Season	Listing Page
③① / p. 731		Scotty Quixx Lounge & Grille	◈◈	$10-$24	768
③② / p. 731		Freemason Abbey	◈◈	$6-$18	766
③③ / p. 731		Asian Grill	◈◈	$6-$15	763
③④ / p. 731		La Galleria	◈◈◈	$13-$44	767
③⑤ / p. 731		Domo	◈◈	$8-$18	765
③⑥ / p. 731		Kincaid's Fish, Chop and Steakhouse	◈◈	$7-$28	767
③⑦ / p. 731		Havana	◈◈	$6-$22	766
③⑧ / p. 731		Empire Little Bar & Bistro	◈◈	$5-$19	765
③⑨ / p. 731		Sterling's	◈◈◈	$20-$30	769
④⓪ / p. 731		Club Soda	◈◈◈	$16-$24	765
④① / p. 731		Granby Street Pizza	◈	$6-$16	766
④② / p. 731		Byrd & Baldwin Brothers Steakhouse	◈◈◈	$20-$42	764
④③ / p. 731		Granby Bistro & Deli	◈	$4-$10	766
④④ / p. 731		The 219	◈◈◈	$5-$23	763
④⑤ / p. 731	AAA	**Todd Jurich's Bistro!**	◈◈◈◈	$9-$32	769
④⑥ / p. 731		Trilogy Bistro	◈◈◈	$20-$30	769
④⑦ / p. 731		D'Egg Diner	◈	$4-$8	765
④⑧ / p. 731		Shula's 347	◈◈◈	$9-$31	768
④⑨ / p. 731		Vintage Kitchen	◈◈◈	$8-$25	770

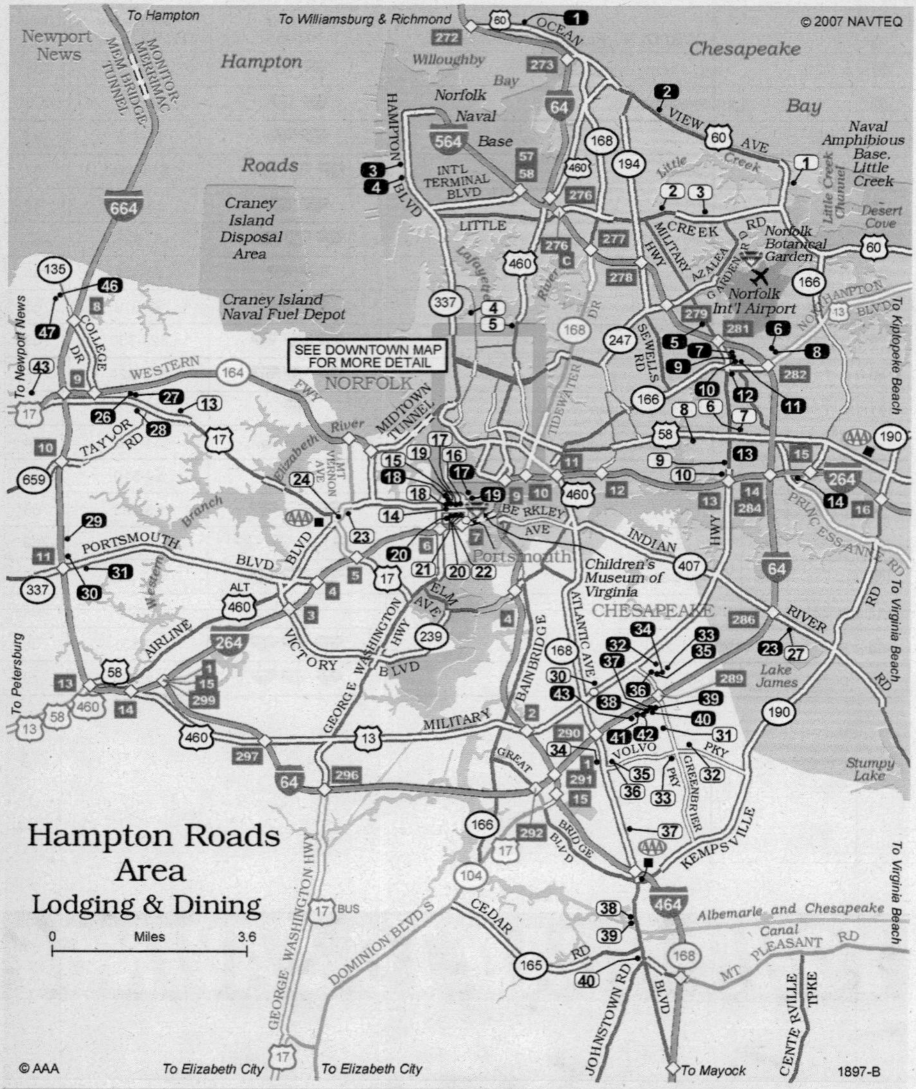

© 2007 NAVTEQ

Newport News

To Hampton

To Williamsburg & Richmond

Hampton

Chesapeake

Willoughby
Bay

Norfolk
Naval
Base

Chesapeake
Bay

Roads

INT'L
TERMINAL
BLVD

Naval
Amphibious
Base.
Little
Creek

Craney
Island
Disposal
Area

LITTLE

Desert
Cove

Craney Island
Naval Fuel Depot

Norfolk
Botanical
Garden

Norfolk
Int'l Airport

SEE DOWNTOWN MAP
FOR MORE DETAIL

NORFOLK

WESTERN

To Kiptopeke Beach

To Newport News

MIDTOWN
TUNNEL

To Virginia Beach

TAYLOR RD

PORTSMOUTH
BLVD

Portsmouth

Children's
Museum of
Virginia

INDIAN

CHESAPEAKE

RIVER
Lake
James

To Petersburg

AIRLINE

VICTORY

GEORGE E. WASHINGTON HWY

MILITARY

Stumpy
Lake

KEMPSVILLE

To Virginia Beach

BAINBRIDGE

ATLANTIC AVE.

VOLVO

GREENBRIER PKY

GREAT

BRIDGE BLVD

Hampton Roads
Area
Lodging & Dining

0   Miles   3.6

Albemarle and Chesapeake
Canal
PLEASANT

CEDAR

DOMINION BLVD S

To Elizabeth City

To Elizabeth City

To Mayock

© AAA

1897-B

JOHNSTOWN RD

CENTERVILLE TPKE

✈ Airport Accommodations

Spotter/Map Page Number	OA	NORFOLK INTERNATIONAL	Diamond Rating	Rate Range High Season	Listing Page
1 / p. 728	AAA	**Comfort Suites Airport, just n**	◇◇◇	$89-$209 SAVE	754
13 / p. 734	AAA	**DoubleTree Hotel-Norfolk, 2.5 mi s of airport**	◇◇◇	$89-$199 SAVE	760
5 / p. 734		Econo Lodge Airport, 1 mi s of airport	◇	$81-$129	760
10 / p. 734	AAA	**Hilton Norfolk Airport, 2 mi s of airport**	◇◇◇	Rates not provided SAVE	760
9 / p. 734		Holiday Inn Select, 2 mi s of airport	◇◇◇	$119-$179	760
12 / p. 734		Ramada Norfolk Airport, 2 mi s of airport	◇◇	$81-$94	761
4 / p. 738	AAA	**Best Western Inn, 2.5 mi n of airport**	◇◇	Rates not provided SAVE	778
5 / p. 738	AAA	**Red Roof Inn VA Beach (Norfolk Airport), 2.5 mi n of airport**	◇◇	Rates not provided SAVE	790
7 / p. 738		Wingate Inn-Norfolk Airport, 3 mi from airport	◇◇◇	$129-$139	797

Hampton Roads Area (Norfolk)

This index helps you "spot" where approved lodgings and restaurants are located on the corresponding detailed maps. Lodging daily rate range is for comparison only and show the property's high season. Restaurant rate range is a combination of lunch and/or dinner. Turn to the listing page for more detailed rate information and consult display ads for special promotions.

Spotter/Map Page Number	OA	NORFOLK - Lodgings	Diamond Rating	Rate Range High Season	Listing Page
1 / p. 734	AAA	**Super 8 Chesapeake Bay** - see color ad p 762	◇◇	Rates not provided SAVE	763
2 / p. 734	AAA	**Best Western Holiday Sands Inn & Suites** - see color ad p 759	◇◇	Rates not provided SAVE	759
3 / p. 734		Hampton Inn Norfolk Naval Base	◇◇◇	Rates not provided	760
4 / p. 734	AAA	**Quality Inn Norfolk Naval Base**	◇◇◇	$99-$159 SAVE	761
5 / p. 734		Econo Lodge Airport	◇	$81-$129	760
6 / p. 734	AAA	**Sleep Inn Lake Wright** - see color ad p 761	◇◇	$89-$139 SAVE	762
7 / p. 734		Residence Inn by Marriott Norfolk Airport	◇◇◇	$158-$186	761
8 / p. 734	AAA	**Quality Suites Lake Wright** - see color ad p 761	◇◇◇	$109-$159 SAVE	761
9 / p. 734		Holiday Inn Select	◇◇◇	$119-$179	760
10 / p. 734	AAA	**Hilton Norfolk Airport**	◇◇◇	Rates not provided SAVE	760
11 / p. 734		Hampton Inn & Suites Norfolk Airport	◇◇◇	Rates not provided	760
12 / p. 734		Ramada Norfolk Airport	◇◇	$81-$94	761
13 / p. 734	AAA	**DoubleTree Hotel-Norfolk**	◇◇◇	$89-$199 SAVE	760
14 / p. 734		SpringHill Suites by Marriott Norfolk/VA Beach	◇◇◇	$131-$175	763
		NORFOLK - Restaurants			
1 / p. 734		Blue Crab Restaurant	◇◇◇	$5-$20	764
2 / p. 734		El Azteca Restaurante Mexicano	◇	$4-$11	765
3 / p. 734		The Azalea Inn	◇◇	$6-$12	763
4 / p. 734		Tanner's Creek Seafood Restaurant & Raw Bar	◇◇	$6-$20	769
5 / p. 734		Mi Hogar Mexican Restaurant	◇	$4-$11	767
6 / p. 734		Wasabi Steakhouse & Sushi Bar	◇◇	$14-$23	770
7 / p. 734		Great Saigon Vietnamese Restaurant	◇◇	$6-$11	766

Spotter/Map Page Number	OA	**NORFOLK - Restaurants (continued)**	Diamond Rating	Rate Range High Season	Listing Page
⑧ / p. 734		The German Pantry	◈◈	$9-$17	766
⑨ / p. 734		Mi Hogar Mexican Restaurant	◈	$4-$13	767
⑩ / p. 734		The Grate Steak	◈◈	$5-$33	766
		PORTSMOUTH - Lodgings			
⑰ / p. 734	AAA	**Holiday Inn-Olde Towne Portsmouth**	◈◈	$110-$130 SAVE	771
⑱ / p. 734	AAA	**Comfort Inn-Olde Towne**	◈◈◈	$89-$135 SAVE	770
⑲ / p. 734		Renaissance Portsmouth Hotel and Waterfront Conference Center	◈◈◈	$148-$180	771
⑳ / p. 734	AAA	**Hawthorn Hotel & Suites at the Governor Dinwiddie**	◈◈◈	$99-$199 SAVE	771
		PORTSMOUTH - Restaurants			
⑬ / p. 734		JoJack's Espresso Bar & Cafe	◈	$5-$7	772
⑭ / p. 734		Breckenridge Restaurant & Lounge	◈◈◈	$7-$31	771
⑮ / p. 734		Fusion 440	◈◈◈	$20-$34	772
⑯ / p. 734		Roger Brown's Restaurant & Sports Bar	◈◈	$6-$17	772
⑰ / p. 734		Brutti's Cafe	◈◈	$5-$27	771
⑱ / p. 734		The Bier Garden	◈◈	$5-$15	771
⑲ / p. 734		Frank and Patty's	◈	$5-$10	772
⑳ / p. 734		New York Deli	◈	$5-$9	772
㉑ / p. 734	AAA	Commodore Theatre	◈	$5-$12	772
㉒ / p. 734		Cafe Europa	◈◈◈	$5-$15	771
㉓ / p. 734		The Circle Steak & Seafood	◈◈	$8-$22	771
㉔ / p. 734		Mario's Italian Restaurant	◈◈	$6-$18	772
		VIRGINIA BEACH - Lodgings			
㉓ / p. 734		The Founders Inn and Spa	◈◈◈	$89-$225	786
		VIRGINIA BEACH - Restaurant			
㉗ / p. 734		Swan Terrace	◈◈◈	$17-$38	810
		CHESAPEAKE - Lodgings			
㉖ / p. 734	AAA	**Sleep Inn & Suites**	◈◈	$105-$125 SAVE	747
㉗ / p. 734		Extended StayAmerica Hotel	◈◈	$95-$145	746
㉘ / p. 734		Hampton Inn Chesapeake	◈◈◈	$89-$129	746
㉙ / p. 734		Holiday Inn Express Hotel & Suites	◈◈◈	$139-$149	746
㉚ / p. 734		SpringHill Suites by Marriott	◈◈◈	$131-$153	747
㉛ / p. 734		Hampton Inn & Suites	◈◈◈	$129-$199	746
㉜ / p. 734		TownePlace Suites By Marriott	◈◈	$120-$153	747
㉝ / p. 734		Wingate Inn-Greenbrier	◈◈◈	$119-$135	747
㉞ / p. 734		Extended StayAmerica Chesapeake-Greenbrier Circle	◈◈	$95-$145	745
㉟ / p. 734		Marriott Hotel Chesapeake	◈◈◈	$139-$189	747
㊱ / p. 734		Hampton Inn Chesapeake	◈◈◈	Rates not provided	746
㊲ / p. 734		Courtyard by Marriott Chesapeake	◈◈◈	$131-$164	745
㊳ / p. 734		Fairfield Inn & Suites Chesapeake	◈◈◈	$120-$142	746

Spotter/Map Page Number	OA	CHESAPEAKE - Lodgings (continued)	Diamond Rating	Rate Range High Season	Listing Page
39 / p. 734		Homewood Suites by Hilton	▽▽▽	Rates not provided	746
40 / p. 734		Hilton Garden Inn-Chesapeake/Greenbrier	▽▽▽	Rates not provided	746
41 / p. 734		Comfort Suites	▽▽▽	$99-$169	745
42 / p. 734		Extended StayAmerica Chesapeake-Crossways Blvd	▽▽	$82-$150	745
43 / p. 734		Residence Inn by Marriott, Chesapeake-Greenbrier	▽▽▽	$153-$186	747
		CHESAPEAKE - Restaurants			
30 / p. 734		Tida Thai Cuisine	▽	$4-$9	749
31 / p. 734		The Angry Chef	▽	$6-$18	748
32 / p. 734		Spice of India	▽▽	$8-$18	749
33 / p. 734		El Loro Mexican Restaurante	▽	$4-$10	748
34 / p. 734		Daikichi Sushi Japanese Bistro	▽▽	$7-$19	748
35 / p. 734		Ms Marian's Restaurant	▽	$4-$11	749
36 / p. 734		Warrior's Mongolian Grill	▽	$6-$10	749
37 / p. 734		Rose Bay Seafood	▽▽	$9-$21	749
38 / p. 734		3 Amigos Restaurante Mexicano	▽	$6-$12	748
39 / p. 734		The Locks Pointe	▽▽	$6-$24	749
40 / p. 734		Courthouse Cafe	▽▽	$7-$20	748
		SUFFOLK - Lodgings			
46 / p. 734		TownePlace Suites by Marriott	▽▽▽	$118-$144	774
47 / p. 734		Courtyard by Marriott	▽▽▽	$128-$156	773
		SUFFOLK - Restaurant			
43 / p. 734		Jersey's Java	▽	$6-$8	774

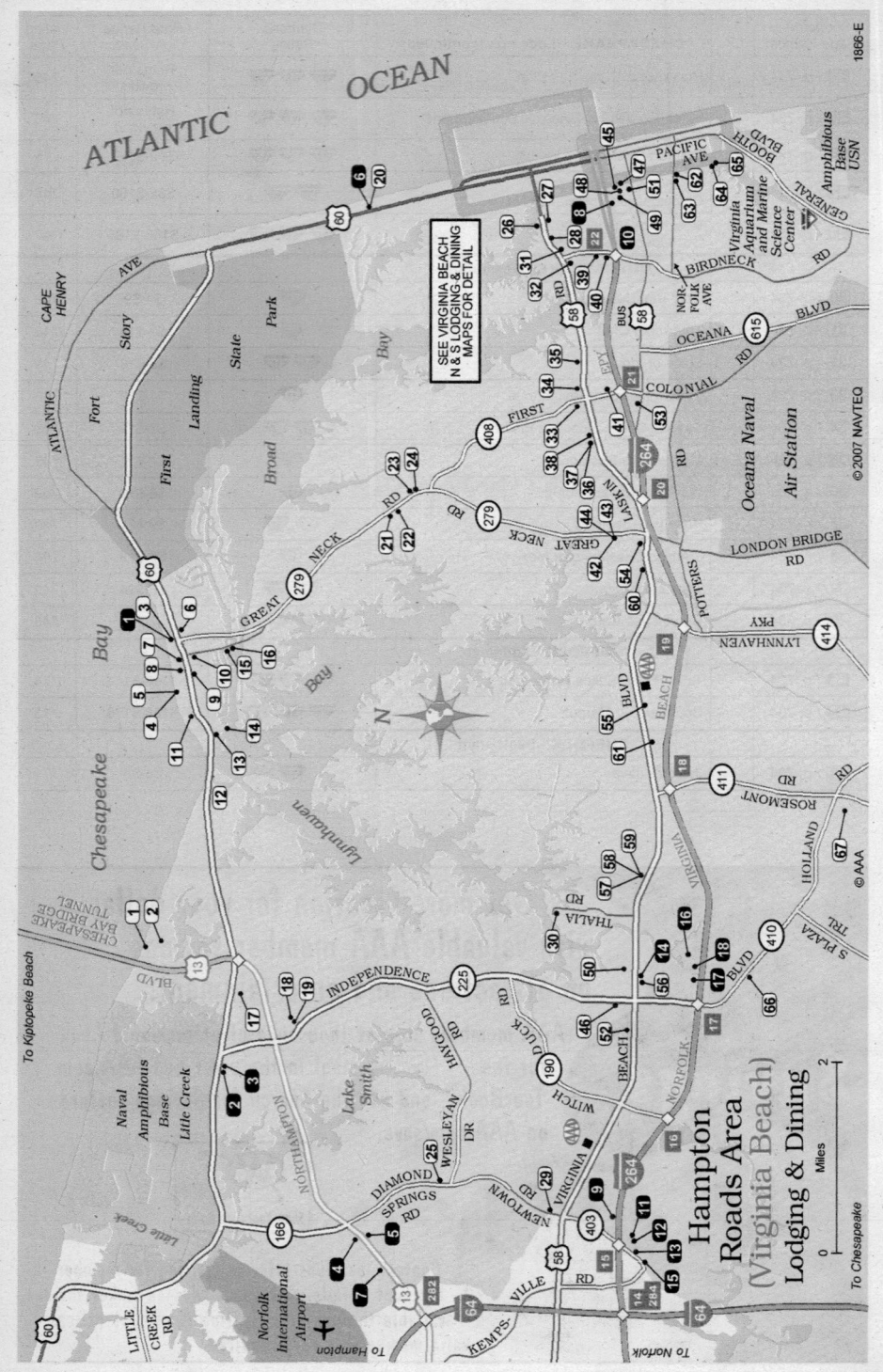

Hampton Roads Area (Virginia Beach)

This index helps you "spot" where approved lodgings and restaurants are located on the corresponding detailed maps. Lodging daily rate range is for comparison only and show the property's high season. Restaurant rate range is a combination of lunch and/or dinner. Turn to the listing page for more detailed rate information and consult display ads for special promotions.

Spotter/Map Page Number	OA	VIRGINIA BEACH - Lodgings	Diamond Rating	Rate Range High Season	Listing Page
1 / p. 738	AAA	Virginia Beach Resort Hotel & Conference Center - see color ad p 798	▽▽▽	$99-$415 SAVE	797
2 / p. 738	AAA	Comfort Inn Little Creek	▽▽	$75-$145 SAVE	781
3 / p. 738		Howard Johnson Inn	▽▽	Rates not provided	788
4 / p. 738	AAA	Best Western Inn	▽▽	Rates not provided SAVE	778
5 / p. 738	AAA	Red Roof Inn VA Beach (Norfolk Airport)	▽▽	Rates not provided SAVE	790
6 / p. 738	AAA	Wyndham Virginia Beach Oceanfront - see color ad p 798, p 776	▽▽▽	$189-$249 SAVE	799
7 / p. 738		Wingate Inn-Norfolk Airport	▽▽▽	$129-$139	797
8 / p. 738	AAA	Quality Inn Pavilion	▽▽	$99-$329 SAVE	790
9 / p. 738		TownePlace Suites By Marriott	▽▽	$147-$164	795
10 / p. 738	AAA	DoubleTree Hotel Virginia Beach	▽▽▽	Rates not provided SAVE	783
11 / p. 738	AAA	Holiday Inn-Executive Center	▽▽▽	$104-$200 SAVE	787
12 / p. 738		Courtyard by Marriott	▽▽▽	$164-$197	781
13 / p. 738		Hampton Inn Virginia Beach	▽▽▽	Rates not provided	786
14 / p. 738		Hilton Garden Inn Virginia Beach, Town Center	▽▽▽	Rates not provided	786
15 / p. 738	AAA	La Quinta Inn Norfolk (Virginia Beach)	▽▽▽	$99-$129 SAVE	788
16 / p. 738		Candlewood Suites	▽▽▽	$69-$199	779
17 / p. 738		Extended StayAmerica-Virginia Beach-Independence Blvd	▽▽	$100-$165	784
18 / p. 738	AAA	Crowne Plaza Virginia Beach - see color ad p 782	▽▽▽	$139-$209 SAVE	782
		VIRGINIA BEACH - Restaurants			
1 / p. 738	AAA	Alexander's on the Bay	▽▽▽	$17-$33	799
2 / p. 738		Zia Marie	▽▽	$8-$20	811
3 / p. 738		Tradewinds	▽▽▽	$7-$27	811
4 / p. 738	AAA	Lynnhaven Fish House Restaurant	▽▽▽	$8-$35	806
5 / p. 738		Pier Cafe	▽▽	$6-$15	807
6 / p. 738		Hot Tuna Bar & Grill	▽▽	$7-$27	804
7 / p. 738		Beale Street	▽▽	$5-$23	800
8 / p. 738		Cabo Cafe	▽▽	$6-$16	801
9 / p. 738		Smokehouse & Cooler	▽▽	$8-$20	809
10 / p. 738		Citrus	▽	$5-$10	802
11 / p. 738		H2O	▽▽	$10-$21	804
12 / p. 738		Croakers	▽▽	$10-$20	802
13 / p. 738		Bubba's Crabhouse & Seafood Restaurant	▽▽	$6-$18	801

Spotter/Map Page Number	OA	VIRGINIA BEACH - Restaurants (continued)	Diamond Rating	Rate Range High Season	Listing Page
(14) / p. 738		Chick's Oyster Bar	◈◈	$8-$23	802
(15) / p. 738		One Fish Two Fish	◈◈◈	$17-$32	807
(16) / p. 738		La Marinella Trattoria Italiana	◈◈	$7-$18	806
(17) / p. 738		Jenna's Mediterranean Deli	◈	$5-$8	805
(18) / p. 738		The Lucky Star	◈◈◈	$7-$35	806
(19) / p. 738		Stella Gourmet Pizzeria	◈◈	$7-$14	809
(20) / p. 738	AAA	**Surf Club Ocean Grille** - see color ad p 798	◈◈◈	$6-$29	809
(21) / p. 738		Coastal Grill	◈◈◈	$13-$23	802
(22) / p. 738		Havana	◈◈	$10-$25	804
(23) / p. 738		Yamato Steak House	◈◈	$6-$30	811
(24) / p. 738		Volcano Sushi Bar	◈◈	$8-$20	811
(25) / p. 738		SurfRider Grill at Cypress Point	◈◈	$6-$18	809
(26) / p. 738		Coyote Cafe & Cantina	◈◈	$6-$23	802
(27) / p. 738		The Purple Cow	◈	$5-$10	808
(28) / p. 738		Beach Pub	◈◈	$5-$14	800
(29) / p. 738		Saigon 1 Restaurant	◈◈	$6-$10	808
(30) / p. 738		Steinhilber's Thalia Acres Inn	◈◈◈	$18-$40	809
(31) / p. 738		La Bella Italia Trattoria	◈◈	$7-$19	805
(32) / p. 738		Bella Monte	◈◈	$6-$22	800
(33) / p. 738		Zinc Brasserie	◈◈◈	$8-$30	811
(34) / p. 738		Cobalt Grille	◈◈	$6-$27	802
(35) / p. 738	AAA	**757 Fire and Vine-Woodfire Cuisine**	◈◈◈	$11-$29	799
(36) / p. 738		Mizuno Japanese Restaurant	◈◈◈	$7-$18	806
(37) / p. 738		Aldo's Ristorante	◈◈◈	$8-$26	799
(38) / p. 738		Plaza Azteca Mexican Restaurant	◈	$6-$13	807
(39) / p. 738		Machismo Burrito Bar	◈	$5-$8	806
(40) / p. 738		Five 0 1 City Grill	◈◈	$7-$21	803
(41) / p. 738		Shogun Japanese Steak House & Seafood	◈	$11-$28	809
(42) / p. 738		Warrior's Grill	◈	$6-$10	811
(43) / p. 738		Sushi & West	◈◈◈	$5-$20	810
(44) / p. 738		Central 111	◈◈	$5-$15	802
(45) / p. 738		Beach Bully	◈	$4-$19	800
(46) / p. 738		Federico's	◈◈	$8-$25	803
(47) / p. 738		Osaka Japanese Restaurant	◈◈	$6-$20	807
(48) / p. 738		Croc's 19th Street Bistro	◈◈	$10-$22	802
(49) / p. 738	AAA	**Zoe's**	◈◈◈◈	$5-$40	812
(50) / p. 738		El Azteca Mexican Restaurant	◈	$5-$14	803

Spotter/Map Page Number	OA	VIRGINIA BEACH - Restaurants (continued)	Diamond Rating	Rate Range High Season	Listing Page
51 / p. 738		Mary's Restaurant	▽	$3-$6	806
52 / p. 738		Pho 79	▽	$3-$8	807
53 / p. 738		The 58 Deli Diner	▽	$3-$10	799
54 / p. 738		Pollard's Chicken	▽	$5-$7	807
55 / p. 738		Conklin's Irish Rover	▽▽	$4-$19	802
56 / p. 738		Zushi Japanese Bistro	▽▽▽	$8-$23	812
57 / p. 738		Bombay Paradise	▽▽	$8-$19	801
58 / p. 738	AAA	**Reginella's Italian Ristorante & Pizzeria**	▽	$5-$15	808
59 / p. 738		Misako Sushi Bar & Grille	▽▽	$5-$18	806
60 / p. 738		Vietnam Garden	▽▽	$6-$19	811
61 / p. 738		Forbidden City Imperial Dining	▽▽	$6-$20	803
62 / p. 738		Tad's Deli	▽	$6-$10	810
63 / p. 738		Gringo's Taqueria	▽	$6-$11	803
64 / p. 738	AAA	**Rockafeller's**	▽▽	$8-$25	808
65 / p. 738	AAA	**Rudee's on the Inlet**	▽▽	$7-$37	808
66 / p. 738		La Casa della Pasta	▽▽	$8-$16	806
67 / p. 738		Imperio Inca	▽▽	$8-$18	805

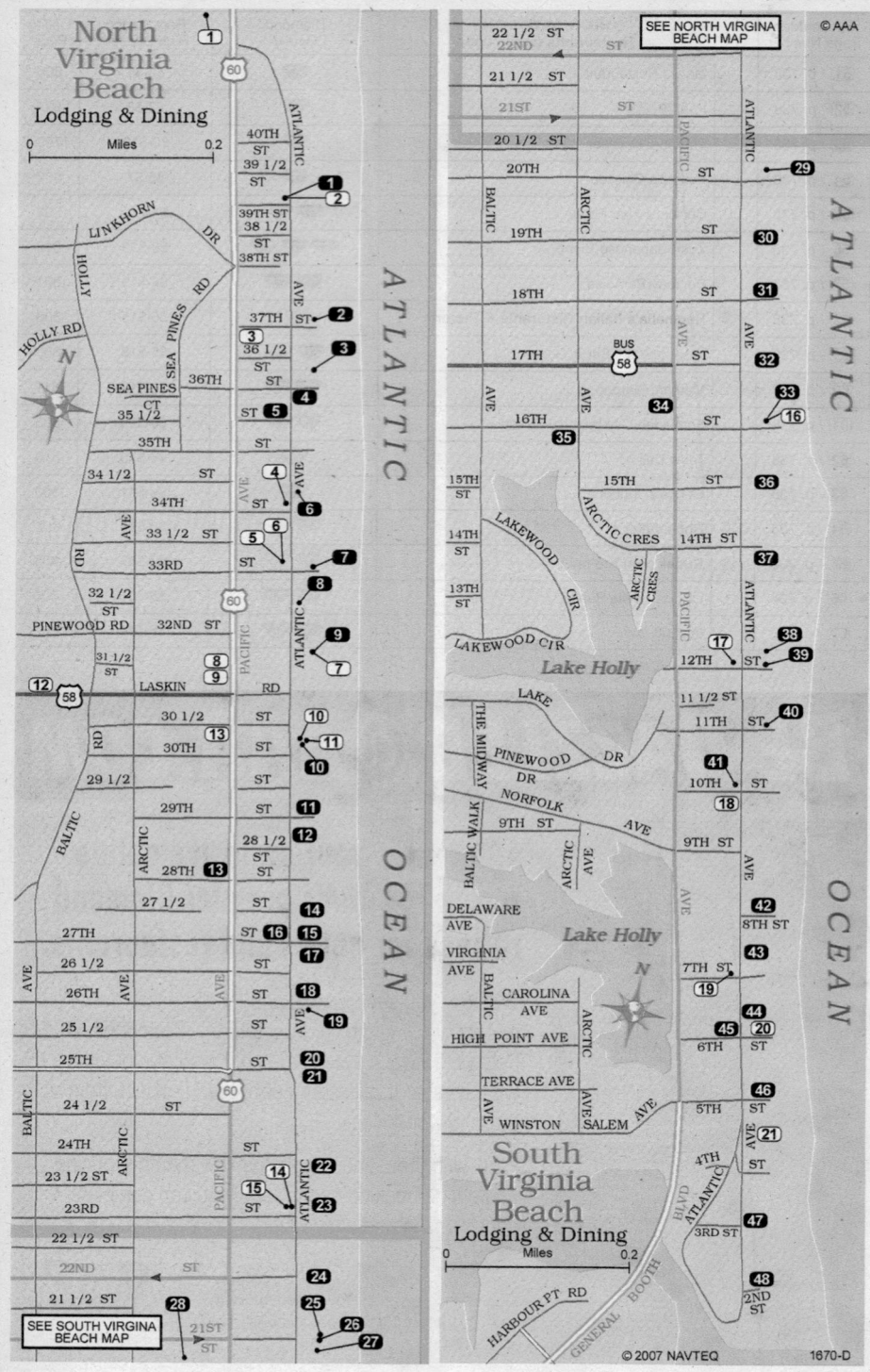

North Virginia Beach Lodging & Dining

South Virginia Beach Lodging & Dining

© 2007 NAVTEQ   1670-D

Hampton Roads Area (Virginia Beach-Beach Area)

This index helps you "spot" where approved lodgings and restaurants are located on the corresponding detailed maps. Lodging daily rate range is for comparison only and show the property's high season. Restaurant rate range is a combination of lunch and/or dinner. Turn to the listing page for more detailed rate information and consult display ads for special promotions.

Spotter/Map Page Number	OA	VIRGINIA BEACH - Lodgings	Diamond Rating	Rate Range High Season	Listing Page
1 / p. 742	AAA	Holiday Inn SunSpree Resort	▽▽▽	$85-$305 SAVE	787
2 / p. 742		Courtyard by Marriott-Oceanfront North	▽▽▽	$169-$252	782
3 / p. 742	AAA	The Belvedere Motel	▽▽	$74-$156 SAVE	776
4 / p. 742		Sheraton Oceanfront Hotel	▽▽▽	$109-$259	795
5 / p. 742	AAA	Royal Clipper Inn & Suites - see color ad p 792	▽▽	$39-$179 SAVE	791
6 / p. 742	AAA	Ocean Beach Club - see color ad p 776	▽▽▽	$89-$359 SAVE	789
7 / p. 742	AAA	Four Sails Resort Hotel - see color ad p 786	▽▽	$79-$219 SAVE	786
8 / p. 742		Residence Inn Virginia Beach Oceanfront	▽▽▽	$235-$351	791
9 / p. 742	AAA	Days Inn Oceanfront - see color ad p 784, p 784	▽▽▽	Rates not provided SAVE	783
10 / p. 742		Hilton Virginia Beach Oceanfront - see color ad p 776, p 787	▽▽▽	Rates not provided	786
11 / p. 742	AAA	The Oceanfront Inn - see color ad p 789	▽▽	$58-$224 SAVE	789
12 / p. 742	AAA	Best Western Oceanfront Va Beach - see color ad p 778	▽▽▽	Rates not provided SAVE	778
13 / p. 742	AAA	La Quinta Inns & Suites - see color ad p 776	▽▽	Rates not provided SAVE	788
14 / p. 742	AAA	Econo Lodge on the Ocean - see color ad p 785	▽▽	$59-$289 SAVE	784
15 / p. 742	AAA	Seaside Motel - see color ad p 794	▽	$50-$150 SAVE	792
16 / p. 742	AAA	The Viking Motel	▽▽	$79-$199 SAVE	796
17 / p. 742	AAA	Sea Gull Motel - see color ad p 794	▽▽	$45-$205 SAVE	792
18 / p. 742	AAA	Holiday Inn Surfside Hotel & Suites	▽▽▽	$109-$319 SAVE	787
19 / p. 742	AAA	Seahawk Motel	▽▽	$49-$189 SAVE	792
20 / p. 742		Courtyard by Marriott-Oceanfront South	▽▽▽	$158-$241	782
21 / p. 742	AAA	Ocean Holiday Hotel	▽▽	$55-$195 SAVE	789
22 / p. 742	AAA	Station One Hotel	▽▽	$199-$350 SAVE	795
23 / p. 742	AAA	Ocean Suites - see color ad p 776, p 790	▽	$49-$249 SAVE	789
24 / p. 742		Marjac Suites - see color ad p 777	▽▽	$49-$239	788
25 / p. 742	AAA	Econo Lodge Oceanfront	▽▽	$59-$259 SAVE	784
26 / p. 742		Holiday Inn Oceanside	▽▽▽	$115-$270	787
27 / p. 742	AAA	Comfort Inn & Suites Oceanfront - see color ad p 780	▽▽▽	$269-$399 SAVE	779
28 / p. 742	AAA	Sundial Motel & Efficiencies - see color ad p 796	▽▽	$49-$229 SAVE	795
29 / p. 742		The Capes Ocean Resort - see color ad p 780	▽▽▽	$45-$320	779
30 / p. 742		Fairfield Inn & Suites Virginia Beach Oceanfront	▽▽▽	$108-$132	785
31 / p. 742		Howard Johnson Oceanfront Hotel - see color ad p 776, p 788	▽▽	$59-$199	788
32 / p. 742	AAA	The Dolphin Inn - see color ad p 776, p 785	▽▽	$89-$359 SAVE	783
33 / p. 742	AAA	Boardwalk Resort Hotel and Villas - see color ad p 776	▽▽▽	$89-$359 SAVE	778
34 / p. 742	AAA	Alamar Resort Inn - see color ad p 775	▽▽▽	$52-$209 SAVE	775

Spotter/Map Page Number	OA	VIRGINIA BEACH - Lodgings (continued)	Diamond Rating	Rate Range High Season	Listing Page
35 / p. 742	AAA	**Barclay Cottage Bed & Breakfast**	◆◆◆	$110-$200 SAVE	775
36 / p. 742	AAA	**The Breakers Resort Inn** - see color ad p 779	◆◆◆	$65-$300 SAVE	778
37 / p. 742	AAA	**Sandcastle Oceanfront Resort Hotel** - see color ad p 793	◆◆	$49-$249 SAVE	791
38 / p. 742	AAA	**Surfside Oceanfront Inn & Suites** - see color ad p 797	◆◆	$49-$249 SAVE	795
39 / p. 742		New Castle Hotel - see color ad p 776	◆◆	Rates not provided	789
40 / p. 742	AAA	**Atlantic Sands Oceanfront Hotel**	◆◆	Rates not provided SAVE	775
41 / p. 742	AAA	**Days Inn at the Beach** - see color ad p 783	◆◆	$39-$189 SAVE	782
42 / p. 742	AAA	**Barclay Towers** - see color ad p 777, p 776	◆◆◆	$69-$269 SAVE	776
43 / p. 742		Quality Inn & Suites - see color ad p 777	◆◆◆	$79-$269	790
44 / p. 742	AAA	**Ramada On the Beach** - see color ad p 776, p 791	◆◆◆	$89-$359 SAVE	790
45 / p. 742	AAA	**Turtle Cay Resort** - see color ad p 776	◆◆◆	$89-$359 SAVE	796
46 / p. 742	AAA	**Clarion Resort** - see color ad p 776	◆◆◆	$89-$359 SAVE	779
47 / p. 742		Best Western Beach Quarters Inn - see color ad p 776	◆◆	Rates not provided	776
48 / p. 742		Schooner Inn - see color ad p 777, p 776	◆◆	$49-$239	791
		VIRGINIA BEACH - Restaurants			
1 / p. 742		The Hunt Room Grill	◆◆◆	$20-$30	804
2 / p. 742		Isle of Capri	◆◆◆	$15-$25	805
3 / p. 742		Sakura Sushi Bar	◆◆	$6-$20	808
4 / p. 742		Mayflower Cafe	◆◆	$5-$21	806
5 / p. 742		Casby's Sea Grill	◆◆	$9-$18	801
6 / p. 742		Pi-zzeria	◆◆	$7-$15	807
7 / p. 742	AAA	**Timbuktu**	◆◆◆	$6-$22	811
8 / p. 742		The Jewish Mother	◆	$5-$10	805
9 / p. 742		The Heritage Health Food Cafe & Deli	◆	$5-$10	804
10 / p. 742		Catch 31 Fish House & Bar	◆◆◆	$8-$22	801
11 / p. 742		Salacia	◆◆◆◆	$25-$45	809
12 / p. 742		Surf Rider Restaurant	◆◆	$5-$17	810
13 / p. 742		Cuisine & Company	◆	$5-$10	803
14 / p. 742		Tautog's	◆◆	$10-$19	810
15 / p. 742		Doc Taylor's	◆	$5-$10	803
16 / p. 742		Rockfish Boardwalk Bar & Sea Grill	◆◆	$6-$22	808
17 / p. 742		The Raven	◆	$6-$20	808
18 / p. 742		IL Giardino	◆◆◆	$11-$47	805
19 / p. 742		Black Angus Restaurant	◆◆	$10-$27	801
20 / p. 742		Mahi Mah's Seafood Restaurant & Sushi Saloon - see color ad p 791	◆◆	$5-$21	806
21 / p. 742	AAA	**Waterman's Surfside Grill**	◆◆	$5-$23	811

CHESAPEAKE pop. 199,184 (See map and index starting on p. 734)

──── WHERE TO STAY ────

COMFORT SUITES

Book at AAA.com

Phone: (757)420-1600 **41**

Small-scale Hotel
$99-$169 All Year

Address: 1550 Crossways Blvd 23320 **Location:** I-64, exit 289B (Greenbrier Pkwy), 0.3 mi s, just w on Jarman Rd (at Crossways Center) to Crossways Blvd, then 0.3 mi n. **Facility:** 124 units. 123 one-bedroom standard units. 1 two-bedroom suite with kitchen. 3 stories, interior corridors. **Parking:** on-site. **Amenities:** high-speed Internet, dual phone lines, voice mail, irons, hair dryers. **Pool(s):** outdoor. **Leisure Activities:** sauna, whirlpool, steamroom, exercise room. **Guest Services:** valet and coin laundry, wireless Internet. **Business Services:** meeting rooms, business center. **Cards:** AX, CB, DC, DS, JC, MC, VI.

ASK SD ☆ ⊺⊺+ CALL 🔊M 🏊 ✕ 📷 🍴 🖨 📺 / SOME UNITS ✕

COUNTRY INN & SUITES

Phone: 757/966-2727

Small-scale Hotel
Rates not provided

Too new to rate. **Address:** 2122 Joliff Rd 23321 **Location:** I-664, exit 11A. **Amenities:** 82 units, coffeemakers, microwaves, refrigerators, pool.

COURTYARD BY MARRIOTT CHESAPEAKE

Book great rates at AAA.com

Phone: 757/420-1700 **37**

Small-scale Hotel
$131-$164 All Year

Address: 1562 Crossways Blvd 23320 **Location:** I-64, exit 289B (Greenbrier Pkwy), just s to Jarman Rd (at Crossway Center), then w. **Facility:** Smoke free premises. 90 units. 87 one-bedroom standard units, some with whirlpools. 3 one-bedroom suites. 3 stories, interior corridors. *Bath:* combo or shower only. **Parking:** on-site. **Amenities:** high-speed Internet, voice mail, irons, hair dryers. **Pool(s):** heated indoor. **Leisure Activities:** whirlpool, exercise room. **Guest Services:** valet and coin laundry, wireless Internet. **Business Services:** meeting rooms, business center. **Cards:** AX, DC, DS, JC, MC, VI.

COURTYARD Marriott

AAA Benefit:
Members save 5%
off of the best
available rate.

ASK SD ☆ ⊺⊺ CALL 🔊M 🏊 ✕ 📷 📺 / SOME UNITS 🍴 🖨

EXTENDED STAYAMERICA CHESAPEAKE-CROSSWAYS BLVD

Book at AAA.com

Phone: (757)424-8600 **42**

Motel
$82-$150 All Year

Address: 1540 Crossways Blvd 23320 **Location:** I-64, exit 289B (Greenbrier Pkwy), 0.3 mi s, just w on Jarman Rd (at Crossways Center) to Crossways Blvd, then 0.3 mi n. **Facility:** 132 one-bedroom standard units with efficiencies. 3 stories (no elevator), exterior corridors. *Bath:* combo or shower only. **Parking:** on-site. **Terms:** office hours 7 am-11 pm. **Amenities:** high-speed Internet (fee), voice mail, irons. **Guest Services:** coin laundry, wireless Internet. **Cards:** AX, DC, DS, JC, MC, VI.

ASK SD ⊺⊺+ CALL 🔊M FEE 🐾+ 📷 🍴 🖨 📺 / SOME UNITS FEE 🐾 ✕

EXTENDED STAYAMERICA CHESAPEAKE-GREENBRIER CIRCLE

Book at AAA.com

Phone: (757)523-7377 **34**

Small-scale Hotel
$95-$145 All Year

Address: 809 Greenbrier Cir 23320 **Location:** I-64, exit 289A (Greenbrier Pkwy), just n. **Facility:** 92 one-bedroom standard units with efficiencies. 4 stories, interior corridors. *Bath:* combo or shower only. **Parking:** on-site. **Amenities:** high-speed Internet, voice mail, irons. **Leisure Activities:** exercise room. **Guest Services:** coin laundry, wireless Internet. **Business Services:** meeting rooms. **Cards:** AX, DC, DS, JC, MC, VI.

ASK SD CALL 🔊M 📷 🍴 🖨 📺 / SOME UNITS FEE 🐾 ✕

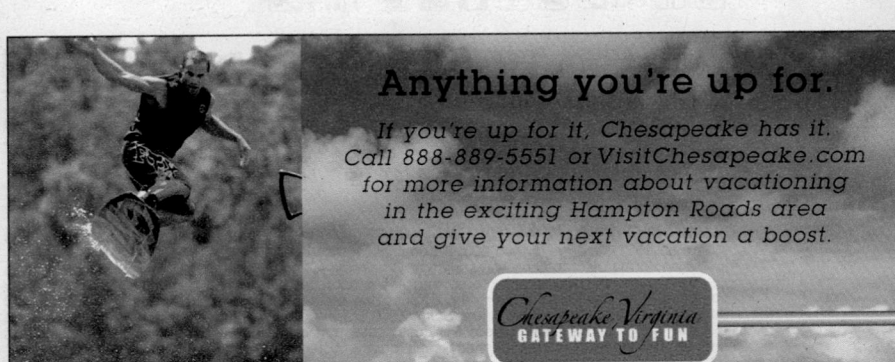

(See map and index starting on p. 734)

EXTENDED STAYAMERICA HOTEL *Book at AAA.com*   Phone: (757)483-9200   **27**

Small-scale Hotel
$95-$145 All Year

Address: 3214 Churchland Blvd 23321 **Location:** I-664, exit 9B northbound; exit 8B southbound, 1 mi s on US 17. **Facility:** 92 one-bedroom standard units with efficiencies. 3 stories, interior corridors. *Bath:* some combo or shower only. **Parking:** on-site. **Terms:** office hours 7 am-11 pm. **Amenities:** high-speed Internet (fee), voice mail, irons. **Guest Services:** coin laundry, wireless Internet. **Cards:** AX, DC, DS, JC, MC, VI.

FAIRFIELD INN & SUITES CHESAPEAKE *Book great rates at AAA.com*   Phone: 757/420-1300   **38**

Small-scale Hotel
$120-$142 3/1-8/31
$98-$120 9/1-2/28

Address: 1560 Crossways Blvd 23320 **Location:** I-64, exit 289B (Greenbrier Pkwy), just s to Greenbrier Mall, then just w on Jarman Rd (at Crossways Center). **Facility:** Smoke free premises. 105 one-bedroom standard units. 3 stories, interior corridors. *Bath:* combo or shower only. **Parking:** on-site. **Amenities:** high-speed Internet, dual phone lines, voice mail, irons, hair dryers. **Leisure Activities:** exercise room. **Guest Services:** valet and coin laundry, wireless Internet. **Business Services:** meeting rooms, business center. **Cards:** AX, DC, DS, JC, MC, VI.

AAA Benefit: Members save 5% off of the best available rate.

HAMPTON INN & SUITES *Book great rates at AAA.com*   Phone: (757)465-7000   **31**

Small-scale Hotel
$129-$199 3/1-10/31
$119-$189 11/1-2/28

Address: 4449 Peek Trail 23321 **Location:** I-664, exit 11B (Portsmouth Blvd E). **Facility:** 86 one-bedroom standard units. 5 stories, interior corridors. *Bath:* combo or shower only. **Parking:** on-site. **Amenities:** high-speed Internet, voice mail, irons, hair dryers. **Pool(s):** heated indoor. **Leisure Activities:** whirlpool, exercise room. **Guest Services:** valet and coin laundry. **Business Services:** meeting rooms, business center. **Cards:** AX, CB, DC, DS, MC, VI.

HAMPTON INN CHESAPEAKE *Book great rates at AAA.com*   Phone: (757)484-5800   **28**

Small-scale Hotel
$89-$129 All Year

Address: 3235 Western Branch Blvd 23321 **Location:** I-664, exit 9B northbound; exit 8B southbound, 1 mi s on US 17. **Facility:** 90 one-bedroom standard units. 4 stories, interior corridors. **Parking:** on-site. **Terms:** check-in 4 pm. **Amenities:** high-speed Internet, voice mail, irons, hair dryers. **Leisure Activities:** sauna, exercise room. **Guest Services:** valet and coin laundry, wireless Internet. **Business Services:** fax. **Cards:** AX, CB, DC, DS, JC, MC, VI.

HAMPTON INN CHESAPEAKE *Book great rates at AAA.com*   Phone: 757/420-1550   **36**

Small-scale Hotel
Rates not provided

Address: 701A Woodlake Dr 23320 **Location:** I-64, exit 289A (Greenbrier Pkwy), just n to Woodlake Dr. **Facility:** 119 one-bedroom standard units. 4 stories, interior corridors. **Parking:** on-site. **Amenities:** video games (fee), high-speed Internet, voice mail, irons, hair dryers. **Pool(s):** outdoor. **Guest Services:** valet laundry, wireless Internet. **Business Services:** PC, fax.

HILTON GARDEN INN-CHESAPEAKE/GREENBRIER *Book great rates at AAA.com*   Phone: 757/420-1212   **40**

Small-scale Hotel
Rates not provided

Address: 1565 Crossways Blvd 23320 **Location:** I-64, exit 289B (Greenbrier Pkwy), just s to Jarman Rd at Crossways Center. **Facility:** 92 one-bedroom standard units, some with whirlpools. 4 stories, interior corridors. *Bath:* combo or shower only. **Parking:** on-site. **Terms:** check-in 4 pm. **Amenities:** video games (fee), high-speed Internet, dual phone lines, voice mail, irons, hair dryers. **Pool(s):** heated indoor. **Leisure Activities:** whirlpool, exercise room. **Guest Services:** valet and coin laundry, area transportation, wireless Internet. **Business Services:** meeting rooms, business center.

HOLIDAY INN EXPRESS HOTEL & SUITES *Book at AAA.com*   Phone: (757)465-2222   **29**

Small-scale Hotel
$139-$149 3/1-9/4
$109-$119 9/5-2/28

Address: 2436 Gum Rd 23321 **Location:** I-664, exit 11B (Portsmouth Blvd E). **Facility:** 90 one-bedroom standard units, some with whirlpools. 5 stories, interior corridors. *Bath:* combo or shower only. **Parking:** on-site. **Terms:** cancellation fee imposed. **Amenities:** high-speed Internet, voice mail, irons, hair dryers. **Pool(s):** heated indoor. **Leisure Activities:** whirlpool, exercise room. **Guest Services:** valet and coin laundry, wireless Internet. **Business Services:** meeting rooms, business center. **Cards:** AX, MC, VI.

HOMEWOOD SUITES BY HILTON *Book at AAA.com*   Phone: 757/213-0808   **39**

Small-scale Hotel
Rates not provided

Address: 1561 Crossways Blvd 23320 **Location:** I-64, exit 289B (Greenbrier Pkwy), 0.3 mi s, then just w on Jarman Rd, to Crossways Center. **Facility:** 100 units. 55 one-bedroom standard units with kitchens. 41 one- and 4 two-bedroom suites with kitchens. 5 stories, interior corridors. *Bath:* combo or shower only. **Parking:** on-site. **Amenities:** video games (fee), high-speed Internet, voice mail, irons, hair dryers. *Some:* DVD players (fee). **Pool(s):** outdoor. **Leisure Activities:** exercise room, sports court. **Guest Services:** valet and coin laundry, area transportation, wireless Internet. **Business Services:** meeting rooms, business center.

(See map and index starting on p. 734)

MARRIOTT HOTEL CHESAPEAKE

Phone: (757)523-1500   **35**

Large-scale Hotel
$139-$189 5/1-11/30
$119-$159 12/1-2/28

Address: 725 Woodlake Dr 23320 **Location:** I-64, exit 289A (Greenbrier Pkwy), n to Woodlake Dr, then just e. Located adjacent to the Chesapeake Conference Center. **Facility:** Smoke free premises. 226 units. 213 one-bedroom standard units. 13 one-bedroom suites. 7 stories, interior corridors. **Parking:** on-site. **Terms:** open 5/1-2/28, cancellation fee imposed. **Amenities:** video games, high-speed Internet, dual phone lines, voice mail, irons, hair dryers. **Pool(s):** heated indoor. **Leisure Activities:** sauna, whirlpool, exercise room. **Guest Services:** valet and coin laundry, area transportation, wireless Internet. **Business Services:** conference facilities, business center. **Cards:** AX, DC, DS, MC, VI.

Marriott
HOTELS & RESORTS

AAA Benefit:
Members save 5% off of the best available rate.

RESIDENCE INN BY MARRIOTT, CHESAPEAKE-GREENBRIER

Book great rates at AAA.com

Phone: 757/502-7300   **43**

Small-scale Hotel
$153-$186 All Year

Address: 1500 Crossways Blvd 23320 **Location:** I-64, exit 289B (Greenbrier Pkwy), just s to Jarman Rd (at Crossways Center) to Crossways Blvd, then 0.6 mi n. **Facility:** Smoke free premises. 121 units. 29 one-bedroom standard units with kitchens. 83 one- and 9 two-bedroom suites with kitchens. 5 stories, interior corridors. **Bath:** combo or shower only. **Parking:** on-site. **Amenities:** high-speed Internet, dual phone lines, voice mail, irons, hair dryers. **Pool(s):** heated indoor. **Leisure Activities:** whirlpool, exercise room, sports court. **Guest Services:** valet and coin laundry, wireless Internet. **Business Services:** meeting rooms, business center. **Cards:** AX, DC, DS, MC, VI.

Residence Inn

AAA Benefit:
Members save 5% off of the best available rate.

SLEEP INN & SUITES

Book great rates at AAA.com

Phone: (757)638-5000   **26**

Small-scale Hotel
$105-$125 7/1-2/28
$99-$115 3/1-6/30

Address: 3280 Western Branch Blvd 23321 **Location:** I-664, exit 9B, 1 mi s on SR 17. **Facility:** 83 one-bedroom standard units, some with whirlpools. 2 stories, interior corridors. **Bath:** combo or shower only. **Parking:** on-site. **Terms:** cancellation fee imposed. **Amenities:** video library (fee). *Some:* high-speed Internet, dual phone lines, voice mail, irons, hair dryers. **Pool(s):** heated indoor. **Leisure Activities:** whirlpool, exercise room. **Guest Services:** valet and coin laundry, wireless Internet. **Business Services:** meeting rooms, business center. **Cards:** AX, DC, DS, MC, VI. **Free Special Amenities:** continental breakfast and high-speed Internet.

SPRINGHILL SUITES BY MARRIOTT

Book great rates at AAA.com

Phone: 757/405-3100   **30**

Small-scale Hotel
$131-$153 All Year

Address: 2424 Gum Rd 23321 **Location:** I-664, exit 11B (Portsmouth Blvd E). **Facility:** Smoke free premises. 93 one-bedroom standard units. 3 stories, interior corridors. **Bath:** combo or shower only. **Parking:** on-site. **Amenities:** high-speed Internet, voice mail, irons, hair dryers. **Pool(s):** heated indoor. **Leisure Activities:** whirlpool, exercise room. **Guest Services:** valet and coin laundry, wireless Internet. **Business Services:** meeting rooms, business center. **Cards:** AX, DC, DS, JC, MC, VI.

SPRINGHILL SUITES Marriott

AAA Benefit:
Members save 5% off of the best available rate.

TOWNEPLACE SUITES BY MARRIOTT

Book great rates at AAA.com

Phone: 757/523-5004   **32**

Small-scale Hotel
$120-$153 All Year

Address: 2000 Old Greenbrier Rd 23320 **Location:** I-64, exit 289A (Greenbrier Pkwy), just n on Greenbrier Pkwy. **Facility:** Smoke free premises. 119 units. 93 one-bedroom standard units with kitchens. 4 one- and 22 two-bedroom suites with kitchens. 3 stories, interior corridors. **Bath:** combo or shower only. **Parking:** on-site. **Amenities:** high-speed Internet, voice mail, irons, hair dryers. **Pool(s):** heated outdoor. **Leisure Activities:** exercise room. **Guest Services:** valet and coin laundry, wireless Internet. **Business Services:** fax. **Cards:** AX, DC, DS, JC, MC, VI.

TownePlace SUITES

AAA Benefit:
Members save 5% off of the best available rate.

WINGATE INN-GREENBRIER

Book at AAA.com

Phone: (757)531-7777   **33**

Small-scale Hotel
$119-$135 All Year

Address: 817 Greenbrier Cir 23320 **Location:** I-64, exit 289A (Greenbrier Pkwy), just n. **Facility:** 100 units. 96 one-bedroom standard units. 4 one-bedroom suites with whirlpools. 4 stories, interior corridors. **Bath:** combo or shower only. **Parking:** on-site. **Amenities:** video games (fee), high-speed Internet, voice mail, safes, irons, hair dryers. **Pool(s):** heated indoor. **Leisure Activities:** whirlpool, exercise room. **Guest Services:** valet and coin laundry, wireless Internet. **Business Services:** meeting rooms, business center. **Cards:** AX, CB, DC, DS, JC, MC, VI.

(See map and index starting on p. 734)

──────── **WHERE TO DINE** ────────

3 AMIGOS RESTAURANTE MEXICANO

Phone: 757/548-4105 (38)

Mexican
$6-$12

Overlooking the Intracoastal Waterway, the eatery is a pleasant spot for sampling such dishes as huevos rancheros and chicken with a savory red mole sauce that derives its richness from cocoa beans. The house specialty is a tasty mix of beef and chicken slices covered in cactus, onions and tomatoes. Casual dress. **Bar:** Full bar. **Hours:** 11 am-10 pm; Fri-11 pm, Sun-9 pm. Closed major holidays. **Address:** 200 N Battlefield Blvd 23320 **Location:** I-64, exit 290B (Battlefield Blvd S), 3.3 mi s. **Parking:** on-site. **Cards:** MC, VI.

THE ANGRY CHEF

Phone: 757/963-7534 (31)

American
$6-$18

He might be angry, but he knows how to cook. Locals drop in to the bright and casual spot for a break from the ordinary such as roasted garlic salad, the drunk burger which is marinated in whiskey, seared crab cakes, fresh soups, and daily changing desserts. Casual dress. **Bar:** Beer & wine. **Hours:** 11 am-9 pm. Closed major holidays. **Address:** 1412 Greenbrier Pkwy, Suite 140 23320 **Location:** I-64, exit 289B (Greenbrier Pkwy), just w; across from Greenbrier Mall; at jct Eden Way; in Crossways Shopping Center. **Parking:** on-site. **Cards:** AX, DS, MC, VI.

CALL 🕭M

ATLAS GRILL & BAR

Phone: 757/420-6222

American
$6-$14

Atlas stakes its claim on "chain row" offering hungry diners heaping portions of comfort food with heavy influences from the South and from traditional diner fare. Great "stick to your ribs" dishes such as meatloaf, chicken pot pie and pork chops, as well as burgers and salad. Casual dress. **Bar:** Full bar. **Reservations:** accepted. **Hours:** 11 am-10 pm, Fri & Sat-11 pm. Closed major holidays. **Address:** 1432 Greenbrier Pkwy 23320 **Location:** I-64, exit 289B (Greenbrier Pkwy), just s; across from Greenbrier Mall. **Parking:** on-site. **Cards:** AX, MC, VI.

CALL 🕭M

BANGKOK GARDEN

Phone: 757/549-9989

Thai
$7-$16

Thai artwork decorates the stylish interior of the cozy restaurant. On the menu is fresh, healthy fare prepared with fresh seafood, chili peppers, curries, coconuts, tropical fruit and vegetables. Casual dress. **Bar:** Full bar. **Reservations:** accepted. **Hours:** 11 am-10 pm, Fri-10:30 pm, Sat noon-10:30 pm, Sun noon-8 pm. Closed major holidays. **Address:** 805 Battlefield Blvd N, #117 23320 **Location:** I-64, exit 290B, 1.6 mi se; in Knell's Ridge Shoppes. **Parking:** on-site. **Cards:** DC, MC, VI.

CALL 🕭M

COURTHOUSE CAFE

Phone: 757/482-7077 (40)

Regional American
$7-$20

Reminiscent of the days when the city was more country than suburbia, the cozy, little spot prepares regional seafood specialties, such as stuffed flounder, she crab soup and Hatteras-style clam chowder. Other favorites include prime rib, burgers and sandwiches. Casual dress. **Bar:** Full bar. **Hours:** 11 am-10 pm, Fri & Sat-10:30 pm. Closed major holidays; also Sun. **Address:** 350 S Battlefield Blvd 23322 **Location:** I-64, exit 290B (Battlefield Blvd S), 4 mi s, jct Johnstown Rd; in Wilson Village Shopping Center. **Parking:** on-site. **Cards:** AX, MC, VI.

DAIKICHI SUSHI JAPANESE BISTRO

Phone: 757/549-0200 (34)

Japanese
$7-$19

A sleek, modern setting in the heart of suburbia offers stylish preparations of fresh sushi—both traditional and the chef's modern additions. Udon noodles and pork katsu are other tasty plates. Rarely seen in America, pure fresh wasabi accompanies sushi plates. Casual dress. **Bar:** Beer & wine. **Hours:** 11:30 am-2 & 5:30-9:30 pm, Fri-10 pm, Sat 5:30 pm-10 pm. Closed major holidays; also Sun. **Address:** 1400 N Battlefield Blvd 23320 **Location:** I-64, exit 290B (Battlefield Blvd S), just s; in Battlefield Marketplace. **Parking:** on-site. **Cards:** MC, VI.

CALL 🕭M

EL LORO MEXICAN RESTAURANTE

Phone: 757/436-3415 (33)

Mexican
$4-$10

Pinatas and colorful paintings add to the festive atmosphere of the traditional Mexican restaurant. The menu is laden with the classics: combination and vegetarian plates, fajitas, tacos, chalupas and, of course, margaritas-in jumbo and Texas-style varieties. Casual dress. **Bar:** Full bar. **Hours:** 10 am-10 pm, Fri-11 pm, Sat noon-10 pm, Sun noon-9 pm. Closed major holidays. **Address:** 801 Volvo Pkwy, Suites 114-115 23320 **Location:** I-64, exit 289B (Greenbrier Pkwy), 0.9 mi s. **Parking:** on-site. **Cards:** AX, MC, VI.

KELLY'S TAVERN

Phone: 757/488-0500

American
$7-$20

The casual chain is a local favorite for such simple specialties as burgers, Buffalo wings, fish tacos, salads and sandwiches. Casual dress. **Bar:** Full bar. **Hours:** 11 am-1 am. Closed: 11/27, 12/25. **Address:** 2400 Ring Rd 23321 **Location:** I-664, exit 11B (Portsmouth Blvd E), just e; adjacent to Chesapeake Square Mall. **Parking:** on-site. **Cards:** AX, DS, MC, VI.

CALL 🕭M

KELLY'S TAVERN

Phone: 757/523-1781

American
$7-$20

The casual chain is a local favorite for such simple specialties as burgers, Buffalo wings, fish tacos, salads and sandwiches. Casual dress. **Bar:** Full bar. **Reservations:** accepted, Mon-Fri. **Hours:** 11 am-1 am. Closed: 11/27, 12/25. **Address:** 1412 Greenbrier Pkwy, Suite 110 23320 **Location:** I-64, exit 289B (Greenbrier Pkwy), just w; across from Greenbrier Mall; in Crossways Shopping Center. **Parking:** on-site. **Cards:** AX, DS, MC, VI.

CALL 🕭M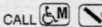

(See map and index starting on p. 734)

THE LOCKS POINTE

Seafood
$6-$24

Phone: 757/547-9618   39

Rooms decorated in rich wood and lots of glass look out onto the Intracoastal Waterway. Traditional, contemporary preparation of predominantly seafood specials, such as tasty scallops with angel hair pasta, make the restaurant popular. Casual dress. **Bar:** Full bar. **Hours:** 11:30 am-9 pm, Fri-10 pm, Sat 4 pm-10 pm, Sun 10:30 am-3 & 4-9 pm, Mon 5 pm-11 pm. Closed: 12/24, 12/25. **Address:** 136 Battlefield Blvd N 23320 **Location:** I-64, exit 290B (Battlefield Blvd S), 3.5 mi s. **Parking:** on-site. **Cards:** AX, DS, MC, VI.

MS MARIAN'S RESTAURANT

Southern
$4-$11

Phone: 757/547-5556   35

All your down-home Southern favorites can be found at Ms. Marian's including fried chicken, barbecue, cornbread, mac n' cheese and even collard greens. Casual dress. **Reservations:** not accepted. **Hours:** 11 am-9 pm. Closed: Sun. **Address:** 1437 Sam's Dr, Suite 104 23320 **Location:** I-64, exit 290B (Battlefield Blvd S); adjacent to Sam's Club. **Parking:** on-site. **Cards:** AX, DS, MC, VI.

CALL 🔊♿

ROSE BAY SEAFOOD

Seafood
$9-$21

Phone: 757/548-9300   37

In a humble strip mall, the restaurant creates a scenic seaside appeal on the inside to accent its extensive selection of fresh local seafood. Specialties of dry-pack scallops, grilled tuna and crab cakes stocked with plenty of crabmeat (not filler) taste great with delicious, steaming-hot hushpuppies. Casual dress. **Bar:** Full bar. **Hours:** 11 am-10 pm, Sat from 4 pm. Closed: Sun. **Address:** 805 N Battlefield Blvd 23320 **Location:** I-64, exit 290B, 1.6 mi se; in Knell's Ridge Square. **Parking:** on-site. **Cards:** AX, DS, MC, VI.

CALL ♿

SILVER DINER

American
$6-$12

Phone: 757/382-0804

The eatery with its chrome and glass plate exterior and the glow of neon, provides the traditional diner setting. Booths with juke boxes, counter service and friendly wait staff add to the diner experience. The menu is extensive with salads, sandwiches and full meals. The desserts are made fresh and the fountain treats, shakes, floats and malts make for a great ending. Breakfast is available all day. Casual dress. **Bar:** Full bar. **Hours:** 6 am-11 pm, Fri & Sat-midnight. Closed: 12/25. **Address:** 1401 Tintern St 23320 **Location:** I-64, exit 290B, just s on Battlefield Blvd. **Parking:** on-site. **Cards:** AX, CB, DC, DS, JC, MC, VI.

CALL ♿

SPICE OF INDIA

Northern Indian
$8-$18

Phone: 757/547-7300   32

Guests enjoy Northern Indian delicacies in a colorful setting that mixes contemporary accents with traditional Indian art and music. Among the many dishes cooked in the clay tandoori oven are flavorful naan and roti breads, as well as marinated seafood and meats. Other offerings include curries, vindaloos and biryanis, which are flavorful and delicately spiced. Casual dress. **Bar:** Full bar. **Hours:** 11:30 am-2:30 & 5-10 pm. **Address:** 1036 Volvo Pkwy, Suite 7 23320 **Location:** I-64, exit 289B (Greenbrier Pkwy), just s to Volvo Pkwy, then just e; in Shoppes at Greenbrier. **Parking:** on-site. **Cards:** AX, DS, MC, VI.

CALL ♿

TASTE UNLIMITED

Deli/Subs
Sandwiches
$5-$10

Phone: 757/424-4583

Casual dress. **Hours:** 10 am-6 pm. Closed: Sun. **Address:** 1580 Crossways Blvd 23320 **Location:** I-64, exit 289B (Greenbrier Pkwy), just s. **Parking:** on-site. **Cards:** AX, MC, VI.

TIDA THAI CUISINE

Thai
$4-$9

Phone: 757/543-9116   30

Traditional dishes are presented in the popular eatery's cozy dining room. Many spicy and exotic flavors await diners in such favorites as crab dumplings and coconut soup. Both the food and friendly, attentive service contribute to this place's regular following. Casual dress. **Bar:** Beer & wine. **Reservations:** accepted. **Hours:** 11 am-3 & 5-10 pm, Sun noon-9 pm. Closed major holidays. **Address:** 1937 S Military Hwy 23320 **Location:** I-64, exit 290A (Battlefield Blvd N), 0.5 mi to Military Hwy, then just n to Chesapeake Crossing Shopping Center. **Parking:** on-site. **Cards:** AX, DS, MC, VI.

WARRIOR'S MONGOLIAN GRILL

Asian
$6-$10

Phone: 757/382-7007   36

Mongolian barbecue is a great alternative to the traditional all-you-can-eat Asian buffet. Diners choose raw vegetables, meats and sauces, then hand them over to the chefs, who grill the tasty fare. Casual dress. **Bar:** Full bar. **Hours:** 11:30 am-9 pm, Fri & Sat-10 pm. Closed major holidays. **Address:** 1437 Sam's Dr, #113 23320 **Location:** I-64, exit 291 (S Battlefield Blvd), just e to Wal-Mart Way Crossing. **Parking:** on-site. **Cards:** AX, DS, MC, VI.

GLOUCESTER

——— **WHERE TO STAY** ———

COMFORT INN GLOUCESTER   *Book at AAA.com*

Small-scale Hotel
$84-$179 3/1-10/31
$84-$149 11/1-2/28

Phone: (804)695-1900

Address: 6639 Forest Hill Ave 23061 **Location:** US 17, just s. **Facility:** 79 one-bedroom standard units, some with whirlpools. 3 stories, interior corridors. *Bath:* combo or shower only. **Parking:** on-site. **Terms:** 2 night minimum stay - weekends. **Amenities:** high-speed Internet, voice mail, irons, hair dryers. **Pool(s):** outdoor. **Guest Services:** valet and coin laundry, wireless Internet. **Business Services:** meeting rooms. **Cards:** AX, CB, DC, DS, JC, MC, VI.

—————— **WHERE TO DINE** ——————

STILLWATER'S ON MAIN
$\bigtriangledown\!\!\bigtriangledown\,\bigtriangledown\!\!\bigtriangledown$
American
$6-$24

Phone: 804/694-5618
The bright storefront overlooks the center of town. The kitchen prepares a delicious array of specialties, such as Urbanna hot smoked salmon, buffalo steak and local seafood, in preparations with Mediterranean influences. Casual dress. **Bar:** Full bar. **Hours:** 11 am-2 & 5-9 pm, Tues from 5 pm. Closed major holidays; also Sun & Mon. **Address:** 6553 Main St 23061 **Location:** Jct Martin St; downtown. **Parking:** on-site. **Cards:** AX, DS, MC, VI.

—————— *The following restaurant has not been evaluated by AAA* ——————
but is listed for your information only.

LEIGH AND NARDOZZI BAKERY
[fyi]

Phone: 804/693-3854
Not evaluated. In the heart of the quaint town is this small bakery, which turns out artisan breads and a short lunch menu of chowders, sandwiches and salads. **Address:** 6672 Main St 23061 **Location:** Downtown.

GLOUCESTER POINT pop. 9,429

—————— **WHERE TO DINE** ——————

RIVER'S INN RESTAURANT & CRAB DECK *Menu on AAA.com*
Ⓐ
$\bigtriangledown\!\!\bigtriangledown\,\bigtriangledown\!\!\bigtriangledown\,\bigtriangledown\!\!\bigtriangledown$
Seafood
$8-$25

Phone: 804/642-9942
Relax in the scenic waterfront setting and crisp indoor decor while sampling a variety of classic regional seafood specialties. Casual, outdoor deck dining focuses on sandwiches, steamed seafood and raw bar offerings. Service is pleasant and well timed. Casual dress. **Bar:** Full bar. **Reservations:** suggested. **Hours:** 11:30 am-3 & 5-9 pm; to 10 pm in season. Closed: 12/25; also 12/31. **Address:** 8109 Yacht Haven Rd 23062 **Location:** From the Coleman Bridge/US 17 N, e on CR 1206/Lafayette Heights Dr to Great Rd N, 0.5 mi e on Terrapin Cove Rd. **Parking:** on-site. **Cards:** AX, DS, MC, VI.

SWEET MADELEINE'S CAFE
$\bigtriangledown\!\!\bigtriangledown\,\bigtriangledown\!\!\bigtriangledown$
American
$5-$18

Phone: 804/642-1780
Homemade soups, gourmet sandwiches and freshly baked desserts fill the bill at the garden-themed cafe. Casual dress. **Bar:** Wine only. **Hours:** 11 am-2:45 & 4-9 pm, Mon & Tues-2:45 pm. Closed major holidays; also Sun. **Address:** 2091 George Washington Memorial Hwy 23062 **Location:** On US 17, 1.5 mi n of Coleman Bridge; jct Tide Mill Rd. **Parking:** on-site. **Cards:** AX, DS, MC, VI.

HAMPTON pop. 146,437   (See map and index starting on p. 728)

—————— **WHERE TO STAY** ——————

CANDLEWOOD SUITES *Book at AAA.com*
$\bigtriangledown\!\!\bigtriangledown\,\bigtriangledown\!\!\bigtriangledown$
Small-scale Hotel
Rates not provided

Phone: 757/766-8976 ㉙
Address: 401 Butler Farm Rd 23666 **Location:** I-64, exit 261B (Hampton Roads Center Pkwy) eastbound; exit 262B (Magruder Blvd) westbound, then e. **Facility:** 98 units. 74 one-bedroom standard units with kitchens. 24 one-bedroom suites with kitchens. 3 stories, interior corridors. **Bath:** combo or shower only. **Parking:** on-site. **Amenities:** video library, DVD players, CD players, high-speed Internet, dual phone lines, voice mail, irons, hair dryers. **Leisure Activities:** exercise room. **Guest Services:** complimentary laundry. **Business Services:** fax.

CLARION HOTEL-HAMPTON ROADS CONVENTION CENTER *Book great rates at AAA.com*
Ⓐ [SAVE]
$\bigtriangledown\!\!\bigtriangledown\,\bigtriangledown\!\!\bigtriangledown\,\bigtriangledown\!\!\bigtriangledown$
Small-scale Hotel
$89-$159 All Year

Phone: (757)838-5011 ㉛
Address: 1809 W Mercury Blvd 23666 **Location:** I-64, exit 263B (Mercury Blvd), jct SR 58. **Facility:** 189 units. 187 one-bedroom standard units. 2 one-bedroom suites. 8 stories, interior corridors. **Bath:** combo or shower only. **Parking:** on-site. **Terms:** check-in 4 pm. **Amenities:** video games, high-speed Internet, voice mail, safes (fee), irons, hair dryers. **Dining:** 2 restaurants. **Pool(s):** heated indoor. **Leisure Activities:** exercise room, game room. **Guest Services:** coin laundry, wireless Internet. **Business Services:** conference facilities, PC. **Cards:** AX, CB, DC, DS, JC, MC, VI. **Free Special Amenities:** early check-in/late check-out.

COMFORT INN *Book at AAA.com*
$\bigtriangledown\!\!\bigtriangledown\,\bigtriangledown\!\!\bigtriangledown$
Small-scale Hotel
$79-$149 All Year

Phone: (757)827-5052 �34
Address: 1916 Coliseum Dr 23666 **Location:** I-64, exit 263B (Mercury Blvd). **Facility:** 66 one-bedroom standard units. 5 stories, interior corridors. **Parking:** on-site. **Terms:** cancellation fee imposed. **Amenities:** high-speed Internet, voice mail, safes (fee), irons, hair dryers. **Pool(s):** outdoor. **Leisure Activities:** exercise room. **Guest Services:** valet and coin laundry, wireless Internet. **Business Services:** PC, fax. **Cards:** AX, CB, DC, DS, MC, VI.

COUNTRY INN & SUITES HAMPTON *Book at AAA.com*
$\bigtriangledown\!\!\bigtriangledown\,\bigtriangledown\!\!\bigtriangledown\,\bigtriangledown\!\!\bigtriangledown$
Small-scale Hotel
$79-$149 All Year

Phone: (757)224-9994 ㉚
Address: 1551 Hardy Cash Dr 23666 **Location:** I-64, exit 261B eastbound, just e on Hampton Rds Center Pkwy, just s on SR 134 (Magruder Blvd), then just e; exit 262B (Nasa/Poquoson) westbound. **Facility:** 96 units. 70 one-bedroom standard units, some with whirlpools. 26 one-bedroom suites. 3 stories, interior corridors. **Bath:** combo or shower only. **Parking:** on-site. **Amenities:** high-speed Internet, dual phone lines, voice mail, irons, hair dryers. **Pool(s):** heated indoor. **Leisure Activities:** whirlpool, exercise room. **Guest Services:** valet and coin laundry, area transportation. **Business Services:** meeting rooms, business center. **Cards:** AX, DC, DS, MC, VI.

(See map and index starting on p. 728)

COURTYARD BY MARRIOTT   *Book great rates at AAA.com*   Phone: 757/838-3300   35

Small-scale Hotel
$142-$164 All Year

Address: 1917 Coliseum Dr 23666 **Location:** I-64, exit 263B (Mercury Blvd) eastbound, just n to Coliseum Dr, then just w; exit 263B westbound. Located adjacent to Hampton Coliseum. **Facility:** Smoke free premises. 146 units. 134 one-bedroom standard units. 12 one-bedroom suites. 3 stories, interior corridors. *Bath:* combo or shower only. **Parking:** on-site. **Amenities:** high-speed Internet, dual phone lines, voice mail, irons, hair dryers. **Pool(s):** outdoor. **Leisure Activities:** whirlpool, exercise room. **Guest Services:** valet and coin laundry. **Business Services:** meeting rooms, business center. **Cards:** AX, DC, DS, MC, VI.

AAA Benefit:
Members save 5% off of the best available rate.

EMBASSY SUITES HAMPTON ROADS HOTEL, SPA, AND CONVENTION CENTER   *Book great rates at AAA.com*   Phone: 757/827-8200   37

Large-scale Hotel
Rates not provided

Address: 1700 Coliseum Dr 23666 **Location:** I-64, exit 263 (Mercury Blvd) eastbound, just n, then just e; exit 263B westbound; adjacent to Hampton Coliseum & Convention Center. **Facility:** 295 one-bedroom suites, some with whirlpools. 10 stories, interior corridors. *Bath:* combo or shower only. **Parking:** on-site. **Amenities:** dual phone lines, voice mail, safes, irons, hair dryers. *Fee:* video games, high-speed Internet. **Pool(s):** heated indoor. **Leisure Activities:** whirlpool, exercise room, spa. **Guest Services:** valet and coin laundry, area transportation-within 5 mi, wireless Internet. **Business Services:** conference facilities, business center. **Free Special Amenities: full breakfast and newspaper.**

EXTENDED STAYAMERICA-HAMPTON COLISEUM   *Book at AAA.com*   Phone: (757)896-3600   38

Motel
$77-$140 All Year

Address: 1915 Commerce Dr 23666 **Location:** I-64, exit 263 (Mercury Blvd), just n, then just e. Located adjacent to Hampton Coliseum. **Facility:** 104 one-bedroom standard units with efficiencies. 3 stories, interior corridors. *Bath:* combo or shower only. **Parking:** on-site. **Terms:** office hours 7 am-11 pm. **Amenities:** high-speed Internet (fee), voice mail, irons. **Guest Services:** coin laundry, wireless Internet. **Cards:** AX, DC, DS, JC, MC, VI.

HILTON GARDEN INN HAMPTON COLISEUM CENTRAL   Phone: 757/310-6323

fyi
Small-scale Hotel
Rates not provided

Too new to rate, opening scheduled for November 2007. **Address:** 1999 Power Plant Pkwy 23666 **Location:** I-64, exit 263 (Mercury Blvd S), just s to Power Plant Pkwy, then just e; exit 263A eastbound. **Amenities:** 149 units, pool.

HOLIDAY INN HAMPTON HOTEL & CONFERENCE CENTER   *Book great rates at AAA.com*   Phone: (757)838-0200   32

Large-scale Hotel
$104-$159 All Year

Address: 1815 W Mercury Blvd 23666 **Location:** I-64, exit 263B (Mercury Blvd) westbound; exit 263 eastbound. **Facility:** 320 units. 318 one-bedroom standard units. 2 one-bedroom suites with whirlpools. 2-4 stories, interior/exterior corridors. *Bath:* combo or shower only. **Parking:** on-site. **Terms:** check-in 4 pm, cancellation fee imposed. **Amenities:** video games (fee), high-speed Internet, voice mail, irons, hair dryers. *Some:* dual phone lines. **Pool(s):** outdoor, heated indoor. **Leisure Activities:** sauna, whirlpool, exercise room. **Guest Services:** valet and coin laundry, airport transportation-Newport News & Williamsburg Airport, area transportation-within 1 mi, wireless Internet. **Business Services:** conference facilities, business center. **Cards:** AX, DS, MC, VI. **Free Special Amenities: newspaper and high-speed Internet.**

QUALITY INN   *Book at AAA.com*   Phone: (757)838-8484   33

Small-scale Hotel
$94-$159 5/1-2/28
$84-$114 3/1-4/30

Address: 1813 W Mercury Blvd 23666 **Location:** I-64, exit 263B (Mercury Blvd), jct SR 58. **Facility:** 129 one-bedroom standard units. 6 stories, interior corridors. **Parking:** on-site. **Terms:** 3 day cancellation notice. **Amenities:** video games (fee), high-speed Internet, voice mail, irons, hair dryers. **Leisure Activities:** exercise room. **Guest Services:** valet laundry. **Business Services:** fax. **Cards:** AX, CB, DC, DS, MC, VI.

RAMADA HAMPTON COLISEUM & CONVENTION CENTER   *Book at AAA.com*   Phone: 757/827-7400   36

Small-scale Hotel
Rates not provided

Address: 1905 Coliseum Dr 23666 **Location:** I-64, exit 263 (Mercury Blvd) eastbound, just n, then just e towards Hampton Coliseum; exit 263B westbound. **Facility:** 131 one-bedroom standard units. 3 stories, interior/exterior corridors. *Bath:* combo or shower only. **Parking:** on-site. **Amenities:** high-speed Internet, voice mail, irons, hair dryers. **Pool(s):** outdoor. **Guest Services:** valet laundry, wireless Internet. **Business Services:** meeting rooms, business center.

(See map and index starting on p. 728)

SPRINGHILL SUITES BY MARRIOTT

Phone: 757/310-6333

(fyi)
Small-scale Hotel
Rates not provided

Too new to rate, opening scheduled for January 2008. **Address:** 1999 Power Plant Pkwy 23666 **Location:** I-64, exit 263 (Mercury Blvd S), just s to Power Plant Pkwy, then just e; exit 263A eastbound. **Amenities:** 148 units, pool.

AAA Benefit:
Members save 5% off of the best available rate.

SUPER 8 MOTEL

Motel
Rates not provided

Book at AAA.com

Phone: 757/723-2888 **39**

Address: 1330 Thomas St 23669 **Location:** I-64, exit 265B westbound; exit 265C eastbound. **Facility:** 66 one-bedroom standard units. 2 stories (no elevator), interior corridors. **Parking:** on-site. **Amenities:** high-speed Internet, safes (fee). **Guest Services:** coin laundry, wireless Internet.

 / SOME UNITS FEE

WHERE TO DINE

CAPTAIN GEORGE'S SEAFOOD RESTAURANT

Phone: 757/826-1435

Seafood
$17-$23

An extensive, all-you-can-eat seafood buffet—which includes everything from Alaskan crab legs and shrimp to prime rib and dessert—satisfies even the heartiest of appetites. Nautical accents such as ropes and fish nets convey the oceanic feel. Casual dress. **Bar:** Full bar. **Reservations:** accepted. **Hours:** 4:30 pm-9:30 pm, Sat from 4 pm, Sun from noon. Closed: 12/25. **Address:** 2710 W Mercury Blvd 23666 **Location:** I-64, exit 263A (Mercury Blvd), 0.5 mi s. **Parking:** on-site. **Cards:** AX, MC, VI.

EL AZTECA RESTAURANTE MEXICANO

Phone: 757/838-4063 **26**

Mexican
$4-$12

The restaurant prepares one of the widest varieties of Mexican cuisine around. In addition to standard favorites, the menu lists more adventurous offerings, including chicken in mole sauce—a rich and savory sauce derived from the cocoa bean. Entrees are fresh, delicious and served quickly. Casual dress. **Bar:** Full bar. **Hours:** 11 am-10 pm, Sat from noon, Sun noon-9 pm. **Address:** 2040 Coliseum Dr 23666 **Location:** I-64, exit 263 (Mercury Blvd), just n to Coliseum Dr, then just w. **Parking:** on-site. **Cards:** AX, DS, MC, VI.

CALL

THE GREY GOOSE

Phone: 757/723-7978 **34**

American
$5-$10

This charming tea room is a quaint spot in which to savor tasty Southern favorites, such as country ham biscuits, Brunswick stew and blue crab soup. Tasty pie and cake selections change daily. The old town nook is filled with porcelain teapots and decorative collectibles. The young ladies who run the show keep things moving with smiles and always a kind word. Dinner theater events are planned intermittently; guests can call for a schedule. Casual dress. **Hours:** 11 am-3 pm. Closed major holidays; also Sun. **Address:** 101-A W Queens Way 23669 **Location:** Olde Merchants Lane in Queens Way Shoppes; downtown. **Parking:** street. **Cards:** AX, DS, MC, VI.

HARPOON LARRY'S OYSTER BAR

Phone: 757/827-0600 **27**

Seafood
$7-$35

Local fliers from Langley make the bar a regular lunch spot. Fresh local seafood is served in enormous portions. Favorites include Hatteras-style clam chowder, a spicy crab cake and excellent Key lime pie, which is the only dessert offered. Casual dress. **Bar:** Full bar. **Hours:** 11 am-2 am. **Address:** 2000 N Armistead Ave 23666 **Location:** I-64, exit 263A (Mercury Blvd), 1 mi ne at Armistead Ave. **Parking:** on-site. **Cards:** AX, DC, DS, MC, VI.

LA BODEGA HAMPTON

Phone: 757/722-8466 **32**

Gourmet Grocery
$4-$7

Hearty sandwiches, daily soups, and gourmet desserts are tasty treats to enjoy either inside or at the sidewalk tables on a sunny day. Casual dress. **Bar:** Beer & wine. **Hours:** 7:30 am-6 pm, Sat 10 am-4 & 7-11 pm. Closed major holidays; also Sun. **Address:** 22 Wine St 23669 **Location:** I-64, exit 267, 1 mi w, then just n; downtown. **Parking:** on-site. **Cards:** AX, DS, MC, VI.

MAMA ROSA'S

Phone: 757/723-3560 **35**

Italian
$6-$15

The simple, family-friendly spot presents a menu of traditional Italian-American favorites, including veal parmigiana, shrimp scampi or fra diavolo, penne alla vodka and, of course, spaghetti with meatballs. Casual dress. **Bar:** Full bar. **Reservations:** accepted. **Hours:** 11 am-11 pm, Fri & Sat-midnight, Sun-10 pm. Closed major holidays. **Address:** 617 E Mercury Blvd 23663 **Location:** I-64, exit 268, just n on Mallory St; in Phoebus. **Parking:** on-site. **Cards:** DS, MC, VI.

CALL

MARKER 20

Phone: 757/726-9410 **31**

American
$6-$16

The casual downtown pub serves traditional American specialties, including burgers and such fresh local seafood as clam chowder, crab cakes and raw bar specialties. Casual dress. **Bar:** Full bar. **Hours:** 11 am-10 pm, Fri & Sat-11 pm. Closed: 11/27, 12/25; also for lunch 11/23. **Address:** 21 E Queens Way 23669 **Location:** Downtown. **Parking:** street. **Cards:** AX, MC, VI.

(See map and index starting on p. 728)

MCFADDEN'S SALOON

American
$7-$27

Phone: 757/896-2220   ㉙

Low-brow and high-brow fare mix on the menu, which lists offerings ranging from filet mignon, seared rockfish and top cut Sterling to burgers, nachos and chicken wings. Lending to the oversize pub's lively atmosphere are a wall of flat-screen televisions, pool tables and video games. Casual dress. **Bar:** Full bar. **Hours:** 11 am-10 pm, Fri & Sat-11 pm, Mon 5 pm-10 pm. Closed major holidays. **Address:** 1990 Power Plant Pkwy 23666 **Location:** I-64, exit 263 (Mercury Blvd S), just s to Power Plant Pkwy, then just e. **Parking:** on-site. **Cards:** AX, DS, MC, VI.

CALL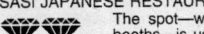

MUSASI JAPANESE RESTAURANT

Japanese
$7-$18

Phone: 757/728-0298   ㉝

The spot—which offers two distinct rooms: the open sushi bar and the other divided into semi-private booths—is usually packed with office workers at lunch but is more peaceful in the evenings. An enormous array of fresh sushi and sashimi is offered, as well as Japanese hot pots and even a few Korean specialties. Casual dress. **Bar:** Full bar. **Hours:** 11 am-2:30 & 5-10:30 pm, Fri-11 pm, Sat 11:30 am-11 pm. Closed major holidays; also Sun. **Address:** 49 W Queens Way 23669 **Location:** I-64, exit 267, 1 mi w to Eaton St, then just n; downtown. **Parking:** street. **Cards:** AX, DC, DS, MC, VI.

PHO 79

Vietnamese
$6-$9

Phone: 757/827-4679   ㉘

At the heart of the menu is pho, a traditional noodle soup sometimes called the national dish of Vietnam. Large bowls of steaming soup, each accented with beef or other meats and seasoned with herbs and sauces, are satisfying and healthy. Several generations of the family are warm and hospitable. Spring rolls, interesting desserts and drinks are also noteworthy. Casual dress. **Hours:** 10 am-9 pm, Fri & Sat-10 pm, Sun-8 pm. **Address:** 1118 W Mercury Blvd 23666 **Location:** I-64, exit 263 (Mercury Blvd), just n; in Riverdale Plaza. **Parking:** on-site.

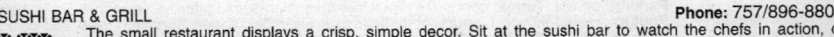

SOYA SUSHI BAR & GRILL

Japanese
$6-$14

Phone: 757/896-8807

The small restaurant displays a crisp, simple decor. Sit at the sushi bar to watch the chefs in action, or select a more quiet table. The menu, heavy on sushi selections, also includes such tempting specialties as teriyaki, udon noodles and soya bento. Casual dress. **Bar:** Beer & wine. **Hours:** 11:30 am-2 & 5-9 pm. Closed major holidays; also Sun. **Address:** 10 Coliseum Crossing 23666 **Location:** I-64, exit 263 (Mercury Blvd), just n to Coliseum Dr, just w to Coliseum Crossing. **Parking:** on-site. **Cards:** AX, DS, MC, VI.

SURFRIDER BLUEWATER

Seafood
$6-$20

Phone: 757/723-9366   ㊱

Fresh, simply prepared seafood is the draw at the casual restaurant, which affords fabulous riverfront views. Local yachters can't get enough of the daily catch, fresh crab cakes and spears of broccoli topped with fresh hollandaise. Casual dress. **Bar:** Full bar. **Hours:** 11 am-9 pm, Fri & Sat-9:30 pm. Closed major holidays. **Address:** 1 Marina Rd 23669 **Location:** I-64, exit 265A, 1.7 mi e on La Salle Ave, 0.5 mi e on Kecoughtan Rd, then just se on Ivy Home, follow signs to marina. **Parking:** on-site. **Cards:** AX, DS, MC, VI.

TOMMY'S RESTAURANT

Regional American
$3-$9

Phone: 757/825-1644   ㉚

Patrons should be prepared to wait, as regulars pack this spot daily for its satisfying all-day breakfast fare and Southern dishes, such as crab cakes, liver and onions, fried chicken and fried catfish. **Hours:** 6 am-3 pm. Closed: 1/1, 11/27, 12/25. **Address:** 3406 W Mercury Blvd 23666 **Location:** I-64, exit 263 (Mercury Blvd), just s of jct Big Bethel Rd. **Parking:** on-site.

NEWPORT NEWS pop. 180,150 (See map and index starting on p. 728)

——— WHERE TO STAY ———

BEST WESTERN NEWPORT NEWS INN & SUITES
Book great rates at AAA.com   Phone: 757/952-1182   **9**

AAA Benefit:
Members save 10% everyday, plus an exclusive frequent stay program.

AAA SAVE

Small-scale Hotel
Rates not provided

Address: 500 Operations Dr 23602 **Location:** I-64, exit 255A, just s on Jefferson Ave. **Facility:** 65 units. 61 one-bedroom standard units. 4 one-bedroom suites. 3 stories, interior corridors. *Bath:* combo or shower only. **Parking:** on-site. **Amenities:** high-speed Internet, voice mail, irons, hair dryers. **Pool(s):** outdoor. **Leisure Activities:** exercise room. **Guest Services:** valet and coin laundry. **Business Services:** meeting rooms, PC. **Free Special Amenities: continental breakfast and high-speed Internet.**

COMFORT INN
Book at AAA.com   Phone: (757)249-0200   **4**

Small-scale Hotel
$109-$149 All Year

Address: 12330 Jefferson Ave 23602 **Location:** I-64, exit 255A, just s on Clarie Ln (mall parking lot). Located adjacent to Patrick Henry Mall. **Facility:** 124 one-bedroom standard units. 3 stories, interior corridors. *Bath:* combo or shower only. **Parking:** on-site. **Terms:** check-in 4 pm. **Amenities:** high-speed Internet, voice mail, irons, hair dryers. **Pool(s):** outdoor. **Guest Services:** valet and coin laundry, area transportation, wireless Internet. **Business Services:** meeting rooms, PC. **Cards:** AX, CB, DC, DS, MC, VI.

COMFORT SUITES AIRPORT
Book great rates at AAA.com   Phone: (757)947-1333   **1**

AAA SAVE

Small-scale Hotel
$89-$209 All Year

Address: 12570 Jefferson Ave 23602 **Location:** I-64, exit 255, 1 mi n. **Facility:** 104 one-bedroom standard units, some with whirlpools. 4 stories, interior corridors. *Bath:* combo or shower only. **Parking:** on-site. **Terms:** check-in 4 pm. **Amenities:** high-speed Internet, voice mail, irons, hair dryers. **Pool(s):** heated indoor. **Leisure Activities:** exercise room. **Guest Services:** valet and coin laundry, wireless Internet. **Business Services:** meeting rooms, business center. **Cards:** AX, CB, DC, DS, JC, MC, VI. **Free Special Amenities: expanded continental breakfast and high-speed Internet.**

COUNTRY INN & SUITES BY CARLSON
Book great rates at AAA.com   Phone: (757)327-0722   **12**

AAA SAVE

Small-scale Hotel
$139-$149 All Year

Address: 1069 J Clyde Morris Blvd 23602 **Location:** I-64, exit 258B, 1 mi n. **Facility:** 64 units. 34 one-bedroom standard units, some with whirlpools. 30 one-bedroom suites. 3 stories, interior corridors. *Bath:* combo or shower only. **Parking:** on-site. **Amenities:** video library (fee), DVD players, high-speed Internet, voice mail, irons, hair dryers. **Pool(s):** heated indoor. **Leisure Activities:** whirlpool, exercise room. **Guest Services:** valet and coin laundry, area transportation-within 5 mi. **Business Services:** meeting rooms, PC. **Cards:** AX, DC, DS, MC, VI. **Free Special Amenities: expanded continental breakfast and high-speed Internet.**

CRESTWOOD SUITES
Book at AAA.com   Phone: 757/951-1017   **11**

Motel
$65-$130 All Year

Address: 11 Old Oyster Point Rd 23602 **Location:** I-64, exit 256A, just s on Oyster Point Rd to Canon Blvd, just e, then just n. **Facility:** 109 one-bedroom standard units with efficiencies. 4 stories, interior corridors. **Parking:** on-site. **Terms:** check-in 4 pm. **Amenities:** high-speed Internet, irons, hair dryers. **Leisure Activities:** exercise room. **Guest Services:** valet and coin laundry. **Business Services:** meeting rooms. **Cards:** AX, DS, MC, VI.

DAYS INN-OYSTER POINT AT CITY CENTER
Book great rates at AAA.com   Phone: (757)873-6700   **18**

AAA SAVE

Small-scale Hotel
$99-$119 3/1-9/30
$89-$99 10/1-2/28

Address: 11829 Fishing Point Dr 23606 **Location:** I-64, exit 255A, 2.5 mi s to Thimble Shoals Dr E, then 1 blk. **Facility:** 125 one-bedroom standard units. 3 stories, interior corridors. **Parking:** on-site. **Amenities:** high-speed Internet, voice mail, safes (fee), irons, hair dryers. *Some:* dual phone lines. **Pool(s):** outdoor. **Leisure Activities:** limited exercise equipment. **Guest Services:** valet and coin laundry, area transportation-within 5 mi, wireless Internet. **Business Services:** meeting rooms, PC, fax. **Cards:** AX, CB, DC, DS, JC, MC, VI. **Free Special Amenities: expanded continental breakfast and high-speed Internet.**

EXTENDED STAYAMERICA NEWPORT NEWS-OYSTER POINT
Book at AAA.com   Phone: (757)873-2266   **20**

Small-scale Hotel
$77-$145 All Year

Address: 11708 Jefferson Ave 23606 **Location:** I-64, exit 258A (Jefferson Ave), 1 mi s. **Facility:** 120 one-bedroom standard units with kitchens. 3 stories, exterior corridors. *Bath:* combo or shower only. **Parking:** on-site. **Terms:** office hours 7 am-11 pm. **Amenities:** high-speed Internet (fee), voice mail. **Guest Services:** coin laundry. **Cards:** AX, DC, DS, JC, MC, VI.

HAMPTON INN
Book great rates at AAA.com   Phone: 757/989-8977   **5**

Small-scale Hotel
Rates not provided

Address: 151 Ottis St 23602 **Location:** I-64, exit 256B, just e on Victory Blvd (US 17). Located in the Kiln Creek Shopping Center. **Facility:** 80 one-bedroom standard units. 5 stories, interior corridors. *Bath:* combo or shower only. **Parking:** on-site. **Amenities:** high-speed Internet, dual phone lines, voice mail, irons, hair dryers. **Pool(s):** heated indoor. **Leisure Activities:** whirlpool, exercise room. **Guest Services:** valet and coin laundry, wireless Internet. **Business Services:** meeting rooms, business center.

(See map and index starting on p. 728)

HAMPTON INN & SUITES

Small-scale Hotel
Rates not provided

Phone: 757/249-0001 **6**

Address: 12251 Jefferson Ave 23602 **Location:** I-64, exit 255A, just s. Located across from Patrick Henry Mall. **Facility:** 120 units. 90 one-bedroom standard units. 30 one-bedroom suites with kitchens. 4 stories, interior corridors. *Bath:* combo or shower only. **Amenities:** video games (fee), high-speed Internet, dual phone lines, voice mail, irons, hair dryers. *Some:* CD players. **Pool(s):** outdoor. **Leisure Activities:** exercise room. **Guest Services:** valet and coin laundry, area transportation, wireless Internet. **Business Services:** meeting rooms, business center.

HILTON GARDEN INN   *Book great rates at AAA.com*

Small-scale Hotel
Rates not provided

Phone: 757/947-1080 **7**

Address: 180 Regal Way 23602 **Location:** I-64, exit 256B, just e on Victory Blvd (US 17); adjacent to Regal Cinemas. **Facility:** 122 one-bedroom standard units. 3 stories, interior corridors. *Bath:* combo or shower only. **Parking:** on-site. **Amenities:** high-speed Internet, dual phone lines, voice mail, irons, hair dryers. **Pool(s):** heated indoor. **Leisure Activities:** whirlpool, exercise room. **Guest Services:** valet and coin laundry, wireless Internet. **Business Services:** meeting rooms, business center.

HOLIDAY INN-EXPRESS   *Book great rates at AAA.com*

Small-scale Hotel
$109-$139 3/1-8/31
$99-$109 9/1-2/28

Phone: (757)887-3300

Address: 16890 Warwick Blvd 23603 **Location:** I-64, exit 250A (SR 105/Ft Eustis Blvd S) to US 60, then 0.3 mi w. **Facility:** 57 one-bedroom standard units, some with efficiencies. 5 stories, interior corridors. *Bath:* combo or shower only. **Parking:** on-site. **Amenities:** high-speed Internet, dual phone lines, voice mail, irons, hair dryers. **Pool(s):** outdoor. **Leisure Activities:** exercise room. **Guest Services:** valet and coin laundry, airport transportation-Newport News/Williamsburg Airport, wireless Internet. **Business Services:** meeting rooms, business center. **Cards:** AX, CB, DC, DS, MC, VI.

HOLIDAY INN HOTEL & SUITES   *Book at AAA.com*

Small-scale Hotel
$129-$219 3/1-8/31
$129-$169 9/1-2/28

Phone: (757)596-6417 **16**

Address: 943 J Clyde Morris Blvd 23601 **Location:** I-64, exit 258B. **Facility:** 122 units. 103 one-bedroom standard units. 19 one-bedroom suites. 5 stories, interior corridors. *Bath:* combo or shower only. **Parking:** on-site. **Terms:** cancellation fee imposed. **Amenities:** DVD players, video games (fee), high-speed Internet, dual phone lines, voice mail, safes, irons, hair dryers. *Some:* fax. **Pool(s):** heated indoor. **Leisure Activities:** exercise room. **Guest Services:** valet and coin laundry, area transportation, wireless Internet. **Business Services:** meeting rooms, PC. **Cards:** AX, DC, DS, MC, VI.

HOST INN

Motel
$45-$59 All Year

Phone: 757/599-3303 **13**

Address: 985 J Clyde Morris Blvd 23601 **Location:** I-64, exit 258B, 0.8 mi n. **Facility:** 50 one-bedroom standard units. 2 stories (no elevator), exterior corridors. **Parking:** on-site. **Pool(s):** outdoor. **Business Services:** fax. **Cards:** AX, DS, MC, VI.

MICROTEL INN   *Book at AAA.com*

Small-scale Hotel
$59-$109 All Year

Phone: (757)249-8355 **8**

Address: 501 Operations Dr 23602 **Location:** I-64, exit 255A, 0.5 mi s to Operations Dr, then just w. **Facility:** 89 one-bedroom standard units. 3 stories, interior corridors. *Bath:* combo or shower only. **Parking:** on-site. **Amenities:** high-speed Internet, voice mail, irons. **Guest Services:** wireless Internet. **Business Services:** fax. **Cards:** AX, DS, MC, VI.

MULBERRY INN   *Book great rates at AAA.com*

Small-scale Hotel
$79-$139 All Year

Phone: (757)887-3000

Address: 16890 Warwick Blvd 23603 **Location:** I-64, exit 250A (SR 105/Ft Eustis Blvd S) s to US 60, then 0.3 mi w. **Facility:** 101 one-bedroom standard units, some with efficiencies. 2 stories (no elevator), interior/exterior corridors. **Parking:** on-site, winter plug-ins. **Terms:** cancellation fee imposed. **Amenities:** high-speed Internet, voice mail, irons, hair dryers. **Pool(s):** outdoor. **Leisure Activities:** exercise room. **Guest Services:** valet and coin laundry, airport transportation-Newport News/Williamsburg Airport, wireless Internet. **Business Services:** meeting rooms, business center. **Cards:** AX, CB, DC, DS, JC, MC, VI. **Free Special Amenities:** expanded continental breakfast and high-speed Internet.

NEWPORT NEWS MARRIOTT AT CITY CENTER   *Book great rates at AAA.com*

Large-scale Hotel
$148-$181 All Year

Phone: 757/873-9299 **19**

Address: 740 Town Center Dr 23606 **Location:** I-64, exit 255A, 2.5 mi s on Jefferson Ave, then just e on Thimble Shoals Dr; in City Center of Oyster Point. **Facility:** Smoke free premises. 256 units. 250 one-bedroom standard units. 6 one-bedroom suites. 11 stories, interior corridors. *Bath:* combo or shower only (fee). **Parking:** on-site (fee). **Terms:** check-in 4 pm, 9 day cancellation notice. **Amenities:** high-speed Internet (fee), dual phone lines, voice mail, safes, irons, hair dryers. **Pool(s):** heated indoor. **Leisure Activities:** whirlpool, exercise room. **Guest Services:** valet and coin laundry, wireless Internet. **Business Services:** conference facilities, business center. **Cards:** AX, DC, DS, JC, MC, VI.

Marriott
HOTELS & RESORTS

AAA Benefit:
Members save 5% off of the best available rate.

(See map and index starting on p. 728)

OMNI NEWPORT NEWS HOTEL   *Book great rates at AAA.com*   Phone: (757)873-6664   **17**

(AAA) (SAVE)

▼▼▼▼
Large-scale Hotel
$136-$159 All Year

Address: 1000 Omni Blvd 23606 **Location:** I-64, exit 258A (US 17), just s to Oyster Point Rd. **Facility:** 182 one-bedroom standard units, some with whirlpools. 9 stories, interior corridors. *Bath:* combo or shower only. **Parking:** on-site. **Terms:** cancellation fee imposed. **Amenities:** video games (fee), high-speed Internet, dual phone lines, voice mail, irons, hair dryers. **Dining:** nightclub, entertainment. **Pool(s):** heated indoor. **Leisure Activities:** whirlpool, exercise room. **Guest Services:** valet and coin laundry, wireless Internet. **Business Services:** conference facilities, business center. **Cards:** AX, DC, DS, MC, VI. **Free Special Amenities: newspaper and high-speed Internet.**

[icons] CALL / SOME UNITS FEE

POINT PLAZA-SUITES AT CITY CENTER   *Book great rates at AAA.com*   Phone: (757)599-4460   **14**

(AAA) (SAVE)

▼▼▼▼
Small-scale Hotel
$69-$139 All Year

Address: 950 J Clyde Morris Blvd 23601 **Location:** I-64, exit 258B, just n on US 17. **Facility:** 150 units. 80 one-bedroom standard units. 70 one-bedroom suites with kitchens, some with whirlpools. 2-4 stories, interior/exterior corridors. **Parking:** on-site. **Terms:** 1-4 night minimum stay - seasonal and/or weekends. **Amenities:** DVD players, high-speed Internet, dual phone lines, voice mail, safes, irons, hair dryers. **Pool(s):** heated indoor/outdoor. **Leisure Activities:** pool games, barbecue pavilion, exercise room. **Guest Services:** valet and coin laundry, area transportation-Amtrak station, wireless Internet. **Business Services:** conference facilities, business center. **Cards:** AX, DC, DS, MC, VI. **Free Special Amenities: local telephone calls and high-speed Internet.**

[icons] CALL / SOME UNITS FEE

SLEEP INN & SUITES   *Book great rates at AAA.com*   Phone: (757)951-1177   **10**

▼▼▼
Small-scale Hotel
$69-$149 3/1-9/30
$54-$109 10/1-2/28

Address: 21 Old Oyster Rd 23602 **Location:** I-64, exit 256A, just s on Oyster Point Rd to Canon Blvd, just e, then just n. **Facility:** 87 one-bedroom standard units. 3 stories, interior corridors. *Bath:* combo or shower only. **Parking:** on-site. **Terms:** check-in 4 pm. **Amenities:** high-speed Internet, voice mail, irons, hair dryers. **Pool(s):** heated indoor. **Leisure Activities:** whirlpool, exercise room. **Guest Services:** valet and coin laundry, wireless Internet. **Business Services:** meeting rooms. **Cards:** AX, DS, MC, VI.

[icons] CALL / SOME UNITS

STUDIOPLUS-NEWPORT NEWS   *Book at AAA.com*   Phone: (757)882-8847   **3**

▼▼▼
Small-scale Hotel
$95-$155 All Year

Address: 12359 Hornsby Ln 23602 **Location:** I-64, exit 255A, just s on Jefferson Ave. **Facility:** 73 one-bedroom standard units with efficiencies. 3 stories, interior corridors. *Bath:* combo or shower only. **Parking:** on-site. **Terms:** office hours 7 am-11 pm. **Amenities:** high-speed Internet (fee), voice mail, irons. *Some:* DVD players. **Pool(s):** outdoor. **Leisure Activities:** exercise room. **Guest Services:** coin laundry, wireless Internet. **Cards:** AX, DC, DS, JC, MC, VI.

[icons] CALL / SOME UNITS FEE

SUPER 8 MOTEL   *Book great rates at AAA.com*   Phone: 757/595-8888   **15**

(AAA) (SAVE)

▼▼
Motel
Rates not provided

Address: 945 J Clyde Morris Blvd 23601 **Location:** I-64, exit 258B, just n. **Facility:** 61 one-bedroom standard units. 3 stories (no elevator), interior corridors. **Parking:** on-site. **Amenities:** high-speed Internet, irons, hair dryers. **Guest Services:** coin laundry, wireless Internet. **Free Special Amenities: continental breakfast and high-speed Internet.**

[icons] / SOME UNITS

TRAVELODGE   *Book at AAA.com*   Phone: 757/874-4100   **2**

▼▼
Motel
Rates not provided

Address: 13700 Warwick Blvd 23602 **Location:** I-64, exit 255B, 1 mi w to Bland Blvd, 1 mi s to Warwick Blvd, then just n. Located in a commercial area. **Facility:** 48 one-bedroom standard units. 2 stories (no elevator), exterior corridors. **Parking:** on-site. **Amenities:** high-speed Internet. **Guest Services:** wireless Internet. **Business Services:** fax.

[icons] CALL / SOME UNITS FEE

─────── **WHERE TO DINE** ───────

99 MAIN   Phone: 757/599-9885   **17**

▼▼▼
American
$16-$30

In the heart of historic Hilton Village, the stylish, sophisticated spot seats diners in cool, paneled booths in the bar or banquettes in the upscale dining room. Fantastic seasonal dishes reflect a decidedly European bistro flair. Dressy casual. **Bar:** Full bar. **Reservations:** suggested. **Hours:** 5 pm-9:30 pm, Fri & Sat-10:30 pm. Closed: 11/27, 12/24, 12/25; also Sun & Mon. **Address:** 99 Main St 23601 **Location:** Jct Warwick Blvd; in Hilton Village. **Parking:** street. **Cards:** AX, MC, VI.

AL FRESCO RISTORANTE   Phone: 757/873-0644   **13**

▼▼▼
Italian
$7-$19

Decorated in soothing shades of pink with a Mediterranean mural lining one wall, the casual and charming spot offers a satisfying menu of Italian favorites. Dressy casual. **Bar:** Full bar. **Reservations:** suggested. **Hours:** 11 am-3 & 5-10 pm, Sat from 5 pm. Closed: 7/4, 11/27, 12/25; also Sun. **Address:** 11710 Jefferson Ave 23606 **Location:** I-64, exit 255A, 2 mi s; in Oyster Point Square. **Parking:** on-site. **Cards:** AX, DS, MC, VI.

AROMAS   Phone: 757/240-4650   **7**

▼▼
Coffee/Espresso
$5-$11

Casual dress. **Bar:** Beer & wine. **Hours:** 7:30 am-10 pm, Fri & Sat-11 pm, Sun 10 am-6 pm. Closed: 1/1, 11/27, 12/25. **Address:** 706 Town Center Dr, Suite 104 23606 **Location:** I-64, exit 255A, 2.5 mi s to Thimble Shoals Dr E; in City Center of Oyster Point. **Parking:** street. **Cards:** MC, VI.

(See map and index starting on p. 728)

THE CRAB SHACK
Phone: 757/245-2722   (18)

Seafood
$6-$18

On the shores of the James River, the restaurant offers prime spots on the deck from which to view sunsets and the parade of fishermen. Representative of local seafood are shrimp and crab cakes. Casual dress. **Bar:** Full bar. **Hours:** 11 am-11:30 pm, Fri & Sat-12:30 am. Closed: 11/27, 12/25. **Address:** 7601 River Rd 23607 **Location:** I-64, exit Mercury Blvd, 3.7 mi s; at foot of James River Bridge at Huntington Park. **Parking:** on-site. **Cards:** AX, DC, DS, MC, VI.

CALL

EL MARIACHI RESTAURANT & CANTINA
Phone: 757/596-4933   (14)

Mexican
$3-$15

Complete with a sunny deck out front, the restaurant has created a cozy spot from a former burger joint. Traditional favorites line the menu on their own or on combination platters. Casual dress. **Bar:** Beer & wine. **Hours:** 11 am-10 pm, Fri-11 pm, Sat noon-11 pm, Sun noon-10 pm. Closed major holidays. **Address:** 660 J Clyde Morris Blvd 23601 **Location:** I-64, exit 258A, 1 mi s. **Parking:** on-site. **Cards:** AX, DC, DS, MC, VI.

FAB FOODS AT MEDIK'S MARKET
Phone: 757/596-8651   (8)

Deli/Subs
Sandwiches
$6-$9

The market and cafe specializes in natural, organic and healthy meals. Overflowing salads, homemade soups and gourmet sandwiches, some of which are grilled, satisfy a hunger, while the luscious desserts tame a sweet tooth. Among specialties are cusabi tuna salad, Greek grilled cheese and the vegetarian d'lite. Casual dress. **Bar:** Beer & wine. **Hours:** 7 am-9 pm, Sun 8 am-6 pm. **Address:** 702 Mariner's Row, Suite 104 23606 **Location:** I-64, exit 255A, 2.5 mi s to Thimble Shoals Dr E; in City Center of Oyster Point. **Parking:** street. **Cards:** AX, DC, DS, MC, VI.

CALL

THE JAMESTOWN PIE COMPANY
Phone: 757/596-3888   (9)

American
$5-$18

All manner of gourmet pies are served here, from pizza pies to pot pies and dessert pies. With a mantra of "round food is good food," the restaurant serves up such gourmet offerings as the $30 pizza topped with lobster and lump crabmeat and the duck breast or Creole pot pie. More traditionalists will also find chicken pot pie and pepperoni pizza. Specialties include the chocolate pecan pie and bumbleberry pie. Casual dress. **Bar:** Beer & wine. **Hours:** 11 am-9 pm, Sun noon-8 pm. Closed: 12/25. **Address:** 11800 Merchants Walk 23606 **Location:** I-64, exit 255A, 2.5 mi s to Thimble Shoals Dr E; in City Center of Oyster Point. **Parking:** street. **Cards:** MC, VI.

KAPPO NARA SEAFOOD & SUSHI RESTAURANT
Phone: 757/249-5395   (5)

Japanese
$5-$20

Excellent, thick pieces of sushi, as well as teriyaki, tempura and other dishes, make up the menu at the quiet, restful restaurant. The professional wait staff in black and white attire provides prompt, friendly service and excellent follow-up. Casual dress. **Bar:** Full bar. **Hours:** 11 am-2 & 5-10 pm, Sat & Sun from 5 pm. Closed: 7/4, 11/27, 12/25. **Address:** 550A Oyster Point Rd 23602 **Location:** I-64, exit 255A, 1 mi s on Jefferson Ave, then just w. **Parking:** on-site. **Cards:** AX, DS, MC, VI.

KYUNG SUNG KOREAN RESTAURANT
Phone: 757/877-2797   (3)

Korean
$6-$16

The setting is simple, but diners are floored by the amount of spicy vegetable sides that come with dishes such as grilled short ribs, chicken bulgogi and kimchee soup. Casual dress. **Bar:** Full bar. **Hours:** 11 am-10 pm. Closed major holidays. **Address:** 13748 Warwick Blvd 23602 **Location:** I-64, exit 255B, 1 mi w to Bland Blvd, 1 mi s to Warwick Blvd, then just n. **Parking:** on-site. **Cards:** AX, DS, MC, VI.

LIGHT
Phone: 757/599-5800   (11)

American
$9-$33

Modern and sleek, the setting includes sidewalk dining when the weather permits. Longtime local chef Michael Toepper has created a unique menu that fuses Southern and European influences. Specialties of the house include the colossal lump crab cake with fried green tomatoes, an artisan cheese plate, wasabi pea-crusted shrimp or venison with butternut ravioli. Delicious breads, ice creams, sorbet and pimento cheese are all made in house. Dressy casual. **Bar:** Full bar. **Reservations:** suggested. **Hours:** 11:30 am-2:30 & 5:30-9:30 pm, Fri & Sat-10 pm. Closed major holidays; also Sun. **Address:** 3150 William Styron Square N 23606 **Location:** I-64, exit 255A, 2.3 mi s on Jefferson Ave, just w on Loftis Blvd; in Port Warwick. **Parking:** on-site. **Cards:** AX, MC, VI.

CALL

THE LUNCH BELL
Phone: 757/873-1839   (10)

American
$5-$8

The casual spot brings a touch of the country to its city environs, both with its laid-back attitude and its menu, which rotates such specials as fried chicken, hot chicken salad, crab cakes and pot roast. Daily choices include salads, sandwiches and heavenly pies. The owners rule the room with friendly smiles and welcomes, and solo diners always feel welcomed at the lunch counter. Casual dress. **Hours:** 6:30 am-4 pm, Sat 8 am-2 pm. Closed major holidays; also Sun. **Address:** 694 Town Center Dr 23606 **Location:** I-64, exit 255A, 2.5 mi s to Thimble Shoals Dr E; in City Center of Oyster Point. **Parking:** street. **Cards:** AX, DC, DS, MC, VI.

CALL

MIKE'S PLACE
Phone: 757/599-5500   (15)

American
$5-$16

The laid-back eatery is serious about satisfying hunger and offering comfort. Customers unwind in leather armchairs in the lounge while noshing on such temptations as juicy one-pound burgers, crab dip, prime rib and local seafood. Casual dress. **Bar:** Full bar. **Hours:** 11 am-10 pm, Fri-11 pm, Sat & Sun 9 am-11 pm. Closed: 11/27, 12/25. **Address:** 11006 Warwick Blvd, Unit 458 23601 **Location:** I-64, exit 258A, 2.5 mi s on J Clyde Morris Blvd, then 1.5 mi e; in Warwick Village Shopping Center. **Parking:** on-site. **Cards:** AX, DC, DS, MC, VI.

(See map and index starting on p. 728)

NAWAB INDIAN CUISINE

Indian
$7-$12

Phone: 757/591-9200

Tandoor specialties and bread baked in a clay oven are at the centerpiece of a traditional menu of curried, lamb and vegetarian dishes. The upscale atmosphere features artwork and instrumental music. A weekday buffet draws a devoted lunch clientele. Casual dress. **Bar:** Full bar. **Hours:** 11:30 am-3 & 5-10 pm, Fri-10:30 pm, Sat noon-3 & 5-10:30 pm, Sun noon-3 & 5-10 pm. Closed major holidays. **Address:** 11712-K Jefferson Ave 23606 **Location:** I-64, exit 255A, 2 mi s; in Oyster Point Square. **Parking:** on-site. **Cards:** AX, DC, DS, MC, VI.

CALL ⓖⓂ

PLAZA AZTECA

Mexican
$6-$13

Phone: 757/249-5299   ⑥

The festive Mexican decor includes serapes and a chandelier crafted from Corona bottles. Choose from among the many combination platters prepared with traditional and unusual Mexican specialties. The atmosphere is welcoming to families. Casual dress. **Bar:** Full bar. **Hours:** 11:30 am-10 pm. Closed major holidays. **Address:** 12099 Jefferson Ave 23606 **Location:** I-64, exit 255, 1.1 mi se. **Parking:** on-site. **Cards:** AX, MC, VI.

PLAZA AZTECA RESTAURANTE MEXICANO

Mexican
$5-$14

Phone: 757/833-0271   ①

The brightly painted Mexican spot serves traditional Mexican-American food, including the popular combination platters, fajitas, carne asada, tacos and, of course, margaritas. Casual dress. **Bar:** Full bar. **Hours:** 11 am-10 pm, Fri-11 pm, Sat noon-10:30 pm, Sun noon-9:30 pm. Closed major holidays. **Address:** 12755 Jefferson Ave 23602 **Location:** I-64, exit 255, 1.7 mi e on US 143; in Denbigh Crossing. **Parking:** on-site. **Cards:** AX, DS, MC, VI.

CALL ⓖⓂ ⓢ

ROCKY MOUNT BARBECUE

Barbecue
$5-$10

Phone: 757/596-0243   ⑯

Down-home favorites, such as meatloaf and Brunswick stew, complement North Carolina-style barbecue pork sandwiches. Country-style side dishes include collard greens and mac 'n' cheese, and the restaurant's fabulous, old-fashioned pies are made in house. Casual dress. **Hours:** 11 am-8:30 pm. Closed major holidays; also Sat & Sun. **Address:** 10113 Jefferson Ave 23605 **Location:** I-64, exit 255A, 5.6 mi s. **Parking:** on-site. **Cards:** AX, DC, DS, MC, VI.

SAMURAI SUSHI & HIBACHI RESTAURANT

Japanese
$8-$28

Phone: 757/249-4400   ④

Patrons can choose from seats at the sushi bar or the teppanyaki tables, where chefs entertain with knife tricks while cooking up delicious shrimp, steak and chicken specialties. Casual dress. **Bar:** Full bar. **Reservations:** accepted. **Hours:** 11:30 am-2 & 4-10 pm, Fri-11 pm, Sat 4 pm-11 pm, Sun & Mon 4 pm-10 pm. **Address:** 12233 Jefferson Ave, Suite 1 23602 **Location:** I-64, exit 255A, just s; in Jefferson Green Shopping Center. **Parking:** on-site. **Cards:** AX, DS, MC, VI.

CALL ⓖⓂ ⓢ

SCHLESINGER'S CHOPHOUSE

Steak House
$7-$55

Phone: 757/599-4700   ⑫

The decor is sleek and sophisticated at the new steakhouse, which carries out a literary twist. Juicy prime steaks, which are at the heart of the menu, are accented by excellent au gratin potatoes, great breads and distinctive salads. A lengthy wine list, skillful staff and cigar lounge round out the offerings. Sunday offers a jazz brunch. Dressy casual. **Bar:** Full bar. **Reservations:** suggested. **Hours:** 11 am-2:30 & 4:30-10 pm, Fri & Sat-11 pm, Sun-9 pm. Closed: 12/25. **Address:** 1106 William Styron Square 23606 **Location:** I-64, exit 255A, 2.4 mi s on Jefferson Ave to Port Warwick. **Parking:** on-site. **Cards:** AX, DC, DS, MC, VI.

CALL ⓖⓂ ⓢ

SILVER DINER

American
$9-$15

Phone: 757/989-6622

The eatery with its chrome and glass plate exterior and the glow of neon, provides the traditional diner setting. Booths with juke boxes, counter service and friendly wait staff add to the diner experience. The menu is extensive with salads, sandwiches and full meals. The desserts are made fresh and the fountain treats, shakes, floats and malts make for a great ending. Breakfast is available all day. Casual dress. **Bar:** Beer & wine. **Reservations:** not accepted. **Hours:** 6 am-11 pm, Fri & Sat-midnight. Closed: 12/25. **Address:** 12581 Jefferson Ave 23602 **Location:** I-64, exit 250B, just se on SR 105 (Ft Eustis Blvd) to SR 143. **Parking:** on-site. **Cards:** AX, DS, MC, VI.

ⓢ

WOK & ROLL

Chinese
$5-$13

Phone: 757/833-6611   ②

The small tidy spot draws a loyal clientele for its tasty homemade Chinese dishes, including a distinctive peppery spring roll, where are served on the lunch buffet. Casual dress. **Hours:** 11 am-10 pm, Fri & Sat-10:30 pm. Closed major holidays. **Address:** 14501-F Warwick Blvd 23608 **Location:** I-64, exit 250A (SR 105/Ft Eustis Blvd), 2.5 mi s to US 60 E (Warwick Blvd), then e; in Denbigh Crossing Shopping area. **Parking:** on-site. **Cards:** AX, DS, MC, VI.

NORFOLK pop. 234,403 (See maps and indexes starting on p. 731, 734)

———— WHERE TO STAY ————

B & B @ HISTORIC PAGE HOUSE INN

AAA SAVE

▼▼▼ ▼▼

Bed & Breakfast
$139-$154 All Year

Phone: (757)625-5033 **1**

Address: 323 Fairfax Ave 23507 **Location:** I-264, exit 9, 1.4 mi n on Waterside Dr to Olney Rd, just w to Mowbray Arch, then just s; in Ghent historic district. Located adjacent to the Chrysler Museum. **Facility:** Once on the verge of condemnation, this Georgian Revival mansion was restored in 1990 and now shines with detailed woodwork and antique appointments. Smoke free premises. 7 units. 5 one-bedroom standard units, some with whirlpools. 2 one-bedroom suites with whirlpools. 3 stories (no elevator), interior corridors. *Bath:* combo or shower only. **Parking:** on-site. **Terms:** 2 night minimum stay - seasonal and/or weekends, 7 day cancellation notice-fee imposed. **Amenities:** video library, CD players, high-speed Internet, irons, hair dryers. **Leisure Activities:** billiards, bicycles, limited exercise equipment. *Fee:* massage. **Guest Services:** valet laundry, wireless Internet. **Business Services:** meeting rooms, business center.

⊠ ⊠ ⊠ / SOME UNITS FEE 🐾 VCR 📶

BEST WESTERN HOLIDAY SANDS INN & SUITES   *Book great rates at AAA.com*

AAA SAVE

▼▼▼ ▼▼

Small-scale Hotel
Rates not provided

Phone: 757/583-2621 **2**

Address: 1330 E Ocean View Ave 23503 **Location:** US 60, 4 mi e of Hampton Roads Bridge-Tunnel. **Facility:** 86 units. 63 one-bedroom standard units, some with efficiencies. 23 one-bedroom suites with kitchens. 2-5 stories, exterior corridors. *Bath:* combo or shower only. **Parking:** on-site. **Amenities:** high-speed Internet, voice mail, irons, hair dryers. **Pool(s):** heated outdoor. **Leisure Activities:** exercise room. **Guest Services:** valet and coin laundry. **Business Services:** business center. **Free Special Amenities:** expanded continental breakfast and high-speed Internet.** *(See color ad below)*

AAA Benefit:
Members save 10% everyday, plus an exclusive frequent stay program.

➕ CALL 📞 🏊 🐾 📶 📠 💻 / SOME UNITS ⊠

COURTYARD BY MARRIOTT   *Book great rates at AAA.com*

▼▼▼ ▼

Small-scale Hotel
$153-$175 All Year

Phone: 757/963-6000 **5**

Address: 520 Plume St 23510 **Location:** Between St Paul's Blvd and Bank St; downtown. **Facility:** Smoke free premises. 140 units. 137 one-bedroom standard units, some with whirlpools. 3 one-bedroom suites. 8 stories, interior corridors. *Bath:* combo or shower only. **Parking:** on-site (fee) and valet. **Amenities:** high-speed Internet, dual phone lines, voice mail, irons, hair dryers. **Pool(s):** heated indoor. **Leisure Activities:** whirlpool, exercise room. **Guest Services:** valet and coin laundry, wireless Internet. **Business Services:** meeting rooms, business center. **Cards:** AX, DC, DS, MC, VI.

AAA Benefit:
Members save 5% off of the best available rate.

ASK 🆒 🍽 🍸 CALL 📞 🏊 ⊠ 📶 📠 💻
/ SOME UNITS FEE 🧳

_____ ▼ See AAA listing above ▼ _____

(See maps and indexes starting on p. 731, 734)

DOUBLETREE HOTEL-NORFOLK   *Book great rates at AAA.com*   Phone: (757)461-9192   🔟🔢

(AAA) [SAVE]
▽▼▽▼▽
Small-scale Hotel
$89-$199 3/1-9/30
$89-$149 10/1-2/28

Address: 880 N Military Hwy, Suite 35 23502 **Location:** I-264, exit 13B (Military Hwy). Located in Military Circle Mall. **Facility:** 199 units. 191 one-bedroom standard units. 8 one-bedroom suites. 14 stories, interior corridors. *Bath:* combo or shower only. **Parking:** on-site. **Terms:** 2 night minimum stay - seasonal and/or weekends, 3 day cancellation notice-fee imposed. **Amenities:** video games (fee), high-speed Internet, dual phone lines, voice mail, irons, hair dryers. **Pool(s):** outdoor. **Leisure Activities:** exercise room. **Guest Services:** valet and coin laundry, wireless Internet. **Business Services:** conference facilities, business center. **Cards:** AX, CB, DS, MC, VI. **Free Special Amenities:** local telephone calls and high-speed Internet.

ECONO LODGE AIRPORT   *Book at AAA.com*   Phone: (757)855-3116   5️⃣

▽▼▽
Motel
$81-$129 3/1-9/14
$59-$79 9/15-2/28

Address: 3343 N Military Hwy 23518 **Location:** I-64, exit 281 (Military Hwy) westbound, just n; exit 281B (Robin Hood Rd) eastbound, just n to Military Hwy, then just ne. **Facility:** 48 one-bedroom standard units. 2 stories (no elevator), exterior corridors. **Parking:** on-site. **Amenities:** high-speed Internet. *Some:* hair dryers. **Guest Services:** coin laundry. **Business Services:** fax. **Cards:** AX, CB, DC, DS, JC, MC, VI.

FREEMASON INN BED & BREAKFAST   Phone: 757/963-7000   3️⃣

(AAA) [SAVE]
▽▼▽▼▽
Historic Bed
& Breakfast
$145-$255 All Year

Address: 411 W York St 23510 **Location:** Jct W Brambleton Ave and Botetourt St. Located in West Freemason Historic District. **Facility:** Set in the historic district, this elegant inn is known for its Victorian decor, an English courtyard garden and sumptuous three-course breakfasts. Smoke free premises. 4 one-bedroom standard units, some with whirlpools. 3 stories (no elevator), interior corridors. **Parking:** on-site and street. **Terms:** 30 day cancellation notice-fee imposed. **Amenities:** DVD players, high-speed Internet, irons, hair dryers. **Guest Services:** wireless Internet. **Cards:** AX, MC, VI.

HAMPTON INN & SUITES NORFOLK AIRPORT   Phone: 757/605-9999   1️⃣1️⃣

▽▼▽▼▽
Small-scale Hotel
Rates not provided

Address: 1511 USAA Dr 23502 **Location:** I-64, exit 281B (Military Hwy), just s at US 13 and SR 165. **Facility:** 88 one-bedroom standard units. 4 stories, interior corridors. *Bath:* combo or shower only. **Parking:** on-site. **Amenities:** video games (fee), high-speed Internet, dual phone lines, irons, hair dryers. **Pool(s):** heated indoor. **Leisure Activities:** exercise room. **Guest Services:** valet laundry, wireless Internet. **Business Services:** meeting rooms, business center.

HAMPTON INN NORFOLK NAVAL BASE   *Book great rates at AAA.com*   Phone: 757/489-1000   3️⃣

▽▼▽▼▽
Small-scale Hotel
Rates not provided

Address: 8501 Hampton Blvd 23505 **Location:** I-64, exit 276 (I-564/Terminal Blvd), 2.5 mi w to Hampton Blvd, then 0.5 mi n. **Facility:** 118 one-bedroom standard units, some with efficiencies (no utensils). 4 stories, interior corridors. **Parking:** on-site. **Amenities:** video games (fee), high-speed Internet, voice mail, irons, hair dryers. **Pool(s):** heated indoor. **Leisure Activities:** whirlpool. **Guest Services:** valet laundry, wireless Internet. **Business Services:** PC, fax.

HILTON NORFOLK AIRPORT   *Book great rates at AAA.com*   Phone: 757/466-8000   1️⃣0️⃣

(AAA) [SAVE]
▽▼▽▼▽
Small-scale Hotel
Rates not provided

Address: 1500 N Military Hwy 23502 **Location:** I-64, exit 281 (Military Hwy), just s at jct US 13 and SR 165. **Facility:** 247 units. 245 one-bedroom standard units, some with whirlpools. 2 two-bedroom suites. 6 stories, interior corridors. *Bath:* combo or shower only. **Parking:** on-site. **Amenities:** video games (fee), high-speed Internet, dual phone lines, voice mail, irons, hair dryers. **Pool(s):** outdoor. **Leisure Activities:** saunas, exercise room. **Guest Services:** valet laundry, beauty salon, wireless Internet. **Business Services:** conference facilities, business center. **Free Special Amenities:** newspaper and high-speed Internet.

HOLIDAY INN SELECT   *Book at AAA.com*   Phone: (757)213-2231   9️⃣

▽▼▽▼▽
Small-scale Hotel
$119-$179 All Year

Address: 1570 N Military Hwy 23502 **Location:** I-64, exit 281 (Military Hwy). **Facility:** 147 units. 129 one-bedroom standard units, some with whirlpools. 18 one-bedroom suites. 5 stories, interior corridors. *Bath:* combo or shower only. **Parking:** on-site. **Amenities:** video games (fee), high-speed Internet, dual phone lines, voice mail, irons, hair dryers. **Pool(s):** heated indoor. **Leisure Activities:** whirlpool, exercise room. **Guest Services:** valet and coin laundry, area transportation, wireless Internet. **Business Services:** conference facilities, business center. **Cards:** AX, CB, DC, DS, JC, MC, VI.

NORFOLK WATERSIDE MARRIOTT HOTEL   *Book great rates at AAA.com*   Phone: 757/627-4200   6️⃣

▽▼▽▼▽
Large-scale Hotel
$207-$253 All Year

Address: 235 E Main St 23510 **Location:** Corner of Main and Atlantic sts; center of downtown. **Facility:** Smoke free premises. 405 units. 404 one-bedroom standard units. 1 one-bedroom suite with whirlpool. 24 stories, interior corridors. *Bath:* some combo or shower only. **Parking:** on-site (fee) and valet. **Terms:** check-in 4 pm. **Amenities:** high-speed Internet (fee), dual phone lines, voice mail, irons, hair dryers. **Dining:** Shula's 347, see separate listing. **Pool(s):** heated indoor. **Leisure Activities:** saunas, whirlpools, exercise room. **Guest Services:** valet and coin laundry, wireless Internet. **Business Services:** conference facilities, business center. **Cards:** AX, DC, DS, JC, MC, VI.

Marriott.
HOTELS & RESORTS

AAA Benefit:
Members save 5% off of the best available rate.

(See maps and indexes starting on p. 731, 734)

QUALITY INN NORFOLK NAVAL BASE   *Book great rates at AAA.com*

Phone: (757)451-0000   **4**

AAA SAVE
◈◈◈
Small-scale Hotel
$99-$159 All Year

Address: 8051 Hampton Blvd 23505 **Location:** I-64, exit 276 (I-564/Terminal Blvd), 2.5 mi w to Hampton Blvd, then 0.5 mi n. **Facility:** 120 one-bedroom standard units. 2 stories (no elevator), exterior corridors. **Parking:** on-site. **Amenities:** video games (fee), high-speed Internet, irons, hair dryers. **Pool(s):** heated indoor. **Leisure Activities:** whirlpool. **Guest Services:** valet and coin laundry, wireless Internet. **Business Services:** fax. **Cards:** AX, CB, DC, DS, JC, MC, VI. **Free Special Amenities: continental breakfast and high-speed Internet.**

[icons] / SOME UNITS ✕

QUALITY SUITES LAKE WRIGHT   *Book great rates at AAA.com*

Phone: (757)461-6251   **8**

AAA SAVE
◈◈◈
Small-scale Hotel
$109-$159 All Year

Address: 6280 Northampton Blvd 23502 **Location:** I-64, exit 282, just w on US 13. **Facility:** 127 one-bedroom suites, some with whirlpools. 5 stories, interior corridors. **Bath:** combo or shower only. **Parking:** on-site. **Amenities:** high-speed Internet, dual phone lines, voice mail, safes (fee), irons, hair dryers. **Pool(s):** heated indoor. **Leisure Activities:** exercise room. **Guest Services:** valet and coin laundry, area transportation-shopping center, wireless Internet. **Business Services:** meeting rooms, business center. **Cards:** AX, CB, DC, DS, JC, MC, VI. **Free Special Amenities: full breakfast and high-speed Internet.** *(See color ad below)*

[icons] CALL / SOME UNITS FEE ✕

RADISSON HOTEL NORFOLK   *Book great rates at AAA.com*

Phone: (757)627-5555   **2**

AAA SAVE
◈◈◈
Small-scale Hotel
$139-$169 3/1-10/31
$129-$169 11/1-2/28

Address: 700 Monticello Ave 23510 **Location:** Jct Brambleton Ave and St. Pauls Blvd; downtown. Located across from Scope Arena. **Facility:** 337 units. 330 one-bedroom standard units. 7 one-bedroom suites. 12 stories, interior corridors. **Bath:** combo or shower only. **Parking:** on-site. **Terms:** cancellation fee imposed. **Amenities:** video games (fee), high-speed Internet, voice mail, irons, hair dryers. **Pool(s):** outdoor. **Leisure Activities:** exercise room. **Guest Services:** valet and coin laundry, area transportation-downtown, barber shop, wireless Internet. **Business Services:** conference facilities, business center. **Cards:** AX, CB, DC, DS, JC, MC, VI. **Free Special Amenities: local telephone calls and high-speed Internet.**

[icons] CALL / SOME UNITS FEE ✕

RAMADA NORFOLK AIRPORT   *Book at AAA.com*

Phone: (757)466-7474   **12**

◈◈
Small-scale Hotel
$81-$94 6/1-2/28
$71-$84 3/1-5/31

Address: 1450 N Military Hwy 23502 **Location:** I-64, exit 281 (Military Hwy S), jct Princess Anne Rd. **Facility:** 130 one-bedroom standard units. 2 stories (no elevator), exterior corridors. **Bath:** combo or shower only. **Parking:** on-site. **Amenities:** video games (fee), high-speed Internet, voice mail, irons, hair dryers. **Pool(s):** outdoor. **Guest Services:** valet laundry, wireless Internet. **Business Services:** fax. **Cards:** AX, DS, MC, VI.

ASK [icons] CALL / SOME UNITS ✕ FEE FEE

RESIDENCE INN BY MARRIOTT NORFOLK AIRPORT   *Book great rates at AAA.com*   Phone: 757/333-3000   **7**

◈◈◈
Small-scale Hotel
$158-$186 All Year

Address: 1590 N Military Hwy 23502 **Location:** I-64, exit 281B (Military Hwy). **Facility:** Smoke free premises. 130 units. 25 one-bedroom standard units with kitchens. 95 one- and 10 two-bedroom suites with kitchens. 5 stories, interior corridors. **Bath:** combo or shower only. **Parking:** on-site. **Amenities:** high-speed Internet, dual phone lines, voice mail, irons, hair dryers. **Pool(s):** heated indoor. **Leisure Activities:** whirlpool, tennis court, exercise room, sports court. **Guest Services:** valet and coin laundry, area transportation, wireless Internet. **Business Services:** meeting rooms, business center. **Cards:** AX, DS, MC, VI.

AAA Benefit:
Members save 5% off of the best available rate.

ASK [icons] CALL / SOME UNITS FEE

(See maps and indexes starting on p. 731, 734)

SLEEP INN LAKE WRIGHT   *Book great rates at AAA.com*   Phone: (757)461-1133   6

Address: 6280 Northampton Blvd 23502 **Location:** I-64, exit 282, just w on US 13. **Facility:** 107 one-bedroom standard units. 3 stories, interior corridors. *Bath:* combo or shower only. **Parking:** on-site. **Amenities:** high-speed Internet, dual phone lines, voice mail, safes (fee), irons, hair dryers. **Pool(s):** heated indoor. **Leisure Activities:** exercise room. **Guest Services:** valet and coin laundry, area transportation-shopping center, wireless Internet. **Business Services:** meeting rooms, business center. **Cards:** AX, CB, DC, DS, JC, MC, VI. **Free Special Amenities:** expanded continental breakfast and high-speed Internet. *(See color ad p 761)*

Small-scale Hotel
$89-$139 All Year

(See maps and indexes starting on p. 731, 734)

SPRINGHILL SUITES BY MARRIOTT NORFOLK/VA BEACH   *Book great rates at AAA.com*   Phone: 757/333-3100

WWWW
Small-scale Hotel
$131-$175 All Year

Address: 6350 Newtown Rd 23502 **Location:** I-64, exit 284B to I-264 (Virginia Beach-Norfolk Expwy), exit Newtown Rd S. **Facility:** Smoke free premises. 131 one-bedroom standard units. 6 stories, interior corridors. *Bath:* combo or shower only. **Parking:** on-site. **Amenities:** high-speed Internet, dual phone lines, voice mail, irons, hair dryers. **Pool(s):** heated indoor. **Leisure Activities:** whirlpool, exercise room. **Guest Services:** valet and coin laundry, wireless Internet. **Business Services:** meeting rooms, business center. **Cards:** AX, DS, MC, VI.

AAA Benefit: Members save 5% off of the best available rate.

SUPER 8 CHESAPEAKE BAY   *Book great rates at AAA.com*   Phone: 757/587-8761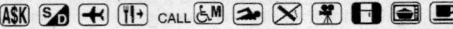

AAA SAVE
WWW
Small-scale Hotel
Rates not provided

Address: 1010 W Ocean View Ave 23503 **Location:** I-64, exit 273. **Facility:** 106 one-bedroom standard units, some with whirlpools. 2 stories (no elevator), exterior corridors. **Parking:** on-site. **Terms:** check-in 4 pm. **Amenities:** high-speed Internet, voice mail, hair dryers. **Pool(s):** outdoor. **Leisure Activities:** beachfront. **Guest Services:** coin laundry, wireless Internet. **Business Services:** fax. *(See color ad p 762)*

TAZEWELL HOTEL AND SUITES   *Book great rates at AAA.com*   Phone: (757)623-6200

AAA SAVE
WWW
Historic
Small-scale Hotel
$109-$269 3/1-9/30
$109-$189 10/1-2/28

Address: 245 Granby St 23510 **Location:** Jct Tazewell St; downtown. **Facility:** In the heart of the restaurants and nightlife of Granby Street, the 1906 hotel mixes historic architecture with updated neoclassical features. 57 units. 50 one-bedroom standard units. 7 one-bedroom suites. 7 stories, interior corridors. *Bath:* combo or shower only. **Parking:** on-site (fee). **Terms:** 2 night minimum stay - seasonal, 3 day cancellation notice-fee imposed. **Amenities:** high-speed Internet, dual phone lines, voice mail, irons, hair dryers. **Dining:** 2 restaurants, also, Empire Little Bar & Bistro, Sterling's, see separate listings. **Leisure Activities:** exercise room. **Guest Services:** valet laundry, wireless Internet. **Business Services:** meeting rooms, business center. **Cards:** AX, CB, DS, MC, VI.

——— WHERE TO DINE ———

THE 219   Phone: 757/627-2896

WWWW
American
$5-$23

Contemporary, upbeat and located on a rejuvenated city block where diners enjoy modern dishes brushed by Asian, Cajun and other regional and international influences. The renowned banana white chocolate macadamia bread pudding is a must! Casual dress. **Bar:** Full bar. **Reservations:** suggested. **Hours:** 11:30 am-2:30 & 5-10 pm, Fri-11 pm, Sat 5 pm-11 pm, Sun 11:30 am-9 pm. Closed major holidays. **Address:** 219 Granby St 23510 **Location:** At Granby and Brook sts; downtown. **Parking:** street. **Cards:** AX, DC, DS, MC, VI.

---

456 FISH   Phone: 757/625-4444

WWWW
Seafood
$15-$37

The high-energy spot sits downtown at the junction of nostalgia and modern. Black-and-white photographs of Norfolk's past line the walls while a wall of water separates the space. Seafood is the specialty, and the menu lines up such favorites as the chefs' Bahamian grouper fingers and pan-seared tuna. Rack of lamb is another good choice. Casual dress. **Bar:** Full bar. **Reservations:** suggested. **Hours:** 5 pm-10 pm, Fri & Sat-11 pm. Closed major holidays. **Address:** 456 Granby St 23510 **Location:** Jct Bute St; downtown. **Parking:** on-site. **Cards:** AX, MC, VI.

AMALFI   Phone: 757/625-1262

WWWW
Italian
$6-$23

This stylish new Italian cafe offers many options for guests. From a full service sit down meal of fresh pasta such as crab ravioli, veal, or other delights to an espresso bar, a market area, and gelato. Casual dress. **Bar:** Full bar. **Reservations:** suggested. **Hours:** 10:30 am-10 pm, Fri & Sat-11 pm. Closed: 11/27, 12/25. **Address:** 2010 Colley Ave 23517 **Location:** Jct 21st St; in Ghent. **Parking:** on-site. **Cards:** AX, DC, DS, MC, VI.

ASIAN GRILL   Phone: 757/625-2222

WWW
Asian
$6-$15

Casual dress. **Bar:** Full bar. **Reservations:** accepted. **Hours:** 11 am-10:30 pm, Fri & Sat-midnight, Sun 2 pm-midnight. Closed major holidays. **Address:** 411 Granby St 23510 **Location:** Between College Pl and Freemason St; downtown. **Parking:** street. **Cards:** AX, MC, VI.

THE AZALEA INN   Phone: 757/587-4649

WWW
Greek
$6-$12

The well-established, family-friendly spot has been offering Greek and American specialties and tasty pizza for as long as anyone in town can remember. Casual dress. **Bar:** Full bar. **Hours:** 10 am-2 am. Closed: 11/27, 12/25. **Address:** 2344 E Little Creek Rd 23518 **Location:** Jct Shore Dr, 1.4 mi w; in Roosevelt Shopping Center. **Parking:** on-site. **Cards:** AX, MC, VI.

(See maps and indexes starting on p. 731, 734)

AZAR'S NATURAL FOODS

Phone: 757/664-7955

Mediterranean
$4-$10

A loyal and growing clientele in search of healthful, well-prepared Middle Eastern fare calls the restaurant home. Roll sandwiches, delicatessen staples and many vegetarian items (although meat is available) are specialties. Try the lentil, orzo and vegetable soup or grab items to go from the market. Casual dress. **Bar:** Full bar. **Hours:** 11 am-9:30 pm, Fri & Sat-10 pm, Sun-8 pm. Closed major holidays. **Address:** 2000 Colley Ave 23517 **Location:** Jct 20th St; in Ghent. **Parking:** on-site. **Cards:** AX, DS, MC, VI.

BAKER'S CRUST BREAD MARKET

Phone: 757/625-3600

American
$6-$20

Baker's offers sandwiches, soup and salad (served in a hollowed-out loaf of bread), or rotisserie-grilled items, supplemented by a short list of appetizers and entrees. In keeping with the bistro ambience, there's a crepe bar in the back. Expect a wait. Casual dress. **Bar:** Full bar. **Hours:** 8 am-10 pm, Fri & Sat-11 pm. Closed: 1/1, 11/27, 12/25. **Address:** 330 W 21st St 23517 **Location:** Jct Colley Ave and W 21st St, just e; in Ghent; in the Palace Shops. **Parking:** on-site. **Cards:** AX, DS, MC, VI.

BANGKOK GARDEN

Phone: 757/622-5047

Thai
$5-$17

Stylish interior decorated with Thai artwork. Menu offers fresh, healthy authentic fare highlighting fresh seafood, chili peppers, curries, coconuts, tropical fruit and vegetarian dishes. Casual dress. **Bar:** Beer & wine. **Hours:** 11 am-10 pm, Fri-10:30 pm, Sat noon-10:30 pm, Sun noon-9 pm. Closed major holidays. **Address:** 339 W 21st St 23517 **Location:** Jct Colley Ave, just e; in Ghent; in the Palace Shops. **Parking:** street. **Cards:** AX, DC, MC, VI.

BARDO EDIBLES & ELIXIRS

Phone: 757/622-7362

Asian
$7-$18

The modern spot mixes an Asian sensibility with the Spanish tapas tradition. The result is a menu of appetizer-size dishes, such as shrimp dumplings, Kobe beef carpaccio and more interesting modern twists. Such menu choices as "the $1 chicken" are evidence of a sense of humor; servers won't offer details, so you have to order it to find out. The lounge is a hot spot to see and be seen. Casual dress. **Bar:** Full bar. **Hours:** 11 am-1:30 am, Sat & Sun from 5 pm. Closed: 12/24, 12/25; also 12/30. **Address:** 430 W 21st St 23517 **Location:** Jct Belmont St; in Ghent. **Parking:** on-site. **Cards:** AX, DS, MC, VI.

BAXTER'S SPORTS LOUNGE

Phone: 757/622-9837   26

American
$7-$20

This swanky, downtown sports bar features more than 100 TVs, both inside and on the sidewalk patio, and all are tuned to all manner of sports. The menu offers such fun bites as nachos, chicken wings and burgers and more upscale fare like crab cakes, steak and pasta Alfredo. Casual dress. **Bar:** Full bar. **Hours:** 11 am-10 pm; limited menu-1 am. Closed: 12/24, 12/25. **Address:** 500 Granby St 23510 **Location:** Between Bute and Charlotte sts; downtown. **Parking:** street. **Cards:** AX, DS, MC, VI.

BLUE CRAB RESTAURANT

Phone: 757/362-3133   1

Seafood
$5-$20

From the veranda of the Florida-inspired restaurant, patrons can watch luxury yachts dock. Fresh Atlantic Ocean seafood is prepared in both traditional and modern ways. Fresh fish stuffed with blue crab dressing is a specialty. Casual dress. **Bar:** Full bar. **Reservations:** accepted. **Hours:** 11 am-10 pm, Fri & Sat-11 pm. Closed major holidays. **Address:** 4521 Pretty Lake Ave 23518 **Location:** Jct Little Creek Rd, just n; in East Beach Marina. **Parking:** on-site. **Cards:** AX, DS, MC, VI.

BOBBYWOOD

Phone: 757/961-5417   27

American
$18-$32

Beloved local chef Bobby Huber has gone uptown with his sophisticated new spot, which showcases fabulous creative cuisine that shows off his French training and Asian and Southern influences. Guests start with any of the small "spoons," bite-size morsels that range from beef bobbaque to fondue with maque choux to shrimp andouille salad. From there, fabulous options such as oyster stew, Peking duck and crab cakes center on only the finest local ingredients. Dressy casual. **Reservations:** required. **Hours:** 5 pm-10 pm, Fri & Sat-11 pm. Closed major holidays; also Mon. **Address:** 435 Monticello Ave 23510 **Location:** Between Freemason and Bute sts; downtown. **Parking:** street. **Cards:** AX, DC, DS, MC, VI.

BODEGA

Phone: 757/622-8527   30

American
$6-$12

A fun place that's great for socializing, the eatery presents a tapas menu that lays out an intriguing array of appetizer choices, enabling diners to share and sample many tastes. The hearty flavors of Mediterranean cuisine, both Spanish and Italian, punctuate delicious dishes such as hearty pasta, spicy meats and tart marinated salads. Casual dress. **Bar:** Full bar. **Hours:** 5 pm-close, Fri & Sat-1:30 am. Closed: 1/1, 12/25; also Sun. **Address:** 442 Granby St 23510 **Location:** Jct Charlotte St; downtown. **Parking:** street. **Cards:** AX, DS, MC, VI.

BYRD & BALDWIN BROTHERS STEAKHOUSE

Phone: 757/222-9191   42

Steak House
$20-$42

You'll find this elegant steak and chophouse behind the impressive, columned stone facade of a lovingly restored, circa 1906 building. The original safe still sits in the wine cellar. Serving only Midwestern-raised, certified prime, grain-fed beef sourced from a single ranch guarantees the best steaks and beef tartare, but the delicious offerings don't end there. Try lobster mac 'n' bleu cheese, oysters Rockefeller, Colorado lamb, veal porterhouse and wild salmon, then pair your meal with a choice from an extensive, sophisticated wine list. Dressy casual. **Bar:** Full bar. **Reservations:** suggested. **Hours:** 5 pm-10 pm, Fri & Sat-11 pm. Closed major holidays. **Address:** 116 Brooke Ave 23518 **Location:** Between Granby and Boush sts; downtown. **Parking:** valet. **Cards:** AX, MC, VI.

(See maps and indexes starting on p. 731, 734)

CLUB SODA
Phone: 757/200-7632   40

International
$16-$24

The sleek, super-cool restaurant brings metropolitan style to the city with its suede banquettes and lighted lounge floor. As modern as the decor is the fare, including such dishes as chilled tuna poke, foie gras stuffed dumplings and lobster pasta. Dressy casual. **Bar:** Full bar. **Reservations:** suggested. **Hours:** 5 pm-10 pm, Fri & Sat-11 pm. Closed major holidays; also Sun & Mon. **Address:** 111 W Tazewell St 23510 **Location:** Between Boush and Granby sts; downtown. **Parking:** street. **Cards:** AX, DS, MC, VI.

COGAN'S
Phone: 757/627-6428   19

Pizza
$5-$15

The music may be loud and the styles alternative, but the pizza, buffalo shrimp and affordable pasta bowls can't be beat. Local bands often play at the small spot. Casual dress. **Bar:** Full bar. **Hours:** 11 am-1 pm, Fri & Sat-2 am. Closed major holidays. **Address:** 1901 Colonial Ave 23517 **Location:** Jct Washington Park; in Ghent. **Parking:** street. **Cards:** AX, DS, MC, VI.

CRACKER'S LITTLE BAR & BISTRO
Phone: 757/640-0200   5

American
$5-$19

The small spot serves numerous tasty dishes in equally small, appetizer-style portions designed for those who like to sample many tastes. Casual dress. **Bar:** Full bar. **Hours:** 11 am-1:30 am. Closed major holidays. **Address:** 4226 Granby St 23505 **Location:** W of downtown at the foot of the Granby St Bridge. **Parking:** on-site. **Cards:** AX, DS, MC, VI.

D'EGG DINER
Phone: 757/626-3447   47

American
$4-$8

The bustling modern diner serves hearty portions of classic American fare, some with a Southern accent, to hungry downtown workers. Among all-day breakfast items is the popular d'eggwich, a fried egg on an onion roll with bacon or sausage and a fried Parmesan tomato. Casual dress. **Hours:** 7 am-3 pm. Closed: 11/27, 12/25. **Address:** 204 E Main St 23510 **Location:** Just n of Waterside Dr; in Selden Arcade. **Parking:** street. **Cards:** AX, DS, MC, VI.

DOG-N-BURGER GRILLE
Phone: 757/623-1667   12

American
$5-$15

Although renovated, the vintage diner retains its nostalgic character, right down to the shiny chrome. Menu choices include delicious barbecue platters, succulent ribs, chili, pitas and, of course, the dogs and burgers that gave this place its name. **Hours:** 11 am-9 pm. Closed major holidays; also Sun. **Address:** 2001 Manteo St 23517 **Location:** Jct 20th St; in Ghent. **Parking:** street. **Cards:** MC, VI.

DOMO
Phone: 757/628-8282   35

Japanese
$8-$18

Sparse and neat is this quintessential sushi bar, a popular spot for downtown workers searching for fresh seafood. Besides great sushi, try dishes such as tuna tataki and tasty noodle soup. Casual dress. **Bar:** Full bar. **Hours:** 11:30 am-3 & 5-10 pm, Fri-11 pm, Sat 5 pm-11 pm. Closed: 11/27; also Sun. **Address:** 273 Granby St 23510 **Location:** Jct College Pl; downtown. **Parking:** street. **Cards:** AX, DC, DS, MC, VI.

DOUMAR'S CONES & BARBECUE
Phone: 757/627-4163   20

Barbecue
$2-$4

Diners can revisit the nostalgic 1950s at this great drive-in, which still offers carhops, tasty barbecue sandwiches and old-fashioned soda fountain favorites. A flash of the headlights prompts a carhop into action. Casual dress. **Hours:** 8 am-11 pm, Fri & Sat-12:30 am. Closed major holidays; also Sun. **Address:** 1919 Monticello Ave 23517 **Location:** Just n of downtown; in Ghent. **Parking:** on-site.

EL AZTECA RESTAURANTE MEXICANO
Phone: 757/587-6016   2

Mexican
$4-$11

The restaurant prepares one of the widest varieties of Mexican cuisine around. In addition to standard favorites, the menu lists more adventurous offerings, including chicken in mole sauce—a rich and savory sauce derived from the cocoa bean. Entrees are fresh, delicious and served quickly. Casual dress. **Bar:** Full bar. **Hours:** 11 am-10 pm, Fri-11 pm, Sat noon-11 pm, Sun noon-10 pm. Closed: 7/4, 11/27, 12/25. **Address:** 1522 E Little Creek Rd 23518 **Location:** Jct Shore Dr, 2.5 mi w. **Parking:** on-site. **Cards:** AX, CB, DC, DS, JC, MC, VI.

EMPIRE LITTLE BAR & BISTRO
Phone: 757/626-3100   38

American
$5-$19

In the heart of the revitalized downtown district, this small, trendy haunt prepares tasty dishes from pasta to filet. This place is a great spot for nibblers who love to sample many items at once. Casual dress. **Bar:** Full bar. **Hours:** 5 pm-1:30 am. Closed major holidays. **Address:** 245A Granby St 23501 **Location:** Jct Tazewell St; downtown; in Tazewell Hotel and Suites. **Parking:** street. **Cards:** AX, DS, MC, VI.

ENRICO'S RISTORANTE
Phone: 757/423-2700   1

Italian
$6-$23

The spicy flavors of Greece and Italy mix on the neighborhood cafe's menu. Regulars return for baked pasta, veal parmigiana, hearty Greek salads and daily specials, including seafood offerings. Casual dress. **Bar:** Full bar. **Reservations:** accepted. **Hours:** 11 am-10 pm, Fri-11 pm, Sat 5 pm-11 pm. Closed major holidays; also Sun. **Address:** 4012 Colley Ave 23508 **Location:** 3 mi n of downtown. **Parking:** on-site. **Cards:** AX, MC, VI.

FELLINI'S
Phone: 757/625-3000   2

Italian
$5-$20

The fun and funky spot has an open, tiled kitchen and intimate booths with chandeliers and draped fabric overhead. The house specialty is individual gourmet pizza, in such varieties as Thai chicken and "killer pie." Also on the menu are homemade pasta dishes, black Angus steak, hearty sandwiches and delicious Greek and Caesar salad. Casual dress. **Bar:** Full bar. **Hours:** 11 am-10 pm, Fri & Sat-11 pm, Sun 4 pm-9:30 pm. Closed major holidays; also Super Bowl Sun. **Address:** 3910 Colley Ave 23508 **Location:** 3 mi n of downtown. **Parking:** on-site. **Cards:** AX, DS, MC, VI.

(See maps and indexes starting on p. 731, 734)

FREEMASON ABBEY

American
$6-$18

Phone: 757/622-3966   **32**

Steak, prime rib, seafood and sandwiches are served in this lofty, restored abbey, complete with an impressive brick and stone exterior. Wooden booths and tables make the atmosphere cozy. Friendly staff members always seem to be wearing smiles. Casual dress. **Bar:** Full bar. **Reservations:** accepted. **Hours:** 11:30 am-10 pm, Fri & Sat-11 pm, Sun 9:30 am-10 pm. Closed major holidays. **Address:** 209 W Freemason St 23510 **Location:** Jct Freemason and Boush sts; downtown. **Parking:** on-site. **Cards:** AX, DC, DS, MC, VI.

THE GERMAN PANTRY

German
$9-$17

Phone: 757/461-5100   **8**

The restaurant is one of the most warm and welcoming spots around. Among German dishes are sauerbraten, knockwurst, apple strudel and Wiener schnitzel. Also offered are delicatessen fare and German market items. Casual dress. **Bar:** Beer & wine. **Reservations:** accepted. **Hours:** 11 am-8:30 pm. Closed: 11/27, 12/25; also Sun & Mon. **Address:** 5329 E Virginia Beach Blvd 23502 **Location:** Just w from jct Military Hwy. **Parking:** on-site. **Cards:** AX, DS, MC, VI.

CALL

GRANBY BISTRO & DELI
Mediterranean
$4-$10

Phone: 757/622-7003   **43**

Another cozy downtown lunch spot, the one shifts the focus to Mediterranean specialties, such as baba ghanoush, falafel, kebabs, gyros and Greek salads. Also on the menu are traditional delicatessen offerings. Casual dress. **Bar:** Full bar. **Hours:** 7:30 am-3 pm. Closed: Sat & Sun. **Address:** 225 Granby St 23510 **Location:** Between Plume and Brooke sts; downtown. **Parking:** street. **Cards:** AX, DS, JC, MC, VI.

GRANBY STREET PIZZA
Pizza
$6-$16

Phone: 757/622-5085   **41**

Casual dress. **Bar:** Beer only. **Hours:** 9 am-9 pm. Closed: 11/27, 12/25. **Address:** 235 Granby St 23510 **Location:** Between Plume and Brooke sts; downtown. **Parking:** street. **Cards:** MC, VI.

THE GRATE STEAK

Steak House
$5-$33

Phone: 757/461-5501   **10**

Locals flock here for prime cuts of Western aged beef that they grill themselves over hot charcoal on the large indoor grill. Casual dress. **Bar:** Full bar. **Hours:** 11:30 am-9 pm, Fri & Sat-10 pm, Sun noon-9 pm. Closed: 11/27, 12/24, 12/25. **Address:** 235 N Military Hwy 23502 **Location:** I-264, exit 13B, on US 13; in Americas Best Value Inn. **Parking:** on-site. **Cards:** AX, DC, DS, MC, VI.

CALL

GREAT SAIGON VIETNAMESE RESTAURANT
Vietnamese
$6-$11

Phone: 757/455-5149   **7**

At the charming spot, diners delight in the flavors of South Asia, which mingle with influences from its French colonization. Light but flavorful dishes include grilled pork over rice noodles, salt and pepper shrimp and soul-warming pho soups. Seasonal seafood specials center on lobster, soft-shell crab and whole flounder. Casual dress. **Hours:** 11:30 am-9:30 pm. **Address:** 5802 E Virginia Beach Blvd, Suite 130 23502 **Location:** I-64, exit 281, 1.6 mi s to Janaf Center; in Janaf Shops. **Parking:** on-site. **Cards:** AX, DS, MC, VI.

THE GREEN ONION
American
$14-$20

Phone: 757/963-1200   **15**

In trendy Ghent, the casual but chic spot has a cozy sidewalk cafe that is heated in the winter. The menu lists creative cuisine that focuses on seasonality. Side dishes show as much flair and attention as entrees, with market-fresh produce shining through. Vegetarian and vegan dishes appeal to herbivores. Casual dress. **Bar:** Full bar. **Reservations:** accepted. **Hours:** 5 pm-10 pm. Closed major holidays; also Sun & Mon. **Address:** 1603 Colley Ave 23517 **Location:** 1 mi n; between Spotswood and Brandon sts. **Parking:** street. **Cards:** AX, MC, VI.

GUADALAJARA CITY CAFE
Mexican
$6-$15

Phone: 757/622-2489

In a chic downtown setting that becomes a hip night spot, the cafe serves a mix of traditional and modern Mexican favorites alongside its specialty frozen tropical drinks. Casual dress. **Bar:** Full bar. **Reservations:** accepted. **Hours:** 11 am-10:30 pm, Fri-1:30 am, Sat noon-1:30 am, Sun 5 pm-10:30 pm. Closed major holidays. **Address:** 411 Granby St 23510 **Location:** Between Freemason and W Charlotte sts; downtown. **Parking:** street. **Cards:** AX, DS, MC, VI.

HAVANA
Latino
$6-$22

Phone: 757/627-5800   **37**

This successful beach eatery opens a new spot with a more urban flair. Expect the same great innovative cuisine with a Cuban accent such as glazed pork loin, Cubano sandwich and grilled seafood. Locals love the communal dining bar as a place to meet new people. Casual dress. **Bar:** Full bar. **Reservations:** accepted. **Hours:** 11:30 am-2 & 5-10 pm, Fri-11 pm. Closed major holidays; also Sun & for lunch Sat. **Address:** 255 Granby St 23510 **Location:** Between College and Tazewell sts, just n. **Parking:** street. **Cards:** AX, DS, MC, VI.

KATANA JAPANESE STEAK HOUSE & SUSHI
Japanese
$7-$25

Phone: 757/640-8898   **11**

Teppanyaki chefs entertain patrons tableside while they grill up good meals. A shrimp appetizer, salad with tangy ginger dressing and soup accompany each entree, including the specialties: savory steaks and seafood accented by delightful dipping sauce. Ghent locals frequent the sushi bar. Kimono-clad waitresses play second to the chefs as they charm and delight diners with high-flying knives and fiery displays. Casual dress. **Bar:** Full bar. **Reservations:** accepted. **Hours:** 11:30 am-2:30 & 4:30-10 pm, Sat from 4:30 pm. Closed major holidays. **Address:** 520 W 21st St, Unit E 23517 **Location:** Between Colley Ave and Granby St; in Ghent. **Parking:** on-site. **Cards:** AX, DS, MC, VI.

CALL

(See maps and indexes starting on p. 731, 734)

KELLY'S BACKSTAGE TAVERN
Phone: 757/622-5915

American

$7-$20

The casual chain is a local favorite for such simple specialties as burgers, Buffalo wings, fish tacos, salads and sandwiches. Casual dress. **Bar:** Full bar. **Hours:** 11 am-1 am. Closed: 11/27, 12/25. **Address:** 320 Granby St 23510 **Location:** Jct College Pl: downtown. **Parking:** street. **Cards:** AX, DS, MC, VI.

KELLY'S TAVERN
Phone: 757/623-3216

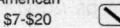

American

$7-$20

The casual chain is a local favorite for such simple specialties as burgers, Buffalo wings, fish tacos, salads and sandwiches. Casual dress. **Bar:** Full bar. **Hours:** 11 am-1 am. Closed: 11/27, 12/25. **Address:** 1408 Colley Ave 23507 **Location:** Just w of downtown; in Ghent. **Parking:** street. **Cards:** AX, DS, MC, VI.

KINCAID'S FISH, CHOP AND STEAKHOUSE
Phone: 757/622-8000　36

Steak & Seafood

$7-$28

This popular restaurant has a bustling, warm ambience. The varied menu includes seafood, steak and excellent prime rib. Ample wine and dessert choices round out the meal. Casual dress. **Bar:** Full bar. **Reservations:** suggested. **Hours:** 11:30 am-10 pm, Fri & Sat-11 pm, Sun 11 am-9 pm. Closed: 12/25. **Address:** 300 Monticello Ave, #147 23510 **Location:** Jct College St; downtown; in MacArthur Center. **Parking:** on-site. **Cards:** AX, CB, DC, DS, MC, VI.

KOTOBUKI
Phone: 757/628-1025　10

Japanese

$9-$20

Crisp lines, an open sushi bar and semi-enclosed tatami tables mark the traditional decor. On the menu are such dishes as maki rolls, nigiri sushi, noodle soups and salmon teriyaki. Casual dress. **Bar:** Full bar. **Reservations:** accepted. **Hours:** 11 am-2:30 & 5-10 pm, Fri-11 pm, Sat 11 am-3 & 5-11 pm, Sun 11 am-3 & 5-9:30 pm. Closed: 11/27, 12/25; also Tues. **Address:** 721 W 21st St 23517 **Location:** Jct Colley Ave, just e; in Ghent. **Parking:** street. **Cards:** AX, DS, MC, VI.

LA GALLERIA
Phone: 757/623-3939　34

Northern Italian

$13-$44

In a renovated warehouse, the restaurant mixes a sleek, modern decor accented by Roman columns with traditional Northern Italian cuisine. Favorites include salmon la Galleria and anything from the brick oven, including pizza and focaccia bread. Casual dress. **Bar:** Full bar. **Reservations:** suggested. **Hours:** 5:30 pm-11 pm, Fri & Sat-midnight. Closed: 11/27, 12/25; also Sun. **Address:** 120 College Pl 23510 **Location:** Between Granby and Boush sts; downtown. **Parking:** valet. **Cards:** AX, DC, MC, VI.

CALL 🛢M 🔲

LUNA MAYA CANTINA
Phone: 757/622-6986　16

Latino

$10-$14

Fresh ingredients and great tasting food prevail on the limited menu in this small hip eatery run by Bolivian sisters. Burritos, quesadillas, and unusual tamales are accented by a wide variety of salsa and peppers. Great guacamole made fresh to order. All meals start with chipotle salsa and fresh chips. Casual dress. **Bar:** Full bar. **Hours:** 5:30 pm-10 pm, Fri & Sat-10:30 pm. Closed major holidays; also Sun & Mon. **Address:** 2000 Colonial Ave 23462 **Location:** Jct 21st St and Princess Anne Rd; in Corner Shoppes; in Ghent. **Parking:** on-site. **Cards:** AX, MC, VI.

CALL 🛢M 🔲

MACHISMO BURRITO BAR
Phone: 757/624-2424　24

Mexican

$5-$8

The simple spot's excellent burritos are custom made to diners' specifications. Guests can choose their favorite meat or meat alternative, vegetables and even flavored wraps. Casual dress. **Hours:** 11 am-9 pm. Closed: 11/27, 12/25. **Address:** 409 W York St 23517 **Location:** Jct W Brambleton Ave and Botetourt St; downtown. **Parking:** street. **Cards:** MC, VI.

MAGNOLIA STEAK
Phone: 757/625-0400　21

Regional American

$8-$33

Southern and international influences support featured menu selections of certified Angus beef, fresh seasonal seafood, vegetables, chicken, pasta, ribs and house-smoked barbecue. Outside dining available, weather permitting. Located in the heart of historic Ghent. Decor is hip and elegant. Casual dress. **Bar:** Full bar. **Reservations:** suggested, weekends. **Hours:** 11:30 am-10:30 pm, Sat & Sun 5 pm-11 pm. Closed: 11/27, 12/25; also Super Bowl Sun. **Address:** 749 W Princess Anne Rd 23517 **Location:** Jct Colley Ave and W Princess Anne Rd; 1 mi n; in Ghent. **Parking:** on-site and street. **Cards:** AX, DS, MC, VI.

🔲

MI HOGAR MEXICAN RESTAURANT
Phone: 757/640-7705　5

Mexican

$4-$11

This bright friendly spot offers Americans' favorites combination plates as well as more authentic Mexican dishes such as chicken mole. Casual dress. **Bar:** Full bar. **Hours:** 11 am-10 pm, Fri & Sat-11 pm. Closed: 7/4, 11/27, 12/25; also Sun. **Address:** 4201 Granby St 23504 **Location:** At foot of Granby St Bridge. **Parking:** on-site. **Cards:** AX, DS, MC, VI.

CALL 🛢M 🔲

MI HOGAR MEXICAN RESTAURANT
Phone: 757/455-5509　9

Mexican

$4-$13

The bright, friendly spot offers the combination plates most Americans favor, as well as more authentic dishes, such as chicken mole. Casual dress. **Bar:** Full bar. **Hours:** 11 am-10 pm, Fri & Sat-11 pm, Sun noon-9:30 pm. Closed major holidays. **Address:** 471 N Military Hwy 23502 **Location:** I-264; exit 13B, just n on US 13. **Parking:** on-site. **Cards:** AX, DS, MC, VI.

🔲

(See maps and indexes starting on p. 731, 734)

NAWAB INDIAN RESTAURANT
Phone: 757/455-8080

Indian
$11-$16

Tandoor specialties and bread baked in a clay oven are at the centerpiece of a traditional menu of curried, lamb and vegetarian dishes. The upscale atmosphere features artwork and instrumental music. A weekday buffet draws a devoted lunch clientele. Casual dress. **Bar:** Full bar. **Hours:** 11:30 am-2:30 & 5-10 pm, Fri-10:30 pm, Sat noon-3 & 5-10:30 pm, Sun noon-3 & 5-10 pm. **Address:** 888 N Military Hwy 23502 **Location:** I-264, exit 13B, 0.5 mi n at jct Virginia Beach Blvd. **Parking:** on-site. **Cards:** AX, DS, MC, VI.

NAZEF CHAR-GRILL
Phone: 757/622-4500   (8)

Greek
$5-$10

The casual spot serves grilled Greek specialties, such as lamb, beef and chicken kebabs, Greek salads and spanakopita to hungry neighbors. Many order for carry out, but a small, neat dining room and large shaded patio allow for on-site eating. Casual dress. **Hours:** 10:30 am-10:30 pm. Closed: Sun. **Address:** 806 Harrington Ave 23517 **Location:** Jct Colley Ave; in Ghent. **Parking:** street. **Cards:** DC, DS, MC, VI.

NEW BELMONT
Phone: 757/623-4477   (13)

American
$14-$30

With exposed brick and contemporary artwork, the restaurant exudes a modern style. Creativity marks the seasonally changing menu. An upstairs lounge offers live music on weekends and billiards always. Dressy casual. Entertainment. **Bar:** Full bar. **Reservations:** suggested. **Hours:** 11 am-10 pm, Sun 11 am-3 & 5-9 pm. Closed major holidays. **Address:** 2117 Colonial Ave 23517 **Location:** Jct 21st St, just n; in Ghent. **Parking:** on-site. **Cards:** AX, DS, MC, VI.

NO FRILL BAR & GRILL
Phone: 757/627-4262

American
$7-$19

This small, brightly decorated spot has a cozy neighborhood feel, particularly on its heated patio. The daily menu lists sandwiches, salad, burgers and house specialties, including award-winning ribs, famous chili and other barbecue dishes. Chalkboard specials shine with creativity and fresh seasonal influences. Casual dress. **Bar:** Full bar. **Hours:** 11 am-10 pm, Fri & Sat-11 pm. Closed major holidays. **Address:** 806 Spotswood Ave 23517 **Location:** Jct Colley Ave, just e; in Ghent. **Parking:** on-site. **Cards:** AX, MC, VI.

THE PAINTED LADY
Phone: 757/623-8872   (22)

Continental
$7-$28

Housed in two colorfully restored Victorian homes, this spot sports an unusual decor of antiques and bric-a-brac. Continental cuisine with a Southern accent is served. Afternoon tea from 2:30 pm-5 pm. Dessert and caesar salad are prepared tableside. Children love the "Teddy Bear Tea." Casual dress. **Reservations:** suggested. **Hours:** 11 am-2:30 & 5-9 pm, Sat 11 am-3 & 5-10 pm, Sun 11 am-9 pm, Mon 11 am-4 pm. Closed: 7/4, 11/27, 12/25. **Address:** 112 E 17th St 23517 **Location:** 1 mi n of downtown, on Monticello to 17th St. **Parking:** on-site. **Cards:** AX, DS, MC, VI.

RAJPUT INDIAN CUISINE
Phone: 757/625-4634   (6)

Indian
$9-$16

Sample many Indian specialties off the buffet for lunch or go straight to the menu for more spicy and unique offerings such as lamb and vegetarian dishes as well as Tandoori-fired bread and meat dishes. Casual dress. **Bar:** Full bar. **Reservations:** accepted. **Hours:** 11:30 am-2:30 & 5-10 pm, Fri & Sat-10:30 pm, Sun noon-3 & 5-10 pm. **Address:** 742 W 21st St 23517 **Location:** Jct Colley Ave, just e; in Ghent; in Center Shops. **Parking:** on-site. **Cards:** AX, DS, MC, VI.

CALL

SCOTTY QUIXX LOUNGE & GRILLE
Phone: 757/625-0008   (31)

American
$10-$24

While the casual lunch menu lists submarine sandwiches, pizza and beloved tuna tacos, dinner fare goes more upscale, with offerings such as lamb chops, crab cakes and gourmet ice cream flavors. During happy hour and on weekends, lively locals crowd the bar and pool table. Casual dress. **Bar:** Full bar. **Reservations:** accepted. **Hours:** 4 pm-1 am. Closed: Sun. **Address:** 436 Granby St 23510 **Location:** Between Bute and Freemason sts; downtown. **Parking:** street. **Cards:** AX, DS, MC, VI.

SHULA'S 347
Phone: 757/282-6347   (48)

Steak House
$9-$31

The ultrasmooth "sports bar" prepares Prime Angus steaks, fresh seafood, rich crab soup and a great burger with thin crispy fries. Diners savor the fine fare while watching sports. Flat-screen TVs are everywhere, including in the restrooms. Casual dress. **Reservations:** suggested. **Hours:** 11 am-11 pm, Sun-10 pm. **Address:** 235 E Main St 23510 **Location:** Corner of Main and Atlantic sts; center of downtown; in Norfolk Waterside Marriott Hotel. **Parking:** on-site (fee). **Cards:** AX, CB, DC, DS, JC, MC, VI.

CALL

SIAM 21
Phone: 757/624-2455   (7)

Thai
$7-$20

The classically French-trained owner-chef returns to his Thai roots with a menu of authentic specialties. The best seats are at tables beside the hearth. Casual dress. **Bar:** Full bar. **Reservations:** suggested. **Hours:** 11:30 am-3 & 5-9:30 pm, Fri & Sat-10 pm, Sun-9 pm. **Address:** 742G W 21st St 23517 **Location:** Jct Colley Ave just e; in Ghent; in Center Shops. **Parking:** on-site. **Cards:** DS, MC, VI.

SIRENA CUCINA ITALIANA
Phone: 757/623-6622   (29)

Italian
$7-$20

The Roman owner and chef turns out fare from his homeland, such as his famed osso buco and gnocchi al Gorgonzola. The interior is sleek and modern. Casual dress. **Bar:** Full bar. **Reservations:** suggested. **Hours:** 11:30 am-2 & 5-9 pm, Sat 5 pm-10 pm, Sun 4 pm-8:30 pm. Closed major holidays. **Address:** 455 Granby St 23510 **Location:** Jct Charlotte St; downtown. **Parking:** street. **Cards:** AX, DS, MC, VI.

(See maps and indexes starting on p. 731, 734)

STERLING'S

Steak House
$20-$30

Phone: 757/625-3366   (39)

The sleek, bilevel spot is the meat lover's downtown choice for fine steak cuts and lamb chops, but the house specialty here, crab cakes, is a seafood aficionado's dream. Casual dress. **Bar:** Full bar. **Reservations:** accepted. **Hours:** 5 pm-9 pm, Fri & Sat-10 pm, Sun 4 pm-8 pm. Closed major holidays; also Mon. **Address:** 245 Granby St 23510 **Location:** Jct Tazewell St; downtown. **Parking:** street. **Cards:** AX, DS, MC, VI.

SURFRIDER-TAYLOR'S LANDING
Seafood
$4-$20

Phone: 757/480-5000

Fresh, simply prepared seafood is the draw at the casual restaurant overlooking a marina in the newly revived East Beach neighborhood. Local boaters and fishermen can't get enough of the daily catch, fresh crab cakes and spears of broccoli topped with fresh hollandaise. Casual dress. **Bar:** Full bar. **Hours:** 11 am-9 pm, Fri & Sat-9:30 pm. Closed major holidays. **Address:** 8180 Shore Dr 23518 **Location:** Just n of jct Little Creek; under Pretty Lake bridge at Taylor's Landing; in Ocean View. **Parking:** on-site. **Cards:** AX, DS, MC, VI.

CALL

SURF RIDER WEST
Seafood
$4-$15

Phone: 757/461-6488

Simply prepared, fresh seafood is the key at this casual restaurant. Locals love the reasonably priced crab cakes, fried flounder and fresh broccoli with hollandaise, as well as the daily assortment of homemade pies. Casual dress. **Bar:** Full bar. **Hours:** 11 am-9:30 pm. Closed major holidays; also Sun. **Address:** 723 Newtown Rd 23502 **Location:** I-64, exit 284B (Newtown Rd N); in Stoney Point Center. **Parking:** on-site. **Cards:** AX, DS, MC, VI.

TANNER'S CREEK SEAFOOD RESTAURANT & RAW BAR
Seafood
$6-$20

Phone: 757/423-2430   (4)

The casual family spot serves fresh local seafood specialties, such as crab cakes, fried shrimp and flounder, as well as such land delicacies as prime rib. Patio seating is a seasonal option. Casual dress. **Bar:** Full bar. **Reservations:** accepted. **Hours:** 11 am-10 pm, Wed-Fri to 2 am, Sat noon-2 am, Sun noon-10 pm. Closed major holidays. **Address:** 5103 Colley Ave 23505 **Location:** 1.5 mi nw of jct W 21st St. **Parking:** on-site. **Cards:** DS, MC, VI.

THE TAP HOUSE GRILL IN GHENT
American
$5-$13

Phone: 757/627-9172   (4)

The funky spot, which has a large patio, offers a huge variety of international specialty brews. Examples of traditional tasty bar fare include burgers, pizza, spicy chicken wings, nachos and hearty chili. Casual dress. **Bar:** Full bar. **Hours:** 4 pm-midnight, Sun-11 pm. **Address:** 931 W 21st St 23505 **Location:** Between Colley Ave and Hampton Blvd; in Ghent. **Parking:** on-site. **Cards:** AX, DC, DS, MC, VI.

TASTE UNLIMITED
Deli/Subs
Sandwiches
$5-$8

Phone: 757/627-3330

The small chain brings in loyal locals who love its sandwiches and salads coated with the specialty house dressing. Folks on the go can grab a boxed lunch and one of the delicious portable desserts, such as cookies and lemon bars. Casual dress. **Hours:** 10 am-5:30 pm. **Address:** 109 E Main St 23510 **Location:** Downtown; in Prince Books. **Parking:** street. **Cards:** MC, VI.

THE TEN TOP
_American
$6-$12

Phone: 757/622-5422   (18)

In the heart of the Ghent area, the small, funky spot is popular among locals for great take-home meals, such as flatbread pizza, Thai noodles, meaty sandwiches and wraps. Pan-roasted salmon is an excellent dinner choice. Casual dress. **Hours:** 11 am-9 pm. Closed major holidays; also Sun. **Address:** 748 Shirley Ave 23517 **Location:** Jct Colley Ave; in Ghent. **Parking:** on-site. **Cards:** AX, MC, VI.

TODD JURICH'S BISTRO!

Regional
American
$9-$32

Phone: 757/622-3210   (45)

Wonderfully flavored creations abound at the upscale restaurant, a picture of restrained, urban elegance. Startling combinations employ fresh local products and evoke influences ranging from Tuscany to Thailand. The wait staff is knowledgeable and smooth. Dressy casual. **Bar:** Full bar. **Reservations:** suggested. **Hours:** 11:30 am-2 & 5:30-10 pm, Sat from 5:30 pm. Closed major holidays; also Sun. **Address:** 150 W Main St, Suite 100 23510 **Location:** Across from Nauticus; downtown. **Parking:** on-site (fee) and valet. **Cards:** AX, DS, MC, VI.

TRILOGY BISTRO
American
$20-$30

Phone: 757/961-0896   (46)

The bistro is set in a renovated bank building on the National Historic Register that retains its impressive soaring stone columns and original bank vault, which now houses the wine cellar. Cuisine is sophisticated and fresh, with such specialties as the fried green tomato tower, pan-seared jumbo lump crab cakes, and cast-iron blackened tuna. Dressy casual. **Bar:** Full bar. **Reservations:** suggested. **Hours:** 4 pm-midnight, Fri & Sat-1 am. **Address:** 101 Granby St 23510 **Location:** At Main St; downtown. **Parking:** on-site (fee) and valet. **Cards:** AX, DC, DS, MC, VI.

(See maps and indexes starting on p. 731, 734)

VELVET LOUNGE
Phone: 757/961-7143   ③

American
$14-$22

Sleek, sensual and hip are words that could describe both the mood and the cuisine at the hot spot. The ever-changing menu highlights exotic gourmet elements with style and creativity. Dressy casual. **Bar:** Full bar. **Reservations:** accepted. **Hours:** 5 pm-10 pm. Closed: 5/26, 11/27, 12/25; also Sun. **Address:** 332 Granby St 23510 **Location:** 3 mi n of jct 25th St; in Ghent. **Parking:** on-site. **Cards:** AX, DC, DS, MC, VI.

VINTAGE KITCHEN
Phone: 757/625-3370   ㊾

Regional American
$8-$25

Vintage Kitchen occupies a stylish spot in the lobby of Dominion Tower and overlooks the Elizabeth River. The chef specializes in serving the freshest and finest regional offerings with a selection of fine Virginia wines. Although the menu changes seasonally, it always lists certain favorites: truffled mac 'n' cheese; pork chops, grilled local fish and the peanut brittle sundae. Dressy casual. **Bar:** Full bar. **Reservations:** accepted. **Hours:** 11 am-6 pm, Thurs-Sat to 10 pm. Closed major holidays; also Sun. **Address:** 999 Waterside Dr 23510 **Location:** Downtown; in Dominion Tower. **Parking:** on-site (fee). **Cards:** AX, DS, MC, VI.

CALL &M

VOILA CUISINE INTERNATIONAL
Phone: 757/640-0343   ㉕

Continental
$7-$36

Sultry and elegant, this tiny restaurant is the ultimate spot for romance. Dine on luscious European- and Moroccan-influenced dishes and sample fine wines while being served by a warm, professional staff. Dressy casual. **Bar:** Full bar. **Reservations:** suggested. **Hours:** 11 am-2:30 & 5-10 pm, Mon-2:30 pm, Sat 5 pm-11 pm, Sun 5 pm-9 pm. Closed major holidays. **Address:** 509 Botetourt St 23510 **Location:** Jct Brambleton Ave; downtown. **Parking:** on-site. **Cards:** AX, MC, VI.

WASABI STEAKHOUSE & SUSHI BAR
Phone: 757/459-2386   ⑥

Japanese
$14-$23

Guests can grab a seat in the small, popular sushi bar in the front or sit at a teppanyaki table to watch skilled Japanese chefs perform and cook simultaneously, turning out delicious steak and seafood dishes. Casual dress. **Bar:** Full bar. **Reservations:** accepted. **Hours:** 4:30 pm-10 pm, Fri-11 pm, Sat noon-11 pm, Sun noon-9 pm. Closed: 11/27, 12/25. **Address:** 5802 E Virginia Beach Blvd, Suite 140 23502 **Location:** I-64, exit 281 (Military Hwy), 1.6 mi s to Janaf Center; in Janaf Shops. **Parking:** on-site. **Cards:** AX, DS, MC, VI.

CALL &M ✎

THE WINEHOUSE IN GHENT
Phone: 757/622-7777   ㉓

American
$13-$26

In a restored Ghent townhouse, the stylish wine bar offers an endless variety of selections from the vineyards and a light menu designed to complement. Dishes, many of which incorporate wine as an ingredient, include international and domestic cheese plates, bruschetta and cassoulet. Casual dress. **Bar:** Full bar. **Hours:** 5 pm-11 pm, Fri & Sat-midnight. Closed major holidays. **Address:** 626 W Olney Rd 23507 **Location:** Jct Colley Ave; in Ghent; across from Eastern Virginia Medical School. **Parking:** on-site. **Cards:** AX, MC, VI.

CALL &M ✎

ZIO'S VINO & CUCINA
Phone: 757/624-1440   ⑰

Italian
$8-$20

Part trattoria and part neighborhood hot spot, Zio's draws a devoted local clientele. House specialties include shrimp alla vodka, stuffed eggplant and osso buco. Examples of dishes typically seen on the blackboard menu are veal saltimbocca and grilled portobello mushrooms. Diners get cozy in wooden booths and drink wine from juice glasses. Casual dress. **Bar:** Full bar. **Hours:** 11:30 am-10 pm, Fri & Sat-11 pm. Closed: 11/27, 12/25. **Address:** 1517 Colley Ave 23517 **Location:** Jct Spottswood Ave; in Ghent. **Parking:** street. **Cards:** AX, CB, DC, DS, JC, MC, VI.

✎

——— *The following restaurant has not been evaluated by AAA* ———
but is listed for your information only.

TASTE UNLIMITED
Phone: 757/623-7770

fyi

Not evaluated. This small chain of gourmet groceries is a local favorite for sandwiches and salads with the specialty house dressing. Box lunches are available for those on the go, and you'll find a nice selection of such delicious desserts as cookies and lemon bars, to name a few. **Address:** 1619 Colley Ave 23517 **Location:** In Ghent.

PORTSMOUTH pop. 100,565 (See map and index starting on p. 734)

——— **WHERE TO STAY** ———

COMFORT INN-OLDE TOWNE
Book great rates at AAA.com   Phone: (757)397-7788   ⑱

AAA SAVE

Small-scale Hotel
$89-$135 All Year

Address: 347 Effingham St 23704 **Location:** 1 mi w on High St, just n. **Facility:** 62 one-bedroom standard units, some with efficiencies and/or whirlpools. 3 stories, interior corridors. *Bath:* combo or shower only. **Parking:** on-site. **Amenities:** high-speed Internet, safes (fee), irons, hair dryers. **Pool(s):** outdoor. **Leisure Activities:** exercise room. **Guest Services:** valet and coin laundry, wireless Internet. **Business Services:** meeting rooms, PC. **Cards:** AX, DC, DS, MC, VI. **Free Special Amenities:** local telephone calls and high-speed Internet.

S📶 ⑪+ CALL &M 🍽 🐾 🔒 🖥 🖨 /SOME UNITS ✕ FEE VCR

(See map and index starting on p. 734)

HAWTHORN HOTEL & SUITES AT THE GOVERNOR
DINWIDDIE   *Book great rates at AAA.com*   Phone: (757)392-1330   **20**

AAA SAVE

◆◆◆

Small-scale Hotel
$99-$199 3/1-9/30
$99-$159 10/1-2/28

Address: 506 Dinwiddie St 23704 **Location:** Jct High St; in Olde Towne. **Facility:** 60 units. 55 one-bedroom standard units, some with efficiencies. 5 one-bedroom suites with kitchens. 7 stories, interior corridors. *Bath:* combo or shower only. **Parking:** on-site. **Terms:** 2 night minimum stay - seasonal, 3 day cancellation notice-fee imposed. **Amenities:** high-speed Internet, dual phone lines, voice mail, irons, hair dryers. *Some:* DVD players (fee). **Leisure Activities:** sauna, exercise room. **Guest Services:** valet and coin laundry, wireless Internet. **Business Services:** meeting rooms, business center. **Cards:** AX, CB, DS, MC, VI. **Free Special Amenities: full breakfast and high-speed Internet.**

[icons]

HOLIDAY INN-OLDE TOWNE PORTSMOUTH   *Book great rates at AAA.com*   Phone: (757)393-2573   **17**

AAA SAVE

◆◆◆

Small-scale Hotel
$110-$130 All Year

Address: 8 Crawford Pkwy 23704 **Location:** Just nw from High St. Located adjacent to the marina. **Facility:** 219 one-bedroom standard units. 4 stories, interior corridors. *Bath:* combo or shower only. **Parking:** on-site. **Terms:** check-in 4 pm, cancellation fee imposed. **Amenities:** high-speed Internet, voice mail, irons, hair dryers. **Dining:** entertainment. **Pool(s):** outdoor. **Leisure Activities:** exercise room. **Guest Services:** valet and coin laundry, wireless Internet. **Business Services:** conference facilities, business center. **Cards:** AX, CB, DC, DS, MC, VI.

[icons]

RENAISSANCE PORTSMOUTH HOTEL AND
WATERFRONT CONFERENCE CENTER   *Book great rates at AAA.com*   Phone: 757/673-3000   **19**

◆◆◆◆

Large-scale Hotel
$148-$181 All Year

Address: 425 Water St 23704 **Location:** Jct Crawford St, just n; downtown. **Facility:** Smoke free premises. 249 one-bedroom standard units. 13 stories, interior corridors. *Bath:* combo or shower only. **Parking:** on-site (fee). **Terms:** check-in 4 pm. **Amenities:** high-speed Internet (fee), dual phone lines, voice mail, irons, hair dryers. **Pool(s):** heated indoor. **Leisure Activities:** whirlpool, exercise room. **Guest Services:** valet laundry, wireless Internet. **Business Services:** conference facilities, business center. **Cards:** AX, DC, DS, JC, MC, VI.

RENAISSANCE.
HOTELS & RESORTS

AAA Benefit:
Members save 5% off of the best available rate.

[icons]

——— WHERE TO DINE ———

THE BIER GARDEN   Phone: 757/393-6022   **18**

◆◆

German
$5-$15

On the menu are German dishes—sauerbraten, spaetzle, bratwurst and hot potato salad—and an extensive list of European brews. The back room with exposed brick walls is cozy and quiet, the garden patio overlooks the sidewalk, and the friendly bar lets guests elbow up among neighbors for hot pretzels and potato soup. Casual dress. **Bar:** Beer & wine. **Hours:** 11 am-9 pm, Fri & Sat-10 pm, Sun noon-9 pm. Closed: 1/1, 11/27, 12/25; also Mon. **Address:** 438 High St 23704 **Location:** Jct Dinwiddie St; center; in Olde Towne. **Parking:** street. **Cards:** AX, CB, DS, JC, MC, VI.

[icon]

BRECKENRIDGE RESTAURANT & LOUNGE   Phone: 757/393-4454   **14**

◆◆◆

American
$7-$31

This friendly, family-run spot offers a charming, unpretentious location for delicious, sophisticated food. Sample colossal crab cakes made exclusively with local lump crab, smoked lamb shanks, black pepper scallops with mango sauce, and chocolate mousse pyramid. Dinner ends early on Friday and Saturday nights, to be replaced by live jazz and light bites. Casual dress. **Bar:** Full bar. **Reservations:** accepted. **Hours:** 11:30 am-3 & 5-8:30 pm, Fri & Sat-8:30 pm, Sun 11:30 am-3 pm. **Address:** 448 Green St 23704 **Location:** Just w of Hight St; in Old Towne. **Parking:** on-site. **Cards:** AX, DS, MC, VI.

[icon]

BRUTTI'S CAFE   Phone: 757/393-1923   **17**

◆◆◆

American
$5-$27

Set in a stylishly restored historic building, the cafe serves its own style of "Ameripean" cuisine in large portions. Specialties include lemon pepper seared tuna, classic steak au poivre, Cajun grilled mahi mahi and wood-fired pizza. Casual dress. **Entertainment. Bar:** Full bar. **Reservations:** suggested. **Hours:** 8:30 am-2:30 & 5:30-9:30 pm, Fri & Sat-10:30 pm, Sun-9 pm, Mon-2:30 pm. Closed major holidays. **Address:** 467 Court St 23704 **Location:** Jct High St; in Olde Towne. **Parking:** street. **Cards:** AX, DS, MC, VI.

CAFE EUROPA   Phone: 757/399-6652   **22**

◆◆◆

Continental
$5-$15

The small, intimate dining room has the feel of romantic French bistro, with a rich wood bar, frosted-glass partitions and exposed brick walls. The menu boasts an impressive mix of European dishes, heaviest on French specialties but incorporating many others. Semi-formal attire. **Bar:** Full bar. **Reservations:** suggested. **Hours:** 11 am-2 & 5-10 pm, Sat from 5 pm. Closed: 11/27, 12/24, 12/25; also Sun & Mon. **Address:** 319 High St 23704 **Location:** Just s of Crawford Pkwy; center. **Parking:** street. **Cards:** MC, VI.

[icon]

THE CIRCLE STEAK & SEAFOOD   Phone: 757/397-8196   **23**

◆◆

Regional American
$8-$22

This 1940's art deco style restaurant features a mural of stars from Hollywood's Golden Era behind the bar, a pianist in the round room on weekends and a wine bar on Mondays. Dinner specialties include local seafood, prime rib, and country vegetables. Casual dress. **Bar:** Full bar. **Reservations:** accepted. **Hours:** 8 am-9 pm, Mon-3 pm. Closed: 5/26, 9/1, 12/25. **Address:** 3010 High St 23707 **Location:** 2 mi w of downtown. **Parking:** on-site. **Cards:** DS, MC, VI.

(See map and index starting on p. 734)

COMMODORE THEATRE   *Menu on AAA.com*   Phone: 757/393-6962   ㉑

American
$5-$12

In the restored 1930s movie house, guests can sit in comfortable armchairs and sample such specialties as delicatessen sandwiches, pizza and cinnamon rolls. Orders are placed via tabletop telephones. Of course, there is popcorn, which is topped with 100 percent pure butter. Casual dress. **Entertainment. Bar:** Beer & wine. **Reservations:** not accepted. **Hours:** 6 pm-close, Fri from 3 pm, Wed, Sat & Sun from 1 pm. **Address:** 421 High St 23704 **Location:** Jct Dinwiddie St; in Olde Towne. **Parking:** street. **Cards:** AX, DS, MC, VI.

CALL ⓢⓜ

FRANK AND PATTY'S   Phone: 757/397-3752   ⑲

American
$5-$10

The fun corner spot is small, but seating is doubled when the large sidewalk patio is used during nice weather. Some of the area's best she crab soup is served alongside gourmet sandwiches, wraps and healthy salads. Leave room for the fabulous cookies and desserts. Casual dress. **Bar:** Beer & wine. **Hours:** 8 am-4 pm. Closed major holidays; also Sun. **Address:** 400 High St 23704 **Location:** Jct Dinwiddie St; in Olde Towne. **Parking:** street. **Cards:** AX, MC, VI.

FUSION 440   Phone: 757/398-0888   ⑮

Continental
$20-$34

Patrons should prepare to be spoiled by culinary indulgence at the chic spot, where even familiar dishes are created in new and imaginative ways. Examples of dishes on the seasonal menu are green tomatoes encrusted with biscotti, chateaubriand with white truffle butter and Caesar salad wrapped in oversized baguette crouton. Dressy casual. **Bar:** Full bar. **Reservations:** suggested. **Hours:** 5 pm-10 pm, Fri & Sat-11 pm, Sun-9 pm. **Address:** 467 Dinwiddie St 23704 **Location:** Jct High St; in Olde Towne. **Parking:** street. **Cards:** AX, DC, DS, MC, VI.

JOJACK'S ESPRESSO BAR & CAFE   Phone: 757/483-1483   ⑬

Coffee/Espresso
$5-$7

The cozy coffee shop presents a menu of gourmet sandwiches, paninis, rich desserts as well as chili and daily soups in bread bowls. A late-afternoon, English-style tea, including scones and cream, also is served. Casual dress. **Hours:** 6:30 am-8 pm, Sat 7:30 am-3 pm. Closed: Sun. **Address:** 5700 Churchland Blvd, Suite 39 23703 **Location:** I-664, exit 11B, 2 mi w on High St; in Churchland Shopping Center. **Parking:** on-site. **Cards:** MC, VI.

MARIO'S ITALIAN RESTAURANT   Phone: 757/399-8970   ㉔

Italian
$6-$18

Since 1952, the homey restaurant has served up hearty Italian-American fare, such as steak pizzaiola, veal Madeira and a fiery shrimp fra diavolo. Casual dress. **Bar:** Full bar. **Hours:** 11 am-2 am, Sat & Sun from 5:30 pm. Closed major holidays. **Address:** 611 Airline Blvd 23707 **Location:** Jct High St and London Blvd, just w. **Parking:** on-site. **Cards:** AX, MC, VI.

NEW YORK DELI   Phone: 757/399-3354   ⑳

Deli/Subs
Sandwiches
$5-$9

The longtime local favorite serves such delicatessen favorites as corned beef, Reubens and BLTs. Daily hot specials often exhibit a Southern influence. Casual dress. **Bar:** Beer only. **Hours:** 8:30 am-4 pm. Closed major holidays; also Sun. **Address:** 509 Court St 23704 **Location:** Jct High St; in Olde Towne. **Parking:** street.

ROGER BROWN'S RESTAURANT & SPORTS BAR   Phone: 757/399-5377   ⑯

American
$6-$17

A famed member of the Los Angeles Rams' "fearsome foursome," local hero Roger Brown turns his attention to delicious dishes from burgers to ribs to seafood. Even non-sports fans can enjoy the fun, multimedia setting. Casual dress. **Bar:** Full bar. **Hours:** 11 am-midnight, Fri & Sat-1 am. Closed: 12/25. **Address:** 316 High St 23704 **Location:** Between Court and Crawford sts; in Olde Towne. **Parking:** street. **Cards:** AX, DS, MC, VI.

SMITHFIELD pop. 6,324

——— WHERE TO STAY ———

CHURCH STREET INN   Phone: (757)357-3176

Bed & Breakfast
$99-$169 All Year

Address: 1607 S Church St 23430 **Location:** 1 mi e on SR 10 business route. **Facility:** 11 one-bedroom standard units, some with whirlpools. 2 stories (no elevator), interior/exterior corridors. **Parking:** on-site. **Terms:** office hours 8 am-7 pm. **Amenities:** DVD players, CD players, high-speed Internet. **Guest Services:** wireless Internet. **Cards:** AX, DS, MC, VI.

(ASK) ⓢ ⓘ ✕ 🛈 🖼 / SOME UNITS 🖵

ECONO LODGE-BENN'S CHURCH   *Book great rates at AAA.com*   Phone: (757)357-9057

(AAA) (SAVE)

Motel
$70-$110 All Year

Address: 20080 Brewers Neck Blvd 23314 **Location:** 3.8 mi s on SR 10, just n on US 258 and SR 32. **Facility:** 72 one-bedroom standard units, some with whirlpools. 2 stories (no elevator), interior corridors. *Bath:* combo or shower only. **Parking:** on-site. **Amenities:** high-speed Internet. **Leisure Activities:** exercise room. **Guest Services:** coin laundry, wireless Internet. **Business Services:** fax. **Cards:** AX, CB, DC, DS, JC, MC, VI. **Free Special Amenities:** continental breakfast and local telephone calls.

SMITHFIELD INN

Historic
Country Inn
$95-$155 All Year

Phone: 757/357-1752

Address: 112 Main St 23430 **Location:** Center. **Facility:** Fronted by a wide veranda, this historic inn in the center of town offers elegant suites furnished with fine antiques and rich fabrics. Smoke free premises. 8 units. 4 one- and 1 two-bedroom standard units. 3 one-bedroom suites. 2 stories, interior corridors. *Bath:* combo or shower only. **Parking:** on-site. **Terms:** office hours 8:30 am-11 pm. **Amenities:** video library, irons, hair dryers. *Some:* high-speed Internet. **Dining:** restaurant, see separate listing. **Guest Services:** valet laundry, wireless Internet. **Cards:** AX, DC, DS, MC, VI. **Free Special Amenities: full breakfast and high-speed Internet.**

SMITHFIELD STATION

Small-scale Hotel
Rates not provided

Phone: 757/357-7700

Address: 415 S Church St 23430 **Location:** 0.5 mi s on SR 10. **Facility:** 22 one-bedroom standard units, some with whirlpools. 3 stories (no elevator), interior/exterior corridors. **Parking:** on-site. **Amenities:** high-speed Internet, dual phone lines, irons, hair dryers. *Some: Fee:* DVD players. **Dining:** restaurant, see separate listing. **Pool(s):** outdoor. **Leisure Activities:** *Fee:* marina. **Guest Services:** wireless Internet. **Business Services:** meeting rooms, fax.

——— WHERE TO DINE ———

SMITHFIELD GOURMET BAKERY AND CAFE

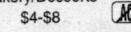

Bakery/Desserts
$4-$8

Phone: 757/357-0045

The lunch spot offers sandwiches, pasta salad, dessert and gourmet coffee. Casual dress. **Hours:** 8 am-5 pm. Closed major holidays. **Address:** 218 Main St 23430 **Location:** Center. **Parking:** street. **Cards:** AX, MC, VI.

SMITHFIELD INN

Regional
American
$7-$29

Phone: 757/357-1752

The elegant dining rooms are draped in sumptuous fabrics and decorated with lots of flowers. Modern twists on Southern favorites characterize such offerings as she-crab soup, sauteed flounder and spoon bread. Light, fluffy biscuits are made every morning. Garden seating is an option during good weather. Dressy casual. **Bar:** Full bar. **Reservations:** suggested, weekends. **Hours:** 11:30 am-3 & 5:30-9 pm, Sun-3 pm. Closed major holidays; also for dinner Mon. **Address:** 112 Main St 23430 **Location:** Center; in Smithfield Inn. **Parking:** on-site. **Cards:** AX, DC, DS, MC, VI. **Country Inn**

SMITHFIELD STATION RESTAURANT

Regional American
$5-$29

Phone: 757/357-7700

Designed to resemble an old Coast Guard station, the restaurant sits on the Pagan River. The menu emphasizes pork and seafood, such as the signature crabmeat Smithfield, sauteed lump crabmeat and ham chunks dripping with melted Monterey Jack cheese. Casual dress. **Bar:** Full bar. **Reservations:** suggested, weekends. **Hours:** 11 am-9:30 pm, Fri-10 pm, Sat 8 am-10 pm, Sun 8 am-9:30 pm. Closed: 12/25. **Address:** 415 S Church St 23430 **Location:** 0.5 mi s on SR 10; in Smithfield Station. **Parking:** on-site. **Cards:** AX, CB, DC, DS, MC, VI.

SUFFOLK pop. 63,677 (See map and index starting on p. 734)

——— WHERE TO STAY ———

COURTYARD BY MARRIOTT   *Book great rates at AAA.com*

Small-scale Hotel
$128-$157 All Year

Phone: 757/483-5777

Address: 8060 Harbour View Blvd 23435 **Location:** I-664, exit 8A (College Dr), just n on SR 135. **Facility:** Smoke free premises. 92 one-bedroom standard units, some with whirlpools. 3 stories, interior corridors. *Bath:* combo or shower only. **Parking:** on-site. **Amenities:** high-speed Internet, dual phone lines, voice mail, irons, hair dryers. **Pool(s):** heated indoor. **Leisure Activities:** whirlpool, exercise room. **Guest Services:** valet and coin laundry, wireless Internet. **Business Services:** meeting rooms, business center. **Cards:** AX, DC, DS, JC, MC, VI.

AAA Benefit:
Members save 5% off the best available rate.

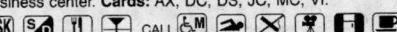

HILTON GARDEN INN & SUFFOLK CONFERENCE CENTER   *Book great rates at AAA.com*

Small-scale Hotel
Rates not provided

Phone: 757/925-1300

Address: 100 E Constance Rd 23434 **Location:** Jct US 58 business and US 460 business/Main St. Adjacent to public park and marina. **Facility:** 150 one-bedroom standard units. 5 stories, interior corridors. *Bath:* combo or shower only. **Parking:** on-site. **Amenities:** video games (fee), high-speed Internet, dual phone lines, voice mail, irons, hair dryers. **Pool(s):** heated indoor. **Leisure Activities:** whirlpool, exercise room. **Guest Services:** valet and coin laundry, wireless Internet. **Business Services:** conference facilities, business center.

(See map and index starting on p. 734)

QUALITY INN   *Book at AAA.com*   **Phone: 757/934-2311**

▼▼▼

Small-scale Hotel
$89-$109 3/1-10/31
$89-$99 11/1-2/28

Address: 2864 Pruden Blvd 23434 **Location:** US 460 at jct US 58 Bypass. **Facility:** 99 one-bedroom standard units. 2 stories (no elevator), exterior corridors. **Parking:** on-site. **Amenities:** high-speed Internet, dual phone lines, voice mail, irons, hair dryers. **Pool(s):** outdoor. **Leisure Activities:** limited exercise equipment. **Guest Services:** valet laundry. **Business Services:** meeting rooms, fax. **Cards:** AX, DC, DS, JC, MC, VI.

ASK SD ⊘ ▢ ▢ CALL ⊘M ⚊ ⊘ ▢ / SOME UNITS FEE ⊘ ✕ FEE ⊘ FEE ⊘

TOWNEPLACE SUITES BY MARRIOTT   *Book great rates at AAA.com*   **Phone: 757/483-5177**   46

▼▼▼

Small-scale Hotel
$118-$145 All Year

Address: 8050 Harbour View Blvd 23435 **Location:** I-664, exit 8A (College Dr), just n. **Facility:** Smoke free premises. 72 units. 55 one-bedroom standard units with kitchens. 4 one- and 13 two-bedroom suites with kitchens. 3 stories, interior corridors. *Bath:* combo or shower only. **Parking:** on-site. **Amenities:** high-speed Internet, dual phone lines, voice mail, irons, hair dryers. **Pool(s):** outdoor. **Leisure Activities:** exercise room. **Guest Services:** valet and coin laundry, wireless Internet. **Business Services:** business center. **Cards:** AX, DS, MC, VI.

ASK SD ▢ CALL ⊘M ⚊ ✕ ⊘ ⊘ ▢ ▢ / SOME UNITS FEE ⊘

AAA Benefit:
Members save 5%
off of the best
available rate.

───── WHERE TO DINE ─────

JERSEY'S JAVA   **Phone: 757/483-9659** 43

▼

Coffee/Espresso
$6-$8

Casual dress. **Hours:** 8 am-8 pm, Sun 10 am-6 pm. **Address:** 5860 A3 Harbour View Blvd 23434 **Location:** I-664, exit 9A, just n on SR 17 to Harbour View Blvd, then just e; in Harbour View West Shoppes. **Parking:** on-site. **Cards:** AX, DS, MC, VI.

KELLY'S TAVERN   **Phone: 757/925-2112**

▼▼ ▼▼

American
$7-$20

The casual chain is a local favorite for such simple specialties as burgers, Buffalo wings, fish tacos, salads and sandwiches. Casual dress. **Bar:** Full bar. **Hours:** 11 am-1 am. Closed: 11/27, 12/25. **Address:** 119 W Constance Rd 23434 **Location:** Jct US 58 business and 460 business/Main St. **Parking:** on-site. **Cards:** AX, DS, MC, VI.

CALL ⊘M ⊘

SURRY pop. 262

───── WHERE TO DINE ─────

SURREY HOUSE RESTAURANT   **Phone: 757/294-3389**

▼▼ ▼▼

Regional American
$4-$18

Traditional Southern comfort foods—fried chicken, country ham, fritters and turnip greens—taste as if Grandma made them. Servers in long, country dresses and a dining room decorated in heavy wallpaper and dark wood reflect a quaint 1960s Americana. Casual dress. **Reservations:** suggested. **Hours:** 8 am-8 pm. Closed: 12/24-12/26; also Mon. **Address:** 11865 Rolfe Hwy 23883 **Location:** Just s of jct SR 10 and 31. **Parking:** on-site. **Cards:** DS, MC, VI.

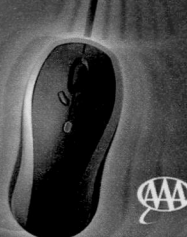

VIRGINIA BEACH pop. 425,257   (See maps and indexes p. 734-736, 738-741, 742-744)

———— WHERE TO STAY ————

ALAMAR RESORT INN

Phone: (757)428-7582   **34**

AAA [SAVE]

Motel
$52-$209 All Year

Address: 311 16th St 23451 **Location:** I-264, terminus to Pacific Ave, just s. **Facility:** Smoke free premises. 22 units. 11 one-bedroom standard units. 11 one-bedroom suites with kitchens. 3 stories (no elevator), exterior corridors. **Parking:** on-site. **Terms:** 21 day cancellation notice-fee imposed. **Amenities:** high-speed Internet, irons, hair dryers. **Pool(s):** heated outdoor. **Leisure Activities:** Fee; game room. **Guest Services:** coin laundry, wireless Internet. **Cards:** AX, DS, MC, VI. **Free Special Amenities:** newspaper and high-speed Internet. *(See color ad below)*

ATLANTIC SANDS OCEANFRONT HOTEL   *Book great rates at AAA.com*

Phone: 757/422-5000   **40**

AAA [SAVE]

Small-scale Hotel
Rates not provided

Address: 1101 Atlantic Ave 23451 **Location:** Oceanfront. I-264, 0.6 mi s of terminus, at 11th St. **Facility:** 110 one-bedroom standard units, some with whirlpools. 8 stories, interior corridors. **Parking:** valet. **Terms:** check-in 4 pm. **Amenities:** voice mail, irons, hair dryers. *Some:* high-speed Internet. **Pool(s):** outdoor. **Guest Services:** coin laundry, wireless Internet. **Business Services:** meeting rooms. **Free Special Amenities:** local telephone calls and early check-in/late check-out.

BARCLAY COTTAGE BED & BREAKFAST

Phone: (757)422-1956   **35**

AAA [SAVE]

Bed & Breakfast
$110-$200 All Year

Address: 400 16th St 23451 **Location:** I-264, just s of terminus to Artic Ave and 16th St. Located in a residential area. **Facility:** Double-decker wraparound verandas add visual appeal to this turn-of-the-20th-century beach cottage, which once functioned as a schoolhouse. Smoke free premises. 5 one-bedroom standard units. 2 stories (no elevator), interior corridors. *Bath:* some shared or private. **Parking:** on-site. **Terms:** 1-14 night minimum stay - seasonal and/or weekends, 21 day cancellation notice-fee imposed. **Amenities:** CD players, high-speed Internet, hair dryers. **Leisure Activities:** beach chairs & umbrellas, boogie chairs, bicycles. **Guest Services:** wireless Internet. **Business Services:** business center. **Cards:** AX, DS, MC, VI. **Free Special Amenities:** full breakfast and high-speed Internet.

(See maps and indexes p. 734-736, 738-741, 742-744)

BARCLAY TOWERS

Small-scale Hotel
$69-$269 All Year

Phone: (757)491-2700 **42**
Address: 809 Atlantic Ave 23451 **Location:** Oceanfront. I-264, 0.8 mi s of terminus; Atlantic Ave and Ninth St. **Facility:** 84 one-bedroom suites with kitchens. 8 stories, interior corridors. **Parking:** on-site. **Terms:** 3 day cancellation notice. **Amenities:** video library (fee), voice mail, safes, irons, hair dryers. **Pool(s):** heated indoor. **Leisure Activities:** sauna, whirlpool, exercise room. *Fee:* game room. **Guest Services:** coin laundry, wireless Internet. **Business Services:** meeting rooms, fax. **Cards:** AX, CB, DC, DS, MC, VI. **Free Special Amenities: expanded continental breakfast and newspaper.**
(See color ad p 777 & below)

THE BELVEDERE MOTEL

Motel
$74-$156 4/4-10/26

Phone: 757/425-0612 **3**
Address: 3603 Atlantic Ave 23451 **Location:** Oceanfront. I-264, 1 mi n of terminus; Atlantic Ave and 36th St. **Facility:** 46 one-bedroom standard units, some with efficiencies. 5 stories, exterior corridors. **Parking:** on-site. **Terms:** open 4/4-10/26, 3-5 night minimum stay - seasonal and/or weekends, 3 day cancellation notice. **Pool(s):** heated outdoor. **Leisure Activities:** bicycles. **Guest Services:** wireless Internet. **Cards:** AX, DS, MC, VI. **Free Special Amenities: local telephone calls.**

BEST WESTERN BEACH QUARTERS INN

Motel
Rates not provided

Phone: 757/437-1200 **47**
Address: 300 Atlantic Ave 23451 **Location:** I-264, 1.2 mi s of terminus at Rudee Inlet. **Facility:** 52 one-bedroom standard units, some with efficiencies (utensils extra charge). 6 stories, exterior corridors. **Parking:** on-site. **Terms:** check-in 4 pm. **Amenities:** voice mail, safes (fee), irons, hair dryers. **Pool(s):** outdoor. **Guest Services:** coin laundry, wireless Internet. **Business Services:** fax.
(See color ad below)

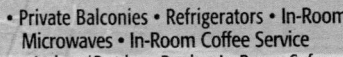

(See maps and indexes p. 734-736, 738-741, 742-744)

BEST WESTERN INN
   Phone: 757/363-2500 **4**

Small-scale Hotel
Rates not provided

Address: 5718 Northampton Blvd 23455 **Location:** I-64, exit 282, 1 mi n on US 13. **Facility:** 59 one-bedroom standard units. 2 stories (no elevator), exterior corridors. **Parking:** on-site. **Amenities:** high-speed Internet, irons, hair dryers. **Pool(s):** outdoor. **Guest Services:** wireless Internet. **Business Services:** fax. **Free Special Amenities: full breakfast and high-speed Internet.**

AAA Benefit:
Members save 10% everyday, plus an exclusive frequent stay program.

BEST WESTERN OCEANFRONT VA BEACH
   Phone: 757/428-5370 **12**

Large-scale Hotel
Rates not provided

Address: 2809 Atlantic Ave 23451 **Location:** Oceanfront. I-264, 0.5 mi n of terminus; jct 28th St. **Facility:** 214 one-bedroom standard units. 2-8 stories, interior/exterior corridors. *Bath:* combo or shower only. **Parking:** on-site. **Terms:** check-in 4 pm. **Amenities:** high-speed Internet, voice mail, safes (fee), irons, hair dryers. **Pool(s):** outdoor, heated indoor. **Leisure Activities:** exercise room. *Fee:* game room. **Guest Services:** coin laundry, wireless Internet. **Business Services:** meeting rooms, business center. **Free Special Amenities: newspaper and high-speed Internet.** *(See color ad below)*

AAA Benefit:
Members save 10% everyday, plus an exclusive frequent stay program.

BOARDWALK RESORT HOTEL AND VILLAS
   Phone: (757)213-3099 **33**

Small-scale Hotel
$89-$359 All Year

Address: 1601 Atlantic Ave 23451 **Location:** Oceanfront. I-264, terminus, just s to 16th St. **Facility:** 106 units. 19 one-bedroom standard units. 85 one- and 2 two-bedroom suites with kitchens. 10 stories, interior corridors. *Bath:* combo or shower only. **Parking:** on-site. **Terms:** check-in 4 pm, 1-4 night minimum stay - seasonal, 3 day cancellation notice. **Amenities:** DVD players, high-speed Internet, voice mail, safes (fee), irons, hair dryers. **Dining:** Rockfish Boardwalk Bar & Sea Grill, see separate listing. **Pool(s):** heated indoor. **Leisure Activities:** whirlpool, exercise room. **Guest Services:** coin laundry, wireless Internet. **Cards:** AX, DC, DS, MC, VI. **Free Special Amenities: newspaper and high-speed Internet.** *(See color ad p 776)*

THE BREAKERS RESORT INN
Phone: (757)428-1821 **36**

Small-scale Hotel
$65-$300 All Year

Address: 1503 Atlantic Ave 23451 **Location:** Oceanfront. I-264, 0.5 mi s of terminus. **Facility:** 56 units. 40 one-bedroom standard units, some with whirlpools. 15 one- and 1 two-bedroom suites, some with efficiencies. 9 stories, interior corridors. *Bath:* combo or shower only. **Parking:** on-site. **Terms:** 3 night minimum stay - seasonal and/or weekends, 3 day cancellation notice-fee imposed. **Amenities:** high-speed Internet, voice mail, irons, hair dryers. **Pool(s):** heated outdoor. **Leisure Activities:** bicycles. **Guest Services:** coin laundry. **Business Services:** fax. **Cards:** AX, DS, MC, VI. **Free Special Amenities: high-speed Internet.** *(See color ad p 779)*

▼ See AAA listing above ▼

(See maps and indexes p. 734-736, 738-741, 742-744)

CANDLEWOOD SUITES
Book at AAA.com   Phone: (757)213-1500    **16**

Small-scale Hotel
$69-$199 All Year

Address: 4437 Bonney Rd 23462 **Location:** I-264, exit 17B (Independence Blvd/Pembroke Area), just n to Bonney Rd, then just e. **Facility:** 83 units. 68 one-bedroom standard units with kitchens. 15 one-bedroom suites with kitchens. 4 stories, interior corridors. **Bath:** combo or shower only. **Parking:** on-site. **Terms:** office hours 7 am-11 pm, 3 day cancellation notice-fee imposed. **Amenities:** video library, DVD players, CD players, high-speed Internet, voice mail, irons, hair dryers. **Leisure Activities:** exercise room. **Guest Services:** complimentary laundry, wireless Internet. **Business Services:** business center. **Cards:** AX, DC, DS, MC, VI.

THE CAPES OCEAN RESORT
                                                       Phone: (757)428-5421   **29**

Small-scale Hotel
$45-$320 3/14-10/12

Address: 2001 Atlantic Ave 23451 **Location:** Oceanfront. I-264, s of terminus; jct 20th St and Atlantic Ave. **Facility:** 59 units. 44 one-bedroom standard units, some with whirlpools. 15 one-bedroom suites, some with whirlpools. 8 stories, interior corridors. **Parking:** on-site. **Terms:** open 3/14-10/12, 1-3 night minimum stay - seasonal and/or weekends, 3 day cancellation notice-fee imposed. **Amenities:** voice mail, irons, hair dryers. *Some:* DVD players (fee). **Pool(s):** heated indoor. **Guest Services:** coin laundry, wireless Internet. **Business Services:** meeting rooms. **Cards:** AX, DS, MC, VI.
(See color ad p 780)

CLARION RESORT
Book great rates at AAA.com   Phone: (757)422-3186   **46**

Small-scale Hotel
$89-$359 All Year

Address: 501 Atlantic Ave 23451 **Location:** Oceanfront. I-264, 1 mi s of terminus; Atlantic Ave and 5th St. **Facility:** 168 units. 48 one-bedroom standard units, some with whirlpools. 120 one-bedroom suites with kitchens. 12 stories, exterior corridors. **Bath:** combo or shower only. **Parking:** on-site. **Terms:** check-in 4 pm, 1-4 night minimum stay - seasonal, 3 day cancellation notice. **Amenities:** voice mail, irons, hair dryers. *Fee:* video games, high-speed Internet, safes. **Pool(s):** heated outdoor, heated indoor. **Leisure Activities:** sauna, whirlpools, lighted tennis court, recreation programs in summer. *Fee:* massage, game room. **Guest Services:** valet and coin laundry, tanning facilities, wireless Internet. **Business Services:** meeting rooms, business center. **Cards:** AX, DC, DS, MC, VI. **Free Special Amenities:** newspaper and high-speed Internet. *(See color ad p 776)*

COMFORT INN & SUITES OCEANFRONT
Book great rates at AAA.com   Phone: (757)425-8200   **27**

Small-scale Hotel
$269-$399 6/1-2/28
$119-$299 3/1-5/31

Address: 2015 Atlantic Ave 23451 **Location:** Oceanfront. I-264, just s of terminus. **Facility:** 83 units. 82 one- and 1 two-bedroom suites, some with whirlpools. 10 stories, interior corridors. **Bath:** combo or shower only. **Parking:** on-site. **Terms:** check-in 4 pm, 2 night minimum stay - seasonal and/or weekends, 3 day cancellation notice. **Amenities:** high-speed Internet, voice mail, irons, hair dryers. *Fee:* video games, safes. **Pool(s):** heated indoor. **Leisure Activities:** whirlpool, exercise room. *Fee:* bicycles. **Guest Services:** valet laundry, wireless Internet. **Business Services:** business center. **Cards:** AX, DS, MC, VI. **Free Special Amenities:** expanded continental breakfast and high-speed Internet. *(See color ad p 780)*

▼ See AAA listing p 778 ▼

(See maps and indexes p. 734-736, 738-741, 742-744)

COMFORT INN LITTLE CREEK   *Book great rates at AAA.com*   Phone: (757)460-5566

Motel
$75-$145 3/1-9/30
$69-$89 10/1-2/28

Address: 5189 Shore Dr 23455 **Location:** Just w of Independence Blvd (SR 225); at Gate 5 of the Naval Amphibious Base. **Facility:** 59 one-bedroom standard units, some with efficiencies. 2 stories (no elevator), exterior corridors. **Parking:** on-site. **Amenities:** high-speed Internet, safes (fee), irons, hair dryers. **Pool(s):** outdoor. **Guest Services:** coin laundry. **Business Services:** fax. **Cards:** AX, CB, DC, DS, JC, MC, VI. **Free Special Amenities:** continental breakfast and high-speed Internet.

COURTYARD BY MARRIOTT   *Book great rates at AAA.com*   Phone: 757/490-2002

Small-scale Hotel
$164-$197 3/1-10/31
$132-$153 11/1-2/28

Address: 5700 Greenwich Rd 23462 **Location:** I-64, exit 284B (Newton Rd S), 0.5 mi e. **Facility:** Smoke free premises. 146 units. 134 one-bedroom standard units. 12 one-bedroom suites. 3 stories, interior corridors. *Bath:* combo or shower only. **Parking:** on-site. **Amenities:** high-speed Internet, dual phone lines, voice mail, irons, hair dryers. *Some:* DVD players (fee). **Pool(s):** heated outdoor. **Leisure Activities:** whirlpool, exercise room. **Guest Services:** valet and coin laundry, wireless Internet. **Business Services:** meeting rooms, business center. **Cards:** AX, DC, DS, MC, VI.

AAA Benefit:
Members save 5% off of the best available rate.

VIRGINIA BEACH

Live the Life

Lose yourself. Find yourself. Start your vacation at vbfun.com or call 1-800-VA-BEACH.

(See maps and indexes p. 734-736, 738-741, 742-744)

COURTYARD BY MARRIOTT-OCEANFRONT NORTH   *Book great rates at AAA.com*   Phone: 757/437-0098   **2**

Small-scale Hotel
$169-$252 3/1-9/3
$142-$169 9/4-2/28

Address: 3737 Atlantic Ave 23451 **Location:** Oceanfront. I-264, at terminus; 1 mi n, jct 37th St. **Facility:** Smoke free premises. 160 units. 100 one-bedroom standard units, some with whirlpools. 60 one-bedroom suites. 10 stories, interior corridors. *Bath:* combo or shower only. **Parking:** on-site. **Terms:** check-in 4 pm, 3 day cancellation notice. **Amenities:** video games (fee), high-speed Internet, dual phone lines, voice mail, irons, hair dryers. **Pool(s):** heated outdoor, heated indoor. **Leisure Activities:** whirlpool, exercise room. **Guest Services:** valet and coin laundry, wireless Internet. **Business Services:** meeting rooms, business center. **Cards:** AX, DS, MC, VI.

AAA Benefit:
Members save 5% off of the best available rate.

COURTYARD BY MARRIOTT-OCEANFRONT SOUTH   *Book great rates at AAA.com*   Phone: 757/491-6222   **20**

Small-scale Hotel
$158-$241 3/1-9/3
$131-$158 9/4-2/28

Address: 2501 Atlantic Ave 23451 **Location:** Oceanfront. I-264, n of terminus; at 25th St and Atlantic Ave. Located adjacent to Norwegian Lady Park. **Facility:** Smoke free premises. 141 units. 113 one-bedroom standard units, some with whirlpools. 28 one-bedroom suites. 11 stories, interior corridors. *Bath:* combo or shower only. **Parking:** on-site. **Terms:** check-in 4 pm, 3 day cancellation notice. **Amenities:** video games (fee), high-speed Internet, dual phone lines, voice mail, irons, hair dryers. *Some: Fee:* safes. **Pool(s):** heated indoor. **Leisure Activities:** exercise room. **Guest Services:** valet and coin laundry, wireless Internet. **Business Services:** meeting rooms, business center. **Cards:** AX, DC, DS, JC, MC, VI.

AAA Benefit:
Members save 5% off of the best available rate.

CROWNE PLAZA VIRGINIA BEACH   *Book great rates at AAA.com*   Phone: (757)473-1700   **18**

Small-scale Hotel
$139-$209 All Year

Address: 4453 Bonney Rd 23462 **Location:** I-264, exit 17B (Independence Blvd), 0.5 mi se. **Facility:** 149 one-bedroom standard units, some with whirlpools. 8 stories, interior corridors. *Bath:* combo or shower only. **Parking:** on-site. **Terms:** 3 day cancellation notice-fee imposed. **Amenities:** video games (fee), high-speed Internet, voice mail, safes, irons, hair dryers. **Pool(s):** heated indoor. **Leisure Activities:** saunas, whirlpool, exercise room. **Guest Services:** valet and coin laundry, wireless Internet. **Business Services:** conference facilities, business center. **Cards:** AX, DC, DS, MC, VI. **Free Special Amenities: newspaper and high-speed Internet.** *(See color ad below)*

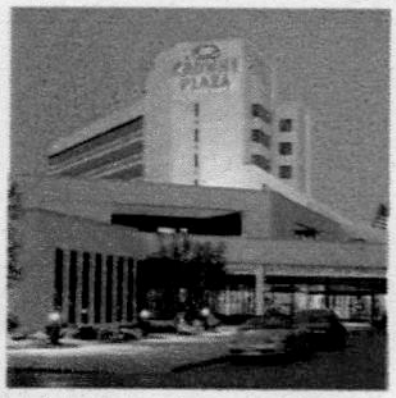

DAYS INN AT THE BEACH   *Book great rates at AAA.com*   Phone: (757)428-6141   **41**

Small-scale Hotel
$39-$189 5/30-2/28
$39-$89 3/1-5/29

Address: 1000 Atlantic Ave 23451 **Location:** I-264, 0.5 mi s of terminus to 10th St. **Facility:** 113 one-bedroom standard units, some with efficiencies and/or whirlpools. 6 stories, exterior corridors. **Parking:** on-site. **Terms:** 3 day cancellation notice. **Amenities:** high-speed Internet, safes, irons, hair dryers. **Pool(s):** heated outdoor. **Leisure Activities:** whirlpool, exercise room. *Fee:* game room. **Guest Services:** coin laundry, wireless Internet. **Business Services:** meeting rooms, PC. **Cards:** AX, CB, DC, DS, MC, VI. **Free Special Amenities: expanded continental breakfast and high-speed Internet.** *(See color ad p 783)*

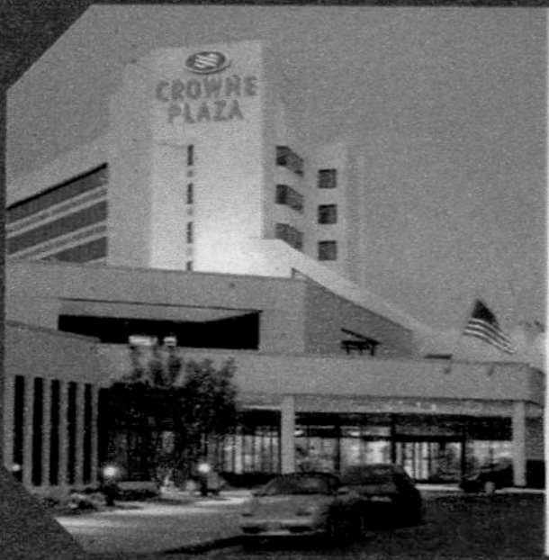

(See maps and indexes p. 734-736, 738-741, 742-744)

DAYS INN OCEANFRONT

 Book great rates at AAA.com   Phone: 757/428-7233 **9**

Small-scale Hotel
Rates not provided

Address: 3107 Atlantic Ave 23451 **Location:** Oceanfront. I-264, 0.8 mi n of terminus; just n of jct Laskin Rd (SR 58) at 32nd St. Adjacent to 31st St Park. **Facility:** 121 one-bedroom standard units, some with whirlpools. 8 stories, interior corridors. **Parking:** on-site. **Amenities:** high-speed Internet, voice mail, safes (fee), irons, hair dryers. **Dining:** Timbuktu, see separate listing. **Pool(s):** heated indoor. **Leisure Activities:** whirlpool. **Guest Services:** coin laundry, wireless Internet. **Business Services:** meeting rooms. **Free Special Amenities: local telephone calls and high-speed Internet.** *(See color ads p 784)*

THE DOLPHIN INN

Book great rates at AAA.com   Phone: (757)491-1420 **32**

Small-scale Hotel
$89-$359 All Year

Address: 1705 Atlantic Ave 23451 **Location:** Oceanfront. I-264, just s of terminus. **Facility:** 54 one-bedroom suites with kitchens and whirlpools. 11 stories, exterior corridors. **Parking:** on-site. **Terms:** 1-4 night minimum stay - seasonal, 3 day cancellation notice. **Amenities:** high-speed Internet, voice mail, safes (fee), irons, hair dryers. **Pool(s):** heated indoor. **Guest Services:** coin laundry, wireless Internet. **Cards:** AX, DC, DS, MC, VI. **Free Special Amenities: high-speed Internet.** *(See color ad p 776 & p 785)*

DOUBLETREE HOTEL VIRGINIA BEACH

Book great rates at AAA.com   Phone: 757/422-8900 **10**

Large-scale Hotel
Rates not provided

Address: 1900 Pavilion Dr 23451 **Location:** I-264, exit 22 (Birdneck Rd). Located adjacent to Virginia Beach Convention Center. **Facility:** 292 units. 286 one-bedroom standard units. 6 one-bedroom suites. 12 stories, interior corridors. *Bath:* combo or shower only. **Parking:** on-site. **Terms:** check-in 4 pm. **Amenities:** high-speed Internet (fee), voice mail, irons, hair dryers. **Pool(s):** heated indoor. **Leisure Activities:** 3 tennis courts, exercise room. *Fee:* game room. **Guest Services:** valet and coin laundry, area transportation-beach. **Business Services:** conference facilities, business center. **Free Special Amenities: newspaper and high-speed Internet.**

▼ See AAA listing p 782 ▼

(See maps and indexes p. 734-736, 738-741, 742-744)

ECONO LODGE OCEANFRONT   *Book great rates at AAA.com*   Phone: (757)428-2403   25

Address: 2109 Atlantic Ave 23451 **Location:** Oceanfront. I-264, just n of terminus; Atlantic Ave and 21st St. **Facility:** 56 one-bedroom standard units, some with efficiencies. 10 stories, interior corridors. **Parking:** on-site. **Terms:** 3 day cancellation notice. **Amenities:** high-speed Internet, safes (fee), irons, hair dryers. **Pool(s):** heated indoor. **Guest Services:** wireless Internet. **Cards:** AX, DC, DS, MC, VI.

Small-scale Hotel
$59-$259 All Year

ECONO LODGE ON THE OCEAN   *Book great rates at AAA.com*   Phone: (757)428-3970   14

Address: 2707 Atlantic Ave 23451 **Location:** Oceanfront. I-264, just n of terminus. **Facility:** 38 units. 36 one-bedroom standard units. 2 one-bedroom suites with kitchens. 3 stories (no elevator), exterior corridors. *Bath:* combo or shower only. **Parking:** on-site. **Terms:** 2-3 night minimum stay - seasonal and/or weekends, 3 day cancellation notice. **Amenities:** high-speed Internet, safes (fee), irons, hair dryers. **Pool(s):** heated outdoor. **Leisure Activities:** bicycles. **Guest Services:** wireless Internet. **Cards:** AX, CB, DC, DS, JC, MC, VI. **Free Special Amenities:** expanded continental breakfast and local telephone calls. *(See color ad p 785)*

Motel
$59-$289 All Year

EXTENDED STAYAMERICA-VIRGINIA BEACH-INDEPENDENCE BLVD   *Book at AAA.com*   Phone: (757)473-9200   17

Address: 4548 Bonney Rd 23462 **Location:** I-264, exit 17B (Independence Blvd/Pembroke Area), just n to Bonney Rd, then just e. **Facility:** 120 one-bedroom standard units with efficiencies. 3 stories, exterior corridors. *Bath:* combo or shower only. **Parking:** on-site. **Terms:** office hours 7 am-11 pm. **Amenities:** high-speed Internet (fee), voice mail, irons. **Guest Services:** coin laundry, wireless Internet. **Cards:** AX, DC, DS, JC, MC, VI.

Motel
$100-$165 All Year

(See maps and indexes p. 734-736, 738-741, 742-744)

FAIRFIELD INN & SUITES VIRGINIA BEACH OCEANFRONT   *Book great rates at AAA.com*

Phone: 757/422-4885   30

Small-scale Hotel
$108-$132 All Year

Address: 1901 Atlantic Ave 23451 **Location:** Oceanfront. I-264, terminus, just s. **Facility:** Smoke free premises. 114 units. 90 one-bedroom standard units, some with whirlpools. 24 one-bedroom suites. 9 stories, interior corridors. *Bath:* combo or shower only. **Parking:** on-site. **Terms:** check-in 4 pm, 3 day cancellation notice. **Amenities:** video games (fee), high-speed Internet, dual phone lines, voice mail, irons, hair dryers. *Some:* CD players. **Pool(s):** heated indoor. **Leisure Activities:** whirlpool, exercise room. **Guest Services:** valet and coin laundry, wireless Internet. **Business Services:** business center. **Cards:** AX, DC, DS, JC, MC, VI.

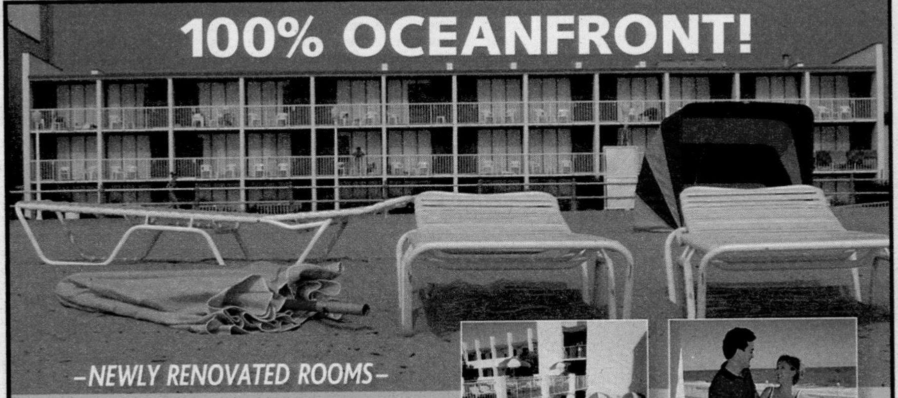

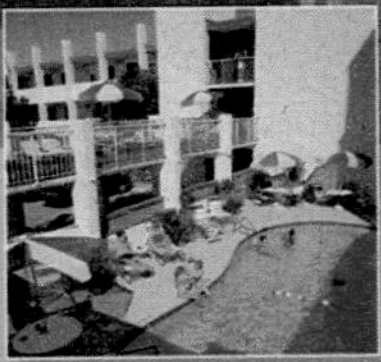

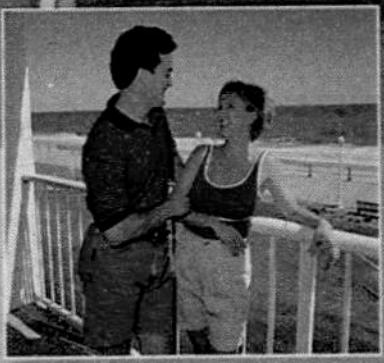

AAA Benefit:
Members save 5% off of the best available rate.

(See maps and indexes p. 734-736, 738-741, 742-744)

THE FOUNDERS INN AND SPA — *Book at AAA.com*

Large-scale Hotel
$89-$225 All Year

Phone: (757)424-5511 **23**

Address: 5641 Indian River Rd 23464 **Location:** I-64, exit 286B, just e; on campus of Christian Broadcasting Network & Regent University. **Facility:** Smoke free premises. 240 units. 234 one-bedroom standard units, some with whirlpools. 3 stories, interior corridors. **Parking:** on-site. **Terms:** check-in 4 pm, 3 day cancellation notice, 4/1-9/30-fee imposed. **Amenities:** high-speed Internet, voice mail, irons, hair dryers. *Some:* CD players. **Dining:** Swan Terrace, see separate listing. **Pool(s):** 2 outdoor, heated indoor. **Leisure Activities:** whirlpool, 4 lighted tennis courts, jogging, playground, exercise room, spa, sports court, volleyball. **Guest Services:** valet laundry, area transportation, wireless Internet. **Business Services:** conference facilities, business center. **Cards:** AX, CB, DC, DS, MC, VI.

FOUR SAILS RESORT HOTEL

Small-scale Hotel
$79-$219 All Year

Phone: 757/491-8100 **7**

Address: 3301 Atlantic Ave 23451 **Location:** Oceanfront. I-264, 1.5 mi n of terminus; Atlantic Ave and 33rd. **Facility:** 55 units. 49 one- and 6 two-bedroom suites with kitchens and whirlpools. 13 stories, interior/exterior corridors. **Parking:** on-site. **Terms:** 2 night minimum stay - weekends, 3 day cancellation notice-fee imposed. **Amenities:** video library (fee), DVD players, CD players, high-speed Internet, voice mail, safes, irons, hair dryers. **Pool(s):** heated indoor. **Leisure Activities:** sauna, bicycles, exercise room. **Guest Services:** coin laundry. **Cards:** AX, DC, DS, MC, VI. **Free Special Amenities:** newspaper. *(See color ad below)*

HAMPTON INN VIRGINIA BEACH — *Book great rates at AAA.com*

Small-scale Hotel
Rates not provided

Phone: 757/490-9800 **13**

Address: 5793 Greenwich Rd 23462 **Location:** I-64, exit 284B to I-264 (Virginia Beach-Norfolk Expwy), then exit Newtown Rd S. **Facility:** 120 one-bedroom standard units. 4 stories, interior corridors. **Parking:** on-site. **Amenities:** video games (fee), high-speed Internet, voice mail, irons, hair dryers. **Pool(s):** outdoor. **Leisure Activities:** exercise room. **Guest Services:** valet laundry, wireless Internet. **Business Services:** business center.

HILTON GARDEN INN VIRGINIA BEACH, TOWN CENTER — *Book great rates at AAA.com*

Small-scale Hotel
Rates not provided

Phone: 757/326-6200 **14**

Address: 252 Town Center Dr 23462 **Location:** I-264, exit 17B (Independence Blvd), just n to Virginia Beach Blvd, then just e; in Town Center. **Facility:** 176 units. 172 one-bedroom standard units, some with whirlpools. 4 one-bedroom suites with whirlpools. 7 stories, interior corridors. *Bath:* combo or shower only. **Parking:** on-site. **Amenities:** video games (fee), high-speed Internet, dual phone lines, voice mail, irons, hair dryers. *Some:* DVD players (fee). **Pool(s):** heated indoor. **Leisure Activities:** whirlpool, exercise room. **Guest Services:** valet and coin laundry, wireless Internet. **Business Services:** meeting rooms, business center.

HILTON VIRGINIA BEACH OCEANFRONT — *Book great rates at AAA.com*

Large-scale Hotel
Rates not provided

Phone: 757/213-3001 **10**

Address: 3001 Atlantic Ave 23451 **Location:** Oceanfront. I-264, 0.5 mi n of terminus. **Facility:** 290 units. 289 one-bedroom standard units, some with whirlpools. 1 one-bedroom suite with whirlpool. 20 stories, interior corridors. *Bath:* combo or shower only. **Parking:** on-site. **Terms:** check-in 4 pm. **Amenities:** high-speed Internet (fee), dual phone lines, voice mail, safes, irons, hair dryers. *Some:* CD players, DVD players (fee). **Dining:** Catch 31 Fish House & Bar, Salacia, see separate listings. **Pool(s):** outdoor, heated indoor. **Leisure Activities:** whirlpool, recreation programs, yoga, water aerobics, spa services. *Fee:* massage. **Guest Services:** valet laundry, area transportation, wireless Internet. **Business Services:** conference facilities, business center. *(See color ad p 776 & p 787)*

(See maps and indexes p. 734-736, 738-741, 742-744)

HOLIDAY INN-EXECUTIVE CENTER   *Book great rates at AAA.com*   **Phone:** (757)499-4400   **11**
AAA SAVE
Address: 5655 Greenwich Rd 23462 **Location:** I-64, exit 284B (Newtown Rd); jct I-64 and 264. **Facility:** 331 units. 327 one-bedroom standard units. 4 one-bedroom suites. 6 stories, interior corridors. *Bath:* combo or shower only. **Parking:** on-site. **Amenities:** video games (fee), high-speed Internet, voice mail, irons, hair dryers. **Pool(s):** outdoor, heated indoor. **Leisure Activities:** sauna, whirlpool, exercise room. **Guest Services:** valet and coin laundry, area transportation-within 5 mi, wireless Internet. **Business Services:** conference facilities, business center. **Cards:** AX, CB, DC, DS, JC, MC, VI. **Free Special Amenities:** newspaper and high-speed Internet.
Large-scale Hotel
$104-$200 All Year

HOLIDAY INN OCEANSIDE   *Book at AAA.com*   **Phone:** (757)491-1500   **26**
Address: 2101 Atlantic Ave 23451 **Location:** Oceanfront. I-264, at terminus; 21st St and Atlantic Ave. **Facility:** 150 one-bedroom standard units. 12 stories, interior corridors. *Bath:* combo or shower only. **Parking:** on-site. **Terms:** 2 night minimum stay - seasonal and/or weekends, 3 day cancellation notice. **Amenities:** video games (fee), high-speed Internet, voice mail, irons, hair dryers. **Pool(s):** heated indoor. **Leisure Activities:** whirlpool, exercise room. **Guest Services:** valet and coin laundry, wireless Internet. **Business Services:** meeting rooms. **Cards:** AX, DC, DS, MC, VI.
Small-scale Hotel
$115-$270 3/1-8/31
$100-$185 9/1-2/28

HOLIDAY INN SUNSPREE RESORT   *Book great rates at AAA.com*   **Phone:** (757)428-1711   **1**
AAA SAVE
Address: 3900 Atlantic Ave 23451 **Location:** Oceanfront. I-264, 2 mi n from terminus; at Atlantic Ave and 39th St. **Facility:** 266 units. 211 one-bedroom standard units, some with whirlpools. 55 one-bedroom suites. 6-7 stories, interior corridors. **Parking:** on-site. **Terms:** check-in 4 pm, 2 night minimum stay - seasonal and/or weekends, 3 day cancellation notice-fee imposed. **Amenities:** video games (fee), high-speed Internet, dual phone lines, voice mail, irons, hair dryers. **Dining:** 2 restaurants, also, Isle of Capri, see separate listing. **Pool(s):** outdoor, heated indoor. **Leisure Activities:** whirlpools, lazy river ride, kids club in season, exercise room. *Fee:* bicycles, game room. **Guest Services:** valet and coin laundry, wireless Internet. **Business Services:** conference facilities. **Cards:** AX, CB, DS, MC, VI. **Free Special Amenities:** local telephone calls and high-speed Internet.
Large-scale Hotel
$85-$305 3/1-8/31
$89-$175 9/1-2/28

HOLIDAY INN SURFSIDE HOTEL & SUITES   *Book great rates at AAA.com*   **Phone:** (757)491-6900   **18**
AAA SAVE
Address: 2607 Atlantic Ave 23451 **Location:** Oceanfront. I-264, n of terminus; at Atlantic Ave and 26th St. **Facility:** 143 units. 125 one-bedroom standard units, some with whirlpools. 18 one-bedroom suites. 10 stories, interior corridors. **Parking:** on-site. **Terms:** check-in 4 pm, 2 night minimum stay - seasonal and/or weekends, 3 day cancellation notice-fee imposed. **Amenities:** video games (fee), high-speed Internet, dual phone lines, voice mail, irons, hair dryers. **Pool(s):** heated indoor. **Leisure Activities:** whirlpool, exercise room. **Guest Services:** valet and coin laundry, wireless Internet. **Business Services:** meeting rooms. **Cards:** AX, CB, DC, DS, MC, VI. **Free Special Amenities:** local telephone calls and high-speed Internet.
Small-scale Hotel
$109-$319 3/1-8/31
$95-$199 9/1-2/28

(See maps and indexes p. 734-736, 738-741, 742-744)

HOWARD JOHNSON INN *Book at AAA.com* **Phone:** 757/460-1151 ❸

Motel
Rates not provided
Address: 5173 Shore Dr 23455 **Location:** Just w of jct Independence Blvd (SR 225) at Gate 5 of Naval Amphibious Base. **Facility:** 52 units. 2 stories (no elevator), exterior corridors. **Parking:** on-site. **Amenities:** high-speed Internet, voice mail, safes (fee), irons, hair dryers. *Some:* DVD players (fee). **Guest Services:** coin laundry.

HOWARD JOHNSON OCEANFRONT HOTEL *Book great rates at AAA.com* **Phone:** (757)437-9100 ㉛

Small-scale Hotel
$59-$199 All Year
Address: 1801 Atlantic Ave 23451 **Location:** Oceanfront. I-264, just s of terminus; jct 18th and Atlantic Ave. **Facility:** 107 units. 106 one-bedroom standard units, some with whirlpools. 1 one-bedroom suite. 8 stories, interior corridors. *Bath:* combo or shower only. **Parking:** on-site. **Terms:** check-in 4 pm, 2-3 night minimum stay - seasonal and/or weekends, 3 day cancellation notice-fee imposed. **Amenities:** high-speed Internet, voice mail, safes (fee), irons, hair dryers. **Pool(s):** heated indoor. **Leisure Activities:** *Fee:* bicycles, game room. **Guest Services:** coin laundry, wireless Internet. **Business Services:** meeting rooms, PC. **Cards:** AX, DC, DS, MC, VI.
(See color ad p 776 & below)

LA QUINTA INN NORFOLK (VIRGINIA BEACH) *Book great rates at AAA.com* **Phone:** (757)497-6620 ⑮

Small-scale Hotel
$99-$129 All Year
Address: 192 Newtown Rd 23462 **Location:** I-64, exit 284B to I-264 (Virginia Beach-Norfolk Expwy), exit Newtown Rd S. **Facility:** 129 units. 126 one-bedroom standard units. 3 one-bedroom suites. 3 stories, interior corridors. **Parking:** on-site. **Amenities:** video games (fee), high-speed Internet, voice mail, irons, hair dryers. **Pool(s):** outdoor. **Guest Services:** wireless Internet. **Business Services:** fax. **Cards:** AX, DC, DS, MC, VI. **Free Special Amenities:** expanded continental breakfast and high-speed Internet.

LAQUINTA
INNS & SUITES
AAA Benefit:
Members save 10% everyday.

LA QUINTA INNS & SUITES *Book great rates at AAA.com* **Phone:** 757/428-2203 ⑬

Small-scale Hotel
Rates not provided
Address: 2800 Pacific Ave 23451 **Location:** I-264, 0.5 mi n of terminus. **Facility:** 137 units. 136 one-bedroom standard units, some with whirlpools. 1 one-bedroom suite. 7 stories, interior corridors. **Parking:** on-site. **Amenities:** high-speed Internet, safes (fee), irons, hair dryers. **Pool(s):** heated outdoor, heated indoor. **Leisure Activities:** whirlpool, bicycles, exercise room. *Fee:* game room. **Guest Services:** valet and coin laundry, wireless Internet. **Business Services:** meeting rooms, business center. **Free Special Amenities:** expanded continental breakfast and high-speed Internet. *(See color ad p 776)*

LAQUINTA
INNS & SUITES
AAA Benefit:
Members save 10% everyday.

MARJAC SUITES **Phone:** 757/425-0100 ㉔

Small-scale Hotel
$49-$239 All Year
Address: 2201 Atlantic Ave 23451 **Location:** Oceanfront. I-264, terminus; just n at 22nd St. **Facility:** 60 one-bedroom suites with kitchens. 6 stories, exterior corridors. **Parking:** on-site. **Terms:** check-in 4 pm, 3 day cancellation notice. **Amenities:** safes (fee), hair dryers. **Pool(s):** outdoor. **Guest Services:** coin laundry. **Cards:** AX, MC, VI. *(See color ad p 777)*

(See maps and indexes p. 734-736, 738-741, 742-744)

NEW CASTLE HOTEL

Small-scale Hotel
Rates not provided

Phone: 757/428-3981 **39**

Address: 1203 Atlantic Ave 23451 **Location:** Oceanfront. I-264, 0.6 mi s of terminus. **Facility:** 83 one-bedroom standard units with whirlpools, some with efficiencies. 10 stories, interior/exterior corridors. **Parking:** on-site. **Amenities:** high-speed Internet, safes (fee), irons, hair dryers. **Pool(s):** heated indoor. **Leisure Activities:** exercise room. **Guest Services:** coin laundry, wireless Internet.
(See color ad p 776)

OCEAN BEACH CLUB

AAA SAVE

Condominium
$89-$359 All Year

Book great rates at AAA.com   **Phone:** (757)213-0601 **6**

Address: 3401 Atlantic Ave 23451 **Location:** Oceanfront. I-264, 0.5 mi n of terminus. **Facility:** Modern one-bedroom apartments and studios are fully equipped at the oceanside, high-rise hotel; a stylish pool with a cabana bar overlooks the beach. 182 units. 86 one-bedroom standard units with efficiencies. 96 one-bedroom suites with kitchens and whirlpools. 18 stories, interior corridors. *Bath:* combo or shower only. **Parking:** on-site. **Terms:** check-in 4 pm, 1-4 night minimum stay - seasonal, 3 day cancellation notice. **Amenities:** DVD players, CD players, voice mail, irons, hair dryers. *Fee:* video library, high-speed Internet, safes. **Pool(s):** heated outdoor. **Leisure Activities:** recreation programs, exercise room privileges. *Fee:* massage. **Guest Services:** coin laundry, wireless Internet. **Cards:** AX, DC, DS, MC, VI. **Free Special Amenities:** high-speed Internet.
(See color ad p 776)

THE OCEANFRONT INN

AAA SAVE

Small-scale Hotel
$58-$224 7/20-2/28
$58-$157 3/1-7/19

Phone: (757)422-0445 **11**

Address: 2901 Atlantic Ave 23451 **Location:** Oceanfront. I-264, n of terminus; at Atlantic Ave and 29th St. **Facility:** 147 one-bedroom standard units. 7 stories, interior corridors. **Parking:** on-site (fee). **Terms:** check-in 4 pm, 2-3 night minimum stay - seasonal and/or weekends. **Amenities:** high-speed Internet, voice mail, irons, hair dryers. **Pool(s):** heated indoor. **Guest Services:** valet laundry, wireless Internet. **Business Services:** meeting rooms. **Cards:** AX, CB, DC, DS, MC, VI. **Free Special Amenities:** newspaper and high-speed Internet.
(See color ad below)

OCEAN HOLIDAY HOTEL

AAA SAVE

Small-scale Hotel
$55-$195 3/1-9/30
$45-$125 10/1-2/28

Phone: (757)425-6920 **21**

Address: 2417 Atlantic Ave 23451 **Location:** Oceanfront. I-264, n of terminus; at Atlantic Ave and 25th St. **Facility:** 105 one-bedroom standard units, some with whirlpools. 7 stories, interior corridors. **Parking:** on-site. **Terms:** 2-3 night minimum stay - seasonal and/or weekends, 3 day cancellation notice-fee imposed. **Amenities:** safes (fee), irons. **Pool(s):** heated indoor. **Leisure Activities:** sun deck. **Business Services:** meeting rooms. **Cards:** AX, DS, MC, VI. **Free Special Amenities:** local telephone calls and newspaper.

OCEAN SUITES

AAA SAVE

Motel
$49-$249 All Year

Phone: (757)428-1111 **23**

Address: 2315 Atlantic Ave 23451 **Location:** Oceanfront. I-264, just n of terminus. **Facility:** 54 one-bedroom suites with kitchens. 8 stories, interior/exterior corridors. **Parking:** on-site. **Terms:** check-in 4 pm, 2-3 night minimum stay - seasonal and/or weekends, 3 day cancellation notice-fee imposed. **Amenities:** safes (fee), hair dryers. **Pool(s):** heated outdoor. **Guest Services:** coin laundry. **Cards:** AX, DS, MC, VI. **Free Special Amenities:** local telephone calls and newspaper.
(See color ad p 776 & p 790)

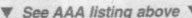

▼ See AAA listing above ▼

(See maps and indexes p. 734-736, 738-741, 742-744)

QUALITY INN & SUITES   *Book great rates at AAA.com*   Phone: (757)428-8935   **43**

Small-scale Hotel
$79-$269 All Year

Address: 705 Atlantic Ave 23451 **Location:** Oceanfront. I-264, 1 mi s of terminus; at Atlantic Ave and 8th St. **Facility:** 124 one-bedroom standard units. 6 stories, interior corridors. **Parking:** on-site. **Terms:** 2-3 night minimum stay - seasonal and/or weekends, 3 day cancellation notice. **Amenities:** high-speed Internet, voice mail, safes (fee), irons, hair dryers. **Pool(s):** outdoor, heated indoor. **Leisure Activities:** *Fee:* bicycles. **Guest Services:** valet laundry, wireless Internet. **Business Services:** conference facilities. **Cards:** AX, CB, DC, DS, JC, MC, VI. *(See color ad p 777)*

QUALITY INN PAVILION   *Book great rates at AAA.com*   Phone: (757)422-3617   **8**

Small-scale Hotel
$99-$329 3/1-9/15
$65-$199 9/16-2/28

Address: 716 21st St 23451 **Location:** I-264, at terminus; jct 21st St and Park Ave. Located adjacent to the Virginia Beach Convention Center. **Facility:** 109 units. 103 one-bedroom standard units. 6 one-bedroom suites, some with kitchens. 2-4 stories, exterior corridors. **Parking:** on-site. **Terms:** 2-3 night minimum stay - weekends, 3 day cancellation notice-fee imposed. **Amenities:** high-speed Internet, irons, hair dryers. **Pool(s):** outdoor. **Guest Services:** area transportation-beach, wireless Internet. **Cards:** AX, CB, DC, DS, MC, VI. **Free Special Amenities: local telephone calls and high-speed Internet.**

RAMADA ON THE BEACH   *Book great rates at AAA.com*   Phone: (757)425-7800   **44**

Small-scale Hotel
$89-$359 All Year

Address: 615 Atlantic Ave 23451 **Location:** Oceanfront. I-264, 1 mi s of terminus; at Atlantic Ave and 6th St. **Facility:** 167 one-bedroom standard units, some with whirlpools. 8 stories, interior corridors. *Bath:* combo or shower only. **Parking:** valet. **Terms:** check-in 4 pm, 1-4 night minimum stay - seasonal, 3 day cancellation notice. **Amenities:** high-speed Internet, voice mail, irons, hair dryers. *Fee:* video games, safes. **Dining:** Mahi Mah's Seafood Restaurant & Sushi Saloon, see separate listing. **Pool(s):** heated indoor. **Leisure Activities:** whirlpool, rental bicycles, exercise room. **Guest Services:** coin laundry, wireless Internet. **Business Services:** conference facilities. **Cards:** AX, DC, DS, MC, VI. **Free Special Amenities: newspaper and high-speed Internet.**
(See color ad p 776 & p 791)

RED ROOF INN VA BEACH (NORFOLK AIRPORT)   *Book great rates at AAA.com*   Phone: 757/460-6700   **5**

Motel
Rates not provided

Address: 5745 Northampton Blvd 23455 **Location:** I-64, exit 282, 1 mi n on US 13 (Northampton Blvd). **Facility:** 148 one-bedroom standard units. 2 stories (no elevator), exterior corridors. **Parking:** on-site. **Amenities:** high-speed Internet (fee). **Pool(s):** outdoor. **Guest Services:** coin laundry, wireless Internet. **Business Services:** fax. **Free Special Amenities: local telephone calls and preferred room (subject to availability with advance reservations).**

▼ See AAA listing p 789 ▼

(See maps and indexes p. 734-736, 738-741, 742-744)

RESIDENCE INN VIRGINIA BEACH OCEANFRONT   *Book great rates at AAA.com*   Phone: 757/425-1141

Small-scale Hotel
$235-$351 3/1-9/3
$186-$235 9/4-2/28

Address: 3217 Atlantic Ave 23451 **Location:** Oceanfront. I-264, 1.5 mi n of terminus; Atlantic Ave and 33rd St. **Facility:** Smoke free premises. 72 one-bedroom suites with kitchens. 13 stories, interior corridors. *Bath:* combo or shower only. **Parking:** on-site. **Terms:** check-in 4 pm, 3 day cancellation notice. **Amenities:** high-speed Internet, voice mail, irons, hair dryers. **Pool(s):** heated indoor, exercise room. **Guest Services:** valet and coin laundry, wireless Internet. **Business Services:** business center. **Cards:** AX, DC, DS, JC, MC, VI.

AAA Benefit:
Members save 5% off of the best available rate.

 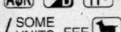 ASK / SOME UNITS FEE

ROYAL CLIPPER INN & SUITES   Phone: (757)428-8992   **5**

AAA SAVE
Motel
$39-$179 3/1-10/31

Address: 3508 Atlantic Ave 23451 **Location:** I-264, exit terminus, 1 mi n. **Facility:** 87 units. 55 one- and 32 two-bedroom standard units, some with efficiencies. 5 stories, exterior corridors. **Parking:** on-site. **Terms:** open 3/1-10/31, 2-3 night minimum stay - seasonal and/or weekends, 3 day cancellation notice-fee imposed. **Amenities:** DVD players, high-speed Internet, voice mail, safes (fee), irons, hair dryers. **Pool(s):** outdoor. **Guest Services:** coin laundry. **Cards:** AX, DS, MC, VI. **Free Special Amenities:** local telephone calls and high-speed Internet. *(See color ad p 792)*

/ SOME UNITS

SANDCASTLE OCEANFRONT RESORT HOTEL   Phone: (757)428-2828   **37**

Small-scale Hotel
$49-$249 3/1-9/2
$49-$129 9/3-2/28

Address: 1307 Atlantic Ave 23451 **Location:** Oceanfront. I-264, 0.5 mi s of terminus; at 14th St. Located adjacent to Lynnhaven Fishing Pier. **Facility:** 150 units. 148 one-bedroom standard units. 2 one-bedroom suites. 9 stories, interior corridors. *Bath:* combo or shower only. **Parking:** on-site. **Terms:** 2-3 night minimum stay - seasonal and/or weekends, 3 day cancellation notice-fee imposed. **Amenities:** DVD players, high-speed Internet, voice mail, safes (fee), irons, hair dryers. **Dining:** 2 restaurants. **Pool(s):** heated indoor. **Leisure Activities:** exercise room. *Fee:* bicycles, game room. **Guest Services:** coin laundry, wireless Internet. **Business Services:** meeting rooms. **Cards:** AX, DC, DS, MC, VI. **Free Special Amenities:** expanded continental breakfast and high-speed Internet. *(See color ad p 793)*

       / SOME UNITS

SCHOONER INN   Phone: 757/425-5222   **48**

Motel
$49-$239 All Year

Address: 215 Atlantic Ave 23451 **Location:** Oceanfront. I-264, 1.4 mi s of terminus. **Facility:** 89 units. 83 one-bedroom standard units and/or whirlpools. 6 one-bedroom suites with kitchens. 6 stories, exterior corridors. *Bath:* combo or shower only. **Parking:** on-site. **Terms:** check-in 4 pm, 3 day cancellation notice. **Amenities:** safes (fee). *Some:* hair dryers. **Pool(s):** heated outdoor. **Guest Services:** coin laundry. **Cards:** AX, DS, MC, VI. *(See color ad p 777 & p 776)*

ASK CALL / SOME UNITS

▼ See AAA listing p 790 ▼

(See maps and indexes p. 734-736, 738-741, 742-744)

SEA GULL MOTEL

AAA SAVE

Small-scale Hotel
$45-$205 All Year

Phone: 757/425-5711 **17**

Address: 2613 Atlantic Ave 23451 **Location:** Oceanfront. I-264, 0.5 mi n of terminus; at Atlantic Ave and 27th St. **Facility:** 51 one-bedroom standard units, some with efficiencies (no utensils). 4 stories, interior/exterior corridors. **Parking:** on-site. **Terms:** check-in 4 pm, 3 day cancellation notice-fee imposed. **Amenities:** irons. **Pool(s):** heated indoor. **Leisure Activities:** whirlpool, sun deck. **Fee:** bicycles. **Cards:** AX, DC, DS, MC, VI. *(See color ad p 794)*

SEAHAWK MOTEL

AAA SAVE

Motel
$49-$189 3/1-11/1

Phone: (757)428-1296 **19**

Address: 2525 Atlantic Ave 23451 **Location:** Oceanfront. I-264, n of terminus; at Atlantic Ave and 26th St. **Facility:** 48 one-bedroom standard units, some with efficiencies. 6 stories, interior corridors. **Parking:** on-site. **Terms:** open 3/1-11/1, 2-3 night minimum stay - seasonal and/or weekends, 3 day cancellation notice-fee imposed. **Amenities:** safes, irons. **Pool(s):** heated indoor. **Leisure Activities:** whirlpool. **Guest Services:** coin laundry. **Cards:** AX, DS, MC, VI. **Free Special Amenities:** local telephone calls and newspaper.

SEASIDE MOTEL

AAA SAVE

Motel
$50-$150 All Year

Phone: 757/428-9341 **15**

Address: 2705 Atlantic Ave 23451 **Location:** Oceanfront. I-264, n of terminus; at Atlantic Ave and 27th St. **Facility:** 46 one-bedroom standard units, some with efficiencies. 4 stories, interior/exterior corridors. **Parking:** on-site. **Terms:** 3 night minimum stay - seasonal, 3 day cancellation notice-fee imposed. **Pool(s):** heated indoor. **Leisure Activities:** sun deck. **Cards:** MC, VI. *(See color ad p 794)*

▼ *See AAA listing p 791* ▼

▼ See AAA listing p 791 ▼

SANDCASTLE
OCEANFRONT RESORT HOTEL

Your Backyard is the Atlantic Ocean

Located in the heart of the resort area at the Oceanfront our deluxe accommodations offer everything you need for the most memorable vacation ever.

Free Deluxe Continental Breakfast

- 150 Rooms • Oceanfront Rooms w/ Private Balcony
- Enclosed Seasonally Heated Pool/Kiddie Pool/Sundeck • Cable TV/HBO, DVD Player • Free High Speed Internet Access • Refrigerator, Microwave, Iron, Ironing Board, Hairdryer & Safe in Every Room • Guest Coin-Operated Laundry • Unlimited Local Calls • 14th Street Fishing Pier • Fitness Room Conference & Meeting Room • On-Site Pier 14 Indoor Mall w/Gift Shops, Restaurants & Bike Rentals • Free On-Site Parking for Vehicles up to 6'2" Non-Smoking Rooms • Group Rates Available

1-800-233-0131
www.sandcastle-vabeach.com
14th St. & Oceanfront • Virginia Beach, VA 23451

(See maps and indexes p. 734-736, 738-741, 742-744)

SHERATON OCEANFRONT HOTEL *Book great rates at AAA.com* Phone: (757)425-9000

Small-scale Hotel
$109-$259 3/1-8/31
$149-$209 9/1-2/28

Address: 3501 Atlantic Ave 23451 **Location:** Oceanfront. I-264, 1 mi n of terminus; jct 36th St. **Facility:** 198 units. 194 one-bedroom standard units, some with whirlpools. 4 one-bedroom suites. 11 stories, interior corridors. *Bath:* combo or shower only. **Parking:** valet. **Terms:** check-in 4 pm, 2 night minimum stay - seasonal and/or weekends, 3 day cancellation notice-fee imposed. **Amenities:** dual phone lines, voice mail, irons, hair dryers. *Fee:* video games, high-speed Internet. **Pool(s):** 2 outdoor, heated indoor. **Leisure Activities:** whirlpools, exercise room. *Fee:* bicycles. **Guest Services:** valet laundry, wireless Internet. **Business Services:** conference facilities, business center. **Cards:** AX, CB, DC, DS, MC, VI.

 Sheraton
AAA Benefit: Members get up to 15% off, plus Starwood Preferred Guest® bonuses.

SPRINGHILL SUITES BY MARRIOTT VIRGINIA BEACH OCEANFRONT **Phone: 757/417-3982**

(fyi)
Small-scale Hotel
$186-$274 3/1-9/27
$131-$158 9/28-2/28

Too new to rate. **Address:** 901 Atlantic Ave 23451 **Location:** Oceanfront. I-264, exit terminus, 1 mi s. **Amenities:** 168 units, coffeemakers, microwaves, refrigerators, pool. **Terms:** 3 day cancellation notice. **Cards:** AX, DC, DS, JC, MC, VI.

 SpringHill
AAA Benefit: Members save 5% off of the best available rate.

STATION ONE HOTEL Phone: (757)491-2400 [22]

Small-scale Hotel
$199-$350 6/16-2/28
$49-$299 3/1-6/15

Address: 2321 Atlantic Ave 23451 **Location:** Oceanfront. I-264, just n of terminus; at Atlantic Ave and 24th St. Adjacent to Old Coast Guard Station. **Facility:** 104 one-bedroom suites with kitchens. 11 stories, exterior corridors. *Bath:* combo or shower only. **Parking:** on-site. **Terms:** 3 day cancellation notice-fee imposed. **Pool(s):** heated outdoor. **Leisure Activities:** whirlpool, exercise room. **Guest Services:** coin laundry. **Cards:** AX, DC, DS, MC, VI.

SUNDIAL MOTEL & EFFICIENCIES *Book great rates at AAA.com* Phone: 757/428-2922 [28]

Motel
$49-$229 3/1-9/30
$39-$149 10/1-2/28

Address: 308 21st St 23451 **Location:** I-264, at terminus; jct 21st St and Pacific Ave. **Facility:** 67 one-bedroom standard units, some with efficiencies. 3-4 stories (no elevator), exterior corridors. **Parking:** on-site. **Terms:** 2-3 night minimum stay - seasonal and/or weekends, 3 day cancellation notice-fee imposed. **Amenities:** high-speed Internet, safes (fee), irons, hair dryers. **Pool(s):** outdoor. **Guest Services:** wireless Internet. **Cards:** AX, DC, DS, MC, VI. **Free Special Amenities:** preferred room (subject to availability with advance reservations) and high-speed Internet. *(See color ad p 796)*

SURFSIDE OCEANFRONT INN & SUITES Phone: (757)428-1183 [38]

Small-scale Hotel
$49-$249 3/1-9/2
$49-$129 9/3-2/28

Address: 1211 Atlantic Ave 23451 **Location:** Oceanfront. I-264, 0.5 mi s of terminus; at Atlantic Ave and 12th St. **Facility:** 99 units. 89 one-bedroom standard units. 10 one-bedroom suites with whirlpools. 9 stories, interior corridors. **Parking:** on-site. **Terms:** 2-3 night minimum stay - seasonal and/or weekends, 3 day cancellation notice-fee imposed. **Amenities:** DVD players, high-speed Internet, voice mail, safes, irons, hair dryers. **Pool(s):** heated indoor. **Leisure Activities:** exercise room. *Fee:* rollerblade, bicycles. **Guest Services:** coin laundry, wireless Internet. **Business Services:** meeting rooms. **Cards:** AX, DC, DS, MC, VI. **Free Special Amenities:** expanded continental breakfast and high-speed Internet. *(See color ad p 797)*

TOWNEPLACE SUITES BY MARRIOTT *Book great rates at AAA.com* Phone: 757/490-9367 [9]

Small-scale Hotel
$147-$164 3/1-9/30
$125-$147 10/1-2/28

Address: 5757 Cleveland St 23462 **Location:** I-64, exit 284B to I-264 (Virginia Beach-Norfolk Expwy), exit Newtown Rd N. **Facility:** Smoke free premises. 95 units. 69 one-bedroom standard units with kitchens. 4 one- and 22 two-bedroom suites with kitchens. 3 stories, interior corridors. *Bath:* combo or shower only. **Parking:** on-site. **Amenities:** high-speed Internet, voice mail, irons, hair dryers. *Some:* DVD players (fee). **Pool(s):** outdoor. **Leisure Activities:** exercise room. **Guest Services:** valet and coin laundry, wireless Internet. **Business Services:** fax. **Cards:** AX, DC, DS, JC, MC, VI.

  TownePlace
AAA Benefit: Members save 5% off of the best available rate.

(See maps and indexes p. 734-736, 738-741, 742-744)

TURTLE CAY RESORT   *Book great rates at AAA.com*   Phone: (757)437-5565   45

(AAA) (SAVE)
▼▼▼ ▼▼
Condominium
$89-$359 All Year

Address: 600 Atlantic Ave 23451 **Location:** I-264, 1 mi s of terminus; jct 6th St and Atlantic Ave. **Facility:** Wraparound verandas and green shingled roofs recall Carolina beach cottages. Efficiencies, one- or two- bedroom suites offer comforts of home with gas-lit fireplaces and pine furniture. 124 units. 33 one-bedroom standard units. 89 one- and 2 two-bedroom suites with kitchens, some with whirlpools. 3 stories, exterior corridors. **Parking:** on-site. **Terms:** check-in 4 pm, 1-4 night minimum stay - seasonal, 3 day cancellation notice. **Amenities:** dual phone lines, voice mail, safes (fee), irons, hair dryers. *Some:* DVD players (fee). **Pool(s):** 2 heated outdoor. **Leisure Activities:** whirlpools, tropical waterfall pool, zero depth pool, indoor pool privileges. **Guest Services:** valet and coin laundry, wireless Internet. **Business Services:** meeting rooms. **Cards:** AX, DC, DS, MC, VI. **Free Special Amenities:** newspaper and high-speed Internet. *(See color ad p 776)*

🅂🄳 🍽📶 🏊 FEE📹 📹 🖥 🖥 💻 / SOME UNITS FEE VCR

THE VIKING MOTEL   Phone: (757)428-7116   16

(AAA) (SAVE)
▼▼▼ ▼▼
Motel
$79-$199 6/10-10/15
$49-$169 3/1-6/9

Address: 2700 Atlantic Ave 23451 **Location:** I-264, 0.5 mi n of terminus; at Atlantic Ave and 27th St. **Facility:** 81 units. 61 one- and 20 two-bedroom standard units, some with efficiencies. 2-3 stories, interior/exterior corridors. **Parking:** on-site. **Terms:** open 3/1-10/15, 2 night minimum stay - seasonal and/or weekends. **Pool(s):** outdoor. **Business Services:** fax. **Cards:** AX, DS, MC, VI. **Free Special Amenities:** local telephone calls and newspaper.

🍽📶 🏊 📹 🖥 / SOME UNITS ⊠ 🖥 💻

▼ *See AAA listing p 795* ▼

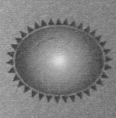

(See maps and indexes p. 734-736, 738-741, 742-744)

VIRGINIA BEACH RESORT HOTEL & CONFERENCE CENTER   *Book great rates at AAA.com*

Phone: (757)481-9000

🔺🔺🔺 (AAA) (SAVE)

Large-scale Hotel
$99-$415 All Year

Address: 2800 Shore Dr 23451 **Location:** US 60, 3.5 mi e of US 13; jct Shore Dr and N Great Neck Rd. Located on the beach of the Chesapeake Bay, in a residential area. **Facility:** 295 units. 282 one- and 13 two-bedroom suites. 9 stories, interior corridors. *Bath:* combo or shower only. **Parking:** on-site. **Terms:** check-in 4 pm, 3 day cancellation notice-fee imposed. **Amenities:** high-speed Internet (fee), dual phone lines, voice mail, irons, hair dryers. **Dining:** Tradewinds, see separate listing. **Pool(s):** outdoor, heated indoor. **Leisure Activities:** sauna, whirlpool, tennis club & golf privileges, recreation programs, bicycles. *Fee:* aqua cycles, personal watercraft, massage. **Guest Services:** valet and coin laundry, area transportation (fee)-oceanfront resort area. **Business Services:** conference facilities, business center. **Cards:** AX, CB, DC, DS, MC, VI. **Free Special Amenities: room upgrade (subject to availability with advance reservations).** *(See color ad p 798)*

(S/D) FEE 🔺 🍽 🍸 👤 CALL 🔺M 🏊 🔺 🔺 🔺 🔺 🔺 / SOME UNITS 🔺

WINGATE INN-NORFOLK AIRPORT   *Book great rates at AAA.com*

Phone: (757)363-2901   ⑦

🔺🔺🔺

Small-scale Hotel
$129-$139 All Year

Address: 5800 Burton Station Rd 23455 **Location:** I-64, exit 282, just ne on US 13 (Northampton Blvd). **Facility:** 101 units. 95 one-bedroom standard units. 6 one-bedroom suites with whirlpools. 4 stories, interior corridors. *Bath:* combo or shower only. **Parking:** on-site. **Amenities:** video games (fee), high-speed Internet, dual phone lines, voice mail, safes, irons, hair dryers. **Pool(s):** heated indoor. **Leisure Activities:** whirlpool, exercise room. **Guest Services:** valet laundry, wireless Internet. **Business Services:** meeting rooms, business center. **Cards:** AX, DC, DS, JC, MC, VI.

(ASK) (S/D) 🔺 🔺 CALL 🔺M 🏊 🔺 🔺 🔺 🔺 / SOME UNITS 🔺

▼ See AAA listing p 797 ▼

(See maps and indexes p. 734-736, 738-741, 742-744)

WYNDHAM VIRGINIA BEACH OCEANFRONT   *Book great rates at AAA.com*   **Phone:** (757)428-7025

Large-scale Hotel
$189-$249 All Year

Address: Atlantic Ave & 57th St 23451 **Location:** Oceanfront. I-264, 2.2 mi n of terminus. Located in a residential area. **Facility:** 245 units. 221 one-bedroom standard units, some with whirlpools. 20 one- and 4 two-bedroom suites. 5-17 stories, interior corridors. *Bath:* combo or shower only. **Parking:** on- site. **Terms:** check-in 4 pm, 3 day cancellation notice-fee imposed. **Amenities:** high-speed Internet, voice mail, irons, hair dryers. *Fee:* video games, safes. *Some:* CD players. **Pool(s):** heated outdoor, heated indoor. **Leisure Activities:** whirlpool, recreation programs in summer, exercise room, volleyball. *Fee:* kayaks, surfboard rentals, bicycles, game room. **Guest Services:** valet and coin laundry, area transportation-resort area, wireless Internet. **Business Services:** conference facilities, business center. **Cards:** AX, DC, DS, MC, VI. **Free Special Amenities:** local telephone calls and newspaper. *(See color ad p 798 & p 776)*

—— WHERE TO DINE ——

THE 58 DELI DINER   **Phone:** 757/226-8493   53

Deli/Subs
Sandwiches
$3-$10

Influenced by the great tradition of New York delis, this retro-style spot offers huge sandwiches and overflowing platters of great meats such as pastrami, corned beef, and roast beef as well as other specialties such as knishes, matzo ball soup, and NY cheesecake. Casual dress. **Hours:** 10:30 am-4 pm. Closed: 11/27, 12/24; also Sun. **Address:** 1716 Virginia Beach Blvd 23454 **Location:** I-264, exit 20, just e. **Parking:** on-site. **Cards:** AX, MC, VI.

---

757 FIRE AND VINE-WOODFIRE CUISINE   **Phone:** 757/428-8463   35

American
$11-$29

Taste delicious cuisine straight from a wood-fired oven. Tasty flatbread pizzas, steaks, lamb, fish and vegetables are grilled over the roaring fire. Vertical skewers inspired by the churrasco cuisine of Brazil offer a fun way to eat. All entrees include an extensive, gourmet antipasto bar overloaded with delicious salads, vegetables, spreads and breads. The wine cellar offers an extensive selection of New World wines. Casual dress. **Bar:** Full bar. **Reservations:** accepted. **Hours:** 11 am-11 pm. Closed major holidays; also Sun. **Address:** 1556 Laskin Rd 23451 **Location:** 3 mi e of oceanfront; in Hilltop East Shopping Center. **Parking:** on-site. **Cards:** AX, MC, VI.

ABERDEEN BARN   **Phone:** 757/464-1580

Steak House
$8-$40

Known for its slow-roasted prime rib of beef prepared on an open charcoal hearth, this rustic steakhouse features post-and-beam construction and attractive barn decor. Other USDA Corn Fed Angus Beef selections, fresh local seafood and mouthwatering desserts round out the menu. Casual dress. Entertainment. **Bar:** Full bar. **Reservations:** accepted. **Hours:** 3 pm-midnight, Sun 11:30 am-11 pm. **Address:** 5805 Northampton Blvd 23455 **Location:** I-64, exit 282, just n on US 13. **Parking:** on-site. **Cards:** AX, CB, DC, DS, JC, MC, VI.

ALDO'S RISTORANTE   **Phone:** 757/491-1111   37

Italian
$8-$26

A hip, local crowd comes for the stylish contemporary decor and the homemade Italian cuisine, prepared fresh daily. Brick-oven pizza, creative and traditional pasta and entrees are dependably well prepared. A pianist entertains Tuesday-Saturday evenings. Casual dress. Entertainment. **Bar:** Full bar. **Reservations:** suggested. **Hours:** 11 am-10:30 pm, Fri & Sat-11:30 pm, Sun 4 pm-10:30 pm. Closed: 11/27, 12/25; also Super Bowl Sun. **Address:** 1860 Laskin Rd 23454 **Location:** I-264, exit Laskin Rd (SR 58), 0.3 mi e; in La Promenade Shops. **Parking:** on-site. **Cards:** AX, DC, DS, MC, VI.

ALEXANDER'S ON THE BAY   **Phone:** 757/464-4999   1

Steak & Seafood
$17-$33

The romantic setting on the shore of Chesapeake Bay is noted for beautiful night views of the illuminated bridge. A breezy deck encourages leisurely dining. Creative preparations of seafood, as well as tender steak and veal, mark an impressive menu. Valet parking weekend and seasonally. Dressy casual. **Bar:** Full bar. **Reservations:** suggested. **Hours:** 5 pm-9 pm, Fri & Sat-10 pm. Closed: 1/1, 12/25. **Address:** 4536 Ocean View Ave 23455 **Location:** Jct US 60 and 13, 0.3 mi w to Pleasure House Rd, 1 mi n to Lookout Rd, then 0.3 mi e to Fentress Rd to end. **Parking:** on-site. **Cards:** AX, DC, DS, MC, VI.

ATLAS GRILL & BAR   **Phone:** 757/430-2839

American
$5-$20

Hungry diners munch on heaping portions of comfort food that shows heavy Southern and diner-style influences. Topping the menu are great stick-to-the-ribs dishes, such as meatloaf, chicken pot pie and pork chops, as well as burgers and salads. Casual dress. **Bar:** Full bar. **Hours:** 11 am-10 pm, Fri & Sat-11 pm. Closed: 11/27, 12/25. **Address:** 2135 General Booth Blvd 23454 **Location:** Jct London Bridge Rd; in Strawbridge Marketplace. **Parking:** on-site. **Cards:** AX, MC, VI.

(See maps and indexes p. 734-736, 738-741, 742-744)

ATLAS GRILL & BAR
Phone: 757/496-3839

American
$6-$17

Hungry diners munch on heaping portions of comfort food that shows heavy Southern and diner-style influences. Topping the menu are great stick-to-the-ribs dishes, such as meatloaf, chicken pot pie and pork chops, as well as burgers and salads. Casual dress. **Bar:** Full bar. **Reservations:** accepted. **Hours:** 11 am-10 pm, Fri & Sat-11 pm. Closed: 11/27, 12/25. **Address:** 2158 Greak Neck Square Shopping Center 23454 **Location:** On Great Neck Rd at jct First Colonial Rd. **Parking:** on-site. **Cards:** AX, MC, VI.

AZAR'S NATURAL FOODS
Phone: 757/486-7778

Middle Eastern
$5-$15

A loyal, growing clientele in search of healthful, well-prepared Middle Eastern fare calls the eatery home. Roll sandwiches, delicatessen offerings and many vegetarian items are specialties, although meat is available. Try the lentil, orzo and vegetable soup, or grab items to go from the market section. Casual dress. **Bar:** Beer & wine. **Hours:** 9 am-8:30 pm, Fri-9:30 pm, Sat 10 am-9:30 pm. Closed major holidays; also Sun. **Address:** 108 Prescott Ave 23452 **Location:** I-264, exit 17B (Independence Blvd), just e on Bonney Rd. **Parking:** on-site. **Cards:** AX, DS, MC, VI.

BAKER'S CRUST BREAD MARKET
Phone: 757/422-6703

American
$5-$16

First and foremost, this place is the home of crusty bread loaves and sweet bakery treats. Lunch favorites include interesting sandwiches and daily soup in edible bread bowl, while dinner offerings lean to more sophisticated fare, such as steak, seafood and rotisserie fowl. Seating at the crepe bar in the rear is a special treat. Casual dress. **Bar:** Full bar. **Hours:** 7 am-9 pm, Fri & Sat-10 pm, Sun-5 pm. Closed: 1/1, 11/27, 12/25. **Address:** 704 Hilltop North Shopping Center 23451 **Location:** I-264, exit 21, just n to Hilltop North; 3 mi w of oceanfront on Laskin Rd. **Parking:** on-site. **Cards:** AX, DS, MC, VI.

BANGKOK GARDEN
Phone: 757/425-4909

Thai
$6-$17

Thai artwork decorates the stylish interior of this cozy restaurant. On the menu is fresh, healthy fare prepared with fresh seafood, chili peppers, curries, coconuts, tropical fruit and vegetables. Casual dress. **Bar:** Full bar. **Hours:** 11 am-10 pm, Fri-10:30 pm, Sat noon-10:30 pm, Sun noon-9 pm. Closed major holidays. **Address:** 737 First Colonial Rd 23451 **Location:** I-264, exit 21, just n; in Hilltop Market Plaza. **Parking:** on-site. **Cards:** DS, MC, VI.

BANGKOK GARDEN
Phone: 757/498-5009

Thai
$6-$17

Thai artwork decorates the stylish interior of this cozy restaurant. On the menu is fresh, healthy fare prepared with fresh seafood, chili peppers, curries, coconuts, tropical fruit and vegetables. Casual dress. **Bar:** Full bar. **Hours:** 11 am-10 pm, Fri-10:30 pm, Sat noon-10:30 pm, Sun noon-9 pm. Closed major holidays. **Address:** 4000 Virginia Beach Blvd 23452 **Location:** I-264, exit 17B (Independence Blvd/Pembroke), just n to US 58, then just e; in Loehmann's Plaza. **Parking:** on-site. **Cards:** AX, DC, DS, MC, VI.

BEACH BULLY
Phone: 757/422-4222 (45)

Barbecue
$4-$19

Locals and tourists alike love the laid-back restaurant for its tangy North Carolina-style barbecue. The establishment is just a few blocks from the oceanfront strip. Casual dress. **Bar:** Beer & wine. **Reservations:** accepted. **Hours:** 10 am-8 pm, Fri & Sat-9 pm; to 9 pm, Fri & Sat-10 pm in summer. Closed: 3/23, 12/25. **Address:** 601 19th St 23451 **Location:** Jct Mediterrenean St; just w of oceanfront. **Parking:** on-site. **Cards:** AX, DC, DS, MC, VI.

BEACH PUB
Phone: 757/422-8817 (28)

Seafood
$5-$14

This is an easy-to-locate eatery near the beach, specializing in ample portions of fresh seafood and American dishes for a good price. Side dishes include steak fries, coleslaw, prepared salad, and vegetables. The family atmosphere is casual. Casual dress. **Bar:** Full bar. **Hours:** 6:30 am-11 pm. Closed: 11/27, 12/24, 12/25. **Address:** 1001 Laskin Rd 23451 **Location:** 1 mi w of oceanfront. **Parking:** on-site. **Cards:** AX, DS, MC, VI.

BEALE STREET
Phone: 757/481-2000 (7)

Barbecue
$5-$23

Tennessee style barbecue in all forms appear here-chicken, ribs, pork, shrimp, and even nachos at this warm and friendly spot where the menu also includes fried catfish and chili. Casual dress. **Bar:** Full bar. **Hours:** 11 am-10 pm, Fri & Sat-11 pm. Closed: 3/23, 11/27, 12/25; also Sun. **Address:** 2916 Shore Dr 23451 **Location:** Jct W Great Neck Rd. **Parking:** on-site. **Cards:** AX, DS, MC, VI.

BELLA MONTE
Phone: 757/425-6290 (32)

Italian
$6-$22

Superlatives abound: "excellent" pasta and salad "marvelous" pastry and "great" gourmet pizza. The gourmet cafe and market offers updated Italian cuisine, including rotisserie, in an artistically stylish dining room. Patio dining is available in season. Casual dress. **Bar:** Full bar. **Reservations:** suggested, Fri & Sat. **Hours:** 11 am-9 pm, Fri & Sat-10 pm. Closed major holidays; also Sun. **Address:** 1201 Laskin Rd, Suite 100 23451 **Location:** 1.5 mi w on US 58 from ocean; in Birdneck Point Commons. **Parking:** on-site. **Cards:** DS, MC, VI.

(See maps and indexes p. 734-736, 738-741, 742-744)

BLACK ANGUS RESTAURANT
Phone: 757/428-7700   (19)

A local favorite for more than 40 years, the restaurant brings the finest steaks to the oceanfront. Those seeking something other than Choice beef might consider crab cakes, local seafood (which comes with shrimp cocktail) and some Greek and Italian specialties. Limited free parking is in the adjacent lot. Casual dress. **Bar:** Full bar. **Hours:** 4:30 pm-10 pm, Fri & Sat-10:30 pm. Closed: 12/25-12/27. **Address:** 706 Atlantic Ave 23451 **Location:** I-264, 1 mi s of terminus; between 7th and 8th sts. **Parking:** on-site (fee). **Cards:** AX, DS, MC, VI.

Steak House
$10-$27

THE BOARDWOK RESTAURANT
Phone: 757-426-1700

Part tropical bar and part Chinese restaurant, the eatery is the spot for everything from Hunan chicken and wonton soup to grilled fish, island-style. Casual dress. **Bar:** Full bar. **Reservations:** accepted. **Hours:** 11:30 am-9 pm. Closed: Sun. **Address:** 1993 Sandbridge Rd 23456 **Location:** Jct Princess Anne and Sandbridge rds. **Parking:** on-site. **Cards:** AX, MC, VI.

Chinese
$5-$22

CALL

BOMBAY PARADISE
Phone: 757/631-2111   (57)

The setting is sultry and exotic at the new Indian restaurant, where diners sample specialties from both Northern and Southern India. Among choices are flavorful curries, vindaloos, lamb and fluffy breads baked in house. Casual dress. **Hours:** 11:30 am-3 & 5-10 pm. **Address:** 4000 Virginia Beach Blvd 23452 **Location:** I-264, exit 17B (Independence Blvd), just n to Virginia Beach Blvd (US 58), 0.5 mi e; in Loehmann's Plaza. **Parking:** on-site. **Cards:** AX, DS, MC, VI.

Indian
$8-$19

CALL

BUBBA'S CRABHOUSE & SEAFOOD RESTAURANT
Phone: 757/481-3513   (13)

This waterfront spot offers prime view of the Lynnhaven Inlet's waters and features the freshest catch from its waters such as crab cakes, shrimp, and even a fresh tuna salad and softshell crabs in season. Casual dress. **Bar:** Full bar. **Hours:** 11 am-10 pm, Fri & Sat-11 pm, Sun 8:30 am-10 pm. Closed: 11/27, 12/25. **Address:** 3323 Shore Dr 23451 **Location:** US 60, 2.5 mi e of jct US 13; at east end of Lynnhaven Inlet Bridge. **Parking:** on-site. **Cards:** AX, DC, DS, MC, VI.

Seafood
$6-$18

CABO CAFE
Phone: 757-216-2095   (8)

The chic lounge gets a crowd of partygoers but also serves great food. Most dishes are served tapas style in appetizer-size portions for sharing. Among house specialties are meatballs, churrasco beef, seviche-style seafood and fried tomatoes with mozzarella. Also offered are burgers, wings and other traditional bar food. Casual dress. **Bar:** Full bar. **Hours:** 5 pm-2 am. **Address:** 2301 Red Tide Rd 23451 **Location:** On Shore Dr, just w of jct N Great Neck Rd. **Parking:** on-site. **Cards:** AX, DC, DS, MC, VI.

American
$6-$16

CALL

CAPTAIN GEORGE'S SEAFOOD RESTAURANT
Phone: 757/428-3494

An extensive, all-you-can-eat seafood buffet—which includes everything from Alaskan crab legs and shrimp to prime rib and dessert—satisfies even the heartiest of appetites. Nautical accents such as ropes and fish nets convey the oceanic feel. Casual dress. **Bar:** Full bar. **Hours:** 4 pm-10:30 pm, Sat 3:30 pm-11 pm, Sun noon-10:30 pm. Closed: 12/25. **Address:** 1956 Laskin Rd 23454 **Location:** I-264, exit Laskin Rd (US 58), 3.5 mi w of oceanfront. **Parking:** on-site. **Cards:** AX, MC, VI.

Seafood
$19-$26

CALL

CASBY'S SEA GRILL
Phone: 757/962-4783   (5)

Casby's offers a large, inviting interior lined with nostalgic resort scenes. Patrons also can choose a table on the covered sidewalk patio to watch the changing street scene. A modern menu offers a wide range of salads, sandwiches and entrees. Specialties include the scallops "Dunn" right, which are pan-seared atop a shrimp potato cake, and a flounder filet topped with lump crab and a white wine sauce. Other delicious options are fried oysters, crab cakes and a traditional she crab soup served with a side of sherry. Casual dress. **Bar:** Full bar. **Reservations:** accepted. **Hours:** 11 am-10 pm, Fri & Sat-11 pm. Closed: 11/27, 12/25. **Address:** 3316 Atlantic Ave 23451 **Location:** I-264, terminus, 1 mi n to 33rd St. **Parking:** on-site. **Cards:** AX, MC, VI.

Seafood
$9-$18

CALL

CATCH 31 FISH HOUSE & BAR
Phone: 757/213-3472   (10)

A favorite night spot, this high-energy establishment offers a large patio overlooking live music at Neptune's Park, the boardwalk and the beach. The menu offers a wide variety of fresh seafood, including favorites from the raw bar. Casual dress. Entertainment. **Bar:** Full bar. **Reservations:** accepted. **Hours:** 6 am-11 pm. **Address:** 3001 Atlantic Ave 23451 **Location:** I-264, 0.5 mi n of terminus; in Hilton Virginia Beach Oceanfront. **Parking:** on-site (fee). **Cards:** AX, CB, DC, DS, JC, MC, VI.

Seafood
$8-$22

CALL

(See maps and indexes p. 734-736, 738-741, 742-744)

CENTRAL 111

American
$5-$15

Phone: 757/222-1022 (44)
The hip new tapas bar presents an all-appetizer menu. A stylish scene of singles sips custom martinis and samples such offerings as baby lamb chops and seared tuna. Casual dress. **Bar:** Full bar. **Reservations:** accepted. **Hours:** 5 pm-3 am. **Address:** 401 N Great Neck Rd, Suite 111 23454 **Location:** Just n of jct US 58/Virginia Beach Blvd; in Renaissance Place. **Parking:** on-site. **Cards:** AX, MC, VI.

CHICK'S OYSTER BAR

Seafood
$8-$23

Phone: 757/481-5757 (14)
Some come by land, while others just tie their boats at one of the restaurant's waterfront decks. Among specialties are fried shrimp, local shellfish and fresh crabs. Not only are the water views spectacular, but the people-watching also is good. Casual dress. **Bar:** Full bar. **Hours:** 11 am-10 pm, Fri & Sat-11 pm, Sun 10 am-9 pm; Sunday brunch. Closed: 11/27, 12/25. **Address:** 2143 Vista Cir 23451 **Location:** US 60, 2.5 mi e of jct US 13; at east end of the Lynnhaven Inlet Bridge, then just s. **Parking:** on-site. **Cards:** AX, DS, MC, VI.

CITRUS
American
$5-$10

Phone: 757/227-3333 (10)
Citrus is a casual lunch and breakfast spot that caters to the local seaside community. Specialties include crab Benedict, omelets, eggwiches, salads, sandwiches and daily soup and blue plate specials. But don't forget the fantastic pancakes, in varieties from potato to citrus-glazed. Casual dress. **Bar:** Full bar. **Hours:** 7 am-3 pm. Closed: 3/23, 12/25. **Address:** 2265 W Great Neck Rd 23451 **Location:** Just s of jct Shore Dr (US 60). **Parking:** on-site. **Cards:** AX, MC, VI.

COASTAL GRILL

American
$13-$23

Phone: 757/496-3348 (21)
Such highlights as lamb with eggplant puree, spinach salad with chicken livers, pepper-crusted tuna and soft-shell crab are served in an understated bistro punctuated by white tablecloths and handsome artwork. Reservations are not accepted, but neighborhood regulars don't seem to mind the wait. Casual dress. **Bar:** Full bar. **Hours:** 5:30 pm-11 pm, Sat from 5 pm, Sun 5 pm-9:45 pm. Closed major holidays. **Address:** 1427 N Great Neck Rd 23454 **Location:** 3 mi n of jct Laskin Rd and US 58; 3 mi s of jct Shore Dr; in Mill Dam Crossing. **Parking:** on-site. **Cards:** AX, MC, VI.

COBALT GRILLE

American
$6-$27

Phone: 757/333-3334 (34)
The stylish and contemporary bistro has quickly become a trendy haunt. From the curved bar up front to the open chrome kitchen, the style is hip and modern. The cuisine also is cutting edge, with global and regional influences. Dressy casual. **Bar:** Full bar. **Reservations:** accepted. **Hours:** 11 am-2:30 & 5-10 pm, Fri & Sat-11 pm. Closed: Sun. **Address:** 1624 Laskin Rd, Suite 762 23451 **Location:** I-264, exit 21, just n in Hilltop North; 3 mi w of Oceanfront/Atlantic Ave via Laskin Rd in Hilltop North Shopping Center. **Parking:** on-site. **Cards:** AX, DC, DS, MC, VI.

CONKLIN'S IRISH ROVER

Irish
$4-$19

Phone: 757/631-1294 (55)
The cozy, family-run neighborhood pub puts forth a menu of more sophisticated "gastro-pub" interpretations of Irish and English specialties, including lamb meatloaf, seared salmon over poached potatoes and cabbage, sauteed mussels and clams, and potato croquettes. Casual dress. **Bar:** Full bar. **Reservations:** accepted. **Hours:** 11 am-2 am, Sun 10 am-midnight. **Address:** 3157 Virginia Beach Blvd 23452 **Location:** I-264, exit 18 (Rosemont Rd), 1 mi e; in Village Shops at Rose Hall. **Parking:** on-site. **Cards:** AX, DS, MC, VI.

COYOTE CAFE & CANTINA

Southwest American
$6-$23

Phone: 757/425-8705 (26)
Unusually modern Southwestern cuisine, often using the region's fresh local seafood, takes the spotlight. Light fare such as quesadillas is offered as well as many tasty, creative entrees. The atmosphere is lively, bustling and fun, with friendly service. Casual dress. **Bar:** Full bar. **Reservations:** suggested. **Hours:** 11:30 am-2:30 & 5-10:30 pm, Fri-midnight, Sat 5 pm-midnight, Sun 5 pm-10:30 pm. Closed: 11/27, 12/24, 12/25. **Address:** 972-A Laskin Rd 23451 **Location:** 1 mi w of oceanfront on 31st/Laskin Rd; in Linkhorn Shoppes. **Parking:** on-site. **Cards:** AX, DC, DS, MC, VI.

CROAKERS

Seafood
$10-$20

Phone: 757/363-2490 (12)
In the heart of the local-favorite beach, the casual restaurant naturally serves the freshest local seafood. Specialties include a seafood roll-up, blackened tuna and fish St. Charles. Casual dress. **Bar:** Full bar. **Reservations:** suggested. **Hours:** 5 pm-10 pm. Closed: 1/1, 11/27, 12/24, 12/25; also Super Bowl Sun. **Address:** 3629 Shore Dr 23455 **Location:** US 60, 2 mi e of jct US 13. **Parking:** on-site. **Cards:** AX, DC, DS, MC, VI.

CROC'S 19TH STREET BISTRO

American
$10-$22

Phone: 757/428-5444 (48)
With environmentally friendly decor, Croc's offers a lively and colorful environment and a nightlife scene to match. The menu shows such traditional favorites as burgers and chicken wings as well as more sophisticated choices like fine steaks and local seafood. Try wonderful crab cakes, five-pepper grilled tuna or choose one of a few Middle Eastern appetizers. A cigar patio and a hookah bar also are available. Casual dress. **Bar:** Full bar. **Reservations:** accepted. **Hours:** 4 pm-10 pm. Closed: 11/27, 12/25. **Address:** 620 19th St 23451 **Location:** I-264 terminus at Cypress Ave, just e of Virginia Beach Convention Center. **Parking:** on-site. **Cards:** AX, DS, MC, VI.

(See maps and indexes p. 734-736, 738-741, 742-744)

CUISINE & COMPANY
American
$5-$10

Phone: 757/428-6700 (13)

Known locally for its elegant catered affairs, the cafe offers similar gourmet delights in a casual setting. Chose from inventive gourmet sandwiches, zesty prepared salad and sinful dessert. Casual dress. **Bar:** Beer & wine. **Hours:** 9 am-7 pm, Sun-6 pm. Closed: 1/1, 11/27, 12/25. **Address:** 3004 Pacific Ave 23451 **Location:** Just w of jct 31st St (Laskin Rd). **Parking:** on-site.

DOC TAYLOR'S
American
$5-$10

Phone: 757/425-1960 (15)

Sitting in a turn-of-the-century clapboard cottage, Doc Taylor's mixes the nostalgia of a beach cottage with a diner-style, open chrome kitchen. Enjoy breakfast all day and such tasty lunch sandwiches and salads as patty melts and crab cakes. A seat on the large front porch affords the chance to watch the sidewalk traffic. Casual dress. **Bar:** Full bar. **Hours:** 7 am-3 pm. **Address:** 207 23rd St 23451 **Location:** I-264, exit terminus, just n; between Pacific and Atlantic aves. **Parking:** on-site. **Cards:** AX, DS, MC, VI.

CALL 🔊M

DOUGH BOY'S CALIFORNIA PIZZA
Pizza
$3-$12

Phone: 757/422-6111

Part of the fun, tropical atmosphere at this spot is its sidewalk patio, which overlooks the activity of Atlantic Avenue. Specialty pizzas come with a variety of creative toppings, from Thai-flavored shrimp to Santa Fe chicken. We recommend you start with Mom's large Greek salad or the cheesy breadsticks. Casual dress. **Bar:** Full bar. **Hours:** 11 am-1 am; to 10 pm off season. Closed: 1/1, 11/27, 12/25. **Address:** 1700 Atlantic Ave 23451 **Location:** I-264, just n of terminus. **Parking:** no self-parking. **Cards:** AX, DC, DS, MC, VI.

🚫

DOUGH BOYS CALIFORNIA PIZZA
Pizza
$5-$20

Phone: 757/425-7108

Casual dress. **Bar:** Full bar. **Hours:** 11 am-1 am; to 9 pm off season. Closed: 11/27, 12/25. **Address:** 2410 Atlantic Ave 23451 **Location:** I-264, just n of terminus. **Parking:** no self-parking. **Cards:** AX, DC, DS, MC, VI.

🚫

EL AZTECA MEXICAN RESTAURANT
Mexican
$5-$14

Phone: 757/473-1746 (50)

The restaurant prepares one of the widest varieties of Mexican cuisine around. In addition to standard favorites, the menu lists more adventurous offerings, including chicken in mole sauce—a rich and savory sauce derived from the cocoa bean. Entrees are fresh, delicious and served quickly. Casual dress. **Bar:** Full bar. **Hours:** 11 am-10 pm, Sun noon-9 pm. Closed major holidays. **Address:** 314 Constitution Dr 23462 **Location:** I-264, exit 17B (Independence Blvd), just n to Virginia Beach Blvd, just e to Constitution Dr, then just n. **Parking:** on-site. **Cards:** DS, MC, VI.

🚫

FEDERICO'S
Italian
$8-$25

Phone: 757/497-1445 (46)

The casually elegant restaurant's menu centers on dependable favorites, such as veal parmigiana and pasta al vodka. Piano music adds to the weekend atmosphere. Casual dress. **Bar:** Full bar. **Reservations:** suggested, weekends. **Hours:** 11 am-9:30 pm, Fri-10:30 pm, Sat noon-10:30 pm, Sun 4 pm-9 pm. Closed major holidays; also Mon. **Address:** 357 Independence Blvd 23462 **Location:** I-264, exit 17B (Independence Blvd), just n; in Pembroke Plaza. **Parking:** on-site. **Cards:** DS, MC, VI.

🚫

FIVE 0 1 CITY GRILL
American
$7-$21

Phone: 757/425-7195 (40)

Enjoy a regularly revised menu of contemporary food, typified by such specialties as Michelob shrimp and baked goat cheese with roasted garlic & prosciutto-wrapped lamb chops. The New York-style restaurant, a hot spot with the trendy beach crowd, lists an impressive inventory of wine. Casual dress. **Bar:** Full bar. **Reservations:** suggested, weekends. **Hours:** 4 pm-10 pm. Closed: 1/1, 11/27, 12/24, 12/25. **Address:** 501 N Birdneck Rd 23451 **Location:** I-264, exit exit 22 (Birdneck Rd), n to Birdneck Shoppes. **Parking:** on-site. **Cards:** AX, MC, VI.

CALL 🔊M 🚫

FORBIDDEN CITY IMPERIAL DINING
Chinese
$6-$20

Phone: 757/747-2388 (61)

Upscale in the dining room and more casual in the lounge, the Chinese restaurant specializes in Cantonese and Szechuan preparations. Offerings include a tasty assortment of stuffed won tons, dim sum and vegetarian dishes. For a special evening, guests can reserve the "tree house" table, which is its own private perch. Casual dress. **Bar:** Full bar. **Reservations:** accepted. **Hours:** 11:30 am-9 pm, Fri & Sat-10 pm. **Address:** 3333 Virginia Beach Blvd, Suite 17 23452 **Location:** I-264, exit 18 (Rosemont Rd), just n to Virginia Beach. **Parking:** on-site. **Cards:** AX, DC, DS, MC, VI.

CALL 🔊M 🚫

GRINGO'S TAQUERIA
Mexican
$6-$11

Phone: 757/961-2987 (63)

This tiny, colorful spot just blocks from the beach offers delicious soft tacos and burritos with stuffings that range from pork to fried fish. Tasty house-made chips are offered with a variety of fresh salsas, including pineapple jalapeno salsa. Casual dress. **Bar:** Beer & wine. **Hours:** 11 am-9 pm. Closed: Sun & Mon. **Address:** 612 Norfolk Ave, Suite 109 23451 **Location:** 0.5 mi w of Atlantic Ave via 9th St. **Parking:** on-site. **Cards:** MC, VI.

(See maps and indexes p. 734-736, 738-741, 742-744)

GUADALAJARA MEXICAN BAR & GRILL
Mexican
$6-$16

Phone: 757/481-5511

A bustling nightlife atmosphere prevails on the neon-lit patio. The menu lists not only traditional Mexican specialties but also coastal dishes, such as grilled fish tacos. Casual dress. **Bar:** Full bar. **Reservations:** accepted. **Hours:** 11 am-2 am. **Address:** 2272 W Great Neck Rd 23451 **Location:** Jct Shore Dr/US 60. **Parking:** on-site. **Cards:** AX, CB, DC, DS, MC, VI.

GUADALAJARA RESTAURANTE MEXICANO
Mexican
$6-$13

Phone: 757/491-1613

This original location of a popular local chain serves as a lively venue for meeting friends and enjoying traditional Mexican cuisine and cocktails. Casual dress. **Bar:** Full bar. **Hours:** 11 am-10 pm. Closed: 11/27, 12/25. **Address:** 509 Hilltop Plaza 23454 **Location:** I-264, exit 20 Laskin Rd (US 58), just e. **Parking:** on-site. **Cards:** AX, DS, MC, VI.

GUADALAJARA RESTAURANTE MEXICANO
Mexican
$6-$16

Phone: 757/433-0140

Just off the main resort strip, the simple spot has a large sidewalk cafe perfect for people-watching. On the menu are Mexican standards, as well as pork carnitas, spinach dip and a wide variety of frozen tropical drinks. Casual dress. **Bar:** Full bar. **Hours:** noon-2 am. Closed: 11/27, 12/25. **Address:** 200 21st St 23451 **Location:** I-264, terminus; between Pacific and Atlantic aves. **Parking:** on-site (fee). **Cards:** AX, DS, MC, VI.

GUADALAJARA TROPICAL CAFE
Mexican
$6-$15

Phone: 757/563-2926

Colorful tropical decor comes together with sleek diner features, including neon lights, glossy tile and a train riding the rails overhead. The menu mixes Mexican dishes and combination plates that are familiar to many but expands to include this place's own specialties: fish, shrimp and pork soft tacos, shrimp seviche and more fresh seafood offerings. Casual dress. **Bar:** Full bar. **Hours:** 11 am-10:30 pm, Sat & Sun noon-10 pm. Closed: 11/27, 12/25. **Address:** 2149 General Booth Blvd 23454 **Location:** Jct London Bridge Rd; in Strawbridge Marketplace. **Parking:** on-site. **Cards:** AX, CB, DS, MC, VI.

H2O
American
$10-$21
(11)

Phone: 757/496-2528

The hot and spicy, down-home operation knocks your socks off with an impressive variety of chilies, cooked in styles ranging from Cincinnati to Texas and vegetarian. Casual dress. **Bar:** Full bar. **Reservations:** suggested. **Hours:** 5 pm-10 pm, Fri & Sat-midnight. Closed major holidays. **Address:** 3152 Shore Dr 23454 **Location:** US 60, 2.8 mi e of jct US 13. **Parking:** on-site. **Cards:** AX, DC, DS, MC, VI.

HAVANA
American
$10-$25
(22)

Phone: 757/496-3333

The hip, innovative menu takes much inspiration from Cuban cuisine but is not centered on traditional fare. Of note is pork tenderloin with soy/citrus glaze and the tropical flavors of the salade de casa. Cigars are welcomed, and a nightly tapas happy hour from 5 pm-7 pm offers a wide range of appetizers. Casual dress. **Bar:** Full bar. **Reservations:** suggested, weekends. **Hours:** 5 pm-10 pm, Fri & Sat-11 pm. Closed: 1/1, 11/27, 12/25; also Sun. **Address:** 1423 Great Neck Rd 23454 **Location:** 3 mi s of Shore Dr; in Mill Dam Crossing. **Parking:** on-site. **Cards:** AX, DS, MC, VI.

THE HERITAGE HEALTH FOOD CAFE & DELI
Vegetarian
$5-$10
(9)

Phone: 757/428-0500

Beachgoers and locals know the grocery and delicatessen is the spot to find many vegetarian and organic favorites, including sandwiches, smoothies and fresh-squeezed juices. A few poultry and seafood offerings are available. Casual dress. **Reservations:** not accepted. **Hours:** 10 am-6:40 pm, Fri-7:40 pm, Sat-6:40 pm, Sun noon-6:40 pm. Closed: 1/1, 11/27, 12/25. **Address:** 314 Laskin Rd 23451 **Location:** Jct 31st St/Laskin Rd and Pacific Ave. **Parking:** on-site. **Cards:** DS, MC, VI.

HOT TUNA BAR & GRILL
Seafood
$7-$27
(6)

Phone: 757/481-2888

The fun spot is colorfully decorated with glittering papier-mache fish hanging from the ceiling and offers a lively crowd and live entertainment on the weekends. Obviously fresh tuna—Parmesan-seared, sesame-fired, sashimi-style or in fajitas—is a specialty. Other house favorites include burgers, crab cakes and grilled steaks. Casual dress. **Bar:** Full bar. **Reservations:** accepted. **Hours:** 4 pm-11 pm, Fri & Sat-midnight. Closed: 11/27, 12/25. **Address:** 2817 Shore Dr 23451 **Location:** Just N Great Neck Rd; in Cape Henry Plaza. **Parking:** on-site. **Cards:** AX, MC, VI.

THE HUNT ROOM GRILL
Regional American
$20-$30
(1)

Phone: 757/425-8555

In the early days of this historic hotel, male guests would retire here after hunting to gather around the enormous hearth, drink brandy and roast game. The roaring fire is still the main draw since the dining room is open only in winter months. The menu centers on hearty fare, such as lamb, duck, steak and, of course, the region's famed seafood. Dressy casual. **Entertainment. Bar:** Full bar. **Reservations:** suggested. **Hours:** Open 3/1-3/31 & 1/3-2/28; 6 pm-10 pm, Fri & Sat-11 pm. Closed: Sun-Tues. **Address:** 42nd and Pacific 23451 **Location:** I-264, terminus, to Pacific Ave, 2 mi n; in The Cavalier on the Hill. **Parking:** on-site. **Cards:** AX, DC, DS, MC, VI.

(See maps and indexes p. 734-736, 738-741, 742-744)

IL GIARDINO
Italian
$11-$47
Phone: 757/422-6464 [18]
A loyal following frequents the exciting, upscale restaurant. An excellent selection of pasta, veal, seafood, chicken and brick-oven pizza appeals to many tastes. The freshly made tiramisu is a rich, decadent delight. A pianist plays on Saturday night. Dressy casual. Entertainment. **Bar:** Full bar. **Reservations:** suggested, weekends. **Hours:** 5 pm-11 pm, Sat-11:30 pm, Sun-10:30 pm. Closed: 11/27, 12/25. **Address:** 910 Atlantic Ave, Suite 200 23451 **Location:** I-264, terminus, 0.5 mi s to 10th St. **Parking:** on-site. **Cards:** AX, CB, DC, DS, MC, VI.

IMPERIO INCA
Peruvian
$8-$18
Phone: 757/486-4622 [67]
In a suburban strip mall, the tiny, humble spot shares the flavors of Peru in affordable dishes. Seviche, an excellent start to the menu, is best accented by pisco sour, the country's official drink. Another good way to kick off the meal is with house-roasted corn nuts and an Inca cola. Diners might follow an entree of rotisserie chicken or adobe pork loin with tres leches cake. Casual dress. **Bar:** Full bar. **Reservations:** accepted. **Hours:** 5 pm-10 pm, Sat 11 am-10 pm, Sun 11 am-8 pm. Closed major holidays; also Mon. **Address:** 865 Chimney Hill Shopping Center 23452 **Location:** I-264, exit 18 (Rosemont Rd), 1 mi s to jct Holland Rd; in Chimney Hill Shopping Center. **Parking:** on-site. **Cards:** MC, VI.

ISLE OF CAPRI
Italian
$15-$25
Phone: 757/428-2411 [2]
Perched six floors up, the upscale, attractive restaurant boasts gorgeous views of the ocean below. Chef Pasqual has been serving up his Mediterranean specialities since 1952, but now in a new home. Menu highlights include Spagetti alla Sangiovannio, Calamerdti di Napoli and Veal Sicilian. Dressy casual. **Bar:** Full bar. **Reservations:** suggested. **Hours:** 5 pm-10 pm. Closed: 11/27, 12/24, 12/25. **Address:** 3900 Atlantic Ave 23451 **Location:** I-264, 2 mi n from terminus; at Atlantic Ave and 39th St; in Holiday Inn SunSpree Resort. **Parking:** valet. **Cards:** AX, DC, DS, MC, VI.

JENNA'S MEDITERRANEAN DELI
Mediterranean
$5-$8
Phone: 757/460-0973 [17]
The decor is decidedly humble, but guests shouldn't let that steer them away. The menu offers excellent Greek dishes from hummus and gyros to baba ghanoush and pita bread. Regulars often buy extra to take home. Casual dress. **Hours:** 10:30 am-8 pm, Thurs-Sat to 9 pm. Closed major holidays; also Sun. **Address:** 2104-I Pleasure House Rd 23455 **Location:** Jct Shore Dr; in Bayside Shopping Center. **Parking:** on-site. **Cards:** DS, MC, VI.

THE JEWISH MOTHER
Deli/Subs
Sandwiches
$5-$10
Phone: 757/422-5430 [8]
The oceanfront mainstay has been serving great delicatessen sandwiches, noshes, smoked fish and thick milkshakes to local teens and music lovers for years. Adding to the lively atmosphere are walls decorated in crayon scribbles and a coloring book menu. Casual dress. Entertainment. **Bar:** Full bar. **Hours:** 8 am-9 pm, Thurs-Sat to 2 am. **Address:** 3108 Pacific Ave 23451 **Location:** I-264, 1 mi n at Pacific Ave, jct 31st St. **Parking:** on-site. **Cards:** AX, DC, DS, MC, VI.

KELLY'S TAVERN
American
$7-$20
Phone: 757/497-3940
The casual chain is a local favorite for such simple specialties as burgers, Buffalo wings, fish tacos, salads and sandwiches. Casual dress. **Bar:** Full bar. **Hours:** 11 am-1 am. Closed: 11/27, 12/25. **Address:** 1830 Kempsville Rd 23464 **Location:** I-64, exit 286B (Indian River Rd), 1 mi s to Kempsville Rd, then 0.5 mi s; in Kemps Wood Shopping Center. **Parking:** on-site. **Cards:** AX, DS, MC, VI.

KELLY'S TAVERN
American
$7-$20
Phone: 757/491-8737
The casual chain is a local favorite for such simple specialties as burgers, Buffalo wings, fish tacos, salads and sandwiches. Casual dress. **Bar:** Full bar. **Hours:** 11 am-1 am. Closed: 11/27, 12/25. **Address:** 1936 Laskin Rd, Suite 201 23454 **Location:** I-264, exit 20 (Laskin Rd), just e; in Regency Hilltop Shopping Center. **Parking:** on-site. **Cards:** AX, DS, MC, VI.

KELLY'S TAVERN
American
$7-$20
Phone: 757/490-7999
The casual chain is a local favorite for such simple specialties as burgers, Buffalo wings, fish tacos, salads and sandwiches. Casual dress. **Bar:** Full bar. **Hours:** 11 am-1 am. Closed: 11/27, 12/25. **Address:** 4554 Virginia Beach Blvd, Suite 790 23462 **Location:** I-264, exit 17B (Independence Blvd), just n to Virginia Beach Blvd, then just e; in Pembroke Mall. **Parking:** on-site. **Cards:** AX, DS, MC, VI.

KELLY'S TAVERN
American
$7-$20
Phone: 757/430-8999
The casual chain is a local favorite for such simple specialties as burgers, Buffalo wings, fish tacos, salads and sandwiches. Casual dress. **Bar:** Full bar. **Hours:** 11 am-1 am. Closed: 11/27, 12/25. **Address:** 2129 General Booth Blvd, Suite 130 23454 **Location:** Jct London Bridge Rd; in Strawbridge Marketplace. **Parking:** on-site. **Cards:** AX, DS, MC, VI.

LA BELLA ITALIA TRATTORIA
Italian
$7-$19
Phone: 757/422-8536 [31]
Patrons who make it past the delightful bakery and deli-case offerings up front will find a peaceful dining room. Traditional flavors punctuate such dishes as black pepper linguine with clams, brick-oven pizzas and veal saltimbocca. Casual dress. **Bar:** Full bar. **Reservations:** suggested. **Hours:** 11:30 am-2:30 & 5-10 pm, Fri & Sat-11 pm. Closed major holidays; also Sun. **Address:** 1065 Laskin Rd 23451 **Location:** 1.2 mi w on US 58 (31st St) from oceanfront; in Laskin Center. **Parking:** on-site. **Cards:** AX, DS, MC, VI.

(See maps and indexes p. 734-736, 738-741, 742-744)

LA CASA DELLA PASTA
Phone: 757/518-2600 66

Italian
$8-$16

This staff starts cooking every morning at 5 a.m. to make Italian breads, cookies, pastries, and mozzarella cheese from scratch. Traditional Italian favorites include pastas, seafood and veal dishes. Casual dress. **Bar:** Full bar. **Reservations:** accepted. **Hours:** 11 am-9 pm, Fri & Sat-10 pm, Sun noon-8 pm. **Address:** 485 S Independence Blvd 23452 **Location:** I-264, 17A (Independence/Princess Anne Area), just s to Larkspur Village. **Parking:** on-site. **Cards:** AX, DS, MC, VI.

CALL M

LA MARINELLA TRATTORIA ITALIANA
Phone: 757/412-0203 16

Italian
$7-$18

In a bustling upscale marina, the restaurant comprises two bars, where locals often opt to eat to best enjoy the scene, and a cozy, wood-paneled dining room with a large stone hearth on one end. Menu options—such as pizza, calzones, pasta dishes and entrees centered on fine meats and fresh seafood—run from casual to fine dining. Casual dress. **Bar:** Full bar. **Reservations:** accepted. **Hours:** 11 am-11 pm, Sat from noon, Sun noon-10 pm. Closed: Mon. **Address:** 2105 W Great Neck Rd 23451 **Location:** Just s of US 60/Shore Dr; in Long Bay Pointe Boating Resort. **Parking:** on-site. **Cards:** MC, VI.

THE LUCKY STAR
Phone: 757/363-8410 18

American
$7-$35

The dining room is casual and coolly elegant, an intimate setting in which to savor seasonally changing dishes, such as mustard-grilled lamb chops and bundled leeks with roast duck and goat cheese. Also delightful are the exciting appetizers and enticing desserts. Casual dress. **Bar:** Full bar. **Reservations:** suggested. **Hours:** 11:30 am-2:30 & 5:30-10 pm, Sat from 5:30. Closed: 1/1, 11/27, 12/25; also Sun. **Address:** 1608 Pleasure House Rd 23455 **Location:** Jct Northampton Blvd, just sw; in Thoroughgood Center. **Parking:** on-site. **Cards:** AX, DS, MC, VI.

LYNNHAVEN FISH HOUSE RESTAURANT
Phone: 757/481-0003 4

Seafood
$8-$35

Perched on the rolling dunes of Chesapeake Bay, the cozy restaurant, a longtime popular spot, has big picture windows that overlook the beach. Fresh, high-quality seafood—much of which is presented in more creative preparations—rarely disappoints. Excellent she crab soup served traditionally with a hint of sherry. Dressy casual. **Bar:** Full bar. **Hours:** 11:30 am-10:30 pm. Closed: 11/27, 12/25. **Address:** 2350 Starfish Rd 23451 **Location:** Just n of US 60; 2.8 mi e of jct US 13. **Parking:** on-site. **Cards:** AX, CB, DC, DS, MC, VI.

CALL M

MACHISMO BURRITO BAR
Phone: 757/422-6010 39

Mexican
$5-$8

The simple spot's excellent burritos are custom made to diners' specifications. Guests can choose their favorite meat or meat alternative, vegetables and even flavored wraps. Tuna is coming soon. Casual dress. **Hours:** 11 am-9 pm. Closed: 11/27, 12/25. **Address:** 525 N Birdneck Rd 23451 **Location:** I-264, exit 22 (Birdneck Rd), just n to Birdneck Shoppes. **Parking:** on-site. **Cards:** MC, VI.

CALL M

MAHI MAH'S SEAFOOD RESTAURANT & SUSHI SALOON
Phone: 757/437-8030 20

Seafood
$5-$21

Loud, hip crowds gather at the oceanfront eatery, which offers traditional and innovative sushi as well as fresh, grilled seafood, pasta, and raw-bar items. Open-air patio seating is in high demand in pleasant weather. Late night menu until 12:30 am. Entertainers perform seasonally. Casual dress. **Bar:** Full bar. **Reservations:** suggested. **Hours:** 7 am-11 pm. Closed: 12/25. **Address:** 615 Atlantic Ave 23451 **Location:** I-264, 1 mi s of terminus; at Atlantic Ave and 6th St; in Ramada On the Beach. **Parking:** valet. **Cards:** AX, DC, DS, MC, VI. *(See color ad p 791)*

MARY'S RESTAURANT
Phone: 757/428-1355 51

American
$3-$6

A local favorite for more than 40 years, the cozy spot offers such down-home favorites as country-fried steak, barbecue and homemade soup. Desserts include a mouthwatering array of cakes and pies. On the all-day breakfast menu are the Old Virginia homemade biscuits, omelets and pancakes. Casual dress. **Hours:** 6 am-3 pm. Closed: 11/27, 12/25. **Address:** 616 Viginia Beach Blvd 23451 **Location:** W of Atlantic Ave, on 17th St. **Parking:** on-site. **Cards:** MC, VI.

MAYFLOWER CAFE
Phone: 757/417-0117 4

Mediterranean
$5-$21

The dining room is small and the kitchen even tinier, but that doesn't stop the chef from turning out great Turkish-Mediterranean fare. Pita bread is fluffy, light and always warm; the gyros savory; and the daily specials always fresh and delicious. Casual dress. **Bar:** Wine only. **Reservations:** accepted. **Hours:** 11 am-9 pm, Sun from 5 pm. Closed: 7/4, 11/27, 12/25. **Address:** 209 34th St 23451 **Location:** I-264, to Pacific Ave, then 1.5 mi n; in Mayflower Apartments. **Parking:** street. **Cards:** DS, MC, VI.

MISAKO SUSHI BAR & GRILLE
Phone: 757/631-6831 59

Japanese
$5-$18

Locals love the weekday lunch buffet of sushi specialties and other Japanese favorites at this stylish spot; dinner offers table service and an even wider array of delicacies. Casual dress. **Bar:** Full bar. **Hours:** 11:30 am-2:30 & 4:30-9:30 pm, Fri & Sat-10:30 pm. **Address:** 4000 Virginia Beach Blvd 23452 **Location:** I-264, exit 17B (Independence Blvd), just n to Virginia Beach Blvd (US 58), then 0.5 mi e; in Loehmann's Plaza. **Parking:** on-site. **Cards:** MC, VI.

CALL M

MIZUNO JAPANESE RESTAURANT
Phone: 757/422-1200 36

Japanese
$7-$18

Elegantly prepared Japanese cuisine is sophisticated but sometimes unfamiliar, as in the case of the seaweed salad. The sparse decor in the front dining room is soothing, and private seating is offered in the back. Sushi lovers flock to the bar to watch the chefs in action. Casual dress. **Bar:** Beer & wine. **Reservations:** suggested, weekends. **Hours:** 11:30 am-2 & 5:30-9:30 pm, Fri & Sat-10 pm. Closed major holidays; also Sun & Mon. **Address:** 1860 Laskin Rd, Suite 120 23454 **Location:** I-264, exit Laskin Rd (US 58), 0.3 mi e; in La Promenade Shops. **Parking:** on-site. **Cards:** AX, MC, VI.

(See maps and indexes p. 734-736, 738-741, 742-744)

NAWAB INDIAN RESTAURANT
Phone: 757/491-8600

Indian
$8-$19

Tandoor specialties and bread baked in a clay oven are at the centerpiece of a traditional menu of curried, lamb and vegetarian dishes. The upscale atmosphere features artwork and instrumental music. A weekday buffet draws a devoted lunch clientele. Casual dress. **Bar:** Full bar. **Reservations:** accepted. **Hours:** 11:30 am-2:30 & 5-10 pm, Fri-10:30 pm, Sat noon-3 & 5-10:30 pm, Sun noon-3 pm. **Address:** 756 First Colonial Rd 23451 **Location:** I-264, exit 21, just n; adjacent to Hilltop North. **Parking:** on-site. **Cards:** AX, DC, DS, MC, VI.

NO FRILL BAR & GRILL
Phone: 757/425-2900

American
$7-$20

The shiny chrome and neon exterior recalls a diner, but inside the offerings are more modern: sandwiches, salads, burgers and such house specialties as award-winning ribs, famous chili and other barbecue dishes. Chalkboard specials shine with creativity and fresh seasonal influences. Casual dress. **Bar:** Full bar. **Hours:** 11 am-10 pm, Fri & Sat-11 pm; Sunday brunch. Closed: 11/27, 12/25. **Address:** 1620 Laskin Rd 23451 **Location:** 3 mi w of oceanfront; at Hilltop North Shopping Center. **Parking:** on-site. **Cards:** AX, MC, VI.

CALL

ONE FISH TWO FISH
Phone: 757/496-4350   (15)

Seafood
$17-$32

Trendy and bright with a distinct Californian feel. Walls of windows showcase excellent views of the Lynnhaven River and passing boats, or sit on the covered open-air patio and enjoy the gentle breezes and lovely sunsets. A shiny chrome exhibition kitchen on the other side of the curved bar turns out market-inspired regional seafood with a creative and modern flair. Dressy casual. **Bar:** Full bar. **Reservations:** suggested. **Hours:** 5 pm-10 pm. Closed: 1/1, 11/27, 12/25. **Address:** 2109 W Great Neck Rd 23454 **Location:** Just s of US 60/Shore Dr; in Long Bay Pointe Boating Resort at the Pier House. **Parking:** on-site. **Cards:** AX, MC, VI.

CALL

OSAKA JAPANESE RESTAURANT
Phone: 757/428-8609   (47)

Japanese
$6-$20

This small sushi bar is conveneintly located blocks from the beach and the convention center. Traditional and creative rolls, noodle soups, and tempura items are favorites of regulars. Casual dress. **Bar:** Full bar. **Hours:** 11:30 am-2:30 & 4:30-10 pm, Fri & Sat-11 pm, Sun 5 pm-10 pm. **Address:** 1807 Mediterranean Ave 23451 **Location:** Jct 19th St. **Parking:** on-site. **Cards:** AX, DS, MC, VI.

PHO 79
Phone: 757/687-7844   (52)

Vietnamese
$3-$8

At the heart of the menu is pho, a traditional noodle soup sometimes called the national dish of Vietnam. Large bowls of steaming soup, each accented with beef or other meats and seasoned with herbs and sauces, are satisfying and healthy. Several generations of the family are warm and hospitable. Spring rolls, interesting desserts and drinks are also noteworthy. Casual dress. **Reservations:** not accepted. **Hours:** 10 am-9 pm, Fri & Sat-10 pm, Sun-8 pm. **Address:** 4816 Virginia Beach Blvd 23462 **Location:** I-264, exit 17B (Independence Blvd), just w. **Parking:** on-site. **Cards:** AX, DC, DS, MC, VI.

PIER CAFE
Phone: 757/481-5950   (5)

Seafood
$6-$15

The most popular seats in the fun and frivolous eatery on the pier are in the open-air area that sits right over the water. Although brief, the menu's good, with raw-bar items, a cheese board for two, fantastic she crab soup and grilled yellowfin tuna. Casual dress. Entertainment. **Bar:** Full bar. **Hours:** Open 5/1-10/31; 11:30 am-10:30 pm. **Address:** 2350 Starfish Rd 23451 **Location:** Just n on US 60, 2.8 mi e of jct US 13; on the Lynnhaven fishing pier. **Parking:** on-site. **Cards:** AX, CB, DC, DS, MC, VI.

PI-ZZERIA
Phone: 757/213-0600   (6)

Pizza
$7-$15

The lively, colorful spot presents a lengthy menu of creative pizzas from the wood-burning oven, pasta dishes and easy-to-share appetizers, such as bruschetta and shrimp dip. The sidewalk patio is the place to watch the scene on Atlantic Avenue. Casual dress. **Bar:** Full bar. **Hours:** 11 am-11 pm; to 10 pm off season. Closed: 11/27, 12/25. **Address:** 3316 Atlantic Ave 23451 **Location:** I-264, 0.5 mi n of terminus. **Parking:** on-site. **Cards:** AX, CB, DS, JC, MC, VI.

CALL

PLAZA AZTECA MEXICAN RESTAURANT
Phone: 757/425-1676   (38)

Mexican
$6-$13

This large restaurant's bright, festive decor includes neon-lit palm trees out front. A big menu includes all your Mexican favorites, from tacos to tamales, combination plates and seafood dishes. Casual dress. **Bar:** Full bar. **Hours:** 11 am-10 pm, Fri-11 pm, Sat noon-11 pm, Sun noon-9:30 pm. Closed: 11/27, 12/25. **Address:** 1824 Laskin Rd 23454 **Location:** I-264, exit 20 Laskin Rd (SR 58), 0.3 mi e. **Parking:** on-site. **Cards:** AX, CB, DC, DS, JC, MC, VI.

CALL

POLLARD'S CHICKEN
Phone: 757/340-2565   (54)

American
$5-$7

There's nothing fancy about the fried chicken, barbecue and seafood on the down-to-earth restaurant's menu, but they sure are good. Inexpensive, casual and enjoyable, the experience here is a great one for families. The honey puffs shouldn't be missed. Casual dress. **Hours:** 10 am-9 pm. Closed: 11/27, 12/25. **Address:** 100 London Bridge Center 23454 **Location:** 4 mi w of Oceanfront via US 58/Virginia Beach Blvd at N Great Neck Rd; in London Bridge Shopping Center. **Parking:** on-site. **Cards:** AX, MC, VI.

(See maps and indexes p. 734-736, 738-741, 742-744)

THE PURPLE COW

American
$5-$10

Phone: 757/233-7269 27

The 1950s-themed rock 'n' roll diner features favorites from the grill—including burgers and wraps—as well as soda fountain standbys. The setting welcomes families. Casual dress. **Bar:** Full bar. **Reservations:** accepted. **Hours:** 11 am-9 pm, Fri-10 pm, Sat 10 am-10 pm, Sun 10 am-9 pm. Closed: 1/1, 11/27, 12/25. **Address:** 981 Laskin Rd 23451 **Location:** Just w of Oceanfront/Atlantic Ave via 31st St. **Parking:** on-site. **Cards:** AX, DS, MC, VI.

CALL M

THE RAVEN

American
$6-$20

Phone: 757/425-1200 17

This long-established "locals" spot offers steak, local seafood, sandwiches and burgers. The patio dining area overlooking "the strip" is great for people watching and makes the lively atmosphere and internationally seen T-shirts a special treat. Casual dress. **Bar:** Full bar. **Hours:** noon-2 am. **Address:** 1200 Atlantic Ave 23451 **Location:** 12th St and Atlantic Ave. **Parking:** on-site. **Cards:** AX, CB, DC, DS, MC, VI.

RED STAR TAVERN

American

Phone: 757/473-3295

The stylish American grill is a popular watering hole for many area office workers. The interior is chic and cool, and the menu offers a modern twist on such American favorites as the wedge salad, skillet corn bread, Angus burgers, seafood macaroni and cheese and roasted salmon. Casual dress. **Bar:** Full bar. **Reservations:** accepted. **Hours:** 11 am-2 am. Closed: 11/27, 12/25. **Address:** 201 Town Center Dr 23462 **Location:** I-261, exit 17B (Independence Blvd), just n to Virginia Beach Blvd, then just e; in Town Center. **Parking:** on-site. **Cards:** AX, CB, DC, DS, JC, MC, VI.

CALL M

REGINELLA'S ITALIAN RISTORANTE & PIZZERIA   *Menu on AAA.com*

Italian
$5-$15

Phone: 757/498-9770 58

Authentic Italian specialties are the offerings at this cozy family spot, which is owned and operated by natives of Napoli. Try excellent pasta, Napoletana or Sicilian pizza and stromboli. Bookend your entree with tempting antipasto and mouthwatering tiramisu. Casual dress. **Bar:** Full bar. **Hours:** 11 am-10 pm, Sun noon-9 pm. Closed major holidays. **Address:** 4000 Virginia Beach Blvd 23452 **Location:** I-264, exit 17B (Independence Blvd) to SR 58, 0.5 mi e to Loehmann's Plaza. **Parking:** on-site. **Cards:** AX, DS, MC, VI.

ROCKAFELLER'S

Seafood
$8-$25

Phone: 757/422-5654 64

Overlooking the sparkling waters and marinas of Rudee Inlet, this restaurant is a beautiful spot in which to enjoy local seafood such as crabcakes, flounder, and more. Casual dress. **Bar:** Full bar. **Reservations:** not accepted. **Hours:** 11 am-10 pm, Sun from 10 am; Sunday brunch. Closed: 11/27, 12/25. **Address:** 308 Mediterranean Ave 23451 **Location:** I-264, terminus, 1.3 mi s to Rudee Inlet. **Parking:** on-site. **Cards:** AX, DC, DS, MC, VI.

CALL M

ROCKFISH BOARDWALK BAR & SEA GRILL

American
$6-$22

Phone: 757/213-7625 16

A rock 'n' roll attitude reigns at the colorful beachside spot, made a fast local favorite for its patio and private "dining pods." Guests can sample any of the three varieties of crab cakes, hushpuppies, burgers and grilled seafood, which are served in mammoth portions, while watching the action both inside and out. Casual dress. **Bar:** Full bar. **Reservations:** suggested. **Hours:** 11 am-1 am, Sat & Sun from 8 am; hours vary off season. Closed: 1/1, 11/27, 12/25; also Mon off season. **Address:** 1601 Atlantic Ave 23451 **Location:** I-264, terminus, just s to 16th St; in Boardwalk Resort Hotel and Villas. **Parking:** no self-parking. **Cards:** AX, DC, DS, MC, VI.

RUDEE'S ON THE INLET   *Menu on AAA.com*

Seafood
$7-$37

Phone: 757/425-1777 65

The open, airy, nautical-themed decor goes well with the menu: fried or broiled fresh seafood served inside or on the outdoor deck overlooking the inlet and marina. The marinated tuna steak and sweet potato chips are delicious at this popular eatery. Casual dress. **Bar:** Full bar. **Hours:** 11 am-midnight, Sun 10 am-11 pm. Closed: 11/27, 12/25. **Address:** 227 Mediterranean Ave 23451 **Location:** I-264, terminus, 1.3 mi s. **Parking:** on-site. **Cards:** AX, DC, DS, MC, VI.

SAIGON 1 RESTAURANT

Vietnamese
$6-$10

Phone: 757/518-0307 29

The setting couldn't be more simple at the humble spot, which serves a wide variety of fresh and healthy Vietnamese fare. Among specialties are pho noodle soups, rice paper rolls and grilled meats, including quail. Wash down the food with a trendy bubble tea. Casual dress. **Bar:** Beer & wine. **Hours:** 11 am-10 pm. Closed major holidays. **Address:** 448 Newtown Rd 23462 **Location:** I-264, exit Newtown Rd, just n at jct Virginia Beach Blvd. **Parking:** on-site. **Cards:** AX, DS, MC, VI.

SAKURA SUSHI BAR

Japanese
$6-$20

Phone: 757/428-2899 3

This bright, airy spot near the oceanfront hotels serves delicious traditional and innovative offerings from the sushi bar, as well as other wonderful Japanese dishes, including tempura, teriyaki and noodle preparations. Casual dress. **Bar:** Beer & wine. **Hours:** noon-3 & 4:30-10:30 pm, Sat & Sun 1 pm-10 pm. **Address:** 3623-3627 Pacific Ave 23451 **Location:** I-264, terminus, 1.5 mi n to 37th St. **Parking:** on-site. **Cards:** DS, MC, VI.

CALL M

(See maps and indexes p. 734-736, 738-741, 742-744)

SALACIA

Steak House
$25-$45

Phone: 757/213-3472 11

Salacia at the Hilton is classic New York steakhouse meets the beach. Sit in on leather banquettes in the cool dining room or at romantic patio tables overlooking the beach. Specialties include steaks, including rare, Kobe-style beef, fresh international seafood and raw bar specialties, and classic tableside preparations of Caesar salad and bananas Foster. Dressy casual. **Bar:** Full bar. **Reservations:** required. **Hours:** 5 pm-11 pm. **Address:** 3001 Atlantic Ave 23451 **Location:** I-264, 0.5 mi n of terminus; in Hilton Virginia Beach Oceanfront. **Parking:** valet. **Cards:** AX, CB, DC, DS, JC, MC, VI.

CALL

SHOGUN JAPANESE STEAK HOUSE & SEAFOOD

Japanese
$11-$28

Phone: 757/422-5150 41

Teppanyaki chefs entertain patrons tableside at the Shogun and cook up quite a good meal. Steak and seafood are the specialties and each entree is accompanied by a shrimp appetizer, salad with ginger dressing, and soup. There's also a sushi bar. Casual dress. **Bar:** Full bar. **Reservations:** suggested, Fri & Sat. **Hours:** 5 pm-10 pm, Fri & Sat-11 pm. **Address:** 550 First Colonial Rd 23451 **Location:** I-264, exit 21 (First Colonial Rd), just n to K-Mart Plaza. **Parking:** on-site. **Cards:** AX, DS, MC, VI.

SILVER DINER

American
$5-$15

Phone: 757/499-3600

The eatery with its chrome and glass plate exterior and the glow of neon, provides the traditional diner setting. Booths with juke boxes, counter service and friendly wait staff add to the diner experience. The menu is extensive with salads, sandwiches and full meals. The desserts are made fresh and the fountain treats, shakes, floats and malts make for a great ending. Breakfast is available all day. Casual dress. **Bar:** Full bar. **Hours:** 6 am-11 pm, Thurs-Sat to midnight, Sun-10 pm. Closed: 12/25. **Address:** 4401 Virginia Beach Blvd 23462 **Location:** I-264, exit 17B (Independence Blvd) eastbound to US 58, just n. **Parking:** on-site. **Cards:** AX, DS, MC, VI.

CALL

SMOKEHOUSE & COOLER

American
$8-$20

Phone: 757/481-9737 9

Although the decor says "casual sports bar," the menu shows a creativity not found elsewhere. Excellent smoked meats—such as chicken and grilled seafood—abound, and even a smoked beef egg roll is a delicious choice. Steak with homemade barbecue sauce is an excellent selection. Casual dress. **Bar:** Full bar. **Reservations:** accepted. **Hours:** 5 pm-1:30 am. **Address:** 2957 Shore Dr 23451 **Location:** Jct Great Neck Rd, just w; in Lynnhaven Beach Square shopping center. **Parking:** on-site. **Cards:** AX, DS, MC, VI.

STEINHILBER'S THALIA ACRES INN

Seafood
$18-$40

Phone: 757/340-1156 30

Family-owned and operated since 1939, the former country club is charming for its mahogany paneling, vaulted ceiling and riverfront location. The signature dish is fried fantail jumbo shrimp, but the fabulous she crab soup and grilled fresh fish are other good choices. Attentive servers show obvious signs of formal training. Patio dining by the water is available in season. Dressy casual. **Bar:** Full bar. **Hours:** 5 pm-10 pm. Closed: 11/27, 12/24, 12/25; also Sun. **Address:** 653 Thalia Rd 23452 **Location:** I-264, exit 18 (Rosemont Rd) westbound; exit 17B (Independence Blvd) eastbound to US 58 (Virginia Beach Blvd), 1 mi n. **Parking:** on-site. **Cards:** AX, CB, DC, DS, MC, VI.

STELLA GOURMET PIZZERIA

Pizza
$7-$14

Phone: 757/963-5883 19

Patrons sit down in a sparse glistening white space to nosh on excellent gourmet pizza with a wide variety of traditional and gourmet toppings, such as pear Gorgonzola, wild mushrooms, and goat cheese and garlic. Also enticing are bountiful salads, big bowls of spaghetti, and gelato for dessert. Casual dress. **Bar:** Beer & wine. **Hours:** 11:30 am-9 pm, Fri & Sat-10 pm. **Address:** 1608 Pleasure House Rd, Suite 101 23455 **Location:** Jct Northampton Blvd, just sw; in Thoroughgood Center. **Parking:** on-site. **Cards:** AX, DS, MC, VI.

CALL

SURF CLUB OCEAN GRILLE

Seafood
$6-$29

Phone: 757/425-5699 20

Dressy casual. **Bar:** Full bar. **Reservations:** suggested. **Hours:** 7 am-9 pm; to 10 pm in summer. Closed major holidays. **Address:** 57th St & Atlantic Ave 23451 **Location:** I-264, 2.2 mi n of terminus; in Wyndham Virginia Beach Oceanfront. **Parking:** on-site. **Cards:** AX, DC, DS, MC, VI. *(See color ad p 798)*

CALL

SURFRIDER GRILL AT CYPRESS POINT

Seafood
$6-$18

Phone: 757/497-3534 25

Patrons of the beloved local chain know they consistently can find fresh local Atlantic Ocean and Chesapeake Bay seafood prepared in the traditional manner. Offerings include grilled tuna, fried or stuffed flounder, fried shrimp and broiled crab cakes, which are made without fillers. All are best accented by crowns of steamed broccoli with fresh hollandaise. Casual dress. **Bar:** Full bar. **Hours:** 11 am-9:30 pm, Fri & Sat-10:30 pm. Closed major holidays. **Address:** 928 Diamond Springs Rd 23455 **Location:** 1.8 mi s of jct Northampton Blvd. **Parking:** on-site. **Cards:** AX, DS, MC, VI.

CALL

SURFRIDER GRILL AT MARINA SHORES

Seafood
$7-$17

Phone: 757/481-5646

Fresh, simply prepared seafood is the draw at the casual open-air restaurant overlooking a marina. Local boaters and fishermen can't get enough of the daily catch, fresh crab cakes and spears of broccoli topped with fresh hollandaise. Casual dress. **Bar:** Full bar. **Hours:** Open 4/1-10/1; 4 pm-10 pm, Sat 11 am-11 pm, Sun 11 am-9 pm. Closed major holidays. **Address:** 2100 Marina Shores Dr 23451 **Location:** Off N Great Neck Rd, just s of jct Shore Dr; in Marina Shores. **Parking:** on-site. **Cards:** AX, CB, DC, DS, JC, MC, VI.

CALL

(See maps and indexes p. 734-736, 738-741, 742-744)

SURF RIDER RESTAURANT

Seafood
$5-$17

Phone: 757/422-1703   ⑫

Simply prepared, fresh seafood is key at this casual restaurant. Locals love the reasonably priced crab cakes, fried flounder and fresh broccoli with hollandaise as well as the daily assortment of homemade pies. Just blocks from the beach, the large deck overlooking a small creek is an ideal spot to wait for your table on busy nights. Casual dress. **Bar:** Full bar. **Hours:** 11 am-9:30 pm, Fri & Sat-10 pm, Sun-9 pm. **Address:** 550 Laskin Rd 23451 **Location:** 0.5 mi w of oceanfront via 31st St. **Parking:** on-site. **Cards:** AX, DS, MC, VI.

CALL 🕭M

SUSHI & WEST

Japanese
$5-$20

Phone: 757/631-1004   ㊸

Patrons can be tame and stick to the traditional sushi rolls, but the real fun here is in being adventurous and sampling the creative dishes chef Kim invents daily. Among the innovations are seafood noodle cocktail, panko-crusted sashimi tuna and tuna dome. Casual dress. **Bar:** Full bar. **Hours:** 11:30 am-2:30 & 5-9:30 pm, Fri & Sat-10 pm, Sun 5 pm-9:30 pm. Closed major holidays. **Address:** 401 N Great Neck Rd 23454 **Location:** 4 mi w of oceanfront via US 58/Virginia Beach Blvd, just n; in Renaissance Shoppes. **Parking:** on-site. **Cards:** AX, DC, DS, MC, VI.

CALL 🕭M

SWAN TERRACE

American
$17-$38

Phone: 757/366-5700   ㉗

The large, Colonial dining room, centered around a warm hearth, is decorated with attractive pine trim. French doors open to a porch that overlooks the lake. Dishes employ fresh, local ingredients. Honest, friendly servers go out of their way to please. Dressy casual. **Bar:** Beer & wine. **Reservations:** accepted. **Hours:** 7-10 am, 11:30-2 & 5:30-9 pm, Mon-2 pm. **Address:** 5641 Indian River Rd 23464 **Location:** I-64, exit 286B, just e; in The Founders Inn and Spa. **Parking:** on-site. **Cards:** MC, VI.

CALL 🕭M

TAD'S DELI

Deli/Subs
Sandwiches
$6-$10

Phone: 757/422-3577   ㉖

The smoker is the star of this small delicatessen, which turns out its own smoked tuna, mahi mahi, roast beef, chicken and pork. Guests can order their favorites in an overstuffed sandwich or straight with sides such as macaroni and cheese, potato salad or baked beans. Casual dress. **Bar:** Beer & wine. **Hours:** 10 am-6 pm. Closed: 11/27, 12/25. **Address:** 600 Norfolk Ave 23451 **Location:** 0.5 mi w of Atlantic Ave, jct Mediterranean Ave. **Parking:** on-site. **Cards:** AX, MC, VI.

CALL 🕭M

TASTE UNLIMITED

Gourmet Grocery
$4-$7

Phone: 757/422-3399

Casual dress. **Hours:** 10 am-7 pm, Sun-6 pm; to 8 pm 5/31-9/5. Closed: 1/1, 11/27, 12/25. **Address:** 3603 Pacific Ave 23451 **Location:** 1 blk w of Atlantic Ave. **Parking:** on-site. **Cards:** AX, MC, VI.

TAUTOG'S
Seafood
$10-$19

Phone: 757/422-0081   ⑭

In a historic cedar-shingle cottage with a wide veranda that provides lots of open-air seating, the small spot presents a casual menu of fresh and tasty seafood, as well as some land specialties. Casual dress. **Bar:** Full bar. **Hours:** 5:30 pm-11:30 pm, Thurs-Sat to 11 pm. Closed: 1/1, 11/27, 12/25; also Super Bowl Sun. **Address:** 205 23rd St 23451 **Location:** Oceanfront; between Atlantic and Pacific aves. **Parking:** on-site. **Cards:** AX, DS, MC, VI.

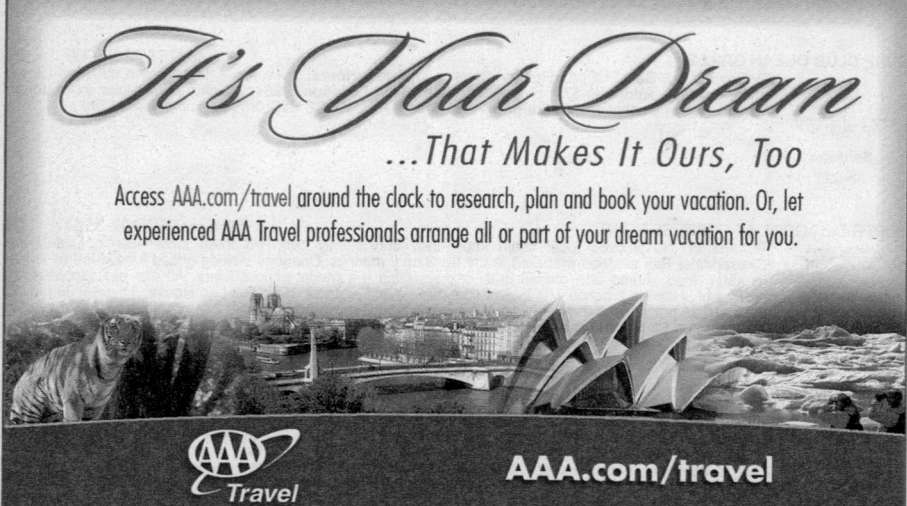

(See maps and indexes p. 734-736, 738-741, 742-744)

TIMBUKTU

American
$6-$22

Phone: 757/491-1800 ⑦

Swift service and incredible food, such as sea creatures and assorted veggies circling a bed of garlic mashed potatoes daubed with basil and chive pesto and tomato vinaigrette. Tempting desserts is an understatement. Valet parking is available in season. Casual dress. **Bar:** Full bar. **Reservations:** suggested, weekends. **Hours:** 7-10:30 am, 11:30-3 & 5-9 pm, Fri & Sat-10 pm. Closed: 12/25. **Address:** 3101 Atlantic Ave 23451 **Location:** I-264, 0.8 mi n of terminus; just n of jct Laskin Rd (SR 58) at 32nd St; in Days Inn Oceanfront. **Parking:** on-site. **Cards:** AX, DC, DS, MC, VI.

TRADEWINDS

Continental
$7-$27

Phone: 757/481-9000 ③

A panorama of Chesapeake Bay is available from the dining room of the intimate restaurant. Splendid dishes include lump crab cakes, shrimp and scallop provencal, poached salmon, & seafood Caesar salad. Mouthwatering pastry, bread and dessert are baked on the premises. Dressy casual. **Bar:** Full bar. **Reservations:** suggested, Fri-Sun. **Hours:** 11 am-3 & 5-10 pm, Sat 8 am-11, noon-3 & 5-10 pm, Sun 10 am-2 & 5-10 pm. Closed: 11/27, 12/25; also Mon. **Address:** 2800 Shore Dr 23451 **Location:** US 60, 3.5 mi e of US 13; jct Shore Dr and N Great Neck Rd; in Virginia Beach Resort Hotel & Conference Center. **Parking:** on-site. **Cards:** AX, DC, DS, MC, VI.

CALL

VIETNAM GARDEN

Vietnamese
$6-$19

Phone: 757/631-8048 ㉠

With a light decor highlighted by bamboo and rice paper lanterns, this small spot serves up some of the freshest and healthiest fare around. Start with sesame pancakes and move on to grilled shrimp over noodles or barbecue pork. Casual dress. **Bar:** Beer & wine. **Hours:** 11 am-3 & 5-10 pm, Sat from noon, Sun noon-3 & 5-9 pm. Closed: 11/27, 12/25; also Mon. **Address:** 2404 Virginia Beach Blvd, Suite 114 23454 **Location:** SR 58, just w of jct W Great Neck Rd; in London Bridge Shoppes. **Parking:** on-site. **Cards:** AX, DS, MC, VI.

VOLCANO SUSHI BAR

Japanese
$8-$20

Phone: 757/481-3141 ㉔

The contemporary spot presents a lengthy menu of traditional and creative Japanese dishes, including tuna tartare, crab and avocado salad, tempura selections and udon noodles. The fun variety of sushi rolls incorporates some distinctive fish combinations. Casual dress. **Bar:** Full bar. **Hours:** 11:30 am-2:30 & 4:30-10 pm, Fri & Sat-11 pm. **Address:** 1328 N Great Neck Rd, Suite 106-107 23451 **Location:** Between First Colonial and Mill Dam rds; in Great Neck Shoppes. **Parking:** on-site. **Cards:** MC, VI.

CALL

WARRIOR'S GRILL

Asian
$6-$10

Phone: 757/498-0323 ㊷

Mongolian barbecue is a great alternative to the traditional all-you-can-eat Asian buffet. Diners choose raw vegetables, meats and sauces, then hand them over to the chefs, who grill the tasty fare. Casual dress. **Bar:** Full bar. **Hours:** 11:30 am-10 pm, Fri-11 pm, Sat noon-11 pm, Sun noon-9:30 pm. Closed: 11/27, 12/25. **Address:** 401 N Great Neck Rd 23454 **Location:** 3 mi w of oceanfront; just n of Laskin Rd (SR 58); in Renaissance Place. **Parking:** on-site. **Cards:** AX, DS, MC, VI.

CALL

WATERMAN'S SURFSIDE GRILL   *Menu on AAA.com*

Seafood
$5-$23

Phone: 757/428-3644 ㉑

Specializing in appetizers, dips, raw-bar specialties and lighter versions of seafood dishes, this eatery sports a casual atmosphere in an oceanfront setting. Great views of the boardwalk can be enjoyed from the patio in season. Sunday brunch is offered from October through May. Casual dress. **Bar:** Full bar. **Reservations:** accepted. **Hours:** 11 am-10 pm, Sun 9 am-11 pm. Closed: 11/27, 12/25. **Address:** 415 Atlantic Ave 23451 **Location:** I-264, 1 mi s of terminus, jct 5th St. **Parking:** on-site and valet. **Cards:** AX, CB, DC, DS, MC, VI.

CALL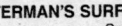

YAMATO STEAK HOUSE

Japanese
$6-$30

Phone: 757/496-8828 ㉓

Skilled teppanyaki chefs entertain guests and cook delicious steak and seafood choices, often highlighting local fresh catches, at the large grill tables. A delightful assortment of sushi also is offered. Casual dress. **Bar:** Full bar. **Reservations:** accepted. **Hours:** 11:30 am-2:30 & 5-10 pm, Sat 5 pm-11 pm. Closed: 11/27. **Address:** 1340 N Great Neck Rd, Suite 1212 23454 **Location:** Between Mill Dam and First Colonial rds. **Parking:** on-site. **Cards:** DS, MC, VI.

ZIA MARIE

Italian
$8-$20

Phone: 757/460-0715 ②

Part trattoria and part barefoot beach cafe, Zia Marie draws a devoted local clientele. House specialties include heaping bowls of pasta, stuffed eggplant and veal saltimbocca. Casual dress. **Bar:** Full bar. **Hours:** 5 pm-10 pm. Closed major holidays. **Address:** 4497 Lookout Rd 23455 **Location:** Jct US 60 and 13, 0.3 mi w to Pleasure House Rd, 1 mi n to Lookout Rd, then just e. **Parking:** on-site. **Cards:** AX, DS, MC, VI.

ZINC BRASSERIE

French
$8-$30

Phone: 757/425-9462 ㉝

This stylish spot emulates the chic brasseries of turn-of-the-century Paris, right down to the imported zinc bar. Authentic French dishes include bouillabaisse, duck confit, escargot, steak tartare, steak au poivre and such nightly specials as cassoulet and coq au vin. The menu also offers a raw bar and diverges into creative territory with dishes like curried lamb shank, olive oil-poached salmon and crab cakes nicoise. Casual dress. **Bar:** Full bar. **Reservations:** required. **Hours:** 11 am-2:30 & 5-10 pm, Sun-9 pm. Closed: 1/1, 11/27, 12/25. **Address:** 741 First Colonial Rd, Suite 107 23451 **Location:** I-264, exit 21B, just n; jct Laskin Rd; in Marketplace at Hilltop. **Parking:** on-site. **Cards:** AX, DS, MC, VI.

CALL

(See maps and indexes p. 734-736, 738-741, 742-744)

ZOE'S　　　　　　　　　　　　　　　　　　　**Phone:** 757/437-3636　　49

Near the oceanfront, the chic and sophisticated new spot presents an intriguing menu of self-proclaimed "fusion steakhouse" fare. A lengthy and distinguished wine list complements the creative, seasonally changing dishes. Dressy casual. **Bar:** Full bar. **Reservations:** suggested. **Hours:** 11:30 am-2:30 & 5-10 pm, Fri & Sat-11 pm, Sun 5 pm-10 pm. Closed: 11/27, 12/25. **Address:** 713 19th St, Suite 102 23451 **Location:** I-264, exit Birdneck Rd, just s to 19th St, then just e; adjacent to Virginia Beach Convention Center. **Parking:** valet. **Cards:** AX, DS, MC, VI.

American
$5-$40

CALL 🖖M

ZUSHI JAPANESE BISTRO　　　　　　　　　**Phone:** 757/321-1495　　56

Casual dress. **Bar:** Full bar. **Reservations:** accepted. **Hours:** 11:30 am-10 pm, Fri-11 pm, Sat noon-11 pm, Sun noon-9 pm. **Address:** 4540 Main St 23462 **Location:** I-264, exit 17B (Independence Blvd), just n to Virginia Beach Blvd, then just e in Town Center. **Parking:** street. **Cards:** MC, VI.

Japanese
$8-$23

————— *The following restaurants have not been evaluated by AAA* —————
but are listed for your information only.

TASTE UNLIMITED　　　　　　　　　　　　**Phone:** 757/425-1858

[fyi]　　Not evaluated. **Address:** 638 Hilltop West 23454 **Location:** 3 mi w of oceanfront; jct Laskin and First Colonial rds; in Hilltop West Shopping Center.

TASTE UNLIMITED-BAYVILLE　　　　　　　**Phone:** 757/464-1566

[fyi]　　Not evaluated. **Address:** 4097 Shore Dr 23455 **Location:** Jct US 13, 1 mi e.

Endview Plantation / Newport News Tourism Development Office

This ends listings for the Hampton Roads Area.
The following page resumes the alphabetical listings of cities in Virginia.

HANOVER —See Richmond p. 880.

HARRISONBURG pop. 40,468

——— WHERE TO STAY ———

BEST WESTERN HARRISONBURG INN   *Book great rates at AAA.com*   Phone: 540/433-6089

Small-scale Hotel
Rates not provided

Address: 45 Burgess Rd 22801 **Location:** I-81, exit 247A, just e on US 33. **Facility:** 98 one-bedroom standard units, some with whirlpools. 3 stories, exterior corridors. *Bath:* combo or shower only. **Parking:** on-site. **Amenities:** high-speed Internet, voice mail, irons, hair dryers. **Pool(s):** heated indoor. **Leisure Activities:** sauna, whirlpool, exercise room. **Guest Services:** valet and coin laundry. **Business Services:** meeting rooms, business center. **Free Special Amenities:** expanded continental breakfast and high-speed Internet.

AAA Benefit:
Members save 10% everyday, plus an exclusive frequent stay program.

COMFORT INN   *Book great rates at AAA.com*   Phone: (540)433-6066

Small-scale Hotel
$79-$130 All Year

Address: 1440 E Market St 22801 **Location:** I-81, exit 247A, just e. **Facility:** 102 one-bedroom standard units, some with whirlpools. 2 stories (no elevator), interior corridors. *Bath:* combo or shower only. **Parking:** on-site. **Amenities:** irons, hair dryers. **Pool(s):** outdoor. **Leisure Activities:** exercise room. **Guest Services:** valet laundry, wireless Internet. **Cards:** AX, CB, DC, DS, JC, MC, VI. **Free Special Amenities:** expanded continental breakfast and high-speed Internet.

COURTYARD BY MARRIOTT-HARRISONBURG   *Book great rates at AAA.com*   Phone: 540/432-3031

Small-scale Hotel
$122-$152 3/1-11/20
$121-$141 11/21-2/28

Address: 1890 Evelyn Byrd Ave 22801 **Location:** I-81, exit 247A, 0.6 mi e on US 33 to University Blvd, then just w. **Facility:** Smoke free premises. 125 one-bedroom standard units, some with whirlpools. 4 stories, interior corridors. *Bath:* combo or shower only. **Parking:** on-site. **Amenities:** high-speed Internet, voice mail, irons, hair dryers. **Pool(s):** heated indoor. **Leisure Activities:** whirlpool, exercise room. **Guest Services:** valet and coin laundry, wireless Internet. **Business Services:** meeting rooms, business center. **Cards:** AX, DC, DS, MC, VI.

AAA Benefit:
Members save 5% off of the best available rate.

DAYS INN HARRISONBURG   *Book great rates at AAA.com*   Phone: (540)433-9353

Small-scale Hotel
$89-$120 3/1-10/31
$79-$110 11/1-2/28

Address: 1131 Forest Hill Rd 22801 **Location:** I-81, exit 245, just e. Truck parking on premises. **Facility:** 89 one-bedroom standard units. 4 stories, interior corridors. **Parking:** on-site. **Amenities:** high-speed Internet, safes, hair dryers. *Some:* irons. **Pool(s):** indoor. **Leisure Activities:** whirlpool, university jogging trail adjacent. **Guest Services:** coin laundry, wireless Internet. **Cards:** AX, DC, DS, MC, VI. **Free Special Amenities:** continental breakfast and newspaper.

HAMPTON INN   *Book great rates at AAA.com*   Phone: 540/432-1111

Small-scale Hotel
Rates not provided

Address: 85 University Blvd 22801 **Location:** I-81, exit 247A, 0.5 mi e on US 33 to University Blvd, then just s. **Facility:** 163 one-bedroom standard units. 4 stories, interior corridors. *Bath:* combo or shower only. **Parking:** on-site. **Amenities:** high-speed Internet, voice mail, irons, hair dryers. *Some:* fax. **Pool(s):** outdoor. **Leisure Activities:** exercise room. **Guest Services:** valet laundry, wireless Internet. **Business Services:** meeting rooms, business center. **Free Special Amenities:** expanded continental breakfast and high-speed Internet.

HARRISONBURG ECONO LODGE   *Book great rates at AAA.com*   Phone: (540)433-2576

Motel
$70-$150 All Year

Address: 1703 E Market St 22801 **Location:** I-81, exit 247A, 0.5 mi e on US 33. **Facility:** 88 one-bedroom standard units, some with whirlpools. 2 stories (no elevator), interior/exterior corridors. **Parking:** on-site. **Amenities:** hair dryers. *Some:.* irons. **Pool(s):** outdoor. **Guest Services:** coin laundry, wireless Internet. **Business Services:** meeting rooms. **Cards:** AX, CB, DC, DS, MC, VI. **Free Special Amenities:** expanded continental breakfast and high-speed Internet.

HOLIDAY INN EXPRESS   *Book great rates at AAA.com*   Phone: 540/433-9999

Small-scale Hotel
Rates not provided

Address: 3325 S Main St 22801 **Location:** I-81, exit 243, just w. **Facility:** 72 one-bedroom standard units, some with whirlpools. 3 stories, interior corridors. *Bath:* combo or shower only. **Parking:** on-site. **Amenities:** high-speed Internet, voice mail, irons, hair dryers. **Pool(s):** heated indoor. **Leisure Activities:** whirlpool, exercise room. **Guest Services:** valet and coin laundry, wireless Internet. **Business Services:** meeting rooms, business center. **Free Special Amenities:** expanded continental breakfast and high-speed Internet.

HOLIDAY INN HARRISONBURG
Book great rates at AAA.com
Phone: 540/433-2521

(AAA) [SAVE]

Small-scale Hotel
Rates not provided

Address: 1400 E Market St 22801 **Location:** I-81, exit 247A, just e on US 33. **Facility:** 140 one-bedroom standard units. 4-5 stories, interior corridors. *Bath:* combo or shower only. **Parking:** on-site. **Amenities:** video games, high-speed Internet, dual phone lines, voice mail, irons, hair dryers. **Dining:** 2 restaurants. **Pool(s):** heated indoor. **Leisure Activities:** exercise room. **Guest Services:** valet laundry, wireless Internet. **Business Services:** conference facilities, business center. **Free Special Amenities:** newspaper and high-speed Internet.

JAMESON INN
Book at AAA.com
Phone: 540/442-1515

Small-scale Hotel
Rates not provided

Address: 1881 Evelyn Byrd Ave 22801 **Location:** I-81, exit 247A, just e. **Facility:** 67 one-bedroom standard units. 3 stories, interior corridors. **Amenities:** high-speed Internet, voice mail, irons, hair dryers. **Pool(s):** outdoor. **Leisure Activities:** exercise room. **Guest Services:** valet laundry. **Business Services:** meeting rooms, business center.

RAMADA LIMITED
Book at AAA.com
Phone: 540/434-9981

Small-scale Hotel
Rates not provided

Address: 1 Pleasant Valley Rd 22801 **Location:** I-81, exit 243, just w, then just n on US 11. **Facility:** 119 one-bedroom standard units. 2 stories (no elevator), exterior corridors. **Parking:** on-site. **Amenities:** voice mail, irons, hair dryers. **Pool(s):** outdoor. **Guest Services:** valet laundry, wireless Internet. **Business Services:** meeting rooms.

SLEEP INN & SUITES
Book great rates at AAA.com
Phone: (540)433-7100

Small-scale Hotel
$85-$185 3/1-11/1
$85-$110 11/2-2/28

Address: 1891 Evelyn Byrd Ave 22801 **Location:** I-81, exit 247A, 0.5 mi e on US 33 to University Blvd, 0.3 mi s to Evelyn Byrd Ave, then just w. **Facility:** 81 one-bedroom standard units. 4 stories (no elevator), interior corridors. *Bath:* combo or shower only. **Parking:** on-site. **Terms:** check-in 4 pm. **Amenities:** high-speed Internet, voice mail, irons, hair dryers. **Leisure Activities:** exercise room. **Guest Services:** coin laundry, wireless Internet. **Business Services:** fax (fee). **Cards:** AX, DS, MC, VI.

STONEWALL JACKSON INN BED & BREAKFAST
Phone: 540/433-8233

Historic Bed
& Breakfast
$119-$179 All Year

Address: 547 E Market St 22801 **Location:** I-81, exit 247, 0.8 mi w on US 33. **Facility:** The inn is centered in the town's historic district in the heart of the Shenandoah Valley; find beautiful garden areas, porches and parlor rooms. 10 one-bedroom standard units. 2 stories (no elevator), interior corridors. *Bath:* shower only. **Parking:** on-site. **Terms:** 3 day cancellation notice-fee imposed. **Amenities:** irons, hair dryers. *Some:* DVD players, CD players. **Leisure Activities:** whirlpool, horseshoes, volleyball. **Guest Services:** wireless Internet. **Business Services:** meeting rooms. **Cards:** AX, DS, MC, VI.

SUPER 8 MOTEL
Book great rates at AAA.com
Phone: 540/433-8888

(AAA) [SAVE]

Motel
Rates not provided

Address: 3330 S Main St 22801 **Location:** I-81, exit 243, just e, then just s on US 11. Located across from truck stop and bus station. **Facility:** 50 one-bedroom standard units. 3 stories (no elevator), interior corridors. **Parking:** on-site. **Amenities:** hair dryers. **Guest Services:** wireless Internet. **Free Special Amenities:** continental breakfast and high-speed Internet.

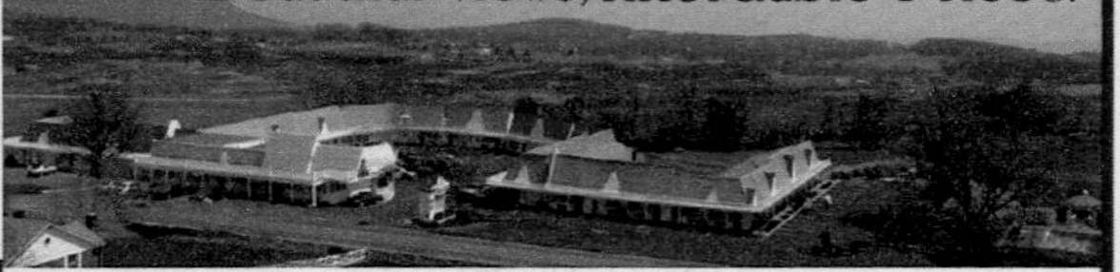

▼ See AAA listing p 815 ▼

THE VILLAGE INN

Small-scale Hotel
$74-$79 All Year

Book great rates at AAA.com **Phone:** (540)434-7355
Address: 4979 S Valley Pike 22801 **Location:** I-81, exit 240 southbound, 0.6 mi w on SR 257, then 1.5 mi n on US 11; exit 243 northbound, just w to US 11, then 1.7 mi s. **Facility:** 37 units. 36 one- and 1 two-bedroom standard units, some with whirlpools. 1 story, exterior corridors. **Parking:** on-site. **Amenities:** DVD players, CD players, high-speed Internet, voice mail, irons, hair dryers. **Pool(s):** outdoor. **Leisure Activities:** whirlpool, putting green, walking trail, playground, shuffleboard. **Guest Services:** valet and coin laundry, wireless Internet. **Business Services:** meeting rooms, fax (fee). **Cards:** AX, CB, DC, DS, JC, MC, VI. **Free Special Amenities:** local telephone calls and preferred room (subject to availability with advance reservations). *(See color ad p 814)*

[icons] FEE ☐ FEE ☐ ☐ / SOME UNITS FEE ☐

The following lodging was either not evaluated or did not meet AAA rating requirements but is listed for your information only.

MASSANUTTEN RESORT HOTEL

[fyi]

Phone: 540/289-4914

Not evaluated. **Address:** Rt 644 (Resort Drive) 22801 **Location:** I-81, exit 247A, 10 mi e on US 33, 2 mi n on SR 644, then 2.5 mi beyond the gatehouse. Facilities, services, and decor characterize a mid-range property.

——— WHERE TO DINE ———

ASIA INN

Chinese
$6-$14

Phone: 540/438-8500

The Asia Inn offers Chinese cuisine with a flair. A huge selection on the menu and a very friendly staff along with a quiet and serene atmosphere. Casual dress. **Bar:** Beer & wine. **Hours:** 11:30 am-10:30 pm, Sun noon-4 pm. **Address:** 2184 John Wayland Hwy 22801 **Location:** 1.7 mi s on SR 42. **Parking:** on-site. **Cards:** AX, CB, DC, DS, JC, MC, VI.

BAR-B-Q RANCH

Barbecue
$5-$15

Phone: 540/434-3296

The barbecue joint goes by the saying, "Pigs are beautiful." Although barbecue dishes stand out, other options also are good. Service is quick and friendly. Casual dress. **Hours:** 11 am-8 pm, Fri & Sat-10:30 pm, Sun noon-9 pm. Closed major holidays. **Address:** 3311 N Valley Pike 22801 **Location:** I-81, exit 251, just w. **Parking:** on-site.

BLUE NILE

Ethiopian
$7-$20

Phone: 540/432-6453

Beautifully decorated mesobs, which are homemade wicker tables, and authentic Ethiopian cuisine await at the restaurant. Casual dress. **Hours:** 11 am-9 pm, Fri & Sat-10 pm, Sun noon-9 pm. Closed: Mon. **Address:** 1251 Virginia Ave 22801 **Location:** 2.1 mi n on SR 42. **Parking:** on-site. **Cards:** MC, VI.

BLUE STONE INN

American
$12-$22

Phone: 540/434-0535

Casual dress. **Bar:** Full bar. **Hours:** 5 pm-9 pm. Closed: 1/1, 12/25; also Sun & Mon. **Address:** 9107 N Valley Pike 22802 **Location:** I-81, exit 251, just w to US 11, then 1.1 mi n on US 11. **Parking:** on-site. **Cards:** AX, CB, DC, DS, JC, MC, VI.

CAESAR'S ITALIAN RESTAURANT

Italian
$10-$25

Phone: 540/433-3456

Casual dress. **Bar:** Full bar. **Hours:** 11:30 am-9:30 pm. Closed: 12/25. **Address:** 243 Neff Ave 22801 **Location:** I-81, exit 247A, just e. **Parking:** on-site. **Cards:** AX, CB, DC, DS, JC, MC, VI.

CALHOUN'S

American
$7-$22

Phone: 540/434-8777

Calhoun's has a large selection of beers, some made on the property, classic American cuisine and a smartly attired wait staff. Casual dress. **Bar:** Full bar. **Hours:** 11 am-10 pm. Closed: 12/25. **Address:** 41 Court Square 22801 **Location:** I-81, exit 247, 2.9 mi w on US 33. **Parking:** on-site. **Cards:** AX, CB, DC, DS, JC, MC, VI.

DAVE'S DOWNTOWN TAVERNA

American
$6-$14

Phone: 540/564-1487

A popular gathering spot for all ages, the cozy downtown brew pub presents a diverse menu. Casual dress. **Bar:** Full bar. **Hours:** 11 am-1 am. Closed: 12/25. **Address:** 121 S Main St 22801 **Location:** I-81, exit 247A, 2.1 mi w on SR 33, just s on SR 11. **Parking:** on-site. **Cards:** AX, CB, DC, DS, JC, MC, VI.

DINNER BELL CAFE AT SHENANDOAH HERITAGE MARKET

American
$4-$12

Phone: 540/437-1901

Hit the bell and head for a good meal at the Dinner Bell Cafe at Shenandoah Heritage Market. Country cooking and friendly surroundings abound. Casual dress. **Hours:** 10 am-6 pm, Sat from 9 am. Closed: 1/1, 11/27, 12/25; also Sun. **Address:** 121 Carpenter Ln 22801 **Location:** I-81, exit 243, just s. **Parking:** on-site.

EL CHARRO

Mexican
$5-$15

Phone: 540/564-0386

Patrons can look forward to a lively atmosphere, friendly service, great chips and salsa, top-notch margaritas and Mexican standbys. Casual dress. **Bar:** Full bar. **Hours:** 11 am-11 pm. Closed: 12/25. **Address:** 1570 E Market St 22801 **Location:** I-81, exit 245, just w on Port Republic Rd, then 0.3 mi s on US 11. **Parking:** on-site. **Cards:** AX, CB, DC, DS, JC, MC, VI.

FINNIGAN'S COVE

American
$5-$18

Phone: 540/433-9874

Finnigan's Cove is fun Brew Pub that specializes in fresh seafood and a lively atmosphere. Casual dress. **Bar:** Full bar. **Hours:** 11 am-2 am. **Address:** 30 W Water St 22801 **Location:** Just w; center. **Parking:** street. **Cards:** AX, CB, DC, DS, JC, MC, VI.

FRANCO'S

Italian
$7-$20

Phone: 540/564-0105

Italian classics are served in a casual atmosphere. The wait staff is knowledgeable, and wines are good. Casual dress. **Bar:** Full bar. **Hours:** 11 am-11 pm. Closed: 1/1, 12/25. **Address:** 225 Burgess Rd 22801 **Location:** I-81, exit 247, just e. **Parking:** on-site. **Cards:** AX, CB, DC, DS, JC, MC, VI.

THE GALLEY

American
$6-$15

Phone: 540/434-3518

The restaurant's diverse menu spans from subs, wraps and salads to spaghetti and burgers. A relaxed setting has helped make this place a regional favorite for years. Casual dress. **Bar:** Beer only. **Hours:** 10 am-10 pm. Closed: 12/25; also Sun. **Address:** 2430 S Main St 22801 **Location:** I-81, exit 243, just w, then 1 mi n on US 11. **Parking:** on-site. **Cards:** MC, VI.

GUZMAN'S MEXICAN RESTAURANT

Mexican
$6-$16

Phone: 540/432-1094

The mood is lively inside the restaurant, where diners linger over Mexican favorites served with some beer and wine choices. Casual dress. **Bar:** Beer & wine. **Hours:** 10 am-9 pm. Closed: 12/25. **Address:** 928 W Market St 22801 **Location:** I-81, exit 247B, 2.3 mi w on SR 33. **Parking:** on-site. **Cards:** MC, VI.

HAM'S RESTAURANT

American
$7-$23

Phone: 540/574-4267

Menu choices range from salads to wraps to steaks. The atmosphere is casual and fun. Casual dress. **Bar:** Full bar. **Hours:** 11 am-11 pm. Closed: 12/25. **Address:** 221 University Blvd 22801 **Location:** I-81, exit 247A, just e. **Parking:** on-site. **Cards:** AX, CB, DC, DS, JC, MC, VI.

JESS' LUNCH #2

American
$5-$14

Phone: 540/434-8280

Tastes of the Shenandoah Valley make up the menu at the casual hometown eatery. Casual dress. **Hours:** 10 am-midnight. **Address:** 1746 E Market St 22801 **Location:** I-81, exit 247A, 0.4 mi e on US 33. **Parking:** on-site.

L'ITALIA RESTAURANT

Italian
$6-$20

Phone: 540/433-0961

Wonderful background music, candles on the tables and attractive murals on the walls make for a cozy, romantic atmosphere. The restaurant enjoys a strong local following. Among favorites is ham- and cheese-stuffed chicken breast sauteed with mushrooms and wine. Fresh bread is served with the salad and meal. Casual dress. **Bar:** Full bar. **Hours:** 11 am-10 pm, Fri & Sat-11 pm. Closed: 12/25. **Address:** 815 E Market St 22801 **Location:** I-81, exit 247, 0.8 mi w on US 33. **Parking:** on-site. **Cards:** AX, CB, DC, DS, MC, VI.

LUIGI'S PIZZA

Pizza
$6-$15

Phone: 540/433-0077

Remarkable pizza and pasta with Old Italian sauces await at the comfortable pizzeria. Good background music contributes to the cozy feel. Casual dress. **Bar:** Beer only. **Hours:** 11 am-10 pm. Closed: 12/25. **Address:** 1059 S High St 22801 **Location:** 2.1 mi s on SR 42. **Parking:** on-site. **Cards:** AX, CB, DC, DS, JC, MC, VI.

THE OLYMPIC ROOM

American
$7-$22

Phone: 540/433-2521

You do not have to be an Olympic athlete to enjoy the classic American cuisine offered at The Olympic Room. Big selections to choose from and huge portions to relish. Casual dress. **Bar:** Full bar. **Reservations:** accepted. **Hours:** 7 am-10 & 6-10 pm, Sat 6:30 am-noon & 5-10 pm; Sunday brunch. **Address:** 1400 E Market St 22801 **Location:** I-81, exit 247A, just e on US 33. **Parking:** on-site. **Cards:** AX, DS, MC, VI.

PHO HA VIETNAMESE NOODLE RESTAURANT

Vietnamese
$5-$12

Phone: 540/438-0999

Guests unwind in a quiet, quaint setting to savor Vietnamese cuisine from an enormous menu. The staff is pleasant. Casual dress. **Hours:** 11 am-9 pm, Sat from 10 am-9 pm, Sun 10 am-8 pm. **Address:** 1015 Port Republic Rd 22801 **Location:** I-81, exit 245, just e. **Parking:** on-site. **Cards:** AX, DS, MC, VI.

RT'S CHICKEN & GRILLE

American
$5-$15

Phone: 540/438-0080
The restaurant employs a friendly wait staff and presents a varied menu. Barbecue chicken is a flavorful choice. Casual dress. **Hours:** 11 am-8 pm. Closed: 11/27, 12/25; also Sun. **Address:** 120 University Blvd 22801 **Location:** I-81, exit 247, just e. **Parking:** on-site. **Cards:** MC, VI.

SAIGON CAFE

Vietnamese
$6-$19

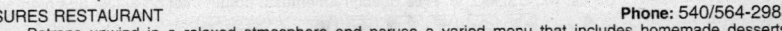

Phone: 540/434-5750
Vietnamese cuisine is served in a charming dining atmosphere. The staff is knowledgeable and friendly. Casual dress. **Bar:** Full bar. **Hours:** 11:30 am-9 pm. Closed: 12/25; also Sun. **Address:** 787 E Market St 22801 **Location:** I-81, exit 247, just w. **Parking:** on-site. **Cards:** AX, CB, DC, DS, JC, MC, VI.

SIMPLE PLEASURES RESTAURANT

American
$7-$26

Phone: 540/564-2988
Patrons unwind in a relaxed atmosphere and peruse a varied menu that includes homemade desserts. Casual dress. **Bar:** Beer & wine. **Hours:** 11 am-9 pm. Closed: 12/25; also Sun. **Address:** 380 University Blvd 22801 **Location:** I-81, exit 247A, just e on US 33 to University Blvd, then 0.3 mi s. **Parking:** on-site. **Cards:** AX, CB, DC, DS, JC, MC, VI.

THE SMOKIN PIG

Barbecue
$4-$12

Phone: 540/433-3917
Wonderful aromas linger in the restaurant's smokin' atmosphere. The menu centers on great barbecue. Casual dress. **Hours:** 11 am-8 pm. Closed major holidays. **Address:** 56 E Wolfe St 22801 **Location:** I-81, exit 247, 2 mi w on SR 33. **Parking:** on-site.

SOUTHSIDE DINER

American
$6-$19

Phone: 540/437-0061
The diner is home to the half-pound burger, hand-cut fries and homemade desserts and pies. Casual and friendly service awaits. Casual dress. **Hours:** 24 hours. Closed: 12/25. **Address:** 3355 S Main St 22801 **Location:** I-81, exit 243, just w. **Parking:** on-site. **Cards:** MC, VI.

TASTE OF THAI

Thai
$8-$18

Phone: 540/801-8878
A city favorite, the ethnic eatery is a great stop for spicy and delicious cuisine. Casual dress. **Bar:** Full bar. **Hours:** 11 am-9:30 pm. Closed: 12/25. **Address:** 917 S High St 22801 **Location:** I-81, exit 245, just w. **Parking:** on-site. **Cards:** AX, CB, DC, DS, JC, MC, VI.

TRADITIONS

American
$9-$17

Phone: 540/438-0301
Known for a family atmosphere and home-style country cuisine, the restaurant lives up to its name as a tradition throughout the Shenandoah Valley. Casual dress. **Hours:** 11 am-3 pm, Thurs-Sat to 9 pm, Sun-4 pm. Closed: 11/27, 12/25. **Address:** 625 Mt Clinton Pike, Suite E 22802 **Location:** 0.7 mi n on SR 42, just w. **Parking:** on-site. **Cards:** MC, VI.

HERNDON —*See District Of Columbia p. 537.*

HILLSVILLE pop. 2,607

——— **WHERE TO STAY** ———

BEST WESTERN FOUR SEASONS SOUTH   *Book great rates at AAA.com*   **Phone: (276)728-4136**

Small-scale Hotel
$65-$140 All Year

Address: 57 Airport Rd 24343 **Location:** I-77, exit 14, just w on US 58 and 221. **Facility:** 48 one-bedroom standard units. 1-2 stories (no elevator), exterior corridors. **Parking:** on-site. **Amenities:** high-speed Internet, irons, hair dryers. **Pool(s):** outdoor. **Guest Services:** wireless Internet. **Business Services:** PC. **Cards:** AX, CB, DC, DS, MC, VI. **Free Special Amenities:** early check-in/late check-out and preferred room (subject to availability with advance reservations).

COMFORT INN-HILLSVILLE   *Book great rates at AAA.com*   **Phone: (276)730-9999**

Small-scale Hotel
$75-$180 3/1-10/31
$75-$90 11/1-2/28

Address: 151 Farmers Market Dr 24343 **Location:** I-77, exit 14, just sw on US 58, then just s. **Facility:** Smoke free premises. 73 one-bedroom standard units, some with whirlpools. 3 stories, interior corridors. **Bath:** combo or shower only. **Parking:** on-site. **Terms:** 7 day cancellation notice-fee imposed. **Amenities:** high-speed Internet, dual phone lines, voice mail, irons, hair dryers, wireless Internet. **Pool(s):** heated indoor. **Leisure Activities:** whirlpool, exercise room. **Guest Services:** valet laundry, wireless Internet. **Business Services:** meeting rooms, business center. **Cards:** AX, CB, DC, DS, JC, MC, VI. **Free Special Amenities:** expanded continental breakfast and high-speed Internet.

HAMPTON INN
Book great rates at AAA.com
Phone: 276/728-2345

Address: 90 Farmers Market Rd 24343 **Location:** I-77, exit 14, just w on US 58. **Facility:** 86 units. 81 one-bedroom standard units. 5 one-bedroom suites with whirlpools. 4 stories, interior corridors. *Bath:* combo or shower only. **Parking:** on-site. **Amenities:** high-speed Internet, dual phone lines, voice mail, irons, hair dryers. **Pool(s):** heated indoor. **Leisure Activities:** whirlpool, exercise room. **Guest Services:** valet laundry, wireless Internet. **Business Services:** meeting rooms, business center.

Small-scale Hotel
Rates not provided

HOLIDAY INN EXPRESS
Book great rates at AAA.com
Phone: (276)728-9100

AAA SAVE

Address: 1994 Carrollton Pike Rd 24343 **Location:** I-77, exit 14, just w. **Facility:** 54 one-bedroom standard units, some with whirlpools. 4 stories, interior corridors. *Bath:* combo or shower only. **Parking:** on-site. **Terms:** cancellation fee imposed. **Amenities:** high-speed Internet, dual phone lines, voice mail, irons, hair dryers. **Pool(s):** heated indoor. **Leisure Activities:** whirlpool, exercise room. **Guest Services:** coin laundry, wireless Internet. **Business Services:** meeting rooms, business center. **Cards:** AX, DS, MC, VI. **Free Special Amenities: continental breakfast and high-speed Internet.**

Small-scale Hotel
$69-$175 All Year

KNOB HILL MOTOR LODGE
Phone: 276/728-2131

AAA SAVE

Address: 305 E Stuart Dr 24343 **Location:** I-77, exit 14, 2.5 mi e on US 58 and 221. **Facility:** 19 one-bedroom standard units. 1 story, exterior corridors. *Bath:* combo or shower only. **Parking:** on-site. **Terms:** 7 day cancellation notice. **Amenities:** hair dryers. **Cards:** AX, DS, MC, VI. **Free Special Amenities: local telephone calls and room upgrade (subject to availability with advance reservations).**

Motel
$40-$120 All Year

QUALITY INN
Book at AAA.com
Phone: (276)728-2120

Address: 85 Airport Rd 24343 **Location:** I-77, exit 14, just w on US 58 and 221. **Facility:** 81 one-bedroom standard units, some with whirlpools. 1-2 stories (no elevator), exterior corridors. *Bath:* combo or shower only. **Parking:** on-site. **Amenities:** high-speed Internet, voice mail, irons, hair dryers. **Pool(s):** outdoor. **Leisure Activities:** limited exercise equipment. **Guest Services:** valet laundry. **Business Services:** meeting rooms, business center. **Cards:** AX, DS, MC, VI.

Small-scale Hotel
$69-$169 All Year

SUPER 8 OF HILLSVILLE
Book great rates at AAA.com
Phone: 276/728-4125

AAA SAVE

Address: 99 Farmers Market Dr 24343 **Location:** I-77, exit 14, just w on US 58 and 221. **Facility:** 65 one-bedroom standard units. 2 stories (no elevator), interior/exterior corridors. **Parking:** on-site. **Amenities:** high-speed Internet, hair dryers. *Some:* irons. **Leisure Activities:** exercise room. **Guest Services:** wireless Internet.

Motel
Rates not provided

--------- WHERE TO DINE ---------

COUNTRYSIDE FAMILY RESTAURANT
Phone: 276/728-4567

Widely varied preparations of fresh Virginia home cooking are served in a family-friendly atmosphere. This place is easily accessible and employs knowledgeable servers. Casual dress. **Hours:** 7 am-9 pm. Closed: 1/1, 12/25. **Address:** 88 Framers Market Rd 24343 **Location:** I-77, exit 14, just w on US 58. **Parking:** on-site. **Cards:** AX, CB, DC, DS, JC, MC, VI.

American
$6-$15

PEKING PALACE
Phone: 276/728-5539

The menu lines up all the favorite Chinese choices. Far East prints are among elements of the quaint decor scheme. The atmosphere is relaxed. Casual dress. **Bar:** Full bar. **Hours:** 11 am-10 pm. Closed: 12/25. **Address:** 2666 Old Galax Pike 24343 **Location:** I-77, exit 14, just e. **Parking:** on-site. **Cards:** AX, CB, DC, DS, JC, MC, VI.

Chinese
$6-$17

HOPEWELL pop. 22,354 (See map and index starting on p. 854)

--------- WHERE TO STAY ---------

CANDLEWOOD SUITES
Book great rates at AAA.com
Phone: (804)541-0200  14

AAA SAVE

Address: 5113 Plaza Dr 23860 **Location:** I-295, exit 9B (SR 36), just w; adjacent to Oak Lawn Plaza. **Facility:** 60 units. 48 one-bedroom standard units with kitchens. 12 one-bedroom suites with kitchens. 3 stories, interior corridors. *Bath:* combo or shower only. **Parking:** on-site, winter plug-ins. **Terms:** office hours 7 am-11 pm, cancellation fee imposed. **Amenities:** video library, DVD players, CD players, high-speed Internet, dual phone lines, voice mail, irons, hair dryers. **Leisure Activities:** gazebo & grills, exercise room. **Guest Services:** complimentary laundry. **Cards:** AX, DC, DS, MC, VI. **Free Special Amenities: local telephone calls and high-speed Internet.**

Small-scale Hotel
$119-$145 All Year

COMFORT INN-PRINCE GEORGE
Book great rates at AAA.com
Phone: (804)452-0022 15

AAA SAVE

Address: 5380 Oaklawn Blvd 23875 **Location:** I-295, exit 9B (SR 36), just w. **Facility:** 125 one-bedroom standard units, some with whirlpools. 2 stories (no elevator), interior corridors. **Parking:** on-site. **Terms:** 3 day cancellation notice. **Amenities:** high-speed Internet, voice mail, irons, hair dryers. **Pool(s):** outdoor. **Leisure Activities:** sauna, whirlpool, exercise room. **Guest Services:** valet and coin laundry, area transportation-Ft Lee, wireless Internet. **Business Services:** meeting rooms, fax. **Cards:** AX, CB, DC, DS, MC, VI. **Free Special Amenities: newspaper and high-speed Internet.**

Small-scale Hotel
$89-$149 All Year

(See map and index starting on p. 854)

ECONO LODGE   *Book great rates at AAA.com*   Phone: 804/541-4849   **11**

Small-scale Hotel
$69-$99 All Year

Address: 4096 Oaklawn Blvd 23860 **Location:** I-295, exit 9A, just e on SR 36. **Facility:** 50 one-bedroom standard units, some with efficiencies and/or whirlpools. 3 stories, interior corridors. *Bath:* combo or shower only. **Parking:** on-site. **Amenities:** high-speed Internet, voice mail, irons, hair dryers. **Guest Services:** coin laundry, wireless Internet. **Business Services:** fax. **Cards:** AX, DS, MC, VI.

FAIRFIELD INN & SUITES BY MARRIOTT   *Book great rates at AAA.com*   Phone: (804)458-2600   **10**

Small-scale Hotel
$99-$129 All Year

Address: 3952 Courthouse Rd 23860 **Location:** I-295, exit 9A, just e on SR 36. **Facility:** Smoke free premises. 89 units. 80 one-bedroom standard units. 9 one-bedroom suites. 3 stories, interior corridors. *Bath:* combo or shower only. **Parking:** on-site. **Terms:** 3 day cancellation notice. **Amenities:** video games (fee), high-speed Internet, voice mail, irons, hair dryers. **Pool(s):** outdoor. **Leisure Activities:** exercise room. **Guest Services:** coin laundry, wireless Internet. **Business Services:** meeting rooms, business center. **Cards:** AX, CB, DC, DS, JC, MC, VI.

AAA Benefit: Members save 5% off of the best available rate.

HAMPTON INN-FT LEE   *Book great rates at AAA.com*   Phone: (804)452-1000   **13**

Small-scale Hotel
$119-$129 All Year

Address: 5103 Plaza Dr 23860 **Location:** I-295, exit 9B (SR 36), just w. **Facility:** 74 one-bedroom standard units, some with whirlpools. 3 stories, interior corridors. **Parking:** on-site. **Amenities:** high-speed Internet, voice mail, irons, hair dryers. **Pool(s):** outdoor. **Leisure Activities:** sauna, exercise room. **Guest Services:** valet and coin laundry, wireless Internet. **Business Services:** meeting rooms, PC, fax. **Cards:** AX, DC, DS, MC, VI.

QUALITY INN AT FT LEE/HOPEWELL   *Book at AAA.com*   Phone: (804)458-1500   **12**

Small-scale Hotel
$90-$100 All Year

Address: 4911 Oaklawn Blvd 23860 **Location:** I-295, exit 9B (SR 36), just w. **Facility:** 115 one-bedroom standard units, some with efficiencies (no utensils) and/or whirlpools. 2 stories (no elevator), exterior corridors. *Bath:* combo or shower only. **Parking:** on-site. **Amenities:** high-speed Internet, voice mail, irons, hair dryers. **Pool(s):** outdoor. **Leisure Activities:** sauna, whirlpool, exercise room. **Guest Services:** valet and coin laundry, area transportation, wireless Internet. **Business Services:** fax. **Cards:** AX, DC, DS, MC, VI.

——— WHERE TO DINE ———

DOCKSIDE RESTAURANT   Phone: 804/541-2600

Seafood
$5-$18

The menu showcases fresh local seafood, such as flounder, swordfish and blackened tuna, pasta, steak and salad. Enjoy a panoramic view through the picture windows that overlook the water. The decor is decidedly nautical, with lots of rich wood. Casual dress. Entertainment. **Bar:** Full bar. **Reservations:** suggested. **Hours:** 11:30 am-10 pm, Fri & Sat-11 pm. Closed: 1/1, 12/25. **Address:** 700 Jordan Point Rd 23860 **Location:** SR 156, just n of jct SR 10; at south end of Benjamin Harrison Bridge. **Parking:** on-site. **Cards:** AX, DS, MC, VI.

HOT SPRINGS

——— WHERE TO STAY ———

THE HOMESTEAD   *Book at AAA.com*   Phone: 540/839-1766

Resort
Large-scale Hotel
Rates not provided

Address: 1766 Homestead Dr 24445 **Location:** Center. Located in a rural area. **Facility:** The 1766 mountain resort offers recreation options from golf to horseback riding; a presidents? lounge displays oil portraits of presidential guests. 483 units. 473 one-bedroom standard units. 10 two-bedroom suites. 7 stories, interior corridors. *Bath:* combo or shower only. **Parking:** on-site and valet. **Terms:** check-in 4 pm. **Amenities:** video games, high-speed Internet, voice mail, safes, honor bars, irons, hair dryers. **Pool(s):** heated outdoor, heated indoor. **Leisure Activities:** sauna, whirlpool, steamroom, canoeing, fishing, recreation programs, hiking trails, jogging, playground, spa. *Fee:* golf-54 holes, 6 tennis courts, downhill & cross country skiing, ice skating, bicycles, horseback riding. **Guest Services:** valet laundry, wireless Internet. **Business Services:** conference facilities, business center.

ROSELOE MOTEL   Phone: (540)839-5373

Motel
$75-$85 All Year

Address: 10849 Sam Snead Hwy 24445 **Location:** 3 mi n. **Facility:** 14 one-bedroom standard units, some with kitchens. 1 story, exterior corridors. **Parking:** on-site. **Terms:** 3 day cancellation notice-fee imposed. **Leisure Activities:** horseshoes. **Cards:** AX, CB, DC, DS, JC, MC, VI.

HUDDLESTON

——— WHERE TO STAY ———

MARINERS LANDING

Book at AAA.com

Phone: (540)297-4900

▽▼▽▼▽▼

Vacation Rental
Condominium

$135-$270 All Year

Address: 1217 Graves Harbor Tr 24104 **Location:** On SR 626; on Smith Mountain Lake. **Facility:** Find condo units, townhomes, villas and large, private homes overlooking the golf course or the lake at this sprawling resort on Smith Mountain Lake. 158 units. 80 one-bedroom standard units with efficiencies, some with whirlpools. 7 one-, 54 two- and 11 three-bedroom suites, some with kitchens and/or whirlpools. 6 vacation homes, some with whirlpools. 1-6 stories, interior/exterior corridors. *Bath:* combo or shower only. **Parking:** on-site. **Terms:** office hours 7 am-9 pm, 7 day cancellation notice-fee imposed. **Amenities:** video library, DVD players, CD players, irons, hair dryers. *Some:* high-speed Internet. **Pool(s):** 2 outdoor, heated outdoor. **Leisure Activities:** whirlpools, waterslide, limited beach access, paddleboats, boat dock, 2 lighted tennis courts, hiking trails, playground, exercise room, sports court, volleyball. *Fee:* golf-18 holes, game room. **Guest Services:** wireless Internet. **Business Services:** conference facilities, fax (fee). **Cards:** AX, MC, VI.

(A$K) (S⌷) (†⍳) CALL (Ġ,M) (🏊) (✕) (✕⃟) (VCR) (🎞) / (🛗) (🖥) (💻) / SOME UNITS FEE (🐾)

——— WHERE TO DINE ———

THE POINTE RESTAURANT

Phone: 540/296-1215

◉◉◉

▽▼▽▼▽▼

American

$9-$38

Casual dress. **Bar:** Full bar. **Reservations:** suggested. **Hours:** 11:30 am-2:30 & 5:30-10 pm. **Address:** 1217 Graves Harbor Tr 24104 **Location:** On SR 626; on Smith Mountain Lake; in Mariner's Landing Lodging. **Parking:** on-site. **Cards:** AX, CB, DC, DS, JC, MC, VI.

IRVINGTON pop. 673

——— WHERE TO STAY ———

THE TIDES INN

Book great rates at AAA.com

Phone: (804)438-5000

◉◉◉ (SAVE)

▽▼▽▼▽▼

Small-scale Hotel

$189-$375 All Year

Address: 480 King Carter Dr 22480 **Location:** 0.3 mi w of CR 200. **Facility:** The gracious riverfront resort offers warm, Southern hospitality amid elegant surroundings; decor is reminiscent of the tropics. 106 one-bedroom standard units. 4 stories, interior/exterior corridors. *Bath:* combo or shower only. **Parking:** on-site. **Terms:** check-in 4 pm, 7 day cancellation notice-fee imposed. **Amenities:** video library, DVD players, CD players, high-speed Internet, dual phone lines, voice mail, safes, honor bars, irons, hair dryers. **Dining:** 3 restaurants, also, The Chesapeake Club, see separate listing, entertainment. **Pool(s):** heated outdoor. **Leisure Activities:** canoeing, paddleboats, marina, beach & sunset cruises, sailing school, 4 tennis courts, recreation programs, croquet, bicycles, playground, exercise room, spa, sports court, shuffleboard. *Fee:* boats, sailboats, fishing, charter fishing, golf-27 holes. **Guest Services:** valet laundry, area transportation-within 5 mi, wireless Internet. **Business Services:** conference facilities, PC, fax. **Cards:** AX, CB, DC, DS, JC, MC, VI. **Free Special Amenities:** newspaper and high-speed Internet.

(S⌷) (†⍳) (24†) (Y) (⌂†) CALL (Ġ,M) (🏊) (✕) (🎞) (💻) / SOME UNITS FEE (🐾) (✕) (VCR) FEE (🖥)

——— WHERE TO DINE ———

THE CHESAPEAKE CLUB

Phone: 804/438-5000

▽▼▽▼▽▼

Regional American

$23-$36

Overlooking Carter's Creek and the marina, the dining room enables guests to sample sophisticated fare prepared with both international and regional Mid-Atlantic influences. Semi-formal attire. **Bar:** Full bar. **Reservations:** required. **Hours:** 7 am-10 pm. **Address:** 480 King Carter Dr 22480 **Location:** 0.3 mi w of CR 200; in The Tides Inn. **Parking:** on-site. **Cards:** AX, MC, VI.

CALL (Ġ,M)

KESWICK

——— WHERE TO STAY ———

KESWICK HALL AT MONTICELLO

Book great rates at AAA.com

Phone: (434)979-3440

◉◉◉ (SAVE)

▽▼▽▼▽▼

Resort
Small-scale Hotel

$325-$425 All Year

Address: 701 Club Dr 22947 **Location:** I-64, exit 129, just n. **Facility:** In a gated community, the service-oriented, upscale resort offers fine views, luxury appointments, a billiards room, afternoon tea and a plunge pool. 48 one-bedroom standard units, some with whirlpools. 3 stories, interior corridors. *Bath:* combo or shower only. **Parking:** on-site and valet. **Terms:** cancellation fee imposed. **Amenities:** video library, DVD players, CD players, high-speed Internet, voice mail, safes, honor bars, irons, hair dryers. **Dining:** 2 restaurants, also, Fossett's, see separate listing. **Pool(s):** heated outdoor, heated indoor, heated indoor/outdoor. **Leisure Activities:** whirlpools, fishing, putting green, 5 lighted tennis courts, recreation programs, archery, billards, croquet, fly fishing school, bicycles, playground, exercise room, basketball, horseshoes, volleyball. *Fee:* golf-18 holes, massage, game room. **Guest Services:** valet laundry, wireless Internet. **Business Services:** conference facilities, business center. **Free Special Amenities:** newspaper and high-speed Internet.

(†⍳) (24†) (Y) CALL (Ġ,M) (🏊) (✕) (✕⃟) (VCR) (🎞) / SOME UNITS FEE (🐾) (🖥) (🖧)

——— WHERE TO DINE ———

FOSSETT'S

Phone: 434/979-3440

◉◉◉

▽▼▽▼▽▼

American

$29-$39

Named after Thomas Jefferson's chief chef at Monticello, the restaurant offers seating in an amazingly elegant dining room that affords estate and golf views. Wonderful plate presentations accentuate many local gourmet ingredients, which are harvested at the peak of flavor. Dressy casual. **Bar:** Full bar. **Reservations:** suggested, weekends. **Hours:** 6 pm-9:30 pm. **Address:** 701 Club Dr 22947 **Location:** I-64, exit 129, just n; in Keswick Hall at Monticello. **Parking:** on-site and valet. **Cards:** AX, CB, DC, DS, JC, MC, VI.

KILMARNOCK pop. 1,244

―――― WHERE TO DINE ――――

LEE'S RESTAURANT

◆◇◆

Regional American
$6-$11

Southern hospitality and delicious bay country cuisine please patrons of this small Main Street spot. On the menu are many preparations of local seafood, homemade pies and daily soups. Casual dress. **Bar:** Beer & wine. **Hours:** 7 am-8 pm. Closed: Sun. **Address:** 30 Main St 22482 **Location:** Center. **Parking:** street. **Cards:** MC, VI.

Phone: 804/435-1255

LAWRENCEVILLE pop. 1,275

―――― WHERE TO STAY ――――

BRUNSWICK MINERAL SPRINGS B & B CIRCA 1785

◆◇◆◇◆

Historic Bed
& Breakfast
$90-$200 All Year

Address: 14910 Western Mill Rd 23868 **Location:** 5 mi e on US 58, 1 mi s on SR 712, then just e. Located in a quiet rural area. **Facility:** Towering oaks shade this Colonial-style plantation home, which has seen many incarnations since its late-1700s inception as a mineral springs resort. Smoke free premises. 4 units. 2 one-bedroom standard units. 1 two-bedroom suite. 1 cottage. 3 stories (no elevator), interior corridors. *Bath:* combo or shower only. **Parking:** on-site. **Terms:** check-in 4 pm, 2 night minimum stay - seasonal, age restrictions may apply, 5 day cancellation notice-fee imposed. **Amenities:** video library, high-speed Internet, hair dryers. *Some:* DVD players, irons. **Leisure Activities:** whirlpool, hiking trails. **Guest Services:** wireless Internet. **Business Services:** business center. **Cards:** MC, VI.

Phone: (434)848-4010

A$K ⊠ 📷 / SOME UNITS FEE 🐾 📺 VCR ☎ 📶 🖨 💻

THREE ANGELS INN AT SHERWOOD

◆◇◆◇◆

Historic Bed
& Breakfast
$95-$110 All Year

Address: 236 Pleasant Grove Rd (SR 681) 23920 **Location:** 1.5 mi w on US 58 to jct SR 681. Located in a quiet rural area. **Facility:** Built in 1883 as a hospital, the inn is surrounded by shady oak and cedar trees best appreciated from the rocking chairs and swings on its porches. Smoke free premises. 4 one-bedroom standard units. 2 stories (no elevator), interior corridors. **Parking:** on-site. **Terms:** age restrictions may apply, 3 day cancellation notice-fee imposed. **Amenities:** hair dryers. **Guest Services:** wireless Internet. **Business Services:** fax. **Cards:** MC, VI.

Phone: 434/848-0830

A$K S/D ⊠ 📺 / SOME UNITS ☎

LEBANON pop. 3,273

―――― WHERE TO STAY ――――

LEBANON SUPER 8 MOTEL *Book at AAA.com*

◆◇◆◇◆

Small-scale Hotel
Rates not provided

Address: 711 Townview Dr 24266 **Location:** Just e on SR 654 from US 19 Bypass. **Facility:** 47 one-bedroom standard units, some with whirlpools. 2 stories (no elevator), interior corridors. **Parking:** on-site. **Amenities:** high-speed Internet, hair dryers. *Fee:* safes. **Guest Services:** coin laundry, wireless Internet. **Business Services:** meeting rooms.

Phone: 276/889-1800

CALL 🖥M 📷 FEE 🖨 💻 / SOME UNITS ⊠

LEESBURG —*See District Of Columbia p. 541.*

LEXINGTON pop. 6,867

―――― WHERE TO STAY ――――

A B&B AT LLEWELLYN LODGE

◆◇◆◇◆

Bed & Breakfast
$95-$179 3/1-11/30
$89-$169 12/1-2/28

Address: 603 S Main St 24450 **Location:** 0.5 mi s on US 11. **Facility:** Close to shops and the famed Virginia Military Institute, this cozy family home is in a serene country setting near many attractions. Smoke free premises. 6 one-bedroom standard units. 2 stories (no elevator), interior corridors. *Bath:* combo or shower only. **Parking:** on-site. **Terms:** age restrictions may apply, 3 day cancellation notice-fee imposed. **Amenities:** high-speed Internet, hair dryers. *Some:* DVD players, irons. **Guest Services:** complimentary laundry, wireless Internet. **Business Services:** business center. **Cards:** AX, DS, MC, VI.

Phone: (540)463-3235

A$K ⊠ / SOME UNITS 📺 ☎ 🖨 💻

BEST WESTERN INN AT HUNT RIDGE *Book great rates at AAA.com*

AAA SAVE

◆◇◆◇◆

Small-scale Hotel
$56-$175 All Year

Address: 25 Willow Spring Rd 24450 **Location:** I-64, exit 55, just n on US 11 to SR 39; I-81, exit 191, 0.6 mi w. **Facility:** 100 one-bedroom standard units. 3 stories, interior corridors. *Bath:* combo or shower only. **Parking:** on-site. **Amenities:** high-speed Internet, irons, hair dryers. **Dining:** G Willaker's, see separate listing. **Pool(s):** heated indoor/outdoor. **Guest Services:** coin laundry, wireless Internet. **Business Services:** conference facilities, PC. **Cards:** AX, CB, DC, DS, JC, MC, VI. **Free Special Amenities:** local telephone calls and high-speed Internet.

Phone: (540)464-1500

AAA Benefit:
Members save 10% everyday, plus an exclusive frequent stay program.

S/D 🍴 🍸 CALL 🖥M 🏊 📷 📶 💻 / SOME UNITS FEE 🐾 ⊠ FEE 🖨 FEE 🖥

BEST WESTERN LEXINGTON INN
Book great rates at AAA.com

Phone: (540)458-3020

Small-scale Hotel
$64-$150 All Year

Address: 850 N Lee Hwy 24450 **Location:** I-64, exit 55, just s on US 11; I-81, exit 191, 1.6 mi w. **Facility:** 72 one-bedroom standard units. 2 stories (no elevator), exterior corridors. *Bath:* combo or shower only. **Parking:** on-site. **Amenities:** high-speed Internet, voice mail, irons, hair dryers. **Leisure Activities:** picnic tables, exercise room. **Guest Services:** valet laundry, wireless Internet. **Business Services:** meeting rooms, PC. **Cards:** AX, CB, DC, DS, JC, MC, VI. **Free Special Amenities:** continental breakfast and high-speed Internet.

AAA Benefit:
Members save 10% everyday, plus an exclusive frequent stay program.

COMFORT INN-VIRGINIA HORSE CENTER
Book great rates at AAA.com

Phone: (540)463-7311

Small-scale Hotel
$64-$175 All Year

Address: 62 Comfort Way 24450 **Location:** I-64, exit 55, just s on US 11; I-81, exit 191, 0.6 mi w. **Facility:** 80 one-bedroom standard units. 4 stories, interior corridors. **Parking:** on-site. **Amenities:** high-speed Internet, irons, hair dryers. **Pool(s):** heated indoor. **Guest Services:** coin laundry, wireless Internet. **Business Services:** fax (fee). **Cards:** AX, CB, DC, DS, JC, MC, VI. **Free Special Amenities:** continental breakfast and high-speed Internet.

COUNTRY INN & SUITES
Book great rates at AAA.com

Phone: (540)464-9000

Small-scale Hotel
$90-$190 3/1-11/30
$69-$130 12/1-2/28

Address: 875 N Lee Hwy 24450 **Location:** I-81, exit 191, just s on US 11. **Facility:** 66 one-bedroom standard units, some with whirlpools. 4 stories, interior corridors. *Bath:* combo or shower only. **Parking:** on-site. **Amenities:** high-speed Internet, voice mail, irons, hair dryers. **Pool(s):** heated indoor. **Leisure Activities:** whirlpool, exercise room. **Guest Services:** coin laundry, wireless Internet. **Business Services:** meeting rooms, business center. **Cards:** AX, DC, DS, MC, VI. **Free Special Amenities:** continental breakfast and high-speed Internet.

DAYS INN
Book great rates at AAA.com

Phone: 540/463-9131

Small-scale Hotel
Rates not provided

Address: 2809 N Lee Hwy 24450 **Location:** I-81, exit 195, just sw on US 11. **Facility:** 149 one-bedroom standard units. 2-3 stories, exterior corridors. **Parking:** on-site. **Amenities:** hair dryers. *Some:* high-speed Internet, irons. **Pool(s):** outdoor. **Leisure Activities:** playground. **Guest Services:** wireless Internet. **Free Special Amenities:** local telephone calls and high-speed Internet.

ECONO LODGE
Book at AAA.com

Phone: (540)463-7371

Motel
$50-$150 All Year

Address: 65 Econo Ln 24450 **Location:** I-81, exit 191, just s on US 11. **Facility:** 48 one-bedroom standard units. 2 stories (no elevator), exterior corridors. **Parking:** on-site. **Amenities:** irons, hair dryers. **Guest Services:** coin laundry, wireless Internet. **Business Services:** fax (fee). **Cards:** AX, DS, MC, VI.

HAMPTON INN-COL ALTO
Book great rates at AAA.com

Phone: 540/463-2223

Small-scale Hotel
Rates not provided

Address: 401 E Nelson St 24450 **Location:** I-81, exit 188B, 2.5 mi w on US 60. **Facility:** 86 one-bedroom standard units, some with whirlpools. 3 stories, interior/exterior corridors. *Bath:* combo or shower only. **Parking:** on-site. **Amenities:** high-speed Internet, voice mail, irons, hair dryers. **Pool(s):** outdoor. **Leisure Activities:** whirlpool, exercise room. **Guest Services:** valet laundry, wireless Internet. **Business Services:** meeting rooms, business center.

HISTORIC COUNTRY INNS OF LEXINGTON

Phone: (540)463-2044

Historic Bed
& Breakfast
$125-$195 All Year

Address: 11 N Main St 24450 **Location:** Between Washington and Henry sts; center of downtown. **Facility:** Find rooms and suites in two historic townhouses, one dating from 1789 and the other from 1809, at this property in the heart of downtown Lexington. 23 one-bedroom standard units, some with whirlpools. 3-4 stories (no elevator), interior/exterior corridors. *Bath:* combo or shower only. **Parking:** on-site. **Terms:** 10 day cancellation notice. **Amenities:** voice mail. *Some:* DVD players. **Guest Services:** wireless Internet. **Business Services:** meeting rooms. **Cards:** DS, MC, VI.

HOLIDAY INN EXPRESS
Book great rates at AAA.com

Phone: (540)463-7351

Small-scale Hotel
$99-$200 All Year

Address: 880 N Lee Hwy 24450 **Location:** I-64, exit 55, just s on US 11; I-81, exit 191, 1 mi w. **Facility:** 79 one-bedroom standard units. 4 stories, interior corridors. *Bath:* combo or shower only. **Parking:** on-site. **Amenities:** high-speed Internet, voice mail, irons, hair dryers. **Guest Services:** valet and coin laundry, wireless Internet. **Business Services:** meeting rooms, PC, fax (fee). **Cards:** AX, CB, DC, DS, JC, MC, VI. **Free Special Amenities:** continental breakfast and high-speed Internet.

HOWARD JOHNSON INN *Book great rates at AAA.com* Phone: 540/463-9181

Small-scale Hotel
Rates not provided

Address: 2836 N Lee Hwy 24450 **Location:** I-81, exit 195, just s on US 11. **Facility:** 100 one-bedroom standard units. 5 stories, interior corridors. **Parking:** on-site. **Amenities:** safes (fee), irons, hair dryers. *Some:* high-speed Internet. **Pool(s):** outdoor. **Leisure Activities:** picnic tables. **Guest Services:** coin laundry, wireless Internet. **Business Services:** meeting rooms, PC, fax (fee). **Free Special Amenities: continental breakfast and high-speed Internet.**

CALL ⬛ᴹ 🏊 🐾 💻 / SOME UNITS FEE 🛏 ✖ 🛗

MAPLE HALL COUNTRY INN Phone: (540)463-6693

Historic
Country Inn
$105-$185 All Year

Address: 3111 N Lee Hwy 24450 **Location:** I-81, exit 195, just ne on US 11. Located in a rural area. **Facility:** Some units overlook a pond and others have fireplaces in this 1850 Greek Revival plantation home with candlelit dining rooms and upscale fixtures. 21 one-bedroom standard units. 3 stories (no elevator), interior corridors. *Bath:* combo or shower only. **Parking:** on-site. **Terms:** 10 day cancellation notice. **Dining:** Maple Hall Dining Room, see separate listing. **Pool(s):** outdoor. **Leisure Activities:** fishing, tennis court, hiking trails. **Business Services:** meeting rooms. **Cards:** DS, MC, VI.

A$K S⬤ 🍴 🏊 ✖ 💻 / SOME UNITS ✖ VCR 🛗 📞

SLEEP INN & SUITES *Book great rates at AAA.com* Phone: (540)463-6000

Small-scale Hotel
$60-$195 3/1-11/15
$50-$150 11/16-2/28

Address: 95 Maury River Rd 24450 **Location:** I-64, exit 55, just n. **Facility:** 71 one-bedroom standard units, some with whirlpools. 4 stories, interior corridors. *Bath:* combo or shower only. **Parking:** on-site. **Amenities:** dual phone lines, voice mail, irons, hair dryers. **Pool(s):** heated indoor. **Leisure Activities:** whirlpool, exercise room. **Guest Services:** valet and coin laundry, wireless Internet. **Business Services:** meeting rooms, administrative services. **Cards:** AX, CB, DC, DS, JC, MC, VI.

S⬤ CALL ⬛ᴹ 🏊 🐾 🛗 🖨 💻 / SOME UNITS ✖

SUPER 8 MOTEL *Book at AAA.com* Phone: 540/463-7858

Motel
Rates not provided

Address: 1139 N Lee Hwy 24450 **Location:** I-64, exit 55, just n. **Facility:** 50 one-bedroom standard units. 3 stories (no elevator), interior corridors. **Parking:** on-site. **Amenities:** safes (fee). *Some:* hair dryers. **Guest Services:** wireless Internet. **Business Services:** fax (fee).

🐾 / SOME UNITS 🛏 ✖ 🛗 🖨 💻

WINGATE INN *Book great rates at AAA.com* Phone: (540)464-8100

Small-scale Hotel
$109-$119 All Year

Address: 1100 N Lee Hwy 24450 **Location:** I-64, exit 55, just n. **Facility:** 86 one-bedroom standard units, some with whirlpools. 4 stories, interior corridors. *Bath:* combo or shower only. **Parking:** on-site. **Amenities:** video games, high-speed Internet, voice mail, safes, irons, hair dryers. **Pool(s):** heated indoor. **Leisure Activities:** whirlpool, exercise room. **Guest Services:** coin laundry, wireless Internet. **Business Services:** meeting rooms, business center. **Cards:** AX, CB, DC, DS, MC, VI. **Free Special Amenities: continental breakfast and high-speed Internet.**

S⬤ CALL ⬛ᴹ 🏊 🐾 🛗 🖨 💻 / SOME UNITS ✖

——— **WHERE TO DINE** ———

BISTRO ON MAIN Phone: 540/464-4888

South American
$7-$20

The cozy little dining establishment presents a menu that incorporates some Lowcountry dishes, including shrimp and grits. The staff provides friendly service. Casual dress. **Bar:** Beer & wine. **Hours:** 11:30 am-2:30 & 5-9 pm. Closed: 12/25; also Sun & Mon. **Address:** 8 N Main St 24450 **Location:** Between Washington and Henry sts; center of downtown historic district. **Parking:** street. **Cards:** MC, VI.

DON TEQUILA MEXICAN RESTAURANT Phone: 540/463-3289

Mexican
$7-$19

Guests can nosh on hot chips and salsa while waiting for their choice from the large menu. Service is good. Casual dress. **Bar:** Full bar. **Hours:** 11 am-10 pm. Closed: 12/25. **Address:** 455 E Nelson St 24450 **Location:** I-81, exit 188B, 2.6 mi w on US 60. **Parking:** on-site. **Cards:** AX, CB, DC, DS, JC, MC, VI.

G WILLAKER'S Phone: 540/464-9499

American
$6-$19

G. Willaker's offers a tremendous place to unwind and enjoy great American classic cuisine. Located close to the Virginia Horse Center. Casual dress. **Hours:** 11 am-10 pm, Fri & Sat-10:30 pm. **Address:** 25 Willow Spring Rd 24450 **Location:** I-64, exit 55, just n on US 11 to SR 39; I-81, exit 191, 0.6 mi w; in Best Western Inn at Hunt Ridge. **Parking:** on-site. **Cards:** AX, DS, MC, VI.

MAPLE HALL DINING ROOM Phone: 540/463-4666

American
$13-$27

Dining rooms in the 1850s plantation home are decorated in period. A glass-enclosed patio overlooks the garden. Although the menu is limited, the ingredients are upscale in such rich, flavorful dishes as lobster bisque. Friendly servers are trained in fine dining. Home-baked bread adds to the salad and meal. Don't miss the weekly changing dessert menu. Dressy casual. **Bar:** Full bar. **Reservations:** suggested. **Hours:** 5:30 pm-close. Closed: 3/23, 12/24, 12/25; also Sun & 1/1-1/7. **Address:** 3111 N Lee Hwy 24450 **Location:** I-81, exit 195, just ne on US 11; in Maple Hall Country Inn. **Parking:** on-site. **Cards:** DS, MC, VI. **Country Inn**

THE PALMS

American
$6-$18

Phone: 540/463-7911
A touch of the Caribbean in Lexington, VA. The Palms has a wide ranging menu and friendly service. Casual dress. **Bar:** Full bar. **Hours:** 11 am-10 pm. Closed: 12/25. **Address:** 101 W Nelson 24450 **Location:** Between Washington and Henry sts; center of downtown. **Parking:** street. **Cards:** AX, CB, DC, DS, JC, MC, VI.

REDWOOD FAMILY RESTAURANT

American
$5-$15

Phone: 540/463-2168
Popular with locals for its home-style country cooking, the restaurant serves affordable family favorites, such as Virginia ham, fried chicken and rib-eye steak. Try tasty broiled catfish with mixed vegetables or one of the many daily specials. Casual dress. **Hours:** 7 am-10 pm. Closed: 12/25. **Address:** 898 N Lee Hwy 24450 **Location:** I-64, exit 55, just s on US 11. **Parking:** on-site.

SHERIDAN LIVERY INN RESTAURANT

American
$8-$29

Phone: 540/464-1887
Nestled in the heart of downtown Lexington, the Sheridan Livery Inn Restaurant is a converted turn of the century stagecoach service stable with an extensive menu. Casual dress. **Bar:** Full bar. **Hours:** 11 am-8 pm, Fri & Sat-9:30 pm. Closed: 1/1, 12/25. **Address:** 35 N Main St 24450 **Location:** Between Washington and Henry sts; center of downtown. **Parking:** street. **Cards:** AX, CB, MC, VI.

THE SOUTHERN INN RESTAURANT

American
$6-$22

Phone: 540/463-3612
This restaurant offers southern hospitality and great food in a wonderfully cozy atmosphere. The people will make you feel welcome and ensure that you will want to come back again and again. Casual dress. **Bar:** Full bar. **Hours:** 11:30 am-10 pm, Sun-9 pm. **Address:** 37 S Main St 24450 **Location:** Between Washington and Henry sts; center. **Parking:** on-site. **Cards:** AX, DS, MC, VI.

TUSCANY ITALIAN RESTAURANT

Northern Italian
$9-$23

Phone: 540/463-9888
Homemade sauces flavor the restaurant's fine Italian dishes, which lead into freshly made desserts. Casual dress. **Bar:** Full bar. **Reservations:** suggested, weekends. **Hours:** 11:30 am-9 pm. Closed: 12/25; also Tues. **Address:** 24 N Main St 24450 **Location:** Between Washington and Henry sts; center of downtown historic district. **Parking:** street. **Cards:** AX, CB, DC, DS, JC, MC, VI.

LIGHTFOOT — See Williamsburg, Jamestown & Yorktown p. 950.

LORTON — See District Of Columbia p. 543.

LOVINGSTON

——— WHERE TO DINE ———

LOVINGSTON CAFE

American
$6-$15

Phone: 434/263-8000
Hometown pride and homemade food reign supreme at the cafe, which presents a varied menu. Servers are friendly. Casual dress. **Hours:** 7 am-9 pm, Tues-Thurs from 10:30 am. Closed: 1/1, 12/25. **Address:** 1 Front St 22949 **Location:** Center. **Parking:** on-site. **Cards:** DS, MC, VI.

LOW MOOR pop. 367

——— WHERE TO DINE ———

THE CAT AND OWL

Steak & Seafood
$9-$29

Phone: 540/862-5808
Choice rib eye, filet mignon and fresh seafood are served in the family-owned, rich-looking, Victorian-style restaurant. The rural location is worth the drive. The selection of Virginia wines is good. Dressy casual. **Bar:** Full bar. **Reservations:** suggested. **Hours:** 5 pm-9 pm. Closed major holidays; also Sun. **Address:** 110 Karnes Rd 24457 **Location:** I-64, exit 21, just s, then just w, follow signs. **Parking:** on-site. **Cards:** AX, DS, MC, VI.

LURAY pop. 4,871

——— WHERE TO STAY ———

BEST WESTERN INTOWN OF LURAY

Small-scale Hotel
$70-$130 All Year

Phone: (540)743-6511
Address: 410 W Main St 22835 **Location:** 0.3 mi w on US 211 business route. **Facility:** 40 one-bedroom standard units. 2 stories (no elevator), exterior corridors. **Parking:** on-site. **Amenities:** high-speed Internet, voice mail, irons, hair dryers. **Pool(s):** outdoor. **Guest Services:** valet laundry, wireless Internet. **Business Services:** meeting rooms. **Cards:** AX, CB, DC, DS, JC, MC, VI. **Free Special Amenities:** local telephone calls and high-speed Internet.

AAA Benefit:
Members save 10% everyday, plus an exclusive frequent stay program.

THE CABINS AT BROOKSIDE

Cabin
Rates not provided

Phone: 540/743-5698
Address: 2978 US Hwy 211 E 22835 **Location:** On US 211 Bypass, 4.8 mi e. Located in a quiet rural area. **Facility:** A mountain stream runs next to this property, which offers varied log cabins, some with front porches, and a great gift shop. 9 cabins, some with whirlpools. 1 story, exterior corridors. **Parking:** on-site. **Terms:** check-in 4 pm. **Amenities:** CD players. **Dining:** Brookside Restaurant, see separate listing. **Leisure Activities:** fishing. **Business Services:** meeting rooms.

THE CARDINAL INN

Motel
$60-$160 All Year

Book at AAA.com
Phone: (540)743-5010
Address: 1005 E Main St 22835 **Location:** 1 mi e on US 211 business route. **Facility:** 27 one-bedroom standard units, some with whirlpools. 1 story, exterior corridors. *Bath:* combo or shower only. **Parking:** on-site. **Terms:** cancellation fee imposed. **Cards:** AX, DC, DS, MC, VI.

DAYS INN-LURAY

Small-scale Hotel
Rates not provided

Book at AAA.com
Phone: 540/743-4521
Address: 138 Whispering Hill Rd 22835 **Location:** US 211 Bypass, 1.7 mi e of jct US 340. **Facility:** 106 one-bedroom standard units, some with whirlpools. 2 stories (no elevator), interior/exterior corridors. **Parking:** on-site. **Amenities:** voice, mail, hair dryers. **Pool(s):** outdoor. **Leisure Activities:** exercise room, horseshoes, volleyball. *Fee:* miniature golf. **Guest Services:** coin laundry, wireless Internet. **Business Services:** meeting rooms, business center.

LURAY CAVERNS MOTEL EAST

Motel
$68-$90 All Year

Phone: (540)743-4531
Address: 831 W Main St 22835 **Location:** 1 mi w on US 211 business route. Located across from Luray Caverns. **Facility:** 44 units. 39 one- and 5 two-bedroom standard units, some with efficiencies (no utensils). 1-2 stories (no elevator), exterior corridors. *Bath:* combo or shower only. **Parking:** on-site. **Amenities:** hair dryers. **Pool(s):** outdoor. **Cards:** AX, DS, MC, VI. **Free Special Amenities:** continental breakfast and local telephone calls.

LURAY CAVERNS MOTEL WEST

Motel
$68-$90 4/1-10/27

Phone: (540)743-4536
Address: 1001 US Hwy 211 W Bypass 22835 **Location:** 1.5 mi w on US 211 Bypass; w of jct US 211 business route. **Facility:** 19 one-bedroom standard units, some with efficiencies (no utensils). 1 story, exterior corridors. *Bath:* combo or shower only. **Parking:** on-site. **Terms:** open 4/1-10/27. **Amenities:** hair dryers. **Pool(s):** outdoor. **Cards:** AX, DS, MC, VI. **Free Special Amenities:** continental breakfast and local telephone calls.

SHADOW MOUNTAIN ESCAPE

Cabin
$155-$250 All Year

Phone: (540)843-0584
Address: 1132 Jewell Hollow Rd 22835 **Location:** I-81, exit 264, 3.7 mi e on US 211. **Facility:** Offering very scenic views, a tranquil setting and unforgettable hospitality, Shadow Mountain Escape is nestled just below the Blue Ridge Mountains. 3 cabins. 1 story, exterior corridors. **Parking:** on-site. **Terms:** 2 night minimum stay - seasonal and/or weekends, 14 day cancellation notice. **Amenities:** DVD players, CD players. *Some:* irons, hair dryers. **Leisure Activities:** fishing, hiking trails, exercise room, horseshoes. **Guest Services:** coin laundry. **Business Services:** meeting rooms.

VILLA BELLA VISTA INN

Bed & Breakfast
Rates not provided

Phone: 540/843-4800
Address: 50 Cottage Dr 22835 **Location:** US 211 Bypass, 1 mi e from Luray Caverns. **Facility:** This upscale, new B&B offers spacious rooms, whirlpools and fireplaces; it boasts modern features all around, so you won[0092]t find antiques here. 6 one-bedroom standard units, some with whirlpools. 2 stories (no elevator), interior/exterior corridors. *Bath:* combo or shower only. **Parking:** on-site. **Terms:** age restrictions may apply. **Amenities:** CD players, hair dryers. *Some:* DVD players. **Leisure Activities:** exercise room. **Guest Services:** valet laundry, wireless Internet. **Business Services:** meeting rooms.

WOODRUFF INNS

Historic Bed
& Breakfast
$169-$299 9/2-2/28
$129-$259 3/1-9/1

Phone: (540)743-1494
Address: 138 E Main St 22835 **Location:** 0.3 mi e on US 211 business route. **Facility:** Chandeliers and collectibles decorate these three stately Victorian homes; elegant meals and the property's own wines are served in the dining room. Designated smoking area. 9 one-bedroom standard units, some with whirlpools. 2-3 stories (no elevator), interior corridors. *Bath:* combo or shower only. **Parking:** on-site. **Terms:** 2 night minimum stay - seasonal and/or weekends, age restrictions may apply, 7 day cancellation notice. **Amenities:** CD players, hair dryers. *Some:* DVD players, irons. **Dining:** The Restaurant at The Victorian Inn, see separate listing. **Leisure Activities:** whirlpools, 2 garden hot tubs. *Fee:* massage. **Business Services:** meeting rooms. **Cards:** AX, DS, MC, VI. **Free Special Amenities:** full breakfast and local telephone calls.

——— WHERE TO DINE ———

ALEXANDER'S

American
$5-$20

Phone: 540/743-6511

Alexander's is family oriented eatery with a wide variety on the menu and friendly wait staff. Don't miss the bread pudding. Casual dress. **Bar:** Beer & wine. **Reservations:** accepted. **Hours:** 6 am-2 & 5-9 pm. **Address:** 410 W Main St 22835 **Location:** 0.3 mi w on US 211 business route. **Parking:** on-site and street. **Cards:** AX, CB, DC, DS, JC, MC, VI.

BROOKSIDE RESTAURANT
American
$4-$17

Phone: 540/743-5698

Diners in the mood for homemade soup or tasty, well-prepared salmon cakes won't be disappointed. The basic eatery prepares a good variety of standard favorites and spreads out a tempting salad bar. Homespun decor and wonderful service are other strengths. Don't miss seeing the brook running beside the restaurant. Casual dress. **Bar:** Beer & wine. **Hours:** Open 3/1-12/31 & 1/18-2/28; 7 am-8:30 pm. **Address:** 2978 US Hwy 211 E 22835 **Location:** On US 211 Bypass, 4.8 mi e; in The Cabins at Brookside. **Parking:** on-site. **Cards:** AX, CB, DC, DS, MC, VI.

DAN'S STEAK HOUSE
American
$10-$22

Phone: 540/743-6285

A Shenandoah Valley tradition, the steakhouse presents a menu that centers on fine-cut steaks. In addition to a friendly atmosphere, the dining room offers great views of the mountains. Casual dress. **Bar:** Full bar. **Hours:** 5 pm-9 pm, Fri & Sat 4 pm-9:30 pm, Sun noon-9 pm. Closed: 11/27, 12/25. **Address:** 8512 US 211 W 22835 **Location:** I-81, exit 264, 9 mi w on US 211. **Parking:** on-site. **Cards:** DS, MC, VI.

THE PARKHURST RESTAURANT ON RAINBOW HILL
American
$5-$14

Phone: 540/743-6009

The well-established, casual restaurant prepares a variety of soups, salads and entrees, including vegetarian dishes. The list of wines and beers is extensive. Casual dress. **Bar:** Beer & wine. **Hours:** 11:30 am-9 pm, Fri & Sat-10 pm. **Address:** 2547 US 211 W 22835 **Location:** US 211, 1.7 mi w of Luray Caverns. **Parking:** on-site. **Cards:** AX, CB, DC, DS, MC, VI.

THE RESTAURANT AT THE VICTORIAN INN
American
$17-$40

Phone: 540/743-1494

In a Victorian inn, the fine-dining establishment presents an excellent wine list to accompany classic American dishes. Background music enhances the relaxed ambience. Service is friendly. Dressy casual. **Bar:** Full bar. **Reservations:** suggested. **Hours:** 5 pm-9 pm; Tues hours vary. Closed: 12/25; also Mon. **Address:** 138 E Main St 22835 **Location:** 0.3 mi e on US 211 business route; in Woodruff Inns. **Parking:** on-site. **Cards:** AX, DC, DS, MC, VI.

LYNCHBURG pop. 65,269

——— WHERE TO STAY ———

BEST WESTERN LYNCHBURG *Book great rates at AAA.com*
Motel
$85-$130 All Year

Phone: (434)237-2986

Address: 2815 Candlers Mountain Rd 24502 **Location:** Jct US 29 and 460. **Facility:** 87 one-bedroom standard units. 2 stories (no elevator), exterior corridors. **Parking:** on-site. **Amenities:** voice mail, irons, hair dryers. *Some:* high-speed Internet. **Pool(s):** outdoor. **Guest Services:** valet laundry, wireless Internet. **Business Services:** meeting rooms. **Cards:** AX, CB, DC, DS, JC, MC, VI. **Free Special Amenities:** expanded continental breakfast and early check-in/late check-out.

AAA Benefit:
Members save 10% everyday, plus an exclusive frequent stay program.

   CALL   / SOME UNITS

COURTYARD BY MARRIOTT *Book great rates at AAA.com*
Small-scale Hotel
$98-$119 All Year

Phone: 434/846-7900

Address: 4640 Murray Pl 24502 **Location:** US 29, exit US 501, just e of SR 29, off Candlers Mountain Rd. Located opposite River Ridge Mall. **Facility:** Smoke free premises. 90 units. 87 one-bedroom standard units. 3 one-bedroom suites. 3 stories, interior corridors. *Bath:* combo or shower only. **Parking:** on-site. **Amenities:** high-speed Internet, dual phone lines, voice mail, irons, hair dryers. **Pool(s):** heated indoor. **Leisure Activities:** whirlpool, exercise room. **Guest Services:** valet and coin laundry, wireless Internet. **Business Services:** meeting rooms, PC. **Cards:** AX, DC, DS, MC, VI.

AAA Benefit:
Members save 5% off of the best available rate.

 CALL / SOME UNITS

DAYS INN OF LYNCHBURG *Book at AAA.com*
Small-scale Hotel
$75-$150 All Year

Phone: (434)847-8655

Address: 3320 Candlers Mountain Rd 24502 **Location:** US 29, exit US 501, just e. Located opposite River Ridge Mall. **Facility:** 131 one-bedroom standard units. 5 stories, interior corridors. **Parking:** on-site. **Terms:** cancellation fee imposed. **Amenities:** high-speed Internet, voice mail, irons, hair dryers. **Pool(s):** outdoor. **Leisure Activities:** exercise room. **Guest Services:** valet and coin laundry, area transportation, wireless Internet. **Business Services:** fax. **Cards:** AX, CB, DC, DS, MC, VI.

 / SOME UNITS FEE

ECONO LODGE

AAA SAVE

Motel
$80-$140 All Year

Phone: (434)847-1045

Address: 2400 Stadium Rd 24501 **Location:** US 29, exit 4 southbound; exit 6 northbound, just w on James St, then just n. **Facility:** 47 one-bedroom standard units, some with whirlpools. 2 stories (no elevator), exterior corridors. **Parking:** on-site. **Terms:** 1-2 night minimum stay - seasonal and/or weekends, 4 day cancellation notice. **Amenities:** high-speed Internet, hair dryers. *Some:* irons. **Guest Services:** wireless Internet. **Cards:** AX, DC, DS, MC, VI. **Free Special Amenities: continental breakfast and high-speed Internet.**

EXTENDED STAYAMERICA - UNIVERSITY BLVD   *Book at AAA.com*

Motel
$77-$175 All Year

Phone: (434)239-8863

Address: 1910 University Blvd 24502 **Location:** US 460, exit Candlers Mountain Rd/University Blvd. Located adjacent to Liberty University. **Facility:** 101 one-bedroom standard units with kitchens. 3 stories, interior corridors. *Bath:* combo or shower only. **Terms:** office hours 7 am-11 pm. **Amenities:** high-speed Internet (fee), voice mail, irons. **Guest Services:** coin laundry, wireless Internet. **Cards:** AX, DC, DS, JC, MC, VI.

FEDERAL CREST INN B&B

Historic Bed
& Breakfast
$135-$210 All Year

Phone: (434)845-6155

Address: 1101 Federal St 24504 **Location:** US 29, exit 1A (Main St), just w to 11th St, then 0.5 mi s. **Facility:** This Georgian Revival mansion, surrounded by mature magnolia trees, features intricate woodwork and a central staircase beneath a leaded-glass window. Smoke free premises. 4 units. 1 one- and 1 two-bedroom standard units. 2 one-bedroom suites, some with whirlpools. 2 stories (no elevator), interior corridors. *Bath:* combo or shower only. **Parking:** on-site. **Terms:** age restrictions may apply, 10 day cancellation notice. **Amenities:** video library, hair dryers. **Leisure Activities:** limited exercise equipment. **Guest Services:** wireless Internet. **Business Services:** meeting rooms. **Cards:** AX, DS, MC, VI.

HAMPTON INN   *Book great rates at AAA.com*

Small-scale Hotel
$99-$114 All Year

Phone: (434)237-2704

Address: 5604 Seminole Ave 24502 **Location:** US 460, exit Candlers Mountain Rd, 0.3 mi w; US 29, exit Candlers Mountain Rd. **Facility:** 65 one-bedroom standard units. 2 stories (no elevator), interior/exterior corridors. *Bath:* combo or shower only. **Parking:** on-site. **Terms:** 3 day cancellation notice. **Amenities:** high-speed Internet, voice mail, irons, hair dryers. **Guest Services:** valet laundry, wireless Internet. **Business Services:** business center. **Cards:** AX, CB, DC, DS, JC, MC, VI.

HOLIDAY INN EXPRESS   *Book at AAA.com*

Small-scale Hotel
$99-$104 All Year

Phone: (434)237-7771

Address: 5600 Seminole Ave 24502 **Location:** US 460, exit Candlers Mountain Rd, 0.3 mi w; US 29, exit Candlers Mountain Rd. **Facility:** 102 one-bedroom standard units, some with whirlpools. 3 stories, interior corridors. **Parking:** on-site. **Terms:** 3 day cancellation notice. **Amenities:** high-speed Internet, dual phone lines, voice mail, irons, hair dryers. **Pool(s):** outdoor. **Guest Services:** valet laundry, wireless Internet. **Business Services:** meeting rooms, business center. **Cards:** AX, CB, DC, DS, JC, MC, VI.

HOLIDAY INN SELECT   *Book at AAA.com*

Small-scale Hotel
$119 All Year

Phone: (434)528-2500

Address: 601 Main St 24504 **Location:** US 29 Expwy, exit 1 (Main St), just w; downtown. **Facility:** 241 one-bedroom standard units, some with whirlpools. 8 stories, interior corridors. *Bath:* combo or shower only. **Parking:** on-site. **Amenities:** video games (fee), high-speed Internet, dual phone lines, voice mail, irons, hair dryers. **Pool(s):** outdoor. **Leisure Activities:** exercise room. **Guest Services:** valet laundry, area transportation, wireless Internet. **Business Services:** conference facilities, business center. **Cards:** AX, DC, DS, MC, VI.

KIRKLEY HOTEL & CONFERENCE CENTER   *Book at AAA.com*

Small-scale Hotel
$90 All Year

Phone: 434/237-6333

Address: 2900 Candlers Mountain Rd 24502 **Location:** US 29 Expwy, exit 8A, just w. **Facility:** 167 units. 163 one-bedroom standard units. 4 two-bedroom suites. 5 stories, interior corridors. **Parking:** on-site. **Amenities:** high-speed Internet, dual phone lines, voice mail, irons, hair dryers. *Some:* DVD players (fee). **Pool(s):** heated indoor. **Leisure Activities:** saunas, whirlpool, exercise room. **Guest Services:** valet laundry, area transportation, wireless Internet. **Business Services:** conference facilities, business center. **Cards:** AX, DS, MC, VI.

LYNCHBURG SUPER 8 MOTEL   *Book at AAA.com*

Small-scale Hotel
Rates not provided

Phone: 434/846-1668

Address: 3736 Candlers Mountain Rd 24502 **Location:** US 29, exit 8B, just e. **Facility:** 59 one-bedroom standard units, some with whirlpools. 3 stories, interior corridors. *Bath:* combo or shower only. **Parking:** on-site. **Amenities:** safes (fee). **Leisure Activities:** exercise room. **Guest Services:** coin laundry, wireless Internet.

QUALITY INN   *Book great rates at AAA.com*

AAA SAVE

Small-scale Hotel
$59-$99 All Year

Phone: (434)847-9041

Address: 3125 Albert Lankford Dr 24501 **Location:** US 29, exit 7, just s. **Facility:** 120 units. 119 one-bedroom standard units. 1 one-bedroom suite. 5 stories, interior corridors. **Parking:** on-site. **Terms:** 15 day cancellation notice. **Amenities:** voice mail, irons, hair dryers. **Pool(s):** outdoor. **Leisure Activities:** exercise room. **Guest Services:** valet and coin laundry, wireless Internet. **Business Services:** meeting rooms, business center. **Cards:** AX, CB, DC, DS, JC, MC, VI. **Free Special Amenities: expanded continental breakfast and early check-in/late check-out.**

THE RESIDENCE BED & BREAKFAST
Phone: 434/845-6565

Historic Bed & Breakfast
$130-$195 All Year

Address: 2460 Rivermont Ave 24503 **Location:** US 29, 2 mi w on Main St (becomes Rivermont Ave). Located in the Rivermont Historic District. **Facility:** Located within walking distance of Randolph College, this grand 1915 Spanish Colonial home is decorated with the owner's European and Asian collections. Smoke free premises. 4 units. 3 one- and 1 two-bedroom standard units. 2 stories (no elevator), interior corridors. *Bath:* some shared or private. **Parking:** on-site. **Terms:** 7 day cancellation notice-fee imposed. **Amenities:** video library, hair dryers. *Some:* DVD players. **Leisure Activities:** bicycles. **Guest Services:** wireless Internet. **Business Services:** fax. **Cards:** MC, VI.

SLEEP INN LYNCHBURG
Book great rates at AAA.com
Phone: (434)846-6900

Small-scale Hotel
$75-$250 All Year

Address: 3620 Candlers Mountain Rd 24502 **Location:** US 29, exit 8B. **Facility:** 75 one-bedroom standard units. 4 stories, interior corridors. *Bath:* combo or shower only. **Parking:** on-site. **Amenities:** high-speed Internet, dual phone lines, voice mail, irons, hair dryers. **Leisure Activities:** exercise room. **Guest Services:** valet and coin laundry. **Business Services:** meeting rooms, fax. **Cards:** AX, CB, DC, DS, JC, MC, VI. **Free Special Amenities:** expanded continental breakfast and high-speed Internet.

WINGATE INN LYNCHBURG
Book at AAA.com
Phone: (434)845-1700

Small-scale Hotel
$119-$219 All Year

Address: 3777 Candlers Mountain Rd 24502 **Location:** Just se of US 460. **Facility:** 131 one-bedroom standard units, some with whirlpools. 5 stories, interior corridors. *Bath:* combo or shower only. **Parking:** on-site. **Amenities:** video games (fee), high-speed Internet, dual phone lines, voice mail, safes, irons, hair dryers. **Pool(s):** heated indoor. **Leisure Activities:** whirlpool, exercise room. **Guest Services:** valet laundry, wireless Internet. **Business Services:** meeting rooms, business center. **Cards:** AX, CB, DC, DS, JC, MC, VI.

———— WHERE TO DINE ————

BULL BRANCH
Phone: 434/847-8477

American
$15-$23

In a half basement dimly lit with candles, the dining room makes guests feel as though they've stepped into a 1930s speakeasy. The distinctive menu, printed on translucent rice paper, lists dishes with a touch of an Eastern influence. Food is accented with tangy curries, chutneys and spices. Among more traditional offerings are smashed potatoes and creamed spinach. Casual dress. **Bar:** Full bar. **Reservations:** accepted. **Hours:** 6 pm-9:30 pm, Fri & Sat-10 pm. Closed: 1/1, 11/27, 12/25; also Sun & Mon. **Address:** 109 11th St 24505 **Location:** Just ne of jct Main St. **Parking:** street. **Cards:** AX, DS, MC, VI.

BULL'S STEAKHOUSE
Phone: 434/385-7581

Steak House
$6-$15

Steak, prime rib, fajitas and Mexican specialties are menu mainstays at the steakhouse, a warm spot that welcomes guests to get comfortable. Dishes are hearty and satisfying. Casual dress. **Bar:** Full bar. **Hours:** 11 am-10 pm, Fri-10:30 pm, Sat 4:30 pm-10 pm. Closed major holidays; also Sun. **Address:** 1887 Graves Mill Rd 24551 **Location:** US 501 N, exit Graves Mill Rd, 2 mi w; in Graves Mill Shopping Center. **Parking:** on-site. **Cards:** AX, DC, DS, MC, VI.

CHARLEY'S
Phone: 434/237-5988

American
$6-$15

Charley's fits into the traditional mold of American bar and grill so expect to find a friendly casual spot and the standard menu of favorites such as burgers, ribs, fajitas, and more. Casual dress. **Bar:** Full bar. **Hours:** 11 am-10 pm, Fri & Sat-midnight. Closed: 1/1, 12/25. **Address:** 707 Graves Mill Rd 24502 **Location:** US 29, exit 11. **Parking:** on-site. **Cards:** AX, DS, MC, VI.

CROWN STERLING
Phone: 434/239-7744

Steak House
$15-$30

Locally owned and operated for more than 30 years, the restaurant provides ample parking and a cozy interior of fireplaces and wood-paneled walls. Diners get an open view of the cooking area. The aroma of charcoal-grilled steaks wafts through the dining area. Other entrees include preparations of lobster, shrimp, tuna and chicken. Formally attired servers are attentive. Dressy casual. **Bar:** Full bar. **Reservations:** accepted. **Hours:** 5:30 pm-9:30 pm, Sat 5 pm-10 pm. Closed major holidays; also Sun & Mon. **Address:** 6120 Fort Ave 24502 **Location:** US 501 N, exit 10A, just e. **Parking:** on-site. **Cards:** AX, CB, DC, DS, MC, VI.

THE DEPOT GRILLE
Phone: 434/846-4464

American
$7-$18

The simplest way to describe the restaurant's feel is to say it's like a Wild West saloon meeting a turn-of-the-20th-century church. Such choices as bison burgers and the savory signature ribs are prepared in the authentic railroad car kitchen. At Lynchburg Riverfront, the restaurant offers traditional American fare at reasonable prices. Casual dress. **Bar:** Full bar. **Hours:** 11 am-10 pm, Fri & Sat-11 pm, Sun-9 pm. Closed: 7/4, 11/27, 12/25. **Address:** 10 Ninth St 24504 **Location:** US 29 N, exit Main St W, just n on Ninth St to the Riverfront. **Parking:** on-site. **Cards:** AX, CB, DC, DS, JC, MC, VI.

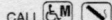

THE FARM BASKET

Deli/Subs
Sandwiches
$4-$7

Phone: 434/528-1107

This place's box lunches grace many a local's picnic or office desk. Delicious sandwiches, Southern specialties and gourmet desserts are the draw. Among favorites are country ham biscuits, apple dapple cake and traditional side salads, such as tomato aspic and marinated coleslaw. Casual dress. **Hours:** 10 am-3 pm. Closed major holidays; also Sun. **Address:** 2008 Langhorne Rd 24501 **Location:** Jct US 29 business route, 2 mi w. **Parking:** on-site. **Cards:** AX, DS, MC, VI.

ISABELLA'S ITALIAN TRATTORIA

Northern Italian
$5-$23

Phone: 434/385-1660

Part warm Italian trattoria and part hip, stylish bistro, Isabella's brings Northern Italian fare and stone oven cooking to Southwest Virginia with a daily changing menu of rustic pasta, chops and seafood based on fresh local produce and imported ingredients. Dishes might include stacked eggplant parmigiana, toasted fresh ravioli, braised lamb shank and Milanese-style tiramisu. Accents of cool cobalt and warm yellow provide punch around the sleek black bar. Casual dress. **Bar:** Full bar. **Reservations:** suggested. **Hours:** 11:30 am-2 & 5-9 pm, Fri-10 pm, Sat 5 pm-10 pm. Closed major holidays; also Sun. **Address:** 3225 Old Forest Rd 24501 **Location:** 1 mi n from US 501; in the Forest Plaza West Shopping Center. **Parking:** on-site. **Cards:** AX, DS, MC, VI.

CALL

JAZZ STREET GRILL

Regional American
$7-$17

Phone: 434/385-0100

As the name implies, the Jazz Street Grill specializes in New Orleans Creole-style cuisine such as plump crawfish etouffee, shrimp po'boys, blackened dishes, andouille and gumbo. Live entertainment jazzes up the place on Friday and Saturday nights. Casual dress. **Bar:** Full bar. **Hours:** 11:30 am-10 pm, Fri & Sat-midnight, Sun 11 am-3 pm. Closed major holidays. **Address:** 2335 Old Forest Rd 24501 **Location:** 1 mi n from US 501; in Forest Plaza West Shopping Center. **Parking:** on-site. **Cards:** AX, DS, MC, VI.

JUI-LIN'S TEA HOUSE, SUSHI & SANDWICH SHOPPE

Asian
$4-$7

Phone: 434/528-5351

The small lunch spot prepares such Pan-Asian specialties as sushi, chicken satay, Vietnamese summer rolls and miso soup, as well as American-style sandwiches. For a fruity treat, try the bubble teas in fun tropical flavors. Casual dress. **Hours:** 10:30 am-6 pm, Sat 11:30 am-3:30 pm. Closed major holidays; also Sun. **Address:** 207 9th St 24504 **Location:** Between Main and Church sts; downtown. **Parking:** street. **Cards:** MC, VI.

LA PLAZA ALEGRE

Latino
$5-$15

Phone: 434/846-0303

Don't let the diner fool you. Inside, authentic Mexican, Spanish and Latin fare awaits. You can't go wrong with the hearty tortilla soup, the fragrant paellas or the popular fajitas. Freshness abounds, and the black beans and rice are pure comfort. Lynchburg's Main St. never had it so good. Casual dress. **Bar:** Full bar. **Reservations:** accepted. **Hours:** 11 am-3 & 5-10 pm, Sun 10 am-9 pm. Closed major holidays. **Address:** 1125 Main St 24504 **Location:** At 12th and Main sts; downtown. **Parking:** on-site. **Cards:** AX, DS, MC, VI.

MACADO'S

Deli/Subs
Sandwiches
$5-$10

Phone: 434/845-6464

The lively student hangout is well-loved for its lengthy list of imaginative overstuffed sandwiches and wraps. Macaroni and cheese, chili and oversized ice cream desserts also are popular. Casual dress. **Bar:** Full bar. **Reservations:** not accepted. **Hours:** 8 am-midnight. Closed: 11/27, 12/25. **Address:** 3744 Candlers Mountain Rd 24502 **Location:** US 29, exit 8B, just e. **Parking:** on-site. **Cards:** AX, MC, VI.

CALL

MAGNOLIA FOODS

Gourmet Grocery
$3-$12

Phone: 434/528-5442

A good spot for picking up picnic fixings, the gourmet market and bakery prepares specialty sandwiches, salads and limited entrees. Casual dress. **Bar:** Beer & wine. **Reservations:** not accepted. **Hours:** 9 am-7 pm, Sat 10 am-5 pm. Closed major holidays; also Sun. **Address:** 2476 Rivermont Ave 24503 **Location:** US 29, 2 mi w on Main St (becomes Rivermont Ave); located adjacent to Randolph College. **Parking:** on-site. **Cards:** AX, DS, MC, VI.

MAIN ST EATERY

Continental
$7-$21

Phone: 434/847-2500

A lively, bustling atmosphere fills the restored historic building. The chef/owner's Swiss lineage is reflected in the interesting, eclectic menu. Among dishes are German rahmschnitzel with spaetzle, almond-crusted scallops and pork loin with chipotle sauce. Casual dress. **Bar:** Full bar. **Reservations:** accepted. **Hours:** 4:30 pm-9:30 pm. Closed major holidays; also Sun. **Address:** 907 Main St 24504 **Location:** US 29, exit Main St; center of downtown. **Parking:** street. **Cards:** AX, DC, DS, MC, VI.

MERIWETHER'S MARKET RESTAURANT

American
$6-$25

Phone: 434/384-3311

The contemporary "city-style" dining area and bar is a showcase for the talents of local artists. A seasonally changing menu appeals to the casual gourmet with a contemporary interpretation of Southern cuisine. Among selections are preparations of fresh seafood, such as shrimp and grits, gourmet pizza and innovative salads. Live jazz drifts in the air on Wednesday evenings. Casual dress. **Bar:** Full bar. **Reservations:** suggested, weekends. **Hours:** 11:30 am-2:30 & 5:30-9:30 pm, Fri & Sat-10 pm. Closed major holidays; also Sun. **Address:** 4925 Boonsboro Rd 24503 **Location:** US 29, exit Main St, 5.7 mi n, then w on Main St, Rivermont Ave and Boonsboro Rd; in Boonsboro Shopping Center. **Parking:** on-site. **Cards:** AX, DS, MC, VI.

CALL

MILAN INDIAN CUISINE

Indian
$6-$16

Phone: 434/237-7990

Tandoori specialties and bread baked in a clay oven are at the centerpiece of the traditional menu of curried, lamb and vegetarian dishes. The exotic atmosphere features artwork and instrumental music. The weekday buffet draws a large lunch clientele. Casual dress. **Bar:** Full bar. **Hours:** 11:30 am-3 & 5-10 pm, Fri-10:30 pm, Sat noon-3 & 5-10:30 pm, Sun noon-3 & 5-10 pm. **Address:** 2124 Wards Rd 24502 **Location:** Just n of jct Candlers Mountain Rd; in strip mall. **Parking:** on-site. **Cards:** AX, DC, DS, MC, VI.

CALL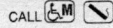

MILANO'S ITALIAN RESTAURANT
Phone: 434/384-3400

Traditional Italian
$6-$15

In a small strip mall on the outskirts of the city, this restaurant sports a semi-formal atmosphere, with a fountain as a centerpiece. Representative of the fare are specialty pizzas, pasta dishes and some classic entrees, including chicken Marsala and veal selections. Casual dress. **Bar:** Full bar. **Hours:** 11:30 am-9:30 pm, Fri-10:30 pm, Sat 4 pm-10:30 pm, Sun noon-9:30 pm. Closed: 1/1, 12/25. **Address:** 5006 Boonsboro Rd 24503 **Location:** Just e of jct US 501; in Oakwood Square. **Parking:** on-site. **Cards:** AX, MC, VI.

MONTE CARLO ITALIAN RESTAURANT
Phone: 434/385-7711

Italian
$5-$18

Diners can expect to find such Italian-American favorites as pasta and pizza, as well as specialties that reflect the chef's Sicilian heritage, including homemade gnocchi with pesto, veal rollatini and fish oreganato. Casual dress. **Bar:** Full bar. **Reservations:** accepted. **Hours:** 11 am-2 & 4-10 pm, Sat 4 pm-11 pm, Sun 4 pm-10 pm. Closed: 11/27, 12/25. **Address:** 3230 Old Forest Rd 24501 **Location:** 1 mi n from US 501; in Forest Plaza West Shopping Center. **Parking:** on-site. **Cards:** AX, DC, DS, MC, VI.

CALL 🅑Ⓜ 🅝

SHADS - UPSTAIRS AT TROTTERS
Phone: 434/846-3545

American
$7-$22

You'll like the casual, neighborhood setting, including patio seating when weather permits. American specialties range from sandwiches, wraps, and steak to shrimp and grits with a spicy Cajun sauce. Be sure to try the house salad with mandarin oranges. Casual dress. **Bar:** Full bar. **Hours:** 7 am-2 pm, Wed & Fri-9 pm, Sun 8 am-8 pm. Closed: 12/24, 12/25. **Address:** 2496 Rivermont Ave 24503 **Location:** US 29, 2 mi w on Main St/Rivermont Ave; adjacent to Randolph College. **Parking:** street. **Cards:** AX, DC, DS, MC, VI.

SPRING HOUSE DINING ROOM & RECEPTION HALL
Phone: 434/993-2475

Southern
$12-$16

Composed entirely of plate-glass windows, the dining room's rear wall affords an expansive view of the lake and woods. Guests feel right at home with family-style service and a prix fixe meal that includes two entrees and five Southern-style side dishes. Casual dress. **Bar:** Full bar. **Hours:** 4:30 pm-9 pm, Sun noon-8 pm. Closed: 12/25; also Mon-Wed. **Address:** 9789 Richmond Hwy 24504 **Location:** 10 mi e on US 460. **Parking:** on-site. **Cards:** AX, DS, MC, VI.

CALL 🅑Ⓜ 🅝

THAI 99
Phone: 434/528-2855

Thai
$7-$9

Thai favorites shape the menu of the cozy family-run spot. Pad thai, panang curry and drunken noodles are predictable favorites, but adventurous diners will be tempted by such chef specialties as lamb two seasons and mixed seafood with choo chee sauce. Casual dress. **Bar:** Beer & wine. **Reservations:** accepted. **Hours:** 11 am-2:30 & 5-9 pm, Fri & Sat-9:30 pm. Closed major holidays; also Sun. **Address:** 21 Wadsworth St, Suite 100 24501 **Location:** Just w of Memorial Ave. **Parking:** on-site. **Cards:** AX, MC, VI.

CALL 🅑Ⓜ

MADISON pop. 210

------ **WHERE TO DINE** ------

THE BAVARIAN CHEF
Phone: 540/948-6505

German
$16-$24

You can't go wrong when ordering the Wiener schnitzel, and it arrives at your table fast and hot. The authentic German atmosphere enhances both the food and the experience. Table spacing can be tight. Costumed staff service is attentive and capable. Casual dress. **Bar:** Full bar. **Reservations:** suggested. **Hours:** 4:30 pm-9 pm; Sun from 11:30 am. Closed: 1/1, 12/24, 12/25; also Mon & Tues. **Address:** US 29 S 22727 **Location:** 4 mi s on US 29; 2.2 mi s of jct SR 230. **Parking:** on-site. **Cards:** AX, MC, VI.

MANAKIN —*See Richmond p. 880.*

MANASSAS —*See District Of Columbia p. 544.*

MARION pop. 6,349

------ **WHERE TO STAY** ------

BEST WESTERN-MARION
Book great rates at AAA.com
Phone: 276/783-3193

AAA SAVE

Small-scale Hotel
Rates not provided

Address: 1424 N Main St 24354 **Location:** I-81, exit 47, 0.3 mi s on US 11. **Facility:** 80 one-bedroom standard units. 2-3 stories (no elevator), exterior corridors. *Bath:* combo or shower only. **Parking:** on-site. **Amenities:** irons, hair dryers. *Some:* high-speed Internet. **Pool(s):** outdoor. **Guest Services:** valet laundry, wireless Internet. **Business Services:** meeting rooms, fax (fee). **Free Special Amenities:** full breakfast and high-speed Internet.

AAA Benefit:
Members save 10% everyday, plus an exclusive frequent stay program.

ECONO LODGE

Small-scale Hotel
$59-$89 All Year

Book at AAA.com

Phone: (276)783-6031

Address: 1420 N Main St 24354 **Location:** I-81, exit 47, 0.3 mi s on US 11. **Facility:** 40 one-bedroom standard units. 2 stories (no elevator), exterior corridors. **Parking:** on-site. **Terms:** 10 day cancellation notice-fee imposed. **Amenities:** *Some:* irons, hair dryers. **Guest Services:** wireless Internet. **Business Services:** fax (fee). **Cards:** AX, DS, MC, VI.

GENERAL FRANCIS MARION HOTEL

(AAA) [SAVE]

Small-scale Hotel
$85-$250 All Year

Phone: 276/783-4800

Address: 107 E Main St 24354 **Location:** I-81, exit 45, 2.1 mi w on SR 16, then 0.4 mi s. **Facility:** 36 one-bedroom standard units. 5 stories, interior corridors. *Bath:* combo or shower only. **Parking:** on-site. **Terms:** 3 day cancellation notice. **Amenities:** high-speed Internet, voice mail, hair dryers. *Some:* DVD players, irons. **Guest Services:** valet laundry, wireless Internet. **Business Services:** meeting rooms, PC, fax (fee). **Cards:** AX, DS, MC, VI. **Free Special Amenities: continental breakfast and high-speed Internet.**

MARTINSVILLE pop. 15,416

──── WHERE TO STAY ────

BEST LODGE

Motel
$48-$68 All Year

Phone: (276)647-3941

Address: 1985 Virginia Ave 24112 **Location:** Jct US 58, 2.5 mi n on US 220 business route. **Facility:** 47 one-bedroom standard units. 2 stories (no elevator), exterior corridors. **Parking:** on-site. **Terms:** cancellation fee imposed. **Guest Services:** coin laundry. **Cards:** AX, DC, DS, MC, VI.

BEST WESTERN MARTINSVILLE INN

(AAA) [SAVE]

Small-scale Hotel
$85 All Year

Book great rates at AAA.com

Phone: (276)632-5611

Address: US 220 Business Rt S 24112 **Location:** Jct US 58, 2.3 mi n. **Facility:** 95 one-bedroom standard units. 2 stories (no elevator), exterior corridors. **Parking:** on-site. **Amenities:** high-speed Internet, voice mail, irons, hair dryers. **Pool(s):** outdoor. **Leisure Activities:** barbecue grill area, exercise room. **Guest Services:** valet and coin laundry, wireless Internet. **Business Services:** meeting rooms, business center. **Cards:** AX, DC, DS, MC, VI. **Free Special Amenities: full breakfast and high-speed Internet.**

AAA Benefit:
Members save 10% everyday, plus an exclusive frequent stay program.

HAMPTON INN

Small-scale Hotel
$99-$134 All Year

Book great rates at AAA.com

Phone: (276)647-4700

Address: 50 Hampton Dr 24112 **Location:** Jct US 58, 2.5 mi n on US 220 business route. **Facility:** 68 one-bedroom standard units, some with whirlpools. 4 stories, interior corridors. *Bath:* combo or shower only. **Parking:** on-site. **Terms:** 3 day cancellation notice. **Amenities:** video games, high-speed Internet, dual phone lines, voice mail, irons, hair dryers. *Some:* DVD players. **Pool(s):** outdoor. **Leisure Activities:** whirlpool, exercise room. **Guest Services:** coin laundry, wireless Internet. **Business Services:** meeting rooms, business center. **Cards:** AX, CB, DC, DS, JC, MC, VI.

HOLIDAY INN EXPRESS

Small-scale Hotel
$76-$97 All Year

Book at AAA.com

Phone: (276)666-6835

Address: 1895 Virgina Ave 24112 **Location:** Jct US 58, 2.4 mi n on US 220 business route. **Facility:** 70 one-bedroom standard units, some with whirlpools. 2 stories (no elevator), interior corridors. *Bath:* combo or shower only. **Parking:** on-site. **Terms:** 3 day cancellation notice. **Amenities:** video games, high-speed Internet, voice mail, irons, hair dryers. **Pool(s):** outdoor. **Guest Services:** valet laundry, wireless Internet. **Business Services:** meeting rooms, PC. **Cards:** AX, CB, DC, DS, JC, MC, VI.

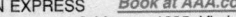

──── WHERE TO DINE ────

CHINA BUFFET

Chinese
$5-$11

Phone: 276/632-8689

The star attraction is the 60-item buffet bar, which is loaded with such popular favorites as General Tso chicken, spareribs and sweet and sour pork. In a setting that values function over form, the family restaurant offers fresh food and prompt, attentive service. Casual dress. **Bar:** Beer only. **Hours:** 11 am-10 pm, Fri & Sat-11 pm, Sun noon-10 pm. **Closed:** 11/27, 12/25. **Address:** 970 Memorial Blvd 24112 **Location:** Jct US 58, 1.5 mi n on US 220 business route. **Parking:** on-site. **Cards:** MC, VI.

PIGS-R-US BAR-B-QUE

Barbecue
$4-$15

Phone: 276/632-1161

Real pit cooked barbeque is offered at this restaurant. Friendly service, racing themed decor and some of the best hushpuppies you'll ever taste. Casual dress. **Bar:** Beer only. **Hours:** 11 am-9 pm. **Closed:** 12/25; also Sun. **Address:** 1014 Liberty St 24112 **Location:** Jct US 58, 1.6 mi n US 220 business route, 1 mi e on Commonweath Blvd, then 1.2 mi n. **Parking:** on-site. **Cards:** MC, VI.

MAX MEADOWS pop. 512

——— WHERE TO STAY ———

GATEWAY MOTEL

Motel
Rates not provided

Phone: 276/637-3119

Address: 5465 E Lee Hwy 24360 **Location:** I-81, exit 86, just w, then 0.5 mi s on service road. **Facility:** 10 one-bedroom standard units. 1 story, exterior corridors. **Parking:** on-site.

HAMPTON INN OF FT. CHISWELL *Book great rates at AAA.com*   **Phone:** 276/637-4027

▽▽▽▽

Small-scale Hotel
Rates not provided

Address: 199 Ft Chiswell Rd 24360 **Location:** I-77/81, exit 80, just w. **Facility:** 63 one-bedroom standard units, some with whirlpools. 4 stories, interior corridors. *Bath:* combo or shower only. **Parking:** on-site. **Amenities:** high-speed Internet, voice mail, irons, hair dryers. **Pool(s):** outdoor. **Leisure Activities:** limited exercise equipment. **Guest Services:** wireless Internet. **Business Services:** meeting rooms, PC.

SUPER 8 MOTEL   *Book great rates at AAA.com*   **Phone:** 276/637-4141

ⒶⒶⒶ [SAVE]

▽▽▽▽

Small-scale Hotel
Rates not provided

Address: 194 Ft Chiswell Rd 24360 **Location:** I-77/81, exit 80, just e. **Facility:** 60 one-bedroom standard units, some with whirlpools. 2 stories (no elevator), exterior corridors. **Parking:** on-site. **Amenities:** *Some:* irons, hair dryers. **Guest Services:** wireless Internet. **Free Special Amenities:** continental breakfast and high-speed Internet.

MCGAHEYSVILLE

——— WHERE TO DINE ———

HANK'S SMOKEHOUSE AND DELI   **Phone:** 540/289-7667

▽▽ ▽▽

Barbecue
$8-$21

The Southern grill centers its menu on numerous choices of barbecue. A delicatessen and wine shop are adjacent to the dining area. Casual dress. **Bar:** Beer only. **Hours:** 11 am-3 & 5-9 pm. Closed major holidays. **Address:** 49 Bloomer Springs Rd 22840 **Location:** I-81, exit 247, 6 mi e on US 33. **Parking:** on-site. **Cards:** MC, VI.

THUNDERBIRD DINER   **Phone:** 540/289-5094

▽▽

American
$6-$18

Homemade cooking, including many breakfast specialties and dessert choices, pleases patrons who eat at the comfortable diner. Casual dress. **Hours:** 6 am-8 pm. Closed: 12/25. **Address:** 42 Island Ford Rd 22840 **Location:** I-81, exit 247, 5.9 mi e on US 33. **Parking:** on-site. **Cards:** MC, VI.

MCLEAN —*See District Of Columbia p. 547.*

MEADOWS OF DAN

——— WHERE TO DINE ———

THE RESTAURANT AT CHATEAU MORRISETTE   **Phone:** 540/593-2865

▽▽▽▽

Continental
$9-$32

Guests can experience elegant dining in a romantic French country atmosphere. The hillside location is scenic and charming.. Nicely presented farm-raised catfish, game and seafood dishes grace the menu, as do some heavenly desserts. Patio seating is an option in nice weather. Dressy casual. **Bar:** Beer & wine. **Reservations:** suggested. **Hours:** 11 am-2 pm, Fri & Sat also 6 pm-9 pm, Sun 11 am-3 pm. Closed: 11/27, 12/24, 12/25; also Mon & Tues. **Address:** 287 Winery Rd SW 24091 **Location:** Blue Ridge Pkwy, between Mileposts 171 and 172, exit w on Black Ridge Rd, just s on CR 777 (Winery Rd), then 0.3 mi; at the winery. **Parking:** on-site. **Cards:** AX, MC, VI.

MECHANICSVILLE —*See Richmond p. 880.*

MIDDLEBURG —*See District Of Columbia p. 551.*

MIDDLETOWN pop. 1,015

——— WHERE TO STAY ———

SUPER 8 MOTEL   *Book at AAA.com*   **Phone:** 540/868-1800

▽▽

Small-scale Hotel
Rates not provided

Address: 2120 Relaince Rd 22645 **Location:** I-81, exit 302. **Facility:** 49 one-bedroom standard units, some with whirlpools. 3 stories, interior corridors. **Parking:** on-site. **Pool(s):** heated indoor. **Guest Services:** coin laundry.

WAYSIDE INN SINCE 1797

Historic
Country Inn
$99-$159 All Year

Phone: (540)869-1797
Address: 7783 Main St 22645 **Location:** I-81, exit 302, just w to US 11, then 0.4 mi s. **Facility:** Said to have been in continuous operation since 1797, the elegantly restored inn offers gracious hospitality and enchanting rooms with antiques. Designated smoking area. 24 one-bedroom standard units. 3 stories (no elevator), interior corridors. *Bath:* combo or shower only. **Parking:** on-site. **Terms:** cancellation fee imposed. **Dining:** restaurant, see separate listing. **Guest Services:** wireless Internet. **Business Services:** meeting rooms. **Cards:** AX, DC, DS, MC, VI. **Free Special Amenities:** continental breakfast and high-speed Internet.

------- WHERE TO DINE -------

THE IRISH ISLE

Irish
$8-$20

Phone: 540/868-9877
Good times await at the restaurant, where a huge selection of ales pairs with varied choices of Irish cuisine. Casual dress. **Bar:** Full bar. **Hours:** 11 am-11 pm, Sun noon-9 pm. Closed: 12/25; also Mon. **Address:** 7843 Main St 22645 **Location:** I-81, exit 302, just w to US 11, then 0.5 mi s. **Parking:** on-site. **Cards:** AX, CB, DC, DS, JC, MC, VI.

WAYSIDE INN SINCE 1797

Regional American
$8-$23

Phone: 540/869-1797
Rich, creamy peanut soup is a Virginia favorite and a house specialty, along with spoon bread and country ham. The historic inn exudes Colonial ambience. Shenandoah Valley products factor heavily on the menu, which lists a wide variety of classic American cuisine. Casual dress. **Bar:** Full bar. **Reservations:** suggested. **Hours:** 11:30 am-2:30 & 5-9 pm, Fri & Sat-10 pm. **Address:** 7783 Main St 22645 **Location:** I-81, exit 302, just w to US 11, then 0.4 mi s; in Wayside Inn Since 1797. **Parking:** on-site. **Cards:** AX, CB, DC, MC, VI. **Historic**

MIDLOTHIAN —See Richmond p. 881.

MINT SPRING

------- WHERE TO STAY -------

DAYS INN-STAUNTON

Book at AAA.com

Motel
Rates not provided

Phone: 540/337-3031
Location: I-81, exit 217, just e on SR 654. **Facility:** 119 one-bedroom standard units. 2 stories (no elevator), exterior corridors. *Bath:* combo or shower only. **Parking:** on-site. **Amenities:** hair dryers. **Pool(s):** outdoor.

MONTCLAIR —See District Of Columbia p. 551.

MOUNT CRAWFORD pop. 254

------- WHERE TO DINE -------

EVERS FAMILY RESTAURANT

American
$6-$10

Phone: 540/433-0993
Value-oriented buffet dining is what the laid-back restaurant is all about. Home-style fare includes ham, chicken and lots of country vegetables, such as hominy. The Friday night buffet is stocked with seafood. Servers are prompt and pleasant. Casual dress. **Hours:** 11 am-8 pm, Fri & Sat-9 pm, Sun-6 pm. Closed major holidays. **Address:** Rt 11 22801 **Location:** I-81, exit 240, 0.6 mi w on SR 257, then 0.3 mi n. **Parking:** on-site. **Cards:** MC, VI.

MOUNT JACKSON pop. 1,664

------- WHERE TO STAY -------

SUPER 8 MOTEL

Book great rates at AAA.com

Small-scale Hotel
Rates not provided

Phone: 540/477-2911
Address: 250 Conicville Blvd 22842 **Location:** I-81, exit 273, just e. **Facility:** 82 one-bedroom standard units. 2 stories (no elevator), exterior corridors. **Parking:** on-site. **Amenities:** high-speed Internet, voice mail, irons, hair dryers. **Pool(s):** outdoor. **Leisure Activities:** tennis court, basketball. **Guest Services:** wireless Internet. **Business Services:** meeting rooms, PC, fax (fee). **Free Special Amenities:** continental breakfast and high-speed Internet.

THE WIDOW KIP'S

Bed & Breakfast
$90-$125 All Year

Phone: (540)477-2400
Address: 355 Orchard Dr 22842-9753 **Location:** I-81, exit 273, 1.5 mi s on US 11, just w on SR 263, then just sw on SR 698. Located in a quiet country setting. **Facility:** In the Shenandoah Valley, the restored 1830 Colonial home offers personal hospitality, a library, recreational opportunities, gardens and a pool. Smoke free premises. 7 units. 6 one- and 1 two-bedroom standard units. 2 stories (no elevator), interior corridors. *Bath:* combo or shower only. **Parking:** on-site. **Terms:** age restrictions may apply, 5 day cancellation notice. **Amenities:** video library. **Pool(s):** outdoor. **Business Services:** meeting rooms. **Cards:** MC, VI.

MOUNT VERNON —See District Of Columbia p. 551.

NASSAWADOX pop. 572

—— WHERE TO DINE ——

THE GREAT MACHIPONGO CLAM SHACK   Phone: 757/442-3800

Seafood
$6-$13

The "Eat & Drive" sign lures many a traveler into the small fish shop for fresh lunch entrees to go. Among choices are steamed clams or shrimp, seafood cake sandwich and stuffed clams. Casual dress. **Bar:** Beer & wine. **Hours:** 9 am-6 pm; to 5 pm off season. Closed: 11/27, 12/25. **Address:** 6468 Lankford Hwy 23413 **Location:** 0.8 mi n on US 13. **Parking:** on-site. **Cards:** DS, MC, VI.

CALL

LITTLE ITALY   Phone: 757/442-7831

Italian
$6-$16

Those who tire of Eastern Shore seafood houses can stop here for favorite Italian specialties, including baked pasta, pizza and hearty, filling subs. Casual dress. **Bar:** Full bar. **Hours:** 11 am-9 pm. Closed major holidays; also Sun & Mon. **Address:** 10227 Rogers Dr 23413 **Location:** On US 13; center. **Parking:** on-site. **Cards:** AX, MC, VI.

NATURAL BRIDGE

—— WHERE TO DINE ——

COLONIAL DINING ROOM   Phone: 540/291-2121

American
$17-$30

The large, elegant dining room is enhanced with brass chandeliers, opulent window treatments and striking red walls. The charming veranda offers spectacular mountain views. The menu favors Southern entrees, accompanied by traditional spoon bread. Classic American cuisine. Casual dress. **Bar:** Full bar. **Reservations:** suggested. **Hours:** 7 am-10 & 5:30-8:30 pm, Fri & Sat-9:30 pm, Sun 7 am-10, noon-3 & 5:30-8:30 pm; hours vary 12/1-3/31. **Address:** 15 Appledore Ln 24578 **Location:** I-81, exit 175, 1.7 mi n on US 11; in The Natural Bridge Hotel. **Parking:** on-site. **Cards:** AX, DS, MC, VI.

FANCY HILL RESTAURANT   Phone: 540/291-2860

American
$6-$15

The casual, informal restaurant, a favorite of families, serves excellent homemade bread and soup and such tasty, traditional fare as grilled chicken. The cheerful, bright dining room is well attended by a friendly staff of thoughtful servers. License plates from most all 50 states adorn the walls. Wonderful scenic mountain views. Casual dress. **Bar:** Beer & wine. **Hours:** 7 am-9 pm, Fri & Sat-9:30 pm; to 8 pm in winter. Closed major holidays; also Wed. **Address:** 4832 S Lee Hwy 24578 **Location:** I-81, exit 180A, just e on US 11. **Parking:** on-site. **Cards:** CB, DC, DS, MC, VI.

PINK CADILLAC DINER   Phone: 540/291-2378

American
$5-$14

The '50s come alive again at this restaurant. From Elvis to Marilyn, nostalgia flows from every corner. And the food-classic American fare-is just as great as the atmosphere. Set aside some room to enjoy selections from the ice cream parlor. Casual dress. **Hours:** 7 am-9 pm. Closed major holidays. **Address:** 4347 S Lee Hwy 24578 **Location:** I-81, exit 180, just n on US 11. **Parking:** on-site. **Cards:** AX, DS, MC, VI.

NELLYSFORD

—— WHERE TO STAY ——

THE MEANDER INN   Phone: (434)361-1121

Historic Bed & Breakfast
$115-$125 All Year

Address: 3100 Berry Hill Rd 22958 **Location:** 2 mi n on SR 151, 0.5 mi e on SR 612. Located in a quiet area. **Facility:** Guests who take to the front porch of this Victorian-era farmhouse are afforded picturesque views of mountains, surrounding water and horse pastures. Smoke free premises. 5 one-bedroom standard units. 2 stories (no elevator), interior corridors. *Bath:* combo or shower only. **Parking:** on-site. **Terms:** 2 night minimum stay - weekends, 14 day cancellation notice. **Amenities:** hair dryers. **Leisure Activities:** whirlpool, fishing, hiking trails. **Guest Services:** wireless Internet. **Cards:** AX, MC, VI.

WINTERGREEN RESORT INC   *Book at AAA.com*   Phone: (434)325-2200

Resort
Large-scale Hotel
$205-$874 12/1-2/28
$190-$778 3/1-11/30

Address: Rt 664 22958 **Location:** SR 664, 4.5 mi w of jct SR 151. Located in a quiet area. **Facility:** Find recreational activities for every age at this all-season resort atop a mountain with great views and reached by a tree-lined drive. 316 units. 158 one- and 98 two-bedroom standard units, some with kitchens. 60 three-bedroom suites with efficiencies. 2-4 stories, interior/exterior corridors. **Parking:** on-site. **Terms:** check-in 4 pm, 2 night minimum stay - weekends, 14 day cancellation notice-fee imposed. **Amenities:** voice mail, irons, hair dryers. *Some:* DVD players, CD players. **Pool(s):** 3 heated outdoor, heated indoor. **Leisure Activities:** saunas, whirlpools, steamrooms, rental canoes, rental paddleboats, fishing, 21 tennis courts (3 indoor, 10 lighted), recreation programs, hiking trails, playground, spa, basketball, horseshoes, volleyball. *Fee:* golf-45 holes, miniature golf, downhill skiing, bicycles, horseback riding, game room. **Guest Services:** coin laundry, area transportation (fee), wireless Internet. **Business Services:** conference facilities, business center. **Cards:** AX, DS, MC, VI.

NEW CHURCH

—— WHERE TO STAY ——

THE GARDEN & THE SEA INN

Historic Bed
& Breakfast

Rates not provided

Phone: 757/824-0672

Address: 4188 Nelson Rd 23415 **Location:** US 13, 0.3 mi n, just w on CR 710 (Nelson Rd). **Facility:** Wraparound porches accent this Victorian home, which offers spacious guest rooms and baths decorated in pastel shades. Smoke free premises. 8 units. 7 one-bedroom standard units, some with whirlpools. 1 one-bedroom suite with whirlpool. 2 stories (no elevator), interior corridors. **Parking:** on-site. **Terms:** open 4/1-11/30. **Amenities:** DVD players, high-speed Internet, hair dryers. **Pool(s):** heated outdoor. **Leisure Activities:** exercise room. **Guest Services:** wireless Internet.

NEW MARKET pop. 1,637

—— WHERE TO STAY ——

BLUE RIDGE INN

Motel

$45-$85 3/1-11/30
$35-$60 12/1-2/28

Phone: (540)740-4136

Address: 2251 Old Valley Pike 22844 **Location:** I-81, exit 264, 1 mi n on US 11. Located in a quiet rural area. **Facility:** 18 one-bedroom standard units. 1 story, exterior corridors. *Bath:* shower only. **Parking:** on-site. **Terms:** 7 day cancellation notice-fee imposed. **Leisure Activities:** barbecue grill, playground. **Cards:** DS, MC, VI. **Free Special Amenities:** local telephone calls and preferred room (subject to availability with advance reservations).

BUDGET INN

Motel

$29-$69 3/1-11/15
$29-$49 11/16-2/28

Phone: (540)740-3105

Address: 2192 Old Valley Pike 22844 **Location:** I-81, exit 264, 1 mi n on US 11. Located in a quiet rural area. **Facility:** 14 one-bedroom standard units. 1 story, exterior corridors. *Bath:* combo or shower only. **Parking:** on-site. **Terms:** 3 day cancellation notice-fee imposed. **Leisure Activities:** playground, basketball. **Cards:** AX, DC, DS, MC, VI. **Free Special Amenities:** local telephone calls and early check-in/late check-out.

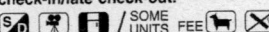

CROSS ROADS INN B&B

Bed & Breakfast

$75-$135 All Year

Phone: 540/740-4157

Address: 9222 John Sevier Rd 22844 **Location:** I-81, exit 264, 0.6 mi e on US 211. Located in a quiet area. **Facility:** The inn offers large lodgings and grounds with flower gardens and a white picket fence in a serene setting near Civil War sites and antiques shops. Smoke free premises. 6 one-bedroom standard units, some with whirlpools. 2 stories (no elevator), interior corridors. *Bath:* combo or shower only. **Parking:** on-site. **Terms:** check-in 4 pm, 7 day cancellation notice-fee imposed. **Amenities:** hair dryers. **Leisure Activities:** whirlpool, playground. **Business Services:** meeting rooms. **Cards:** MC, VI.

DAYS INN   *Book great rates at AAA.com*

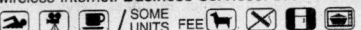

Small-scale Hotel

Rates not provided

Phone: 540/740-4100

Address: 9360 George Collins Pkwy 22844 **Location:** I-81, exit 264, just w on US 211. **Facility:** 85 one-bedroom standard units, some with whirlpools. 2 stories (no elevator), exterior corridors. **Parking:** on-site. **Amenities:** safes (fee), irons, hair dryers. **Pool(s):** outdoor. **Guest Services:** coin laundry, wireless Internet. **Business Services:** business center.

▼ See AAA listing p 836 ▼

QUALITY INN SHENANDOAH VALLEY

Book great rates at AAA.com

Phone: (540)740-3141

Small-scale Hotel
$59-$119 3/1-11/2
$49-$85 11/3-2/28

Address: 162 W Old Cross Rd 22844 **Location:** I-81, exit 264, just e on US 11/211, then just n. **Facility:** 100 one-bedroom standard units. 2 stories (no elevator), interior/exterior corridors. **Parking:** on-site. **Amenities:** high-speed Internet, irons, hair dryers. **Pool(s):** outdoor. **Leisure Activities:** playground, exercise room. *Fee:* miniature golf. **Guest Services:** coin laundry, wireless Internet. **Business Services:** meeting rooms. **Cards:** AX, DC, DS, MC, VI. *(See color ad p 835)*

─────── WHERE TO DINE ───────

SOUTHERN KITCHEN

Phone: 540/740-3514

American
$6-$14

The restaurant takes patrons on a nostalgic trip back in time, with jukeboxes, bright colors and an all-American menu. Casual dress. **Bar:** Beer & wine. **Hours:** 7 am-9 pm. Closed: 11/27, 12/25, 12/26. **Address:** 9576 S Congress St 22844 **Location:** I-81, exit 264, 1 mi s on US 11. **Parking:** on-site. **Cards:** DS, MC, VI.

NEWPORT NEWS —*See Hampton Roads Area p. 754.*

NORFOLK —*See Hampton Roads Area p. 759.*

NORTON pop. 3,904

─────── WHERE TO STAY ───────

DAYS INN   *Book at AAA.com*

Phone: 276/679-5340

Small-scale Hotel
Rates not provided

Address: 375 Wharton Ln 24273 **Location:** Jct US 58 and 23. **Facility:** 58 one-bedroom standard units, some with whirlpools. 3 stories, interior corridors. *Bath:* combo or shower only. **Parking:** on-site. **Amenities:** dual phone lines, voice mail, irons, hair dryers. **Leisure Activities:** exercise room. **Guest Services:** coin laundry, wireless Internet. **Business Services:** meeting rooms, business center.

SUPER 8 MOTEL-NORTON   *Book at AAA.com*

Phone: 276/679-0893

Motel
Rates not provided

Address: 425 Wharton Ln 24273 **Location:** Jct US 58 and 23. **Facility:** 56 one-bedroom standard units. 2 stories (no elevator), interior corridors. **Parking:** on-site. **Amenities:** high-speed Internet, safes (fee), hair dryers. **Guest Services:** coin laundry, wireless Internet. **Business Services:** meeting rooms.

OAKTON —*See District Of Columbia p. 551.*

ONANCOCK pop. 1,525

─────── WHERE TO STAY ───────

CHARLOTTE HOTEL

Phone: 757/787-7400

Country Inn
$120-$175 3/1-9/30
$110-$160 10/1-2/28

Address: 7 North St 23417 **Location:** Just n of jct Market (SR 179) and North sts; downtown. **Facility:** A charming property offering painted plank floors, custom-made furniture and extended amenities, like a rain shower head, in all the guest units. Smoke free premises. 8 one-bedroom standard units. 3 stories (no elevator), interior corridors. *Bath:* shower only. **Parking:** street. **Terms:** office hours 8 am-11 pm, age restrictions may apply, 3 day cancellation notice. **Amenities:** video library, DVD players, CD players, high-speed Internet, hair dryers. **Dining:** Charlotte Restaurant, see separate listing. **Guest Services:** wireless Internet. **Business Services:** meeting rooms. **Cards:** AX, DS, MC, VI.

THE INN & GARDEN CAFE

Phone: 757/787-8850

Country Inn
$95-$130 All Year

Address: 145 Market St 23417 **Location:** On SR 179, just w of US 13. **Facility:** Smoke free premises. 4 one-bedroom standard units. 2 stories, interior corridors. *Bath:* shower only. **Parking:** on-site. **Terms:** cancellation fee imposed. **Amenities:** video library, DVD players, CD players, high-speed Internet, hair dryers. **Leisure Activities:** golf privileges. **Guest Services:** airport transportation-Accomack airport, area transportation-County Wharf, wireless Internet. **Business Services:** meeting rooms. **Cards:** AX, MC, VI. **Free Special Amenities:** full breakfast and high-speed Internet.

SPINNING WHEEL BED & BREAKFAST

Phone: (757)787-7311

Historic Bed
& Breakfast
$95-$125. 3/1-10/31
$75-$110 11/1-2/28

Address: 31 North St 23417 **Location:** Just n of jct Market (SR 179) and North sts. Located in a quiet area. **Facility:** This 1890's home is decorated in a folk-Victorian style and offers a large back yard equipped with lawn games such as croquet and badminton. Smoke free premises. 5 one-bedroom standard units. 3 stories (no elevator), interior corridors. *Bath:* shower only. **Parking:** on-site. **Terms:** age restrictions may apply, 3 day cancellation notice-fee imposed. **Leisure Activities:** croquet, badminton, bicycles, volleyball. **Guest Services:** airport transportation-Accomack Airport, area transportation-county wharf. **Cards:** MC, VI.

——— WHERE TO DINE ———

BIZZOTTO'S GALLERY-CAFFE   Phone: 757/787-3103

Continental
$6-$25

The owner is both a chef and an artist, so this combination gallery and cafe proves ideal to display his creations on the walls and the plates. Local seafood flavors meet European influences in dishes such as shrimp and spinach bisque, crab cakes on focaccia bread and cod meuniere. Casual dress. **Bar:** Full bar. **Reservations:** suggested. **Hours:** 11 am-3 & 5-9 pm, Fri & Sat-9:30 pm; Sun from 5 pm in summer. Closed: 12/25; also Sun off season. **Address:** 41 Market St 23417 **Location:** 1 mi w of US 13; center. **Parking:** street. **Cards:** MC, VI.

CHARLOTTE RESTAURANT   Phone: 757/787-7400

American
$15-$30

CALL 🔲

French elegance meets coastal casual at the intimate inn. The chef skillfully integrates Continental and Southern traditions with fresh local ingredients, including the region's great seafood. Homemade ice creams are a specialty. Casual dress. **Bar:** Full bar. **Reservations:** suggested. **Hours:** 8 am-11 & 5:30-9 pm. Closed: 1/1, 11/27, 12/25; also Mon & Tues. **Address:** 7 North St 23417 **Location:** Just n of jct Market (SR 179) and North sts; downtown; in Charlotte Hotel. **Parking:** street. **Cards:** AX, DC, DS, MC, VI.

MALLARD'S ON THE WHARF   Phone: 757/787-8558

Seafood
$8-$19

In the historic former Hopkins & Brothers general store, the casual restaurant overlooks the harbor. In good weather, guests often sit on the patio to sample crab-stuffed oysters, mussels, grilled salmon over spinach greens, spicy sweet chicken wings and large salads. After 5 p.m., entrees include shrimp skewers, fajitas and preparations of Certified Angus beef. Casual dress. **Bar:** Full bar. **Reservations:** accepted. **Hours:** 11:30 am-9 pm. Closed: 11/27, 12/25. **Address:** 2 Market St 23417 **Location:** SR 179; at the public dock. **Parking:** on-site. **Cards:** AX, DS, MC, VI.

STELLA'S   Phone: 757/789-5045

Italian
$5-$19

🔲

This festive downtown spot offers a family friendly atmosphere downstairs and a more adult-oriented atmosphere upstairs. Italian-American favorites mingle with great local seafood in dishes such as spicy shrimp pasta, crab-stuffed pretzels, fried seafood baskets, and linguine with clam sauce. Casual dress. **Bar:** Full bar. **Reservations:** accepted. **Hours:** 11 am-10 pm, Sun noon-11 pm; to 9 pm in winter. Closed major holidays. **Address:** 57 Market St 23417 **Location:** Jct North St; downtown. **Parking:** street. **Cards:** AX, DS, MC, VI.

*——— The following restaurant has not been evaluated by AAA ———
but is listed for your information only.*

THE INN & GARDEN CAFE   Phone: 757/787-8850

[fyi]

Not evaluated. The charming sunny dining room is known for specialties such as lump crab cakes, "Steak Dad's Way", Seafood saute over angel hair pasta, and Bird's favorite salad. **Address:** 145 Market St 23417 **Location:** On Market St (SR 179); just w of US 13.

ONLEY pop. 496

——— WHERE TO STAY ———

COMFORT INN    *Book great rates at AAA.com*   Phone: (757)787-7787

Small-scale Hotel
$83-$235 All Year

Address: 25297 Lankford Hwy 23418 **Location:** US 13 at SR 179. **Facility:** 80 one-bedroom standard units, some with whirlpools. 2 stories (no elevator), exterior corridors. **Parking:** on-site. **Amenities:** high-speed Internet, irons, hair dryers. *Some:* DVD players. **Pool(s):** outdoor. **Leisure Activities:** limited exercise equipment. **Guest Services:** wireless Internet. **Cards:** AX, CB, DC, DS, JC, MC, VI. **Free Special Amenities:** expanded continental breakfast and high-speed Internet.

ORANGE pop. 4,123

——— WHERE TO STAY ———

GREENOCK HOUSE INN   Phone: 540/672-3625

Historic Bed
& Breakfast
Rates not provided

Address: 249 Caroline St 22960 **Location:** US 15, just s of jct SR 20. **Facility:** The 1890 country Victorian farmhouse is in historic Orange County close to such notable sites as Jefferson's Monticello and Madison's Montpelier. Smoke free premises. 5 one-bedroom standard units, some with whirlpools. 2 stories (no elevator), interior corridors. *Bath:* combo or shower only. **Parking:** on-site. **Terms:** check-in 4:30 pm. **Amenities:** CD players, hair dryers. **Business Services:** meeting rooms.

HOLIDAY INN EXPRESS    *Book great rates at AAA.com*   Phone: (540)672-6691

Small-scale Hotel
$135-$155 3/1-11/15
$100-$110 11/16-2/28

Address: 750 Round Hill Dr 22960 **Location:** US 15, 2.1 mi n of jct SR 20. **Facility:** 65 one-bedroom standard units, some with kitchens and/or whirlpools. 2 stories, interior corridors. *Bath:* combo or shower only. **Parking:** on-site. **Amenities:** high-speed Internet, voice mail, irons, hair dryers. **Pool(s):** outdoor. **Leisure Activities:** picnic area, barbecue pit, exercise room. **Guest Services:** coin laundry, wireless Internet. **Business Services:** meeting rooms, business center. **Cards:** AX, CB, DC, DS, JC, MC, VI. **Free Special Amenities:** full breakfast and high-speed Internet.

MAYHURST INN

Historic Bed
& Breakfast
$155-$235 All Year

Phone: 540/672-5597

Address: 12460 Mayhurst Ln 22960 **Location:** On US 15, 0.5 mi s of town from SR 20 at the divided highway. **Facility:** A Virginia landmark, the 1859 Italianate plantation mansion sits amid 200-year-old ash trees and is near many wineries and James Madison's Montpelier. Smoke free premises. 8 one-bedroom standard units, some with kitchens and/or whirlpools. 4 stories (no elevator), interior corridors. *Bath:* combo or shower only. **Parking:** on-site. **Terms:** check-in 4 pm, 10 day cancellation notice-fee imposed. **Amenities:** hair dryers. *Some:* DVD players, CD players. **Leisure Activities:** fishing, jogging. **Guest Services:** wireless Internet. **Business Services:** meeting rooms. **Cards:** AX, MC, VI.

(A$K) CALL (&M) ⊠ (☎) / SOME UNITS (W) (VCR) 🔲 🖿 💻

─────── **WHERE TO DINE** ───────

CAPE PORPOISE LOBSTER HOUSE

American
$5-$20

Phone: 540/672-0800

The fun, casual eatery has an unusual name, but the seafood is fresh, and the staff is friendly. Casual dress. **Bar:** Full bar. **Hours:** 11:30 am-9 pm, Sat-10 pm, Sun 10:30 am-9 pm; Sunday brunch. Closed: 12/25. **Address:** 182 Byrd St 22960 **Location:** 0.2 mi n on SR 20 (Byrd St). **Parking:** on-site. **Cards:** AX, DS, MC, VI.

(N)

SILK MILL GRILLE

American
$7-$20

Phone: 540/672-4010

A city tradition, the restaurant prepares steaks, sandwiches and seafood. In the historic area, this place is near many attractions. Casual dress. **Bar:** Full bar. **Reservations:** suggested, weekends. **Hours:** 11 am-9 pm, Fri & Sat-10 pm, Sun noon-8 pm. Closed: 1/1, 12/25; also Mon. **Address:** 101-A Woodmark St 22960 **Location:** US 15, 2 mi n of jct SR 20, just e. **Parking:** on-site. **Cards:** AX, MC, VI.

(N)

PEMBROKE pop. 1,134

─────── **WHERE TO STAY** ───────

MOUNTAIN LAKE HOTEL

(AAA) (SAVE)

Resort
Small-scale Hotel
$200-$355 5/2-11/1

Phone: (540)626-7121

Address: 115 Hotel Cir 24136 **Location:** Jct US 460, 6.6 mi n on SR 700; caution steep, narrow paved mountain road. Located in remote area. **Facility:** In a remote mountaintop location that was the setting for the movie "Dirty Dancing," the hotel offers rustic to deluxe lodge and cottage units. 101 units. 81 one-bedroom standard units, some with whirlpools. 20 cottages. 1-2 stories (no elevator), interior/exterior corridors. **Parking:** on-site. **Terms:** open 5/2-11/1, check-in 5 pm, 2-5 night minimum stay - seasonal and/or weekends, 21 day cancellation notice-fee imposed. **Amenities:** *Some:* DVD players, hair dryers. **Pool(s):** outdoor. **Leisure Activities:** sauna, whirlpools, boating, canoeing, paddleboats, boat dock, fishing, kayaks, water trampoline, tennis court, recreation programs in summer, archery, bocci, croquet, disc golf, hayrides, mountain bikes, hiking trails, playground, exercise room, horseshoes, shuffleboard, volleyball. *Fee:* massage, game room. **Guest Services:** coin laundry. **Business Services:** meeting rooms, PC. **Cards:** AX, CB, DC, DS, MC, VI. **Free Special Amenities: room upgrade and preferred room (each subject to availability with advance reservations).**

(S🚭) (❘❘) ⊠ ⊠ (X) (🎬) 💻 / SOME UNITS (W) 🔲 🖿

PETERSBURG pop. 33,740   (See map and index starting on p. 854)

─────── **WHERE TO STAY** ───────

COMFORT INN-PETERSBURG SOUTH   *Book at AAA.com*

Small-scale Hotel
$59-$119 All Year

Phone: (804)732-2000   **5**

Address: 12001 S Crater Rd 23805 **Location:** I-95, exit 45, jct US 301. **Facility:** 97 one-bedroom standard units, some with whirlpools. 2 stories (no elevator), interior corridors. **Parking:** on-site. **Terms:** cancellation fee imposed. **Amenities:** high-speed Internet, voice mail, irons, hair dryers. **Pool(s):** outdoor. **Leisure Activities:** playground, limited exercise equipment. **Guest Services:** coin laundry, wireless Internet. **Business Services:** fax. **Cards:** AX, CB, DC, DS, JC, MC, VI.

(A$K) (S🚭) (❘❘+) CALL (&M) 🌀 (🎬) 🔲 🖿 💻 / SOME UNITS ⊠

DAYS INN   *Book great rates at AAA.com*

(AAA) (SAVE)

Small-scale Hotel
Rates not provided

Phone: 804/733-4400   **7**

Address: 12208 S Crater Rd 23805 **Location:** I-95, exit 45, jct US 301. **Facility:** 155 one-bedroom standard units, some with efficiencies (no utensils). 2 stories (no elevator), exterior corridors. **Parking:** on-site. **Amenities:** high-speed Internet, voice mail, irons, hair dryers. **Pool(s):** outdoor. **Leisure Activities:** playground, exercise room. **Guest Services:** coin laundry, wireless Internet. **Business Services:** PC, fax. **Free Special Amenities: expanded continental breakfast and newspaper.** *(See color ad p 839)*

(❘❘+) 🌀 (🎬) 💻 / SOME UNITS FEE (🐾) ⊠ 🔲 🖿

HAMPTON INN   *Book great rates at AAA.com*

(AAA) (SAVE)

Small-scale Hotel
Rates not provided

Phone: 804/732-1400   **3**

Address: 11909 S Crater Rd 23805 **Location:** I-95, exit 45, jct US 301. **Facility:** 77 one-bedroom standard units, some with whirlpools. 4 stories, interior corridors. *Bath:* combo or shower only. **Parking:** on-site. **Amenities:** high-speed Internet, dual phone lines, voice mail, irons, hair dryers. **Pool(s):** outdoor. **Guest Services:** valet and coin laundry, wireless Internet. **Business Services:** meeting rooms, business center. **Free Special Amenities: continental breakfast and high-speed Internet.**

(❘❘+) CALL (&M) 🌀 (🎬) 🔲 🖿 💻 / SOME UNITS ⊠

(See map and index starting on p. 854)

HOLIDAY INN EXPRESS HOTEL & SUITES *Book great rates at AAA.com* **Phone:** (804)518-1800

Small-scale Hotel
$129-$299 3/1-11/1
$119-$199 11/2-2/28

Address: 11979 S Crater Rd 23805 **Location:** I-95, exit 45, jct US 301, then just n. **Facility:** 104 units. 33 one-bedroom standard units. 71 one-bedroom suites, some with efficiencies and/or whirlpools. 5 stories, interior corridors. *Bath:* combo or shower only. **Parking:** on-site. **Amenities:** high-speed Internet, dual phone lines, voice mail, safes (fee), irons, hair dryers. **Pool(s):** heated indoor. **Leisure Activities:** exercise room. **Guest Services:** valet and coin laundry, wireless Internet. **Business Services:** business center. **Cards:** AX, DS, MC, VI. **Free Special Amenities:** expanded continental breakfast and high-speed Internet.

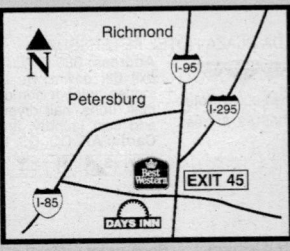
▼ See AAA listing p 711 ▼

(See map and index starting on p. 854)

HOWARD JOHNSON STEVEN KENT *Book great rates at AAA.com* Phone: 804/733-0600 **6**

△△△ SAVE
▽▽▽ ▽▽
Small-scale Hotel
Rates not provided

Address: 12205 S Crater Rd 23805 **Location:** I-95, exit 45, jct US 301. **Facility:** 135 units. 130 one-bedroom standard units. 5 one-bedroom suites. 2 stories (no elevator), interior/exterior corridors. **Parking:** on-site. **Amenities:** voice mail, irons, hair dryers. *Some:* high-speed Internet. **Dining:** restaurant, see separate listing. **Pool(s):** outdoor. **Leisure Activities:** playground, sports court. **Guest Services:** coin laundry, wireless Internet. **Business Services:** meeting rooms, PC, fax. **Free Special Amenities:** continental breakfast and high-speed Internet. *(See color ad p 839)*

🍴 CALL 🔊M 🏊 ⚙ 📺 / SOME UNITS FEE 🐾 ✕ 🔲 🖥

QUALITY INN *Book great rates at AAA.com* Phone: (804)732-2900 **4**

▽▽▽ ▽▽▽
Small-scale Hotel
$60-$139 All Year

Address: 11974 S Crater Rd 23805 **Location:** I-95, exit 45, just n. **Facility:** 96 one-bedroom standard units, some with efficiencies (no utensils) and/or whirlpools. 2 stories (no elevator), exterior corridors. **Parking:** on-site. **Amenities:** high-speed Internet, irons, hair dryers. **Pool(s):** outdoor. **Guest Services:** coin laundry, wireless Internet. **Cards:** AX, DS, MC, VI. *(See color ad below)*

ASK 🔊🍴 🏊 ⚙ 🔲 🖥 📺 / SOME UNITS FEE 🐾 ✕

RAMADA PLAZA HOTEL PETERSBURG Phone: (804)733-0000 **1**

▽▽▽ ▽▽▽
Small-scale Hotel
$119-$169 All Year

Address: 380 E Washington St 23803 **Location:** I-95, exit 52 southbound; exit 50D northbound; I-85, exit 69; downtown. Located in historic Olde Towne. **Facility:** 192 one-bedroom standard units. 9 stories, interior corridors. **Parking:** on-site. **Amenities:** high-speed Internet, dual phone lines, voice mail, irons, hair dryers. **Pool(s):** outdoor. **Leisure Activities:** exercise room. **Guest Services:** valet and coin laundry, area transportation, wireless Internet. **Business Services:** conference facilities. **Cards:** AX, DC, DS, MC, VI.

ASK 🔊🍴 🍴 🍸 🏊 ⚙ 🔲 🖥 📺 / SOME UNITS ✕

SUPER 8 MOTEL *Book great rates at AAA.com* Phone: 804/732-6020 **8**

△△△ SAVE
▽▽▽ ▽▽
Motel
Rates not provided

Address: 3138 S Crater Rd 23805 **Location:** I-95, exit 48B (Wagner Rd), 0.7 mi w. **Facility:** 32 one-bedroom standard units, some with whirlpools. 2 stories (no elevator), exterior corridors. **Parking:** on-site. **Amenities:** high-speed Internet, hair dryers. **Guest Services:** wireless Internet. **Free Special Amenities:** continental breakfast and high-speed Internet.

🍴 ⚙ 🔲 🖥 📺 / SOME UNITS ✕

▼ *See AAA listing above* ▼

(See map and index starting on p. 854)

——— WHERE TO DINE ———

ALEXANDER'S FINE FOOD
Phone: 804/733-7134

Greek
$5-$14
A simple, little Greek spot, the restaurant serves pasta, subs, salad and assorted entrees. The white walls of the front of the dining room boast an attractive decorative border. Nothing here's too fancy, but everything's plentiful and tasty. Casual dress. **Bar:** Beer & wine. **Hours:** 11 am-9 pm, Mon & Tues-3 pm. Closed major holidays; also Sun. **Address:** 101 W Bank St 23803 **Location:** Just e of Sycamore St; center; in Olde Towne Historic District. **Parking:** street. **Cards:** AX, DS, MC, VI.

THE BRICKHOUSE RUN
Phone: 804/862-1815
American
$12-$25
Traditional British and regional specialties are served in the appropriately decorated English-style pub on a cobblestone lane in Olde Towne. Casual dress. **Bar:** Full bar. **Hours:** 5 pm-9 pm, Fri & Sat-10 pm. Closed major holidays; also Sun & Mon. **Address:** 407-409 Cockade Alley 23803 **Location:** Between Olde St and Bollingbrook; in Olde Towne; adjacent to visitor's center. **Parking:** street. **Cards:** AX, MC, VI.

KINGS BARBEQUE
Phone: 804/732-0975
Regional American
$5-$15
Think "Southern country diner circa 1965" and you've captured the personality of the cozy, familiar restaurant. Great vinegar-based barbecue, most notably pork, is the highlight of the menu although burgers and sandwiches also are offered. End with their homemade apple pie just like Grandma made. Casual dress. **Reservations:** accepted. **Hours:** 11 am-8:30 pm. Closed: 1/1, 11/27, 12/25; also Mon & Tues. **Address:** 2910 S Crater Rd 23805 **Location:** I-95, exit 48B, just e on Wagner Rd, then just n. **Parking:** on-site. **Cards:** AX, DS, MC, VI.

LONGSTREET'S DELICATESSEN
Phone: 804/722-4372
Deli/Subs
Sandwiches
$5-$8
Decorated with American and Oriental antiques, the eatery is a charming mix of gourmet delicatessen and soda fountain. Also offered is a large selection of specialty draft beer. A player piano and a waitress on wheels set the mood. Casual dress. **Bar:** Beer & wine. **Hours:** 11 am-9 pm. Closed major holidays; also Sun & Mon. **Address:** 302 N Sycamore St 23803 **Location:** I-95, exit 52, just w to Sycamore St. **Parking:** street. **Cards:** AX, CB, DS, MC, VI.

NANNY'S FAMILY RESTAURANT
Phone: 804/733-6619
Southern
$4-$10
The simple spot in the country has become a local favorite for its plentiful buffet of Southern favorites, such as pork barbecue, fried chicken, collard greens, cornbread and fruit cobblers. Casual dress. **Hours:** 11 am-2:30 pm, Fri-9 pm, Sat 4 pm-9 pm. Closed: Sun & Mon. **Address:** 11900 S Crater Rd 23805 **Location:** I-95, exit 45, just n on US 301. **Parking:** on-site. **Cards:** MC, VI.

STEVEN KENT RESTAURANT
Phone: 804/733-0500
American
$3-$19
This quiet, family-oriented restaurant sits amid comfortable, quaint surroundings. Paintings by local artists decorate the walls. The menu focuses on Southern favorites—liver and pork chops among them. Servers are quick and "country friendly". Casual dress. **Bar:** Full bar. **Hours:** 6:30 am-10 pm. **Address:** 12205 S Crater Rd 23805 **Location:** I-95, exit 45, jct US 301; in Howard Johnson Steven Kent. **Parking:** on-site. **Cards:** AX, CB, DC, DS, MC, VI.
CALL

WABI-SABI
Phone: 804/862-1365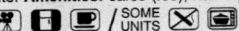
Japanese
$6-$20
Despite its setting in a 19th-century brick townhouse in the heart of Olde Towne, the eatery focuses on the modern in everything from its decor to its menu, which fuses traditional Japanese cuisine with New American touches. Favorites include crab cakes, seared seafood, distinctive salads, stir-fries and, of course, sushi. Tempting desserts include such intriguing ice cream flavors as coconut and green tea. Casual dress. **Bar:** Full bar. **Reservations:** accepted. **Hours:** 11:30 am-2 & 5-9 pm, Fri-10 pm, Sat 11:30 am-10 pm; Sunday brunch 11 am-2 pm. Closed major holidays; also Mon. **Address:** 29 Bollingbrook St 23803 **Location:** Just e of Sycamore St; in Old Towne Historic District. **Parking:** street. **Cards:** MC, VI.

PORTSMOUTH —See Hampton Roads Area p. 770.

POUNDING MILL

——— WHERE TO STAY ———

CLAYPOOL HILL HOLIDAY INN EXPRESS HOTEL & SUITES   *Book at AAA.com*
Phone: 276/596-9880
Small-scale Hotel
$140-$160 All Year
Address: 180 Clay Dr 24637 **Location:** 0.5 mi e of US 460 and 19. **Facility:** 63 one-bedroom standard units, some with whirlpools. 3 stories, interior corridors. **Bath:** combo or shower only. **Parking:** on-site. **Terms:** cancellation fee imposed. **Amenities:** high-speed Internet, irons, hair dryers. **Pool(s):** heated indoor. **Leisure Activities:** whirlpool, exercise room. **Guest Services:** coin laundry, wireless Internet. **Business Services:** meeting rooms, fax (fee). **Cards:** AX, CB, DC, DS, MC, VI.

CLAYPOOL HILL SUPER 8 MOTEL   *Book at AAA.com*
Phone: 276/964-9888
Small-scale Hotel
Rates not provided
Address: 12367 Governor GC Peery Hwy 24637 **Location:** 0.3 mi w on US 19/460. **Facility:** 46 one-bedroom standard units, some with whirlpools. 2 stories (no elevator), interior corridors. **Parking:** on-site. **Amenities:** safes (fee), hair dryers. **Guest Services:** wireless Internet.

QUICKSBURG

─── WHERE TO STAY ───

STRATHMORE HOUSE BED & BREAKFAST ON THE SHENANDOAH

Bed & Breakfast
$135-$175 All Year

Phone: 540/477-4141

Address: 658 Wissler Rd 22847 **Location:** I-81, exit 269, just e to SR 11, 1.1 mi n to Wissler Rd, then just w over covered bridge. **Facility:** Nestled near a covered bridge and within walking distance to Civil War sites, the B&B offers a retreatlike setting with attractive rooms and gardens. 4 one-bedroom standard units. 2 stories (no elevator), interior corridors. *Bath:* combo or shower only. **Parking:** on-site. **Terms:** age restrictions may apply, 7 day cancellation notice-fee imposed. **Amenities:** irons, hair dryers.

RADFORD pop. 15,859

─── WHERE TO STAY ───

BEST WESTERN RADFORD INN   *Book great rates at AAA.com*

Small-scale Hotel
$69-$119 All Year

Phone: (540)639-3000

Address: 1501 Tyler Ave 24141 **Location:** I-81, exit 109, 2.7 mi nw on SR 177. **Facility:** 104 one-bedroom standard units, some with whirlpools. 2 stories, interior corridors. **Parking:** on-site. **Amenities:** voice mail, irons, hair dryers. *Some:* high-speed Internet. **Pool(s):** heated indoor. **Leisure Activities:** saunas, whirlpool, exercise room. **Guest Services:** valet and coin laundry, wireless Internet. **Business Services:** meeting rooms, business center. **Cards:** AX, CB, DC, DS, JC, MC, VI. **Free Special Amenities: expanded continental breakfast and high-speed Internet.** *(See color ad below)*

AAA Benefit:

Members save 10% everyday, plus an exclusive frequent stay program.

COMFORT INN & SUITES   *Book great rates at AAA.com*

Small-scale Hotel
$64-$150 All Year

Phone: (540)639-3333

Address: 2331 Tyler Rd 24143 **Location:** I-81, exit 109, just w. **Facility:** 72 one-bedroom standard units, some with whirlpools. 3 stories, interior corridors. *Bath:* combo or shower only. **Parking:** on-site. **Amenities:** high-speed Internet, voice mail, safes (fee), irons, hair dryers. **Pool(s):** heated indoor. **Leisure Activities:** whirlpool, exercise room. **Guest Services:** coin laundry, wireless Internet. **Business Services:** conference facilities, business center. **Cards:** AX, CB, DC, DS, JC, MC, VI. **Free Special Amenities: expanded continental breakfast and room upgrade (subject to availability with advance reservations).**

SUPER 8 MOTEL-RADFORD   *Book at AAA.com*

Motel
Rates not provided

Phone: 540/731-9355

Address: 1600 Tyler Ave 24141 **Location:** I-81, exit 109, just w. **Facility:** 58 one-bedroom standard units. 2 stories (no elevator), interior corridors. **Parking:** on-site. **Amenities:** safes (fee), hair dryers. **Guest Services:** wireless Internet.

——— **WHERE TO DINE** ———

SAL'S RISTORANTE ITALIANO   **Phone:** 540/639-9669

Sal's Ristorante Italiano is a family operated eatery that has been serving quality Italian cuisine over 25 years in the Radford area. Casual dress. **Bar:** Full bar. **Hours:** 11 am-11 pm, Sun noon-10 pm. Closed:
Italian   12/25; also Mon. **Address:** 709 W Main St 24141 **Location:** I-81, exit 105, just w. **Parking:** on-site.
$7-$22   **Cards:** AX, CB, DC, DS, JC, MC, VI.

RESTON —*See District Of Columbia p. 552.*

Destination Richmond
pop. 197,790

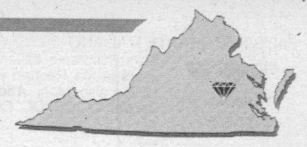

*A*t the falls of the James River, Richmond was a destination for the purposeful. Traders built warehouses in the Shockoe Slip district; farmers hawked goods on 17th Street; and statesmen convened at the capitol to shape a nation.

*M*ake it your destination for a good time. The Farmer's Market still thrives on 17th Street. Revitalized Shockoe Bottom is where nightlife is the liveliest. And museums of art, history and culture dot downtown Richmond.

Bob Krist / Virginia Tourism Corp

Richmond skyline. Modern towers cast reflections upon the James River.

Shopping at the 17th Street Farmers' Market, Richmond. Enjoy local produce and crafts at one of the country's oldest public marketplaces. (See mention page 288)

Richmond Metropolitan CVB

See Vicinity map page 848

Richmond Metropolitan CVB

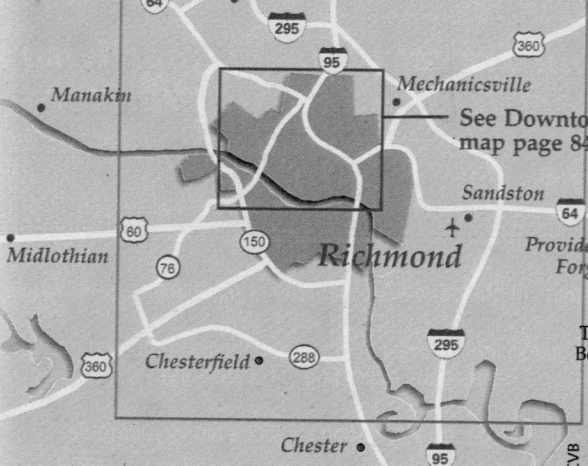

See Downtown map page 845

Richmond International Raceway. Relish the excitement during race season, May through September. (See listing page 298)

Richmond Braves. This minor league team plays ball at The Diamond on the Boulevard. (See mention page 297)

Richmond Metropolitan CVB

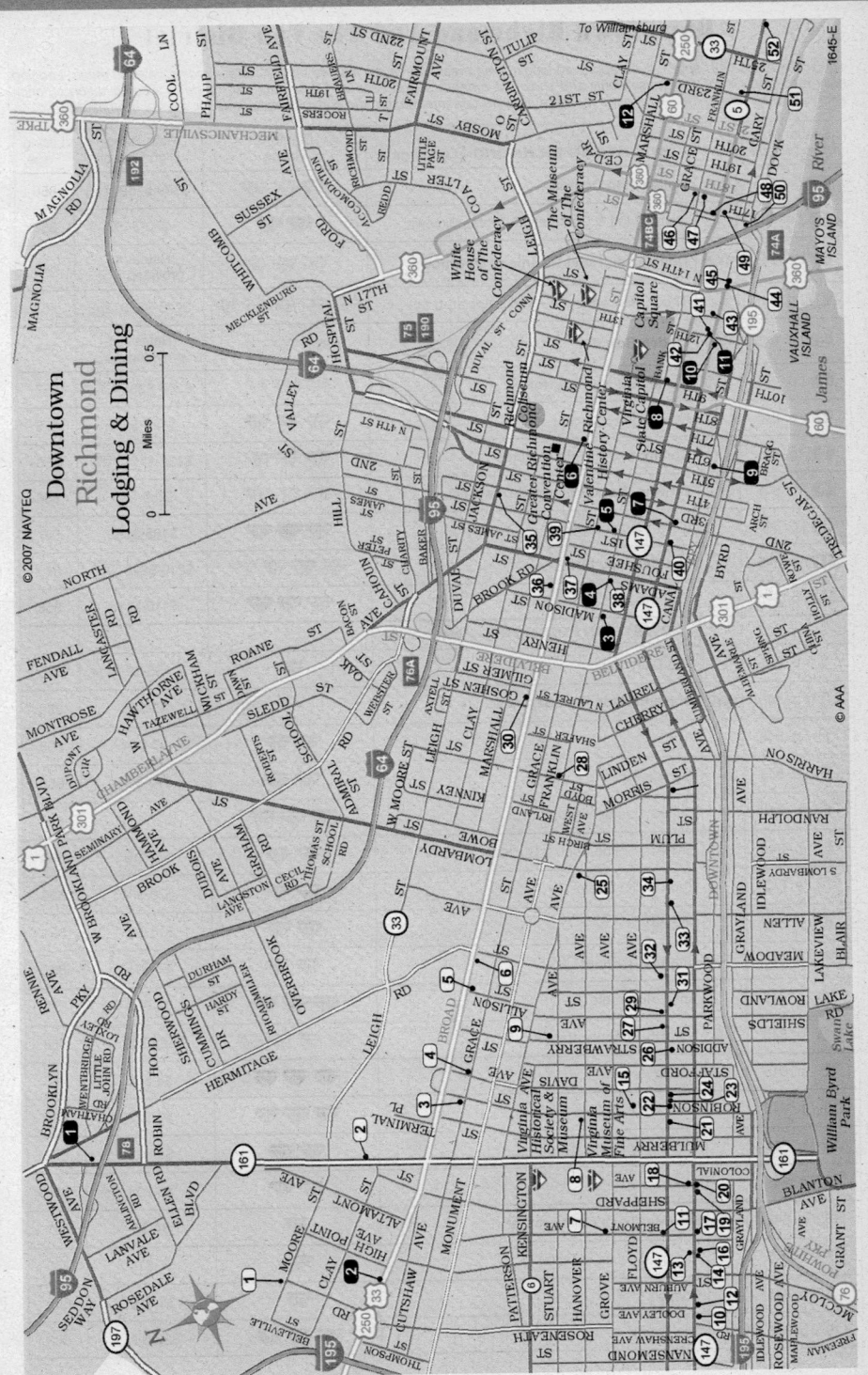

Downtown
Richmond
Lodging & Dining

© 2007 NAVTEQ

To Williamsburg

Downtown Richmond And The Fan District

This index helps you "spot" where approved lodgings and restaurants are located on the corresponding detailed maps. Lodging daily rate range is for comparison only and show the property's high season. Restaurant rate range is a combination of lunch and/or dinner. Turn to the listing page for more detailed rate information and consult display ads for special promotions.

Spotter/Map Page Number	OA	DOWNTOWN RICHMOND - Lodgings	Diamond Rating	Rate Range High Season	Listing Page
❶ / p. 845	AAA	**Holiday Inn Central**	◈◈◈	$109-$159 SAVE	856
❷ / p. 845		Comfort Inn & Conference Center-Midtown	◈◈	$80-$150	856
❸ / p. 845	AAA	**DoubleTree Hotel Richmond Downtown**	◈◈◈	Rates not provided SAVE	856
❹ / p. 845	AAA	**The Jefferson Hotel** - see color ad p 857	◈◈◈◈◈	$245-$375 SAVE	857
❺ / p. 845	AAA	**Linden Row Inn**	◈◈◈	Rates not provided SAVE	857
❻ / p. 845	AAA	**Richmond Marriott Hotel**	◈◈◈	$253-$285 SAVE	857
❼ / p. 845		Holiday Inn Express	◈◈◈	$129-$249	856
❽ / p. 845	AAA	**Commonwealth Park Suites**	◈◈◈	$139-$189 SAVE	856
❾ / p. 845	AAA	**Crowne Plaza Richmond Downtown**	◈◈◈	$259 SAVE	856
❿ / p. 845		Omni Richmond Hotel	◈◈◈	$169-$299	857
⓫ / p. 845	AAA	**The Berkeley Hotel**	◈◈◈◈	$219-$249 SAVE	856
⓬ / p. 845		The William Catlin House	◈◈◈	$110-$115	858
		DOWNTOWN RICHMOND - Restaurants			
① / p. 845		The Dairy Bar	◈	$5-$9	860
② / p. 845	AAA	**Buz and Neds Real Barbecue**	◈	$5-$20	859
③ / p. 845		Akida	◈◈	$7-$14	858
④ / p. 845		Avenue 805	◈◈	$10-$24	858
⑤ / p. 845		Cabo's Corner Bistro	◈◈◈	$17-$37	859
⑥ / p. 845		Enoteca Sogno, Vino e Cucina	◈◈	$7-$16	860
⑦ / p. 845		Zeus Gallery Cafe	◈◈	$20-$35	863
⑧ / p. 845		Racine	◈◈	$18-$28	861
⑨ / p. 845		Strawberry Street Cafe	◈◈	$5-$15	862
⑩ / p. 845		Amici Ristorante	◈◈◈	$8-$30	858
⑪ / p. 845	AAA	**1 North Belmont Restaurant**	◈◈◈◈	$28-$42	858
⑫ / p. 845		Acacia	◈◈◈	$5-$23	858
⑬ / p. 845		Can Can Brasserie	◈◈◈	$8-$22	859
⑭ / p. 845		Thai Curry House	◈◈	$8-$20	862
⑮ / p. 845		Carlton's	◈◈	$6-$23	859
⑯ / p. 845		Mrs. Marshall's Carytown Cafe	◈	$4-$8	861
⑰ / p. 845		Farouk's House of India	◈	$5-$14	860
⑱ / p. 845		Coppola's	◈	$5-$10	859
⑲ / p. 845		The Track	◈◈◈	$22-$30	863

Spotter/Map Page Number	OA	DOWNTOWN RICHMOND - Restaurants (continued)	Diamond Rating	Rate Range High Season	Listing Page
20 / p. 845		Double T's Real Smoked Barbecue	◇	$6-$18	860
21 / p. 845	AAA	**Avalon**	◇◇	$14-$22	858
22 / p. 845		Helen's	◇◇◇	$17-$25	861
23 / p. 845		3 Monkeys Bar & Grill	◇◇	$7-$18	858
24 / p. 845		Davis & Main	◇◇	$12-$23	860
25 / p. 845		Kuba Kuba	◇◇	$6-$18	861
26 / p. 845		The White Dog	◇◇	$15-$26	863
27 / p. 845		Sticky Rice	◇◇	$7-$20	862
28 / p. 845		Edo's Squid	◇◇	$8-$25	860
29 / p. 845		Rowland Fine Dining	◇◇◇	$20-$30	862
30 / p. 845		Taqueria Loco	◇	$3-$6	862
31 / p. 845		Sidewalk Cafe	◇	$5-$17	862
32 / p. 845		Bacchus	◇◇◇	$12-$30	858
33 / p. 845		Dogwoods Grille & Spirits	◇◇◇	$18-$32	860
34 / p. 845		The Six Burner Restaurant & Bar	◇◇	$6-$22	862
35 / p. 845		Croaker's Spot	◇	$9-$33	860
36 / p. 845		Comfort	◇◇	$6-$18	859
37 / p. 845		Twenty Seven	◇◇◇	$6-$23	863
38 / p. 845		T. J.'s Restaurant and Lounge	◇◇◇	$10-$30	863
39 / p. 845		Perly's	◇◇	$5-$9	861
40 / p. 845		The Thai Room at Beauregard's	◇◇	$4-$14	863
41 / p. 845	AAA	**La Grotta Ristorante**	◇◇◇	$8-$27	861
42 / p. 845	AAA	**The Dining Room at The Berkeley Hotel**	◇◇◇◇	$9-$40	860
43 / p. 845		Peking Pavilion	◇◇	$6-$14	861
44 / p. 845		Europa Mediterranean Cafe and Tapas Bar	◇◇	$5-$25	860
45 / p. 845		The Hard Shell	◇◇◇	$7-$30	861
46 / p. 845		Zuppa	◇	$5-$8	863
47 / p. 845		Julep's, New Southern Cuisine	◇◇◇	$18-$30	861
48 / p. 845		Cafe' Gutenberg	◇◇	$3-$15	859
49 / p. 845		Sumo San	◇◇	$7-$14	862
50 / p. 845		Bottoms Up Pizza	◇◇	$5-$10	859
51 / p. 845		Sette	◇◇	$7-$14	862
52 / p. 845		Millie's Diner	◇◇	$6-$28	861

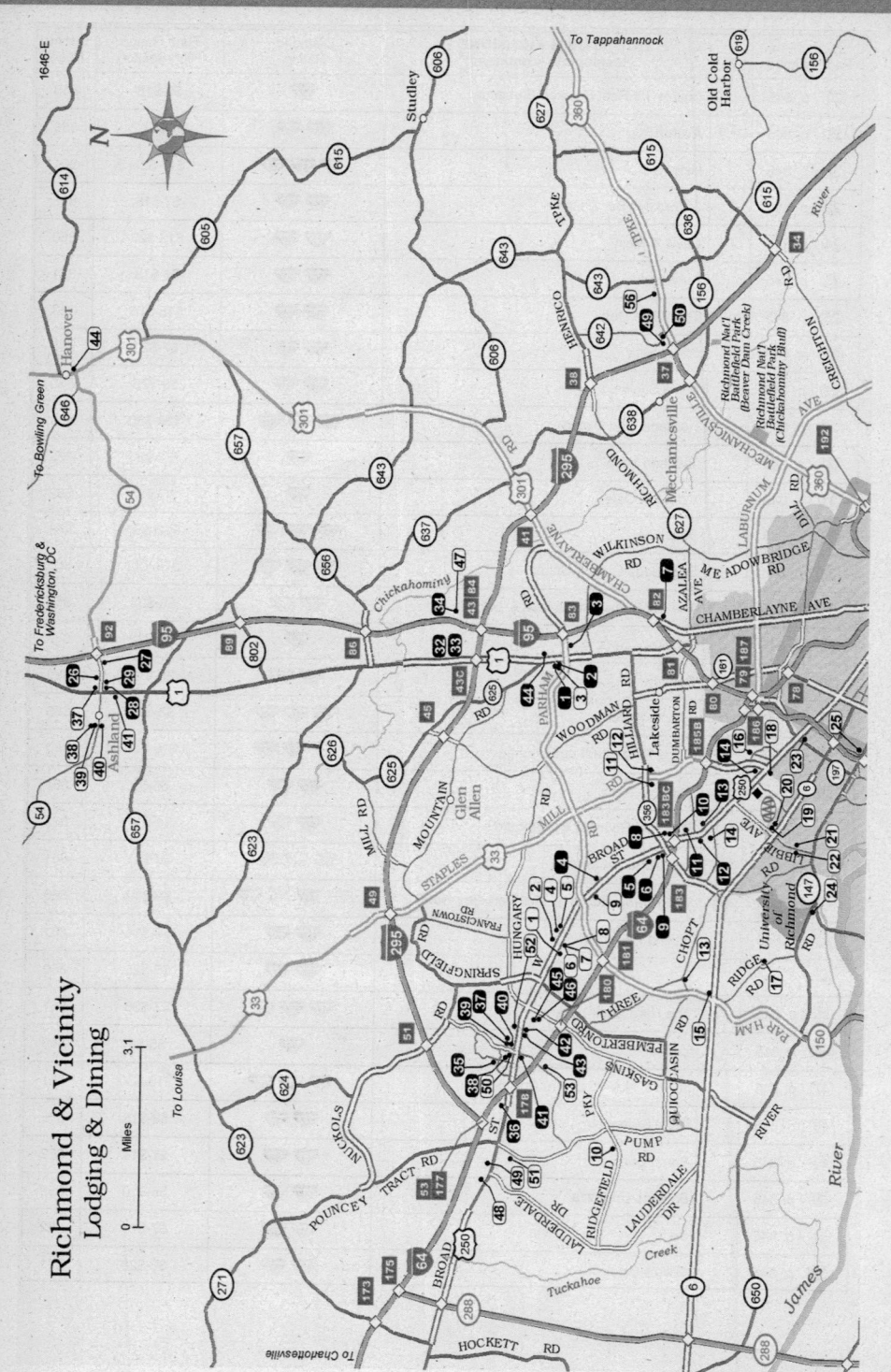

Richmond & Vicinity
Lodging & Dining

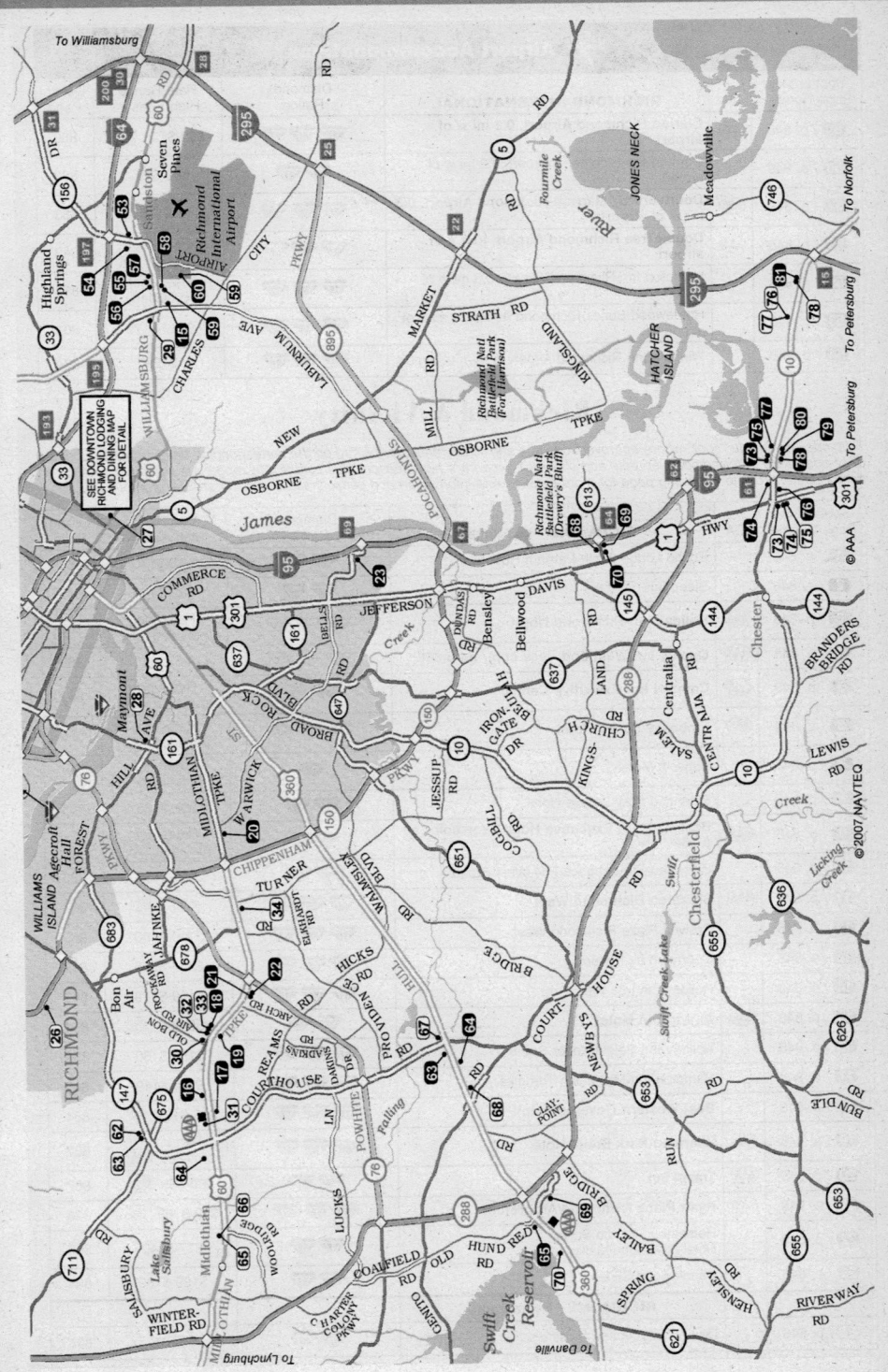

✈ Airport Accommodations

Spotter/Map Page Number	OA	RICHMOND INTERNATIONAL	Diamond Rating	Rate Range High Season	Listing Page
59 / p. 848	AAA	Clarion Richmond Airport, 0.3 mi w of airport	▽▽▽	$89-$139 SAVE	883
56 / p. 848		Comfort Inn Richmond Airport, 0.3 mi w of airport	▽▽	$80-$100	883
57 / p. 848	AAA	Courtyard by Marriott-Richmond Airport, 0.3 mi w of airport	▽▽▽	$144-$176 SAVE	883
60 / p. 848	AAA	DoubleTree Richmond Airport, just n of airport	▽▽▽	Rates not provided SAVE	883
55 / p. 848		Hampton Inn-Richmond Airport, 0.3 mi w of airport	▽▽▽	Rates not provided	883
53 / p. 848		Homewood Suites Richmond Airport, 1 mi n of airport	▽▽▽	$169-$179	883
54 / p. 848		Wingate Inn Richmond Airport, 1 mi n of airport	▽▽▽	$129	884

Richmond & Vicinity

This index helps you "spot" where approved lodgings and restaurants are located on the corresponding detailed maps. Lodging daily rate range is for comparison only and show the property's high season. Restaurant rate range is a combination of lunch and/or dinner. Turn to the listing page for more detailed rate information and consult display ads for special promotions.

Spotter/Map Page Number	OA	RICHMOND - Lodgings	Diamond Rating	Rate Range High Season	Listing Page
1 / p. 848		Econo Lodge North-Parham Rd	▽▽	$45-$170	865
2 / p. 848		Sleep Inn	▽▽	$82-$144	867
3 / p. 848	AAA	Holiday Inn-Richmond North	▽▽▽	Rates not provided SAVE	866
4 / p. 848	AAA	Quality Inn West End - see color ad p 866	▽▽▽	$79-$159 SAVE	866
5 / p. 848	AAA	Comfort Inn Executive Center	▽▽	Rates not provided SAVE	864
6 / p. 848	AAA	Embassy Suites Hotel	▽▽▽	Rates not provided SAVE	865
7 / p. 848		Super 8 Motel	▽	Rates not provided	867
8 / p. 848		Extended Stay Deluxe Hotel	▽▽	$95-$165	865
9 / p. 848	AAA	Best Western Executive Hotel - see color ad p 864	▽▽	Rates not provided SAVE	864
10 / p. 848		Extended StayAmerica-I-64-West Broad	▽▽	$64-$135	865
11 / p. 848	AAA	Sheraton Richmond West	▽▽▽	$255 SAVE	867
12 / p. 848		Crowne Plaza Richmond West	▽▽▽	$110-$160	865
13 / p. 848		Courtyard by Marriott	▽▽▽	$167-$205	865
14 / p. 848		Holiday Inn I-64 West End	▽▽▽	$109-$179	865
15 / p. 848	AAA	Airport Inn Motel	▽▽	$55-$85 SAVE	864
16 / p. 848		Holiday Inn Select-Koger South	▽▽▽	$150-$180	866
17 / p. 848		Hampton Inn-Midlothian Turnpike	▽▽▽	$139-$149	865
18 / p. 848	AAA	Best Western Governor's Inn	▽▽▽	$85-$189 SAVE	864
19 / p. 848	AAA	Sheraton Park South Hotel	▽▽▽	Rates not provided SAVE	867
20 / p. 848	AAA	Travel Inn	▽	$50-$65 SAVE	867
21 / p. 848	AAA	Hyatt Place Richmond/Arboretum	▽▽▽	$99-$189 SAVE	866
22 / p. 848		Homestead Studio Suites Hotel-Richmond/Midlothian	▽▽	$77-$140	866
23 / p. 848		Candlewood Suites	▽▽	$129-$189	864
		RICHMOND - Restaurants			
1 / p. 848		Da Lat Vietnamese Cuisine	▽▽	$6-$15	868

Spotter/Map Page Number	OA	**RICHMOND** - Restaurants (continued)	Diamond Rating	Rate Range High Season	Listing Page
(2) / p. 848		Zorba's	◆◆	$5-$15	871
(3) / p. 848		Bella Luna Ristorante Italiano	◆◆	$6-$18	868
(4) / p. 848		Peking Restaurant	◆◆	$6-$14	870
(5) / p. 848		Pasta Luna	◆◆	$8-$22	870
(6) / p. 848		Franco's Ristorante	◆◆◆	$18-$26	869
(7) / p. 848		Manila! Manila! Cafe & Grille	◆◆	$9-$15	870
(8) / p. 848		Akida Japanese Restaurant	◆◆	$7-$25	867
(9) / p. 848		Thai Diner	◆◆	$6-$10	871
(10) / p. 848		Shackleford's Restaurant	◆◆	$5-$25	871
(11) / p. 848		Vietnam Garden	◆◆	$6-$13	871
(12) / p. 848		Pho 79	◆	$6-$9	871
(13) / p. 848		Melito's	◆◆	$5-$23	870
(14) / p. 848		Full Kee Restaurant	◆◆	$5-$15	869
(15) / p. 848		Buckhead's	◆◆◆	$27-$48	868
(16) / p. 848		La Petite France	◆◆◆	$9-$36	869
(17) / p. 848		Grafiti Grille	◆◆	$5-$23	869
(18) / p. 848		The Crazy Greek	◆	$5-$13	868
(19) / p. 848		Super Stars Gourmet Pizza	◆	$4-$10	871
(20) / p. 848		Yum Yum Good	◆◆	$5-$15	871
(21) / p. 848		Peking	◆◆	$7-$23	870
(22) / p. 848		Escabar	◆◆◆	$8-$25	869
(23) / p. 848		Su Casa Mexican Restaurant	◆	$5-$15	871
(24) / p. 848		Azzurro	◆◆◆	$9-$32	867
(25) / p. 848	AAA	**Carytown Burger & Fries**	◆	$4-$7	868
(26) / p. 848		Brio Tuscan Grill	◆◆◆	$10-$29	868
(27) / p. 848		The Hill Cafe	◆◆	$6-$21	869
(28) / p. 848		Maldini's	◆◆	$6-$16	870
(29) / p. 848		Grand Dynasty Restaurant	◆	$5-$14	869
(30) / p. 848		Little Saigon	◆◆	$4-$15	870
(31) / p. 848		Dena's Grecian Restaurant	◆◆	$4-$15	868
(32) / p. 848		Ruchee Indian Restaurant	◆◆	$4-$16	871
(33) / p. 848		La Siesta Mexican Restaurant	◆◆	$4-$12	870
(34) / p. 848		La Palmera	◆	$5-$13	869
		ASHLAND - Lodgings			
(26) / p. 848	AAA	**Days Inn Ashland**	◆◆	Rates not provided [SAVE]	872
(27) / p. 848		Holiday Inn Express Hotel & Suites	◆◆◆	$99-$139	872
(28) / p. 848		Hampton Inn	◆◆◆	Rates not provided	872
(29) / p. 848	AAA	**Sleep Inn & Suites**	◆◆◆	$75-$174 [SAVE]	872
		ASHLAND - Restaurants			
(37) / p. 848		El Azteca	◆	$5-$17	872

Spotter/Map. Page Number	OA	ASHLAND - Restaurants (continued)	Diamond Rating	Rate Range High Season	Listing Page
38 / p. 848		Ashland Coffee & Tea	◆	$5-$12	872
39 / p. 848		Homemades by Suzanne	◆	$5-$8	872
40 / p. 848		The Ironhorse Restaurant	◆◆	$7-$32	872
41 / p. 848		The Smokey Pig	◆	$4-$16	873
		GLEN ALLEN - Lodgings			
32 / p. 848		Hampton Inn & Suites	◆◆◆	Rates not provided	877
33 / p. 848		SpringHill Suites by Marriott	◆◆◆	$148-$180	878
34 / p. 848	(AAA)	**Virginia Crossings Resort**	◆◆◆◆	$159-$209 [SAVE]	878
35 / p. 848		Richmond Marriott West	◆◆◆	$175-$213	878
36 / p. 848		Candlewood Suites Richmond-West	◆◆	$109-$179	876
37 / p. 848		Homewood Suites by Hilton Richmond West End-Innsbrook	◆◆◆	Rates not provided	877
38 / p. 848		Hilton Garden Inn Richmond Innsbrook	◆◆◆	$179	877
39 / p. 848		Comfort Suites-Innsbrook	◆◆◆	$133	876
40 / p. 848		Hampton Inn-Richmond West	◆◆◆	Rates not provided	877
41 / p. 848		Homestead Studio Suites Hotel-Richmond-Innsbrook	◆◆	$77-$140	877
42 / p. 848		Courtyard by Marriott Richmond Northwest	◆◆◆	$167-$205	876
43 / p. 848		Residence Inn by Marriott	◆◆◆	$204-$234	878
44 / p. 848		Howard Johnson Express Inn	◆◆	Rates not provided	877
45 / p. 848		Fairfield Inn & Suites by Marriott	◆◆◆	$119-$144	877
46 / p. 848		Holiday Inn Express	◆◆◆	$119-$134	877
		GLEN ALLEN - Restaurants			
47 / p. 848		The Glen Restaurant	◆◆◆	$13-$33	879
48 / p. 848		Firebirds Wood Fired Grill	◆◆◆	$6-$26	879
49 / p. 848		Osaka Sushi & Steak	◆◆	$8-$20	879
50 / p. 848		Mama Cucina	◆◆◆	$7-$18	879
51 / p. 848		House of Vietnam	◆◆	$7-$16	879
52 / p. 848		Bistro R	◆◆◆	$8-$30	878
53 / p. 848		The Grapevine II	◆◆◆	$5-$20	879
		MECHANICSVILLE - Lodgings			
49 / p. 848		Holiday Inn Express-Richmond-Mechanicsville	◆◆◆	$99-$149	880
50 / p. 848		Hampton Inn	◆◆◆	$99-$159	880
		MECHANICSVILLE - Restaurant			
56 / p. 848		Peking Restaurant	◆◆	$6-$23	880
		SANDSTON - Lodgings			
53 / p. 848		Homewood Suites Richmond Airport	◆◆◆	$169-$179	883
54 / p. 848		Wingate Inn Richmond Airport	◆◆◆	$129	884
55 / p. 848		Hampton Inn-Richmond Airport	◆◆◆	Rates not provided	883
56 / p. 848		Comfort Inn Richmond Airport	◆◆	$80-$100	883
57 / p. 848	(AAA)	**Courtyard by Marriott-Richmond Airport**	◆◆◆	$144-$176 [SAVE]	883
58 / p. 848	(AAA)	**Red Roof Inn**	◆◆	$49-$79 [SAVE]	883
59 / p. 848	(AAA)	**Clarion Richmond Airport**	◆◆◆	$89-$139 [SAVE]	883

Spotter/Map Page Number	OA		Diamond Rating	Rate Range High Season	Listing Page
60 / p. 848	AAA	**DoubleTree Richmond Airport**	◆◆◆	Rates not provided SAVE	883
		SANDSTON - Restaurant			
59 / p. 848	AAA	**Wings**	◆◆	$5-$20	884
		MIDLOTHIAN - Lodgings			
63 / p. 848	AAA	**Super 8 Motel**	◆◆	Rates not provided SAVE	881
64 / p. 848		Hampton Inn-Richmond-South West-Hull Street	◆◆◆	$139-$149	881
65 / p. 848		Holiday Inn Express Hotel & Suites-Brandermill	◆◆◆	$129-$169	881
		MIDLOTHIAN - Restaurants			
62 / p. 848		Bottega Bistro	◆◆◆	$6-$27	881
63 / p. 848		Ruth's Chris Steak House	◆◆◆	$20-$40	882
64 / p. 848		Bookbinder's Grill	◆◆◆	$9-$30	881
65 / p. 848	AAA	**Pescados**	◆◆◆	$15-$25	882
66 / p. 848		Peking	◆◆	$9-$16	882
67 / p. 848		Andre's Grille	◆◆	$7-$20	881
68 / p. 848		Saigon Gourmet Restaurant	◆◆	$5-$14	882
69 / p. 848		Pasta Luna	◆◆	$6-$20	882
70 / p. 848		Bonefish Grill	◆◆◆	$14-$25	881
		CHESTERFIELD - Lodgings			
68 / p. 848		Chester Inn & Suites	◆◆	$80-$180	875
69 / p. 848	AAA	**Country Inn & Suites, Richmond I-95S**	◆◆◆	$89-$169 SAVE	875
70 / p. 848	AAA	**Sleep Inn**	◆◆	$69-$99 SAVE	875
		CHESTER - Lodgings			
73 / p. 848	AAA	**Hampton Inn**	◆◆◆	Rates not provided SAVE	873
74 / p. 848		Fairfield Inn By Marriott	◆◆◆	$118-$144	873
75 / p. 848	AAA	**Comfort Inn-Richmond/Chester**	◆◆◆	$90-$153 SAVE	873
76 / p. 848		Clarion Hotel	◆◆◆	$59-$129	873
77 / p. 848		Quality Inn & Suites	◆◆	$59-$129	874
78 / p. 848		Courtyard by Marriott Richmond/Chester	◆◆◆	$127-$157	873
79 / p. 848		Holiday Inn Express	◆◆◆	$99-$169	873
80 / p. 848		Homewood Suites by Hilton Richmond/Chester	◆◆◆	$159-$179	874
81 / p. 848	AAA	**Hyatt Place Richmond/Chester**	◆◆◆	$99-$299 SAVE	874
		CHESTER - Restaurants			
73 / p. 848		Peking Restaurant	◆◆	$5-$14	875
74 / p. 848		Central Park Deli	◆	$5-$7	874
75 / p. 848		Don Papa Grande Mexican Restaurant	◆	$4-$13	874
76 / p. 848		Narita Japanese Restaurant	◆◆	$6-$50	874
77 / p. 848		Cesare's Restaurant & Pizzeria	◆◆	$6-$14	874
78 / p. 848		Jalapenos	◆	$5-$14	874
		HANOVER - Restaurant			
44 / p. 848		Houndstooth Cafe	◆◆	$4-$24	880

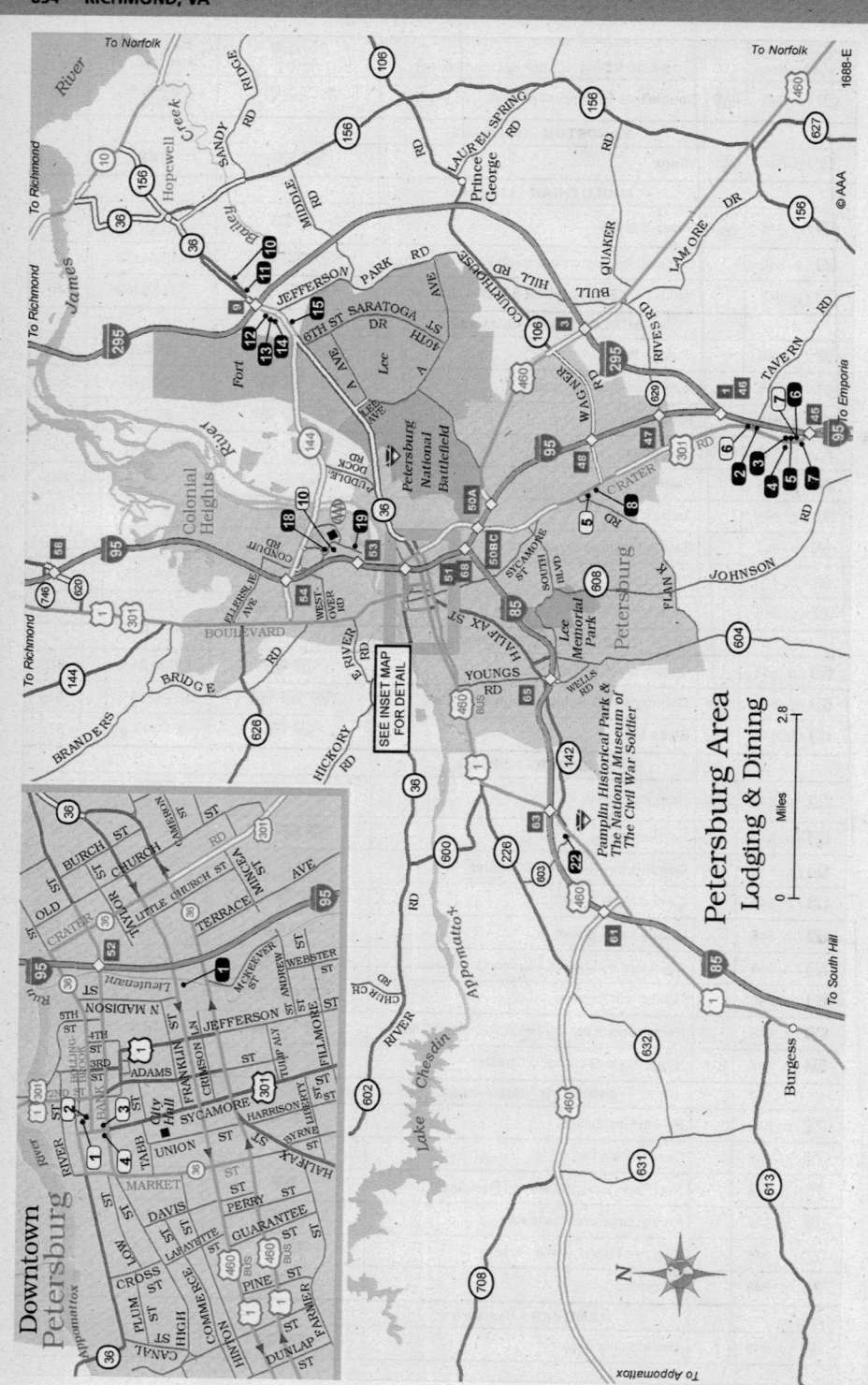

Petersburg Area
Lodging & Dining

Downtown
Petersburg

Petersburg

This index helps you "spot" where approved lodgings and restaurants are located on the corresponding detailed maps. Lodging daily rate range is for comparison only and show the property's high season. Restaurant rate range is a combination of lunch and/or dinner. Turn to the listing page for more detailed rate information and consult display ads for special promotions.

Spotter/Map Page Number	OA	PETERSBURG - Lodgings	Diamond Rating	Rate Range High Season	Listing Page
1 / p. 854		Ramada Plaza Hotel Petersburg	▽▽▽	$119-$169	840
2 / p. 854	AAA	**Holiday Inn Express Hotel & Suites**	▽▽▽	$129-$299 SAVE	839
3 / p. 854	AAA	**Hampton Inn**	▽▽▽	Rates not provided SAVE	838
4 / p. 854		Quality Inn - see color ad p 840	▽▽	$60-$139	840
5 / p. 854		Comfort Inn-Petersburg South	▽▽	$59-$119	838
6 / p. 854	AAA	**Howard Johnson Steven Kent** - see color ad p 839	▽▽	Rates not provided SAVE	840
7 / p. 854	AAA	**Days Inn** - see color ad p 839	▽▽	Rates not provided SAVE	838
8 / p. 854	AAA	**Super 8 Motel**	▽▽	Rates not provided SAVE	840
		PETERSBURG - Restaurants			
①/ p. 854		Wabi-Sabi	▽▽	$6-$20	841
②/ p. 854		The Brickhouse Run	▽▽▽	$12-$25	841
③/ p. 854		Alexander's Fine Food	▽	$5-$14	841
④/ p. 854		Longstreet's Delicatessen	▽	$5-$8	841
⑤/ p. 854		Kings Barbeque	▽	$5-$15	841
⑥/ p. 854		Nanny's Family Restaurant	▽	$4-$10	841
⑦/ p. 854		Steven Kent Restaurant	▽▽	$3-$19	841
		HOPEWELL - Lodgings			
10 / p. 854		Fairfield Inn & Suites by Marriott	▽▽▽	$99-$129	819
11 / p. 854	AAA	**Econo Lodge**	▽▽	$69-$99 SAVE	819
12 / p. 854		Quality Inn at Ft Lee/Hopewell	▽▽	$90-$100	819
13 / p. 854		Hampton Inn-Ft Lee	▽▽▽	$119-$129	819
14 / p. 854	AAA	**Candlewood Suites**	▽▽	$119-$145 SAVE	818
15 / p. 854	AAA	**Comfort Inn-Prince George**	▽▽	$89-$149 SAVE	818
		COLONIAL HEIGHTS - Lodgings			
18 / p. 854		Hilton Garden Inn-Southpark	▽▽▽	$109-$199	875
19 / p. 854	AAA	**Comfort Suites Southpark**	▽▽▽	$109-$259 SAVE	875
		COLONIAL HEIGHTS - Restaurant			
⑩/ p. 854		Koreana Oriental Restaurant	▽▽	$6-$17	875
		DINWIDDIE - Lodgings			
22 / p. 854	AAA	**Holiday Inn Express Hotel & Suites** - see color ad p 839	▽▽▽	$105-$133 SAVE	711

DOWNTOWN RICHMOND (See map and index starting on p. 845)

———— WHERE TO STAY ————

THE BERKELEY HOTEL
Book great rates at AAA.com

Phone: (804)780-1300 **11**

Address: 1200 E Cary St 23219 **Location:** Just s of State Capitol; in Shockoe Slip at jct 12th St. Located in Historic Shockoe Slip District. **Facility:** In the tradition of the boutique hotel, the petite Berkeley offers guests highly personalized service and elegant suites in the heart of Shockoe Slip. 55 units. 54 one-bedroom standard units. 1 one-bedroom suite. 6 stories, interior corridors. *Bath:* combo or shower only. **Parking:** on-site (fee) and valet. **Terms:** cancellation fee imposed. **Amenities:** CD players, voice mail, safes, irons, hair dryers. *Some:* DVD players. **Dining:** restaurant, see separate listing. **Guest Services:** valet laundry, area transportation-downtown, wireless Internet. **Business Services:** meeting rooms, administrative services, PC. **Cards:** AX, CB, DC, DS, MC, VI. **Free Special Amenities: newspaper and high-speed Internet.**

Small-scale Hotel
$219-$249 All Year

COMFORT INN & CONFERENCE CENTER-MIDTOWN
Book at AAA.com

Phone: (804)359-4061 **2**

Address: 3200 W Broad St 23230 **Location:** Jct Broad St and I-95, just e. **Facility:** 189 units. 183 one-bedroom standard units. 6 one-bedroom suites. 6 stories, interior corridors. *Bath:* combo or shower only. **Parking:** on-site. **Terms:** 1-2 night minimum stay, 30 day cancellation notice-fee imposed. **Amenities:** high-speed Internet, voice mail, irons, hair dryers. **Pool(s):** outdoor. **Leisure Activities:** exercise room. **Guest Services:** valet and coin laundry, area transportation, wireless Internet. **Business Services:** meeting rooms. **Cards:** AX, CB, DC, DS, JC, MC, VI.

Small-scale Hotel
$80-$150 All Year

COMMONWEALTH PARK SUITES
Book great rates at AAA.com

Phone: (804)343-7300 **8**

Address: 901 Bank St 23219 **Location:** Jct 9th and Bank sts; across the green from the state capitol. **Facility:** 59 units. 10 one-bedroom standard units. 49 one-bedroom suites. 11 stories, interior corridors. *Bath:* combo or shower only. **Parking:** on-site (fee) and valet. **Terms:** cancellation fee imposed. **Amenities:** high-speed Internet (fee), voice mail, irons, hair dryers. *Some:* CD players. **Leisure Activities:** sauna, exercise room. **Guest Services:** valet and coin laundry, wireless Internet. **Business Services:** meeting rooms. **Cards:** AX, DC, DS, MC, VI. **Free Special Amenities: local telephone calls and high-speed Internet.**

Small-scale Hotel
$139-$189 All Year

CROWNE PLAZA RICHMOND DOWNTOWN
Book great rates at AAA.com

Phone: 804/788-0900 **9**

Address: 555 E Canal St 23219 **Location:** I-95, exit 74A (downtown expwy I-195), exit Canal St. **Facility:** 298 one-bedroom standard units. 16 stories, interior corridors. *Bath:* combo or shower only. **Parking:** on-site (fee) and valet. **Amenities:** CD players, high-speed Internet, voice mail, irons, hair dryers. *Some:* dual phone lines. **Pool(s):** heated indoor. **Leisure Activities:** saunas, whirlpool, exercise room. **Guest Services:** valet laundry, area transportation-within downtown, wireless Internet. **Business Services:** conference facilities, business center. **Cards:** AX, CB, DC, DS, JC, MC, VI. **Free Special Amenities: local telephone calls and high-speed Internet.**

Large-scale Hotel
$259 All Year

DOUBLETREE HOTEL RICHMOND DOWNTOWN
Book great rates at AAA.com

Phone: 804/644-9871 **3**

Address: 301 W Franklin St 23220 **Location:** Franklin St at Madison. **Facility:** 230 units. 228 one-bedroom standard units. 2 one-bedroom suites. 16 stories, interior corridors. *Bath:* combo or shower only. **Parking:** on-site (fee). **Amenities:** high-speed Internet, voice mail, irons, hair dryers. **Pool(s):** outdoor. **Leisure Activities:** exercise room. **Guest Services:** valet and coin laundry, area transportation-within 3 mi, wireless Internet. **Business Services:** meeting rooms, business center. **Free Special Amenities: high-speed Internet.**

Small-scale Hotel
Rates not provided

HOLIDAY INN CENTRAL
Book great rates at AAA.com

Phone: (804)359-9441 **1**

Address: 3207 N Boulevard 23230 **Location:** I-64/95, exit 78, just n. **Facility:** 179 units. 176 one-bedroom standard units. 3 one-bedroom suites. 3-4 stories, interior/exterior corridors. *Bath:* combo or shower only. **Parking:** on-site. **Amenities:** high-speed Internet, voice mail, irons, hair dryers. **Pool(s):** outdoor. **Leisure Activities:** exercise room. **Guest Services:** valet laundry, area transportation-train & bus stations, wireless Internet. **Business Services:** meeting rooms, business center. **Cards:** AX, CB, DC, DS, MC, VI. **Free Special Amenities: newspaper and high-speed Internet.**

Small-scale Hotel
$109-$159 All Year

HOLIDAY INN EXPRESS
Book at AAA.com

Phone: (804)788-1600 **7**

Address: 201 E Cary St 23219 **Location:** Jct 2nd St. **Facility:** 100 units. 80 one-bedroom standard units, some with whirlpools. 20 one-bedroom suites, some with whirlpools. 6 stories, interior corridors. *Bath:* combo or shower only. **Parking:** on-site (fee). **Amenities:** high-speed Internet, dual phone lines, voice mail, safes, irons, hair dryers. **Leisure Activities:** exercise room. **Guest Services:** valet laundry, wireless Internet. **Business Services:** meeting rooms, business center. **Cards:** AX, DC, DS, MC, VI.

Small-scale Hotel
$129-$249 All Year

(See map and index starting on p. 845)

THE JEFFERSON HOTEL
Book great rates at AAA.com **Phone:** (804)788-8000 **4**

AAA [SAVE]

◆◆◆◆◆

Classic Historic
Large-scale Hotel
$245-$375 All Year

Address: 101 W Franklin St 23220 **Location:** Franklin and Adams sts; center. **Facility:** This ornate 1895 Beaux Arts hotel is a historic landmark with a wealth of architectural details including a Tiffany stained-glass rotunda. 262 units. 222 one-bedroom standard units. 40 one-bedroom suites, some with whirlpools. 5-6 stories; interior corridors. **Parking:** on-site (fee) and valet. **Amenities:** video library, video games, CD players, dual phone lines, voice mail, safes, honor bars, irons, hair dryers. *Some:* DVD players, fax. **Dining:** 2 restaurants, also, T. J.'s Restaurant and Lounge, see separate listing, entertainment. **Pool(s):** heated indoor. **Leisure Activities:** *Fee:* massage. **Guest Services:** valet laundry, area transportation-within 3 mi, wireless Internet. **Business Services:** conference facilities, business center. **Cards:** AX, DC, DS, MC, VI. **Free Special Amenities:** newspaper and high-speed Internet. *(See color ad below)*

LINDEN ROW INN
Book great rates at AAA.com **Phone:** 804/783-7000 **5**

AAA [SAVE]

◆◆◆◆◆

Historic
Small-scale Hotel
Rates not provided

Address: 100 E Franklin St 23219 **Location:** At 1st and Franklin sts. **Facility:** The property includes a series of Greek Revival townhouses plus carriage houses in a walled garden. 70 units. 63 one-bedroom standard units. 4 stories, interior/exterior corridors. *Bath:* combo or shower only. **Parking:** on-site (fee). **Amenities:** high-speed Internet, voice mail, irons, hair dryers. **Guest Services:** valet laundry, area transportation-downtown & VCU. **Business Services:** meeting rooms. **Free Special Amenities:** continental breakfast and high-speed Internet.

OMNI RICHMOND HOTEL
Book at AAA.com **Phone:** (804)344-7000 **10**

◆◆◆

Large-scale Hotel
$169-$299 All Year

Address: 100 S 12th St 23219 **Location:** I-95, exit 74A; I-195, exit Canal St. Located near the Historic Shockoe Slip District. **Facility:** 361 units. 357 one-bedroom standard units. 4 one-bedroom suites. 19 stories, interior corridors. *Bath:* combo or shower only. **Parking:** on-site (fee) and valet. **Terms:** cancellation fee imposed. **Amenities:** video games (fee), voice mail, honor bars, irons, hair dryers. *Some:* dual phone lines. **Pool(s):** heated indoor. **Guest Services:** valet laundry, area transportation, wireless Internet. **Business Services:** conference facilities, business center. **Cards:** AX, CB, DC, DS, JC, MC, VI.

RICHMOND MARRIOTT HOTEL
Book great rates at AAA.com **Phone:** 804/643-3400 **6**

AAA [SAVE]

◆◆◆◆

Large-scale Hotel
$253-$285 All Year

Address: 500 E Broad St 23219 **Location:** I-95, exit 74C, at 5th and E Broad sts. Located adjacent to the Richmond Coliseum and Richmond Center. **Facility:** Smoke free premises. 401 one-bedroom standard units. 18 stories, interior corridors. *Bath:* combo or shower only. **Parking:** on-site (fee). **Terms:** check-in 4 pm. **Amenities:** dual phone lines, voice mail, irons, hair dryers. *Fee:* video games, high-speed Internet. **Pool(s):** heated indoor. **Leisure Activities:** whirlpool, sun deck, exercise room. **Guest Services:** valet and coin laundry, area transportation-downtown, wireless Internet. **Business Services:** conference facilities, business center. **Cards:** AX, DC, DS, JC, MC, VI. **Free Special Amenities:** newspaper and preferred room (subject to availability with advance reservations).

Marriott
HOTELS & RESORTS

AAA Benefit:
Members save 5% off of the best available rate.

▼ See AAA listing above ▼

Our attentive staff is trained to catch bags, and jaws, before either hits the floor.

(See map and index starting on p. 845)

THE WILLIAM CATLIN HOUSE

Historic Bed
& Breakfast

$110-$115 3/1-11/30
$105-$110 12/1-2/28

Phone: (804)780-3746 12

Address: 2304 E Broad St 23223 **Location:** Between 22nd and 23rd sts; in the Church Hill Historic District. **Facility:** This richly appointed house in a historic district features Civil War history books, family heirlooms and period furniture including canopy beds. Smoke free premises. 4 units. 2 one- and 2 two-bedroom standard units. 3 stories (no elevator), interior/exterior corridors. **Bath:** some shared or private, combo or shower only. **Parking:** street. **Terms:** 3 day cancellation notice. **Cards:** DS, MC, VI.

 / SOME UNITS

——— WHERE TO DINE ———

1 NORTH BELMONT RESTAURANT

French
$28-$42

Phone: 804/358-0050 11

The classically trained chef's fine specialties—which include whole Dover sole filleted tableside, lobster salad martini, beef tenderloin in brioche with foie gras and a traditional cheese course—pair with choices from a Euro-centric wine list. The French bistro setting is ideal for intimate dining. Dressy casual. **Bar:** Full bar. **Reservations:** suggested. **Hours:** 5:30 pm-10 pm. Closed major holidays; also Sun. **Address:** 1 N Belmont Ave 23221 **Location:** Jct Ellwood St, just w of Boulevard; in Historic Fan District. **Parking:** on-site. **Cards:** AX, DC, DS, MC, VI.

3 MONKEYS BAR & GRILL

American
$7-$18

Phone: 804/204-2525 23

Yet another cozy Fan neighborhood bar, this place serves delicious food that's miles from the standard pub grub. Mediterranean and Asian influences mingle on the lengthy, eclectic menu, with such house specialties as falafel sliders, baked goat cheese pizzas, Asian grilled chicken salad, steaks and burgers. This small spot's large sidewalk patio is a favorite spot for locals. Casual dress. **Bar:** Full bar. **Hours:** 11 am-1 am, Sat & Sun from 9:30 am. Closed: 11/27, 12/25. **Address:** 2525 W Main St 23221 **Location:** Jct Robinson St; in Historic Fan District. **Parking:** street. **Cards:** AX, MC, VI.

ACACIA

Regional American
$5-$23

Phone: 804/354-6060 12

Acacia was first noticed for their unique setting in the nave of a restored church but recently it's the culinary skills of the chef, Dale Reitzer, which has garnered national acclaim. The menu changes seasonally taking advantage of the freshest regional fare in creative and light combinations. Tables on the raised patio above the street are a nice spot to enjoy the streetscape. Dressy casual. **Bar:** Full bar. **Reservations:** suggested. **Hours:** 11:30 am-2:30 & 5:30-9 pm, Fri & Sat-9:30 pm. Closed: 11/27, 12/25; also Sun. **Address:** 3325 W Cary St 23221 **Location:** I-195, exit W Cary St, just e; in Carytown. **Parking:** street. **Cards:** AX, DC, DS, MC, VI.

AKIDA

Japanese
$7-$14

Phone: 804/359-8036 3

Because seating is limited in the tiny and much-loved Fan spot, take-out service is a popular option. Offerings include great traditional and creative sushi, udon noodle soups, tempuras and teriyakis. The lunch box provides a great way to sample several tastes. Casual dress. **Bar:** Full bar. **Hours:** 11:30 am-2:30 & 5-10 pm, Fri-11 pm, Sat 5 pm-11 pm. Closed: Sun. **Address:** 814 N Robinson St 23220 **Location:** Just s of Broad St; in Historic Fan District. **Parking:** street. **Cards:** AX, MC, VI.

AMICI RISTORANTE

Northern Italian
$8-$30

Phone: 804/353-4700 10

In a converted turn-of-the-20th-century townhouse, the intimate restaurant has preferred tables set amid the twinkling lights of the sidewalk patio. Although the upscale Italian cuisine changes seasonally, some constant specialties include fresh fennel salad, agnolotti pasta stuffed with spinach and ricotta, and baby rack of lamb with rosemary and garlic. Service is smooth and professional, and wine choices are excellent. Dressy casual. **Bar:** Full bar. **Reservations:** suggested. **Hours:** 11:30 am-2:30 & 5:30-10 pm. Closed major holidays; also Sun. **Address:** 3343 W Cary St 23221 **Location:** I-195, exit W Cary St, just e; in Carytown. **Parking:** street. **Cards:** AX, DS, MC, VI.

AVALON   *Menu on AAA.com*

American
$14-$22

Phone: 804/353-9709 21

The seasonally changing menu shows a real flair, taking advantage of the freshest ingredients in imaginative ways. Out-of-the-ordinary dishes incorporate plenty of fruit, cheese and veggies. Photographs from the '40s and '50s capture notables of the time. Noisy bar crowd later in the evenings. Casual dress. **Bar:** Full bar. **Reservations:** suggested. **Hours:** 5 pm-1 am. Closed: 11/27, 12/24, 12/25. **Address:** 2619 W Main St 23220 **Location:** Just e of Boulevard (SR 161) on W Main St (SR 147); in Historic Fan District. **Parking:** street. **Cards:** AX, DC, DS, MC, VI.

AVENUE 805

American
$10-$24

Phone: 804/353-2505 4

A light-hearted attitude prevails at the fun little spot. The constantly changing list of creative specials might include potato-crusted rockfish, seared duck or what the owner dubs the "menu du always" of "inspired" Italian dishes, such as veal or chicken scaloppine, varied pasta dishes and delightful shrimp, scallop and crab cakes. Casual dress. **Bar:** Full bar. **Hours:** 5:30 pm-10 pm, Fri & Sat-11 pm; Sunday brunch 11 am-2 pm. Closed: 11/27, 12/24, 12/25; also 1st week in Jan & Jul. **Address:** 805 N Davis Ave 23220 **Location:** Just s of jct W Broad St; in Historic Fan District. **Parking:** street. **Cards:** AX, DS, MC, VI.

BACCHUS

Continental
$12-$30

Phone: 804/355-9919 32

The charming bistro is tucked in a narrow spot with an elaborately carved bar and Roman-themed mural. Modern, creative dishes reflect Mediterranean influences. Start with classic antipasto or carpaccio, then choose from such well-prepared options as roasted duck, seared tuna or bouillabaisse. Parking is available across the street after 6 pm. Casual dress. **Bar:** Full bar. **Reservations:** suggested. **Hours:** 5 pm-11 pm. Closed major holidays; also Sun. **Address:** 2 N Meadow St 23220 **Location:** Jct W Main St; in Historic Fan District. **Parking:** street. **Cards:** AX, MC, VI.

(See map and index starting on p. 845)

BOTTOMS UP PIZZA

Pizza
$5-$10

Phone: 804/644-4400   **50**

Diners can choose from such creative toppings as seafood and vegetables when ordering thick-crust pizza either whole or by the slice. An ideal place to wait while the pizza is baking is in the lively bar, which caters to a young crowd. Popular starters include wings and fried mozzarella. Casual dress. **Bar:** Full bar. **Hours:** 11 am-11 pm, Fri & Sat-2 am, Mon & Tues-10 pm. Closed: 11/27, 12/25. **Address:** 1700 Dock St 23223 **Location:** Jct 17th and Dock sts; just s of E Main St; in Shockoe Bottom District. **Parking:** on-site (fee). **Cards:** AX, DS, MC, VI.

BUZ AND NEDS REAL BARBECUE

Barbecue
$5-$20

Phone: 804/355-6055   **2**

After traveling the country researching the world of barbecue, Buz and Ned have perfected their spicy-sweet version. Guests can sample brisket, pork, chicken and even buffalo ribs with such traditional Southern sides as baked beans, macaroni and cheese and jalapeno corn fries. Casual dress. **Bar:** Full bar. **Hours:** 11 am-9 pm, Fri & Sat-10 pm, Sun noon-8 pm. Closed major holidays. **Address:** 1119 N Boulevard 23230 **Location:** Just n of W Broad St. **Parking:** no self-parking. **Cards:** AX, DS, MC, VI.

CABO'S CORNER BISTRO

Continental
$17-$37

Phone: 804/355-1144   **5**

Stylish art deco interior with dining in the more social lounge as well. Eclectic cuisine mixing European traditions with Southern influences. Entertainment nightly specializing in swing jazz and blues. Casual dress. **Bar:** Full bar. **Reservations:** accepted. **Hours:** 5 pm-10:30 pm. Closed major holidays; also Sun & Mon. **Address:** 2053 W Broad St 23220 **Location:** Just e of Science Museum of Virginia. **Parking:** on-site. **Cards:** AX, CB, DC, MC, VI.

CAFE' GUTENBERG

Coffee/Espresso
$3-$15

Phone: 804/497-5000   **48**

If sitting down with a great cup of joe and a good book is your thing, then you'll like this bohemian cafe, which houses an eclectic selection of books and magazines for your reading pleasure. But this is no ordinary coffee joint. There's also beer and wine, as well as soups, salads, tapas, panini sandwiches and dessert. And if you're an early riser, there's breakfast, and the morning paper, too. Casual dress. **Bar:** Beer & wine. **Reservations:** accepted. **Hours:** 11 am-11 pm, Sat & Sun from 8 am. Closed: 11/27, 12/25. **Address:** 1700 E Main St 23223 **Location:** Jct 17th St; across from the Farmer's Market; in Shockoe Bottom. **Parking:** street. **Cards:** DS, MC, VI.

CAN CAN BRASSERIE

French
$8-$22

Phone: 804/358-7274   **13**

The brasserie's turn-of-the-20th-century Parisian setting oozes style with such touches as pressed-tin ceilings and a 50-foot zinc bar. Dishes on the classic French cafe menu may not sound familiar, but they translate into well-known flavors. Specialties include gougeres (a type of cheese puff), oyster and raw-bar offerings, coq au vin and hamburgers elegantly topped with Gruyere cheese. Also popular are savory crepes for lunch or brunch and artisan breads and pastries from the coffee bar. Casual dress. **Bar:** Full bar. **Reservations:** accepted. **Hours:** 11:30 am-3 & 5:30-10 pm, Fri & Sat-11 pm, Sun 9 am-3 & 5:30-10 pm. Closed: 11/27, 12/25. **Address:** 3120 W Cary St 23221 **Location:** I-195, exit Cary St, just w; in Cary Court; in Carytown. **Parking:** on-site. **Cards:** AX, DS, MC, VI.

CALL

CAPITAL ALE HOUSE

American
$7-$20

Phone: 804/780-2537

Ice troughs shaped to fit drink glasses at the bar show where the priorities lie. However, the food isn't taken for granted either. Menu selections range from sandwiches to snack-size appetizers to sophisticated entrees. Casual dress. **Bar:** Full bar. **Hours:** 11 am-1 am. Closed: 11/27, 12/25. **Address:** 623 E Main St 23219 **Location:** Between 6th and 7th sts. **Parking:** street. **Cards:** AX, DC, DS, MC, VI.

CARLTON'S

Continental
$6-$23

Phone: 804/359-3122   **15**

With murals, rich cherry wood, Italian green marble and lots of stained glass, the setting inside is cool. Interesting menu choices—including Lowcountry crab maki rolls, pulled pork spring rolls, crab cakes and chili-glazed pork shanks—show influences from Asia, Greece and the South. Casual dress. **Bar:** Full bar. **Reservations:** suggested. **Hours:** 11 am-2:30 & 5-10 pm, Sat from 5 pm. Closed major holidays; also Sun. **Address:** 2526 Floyd Ave 23221 **Location:** Jct Robinson St and Floyd Ave; in Historic Fan District. **Parking:** on-site. **Cards:** AX, MC, VI.

COMFORT

Regional American
$6-$18

Phone: 804/780-0004   **36**

As the name implies, this spot specializes in comfort foods of the Southern variety. Among specialties are fried catfish, braised short ribs and roasted duck, which are served with plentiful country sides, such as fried green tomatoes, creamed spinach and cheese grits. Casual dress. **Bar:** Full bar. **Hours:** 11:30 am-2:30 & 5:30-10:30 pm, Sat 5:30 pm-11 pm. Closed major holidays; also Sun. **Address:** 200 W Broad St 23220 **Location:** Jct Jefferson St. **Parking:** street. **Cards:** AX, DS, MC, VI.

COPPOLA'S

Deli/Subs
Sandwiches
$5-$10

Phone: 804/359-6969   **18**

Self described as a "taste of lil' Italy" this cozy New York-style delicatessen is on a busy corner complete with sidewalk tables. Awesome overstuffed sandwiches such as the Industrial Hero, the Mediterranean Magic, or the South Bronx Club. All lunches end well with the NY cannoli. Casual dress. **Bar:** Beer & wine. **Hours:** 10 am-8 pm, Thurs-Sat to 9 pm, Sun 11 am-4 pm. Closed major holidays. **Address:** 2900 W Cary St 23221 **Location:** I-95, exit W Cary St, 1 mi e, then just w of jct Boulevard; in Carytown. **Parking:** street. **Cards:** MC, VI.

(See map and index starting on p. 845)

CROAKER'S SPOT

Soul Food
$9-$33

Phone: 804/421-0560 (35)

Tucked on a busy corner in historic Jackson Ward, the restaurant serves some of the city's best and most affordable seafood dishes, such as shrimp and grits, shrimp curry and an overflowing seafood platter. Delicious cornbread is a side for all dishes. Casual dress. **Bar:** Full bar. **Hours:** 11 am-9 pm, Thurs-10 pm, Fri-11 pm, Sat noon-11 pm, Sun noon-7 pm. Closed major holidays. **Address:** 119 E Leigh St 23219 **Location:** Jct 2nd St; in Jackson Ward. **Parking:** street. **Cards:** AX, DC, DS, MC, VI.

THE DAIRY BAR

Deli/Subs
Sandwiches
$5-$9

Phone: 804/355-1937 (1)

Casual dress. **Hours:** 7 am-3 pm. Closed major holidays; also Sun. **Address:** 1602 Roseneath Rd 23230 **Location:** Just n of W Broad St. **Parking:** street. **Cards:** DS, MC, VI.

DAVIS & MAIN

American
$12-$23

Phone: 804/353-6641 (24)

Termed "American Grill Cuisine" which means using the grill to enhance the freshest ingredients and natural flavors including chicken, seafood and beef choices. Known for their grilled pork tenderloin with Southern chutney, smoked trout appetizer, or spinach and sweet potato salad, as well as nightly blackboard specials. Charming atmosphere in historic district; dark woods, cozy high-backed booths, long friendly bar. Casual dress. **Bar:** Full bar. **Hours:** 4 pm-midnight. Closed major holidays. **Address:** 2501 W Main St 23220 **Location:** Jct Davis and W Main sts; in Historic Fan District. **Parking:** street. **Cards:** AX, DC, MC, VI.

THE DINING ROOM AT THE BERKELEY HOTEL   Menu on AAA.com

Continental
$9-$40

Phone: 804/225-5105 (42)

Wonderful menu choices of regional fare are both visually impressive and delicious tasting at this richly appointed downtown dining room. Diners at many tables enjoy a sidewalk view of the cobblestone streets of Shockoe Slip. Dressy casual. **Bar:** Full bar. **Reservations:** suggested. **Hours:** 7-10:30 am, 11:30-2 & 5:30-10 pm, Sun 7:30-10:30 am, 11:30-2 & 5:30-9 pm. Closed: 12/25. **Address:** 1200 E Cary St 23219 **Location:** Just w of state capitol; in The Berkeley Hotel; in Historic Shockoe Slip District. **Parking:** valet. **Cards:** AX, CB, DC, DS, MC, VI.

DOGWOODS GRILLE & SPIRITS

American
$18-$32

Phone: 804/340-1984 (33)

Underneath a casual neighborhood ambience lies a sophisticated urban menu. The highest-quality ingredients combine in a fusion of Continental and Southern accents, with a touch of Asian flavor thrown in for exotic measure. Casual dress. **Bar:** Full bar. **Reservations:** suggested. **Hours:** 5 pm-9:30 pm, Fri & Sat-10 pm. Closed major holidays; also Sun & Mon. **Address:** 1731 W Main St 23220 **Location:** Jct S Allen St; in Fan Historic District. **Parking:** street. **Cards:** AX, DC, DS, MC, VI.

DOUBLE T'S REAL SMOKED BARBECUE

Barbecue
$6-$18

Phone: 804/353-9861 (20)

This casual rough-hewn spot with an inviting sidewalk patio features all manner of barbecue specialties from chicken to ribs and 4 different sauces to top it with. Casual dress. **Bar:** Full bar. **Hours:** 11 am-10 pm, Fri & Sat-11 pm. Closed major holidays. **Address:** 2907 W Cary St 23221 **Location:** I-195, exit W Cary St, 1 mi e; just w of jct Boulevard; in Carytown Shopping District. **Parking:** street. **Cards:** AX, DS, MC, VI.

EDO'S SQUID

Italian
$8-$25

Phone: 804/864-5488 (28)

Locals have long loved the pastas—such as rich, savory carbonara—as well as the fresh fish and osso buco. The cozy, second-floor, brick-walled retreat above the Virginia Commonwealth University campus is a fresh spot in which to savor the food. Casual dress. **Bar:** Full bar. **Reservations:** accepted. **Hours:** 11 am-11 pm, Fri & Sat-midnight, Sun 5:30 pm-11 pm. Closed major holidays. **Address:** 411 N Harrison St 23220 **Location:** Between W Grace and Franklin sts; adjacent to the Virginia Commonwealth University campus; 2nd floor. **Parking:** street. **Cards:** AX, MC, VI.

ENOTECA SOGNO, VINO E CUCINA

Italian
$7-$16

Phone: 804/355-8466 (6)

This casual wine bar offers an extensive selection of Italian and Spanish wines, which pair well with distinctive appetizers of tuna carpaccio, tuna croquettes and cheese and antipasti platters. The menu lists traditional fresh pasta and scaloppine dishes, as well as daily specials that can run from steaks to branzino. Among mouthwatering homemade desserts are tiramisu, panna cotta and cannoli. Casual dress. **Bar:** Beer & wine. **Hours:** 5:30 pm-10 pm, Fri & Sat-11 pm. Closed: Sun & Mon. **Address:** 2043 W Broad St 23220 **Location:** Just w of jct Chamberlyne Rd. **Parking:** on-site. **Cards:** AX, DC, DS, MC, VI.

EUROPA MEDITERRANEAN CAFE AND TAPAS BAR

Ethnic
$5-$25

Phone: 804/643-0911 (44)

The lively downtown spot specializes in tapas, a fun and social Spanish tradition that features multiple plates of savory appetizers. Hot and cold dishes reflect multicultural influences. Among full entrees are several varieties of paella. Casual dress. **Bar:** Full bar. **Reservations:** accepted. **Hours:** 11:30 am-2:30 & 5:30-10 pm, Fri-11 pm, Sat 5:30 pm-11 pm, Sun 5:30 pm-10 pm. **Address:** 1409 E Cary St 23219 **Location:** Just e of jct 14th St; in Shockoe Bottom District. **Parking:** street. **Cards:** AX, DC, DS, MC, VI.

FAROUK'S HOUSE OF INDIA

Ethnic
$5-$14

Phone: 804/355-0378 (17)

Indian cuisine, traditional vindaloos and biryanis and a large selection of curry dishes makes this restaurant a crowd pleaser. The all-you-can-eat lunch buffet offers a good variety of fresh, hot dishes, bread, vegetables, salad and rice pudding. Casual dress. **Bar:** Beer & wine. **Hours:** 11:30 am-3 & 5-10:30 pm. **Address:** 3033 W Cary St 23221 **Location:** I-195, exit Cary St, 0.5 mi e; in Carytown Shopping District. **Parking:** street. **Cards:** AX, DC, DS, MC, VI.

(See map and index starting on p. 845)

THE HARD SHELL
Phone: 804/643-2333   45

Seafood
$7-$30

Exposed brick walls and frequent live jazz performances add to the casual ambience. Patrons are drawn by sophisticated preparations of fresh local and international seafood, as well as raw bar items. Oysters Michelle are a signature dish. The courtyard patio is inviting. Casual dress. Entertainment. **Bar:** Full bar. **Reservations:** suggested. **Hours:** 11:30 am-4 & 5-10 pm, Fri & Sat-11 pm, Sun 10:30 am-2:30 & 5-9 pm; Sunday brunch. Closed major holidays. **Address:** 1411 E Cary St 23219 **Location:** Just e of jct 14th St; in Shockoe Bottom District. **Parking:** on-site (fee). **Cards:** AX, DC, DS, MC, VI.

HELEN'S
Phone: 804/358-4370   22

American
$17-$25

The casual atmosphere is set by the nostalgic surroundings of this former lunch counter complete with swivel seats at the counter and pressed tin ceilings. The menu sets a decidedly more sophisticated tone with seasonally changing gourmet offerings. Casual dress. **Bar:** Full bar. **Reservations:** accepted. **Hours:** 5:30 pm-10 pm, Fri & Sat-11 pm; Sunday brunch. 10:30 am-2:30 pm. Closed major holidays; also Mon. **Address:** 2527 W Main St 23220 **Location:** Jct Robinson St; in Fan Historic District. **Parking:** street. **Cards:** AX, DC, DS, MC, VI.

JULEP'S, NEW SOUTHERN CUISINE
Phone: 804/377-3968   47

Regional American
$18-$30

Housed in one of Richmond's oldest commercial buildings in Shockoe Slip, Julep's, with its spiral staircase and open attic with exposed beams, is a true Southern belle. But her beauty goes way beyond the surface. The tart and oh-so-good fried green tomatoes only add to her charm, as does the hearty blackened bouillabaisse, and the super creamy cheese grits. The regional menu changes seasonally, but its delightful Southern fare will never go out of style. Dressy casual. **Bar:** Full bar. **Reservations:** suggested. **Hours:** 5:30 pm-9:30 pm, Fri & Sat-10 pm. Closed major holidays; also Sun. **Address:** 1719-21 E Franklin St 23219 **Location:** Jct 18th St; in Shockoe Bottom. **Parking:** street. **Cards:** AX, DC, DS, MC, VI.

KUBA KUBA
Phone: 804/355-8817   25

Cuban
$6-$18

You'll delight in the coziness of this Cuban diner/bodega, located in a small, restored pharmacy/lunch counter. Authentic Cuban roast pork, three paellas and Cuban sandwiches, rich coffee and dessert are menu highlights. There's a market on the premises. Casual dress. **Bar:** Beer & wine. **Hours:** 9 am-9:30 pm, Fri & Sat-10 pm, Sun-8 pm. Closed major holidays. **Address:** 1601 Park Ave 23220 **Location:** Jct Park Ave and Lombardy St, 0.5 mi s of W Broad St; in Historic Fan District. **Parking:** street. **Cards:** AX, DS, MC, VI.

LA GROTTA RISTORANTE
Phone: 804/644-2466   41

Italian
$8-$27

The quaint restaurant has the feel of entering a cozy wine cellar. Start off with homemade bread with crushed olives and sun-dried tomatoes or fresh pesto. Caesar salad served tableside, roasted quail, excellent carpaccio and rich tiramisu are examples of the savory Italian cucina-style cuisine. Casual dress. **Bar:** Full bar. **Reservations:** suggested. **Hours:** 11:30 am-2:30 & 5:30-10 pm, Fri-11 pm, Sat 5:30 pm-11 pm, Sun 5 pm-9 pm. Closed major holidays. **Address:** 1218 E Cary St 23219 **Location:** Jct 13th and E Cary sts; in Historic Shockoe Slip District. **Parking:** street. **Cards:** AX, DC, DS, MC, VI.

MILLIE'S DINER
Phone: 804/643-5512   52

American
$6-$28

Once a lunch spot for tobacco plant workers, the restaurant is now a retro '50s diner, with individual jukeboxes that play vintage music. An often changing, eclectic menu includes dishes made with only fresh ingredients. The wine and beer list is lengthy. Popular brunch spot for the "Devil's Mess". Casual dress. **Bar:** Full bar. **Hours:** 11 am-2:30 & 5:30-10:30 pm, Sat 11 am-3 & 5:30-10:30 pm, Sun 9 am-3 & 5:30-9:30 pm. Closed: 11/27, 12/24, 12/25; also Mon. **Address:** 2603 E Main St 23223 **Location:** Jct 26th and E Main sts; in Shockoe Bottom District. **Parking:** street. **Cards:** AX, DS, MC, VI.

MRS. MARSHALL'S CARYTOWN CAFE
Phone: 804/355-1305   16

Deli/Subs
Sandwiches
$4-$8

Known for potato salad and boxed lunches, the small spot is beloved by Richmonders. Tasty soups, sandwiches and old-fashioned deviled eggs round out the short lunch menu. Casual dress. **Hours:** 10 am-4 pm. Closed major holidays; also Sun. **Address:** 3125 W Cary St 23221 **Location:** In Carytown; between Addison and Shields sts. **Parking:** street. **Cards:** AX, MC, VI.

PEKING PAVILION
Phone: 804/649-8888   43

Chinese
$6-$14

Traditional dishes—General Tso's chicken, crispy duck and shrimp velvet among them—make up the menu at the quiet, laid-back restaurant. Wood carvings, art and music all show Oriental influences. The place does a hopping business at lunchtime. Casual dress. **Bar:** Full bar. **Reservations:** accepted. **Hours:** 11:30 am-2 & 5-9:30 pm, Fri-10:30 pm, Sat 5 pm-10:30 pm, Sun 11 am-2 & 5-9:30 pm. Closed major holidays. **Address:** 1302 E Cary 23219 **Location:** Corner of E Cary and Shockoe Slip; in the Historic Shockoe Slip District. **Parking:** on-site (fee). **Cards:** AX, MC, VI.

PERLY'S
Phone: 804/649-2779   39

American
$5-$9

In a nostalgic turn-of-the-20th-century setting, the restaurant keeps downtowners packing in for warm service and great overstuffed sandwiches, homemade biscuits and rolls and extensive vegetarian offerings, such as curry and chili. A country flavor infuses some of the daily changing specials and soups, which may include chicken and dumplings, smothered pork chops with homemade stuffing and homemade barbecue on Fridays. Casual dress. **Bar:** Beer & wine. **Hours:** 7 am-3 pm, Sat & Sun from 8 am. Closed major holidays. **Address:** 111 E Grace St 23219 **Location:** Between 1st and 2nd sts; downtown. **Parking:** street. **Cards:** AX, DS, MC, VI.

RACINE
Phone: 804/340-2884   8

French
$18-$28

The tiny Fan bistro sets a romantic mood with rich burgundy walls, romantic music and a charming French server. From a closet-sized kitchen, the owner-chef turns out such dishes as sweetbreads, cassoulet and lamb chops with seasonal vegetable side dishes. Casual dress. **Bar:** Full bar. **Reservations:** accepted. **Hours:** 5:30 pm-11 pm. Closed major holidays; also Sun & Mon. **Address:** 304 N Robinson St 23220 **Location:** Just n of Hanover Ave; in Historic Fan District. **Parking:** street. **Cards:** AX, DS, MC, VI.

(See map and index starting on p. 845)

ROWLAND FINE DINING

Phone: 804/257-9885 ㉙

American
$20-$30

This husband and wife team turns out sophisticated dishes at the casual corner spot. She bakes the breads and desserts, and makes the salad dressings while Mr. Rowland turns out interesting dishes that mix international and Southern influences. Items on the seasonally changing menu might include pumpkin ravioli with duck breast, chipotle mustard-glazed pork loin with goat cheese tamale or seared rockfish on any given night. Casual dress. **Bar:** Full bar. **Hours:** 5 pm-10 pm. Closed major holidays; also Mon. **Address:** 2132 W Main St 23220 **Location:** Jct Shields St; in Historic Fan District. **Parking:** street. **Cards:** AX, DS, MC, VI.

SETTE

Phone: 804/788-7077 (51)

Pizza
$7-$14

Mixing an industrial decor of sleek steel and exposed brick in a historic carriage house at the base of Church Hill in Shockoe Bottom, the restaurant serves gourmet pizza from its wood-burning oven with a wide variety of fancy toppings. Pastas, focaccia sandwiches and excellent crisp calamari round out the menu at this trendy spot, which also offers a courtyard patio and sophisticated wine options. Casual dress. **Bar:** Full bar. **Hours:** 11 am-10 pm, Fri & Sat-11 pm, Sun noon-9 pm. Closed major holidays. **Address:** 7 N 23rd St 23223 **Location:** Just n of E Main St; in Shockoe Bottom District. **Parking:** on-site. **Cards:** AX, MC, VI.

SIDEWALK CAFE

Phone: 804/358-0645 ㉛

Greek
$5-$17

Buffalo wings and Greek nachos are staples at the neighborhood bar, a favorite despite the often-rowdy crowds and loud music. Casual dress. **Bar:** Full bar. **Hours:** 11 am-2 am, Sat & Sun from 9:30 am. **Address:** 2101 W Main St 23220 **Location:** Jct W Main and Rowland sts; in Historic Fan District. **Parking:** street. **Cards:** AX, MC, VI.

THE SIX BURNER RESTAURANT & BAR

Phone: 804/353-4060 ㉞

American
$6-$22

Exposed brick walls and a large bar set a casual tone for the Fan spot. Representative of slightly more upscale comfort foods are lamb shank with cheese grits, hanger steak with seasoned squash and soft-shell crabs in season. Casual dress. **Bar:** Full bar. **Reservations:** accepted. **Hours:** 11:30 am-2 & 5:30-10 pm, Fri & Sat-11 pm. Closed major holidays; also Sun. **Address:** 1627 W Main St 23220 **Location:** Jct Vine St; in Historic Fan District. **Parking:** street. **Cards:** AX, MC, VI.

STICKY RICE

Phone: 804/358-7870 ㉗

Japanese
$7-$20

A lively spot in the evenings, the small bar serves great traditional sushi, as well as creative takes on such Japanese dishes as ponzu tuna with pineapple salsa. Also on the menu are varied noodle bowls, soba spinach salad and funky sushi offerings, such as the chili roll. This place even serves tater tots. Casual dress. **Bar:** Full bar. **Hours:** 11:30 am-10:30 pm, Sat & Sun from 5 pm. Closed major holidays. **Address:** 2232 W Main St 23220 **Location:** Jct Stafford St; in Historic Fan District. **Parking:** street. **Cards:** AX, DC, DS, MC, VI.

STRAWBERRY STREET CAFE

Phone: 804/353-6860 ⑨

American
$5-$15

This long-standing neighborhood favorite boasts a "famous bathtub salad bar" and its large variety of choices. The menu ranges from sandwiches and salad to steak and pasta. Specialties include sun-dried tomato bisque and eggs a la Richmond for brunch. Casual dress. **Bar:** Full bar. **Hours:** 11 am-3 & 5-10:30 pm, Fri-11 pm, Sat 10 am-11 pm, Sun 10 am-10:30 pm. Closed: 11/27, 12/24, 12/25. **Address:** 421 N Strawberry St 23220 **Location:** Jct W Monument Ave, 2 blks s; in Historic Fan District. **Parking;** street. **Cards:** AX, MC, VI.

SUMO SAN

Phone: 804/643-6500 ㊾

Japanese
$7-$14

Modern and traditional sushi is served with a rock 'n' roll attitude in the lively Shockoe Bottom spot. Creative menu options include ginger-lime pork, grilled salmon curry, portobello mushrooms stuffed with a spicy seafood mixture and the caterpillar sushi roll. Casual dress. **Bar:** Full bar. **Reservations:** accepted. **Hours:** 11:30 am-2:30 & 5-10 pm, Sat from 5 pm. Closed major holidays; also Sun. **Address:** 1725 E Main St 23223 **Location:** Between 17th and 18th sts; in Shockoe Bottom. **Parking:** street. **Cards:** AX, MC, VI.

TAQUERIA LOCO

Phone: 804/648-5626 ㉚

Mexican
$3-$6

Students and hipsters frequent this small funky spot, looking to fill up on delicious "mission-style" tacos, burritos and salads with fresh fillings such as chicken, steak, pork and fish. Casual dress. **Bar:** Full bar. **Hours:** 10 am-10 pm, Fri-3 am, Sat noon-3 am. Closed major holidays; also Sun. **Address:** 818 W Broad St 23220 **Location:** Just w of downtown; adjacent to VCU campus. **Parking:** street. **Cards:** MC, VI.

THAI CURRY HOUSE

Phone: 804/358-7027 ⑭

Thai
$8-$20

In the charming Carytown shopping district, the restaurant has two small dining rooms decorated in warm shades of gold and purple and with authentic Thai art. The menu touches on many specialties, such as pad thai, dumplings and many curry dishes. Casual dress. **Bar:** Full bar. **Hours:** 11:30 am-9:30 pm, Fri & Sat-10 pm. **Address:** 3129 W Cary St 23231 **Location:** I-195, exit W Cary St, just e; in Carytown. **Parking:** street. **Cards:** AX, DS, MC, VI.

(See map and index starting on p. 845)

THE THAI ROOM AT BEAUREGARD'S

Thai
$4-$14

Phone: 804/644-2328 (40)

Fresh, traditional Thai cuisine is served in this 19th-century townhouse's upscale dining room, graced by lovely artwork. Try the spicy shrimp soup and Pad Thai. The menu also features luscious homemade ice cream, such as chocolate Kevorkian. Casual dress. **Bar:** Full bar. **Reservations:** suggested. **Hours:** 11 am-2:30 & 4:30-10 pm, Fri & Sat-11 pm. Closed: Sun. **Address:** 103 E Cary St 23219 **Location:** At 1st and E Cary sts. **Parking:** on-site. **Cards:** AX, DS, MC, VI.

T. J.'S RESTAURANT AND LOUNGE

American
$10-$30

Phone: 804/649-4672 (38)

Guests can dine in the garden-themed dining room or choose a bar side table overlooking the glorious lower lobby of the grand hotel. Menu offerings range from sandwiches and Angus burgers to peanut soup and crab cakes. Servers are gracious. Semi-formal attire. **Bar:** Full bar. **Reservations:** accepted. **Hours:** 11 am-midnight, Sun 10:30 am-1:30 & 4-11 pm. **Address:** 101 W Franklin St 23220 **Location:** Franklin and Adams sts; center; in The Jefferson Hotel. **Parking:** on-site (fee) and valet. **Cards:** AX, CB, DC, DS, MC, VI.

CALL

THE TRACK

Regional American
$22-$30

Phone: 804/359-4781 (19)

A Richmond mainstay for 20 years, The Track still impresses regulars with their creative fare served in an intimate setting. The Bounty from local waters' is a specialty served up in new ways alongside lamb, beef, and more. Casual dress. **Bar:** Full bar. **Reservations:** suggested. **Hours:** 5 pm-9:30 pm, Fri & Sat-10:30 pm. Closed major holidays; also Sun & Mon. **Address:** 2915 W Cary St 23221 **Location:** I-195, exit W Cary St, just e; in Carytown. **Parking:** street. **Cards:** AX, MC, VI.

TWENTY SEVEN

American
$6-$23

Phone: 804/780-0086 (37)

Casual dress. **Bar:** Full bar. **Reservations:** accepted. **Hours:** 11:30 am-2 & 5-10 pm, Fri & Sat-11 pm. Closed: 11/27, 12/25; also Sun. **Address:** 27 W Broad St 23219 **Location:** Jct Adams St. **Parking:** street. **Cards:** AX, DS, MC, VI.

THE WHITE DOG

American
$15-$26

Phone: 804/340-1975 (26)

The small corner in the Fan has hosted many a dining spot but has found a winner in The White Dog. The setting is warm and welcoming, and the menu lists both modern and traditional dishes. Local favorites include the big salad, which can be topped with steak or other options, as well as pasta, barbecue shrimp, pork chops and more. The owner's colorful paintings decorate the walls. Casual dress. **Bar:** Full bar. **Hours:** 5 pm-11 pm, Fri & Sat-midnight. Closed major holidays; also Mon. **Address:** 2329 W Main St 23220 **Location:** Jct Stafford St; in the Historic Fan. **Parking:** street. **Cards:** AX, DS, MC, VI.

ZEUS GALLERY CAFE

Nouvelle American
$20-$35

Phone: 804/359-3219 (7)

Near the Virginia Museum, the charming, intimate cafe displays the work of local artists. Dishes on the often-changing menu use the freshest seasonal ingredients. Interesting, creative presentation marks the mostly pasta, fish, chicken and beef entrees. Casual dress. **Bar:** Full bar. **Reservations:** accepted. **Hours:** 5:30 pm-10 pm, Fri noon-2 & 5:30-11 pm, Sat 5:30 pm-11 pm, Sun 9 am-2 & 5:30-9:30 pm. Closed: 11/27, 12/24, 12/25. **Address:** 201 N Belmont Ave 23221 **Location:** Jct Grove Ave, just n; in Historic Fan District. **Parking:** street. **Cards:** AX, CB, DC, DS, MC, VI.

ZUPPA

American
$5-$8

Phone: 804/249-8831 (46)

This tiny spot is the place to grab a delicious cup of steaming soup. Among selections are she-crab, lobster bisque and black bean served with freshly baked focaccia bread. Warmer weather brings chilled soups to the menu. Other options include sandwiches, focaccia pizzas, salads and delicious bread pudding. Casual dress. **Bar:** Full bar. **Hours:** 11 am-10 pm, Fri & Sat-11 pm, Mon-3 pm. Closed major holidays; also Sun. **Address:** 101 N 18th St 23223 **Location:** Just n of Main St; in Shockoe Bottom. **Parking:** street. **Cards:** AX, DS, MC, VI.

The following restaurant has not been evaluated by AAA
but is listed for your information only.

SALLY BELL'S KITCHEN

(fyi)

Phone: 804/644-2838

Not evaluated. Since 1924, the local landmark has been serving boxed lunches full of old-fashioned homemade specialties. Not only does this place bake its own breads, but it also makes its own mayonnaise. Offerings are purely Southern: deviled eggs, cheese wafers, upside-down cupcakes and potato, macaroni and chicken salads. **Address:** 708 W Grace St 23220 **Location:** Just w of jct Belvidere; adjacent to Virginia Commonwealth University.

RICHMOND pop. 197,790   (See map and index starting on p. 848)

———— WHERE TO STAY ————

AIRPORT INN MOTEL

Motel
$55-$85 All Year

Address: 5121 S Laburnum Ave 23231 **Location:** I-64, exit 195, 1.4 mi s. **Facility:** 17 one-bedroom standard units, some with whirlpools. 1 story, exterior corridors. **Parking:** on-site. **Terms:** 7 day cancellation notice-fee imposed. **Amenities:** high-speed Internet, irons, hair dryers. **Guest Services:** wireless Internet. **Business Services:** fax. **Cards:** AX, CB, DC, DS, JC, MC, VI. **Free Special Amenities: continental breakfast and high-speed Internet.**

Phone: 804/222-4200   **15**

BEST WESTERN EXECUTIVE HOTEL   *Book great rates at AAA.com*

Small-scale Hotel
Rates not provided

Address: 7007 W Broad St 23294 **Location:** I-64, exit 183C (US 250 W), jct Glenside Dr. **Facility:** 117 one-bedroom standard units. 4 stories, interior corridors. **Parking:** on-site. **Amenities:** high-speed Internet, voice mail, irons, hair dryers. **Pool(s):** outdoor. **Leisure Activities:** exercise room. **Guest Services:** coin laundry, wireless Internet. **Business Services:** meeting rooms, business center. **Free Special Amenities: expanded continental breakfast and high-speed Internet.**
(See color ad below)

Phone: 804/672-7007   **9**

AAA Benefit:
Members save 10% everyday, plus an exclusive frequent stay program.

BEST WESTERN GOVERNOR'S INN   *Book great rates at AAA.com*

Small-scale Hotel
$85-$189 All Year

Address: 9826 Midlothian Tpke 23235 **Location:** US 60, 1.5 mi w of jct Powhite Pkwy. **Facility:** 80 units. 77 one-bedroom standard units, some with whirlpools. 3 one-bedroom suites. 3 stories, interior corridors. **Parking:** on-site. **Terms:** 7 day cancellation notice. **Amenities:** high-speed Internet, dual phone lines, voice mail, safes, irons, hair dryers. **Pool(s):** outdoor. **Leisure Activities:** exercise room. **Guest Services:** wireless Internet. **Business Services:** meeting rooms, fax. **Cards:** AX, CB, DC, DS, MC, VI. **Free Special Amenities: early check-in/late check-out and room upgrade (subject to availability with advance reservations).**

Phone: (804)323-0007   **18**

AAA Benefit:
Members save 10% everyday, plus an exclusive frequent stay program.

CANDLEWOOD SUITES   *Book at AAA.com*

Small-scale Hotel
$129-$189 All Year

Address: 4301 Commerce Rd 23234 **Location:** I-95, exit 69, just n. **Facility:** 104 units. 92 one-bedroom standard units with kitchens. 12 one-bedroom suites with kitchens. 3 stories, interior corridors. *Bath:* combo or shower only. **Parking:** on-site. **Terms:** office hours 7 am-11 pm. **Amenities:** video library, DVD players, high-speed Internet, dual phone lines, voice mail, irons, hair dryers. **Leisure Activities:** exercise room. **Guest Services:** complimentary laundry, wireless Internet. **Cards:** AX, DC, DS, MC, VI.

Phone: (804)271-0016   **23**

COMFORT INN EXECUTIVE CENTER   *Book great rates at AAA.com*

Small-scale Hotel
Rates not provided

Address: 7201 W Broad St 23294 **Location:** I-64, exit 183C(250 W) westbound; exit 183 eastbound. **Facility:** 123 units. 122 one-bedroom standard units, some with whirlpools. 1 one-bedroom suite. 2 stories (no elevator), interior corridors. **Parking:** on-site. **Amenities:** *Some:* high-speed Internet, voice mail, safes (fee), irons, hair dryers. **Pool(s):** outdoor. **Leisure Activities:** exercise room. **Guest Services:** valet and coin laundry, wireless Internet. **Business Services:** meeting rooms, PC.

Phone: 804/672-1108   **5**

(See map and index starting on p. 848)

COURTYARD BY MARRIOTT   *Book great rates at AAA.com*   Phone: 804/282-1881   **13**

Small-scale Hotel
$168-$205 All Year

Address: 6400 W Broad St 23230 **Location:** I-64, exit 183B westbound; exit 183 eastbound; jct US 250, 0.5 mi e. **Facility:** Smoke free premises. 145 units. 132 one-bedroom standard units. 13 one-bedroom suites. 2-3 stories, interior corridors. *Bath:* combo or shower only. **Parking:** on-site. **Amenities:** high-speed Internet, dual phone lines, voice mail, irons, hair dryers. **Pool(s):** outdoor. **Leisure Activities:** whirlpool, exercise room. **Guest Services:** valet and coin laundry. **Business Services:** meeting rooms, business center. **Cards:** AX, DC, DS, JC, MC, VI.

AAA Benefit: Members save 5% off of the best available rate.

CROWNE PLAZA RICHMOND WEST   *Book at AAA.com*   Phone: (804)285-9951   **12**

Small-scale Hotel
$110-$160 1/1-2/28
$100-$150 3/1-12/31

Address: 6531 W Broad St 23230 **Location:** I-64, exit 183B, just e; jct Glenside Dr, just e. **Facility:** 282 one-bedroom standard units. 7 stories, interior corridors. *Bath:* combo or shower only. **Parking:** on-site. **Amenities:** CD players, high-speed Internet, dual phone lines, voice mail, irons, hair dryers. **Pool(s):** heated indoor. **Leisure Activities:** whirlpool, exercise room. **Guest Services:** valet and coin laundry, wireless Internet. **Business Services:** conference facilities, business center. **Cards:** AX, CB, DC, DS, JC, MC, VI.

ECONO LODGE NORTH-PARHAM RD   *Book at AAA.com*   Phone: (804)262-7070   **1**

Motel
$45-$170 3/1-9/30
$40-$170 10/1-2/28

Address: 8350 Brook Rd 23227 **Location:** I-95, exit 83B, 0.5 mi w. Located adjacent to Hungary Brook Shopping Center. **Facility:** 31 one-bedroom standard units. 2 stories (no elevator), exterior corridors. **Parking:** on-site. **Amenities:** high-speed Internet. **Guest Services:** wireless Internet. **Cards:** AX, DC, DS, MC, VI.

EMBASSY SUITES HOTEL   *Book great rates at AAA.com*   Phone: 804/672-8585   **6**

Large-scale Hotel
Rates not provided

Address: 2925 Emerywood Pkwy 23294 **Location:** I-64, exit 183C, just s of W Broad St. **Facility:** 224 one-bedroom suites. 8 stories, interior corridors. **Parking:** on-site. **Amenities:** video games (fee); high-speed Internet, voice mail, irons, hair dryers. **Pool(s):** heated indoor. **Leisure Activities:** sauna, whirlpool, exercise room. **Guest Services:** valet and coin laundry, area transportation-within 5 mi, wireless Internet. **Business Services:** conference facilities, business center. **Free Special Amenities:** full breakfast and high-speed Internet.

EXTENDED STAYAMERICA-I-64-WEST BROAD   *Book at AAA.com*   Phone: (804)285-2065   **10**

Motel
$64-$135 All Year

Address: 6811 Paragon Pl 23230 **Location:** I-64, exit 183C (W Broad St), just w to Glenside Dr, just n. **Facility:** 108 one-bedroom standard units with efficiencies. 3 stories, exterior corridors. **Parking:** on-site. **Terms:** office hours 7 am-11 pm. **Amenities:** high-speed Internet (fee), voice mail, irons. **Leisure Activities:** exercise room privileges. **Guest Services:** coin laundry, wireless Internet. **Cards:** AX, DC, DS, JC, MC, VI.

EXTENDED STAY DELUXE HOTEL   *Book at AAA.com*   Phone: (804)285-7050   **8**

Small-scale Hotel
$95-$165 All Year

Address: 6807 Paragon Pl 23230 **Location:** I-64, exit 183C (W Broad St), just w to Glenside Dr, just n. **Facility:** 82 units. 81 one-bedroom standard units with kitchens. 1 two-bedroom suite with kitchen. 3 stories, interior corridors. *Bath:* combo or shower only. **Parking:** on-site. **Terms:** office hours 7 am-11 pm. **Amenities:** DVD players, high-speed Internet (fee), voice mail, irons, hair dryers. **Pool(s):** outdoor. **Leisure Activities:** exercise room. **Guest Services:** coin laundry, wireless Internet. **Cards:** AX, DC, DS, JC, MC, VI.

HAMPTON INN-MIDLOTHIAN TURNPIKE   *Book great rates at AAA.com*   Phone: 804/897-2800   **17**

Small-scale Hotel
$139-$149 All Year

Address: 800 Research Rd 23236 **Location:** 1.5 mi w of jct Powhite Pkwy (US 76) and Midlothian Tpke (US 60). Located across from Chesterfield Towne Center. **Facility:** 80 one-bedroom standard units. 3 stories, interior corridors. *Bath:* combo or shower only. **Parking:** on-site. **Amenities:** high-speed Internet, dual phone lines, voice mail, irons, hair dryers. **Pool(s):** heated indoor. **Leisure Activities:** exercise room. **Guest Services:** valet laundry. **Business Services:** meeting rooms. **Cards:** AX, DC, DS, MC, VI.

HOLIDAY INN I-64 WEST END   *Book at AAA.com*   Phone: (804)359-6061   **14**

Small-scale Hotel
$109-$179 All Year

Address: 2000 Staples Mill Rd 23230 **Location:** I-64, exit 185, 0.8 mi e. **Facility:** 142 one-bedroom standard units. 8 stories, interior corridors. *Bath:* combo or shower only. **Parking:** on-site. **Terms:** cancellation fee imposed. **Amenities:** high-speed Internet, dual phone lines, voice mail, irons, hair dryers. **Pool(s):** outdoor. **Leisure Activities:** exercise room. **Guest Services:** valet and coin laundry, wireless Internet. **Business Services:** conference facilities, business center. **Cards:** AX, DS, MC, VI.

(See map and index starting on p. 848)

HOLIDAY INN-RICHMOND NORTH
Book great rates at AAA.com   Phone: 804/266-8753   **3**

Small-scale Hotel
Rates not provided

Address: 801 E Parham Rd 23227 **Location:** I-95, exit 83B. **Facility:** 82 one-bedroom standard units. 2 stories (no elevator), interior corridors. *Bath:* combo or shower only. **Parking:** on-site. **Amenities:** high-speed Internet, voice mail, irons, hair dryers. **Dining:** River City Diner, see separate listing. **Pool(s):** outdoor. **Leisure Activities:** exercise room. **Guest Services:** valet laundry, wireless Internet. **Business Services:** meeting rooms. **Free Special Amenities:** newspaper and high-speed Internet.

〔❙❙〕 CALL 〔&M〕 〔🏊〕 〔📷〕 〔💻〕 / SOME UNITS 〔✕〕 FEE 〔🔌〕

HOLIDAY INN SELECT-KOGER SOUTH
Book at AAA.com   Phone: (804)379-3800   **16**

Small-scale Hotel
$150-$180 All Year

Address: 10800 Midlothian Tpke 23235 **Location:** Jct Powhite Pkwy (US 76) and Midlothian Tpke (US 60), 1 mi w. Located adjacent to Johnston Willis Hospital. **Facility:** 237 units. 231 one-bedroom standard units. 6 one-bedroom suites with whirlpools. 8 stories, interior corridors. *Bath:* combo or shower only. **Parking:** on-site. **Amenities:** video games (fee), high-speed Internet, voice mail, irons, hair dryers. **Pool(s):** heated indoor/outdoor. **Leisure Activities:** exercise room. **Guest Services:** valet and coin laundry, area transportation, wireless Internet. **Business Services:** conference facilities, business center. **Cards:** AX, CB, DC, DS, JC, MC, VI.

〔A$K〕 〔❙❙〕 〔🍽〕 CALL 〔&M〕 〔🏊〕 〔📷〕 〔🔌〕 〔🖥〕 〔💻〕 / SOME UNITS 〔✕〕

HOMESTEAD STUDIO SUITES
HOTEL-RICHMOND/MIDLOTHIAN
Book at AAA.com   Phone: (804)272-1800   **22**

Small-scale Hotel
$77-$140 All Year

Address: 241 Arboretum Pl 23236 **Location:** Jct Powhite Pkwy (US 76) and Midlothian Tpke (US 60), just w. **Facility:** 123 units. 113 one-bedroom standard units with kitchens. 10 one-bedroom suites with kitchens. 3 stories, interior corridors. *Bath:* combo or shower only. **Parking:** on-site. **Terms:** office hours 6:30 am-11 pm. **Amenities:** high-speed Internet (fee), voice mail, irons, hair dryers. *Some:* dual phone lines. **Guest Services:** coin laundry, wireless Internet. **Business Services:** meeting rooms, fax. **Cards:** AX, DC, DS, JC, MC, VI.

〔A$K〕 〔S🐾〕 〔❙❙→〕 CALL 〔&M〕 FEE 〔🏊〕 〔📷〕 〔🔌〕 〔🖥〕 〔💻〕 / SOME UNITS FEE 〔🐾〕 〔✕〕 FEE 〔VCR〕

HYATT PLACE RICHMOND/ARBORETUM
Book great rates at AAA.com   Phone: (804)560-1566   **21**

Small-scale Hotel
$99-$189 All Year

Address: 201 Arboretum Pl 23236 **Location:** Jct Powhite Pkwy (US 76) and Midlothian Tpke (US 60), just w. **Facility:** 128 one-bedroom standard units. 6 stories, interior corridors. *Bath:* combo or shower only. **Parking:** on-site. **Terms:** cancellation fee imposed. **Amenities:** high-speed Internet, voice mail, safes (fee), irons, hair dryers. *Some:* dual phone lines. **Pool(s):** heated outdoor. **Leisure Activities:** exercise room. **Guest Services:** valet and coin laundry, wireless Internet. **Business Services:** meeting rooms, fax. **Cards:** AX, CB, DC, DS, JC, MC, VI. **Free Special Amenities:** continental breakfast and high-speed Internet.

〔❙❙→〕 CALL 〔&M〕 〔🏊〕 〔📷〕 〔🔌〕 〔🖥〕 〔💻〕 / SOME UNITS FEE 〔🐾〕 〔✕〕 〔VCR〕

HYATT PLACE

AAA Benefit:
Ask for the AAA rate and save 10%.

QUALITY INN WEST END
Book great rates at AAA.com   Phone: (804)346-0000   **4**

Small-scale Hotel
$79-$159 All Year

Address: 8008 W Broad St 23294 **Location:** I-64, exit 183C westbound; exit 183 eastbound, 1.5 mi w. **Facility:** 191 one-bedroom standard units. 6 stories, interior corridors. *Bath:* combo or shower only. **Parking:** on-site. **Amenities:** high-speed Internet, voice mail, irons, hair dryers. *Fee:* video games, safes. **Pool(s):** outdoor. **Guest Services:** coin laundry, wireless Internet. **Business Services:** meeting rooms, fax. **Cards:** AX, CB, DC, DS, JC, MC, VI. **Free Special Amenities:** expanded continental breakfast and early check-in/late check-out. *(See color ad below)*

〔S🐾〕 〔❙❙→〕 CALL 〔&M〕 〔🏊〕 FEE 〔🐾〕 〔📷〕 〔🔌〕 / SOME UNITS FEE 〔🐾〕 〔✕〕 〔🖥〕 〔💻〕

(See map and index starting on p. 848)

SHERATON PARK SOUTH HOTEL   *Book great rates at AAA.com*   Phone: 804/323-1144

Small-scale Hotel
Rates not provided

Address: 9901 Midlothian Tpke 23235 **Location:** US 60, 1 mi w of Powhite Pkwy (US 76). **Facility:** 194 units. 193 one-bedroom standard units. 1 one-bedroom suite. 7 stories, interior corridors. *Bath:* combo or shower only. **Parking:** on-site. **Amenities:** high-speed Internet, dual phone lines, voice mail, irons, hair dryers. **Pool(s):** heated indoor/outdoor. **Leisure Activities:** whirlpool, jogging, exercise room. **Guest Services:** valet laundry, area transportation-within 3 mi, wireless Internet. **Business Services:** conference facilities, PC. **Free Special Amenities: newspaper and high-speed Internet.**

Ⓢ Sheraton
HOTELS & RESORTS

AAA Benefit:
Members get up to 15% off, plus Starwood Preferred Guest® bonuses.

SHERATON RICHMOND WEST   *Book great rates at AAA.com*   Phone: (804)285-2000

Large-scale Hotel
$255 1/1-2/28
$249 3/1-12/31

Address: 6624 W Broad St 23230 **Location:** I-64, exit 183 eastbound; exit 183B westbound. **Facility:** 372 one-bedroom standard units. 8 stories, interior corridors. *Bath:* combo or shower only. **Parking:** on-site. **Terms:** cancellation fee imposed. **Amenities:** dual phone lines, voice mail, irons, hair dryers. *Fee:* video games, high-speed Internet. **Dining:** 2 restaurants. **Pool(s):** outdoor, heated indoor. **Leisure Activities:** 2 lighted tennis courts, jogging, exercise room. **Guest Services:** valet laundry, area transportation-within 5 mi, wireless Internet. **Business Services:** conference facilities, business center. **Cards:** AX, DC, DS, MC, VI. **Free Special Amenities: newspaper and early check-in/late check-out.**

Ⓢ Sheraton
HOTELS & RESORTS

AAA Benefit:
Members get up to 15% off, plus Starwood Preferred Guest® bonuses.

SLEEP INN   *Book great rates at AAA.com*   Phone: (804)515-7800

Small-scale Hotel
$82-$144 All Year

Address: 950 E Parham Rd 23228 **Location:** I-95, exit 83B, 0.5 mi; adjacent to Hungary Brook Shopping Center. **Facility:** 72 one-bedroom standard units. 4 stories, interior corridors. *Bath:* combo or shower only. **Parking:** on-site. **Amenities:** high-speed Internet, dual phone lines, voice mail, irons, hair dryers. **Guest Services:** valet and coin laundry, wireless Internet. **Business Services:** meeting rooms, fax. **Cards:** AX, DC, DS, MC, VI.

SUPER 8 MOTEL   *Book at AAA.com*   Phone: 804/262-8880

Motel
Rates not provided

Address: 5615 Chamberlayne Rd 23227 **Location:** I-95, exit 82. **Facility:** 57 one-bedroom standard units. 3 stories, interior corridors. **Parking:** on-site. **Amenities:** high-speed Internet, hair dryers. **Guest Services:** wireless Internet.

TRAVEL INN   Phone: (804)745-7500

Motel
$50-$65 All Year

Address: 6511 Midlothian Tpke 23225 **Location:** 0.3 mi e of jct SR 150 and US 60, exit 60E; off Chippenham Pkwy. **Facility:** 17 one-bedroom standard units. 2 stories (no elevator), exterior corridors. **Parking:** on-site. **Amenities:** irons, hair dryers. **Business Services:** fax. **Cards:** AX, DC, DS, MC, VI.

--- **WHERE TO DINE** ---

AKIDA JAPANESE RESTAURANT   Phone: 804/762-8878

Japanese
$7-$25

Diners can slip into this narrow spot and choose a wooden bench with a good view of the chefs at the sushi bar. Options range from colorful bites of traditional, innovative sushi to tamer standbys, such as noodle soups and pork katsu. Casual dress. **Bar:** Beer & wine. **Reservations:** accepted. **Hours:** 11:30 am-2:30 & 5-10 pm, Fri-11 pm, Sat 5 pm-11 pm. Closed: 11/27, 12/25; also Sun. **Address:** 9039-3 W Broad St 23294 **Location:** I-64, exit Parham Rd N, 1 mi w on W Broad St at jct Tuckernuck; in Sassafras Square. **Parking:** on-site. **Cards:** AX, MC, VI.

AZZURRO   Phone: 804/282-1509

Italian
$9-$32

Located in an upscale strip mall, Azzurro has quickly become a trendy spot for fine Italian food in casual trattoria setting enhanced by sunny mosaics. Unique homemade pasta, wood-fired pizza, veal and daily fresh fish. With seating by a roaring fire in the winter or a garden patio in spring, it's right for all seasons. Casual dress. **Bar:** Full bar. **Reservations:** suggested. **Hours:** 11:30 am-3 & 5:30-10 pm, Fri-11 pm, Sat 11:30 am-2:30 & 5:30-11 pm, Sun 5:30 pm-9:30 pm. Closed major holidays. **Address:** 6221 River Rd 23229 **Location:** 6 mi w of downtown; Chippenham Pkwy/SR 150, exit Huguenot Rd, 1.8 mi ne; in River Road Center. **Parking:** on-site. **Cards:** AX, MC, VI.

(See map and index starting on p. 848)

BAKER'S CRUST BREAD MARKET

American
$6-$20

Phone: 804/213-0800

First and foremost, this place is the home of crusty bread loaves and sweet bakery treats. Lunch favorites include interesting sandwiches and daily soup in edible bread bowl, while dinner offerings lean to more sophisticated fare, such as steak, seafood and rotisserie fowl. Seating at the crepe bar in the rear is a special treat. Casual dress. **Bar:** Full bar. **Hours:** 8 am-10 pm, Fri & Sat-11 pm. Closed: 11/27, 12/25. **Address:** 3553 W Cary St 23221 **Location:** Just e of jct I-195; in International Shopping Center; in Carytown. **Parking:** on-site. **Cards:** AX, DS, MC, VI.

BELLA LUNA RISTORANTE ITALIANO

Italian
$6-$18

Phone: 804/497-4681   ③

Fresh fare straight from Sicily is the specialty at the casual Northside spot. Diners choose from a variety of delicious pasta, veal and seafood dishes. The friendly, mostly Italian staff is eager to offer suggestions from the lengthy menu. Top choices include delicious penne al vodka, fried calamari and mussels in a light marinara sauce. Casual dress. **Bar:** Full bar. **Reservations:** accepted. **Hours:** 11 am-10 pm, Sat 5 pm-11 pm. Closed major holidays; also Sun. **Address:** 1212 Concord Ave 23228 **Location:** I-95, exit 83B, 0.5 mi w; in Hungary Brook Shopping Center. **Parking:** on-site. **Cards:** AX, DS, MC, VI.

BRIO TUSCAN GRILL

Italian
$10-$29

Phone: 804/272-2255   ㉖

While the atmosphere is casual, upscale Tuscan villa-style decor lends a sophisticated touch to the dining experience. Both lunch and dinner offer all the attentiveness a diner expects. From the garlic, spinach and artichoke dip starter to beef, chicken, veal, seafood and homemade pasta entrees, there is a selection to satisfy all tastes. Among specialties are home-made mozzarella, crisp flat breads and wood-fired oven-baked pizza, in addition to a selection of steak. Casual dress. **Bar:** Full bar. **Reservations:** accepted. **Hours:** 11 am-10 pm, Fri & Sat-11 pm. **Address:** 9210 Stony Point Pkwy 23235 **Location:** Off US 150/Chippenham Pkwy; in Stony Point Fashion Park. **Parking:** on-site. **Cards:** AX, CB, DC, DS, JC, MC, VI.

CALL

BUCKHEAD'S

Steak House
$27-$48

Phone: 804/750-2000   ⑮

A dark, club-like setting—with rich wood paneling and wine bottles lining the walls—sets an upscale mood. The specialty here is prime aged beef and chops, although selected seafood specialties are offered nightly. The classic lobster bisque's rich stock simmers for days. The award-winning extensive wine book is accented at the dessert course by fine ports and single malts. Dressy casual. **Bar:** Full bar. **Reservations:** suggested. **Hours:** 5 pm-10 pm, Sun-9 pm. Closed major holidays. **Address:** 8510 Patterson Ave 23229 **Location:** I-64, exit 181A (Parham Rd), 2.1 mi s; in Beverly Hills Shopping Center. **Parking:** on-site. **Cards:** AX, DC, DS, MC, VI.

CARYTOWN BURGER & FRIES

American
$4-$7

Phone: 804/358-5225   ㉕

The simple spot lists a lengthy selection of specialty burgers from Hawaiian to Greek, which go well with cheese fries, tater tots, chili and milk shakes. Chicken and grilled portobello sandwiches are good light bites. Casual dress. **Bar:** Beer only. **Hours:** 11 am-10 pm, Fri & Sat-10:30 pm. Closed major holidays. **Address:** 3500 1/2 W Cary St 23221 **Location:** I-195, exit Cary St Rd, just w; in Ukrop's Center. **Parking:** on-site. **Cards:** AX, DS, MC, VI.

THE CRAZY GREEK

Greek
$5-$13

Phone: 804/355-3786   ⑱

The long-standing Richmond mainstay offers great, affordable Greek food in a family-friendly setting. Delicious favorites include souvlaki, moussaka, gyros and Greek pizza, as well as a smattering of Italian pasta dishes. Try the Greek spaghetti and baklava. Casual dress. **Bar:** Full bar. **Hours:** 11 am-10 pm. Closed: 7/4, 11/27, 12/25. **Address:** 1903 Staples Mill Rd 23230 **Location:** Jct W Broad St, just s. **Parking:** on-site. **Cards:** AX, DC, DS, MC, VI.

DA LAT VIETNAMESE CUISINE

Vietnamese
$6-$15

Phone: 804/762-9330   ①

Da Lat is known for its delicious food as well as the warmth and hospitality of its staff. Any questions you have about Vietnamese food, staff members can answer. Try such delicacies as pork cooked in a clay pot, crispy whole rockfish, rice noodle crepes rolled with delicious stuffings or marinated grilled quail. Casual dress. **Bar:** Full bar. **Hours:** 11 am-9:30 pm, Fri-Sun to 10 pm. **Address:** 9125 W Broad St 23294 **Location:** I-64, exit 183C westbound; exit 183 eastbound, 2 mi w; in TJ Maxx Shopping Center. **Parking:** on-site. **Cards:** AX, DC, DS, MC, VI.

CALL

DENA'S GRECIAN RESTAURANT

Greek
$4-$15

Phone: 804/794-9551   ㉛

Robust flavors result when the restaurant mingles Greek and Italian flavors in its intricate dishes, such as the popular Greek spaghetti. The atmosphere is comfortable, and the prices great for the generous portions and great tastes served. Casual dress. **Bar:** Full bar. **Hours:** 11:30 am-2:30 & 5-9 pm, Fri & Sat-10 pm, Mon 5 pm-9 pm. Closed: Sun. **Address:** 11374 Mall Dr 23235 **Location:** Midlothian Tpke (US 60), just e of jct Huguenot Rd; in Towne Center Plaza; adjacent to Chesterfield Towne Center. **Parking:** on-site. **Cards:** AX, DC, DS, MC, VI.

(See map and index starting on p. 848)

ESCABAR

American
$8-$25

Phone: 804/288-4885 [22]

Tucked in a trendy shopping area called "The Avenues," this small spot offers an intimate dining room and bar with ever-changing mood lighting and a large sidewalk patio that's heated in inclement weather. The menu showcases sophisticated dishes that pick up on Asian, European, Deep American South and other global influences. Casual dress. **Bar:** Full bar. **Reservations:** accepted. **Hours:** 11 am-2 & 5-11 pm, Mon from 5 pm. Closed major holidays; also Sun. **Address:** 5806 Grove Ave 23226 **Location:** Just w of jct Libbie Ave. **Parking:** street. **Cards:** AX, MC, VI.

FRANCO'S RISTORANTE

Regional Italian
$18-$26

Phone: 804/270-9124 [6]

Searching for excellent classic Italian cuisine served in either a formal dining room or a more casual cafe? You've come to the right place. This restaurant specializes in veal and seasonal menu specials. An extensive wine list is also available. Dressy casual. Entertainment. **Bar:** Full bar. **Reservations:** suggested. **Hours:** 5 pm-10 pm, Fri & Sat-10:30 pm. Closed major holidays; also Sun. **Address:** 9031 W Broad St, Suite 1 23294 **Location:** I-64, exit Parham Rd N, 1 mi w on W Broad St, jct W Broad St and Tuckermuck; in West Broad Commons. **Parking:** on-site. **Cards:** AX, DC, DS, MC, VI.

FULL KEE RESTAURANT

Chinese
$5-$15

Phone: 804/673-2233 [14]

Catering to a nearby Chinese population, the restaurant mingles Cantonese, Hunan, Szechuan and Mandarin cuisines on its often-exotic menu. Traditional favorites—such as lemon chicken and Peking duck—also are plentiful. A dim sum lunch is served daily. Casual dress. **Bar:** Full bar. **Hours:** 11 am-10:30 pm, Fri & Sat-11 pm. **Address:** 6400 Horsepen Rd 23226 **Location:** Jct W Broad St, just s. **Parking:** on-site. **Cards:** AX, DC, MC, VI.

GLORY DAYS GRILL, GLENEAGLES

Phone: 804/754-3710

American
$7-$18

Lending to the casual restaurant's sports-themed atmosphere are memorabilia decorating the dining area and 25 TVs with control centers at each table and booth. Food selections range from wings and ribs to seafood, beef and pasta dishes. Casual dress. **Bar:** Full bar. **Reservations:** not accepted. **Hours:** 4 pm-midnight, Fri & Sat from 11:30 am, Sun 11:30 am-11 pm. Closed: 11/27, 12/25. **Address:** 10466 Ridgefield Pkwy 23233 **Location:** I-64, exit 180A (Gaskins Rd S), 1 mi s to Ridgefield Pkwy, then 1.5 mi w; in Gleneagles Center. **Parking:** on-site. **Cards:** AX, DS, MC, VI.

GRAFITI GRILLE

American
$5-$23

Phone: 804/288-0633 [17]

A twist on the typical neighborhood grill, this spot in the 'burbs is bright and fun with humorous spray-painted artwork. The food is self-styled "California eclectic," with such seasonally changing specialties as veal meatloaf and blackberry-glazed tuna. Menu options are hearty in the winter and lighter in the summer. Sunday's jazz brunch is popular with locals. Casual dress. **Bar:** Full bar. **Reservations:** accepted. **Hours:** 11:30 am-2:30 & 5:30-9:30 pm, Fri-10:30 pm, Sat 5:30 pm-10:30 pm; Sunday brunch 10:30 am-2:30 pm. Closed: 7/4, 11/27. **Address:** 403-B N Ridge Rd 23229 **Location:** Jct Patterson Ave, 3 mi s; in Tuckahoe Shopping Center. **Parking:** on-site. **Cards:** AX, MC, VI.

CALL

GRAND DYNASTY RESTAURANT

Chinese
$5-$14

Phone: 804/222-8545 [29]

The restaurant has stayed away from the buffet formula that seems to overrun Chinese food in the states and sticks to offering freshly made Hunan and Szechuan specialties. Casual dress. **Bar:** Full bar. **Hours:** 11:30 am-10 pm. Closed: 11/27, 12/25. **Address:** 4734 Finlay St 23231 **Location:** I-64, exit 195, 1.4 mi s on Laburnum Ave, jct Williamsburg Rd; in Laburnum Square Shopping Center. **Parking:** on-site. **Cards:** AX, DS, MC, VI.

THE HILL CAFE

American
$6-$21

Phone: 804/648-0360 [27]

Amid the restored row houses of historic Church Hill, the restaurant and bar is known for classic eats with a twist. Among choices are corn and crab chowder and the chicken salad BLT. Casual dress. **Bar:** Full bar. **Hours:** 11 am-11 pm, Fri & Sat-midnight, Sun 10:30 am-10 pm. Closed: 11/27, 12/24, 12/25. **Address:** 2800 E Broad St 23223 **Location:** Just e at jct 28th St; in Church Hill Historic District. **Parking:** street. **Cards:** AX, DS, MC, VI.

LA PALMERA

Mexican
$5-$13

Phone: 804/330-9234 [34]

The casual restaurant's menu comprises fresh Latin fare. Included on a long list of exotic specialties are empanadas, tripe soup, fried pork chicharrones, fried plantains and the most authentic tamales likely to be found this far north of the border. Casual dress. **Hours:** 9 am-8 pm, Sat from 8 am, Sun 3 pm-7 pm. Closed major holidays. **Address:** 7701 Midlothian Tpke 23225 **Location:** 0.7 mi w of Chippenham Pkwy. **Parking:** on-site.

LA PETITE FRANCE

French
$9-$36

Phone: 804/353-8729 [16]

Attentive, professional service is emphasized in the intimate, candlelit dining room, a sumptuous setting for fabulous French cuisine. A loyal local following patronizes the 30-year-old restaurant. For dessert, consider the fabulous strawberry souffle. Semi-formal attire. **Bar:** Full bar. **Reservations:** suggested, Fri & Sat. **Hours:** 11:30 am-2 & 5:30-10 pm, Sat from 5:30 pm. Closed major holidays; also Sun & Mon. **Address:** 2108 Maywill St 23230 **Location:** I-64, exit Staples Mill Rd, just s to Thalbro Rd, then just e. **Parking:** on-site. **Cards:** AX, CB, DC, DS, MC, VI.

(See map and index starting on p. 848)

LA SIESTA MEXICAN RESTAURANT

Mexican
$4-$12

Phone: 804-272-7333 (33)

For more than 30 years, the Zajur family has been satisfying locals with family recipes such as zacatecanas (savory pork tortillas), and carne Tampiquena (tender, grilled and marinated steak). Casual dress. **Bar:** Full bar. **Hours:** 11:30 am-10 pm, Fri & Sat-11 pm, Sun-9 pm. Closed major holidays; also Mon. **Address:** 9900 Midlothian Tpke 23235 **Location:** Midlothian Tpke (US 60), 1.5 mi w of jct Powhite Pkwy. **Parking:** on-site. **Cards:** AX, DS, MC, VI.

CALL

LITTLE SAIGON

Vietnamese
$4-$15

Phone: 804/320-6098 (30)

Enjoy an extensive selection of specialties, such as noodle soup, rice crepes, garden rolls and grilled dishes as well as many healthful choices showcasing fresh produce and seafood. The large, open dining room is crisp and sparsely decorated. Casual dress. **Bar:** Full bar. **Hours:** 11 am-2:30 & 5-9:30 pm. Closed: 7/4, 11/27, 12/25. **Address:** 10012 Robious Rd 23235 **Location:** Jct Midlothian Tpke (US 60) and Robious Rd; in Robious Hall Shopping Center. **Parking:** on-site. **Cards:** AX, DS, MC, VI.

MALDINI'S

Italian
$6-$16

Phone: 804/230-9055 (28)

The Southside spot nurtures a true neighborhood ambience. Patrons dine alongside families enjoying delicious New York- or Sicilian-style pizza, couples dining romantically on sauteed fish and veal Marsala and single diners happily munching on pasta dishes, such as spaghetti carbonara and gnocchi al pesto, and sipping wine at the bar. Casual dress. **Bar:** Full bar. **Reservations:** accepted. **Hours:** 11 am-10 pm. Closed: 3/23, 11/27, 12/25. **Address:** 4811 Forest Hill Ave 23225 **Location:** Jct Boulevard (SR 161). **Parking:** on-site. **Cards:** MC, VI.

MANILA! MANILA! CAFE & GRILLE

Philippine
$9-$15

Phone: 804/346-9928 (7)

Diners can experience the taste of the Philippines in a semi-tropical setting. Savory stew, spicy empanadas, crisp lumpia and grilled fish lead the tasty delicacies. Casual dress. **Bar:** Full bar. **Hours:** 11:30 am-2:30 & 5:30-9 pm, Fri-10 pm, Sat 11:30-midnight. Closed: Mon. **Address:** 9047 W Broad St, Suite 1 23294 **Location:** I-64, exit Parham Rd N, 1 mi w on W Broad St at Tuckernuck; in West Broad Commons. **Parking:** on-site. **Cards:** AX, DS, MC, VI.

MELITO'S

American
$5-$23

Phone: 804/285-1899 (13)

Although the daily specials show more creativity, there's a good selection of tasty sandwiches and salad on the menu. This very popular neighborhood spot features homemade rolls, great soup and rich dessert. Grilled pork tenderloin is a specialty. Casual dress. **Bar:** Full bar. **Hours:** 11 am-midnight. Closed major holidays; also Sun. **Address:** 8815 Three Chopt Rd 23229 **Location:** Jct Ridge and Three Chopt Rd; in Westbury Shopping Center. **Parking:** on-site. **Cards:** AX, MC, VI.

CALL

MEXICO RESTAURANT

Mexican
$4-$12

Phone: 804/282-7357

The family-owned chain is a favorite of locals for reliable Mexican fare and a friendly atmosphere. Most opt for the expected combination dinners, but the more adventurous will be pleased by the delicious rendition of mole poblano sauce, a traditional sauce made from cocoa beans. Casual dress. **Bar:** Full bar. **Hours:** 11 am-2:30 & 5-10 pm, Sat & Sun noon-10 pm. **Address:** 6406 Horsepen Rd 23226 **Location:** Jct W Broad St, just s. **Parking:** on-site. **Cards:** AX, DC, DS, MC, VI.

PASTA LUNA

Northern Italian
$8-$22

Phone: 804/762-9029 (5)

Pasta, salad, antipasto, veal dishes and all manner of other traditional Italian specialties beckon from the menu. Large portions are served family-style in sizzling copper skillets that invite sharing and sampling. A great beginning is the antipasto plate with a mix of marinated vegetables. Casual dress. **Bar:** Full bar. **Reservations:** suggested. **Hours:** 11:30 am-2 & 5-10 pm, Sat 11:30 am-3 & 5-10 pm, Sun 11:30 am-3 & 5-9 pm. Closed: 11/27, 12/25. **Address:** 8902-D W Broad St 23294 **Location:** Just w of jct Parham Rd; in Gold's Gym Plaza. **Parking:** on-site. **Cards:** AX, CB, DC, DS, MC, VI.

CALL

PEKING

Chinese
$7-$23

Phone: 804/288-8371 (21)

The small chain is a local favorite for its wide selection of dishes, including such specialties as crispy duck, velvet shrimp and dry sauteed green beans. The atmosphere is refined. Casual dress. **Bar:** Full bar. **Hours:** 11:30 am-2 & 5-10 pm, Sat from 5 pm. **Address:** 5710 Grove Ave 23226 **Location:** "On the Avenues"; in Near West End; between Libbie and Granite aves. **Parking:** on-site. **Cards:** AX, MC, VI.

PEKING RESTAURANT

Chinese
$6-$14

Phone: 804/270-9898 (4)

The small chain is a local favorite for its wide selection of dishes, including such specialties as crispy duck, velvet shrimp and dry sauteed green beans. The atmosphere is refined. Casual dress. **Bar:** Full bar. **Hours:** 11:30 am-2:15 & 4:45-10:30 pm, Sat from 4:45 pm, Sun 11:30 am-2 & 4:45-9:30 pm; Sunday brunch. Closed: 11/27. **Address:** 8904-F W Broad St 23294 **Location:** Just w of jct Parham Rd; in Gold's Gym Plaza. **Parking:** on-site. **Cards:** AX, MC, VI.

CALL

(See map and index starting on p. 848)

PHO 79
Phone: 804/627-2200 ⑫

Vietnamese
$6-$9

At the heart of the menu is pho, a traditional noodle soup sometimes called the national dish of Vietnam. Large bowls of steaming soup, each accented with beef or other meats and seasoned with herbs and sauces, are satisfying and healthy. Several generations of the family are warm and hospitable. Spring rolls, interesting desserts and drinks are also noteworthy. Casual dress. **Hours:** 10 am-9 pm, Fri & Sat-10 pm, Sun-8 pm. **Address:** 6909 Staples Mill Rd 23228 **Location:** I-64, exit 185B (Staples Mill Rd), 1 mi w. **Parking:** on-site. **Cards:** AX, DS, MC, VI.

RIVER CITY DINER
Phone: 804/266-1500

American
$5-$11

The lively diner is likely to make you nostalgic for poodle skirts and sock hops. Kitschy decor and shiny chrome enliven the dining room. Order from the all-day breakfast menu or enjoy old favorites such as burgers, sandwiches and soda fountain treats. Casual dress. **Bar:** Full bar. **Hours:** 7:30 am-9 pm, Tues-Thurs to 10 pm, Fri & Sat-11 pm. Closed: 11/27, 12/25. **Address:** 803 E Parham Rd 23227 **Location:** I-95, exit 83B; adjacent to Holiday Inn-Richmond North. **Parking:** on-site. **Cards:** AX, DS, MC, VI.

RUCHEE INDIAN RESTAURANT
Phone: 804/323-5999 ㉜

Indian
$4-$16

The restaurant occupies a charming setting accented by wood paneling and pale shades of pink. The food, including tandoori specialties, shows off the fresh flavors of Northern and Southern Indian cuisine. Locals love the luncheon buffet. The spicy tastes are even better washed down with a cool strawberry or mango lassi. Casual dress. **Bar:** Beer & wine. **Hours:** 11:30 am-2:30 & 5-9:30 pm, Fri-10 pm, Sat noon-3 & 5-10 pm, Sun noon-3 & 5-9:30 pm. Closed major holidays. **Address:** 9930 Midlothian Tpke 23235 **Location:** 1.5 mi w of jct Powhite Pkwy; in Midlothian Green. **Parking:** on-site. **Cards:** AX, DC, DS, MC, VI.

SHACKLEFORD'S RESTAURANT
Phone: 804/741-9900 ⑩

American
$5-$25

In addition to a raw bar, the popular, neighborhood restaurant focuses on regional seafood entrees, such as trout stuffed with seafood and spinach. Creativity is a big strength of the menu. A great selection of beer and microbrew is available. Casual dress. **Bar:** Full bar. **Reservations:** accepted. **Hours:** 11 am-midnight. Closed major holidays. **Address:** 10496 Ridgefield Pkwy 23233 **Location:** I-64, exit 180A (Gaskins Rd S), 1 mi s to Ridgefield Pkwy, then 1.5 mi w; in Gleneagle Center. **Parking:** on-site. **Cards:** AX, DS, MC, VI.

SU CASA MEXICAN RESTAURANT
Phone: 804/355-6805 ㉓

Mexican
$5-$15

This small neighborhood restaurant offers classic Mexican favorites, including great fresh guacamole with a special twist. The Greek owners also pep up the menu with delicious Greek pastries, such as baklava, and occasional specials of marinated chicken or pastittsio. Casual dress. **Bar:** Beer & wine. **Hours:** 11 am-9:30 pm, Fri & Sat-10:30 pm. Closed: Sun. **Address:** 4013 W Broad St 23230 **Location:** Between jct Westwood Ave and N Hamilton St. **Parking:** on-site. **Cards:** AX, DS, MC, VI.

SUPER STARS GOURMET PIZZA
Phone: 804/673-3663 ⑲

Pizza
$4-$10

Locals love the quirky little pizza spot both for its sunny patio and "take and bake" pizzas. Gourmet toppings include pesto, barbecue chicken and the beloved "cheeseburger in paradise." Hot subs such as the veggie monster also are popular. Casual dress. **Bar:** Beer only. **Hours:** 11 am-9 pm. Closed: 7/4, 11/27, 12/25. **Address:** 5700 Patterson Ave 23226 **Location:** Jct Libbie and Willow Lawn rds. **Parking:** street.

THAI DINER
Phone: 804/270-2699 ⑨

Thai
$6-$10

Thai food is served in a modern, almost-space-age atmosphere. Specialties on a menu nearly the size of a book include fish with basil, noodle soup and spicy dishes. Sundaes are available. Casual dress. **Bar:** Full bar. **Hours:** 11:30 am-3 & 5-10 pm, Sat from noon. Closed: Sun. **Address:** 8059 W Broad St 23294 **Location:** Jct Parham Rd, just e; in Westland Shopping Center. **Parking:** on-site. **Cards:** AX, DC, DS, MC, VI.

VIETNAM GARDEN
Phone: 804/262-6114 ⑪

Vietnamese
$6-$13

Diners can sample Vietnamese fare amid soft lighting and a simple but soothing decor. Favorite menu choices include grilled shrimp on sugar cane, spicy seafood hot pot and barbecue pork on rice noodles. Flavors are spicy and fresh, with delicate flavorings such as cilantro, lemon grass and crunchy peanuts. Casual dress. **Bar:** Full bar. **Hours:** 11 am-10 pm, Fri-11 pm, Sun 5 pm-11 pm. Closed: 7/4, 11/27. **Address:** 3991 Glenside Dr 23228 **Location:** Jct Glenside Dr and Staples Mill Rd, just w. **Parking:** on-site. **Cards:** AX, DS, MC, VI.

YUM YUM GOOD
Phone: 804/673-9226 ⑳

Chinese
$5-$15

The dining room functions as a simple, elegant setting. Menu choices include hearty portions of traditional favorites, with sauce that tend to be sweeter than average. Servers don't speak much English, but they're efficient and unflaggingly friendly. Casual dress. **Bar:** Full bar. **Reservations:** accepted. **Hours:** 11 am-9:30 pm, Fri-10:30 pm, Sat noon-10:30 pm, Sun noon-9:30 pm. Closed: 11/27, 12/25. **Address:** 5612 Patterson Ave 23226 **Location:** Jct Willow Lawn Rd, just w. **Parking:** on-site and street. **Cards:** AX, DS, MC, VI.

ZORBA'S
Phone: 804/270-6026 ②

Greek
$5-$15

The casual spot presents an everyday menu of standard Greek favorites, from pasticcio to spanakopita. Daily specials can veer more upscale, with options such as leg of lamb and fresh seafood. Casual dress. **Bar:** Full bar. **Hours:** 11 am-10 pm, Fri & Sat-11 pm. Closed major holidays. **Address:** 9068 W Broad St 23294 **Location:** I-64, exit 181B, 1 mi n on Parham Rd, 0.7 mi w on Broad St; in Tuckernuck Square. **Parking:** on-site. **Cards:** AX, DC, DS, MC, VI.

The Richmond Vicinity

ASHLAND pop. 6,619 (See map and index starting on p. 848)

─────── WHERE TO STAY ───────

DAYS INN ASHLAND
(AAA) [SAVE]
▼▼ ▼▼
Motel
Rates not provided

Book great rates at AAA.com   Phone: 804/798-4262   [26]
Address: 806 England St 23005 **Location:** I-95, exit 92B, just w on SR 54. **Facility:** 90 one-bedroom standard units. 2 stories (no elevator), exterior corridors. **Parking:** on-site. **Amenities:** high-speed Internet, dual phone lines, hair dryers. **Pool(s):** outdoor. **Business Services:** fax. **Free Special Amenities:** continental breakfast and high-speed Internet.

[⊺↦] [🛁] [☕] / SOME UNITS FEE [🐾] [✕] [🗐] [🖵]

HAMPTON INN
▼▼▼▼▼▼
Small-scale Hotel
Rates not provided

Book great rates at AAA.com   Phone: 804/752-8444   [28]
Address: 705 England St 23005 **Location:** I-95, exit 92B northbound; exit 92 southbound, 0.5 mi w on SR 54. **Facility:** 74 units. 72 one-bedroom standard units, some with whirlpools. 2 one-bedroom suites with whirlpools. 3 stories, interior corridors. *Bath:* combo or shower only. **Parking:** on-site. **Amenities:** high-speed Internet, dual phone lines, voice mail, irons, hair dryers. **Pool(s):** heated outdoor. **Leisure Activities:** exercise room. **Guest Services:** valet and coin laundry, wireless Internet. **Business Services:** meeting rooms, business center.

[⊺↦] CALL [&M] [🛁] [☕] [🗐] [🖵] [🖵] / SOME UNITS [✕]

HOLIDAY INN EXPRESS HOTEL & SUITES   *Book at AAA.com*   Phone: (804)752-7889   [27]
▼▼▼▼▼▼
Small-scale Hotel
$99-$139 All Year

Address: 107 S Carter Rd 23005 **Location:** I-95, exit 92, just w. **Facility:** 115 units. 49 one-bedroom standard units, some with whirlpools. 66 one-bedroom suites. 3 stories, interior corridors. *Bath:* combo or shower only. **Parking:** on-site. **Amenities:** high-speed Internet, dual phone lines, irons, hair dryers. **Pool(s):** heated indoor. **Leisure Activities:** whirlpool, exercise room. **Guest Services:** valet and coin laundry, wireless Internet. **Business Services:** meeting rooms, business center. **Cards:** AX, DC, DS, MC, VI.

[A$K] [S◐] [⊺↦] CALL [&M] [🛁] [☕] [🗐] [🖵] [🖵] / SOME UNITS [✕]

SLEEP INN & SUITES   *Book great rates at AAA.com*   Phone: (804)752-2355   [29]
(AAA) [SAVE]
▼▼▼▼▼▼
Small-scale Hotel
$75-$174 All Year

Address: 80 Cottage Green Dr 23005 **Location:** I-95, exit 92B northbound; exit 92 southbound, 0.5 mi w on SR 54. **Facility:** 69 one-bedroom standard units, some with whirlpools. 3 stories, interior corridors. *Bath:* combo or shower only. **Parking:** on-site. **Amenities:** high-speed Internet, dual phone lines, voice mail, irons, hair dryers. **Pool(s):** heated indoor. **Leisure Activities:** whirlpool, exercise room. **Guest Services:** valet and coin laundry, wireless Internet. **Business Services:** meeting rooms, business center. **Cards:** AX, CB, DC, DS, JC, MC, VI. **Free Special Amenities:** expanded continental breakfast and high-speed Internet.

[S◐] [⊺↦] CALL [&M] [🛁] [☕] [🗐] [🖵] [🖵] / SOME UNITS [✕]

─────── WHERE TO DINE ───────

ASHLAND COFFEE & TEA   Phone: 804/798-1702   [38]
▼▼
American
$5-$12

In the heart of a quaint college town, the quirky coffeehouse serves overstuffed sandwiches, daily soups and a wide array of delicious coffee drinks. Live music often is scheduled for weekend evenings. Shelves line up books and other reading materials, and murals color the walls. A young staff of local college students gives the spot a lighthearted and fun atmosphere. Casual dress. Entertainment. **Bar:** Beer & wine. **Hours:** 7 am-8 pm, Thurs & Fri-11 pm, Sat 7:30 am-11 pm, Sun 8:30 am-2 pm. Closed major holidays. **Address:** 100 N Railroad Ave 23005 **Location:** Just w of railroad track, entrance on England St. **Parking:** on-site. **Cards:** AX, DS, MC, VI.

EL AZTECA   Phone: 804/798-4652   [37]
▼▼
Mexican
$5-$17

The restaurant prepares one of the widest varieties of Mexican cuisine around. In addition to standard favorites, the menu lists more adventurous offerings, including chicken in mole sauce—a rich and savory sauce derived from the cocoa bean. Entrees are fresh, delicious and served quickly. Casual dress. **Bar:** Full bar. **Hours:** 11 am-10 pm, Fri-11 pm, Sat noon-11 pm, Sun noon-9 pm. Closed major holidays. **Address:** 103 N Washington Hwy 23005 **Location:** I-95, exit 92B, 0.5 mi w on SR 54. **Parking:** on-site. **Cards:** AX, DS, MC, VI.

HOMEMADES BY SUZANNE   Phone: 804/798-8331   [39]
▼▼
Regional American
$5-$8

A great stop for lunch or picnic-packing, the eatery specializes in homestyle American and Southern favorites, which are served cafeteria style. Boxed lunches, homemade bread and numerous fabulous desserts—cream puffs, pies, cakes and more—fill the menu. Casual dress. **Hours:** 9 am-2 pm, Sat-3 pm. Closed major holidays; also Sun. **Address:** 102 N Railroad Ave 23005 **Location:** I-95, exit 92, 1.5 mi w on SR 54, then just n. **Parking:** on-site. **Cards:** AX, DS, MC, VI.

THE IRONHORSE RESTAURANT   Phone: 804/752-6410   [40]
▼▼ ▼▼
Regional American
$7-$32

The 1903 storefront retains many original architectural details, such as the pressed-tin ceiling. Picture windows overlook the railroad tracks, and the decor—including prominently displayed railroad collectibles—reflects the town's heritage. Monthly changing specialties use local market produce, seafood and certified Angus beef and reflect creative international and Southern influences. Dressy casual. **Bar:** Full bar. **Reservations:** suggested. **Hours:** 11:30 am-2:30 & 5:30-9 pm, Fri & Sat-10 pm. Closed: Sun. **Address:** 100 S Railroad Ave 23005 **Location:** I-95, exit 92, 1.5 mi w on SR 54. **Parking:** street. **Cards:** AX, DS, MC, VI.

(See map and index starting on p. 848)

THE SMOKEY PIG

Barbecue
$4-$16

Phone: 804/798-4590 [41]

As the name implies, this restaurant specializes in Southern barbecue ribs, chicken, beef and pork. Add a few of the traditional fixings like greens, sweet potatoes and hush puppies, and you've got a good, satisfying meal. Prime rib is served Saturday and Sunday. Casual dress. **Bar:** Beer & wine. **Hours:** 11 am-9 pm, Mon-3 pm. **Address:** 212 S Washington Hwy 23005 **Location:** I-95, exit 92B, just s of jct SR 54; on US 1. **Parking:** on-site. **Cards:** AX, MC, VI.

CALL [symbols]

CHESTER pop. 17,890 (See map and index starting on p. 848)

——— **WHERE TO STAY** ———

CLARION HOTEL

Book at AAA.com

Small-scale Hotel
$59-$129 All Year

Phone: (804)748-6321 [76]

Address: 2401 W Hundred Rd 23831 **Location:** I-95, exit 61B, just w on SR 10. **Facility:** 165 one-bedroom standard units. 2 stories (no elevator), interior corridors. **Parking:** on-site. **Terms:** cancellation fee imposed. **Amenities:** high-speed Internet, voice mail, irons, hair dryers. **Pool(s):** outdoor. **Leisure Activities:** exercise room. **Guest Services:** valet and coin laundry, wireless Internet. **Business Services:** meeting rooms, business center. **Cards:** AX, CB, DC, DS, JC, MC, VI.

[symbols] / SOME UNITS [symbol]

COMFORT INN-RICHMOND/CHESTER

Book great rates at AAA.com

[AAA] [SAVE]

Small-scale Hotel
$90-$153 All Year

Phone: 804/751-0000 [75]

Address: 2100 W Hundred Rd 23836 **Location:** I-95, exit 61A, just e on SR 10. **Facility:** 122 units. 112 one-bedroom standard units. 10 one-bedroom suites. 5 stories, interior corridors. *Bath:* combo or shower only. **Parking:** on-site. **Amenities:** high-speed Internet, voice mail, irons, hair dryers. **Pool(s):** heated outdoor. **Leisure Activities:** exercise room. **Guest Services:** valet and coin laundry, wireless Internet. **Business Services:** business center. **Cards:** AX, DC, DS, MC, VI. **Free Special Amenities: continental breakfast and high-speed Internet.**

[symbols] / SOME UNITS [symbol]

COURTYARD BY MARRIOTT RICHMOND/CHESTER

Book great rates at AAA.com Phone: 804/414-1010 [78]

Small-scale Hotel
$127-$157 All Year

Address: 2001 W Hundred Rd 23836 **Location:** I-95, exit 61A; I-295, exit 15B, 4 mi nw. **Facility:** Smoke free premises. 135 units. 124 one-bedroom standard units, some with whirlpools. 11 one-bedroom suites. 6 stories, interior corridors. *Bath:* combo or shower only. **Parking:** on-site. **Amenities:** high-speed Internet, dual phone lines, voice mail, irons, hair dryers. **Pool(s):** heated indoor. **Leisure Activities:** whirlpool, exercise room. **Guest Services:** valet and coin laundry, wireless Internet. **Business Services:** meeting rooms, business center. **Cards:** AX, DS, MC, VI.

AAA Benefit:
Members save 5% off of the best available rate.

[symbols] / SOME UNITS FEE [symbol]

FAIRFIELD INN BY MARRIOTT

Book great rates at AAA.com

Small-scale Hotel
$118-$145 All Year

Phone: 804/778-7500 [74]

Address: 12400 Redwater Creek Rd 23831 **Location:** I-95, exit 61B, just w of jct SR 10. **Facility:** Smoke free premises. 115 one-bedroom standard units, some with whirlpools. 4 stories, interior corridors. *Bath:* combo or shower only. **Parking:** on-site. **Amenities:** video games (fee), high-speed Internet, voice mail, irons, hair dryers. **Pool(s):** heated indoor. **Leisure Activities:** whirlpool, exercise room. **Guest Services:** valet laundry, wireless Internet. **Business Services:** fax. **Cards:** AX, DC, DS, MC, VI.

AAA Benefit:
Members save 5% off of the best available rate.

[symbols] / SOME UNITS FEE [symbol] FEE [symbol]

HAMPTON INN

Book great rates at AAA.com

[AAA] [SAVE]

Small-scale Hotel
Rates not provided

Phone: 804/768-8888 [73]

Address: 12610 Chestnut Hill Rd 23836 **Location:** I-95, exit 61A, jct SR 10. Located behind Comfort Inn. **Facility:** 65 units. 63 one-bedroom standard units. 2 one-bedroom suites. 2 stories, interior corridors. *Bath:* combo or shower only. **Parking:** on-site. **Amenities:** high-speed Internet, voice mail, irons, hair dryers. *Some:* safes (fee). **Leisure Activities:** pool privileges, exercise room. **Guest Services:** valet and coin laundry, wireless Internet. **Business Services:** business center. **Free Special Amenities: full breakfast and newspaper.**

[symbols] / SOME UNITS [symbol] [VCR]

HOLIDAY INN EXPRESS

Book at AAA.com

Small-scale Hotel
$99-$169 All Year

Phone: (804)751-0123 [79]

Address: 1911 W Hundred Rd 23836 **Location:** I-95, exit 61A, just e. **Facility:** 95 one-bedroom standard units. 4 stories, interior corridors. *Bath:* combo or shower only. **Parking:** on-site. **Amenities:** high-speed Internet, voice mail, irons, hair dryers. **Leisure Activities:** exercise room. **Guest Services:** valet and coin laundry, wireless Internet. **Business Services:** meeting rooms, fax (fee). **Cards:** AX, CB, DC, DS, JC, MC, VI.

[symbols] / SOME UNITS [symbol]

(See map and index starting on p. 848)

HOMEWOOD SUITES BY HILTON RICHMOND/CHESTER

Small-scale Hotel
$159-$179 All Year

Book at AAA.com   Phone: (804)751-0010   80

Address: 12810 Old Stage Rd 23836 **Location:** I-95, exit 61A; I-295, exit 15B, 4 mi w. **Facility:** 118 units. 62 one-bedroom standard units with kitchens. 55 one- and 1 two-bedroom suites with kitchens, some with whirlpools. 7 stories, interior corridors. **Bath:** combo or shower only. **Parking:** on-site. **Terms:** cancellation fee imposed. **Amenities:** high-speed Internet, dual phone lines, voice mail, irons, hair dryers. **Pool(s):** heated indoor. **Leisure Activities:** whirlpool, exercise room, sports court. **Guest Services:** valet and coin laundry. **Business Services:** meeting rooms, business center. **Cards:** AX, DC, DS, MC, VI.

HYATT PLACE RICHMOND/CHESTER

AAA SAVE

Small-scale Hotel
$99-$299 All Year

Book great rates at AAA.com   Phone: (804)530-4600   81

Address: 13148 Kingston Ave 23836 **Location:** I-295, exit 15B, just w; I-95, exit 61A, 4.5 mi e; in River's Bend. **Facility:** 80 one-bedroom standard units. 4 stories, interior corridors. **Parking:** on-site. **Terms:** cancellation fee imposed. **Amenities:** video games, high-speed Internet, voice mail, irons, hair dryers. **Some:** dual phone lines. **Pool(s):** heated outdoor. **Leisure Activities:** golf privileges, exercise room. **Guest Services:** valet and coin laundry, area transportation-within 5 mi. **Business Services:** meeting rooms, fax. **Cards:** AX, DC, DS, MC, VI.

HYATT PLACE™

AAA Benefit:
Ask for the AAA rate and save 10%.

QUALITY INN & SUITES

Small-scale Hotel
$59-$129 All Year

Book at AAA.com   Phone: (804)796-5200   77

Address: 12711 Old Stage Rd 23836 **Location:** I-95, exit 61A, just e on SR 10/W Hundred Rd; I-295, exit 15B, 4 mi nw. **Facility:** 70 one-bedroom standard units. 3 stories, interior corridors. **Bath:** combo or shower only. **Parking:** on-site. **Terms:** cancellation fee imposed. **Amenities:** high-speed Internet, voice mail, irons, hair dryers. **Some:** dual phone lines. **Pool(s):** heated indoor. **Leisure Activities:** exercise room. **Guest Services:** valet and coin laundry, wireless Internet. **Business Services:** meeting rooms, fax. **Cards:** AX, CB, DC, DS, JC, MC, VI.

──── WHERE TO DINE ────

CENTRAL PARK DELI

Deli/Subs
Sandwiches
$5-$7

Phone: 804-796-9660   74

Regulars can't last a few days without a patty melt or corned beef sandwich from the casual spot. Also on offer are delicious daily soups, pickles, a glass case full of desserts and cookies and barbecue ribs in the evening. Casual dress. **Bar:** Beer & wine. **Hours:** 11 am-8 pm, Fri-9 pm, Sat-3 pm. Closed major holidays. **Address:** 12744 Jefferson Davis Hwy 23831 **Location:** I-95, exit 61B, 1 mi w; in Breckenridge Shopping Center. **Parking:** on-site. **Cards:** AX, MC, VI.

CESARE'S RESTAURANT & PIZZERIA

Italian
$6-$14

Phone: 804/530-1047   77

Diners can catch a glimpse of their pizza being made or choose from such daily specials as calzones, baked manicotti, vegetable-stuffed shells and Italian hoagies. The setting is casual, and the service friendly and attentive. Casual dress. **Bar:** Beer & wine. **Hours:** 11 am-10 pm, Fri & Sat-11 pm, Sun noon-10 pm. Closed major holidays. **Address:** 13127 River's Bend Blvd 23831 **Location:** I-95, exit 61A, 2 mi e; in River's Bend Shopping Center. **Parking:** on-site. **Cards:** AX, DC, DS, MC, VI.

DON PAPA GRANDE MEXICAN RESTAURANT

Mexican
$4-$13

Phone: 804/796-7988   75

Walls are painted with colorful, festive murals at the neighborhood spot. Patrons can order all the favorite Mexican combination plates, as well as more authentic specialties, such as tostadas de ceviche on weekends, chile Colorado and carne asada. Casual dress. **Bar:** Full bar. **Hours:** 11 am-2:30 & 5-10 pm, Sun-9 pm. Closed major holidays. **Address:** 12806 Jefferson Davis Hwy 23831 **Location:** I-95, exit 61B, 1 mi w; in Breckenridge Shopping Center. **Parking:** on-site. **Cards:** AX, DS, MC, VI.

JALAPENOS

Mexican
$5-$14

Phone: 804/530-2787   78

In addition to Mexican standards, the bright, cheerful spot serves some more creative dishes, such as marinated shrimp cocktail, tortilla soup and chile Colorado. Casual dress. **Bar:** Full bar. **Hours:** 11:30 am-10 pm, Fri-11 pm, Sun-9 pm. Closed: 7/4, 11/27, 12/25. **Address:** 13130 Kingston Ave 23836 **Location:** I-295, exit 15B, just w; in River's Bend. **Parking:** on-site. **Cards:** AX, DS, MC, VI.

NARITA JAPANESE RESTAURANT

Japanese
$6-$50

Phone: 804/530-0013   76

In a cool, uncluttered setting, the restaurant serves fresh, colorful sushi, along with other specialties ranging from soups to teriyakis. Casual dress. **Bar:** Beer & wine. **Hours:** 11 am-10 pm, Fri & Sat-10 pm. Closed major holidays; also Sun. **Address:** 13115 River's Bend Blvd 23836 **Location:** I-95, exit 61A, 2 mi e; in River's Bend Shopping Center. **Parking:** on-site. **Cards:** AX, DS, MC, VI.

(See map and index starting on p. 848)

PEKING RESTAURANT

Chinese
$5-$14

Phone: 804/751-9898   [73]

You'll find all your favorites on the extensive menu, from lo mein to chicken imperial and everything in between. Chinese, Hunan, Mandarin and Szechuan cuisines are the highlights. A good choice is the hot and sour soup and the tasty Hunan chicken entree. Casual dress. **Bar:** Full bar. **Hours:** 11:30 am-2 & 5-9 pm, Fri & Sat-10:30 pm, Sun-9:30 pm. Closed: 11/27. **Address:** 12730 Jefferson Davis Hwy 23831 **Location:** I-95, exit 61B, 1 mi w; in Breckenridge Shopping Center. **Parking:** on-site. **Cards:** AX, MC, VI.

CHESTERFIELD   (See map and index starting on p. 848)

———— WHERE TO STAY ————

CHESTER INN & SUITES

Small-scale Hotel
$80-$180 3/1-10/31
$70-$150 11/1-2/28

Phone: (804)743-0770   [68]

Address: 9040 Pams Ave 23237 **Location:** I-95, exit 64, just w. **Facility:** 50 one-bedroom standard units, some with whirlpools. 3 stories, interior corridors. *Bath:* combo or shower only. **Parking:** on-site. **Amenities:** high-speed Internet, voice mail, irons, hair dryers. **Leisure Activities:** exercise room. **Guest Services:** coin laundry, wireless Internet. **Business Services:** fax. **Cards:** AX, DS, MC, VI.

ASK SØ ↑↓ CALL &M ⊞ ⊟ ☞ ▭ / SOME UNITS ✕

COUNTRY INN & SUITES, RICHMOND I-95S   *Book great rates at AAA.com*
AAA SAVE

Small-scale Hotel
$89-$169 3/1-8/31
$75-$135 9/1-2/28

Phone: (804)275-5900   [69]

Address: 2401 Willis Rd 23237 **Location:** I-95, exit 64, just w. **Facility:** 50 units. 37 one-bedroom standard units, some with whirlpools. 13 one-bedroom suites. 2 stories, interior corridors. **Parking:** on-site. **Amenities:** high-speed Internet, dual phone lines, voice mail, irons, hair dryers. **Guest Services:** coin laundry, wireless Internet. **Business Services:** PC, fax. **Cards:** AX, CB, DC, DS, JC, MC, VI. **Free Special Amenities:** continental breakfast and high-speed Internet.

SØ 🎦 ⊞ ⊟ ▭ / SOME UNITS ✕ VCR

SLEEP INN   *Book great rates at AAA.com*
AAA SAVE

Small-scale Hotel
$69-$99 5/1-2/28
$59-$89 3/1-4/30

Phone: (804)275-8800   [70]

Address: 2321 Willis Rd 23237 **Location:** I-95, exit 64, just w. **Facility:** 51 one-bedroom standard units. 3 stories, interior corridors. *Bath:* combo or shower only. **Parking:** on-site. **Amenities:** high-speed Internet, voice mail, irons, hair dryers. **Business Services:** fax. **Cards:** AX, CB, DC, DS, JC, MC, VI. **Free Special Amenities:** continental breakfast and high-speed Internet.

SØ ↑↓ CALL &M 🎦 ⊞ ⊟ / SOME UNITS ✕

COLONIAL HEIGHTS pop. 16,897   (See map and index starting on p. 854)

———— WHERE TO STAY ————

COMFORT SUITES SOUTHPARK   *Book great rates at AAA.com*
AAA SAVE

Small-scale Hotel
$109-$259 3/1-10/1
$89-$229 10/2-2/28

Phone: (804)520-8900   [19]

Address: 931 South Ave 23834 **Location:** I-95, exit 53, just n. Located adjacent to Southpark Mall. **Facility:** Smoke free premises. 92 units. 91 one-bedroom standard units, some with whirlpools. 1 two-bedroom suite. 5 stories, interior corridors. *Bath:* combo or shower only. **Parking:** on-site. **Terms:** cancellation fee imposed. **Amenities:** high-speed Internet, dual phone lines, voice mail, safes (fee), irons, hair dryers. **Pool(s):** heated indoor. **Leisure Activities:** whirlpool, limited exercise equipment. **Guest Services:** valet and coin laundry, area transportation-within 5 mi, wireless Internet. **Business Services:** meeting rooms, business center. **Cards:** AX, CB, DC, DS, JC, MC, VI. **Free Special Amenities:** expanded continental breakfast and high-speed Internet.

SØ CALL &M 🛬 ✕ ⊞ ⊟ ▭ / SOME UNITS VCR

HILTON GARDEN INN-SOUTHPARK   *Book great rates at AAA.com*

Small-scale Hotel
$109-$199 All Year

Phone: (804)520-0600   [18]

Address: 800 Southpark Blvd 23834 **Location:** I-95, exit 53, just n. Located adjacent to Southpark Mall. **Facility:** 155 units. 145 one-bedroom standard units, some with whirlpools. 10 one-bedroom suites. 6 stories, interior corridors. *Bath:* combo or shower only. **Parking:** on-site. **Amenities:** video games (fee), high-speed Internet, dual phone lines, voice mail, irons, hair dryers. **Pool(s):** heated indoor. **Leisure Activities:** whirlpool, exercise room. **Guest Services:** valet and coin laundry, wireless Internet. **Business Services:** meeting rooms, business center. **Cards:** AX, CB, DC, DS, MC, VI.

↑↓ CALL &M 🛬 🎦 ⊞ ⊟ ▭ / SOME UNITS ✕

———— WHERE TO DINE ————

KOREANA ORIENTAL RESTAURANT

Korean
$6-$17

Phone: 804/520-8989   [10]

For years, the restaurant has introduced southside Virginia to the flavors of Korea. Barbecue beef and pork, steaming noodle soups and stir-fried dishes come with that ubiquitous Korean condiment: spicy kimchee. The daily lunch buffet lines up a good sampling. Casual dress. **Bar:** Beer & wine. **Hours:** 11:30 am-10 pm, Fri & Sat-11 pm, Sun noon-10 pm. Closed major holidays. **Address:** 168 Southgate Sq 23834 **Location:** I-95, exit 53, just n. **Parking:** on-site. **Cards:** MC, VI.

CALL &M ▣

(See map and index starting on p. 854)

SAGEBRUSH STEAKHOUSE   Phone: 804/520-8216

American
$5-$19

Born from the spirit of Texas cattle drives, the restaurant presents a menu of hearty steaks, prime rib, chicken, seafood and baby back ribs. Yummy desserts merit a splurge. Guests can call ahead to facilitate seating. Casual dress. **Bar:** Full bar. **Hours:** 11 am-10 pm, Fri & Sat-11 pm. Closed: 12/25. **Address:** 204 Southgate Square Shopping Center 23834 **Location:** I-95, exit 53, just e, then just n. **Parking:** on-site. **Cards:** AX, DC, DS, MC, VI.

CALL 🔲M 🔲

DOSWELL

———— **WHERE TO STAY** ————

BEST WESTERN-KINGS QUARTERS   *Book great rates at AAA.com*   Phone: (804)876-3321

Small-scale Hotel
$59-$189 3/1-11/1
$59-$99 11/2-2/28

Address: 16102 Theme Park Way 23047 **Location:** I-95, exit 98, just e on SR 30; entrance to theme park. Located adjacent to King's Dominion. **Facility:** 248 units. 247 one-bedroom standard units. 1 one-bedroom suite. 2 stories (no elevator), exterior corridors. *Bath:* combo or shower only. **Parking:** on-site. **Terms:** 3 day cancellation notice-fee imposed. **Amenities:** high-speed Internet, safes (fee), irons, hair dryers. **Pool(s):** outdoor. **Leisure Activities:** putting green, 2 lighted tennis courts, playground, shuffleboard, volleyball. *Fee:* game room. **Guest Services:** coin laundry, area transportation-theme park, wireless Internet. **Business Services:** meeting rooms. **Cards:** AX, DS, MC, VI. **Free Special Amenities:** local telephone calls and high-speed Internet.

AAA Benefit:

Members save 10% everyday, plus an exclusive frequent stay program.

S🔲D 🍽 CALL 🔲M 🏊 🚫 🎮 🔲 / SOME UNITS FEE 🐾 ✖ FEE 🔲 FEE 🔲

ECONO LODGE AT KING'S DOMINION   *Book at AAA.com*   Phone: 804/876-3712

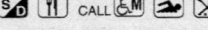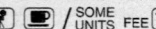

Small-scale Hotel
Rates not provided

Address: 10222 Kings Dominion Blvd 23047 **Location:** I-95, exit 98, just e; at All American Travel Plaza. Near King's Dominion. **Facility:** 85 one-bedroom standard units. 2 stories (no elevator), exterior corridors. **Parking:** on-site. **Amenities:** high-speed Internet (fee). **Pool(s):** outdoor. **Leisure Activities:** *Fee:* game room. **Guest Services:** coin laundry, wireless Internet. **Business Services:** meeting rooms, PC.

🍽 🏊 🎮 🔲 / SOME UNITS ✖

GLEN ALLEN pop. 12,562   (See map and index starting on p. 848)

———— **WHERE TO STAY** ————

CANDLEWOOD SUITES RICHMOND-WEST   *Book at AAA.com*   Phone: 804/364-2000 **36**

Small-scale Hotel
$109-$179 All Year

Address: 4120 Brookriver Dr 23060 **Location:** I-64, exit 178, just w on W Broad St. **Facility:** 122 units. 98 one-bedroom standard units with kitchens. 24 one-bedroom suites with kitchens. 3 stories, interior corridors. *Bath:* combo or shower only. **Parking:** on-site. **Terms:** office hours 7 am-11 pm, cancellation fee imposed. **Amenities:** video library, DVD players, high-speed Internet, dual phone lines, voice mail, irons, hair dryers. **Leisure Activities:** exercise room. **Guest Services:** complimentary laundry. **Business Services:** fax. **Cards:** AX, DC, DS, MC, VI.

ASK CALL 🔲M VCR 🎮 🔲 🔲 🔲 / SOME UNITS FEE 🐾 ✖

COMFORT SUITES-INNSBROOK   *Book at AAA.com*   Phone: (804)217-9200 **39**

Small-scale Hotel
$133 All Year

Address: 4051 Innslake Dr 23060 **Location:** I-64, exit 178B, just e on W Broad St to Cox Rd, then just n. **Facility:** 125 units. 118 one-bedroom standard units. 7 one-bedroom suites with whirlpools. 5 stories, interior corridors. *Bath:* combo or shower only. **Parking:** on-site. **Terms:** 3 day cancellation notice-fee imposed. **Amenities:** video games (fee), high-speed Internet, dual phone lines, voice mail, irons, hair dryers. **Pool(s):** heated indoor. **Leisure Activities:** exercise room. **Guest Services:** valet and coin laundry, wireless Internet. **Business Services:** meeting rooms, business center. **Cards:** AX, DS, MC, VI.

ASK S🔲D 🍽 CALL 🔲M 🏊 🎮 🔲 🔲 🔲 / SOME UNITS ✖

COURTYARD BY MARRIOTT RICHMOND NORTHWEST   *Book great rates at AAA.com*   Phone: 804/346-5427 **42**

Small-scale Hotel
$168-$205 All Year

Address: 3950 Westerre Pkwy 23233 **Location:** I-64, exit 178B, 0.5 mi e; jct W Broad St and Westerre Pkwy. **Facility:** Smoke free premises. 154 units. 146 one-bedroom standard units, some with whirlpools. 8 one-bedroom suites. 4 stories, interior corridors. *Bath:* combo or shower only. **Parking:** on-site. **Amenities:** video games (fee), CD players, high-speed Internet, dual phone lines, voice mail, irons, hair dryers. **Pool(s):** heated indoor. **Leisure Activities:** whirlpool, exercise room. **Guest Services:** valet and coin laundry, wireless Internet. **Business Services:** meeting rooms, business center. **Cards:** AX, DC, DS, MC, VI.

AAA Benefit:

Members save 5% off of the best available rate.

ASK S🔲D 🍽 CALL 🔲M 🏊 🚫 🎮 🔲 / SOME UNITS 🔲 🔲

(See map and index starting on p. 848)

FAIRFIELD INN & SUITES BY MARRIOTT

Book great rates at AAA.com   **Phone: (804)545-4200**   45

Small-scale Hotel
$119-$144 All Year

Address: 9937 Mayland Dr 23233 **Location:** I-64, exit 180B, just n on Gaskins Rd. **Facility:** Smoke free premises. 83 one-bedroom standard units. 3 stories, interior corridors. *Bath:* combo or shower only. **Parking:** on-site. **Terms:** 3 day cancellation notice. **Amenities:** video games (fee), high-speed Internet, voice mail, irons, hair dryers. *Some:* CD players. **Pool(s):** heated indoor. **Leisure Activities:** whirlpool, exercise room. **Guest Services:** valet and coin laundry, wireless Internet. **Business Services:** business center. **Cards:** AX, CB, DC, DS, JC, MC, VI.

AAA Benefit:
Members save 5% off of the best available rate.

HAMPTON INN & SUITES

Phone: 804-261-2266   32

Small-scale Hotel
Rates not provided

Address: 1101 Technology Park Dr 23059 **Location:** I-295, exit 43C, just n on US 7; I-95, exit 86B (SR 656 Elmont); just w to US 1, 1.1 mi s; in Virginia Center Station. Located near Virginia Center Commons. **Facility:** 72 one-bedroom standard units, some with whirlpools. 4 stories, interior corridors. *Bath:* combo or shower only. **Parking:** on-site. **Amenities:** high-speed Internet, voice mail, irons, hair dryers. **Pool(s):** heated indoor. **Leisure Activities:** whirlpool, exercise room. **Guest Services:** valet and coin laundry, wireless Internet. **Business Services:** meeting rooms, business center.

HAMPTON INN-RICHMOND WEST

Book great rates at AAA.com   **Phone: 804-747-7777**   40

Small-scale Hotel
Rates not provided

Address: 10800 W Broad St 23060 **Location:** I-64, exit 178B, just e, jct Cox Rd. Located in Innsbrook shopping and corporate complex. **Facility:** 136 one-bedroom standard units. 3 stories, interior corridors. *Bath:* combo or shower only. **Amenities:** high-speed Internet, dual phone lines, voice mail, irons, hair dryers. *Some:* DVD players (fee). **Pool(s):** outdoor. **Leisure Activities:** exercise room. **Guest Services:** valet laundry, wireless Internet. **Business Services:** meeting rooms, business center.

HILTON GARDEN INN RICHMOND INNSBROOK

Book great rates at AAA.com   **Phone: (804)521-2900**   38

Small-scale Hotel
$179 All Year

Address: 4050 Cox Rd 23060 **Location:** I-64, exit 178B, just e on W Broad St to Dominion Blvd, then just n. Located in Innsbrook Corporate Center. **Facility:** Smoke free premises. 155 one-bedroom standard units, some with whirlpools. 6 stories, interior corridors. *Bath:* combo or shower only. **Parking:** on-site. **Amenities:** high-speed Internet, dual phone lines, voice mail, irons, hair dryers. **Pool(s):** heated indoor. **Leisure Activities:** whirlpool, exercise room. **Guest Services:** valet and coin laundry, wireless Internet. **Business Services:** meeting rooms, business center. **Cards:** AX, CB, DC, DS, JC, MC, VI.

HOLIDAY INN EXPRESS

Book at AAA.com   **Phone: (804)934-9300**   46

Small-scale Hotel
$119-$134 All Year

Address: 9933 Mayland Dr 23233 **Location:** I-64, exit 180B, just n to Mayland Dr, then just w. **Facility:** 113 one-bedroom standard units. 4 stories, interior corridors. *Bath:* combo or shower only. **Parking:** on-site. **Terms:** 3 day cancellation notice. **Amenities:** video games (fee), high-speed Internet, dual phone lines, voice mail, irons, hair dryers. **Pool(s):** outdoor. **Guest Services:** valet and coin laundry, area transportation. **Business Services:** meeting rooms, business center. **Cards:** AX, CB, DC, DS, JC, MC, VI.

HOMESTEAD STUDIO SUITES HOTEL-RICHMOND-INNSBROOK

Book at AAA.com   **Phone: (804)747-8898**   41

Motel
$77-$140 All Year

Address: 10961 W Broad St 23060 **Location:** I-64, exit 178B, just e on W Broad St, then just s on Cox Rd. **Facility:** 142 one-bedroom standard units with kitchens. 2 stories (no elevator), exterior corridors. *Bath:* combo or shower only. **Parking:** on-site. **Terms:** office hours 7 am-11 pm. **Amenities:** high-speed Internet (fee), voice mail, irons, hair dryers. **Guest Services:** valet and coin laundry. **Business Services:** fax. **Cards:** AX, DC, DS, JC, MC, VI.

HOMEWOOD SUITES BY HILTON RICHMOND WEST END-INNSBROOK

Book at AAA.com   **Phone: 804-217-8000**   37

Small-scale Hotel
Rates not provided

Address: 4100 Innslake Dr 23060 **Location:** I-64, exit 178B, just e on W Broad St to Cox Rd, then just n. **Facility:** 123 units. 116 one- and 7 two-bedroom suites with kitchens. 4 stories, interior corridors. *Bath:* combo or shower only. **Parking:** on-site. **Amenities:** video library, video games (fee), high-speed Internet, dual phone lines, voice mail, irons, hair dryers. *Some:* DVD players. **Pool(s):** outdoor. **Leisure Activities:** exercise room. **Guest Services:** valet and coin laundry, area transportation, wireless Internet. **Business Services:** meeting rooms, business center.

HOWARD JOHNSON EXPRESS INN

Book at AAA.com   **Phone: 804/261-0188**   44

Small-scale Hotel
Rates not provided

Address: 8613 Brook Rd 23060 **Location:** I-95, exit 83B, 0.5 mi w to Brook Rd, then just n. **Facility:** 36 one-bedroom standard units, some with efficiencies (no utensils) and/or whirlpools. 2 stories, interior corridors. **Parking:** on-site. **Amenities:** high-speed Internet, voice mail, safes (fee), irons, hair dryers. **Leisure Activities:** limited exercise equipment. **Guest Services:** wireless Internet.

(See map and index starting on p. 848)

RESIDENCE INN BY MARRIOTT   *Book great rates at AAA.com*

Phone: 804/762-9852   **43**

Small-scale Hotel
$204-$234 All Year

Address: 3940 Westerre Pkwy 23233 **Location:** I-64, exit 180, n on Gaskins Rd to W Broad St. **Facility:** Smoke free premises. 103 units. 44 one-bedroom standard units with kitchens. 43 one- and 16 two-bedroom suites. 4 stories, interior corridors. *Bath:* combo or shower only. **Parking:** on-site. **Amenities:** video games (fee), high-speed Internet, dual phone lines, voice mail, irons, hair dryers. **Pool(s):** heated outdoor. **Leisure Activities:** whirlpool, exercise room, sports court. **Guest Services:** valet and coin laundry, wireless Internet. **Business Services:** meeting rooms, PC. **Cards:** AX, DC, DS, JC, MC, VI.

AAA Benefit:
Members save 5% off of the best available rate.

RICHMOND MARRIOTT WEST   *Book great rates at AAA.com*

Phone: 804/965-9500   **35**

Small-scale Hotel
$175-$214 All Year

Address: 4240 Dominion Blvd 23060 **Location:** I-64, exit 178B, 0.5 mi e to Dominion Blvd, then just n. Located in the Innsbrook Corporate Center. **Facility:** Smoke free premises. 242 units. 234 one-bedroom standard units. 8 one-bedroom suites. 6 stories, interior corridors. *Bath:* combo or shower only. **Parking:** on-site. **Amenities:** high-speed Internet, dual phone lines, voice mail, irons, hair dryers. **Pool(s):** heated indoor. **Leisure Activities:** whirlpool, exercise room. **Guest Services:** valet laundry, wireless Internet. **Business Services:** conference facilities, business center. **Cards:** AX, DC, DS, JC, MC, VI.

AAA Benefit:
Members save 5% off of the best available rate.

SPRINGHILL SUITES BY MARRIOTT   *Book great rates at AAA.com*

Phone: 804/266-9403   **33**

Small-scale Hotel
$148-$181 All Year

Address: 9701 Brook Rd 23059 **Location:** I-295, exit 43C, just n on US 1; I-95, exit 86B (SR 656-Elmont), just w to US 1, then 1.2 mi s. Located near the Virginia Center Commons. **Facility:** Smoke free premises. 136 one-bedroom standard units. 4 stories, interior corridors. *Bath:* combo or shower only. **Parking:** on-site. **Amenities:** video games (fee), high-speed Internet, dual phone lines, voice mail, irons, hair dryers. **Pool(s):** heated indoor. **Leisure Activities:** exercise room. **Guest Services:** valet and coin laundry. **Business Services:** meeting rooms, business center. **Cards:** AX, DC, DS, MC, VI.

AAA Benefit:
Members save 5% off of the best available rate.

VIRGINIA CROSSINGS RESORT   *Book great rates at AAA.com*

Phone: (804)727-1400   **34**

Large-scale Hotel
$159-$209 All Year

Address: 1000 Virginia Center Pkwy 23059 **Location:** I-295, exit 43C, just n on US 1, then 1 mi e. **Facility:** The state's Colonial legacy sets the theme in this elegant hotel perched atop a hillside overlooking the rolling fields of the resort's golf course. 183 units. 178 one-bedroom standard units. 5 one-bedroom suites, some with whirlpools. 5 stories, interior corridors. *Bath:* combo or shower only. **Parking:** on-site. **Terms:** check-in 4 pm, cancellation fee imposed. **Amenities:** dual phone lines, voice mail, irons, hair dryers. **Fee:** video games, high-speed Internet. *Some:* DVD players (fee), CD players. **Dining:** 2 restaurants, also, The Glen Restaurant, see separate listing. **Pool(s):** heated outdoor. **Leisure Activities:** whirlpool, driving range, racquetball court, jogging, exercise room, sports court, horseshoes, volleyball. *Fee:* golf-18 holes, massage. **Guest Services:** valet laundry, area transportation-within 5 mi, wireless Internet. **Business Services:** conference facilities, business center. **Cards:** AX, CB, DC, DS, MC, VI.

WHERE TO DINE

BAKER'S CRUST BREAD MARKET

Phone: 804/377-9060

American
$8-$20

A short list of appetizers and entrees complements the eatery's sandwiches, soups, rotisserie-grilled items and salads served in a hollowed-out loaf of bread. In keeping with the bistro atmosphere, there's a crepe bar in the back. Among pleasing dinner specialties are roasted chicken, lasagna and other pastas, as well as rich seafood chowder served over a mound of buttery mashed potatoes. Casual dress. **Bar:** Full bar. **Hours:** 11 am-9 pm, Fri-10 pm, Sat 9 am-10 pm, Sun 9 am-7 pm. Closed: 11/27, 12/25. **Address:** 11800 W Broad St, Suite 1102 23235 **Location:** I-64, exit 178, just w; in Short Pump Town Center. **Parking:** on-site. **Cards:** AX, DC, DS, MC, VI.

BISTRO R

Phone: 804/747-9484   **52**

French
$8-$30

Attentive servers present such discriminating mostly French fare as escargots bourguignon, braised lamb shank and veal blanketed in a sauce of caramelized shallots and white wine. The atmosphere is casual cafe bistro, the service knowledgeable and sure. Semi-formal attire. **Bar:** Full bar. **Reservations:** suggested. **Hours:** 11:30 am-2:30 & 5:30-9 pm, Fri-9:30 pm, Sat 5:30 pm-9:30 pm. Closed major holidays; also Sun. **Address:** 10190 W Broad St 23060 **Location:** I-64, exit 178B, 1.5 mi e; in Lexington Commons. **Parking:** on-site. **Cards:** AX, DC, MC, VI.

(See map and index starting on p. 848)

CAPITAL ALE HOUSE

American
$7-$20

Phone: 804/780-2537

Although the bar's ice troughs, which are shaped to fit drink glasses, show where the priorities lie, the food isn't taken for granted. Menu selections range from sandwiches to snack-size appetizers to sophisticated entrees. Casual dress. **Bar:** Full bar. **Hours:** 11 am-1 am. Closed: 11/27, 12/25. **Address:** 4024-A Cox Rd 23060 **Location:** I-64, exit 178B, 0.5 mi e to Dominion Blvd, just n; in Innsbrook Shoppes. **Parking:** on-site. **Cards:** AX, DC, DS, MC, VI.

FIREBIRDS WOOD FIRED GRILL

American
$6-$26

Phone: 804/364-9744   48

The restaurant re-creates the atmosphere of a mountain lodge. Hand-cut steaks and seafood dominate the menu, which also lists a few pork and chicken entrees, as well as elk tenderloin medallions and buffalo meatloaf. The kitchen uses wood grilling, and pizzas bake in a wood-burning oven. Flavorful food, enhanced presentations and a skilled, knowledgeable and attentive staff, together with distinctive physical elements, make this place appealing. Casual dress. **Bar:** Full bar. **Hours:** 11 am-10 pm, Fri & Sat-11 pm. Closed: 11/27, 12/25. **Address:** 11800 W Broad St, #1068 23233 **Location:** I-64, exit 178, just w; in Short Pump Town Center. **Parking:** on-site. **Cards:** AX, DC, DS, MC, VI.

THE GLEN RESTAURANT

American
$13-$33

Phone: 804/727-1480   47

Guests dine in Colonial elegance as they look out over the rolling fields of the resort's golf course. The chef's regional specialties range from crab cakes to venison. A complimentary chef's bar of assorted cold appetizers is an extra treat. Dressy casual. **Bar:** Full bar. **Reservations:** suggested. **Hours:** 6:30-10 am, 11:30-2 & 5:30-9:30 pm, Sat from 7 am, Sun 7 am-10 & 11:30-2 pm. **Address:** 1000 Virginia Center Pkwy 23059 **Location:** I-295, exit 43C, just n on US 1, then 1 mi e; in Virginia Crossings Resort. **Parking:** on-site. **Cards:** AX, CB, DC, DS, MC, VI.

THE GRAPEVINE II

Greek
$5-$20

Phone: 804/440-9100   53

Motifs of Grecian columns and grapevines deck the walls at the intimate spot. The owners serve a delightful array of Greek and Italian specialties, from pizza to seafood to baked pasta dishes. Casual dress. **Bar:** Full bar. **Reservations:** accepted. **Hours:** 11:30 am-9:45 pm, Sat 5 pm-10:45 pm, Sun noon-9 pm. Closed major holidays. **Address:** 11055 Three Chopt Rd 23233 **Location:** I-64, exit 178B, just e on Broad St, then just s; in Granville Square. **Parking:** on-site. **Cards:** AX, DC, DS, MC, VI.

HOUSE OF VIETNAM

Vietnamese
$7-$16

Phone: 804/364-1888   51

The small spot serves tasty and healthy fare with Vietnamese origins. Diners experience soothing pho noodle soup, lemon-grass grilled seafood, fresh rice-paper rolls and broken rice platters with grilled meats. Casual dress. **Bar:** Beer & wine. **Hours:** 11:30 am-2:10 & 4:30-9:15 pm, Fri-10 pm, Sat 4:30 pm-10 pm, Sun noon-2:10 & 4:30-9 pm. Closed major holidays. **Address:** 3402 Pump Rd 23233 **Location:** I-64, exit 177, 0.8 mi w on W Broad St; in Short Pump Crossing. **Parking:** on-site. **Cards:** AX, MC, VI.

MAMA CUCINA

Italian
$7-$18

Phone: 804/346-3350   50

The warm, welcoming restaurant treats diners to heaping plates of freshly made pasta with savory sauces, as well as numerous other Italian specialties. Casual dress. **Bar:** Full bar. **Reservations:** suggested. **Hours:** 11:30 am-2:30 & 5-10 pm, Sat from 5 pm. Closed major holidays; also Sun. **Address:** 4028-O Cox Rd 23060 **Location:** I-64, exit 178B, 0.5 mi e to Dominion Blvd, then just n; in Innsbrook Shoppes. **Parking:** on-site. **Cards:** AX, MC, VI.

MEXICO RESTAURANT

Mexican
$4-$11

Phone: 804/290-0400

The family-owned chain is a favorite of locals for reliable Mexican fare and a friendly atmosphere. Most opt for the expected combination dinners, but the more adventurous will be pleased by the delicious rendition of mole poblano sauce, a traditional sauce made from cocoa beans. Casual dress. **Bar:** Full bar. **Hours:** noon-10 pm. Closed major holidays. **Address:** 4040-G Cox Rd 23060 **Location:** I-64, exit 178B, just e; in Innsbrook Shoppes. **Parking:** on-site. **Cards:** AX, DC, DS, MC, VI.

OSAKA SUSHI & STEAK

Japanese
$8-$20

Phone: 804/364-8800   49

The decisions here are endless: Watch teppanyaki chefs cook at hibachi grills; watch sushi chefs prepare fine, fresh fish delicacies; or grab a booth and sample from teriyaki, gyoza dumplings, udon soup and more. Casual dress. **Bar:** Full bar. **Hours:** 11:30 am-3 & 5-10 pm, Fri & Sat-10:30 pm, Sun noon-10 pm. **Address:** 11674 W Broad St 23233 **Location:** Just w of jct I-64 and 295, on US 250; downtown Short Pump. **Parking:** on-site. **Cards:** AX, MC, VI.

GOOCHLAND

—— **WHERE TO DINE** ——

TANGLEWOOD ORDINARY COUNTRY RESTAURANT
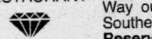
Regional American

Phone: 804/556-3284

Way out in the country, the homey log cabin is a quaint, charming place in which to enjoy home-style Southern cooking. All-you-can-eat specials are served family style. Casual dress. **Bar:** Full bar. **Reservations:** accepted. **Hours:** 5 pm-9 pm, Sun noon-8 pm; holiday hours vary. Closed: 12/25; also Mon-Wed. **Address:** 2210 River Rd W 23102-2705 **Location:** I-64, exit 173, 1 mi s to US 250, just w to SR 623, 5.2 mi s, then 9.5 mi w on SR 6. **Parking:** on-site.

HANOVER (See map and index starting on p. 848)

──────── **WHERE TO DINE** ────────

HOUNDSTOOTH CAFE

▽▽▽ ▽▽▽

Regional American
$4-$24

Phone: 804/537-5404 **44**

This is a very popular country spot for succulent Southern barbecue including ribs, pork, beef, and chicken as well as the freshest local seafood such as fried flounder and shrimp, famous crabcakes, and she-crab soup. Expect a wait. Casual dress. **Bar:** Beer & wine. **Hours:** 11:30 am-2 & 5-8 pm, Fri-9 pm, Sat 5 pm-9 pm. Closed: Sun & Mon. **Address:** 13271 Hanover Courthouse Rd 23069 **Location:** I-95, exit 92A, 5 mi e; at jct US 54 and 301. **Parking:** on-site. **Cards:** AX, DC, MC, VI.

MANAKIN

──────── **WHERE TO DINE** ────────

THE FOX HEAD INN

AAA

▽▽▽ ▽▽▽

French
$58-$68

Phone: 804/784-5126

The hunt room atmosphere is intimate and romantic in this restored country farmhouse. What better then to savor superb French cuisine that showcases fresh Virginia products, often from the chef's garden? The menu changes seasonally, and the wine list is extensive. Dressy casual. **Bar:** Full bar. **Reservations:** required. **Hours:** 5:30 pm-9:30 pm, Fri & Sat-10 pm. Closed: 12/25; also Mon & Tues. **Address:** 1840 Manakin Rd 23103 **Location:** I-64, exit 173, 1 mi s on SR 623, 1 mi w on US 250, then just s on SR 621. **Parking:** on-site. **Cards:** MC, VI.

MECHANICSVILLE pop. 30,464 (See map and index starting on p. 848)

──────── **WHERE TO STAY** ────────

HAMPTON INN

Book great rates at AAA.com

▽▽▽

Small-scale Hotel
$99-$159 All Year

Phone: (804)559-0559 **50**

Address: 7433 Bell Creek Rd 23111 **Location:** I-295, exit 37A (US 360 E) to Bell Creek Rd, just n. **Facility:** 80 one-bedroom standard units, some with whirlpools. 3 stories, interior corridors. *Bath:* combo or shower only. **Parking:** on-site. **Amenities:** high-speed Internet, voice mail, irons, hair dryers. **Pool(s):** heated indoor. **Leisure Activities:** exercise room. **Guest Services:** valet laundry, wireless Internet. **Business Services:** meeting rooms, fax. **Cards:** AX, DC, DS, MC, VI.

HOLIDAY INN
EXPRESS-RICHMOND-MECHANICSVILLE

Book at AAA.com

▽▽▽

Small-scale Hotel
$99-$149 All Year

Phone: (804)559-0022 **49**

Address: 7441 Bell Creek Rd 23111 **Location:** I-295, exit 37A (US 360 E) to Bell Creek Rd, just n. **Facility:** 105 units. 101 one-bedroom standard units. 4 one-bedroom suites. 5 stories, interior corridors. *Bath:* combo or shower only. **Parking:** on-site. **Amenities:** high-speed Internet, voice mail, irons, hair dryers. **Pool(s):** outdoor. **Leisure Activities:** exercise room. **Guest Services:** valet and coin laundry, wireless Internet. **Business Services:** fax. **Cards:** AX, DC, DS, MC, VI.

──────── **WHERE TO DINE** ────────

JOE'S INN

▽▽▽ ▽▽▽

American
$5-$10

Phone: 804/569-0411

An offshoot of the longtime Fan neighborhood favorite, this suburban outpost serves all of its specialties, including baked spaghetti and submarine sandwiches, in the enormous portions that made the place famous. Casual dress. **Bar:** Full bar. **Reservations:** accepted. **Hours:** 9 am-10 pm. Closed: 5/26, 11/27, 12/24, 12/25. **Address:** 7140 Mechanicsville Tpke 23111 **Location:** I-295, exit 37A (US 360 E), just w; in Spring Center. **Parking:** on-site. **Cards:** AX, CB, DC, DS, JC, MC, VI.

MEXICO RESTAURANT

▽▽▽

Mexican
$5-$15

Phone: 804/559-8126

The family-owned chain is a favorite of locals for reliable Mexican fare and a friendly atmosphere. Most opt for the expected combination dinners, but the more adventurous will be pleased by the delicious rendition of mole poblano sauce, a traditional sauce made from cocoa beans. Casual dress. **Bar:** Full bar. **Hours:** 11 am-10 pm, Fri-11 pm, Sat & Sun noon-10 pm. Closed major holidays; also 12/24. **Address:** 7162 Mechanicsville Tpke 23111 **Location:** I-295, exit 34A (US 360 E), just ne. **Parking:** on-site. **Cards:** AX, DC, DS, MC, VI.

PEKING RESTAURANT

▽▽▽ ▽▽▽

Chinese
$6-$23

Phone: 804/730-9898 **56**

The small chain is a local favorite for its wide selection of dishes, including such specialties as crispy duck, velvet shrimp and dry sauteed green beans. The atmosphere is refined. Casual dress. **Bar:** Full bar. **Reservations:** accepted. **Hours:** 11:30 am-2:15 & 4:30-9:30 pm, Fri-10:15 pm, Sat 4:30 pm-10:15 pm. Closed major holidays. **Address:** 7100 Mechanicsville Tpke 23111 **Location:** I-295, exit 37A (US 360 E), 0.5 mi e. **Parking:** on-site. **Cards:** AX, MC, VI.

MIDLOTHIAN   (See map and index starting on p. 848)

---------- **WHERE TO STAY** ----------

HAMPTON INN-RICHMOND-SOUTH WEST-HULL
STREET *Book great rates at AAA.com*

Phone: (804)675-0000 [64]

WWWW

Small-scale Hotel
$139-$149 All Year

Address: 3620 Price Club Blvd 23112 **Location:** On Hull Street Rd (US 360), 5 mi w of jct SR 150. **Facility:** 68 one-bedroom standard units, some with whirlpools. 3 stories, interior corridors. *Bath:* combo or shower only. **Parking:** on-site. **Amenities:** high-speed Internet, voice mail, irons, hair dryers. **Pool(s):** heated indoor. **Leisure Activities:** exercise room. **Guest Services:** valet laundry. **Business Services:** meeting rooms, fax. **Cards:** AX, DC, DS, MC, VI.

HOLIDAY INN EXPRESS HOTEL &
SUITES-BRANDERMILL *Book at AAA.com*

Phone: (804)744-7303 [65]

WWWW

Small-scale Hotel
$129-$169 All Year

Address: 5030 W Village Green Dr 23112 **Location:** From SR 288, just w on Hull Street Rd. **Facility:** 96 one-bedroom standard units, some with whirlpools. 4 stories, interior corridors. *Bath:* combo or shower only. **Parking:** on-site. **Amenities:** high-speed Internet, dual phone lines, voice mail, irons, hair dryers. **Leisure Activities:** exercise room. **Guest Services:** valet and coin laundry. **Business Services:** meeting rooms, business center. **Cards:** AX, DC, DS, MC, VI.

SUPER 8 MOTEL   *Book great rates at AAA.com*

Phone: 804-276-3900 [63]

AAA [SAVE]

WWW WW

Small-scale Hotel
Rates not provided

Address: 10300 Hull St Rd 23112 **Location:** US 360, 4 mi e of SR 288; 5 mi w of US 150 (Chippenham Pkwy). **Facility:** 41 one-bedroom standard units, some with whirlpools. 2 stories (no elevator), interior corridors. **Parking:** on-site. **Amenities:** high-speed Internet, irons, hair dryers. **Guest Services:** wireless Internet. **Business Services:** fax. **Free Special Amenities: continental breakfast and high-speed Internet.**

---------- **WHERE TO DINE** ----------

ANDRE'S GRILLE

Phone: 804/276-8677 [67]

WWW

American
$7-$20

Hidden in a tiny shopping center, the restaurant shouldn't be overlooked. Burgundy walls and rich wooden booths illuminated by candle sconces highlight the cozy eatery's warmth. Widely varied dishes please nearly every palate and budget. Pasta, sandwiches, chops and curry dishes reflect influences from Asian and Continental cooking. Casual dress. **Bar:** Full bar. **Hours:** 11:30 am-2:30 & 5-9:30 pm, Sat from 5 pm, Sun 11 am-2:30 & 5-9:30 pm. Closed: 11/27, 12/25; also Mon. **Address:** 3511 Courthouse Rd 23236 **Location:** Jct Hull Street Rd; in Rockwood Plaza. **Parking:** on-site. **Cards:** MC, VI.

BONEFISH GRILL

Phone: 804/639-2747 [70]

WWWW

Seafood
$14-$25

Fish is the house specialty, and the menu and nightly specials offer a variety of choices. Well-prepared food is cooked to perfection. Service is casual in nature, and the staff is skilled and attentive. Casual dress. **Bar:** Full bar. **Reservations:** accepted. **Hours:** 4 pm-10:30 pm, Fri & Sat-11:30 pm, Sun-10 pm. Closed: 11/27, 12/25. **Address:** 6081 Harbour Park Dr 23112 **Location:** 1 mi w of SR 288 via Hull Street Rd/US 360. **Parking:** on-site. **Cards:** AX, CB, DC, DS, JC, MC, VI.

BOOKBINDER'S GRILL

Phone: 804/379-3338 [64]

WWWW

Seafood
$9-$30

Inspired by the historic landmark restaurant in Philadelphia, this more modern interpretation presents a large menu of fresh seafood, steaks and more in a crisply styled spot. Casual dress. **Bar:** Full bar. **Reservations:** accepted. **Hours:** 11:30 am-2:30 & 5-10 pm, Sat from 5 pm, Sun 5 pm-9 pm. Closed major holidays. **Address:** 1244 Alverser Plaza 23113 **Location:** Just nw of jct Midlothian Tpke and Huguenut Rd on Alverser Rd. **Parking:** on-site. **Cards:** AX, MC, VI.

BOTTEGA BISTRO

Phone: 804/379-9899 [62]

WWWW

American
$6-$27

A cozy gas-light lantern ambience envelops the eclectic, American-style bistro, which offers an appealing menu of innovative beef, pasta, salad, fish and veal preparations, as well as pizza made in a wood-burning oven. During nice weather, the iron tables lining the sidewalk are a popular seating option. Casual dress. **Bar:** Full bar. **Reservations:** suggested. **Hours:** 11:30 am-3 & 5-10 pm, Fri & Sat-11 pm, Sun 5 pm-9 pm; Sunday brunch 11 am-2 pm. Closed: 1/1, 11/27, 12/25. **Address:** 11400 W Huguenot Rd 23113 **Location:** Jct Midlothian Tpke, 1.3 mi n; in The Shoppes at Bellgrade. **Parking:** on-site. **Cards:** AX, CB, DC, DS, MC, VI.

(See map and index starting on p. 848)

GLORY DAYS GRILL, HARBOURSIDE   **Phone:** 804/608-8350

American
$7-$18
Lending to the casual restaurant's sports-themed atmosphere are memorabilia decorating the dining area and 25 TVs with control centers at each table and booth. Food selections range from wings and ribs to seafood, beef and pasta dishes. Casual dress. **Bar:** Full bar. **Hours:** 4 pm-midnight, Fri & Sat from 11:30 am, Sun 11:30 am-11 pm. Closed: 11/27, 12/25. **Address:** 6151 Harbourside Centre Loop 23112 **Location:** On US 360/Hull Street Rd, 1 mi w SR 288. **Parking:** on-site. **Cards:** AX, DS, MC, VI.

PASTA LUNA   **Phone:** 804/763-3211   (69)

Italian
$6-$20
Large portions of Italian dishes are served family style in sizzling copper skillets that invite sharing and sampling. Among traditional specialties are salads, pasta, veal and an antipasto plate that includes a mix of marinated vegetables. Casual dress. **Bar:** Full bar. **Reservations:** accepted. **Hours:** 11:30 am-3 & 4:30-10 pm, Fri 11:30 am-3 & 3:30-11 pm, Sat 11:30 am-2 & 4-11 pm, Sun 11:30 am-2 & 4:30-9 pm. Closed major holidays. **Address:** 5000 Commonwealth Centre Pkwy 23112 **Location:** From SR 288, just w on Hull Street Rd (US 360), just s. **Parking:** on-site. **Cards:** AX, DC, DS, MC, VI.

PEKING   **Phone:** 804/794-1799   (66)

Chinese
$9-$16
Locals frequent the small chain for such specialties as crispy duck, velvet shrimp and dry-sauteed green beans. The atmosphere is refined. Casual dress. **Bar:** Full bar. **Hours:** 11:30 am-2 & 5-9 pm, Fri-10:30 pm, Sat 5 pm-10:30 pm, Sun 11:30 am-2 & 5-9:30 pm. Closed major holidays. **Address:** 13132 Midlothian Tpke 23113 **Location:** 1.6 mi w of jct Huguenot/Courthouse rds; in Village Marketplace. **Parking:** on-site. **Cards:** AX, MC, VI.

PESCADOS   **Phone:** 804/379-7121   (65)
(AAA)

Latino
$15-$25
Latin inspiration punctuates seafood dishes on the suburban eatery's innovative menu. Daily trips to local markets to find the freshest meats, vegetables and fruits pay off in the flavorful fare. Everything is made from scratch, and the chefs happily boast of their desire to suit the dietary needs of their clientele. The avocado taco dessert, which is likened to a Latin Key lime pie, is not to be missed. Casual dress. **Bar:** Full bar. **Hours:** 5 pm-10 pm. Closed: 7/4, 11/27, 12/24, 12/25; also Sun. **Address:** 13126 Midlothian Tpke 23113 **Location:** 1.6 mi w of Huguenot and Courthouse rds. **Parking:** on-site. **Cards:** AX, DS, MC, VI.

RIVER CITY DINER   **Phone:** 804/897-9518

American
$5-$11
The lively diner is likely to make you nostalgic for poodle skirts and sock hops. Kitschy decor and shiny chrome enliven the dining room. Order from the all-day breakfast menu or enjoy old favorites such as burgers, sandwiches and soda fountain treats. Casual dress. **Bar:** Full bar. **Hours:** 8 am-10 pm, Fri & Sat-11 pm, Sun & Mon-9 pm. Closed: 11/27, 12/25. **Address:** 11430 W Huguenot Rd 23113 **Location:** 1.4 mi n of jct Midlothian Tpke; in Shoppes at Bellgrade Plantation. **Parking:** on-site. **Cards:** MC, VI.

RUTH'S CHRIS STEAK HOUSE   **Phone:** 804/378-0600   (63)

Steak House
$20-$40
The main fare is steak, which is prepared from several cuts of prime beef and cooked to perfection, but the menu also lists lamb, chicken and seafood dishes. Guests should come hungry because the side dishes, which are among the a la carte offerings, could make a meal in themselves. Dressy casual. Entertainment. **Bar:** Full bar. **Reservations:** suggested. **Hours:** 5 pm-10 pm, Mon-9 pm, Fri & Sat-11 pm, Sun 4 pm-9 pm. Closed: 1/1, 11/27, 12/25; also Super Bowl Sun. **Address:** 11500 W Huguenot Rd 23113 **Location:** 1.4 mi n of jct Midlothian Tpke; in Shoppes at Bellgrade Plantation. **Parking:** on-site. **Cards:** AX, DC, DS, MC, VI.

SAIGON GOURMET RESTAURANT   **Phone:** 804/745-0199   (68)

Vietnamese
$5-$14
Tinted in soothing shades of green, the calming dining room is a great spot to sample the fresh, flavorful tastes of Vietnam. Favorites include grilled meats on rice noodles, pho noodle soups, rice paper rolls and peppery hot and sour soup. Casual dress. **Hours:** 11 am-3 & 4:30-9:30 pm, Fri-10:30 pm, Sat 11:30 am-10:30 pm, Sun 11:30 am-9 pm, Mon 5 pm-9:30 pm. **Address:** 11033 Hull St Rd 23113 **Location:** 0.5 mi w of Courthouse Rd. **Parking:** on-site. **Cards:** AX, DS, MC, VI.

SOYA SUSHI BAR & GRILL   **Phone:** 804/622-9887

Japanese
$7-$20
Difficult choices start when guests enter: Sit at the sushi bar or at one of the hibachi tables to watch the chefs in action? The menu, heavy on sushi selections, also includes such tempting specialties as teriyaki, udon noodles and soya bento. Casual dress. **Bar:** Beer only. **Hours:** 11 am-2 & 5-9 pm, Sat 5 pm-10 pm. Closed major holidays; also Sun. **Address:** 4508 Commonwealth Centre Pkwy 23112 **Location:** just sw of jct US 360 and SR 288. **Parking:** on-site. **Cards:** AX, DS, MC, VI.
CALL &M

SANDSTON   (See map and index starting on p. 848)

──── WHERE TO STAY ────

CLARION RICHMOND AIRPORT   *Book great rates at AAA.com*
Phone: (804)222-6450   59

AAA SAVE

Small-scale Hotel
$89-$139 All Year

Address: 5203 Williamsburg Rd 23150 **Location:** I-64, exit 195, 1.5 mi s to Williamsburg Rd, then just e. **Facility:** 116 units. 110 one-bedroom standard units, some with efficiencies (no utensils) and/or whirlpools. 6 one-bedroom suites with kitchens (no utensils). 3-6 stories, interior/exterior corridors. *Bath:* combo or shower only. **Parking:** on-site. **Amenities:** high-speed Internet, dual phone lines, voice mail, irons, hair dryers. **Pool(s):** outdoor. **Leisure Activities:** exercise room. **Guest Services:** valet and coin laundry, area transportation-within 10 mi, wireless Internet. **Business Services:** conference facilities, business center. **Cards:** AX, CB, DC, DS, JC, MC, VI. **Free Special Amenities: local telephone calls and high-speed Internet.**

COMFORT INN RICHMOND AIRPORT   *Book at AAA.com*
Phone: (804)226-1800   56

Small-scale Hotel
$80-$100 All Year

Address: 5240 Airport Square Ln 23150 **Location:** I-64, exit 197A (Sandston-RIC Airport), 0.3 mi s to Williamsburg Rd, then 1 mi w. **Facility:** 61 one-bedroom standard units. 2 stories (no elevator), interior corridors. *Bath:* combo or shower only. **Amenities:** voice mail, irons, hair dryers. **Leisure Activities:** exercise room. **Guest Services:** valet laundry, wireless Internet. **Cards:** AX, DC, DS, MC, VI.

COURTYARD BY MARRIOTT-RICHMOND AIRPORT   *Book great rates at AAA.com*
Phone: 804/652-0500   57

AAA SAVE

Small-scale Hotel
$144-$176 All Year

Address: 5400 Williamsburg Rd 23150 **Location:** I-64, exit 197A (Sandston-RIC Airport), just s to Williamsburg Rd E, then 1 mi w. **Facility:** Smoke free premises. 142 units. 136 one-bedroom standard units, some with whirlpools. 6 one-bedroom suites. 3 stories, interior corridors. *Bath:* combo or shower only. **Parking:** on-site. **Amenities:** high-speed Internet, dual phone lines, voice mail, irons, hair dryers. **Pool(s):** heated indoor. **Leisure Activities:** whirlpool, exercise room. **Guest Services:** valet and coin laundry, wireless Internet. **Business Services:** meeting rooms, business center. **Cards:** AX, DC, DS, JC, MC, VI. **Free Special Amenities: newspaper and high-speed Internet.**

> **COURTYARD** Marriott
>
> **AAA Benefit:**
> Members save 5% off of the best available rate.

DOUBLETREE RICHMOND AIRPORT   *Book great rates at AAA.com*
Phone: 804/226-6400   60

AAA SAVE

Small-scale Hotel
Rates not provided

Address: 5501 Eubank Rd 23150 **Location:** I-64, exit 197A (Sandston-RIC Airport), 1 mi s. **Facility:** 160 units. 38 one-bedroom standard units. 122 one-bedroom suites. 5 stories, interior corridors. *Bath:* combo or shower only. **Parking:** on-site. **Amenities:** video games (fee), high-speed Internet, dual phone lines, voice mail, irons, hair dryers. **Pool(s):** outdoor. **Leisure Activities:** whirlpool, exercise room, volleyball. **Dining:** Wings, see separate listing. **Guest Services:** valet laundry, area transportation-within 3 mi, wireless Internet. **Business Services:** conference facilities, business center. **Free Special Amenities: newspaper and high-speed Internet.**

HAMPTON INN-RICHMOND AIRPORT
Phone: 804/222-8200   55

Small-scale Hotel
Rates not provided

Address: 5300 Airport Square Ln 23150 **Location:** I-64, exit 197A (Sandston-RIC Airport), just s to Williamsburg Rd, then 1 mi w. **Facility:** 124 one-bedroom standard units. 4 stories, interior corridors. **Parking:** on-site. **Amenities:** video games (fee), high-speed Internet, voice mail, irons, hair dryers. *Some Fee:* DVD players. **Pool(s):** outdoor. **Leisure Activities:** exercise room. **Guest Services:** valet laundry, wireless Internet. **Business Services:** meeting rooms, business center.

HOMEWOOD SUITES RICHMOND AIRPORT   *Book at AAA.com*
Phone: (804)737-1600   53

Small-scale Hotel
$169-$179 All Year

Address: 5996 Audubon Dr 23150 **Location:** I-64, exit 197A (Sandston-RIC Airport), just s. **Facility:** 125 units. 52 one-bedroom standard units with kitchens. 72 one- and 1 two-bedroom suites with kitchens, some with whirlpools. 6 stories, interior corridors. *Bath:* combo or shower only. **Parking:** on-site. **Terms:** 2-5 night minimum stay - seasonal, cancellation fee imposed. **Amenities:** high-speed Internet, dual phone lines, voice mail, irons, hair dryers. **Pool(s):** heated indoor. **Leisure Activities:** whirlpool, exercise room, basketball. **Guest Services:** valet and coin laundry, area transportation, wireless Internet. **Business Services:** meeting rooms, business center. **Cards:** AX, CB, DC, DS, JC, MC, VI.

RED ROOF INN   *Book great rates at AAA.com*
Phone: (804)440-5770   58

AAA SAVE

Motel
$49-$79 All Year

Address: 5209 Williamsburg Rd 23150 **Location:** I-64, exit 195, 1.5 mi s to Williamsburg Rd, then just e. **Facility:** 105 one-bedroom standard units. 3 stories, exterior corridors. **Parking:** on-site. **Amenities:** high-speed Internet, voice mail, irons, hair dryers. **Guest Services:** coin laundry, area transportation-within 10 mi, wireless Internet. **Cards:** AX, CB, DC, DS, JC, MC, VI. **Free Special Amenities: local telephone calls and newspaper.**

(See map and index starting on p. 848)

WINGATE INN RICHMOND AIRPORT   *Book at AAA.com*   Phone: (804)222-1499   54

Small-scale Hotel
$129 All Year

Address: 491 International Centre Dr 23150 **Location:** I-64, exit 197A (Sandston-RIC Airport), just s to Audobon Dr, then just n. **Facility:** 100 one-bedroom standard units. 4 stories, interior corridors. *Bath:* combo or shower only. **Parking:** on-site. **Amenities:** video games (fee), high-speed Internet, dual phone lines, voice mail, safes, irons, hair dryers. **Pool(s):** heated indoor. **Leisure Activities:** whirlpool, exercise room. **Guest Services:** valet laundry, wireless Internet. **Business Services:** meeting rooms, business center. **Cards:** AX, DC, DS, MC, VI.

──────── **WHERE TO DINE** ────────

MEXICO RESTAURANT   Phone: 804/226-2388

Mexican
$4-$7

The family-owned chain is a favorite of locals for reliable Mexican fare and a friendly atmosphere. Most opt for the expected combination dinners, but the more adventurous will be pleased by the delicious rendition of mole poblano sauce, a traditional sauce made from cocoa beans. Casual dress. **Bar:** Full bar. **Hours:** 11 am-10 pm, Fri-11 pm, Sat & Sun noon-10 pm. Closed major holidays. **Address:** 5213 Williamsburg Rd 23150 **Location:** I-64, exit 195, 1.5 mi s to Williamsburg Rd, then just e. **Parking:** on-site. **Cards:** AX, DC, DS, MC, VI.

WINGS   *Menu on AAA.com*   Phone: 804/226-6400   59

American
$5-$20

The house specialties are endless: New York sirloin, chicken cordon bleu, seafood sampler, crabcakes and a variety of dessert. Glass and greenery prevail, lending to a contemporary ambience. The buffet breakfast and pasta bar are available Monday-Friday. Casual dress. **Bar:** Full bar. **Reservations:** accepted. **Hours:** 6 am-11 pm. **Address:** 5501 Eubank Rd 23150 **Location:** I-64, exit 197A (Sandston-RIC Airport), 1 mi s; in DoubleTree Richmond Airport. **Parking:** on-site. **Cards:** AX, DC, DS, MC, VI.

Capitol Square / © Lynn Seldon / Danita Delimont Stock Photography

This ends listings for the Richmond Vicinity.
The following page resumes the alphabetical listings of cities in Virginia.

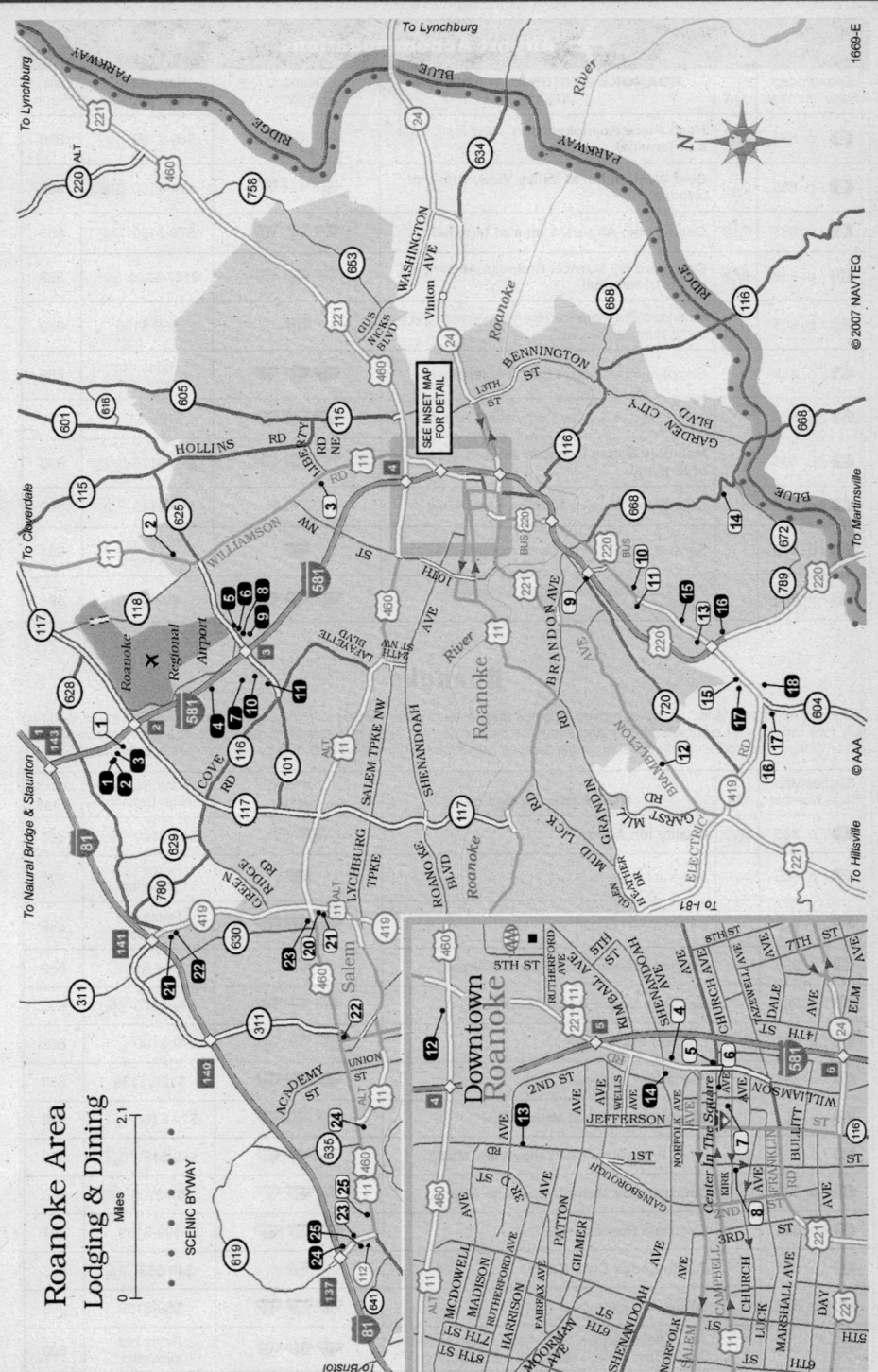

✈ Airport Accommodations

Spotter/Map Page Number	OA	ROANOKE REGIONAL-WOODRUM FIELD	Diamond Rating	Rate Range High Season	Listing Page
9 / p. 885	AAA	Hyatt Place Roanoke/Valley View Mall, 1 mi s of terminal	♦♦♦	$89-$189 SAVE	890
8 / p. 885	AAA	Best Western Inn at Valley View, 1 mi s of terminal	♦♦♦	$74-$180 SAVE	888
6 / p. 885	AAA	Comfort Inn Airport, 1 mi s of terminal	♦♦♦	$79-$190 SAVE	888
10 / p. 885	AAA	Courtyard By Marriott Roanoke Airport, 1.4 mi sw of terminal	♦♦♦	$167-$205 SAVE	888
4 / p. 885		Extended StayAmerica Roanoke-Airport, 1.4 mi sw of terminal	♦	$68-$135	889
3 / p. 885		Hampton Inn Airport, 1.5 mi n of terminal	♦♦♦	Rates not provided	889
7 / p. 885		Holiday Inn Roanoke, 1.5 mi sw of terminal	♦♦♦	$129-$139	889
5 / p. 885	AAA	MainStay Suites Roanoke Airport, 1.1 mi s of terminal	♦♦♦	$99-$175 SAVE	890
1 / p. 885	AAA	Quality Inn Airport, 1.5 mi n of terminal	♦♦	$59-$149 SAVE	890
2 / p. 885		Super 8 Motel, 1.4 mi sw of terminal	♦	Rates not provided	891
11 / p. 885		Wyndham Roanoke Hotel, 1.5 mi sw of terminal	♦♦♦	$99-$169	891

Roanoke

This index helps you "spot" where approved lodgings and restaurants are located on the corresponding detailed maps. Lodging daily rate range is for comparison only and show the property's high season. Restaurant rate range is a combination of lunch and/or dinner. Turn to the listing page for more detailed rate information and consult display ads for special promotions.

Spotter/Map Page Number	OA	ROANOKE - Lodgings	Diamond Rating	Rate Range High Season	Listing Page
1 / p. 885	AAA	Quality Inn Airport	♦♦	$59-$149 SAVE	890
2 / p. 885		Super 8 Motel	♦	Rates not provided	891
3 / p. 885		Hampton Inn Airport	♦♦♦	Rates not provided	889
4 / p. 885		Extended StayAmerica Roanoke-Airport	♦	$68-$135	889
5 / p. 885	AAA	MainStay Suites Roanoke Airport	♦♦♦	$99-$175 SAVE	890
6 / p. 885	AAA	Comfort Inn Airport	♦♦♦	$79-$190 SAVE	888
7 / p. 885		Holiday Inn Roanoke	♦♦♦	$129-$139	889
8 / p. 885	AAA	Best Western Inn at Valley View	♦♦♦	$74-$180 SAVE	888
9 / p. 885	AAA	Hyatt Place Roanoke/Valley View Mall	♦♦♦	$89-$189 SAVE	890
10 / p. 885	AAA	Courtyard By Marriott Roanoke Airport	♦♦♦	$167-$205 SAVE	888
11 / p. 885		Wyndham Roanoke Hotel	♦♦♦	$99-$169	891
12 / p. 885	AAA	Econo Lodge Civic Center	♦	$49-$89 SAVE	888
13 / p. 885		Holiday Inn Express	♦♦♦	$89-$159	889
14 / p. 885		The Hotel Roanoke & Conference Center, A DoubleTree Hotel - see color ad p 890	♦♦♦	Rates not provided	890

Spotter/Map Page Number	OA	ROANOKE - Lodgings (continued)	Diamond Rating	Rate Range High Season	Listing Page
15 / p. 885		Colony House Motor Lodge	◆◆	$63-$75	888
16 / p. 885	AAA	**Quality Inn/Tanglewood**	◇◇◇	$65-$75 SAVE	890
17 / p. 885	AAA	**Holiday Inn Hotel Tanglewood**	◆◆	$99-$149 SAVE	889
18 / p. 885		Sleep Inn Tanglewood	◆◆	$56-$140	891
		ROANOKE - Restaurants			
1 / p. 885		El Toreo	◆	$5-$11	892
2 / p. 885		Coach and Four	◆◆◆	$10-$21	891
3 / p. 885		New Yorker Delicatessen and Restaurant	◆	$4-$10	893
4 / p. 885		The Regency Room	◆◆◆	$10-$35	893
5 / p. 885		Arzu	◆◆◆	$8-$30	891
6 / p. 885		Green Dolphin Grille	◆◆	$7-$20	892
7 / p. 885		Wertz's Restaurant	◆◆◆	$8-$25	893
8 / p. 885		Swagat Indian Cuisine	◆◆	$7-$18	893
9 / p. 885	AAA	**The Roanoker Restaurant**	◆	$5-$11	893
10 / p. 885		Stephen's	◆◆	$18-$30	893
11 / p. 885		The Library Restaurant	◆◆◆	$20-$40	892
12 / p. 885		Luigi's	◆◆◆	$11-$27	892
13 / p. 885	AAA	**Montano's International Gourmet**	◆◆	$7-$20	892
14 / p. 885		Brugh Tavern	◆◆◆	$9-$25	891
15 / p. 885		Carlos Brazilian International Cuisine	◆◆◆	$7-$28	891
16 / p. 885		419 West	◆◆◆	$9-$25	891
17 / p. 885		Szechuan Restaurant	◆◆	$5-$14	893
		SALEM - Lodgings			
21 / p. 885	AAA	**Quality Inn Roanoke/Salem**	◆◆◆	Rates not provided SAVE	895
22 / p. 885	AAA	**Baymont Inn Roanoke-Salem**	◆◆◆	$89-$99 SAVE	895
23 / p. 885	AAA	**Days Inn**	◆◆◆	Rates not provided SAVE	895
24 / p. 885	AAA	**Econo Lodge-Roanoke/Salem**	◆◆	$34-$99 SAVE	895
25 / p. 885	AAA	**Comfort Inn**	◆◆◆	$89-$94 SAVE	895
		SALEM - Restaurants			
20 / p. 885		Sake House	◆◆	$6-$20	896
21 / p. 885		Picaso's Italian Grill	◆◆	$7-$20	896
22 / p. 885		Mac-and-Bob's Restaurant	◆◆	$6-$20	896
23 / p. 885		El Rodeo	◆	$5-$11	896
24 / p. 885		Fast Freddy's	◆	$4-$15	896
25 / p. 885	AAA	**Mamma Maria's Italian Restaurant**	◆	$6-$20	896

ROANOKE pop. 94,911 (See map and index starting on p. 885)

──────── WHERE TO STAY ────────

BEST WESTERN INN AT VALLEY VIEW
Book great rates at AAA.com
Phone: (540)362-2400 **8**

 (AAA) [SAVE]
▽▽▽
Small-scale Hotel
$74-$180 All Year

Address: 5050 Valley View Blvd 24012 **Location:** I-581, exit 3E, just e, then just s via shopping center exit. **Facility:** 85 one-bedroom standard units. 3 stories, interior corridors. *Bath:* combo or shower only. **Parking:** on-site. **Amenities:** high-speed Internet, irons, hair dryers. **Pool(s):** heated indoor. **Guest Services:** valet laundry, wireless Internet. **Business Services:** meeting rooms, PC. **Cards:** AX, CB, DC, DS, JC, MC, VI. **Free Special Amenities: continental breakfast and high-speed Internet.**

AAA Benefit: Members save 10% everyday, plus an exclusive frequent stay program.

COLONY HOUSE MOTOR LODGE
Phone: 540/345-0411 **15**

▽▽ ▽▽
Motel
$63-$75 All Year

Address: 3560 Franklin Rd SW 24014 **Location:** I-581/US 220, exit Franklin Rd/Salem, 0.5 mi n on US 220 business route. **Facility:** 67 one-bedroom standard units, some with whirlpools. 2 stories (no elevator), interior/exterior corridors. **Parking:** on-site. **Terms:** 3 day cancellation notice. **Amenities:** *Some:* irons. **Pool(s):** outdoor. **Leisure Activities:** exercise room. **Guest Services:** valet and coin laundry, wireless Internet. **Business Services:** meeting rooms, business center. **Cards:** AX, CB, DC, DS, MC, VI.

COMFORT INN AIRPORT
Book great rates at AAA.com
Phone: (540)527-2020 **6**

(AAA) [SAVE]
▽▽ ▽▽
Small-scale Hotel
$79-$190 All Year

Address: 5070 Valley View Blvd 24012 **Location:** I-81, exit 143 to I-581, exit 3, e to Hershberger Rd. **Facility:** 96 one-bedroom standard units. 4 stories, interior corridors. *Bath:* combo or shower only. **Parking:** on-site. **Amenities:** voice mail, irons, hair dryers. *Some:* DVD players, CD players, high-speed Internet. **Pool(s):** outdoor. **Leisure Activities:** exercise room. **Guest Services:** coin laundry, wireless Internet. **Business Services:** meeting rooms, PC. **Cards:** AX, CB, DC, DS, JC, MC, VI. **Free Special Amenities: continental breakfast and high-speed Internet.**

COUNTRY INN & SUITES BY CARLSON
Book at AAA.com
Phone: 540/366-5678

▽▽▽
Small-scale Hotel
Rates not provided

Address: 7860 Plantation Rd 24019 **Location:** I-81, exit 146, just se on SR 115. **Facility:** 77 one-bedroom standard units, some with whirlpools. 2-3 stories, interior corridors. **Parking:** on-site. **Amenities:** high-speed Internet, voice mail, irons, hair dryers. **Pool(s):** indoor. **Leisure Activities:** whirlpool, exercise room. *Fee:* game room. **Guest Services:** coin laundry, wireless Internet. **Business Services:** meeting rooms, PC, fax (fee).

COURTYARD BY MARRIOTT ROANOKE AIRPORT
Book great rates at AAA.com
Phone: 540/563-5002 **10**

(AAA) [SAVE]
▽▽ ▽▽
Small-scale Hotel
$168-$205 All Year

Address: 3301 Ordway Dr 24017 **Location:** I-581, exit 3W, just w to Ordway Dr. **Facility:** Smoke free premises. 135 one-bedroom standard units, some with whirlpools. 4 stories, interior corridors. *Bath:* combo or shower only. **Parking:** on-site. **Amenities:** video games, high-speed Internet, voice mail, irons, hair dryers. **Pool(s):** heated indoor. **Leisure Activities:** whirlpool, sun deck, picnic & grill area, exercise room. **Guest Services:** valet and coin laundry, airport transportation-Roanoke Municipal Airport, area transportation-within 5 mi, wireless Internet. **Business Services:** meeting rooms, business center. **Cards:** AX, DC, DS, JC, MC, VI. **Free Special Amenities: newspaper and high-speed Internet.**

AAA Benefit: Members save 5% off of the best available rate.

DAYS INN
Book great rates at AAA.com
Phone: 540/366-0341

(AAA) [SAVE]
▽▽ ▽▽
Small-scale Hotel
Rates not provided

Address: 8118 Plantation Rd 24019 **Location:** I-81, exit 146, just e on SR 115. **Facility:** 121 one-bedroom standard units, some with whirlpools. 2 stories (no elevator), interior/exterior corridors. **Parking:** on-site. **Amenities:** video library (fee), high-speed Internet, hair dryers. **Pool(s):** outdoor. **Leisure Activities:** exercise room. **Guest Services:** valet laundry, wireless Internet. **Business Services:** meeting rooms, PC.

ECONO LODGE CIVIC CENTER
Book great rates at AAA.com
Phone: (540)343-2413 **12**

(AAA) [SAVE]
▽

Motel
$49-$89 All Year

Address: 308 Orange Ave 24016 **Location:** I-581, exit 4E, just e on US 460. Located in a commercial area. **Facility:** 46 one-bedroom standard units. 2 stories (no elevator), exterior corridors. **Parking:** on-site. **Business Services:** fax (fee). **Cards:** AX, DS, MC, VI.

(See map and index starting on p. 885)

EXTENDED STAYAMERICA ROANOKE-AIRPORT   *Book at AAA.com*   Phone: (540)366-3216   4

Motel
$68-$135 All Year

Address: 2705 W Frontage Rd NW 24017 **Location:** I-581, exit 3W, just w to Ordway Dr, then 0.4 mi n via service frontage road. **Facility:** 90 one-bedroom standard units with kitchens. 3 stories, exterior corridors. *Bath:* combo or shower only. **Parking:** on-site. **Terms:** office hours 7 am-11 pm. **Amenities:** voice mail, irons. **Guest Services:** coin laundry, wireless Internet. **Business Services:** fax (fee). **Cards:** AX, DC, DS, JC, MC, VI.

FAIRFIELD INN & SUITES ROANOKE NORTH   *Book great rates at AAA.com*   Phone: 540/362-4200

Small-scale Hotel
$99-$120 All Year

Address: 7944 Plantation Rd 24019 **Location:** I-81, exit 146, just e. **Facility:** Smoke free premises. 76 one-bedroom standard units, some with whirlpools. 4 stories, interior corridors. *Bath:* combo or shower only. **Parking:** on-site. **Amenities:** video games, high-speed Internet, dual phone lines, voice mail, irons, hair dryers. *Some:* CD players. **Pool(s):** outdoor. **Leisure Activities:** whirlpool, exercise room. **Guest Services:** valet and coin laundry, wireless Internet. **Business Services:** meeting rooms, business center. **Cards:** AX, DS, MC, VI.

AAA Benefit:
Members save 5% off of the best available rate.

HAMPTON INN AIRPORT   *Book great rates at AAA.com*   Phone: 540/265-2600   3

Small-scale Hotel
Rates not provided

Address: 6621 Thirlane Rd NW 24019 **Location:** I-581, exit 2S, just s on SR 117 (Peters Creek Rd), then just w. **Facility:** 79 one-bedroom standard units, some with whirlpools. 2 stories (no elevator), exterior corridors. *Bath:* combo or shower only. **Parking:** on-site. **Amenities:** video games, high-speed Internet, voice mail, irons, hair dryers. **Pool(s):** outdoor. **Leisure Activities:** exercise room. **Guest Services:** coin laundry, wireless Internet. **Business Services:** meeting rooms, business center.

HAMPTON INN ROANOKE/HOLLINS   *Book great rates at AAA.com*   Phone: 540/563-5656

Small-scale Hotel
Rates not provided

Address: 7922 Plantation Rd 24019 **Location:** I-81, exit 146, 0.3 mi e on SR 115. **Facility:** 60 one-bedroom standard units, some with whirlpools. 3 stories, interior corridors. *Bath:* combo or shower only. **Parking:** on-site. **Amenities:** video games, high-speed Internet, voice mail, irons, hair dryers. **Pool(s):** indoor. **Leisure Activities:** exercise room. **Guest Services:** coin laundry, wireless Internet. **Business Services:** meeting rooms, fax (fee).

HOLIDAY INN EXPRESS   *Book at AAA.com*   Phone: (540)982-0100   13

Small-scale Hotel
$89-$159 All Year

Address: 815 Gainsboro Rd 24016 **Location:** I-581, exit 4W, just w, then just s. **Facility:** 97 one-bedroom standard units, some with whirlpools. 3 stories, interior corridors. *Bath:* combo or shower only. **Parking:** on-site. **Amenities:** high-speed Internet, irons, hair dryers. **Pool(s):** outdoor. **Guest Services:** valet laundry, wireless Internet. **Business Services:** business center. **Cards:** AX, CB, DC, DS, JC, MC, VI.

HOLIDAY INN HOTEL TANGLEWOOD   *Book great rates at AAA.com*   Phone: 540/774-4400   17

Small-scale Hotel
$99-$149 All Year

Address: 4468 Starkey Rd 24018 **Location:** I-581, exit Franklin Rd/Salem, 0.8 mi n on SR 419. **Facility:** 196 one-bedroom standard units, some with whirlpools. 5 stories, interior corridors. *Bath:* combo or shower only. **Parking:** on-site. **Amenities:** voice mail, irons, hair dryers. **Pool(s):** outdoor. **Leisure Activities:** exercise room. **Guest Services:** valet and coin laundry, airport transportation-Roanoke Regional-Woodrum Field Airport, area transportation-within 5 mi, wireless Internet. **Business Services:** conference facilities, business center. **Cards:** AX, CB, DC, DS, JC, MC, VI. **Free Special Amenities:** preferred room (subject to availability with advance reservations) and high-speed Internet.

HOLIDAY INN ROANOKE   *Book at AAA.com*   Phone: (540)362-4500   7

Small-scale Hotel
$129-$139 All Year

Address: 3315 Ordway Dr 24017 **Location:** I-581, exit 3W, just w to Ordway Dr, then 0.6 mi n via service road. **Facility:** 153 one-bedroom standard units. 5 stories, interior corridors. *Bath:* combo or shower only. **Parking:** on-site. **Terms:** check-in 4 pm. **Amenities:** high-speed Internet, voice mail, irons, hair dryers. **Pool(s):** heated indoor/outdoor. **Leisure Activities:** whirlpool, exercise room, basketball, horseshoes, volleyball. **Guest Services:** valet and coin laundry, area transportation, wireless Internet. **Business Services:** conference facilities, business center. **Cards:** AX, CB, DC, DS, JC, MC, VI.

(See map and index starting on p. 885)

THE HOTEL ROANOKE & CONFERENCE CENTER, A DOUBLETREE HOTEL　　*Book great rates at AAA.com*

Classic Historic
Large-scale Hotel
Rates not provided

Phone: 540/985-5900　**14**

Address: 110 Shenandoah Ave 24016 **Location:** I-581, exit 5 southbound; exit 4E northbound, 0.5 mi s oh US 11/221/SR 16, then just w on Wells Ave. **Facility:** Historic elegance and a variety of room types characterize this longstanding property; a walkway to the downtown area accesses restaurants and shops. 331 one-bedroom standard units. 7 stories, interior corridors. *Bath:* combo or shower only. **Parking:** on-site (fee). **Terms:** check-in 4 pm. **Amenities:** video games, high-speed Internet, dual phone lines, voice mail, irons, hair dryers. *Some:* DVD players. **Dining:** The Regency Room, see separate listing. **Pool(s):** outdoor. **Leisure Activities:** whirlpool, exercise room. *Fee:* massage. **Guest Services:** valet laundry, area transportation, wireless Internet. **Business Services:** conference facilities, business center. *(See color ad below)*

HYATT PLACE ROANOKE/VALLEY VIEW MALL　　*Book great rates at AAA.com*

Small-scale Hotel
$89-$189 All Year

Phone: (540)366-4700　**9**

Address: 5040 Valley View Blvd 24012 **Location:** I-581, exit 3E, just e, then just s via shopping center exit. **Facility:** 128 one-bedroom standard units. 6 stories, interior corridors. *Bath:* combo or shower only. **Parking:** on-site. **Terms:** cancellation fee imposed. **Amenities:** high-speed Internet, voice mail, safes (fee), irons, hair dryers. **Pool(s):** heated indoor. **Leisure Activities:** exercise room. **Guest Services:** coin laundry, wireless Internet. **Business Services:** meeting rooms, business center. **Cards:** AX, CB, DC, DS, JC, MC, VI. **Free Special Amenities:** full breakfast and high-speed Internet.

HYATT
PLACE

AAA Benefit:
Ask for the AAA rate
and save 10%.

MAINSTAY SUITES ROANOKE AIRPORT　　*Book great rates at AAA.com*

Small-scale Hotel
$99-$175 All Year

Phone: (540)527-3030　**5**

Address: 5080 Valley View Blvd 24012 **Location:** I-581, exit 3E, just n. **Facility:** 77 one-bedroom standard units with kitchens. 4 stories, interior corridors. *Bath:* combo or shower only. **Parking:** on-site. **Amenities:** high-speed Internet, voice mail, irons, hair dryers. **Leisure Activities:** putting green, exercise room. **Guest Services:** coin laundry, wireless Internet. **Business Services:** meeting rooms, business center. **Cards:** AX, CB, DC, DS, JC, MC, VI. **Free Special Amenities:** continental breakfast and high-speed Internet.

QUALITY INN AIRPORT　　*Book great rates at AAA.com*

Small-scale Hotel
$59-$149 All Year

Phone: (540)366-8861　**1**

Address: 6626 Thirlane Rd 24019 **Location:** I-581, exit 2 southbound, just s on SR 117 (Peters Creek Rd), then just w. **Facility:** 161 one-bedroom standard units. 2 stories (no elevator), exterior corridors. *Bath:* combo or shower only. **Parking:** on-site. **Amenities:** video games, voice mail, irons, hair dryers. **Pool(s):** outdoor. **Leisure Activities:** exercise room, horseshoes. *Fee:* game room. **Guest Services:** valet and coin laundry, wireless Internet. **Business Services:** meeting rooms, PC, fax (fee). **Cards:** AX, CB, DC, DS, MC, VI. **Free Special Amenities:** continental breakfast and high-speed Internet.

QUALITY INN/TANGLEWOOD　　*Book great rates at AAA.com*

Small-scale Hotel
$65-$75 3/1-10/31
$55-$65 11/1-2/28

Phone: 540/989-4000　**16**

Address: 3816 Franklin Rd SW 24014 **Location:** I-581/US 220, exit Franklin Rd/Salem, just n on US 220 business route, then w on Frontage Rd. **Facility:** 58 one-bedroom standard units, some with efficiencies. 2 stories (no elevator), exterior corridors. **Parking:** on-site. **Terms:** cancellation fee imposed. **Amenities:** high-speed Internet, voice mail, irons, hair dryers. **Leisure Activities:** whirlpool, exercise room. **Guest Services:** coin laundry, wireless Internet. **Business Services:** meeting rooms, business center. **Cards:** AX, CB, DC, DS, JC, MC, VI. **Free Special Amenities:** continental breakfast and high-speed Internet.

▼ See AAA listing above ▼

(See map and index starting on p. 885)

RESIDENCE INN ROANOKE AIRPORT

[fyi]
Small-scale Hotel
$149-$179 All Year

Too new to rate, opening scheduled for September 2007. **Address:** 3305 Ordway Dr NW 24017 **Location:** I-581, exit 3W. **Amenities:** 79 units, coffeemakers, microwaves, refrigerators, pool. **Cards:** AX, DC, DS, JC, MC, VI.

AAA Benefit:
Members save 5% off of the best available rate.

SLEEP INN TANGLEWOOD
Book great rates at AAA.com   Phone: (540)772-1500 [18]

Small-scale Hotel
$56-$140 All Year

Address: 4045 Electric Rd 24018 **Location:** I-581/US 220, exit Franklin Rd/Salem, 0.7 mi n on SR 419. **Facility:** 82 one-bedroom standard units. 2-3 stories (no elevator), interior corridors. *Bath:* shower only. **Parking:** on-site. **Amenities:** high-speed Internet, irons, hair dryers. **Guest Services:** valet laundry, wireless Internet. **Business Services:** meeting rooms, PC. **Cards:** AX, CB, DC, DS, JC, MC, VI.

SUPER 8 MOTEL
Book at AAA.com   Phone: 540-563-8888 [2]

Small-scale Hotel
Rates not provided

Address: 6616 Thirlane Rd 24019 **Location:** I-581, exit 25, s on SR 117 (Peters Creek Rd), then just w. **Facility:** 59 one-bedroom standard units. 2-3 stories (no elevator), interior corridors. **Parking:** on-site. **Amenities:** safes (fee), hair dryers. **Guest Services:** wireless Internet. **Business Services:** fax (fee).

WYNDHAM ROANOKE HOTEL
Book at AAA.com   Phone: (540)563-9300 [11]

Large-scale Hotel
$99-$169 All Year

Address: 2801 Hershberger Rd 24017 **Location:** I-581, exit 3W, just w to Ordway Dr, then just n via service road. **Facility:** 320 one-bedroom standard units. 7-8 stories, interior corridors. *Bath:* combo or shower only. **Parking:** on-site. **Amenities:** high-speed Internet, dual phone lines, voice mail, irons, hair dryers. *Some:* CD players. **Pool(s):** outdoor, indoor. **Leisure Activities:** sauna, whirlpool, 2 lighted tennis courts, exercise room. **Guest Services:** valet and coin laundry, wireless Internet. **Business Services:** conference facilities, PC, fax. **Cards:** AX, DC, DS, JC, MC, VI.

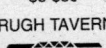

——— WHERE TO DINE ———

419 WEST
Phone: 540/776-0419 [16]

American
$9-$25

The restaurant features a spacious dining room, seasonal outdoor seating and a large, stylish bar. Fresh seafood, pasta and steaks are prepared in the open-air kitchen. Casual dress. **Bar:** Full bar. **Reservations:** suggested, weekends. **Hours:** 11:30 am-10 pm, Fri & Sat-11 pm, Sun 4 pm-10 pm. Closed: 12/25. **Address:** 3865 Electric Rd 24014 **Location:** I-581, Franklin Rd/Salem, 1.1 mi n on SR 419. **Parking:** on-site. **Cards:** AX, CB, DC, DS, JC, MC, VI.

ARZU
Phone: 540/982-7160 [5]

Mediterranean
$8-$30

A combination of classic French and Turkish cuisine is served in an upscale atmosphere. Casual dress. **Bar:** Full bar. **Hours:** 11 am-9 pm, Fri & Sat-10 pm, Sun noon-8 pm. Closed major holidays; also Mon. **Address:** 213 Williamson Rd SE 24011 **Location:** Between Kirk and Campbell sts; center of downtown. **Parking:** on-site. **Cards:** AX, DC, DS, MC, VI.

BRUGH TAVERN
Phone: 540/427-2440 [14]

American
$9-$25

In a historic log cabin, the tavern occupies a remote location off the Blue Ridge Parkway. The menu comprises surprisingly chic, inventive presentations of popular fare. Casual dress. **Bar:** Full bar. **Reservations:** required. **Hours:** 11:30 am-3 & 5-9 pm, Sun 11 am-3 pm. Closed major holidays; also Mon. **Address:** Milepost 115 Blue Ridge Pkwy 24014 **Location:** Blue Ridge Pkwy, MM 115; jct US 220, 7.9 mi n; in Virginia's Explore Park. **Parking:** on-site. **Cards:** MC, VI. **Historic**

CARLOS BRAZILIAN INTERNATIONAL CUISINE
Phone: 540/776-1117 [15]

Brazilian
$7-$28

Cuisine is prepared with an unusual flair, as evidenced by such selections as grilled chicken breast with a sweet sauce and fried bananas, fruit and steamed vegetables. The atmosphere is informal, and service is attentive and pleasant. Casual dress. **Bar:** Full bar. **Reservations:** suggested, for dinner. **Hours:** 11:30 am-2 & 5-9:30 pm, Fri-10 pm, Sat 5 pm-10 pm, Mon & Tues 5 pm-9:30 pm. Closed major holidays; also Sun. **Address:** 4167 Electric Rd 24014 **Location:** I-581, exit US 220 (Franklin Rd/Salem), 0.6 mi n on SR 419. **Parking:** street. **Cards:** AX, MC, VI.

COACH AND FOUR
Phone: 540/362-4220 [2]

American
$10-$21

A favorite with the locals, the traditional restaurant is known for its exciting gourmet entrees. Patrons can mingle in the large lounge or enjoy quiet, elegant dining. Little extras, such as a single meatball with salad, enhance the overall experience. Casual dress. **Hours:** 4 pm-10 pm, Fri & Sat-11 pm, Sun 11:30 am-10 pm. Closed: 11/27, 12/24, 12/25. **Address:** 5206 Williamson Rd 24012 **Location:** I-81, exit 146, 1.5 mi e on SR 115, then 1 mi right. **Parking:** on-site. **Cards:** AX, DC, DS, MC, VI.

(See map and index starting on p. 885)

EL TOREO

Mexican
$5-$11

Phone: 540/265-9116   ①

A lengthy list of Mexican favorites tempts patrons. Prompt, courteous service is the norm, as are ample portions. Casual dress. **Bar:** Full bar. **Hours:** 11 am-10 pm, Sat from noon, Sun noon-9 pm. Closed major holidays. **Address:** 6617 Thirlane Rd 24019 **Location:** I-581, exit 2S, just s on SR 117, then just w. **Parking:** on-site. **Cards:** AX, DS, MC, VI.

FAMOUS ANTHONY'S FAMILY RESTAURANT

American
$6-$14

Phone: 540/362-1400

Casual dress. **Hours:** 6 am-10 pm. Closed: 12/25. **Address:** 6499 Williamson Rd 24019 **Location:** I-81, exit 146, just e. **Parking:** on-site. **Cards:** MC, VI.

GREEN DOLPHIN GRILLE

Seafood
$7-$20

Phone: 540/857-0688   ⑥

The service-oriented staff brings out fresh seafood assembled in creative and colorful presentations, as well as daily specials. Casual dress. **Bar:** Full bar. **Hours:** 11:30 am-2 am, Sun & Mon 4:30 pm-10 pm. Closed: 12/25. **Address:** 127 Campbell Ave 24011 **Location:** Between 1st and Jefferson sts; center. **Parking:** on-site. **Cards:** AX, CB, DC, DS, JC, MC, VI.

HARBOR INN SEAFOOD RESTAURANT

Seafood
$8-$15

Phone: 540/563-0001

The restaurant is popular for its good selection of flavorful, affordably priced seafood selections. The atmosphere is welcoming to families. Landlubbers may choose from a handful of steak and chicken entrees. Portions are ample. Casual dress. **Bar:** Beer & wine. **Hours:** 4 pm-9 pm, Fri & Sat-10 pm, Sun 11 am-9 pm. Closed: 1/1, 11/27, 12/25; also Mon. **Address:** 7416 Williamson Rd NE 24019 **Location:** I-81, exit 146, 1 mi se on SR 115, then just s on US 11. **Parking:** on-site. **Cards:** MC, VI.

HOLLYWOOD'S RESTAURANT &
BAKERY

American
$7-$21

Phone: 540/362-1812

Fresh food is prepared from family recipes. Servers are friendly, courteous and attentive. Casual dress. **Bar:** Beer & wine. **Hours:** 11 am-10 pm. Closed: 1/1, 12/25; also Sun. **Address:** 7770 Williamson Rd 24019 **Location:** I-81, exit 146, 0.6 mi e on SR 115, then 0.3 mi n. **Parking:** on-site. **Cards:** AX, DS, MC, VI.

THE LIBRARY RESTAURANT

French
$20-$40

Phone: 540/985-0811   ⑪

French cuisine is at the heart of the intimate restaurant's menu. A few walls with shelves of books help this place live up to its name. Attractive artwork and tables set with a candle and fresh flower in slim brass vase add to the sophistication. The dining room is nice for celebrating an anniversary or other special occasion. Dressy casual. **Bar:** Full bar. **Reservations:** suggested. **Hours:** 5:30 pm-close. Closed: 11/27, 12/25; also Sun. **Address:** 3117 Franklin Rd SW 24014 **Location:** I-581, exit US 220 (Franklin Rd/Salem), 1 mi n on US 220 business route; in Piccadilly Square Shopping Center. **Parking:** on-site. **Cards:** AX, CB, DC, DS, MC, VI.

LUIGI'S

Italian
$11-$27

Phone: 540/989-6277   ⑫

Luigi's offers authentic Italian gourmet specialties such as veal bella bola and steak-n-such. Intimate surroundings,wonderful background music and a knowledgeable friendly staff. Casual dress. **Bar:** Full bar. **Reservations:** suggested, weekends. **Hours:** 4:30 pm-11 pm, Fri & Sat-midnight. Closed: 1/1, 11/27, 12/25. **Address:** 3301 Brambleton Ave SW 24018 **Location:** I-581, exit US 220 (Franklin Rd/Salem), 2.1 mi nw on SR 419, then 1 mi n. **Parking:** on-site. **Cards:** AX, DS, MC, VI.

MACADO'S

American
$4-$14

Phone: 540/776-9884

The loud, lively college hangout sports a lengthy menu of creatively prepared sandwiches and wraps. Among enjoyable choices are the grilled chicken wrap, stuffed with flavorful vegetables and melted provolone cheese, and French onion soup served in a cup. Casual dress. **Bar:** Full bar. **Hours:** 8 am-12:30 am, Fri & Sat-1:30 am. Closed: 11/27, 12/25. **Address:** 4237 Electric Rd 24014 **Location:** I-581, exit US 220 (Franklin Rd/Salem), 0.4 mi n on SR 419; at Grand Pavillion Shopping Center. **Parking:** on-site. **Cards:** AX, DC, MC, VI.

MONTANO'S INTERNATIONAL
GOURMET

Continental
$7-$20

Phone: 540/344-8960   ⑬

Popular at lunch with the local business crowd, the extensive menu features soup, salad and sandwiches. House specials at the family-owned eatery include paella, surf and turf and some pasta dishes. The delicatessen serves quality meat and cheese. Casual dress. **Bar:** Full bar. **Hours:** 10 am-10:30 pm. Closed: 1/1, 11/27, 12/25; also Sun. **Address:** 3733 Franklin Rd SW 24014 **Location:** I-581, exit US 220 (Franklin Rd/Salem), just n on US 220 business route; in Townside Festival Mall. **Parking:** on-site. **Cards:** AX, DS, MC, VI.

(See map and index starting on p. 885)

NAWAB INDIAN CUISINE
Phone: 540/345-5150

Tandoori specialties and bread baked in a clay oven are at the centerpiece of a traditional menu of curried, lamb and vegetarian dishes. The upscale atmosphere features artwork and instrumental music. A weekday buffet draws a devoted lunch clientele. Casual dress. **Bar:** Full bar. **Hours:** 11:30 am-2:30 & 5-10 pm, Sat from 5 pm. **Address:** 118 A Campbell Ave SE 24011 **Location:** Center; between 1st & Jefferson Sts. **Parking:** on-site. **Cards:** AX, DS, MC, VI.

Indian
$7-$25

NEW YORKER DELICATESSEN AND RESTAURANT
Phone: 540/366-0935   ③

In operation here for more than 40 years, the delicatessen has the atmosphere of a big-city operation. Meat cases are visible from the entrance, and the many selections of shaven sandwich meats and knockwursts will get the appetite juices flowing. Lunch is busy, but the price is right. Casual dress. **Bar:** Full bar. **Hours:** 11 am-10 pm, Fri & Sat-11 pm. Closed: 11/27, 12/25; also Mon. **Address:** 2802 Williamson Rd 24012 **Location:** I-581, exit 4E, just e, then 1 mi n. **Parking:** on-site.

American
$4-$10

THE REGENCY ROOM
Phone: 540/853-8280   ④

The circular, open dining room is considered a regional landmark. The historic lobby opens into the lovely dining room, where the charming staff tends to diners' needs. Dressy casual. Entertainment. **Bar:** Full bar. **Reservations:** suggested. **Hours:** 6:30-10:30 am, 11:30-2 & 5-10 pm, Sat from 7 am, Sun 7-10:30 am, 11:30-2 & 5-9 pm. **Address:** 110 Shenandoah Ave 24016 **Location:** I-581, exit 5 southbound; exit 4E northbound, 0.5 mi s on US 11/221/SR 16, then just w on Wells Ave; in The Hotel Roanoke & Conference Center, A DoubleTree Hotel. **Parking:** on-site (fee) and valet. **Cards:** AX, CB, DC, DS, MC, VI. **Historic**

American
$10-$35

THE ROANOKER RESTAURANT
Phone: 540/344-7746   ⑨

Near many downtown businesses, the long-established eatery is popular for its well-priced, homemade country cooking, which is dished up in large, simply presented portions. There's no putting on airs here, as this informal and relaxed spot registers on the basic end of the decor spectrum. Patrons enjoy excellent breakfasts, as well as such dishes as pork tenderloin accompanied by country vegetables and sweet, moist corn sticks. Perky servers aim to please. Casual dress. **Bar:** Full bar. **Hours:** 7 am-9 pm, Sun from 8 am. Closed: 12/25, 12/26; also Mon. **Address:** 2522 Colonial Ave SW 24015 **Location:** I-581, exit Colonial Ave, just sw. **Parking:** on-site. **Cards:** MC, VI.

American
$5-$11

STEPHEN'S
Phone: 540/344-7203   ⑩

Tall ceilings and lots of wrought iron give the multilevel restaurant the feeling of south Louisiana. The chef's specialties, which emphasize seafood but also include lamb and duck, reflect the same influences. The atmosphere is relaxed and subdued. Dressy casual. **Bar:** Full bar. **Reservations:** suggested. **Hours:** 5 pm-9 pm. Closed major holidays; also 12/24, Sun & Mon. **Address:** 2926 Franklin Rd SW 24014 **Location:** I-581, exit US 220 (Franklin Rd/Salem), 1.2 mi n on US 220 business route. **Parking:** on-site. **Cards:** AX, DC, DS, MC, VI.

Regional American
$18-$30

SWAGAT INDIAN CUISINE
Phone: 540/342-4887   ⑧

Swagat Indian Cuisine has a huge menu, friendly wait staff and cozy and warm dining surroundings. Casual dress. **Bar:** Full bar. **Hours:** 11:30 am-10 pm. **Address:** 303 First St 24011 **Location:** Between Church and Kirk aves; center. **Parking:** street. **Cards:** AX, CB, DC, DS, JC, MC, VI.

Indian
$7-$18

SZECHUAN RESTAURANT
Phone: 540/989-7947   ⑰

Excellent chicken, beef, seafood and vegetarian entrees are served in a family-friendly atmosphere. Artfully presented on a bed of lettuce, shrimp toast is more than tasty. Guests can sample a little bit of everything at the lunch buffet, available Sunday through Friday. Casual dress. **Bar:** Full bar. **Hours:** 11:30 am-10 pm, Fri & Sat-11 pm. Closed: 11/27, 12/25. **Address:** 5207 Bernard Dr 24018 **Location:** I-581, exit US 220 (Franklin Rd/Salem), 1 mi w on SR 419; in The Corners Shopping Center. **Parking:** on-site. **Cards:** AX, DC, DS, MC, VI.

Chinese
$5-$14

TUDOR'S BISCUIT WORLD
Phone: 540/344-2008

Serving breakfast all day folks can stop into Tudor's Biscuit World to sample their many varieities of homemade biscuit sandwiches. Known for fast and friendly service in a clean casual atmosphere. Casual dress. **Hours:** 5:30 am-2 pm, Sun from 7 am. Closed: 12/25. **Address:** 23 Church Ave SW 24011 **Location:** I-81, exit 141, just e. **Parking:** on-site.

American
$5-$10

WERTZ'S RESTAURANT
Phone: 540/342-5133   ⑦

In the heart of downtown, the restaurant enjoys a strong local following for lunch and dinner. The huge wine list is something to savor. Casual dress. **Bar:** Full bar. **Hours:** 11 am-2:30 & 5:30-10 pm, Mon-2:30 pm. Closed: 1/1, 12/25; also Sun. **Address:** 215 Market St 24011 **Location:** I-581, exit 5, just s. **Parking:** street. **Cards:** AX.

American
$8-$25

ROCKY MOUNT pop. 4,066

—— WHERE TO STAY ——

COMFORT INN-ROCKY MOUNT
Book at AAA.com
Phone: (540)489-4000

Address: 1730 N Main St 24151 **Location:** 1.5 mi n on US 220 business route. **Facility:** 61 one-bedroom standard units. 2 stories, interior corridors. **Parking:** on-site. **Amenities:** safes (fee), irons, hair dryers. *Some:* high-speed Internet. **Pool(s):** outdoor. **Guest Services:** coin laundry, wireless Internet. **Business Services:** meeting rooms. **Cards:** AX, CB, DC, DS, JC, MC, VI.

Small-scale Hotel
$77-$87 All Year

FRANKLIN MOTEL

Motel

$45-$90 All Year

Phone: (540)483-9962

Address: 20281 Virgil H Goode Hwy 24151 **Location:** 6.5 mi n on US 220. **Facility:** 22 one-bedroom standard units, some with whirlpools. 1 story, exterior corridors. **Parking:** on-site. **Terms:** cancellation fee imposed. **Cards:** AX, DS, MC, VI.

ROCKY MOUNT HOLIDAY INN EXPRESS HOTEL &
SUITES   *Book at AAA.com*

Small-scale Hotel

$90-$175 All Year

Phone: 540/489-5001

Address: 395 Old Franklin Tpke 24151 **Location:** US 220 S and SR 40, 0.3 mi e. **Facility:** 63 one-bedroom standard units, some with whirlpools. 3 stories, interior corridors. *Bath:* combo or shower only. **Parking:** on-site. **Amenities:** voice mail, irons, hair dryers. **Pool(s):** heated indoor. **Leisure Activities:** whirlpool, exercise room. **Guest Services:** coin laundry, wireless Internet. **Business Services:** meeting rooms, PC, fax (fee). **Cards:** AX, CB, DC, DS, JC, MC, VI.

------- **WHERE TO DINE** -------

FISHERMAN'S GALLEY

Seafood

$5-$16

Phone: 540/483-3474

Fisherman's Galley is a family owned and operated restaurant that is known far and wide for fresh seafood. Do not miss the hushpuppies. Casual dress. **Bar:** Full bar. **Hours:** 11 am-9 pm, Sat 3 pm-9:30 pm, Sun noon-8 pm. Closed: 3/23, 12/25; also Mon. **Address:** 17890 Virgil H Goode Hwy 24151 **Location:** 2.1 mi n on US 220. **Parking:** on-site. **Cards:** MC, VI.

IPPY'S UNCLE TOM'S RESTAURANT

American

$6-$20

Phone: 540/489-5600

A unique and plave that serves all the classic American favorites from ribs to steaks and everything in between. Casual dress. **Bar:** Full bar. **Hours:** 11 am-2 & 5-9 pm, Thurs & Fri-10 pm, Sat 5 pm-10 pm. Closed: 12/25; also Sun. **Address:** 1760 N Main St 24151 **Location:** 1.8 mi n on US 220 business route. **Parking:** on-site. **Cards:** AX, CB, DC, DS, JC, MC, VI.

OLDE VIRGINIA BARBECUE

American

$5-$15

Phone: 540/489-1788

A city tradition, the eatery satisfies diners with delicious, hickory wood-smoked beef and pork, as well as succulent ribs. Casual dress. **Bar:** Beer only. **Hours:** 11 am-9 pm. Closed: 11/27, 12/25. **Address:** 35 Meadowview Ave 24151 **Location:** 1.6 mi n on US 220 business route. **Parking:** on-site. **Cards:** MC, VI.

ROUND HILL —*See District Of Columbia p. 553.*

RUCKERSVILLE

------- **WHERE TO STAY** -------

**BEST WESTERN CHARLOTTESVILLE AIRPORT INN
& SUITES**   *Book great rates at AAA.com*

Small-scale Hotel

$109-$159 3/1-11/30
$89-$109 12/1-2/28

Phone: (434)985-1855

Address: 5920 Seminole Tr 22968 **Location:** I-64, exit 118B (US 29), 4.1 mi n of jct US 250 Bypass. **Facility:** 122 one-bedroom standard units. 4 stories, interior corridors. *Bath:* combo or shower only. **Parking:** on-site. **Terms:** cancellation fee imposed. **Amenities:** high-speed Internet, voice mail, safes, irons, hair dryers. **Pool(s):** outdoor. **Leisure Activities:** exercise room. **Guest Services:** valet and coin laundry, wireless Internet. **Business Services:** meeting rooms, business center. **Cards:** AX, DC, DS, MC, VI. **Free Special Amenities:** continental breakfast and local telephone calls.

AAA Benefit:
Members save 10% everyday, plus an exclusive frequent stay program.

------- **WHERE TO DINE** -------

BLUE RIDGE CAFE

American

$6-$20

Phone: 434/985-3633

Casual dress. **Bar:** Full bar. **Hours:** 11 am-9 pm. Closed: 1/1, 12/25. **Address:** 8315 Seminole Tr 22968 **Location:** I-64, exit 118B (US 29), 5.3 mi n of jct US 250 Bypass. **Parking:** on-site. **Cards:** MC, VI.

RUTHER GLEN

------- **WHERE TO STAY** -------

COMFORT INN & SUITES   *Book at AAA.com*

Small-scale Hotel

$68-$199 All Year

Phone: (804)448-1144

Address: 24058 Welcome Way Dr 22546 **Location:** I-95, exit 104 (SR 207), just w. **Facility:** 64 one-bedroom standard units. 3 stories, interior corridors. *Bath:* combo or shower only. **Parking:** on-site. **Terms:** cancellation fee imposed. **Amenities:** high-speed Internet, dual phone lines, irons, hair dryers. **Pool(s):** heated indoor. **Leisure Activities:** exercise room. **Guest Services:** wireless Internet. **Business Services:** meeting rooms, fax. **Cards:** AX, DC, DS, MC, VI.

SUPER 8 MOTEL-RUTHER GLEN *Book at AAA.com*
Phone: 804/448-2608
▼▼▼ ▼▼▼
Small-scale Hotel
Rates not provided
Address: 24011 Ruther Glen Rd 22546 **Location:** I-95, exit 104 (SR 207), just e on Rogers Clark Blvd. **Facility:** 62 one-bedroom standard units. 2 stories, exterior corridors. *Bath:* combo or shower only. **Parking:** on-site. **Amenities:** high-speed Internet, irons, hair dryers. **Pool(s):** outdoor. **Guest Services:** wireless Internet.
CALL 🄶M 🏊 📺 🛏 💻 / SOME UNITS FEE 🐾 ✖

SALEM pop. 24,747 (See map and index starting on p. 885)

—— **WHERE TO STAY** ——

BAYMONT INN ROANOKE-SALEM *Book great rates at AAA.com*
Phone: (540)562-2717 **22**
🄰🄰🄰 SAVE
▼▼▼ ▼▼▼
Small-scale Hotel
$89-$99 11/1-2/28
$84-$94 3/1-10/31
Address: 140 Sheraton Dr 24153 **Location:** I-81, exit 141, 0.5 mi se on SR 419. **Facility:** 67 one-bedroom standard units, some with whirlpools. 3 stories, interior corridors. *Bath:* combo or shower only. **Parking:** on-site. **Terms:** cancellation fee imposed. **Amenities:** video games, high-speed Internet, voice mail, irons, hair dryers. **Pool(s):** outdoor. **Leisure Activities:** exercise room. **Guest Services:** coin laundry, wireless Internet. **Business Services:** meeting rooms, business center. **Cards:** AX, CB, DC, DS, MC, VI. **Free Special Amenities: continental breakfast and high-speed Internet.**
🆂🄳 🍴 CALL 🄶M 🏊 📺 FEE 🛏 FEE 💻 / SOME UNITS ✖

COMFORT INN *Book great rates at AAA.com*
Phone: (540)387-1600 **25**
🄰🄰🄰 SAVE
▼▼▼ ▼▼▼
Small-scale Hotel
$89-$94 All Year
Address: 151 Wildwood Rd 24153 **Location:** I-81, exit 137, 0.3 mi e on SR 112. **Facility:** 50 one-bedroom standard units, some with whirlpools. 2 stories (no elevator), exterior corridors. **Parking:** on-site. **Amenities:** high-speed Internet, voice mail, irons, hair dryers. *Some:* DVD players. **Pool(s):** outdoor. **Guest Services:** valet laundry, wireless Internet. **Business Services:** business center. **Cards:** AX, CB, DC, DS, JC, MC, VI. **Free Special Amenities: continental breakfast and high-speed Internet.**
🆂🄳 🍴 🏊 🛏 💻 / SOME UNITS ✖ VCR

COMFORT SUITES INN AT RIDGEWOOD FARM *Book great rates at AAA.com*
Phone: (540)375-4800
🄰🄰🄰 SAVE
▼▼▼ ▼▼▼
Small-scale Hotel
$80-$130 All Year
Address: 2898 Keagy Rd 24153 **Location:** I-81, exit 141, 4.7 mi s on SR 419, then just w. **Facility:** 78 one-bedroom standard units, some with whirlpools. 3 stories, interior corridors. *Bath:* combo or shower only. **Parking:** on-site. **Terms:** cancellation fee imposed. **Amenities:** high-speed Internet, voice mail, irons, hair dryers. **Pool(s):** outdoor. **Leisure Activities:** whirlpool, exercise room. **Guest Services:** coin laundry, wireless Internet. **Business Services:** meeting rooms, business center. **Cards:** AX, DS, MC, VI. **Free Special Amenities: expanded continental breakfast and high-speed Internet.**
CALL 🄶M 🏊 📺 🛏 💻 / SOME UNITS FEE 🐾 ✖

DAYS INN *Book great rates at AAA.com*
Phone: 540/986-1000 **23**
🄰🄰🄰 SAVE
▼▼▼ ▼▼▼
Small-scale Hotel
Rates not provided
Address: 1535 E Main St 24153 **Location:** I-81, exit 141, 2 mi s on SR 419, then just w on US 460. Located across from a shopping center. **Facility:** 70 one-bedroom standard units, some with whirlpools. 3 stories (no elevator), interior/exterior corridors. **Parking:** on-site. **Amenities:** high-speed Internet, voice mail, irons, hair dryers. **Guest Services:** coin laundry, wireless Internet. **Business Services:** meeting rooms, business center. **Free Special Amenities: expanded continental breakfast and high-speed Internet.**
🍴 FEE 🔧 VCR 📺 🛏 💻 / SOME UNITS FEE 🐾 ✖

ECONO LODGE-ROANOKE/SALEM *Book great rates at AAA.com*
Phone: (540)389-0280 **24**
🄰🄰🄰 SAVE
▼▼▼ ▼▼▼
Motel
$34-$99 3/1-10/31
$34-$79 11/1-2/28
Address: 301 Wildwood Rd 24153 **Location:** I-81, exit 137, just e on SR 112. **Facility:** 64 one-bedroom standard units, some with whirlpools. 1 story, exterior corridors. **Parking:** on-site. **Amenities:** hair dryers. **Cards:** AX, DS, MC, VI.
🆂🄳 🍴 📺 🛏 💻 / SOME UNITS FEE 🐾 ✖ 💻

HAMPTON INN SALEM *Book great rates at AAA.com*
Phone: (540)776-6500
▼▼▼ ▼▼▼
Small-scale Hotel
$99-$159 All Year
Address: 1886 Electric Rd 24153 **Location:** I-81, exit 141, 4.6 mi s on SR 419. Located adjacent to hospital, connected by pedestrian walkway. **Facility:** 113 one-bedroom standard units, some with whirlpools. 6 stories, interior corridors. *Bath:* combo or shower only. **Parking:** on-site. **Terms:** 2 night minimum stay - seasonal, 10 day cancellation notice. **Amenities:** high-speed Internet, dual phone lines, voice mail, irons, hair dryers. **Pool(s):** outdoor. **Leisure Activities:** exercise room. **Guest Services:** coin laundry, wireless Internet. **Business Services:** meeting rooms, business center. **Cards:** AX, CB, DC, DS, JC, MC, VI.
A$K 🆂🄳 CALL 🄶M 🏊 VCR 📺 🛏 💻 / SOME UNITS ✖

QUALITY INN ROANOKE/SALEM *Book great rates at AAA.com*
Phone: 540-562-1912 **21**
🄰🄰🄰 SAVE
▼▼▼ ▼▼▼
Small-scale Hotel
Rates not provided
Address: 179 Sheraton Dr 24153 **Location:** I-81, exit 141, 0.4 mi e on SR 419. Truck parking on premises. **Facility:** 120 one-bedroom standard units. 2 stories (no elevator), interior corridors. **Parking:** on-site. **Amenities:** high-speed Internet, irons, hair dryers. **Pool(s):** outdoor. **Leisure Activities:** picnic tables, exercise room. **Guest Services:** coin laundry, wireless Internet. **Business Services:** meeting rooms, business center. **Free Special Amenities: continental breakfast and high-speed Internet.**
🏊 📺 💻 / SOME UNITS FEE 🐾 ✖ 🛏 💻

(See map and index starting on p. 885)

——— WHERE TO DINE ———

AFTON'S RESTAURANT
Phone: 540/380-2476

American
$5-$14

Wholesome country cooking and a warm atmosphere characterize the homey restaurant. Casual dress. **Hours:** 6 am-10 pm, Fri & Sat-11 pm. Closed: 1/1, 12/25; also Mon. **Address:** 5383 W Main St 24153 **Location:** I-81, exit 132, just e. **Parking:** on-site. **Cards:** AX, MC, VI.

CHIP & JO'S RESTAURANT
Phone: 540/387-9585

American
$5-$12

Chip & Jo's is a family operated eatery that serves breakfast all day. A wide variety menu of classic American cuisine. Casual dress. **Hours:** 6 am-8 pm, Sat 7 am-3 pm. Closed: 12/25; also Sun. **Address:** 315 8th St 24153 **Location:** I-81, exit 141, 4.1 mi s on SR 419. **Parking:** on-site. **Cards:** MC, VI.

EL RODEO
Phone: 540/387-4045   23

Mexican
$5-$11

Traditional favorites are menu mainstays at the family eatery. The lengthy list of selections includes chips and salsa, chiles rellenos and hot and tasty beef enchiladas. Portions are large, and service is prompt and courteous. Casual dress. **Bar:** Full bar. **Hours:** 11 am-10 pm, Sat from noon, Sun noon-9 pm. Closed major holidays. **Address:** 260 Wildwood Rd 24153 **Location:** I-81, exit 137, 0.3 mi e on SR 112. **Parking:** on-site. **Cards:** AX, DS, MC, VI.

FAST FREDDY'S
Phone: 540/389-5409   24

American
$4-$15

This place is a fast-food restaurant without the fast-food mentality. On the menu is a huge variety of dishes. Service is quick and friendly. Casual dress. **Hours:** 11 am-10 pm. Closed major holidays. **Address:** 816 W Main St 24153 **Location:** I-81, exit 137, just e. **Parking:** on-site.

MAC-AND-BOB'S RESTAURANT
Phone: 540/389-5999   22

American
$6-$20

Mac and Bob's restaurant is a lively setting complete with all your favorite American cuisine classics and an upbeat wait staff. Casual dress. **Bar:** Full bar. **Hours:** 11:30 am-midnight. Closed: 12/25. **Address:** 316 E Main St 24153 **Location:** I-81, exit 140, 1.6 mi s on SR 311, then just e. **Parking:** on-site. **Cards:** AX, CB, DC, DS, JC, MC, VI.

MAMMA MARIA'S ITALIAN RESTAURANT
Phone: 540/389-2848   25

Italian
$6-$20

A Southern Virginia favorite, the restaurant prepares a wide variety of pizza and pasta dishes. Service is friendly. Casual dress. **Bar:** Full bar. **Hours:** 11 am-10 pm. Closed: 1/1, 12/25; also Mon. **Address:** 2025 W Main St 24153 **Location:** I-81, exit 137, just e. **Parking:** on-site. **Cards:** MC, VI.

PICASO'S ITALIAN GRILL
Phone: 540/986-0320   21

Italian
$7-$20

Pasta and desserts are works of art. Selections are plentiful, and the atmosphere is homey. Casual dress. **Bar:** Beer & wine. **Hours:** 11 am-10 pm. Closed: 12/25; also Sun. **Address:** 151 Electric Rd 24153 **Location:** I-81, exit 141, 2 mi s on SR 419, then just w on US 460. **Parking:** on-site. **Cards:** AX, CB, DC, DS, JC, MC, VI.

SAKE HOUSE
Phone: 540/986-1207   20

Japanese
$6-$20

The menu centers on Japanese tempura, teriyaki and sushi preparations, highlights of which include miso soup to open and a lovely dessert of deep-fried sesame balls with sweet sesame paste to close. Tea room seating is available. Casual dress. **Bar:** Full bar. **Hours:** 11:30 am-3 & 5-10 pm, Fri & Sat-10:30 pm, Sun 5 pm-9 pm. Closed major holidays; also Mon. **Address:** 141 Electric Rd 24153 **Location:** I-81, exit 141, 2 mi s on SR 419, then just w on US 460; in Lakeside Plaza. **Parking:** on-site. **Cards:** AX, MC, VI.

SZECHUAN RESTAURANT
Phone: 540/387-9869

Chinese
$6-$12

A wide range of traditional favorites is authentically prepared and served promptly. Among choices on the daily lunch buffet are General Tso's chicken, beef with broccoli, seafood, spare ribs, soup and Szechwan-style green beans. Casual dress. **Bar:** Full bar. **Hours:** 11:30 am-10 pm, Fri & Sat-11 pm. Closed: 11/27, 12/25. **Address:** 1923-G Electric Rd 24153 **Location:** I-81, exit 141, 4.6 mi s on SR 419. **Parking:** on-site. **Cards:** AX, DC, DS, MC, VI.

(See map and index starting on p. 885)

SANDSTON —*See Richmond p. 883.*

SMITHFIELD —*See Hampton Roads Area p. 772.*

SOUTH BOSTON pop. 8,491

——— **WHERE TO STAY** ———

HOLIDAY INN-EXPRESS *Book at AAA.com* Phone: 434/575-4000
Address: 1074 Bill Tuck Hwy 24592 **Location:** Just e on US 58, from jct US 501. **Facility:** 66 one-bedroom standard units, some with whirlpools. 2 stories (no elevator), interior corridors. *Bath:* combo or shower only. **Parking:** on-site. **Terms:** 14 day cancellation notice. **Amenities:** high-speed Internet, dual phone lines, voice mail, irons, hair dryers. **Pool(s):** outdoor. **Leisure Activities:** limited exercise equipment. **Guest Services:** valet and coin laundry, wireless Internet. **Business Services:** meeting rooms, business center. **Cards:** AX, DC, DS, MC, VI.

Small-scale Hotel
$90-$129 All Year

QUALITY INN SOUTH BOSTON *Book great rates at AAA.com* Phone: (434)572-4311
Address: 2001 Seymour Dr 24592 **Location:** Jct US 58, 501 and 360, 1 mi e on US 360. **Facility:** 52 one-bedroom standard units. 2 stories (no elevator), exterior corridors. **Parking:** on-site. **Terms:** cancellation fee imposed. **Amenities:** high-speed Internet, irons, hair dryers. **Pool(s):** outdoor. **Guest Services:** valet laundry, wireless Internet. **Business Services:** meeting rooms, fax. **Cards:** AX, CB, DC, DS, JC, MC, VI. **Free Special Amenities:** continental breakfast and high-speed Internet.

Small-scale Hotel
$80-$100 3/1-10/30
$60-$80 10/31-2/28

SUPER 8 MOTEL *Book at AAA.com* Phone: 434/572-8868
Address: 1040 Bill Tuck Hwy 24592 **Location:** Just e on US 58, from jct US 501. **Facility:** 58 one-bedroom standard units. 2 stories (no elevator), interior corridors. **Parking:** on-site, winter plug-ins. **Amenities:** high-speed Internet, safes (fee). **Guest Services:** wireless Internet. **Business Services:** fax.

Motel
Rates not provided

——— **WHERE TO DINE** ———

BISTRO 1888 Phone: 434/572-1888
The chic interior mixes urban cool with turn-of-the-20th-century charm at the refurbished downtown building. The menu shows sophistication and creativity with influences as wide-ranging as the Pacific Northwest, Asia, Europe and, of course, the South. Dressy casual. **Bar:** Full bar. **Reservations:** suggested, weekends. **Hours:** 5 pm-10 pm. Closed major holidays; also Sun & Mon. **Address:** 221 Main St 24592 **Location:** Between Arch and Seymoure sts; downtown. **Parking:** street. **Cards:** AX, DS, MC, VI.

American
$11-$20

ERNIE'S RESTAURANT Phone: 434/572-3423
Since 1958, the Green family has been serving Southside locals and travelers such country-style favorites as Brunswick stew, biscuits, succotash, barbecue and fried seafood on the weekends and more. Casual dress. **Bar:** Full bar. **Hours:** 11 am-9 pm. Closed: 7/4; also Mon & 12/23-1/4. **Address:** 1010 John Randolph Blvd 24592 **Location:** From US 58, 1.5 mi ne on US 360. **Parking:** on-site. **Cards:** AX, CB, DC, MC, VI.

Southern
$4-$13

THE VINTNERS CELLAR CAFE Phone: 434/575-5645
The gourmet food and wine shop offers a tasty selection of soups, salads, sandwiches and pastries for breakfast and lunch. Pate and cheese platters make a nice snack to sample with a choice from the wine variety. A cozy seating section overlooks Main Street. Casual dress. **Bar:** Beer & wine. **Hours:** 9 am-3:30 pm. Closed major holidays; also Sun. **Address:** 303 Main St 24592 **Location:** Just n of US 58; center. **Parking:** street. **Cards:** AX, MC, VI.

Deli/Subs
Sandwiches
$6-$9

SOUTH HILL pop. 4,403

——— **WHERE TO STAY** ———

COMFORT INN *Book great rates at AAA.com* Phone: 434/447-2600
Address: 918 E Atlantic St 23970 **Location:** I-85, exit 12B, just w. **Facility:** 50 one-bedroom standard units, some with whirlpools. 2 stories (no elevator), exterior corridors. **Parking:** on-site, winter plug-ins. **Amenities:** high-speed Internet, irons, hair dryers. **Leisure Activities:** exercise room. **Guest Services:** coin laundry, wireless Internet. **Business Services:** business center. **Cards:** AX, CB, DC, DS, JC, MC, VI. **Free Special Amenities:** expanded continental breakfast and high-speed Internet.

Small-scale Hotel
$60-$90 3/1-9/15
$60-$80 9/16-2/28

FAIRFIELD INN & SUITES

[fyi]
Small-scale Hotel
$94-$119 All Year

Too new to rate, opening scheduled for September 2007. **Address:** 150 Arnold Dr 23950 **Location:** I-85, exit 12A, just e on US 58. **Amenities:** 68 units. **Cards:** AX, CB, DC, DS, JC, MC, VI.

Phone: 434/447-6800

HAMPTON INN

(AAA) (SAVE)
▽▽▽▽
Small-scale Hotel
$88-$155 All Year

Book great rates at AAA.com
Phone: 434/447-4600
Address: 200 Thompson St 23970 **Location:** I-85, exit 12A, just e on US 58. **Facility:** 55 units. 53 one-bedroom standard units, some with whirlpools. 2 one-bedroom suites with whirlpools. 3 stories, interior corridors. *Bath:* combo or shower only. **Parking:** on-site, winter plug-ins. **Terms:** cancellation fee imposed. **Amenities:** high-speed Internet, voice mail, irons, hair dryers. **Pool(s):** outdoor. **Leisure Activities:** exercise room. **Guest Services:** valet and coin laundry, wireless Internet. **Business Services:** meeting rooms, business center. **Cards:** AX, DC, DS, MC, VI. **Free Special Amenities: expanded continental breakfast and newspaper.**

[†↑] CALL [&M] [⊠] [⊡] [▣] / SOME UNITS [✕] [VCR] [▤] [▭]

HOLIDAY INN EXPRESS

▽▽▽▽
Small-scale Hotel
$74-$99 All Year

Book at AAA.com
Phone: (434)955-2777
Address: 101 Thompson St 23950 **Location:** I-85, exit 12A, just e on US 58. **Facility:** 58 one-bedroom standard units, some with efficiencies and/or whirlpools. 2 stories, interior corridors. *Bath:* combo or shower only. **Parking:** on-site, winter plug-ins. **Amenities:** high-speed Internet, dual phone lines, voice mail, irons, hair dryers. **Pool(s):** outdoor. **Leisure Activities:** exercise room. **Guest Services:** valet and coin laundry, wireless Internet. **Business Services:** meeting rooms, business center. **Cards:** AX, CB, DC, DS, JC, MC, VI.

[ASK] [S/D] CALL [&M] [⊠] [⊡] [▤] [▭] [▣] / SOME UNITS [✕] [VCR]

SUPER 8 MOTEL

▽▽
Small-scale Hotel
Rates not provided

Book at AAA.com
Phone: 434/447-2313
Address: 250 Thompson St 23950 **Location:** I-85, exit 12A, just n. **Facility:** 52 one-bedroom standard units, some with whirlpools. 3 stories, interior corridors. *Bath:* combo or shower only. **Parking:** on-site, winter plug-ins. **Amenities:** high-speed Internet, safes (fee), hair dryers. **Guest Services:** coin laundry, wireless Internet. **Business Services:** meeting rooms.

CALL [&M] [⊡] / SOME UNITS FEE [🐾] [✕] [▤] [▭]

—— WHERE TO DINE ——

KAHILL'S

▽▽▽
American
$5-$15

Phone: 434/447-6941
Rustic dining room with wood pegged floors and log walls. Casual setting, entrees include pasta, regional seafood and steak. Also known for our Cowboy Chili breakfast. Casual dress. **Bar:** Full bar. **Hours:** 7 am-10 pm. Closed: 11/27, 12/25. **Address:** 1791 N Mecklenburg Ave 23950 **Location:** I-85, exit 15, just s; 2 mi n of downtown. **Parking:** on-site. **Cards:** AX, DS, MC, VI.

[⊘]

SPERRYVILLE

—— WHERE TO DINE ——

THORNTON RIVER GRILLE

▽▽▽
American
$6-$20

Phone: 540/987-8790
Sharing menu space with classic American favorites are beef and seafood entrees. Diners can expect friendly hometown service. Casual dress. **Bar:** Full bar. **Hours:** 11 am-3 & 5-9 pm, Sun 10 am-3 pm. Closed: 1/1, 11/27, 12/25; also Mon. **Address:** 3710 Sperryville Pike 22740 **Location:** Just n on SR 522. **Parking:** on-site. **Cards:** AX, CB, DC, DS, JC, MC, VI.

[⊘]

SPRINGFIELD —See District Of Columbia p. 553.

STAFFORD

—— WHERE TO STAY ——

COMFORT INN

▽▽▽
Small-scale Hotel
$99-$159 3/1-10/31
$99-$119 11/1-2/28

Book at AAA.com
Phone: (540)659-8999
Address: 20 Salisbury Dr 22554 **Location:** I-95, exit 143B, w on Garrisonville Rd. **Facility:** 83 one-bedroom standard units, some with whirlpools. 4 stories, interior corridors. *Bath:* combo or shower only. **Parking:** on-site. **Amenities:** high-speed Internet, dual phone lines, voice mail, safes, irons, hair dryers. *Some:* DVD players (fee). **Pool(s):** outdoor. **Leisure Activities:** exercise room. **Guest Services:** valet and coin laundry, wireless Internet. **Business Services:** meeting rooms, business center. **Cards:** AX, CB, DC, DS, JC, MC, VI.

[ASK] [S/D] [†↑] CALL [&M] [⊠] [⊡] [▤] [▭] [▣] / SOME UNITS [✕] FEE [VCR]

COUNTRY INN BY CARLSON

Book great rates at AAA.com

AAA SAVE

Small-scale Hotel
$84-$150 All Year

Phone: (540)659-4330

Address: 153 Garrisonville Rd 22554 **Location:** I-95, exit 143B, just w. **Facility:** 58 one-bedroom standard units, some with whirlpools. 2 stories (no elevator), interior corridors. *Bath:* combo or shower only. **Parking:** on-site. **Terms:** cancellation fee imposed. **Amenities:** high-speed Internet, dual phone lines, voice mail, safes (fee), irons, hair dryers. **Leisure Activities:** exercise room. **Guest Services:** valet and coin laundry, wireless Internet. **Business Services:** meeting rooms, fax. **Cards:** AX, CB, DC, DS, MC, VI. **Free Special Amenities: expanded continental breakfast and high-speed Internet.**

SD ¶↑ CALL ⓛM 🐾 📷 🍴 🖥 💻 / SOME UNITS ✕ FEE VCR

HAMPTON INN

Book great rates at AAA.com

Small-scale Hotel
Rates not provided

Phone: 540/657-0999

Address: 2925 Jefferson Davis Hwy 22554 **Location:** I-95, exit 143A, just n of jct Garrisonville Rd. **Facility:** 88 one-bedroom standard units, some with whirlpools. 4 stories, interior corridors. *Bath:* combo or shower only. **Parking:** on-site. **Amenities:** high-speed Internet, dual phone lines, voice mail, irons, hair dryers. **Pool(s):** outdoor. **Leisure Activities:** exercise room. **Guest Services:** wireless Internet. **Business Services:** meeting rooms, business center.

CALL ⓛM 🏊 📷 🍴 🖥 💻 / SOME UNITS ✕

HOLIDAY INN EXPRESS

Book at AAA.com

Small-scale Hotel
$109-$139 3/1-9/30
$99-$129 10/1-2/28

Phone: (540)657-5566

Address: 28 Greenspring Dr 22554 **Location:** I-95, exit 143B, just w on Garrisonville Rd. **Facility:** 54 units. 50 one-bedroom standard units, some with whirlpools. 4 one-bedroom suites. 2 stories, interior corridors. *Bath:* combo or shower only. **Parking:** on-site. **Amenities:** high-speed Internet, dual phone lines, voice mail, irons, hair dryers. **Leisure Activities:** limited exercise equipment. **Guest Services:** valet laundry, wireless Internet. **Business Services:** PC, fax (fee). **Cards:** AX, CB, DC, DS, MC, VI.

ASK SD ¶↑ CALL ⓛM 🐾 📷 🍴 🖥 💻 / SOME UNITS FEE 🐾 ✕ FEE VCR

TOWNEPLACE SUITES BY MARRIOTT

Book great rates at AAA.com

Small-scale Hotel
$79-$96 All Year

Phone: 540/657-1990

Address: 2772 Jefferson Davis Hwy 22554 **Location:** I-95, exit 143A, just s on US 1. **Facility:** Smoke free premises. 93 units. 70 one-bedroom standard units with whirlpools. 10 one- and 13 two-bedroom suites with kitchens. 3 stories, interior corridors. *Bath:* combo or shower only. **Parking:** on-site. **Amenities:** high-speed Internet, voice mail, irons, hair dryers. **Pool(s):** heated outdoor. **Leisure Activities:** exercise room. **Guest Services:** valet and coin laundry, wireless Internet. **Business Services:** meeting rooms, business center. **Cards:** AX, DC, DS, JC, MC, VI.

AAA Benefit:
Members save 5% off of the best available rate.

ASK SD CALL ⓛM 🐾 ✕ 📷 🍴 🖥 💻 / SOME UNITS FEE 🐾

WINGATE INN STAFFORD

Book at AAA.com

Small-scale Hotel
$105-$115 All Year

Phone: (540)659-3600

Address: 15 Salisbury Dr 22554 **Location:** I-95, exit 143B, just w on Garrisonville Rd. **Facility:** 99 one-bedroom standard units, some with whirlpools. 4 stories, interior corridors. *Bath:* combo or shower only. **Parking:** on-site. **Terms:** 2-5 night minimum stay. **Amenities:** video games (fee), high-speed Internet, dual phone lines, voice mail, safes, irons, hair dryers. **Pool(s):** heated indoor. **Leisure Activities:** whirlpool, exercise room. **Guest Services:** valet and coin laundry, wireless Internet. **Business Services:** meeting rooms, business center. **Cards:** AX, CB, DC, DS, JC, MC, VI.

ASK SD ¶↑ CALL ⓛM 🐾 📷 🍴 🖥 💻 / SOME UNITS ✕

WHERE TO DINE

IMPERIAL GARDEN RESTAURANT

Chinese
$5-$19

Phone: 540/720-2200

A stately grand piano sits in the center of the dining room, which has a more upscale feel than most restaurants of its type. Exceptional, well-presented entrees are offered with such special complements as enticing plates of flavorful hors d'oeuvres and a fine hot and sour soup. Casual dress. **Bar:** Full bar. **Hours:** 11:30 am-10 pm. Closed: 11/27, 12/25. **Address:** 2848 Jefferson Davis Hwy, Suite 806 22554 **Location:** I-95, exit 143A, jct SR 610; in Aquia Town Center. **Parking:** on-site. **Cards:** AX, DC, DS, MC, VI.

CALL ⓛM 🅺 🍸

KING STREET BLUES

American
$7-$14

Phone: 540/288-1100

The atmosphere is joyful and exuberant with colorful papier mache figures popping out from all corners; the menu is lively as well with barbecue and ribs a specialty but a large list of other offerings as well from salads to macaroni bowls. Casual dress. **Bar:** Full bar. **Hours:** 11 am-10 pm, Fri & Sat-11 pm, Sun-9:30 pm. Closed major holidays. **Address:** 2866 Jefferson Davis Hwy 22554 **Location:** I-95, exit 143A, jct US 1 and SR 610; in Days Inn Aquia-Quantico. **Parking:** on-site. **Cards:** AX, DC, DS, MC, VI.

CALL ⓛM 🍸

THE LOG CABIN

Seafood
$16-$50

Phone: 540/659-5067

The natural bark log interior and brick fireplace contribute to the warm, cozy ambience of the rustic dining room. Steak, pasta and seafood choices, including many dishes with fresh Chesapeake blue crab and Maine lobster, make up an interesting, tempting menu. Dressy casual. **Bar:** Full bar. **Reservations:** suggested. **Hours:** 4 pm-9 pm, Fri & Sat-10 pm. Closed major holidays; also 12/24. **Address:** 1749 Jefferson Davis Hwy 22554 **Location:** I-95, exit 140, 1.5 mi e to US 1, then 1 mi s. **Parking:** on-site. **Cards:** AX, MC, VI.

VINNY'S ITALIAN GRILL & PIZZERIA

▼▼▼ ▼▼▼
Italian
$5-$15

Phone: 540/657-8400
Whether taking-out or eating-in, patrons can choose from many tasty options, including pasta and fish dishes, veal parmigiana and pizza—by the slice or by the pie. The dining room is cozy. Casual dress. **Bar:** Beer & wine. **Hours:** 11 am-10 pm, Fri & Sat-11 pm, Sun 11:30 am-9:30 pm. Closed major holidays; also 12/24. **Address:** 397 Garrisonville Rd 22554 **Location:** I-95, exit 143B, 1.5 mi w; in Garrison Village Center. **Parking:** on-site. **Cards:** AX, DS, MC, VI.

ZUM RHEINGARTEN RESTAURANT

▼▼▼ ▼▼▼
German
$17-$25

Phone: 703/221-4635
The restaurant is housed in a quaint stone farmhouse whose stone terrace serves as a summer beer garden. Dining rooms center around a stone hearth and whimsical murals highlight some of the walls. The menu offers authentic dishes such as sauerbraten, Wiener schnitzel, bratwurst, and spatzle. Traditional side dishes include red cabbage, potato dumplings, and potato pancakes. Don't forget the traditional dessert of apple streudel and black forest cake. Dressy casual. **Bar:** Full bar. **Reservations:** suggested, weekends. **Hours:** 5 pm-9 pm, Sun 4 pm-8 pm. Closed: 7/4, 12/24, 12/25; also Mon, Tues, 8/20-8/30 & Super Bowl Sun. **Address:** 3998 Jefferson Davis Hwy 22554 **Location:** I-95, exit 150A southbound, 3 mi s on US 1; exit 143A northbound, 4.5 mi n on US 1. **Parking:** on-site. **Cards:** AX, DC, MC, VI.

STANLEY pop. 1,326

--- **WHERE TO DINE** ---

HAWKSBILL DINER

▼▼ ▼▼
American
$6-$18

Phone: 540/778-2006
A slice of the Shenandoah Valley can be found at the diner, which presents a menu of home-style cooking and nurtures a friendly atmosphere. Casual dress. **Hours:** 9 am-8 pm. Closed: 12/25. **Address:** 1388 Main St 22851 **Location:** 0.3 mi w on US 340 business route; center. **Parking:** on-site. **Cards:** MC, VI.

STAUNTON pop. 23,853

--- **WHERE TO STAY** ---

THE BELLE GRAE INN AND RESTAURANT

▼▼▼ ▼▼▼
Historic
Country Inn
$149-$209 All Year

Phone: (540)886-5151
Address: 515 W Frederick St 24401-3333 **Location:** Between N Madison and N Jefferson sts. **Facility:** Private baths adjoin rooms at this restored Victorian mansion in an urban neighborhood of historic homes within walking distance to shops. Smoke free premises. 14 one-bedroom standard units, some with whirlpools. 2 stories (no elevator), interior/exterior corridors. **Bath:** combo or shower only. **Parking:** on-site. **Terms:** age restrictions may apply, 10 day cancellation notice-fee imposed. **Amenities:** hair dryers. *Some:* irons. **Dining:** restaurant, see separate listing. **Guest Services:** coin laundry. **Business Services:** meeting rooms, fax (fee). **Cards:** AX, DC, DS, MC, VI.

BEST WESTERN STAUNTON INN   *Book great rates at AAA.com*

(AAA) (SAVE)
▼▼▼ ▼▼▼
Small-scale Hotel
$64-$175 All Year

Phone: (540)885-1112
Address: 92 Rowe Rd 24401 **Location:** I-81, exit 222, just e on US 250. **Facility:** 80 one-bedroom standard units. 4 stories, interior corridors. **Parking:** on-site. **Amenities:** high-speed Internet, irons, hair dryers. **Pool(s):** heated indoor. **Guest Services:** wireless Internet. **Business Services:** meeting rooms. **Cards:** AX, CB, DC, DS, JC, MC, VI. **Free Special Amenities:** continental breakfast and high-speed Internet.

AAA Benefit:
Members save 10% everyday, plus an exclusive frequent stay program.

▼ See AAA listing p 901 ▼

COMFORT INN

AAA [SAVE]

▽▽▽ ▽▽▽

Small-scale Hotel
$72-$135 All Year

Book great rates at AAA.com

Phone: (540)886-5000

Address: 1302 Richmond Ave 24401 **Location:** I-81, exit 222, just w on US 250. **Facility:** 97 one-bedroom standard units, some with whirlpools. 5 stories, interior corridors. **Parking:** on-site. **Amenities:** high-speed Internet, voice mail, safes (fee), irons, hair dryers. **Pool(s):** outdoor. **Guest Services:** valet laundry, wireless Internet. **Business Services:** PC, fax (fee). **Cards:** AX, CB, DC, DS, JC, MC, VI. **Free Special Amenities:** expanded continental breakfast and high-speed Internet.

[S/D] [↑↓] CALL [&M] [icons] / SOME UNITS FEE [icons]

ECONO LODGE STAUNTON

AAA [SAVE]

▽▽▽ ▽▽▽

Small-scale Hotel
$70-$109 3/1-10/31
$45-$109 11/1-2/28

Book great rates at AAA.com

Phone: (540)885-5158

Address: 1031 Richmond Ave 24401 **Location:** I-81, exit 222, 0.7 mi w on US 250. **Facility:** 88 one-bedroom standard units. 2 stories (no elevator), interior/exterior corridors. **Parking:** on-site. **Terms:** 3 day cancellation notice-fee imposed. **Amenities:** irons, hair dryers. **Guest Services:** coin laundry, wireless Internet. **Business Services:** meeting rooms, fax (fee). **Cards:** AX, CB, DC, DS, MC, VI. **Free Special Amenities:** continental breakfast and high-speed Internet.

[S/D] [↑↓] [icons] / SOME UNITS FEE [icons]

FREDERICK HOUSE

AAA [SAVE]

▽▽▽ ▽▽▽

Historic
Small-scale Hotel
$99-$239 All Year

Phone: (540)885-4220

Address: 28 N New St 24401 **Location:** I-81, exit 222, New and Frederick sts; 2 mi w on US 250; downtown. **Facility:** A tremendous breakfast is served in the main building of this property comprising five 19th-century townhouses with antiques and reproductions. Smoke free premises. 23 units. 19 one- and 4 two-bedroom standard units. 2-3 stories (no elevator), interior/exterior corridors. **Bath:** combo or shower only. **Parking:** on-site. **Terms:** cancellation fee imposed. **Amenities:** hair dryers. **Guest Services:** valet laundry, wireless Internet. **Business Services:** meeting rooms. **Cards:** AX, DS, MC, VI. **Free Special Amenities:** full breakfast and newspaper. *(See color ad p 900)*

[S/D] [↑↓] [✕] / SOME UNITS [VCR]

GUESTHOUSE INTERNATIONAL INN

▽▽▽ ▽▽▽

Small-scale Hotel
$60-$120 All Year

Book at AAA.com

Phone: 540/885-3117

Address: 42 Sangers Ln 24401 **Location:** I-81, exit 222, just e on US 250. Truck and camper parking. **Facility:** 84 one-bedroom standard units, some with whirlpools. 2 stories (no elevator), exterior corridors. *Bath:* combo or shower only. **Parking:** on-site. **Amenities:** high-speed Internet. *Some:* hair dryers. **Pool(s):** heated indoor. **Leisure Activities:** sauna, whirlpool, exercise room. **Guest Services:** valet laundry, wireless Internet. **Cards:** AX, DS, MC, VI.

[ASK] [S/D] [↑↓] CALL [&M] [icons] [✕] / SOME UNITS FEE [icons]

▼ See AAA listing p 902 ▼

▼ See AAA listing p 902 ▼

HAMPTON INN

▼▼▼

Small-scale Hotel
Rates not provided

Phone: 540/886-7000

Address: 40 Payne Ln 24401 **Location:** I-81, exit 220, 0.6 mi w, then just n on US 11. **Facility:** 76 one-bedroom standard units. 3 stories, interior corridors. *Bath:* combo or shower only. **Parking:** on-site. **Amenities:** high-speed Internet, voice mail, irons, hair dryers. *Some:* DVD players. **Pool(s):** outdoor. **Leisure Activities:** exercise room. **Guest Services:** valet laundry, wireless Internet. **Business Services:** meeting rooms, business center.

[Symbols] CALL ⑤M ⊠ SOME UNITS FEE VCR FEE FEE

HOLIDAY INN GOLF & CONFERENCE CENTER

(AAA) SAVE
▼▼▼

Small-scale Hotel
$99-$200 All Year

Phone: (540)248-6020

Address: 152 Fairway Ln 24401 **Location:** I-81, exit 225, 0.3 mi w on SR 275 (Woodrow Wilson Pkwy). **Facility:** 114 one-bedroom standard units. 6 stories, interior corridors. **Parking:** on-site. **Amenities:** high-speed Internet, voice mail, irons, hair dryers. **Dining:** Cafe on the Green, see separate listing. **Pool(s):** outdoor, heated indoor. **Leisure Activities:** exercise room. *Fee:* golf & tennis privileges. **Guest Services:** valet laundry, airport transportation-Shenandoah Regional Airport, area transportation-Amtrak & bus station, wireless Internet. **Business Services:** conference facilities, fax (fee). **Cards:** AX, CB, DC, DS, JC, MC, VI. **Free Special Amenities:** local telephone calls and high-speed Internet. *(See color ad p 901)*

[Symbols] CALL ⑤M / SOME UNITS FEE ⊠

HOWARD JOHNSON EXPRESS INN

▼▼

Small-scale Hotel
Rates not provided

Phone: 540/886-5330

Address: 268 N Central Ave 24401 **Location:** I-81, exit 222, 2.2 mi w on SR 250 into downtown; between Pine and Baldwin sts. **Facility:** 101 one-bedroom standard units, some with whirlpools. 4 stories, exterior corridors. *Bath:* combo or shower only. **Parking:** on-site. **Amenities:** irons, hair dryers. **Pool(s):** outdoor. **Guest Services:** coin laundry.

CALL ⑤M / SOME UNITS FEE ⊠

MICROTEL INN

(AAA) SAVE
▼▼

Small-scale Hotel
$60-$99 3/1-10/31
$48-$54 11/1-2/28

Phone: 540/887-0200

Address: 200 Frontier Dr 24401 **Location:** I-81, exit 222, 0.4 mi w on US 250, then 0.3 mi s. **Facility:** Smoke free premises. 58 one-bedroom standard units. 2 stories, interior corridors. *Bath:* combo or shower only. **Parking:** on-site. **Terms:** cancellation fee imposed. **Amenities:** high-speed Internet. **Pool(s):** heated outdoor. **Leisure Activities:** playground. **Guest Services:** coin laundry, wireless Internet. **Business Services:** meeting rooms. **Cards:** AX, DC, DS, MC, VI. **Free Special Amenities:** continental breakfast and high-speed Internet. *(See color ad p 901)*

S⃝D CALL ⑤M ⊠ / SOME UNITS

QUALITY INN-CONFERENCE CENTER

(AAA) SAVE
▼▼▼

Small-scale Hotel
$59-$139 All Year

Phone: (540)248-5111

Address: 96 Baker Ln 24401 **Location:** I-81, exit 225, just e on SR 275 (Woodrow Wilson Pkwy). **Facility:** 100 one-bedroom standard units. 2 stories (no elevator), exterior corridors. **Parking:** on-site. **Terms:** cancellation fee imposed. **Amenities:** high-speed Internet, irons, hair dryers. **Pool(s):** outdoor. **Guest Services:** coin laundry, wireless Internet. **Business Services:** meeting rooms, business center. **Cards:** AX, DS, MC, VI. **Free Special Amenities:** continental breakfast and high-speed Internet.

S⃝D / SOME UNITS FEE ⊠

SLEEP INN

(AAA) SAVE
▼▼▼

Small-scale Hotel
$69-$125 All Year

Phone: (540)887-6500

Address: 222 Jefferson Hwy 24401 **Location:** I-81, exit 222, just e on US 250. **Facility:** 87 one-bedroom standard units. 4 stories, interior corridors. *Bath:* combo or shower only. **Parking:** on-site. **Terms:** 7 day cancellation notice. **Amenities:** high-speed Internet, voice mail, irons, hair dryers. **Leisure Activities:** pool privileges. **Guest Services:** valet laundry, wireless Internet. **Cards:** AX, CB, DC, DS, JC, MC, VI. **Free Special Amenities:** continental breakfast and high-speed Internet.

S⃝D [Symbols] CALL ⑤M / SOME UNITS ⊠

For Reservations Call 1-800-762-

--- **WHERE TO DINE** ---

THE BELLE GRAE INN AND RESTAURANT

▼▼▼

Regional American
$17-$29

Phone: 540/886-5151

Creaky wooden floors are expected in the historic inn, and so is the stylish fare. Picnic dinner baskets for two, $50, with wine are available on Monday. The premises are smoke-free. Formal attire. **Bar:** Full bar. **Reservations:** suggested. **Hours:** 5:30-9 pm. Closed: Mon & Tues. **Address:** 515 W Frederick St 24401-3333 **Location:** Between N Madison and N Jefferson sts; in The Belle Grae Inn and Restaurant. **Parking:** on-site and street. **Cards:** AX, DS, MC, VI. **Historic**

THE BEVERLEY RESTAURANT

▼

American
$5-$14

Phone: 540/886-4317

A Staunton tradition for almost 40 years. The Beverley Restaurant serves breakfast all day and has many salad and sandwich selections. Casual dress. **Hours:** 7 am-7 pm, Sat 8 am-3 pm. Closed: 1/1, 12/25; also Sun. **Address:** 12 E Beverley St 24401 **Location:** Between New and Augusta sts; center of downtown. **Parking:** street. **Cards:** DS, MC, VI.

CAFE ON THE GREEN

▼▼▼

American
$4-$18

Phone: 540/248-6020

The "hen house," chicken salad in cantaloupe, is fresh and incorporates a generous array of four fruits. French onion soup is tasty and hot. Beef is the house specialty. Popular, too, is the golf course view, with some tables affording better views than others. Casual dress. **Bar:** Full bar. **Hours:** 6:30 am-2 & 5-10 pm, Sat from 7 am. Closed: 12/25. **Address:** 152 Fairway Ln 22401 **Location:** I-81, exit 225, 0.3 mi w on SR 275 (Woodrow Wilson Pkwy); in Holiday Inn Golf & Conference Center. **Parking:** on-site. **Cards:** AX, CB, DC, DS, JC, MC, VI.

THE DEPOT GRILLE

Phone: 540/885-7332

American
$6-$24

The Depot Grille is set at a converted train station with wonderful ambience and a diverse menu. Casual dress. **Bar:** Full bar. **Hours:** 11 am-11 pm. Closed: 11/27, 12/25. **Address:** 42 Middlebrook Ave 24401 **Location:** I-81, exit 222; downtown; in the Wharf Historic District; at train station. **Parking:** on-site. **Cards:** AX, CB, DC, DS, JC, MC, VI.

THE DINING ROOM

Phone: 540/213-0606

American
$8-$37

In historic old downtown, the dining area displays a cozy and elegant decor. Formally attired staff members present an upscale menu and wine list. Dressy casual. **Bar:** Full bar. **Reservations:** accepted. **Hours:** 11 am-2:30 & 4:30-9 pm, Thurs-Sat to 10 pm. Closed: 12/25; also Sun & Mon. **Address:** 29 N Augusta St 24401 **Location:** Augusta and Frederick sts; 2 mi w of US 250; downtown. **Parking:** street. **Cards:** DS, MC, VI.

EL PUERTO MEXICAN RESTAURANT

Phone: 540/886-3578

Mexican
$7-$20

A festive feel is part of the appeal at this place, which presents a huge menu of Mexican favorites. Casual dress. **Bar:** Full bar. **Hours:** 11 am-10 pm. Closed: 12/25. **Address:** 830 Greenville Ave 24401 **Location:** I-81, exit 220, 0.6 mi w, then 0.4 mi n on US 11. **Parking:** on-site. **Cards:** AX, CB, DC, DS, JC, MC, VI.

L'ITALIA RESTAURANT

Phone: 540/885-0102

Italian
$6-$22

Attractive paintings, plants and soft music set a relaxed mood in the cozy restaurant. Veal, pasta and seafood dishes as well as such specialties as chicken rolatini make up a thoughtful, pleasing menu. Servers are knowledgeable and professional. Casual dress. **Bar:** Full bar. **Hours:** 11 am-10 pm, Fri & Sat-11 pm, Sun-9 pm. Closed major holidays; also Mon. **Address:** 23 E Beverly St 24401 **Location:** I-81, exit 222, just w. **Parking:** street. **Cards:** AX, CB, DC, DS, MC, VI.

CALL

MILL STREET GRILL

Phone: 540/886-0656

American
$10-$20

This restaurant is a contemporary environment with many American favorites. Do not miss the ribs. Casual dress. **Bar:** Full bar. **Reservations:** suggested, weekends. **Hours:** 4 pm-10 pm, Fri & Sat-10:30 pm, Sun 11:30 am-10 pm. Closed: 11/27, 12/25. **Address:** 1 Mill St 24401 **Location:** I-81, exit 222, just w. **Parking:** on-site. **Cards:** AX, CB, DC, DS, JC, MC, VI.

MRS ROWE'S FAMILY RESTAURANT & BAKERY

Phone: 540/886-1833

American
$7-$18

Reliable country specialties range from spoon bread to baked tomatoes to rich homemade pie. Family-owned and operated since 1947, the wonderful eatery—and Mrs. Rowe—are popular and with good reason. Peak hours can be busy. Casual dress. **Bar:** Beer & wine. **Hours:** 7 am-9 pm, Sun-7 pm. Closed major holidays. **Address:** Rowe Rd 24401 **Location:** I-81, exit 222, just e on US 250. **Parking:** on-site. **Cards:** DS, MC, VI.

THE PULLMAN RESTAURANT

Phone: 540/885-6612

American
$6-$20

In the restored C&O Railroad Station, the restaurant welcomes diners back to the days of Victorian-style soda fountains and ice cream parlors. A daily changing menu is offered. Casual dress. **Bar:** Full bar. **Hours:** 11 am-11 pm, Sun-9 pm. Closed: 11/27, 12/25. **Address:** 36 Middlebrook Ave 24401 **Location:** I-81, exit 222; downtown; in the Wharf Historic District; at train station. **Parking:** on-site. **Cards:** AX, CB, DC, DS, MC, VI. **Historic**

WRIGHT'S DAIRY-RITE FAMILY RESTAURANT

Phone: 540/886-0435

American
$5-$12

The nostalgic restaurant has been family owned and operated since 1952 and offers exceedingly friendly service. Casual dress. **Hours:** 9 am-9 pm, Fri & Sat-11 pm. Closed: 1/1, 12/25. **Address:** 346 Greenville Ave 24401 **Location:** I-81, exit 222, 1.7 mi w on US 250, then just s. **Parking:** on-site.

STEPHENS CITY pop. 1,146

---- WHERE TO STAY ----

COMFORT INN-STEPHENS CITY

Book great rates at AAA.com

Phone: (540)869-6500

Small-scale Hotel
$85-$125 All Year

Address: 167 Town Run Ln 22655 **Location:** I-81, exit 307, just se. **Facility:** 60 one-bedroom standard units, some with whirlpools. 2 stories (no elevator), interior corridors. **Parking:** on-site. **Amenities:** high-speed Internet, voice mail, irons, hair dryers. **Pool(s):** outdoor. **Guest Services:** wireless Internet. **Cards:** AX, CB, DC, DS, JC, MC, VI. **Free Special Amenities:** continental breakfast and high-speed Internet.

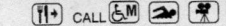

HOLIDAY INN EXPRESS

Book at AAA.com

Phone: 540/869-0909

Small-scale Hotel
Rates not provided

Address: 165 Town Run Ln 22655 **Location:** I-81, exit 307, just se. **Facility:** 69 one-bedroom standard units, some with whirlpools. 3 stories, interior corridors. *Bath:* combo or shower only. **Parking:** on-site. **Amenities:** high-speed Internet, voice mail, irons, hair dryers. **Pool(s):** outdoor. **Leisure Activities:** exercise room. **Guest Services:** coin laundry, wireless Internet. **Business Services:** meeting rooms, business center.

——— **WHERE TO DINE** ———

NEW TOWN TAVERN   Phone: 540/868-0111

American
$6-$20

The restaurant sets forth a winning combination of friendly service, a fun atmosphere and award-winning ribs that shouldn't be missed. The menu is lengthy. Casual dress. **Bar:** Full bar. **Hours:** 11 am-1 am, Sun noon-11 pm. Closed major holidays. **Address:** 356 Fairfax Pike 22655 **Location:** I-81, exit 307, just e. **Parking:** on-site. **Cards:** AX, CB, DC, DS, MC, VI. **Historic**

STERLING —See District Of Columbia p. 556.

STONY CREEK pop. 202

——— **WHERE TO STAY** ———

HAMPTON INN-STONY CREEK   *Book great rates at AAA.com*   Phone: 434/246-5500

Small-scale Hotel
Rates not provided

Address: 10476 Blue Star Hwy 23882 **Location:** I-95, exit 33, 0.3 mi s on SR 301. **Facility:** 71 one-bedroom standard units. 3 stories, interior corridors. *Bath:* combo or shower only. **Parking:** on-site. **Amenities:** video games (fee), high-speed Internet, voice mail, irons, hair dryers. **Pool(s):** outdoor. **Leisure Activities:** exercise room. **Guest Services:** coin laundry, wireless Internet. **Business Services:** meeting rooms, business center. **Free Special Amenities: expanded continental breakfast and high-speed Internet.**

SLEEP INN & SUITES   *Book great rates at AAA.com*   Phone: (434)246-5100

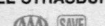
Small-scale Hotel
$69-$149 All Year

Address: 11019 Blue Star Hwy 23882 **Location:** I-95, exit 33, 0.3 mi s on SR 301. **Facility:** 64 one-bedroom standard units. 3 stories, interior corridors. *Bath:* combo or shower only. **Parking:** on-site. **Terms:** cancellation fee imposed. **Amenities:** high-speed Internet, voice mail, irons, hair dryers. **Pool(s):** heated indoor. **Leisure Activities:** playground, exercise room. **Guest Services:** coin laundry, wireless Internet. **Business Services:** business center. **Cards:** AX, CB, DS, MC, VI. **Free Special Amenities: continental breakfast and high-speed Internet.**

STRASBURG pop. 4,017

——— **WHERE TO STAY** ———

HOTEL STRASBURG   Phone: (540)465-9191

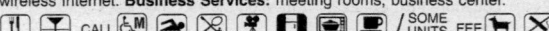

Historic
Country Inn
$83-$180 All Year

Address: 213 S Holliday St 22657 **Location:** I-81, exit 298, 2.2 mi s on US 11, then just s. **Facility:** A tavern, dining room, many gathering areas and an impressive antiques collection create a wonderful setting at this service-oriented Victorian inn. 29 one-bedroom standard units, some with whirlpools. 3 stories (no elevator), interior corridors. *Bath:* combo, shower or tub only. **Parking:** on-site. **Terms:** cancellation fee imposed. **Amenities:** high-speed Internet, hair dryers. **Dining:** restaurant, see separate listing. **Guest Services:** wireless Internet. **Business Services:** meeting rooms, fax (fee). **Cards:** AX, CB, DC, DS, MC, VI.

RAMADA   *Book at AAA.com*   Phone: 540/465-2444

Small-scale Hotel
Rates not provided

Address: 21 Signal Knob Dr 22657 **Location:** I-81, exit 298, just e. **Facility:** 89 one-bedroom standard units, some with whirlpools. 3 stories, interior corridors. *Bath:* combo or shower only. **Parking:** on-site. **Amenities:** high-speed Internet, voice mail, irons, hair dryers. **Pool(s):** heated indoor. **Leisure Activities:** whirlpool, exercise room. *Fee:* game room. **Guest Services:** coin laundry, wireless Internet. **Business Services:** meeting rooms, business center.

—— WHERE TO DINE ——

CHRISTINA'S MEXICAN RESTAURANT
Phone: 540/465-5300

Great background music lends to the wonderful atmosphere. Many drink selections complement the amazing chips and salsa and Mexican cuisine. Casual dress. **Bar:** Full bar. **Hours:** 11 am-9:30 pm. Closed: 12/25; also Tues. **Address:** 348 E King St 22657 **Location:** I-81, exit 298, 2.2 mi s on US 11, then just n. **Parking:** on-site. **Cards:** AX, CB, DC, DS, JC, MC, VI.

Mexican
$5-$15

HOTEL STRASBURG RESTAURANT
Phone: 540/465-9191

Victorian-period antiques and quaint decor set a casual, relaxed tone. The sophisticated menu focuses on pasta and veal specialties, such as sauteed veal scaloppine with diced tomatoes, fresh mozzarella and wine sauce. The weekday lunch buffet is popular. The large lounge is perfect for pre-dinner meetings or after-dinner drinks. Visitors should take a look at the inn. Casual dress. **Bar:** Full bar. **Reservations:** suggested. **Hours:** 11:30 am-2:30 & 5-9 pm, Fri & Sat 8-10:30 am, 11:30-2:30 & 5-10 pm, Sun 8-10:30 am, 11-2:30 & 3-9 pm. **Address:** 213 Holliday St 22657 **Location:** I-81, exit 298, 2.2 mi s on US 11, then just s; in Hotel Strasburg. **Parking:** on-site. **Cards:** AX, CB, DC, DS, MC, VI. **Country Inn**

Regional American
$7-$24

SUFFOLK —*See Hampton Roads Area p. 773.*

SURRY —*See Hampton Roads Area p. 774.*

TANGIER pop. 604

—— WHERE TO STAY ——

—— *The following lodging was either not evaluated or did not* ——
meet AAA rating requirements but is listed for your information only.

BAY VIEW INN
Phone: 757/891-2396

Not evaluated. **Address:** W Ridge Rd 23440 **Location:** West side of island. Facilities, services, and decor characterize a basic property.

[fyi]

—— WHERE TO DINE ——

—— *The following restaurant has not been evaluated by AAA* ——
but is listed for your information only.

CHESAPEAKE HOUSE
Phone: 757/891-2331

Not evaluated. This is the spot to stop for meals any Southern grandmother would be proud to serve. All served family style at long tables; heaping platters of crabcakes, clam fritters, baked ham, hot rolls, corn pudding, potato salad, and more. **Address:** 16243 Main Ridge Rd 23440

[fyi]

TAPPAHANNOCK pop. 2,068

—— WHERE TO STAY ——

THE ESSEX INN
Phone: (804)443-9900

Address: 203 Duke St 22560 **Location:** 0.3 mi s on US 17, then just e. **Facility:** 8 one-bedroom standard units, some with kitchens. 3 stories (no elevator), interior/exterior corridors. **Parking:** on-site. **Terms:** 7 day cancellation notice. **Amenities:** DVD players, CD players, irons, hair dryers. **Guest Services:** wireless Internet. **Business Services:** meeting rooms. **Cards:** AX, MC, VI.

Bed & Breakfast
$145-$200 All Year

SUPER 8 MOTEL
Book at AAA.com
Phone: 804/443-3888

Address: 1800 Tappahannock Blvd 22560 **Location:** US 17 and 360. **Facility:** 43 one-bedroom standard units. 2 stories (no elevator), interior corridors. **Parking:** on-site. **Amenities:** high-speed Internet, safes (fee), hair dryers. **Guest Services:** wireless Internet.

Motel
Rates not provided

—— WHERE TO DINE ——

LOWERY'S SEAFOOD RESTAURANT
Phone: 804/443-4314

Established in 1938, the family-run spot sits along the Rappahannock River. Regional fresh seafood, Southern-style vegetables, delightful corn muffins and such sinful desserts as hot fudge cake and bread pudding make for a pleasing and satisfying menu. Casual dress. **Bar:** Beer & wine. **Hours:** 11 am-9 pm, Sat & Sun also 8-10:30 am. Closed: 12/24, 12/25. **Address:** 528 Church Ln 22560 **Location:** On US 17/360; center. **Parking:** on-site. **Cards:** AX, DS, MC, VI.

Regional Seafood
$5-$25

THORNBURG

─── WHERE TO STAY ───

QUALITY INN *Book at AAA.com*
◆◆
Small-scale Hotel
Rates not provided

Address: 6409 Dan Bell Ln 22565 **Location:** I-95, exit 118 (SR 606), just w. **Facility:** 54 one-bedroom standard units, some with whirlpools. 2 stories (no elevator), exterior corridors. *Bath:* combo or shower only. **Parking:** on-site. **Amenities:** high-speed Internet, voice mail, irons, hair dryers. **Pool(s):** outdoor. **Guest Services:** wireless Internet. **Business Services:** fax.

Phone: 540/582-1097

CALL 🚪M 🏊 📷 🔲 🖥 / SOME UNITS FEE 🐾 ✕

TROUTVILLE pop. 432

─── WHERE TO STAY ───

COMFORT INN TROUTVILLE *Book great rates at AAA.com*
AAA SAVE
◆◆◆
Small-scale Hotel
$64-$125 All Year

Address: 2545 Lee Hwy S 24175 **Location:** I-81, exit 150A, just s on US 11. **Facility:** 72 one-bedroom standard units. 2 stories (no elevator), interior corridors. **Parking:** on-site. **Amenities:** high-speed Internet, irons, hair dryers. **Pool(s):** outdoor. **Guest Services:** valet laundry, wireless Internet. **Business Services:** PC. **Cards:** AX, CB, DC, DS, JC, MC, VI. **Free Special Amenities:** continental breakfast and high-speed Internet.

Phone: (540)992-5600

S/D 🍴 🏊 📷 🖥 / SOME UNITS FEE 🐾 ✕ 🔲 🖥

HOLIDAY INN EXPRESS *Book great rates at AAA.com*
AAA SAVE
◆◆◆
Small-scale Hotel
$89-$129 All Year

Address: 3139 Lee Hwy S 24175 **Location:** I-81, exit 150A, just ne on US 11. **Facility:** 82 one-bedroom standard units, some with whirlpools. 2 stories (no elevator), interior/exterior corridors. *Bath:* combo or shower only. **Parking:** on-site. **Amenities:** high-speed Internet, dual phone lines, voice mail, irons, hair dryers. **Pool(s):** outdoor. **Leisure Activities:** whirlpool, exercise room. **Guest Services:** coin laundry, wireless Internet. **Business Services:** meeting rooms, fax (fee). **Cards:** AX, CB, DC, DS, JC, MC, VI. **Free Special Amenities:** newspaper and high-speed Internet.

Phone: 540/966-4444

🍴 CALL 🚪M 🏊 📷 🔲 🖥 🖥 / SOME UNITS ✕

─── WHERE TO DINE ───

COUNTRY PRIDE RESTAURANT
AAA
◆
American
$6-$15

Diners get just what they would expect from the popular truck stop: fast service, cheerful servers and good food. The all-you-can-eat buffet is loaded with hot and cold fare. Chicken, chops, lasagna and sausage with peppers are favorites. Casual dress. **Hours:** 24 hours. **Address:** US 220 24175 **Location:** I-81, exit 150A, just e on US 220, at jct US 11; in Travel Centers of America. **Parking:** on-site. **Cards:** AX, DC, DS, MC, VI.

Phone: 540/992-3100

🔲

THE GREENWOOD RESTAURANT
◆
American
$5-$10

The restaurant has been serving home-style cooking since 1952. Servers are friendly. Casual dress. **Hours:** 7 am-8 pm, Fri & Sat-9 pm. Closed: 12/25. **Address:** 8176 Lee Hwy 24175 **Location:** I-81, exit 156, 0.5 mi e on SR 640, 1 mi s on US 11. **Parking:** on-site.

Phone: 540/992-3550

URBANNA pop. 543

─── WHERE TO DINE ───

SOMETHING DIFFERENT COUNTRY STORE
◆
Deli/Subs
Sandwiches
$5-$8

The simple country store focuses on great Southern fare, such as hearty breakfasts with homemade sausage, North Carolina-style pork barbecue, she-crab soup, clam chowder, homemade rolls and the specialty sandwich made with smoked turkey and country ham salad. Casual dress. **Hours:** 9 am-6 pm, Fri & Sat-8 pm, Sun-5 pm. Closed major holidays; also Tues. **Address:** 3617 Old Virginia St 23175 **Location:** 1.7 mi w of jct SR 602 and 603. **Parking:** on-site. **Cards:** MC, VI.

Phone: 804/758-8000

VERONA pop. 3,638

─── WHERE TO STAY ───

KNIGHTS INN *Book great rates at AAA.com*
AAA SAVE
◆◆
Small-scale Hotel
Rates not provided

Address: 70 Lodge Ln 24482 **Location:** I-81, exit 227, just w, then just n. **Facility:** 100 one-bedroom standard units. 2 stories (no elevator), exterior corridors. **Parking:** on-site. **Amenities:** voice mail, irons, hair dryers. **Pool(s):** outdoor. **Guest Services:** coin laundry. **Business Services:** meeting rooms, fax (fee). **Free Special Amenities:** continental breakfast and high-speed Internet.

Phone: 540/248-8981

CALL 🚪M 🏊 📷 🖥 / SOME UNITS FEE 🐾 ✕ 🔲

VESUVIUS

──── **WHERE TO STAY** ────

SUGAR TREE INN

Historic
Country Inn
$145-$265 3/1-12/15 &
2/10-2/28

Phone: 540/377-2197

Address: 145 Lodge Tr 24483 **Location:** SR 56, 3 mi e; 0.9 mi w of jct Blue Ridge Pkwy; very narrow, steep, one-lane winding mountain road; in George Washington National Forest. **Facility:** Follow a winding drive to this tree-lined property with picturesque views, gardens, antiques, a parlor with books and a professional staff. 13 one-bedroom standard units, some with whirlpools. 2 stories (no elevator), interior/exterior corridors. *Bath:* combo or shower only. **Parking:** on-site. **Terms:** open 3/1-12/15 & 2/10-2/28, cancellation fee imposed. **Amenities:** CD players, hair dryers. *Some:* DVD players. **Leisure Activities:** whirlpool, fishing, hiking trails. **Guest Services:** wireless Internet. **Business Services:** meeting rooms.

VIENNA — *See District Of Columbia p. 562.*

VIRGINIA BEACH — *See Hampton Roads Area p. 775.*

WAKEFIELD pop. 1,038

──── **WHERE TO DINE** ────

VIRGINIA DINER

Regional American
$4-$15

Phone: 757/899-3106

In the heart of Virginia's peanut country, the long-standing Southern diner is a regional favorite that started in 1929 in a renovated railroad car. Look for specialties such as peanut soup, country ham, Brunswick stew and Southern fried chicken. Casual dress. **Bar:** Beer only. **Reservations:** accepted. **Hours:** 6 am-8 pm; to 9 pm in summer. Closed: 12/25; also for dinner 12/24. **Address:** 322 W Main St 23888 **Location:** SR 460; center. **Parking:** on-site. **Cards:** AX, DS, MC, VI.

WARM SPRINGS

──── **WHERE TO STAY** ────

THE INN AT GRISTMILL SQUARE

Historic
Country Inn
$95-$160 All Year

Phone: (540)839-2231

Address: Rt 645 Old Mill Rd 24484 **Location:** US 220, 0.4 mi w on SR 619. **Facility:** Centered around a circa 1900 gristmill, this cluster of historic buildings offers such rooms as the Silo, tennis courts, a stream and rocking chairs. 20 one-bedroom standard units, some with efficiencies, kitchens and/or whirlpools. 2 stories (no elevator), interior/exterior corridors. **Parking:** on-site. **Terms:** 3 day cancellation notice. **Amenities:** irons, hair dryers. Dining: Waterwheel Restaurant, see separate listing. **Pool(s):** outdoor. **Leisure Activities:** 3 tennis courts, exercise room. *Fee:* massage. **Business Services:** meeting rooms. **Cards:** MC, VI.

──── **WHERE TO DINE** ────

WATERWHEEL RESTAURANT

American
$18-$26

Phone: 540/839-2231

Cozy, relaxed fine dining is the mode in the restored circa 1900 grist mill. Included in the good selection of specialties is mountain trout with cornmeal breading and black walnuts, snap peas and red potatoes. Service is attentive and professional. Casual dress. **Bar:** Full bar. **Reservations:** suggested. **Hours:** 6 pm-9 pm, Fri & Sat-10 pm, Sun 11 am-2 & 6-9 pm; hours vary in winter. Closed: Tues 11/1-5/1. **Address:** Old Mill Rd (Rt 645) 24484 **Location:** US 220, 0.4 mi w on SR 619; in The Inn at Gristmill Square. **Parking:** on-site. **Cards:** DS, MC, VI. **Historic**

WARRENTON pop. 6,670

──── **WHERE TO STAY** ────

BLACK HORSE INN

Bed & Breakfast
Rates not provided

Phone: 540/349-4020

Address: 8393 Meetze Rd 20187 **Location:** US 15/29 and 17, exit Meetz Rd, 1.6 mi e. Located in a rural area. **Facility:** The inn, which carries an equine theme throughout its main house and grounds, offers named guest rooms and a gazebo where readers may retreat. Smoke free premises. 9 one-bedroom standard units, some with whirlpools. 2 stories (no elevator), interior/exterior corridors. *Bath:* combo or shower only. **Parking:** on-site. **Terms:** office hours 9 am-5 pm, check-in 4 pm. **Amenities:** video library, hair dryers. *Some:* CD players, irons. **Guest Services:** wireless Internet. **Business Services:** meeting rooms.

COMFORT INN

Motel
$129-$179 All Year

Book great rates at AAA.com

Phone: (540)349-8900

Address: 7379 Comfort Inn Dr 20187 **Location:** 1.5 mi n on US 15/29, on service road. **Facility:** 97 one-bedroom standard units, some with efficiencies (no utensils) and/or whirlpools. 2 stories (no elevator), interior/exterior corridors. **Parking:** on-site. **Terms:** cancellation fee imposed. **Amenities:** voice mail, irons, hair dryers. **Pool(s):** outdoor. **Leisure Activities:** picnic tables, grills, limited exercise equipment, basketball. **Guest Services:** coin laundry, wireless Internet. **Business Services:** meeting rooms. **Cards:** AX, DC, DS, MC, VI. **Free Special Amenities:** expanded continental breakfast and high-speed Internet.

HOLIDAY INN EXPRESS HOTEL & SUITES   *Book at AAA.com*   Phone: 540/341-3461

Small-scale Hotel
Rates not provided

Address: 410 Holiday Ct 20186 **Location:** US 15/29 and 17, exit Meetze Rd (SR 643), just w, then 0.8 mi n on Walker Rd. **Facility:** Smoke free premises. 85 one-bedroom standard units. 3 stories, interior corridors. *Bath:* combo or shower only. **Parking:** on-site. **Amenities:** high-speed Internet, voice mail, irons, hair dryers. *Some:* DVD players (fee). **Pool(s):** outdoor. **Leisure Activities:** exercise room. **Guest Services:** valet and coin laundry, wireless Internet. **Business Services:** meeting rooms, business center.

CALL

----------- **WHERE TO DINE** -----------

GRANPA GROOVEY'S   Phone: 540/347-5757

American
$7-$30

The modest dining room in this shopping center restaurant is comfortable. The specialty is fresh, flavorful seafood, which is available in a large variety. All-you-can-eat offerings are available daily. Casual dress. **Bar:** Full bar. **Reservations:** accepted. **Hours:** 11:30 am-10 pm, Sun noon-8 pm. Closed major holidays; also Mon. **Address:** 573 Frost Ave 20186 **Location:** US 17/29 business route, just w on US 211 W; in Warrenton Towne Center. **Parking:** on-site. **Cards:** AX, DS, MC, VI.

NAPOLEON'S RESTAURANT   Phone: 540/347-4300

Continental
$9-$25

In an 1830 Greek Revival home in the historic district, the restaurant affords seating in the casual ground-level dining room, in the more formal upstairs dining rooms or on the seasonal patio. Global cuisine incorporates high-quality ingredients and draws on worldwide influences. Many ingredients are organic. Angus beef stands out among offerings in the more formal upstairs area, referred to as "67 Chop House.". Casual dress. **Bar:** Full bar. **Reservations:** suggested, weekends. **Hours:** 11 am-9 pm, Fri & Sat-10 pm. Closed: 12/25. **Address:** 67 Waterloo St 20186 **Location:** At Waterloo and Diagonal sts; in historic district. **Parking:** on-site. **Cards:** AX, DS, MC, VI. **Historic**

WARSAW pop. 1,375

----------- **WHERE TO STAY** -----------

BEST WESTERN WARSAW   *Book great rates at AAA.com*   Phone: 804/333-1700

Small-scale Hotel
Rates not provided

Address: 4522 Richmond Rd 22572 **Location:** US 360, just w of town. **Facility:** 38 units. 37 one-bedroom standard units. 1 one-bedroom suite. 2 stories, interior corridors. *Bath:* combo or shower only. **Parking:** on-site. **Amenities:** high-speed Internet, irons, hair dryers. **Pool(s):** outdoor. **Leisure Activities:** limited exercise equipment. **Guest Services:** wireless Internet.

CALL

/ SOME UNITS   FEE   FEE VCR   FEE   FEE

Best Western

AAA Benefit:

Members save 10% everyday, plus an exclusive frequent stay program.

WASHINGTON pop. 183

----------- **WHERE TO STAY** -----------

FOSTER HARRIS HOUSE   Phone: (540)675-3757

Historic Bed
& Breakfast
$195-$335 All Year

Address: 189 Main St 22747 **Location:** 0.5 mi w on US 211 business route. Located in a quiet area. **Facility:** In the tiny town of Washington near many antiques shops, this turn-of-the-20th-century house is nestled in the foothills of the Blue Ridge Mountains. Smoke free premises. 5 one-bedroom standard units, some with whirlpools. 2 stories (no elevator), interior corridors. *Bath:* combo or shower only. **Parking:** on-site. **Terms:** age restrictions may apply, 14 day cancellation notice-fee imposed. **Amenities:** irons, hair dryers. **Leisure Activities:** horseshoes. **Business Services:** meeting rooms, PC, fax. **Cards:** AX, MC, VI.

HERITAGE HOUSE BED & BREAKFAST   Phone: 540/675-3207

Historic Bed
& Breakfast
$175-$295 All Year

Address: 291 Main St 22747 **Location:** Just w on US 211 business route. **Facility:** The elegant 1837 manor house is located in the heart of the historic district; the club house is kept stocked with refreshments. Smoke free premises. 5 units. 4 one-bedroom standard units. 1 one-bedroom suite. 2 stories (no elevator), interior corridors. *Bath:* combo or shower only. **Parking:** on-site. **Terms:** age restrictions may apply, 14 day cancellation notice-fee imposed. **Amenities:** CD players. **Leisure Activities:** croquet. **Guest Services:** wireless Internet. **Business Services:** meeting rooms. **Cards:** AX, MC, VI. **Free Special Amenities:** full breakfast and local telephone calls.

THE INN AT LITTLE WASHINGTON   Phone: 540/675-3800

Country Inn
$410-$755 All Year

Address: Middle and Main Sts 22747 **Location:** Jct of Middle and Main sts. **Facility:** European fabrics and antiques create a sumptuous ambience in this service-oriented inn's units and such public areas as a koi fish pond and tea area. Designated smoking area. 18 units. 16 one-bedroom standard units, some with whirlpools. 1 vacation home and 1 cottage. 3 stories, interior corridors. *Bath:* combo or shower only. **Parking:** on-site and valet. **Terms:** 14 day cancellation notice-fee imposed. **Amenities:** video library, DVD players, CD players, high-speed Internet, voice mail, safes, irons, hair dryers. **Dining:** restaurant, see separate listing. **Leisure Activities:** bicycles. *Fee:* massage. **Guest Services:** valet laundry, wireless Internet. **Business Services:** meeting rooms, PC. **Cards:** AX, MC, VI. **Free Special Amenities:** continental breakfast and high-speed Internet.

/ SOME UNITS

MIDDLETON INN

AAA [SAVE]

▽△▽ ▽△▽ ▽△▽

Historic Bed
& Breakfast

$235-$595 All Year

Phone: 540/675-2020

Address: 176 Main St 22747 **Location:** 0.5 mi w on US 211 business route. **Facility:** Afternoon tea and greetings by friendly resident dogs, cats and horses await arrivals to this Federal-style manor fronted by a long, winding driveway. Smoke free premises. 7 units. 4 one-bedroom standard units. 3 cottages, some with whirlpools. 2 stories (no elevator), interior/exterior corridors. *Bath:* combo or shower only. **Parking:** on-site. **Terms:** age restrictions may apply, cancellation fee imposed. **Amenities:** DVD players, CD players, irons, hair dryers. **Leisure Activities:** croquet, badminton. *Fee:* massage. **Guest Services:** valet laundry, wireless Internet. **Business Services:** meeting rooms, fax. **Cards:** AX, MC, VI. **Free Special Amenities: full breakfast and high-speed Internet.**

 ⊠ 🎦 / SOME UNITS 🅦 🍴 🖥 🖨

------ WHERE TO DINE ------

COUNTRY CAFE

▽△▽

American

$6-$18

Phone: 540/675-1066

A local favorite for many years, the cafe serves excellent food at affordable prices. The ice cream desserts shouldn't be missed. Casual dress. **Hours:** 8 am-9 pm. Closed: 12/25; also Sun. **Address:** 389A Main St 22747 **Location:** Just w on US 211 business route. **Parking:** on-site. **Cards:** MC, VI.

THE INN AT LITTLE WASHINGTON
DINING ROOM

AAA

▽△▽ ▽△▽ ▽△▽

Regional
American

$148-$188

Phone: 540/675-3800

Uncompromising cuisine with a prix-fixe menu representing the freshest of premium ingredients artfully prepared and presented is what makes this restaurant shine. The opulent atmosphere, world-class wine list and gracious staff are well orchestrated by chef/owner Patrick O'Connell. Don't miss the opportunity to tour the kitchen and the outside garden area. One of a kind. Dressy casual. **Bar:** Full bar. **Reservations:** required, 2-3 weeks advance. **Hours:** seatings 6 pm-9:30 pm, Fri & Sat from 5:30 pm, Sun 4 pm-8:30 pm. Closed: Tues except 4/20-6/15 & 9/21-12/21. **Address:** Business Rt US 211 22747 **Location:** Jct of Middle and Main sts; in The Inn at Little Washington. **Parking:** on-site and valet. **Cards:** AX, MC, VI. **Country Inn**

WAVERLY pop. 2,309

------ WHERE TO DINE ------

COWLINGS BARBEQUE

▽△▽

Barbecue

$3-$11

Phone: 804/834-3100

For more than 20 years, lovers of North Carolina-style barbecue have traveled from far and wide to the simple spot for delicious pork barbecue, cornbread and homemade pies. Casual dress. **Bar:** Beer only. **Hours:** 11 am-8 pm. Closed major holidays; also Tues. **Address:** 7019 General Mahone Hwy 23890 **Location:** Just e of center on US 460. **Parking:** on-site. **Cards:** MC, VI.

WAYNESBORO pop. 19,520

------ WHERE TO STAY ------

BELLE HEARTH BED & BREAKFAST

▽△▽ ▽△▽

Bed & Breakfast

$95-$140 All Year

Phone: 540/943-1910

Address: 320 S Wayne Ave 22980 **Location:** 0.3 mi s from Main St. **Facility:** A gabled roof and heart-pine floors enhance the ambience at this 1909 Victorian home with a wrap-around porch, antiques and country breakfasts. 4 one-bedroom standard units. 2 stories (no elevator), interior corridors. *Bath:* combo or shower only. **Parking:** on-site. **Terms:** 2 night minimum stay - seasonal and/or weekends, age restrictions may apply, 10 day cancellation notice. **Amenities:** *Some:* DVD players, CD players. **Pool(s):** outdoor. **Guest Services:** wireless Internet. **Cards:** MC, VI.

 A$K S🄳 🏊 ⊠ / SOME UNITS VCR 🍴 🖨

COMFORT INN WAYNESBORO   *Book great rates at AAA.com*

AAA [SAVE]

▽△▽ ▽△▽

Small-scale Hotel

$80-$130 All Year

Phone: (540)932-3060

Address: 15 Windigrove Dr 22980 **Location:** I-64, exit 94, 0.5 mi n on US 340, then just e. **Facility:** 56 one-bedroom standard units, some with whirlpools. 3 stories, interior corridors. *Bath:* combo or shower only. **Parking:** on-site. **Terms:** 30 day cancellation notice-fee imposed. **Amenities:** high-speed Internet, voice mail, irons, hair dryers. **Pool(s):** outdoor. **Leisure Activities:** limited exercise equipment. **Guest Services:** coin laundry, wireless Internet. **Business Services:** meeting rooms. **Cards:** AX, CB, DC, DS, JC, MC, VI. **Free Special Amenities: expanded continental breakfast and high-speed Internet.**

S🄳 🍴📶 CALL 🄼 🏊 🎦 🍴 🖨 🖥 / SOME UNITS ⊠

DAYS INN WAYNESBORO   *Book great rates at AAA.com*

AAA [SAVE]

▽△▽

Small-scale Hotel

Rates not provided

Phone: 540/943-1101

Address: 2060 Rosser Ave 22980 **Location:** I-64, exit 94, 0.5 mi n on US 340. **Facility:** 97 one-bedroom standard units. 2 stories (no elevator), exterior corridors. **Parking:** on-site. **Amenities:** high-speed Internet, hair dryers. **Pool(s):** outdoor. **Guest Services:** valet laundry, wireless Internet. **Business Services:** meeting rooms, fax (fee). **Free Special Amenities: newspaper and high-speed Internet.**

 🍴📶 🏊 🎦 FEE 🍴 🖥 🖨 / SOME UNITS FEE 🐾 ⊠

DELUXE BUDGET MOTEL   *Book great rates at AAA.com*

AAA [SAVE]

▽△▽

Motel

$50-$80 3/1-10/31
$40-$60 11/1-2/28

Phone: 540/949-8253

Address: 2112 W Main St 22980 **Location:** I-64, exit 94, 0.5 mi n on US 340, 1 mi w on Lew Dewitt Blvd, then 0.8 mi e on US 250. **Facility:** 25 one-bedroom standard units. 1 story, exterior corridors. *Bath:* combo or shower only. **Parking:** on-site. **Terms:** 3 day cancellation notice-fee imposed. **Leisure Activities:** playground. **Cards:** AX, DS, MC, VI. **Free Special Amenities: local telephone calls and room upgrade (subject to availability with advance reservations).**

S🄳 🍴📶 🎦 🍴 🖥 / SOME UNITS ⊠ 🖨

HOLIDAY INN EXPRESS   *Book at AAA.com*

Small-scale Hotel
$114-$134 All Year

Phone: 540/932-7170

Address: 20 Windigrove Dr 22980 **Location:** I-64, exit 94, 0.5 mi n on US 340, then just e. **Facility:** 80 one-bedroom standard units, some with whirlpools. 3 stories, interior corridors. *Bath:* combo or shower only. **Parking:** on-site. **Terms:** cancellation fee imposed. **Amenities:** high-speed Internet, voice mail, irons, hair dryers. *Some:* DVD players. **Pool(s):** heated indoor. **Leisure Activities:** sauna, whirlpool, exercise room. **Guest Services:** coin laundry, wireless Internet. **Business Services:** meeting rooms, business center. **Cards:** AX, CB, DC, DS, MC, VI.

THE IRIS INN

Bed & Breakfast
$120-$285 3/1-11/30
$110-$250 12/1-2/28

Phone: 540/943-1991

Address: 191 Chinquapin Dr 22980 **Location:** I-64, exit 96, just s on SR 624, then just e. Located in a quiet rural area. **Facility:** With observation decks, a high level of service and special breakfasts, this lodge-type inn is in a wooded tract on the Blue Ridge's western slope. Smoke free premises. 10 one-bedroom standard units, some with whirlpools. 2 stories (no elevator), interior/exterior corridors. *Bath:* combo or shower only. **Parking:** on-site. **Terms:** age restrictions may apply, 7 day cancellation notice-fee imposed. **Amenities:** hair dryers. *Some:* DVD players, irons. **Leisure Activities:** whirlpools. **Guest Services:** wireless Internet. **Business Services:** meeting rooms. **Cards:** AX, DS, MC, VI.

QUALITY INN WAYNESBORO   *Book great rates at AAA.com*

Small-scale Hotel
$66-$130 All Year

Phone: 540/942-1171

Address: 640 W Broad St 22980 **Location:** I-64, exit 96, 3 mi w on SR 624; jct US 250 and 340. **Facility:** 75 one-bedroom standard units. 2 stories (no elevator), interior/exterior corridors. **Parking:** on-site. **Amenities:** irons, hair dryers. *Some:* high-speed Internet. **Pool(s):** outdoor. **Business Services:** valet laundry, wireless Internet. **Business Services:** fax (fee). **Cards:** AX, CB, DC, DS, JC, MC, VI. **Free Special Amenities:** expanded continental breakfast and high-speed Internet.

SUPER 8 MOTEL   *Book great rates at AAA.com*

Small-scale Hotel
Rates not provided

Phone: 540/943-3888

Address: 2045 Rosser Ave 22980 **Location:** I-64, exit 94, n on US 340 to Lew Dewitt Blvd, then just w to Apple Tree Ln. **Facility:** 48 one-bedroom standard units. 3 stories (no elevator), interior corridors. **Parking:** on-site. **Amenities:** high-speed Internet, hair dryers. **Guest Services:** wireless Internet. **Business Services:** PC. **Free Special Amenities:** local telephone calls and high-speed Internet.

--- **WHERE TO DINE** ---

GAVIDS STEAK HOUSE FAMILY GRILL

American
$6-$18

Phone: 540/949-6353

A city favorite for many years, the restaurant nurtures a family-friendly atmosphere. Wholesome American food is value-priced. Casual dress. **Hours:** 11 am-9 pm. Closed: 1/1, 12/25. **Address:** 1501 W Broad St 22980 **Location:** I-64, exit 96, 3 mi w on SR 624; jct US 250 and 340. **Parking:** on-site. **Cards:** MC, VI.

MI RANCHO MEXICAN RESTAURANT

Mexican
$7-$17

Phone: 540/941-5980

Patrons browse a large and diverse menu of standard favorites at the lively restaurant. Casual dress. **Bar:** Full bar. **Hours:** 11 am-10 pm. **Address:** 408 E Main St 22980 **Location:** Just e. **Parking:** on-site. **Cards:** AX, CB, DC, DS, JC, MC, VI.

SOUTH RIVER GRILL   *Menu on AAA.com*

American
$6-$21

Phone: 540/942-5567

The open-air, equestrian-themed restaurant offers many choices of classic American cuisine. Upscale design elements enhance the relaxed atmosphere. Seating is laid-back on the two porches and in the large lounge. Try the pork platter with homemade barbecue sauce. Casual dress. **Bar:** Full bar. **Hours:** 11 am-11 pm. Closed: 11/27, 12/24, 12/25. **Address:** 23 Windigrove Dr 22980 **Location:** I-64, exit 94, 0.5 mi n on US 340, then just e. **Parking:** on-site. **Cards:** AX, DS, MC, VI.

ZERO'S

Deli/Subs
Sandwiches
$4-$11

Phone: 540/941-1000

As Zero's says, "They are hot and on a roll." The fun, peppy and casual eatery prepares a large selection of delicatessen favorites. Casual dress. **Hours:** 11:30 am-9:30 pm. Closed: 12/25. **Address:** 125A Lucy Ln 22980 **Location:** I-64, exit 94, 0.6 mi n on US 340, then just w. **Parking:** on-site. **Cards:** MC, VI.

WEYERS CAVE pop. 1,225

--- **WHERE TO STAY** ---

THE INN AT KEEZLETOWN ROAD

Historic Bed
& Breakfast
Rates not provided

Phone: 540/234-0644

Address: 1224 Keezletown Rd 24486 **Location:** I-81, exit 235, 1 mi e, then just n. **Facility:** In a quiet town, the Victorian inn has hardwood floors, fireplaces, antiques, spectacular bedding atop large beds and a daily home-style breakfast. Smoke free premises. 4 one-bedroom standard units. 2 stories (no elevator), interior corridors. *Bath:* combo or shower only. **Parking:** on-site. **Terms:** age restrictions may apply. **Amenities:** hair dryers. **Business Services:** meeting rooms.

WHITE HALL

——— WHERE TO STAY ———

THE INN AT SUGAR HOLLOW FARM

Phone: 434/823-7086

Bed & Breakfast
Rates not provided

Address: 6051 Sugar Hollow Rd 22905 **Location:** SR 614, 2.5 mi w of jct SR 810. Located in a secluded rural area. **Facility:** A series of small bridges must be crossed to access this secluded property set back in the woods; a rooftop deck offers celestial views. Smoke free premises. 5 one-bedroom standard units, some with whirlpools. 2 stories (no elevator), interior corridors. *Bath:* combo or shower only. **Parking:** on-site. **Terms:** check-in 4 pm, age restrictions may apply. **Amenities:** CD players, hair dryers. **Leisure Activities:** fishing, bicycles, hiking trails. **Guest Services:** complimentary laundry. **Business Services:** meeting rooms.

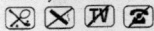

WHITE POST

——— WHERE TO STAY ———

L'AUBERGE PROVENCALE FRENCH COUNTRY INN

Phone: (540)837-1375

Historic
Country Inn
$165-$350 All Year

Address: 13630 Lord Fairfax Hwy 22663 **Location:** US 340, 1 mi s of jct US 50 and 17. **Facility:** In the heart of Virginia hunting and wine country, the inn reflects European influences in its food service, furnishings and decor. Smoke free premises. 14 one-bedroom standard units, some with whirlpools. 2 stories (no elevator), interior/exterior corridors. *Bath:* combo or shower only. **Parking:** on-site. **Terms:** age restrictions may apply, 10 day cancellation notice. **Amenities:** CD players, hair dryers. *Some:* DVD players, irons. **Dining:** L'Auberge Provencale, see separate listing. **Leisure Activities:** *Fee:* massage. **Guest Services:** valet laundry, wireless Internet. **Business Services:** meeting rooms. **Cards:** AX, DC, DS, MC, VI.

——— WHERE TO DINE ———

L'AUBERGE PROVENCALE

Phone: 540/837-1375

Regional French
$92

Dinner is deliberately lengthy, as a five-course event evokes the traditions of Southern France. Chef/owner Alain Borel artfully presents "cuisine Provencal moderne" in the 1753 fieldstone home, which is appointed in lovely decor. Professional and knowledgeable service is notable. The atmosphere is soothing and relaxed. Guests can unwind in the large parlor room with pre-dining cocktails. Semi-formal attire. **Bar:** Full bar. **Reservations:** suggested. **Hours:** 6 pm-10 pm, Sun 5 pm-9 pm. Closed: 12/25; also Mon, Tues & 1/1-1/21. **Address:** 13630 Lord Fairfax Hwy 22663 **Location:** US 340, 1 mi s of jct US 50 and 17; in L'Auberge Provencale French Country Inn. **Parking:** on-site. **Cards:** AX, CB, DC, DS, MC, VI. **Historic**

WHITE STONE pop. 358

——— WHERE TO DINE ———

THE SANDPIPER

Phone: 804/435-6176

Seafood
$15-$30

This family-run spot offers several cozy dining rooms and a great selection of delicious dishes. Specialties include shrimp with champagne sauce, grilled lamb chops, seafood chowder, fried oysters and other seasonal specialties from the sea. Casual dress. **Bar:** Full bar. **Hours:** 5 pm-9 pm, Fri & Sat-10 pm. Closed major holidays; also Sun & Mon. **Address:** 850 Rappahannock Dr 22578 **Location:** Just s on SR 3. **Parking:** on-site. **Cards:** DS, MC, VI.

WILLABY'S

Phone: 804/435-0044

Regional American
$5-$10

The casual spot is a local favorite for large burgers, waffle fries, homemade pie and fresh Chesapeake Bay seafood, including crab cakes and seasonal fried oysters. This place is well-known for its line of bottled sauces. Casual dress. **Hours:** 11 am-3 pm. Closed major holidays; also Sun & 12/24-1/2. **Address:** 453 Rappahannock Dr 22578 **Location:** On SR 3; center. **Parking:** on-site. **Cards:** AX, MC, VI.

WILLIAMSBURG —See Williamsburg, Jamestown & Yorktown p. 919.

Destination Williamsburg, Jamestown & Yorktown

*T*ime—whether you spend it in the past or the present—is on your side when you visit Virginia's Historic Triangle. In this compact heritage region you're only minutes from the next diversion of choice.

*S*hop for the old in Williamsburg's historic district or seek out the new in outlet malls. Take your golf clubs to the nearest course. Pack a picnic lunch and drive Colonial Parkway, end to end.

Len Kaufman / Virginia Tourism Corp

Susan Constant at Jamestown Settlement. This reproduction of the 17th-century sailing vessel is moored in the James River. (See listing page 319)

Shopping in Yorktown. Whether you fancy bonnets or baubles, charming shops offer a pleasant shopping experience.

Bill Boxer / Virginia Tourism Corp

© Richard I'Anson / Lonely Planet Images

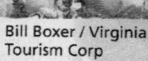

Colonial Williamsburg Historic Area living-history demonstrations. Costumed interpreters bring 18th-century traditions to life. (See listing page 322)

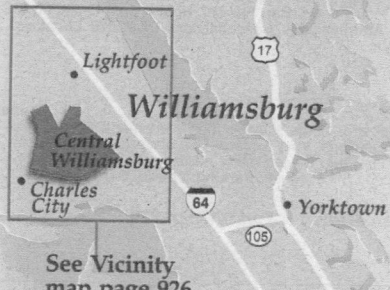

Lightfoot

Williamsburg

Central Williamsburg

Charles City

Yorktown

See Vicinity map page 926

*P*laces included in this AAA Destination Area:

© David R. Frazier Photolibrary, Inc. / Alamy

Dining in Historic Yorktown. Restaurants with handsome Colonial architecture set the tone for unforgettable dining experiences.

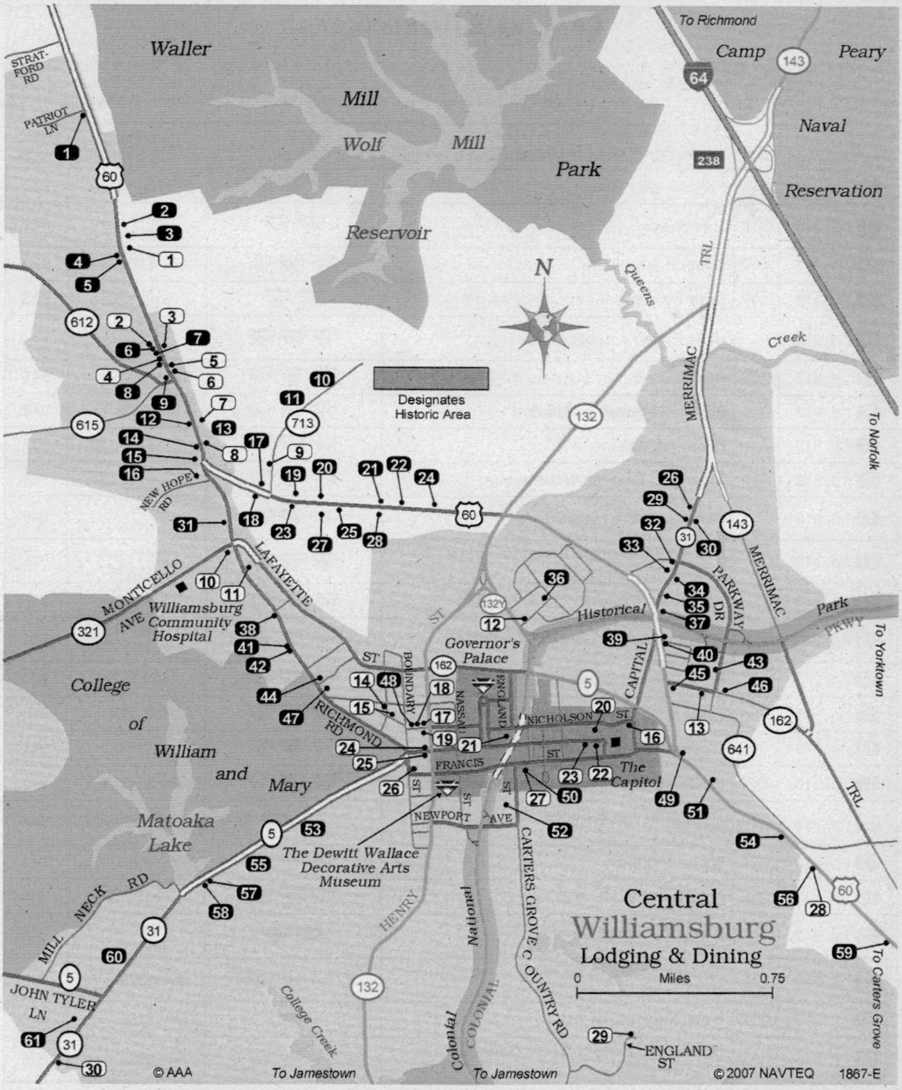
Central
Williamsburg
Lodging & Dining
Miles
0
0.75
Designates Historic Area
N
Waller
Mill
Wolf
Mill
Park
Reservoir
To Richmond
Camp
Peary
Naval
Reservation
STRAT-FORD RD
PATRIOT LN
NEW HOPE RD
MONTICELLO AVE
LAFAYETTE
Williamsburg Community Hospital
College
of
William
and
Mary
Matoaka
Lake
MILL
NECK
RD
JOHN TYLER LN
RICHMOND RD
BOUNDARY
NASSAU
ENGLAND
NICHOLSON ST
FRANCIS
ST
NEWPORT AVE
Governor's Palace
The Capitol
The Dewitt Wallace Decorative Arts Museum
HENRY
National
Colonial
COLONIAL
CARTERS GROVE COUNTRY RD
ENGLAND ST
Historical
Park
PKWY
CAPITAL
PARKWAY DR
MERRIMAC TRL
MERRIMAC
TRL
Queens
Creek
College Creek
To Norfolk
To Yorktown
To Carters Grove
To Jamestown
To Jamestown
© AAA
© 2007 NAVTEQ
1867-E

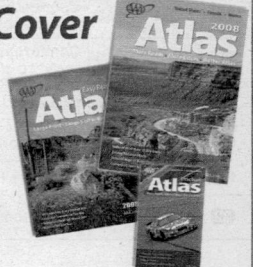

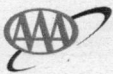

Central Williamsburg

This index helps you "spot" where approved lodgings and restaurants are located on the corresponding detailed maps. Lodging daily rate range is for comparison only and show the property's high season. Restaurant rate range is a combination of lunch and/or dinner. Turn to the listing page for more detailed rate information and consult display ads for special promotions.

Spotter/Map Page Number	OA	CENTRAL WILLIAMSBURG - Lodgings	Diamond Rating	Rate Range High Season	Listing Page
1 / p. 913	AAA	Holiday Inn Patriot - see color ad p 938	◆◆◆	$109-$149 SAVE	939
2 / p. 913	AAA	Travelodge	◆◆	Rates not provided SAVE	943
3 / p. 913	AAA	Comfort Inn Central - see color ad p 930	◆◆◆	$59-$129 SAVE	930
4 / p. 913	AAA	Days Inn Central - see color ad p 933	◆◆	$109 SAVE	933
5 / p. 913		Hampton Inn & Suites	◆◆◆	Rates not provided	937
6 / p. 913	AAA	Residence Inn by Marriott Williamsburg	◆◆◆	$153-$241 SAVE	941
7 / p. 913	AAA	SpringHill Suites by Marriott	◆◆◆	$109-$208 SAVE	943
8 / p. 913	AAA	Hilton Garden Inn	◆◆◆	$79-$199 SAVE	937
9 / p. 913	AAA	America's Best Inn Williamsburg	◆◆◆	$49-$109 SAVE	928
10 / p. 913		Wyndham Governor's Green	◆◆◆	Rates not provided	945
11 / p. 913		Fairfield Williamsburg Condo Rentals at Kingsgate	◆◆◆	Rates not provided	936
12 / p. 913		Holiday Inn Express Hotel & Suites	◆◆◆	$89-$199	937
13 / p. 913	AAA	Embassy Suites - see color ad p 919	◆◆◆	Rates not provided SAVE	934
14 / p. 913		Patriot Inn and Suites	◆◆◆	$69-$119	940
15 / p. 913		Fairfield Inn & Suites by Marriott	◆◆◆	$98-$175	936
16 / p. 913		Quality Suites Williamsburg	◆◆◆	$132	941
17 / p. 913	AAA	La Quinta Inn Williamsburg (Historic Area)	◆◆◆	$85-$115 SAVE	940
18 / p. 913	AAA	Travelodge Inn & Suites - see color ad p 943	◆◆	$69-$99 SAVE	944
19 / p. 913	AAA	Waller Mill Inn	◆◆◆	$69-$129 SAVE	944
20 / p. 913	AAA	Days Inn Historic Area - see color ad p 935	◆◆◆	$39-$99 SAVE	933
21 / p. 913		Ramada Inn 1776	◆◆	Rates not provided	941
22 / p. 913	AAA	Homewood Suites by Hilton - see color ad p 939	◆◆◆	$99-$379 SAVE	939
23 / p. 913	AAA	Sleep Inn-Historic - see color ad p 924	◆◆	$49-$159 SAVE	943
24 / p. 913	AAA	Holiday Inn Hotel & Suites Gateway - see color ad p 938	◆◆◆	$69-$499 SAVE	938
25 / p. 913	AAA	Quality Inn Historic Area Hotel - see color ad p 942	◆◆◆	$59-$179 SAVE	941
26 / p. 913	AAA	Colonel Waller Inn & Suites	◆	$27-$99 SAVE	929
27 / p. 913	AAA	Country Inn and Suites by Carlson Historic Area - see color ad p 932	◆◆◆	$69-$329 SAVE	932
28 / p. 913	AAA	Comfort Inn King George Historic - see color ad p 931	◆◆◆	$64-$169 SAVE	930
29 / p. 913		Hampton Inn & Suites Historic	◆◆◆	Rates not provided	937
30 / p. 913	AAA	White Lion Motel	◆◆	$85-$175 SAVE	945
31 / p. 913	AAA	Westgate Historic Williamsburg	◆◆◆	$149-$209 SAVE	945
32 / p. 913		Quality Inn Lord Paget	◆◆	Rates not provided	941

Spotter/Map Page Number	OA	CENTRAL WILLIAMSBURG - Lodgings (continued)	Diamond Rating	Rate Range High Season	Listing Page
33 / p. 913	AAA	Econo Lodge-Historic Area - see color ad p 936	◇◇	$59-$119 SAVE	934
34 / p. 913	AAA	TraveLodge-King William Inn - see color ad p 944	◇◇	Rates not provided SAVE	944
35 / p. 913		Red Roof Inn-Williamsburg	◇◇	Rates not provided	941
36 / p. 913		Colonial Williamsburg-Woodlands Hotel & Suites - see color ad p 321	◇◇◇	$79-$209	929
37 / p. 913	AAA	Holiday Inn-Downtown & Holidome	◇◇◇	$99-$139 SAVE	937
38 / p. 913	AAA	Days Inn Colonial Downtown - see color ad p 934	◇◇	$69-$129 SAVE	933
39 / p. 913		Fox & Grape Bed & Breakfast	◇◇◇	Rates not provided	937
40 / p. 913		Hite's Bed & Breakfast	◇◇◇	$95-$125	937
41 / p. 913		A Boxwood Inn of Williamsburg	◇◇◇	$119-$225	928
42 / p. 913		A Primrose Cottage	◇◇◇	Rates not provided	928
43 / p. 913	AAA	Econo Lodge Colonial	◇◇	$55-$99 SAVE	933
44 / p. 913	AAA	Colonial Capital Bed & Breakfast	◇◇◇	$137-$187 SAVE	929
45 / p. 913	AAA	Quality Inn Colony - see color ad p 940	◇◇	$49-$179 SAVE	941
46 / p. 913	AAA	Super 8 Motel-Historic	◇◇	Rates not provided SAVE	943
47 / p. 913	AAA	Williamsburg Hospitality House	◇◇◇	$99-$229 SAVE	945
48 / p. 913		The Fife and Drum Inn	◇◇◇	$165-$295	936
49 / p. 913	AAA	Patrick Henry Inn	◇◇	$64-$104 SAVE	940
50 / p. 913		Colonial Williamsburg-Williamsburg Inn - see color ad p 321	◇◇◇◇	$279-$799	929
51 / p. 913	AAA	Four Points by Sheraton Hotel & Suites Williamsburg Historic District	◇◇◇	$50-$160 SAVE	937
52 / p. 913		Colonial Williamsburg-Williamsburg Lodge - see color ad p 321	◇◇◇	$119-$299	929
53 / p. 913		Cedars of Williamsburg Bed & Breakfast	◇◇◇	$165-$440	929
54 / p. 913		Quarterpath Inn	◇◇	$39-$109	941
55 / p. 913		Inn at 802	◇◇◇	$145-$175	939
56 / p. 913	AAA	Crowne Plaza Williamsburg at Fort Magruder	◇◇◇	$99-$279 SAVE	933
57 / p. 913		Williamsburg Sampler Bed & Breakfast Inn	◇◇◇	$165-$225	945
58 / p. 913		Legacy of Williamsburg Bed & Breakfast Inn	◇◇◇	$185-$225	940
59 / p. 913	AAA	Country Inn & Suites by Carlson East - see color ad p 932	◇◇◇	$59-$179 SAVE	930
60 / p. 913		Liberty Rose Bed & Breakfast	◇◇◇◇	$185-$275	940
61 / p. 913		Colonial Gardens Bed & Breakfast	◇◇◇	$145-$195	929
		CENTRAL WILLIAMSBURG - Restaurants			
1 / p. 913	AAA	Fireside Chophouse - see color ad p 930	◇◇◇	$10-$25	947
2 / p. 913		Casa Maya Mexican Restaurant	◇	$7-$15	946
3 / p. 913		Food For Thought	◇◇	$8-$19	947
4 / p. 913	AAA	Seafare Restaurant - see color ad p 931	◇◇◇	$13-$23	948
5 / p. 913	AAA	Kyoto Japanese Steak & Seafood House	◇◇	$10-$24	947
6 / p. 913	AAA	Aberdeen Barn	◇◇	$17-$35	945

Spotter/Map Page Number	OA	CENTRAL WILLIAMSBURG - Restaurants (continued)	Diamond Rating	Rate Range High Season	Listing Page
⑦ / p. 913	🔺🔺🔺	The Jefferson	◈◈	$12-$20	947
⑧ / p. 913	🔺🔺🔺	The Black Angus Grille	◈◈◈	$11-$37	946
⑨ / p. 913		Peking & Mongolian Grill	◈	$5-$10	948
⑩ / p. 913		Chez Trinh	◈◈	$5-$16	946
⑪ / p. 913		Three Olives Greek Restaurant	◈◈	$9-$20	948
⑫ / p. 913		Huzzah!	◈◈	$7-$18	947
⑬ / p. 913		La Tolteca Mexican Restaurante	◈	$4-$10	947
⑭ / p. 913	🔺🔺🔺	Alize Bistro	◈◈◈ .	$8-$47	945
⑮ / p. 913		Friends Cafe	◈	$3-$7	947
⑯ / p. 913		Christiana Campbell's Tavern - see color ad p 323	◈◈	$21-$32	946
⑰ / p. 913		Aromas	◈	$5-$7	945
⑱ / p. 913		Retro's-Good Eats	◈	$2-$4	948
⑲ / p. 913		Blue Talon Bistro	◈◈◈	$7-$20	946
⑳ / p. 913		Shields Tavern - see color ad p 323	◈	$5-$9	948
㉑ / p. 913		Chowning's Tavern - see color ad p 323	◈	$6-$8	946
㉒ / p. 913		King's Arms Tavern - see color ad p 323	◈◈	$9-$38	947
㉓ / p. 913		The Cheese Shop	◈	$5-$9	946
㉔ / p. 913	🔺🔺🔺	The Trellis Restaurant	◈◈◈	$7-$32	948
㉕ / p. 913		Fat Canary	◈◈◈◈	$23-$37	946
㉖ / p. 913	🔺🔺🔺	Berret's Seafood Restaurant and Taphouse Grill	◈◈◈	$10-$35	946
㉗ / p. 913		The Regency Dining Room	◈◈◈◈	$9-$37	948
㉘ / p. 913		Veranda Dining Room	◈◈	$7-$24	948
㉙ / p. 913		Golden Horseshoe Gold Course Grill	◈◈	$8-$15	947
㉚ / p. 913		Old Chickahominy House	◈◈	$3-$7	948

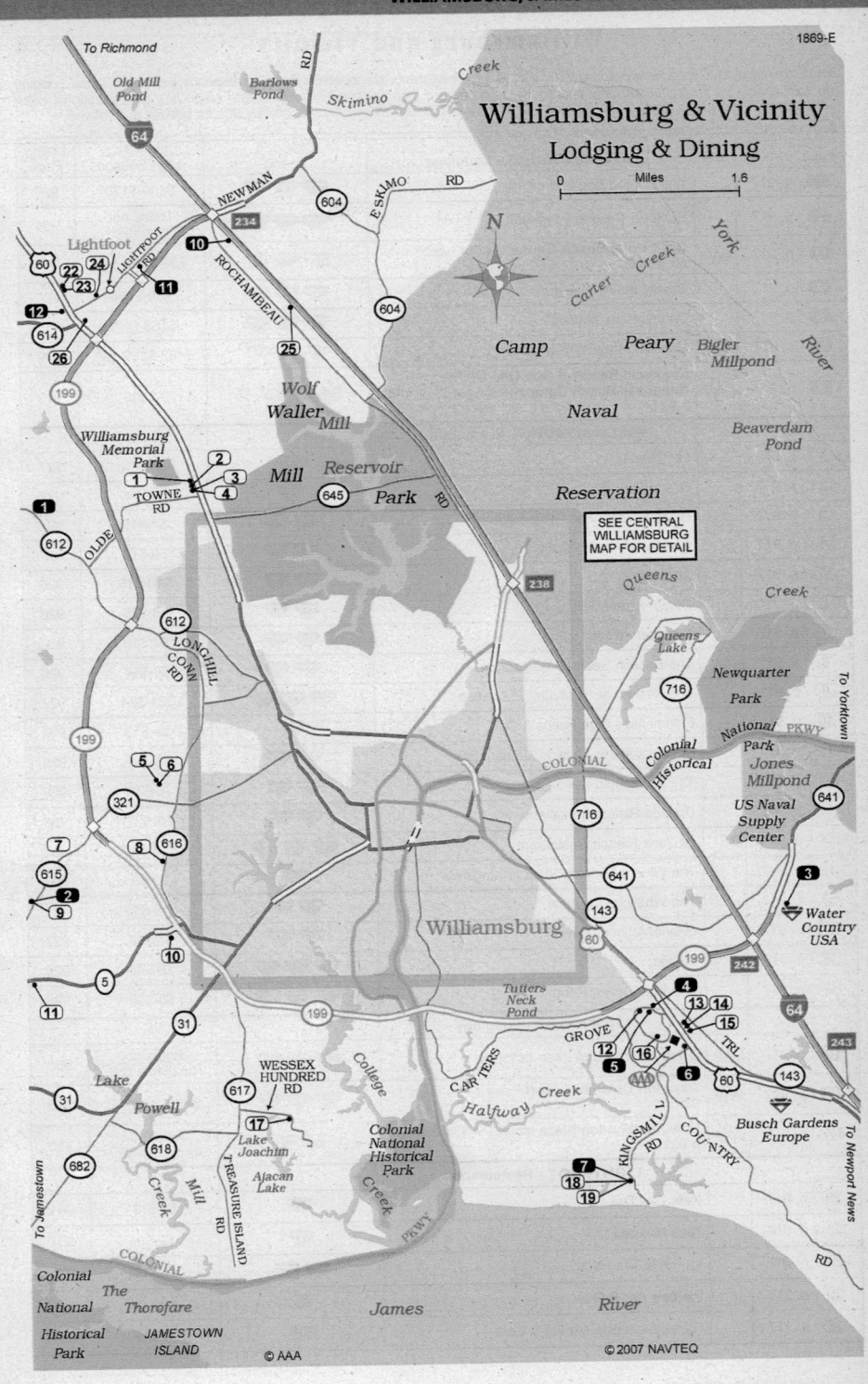

1869-E

Williamsburg & Vicinity
Lodging & Dining

0   Miles   1.6

To Richmond

Old Mill Pond

Barlows Pond

Skimino Creek

NEWMAN RD

ESKIMO RD

604

604

N

York River

Carter Creek

Camp Peary

Bigler Millpond

Naval

Beaverdam Pond

Reservation

Lightfoot

60
22 24
23
11
12
614
26

10

ROCHAMBEAU

25

199

Wolf Waller Mill

Mill Reservoir

Park RD

645

238

SEE CENTRAL WILLIAMSBURG MAP FOR DETAIL

Queens Creek

Williamsburg Memorial Park

2
1   3
4
TOWNE RD

Queens Lake

716

Newquarter Park

199

612

OLDE

612

LONGHILL CONN RD

Colonial National Historical Park

Jones Millpond

US Naval Supply Center

641

5   6

321

716

7
615
2
9

8   616

641

143

3

Water Country USA

60

199

242

64

Williamsburg

10

5

11

31

243

4
13 14
15

Tutters Neck Pond

GROVE

12
5

16
AAA
6

80

143

TRL

31

Lake Powell

617

WESSEX HUNDRED RD

17
Lake Joachim

Colonial National Historical Park

CARTERS

Halfway Creek

Busch Gardens Europe

KINGSMILL RD

COUNTRY

To Newport News

682

818

Ajacan Lake

College Creek

7
18
19

To Jamestown

Mill Creek

TREASURE ISLAND RD

PKWY

RD

COLONIAL

Colonial
National
Historical
Park

The Thorofare

JAMESTOWN ISLAND

James River

© AAA

© 2007 NAVTEQ

Williamsburg and Vicinity

This index helps you "spot" where approved lodgings and restaurants are located on the corresponding detailed maps. Lodging daily rate range is for comparison only and show the property's high season. Restaurant rate range is a combination of lunch and/or dinner. Turn to the listing page for more detailed rate information and consult listing ads for special promotions.

Spotter/Map Page Number	OA	WILLIAMSBURG - Lodgings	Diamond Rating	Rate Range High Season	Listing Page
1 / p. 917		War Hill Inn Bed & Breakfast	▽▽▽	$100-$170	926
2 / p. 917		Sunterra Resorts Powhatan Plantation	▽▽▽	Rates not provided	924
3 / p. 917	AAA	**Days Hotel Busch Gardens Area** - see color ad p 920	▽▽▽	$39-$119 SAVE	919
4 / p. 917		Quality Inn At Kingsmill	▽▽▽	$69-$134	924
5 / p. 917		Courtyard by Marriott	▽▽▽	$153-$175	919
6 / p. 917	AAA	**Marriott Hotel Williamsburg**	▽▽▽	$165-$209 SAVE	919
7 / p. 917	AAA	**Kingsmill Resort & Spa One Of The Anheuser-Busch Companies** - see color ad p 921	▽▽▽▽	$179-$999 SAVE	919
		WILLIAMSBURG - Restaurants			
① / p. 917		La Tolteca	▽	$4-$12	927
② / p. 917		Grand Shanghai	▽	$4-$15	927
③ / p. 917		Hayashi Japanese Restaurant	▽▽	$7-$19	927
④ / p. 917		Giuseppe's Italian Cafe	▽▽	$6-$18	927
⑤ / p. 917		Art Cafe 26	▽▽	$10-$15	926
⑥ / p. 917		Center Street Grill	▽▽	$8-$25	926
⑦ / p. 917		Shackleford's II	▽▽	$7-$18	927
⑧ / p. 917		The Backfin Seafood Restaurant	▽▽	$5-$17	926
⑨ / p. 917		The Kitchen at Powhatan Plantation	▽▽▽	$21-$34	927
⑩ / p. 917		Florimonte's Fine Foods & Deli	▽	$5-$13	927
⑪ / p. 917		Soya Japanese Cuisine & Sushi Bar	▽▽	$8-$25	928
⑫ / p. 917		The Sportsman's Grille	▽▽	$5-$16	928
⑬ / p. 917		Doraldo Ristorante Italiano	▽▽	$5-$22	926
⑭ / p. 917		Le Yaca French Restaurant	▽▽▽	$10-$40	927
⑮ / p. 917		The Wine & Cheese Shop at Kingsmill	▽	$3-$9	928
⑯ / p. 917		The Whaling Company	▽▽	$13-$19	928
⑰ / p. 917		Gabriel Archer Tavern	▽▽	$7-$14	927
⑱ / p. 917		Eagles	▽▽▽	$8-$45	926
⑲ / p. 917		The Bray Dining Room	▽▽▽	$8-$40	926
		LIGHTFOOT - Lodgings			
10 / p. 917	AAA	**Great Wolf Lodge** - see color ad p 923	▽▽▽	Rates not provided SAVE	950
11 / p. 917	AAA	**Days Inn Colonial Resort** - see color ad p 925	▽▽▽	$39-$119 SAVE	950
12 / p. 917	AAA	**Howard Johnson Plaza Hotel** - see color ad p 922	▽▽	Rates not provided SAVE	950
		LIGHTFOOT - Restaurants			
㉒ / p. 917		New York Deli	▽	$4-$12	951
㉓ / p. 917		Taco Mexicali	▽	$2-$9	951
㉔ / p. 917		La Petite Tea Room	▽▽	$7-$14	951
㉕ / p. 917		Pierce's Bar-B-Que	▽	$3-$15	951
㉖ / p. 917		Carmine's Italian Market & Cafe	▽	$6-$13	951

WILLIAMSBURG pop. 11,998 (See map and index starting on p. 917)

──── WHERE TO STAY ────

COURTYARD BY MARRIOTT *Book great rates at AAA.com* Phone: 757/221-0700 **5**

Small-scale Hotel
$153-$175 All Year

Address: 470 McLaws Cir 23185 **Location:** I-64, exit 242A, just e of jct SR 199 on US 60. Located in the Busch Corporate Center. **Facility:** Smoke free premises. 151 units. 139 one-bedroom standard units. 12 one-bedroom suites. 4 stories, interior corridors. *Bath:* combo or shower only. **Parking:** on-site. **Amenities:** high-speed Internet, voice mail, irons, hair dryers. **Pool(s):** heated indoor/outdoor. **Leisure Activities:** whirlpool, exercise room. *Fee:* game room. **Guest Services:** valet and coin laundry, wireless Internet. **Business Services:** meeting rooms, business center. **Cards:** AX, DC, DS, JC, MC, VI.

AAA Benefit:
Members save 5% off of the best available rate.

DAYS HOTEL BUSCH GARDENS AREA *Book great rates at AAA.com* Phone: 757/253-6444 **3**

Small-scale Hotel
$39-$119 All Year

Address: 201 Water Country Pkwy 23185 **Location:** I-64, exit 24B, just w on SR 199; facing Water Country. **Facility:** 210 one-bedroom standard units. 8 stories, interior corridors. **Parking:** on-site. **Amenities:** DVD players, high-speed Internet, voice mail, safes (fee), irons, hair dryers. **Pool(s):** outdoor. **Leisure Activities:** playground, exercise room, volleyball. *Fee:* game room. **Guest Services:** valet and coin laundry, wireless Internet. **Business Services:** meeting rooms, business center. **Cards:** AX, CB, DC, DS, JC, MC, VI. **Free Special Amenities:** local telephone calls and newspaper. *(See color ad p 920)*

KINGSMILL RESORT & SPA ONE OF THE ANHEUSER-BUSCH COMPANIES *Book great rates at AAA.com* Phone: (757)253-1703 **7**

Resort Condominium
$179-$999 All Year

Address: 1010 Kingsmill Rd 23185 **Location:** I-64, exit 242A to US 60, 1 mi e, follow signs. **Facility:** This sprawling resort on the banks of the James River offers extensive golf and tennis facilities, a full-service spa and full conference facilities. 425 units. 235 one-bedroom standard units. 190 one-bedroom suites with kitchens. 3 stories (no elevator), exterior corridors. *Bath:* combo or shower only. **Parking:** on-site. **Terms:** check-in 4 pm, 3 day cancellation notice. **Amenities:** CD players, high-speed Internet (fee), dual phone lines, voice mail, safes, irons, hair dryers. *Some:* DVD players (fee), fax. **Dining:** 5 restaurants, also, The Bray Dining Room, Eagles, see separate listings, nightclub, entertainment. **Pool(s):** 2 outdoor, heated indoor. **Leisure Activities:** saunas, whirlpools, marina, fishing, kayaks, golf academy, racquetball courts, recreation programs, hiking trails, jogging, playground, spa, sports court. *Fee:* boats, paddleboats, golf-63 holes, 15 tennis courts (2 lighted), bicycles, game room. **Guest Services:** valet laundry, area transportation-attractions & in resort, wireless Internet. **Business Services:** conference facilities, business center. **Cards:** AX, CB, DC, DS, MC, VI. **Free Special Amenities:** newspaper. Affiliated with A Preferred Hotel. *(See color ad p 921)*

MARRIOTT HOTEL WILLIAMSBURG *Book great rates at AAA.com* Phone: 757/220-2500 **6**

Large-scale Hotel
$165-$209 All Year

Address: 50 Kingsmill Rd 23185 **Location:** I-64, exit 242A, 0.5 mi e on SR 199 to US 60; just w of Busch Gardens. **Facility:** Smoke free premises. 295 units. 291 one-bedroom standard units. 6 one-bedroom suites. 6 stories, interior corridors. *Bath:* combo or shower only. **Parking:** on-site. **Terms:** check-in 4 pm. **Amenities:** high-speed Internet (fee), voice mail, irons, hair dryers. **Pool(s):** heated indoor/outdoor. **Leisure Activities:** whirlpool, 2 tennis courts, exercise room. *Fee:* game room. **Guest Services:** valet and coin laundry, wireless Internet. **Business Services:** conference facilities, business center. **Cards:** AX, DC, DS, JC, MC, VI.

AAA Benefit:
Members save 5% off of the best available rate.

▼ See AAA listing p 934 ▼

▼ *See AAA listing p 919* ▼

▼ See AAA listing p 919 ▼

Stay. Play.
Getaway.

There's a destination along the James River where the whole family comes to play. Where you'll cozy into the comfortable luxury of our guestrooms and suites. Take a swim in the pool. Or a swing on our recently renovated, world-famous River Course. Join our Kids Kamp or visit Busch Gardens.® Get a massage. Or a steak dinner at Eagles. It's everything your family wants, all at one place. And all just a phone call away.

KINGSMILL
Resort & Spa

ONE OF THE ANHEUSER-BUSCH COMPANIES

WILLIAMSBURG, VIRGINIA

Preferred
HOTELS & RESORTS

Four Diamond Award

Great vacation packages are available for everything from golf and spa to family getaways.
800.832.5665 • kingsmill.com

THREE CHAMPIONSHIP GOLF COURSES   FULL-SERVICE MARINA   FINE & CASUAL DINING
EUROPEAN-STYLE SPA   CONTEMPORARY SPORTS CLUB   WORLD-CLASS AMENITIES

▼ See AAA listing p 950 ▼

(See map and index starting on p. 917)

QUALITY INN AT KINGSMILL   *Book great rates at AAA.com*   Phone: (757)220-1100   **4**

Small-scale Hotel
$69-$134 3/1-10/31
$49-$89 11/1-2/28

Address: 480 McLaws Cir 23185 **Location:** I-64, exit 242A, just e of jct SR 199 to US 60 E. **Facility:** 111 one-bedroom standard units, some with whirlpools. 3 stories, interior corridors. **Parking:** on-site. **Amenities:** high-speed Internet, voice mail, irons, hair dryers. **Pool(s):** heated indoor/outdoor. **Leisure Activities:** *Fee:* game room. **Guest Services:** valet laundry, wireless Internet. **Business Services:** business center. **Cards:** AX, CB, DC, DS, MC, VI.

ASK SD Y+ CALL &M 🏊 🎥 💻 /SOME UNITS ✖ VCR 🔒 🖨

SUNTERRA RESORTS GREENSPRINGS
PLANTATION   *Book at AAA.com*   Phone: 757/253-1177

Condominium
Rates not provided

Address: 3500 Ludwell Pkwy 23188 **Location:** 3 mi w on SR 5 from jct SR 199, just n on Greensprings Plantation Dr. **Facility:** Bordered by the golf course in a wooded community sits spacious two-bedroom apartments with a washer and dryer. 296 two-bedroom suites with kitchens and whirlpools. 4 stories (no elevator), exterior corridors. **Parking:** on-site. **Terms:** check-in 4 pm. **Amenities:** DVD players, voice mail, irons, hair dryers. *Fee:* video library, high-speed Internet. *Some:* safes (fee). **Pool(s):** outdoor, heated indoor. **Leisure Activities:** whirlpools, 2 lighted tennis courts, recreation programs, playground, exercise room, basketball, horseshoes, shuffleboard, volleyball. *Fee:* golf-18 holes, miniature golf, bicycles. **Guest Services:** complimentary laundry, wireless Internet. **Business Services:** business center.

CALL &M 🏊 ✖ 🔒 📷 💻 /SOME UNITS ✖

SUNTERRA RESORTS POWHATAN PLANTATION   *Book at AAA.com*   Phone: 757/220-1200   **2**

Resort Condominium
Rates not provided

Address: 3601 Ironbound Rd 23188 **Location:** Jct SR 5, just n. **Facility:** Geese linger around ponds on the landscaped grounds of this restored 17th-century plantation; townhouse units include fireplaces. 845 units. 48 one- and 797 two-bedroom suites, some with efficiencies, kitchens and/or whirlpools. 2 stories (no elevator), exterior corridors. **Parking:** on-site. **Terms:** check-in 4 pm. **Amenities:** video library (fee). *Some:* DVD players, high-speed Internet (fee), voice mail, irons, hair dryers. **Dining:** The Kitchen at Powhatan Plantation, see separate listing. **Pool(s):** 3 outdoor, heated indoor. **Leisure Activities:** sauna, whirlpool, fishing, 2 lighted tennis courts, racquetball courts, recreation programs, hiking trails, jogging, playground, exercise room, basketball, horseshoes, volleyball. *Fee:* miniature golf, bicycles, massage, game room. **Guest Services:** complimentary laundry, beauty salon, wireless Internet. **Business Services:** meeting rooms, business center.

🍴 CALL &M 🏊 ✖ 🎥 /SOME UNITS 🅰 📶 🔒 🖨 💻

(See map and index starting on p. 917)

WAR HILL INN BED & BREAKFAST
Phone: 757/565-0248

Bed & Breakfast
$100-$170 All Year

Address: 4560 Longhill Rd 23188-1533 **Location:** I-64, exit 234, just e on SR 199, 1.4 mi nw. Located in a quiet rural area. **Facility:** A large working farm serves as a backdrop for this Colonial-style home featuring country furnishings in cottages; two rooms have gas fireplaces. Smoke free premises. 6 units. 4 one-bedroom standard units. 2 cottages with whirlpools. 2 stories (no elevator), interior/exterior corridors. **Parking:** on-site. **Terms:** check-in 4 pm, 2-3 night minimum stay - weekends, 14 day cancellation notice. **Amenities:** hair dryers. **Cards:** MC, VI.

The following lodging was either not evaluated or did not
meet AAA rating requirements but is listed for your information only.

COLONIAL WILLIAMSBURG-COLONIAL HOUSES
Phone: 757/565-8440

[fyi]

Not evaluated. **Address:** 136 E Francis St 23187 **Location:** In Colonial Willamsburg restored area; registration on Francis St. Facilities, services, and decor characterize a mid-range property.

——— WHERE TO DINE ———

ART CAFE 26
Phone: 757/565-7788   5

Natural/Organic
$10-$15

This stylish spot features a rotating gallery of worldly art collections amid its feng shui design. European chefs, who rotate every few months, concoct European breakfasts, daily specials and homemade soups using healthy, organic ingredients. Casual dress. **Bar:** Beer & wine. **Hours:** 8:30 am-5 pm, Sat-4 pm. Closed major holidays; also Sun. **Address:** 5107-2 Center St 23188 **Location:** SR 199, exit Monticello Ave, just e to New Town; jct Courthouse St. **Parking:** street. **Cards:** AX, DS, MC, VI.

CALL

THE BACKFIN SEAFOOD RESTAURANT
Phone: 757/565-5430   8

Seafood
$5-$17

Hand-painted murals of sea birds on the beach, tinted-wood walls and airy sails suspended from the ceiling set the casual restaurant apart from many other area seafood establishments. Diners can munch on healthy servings of fried or broiled oysters, scallops and shrimp and excellent crab cakes. Seating options include the dining room and new deck. **Bar:** Full bar. **Hours:** 11 am-3 & 4:30-9 pm. Closed major holidays; also Sun. **Address:** 3701 Strawberry Plains Rd 23188 **Location:** Jct Ironbound Rd, 0.6 mi s. **Parking:** on-site. **Cards:** MC, VI.

CALL

THE BRAY DINING ROOM
Phone: 757/253-3900   19

Continental
$8-$40

Classic dishes with modern, creative influences from Europe and the Chesapeake Bay region are served in contemporary surroundings in the Kingsmill Resort, overlooking the James River. Jackets are required during winter. Dressy casual. **Bar:** Full bar. **Reservations:** suggested, for dinner. **Hours:** 6:30-10 am, 11:30-2 & 6-10 pm. **Address:** 1010 Kingsmill Rd 23185 **Location:** I-64, exit 242A to US 60, 1 mi e, follow signs; in Kingsmill Resort & Spa One Of The Anheuser-Busch Companies. **Parking:** on-site. **Cards:** AX, DC, DS, MC, VI.

CENTER STREET GRILL
Phone: 757/220-4600   6

American
$8-$25

In the popular New Town development, the grill puts forth a menu that mixes tasty traditional American standards with Southern and Asian influences. Pan-seared ahi tuna, smothered pork over spoon bread, hoisin duck tacos and Waldorf chicken salad can be enjoyed in the bright yellow dining room lined with local artwork or on the sidewalk patio. **Bar:** Full bar. **Hours:** 11 am-10 pm, Fri & Sat-11 pm, Sun 10 am-10 pm. Closed: 11/27, 12/25. **Address:** 5101 Center St 23188 **Location:** SR 199, exit Monticello Ave, just e to New Town, jct Courthouse St. **Parking:** street. **Cards:** AX, MC, VI.

CITIES GRILLE
Phone: 757/564-3955

Regional American
$6-$20

Casual dress. **Bar:** Full bar. **Reservations:** suggested. **Hours:** 11:30 am-3 & 5-9 pm, Fri & Sat-10 pm, Sun noon-3 & 5-9 pm. Closed major holidays. **Address:** 4511 C John Tyler Hwy 23185 **Location:** Jct SR 5 and Ironbound Rd; in Governor's Green Shopping Center. **Parking:** on-site. **Cards:** AX, DC, DS, MC, VI.

DORALDO RISTORANTE ITALIANO
Phone: 757/220-0795   13

Italian
$5-$22

The casual, family restaurant has a menu of a wide variety of Italian favorites. Seating is cozy and intimate on the covered patio. For dessert, try cannoli or tartuffo. Casual dress. **Bar:** Full bar. **Hours:** 11:30 am-2:30 & 5-9 pm, Sat 5 pm-10 pm. Closed major holidays; also Sun. **Address:** 1915 Pocahontas Tr, Suite D2 23185 **Location:** I-64, exit 242A to US 60, just e of SR 199; in Village Shoppes at Kingsmill, just w of Busch Gardens. **Parking:** on-site. **Cards:** AX, MC, VI.

EAGLES
Phone: 757/253-3900   18

Steak House
$8-$45

Steaks and chops are cold-smoked over beechwood chips straight from the Anheuser-Busch brewery, resulting in a distinctive flavor. The dining room overlooks the championship river golf course. Dressy casual. **Bar:** Full bar. **Reservations:** suggested, for dinner. **Hours:** 6 am-11 pm. **Address:** 1010 Kingsmill Rd 23185 **Location:** I-64, exit 242A to US 60, 1 mi e, follow signs; in Kingsmill Resort & Spa One Of The Anheuser-Busch Companies. **Parking:** on-site. **Cards:** AX, DC, DS, MC, VI.

(See map and index starting on p. 917)

FLORIMONTE'S FINE FOODS & DELI
Phone: 757/253-2266

Deli/Subs
Sandwiches
$5-$13

In the heart of Colonial Virginia, the New York-style delicatessen prepares both thin-crust and Sicilian pizza to order and great hot and cold sandwiches, including the delicious turkey a la Karen, which includes grilled onions and fresh mozzarella. The daily hot special ranges from a pasta dish to osso buco. Cases display fabulous take-home meals, from fresh pasta and sauce, dressings and refined entrees to seafood and steak. Also offered are freshly baked bread, Italian pastries and desserts. Casual dress. **Bar:** Beer & wine. **Reservations:** not accepted. **Hours:** 8 am-7 pm. Closed: Sun. **Address:** 5251 John Tyler Hwy 23185 **Location:** Jct SR 199 and 5; in Williamsburg Crossing. **Parking:** on-site. **Cards:** AX, DS, MC, VI.

GABRIEL ARCHER TAVERN
Phone: 757/229-0999

American
$7-$14

The tiny tavern is a pleasant spot to enjoy an afternoon meal. Patrons can sit in the wood-floored tavern or on the trellis-covered patio overlooking the vineyards while sipping the house wines. Menu offerings include cheese and pate platters, baguette sandwiches and tasty salads. Casual dress. **Bar:** Wine only. **Hours:** 6 pm-9 pm, Tues & Wed 11 am-4 pm. Closed: 1/1, 11/27, 12/25. **Address:** 5800 Wessex Hundred 23185 **Location:** SR 199, 0.5 mi nw to Brookwood Ln; at Williamsburg Winery. **Parking:** on-site. **Cards:** AX, DC, DS, MC, VI.

CALL 🚗M

GIUSEPPE'S ITALIAN CAFE
Phone: 757/565-1977

Italian
$6-$18

Well-prepared, hearty offerings, including a lentil soup that was featured in Bon Appetit Magazine, make up a varied, traditional menu with lots of interesting pasta and pizza. Photographs and prints decorate the walls of the comfortable cafe. Casually dressed servers are friendly and prompt. Casual dress. **Bar:** Full bar. **Reservations:** accepted. **Hours:** 11:30 am-2 & 5-9 pm, Fri & Sat-9:30 pm. Closed major holidays; also Sun. **Address:** 5601 Richmond Rd 23188 **Location:** 3 mi w on US 60; in Ewell Station Shopping Center. **Parking:** on-site. **Cards:** AX, MC, VI.

GRAND SHANGHAI
Phone: 757/565-1212

Chinese
$4-$15

An extensive selection of Asian specialties lines up on the restaurant's buffet. Diners also can take advantage of the Mongolian grill, where they combine vegetables, meats, spices and sauces for the chef to stir-fry as they watch. In the evenings, crab legs are a tasty option. Casual dress. **Bar:** Beer & wine. **Hours:** 11 am-9 pm. **Address:** 5601-12 Richmond Rd 23185 **Location:** 3 mi w on US 60; in Ewell Station Shopping Center. **Parking:** on-site. **Cards:** MC, VI.

CALL 🚗M

HAYASHI JAPANESE RESTAURANT
Phone: 757/253-0282

Japanese
$7-$19

Traditional Japanese dishes such as teriyaki, tempura, gyoza dumplings and noodle soup are featured as well as a full sushi bar. The atmosphere is warm and contemporary, and noticeably and nicely bereft of the standardized decor. The service is friendly. Casual dress. **Bar:** Full bar. **Reservations:** suggested. **Hours:** 11:30 am-2:30 & 5-9:30 pm, Fri & Sat-10:30 pm. Closed: 1/1, 11/27, 12/25. **Address:** 5601 Richmond Rd 23188 **Location:** 2 mi w on US 60; in Ewell Station Shopping Center. **Parking:** on-site. **Cards:** AX, DC, DS, MC, VI.

CALL 🚗M

THE KITCHEN AT POWHATAN PLANTATION
Phone: 757/253-7893

Regional American
$21-$34

A Colonial atmosphere combines with a cutting-edge contemporary menu that showcases regional food and farm-raised game. The innovative and excellent menu, which changes frequently, includes a la carte, prix fixe and five-course tasting choices. Dressy casual. **Bar:** Full bar. **Reservations:** suggested. **Hours:** 5:30 pm-9 pm. Closed: 12/25; also Mon. **Address:** 3601 Ironbound Rd 23188 **Location:** Jct SR 5, just n; in Sunterra Resorts Powhatan Plantation. **Parking:** on-site. **Cards:** AX, DC, DS, MC, VI.

LA TOLTECA
Phone: 757/253-2939   ①

Mexican
$4-$12

The restaurant breaks out of the mold of other Mexican eateries with its daily buffets. Diners can make their own burritos, fajitas, nachos and more. Casual dress. **Bar:** Full bar. **Hours:** 11 am-10 pm, Sat noon-10:30 pm, Sun noon-9:30 pm. Closed major holidays. **Address:** 3048 Richmond Rd 23185 **Location:** I-64, exit 234 (SR 199 E) to US 60, 1.5 mi e. **Parking:** on-site. **Cards:** AX, DS, MC, VI.

LE YACA FRENCH RESTAURANT
Phone: 757/220-3616   ⑭

French
$10-$40

French country elegance reigns as does a signature entree of leg of lamb prepared over an open hearth. Marquise au chocolate dessert is delightful. Four prix fixe menus with ten entree selections are offered. Casual dress. **Bar:** Full bar. **Reservations:** suggested. **Hours:** 11:30 am-2:30 & 5:45-9:30 pm, Sat from 5:45 pm. Closed: 1/1, 12/25; also Sun, except holidays. **Address:** 1915 Pocahontas Tr 23185 **Location:** US 60, just e of jct SR 199; in the Village Shops at Kingsmill. **Parking:** on-site. **Cards:** AX, CB, DC, DS, MC, VI.

SHACKLEFORD'S II
Phone: 757/258-5559   ⑦

Regional American
$7-$18

The focus of the inviting neighborhood bar and grill is on regional American cuisine, particularly seafood selections from Chesapeake Bay and choices from the great raw bar. Among the more creative and original dishes are crab and shrimp sofrito or pork loin attakas. Casual dress. **Bar:** Full bar. **Reservations:** accepted, except Tues. **Hours:** 4 pm-close. Closed major holidays. **Address:** 4640-7 Monticello Ave 23188 **Location:** SR 199, exit Monticello Ave; in Monticello Marketplace. **Parking:** on-site. **Cards:** AX, DS, MC, VI.

CALL 🚗M

(See map and index starting on p. 917)

SOYA JAPANESE CUISINE & SUSHI BAR

Japanese
$8-$25

Phone: 757/229-1212 ⑪

Difficult choices start when guests enter: Sit at the sushi bar or at one of the hibachi tables to watch the chefs in action. The menu, heavy on sushi selections, also includes such tempting specialties as teriyaki, udon noodles and soya bento. Casual dress. **Bar:** Full bar. **Reservations:** accepted. **Hours:** 11:30 am-2 & 5-9:30 pm, Sat & Sun from 5 pm. Closed major holidays. **Address:** 4511 John Tyler Hwy 23185 **Location:** Jct SR 5 and Ironbound Rd; in Governor's Green Shopping Center. **Parking:** on-site. **Cards:** AX, CB, DS, MC, VI.

CALL [image]

THE SPORTSMAN'S GRILLE

American
$5-$16

Phone: 757/221-8002 ⑫

More than your average sports bar, this restaurant has a neighborly feel. Try such specialties as chef's lasagna, burgers, nachos, pot roast sandwich, large salad and daily soup which watching kids sort through the fish tank of trading cards. Decoys and fish trophies hint at the real favorite sport around here. Casual dress. **Bar:** Full bar. **Hours:** 11 am-10 pm. Closed major holidays; also Sun. **Address:** 240 McLaws Cir, Suite 154 23185 **Location:** I-64, exit 242A, just w on SR 199, then e on US 60; in Busch Corporate Center. **Parking:** on-site. **Cards:** AX, DS, MC, VI.

THE WHALING COMPANY

Steak & Seafood
$13-$19

Phone: 757/229-0275 ⑯

Divided into cozy rooms with wood and nautical accents, the large space is appropriately relaxed. Although delightful seafood specialties include tilapia Norfolk, seafood skillet and combination platters. Casual dress. **Bar:** Full bar. **Reservations:** accepted. **Hours:** 4:30 pm-10 pm. Closed: 12/25. **Address:** 494 McLaws Cir 23185 **Location:** I-64, exit 242A, just e of jct SR 199 and US 60. **Parking:** on-site. **Cards:** AX, DC, DS, MC, VI.

CALL [image]

THE WINE & CHEESE SHOP AT KINGSMILL

Gourmet Grocery
$3-$9

Phone: 757/229-6754 ⑮

Hearty sandwiches, daily soups, and gourmet desserts are tasty treats to enjoy either inside or at the sidewalk tables on a sunny day. Casual dress. **Bar:** Beer & wine. **Hours:** 9:30 am-6 pm, Sun noon-5 pm; to 7 pm 5/1-12/1. Closed major holidays. **Address:** 1915 Pocahontas Tr 23185 **Location:** I-64, exit 242A, just e of jct SR 199 on US 60; in Village Shops at Kingsmill. **Parking:** on-site. **Cards:** AX, DS, MC, VI.

The following restaurant has not been evaluated by AAA but is listed for your information only.

VIRGINIA HAM SHOPPE

[fyi]

Phone: 757/220-6618

Not evaluated. The shop specializes in Virginia's famed salty country ham and other specialty gourmet products. Patrons can step to the counter in the back for a tasty to-go lunch of ham rolls, Brunswick stew, peanut pie, tasty sandwiches and other local specialties. **Address:** 1814 Richmond Rd 23185 **Location:** 0.5 mi w of jct Bypass Rd.

CENTRAL WILLIAMSBURG (See map and index starting on p. 913)

--- **WHERE TO STAY** ---

A BOXWOOD INN OF WILLIAMSBURG

Bed & Breakfast
$119-$225 All Year

Phone: 757/221-6607 ㊶

Address: 708 Richmond Rd 23185 **Location:** Just w of Colonial Williamsburg restored area on US 60/Richmond Rd. Located in a residential area. **Facility:** This B&B is housed in a charming 1928 Dutch Colonial and features a spacious sunroom and rear porch overlooking picturesque perennial gardens. Smoke free premises. 4 one-bedroom standard units, some with whirlpools. 2 stories (no elevator), interior corridors. **Bath:** combo or shower only. **Parking:** on-site. **Terms:** 2 night minimum stay - weekends, age restrictions may apply, 30 day cancellation notice-fee imposed. **Amenities:** CD players, hair dryers. **Cards:** AX, MC, VI.

ASK [image] / SOME UNITS VCR

AMERICA'S BEST INN WILLIAMSBURG *Book great rates at AAA.com*

Small-scale Hotel
$49-$109 All Year

Phone: (757)229-1134 ⑨

Address: 1600 Richmond Rd 23185 **Location:** Jct US 60/Richmond Rd and SR 612 (Ironbound Rd). **Facility:** 163 units. 159 one-bedroom standard units. 4 one-bedroom suites. 2-3 stories (no elevator), interior/exterior corridors. **Bath:** combo or shower only. **Parking:** on-site. **Some:** Fee: high-speed Internet. **Pool(s):** heated indoor. **Leisure Activities:** Fee: game room. **Guest Services:** valet and coin laundry. **Business Services:** meeting rooms, fax. **Cards:** AX, DC, DS, MC, VI. **Free Special Amenities:** continental breakfast and high-speed Internet.

 CALL [images] / SOME UNITS FEE [images] FEE [images]

A PRIMROSE COTTAGE

[image]

Bed & Breakfast
Rates not provided

Phone: 757/229-6421 ㊷

Address: 706 Richmond Rd 23185 **Location:** Just w of Colonial Williamsburg restored area on US 60/Richmond Rd. **Facility:** Overflowing gardens surround this cozy Cape Cod-style cottage decorated with German folk-art accents. Smoke free premises. 4 one-bedroom standard units, some with whirlpools. 2 stories, interior corridors. **Parking:** on-site. **Terms:** check-in 4 pm, age restrictions may apply. **Amenities:** hair dryers. *Some:* irons.

[images]

(See map and index starting on p. 913)

CEDARS OF WILLAMSBURG BED & BREAKFAST
Phone: 757/229-3591 **53**

Historic Bed
& Breakfast
$165-$440 All Year

Address: 616 Jamestown Rd 23185 **Location:** SR 31 and 5 (Jamestown Rd). Located across from William and Mary College. **Facility:** Colonial-style appointments decorate this brick Georgian home which is one of the town's longest-operating B&Bs. Smoke free premises. 9 units. 7 one- and 1 two-bedroom standard units. 1 one-bedroom suite. 3 stories (no elevator), interior/exterior corridors. *Bath:* combo or shower only. **Parking:** on-site. **Terms:** 30 day cancellation notice-fee imposed. **Amenities:** high-speed Internet, hair dryers. *Some:* CD players. **Leisure Activities:** *Fee:* massage. **Guest Services:** wireless Internet. **Cards:** AX, MC, VI.

COLONEL WALLER INN & SUITES
Phone: (757)253-0999 **26**

Motel
$27-$99 All Year

Address: 917 Capitol Landing Rd 23185 **Location:** I-64, exit 238, 1.5 mi e on SR 143, then just w on SR 5 (Jamestown Rd). **Facility:** 28 one-bedroom suites. 2 stories (no elevator), exterior corridors. **Parking:** on-site. **Terms:** 3 day cancellation notice. **Amenities:** irons, hair dryers. **Pool(s):** outdoor. **Guest Services:** coin laundry. **Cards:** AX, DS, MC, VI.

COLONIAL CAPITAL BED & BREAKFAST
Phone: 757/229-0233 **44**

Historic Bed
& Breakfast
$137-$187 All Year

Address: 501 Richmond Rd 23185 **Location:** Just w of Colonial Williamsburg and William and Mary College. Located across from the stadium. **Facility:** This 1926 Colonial Revival home offers gracious units furnished with canopy beds; a private third-floor suite includes a seating area. Designated smoking area. 5 units. 4 one-bedroom standard units. 1 one-bedroom suite. 2 stories (no elevator), interior corridors. *Bath:* combo or shower only. **Parking:** on-site. **Terms:** 2 night minimum stay - weekends, age restrictions may apply, 14 day cancellation notice-fee imposed. **Amenities:** video library, high-speed Internet, hair dryers. **Business Services:** fax. **Cards:** AX, DS, MC, VI. **Free Special Amenities: full breakfast and local telephone calls.**

COLONIAL GARDENS BED & BREAKFAST
Phone: (757)220-8087 **61**

Bed & Breakfast
$145-$195 All Year

Address: 1109 Jamestown Rd 23185 **Location:** Just ne of jct SR 5 and 31; jct SR 199. **Facility:** Original artwork and 18th- and 19th-century antiques decorate the large guest rooms at this Colonial-style home with wooded gardens. Smoke free premises. 4 units. 3 one-bedroom standard units. 1 one-bedroom suite. 2 stories, interior corridors. *Bath:* combo or shower only. **Parking:** on-site. **Terms:** check-in 4 pm, age restrictions may apply, 14 day cancellation notice-fee imposed. **Amenities:** video library, CD players, high-speed Internet, hair dryers. **Guest Services:** wireless Internet. **Cards:** AX, DS, MC, VI.

COLONIAL WILLIAMSBURG-WILLIAMSBURG INN
Phone: (757)220-7978 **50**

Classic
Small-scale Hotel
$279-$799 3/1-12/31
$279-$629 1/1-2/28

Address: 136 E Francis St 23187 **Location:** In Colonial Williamsburg restored area. **Facility:** Constructed in 1936 in Regency-style. Decor reflects a bygone era; public rooms have warmth and charm. 40 units in Providence wing offer a more modern decor, some with balcony overlooking a fountain pond. 105 units. 97 one-bedroom standard units. 8 one-bedroom suites. 3 stories (no elevator), interior corridors. **Parking:** valet. **Terms:** check-in 4 pm, cancellation fee imposed. **Amenities:** CD players, high-speed Internet, dual phone lines, voice mail, safes, irons, hair dryers. *Some:* DVD players, honor bars. **Dining:** The Regency Dining Room, see separate listing. **Pool(s):** outdoor, heated indoor/outdoor. **Leisure Activities:** recreation programs, spa. *Fee:* golf-45 holes, 8 tennis courts, bicycles. **Guest Services:** valet laundry, area transportation, wireless Internet. **Business Services:** conference facilities, business center. **Cards:** AX, DC, DS, MC, VI.
(See color ad p 321)

COLONIAL WILLIAMSBURG-WILLIAMSBURG LODGE
Book great rates at AAA.com Phone: (757)220-7976 **52**

Large-scale Hotel
$119-$299 3/1-12/31
$119-$259 1/1-2/28

Address: 310 S England St 23187 **Location:** Just s of jct Francis St and restored area. **Facility:** 323 units. 299 one-bedroom standard units. 24 one-bedroom suites. 4 stories, interior corridors. *Bath:* combo or shower only. **Parking:** on-site. **Terms:** check-in 4 pm, cancellation fee imposed. **Amenities:** high-speed Internet, voice mail, irons, hair dryers. *Some:* DVD players (fee), safes. **Pool(s):** heated outdoor, heated indoor. **Leisure Activities:** jogging, spa. *Fee:* golf-45 holes, 8 tennis courts, bicycles. **Guest Services:** valet laundry, area transportation, wireless Internet. **Business Services:** conference facilities, business center. **Cards:** AX, DC, DS, MC, VI. *(See color ad p 321)*

COLONIAL WILLIAMSBURG-WOODLANDS HOTEL & SUITES
Book great rates at AAA.com Phone: (757)220-7960 **36**

Small-scale Hotel
$79-$209 3/1-12/31
$79-$199 1/1-2/28

Address: 105 Visitor Center Dr 23185 **Location:** I-64, exit 238, s on SR 143 to SR 132. Located in Colonial Williamsburg Visitor Center Complex. **Facility:** 300 units. 204 one-bedroom standard units. 96 one-bedroom suites. 3 stories, interior corridors. *Bath:* combo or shower only. **Parking:** on-site. **Terms:** check-in 4 pm, cancellation fee imposed. **Amenities:** high-speed Internet, dual phone lines, voice mail, irons, hair dryers. **Dining:** Huzzah!, see separate listing. **Pool(s):** outdoor. **Leisure Activities:** miniature golf, playground, exercise room, shuffleboard, volleyball. *Fee:* bicycles. **Guest Services:** valet and coin laundry, area transportation, wireless Internet. **Business Services:** conference facilities, business center. **Cards:** AX, DC, DS, MC, VI. *(See color ad p 321)*

(See map and index starting on p. 913)

COMFORT INN CENTRAL — *Book great rates at AAA.com*   Phone: (757)220-3888   3

Small-scale Hotel
$59-$129 3/1-9/6
$49-$99 9/7-2/28

Address: 2007 Richmond Rd 23185 **Location:** I-64, exit 234, 2 mi s to US 60/Richmond Rd, then 3 mi e. **Facility:** 128 one-bedroom standard units, some with whirlpools. 5 stories, interior corridors. **Parking:** on-site. **Terms:** cancellation fee imposed. **Amenities:** high-speed Internet, dual phone lines, voice mail, irons, hair dryers. **Dining:** 2 restaurants, also, Fireside Chophouse, see separate listing. **Pool(s):** heated indoor. **Guest Services:** valet laundry, wireless Internet. **Business Services:** fax. **Cards:** AX, CB, DC, DS, JC, MC, VI. **Free Special Amenities:** expanded continental breakfast and high-speed Internet. *(See color ad below)*

COMFORT INN KING GEORGE HISTORIC   *Book great rates at AAA.com*   Phone: (757)229-9230   28

Small-scale Hotel
$64-$169 3/1-9/5
$49-$109 9/6-2/28

Address: 706 Bypass Rd 23185 **Location:** US 60 Bypass, 0.5 mi w of jct SR 132. **Facility:** 157 one-bedroom standard units, some with whirlpools. 3-4 stories, interior/exterior corridors. **Parking:** on-site. **Terms:** cancellation fee imposed. **Amenities:** high-speed Internet, voice mail, irons, hair dryers. **Pool(s):** outdoor, heated indoor. **Leisure Activities:** sauna, whirlpool, limited exercise equipment. **Guest Services:** valet laundry, wireless Internet. **Business Services:** meeting rooms, fax. **Cards:** AX, DC, DS, MC, VI. **Free Special Amenities:** expanded continental breakfast and high-speed Internet. *(See color ad p 931)*

COUNTRY INN & SUITES BY CARLSON EAST   *Book great rates at AAA.com*   Phone: (757)229-6900   59

Small-scale Hotel
$59-$179 All Year

Address: 7135 Pocahontas Tr 23185 **Location:** I-64, exit 242 (SR 199), 0.5 mi w on US 60. **Facility:** 88 units. 76 one- and 4 two-bedroom standard units. 8 one-bedroom suites. 5 stories, interior corridors. *Bath:* combo or shower only. **Parking:** on-site. **Terms:** 2 night minimum stay - seasonal and/or weekends. **Amenities:** video library, high-speed Internet, voice mail, irons, hair dryers. *Some: Fee:* DVD players. **Pool(s):** outdoor. **Leisure Activities:** picnic area, exercise room. *Fee:* game room. **Guest Services:** valet and coin laundry, wireless Internet. **Business Services:** meeting rooms, business center. **Cards:** AX, CB, DC, DS, MC, VI. **Free Special Amenities:** expanded continental breakfast and high-speed Internet. *(See color ad p 932)*

Comfort Inn
King George
Historic Area

King George
COMFORT INN

Our 157 room hotel is nestled in a wooded setting just 1/2 mile from Colonial Williamsburg's Visitor Center and 3 miles from Busch Gardens. Meeting facilities, indoor pool with sauna and Jacuzzi®, color cable TV and seasonal outdoor pool. Free continental breakfast and free wireless high-speed Internet. Luxury designed for the economy minded. 706 Bypass Rd., Route 60, Williamsburg, VA 23185. (757)229-9230.

Our terrific package includes...

2 nights lodging at the Comfort Inn Historic, 2 dinners at one of Williamsburg's finest restaurants, The Seafare, 4 breakfasts at your choice of 2 different pancake houses. Total food value is $64.00. Your choice of attractions to Colonial Williamsburg or Busch Gardens. Call us for details on rates and other great packages.

The Seafare

Fine Seafood, Prime Beef, Entrees, Ethnic and Local Dishes are served in a sophisticated, nautical setting. Children's menu. Cocktails.
VISA, MC, AE
1632 Richmond Rd.
(757) 229-0099

TOLL FREE RESERVATIONS 800-358-8003
www.comfortinn.com/hotel/va223

(See map and index starting on p. 913)

COUNTRY INN AND SUITES BY CARLSON
HISTORIC AREA *Book great rates at AAA.com*   Phone: (757)259-7990 (27)

Address: 400 Bypass Rd 23185 **Location:** US 60 Bypass, just e of jct Richmond Rd; 0.7 mi w of jct SR 132. **Facility:** 66 units. 50 one-bedroom standard units. 16 one-bedroom suites. 3 stories, interior corridors. *Bath:* combo or shower only. **Parking:** on-site. **Terms:** cancellation fee imposed. **Amenities:** video library (fee), DVD players, high-speed Internet, voice mail, irons, hair dryers. *Some:* dual phone lines. **Pool(s):** heated indoor. **Leisure Activities:** whirlpool, exercise room, game room. **Guest Services:** valet and coin laundry, wireless Internet. **Business Services:** meeting rooms. **Cards:** AX, DC, DS, MC, VI. **Free Special Amenities:** expanded continental breakfast and high-speed Internet. *(See color ad below)*

Small-scale Hotel
$69-$329 All Year

(See map and index starting on p. 913)

CROWNE PLAZA WILLIAMSBURG AT FORT MAGRUDER
Book great rates at AAA.com

Phone: (757)220-2250   **56**

AAA SAVE
◆◆◆

Large-scale Hotel
$99-$279 3/1-10/31
$69-$199 11/1-2/28

Address: 6945 Pocahontas Tr 23185 **Location:** US 60, 0.8 mi e of jct SR 5 and 31. **Facility:** 303 units. 290 one-bedroom standard units. 13 one-bedroom suites, some with whirlpools. 4 stories, interior corridors. *Bath:* combo or shower only. **Parking:** on-site. **Terms:** check-in 4 pm. **Amenities:** video games (fee), high-speed Internet, voice mail, irons, hair dryers. **Dining:** Veranda Dining Room, see separate listing. **Pool(s):** outdoor, heated indoor. **Leisure Activities:** saunas, whirlpool, 2 lighted tennis courts, exercise room. *Fee:* game room. **Guest Services:** valet and coin laundry. **Business Services:** conference facilities, business center. **Cards:** AX, CB, DC, DS, JC, MC, VI.

🍽 🍸 CALL 📲 🏊 ✕ 🎥 🖥 💻 / SOME UNITS FEE 🐾 ✕ FEE 📷

DAYS INN CENTRAL
Book great rates at AAA.com

Phone: (757)229-6600   **4**

AAA SAVE
◆◆◆

Motel
$109 3/1-9/1
$79 9/2-2/28

Address: 1900 Richmond Rd 23185 **Location:** US 60, 2 mi w of jct W Bypass Rd. **Facility:** 85 one-bedroom standard units. 2 stories (no elevator), exterior corridors. **Parking:** on-site. **Terms:** 1-7 night minimum stay. **Amenities:** high-speed Internet, irons. **Pool(s):** outdoor. **Guest Services:** wireless Internet. **Business Services:** fax. **Cards:** AX, CB, DC, DS, JC, MC, VI. **Free Special Amenities:** continental breakfast and newspaper. *(See color ad below)*

📲 🍽 🏊 🎥 🖥 💻 / SOME UNITS ✕

DAYS INN COLONIAL DOWNTOWN
Book great rates at AAA.com

Phone: (757)229-5060   **38**

AAA SAVE
◆◆◆

Small-scale Hotel
$69-$129 3/1-9/8
$39-$89 9/9-2/28

Address: 902 Richmond Rd 23185 **Location:** Just w of Colonial Williamsburg on US 60. **Facility:** 100 one-bedroom standard units. 2 stories (no elevator), exterior corridors. **Parking:** on-site. **Terms:** cancellation fee imposed. **Amenities:** high-speed Internet, safes (fee), irons, hair dryers. **Pool(s):** outdoor. **Guest Services:** valet laundry, wireless Internet. **Business Services:** meeting rooms, PC, fax. **Cards:** AX, CB, DC, DS, MC, VI. **Free Special Amenities:** expanded continental breakfast and high-speed Internet. *(See color ad p 934)*

📲 🍽 🏊 🎥 / SOME UNITS FEE 🐾 ✕ FEE 🖥 FEE 📷

DAYS INN HISTORIC AREA
Book great rates at AAA.com

Phone: 757-253-1166   **20**

AAA SAVE
◆◆◆

Small-scale Hotel
$39-$99 All Year

Address: 331 Bypass Rd 23185 **Location:** US 60 Bypass Rd, 0.5 mi w of just SR 132. **Facility:** 120 units. 117 one-bedroom standard units. 3 one-bedroom suites with whirlpools. 4 stories, interior corridors. **Parking:** on-site. **Amenities:** high-speed Internet, voice mail, irons, hair dryers. *Fee:* DVD players, safes. **Pool(s):** heated outdoor. **Leisure Activities:** whirlpool, picnic area, volleyball. *Fee:* game room. **Guest Services:** valet laundry, wireless Internet. **Business Services:** meeting rooms, business center. **Cards:** AX, CB, DC, DS, JC, MC, VI. **Free Special Amenities:** continental breakfast and high-speed Internet. *(See color ad p 935)*

📲 🍽 🏊 ✕ 🎥 💻 / SOME UNITS ✕ 🖥 📷

ECONO LODGE COLONIAL
Book great rates at AAA.com

Phone: (757)253-6450   **43**

AAA SAVE
◆◆◆

Motel
$55-$99 3/1-9/6
$40-$55 9/7-2/28

Address: 216 Parkway Dr 23185 **Location:** Just n of 2nd St. **Facility:** 48 one-bedroom standard units, some with efficiencies (no utensils). 2 stories (no elevator), interior/exterior corridors. **Parking:** on-site. **Amenities:** hair dryers. **Pool(s):** outdoor. **Leisure Activities:** picnic area. **Guest Services:** wireless Internet. **Business Services:** fax. **Cards:** AX, DC, DS, MC, VI. **Free Special Amenities:** continental breakfast and high-speed Internet.

📲 🏊 🎥 🖥 / SOME UNITS ✕ FEE 📷 💻

─────────── ▼ *See AAA listing above* ▼ ───────────

(See map and index starting on p. 913)

ECONO LODGE-HISTORIC AREA *Book great rates at AAA.com*   Phone: 757/229-7564

Motel
$59-$119 3/1-9/6
$29-$59 9/7-2/28

Address: 442 Parkway Dr 23185 **Location:** I-64, exit 238 to SR 143 E, 2 mi to SR 5, then 1 blk. **Facility:** 47 one-bedroom standard units. 2 stories (no elevator), exterior corridors. **Parking:** on-site. **Amenities:** irons, hair dryers. **Pool(s):** outdoor. **Guest Services:** coin laundry, wireless Internet. **Business Services:** fax. **Cards:** AX, CB, DC, DS, JC, MC, VI. **Free Special Amenities: continental breakfast and high-speed Internet.** *(See color ad p 936)*

EMBASSY SUITES   *Book great rates at AAA.com*   Phone: 757/229-6800

Small-scale Hotel
Rates not provided

Address: 3006 Mooretown Rd 23185 **Location:** US 60 (Bypass Rd), just w of jct Richmond Rd. Located adjacent to Kingsgate Shopping Center. **Facility:** 168 one-bedroom suites, some with whirlpools. 5 stories, interior corridors. *Bath:* combo or shower only. **Parking:** on-site. **Terms:** check-in 4 pm. **Amenities:** video games (fee), high-speed Internet, voice mail, irons, hair dryers. **Pool(s):** heated indoor. **Leisure Activities:** whirlpool, exercise room. **Guest Services:** valet and coin laundry, wireless Internet. **Business Services:** meeting rooms, business center. **Free Special Amenities: full breakfast and newspaper.** *(See color ad p 919)*

 CALL

▼ See AAA listing p 933 ▼

Southern Elegance

1-800-759-1166

- Heated outdoor pool & spa (seasonal)
- Fitness Room
- High speed wireless internet
- Suites & Deluxe rooms with whirlpool tubs
- Volleyball & picnic area
- Continental Breakfast

- Award-winning exterior
- Custom golf packages available
- Children 17 & under stay free

DAYS INN
Historic Area

331 Bypass Rd., Rt. 60W
Williamsburg, VA 23185

Located in the heart of Colonial Williamsburg and minutes from Busch Gardens and outlet shopping

"... it is absolutely beautiful. The service was great and I would definitely recommend this hotel." —AAA of Massachusetts

"The staff is the best at this hotel ... I would recommend this hotel to everyone." —AAA Ohio

The most frequently heard comment from our guests:
"It looks just like the picture!"

Managed by
Carlton Group

SAVE
Program

www.williamsburgvacations.com

(See map and index starting on p. 913)

FAIRFIELD INN & SUITES BY MARRIOTT   *Book great rates at AAA.com*   Phone: 757/645-3600   **15**

Small-scale Hotel
$98-$175 3/1-9/7
$71-$97 9/8-2/28

Address: 1402 Richmond Rd 23185 **Location:** US 60, jct Richmond and Bypass rds. **Facility:** Smoke free premises. 148 units. 118 one-bedroom standard units. 30 one-bedroom suites. 4 stories, interior corridors. *Bath:* combo or shower only. **Parking:** on-site. **Terms:** check-in 4 pm. **Amenities:** high-speed Internet, dual phone lines, voice mail, irons, hair dryers. *Some:* CD players. **Pool(s):** heated indoor. **Leisure Activities:** exercise room. **Guest Services:** valet and coin laundry, wireless Internet. **Business Services:** meeting rooms, business center. **Cards:** AX, DS, MC, VI.

AAA Benefit:
Members save 5% off of the best available rate.

FAIRFIELD WILLIAMSBURG CONDO RENTALS AT
     KINGSGATE   *Book at AAA.com*   Phone: 757/220-5702   **11**

Condominium
Rates not provided

Address: 619 Georgetown Crescent 23185 **Location:** US 60 (Bypass Rd), just n on Waller Mill Rd. **Facility:** A time-share community spread over well-landscaped grounds; a family entertainment center offers space to gather. 600 units. 300 one- and 300 two-bedroom suites, some with efficiencies or kitchens. 2-3 stories (no elevator), exterior corridors. **Parking:** on-site. **Terms:** office hours 7 am-11 pm, check-in 4 pm. **Amenities:** CD players, voice mail, safes, irons, hair dryers. *Some:* DVD players. **Pool(s):** 2 outdoor, heated indoor. **Leisure Activities:** sauna, whirlpool, miniature golf, 2 lighted tennis courts, recreation programs, playground, exercise room. **Fee:** massage, game room. **Guest Services:** complimentary laundry, area transportation (fee). **Business Services:** meeting rooms, business center.

THE FIFE AND DRUM INN   *Book at AAA.com*   Phone: (757)345-1776   **48**

Bed & Breakfast
$165-$295 All Year

Address: 441 Prince George St 23185 **Location:** Between Henry and Boundary sts; center; at Merchants Square. Located on the second floor. **Facility:** Tucked away on the second floor of Merchants Square, this B&B features a stylish, modern interpretation of Colonial decor. Smoke free premises. 10 units. 7 one- and 1 two-bedroom standard units. 1 one-bedroom suite. 1 cottage. 2 stories (no elevator), interior/exterior corridors. *Bath:* combo or shower only. **Parking:** on-site. **Terms:** cancellation fee imposed. **Amenities:** video library, high-speed Internet, voice mail, hair dryers. **Guest Services:** wireless Internet.

(See map and index starting on p. 913)

FOUR POINTS BY SHERATON HOTEL & SUITES
WILLIAMSBURG HISTORIC DISTRICT   *Book great rates at AAA.com*   Phone: (757)229-4100   **51**

Small-scale Hotel
$50-$160 All Year

Address: 351 York St 23185 **Location:** US 60 E, 0.3 mi se of jct SR 5 and 31. **Facility:** 199 units. 143 one-bedroom standard units. 56 two-bedroom suites with kitchens. 4 stories, interior/exterior corridors. *Bath:* combo or shower only. **Parking:** on-site. **Terms:** check-in 4 pm. **Amenities:** video games (fee), dual phone lines, voice mail, irons, hair dryers. *Some:* high-speed Internet, safes. **Pool(s):** heated indoor. **Leisure Activities:** whirlpool, picnic tables, exercise room, game room. **Guest Services:** valet and coin laundry, wireless Internet. **Business Services:** meeting rooms, fax. **Cards:** AX, DC, DS, MC, VI.

FOUR POINTS
BY SHERATON

AAA Benefit:
Members get up to 15% off, plus Starwood Preferred Guest® bonuses.

FOX & GRAPE BED & BREAKFAST   Phone: 757/229-6914   **39**

Bed & Breakfast
Rates not provided

Address: 701 Monumental Ave 23185 **Location:** I-64, exit 238, s on SR 143 to SR 5, 0.8 mi w, then just n. Located in a residential area. **Facility:** The owners' own quilts, cross-stitch samplers, hand-carved walking sticks and decoys decorate this Colonial-style home with wraparound porch. Smoke free premises. 4 one-bedroom standard units. 2 stories (no elevator), interior corridors. **Parking:** on-site. **Terms:** age restrictions may apply. **Amenities:** video library, high-speed Internet. **Guest Services:** wireless Internet. **Business Services:** fax.

HAMPTON INN & SUITES   Phone: 757/229-4900   **5**

Small-scale Hotel
Rates not provided

Address: 1880 Richmond Rd 23185 **Location:** On US 60, 2 mi w of jct W Bypass Rd. **Facility:** 100 units. 76 one-bedroom standard units, some with whirlpools. 24 one-bedroom suites with kitchens. 4 stories, interior corridors. *Bath:* combo or shower only. **Parking:** on-site. **Amenities:** high-speed Internet, voice mail, irons, hair dryers. *Some:* dual phone lines. **Pool(s):** heated indoor. **Leisure Activities:** exercise room. **Guest Services:** coin laundry, wireless Internet. **Business Services:** business center.

HAMPTON INN & SUITES HISTORIC   Phone: 757/941-1777   **29**

Small-scale Hotel
Rates not provided

Address: 911 Capitol Landing Rd 23185 **Location:** I-64, exit 238, 1 mi e on SR 143, then just w on SR 5. **Facility:** 109 one-bedroom standard units. 4 stories, interior corridors. *Bath:* combo or shower only. **Parking:** on-site. **Amenities:** high-speed Internet, voice mail, safes, irons, hair dryers. **Pool(s):** heated indoor. **Leisure Activities:** whirlpool, exercise room. **Guest Services:** valet and coin laundry, wireless Internet. **Business Services:** meeting rooms, business center.

HILTON GARDEN INN   *Book great rates at AAA.com*   Phone: (757)253-9400   **8**

Small-scale Hotel
$79-$199 All Year

Address: 1624 Richmond Rd 23185 **Location:** On US 60, w of jct Bypass Rd. **Facility:** 119 one-bedroom standard units. 4 stories, interior corridors. *Bath:* combo or shower only. **Parking:** on-site. **Terms:** cancellation fee imposed. **Amenities:** high-speed Internet, dual phone lines, voice mail, irons, hair dryers. **Pool(s):** heated indoor. **Leisure Activities:** whirlpool, exercise room. **Guest Services:** valet and coin laundry, wireless Internet. **Business Services:** meeting rooms, business center. **Cards:** AX, CB, DC, DS, JC, MC, VI.

HITE'S BED & BREAKFAST   Phone: 757/229-4814   **40**

Bed & Breakfast
$95-$125 All Year

Address: 704 Monumental Ave 23185 **Location:** I-64, exit 238, s on SR 143 to SR 5, 0.8 mi w, then just n. Located in a residential area. **Facility:** A charming garden adds curb appeal to this Cape Cod-style B&B, which is furnished with collectibles and antiques. Smoke free premises. 2 one-bedroom standard units. 2 stories (no elevator), interior corridors. **Parking:** on-site. **Terms:** 14 day cancellation notice. **Amenities:** irons, hair dryers.

HOLIDAY INN-DOWNTOWN & HOLIDOME   *Book great rates at AAA.com*   Phone: (757)229-0200   **37**

Small-scale Hotel
$99-$139 3/1-8/31
$79-$99 9/1-2/28

Address: 814 Capital Landing Rd 23185 **Location:** SR 5, just e of jct US 60. **Facility:** 136 one-bedroom standard units. 1 one-bedroom suite. 3 stories, interior corridors. *Bath:* combo or shower only. **Parking:** on-site. **Terms:** cancellation fee imposed. **Amenities:** high-speed Internet, voice mail, irons, hair dryers. **Dining:** 2 restaurants. **Pool(s):** heated indoor. **Leisure Activities:** sauna, whirlpool, limited exercise equipment. **Guest Services:** valet and coin laundry. **Business Services:** conference facilities, business center. **Cards:** AX, CB, DC, DS, JC, MC, VI. **Free Special Amenities:** local telephone calls and newspaper.

HOLIDAY INN EXPRESS HOTEL & SUITES   *Book at AAA.com*   Phone: (757)941-1057   **12**

Small-scale Hotel
$89-$199 All Year

Address: 1452 Richmond Rd 23185 **Location:** On US 60, just w of jct Bypass Rd. **Facility:** 93 one-bedroom standard units. 4 stories, interior corridors. *Bath:* combo or shower only. **Parking:** on-site. **Amenities:** high-speed Internet, voice mail, irons, hair dryers. **Pool(s):** heated indoor. **Leisure Activities:** exercise room. **Guest Services:** valet and coin laundry. **Business Services:** business center. **Cards:** AX, CB, DC, DS, JC, MC, VI.

(See map and index starting on p. 913)

HOLIDAY INN HOTEL & SUITES GATEWAY   *Book great rates at AAA.com*   **Phone:** (757)229-9990   [24]

Small-scale Hotel
$69-$499 All Year

Address: 515 Bypass Rd 23185 **Location:** US 60 Bypass, 1 mi e of jct Richmond Rd. **Facility:** Smoke free premises. 96 units. 50 one-bedroom standard units. 40 one- and 6 two-bedroom suites. 5 stories, interior corridors. **Bath:** combo or shower only. **Parking:** on-site. **Terms:** check-in 4 pm, cancellation fee imposed. **Amenities:** high-speed Internet, dual phone lines, voice mail, irons, hair dryers. **Pool(s):** heated outdoor. **Leisure Activities:** whirlpool, exercise room. **Guest Services:** valet and coin laundry, wireless Internet. **Business Services:** meeting rooms, business center. **Cards:** AX, DC, DS, MC, VI. **Free Special Amenities:** newspaper and high-speed Internet.
(See color ad below)

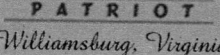

(See map and index starting on p. 913)

HOLIDAY INN PATRIOT   *Book great rates at AAA.com*   Phone: (757)565-2600

Small-scale Hotel
$109-$149 3/1-9/30
$79-$129 10/1-2/28

Address: 3032 Richmond Rd 23185 **Location:** I-64, exit 234 (SR 199 E) to US 60, 2.5 mi e. **Facility:** 160 one-bedroom standard units. 4 stories, interior corridors. **Parking:** on-site. **Terms:** check-in 4 pm. **Amenities:** high-speed Internet, dual phone lines, voice mail, irons, hair dryers. **Dining:** entertainment. **Pool(s):** heated indoor/outdoor. **Leisure Activities:** whirlpool, bicycles, playground, exercise room. *Fee:* golf privileges. **Guest Services:** valet laundry, wireless Internet. **Business Services:** conference facilities, PC, fax. **Cards:** AX, CB, DC, DS, JC, MC, VI. **Free Special Amenities:** room upgrade and preferred room (each subject to availability with advance reservations).
(See color ad p 938)

HOMEWOOD SUITES BY HILTON   *Book great rates at AAA.com*   Phone: (757)259-1199   22

Small-scale Hotel
$99-$379 All Year

Address: 601 Bypass Rd 23185 **Location:** US 60 Bypass, 0.5 mi w of jct SR 132. **Facility:** 61 units. 43 one- and 18 two-bedroom suites with kitchens, some with whirlpools. 5 stories, interior corridors. **Parking:** on-site. **Terms:** check-in 4 pm. **Amenities:** video library (fee), DVD players, high-speed Internet, dual phone lines, voice mail, irons, hair dryers. **Pool(s):** heated indoor. **Leisure Activities:** gas grills, exercise room. *Fee:* game room. **Guest Services:** valet and coin laundry. **Business Services:** meeting rooms, fax. **Cards:** AX, DC, DS, MC, VI. **Free Special Amenities:** expanded continental breakfast and high-speed Internet. *(See color ad below)*

INN AT 802   Phone: 757/345-3316   55

Bed & Breakfast
$145-$175 All Year

Address: 802 Jamestown Rd 23185 **Location:** Just w of SR 199; 1 mi ne of SR 31 and 5. Located across from William and Mary College's Phi Beta Kappa Hall. **Facility:** Comfort features at this brick Cape Cod include goose-down comforters with handmade covers and a sunroom overlooking the garden. Smoke free premises. 4 one-bedroom standard units. 2 stories, interior corridors. **Parking:** on-site. **Terms:** age restrictions may apply, 14 day cancellation notice-fee imposed. **Amenities:** video library, DVD players, high-speed Internet, irons, hair dryers. **Guest Services:** wireless Internet. **Business Services:** business center. **Cards:** AX, DS, MC, VI.

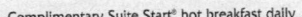

▼ *See AAA listing above* ▼

(See map and index starting on p. 913)

LA QUINTA INN WILLIAMSBURG (HISTORIC AREA)

Book great rates at AAA.com   **Phone:** (757)253-1663   **17**

Small-scale Hotel
$85-$115 All Year

Address: 119 Bypass Rd 23185 **Location:** US 60 Bypass Rd, 0.3 mi e of Richmond Rd. **Facility:** 131 one-bedroom standard units. 2 stories (no elevator), exterior corridors. **Parking:** on-site. **Amenities:** high-speed Internet, dual phone lines, voice mail, safes (fee), irons, hair dryers. **Pool(s):** outdoor. **Guest Services:** valet laundry, wireless Internet. **Business Services:** meeting rooms, fax. **Cards:** AX, DS, VI. **Free Special Amenities:** expanded continental breakfast and high-speed Internet.

AAA Benefit:
Members save 10% everyday.

LEGACY OF WILLIAMSBURG BED & BREAKFAST INN

Phone: 757/220-0524   **58**

Bed & Breakfast
$185-$225 All Year

Address: 930 Jamestown Rd 23185 **Location:** SR 31 and 5, just ne of jct SR 199. Located in a residential area bordering William and Mary College. **Facility:** This B&B, which offers three fireplace suites, evokes the style of the 18th-century with antique furnishings, reproduction fabrics and canopy beds. Smoke free premises. 4 units. 1 one-bedroom standard unit. 3 one-bedroom suites. 3 stories (no elevator), interior corridors. *Bath:* combo or shower only. **Parking:** on-site. **Terms:** 2 night minimum stay - weekends, age restrictions may apply, 30 day cancellation notice-fee imposed. **Amenities:** irons, hair dryers. **Business Services:** fax. **Cards:** MC, VI.

LIBERTY ROSE BED & BREAKFAST

Phone: 757/253-1260   **60**

Historic Bed & Breakfast
$185-$275 All Year

Address: 1022/1025 Jamestown Rd 23185 **Location:** SR 31 and 5, just ne of jct SR 199. **Facility:** This charming Cape Cod home, set on a wooded hillside, reflects English, French and Victorian influences in its richly romantic decor. Smoke free premises. 4 units. 3 one-bedroom standard units. 1 one-bedroom suite. 2 stories (no elevator), interior corridors. *Bath:* combo, shower or tub only. **Parking:** on-site. **Terms:** age restrictions may apply, 18 day cancellation notice-fee imposed. **Amenities:** video library, high-speed Internet, irons, hair dryers. *Some:* DVD players. **Guest Services:** area transportation, wireless Internet. **Cards:** AX, MC, VI.

PATRICK HENRY INN

Phone: (757)229-9540   **49**

Small-scale Hotel
$64-$104 All Year

Address: 249 York St 23185 **Location:** E on US 60/Richmond Rd at jct SR 5 and 31; 1 blk from Colonial Williamsburg. **Facility:** Smoke free premises. 158 units. 82 one-bedroom standard units. 76 two-bedroom suites with kitchens. 4 stories, interior corridors. *Bath:* combo or shower only. **Parking:** on-site. **Amenities:** voice mail, safes, irons, hair dryers. **Pool(s):** heated outdoor. **Leisure Activities:** playground. **Guest Services:** valet and coin laundry. **Business Services:** meeting rooms, fax. **Cards:** AX, DS, MC, VI. **Free Special Amenities:** expanded continental breakfast and early check-in/late check-out.

PATRIOT INN AND SUITES

Book at AAA.com   **Phone:** (757)229-2981   **14**

Small-scale Hotel
$69-$119 3/1-9/4
$49-$79 9/5-2/28

Address: 1420 Richmond Rd 23185 **Location:** 1.5 mi nw of Colonial Williamsburg on US 60/Richmond Rd; jct Bypass Rd. **Facility:** 110 units. 89 one-bedroom standard units, some with whirlpools. 21 one-bedroom suites. 3 stories, interior/exterior corridors. **Parking:** on-site. **Amenities:** voice mail, safes, irons, hair dryers. **Guest Services:** valet and coin laundry. **Business Services:** business center. **Cards:** DC, DS, MC, VI.

▼ *See AAA listing p 941* ▼

(See map and index starting on p. 913)

QUALITY INN COLONY   *Book great rates at AAA.com*   Phone: (757)229-1855   **45**

AAA SAVE

Small-scale Hotel
$49-$179 3/1-8/31
$49-$119 9/1-2/28

Address: Page & 2nd 23187 **Location:** US 60 E and SR 5; jct SR 162. **Facility:** 58 one-bedroom standard units, some with whirlpools. 1 story, exterior corridors. **Parking:** on-site. **Terms:** cancellation fee imposed. **Amenities:** video library (fee), DVD players, high-speed Internet, irons, hair dryers. **Pool(s):** outdoor. **Guest Services:** valet laundry, wireless Internet. **Business Services:** fax. **Cards:** AX, CB, DC, DS, JC, MC, VI. **Free Special Amenities: expanded continental breakfast and high-speed Internet.** *(See color ad p 940)*

QUALITY INN HISTORIC AREA HOTEL   *Book great rates at AAA.com*   Phone: (757)220-2800   **25**

AAA SAVE

Small-scale Hotel
$59-$179 3/1-9/5
$39-$109 9/6-2/28

Address: 600 Bypass Rd 23185 **Location:** US 60 Bypass, 0.5 mi w of jct SR 132. **Facility:** 141 one-bedroom standard units. 5 stories, interior corridors. **Bath:** combo or shower only. **Parking:** on-site. **Terms:** cancellation fee imposed. **Amenities:** high-speed Internet, dual phone lines, voice mail, irons, hair dryers. **Pool(s):** outdoor. **Leisure Activities:** *Fee:* game room. **Guest Services:** valet and coin laundry, wireless Internet. **Cards:** AX, CB, DC, DS, JC, MC, VI. **Free Special Amenities: continental breakfast and high-speed Internet.** *(See color ad p 942)*

QUALITY INN LORD PAGET   *Book great rates at AAA.com*   Phone: 757/229-4444   **32**

Motel
Rates not provided

Address: 901 Capitol Landing Rd 23185 **Location:** I-64, exit 238, 0.5 mi s to SR 5, then 0.5 mi s. **Facility:** 94 units. 93 one-bedroom standard units. 1 one-bedroom suite. 2 stories (no elevator), exterior corridors. **Bath:** combo or shower only. **Parking:** on-site. **Amenities:** video library, high-speed Internet, voice mail, irons. **Pool(s):** outdoor. **Leisure Activities:** fishing, putting green. **Guest Services:** coin laundry, wireless Internet. **Business Services:** fax.

QUALITY SUITES WILLIAMSBURG   *Book at AAA.com*   Phone: (757)220-9304   **16**

Small-scale Hotel
$132 3/1-9/30
$99 10/1-2/28

Address: 1406 Richmond Rd 23185 **Location:** US 60, jct Bypass Rd. **Facility:** 118 units. 6 one-bedroom standard units. 112 one-bedroom suites, some with whirlpools. 4 stories, interior corridors. **Bath:** combo or shower only. **Parking:** on-site. **Amenities:** video library (fee), high-speed Internet, voice mail, safes, irons, hair dryers. *Some:* CD players. **Pool(s):** heated indoor. **Leisure Activities:** exercise room. *Fee:* game room. **Guest Services:** valet and coin laundry, wireless Internet. **Business Services:** business center. **Cards:** AX, CB, DC, DS, JC, MC, VI.

QUARTERPATH INN   *Book at AAA.com*   Phone: (757)220-0960   **54**

Motel
$39-$109 All Year

Address: 620 York St 23185 **Location:** I-64, exit 242 (SR 199 W), 0.6 mi w to US 60 E, then just w. Located adjacent to a public park. **Facility:** 130 one-bedroom standard units, some with whirlpools. 2 stories (no elevator), exterior corridors. **Parking:** on-site. **Terms:** cancellation fee imposed. **Amenities:** *Some:* high-speed Internet (fee). **Pool(s):** outdoor. **Guest Services:** wireless Internet. **Business Services:** fax. **Cards:** AX, CB, DC, DS, MC, VI.

RAMADA INN 1776   *Book at AAA.com*   Phone: 757/220-1776   **21**

Small-scale Hotel
Rates not provided

Address: 725 Bypass Rd 23185 **Location:** US 60 (Bypass Rd), 0.5 mi w of jct SR 132. **Facility:** 194 units. 186 one-bedroom standard units. 5 one- and 3 two-bedroom suites. 2 stories (no elevator), interior corridors. **Parking:** on-site. **Terms:** check-in 4 pm. **Amenities:** voice mail, irons, hair dryers. **Pool(s):** outdoor. **Leisure Activities:** *Fee:* game room. **Guest Services:** valet and coin laundry, wireless Internet. **Business Services:** conference facilities, fax.

RED ROOF INN-WILLIAMSBURG   *Book great rates at AAA.com*   Phone: 757/259-1948   **35**

Motel
Rates not provided

Address: 824 Capitol Landing Rd 23185 **Location:** I-64, exit 238, 0.9 mi se on SR 143, then just w on SR 5. **Facility:** 72 one-bedroom standard units. 2 stories (no elevator), exterior corridors. **Parking:** on-site. **Amenities:** safes, hair dryers. **Pool(s):** outdoor. **Guest Services:** coin laundry.

RESIDENCE INN BY MARRIOTT WILLIAMSBURG   *Book great rates at AAA.com*   Phone: 757/941-2000   **6**

AAA SAVE

Small-scale Hotel
$153-$241 3/1-9/3
$110-$131 9/4-2/28

Address: 1648 Richmond Rd 23185 **Location:** US 60, just w of jct Bypass Rd. **Facility:** Smoke free premises. 108 units. 16 one-bedroom standard units with efficiencies. 68 one- and 24 two-bedroom suites, some with kitchens. 4 stories, interior corridors. **Bath:** combo or shower only. **Parking:** on-site. **Terms:** check-in 4 pm. **Amenities:** high-speed Internet, dual phone lines, voice mail, irons, hair dryers. **Pool(s):** heated outdoor. **Leisure Activities:** whirlpool, exercise room, sports court. **Guest Services:** valet and coin laundry. **Business Services:** fax. **Cards:** AX, DC, DS, JC, MC, VI. **Free Special Amenities: full breakfast and high-speed Internet.**

AAA Benefit:
Members save 5% off of the best available rate.

▼ See AAA listing p 941 ▼

(See map and index starting on p. 913)

SLEEP INN-HISTORIC *Book great rates at AAA.com* **Phone:** (757)259-1700 23

AAA SAVE

Small-scale Hotel
$49-$159 All Year

Address: 220 Bypass Rd 23185 **Location:** US 60 (Bypass Rd), just e of jct Richmond Rd. **Facility:** 66 one-bedroom standard units, some with whirlpools. 3 stories, interior corridors. *Bath:* combo or shower only. **Parking:** on-site. **Amenities:** video library (fee), DVD players, high-speed Internet, voice mail, irons, hair dryers. **Pool(s):** heated indoor. **Leisure Activities:** exercise room. **Guest Services:** valet and coin laundry, wireless Internet. **Business Services:** meeting rooms. **Cards:** AX, DS, MC, VI. **Free Special Amenities: continental breakfast and high-speed Internet.** *(See color ad p 924)*

CALL / SOME UNITS FEE FEE

SPRINGHILL SUITES BY MARRIOTT *Book great rates at AAA.com* **Phone:** 757/941-3000 7

AAA SAVE

Small-scale Hotel
$109-$208 3/1-9/3
$88-$108 9/4-2/28

Address: 1644 Richmond Rd 23185 **Location:** US 60, just w of jct Bypass Rd. **Facility:** Smoke free premises. 120 one-bedroom standard units. 4 stories, interior corridors. *Bath:* combo or shower only. **Parking:** on-site. **Terms:** check-in 4 pm. **Amenities:** high-speed Internet, dual phone lines, voice mail, irons, hair dryers. **Pool(s):** heated indoor. **Leisure Activities:** whirlpool, exercise room. **Guest Services:** valet and coin laundry, wireless Internet. **Business Services:** fax. **Cards:** AX, DC, DS, MC, VI. **Free Special Amenities: full breakfast and high-speed Internet.**

CALL

AAA Benefit:
Members save 5% off of the best available rate.

SUPER 8 MOTEL-HISTORIC *Book great rates at AAA.com* **Phone:** 757/229-0500 46

AAA SAVE

Motel
Rates not provided

Address: 304 2nd St 23185 **Location:** I-642, exit 242 (SR 199 W), 0.6 mi w on SR 199 to SR 143, 1.6 mi w to SR 162, then just w. **Facility:** 107 one-bedroom standard units, some with efficiencies (no utensils). 2 stories (no elevator), exterior corridors. **Parking:** on-site. **Amenities:** high-speed Internet, irons, hair dryers. **Pool(s):** outdoor. **Leisure Activities:** poolside grills. **Guest Services:** coin laundry, wireless Internet. **Free Special Amenities: continental breakfast and high-speed Internet.**

/ SOME UNITS FEE

TRAVELODGE *Book great rates at AAA.com* **Phone:** 757/220-0710 2

AAA SAVE

Motel
Rates not provided

Address: 2225 Richmond Rd 23185 **Location:** On US 60, 2 mi w of jct Bypass Rd. **Facility:** 68 one-bedroom standard units. 2 stories (no elevator), exterior corridors. **Parking:** on-site. **Amenities:** high-speed Internet, safes, hair dryers. **Pool(s):** outdoor. **Leisure Activities:** *Fee:* game room. **Guest Services:** wireless Internet. **Free Special Amenities: expanded continental breakfast and high-speed Internet.**

/ SOME UNITS FEE

▼ See AAA listing p 944 ▼

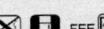

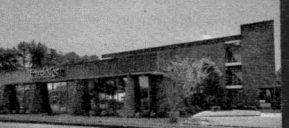

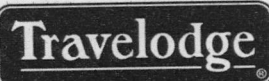

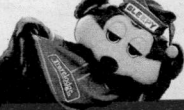

(See map and index starting on p. 913)

TRAVELODGE INN & SUITES *Book great rates at AAA.com* **Phone:** (757)229-2000 18

AAA SAVE

Small-scale Hotel

$69-$99 6/1-2/28

$39-$59 3/1-5/31

Address: 120 Bypass Rd 23185 **Location:** US 60 Bypass Rd, just e of jct Richmond Rd. **Facility:** 122 units. 94 one-bedroom standard units. 28 one-bedroom suites. 3 stories, exterior corridors. **Parking:** on-site. **Terms:** cancellation fee imposed. **Amenities:** high-speed Internet, voice mail, safes (fee), irons, hair dryers. **Pool(s):** outdoor. **Guest Services:** coin laundry, wireless Internet. **Business Services:** business center. **Cards:** AX, DS, MC, VI. **Free Special Amenities: continental breakfast and high-speed Internet.** *(See color ad p 943)*

/ SOME UNITS FEE FEE

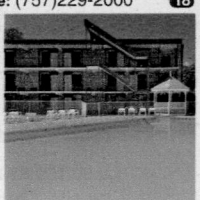

TRAVELODGE-KING WILLIAM INN *Book great rates at AAA.com* **Phone:** 757/229-4933 34

AAA SAVE

Motel

Rates not provided

Address: 834 Capitol Landing Rd 23185 **Location:** On SR 5 and 31, just e of jct US 60. **Facility:** 108 one-bedroom standard units. 3 stories, exterior corridors. **Parking:** on-site. **Amenities:** high-speed Internet, safes (fee), irons, hair dryers. **Pool(s):** outdoor. **Guest Services:** coin laundry, wireless Internet. **Free Special Amenities: continental breakfast and high-speed Internet.** *(See color ad below)*

/ SOME UNITS

WALLER MILL INN *Book great rates at AAA.com* **Phone:** (757)220-0880 19

AAA SAVE

Small-scale Hotel

$69-$129 3/1-8/31

$59-$99 9/1-2/28

Address: 201 Bypass Rd 23185 **Location:** US 60 (Bypass Rd), just se of jct Richmond Rd. **Facility:** 121 one-bedroom standard units, some with whirlpools. 4 stories, interior corridors. **Parking:** on-site. **Terms:** check-in 4 pm. **Amenities:** high-speed Internet, voice mail, irons, hair dryers. **Pool(s):** heated indoor. **Leisure Activities:** whirlpool. *Fee:* game room. **Guest Services:** valet and coin laundry, wireless Internet. **Cards:** AX, CB, DC, DS, MC, VI. **Free Special Amenities: expanded continental breakfast and high-speed Internet.**

CALL / SOME UNITS

▼ See AAA listing above ▼

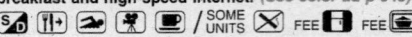

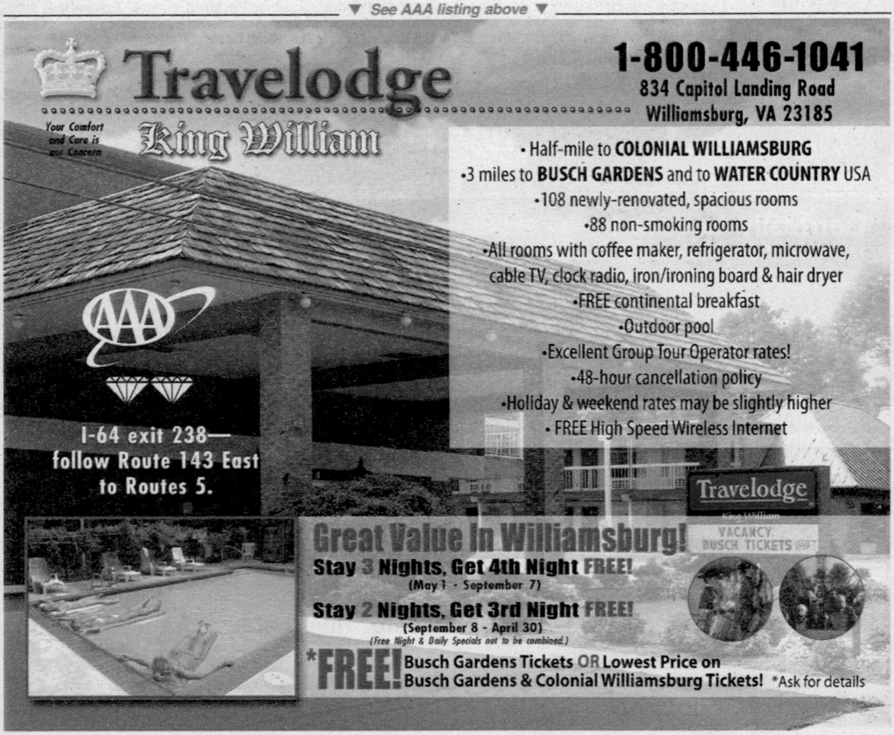

(See map and index starting on p. 913)

WESTGATE HISTORIC WILLIAMSBURG   *Book great rates at AAA.com*   Phone: (757)229-6220   **31**

AAA SAVE

▽▽▽▽

Small-scale Hotel
$149-$209 All Year

Address: 1324 Richmond Rd 23185 **Location:** Just e of jct Richmond and Bypass rds. **Facility:** Smoke free premises. 89 units. 30 one-bedroom standard units, some with efficiencies and/or whirlpools. 47 one-, 7 two- and 5 three-bedroom suites, some with kitchens and/or whirlpools. 3 stories, interior/exterior corridors. *Bath:* combo or shower only. **Parking:** on-site. **Terms:** check-in 4 pm. **Amenities:** CD players, dual phone lines, voice mail, irons, hair dryers. *Fee:* video library, DVD players. *Some:* safes. **Pool(s):** outdoor. **Leisure Activities:** whirlpool, recreation programs, playground, exercise room. *Fee:* game room. **Cards:** AX, DC, DS, MC, VI.

WHITE LION MOTEL   Phone: (757)229-3931   **30**

AAA SAVE

▽▽▽▽

Motel

$85-$175 3/1-9/15
$35-$75 9/16-2/28

Address: 912 Capitol Landing Rd 23185 **Location:** I-64, exit 238, 1 mi e on SR 143, then just w on SR 5. **Facility:** 37 units. 36 one-bedroom standard units. 1 two-bedroom suite. 3 stories (no elevator), exterior corridors. *Bath:* combo or shower only. **Parking:** on-site. **Terms:** office hours 8 am-midnight, 3 day cancellation notice-fee imposed. **Amenities:** *Some:* high-speed Internet. **Pool(s):** outdoor. **Leisure Activities:** picnic area, grills. **Guest Services:** wireless Internet. **Cards:** AX, DC, DS, JC, MC, VI. **Free Special Amenities:** continental breakfast and high-speed Internet.

WILLIAMSBURG HOSPITALITY HOUSE   *Book great rates at AAA.com*   Phone: (757)229-4020   **47**

AAA SAVE

▽▽▽▽

Small-scale Hotel
$99-$229 All Year

Address: 415 Richmond Rd 23185 **Location:** Just w of Colonial Williamsburg restored area on US 60/Richmond Rd. Located across from William and Mary College Stadium. **Facility:** 295 units. 284 one-bedroom standard units. 11 one-bedroom suites. 4 stories, interior corridors. **Parking:** on-site. **Terms:** 3 day cancellation notice-fee imposed. **Amenities:** high-speed Internet (fee), voice mail, irons, hair dryers. **Dining:** 2 restaurants. **Pool(s):** outdoor. **Leisure Activities:** exercise room. *Fee:* game room. **Guest Services:** valet laundry, wireless Internet. **Business Services:** conference facilities, business center. **Cards:** AX, DC, DS, MC, VI. **Free Special Amenities:** early check-in/late check-out.

WILLIAMSBURG SAMPLER BED & BREAKFAST INN   Phone: (757)253-0398   **57**

▽▽▽

Bed & Breakfast
$165-$225 All Year

Address: 922 Jamestown Rd 23185 **Location:** Jct SR 199, 1 mi ne on SR 5; just w of William and Mary College. Located in a residential area. **Facility:** Samplers, pewter pieces and an antique organ in the game room contribute to the rich decor of this B&B. 4 units. 2 one-bedroom standard units. 2 one-bedroom suites. 3 stories (no elevator), interior corridors. *Bath:* shower only. **Parking:** on-site. **Terms:** check-in 4 pm, 2 night minimum stay - weekends, age restrictions may apply, 14 day cancellation notice-fee imposed. **Amenities:** video library, irons, hair dryers. **Leisure Activities:** sauna, exercise room. **Guest Services:** wireless Internet. **Business Services:** fax. **Cards:** MC, VI.

WYNDHAM GOVERNOR'S GREEN   *Book at AAA.com*   Phone: 757/564-2420   **10**

▽▽▽

Condominium
Rates not provided

Address: 4600 Mooretown Rd 23185 **Location:** US 60 (Bypass Rd), just n to Willer Mill Rd, then 0.5 mi n on Mooretown Rd. **Facility:** This large resort offers spacious and stylish apartments which are fully equipped and a large family activity center which includes a walk-in pool. 198 units. 5 one-bedroom standard units with kitchens. 8 one-, 91 two- and 94 three-bedroom suites with kitchens and whirlpools. 3 stories, exterior corridors. **Parking:** on-site. **Terms:** office hours 7 am-11 pm, check-in 4 pm. **Amenities:** DVD players, CD players, voice mail, safes, irons, hair dryers. **Pool(s):** 2 outdoor, heated indoor. **Leisure Activities:** whirlpools, putting green, miniature golf, lighted tennis court, recreation programs, playground, exercise room, spa, horseshoes, volleyball. **Guest Services:** complimentary laundry, wireless Internet. **Business Services:** meeting rooms, business center.

—————— **WHERE TO DINE** ——————

ABERDEEN BARN   *Menu on AAA.com*   Phone: 757/229-6661   **6**

AAA

▽▽ ▽▽

Steak House
$17-$35

Known for its slow-roasted prime rib of beef prepared on an open charcoal hearth, this rustic steakhouse features post-and-beam construction and attractive barn decor. Other USDA Corn Fed Angus Beef selections, fresh local seafood and mouthwatering desserts round out the menu. Casual dress. **Bar:** Full bar. **Reservations:** suggested. **Hours:** 5 pm-9:30 pm, Fri & Sat-10 pm. Closed: 11/27, 12/25; also 1/1-1/15. **Address:** 1601 Richmond Rd 23185 **Location:** 1.8 mi nw on US 60, just w of jct Bypass Rd. **Parking:** on-site. **Cards:** AX, DS, MC, VI.

ALIZE BISTRO   Phone: 757/258-8882   **14**

AAA

▽▽▽▽

American
$8-$47

On the edge of the restored area, the stylish spot serves a mix of modern and traditional American dishes. Dressy casual. **Bar:** Full bar. **Reservations:** suggested. **Hours:** 11:30 am-2 & 5:30-10 pm, Fri-11 pm, Sat 5:30 pm-11 pm, Sun 11 am-2 & 5:30-9 pm. Closed major holidays. **Address:** 601 Prince George St 23185 **Location:** Just w of Merchants Square at jct Armistead. **Parking:** on-site. **Cards:** AX, DS, MC, VI.

AROMAS   Phone: 757/221-6676   **17**

▽▽

Coffee/Espresso
$5-$7

Locals, students and tourists who visit this cozy coffee shop find a lot more besides gourmet coffee and teas. Delicious breakfasts include crepes and homemade granola, and the menu has a long list of wonderful sandwiches and wraps, daily soup specials, gourmet cakes, cookies and desserts. After 5, sample such fondues as crab asiago or a small variety of delicious tapas dinners like sesame tuna bites or shrimp and grits. Casual dress. **Bar:** Beer & wine. **Entertainment. Hours:** 7 am-10 pm, Fri & Sat-11 pm, Sun 8 am-8 pm. Closed: 1/1, 11/27, 12/25. **Address:** 431 Prince George St 23185 **Location:** Between Henry and Boundary; at Merchants Square; center. **Parking:** street. **Cards:** MC, VI.

(See map and index starting on p. 913)

BERRET'S SEAFOOD RESTAURANT AND TAPHOUSE GRILL   *Menu on AAA.com*   Phone: 757-253-1847   [26]

Seafood
$10-$35

Berret's is centrally located and offers contemporary fine dining with emphasis on fresh Chesapeake Bay seafood. The seasonal patio offers raw bar favorites, steamed seafood and sandwiches in a very casual setting. Service is friendly and attentive. Casual dress. **Bar:** Full bar. **Reservations:** suggested. **Hours:** 11:30 am-3:30 & 5:30-10 pm. Closed major holidays; also Mon 1/1-2/28. **Address:** 199 S Boundary St 23185 **Location:** Center; in Merchants Square. **Parking:** on-site. **Cards:** AX, DS, MC, VI.

THE BLACK ANGUS GRILLE   Phone: 757/229-6823   [8]

Steak & Seafood
$11-$37

The menu features a selection of seafood, black Angus steak and Southwestern dishes, as well as some vegetarian entrees. Grilled salmon over black beans with the soup sampler is a pleasing choice. Casual dress. **Bar:** Full bar. **Reservations:** suggested. **Hours:** 4:30 pm-10 pm, Fri & Sat-10:30 pm. Closed: 12/24. **Address:** 1433 Richmond Rd 23185 **Location:** 1.5 mi nw on US 60. **Parking:** on-site. **Cards:** AX, DC, DS, MC, VI.

BLUE TALON BISTRO   Phone: 757/476-2583   [19]

French
$7-$20

Julia Child videos play on the flat screen over the chic yet casual bistro's bar, which also displays portraits of some of the most famed French chefs. The menu lists many affordable French classics—such as steak and frites, roasted chicken, coq au vin and even a classic hamburger topped with a fried egg—alongside "expensive stuff," such as foie gras. Casual dress. **Bar:** Full bar. **Reservations:** accepted. **Hours:** 11 am-9 pm. **Address:** 420 Prince George St 23185 **Location:** Downtown; in Merchant's Square. **Parking:** street. **Cards:** DC, DS, MC, VI.

CAPTAIN GEORGE'S SEAFOOD RESTAURANT   Phone: 757/565-2323

Seafood

An extensive, all-you-can-eat seafood buffet—which includes everything from Alaskan crab legs and shrimp to prime rib and dessert—satisfies even the heartiest of appetites. Nautical accents such as ropes and fish nets convey the oceanic feel. Casual dress. **Bar:** Full bar. **Reservations:** accepted. **Hours:** 4 pm-10 pm, Sat from 3:30 pm, Sun from noon. Closed: 12/25. **Address:** 5363 Richmond Rd 23188 **Location:** 3 mi w on US 60. **Parking:** on-site. **Cards:** AX, MC, VI.

CASA MAYA MEXICAN RESTAURANT   Phone: 757/259-2470   [2]

Mexican
$7-$15

CALL

The popular spot serves combination plates that diners know and love, as well as dishes that draw on more regional flavors, such as chilaquiles (marinated tortillas mixed with chicken), calabacitas (stuffed zucchini), seviche and shrimp mojo. Casual dress. **Bar:** Full bar. **Hours:** 11 am-10 pm. **Address:** 1660 Richmond Rd 23185 **Location:** 1.6 mi w of jct Bypass Rd. **Parking:** on-site. **Cards:** MC, VI.

THE CHEESE SHOP   Phone: 757/229-0298   [23]

Gourmet Grocery
$5-$9

The shop offers a wide range of specialty food products, Virginia delicacies, wines and sandwiches with their famed house dressing. Casual dress. **Bar:** Beer & wine. **Hours:** 10 am-8 pm, Sun 11 am-6 pm. Closed major holidays. **Address:** 410 Duke of Glouchester St 23185 **Location:** In Merchants Square; downtown. **Parking:** no self-parking. **Cards:** AX, DS, MC, VI.

CHEZ TRINH   Phone: 757/253-1888   [10]

Vietnamese
$5-$16

Vietnamese dishes and nightly specials—including excellent noodle soup and fresh, not fried, rice paper rolls—are presented in a casual setting within a local shopping center. The crowd comprises mostly locals and students. Casual dress. **Bar:** Full bar. **Hours:** 11:30 am-3 & 5-10 pm. Closed major holidays. **Address:** 157 Monticello Ave 23185 **Location:** On Lafayette Ave, just s of jct Richmond Rd; in Williamsburg Shopping Center. **Parking:** on-site. **Cards:** MC, VI.

CHOWNING'S TAVERN   Phone: 757/220-7012   [21]

American
$6-$8

The menu in the historic tavern and summer garden centers on lighter fare at lunchtime and from 9 p.m. to 1 a.m. Pub foods are served evenings, when an ale pub ambience prevails. Southern specialties range from chicken pot pie and crab soup to Sally Lunn bread. The service staff dons period costumes and performs Colonial entertainment. Casual dress. Entertainment. **Bar:** Full bar. **Hours:** 11 am-10 pm; seasonal hours vary. **Address:** 109 E Duke of Gloucester St 23185 **Location:** In Colonial Williamsburg restored area. **Parking:** on-site. **Cards:** AX, DS, MC, VI. **Historic** *(See color ad p 323)*

CHRISTIANA CAMPBELL'S TAVERN   Phone: 757/220-7015   [16]

Seafood
$21-$32

The charming, Old World atmosphere is very popular in this 18th-century tavern, replete with roving balladeers, costumed wait staff and Southern seafood specialties, some diligently made from scratch using authentic 17th-century family recipes. Casual dress. Entertainment. **Bar:** Full bar. **Reservations:** suggested. **Hours:** 5 pm-9 pm. Closed: Sun & Mon off season. **Address:** 120 E Waller St 23185 **Location:** In Colonial Williamsburg restored area. **Parking:** on-site. **Cards:** AX, DC, DS, MC, VI. **Historic** *(See color ad p 323)*

FAT CANARY   Phone: 757/229-3333   [25]

Regional American
$23-$37

This stylish new spot overlooks historic Merchants Square but is all modern inside with crisp lines and creative gourmet fare which changes seasonally so as to offer the freshest regional ingredients. The South is a heavy influence but one will find the chef has also drawn inspiration from around the world. An excellent complement of wines is offered. Dressy casual. **Bar:** Full bar. **Reservations:** required. **Hours:** 5 pm-10 pm. Closed major holidays. **Address:** 410 Duke of Gloucester St 23185 **Location:** At Merchants Square. **Parking:** on-site. **Cards:** AX, DS, MC, VI.

(See map and index starting on p. 913)

FIRESIDE CHOPHOUSE

Phone: 757/229-3310 ①

Prime rib, seafood and grilled, aged steak are house specialties at the casual, family-oriented restaurant. The owners' Greek heritage makes an appearance in a few dishes, such as the salad, appetizers and baklava for dessert. Casual dress. **Bar:** Full bar. **Reservations:** suggested, weekends. **Hours:** 4:30 pm-11 pm, Sun noon-10 pm. **Address:** 1995 Richmond Rd 23185 **Location:** I-64, exit 234, 2 mi s to US 60/Richmond Rd, then 3 mi e; in Comfort Inn Central. **Parking:** on-site. **Cards:** AX, MC, VI.

Steak House
$10-$25

(See color ad p 930)

FOOD FOR THOUGHT

Phone: 757/645-4665 ③

The eatery mixes home-style classics of pot roast, meatloaf, and baby back ribs with modern ideas, such as grilled portobellos, cilantro-lime chicken and sweet potato fries. Casual dress. **Bar:** Full bar. **Hours:** 11:30 am-9:30 pm, Sat-11 pm, Sun-9 pm. Closed: 11/27, 12/25. **Address:** 1647 Richmond Rd 23185 **Location:** On US 60, just w of jct Bypass Rd. **Parking:** on-site. **Cards:** AX, MC, VI.

American
$8-$19

CALL

FRIENDS CAFE

Phone: 757/645-3100 ⑮

Just steps from campus and the Colonial district, this small, bright cafe offers an extensive menu of sandwiches, salads, fruit smoothies and coffee drinks. Tasty specialties include the steak and cheese sandwich with special Korean barbecue marinade, the "pizza on a sub," an avocado and seafood salad sandwich and the Harmony snow ice. Casual dress. **Hours:** 8:30 am-10 pm. Closed: 11/27, 12/25; also Sun. **Address:** 603 Prince George St 23185 **Location:** Just w of Merchants Square at Armistead. **Parking:** on-site. **Cards:** AX, DS, MC, VI.

Deli/Subs
Sandwiches
$3-$7

GOLDEN HORSESHOE GOLD COURSE GRILL

Phone: 757/565-8460 ㉙

On a sunny day, a table on the patio can't be beat. Guests can enjoy the view of the inn's golf course and duck pond while dining on juicy burgers, grilled panini sandwiches, daily pasta and entree specials and delicious, freshly made ice cream. Casual dress. **Bar:** Full bar. **Hours:** 11:30 am-5 pm. **Address:** 401 S England St 23185 **Location:** Jct Francis St, just s. **Parking:** on-site. **Cards:** AX, DS, MC, VI.

American
$8-$15

HUZZAH!

Phone: 757/220-7692 ⑫

A break from all things Colonial can be found at the casual visitor center eatery. Families enjoy snacking on turkey chili, burgers, Brunswick stew and other American favorites. Casual dress. **Bar:** Full bar. **Hours:** 8 am-10 pm; hours may vary in winter. **Address:** 113 Visitor Center Dr 23188 **Location:** I-64, exit 238, s on SR 143 to SR 132; in Colonial Williamsburg-Woodlands Hotel & Suites. **Parking:** on-site. **Cards:** AX, DC, DS, MC, VI.

American
$7-$18

THE JEFFERSON

Phone: 757/229-2296 ⑦

Family-owned and operated since 1956, the restaurant specializes in Southern favorites such as fried chicken, Smithfield ham and homemade Virginia peanut soup. Steak and seafood also are good choices as are a few Greek dishes that reflects the family's heritage. An English country decor sets a cozy, relaxed mood. Casual dress. **Bar:** Full bar. **Reservations:** suggested. **Hours:** 3 pm-10 pm. Closed: 11/27, 12/25. **Address:** 1453 Richmond Rd 23185 **Location:** On US 60 W (Richmond Rd), just w of jct Bypass Rd. **Parking:** on-site. **Cards:** AX, CB, DC, MC, VI.

Regional
American
$12-$20

KING'S ARMS TAVERN

Phone: 757/220-7744 ㉒

This Colonial eatery was reconstructed on the site of the original King's Arms, opened in 1772. Servers don Colonial attire and roving balladeers entertain. Garden seating is offered, weather permitting. Lamb, game, meat and vegetable pies are served. Casual dress. Entertainment. **Bar:** Full bar. **Reservations:** suggested, for dinner. **Hours:** 11:30 am-2:30 & 5-9:30 pm. **Address:** 416 E Duke of Gloucester St 23187 **Location:** In Colonial Williamsburg restored area. **Parking:** on-site. **Cards:** AX, DS, MC, VI. **Historic**

American
$9-$38

(See color ad p 323)

KYOTO JAPANESE STEAK & SEAFOOD HOUSE

Phone: 757/220-8888 ⑤

Kyoto offers a fun and filling family-friendly dinner. In the front room, sit at the teppanyaki grill tables as Japanese chefs prepare steak and seafood specialties in an entertaining show. Or sit in the rear room and try traditional sushi specialties in artful arrangements. Casual dress. **Bar:** Full bar. **Reservations:** suggested, weekends. **Hours:** 4 pm-10 pm. Closed: 1/1, 11/27, 12/25. **Address:** 1621 Richmond Rd 23185 **Location:** 2 mi nw on US 60; just w of jct Bypass Rd. **Parking:** on-site. **Cards:** AX, DC, DS, MC, VI.

Japanese
$10-$24

LA TOLTECA MEXICAN RESTAURANTE

Phone: 757/259-0598 ⑬

Authentic Mexican cuisine, lunch specials and combination dinners are served in the festive atmosphere of La Tolteca. The menu is categorized with both a vegetarian section and glossary of terms for those less familiar with the cuisine and ingredients. Casual dress. **Bar:** Full bar. **Hours:** 11 am-10 pm, Sat noon-10:30 pm, Sun noon-9:30 pm. Closed: 11/27, 12/24, 12/25. **Address:** 135 Second St 23185 **Location:** Just e of jct Page St (US 5 and 31). **Parking:** on-site. **Cards:** AX, DS, MC, VI.

Mexican
$4-$10

CALL

NAWAB INDIAN CUISINE

Phone: 757/565-3200

Tandoor specialties and bread baked in a clay oven are at the centerpiece of a traditional menu of curried, lamb and vegetarian dishes. The upscale atmosphere features artwork and instrumental music. A weekday buffet draws a devoted lunch clientele. Casual dress. **Bar:** Full bar. **Hours:** 11:30 am-2:30 & 5-10 pm, Fri-10:30 pm, Sat noon-3 & 5-10:30 pm, Sun noon-3 pm. **Address:** 204 Monticello Ave 23185 **Location:** Just w of jct Richmond Rd; in Monticello Shopping Center. **Parking:** on-site. **Cards:** AX, DS, MC, VI.

Indian
$7-$16

CALL

(See map and index starting on p. 913)

OLD CHICKAHOMINY HOUSE
Phone: 757/229-4689   30
Regional American
$3-$7

The small menu offers traditional Southern favorites like country ham and biscuits, Brunswick stew and buttermilk pie in a restored 18th-century cottage. Even the dumplings will remind you, if you grew up lucky, of Grandma's cooking. Casual dress. **Bar:** Beer & wine. **Hours:** 8:30 am-10:30 & 11:30-2:30 pm. Closed major holidays. **Address:** 1211 Jamestown Rd 23185 **Location:** SR 31 (Jamestown Rd), just sw of jct SR 199. **Parking:** on-site. **Cards:** MC, VI.

PEKING & MONGOLIAN GRILL
Phone: 757/229-2288   9
Chinese
$5-$10

The decor is somewhat standard but the cuisine tastes are varied, from Cantonese and Hunan to Peking Szechuan and Shanghai. A new addition included a lengthy buffet and Mongolian grill where one chooses their favorite meat, seafood, vegetables and sauce that chefs prepare in front of them. Casual dress. **Bar:** Full bar. **Reservations:** suggested. **Hours:** 11 am-10 pm, Fri & Sat-11 pm. Closed: 11/27. **Address:** 120 J Waller Mill Rd 23185 **Location:** US 60 Bypass Rd; in K-Mart Shopping Center. **Parking:** on-site. **Cards:** AX, DS, MC, VI.

THE REGENCY DINING ROOM
Phone: 757/220-7978   27
Regional American
$9-$37

Sophisticated dishes are matched with choices from the lengthy wine list at the elegant dining room, which remains much the same as it was when first opened in 1938. Semi-formal attire. Entertainment. **Bar:** Full bar. **Reservations:** suggested, for dinner. **Hours:** 7:30 am-10, noon-2 & 6-9 pm. **Address:** 136 E Francis St 23185 **Location:** In Colonial Williamsburg restored area; in Colonial Williamsburg-Williamsburg Inn. **Parking:** valet. **Cards:** AX, CB, DC, DS, MC, VI.

RETRO'S-GOOD EATS
Phone: 757/253-8816   18
American
$2-$4

Both modern and nostalgic with cool design and chrome accents, the restaurant whips up great hot dogs with a wide variety of traditional and gourmet toppings, such as blue cheese slaw; turkey corn dogs; Carolina barbecue, freshly cut fries and chicken sandwiches. Limeade, real fruit milk shakes and root beer floats made with frozen custard wash it all down. Casual dress. **Bar:** Beer only. **Hours:** 11 am-9 pm. Closed: 1/1, 11/27, 12/25. **Address:** 435 Prince George St 23185 **Location:** At Merchant's Square; between Henry & Boundary sts. **Parking:** street. **Cards:** AX, DS, MC, VI.

SEAFARE RESTAURANT
Phone: 757/229-0099   4
Seafood
$13-$23

Diners who crave Atlantic or Chesapeake Bay seafood and prime beef are likely to enjoy this casual, nautical spot. There are many seafood dishes from which to choose, in addition to good bread and excellent homemade Caesar salad. Expect more formal service than is the norm. Casual dress. **Bar:** Full bar. **Reservations:** suggested. **Hours:** 4 pm-11 pm, Sun noon-10 pm. **Address:** 1632 Richmond Rd 23185 **Location:** 2 mi nw on US 60. **Parking:** on-site. **Cards:** AX, MC, VI. *(See color ad p 931)*

SHIELDS TAVERN
Phone: 757/220-7765   20
American
$5-$9

In the heart of the restored Colonial Williamsburg area, the tavern was re-created in meticulous detail on the spot where it once stood. Costumed staffers serve as interpreters of the past. The simple coffeehouse menu lists sandwiches, wraps, Smithfield ham biscuits, sausage gumbo, peanut pie and various pastries. Garden service is available, weather permitting. Casual dress. Entertainment. **Bar:** Full bar. **Reservations:** accepted. **Hours:** 8 am-5 pm; hours may vary off season. **Address:** 422 E Duke of Gloucester St 23185 **Location:** In Colonial Williamsburg restored area. **Parking:** on-site. **Cards:** AX, DC, DS, MC, VI. **Historic** *(See color ad p 323)*

THREE OLIVES GREEK RESTAURANT
Phone: 757/259-7300   11
Greek
$9-$20

Flavors from the owner's Greek hillside village show up on the menu, which lists distinctive dishes along the lines of octopus salad, braised dandelion greens, fried smelt and loukanico-Greek sausages flavored with orange rind. Also of note are traditional Greek favorites, such as souvlaki, spanakopita and moussaka. Lending to the atmosphere are belly dancing on Friday and Saturday nights and hookah pipes in the lounge. Casual dress. **Bar:** Full bar. **Reservations:** suggested. **Hours:** 4:30 pm-10 pm. Closed: 11/27, 12/25; also 1/1-1/7. **Address:** 1203 Richmond Rd 23185 **Location:** Jct Monticello Ave. **Parking:** on-site. **Cards:** AX, MC, VI.

CALL ⟨M⟩

THE TRELLIS RESTAURANT   *Menu on AAA.com*
Phone: 757/229-8610   24
Regional American
$7-$32

The owner/chef, who boasts many best-selling cookbooks, conceives an imaginative, seasonally changing menu with innovative food preparations. Desserts are creative and decadent, such as his famous 'Death by Chocolate'. Each dining area, including the airy patio, has a different personality. Nationally renowned. Dressy casual. **Bar:** Full bar. **Reservations:** suggested. **Hours:** 11 am-3 & 5-10 pm. Closed: 1/1, 11/27, 12/25. **Address:** 403 Duke of Gloucester St 23185 **Location:** In Merchants Square at Duke of Gloucester and Henry sts. **Parking:** on-site. **Cards:** AX, DC, DS, MC, VI.

VERANDA DINING ROOM
Phone: 757/220-2250   28
Regional American
$7-$24

Patrons are attracted to the soup, salad and pasta bars that are part of the buffet lunch served weekdays overlooking the pool. The spacious main dining room supports an older crowd at breakfast, lunch and dinner. Casual dress. **Bar:** Full bar. **Hours:** 7 am-10 pm. **Address:** 6945 Pocahontas Tr 23187 **Location:** US 60, 0.8 mi e of jct SR 5 and 31; in Crowne Plaza Williamsburg at Fort Magruder. **Parking:** on-site. **Cards:** AX, DC, DS, MC, VI.

CALL ⟨M⟩

The Williamsburg Vicinity

CHARLES CITY

——— WHERE TO STAY ———

EDGEWOOD PLANTATION BED & BREAKFAST
Phone: 804/829-2962

Historic Bed
& Breakfast
$139-$198 All Year

Address: 4800 John Tyler Memorial Hwy 23030 **Location:** Jct SR 609, just e; on SR 5. **Facility:** This 1849 Gothic Revival-style home on the site of what was once a working plantation features manicured grounds and tasteful decor. Smoke free premises. 8 units. 5 one-bedroom standard units, some with whirlpools. 1 one- and 2 two-bedroom suites. 3 stories (no elevator), interior/exterior corridors. *Bath:* some shared or private, combo, shower or tub only. **Parking:** on-site. **Terms:** age restrictions may apply, cancellation fee imposed. **Amenities:** video library. *Some:* CD players, irons, hair dryers. **Pool(s):** outdoor. **Cards:** MC, VI.

NORTH BEND PLANTATION BED & BREAKFAST
Phone: 804/829-5176

Historic Bed
& Breakfast
Rates not provided

Address: 12200 Weyanoke Rd 23030 **Location:** Jct SR 5 and 619, 1 mi s on SR 619. **Facility:** On the grounds of this Bed and Breakfast are trenches said to have been used by soldiers in the Civil War; inside, many artifacts from that era are displayed. Smoke free premises. 4 units. 3 one- and 1 two-bedroom standard units. 2 stories (no elevator), interior corridors. *Bath:* combo or shower only. **Parking:** on-site. **Terms:** age restrictions may apply. **Amenities:** video library, high-speed Internet, irons, hair dryers. **Pool(s):** outdoor. **Leisure Activities:** hiking trails, horseshoes, volleyball. **Guest Services:** wireless Internet. **Business Services:** fax.

PINEY GROVE AT SOUTHALL'S PLANTATION-1790
Phone: (804)829-2480

Historic Bed
& Breakfast
$140-$280 All Year

Address: 16920 Southall Plantation Ln 23030 **Location:** 1 mi e on SR 5, 8 mi n on SR 615. **Facility:** Flower beds peppered with perennials surround the meandering red-brick walkway at this plantation inn, which features numerous outbuildings. Smoke free premises. 5 units. 4 one-bedroom standard units. 1 two-bedroom suite. 2 stories (no elevator), interior corridors. **Parking:** on-site. **Terms:** check-in 4 pm, 1-14 night minimum stay, 30 day cancellation notice-fee imposed. **Amenities:** hair dryers. **Pool(s):** outdoor. **Leisure Activities:** hiking trails.

——— WHERE TO DINE ———

INDIAN FIELDS TAVERN
Phone: 804/829-5004

Regional American
$7-$29

The menu features "new" Southern cuisine, with emphasis on regional specialties, and features ample portions. This charming restored farmhouse in the historic plantation region boasts quaint screened porches overlooking the gardens for seasonal dining. Casual dress. **Bar:** Full bar. **Reservations:** suggested. **Hours:** 11 am-3:30 & 5-9 pm, Fri & Sat-10 pm. Closed: 1/1, 7/4, 12/24, 12/25; also Mon 1/1-2/28. **Address:** 9220 John Tyler Memorial Hwy 23030 **Location:** On SR 5. **Parking:** on-site. **Cards:** AX, DS, MC, VI.

LIGHTFOOT   (See map and index starting on p. 917)

──── WHERE TO STAY ────

DAYS INN COLONIAL RESORT   *Book great rates at AAA.com*   Phone: 757/220-0062   **11**

AAA [SAVE]

▼▼▼

Small-scale Hotel
$39-$119 All Year

Address: 720 Lightfoot Rd 23188 **Location:** I-64, exit 234 (SR 199 E), 0.5 mi s to International Pkwy. **Facility:** 120 units. 117 one-bedroom standard units, some with whirlpools. 3 one-bedroom suites. 5 stories, interior corridors. **Bath:** combo or shower only. **Parking:** on-site. **Amenities:** voice mail, safes (fee), hair dryers. *Some:* Fee: DVD players. **Pool(s):** heated indoor. **Leisure Activities:** exercise room. Fee: game room. **Guest Services:** valet and coin laundry. **Business Services:** meeting rooms, business center. **Cards:** AX, CB, DC, DS, JC, MC, VI. **Free Special Amenities: continental breakfast and room upgrade (subject to availability with advance reservations).** *(See color ad p 925)*

[S/D] CALL [&M] 🏊 🐾 / SOME UNITS ✖ FEE 🖥 FEE 📷 ☕

ECONO LODGE-POTTERY   *Book great rates at AAA.com*   Phone: (757)564-3341

AAA [SAVE]

▼▼▼

Motel
$45-$99 3/1-9/1
$45-$75 9/2-2/28

Address: 7051 Richmond Rd 23188 **Location:** I-64, exit 231A, 1 mi s on SR 607, then 2.4 mi e on US 60. **Facility:** 74 one-bedroom standard units, some with whirlpools. 2 stories (no elevator), exterior corridors. **Parking:** on-site. **Terms:** cancellation fee imposed. **Pool(s):** outdoor. **Business Services:** fax. **Cards:** AX, DS, MC, VI. **Free Special Amenities: continental breakfast and local telephone calls.** *(See color ad below)*

[S/D] [✚] 🏊 🐾 / SOME UNITS ✖ FEE 🖥 FEE 📷 ☕

GREAT WOLF LODGE   *Book great rates at AAA.com*   Phone: 757/229-9700   **10**

AAA [SAVE]

▼▼▼

Large-scale Hotel
Rates not provided

Address: 549 E Rochambeau Dr 23188 **Location:** I-64, exit 234A (SR 199 E), 0.5 mi s to Mooretown Rd, just e to Rochambeau Dr, then 1 mi ne. **Facility:** Smoke free premises. 405 units. 335 one-bedroom standard units. 38 one- and 32 two-bedroom suites, some with whirlpools. 4 stories, interior corridors. **Bath:** combo or shower only. **Parking:** on-site. **Terms:** check-in 4 pm. **Amenities:** video games (fee), high-speed Internet, voice mail, safes, irons, hair dryers. **Dining:** 4 restaurants. **Pool(s):** heated outdoor, heated indoor. **Leisure Activities:** whirlpools, waterslide, poolside cabana rentals, recreation programs, kids club, exercise room, spa. Fee: miniature golf, game room. **Guest Services:** valet and coin laundry, wireless Internet. **Business Services:** conference facilities, business center. *(See color ad p 923)*

[🍴] CALL [&M] 🏊 ✖ ✖ 🐾 🖥 📷 ☕

HOWARD JOHNSON PLAZA HOTEL   *Book great rates at AAA.com*   Phone: 757/220-5550   **12**

AAA [SAVE]

▼▼▼

Small-scale Hotel
Rates not provided

Address: 6483 Richmond Rd 23188 **Location:** I-64, exit 234 (SR 199), 1 mi se; just w on US 60. **Facility:** 189 one-bedroom standard units, some with whirlpools. 7 stories, interior corridors. **Parking:** on-site. **Amenities:** high-speed Internet, voice mail, irons, hair dryers. **Pool(s):** heated indoor. **Leisure Activities:** whirlpool, exercise room. **Guest Services:** valet and coin laundry, wireless Internet. **Business Services:** meeting rooms. **Free Special Amenities: local telephone calls and high-speed Internet.** *(See color ad p 922)*

[🍴] 🏊 🐾 ☕ / SOME UNITS ✖ 🖥 📷

(See map and index starting on p. 917)

——————— **WHERE TO DINE** ———————

CARMINE'S ITALIAN MARKET & CAFE

Deli/Subs
Sandwiches
$6-$13

Phone: 757/259-6844   (26)
Casual dress. **Hours:** 10 am-8 pm, Sat-5 pm. Closed major holidays; also Sun. **Address:** 6380-F Richmond Rd 23188 **Location:** I-64, exit 234A (SR199 E), 1.7 mi s on SR 199, exit US 60, just w. **Parking:** on-site. **Cards:** AX, MC, VI.

LA PETITE TEA ROOM

Specialty
$7-$14

Phone: 757/565-3422   (24)
This tea room is super tiny, tucked in a corner of a busy antique mall, and the menu is small as well but full of flavor from the tea sandwiches, famous chowders, scones, and luscious desserts such as chocolate cream puffs. Casual dress. **Hours:** 11 am-5 pm, Sun from noon. Closed major holidays. **Address:** 500 Lightfoot Rd 23188 **Location:** I-64, exit 234A (SR 199 E), s on SR 199, then just w; in the Williamsburg Antique Mall. **Parking:** on-site.

NEW YORK DELI

Deli/Subs
Sandwiches
$4-$12

Phone: 757/564-9258   (22)
The oversized delicatessen offers an equally oversized menu of typical Greek and Italian favorites, such as cold or hot submarine sandwiches (including parmigiana choices), gyros, pasta dishes and calzones. Casual dress. **Bar:** Beer & wine. **Hours:** 11 am-10 pm. Closed major holidays. **Address:** 6546 Richmond Rd 23185 **Location:** I-64, exit 234A (SR 199 E), 1 mi s to US 60, then 0.5 mi w. **Parking:** on-site. **Cards:** MC, VI.

PIERCE'S BAR-B-QUE

Barbecue
$3-$15

Phone: 757/565-2955   (25)
Nationally known and beloved for its sweet and tangy barbecue sauce—which is great on chopped pork sandwiches, chicken and ribs—the restaurant also is a good spot for hushpuppies, catfish and Brunswick stew. Casual dress. **Hours:** 10 am-9 pm. Closed: 1/1, 11/27, 12/25. **Address:** 447 E Rochambeau Dr 23185 **Location:** I-64, exit 238A westbound, just s to E Rochambeau Dr, then 3 mi w; exit 234A eastbound, 1.2 mi s on SR 199, then 3 mi e on F137. **Parking:** on-site. **Cards:** AX, MC, VI.

TACO MEXICALI

Mexican
$2-$9

Phone: 757/220-3116   (23)
The casual, quick-serve spot treats patrons to delicious tacos, burritos and other dishes made with eight meat choices—including green or red chili pork, chorizo (Cuban sausage), steak and grilled chicken—and varied toppings from the salsa bar. The freshly made guacamole is excellent. Casual dress. **Bar:** Beer & wine. **Hours:** 11 am-10 pm. Closed: 11/27, 12/24, 12/25; also 12/31. **Address:** 6572 Richmond Rd 23188 **Location:** I-64, exit 234A, 1.2 mi s on SR 199 E, exit US 60, just w. **Parking:** on-site. **Cards:** AX, DC, DS, MC, VI.

YORKTOWN pop. 203   (See map and index starting on p. 728)

——————— **WHERE TO STAY** ———————

CANDLEWOOD SUITES-YORKTOWN   *Book at AAA.com*

Small-scale Hotel
Rates not provided

Phone: 757/952-1120   (26)
Address: 329 Commonwealth Dr 23693 **Location:** I-64, exit 256B, just n, then just e. **Facility:** 59 units. 47 one-bedroom standard units. 10 one- and 2 two-bedroom suites with kitchens. 3 stories, interior corridors. *Bath:* combo or shower only. **Parking:** on-site. **Amenities:** video library, DVD players, CD players, high-speed Internet, dual phone lines, voice mail, irons, hair dryers. **Pool(s):** outdoor. **Leisure Activities:** exercise room. **Guest Services:** valet and coin laundry. **Business Services:** meeting rooms, fax.

COURTYARD BY MARRIOTT   *Book great rates at AAA.com*

Small-scale Hotel
$143-$174 All Year

Phone: 757/874-9000   (25)
Address: 105 Cybernetics Way 23693 **Location:** I-64, exit 256B, just n to Kiln Creek Pkwy. Located in a residential area. **Facility:** Smoke free premises. 90 units. 87 one-bedroom standard units, some with whirlpools. 3 one-bedroom suites. 3 stories, interior corridors. *Bath:* combo or shower only. **Parking:** on-site. **Amenities:** high-speed Internet, voice mail, irons, hair dryers. **Pool(s):** heated indoor. **Leisure Activities:** whirlpool, exercise room. **Guest Services:** valet and coin laundry, wireless Internet. **Business Services:** meeting rooms, business center. **Cards:** AX, DC, DS, MC, VI.

AAA Benefit:
Members save 5% off of the best available rate.

DAYS INN   *Book at AAA.com*

Small-scale Hotel
Rates not provided

Phone: 757/283-1111   (23)
Address: 4531 George Washington Memorial Hwy 23692 **Location:** I-64, exit 256B, 0.8 mi ne on Victory Blvd (SR 171), 2.4 mi n on US 17. **Facility:** 43 one-bedroom standard units, some with whirlpools. 3 stories, interior corridors. **Parking:** on-site. **Amenities:** high-speed Internet, voice mail, irons, hair dryers. **Pool(s):** outdoor. **Guest Services:** coin laundry, wireless Internet.

DUKE OF YORK HOTEL

Small-scale Hotel
$69-$189 All Year

Phone: 757/898-3232
Address: 508 Water St 23690 **Location:** SR 238; downtown; on waterfront. **Facility:** 57 units. 56 one- and 1 two-bedroom standard units, some with whirlpools. 2-3 stories, interior/exterior corridors. *Bath:* combo or shower only. **Parking:** on-site. **Amenities:** safes (fee), hair dryers. *Some:* high-speed Internet. **Pool(s):** outdoor. **Guest Services:** wireless Internet. **Cards:** AX, DC, DS, MC, VI.

(See map and index starting on p. 728)

TOWNEPLACE SUITES BY MARRIOTT   *Book great rates at AAA.com*   Phone: 757/874-8884

Small-scale Hotel
$154-$185 All Year

Address: 200 Cybernetics Way 23693 **Location:** I-64, exit 256B, e to Kiln Creek Pkwy. **Facility:** Smoke free premises. 95 units. 68 one-bedroom standard units with kitchens. 4 one- and 23 two-bedroom suites with kitchens. 3 stories, interior corridors. *Bath:* combo or shower only. **Parking:** on-site. **Amenities:** high-speed Internet, voice mail, irons, hair dryers. **Pool(s):** heated outdoor. **Leisure Activities:** exercise room. **Guest Services:** valet and coin laundry, wireless Internet. **Business Services:** fax. **Cards:** AX, DC, DS, JC, MC, VI. **Free Special Amenities:** continental breakfast and high-speed Internet.

AAA Benefit:
Members save 5% off of the best available rate.

YORKTOWN MOTOR LODGE   *Book great rates at AAA.com*   Phone: (757)898-5451

Motel
$80-$120 3/1-9/1
$70-$80 9/2-2/28

Address: 8829 George Washington Memorial Hwy 23692 **Location:** 3 mi s of York River bridge on US 17. **Facility:** 42 one-bedroom standard units. 1 story, exterior corridors. **Parking:** on-site. **Terms:** office hours 7 am-11 pm, 3 day cancellation notice-fee imposed. **Amenities:** irons, hair dryers. **Pool(s):** outdoor. **Guest Services:** wireless Internet. **Business Services:** fax. **Cards:** AX, DS, MC, VI. **Free Special Amenities:** expanded continental breakfast and room upgrade (subject to availability with advance reservations).

———— WHERE TO DINE ————

CARROT TREE KITCHEN AT THE COLE DIGGS HOUSE   Phone: 757/246-9559

Regional American
$5-$11

In the center of a Colonial village, the charming historic cottage employs a staff that serves tasty lunch specialties made with a Southern flair. Examples include tomato basil soup, ham biscuits, hot crab dip and rich desserts, including, of course, the specialty carrot cake. Casual dress. **Bar:** Beer & wine. **Reservations:** accepted. **Hours:** 10 am-5 pm, Fri & Sat-9 pm. Closed: 3/23, 11/27, 12/24, 12/25. **Address:** 411 Main St 23692 **Location:** Jct Read St; in Colonial District. **Parking:** street. **Cards:** AX, DS, MC, VI.

EMPRESS RESTAURANT   Phone: 757/875-5460   23

Chinese
$6-$13

The bountiful lunch and dinner buffets line up a wide range of Chinese specialties and a few Japanese and Korean ones as well. A la carte dishes also are available. Casual dress. **Hours:** 11 am-10 pm, Fri & Sat-11 pm. Closed: 11/27, 12/25. **Address:** 5005 Victory Blvd 23606 **Location:** I-64, exit 256B, just e; in K-Mart Shopping Plaza. **Parking:** on-site. **Cards:** AX, DC, DS, MC, VI.

THE GLASS PHEASANT ENGLISH TEA ROOM   Phone: 757/595-9012   22

American
$5-$9

The tea room offers a menu of sandwiches, soup, salad and quiche in a setting of antiques and English china. Casual dress. **Hours:** 11 am-2 pm. Closed: Sun. **Address:** 1215Q SR 17 23693 **Location:** I-64, exit 258B, 2 mi n on US 17; in Kiln Creek Shopping Center. **Parking:** on-site. **Cards:** DC, MC, VI.

NICK'S RIVERWALK RESTAURANT   Phone: 757/875-1522

Seafood
$9-$29

Nick's Riverwalk overlooks the wide York River on the beach in this town entrenched in history. Guests can dine in both its casual cafe and raw bar as well as in a sophisticated modern dining room. Local Chesapeake Bay seafood occupies prime placement on the menu, but other delicious choices mix flavors of both Virginia and the deeper South; the gumbo is one example. Sample duck confit, local crab cakes, grilled tuna, pepper-seared filet mignon, lobster bisque and prosciutto-wrapped grouper. Casual dress. **Bar:** Full bar. **Reservations:** accepted. **Hours:** 11:30 am-2 & 5-10 pm. Closed: 1/1, 12/25; also for dinner 12/24. **Address:** 323 Water St, Suite A1 23690 **Location:** SR 238; downtown; on the waterfront. **Parking:** on-site. **Cards:** AX, DS, MC, VI.

SMOKIN' JOE'S BARBEQUE   Phone: 757/875-7774

Barbecue
$6-$15

The bright and clean roadside spot serves lots of tasty barbecue and country sides to hungry patrons. Pork and ribs the specialty, but yummy wraps and salads are find a place on the menu. Casual dress. **Hours:** 11 am-8 pm, Fri & Sat-9 pm, Sun noon-4 pm. Closed: 11/27, 12/25. **Address:** 5619 George Washington Memorial Hwy 23692 **Location:** On US 17, 2 mi n of SR 134. **Parking:** on-site. **Cards:** MC, VI.

(See map and index starting on p. 728)

SPRING GARDEN   **Phone:** 757/599-0088

Chinese

$5-$13

Inside, the pleasant little spot has the feel of a greenhouse, with plenty of plants and cozy pink bistro curtains. The menu is all Chinese, from the fresh and tasty lunch buffet to seasonal dinner specialties of Mandarin roast duck and soft-shell crabs. Casual dress. **Bar:** Beer & wine. **Hours:** 11 am-9:30 pm, Fri-10 pm, Sat 4:30 pm-10 pm, Sun 4:30 pm-9 pm. Closed major holidays. **Address:** 1215-X George Washington Memorial Hwy 23963 **Location:** I-64, exit 258B, 1 mi n on US 17; in Kiln Creek Shopping Center. **Parking:** on-site. **Cards:** DS, MC, VI.

WATERSTREET LANDING   **Phone:** 757/886-5890

Seafood

$5-$21

The simple spot offers panoramic views of the riverfront from its beachside perch. On the basic menu are such local favorites as she crab soup, crab cakes and baked apple dumplings, as well as ice cream novelties for the kids. Casual dress. **Bar:** Full bar. **Reservations:** accepted. **Hours:** 11 am-9 pm, Fri & Sat-10 pm; 10 am-10 pm, Fri & Sat-11 pm in summer. Closed: 1/1, 11/27, 12/25. **Address:** 114 Water St 23690 **Location:** Downtown; on the waterfront. **Parking:** on-site. **Cards:** MC, VI.

![Yorktown Victory Center photograph]

Yorktown Victory Center, Yorktown / Jeff Greenberg / Virginia Tourism Corporation

This ends listings for the Williamsburg Vicinity.
The following page resumes the alphabetical listings of cities in Virginia.

WILLIAMSVILLE

——— WHERE TO STAY ———

FORT LEWIS LODGE

Country Inn
$190-$295 4/4-11/8

Phone: (540)925-2314

Address: SR 625 (River Rd) 24460 **Location:** 5.8 mi s on SR 678, just w on SR 625; from SR 39, just w on SR 625, then 11 mi n. Located in rural area. **Facility:** The owner's friendly dog roams the grounds of this mountain farm which houses guests in converted silo rooms, standard lodge rooms and two cabins. Smoke free premises. 19 units. 15 one- and 1 two-bedroom standard units. 3 cabins. 2-3 stories (no elevator), interior/exterior corridors. *Bath:* combo or shower only. **Parking:** on-site. **Terms:** open 4/4-11/8, 2 night minimum stay - weekends, 10 day cancellation notice-fee imposed. **Amenities:** irons, hair dryers. **Leisure Activities:** whirlpool, canoeing, fishing, basketball, horseshoes, volleyball. **Business Services:** meeting rooms. **Cards:** MC, VI.

WINCHESTER pop. 23,585

——— WHERE TO STAY ———

BEST WESTERN LEE-JACKSON MOTOR INN   *Book great rates at AAA.com*

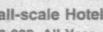

Small-scale Hotel
$69-$72 3/1-10/31
$62-$65 11/1-2/28

Phone: (540)662-4154

Address: 711 Millwood Ave 22601 **Location:** I-81, exit 313B, just nw on US 50/522/17. **Facility:** 139 one-bedroom standard units. 2 stories (no elevator), exterior corridors. **Parking:** on-site. **Amenities:** high-speed Internet, voice mail, irons, hair dryers. **Pool(s):** outdoor. **Leisure Activities:** exercise room. **Guest Services:** valet and coin laundry, airport transportation-Winchester Regional Airport, area transportation-hospital, wireless Internet. **Business Services:** conference facilities, fax (fee). **Cards:** AX, DC, DS, MC, VI. **Free Special Amenities:** local telephone calls and newspaper. *(See color ad below)*

AAA Benefit:
Members save 10% everyday, plus an exclusive frequent stay program.

COMFORT INN   *Book great rates at AAA.com*

Small-scale Hotel
$69-$99 All Year

Phone: (540)667-8894

Address: 1601 Martinsburg Pike 22603 **Location:** I-81, exit 317, just s on US 11. **Facility:** 82 one-bedroom standard units. 2 stories (no elevator), interior corridors. *Bath:* combo or shower only. **Parking:** on-site. **Amenities:** high-speed Internet, voice mail, irons, hair dryers. **Pool(s):** outdoor. **Leisure Activities:** picnic and grill area, exercise room, horseshoes. **Guest Services:** coin laundry, wireless Internet. **Business Services:** meeting rooms, PC. **Cards:** AX, CB, DC, DS, MC, VI. **Free Special Amenities:** expanded continental breakfast and high-speed Internet.

COUNTRY INN & SUITES-WINCHESTER

(fyi)

Small-scale Hotel
$99-$115 All Year

Phone: 540/869-7657

Too new to rate. **Address:** 141 Kernstown Commons Blvd 22602 **Location:** I-81, exit 310. **Amenities:** 81 units, coffeemakers, microwaves, refrigerators, pool. **Cards:** AX, DS, MC, VI.

▼ *See AAA listing above* ▼

COURTYARD BY MARRIOTT WINCHESTER MEDICAL CENTER   *Book great rates at AAA.com*

Phone: 540/678-8822

Small-scale Hotel
$108-$132 All Year

Address: 300 Marriott Dr 22603 **Location:** I-81, exit 310, 4.1 mi w on SR 37, then just nw on US 50. **Facility:** Smoke free premises. 136 one-bedroom standard units. 5 stories, interior corridors. **Parking:** on-site. **Amenities:** high-speed Internet, dual phone lines, voice mail, irons, hair dryers. *Some:* CD players. **Pool(s):** heated indoor. **Leisure Activities:** whirlpool, exercise room. **Guest Services:** valet and coin laundry, area transportation, wireless Internet. **Business Services:** conference facilities, business center. **Cards:** AX, DS, MC, VI.

AAA Benefit:
Members save 5% off of the best available rate.

ASK SD [icons] CALL [icons] / SOME UNITS [icon]

DAYS INN   *Book great rates at AAA.com*

Phone: 540/667-1200

AAA SAVE

Small-scale Hotel
Rates not provided

Address: 2951 Valley Ave 22601 **Location:** I-81, exit 310, just w, then 1.8 mi n on US 11. **Facility:** 81 one-bedroom standard units. 2 stories (no elevator), interior/exterior corridors. *Bath:* combo or shower only. **Parking:** on-site. **Amenities:** hair dryers. *Some:* safes. **Pool(s):** outdoor. **Guest Services:** valet and coin laundry, wireless Internet. **Business Services:** business center. **Free Special Amenities:** continental breakfast and high-speed Internet.

CALL [icons] / SOME UNITS FEE [icons]

ECONO LODGE NORTH   *Book great rates at AAA.com*

Phone: (540)662-4700

AAA SAVE

Small-scale Hotel
$65-$75 3/1-10/31
$60-$65 11/1-2/28

Address: 1593 Martinsburg Pike 22603 **Location:** I-81, exit 317, 0.3 mi sw on US 11. **Facility:** 49 one-bedroom standard units. 2 stories (no elevator), interior corridors. **Parking:** on-site. **Amenities:** *Some:* hair dryers. **Leisure Activities:** pool privileges, horseshoes. **Guest Services:** valet laundry, wireless Internet. **Business Services:** PC, fax (fee). **Cards:** AX, CB, DC, DS, JC, MC, VI. **Free Special Amenities:** continental breakfast and local telephone calls.

SD [icons] CALL [icons] / SOME UNITS [icons]

FAIRFIELD INN AND SUITES BY MARRIOTT IN WINCHESTER

Phone: 540/665-8881

Small-scale Hotel
$90-$109 All Year

Address: 250 Front Royal Pike 22602 **Location:** I-81, exit 313 northbound; exit 313A southbound, just s on US 522. **Facility:** Smoke free premises. 85 one-bedroom standard units. 3 stories, interior corridors. *Bath:* combo or shower only. **Parking:** on-site. **Amenities:** high-speed Internet, voice mail, irons, hair dryers. *Some:* CD players. **Pool(s):** heated indoor. **Leisure Activities:** whirlpool, exercise room. **Guest Services:** valet and coin laundry, wireless Internet. **Business Services:** meeting rooms, business center. **Cards:** AX, DS, MC, VI.

AAA Benefit:
Members save 5% off of the best available rate.

ASK SD CALL [icons] [icons]

THE GEORGE WASHINGTON HOTEL, A WYNDHAM HISTORIC HOTEL

Phone: 540/678-4700

fyi

Historic
Small-scale Hotel
$169 All Year

Too new to rate. **Address:** 103 E Piccadilly St 22601 **Location:** I-81, exit 313, just w. **Amenities:** 90 units, restaurant, coffeemakers, microwaves, refrigerators, pool. **Terms:** cancellation fee imposed. **Cards:** AX, DC, DS, MC, VI.

HAMPTON INN NORTH   *Book great rates at AAA.com*

Phone: 540/678-4000

Small-scale Hotel
Rates not provided

Address: 1204 Berryville Ave 22601 **Location:** I-81, exit 315, just w. **Facility:** 100 one-bedroom standard units, some with whirlpools. 4 stories, interior corridors. *Bath:* combo or shower only. **Parking:** on-site. **Amenities:** video games, high-speed Internet, voice mail, irons, hair dryers. **Pool(s):** outdoor. **Leisure Activities:** exercise room. **Guest Services:** valet and coin laundry, wireless Internet. **Business Services:** meeting rooms, business center.

CALL [icons] / SOME UNITS [icon]

HAMPTON INN WINCHESTER UNIVERSITY MALL   *Book great rates at AAA.com*

Phone: 540/667-8011

Small-scale Hotel
Rates not provided

Address: 1655 Apple Blossom Dr 22601 **Location:** I-81, exit 313 northbound; exit 313B southbound, 0.5 mi nw on US 50/522/17. **Facility:** 100 one-bedroom standard units. 4 stories, interior corridors. **Parking:** on-site. **Amenities:** video games, high-speed Internet, voice mail, irons, hair dryers. **Pool(s):** outdoor. **Leisure Activities:** exercise room. **Guest Services:** valet and coin laundry, wireless Internet. **Business Services:** meeting rooms, business center.

[icons] CALL [icons] / SOME UNITS [icons]

Leading the Way

AAA is the No. 1 choice for emergency road service and maps. But AAA members receive so much more:

- Battery delivery and installation
- Expert travel planning
- Special rates on hotels
- Financial services products
- Savings at thousands of merchants worldwide

Make the most of your membership! Visit AAA.com for details.

AAA. Delivering high performance service.

Proud Sponsor of the No. 6 AAA Ford Fusion

Roush Fenway Racing trademarks used by authority of Roush Fenway LLC. The AAA logo is a trademark of the American Automobile Association.

HOLIDAY INN EXPRESS & SUITES WINCHESTER

Book at AAA.com

Phone: (540)667-7050

WWWW

Small-scale Hotel
$89-$120 All Year

Address: 142 Fox Ridge Ln 22603 **Location:** I-81, exit 317, 2.7 mi w on SR 37. **Facility:** 81 one-bedroom standard units. 3 stories, interior corridors. *Bath:* combo or shower only. **Parking:** on-site. **Amenities:** high-speed Internet, voice mail, irons, hair dryers. **Pool(s):** heated indoor. **Leisure Activities:** whirlpool, exercise room. **Guest Services:** valet and coin laundry, wireless Internet. **Business Services:** meeting rooms, business center. **Cards:** AX, CB, DC, DS, MC, VI.

ASK SD CALL M 🏊 📷 🍽 🖥 🖥 / SOME UNITS ✕

HOLIDAY INN WINCHESTER

Book great rates at AAA.com

Phone: (540)667-3300

AAA SAVE

WWWW

Small-scale Hotel
$79-$99 All Year

Address: 1017 Millwood Pike 22602 **Location:** I-81, exit 313 northbound; exit 313A southbound, just se on US 50/17, at US 522. **Facility:** 120 one-bedroom standard units. 2 stories (no elevator), interior/exterior corridors. *Bath:* combo or shower only. **Parking:** on-site. **Amenities:** video games, high-speed Internet, voice mail, irons, hair dryers. **Pool(s):** outdoor. **Leisure Activities:** exercise room. **Guest Services:** valet laundry, airport transportation-Winchester Regional Airport, area transportation-within 5 mi, wireless Internet. **Business Services:** meeting rooms. **Cards:** AX, CB, DC, DS, JC, MC, VI. **Free Special Amenities:** early check-in/late check-out and room upgrade (subject to availability with advance reservations).

SD 🛏 🍽 🍸 CALL M 🏊 📷 🖥 / SOME UNITS 🐕 ✕ 🖥 🖥

RED ROOF INN

Book great rates at AAA.com

Phone: 540/667-5000

AAA SAVE

WW

Small-scale Hotel
Rates not provided

Address: 991 Millwood Pike 22602 **Location:** I-81, exit 313 northbound; exit 313A southbound, just se on US 50/17. **Facility:** 113 one-bedroom standard units. 2 stories (no elevator), exterior corridors. **Parking:** on-site. **Amenities:** irons, hair dryers. **Guest Services:** coin laundry, wireless Internet. **Business Services:** meeting rooms.

🍽 🛗 📷 / SOME UNITS 🐕 ✕ FEE 🖥 FEE 🖥

ROYAL INN

Phone: (540)667-8881

AAA SAVE

W

Motel
$42-$49 All Year

Address: 2930 Valley Ave 22601 **Location:** I-81, exit 310, just w, then 1.9 mi n on US 11. **Facility:** 16 one-bedroom standard units. 1 story, exterior corridors. **Parking:** on-site. **Leisure Activities:** picnic area. **Cards:** AX, DS, MC, VI.

SD 📷 🖥 / SOME UNITS ✕ 🖥

SLEEP INN & SUITES

Book great rates at AAA.com

Phone: (540)667-7636

AAA SAVE

WWWW

Small-scale Hotel
$75-$149 3/1-10/31
$75-$99 11/1-2/28

Address: 140 Costello Dr 22602 **Location:** I-81, exit 313, s on US 522, then left. **Facility:** 72 one-bedroom standard units, some with whirlpools. 4 stories, interior corridors. *Bath:* combo or shower only. **Parking:** on-site. **Amenities:** high-speed Internet, voice mail, irons, hair dryers. *Some:* safes. **Pool(s):** heated indoor. **Leisure Activities:** exercise room. **Guest Services:** valet and coin laundry, wireless Internet. **Business Services:** meeting rooms, business center. **Cards:** AX, DC, DS, MC, VI. **Free Special Amenities:** expanded continental breakfast and high-speed Internet.

SD CALL M 🏊 📷 🖥 🖥 🖥 / SOME UNITS ✕

SUPER 8 MOTEL

Book great rates at AAA.com

Phone: 540/665-4450

AAA SAVE

WWWW

Small-scale Hotel
Rates not provided

Address: 1077 Millwood Pike 22602 **Location:** I-81, exit 313 northbound; exit 313A southbound, 0.3 mi se on US 50/17. **Facility:** 62 one-bedroom standard units. 2 stories (no elevator), interior corridors. **Parking:** on-site. **Amenities:** hair dryers. *Some:* high-speed Internet. **Guest Services:** wireless Internet. **Free Special Amenities:** continental breakfast and high-speed Internet.

🍽 📷 🖥 🖥 / SOME UNITS FEE 🐕 ✕

TOURIST CITY MOTEL

Phone: 540/662-9011

W

Motel
Rates not provided

Address: 214 Millwood Ave 22601 **Location:** I-81, exit 313 northbound; exit 313B southbound, 1 mi nw on US 50/522. **Facility:** 11 one-bedroom standard units. 1 story, exterior corridors. *Bath:* shower only. **Parking:** on-site.

🍽 / SOME UNITS FEE 🐕 ✕ FEE 🖥 🖥

TRAVELODGE OF WINCHESTER

Book at AAA.com

Phone: 540/665-0685

WWW

Small-scale Hotel
Rates not provided

Address: 160 Front Royal Pike 22602 **Location:** I-81, exit 313 northbound; exit 313A southbound, just s on US 522. **Facility:** 145 one-bedroom standard units, some with kitchens and/or whirlpools. 3 stories, interior corridors. **Parking:** on-site. **Amenities:** video library, voice mail, hair dryers. *Some:* irons. **Pool(s):** outdoor. **Guest Services:** coin laundry, wireless Internet. **Business Services:** meeting rooms, fax (fee).

🍽 CALL M 🏊 FEE 🛗 📷 🖥 / SOME UNITS FEE 🐕 ✕ FEE VCR 🖥 🖥

WINGATE INN

Book great rates at AAA.com

Small-scale Hotel
$99-$119 All Year

Address: 150 Wingate Dr 22601 **Location:** I-81, exit 313 northbound; 313B southbound, 0.6 mi nw, then just s. **Facility:** 84 one-bedroom standard units, some with whirlpools. 4 stories, interior corridors. *Bath:* combo or shower only. **Parking:** on-site. **Amenities:** CD players, high-speed Internet, voice mail, safes, irons, hair dryers. **Pool(s):** indoor. **Leisure Activities:** whirlpool, exercise room. **Guest Services:** valet and coin laundry, wireless Internet. **Business Services:** meeting rooms, business center. **Cards:** AX, CB, DC, DS, JC, MC, VI. **Free Special Amenities: expanded continental breakfast and high-speed Internet.**

Phone: (540)678-4283

——— WHERE TO DINE ———

BREWBAKER'S RESTAURANT

American
$6-$20

The casual restaurant's slow pace gives diners plenty of time to unwind with any of many beverages and choices from a diverse menu. Upbeat servers boost the mood. Casual dress. **Bar:** Full bar. **Hours:** 11 am-2 am. Closed: 12/25; also Sun & Mon. **Address:** 168 N Loudoun St 22601 **Location:** Between Boscowan and Piccadilly sts; center of downtown; in Historic Old Town Mall District. **Parking:** street. **Cards:** AX, CB, DC, DS, JC, MC, VI.

Phone: 540/535-0111

CANTINA D'ITALIA

Italian
$8-$21

Casual dress. **Bar:** Full bar. **Hours:** 11 am-10 pm, Sun noon-9 pm. Closed: 12/25. **Address:** 242 Millwood Ave 22601 **Location:** I-81, exit 313 northbound; 313B southbound, 0.8 mi nw on US 50/522. **Parking:** on-site. **Cards:** AX, CB, DC, DS, JC, MC, VI.

Phone: 540/535-2055

CASTIGLIA'S

Italian
$6-$20

Castiglia's Italian Eatery offers delicious Italian Cuisine in a family friendly atmosphere. Outstanding bread selections. Casual dress. **Bar:** Beer & wine. **Hours:** 11 am-10 pm. Closed major holidays. **Address:** 2100 S Pleasant Valley Rd 22601 **Location:** I-81, exit 315, just w. **Parking:** on-site. **Cards:** MC, VI.

Phone: 540/722-6084

CORK STREET TAVERN

Menu on AAA.com

American
$7-$24

Flavorful specialties are served in a cozy tavern, with some areas dating to the 1830s. The atmosphere is casual and laid-back. Sandwiches, salads, seafood, steak and barbecue dishes grace the downtown eatery's varied menu. Be sure to ask for a brief history of the building while dining. Casual dress. **Bar:** Full bar. **Hours:** 11 am-midnight, Sun noon-11 pm. Closed major holidays. **Address:** 8 W Cork St 22601 **Location:** Between Braddock and Loudoun sts; in historic district. **Parking:** on-site. **Cards:** AX, DC, DS, MC, VI. **Historic**

Phone: 540/667-3777

GLORY DAYS GRILL, WINCHESTER

American
$7-$18

Lending to the casual restaurant's sports-themed atmosphere are memorabilia decorating the dining area and 25 TVs with control centers at each table and booth. Food selections range from wings and ribs to seafood, beef and pasta dishes. Casual dress. **Bar:** Full bar. **Reservations:** not accepted. **Hours:** 4 pm-midnight, Fri & Sat from 11:30 am, Sun 11:30 am-11 pm. Closed: 11/27, 12/25. **Address:** 130 Featherbed Ln 22601 **Location:** Just w of S Pleasant Valley Rd; opposite Apple Blossom Mall. **Parking:** on-site. **Cards:** AX, DS, MC, VI.

Phone: 540/662-9922

PARGO'S

American
$6-$18

Casual dress. **Bar:** Full bar. **Hours:** 11 am-11 pm, Fri & Sat-midnight, Sun 10:30 am-11 pm. Closed major holidays. **Address:** 645 E Jubal Early Dr 22601 **Location:** I-81, exit 313 northbound; exit 313B southbound, 0.5 mi nw on US 50/522/17; in Apple Blossom Mall. **Parking:** on-site. **Cards:** AX, CB, DC, DS, MC, VI.

Phone: 540/678-8800

VENICE ITALIAN RESTAURANT

Italian
$7-$20

Patrons don't need a gondola or even a passport to journey to Venice and enjoy the sights, sounds and cuisine of Italy. The restaurant offers a taste of it all in its decor, background music and great menu. Casual dress. **Bar:** Full bar. **Hours:** 10:30 am-10 pm. Closed major holidays; also Sun. **Address:** 1490 N Frederick Pike 22601 **Location:** 1 mi n on US 522, just e. **Parking:** on-site. **Cards:** AX, CB, DC, DS, JC, MC, VI.

Phone: 540/722-0992

VIOLINO RISTORANTE ITALIANO

Northern Italian
$10-$25

Attention to detail marks the creative contemporary cuisine at the family-run establishment. Casual dress. **Bar:** Full bar. **Reservations:** suggested, weekends. **Hours:** 11:30 am-2 & 5-9 pm, Sat from noon. Closed: 12/25; also Sun. **Address:** 181 N Loudoun St 22601 **Location:** Corner of Loudoun and Picadilly sts; center. **Parking:** street. **Cards:** AX, CB, DC, DS, JC, MC, VI.

Phone: 540/667-8006

WOODBRIDGE —*See District Of Columbia p. 566.*

WOODSTOCK pop. 3,952

——— **WHERE TO STAY** ———

BUDGET HOST INN

Motel
$55-$77 3/1-11/30
$50-$70 12/1-2/28

Phone: (540)459-4086
Address: 1290 S Main St 22664 **Location:** I-81, exit 283, 0.8 mi se on SR 42, then 0.6 mi s on US 11. **Facility:** 43 one-bedroom standard units. 1-2 stories (no elevator), exterior corridors. **Parking:** on-site. **Pool(s):** outdoor. **Leisure Activities:** picnic tables. **Guest Services:** coin laundry. **Cards:** AX, DC, DS, MC, VI. **Free Special Amenities:** local telephone calls and high-speed Internet.

COMFORT INN SHENANDOAH   *Book great rates at AAA.com*

Small-scale Hotel
$72-$139 All Year

Phone: (540)459-7600
Address: 1011 Motel Dr 22664 **Location:** I-81, exit 283, just e. **Facility:** 66 one-bedroom standard units, some with whirlpools. 3 stories, interior corridors. *Bath:* combo or shower only. **Parking:** on-site. **Amenities:** high-speed Internet, safes (fee), irons, hair dryers. **Pool(s):** outdoor. **Leisure Activities:** exercise room. **Guest Services:** coin laundry, wireless Internet. **Business Services:** meeting rooms, PC, fax (fee). **Cards:** AX, CB, DC, DS, JC, MC, VI. **Free Special Amenities: expanded continental breakfast and high-speed Internet.**

HOLIDAY INN EXPRESS WOODSTOCK   *Book great rates at AAA.com*

Small-scale Hotel
$79-$129 3/1-11/30
$69-$129 12/1-2/28

Phone: (540)459-5000
Address: 1130 Motel Dr 22664 **Location:** I-81, exit 283, just e on SR 42. **Facility:** 119 one-bedroom standard units, some with whirlpools. 3 stories, interior corridors. *Bath:* combo or shower only. **Parking:** on-site. **Terms:** cancellation fee imposed. **Amenities:** high-speed Internet, voice mail, irons, hair dryers. *Some:* DVD players, CD players. **Pool(s):** outdoor. **Leisure Activities:** exercise room. **Guest Services:** coin laundry, wireless Internet. **Business Services:** meeting rooms, business center. **Cards:** AX, DS, MC, VI. **Free Special Amenities: expanded continental breakfast and high-speed Internet.**

THE INN AT NARROW PASSAGE

Historic Bed
& Breakfast
$110-$175 All Year

Phone: (540)459-8000
Address: 30 Chapman Landing Rd 22664 **Location:** I-81, exit 283, just e to US 11, 1.7 mi s to SR 672, then just e. Located in a rural area. **Facility:** Handmade furnishings and some rooms with fireplaces reflect a Colonial-style ambience at this 1740 inn set on grounds with a river, bridge and garden. Smoke free premises. 12 one-bedroom standard units. 2 stories (no elevator), interior/exterior corridors. *Bath:* combo or shower only. **Parking:** on-site. **Terms:** 3 day cancellation notice. **Amenities:** hair dryers. *Some:* irons. **Leisure Activities:** canoeing, fishing, hiking trails, horseshoes. *Fee:* horseback riding. **Business Services:** meeting rooms. **Cards:** MC, VI.

——— **WHERE TO DINE** ———

CHAPPALINO'S

Italian
$6-$15

Phone: 540/459-7332
Patrons can unwind in the casual, fun atmosphere and choose from a wide variety of Italian specialties. Don't pass up the chance to sample the "doughboys". Casual dress. **Bar:** Beer only. **Hours:** 11 am-11 pm, Fri & Sat-midnight, Sun-10 pm. **Closed:** 12/25. **Address:** 121 S Main St 22664 **Location:** I-81, exit 283, just e. **Parking:** street. **Cards:** MC, VI.

PAISANO'S

Italian
$6-$21

Phone: 540/459-8756
Paisano's offers a relaxing atmosphere with authentic Italian Cuisine. You'll make friends quickly at this restaurant and don't miss the bruscette. Casual dress. **Bar:** Beer & wine. **Hours:** 10:30 am-10 pm. **Closed:** 1/1, 12/25. **Address:** 483 W Reservoir Rd 22664 **Location:** I-81, exit 283, just w. **Parking:** on-site. **Cards:** AX, CB, DC, DS, JC, MC, VI.

SPRING HOUSE TAVERN

American
$5-$20

Phone: 540/459-4755
Plenty of choices line the relaxed restaurant's menu of American cuisine. The staff is friendly and the atmosphere nice. Casual dress. **Bar:** Full bar. **Hours:** 11 am-midnight, Sun noon-10 pm. **Closed:** major holidays. **Address:** 325 S Main St 22664 **Location:** I-81, exit 283, just e. **Parking:** on-site. **Cards:** AX, CB, DC, DS, JC, MC, VI. **Historic**

WOODSTOCK CAFE

American
$6-$14

Phone: 540/459-8888
Woodstock Cafe has great food, a gift and wine shop and a fun casual atmosphere. **Bar:** Beer & wine. **Hours:** 8 am-6 pm, Sat & Sun 9 am-5 pm. **Closed:** 12/25. **Address:** 117 S Main St 22664 **Location:** I-81, exit 283, just e to US 11, then 2.1 mi n on US 11. **Parking:** street. **Cards:** MC, VI.

WOOLWINE

—————— **WHERE TO STAY** ——————

THE MOUNTAIN ROSE INN

Historic Bed
& Breakfast
$125-$155 All Year

Phone: 276/930-1057

Address: 1787 Charity Hwy 24185 **Location:** SR 8, 1.8 mi e on SR 40; Blue Ridge Pkwy, Milepost 165.2, 6.5 mi s on SR 8, then 1.8 mi e on SR 40. Located in a quiet area. **Facility:** Once a distillery, the 1901 Victorian inn is off the Blue Ridge Parkway in a mountain meadow; find cozy rooms appointed with antiques and fireplaces. Smoke free premises. 5 one-bedroom standard units. 2 stories (no elevator), interior corridors. *Bath:* shower only. **Parking:** on-site. **Terms:** check-in 4 pm, 2 night minimum stay - weekends, age restrictions may apply, 10 day cancellation notice-fee imposed. **Amenities:** DVD players, CD players, irons, hair dryers. **Pool(s):** outdoor. **Leisure Activities:** fishing, hiking trails. **Guest Services:** wireless Internet. **Business Services:** meeting rooms. **Cards:** AX, DS, MC, VI.

[ASK] [SD] [icons] / SOME UNITS [icons]

WYTHEVILLE pop. 7,804

—————— **WHERE TO STAY** ——————

BEST WESTERN WYTHEVILLE INN   *Book great rates at AAA.com*

(AAA) [SAVE]
[diamond icons]

Small-scale Hotel
Rates not provided

Phone: 276/228-7300

Address: 355 Nye Rd 24382 **Location:** I-77, exit 41, just e. **Facility:** 99 one-bedroom standard units, some with whirlpools. 2 stories (no elevator), interior corridors. **Parking:** on-site. **Amenities:** voice mail, safes, irons, hair dryers. **Pool(s):** outdoor. **Leisure Activities:** exercise room. **Guest Services:** wireless Internet. **Free Special Amenities:** continental breakfast and early check-in/late check-out.

AAA Benefit:
Members save 10%
everyday, plus an
exclusive frequent
stay program.

[icons] / SOME UNITS FEE [icons]

BUDGET HOST INN/INTERSTATE INN   *Book at AAA.com*

[diamond icon]
Motel
$59-$155 3/1-10/31
$55-$75 11/1-2/28

Phone: (276)228-8618

Address: 705 Chapman Rd 24382 **Location:** I-77/81, exit 73, just w. **Facility:** 42 one-bedroom standard units. 2 stories (no elevator), exterior corridors. **Parking:** on-site. **Amenities:** voice mail. **Guest Services:** wireless Internet. **Cards:** AX, DC, DS, MC, VI.

[ASK] [SD] [icons] / SOME UNITS FEE [icons]

COMFORT INN   *Book great rates at AAA.com*

(AAA) [SAVE]
[diamond icons]

Small-scale Hotel
Rates not provided

Phone: 276/637-4281

Address: 2594 E Lee Hwy 24382 **Location:** I-77/81, exit 80, just w. **Facility:** 60 one-bedroom standard units, some with whirlpools. 3 stories, interior corridors. **Parking:** on-site. **Amenities:** high-speed Internet, irons, hair dryers. **Pool(s):** indoor. **Leisure Activities:** exercise room. **Guest Services:** coin laundry, wireless Internet. **Business Services:** meeting rooms, business center.

[icons] CALL [GM] [icons] / SOME UNITS FEE [icons]

COMFORT INN   *Book great rates at AAA.com*

(AAA) [SAVE]
[diamond icons]

Small-scale Hotel
$75-$150 All Year

Phone: 276/228-4488

Address: 315 Holston Rd 24382 **Location:** I-81, exit 70, just w. **Facility:** 78 one-bedroom standard units. 2 stories (no elevator), interior corridors. **Parking:** on-site. **Amenities:** high-speed Internet, voice mail, irons, hair dryers. **Pool(s):** outdoor. **Leisure Activities:** exercise room. **Guest Services:** wireless Internet. **Business Services:** PC, fax (fee). **Cards:** AX, CB, DC, DS, JC, MC, VI. **Free Special Amenities:** expanded continental breakfast and high-speed Internet.

[SD] [icons] / SOME UNITS [icons]

COMFORT SUITES   *Book great rates at AAA.com*

(AAA) [SAVE]
[diamond icons]

Small-scale Hotel
$90-$250 All Year

Phone: 276/228-1234

Address: 695 Peppers Ferry Rd 24382 **Location:** I-77, exit 41, just e. **Facility:** 56 one-bedroom standard units, some with whirlpools. 3 stories, interior corridors. *Bath:* combo or shower only. **Parking:** on-site. **Terms:** 30 day cancellation notice-fee imposed. **Amenities:** voice mail, irons, hair dryers. *Some:* CD players. **Guest Services:** valet and coin laundry, wireless Internet. **Business Services:** meeting rooms, business center. **Cards:** AX, CB, DC, DS, JC, MC, VI. **Free Special Amenities:** full breakfast and high-speed Internet.

[SD] CALL [GM] [icons] / SOME UNITS [icons]

COUNTRY INN & SUITES BY CARLSON, WYTHEVILLE

[fyi]
Small-scale Hotel
$85-$195 All Year

Too new to rate, opening scheduled for December 2007. **Address:** 697 Peppers Ferry Rd 24382 **Location:** I-81, exit 71. **Amenities:** 60 units, coffeemakers, microwaves, refrigerators, pool. **Cards:** AX, CB, DC, DS, JC, MC, VI.

DAYS INN

Small-scale Hotel
Rates not provided

Phone: 276/228-5500

Address: 150 Malin Dr 24382 **Location:** I-81, exit 73, just w. **Facility:** 118 one-bedroom standard units. 2-3 stories (no elevator), exterior corridors. **Parking:** on-site. **Amenities:** irons, hair dryers. **Guest Services:** wireless Internet. **Business Services:** business center.

HAMPTON INN *Book great rates at AAA.com*

Small-scale Hotel
Rates not provided

Phone: 276/228-6090

Address: 950 Peppers Ferry Rd 24382 **Location:** I-77, exit 41, just w. **Facility:** 97 one-bedroom standard units, some with whirlpools. 3 stories, interior corridors. *Bath:* combo or shower only. **Parking:** on-site. **Amenities:** high-speed Internet, voice mail, irons, hair dryers. **Pool(s):** heated outdoor. **Leisure Activities:** sauna, whirlpool, exercise room. **Guest Services:** valet and coin laundry, wireless Internet. **Business Services:** meeting rooms, business center.

LA QUINTA INN *Book great rates at AAA.com*

Small-scale Hotel
$89-$129 All Year

Phone: (276)228-7400

Address: 1800 E Main 24382 **Location:** I-77/81, exit 73, just w. **Facility:** 79 one-bedroom standard units, some with whirlpools. 4 stories, interior corridors. **Parking:** on-site. **Amenities:** irons, hair dryers. **Pool(s):** heated indoor. **Leisure Activities:** whirlpool, exercise room. **Business Services:** meeting rooms, PC. **Cards:** AX, DC, DS, MC, VI. **Free Special Amenities:** expanded continental breakfast and high-speed Internet.

AAA Benefit:
Members save 10%
everyday.

QUALITY INN & SUITES *Book great rates at AAA.com*

Small-scale Hotel
$50-$165 All Year

Phone: 276/228-4241

Address: 2015 E Main St 24382 **Location:** I-77/81, exit 73, just e. **Facility:** 61 one-bedroom standard units, some with whirlpools. 4 stories, interior corridors. *Bath:* combo or shower only. **Parking:** on-site. **Amenities:** high-speed Internet, irons, hair dryers. **Pool(s):** indoor. **Leisure Activities:** whirlpool. **Guest Services:** coin laundry, wireless Internet. **Business Services:** fax (fee). **Cards:** AX, DC, DS, JC, MC, VI. **Free Special Amenities:** expanded continental breakfast and high-speed Internet.

RAMADA *Book great rates at AAA.com*

Small-scale Hotel
Rates not provided

Phone: 276/228-6000

Address: 955 Peppers Ferry Rd 24382 **Location:** I-77, exit 41, just e. **Facility:** 154 one-bedroom standard units. 2 stories (no elevator), exterior corridors. **Parking:** on-site. **Amenities:** voice mail, irons, hair dryers. **Pool(s):** outdoor. **Guest Services:** valet and coin laundry, wireless Internet. **Business Services:** meeting rooms, fax (fee). **Free Special Amenities:** full breakfast and high-speed Internet.

RED CARPET INN *Book great rates at AAA.com*

Motel
$45-$90 All Year

Phone: 276/228-5525

Address: 280 Lithia Rd 24382 **Location:** I-77/81, exit 73, just w. **Facility:** 34 one-bedroom standard units. 2 stories (no elevator), exterior corridors. **Parking:** on-site. **Terms:** 7 day cancellation notice-fee imposed. **Amenities:** high-speed Internet, hair dryers. **Cards:** AX, DS, MC, VI. **Free Special Amenities:** continental breakfast and local telephone calls.

RED ROOF INN & SUITES *Book at AAA.com*

Small-scale Hotel
$53-$129 All Year

Phone: (276)223-1700

Address: 1900 E Main St 24382 **Location:** I-77/81, exit 73, just w. **Facility:** 102 one-bedroom standard units. 2 stories (no elevator), exterior corridors. **Parking:** on-site. **Pool(s):** outdoor. **Guest Services:** wireless Internet. **Cards:** AX, CB, DC, DS, JC, MC, VI.

SLEEP INN *Book great rates at AAA.com*

Small-scale Hotel
Rates not provided

Phone: 276/625-0667

Address: 135 Nye Cir 24382 **Location:** I-77, exit 41, just e. **Facility:** 72 one-bedroom standard units. 3 stories, interior corridors. *Bath:* combo or shower only. **Parking:** on-site. **Amenities:** high-speed Internet, irons, hair dryers. **Leisure Activities:** exercise room. **Guest Services:** coin laundry, wireless Internet. **Business Services:** meeting rooms, fax (fee). **Free Special Amenities:** continental breakfast and high-speed Internet.

SUPER 8 MOTEL *Book at AAA.com*

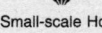

Small-scale Hotel
Rates not provided

Phone: 276/228-6620

Address: 130 Nye Cir 24382 **Location:** I-77, exit 41, just e. **Facility:** 92 one-bedroom standard units. 2 stories (no elevator), exterior corridors. **Parking:** on-site. **Amenities:** irons, hair dryers. **Guest Services:** wireless Internet.

———— **WHERE TO DINE** ————

1776 LOG HOUSE

WWW

American

$7-$25

Phone: 276/228-4139

Enjoy a trip back in time to the beginning of our great nation at this restaurant. Fine dining with a history. Casual dress. **Bar:** Full bar. **Hours:** 11 am-3 & 4-10 pm. Closed: 1/1, 12/25; also Sun. **Address:** 520 E Main St 24382 **Location:** I-77/81, exit 73, 2.1 mi e. **Parking:** on-site. **Cards:** AX, CB, DC, MC, VI.

OCEAN BAY RESTAURANT

WW

American

$5-$20

Phone: 276/228-5300

Welcoming to families, the restaurant serves seafood, steaks and spaghetti. Friendly servers contribute to the casual, comfortable atmosphere. Easy access from the interstate makes it a good stop for travelers. Good food is reasonably priced. Casual dress. **Bar:** Full bar. **Hours:** 11:30 am-10 pm, Sun-9 pm. Closed: 11/27, 12/25; also Mon. **Address:** 1505 E Main St 24382 **Location:** I-77/81, exit 73, just e. **Parking:** on-site. **Cards:** MC, VI.

PEKING RESTAURANT

AAA

WW WW

Chinese

$6-$15

Phone: 276/228-5515

Atop a small hill immediately off the busy interstate, the restaurant occupies a brick structure with large, round windows and a pagoda-type green roof. Canadians and Northerners who frequent the interstate often stop in for tasty food. The traditional theme employs lots of dragons and splashes of red. Casual dress. **Bar:** Full bar. **Reservations:** suggested, weekends. **Hours:** 11 am-9:30 pm, Sat-10 pm. Closed: 11/27, 12/25. **Address:** 105 Malin Dr 24382 **Location:** I-77/81, exit 73, just e. **Parking:** on-site. **Cards:** AX, DS, MC, VI.

SAGEBRUSH STEAKHOUSE

WW WW

Steak House

$5-$19

Phone: 276/228-7103

Born from the spirit of Texas cattle drives, the restaurant presents a menu of hearty steaks, prime rib, chicken, seafood and baby back ribs. Yummy desserts merit a splurge. Guests can call ahead to facilitate seating. Casual dress. **Bar:** Full bar. **Hours:** 11 am-10 pm, Fri & Sat-11 pm. Closed: 12/25. **Address:** 190 Nye Cir 24382 **Location:** I-77, exit 41, just e. **Parking:** on-site. **Cards:** AX, DC, DS, MC, VI.

SKEETERS

W

American

$4-$10

Phone: 276/228-2611

Skeeters is family friendly and has been serving hot dogs and sandwiches since the 1920's. A Wytheville favorite. Casual dress. **Hours:** 8 am-5:30 pm. Closed major holidays; also Sun. **Address:** 165 E Main St 24382 **Location:** I-77/81, exit 73, 2.8 mi w on US 11. **Parking:** street.

WOHLFAHRT HAUS DINNER THEATRE

AAA

WWW

American

$35-$41

Phone: 276/223-0891

America's musicals in the mountains. This restaurant offers great cuisine combined with live theater. **Bar:** Full bar. **Hours:** 6 pm seating, Sun 1 pm seating. Closed: 1/1, 11/27, 12/25; also Mon-Wed. **Address:** 170 Malin Dr 24382 **Location:** I-77/81, exit 73, just e. **Parking:** on-site. **Cards:** AX, MC, VI.

CALL M

YORKTOWN —*See Williamsburg, Jamestown & Yorktown p. 951.*

West Virginia

Monongahela
National Forest
© Laurence Parent

ANSTED pop. 1,576

———— WHERE TO STAY ————

HAWKS NEST LODGE

Small-scale Hotel
$72-$107 3/1-10/31
$53-$87 11/1-2/28

Phone: 304/658-5212

Address: 177 W Main St 25812 **Location:** 1.7 mi w. Located in Hawks Nest State Park. **Facility:** 31 one-bedroom standard units. 2-4 stories, interior/exterior corridors. **Parking:** on-site. **Amenities:** *Some:* irons, hair dryers. **Pool(s):** outdoor. **Leisure Activities:** tennis court, hiking trails, playground, basketball, horseshoes, volleyball. **Business Services:** meeting rooms, fax (fee). **Cards:** AX, DC, DS, MC, VI.

———— WHERE TO DINE ————

TUDOR'S BISCUIT WORLD

American
$5-$12

Phone: 304/658-5235

Serving breakfast all day folks can stop into Tudor's Biscuit World to sample their many varieities of homemade biscuit sandwiches. Known for fast and friendly service in a clean casual atmosphere. Casual dress. **Hours:** 6 am-9 pm. Closed: 12/25. **Address:** 126 W Main St 25812 **Location:** Just w on US 60; center. **Parking:** on-site.

BARBOURSVILLE pop. 3,183

———— WHERE TO STAY ————

BEST WESTERN HUNTINGTON MALL INN   *Book great rates at AAA.com*

Small-scale Hotel
Rates not provided

Phone: 304/736-9772

Address: 3441 US 60 E 25504 **Location:** I-64, exit 20A eastbound; exit 20 westbound, 0.3 mi s. **Facility:** 129 one-bedroom standard units. 2 stories (no elevator), interior corridors. *Bath:* combo or shower only. **Parking:** on-site. **Amenities:** high-speed Internet, irons, hair dryers. **Pool(s):** outdoor. **Leisure Activities:** exercise room. **Guest Services:** wireless Internet. **Business Services:** meeting rooms, PC.

AAA Benefit:
Members save 10% everyday, plus an exclusive frequent stay program.

COMFORT INN BY CHOICE HOTELS   *Book at AAA.com*

Small-scale Hotel
Rates not provided

Phone: 304/733-2122

Address: 249 Mall Rd 25504 **Location:** I-64, exit 20, 0.4 mi n. Located at a shopping mall. **Facility:** 58 one-bedroom standard units. 3 stories, interior corridors. *Bath:* combo or shower only. **Parking:** on-site. **Amenities:** high-speed Internet, irons, hair dryers. **Pool(s):** heated indoor. **Leisure Activities:** whirlpool. **Guest Services:** valet laundry. **Business Services:** meeting rooms.

HAMPTON INN HUNTINGTON/BARBOURSVILLE   *Book great rates at AAA.com*

Small-scale Hotel
Rates not provided

Phone: 304/733-5300

Address: 1 Cracker Barrel Dr 25504 **Location:** I-64, exit 20, just s. **Facility:** 90 one-bedroom standard units, some with whirlpools. 5 stories, interior corridors. *Bath:* combo or shower only. **Parking:** on-site. **Amenities:** video games, high-speed Internet, voice mail, irons, hair dryers. **Pool(s):** outdoor. **Leisure Activities:** exercise room. **Guest Services:** coin laundry, wireless Internet. **Business Services:** meeting rooms, fax (fee).

———— WHERE TO DINE ————

TASCALI'S

Italian
$6-$20

Phone: 304/736-0504

A West Virginia tradition for many years, the restaurant prepares wonderful, homespun choices. The staff is friendly. Casual dress. **Bar:** Full bar. **Hours:** 11 am-9 pm, Fri & Sat-10 pm. Closed major holidays. **Address:** 5505 Rt 60 E 25504 **Location:** I-64, exit 15, just e. **Parking:** on-site. **Cards:** AX, CB, DC, DS, JC, MC, VI.

BEAVER pop. 1,378

———— WHERE TO STAY ————

SLEEP INN   *Book great rates at AAA.com*

Small-scale Hotel
$59-$105 All Year

Phone: (304)255-4222

Address: 1124 Airport Rd 25813 **Location:** I-64, exit 125B eastbound; exit 125 westbound, 0.4 mi n. **Facility:** 104 one-bedroom standard units. 2 stories (no elevator), interior corridors. *Bath:* combo or shower only. **Parking:** on-site, winter plug-ins. **Amenities:** high-speed Internet, irons, hair dryers. *Fee:* safes. **Guest Services:** coin laundry, wireless Internet. **Business Services:** meeting rooms, fax (fee). **Cards:** AX, CB, DC, DS, JC, MC, VI.

WHERE TO DINE

PADRINO'S

Italian
$6-$16

Phone: 304/255-7755
Real Italian food is prepared and served in a comfortable, family-friendly setting. Casual dress. **Bar:** Beer & wine. **Hours:** 10:30 am-10 pm. Closed major holidays; also Sun. **Address:** 167 Beaver Plaza 25813 **Location:** I-64, exit 125B eastbound; exit 125 westbound, 1.8 mi s. **Parking:** on-site. **Cards:** MC, VI.

TUDOR'S BISCUIT WORLD

American
$5-$12

Phone: 304/252-7590
Serving breakfast all day folks can stop into Tudor's Biscuit World to sample their many homemade biscuit sandwiches. Known for fast and friendly service in a clean casual atmosphere. Casual dress. **Hours:** 6 am-7 pm. Closed: 12/25. **Address:** 1125 Airport Rd 25813 **Location:** I-64, exit 125, just n. **Parking:** on-site.

BECKLEY pop. 17,254

WHERE TO STAY

BEST WESTERN FOUR SEASONS INN   *Book great rates at AAA.com*   **Phone:** (304)252-0671

Small-scale Hotel
$63-$110 All Year

Address: 1939 Harper Rd 25801 **Location:** I-64/77, exit 44, just e on SR 3. **Facility:** 80 one-bedroom standard units. 2 stories (no elevator), interior/exterior corridors. **Parking:** on-site. **Terms:** 7 day cancellation notice. **Amenities:** irons, hair dryers. **Leisure Activities:** whirlpool. **Cards:** AX, CB, DC, DS, MC, VI. **Free Special Amenities:** continental breakfast and newspaper.

AAA Benefit:
Members save 10% everyday, plus an exclusive frequent stay program.

COMFORT INN   *Book at AAA.com*   **Phone:** 304/255-5291

Small-scale Hotel
Rates not provided

Address: 300 Harper Park Dr 25801 **Location:** I-64/77, exit 44, just w, then 0.4 mi s. **Facility:** 120 one-bedroom standard units. 2 stories (no elevator), interior corridors. **Parking:** on-site. **Amenities:** high-speed Internet, safes (fee), irons, hair dryers. **Pool(s):** outdoor. **Guest Services:** wireless Internet. **Business Services:** meeting rooms.

COUNTRY INN & SUITES BY CARLSON   *Book great rates at AAA.com*   **Phone:** (304)252-5100

Small-scale Hotel
$99-$199 All Year

Address: 2120 Harper Rd 25801 **Location:** I-64/77, exit 44, just w on SR 3. **Facility:** 156 one-bedroom standard units, some with whirlpools. 3 stories, interior corridors. *Bath:* combo or shower only. **Parking:** on-site. **Amenities:** video games, high-speed Internet, dual phone lines, voice mail, irons, hair dryers. **Pool(s):** heated indoor/outdoor. **Leisure Activities:** whirlpools, exercise room. *Fee:* game room. **Guest Services:** coin laundry, wireless Internet. **Business Services:** conference facilities, fax (fee). **Cards:** AX, DS, MC, VI. **Free Special Amenities:** expanded continental breakfast and newspaper. *(See color ad below)*

COURTYARD BY MARRIOTT   *Book great rates at AAA.com*   Phone: 304/252-9800

Small-scale Hotel
$96-$126 All Year

Address: 124 Hylton Ln 25801 **Location:** I-64/77, exit 44, just e. **Facility:** Smoke free premises. 106 one-bedroom standard units, some with whirlpools. 4 stories, interior corridors. *Bath:* combo or shower only. **Parking:** on-site. **Amenities:** high-speed Internet, voice mail, irons, hair dryers. **Pool(s):** indoor. **Leisure Activities:** whirlpool, exercise room. **Guest Services:** coin laundry, wireless Internet. **Business Services:** meeting rooms, PC, fax (fee). **Cards:** AX, DC, DS, MC, VI.

AAA Benefit:
Members save 5% off of the best available rate.

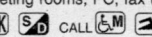

ECONO LODGE   *Book at AAA.com*   Phone: (304)255-2161

Small-scale Hotel
$49-$100 All Year

Address: 1909 Harper Rd 25801 **Location:** I-64/77, exit 44, 0.3 mi e on SR 3. **Facility:** 130 one-bedroom standard units. 2-3 stories, interior/exterior corridors. **Parking:** on-site. **Amenities:** high-speed Internet, safes (fee), irons, hair dryers. **Leisure Activities:** exercise room. **Guest Services:** coin laundry, wireless Internet. **Business Services:** meeting rooms. **Cards:** AX, DC, DS, MC, VI.

    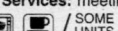

FAIRFIELD INN   *Book great rates at AAA.com*   Phone: 304/252-8661

Small-scale Hotel
Rates not provided

Address: 125 Hylton Ln 25801 **Location:** I-64/77, exit 44, just e. **Facility:** Smoke free premises. 89 one-bedroom standard units. 5 stories, interior corridors. *Bath:* combo or shower only. **Parking:** on-site. **Amenities:** high-speed Internet, voice mail, irons, hair dryers. **Pool(s):** outdoor. **Leisure Activities:** whirlpool, exercise room. *Fee:* game room. **Guest Services:** coin laundry, wireless Internet. **Business Services:** PC, fax (fee).

AAA Benefit:
Members save 5% off of the best available rate.

HAMPTON INN   *Book great rates at AAA.com*   Phone: (304)252-2121

Small-scale Hotel
$75-$130 All Year

Address: 110 Harper Park Dr 25801 **Location:** I-64/77, exit 44, just w on SR 3. **Facility:** 108 one-bedroom standard units. 5 stories, interior corridors. **Parking:** on-site. **Amenities:** voice mail, irons, hair dryers. **Pool(s):** outdoor. **Guest Services:** valet laundry, wireless Internet. **Business Services:** meeting rooms, fax (fee). **Cards:** AX, DC, DS, MC, VI. *(See color ad below)*

HOLIDAY INN HOTEL & SUITES *Book great rates at AAA.com*

Phone: (304)252-2250

Small-scale Hotel
$71-$250 All Year

Address: 114 Dry Hill Rd 25801 **Location:** I-64/77, exit 44, just w. **Facility:** 110 one-bedroom standard units. 4 stories, interior corridors. *Bath:* combo or shower only. **Parking:** on-site. **Terms:** check-in 4 pm, cancellation fee imposed. **Amenities:** high-speed Internet, dual phone lines, voice mail, irons, hair dryers. **Pool(s):** heated indoor. **Leisure Activities:** whirlpool, exercise room. *Fee:* game room. **Guest Services:** valet and coin laundry, wireless Internet. **Business Services:** meeting rooms, business center. **Cards:** AX, DC, DS, MC, VI. **Free Special Amenities:** newspaper and high-speed Internet.
(See color ad below)

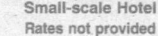

HOWARD JOHNSON EXPRESS INN *Book great rates at AAA.com*

Phone: 304/255-5900

Small-scale Hotel
Rates not provided

Address: 1907 Harper Rd 25801 **Location:** I-64/77, exit 44, 0.4 mi e on SR 3. **Facility:** 50 one-bedroom standard units. 2 stories (no elevator), interior corridors. **Amenities:** high-speed Internet, voice mail, safes, irons, hair dryers. **Pool(s):** outdoor. **Guest Services:** coin laundry. **Free Special Amenities:** continental breakfast and local telephone calls.

MICROTEL INN *Book great rates at AAA.com*

Phone: (304)256-2000

Small-scale Hotel
$55-$129 All Year

Address: 2130 Harper Rd 25801 **Location:** I-64/77, exit 44. **Facility:** 75 one-bedroom standard units. 3 stories, interior corridors. *Bath:* combo or shower only. **Parking:** on-site. **Terms:** 3 day cancellation notice. **Amenities:** high-speed Internet, irons, hair dryers. **Pool(s):** indoor. **Leisure Activities:** whirlpool. **Guest Services:** coin laundry, wireless Internet. **Business Services:** fax (fee). **Free Special Amenities:** continental breakfast and high-speed Internet.

▼ See AAA listing above ▼

▼ See AAA listing p 968 ▼

MICROTEL INN & SUITES

[fyi]

Small-scale Hotel
Rates not provided

Phone: 304/225-2200

Too new to rate, opening scheduled for September 2007. **Address:** 1001 S Eisenhower Dr 25801 **Location:** I-64, exit 124. **Amenities:** 64 units.

PARK INN & SUITES

[AAA] [SAVE]

▼▼▼ ▼▼▼

Small-scale Hotel
$69-$109 All Year

Book great rates at AAA.com   **Phone: (304)255-9091**

Address: 134 Harper Park Dr 25801 **Location:** I-64/77, exit 44, just w on SR 3. **Facility:** 55 one-bedroom standard units, some with whirlpools. 3 stories, interior corridors. **Parking:** on-site. **Amenities:** voice mail, irons, hair dryers. **Pool(s):** outdoor. **Guest Services:** valet laundry, wireless Internet. **Cards:** AX, DC, DS, MC, VI. **Free Special Amenities: continental breakfast and high-speed Internet.**

[S⊘] [†↑⁺] [⌁] [🎥] [🗄] [📠] [💻] / SOME UNITS [✕]

QUALITY INN OF BECKLEY

▼▼▼

Small-scale Hotel
$89-$119 All Year

Book great rates at AAA.com   **Phone: (304)255-1511**

Address: 1924 Harper Rd 25801 **Location:** I-64/77, exit 44, 0.3 mi e on SR 3. **Facility:** 103 one-bedroom standard units, some with whirlpools. 3 stories (no elevator), interior corridors. **Parking:** on-site. **Amenities:** high-speed Internet, dual phone lines, voice mail, irons, hair dryers. **Pool(s):** heated outdoor. **Leisure Activities:** exercise room. **Guest Services:** coin laundry, wireless Internet. **Business Services:** meeting rooms. **Cards:** AX, DC, DS, MC, VI. *(See color ad p 967)*

[ASK] [S⊘] [†↑] [Ⓨ] [⌁] [🎥] [💻] / SOME UNITS [✕] FEE [🔌] FEE [🗄]

SUPER 8 MOTEL

[AAA] [SAVE]

▼▼

Small-scale Hotel
Rates not provided

Phone: 304/253-0802

Address: 2014 Harper Rd 25801 **Location:** I-64/77, exit 44, just e. **Facility:** 71 one-bedroom standard units, some with whirlpools. 3 stories, interior corridors. *Bath:* combo or shower only. **Parking:** on-site. **Amenities:** hair dryers. **Guest Services:** wireless Internet. **Business Services:** fax (fee). **Free Special Amenities: continental breakfast and high-speed Internet.**

CALL [🔗M] [🎥] [🔌] [🗄] / SOME UNITS FEE [🐾] [✕]

─────── **WHERE TO DINE** ───────

THE CHAR

[AAA]

▼▼▼ ▼▼

American
$12-$38

Phone: 304/253-1760

Known for quality steaks, seafood and Italian specialties, the restaurant boasts brascioli—a beef filet with bread crumbs and cheese—as its specialty. The atmosphere, enhanced by soothing background music, and service are great. Casual dress. **Bar:** Full bar. **Hours:** 5 pm-10 pm, Mon-9 pm. Closed major holidays; also Sun. **Address:** 100 Char Dr 25801 **Location:** I-64/77, exit 44, 0.3 mi w on SR 3, then 0.5 mi n on Dry Hill Rd. **Parking:** on-site and valet. **Cards:** AX, DS, MC, VI.

[◣]

PASQUALE MIRA'S ITALIAN RESTAURANT

▼▼▼ ▼▼

Italian
$7-$20

Phone: 304/255-5253

Excellent specialties, including veal and seafood dishes, are offered in two dining rooms—one casual and one more formal—and on the patio. Family owned since 1960, the restaurant prepares fare with a welcomed homemade flavor. Don't miss the aquarium. Casual dress. **Bar:** Full bar. **Hours:** 11 am-10 pm. Closed: 11/27, 12/25. **Address:** 224 Harper Park Dr 25801 **Location:** I-64/77, exit 44, just w, then 0.3 mi s. **Parking:** on-site. **Cards:** AX, DS, MC, VI.

[◣]

TUDOR'S BISCUIT WORLD

▼▼

American
$5-$12

Phone: 304/253-9471

Serving breakfast all day folks can stop into Tudor's Biscuit World to sample their many varieities of homemade biscuit sandwiches. Known for fast and friendly service in a clean casual atmosphere. Casual dress. **Hours:** 6 am-7 pm. Closed: 12/25. **Address:** 102 4th St 25801 **Location:** I-64/77, exit 44, just w. **Parking:** on-site.

[◣]

TUDOR'S BISCUIT WORLD

▼▼

American
$5-$12

Phone: 304/253-3330

Serving breakfast all day folks can stop into Tudor's Biscuit World to sample their many varieities of homemade biscuit sandwiches. Known for fast and friendly service in a clean casual atmosphere. Casual dress. **Hours:** 6 am-7 pm. Closed: 12/25. **Address:** 1334 Harper Rd 25801 **Location:** I-64/77, exit 44, just e. **Parking:** on-site.

YOUNG CHOW'S

[AAA]

▼▼ ▼▼

Chinese
$6-$20

Phone: 304/253-2469

The restaurant has wonderful cuisine and a lovely setting in which to dine. The atmosphere begins with the shrub-lined walkway up to the entrance and is rounded out by artwork on display inside. Casual dress. **Bar:** Full bar. **Hours:** 11 am-10 pm. Closed major holidays. **Address:** 219 Pikeview Dr 25801 **Location:** I-64/77, exit 44, just e on SR 3, then 0.7 mi n. **Parking:** on-site. **Cards:** AX, DC, MC, VI.

[◣]

BENWOOD pop. 1,585

——— WHERE TO DINE ———

UNDO'S FAMILY RISTORANTE
Phone: 304/233-0560

Italian
$7-$22

Italian and American specialties are served in the family-oriented restaurant. Casual dress. **Bar:** Full bar. **Hours:** 11:30 am-10 pm, Fri & Sat-11 pm. Closed: 1/1, 12/25; also Mon. **Address:** 753 Main St 26031 **Location:** SR 2, exit 4th St, just sw. **Parking:** on-site. **Cards:** AX, DC, DS, MC, VI.

BERKELEY SPRINGS pop. 663

——— WHERE TO DINE ———

MARIA'S GARDEN & INN
Phone: 304/258-2021

Italian
$5-$15

Religious-themed artwork, an attractive garden room and a setting at the foot of the mountains give the restaurant a peaceful, serene ambience. Traditional dishes are well-prepared, well-presented and flavorful. Servers are knowledgeable and pleasant. Casual dress. **Bar:** Beer & wine. **Reservations:** suggested, weekends. **Hours:** 11 am-8 pm, Fri-9 pm, Sat 8 am-9 pm, Sun 8 am-8 pm. Closed: 11/27, 12/25; also Wed. **Address:** 42 Independence St 25411 **Location:** Just w of US 522. **Parking:** on-site. **Cards:** AX, DS, MC, VI.

BLUEFIELD pop. 11,451

——— WHERE TO STAY ———

DIAN-LEE HOUSE BED & BREAKFAST
Phone: 304/327-6370

Historic Bed & Breakfast
$85-$100 All Year

Address: 2109 Jefferson St 24701 **Location:** I-77, exit 1, 1 mi w on SR 52, 4 mi nw on SR 460 to Washington St exit, then just n. **Facility:** Built in 1900, the Dian-Lee House offers large parlor rooms, a porch swing, a small garden area perfect for meandering, beautiful artwork and themed, named rooms. 6 one-bedroom standard units. 3 stories (no elevator), interior/exterior corridors. **Parking:** on-site. **Terms:** 7 day cancellation notice. **Amenities:** irons, hair dryers. *Some:* DVD players. **Guest Services:** valet laundry, wireless Internet. **Business Services:** meeting rooms. **Cards:** AX, DS, MC, VI. **Free Special Amenities:** expanded continental breakfast and high-speed Internet.

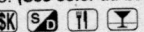 / SOME UNITS VCR

HOLIDAY INN BLUEFIELD-ON THE HILL   *Book great rates at AAA.com*
Phone: (304)325-6170

Small-scale Hotel
$85-$110 6/1-2/28
$80-$95 3/1-5/31

Address: 3350 Big Laurel Hwy 24701 **Location:** I-77, exit 1, 3.8 mi nw via US 52/460. **Facility:** 120 one-bedroom standard units. 2 stories (no elevator), interior corridors. *Bath:* combo or shower only. **Parking:** on-site. **Terms:** check-in 4 pm. **Amenities:** voice mail, safes (fee), irons, hair dryers. **Pool(s):** heated outdoor. **Leisure Activities:** sauna, exercise room. *Fee:* game room. **Guest Services:** valet laundry, wireless Internet. **Business Services:** conference facilities, administrative services (fee), PC. *(See color ad below)*

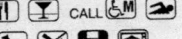

——— WHERE TO DINE ———

TUDOR'S BISCUIT WORLD
Phone: 304/589-3383

American
$5-$12

Serving breakfast all day folks can stop into Tudor's Biscuit World to sample their many varieties of homemade biscuit sandwiches. Known for fast and friendly service in a clean casual atmosphere. Casual dress. **Hours:** 6 am-2 pm, Sun from 7 am. Closed: 12/25. **Address:** SR 52 24701 **Location:** I-77, exit 1, just w. **Parking:** on-site.

BRIDGEPORT pop. 7,306

——— WHERE TO STAY ———

DAYS INN & SUITES CLARKSBURG   *Book at AAA.com*
Phone: 304/842-7371
▼▼ ▼▼
Small-scale Hotel
Rates not provided

Address: 112 Tolley Dr 26330 **Location:** I-79, exit 119, just e. Located in a busy commercial area. **Facility:** 98 one-bedroom standard units, some with kitchens. 2 stories (no elevator), interior corridors. *Bath:* combo or shower only. **Parking:** on-site. **Amenities:** safes (fee), hair dryers. *Some:* irons. **Pool(s):** heated indoor. **Guest Services:** valet and coin laundry. **Business Services:** meeting rooms, business center.

CALL 🔲🅼 🏊 🏨 🎥 💻 / SOME UNITS ✕ 🔒 🖥

HOLIDAY INN CLARKSBURG-BRIDGEPORT   *Book great rates at AAA.com*
Phone: 304/842-5411
(AAA) [SAVE]

▼▼ ▼▼
Small-scale Hotel
Rates not provided

Address: 100 Lodgeville Rd 26330 **Location:** I-79, exit 119, just e on US 50. Located in a busy commercial area. **Facility:** 158 one-bedroom standard units. 2 stories (no elevator), interior corridors. *Bath:* combo or shower only. **Parking:** on-site. **Amenities:** voice mail, irons, hair dryers. **Pool(s):** outdoor. **Guest Services:** valet laundry, wireless Internet. **Business Services:** meeting rooms, business center. **Free Special Amenities:** newspaper and high-speed Internet.

🍴 🍸 CALL 🔲🅼 🏊 FEE 🏨 🎥 💻 / SOME UNITS 🐾 ✕ FEE 🔒 FEE 🖥

MICROTEL INN & SUITES   *Book at AAA.com*
Phone: (304)808-2000
▼▼ ▼▼
Small-scale Hotel
$74-$89 All Year

Address: 201 Conference Center Way 26330 **Location:** I-79, exit 124, 0.5 mi e on SR 279. **Facility:** 86 one-bedroom standard units. 3 stories, interior corridors. **Parking:** on-site. **Terms:** cancellation fee imposed. **Amenities:** high-speed Internet, irons, hair dryers. **Leisure Activities:** exercise room. **Guest Services:** coin laundry, wireless Internet. **Business Services:** meeting rooms, fax (fee). **Cards:** AX, CB, DC, DS, JC, MC, VI.

[A$K] CALL 🔲🅼 🎥 / SOME UNITS ✕ 🔒 🖥 💻

SLEEP INN   *Book great rates at AAA.com*
Phone: (304)842-1919
▼▼ ▼▼
Small-scale Hotel
$79 All Year

Address: 115 Tolley Dr 26330 **Location:** I-79, exit 119, just e on US 50. Located in an industrial area. **Facility:** 73 one-bedroom standard units. 2 stories (no elevator), interior corridors. *Bath:* combo or shower only. **Parking:** on-site. **Amenities:** voice mail, safes (fee), irons, hair dryers. **Guest Services:** valet and coin laundry, wireless Internet. **Business Services:** meeting rooms, fax (fee). **Cards:** AX, CB, DC, DS, JC, MC, VI.

[A$K] [S🔲] 🍴 CALL 🔲🅼 🎥 💻 / SOME UNITS 🐾 ✕ 🔒 🖥

WINGATE INN-BRIDGEPORT   *Book at AAA.com*
Phone: (304)808-1000
▼▼ ▼▼
Small-scale Hotel
$104-$115 All Year

Address: 350 Conference Center Way 26330 **Location:** I-79, exit 124, just e. **Facility:** 116 one-bedroom standard units, some with whirlpools. 4 stories, interior corridors. *Bath:* combo or shower only. **Parking:** on-site. **Terms:** check-in 4 pm. **Amenities:** high-speed Internet, dual phone lines, voice mail, safes, irons, hair dryers. **Pool(s):** heated indoor. **Leisure Activities:** whirlpool, exercise room. **Guest Services:** valet laundry, wireless Internet. **Business Services:** meeting rooms, business center. **Cards:** AX, DC, DS, MC, VI.

[A$K] [S🔲] CALL 🔲🅼 🏊 🎥 🔒 🖥 💻 / SOME UNITS ✕

——— WHERE TO DINE ———

OLIVERIO'S RISTORANTE
Phone: 304/842-7388
▼▼ ▼▼
Italian
$7-$25

The family-run-and-oriented restaurant offers amazing cuisine choices and a knowledgeable staff. Casual dress. **Bar:** Full bar. **Hours:** 11 am-10 pm, Sat from 4 pm, Sun 4 pm-9 pm. Closed: 12/25. **Address:** 507 E Main St 26330 **Location:** I-79, exit 119, 2.9 mi e on US 50. **Parking:** on-site. **Cards:** AX, CB, DC, DS, JC, MC, VI.

BRUCETON MILLS pop. 74

——— WHERE TO DINE ———

TWILA'S RESTAURANT
Phone: 304/379-8080
▼▼ ▼▼
American
$5-$15

Homespun country goodness comes standard with all of the menu items. Families are welcomed with truly friendly service. Casual dress. **Hours:** 7 am-10 pm. Closed: 12/25. **Address:** Rt 26 26525 **Location:** I-68, exit 23, just n. **Parking:** on-site.

BUCKHANNON pop. 5,725

——— WHERE TO STAY ———

THE BICENTENNIAL INN
Phone: 304/472-5000
(AAA) [SAVE]

▼▼ ▼▼
Small-scale Hotel
$66-$87 All Year

Address: 90 E Main St 26201 **Location:** Just e on Main St. **Facility:** 51 one-bedroom standard units. 2 stories (no elevator), interior corridors. *Bath:* combo or shower only. **Parking:** on-site. **Terms:** cancellation fee imposed. **Amenities:** hair dryers. *Some:* irons. **Leisure Activities:** croquet, horseshoes, volleyball. **Guest Services:** valet and coin laundry, wireless Internet. **Business Services:** meeting rooms, business center. **Cards:** AX, DC, DS, MC, VI.

🍴 🍸 CALL 🔲🅼 🏊 / SOME UNITS ✕ 🔒 🖥

HAMPTON INN

Small-scale Hotel
Rates not provided

Book great rates at AAA.com

Phone: 304/473-0900

Address: 1 Commerce Blvd 26201 **Location:** I-79, exit 99, 9 mi e on US 33. **Facility:** 62 one-bedroom standard units, some with whirlpools. 3 stories, interior corridors. *Bath:* combo or shower only. **Parking:** on-site. **Terms:** check-in 4 pm. **Amenities:** high-speed Internet, voice mail, irons, hair dryers. **Pool(s):** heated indoor. **Leisure Activities:** exercise room. **Guest Services:** valet laundry, wireless Internet. **Business Services:** meeting rooms, fax (fee).

CALL ⓜ 🛏 🐕 🖥 🖨 📺 / SOME UNITS ✕

——— **WHERE TO DINE** ———

AUDREY'S RESTAURANT

American
$5-$15

Phone: 304/472-9131

Home-style dishes include a good choice of American classics, in addition to all-day breakfast items. Casual dress. **Hours:** 6:30 am-10 pm. Closed major holidays. **Address:** 95 Clarksburg Rd 26201 **Location:** 2.2 mi n on SR 119. **Parking:** on-site. **Cards:** MC, VI.

✕

CEREDO pop. 1,675

——— **WHERE TO DINE** ———

TUDOR'S BISCUIT WORLD

American
$5-$10

Phone: 304/453-2850

Serving breakfast all day folks can stop into Tudor's Biscuit World to sample their many varieities of homemade biscuit sandwiches. Known for fast and friendly service in a clean casual atmosphere. Casual dress. **Hours:** 5:30 am-2 pm. Closed: 12/25. **Address:** C St & Main St 25507 **Location:** Center. **Parking:** on-site.

✕

CHAPMANVILLE pop. 1,211

——— **WHERE TO STAY** ———

BEST WESTERN LOGAN INN

AAA SAVE

Small-scale Hotel
Rates not provided

Book great rates at AAA.com

Phone: 304/831-2345

Address: 2 Central Ave 25508 **Location:** Just s on US 119. **Facility:** 60 one-bedroom standard units, some with whirlpools. 3 stories, interior corridors. *Bath:* combo or shower only. **Parking:** on-site. **Amenities:** high-speed Internet, voice mail, irons, hair dryers. **Pool(s):** heated indoor. **Leisure Activities:** exercise room. **Guest Services:** coin laundry, wireless Internet. **Business Services:** meeting rooms, PC, fax (fee). **Free Special Amenities:** expanded continental breakfast and high-speed Internet.

🍴 CALL ⓜ 🛏 🐕 🖥 🖨 📺 / SOME UNITS ✕

AAA Benefit:
Members save 10% everyday, plus an exclusive frequent stay program.

CHARLESTON pop. 53,421—See also SOUTH CHARLESTON.

——— **WHERE TO STAY** ———

BUDGET HOST INN

AAA SAVE

Motel
$39-$70 All Year

Book great rates at AAA.com

Phone: 304/925-2592

Address: 3313 Kanawha Blvd E 25306 **Location:** I-64/77, exit 96. **Facility:** 26 one-bedroom standard units. 1 story, exterior corridors. **Parking:** on-site. **Amenities:** hair dryers. **Cards:** AX, DS, MC, VI. **Free Special Amenities:** local telephone calls and early check-in/late check-out.

🅢 🍴 VCR 🐕 / SOME UNITS ✕ 🖥

CHARLESTON COMFORT SUITES

Small-scale Hotel
$110-$130 All Year

Book at AAA.com

Phone: (304)925-1171

Address: 107 Alex Ln 25304 **Location:** I-77, exit 95, just s on SR 61. **Facility:** 67 one-bedroom standard units, some with whirlpools. 3 stories, interior corridors. *Bath:* combo or shower only. **Parking:** on-site. **Terms:** cancellation fee imposed. **Amenities:** high-speed Internet, voice mail, safes (fee), irons, hair dryers. **Pool(s):** heated indoor. **Leisure Activities:** whirlpool, exercise room. **Guest Services:** coin laundry, wireless Internet. **Business Services:** fax (fee). **Cards:** AX, CB, DC, DS, JC, MC, VI.

ASK 🅢 🛏 🐕 🖥 🖨 📺 / SOME UNITS 🐾 ✕

CHARLESTON MARRIOTT TOWN CENTER HOTEL

Book great rates at AAA.com

Phone: 304/345-6500

Large-scale Hotel
$158-$193 All Year

Address: 200 Lee St E 25301 **Location:** I-64, exit 58C; downtown. Located opposite Charleston Civic Center. **Facility:** Smoke free premises. 352 one-bedroom standard units. 16 stories, interior corridors. **Parking:** on-site (fee). **Terms:** check-in 4 pm. **Amenities:** video games, high-speed Internet, voice mail, irons, hair dryers. *Some:* CD players. **Pool(s):** heated indoor. **Leisure Activities:** saunas, whirlpool, exercise room. **Guest Services:** coin laundry, tanning facilities, wireless Internet. **Business Services:** conference facilities, business center. **Cards:** AX, DC, DS, JC, MC, VI.

COUNTRY INN & SUITES BY CARLSON

Book at AAA.com

Phone: (304)925-4300

Small-scale Hotel
$110-$130 All Year

Address: 105 Alex Ln 25304 **Location:** I-77, exit 95, just s on SR 61. **Facility:** 64 one-bedroom standard units. 3 stories, interior corridors. *Bath:* combo or shower only. **Parking:** on-site. **Terms:** cancellation fee imposed. **Amenities:** high-speed Internet, voice mail, irons, hair dryers. **Pool(s):** heated indoor. **Leisure Activities:** whirlpool, exercise room. **Guest Services:** coin laundry, wireless Internet. **Business Services:** meeting rooms, business center. **Cards:** AX, DC, DS, MC, VI.

DAYS INN CHARLESTON EAST

Book at AAA.com

Phone: 304/925-1010

Motel
Rates not provided

Address: 6400 MacCorkle Ave SE 25304 **Location:** I-77, exit 95, just s on SR 61. **Facility:** 147 one-bedroom standard units, some with whirlpools. 3 stories, interior corridors. *Bath:* combo or shower only. **Parking:** on-site. **Amenities:** high-speed Internet, irons, hair dryers. **Pool(s):** outdoor. **Leisure Activities:** exercise room. **Guest Services:** coin laundry. **Business Services:** meeting rooms.

EMBASSY SUITES HOTEL

Book great rates at AAA.com

Phone: 304/347-8700

Large-scale Hotel
Rates not provided

Address: 300 Court St 25301 **Location:** I-64, exit 58C; center. **Facility:** 253 one-bedroom standard units, some with whirlpools. 9 stories, interior corridors. *Bath:* combo or shower only. **Parking:** on-site (fee). **Terms:** check-in 4 pm. **Amenities:** video games, high-speed Internet, dual phone lines, voice mail, irons, hair dryers. **Pool(s):** heated indoor. **Leisure Activities:** sauna, whirlpool. **Guest Services:** valet and coin laundry, area transportation-within 5 mi, wireless Internet. **Business Services:** meeting rooms, business center. **Free Special Amenities:** full breakfast and newspaper.

▼ *See AAA listing p 973* ▼

FAIRFIELD INN BY MARRIOTT   *Book great rates at AAA.com*

Small-scale Hotel
$69-$129 All Year

Phone: (304)343-4661

Address: 1000 Washington St 25301 **Location:** I-64/77, exit 100, 0.5 mi w. **Facility:** Smoke free premises. 136 one-bedroom standard units. 9 stories, interior corridors. *Bath:* combo or shower only. **Parking:** on-site. **Terms:** 3 day cancellation notice. **Amenities:** high-speed Internet, voice mail, irons, hair dryers. **Pool(s):** heated outdoor. **Leisure Activities:** whirlpool, exercise room. **Guest Services:** coin laundry. **Business Services:** business center. **Cards:** AX, CB, DC, DS, JC, MC, VI. **Free Special Amenities:** continental breakfast and high-speed Internet. *(See color ad p 972)*

AAA Benefit:
Members save 5% off of the best available rate.

HAMPTON INN SOUTHRIDGE   *Book great rates at AAA.com*

Small-scale Hotel
Rates not provided

Phone: 304/746-4646

Address: 1 Preferred Pl 25309 **Location:** I-64, exit 58A, 4 mi s on US 119. Located adjacent to a shopping center. **Facility:** 104 one-bedroom standard units, some with whirlpools. 6 stories, interior corridors. *Bath:* combo or shower only. **Parking:** on-site. **Amenities:** video games, high-speed Internet, voice mail, irons, hair dryers. **Pool(s):** heated indoor. **Leisure Activities:** whirlpool, playground, exercise room, basketball. **Guest Services:** valet and coin laundry, wireless Internet. **Business Services:** meeting rooms, business center.

HOLIDAY INN DOWNTOWN CHARLESTON HOUSE   *Book at AAA.com*

Large-scale Hotel
$90-$119 All Year

Phone: (304)344-4092

Address: 600 Kanawha Blvd E 25301 **Location:** I-64, exit 58B eastbound; exit 58C westbound, Virginia St to corner of Laidley and Kanawha Blvd; I-64/77, exit 97, 4.5 mi w on US 60 (Kanawha Blvd); downtown. **Facility:** 256 one-bedroom standard units. 12 stories, interior corridors. *Bath:* combo or shower only. **Parking:** on-site (fee). **Amenities:** high-speed Internet, voice mail, irons, hair dryers. **Pool(s):** outdoor. **Leisure Activities:** exercise room. **Guest Services:** valet laundry, area transportation, wireless Internet. **Business Services:** conference facilities, business center. **Cards:** AX, DC, DS, MC, VI.

HOLIDAY INN EXPRESS CIVIC CENTER   *Book at AAA.com*

Small-scale Hotel
$80-$100 All Year

Phone: (304)345-0600

Address: 100 Civic Center Dr 25301 **Location:** I-64, exit 58B eastbound; exit 58C westbound, just s; downtown. **Facility:** 196 one-bedroom standard units. 6 stories, interior corridors. *Bath:* combo or shower only. **Parking:** on-site. **Amenities:** video games, high-speed Internet, dual phone lines, voice mail, irons, hair dryers. **Leisure Activities:** exercise room. **Guest Services:** valet and coin laundry, wireless Internet. **Business Services:** meeting rooms, business center. **Cards:** AX, CB, DC, DS, JC, MC, VI.

KNIGHTS INN-CHARLESTON EAST   *Book great rates at AAA.com*

Motel
$50-$57 3/1-8/31
$47-$50 9/1-2/28

Phone: (304)925-0451

Address: 6401 MacCorkle Ave SE 25304 **Location:** I-77, exit 95, just s on SR 61. **Facility:** 128 one-bedroom standard units, some with kitchens and/or whirlpools. 1 story, exterior corridors. **Parking:** on-site. **Terms:** cancellation fee imposed. **Amenities:** *Some:* high-speed Internet. **Pool(s):** outdoor. **Guest Services:** coin laundry. **Cards:** AX, DS, MC, VI. **Free Special Amenities:** continental breakfast and local telephone calls.

RED ROOF INN-KANAWHA CITY   *Book at AAA.com*

Motel
Rates not provided

Phone: 304/925-6953

Address: 6305 SE MacCorkle Ave 25304 **Location:** I-77, exit 95, just s on SR 61. **Facility:** 108 one-bedroom standard units. 2 stories (no elevator), exterior corridors. *Bath:* combo or shower only. **Parking:** on-site. **Amenities:** video games, voice mail. **Guest Services:** valet laundry.

SLEEP INN   *Book great rates at AAA.com*

Small-scale Hotel
$79-$149 All Year

Phone: (304)345-5111

Address: 2772 Pennsylvania Ave 25302 **Location:** I-79, exit 1, just e. **Facility:** 81 one-bedroom standard units. 3 stories, interior corridors. *Bath:* combo or shower only. **Parking:** on-site. **Amenities:** high-speed Internet, irons, hair dryers. **Leisure Activities:** exercise room. **Guest Services:** valet and coin laundry, wireless Internet. **Business Services:** meeting rooms, PC, fax (fee). **Cards:** AX, CB, DC, DS, JC, MC, VI.

─── WHERE TO DINE ───

THE CHOP HOUSE
Phone: 304/344-3954

American
$26-$42

An elegant restaurant with upscale surroundings, a fine wine list and superb menu. Formally attired wait staff help in selections. Casual dress. **Bar:** Full bar. **Reservations:** suggested, weekends. **Hours:** 5 pm-10 pm. Closed major holidays. **Address:** 1003 Charleston Town Center 25389 **Location:** I-64, exit 58C; center of downtown. **Parking:** on-site (fee) and street. **Cards:** AX, CB, DC, DS, JC, MC, VI.

COZUMEL MEXICAN RESTAURANT
Phone: 304/342-0113

Mexican
$7-$20

Great salsa and a wide selection of traditional favorites satisfy the palate at the lively restaurant. Casual dress. **Bar:** Full bar. **Hours:** 11 am-11 pm. Closed: 12/25. **Address:** 1120 Fledderjohn Rd 25314 **Location:** I-64, exit 58A, 3 mi s on US 119. **Parking:** on-site. **Cards:** AX, CB, DC, DS, JC, MC, VI.

FAZIO'S
Phone: 304/344-3071

Italian
$13-$25

A city landmark and mainstay since 1934, the casual restaurant prepares delicious Italian fare that's worth every "penne". Casual dress. **Bar:** Full bar. **Hours:** 5 pm-10 pm. Closed: 1/1, 12/25; also Mon. **Address:** 1008 Bullitt St 25301 **Location:** I-64, exit 58C, just s. **Parking:** on-site. **Cards:** AX, CB, DC, DS, JC, MC, VI.

FIFTH QUARTER STEAK HOUSE
Phone: 304/345-3933

Steak & Seafood
$7-$20

Prime rib is the big seller at the rustic steakhouse, decorated in an attractive Early American motif. Fish and fowl dishes, such as chicken Monterey, also are on the menu. The restaurant's casual atmosphere makes it a popular place with families. Casual dress. **Bar:** Full bar. **Hours:** 11 am-10 pm, Fri & Sat-11 pm. Closed: 12/24, 12/25. **Address:** 201 Clendenin St 25301 **Location:** Jct Quarrier and Clendenin sts; adjacent to Civic Center. **Parking:** on-site. **Cards:** AX, CB, DC, DS, MC, VI.

GRATZI RISTORANTE
Phone: 304/344-4824

Italian
$8-$26

Spicy red sauces and grilled dishes of Tuscany are fresh and uncomplicated. Casual dress. **Bar:** Full bar. **Hours:** 11 am-11 pm, Sun noon-9 pm. Closed: 12/25. **Address:** 1061 Charleston Town Center 25389 **Location:** I-64, exit 58C; center of downtown. **Parking:** street. **Cards:** AX, CB, DC, DS, JC, MC, VI.

HARDING'S FAMILY RESTAURANT
Phone: 304/344-5044

American
$5-$16

The restaurant's laid-back atmosphere is welcoming to families. The menu offers breakfast, lunch and dinner selections. Casual dress. **Hours:** 6 am-11 pm, Sun from 7 am. Closed: 12/25. **Address:** 2772 Pennslyvania Ave 25302 **Location:** I-79, exit 1, just e. **Parking:** on-site. **Cards:** AX, CB, DC, DS, JC, MC, VI.

THE RIVERSIDE ANCHOR
Phone: 304/925-9902

American
$5-$18

Serving the Kanawha Valley since 1936, the restaurant affords wonderful river views. The food is great, and service is friendly. Casual dress. **Bar:** Beer only. **Hours:** 11 am-11 pm, Sun 5 pm-10 pm, Mon 11 am-10 pm. Closed: 3/23, 11/27, 12/25. **Address:** 3315 Kanawha Blvd E 25306 **Location:** I-64/77, exit 96, just sw. **Parking:** on-site. **Cards:** AX, DS, MC, VI.

SOHO'S
Phone: 304/720-7646

Italian
$7-$25

Italian cuisine is served in a modern comfortable setting with a large selection of wines. The wait staff is friendly. Casual dress. **Bar:** Full bar. **Reservations:** suggested, weekends. **Hours:** 11 am-3 & 5-9 pm, Fri & Sat 5 pm-10 pm, Sun noon-4 pm. Closed: 12/25. **Address:** 800 Smith St 25301 **Location:** Between Leon Sullivan Way and Shrewsberry St; center of downtown. **Parking:** on-site. **Cards:** AX, CB, DC, DS, JC, MC, VI.

TIDEWATER GRILL
Phone: 304/345-2620

American
$7-$21

This restaurant is fun and casual, has an exciting contemporary menu and is close to all the action at the Town Center. Casual dress. **Bar:** Full bar. **Hours:** 11 am-10 pm, Fri & Sat-11 pm, Sun noon-9 pm. Closed: 12/25. **Address:** 1060 Charleston Town Center 25389 **Location:** I-64, exit 58C; center of downtown. **Parking:** street. **Cards:** AX, CB, DC, DS, JC, MC, VI.

TUDOR'S BISCUIT WORLD
Phone: 304/949-2088

American
$5-$12

Serving breakfast all day folks can stop into Tudor's Biscuit World to sample their many varieities of homemade biscuit sandwiches. Known for fast and friendly service in a clean casual atmosphere. Casual dress. **Hours:** 7 am-7 pm. Closed: 12/25. **Address:** 10501 MacCorkle Ave 25315 **Location:** I-77, exit 95, 2.3 n on SR 61. **Parking:** on-site.

TUDOR'S BISCUIT WORLD

American
$5-$12

Phone: 304/768-0782

Serving breakfast all day folks can stop into Tudor's Biscuit World to sample their many varieities of homemade biscuit sandwiches. Known for fast and friendly service in a clean casual atmosphere. Casual dress. **Hours:** 6 am-2 pm. **Closed:** 12/25. **Address:** 5403 MacCorkle Ave SW 25304 **Location:** I-64, exit 95, just n. **Parking:** on-site.

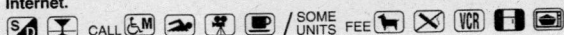

CHARLES TOWN pop. 2,907

———— WHERE TO STAY ————

COTTONWOOD INN

Historic Bed
& Breakfast
$95-$140 All Year

Phone: (304)725-3371

Address: 199 Mill Ln 25414 **Location:** Jct US 340 and SR 9 E, 1.3 mi e on SR 9, 3.1 mi s on CR 25 (Kabletown Rd), then 0.3 mi w. Located in a quiet rural area. **Facility:** Nestled in the farmlands of the Shenandoah Valley, the inn is decorated with quilts and Colonial-style furnishings and sits in a wooded area. Smoke free premises. 6 one-bedroom standard units. 3 stories (no elevator), interior/exterior corridors. **Bath:** combo, shower or tub only. **Parking:** on-site. **Terms:** age restrictions may apply, 3 day cancellation notice. **Business Services:** meeting rooms. **Cards:** AX, DS, MC, VI.

WASHINGTON HOUSE INN BED & BREAKFAST

Historic Bed
& Breakfast
$125-$250 All Year

Phone: (304)725-7923

Address: 216 S George St 25414 **Location:** SR 115, just e of jct Washington St. **Facility:** Fireplaces, antique furnishings and carved oak mantels grace this turn-of-the-20th-century Victorian inn tucked in the Blue Ridge Mountains. Smoke free premises. 8 one-bedroom standard units, some with whirlpools. 3 stories (no elevator), interior corridors. **Bath:** shower only. **Parking:** on-site. **Terms:** age restrictions may apply, 5 day cancellation notice. **Amenities:** hair dryers. *Some:* DVD players, CD players. **Guest Services:** valet laundry, wireless Internet. **Cards:** AX, DS, MC, VI. **Free Special Amenities:** full breakfast and high-speed Internet.

———— WHERE TO DINE ————

AVANTI RISTORANTE

Italian
$7-$23

Phone: 304-728-8880

The restaurant offers patrons an escape from the mundane. Splashed in large murals, the dining room nurtures an inviting atmosphere. The friendly wait staff serves great Italian cuisine. Casual dress. **Bar:** Full bar. **Hours:** 11:30 am-9:30 pm, Fri & Sat-10:30 pm, Sun noon-9:30 pm. **Closed:** 12/25. **Address:** 119 E Washington St 25414 **Location:** SR 9, just e. **Parking:** on-site. **Cards:** AX, CB, DC, DS, JC, MC, VI.

CHESTER pop. 2,592

———— WHERE TO STAY ————

MOUNTAINEER RACETRACK & GAMING RESORT

Large-scale Hotel
$123-$229 All Year

Phone: (304)387-8000

Address: Rt 2 26034 **Location:** On SR 2, 6 mi s. **Facility:** With horse racing, a casino, concert events, a grand spa, many restaurants and gift shops, this river-view property provides a plethora of diversions. 359 one-bedroom standard units, some with whirlpools. 2-6 stories, interior/exterior corridors. **Bath:** combo or shower only. **Parking:** on-site and valet. **Terms:** check-in 4 pm. **Amenities:** video games, voice mail, irons, hair dryers. *Some:* CD players, high-speed Internet, safes, honor bars. **Pool(s):** 2 outdoor, heated indoor. **Leisure Activities:** whirlpools, steamrooms, 2 lighted tennis courts, exercise room, spa, horseshoes. *Fee:* golf-18 holes. **Guest Services:** valet laundry, area transportation. **Business Services:** conference facilities, business center. **Cards:** AX, DC, DS, MC, VI.

CLARKSBURG pop. 16,743

———— WHERE TO DINE ————

MINARD'S SPAGHETTI INN

Italian
$8-$16

Phone: 304/623-1711

The fare consists of popular homemade pasta, especially the spaghetti dishes, specially baked Italian bread and beef cacciatore. Some American cuisine also is served in the homey, family-oriented atmosphere. The service staff is friendly and prompt. Casual dress. **Bar:** Full bar. **Reservations:** accepted. **Hours:** 11 am-10 pm, Fri & Sat-11 pm. **Closed** major holidays. **Address:** 813 E Pike St 26301 **Location:** I-79, exit 119, 2 mi w on US 50, exit Joyce St, just n, then just e. **Parking:** on-site. **Cards:** AX, DS, MC, VI.

CROSS LANES pop. 10,353

———— WHERE TO STAY ————

COMFORT INN WEST CHARLESTON *Book great rates at AAA.com*

Small-scale Hotel
$88 All Year

Phone: (304)776-8070

Address: 102 Racer Dr 25313 **Location:** I-64, exit 47, just s. **Facility:** 112 one-bedroom standard units, some with kitchens. 2 stories (no elevator), interior corridors. **Bath:** combo or shower only. **Parking:** on-site. **Amenities:** video games, high-speed Internet, voice mail, irons, hair dryers. **Pool(s):** heated outdoor. **Leisure Activities:** whirlpool, exercise room. **Guest Services:** valet laundry, area transportation-dog track. **Business Services:** meeting rooms, business center. **Cards:** AX, CB, DC, DS, JC, MC, VI. **Free Special Amenities:** expanded continental breakfast and high-speed Internet.

--------- **WHERE TO DINE** ---------

TUDOR'S BISCUIT WORLD   **Phone:** 304/776-0368

American
$5-$12

Serving breakfast all day folks can stop into Tudor's Biscuit World to sample their many varieties of homemade biscuit sandwiches. Known for fast and friendly service in a clean casual atmosphere. Casual dress. **Hours:** 6 am-2 pm. Closed: 12/25. **Address:** 106 Goff Mountain Rd 25313 **Location:** I-64, exit 47, just n. **Parking:** on-site.

DANIELS pop. 1,846

--------- **WHERE TO STAY** ---------

THE RESORT AT GLADE SPRINGS   *Book great rates at AAA.com*

Phone: (304)763-2000

Resort
Small-scale Hotel
$138-$332 All Year

Address: 255 Resort Dr 25832 **Location:** I-64, exit 125, 1.5 mi w on SR 307, then 2.8 mi w on US 19. **Facility:** On extensive grounds with ponds and trails, the property offers high-rise, hotel-style rooms and bungalow-style rooms and recreational activities. 186 units. 169 one- and 12 two-bedroom standard units, some with kitchens. 4 three-bedroom suites. 1 vacation home. 2-3 stories (no elevator), interior/exterior corridors. *Bath:* combo or shower only. **Parking:** on-site. **Terms:** 7 day cancellation notice-fee imposed. **Amenities:** video games, voice mail, honor bars, irons, hair dryers. *Some:* DVD players, safes. **Dining:** Glade's Grill & Bar, see separate listing. **Pool(s):** outdoor, indoor. **Leisure Activities:** saunas, whirlpools, steamrooms, canoeing, paddleboats, 7 tennis courts (1 indoor), recreation programs, bowling lanes, hiking trails, jogging, playground, basketball, horseshoes, volleyball. *Fee:* fishing, golf-36 holes, bicycles, horseback riding, massage, game room. **Guest Services:** valet laundry, area transportation-within 10 mi, wireless Internet. **Business Services:** conference facilities, business center. **Cards:** AX, DC, DS, MC, VI. **Free Special Amenities: full breakfast and newspaper.** *(See color ad below)*

   CALL   / SOME UNITS FEE

--------- ▼ *See AAA listing above* ▼ ---------

—— **WHERE TO DINE** ——

GLADE'S GRILL & BAR
Phone: 304/763-3033

American
$7-$28

Fantastic artwork and table settings enhance the atmosphere at the fine-dining establishment. Large picture windows afford wonderful woodland and golf views. The highly trained staff will assist with wine and food selections. Casual dress. **Bar:** Full bar. **Hours:** 5:30 pm-9:30 pm, Sat & Sun 7 am-10:30 & 11-2 pm. **Address:** 200 Lake Dr 25832 **Location:** I-64, exit 125, 1.5 mi w on SR 307, then 2.8 mi w on US 19; in The Resort at Glade Springs. **Parking:** on-site. **Cards:** AX, DC, DS, MC, VI.

DANVILLE pop. 550

—— **WHERE TO DINE** ——

TUDOR'S BISCUIT WORLD
Phone: 304/369-2003

American
$5-$14

Serving breakfast all day folks can stop into Tudor's Biscuit World to sample their many varieities of homemade biscuit sandwiches. Known for fast and friendly service in a clean casual atmosphere. Casual dress. **Hours:** 5:30 am-7 pm, Sun from 7 am. Closed: 12/25. **Address:** 209 Smooth St 25053 **Location:** 0.4 mi s on US 119, then just e. **Parking:** on-site.

DAVIS pop. 624

—— **WHERE TO STAY** ——

BLACK BEAR RESORT
Phone: 304/866-4391

Cabin
$90-$510 All Year

Address: Cortland Rd, Canaan Valley 26260 **Location:** 7.4 mi s on SR 32. **Facility:** 60 units. 12 one-bedroom standard units with kitchens and whirlpools. 48 cabins, some with whirlpools. 2 stories (no elevator), exterior corridors. **Parking:** on-site. **Terms:** check-in 4 pm, 2 night minimum stay, cancellation fee imposed. **Amenities:** DVD players. *Some:* CD players. **Pool(s):** outdoor. **Leisure Activities:** whirlpool, fishing, tennis court, hiking trails, playground, basketball, horseshoes, volleyball. *Fee:* miniature golf, game room. **Guest Services:** coin laundry, wireless Internet. **Business Services:** meeting rooms. **Cards:** AX, DS, MC, VI. *(See color ad below)*

—— **WHERE TO DINE** ——

HICKORY ROOM
Phone: 304/866-4121

American
$10-$28

This restaurant affords stunning views of the mountains, nature and golf course. A huge fireplace sits in the center of the dining area. On the menu are classic American favorites. Casual dress. **Bar:** Full bar. **Hours:** 8 am-9 pm. **Address:** SR 32 26260 **Location:** On SR 32, 10 mi s; 2 mi w off SR 32, follow signs; in Canaan Valley Resort & Conference Center. **Parking:** on-site. **Cards:** AX, CB, DC, DS, JC, MC, VI.

DUNBAR pop. 8,154

―――――― WHERE TO STAY ――――――

DUNBAR SUPER 8 MOTEL   *Book at AAA.com*   Phone: 304/768-6888

Small-scale Hotel
Rates not provided

Address: 911 Dunbar Ave 25064 **Location:** I-64, exit 53, just w. **Facility:** 62 one-bedroom standard units. 3 stories (no elevator), interior corridors. **Parking:** on-site. **Amenities:** safes (fee), hair dryers. **Guest Services:** coin laundry, wireless Internet. **Business Services:** fax (fee).

―――――― WHERE TO DINE ――――――

TUDOR'S BISCUIT WORLD   Phone: 304/768-2046

American
$5-$12

Serving breakfast all day folks can stop into Tudor's Biscuit World to sample their many varieities of homemade biscuit sandwiches. Known for fast and friendly service in a clean casual atmosphere. Casual dress. **Hours:** 5:30 am-7 pm. Closed: 12/25. **Address:** 1305 Fairlawn Ave 25064 **Location:** I-64, exit 53, just sw. **Parking:** on-site.

DUNMORE

―――――― WHERE TO STAY ――――――

THE INN AT MOUNTAIN QUEST   Phone: 304/799-7267

Country Inn
$130-$150 All Year

Address: Rt 92 Frost 24954 **Location:** On SR 92, 0.4 mi n. **Facility:** The inn offers an observation tower, a billiard room, lounge and a large, award-winning library as well as ponds, miles for hiking and great views. 12 one-bedroom standard units. 2-3 stories (no elevator), exterior corridors. **Parking:** on-site. **Terms:** cancellation fee imposed. **Amenities:** video library, DVD players, CD players, high-speed Internet, irons, hair dryers. **Leisure Activities:** whirlpool, fishing, hiking trails, exercise room, basketball, horseshoes. **Guest Services:** complimentary laundry. **Business Services:** conference facilities, business center. **Cards:** MC, VI.

ELKINS pop. 7,032

―――――― WHERE TO STAY ――――――

CHEAT RIVER LODGE & INN   Phone: 304/636-2301

Cabin
$73-$88 All Year

Address: Rt 1, Box 115, Faulkner Rd 26241 **Location:** 4.8 mi e on US 33, then 1.5 mi ne. **Facility:** In a serene setting, the property offers wonderful river views as well as a gift shop with fine jewelry, an eatery and recreational opportunities. 13 units. 7 one-bedroom standard units, some with whirlpools. 6 cabins with whirlpools. 1 story, exterior corridors. **Parking:** on-site. **Terms:** 2 night minimum stay - weekends, cancellation fee imposed. **Amenities:** *Some:* CD players. **Leisure Activities:** whirlpool, fishing, bicycles, hiking trails. *Fee:* massage. **Business Services:** fax (fee). **Cards:** MC, VI.

ECONO LODGE   *Book at AAA.com*   Phone: 304/636-5311

Motel
Rates not provided

Address: US 33 E 26241 **Location:** 1 mi e. **Facility:** 72 one-bedroom standard units, some with whirlpools. 1-2 stories (no elevator), interior/exterior corridors. **Parking:** on-site. **Terms:** check-in 4 pm. **Pool(s):** heated indoor. **Leisure Activities:** whirlpool. **Guest Services:** coin laundry. **Business Services:** meeting rooms, fax (fee).

ELKINS SUPER 8 MOTEL   *Book at AAA.com*   Phone: 304/636-6500

Small-scale Hotel
Rates not provided

Address: 350 Beverly Pike 26241 **Location:** 0.8 mi s on SR 219. **Facility:** 44 one-bedroom standard units. 2 stories (no elevator), interior corridors. **Parking:** on-site. **Amenities:** safes (fee), hair dryers. **Guest Services:** coin laundry, wireless Internet. **Business Services:** fax (fee).

―――――― WHERE TO DINE ――――――

CHEAT RIVER INN   *Menu on AAA.com*   Phone: 304/636-6265

American
$14-$26

The comfortable and exquisite setting is on the banks of the Cheat River. A balanced menu and knowledgeable staff can be expected. Casual dress. **Bar:** Full bar. **Reservations:** suggested, weekends. **Hours:** 5 pm-9 pm, Fri & Sat-10 pm. Closed: Tues 11/1-5/31 & Mon. **Address:** Rt 1, Box 115, Faulkner Rd 26241 **Location:** 4.8 mi e on US 33, 1.5 mi ne on Faulkner Rd. **Parking:** on-site. **Cards:** CB, DS, MC, VI.

THE LODGE AT KELLY MOUNTAIN   Phone: 304/635-0300

Casual dress. **Bar:** Full bar. **Reservations:** suggested. **Hours:** 11 am-2 & 6-10 pm, Sat from 6 pm. Closed major holidays; also Sun. **Address:** Kelly Mountain Rd 26241 **Location:** 4.1 mi e on US 33, just s. **Parking:** on-site. **Cards:** AX, CB, DC, DS, JC, MC, VI.

American
$10-$28

ELKVIEW pop. 1,182

———— **WHERE TO STAY** ————

COUNTRY INN & SUITES BY CARLSON   *Book great rates at AAA.com*   Phone: (304)965-9200

Address: 101 The Crossings Shopping Center 25071 **Location:** I-79, exit 9, just e. **Facility:** 90 one-bedroom standard units, some with whirlpools. 5 stories, interior corridors. *Bath:* combo or shower only. **Parking:** on-site. **Terms:** cancellation fee imposed. **Amenities:** high-speed Internet, voice mail, irons, hair dryers. **Pool(s):** heated indoor. **Leisure Activities:** whirlpool, exercise room. **Guest Services:** valet and coin laundry, wireless Internet. **Business Services:** meeting rooms. **Cards:** AX, DS, MC, VI. **Free Special Amenities: continental breakfast and high-speed Internet.**

Small-scale Hotel
$90 All Year

FAIRMONT pop. 19,097

———— **WHERE TO STAY** ————

COMFORT INN & SUITES   *Book great rates at AAA.com*   Phone: (304)367-1370

Address: 1185 Airport Rd 26554 **Location:** I-79, exit 133, just w. **Facility:** 82 one-bedroom standard units, some with whirlpools. 2 stories (no elevator), interior corridors. **Parking:** on-site. **Amenities:** high-speed Internet, irons, hair dryers. **Pool(s):** outdoor. **Leisure Activities:** exercise room. **Guest Services:** coin laundry, wireless Internet. **Business Services:** meeting rooms. **Cards:** AX, CB, DC, DS, JC, MC, VI. **Free Special Amenities: continental breakfast and high-speed Internet.**

Small-scale Hotel
$70-$150 All Year

COUNTRY CLUB MOTOR LODGE   Phone: (304)366-4141

Address: 1499 Locust Ave 26554 **Location:** I-79, exit 132, 3 mi n on US 250, then 1 mi w on Country Club Rd. Located at a busy high-traffic intersection. **Facility:** 27 one-bedroom standard units. 2 stories (no elevator), exterior corridors. **Parking:** on-site. **Guest Services:** wireless Internet. **Cards:** AX, DS, MC, VI. **Free Special Amenities: local telephone calls and high-speed Internet.**

Motel
$33-$49 All Year

DAYS INN   *Book great rates at AAA.com*   Phone: 304/366-5995

Address: 228 Middletown Rd 26554 **Location:** I-79, exit 132, just se on US 250, then just s. Located in an industrial area. **Facility:** 46 one-bedroom standard units. 2 stories (no elevator), interior/exterior corridors. **Parking:** on-site. **Amenities:** high-speed Internet, hair dryers. **Guest Services:** wireless Internet. **Free Special Amenities: continental breakfast and high-speed Internet.**

Small-scale Hotel
Rates not provided

FAIRFIELD INN & SUITES   *Book great rates at AAA.com*   Phone: 304/367-9150

Address: 27 Southland Dr 26554 **Location:** I-79, exit 132, just e. **Facility:** Smoke free premises. 80 one-bedroom standard units. 3 stories, interior corridors. *Bath:* combo or shower only. **Parking:** on-site. **Terms:** check-in 4 pm. **Amenities:** high-speed Internet, voice mail, irons, hair dryers. *Some:* CD players. **Pool(s):** heated indoor. **Leisure Activities:** whirlpool, exercise room. **Guest Services:** valet and coin laundry, wireless Internet. **Business Services:** meeting rooms, business center. **Cards:** AX, DS, MC, VI.

Small-scale Hotel
$93-$114 All Year

AAA Benefit:
Members save 5% off of the best available rate.

HOLIDAY INN FAIRMONT   *Book at AAA.com*   Phone: (304)366-5500

Address: 930 E Grafton Rd 26554 **Location:** I-79, exit 137, just e. **Facility:** 106 one-bedroom standard units. 2 stories (no elevator), interior corridors. *Bath:* combo or shower only. **Parking:** on-site. **Amenities:** voice mail, irons, hair dryers. *Some:* high-speed Internet. **Pool(s):** outdoor. **Guest Services:** valet laundry, wireless Internet. **Business Services:** meeting rooms, fax (fee). **Cards:** AX, DS, MC, VI.

Small-scale Hotel
$75-$85 All Year

SUPER 8 MOTEL
Book at AAA.com
Phone: 304/363-1488

Small-scale Hotel
Rates not provided

Address: 2208 Pleasant Valley Rd 26554 **Location:** I-79, exit 133, just e. **Facility:** 54 one-bedroom standard units, some with whirlpools. 2 stories (no elevator), interior corridors. **Parking:** on-site. **Amenities:** irons, hair dryers. **Guest Services:** wireless Internet. **Business Services:** meeting rooms.

─────── **WHERE TO DINE** ───────

DJ'S 50'S & 60'S DINER
Phone: 304/366-8110

American
$6-$12

Decorated in a 1950s and '60s style, the retro diner prepares tried-and-true American favorites. Casual dress. **Hours:** 7 am-10 pm, Fri & Sat-midnight. **Closed:** 12/25. **Address:** 1181 Airport Rd 26554 **Location:** I-79, exit 133, just n. **Parking:** on-site. **Cards:** AX, DS, MC, VI.

MURIALE'S RESTAURANT
Phone: 304/363-3190

Italian
$7-$22

On the Tiger River, the casual restaurant makes its own excellent pasta and sauce. Photographs of Italian singers decorate the walls of the indoor dining area, the outdoor deck is laid-back and bright, and the large lounge is the newest area in which to unwind. Private inlet rooms also are available. Save room for Italian rum cake. Casual dress. **Bar:** Full bar. **Hours:** 11 am-9 pm, Fri & Sat-10 pm, Sun-8 pm. **Closed:** 3/23, 7/4, 12/25. **Address:** 1742 Fairmont Ave Ext 26554 **Location:** I-79, exit 132, 1.5 mi n on US 250. **Parking:** on-site. **Cards:** AX, DC, DS, MC, VI.

POKY DOT
Phone: 304/366-3271

American
$5-$12

An area tradition, the restaurant blends '50s nostalgia and quick, but tasty, meals. The friendly atmosphere is welcoming to families. Casual dress. **Hours:** 7 am-11 pm, Fri & Sat-midnight. **Closed:** 1/1, 11/27, 12/25. **Address:** 1111 Fairmont Ave 26554 **Location:** I-79, exit 132, 3.3 mi n on US 250. **Parking:** on-site. **Cards:** DS, MC, VI.

SAY-BOY RESTAURANT
Phone: 304/366-7252

American
$7-$22

Sizzling steaks, pasta choices and roasted chicken are among popular choices at the family-operated restaurant. Casual dress. **Bar:** Full bar. **Hours:** 11 am-9 pm. **Closed:** 12/25. **Address:** 905 Country Club Rd 26554 **Location:** I-79, exit 132, 3 mi n US 250, then 0.8 mi w. **Parking:** on-site. **Cards:** AX, CB, DC, DS, JC, MC, VI.

THE SIMMERING POT FAMILY RESTAURANT
Phone: 304/366-5500

American
$8-$20

This restaurant is boiling over with classic American favorites, friendly service and a home-spun cozy family friendly atmosphere. Casual dress. **Bar:** Full bar. **Hours:** 6 am-10 & 5-10 pm. **Address:** 930 E Grafton Rd 26554 **Location:** I-79, exit 137, just e. **Parking:** on-site. **Cards:** AX, CB, DC, DS, JC, MC, VI.

FALLING WATERS

─────── **WHERE TO STAY** ───────

HOLIDAY INN EXPRESS MARTINSBURG NORTH   *Book at AAA.com*
Phone: 304/274-6100

Small-scale Hotel
Rates not provided

Address: 1220 TJ Jackson Dr 25419 **Location:** I-81, exit 20, just w. **Facility:** 71 one-bedroom standard units. 3 stories, interior corridors. *Bath:* combo or shower only. **Parking:** on-site. **Amenities:** voice mail, irons, hair dryers. *Some:* high-speed Internet. **Pool(s):** outdoor. **Guest Services:** coin laundry, wireless Internet. **Business Services:** fax (fee).

FAYETTEVILLE pop. 2,754

─────── **WHERE TO DINE** ───────

TUDOR'S BISCUIT WORLD
Phone: 304/574-3820

American
$5-$12

Serving breakfast all day folks can stop into Tudor's Biscuit World to sample their many varieities of homemade biscuit sandwiches. Known for fast and friendly service in a clean casual atmosphere. Casual dress. **Hours:** 6 am-7 pm. **Closed:** 12/25. **Address:** 323 N Court St 25840 **Location:** 0.5 mi n on US 19, then just e. **Parking:** on-site.

FLATWOODS pop. 348

─────── **WHERE TO STAY** ───────

DAYS HOTEL   *Book at AAA.com*
Phone: (304)765-5055

Small-scale Hotel
$79-$99 All Year

Address: 2000 Sutton Ln 26601 **Location:** I-79, exit 67, just e. **Facility:** 200 one-bedroom standard units, some with whirlpools. 5 stories, interior corridors. **Parking:** on-site. **Amenities:** irons, hair dryers. **Pool(s):** outdoor, heated indoor. **Leisure Activities:** sauna, whirlpool, exercise room. **Guest Services:** wireless Internet. **Business Services:** conference facilities, business center. **Cards:** AX, CB, DC, DS, JC, MC, VI.

GASSAWAY pop. 901

——— WHERE TO STAY ———

MICROTEL INN AND SUITES
Phone: 304/364-6100

[fyi]
Small-scale Hotel
$70-$120 All Year

Too new to rate. **Address:** 115 Reston Pl 26624 **Location:** I-79, exit 62. **Amenities:** 75 units. **Cards:** AX, CB, DC, DS, MC, VI.

GLEN DALE pop. 1,552

——— WHERE TO STAY ———

BONNIE DWAINE BED & BREAKFAST
Phone: (304)845-7250

▼▼▼
Bed & Breakfast
$89-$125 All Year

Address: 505 Wheeling Ave 26038 **Location:** I-470, exit 1, 7 mi s on SR 2. **Facility:** Breakfast is served by candlelight at this renovated Victorian home located 7 miles south of Wheeling; the B&B boasts great porch and garden areas. Smoke free premises. 5 one-bedroom standard units with whirlpools. 3 stories (no elevator), interior corridors. **Parking:** on-site. **Amenities:** hair dryers. *Some:* DVD players, irons. **Guest Services:** complimentary laundry, wireless Internet. **Cards:** AX, CB, DC, DS, JC, MC, VI.

ASK SⱭ Ⓨ⁺ ☒ VCR / SOME UNITS ▣ ▣

GLENVILLE pop. 1,544

——— WHERE TO STAY ———

BEST WESTERN GLENVILLE INN & CONFERENCE
CENTER   *Book great rates at AAA.com*
Phone: 304/462-5511

ⒶⒶⒶ SAVE
▼▼▼
Small-scale Hotel
Rates not provided

Address: 61 Best Western Dr 26351 **Location:** 1.5 mi e on SR 5. **Facility:** 57 one-bedroom standard units, some with whirlpools. 3 stories, interior corridors. **Amenities:** high-speed Internet, voice mail, irons, hair dryers. **Leisure Activities:** sauna, exercise room. *Fee:* game room. **Parking:** on-site. **Business Services:** meeting rooms, business center. **Free Special Amenities: continental breakfast and high-speed Internet.**

CALL ⒼⓂ ☒ 🎦 ▣ / SOME UNITS ☒ ▣ ▣

AAA Benefit:
Members save 10% everyday, plus an exclusive frequent stay program.

HAMLIN pop. 1,119

——— WHERE TO DINE ———

TUDOR'S BISCUIT WORLD
Phone: 304/824-7377

▼▼
American
$5-$12

Serving breakfast all day folks can stop into Tudor's Biscuit World to sample their many varieities of homemade biscuit sandwiches. Known for fast and friendly service in a clean casual atmosphere. Casual dress. **Hours:** 5:30 am-2 pm, Sun from 7 am. Closed: 12/25. **Address:** 1 Court Ave 25523 **Location:** 0.7 mi w on SR 3. **Parking:** on-site.

✎

HARPERS FERRY pop. 307

———— WHERE TO STAY ————

COMFORT INN

Phone: (304)535-6391

AAA SAVE

▽▽▽▽

Small-scale Hotel
$85-$150 3/1-12/31
$85-$125 1/1-2/28

Address: 25 Union St 25425 **Location:** On US 340, just e. **Facility:** 50 one-bedroom standard units. 2 stories (no elevator), interior corridors. *Bath:* combo or shower only. **Parking:** on-site. **Terms:** cancellation fee imposed. **Amenities:** video library (fee), high-speed Internet, voice mail, irons, hair dryers. **Guest Services:** valet laundry, wireless Internet. **Business Services:** fax (fee). **Cards:** AX, CB, DC, DS, JC, MC, VI. **Free Special Amenities:** expanded continental breakfast and high-speed Internet.

[icons] CALL / SOME UNITS FEE VCR

———— WHERE TO DINE ————

ANVIL RESTAURANT

Phone: 304/535-2582

AAA

▽▽▽▽

American
$5-$23

Steak, chicken, veal and seafood, including the specialty crab cakes, share menu space with several dessert offerings and a nice selection of children's dishes. The surroundings are rustic—with fireplaces, brick walls and soft lighting—and the atmosphere casual. Casual dress. **Bar:** Full bar. **Reservations:** suggested, Fri-Sun. **Hours:** 11 am-9 pm. Closed: 11/27, 12/25; also Mon & Tues. **Address:** 1290 W Washington St 25425 **Location:** Washington St and Old Furnace Rd; center. **Parking:** on-site. **Cards:** AX, DC, MC, VI.

[icon]

HICO

———— WHERE TO STAY ————

COUNTRY ROAD CABINS

Phone: (304)658-5266

AAA SAVE

▽▽▽▽

Cabin
$150-$500 All Year

Address: Sunday Rd 25854 **Location:** SR 19 to US 60 (Midland Trail), just w. **Facility:** The cabins are close to two national recreation areas offering such activities as golf, rafting, hiking and skiing; most rooms have whirlpools. 18 cabins with whirlpools. 1-3 stories (no elevator), exterior corridors. *Bath:* combo or shower only. **Parking:** on-site. **Terms:** cancellation fee imposed. **Amenities:** DVD players, irons, hair dryers. *Some:* CD players. **Leisure Activities:** volleyball. **Guest Services:** coin laundry. **Business Services:** meeting rooms, fax. **Free Special Amenities:** local telephone calls. *(See color ad p 344)*

[icons] VCR

HUNTINGTON pop. 51,475

———— WHERE TO STAY ————

HOLIDAY INN HOTEL & SUITES   *Book at AAA.com*   **Phone:** 304/523-8880

Small-scale Hotel
$99 All Year

Address: 800 3rd Ave 25701 **Location:** I-64, exit 11, 3 mi n on SR 10, then 0.9 mi w; downtown. **Facility:** 135 one-bedroom standard units, some with whirlpools. 5 stories, interior corridors. *Bath:* combo or shower only. **Pool(s):** heated indoor. **Leisure Activities:** exercise room. **Guest Services:** coin laundry, wireless Internet. **Business Services:** meeting rooms, business center. **Cards:** AX, DC, DS, MC, VI.

PULLMAN PLAZA HOTEL   *Book great rates at AAA.com*   **Phone:** (304)525-1001

Large-scale Hotel
$83 All Year

Address: 1001 3rd Ave 25701 **Location:** I-64, exit 11, 3 mi n on SR 10, then 0.7 mi w; downtown. **Facility:** 202 one-bedroom standard units, some with whirlpools. 11 stories, interior corridors. **Parking:** on-site. **Terms:** 14 day cancellation notice. **Amenities:** video games, high-speed Internet, voice mail, irons, hair dryers. *Some:* DVD players. **Dining:** 2 restaurants. **Pool(s):** heated outdoor. **Guest Services:** valet laundry, area transportation-within 10 mi, tanning facilities, wireless Internet. **Business Services:** conference facilities, fax (fee). **Cards:** AX, DC, DS, MC, VI. **Free Special Amenities:** full breakfast and high-speed Internet.

RAMADA LIMITED AND CONFERENCE CENTER   *Book at AAA.com*   **Phone:** (304)523-4242

Small-scale Hotel
$92-$150 All Year

Address: 3094 16th Street Rd 25701 **Location:** I-64, exit 11, just n. **Facility:** 68 one-bedroom standard units, some with whirlpools. 3 stories, interior corridors. *Bath:* combo or shower only. **Parking:** on-site. **Amenities:** high-speed Internet, voice mail, irons, hair dryers. *Some:* CD players. **Pool(s):** heated indoor. **Leisure Activities:** whirlpool, exercise room. *Fee:* massage. **Guest Services:** coin laundry, wireless Internet. **Business Services:** conference facilities, business center. **Cards:** AX, DC, DS, MC, VI.

RED ROOF INN   *Book at AAA.com*   **Phone:** 304/733-3737

Small-scale Hotel
Rates not provided

Address: 5190 US Rt 60 E 25705 **Location:** I-64, exit 15, just s. **Facility:** 108 one-bedroom standard units. 2 stories (no elevator), exterior corridors. *Bath:* combo or shower only. **Parking:** on-site. **Amenities:** video games, voice mail. **Guest Services:** valet laundry.

SUPER 8 MOTEL   *Book at AAA.com*   **Phone:** 304/525-1410

Small-scale Hotel
Rates not provided

Address: 3090 16th Street Rd 25701 **Location:** I-64, exit 11, just n. **Facility:** 78 one-bedroom standard units, some with whirlpools. 3 stories, interior corridors. *Bath:* combo or shower only. **Parking:** on-site. **Amenities:** high-speed Internet, irons, hair dryers. **Pool(s):** heated indoor. **Leisure Activities:** whirlpool, exercise room. *Fee:* massage. **Guest Services:** coin laundry, wireless Internet. **Business Services:** meeting rooms, business center.

———— WHERE TO DINE ————

JIM'S RESTAURANT   **Phone:** 304/696-9788

American
$6-$16

Homemade pie and award-winning spaghetti are just two of the cuisine choices at the family-owned-and-operated restaurant. Casual dress. **Hours:** 11 am-9 pm. Closed major holidays; also Sun & Mon. **Address:** 920 Fifth Ave 25701 **Location:** I-64, exit 11, 3 mi n on SR 10, then 0.4 mi w; downtown. **Parking:** street.

THE MARSHALL HALL OF FAME CAFE   **Phone:** 304/697-9800

American
$6-$18

The charming cafe appeals to nearly everyone, not just fans of the Thundering Herd. A wide variety of classic American favorites and friendly service abound. Casual dress. **Bar:** Full bar. **Hours:** 11 am-11 pm. Closed: 1/1, 12/25. **Address:** 857 3rd Ave 25701 **Location:** I-64, exit 11, 3 mi n on SR 10, then 0.9 mi w; downtown. **Parking:** on-site. **Cards:** AX, CB, DC, DS, JC, MC, VI.

———— The following restaurant has not been evaluated by AAA ————
but is listed for your information only.

SAVANNAH'S   **Phone:** 304/529-0919

[fyi]

Not evaluated. Savannah's offers Southern charm and elegance along with gourmet cuisine and an exquisite wine and martini bar. **Address:** 1208 6th Ave 25701 **Location:** I-64, exit 11, 3 mi n on SR 10, then 0.4 mi w; downtown.

HURRICANE pop. 5,222

———— WHERE TO STAY ————

HOLIDAY INN EXPRESS *Book at AAA.com* **Phone:** 304/757-7177
▼▼▼▼▼
Address: 4218 SR 34 25526 **Location:** I-64, exit 39, just n. **Facility:** 68 one-bedroom standard units, some with whirlpools. 3 stories, interior corridors. *Bath:* combo or shower only. **Parking:** on-site.
Small-scale Hotel
Amenities: high-speed Internet, voice mail, irons, hair dryers. **Pool(s):** indoor. **Leisure Activities:** whirlpool, exercise room. **Guest Services:** valet and coin laundry, wireless Internet. **Business Services:** meeting rooms, business center.
Rates not provided

[Ⓣ] CALL [Ⓜ] [⤢] [✱] [▤] [▦] [▯] / SOME UNITS [✕]

RED ROOF INN *Book at AAA.com* **Phone:** 304/757-6392
▼▼▼▼
Address: 500 Putnam Village Dr 25526 **Location:** I-64, exit 39, just n on SR 34, then just e. Located behind Liberty Square Shopping Center. **Facility:** 79 one-bedroom standard units. 2 stories (no elevator), exterior corridors. *Bath:* combo or shower only. **Parking:** on-site. **Amenities:** video games, voice mail. **Guest Services:** coin laundry.
Motel
Rates not provided

[Ⓣ] CALL [Ⓜ] [✱] / SOME UNITS [🐾] [✕] FEE [▤] FEE [▱]

INWOOD pop. 2,084

———— WHERE TO DINE ————

VIVA MEXICO FAMILY RESTAURANT **Phone:** 304/229-1122
▼▼▼
Just off the interstate, the family-oriented restaurant focuses on Mexican food, fabulous salsa and varied drinks. Casual dress. **Bar:** Full bar. **Hours:** 11 am-10 pm, Sat from noon, Sun noon-9 pm. Closed: 12/25.
Mexican
Address: 24 Annex Dr 25428 **Location:** I-81, exit 5, just e. **Parking:** on-site. **Cards:** AX, CB, DC, DS, JC, MC, VI.
$6-$18
[◩]

KEARNEYSVILLE

———— WHERE TO STAY ————

COMFORT SUITES *Book great rates at AAA.com* **Phone:** (304)263-8888
[AAA] [SAVE]
Address: 1937 Short Rd 25401 **Location:** I-81, exit 12, 1.1 mi e on SR 45, then 4.5 mi e. **Facility:** 76 one-bedroom standard units, some with whirlpools. 2-3 stories (no elevator), interior corridors. *Bath:* combo or shower only. **Parking:** on-site. **Terms:** check-in 4 pm, cancellation fee imposed.
▼▼▼▼▼
Amenities: high-speed Internet, dual phone lines, voice mail, safes (fee), irons, hair dryers.
Small-scale Hotel
Pool(s): outdoor. **Leisure Activities:** exercise room. **Guest Services:** valet and coin laundry, wireless
$79-$159 All Year
Internet. **Business Services:** meeting rooms, PC, fax (fee). **Cards:** AX, CB, DC, DS, JC, MC, VI. **Free Special Amenities:** expanded continental breakfast and high-speed Internet.

[Ⓢ] CALL [Ⓜ] [⤢] [✱] [▤] [▦] [▯] / SOME UNITS [✕]

KEYSER pop. 5,303

———— WHERE TO STAY ————

KEYSER INN **Phone:** 304/788-0913
[AAA] [SAVE]
Address: Rt 220 S 26726 **Location:** On US 220, 2.3 mi s. Located next to Wal-Mart. **Facility:** 44 one-bedroom standard units, some with whirlpools. 2 stories (no elevator), interior corridors. **Parking:** on-site. **Terms:** check-in 4 pm. **Amenities:** hair dryers. **Guest Services:** wireless Internet. **Cards:** AX,
▼▼▼▼
DC, DS, MC, VI. **Free Special Amenities:** continental breakfast and high-speed Internet.
Small-scale Hotel
$54-$60 All Year

[Ⓢ] [🍸] [✱] [▯] / SOME UNITS [🐾] [✕] FEE [VCR] [▤] [▱]

LAVALETTE

———— WHERE TO DINE ————

TUDOR'S BISCUIT WORLD **Phone:** 304/523-4808
▼▼▼
Serving breakfast all day folks can stop into Tudor's Biscuit World to sample their many varieities of homemade biscuit sandwiches. Known for fast and friendly service in a clean casual atmosphere. Casual
American
dress. **Hours:** 5:30 am-2 pm, Sun from 7 am. Closed: 12/25. **Address:** 4540 SR 152 25535 **Location:** 1.8
$5-$10
mi s on SR 152. **Parking:** on-site.
[◩]

LEWISBURG pop. 3,624

———— WHERE TO STAY ————

AMERICAS BEST VALUE INN *Book great rates at AAA.com* **Phone:** 304/645-7070
[AAA] [SAVE]
Address: 107 W Fair St 24901 **Location:** I-64, exit 169, 3.1 mi s on US 219. **Facility:** 31 one-bedroom standard units, some with kitchens (no utensils). 2 stories (no elevator), exterior
▼▼▼
corridors. **Parking:** on-site. **Leisure Activities:** whirlpool. **Guest Services:** coin laundry. **Free Special**
Motel
Amenities: continental breakfast and high-speed Internet.
Rates not provided

[Ⓣ] [✱] [▤] [▦] [▯] / SOME UNITS FEE [🐾] [✕]

BRIER INN

Small-scale Hotel
$64-$110 All Year

Phone: (304)645-7722
Address: 540 N Jefferson St 24901 **Location:** I-64, exit 169, just s on US 219. Truck parking on site. **Facility:** 162 one-bedroom standard units, some with whirlpools. 2 stories (no elevator), exterior corridors. *Bath:* combo or shower only. **Parking:** on-site. **Amenities:** video library (fee), high-speed Internet, voice mail, irons, hair dryers. *Some:* DVD players, honor bars. **Pool(s):** outdoor. **Guest Services:** valet laundry, airport transportation-Greenbrier Valley Airport, wireless Internet. **Business Services:** conference facilities. **Cards:** AX, DC, DS, MC, VI.

GENERAL LEWIS INN

Historic
Country Inn
$135-$165 All Year

Phone: 304/645-2600
Address: 301 E Washington St 24901 **Location:** I-64, exit 169, 1.4 mi s on US 219, then just e on US 60. **Facility:** Pioneer tools and memorabilia are displayed in the inn's 1834 original building and its 1928 addition; an extensive garden surrounds both structures. Smoke free premises. 25 units. 23 one- and 2 two-bedroom standard units. 2 stories (no elevator), interior corridors. **Parking:** on-site. **Terms:** 10 day cancellation notice-fee imposed. **Amenities:** high-speed Internet, hair dryers. **Dining:** The General Lewis Inn Dining Room, see separate listing. **Guest Services:** wireless Internet. **Cards:** AX, DS, MC, VI.

HAMPTON INN LEWISBURG   *Book great rates at AAA.com*

Small-scale Hotel
Rates not provided

Phone: 304/645-7300
Address: 30 Coleman Dr 24901 **Location:** I-64, exit 169, just s. **Facility:** 60 one-bedroom standard units, some with whirlpools. 3 stories, interior corridors. *Bath:* combo or shower only. **Parking:** on-site. **Amenities:** high-speed Internet, voice mail, irons, hair dryers. **Pool(s):** heated indoor. **Leisure Activities:** whirlpool, exercise room. **Guest Services:** valet laundry, wireless Internet. **Business Services:** meeting rooms, PC. **Free Special Amenities: expanded continental breakfast and local telephone calls.**

LEWISBURG HOLIDAY INN EXPRESS HOTEL & SUITES

[fyi]

Small-scale Hotel

Under construction, scheduled to open July 2008. **Address:** Hunter Ln 24901 **Location:** I-64, exit 169. **Amenities:** pets, coffeemakers, pool.

SUPER 8 MOTEL   *Book at AAA.com*

Small-scale Hotel
Rates not provided

Phone: 304/647-3188
Address: 550 N Jefferson St 24901 **Location:** I-64, exit 169, just s on US 219. **Facility:** 53 one-bedroom standard units. 2 stories (no elevator), interior corridors. **Parking:** on-site. **Amenities:** safes (fee), hair dryers. **Guest Services:** wireless Internet. **Business Services:** meeting rooms, fax (fee).

——— WHERE TO DINE ———

FOOD & FRIENDS

American
$7-$20

Phone: 304/645-4548
Busily decorated with lots of memorabilia on the walls, the relaxed downtown restaurant builds its menu around steaks and seafood. Many dining areas derive their atmosphere from enhanced lighting and piped-in jazz music. A difficult-to-resist counter case of chocolates and bonbons tempts at the checkout. Casual dress. **Bar:** Full bar. **Reservations:** suggested, weekend evening. **Hours:** 11 am-9 pm. Closed major holidays; also Sun. **Address:** 213 W Washington St 24901 **Location:** I-64, exit 169, 1.4 mi s on US 219, then just w on US 60. **Parking:** street. **Cards:** AX, DC, DS, MC, VI.

THE GENERAL LEWIS INN DINING ROOM

American
$6-$23

Phone: 304/645-2600
Not only can guests sample the restaurant's tasty entrees and homemade soup, bread and cobbler, they also can tour the inn and gardens, listed on the National Register of Historic Places; relax in a front-porch rocking chair; or view the scenic garden pond. Many antiques furnish the dining room and waiting area. Dressy casual. **Bar:** Full bar. **Reservations:** suggested. **Hours:** 7-11 am, 11:30-2 & 6-9 pm, Sun 7:30 am-9 pm. **Address:** 301 E Washington St 24901 **Location:** I-64, exit 169, 1.4 mi s on US 219, then just e on US 60; in General Lewis Inn. **Parking:** on-site. **Cards:** AX, DS, MC, VI. **Historic**

LOGAN pop. 1,630

——— WHERE TO STAY ———

SUPER 8 MOTEL-LOGAN

Motel
Rates not provided

Phone: 304/752-8787
Address: 316 Riverview Ave 25601 **Location:** 1.8 mi e on SR 73. **Facility:** 59 one-bedroom standard units, some with whirlpools. 3 stories, interior corridors. **Parking:** on-site. **Amenities:** hair dryers. **Guest Services:** wireless Internet. **Business Services:** fax (fee).

MARLINTON pop. 1,204

——— WHERE TO STAY ———

MARLINTON MOTOR INN

Motel
$65-$115 All Year

Phone: 304/799-4711
Address: US 219 N 24954 **Location:** Center. **Facility:** 69 one-bedroom standard units, some with whirlpools. 2 stories (no elevator), exterior corridors. **Parking:** on-site. **Terms:** 3 day cancellation notice-fee imposed. **Pool(s):** outdoor. **Business Services:** meeting rooms. **Cards:** AX, CB, DC, DS, MC, VI. **Free Special Amenities: local telephone calls and early check-in/late check-out.**

MARTINSBURG pop. 14,972

———— WHERE TO STAY ————

COMFORT INN AIKENS CENTER   *Book at AAA.com*   Phone: (304)263-6200
Small-scale Hotel
$88-$125 3/1-10/31
$79-$125 11/1-2/28
Address: 1872 Edwin Miller Blvd 25404 **Location:** I-81, exit 16E, 0.5 mi e on SR 9. **Facility:** 110 one-bedroom standard units, some with whirlpools. 4 stories, interior corridors. **Parking:** on-site. **Amenities:** high-speed Internet, voice mail, irons, hair dryers. **Pool(s):** outdoor. **Leisure Activities:** exercise room. *Fee:* game room. **Guest Services:** coin laundry, wireless Internet. **Business Services:** meeting rooms, business center. **Cards:** AX, CB, DC, DS, JC, MC, VI.

DAYS INN MARTINSBURG   *Book at AAA.com*   Phone: 304/263-1800
Small-scale Hotel
Rates not provided
Address: 209 Viking Way 25401 **Location:** I-81, exit 13, just e on W King St (CR 15). **Facility:** 62 one-bedroom standard units. 3 stories, interior/exterior corridors. **Parking:** on-site. **Amenities:** voice mail, irons, hair dryers. *Some:* high-speed Internet. **Leisure Activities:** exercise room. **Guest Services:** coin laundry, wireless Internet.

ECONO LODGE   *Book at AAA.com*   Phone: (304)274-2181
Motel
$60-$62 All Year
Address: 5595 Hammonds Mill Rd 25401 **Location:** I-81, exit 20, just e. **Facility:** 48 one-bedroom standard units. 2 stories (no elevator), interior/exterior corridors. **Parking:** on-site. **Guest Services:** wireless Internet. **Cards:** AX, CB, DC, DS, MC, VI.

HAMPTON INN MARTINSBURG   *Book great rates at AAA.com*   Phone: (304)267-2900
Small-scale Hotel
$99-$139 All Year
Address: 975 Foxcroft Ave 25401 **Location:** I-81, exit 12, just e on SR 45, then just n. **Facility:** 99 one-bedroom standard units, some with whirlpools. 5 stories, interior corridors. *Bath:* combo or shower only. **Parking:** on-site. **Terms:** cancellation fee imposed. **Amenities:** high-speed Internet, voice mail, irons, hair dryers. **Pool(s):** outdoor. **Leisure Activities:** exercise room. **Guest Services:** coin laundry, wireless Internet. **Business Services:** business center. **Cards:** AX, CB, DC, DS, JC, MC, VI.

HOLIDAY INN MARTINSBURG   *Book at AAA.com*   Phone: (304)267-5500
Small-scale Hotel
$109-$149 All Year
Address: 301 Foxcroft Ave 25401 **Location:** I-81, exit 13, just e on W King St (CR 15). **Facility:** 120 one-bedroom standard units, some with whirlpools. 5 stories, interior corridors. *Bath:* combo or shower only. **Parking:** on-site. **Amenities:** CD players, high-speed Internet, voice mail, safes, irons, hair dryers. **Pool(s):** heated indoor. **Leisure Activities:** exercise room. **Guest Services:** valet and coin laundry, wireless Internet. **Business Services:** meeting rooms, PC. **Cards:** AX, CB, DC, DS, JC, MC, VI.

KNIGHTS INN-MARTINSBURG   *Book great rates at AAA.com*   Phone: 304/267-2211
Motel
Rates not provided
Address: 1997 Edwin Miller Blvd 25404 **Location:** I-81, exit 16E, 0.4 mi e on SR 9. **Facility:** 59 one-bedroom standard units. 1 story, exterior corridors. **Parking:** on-site. **Amenities:** video library, irons, hair dryers. **Guest Services:** wireless Internet. **Free Special Amenities:** continental breakfast and high-speed Internet.

RODEWAY INN   *Book great rates at AAA.com*   Phone: (304)263-8811
Small-scale Hotel
$65-$80 3/1-10/31
$55-$60 11/1-2/28
Address: 94 McMillan Ct 25404 **Location:** I-81, exit 16E, just e. **Facility:** 114 one-bedroom standard units. 1-2 stories (no elevator), interior/exterior corridors. *Bath:* combo or shower only. **Parking:** on-site. **Terms:** check-in 4 pm, cancellation fee imposed. **Amenities:** high-speed Internet, voice mail, irons, hair dryers. **Pool(s):** indoor. **Leisure Activities:** whirlpool. *Fee:* game room. **Guest Services:** coin laundry, wireless Internet. **Business Services:** meeting rooms. **Cards:** AX, DS, MC, VI. **Free Special Amenities:** newspaper and high-speed Internet.

SUPER 8 MOTEL-MARTINSBURG   *Book at AAA.com*   Phone: (304)263-0801
Small-scale Hotel
Rates not provided
Address: 2048 Edwin Miller Blvd 25401 **Location:** I-81, exit 16E, just e on SR 9. **Facility:** 41 one-bedroom standard units. 3 stories (no elevator), interior corridors. **Parking:** on-site. **Amenities:** safes, hair dryers. **Guest Services:** wireless Internet.

———— WHERE TO DINE ————

CASA GONZALEZ   Phone: 304/262-0884
Mexican
$6-$18
The restaurant takes a spin through Old Mexico with traditional food, which tastes great with tempting margaritas. Fried ice cream tops the dessert menu. Both the staff and the setting are lively. Casual dress. **Bar:** Full bar. **Hours:** 11 am-10 pm. **Closed:** 12/25. **Address:** 1350 Edwin Miller Blvd 25401 **Location:** I-81, exit 16E, 1.1 mi e on SR 9. **Parking:** on-site. **Cards:** AX, CB, DC, DS, JC, MC, VI.

LA TRATTORIA ITALIAN EATERY

Italian
$7-$20

Phone: 304/262-6925

Family recipes and traditions abound at the restaurant, which serves many homemade pasta and dessert items. Casual dress. **Bar:** Beer & wine. **Hours:** 4 pm-10 pm, Fri & Sat-11 pm, Sun noon-10 pm. Closed: 12/25. **Address:** 240 Lutz Ave 25401 **Location:** I-81, exit 16E, 0.3 mi e on SR 9. **Parking:** on-site. **Cards:** AX, CB, DC, DS, JC, MC, VI.

TOSCANA, AN ITALIAN BISTRO

Italian
$7-$21

Phone: 304/260-9099

A quaint Italian Bistro located in the downtown area of Martinsburg. Cozy atmosphere and do not miss the bread and virgin olive oil. Casual dress. **Bar:** Full bar. **Hours:** 11 am-2 & 5:30-9 pm, Sat from 5:30 pm. Closed major holidays; also Sun. **Address:** 301 W King St 25401 **Location:** I-81, exit 13, 2.8 mi e. **Parking:** street. **Cards:** AX, CB, DC, DS, JC, MC, VI.

MEADOW BRIDGE pop. 321

——— WHERE TO STAY ———

DAWSON INN

Small-scale Hotel
$55-$63 All Year

Phone: 304/392-6661

Address: 2625 Lawn Rd 25976 **Location:** I-64, exit 150, just s. **Facility:** 24 one-bedroom standard units. 2 stories (no elevator), interior corridors. **Parking:** on-site. **Terms:** cancellation fee imposed. **Amenities:** hair dryers. **Cards:** AX, DS, MC, VI.

MINERAL WELLS pop. 1,860

——— WHERE TO STAY ———

AMERIHOST INN PARKERSBURG SOUTH AT I-77 · *Book at AAA.com*

Small-scale Hotel
Rates not provided

Phone: 304/489-3111

Address: 201 Hospitality Ln 26150 **Location:** I-77, exit 170, just w. **Facility:** 61 one-bedroom standard units, some with whirlpools. 2 stories (no elevator), interior corridors. *Bath:* combo or shower only. **Parking:** on-site. **Amenities:** high-speed Internet, voice mail, safes (fee), irons, hair dryers. *Some:* DVD players. **Pool(s):** heated indoor. **Leisure Activities:** whirlpool, exercise room. **Guest Services:** valet and coin laundry, wireless Internet. **Business Services:** meeting rooms, fax (fee).

COMFORT SUITES *Book at AAA.com*

Small-scale Hotel
$84-$160 All Year

Phone: (304)489-9600

Address: 167 Elizabeth Pike 26150 **Location:** I-77, exit 170, 0.3 mi se. **Facility:** 114 one-bedroom standard units, some with efficiencies and/or whirlpools. 3 stories, interior/exterior corridors. **Parking:** on-site. **Terms:** check-in 4 pm. **Amenities:** voice mail, irons, hair dryers. **Pool(s):** heated indoor/outdoor. **Leisure Activities:** sauna, whirlpool, exercise room. **Guest Services:** coin laundry, wireless Internet. **Business Services:** meeting rooms, PC, fax. **Cards:** AX, CB, DC, DS, JC, MC, VI.

HAMPTON INN-PARKERSBURG *Book great rates at AAA.com*

Small-scale Hotel
Rates not provided

Phone: 304/489-2900

Address: 64 Elizabeth Pike 26150 **Location:** I-77, exit 170, just e on SR 14. **Facility:** 68 one-bedroom standard units. 3 stories, interior corridors. *Bath:* combo or shower only. **Parking:** on-site. **Amenities:** high-speed Internet, voice mail, irons, hair dryers. **Pool(s):** outdoor. **Leisure Activities:** exercise room. **Guest Services:** valet and coin laundry, wireless Internet. **Business Services:** meeting rooms, fax (fee).

HOLIDAY INN EXPRESS HOTEL & SUITES
PARKERSBURG/MINERAL WELLS

[fyi]

Small-scale Hotel
$95-$109 All Year

Phone: 304/489-4111

Too new to rate. **Address:** 80 Nicholette Rd 26150 **Location:** I-77, exit 170. **Amenities:** 86 units, coffeemakers, microwaves, refrigerators, pool. **Cards:** AX, DC, DS, MC, VI.

——— WHERE TO DINE ———

NAPOLI'S

Italian
$6-$15

Phone: 304/422-1111

A tradition for 37 years, the family restaurant serves fresh pasta and other Italian entrees in its six West Virginia locations. Casual dress. **Bar:** Beer & wine. **Hours:** 11 am-10 pm. Closed: 12/25. **Address:** 102 Nicollette Rd 26150 **Location:** I-77, exit 170, just w. **Parking:** on-site. **Cards:** MC, VI.

MOOREFIELD pop. 2,375

——— WHERE TO STAY ———

SOUTH BRANCH INN

Small-scale Hotel
$72-$116 All Year

Phone: 304/538-2033

Address: 1500 US 220 N 26836 **Location:** On US 220/SR 28, 1.3 mi n. **Facility:** 100 one-bedroom standard units, some with whirlpools. 2 stories (no elevator), interior corridors. *Bath:* combo or shower only. **Parking:** on-site. **Terms:** check-in 4 pm. **Amenities:** hair dryers. **Leisure Activities:** exercise room. **Guest Services:** coin laundry, wireless Internet. **Business Services:** meeting rooms, fax (fee). **Cards:** AX, DC, DS, MC, VI.

--- **WHERE TO DINE** ---

O'NEILLS

American
$6-$22

Phone: 304/530-2727

A wonderful place to escape, the restaurant invites guests to unwind with varied selections of flavorful food. Servers are outgoing. Casual dress. **Bar:** Full bar. **Hours:** 7 am-9 pm. Closed: 12/25; also Sun. **Address:** 614 N Main St 26836 **Location:** 1.1 mi n on US 220/SR 28. **Parking:** on-site. **Cards:** AX, DS, MC, VI.

MORGANTOWN pop. 26,809—*See also STAR CITY.*

--- **WHERE TO STAY** ---

COMFORT INN-MORGANTOWN   *Book great rates at AAA.com*

  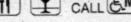

Small-scale Hotel
$69-$125 All Year

Phone: (304)296-9364

Address: 225 Comfort Inn Dr 26508 **Location:** I-68, exit 1, 0.3 mi n on US 119. **Facility:** 80 one-bedroom standard units, some with whirlpools. 2 stories (no elevator), interior corridors. **Parking:** on-site. **Amenities:** high-speed Internet, safes (fee), irons, hair dryers. **Pool(s):** outdoor. **Leisure Activities:** whirlpool, exercise room. **Guest Services:** valet laundry, wireless Internet. **Business Services:** meeting rooms. **Cards:** AX, CB, DC, DS, JC, MC, VI. **Free Special Amenities: continental breakfast and high-speed Internet.**

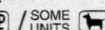

EURO-SUITES HOTEL   *Book great rates at AAA.com*

Small-scale Hotel
$109-$259 All Year

Phone: (304)598-1000

Address: 501 Chestnut Ridge Rd 26505 **Location:** I-79, exit 155, 2 mi s on US 19, then 1 mi e on SR 705. **Facility:** 79 one-bedroom standard units, some with kitchens. 5 stories, interior corridors. *Bath:* combo or shower only. **Parking:** on-site. **Amenities:** high-speed Internet, voice mail, irons, hair dryers. *Some:* DVD players, CD players. **Guest Services:** valet laundry, area transportation-hospital, wireless Internet. **Business Services:** meeting rooms, business center. **Cards:** AX, CB, DC, DS, MC, VI. **Free Special Amenities: full breakfast and high-speed Internet.**

FRIENDS INN

Motel
$50-$150 All Year

Phone: (304)599-4850

Address: 452 Country Club Rd 26505 **Location:** I-79, exit 155, s on US 19 to SR 705, then e on University Ave. Located adjacent to University Health Center. **Facility:** 54 one-bedroom standard units, some with whirlpools. 2 stories (no elevator), exterior corridors. *Bath:* combo or shower only. **Parking:** on-site. **Terms:** 2 night minimum stay - seasonal, 14 day cancellation notice-fee imposed. **Amenities:** hair dryers. *Some:* irons. **Guest Services:** wireless Internet. **Business Services:** fax (fee). **Cards:** AX, CB, DC, DS, JC, MC, VI. **Free Special Amenities: local telephone calls and newspaper.**

HAMPTON INN   *Book great rates at AAA.com*

Small-scale Hotel
$119-$149 All Year

Phone: 304/599-1200

Address: 1053 Van Voorhis Rd 26505 **Location:** I-79, exit 155, 2 mi s on US 19, then 0.7 mi e on SR 705. **Facility:** 107 one-bedroom standard units. 5 stories, interior corridors. *Bath:* combo or shower only. **Parking:** on-site. **Terms:** cancellation fee imposed. **Amenities:** high-speed Internet, voice mail, irons, hair dryers. **Guest Services:** valet laundry, wireless Internet. **Business Services:** meeting rooms, business center. **Cards:** AX, DS, MC, VI. *(See color ad below)*

--- ▼ *See AAA listing above* ▼ ---

HISTORIC CLARION HOTEL MORGAN

Book at AAA.com

Phone: (304)292-8200

Historic
Small-scale Hotel
$99-$210 All Year

Address: 127 High St 26505 **Location:** On High St between Pleasant and Kirk sts; downtown; center. **Facility:** Built in the 1920s, the hotel has retained many elegant features; its comfortable, modern amenities offer a touch of old-time style and class. 76 one-bedroom standard units, some with whirlpools. 7 stories, interior corridors. **Parking:** on-site. **Terms:** cancellation fee imposed. **Amenities:** high-speed Internet, voice mail, safes (fee), irons, hair dryers. **Leisure Activities:** exercise room. **Guest Services:** valet laundry, area transportation, wireless Internet. **Business Services:** meeting rooms, business center. **Cards:** AX, DC, DS, MC, VI.

HOLIDAY INN EXPRESS

Book at AAA.com

Phone: 304/291-2600

Small-scale Hotel
Rates not provided

Address: 605 Venture Dr 26508 **Location:** I-68, exit 7, just n. **Facility:** 68 one-bedroom standard units, some with whirlpools. 3 stories, interior corridors. **Bath:** combo or shower only. **Amenities:** high-speed Internet, dual phone lines, voice mail, irons, hair dryers. **Pool(s):** heated indoor. **Leisure Activities:** whirlpool, exercise room. **Guest Services:** valet laundry, wireless Internet. **Business Services:** meeting rooms, business center.

MORGANTOWN ECONO LODGE

Book great rates at AAA.com

Phone: (304)296-8774

Motel
$65 All Year

Address: 15 Commerce Dr 26502 **Location:** I-79, exit 152, 0.4 mi e on US 19. Located adjacent to shopping plaza. **Facility:** 78 one-bedroom standard units. 2 stories (no elevator), interior corridors. **Parking:** on-site. **Amenities:** high-speed Internet. **Guest Services:** valet and coin laundry. **Cards:** AX, DC, DS, MC, VI. **Free Special Amenities:** continental breakfast and high-speed Internet.

RAMADA CONFERENCE CENTER

Book great rates at AAA.com

Phone: 304/296-3431

Small-scale Hotel
Rates not provided

Address: 20 Scott Ave 26508 **Location:** I-68, exit 1, 0.3 mi n. **Facility:** 149 one-bedroom standard units, some with whirlpools. 4 stories, interior corridors. **Bath:** combo or shower only. **Parking:** on-site. **Amenities:** high-speed Internet, voice mail, safes (fee), irons, hair dryers. **Pool(s):** heated outdoor. **Leisure Activities:** exercise room, volleyball. **Guest Services:** valet and coin laundry, airport transportation-Morgantown Airport, area transportation-bus station, wireless Internet. **Business Services:** meeting rooms, business center. **Free Special Amenities:** full breakfast and high-speed Internet.

RESIDENCE INN BY MARRIOTT MORGANTOWN

Book great rates at AAA.com

Phone: 304/599-0237

Small-scale Hotel
$128-$157 All Year

Address: 1046 Willowdale Rd 26505 **Location:** I-79, exit 155, 2 mi s on US 19, then 0.9 mi e on SR 705. **Facility:** Smoke free premises. 104 one-bedroom standard units with kitchens. 4 stories, interior corridors. **Bath:** combo or shower only. **Parking:** on-site. **Terms:** check-in 4 pm. **Amenities:** high-speed Internet, dual phone lines, voice mail, irons, hair dryers. **Pool(s):** heated indoor. **Leisure Activities:** whirlpool, exercise room, sports court. **Guest Services:** coin laundry, wireless Internet. **Business Services:** meeting rooms, business center. **Cards:** AX, DS, MC, VI.

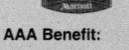

AAA Benefit:

Members save 5% off of the best available rate.

▼ See AAA listing p 990 ▼

WATERFRONT PLACE HOTEL

Large-scale Hotel
$89-$279 All Year

Book great rates at AAA.com

Phone: (304)296-1700

Address: 2 Waterfront Pl 26501 **Location:** I-68, exit 1, just n. **Facility:** 205 one-bedroom standard units. 11 stories, interior corridors. *Bath:* combo or shower only. **Parking:** on-site and valet. **Terms:** cancellation fee imposed. **Amenities:** video games, high-speed Internet, dual phone lines, voice mail, irons, hair dryers. **Dining:** The Regatta Bar & Grille, see separate listing. **Pool(s):** indoor. **Leisure Activities:** whirlpool, exercise room, spa. **Guest Services:** valet laundry, area transportation-within 5 mi, wireless Internet. **Business Services:** conference facilities, business center. **Cards:** AX, DS, MC, VI. **Free Special Amenities:** newspaper and high-speed Internet. *(See color ad p 989)*

——— WHERE TO DINE ———

ASIAN GARDEN RESTAURANT

Chinese
$5-$15

Phone: 304/599-1888

The laid-back restaurant serves such flavorful dishes as phai pepper chicken and stir-fried scallops with snow peas, shiitake mushrooms, carrots, broccoli and bamboo shoots in a garlic brown sauce. The lengthy menu also offers Thai and Malaysian cuisine. The relaxed dining area displays Asian artwork and collectibles. Casual dress. **Bar:** Beer & wine. **Reservations:** suggested, weekends. **Hours:** 11 am-2 & 4:30-9:30 pm, Fri-10 pm, Sat 4:30 pm-10 pm. Closed major holidays; also Sun. **Address:** 3109 University Ave, Suite D 26505 **Location:** I-79, exit 155, 1.3 mi s on US 19, just e on Boyers Ave, then 1 mi s; in Sellaro Plaza. **Parking:** on-site. **Cards:** AX, DC, DS, MC, VI.

FLYING FISH AND CO.

Seafood
$5-$12

Phone: 304/225-3474

This restaurant has a wonderful, casual atmosphere and incredibly fresh seafood. Casual dress. **Bar:** Beer only. **Hours:** 11 am-8 pm. Closed: Sun. **Address:** 1111 Van Voorhis Rd 26505 **Location:** I-79, exit 155, 2 mi s on US 19, then 0.8 mi e on SR 705. **Parking:** on-site. **Cards:** AX, DC, DS, MC, VI.

THE GLASSHOUSE GRILLE

American
$8-$24

Phone: 304/296-8460

The relaxed restaurant entices diners interested in fine dining in a cozy, candlelit setting. On the varied menu are fresh seafood, chargrilled steaks and a generous array of homemade fare: soups, sauces, dressing and desserts. The wine list has received awards. Casual dress. **Bar:** Full bar. **Reservations:** suggested. **Hours:** 11 am-2 & 5-9 pm. Closed major holidays; also Sun. **Address:** 709 Beechurst Ave 26505 **Location:** I-79, exit 155, 3.5 mi e on US 19/SR 7; in Seneca Center. **Parking:** on-site. **Cards:** AX, DC, DS, MC, VI.

PEKING HOUSE

Chinese
$5-$14

Phone: 304/598-3333

You can enjoy all your Chinese favorites in a warm Oriental atmosphere that is a Morgantown staple for meals. Casual dress. **Bar:** Full bar. **Hours:** 11:30 am-2 & 4:30-9:30 pm. **Address:** 1125 Van Voorhis Rd 26505 **Location:** I-79, exit 155, 2 mi s on US 19, then 0.9 mi e on SR 705. **Parking:** on-site. **Cards:** AX, CB, DC, DS, JC, MC, VI.

PRIME THYME

American
$6-$20

Phone: 304/292-9190

Prime Thyme has all the classic American favorites. No need to just go at prime time, they are opne for lunch also. Friendly wait staff abound. Casual dress. **Bar:** Full bar. **Hours:** 11 am-10 pm. Closed: Mon. **Address:** 226 Comfort Inn Dr 26508 **Location:** I-68, exit 1, 0.3 mi n on US 119. **Parking:** on-site. **Cards:** AX, CB, DC, DS, JC, MC, VI.

THE REGATTA BAR & GRILLE

American
$8-$24

Phone: 304/284-9850

The riverside restaurant affords wonderful views. The dining room carries out a regatta and nautical theme. On the menu are all the American classics. Casual dress. **Bar:** Full bar. **Hours:** 11 am-10 pm. **Address:** 2 Waterfront Pl 26501 **Location:** I-68, exit 1, just n; in Waterfront Place Hotel. **Parking:** on-site and valet. **Cards:** AX, CB, DC, DS, JC, MC, VI.

NEW MARTINSVILLE pop. 5,984

——— WHERE TO STAY ———

AMERIHOST INN-NEW MARTINSVILLE

Small-scale Hotel
Rates not provided

Book great rates at AAA.com

Phone: 304/455-6100

Address: 166 N SR 2 26155 **Location:** 1.5 mi n on SR 2; 0.3 mi n of bridge. **Facility:** 60 one-bedroom standard units, some with whirlpools. 2 stories (no elevator), interior corridors. *Bath:* combo or shower only. **Parking:** on-site. **Amenities:** voice mail, safes (fee), irons, hair dryers. *Some:* high-speed Internet. **Pool(s):** heated indoor. **Leisure Activities:** whirlpool, limited exercise equipment. **Guest Services:** valet laundry, wireless Internet. **Business Services:** PC, fax (fee). **Free Special Amenities:** expanded continental breakfast and local telephone calls.

NITRO pop. 6,824

———— WHERE TO STAY ————

ECONO LODGE *Book at AAA.com*   Phone: (304)755-8341

Motel
$50-$60 All Year

Address: 4115 1st Ave 25143 **Location:** I-64, exit 45, 0.8 mi e on SR 25. **Facility:** 42 one-bedroom standard units. 2-3 stories (no elevator), exterior corridors. **Parking:** on-site. **Amenities:** irons, hair dryers. **Business Services:** meeting rooms. **Cards:** AX, DC, DS, MC, VI.

———— WHERE TO DINE ————

TUDOR'S BISCUIT WORLD   Phone: 304/755-2001

American
$5-$12

Serving breakfast all day folks can stop into Tudor's Biscuit World to sample their many varieities of homemade biscuit sandwiches. Known for fast and friendly service in a clean casual atmosphere. Casual dress. **Hours:** 24 hours. Closed: 12/25. **Address:** 4113 1st Ave 25143 **Location:** I-64, exit 45, 0.9 mi e on SR 25. **Parking:** on-site.

OAK HILL pop. 7,589

———— WHERE TO STAY ————

HOLIDAY INN *Book great rates at AAA.com*   Phone: (304)465-0571

Small-scale Hotel
$125 All Year

Address: 340 Oyler Ave 25901 **Location:** US 19, exit Oyler Ave, just w. **Facility:** 119 one-bedroom standard units. 3 stories, interior corridors. **Parking:** on-site. **Terms:** 7 day cancellation notice. **Amenities:** high-speed Internet, voice mail, safes, irons, hair dryers. **Pool(s):** heated indoor. **Leisure Activities:** whirlpool. **Guest Services:** coin laundry, wireless Internet. **Business Services:** conference facilities. **Cards:** AX, DC, DS, MC, VI. *(See color ad below)*

    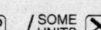

PARKERSBURG pop. 33,099

———— WHERE TO STAY ————

THE BLENNERHASSETT *Book at AAA.com*   Phone: (304)422-3131

Small-scale Hotel
$109-$269 All Year

Address: 320 Market St 26101 **Location:** Between Fourth and Fifth sts; downtown. **Facility:** 89 one-bedroom standard units, some with whirlpools. 4 stories, interior corridors. *Bath:* combo or shower only. **Parking:** on-site and valet. **Terms:** cancellation fee imposed. **Amenities:** high-speed Internet, voice mail, irons, hair dryers. *Some:* DVD players, CD players. **Leisure Activities:** exercise room. **Guest Services:** valet laundry, wireless Internet. **Business Services:** meeting rooms, business center. **Cards:** AX, DS, MC, VI.

COMFORT INN *Book great rates at AAA.com*   Phone: 304/424-5300

Small-scale Hotel
Rates not provided

Address: 401 37th St 26101 **Location:** 2.4 mi n on SR 14, via SR 14 and 68; 0.9 mi n of Memorial Bridge. **Facility:** 78 one-bedroom standard units, some with whirlpools. 2 stories (no elevator), interior corridors. *Bath:* combo or shower only. **Parking:** on-site. **Amenities:** high-speed Internet, voice mail, safes (fee), irons, hair dryers. **Pool(s):** heated indoor. **Leisure Activities:** whirlpool, board games. **Guest Services:** valet laundry, wireless Internet. **Business Services:** meeting rooms, PC, fax. **Free Special Amenities:** expanded continental breakfast and high-speed Internet.

▼ See AAA listing above ▼

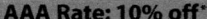

HOLIDAY INN PARKERSBURG

Phone: 304/485-6200

Small-scale Hotel
Rates not provided

Address: 225 Holiday Hills Dr 26104 **Location:** I-77, exit 176, just e. **Facility:** 149 one-bedroom standard units, some with efficiencies. 2 stories (no elevator), interior corridors. **Parking:** on-site. **Amenities:** video games, high-speed Internet, irons, hair dryers. **Pool(s):** heated indoor. **Leisure Activities:** saunas, whirlpool, exercise room. **Guest Services:** valet and coin laundry, wireless Internet. **Business Services:** meeting rooms.

KNIGHTS INN   *Book at AAA.com*

Phone: 304/420-2420

Motel
Rates not provided

Address: 3604 1/2 7th St 26104 **Location:** I-77, exit 176, just w. **Facility:** 51 one-bedroom standard units, some with whirlpools. 1 story, exterior corridors. **Parking:** on-site. **Guest Services:** wireless Internet. **Business Services:** meeting rooms, fax.

RED CARPET INN   *Book great rates at AAA.com*

Phone: (304)485-1851

Motel
$45-$65 All Year

Address: 6333 Emerson Ave 26101 **Location:** I-77, exit 179, 0.4 mi sw on SR 68. **Facility:** 46 one-bedroom standard units, some with whirlpools. 2 stories (no elevator), exterior corridors. **Parking:** on-site. **Terms:** 1-7 night minimum stay - seasonal. **Business Services:** fax. **Cards:** AX, DS, MC, VI. **Free Special Amenities:** continental breakfast and high-speed Internet.

RED ROOF INN   *Book at AAA.com*

Phone: 304/485-1741

Motel
Rates not provided

Address: 3714 E 7th St 26104 **Location:** I-77, exit 176, just w on US 50. **Facility:** 105 one-bedroom standard units. 2 stories (no elevator), exterior corridors. **Parking:** on-site. **Amenities:** video games, voice mail. *Some:* irons, hair dryers. **Leisure Activities:** exercise room. **Guest Services:** coin laundry. **Business Services:** meeting rooms, fax (fee).

TRAVELODGE PARKERSBURG   *Book at AAA.com*

Phone: 304/424-5100

Motel
Rates not provided

Address: 3604 E 7th St 26104 **Location:** I-77, exit 176, just w. **Facility:** 95 one-bedroom standard units, some with whirlpools. 1 story, exterior corridors. **Parking:** on-site. **Amenities:** hair dryers. **Pool(s):** outdoor. **Leisure Activities:** exercise room. **Guest Services:** coin laundry, wireless Internet. **Business Services:** meeting rooms, fax (fee).

── **WHERE TO DINE** ──

J. P. HENRY'S

Phone: 304/485-9390

American
$8-$22

At this restaurant they do all the work, so you can have all the fun. Friendly service and a very diverse menu. Casual dress. **Bar:** Full bar. **Hours:** 4 pm-11 pm, Sat & Sun from 1 pm. Closed: 12/25. **Address:** 5106 Emerson Ave 26101 **Location:** I-77, exit 179, 2.4 mi sw on SR 86. **Parking:** on-site. **Cards:** AX, CB, DC, DS, JC, MC, VI.

MOUNTAINEER FAMILY RESTAURANT

Phone: 304/422-0101

American
$5-$12

With the restaurant being open 24 hours a day, it gives the guest great freedom to come and dine anytime, and that is their motto: Mountaineers are always free. Casual dress. **Hours:** 24 hours. Closed: 12/25. **Address:** 4006 7th St 26101 **Location:** I-77, exit 176, just w. **Parking:** on-site. **Cards:** AX, CB, DC, DS, MC, VI.

THE RIVER CITY TAVERN & GRILL

Phone: 304/865-2400

American
$7-$20

Guests can peruse a diverse men while relaxing in the casually fun setting. The award-winning ribs are a popular choice. Casual dress. **Bar:** Full bar. **Hours:** 11 am-11 pm. Closed: 12/25. **Address:** 3420 Murdoch Ave 26101 **Location:** 1.1 mi n on SR 14. **Parking:** on-site. **Cards:** AX, CB, DC, DS, JC, MC, VI.

PETERSBURG pop. 2,423

── **WHERE TO STAY** ──

HERMITAGE MOTOR INN

Phone: (304)257-1711

Small-scale Hotel
$63-$65 All Year

Address: 203 Virginia Ave 26847 **Location:** 0.3 mi n on US 220/SR 28/55. **Facility:** 38 one-bedroom standard units. 2 stories (no elevator), interior/exterior corridors. *Bath:* combo or shower only. **Parking:** on-site. **Dining:** Hermitage Inn Restaurant, see separate listing. **Pool(s):** outdoor. **Leisure Activities:** whirlpool. **Guest Services:** wireless Internet. **Business Services:** meeting rooms, fax (fee). **Cards:** AX, DC, DS, MC, VI.

HOMESTEAD INN AND MOTEL   Phone: 304/257-1049

(AAA) [SAVE]

Motel
$59-$65 All Year

Address: SR 28/55 26847 **Location:** On SR 55 and 28, 1.5 mi w. Located in a rural area. **Facility:** 12 one-bedroom standard units. 2 stories (no elevator), exterior corridors. **Parking:** on-site. **Amenities:** voice mail. **Business Services:** fax (fee). **Cards:** AX, CB, DC, DS, MC, VI.

------- WHERE TO DINE -------

HERMITAGE INN RESTAURANT   Phone: 304/257-4800

American
$5-$20

Homespun goodness, country cooking and friendly service await patrons of the restaurant. Casual dress. **Hours:** 11 am-9 pm, Sat from 4 pm, Sun 11 am-2 pm. Closed: 12/25. **Address:** 203 Virginia Ave 26847 **Location:** 0.3 mi n on US 220/SR 28/55; in Hermitage Motor Inn. **Parking:** on-site. **Cards:** AX, CB, DC, DS, JC, MC, VI.

PHILIPPI pop. 2,870

------- WHERE TO STAY -------

PHILIPPI LODGING   Phone: (304)457-5888

Motel
$46-$83 All Year

Address: Rt 4, Box 155 26416 **Location:** 2.5 mi s on US 250. **Facility:** 39 one-bedroom standard units, some with whirlpools. 2 stories (no elevator), interior corridors. **Parking:** on-site. **Guest Services:** wireless Internet. **Cards:** AX, DC, DS, MC, VI.

------- WHERE TO DINE -------

PHILIPPI INN RESTAURANT   Phone: 304/457-1733

American
$5-$17

This restaurant thrives on home cooking, a huge menu selection and a friendly, welcoming staff. Casual dress. **Hours:** 6 am-8 pm, Fri & Sat-9 pm, Sun 7 am-8 pm. Closed: 11/27, 12/25. **Address:** Rt 250 S 26416 **Location:** On US 250, 2.5 mi s. **Parking:** on-site. **Cards:** MC, VI.

POINT PLEASANT pop. 4,637

------- WHERE TO DINE -------

TUDOR'S BISCUIT WORLD   Phone: 304/675-6166

American
$5-$10

Serving breakfast all day folks can stop into Tudor's Biscuit World to sample their many varieities of homemade biscuit sandwiches. Known for fast and friendly service in a clean casual atmosphere. Casual dress. **Hours:** 5:30-2 pm, Sun from 7 am. Closed: 12/25. **Address:** 2322 Jackson Ave 25550 **Location:** 1.8 mi e on SR 2. **Parking:** on-site.

PRINCETON pop. 6,347

------- WHERE TO STAY -------

COMFORT INN-PRINCETON   *Book at AAA.com*   Phone: (304)487-6101

Small-scale Hotel
$65-$85 All Year

Address: 136 Ambrose Ln 24740 **Location:** I-77, exit 9, 0.3 mi w on US 460. **Facility:** 51 one-bedroom standard units, some with whirlpools. 2 stories (no elevator), interior corridors. **Parking:** on-site. **Amenities:** high-speed Internet, safes (fee), irons, hair dryers. **Leisure Activities:** whirlpool. **Guest Services:** valet laundry, wireless Internet. **Cards:** AX, CB, DC, DS, JC, MC, VI.

DAYS INN   *Book great rates at AAA.com*   Phone: 304/425-8100

(AAA) [SAVE]

Small-scale Hotel
Rates not provided

Address: 347 Meadowfield Ln 24740 **Location:** I-77, exit 9, 0.3 mi w on US 460, just s on Ambrose Ln, then just e. Graveled truck and camper parking on site. **Facility:** 122 one-bedroom standard units. 2 stories (no elevator), exterior corridors. **Parking:** on-site. **Amenities:** voice mail, hair dryers. *Some:* irons. **Pool(s):** indoor. **Leisure Activities:** whirlpool. **Guest Services:** valet and coin laundry, wireless Internet. **Business Services:** meeting rooms. **Free Special Amenities:** expanded continental breakfast and local telephone calls.

HAMPTON INN   *Book great rates at AAA.com*   Phone: 304/431-2580

Small-scale Hotel
Rates not provided

Address: 277 Meadowfield Ln 24740 **Location:** I-77, exit 9, 0.3 mi w on US 460, just s on Ambrose Ln, then just e. **Facility:** 112 one-bedroom standard units. 5 stories, interior corridors. **Bath:** combo or shower only. **Parking:** on-site. **Amenities:** voice mail, irons, hair dryers. **Pool(s):** heated indoor. **Leisure Activities:** whirlpool, exercise room. **Guest Services:** valet laundry, wireless Internet. **Business Services:** meeting rooms, business center.

HOLIDAY INN EXPRESS PRINCETON *Book great rates at AAA.com* Phone: (304)425-8156

Small-scale Hotel
$85-$125 All Year

Address: 805 Oakvale Rd 24740 **Location:** I-77, exit 9, just w. **Facility:** 70 one-bedroom standard units. 3 stories, interior corridors. *Bath:* combo or shower only. **Parking:** on-site. **Amenities:** high-speed Internet, voice mail, irons, hair dryers. **Pool(s):** heated indoor. **Leisure Activities:** whirlpool, limited exercise equipment. **Guest Services:** valet and coin laundry, wireless Internet. **Business Services:** meeting rooms, business center. **Cards:** AX, DS,. MC, VI. **Free Special Amenities: continental breakfast and high-speed Internet.**

SLEEP INN & SUITES *Book great rates at AAA.com* Phone: (304)431-2800

Small-scale Hotel
$99-$225 All Year

Address: 1015 Oakvale Rd 24740 **Location:** I-77, exit 9, just w on US 460, then just n via service road. **Facility:** 109 one-bedroom standard units. 3 stories, interior corridors. *Bath:* combo or shower only. **Parking:** on-site. **Amenities:** high-speed Internet, safes (fee), irons, hair dryers. **Pool(s):** heated indoor. **Leisure Activities:** whirlpool. **Guest Services:** valet laundry, wireless Internet. **Business Services:** meeting rooms. **Cards:** AX, CB, DC, DS, JC, MC, VI.

----------- **WHERE TO DINE** -----------

EL MARIACHI Phone: 304/431-2059

Mexican
$6-$14

The restaurant features authentic Mexican cuisine at very affordable prices along with a huge drink and dessert menu and a fun, casual setting. Casual dress. **Bar:** Full bar. **Hours:** 11 am-9 pm. Closed: 12/25. **Address:** 1025 Stafford Dr 24740 **Location:** I-77, exit 9, just w. **Parking:** on-site. **Cards:** AX, CB, DC, DS, JC, MC, VI.

VINCENZA'S Phone: 304/425-0214

Italian
$8-$25

Choice steaks and seafood, as well as Italian dishes, are prepared in a fine-dining atmosphere. Guests can expect friendly service. Homemade desserts are tempting. Casual dress. **Bar:** Full bar. **Hours:** 11 am-10 pm. Closed: 12/25; also Mon. **Address:** 801 Oakvale Rd 24740 **Location:** I-77, exit 9, just w. **Parking:** on-site. **Cards:** AX, CB, DC, DS, JC, MC, VI.

RIPLEY pop. 3,263

----------- **WHERE TO STAY** -----------

BEST WESTERN MCCOYS INN & CONFERENCE CENTER *Book great rates at AAA.com* Phone: 304/372-9122

Small-scale Hotel
Rates not provided

Address: 701 W Main St 25271 **Location:** I-77, exit 138, just e. **Facility:** 137 one-bedroom standard units, some with whirlpools. 2 stories (no elevator), interior/exterior corridors. *Bath:* combo or shower only. **Parking:** on-site. **Amenities:** voice mail, irons, hair dryers. **Pool(s):** heated outdoor. **Leisure Activities:** whirlpool, horseshoes. **Guest Services:** valet and coin laundry, wireless Internet. **Business Services:** conference facilities, administrative services, PC. **Free Special Amenities: full breakfast and local telephone calls.**

AAA Benefit:
Members save 10% everyday, plus an exclusive frequent stay program.

HOLIDAY INN EXPRESS *Book great rates at AAA.com* Phone: 304/372-5000

Small-scale Hotel
$89 All Year

Address: 1 Hospitality Dr 25271 **Location:** I-77, exit 138, just w on SR 33, then 0.3 mi n. **Facility:** 65 one-bedroom standard units, some with whirlpools. 2 stories (no elevator), interior/exterior corridors. *Bath:* combo or shower only. **Parking:** on-site. **Amenities:** dual phone lines, voice mail, irons, hair dryers. *Some:* high-speed Internet. **Leisure Activities:** exercise room. **Guest Services:** coin laundry, wireless Internet. **Business Services:** meeting rooms, fax (fee). **Cards:** AX, CB, DC, DS, JC, MC, VI. **Free Special Amenities: expanded continental breakfast and high-speed Internet.**

RIPLEY SUPER 8 MOTEL *Book at AAA.com* Phone: 304/372-8880

Motel
Rates not provided

Address: 102 Duke Dr 25271 **Location:** I-77, exit 138, just e on SR 33. **Facility:** 44 one-bedroom standard units. 2 stories (no elevator), interior corridors. **Parking:** on-site. **Amenities:** hair dryers. **Guest Services:** wireless Internet.

----------- **WHERE TO DINE** -----------

FRATELLO'S Phone: 304/373-0070

Italian
$5-$25

The diverse menu lists award-winning pasta dishes and other Italian favorites. Families appreciate the pleasant atmosphere. Homemade ice cream is a delicious meal-ender. Casual dress. **Bar:** Beer & wine. **Reservations:** accepted. **Hours:** 11 am-9 pm, Fri & Sat-10 pm, Sun noon-9 pm. Closed: 1/1, 11/27, 12/25. **Address:** 1825 Rt 21 S & I-77 25271 **Location:** I-77, exit 132, just ne. **Parking:** on-site. **Cards:** AX, DC, MC, VI.

RIPPON

------- **WHERE TO DINE** -------

JOHN'S FAMILY RESTAURANT   **Phone:** 304/725-4348
This restaurant has a family atmosphere, home cooking and friendly people. Casual dress. **Hours:** 7 am-
9:30 pm. Closed: 1/1, 3/23, 12/25; also Sun. **Address:** Rt 340 25441 **Location:** Center. **Parking:** on-site.
American   **Cards:** MC, VI.
$5-$18

ROANOKE

------- **WHERE TO STAY** -------

STONEWALL RESORT   *Book great rates at AAA.com*   **Phone:** (304)269-7400

AAA SAVE

Resort
Large-scale Hotel
$99-$179 All Year

Address: 940 Resort Dr 26447 **Location:** I-79, exit 91, just e.
Facility: Nestled in the mountains, this resort brings guests close to
nature with a retreatlike ambience enhanced by many dining and
recreational choices. 208 units. 198 one-bedroom standard units, some
with whirlpools. 10 cottages. 3 stories, interior/exterior corridors. *Bath:*
combo or shower only. **Parking:** on-site and valet. **Terms:** check-in 4
pm, 2-3 night minimum stay - seasonal and/or weekends, 3 day
cancellation notice-fee imposed. **Amenities:** video games, high-speed
Internet, voice mail, irons, hair dryers. *Some:* CD players.
Dining: Stillwaters Restaurant, see separate listing. **Pool(s):** heated
indoor/outdoor. **Leisure Activities:** saunas, whirlpools, steamrooms,
boating, marina, waterskiing, fishing, excursion tour boat, recreation
programs, badminton, hiking trails, playground, exercise room, spa,
basketball, horseshoes, volleyball. *Fee:* canoes, paddleboats, golf-18
holes, bicycles, game room. **Guest Services:** valet laundry, area transportation-within 10 mi.
Business Services: conference facilities, business center. **Cards:** AX, DS, MC, VI.
(See color ad below)

 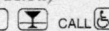 CALL   / SOME UNITS

------- ▼ See AAA listing above ▼ -------

——— WHERE TO DINE ———

STILLWATERS RESTAURANT   Phone: 304/269-7400

As the name implies, the restaurant nurtures a tranquil setting. Lakeside seating is a seasonal option. Casual dress. **Bar:** Full bar. **Hours:** 7 am-11 pm. **Address:** 940 Resort Dr 26447 **Location:** I-79, exit 91, just e; in Stonewall Resort. **Parking:** on-site. **Cards:** AX, CB, DC, DS, JC, MC, VI.

American
$9-$26

ROMNEY pop. 1,940

——— WHERE TO STAY ———

HAMPSHIRE HOUSE 1884   Phone: (304)822-7171

Historic Bed
& Breakfast
$95-$275 All Year

Address: 165 N Grafton St 26757 **Location:** Just ne of jct US 50 and SR 28; center. **Facility:** Very close to the Potomac Eagle train attraction, this restored, 1880s-era inn set in West Virginia's oldest hamlet includes many antiques. Designated smoking area. 5 one-bedroom standard units. 2 stories (no elevator), interior corridors. **Parking:** on-site. **Terms:** 3 day cancellation notice. **Amenities:** video library. **Guest Services:** wireless Internet. **Business Services:** meeting rooms. **Cards:** AX, DC, DS, MC, VI.

SOUTH BRANCH INN-ROMNEY   Phone: 304/822-2444

Small-scale Hotel
$72-$116 All Year

Address: US Rt 50 E 26757 **Location:** Just n on US 50; center. **Facility:** 61 one-bedroom standard units, some with whirlpools. 3 stories, interior corridors. *Bath:* combo or shower only. **Parking:** on-site. **Terms:** check-in 4 pm, cancellation fee imposed. **Amenities:** high-speed Internet, voice mail, irons, hair dryers. **Guest Services:** coin laundry. **Business Services:** meeting rooms, fax (fee). **Cards:** AX, DC, DS, MC, VI.

——— WHERE TO DINE ———

MARIO'S ITALIAN CUISINE   Phone: 304/822-7776

Italian
$6-$18

The fun and casual hometown place prepares many homemade pasta and desserts with care. Casual dress. **Bar:** Beer only. **Hours:** 11 am-9 pm. Closed: 12/25; also Mon. **Address:** 33 S High St 26757 **Location:** Just s. **Parking:** street. **Cards:** AX, CB, DC, DS, JC, MC, VI.

ST. ALBANS pop. 11,567

——— WHERE TO DINE ———

TUDOR'S BISCUIT WORLD   Phone: 304/722-2007

American
$5-$11

Serving breakfast all day folks can stop into Tudor's Biscuit World to sample their many varieities of homemade biscuit sandwiches. Known for fast and friendly service in a clean casual atmosphere. Casual dress. **Hours:** 5:30 am-2 pm, Sun from 6 am. Closed: 12/25. **Address:** 113 W Main St 25177 **Location:** 1.5 mi s on SR 35. **Parking:** on-site.

TUDOR'S BISCUIT WORLD   Phone: 304/722-2044

American
$5-$10

Serving breakfast all day folks can stop into Tudor's Biscuit World to sample their many varieities of homemade biscuit sandwiches. Known for fast and friendly service in a clean casual atmosphere. Casual dress. **Hours:** 5:30 am-2 pm, Sun from 7 am. Closed: 12/25. **Address:** 2503 MacCorkle Ave 25177 **Location:** I-64, exit 54, 1.2 mi w on US 60. **Parking:** on-site.

SCOTT DEPOT

——— WHERE TO DINE ———

TUDOR'S BISCUIT WORLD   Phone: 304/757-6868

American
$5-$12

Serving breakfast all day folks can stop into Tudor's Biscuit World to sample their many varieities of homemade biscuit sandwiches. Known for fast and friendly service in a clean casual atmosphere. Casual dress. **Hours:** 5:30 am-2 pm, Sun from 7 am. Closed: 12/25. **Address:** Great Teays Blvd 25560 **Location:** I-64, exit 39, just s. **Parking:** on-site.

SHEPHERDSTOWN pop. 803

———— WHERE TO STAY ————

BAVARIAN INN

Phone: 304/876-2551

Small-scale Hotel
$125-$355 All Year

Address: 164 Shepherd Grade Rd 25443 **Location:** 0.3 mi n on SR 480 at south end of Potomac River Bridge. **Facility:** A gazebo and walkways add appeal to the gardens around these alpine-style chalets, all of which offer good views of the Potomac River. 72 one-bedroom standard units, some with whirlpools. 3-4 stories, interior/exterior corridors. **Parking:** on-site. **Amenities:** CD players, high-speed Internet, voice mail, irons, hair dryers. *Some:* DVD players. **Dining:** restaurant, see separate listing. **Pool(s):** outdoor. **Leisure Activities:** putting green, lighted tennis court, hiking trails, exercise room. *Fee:* golf & tennis privileges, bicycles. **Guest Services:** valet laundry, wireless Internet. **Business Services:** meeting rooms, fax (fee). **Free Special Amenities: high-speed Internet.**
(See color ad p 982)

CLARION HOTEL & CONFERENCE CENTER   *Book great rates at AAA.com*
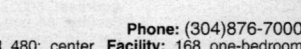

Phone: (304)876-7000

Small-scale Hotel
$130-$170 3/1-10/31
$100-$140 11/1-2/28

Address: 233 Lowe Dr 25443 **Location:** Just s on SR 480; center. **Facility:** 168 one-bedroom standard units, some with whirlpools. 4 stories, interior corridors. *Bath:* combo or shower only. **Parking:** on-site. **Terms:** check-in 4 pm, cancellation fee imposed. **Amenities:** high-speed Internet, voice mail, safes, irons, hair dryers. **Pool(s):** outdoor. **Leisure Activities:** sauna, whirlpool, steamroom, aerobic instruction, indoor walking & running track, hiking trails, exercise room, basketball, volleyball. *Fee:* golf & tennis privileges. **Guest Services:** coin laundry, area transportation-within 5 mi, wireless Internet. **Business Services:** conference facilities, business center. **Cards:** AX, DC, DS, MC, VI.

DAYS INN   *Book at AAA.com*

Phone: 304/876-3160

Small-scale Hotel
Rates not provided

Address: 70 Maddex Square Dr 25443 **Location:** Just w on SR 45; center. **Facility:** 51 one-bedroom standard units. 3 stories, interior corridors. *Bath:* combo or shower only. **Parking:** on-site. **Amenities:** voice mail, hair dryers. **Guest Services:** wireless Internet. **Business Services:** meeting rooms.

———— WHERE TO DINE ————

BAVARIAN INN DINING ROOM

Phone: 304/876-2551

Continental
$8-$35

German and American cuisine is served in a 1930s gray stone residence surrounded by well-manicured grounds. Wiener schnitzel is notably flavorful, and the well-presented torte is tasty and light. Service is courteous and prompt. Dressy casual. **Bar:** Full bar. **Reservations:** suggested. **Hours:** 7-10:30 am, 11:30-2:30 & 5-10 pm, Sat 7-10:30 am, 11:30-2:30 & 4-10 pm, Sun 7 am-10:30 & noon-9 pm. **Address:** 164 Shepherd Grade Rd 25443 **Location:** 0.3 mi n on SR 480 at south end of Potomac River Bridge; in Bavarian Inn. **Parking:** on-site. **Cards:** AX, CB, DC, DS, MC, VI. **Country Inn** *(See color ad p 982)*

THREE ONIONS

Phone: 304/876-8000

American
$6-$25

In historic downtown, the restaurant presents an ever-changing menu of dishes that pair with choices from the fine wine list. Casual dress. **Bar:** Full bar. **Hours:** 11:30 am-10 pm. Closed: 12/25; also Mon. **Address:** 117 E German St 25443 **Location:** Just e on German St; center. **Parking:** street. **Cards:** AX, CB, DC, DS, JC, MC, VI.

THE YELLOW BRICK BANK RESTAURANT

Phone: 304/876-2208

American
$6-$25

Set in an old bank with a bright new atmosphere, the restaurant has a wide variety on the menu and friendly service. Casual dress. **Bar:** Full bar. **Hours:** 11 am-9 pm. Closed: 11/27, 12/25. **Address:** 201 German St 25443 **Location:** Just e on German St; center. **Parking:** street. **Cards:** CB, DC, MC, VI.

SNOWSHOE

———— WHERE TO STAY ————

INN AT SNOWSHOE

Phone: 304/572-6520

Resort
Small-scale Hotel
Rates not provided

Address: SR 66 26209 **Location:** 0.5 mi e on SR 66, from US 219 jct, follow signs. **Facility:** Recreational opportunities abound at the sprawling complex, where visitors can ski, golf or stroll to nearby shops as well as spot wildlife. 151 one-bedroom standard units, some with whirlpools. 2 stories, interior corridors. **Parking:** on-site. **Terms:** check-in 5 pm. **Amenities:** voice mail, irons, hair dryers. **Pool(s):** heated indoor. **Leisure Activities:** whirlpools, exercise room, game room. **Guest Services:** coin laundry. **Business Services:** meeting rooms, fax (fee).

SOUTH CHARLESTON pop. 13,390—*See also CHARLESTON.*

——— WHERE TO STAY ———

HOLIDAY INN EXPRESS HOTEL & SUITES   *Book at AAA.com*   **Phone:** (304)746-4748
▼▼▼
Small-scale Hotel
$79-$189 All Year

Address: 95 RHL Blvd 25309 **Location:** I-64, exit 58A, 3.5 mi s. **Facility:** 84 one-bedroom standard units, some with whirlpools. 5 stories, interior corridors. *Bath:* combo or shower only. **Parking:** on-site. **Terms:** 14 day cancellation notice-fee imposed. **Amenities:** high-speed Internet, dual phone lines, voice mail, irons, hair dryers. **Pool(s):** heated indoor. **Leisure Activities:** whirlpool, exercise room. **Guest Services:** valet and coin laundry, wireless Internet. **Business Services:** meeting rooms, business center. **Cards:** AX, CB, DC, DS, JC, MC, VI.

(ASK) (S/D) (†↑) CALL (&M) (≈) (†) (▪) (▤) (▯) / SOME UNITS (✕)

MICROTEL INN   *Book great rates at AAA.com*   **Phone:** 304/744-4900
(AAA) (SAVE)
▼▼ ▼▼
Small-scale Hotel
$70-$130 All Year

Address: 600 2nd Ave 25303 **Location:** I-64, exit 56, just ne. Located in an industrial area. **Facility:** 84 one-bedroom standard units. 3 stories, interior corridors. *Bath:* combo or shower only. **Parking:** on-site. **Amenities:** hair dryers. **Leisure Activities:** exercise room. **Guest Services:** coin laundry, wireless Internet. **Business Services:** fax (fee). **Cards:** AX, DS, MC, VI. **Free Special Amenities: continental breakfast and high-speed Internet.**

CALL  / SOME UNITS (✕) FEE (▪) FEE (▤)

RAMADA PLAZA HOTEL CHARLESTON   *Book at AAA.com*   **Phone:** (304)744-4641
▼▼▼
Small-scale Hotel
$89-$139 All Year

Address: 400 2nd Ave 25303 **Location:** I-64, exit 56, just nw. Located in an industrial area. **Facility:** 170 one-bedroom standard units, some with whirlpools. 6 stories, interior corridors. **Parking:** on-site. **Amenities:** video games, dual phone lines, voice mail, irons, hair dryers. *Some:* high-speed Internet. **Pool(s):** heated indoor. **Leisure Activities:** whirlpool, exercise room. **Guest Services:** valet and coin laundry, wireless Internet. **Business Services:** conference facilities, business center. **Cards:** AX, CB, DC, DS, JC, MC, VI.

(ASK) (S/D) (✦) (†↑) (Ⓨ) CALL (&M) (≈) (†) (▯) / SOME UNITS FEE (†) (✕) (▪) (▤)

WINGATE INN-CHARLESTON   *Book at AAA.com*   **Phone:** (304)744-4444
▼▼▼
Small-scale Hotel
$99-$119 All Year

Address: 402 2nd Ave 25303 **Location:** I-64, exit 56, just nw. Located in an industrial area. **Facility:** 94 one-bedroom standard units, some with whirlpools. 6 stories, interior corridors. *Bath:* combo or shower only. **Parking:** on-site. **Amenities:** video games, high-speed Internet, voice mail, safes, irons, hair dryers. **Leisure Activities:** whirlpool, exercise room. **Guest Services:** coin laundry, wireless Internet. **Business Services:** meeting rooms, business center. **Cards:** AX, DC, DS, MC, VI.

(ASK) (S/D) (✦) (†↑) CALL (&M) (†) (▪) (▤) (▯) / SOME UNITS (✕)

STAR CITY pop. 1,366—*See also MORGANTOWN.*

——— WHERE TO STAY ———

BEST WESTERN MOUNTAINEER INN   *Book great rates at AAA.com*   **Phone:** 304/599-5399
(AAA) (SAVE)
▼▼ ▼▼
Small-scale Hotel
Rates not provided

Address: 366 Boyers Ave 26505 **Location:** I-79, exit 155, 1.4 mi e on SR 7. **Facility:** 100 one-bedroom standard units, some with whirlpools. 3 stories, interior corridors. **Parking:** on-site. **Amenities:** irons, hair dryers. **Pool(s):** heated indoor. **Leisure Activities:** exercise room. **Guest Services:** wireless Internet. **Business Services:** meeting rooms, business center. **Free Special Amenities: continental breakfast and early check-in/late check-out.**

(≈) (†) (▪) (▤) (▯) / SOME UNITS (✕)

AAA Benefit:
Members save 10% everyday, plus an exclusive frequent stay program.

ECONO LODGE-COLISEUM   *Book great rates at AAA.com*   **Phone:** (304)599-8181
(AAA) (SAVE)
▼▼
Small-scale Hotel
$64-$75 All Year

Address: 3506 Monongahela Blvd 26505 **Location:** I-79, exit 155, 1.4 mi s on US 119/SR 7. **Facility:** 72 one-bedroom standard units, some with whirlpools. 2 stories (no elevator), exterior corridors. *Bath:* combo or shower only. **Parking:** on-site. **Amenities:** hair dryers. **Guest Services:** wireless Internet. **Business Services:** fax (fee). **Cards:** AX, DS, MC, VI. **Free Special Amenities: continental breakfast and high-speed Internet.**

(S/D) (†) / SOME UNITS (†) (✕) (▪) (▤) (▯)

SUMMERSVILLE pop. 3,294

———— WHERE TO STAY ————

BEST WESTERN SUMMERSVILLE LAKE MOTOR
LODGE   *Book great rates at AAA.com*   Phone: 304/872-6900

Small-scale Hotel
Rates not provided

Address: 1203 S Broad St 26651 **Location:** US 19 and Broad St; 0.6 mi s of jct SR 39. Located in busy industrial area. **Facility:** 57 one-bedroom standard units. 3 stories, exterior corridors. **Parking:** on-site. **Amenities:** irons, hair dryers. **Guest Services:** coin laundry, wireless Internet. **Business Services:** fax (fee). **Free Special Amenities: full breakfast and high-speed Internet.**

AAA Benefit:
Members save 10% everyday, plus an exclusive frequent stay program.

COMFORT INN   *Book great rates at AAA.com*   Phone: (304)872-6500

Small-scale Hotel
$75-$180 All Year

Address: 903 Industrial Dr N 26651 **Location:** US 19, 1.9 mi n of jct SR 39. **Facility:** 99 one-bedroom standard units, some with whirlpools. 2 stories (no elevator), interior corridors. **Parking:** on-site. **Amenities:** irons, hair dryers. **Pool(s):** heated outdoor. **Leisure Activities:** sauna, racquetball courts, recreation programs, exercise room. **Guest Services:** coin laundry, wireless Internet. **Business Services:** meeting rooms, fax (fee). **Cards:** AX, DC, DS, MC, VI.

COUNTRY INN & SUITES   *Book great rates at AAA.com*   Phone: (304)872-0555

Small-scale Hotel
$89-$139 3/1-10/31
$79-$119 11/1-2/28

Address: 106 Merchants Walk 26651 **Location:** US 19, just w. **Facility:** 106 one-bedroom standard units, some with whirlpools. 4 stories, interior corridors. *Bath:* combo or shower only. **Parking:** on-site. **Terms:** cancellation fee imposed. **Amenities:** high-speed Internet, voice mail, irons, hair dryers. **Pool(s):** heated indoor. **Leisure Activities:** whirlpool, exercise room. **Guest Services:** coin laundry. **Business Services:** meeting rooms, fax (fee). **Cards:** AX, CB, DC, DS, MC, VI.

HAMPTON INN   *Book great rates at AAA.com*   Phone: 304/872-7100

Small-scale Hotel
Rates not provided

Address: 5400 Webster Rd 26651 **Location:** Just s on SR 41 from US 19. **Facility:** 75 one-bedroom standard units. 3 stories, interior corridors. **Amenities:** voice mail, irons, hair dryers. *Some:* DVD players. **Pool(s):** outdoor. **Leisure Activities:** playground, exercise room, horseshoes. **Guest Services:** valet laundry, wireless Internet. **Business Services:** meeting rooms, business center.

SLEEP INN OF SUMMERSVILLE   *Book great rates at AAA.com*   Phone: (304)872-4500

Small-scale Hotel
$65-$155 All Year

Address: 701 Professional Park Dr 26651 **Location:** US 19, 1.7 mi n of jct SR 39. Located at Northside Plaza. **Facility:** 95 one-bedroom standard units. 2 stories (no elevator), interior corridors. *Bath:* combo or shower only. **Parking:** on-site. **Amenities:** irons, hair dryers. **Pool(s):** heated outdoor. **Leisure Activities:** horseshoes, volleyball. **Guest Services:** coin laundry, wireless Internet. **Cards:** AX, DC, DS, MC, VI.

SUPER 8 MOTEL-SUMMERSVILLE   *Book at AAA.com*   Phone: 304/872-4888

Small-scale Hotel
Rates not provided

Address: 306 Merchants Walk 26651 **Location:** US 19, just n. **Facility:** 56 one-bedroom standard units. 3 stories (no elevator), interior corridors. **Parking:** on-site. **Amenities:** safes (fee), hair dryers. **Guest Services:** coin laundry, wireless Internet. **Business Services:** fax (fee).

TEAYS

———— WHERE TO STAY ————

DAYS INN TEAYS   *Book great rates at AAA.com*   Phone: 304/729-3006

Motel
Rates not provided

Address: Putnam Village Dr 25569 **Location:** I-64, exit 39, just n on SR 34, then just e. Located behind Liberty Square Shopping Center. **Facility:** 89 one-bedroom standard units. 1 story, exterior corridors. *Bath:* combo or shower only. **Parking:** on-site. **Amenities:** hair dryers. **Pool(s):** outdoor. **Free Special Amenities: continental breakfast and local telephone calls.**

TRIADELPHIA pop. 817

─────── **WHERE TO STAY** ───────

COMFORT INN-WHEELING   *Book great rates at AAA.com*   Phone: (304)547-0610

AAA [SAVE]

▽▽▽▽ ▽▽▽

Small-scale Hotel
$69-$129 All Year

Address: 675 Fort Henry Rd 26059 **Location:** I-70, exit 11, just n. **Facility:** 106 one-bedroom standard units, some with whirlpools. 2 stories (no elevator), interior corridors. **Parking:** on-site. **Amenities:** high-speed Internet, voice mail, irons, hair dryers. **Pool(s):** indoor. **Leisure Activities:** whirlpool, exercise room. **Guest Services:** coin laundry, wireless Internet. **Business Services:** meeting rooms, PC. **Cards:** AX, CB, DC, DS, JC, MC, VI. **Free Special Amenities: expanded continental breakfast and high-speed Internet.**

[icons] / SOME UNITS FEE [icons]

HOLIDAY INN EXPRESS WHEELING EAST   *Book great rates at AAA.com*   Phone: 304/547-1380

AAA [SAVE]

▽▽▽▽ ▽▽▽

Small-scale Hotel
$79-$145 All Year

Address: RR 1 26059 **Location:** I-70, exit 11. **Facility:** 115 one-bedroom standard units. 2 stories (no elevator), interior corridors. *Bath:* combo or shower only. **Parking:** on-site. **Amenities:** high-speed Internet, voice mail, irons, hair dryers. **Pool(s):** outdoor. **Leisure Activities:** exercise room. **Guest Services:** valet and coin laundry, wireless Internet. **Business Services:** meeting rooms, business center. **Cards:** AX, DS, MC, VI. **Free Special Amenities: expanded continental breakfast and high-speed Internet.**

[icons] CALL [icons] / SOME UNITS FEE [icons]

VIENNA pop. 10,861

─────── **WHERE TO STAY** ───────

WINGATE INN VIENNA/PARKERSBURG   *Book at AAA.com*   Phone: (304)295-5501

▽▽ ▽▽ ▽▽

Small-scale Hotel
$119-$129 All Year

Address: 1502 Grand Central Ave 26105 **Location:** I-77, exit 179, 3.9 mi w on SR 68. **Facility:** 76 one-bedroom standard units, some with whirlpools. 3 stories, interior corridors. *Bath:* combo or shower only. **Parking:** on-site. **Amenities:** video games, high-speed Internet, voice mail, safes, irons, hair dryers. **Pool(s):** heated indoor. **Leisure Activities:** whirlpool, exercise room. **Guest Services:** valet and coin laundry, wireless Internet. **Business Services:** meeting rooms, business center. **Cards:** AX, CB, DC, DS, JC, MC, VI.

[ASK] [icons] CALL [icons] / SOME UNITS [icons]

WEIRTON pop. 20,411

─────── **WHERE TO STAY** ───────

BAYMONT INN & SUITES WEIRTON   *Book at AAA.com*   Phone: (304)723-0050

▽▽ ▽▽ ▽▽

Small-scale Hotel
$85-$125 All Year

Address: 1 AmeriHost Dr 26062 **Location:** US 22, exit 4. **Facility:** 79 one-bedroom standard units, some with whirlpools. 3 stories, interior corridors. *Bath:* combo or shower only. **Parking:** on-site. **Amenities:** high-speed Internet, voice mail, safes (fee), irons, hair dryers. **Pool(s):** heated indoor. **Leisure Activities:** whirlpool, exercise room. **Guest Services:** valet laundry, wireless Internet. **Business Services:** meeting rooms, PC, fax (fee). **Cards:** AX, DC, DS, JC, MC, VI.

[ASK] [icons] CALL [icons] / SOME UNITS [icons]

HOLIDAY INN   *Book at AAA.com*   Phone: (304)723-5522

▽▽ ▽▽ ▽▽

Small-scale Hotel
$109 5/1-2/28
$105 3/1-4/30

Address: 350 Three Springs Dr 26062 **Location:** 4.5 mi e on US 22, exit Three Springs Dr. **Facility:** 118 units. 114 one-bedroom standard units, some with whirlpools. 4 one-bedroom suites. 5 stories, interior corridors. *Bath:* combo or shower only. **Parking:** on-site. **Amenities:** video games, voice mail, irons, hair dryers. *Some:* high-speed Internet. **Pool(s):** outdoor. **Leisure Activities:** exercise room, horseshoes, volleyball. **Guest Services:** valet and coin laundry, wireless Internet. **Business Services:** meeting rooms, PC, fax (fee). **Cards:** AX, DC, DS, MC, VI.

[ASK] [icons] CALL [icons] / SOME UNITS FEE [icons]

─────── **WHERE TO DINE** ───────

MARIO'S ITALIAN RESTAURANT   Phone: 304/748-1179

▽▽ ▽▽

Italian
$6-$16

Open since 1970, the restaurant is known for homemade spaghetti, gnocchi, chicken and steak. The wait staff is welcoming and efficient. Casual dress. **Bar:** Beer & wine. **Hours:** 11 am-9 pm, Fri & Sat-10 pm, Sun noon-9 pm. Closed major holidays. **Address:** 3810 Main St 26062 **Location:** 2.5 mi e on US 22. **Parking:** on-site. **Cards:** MC, VI.

[icon]

WEST HAMLIN pop. 696

─────── **WHERE TO DINE** ───────

TUDOR'S BISCUIT WORLD   Phone: 304/824-7979

▽▽▽

American
$5-$12

Serving breakfast all day folks can stop into Tudor's Biscuit World to sample their many varieties of homemade biscuit sandwiches. Known for fast and friendly service in a clean casual atmosphere. Casual dress. **Hours:** 5:30 am-2, Sun from 7 am. Closed: 12/25. **Address:** SR 10 25571 **Location:** 2 mi w. **Parking:** on-site.

WESTON pop. 4,317

———— WHERE TO STAY ————

COMFORT INN
AAA (SAVE)
▽▽▽▽
Small-scale Hotel
$65-$130 All Year

Book great rates at AAA.com
Phone: 304/269-7000
· **Address:** 2906 US Hwy 33 E 26452 **Location:** I-79, exit 99, just e. **Facility:** 70 one-bedroom standard units, some with whirlpools. 2 stories (no elevator), exterior corridors. *Bath:* combo or shower only. **Parking:** on-site. **Amenities:** voice mail, irons, hair dryers. **Pool(s):** heated outdoor. **Guest Services:** wireless Internet. **Business Services:** meeting rooms, fax (fee). **Cards:** AX, CB, DC, DS, JC, MC, VI. **Free Special Amenities: expanded continental breakfast and high-speed Internet.**

CALL &M ⊘ ⊠ ▢ / SOME UNITS FEE ⊡ ⊠ ⊟ ⊡

WESTON HOLIDAY INN EXPRESS HOTEL & SUITES
[fyi]
Small-scale Hotel
$90-$140 All Year

Phone: 304/269-3550
Too new to rate, opening scheduled for September 2007. **Address:** 215 Staunton Dr 26452 **Location:** I-79, exit 99. **Amenities:** 63 units, pets, coffeemakers, pool. **Cards:** AX, CB, DC, DS, JC, MC, VI.

WESTON SUPER 8 MOTEL
▽▽▽
Small-scale Hotel
Rates not provided

Book at AAA.com
Phone: 304/269-1086
Address: 100 Market Place Mall, Suite 12 26452 **Location:** I-79, exit 99, just e. **Facility:** 62 one-bedroom standard units. 2 stories (no elevator), interior corridors. *Bath:* combo or shower only. **Parking:** on-site. **Amenities:** safes (fee). **Guest Services:** coin laundry.

CALL &M ⊠ / SOME UNITS ⊡ ⊠ ⊟ ⊡

WHEELING pop. 31,419

———— WHERE TO STAY ————

HAMPTON INN
▽▽▽
Small-scale Hotel
$109-$129 All Year

Book great rates at AAA.com
Phone: (304)233-0440
Address: 795 National Rd 26003 **Location:** I-70, exit 2A (SR 88 N), just e on US 40. **Facility:** 104 one-bedroom standard units. 5 stories, interior corridors. **Amenities:** high-speed Internet, dual phone lines, voice mail, irons, hair dryers. **Leisure Activities:** exercise room. **Guest Services:** valet laundry, wireless Internet. **Business Services:** meeting rooms. **Cards:** AX, CB, DC, DS, MC, VI.

(ASK) (S/D) (Y+) CALL &M ⊠ ▢ / SOME UNITS ⊠ (VCR) ⊟

OGLEBAY RESORT
▽▽▽
Resort
Small-scale Hotel
$135-$1500 All Year

Phone: 304/243-4000
Address: Rt 88 N 26003 **Location:** I-70, exit 2A (SR 88 N), 4 mi s. **Facility:** In addition to spectacular mountain vistas, the lodge offers recreational activities, incredible touches, amenities and an attentive staff. 265 one-bedroom standard units. 3 stories, interior/exterior corridors. *Bath:* combo or shower only. **Parking:** on-site. **Terms:** 2-3 night minimum stay - seasonal and/or weekends, 10 day cancellation notice-fee imposed. **Amenities:** voice mail, irons, hair dryers. *Some:* DVD players, CD players. **Pool(s):** heated outdoor, heated indoor. **Leisure Activities:** sauna, whirlpool, paddleboats, boat dock, fishing, snowmobiling, recreation programs, hiking trails, playground, exercise room, basketball, volleyball. *Fee:* golf-72 holes, miniature golf, 9 lighted tennis courts, horseback riding, massage, game room. **Guest Services:** valet and coin laundry, wireless Internet. **Business Services:** conference facilities, PC, fax (fee). **Cards:** AX, DS, MC, VI.

(Y¶) (Y) CALL &M ⊘ (X) ⊠ ⊠ ▢ / SOME UNITS (VCR) ⊟

WHEELING ISLAND RACE TRACK & GAMING CENTER
▽▽▽
Small-scale Hotel
$135-$225 All Year

Phone: 304/232-5050
Address: 1 S Stone St 26003 **Location:** I-70, exit 0, just s. **Facility:** The property offers dog racing and gaming as well as many shopping and dining opportunities. 151 one-bedroom standard units. 7 stories, interior corridors. *Bath:* combo or shower only. **Parking:** on-site and valet. **Amenities:** video games, voice mail, safes, irons, hair dryers. **Leisure Activities:** *Fee:* exercise room, game room. **Guest Services:** valet laundry, wireless Internet. **Business Services:** meeting rooms, fax (fee). **Cards:** AX, DS, MC, VI.

⊗ (ASK) (S/D) (Y¶) (Y) CALL &M ⊠ ▢ / SOME UNITS ⊠

WHEELING SUPER 8 MOTEL
▽▽▽
Motel
Rates not provided

Book at AAA.com
Phone: 304/243-9400
Address: 2400 National Rd 26003 **Location:** I-70, exit 5, just e. **Facility:** 55 one-bedroom standard units, some with whirlpools. 3 stories, interior corridors. *Bath:* combo or shower only. **Parking:** on-site. **Amenities:** high-speed Internet, safes (fee), hair dryers. **Leisure Activities:** exercise room. **Guest Services:** coin laundry, wireless Internet. **Business Services:** meeting rooms.

CALL &M ⊠ ⊟ ▢ / SOME UNITS ⊠ ⊡

──────── **WHERE TO DINE** ────────

ABBEY'S RESTAURANT **Phone: 304/233-0729**

This restaurant is known locally for its steak, seafood, chicken and ribs. Friendly servers do what they can to ensure no one leaves a stranger. Casual dress. **Bar:** Full bar. **Hours:** 11 am-11 pm. Closed major holidays. **Address:** 145 Zane St 26003 **Location:** I-70, exit 0, just n. **Parking:** on-site. **Cards:** AX, DC, MC, VI.

American
$5-$22

BELLA VIA RESTAURANT **Phone: 304/242-8181**

An Old World atmosphere prevails in the relaxed restaurant, which serves homemade Italian and American dishes. Servers are outgoing. Casual dress. **Bar:** Full bar. **Reservations:** suggested, weekends. **Hours:** 11 am-10 pm, Sat from 4 pm. Closed major holidays. **Address:** 1 Burkham Ct 26003 **Location:** I-70, exit 5, just n. **Parking:** on-site. **Cards:** AX, CB, DC, DS, JC, MC, VI.

Italian
$6-$20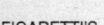

ENZIO'S BRICK OVEN PIZZA & PASTA **Phone: 304/242-3694**

Diners find great food, fun and a family atmosphere at the restaurant. A family tradition, this place serves homemade pizza and pasta. Casual dress. **Bar:** Full bar. **Hours:** 11 am-10 pm. Closed: 12/25. **Address:** 2053 National Rd 26003 **Location:** I-70, exit 2, just e. **Parking:** on-site. **Cards:** AX, CB, DC, DS, JC, MC, VI.

Italian
$6-$20

FIGARETTI'S **Phone: 304/243-5625**

The family-owned-and-operated restaurant has been part of the city landscape since 1948. Homemade pasta dishes and salads make up the menu. Casual dress. **Bar:** Full bar. **Reservations:** suggested, weekends. **Hours:** 11 am-10 pm. Closed: 12/25. **Address:** 1035 Mt. DeChantal Rd 26003 **Location:** I-70, exit 2D, just w. **Parking:** on-site. **Cards:** AX, CB, DC, DS, JC, MC, VI.

Italian
$8-$20

RIVER CITY ALE WORKS **Phone: 304/233-4555**

In historic downtown's Wheeling Artisan Center, the spacious and sunny atrium restaurant prepares varied dishes, most notably the Thai peanut wings appetizer, homemade gnocchi entree and pizza. Service is prompt. Organic micro-brewed beer is available. Casual dress. **Bar:** Full bar. **Hours:** 11 am-9 pm, Fri & Sat-midnight. Closed: 12/25; also Sun. **Address:** 1400 Main St 26003 **Location:** Corner of Main and 14th St; downtown. **Parking:** street. **Cards:** AX, DC, DS, MC, VI.

American
$7-$20

STRATFORD SPRINGS RESTAURANT **Phone: 304/233-5100**
Built in 1906 and listed on the National Register of Historic Places, the historic inn, nestled on 30 acres of rolling hills near Oglebay Park, is an elegant place for fine dining. Menu selections include well-prepared dishes of chicken, steak, seafood and lamb. Don't skip the dessert tray. Dressy casual. **Bar:** Full bar. **Reservations:** suggested. **Hours:** 11:30 am-2 & 5-9 pm, Sun-8:30 pm. Closed: 1/1, 12/24, 12/25. **Address:** 100 Kensington Dr 26003 **Location:** I-70, exit 2A, 0.5 mi e on US 40, then 1.5 mi n on SR 88. **Parking:** on-site. **Cards:** AX, DC, MC, VI. **Historic**

American
$7-$25

TJ'S SPORTS GARDEN RESTAURANT **Phone: 304/232-9555**
Geared toward families, the restaurant has a sporty feel, with pool tables and game rooms. Casual dress. **Bar:** Full bar. **Hours:** 11 am-1 am. Closed: 12/25. **Address:** 808 National Rd 26003 **Location:** I-70, exit 2A, just n. **Parking:** on-site. **Cards:** AX, DS, MC, VI.

American
$7-$16

WHITE SULPHUR SPRINGS pop. 2,315

——— WHERE TO STAY ———

THE GREENBRIER

AAA SAVE

◆◆◆◆◆

Classic Historic
Large-scale Hotel
$299-$729 All Year

Book great rates at AAA.com

Phone: (304)536-1110

Address: 300 W Main St 24986 **Location:** I-64, exit 181 westbound, 1.8 mi w on US 60; exit 175 eastbound, just n, then 3.2 mi e on US 60. **Facility:** The grand resort's flamboyant interior design spans a range of eras, employs vibrant colors and patterns and conceals an underground hideaway. Smoke free premises. 721 units. 398 one-bedroom standard units. 82 one-bedroom suites. 241 cottages, some with whirlpools. 1-6 stories, interior/exterior corridors. *Bath:* combo or shower only. **Parking:** on-site and valet. **Terms:** check-in 4 pm, 15 day cancellation notice. **Amenities:** video games (fee), CD players, high-speed Internet, dual phone lines, voice mail, safes, irons, hair dryers. *Some: Fee:* DVD players. **Dining:** 5 restaurants, nightclub, entertainment. **Pool(s):** heated outdoor, heated indoor. **Leisure Activities:** steamrooms, putting green, recreation programs, rental bicycles, hiking trails, jogging, playground, spa, basketball, horseshoes, shuffleboard. *Fee:* saunas, canoes, fishing, sulphur baths, mineral water spa, kayaking, white-water rafting, golf-54 holes, Golf Digest Academy, 10 tennis courts (5 indoor, 5 lighted), Falconry Academy, hunting preserve, Greenbrier Driving School, billiards, bowling, carriage ride, horse drawn sleighs, cooking classes, croquet, movie theater, meditation trail, horseback riding, trap, skeet shooting, sporting clay course, game room. **Guest Services:** valet laundry, airport transportation (fee)-Greenbrier Valley Airport, area transportation-within 5 mi, wireless Internet. **Business Services:** conference facilities, business center. **Cards:** AX, DC, DS, MC, VI. *(See color ad below)*

FEE ✈ ▮▮ 24▮ ▯ 𝄞 CALL Ⓜ 🛁 ▮▮ ✗ ✕ 🎥 ▮ ▯
/SOME UNITS FEE ▮ FEE ▯

——— WHERE TO DINE ———

GRANNY'S HOUSE RESTAURANT

◆◆◆

American
$6-$17

🚭

Phone: 304/536-2361

Country cooking is done right at the hospitable restaurant, where breakfast specials and homemade desserts are served all the time. Casual dress. **Hours:** 24 hours. Closed: 12/25. **Address:** US 60 - White Sulphur Springs 24986 **Location:** I-64, exit 175, just n. **Parking:** on-site. **Cards:** MC, VI.

WILLIAMSTOWN pop. 2,996

———— WHERE TO STAY ————

DAYS INN *Book at AAA.com*

Small-scale Hotel
Rates not provided

Phone: 304/375-3730
Address: 1339 Highland Ave 26187 **Location:** I-77, exit 185, just w on SR 31. **Facility:** 110 one-bedroom standard units. 2 stories (no elevator), interior corridors. **Parking:** on-site. **Amenities:** hair dryers. **Pool(s):** outdoor. **Leisure Activities:** exercise room, horseshoes. **Guest Services:** coin laundry, wireless Internet. **Business Services:** meeting rooms, fax (fee).

———— WHERE TO DINE ————

DA VINCI'S

Italian
$6-$20

Phone: 304/375-3633
Homemade dessert and the unusual spaghetti Mona Lisa—baked capellini topped with meat sauce, green peppers, mushrooms, pepperoni and cheese—are wonderful offerings at the cheerful restaurant. The four dining rooms are inviting, and the atmosphere is great with large, inviting booths, good background music and warm greeting and seating. The chef prepares weekly specials; a variety including duck and lamb. Casual dress. **Bar:** Full bar. **Hours:** 11 am-10 pm, Fri & Sat-11 pm. Closed: 3/23, 11/27, 12/24, 12/25; also Mon. **Address:** 215 Highland Ave 26187 **Location:** I-77, exit 185, 1.4 mi w on SR 14. **Parking:** on-site. **Cards:** AX, DS, MC, VI.

WINFIELD pop. 1,858

———— WHERE TO DINE ————

TUDOR'S BISCUIT WORLD

American
$5-$12

Phone: 304/586-4885
Serving breakfast all day folks can stop into Tudor's Biscuit World to sample their many varieities of homemade biscuit sandwiches. Known for fast and friendly service in a clean casual atmosphere. Casual dress. **Hours:** 5:30 am-8 pm, Sun from 7 am. Closed: 12/25. **Address:** SR 35 25213 **Location:** 1.5 mi w. **Parking:** on-site.

Offices

Cities with main offices are listed in **BOLD TYPE** and toll-free member service numbers in *ITALIC TYPE*.
All are closed Saturdays, Sundays and holidays unless otherwise indicated.
The type of service provided is designated below the name of the city where the office is located:

+ ✚ Auto travel services, including books/maps, marked maps and on-demand TripTik® maps
+ ● Auto travel services, including books/maps, marked maps, but no on-demand TripTik® maps
+ ■ Provides books/maps only. No marked maps or on-demand TripTik® maps available
+ ▲ Travel agency services

AAA NATIONAL OFFICE: 1000 AAA DRIVE, HEATHROW, FLORIDA 32746-5063, (407) 444-7000

DELAWARE

DOVER—AAA MID-ATLANTIC, 55 GREENTREE DR RT 8, 19904.
MON-FRI 9-6, SAT 9-3. (302) 674-8020. ✚▲

NEWARK—AAA MID-ATLANTIC, 1201 CHURCHMAN'S RD,
19713. MON-FRI 9-6, SAT 9-3. (302) 292-6360. ✚▲

WILMINGTON—AAA MID-ATLANTIC, ONE RIVER PL, 19801.
MON-FRI 9-6, SAT 9-3. (302) 299-4700. ✚▲

DISTRICT OF COLUMBIA

WASHINGTON—AAA MID-ATLANTIC, 701 15TH ST NW STE
100, 20005. MON-FRI 9-5:30. (202) 331-3000. ✚▲

MARYLAND

ARNOLD—AAA MID-ATLANTIC, 1450 RITCHIE HWY #110,
21012. MON-FRI 9-6, SAT 9-3. (410) 757-7400. ✚▲

BEL AIR—AAA MID-ATLANTIC, 520 BALTIMORE PIKE, 21014.
MON-FRI 9-6, SAT 9-3. (410) 838-5121. ✚▲

FREDERICK—AAA MID-ATLANTIC, 1305 W 7TH ST, 21702.
MON-FRI 9-6, SAT 9-3. (301) 663-4161. ✚▲

FULTON—AAA MID-ATLANTIC, 8170 MAPLE LAWN BLVD,
20759. MON-FRI 9-6, SAT 9-3. (301) 362-2380. ✚▲

GERMANTOWN—AAA MID-ATLANTIC, 19847 CENTURY BLVD
STE A, 20874. MON-FRI 9-6, SAT 9-3. (301) 944-9519. ✚▲

HAGERSTOWN—AAA MID-ATLANTIC, 1580 WESEL BLVD STE
9, 21740. MON-FRI 9-6, SAT 9-3. (240) 313-7009. ✚▲

LARGO—AAA MID-ATLANTIC, 10412 CAMPUS WAY S, 20774.
MON-FRI 9-6, SAT 9-3. (301) 909-9519. ✚▲

SALISBURY—AAA MID-ATLANTIC, 8245F DICKERSON LN,
21804. MON-FRI 9-6, SAT 9-3. (410) 860-2885.
(800) 492-0282. ✚▲

TIMONIUM—AAA MID-ATLANTIC, 2133 YORK RD, 21093.
MON-FRI 9-6, SAT 9-3. (410) 616-1000. ✚▲

WESTMINSTER—AAA MID-ATLANTIC, 1030 BALTIMORE BLVD
#140, 21157. MON-FRI 9-6, SAT 9-3. (410) 848-8500. ✚▲

WHEATON—AAA MID-ATLANTIC, 2730 UNIVERSITY BLVD,
20902. MON-FRI 9-6, SAT 9-3. (301) 946-5200. ✚▲

VIRGINIA

ALEXANDRIA—AAA MID-ATLANTIC, 801 N FAIRFAX ST,
22314. MON-FRI 9-6, SAT 9-3. (703) 549-1080. ✚▲

CHARLOTTESVILLE—AAA MID-ATLANTIC, 1820 RIO HILL CTR,
22901. MON-FRI 9-6, SAT 9-3. (434) 974-1426. ✚▲

CHESAPEAKE—AAA OF TIDEWATER VIRGINIA, 111
KEMPSVILLE RD, 23320. MON-FRI 8:30-5:30, SAT 8:30-12:30.
(757) 547-9741. ✚▲

COLONIAL HEIGHTS—AAA MID-ATLANTIC, 707 SOUTHPARK
BLVD #7, 23834. MON-FRI 9-6, SAT 9-3. (804) 520-7388. ✚▲

FAIRFAX—AAA MID-ATLANTIC, 4100 MONUMENT CORNER
DR, 22030. MON-FRI 9-6, SAT 9-3. (703) 222-4200. ✚▲

FOREST—AAA MID-ATLANTIC, 18013 FOREST RD STE A,
24551. MON-FRI 9-6, SAT 9-3. (434) 385-0091. ✚▲

FREDERICKSBURG—AAA MID-ATLANTIC, 1171 CENTRAL PARK
BL #100, 22401. MON-FRI 9-6, SAT 9-3. (540) 785-0282. ✚▲

HAMPTON—AAA OF TIDEWATER VIRGINIA, 1520 ABERDEEN
RD, 23666. MON-FRI 8:30-5:30, SAT 8:30-12:30.
(757) 826-1061. ✚▲

LEESBURG—AAA MID-ATLANTIC, 19317 WINMEADE, 20176.
MON-FRI 9-6, SAT 9-3. (571) 223-2262. ●▲

MIDLOTHIAN—AAA MID-ATLANTIC, 13241 RITTENHOUSE DR,
23112. MON-FRI 9-6, SAT 9-3. (804) 744-1513. ■▲

NEWPORT NEWS—AAA OF TIDEWATER VIRGINIA, 733 J
CLYDE MORRIS BLVD, 23601. MON-FRI 8:30-5:30, SAT
8:30-12:30. (757) 246-4746. ✚▲

NORFOLK—AAA OF TIDEWATER VIRGINIA, 141 W VIRGINIA
BEACH BLVD, 23510. MON-FRI 8:30-5:30, SAT 8:30-12:30.
(757) 622-5634. ✚▲

NORTON—AAA ALLIED GROUP INC, 613 PARK AVE NW,
24273. MON-FRI 8:30-5. (276) 679-5160. ✚▲

PORTSMOUTH—AAA OF TIDEWATER VIRGINIA, 3521
WESTERN BRANCH BLVD, 23707. MON-FRI 8:30-5:30, SAT
8:30-12:30. (757) 397-5941. ✚▲

RICHMOND—AAA MID-ATLANTIC, 1201 MALL DR, 23235.
MON-FRI 9-6, SAT 9-3. (804) 379-4487. ✚▲

RICHMOND—AAA MID-ATLANTIC, 1601 WILLOW LAWN DR
#700, 23230. MON-FRI 9-6, SAT 9-3. (804) 281-7100. ✚▲

ROANOKE—AAA MID-ATLANTIC, 707 5TH ST NE, 24016.
MON-FRI 9-6, SAT 9-3. (540) 344-0943. ✚▲

VIENNA—AAA MID-ATLANTIC, 8300 OLD COURTHOUSE RD,
22182. MON-FRI 9-6, SAT 9-3. (703) 790-2600. ✚▲

VIRGINIA BEACH—**AAA OF TIDEWATER VIRGINIA**, 5366
VIRGINIA BEACH BLVD, 23462. MON-FRI 8:30-5:30, SAT
8:30-12:30. (757) 233-3800. ✚▲

VIRGINIA BEACH—AAA OF TIDEWATER VIRGINIA, 296 KINGS
GRANT RD, 23452. MON-FRI 8:30-5:30, SAT 8:30-12:30.
(757) 340-7271. ✚▲

WILLIAMSBURG—AAA OF TIDEWATER VIRGINIA, 260
MCLAWS CIR, 23185. MON-FRI 8:30-5:30, SAT 8:30-12:30.
(757) 564-7711. ✚▲

WEST VIRGINIA

BECKLEY—AAA ALLIED GROUP INC, 1004 N EISENHOWER DR,
25801. MON-FRI 9-6, SAT 9-3. (304) 255-4147. ✚▲

BLUEFIELD—AAA ALLIED GROUP INC, 622 COMMERCE ST,
24701. MON-FRI 8:30-5. (304) 327-8187. ✚▲

BRIDGEPORT—AAA EAST CENTRAL, 169 BARNETT RUN RD,
26330. MON-FRI 9-5:30. (304) 842-2221. ✚▲

CHARLESTON—AAA ALLIED GROUP INC, 1000 PKY RD STE A,
25309. MON-FRI 9-6, SAT 9-3. (304) 925-6681. ✚▲

HUNTINGTON—AAA EAST CENTRAL, 1126 SIXTH AVE, 25701.
MON-FRI 9-5. (304) 523-6423. ✚▲

MARTINSBURG—AAA EAST CENTRAL, 135 N QUEEN ST,
25401. MON-FRI 9-5. (304) 263-4619. ✚▲

MORGANTOWN—AAA EAST CENTRAL, 6520 MALL RD, 26501.
MON-FRI 10-6, SAT 10-2. (304) 983-6480. ✚▲

VIENNA—AAA EAST CENTRAL, 1107 NINTH ST STE K, 26105.
MON-FRI 9-5:30. (304) 295-9715. ✚▲

WEIRTON—AAA EAST CENTRAL, 3126 WEST ST, 26062.
MON-FRI 9-5, SAT 9-12. (304) 748-1616. ✚▲

WHEELING—AAA EAST CENTRAL, 846 NATIONAL RD, 26003.
MON-FRI 8:30-5:30. (304) 233-1810. ✚▲

At 60 mph, if you reach down to change the radio station you can travel the length of a football field.
Stay Focused
Keep your mind on the road.

Metric Equivalents Chart

TEMPERATURE

To convert Fahrenheit to Celsius, subtract 32 from the Fahrenheit temperature, multiply by 5 and divide by 9.
To convert Celsius to Fahrenheit, multipy by 9, divide by 5 and add 32.

ACRES

1 acre = 0.4 hectare (ha)   1 hectare = 2.47 acres

MILES AND KILOMETRES

Note: A kilometre is approximately 5/8 or 0.6 of a mile.
To convert kilometres to miles multiply by 0.6.

Miles/Kilometres		Kilometres/Miles	
15	24.1	30	18.6
20	32.2	35	21.7
25	40.2	40	24.8
30	48.3	45	27.9
35	56.3	50	31.0
40	64.4	55	34.1
45	72.4	60	37.2
50	80.5	65	40.3
55	88.5	70	43.4
60	96.6	75	46.6
65	104.6	80	49.7
70	112.7	85	52.8
75	120.7	90	55.9
80	128.7	95	59.0
85	136.8	100	62.1
90	144.8	105	65.2
95	152.9	110	68.3
100	160.9	115	71.4

Temperature Chart

Celsius°		Fahrenheit°
100	BOILING	212
37		100
35		95
32		90
29		85
27		80
24		75
21		70
18		65
16		60
13		55
10		50
7		45
4		40
2		35
0	FREEZING	32
-4		25
-7		20
-9		15
-12		10
-15		5
-18		0
-21		-5
-24		-10
-27		-15

LINEAR MEASURE

Customary	Metric
1 inch = 2.54 centimetres	1 centimetre = 0.4 inches
1 foot = 30 centimetres	1 metre = 3.3 feet
1 yard = 0.91 metres	1 metre = 1.09 yards
1 mile = 1.6 kilometres	1 kilometre = .62 miles

LIQUID MEASURE

Customary	Metric
1 fluid ounce = 30 millilitres	1 millilitre = .03 fluid ounces
1 cup = .24 litres	1 litre = 2.1 pints
1 pint = .47 litres	1 litre = 1.06 quarts
1 quart = .95 litres	1 litre = .26 gallons
1 gallon = 3.8 litres	

WEIGHT

If You Know:	Multiply By:	To Find:
Ounces	28.000	Grams
Pounds	0.450	Kilograms
Grams	0.035	Ounces
Kilograms	2.200	Pounds

PRESSURE

Air pressure in automobile tires is expressed in kilopascals. Multiply pound-force per square inch (psi) by 6.89 to find kilopascals (kPa).

24 psi = 165 kPa	28 psi = 193 kPa
26 psi = 179 kPa	30 psi = 207 kPa

GALLON AND LITRES

Gallons/Litres				Litres/Gallons			
5	19.0	12	45.6	10	2.6	40	10.4
6	22.8	14	53.2	15	3.9	50	13.0
7	26.6	16	60.8	20	5.2	60	15.6
8	30.4	18	68.4	25	6.5	70	18.2
9	34.2	20	76.0	30	7.8	80	20.8
10	38.0	25	95.0	35	9.1	90	23.4

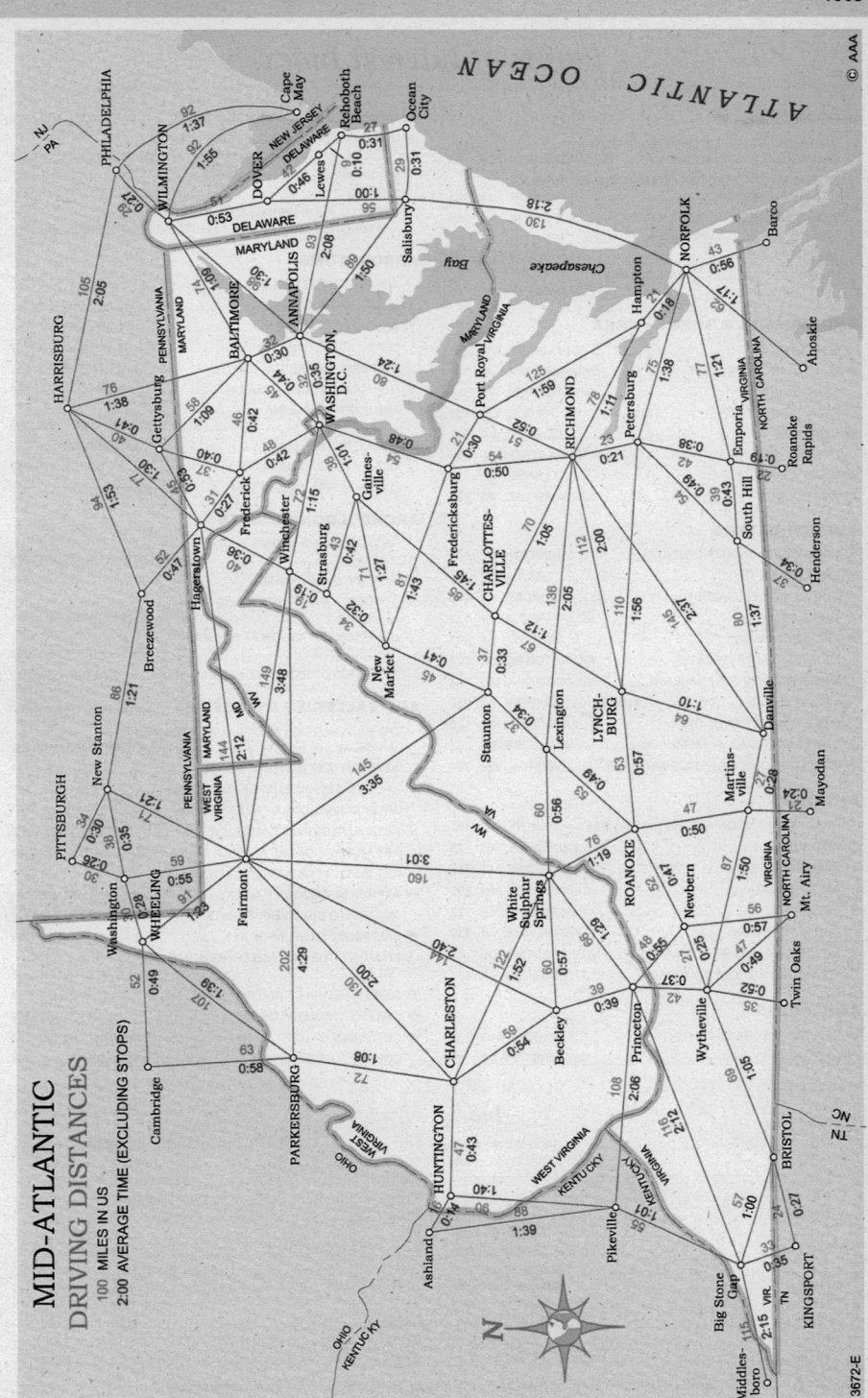

MID-ATLANTIC
DRIVING DISTANCES
100 MILES IN US
2:00 AVERAGE TIME (EXCLUDING STOPS)

© AAA

ATLANTIC OCEAN

3672-E

Points of Interest Index

Index Legend

NB.	national battlefield	NR.	national river
NBP.	national battlefield park	NS.	national seashore
NC.	national cemetery	NWR.	national wildlife refuge
NF.	national forest	PHP.	provincial historic(al) park
NHM.	national historic(al) monument	PHS.	provincial historic(al) site
NHP.	national historic(al) park	PP.	provincial park
NHS.	national historic(al) site	SF.	state forest
NL.	national lakeshore	SHM.	state historic(al) monument
NME.	national memorial	SHP.	state historic(al) park
NMO.	national monument	SHS.	state historic(al) site
NMP.	national military park	SME.	state memorial
NP.	national park	SP.	state park
NRA.	national recreation area	SRA.	state recreation area

☟ GEM: Points of Interest Offering a *Great Experience for Members*®

CHILDREN'S ATTRACTIONS

CHURCHES, CATHEDRALS & BASILICAS

CHURCHES-CHAPELS

CHURCHES-MEETING HOUSES

CHURCHES-SHRINES

CHURCHES-TEMPLES & SYNAGOGUES

EXHIBITS & COLLECTIONS-AVIATION

EXHIBITS & COLLECTIONS-CIVIL WAR

FOSSILS

FOUNTAINS

FURNACES, SHOT TOWERS

GAMBLING ESTABLISHMENTS

GAPS & PASSES

GARDENS

HISTORIC DOCUMENTS, MANUSCRIPTS & RARE BOOKS

HISTORIC SITES

MUSIC HALLS & OPERA HOUSES

PARKS, NATIONAL

PERFORMING ARTS ORGANIZATIONS

RECREATION-WINTER ACTIVITIES

RESEARCH ORGANIZATIONS

RESTORED VILLAGES & SETTLEMENTS

RIVERS

ROCKS

RUINS

SHIPS & BOATS

SHOPS, FIRMS & STORES

SIGHTSEEING TOURS

SIGHTSEEING TOURS-ARCHITECTURAL

SIGHTSEEING TOURS-BOATS

SIGHTSEEING TOURS-BUS & TROLLEY

VISITOR INFORMATION

SAVE Attraction Admission Discount Index

Bed & Breakfast Lodgings Index

Some bed and breakfasts listed below might have historical significance.
Those properties are also referenced in the Historical index.

Country Inns Index

Some of the following country inns can also be considered as bed-and-breakfast operations.

Historical Lodgings & Restaurants Index

Some of the following historical lodgings can also be considered as bed-and-breakfast operations.

Resorts Index

Many establishments are located in resort areas; however, the following places have extensive on-premises recreational facilities:

Comprehensive City Index

Here is an alphabetical list of all cities appearing in this TourBook® guide. Cities are presented by state/province. Page numbers under the POI column indicate where points of interest text begins. Page numbers under the L&R column indicate where lodging and restaurant listings begin.

Comprehensive City Index (cont'd)

Comprehensive City Index (cont'd)

Comprehensive City Index (cont'd)